European Commentaries
on Private International Law
ECPIL

Commentary

Volume I
Brussels Ibis Regulation

s|e|l|p sellier european law publishers

European Commentaries on Private International Law ECPIL

Commentary

Volume I
Brussels Ibis Regulation
2016

edited by

Ulrich Magnus
Peter Mankowski

ottoschmidt

Brussels Ibis Regulation is Volume 1 of the Series European Commentaries
on Private International Law edited by Ulrich Magnus and Peter Mankowski,
written by

Introduction:	Ulrich Magnus	Arts. 27-28:	Ilaria Queirolo
Art. 1:	Pippa Rogerson	Arts. 29-34:	Richard Fentiman
Art. 2:	Louise Merrett	Art. 35:	Marta Pertegás Sender / Thomas Garber
Art. 3:	Peter Mankowski		
Arts. 4-6:	Paul Vlas	Arts. 36-38:	Patrick Wautelet
Art. 7:	Peter Mankowski	Arts. 39-44:	Isabelle Rueda / Gilles Cuniberti
Arts. 8-9:	Horatia Muir Watt		
Arts. 10-16:	Helmut Heiss	Art. 45:	Stéphanie Francq / Peter Mankowski
Arts. 17-19:	Peter Arnt Nielsen / Peter Mankowski		
		Arts. 46-51:	Isabelle Rueda / Gilles Cuniberti
Arts. 20-23:	Carlos Esplugues Mota		
Art. 24:	Luís de Lima Pinheiro	Art. 52:	Peter Mankowski
Art. 25:	Ulrich Magnus	Arts. 53-61:	Xandra Kramer
Art. 26:	Alfonso-Luis Calvo Caravaca / Javier Carrascosa González	Arts. 62-63:	Paul Vlas
		Arts. 64-81:	Peter Mankowski

To be cited as:

Magnus / Mankowski / *Author*, Brussels Ibis Regulation (2016) Art. #note#

The Deutsche Nationalbibliothek lists this publication in the
Deutsche Nationalbibliografie; detailed bibliographic data are
available on the Internet at http://dnb.dnb.de.

Verlag Dr. Otto Schmidt KG
Gustav-Heinemann-Ufer 58, 50968 Köln
Tel. +49 221 / 9 37 38-01, Fax +49 221 / 9 37 38-943
info@otto-schmidt.de, www.otto-schmidt.de

ISBN (print) 978-3-504-08005-1
ISBN (eBook) 978-3-504-38480-7

The paper used is made from chlorine-free bleached materials, wood
and acid free, age resistant and environmentally friendly.

Typesetting: fidus Publikations-Service GmbH, Nördlingen
Printing and binding: Friedrich Pustet, Regensburg
Printed in Germany.

Preface

Brussels I is dead, long live Brussels Ibis! The European legislator deemed it both appropriate and necessary to promulgate a recast of the Brussels I Regulation only twelve years after the original Regulation had become effective. The eventual outcome of the recast process is even less revolutionary and more evolutionary than the Proposal which the Commission had tabled initially. Some of the major weaknesses and shortcomings of the original Brussels I regime have not been extinguished but retained. Others have been remedied. The future will have to show whether the cure in some instances might be worse than the illness. The relatively most revolutionary feature of the recast is abandoning the time-honoured institution of *exequatur* – if only to revive its substance at another stage, namely within the framework of enforcement proceedings.

Of course, the Commentary had to follow suit to the advance in European legislation. Its first two editions, then on the Brussels I Regulation, have been exceptionally well received and have established it as one of the leading works on the Brussels I Regulation. Hence, it is an obligation, a pleasure and a honour to continue it on the Brussels Ibis Regulation. We hope that it will provide guidance on the new Regulation in the same quality and depth as previously on the old Regulation.

The proven team of commentators has undergone only few changes: *Gilles Cuniberti* and *Isabel Rueda* have replaced *Konstantinos Kerameus* and *Lennart Pålsson* who deplorably were not able to participate anymore, and *Xandra Kramer* has substituted for *Lajos Vékás*. *Thomas Garber* teamed with *Marta Pertegás*, and *Peter Mankowski* joined *Peter Arnt Nielsen*. The publishers underwent minor changes, too: sellier european law publishers now have become a division of Verlag Dr. Otto Schmidt.

The indefatigable backing team in Hamburg to which all too well deserved thanks are due, this time consisted of *Marie-Thérèse Hölscher, Anca David, Helen Loose* and *Antonia Sommerfeld* with secretarial support rendered by *Helga Jakobi*. Sellier publishers, now part of Otto Schmidt publishers, were amiably and most aptly represented by *Andreas Pittrich, Anna Rosch* and *Karina Hack*; the editors are once more most grateful to them for their almost incredible patience.

Ulrich Magnus
Peter Mankowski

List of Authors

Professor Dr. Alfonso-Luis Calvo Caravaca
Area de derecho internacional privado de Universidad Carlos III de Madrid

Professor Dr. Javier Carrascosa González
Catedrático de derecho internacional privado, Universidad de Murcia Facultad de Derecho

Professor Dr. Gilles Cuniberti
Université de Luxembourg

Professor Dr. Carlos Esplugues Mota
Departemento de Derecho Internacional de Universitat de Valencia

Professor Richard Fentiman
Faculty of Law, University of Cambridge

Professor Dr. Stéphanie Francq
UCL – Université catholique de Louvain CeDIE – Centre Charles de Visscher pour le droit international et européen

Assistant Professor Dr. Thomas Garber
Institut für Zivilverfahrensrecht und Insolvenzrecht, Karl-Franzens-Universität Graz

Professor Dr. Helmut Heiss
Rechtswissenschaftliches Institut, Lehrstuhl für Privatrecht, Rechtsvergleichung und Internationales Privatrecht der Universität Zürich

Professor Dr. Xandra Kramer
Erasmus School of Law, Erasmus Universiteit Rotterdam

Professor Luís de Lima Pinheiro
Faculdade de Direito de Universidade de Lisboa

Professor Dr. Ulrich Magnus
Fakultät für Rechtswissenschaft, Seminar für ausländisches und internationales Privat- und Prozessrecht der Universität Hamburg

Professor Dr. Peter Mankowski
Fakultät für Rechtswissenschaft, Seminar für ausländisches und internationales Privat- und Prozessrecht der Universität Hamburg

Dr. Louise Merrett
Faculty of Law, Trinity College, University of Cambridge

Professor Dr. Horatia Muir Watt
Sciences Po, École de droit, Paris

Professor Dr. Peter Arnt Nielsen
Copenhagen Business School Juridisk Institut/Law Department

Professor Dr. Guillermo Palao Moreno
Departamento de Derecho Internacional de Universitat de Valencia

Professor Dr. Marta Pertegás Sender
Universiteit Antwerpen – Faculteit Rechten Secretary of the Hague Conference for Private International Law

Professor Dr. Ilaria Queirolo
Università degli Studi di Genova

Professor Dr. Pippa Rogerson
Faculty of Law, University of Cambridge

Dr. Isabelle Rueda
School of Law, University of Sheffield

Professor Dr. Paul Vlas
Faculteit der Rechtsgeleerdheid, Afdeling Privaatrecht, Vrije Universiteit Amsterdam Advocaat Generaal Hoge Raad der Nederlanden

Professor Dr. Patrick Wautelet
Département de Droit international privé de Université de Liege

To the First Edition of the Commentary on the Brussels I Regulation (2007)

The Brussels I Regulation is by far the most prominent cornerstone of the European law of international civil procedure. Its imminence could be easily ascertained by every practitioner even remotely concerned with cross-border work in Europe. However arcane private international law in general might appear to practitioners – the Brussels I Regulation is a well-known and renowned instrument. It is heir to the Brussels Convention which has proven its immeasurable and incomparable value for over thirty years. The European Court of Justice and the national courts of the Member States have produced an abundance and a treasure of judgments interpreting the Convention and now the Regulation. Legal writing on the Brussels system is thorough and virtually uncountable throughout Europe. Yet no-one has so far taken the effort of completing a truly pan-European commentary mirroring the pan-European nature of its fascinating object. The existing commentaries clearly each stem from certain national perspectives and more or less deliberately reflect certain national traditions. The co-operation across and bridging borders had not truly reached European jurisprudence in this regard. This is why the idea of this commentary was conceived. This commentary for the first time assembles a team of very prominent and renowned authors from total Europe. The authors' geographical provenience stretches from Sweden in the North to Italy in the South and from Portugal and the United Kingdom in the West to Hungary and Greece in the East. Perhaps fittingly, both of the general editors are located in Hamburg now somewhere near the geographical centre of the extended European Union. The idea of a pan-European commentary met an overwhelmingly warm welcome by almost everyone who was invited to participate and to contribute a commentary on some articles. Apparently now the time is ripe to give such a project a try. It was, and still should be, beyond even the slightest doubt that the proper language of such a project should be English, the current *lingua franca* of transnational legal communication in Europe. Sellier European Law Publishers were as daring and courageous (if not adventurous) as to embrace the idea. Patrick Sellier in particular provided the support sometimes necessary to keep daunting projects afloat in difficult waters. May the future show that is was right to endeavour and to go for the stars!

Everyone who has ever undertaken the venture to edit a multi-author work only too well knows about the absolute necessity of competent assistance. The editors thus are absolutely grateful and cannot remotely express the thanks and accolades due to our backing team at Hamburg in a proper fashion. Without them it would have been virtually impossible to complete this commentary. *Stefanie Bock* and Dr. *Oliver Knöfel* with sheer and utter indefatigability undertook the burdensome task of unifying the style of citations in the contributions. Dr. *Klaus Bitterich* participated in this task. He and Dr. *Knöfel* share the responsibility for the index whereas Ms. *Bock* and *Jan Lüsing* compiled the Table of Cases of decisions by national courts and Ms. *Bock* alone accomplished the Table of Cases by the

To the First Edition of the Commentary on the Brussels I Regulation (2007)

ECJ. The list of Abbreviations was prepared by Professor *Mankowski*, once again with Dr. *Knöfel's* invaluable assistance. Secretarial support was rendered by *Inga Burmeister*. Last but not least, a very special thank is due to *John Blakeley*. He took the pain of revising the linguistical niceties of contributions written in English by authors who in their majority are not native speakers – and he kept his good (Australian) humour till the very end!

Ulrich Magnus
Peter Mankowski

Table of Contents

Regulation (EU) No. 1215/2012 of the European Parliament and of the Council of 12 December 2012 on jurisdiction and enforcement of judgments in civil and commercial matters (Recast)

Official Reports

Amended Commission Proposal COM (2000) 689 final = Commission of the European
  Communities – Amended Proposal for a Council Regulation (EC) on jurisdiction
  and the recognition and enforcement of judgments in civil and commercial matters,
  COM (2000) 689 final

Commission Proposal COM (1999) 348 final = Commission of the European Communities – Proposal for a Council Regulation (EC) on jurisdiction and the recognition and
  enforcement of judgments in civil and commercial matters, COM (1999) 348 final

Commission Proposal Brussels Ibis Regulation COM (2010) 748/3 = Proposal for a
  Regulation of the European Parliament and of the Council on jurisdiction and the
  recognition and enforcement of judgments in civil and commercial matters, COM
  (2010) 748/3

Commission Report = Report from the Commission to the European Parliament, the
  Council and the Economic and Social Committee on the application of Council
  Regulation (EG) No. 44/2001 on jurisdiction and the recognition and enforcement of
  judgments in civil and commercial matters, 21 April 2009, COM (2009) 174 final

Draft Report Zwiefka = Draft Report on the Proposal for a Regulation of the European
  Parliament and of the Council on jurisdiction and the recognition and enforcement of
  judgments in civil and commercial matters (recast), Committee on Legal Affairs,
  Rapporteur: *Tadeusz Zwiefka*, 28 June 2011, PR\869709.EN

Green Paper = Green Paper on the review of Council Regulation (EG) No. 44/2001 on
  jurisdiction and the recognition and enforcement of judgments in civil and commercial matters, 21 April 2009, COM (2009) 175 final

Heidelberg Report = *Hess/Pfeiffer/Schlosser*, The Brussels I Regulation 44/2001.
  Application and Enforcement in the EU (München 2008)

Report *Almeida Cruz/Desantes Real/Jenard* = Almeida Cruz/Desantes Real/Jenard,
  Report on the accession of the Kingdom of Spain and the Portuguese Republic to the
  1968 Convention on jurisdiction and the enforcement of judgments in civil and
  commercial matters, OJ 1990 C 189/35

Report *Evrigenis/Kerameus* = Evrigenis/Kerameus, Report on the accession of the
  Hellenic Republic to the Community Convention on jurisdiction and enforcement
  of judgments in civil and commercial matters, OJ 1986 C 298/1

Official Reports

Report *Jenard* = *Jenard*, Report on the Convention on jurisdiction and the enforcement of judgments in civil and commercial matters, OJ 1979 C 59/1

Report *Jenard/Möller* = *Jenard/Möller*, Report on the Convention on jurisdiction and the enforcement of judgments in civil and commercial matters done at Lugano on 16 September 1988, OJ 1990 C 189/57

Report *Pocar* = *Pocar*, Report on the Convention on jurisdiction and the enforcement of judgments in civil and commercial matters done at Lugano on 30 October 2007, OJ EU 2009 C 319/1

Report *Schlosser* = *Schlosser*, Report on the Convention on the Association of the Kingdom of Denmark, Ireland and the United Kingdom of Great Britain and Northern Ireland to the Convention on jurisdiction and the enforcement of judgments in civil and commercial matters and to the protocol on its interpretation by the Court of Justice, OJ 1979 C 59/71

Report *Zwiefka* = Report on the implementation and review of Council Regulation (EG) No. 44/2001 on jurisdiction and the recognition and enforcement of judgments in civil and commercial matters, Committee on Legal Affairs, Rapporteur: *Tadeusz Zwiefka*, 29 June 2010, A7-0219/2010

Revised Commission Proposal COM (1999) 348 final = Commission of the European Communities – Revised Proposal for a Council Regulation (EC) on jurisdiction and the recognition and enforcement of judgments in civil and commercial matters, COM (2000) 689 final.

List of Principal Works

Referred to by author alone

Adolphsen, Europäisches Zivilprozessrecht (Berlin 2011)
Alexandre, Encyclopédie Dalloz Droit Communautaire, V° Règlement Bruxelles I (2003)
Anton/Beaumont, Civil Jurisdiction in Scotland (2nd ed. Edinburgh 1995)

Basler Kommentar zum Lugano-Übereinkommen (Basel 2011)
Beraudo, J-Cl. Europe, fasc. 3000-3031
Bonomi/Christina Schmid (éds.), Revision der Verordnung 44/2001 (Brüssel I) –
Welche Folgen für das Lugano-Übereinkommen (Zürich 2011)
Borrás (ed.), Revisión de los convenios de Bruselas de 1968 y de Lugano de 1988 sobre
competencia judicial y ejecución de resoluciones judiciales – una reflexión preliminar
de la práctica española (Madrid/Barcelona 1998)
Brenn, Europäischer Zivilprozess (Wien 2005)
Briggs, Civil Jurisdiction and Judgments (6th ed. Abingdon, Oxon. 2015)
Briggs, Private International Law in British Courts (Oxford 2014) (cited as *Briggs*, PIL)
Briggs/Rees, Civil Jurisdiction and Judgments (5th ed. London 2008)
Andreas Bucher (dir.), Loi sur le dorit international privé/Convention de Lugano
(Commentaire Romand) (Basel 2011)
Bülow/Böckstiegel/Geimer/Schütze, Internationaler Rechtsverkehr in Zivil- und Handels-
sachen (looseleaf München 1954/1073-ongoing)
Burgstaller/Neumayr/Geroldinger/Schmaranzer, Internationales Zivilverfahrensrecht
(looseleaf Wien 2000-ongoing)
Byrne, The European Union and Lugano Conventions on Jurisdiction and the Enforcement
of Judgments (Dublin 1994)

Calvo Caravaca, Comentario al convenio de Bruselas relativo a la competencia judicial
y a la ejecución de resoluciones judiciales en materia civil y mercantil (Madrid 1994)
Carbone, Lo spazio giudiziario europeo in matericia civile e commerciale – Da Bruxelles I
al Regolamento CE n. 805/2004 (6th ed. Torino 2009)
Cheshire/North/Fawcett/Carruthers, Private International Law (14th ed. Oxford 2009)
Ciszewski, Konwencja z Lugano (2nd ed. Warszawa 2004)
Collins, The Civil Jurisdiction and Judgments Act 1982 (London 1983)
Czernich/Kodek/Mayr, Europäisches Gerichtsstands- und Vollstreckungsrecht
(4th ed. Wien 2015)
Czernich/Tiefenthaler/Kodek, Kurzkommentar zum Europäischen Gerichtsstands- und
Vollstreckungsrecht (3rd ed. Wien 2009)

Dashwood/Halcon/White, A Guide to the Civil Jurisdiction and Judgments Convention
(Deventer/Antwerpen 1987)
Dasser/Oberhammer, Lugano-Übereinkommen (2nd ed. Bern 2011)
Dicey/Morris, The Conflict of Laws (15h ed. London 2012, annual Supplements)

List of Principal Works

Dickinson/Lein (eds.), The Brussels I Regulation Recast (Oxford 2015)
Donzallaz, La Convention de Lugano du 16 septembre 1988 concernant la compétence judiciaire et l'exécution des décisions en matière civile et commerciale, Vol I-III (Bern 1996–1998)
Droz, Compétence judiciaire et effets des jugements dans le Marché Commun (Paris 1972)

ECJ (ed.), Civil Jurisdiction and Judgments in Europe (London 1992)

Fasching/Konecny, Kommentar zu den Zivilprozessgesetzen, vol. 5/1 (2nd ed. Wien 2008)
Fawcett/Harris/Bridge, International Sale of Goods in the Conflict of Laws (Oxford 2005)
Fentiman, International Commercial Litigation (Oxford 2010)
Fentiman/Nuyts/Tagaras/Watté (eds.), L'espace judiciare européen en matières civiles et commerciales (Bruxelles 1999)

Gaudemet-Tallon, Compétence et exécution des jugements en Europe (4th ed. Paris 2010)
Gaudemet-Tallon, Compétence et exécution des jugements en Europe (5th ed. Paris 2015) (cited as *Gaudemet-Tallon* 5th ed.)
Geimer/Schütze, Internationale Urteilsanerkennung, Vol. I/1 (München 1983)
Geimer/Schütze, Europäisches Zivilverfahrensrecht (3rd ed. München 2010)
Geimer/Schütze (eds.), Internationaler Rechtsverkehr in Zivil- und Handelssachen (looseleaf München 1973-ongoing)
Gillard/Voyame (eds.), L'espace judiciaire européen – La Convention de Lugano du 16 septembre 1988 (Lausanne 1992)
Gothot/Holleaux, La Convention de Bruxelles du 28 septembre 1968 (Paris 1985)

Handbuch des Internationalen Zivilverfahrensrechts Vol. I (Tübingen 1982)
Handkommentar zur ZPO (4th ed. Baden-Baden 2011)
Hartley, Civil Jurisdiction and Judgments (London 1984)
Hartley, International Commercial Litigation (Oxford 2009)
Hess, Europäisches Zivilprozessrecht (Heidelberg 2010)

Jonathan Hill/Chong, International Commercial Disputes (4th ed. London 2010)
van Houtte/Pertegás Sender (eds.), Het nieuwe Europese IPR: van verdrag naar verordening (Antwerpen/Apeldoorn 2001)

Kaye, Civil Jurisdiction and Enforcement of Foreign Judgments (Abingdon, Oxon. 1987)
Kaye, European Case Law on the Judgments Conventions (Chichester/Weinheim 1998) (*Kaye*, Case Law)
Kaye, Law of the European Judgments Convention (London/Chichester 1999)
Kennett, The Enforcement of Judgments in Europe (Oxford 2000)
Kerameus/Kremlis/Tagaras, The Brussels Convention on Jurisdiction and Recognition and Enforcement of Judgments as in Force in Greece [Translation from Greek] (Athinai 1989), Supplement (Athinai 1996)
Klauser, EuGVÜ und EVÜ (Wien 1999)
Kreuzer/Rolf Wagner, Europäisches Internationales Zivilverfahrensrecht (ch. Q) (June 2007), in: *Dauses* (ed.), Handbuch des EU-Wirtschaftsrechts (München looseleaf 1993-ongoing)
Kropholler, Europäisches Zivilprozessrecht (8th ed. Heidelberg 2005)

Kropholler/von Hein, Europäisches Zivilprozessrecht (9th ed. Heidelberg 2011)

Layton/Mercer, European Civil Practice (2nd ed. London 2004)
Lein (ed.), The Brussels I Review Proposal Uncovered (London 2012)
de Lima Pinheiro, Direito Internacional Privado, Vol. III: Compêtencia internacional e reconhecimento de decisões estrangeiras (Lisboa 2002)
van Lith, International Jurisdiction and Commercial Litigation (The Hague 2009)
Lupoi, Conflitti transnazionali di giurisdizioni (Milano 2002)

Mari, Il diritto processuale civile della Convenzione di Bruxelles – Il sistema della competenza (Padova 1999)
Mayr, Europäisches Zivilprozessrecht (Wien 2011)
Mayr/Czernich, Das neue europäische Zivilprozessrecht (Wien 2002)
Münchener Kommentar zur ZPO, Vol. III (4th ed. München 2013)
Musielak, ZPO (9th ed. München 2012)

Nagel/Gottwald, Internationales Zivilprozessrecht (7th ed. Köln 2013)
Newton, The Uniform Interpretation of the Brussels and Lugano Conventions (Oxford/ Portland, Oreg. 2002)
Nuyts/Watté (eds.), International Civil Litigation in Europe and Relations with Third States (Bruxelles 2005)

O'Malley/Layton, European Civil Practice (London 1989)

Pålsson, Brysselkonventionen, Luganokonventionen och Bryssel I-förordningen (Stockholm 2002)
Pocar, La Convenzione di Bruxelles sulla giurisdizione e l'esecuzione delle sentenze (3rd ed. Milano 1995)
Pocar/Viarengo/Villata (eds.), Recasting Brussels I (Padova 2012)
Pontier/Burg, EU Principles on Jurisdiction and Recognition and Enforcement of Judgments in Civil and Commercial Matters according to the Case Law of The European Court of Justice (The Hague 2004)

Rauscher, Europäisches Zivilprozess- und Kollisionsrecht, vol.: Brüssel I-VO; LugÜbk 2007 (3rd ed. München 2011)
Rauscher, EuZPR/EuIPR, vol. I: Brüssel Ia-VO; LugÜbk 2007 (4th ed. Köln 2015) (cited as *Rauscher*, 4th ed.)
Rognlien, Lugano-Konvensjonen (Oslo 1993)
Rosner, Cross-Border Recognition and Enforcement of Foreign Money Judgments in Civil and Commercial Matters (Groningen 2004)

Salerno, Giurisdizione ed efficacia delle decisioni stranieri nel Regolamento (CE) n. 44/2001 (3rd ed. Padova 2006)
Schack, Internationales Zivilverfahrensrecht (5th ed. München 2010)
Schlosser, EU-Zivilprozessrecht (3rd ed. München 2009)
Schnyder, Lugano-Übereinkommen zum internationalen Zivilverfahrensrecht (Zürich/St. Gallen 2011)
Schwander (ed.), Das Lugano-Übereinkommen (St. Gallen 1990)

Stein/Jonas, ZPO, Vol. 10: EuGVVO; GVG (22nd ed. Tübingen 2011)
Stone, Civil Jurisdiction and Judgments in Europe (London 1998)
Storme/de Leval (eds.), Le droit processuel et judiciaire européen (Brugge 2003)

Teixeira de Sousa/Moura Vicente, Comentário à Convenção de Bruxelas de 27 de septembro de 1968 relativa à competência judiciária e à execução de decisões em matéria civil e comercial e textos complementarias (Lisboa 1994)
Thomas/Putzo, ZPO (36th ed. München 2015)
Tirado Robles, La competencia judicial en la Union Europea: comentarios al Convenio de Bruselas (Barcelona 1996)

Virgós Soriano/Garcimartín Alférez, Derecho procesal internacional (Madrid 2000)
Vittoria, La competenza internazionale e l'esecuzione delle decisioni in materia civile e commericale nella giurisprudenza della Corte di giustizia (Milano 2005)
Vlas, Rechtspersonen, Praktijkreeks IPR, del 9 (Deventer 2002)
Vlas, EEX-Verordening, in: Wetboek van Burgerlijke Rechtsvordering, Verdragen en Verordeningen (Deventer loose leaf 2004)

Weser, Convention communautaire sur la compétence judiciaire et l'exécution des décisions (Bruxelles 1975)
Wieczorek/Schütze, ZPO, Vol. I/1: §§ 1-49 ZPO; EuGVÜ (3rd ed. Berlin/New York 1994)

Zöller, ZPO (31st ed. Köln 2015).

For an additional bibliography listing articles which covered the Brussels I Regulation in its entirety, in its ascendancy or its infant years please see pp. XV-XVII of the first edition.

Additional Bibliography

Alio, Die Neufassung der Brüssel I-Verordnung, NJW 2014, 2395
Arenas García, Del reglamento Bruselas I al Reglamento Bruselas Ibis, REDI 2013 (2), 377
d'Avout, La refonte du règlement Bruxelles I, D. 2013, 1014
Azcárraga Monzonís, El Reglamento Bruselas I como hito en el proceso armonizador del Derecho internacional privado europeo: banace y revisión, con especial atención a la eliminación del exequátur, in: Liber amicorum José Luis Iglesias Buhigues (2012), p. 163

Bach, Drei Entwicklungsschritte im europäischen Zivilprozessrecht, ZRP 2011, 97
Baumgartner, Changes in the European Union's Regime of Recognizing and Enforcing Foreign Judgments and Transnational Litigation in the United States, 18 Sw. J. Int'l. L. 567 (2012)
Beraudo, Regards sur le nouveau règlement Bruxelles I sur la compétence judiciaire, la reconnaissance et l'exécution des décisions en matière civile et commerciale, Clunet 140 (2013), 741
Bonomi/Christina Schmid (eds.), Revision der Verordnung 44/2001 (Brüssel I) – Welche Folgen für das Lugano-Übereinkommen? (Zürich 2011)
Boularbah/Francq/Nuyts/van Drooghenbroeck, De Bruxelles I à Bruxelles Ibis, J. trib. 2015, 89
Briggs, The Brussels Ibis Regulation appears on the horizon, [2011] LMCLQ 157

Cachia, Recent Developments in the Sphere of Jurisdiction in Civil and Commercial Matters, [2011] ELŞA Malta L. Rev. 69
Cadet, Le nouveau règlement Bruxelles I ou l'itinéraire d'un enfant gâté, Clunet 140 (2013), 765
Cadet, Main Features of the Revised Brussels I Regulation, EuZW 2013, 218
Carruthers, The Brussels I Regulation Recast, SLT 2011 art. 31
Castell/de Lapasse, La révision du règlement Bruxelles I à la suite de la publication du livre vert de la Commission, Gaz. Pal. 28-29 mai 2010, p. 26
Crawford/Carruthers, Brussels Ibis – the Brussels Regulation Recast: Closure (for the Foreseeable Future), SLT 2013 art. 89
Cuniberti, La réforme du règlement Bruxelles I, Dr. et proc. 2013, 26

Delebecque, Quelques observations sur la révision du Règlement 44/2001, DMF 2009, 815
Deumier/Laazouzi/Treppoz, Le règlement Bruxelles I bis et la géométrie dans l'espace, RDC 2013, 1037
Dickinson, Surveying the Proposed Brussels Ibis Regulation – Solid foundations, but renovations needed, YbPIL 12 (2010), 247
Domej, EuGVVO-Reform: Die angekündigte Revolution, ecolex 2011, 124
Domej, Die Neufassung der EuGVVO, RabelsZ 78 (2014), 509
Durán Ayago, Europeización del Derecho internacional privado: del Convenio de Bruselas de 1968 als Reglamento (EU) 1215/2012, Rev. gen. der. eur. 29 (2013), 1

Additional Bibliography

Francq, La refonte du Règlement Bruxelles I – Champ d'application et compétence, TBH 2013, 307

Garcimartín Alférez/Sara Sánchez, El nuevo Reglamento Bruselas I: Qué ha cambiado en el ámbito de la competencia judicial, REDE 48 (2013), 9
Gaudemet-Tallon, La refonte du règlement Bruxelles I, in: *Douchy-Oudot/Emmanuel Guinchard* (dir.), La justice civile européenne en marche (2012), p. 21
Gaudemet-Tallon, Quelques propos autour du règlement Bruxelles Ibis, J. trib. 2015, 453
Gaudemet-Tallon/Kessedjian, La refonte du règlement Bruxelles I, Rev. trim. dr. eur. 49 (2013), 435
Geimer, Bemerkungen zur Brüssel I-Reform, in: FS Daphne-Ariane Simotta (2012), p. 163
Geimer, Die neue Brüssel I-Verordnung, in: FS Gert Delle Karth (2013), p. 319
Geimer, Das Anerkennungsregime der neuen Brüssel I-Verordnung (EU) Nr 1215/2012, in: FS Hellwig Torggler (2013), p. 311
Geimer, Neues und Altes im Kompetenzsystem der reformierten Brüssel I-Verordnung, in: FS Peter Gottwald (2014), p. 175
Geimer, Unionsweite Titelvollstreckung ohne Exequatur nach der Reform der Brüssel I-Verordnung, in: FS Rolf Schütze zum 80. Geb. (2014), p. 109
Grohmann, Die Reform der EuGVVO, ZIP 2015, 16
Emmanuel Guinchard, Votre cadeau de No.ël est arrivé! Vous sérez invité à l'échanger dans 10 ans, Rev. trim. dr. eur. 49 (2013), 329
Emmanuel Guinchard (dir.), Le nouveau règlement Bruxelles I*bis* – Règlement n°1215/2012 du 12 décembre 2012 concernant la compétence judiciaire, la reconnaissance et l'exécution des décisions en matière civile et commerciale (Bruxelles 2014)

Harris, The recast Judgments Regulation: imminent reform of the rules of jurisdiction and enforcement of foreign judgments in the EU, [2014] JIBFL 709
Hay, Notes on the European Union's Brussels-I "Recast" Regulation, EuLF 2013, 1
von Hein, Die Neufassung der Europäischen Gerichtsstands- und Vollstreckungsverord-nung (EuGVVO), RIW 2013, 97
von Hein, Wirtschaftsrechtlich bedeutende Neuerungen in der Europäischen Gerichtsstands- und Vollstreckungsverordnung von 2012, in: *Hopt/Tzouganatos* (eds.), Das Europäische Wirtschaftsrecht vor neuen Herausforderungen (2014), p. 233
Hess, Die Reform der EuGVVO und die Zukunft des Europäischen Zivilprozessrechts, IPRax 2011, 125
Hess, The Brussels I Regulation: Recent case law of the Court of Justice and proposed recast, (2012) 49 CML Rev. 1075

van het Kaar, EEX op de schop: het nieuwe Commissievoorstel tot wijzijging van het EEX-Verordening, NTHR 2011, 149
Kessedjian, Commentaire de la refonte du règlement n° 44/2001, Rev. trim. dr. eur. 47 (2011), 117
Kessedjian, Le règlement "Bruxelles I révisé": Much ado about ... what?, Europe 2013 étude 3
Kiesselbach, The Brussels I Review Proposal – An Overview, in: *Lein* (ed.), The Brussels I Review Proposal Uncovered (2012), p. 1
Knot, Herschikking Brussels I, NTER 2013, 145

Kodek, EuVVO 2012 – neue Regeln für die internationale Urteilsanerkennung und -vollstreckung, Zak 2014, 424

Legrand, Compétence internationale, reconnaissance et exécution des jugements en matière civile et commercial dans l'espace communautaire: Quels changements en 2015?, Petites affiches N°. 4, 7 janvier 2015, p. 7
Leandro, Prime osservazioni sul regolamento (UE) n. 1215/2012 ("Bruxelles I bis"), Giust. proc. civ. 2013, 583
Leible, Die Zukunft des Europäischen Zivilprozessrechts, in: FS Peter Gottwald (2014) p. 381
Lupoi, La proposta di modifica del regolamento n. 44 del 2011: le norme sulla giurisdizione, in: Studi offerti a Federico Carpi (2012), p. 281

Magnus/Mankowski, Brussels I on the Verge of Reform, ZvglRWiss 109 (2010), 1
Magnus/Mankowski, The Proposal for the Reform of Brussels I – Brussels Ibis *ante portas*, ZvglRWiss 110 (2011), 252
Mankowski, Die Brüssel I-Verordnung vor der Reform, IGKK/IACPIL 1 (2010), 31
Markus, Probleme der EuGVVO-Revision: Begriff der Entscheidung und Abschaffung des Exequaturverfahrens, in: FS Ivo Schwander (St Gallen 2011), p. 747
Markus, Die Revision der Europäischen Gerichtsstandsverordnung und das Lugano-Übereinkommen von 2007, Jusletter 16.4.2012
Markus, Die revidierte europäische Gerichtsstandsverordnung – Eine "Lugano-Sicht", AJP 2014, 800
Niklaus Meier, Brüssel I-VO bis vs. LugÜ 2007 – eine Gegenüberstellung, Jusletter 14.1.2013
de Miguel Asensio, El nuevo Reglamento sobre competencia judicial y reconocimiento y ejecución des resoluciónes, La Ley/Unión Europea 8013 (31 de enero de 2013), 1

Peter Arnt Nielsen, The Recast of the Brussels I Regulation, in: Liber amicorum Ole Lando (2012), p. 257
Peter Arnt Nielsen, The State of Play of the Recast of the Brussels I Regulation, Nordic J. Int. L. 81 (2012), 585
Peter Arnt Nielsen, The New Brussels I Regulation, (2013) 50 C. M. L. Rev 503
Peter Arnt Nielsen, Den nye Bruxelles I-forordning, TfR 2013, 289
Peter Arnt Nielsen, The Recast Brussels I Regulation, Nordic J. Int. L. 83 (2014), 61
Nourissat, Refonte du règlement "Bruxelles I": much ado about nothing …, Procédures N° 3, mars 2013, alerte 26
Nuyts, La refonte du règlement Bruxelles I, RCDIP 102 (2013), 1
Nuyts, Bruxelles Ibis: présentation des nouvelles règles sur la compétence et l'exécution des décisions en matière civile et commerciale, in: *Nuyts* (éd.), Actualités en droit international privé (Bruxelles 2013), p. 77
Nuyts/Boularbah, Chronique Droit international privé européen, J. dr. eur. 2013, 405

Penasa, Il (lungo) cammino della riforma del Reg. Bruxelles I, Int'l. Lis 2010, 57
Penasa, Altre due tappe verso la riforma del Reg. Bruxelles I: la delibera del Parlamento Europeo e la proposta della Commissione, Int'l. Lis 2011, 4
Penasa, Ancora sulla revisione del Reg. Bruxelles I: la parola al Parlamento Europeo, Int'l. Lis 2011, 117
Penasa, La storia … infinita della revisione dell Regolamento Bruxelles I: l'orientamento generale del Consiglio UE, Int'l. Lis 2012, 114

Additional Bibliography

Miriam Pohl, Die Neufassung der EuGVVO – im Spannungsfeld zwischen Vertrauen und Kontrolle, IPRax 2013, 109

Rechberger, Über wiederkehrende Paradigmenwechsel im Europäischen Zivilprozessrecht, in: FS Peter Gottwald (2014), p. 517
Reinmüller, Neufassung der EuGVVO ("Brüssel Ia-VO") seit 10. Januar 2015, IHR 2015, 1
Rouchaud-Joët, Le nouveau règlement "Bruxelles I": réfonte des règles sur la compétence judiciaire, la reconnaissance et l'exécution des décisions en matière civil et commerciale, J. dr. eur. 2014, 2

Sagaut, La refonte du règlement Bruxelles I et l'exécution de l'acte authentique. "Et bien, circulez maintenant!", Defrénois 2013, 83
Saupe, Reform der Brüssel I-Verordnung, öAnwBl 2011, 137
Florian Scholz, Alles neu im Europäischen Zivilprozessrecht?, ecolex 2015, 4
Selie, De nieuwe Brussel Ibis-Vo op het vlak van de exequaturprocedere en de openbare orde-exceptie: meer praktische problemen dan praktische relevantie, TBH 2013, 334
Senoner/Weber-Wilfert, EuGVVO neu – praxisrelevante Aspekte, RZ 2015, 50
Silvestri, "Recasting Brussels I": Il nuovo regolamento n. 1215 del 2012, Riv. trim. dir. proc. civ. 2013, 677
Alexandra Simotta, Die Revision der EuGVVO – Ein Überblick, in: FS Daphne-Ariane Simotta (2012), p. 527
Ansgar Staudinger/Steinrötter, Zuständigkeit bei zivilrechtlichen Sachverhalten nach der Brüssel Ia-VO, JuS 2015, 1

Rolf Wagner, Die Brüssel Ia-Verordnung, TranspR 2015, 45
Matthias Weller, Der Kommissionsentwurf zur Reform der Brüssel I-VO, GPR 2012, 34
Matthias Weller, Der Ratsentwurf und der Parlamentsentwurf zur Reform der Brüssel I-VO, GPR 2012, 328
Zilinsky, De herschikte EEX-Verordening: een overzicht en de gevolgen voor de Nederlandse rechtspraktijk, NIPR 2014, 3.

List of Abbreviations

AA	Ars Aequi
AC	The Law Reports, Appeal Cases
Act. Dr.	Actualités de droit
AdvBl	Advocatenblad
AEDIPr	Anuario Español de Derecho Internacional Privado
AfP	Archiv für Presserecht
Afr. J. Int. Comp. L.	African Journal of International and Comparative Law
A-G	Advocate General (EU)
A-G	Attorney-General (Commonwealth)
A-G	Advocaat-Generaal (Netherlands)
AG	Amtsgericht
AG	Die Aktiengesellschaft
AIDA	Annali italiani de diritto d'autore, della Cultura e dello spettaculo
AJ	Actualités juridiques
AJT	Allgemeen Juridisch Tijdschrift
AktG	Aktiengesetz
All ER	The All England Law Reports
All ER (Comm.)	The All England Law Reports (Commercial Cases)
Am. Econ. Rev.	American Economic Review
Am. J. Comp. L.	American Journal of Comparative Law
Am. J. Int'l. L.	American Journal of International Law
Am. L. & Econ. Rev.	American Law and Economics Review
An. Der. Mar.	Anuario de derecho maritimo
Anh.	Anhang
Anm.	Anmerkung
Ann. Inst. dr. int.	Annales de l'Institute de droit international
AnwBl	Anwaltsblatt
AP	Arbeitsrechtliche Praxis
App.	Corte di appello (or: d'appello)
App. Cogn. Psych.	Applied Cognitive Psychology
Arb. Int.	Arbitration International
ArbG	Arbeitsgericht
Arm.	Armenopoulos
Arr. Cass.	Arresten van het Hof van Cassatie
Arr.Rb.	Arrondissementsrechtbank
Art.	Article
Aud. Prov.	Audiencia Provincial
AVAG	Anerkennungs- und Vollstreckungsausführungsgesetz
AWD	Außenwirtschaftsdienst des Betriebsberaters
BAG	Bundesarbeitsgericht
BAGE	Amtliche Sammlung der Entscheidungen des Bundesarbeitsgerichts

List of Abbreviations

BayObLG	Bayerisches Oberstes Landesgericht
BayObLGZ	Amtliche Sammlung der Entscheidungen des Bayerischen Obersten Landesgerichts in Zivilsachen
BayVBl	Bayerisches Verwaltungsblatt
BB	Betriebs-Berater
B2B	Business-to-Business
BBGS	Bülow/Böckstiegel/Geimer/Schütze, Internationaler Rechtsverkehr in Zivil- und Handelssachen (looseleaf München 1954-ongoing)
BC	Brussels Convention
B2C	Business-to-Consumer
BeckRS	Beck-Rechtsprechung
BerDGesVR	Berichte der Deutschen Gesellschaft für Völkerrecht
BerDGfIR	Berichte der Deutschen Gesellschaft für Internationales Recht
Berkeley J. Int'l. L.	Berkeley Journal of International Law
BezG	Bezirksgericht
BG	Bundesgericht
BGB	Bürgerliches Gesetzbuch
BGBl.	Bundesgesetzblatt
BGE	Entscheidungen des Schweizerischen Bundesgerichts – Amtliche Sammlung
BGH	Bundesgerichtshof
BGH-Report	Schnelldienst zur Zivilrechtsprechung des Bundesgerichtshofs
BGHZ	Amtliche Sammlung der Entscheidungen des Bundesgerichtshofs in Zivilsachen
BIE	Berichten intellectuële eigendom
BKR	Zeitschrift für Bank- und Kapitalmarktrecht
Bl.	Blatt
BOE	Bolétin Oficiál Español
BR-Drs.	Deutscher Bundesrat – Drucksachen
Brooklyn J. Int'l. L.	Brooklyn Journal of International Law
BT-Drs.	Deutscher Bundestag – Drucksachen
Bull. civ.	Bulletin des arrêts civiles
Bull. dr. banq.	Bulletin de droit et banque
B. U. L. Rev.	Boston University Law Review
Bus. & Leg. Prac.	Business and Legal Practice
BYIL	British Yearbook of International Law
CA	Cour d'appel
C. A.	Court of Appeal
Cal. L. Rev.	California Law Review
Cambridge L. J.	Cambridge Law Journal
Cambridge Yb. Eur. L.	Cambridge Yearbook of European Law
Cass.	Cour de Cassation
Cassaz.	Corte di Cassazione
CB	Convenio de Bruselas
CCC	Contrats concurrence consommation
C. civ.	Code civil

C. comm.	Code de commerce
CDE	Cahiers de droit européen
CDT	Cuadernos de derecho transnacional
cf.	*confer* [compare]
Ch.	Chapter
Ch. D.	Chancery Division
Chron.	Chronique
CID	Chronika Idiotikou Dikaiou
Cir.	US Court of Appeals for the Circuit
CISG	United Nations Convention on the International Sale of Goods
Civ. Just. Q.	Civil Justice Quarterly
C.J.	Chief Justice
CJEU	Court of Justice of the European Union
cl.	clause
CLC	Company Law Cases
Clunet	Journal du droit international, fondée par *E. Clunet*
C. M.L. Rev.	Common Market Law Review
Co.	Company
col.	columna
Col. J. Eur. L.	Columbia Journal of European Law
Col. J. Trans. L.	Columbia Journal of Transnational Law
Col. Jur.	Colectânea de Jurisprudência
Col. L. Rev.	Columbia Law Review
COM	Document of the Commission
Colo. L. Rev.	Colorado Law Review
Cornell Int'l. L. J.	Cornell International Law Journal
Cornell L. Rev.	Cornell Law Review
Corr. giur.	Corriere giuridico
Cour sup.	Cour superieure
CPR	Rules of Civil Procedure
CR	Computer und Recht
Ct.	Court
Cuad. der. trans.	Cuadernos de derecho transnacional
CYELS	Cambridge Yearbook of European Law Studies
Czech Yb. Int. L.	Czech Yearbook of International Law
D.	Recueil Dalloz Sirey
DAVorm	Der Amtsvormund
DB	Der Betrieb
D.C.	District of Columbia
DCCR	Droit de la consommation/Consumentenrecht
DEE	Dikaio Epicheirisseon kai Etairion
Denver J. Int'l. L. & Pol'y.	Denver Journal of International Law and Policy
Dickinson L. Rev.	Dickinson Law Review
Digest	Digest of case-law relating to the European Communities, Series D: Convention of 27 September 1968
DIN	Deutsche Industrie-Norm

List of Abbreviations

Dir. comm. int.	Diritto del commercio internazionale
Dir. com. scambi int.	Diritto comunitario e degli scambi internazionali
Dir. e giur.	Diritto e giurisprudenza
Dir. ind.	Diritto industriale
Dir. mar.	Diritto marittimo
Dir. scambi int.	Diritto comunitario e degli scambi internazionali
Div. Act.	Divorce: actualité juridique, sociale et fiscale
DMF	Droit maritime français
DNotZ	Deutsche Notar-Zeitschrift
Doc. Dir. Comp.	Documentação e Direito Comparado (Boletim do Ministério da Justiça)
D. R.	European Commission of Human Rights Decisions & Reports
Dr. & Patr.	Droit et Patrimoine
Dr. aff.	Droit des affaires
Dr. imm.	Droit de l'immateriél: informatique, médias, communication
Dr. soc.	Droit social
Dr. sociétés	Droit des sociétés
DStR	Deutsches Steuerrecht
DVBl	Deutsches Verwaltungsblatt
DWW	Deutsche Wohnungswirtschaft
DZWiR	Deutsche Zeitschrift für Wirtschaftsrecht
DZWIR	Deutsche Zeitschrift für Wirtschafts- und Insolvenzrecht
ead.	eadem (the same, female)
EAT	Employment Appeal Tribunal
EBLR	European Business Law Review
EBOR	European Business Organization Law Review
EC	European Community
ECHR	European Court on Human Rights
ECJ	European Court of Justice
ECLI	European Case Law Identifier
ECR	Reports of Judgments of the European Court of Justice
ed.	edition
ed.	Editor
éd.	éditeur
Edinburgh L. Rev.	Edinburgh Law Review
eds.	Editors
éds.	éditeurs
EF-Z	Zeitschrift für Ehe- und Familienrecht
EHRR	European Human Rights Reports
EIPR	European Intellectual Property Review
EJCCL	European Journal of Commercial Contract Law
EJN	European Judicial Network
Ell. Dik.	Elleniki Dikaiossyni
ELSA	European Law Students' Association
ELSA Malta L. Rev.	ELSA Malta Law Review
END	Epitheorissi Naftiliakou Dikaiou
ERCL	European Review of Contract Law

ERPL	European Review of Private Law
et al.	et alii
ETL	European Transport Law
ETS	European Treaty Series
EuGVÜ	Brussels Convention
EuLF	European Legal Forum
Eur. Hum. Rights J.	European Journal of Human Rights
Eur. J. L. & Econ.	European Journal of Law and Economics
Eur. J. L. Reform	European Journal of Law Reform
Eur. Lawyer	The European Lawyer
Eur. L. Rev.	European Law Review
Eur. L. Rptr.	European Law Reporter
Europa e dir. priv.	Europa e diritto privato
Europe	Juris-Classeur Europe
Eur. Rev. Publ. L.	European Review of Public Law
euvr	Zeitschrift für Europäisches Unternehmens- und Verbraucherrecht
EuZW	Europäische Zeitschrift für Wirtschaftsrecht
EvBl	Evidenzblatt
EWCA	England and Wales Court of Appeal
EWHC	England and Wales High Court
EWiR	Entscheidungen zum Wirtschaftsrecht
EWS	Europäisches Wirtschafts- und Steuerrecht
F. 2d	Federal Reporter, Second Series
Fam. L.	Family Law
FamPra.ch	Die Praxis des Familienrechts
FamRZ	Zeitschrift für das gesamte Familienrecht
fasc.	fascicule
FCR	Family Court Reports
F.D.	Family Division
FG	Festgabe
FGPrax	Praxis der freiwilligen Gerichtsbarkeit
FLR	Family Law Reports
fn.	footnote
Foro it.	Foro italiano
FPR	Familie Partnerschaft Recht
FS	Festschrift
F.S.R.	Fleet Street Reports
FuR	Familie und Recht
GATS	General Agreement on Trade in Services
Ga. L. Rev.	Georgia Law Review
Gaz. Pal.	Gazette du Palais
Geb.	Geburtstag (anniversary)
gen. ed.	general editor
gen. eds.	general editors
Geo. L.J.	Georgetown Law Journal
Giur. it.	Giurisprudenza italiana

Giur. mer.	Giurisprudenza di merito
Giust. civ.	Giustizia civile
Giust. proc. civ.	Il giusto processo civile
GmbH	Gesellschaft mit beschränkter Haftung
GmbHG	Gesetz betreffend die Gesellschaften mit beschränkter Haftung
GmbHR	GmbH-Rundschau
GPR	Zeitschrift für Gemeinschaftsprivatrecht
GRUR	Gewerblicher Rechtsschutz und Urheberrecht
GRUR Int.	Gewerblicher Rechtsschutz und Urheberrecht, Internationaler Teil
GRUR-Prax	Gewerblicher Rechtsschutz und Urheberrecht Praxis im Immaterialgüter- und Wettbewerbsrecht
GRUR-RR	Gewerblicher Rechtsschutz und Urheberrecht Rechtsprechungs-Report
GS	Gedächtnisschrift
GWR	Gesellschafts- und Wirtschaftsrecht
HAVE	Haftpflicht- und Versicherungsrecht
H. C.	High Court
HD	Højesterets Domme (Denmark) or Högsta Domstolen (Sweden)
HG	Handelsgericht
HGB	Handelsgesetzbuch
H. L.	House of Lords
Hof	Gerechtshof (Netherlands) or Hof van Beroep (Belgium)
Hof van Cass.	Hof van Cassatie
ibid.	ibidem
ICC	International Chamber of Commerce
ICCLR	International Company and Commercial Law Law
ICJ	International Court of Justice
ICLQ	International and Comparative Law Quarterly
id.	Idem (the same, masculine; also plural: the sames)
IGKK/IACPIL	Interdisziplinäre Studien zur Komparatistik und zum Kollisionsrecht/Interdisciplinary Studies of Comparative and Private International Law
IHR	Internationales Handelsrecht
IIC	International Review of Industrial Property and Copyright Law
ILM	International Legal Materials
I.L.Pr.	International Litigation Procedure
ILRM	Irish Law Reports Monthly
ILT	Irish Law Times
Inc.	Incorporated
Indiana J. Global Leg. Stud.	Indiana Journal of Global Legal Studies
Indiana L. Rev.	Indiana Law Review
InsO	Insolvenzordnung
InstGE	Entscheidungen der Instanzgerichte zum Geistigen Eigentum
Int. J. L. & Info. Tech.	International Journal of Law and Information Technology

Int'l. Bus. Law.	The International Business Lawyer
Int'l. Lawyer	The International Lawyer
Int'l. Lis	International lis
Int. Mar. & Comm L. Yb.	International Maritime and Commercial Law Yearbook
Int. Rev. IP. & Compet. L.	International Review of Intellectual Property and Competition Law
Int. Rev. L. & Econ.	International Review of Law and Economics
InVo	Insolvenz & Vollstreckung
IPR	Internationales Privatrecht
IPRax	Praxis des Internationalen Privat- und Verfahrensrechts
IPRE	Entscheidungen zum Internationalen Privatrecht (Austria)
IPRspr.	Deutsche Rechtsprechung auf dem Gebiete des Internationalen Privatrechts
IR	Informations rapides
I. R.	Irish Reports
ITRB	IT-Rechtsberater
J.	Justice
JA	Juristische Arbeitsblätter
J. App. Soc. Psych.	Journal of Applied Social Psychology.
JBl	Juristische Blätter
JBL	Journal of Business Law
JbPraxSch	Jahrbuch für die Praxis der Schiedsgerichtsbarkeit
J-Cl.	Juris-Classeur (répertoire)
JCP	Juris-Classeur Périodique, La Sémaine Juridique
J. dr. eur.	Journal de droit européen
J. Empir. Leg. Stud.	Journal of Empirical Legal Studies
J. Finance	Journal of Finance
J. Fin. Econ.	Journal of Financial Economics
JIBFL	Journal of International Banking and Financial Law
JIML	Journal of International Maritime Law
J. Int. Arb.	Journal of International Arbitration
J. IP Law & Practice	Journal of Intellectual Property Law and Practice
J. Corp. L.	Journal of Corporate Law
J. Econ. Behav. & Org.	Journal of Economic Behavior and Organizations
J. L. & Com.	Journal of Law and Commerce
J. L., Econ. & Org.	Journal of Law, Economics and Organization
J. Leg. Stud.	Journal of Legal Studies
jM	Juris Monatszeitschrift
JMLB	Jurisprudence de Mons, Liège et Bruxelles
JMLC	Journal of Maritime Law and Commerce
J. Personality & Soc. Psych.	Journal of Personality and Social Psychology
J. Pol. Econ.	Journal of Political Economy
JR	Juristische Rundschau
J. Risk & Uncert.	Journal of Risk and Uncertainty

JT	Juridisk Tidskrift vid Stockholms Universitet
J. trib.	Journal des tribunaux
J. trib. dr. eur.	Journal des tribunaux de droit européen
Jura	Juristische Ausbildung
jurisPR-ITR	juris PraxisReport IT-Recht
jurisPR-ZivilR	juris PraxisReport Zivilrecht
Jur. Rev.	Juridical Review
JuS	Juristische Schulung
JutD	Juridisch up to Date
JZ	Juristenzeitung
KantonsG	Kantonsgericht
KG	Kammergericht
King's Coll. L.J.	King's College Law Journal
K&R	Kommunikation und Recht
Kyungpook Nat. U. IT & L. Rev.	Kyungpook National University Information Techonoly & Law Review
LAG	Landesarbeitsgericht
LAGE	Entscheidungen der Landesarbeitsgerichte
L. & Contemp. Prbls.	Law and Contemporary Problems
LG	Landgericht (Germany), Landesgericht (Austria)
LIEI	Legal Issues of Economic Integration
lit.	littera
L. J.	Lord Justice
Lloyd's IR	Lloyd's Insurance Law Reports
Lloyd's Rep.	Lloyd's Law Reports
LLP	Limited Liability Partnership
LM	Lindenmaier, Fritz/Möhring, Philipp, Nachschlagewerk des Bundesgerichtshofs – Entscheidungen in Zivilsachen mit Leitsätzen, Sachverhalt und Gründen (München 1951 *et seq.*)
LMCLQ	Lloyd's Maritime and Commercial Law Quarterly
LMK	Lindenmaier/Möhring Kommentierte Rechtsprechung
LMLN	Lloyd's Maritime Law Newsletter
loc. cit.	loco citato
L. Q.Rev.	Law Quarterly Review
LRLR	Lloyd's Reinsurance Law Reports
Ltd.	Limited
Maastricht J. Eur. & Comp. L.	Maastricht Journal of European and Comparative Law
MarkenR	Markenrecht
Mass.	Massimario
M. B.	Moniteur belge
MDR	Monatsschrift für deutsches Recht
Melbourne U. L. Rev.	Melbourne University Law Review
Mich. J. Int'l. L.	Michigan Journal of International Law
MittBayNot	Mitteilungen für das Bayerische Notariat

MittPat	Mitteilungen der Deutschen Patentanwälte
M.L.Rev.	Modern Law Review
MMR	Multimedia und Recht
MNE	Multinational Enterprises
Mod. L. Rev.	Modern Law Review
M.R.	Master of the Rolls
MR	Medien und Recht
n.	numero
NB	Nomiko Vima
ncpc	Nouveau Code de Procedure Civile
NFL	National Football League
NGCC	Nuova giurisprudenza civile commentata
NILR	Netherlands International Law Review
NIPR	Nederlands Internationaal Privaatrecht
NIR	Nordiskt Immateriellt Rättsskydd
NJ	Nederlandse Jurisprudentie (Netherlands), Neue Justiz (Germany)
NJA	Nytt Juridisk Arkiv
NJOZ	Neue Juristische Online-Zeitschrift
NJW	Neue Juristische Wochenschrift
NJW-RR	NJW-Rechtsprechungsreport Zivilrecht
NLCC	Le nuove leggi civili commentate
no.	number (English) or numéro (French)
nr.	number
n. r.	not reported
Nr.	Nummer
NRt	Norsk Retstidende
NTBR	Nederlands Tijdschrift voor Burgerlijk Recht
NTER	Nederlands Tijdschrift voor Europees Recht
NTHR	Nederlands Tijdschrift voor Handelsrecht
NTIR	Nordisk Tidskrift for International Ret
núm.	número
Nw. J. Int'l. L. & Bus.	Northwestern Journal of International Law and Business
Nw. U. L. Rev.	Northwestern University Law Review
NVwZ	Neue Zeitschrift für Verwaltungsrecht
nyr.	not yet reported
N.Y. U. J. Int'l. L. & Pol.	New York University Journal of International Law and Politics
NZA	Neue Zeitschrift für Arbeitsrecht
NZA-RR	Neue Zeitschrift für Arbeitsrecht, Rechtsprechungs-Report
NZBau	Neue Zeitschrift für Baurecht
NZG	Neue Zeitschrift für Gesellschaftsrecht
NZI	Neue Zeitschrift für Insolvenz und Sanierung
NZKart	Neue Zeitschrift für Kartellrecht
NZM	Neue Zeitschrift für Miet- und Immobilienrecht

ObG	Obergericht
obs.	observations
öAnwBl	Österreichisches Anwaltsblatt
ÖBA	Österreichisches Bank-Archiv
ÖBl	Österreichische Blätter für gewerblichen Rechtsschutz und Urheberrecht
ÖJZ	Österreichische Juristenzeitung
ÖJZ-LSK	Österreichische Juristenzeitung – Leitsatz-Kartei
ØLD	Østre Landsrets Domme
ØLK	Østre Landsrets Kendelse
OGH	Österreichischer Oberster Gerichtshof
O. H.	Court of Sessions, Outer House
OJ	Official Journal of the European Community (or, since 2003, European Union)
OLG	Oberlandesgericht
OLG-NL	OLG-Rechtsprechung Neue Länder
OLG-Report	Schnelldienst zur Zivilrechtsprechung der Oberlandesgerichte (regional editions)
OLGZ	Rechtsprechung der Oberlandesgerichte in Zivilsachen
op. cit.	opere citato
Org. Behav. & Hum. Decision	Organization, Behavior and Human Decision
Oss. cost. Assoc. It. Cost.	Osservatorio costituzionale dell'Associazione Italiana del Costituzionalisti
p.	pagina
para.	Paragraph
Pas. belge	Pasicrisie belge
Pas. lux.	Pasicrisie luxembourgeoise
PHI	Produkt-Haftpflicht International
P & I	Protection and Indemnity
PIL	Private International Law
pp.	paginae (pages)
pr.	principio (at the beginning)
Pres.	President
Pret.	Pretore
Propr. Ind.	Proprietà Industriale
Psych. Rev.	Psychological Review
QB	The Law Reports, Queen's Bench Division
Q.B.D.	Queen's Bench Division
Q.C.	Queen's Counsel
Queen Mary J. IP	Queen Mary Journal of Intellectual Property
RabelsZ	Rabels Zeitschrift für ausländisches und internationales Privatrecht
Rb.	Rechtbank
RBDI	Revue belge de droit international
Rb. Kh.	Rechtbank voor Koophandel

RCDIP	Revue critique de droit international privé
RdA	Recht der Arbeit (Germany)
RDAI	Revue des affaires internationales
RDC	Revue des contrats
RDIPP	Rivista di diritto internazionale privato e processuale
RdTW	Recht der Transportwirtschaft
RdW	Recht der Wirtschaft (Austria)
Rec.	Recueil
Rec. des Cours	Recueil des Cours de l'Académie de Droit International de La Haye
REDE	Revista Española de Derecho Europeo
REDI	Revista Española de Derecho Internacional
Rel.	Tribunal da Relação
Rép.	Répertoire
Resp. civ. e prev.	Responsabilità civile e previdenza oggi
Rev. der. com. eur.	Revista de derecho comunitario europeo
Rev. dr. aff. int.	Revue de droit des affaires internationales
Rev. dr. comm. belge	Revue de droit commercial belge
Rev. dr. int. dr. comp.	Revue de droit international et de droit comparé
Rev. dr. transp.	Revue du droit de transport
Rev. jur. comm.	Revue de jurisprudence commerciale
Rev. not. belge	Revue du notariat belge
Rev. dr. ULB	Revue de droit de l'Université Libre de Bruxelles
Rev. Fac. Dir. Univ. Lisboa	Revista da Faculdade de Direito da Universidade de Lisboa
Rev. gen. Der. eur.	Revista general de Derecho europeo
Rev. héll. dr. int.	Revue héllenique de droit international
Rev. int. dr. écon.	Revue international de droit économique
Rev. jur. comm.	Revue de jurisprudence commerciale
Rev. Lamy dr. aff.	Revue Lamy droit des affaires
RLDA	Revue Lamy droit des affaires
Rev. Scapel	Revue du droit maritime, fondée par *Scapel*
RGDC	Revue génerale du droit civil
Riv. dir. ind.	Rivista di diritto industriale
Riv. dir. int.	Rivista di diritto internazionale
Riv. dir. proc.	Rivista di diritto processuale
Riv. it. dir. lav.	Rivista italiana di diritto di lavoro
Riv. not.	Rivista notarile
RIW	Recht der Internationalen Wirtschaft
RJC	Revista juridica de Cataluña
RJcom	Revue de jurisprudence commerciale
RNotZ	Rheinische Notar-Zeitschrift
RRa	ReiseRecht aktuell
r+s	Recht und Schaden
RSC	Rules of the Supreme Court
Rt.	Retstidning
RTDciv	Revue trimestrielle de droit civil
RTDcom	Revue trimestrielle de droit commercial

List of Abbreviations

RTDE	Revue trimestrielle de droit européen
RTDeur	Revue trimestrielle de droit européen
RTDF	Revue trimestrielle de droit financier
RTD fam.	Revue trimestrielle de droit familial
RvdW	Rechtspraak van de Week
R. W.	Rechtskundig Weekblad
S. C.	Supreme Court (United Kingdom or Ireland)
SchiedsVZ	Zeitschrift für Schiedsverfahren
sec.	section
sent.	sentence
seq.	sequens (if singular), sequentes (if plural)
sess.	session
S. I.	Statutory Instrument
sic!	Schweizerische Zeitschrift für Immaterialgüterrecht
Sh. Ct.	Sheriff Court
SJZ	Schweizerische Juristen-Zeitung
SLT	Scots Law Times
SLT (Sh Ct)	Scots Law Times (Sheriff Court)
SME	Small and Medium Enterprise
somm.	sommaires commentées
S & S	Schip en Schade
Stan. L. Rev.	Stanford Law Review
StAZ	Das Standesamt – Zeitschrift für das gesamte Standesamtswesen
STJ	Supremo Tribunal de Justiçia
sup.	superieur
Sup. Ct.	Supreme Court (USA)
SvJT	Svensk Juristtidning
Sw. J. Int'l. L.	Southwestern Journal of International Law
SZ	Sammlung in Zivilsachen (Austria)
SZIER	Schweizerische Zeitschrift für internationales und europäisches Recht
SZW	Schweizerische Zeitschrift für Wirtschaftsrecht
SZZP	Schweizerische Zeitschrift für Zivilprozessrecht
TBH	Tijdschrift voor Belgisch Handelsrecht/Revue de droit commercial belge
TGI	Tribunal de grande instance
TranspR	Transportrecht
Trib.	Tribunale
Trib. arr.	Tribunal d'arrondissement
Trib. civ.	Tribunal civil
Trib. comm.	Tribunal de commerce
TS	Tribunal Supremo
Trust L.J.	Trust Law Journal
Tulane J. Int'l. & Comp. L.	Tulane Journal of International and Comparative Law
TvA	Tijdschrift voor Arbitrage

TVR	Tijdschrift Vervoer en Recht
U. Chi. L. Rev.	University of Chicago Law Review
UCLA L. Rev.	University of California Los Angeles Law Review
UfR	Ugeskrift for Retsvæsen
U. Ill. L. Rev.	University of Illinois Law Review
U. Kan. L. Rev.	University of Kansas Law Review
UKSC	United Kingdom Supreme Court
UNIDROIT	International Institute for the Unification of Private Law
Unif. L. Rev.	Uniform Law Review
UNTS	United Nations Treaty Series
UPC	Unified Patent Court
U. Penn. J. Int'l. Econ. L.	University of Pennsylvania Journal of International Economic Law
ur.	editor
US	United States Reporter
v.	versus
Va. J. Int'l. L.	Virginia Journal of International Law
Va. L. Rev.	Virginia Law Review
Vand. J. Transnat'l. L.	Vanderbilt Journal of Transnational Law
VAT	Value Added Tax
V-C	Vice-Chancellor
VersR	Versicherungsrecht
VOB/B	Verdingungsordnung für Bauleistungen Part B
vol.	volume
VOL	Verdingungsordnung für Leistungen
VuR	Verbraucher und Recht
VVG	Versicherungsvertragsgesetz (German or Austrian Insurance Contracts Act)
Vzngr.	Voorzieningenrechter
Wash. U. L. Q.	Washington University Law Quarterly
WBl	Wirtschaftsrechtliche Blätter
WiB	Wirtschaftsrechtliche Beratung
WiRO	Wirtschaft und Recht in Osteuropa
WLR	The Weekly Law Reports
WM	Wertpapier-Mitteilungen
WPNR	Weekblad voor Privaatrecht, Notariaat en Registratie
WRP	Wettbewerb in Recht und Praxis
WuB	Entscheidungen zum Wirtschafts- und Bankrecht
WuW	Wirtschaft und Wettbewerb
Yale J. Int'l. L.	Yale Journal of International Law
Yale L.J.	Yale Law Journal
Yb. Eur. L.	Yearbook of European Law
Yb. PIL	Yearbook for Private International Law

List of Abbreviations

Zak	Zivilrecht aktuell
ZEuP	Zeitschrift für Europäisches Privatrecht
ZEuS	Zeitschrift für Europäische Studien
ZfJ	Zentralblatt für Jugendrecht
ZfRV	Zeitschrift für Rechtsvergleichung
ZfS	Zeitschrift für Schadensrecht
ZGE	Zeitschrift für Geistiges Eigentum
ZGR	Zeitschrift für Unternehmens- und Gesellschaftsrecht
ZGS	Zeitschrift für das gesamte Schuldrecht
ZHR	Zeitschrift für das gesamte Handels- und Wirtschaftsrecht
ZInsO	Zeitschrift für das gesamte Insolvenzrecht
ZIP	Zeitschrift für Wirtschaftsrecht und Insolvenzpraxis
ZLR	Zeitschrift für Lebensmittelrecht
ZPO	Zivilprozessordnung
ZR	Blätter für Zürcherische Rechtsprechung
ZRP	Zeitschrift für Rechtspolitik
ZSR	Zeitschrift für schweizerisches Recht
ZUM	Zeitschrift für Urheber- und Medienrecht
ZUM-RD	Zeitschrift für Urheber- und Medienrecht Rechtsprechungs-Dienst
ZVertriebsR	Zeitschrift für Vertriebsrecht
ZVglRWiss	Zeitschrift für vergleichende Rechtswissenschaft
ZVR	Zeitschrift für Verkehrsrecht
ZWeR	Zeitschrift für Wettbewerbsrecht (Journal for Competition Law)
ZZP	Zeitschrift für Zivilprozess
ZZP Int.	Zeitschrift für Zivilprozess International
ZZZ	Schweizerische Zeitschrift für Zivilprozess- und Zwangsvollstreckungsrecht

Regulation (EU) No. 1215/2012 of the European Parliament and of the Council of 12 December 2012 on jurisdiction and enforcement of judgments in civil and commercial matters (Recast)

Official Journal no. L 351, 20 December 2012, p. 1–32

THE EUROPEAN PARLIAMENT AND THE COUNCIL OF THE EUROPEAN UNION,

Having regard to the Treaty on the Functioning of the European Union, and in particular Article 67(4) and points (a), (c) and (e) of Article 81(2) thereof,

Having regard to the proposal from the European Commission,

After transmission of the draft legislative act to the national parliaments,

Having regard to the opinion of the European Economic and Social Committee,[1]

Acting in accordance with the ordinary legislative procedure,[2]

Whereas:

(1) On 21 April 2009, the Commission adopted a report on the application of Council Regulation (EC) No. 44/2001 of 22 December 2000 on jurisdiction and the recognition and enforcement of judgments in civil and commercial matters.[3] The report concluded that, in general, the operation of that Regulation is satisfactory, but that it is desirable to improve the application of certain of its provisions, to further facilitate the free circulation of judgments and to further enhance access to justice. Since a number of amendments are to be made to that Regulation it should, in the interests of clarity, be recast.

(2) At its meeting in Brussels on 10 and 11 December 2009, the European Council adopted a new multiannual programme entitled 'The Stockholm Programme – an open and secure Europe serving and protecting citizens'.[4] In the Stockholm Programme the European Council considered that the process of abolishing all intermediate measures (the exequatur) should be continued during the period covered by that Programme. At the same time the abolition of the exequatur should also be accompanied by a series of safeguards.

(3) The Union has set itself the objective of maintaining and developing an area of freedom, security and justice, inter alia, by facilitating access to justice, in particular through the principle of mutual recognition of judicial and extra-judicial decisions in civil matters. For the gradual establishment of such an area, the Union is to adopt measures relating to judicial cooperation in civil matters having cross-border implications, particularly when necessary for the proper functioning of the internal market.

(4) Certain differences between national rules governing jurisdiction and recognition of judgments hamper the sound operation of the internal market. Provisions to unify the rules of conflict of

---

[1] OJ C 218, 23.7.2011, p. 78.

[2] Position of the European Parliament of 20.11.2012 (not yet published in the Official Journal) and Decision of the Council of 6.12.2012.

[3] OJ L 12, 16.1.2001, p. 1.

[4] OJ C 115, 4.5.2010, p. 1.

jurisdiction in civil and commercial matters, and to ensure rapid and simple recognition and enforcement of judgments given in a Member State, are essential.

(5) Such provisions fall within the area of judicial cooperation in civil matters within the meaning of Article 81 of the Treaty on the Functioning of the European Union (TFEU).

(6) In order to attain the objective of free circulation of judgments in civil and commercial matters, it is necessary and appropriate that the rules governing jurisdiction and the recognition and enforcement of judgments be governed by a legal instrument of the Union which is binding and directly applicable.

(7) On 27 September 1968, the then Member States of the European Communities, acting under Article 220, fourth indent, of the Treaty establishing the European Economic Community, concluded the Brussels Convention on Jurisdiction and the Enforcement of Judgments in Civil and Commercial Matters, subsequently amended by conventions on the accession to that Convention of new Member States[5] ('the 1968 Brussels Convention'). On 16 September 1988, the then Member States of the European Communities and certain EFTA States concluded the Lugano Convention on Jurisdiction and the Enforcement of Judgments in Civil and Commercial Matters[6] ('the 1988 Lugano Convention'), which is a parallel convention to the 1968 Brussels Convention. The 1988 Lugano Convention became applicable to Poland on 1 February 2000.

(8) On 22 December 2000, the Council adopted Regulation (EC) No. 44/2001, which replaces the 1968 Brussels Convention with regard to the territories of the Member States covered by the TFEU, as between the Member States except Denmark. By Council Decision 2006/325/EC,[7] the Community concluded an agreement with Denmark ensuring the application of the provisions of Regulation (EC) No. 44/2001 in Denmark. The 1988 Lugano Convention was revised by the Convention on Jurisdiction and the Recognition and Enforcement of Judgments in Civil and Commercial Matters,[8] signed at Lugano on 30 October 2007 by the Community, Denmark, Iceland, Norway and Switzerland ('the 2007 Lugano Convention').

(9) The 1968 Brussels Convention continues to apply to the territories of the Member States which fall within the territorial scope of that Convention and which are excluded from this Regulation pursuant to Article 355 of the TFEU.

(10) The scope of this Regulation should cover all the main civil and commercial matters apart from certain well-defined matters, in particular maintenance obligations, which should be excluded from the scope of this Regulation following the adoption of Council Regulation (EC) No. 4/2009 of 18 December 2008 on jurisdiction, applicable law, recognition and enforcement of decisions and cooperation in matters relating to maintenance obligations.[9]

(11) For the purposes of this Regulation, courts or tribunals of the Member States should include courts or tribunals common to several Member States, such as the Benelux Court of Justice when it exercises jurisdiction on matters falling within the scope of this Regulation. Therefore, judgments given by such courts should be recognised and enforced in accordance with this Regulation.

(12) This Regulation should not apply to arbitration. Nothing in this Regulation should prevent the courts of a Member State, when seised of an action in a matter in respect of which the parties have entered into an arbitration agreement, from referring the parties to arbitration, from

---

5   OJ L 299, 31.12.1972, p. 32, OJ L 304, 30.10.1978, p. 1, OJ L 388, 31.12.1982, p. 1, OJ L 285, 3.10.1989, p. 1, OJ C 15, 15.1.1997, p. 1. For a consolidated text see OJ C 27, 26.1.1998, p. 1.

6   OJ L 319, 25.11.1988, p. 9.

7   OJ L 120, 5.5.2006, p. 22.

8   OJ L 147, 10.6.2009, p. 5.

9   OJ L 7, 10.1.2009, p. 1.

staying or dismissing the proceedings, or from examining whether the arbitration agreement is null and void, inoperative or incapable of being performed, in accordance with their national law.

A ruling given by a court of a Member State as to whether or not an arbitration agreement is null and void, inoperative or incapable of being performed should not be subject to the rules of recognition and enforcement laid down in this Regulation, regardless of whether the court decided on this as a principal issue or as an incidental question.

On the other hand, where a court of a Member State, exercising jurisdiction under this Regulation or under national law, has determined that an arbitration agreement is null and void, inoperative or incapable of being performed, this should not preclude that court's judgment on the substance of the matter from being recognised or, as the case may be, enforced in accordance with this Regulation. This should be without prejudice to the competence of the courts of the Member States to decide on the recognition and enforcement of arbitral awards in accordance with the Convention on the Recognition and Enforcement of Foreign Arbitral Awards, done at New York on 10 June 1958 ('the 1958 New York Convention'), which takes precedence over this Regulation.

This Regulation should not apply to any action or ancillary proceedings relating to, in particular, the establishment of an arbitral tribunal, the powers of arbitrators, the conduct of an arbitration procedure or any other aspects of such a procedure, nor to any action or judgment concerning the annulment, review, appeal, recognition or enforcement of an arbitral award.

(13) There must be a connection between proceedings to which this Regulation applies and the territory of the Member States. Accordingly, common rules of jurisdiction should, in principle, apply when the defendant is domiciled in a Member State.

(14) A defendant not domiciled in a Member State should in general be subject to the national rules of jurisdiction applicable in the territory of the Member State of the court seised.

However, in order to ensure the protection of consumers and employees, to safeguard the jurisdiction of the courts of the Member States in situations where they have exclusive jurisdiction and to respect the autonomy of the parties, certain rules of jurisdiction in this Regulation should apply regardless of the defendant's domicile.

(15) The rules of jurisdiction should be highly predictable and founded on the principle that jurisdiction is generally based on the defendant's domicile. Jurisdiction should always be available on this ground save in a few well-defined situations in which the subject-matter of the dispute or the autonomy of the parties warrants a different connecting factor. The domicile of a legal person must be defined autonomously so as to make the common rules more transparent and avoid conflicts of jurisdiction.

(16) In addition to the defendant's domicile, there should be alternative grounds of jurisdiction based on a close connection between the court and the action or in order to facilitate the sound administration of justice. The existence of a close connection should ensure legal certainty and avoid the possibility of the defendant being sued in a court of a Member State which he could not reasonably have foreseen. This is important, particularly in disputes concerning non-contractual obligations arising out of violations of privacy and rights relating to personality, including defamation.

(17) The owner of a cultural object as defined in Article 1(1) of Council Directive 93/7/EEC of 15 March 1993 on the return of cultural objects unlawfully removed from the territory of a Member State[10] should be able under this Regulation to initiate proceedings as regards a civil claim for the recovery, based on ownership, of such a cultural object in the courts for the place where the

---

[10]   OJ L 74, 27.3.1993, p. 74.

cultural object is situated at the time the court is seised. Such proceedings should be without prejudice to proceedings initiated under Directive 93/7/EEC.

(18) In relation to insurance, consumer and employment contracts, the weaker party should be protected by rules of jurisdiction more favourable to his interests than the general rules.

(19) The autonomy of the parties to a contract, other than an insurance, consumer or employment contract, where only limited autonomy to determine the courts having jurisdiction is allowed, should be respected subject to the exclusive grounds of jurisdiction laid down in this Regulation.

(20) Where a question arises as to whether a choice-of-court agreement in favour of a court or the courts of a Member State is null and void as to its substantive validity, that question should be decided in accordance with the law of the Member State of the court or courts designated in the agreement, including the conflict-of-laws rules of that Member State.

(21) In the interests of the harmonious administration of justice it is necessary to minimise the possibility of concurrent proceedings and to ensure that irreconcilable judgments will not be given in different Member States. There should be a clear and effective mechanism for resolving cases of lis pendens and related actions, and for obviating problems flowing from national differences as to the determination of the time when a case is regarded as pending. For the purposes of this Regulation, that time should be defined autonomously.

(22) However, in order to enhance the effectiveness of exclusive choice-of-court agreements and to avoid abusive litigation tactics, it is necessary to provide for an exception to the general lis pendens rule in order to deal satisfactorily with a particular situation in which concurrent proceedings may arise. This is the situation where a court not designated in an exclusive choice-of-court agreement has been seised of proceedings and the designated court is seised subsequently of proceedings involving the same cause of action and between the same parties. In such a case, the court first seised should be required to stay its proceedings as soon as the designated court has been seised and until such time as the latter court declares that it has no jurisdiction under the exclusive choice-of-court agreement. This is to ensure that, in such a situation, the designated court has priority to decide on the validity of the agreement and on the extent to which the agreement applies to the dispute pending before it. The designated court should be able to proceed irrespective of whether the non-designated court has already decided on the stay of proceedings.

This exception should not cover situations where the parties have entered into conflicting exclusive choice-of-court agreements or where a court designated in an exclusive choice-of-court agreement has been seised first. In such cases, the general lis pendens rule of this Regulation should apply.

(23) This Regulation should provide for a flexible mechanism allowing the courts of the Member States to take into account proceedings pending before the courts of third States, considering in particular whether a judgment of a third State will be capable of recognition and enforcement in the Member State concerned under the law of that Member State and the proper administration of justice.

(24) When taking into account the proper administration of justice, the court of the Member State concerned should assess all the circumstances of the case before it. Such circumstances may include connections between the facts of the case and the parties and the third State concerned, the stage to which the proceedings in the third State have progressed by the time proceedings are initiated in the court of the Member State and whether or not the court of the third State can be expected to give a judgment within a reasonable time.

That assessment may also include consideration of the question whether the court of the third State has exclusive jurisdiction in the particular case in circumstances where a court of a Member State would have exclusive jurisdiction.

(25) The notion of provisional, including protective, measures should include, for example, protective orders aimed at obtaining information or preserving evidence as referred to in Articles 6 and 7 of Directive 2004/48/EC of the European Parliament and of the Council of 29 April 2004 on the enforcement of intellectual property rights.[11] It should not include measures which are not of a protective nature, such as measures ordering the hearing of a witness. This should be without prejudice to the application of Council Regulation (EC) No. 1206/2001 of 28 May 2001 on cooperation between the courts of the Member States in the taking of evidence in civil or commercial matters.[12]

(26) Mutual trust in the administration of justice in the Union justifies the principle that judgments given in a Member State should be recognised in all Member States without the need for any special procedure. In addition, the aim of making cross-border litigation less time-consuming and costly justifies the abolition of the declaration of enforceability prior to enforcement in the Member State addressed. As a result, a judgment given by the courts of a Member State should be treated as if it had been given in the Member State addressed.

(27) For the purposes of the free circulation of judgments, a judgment given in a Member State should be recognised and enforced in another Member State even if it is given against a person not domiciled in a Member State.

(28) Where a judgment contains a measure or order which is not known in the law of the Member State addressed, that measure or order, including any right indicated therein, should, to the extent possible, be adapted to one which, under the law of that Member State, has equivalent effects attached to it and pursues similar aims. How, and by whom, the adaptation is to be carried out should be determined by each Member State.

(29) The direct enforcement in the Member State addressed of a judgment given in another Member State without a declaration of enforceability should not jeopardise respect for the rights of the defence. Therefore, the person against whom enforcement is sought should be able to apply for refusal of the recognition or enforcement of a judgment if he considers one of the grounds for refusal of recognition to be present. This should include the ground that he had not had the opportunity to arrange for his defence where the judgment was given in default of appearance in a civil action linked to criminal proceedings. It should also include the grounds which could be invoked on the basis of an agreement between the Member State addressed and a third State concluded pursuant to Article 59 of the 1968 Brussels Convention.

(30) A party challenging the enforcement of a judgment given in another Member State should, to the extent possible and in accordance with the legal system of the Member State addressed, be able to invoke, in the same procedure, in addition to the grounds for refusal provided for in this Regulation, the grounds for refusal available under national law and within the time-limits laid down in that law.

The recognition of a judgment should, however, be refused only if one or more of the grounds for refusal provided for in this Regulation are present.

(31) Pending a challenge to the enforcement of a judgment, it should be possible for the courts in the Member State addressed, during the entire proceedings relating to such a challenge, including any appeal, to allow the enforcement to proceed subject to a limitation of the enforcement or to the provision of security.

(32) In order to inform the person against whom enforcement is sought of the enforcement of a judgment given in another Member State, the certificate established under this Regulation, if necessary accompanied by the judgment, should be served on that person in reasonable time

---

[11]   OJ L 157, 30.4.2004, p. 45.
[12]   OJ L 174, 27.6.2001, p. 1.

before the first enforcement measure. In this context, the first enforcement measure should mean the first enforcement measure after such service.

(33) Where provisional, including protective, measures are ordered by a court having jurisdiction as to the substance of the matter, their free circulation should be ensured under this Regulation. However, provisional, including protective, measures which were ordered by such a court without the defendant being summoned to appear should not be recognised and enforced under this Regulation unless the judgment containing the measure is served on the defendant prior to enforcement. This should not preclude the recognition and enforcement of such measures under national law. Where provisional, including protective, measures are ordered by a court of a Member State not having jurisdiction as to the substance of the matter, the effect of such measures should be confined, under this Regulation, to the territory of that Member State.

(34) Continuity between the 1968 Brussels Convention, Regulation (EC) No. 44/2001 and this Regulation should be ensured, and transitional provisions should be laid down to that end. The same need for continuity applies as regards the interpretation by the Court of Justice of the European Union of the 1968 Brussels Convention and of the Regulations replacing it.

(35) Respect for international commitments entered into by the Member States means that this Regulation should not affect conventions relating to specific matters to which the Member States are parties.

(36) Without prejudice to the obligations of the Member States under the Treaties, this Regulation should not affect the application of bilateral conventions and agreements between a third State and a Member State concluded before the date of entry into force of Regulation (EC) No. 44/ 2001 which concern matters governed by this Regulation.

(37) In order to ensure that the certificates to be used in connection with the recognition or enforcement of judgments, authentic instruments and court settlements under this Regulation are kept up-to-date, the power to adopt acts in accordance with Article 290 of the TFEU should be delegated to the Commission in respect of amendments to Annexes I and II to this Regulation. It is of particular importance that the Commission carry out appropriate consultations during its preparatory work, including at expert level. The Commission, when preparing and drawing up delegated acts, should ensure a simultaneous, timely and appropriate transmission of relevant documents to the European Parliament and to the Council.

(38) This Regulation respects fundamental rights and observes the principles recognised in the Charter of Fundamental Rights of the European Union, in particular the right to an effective remedy and to a fair trial guaranteed in Article 47 of the Charter.

(39) Since the objective of this Regulation cannot be sufficiently achieved by the Member States and can be better achieved at Union level, the Union may adopt measures in accordance with the principle of subsidiarity as set out in Article 5 of the Treaty on European Union (TEU). In accordance with the principle of proportionality, as set out in that Article, this Regulation does not go beyond what is necessary in order to achieve that objective.

(40) The United Kingdom and Ireland, in accordance with Article 3 of the Protocol on the position of the United Kingdom and Ireland, annexed to the TEU and to the then Treaty establishing the European Community, took part in the adoption and application of Regulation (EC) No. 44/2001. In accordance with Article 3 of Protocol No. 21 on the position of the United Kingdom and Ireland in respect of the area of freedom, security and justice, annexed to the TEU and to the TFEU, the United Kingdom and Ireland have notified their wish to take part in the adoption and application of this Regulation.

(41) In accordance with Articles 1 and 2 of Protocol No. 22 on the position of Denmark annexed to the TEU and to the TFEU, Denmark is not taking part in the adoption of this Regulation and is not bound by it or subject to its application, without prejudice to the possibility for Denmark of

applying the amendments to Regulation (EC) No. 44/2001 pursuant to Article 3 of the Agreement of 19 October 2005 between the European Community and the Kingdom of Denmark on jurisdiction and the recognition and enforcement of judgments in civil and commercial matters,[13]

HAS ADOPTED THIS REGULATION:

Introduction

---

[13] OJ L 399, 16.11.2005, p. 62.

Bibliography

1. To the Brussels Ibis Regulation and the reform
Bach, Drei Entwicklungsschritte im europäischen
Zivilprozessrecht ZRP 2011, 97
Biddell, Die Erstreckung der Zuständigkeiten der
EuGVO auf Drittstaatensachverhalte – Unter be-
sonderer Berücksichtigung des Kommissionsvor-
schlags KOM (2010) 748 endg. (2014)
Bonomi/Schmid (eds.), Revision der Verordnung 44/
2001 (Brüssel I) – Welche Folgen für das Lugano-
Übereinkommen? (2011)
Boschiero, Il funzionamento del regolamento Brux-
elles I nell' ordinamento internazionale: note sulle
modifiche contenuto nella proposta di rifusione
des 2011, Dir. Comm. Int. 2012, 271
Cadet, Main features of the revised Brussels I
Regulation, EuZW 2013, 218
d'Avout, La refonte du règlement Bruxelles I, D.
2013, 1014
Dickinson, Surveying the Proposed Brussels Ibis
Regulation: Solid Foundations but Renovation
Needed, Yb. PIL 12 (2010) 247
Domej, EuGVVO-Reform, ecolex 2011, 124
Gaudemet-Tallon, in: Douchy-Oudot/Guinchard
(eds.), La justice civile européenne en marche (2012)
21
von Hein, Die Neufassung der Europäischen
Gerichtsstands- und Vollstreckungsverordnung
(EuGVVO), RIW 2013, 97
Hess, Die Reform der EuGVVO und die Zukunft des
Europäischen Zivilprozessrechts, IPRax 2011, 125
Lein (ed.), The Brussels I Review Proposal Uncov-
ered (2012)
Lenaerts/Stapper, Die Entwicklung der Brüssel
I-Verordnung im Dialog des Europäischen Ge-
richtshofs mit dem Gesetzgeber, RabelsZ 78 (2014)
252
Linton, The Brussels Ibis Regulation – Status quo or
A New Order for Enforcement, in: Essays in honour
of Michael Bogdan (2013) 275

Magnus/Mankowski, Brussels I on the Verge of Reform – A Response to the Green Paper on the Review
of the Brussels I Regulation, ZVglRWiss 109 (2010) 1
Magnus/Mankowski, The Proposal for the Reform of
Brussels I – Brussels Ibis ante portas, ZVglRWiss 110
(2011) 252
Mankowski, Die Brüssel I-Verordnung vor der Reform, in: *Verschraegen* (ed.), Interdisziplinäre Studien zur Komparatistik und zum Kollisionsrecht
Bd. 1 (2010) 31
de Miguel Asensio, El nuevo Reglamento sobre
competencia judicial y reconocimiento y ejecución
de resoluciones, La Ley, XXXIV, No. 8013, 31 Jan-
uary 2013, p. 1
Nielsen, The Recast of the Brussels I Regulation, in:
Liber amicorum Ole Lando (2012) 257
Nielsen, The New Brussels I Regulation, C.M.L.Rev.
2013, 503
Nuyts, La refonte du règlement Bruxelles I, RCDIP
2013, 50
Pertegas, The Revision of the Brussels I Regulation: A
View from the Hague Conference, in: Lein (ed.), The
Brussels I Review Proposal Uncovered (2012) 193
Pocar/Viarengo/Villata (eds.), Recasting Brussels I
(2012)
Pohl, Die Neufassung der EuGVVO – im Span-
nungsfeld zwischen Vertrauen und Kontrolle, IPRax
2013, 109
Reinmüller, Neufassung der EuGVVO ("Brüssel
Ia-VO") seit 10. Januar 2015, IHR 2015, 1
Solenik, Different legal traditions of procedural law
in international jurisdictions: the ECJ's approaches,
in: Picker/Heckendorn Urscheler/Solenik (eds.),
Comparative Law and International Organisations.
Cooperation, Competition and
Connections (2014) 73
Matthias Weller, Der Kommissionsentwurf zur
Reform der Brüssel I-VO, GPR 2012, 34.

2. To the former Brussels I Regulation

Anweiler, Die Auslegungsmethoden des Gerichtshofs der Europäischen Gemeinschaften (1997)

Bitter, Auslegungszusammenhang zwischen der Brüssel I-Verordnung und der Rom I-Verordnung, IPRax 2008, 96

Borrás, Legislation through Individual Case Law. The ECJ's Handwriting in the Brussels I Regulation, EuLF 2010, I-241

Brückner, Bindungswirkung an die Entscheidungen des EuGH im EuGVÜ und der Luganer Konvention, in: Hommelhoff/Jayme/Mangold (eds.), Europäischer Binnenmarkt. IPR und Rechtsangleichung (1995), p. 263

Buck, Über die Auslegungsmethoden des Gerichtshofs der Europäischen Gemeinschaft (1998)

Calvo Caravaca/Carrascosa González, Derecho Internacional Privado I (10th ed. 2009)

Colneric, Auslegung des Gemeinschaftsrechts und gemeinschaftsrechtskonforme Auslegung, ZEuP 2005, 225

Dasser/Oberhammer (eds.), Kommentar zum Lugano-Übereinkommen (LugÜ) (2008)

Duintjer Tebbens, L'interprétation dynamique, par la Cour de Justice Européenne, de la compétence en matière contractuelle (l'art. 5, 1° de la Convention de Bruxelles de 1968), in: Contributions in Honour of Jean Georges Sauveplanne (1984), p. 65

Duintjer Tebbens, Die einheitliche Auslegung des LugÜ, in: Reichelt (ed.), Europäisches Kollisionsrecht (1993), p. 49

Economides-Apostolidis, Brussels I in the European practice. How autonomous European concepts are developed by the ECJ, EuLF 2010, I-256

Freudenthal/van der Velden, La base juridique du droit processuel européen, in: FS Konstatinos Kerameus (2009), p. 1495

Hausmann, Die Revision des Brüsseler Übereinkommens von 1968, EuLF (D) 2000/2001, 40

Heidelberg Report see *Hess/Pfeiffer/Schlosser*

Hess, Methoden der Rechtsfindung im Europäischen Zivilprozessrecht, IPRax 2006, 346

Hess, Europäisches Zivilprozessrecht (2010)

Hess/Pfeiffer/Schlosser, The Brussels I Regulation – Report on its Application in 25 Member States (2008) (cited: Heidelberg Report)

Jayme/Kohler, Europäisches Kollisionsrecht 2005: Hegemonialgesten auf dem Weg zu einer Gesamtvereinheitlichung, IPRax 2005, 481

Junker, Vom Brüsseler Übereinkommen zur Brüsseler Verordnung – Wandlungen des Internationalen Zivilprozessrechts, RIW 2002, 569

Kennett, The Brussels I Regulation, (2001) 50 ICLQ 725

Kindler, Brussels I and the Principles of Autonomous Interpretation of EU Law, EuLF 2010, I-252

Kohler, Vom EuGVÜ zur EuGVVO: Grenzen und Konsequenzen der Vergemeinschaftung, in: FS Reinhold Geimer (2002), p. 461

Kropholler, Internationales Einheitsrecht (1975)

Kropholler, Die Auslegung von EG-Verordnungen zum Internationalen Privat- und Verfahrensrecht, in: FS 75 Jahre Max-Planck-Institut für Privatrecht (2001), p. 583

Lando, Vorabentscheidungsverfahren und Auslegungsprotokoll des EuGVÜ, in: Reichelt (ed.), Vorabentscheidungsverfahren vor dem EuGH (1998), p. 31

Lechner/Mayr, Das Übereinkommen von Lugano (1993)

Leible/Staudinger, Art. 65 EGV im System der EG-Kompetenzen, EuLF (D) 2000/2001, 225

Mankowski, Wie viel Bedeutung verliert die EuGVVO durch den Europäischen Vollstreckungstitel?, in: FS Kropholler (2009), p. 829

Martiny/Ulrich Ernst, Der Beitritt Polens zum Luganer Übereinkommen, IPRax 2001, 29

Micklitz/Rott, Vergemeinschaftung des EuGVÜ in der Verordnung (EG) Nr. 44/2001, EuZW 2001, 325 and EuZW 2002, 15

Moura Ramos, The New EC Rules on Jurisdiction and the Recognition and Enforcement of Judgments, in: Essays in honor of Arthur T. von Mehren (2002), p. 199

Nielsen, Brussels I and Denmark, IPRax 2007, 506

Oppermann/Classen/Nettesheim, Europarecht (4th ed. 2009)

Pålsson, Luganokonventionen (1992)

Pålsson, Revisionen av Bryssel- och Luganokonventionerna, SvJT 2001, 373

Pfeiffer, Internationale Zuständigkeit und prozessuale Gerechtigkeit (1995)

Piltz, Vom EuGVÜ zur Brüssel I-Verordnung, NJW 2002, 789

Reich, Understanding EU Law. Objectives, Principles and Methods of Community Law (2nd ed. 2005)

Rognlien, Luganokonvensjonen (1993)

Rühl, Das Haager Übereinkommen über die Vereinbarung gerichtlicher Zuständigkeiten: Rückschritt oder Fortschritt?, IPRax 2005, 410

Schack, Hundert Jahre Haager Konferenz für IPR. Ihre Bedeutung für die Vereinheitlichung des Internationalen Zivilverfahrensrechts, RabelsZ 57 (1993) 224

Schack, Die EG-Kommission auf dem Holzweg von Amsterdam, ZEuP 1999, 805

Schmidt-Parzefall, Die Auslegung des Parallelübereinkommens von Lugano (1995)

Schoibl, Vom Brüsseler Übereinkommen zur Brüssel-I-Verordnung: Neuerungen im europäischen Zivilprozessrecht, JBl 2003, 149

Scholz, Das Problem der autonomen Auslegung des EuGVÜ (1998)

Schwander (ed.), Das Lugano-Übereinkommen (1990)

Vandekerckhove, De interpretatie van europees bevoegdheids- en executierecht, in: van Houtte/Pertegás Sender (eds.), Het nieuwe Europese IPR: van verdrag naar verordening (2001), p. 11

Rolf Wagner, Zum zeitlichen Anwendungsbereich des LugÜ, ZIP 1994, 81

Rolf Wagner, Das Haager Übereinkommen vom 30.6. 2005 über Gerichtsstandsvereinbarungen, RabelsZ 73 (2009) 100

Watté, Les relations des Conventions de Bruxelles et de Lugano sur la compétence internationale et les effets des jugements, in: Fentiman/Nuyts/Tagaras/Watté (eds.), L'espace judiciaire européen en matière civile et commerciale (1999), p. 3.

I. The purposes of the Brussels *Ibis* Regulation

1 The Regulation on jurisdiction and the recognition and enforcement of judgments in civil and commercial matters, the so-called Brussels *Ibis* Regulation (in the following: the Regulation)[1] which is the subject of this commentary pursues a number of purposes. Its objectives are enshrined in the Recitals to the Regulation and they are further detailed in many judgments of the European Court of Justice. Though many of the fundamental judgments were rendered on the basis of the Brussels Convention of 1968 or of the Brussels I Regulation of 2001[2] they continue to be relevant also for the understanding and interpretation of the recasted Regulation.[3]

2 The ECJ has summarised the principles underlying the prior Brussels I Regulation (and its predecessor) as comprising the "free movement of judgments in civil and commercial matters, predictability as to the courts having jurisdiction and therefore legal certainty for litigants, sound administration of justice, minimisation of the risk of concurrent proceedings, and mutual trust in the administration of justice in the European Union."[4] These aims and principles continue to underlay the Brussels *Ibis* Regulation as well. The recasted Regulation intends to further these aims even more intensely than its predecessor, in particular

---

[1]   Regulation No. 1215/2012, OJ L 351, p. 1. A first amendment which brings the Unified Patent Court and the Benelux Court of Justice under the regime of Brussels *Ibis* has been adopted on 6 May 2014 by the Council and will enter into force soon.

[2]   Regulation No. 44/2001, OJ 2001 L 12, p. 1; last amendment: Regulation No. 416/2010 of 12 May 2010 amending Annexes I, II and III of the Brussels I Regulation, OJ 2010 L 119, p. 7.

[3]   As to the interpretation of the Regulation see *infra* Introduction note 91 (*Magnus*).

[4]   *TNT Express Nederland BV v. AXA Versicherung AG* (Case C-533/08) (2010) ECR I-4107 para. 49 (the Court referred to Recitals 6, 11, 12 and 15 to 17 in the Preamble to the former Brussels I Regulation.

through the abolition of the exequatur procedure and a better coordination of concurrent proceedings.[5] In addition, the Recast aimed at enhancing the effectiveness of choice-of-court agreements.[6] The further aim of the Recast Proposal,[7] to introduce far-reaching provisions for proceedings with links to third (Non-EU and Non-Lugano) states[8] was not realised.

Primarily, the Regulation intends to facilitate the judicial treatment of suits and judgments **2a** among the Member States. The Regulation aims at easier and more uniform rules and faster and simpler procedures for civil cross-border litigation within the EU.[9] It is based on the conviction that differences between national laws on jurisdiction and recognition of judgments and differing procedural formalities impede the judicial cooperation within the internal market. Difficulties to enforce civil claims in other Member States discourage persons to establish cross-border trade relations and hamper thereby considerably the sound operation of the internal market.[10] With the abolition of the exequatur procedure the Regulation makes another important step to remove a great deal of these differences and difficulties and attempts to enable and ensure the free movement of judgments almost as within a single state.[11] The Regulation is based on the principle of mutual trust in the legal system and judicial institutions of each other Member State, in the legality and correctness of judicial procedures taken, and decisions rendered, in other Member States.[12] The mutual trust includes the expectation that each Member State is willing to strictly obey to the provisions of the Regulation and to unhesitatingly enforce them through the national courts. The mutual trust argument was put to a hard test following the ECJ's rulings on different occasions, in particular in *Gasser*,[13] where the Court forced parties to endure delaying tactics in notoriously slow Member State jurisdictions. The Recast tried to remedy this shortcoming.[14]

A further purpose is to base jurisdiction, and thereby the defendant's obligation to submit to **3** the competent court's jurisdiction,[15] on uniform and fair connecting factors. The defendant must defend him- or herself only at places to which the dispute is sufficiently related to. For this reason the Regulation has abolished a number of national provisions on jurisdiction

---

5   See Recitals 1, 6, 15, 16, 21 and 26 Brussels I*bis* Regulation.

6   See Recital 22.

7   Proposal for a Regulation of the European Parliament and the Council on jurisdiction and the recognition and enforcement of judgments in civil and commercial matters (Recast) of 14 December 2010, COM (2010) 748 fin.

8   See Explanatory Memorandum to the Proposal, COM (2010) 748 fin. p. 1. and 8 *et seq.*

9   See Recitals 1 and 2.

10   Recitals 4 to the Regulation; see already to the prior law *Geimer/Schütze* A. 1 Einl. note 15; *Pfeiffer*, Internationale Zuständigkeit und prozessuale Gerechtigkeit (1995), p. 349, 762.

11   See Recital 26.

12   See Recitals 26; see also the ECJ in *Erich Gasser GmbH v. MISAT Srl*, (Case C-116/02) (2003) ECR I-14693, I-14746 *et seq.* para. 72; *Gregory Paul Turner v. Felix Fareed Ismail Grovit, Harada Ltd. and Changepoint SA*, (Case C-159/02) (2004) ECR I-3565 para. 24; *TNT Express Nederland BV v. AXA Versicherung AG* (Case C-533/08) (2010) ECR I-4107 para. 49; see further *Layton/Mercer* para. 11.015.

13   *Erich Gasser GmbH v. MISAT Srl*, (Case C-116/02) (2003) ECR I-14693.

14   See Recital 22 and the new Art. 31 (2) Brussels I*bis*.

15   Rather than with an obligation in the strict sense the defendant is only burdened with disadvantages (judgment by default etc.) if s/he omits to react to a suit instituted by the claimant.

which are regarded as exorbitant because they extend a court's competence too far.[16] Fairness is also granted by specific protective rules on jurisdiction in the interest of certain socially or economically weaker parties, namely insured persons, employees and consumers who in essence can only be sued in "their" forum.[17]

4 Another main objective is to secure the principle of legal certainty with respect to jurisdiction and the recognition and enforcement of judgments. The Regulation establishes a system of provisions, in particular on jurisdiction, the outcome of which must be "highly predictable".[18] This aims at the highest possible foreseeability and certainty in the application and interpretation of the provisions of the Regulation so that the parties can as far as possible rely in advance on these rules. In particular, a reasonable defendant should be able to foresee in which courts in the EU s/he could be sued.[19] Therefore, it is not a matter of discretion for the court seised whether to entertain a suit or not; the court is bound by the provisions of the Regulation. The doctrine of *forum non conveniens* so well known in Common Law jurisdictions had not survived under the Brussels I Regulation.[20] The Recast has introduced a certain degree of discretion, however only if proceedings within the EU concur with proceedings in third states.[21] Then the court in the EU may stay its proceedings under certain conditions.

5 While the Regulation aims on the one hand at security and certainty in cross-border litigation it pursues on the other hand also the objective to grant the parties the widest possible freedom to select the competent court.[22] Choice of court agreements are widely recognised

---

[16] See Artt. 5 (2) and 6 (2) in connection with Art. 76 (1) (a); thereto *von Hein*, RIW 2013, 102. However, towards persons domiciled in third states these exorbitant national jurisdiction provisions of the Member States remain applicable and respective judgments have to be recognised and enforced in the EU; see also Recital 27.

[17] See Artt. 10 *et seq.*, Artt. 17 *et seq.*, Artt. 20 *et seq.*

[18] See Recital 15; for statements of the ECJ to the same avail compare: *Owens Bank Ltd. v. Fulvio Bracco and Bracco Industria Chimica SpA*, (Case 129/92) (1994) ECR I-117, I-155 para. 32; *Custom Made Commercial Ltd. v. Stawa Metallbau GmbH* (Case 288/92) (1994) ECR I-2913, I-2956 paras. 15, 18; *Benincasa v. Dentalkit Srl*, (Case C-269/95) (1997) ECR I-3767, I-3798 para. 28; *Réunion européenne SA v. Spliethoff's Bevrachtingskantoor BV and Master of the vessel "Alblasgracht 002"*, (Case C-51/97) (1998) ECR I-6511, I-6548 para. 46; *TNT Express Nederland BV v. AXA Versicherung AG* (Case C-533/08) (2010) ECR I-4107 paras. 49, 53; see further *Layton/Mercer* para. 11.020.

[19] See the ECJ statements in *Jakob Handte & Co. GmbH v. Traitements Mécano-chimiques des surfaces SA*, (Case 26/91) (1992) ECR I-3967, I-3995 para. 18; *GIE Groupe Concorde et al. v. Master of the Vessel "Suhadiwarno Panjan"*, (Case C-440/97) (1999) ECR I-6307, I-6350 para. 24; *Besix SA v. Wasserreinigungsbau Alfred Kretzschmar GmbH & Co. KG (WABAG) and Planungs- und Forschungsgesellschaft Dipl. Ing. W. Kretzschmar GmbH &KG (Plafog)*, (Case C-256/00) (2002) ECR I-1699, I-1732 para. 52; *Andrew Owusu v. Nugent B. Jackson, trading as "Villa Holidays Bal-Inn Villas", Mammee Bay Resorts Ltd., Mammee Bay Club Ltd., The Enchanted Garden Resorts & Spa Ltd., Consulting Services Ltd., Town & Country Resorts Ltd.*, (Case C-281/02) (2005) ECR I-1383 para. 38; *TNT Express Nederland BV v. AXA Versicherung AG* (Case C-533/08) (2010) ECR I-4107 paras. 49, 53.

[20] *Andrew Owusu v. Nugent B. Jackson, trading as "Villa Holidays Bal-Inn Villas", Mammee Bay Resorts Ltd., Mammee Bay Club Ltd., The Enchanted Garden Resorts & Spa Ltd., Consulting Services Ltd., Town & Country Resorts Ltd.*, (Case C-281/02) (2005) ECR I-1383 paras. 37 *et seq.*

[21] See Artt. 33 and 34.

(Art. 25) and find their limits only where the Regulation provides for exclusive or protective jurisdiction.[23] Moreover, a defendant can always submit to an incompetent court's jurisdiction except where another Member State court has exclusive jurisdiction (Art. 26).

It is not a mere technical matter but is of high practical importance that the Regulation aims **6** at the widest possible avoidance of concurrent proceedings in different courts and of differing judgments on the same matter.[24] The Recast has improved the situation with respect to exclusive jurisdiction agreements. Contrary to the prior solution the chosen court now enjoys priority even if seised second.[25]

As regards the recognition and enforcement of judgments the Regulation is governed by the **7** principle of automatic recognition which can be refused for few reasons only and by the further principle that enforcement must be efficient and rapid.[26] That the Recast abolished the former exequatur procedure further facilitates the enforcement.

Last but not least the Brussels I*bis* Regulation aims at continuity with respect to its prede- **8** cessors, the Brussels Convention on Jurisdiction and the Recognition and Enforcement of Judgments in Civil and Commercial Matters and the Brussels I Regulation.[27] This continuity is further secured by the fact that the ECJ was already competent to interpret the Brussels Convention and remained and still remains competent to interpret the Regulation. Since the Brussels I Regulation modified the text and substance of the Convention only modestly[28] and since also Brussels I*bis* is a soft evolution of Brussels I most ECJ judgments on the Convention and on Brussels I remain valid under the recasted Regulation. The ECJ decisions can be found on the internet under www.europa.eu.int or under www.curia.eu.int.

II. The Brussels I*bis* Regulation as part of the European law of international civil procedure

1. The development of a European law of international civil procedure

The last one and half decades saw a true outburst of legislative activities of the European **9** Community in the field of international procedural law. Numerous Regulations and Directives on this subject where enacted since the Treaty of Amsterdam of 1997 amended the EC Treaty, established a single area of freedom, security and justice[29] and clothed the European Union with new competences in matters of administration of justice.[30] Except Denmark all

---

22   See Recital 19.

23   See Art. 24 (exclusive jurisdiction) and Art. 15, Art. 19, Art. 23 (protective jurisdiction).

24   Recital 21.

25   See Art. 31 (2) and Recital 22.

26   Recital 26.

27   See in particular Recital 34. As to the Brussels Convention see *infra* Introduction notes 9 *et seq.* (*Magnus*).

28   See thereto *infra* Introduction note 25 (*Magnus*).

29   Art. 67 Treaty on the Functioning of the European Union (TFEU; ex Art. 61 EC Treaty).

30   Art. 81 TFEU (ex Art. 65 EC Treaty); as to the legal base of the Community's competences in the field of international procedural law see *Freudenthal/van der Velden*, in: FS Konstantinos Kerameus (2009), p. 1495 *et seq.*

Member States of the Union accepted this extension[31] and are now directly bound by those Regulations and have to implement the respective Directives. This is also true for the new Member States which joined the EU in 2004, 2007 and 2013.

10 The main new instruments which have been created in the field of civil procedure since the Treaty of Amsterdam entered into force are the following (in the order of the time of their enactment):
– Regulation No. 1347/2000 on jurisdiction and the recognition and enforcement of judgments in matrimonial matters and in matters of parental responsibility for children of both spouses (29 May 2000; *so-called Brussels II Regulation*);
– Regulation No. 1348/2000 on the service in the Member States of judicial and extrajudicial documents in civil and commercial matters (29 May 2000; *Service Regulation*);
– Regulation No. 1346/2000 on insolvency proceedings (29 May 2000; *Insolvency Regulation*);
– Regulation No. 44/2001 on jurisdiction and the recognition and enforcement of judgments in civil and commercial matters (22 December 2000; *Brussels I Regulation*);
– Regulation No. 1206/2001 on cooperation between the courts of the Member States in the taking of evidence in civil and commercial matters (28 May 2001; *Evidence Regulation*);
– Council Decision establishing a European Judicial Network in civil and commercial matters (28 May 2001);
– Charter of fundamental rights of the European Union (2001);
– Directive No. 2003/8/EC to improve access to justice in cross-border disputes by establishing minimum common rules relating to legal aid and other financial aspects of civil proceedings (27 January 2003);
– Regulation No. 2201/2003 concerning jurisdiction and the recognition and enforcement of judgments in matrimonial matters and matters of parental responsibility (27 November 2003; *so-called Brussels IIbis Regulation*);
– Regulation No. 805/2004 creating a European enforcement order for uncontested claims (21 April 2004; *Enforcement Order Regulation*);
– Regulation No. 1896/2006 creating a European order for payment procedure (12 December 2006);
– Regulation No. 861/2007 establishing a European Small Claims Procedure (11 July 2007; *Small Claims Regulation*);
– Regulation No. 1393/2007 on the service in the Member States of judicial and extrajudicial documents in civil or commercial matters (service of documents), and repealing Council Regulation (EC) No. 1348/2000 (13 November 2007; new *Service Regulation*);
– Directive No. 2008/52/EC on certain aspects of mediation in civil and commercial matters (21 May 2008; *Mediation Directive*);

---

[31] According to the Protocol on the Position of Denmark to the Treaty on the European Union as revised by the Treaty of Amsterdam Denmark does not participate in, and is not bound by, measures in pursuance of the new competence. The EU and Denmark have, however, prepared separate instruments by which Denmark will take over single Regulations or Directives concerning judicial measures; a respective Treaty concerning the application of the Brussels I Regulation in Denmark entered into force on 1 July 2007: see Nielsen, IPRax 2007, 506 *et seq.*; since then the Brussels I Regulation was applicable in Denmark as well; by letter of 20 December 2012 Denmark notified the Commission of its decision to implement also the Brussels *Ibis* Regulation which thus also applies in Denmark; see *Nielsen*, in: FS Lando 90; see further *infra* Introduction notes 53 *et seq.* (*Magnus*).

- Regulation No. 4/2009 on jurisdiction, applicable law, recognition and enforcement of decisions and cooperation in matters relating to maintenance obligations (18 December 2008, *Maintenance Regulation*); Art. 68 (1) of this Regulation replaces those provisions of the Brussels I Regulation on maintenance (in particular Art. 5 No. 2 Brussels I Regulation);
- Regulation No. 650/2012 on jurisdiction, applicable law, recognition and enforcement of decisions and acceptance and enforcement of authentic instruments in matters of succession and on the creation of a European Certificate of Succession (4 July 2012, Succession Regulation);
- Regulation No. 1215/2012 on jurisdiction and the recognition and enforcement of judgments in civil and commercial matters (Recast) (12 December 2012, Brussels I*bis* Regulation) which replaces the Brussels I Regulation;
- Regulation No. 606/2013 on mutual recognition of protection measures in civil matters (12 June 2013, Protection Measures Regulation);
- Regulation No. 655/2014 of the European Parliament and of the Council establishing a European Account Preservation Order procedure to facilitate cross-border debt recovery in civil and commercial matters (15 May 2014, Preservation Order Regulation).

It is clear from this list which could be, and will be, still enlarged by further present[32] and **11** future[33] enactments that Europe faces the rapid emergence of a common European law of civil procedure.[34] Already now, almost all aspects which can arise in international civil litigation apart from arbitration[35] are dealt with by these instruments: jurisdiction, recognition and enforcement of judgments, service of claims, evidence abroad, legal aid, specific proceedings for payment orders, for uncontested and for small claims, insolvency proceedings and mediation. Yet, the different instruments do not cover all kinds of civil and com-

---

[32] Further Directives exist in special fields like for the reorganisation and winding-up of both insurance undertakings and credit institutions (Directive 2001/17/EC of the European Parliament and of the Council of 19 March 2001 on the reorganisation and winding-up of insurance undertakings, OJ 2001 L 110/28 and Directive 2001/24/EC of the European Parliament and of the Council of 4 April 2001 on the reorganisation and winding up of credit institutions, OJ 2001 L 125/15), on insurance mediation (Directive 2002/92/EC of the European Parliament and of the Council of 9 December 2002 on insurance mediation, OJ 2003 L 9/3) or on injunctions for the protection of consumers' interest (Directive 98/27/EC of the European Parliament and of the Council of 19 May 1998, OJ 1998 L 166/51). Also a Council Recommendation of 4 April 2001 on the principles for out-of-court bodies involved in the consensual resolution of consumer disputes, OJ 2001 L 109/56 can be mentioned. See also COM (2004) 718 final.

[33] See Proposal on a Regulation on jurisdiction, applicable law and the recognition and enforcement of decisions in matters or matrimonial property regimes, COM (2011) 126 fin. (of 16 March 2011); Proposal on a Regulation on jurisdiction, applicable law and the recognition and enforcement of decisions regarding the property consequences of registered partnerships, COM (2011) 127 fin. (of 16 March 2011); Proposal for a Regulation of the European Parliament and of the Council on promoting the free movement of citizens and businesses by simplifying the acceptance of certain public documents in the European Union and amending Regulation (EU) No. 1024/2012, COM (2013) 228 fin. (of 24 April 2013).

[34] And in the law of criminal procedure, too, a similar development can be observed as the Directive on the European seize order exemplifies.

[35] The most important aspects of arbitration are uniformly regulated on a global level by the United Nations Convention on the Recognition and Enforcement of Foreign Arbitral Awards of 1958.

mercial law disputes[36] nor have the instruments been enacted in a fully coordinated and systematic way. Nonetheless taken together they form at least a nucleus of a uniform code of international civil procedure for the EU. And it is evident that the development is still in the beginning and will continue.

2. Brussels I*bis* Regulation as the fundament of a European law of international civil procedure

12 Among the presently existing instruments on European international civil procedure the Brussels I*bis* Regulation is certainly the most important one. As compared to the other instruments it concerns the most important questions of international civil litigation, namely jurisdiction and recognition and enforcement of judgments. It has the widest scope of application since it covers almost all civil and commercial matters. Of all mentioned instruments it is most often applied: this is evidenced by much more than hundred judgments of the ECJ[37] and probably some thousand decisions of national courts (though many still on the Brussels Convention). It is best known due to the fact that it had two predecessors of identical structure and often same wording, the Brussels Convention on Jurisdiction and the Recognition and Enforcement of Judgments in Civil and Commercial Matters of 27 September 1968 and the Brussels I Regulation, and that these predecessors had been uniformly interpreted by the European Court of Justice since more than forty years. Within the European law of international civil procedure the Brussels I*bis* Regulation therefore constitutes the fundament on which all further development has built in the past and has to build also in the future.

3. Further surrounding international treaties

13 However, the European law of cross-border civil procedure as Community law is surrounded and supplemented by further international treaties on same matters. The mentioned Brussels Convention was superseded by the Brussels I Regulation (now replaced by the Brussels I*bis* Regulation)[38] already in 2001 as between all other Member States[39] and a little later even with respect to Denmark.[40] The Lugano Convention,[41] a treaty first (1988) enacted in parallel to the Brussels Convention, in 2007 adapted to the Brussels I Regulation, regulates the jurisdiction and recognition and enforcement of judgments between the EU Member States and the remaining Member States of the European Free Trade Association (EFTA), namely Iceland, Norway and Switzerland (Liechtenstein abstaining). The two Treaties together with the Brussels I*bis* Regulation constitute what is sometimes called the Brussels-Lugano Regime[42] which is more or less one single scheme of rules for international civil

---

[36] See still some of the exclusions listed in Art. 1 (1) and (2) Brussels I*bis*.

[37] Compare *infra* the register of ECJ judgments in the Table of Cases.

[38] Art. 80 Brussels I*bis* Regulation.

[39] Art. 68 Regulation. The Brussels Convention remains in force in those territories of the Member States to which the Brussels Convention was extended by its former Art. 60 or by special declaration of the respective Member State and to which the Regulation does not extend due to Art. 355 (2) TFEU (ex 299 (3) EC Treaty) in connection with Schedule II of the Treaty; see further *infra* notes 48 *et seq.* and the comments to Art. 68 (*Mankowski*).

[40] See thereto *infra* notes 53 *et seq.* (*Magnus*).

[41] See thereto *infra* notes 29 *et seq.* (*Magnus*).

litigation for the European Economic Area formed of the EU and the remaining EFTA Member States. However, after Lugano 2007 followed slavishly the Brussels I Regulation the new Brussels I*bis* Regulation opened again a certain gap between the Brussels and the Lugano instrument.

On the other hand did the former Brussels I Regulation not supersede existing conventions **14** to which a Member State of the Regulation was already a party and which in relation to particular matters governed also jurisdiction or the recognition or enforcement of judgments – like for instance the CMR or the Warsaw Convention.[43] Art. 71 (1) Brussels I*bis* Regulation upholds and continues this solution. But the competence to ratify, or accede to, new international conventions which contain provisions on jurisdiction or the recognition or enforcement of judgments has passed to the Community. The Community may, however, authorise the Member States to adopt respective conventions.[44]

4. A global Brussels I Convention?

Since long attempts had been undertaken to achieve a worldwide Convention on Jurisdic- **15** tion and the Recognition and Enforcement of Judgments in Civil and Commercial Matters. In 1992 the Hague Conference on Private International Law (HCCH) revived this ambitious venture. But again this project whose first attempts go back to 1925[45] failed due to irreconcilable differences between the United States and the EU countries, in particular with respect to the extent of jurisdiction. As a minimum compromise the Hague Conference prepared a rather limited project, namely a worldwide Convention on Choice of Court Agreements. It was finally concluded on 30 June 2005 on a diplomatic conference.[46] The Convention defines the requirements necessary for a valid jurisdiction agreement;[47] it regulates which consequences follow from a jurisdiction agreement with respect to the jurisdiction of the designated court and of other – derogated – courts;[48] and it deals with the recognition and enforcement of judgments rendered by a court designated by a jurisdiction agreement.[49] It remains to be seen how successful this Convention will be. The Convention gives priority to the Brussels I Regulation where the parties to the dispute are residents of a Regulation Member State or where the recognition or enforcement of a judgment based on a jurisdiction agreement between parties domiciled in these Member States is concerned.[50] In 2011 the Hague Conference on Private International Law resumed work on the 'Judgments Project' which is still in progress.[51]

---

[42]   Cf. for instance *Layton/Mercer* para. 11.001.

[43]   See Art. 71 (1) Brussels I Regulation. As to such Conventions see Art. 71 note 6 (*Mankowski*).

[44]   This has been so done, e.g., with respect to the Montreal Convention.

[45]   See *Schack*, RabelsZ 57 (1993) 224, 234 *et seq.*

[46]   The text is available under www.hcch.net/index_en.php?act=conventions.text&cid=98; see thereto *Brand/Herrup*, The 2005 Hague Convention on Choice of Court Agreements (2008); *R Wagner*, RabelsZ 73 (2009) 100 *et seq.*; for a survey *Rühl*, IPRax 2005, 410. A prior Draft of the Convention was published in 2004 (Work. Doc. No. 110 E of May 2004, also available under www.hcch.net).

[47]   See Art. 3 (c) of the Convention.

[48]   See Art. 5 and 6 of the Convention.

[49]   Artt. 8–15 of the Convention.

[50]   See Art. 26 (6) of the Convention.

[51]   See the information on the website of the Hague conference (www.hcch.net).

III. Historical background of the Brussels *Ibis* Regulation

16 The way to the present Regulation proceeded in several steps over now more than four decades. The second half of this phase brought about dramatic political changes in Europe and in its wake a rising interest of countries to join the EU which more than doubled the number of its Member States since 1989. This had repercussions also on the Community's policy concerning cross-border civil litigation and led to the insight that in a greater Community international treaties could not settle the problems of international civil procedure and provide the intended unification any longer in a satisfactory way but that directly applicable Community instruments were needed.[52] For, it became apparent that the method to adapt the original Brussels Convention with each new accession by a new international treaty which had to be ratified by each Member State was too slow and inflexible. This method caused troubling disharmony instead of the intended unification since while some Contracting States had already ratified the newest version others still adhered to the former or even older version.

1. The Brussels Convention of 1968

17 The development started with the Brussels Convention which was concluded as an international treaty on 27 September 1968. The Treaty was open only to Member States of the then European Economic Community (EEC) and came into force among them on 1 February 1973. The original Member States were the six founding members of the EEC, namely Belgium, France, Germany, Italy, Luxembourg and the Netherlands. The Convention was based on Art. 220 (the later Art. 293 EC Treaty which is now deleted from the TFEU) which obliged the EEC Member States to enter into negotiations "with a view to securing for the benefit of their nationals the simplification of formalities governing the reciprocal recognition and enforcement of judgments of courts or tribunals and of arbitration awards."[53] To come up to this mandate the six Member States instituted a Committee of Experts in 1960 which delivered a draft convention in 1964. However, in its draft the Committee did not confine itself to the preparation of rules on recognition and enforcement of judgments but formulated in a courageous step forward also rules on direct jurisdiction for international cases with a defendant domiciled in a Contracting State. These rules were intended to replace the respective national rules. This step was prompted by the insight that judgments could only be recognised and enforced if they were granted on the basis of the fair and reasonable jurisdiction of the court. Former concepts characteristic of the era of the nation state like reciprocity as well as nationality as a connecting factor were abandoned[54] and instead a Community approach was adopted which regarded the Member States merely as parts of one single greater unit. This new approach laid the foundation for the success of the Brussels Convention.[55] A further reason for the Convention's success was the fact that the

---

[52]   See also Recital 6.

[53]   It must be reminded that when Art. 220 was included into the EEC-Treaty of 1957 the UN Convention on the Recognition and Enforcement of Foreign Arbitral Awards of 1958 was still ahead. After its conclusion and after its success became apparent the Community refrained from preparing a rival convention although many European countries concluded and ratified the (Geneva) European Convention on International Commercial Arbitration of 21 April 1961.

[54]   See thereto Report *Jenard* paras. 63 *et seq.*

[55]   For a similar evaluation see *Layton/Mercer* para. 11.002; *Schlosser* Einl. note 4.

European Court of Justice was given jurisdiction to interpret the Convention by a separate Protocol[56] and that any national court could refer questions of interpretation to the ECJ. A still useful instrument of understanding the Convention is also the accompanying Report by *Jenard.*[57]

2. The revision of 1978

Each time that the Community was enlarged a revision of the Brussels Convention took **18** place (however, with the exception of the last enlargements in 2004 and 2007). The first of these occasions was the accession of Denmark, Ireland and the United Kingdom in 1973. Apart from necessary technical adaptations certain matters of substance in the original Brussels Convention were modified, in particular concerning jurisdiction over insurance and consumer disputes and commercial usages in connection with jurisdiction agreements. The first Accession Convention was concluded in 1978 and had to be ratified by all then nine Member States. This procedure lasted until 1988. A Report by *Schlosser* explains the Accession Convention of 1978.[58]

3. The revision of 1982

The next round was the Greek accession to the EEC in 1981. This led to a second Accession **19** Convention which was concluded on 25 October 1982 and finally ratified by all Member States in 1989. This time no further substantive changes of the Brussels Convention were made. *Evrigenis* and *Kerameus* delivered the explaining Report.[59]

4. The revision of 1989

In 1986 Portugal and Spain joined the EEC and the next Accession Convention became **20** necessary. It was concluded on 26 May 1989. The last ratification of this Accession Convention by the then twelve Member States occurred in 1997.[60] This third Accession Convention brought about a number of substantive changes in order to adapt the Brussels Convention to the Lugano Convention which had been meanwhile concluded.[61] The most important modifications were a new jurisdiction provision on employment contracts and a specification of the form in which in international trade and commerce jurisdiction agreements can be concluded. The accompanying Report was prepared by *Almeida Cruz, Desantes Real* and *Jenard.*[62]

5. The Lugano Convention of 1988

In 1988 the then EC and the Member States of the European Free Trade Association **21**

---

[56]   The Protocol on the Interpretation of the Brussels Convention by the European Court of Justice was concluded on 3 June 1971 and entered into force on 1 September 1975.

[57]   OJ of 5 March 1979 C 59/1.

[58]   OJ of 5 March 1979 C 59/71.

[59]   OJ of 24 November 1986 C 298/1.

[60]   On 1 October 1997 by Belgium (see BGBl 1998 II 230).

[61]   See thereto *infra* Introduction notes 29 *et seq.* (*Magnus*).

[62]   OJ of 28 July 1990 C 189/35.

(EFTA)[63] agreed on the Lugano Convention[64] which was designed as a parallel convention to the Brussels Convention in order to unify the jurisdiction rules and to enable the free movement of judgments also among the Member States of both organisations which together form the European Economic Area (EEA). Also other states were, and are, allowed to join the Lugano Convention. Poland was the first (and thus far only) state from outside the former EC and EFTA to ratify the Lugano Convention and did so in 2000; but in 2004 Poland joined also the EU. *Jenard* and *Möller* prepared the accompanying Report of the Lugano Convention.[65]

6. The revision of the Brussels Convention of 1996

22 The last and fourth Accession Convention followed the so-called northern enlargement of the European Union when Austria, Finland and Sweden joined the EU in 1995. This Accession Convention was concluded on 29 November 1996 and had been ratified by all – then fifteen – Member States except Belgium until 1 March 2002 when the Regulation replaced the Brussels Convention. As in the case of Greece's accession, also the Accession Convention of 1996 brought about mere technical adaptations but no substantial modifications of the Brussels Convention.

7. The Brussels I Regulation of 2001

23 In the mid-nineties of the last century a more extended revision of the Brussels Convention and the Lugano Convention and their full alignment was felt necessary. In order not to overburden and delay the Accession Convention of 1996 it was decided to pursue this reform of the Brussels-Lugano Regime separately. The Commission prepared a Proposal for a fifth Revision Treaty of the Brussels Convention;[66] but that was overtaken by the new policy under the Treaty of Amsterdam which integrated the so-called *third pillar* – the intergovernmental cooperation in matters of police and administration of justice – into the Treaty (Art. 61 *et seq.* EC Treaty; now Art. 67 *et seq.* TFEU), made it a Community policy *(first pillar)* and created a Community competence to act by the instrument of regulation in this field. The Commission brought then forward a Draft Regulation with an Explanatory Memorandum on 14 July 1999.[67] After the Parliament had proposed several amendments,[68] the Commission published on 26 October 2000 a slightly amended Draft Proposal again with a (short) Explanatory Memorandum.[69] With few further adjustments this Draft was

---

[63] The European Free Trade Association was founded in 1960. Its present members are Iceland, Liechtenstein, Norway and Switzerland. Together, the EFTA and the EU States form the European Economic Area (EEA).

[64] See on the Lugano Convention also *infra* Introduction notes 29 *et seq.* (*Magnus*).

[65] OJ of 28 July 1990 C 189/57.

[66] COM (1997) 609 final, OJ 1998 C 33/20.

[67] COM (1999) 348 final, OJ 1999, C 376E/1.

[68] See Proposal for a Council regulation on jurisdiction and the recognition and enforcement of judgements in civil and commercial matters (COM (1999) 348 – C5-0169/1999 – 1999/0154(CNS)), OJ 2001 C 146/94.

[69] COM (2000) 689 final, OJ 2001 C 62E/243.

adopted by the Council on 22 December 2000 as Regulation No. 44/2001[70] and entered into force on 1 March 2002. The basis of the Regulation is the Brussels Convention in its last version of 1996. But the Regulation introduced also a number of changes.

Since not all EU States favoured the unifying approach of Artt. 61 *et seq.* EC Treaty the **24** possibility of specific reservations was provided for. Art. 69 EC Treaty and accompanying protocols reserve an "opt-in" solution for the United Kingdom and Ireland and allow Denmark totally to abstain. The United Kingdom and Ireland have opted in; between Denmark and the EU a separate treaty[71] has been concluded for the more or less full application of the Brussels I Regulation in Denmark. This treaty entered into force on 1 July 2007.[72]

8. The main differences between the Brussels I Regulation and the Brussels Convention and the 1988 Lugano Convention

The main amendments which the Brussels I Regulation brought about as compared to the **25** Brussels Convention and the 1988 Lugano Convention were the following ones:
- Art. 5 (1) – autonomous definition of the place of performance for supply and service contracts;[73]
- Art. 5 (3) – extension of tort jurisdiction to threatened damage;[74]
- Art. 6 no. 1 – jurisdiction in case of several defendants only if close connection between the claims;[75]
- Art. 9 (1) (b) – jurisdiction for claims not only of the policyholder but now also of the insured and of a beneficiary at his domicile;[76]
- Art. 15 (1) (c) and (3) – extension of protective jurisdiction to all consumer contracts, including package tour contracts; sufficient for jurisdiction that offer or directed activities to state of consumer's domicile;[77]
- Art. 16 (1) – regulates not only the international but also the local jurisdiction;[78]
- Artt. 18–21 – a separate section now provides for the jurisdiction over employment contracts and for specific protection of employees who can only be sued at their domicile;[79]

---

[70] Council Regulation (EC) No. 44/2001 of 22 December 2000 on jurisdiction and the recognition and enforcement of judgments in civil and commercial matters, OJ 2001 L 12/1.

[71] As to the text see OJ 2005 L 299/62.

[72] OJ 2007 L 94/70; see thereto *Nielsen*, IPRax 2007, 506 *et seq.*

[73] No equivalent in Art. 5 (1) Brussels and Lugano Conventions.

[74] No equivalent in Art. 5 (3) Brussels and Lugano Conventions.

[75] No equivalent in Art. 6 (1) Brussels and Lugano Conventions but practice of the ECJ: *Athanasios Kalfelis v. Bankhaus Schröder Münchmeyer Hengst & Cie.* (Case 189/87) (1988) ECR 5565.

[76] No equivalent in Art. 8 (1) (2) Brussels and Lugano Conventions.

[77] Art. 13 Brussels and Lugano Conventions confines consumer protection to contracts for the supply of goods and services, excludes generally contracts of transport and requires that the offer or approached the consumer in the latter's State of domicile.

[78] Art. 14 Brussels and Lugano Conventions regulate only the international jurisdiction.

[79] Artt. 5 (1) and 17 (5) Brussels and Lugano Conventions prescribe only a specific place of performance for employment contracts and allow jurisdiction agreements for employment contracts only after the dispute has arisen or, under Art. 17 (5) Brussels Convention, the employee invokes it.

- Art. 22 no. 1 – the tenancy exception applies only where the tenant is a natural person;[80]
- Art. 23 – a jurisdiction agreement has exclusive effect only if not otherwise agreed (par. 1 sent. 2);[81] electronic communication is equivalent to writing (par. 2);[82] jurisdiction agreements for the benefit of only one of the parties are no longer specifically mentioned;[83]
- Art. 26 (3) – reference is now made to the Service Regulation;[84]
- Art. 28 (2) – instead of the law of the court later seised[85] it is now the law of the court first seised which must permit the consolidation of the related actions;
- Art. 30 – autonomous definition of when a court is deemed to be seised;[86]
- Art. 34 – the grounds for non-recognition of judgments have been reduced: the requirement of conformity with conflicts rules has been removed;[87] the public policy clause (no. 1) is formulated in a stricter way (*"manifestly* contrary to public policy");[88] lack of service or failure of correct service does not hinder recognition of default judgments if the defendant did not attack the judgment itself though this was possible for him (no. 2);[89] in no. 4 now also judgments of other Member States are mentioned;[90]
- Art. 35 – does not contain the grounds listed in Art. 28 (2) and (4) Lugano Convention;
- Artt. 41 *et seq.* – examination of formalities only (Art. 53) for immediate enforcement without regard to grounds for non-recognition; examination of those grounds only on appeal (Art. 43 and 45);[91]
- Art. 60 (1) – autonomous definition of the place of domicile;[92]
- Art. 71 (1) – future international conventions on particular matters containing rules on jurisdiction or recognition or enforcement do not prevail over the Regulation as they did with respect to the Brussels and 1988 Lugano Convention.[93]

---

[80]   This corresponds to Art. 16 (1) (b) Lugano Convention but modifies Art. 16 (1) (b) Brussels Convention which required that both landlord and tenant were natural persons.

[81]   Art. 17 (1) sent 1 Brussels and Lugano Convention does not mention that the parties may agree otherwise.

[82]   No equivalent in Art. 17 Brussels and Lugano Conventions.

[83]   In contrast to Art. 17 (4) Brussels and Lugano Conventions.

[84]   But the Hague Service Convention of 15 November 1965 – mentioned by Art. 20 (3) Brussels and Lugano Conventions – remains applicable where the Service Regulation does not apply (Art. 26 (4) Brussels Regulation; now Art. 28 (4) Brussels *Ibis* Regulation).

[85]   As under Art. 22 (2) Brussels and Lugano Conventions.

[86]   No equivalent in Artt. 21–23 Brussels and Lugano Conventions; under the Conventions the question is therefore to be answered according to the *lex fori* of the court seised; see *Siegfried Zelger v. Sebastiano Salinitri*, (Case 56/79) (1980) ECR 89.

[87]   It is contained in Art. 27 (4) Brussels and Lugano Conventions.

[88]   In contrast to Art. 27 (1) Brussels and Lugano Conventions ("contrary to public policy").

[89]   Art. 27 (2) Brussels and Lugano Conventions requires due service and disregards the possibility to challenge the default judgment itself.

[90]   In contrast to Art. 27 (5) Brussels and Lugano Conventions.

[91]   Artt. 31 *et seq.* Brussels and Lugano Conventions provide for an entirely different scheme under which a declaration of enforceability must be sought for which the grounds for non-recognition have to be examined (Art. 34 (2)).

[92]   Whereas under Art. 53 (1) sent. 2 Brussels and Lugano Conventions the seat of a company or other legal person or association is to be determined according to the rules of private international law.

[93]   Since the accession to such conventions is now the competence of the Community which may authorise the Member States to accede.

In essence, the amendments extended the field where the Regulation autonomously governs; **26** they strengthened the protection of the weaker party and they simplified the recognition of judgments rendered in other Member States and the procedure of their enforcement.

9. The Brussels I*bis* Regulation of 2012 (Recast)

On the whole, the Brussels I Regulation worked quite satisfactorily. Nonetheless, some **26a** shortcomings were complained of: in particular the Gasser decision of the ECJ[94] aroused criticism.[95] In that case a negative declaratory claim in Italy trumped the choice-of-court agreement by which the parties had selected Austrian jurisdiction. In the view of the ECJ the priority rules of the Brussels I Regulation obliged the Austrian party to wait until the Italian court had decided on its jurisdiction. It was no counter-argument that Italian courts were notoriously slow and delayed decisions for years so that suits there could be easily used – or better misused – for tactical purposes to avoid payments. So-called Italian torpedoes became known as a procedural weapon. Since the ECJ also denied the possibility to raise anti-suit injunctions against such torpedo suits[96] a party could stop this misuse only by the immediate institution of a lawsuit in a reasonably quick jurisdiction which was competent. In the interest of out-of-court settlements this procedural race to the courthouse was hardly desirable. On the contrary, there was some urgency to change this solution and to strengthen the effectiveness of jurisdiction agreements. It was therefore no surprise that one of the most prominent objectives of the Recast aimed at the remedial of this situation.[97] The reversal of the priority rule in case of an exclusive jurisdiction agreement (now Art. 31 (2)) indeed remedies the Gasser-situation.

The Proposal for the Recast had further aims: to abolish the exequatur procedure, to extend **26b** the Regulation's jurisdiction rules to third country defendants, to improve the interface between the Regulation and arbitration, to better coordinate proceedings before the courts of the Member States, to improve the access to justice for certain specific disputes and to clarify the conditions under which provisional and protective measures can circulate in the EU.[98] The Recast[99] realised only few of them. Many of the modifications are – like in Gasser – a reaction to the case law of the ECJ.[100]

Apart from a renumbering and mere technical changes the main modifications of Brussels **26c** I*bis* in comparison to Brussels I are the following:
- Art. 1 (2) (d) – the exclusion of arbitration is now further explained and specified in Recital 12;
- Art. 2 – assembles definitions which were spread over the former Regulation and adds some which had developed over time;
- Art. 6 (1) – extends the applicability of the Regulation to further cases where the defendant is not seated in the EU (claims of consumers and employees);

---

[94] *Erich Gasser GmbH v. MISAT Srl*, (Case C-116/02,) (2003) ECR I-14693.
[95] See the Heidelberg Report notes 388 ss., 715 ss.
[96] See *Allianz S.p.A. a. o. v. West Tankers Inc.*, (Case C-185/07) (2009) ECR I-663.
[97] See Explanatory Memorandum to the Proposal (COM (2010) 748 fin.) p. 4, 9 s.
[98] See Explanatory Memorandum to the Proposal (COM (2010) 748 fin.) p. 4 s.
[99] For a concise survey on the different preparatory steps of the Recast see *von Hein*, RIW 2013, 97 s.
[100] See *Lenaerts/Stapper*, RabelsZ 78 (2014) 252 ss.

- Art. 7 – the former provision on the special jurisdiction in maintenance matters has been deleted due to the Maintenance Regulation no. 4/2009;
- Art. 7 no. 4 – adds a new special jurisdiction for the recovery of cultural goods;
- Art. 18 (1) and 21 (1) – consumers and employees can sue the other party at the consumer's/employee's domicile irrespective whether the other party is domiciled in a Member State or not;
- Art. 20 (1) – allows the employee in case of closely connected claims to sue several employers in the courts at the place where one of them is domiciled;
- Art. 21 (1) (b) (i) – has inserted "or from where" the employee habitually carries out his work and aligns the provision with Art. 8 (2) Rome I Regulation;
- Art. 24 no. 4 – codifies the ECJ jurisprudence[101] that the exclusive jurisdiction at the place of the necessary deposit or registration of immaterial property rights is engaged even if the lack of validity of the patent etc. is merely raised as defence;
- Art. 25 (1) – abandons the requirement of the domicile of one party of a jurisdiction agreement in a Member State and introduces a conflicts rule for the substantive validity of such agreement;
- Art. 25 (5) – expressly stresses the independence of the jurisdiction agreement from the main contract;
- Art. 26 (2) – obliges the court to inform defendants who are insured (etc.) persons, consumers or employees of their right to contest the jurisdiction before they submit to an incompetent court;
- Art. Art. 29 (2) – obliges the courts of concurrent proceedings to inform each other – on request – of the date when they were seised;
- Art. 31 (2)-(4) – changes the general priority rule in cases of exclusive jurisdiction agreements except where the agreement violates the protective jurisdiction for insured (etc.) persons, consumers and employees;
- Artt. 33 and 34 – are entirely new; they regulate the concurrence of proceedings in Member States and third states on the same matter or on related actions and grant the Member States' courts discretion to stay proceedings under certain conditions;
- Art. 36 ss. – the whole part on recognition and enforcement has been restructured although the substantive modifications are limited;
- Art. 39 – abolishes the former exequatur procedure; however, a right to attack the recognition and enforcement of a judgment for certain grounds remains available (Artt. 45 ss.);
- Art. 45 (1) (e) (i) – adds the violation of the protective jurisdiction for employees to the grounds for the non-recognition and non-enforcement of a judgment;
- Art. 54 (1) – obliges the court of the enforcement state to adapt unknown measures in the judgement to equivalent measures known in the enforcement state;
- Art. 55 – provides that judgments on penalties are enforceable if the court of origin finally fixed the amount of the penalty;
- Art. 58 and 59 – prescribes that authentic instruments and court settlements which are enforceable in the (EU) state of origin are also enforceable without further procedure in the other Member States; however, their enforcement may be attacked for the same reasons as judgments; in addition, the enforcement court can – as before[102] – refuse

---

[101] *GAT v. LuK* (C-4/03) (2006) ECR I-6509.
[102] Art. 57 (1) sent. 2 Brussels I Regulation.

the enforcement without a party's application where the enforcement would be "manifestly contrary to public policy";
- Art. 63 and 64 – deletes the former privileges for Luxembourg, Greece and Portugal which were granted for a certain time which had run out;
- Art. 65 (1) – generalises the possibility to invite third parties to join proceedings under Art. 8 no. 2 and Art. 13;
- Art. 73 – explicitly leaves the Lugano Convention of 2007 as well as the New York Convention on Arbitration of 1958 unaffected.

Meanwhile the Brussels Ibis Regulation itself already underwent changes (see *infra* paras. 131 **26d** *et seq.*).

10. The remaining relevance of the Brussels Convention

The Brussels Convention although still in force has almost no practical importance. Its only **27** practical significance concerns those territories of EU Member States to which the Brussels Ibis Regulation does not extend due to Art. 355 (2) TFEU and where the Brussels Convention once had been introduced.[103] However, for the interpretation of the Brussels Ibis Regulation the Convention and the case law under it continue to matter.

11. The Lugano Convention of 2007

After the revision and conversion of the Brussels Convention into the Brussels I Regulation **28** the same differences as between these two instruments emerged between the Regulation and the Lugano Convention of 1988. The intended uniformity within the European Economic Area concerning international procedural law no longer existed. Therefore a revision of the Lugano Convention to align it to the Brussels I Regulation was initiated. In 2007, the EU as such,[104] Denmark,[105] Iceland, Norway and Switzerland concluded a revised Lugano Convention which replaced the old one of 1988 and adapted it to the Brussels I Regulation with which it is identical in all relevant aspects. The uniformity of international procedural law was re-established within the EU and the EFTA-States. In the EU (including all Member States except Denmark), Denmark and Norway the 2007 Lugano Convention entered into force on 1 January 2010, in Switzerland on 1 January 2011 and in Iceland on 1 May 2011. Liechtenstein remains the only EFTA-State being not a 2007 Lugano State. With the Brussels I Recast new discrepancies between the Brussels and the Lugano instrument emerge: all differences between Brussels Ibis and Brussels I as listed *supra* in note 26c now exist between Brussels Ibis and Lugano 2007. Whether a new alignment of Lugano to the Brussels regime can be reached, remains to be seen. The enthusiasm of the EFTA countries to follow 'on leash' each reversion of Brussels I is decreasing the more frequently such reversions or recasts occur and the less, if at all, they are involved in the preparation of any reversion or recast.

---

[103] See Art. 68 and the comment thereon (*Mankowski*).

[104] The EU as such could act for its Member States (except Denmark) after the ECJ, in an opinion of 7 February 2006 (Opinion 1/03), had decided that the EU had an exclusive competence for concluding the new Lugano Convention.

[105] Because of its special (rejecting) position towards the EU measures on judicial cooperation Denmark is a separate Contracting State.

12. The relevance of the Lugano Convention

a) In general

29 The 1988 Lugano Convention[106] expanded the regime of the Brussels Convention to Non-EU Member States.[107] It was only ratified by the 15 "old" EU Member States,[108] as well as by Poland[109] and further – from outside the EU – by the EFTA-States Iceland, Norway and Switzerland. The revised Lugano Convention of 2007 expanded the Brussels I Regulation to these EFTA-States. It is now in force in all 27 EU Member States and in the mentioned EFTA States. There, it replaces the 1988 Lugano Convention from the date of its entering into force (Art. 69 (6) Lugano Convention of 2007). However, its practical importance is limited because of the small number of "pure" Lugano States (which are not Member States of the EU).

b) Scope of application

30 Concerning the material respect of application the Lugano Convention of 2007 has almost the same scope as the Brussels *Ibis* Regulation: Art. 1 Lugano Convention does not yet exclude maintenance matters. The personal scope of application is widely but not entirely identical (see Art. 2 (1) Lugano Convention):The abolition of the domicile requirement in Art. 25 Brussels *Ibis* and the extension of the jurisdiction for consumers' and employees' claims against third country defendants (Art. 18 (2) and Art. 21 (2) Brussels *Ibis*) cannot be found in the Lugano Convention, yet. Also, the territorial and the temporal scope of application differ. The 2007 Lugano Convention is in force in all EU Member States and Iceland, Norway and Switzerland but only since 2010 resp. 2011. Like the Regulation and the Brussels Convention it applies to all suits which have been instituted on or after the day the Convention entered into force in the relevant state (Art. 63 Lugano Convention).

c) Interpretation

31 The Lugano Convention is an international treaty for whose interpretation the general rules on the interpretation of such instruments are applicable.[110] But in order to ensure the parallel character of the Lugano Convention this Convention should be interpreted in the same way as the Brussels Convention and thus as the Regulation with the qualification that the Lugano Convention is no Community law. The Protocol No. 2 to the Lugano Convention intends to safeguard that the courts of the Non-EU Lugano Member States also take into account and more or less follow the decisions of the ECJ though these decisions cannot be directly

---

[106] For commentaries to the 1988 and the 2007 Lugano Convention see in particular *Czernich/Kodek/Tiefenthaler*, Europäisches Gerichtsstands- und Vollstreckungsrecht (3rd ed. 2009); *Dasser/Oberhammer* (eds.), Kommentar zum Lugano-Übereinkommen (LugÜ) (2008); *Donzallaz*, La Convention de Lugano I, II, III (1996, 1997, 1998); *Lechner/Mayr*, Das Übereinkommen von Lugano (1996); *Pålsson*, Brysselförordningen jämte Bryssel- och Luganokonventionerna (2008); *Rognlien*, Luganokonvensjonen (1993); *Schnyder*, Lugano-Übereinkommen (LugÜ) zum internationalen Zivilverfahrensrecht (2011); *Schwander* (ed.), Das Lugano-Übereinkommen (1990); *Werro* (ed.), Lugano-Übereinkommen (LugÜ) (2011).

[107] See *supra* Introduction note 21 (*Magnus*).

[108] Austria, Belgium, Denmark, Finland, France, Germany, Greece, Ireland, Italy, Luxembourg, Netherlands, Portugal, Sweden, Spain, United Kingdom.

[109] See thereto *Martiny/Ernst*, IPRax 2001, 29.

[110] See in particular Artt. 31–33 Vienna Convention on the Law of Treaties of 1969. A further source for the interpretation is the Report *Jenard/Möller* to the 1988 Lugano Convention (OJ 1990 C 189/57 *et seq.*) and the Report Pocar to the 2007 Lugano Convention (OJ 2009 C 319/ 1 *et seq.*).

binding on them.[111] Vice versa also the courts of the EU Member States have to take notice of relevant decisions of courts in 'pure' Lugano states.[112] Furthermore, courts in EU Member States can – and if they are last instance courts, must[113] – refer preliminary questions on the interpretation of the Lugano Convention to the ECJ.[114]

d) Relationship to the Brussels I*bis* Regulation

The relationship between the Lugano Convention and the Brussels I Regulation is dealt with **32** by Art. 64 Lugano Convention 2007. According to Art. 68 (2) and Art. 73 (1) Brussels I*bis* Regulation this provision is now to be regarded as to apply to the relationship between the Lugano Convention and the present Regulation.

Among the Member States of the EU which are now at the same time all Member States of **33** the Lugano Convention the Regulation prevails while the Lugano Convention has no application (Art. 64 (1) Lugano Convention). This is also true with respect to Denmark and to those third states which are not EFTA Member States.[115]

With respect to the EFTA States (except Liechtenstein), namely the Non-EU Member States **34** of the Lugano Convention Iceland, Norway and Switzerland, the Lugano Convention of 2007 prevails over the Brussels I Regulation under the conditions as defined by Art. 64 (2) Lugano Convention: for purposes of jurisdiction if the defendant has its domicile in one of the Non-EU Lugano States or if the courts of that State have jurisdiction according to Artt. 22, 23 Lugano Convention (the equivalents to Artt. 24, 25 Brussels I*bis* Regulation); for the purposes of *lis pendens* under Artt. 27, 28 Lugano Convention (equivalents to Artt. 29, 30 Brussels I*bis* Regulation) if proceedings are pending or instituted both in a Non-EU Lugano State and in an EU-Lugano State;[116] for the purposes of recognition and enforcement if either the judgment state or the recognition state is a Non-EU Lugano State.[117]

IV. The Regulation as Community law

1. Competence of the EU?

As already indicated the Regulation has been enacted on the basis of Artt. 67 (4) and 81 (2) **35** (a), (c) and (e) TFEU.[118] The predecessors of these Articles (Artt. 61 (c), 65 and 67 (1) EC

---

[111] See Art. 1 Protocol No. 2 to the 2007 Lugano Convention. For further details see *Domej*, in: Dasser/Oberhammer (*supra* fn. 126) Präambel Protokoll Nr. 2 notes 1 *et seq.*; *Kropholler/von Hein* Einl. notes 73 *et seq.*; *Schmidt-Parzefall*, Die Auslegung des Parallelübereinkommens von Lugano (1995), p. 57 *et seq.*

[112] Art. 1 (2) Protocol No. 2 to the 2007 Lugano Convention.

[113] See Art. 267 TFEU.

[114] See the Preamble to, and Art. 2 of, Protocol No. 2 to the 2007 Lugano Convention; further *Domej*, in: Dasser/Oberhammer (*supra* fn. 126) Präambel Protokoll 2 note 3; *Grolimund/Bachofner*, in: Schnyder (*supra* fn. 126) Protokoll 2 note 3; *Hausmann*, in: Simons/Hausmann Einleitung note 87.

[115] *Jenard/Möller* Report para. 15; *Gottwald*, in: Münchener Kommentar zur ZPO, LugÜ Art. 54b note 2.

[116] Art. 31 (2) Brussels I*bis* Regulation should however lead to the priority of the chosen court irrespective whether it is located in an EU Member State or a pure Lugano State.

[117] See thereto *Domej*, in: Dasser/Oberhammer (*supra* fn. 126) Art. 64 LugÜ notes 3 *et seq.*; *Siehr*, in: Schnyder (*supra* fn. 126) Art. 64 LugÜ notes 13 *et seq.*

[118] See Preamble and Recital 5.

Treaty) formed part of Title IV of Part III of the EC Treaty on "Visa, Asylum, Immigration and other Policies related to the Free Movement of Persons." By then it had been doubted whether they constituted a sufficient basis for a legislative competence of the Community to enact the Brussels I Regulation[119] and it had been particularly argued that Title IV was confined to measures which were related to the free movement of persons but did not include the free movement of judgments.[120] However, already Art. 65 (a) EC Treaty provided expressly for a competence concerning among others the recognition and enforcement of judgments; Art. 65 (b) EC Treaty allowed measures concerning also jurisdiction, and Art. 65 (c) EC Treaty permitted even measures concerning the domestic law of civil procedure of the Member States if necessary in order to eliminate obstacles to the proper functioning of civil proceedings. Neither the wording of the cited Articles nor the legislative history showed that the purposes which had been pursued before by the Brussels Convention should in any way be restricted. Thus, despite the too narrow title "Visa, Asylum, Immigration and other Policies related to the Free Movement of Persons" already Articles 61–69 EC Treaty introduced a rather far-reaching general competence of the EU in the field of international procedural law which was limited only by two qualifications: Art. 65 EC Treaty itself provided that the competence was only granted with respect to measures "having cross-border implications"; moreover, the competence extended to measures "insofar as necessary for the proper functioning of the internal market". And as always the subsidiarity principle (Art. 5 EC Treaty) had to be observed. The TFEU has even broadened and strengthened the EU competence insofar as its Art. 81 (1) now provides that "(t)he Union shall develop judicial cooperation in civil matters having cross-border implications". In this respect Art. 81 (2) permits legislative "measures, particularly when necessary for the proper functioning of the internal market, aimed at ensuring (a) the mutual recognition and enforcement between Member States of judgments ... (c) the compatibility of the rules ... of jurisdiction". The Union is now obliged to develop international judicial cooperation; the necessity of furthering the proper functioning of the internal market is no longer the exclusive precondition for respective measures but only a prominent one ("particularly").

36 While it can hardly be questioned that the Regulation focuses on the cross-border aspect yet, its necessity for the proper functioning of the internal market might be less apparent – and is less important under the TFEU. But as mentioned above[121] procedural obstacles to enforce existing rights in cross-border trade and other relations will at the same time discourage such cross-border relations and thereby impede the proper functioning of the internal market, though to an extent which admittedly cannot be specified with final precision. The subsidiarity principle does not stand in the way either since it is rather apparent that only a Community measure can satisfactorily regulate the cross-border aspects within the EU. In the light of both the *Tobacco Advertising* case[122] which highlighted the strictness of the competence rules and the *Ingmar* case[123] which interpreted the functioning market requirement in a rather generous and wide manner it is, however, most unlikely that the ECJ when

---

[119] See, for instance, *Schack*, ZEuP 1999, 805, 807 ("weder zulässig noch geeignet" ["neither admissible nor apt"]); see further the discussion by *Ansgar Staudinger*, in: Rauscher Einl. Brüssel I-VO note 10.

[120] *Schack*, ZEuP 1999, 805, 807.

[121] See *supra* Introduction note 2 (*Magnus*).

[122] *Federal Republic of Germany v. European Parliament and Council of the European Union*, (Case C-376/98) ECR (2000) I-8419.

[123] *Ingmar GB Ltd. v. Eaton Leonard Technologies Inc.*, (Case C-381/98) (2000) ECR I-9305.

ever called upon would quash the Brussels I*bis* Regulation as being based on an insufficient legislative competence of the Community.[124] In my view such a decision would be unjustified.

2. Direct applicability and precedence of the Regulation

The Regulation constitutes secondary Community law. In contrast to Directives the Regu- **37** lation is directly applicable and needs no further implementation into national law (Art. 288 TFEU; ex Art. 249 EC Treaty). As far as the Regulation reaches all Member States (even Denmark by virtue of a special regulation, see *infra* notes 53 *et seq.*) are now immediately bound by it. This is also true for each new Member State which joins the EU. From the date the accession becomes effective the Regulation is directly applicable also there.

The Regulation takes further precedence over all non-conforming national law. Any con- **38** tradicting rule of national law cannot be applied any longer. It does not matter whether the conflicting national law has been enacted before or after the entering into force of the Regulation in the respective Member State.

In regards to Community law the ECJ is competent to interpret the Regulation in accord- **39** ance with the general methods and standards applicable to Community law.[125] Under Art. 68 EC Treaty – and in contrast to Art. 234 EC Treaty – only courts of last instance were entitled but not obliged to refer questions of interpretation of the Regulation to the ECJ.[126] The TFEU abolished this specificity and restored the normal reference procedure under which all courts may and courts of last instance must refer those questions to the ECJ for a preliminary ruling (Art. 267 TFEU).

3. EU external competence

Where the EU possesses an internal competence it also possesses an implied external com- **40** petence as far as necessary for the effective use of the internal competence.[127] This implied power of the EU concerns in particular the conclusion of treaties with third states on matters for which an internal competence exists. If the EU has made use of its internal competence its implied external competence to conclude respective treaties may become even an exclusive competence.[128]

With respect to the Brussels I*bis* Regulation the EU Member States are now no longer **41** entitled to conclude international treaties which are in conflict with the rules of the Regu-

---

[124] In the same sense *Leible/Ansgar Staudinger*, EuLF (D) 2000-01, 225, 228 *et seq.*; *Ansgar Staudinger*, in: Rauscher Einl. Brüssel I-VO note 10.

[125] See *infra* Introduction notes 91 *et seq.* (*Magnus*).

[126] See thereto *infra* Introduction notes 112 *et seq.* (*Magnus*).

[127] *Commission of the European Communities* v. *Council of the European Communities(AETR)*, (Case 22/70) (1971) ECR 263; Draft Agreement establishing a European laying-up fund for inland waterway vessels, (Opinion 1/76) (1977) ECR 741, and standing practice of the Court; see thereto *Oppermann/Classen/ Nettesheim* § 30 note 19; *Reich*, Understanding EU Law, p. 43.

[128] See *Oppermann/Classen/Nettesheim* § 30 note 21.

lation.[129] In a Common Declaration of 14 December 2000 the Council and the Commission have expressly adopted this view and stated that the Regulation does not hinder a Member State to conclude international treaties on matters falling within the scope of the Regulation as long as the treaties leave the Regulation untouched.[130] The Member States themselves can therefore ratify, or accede to, such international treaties on jurisdiction and the recognition and enforcement of judgments which give priority to the Brussels I*bis* Regulation in cases where the Regulation is applicable. The Hague Convention on Choice of Court Agreements of 30 June 2005[131] which is one of the practically relevant examples of a competing convention can therefore be adopted by the Member States of the Regulation[132] since this Convention acknowledges the priority of the Regulation.[133] But the EU as such is also entitled, and willing, to join this Hague Convention.[134]

V. The scope of application of the Regulation

1. The territorial scope of application

a) In general

42 The territorial scope of application of the Regulation corresponds regularly to that of Community law in general.[135] Subject to the exceptions provided for by Art. 355 TFEU (ex Art. 299 EC Treaty) the Regulation applies in the territory of all 27 present Member States now directly bound by the Regulation. This followed from Art. 299 (1) EC Treaty for the "old" Member States listed by that provision (except Denmark). For the thirteen new Member States which joined the EU in 2004, in 2007 and in 2013 it followed from the Accession Treaties of 16 April 2003, of 25 April 2005 and of 9 December 2011.[136]

43 Whether a certain place belongs to the territory of a Member State is not determined by the Regulation or the European Union Treaty or the TFEU but by the principles of public international law.[137] Therefore if the continental shelf before the coast line of a Member State still belongs to the territory of this state must be decided in conformity with the respective international treaties and, in their absence, with general principles of public international law.[138] However, certain Extra-European territories of certain Member States are not subjected to the Brussels I*bis* Regulation (see *infra* notes 46 *et seq.*).

---

[129] *Kropholler/von Hein* Art. 71 note 2; *Layton/Mercer* para. 11.060; *Mankowski*, in: Rauscher Art. 71 note 3; *Ansgar Staudinger*, in: Rauscher Einl. Brüssel I-VO note 21.

[130] See Common Declaration Sched. I no. 5 (German text in IPRax 2001, 259, 261).

[131] See thereto *supra* Introduction note 15 (*Magnus*).

[132] In the same sense *Ansgar Staudinger*, in: Rauscher Einl. Brüssel I-VO note 21.

[133] See *supra* Introduction note 15 (*Magnus*).

[134] See thereto the Decision of the Council of 26 February 2009 which authorises the signing of the Hague Convention, OJ 2009 L 133/1.

[135] See Art. 52 Treaty on the European Union in connection with Art. 355 TFEU.

[136] OJ 2003 L 236/17.OJ 2005 L 157/11 and OJ 2012 L 112/10.

[137] See *Herbert Weber v. Universal Ogden Services Ltd.*, (Case C-37/00) (2002) ECR I-2013.

[138] *Herbert Weber v. Universal Ogden Services Ltd.*, (Case C-37/00) (2002) ECR I-2013 (cook working on an oil drilling platform on the continental shelf in front of the Dutch coast = habitual place of employment under Art. 5 (1) Brussels Convention in the Netherlands).

With respect to jurisdiction the necessary territorial element connecting the dispute with the **44** forum seised is regularly the domicile of the defendant which must be located in a Member State (Art. 4). This is even sufficient where the plaintiff's domicile is located outside the EU.[139] This basic rule is, however, rather widely varied for reasons of procedural justice and efficiency of litigation. The Regulation provides for many exceptions where other more apt connecting factors than the defendant's domicile are decisive: this is the case with the exclusive jurisdiction (Art. 24) where the dispute is so closely linked to a certain place that the courts there are exclusively competent; with the protective jurisdiction (Art. 15, 19, 23) where the weaker party's place prevails; with the agreed jurisdiction (Art. 25) where the parties' consented intention determines which courts are to decide and with the special jurisdictions (Art. 7 *et seq.*) where there is another sufficiently close connection between the dispute and a place different from the defendant's domicile.

With respect to the recognition and enforcement of judgments the required territorial **45** connecting factor is that the judgment must have been rendered by a court situated in a territory to which the Regulation extends.

b) Application in the Member States

In general the Regulation applies in the entire territory of the respective Member State and **46** also in those autonomous parts in Europe for whose external relations the Member State is responsible (Art. 355 (3) TFEU [ex Art. 299 (4) EC Treaty]). However, to some of the EU Member States there belong separate territories located outside Europe, for whose international relations the Member State is also responsible; in certain cases the Regulation applies even there. This depends on whether or not the territorial unit is listed in Annex II to the TFEU to which Art. 355 (2) (ex Art. 299 (3) EC Treaty) refers. Overseas territories listed there are not governed by Community law in its entirety but by the special association system provided for by Part IV of the Lisbon Treaty (Artt. 198–204; ex Arts. 182–187 EC Treaty). The Regulation does not apply in the listed territories (though the Brussels Convention remains applicable in some of the territories).[140]

On the other hand on the territory of some Member States there are separate territorial units **47** located which enjoy a certain or full independence and neither Community law nor the Regulation applies there. It differs therefore considerably between the Member States whether and to which of their separate territorial units the Regulation extends.

(1) Austria

The Regulation is in force in the entire territory of Austria. Austria has also ratified the **48** Brussels Convention and the 1988 Lugano Convention. The 2007 Lugano Convention is in force and has replaced the 1988 version.

(2) Belgium

The Regulation is directly applicable in Belgium. The Brussels Convention as well as the **49** 1988 Lugano Convention were also in force in Belgium. The latter is now replaced by the 2007 Lugano Convention.

---

[139] *Group Josi Reinsurance Company SA v. Universal General Insurance Company (UGIC)*, (Case C-412/98) (2000) ECR I-5925.

[140] See also Art. 68 note 3 (*Mankowski*).

(3) Bulgaria

49a As of 1 January 2007 Bulgaria has joined the EU and since then the Brussels I Regulation is in force there.

49b Bulgaria was never a Contracting State of the Brussels or the 1988 Lugano Convention. However, the 2007 Lugano Convention is now in force there since 1 January 2010.

(4) Croatia

49c Croatia is the youngest EU Member State (since 1 July 2013). The Brussels *Ibis* Regulation is directly applicable as of that date and extends to the entire territory of Croatia. Since the EU as such is Contracting State of the 2007 Lugano Convention also this Convention is applicable in Croatia since the date when the accession became effective. The Brussels Convention and the 1988 Lugano Convention had never entered into force in Croatia.

(5) Cyprus

50 The Regulation extends to the Greek part of Cyprus only. The British base areas on Cyprus – Akrotiri and Dhekelia – are, however, excluded from the scope of the Regulation by virtue of Art. 355 (5) (b) TFEU (ex Art. 299 (6) (b) EC Treaty).[141]

51 Neither the Brussels Convention nor the 1988 Lugano Convention had been ratified by (Greek) Cyprus. The 2007 Lugano Convention is now in force there.

(6) Czech Republic

52 The Regulation is in force in Czech Republic since 1 May 2004 but the country was neither Contracting State of the Brussels Convention nor of the 1988 Lugano Convention. The 2007 Lugano Convention is now in force there since 1 January 2010.

(7) Denmark

53 As already mentioned Denmark abstained from the communitarisation of the measures under Title IV of Part III of the EC Treaty (now Title V of Part III of the TFEU). The Brussels I Regulation was therefore not applicable in Denmark (see also Art. 1 (3) Brussels I Regulation). Denmark reserved this position in a Protocol on the Position of Denmark to the Treaty of Amsterdam. Art. 1 of the Protocol states that Denmark does not participate in such measures and Art. 2 provides that such Community measures are "not applicable nor binding" in Denmark.

54 However, in 2005 the EU and Denmark concluded a separate treaty which entailed the more or less full application of the Brussels I Regulation in Denmark. This treaty entered into force on 1 July 2007.[142] Since then the Brussels I Regulation had to be applied between Denmark and the other EU Member States. Under this treaty, Denmark is entitled, but not obliged to accept modifications and amendments of the Brussels I Regulation.[143] In accordance with the procedure laid down in the separate Treaty Denmark notified the Commission in time by letter of 20 December 2012 of its decision to implement Regulation (EU) No. 1215/2012. Thus, the Brussels *Ibis* Regulation is fully applicable in Denmark. The former Art. 1 (3)

---

[141] Also *Layton/Mercer* para. 11.070.

[142] OJ 2007 L 94/70; see thereto *Nielsen*, IPRax 2007, 506 *et seq.*; see also *supra* note 24 (*Magnus*).

[143] See Art. 3 and 5 of the EU-Danish Treaty.

Brussels I Regulation that Denmark was not a Member State of that Regulation has been deleted from the present Regulation text.

The territorial scope of the Brussels I*bis* Regulation includes the Danish territory with **55** Bornholm but does not extend to Greenland and the Faroe Islands.[144] Although both belong to Denmark they enjoy a certain autonomy and they were excluded already from the operation of the Brussels Convention.

Denmark had ratified the 1988 Lugano Convention and is now one of the five separate **56** Contracting States of the 2007 Lugano Convention where the EU represents the 27 other EU Member States.

(8) Estonia
The Regulation applies directly in Estonia since the accession on 1 May 2004 but the country **57** was neither Contracting State of the Brussels Convention nor of the 1988 Lugano Convention. The 2007 Lugano Convention is now in force there since 1 January 2010.

(9) Finland
The Regulation applies to the entire territory of Finland. As is the case with Community law **58** in general the Regulation is therefore also in force on the Åland Islands (see Art. 355 (4) TFEU [ex Art. 299 (5) EC Treaty]) which formally belong to Finland but enjoy a far-reaching autonomy.

Finland was also Member State of both the Brussels and the 1988 Lugano Convention. The **59** 2007 Lugano Convention is in force since 1 January 2010.

(10) France
The Regulation is applicable in the entire European territory of France. But though France is **60** partly responsible for the external relations of Monaco neither Community law as such nor the Regulation applies in Monaco which in this respect is independent.[145] Also Andorra[146] whose formal head of state is still the French president together with the Spanish Bishop of Urgel lies outside the territorial scope of the Regulation and the Conventions.

According to Art. 355 (1) TFEU (ex Art. 299 (2) EC Treaty) Community Law and thus the **61** Regulation applies also to the French overseas departments (*départements et régions d'outre mer*). These departments comprise Guadeloupe, French Guiana, Martinique, Mayotte and Réunion but not the French overseas territories (*collectivités d'outre mer*), namely New Caledonia, French Polynesia, the Wassis and Futuna Islands, St. Pierre and Miquelon, the French Southern Antarctic territories. These territories fall under the regime of Art. 355 (2) TFEU (ex Art. 299 (3) EC Treaty) in connection with Annex II of the Treaty; they are governed by the specific association rules of Part IV of the Treaty (Artt. 198 *et seq.* TFEU [ex Artt. 182 *et seq.* EC Treaty]). The Regulation does not apply there.[147]

---

[144] Art. 355 (5) (a) TFEU.

[145] See also Cass. RCDIP 88 (1999), 759 with note *Ancel*.

[146] Andorra is de facto independent since 1993 only and was until that time governed by France and the Bishop of Urgel.

[147] See also *Kropholler/von Hein* Einl. note 25; *Layton/Mercer* para. 11.066.

62 Both the Brussels Convention and the Lugano Convention were in force in France and extended to the French overseas territories.[148] But they are neither in force in Andorra nor in Monaco. The 2007 Lugano Convention is in force in France since 1 January 2010.

(11) Germany

63 The application of the Regulation extends to the whole territory of Germany including the territory of the former German Democratic Republic (GDR). The federal structure of Germany with 16 *Bundesländer* does not affect the applicability of the Regulation.

64 Germany was also Member State of the Brussels Convention and the Lugano Convention, now of the 2007 Lugano Convention.

(12) Greece

65 The Regulation is in force in Greece including its islands. Greece had also ratified the Brussels Convention and the Lugano Convention. It is now Member State of the 2007 Lugano Convention.

(13) Hungary

66 Hungary belongs to those EU Member States where the Regulation is in force since 1 May 2004; but neither the Brussels Convention nor the 1988 Lugano Convention were in force in the time before. The 2007 Lugano Convention applies since 1 January 2010.

(14) Ireland

67 Like Denmark and the United Kingdom also Ireland reserved its right not to participate in the adoption of measures enacted under Artt. 61 *et seq.* EC Treaty.[149] But like the United Kingdom – and unlike Denmark – Ireland has declared that it joins the judicial cooperation set forth by the Regulation and further instruments. Therefore the Regulation (and the other instruments enacted under Artt. 61 and 65 EC Treaty [now Art. 81 TFEU]) is in force in Ireland.

68 Ireland was also a Member State of the Brussels Convention and it had ratified the 1988 Lugano Convention which is now replaced by the 2007 Lugano Convention.

(15) Italy

69 The Regulation is in force in Italy but neither in the Vatican which is an independent state nor in San Marino which itself is responsible for its external relations in the sense of Art. 355 (3) TFEU (ex Art. 299 (4) EC Treaty) although San Marino is else under the protective friendship of Italy.[150]

70 The Brussels Convention and the 1988 Lugano Convention were both in force in Italy but neither in the Vatican nor in San Marino. The 2007 Lugano Convention is now applicable in Italy since 1 January 2010.

---

[148] See Report *Almeida Cruz/Desantes Real/Jenard* para. 33; *Geimer/Schütze* A. 1 Einl. note 223 *et seq.*; *Kropholler/von Hein*, Europäisches Zivilprozessrecht (6th ed. 1998), Art. 60 EuGVÜ note 8.

[149] See Protocol on the position of the United Kingdom and Ireland to the Treaty on the European Union and the EC Treaty.

[150] See *Kropholler/von Hein* Einl. note 22; *Layton/Mercer* para. 11.067.

(16) Latvia

Latvia is an EU Member State where the Regulation is in force since 1 May 2004. The **71** country had adopted neither the Brussels Convention nor the 1988 Lugano Convention. The 2007 Lugano Convention is in force since 1 January 2010.

(17) Lithuania

In Lithuania the Regulation applies since 1 May 2004 whereas neither the Brussels Con- **72** vention nor the 1988 Lugano Convention had been adopted. The 2007 Lugano Convention applies since 1 January 2010.

(18) Luxembourg

In Luxembourg the Regulation is in force as well as were the Brussels Convention and the **73** 1988 Lugano Convention. The latter is now replaced by the 2007 Lugano Convention.

(19) Malta

The Regulation is in force in Malta since 1 May 2004 but neither the Brussels Convention **74** nor the Lugano Convention had been ratified there. The 2007 Lugano Convention applies since 1 January 2010.

(20) The Netherlands

The Regulation extends to the European territory of the Netherlands but neither to Aruba **75** nor the Netherlands Antilles for which the association system of Art. 355 (2) TFEU (ex Art. 299 (3) EC Treaty) in connection with Schedule II to the Treaty applies.[151]

The Brussels Convention and the 1988 Lugano Convention were in force in the Netherlands. **76** The latter is now replaced by the 2007 Lugano Convention. The application of the Brussels Convention had been extended to Aruba by a declaration of the Netherlands under the former Art. 60 of the Brussels Convention. Despite the later deletion of the Article the effect of the Dutch declaration remains in force so that the Brussels Convention still applies to Aruba.[152]

(21) Poland

Besides the Regulation which directly applies since 1 May 2004 Poland had ratified the 1988 **77** Lugano Convention but not the Brussels Convention. The old Lugano Convention is now replaced by the 2007 version.

(22) Portugal

The Regulation is directly applicable in Portugal and, due to the express provision of Art. 355 **78** (1) TFEU (ex Art. 299 (2) EC Treaty), also on the Azores and Madeira. The provision in Art. 349 TFEU (ex Art. 299 (2) EC Treaty) that specific measures may be applied to the Azores and Madeira does not affect the applicability of the Regulation there.[153]

Portugal with the Azores and Madeira was also Member State of the Brussels Convention **79**

---

[151] Also *Kropholler/von Hein* Einl. note 26; *Layton/Mercer* para. 11.068.
[152] See also Art. 68 note 3 (*Mankowski*).
[153] See also *Kropholler/von Hein* Einl. note 27; *Layton/Mercer* para. 11.069.

and of the 1988 Lugano Convention, the latter being replaced by the 2007 Lugano Convention.

(23) Romania

79a   As of 1 January 2007 Romania joined the EU and since then the Brussels I Regulation is in force there.

79b   Romania was never a Contracting State of the Brussels or the Lugano Convention. Now, the 2007 Lugano Convention applies there since 1 January 2010.

(24) Slovakia

80   The Regulation is directly applicable in Slovakia since 1 May 2004 but the country had adopted neither the Brussels Convention nor the 1988 Lugano Convention. The 2007 Lugano Convention is in force since 1 January 2010.

(25) Slovenia

81   In Slovenia the Regulation applies since 1 May 2004 whereas neither the Brussels Convention nor the Lugano Convention had been ratified. The 2007 Lugano Convention is in force since 1 January 2010.

(26) Spain

82   The Regulation is applicable in Spain, in Gibraltar (however, Gibraltar being under British rule)[154] and also on the Canary Islands which belong to Spain (Art. 355 (1) TFEU [ex Art. 299 (2) EC Treaty]). The same is true for the Spanish exclaves Ceuta and Melilla in Morocco.[155]

83   Spain was a Member State both of the Brussels Convention and the 1988 Lugano Convention. The latter has been replaced by the 2007 Lugano Convention which is applicable since 1 January 2010.

(27) Sweden

84   The Regulation applies directly to the whole territory of Sweden including the islands Gotland and Öland. Sweden was also a Contracting State of the Brussels Convention and the 1988 Lugano Convention (now replaced by the 2007 Lugano Convention).

(28) United Kingdom

85   Also the United Kingdom reserved its right not to participate in the adoption of measures enacted under Artt. 61 *et seq.* EC Treaty (now Artt. 67 *et seq.* TFEU) – like Denmark and Ireland did.[156] But in contrast to Denmark the United Kingdom as well as Ireland[157] declared to join the judicial cooperation set forth by the Regulation and further instruments. Therefore the Regulation (and the other instruments enacted under Artt. 61 and 65 EC Treaty

---

[154]   See the Accord of 18 October 2000 between Spain and the United Kingdom (OJ 2001 C 13/1 and BOE 2001, 2508); see further *Calvo Caravaca/Carrascosa González* p. 67; *Kropholler/von Hein* Einl. note 29; *Layton/Mercer* para. 11.070.

[155]   *Calvo Caravaca/Carrascosa González* p. 67; *Kropholler/von Hein* Einl. note 28.

[156]   See Protocol on the position of the United Kingdom and Ireland annexed to the Treaty on the European Union and the EC Treaty.

[157]   See *supra* Introduction note 67 (*Magnus*).

[now Art. 81 TFEU]) is in force in most parts of the United Kingdom, in particular in England and Wales, Northern Ireland and Scotland.[158] It is also in force in Gibraltar[159] but, due to Art. 355 (5) (c) TFEU (ex Art. 299 (6) (c) EC Treaty), *not* on the Channel Islands (Jersey, Guernsey, Alderney, Sark) and *not* on the Isle of Man though these islands are British dependencies.[160] Also the British bases Akrotiri and Dhekelia on Cyprus do not fall within the territorial scope of Community law (Art. 355 (5) (b) TFEU [ex Art. 299 (6) (b) EC Treaty]) and are thus excluded from the scope of the Regulation.[161]

In contrast to France the Regulation does not extend to territories outside Europe for whose **86** international relations the United Kingdom is still responsible.

The United Kingdom had ratified both the Brussels Convention and the 1988 Lugano **87** Convention. The latter is now replaced by the 2007 Lugano Convention.

2. Material scope of application

The Regulation deals only with the jurisdiction of the courts in its Member States and with **88** the recognition and enforcement of judgments rendered by these courts and of authentic instruments and court settlements set up in a Member State. Since the Recast also the concurrence of lawsuits inside and outside the EU is regulated.[162] Moreover, the Regulation restricts itself to civil and commercial law matters and provides even there for a number of exclusions, for instance of many family law matters, to which the Regulation does not apply.[163]

3. Personal scope of application

The Regulation does not prescribe specific personal requirements. The basic rule that the **89** defendant must have its domicile in a Member State (Art. 4) concerns rather the necessary territorial connection between the dispute and the forum seised. The nationality of the parties is irrelevant (Art. 4 (1)).

4. Temporal scope of application

The Regulation applies to all suits brought and judgments or other covered titles rendered **90** on or after the day it entered into force, namely the 10 January 2015.[164] This date is applicable to all EU Member States, even to Denmark. For proceedings instituted, and judgments and other titles rendered before that date the former Brussels I Regulation still applies,[165] with respect to the recognition and enforcement of judgments and other enforceable titles how-

---

[158] *Kropholler/von Hein* Einl. note 29; *Layton/Mercer* para. 11.070.
[159] See *supra* Introduction note 82 (*Magnus*).
[160] *Kropholler/von Hein* Einl. note 29; *Layton/Mercer* para. 11.070.
[161] *Kropholler/von Hein* Einl. note 29; *Layton/Mercer* para. 11.070.
[162] See Artt. 33 and 34 Brussels I*bis* Regulation and the commentary thereto (*Fentiman*).
[163] See Art. 1 and the commentary thereto (*Rogerson*).
[164] See Artt. 66 and 80 and the commentaries thereto (*Mankowski*).
[165] Art. 66 (2).

ever only if the old Regulation was in force in both the judgment and the enforcement state at the date the judgment – or other title – was rendered.[166]

VI. Interpretation of the Regulation

1. In general

91   The Regulation is Community law. In principle, it has to be interpreted according to the specific interpretation methods of Community law.[167] However, tradition has it that there are some specifities in the interpretation of the Regulation. The Regulation's pre-predecessor – the Brussels Convention – had been already interpreted, as an international treaty, by the ECJ and national courts over a time span of more than thirty years. It was the intention of the lawgivers of the Brussels I Regulation of 2000 that the transformation of the Convention into a Regulation should not lead to a disruption between the old and the new law but that there should be continuity as far as possible.[168] This aim is maintained by the Recast as well.[169] The Regulation can and should therefore be interpreted in line with the Brussels Convention.[170] The case law under the Brussels Convention, in particular the ECJ decisions but also the accompanying reports to the Convention remain valid. The same is true for the ECJ decisions rendered under the Brussels I Regulation. Only where the recasted Regulation deliberately deviates from the wording of the Brussels Convention or of the former Brussels I Regulation has one to be cautious to rely on former material.

91a Moreover, there is a particular need that the Brussels *Ibis* Regulation should be interpreted in a way that takes account of its model function for the 2007 Lugano Convention. According to Protocol No. 2 to the 2007 Lugano Convention courts in applying that Convention "shall pay due account to the principles laid down by any relevant decision",[171] in particular of the ECJ. Perhaps because of this close interrelation between the Regulation and the Lugano Convention the ECJ appears to be reluctant to base its interpretation of provisions of the Regulation too much on other Community instruments which are not in force and are not binding for the pure Lugano States (Iceland, Norway and Switzerland). In Kainz v. Pantherwerke AG the Court held: "It must be stated next that, although it is apparent from recital 7 in the preamble to [Rome II Regulation] that the European Union legislature sought to ensure consistency between [Brussels I], on the one hand, and the substantive scope and the provisions of [Rome II Regulation], on the other, that does not mean, however, that the provisions of [Brussels I] must for that reason be interpreted in the light of the provisions of [Rome II]. The objective of consistency cannot, in any event, lead to the provisions of [Brussels I] being interpreted in a manner which is unconnected to the scheme and objectives pursued by that regulation."[172] Although Rome I and Rome II Regulations form a far-

---

[166] *Wolf Naturprodukte GmbH v. SEWAR spol.s.r.o.*, (C-514/10) (2012) ECR nyr.

[167] As to these methods see *infra* Introduction notes 98 *et seq.* (*Magnus*).

[168] See Recital 19.

[169] See Art. 68 and the commentary thereto (*Mankowski*).

[170] For this aim under the former Regulation: see the ECJ in *Verein für Konsumenteninformation v. Karl Heinz Henkel*, (Case C-167/00) (2002) ECR I-8111, I-8143 para. 49; in the same sense *Kropholler/von Hein* Einl. note 40; *Francesco Benincasa v. Dentalkit Srl.*, (Case C-269/95) (1997) ECR I-3767, I-3794 para. 12; *Layton/Mercer* para. 11.034; *Ansgar Staudinger*, in: Rauscher Einl. Brüssel I-VO note 35.

[171] Art. 1 (1) Protocol No. 2 to the 2007 Lugano Convention.

reaching unity with Brussels I*bis* and as desirable as their uniform interpretation appears to be,[173] the ECJ rightly insists on the specific nature of the Brussels I(bis) Regulation which prohibits its pure infiltration by the Rome Regulations. One of the specific features of the Brussels I*bis* Regulation is the model function of its interpretation for the Lugano States which themselves are not bound by, or subjected to, other Community law. And while the Recitals to Rome I and Rome II expressly require an application consistent with the Brussels I Regulation,[174] a comparable Recital of the later enacted Brussels I*bis* Regulation is – evidently deliberately – lacking. It is therefore not surprising that the ECJ referred rather to international materials (the CISG etc.) for the interpretation of the Regulation, for instance, when deciding whether a contract to buy manufactured goods is a sales contract in the sense of the former Art. 5 (1)(b) first indent (now Art. 7 (1) (b) first indent).[175] Nonetheless, the interpretative connection between Brussels I*bis* and Rome I and II is no one-way road. As far as possible and in particular as far as the objectives of provisions or expressions in the three instruments are identical or similar their interpretation should also be identical.

The Vienna Convention on the Law of Treaties of 23 May 1969 cannot be applied in the **92** interpretation of the Regulation, at least not directly, since the Regulation is no international treaty but Community law. But since the Vienna Convention was and still is relevant for the interpretation of the Brussels Convention[176] and the Lugano Convention it has at least indirect relevance for the interpretation also of the Regulation. Anyhow, the Vienna Convention codifies in its Artt. 31–33 well known and internationally recognised principles of interpretation of international instruments which can be taken into account in any event.

2. Autonomous interpretation

Under the Brussels Convention which was, however, an international treaty the ECJ pre- **93** ferred generally an autonomous interpretation of this legislative instrument. That meant two different aspects: First, questions of doubt were principally to be answered without redress to a specific national law but from an insofar autonomous, to some extent supranational viewpoint.[177] The ECJ reiterated on various occasions that "[i]t is settled law that, as far as possible, the Court of Justice will interpret the terms of the Convention autonomously

---

[172] *Kainz v. Pantherwerke AG*, (Case C-45/13) ECR (2014) nyr. para. 20 (the Court refused any redress to Art. 5 Rome II Regulation although the case raised the question where the place was where the manufacturer had marketed the defective good and although Art. 5 addresses this problem).

[173] See also Recitals 7, 17 and 24 Rome I Regulation as well as Recital 7 Rome II Regulation.

[174] See preceding fn. 186.

[175] *Car Trim GmbH v.KeySafety Systems Srl*, (C-381/08) ECR (2010) I-1255 paras. 36 *et seq.* (although the Court also and in the first instance referred to the Consumer Sales Directive; para. 35).

[176] The ECJ referred to it in *Herbert Weber v. Universal Ogden Services Ltd.*, (Case C-37/00) (2002) ECR I-2013.

[177] See for instance *Industrie Tessili Italiana Como v. Dunlop AG*, (Case 12/76) (1976) ECR 1473 where the ECJ stated that only by way of exception and in contrast to the general rule of autonomous interpretation the place of performance was to be determined according to the applicable national law. Also for an autonomous European interpretation *Mulox IBC Ltd. v. Hendrick Geels*, (Case C-125/92) (1993) ECR I-4075, I-4102 para. 10; *GIE Groupe Concorde et al. v. Master of the Vessel "Suhadiwarno Panjan"*, (Case C-440/97) (1999) ECR I-6307, I-6347 et seq. para. 11; *Gemeente Steenbergen v. Luc Baten*, (Case C-271/00) (2002) ECR I-10489, I-10519 para. 28; further *Hess*, IPRax 2006, 351 *et seq.*

so as to ensure that it is fully effective ..."[178] Secondly, the construction of terms and the gap-filling of the Convention was to be inferred from the Convention itself generally also without any redress to other national legislative instruments[179] or in the words of the ECJ: "... the concepts used in the Convention, which may have a different content depending on the national law of the Contracting States, must be interpreted independently, by reference principally to the system and objectives of the Convention ..."[180] Under the Brussels I Regulation the ECJ's standard formulation was the same: "(T)he provisions of the Regulation ... must be interpreted independently, by reference to its scheme and purpose".[181] It has to guide the interpretation of the Brussels *Ibis* Regulation as well. The reason behind the autonomous interpretation is to secure that parties should be able to deduce from nothing else than the Convention itself where they can sue and be sued and under which conditions they can enforce, and have to obey to, judgments from other Convention States.[182] This is to further legal certainty and transparency. A further reason is that the rights and obligations created by the Brussels Convention and now by the Regulation should be understood and applied in a uniform way in all Member States so that parties have as far as possible the same obligations and enjoy the same rights in all Member States with respect to the subjects dealt with by the Regulation.[183]

94 However, since the Brussels Convention was based on Art. 220 (later Art. 293)EC Treaty it had from its very beginning a strong connection with Community law even deepened by the fact that the ECJ was competent to interpret the Brussels Convention. This resulted in an autonomous interpretation under which the autonomous point of reference was not only the Convention itself but also Community law as such.[184]

95 After the transformation of the Brussels Convention into the Brussels I Regulation the autonomous interpretation[185] without redress to a specific national law but with reference

---

[178] *Mulox IBC Ltd. v. Hendrick Geels*, (Case C-125/92) (1993) ECR I-4075, I-4102 para. 10; repeated in *Petrus Wilhelmus Rutten v. Cross Medical Ltd.*, (Case C-383/95) (1997) ECR I-57, I-74 para. 12 and *Jackie Farrell v. James Long*, (Case C-295/95) (1997) ECR I-1683, I-1704 para. 12.

[179] Examples are *Arcado SPRL v. Haviland SA*, (Case 9/87) (1988) ECR 1539, 1554 para. 10; *Anastasios Kalfelis v. Bankhaus Schröder Münchmeyer Hengst and Co. and others*, (Case 189/87) (1988) ECR 5565, 5584 para. 15.

[180] *Shearson Lehman Hutton v. TVB Treuhandgesellschaft für Vermögensverwaltung und Beteiligungen mbH*, (Case C-89/91) (1993) ECR I-139, I-186 para. 13; repeated in *Francesco Benincasa v. Dentalkit Srl.*, (Case C-269/95) (1997) ECR I-3767, I-3794 para. 12.

[181] See ECJ, for instance, in: Reisch Montage, (C-103/05) (2006) ECR I-6827 para. 29; *Draka NK Cables a.o.*, (C-167/08) (2009)ECR I-3477 para.19; *Zuid-Chemie*, (C-189/08) (2009) ECR I-6917 para. 17; *Gothaer Allgemeine Versicherung AG v. Samskip GmbH*, (C-456/11) (2013) ECR nyr. para. 25; *Kainz v. Pantherwerke AG*, (C-45/13) (2014) ECR nyr. para. 19.

[182] See the decisions of the ECJ in fn. 200.

[183] See again the decisions of the ECJ in fn. 200 and 201.

[184] See for instance *Arcado SPRL v. Haviland SA*, (Case 9/87) (1988) ECR 1539, 1555 para. 14 where the ECJ referred to the Commercial Agents Directive for the contractual qualification of an agent's compensation claim against the principal; in *Gemeente Steenbergen v. Luc Baten*, (Case C-271/00) (2002) ECR I-10489, I-10523 para. 45 the Court referred to the Council Regulation 1408/71/EEC of 14 June 1971 on the application of social security schemes to employed persons and their families moving within the Community, OJ 1971 L 149/2 for the definition of the term "social security".

to the Community law as a whole actually appeared even more apt than under the Convention since the Regulation is formally part of the – secondary – Community law with the ECJ also being the final instance for its interpretation. The cited reasons advanced in favour of an autonomous interpretation apply equally if not stronger to the Regulation. Therefore, the transformation of the Brussels Convention into a Regulation did not virtually change the method of autonomous interpretation. It only strengthened the approach to follow principally an autonomous European interpretation of the Regulation. However, as pointed out *supra* (note 91a) the ECJ seems to focus on a truly autonomous interpretation which reduces the recourse to other Community law to a minimum and, where possible, the Court resorts to international materials. A further characteristic of the autonomous method is the extensive, if not excessive redress to the ECJ's own precedents which is by far the most often used source.[186] This does not mean, however, that any redress to national law is now excluded. Where the Regulation so orders (for instance in Art. 7(3) or Art. 62) the applicable national law has still to be determined and applied.[187] But this remains the exception.

The autonomous interpretation does not exclude the use of the material on which the **96** Regulation is based. In the first line these are the Recitals to the Regulation and also those to its predecessor. They have not the same weight as the text of the Regulation itself but are a useful means for its interpretation. Further helpful sources are the Explanatory Memoranda accompanying the Draft Proposal and the Amended Draft Proposal of the Commission.[188] But as already indicated also the Official Reports to the Brussels Convention and to the later Accession Conventions and to the Lugano Convention are useful aids for the interpretation of the Regulation. Moreover almost all decisions of the ECJ on the Brussels Convention continue to remain meaningful (except where the text of the regulation deviates from the Brussels Convention).

The autonomous interpretation of the Regulation should also allow the making of reference **97** to such other international instruments and their interpretation which either have influenced the wording of the Regulation – like for instance Art. 9 (2) Vienna Sales Convention (CISG) which was the model for Art. 25 (1) lit. c Regulation[189] – or which concern same basic questions also to be solved in the Regulation and/or require decisions on fundamental civil or commercial concepts like contract, tort, consumer, causation etc. The reason for such a broad interinstrumental approach of interpretation is to avoid that for each international instrument separate and specific concepts for these basic terms develop.[190] A further reason is that these other international instruments are in force in many if not in all EU Member States and also in the Lugano States. They therefore form in a wide sense part of the *acquis*

---

185   See thereto *Economides-Apostolidis*, EuLF 2010, I-256 *et seq.*; *Gottwald*, in: Münchener Kommentar zur ZPO, EuGVO Vorbem. note 39 *et seq.*; *Hess*, IPRax 2006, 348 (351 *et seq.*); *Kindler*, EuLF 2010, I-252 *et seq.*; *Kropholler*, in: FS 75 Jahre Max-Planck-Institut für Privatrecht (2001) 583 *et seq.*; *Staudinger*, in: Rauscher, Einl. notes 35 *et seq.*

186   See, for instance, the ECJ decisions cited in fn. 199 and 200.

187   As to the disputed question whether the *Tessili* doctrine of the ECJ (*supra* fn. 197) has still some application under Art. 7 (1), see Art. 7 notes 96 *et seq.* (*Mankowski*).

188   See *supra* Introduction note 23 (*Magnus*).

189   See further Art. 25 note 116 (*Magnus*).

190   See *Ferrari*, Riv. dir. int. 2000, 669 *et seq.*; *Magnus*, in: FS 75 Jahre Max-Planck-Institut für Privatrecht (2001), p. 571, 579 *et seq.*; see also *Hess*, IPRax 2006, 355.

communautaire as well as of an international acquis. Insofar in the first line the CISG and the case law and doctrine under this Convention should be taken into account for the interpretation of corresponding terms in the Regulation but also, for instance, the Ottawa Convention on International Factoring, the CMR, the Warsaw and Montreal Convention on air carriage.

3. The interpretation criteria

98   The Regulation has to be interpreted according to the methods required for Community law. The interpretation methods of Community law used by the ECJ are in principle the classical tools of verbal, historic, systematic and purposive interpretation known to probably all legal systems but given different weight by the different national laws.[191] But under Community law they have some specifities. Moreover, the comparative interpretation, the general conformity with Community law as such, the conformity with Human Rights and the special relationship with the Lugano Convention have to be taken into account, too. All these tools have now to be applied to the interpretation of the Regulation.

99   The interpretation method as used by the European Court of Justice has also to be followed by the national courts when applying the Regulation.[192]

100   Among the different interpretation aspects there is no strict hierarchy. The courts have a certain discretion although they must avoid any arbitrary use of the interpretation instruments. However, in case of doubt the reasonable purpose of the provision should finally govern the interpretation. This is the attitude of the ECJ[193] shared by legal doctrine.[194]

a) The verbal interpretation

101   The verbal interpretation tries to reveal the sense of the wording of a text as it would normally be understood. As in general with legal texts also under Community law the wording is the starting point of any interpretation.[195] Where the wording is unambiguous and clear legal certainty and a uniform application of the Regulation generally require to keep to the wording. Like generally with international law instruments which intend to unify previously differing national views the wording has a rather strong weight which it might not have under specific national traditions.[196] Thus, the text of the Regulation should be first

---

[191]   See, e.g., *Falco Privatstiftung, Thomas Rabitsch v. Gisela Weller-Lindhorst*, (Case C-533/07) (2009) ECR I-3327 paras. 19 *et seq.*; see also *Hess*, Europäisches Zivilprozessrecht § 4 notes 52 *et seq.*; generally on the interpretation of uniform law still the classical work of *Kropholler*, Internationales Einheitsrecht (1975).

[192]   As to the binding effect of decisions of the ECJ see *infra* Introduction note 127 (*Magnus*).

[193]   See, for instance, *A. de Bloos SPRL v. Société en commandite par actions Bouyer*, (Case 14/76) (1976) ECR 1497, 1508 paras. 9/12; *Jozef de Wolf v. Harry Cox BV*, (Case 42/76) (1976) ECR 1759, 1767 paras. 9/10; *Effer SpA v. Hans-Joachim Kantner*, (Case 38/81) (1982) ECR 825, 834 paras. 5 *et seq.*; *Gubisch Maschinenfabrik KG v. Giulio Palumbo*, (Case 144/86) (1987) ECR 4861, 4874 paras. 8 *et seq.*; *Société financière et industrielle du Peloux (SFIP) v. Axa Belgium*, (Case C-112/03) (2005) ECR I-3707, paras. 28, 36. As to the specific doctrine of "effet utile" see *infra* Introduction note 107 (*Magnus*).

[194]   Hausmann, in: Simons/Hausmann, Einleitung note 48; *Kropholler/von Hein* Einl. note 42, 46; *Layton/Mercer* para. 11.032; *Ansgar Staudinger*, in: Rauscher Einl. Brüssel I-VO note 40.

[195]   See for instance *TNT Express Nederland BV v. Axa Versicherung AG*, (C-533/08) (2010) ECR I-4107 paras. 44 *et seq.*

given its plain meaning and it should be understood in this sense. But since there is no single Community language and since the versions in the different national languages, which have all the same weight may vary, the court or other interpreter should consult not only the version in the home language but also other language versions. Sometimes doubts can be removed by this procedure.[197] On the other hand, a comparison of different language versions can sometimes cast doubts on a provision.[198] They must then be removed by other instruments of interpretation, in particular by a purposive interpretation.[199] "The different language versions of a Community text must be given a uniform interpretation and hence in the case of divergence between the versions the provision in question must be interpreted by reference to the purpose and general scheme of the rules of which it forms a part."[200]

b) The historic interpretation

The historic interpretation tries to reveal the intention of the lawgiver. For the Regulation   **102** the Recitals[201] as well as the Reports to the Drafts both of the Brussels I[202] and the Brussels I*bis* Regulation[203] prepared by the Commission deliver helpful explanations. But also the accompanying Official Reports to the Brussels Convention and to the later Accession Conventions[204] can still be used at least where the wording of the respective provision remained unchanged. The same is true for the Report to the Lugano Convention.[205] It has, however, rightly been pointed out that with the increasing time distance the intentions of the lawgivers lose their weight.[206] A special kind of historic interpretation is the ECJ's method to give the own precedents the greatest weight in interpreting the Regulation. The Court always tries to establish undisturbed continuity of its case law unless the legislator clearly interferes.[207]

---

[196]   See thereto *Kropholler/von Hein*, Internationales Einheitsrecht p. 263 *et seq.*; *Kropholler/von Hein*, in: 75 Jahre Max-Planck-Institut für Privatrecht (2001), p. 583, 590 *et seq.*

[197]   See for instance *A. de Bloos SPRL v. Société en commandite par actions Bouyer*, (Case 14/76) (1976) ECR 1497, 1508 paras. 9/12 (doubts under Art. 5 no. 1 (now Art. 7 (1)) as to whether the place of performance of the disputed obligation or of any obligation was decisive were removed by the consultation of the German and Italian version); with scepticism *Hess*, IPRax 2006, 353 *et seq.*

[198]   See the English decisions with respect to Art. 16 no. 2 Brussels Convention: *Newtherapeutics v. Katz* (1991) 2 All E. R. 151, 163 *et seq.* (Ch. D.); *Grupo Torras v. Al-Sabah* (1995) 1 Lloyd's Rep. 374, 401 *et seq.* (Q. B.).

[199]   In the same sense *Hausmann*, in: Simons/Hausmann, Einleitung note 52; *Kropholler/von Hein* Einl. note 43.

[200]   *Pierre Bouchereau*, (Case 30/77) (1977) ECR 1999, 2010 paras.13/14.

[201]   See for instance *TNT Express Nederland BV v. Axa Versicherung AG*, (C-533/08) (2010) ECR I-4107 paras. 49.

[202]   In particular COM (1999) 348 fin.

[203]   In particular COM (2010) 748 fin.

[204]   See *supra* Introduction notes 16 *et seq.* (*Magnus*).

[205]   Also *Hausmann*, in: Simons/Hausmann, Einleitung note 53; as to the interpretation of the Lugano Convention see *Schmidt-Parzefall*, Die Auslegung des Parallelübereinkommens von Lugano (1995).

[206]   *Kropholler/von Hein* Einl. note 45; for further discussion see *Hess*, IPRax 2006, 354 *et seq.*

[207]   As to the interaction between Court and EU legislator with *many examples* see *Lenaerts/Stapper*, RabelsZ 78 (2014) 252 *et seq.*

c) The systematic interpretation

103 The systematic interpretation tries to infer the meaning of a provision from the surrounding system of rules and provisions either within the same legislative act or even from other neighbouring regulations. The Regulation constitutes a system of its own from which conclusions can be drawn for the understanding of single provisions or terms.[208] The ECJ has drawn conclusions also from other legislative acts of Community law if they contain general definitions or rules which should be applied in the same sense wherever they are used in Community law. This has been for instance the case with the definition of the term "social security" as used in Art. 1 (2) (c). This term has to be understood in the sense as defined by Art. 4 of Regulation No. 1408/71 on social security.[209] For the contractual qualification of the compensation claim of a commercial agent against its principal the ECJ relied on the respective qualification in the Directive on commercial agents.[210] However, under an overall perspective the Court has been rather reluctant to resort to other instruments of Community law.[211]

104 As already outlined[212] other international regulations like the CISG, the CMR etc. and their interpretation by the courts and by legal doctrine can and should also be taken into account as far as these instruments use identical terms and concepts. For instance, the question should be decided under all these instruments including the Regulation in the same way whether and when consumer protecting provisions can be invoked where goods are partly used for private purposes and partly for professional purposes (dual use goods).[213]

105 The systematic interpretation is in particular helpful with respect to questions of general rule and exception. In case of doubt, the general rule can and should be understood in a wide sense whereas the exception must be interpreted restrictively.[214] Thus, for instance, the special jurisdictions in Artt. 7 deviate from the general rule of Art. 4 which requires the defendant's domicile in the forum state. The Court held on many occasions that the exceptions from that rule must be interpreted restrictively.[215] The systematic interpretation also

---

[208] See for an example of systematic interpretation: *Siegfried Zelger v. Sebastiano Salinitri*, (Case 56/79) (1980) ECR 89, where the ECJ held that agreements on the place of performance need not meet the form of jurisdiction agreements because then still the Brussels Convention (now the Regulation) systematically distinguishes between both kinds of agreements; but as to the different solution for agreements on the place of performance which pursue merely procedural purposes see *Mainschiffahrts-Genossenschaft eG (MSG) v. Les Gravières Rhénanes SARL*, (Case C-106/95) (1997) ECR I-911, I-943 *et seq.* paras. 31–35; confirmed by *GIE Groupe Concorde v. Master of the Vessel "Suhadiwarno Panjan"*, (Case C-440/97) (1999) ECR I-6307, I-6351 *et seq.* para. 28; for a full discussion see Art. 7 notes 145 *et seq.* (*Mankowski*) and Art. 23 note 41 *et seq.* (*Magnus*).

[209] *Gemeente Steenbergen v. Luc Baten*, (Case C-271/00) (2002) ECR I-10489, I-10523 para. 45.

[210] *Arcado SPRL v. Haviland SA*, (Case 9/87) (1988) ECR 1539.

[211] See in particular, *Kainz v. Pantherwerke AG*, (C-45/13) (2014) ECR para. 20 *et seq.*; see also *supra* notes 91a and 95.

[212] *Supra* Introduction notes 96 *et seq.* (*Magnus*).

[213] See thereto *Johann Gruber v. BayWa AG*, (Case C-464/01) (2005) ECR I-439.

[214] See for instance ÖFAB, Östergötlands Fastigheter AB v. Frank Koot and Ervergreen Investments BV (C-147/12) (2013) ECR paras. 30 *et seq.*; *Kainz v. Pantherwerke AG*, (C-45/13) (2014) ECR paras. 21 *et seq.*

[215] See the preceding fn. (paras. 31 and 22 respectively: "… those rules of special jurisdiction must be

allows to draw conclusions for the interpretation of the Regulation and even fill its gaps by way of analogy. The analogy can be drawn to provisions of other instruments belonging to those listed above as far as they deal with the same problem which is relevant under the Regulation.[216]

d) The purposive interpretation

The purposive or teleological interpretation tries to reveal the purpose of a provision and **106** then interprets the provision in the light of that purpose. This method has been frequently applied by the ECJ and the purposive approach is often decisive.[217] Nonetheless the wording of the respective provision and the principle of legal certainty restrict too free a purposive interpretation.[218] To reveal the purpose of a provision again the Recitals of the Regulation, the Explanatory Memoranda to the Draft Proposals prepared by the Commission, the Official Reports to the Brussels Convention and the later Accession Conventions are useful aids. The purposive interpretation runs however always the danger that the interpreter infers a purpose from the respective provision which is influenced by the own national perspective. In the ECJ this danger is practically excluded by the composition of the Court where judges of all Member States safeguard that all national views are represented and taken into account. National courts when applying the Regulation do not have this advantage. They have to be careful not to import into the interpretation of the Regulation purposes and transplants from the own national law.

A specific aspect of the purposive interpretation under Community law is the "effet utile" **107** doctrine which the ECJ applies to all fields of Community law.[219] The "effet utile" doctrine requires to interpret a provision in a sense that its purpose is effectively achieved and that the general aim of Community law to integrate the national systems in a single area of freedom, security and justice is as effectively as possible supported; this leads to a "dynamic" interpretation of Community law.[220] The interpreter has to choose that interpretation which serves the integration goal and the goal of full effectiveness best. Again, the interrelationship

---

interpreted restrictively and cannot give rise to an interpretation going beyond the cases expressly envisaged by the regulation …").

[216] In the same sense *Ansgar Staudinger*, in: Rauscher Einl. Brüssel I-VO note 37.

[217] See, for instance, *A. de Bloos SPRL v. Société en commandite par actions Bouyer*, (Case 14/76) (1976) ECR 1497, 1508 paras. 9/12; *Jozef de Wolf v. Harry Cox BV*, (Case 42/76) (1976) ECR 1759, 1767 paras. 9/10; *Effer SpA v. Hans-Joachim Kantner*, (Case 38/81) (1982) ECR 825, 834 paras.5 *et seq.*; *Gubisch Maschinenfabrik KG v. Giulio Palumbo*, (Case 144/86) (1987) ECR 4861, 4874 paras. 8 *et seq.*; *Société financière et industrielle du Peloux (SFIP) v. Axa Belgium*, (Case C-112/03) (2005) ECR I-3707 paras. 28, 36.

[218] A rather far-reaching example of a purposive interpretation is however *Fiona Shevill v. Presse Alliance SA*, (Case C-68/93) (1995) ECR I-415 where the ECJ limited the jurisdiction under the old Art. 5 (3) at the *locus delicti* to the damage suffered there; see further Art. 7 notes 190 *et seq.* (*Mankowski*).

[219] See for instance in general *Jean Noel Royer*, (Case 48/75) (1976) ECR 497; with respect to the Brussels Convention *Ferdinand M. J. J. Duijnstee v. Lodewijk Goderbauer*, (Case 288/82) (1983) ECR 3663, 3674 *et seq.* para. 13; further to the "effet utile" doctrine *Streinz*, in: FS Ulrich Everling II (1995), p. 149 *et seq.*; *Hausmann*, in: Simons/Hausmann, Einleitung note 59; *Hausmann*, in: Simons/Hausmann, Einleitung note 53; *Layton/Mercer* para. 11.053; *Hess*, IPRax 2006, 357 *et seq.*

[220] Thereto *Duintjer Tebbens*, in: Contributions in Honour of Sauveplanne p. 65 *et seq.*; *Kropholler/von Hein* Einl. note 47; *Ansgar Staudinger*, in: Rauscher Einl. Brüssel I-VO note 40.

between Brussels *Ibis* and the 2007 Lugano Convention warns of a too far-reaching recognition and application of other *Community* goals.

e) The comparative interpretation

108 The comparative method supports the interpretation of a provision by comparing it with solutions taken from national legal systems. On several occasions the ECJ has used this method openly: partly by referring to general principles underlying the national laws of all or most Member States,[221] partly by identifying divergences between the national laws and drawing conclusions from this fact.[222] In particular, national courts when applying the Regulation should in case of doubt and where a decision of the ECJ is still lacking consult whether and how other Member State courts have decided the relevant question.[223] Also legal doctrine should be consulted.[224] Comparative material has no binding force. It can only become influential by its persuasive authority when its reasoning and arguments are convincing.

f) Conformity with Community law

109 Since the Regulation is (secondary) Community law it has to be interpreted in conformity with the fundamental principles of Community law, in particular with higher ranking Community law.[225] Therefore the fundamental principles of the TFEU have to be observed like the principle of non-discrimination (Art. 18 TFEU [ex Art. 12 EC Treaty])[226] or the

---

[221] See for instance *LTU Lufttransportunternehmen GmbH & Co. KG v. Eurocontrol*, (Case 29/76) (1976) ECR 1541, 1550 para. 3; *Henri Gourdain v. Franz Nadler*, (Case 133/78) (1979) ECR 733, 743 para. 3; *Netherlands State v. Reinhold Rüffer*, (Case 814/79) (1980) ECR 3807, 3819 paras. 7 *et seq.*; *Criminal proceedings against Siegfried Ewald Rinkau*, (Case 157/80) (1981) ECR 1391, 1400 para. 11; *Ferdinand M. J.J. Duijnstee v. Lodewijk Goderbauer*, (Case 288/82) (1983) 3663, 3675 *et seq.* para. 17; *Volker Sonntag v. Hans Waidmann*, (Case C-172/91) (1993) ECR I-1963, 1996 para. 18; *Gemeente Steenbergen v. Luc Baten*, (Case C-271/00) (2002) ECR I-10489, 10519 para. 28; for a discussion see *Hess*, IPRax 2006, 352 *et seq.*; see also *Economides-Apostolidis*, EuLF 2010, I-256 *et seq.*

[222] From these divergences the ECJ has rather often inferred that an independent interpretation should be adopted: *Handelswekerij G. J. Bier B. V. v. Mines de Potasse d'Alsace S. A.*, (Case 21/76) (1976) ECR 1735, 1747 paras. 20/23; *Industrial Diamond Supplies v. Luigi Riva*, (Case 43/77) (1977) ECR 2175, 2187 *et seq.* paras. 22/27; *Ferdinand M. J. J. Duijnstee v. Lodewijk Goderbauer*, (Case 288/82) (1983) 3663, 3675 *et seq.* para. 17; *Gubisch Maschinenfabrik KG v. Giulio Palumbo*, (Case 144/86) (1987) ECR 4861; on few occasions the Court has inferred that the applicable national law should decide: *Industrie Tessili Italiana Como v. Dunlop AG*, (Case 12/76) (1976) ECR 1473; *Siegfried Zelger v. Sebastiano Salinitri (No. 2)*, (Case 129/83) (1984) ECR 2397, 2407 paras. 10 *et seq.*

[223] In the same sense *Layton/Mercer* para. 11.037. Decisions of other European jurisdictions rendered after 1997 can be found on the internet under http://curia.eu.int/de/coopju/conventions.htm; prior decisions have been published by the ECJ in its collection of jurisprudence on Community law; see also the collection of national decisions in *Kaye*, European Case Law on the Judgments Conventions (1998) and the national sections in *Layton/Mercer* vol. II (2004).

[224] In the same sense *Kropholler/von Hein* Einl. note 48.

[225] For a survey over relevant principles of Community law see also *Layton/Mercer* paras. 11.045 *et seq.*

[226] As to this principle no discrimination according to nationality is allowed among the Member States; thus far no case law on the non-discrimination principle with respect to the matters covered by the Regulation exists since the Brussels Convention did not directly fall under Art. 12 EC Treaty; but as to the principle in general see *Phil Collins v. Imtrat Handelsgesellschaft mbH and Patricia Im- und Export Verwaltungs-*

freedom of movement of persons, goods, services and capital. Moreover the interpretation of the Regulation cannot transgress the limits of the competences granted to the Community in the field of international procedural law by Artt. 67 *et seq.*, 81 TFEU (ex Artt. 61 and 65 EC Treaty).[227]

g) Conformity with Human Rights

The interpretation of the Regulation has finally to conform to the standards of the European **110** Convention for the Protection of Human Rights and Fundamental Freedoms of 4 November 1950[228] which the EU is obliged to observe (see Art. 6 (2) EU Treaty) and which is more or less taken over by the EU Charta on Fundamental Rights. Also the ECJ[229] has already referred to the European Convention on Human Rights whose Art. 6 is particularly relevant for fundamental procedural rights.

VII. The reference procedure

1. In general

Without a central and finally competent court a uniform understanding and application of a **111** legal instrument in different jurisdictions can hardly be achieved, let alone upheld over a longer period of time. The uniform interpretation and application of the Regulation is safeguarded by the European Court of Justice. The Court is competent to finally and solely decide all questions concerning the interpretation of the Regulation by a preliminary ruling which is binding on the parties of the original dispute.[230] The ECJ's competence follows directly from Art. 267 TFEU (ex Art. 234 EC Treaty); a separate protocol granting the ECJ this competence as under the Brussels Convention[231] is no longer necessary since the transformation of the Convention into a Regulation brought the Regulation under the reign of general Community law (albeit the Protocol under the Brussels Regulation is still in force and of relevance with respect to those few non-European territories to which the Regulation does not apply[232]). General Community law provides for a special reference procedure to the ECJ which then renders in the form of a preliminary ruling a final decision on the referred interpretation issue: under Art. 267 TFEU (ex Art. 234 EC Treaty) any national court may

---

gesellschaft mbH and Leif Emanuel Kraul v. Emi Electrola GmbH, (Joined Cases C-92/92 & 392/92) (1993) ECR I-5145; *Anthony Hubbard (Testamentvollstrecker) v. Peter Hamburger*, (Case C-20/92) (1993) ECR I-3777; *Data Delecta Aktiebolag and Ronny Forsberg v. MSL Dynamics Ltd.*, (Case C-43/95) (1996) ECR I-4661; *Stephen Austin Saldanha and MTS Securities Corporation v. Hiross Holding AG*, (Case C-122/96) (1997) ECR I-5325.

[227] See also *Ansgar Staudinger*, in: Rauscher Einl. Brüssel I-VO note 41.

[228] See also *Geimer/Schütze* Einl. A. 1 note 155 *et seq.*; *Kropholler/von Hein* Einl. note 50; *Ansgar Staudinger*, in: Rauscher Einl. Brüssel I-VO note 42.

[229] In *Dieter Krombach v. André Bamberski*, (Case C-7/98) (2000) ECR I-1935, I-1966 para. 27.

[230] It has to be borne in mind that the ECJ is also competent to finally interpret the 2007 Lugano Convention which via the ratification by the EU has become EU law so that courts of the EU Member States can refer interpretation questions for a preliminary ruling.

[231] Protocol on the Interpretation of the Brussels Convention by the European Court of Justice of 3 June 1971.

[232] See *supra* note 46 (*Magnus*); until 30 June 2007 the Brussels Regulation and its Protocols were further applicable to Denmark; see also Recital 22.

---

and any national court of last instance must refer questions of interpretation of Community law to the European Court of Justice if the question is relevant for the decision of the dispute, if the question is still undecided by the ECJ and if the answer is not clear beyond reasonable doubt.[233] However, until 30 November 2009 Art. 68 EC Treaty specified and qualified the reference procedure for all legislative measures taken under Art. 65 EC Treaty (now Art. 81 TFEU) on which provision also the Regulation is based. Art. 68 EC Treaty restricted considerably the ambit of the former Art. 234 EC Treaty.[234]

2. Requirements of the reference procedure under Art. 267 TFEU

112 Art. 267 TFEU replaced the special provision of Art. 68 EC Treaty which applied until the TFEU entered into force on 1 December 2009.

a) No interpretation of national law

113 The reference procedure concerns only the interpretation of the Regulation. Questions of national law even if disguised in the reference question cannot be referred.[235] Therefore a reference is generally inadmissible if it asks for the interpretation of provisions of the Regulation which have been voluntarily implemented into national law, for instance into national interlocal procedural law.[236] Also, where the Regulation explicitly refers to national law (see Artt. 6 (1), 35, 62) the ECJ cannot be called upon to interpret the provisions of the applicable national law or whether those provisions conform to the Regulation; however the Court is competent to determine the precise scope of the provision of the Regulation which refers to national law.[237] Likewise a referral to the ECJ is admissible to determine the meaning and scope of the notion "public policy" where the Regulation uses the term, as in Art. 45 (1) (a) (though the Court is not competent to decide on the contents of the public policy of the applicable national law).[238] Additionally, the question whether an expression of the Regulation is to be interpreted autonomously or refers to national law can itself be referred to the ECJ.[239]

b) Pending procedure

114 An admissible referral further requires that the interpretation issue arises during a pending proceeding. The proceeding must have been formally begun and must not have been already ended, by judgment or settlement, before the referring court.[240] The nature of the proceed-

---

[233] *Srl CILFIT and Lanificio di Gavardo SpA v. Ministry of Health*, (Case 283/81) (1982) ECR 3415.

[234] As to the details see *infra* Introduction notes 112 *et seq.* (*Magnus*).

[235] *Kleinwort Benson Ltd. v. Glasgow City District Council*, (Case C-346/93) (1995) ECR I-615; but see also *Banque internationale pour l'Afrique occidentale SA (BIAO) v. Finanzamt für Großunternehmen in Hamburg*, (Case C-306/99) (2003) ECR I-1; see further *Kropholler/von Hein* Einl. note 32; *Ansgar Staudinger*, in: Rauscher Einl. Brüssel I-VO note 47.

[236] See *Kleinwort Benson Ltd. v. Glasgow City District Council*, (Case C-346/93) (1995) ECR I-615.

[237] See also *Kropholler/von Hein* Einl. note 32.

[238] See *Dieter Krombach v. André Bamberski*, (Case C-7/98) (2000) ECR I-1935, I-1965 para. 23; *Régie nationale des usines Renault SA v. Maxicar SpA and Orazio Formento*, (Case C-38/98) (2000) ECR I-2973, I-3020 para. 28.

[239] An example is *Industrie Tessili Italiana Como v. Dunlop AG*, (Case 12/76) (1976) ECR 1473 concerning the question whether the place of performance is to be determined autonomously or by redress to the applicable national law and deciding that question in the latter sense.

ings – contentious or non-contentious – and also the nature of the court or tribunal is irrelevant.[241] Even in proceedings on preliminary measures, including protective measures, a referral is admissible since otherwise the interpretation of Art. 35 and its relation to other provisions of the Regulation could not be finally decided by the ECJ.[242] But again, interpretation questions of national law to which Art. 35 mainly refers cannot be brought before the Court.

The court or tribunal which refers the issue to the ECJ must, however, have acted in the **115** original dispute in its judicial capacity. Where it acted merely in an administrative capacity, for instance as a mere registry, it is neither entitled nor obliged to refer.[243]

Arbitration courts do not belong to the courts meant by Art. 267 TFEU. The provision **116** concerns only state courts. Arbitration as such falls outside the scope of the Regulation (Art. 1 (2) (d) Regulation). Arbitration courts are therefore not entitled to referrals to the ECJ.[244]

c) Court of last instance
Under Art. 267 TFEU any court of a Member State is entitled to refer questions of inter- **117** pretation of the Regulation to the European Court of Justice for a preliminary ruling and the courts of last instance are obliged to refer. Similarly under the Interpretation Protocol to the Brussels Convention at least all courts of appeal were entitled and the courts of last instance were obliged to refer. Under the former Art. 68 (1) EC Treaty only courts of last instance could make references to the ECJ but were not obliged to refer. References of all other courts were inadmissible. This restriction was evidently dictated by the fear that the number of references would overflow the ECJ if each court in the Community could seise the ECJ with preliminary rulings. The restricted access of national courts to the ECJ due to Art. 68 EC Treaty met with considerable critique.[245] The TFEU remedied this shortcoming by deleting Art. 68 EC Treaty.

The court or tribunal which is obliged to refer the issue to the ECJ must be a court against **118** whose decision there is no further remedy available.[246] This is almost unanimously understood in the sense that it is necessary but also sufficient that in the concrete case no ordinary judicial remedy would be given when the referring court renders its final decision.[247] It is not

---

[240] Also *Hausmann*, in: Simons/Hausmann, Einleitung note 69.

[241] See Art. 1 (1); further *Kropholler/von Hein* Einl. note 33; *Ansgar Staudinger*, in: Rauscher Einl. Brüssel I-VO note 48.

[242] In the same sense *Kropholler/von Hein* Einl. note 33; contra *Ansgar Staudinger*, in: Rauscher Einl. Brüssel I-VO note 47.

[243] *HSB-Wohnbau GmbH, (Case C-86/00) (2001) ECR I-5353.*

[244] *Nordsee Deutsche Hochseefischerei GmbH v. Reederei Mond Hochseefischerei Nordstern AG & Co. KG and Reederei Friedrich Busse Hochseefischerei Nordstern AG & Co. KG, (Case 102/81) (1982) ECR 1095; Eco Swiss China Time Ltd. v. Benetton Int., (Case C-126/97) (1999) I-3055.*

[245] For further critique see *Basedow*, ZEuP 2001, 437; *Kropholler/von Hein*, in: 75 Jahre Max-Planck-Institut für Privatrecht (2001), p. 583, 587 *et seq.*; *Layton/Mercer* para. 11.030.

[246] See *Lyckeskog* (C-99/00) (2002) ECR I-4839 para.16; *Cartesio* (C-210/06) (2008) ECR I-9641 paras.75 *et seq.*

[247] See; *Wegener*, in: Callies/Ruffert (eds.), EUV. AEUV. Kommentar (4th ed. 2011) Art. 267 note 27; *Geimer/*

necessary that there would be generally – in abstracto – no judicial remedy against a decision of the referring court. The national law prescribes which ordinary remedies lie (Art. 267 sent. 3 TFEU [ex Art. 68 (1) EC Treaty]). In any case the highest national courts in civil matters are obliged to referrals to the ECJ.[248] It does not matter that their decisions may be subject to attack by an eventual remedy to the constitutional court of the country.[249] But even lower courts must make a reference insofar as national law provides that there is no judicial remedy against their decision in the concrete case be it that the sum is not reached which is needed to entitle to appeal, be it otherwise. Where the first instance is at the same time the last instance this court is obliged to a reference to the ECJ.[250]

119 Where it is the court's discretion to permit a remedy to a higher instance the court remains nonetheless a court of last instance if the court refuses the permission.[251] Where the court on the contrary either permits the remedy or where its refusal can be attacked by a separate remedy then the court is not a court of last instance and is not obliged to make a reference.[252]

120 The restriction of Art. 68 (1) EC Treaty could not be circumvented by basing the reference also on interpretation issues of general Community law and invoking the then Art. 234 EC Treaty.[253] Art. 68 (1) EC Treaty prevailed over this latter section. Art. 267 TFEU made this difficulty superfluous.

d) Relevance for the original dispute

121 A reference for a preliminary ruling of the ECJ is inadmissible where the interpretation issue has no bearing on the outcome of the original dispute before the referring court. The referring court must consider that a decision on the referred question is necessary to enable it to give judgment (Art. 267 sent. 2 TFEU [ex Art. 68 (1) EC Treaty]). The ECJ is neither competent nor obliged to answer mere hypothetical questions concerning the interpretation of the Regulation nor does the Court render legal opinions on such issues. References to that effect are thus inadmissible. The referring court must therefore explain in its referral why the answer to the interpretation issue is decisive for the final judgment.[254] The interpretation issue is for instance irrelevant where all possible interpretations lead to the same result[255] or where a party is already precluded to raise the interpretation issue.[256]

Schütze Einl. A.1 note 162; *Kropholler/von Hein* Einl. note 34; *Ansgar Staudinger*, in: Rauscher Einl. Brüssel I-VO note 45; probably also *Layton/Mercer* para. 11.029.

[248] For instance in England the Supreme Court (the former House of Lords), in France the Cour de Cassation, in Germany the Bundesgerichtshof and the Bundesarbeitsgericht.

[249] See *Ansgar Staudinger*, in: Rauscher Einl. Brüssel I-VO note 45 and fn. 180.

[250] *Danmarks Rederiforening, acting on behalf of DFDS Torline A/S v. LO Landsorganisationen i Sverige, acting on behalf of SEKO Sjöfolk Facket för Service och Kommunikation,* (Case C-18/02) (2004) ECR I-1417, I-1450 para. 17.

[251] See thereto *Geimer/Schütze* Einl. A.1 note 162 with further references.

[252] See also *Criminal proceedings against Kenny Roland Lyckeskog,* (Case C-99/00) (2002) ECR I-4839, I-4885 para. 16; *Ansgar Staudinger*, in: Rauscher Einl. Brüssel I-VO note 58.

[253] *Marseille Fret SA. v. Seatrano Shipping Company Ltd.,* (Case C-24/02) (2002) ECR I-3383.

[254] *Gantner Electronic GmbH v. Baasch Exploitatie Maatschappij BV,* (Case C-111/01) (2003) ECR I-4207.

[255] In this sense at least BGH IPRax 2003, 346, 349; also *Kropholler/von Hein* Einl. note 35; but doubting *Ansgar Staudinger*, in: Rauscher Einl. Brüssel I-VO note 50.

[256] *Kropholler/von Hein* Einl. note 35.

It is the referring court's discretion to regard an interpretation issue as doubtful. Only if the **122** issue is clear beyond reasonable doubt a referral becomes inadmissible (acte clair doctrine).[257] But the ECJ accepted even a reference on the matter whether under an EU regulation sheep's wool had to be regarded as a product gained from animals.[258]

e) Obligation to refer

Where the mentioned requirements are met the court is entitled and being a court of last **123** instance also obliged to refer the interpretation issue to the ECJ.[259] Without such obligation at least of the national courts of last instance the ECJ could not effectively fulfil its function to unify the interpretation of the Regulation. It is however only the national court which can make a reference to the ECJ. The parties may urge the court to do so but they themselves are not entitled to a referral and they have no remedy under Community law if the national court refuses a reference (though under national law a remedy may lie).[260]

Only in exceptional circumstances is the national court of last instance not obliged to refer **124** an interpretation issue. One such situation is where the ECJ has already decided that issue.[261] But even if an ECJ ruling already exists a court is nonetheless entitled to a reference. It can be expected that in such a case the referring court explains in detail why it considers the previous decision of the ECJ as unsatisfactory.

There is also no obligation to refer and, as mentioned above, a reference becomes inad- **125** missible if the interpretation issue is clear beyond reasonable doubt.[262] However courts should be cautious to consider interpretation issues as so clear. Courts of other jurisdictions and in particular the ECJ might take another view on the interpretation. In order to support the ECJ's function to unify the interpretation of the Regulation national courts should rather refer than avoid referrals.

f) Formal requirements

In its referral the court must formulate concrete questions which the ECJ is asked to answer. **126** The referring court must further give a survey of the facts and of the legal background of the dispute – the facts must therefore already have been established[263] – and it must explain why the interpretation issue is relevant for its decision.[264] In cases of particular urgency the national courts may apply for the special urgent procedure provided for in Art. 104b of the Rules of Procedure of the Court of Justice.[265] According to para (1) of this provision the

---

[257] *Srl CILFIT and Lanificio di Gavardo SpA v. Ministry of Health*, (Case 283/81) (1982) ECR 3415.

[258] See *Srl CILFIT and Lanificio di Gavardo SpA v. Ministry of Health*, (Case 283/81) (1982) ECR 3415.

[259] Also *Kropholler/von Hein* Einl. note 36; *Layton/Mercer* para. 11.029; *Ansgar Staudinger*, in: Rauscher Einl. Brüssel I-VO note 43 with further references.

[260] See *Geimer/Schütze* Einl. A.1 note 164; *Kropholler/von Hein* Einl. note 36.

[261] *Da Costa en Schaake NV, Jacob Meijer NV, Hoechst-Holland NV v. Netherlands Inland Revenue Administration*, (Joined Cases 28–30/62) (1963) ECR 63, 80 et seq.; *Srl CILFIT and Lanificio di Gavardo SpA v. Ministry of Health*, (Case 283/81) (1982) ECR 3415, 3429 para. 10.

[262] *Srl CILFIT and Lanificio di Gavardo SpA v. Ministry of Health*, (Case 283/81) (1982) ECR 3415.

[263] *Gantner Electronic GmbH v. Baasch Exploitatie Maatschappij BV*, (Case C-111/01) (2003) ECR I-4207, I-4238 paras. 35 et seq.; see also *Geimer/Schütze* Einl. A.1 note 167.

[264] *Gantner Electronic GmbH v. Baasch Exploitatie Maatschappij BV*, (Case C-111/01) (2003) ECR I-4207.

[265] See OJ 2008 L 24/39.

national court "shall set out, in its request, the matters of fact and law which establish the urgency and justify the application of that exceptional procedure and shall, insofar as possible, indicate the answer it proposes to the questions referred."

3. The effects of decisions of the ECJ

127 The preliminary ruling of the ECJ decides the interpretation issue with binding effect for the court and the parties of the referred dispute. But the ruling is neither a final decision of the original dispute nor has it a formally binding effect on other parties or other disputes.[266] Even the referring court can refer the same issue in another dispute again to the ECJ.[267] Nonetheless, once the ECJ has decided on an interpretation issue this decision has a wide factual effect and is regularly followed by the national courts of the Member States.

4. The reference procedure under the former Art. 68 (3) EC Treaty

128 As a kind of compensation measure for the restricted access of national courts to the ECJ Art. 68 (3) sent. 1 EC Treaty entitled the Council, the Commission and each Member State to refer interpretation issues concerning legislative acts based on Title IV of Part III of the EC Treaty – and thus concerning also the Regulation – to the European Court of Justice. It was a procedure by which abstract and hypothetical questions could be posed. A connection with a concrete dispute was not required. The TFEU abolished this special procedure.

129 Decisions ever rendered by the ECJ under the former Art. 68 (3) EC Treaty could not affect in any respect final and binding judgments which had been delivered before by national courts even if these judgments would now have to be decided to the contrary (see Art. 68 (3) sent. 2 EC Treaty). The ECJ decision gave also no justification to resume the prior proceedings.[268]

130 As far as visible the procedure under Art. 68 (3) EC Treaty was never used. The procedure was no adequate equivalent for the necessary cooperation and dialogue between the ECJ and the national courts in applying the Regulation.

VIII. Updating and reform of the Brussels *Ibis* Regulation

1. Updating

131 Artt. 77 and 78 Brussels I*bis* Regulation empowers the Commission to adopt delegated acts concerning amendments of the Annexes I and II to the Regulation. The Annexes concern the certificates required for the recognition and enforcement of judgments and the other

---

[266] *Geimer/Schütze* Einl. A.1 note 174; *Hausmann*, in: Simons/Hausmann Einleitung note 74; *Kropholler/von Hein* Einl. note 38; *Schmidt-Parzefall* 35 *et seq.*; *Ansgar Staudinger*, in: Rauscher Einl. Brüssel I-VO note 62; for a wider binding effect however *Brückner*, in: Hommelhoff/Jayme/Mangold (eds.), Europäischer Binnenmarkt, IPR und Rechtsangleichung (1995), p. 263, 267 *et seq.*

[267] See *Da Costa en Schaake NV, Jacob Meijer NV, Hoechst-Holland NV v. Netherlands Inland Revenue Administration*, (Joined Cases 28–30/62) (1963) ECR 63, 81.

[268] *Geimer/Schütze* Einl. A.1 note 179; *Kohler*, in: FS Geimer p. 469; *Kropholler/von Hein* Einl. note 31; *Ansgar Staudinger*, in: Rauscher Einl. Brüssel I-VO note 63.

enforceable titles. Although the Commission's power seems to concern mere formalities it allows a certain form of practical updating of the Regulation without great legislative effort. The Commission is so empowered as of 9 January 2013 for an indeterminate period of time.[269] The first updating of this kind is Regulation (EU) 2015/281[270] which replaced Annexes I and II of the original Brussels I*bis* Regulation by new Annexes. The new ones adapt the form of the certificates under Art. 53 and 60 of the Brussels I*bis* Regulation to the facts that Latvia and Lithuania joined the Euro system, that Croatia became an EU Member State and that Denmark implemented the contents of Brussels I*bis*. All this is now mirrored in the new certificate forms. Regulation 2015/281 entered into force on the day after its publication in the Official Journal (25 February 2015).[271] It is thus in force since 26 February 2015.

2. Constant reform

Even before the Brussels I*bis* Regulation became applicable (on 10 January 2015) already an amendment had been prepared.[272] Its purpose is to bring the so-called "patent package" and the Benelux Court under the roof of the Regulation. The Unified Patent Court and the Benelux Court shall be regarded as courts in the sense of the Brussels I*bis* Regulation. Special provisions on the jurisdiction of these courts, their concurrence with other pending proceedings and the recognition and enforcement of their judgments shall be regulated by new Artt. 71a–d.   **132**

Further reform is scheduled by Art. 79 Brussels I*bis* Regulation: Until 11 January 2022 the Commission has to present an assessment report on the functioning of the Regulation and, where appropriate, make amendment proposals. After seven years of experience next steps shall be considered. The pace of the production of European procedural law remains rather high.   **133**

Chapter I: **Scope and Definitions**

Article 1

1. This Regulation shall apply in civil and commercial matters whatever the nature of the court or tribunal. It shall not extend, in particular, to revenue, customs or administrative matters or to the liability of the State for acts and omissions in the exercise of State authority (acta iure imperii).
2. This Regulation shall not apply to:
   (a) the status or legal capacity of natural persons, rights in property arising out of a matrimonial relationship or out of a relationship deemed by the law applicable to such relationship to have comparable effects to marriage;

---

[269] See Art. 78 (2).
[270] See OJ of 25 February 2015, L 54 p. 1.
[271] See Art. 2 Regulation 2015/281.
[272] COM (2013) 554 fin. of 26 July 2013.

(b) bankruptcy, proceedings relating to the winding-up of insolvent companies or other legal persons, judicial arrangements, compositions and analogous proceedings;

(c) social security;

(d) arbitration;

(e) maintenance obligations arising from a family relationship, parentage, marriage or affinity;

(f) wills and succession, including maintenance obligations arising by reason of death.

Recital (12)

This Regulation should not apply to arbitration. Nothing in this Regulation should prevent the courts of a Member State, when seised of an action in a matter in respect of which the parties have entered into an arbitration agreement, from referring the parties to arbitration, from staying or dismissing the proceedings, or from examining whether the arbitration agreement is null and void, inoperative or incapable of being performed, in accordance with their national law.

A ruling given by a court of a Member State as to whether or not an arbitration agreement is null and void, inoperative or incapable of being performed should not be subject to the rules of recognition and enforcement laid down in this Regulation, regardless of whether the court decided on this as a principal issue or as an incidental question.

On the other hand, where a court of a Member State, exercising jurisdiction under this Regulation or under national law, has determined that an arbitration agreement is null and void, inoperative or incapable of being performed, this should not preclude that court's judgment on the substance of the matter from being recognised or, as the case may be, enforced in accordance with this Regulation. This should be without prejudice to the competence of the courts of the Member States to decide on the recognition and enforcement of arbitral awards in accordance with the Convention on the Recognition and Enforcement of Foreign Arbitral Awards, done at New York on 10 June 1958 ('the 1958 New York Convention'), which takes precedence over this Regulation.

This Regulation should not apply to any action or ancillary proceedings relating to, in particular, the establishment of an arbitral tribunal, the powers of arbitrators, the conduct of an arbitration procedure or any other aspects of such a procedure, nor to any action or judgment concerning the annulment, review, appeal, recognition or enforcement of an arbitral award.

Bibliography

1. On EC Reg. 1215/2012

Camilleri, Recital (12) of the recast Regulation: a new hope?, [2013] ICLQ 899

Carducci, Arbitration, anti-suit injunctions and *lis pendens* under the European Jurisdiction Regulation and the New York Convention, [2011] Arb. Int. 171

Dowers, The anti-suit injunction and the EU: legal tradition and Europeanisation in international private law, [2013] Cam. J. Int. & Comp. L. 960

Dowers/Holloway, Brussels I recast passed [2013] Int. Arb. Law Rev. 18

Estrup Ippolito/Adler-Nissen, West Tankers revisited: has the new Brussels I Regulation brought anti-suit injunctions back into the procedural armoury?, [2013] Arb. 158

Radicati di Brozolo, Arbitration and the Draft Revised Brussels I Regulation: Seeds of Home Country Control and of Harmonisation?, [2013] JPrIL 423.

2. On EC Reg. 44/2001

Ambrose, Arbitration and the Free Movement of Judgments, (2003) 19 Arb. Int. 1

Ambrose, English Arbitration Law (2008) International Maritime and Commercial Law Yearbook 27–34

Audit, Arbitration and the Brussels Convention, (1993) 9 Arb. Int. 1

Baatz, A jurisdiction race in the dark: the Wadi Sudr [2010] LMCLQ 364

Barthet, On-line Gambling and the Further Displacement of State Regulation [2008] ICLQ 417

Benedettelli, 'Communitarization' of International Arbitration: A New Spectre Haunting Europe? [2011] Arb. Int. 582

Beraudo, The Arbitration Exception of the Brussels and Lugano Conventions, (2001) 18 (1) J. Int. Arb. 13 (2001)

Carducci, Arbitration, anti-suit injunctions and *lis pendens* under the European Jurisdiction Regulation and the New York Convention [2011] Arb. Int. 171

Dutson/Howarth, National Navigation Co v. Endesa Generacion SA (The Wadi Sudr); dead ahead? West Tankers sails on in the Court of Appeal in The Wadi Sudr [2010] Arbitration 374

Dutta, Jurisdiction for Insolvency-related Proceedings Caught Between European Legislation [2008] Lloyds Mar. & Comm. L.Q. 88

van Haersolte-van Hof, The Arbitration Exception in the Brussels Convention: Further Comment, 18 (1) J. Int. Arb. 27 (2001)

Hartley, The Scope of the Convention: Proceedings for the Appointment of an Arbitrator, (1991) 16 Eur. L. Rev. 529

Hess, Pfeiffer and *Schlosser*, Study JLS/C4/2005/03 Report on the Application of Regulation Brussels 1 in the Member States

van Houtte, May Court Judgments that Disregard Arbitration Clauses and Awards be Enforced under the Brussels and Lugano Conventions?, (1997) 13 Arb. Int. 85

Illmer and *Naumann*, Yet Another Blow: Anti-suit Injunctions in Support of Arbitration Agreements Within the European Union [2007] Int. Arb. LR 147

Kaye, The EEC and Arbitration: The Unsettled Wake of *The Atlantic Emperor*, (1993) 9 Arb. Int. 27

T. Kruger, Civil jurisdiction and the issue of legislating for the EU [2010] Jo. Priv. Int. L. 499

Noussia, Antisuit injunctions and arbitration proceedings: What does the future hold? [2009] 26 Jo. Int. Arb. 311

Nurmela, Sanctity of Dispute Resolution Clauses: Strategic Coherence of the Brussels System [2005] JPrIL 115

Santomauro, Sense and sensibility: reviewing West Tankers and dealing with its implications in the wake of the reform of EC Regulation [2010] JPrIL 281

Schlosser, The 1968 Convention and Arbitration, (1991) 7 Arb. Int. 227

Schlosser, Die Erstreckung von Brüssel I auf die Schiedsgerichtsbarkeit?, SchiedsV 2007, 149

Schlosser, Europe – Is it Time to Reconsider the Arbitration Exception from the Brussels Regulation? [2009] Int. Arb. L. Rev. 45

Smart, Insolvency Proceedings and the Civil Jurisdiction and Judgments Act 1982, [1998] CJQ 149

Steinbrück, The impact of EU law on anti-suit injunctions in aid of English arbitration proceedings [2007] CJQ 358.

I. Introduction and Purpose

1   Art. 1 is critical to understanding the Brussels I Regulation (Recast). It sets the boundaries of
the Brussels I*bis* Regulation and is the trigger for its application to disputes being heard
before Member States' courts. Art. 1 determines whether or not aspects of a case must or may
be decided in particular Member States' courts,[1] whether other Member States' courts can
also exercise jurisdiction or must decline to do so,[2] and whether a judgment from the court of
another Member State is entitled to automatic recognition and then enforcement.[3] The first
question any Member State's court must ask itself is whether the dispute falls within the
scope of the Brussels I*bis* Regulation. This may well be to put the question too simply. There
can be considerable argument over the content of the dispute. Member States' courts may
not agree as to the extent of the matters in dispute and whether all or any of the issues raised
are within the scope of the Brussels I*bis* Regulation. There can also be disagreement over the
consequences of a decision that some issues in a case are excluded from the Brussels I*bis*
Regulation. Traditionally, Art. 1 sets the scope *ratione materiae* of the Recast Brussels I
Regulation.[4] If the dispute falls outwith the Brussels I*bis* Regulation, then matters of jurisdiction, *lis pendens* and recognition and enforcement of the judgment in that dispute have to
be answered by reference to different rules. These may be found in the traditional local law
rules (not arising from EU legislation), treaties[5] and other EU legislation.[6] EU instruments
dealing with specific matters have increased over recent years and as a result, the Brussels

---

[1]   See, for example, Artt. 4 to 6 *et seq.*

[2]   See, for example, Artt. 24, 25, 29–34.

[3]   Chapter III.

[4]   The scope of the Brussels I*bis* Regulation *ratione temporis* (it applies to all proceedings commenced on or
after 10 January 2015, Artt. 66); over particular persons (e.g. third States as a party to the proceedings);
and its territorial scope (e.g. the relationship to Denmark, the Lugano Convention, and the non European
possessions of France and third Member States) is discussed elsewhere, see Introduction paras. 42, 87.

[5]   For example, the New York Convention on the Recognition and Enforcement of Foreign Arbitral Awards
adopted by the United Nations Conference on International Commercial Arbitration on 10th June 1958;
the Hague Convention on Choice of Court Agreements of 30th June 2005 (ratified by the European Justice
Ministers on 10th October 2014 and which is likely shortly to come into force following adoption by the
European Council of Ministers); the Berne Convention concerning international carriage by rail 9 May
1980, as amended by the Vilnius Protocol of 3 June 1999 (COTIF); the Montreal Convention 28 May
1999; the Cape Town Convention on International Interests in mobile Equipment of 16 November 2001.

[6]   Such as Council Regulation (EC) No. 1346/2000 on Insolvency Proceedings 2000 OJ L 338/1(amended
2003 OJ L 236/33, 2005 OJ L 100/1, 2006 OJ L 121/1, 2007 OJ L 159/1, 2008 OJ L 213/1, 2010 OJ L 65/1,
2011 OJ L 160/52; [2014] OJ L 179/4); Council Regulation (EC) No. 4/2009 on jurisdiction, applicable
law, recognition and enforcement of decisions and cooperation in matters relating to maintenance
obligations [2009] OJ L 7/1); Regulation (EC) No. 805/2004 establishing a European Enforcement Order
for uncontested claims 2004 OJ L 143/15 (amended 2005 OJ L 97/64, 2005 OJ L 168/50, 2008 OJ L 304/
80); Regulation (EC) No. 1896/2006 establishing a European Payment Order 2006 OJ L 399/1 (amended
2012 OJ L 283/1); Regulation (EC) No. 861/2007 establishing a European Small Claims Procedure 2007
OJ L 199/1; Regulation (EC) No. 4/2009 on jurisdiction, applicable law, recognition and enforcement of
decisions and cooperation in matters relating to maintenance obligations 2009 OJ L 7/1 (amended 2011
OJ L 293/24); Regulation (EU) No. 650/2012 on jurisdiction, applicable law, recognition and enforcement
of decisions and acceptance and enforcement of authentic instruments in matters of succession and on
the creation of a European Certificate of Succession 2012 OJ L 201/107.

I*bis* Regulation is becoming a residual instrument.[7] The overlaps and gaps between these various instruments and the Brussels I*bis* Regulation require careful consideration. In addition, the Brussels I*bis* Regulation is part of the Area of Freedom, Justice and Security that requires judicial cooperation in civil matters having cross border implications.[8] The CJEU has interpreted the newer instruments as a means of implementing that wider policy of integration.[9] Some of the older jurisprudence on the scope of Regulation and its preceding Brussels Convention may therefore be inappropriate.

The purposes of the Brussels I*bis* Regulation must be reflected in Art. 1, which delimits the **2** scope of the Brussels I Regulation. The purposes of Art. 1 can therefore be found generally in the Recitals to the Brussels I*bis* Regulation. As originally conceived in the Brussels Convention of 1968 and taken through its various amendments by Accession States, the apparent primary purpose was the automatic recognition and easy enforcement of judgments within Member States.[10] The difficulty of recognising and enforcing foreign judgments was believed to hamper the single market. Any argument that the scope of the Brussels I*bis* Regulation could be interpreted only narrowly to achieve the original aim of the recognition and enforcement of judgments would be too narrow. First, in order to further its primary aim, the Brussels Convention laid down rules of international jurisdiction to allocate jurisdiction in various disputes covered by the Convention to the courts of a Contracting States. The jurisdictional rules give rise to the greatest number of references to the CJEU and have taken on various purposes of their own. So, although the words of Art. 1 remain substantially unchanged from the original Brussels Convention of 1968 and from the Brussels I Regulation, the purposes of the Brussels I*bis* Regulation have reflected developments in the jurisprudence of the CJEU in relation to the Brussels Convention and the Brussels I Regulation. Secondly, following the Treaty of Amsterdam and the Treaty on the Functioning of the European Union[11] competence in the field of judicial cooperation in civil matters has been both refined and adapted. Judicial cooperation in civil and commercial matters has been disengaged from the original purpose of the recognition and enforcement of judgments. The Brussels I*bis* Regulation therefore refers to the broader objective of "maintaining and developing an area of freedom, security and justice, inter alia, by facilitating access to justice ... particularly when necessary for the proper functioning of the internal market".[12] Equal treatment for all litigants throughout the European Union is therefore essential. The purposes of the Brussels I*bis* Regulation, and thus Art. 1, have been further elaborated to include predictability in jurisdiction,[13] respect for the autonomy of the parties,[14] minimising con-

---

7   See *Hess, Pfeiffer* and *Schlosser* at para. 65.

8   COM (1997) 609 final, [1998] OJ C 33 of 1/31/1998 and Tampere Summit. See too *Fiorini*, The evolution of European private international law [2008] ICLQ 969.

9   See for example, *Götz Leffler v. Berlin Chemie* (Case 443-03) [2005] ECR I-9611. The ECJ stressed the importance of the requirement to give full effectiveness to Community law in interpreting Regulation (EC) 1348/2000 on the service in Member States of judicial and extrajudicial documents in civil and commercial matters 2006 OJ L 160/37 followed in *Civil proceedings concerning Roda Golf & Beach Resort SL* (Case 14/08) and *Vereiniging Nationaal Overlegorgaan Sociale Werkvoorziening v. Minister van Sociale Zaken en Werkgelegenheid* (Joined Cases C-383/06 to C-385/06).

10 Preamble to the Brussels Convention 1968 [1972] OJ L 299/32.

11 Artt. 67 and 81 Treaty on the Functioning of the European Union.

12 Recital (3).

13 Recital (15).

current proceedings and irreconcilable judgments,[15] and mutual trust in the administration of justice.[16] There is an argument that the Brussels I*bis* Regulation must be interpreted as an instrument of the integration of procedural law in order to implement a comprehensive policy of a European Judicial Area.[17] This raises the application of wider considerations of European law, such as access to justice[18] and unification of the rules of conflict of jurisdiction.[19] Nevertheless, Recital (4) recognises that the sound operation of the internal market would be hampered by differences in national rules governing jurisdiction and the recognition of judgments so this purpose remains important.[20]

3   The difficulty in using the various purposes as aids to interpretation can be seen where the purposes conflict. For example, where a case raises a question of the interpretation of "arbitration". This can be seen as a matter of party autonomy but in some circumstances, such as where the court of another Member State is hearing the substance of the case, the purposes of minimising concurrent proceedings and irreconcilable judgments point to a different interpretation. CJEU jurisprudence tentatively indicates a hierarchy of purposes where they conflict, headed by the mutual trust in other courts' decisions.[21] In *Allianz SpA Generali Assicurazioni Generali SpA v. West Tankers*[22] (a case on the Brussels I Regulation) the highest importance of mutual trust in other courts' decisions resulted in a narrower interpretation of the "arbitration" exception, even if the result was concurrent proceedings and likely irreconcilable judgments.[23]

4   The Brussels I*bis* Regulation is only invoked where "an international element is involved".[24] It is not clear how this is to be interpreted. Does any international connection suffice? Does it

---

[14]   Recital (19), except in certain cases. Recital (22) refers to the purpose of enhancing the effectiveness of exclusive choice-of-court agreements and avoiding abusive litigation tactics.

[15]   Recital (21).

[16]   Recitals (16), (17) and (26).

[17]   *Hess, Pfeiffer, Schlosser* at para. 62, citing *Götz Leffler v. Berlin Chemie AG* (Case C-443/03) [2005] ECR I-9611 a case not on this Regulation but on Council Regulation (EC) No. 1348/2000 of 29 May 2000 on the service in the Member States of judicial and extrajudicial documents in civil or commercial matters (OJ 2000 L 160, p. 37).

[18]   *Andrew Owusu v. Nugent B. Jackson, trading as "Villa Holidays Bal-Inn Villas", Mammee Bay Resorts Ltd., Mammee Bay Club Ltd., The Enchanted Garden Resorts & Spa Ltd., Consulting Services Ltd., Town & Country Resorts Ltd.*, (Case C-281/02) [2005] ECR I-1363.

[19]   *Allianz SpA, Generali Assicurazioni Generali Spa v West Tankers Inc, The Front Comor* (Case C-185/07) [2009] ECR I 663 para. 24.

[20]   Recital (4).

[21]   *Erich Gasser GmbH v. MISAT srl*, (Case C-116/02) [2003] ECR I-14693; *Gregory Paul Turner v. Felix Fareed Ismail Grovit, Harada Ltd and Changepoint SA*, (Case C-159/02) [2004] ECR I-3565.

[22]   *Allianz SpA, Generali Assicurazioni Generali Spa v. West Tankers Inc, The Front Comor* (Case C-185/07) [2009] ECR I 663.

[23]   The provisions of Art. 1 Brussels I*bis* Regulation are little changed, although there is an expansive new Recital and an express reference to the New York Convention on the recognition and enforcement of foreign arbitral awards of 1958 in Art. 73(2) which may reverse some of the effects of *Allianz SpA, Generali Assicurazioni Generali Spa v. West Tankers Inc, The Front Comor* (Case C-185/07) [2009] ECR I 663 (see further paras. 49–50 of this chapter).

[24]   Report *Jenard* p. 8, Report *Schlosser* para. 21.

have to be substantial? Does the connection have to be relevant or significant to the dispute? For example, where two parties to a contract both are domiciled in the same Member State in which proceedings are commenced but the goods supplied under the contract are delivered to another Member State, is the mere fact of delivery elsewhere sufficient to invoke the Brussels I*bis* Regulation? Even if the dispute is concerned only with liability for an allegedly late payment in the parties' Member State and delivery is not in dispute? The Brussels I*bis* Regulation would operate to permit the Member State's courts of the place of delivery to take jurisdiction, but does it also apply in the courts where the proceedings are commenced?[25] It is important that this requirement is interpreted uniformly across the European Union.

The CJEU in *Color Drack GmbH* v. *Lexx International Vertriebs GmbH*[26] applied Art. 5 (1)   **5** Brussels I Regulation (now Art. 7 (1) Brussels I*bis* Regulation) to identify a place of per- formance in a case in which all the deliveries were made within one Member State. No question was raised about the applicability of the Brussels I Regulation. It can be noted that despite all the deliveries being in one Member State, the seller came from another Member State and it is possible that the place of payment would be another international connecting factor.

In *British Sugar Plc v. Fratelli Babbini*[27] the English court applied the rules of the Brussels I   **6** Regulation to a case involving an Italian jurisdiction agreement allocating jurisdiction to a particular Italian court made between two Italian parties to an Italian law contract. The necessary international element was supplied by the case being commenced in England against another party to the litigation. Certain factors are likely to be found to significant in a case even if not specifically in dispute as the factor could be relied on to provide jurisdiction in another Member State. These factors might include the place of the parties' domiciles, the place of delivery, the place of payment, the place where the events occurred, and any choice of another court.

The Brussels I*bis* Regulation provides rules for the regulation of jurisdiction and the rec-   **7** ognition and enforcement of judgments, it does not extend to matters of procedure.[28] The distinction between jurisdiction and procedure might appear to be clear. Nevertheless, in common law Member States the jurisdictional rules are often contained in the rules govern- ing procedure in the courts, such as Rule 6 of the Civil Procedure Rules in England. Member State's courts cannot use their own rules of domestic procedure to impair the effectiveness of the Brussels I*bis* Regulation.[29] As Lord Clarke in the English Supreme Court has noted, the

---

[25]   It is clear that the Brussels I*bis* Regulation does not apply to purely internal situations such as the conflict of territorial jurisdiction between the courts of one Member State (A-G *Tesauro*, Opinion in Case C-346/ 93 [1995] ECR I-617, I-627 para. 20).

[26]   Case C-386/05 [2007] E.C.R. I 3699.

[27]   [2004] EWHC 2560 (TCC).

[28]   *KongressAgentur Hagen GmbH v. Zeehaghe BV*, (Case C-365/88) [1990] ECR I-1845; *Fiona Shevill v. Presse Alliance SA*, (Case C-68/98) [1995] ECR I-415.

[29]   *Fiona Shevill v. Presse Alliance SA*, (Case C-68/98)[1995] ECR I-415, I-464 para. 39; *GIE Reunion Européene v.Zurich España* [2005] ECR I-4509 para. 35; *Gregory Paul Turner v. Felix Fareed Ismail Grovit, Harada Ltd and Changepoint SA*, (Case C-159/02) [2004] ECR I-3565 para. 29; *Freeport plc v. Arnoldsson* (Case C-98/06) [2008] ECR I-8319 para. 63; *Allianz SpA, Generali Assicurazioni Generali Spa v. West Tankers Inc, The Front Comor* (Case C-185/07) [2009] ECR I 663 para. 24.

principle of effectiveness requires considering whether the rule of procedure can operate consistently with the Brussels I*bis* Regulation or is incompatible with it.[30] Therefore the English practice of granting an anti-suit injunction to prevent proceedings continuing in another Member State's courts is impermissible even where the proceedings in England are outwith the scope of the Brussels I*bis* Regulation, such as proceedings to support arbitration in England.[31]

II. Legislative History of Art. 1

8 The wording of Art. 1 has not been greatly altered from that of the same Art. in the Brussels I Regulation which was substantially similar to the 1978 Accession Convention.[32] The changes are largely the result of an abundance of caution. Art. 1(1) has been expanded so that liability of the State for acts and omissions in the exercise of State authority *(acta iure imperii)* are specifically excluded from the scope of the Brussels I*bis* Regulation.[33] Art. 1 (2) (a) has been expanded to exclude also from the Brussels I*bis* Regulation rights in property arising out of "a relationship deemed by the law applicable to such relationship to have comparable effects to marriage".[34] Two new additional specific exclusions from the scope of the Brussels I*bis* Regulation have been added to reflect EU legislation. Art. 1 (2) (e) excludes "maintenance obligations arising from a family relationship, parentage, marriage or affinity";[35] and Art. 1(2)(f) excludes "wills and succession, including maintenance obligations arising by reason of death".[36] Art. 67 expressly gives priority to the provisions governing jurisdiction and the recognition and enforcement of judgments in specific matters contained in EU legislation.

III. Autonomous interpretation

9 The CJEU has held that interpretation of Art. 1, as with many of the provisions of the Brussels I*bis* Regulation, requires independent, community wide, autonomous principles.[37]

---

[30] *Starlight Shipping Co v.Allianz Marine & Aviation Versicherungs AG, The Alexandros T* [2013] UKSC 70, [2014] 1 Lloyd's Rep. 223 at [118].

[31] *Allianz SpA, Generali Assicurazioni Generali Spa v. West Tankers Inc, The Front Comor* (Case C-185/07) [2009] ECR I 663 para. 30.

[32] 78/884/EEC, Convention of Accession of 9 October 1978 of the Kingdom of Denmark, of Ireland and of the United Kingdom of Great Britain and Northern Ireland to the Convention on jurisdiction and enforcement of judgments in civil and commercial matters and to the Protocol on its interpretation by the Court of Justice OJ 1978 L 304/1.

[33] As was decided by the CJEU in *Lechouritou v. Greece* Case C-292/05 [2007] ECR I-1519.

[34] As was suggested by an earlier edition of this work.

[35] Council Regulation (EC) No. 2201/2003 concerning jurisdiction and the recognition and enforcement of judgments in matrimonial matters and the matters of parental responsibility 2003 OJ L 338/1 (amended 2004 OJ L 367/1).

[36] Reflecting Regulation (EU) No. 650/2012 on jurisdiction, applicable law, recognition and enforcement of decisions and acceptance and enforcement of authentic instruments in matters of succession and on the creation of a European Certificate of Succession 2012 OJ L 201/107.

[37] *Re Schneider* (C-386/12) [2013] ECR I nyr. [18], *Orams v. Apostolides* (Case C-420/07) [2009] ECR I 3571 [42]; *Netherlands State v. Rüffer* (Case 814/79) [1980] ECR 3807 [14]; *Préservatrice foncière TIARD SA v. Staat der Nederlanden*, (Case C-266/01) [2003] ECR I-4867 [21]; *Land Oberösterreich v. Čez as* (Case

This involves an interpretation of Art. 1 that is not solely limited by reference to national law on the matter in dispute. An autonomous interpretation is essential to ensure equal and uniform operation of the Brussels I*bis* Regulation.[38] The Court arrives at the autonomous interpretation, first by reference to the objectives and scheme of the Brussels I*bis* Regulation and then to the "general principles which stem from the corpus of the national legal systems".[39]

There are multiple objectives of the Brussels I*bis* Regulation.[40] First is the objective to **10** maintain and develop an area of freedom, security and justice by facilitating access to justice, in particular through mutual recognition and enforcement of judgments.[41] Other objectives include ensuring certainty in the clear allocation of jurisdiction between Member States,[42] protection of parties established in the European Union,[43] mutual trust and confidence between Member States, party autonomy, and so on. On many issues authoritative guidance can only be given by the CJEU. First, by deciding in what cases the objectives of the Brussels I*bis* Regulation are engaged at all.[44] Secondly, in identifying the limits of the objectives of the Brussels I*bis* Regulation. Thirdly, by establishing hierarchy of the objectives of the Brussels I*bis* Regulation. Fourthly, by deciding what the "general principles" are to be in any case. And fifthly, in particular by establishing what should happen when any of these objectives or general principles conflict.

It is even more difficult to pin down accurately any definition of the general principles **11** derived from the corpus of national legal systems. The European Union now has many more members from a variety of legal traditions. Beyond concepts common to all European legal systems, described at such a general level as to be unhelpful, this exhortation is close to meaningless. As with any legal interpretation one would hope that Art. 1 will be interpreted in accordance with broad conceptions of reasonable certainty, justice, objectivity, fairness

---

C-343/04) [2006] ECR I-4557 para. 22. *LTU Lufttransportunternehmen GmbH & Co. KG v. Eurocontrol*, (Case 29/76) [1976] ECR 1541.

[38] *LTU Lufttransportunternehmen GmbH & Co. KG v. Eurocontrol*, (Case 29/76) [1976] ECR 1541, 1550 *et seq.* paras. 3 *et seq.*

[39] *LTU Lufttransportunternehemen GmbH & Co KG v. Eurocontrol* (Case 29/76) [1976] ECR 1541 [3]; *Netherlands State v. Rüffer*(Case 814/79) [1980] ECR 3807, [7]; *Sonntag v. Waidmann* (Case C-172/91) [1993] ECR I-1963 [18]; *Préservatrice foncière TIARD SA v. Staat der Nederlanden* (Case C-266/01) [2003] ECR I-4867, para. 20; *Land Oberösterreich v. CEZ as* (Case C-343/04) [2006] ECR I-4557[22] and *Lechouritou v. Dimosio tis Omospondiakis Dimokratias tis Germanias* (Case C-292/05) [2007] ECR I-1519, [29].

[40] See discussion above.

[41] Recital (3).

[42] *Andrew Owusu v. Nugent B. Jackson, trading as "Villa Holidays Bal-Inn Villas", Mammee Bay Resorts Ltd., Mammee Bay Club Ltd., The Enchanted Garden Resorts & Spa Ltd., Consulting Services Ltd., Town & Country Resorts Ltd.*, (Case C-281/02) [2005] ECR I-1383.

[43] *Andrew Owusu v. Nugent B. Jackson, trading as "Villa Holidays Bal-Inn Villas", Mammee Bay Resorts Ltd., Mammee Bay Club Ltd., The Enchanted Garden Resorts & Spa Ltd., Consulting Services Ltd., Town & Country Resorts Ltd.*, (Case C-281/02) [2005] ECR I-1383 para. 3.

[44] For instance, where there are connections with third States. The Brussels I*bis* Regulation now specifically permits engagement of the Brussels I*bis* Regulation where proceedings are continuing in third States, see for example Artt. 33 and 34.

between the parties, and so on. However, none of these conceptions help at the more discrete level of identifying a proper resolution to a problem of what exactly is covered by, for example, arbitration. This reference to the corpus of national legal systems has not been very illuminating. There is no systematic investigation of the national legal systems when cases arise but the CJEU relies on the observations (if any) submitted by Member States and by the Commission. It is possible that these observations might be submitted haphazardly or for particular national reasons. For example, in *Schneider*[45] a Hungarian national who had been placed under guardianship by a Hungarian court applied to a Bulgarian court through his official guardian for authorisation to sell his half-share in Bulgarian immovable property. The Bulgarian court refused authorisation on the basis that the disposal of the property was not in the interests of the person lacking full capacity. The CJEU had to decide if these proceedings concerned the legal capacity of natural persons and so excluded from the scope of Brussels I Regulation. If the proceedings had come within the scope of the Brussels I Regulation, the further question arose as to whether Art. 22(1) (now Art. 24(1) Brussels I*bis* Regulation) applied. As these proceedings had been framed solely to seek judicial authorisation for the disposal of the property the CJEU held that Art. 22(1) did not apply and in any event the proceedings fell outside the scope of the Brussels I Regulation. The proceedings were non-contentious and all the Member States which had submitted observations[46] were of the opinion that such proceedings are concerned with the legal capacity of natural persons.

12   The CJEU has also had regard to the definition of concepts which appear elsewhere in Community law to interpret the same concept in the Brussels I Regulation. For example, in *Gemeente Steenbergen v. Luc Baten*[47] the concept of "social security" had to be considered in the light of Regulation 1408/71.[48] In *Lechouritou v. Germany*[49] the CJEU referred to both Regulation 805/2000 and Regulation 1896/2006 which expressly exclude *acta iure imperii* in order to decide that the scope of Brussels I Regulation also excluded such acts.[50] In addition, some lines may have to be drawn between different EU instruments (Artt.67). These EU instruments are growing in number[51] which will necessitate an investigation of the relative purposes of each instrument. In contrast, the different objectives of the instruments may

---

45   *Proceedings Brought by Schneider* (Case C-386/12) [2013] ECR I nyr.
46   Those Member States were only Germany, Hungary, Austria and the UK.
47   *Gemeente Steenbergen v. Luc Baten*, (Case C-271/00) [2002] ECR I-10489.
48   *Gemeente Steenbergen v. Luc Baten*, (Case C-271/00) [2002] ECR I-10489, I-10523 para. 45.
49   Case C-292/05 [2007] ECR I-1519, para. 45.
50   The Brussels *Ibis* Regulation has made this exception for *acta iure imperii* explicit (Art. 1(1)).
51   See Council Regulation (EC) No. 2201/2003 concerning jurisdiction and the recognition and enforcement of judgments in matrimonial matters and the matters of parental responsibility, OJ 2003 L 338/1 (amended [2004] OJ L 367/1); Regulation (EC) No. 805/2004 establishing a European Enforcement Order for uncontested claims 2004 OJ L 143/15 (amended 2005 OJ L 97/64, 2005 OJ L 168/50, 2008 OJ L 304/80); Regulation (EC) No. 1896/2006 establishing a European Payment Order 2006 OJ L 399/1 (amended 2012 OJ L 283/1); Regulation (EC) No. 861/2007 establishing a European Small Claims Procedure 2007 OJ L 199/1; Regulation (EC) No. 4/2009 on jurisdiction, applicable law, recognition and enforcement of decisions and cooperation in matters relating to maintenance obligations 2009 OJ L 7/1 (amended 2011 OJ L 293/24); Regulation (EU) No. 650/2012 on jurisdiction, applicable law, recognition and enforcement of decisions and acceptance and enforcement of authentic instruments in matters of succession and on the creation of a European Certificate of Succession 2012 OJ L 201/107.

lead to distinct interpretations of civil and commercial matters.[52] The concept of civil and commercial matters is also used in conventions to which Member States or the EU are parties.[53] The provisions of such conventions are given precedence over the Brussels I*bis* Regulation in some circumstances by Artt. 71 and 73. Again, questions could be asked whether civil and commercial matters must have the same interpretation in all circumstances.

IV. Civil and Commercial Matters, (1)

The Brussels I*bis* Regulation is limited to jurisdiction and judgments in "civil and commer-   **13** cial matters". This term is not defined in the Brussels I*bis* Regulation although as can be seen from the argument above, it is given an autonomous meaning. The domestic law of civilian law countries generally recognise the distinction between public and private law, and civil and commercial matters are included within private law.[54] However, not all Member States agree on the exact line to be drawn.[55] Common law countries do not have such a firm conception of a distinction between public and private law.[56] The amendment of Art. 1 (1) in the1978 Accession Convention specifies that civil and commercial matters do not apply to "revenue, customs or administrative matters". The extra words were added merely to make it plain that civil and commercial matters did not extend to these revenue, customs or administrative matters. Additionally, the Brussels I*bis* Regulation explicitly does not extend to liability of the State for acts and omissions in the exercise of State authority *(acta iure imperii)*. Arguably, both these amendments were made for the avoidance of doubt and as a matter of clarity, rather than to cut down the scope of "civil and commercial matters". The exclusions apply whether a public authority or a private individual is the party to the litigation.

An obvious example of an *actum iure imperii* falling outside the Brussels I*bis* Regulation is   **14** *Lechouritou v. Germany*.[57] The CJEU agreed with AG *Colomer* to hold that actions by injured parties against a State for damages caused by the armed forces during the Second World War were not civil and commercial matters. These actions were to recover losses resulting from warfare which is an obvious exercise of sovereign public powers. Those powers were exercised outside the ordinary legal rules determining relationships between private parties; the decisions were unilateral, binding and inextricable from State's foreign and defence policy. Despite the form of the actions in private law for losses, the damage arose

---

[52] See *Re C* (Case C-435-06) [2008] ECR I 10141 paras. 36–38, a case on Regulation 2201/2003 (amended [2004] OJ L 367/1). In that case a decision taken by a social welfare board to take children into care was within "civil matters" despite the decision being an exercise of public powers. The objectives described in the Brussels II*bis* Regulation are different from those in this Regulation and the caselaw on this Regulation was distinguished by the ECJ.

[53] Such as the Hague Convention on choice of court agreements of 30 June 2005 and the Lugano Convention on jurisdiction and the recognition and enforcement of judgments in civil and commercial matters of 30 October 2007.

[54] Report *Schlosser* para. 23.

[55] Report *Schlosser* paras. 23, 26–28.

[56] See Report *Schlosser* para. 24. For an English law example, *O'Reilly v. Mackman* [1982] 3 WLR 1096 (H.L.) and cases following it.

[57] Case C-292/05 [2007] ECR I-1519.

out of sovereign activity. The claimants tried to make a link with sovereign immunity doctrine in public international law under which wrongful acts by a sovereign may be considered not to be *de jure imperii* and therefore actionable in domestic courts. However, both the Advocate General and the CJEU disagreed that this brought the actions within the scope of the Brussels I Regulation. The form of the actions is irrelevant;[58] it is the nature of the acts and how the powers were exercised that is key.[59]

15 In contrast, in *Land Berlin v. Sapir*[60] the CJEU held that an action by a public authority to recover overpayments made by mistake in compensation to successors of landowners wrongly deprived of their land under the Nazi regime was within the scope of the Brussels I Regulation. In this case the public authority exercised its powers of compensation outside the administrative procedure of national law and the action was based on provisions of national law which were identical for all owners of property. Here, the CJEU focussed on the nature of the claim in private law and the origin of the substantive right, also in private law.

16 Litigation between private individuals generally falls within the scope of the Brussels I*bis* Regulation as such cases relate to property rights, or contractual or non-contractual obligations,[61] except insofar as the case is excluded by subject matter.[62] The CJEU has accepted that litigation involving a public authority as a party can fall within the scope of the Brussels I*bis* Regulation where the nature of the legal relationship between the parties is not excluded. Cases come within the Brussels I*bis* Regulation where the public authority has acted in a private law capacity: such as by entering a commercial contract,[63] an employment contract,[64] or by incurring tortious liability for damage. In *LTU v. Eurocontrol*[65] Eurocontrol, a body formed under public law, obtained a judgment in Belgium against a German company for payment of various charges. Eurocontrol sought enforcement of that judgment in Germany and the German court referred the question of whether the definition of a civil and commercial matter was to be determined according to German or Belgian law. The ECJ held an autonomous definition had to be applied to the scope of the Convention rather than either domestic law interpretation. In this case, Eurocontrol was acting in accordance with public law powers, despite the charges appearing to be of a private law nature. The public law nature of the relationship was found as "the use of equipment and services, provided by such

---

58 See too *Grovit v. De Nederlandsche Bank NV* [2007] EWCA Civ 953 [2008] 1 WLR 151 in which an action in libel against the Dutch Central Bank was dismissed as the bank was protected by state immunity. This was not a "civil and commercial matter" as the alleged libel in the bank's letter refusing to register the claimants was an exercise of public law powers of the supervision of the banking system.

59 "Civil and commercial matters" is also used in the Enforcement Regulation (Regulation (EC) No. 805/ 2004) and the Payment Regulation (Regulation (EC) No. 1896/2006), in these cases explicitly excluding *acta iure imperii*. Hess, *Pfeiffer* and *Schlosser* argue that this basic concept must be construed in such a way as to allow the same definition in all these parallel instruments (para. 66).

60 *Land Berlin v. Sapir* (Case C-645/11) [2013] ECR I nyr.

61 See *Verein für Konsumenteninformation v. Karl Heinz Henkel*, (Case C-167/00) [2002] ECR I-8111 and *Apostolides v.Orams* (Case C-420/07) [2009] ECR I- 3571 para. 45.

62 Report *Jenard* p. 10.

63 Though even this may not be entirely clear, see Report *Schlosser* paras. 26 and 27.

64 *Mahamdia v. People's Democratic Republic of Algeria* (Case C-154/11) [2012] ECR I nyr.

65 *LTU Lufttransportunternehmen GmbH & Co. KG v. Eurocontrol*, (Case 29/76) [1976] ECR 1541.

body ... [was] obligatory and exclusive" and also because of the unilateral nature of the relationship.

Likewise in *Netherlands State v. Rüffer*[66] the action of the agent of the State of the Nether- **17** lands in recovering a wreck from an international waterway and then seeking payment from the owner was outside Art. 1. Even though the claim was brought before the civil courts it concerned a public authority acting in exercise of its public authority powers. These public powers were administered in performance both of an international obligation and also under the Netherlands national law. Other national laws also considered that administering waterways was an exercise of public authority. Jurisdiction in the Netherlands court could not therefore be established by reference to the Brussels Convention.

On the other hand, in *Sonntag v. Waidmann*,[67] an Italian judgment against a German teacher **18** found negligently liable for the death of a pupil on a school trip was held by the CJEU to come within civil and commercial matters. Although the teacher had been employed in a publicly funded school and could be argued to be acting in some sense on behalf of the state, the right to compensation for criminally culpable conduct "is generally recognised as being a civil law right".[68] In addition, the teacher's exercise of the powers were only those "existing under the rules applicable to relations between private individuals", which would be the same whether the school was a state-funded or private school.[69]

The Regulation also covers an action by a public authority against a private individual to **19** recover sums paid by way of social assistance to the divorced spouse and child of the individual.[70] A distinction has been drawn in this case between two types of actions. First, those which are brought under the rules of "ordinary law in regard to maintenance obligations" are matters of private law and therefore fall within the Brussels I Regulation. Secondly, those brought under provisions "by which the legislature conferred on the public body a prerogative of its own" fall outside the Brussels I Regulation. The CJEU had to investigate carefully the provisions of Netherlands law relied on by the public authority to determine which side of the line this action fell. Therefore there has to be some reference to national, domestic law, to determine whether the public body is acting under a prerogative power or a private law right. The distinction is not always easy to draw and may depend entirely on the framing of the claim in the domestic courts.

Similarly, in *Préservatrice foncière TIARD SA v. Netherlands State*[71] a French insurance **20** company had issued a contract of guarantee to the government of the Netherlands for customs duties owed by those hauliers licensed to issue TIR carnets. These carnets generally exempt goods carried by road from customs duties. If there has been some irregularity, however, the customs duties become payable by the carrier. The guarantee was governed by

---

66 *Netherlands State v. Reinhold Rüffer*, (Case 814/79) [1980] ECR 3807.
67 *Volker Sonntag v. Hans Waidmann*, (Case C-172/91) [1993] ECR I-1963.
68 *Volker Sonntag v. Hans Waidmann*, (Case C-172/91) [1993] ECR I-1963, I-1995 para. 16.
69 *Volker Sonntag v. Hans Waidmann*, (Case C-172/91) [1993] ECR I-1963, I-1997 paras. 22–23.
70 *Gemeente Steenbergen v. Luc Baten*, (Case C-271/00) [2002] ECR I-10489, see too Regulation (EC) 4/2009 on jurisdiction, applicable law, recognition and enforcement of decisions and cooperation in matters relating to maintenance obligations [2009] OJ L 7/1.
71 *Préservatrice foncière TIARD SA v. Staat der Nederlanden*, (Case C-266/01) [2003] ECR I-4867.

private law rules. The Netherlands contended that certain customs duties were due and started proceedings against PFA for payment. PFA argued that this claim was within Art. 1 and so the Netherlands court did not have jurisdiction. The CJEU held that in determining whether the claim was in the nature of the exercise of public law powers, the court had to assess whether the guarantee contract entailed "the exercise of powers going beyond those existing under the rules applicable to relations between private individuals".[72] The court also articulated various factors to take into consideration to decide that matter. For example, the source of the legal relationship between the parties,[73] and whether the contract was freely undertaken.[74] It noted that the mere existence of a State as a party to a contract is not conclusive of an exercise of public powers.[75] This case was followed in *Freistaat Bayern* v. *Blijdenstein*[76] where a German public body sought recovery of sums paid by way of education grant to the child of the defendant. Under German Civil Code the child had a maintenance claim against his or her parents in private law, to which the German public body was statutorily subrogated where it had paid the education grant. As this was a claim governed by rules of ordinary law it fell within the Brussels I Regulation.[77]

21   Actions regarding environmental matters and other types of private law enforcement are beginning to raise concerns.[78] Characterisation of these mixed public-private law actions vary in the Member States. For example, the regulation of gambling is not uniformly regarded by Member States as a civil law matter. At least some aspects are regarded as deriving from public or administrative law.[79] Likewise an imposition of liability for misleading information in a prospectus is not necessarily wholly a private law matter. Although many of these actions have a private law form, as for example an injunction to prevent the escape of ionising radiation from a power plant in another State,[80] they raise issues of policy and public law which need careful consideration. Whether to include such cases within "civil and commercial matters" and bringing them within the scope of the Brussels I Regulation is a

---

[72] *Préservatrice foncière TIARD SA v. Staat der Nederlanden*, (Case C-266/01) [2003] ECR I-4867, I-4892 para. 30.

[73] *Préservatrice foncière TIARD SA v. Staat der Nederlanden*, (Case C-266/01) [2003] ECR I-4867, I-4892 para. 32. Here the claim arose out of a private law guarantee not governed by the TIR Convention (Convention on the International Transport of Goods under Cover of TIR Carnets, 1975).

[74] *Préservatrice foncière TIARD SA v. Staat der Nederlanden*, (Case C-266/01) [2003] ECR I-4867, I-4892 *et seq.* para. 33. Unlike in *LTU Lufttransportunternehmen GmbH & Co. KG v. Eurocontrol*, (Case 29/76) [1976] ECR 1541 where the dues were compulsory.

[75] *Préservatrice foncière TIARD SA v. Staat der Nederlanden*, (Case C-266/01) [2003] ECR I-4867, I-4893 para. 34.

[76] *Freistaat Bayern* v. *Jan Blijdenstein*, (Case C-433/01) [2004] ECR I-981.

[77] The claim however, did not fall within Art. 5 (2) jurisdiction.

[78] See *Hess, Pfeiffer* and *Schlosser* para. 75–78.

[79] See *GIE Pari Mutuel Urbain v. Zeturf Ltd* in France (Cour de cassation Cour de Cassation, Chambre Commerciale, Financière et Économique, Arrêt No. 1023 du 10 juillet 2007, GIE Pari Mutuel Urbain (PMU)/Zeturf, Eturf) and in Malta (Civil Court (First Hall) Application 82/2007 *GIE Pari Mutuel Urbain (PMU) v. Zeturf* (2 Mar 2007)).

[80] See, for example, *Land Oberösterreich v. Čez as* (Case C-343/04) [2006] ECR I-4557 where such an action was excluded from Art. 16. However, the prior question of whether the Brussels I Regulation applied was not taken. An implicit assumption of the application of the Brussels I Regulation had been made by all concerned.

political question, arguably would more properly be answered by amendment of the Brussels *Ibis* Regulation than piecemeal by the CJEU. In addition some actions in these areas are commenced to impose criminal penalties, which were originally considered not to be within civil and commercial matters[81] although an ancillary civil damages remedy would be a civil and commercial law matter.

More recent cases appear to be expanding the scope of "civil and commercial matters" to **22** permit actions by public authorities to recover for what appear to be breaches of public law. In *Realchemie Nederland BV v. Bayer Crop Science AG*[82] the question was raised whether a fine for non-compliance with a court order in the course of proceedings that was to be paid to the German State was within the Brussels I Regulation such that it could be enforced in another Member State. The CJEU held that such a fine did fall within civil and commercial matters despite the clearly penal nature of the national law. One must inspect "the factors characterising the nature of the legal relationships between the parties to the action or the subject-matter of the action" to determine if the judgment fell within the scope of the Brussels I Regulation. In this case the substantive exclusive right to exploit a patent was clearly within civil and commercial matters and that justified bringing this judgment within the scope of the Brussels I Regulation. Similarly, in *Revenue and Customs Commissioners v. Sunico ApS*[83] the revenue authorities of the United Kingdom claimed in damages against the defendants who had allegedly taken part in a tortious conspiracy to defraud the revenue of VAT. The amount of the damages was equivalent to the VAT unpaid. A straightforward action in criminal law for non-payment of the tax would obviously fall outside the scope of the Brussels I Regulation. However, the CJEU held that this action was within the scope of the Brussels I Regulation. The legal basis of this claim was in the domestic law of tort, the commissioners were not exercising any powers beyond those available to private persons and had brought the action in the civil courts. These cases open the door to a more extensive enforcement of revenue, quasi-criminal and regulatory judgments.

Préservatrice foncière TIARD SA v. Netherlands State[84] raised the further question, whether **23** the case was excluded from the scope of Art. 1 by virtue of being within "customs matters". The CJEU used a similar reasoning. The delimitation between "civil and commercial matters" and the excluded non-civil and commercial matters exemplified by the concepts of "customs, revenue or administrative matters" required an application of the same criterion. So in order to be excluded from the rules of the Brussels *Ibis* Regulation, the claim must arise out of a legal relationship entailing the "exercise of public powers going beyond those existing under the rules applicable to relations between private individuals".[85] This case was one of a civil and commercial matter even though the customs debt might have to be investigated as part of it. Any investigation of the customs debt would apparently only be of a

---

81 For example, if a penalty is imposed by the State authorities against an unregulated provider of gambling services. The State penalty may be contrary to freedom of establishment under EU law (see *Gambelli* [Case C-243/01] [2003] ECR I-13031) but the penalty would not be a "civil and commercial matter" within the Brussels I Regulation. The penalty is therefore not enforceable under the Brussels I Regulation.

82 *Realchemie Nederland BV v. Bayer Crop Science AG* (Case C-409/09) [2011] ECR I 9773.

83 *Revenue and Customs Commissioners v. Sunico ApS* (Case C-49/12), ECLI:EU:C:2013:545.

84 *Préservatrice foncière TIARD SA v. Staat der Nederlanden,* (Case C-266/01) [2003] ECR I-4867.

85 *Préservatrice foncière TIARD SA v. Staat der Nederlanden,* (Case C-266/01 [2003] ECR I-4867, I-4895 para. 40.

preliminary issue which could be raised at any time. Therefore the existence of preliminary issues which are excluded matters do not necessarily prevent the applicability of the Brussels I*bis* Regulation. This is a contrary conclusion to the one the court came to in two other cases where it held that if the substance of the dispute was an excluded matter, then even if some preliminary matters could have been thought to be determinable within the Brussels I Regulation, the Brussels I Regulation was not invoked.[86] The two views may be reconcilable by identifying the substance of the dispute. If the substance is an excluded matter, the whole dispute is excluded. Where, however, the substance is not excluded, but some preliminary or incidental issue is raised which is without the scope of the Brussels I*bis* Regulation, then the whole dispute is within it.[87] This is not very satisfactory. Whether a dispute "in substance" raises an excluded matter is often dependent on national law rules of procedure (such as pleading) and on which party raises the claim or defence. Such distinctions do the law no service.

24 *Préservatrice foncière TIARD SA v. Netherlands State*[88] was followed by the CJEU in *Frahuil SA v. Assitalia SpA*[89] the claimant sought reimbursement of customs duties which it had paid as guarantor. The claimant had undertaken the contract of guarantee with the customs authorities unknown to the defendant who alleged it had already paid a sum for the customs duties to the debtor under the guarantee. The CJEU only focussed on the relationship between the two parties in dispute and found that their relationship was governed by private law.[90] The exercise of powers of subrogation under the guarantee was provided for in Italian private law and therefore this action was within "civil and commercial matters". This is entirely consistent with the view taken by the CJEU in *Revenue and Customs Commissioners v. Sunico ApS*.[91]

25 The nature of the court or tribunal in which proceedings are brought is not relevant to the question of whether the proceedings themselves fall within the scope of the Brussels I*bis* Regulation.[92] It therefore covers civil claims brought before criminal courts[93] as well as civil and commercial matters which are brought before administrative tribunals.[94] Also penalties for the benefit of private individuals fall within the scope of the Brussels I Regulation.[95] As has already been discussed, this has been expanded to include some payments to a State ordered by a court so long as the nature of the claim is in private law.[96]

---

[86] *Marc Rich & Co AG v. Societa Italiana Impianti PA*, (Case C-190/89) [1991] ECR I-3855, I-3902 *et seq.* paras. 26 *et seq.*; *Owens Bank Ltd. v. Fulvio Bracco and Bracco Industria Chimica SpA*, (Case C-129/92) [1994] ECR I-117, I-155 para. 34.

[87] See too *Allianz SpA, Generali Assicurazioni Generali Spa v. West Tankers Inc, The Front Comor* (Case C-185/07) [2009] ECR I 663 para. 26.

[88] *Préservatrice foncière TIARD SA v. Staat der Nederlanden*, (Case C-266/01) [2003] ECR I-4867.

[89] *Frahuil SA v. Assitalia SpA*, (Case C-265/02) [2004] ECR I-1543.

[90] *Frahuil SA v. Assitalia SpA*, (Case C-265/02) [2004] ECR I-1543, I-1554 para. 21.

[91] *Revenue and Customs Commissioners v. Sunico ApS* (Case C-49/12), ECLI:EU:C:2013:545.

[92] Art. 2, note Art. 3 which specifies particular national authorities as being "courts" for the purposes of the Brussels I*bis* Regulation.

[93] Art. 7(3) expressly permits a person domiciled in a Member State to be sued in another Member State in such cases; *Volker Sonntag v. Hans Waidmann*, (Case C-172/91) [1993] ECR I-1963.

[94] Report *Jenard* p. 9.

[95] Report *Schlosser* para. 29.

Employment law issues fall within the Brussels I*bis* Regulation.[97] This is the case even in 26
courts or tribunals which would not be considered by local law to have power to determine
private law rights.

Issues arising out of the recognition and enforcement of judgments from courts of third 27
States were not within the definition of "civil and commercial matters" in Brussels I Regulation. In *Owens Bank v. Fulvio Bracco and Bracco Industria Chimica SpA*[98] the claimant
bank had obtained a judgment from a non Contracting State to the Brussels Convention. It
applied to the Italian courts for enforcement of that judgment and the defendant alleged it
had been obtained by fraud. The claimant bank also applied to the English courts for a
declaration that the judgment was enforceable and the defendants sought to rely on the *lis
pendens* provisions such that the English court should decline to hear the case until the
Italian proceedings were concluded. The same issue of fraud had been raised in both the
English and the Italian proceedings. The CJEU held, however, that these proceedings in Italy
and England were not "civil and commercial matters". The recognition and enforcement
rules are only concerned with judgments from courts of Member States and not with
judgments from third States.[99] There are no jurisdictional rules for the recognition and
enforcement of judgments from courts of third States. Therefore the Brussels I Regulation
did not apply.[100] The CJEU would not accept an argument that the issue raised in both sets of
proceedings was either severable or, as a mere preliminary issue, within the scope of civil and
commercial matters. The CJEU followed *Marc Rich & Co AG v. Societa Italiana Impianti
PA*[101] to hold "that if, by virtue of its subject matter, a dispute falls outside the scope of the
[Regulation], the existence of a preliminary issue which the court must resolve in order to
determine the dispute cannot, whatever that issue may be, justify application of the [Regu-
lation]".[102] It might be argued that this position may not continue under the Brussels I*bis*
Regulation. First, there is evidence of a broadening of the scope of the Brussels I Regulation
following *Allianz SpA, Generali Assicurazioni Generali Spa v.West Tankers Inc.*[103] A judgment from a Member State on the substantive issue allegedly subject to arbitration proceedings continuing in another Member State would be enforceable in that other Member State
(thus making the arbitration proceedings ineffective).[104] This particular issue is the subject of

---

[96] *Revenue and Customs Commissioners v. Sunico ApS* (Case C-49/12), ECLI:EU:C:2013:545.

[97] Artt. 20–23 provide special grounds for jurisdiction in such cases. See too Report *Jenard* p. 9, *Sanicentral
      GmbH v. René Collin*, (Case 25/79) [1979] ECR 3423; *Roger Ivenel* v. *Helmut Schwab*, (Case 133/81)
      [1982] ECR 1891; *Mahamdia v. Algeria* (Case C-154/11) [2012] ECR I nyr.

[98] *Owens Bank Ltd. v. Fulvio Bracco and Bracco Industria Chimica SpA*, (Case C-129/92) [1994] ECR I-117.

[99] *Owens Bank Ltd. v. Fulvio Bracco and Bracco Industria Chimica SpA*, (Case C-129/92) [1994] ECR I-117,
      I-152 *et seq.* paras. 20–23.

[100] *Owens Bank Ltd. v. Fulvio Bracco and Bracco Industria Chimica SpA*, (Case C-129/92) [1994] ECR I-117,
      I-153 para. 25.

[101] *Marc Rich & Co AG v. Societa Italiana Impianti PA*, (Case C-190/89) [1991] ECR I-3855, I-3902 para. 26.

[102] *Owens Bank Ltd. v. FulvioBracco and Bracco Industria Chimica SpA*, (Case C-129/92) [1994] ECR I-117,
      I-155 para. 34.

[103] *Allianz SpA, Generali Assicurazioni Generali Spa v.West Tankers Inc, The Front Comor* (Case C-185/07)
      [2009] ECR I 663.

[104] See the English case *National Navigation Co v. Endesa Generacion SA* [2009] EWCA Civ 1397; [2010] 1
      Lloyd's Rep 193 noted *Fentiman* [2010] C.L.J. 242.

discussion later in this work.[105] Secondly, the Brussels I*bis* Regulation itself makes provision for the staying of proceedings in a Member State when proceedings are continuing in another Member State provided that those third State proceedings will give rise to a recognisable judgment.[106] By explicitly referring to the recognition of a third State judgment such judgments have some relevance within the operation of the Brussels I*bis* Regulation even though the rules of recognition of third State judgments are left to national law.

V. Specified Exclusions, (2)

28 Art. 1(2) expressly excludes certain issues from the Brussels I*bis* Regulation, which would otherwise raise questions of "civil and commercial matters". The reports explain that these issues were excluded as there is considerable divergence in both domestic and private international law among the Member States and also because some of the issues are the subject of other international conventions[107] and other European instruments.[108] The application of international conventions and European instruments are explicitly unaffected by the Brussels I*bis* Regulation.[109]

1. The status or legal capacity of natural persons, rights in property arising out of a matrimonial relationship or out of a relationship deemed by the law applicable to such relationship to have comparable effects to marriage, (2) (a)

29 The definitions in this exclusion to the scope of the Brussels I*bis* Regulation must be autonomous. Proceedings with respect to the status or legal capacity of natural persons would cover questions of minority or mental capacity, for example. In *Schneider*[110] the CJEU

---

[105] See paras. 50–52 of this chapter.

[106] Artt. 33 and 34, see further Chapter 2.

[107] Report *Jenard* p. 10, for example, the New York Convention on the Recognition and Enforcement of Foreign Arbitral Awards adopted by the United Nations Conference on International Commercial Arbitration on 10th June 1958 (now explicitly referred to in Art. 73 Brussels I*bis* Regulation); the Hague Convention on Choice of Court Agreements of 30 June 2005; the Berne Convention concerning international carriage by rail 9 May 1980, as amended by the Vilnius Protocol of 3 June 1999 (COTIF); the Montreal Convention 28 May 1999; the Cape Town Convention on International Interests in mobile Equipment of 16 November 2001.

[108] Such as Council Regulation (EC) No. 1346/2000 on Insolvency Proceedings 2000 OJ L 338/1(amended 2003 OJ L 236/33, 2005 OJ L 100/1, 2006 OJ L 121/1, 2007 OJ L 159/1, 2008 OJ L 213/1, 2010 OJ L 65/1, 2011 OJ L 160/52; [2014] OJ L 179/4); Council Regulation (EC) No. 4/2009 on jurisdiction, applicable law, recognition and enforcement of decisions and cooperation in matters relating to maintenance obligations [2009] OJ L 7/1; Regulation (EC) No. 805/2004 establishing a European Enforcement Order for uncontested claims 2004 OJ L 143/15 (amended 2005 OJ L 97/64, 2005 OJ L 168/50, 2008 OJ L 304/80); Regulation (EC) No. 1896/2006 establishing a European Payment Order 2006 OJ L 399/1 (amended 2012 OJ L 283/1); Regulation (EC) No. 861/2007 establishing a European Small Claims Procedure 2007 OJ L 199/1; Regulation (EC) No. 4/2009 on jurisdiction, applicable law, recognition and enforcement of decisions and cooperation in matters relating to maintenance obligations 2009 OJ L 7/1 (amended 2011 OJ L 293/24); Regulation (EU) No. 650/2012 on jurisdiction, applicable law, recognition and enforcement of decisions and acceptance and enforcement of authentic instruments in matters of succession and on the creation of a European Certificate of Succession 2012 OJ L 201/107.

[109] See Artt. 69–73 discussed Chapter 7.

held that proceedings in Bulgaria which sought authorisation of the court to permit a person under guardianship to sell his half-share in Bulgarian property fell within this exception. The proceedings were non-contentious and the Member States that had submitted observations all concluded that these sorts of proceedings were concerned with the legal capacity of natural persons. That was not a direct reference to national law but perhaps a use of national law concepts to attempt to arrive at some autonomous meaning of legal capacity.

The framers of the original Brussels Convention intended to exclude all family law matters, **30** apart from maintenance issues.[111] Maintenance issues are now also specifically excluded from the scope of the Brussels I*bis* Regulation by Art. 1(2)(e).The Maintenance Regulation[112] applies to "maintenance obligations arising from a family relationship, parentage, marriage or affinity". Only proprietary issues arising out of a matrimonial relationship etc. are excluded from the Brussels I*bis* Regulation, rights in property which are generally available irrespective of marriage are within the scope of the Brussels I*bis* Regulation. This exclusion is not necessarily straightforward as the concept of rights in property arising out of a matrimonial relationship etc. is unknown in some Member States and interpreted differently in others. In *De Cavel v. De Cavel (No. 1)*[113] divorce proceedings were continuing in France, in which the husband had obtained an interim order protecting assets of the couple and freezing bank accounts. He sought enforcement of that order in Germany. The German court asked whether the order was required to be enforced under the Brussels Convention. The CJEU held that disputes relating to assets of spouses which concerned or were closely connected with "(1) questions relating to the legal status of persons; or (2) proprietary legal relationships between spouses resulting directly from the matrimonial relationship or the dissolution thereof"[114] were excluded. Likewise in *CHW v. GJH*[115] the application by a husband to the Netherlands court for a provisional measure to return and not to use in evidence a document intended to exempt the wife's property from the management of her husband was held to be excluded. The management of the property (the subject of the dispute to which the provisional measure was support) was closely connected with the property relationships which arose directly from the marriage. Whether rights or claims or proceedings arise directly from the matrimonial relationship seems to be a matter that can only be referred to the national law. On the other hand, proceedings concerning "proprietary legal relations existing between the spouses which have no connexion with the marriage (including relationships deemed by law to have comparable effects to marriage)" fall within the Brussels I*bis* Regulation.[116]

The previous edition of this work pointed out that the exception from the scope of the **31** Brussels I Regulation only for matrimonial relationships was too narrow. The Brussels I*bis* Regulation has been amended to exclude not merely matrimonial relationships but also

---

110 Proceedings brought by *Schneider* (Case 386/12) [2013] ECR I nyr.
111 Report *Jenard* p. 10. Regulation 2201/2003 on jurisdiction in matrimonial matters deals with the question of jurisdiction, although it does not cover the financial consequences of the decrees.
112 Council Regulation (EC) No. 4/2009 on jurisdiction, applicable law, recognition and enforcement of decisions and cooperation in matters relating to maintenance obligations [2009] OJ L 7/1.
113 *Jacques de Cavel v. Louise de Cavel*, (Case 143/78) [1979] ECR 1055.
114 *Jacques de Cavel v. Louise de Cavel*, (Case 143/78) [1979] ECR 1055, 1066 para. 7.
115 *C.H.W. v. G.J.H.* (Case 25/81) [1982] ECR 1189.
116 *Jacques de Cavel v. Louise de Cavel*, (Case 143/78) [1979] ECR 1055, 1066 para. 7.

other relationships deemed by the law applicable to such relationship to have comparable effects to marriage.

2. Bankruptcy, proceedings relating to the winding-up of insolvent companies or other legal persons, judicial arrangements, compositions and analogous proceedings, (2) (b)

32 This exclusion must be read in conjunction with Regulation 1346/2000 on Insolvency. As the Report Schlosser contemplated, the two Regulations should be interpreted so that proceedings should fall within one or the other, but not both and leaving no gap between them.[117] The Report *Jenard* defined bankruptcy proceedings as those which "depending on the system of law involved, are based on the suspension of payments, the insolvency of the debtor or his inability to raise credit, and which involve the judicial authorities for the purpose either of compulsory and collective liquidation of the assets or simply of supervision."[118] Unlike the arbitration exception, where there is no corresponding EU arbitration legislation, the Report Schlosser's interpretation of the mutually exclusive nature of these two Regulations means that all civil and commercial matters should be decided in accordance with one of the Brussels I Regulations. The interpretation of this exclusion from the Brussels I*bis* Regulation therefore might be argued to be less problematic than that of arbitration. However, it is possible to argue that the insolvency exception to the Brussels I*bis* Regulation is not limited to those insolvency issues covered in Regulation 1346/2000 on Insolvency as not all insolvency proceedings are covered by that latter Regulation. Also, although insolvency proceedings are excluded from the Brussels I*bis* Regulation, the rules of that Regulation are used to enforce the judgments given in the context of Regulation 1346/2000 with limited grounds for the refusal of recognition.[119]

33 The CJEU in *Gourdain v. Nadler*[120] decided that an order of the French court requiring a de facto manager of an insolvent company to contribute to the company's assets was within the exclusion. It held that the exclusion had to be given an autonomous definition, not merely decided by reference to national law. In this case, the French court order derived directly from the bankruptcy[121] and was closely connected to the "liquidation des biens". This was due to the application for the order only being made to the court making the liquidation des biens, the order could only be made by that court (or by the manager of the liquidation), the period of limitation ran from a date when the final list of claims was drawn up and the reimbursement from the manager was for the benefit of all creditors rather than any individual creditor being able to take this action for itself. On the other hand, an action by a liquidator to recover debts due to the company comes within the Brussels I*bis* Regulation, not the exclusion. Such an action does not derive directly from the winding up, but comes from the general law.[122] Nevertheless, actions by a liquidator to recover money wrongfully

---

[117] Report *Schlosser* para. 53.

[118] Report *Jenard* p. 12.

[119] Artt. 25 and 26 Regulation 1346/2000.

[120] *Henri Gourdain v. Franz Nadler*, (Case 133/78) [1979] ECR 733.

[121] See too Report *Jenard* p. 12.

[122] In *Powell Duffryn Plc v. Wolfgang Petereit*, (Case C-214/89) [1992] ECR I-1745 the liquidator brought an action to recover calls on shares and improperly paid dividends from a shareholder. This action would be within the scope of the Brussels I*bis* Regulation. Two English cases are to similar effect *In Re Hayward dec'd* [1997] Ch 45 (Ch.D. Rattee J.) and *Ashurst v. Pollard* [2001] Ch 595 (C.A.), in neither case did the

paid away by the debtor in fraud of creditors are excluded as the source of the liquidator's right to recover is in bankruptcy law and the debtor would not have had an action.[123]

The relationship between the two Regulations can be problematic[124] and national courts **34** have found difficulty in interpreting the requirement that the action must derive directly from the bankruptcy in order to be excluded from the Brussels I Regulation.[125] The CJEU has held that the scope of the Insolvency Regulation 1346/2000 was to be interpreted narrowly compared with that of the Brussels I Regulation.[126] In *German Graphics Graphische Maschinen GmbH*[127] the German seller had obtained a German judgment based upon a reservation of title clause. The Dutch liquidator of the Dutch purchaser challenged the enforcement under the Brussels I Regulation of the German judgment. In order for the German judgment to be excluded from recognition on the grounds of being related to the winding up of an insolvent company, there would have to be a sufficiently direct and close link between the proceedings and the insolvency. In this case the action on the reservation of title clause was an independent claim, not based upon the law of the insolvency proceedings and did not require the involvement of a liquidator. It therefore fell within the Brussels I Regulation and was to be enforced in the Netherlands, even though a liquidator had been appointed there and the company was insolvent. Similarly, in *F-Tex SIA*[128] a liquidator had assigned claims to recover debts owed to the company to the creditor of the company to enforce directly against the debtor. The claims arose out of the law of the insolvency to have transactions between the company and the debtor set aside. The CJEU held that these proceedings did not derive directly from the bankruptcy or winding up and the proceedings therefore fell within the Brussels I Regulation. Once the assignment had taken place the assignee could freely decide whether to exercise the right to set the transaction aside. Also, the assignee could keep the proceeds for the assignee's personal benefit rather than having to share with other creditors in the insolvency. The fact that as part of the assignment the assignee agreed to return to the liquidator 33% any proceeds recovered by the assignee did not alter that conclusion.

In *Coursier v. Fortis Bank*[129] the Luxembourg court was faced with a judgment obtained in **35** France. In further French insolvency proceedings that judgment had been rendered unenforceable in France by provisions preventing creditors acting individually against the debtor. The later judgment was clearly within the exclusion for bankruptcy but what of the earlier judgment? The parties conceded that earlier judgment was within the scope and the CJEU decided that the effect of the later judgment fell outside the scope. The relationship between the two judgments then had to be decided according to the Luxembourg rules of private

---

    liquidator's action derive directly from the bankruptcy and were actions the bankrupt could have taken himself.

[123] For example, actions under s. 423 Insolvency Act 1986 in England. See *Smart*, [1998] CJQ 149.

[124] *Hess, Pfeiffer* and *Schlosser* note that "forum shopping in the borderline between insolvency and litigation has become a broad phenomenon in the European Judicial Area" para. 88. See too, *Dutta*, Jurisdiction for Insolvency Related Proceedings [2008] L.M.C.L.Q. 88.

[125] See *Layton/Mercer* p. 358–9.

[126] *German Graphics Graphische Maschinen GmbH v. Alice van de Schee* (Case C-292/08) [2009] ECR I 8421.

[127] Case C-292/08 [2009] ECR I-8421.

[128] *F-Tex SIA v. Lietuvos-Anglijos UAB Jadecloud-Vilma* (Case C-213/10) ECLI:EU:C:2012:215.

[129] *Eric Coursier v. Fortis Bank and Martine Coursier, née Bellami*, (Case C-267/97) [1999] ECR I-2543.

---

international law. In *SCT Industri AB in likvidation v. Alpenblume AB*[130] the CJEU decided that a judgment of the Austrian court fell within the insolvency exception and was not enforceable in Sweden. The Austrian court had declared the original transfer of shares in a Swedish company invalid and ordered their re-transfer. As the original transfer had been ordered by a Swedish liquidator the issue was found to be directly and intimately linked to the conduct of insolvency proceedings.

Solvent schemes of arrangement which are entered into between a debtor and creditors out of court would, however, fall within the Brussels *Ibis* Regulation.[131] Also within the Brussels *Ibis* Regulation are proceedings to wind up solvent companies.[132] If the company is in fact insolvent, any proceedings fall outside the Brussels *Ibis* Regulation. It is up to the enforcing court to determine whether or not the company was solvent.[133]

36 Special problems can arise with particular types of claim. The *action pauliana* in civil law countries enables a creditor to pursue a remedy against a debtor into an asset once it has passed from the debtor to a third party, or sometimes as a personal remedy against the third party. It is somewhat comparable in common law countries to an action taken to enforce a security interest in an asset. These actions can arise on the debtor's bankruptcy or within a prior "period of suspicion"; or they may more generally be available, depending on the intention of the debtor or on the knowledge of the third party. Usually such an action would be destroyed by the acquisition of the asset in good faith by a third party. Those actions which derive from the general law are difficult to classify as arising directly out of a bankruptcy. *Actiones paulianae* which arise out of bankruptcy proceedings fall outside the scope of the Brussels *Ibis* Regulation, despite being initiated by an individual creditor, as the action derives from the bankruptcy and should be determined in accordance with the Brussels Regulation 1346/2000 on Insolvency. This proposition has been recently confirmed by the CJEU in *Seagon v. Deko Marty Belgium NV*.[134] The German liquidator wished to pursue an action in Germany to set aside a transfer of money from the insolvent company to Deko Marty, a Belgian company. The court was asked the question whether the courts which have jurisdiction under the Brussels Regulation 1346/2000 on Insolvency had jurisdiction over the action to set aside or, if not, whether the action fell within the Brussels I Regulation. The CJEU decided that this German action derived directly from the bankruptcy as it was brought by a liquidator and under the German code was intended to increase the assets available to all creditors.[135] It fell within Article 3(1) of the Brussels Regulation 1346/2000 on Insolvency and not within the Brussels I Regulation.[136] Jurisdiction was therefore established in the court with jurisdiction to open insolvency proceedings, which was Germany in this case. Although not expressly decided, the CJEU interpretation of the Brussels Regulation 1346/2000 on Insolvency confirms a broad interpretation of Art. 1(1)(d) of the Brussels I Regulation excluding insolvency and insolvency related proceedings from the jurisdictional rules of the latter Regulation.

---

[130] Case C-111/08 [2009] ECR I-5655.

[131] Report *Jenard* p. 12.

[132] Report *Schlosser* para. 55.

[133] Report *Schlosser* para. 57.

[134] *Seagon v. Deko Marty Belgium NV* Case C-339/07 [2009] ECR I-767.

[135] [2009] ECR I-767 paras. 16, 17.

[136] For a contrary view, written before this judgment was given, see *Dutta*, [2008] LMCLQ 88.

However, *actiones paulianae* which derive from the general law may be argued to fall within   **37**
the Brussels I*bis* Regulation as they do not derive directly from the bankruptcy, the power is
not in a liquidator but in a creditor personally and the creditor personally benefits rather
than general creditors.[137] It is clear that all such actions which fall within the Brussels I
Regulation 1346/2000 on Insolvency via Annex A and Art. 4 (2) (m) must be excluded and,
drawing on the Report *Schlosser*, one might argue that all actions which are not within the
Brussels I Regulation 1346/2000 on Insolvency should fall within the scope of this Regulation.[138] Nevertheless, this distinction is not without practical problems and does not answer
the difficult cases. First, even actions available under the general law are often temporally
and procedurally tied into bankruptcy proceedings. Secondly, those actions may be affected
by a later bankruptcy, in that the right becomes unavailable or must be shared with other
creditors. Thirdly, an *action pauliana* may derive from bankruptcy law but may be initiated
without actual bankruptcy of the debtor. Because different jurisdictional rules (and consequently choice of law rules) would apply to the actions, inconsistent judgments may arise. A
further complication would arise if a third party sought a declaratory judgment that the asset
was free of any such claims. Although the possible claims (which may be known to the third
party) could include those arising from a likely later bankruptcy, it does not make practical
sense to separate the issues and decide them in more than one court, but that is presently
permitted. As with arbitration, a well advised party can take advantage of the confusion and
locate the most attractive forum, splitting the action to its own benefit.[139]

The result of the decision of the CJEU in *F-Tex SIA*[140] also permits creditors of the company   **38**
to pursue actions against the company's debtors by way of assignment from the liquidator.
Such claims are then brought within the scope of the Brussels I*bis* Regulation. The fact of
assignment often breaks the direct link with the insolvency proceedings (despite the fact that
the claim may only be available due to insolvency). The second criterion for exclusion from
the Recast is also not satisfied as assignment generally means that the assignee can act in the
assignee's own interest.

Insolvency matters have to be distinguished from other matters concerning companies as   **39**
insolvency is excluded from the Brussels I*bis* Regulation but other company matters are
within its scope, many falling within Art. 24 (2). The CJEU decisions in cases such as *Centros
Ltd v. Erhvervs- og Selskabsstyrelsen*,[141] *Überseering BV v. Nordic Construction Company
Baumanagement GmbH*[142] and *Kamer van Koophandel en Fabrieken voor Amsterdam v.
Inspire Art Ltd.*[143] allow Member States to introduce very limited measures which protect

---

[137] *Reichert and Kockler v. Dresdner Bank* Case C-115/88 [1990] ECR I-27 and *Reichert and Kockler* Case
C-261/90 [1992] ECR I-2149 as explained by A-G Ruiz-Jarabo Colomer in *Seagon v. Deko Marty NV*
Case C-339/07 [2009] ECR I-767.

[138] Report *Schlosser* para. 53.

[139] For an example of the complicated litigation which arises in the case of insolvencies see *Mazur Media Ltd
v. Mazur Media GmbH* [2004] EWHC 1566 [2004] 1 W.L.R. 2966.

[140] *F-Tex SIA v. Lietuvos-Anglijos UAB Jadecloud-Vilma* (Case C-213/10) ECLI:EU:C:2012:215.

[141] *Centros Ltd. v. Erhvervs- og Selskabsstyrelsen*, (Case C-212/97) [1999] ECR I-1459.

[142] *Überseering BV v. Nordic Construction Company Baumanagement GmbH (NCC)*, (Case C-208/00)
[2002] ECR I-9919.

[143] *Kamer van Koophandel en Fabrieken voor Amsterdam v. Inspire Art Ltd.*, (Case C-167/01) [2003] ECR
I-10155.

domestic creditors, consumers, employees and minority shareholders when dealing with companies formed or registered in other Member States. Enforcement of such measures via civil actions should fall within the Brussels *Ibis* Regulation if they are not classified as insolvency matters within the Brussels Regulation 1346/2000 on Insolvency.[144] Issues such as the potential liability of managers or shareholders for activities of the company may well arise around the time of impending insolvency of the company, although not necessarily requiring a liquidation. The action may well derive from area of domestic law characterised as bankruptcy, for example, in the rules relating to minimum capital requirements. However, unless the issue arises in an actual insolvency (in which case the matter must be excluded from the Brussels *Ibis* Regulation) there is an argument that the action merely deriving from bankruptcy law is insufficient to exclude the matter from the Brussels *Ibis* Regulation. This argument may be stronger where an individual creditor is taking action for its own benefit.

3. Social security, (2) (c)

40 As with other excluded concepts, the CJEU has held that "social security" is to have an autonomous definition, determined by reference to the objectives of the Brussels *Ibis* Regulation. The Report *Jenard* noted that this exclusion was to be limited to disputes between the administrative authorities and employers or employees.[145] In *Gemeente Steenbergen v. Baten*[146] the CJEU noted Regulation (EEC) No. 1408/71[147] lays down certain rules regarding social security and the concept of social security in this Brussels *Ibis* Regulation must be interpreted in the light of the substance of the concept in community law.[148] However, public authorities' actions against third parties or in subrogation to the rights of an injured party may fall within the Brussels *Ibis* Regulation. Therefore, where the public body which has paid out benefits to an assisted person has a right of recourse against a third person, the proceedings for recourse may be within the Brussels *Ibis* Regulation. It is important that the third person has an obligation under private law to the assisted person as it is this private law foundation which gives rise to the "civil and commercial" nature of the claim.[149] However, where the obligation under private law is a matter of maintenance falling within the Maintenance Regulation, the proceedings for recourse are excluded from the Brussels *Ibis* Regulation by Art. 1(1)(e).

4. Arbitration, (2) (d)

41 As with the Brussels Convention of 1968 and the Brussels I Regulation, the Brussels *Ibis* Regulation excludes arbitration. The wording of Art. 1 (2) (d) has not changed but an extensive new Recital (12) has been included and Art. 73 makes specific imperative that Brussels *Ibis* Regulation "shall not affect the application of the 1958 New York Convention". It remains to be seen whether these amendments make the arbitration exception more clear.

---

[144] Report *Schlosser* para. 53.

[145] Report *Jenard* p. 13.

[146] *Gemeente Steenbergen v. Luc Baten*, (Case C-271/00) [2002] ECR I-10489.

[147] Now replaced with Regulation (EC) No. 883/2004.

[148] *Gemeente Steenbergen v. Luc Baten*, (Case C-271/00) [2002] ECR I-10489, I-10523 paras. 43–44.

[149] *Gemeente Steenbergen v. Luc Baten*, (Case C-271/00) [2002] ECR I-10489, I-10523 *et seq.* para. 46, I-10524 para. 48. See too Regulation EC No. 883/2004 Recital (36), Art. 1 (z), and Annex 1.

The exclusion of proceedings concerning arbitration matters from the Brussels I Regulation **42**
gave rise to considerable difficulties in Member States.[150] Resolving these difficulties was at
the forefront of the reform proposals.[151] The intention of the original framers of the Brussels
Convention 1968 was to exclude arbitration matters entirely as there were many international agreements on arbitration to which the Contracting States were parties.[152] At that
time, it had been hoped that there might be a separate European agreement for a uniform
law of arbitration, which has never come to fruition. The Report *Jenard* noted "The Brussels
Convention does not apply to the recognition and enforcement of arbitral awards ...; it does
not apply for the purpose of determining the jurisdiction of courts and tribunals in respect of
litigation relating to arbitration – for example, proceedings to set aside an arbitral award;
and, finally, it does not apply to the recognition of judgments given in such proceedings".[153]

Nevertheless, a division of opinion between the Member States on the width of the exception **43**
can be seen the Report *Schlosser*[154] but no agreement was reached to amend the text of the
Brussels I Regulation; nor was the text of Art. 1(2)(d) of the Brussels I*bis* Regulation amend-

---

[150] See discussion in *Ambrose*, (2003) 19 Arb. Int. 1; *Ambrose*, (2008) Int. Mar. & Comm. L. Yb. 27–34; *B. Audit, Arbitration and the Brussels Convention* (1993) 9 Arb. Int. 1; *Baatz*, [2010] LMCLQ 364; *Beraudo*, 18 (1) J. Int. Arb. 13 (2001); *Briggs*, (1991) Yb. Eur. L. 521, 527; *Camillieri*, [2013] ICLQ 899; *Dowers*, [2013] Cam. J. Int. & Comp. L. 960; *Dowers/Holloway*, [2013] Int. Arb. L. Rev. 18; *Dutson/Howarth*, [2010] Arb. 374; *Estrup Ippolito/Adler-Nissen*, [2013] Arb. 158; *van Haersolte-van Hof*, 18 (1) J. Int. Arb. 27 (2001); *Hartley*, (1991) 16 Eur. L. Rev. 529; *van Houtte*, (1997) 13 Arb. Int. 85; *Hess*, in: Heidelberg Report paras. 106–138; *Illmer/Naumann*, [2007] Int. Arb. L. Rev. 147; *Kaye*, (1993) 9 Arb. Int. 27; *Kruger*, [2010] JPrIL 499; *Nurmela*, [2005] JPrIL 115; *Santomauro*, [2010] JPrIL 281; *Schlosser*, (1991) 7 Arb. Int. 227; *Schlosser*, SchiedsVZ 2007, 149; *Schlosser*, [2009] Int. Arb. L. Rev. 45; *Steinbrück*, [2007] C.J.Q. 358. The case law in England has been ample and contradictory, see for example and contradictory, case-law in England. See for example *National Navigation Co v. Endesa Generacion SA* [2009] EWCA Civ 1397; *Youellv. La Reunion Arienne* [2009] EWCA Civ 175; *West Tankers v. RAS Riunione Adriatica de Sicurta SpA* [2007] UKHL 4, decided by the CJEU as *Allianz SpA, Generali Assicurazioni Generali Spa v. West Tankers Inc, The Front Comor* (Case C-185/07) [2009] ECR I 663; *Through Transport Mutual Insurance Association (Eurasia) Ltd v. New India Assurance Co Ltd (The Hari Bhum)* [2005] 1 Lloyds Reports 67 (C. A.); *Navigation Maritime Bulgare v. Rustal Trading Ltd (The Ivan Zagubanski)* [2002] 1 Lloyd's Reports 106 (Q.B.D., *Aikens* J.); *Welex AG v. Rosa Maritime Ltd (The Epsilon Rosa) (No. 2)* [2003] 2 Lloyd's Reports 509 (C.A.); *Vale do Rio doce Navegacao SA v. Shanghai Bao Steel Ocean Shipping Co Ltd (t/a Bao Steel Ocean Shipping Co)* [2000] 2 Lloyd's Reports 1 (Q.B.D., *Thomas* J.); *Alfred C Toepfer International GmbH v. Societe Cargill France* [1998] 1 Lloyd's Reports 379 (C.A.); *Lexmar Corp and Steamship Mutual Underwriting Association (Bermuda) Ltd v. Nordisk Skibsrederforening* [1997] 1 Lloyd's Report 289 (Q.B. D., *Colman* J.); *Alfred C Toepfer International GmbH v. Molino BoschiSrl* [1996] 1 Lloyd's Reports 510; *Partenreederei M/S Heidberg v.Grosvenor Grain & Feed Co Ltd (The Heidberg) (No. 2)* [1994] 2 Lloyd's Reports 287 (Q.B.D., Judge *Diamond* Q.C.).

[151] See Report from the Commission to the European Parliament, the Council and the European Economic and Social Committee on the application of Council Regulation (EC) No on jurisdiction and the recog-nition and enforcement of judgments in civil and commercial matters, 21.04.2009, COM (2009) 174 final para [3.7].

[152] Notably the New York Convention on the Recognition and Enforcement of Foreign Arbitral Awards adopted by the United Nations Conference on International Commercial Arbitration on 10th June 1958.

[153] Report *Jenard* p. 13.

[154] Report *Schlosser* para. 61.

Pippa Rogerson

ed. The Report *Schlosser* notes the difficulties where national courts take decisions on the subject matter of a dispute despite an arbitration agreement but does not decide between the two options.[155] The Report *Schlosser* does unequivocally state that parties are free to submit disputes to arbitration and national law is able to invalidate arbitration agreements despite the Brussels Convention;[156] that court proceedings which are ancillary to arbitration proceedings are excluded from the Convention;[157] and that proceedings and decisions concerning application for the revocation, amendment, recognition and enforcement of arbitration awards are likewise excluded.[158]

44 A very wide exclusion of arbitration was apparently accepted by the CJEU in *Marc Rich & Co AG v. Società Italiana Impianti*.[159] Proceedings were started in England between a Swiss claimant and an Italian defendant under which the Swiss claimant asked the English court to appoint an arbitrator under an agreement allegedly requiring arbitration of substantive contractual disputes between the parties in England. The Italian defendants had already commenced proceedings in Italy for a declaration that they were not liable to the claimants. The defendants disputed the validity of the arbitration agreement in the English proceedings and the claimants relied on the arbitration agreement in the Italian proceedings to challenge the jurisdiction of the Italian courts. The English Court of Appeal referred the question whether the English proceedings were within or without the scope of the Brussels Convention to the CJEU. The CJEU held that the intention was "to exclude arbitration in its entirety". Particularly, ancillary proceedings such as these proceedings for the appointment of arbitrators fell outside the scope of the Convention. This would be so even if in such proceedings a national court would have to determine the validity of the arbitration agreement as a preliminary issue.[160] This apparently answered the English court's question to the CJEU's satisfaction but its exact effect was rather unclear.

45 Where the proceedings in a national court are for the purpose of appointing or removing an arbitrator,[161] or for referring the parties to arbitration,[162] or for fixing the place of the arbitration, enforcing or setting aside an arbitral award itself,[163] or are declaratory proceedings as to the validity and effect of the arbitration agreement,[164] or answer some point of law raised in an arbitration then those proceedings fall outside the Brussels *Ibis* Regulation.[165] In

---

[155] Report *Schlosser* para. 62.

[156] Report *Schlosser* para. 63.

[157] Report *Schlosser* para. 64.

[158] Report *Schlosser* para. 65.

[159] *Marc Rich & Co AG v. Società Italiana Impianti PA*, (Case C-190/89) [1991] ECR I-3855.

[160] *Marc Rich & Co AG v. Società Italiana Impianti PA*, (Case C-190/89) [1991] ECR I-3855, I-3902 para. 26.

[161] Recital (12) para. 4.

[162] Recital (12) para. 1.

[163] Recital (12) para. 4 and Art. 73.

[164] See Recital (12) paras. 1 and 2. The ECJ in *Allianz SpA, Generali Assicurazioni Generali Spa v. West Tankers Inc, The Front Comor* (Case C-185/07) [2009] ECR I-663 decided that an anti suit injunction to support the arbitration agreement was impermissible but the proceedings by which the injunction was granted were outside the scope of the Brussels I Regulation, these proceedings included a request for a declaration as to the effect of the arbitration agreement binding the insurer (para. 23).

[165] Report *Schlosser* para. 65; *Marc Rich & Co AG v. Società Italiana Impianti PA*, (Case C-190/89) [1991] ECR I-3855, I-3902 para. 26.

such a case the Member State's court can assume jurisdiction under its national rules and ignore any proceedings continuing in another Member State on the same issue. The issues of recognition and enforcement of any judgment on the substance of the dispute in those cases are not so straightforward.[166] Other unclear cases include: proceedings in which the arbitration agreement is used to challenge jurisdiction;[167] proceedings for damages for breach of the arbitration agreement; proceedings to require the taking of evidence or the protection of evidence; proceedings as to awards of costs or security in arbitration; and proceedings to recognise or enforce a judgment which has been given in violation of an arbitration agreement[168] (whether the validity of the arbitration agreement was decided in that judgment or not).[169] Until the decision of the CJEU in *Allianz SpA Assicurazioni Generali Spa v. West Tankers*[170] the prevailing view of English lawyers was that the arbitration exception should be given a wide interpretation to ensure that all these cases would likewise fall outside the scope of the Brussels I*bis* Regulation.[171]

The scope of the arbitration exception has been somewhat cut down by developments on **46** other exclusions in the Brussels I*bis* Regulation. Although it is clear that arbitration awards themselves are neither recognisable nor enforceable under the rules of the Brussels I*bis* Regulation,[172] other matters that raise questions of arbitration could be argued to come within the Brussels I*bis* Regulation. The *Evrigenis/Kerameus* Report notes that "the verification as an incidental question of an arbitration agreement which is cited by a litigant in order to contest the jurisdiction of the court before which he is being sued pursuant to the Convention, must be considered as falling within its scope".[173] On that reasoning, where arbitration has been raised as an incidental issue in proceedings which are otherwise within the scope of the Brussels I*bis* Regulation, the Brussels I Regulation's rules on jurisdiction, *lis pendens* and recognition and enforcement nonetheless apply. Advocate General Darmon in *Marc Rich AG v. Società Italiana Impianti SpA* criticised that interpretation of the paragraph unless it was only to be regarded as applying to the question of recognition of a judgment obtained in disregard of a valid arbitration agreement. He regarded that question, too, as open.

In the *van Uden* decision[174] the CJEU reiterated that arbitration was to be excluded from the **47** Brussels I Regulation, provided that the proceedings were in substance issues of arbitration

---

166   See Recital (12) para. 3.

167   This might be seen as an incidental question, which could be argued to be within the Brussels I Regulation as the primary purpose of the proceedings is not the arbitration agreement. Recital (12) paras. 3 and 4 complicates this question further. See further para. 50.

168   Recital (12) paras. 3–4.

169   *Illmer* and *Naumann* suggest a functional analysis which would place a number of these within the arbitration exception.

170   *Allianz SpA, Generali Assicurazioni Generali Spa v. West Tankers Inc, The Front Comor* (Case C-185/07) [2009] ECR I 663.

171   Cf. *Schlosser*, (1991) 7 Arb. Int. 227, who argued that only arbitral proceedings themselves come within the exception.

172   Recital (12) and Art. 73.

173   Report *Evrigenis/Kerameus* para. 35.

174   *van Uden Maritime BV, trading as van Uden Africa Line v. Kommanditgesellschaft in Firma Deco-Line*, (Case C-391/95) [1998] ECR I-7091.

or ancillary to arbitration. Proceedings which were parallel to the arbitration were not necessarily excluded. In this case provisional measures sought from a Member State's court in support of arbitration proceedings would fall within the scope of the Brussels I Regulation for the purposes of providing provisional or protective measures under Art. 35 (formerly Art. 31). Allowing some matters which could be said to be related to arbitration to come within the Brussels I*bis* Regulation in this way could be argued to pave the way for the narrow interpretation of the arbitration exception. On this analysis, unless the arbitration is directly and primarily the subject matter of the proceedings, any other proceedings come within the scope of the Brussels I*bis* Regulation. Art. 29 and the automatic recognition and enforcement provisions would then apply to those other proceedings. Other commentators[175] argue that the recognising court is permitted to make its own decision on the scope of the Brussels I*bis* Regulation. This is hardly consistent with a uniform interpretation of the exception and is contrary to the prohibition on reviewing the judgment granting court's jurisdiction found in Art. 52.

48 Some commentators have argued that it might be possible to define the arbitration exception by reference to the scope of the New York Convention on the Recognition and Enforcement of Foreign Arbitral Awards.[176] If the matter comes within the scope of the New York Convention it falls outside the scope of the Brussels I*bis* Regulation.[177] This argument takes account of the purpose of the exception for arbitration. As the New York Convention requires national courts to decide matters of existence, scope and validity of an arbitration agreement such matters are outside the scope of the Brussels I*bis* Regulation.

49 Criticisms of the operation of the exception from the scope of the Brussels I Regulation for arbitration arose after the decision of the CJEU in *Allianz SpA, Generali Assicurazioni Generali Spa v.West Tankers Inc, The Front Comor*.[178] The English courts were requested to grant an anti-suit injunction to restrain an insurer from continuing proceedings in Italy to recover amounts already paid to an insured. Those Italian proceedings were allegedly in breach of an arbitration agreement between the defendant in Italy (the petitioner in the English proceedings) and the insured. Arbitration on the same matter was continuing in England. The English proceedings were also declaratory as to the effect of the arbitration agreement and its breach by the Italian proceedings. The CJEU found the English proceedings fell outwith the scope of the Brussels I Regulation as their subject matter was the right to arbitrate. However, the Italian proceedings fell within the Brussels I Regulation as the validity and effect of the arbitration agreement was only a preliminary matter. The CJEU relied on paragraph 35 of the *Kerameus/Evrigenis* Report but did not answer the criticism of that opinion made by A-G *Darmon* in the earlier case of *Marc Rich*. The substance of the Italian proceedings was the dispute over liability and jurisdiction for those proceedings could be established under the rules of the Brussels I Regulation. The CJEU also held that the English court could not grant an anti-suit injunction over the Italian proceedings as to do so would interfere with the Italian court's determination of its own jurisdiction under the Brussels I Regulation. This solution, however compatible with other CJEU cases which uphold mutual trust and confidence and apply *effet utile*,[179] had very unfortunate conse-

---

[175] For example, *Briggs/Rees* p. 48–50, 434–436.

[176] Adopted by the United Nations Conference on International Commercial Arbitration on 10th June 1958.

[177] *Ambrose*, (2003) 19 Arb. Int. 3, 12.

[178] Case C-185/07 [2009] ECR I-663.

quences. The English proceedings, even if commenced first, were not within Artt. 29 and 30 (formerly Artt. 27 and 28), so inevitably there was the risk of irreconcilable decisions on the validity and effect of the arbitration agreement as well as the expense of two sets of proceedings in which the same matter is in issue. Also, the judgment of the Italian court on the substance of the dispute is enforceable within the Brussels I Regulation throughout the EU. An irreconcilable decision of the English court is not within the Brussels I Regulation, although the Italian judgment would not be recognised or enforced in England.[180] The judgment of the Italian court would compete with the arbitration award, necessarily,[181] but there will also be competing judgments on the effect of the arbitration agreement.[182]

Recital (12) of the Brussels I*bis* Regulation was inserted to answer many of these questions. **50** The Brussels I*bis* Regulation should not apply to arbitration by Recital (12) paragraph 1. That paragraph continues to explain that nothing in the Brussels I*bis* Regulation prevents the courts of a Member State (seised of a matter which the parties have agreed to refer to arbitration) from referring parties to arbitration, or from staying or dismissing the proceedings, or from examining the validity of the agreement in accordance with national law. (2) provides that a ruling, whether or not as a principal or incidental question, that an arbitration agreement is null and void, inoperative or incapable of being performed should not be subject to the rules of recognition and enforcement of the Brussels I Regulation. This covers some of the points made above in relation to *van Uden*[183] but only in respect of the part of any judgment that deals with the validity of the arbitration agreement. On the other hand, paragraph 3 provides that the decision on the substantive issues following a ruling that an arbitration agreement is null and void, inoperative or incapable of being performed may be recognised or enforced in accordance with the Brussels I*bis* Regulation. Member States are reminded by the last sentence of this paragraph of their obligations under the 1958 New York Convention and that that Convention takes precedence over the Brussels I*bis* Regulation.[184] The final paragraph of Recital (12) declares that the Brussels I*bis* Regulation should not apply to actions or ancillary proceedings which relate, in particular, to establishment of the arbitral tribunal, the powers of arbitrators, or the conduct of an arbitration procedure. The Brussels I*bis* Regulation also should not apply to actions or judgments concerning the annulment, review, appeal, recognition or enforcement of arbitral awards by paragraph 4 of Recital (12). Neither Recital (12) nor any provision of the Brussels I*bis* Regulation makes it clear that the automatic stay of proceedings in Art. 29 does not operate where the parties

---

[179] *Turner v. Grovit* Case C-159/02 [2004] ECR I-3565; *van Uden Maritime BV, trading as van Uden Africa Line v. Kommanditgesellschaft in Firma Deco-Line*, (Case C-391/95) [1998] ECR I-7091; *Erich Gasser GmbH v. MISAT srl*, (Case C-116/02) [2003] ECR I-14693.

[180] Art. 45(1)(c).

[181] There are already examples of conflicting judgments and arbitral awards *Gouvernement du Pakistan v. SociétéDallah Real Estate & Tourism Holding Co*, CA Paris 17 February 2011, [2011] Les Cahiers de l'arbitrage/Paris Journal of International Arbitration and *Dallah Estate and Tourism Holding Company v. The Ministry of Religious Affairs, Government of Pakistan* [2010] UKSC 46, on appeal from [2009] EWCA Civ 755 cited in: Radicati di Brozolo, [2013] JPrIL 423, 428.

[182] The litigation has continued in England, see *West Tankers Inc v. Allianz SpA (The Front Comor)* [2012] EWCA Civ 27 [2012] 1 Lloyd's Rep. 398.

[183] *van Uden Maritime BV, trading as van Uden Africa Line v. Kommanditgesellschaft in Firma Deco-Line*, (Case C-391/95) [1998] ECR I-7091.

[184] See too Art. 73.

---

have agreed to arbitration.[185] Such a provision was envisaged in one of the earlier proposals for the Brussels *Ibis* Regulation[186] but was not in the final text. A party which wishes to 'torpedo' a dispute which should be subject to arbitration can still commence proceedings in the courts of a Member State and by doing so prevent the same cause of action being heard in another Member State, say at the seat of the arbitration.

51 Problems could arise where a court at the seat of the arbitration has ruled that the dispute must go to arbitration and the court of another Member State has made order that the arbitration agreement invalid and decided the substance of the dispute. The part of judgment relating to the validity of the arbitration agreement does not have to be recognised and enforced but the actual judgment on the substance must be recognised and enforced generally. This result nullifies the effect of the arbitration unless an award has been already made and a judgment to enforce the award already granted. Does this requirement to recognise and enforce the substantive decision also apply to the courts of the Member State at the seat of the arbitration? Art. 45 (1) (c) permits refusal of recognition or enforcement if there was already a conflicting judgment of the Member State at the seat of the arbitration as to the substance of the dispute. What if there has not been such a judgment as the arbitrators' award has not yet been made or not yet made enforceable? There may be a question as to whether the courts of a Member State at the seat of the arbitration can enforce the arbitration award in precedence to the judgment of another Member State, as the New York Convention only applies to "foreign" arbitral awards. However, it must be right that the courts of a Member State at the seat of the arbitration must not be at a disadvantage to those of a third Member State. Also, an arbitral tribunal sitting in a Member State may be bound by the decision of the court of the other Member State where the conflict of laws rules of the seat of the arbitration require recognition of the judgment of the other Member State.[187] That also robs an arbitration agreement of much of its utility. It is unlikely that the amendments in the Brussels *Ibis* Regulation will prevent a race to the courts in an attempt to disrupt arbitration agreements.

52 It has been argued that the last paragraph of Recital (12) may permit the courts of a Member State to grant injunctive relief in support of arbitration proceedings.[188] However, this is most unlikely. First, anti-suit injunctions generally offend the principle of mutual trust underpinning the whole regime.[189] The third paragraph of Recital (12) makes a ruling on the substance of the dispute allegedly subject to arbitration recognisable and enforceable in other Member States and no other court is in a better position to determine the jurisdiction of the court giving the judgment on the substance.[190] The anti-suit injunction is also arguably unnecessary as paragraph 3 of Recital (12) refers specifically to the New York Convention.

---

[185] Compare with Arts. 29; 31 (2) which explicitly protect exclusive jurisdiction agreements (if only to a certain extent).

[186] See *Radicati di Brozolo*, (2011) 7 JPrIL 423, 436 *et seq.*; *Carducci*, [2011] Arb. Int. 171, 192 *et seq.*

[187] As happened in *National Navigation Co v. Endesa Generacion SA* [2009] EWCA Civ 1397; [2010] 1 Lloyd's Rep 193 (C.A.).

[188] See *Camilleri*, [2013] ICLQ 899, 903 *et seq.*

[189] *Gregory Paul Turner v. Felix Fareed Ismail Grovit, Harada Ltd and Changepoint SA*, (Case C-159/02) [2004] ECR I-3565. See too Recital (26).

[190] *Allianz SpA, Generali Assicurazioni Generali Spa v. West Tankers Inc.* (Case C-185/07) [2009] ECR I 663 para. [29].

This paragraph, along with Art. 73, appears to permit the courts of a Member State to recognise or enforce an arbitral award in precedence to a judgment of a court of a Member State. The enforcement of a judgment on the substance of the dispute is "without prejudice" to the New York Convention. An anti-enforcement injunction protecting an arbitral award from peril of the enforcement of a competing Member State's judgment may, nevertheless, be possible.[191]

5. Maintenance obligations arising from a family relationship, parentage, marriage or affinity, (2) (e)

The Maintenance Regulation[192] applies to all maintenance obligations arising from a family   **53** relationship, parentage, marriage or affinity. These matters are therefore outwith the scope of the Brussels I*bis* Regulation. This was not the case in the Brussels I Regulation or the Brussels Convention where maintenance was within the scope of those instruments.[193] The definition of maintenance obligations arising from a family relationship, parentage, marriage or affinity must be autonomous so that both Regulations are similarly interpreted.[194] It is possible that similar problems to those already encountered in the exclusion of insolvency due to a specific Regulation might result.[195]

6. Wills and succession, including maintenance obligations arising by reason of death, (2) (f)

Proceedings concerning wills and succession are excluded by this paragraph, along with   **54** maintenance obligations arising by reason of death. Disputes as to the interpretation or validity of a will or codicil, or claims to testate or intestate succession to property, and the appointment and removal of trustees or administrators to administer the succession are excluded from the scope of the Brussels I*bis* Regulation. The jurisdiction and enforcement rules of the Succession Regulation apply to the estates of deceased persons.[196] However, the matter may fall within the Brussels I*bis* Regulation where the dispute is between a trustee or administrator and someone other than a beneficiary, such as a debtor to the estate.[197] A very difficult question might arise in such cases where the debtor seeks as a matter of defence to assert that the trustee does not have power as the will is invalid. The main subject matter of the proceedings would be within the Brussels I*bis* Regulation, but the defence directly raises an excluded matter.[198] Although the jurisdiction of the court could be said to have been

---

[191] See *S Camilleri* Recital (12) of the recast Regulation: a new hope? [2013] ICLQ 899 at pp. 906 *et seq.*

[192] Regulation (EC) No. 4/2009 on jurisdiction, applicable law, recognition and enforcement of decisions and cooperation in matters relating to maintenance obligations 2009 OJ L 7/1 (amended 2011 OJ L 293/24).

[193] See for example, *Louise de Cavel v. Jacques de Cavel*, (Case 120/79) [1980] ECR 731.

[194] See too Recital (11) Maintenance Regulation.

[195] See further paras. 32–35 of this chapter.

[196] Art. 1 Regulation (EU) No. 650/2012 on jurisdiction, applicable law, recognition and enforcement of decisions and acceptance and enforcement of authentic instruments in matters of succession and on the creation of a European Certificate of Succession 2012 OJ L 201/107.

[197] Report *Schlosser* para. 52.

[198] The mere possibility of defences does not generally exclude the claim from the scope, see *Préservatrice foncière TIARD SA v. Staat der Nederlanden*, (Case C-266/01) [2003] ECR I-4867.

properly established under the Brussels I*bis* Regulation,[199] any enforcement of the judgment (either accepting or denying the defence) might be more problematic. Proceedings relating to gifts *inter vivos* are within the Brussels I*bis* Regulation as are disputes over some trusts.[200]

VI. Cases involving some aspects which may fall outside the scope of the Brussels I*bis* Regulation (Principal or Ancillary Claims, Preliminary, Incidental or Indirect Issues)

55 More complex cases which raise several intertwined issues either as a matter of claim or as defence where some of the issues could fall outside the scope of the Brussels I*bis* Regulation are difficult. The case-law is not consistent and the problems particularly intricate. How should ancillary matters, indirectly raised claims, preliminary issues or preliminary proceedings, defences, incidental questions and provisional measures be dealt with?

56 The cases seem to indicate the following principles. First, if the principal subject matter of the dispute is an excluded matter, for example, arbitration, then the entire dispute is excluded from the ambit of the Brussels I*bis* Regulation, including any incidental or preliminary matter that would otherwise be included.[201] However, severable ancillary claims can be included.[202] Provisional measures in support of civil and commercial claims that would otherwise be excluded under Art. 1(2) are within the scope of the Brussels I*bis* Regulation.[203]

57 If the principal subject matter of the proceedings is not an excluded matter, it appears that the proceedings are within the scope of the Brussels I Regulation. This is so despite the possibility of incidental, preliminary or ancillary matters falling outside the scope of the Brussels I Regulation.[204] This proposition includes any defences raised; i.e. the possibility of raising an excluded matter as a defence does not affect the scope of the Brussels I*bis* Regulation.[205] Proceedings which do not directly derive from an excluded matter are included within the scope of the Brussels I Regulation,[206] for example, proceedings which only indirectly concern matters of bankruptcy.[207] Given that the Brussels I*bis* Regulation allows declaratory proceedings,[208] a well advised litigant may take advantage of local law to frame

---

[199] For example, under Art. 7 (6) as an alternative to Art. 4 jurisdiction.

[200] Report *Jenard* p. 11 and Art. 7 (6).

[201] *Marc Rich & Co AG v. Societa Italiana Impianti PA*, (Case C-190/89) [1991] ECR I-3855; *Owens Bank Ltd. v. Fulvio Bracco and Bracco Industria Chimica SpA*, (Case C-129/92) [1994] ECR I-117; *Allianz SpA, Generali Assicurazioni Generali Spa v. West Tankers Inc, The Front Comor* (Case C-185/07) [2009] ECR I 663.

[202] *Louise de Cavel v. Jacques de Cavel*, (Case 120/79) [1980] ECR 731.

[203] *van Uden Maritime BV, trading as van Uden Africa Line v. Kommanditgesellschaft in Firma Deco-Line*, (Case C-391/95) [1998] ECR I-7091.

[204] Report *Jenard* p. 10; *Louise de Cavel v. Jacques de Cavel*, (Case 120/79), [1980] ECR 731; *Préservatrice foncière TIARD SA v. Staat der Nederlanden*, (Case C-266/01) [2003] ECR I-4867; *Gemeente Steenbergen v. Luc Baten*, (Case C-271/00) [2002] ECR I-10489.

[205] *Préservatrice foncière TIARD SA v. Staat der Nederlande*, (Case C-266/01) [2003] ECR I-4867.

[206] Report *Jenard* p. 12.

[207] *Henri Gourdain v. Franz Nadler*, (Case 133/78) [1979] ECR 733 and by implication *Seagon v.Deko Marty Belgium NV* (case C-339/07) [2009] ECR I-767.

[208] *The owners of the cargo lately laden on board the ship "Tatry" v. The owners of the ship "Maciej Rataj"*, (Case C-406/92) [1994] ECR I-5439.

the issues in the proceedings to fall within or without the Brussels I*bis* Regulation to its benefit.[209]

This is a very unsatisfactory conclusion. Although it might be possible to justify these **58** principles in relation to the assumption of jurisdiction under the Brussels I*bis* Regulation, the problem is merely then postponed to the question of recognition and enforcement of any judgment given. Is the recognising Member State's court entitled to determine afresh the matter of the scope of the Brussels I*bis* Regulation? Is it bound by any decision on this question given by the judgment granting court? An affirmative answer to the latter question is the only one consistent with aim of mutual trust and confidence. Recital (12) complicates this position a little. The Recital explicitly excludes from the operation of the Brussels I*bis* Regulation a ruling as to whether an arbitration agreement is null and void, inoperative or incapable of being performed whether decided as a principal or an ancillary matter. However, this is only for the purposes of recognition and enforcement. Therefore if the courts another Member State have determined that an arbitration agreement does not cover a dispute (ie is inoperative in the circumstances), that decision does not have to be recognised or enforced even if it was only an incidental issue in the dispute. For all other excluded matters the rules of the Brussels I*bis* Regulation do not apply only if the excluded matter is the principal subject matter of the dispute.

The relationship between the excluded proceedings and Artt. 29 and 30 is opaque and will **59** continue to lead to a multiplicity of proceedings with the consequent expense. First, a court other than the seat of arbitration can usurp the arbitration by hearing the substantive dispute. Proceedings commenced on the substantive dispute then prevent any proceedings on the same cause of action in other Member States (Art. 29 formerly Art. 27). Secondly the court hearing the substantive dispute is not bound to recognise the decision of the court of the seat as the decision of the court of the seat are excluded from the Brussels I*bis* Regulation. There are examples in the English courts under the Brussels I*bis* Regulation of a well-advised litigant using the uncertainty created by the exception to his or her own advantage. Tactical litigation was thereby increased. In *National Navigation Co v. Endesa Generacion SA*[210] there were initial Spanish proceedings relating to the substance of the dispute which decided that the arbitration clause had not been incorporated into the Bill of Lading. The Court of Appeal found that those Spanish proceedings were within the Brussels I Regulation as arbitration was only an ancillary question in them and the English court was bound by the Spanish decision under Art. 33 (now Art. 36). It therefore denied the declaration that the arbitration clause was binding, despite the clause being effective under English law. In contrast, in *Youell v. La Reunion Aerienne*[211] the Court of Appeal continued English proceedings as to the substance of the dispute despite arbitration having been commenced in France. The court held that it could take jurisdiction pursuant to Art. 5(1) (now Art. 7(1)) of the Brussels I Regulation and that it could come to its own decision as to the scope of the arbitration agreement. Even proceedings in France to uphold the French arbitration agreement would not have altered this conclusion as these were excluded from the recognition rules of the Brussels I Regulation. In that case there would be competing arbitration awards and a judgment from the courts of a Member State. These cases would be decided only a little

---

[209]   See Art. 29–34 paras. 19–20 (Chapter 2).
[210]   [2009] EWCA Civ 1397; [2010] 1 Lloyd's Rep 193 noted Fentiman [2010] C.L.J. 242.
[211]   [2009] EWCA Civ 175; [2009] 1 Lloyd's Rep 586.

differently under the Brussels I*bis* Regulation. In *National Navigation Co v. Endesa Generacion SA*[212] the Spanish decision as to the operation of the arbitration agreement would not have to be recognised in England (Recital (12) paragraph 2). However, the Spanish proceedings as they were commenced first would prevent any English proceedings on the same issue (Article 29). In *Youell v. La Reunion Aerienne*[213] the English court could continue to hear the substantive dispute and any decision of the court as to the substance would be recognisable and enforceable in other Member States. In both cases there would be competing enforcement of national judgments and arbitration awards.

Article 2

For the purposes of this Regulation:

(a) 'judgment' means any judgment given by a court or tribunal of a Member State, whatever the judgment may be called, including a decree, order, decision or writ of execution, as well as a decision on the determination of costs or expenses by an officer of the court.
For the purposes of Chapter III, 'judgment' includes provisional, including protective, measures ordered by a court or tribunal which by virtue of this Regulation has jurisdiction as to the substance of the matter. It does not include a provisional, including protective, measure which is ordered by such a court or tribunal without the defendant being summoned to appear, unless the judgment containing the measure is served on the defendant prior to enforcement;

(b) 'court settlement' means a settlement which has been approved by a court of a Member State or concluded before a court of a Member State in the course of proceedings;

(c) 'authentic instrument' means a document which has been formally drawn up or registered as an authentic instrument in the Member State of origin and the authenticity of which:
   i) relates to the signature and the content of the instrument; and
   ii) has been established by a public authority or other authority empowered for that purpose;

(d) 'Member State of origin' means the Member State in which, as the case may be, the judgment has been given, the court settlement has been approved or concluded, or the authentic instrument has been formally drawn up or registered;

(e) 'Member State addressed' means the Member State in which the recognition of the judgment is invoked or in which the enforcement of the judgment, the court settlement or the authentic instrument is sought;

(f) 'court of origin' means the court which has given the judgment the recognition of which is invoked or the enforcement of which is sought.

---

[212] [2009] EWCA Civ 1397; [2010] 1 Lloyd's Rep 193.
[213] [2009] EWCA Civ 175; [2009] 1 Lloyd's Rep 586.

I. General outline and legislative history

Art. 2 is a new Article setting out a series of definitions for the purposes of the Regulation. As 1
well as becoming increasingly common in EU legislation,[1] modern statutes in many common law countries frequently contain (in English statutes usually at the end) a set of provisions concerning interpretation.[2] Legislators often find it convenient to lay down limited
rules of construction in the statute itself and the use of such definitions can lead to economy
and simplicity in drafting. Legislative definitions take a variety of different forms, many of
which are present in the new Art. 2.[3]

Some definitions are "labelling" definitions which use a term as a label denoting a concept, 2
perhaps complex, that can be referred to merely by use of that label. This seems to be the case
for the definitions introduced in Art. 2 (d)-(f). These are also compound definitions in that
they include terms (for example, 'judgment,' 'court settlement' and 'authentic instrument')
which have themselves received a definition of their own.

In other cases, definitions perform a more significant role in clarifying the meaning of a 3
term; through either enlarging or excluding a meaning which the term might otherwise have
had. For example, Art. 2 (a) makes it clear that in the Regulation 'judgments' include decrees,
orders etc which may or may not otherwise have been taken to have been included within
that term. This enlarging function may be particularly important in a European context as it
emphasises that a broad European meaning of a concept is not limited by the meaning that
term would have in individual Member States. Art. 2 (a) is also an exclusionary definition in
that it makes it clear that 'judgments' do not include provisional measures given without
notice unless the judgment is served on the defendant prior to enforcement. Finally, definitions can also be comprehensive in that they provide a full and exhaustive statement of the
meaning of a term. Thus, Art. 2 (b) and (c) makes it clear that *only* 'court settlements' and
'authentic instruments' which come within the terms set out in those definitions fall within
the rules for recognition and enforcement under the Regulation.

Art. 2 is not comprehensive. The article focuses on issues concerning recognition and 4

---

[1] Regulation (EC) No. 805/04 creating a European Enforcement Order for Uncontested Claims contains
   a similar definition section in Art. 4. Definition sections are also found in Art. 3 Rome III Regulation;
   Art. 3 Succession Regulation and in proposed Regulations concerning Matrimonial Property and Partnership.
[2] See *J. Bell/Engle*, Cross Statutory Interpretation (2nd ed. 1987) pp. 117–118.
[3] Halsbury's Laws of England (4th ed. 1995) Vol 44 (1) para. 1389.

enforcement in the narrow sense (as opposed to jurisdiction more generally). Furthermore, although the form is new, many of the ideas were express or inherent in the Brussels I Regulation. The basic definition of 'judgment' (Art. 2 (a)) is almost identical to that which previously appeared as a definition in Art. 32 Brussels I Regulation (which itself closely mirrored Art. 25 Brussels Convention and Art. 26 1988 Lugano Convention); it has simply been extracted from that article and moved to Art. 2. However, clarification of the position in relation to provisional including protective measures is provided which, to some extent, modifies the existing position. The definitions of 'court settlements' (Art. 2 (b)) and 'authentic instruments' (Art. 2 (c)) are drawn from Articles 57 and 58 Brussels I Regulation which provided rules for the enforcement of such instruments. Although they were not framed in the form of a definition in those provisions but were expressed indirectly, they had a defining effect and could be referred to as oblique definitions.[4] The concept of 'Member State of origin', 'Member State addressed', and 'court of origin' are new[5] and differentiate the different possible Member States and courts at issue in the new procedure for the enforcement of judgments following the abolition of *exequatur* proceedings.

II. Judgments

5   The first sentence of Art. 2 (a) repeats, almost identically,[6] the definition of 'judgment' previously found in Art. 32 Brussels I Regulation. This definition is crucial in identifying the measures which potentially benefit from the automatic recognition and enforcement which the Regulation provides.[7] The judgment must also fall within the material scope of the Regulation, set out in Art. 1, that is, it must relate to a civil and commercial matter and not be excluded by Art. 1(2).[8] The enforcing court is entitled to take its own view on whether the provisions of Art. 1 are satisfied.[9] In determining whether an order falls within Art. 1 for the purposes of enforcement, reference must be made to the factors characterising the nature of the legal relationship between the parties to the action or the subject matter of the action. Thus, even a fine payable to the state can be enforced where it was made in proceedings between private persons and was intended to protect private rights (for example, a patent).[10]

---

4   Halsbury's Laws of England, para. 1389.

5   Similar definitions appear in Art. 4(4)-(6) of Regulation 805/04.

6   The Brussels *Ibis* Regulation refers to 'a decision' on the determination of costs.

7   The Heidelberg Report notes (para. 536) that in the cross-border context, it seems likely that Regulation (EC) No. 805/04 creating a European Enforcement Order for uncontested claims and the new instruments creating the European Order for Payments and for Small Claims (EC Reg No. 1896/2006 creating a European procedure for payment and EC Reg No. 861/2007 establishing a European Small Claims procedure) will facilitate the application of what was Art. 32 Brussels I Regulation.

8   The test is the same as that applied for the purposes of jurisdiction: see commentary on Art. 1.

9   Sometimes the judgment granting court will not itself have considered the issue. Even if it has, it should be open to the enforcing court to establish for itself that the judgment is within Art. 1 (see *Briggs/Rees* para. 7.07 and *Cheshire/North/Fawcett/Carruthers* p. 601. But compare *Layton/Mercer* para. 25.003.

10 *Realchemie Nederland BV v. Bayer CropScience AG* (Case 406/09), [2011] ECR I-9773. In the *Stolzenberg case*, the French Cour de Cassation held that a *Mareva* injunction (now renamed as freezing injunction) could fall within the Regulation even if it gave rise to criminal sanctions (Cass. RCDIP 93 [2004], 815).

1. "Any judgment, ... whatever the judgment may be called"

In order to ensure the widest possible scope for the free movement of judgments, Art. 2 (a)   **6**
provides a broad autonomous definition of judgment.[11] The definition is autonomous in that
it does not depend on how a measure is described or treated as a matter of national law. For
example, in *Gothaer v. Samskip*,[12] a Belgian court had dismissed an action for compensation
on the basis that the claim was subject to an exclusive jurisdiction agreement in favour of
Iceland (enforceable under the Lugano Convention). The question was whether that decision was enforceable in subsequent German proceedings. According to German law it was a
'judgment on a procedural matter' ('Prozessurteil') and, generally speaking, accordingly
unenforceable. The ECJ confirmed that the concept of 'judgment'(under Art. 32 Brussels I
Regulation) had to be interpreted independently of any national law.[13] Furthermore, the
autonomous definition was a broad one. Art. 32 Brussels I Regulation covered 'any' judgment without any distinction being drawn according to the content of the judgment.[14] The
ECJ also confirmed that the definition is not limited to decisions which terminate a dispute
in whole or in part, but also applied to provisional or interlocutory decisions (the enforcement of provisional and protective measures is now dealt with expressly in Art. 2 (a) as
considered further below).[15] Thus, the decision of the Belgian court was a binding judgment
within the meaning of the Regulation.[16]

There is no requirement that the judgment be *res judicata* or final and conclusive.[17]   **7**

The broad definition of 'judgment' includes a decree establishing a limitation fund.[18] It can   **8**
also include an order decreeing a periodic payment by way of a penalty for non-compliance
with the order of a court.[19] Contrary to the position under some national laws (for example,
English law) judgments are not limited to money judgments: enforcement extends to other
types of order such as orders for specific performance or injunctions.[20] However, the defi-

---

[11] Heidelberg Report para. 527.

[12] *Gothaer Allgemeine Versicherung AG v. Samskip GmbH* (Case 456/11), EU:C:2012:719.

[13] *Gothaer Allgemeine Versicherung AG v. Samskip GmbH* (Case 456/11), EU:C:2012:719 paras. 25, 26.

[14] *Gothaer Allgemeine Versicherung AG v. Samskip GmbH* (Case 456/11), EU:C:2012:719 para. 23.

[15] *Gothaer Allgemeine Versicherung AG v. Samskip GmbH* (Case 456/11), EU:C:2012:719 para. 24.

[16] The ECJ held that the concept of *res judicata* attaches not only to the operative part of the judgment but
      also to the *ratio*; thus, the finding in favour of the Icelandic jurisdiction clause, as well as the decision
      declining jurisdiction, was binding.

[17] See *Layton/Mercer* para. 24.021. The concept of *res iudicata* has a different meaning in different Member
      States and is also separate from the question of whether the judgment is 'final' or 'conclusive'. The Report
      Jenard commentary on Art. 26 Brussels Convention noted that the words 'res judicata' which appear in a
      number of existing conventions relating to enforcement were expressly omitted from the Brussels Con-
      vention.

[18] *Mærsk Olie & Gas A/S v. Firma M. de Haan en W. de Boer* (Case 39/02), [2004] ECR I-9657. The
      Heidelberg Report para. 533 notes that in the Netherlands the Regional Court of Rotterdam has decided
      that the Swedish limitation procedure fell within the scope of Art. 1 Brussels I Regulation and was,
      therefore, a decision according to Art. 32 Brussels I Regulation *VznGr Rotterdam*, SES 2003/126.

[19] Sometimes referred to as *an astreinte*: see *Briggs/Rees* para. 7.06.

[20] In *Barratt International Resorts Ltd v. Martin* 1994 SLT 434, a Scottish court held that a decree for
      interdict issued by the Scottish court would be a judgment which would be enforceable in Spain.

nition of 'judgments' which are enforceable under the Regulation, does not include interlocutory directions of a procedural nature, such as, orders relating to the conduct of proceedings or the taking of evidence.

9 Decisions which are not intended to govern the legal relationships of the parties, but to
arrange the further conduct of the proceedings, are excluded from the scope of Chapter III.[21]
Many procedural decisions, such as, an order to set a hearing date or to establish how
evidence is to be given during proceedings, are irrelevant to any other country in any event.
However, in *CFEM Façades SA v. Bovis Construction Ltd*[22] the English High Court was asked
to register an order of a French court ordering inspection of an office building in London.
Having referred to the test set out in the Report *Schlosser*, the court held that procedural
orders were those which were not intended to govern the legal relationships of the parties
nor to affect proprietary rights. While certain parts of the order were procedural, in so far as
experts were appointed to visit buildings and in so far as the plaintiffs were authorised under
certain conditions to carry out works on the building, it was not clear that the orders did not
govern the legal relationship of the parties or affect their property rights and accordingly the
order was in part an enforceable judgment.[23]

2. "Including a decree, order, decision or writ of execution, as well as a decision on the determination of costs or expenses by an officer of the court"

10 The definition in Art. 2 (a) expressly encompasses decrees, orders, decisions and writs as
well as decisions on costs. The definition includes writs of execution issued by a court
registrar,[24] but is unlikely to include 'protêts' whereby the holder of a commercial paper
may under French or Belgian law request that a bailiff formally records that the commercial
debt remains unpaid. The judicial assignment of wages to the maintenance of the creditor
must be recognised whenever the latter sues the employer provided that there has been an
inter partes hearing of the relevant parties.[25]

11 National courts are often asked to recognise and enforce costs orders which are not always
given by judicial authorities of other Member States. Art. 2(a) makes it clear that a decision
on costs by an officer of the court can be enforced under the Regulation including decisions
of a registrar acting as an officer of the court.[26] A decision of a French president of a *Tribunal
de Grande Instance* fixing costs can accordingly be enforced. Similarly, under the German
Code of Civil Procedure, a costs registrar acts as an officer of the court which decided on the

---

[21]   Report *Schlosser* (para. 184). See also *Layton/Mercer* para. 24.032. Many such orders fall within other
        instruments such as the EU Service Regulation, the EU Evidence Regulation or the Hague Convention on
        service or the taking of evidence abroad.

[22]   [1992] I.L.Pr 561.

[23]   Compare OLG of Hamm 14 June 1988 referred to in *Kaye* para. 513 where a French order ordering an
        expert to inspect premises and to investigate was held not to be enforceable.

[24]   Vollstreckungsbefehl, § 699 German ZP: Report *Jenard* p. 42.

[25]   See *Heidelberg Report* (para. 528) referring to the practice of the Dutch *Hoge Raad*. Such hearings do not
        regularly take place in garnishment proceedings: *Hess*, Study JAI A3/03/2002 on Making More Efficient
        the Enforcement of Judicial Decisions in Europe, pp. 58 *et seq.*

[26]   Heidelberg Report para. 528. The *BGH* has stated that the term judgment has to be construed broadly and
        autonomously (Judgment of 9/22/2005 – X ZB 7/04).

substance of the matter, and in the event of a challenge to the registrar's decision, the court decides the issue. Costs orders made by German costs registrars will be enforceable under the Regulation.[27]

3. Given by a court or tribunal of a Member State

The requirement that the judgment must be given by a court or tribunal of a Member State **11a** encompasses two separate principles. One is a territorial requirement; the judgment must originate in a Member State. Secondly, the decision must come from a court or tribunal exercising judicial functions of that state. This means that the judgment must be a decision which emanates from a judicial body deciding on its own authority the issues between the parties.[28] Courts are also broadly defined as including courts or tribunals of a Member State. This includes courts or tribunals common to several Member States, such as the Benelux ECJ when it exercises jurisdiction on matters falling within the scope of the Regulation.[29] Decisions of criminal courts are included.[30] The definition in Art. 2 (a) may also encompass orders of inferior tribunals, including tribunals where the judge is not legally qualified, such as *Tribunals de Commerce* in France, and bodies designated as tribunals if exercising judicial powers, such as English employment tribunals.[31] Private tribunals, in particular arbitration tribunals, are not tribunals 'of a Member State'. Thus the rules do not apply to arbitral awards (even if Art. 1 (2) (d) did not exist). Decisions rendered by international courts or tribunals are also excluded.

The Regulation only applies to a judgment when the merits have been determined in that **12** Member State. Thus, a judgment of a Member State enforcing a judgment obtained in another Member State is not in turn enforceable in a third Member State. Nor is a judgment of a Member State enforcing a judgment obtained in a non-Member State enforceable in a third Member State.[32] The same principle is likely to apply if the proceedings lead to the issue of a new judgment incorporating the first decision *(actio judicati)*. This is because when a court authorizes the enforcement of a foreign judgment it will consider only whether the judgment complies with the requirements for recognition or enforcement in that state.[33] The same principle applies to a judgment declaring an arbitration award enforceable.[34] This

---

[27] *Solo Kleinmotoren GmbH v. Emilio Boch* (Case 414/92), [1994] ECR I-2237. The German procedure is also referred to at p. 42 of the Report *Jenard*.

[28] *Mærsk Olie & Gas A/S v. Firma M. de Haan en W. de Boer* (Case 39/02), [2004] ECR I-9657 citing *Solo Kleinmotoren GmbH v. Emilio Boch* (Case 414/92), [1994] ECR I-2237.

[29] Brussels *Ibis* Regulation Recital (11).

[30] The Heidelberg Report para. 532 notes that a Belgian court has held that a decision issued by a foreign criminal court could be qualified as a judgment under Art. 32 Brussels I Regulation *(Court of Appeal of Mons*, 15 January 1998). See also the Report *Jenard* p. 42 noting that Art. 1 provides that the Convention shall apply in civil and commercial matters whatever the nature of the court or tribunal and that it followed that judgments given in a Contracting State in civil and commercial matters by a criminal court or administrative tribunal must be recognized and enforced.

[31] *Briggs/Rees* p. 675.

[32] *Owens Bank Ltd v. Fulvio Bracco and Bracco Industria Chimica SpA* (Case C-129/92), [1994] ECR I-117.

[33] Although findings of the court asked originally asked to enforce the judgment may be taken into account, the question for the second enforcing court will not be identical. For example, in *Yukos Capital Sarl v. OJSC Rosneft Oil Co* [2012] EWCA Civ 855, [2014] QB 455 a Dutch court had refused to recognise a

---

principle preventing double enforcement has been referred to under the observation that *'exequatur sur exequatur ne vaut'*: enforcement upon enforcement is not permitted.[35]

4. Judgments in default

13 Judgments given in default of appearance are capable of being judgments within the definition in Art. 2 (a), but a number of different issues arise. First, a judgment is not excluded from the definition simply because it was given in default of appearance. It may be that there will be a defence to enforcement under the rules in Part III, but a default judgment is a judgment which is capable of enforcement according to the definition in Art. 2 (a).[36] A judgment in default may be given either because the defendant chooses not to appear or because the defendant is debarred from appearing(for example, because the defendant is in breach of an order in the proceedings). In either case, such a judgment is still a judgment within the meaning of Art. 2 (a).[37] It is sufficient that it is a decision which has been or was capable of being the subject in the state of origin of an inquiry in adversarial proceedings.

14 However, a distinction may need to be drawn between cases where a defendant did not appear (referred to above and described here as judgments in default) and cases where the very nature of the procedure was designed so that the defendant *could not* appear *(ex parte proceedings)*. The position in relation to the latter types of procedure, which arise primarily in the context of provisional and protective measures, is considered further below.[38]

15 Secondly, it is also a feature of this type of judgment that it is often given without a full hearing on the merits and accordingly without a fully reasoned judgment on the merits. But, this will also not prevent the judgment from being a judgment within the definition in Art. 2 (a).[39] Although the right to a fair trial includes the right to have a reasoned decision, this is not an unfettered right. Thus, a judgment given without detailed reasons may still be a judgment and may also be enforceable if the restriction on the right to a fair trial can be justified and is proportionate. In *Trade Agency Ltd v. Seramico Investments Ltd*,[40] the ECJ considered the enforceability of an English default judgment and accepted that, in the

---

Russian judgment on the ground that it infringed Dutch public policy. When the same judgment came to be enforced in England the issue was whether it accorded with English public policy.

[34]   *Arab Business Consortium v. Banque Franco* [1996] 1 Lloyd's Rep. 485 and Report *Schlosser* para. 65.

[35]   See *Briggs/Rees* p. 675 and A-G *Lenz* in *Owens Bank Ltd v. Fulvio Bracco and Bracco Industria Chimica SpA* (Case C-129/92), [1994] ECR I-117 discussing the arguments against 'double execution'. See also *Kaye* The Law of the European Judgments Convention Vol 4 pp. 3105–3110.

[36]   It is sometimes unclear whether the court is addressing the first or second of these issues: see *Layton/Mercer* para. 24.021.

[37]   *Trade Agency Ltd v. Seramico Investments Ltd*,(Case C-619/10) (judgment in default) and *Gambazziv. DaimlerChrysler Canada Inc.* (Case 394/07), [2009] ECR I-2563 (judgment in default where defendant debarred from appearing).

[38]   For example, an *ex parte* freezing order or other provisional measure: *Denilauler v. SNC Couchet Frères* (Case C-125/79), [1980] ERC 1553, discussed further below.

[39]   In the case of a judgment in default there will usually be reference to a detailed statement of claim, but the reason for the judgment is essentially a procedural one ie the defendant chose not to or was debarred from denying the claim: see *Layton/Mercer* para. 25–005.

[40]   Case C-619/10, EU:C:2012:531.

English procedural system, the adoption of such a default judgment is intended to ensure the swift, efficient and cost effective handling of proceedings brought for the recovery of uncontested claims, for the sound administration of justice. That objective was likely to justify a restriction of the right to a fair trial in so far as that right requires that judgments be reasoned. It would then be for the enforcing court to verify, in the light of the specific circumstances in the proceedings, whether the restriction is not manifestly disproportionate as compared with the aim pursued.[41]

In some Member States, special procedures exist to allow the summary enforcement of **16** specific forms of payment order. In *Klomps v. Michel*,[42] the ECJ considered the summary procedure for the recovery of debts or liquidated demands in German law, known as '*Mahnverfahren*.' Under this procedure an order for payment ('*Zahlungsbefehl*') is served on the defendant, enabling the claimant, in default of appropriate action being taken by the defendant, to obtain an enforcement order ('*Vollstreckungsbefehl*'). The ECJ made it clear that the enforcement order would be an enforceable judgment.[43] In *Hengst Import v. Campese*[44] a similar Italian summary procedure for the recovery of debts was at issue (the '*procedimento d'ingiunzione*'). The creditor had applied to the Italian court for an order for payment ('*decreto ingicentivo*'). After expiry of the period for opposing the order, the court had authorized the order to make it enforceable. The ECJ held[45] that the order at issue was undoubtedly a judgment capable of recognition or enforcement since there could have been an inter partes hearing in the state where it was made before recognition and enforcement was sought.[46]

5. Judgments by consent and court settlements

Judgments by consent are included within the definition of judgments, but must be differ- **17** entiated from judicially approved settlements which are essentially contractual. The dis-

---

[41] The Court adopted its reasoning in the earlier case of *Gambazzi v. DaimlerChrysler Canada Inc*, (Case C-394/07) [2009] ECR I-2563, at para. 34, where a defendant had been debarred from appearing for breach of an earlier court order.

[42] Case C-166/80 [1981] ECR 1593.

[43] The actual issue for the court was which of the two documents were covered by the words 'the document which instituted the proceedings' in Art. 27(2) Brussels Convention.

[44] Case C-474/93 [1995] ECR I-2133.

[45] At para. 14: again the actual issue was whether the document which instituted the proceedings had been served in sufficient time pursuant to Art. 27(2) Brussels Convention.

[46] The Heidelberg Report (para. 528) refers to German practice concerning Italian orders for payment: The *OLG Zweibrücken*, 01/25/2006 – 3 W 239/05 held that an Italian provisionally enforceable payment order constitutes a 'judgment' in terms of Art. 32 Brussels I Regulation. However, as the same court points out, in its decision of 09/22/2005 – 3 W 175/05, an Italian provisionally enforceable payment order *(decreto ingiuntivo)* does not constitute a 'judgment' in terms of Art. 32 Brussels I Regulation if it has been rendered as an *ex parte* decision, ie without the defendant being heard. Nevertheless, a *decreto ingiuntivo*, which has been issued in a normal contentious procedure was classified as a decision in terms of Art. 32 Brussels I Regulation by the *OLG*, 11/17/2004 – 16 W 31/04. *LG Düsseldorf* also qualified a *decreto ingiuntivo* as a decision in the terms of Art. 32 Brussels I Regulation (08/08/2006 – I-3 W 118/06). The Report also refers to *CA Bourges* 02/22/2005, French report Annex 4.1.3, expressing the same opinion.

tinction can be difficult to draw. 'Court settlements' are defined in Art. 2 (b) (see further below). The fundamental difference is that "the authority of the law does not lie behind a court settlement as it does in the case of a court judgment".[47] In *Solo Kleinmotoren GmbH v. Boch*[48] the ECJ held that in order to be a 'judgment' for the purposes of the Convention, the decision must emanate from a judicial body of a Contracting State deciding on its own authority on the issues between the parties. That condition is not fulfilled in the case of a settlement, even if it was reached in a court of a Contracting State and brings legal proceedings to an end. Settlements in court are essentially contractual in that their terms depend first and foremost on the parties' intention.

6. Provisional including protective measures

18 The second paragraph of Art. 2 (a) deals with provisional, including protective, measures. This provision seeks to clarify the conditions under which provisional and protective measures can circulate in the EU.[49] It needs to be read in conjunction with Recital 33 which provides:

(33) Where provisional, including protective, measures are ordered by a court having jurisdiction as to the substance of the matter, their free circulation should be ensured under this Regulation. However, provisional, including protective, measures which were ordered by such a court without the defendant being summoned to appear should not be recognised or enforced under this Regulation unless the judgment containing the measure is served on the defendant prior to enforcement. This should not preclude the recognition and enforcement of such measures under national law. Where provisional, including protective, measures are ordered by a court of a Member State not having jurisdiction as to the substance of the matter, the effect of such measures should be confined, under this Regulation, to the territory of that Member State.

19 As is clear from the existing case law, and is reflected in Art. 2 (a) and Recital 33,when considering provisional, including protective, measures under the Regulation two situations must be distinguished. Such measures can be ordered by the court which also has jurisdiction as to the substance of the matter. In those cases, no additional issues of jurisdiction arise, the court with jurisdiction over the substance of the claim can make whatever provisional orders it considers appropriate.[50] However, the Regulation also allows for such orders to be made by courts which do not have jurisdiction over the substance of the case. Because of the danger that the Regulation rules on substantive jurisdiction might be circumvented, the ECJ has in its case law developed restrictions on the grant of provisional measures in such cases.

20 In summary, the effect of the Regulation is to provide for the free circulation of measures granted by a court having jurisdiction on the substance of the case. Such orders are treated as 'judgments' within the definition in Art. 2 (a). By contrast, the Regulation prevents circula-

---

[47] A-G Gulmann in *Solo Kleinmotoren GmbH v. Emilio Boch*, (Case C-414/92) [1994] ECR I-2237 at para. 29.

[48] Case C-414/92 [1994] ECR I-2237.

[49] See Proposal for a Regulation, Commission 14.12.2010 COM (2010) 748 final at para. 3.1.

[50] *Reichert v. Dresdner Bank (No. 2)*, (Case C-261/90) [1992] ECR I-2149, *van Uden Maritime BV (t/a van Uden Africa Line) v. Kommanditgesellschaft in Firma Deco-Line*, (Case C-391/95) [1998] ECR I-7091 and *Mietz v. Internship Yachting Sneek BV*, (Case C-99/96) [1999] ECR I-2277.

tion of provisional measures granted by other courts as the effect of these measures should be limited to the territory of the Member State where they were granted (Recital (33)).[51] Such orders are not 'judgments' entitled to free circulation. To this extent, the Brussels I*bis* Regulation narrows the definition of judgment. Under the Brussels I Regulation provisional measures were regarded as judgments whether or not they were ordered by the court having jurisdiction over the substance.[52] However, case law imposed certain restrictions on the granting and enforcement of such measures. Under the Brussels I*bis* Regulation, rather than codify these restrictions,[53] the cross-border enforcement of provisional measures is restricted to those granted by the court with jurisdiction over the substance of the case.

a) The definition of provisional including protective measures

Measures must be both provisional and protective: provisional in the sense that they are   21
interlocutory and reversible and protective in that they seek to preserve the existing situation.[54] Thus, in *Reichert v. Dresdner Bank (No. 2)*[55] the ECJ held that: "The expression 'provisional, including protective, measures' within the meaning of Art. 24 [Brussels Convention] must therefore be understood as referring to measures which, within the scope of the Convention, are intended to preserve a factual or legal situation so as to safeguard rights the recognition of which is sought elsewhere from the court having jurisdiction as to the substance of the matter".[56] Applying this definition, the ECJ held that an *action paulienne* under French law was not a provisional and protective measure. The action allowed for the revocation of transactions on certain grounds. The ECJ held that while the action enabled the creditor's security to be protected by preventing dissipation of his debtor's assets; its purpose was that the court could vary the legal situation of the assets, of the debtor and that of the beneficiary of the disposition effected by the debtor and, as such, could not be described as a provisional or protective measure. Provisional and protective measures within the meaning of Art. 2 (a) can include freezing injunctions, orders for arrest and interim payments in certain circumstances. But an order to examine a witness in order to establish facts to enable the applicant to decide whether to bring proceedings is not a provisional and protective measure.[57]

---

[51] Proposal for a Regulation Commission 14.12.2010 COM (2010) 748 final at para. 3.1.5. See also Commission Proposal for a Regulation creating a European Account Preservation Order (2011) COM (2011) 445 final discussed *Kyriakides* [2014] Civ. Just. Q 93.

[52] Both *Mietz v. Internship Yachting Sneek BV*, (Case 99/96) [1999] ECR I-2277 and *Italian Leather SpA v. Weco Polstermöbel GmbH Co*, (Case 80/00) [2001] ECR I-4995 proceeded on the basis that such judgments were in principle enforceable.

[53] Or, for example, introduce a power in the court with jurisdiction over the substance to discharge such measures when ordered by a different court. The absence of such a power was identified as a shortcoming in the current regime concerning provisional measures in the Heidelberg Report at p. 761.

[54] The definition includes protective orders aimed at obtaining information or preserving evidence as referred to in Arts 6 and 7 of Directive 2004/48/EC of the European Parliament and of the Council of 29 April 2004 on the enforcement of intellectual property rights (Brussels I*bis* Regulation Recital (25)).

[55] Case 261/90 [1992] ECR I-2149.

[56] At para. 34.

[57] *St Paul Dairy Industries NV v. Unibel Exser BVBA*, (Case C-104/03) [2005] ECR I-3481. See also Recital (25) Brussels I*bis* Regulation: shall not include measures which are not of a protective nature, such as measures ordering the hearing of a witness. This should be without prejudice to the application of

22   The measures must also come within the material scope of the Regulation set out in Art. 1.[58]

b) Provisional including protective measures under the Brussels I Regulation

23   Where a court which does not have jurisdiction over the substance of the case wishes to make provisional measures, special jurisdictional rules are needed. Such orders are possible under Brussels I*bis* Regulation Art. 35 (see the commentary on Art. 35, which mirrors almost exactly Art. 31 Brussels I Regulation).[59] Art. 35 provides that applications may be made to the courts of a Member State for such provisional, including protective, measures as may be available under the laws of that State, even if, under the Regulation, the courts of another Member State have jurisdiction as to the substance of the matter. On its face, this provision is permissive; it does not positively provide jurisdiction, it simply removes any jurisdictional hurdle which would otherwise be created by the rules in the Regulation which govern jurisdiction as to the substance of the case. Nor does this provision require such measures to be available. It simply allows for the making of such orders as may be available under the national law of the particular Member State. Nor does this provision on its face say anything about how such orders are to be enforced.

24   However, because the use of national rules for provisional relief could pre-empt the decision on the substance of the case, and thereby undermine the rules on substantive jurisdiction, the ECJ has imposed additional requirements in relation to measures based on Art. 31 Brussels I Regulation (now Art. 35 of the Brussels I*bis* Regulation). In particular, the cases have established the need for: (1) the existence of a real connecting link, and (2) an autonomous definition of provisional measures.

25   The ECJ in *van Uden Maritime BV (t/a van Uden Africa Line) v. Kommanditgesellschaft in Firma Deco-Line*[60] held that the granting of this type of measure requires particular care on the part of the court in question and detailed knowledge of the actual circumstances in which the measures sought are to take effect. It followed that:

"the granting of protective or provisional measures on the basis of Article[31] is conditional on, inter alia, the existence of a real connecting link between the subject matter of the measures sought and the territorial jurisdiction of the contracting state of the court before which these measures are sought."[61]

Regulation (EC) No. 1206.2001 of 28 May 2001 on cooperation between the courts of Member States in the taking of evidence in civil or commercial matters.

[58]   See the commentary on Art. 1. Whether interim measures fall within the scope of the Regulation depends on the nature of the rights which they serve to protect *(De Cavel v. De Cavel (No. 1)*, (Case C-143/78) [1979] ECR 1055; *De Cavel v. De Cavel (No. 2)*, (Case C-120/79) [1980] ECR 371; *van Uden Maritime BV (t/a van Uden Africa Line) v. Kommanditgesellschaft in Firma Deco-Line*, (Case C-391/95) [1998] ECR I-7091 applied in *Realchemie Nederland BV v. Bayer CropScience AG* (Case C-406/09) [2011] ECR I-9773 at para. 39. In *CWH v. CJH* Case C-25/81 [1982] ECR 1189 an application for the issuing of a document to be used in evidence in an action concerning a husband's management of his wife's property directly on the basis of a marriage bond did not come within the scope of the regime.

[59]   Which in turn closely mirrors Art. 24 of the Brussels Convention and Lugano Convention.

[60]   *van Uden Maritime BV (t/a van Uden Africa Line) v. Kommanditgesellschaft in Firma Deco-Line* (Case C-391/95), [1998] ECR I-7091.

The ECJ also held that while interim payment orders could, in an appropriate case, qualify, **26** special care must be taken in such cases:

"[…] an order for interim payment of money is, by its very nature, such that it may pre-empt the decision on the substance of the case […]."[62]

Consequently, interim payment of a contractual consideration does not constitute a provi- **27** sional measure within the meaning of Article 24 unless, first, repayment to the defendant of the sum awarded is guaranteed if the plaintiff is unsuccessful as regards the substance of his claim and, second, the measure sought relates only to specific assets of the defendant located or to be located within the confines of the territorial jurisdiction of the court to which application is made.[63]

These conditions were applied in *Mietz v. Intership Yachting Sneek BV*[64] in relation to *kort* **28** *geding* proceedings under Netherlands law. The ECJ held that where relief is granted under Art. 31 and the claimant relies on such relief in another Member State, the courts of that State may decline to recognise the order if it exceeds the limitations imposed by Art. 31. In this case the conditions set out in *van Uden* were not satisfied.

The Brussels I*bis* Regulation does not seek to codify the real connecting link requirement, **29** rather, the solution is left to the enforcement stage. Judgments under Art. 2 (a) which can be enforced under the Regulation are limited that those measures which have been ordered by a court with jurisdiction over the substance of the matter (Art. 2 (a)).[65] Provisional measures adopted by other courts "should be confined to the territory of that Member State" (Recital (33)).

c) Provisional and protective measures ordered without notice
As explained above, Art. 2 (a) confirms that an order for provisional and protective relief **30** ordered by a court with jurisdiction over the substance of the case can satisfy the broad definition of judgment. However, in *Denilauler v. SNC Couchet Frères*[66] the ECJ held that under the Brussels I Regulation, provisional, including protective, measures ordered without notice to the defendant will not be enforced:

---

[61] *van Uden Maritime BV (t/a van Uden Africa Line) v. Kommanditgesellschaft in Firma Deco-Line* (Case C-391/95), [1998] ECR I-7091 para. 40.

[62] *van Uden Maritime BV (t/a van Uden Africa Line) v. Kommanditgesellschaft in Firma Deco-Line* (Case C-391/95), [1998] ECR I-7091 para. 46.

[63] *van Uden Maritime BV (t/a van Uden Africa Line) v. Kommanditgesellschaft in Firma Deco-Line* (Case C-391/95), [1998] ECR I-7091 para. 47.

[64] *Mietz v. Intership Yachting Sneek BV* (Case C-99/96), [1999] ECR I-2277.

[65] Brussels I*bis* Regulation Art. 42 (2) sets out rules for the enforcement in a Member State of a judgment given in another Member State ordering a provisional, including a protective, measure. The rules only apply where the court granting the provisional measure has jurisdiction over the substance of the case.

[66] *Denilauler v. SNC Couchet Frères*, (Case C-125/79) [1980] ERC 1553 at para. 18. The conditions for enforcement in Art. 27(2) of Title III of the Brussels Convention, which were the provisions in force at the time, prevented the enforcement of judgments where the defendant had not been summoned to appear and which were intended to be enforced without prior service and the ECJ held that a similar restriction applied to the enforcement of provisional measures.

"Judicial decisions authorizing provisional or protective measures, which are delivered without the party against which they are directed having been summoned to appear and which are intended to be enforced without prior service do not come within the system of recognition and enforcement provided for by chapter [III]."[67]

31 However, this does not mean that 'judgments' can never be given in uncontested proceedings. As explained above, the situation is different in the case of judgments in default where the defendant chooses not to appear or is barred from appearing. Furthermore, if an order initially granted without notice if the order could have been the subject of submissions by both parties before the issue of its recognition or enforcement comes to be addressed (such as an order which has no effect until notified to the other party who may then challenge or appeal the order) then it can qualify as a judgment.[68] This is the case in relation to certain procedures for the summary enforcement of debts (discussed above) where an order for payment is initially made *ex parte* but is served on the defendant before enforcement is ordered. The fact that the defendant chooses not to appear and the enforcement is ordered in default is irrelevant (at this stage what matters is not whether the proceedings have been adversarial but rather whether they could have been). It also follows that if the defendant has sought to have the order set aside in *inter partes* proceedings, the confirmed or continued order becomes a judgment.[69]

32 The definition in Art. 2 (a) confirms this position. 'Judgments' will include provisional measure even those ordered without the defendant being summoned to appear *if the judg-*

---

[67] In *EMI Records v. Modern Music* [1992] 1 All ER 616 the English High Court confirmed that an injunction obtained in an *ex parte* application in a foreign jurisdiction without prior notice or service of documents on the defendant is not a judgment within the Convention. The court set aside registration of a judgment of the Berlin Land Court which had made an *ex parte* order restraining the defendant from reproducing or distributing recordings.

[68] *Mærsk Olie & Gas A/S v. Firma M. de Haan en W. de Boer*, (Case C-39/02) [2004] ECR I-9657 para. 50. In *Stolzenburg* the French Cour de Cassation RCDIP 93 (2004), 815 (discussed in the Heidelberg Report at para. 753) held that a *Mareva* injunction could be recognised and enforced in France because it was obtained after a preliminary hearing at which the defendant was heard. In *Normaco v. Lundman* [1999] I L Pr 381 the English High Court explained that a *Mareva* injunction could be certified for enforcement under the Lugano Convention on the basis that it satisfied the wide definition of judgment because while originally made *ex parte*, the order was continued following notice to the defendant and an opportunity for the defendant to appear and contest the order. See also *Micciche v. Banco di Silicia*, RCDIP 83 (1994), 688 where the *Cour de Cassation* held that an Italian judgment which was enforceable under Italian law even before notification to the debtor was not enforceable under the Brussels Convention (see *Kaye* para. 428).

[69] This assumption was made by a German court in *European Consulting Unternehmensberatung AG v. Refco Overseas Ltd* (OLG Karlsruhe, 19.12.94 – Case 9 W 32/94 (referred to in *Briggs/Rees* para. 7.06 and the Heidelberg Report para. 675). Compare a case referred to in the Heidelberg Report (at para. 718) where the IXth Senate refused to recognise a Swedish arrestment which had been ordered without a preliminary hearing of the German defendant. The court referred to the ECJ's judgment in *Denilauler* and held that recognition under Art. 32 Brussels I Regulation presupposes the prior service of the complaint. The Report comments that with all due respect, this judgment is regrettable. For the protection of the debtor, the availability of an effective remedy against the decision (even at a later stage of the proceedings) seems sufficient. This position is that adopted in the definition in Art. 2.

ment containing the measure is served on the defendant prior to enforcement. This also reflects the fact that, in a change from the position under Brussels Convention, a judgment will not be enforced under Part III where it was given in default of appearance if the defendant was not served, *unless the defendant failed to commence proceedings to challenge the judgment when it was possible for him to do so.*[70] Thus, default judgments must be recognised if the defendant did not take the initiative to appeal against that judgment when it was possible for him to do so because the order was served on the defendant before enforcement.[71]

III. Court settlements

1. Overview and legislative history

Court approved settlements are known in all Member States, but the form of those settle-   **33** ments may differ. A distinction must be drawn between consent judgments, which fall within the definition of 'judgments' in Art. 2 (a), already discussed, and court settlements. 'Court settlements,' while not judgments for the purposes of Chapter III, are enforceable under Chapter IV of the Regulation under the same conditions as authentic instruments (see commentary on Arts 58 and 59).[72] Private settlements between the parties themselves fall outside all of the procedures for enforcement under the Regulation. In the Brussels I*bis* Regulation, the definition of 'court settlement' has been extracted from the provisions concerning enforcement and included as a new definition in Art. 2 (b).[73]

The definition of a court settlement was considered in *Solo Kleinmotoren v. Bosch.*[74] A-G   **34** *Gulmann* noted that proceedings in all Contracting States can be terminated by common agreement of the parties. But in some contracting states this happens by way of 'court settlement' whereas in others (such as Belgium, Luxembourg, Ireland and the United Kingdom) the result is a 'consent judgment'. The A-G rejected the argument that as the result was the same in practice, such measures should be treated in the same way for the purposes of the Regulation. He also rejected the suggestion[75] that the two alternative ways of concluding disputes differ from each other merely on minor details. In particular, the A-G noted that:

---

[70] Art. 45 (1) (b) (and Art. 34 (4) Brussels I Regulation). Thus, as recognised by the ECJ in *Orams v. Apostilides* (Case C-420/07), [2009] ECR I-3571, Art. 34 (2) Brussels I Regulation – unlike the equivalent provision in Art. 27 (2) Brussels Convention – does not necessarily require the document which instituted the proceedings to be duly served, but does require that the rights of the defence are effectively respected.

[71] If no appeal is possible under the law of the judgment granting state, this might be a ground for invoking the public policy defence under Art. 45 (1) (a) but that would no longer be strictly speaking a case about appearance. See also *Layton/Mercer* para. 23–022.

[72] The Report *Jenard* p. 57 noted that a provision covering court settlements was considered necessary on account of the German and Netherlands legal systems where such settlements were enforceable without further formality.

[73] The provisions for the enforcement of authentic instruments are found in Arts. 58–60. These rules closely mirror those previously set out in Arts. 57 and 58 of the Brussels I Regulation and Arts. 50 and 51 of the Brussels Convention [and Lugano Convention].

[74] Case C-414/92 [1994] ECR I-2237.

[75] At para. 30.

"on the evidence there are currently no Contracting States whose legal systems accord the status of res judicata to court settlements, whereas 'consent judgments' can acquire that status ... .Furthermore, there is the point that a settlement will typically not be afforded all the guarantees of a judgment and the authority of the law does not lie behind a court settlement as it does in the case of a court judgment."

35   The ECJ, confirming that court settlements are different from consent judgments, held:[76]

"in order to be a 'judgment' for the purposes of the Convention the decision must emanate from a judicial body of a Contracting State deciding on its own authority on the issues between the parties. That condition is not fulfilled in the case of a settlement, even if it was reached in a court of a Contracting State and brings legal proceedings to an end. Settlements in court are essentially contractual in that their terms depend first and foremost on the parties' intention."[77]

36   Art. 2 (b) refers to a settlement which 'has been approved by a court' or 'concluded before a court in the course of proceedings'. By contrast, Art. 58 Brussels I Regulation referred only to a settlement 'which has been approved by a court in the course of proceedings'.

37   This change was partly to solve an ambiguity between different language versions of the text in the Brussels I Regulation, and makes it clear that an settlement can be approved by the court even in the absence of substantive court proceedings.[78] This definition would include out of court settlements which are concluded in out-of-court proceedings (for example, mediation), but at a later stage formally approved by a competent court.[79]

38   The court settlement must be in relation to a civil and commercial matter so as to come within the material scope of the Regulation set out in Art. 1.[80]

IV. Authentic instruments

39   An authentic instrument is a public document which formally and authoritatively records

---

[76]   At paras. 17 and 18.

[77]   The distinction is not always easy to draw. In *Landhurst Leasing Plc v. Marcq* [1998] I L Pr 822 CA the English Court of Appeal held that a Belgian judgment was a 'judgment' (not simply a court settlement) refusing to hold that the decision in *Solo Kleinmotoren* required a different conclusion and noting (at para. 37 per *Beldham* LJ) that "a judgment entered into by consent or in default is nevertheless a judgment ... If a party agrees to a judgment being entered by conceding the issues, the judgment is no less an authoritative judgment than a judgment entered in default".

[78]   The Heidelberg Report (para. 624) notes that the English text of Art. 58 Brussels I Regulation is misleading. While the French text presupposes that the settlement had been agreed in the presence of the judge in the course the proceedings ('les transactions concludes devant un juge au cours d'unprocès'), the English wording states that the settlement must have been approved by the court in the course of the proceedings. The German text equally corresponds to the French wording ('Vergleiche, die vor einem Gericht im Verlauf des Verfahrens geschlossen wurden').

[79]   The definition in Art. 2 (b) of the Brussels *Ibis* Regulation accords with Arts. 3 (1) (a) and 24 (1) of Reg. (EC) 805/04 creating a European Enforcement Order for uncontested claims.

[80]   See the commentary on Art. 1.

---

declarations made by the parties so as to constitute those declarations as legal obligations.[81] Authentic instruments which satisfy this definition are enforceable in other Member States under the conditions laid down in Art. 58 (which rules are also applied to court settlements both being contractual in nature).[82] While court approved settlements are known in all Member States, notarial deeds (and similar authentic instruments) are unknown in England, Wales and Ireland.[83]

Provisions for the enforcement of authentic instruments were previously contained in **40** Art. 57 Brussels I Regulation and Art. 50 Brussels Convention. The definition in Art. 2 (c) draws on and makes express the further conditions laid down by the ECJ in *Unibank A/S v. Christensen*.[84] In that case, the ECJ noted that since the instruments covered by Art. 50 Brussels Convention are enforced in the same way as judgments, the authentic nature of such judgments must be established beyond dispute. Since instruments drawn up by private parties are not inherently authentic, the involvement of a public authority, or any other authority empowered for that purpose by the State of Origin, is needed in order to endow them with the character of authentic instruments.[85] Authentic instruments will not be enforceable under the Regulation unless this condition is satisfied even if national law (here the law Denmark) did not require such authentication.[86] The ECJ also drew on the conditions referred to in the *Jenard/Möller* Report on the Lugano Convention[87] which referred firstly to the fact that authenticity should have been established by a public authority, and secondly to the fact that this authenticity should relate to the content of the instrument and not only, for example, the signature. Both of these conditions are incorporated into the definition of authentic instruments in Art. 2 (c).[88]

---

[81] *Fitchen* (2011) 7 JPrIL 33. In practice, most commonly notarially validated documents but also including documents authenticated by other public officers or by registration in a special register (see *Layton/Mercer* para. 29.002). An Italian decreto ingiuntuo (referred to above and considered by the ECJ in *Hengst Import v. Campese*, (Case C-474/93) [1995] ECR I-2133 does not constitute an authentic instrument, but once the defendant has been given a chance to challenge the order for payment it can be a judgment under Art. 2 (a).

[82] Report *Jenard* comments on Art. 51 Brussels Convention, p. 57.

[83] The Report *Schlosser* (para. 226) noted that in Scotland, instruments establishing a clearly defined obligation to perform a contract can be entered in a public register. An extract from the public register can then serve as a basis for enforcement in the same way as a court judgment. The Report concluded that such an extract would be covered by Art. 50 Brussels Convention.

[84] *Unibank A/S v. Christensen*, (Case C-260/97) [1999] ECR I-3715.

[85] *Unibank A/S v. Christensen*, (Case C-260/97) [1999] ECR I-3715 para. 15.

[86] See: § 794 ZPO; CA Paris Clunet 118 (1991), 162; Cass. *Tonon v. Office Cantonal de la Jeunesse de Tutligen* [1995] I.L.Pr. 23 which concerned a German paternity declaration which included an obligation to pay maintenance (discussed by *Briggs/Rees* p. 712) and a German formal acknowledgement of a debt, Schuld-anerkenntnis (which was the subject of enforcement in England in *Bautrading v. Nordling* [1997] 3 All ER 718 [C.A.]). See also the two Dutch cases discussed in *Kaye* paras. 740 and 741 holding that a German kostenrechnung (a statement of costs drawn up by civil law notaries for themselves) was not an authentic instrument whatever its status in German law, whereas a German urkunde recording an agreement to pay maintenance was.

[87] Report *Jenard/Möller* para. 72.

[88] And also form the basis of the definition in Art. 4 (3) Regulation 804/2005 on Uncontested Claims. The Heidelberg Report para. 629 notes that the practical impact of these provisions will be diminished by the

41 The instrument must also fall within the general material scope of the Regulation set out in Art. 1.[89] So long as the subject matter of the instrument falls within that scope, it does not matter if the document itself has public law characteristics in its state of origin.[90]

42 Orders have been refused enforcement on the ground that the party against whom the enforcement was sought was not a party to the creation of the instrument. It is unclear whether this is a requirement under Art. 2 (c).[91]

V. Member State of origin

43 Art. 2 (d)-(f) appeared, with some modifications, in the original Commission Proposal.[92] As a consequence of the abolition of exequatur proceedings, it becomes important to define the various potential Member States involved in the recognition or enforcement process. This is illustrated by the fact that similar definitions were introduced in Art. 4 (4)-(6) Regulation 805/2004 which abolished exequatur proceedings for uncontested claims.

44 The definition of 'Member State of origin' in Art. 2 (d) draws on the definitions of 'judgment', 'court settlement' and 'authentic instrument' referred to earlier in Art. 2 (see above). The Member State of origin is the Member State where the judgment or instrument originated, thus in the case of a judgment where the judgment was given, in the case of a court settlement where it was approved or concluded and in the case of an authentic instrument where it was drawn up or registered.

VI. Member State addressed

45 The Green Paper on the review of the Brussels I Regulation[93] and the original Commission Proposal[94] both referred to the Member State *of enforcement* rather than the Member State addressed which is the definition which appears in Art. 2 (e).[95] The change was one of the amendments introduced following the European Parliament's adoption of the report of the Legal Affairs Committee on the Commission's original proposal.[96] The change is intended to allow for the possibility of the recognition, as well as enforcement of judgments, court settlements and authentic instruments. Art. 2 (e) draws on the definitions of 'judgment', 'court settlement' and 'authentic instrument' referred to earlier in Art. 2 (a) to (c). The Member State addressed is the Member State in which the judgment or instrument is sought to be recognised or enforced.

---

new instruments in this field as the cross-border enforcement of notarial deeds will mainly be effected through that Regulation.

[89] See commentary on Art. 1.

[90] For example, the executory copy of a paternity declaration in Cass. *Tonon v. Office Cantonal de la Jeunesse de Tutligen* [1995] I. L. Pr 23. See further *Layton/Mercer* para. 29.006.

[91] See *Layton/Mercer* para. 29.004.

[92] 14.12.10 COM (2010) 748 final.

[93] 21.4.2009 COM (2009) 175 final.

[94] 14.12.10 COM (2010) 748 final.

[95] Art. 4 (5) Regulation 805/04 also refers to the Member State of enforcement.

[96] 15. 10. 12 A7-0320/2012.

VII. Court of origin

The notion "court of origin" refers to the court which has given the judgment which is   **46** sought to be recognised or enforced. Art. 45 (2) and (3) makes it clear that the jurisdiction of the court of origin generally cannot be challenged. As has been described, the definition of judgment in Art. 2 (a) is broad and includes a judgment given by a 'court or tribunal'. In the case of a judgment of a tribunal, the provisions in Art. 45 (2) and (3) which prohibit review of the jurisdiction of the 'court' of origin would presumably apply in the same way to the judgment of a tribunal.

Article 3

For the purposes of this Regulation, the 'court' includes the following authorities to the extent that they have jurisdiction in matters falling within the scope of this Regulation:
(a) in Hungary, in summary proceedings concerning orders to pay (fizetési meghagyásos eljárás), the notary (közjegyzö);
(b) in Sweden, in summary proceedings concerning orders to pay (betalningsföreläggande) and assistance (handräckning), the Enforcement Authority (Kronofogdemyndigheten).

In principle, Arts. 4–35 are only concerned with court proceedings, i.e. proceedings before a   **1** court of justice. Proceedings before mere administrative bodies or other government officials following their own rules are generally excluded mainly as they are not for not being civil and commercial affairs. Yet in some rare instances administrative bodies are also involved in the sound administration of justice, also. Accordingly they should be included. Art. 3 expressly does so in three instances extending the rules on jurisdiction to them,[1] namely for summary proceedings concerning orders to pay in Hungary before a notary and two kinds of Swedish summary proceedings before the kronofogdemyndighet.[2] Both the Hungarian notary insofar as he assumes tasks in other Member States fulfilled by courts, namely in summary proceedings concerning orders to pay (fizetési meghagyásos eljárás), and the kronofogdemyndighet which has to perform tasks in other Member States fulfilled by courts[3] expressly gain a status equivalent to that of a court. Art. 3 supplements Art. 2 although an express definition of "court" is lacking in Art. 2.

The list of bodies elevated to the rank of "courts" as contained in Art. 3 is exhaustive. Other   **2** administrative bodies, other institutions or notaries in other Member States are not to be deemed as courts even if they perform genuine judicial tasks with which proper (and properly so denominated) courts would be charged. *A maiore ad minus*, other administrative authorities than those expressly listed in Art. 3 do not qualify as "courts" and cannot render "decisions" in the Regulation sense[4] in the first place.[5]

---

[1]   *Ansgar Staudinger*, in: Rauscher Art. 62 note 1.
[2]   *Layton/Mercer* para. 30.038 are roughly equating this expression with a bailiff.
[3]   *Geimer/Schütze* Art. 62 note 1.
[4]   *Bariatti*, in: Omaggio Aldo Attardi (2009), p. 831, 833.
[5]   But cf. *infra* Art. 3 note 5.

3 Consequentially, the decisions of the Hungarian notary in in summary proceedings concerning orders to pay (fizetési meghagyásos eljárás) and of the Swedish kronofogdemyndighet are decisions under Arts. 2 (a) subpara. 1; 36 and are privileged with regard to recognition and enforcement according to the provisions of Art. 3 as well, too.[6] The main purpose of Art. 3 is to widen the notion of "court" also under Arts. 2 (a) subpara. 1; 36.[7] The predecessor to Art. 3, Art. 62 Brussels Regulation, was provoked by particularities of Swedish procedural law, and it in turn had its immediate predecessor in Art. Va Protocol Brussels Convention.[8] Since this latter provision also covers a Danish body it still is applicable with regard to Denmark. The addition of the Hungarian notary in summary proceedings concerning orders to pay (fizetési meghagyásos eljárás) is a novelty appearing in the Brussels I*bis* Regulation for the first time. Hungary had not seized upon any occasion to add her notaries previously, even not when the 2003 Accession Act was negotiated (although it successfully urged for an addition in the then Art. 65 Brussels I Regulation).

4 A parallel special provision could be found in Art. Va Protocol No. 1 Lugano Convention 1988:[9] According to this provision, in maintenance matters the notion of "court" also covers certain Danish, Icelandic and Norwegian administrative bodies. This provision lists the Finnish "ulosotonhaltija/överexekutor" as well. Yet the latter did not make its way in Art. 62 Brussels I Regulation and onwards in Art. 3, for whichever reason. Art. 2 (2) (c) EC-Denmark Agreement[10] supplements Art. 62 Brussels I Regulation by a second paragraph which reads: "In matters relating to maintenance, the expression 'court' includes the Danish administrative authorities."

5 Art. 62 Lugano Convention 2007 goes a sensible step further; It does not refer to certain listed official bodies of single States but adopts a general approach extending the notion of "court" to any authorities designated by a Contracting State as having jurisdiction in matters falling into the scope of the 2007 Lugano Convention. At first glance both Lugano solutions, the old and the new one, appear to support an ***argumentum e contrario*** for the interpretation of Art. 3 whereas in substance an analogy to Art. 62 Lugano Convention 2007 appears more appropriate and better justified. Editorial neglect should not alter substance. Under Art. 62 Lugano Convention 2007 functionality alone matters, not terminology or organisational structure.[11] Where in some States administrative bodies perform functions which in other States are reserved to the judiciary, it is fully justified to treat both phenomena as equivalent.[12] Art. 2 (c) Proposal Brussels I*bis* Regulation set out to continue this line, with the additional advantage of keeping pace with Art. 62 Lugano Convention.[13] Modern procedural law observes the rise of administrative bodies at the expense of the judiciary. Art. 2 (c)

---

6   *Ansgar Staudinger*, in: Rauscher Art. 62 note 1.

7   *Layton/Mercer* para. 30.038.

8   *Kropholler/von Hein* Art. 62 note 1.

9   *Kropholler/von Hein* Art. 62 note 2; *Geimer/Schütze* Art. 62 note 2.

10 Agreement between the European Community and the Kingdom of Denmark on jurisdiction and the recognition and enforcement of judgments in civil and commercial matters of 19 October 2005, OJ EU 2005 L 299/62.

11 Report *Pocar* para. 175; *Acocella*, in: FS Ivo Schwander (2011), p. 643, 653.

12 *Domej*, ZZP Int. 2008, 168; *Acocella*, in: FS Ivo Schwander (2011), p. 643, 653.

13 *Markus*, in: FS Ivo Schwander (2011), p. 747, 753.

Proposal Brussels I*bis* Regulation mirrored that development aptly.[14] Yet it was not to be eventually.

With maintenance having been virtually excluded from the scope of the Brussels I Regula- **6** tion by the Maintenance Regulation[15] for cases made pending on or after 18 June 2011 and being formally excluded from the scope of the Brussels I*bis* Regulation by virtue of Art. 1 (2) (e), Art. 3 like Art. 62 Brussels I Regulation has lost much of its relevance. This relevance with regard to maintenance is in principle inherited by Art. 2 (2) Maintenance Regulation. Pursuant to this rule, for the purposes of the Maintenance Regulation the term "court" shall include administrative authorities of the Member States with competence in matters relating to maintenance obligations provided that such authorities offer guarantees with regard to impartiality and the right of all parties to be heard and provided that their decisions under the law of the Member State where they are established, (i) may be made the subject of an appeal to review by a judicial authority; and (ii) have a similar force and effect as a decision of a judicial authority on the same matter. Yet Annex X to the Maintenance Regulation which should contain the list of administrative authorities referred to, is blank in the issue of the Official Journal in which the Maintenance Regulation was originally published. It should not go unnoticed and unremarked that Art. 2 (2) Maintenance Regulation endorses the same technique as Art. 62 Lugano Convention 2007.

For general purposes and for purposes not expressly mentioned in Art. 3, the kronofogdo- **7** myndighet remains an administrative body, though.[16] It is a kind of enforcement service.[17] In proceedings other than those referred to in Art. 3, it cannot be classified as a court or tribunal.[18] For instance, a debt relief decision adopted by a public authority like the krono-fogdomyndighet is excluded from the scope of application of the Brussels I*bis* Regulation[19] for it is an intervention and administrative act taken in the exercise of public powers, that extinguishes (part of) a debt as a matter of private law.[20]

---

[14] *Markus*, in: FS Ivo Schwander (2011), p. 747, 753.

[15] Council Regulation (EC) No. 4/2009 of 18 December 2008 on jurisdiction, applicable law, recognition and enforcement of decisions and cooperation in matters relating to maintenance obligations, OJ EU 2009 L 7/1, with Corrigendum, OJ EU 2009 L 131/26.

[16] *Ulf Kazimierz Radziéjewski v. Kronofogdemyndigheten i Stockholm* (Case C-461/11), nyr. para. 25 (commented upon by *Michel*, Europe 2013 janvier comm. n° 1 p. 32; *Raphael Koch*, EWS 2013, 74; *Bellil*, Petites affiches 2013 n° 211 p. 16; *Linna*, Lakimies 2013, 790; *Carlier*, J. dr. eur. 2013 n° 197 p. 103); A-G *Sharpston*, Opinion of 13 september 2012 in Case C-461/11, nyr. para. 41; *Acocella*, in: FS Ivo Schwander (2011), p. 643, 653.

[17] *Golaczynski*, Anerkennung und Bestätigung der Vollstreckbarkeit nach der Verordnung 44/2011 über die gerichtliche Zuständigkeit und die Anerkennung und Vollstreckung von gerichtlichen Entscheidungen in Zivil- und Handelssachen http://www.wroclaw.so.gov.pl/grant2007/data/BrusselsI-Poland_DE.doc; *Markus*, in: Kren Kostkiewicz/Markus/Rodrigo Rodriguez, Internationaler Zivilprozess 2011 (2010) p. 33, 61.

[18] *Ulf Kazimierz Radziéjewski v. Kronofogdemyndigheten i Stockholm* (Case C-461/11), nyr. para. 25; A-G *Sharpston*, Opinion of 13 september 2012 in Case C-461/11, nyr. para. 41.

[19] *Ulf Kazimierz Radziéjewski v. Kronofogdemyndigheten i Stockholm* (Case C-461/11), nyr. para. 26.

[20] A-G *Sharpston*, Opinion of 13 september 2012 in Case C-461/11, nyr. para. 41.

Chapter II: **Jurisdiction**

Section 1: **General provisions**

Article 4

1. Subject to this Regulation, persons domiciled in a Member State shall, whatever their nationality, be sued in the courts of that Member State.
2. Persons who are not nationals of the Member State in which they are domiciled shall be governed by the rules of jurisdiction applicable to nationals of that Member State.

Bibliography

Aull, Der Geltungsanspruch des EuGVÜ: "Binnensachverhalte" und Internationales Zivilverfahrensrecht in der Europäischen Union (1996)

Benecke, Die teleologische Reduktion des räumlich-persönlichen Anwendungsbereichs von Art. 2 ff. und Art. 17 EuGVÜ (1993)

Bernasconi/Gerber, Der räumlich-persönliche Anwendungsbereich des Lugano-Übereinkommens, SZIER 1993, 39

Bork, Die Aufrechnung des Beklagten im internationalen Zivilverfahren, in: FS Kostas Beys (2003), p. 113

Briggs, The Death of Harrods: Forum Non Conveniens and the European Court, L.Q. Rev. 2005, 535

Burgstaller/Neumayr, Beobachtungen zu Grenzfragen der internationalen Zuständigkeit: Von forum non conveniens bis Notzuständigkeit, in: FS Peter Schlosser (2005), p. 119

Chalas, L'exercice discrétionnaire de la compétence juridictionnelle en droit international privé (2000)

Coester-Waltjen, Die Bedeutung des EuGVÜ und des Luganer Abkommens für Drittstaaten, in: FS Hideo Nakamura (1996), p. 89

Duintjer Tebbens, From Jamaica with Pain. Enkele aantekeningen bij het arrest van 1 maart 2005 van het Hof van Justitie in de zaak Owusu, in: FS Frans van der Velden (2006), p. 95

Erwand, Forum non conveniens und EuGVÜ (1996)

Fentiman, Ousting Jurisdiction and the European Conventions, (2000) 3 Cambridge Yb. Eur. Leg. Stud. 107

Fentiman, Civil jurisdiction and third States: *Owusu* and after, (2006) 43 CML Rev. 705

Gaudemet-Tallon, Le "forum non conveniens", une menace pour la convention de Bruxelles?, RCDIP 80 (1991) 491

Gebauer, Drittstaaten- und Gemeinschaftsbezug im europäischen Recht der internationalen Zuständigkeit, ZEuP 2001, 943

Gebauer, Internationale Zuständigkeit und Prozessaufrechnung, IPRax 1998, 79

Geimer, Ungeschriebene Anwendungsgrenzen des EuGVÜ: Müssen Berührungspunkte zu mehreren Vertragsstaaten bestehen?, IPRax 1991, 31

Gottwald, Anerkennungszuständigkeit und doppelrelevante Tatsachen, IPRax 1995, 75

Grolimund, Drittstaatenproblematik des europäischen Zivilverfahrensrechts (2000)

Urs Peter Gruber, Ungeklärte Zuständigkeitsprobleme bei der Prozessaufrechnung, IPRax 2002, 285

Hare, Forum non conveniens in Europe: Game Over or Time for "Reflexion"?, [2006] JBL 157

Harris, Stay of Proceedings and the Brussels Convention, (2005) 54 ICLQ 933

Hartley, The Brussels Convention and forum non conveniens, (1992) 17 Eur. L. Rev. 553

Hartley, The European Union and the Systematic Dismantling of the Common Law of Conflict of Laws, ICLQ 2005, 813

Heinze/Dutta, Ungeschriebene Grenzen für europäische Zuständigkeiten bei Streitigkeiten mit Drittstaatenbezug, IPRax 2005, 224

Hess, Europäisches Zivilprozessrecht (2010)

Hess/Gregor Vollkommer, Die begrenzte Freizügigkeit einstweiliger Maßnahmen nach Art. 24 EuGVÜ, IPrax 1999, 220

Hess/Pfeiffer/Schlosser, The Brussels I Regulation 44/
2001, Application and Enforcement in the EU (2008)
Peter Huber, Forum non conveniens und EuGVÜ,
RIW 1993, 977
Ibili, De verweerder met onbekende woonplaats in
de EEX-Verordening, in: FS Paul Vlas (2012), p. 89
Ibili, The Court of Justice of the European Union on
Forum Non Conveniens, NILR 2006, 127
Jayme, Das Europäische Gerichtsstands- und Voll-
streckungsübereinkommen und die Drittländer –
das Beispiel Österreich, in: Schwind (ed.), Europa-
recht, IPR, Rechtsvergleichung (1988), p. 97
Jan Krause, Turner/Grovit – Der EuGH erklärt
Prozessführungsverbote für unvereinbar mit dem
EuGVÜ, RIW 2004, 533
Kropholler, Problematische Schranken der europä-
ischen Zuständigkeitsordnung gegenüber Drittstaa-
ten, in: FS Murad Ferid (1988), p. 239
Kropholler, Das Unbehagen am forum shopping, in:
FS Karl Firsching (1985), p. 165
Kruger, Civil Jurisdiction Rules of the EU and their
Impact on Third States (2008)
van Lith, International Jurisdiction and Commercial
Litigation (2009)
Lupoi, Convenzione di Bruxelles ed esercizio dis-
crezionale della giurisidizione, Riv. trim. dir. proc.
civ. 1995, 997
McClean, The Right to a Fair Trial, *Forum Non
Conveniens* and the Limits of the Possible, in: FS
Hans van Loon (20130, p. 357

Nadelmann, A Common Market Assimilation of
Laws and the Outer World, (1964) 58 AJIL 764
Nadelmann, Jurisdictionally Improper Fora in
Treaties on Recognition of Judgments: the Common
Market Draft, (1967) 67 Col. L. Rev. 995
North, The Brussels Convention and Forum Non
Conveniens, IPRax 1992, 183
Konrad Ost, Doppelrelevante Tatsachen im Inter-
nationalen Zivilverfahrensrecht (2002)
Pohl, Die Neufassung der EuGVVO – im Span-
nungsfeld zwischen Vertrauen und Kontrolle,
IPRax 2013, 109.
Queirolo, Forum non conveniens e Convenzione di
Bruxelles: un rapporto possibile?, RDIPP 1996, 673
Rüßmann, Die internationale Zuständigkeit für
Widerklage und Prozessaufrechnung, in: FS Akira
Ishikawa (2001), p. 455
Schillig, Die ausschließliche Zuständigkeit für ge-
sellschaftsrechtliche Streitigkeiten vor dem Hinter-
grund der Niederlassungsfreiheit – zur Anwendung
des Art. 22 Nr. 2 EuGVVO auf eine englische limited
mit Verwaltungssitz in Deutschland, IPRax 2005,
208
Götz Schulze, Internationale Annexzuständigkeit
nach dem EuGVÜ, IPRax 1999, 21
Ansgar Staudinger, Vertragsstaatenbezug und
Rückversicherungsverträge im EuGVÜ, IPRax 2000,
483
Christian Thiele, Forum non conveniens im Lichte
europäischen Gemeinschaftsrechts, RIW 2002, 696.

I. Introduction

Chapter 2 of the Brussels I*bis* Regulation has as its heading "Jurisdiction". This Chapter **1**
contains ten sections, dealing from general provisions (Section 1), special grounds of jurisdiction (Section 2), autonomous jurisdiction in matters of insurance, consumer contracts
and individual contracts of employment (Sections 3 to 5), exclusive jurisdiction (Section 6),
prorogation of jurisdiction (Section 7), examination as to jurisdiction and admissibility
(Section 8), *lis pendens* and related actions (Section 9) to provisional, including protective,
measures (Section 10).

Section 1 (General provisions) contains three provisions. The general rule of jurisdiction is **2**

laid down in Art. 4. Art. 5 deals with the prohibition of using exorbitant grounds of jurisdiction against defendants domiciled in the Member States. Art. 6 provides for the application of the national rules of jurisdiction, if the defendant is not domiciled in a Member State.

II. Article 4: general rule of jurisdiction

3   Art. 4 gives the general rule of jurisdiction. The same provision can be found in Art. 2
Brussels Convention and in Art. 2 Lugano Convention. The defendant having his domicile
in a Member State shall, whatever his nationality, be sued in the courts of that Member State.
This provision gives expression to the notion *actor sequitur forum rei*, according to which
the plaintiff has to sue the defendant before the courts of the latter's domicile.[1] Where the
plaintiff is domiciled is of no consequence for the application of the Brussels I Regulation.
Art. 4 can be seen as the cornerstone of the jurisdictional regime. In the *Group Josi* decision
the ECJ reaffirmed its settled case-law that jurisdiction rules which depart from the general
principle of Art. 2 Brussels Convention can only be used in the specific cases as expressly
provided for in the Brussels Convention. The same applies under Art. 4 of the Brussels I*bis*
Regulation.

4   The Regulation will apply, if the defendant is domiciled in a Member State. However, there
are exceptions to this general rule of jurisdiction.[2] The defendant *may* be sued in a Member
State other than the Member State where he is domiciled in the cases mentioned in Artt. 7 to
9 (special rules of jurisdiction), and *must* be sued regardless of domicile in the courts of the
Member State determined by Art. 24 in matters of exclusive jurisdiction. Furthermore, Art. 4
can be put aside by virtue of a forum choice agreement between the respective parties
(Art. 25) and by tacit prorogation if the defendant enters an appearance without contesting
the court's jurisdiction (Art. 26).

III. General jurisdiction

5   According to Art. 4 defendants that are domiciled in a Member State shall be sued in the
courts of that Member State. Art. 4 does not confer jurisdiction upon the court of the place
where the defendant is domiciled. He may be sued in any court of that Member State, which
has jurisdiction under the national law of that State. Art. 4 does not touch upon the national
rules of venue.[3] In most cases the court of the place where the defendant is domiciled, has
jurisdiction under these national rules. In legal practice the application of Art. 4 has the same
effect.

---

[1]   *Group Josi Reinsurance Company SA* v. *Universal General Insurance Company (UGIC)*, (Case C-412/98)
ECLI:EU:C:2000:399, (2000) ECR I-5925, I-5952 para. 35. Published in Clunet 129 (2002), 623 with
note *Leclerc* and NJ 2003/597 with note *Vlas*. See also Report *Jenard* p. 18. In *A-S Autoteile Service GmbH*
v. *Malhé*, (Case C-220/84) ECLI:EU:C:1985:302, (1985) ECR 2267, para. 15, the ECJ considered that
Art. 2 is intended to protect the rights of the defendant.

[2]   In the Commission's proposal for a recast of the Brussels I Regulation the jurisdiction rules of the revised
Regulation were also to be applied as regards defendants domiciled in third states (Brussels 14/12/2010,
COM (2010) 748/3). During the negotiations of the recast the extention to defendants domiciled in third
States was rejected and the situation stayed as it was under the Brussels I Regulation.

[3]   The same applies under Art. 2 Brussels Convention, see Report *Jenard* p. 18; *Droz* para. 57.

IV. Forum non conveniens

According to the doctrine of *forum non conveniens*, which is known in common law sys- **6**
tems, a court can decline its jurisdiction if it is of the opinion that a court of another
jurisdiction would be a more appropriate forum for the trial of the action. The application
of *forum non conveniens* is not allowed in the context of the Brussels I*bis* Regulation. The
ECJ has denied the application of this doctrine under the Brussels Convention.[4] Under the
Brussels I*bis* Regulation there is no reason to deviate from this preliminary ruling. The ECJ
emphasised that nothing in the wording of Art. 2 Brussels Convention suggests that its
application is subject to the condition that there should be a legal relationship involving a
number of Contracting States.[5] As the ECJ pointed out, the existence of an international
element is required for the application of the jurisdiction rules of the Brussels Convention.
In later decisions the ECJ reaffirmed the *Owusu* decision with respect to the existence of an
international requirement for the application of the jurisdiction rules.[6] In the *Maletic* decision the ECJ reiterated that the international nature of the legal relationship at issue need not
necessarily derive, for the purposes of the application of Art. 2 Brussels I Regulation (now
Art. 4 Brussels I*bis* Regulation), from the involvement, either because of the subject-matter
of the proceedings or the respective domiciles of the parties, of a number of Member States.[7]

Under the Brussels I*bis* Regulation the requirement of an international element may follow **7**
from Recital (3), where mention is made that for the gradual establishment of an area of
freedom, security and justice, the Union is to adopt measures relating to judicial cooperation
in civil matters having cross-border implications, particularly when necessary for the proper
functioning of the internal market. Furthermore, recital 13 also states that there must be a
connection between proceedings to which the Brussels I*bis* Regulation applies and the
territory of the Member States. In order to become operable, Art. 4 does not only require
that the defendant is domiciled in the Member State of the court seised, but also that the case
has an international element. If the case is purely national and without international elements, either within the EU or outside the Member States, Art. 4 is not operable.

---

4   *Andrew Owusu* v. *Nugent B. Jackson, trading as "Villa Holidays Bal-Inn Villas", Mammee Bay Resorts*
    Ltd., Mammee Bay Club Ltd., The Enchanted Garden Resorts & Spa Ltd., Consulting Services Ltd., Town &
    Country Resorts Ltd., (Case C-281/02) ECLI:EU:C:2005:120, (2005) ECR I-1383. Published in RCDIP 94
    (2005), 699 with note *Chalas*, Clunet 132 (2005), 1177 with note *Cuniberti/M. M. Winkler* and NJ 2007/
    152 note *Vlas*. See in addition the comments by *Heinze/Dutta*, IPRax 2005, 224, *Hartley*, ICLQ 2005, 813;
    Fentiman, CMLR 2006, 705, *Ibili*, NILR 2006, 127 and *van Lith*, p. 50–54.
5   See *Andrew Owusu* v. *Nugent B. Jackson, trading as "Villa Holidays Bal-Inn Villas", Mammee Bay Resorts*
    Ltd., Mammee Bay Club Ltd., The Enchanted Garden Resorts & Spa Ltd., Consulting Services Ltd., Town &
    Country Resorts Ltd., (Case C-281/02) ECLI:EU:C:2005:120, (2005) ECR I-1383 para. 24.
6   See *Hypoteční banka a.s* v. *Udo Mike Lindner*, (Case C-327/10) ECLI:EU:C:2011:745, paras. 29–30, NJ
    2012/225 note Polak. See in addition the comments by Vlek, NIPR 2012, 202, Grimm, GPR 2012, 87,
    Corneloup, Rev crit dr int priv 2011, 411. See also *Armin Maletic, Marianne Maletic* v. *lastminute.com*
    GmbH, TUI Österreich GmbH, (Case C-478/12) ECLI:EU:C:2013:735, paras. 26–28, NJ 2014/234 with
    note *Strikwerda*; *Corman-Collins SA* v. *La Maison du Whisky SA* (Case C-9/12) ECLI:EU:C:2013:860,
    para. 18.
7   *Armin Maletic, Marianne Maletic* v. *lastminute.com GmbH, TUI Österreich GmbH*, (Case C-478/12)
    ECLI:EU:C:2013:735, paras. 26–28.

8 In the case of the *Owusu* decision, the claimant, Mr Owusu, was a British national domiciled in the United Kingdom, who suffered a serious accident during a holiday in Jamaica. Mr Owusu brought an action for breach of contract against Mr Jackson, who was also domiciled in the United Kingdom and who had let to Mr Owusu a holiday home in Jamaica. The claimant brought also an action in tort against several Jamaican companies. The defendants asked for a declaration that the English court should not exercise its jurisdiction, because the case had closer links with Jamaica and that the Jamaican courts were a forum with jurisdiction in which the case might be tried more suitably in the interests of all the parties and the ends of justice. The question was whether Art. 2 Brussels Convention would still apply, where the claimant and one of the defendants are domiciled in the same Contracting State and the case between them has certain connecting factors with a non-Contracting State. The ECJ ruled that a court of a Member State cannot deny jurisdiction on the ground that the proceedings have more connecting factors to any other (Member) State.[8]

9 In the case of the *Maletic* decision, the claimants, Mr and Mrs Maletic, both Austrian nationals and domiciled in Austria, booked and paid for a package holiday to Egypt on the website of lastminute.com GmbH, a German company having its registered office in Munich. The German company stated on its website that it acted as a travel agent and that the trip to Egypt was organised by TUI Österreich GmbH, an Austrian company having its registered office in Vienna. Upon arrival in Egypt the Maletics noticed a mistake concerning the hotel. In order to be able to stay in the hotel initially booked on lastminute.com's website, they had to pay a surcharge. Afterwards the claimants started proceedings before the Austrian *Bezirksgericht* Bludenz against lastminute.com and TUI for recovering of the surcharge and for compensation of the inconvenience which affected their holiday. The *Bezirksgericht* held that it lacked local jurisdiction to hear the case against TUI, because the Brussels I Regulation was not applicable, since the dispute between the claimants and TUI was purely domestic. In appeal proceedings the Maletics stated that Art. 15 (3) and 16 (1) of the Brussels I Regulation concerning consumer contracts were applicable and that these provisions were also applicable against TUI, whereas TUI contended that the dispute should be brought before the *Bezirksgericht* of Vienna according to the Austrian rules of local jurisdiction. The *Landesgericht* Feldkirch asked the ECJ for a preliminary ruling on the interpretation of Art. 16 (1) Brussels I Regulation and on the existence of an international requirement in this case. The ECJ ruled that the international element is present not only as regards lastminute.com, but also as regards TUI. The contractual relationship with TUI cannot be classified as purely domestical since it was inseparably linked to the contractual relationship between the Maletics and the travel agent.[9] No general rules on the requirement of internationality can be deducted from this preliminary decision. However, it is clear that there is the requirement of an international element for the application of the jurisdiction rules of (now) the Brussels *Ibis* Regulation.

10 In the *Corman-Collins* case a Belgian company (Corman-Collins SA) sued a French company (La Maison du Whisky SA) before a Belgian court asking for compensation under the Belgian Law of 27 July 1961 on Unilateral Termination of Exclusive Distribution Agree-

---

[8]   See also *Kropholler/von Hein, Before* Art. 2 note 20; *Gaudemet-Tallon* p. 58; *McClean*, in: FS Hans van Loon p. 358.

[9]   *Armin Maletic, Marianne Maletic* v. *lastminute.com GmbH, TUI Österreich GmbH*, (Case C-478/12) ECLI:EU:C:2013:735, para. 29.

ments of Infinite Duration. According to Article 4 of this Statute Belgian courts have jurisdiction if a distributor has suffered damage further to the termination of a distribution agreement covering all or part of Belgian territory. The French defendant company challenged the jurisdiction of the Belgian court on the ground that the French courts had jurisdiction under Art. 2 Brussels I Regulation. The Belgian Court of Commerce dealing with this question in first instance asked the ECJ for a preliminary ruling, a.o. on the question whether Art. 2 Brussels I Regulation precludes the application of a national rule of jurisdiction such as Art. 4 of the Belgian Act of 27 July 1961. In its decision, the ECJ reaffirmed the requirement of the existence of an international element in view of the application of the jurisdiction rules of the Brussels I Regulation. It follows that, if a case presenting an international element falls within the scope *ratione materiae* of the Regulation and if the defendant is domiciled in a Member State the rules of the jurisdiction laid down by the Regulation must in principle be applied and prevail over national rules of jurisdiction. According to the ECJ Art. 2 Brussels I Regulation must be interpreted as meaning that, where the defendant is domiciled in a Member State other than in which the court seised is situated, it precludes the application of a national rules of jurisdiction.[10] This preliminary judgment also preserves its importance under the Brussels I*bis* Regulation.

V. Domicile

What is to be understood by the notion "domicile" for the purposes of the Brussels I*bis*   **11** Regulation, is provided for in Art. 62 (for natural persons) and Art. 63 (for legal persons). Art. 62 provides a conflicts rule in order to determine whether a party is domiciled in the Member State whose courts are seised of the matter and provides for the application of the lex fori. If a court of a Member State is seised of a matter, that court shall apply its internal law to decide whether a party is domiciled in that State. Should the court of that State decide that a party is domiciled in another Member State, the law of the latter State ought to be applied (Art. 62 (2)). Art. 62 does not give an autonomous definition of domicile.[11] However, Art. 63 gives an autonomous definition regarding the domicile of a company or other legal person or association of natural or legal persons. According to Recital (15) the domicile of a legal person must be defined autonomously so as to make the common rules more transparent and to avoid conflicts of jurisdiction.[12] According to Art. 63 a company or legal person is domiciled at the place where it has its statutory seat, its central administration, or its principal place of business. However, there is an exception to this rule: for the purposes of the application of Art. 24 (2) regarding exclusive jurisdiction in proceedings concerning certain matters of company law, the domicile of the company or legal person should be determined in accordance with the rules of private international law of the forum.

Since the notion "statutory seat" is unknown in Cyprus, Ireland and the United Kingdom,   **12** Art. 63 (2) gives a special rule regarding the use of this notion.

---

[10]   *Cormin-Collins SA* v. *La Maisin du Whisky SA*, (Case C-9/12) ECLI:EU:C:2013:860, paras. 18–22.

[11]   Neither does Art. 52 Brussels Convention nor Art. 59 of the 2007 Lugano Convention.

[12]   See also *Hassett* v. *MDU Services*, (Case C-372/07) ECLI:EU:C:2008:534, (2008) ECR I-7403, para. 18, NJ 2009/192 with note *Vlas*. See in addition the comments by *Sujecki*, EuZW 2008, 667, *Ancel*, RCDIP 2009, 76.

13   The domicile of a trust is to be determined in accordance with the rules of private international law of the forum (Art. 63 (3)).

VI. No discrimination based on nationality

14   The general rule of jurisdiction laid down in Art. 4 is based on the connecting factor of domicile (within the meaning of Arts. 62 and 63) in a Member State. Nationality is of no importance. A Russian citizen who is domiciled in Germany, shall be sued in accordance with the provisions of the Brussels *Ibis* Regulation, in the German courts, just as a Liberian company having its central place of business in Greece, shall be sued according to Art. 4 in the Greek courts. Nationality of the defendant is of no importance, unless the defendant is domiciled outside the Member States. In the latter case the rules of national jurisdiction have to be applied (Art. 6) including the rules of exorbitant jurisdiction mentioned in Art. 5 (2). The national grounds of exorbitant jurisdiction can not be exercised against persons domiciled in a Member State. The Member States are to notify the Commission which rules of exorbitant jurisdiction shall not be applicable against the persons domiciled in a Member State (see Art. 76 (1) (a)).

15   Discrimination on the ground of nationality is prohibited against defendants domiciled in a Member State. This follows from Art. 18 TFEU and from the case-law of the ECJ.[13]

VII. Article 4 (2): assimilation

16   Art. 4 (2) provides for an assimilation between persons not having the nationality of the Member States with those who have. Persons without the nationality of the Member State in which they are domiciled, shall be treated in accordance with the rules of national (local) jurisdiction applicable to nationals of that State. The same provision can be found in Art. 2 (2) Brussels Convention and Art. 2 (2) Lugano Convention. The Report *Jenard* explains that the same rules of jurisdiction apply to a foreigner domiciled in the Member State of the forum as those rules that are applicable to nationals of that forum state.[14]

17   Art. 6(2) provides for the same assimilation regarding the application of exorbitant rules of jurisdiction against defendants domiciled outside the Member States.

Article 5

1. Persons domiciled in a Member State may be sued in the courts of another Member State only by virtue of the rules set out in Sections 2 to 7 of this Chapter.
2. In particular, the rules of national jurisdiction of which the Member States are to notify the Commission pursuant to point (a) of Article 76(1) shall not be applicable as against the persons referred to in paragraph 1.

---

[13]   E.g., *Mund & Fester* v. *Hatrex Internationaal Transport*, (Case C-398/92) ECLI:EU:C:1994:52 (1994) ECR I-467, 479 para. 14.

[14]   Report *Jenard* p. 18, referring to Artt. 14 and 15 of the French *Code Civil.*

I. Jurisdiction over persons domiciled in a Member State

Art. 5 (1) states that persons domiciled in a Member State may be sued in the courts of **1** another Member State only by virtue of the rules set out in Sections 2 to 7 of Chapter II of the Regulation. From this provision it follows that the rules of jurisdiction as laid down in the Regulation are exhaustive. The rules of national jurisdiction shall not be used against defendants domiciled in a Member State.

II. Exorbitant rules of jurisdiction

Art. 5 (2) explicitly provides for the non-applicability of the rules of national jurisdiction. **2** According to Art. 76 (1) (a) Brussels I*bis* Regulation the Member States shall notify the Commission about the national rules of jurisdiction which shall not be applicable as against the persons domiciled in a Member State. These rules can be described as exorbitant grounds of jurisdiction, which are internationally not acceptable, because they are based on, for instance, nationality of the plaintiff, the localisation of property within the forum state or the detention of property in the forum state. On the basis of the notifications received from the Member States, the Commission shall establish a list with these exorbitant national provisions (Art. 76 (2) Brussels I*bis* Regulation). Under the Brussels I Regulation the exorbitant grounds of jurisdiction were mentioned in Annex I to the Brussels I Regulation, where the new system of information gathering under Article 76 Brussels I*bis* Regulation is more flexible. Whether or not notification by a Member State has taken place and whether a Member State mentions all possible exorbitant rules of national jurisdiction, is not decisive for the non-applicability of these rules, since Art. 5 (2) uses the words 'in particular'. However, the use of a national (exorbitant) ground of jurisdiction is not prohibited, if it is a ground for provisional measures according to Art. 35. If the court seised cannot base its jurisdiction for provisional measures on Art. 4 or Arts. 7 to 26, the court can use its national rules of jurisdiction, including possible exorbitant rules.[1]

In January 2015 the list as announced by (2) was promulgated in accordance with Art. 76.[2] It **3** reads:

"List 1

The rules of jurisdiction referred to in Articles 5(2) and 6(2) are the following:
- in Belgium, none,
- in Bulgaria, Article 4(1)(2) of the International Private Law Code,
- in Czech Republic, Act No. 91/2012 on private international law, in particular, its Article 6,
- in Denmark, Article 246(2) and (3) of the Administration of Justice Act,
- in Germany, Section 23 of the Code of Civil Procedure,
- in Estonia, Article 86 (jurisdiction at the location of property) of Code of Civil Procedure, insofar as the claim is unrelated to that property of the person; Article 100 (claim for termination of

---

[1]   *van Uden Maritime BV, trading as van Uden Africa Line* v. *Kommanditgesellschaft in Firma Deco-Line and Another*, (Case C-391/95) ECLI:EU:C:1998:543, (1998) ECR I-7091, I-7135 para. 42.

[2]   The information referring to Article 76 of Regulation (EU) No. 1215/2012 of the European Parliament and of the Council on jurisdiction and recognition and enforcement of judgments in civil and commercial matters, OJ EU 2015 C 4/2.

application of standard terms) of Code of Civil Procedure, insofar as the action is to be lodged with the court in whose territorial jurisdiction the standard term was applied,
- in Greece, Article 40 of the Code of Civil Procedure,
- in Spain, none,
- in France, Articles 14 and 15 of the Civil Code,
- in Croatia, Article 54 of the Act on the Resolution of Conflicts of Laws with the Regulations of Other Countries in Specific Relations,
- in Ireland, the rules which enable jurisdiction to be founded on the document instituting the proceedings having been served on the defendant during his temporary presence in Ireland,
- in Italy, Articles 3 and 4 of Law No. 218 of 31 May 1995,
- in Cyprus, Article 21 of the Law on Courts (Law 14/60),
- in Latvia: Articles 27(2), 28 (3), 28 (5), 28 (6) and 28 (9) of the Law on Civil Procedure,
- in Lithuania, Articles 783(3), 787, 789(3) of the Code of Civil Procedure,
- in Luxembourg, Articles 14 and 15 of the Civil Code,
- in Hungary, Article 57(a) of Legislative Decree No. 13 of 1979 on International Private Law,
- in Malta, Article 742, 743 and 744 of the Code of Organization and Civil Procedure (Chapter 12 of the Laws of Malta) and Article 549 of the Commercial Code (Chapter 13 of the Laws of Malta),
- in the Netherlands, none,
- in Austria, Article 99 of the Law on court jurisdiction,
- in Poland, Article 11037(4) of the Code of Civil Procedure and Article 1110 of the Code of Civil Procedure, insofar as it provides for jurisdiction for the Polish courts exclusively on the basis of one of the following circumstances concerning the applicant: Polish citizenship, domicile, habitual residence or registered office in Poland,
- in Portugal, Article 63(1) of the Code of Civil Procedure in so far as it provides for courts to have extraterritorial jurisdiction, for instance, the court at the seat of the branch, agency, office, delegation or representation (if located in Portugal) where application is made for service on the head office (if located abroad) and Article 10 of the Code of Labour Procedure in so far as it provides for courts to have extraterritorial jurisdiction, for instance, the court at the domicile of the applicant for proceedings arising from an employment contract brought by a worker against an employer,
- in Romania, Articles 1065–1081 under Title I 'International jurisdiction of Romanian courts' in Book VII 'International civil procedure' of Act No. 134/2010 on the Code of Civil Procedure,
- in Slovenia, Article 58 of the Private International Law and Procedure Act,
- in Slovakia, § 37 to § 37e of the Act No. 97/1963 Coll. on Private International Law and the Rules of Procedure relating thereto,
- in Finland, Subparagraphs 1 and 2 of Section 18(1) of Chapter 10 of the Code of Judicial Procedure,
- in Sweden, Chapter 10, Section 3, first sentence of the Code of Judicial Procedure,
- in the United Kingdom:
  - (a) the document instituting the proceedings having been served on the defendant during his temporary presence in the United Kingdom; or
  - (b) the presence within the United Kingdom of property belonging to the defendant; or
  - (c) the seizure by the plaintiff of property situated in the United Kingdom.

The same principles apply in Gibraltar."

Article 6

1. If the defendant is not domiciled in a Member State, the jurisdiction of the courts of each Member State shall, subject to Article 18(1), Article 21(2) and Articles 24 and 25, be determined by the law of that Member State.

2. As against such a defendant, any person domiciled in a Member State may, whatever his nationality, avail himself in that Member State of the rules of jurisdiction there in force, and in particular those of which the Member States are to notify the Commission pursuant to point (a) of Article 76 (1), in the same way as nationals of that Member State.

Bibliography

Bonomi, Sull'opportunità e le possibili modalità di una regolamentazione comunitaria della competenza giurisdizionale applicabile erga omnes, RDIPP 2007, 313

Domej, Die Neufassung der EuGVVO, Quantensprünge im europäischen Zivilprozessrecht, RabelsZ 78 (2014) 508

Fallon, L'applicabilité du règlement Bruxelles I aux situations externes après l'avis 1/03, in: Liber amicorum Hélène Gaudemet-Tallon (2008), p. 241

Gaudemet-Tallon, De quelques aspects de la concentration des contentieux en droit communautaire: les litiges impliquant des juridictions d'États tiers, in: Mélanges en l'honneur de Serge Guinchard (2010), p. 465

Grolimund, Drittstaatenproblematik des europäischen Zivilverfahrensrechts (2000)

Grolimund, Drittstaatenproblematik des europäischen Zivilverfahrensrechts – Eine Never-Ending-Story?, ZVR-Jb 2010, 79

Ibili, Toepassing van de EEX-bevoegdheidsregels op verweerders uit derde landen: naar een universeel formeel toepassingsgebied, WPNR 6892 (2011) 533

Jayme, Das Europäische Gerichtsstands- und Vollstreckungsübereinkommen und die Drittländer – Das Beispiel Österreich, in: Schwind (Hrsg), Europarecht, IPR, Rechtsvergleichung (1988), p. 97

Kropholler, Problematische Schranken der europäischen Zuständigkeitsordnung gegenüber Drittstaaten, in: FS Murad Ferid zum 80. Geb (1988), p. 239

Kruger, Wanneer is een zaak "internationaal" vor het Europese IPR?, TBH 2006, 941

Kruger, Civil Jurisdiction Rules of the European Union and Their Impact on Third States (2008)

Nuyts, Study on residual jurisdiction, 3 September 2007 http:ec.europa.eu/justice_home/doc_centre/civil/studies/doc/study_residual_jurisdiction.en

Pataut, Qu'est-ce qu'un litige "intracommunautaire"? – Réflexions autour de l'article 4 du Règlement Bruxelles I, in: Études offertes à Jacques Normand (2003), p. 365

Pataut, L'espace judiciaire européen: un espace cohérent?, in: Leroyer/Jeuland (dir.), Quelle cohérence pour l'espace judiciaire européen? (2004), p. 31

Pocar, Faut-il replacer le renvoi au droit national par des règles uniformes dans l'article 4 du Règlement n° 44/2001?, in: Liber amicorum Hélène Gaudemet-Tallon (2008), p. 573

Schlosser, Das internationale Zivilprozessrecht der Europäischen Wirtschaftsgemeinschaft und Österreich, in: FS Winfried Kralik (1986), p. 287

Schlosser, Unzulässige Diskriminierung nach Bestehen oder Fehlen eines EG-Wohnsitzes im europäischen Zivilprozessrecht, in: FS Andreas Heldrich (2005), p. 1007

de Vareilles-Sommières, La compétence internationale de l'espace judiciaire européen, in: Liber amicorum Hélène Gaudemet-Tallon (2008), p. 397

Johannes Weber, Universal Jurisdiction and Third States in the Reform of the Brussels I Regulation, RabelsZ 75 (2011) 619

Weitz, Die geplante Erstreckung der Zuständigkeitsordnung der Brüssel I-Verordnung auf drittstaatsansässige Beklagte, in: FS Daphne-Ariane Simotta (2012), p. 679.

I. Defendant domiciled outside the Member States

1   Art. 6 is a very important provision. It does not give jurisdiction to the courts of a Member State, but it demarcates the application of the jurisdiction rules set out in the Regulation vis-à-vis defendants domiciled outside the Member States. In that case the rules of national jurisdiction have to be applied in order to determine whether the court of the forum state has jurisdiction. However, there are a few exceptions to this rule. The national rules of jurisdiction do not apply, if the matter falls within the scope of Art. 18 (1) (if the consumer starts legal proceedings against the other party to the contract, regardless of the domicile of that other party), 21 (2) (if the employee starts legal proceedings against his employer who is not domiciled in a Member State), 24 (exclusive jurisdiction) and Art. 25 (choice of forum). Art. 24 applies irrespective of domicile of the parties. Art. 25 also applies irrespective of domicile of the parties which have agreed to a choice of forum. In this regard Art. 25 Brussels *Ibis* Regulation differs from its predecessor Art. 23 Brussels I Regulation. According to Art. 23 Brussels I Regulation one of the parties to a choice of forum is to be domiciled in a Member State. Under Art. 25 Brussels *Ibis* Regulation this requirement is deleted. The choice of forum, however, shall be made in favour of a court or the courts of a Member State. Art. 25 regarding tacit submission could also be seen as an exception to Art. 6, although this is not explicitly mentioned. Art. 25 also applies irrespective of the domicile of the parties, which can be derived from the *Group Josi* decision of the ECJ.[1]

2   The autonomous rules of jurisdiction laid down in Section 3 (insurance) do not prejudice the application of Art. 6. For instance, an insurer without domicile in a Member State can be sued in the courts of a Member State according to the national rules of jurisdiction of that State. However, if the insurer has a branch, agency or other establishment in one of the Member States, he shall be deemed to be domiciled in that Member State for disputes within the scope of Section 3 (see Art. 11 (2)).

3   The autonomous rules of jurisdiction of Sections 4 (consumer contracts) and 5 (individual contracts of employment) do affect the application of Art. 6. According to Art. 18 (1) the consumer can start legal proceedings against the other party to the consumer contract in the courts of the Member State in which the consumer is domiciled. The domicile of the other party is irrelevant in this respect. The ratio of this provision is the protection of the consumer as weaker party.[2] Hence, Art. 6 explicitly mentions Art. 18 (1) as an exception to the rule that a defendant without domicile in a Member State can be sued before the courts of that Member State according to its national rules of jurisdiction. If the other party, which is not domiciled in a Member State, has a branch, agency or other establishment in one of the Member States, that party shall, in disputes arising out of the operations of that branch, agency or establishment, be deemed to be domiciled in that Member State (Art. 17 (2)). The same applies for the autonomous rules of jurisdiction to individual contracts of employment as set out in Artt. 20–23. According to Art. 21 (2) an employer not domiciled in a Member State may be sued in a court of a Member State where the employee habitually carries out his work or in the courts for the last place where he did so (Art. 21 (1) (a)), or if there is no place where the employee habitually carries or carried out his work in any one country, in the

---

[1]   *Group Josi Reinsurance Company SA* v. *Universal General Insurance Company*, (Case C-412/98) ECLI: EU:C:2000:399, (2000) ECR I-5925.

[2]   See also Recital (18).

courts of the place where the business is or was situated which engaged the employee (Art. 21 (1) (b)). Art. 21 (2) is therefore also an exception to Art. 6. Art. 20 (2) contains a similar provision as Art. 17 (2), which also can be seen as exceptions to Art. 6.

In the Green Paper on the review of the Brussels I Regulation the question was asked **4** whether the Regulation should be extended to third States defendants in view of equal access to justice.[3] Since the jurisdictional rules for defendants in third states differ from one Member State to another, the Green Paper stated that 'a common approach would strengthen the legal protection of Community citizens and economic operators and guarantee the application of mandatory Community legislation'.[4] The operation of the Brussels I Regulation vis-à-vis third states was also discussed by the European Group for Private International Law, which proposed the deletion of Art. 4 Brussels I Regulation and the application of the rules of jurisdiction of the Brussels I Regulation to all external relations.[5] In the Commission's proposal for a recast of the Brussels I Regulation,[6] the jurisdiction rules of the proposed Regulation were designed to be applied against defendants domiciled in third States in the same way as they are applicable to defendants domiciled in Member States. Although the rationale behind this proposal, i.e. the diversity of national laws regarding third States defendants, can be underlined, the application of the jurisdiction rules of the Brussels I Regulation to these defendants is not without problems. In the resolution of the European Parliament of 7 September 2010, the Parliament criticized the Commission's proposals in this respect as premature, because the 'reflexive effect' of the jurisdiction rules has not been given 'much study, wide-ranging consultations and political debate, in which Parliament should play a leading role'. The Parliament asked for a global solution in cooperation with the Hague Conference on Private International Law within the framework of the resumption of the negotiations on an international judgments convention.[7] In the final text of the Brussels I*bis* Regulation Article 4 was retained and renumbered to Article 6. Only a few changes have been made in respect to the application of Articles 18 (1) and 21 (2), as discussed above.

---

3   Green Paper, Brussels 21 April 2009, COM (2009) 175 final; see also the Report from the Commission to the European Parliament, the Council and the European Economic and Social Committee, Brussels 21 April 2009, COM (2009) 174 final. The latter Report is based on the Heidelberg Report on the application of the Brussels I Regulation (*Hess/Pfeifer/Schlosser*, 2008) and on the study on residual jurisdiction by A. *Nuyts*, (2007), available at: http://ec.europa.eu.

4   Green Paper, p. 3. According to the Commission's Report (op. cit., p. 5) the study on residual jurisdiction shows that "the absence of common rules determining jurisdiction may jeopardize the application of mandatory Community legislation, for example on consumer protection (e.g. time share), commercial agents, data protection or product liability".

5   See European Group for Private International Law, Proposed Amendment of Regulation 44/2001 in order to apply it to external situations (Bergen, 21 September 2008), http://gedip-eugpil.eu also published in IPRax 2009, p. 283–284; see also *Alegría Borrás*, Application of the Brussels I Regulation to External Situations, Yb. PIL 12 (2010) 333.

6   Proposal for a Regulation of the European Parliament and of the Council on jurisdiction and the recognition and enforcement of judgments in civil and commercial matters (Recast), Brussels 14/12/2010, COM (2010) 748/3.

7   European Parliament resolution of 7 September 2010 on the implementation and review of Council Regulation (EC) No. 44/2001 (…), 2009/2140 (INI). See also *Tanja Domej*, RabelsZ 78 (2014) 522 with further references to literature in favour of extending the jurisdiction rules to defendants in third States.

II. Unknown domicile of the defendant

5 The question has arisen what to do if the defendant's domicile is unknown. In the *Hypoteční banka* preliminary ruling the ECJ had to decide whether the courts of a Member State (i.e. Czech Republic) have jurisdiction if the defendant has the nationality of another Member State (i.e. Germany), having his last known domicile in the Czech Republic, but an unknown domicile at the time of instituting the court proceedings.[8] In this case a Czech bank brought an action before the Czech court against Mr Lindner, a German national, for payment of the arrears on the mortgage loan which was granted to Mr Lindner by the bank. At the time of the conclusion of the mortgage loan agreement Mr Lindner was deemed to be domiciled in the Czech Republic. At the time the court proceedings against Mr Lindner were instituted, the defendant's address was unknown and the court was unable to establish any other place of residence of Mr Lindner in the Czech Republic. The Czech District Court assigned a guardian *ad litem* according to the Rules of Civil Procedure of the Czech Republic, since the defendant was considered to be a person whose domicile was unknown. The District Court asked the ECJ for a preliminary ruling whether the Brussels I Regulation was applicable in the circumstances of the case and whether the Brussels I Regulation must be interpreted as precluding a provision of national law of a Member State which enables proceedings to be brought against persons whose domicile is unknown.

6 The ECJ considered that the international nature of a legal relationship may derive from the fact that the situation at issue in the proceedings is such as to raise questions relating to the determination of international jurisdiction (para. 30) and that the foreign nationality of the defendant, although not taken into account by the rules of jurisdiction of the Brussels I Regulation, may raise questions relating to the determination of the international jurisdiction of the court seised (para. 32). The ECJ held that in a case in which the defendant is a foreign national and has no known place of domicile in the State of the court seised, the rules of jurisdiction of the Brussels I Regulation may be applicable (para. 34).

7 As for the question whether the Brussels I Regulation precludes a national provision of a Member State enabling the assignment of a guardian *ad litem*, the ECJ held that if proceedings are brought against a consumer – Mr Lindner is a consumer falling within the ambit of Art. 16 (2) Brussels I Regulation (now Art. 18 (2) Brussels *Ibis* Regulation) – the national court has to determine whether the defendant is domiciled in a Member State. The court has first to apply (now) Art. 62 (1) Brussels *Ibis* Regulation and secondly, where the defendant has no domicile in the Member State of the court addressed, to examine whether the defendant is domiciled in another Member State in accordance with (now) Art. 62 (2) Brussels *Ibis* Regulation (paras. 39–41). Lastly, the ECJ considered that where the national court is still unable to identify the place of domicile of the consumer and has no firm evidence to support the conclusion that the defendant is in fact domiciled outside the European Union, a situation in which Art. 6 Brussels *Ibis* Regulation may be applicable, it is necessary to examine whether (now) Art. 18 (2) Brussels *Ibis* Regulation may be interpreted as meaning that the rule on jurisdiction of the courts of the Member State in which the consumer is domiciled also covered the consumer's last known domicile (para. 42).

---

[8] *Hypoteční banka a.s* v. *Udo Mike Lindner*, (Case C-327/10) [2011] ECR I-11543 paras. 29–30 = NJ 2012 Nr. 225 with note *Polak*. See in addition the comments by *Vlek*, NIPR 2012, 202, *Grimm*, GPR 2012, 87, *Corneloup*, RCDIP 110 (2011), 411.

According to the ECJ the criterion of the consumer's last known domicile ensures a fair balance between the rights of the other party and those of the defendant (para. 46). From this decision it derives that in case of consumer contracts – falling with the ambit of the autonomous provisions of Section 4 of Chapter II Brussels I*bis* Regulation – the last known domicile of the consumer may be taken into account, if at the time of the court proceedings the consumer's domicile is unknown.

Another question is whether Art. 6 applies if the domicile of the defendant is unknown, **8** however, it is said that the defendant might have his domicile in another Member State. In this respect regard has to be had to a preliminary decision of the ECJ of 15 March 2012.[9] The *Landgericht* Regensburg (Germany) asked the ECJ for a preliminary ruling whether e.g. Art. 4 (1) Brussels I Regulation (now Art. 6 (1) Brussels I*bis* Regulation) is applicable "in cases in which the whereabouts of the defendant in a civil action, who has been sued for an injunction, information and compensation for pain and suffering because of the operation of a website, who is (presumed to be) a Union citizen within the meaning of the second sentence of Art. 9 TEU, are unknown, it therefore being conceivable, but by no means certain, that he is currently residing outside the Union territory and also outside the residual treaty area governed by the Lugano Convention, and the precise location of the server on which the website is stored is also unknown, although it seems logical to assume that it is the Union territory?" The ECJ reaffirmed the *Hypoteční banka* decision and that the expression 'is not domiciled in a Member State' used in (now) Art. 6 (1) of the Brussels I*bis* Regulation, must be understood as meaning that the application of the national rules rather than the uniform rules of jurisdiction is possible only if the court seised of the case holds firm evidence to support the conclusion that the defendant, a citizen of the European Union not domiciled in the Member State of that court, is in fact domiciled outside the European Union (para. 40). If there is no such firm evidence, the international jurisdiction of a court of a Member State is established on the basis of (now) the Brussels I*bis* Regulation, when the conditions for application of the rules of jurisdiction of the Regulation are met, including in particular that in (now) Art. 7 (2) Brussels I*bis* Regulation, in matters of tort, delict or quasi-delict (para. 41). Hence, if the defendant is a Union citizen, the domicile of the defendant is unknown and it cannot be ascertained that the defendant is domiciled outside the European Union, the jurisdiction of the court of a Member State is to be established according to rules of jurisdiction of the Brussels I*bis* Regulation.

Art. 4 does not require the defendant having a (known) domicile in a third State, it only **9** states that the defendant is not domiciled in a Member State. If it is established that the defendant is not domiciled in a Member State, although the domicile of the defendant is unknown, the national rules of jurisdiction shall apply.[10]

III. Effect of Article 6

If the defendant is not domiciled in a Member State, the rules of national jurisdiction shall **10** apply. A judgment rendered against such a defendant will be recognised and enforced in all Member States under the rules of the Brussels I*bis* Regulation. The scope of application of

---

[9] G v. *Cornelius de Visser* (Case C-292/10) ECLI:EU:C:2012:142, nyr. = NJ 2012 Nr. 286 with note *Polak.* Additional comments by *Bach*, EuZW 2012, 381, *Cuniberti*, J. dr. eur. 2012, 187.

[10] See G v. *Cornelius de Visser* (Case C-292/10) ECLI:EU:C:2012:142.

Chapter III of the Regulation regarding recognition and enforcement does not depend on the defendant's domicile. It is only required that the judgment is given in a Member State (Art. 36). This also means that a judgment given against a defendant domiciled outside the Member States, in which jurisdiction is based on an exorbitant ground of national jurisdiction, shall be recognised and enforced under the rules of the Regulation.[11] Jurisdiction of the court of the Member State that rendered the decision may not be reviewed (Art. 45 (3)). In this respect the Regulation does not deviate from the Brussels Convention. The effect that a judgment rendered against a defendant domiciled outside the EU could be recognised and enforced within the Member States received much criticism at the time the Brussels Convention was drafted.[12] However, the drafting committee took a firm stand in this respect and justified the extension of these exorbitant 'privileges' of jurisdiction against defendants domiciled outside the (then) Contracting States.[13]

11 In this respect regard should be had to Art. 72, which refers to Art. 59 Brussels Convention. The Regulation shall not affect agreements by which Member States undertook, prior to the entry into force of the Brussels I Regulation, pursuant to Art. 59 Brussels Convention, not to recognise judgments given, in particular in other Contracting States to that Convention, against defendants domiciled or habitually resident in a third country, where, in cases provided for in Art. 4 Brussels Convention, the judgment could only be founded on an exorbitant ground of jurisdiction specified in the Art. 3 (2) Brussels Convention. Such agreements are concluded between the United Kingdom and Canada, and the United Kingdom and Australia.[14] Art. 59 Brussels Convention has no equivalent in the Brussels I Regulation, due to the fact that under EU law the individual Member States are no longer exclusively competent to conclude agreements on recognition and enforcement of judgments in civil and commercial matters.

IV. Article 6 (2): assimilation

12 Art. 6 (2) is more or less a repetition of Art. 4 (2). If the defendant is not domiciled in a Member State, the claimant domiciled in a Member State may, whatever his nationality, avail himself in that state of the rules of jurisdiction there in force, including the rules of which the Member States are to notify the Commission pursuant to point (a) of Art. 76 (1), in the same way as the nationals of that State. In this respect mention should be made of Art. 14 French Civil Code.[15] This exorbitant ground of jurisdiction is, for instance, available to an American national domiciled in Paris against another American national domiciled in New York.

---

11   See also *Kruger*, paras. 2.58 and 2.77.

12   See *e.g. Nadelmann*, (1964) 58 AJIL 764; *Nadelmann*, (1967) 67 Colum. L. Rev. 995.

13   Report *Jenard* p. 21.

14   See *Kaye*, Civil Jurisdiction and Enforcement of Foreign Judgments (1987) p. 1524; *Dicey/Morris/Collins* para. 14–188; *Gaudemet-Tallon* p. 68.

15   Art. 14 CC: "L'étranger, même non résident en France, pourra être cité devant les tribunaux français, pour l'exécution des obligations par lui contractées en France avec un Français; il pourra être traduit devant les tribunaux de France, pour les obligations par lui contractées en pays étranger envers des Français."

Section 2: **Special jurisdiction**

Article 7

A person domiciled in a Member State may be sued in another Member State:
(1) (a) in matters relating to a contract, in the courts for the place of performance of the obligation in question;
  (b) for the purpose of this provision and unless otherwise agreed, the place of performance of the obligation in question shall be:
    – in the case of the sale of goods, the place in a Member State where, under the contract, the goods were delivered or should have been delivered,
    – in the case of provision of services, the place in a Member State where, under the contract, the services were provided or should have been provided;
  (c) if point (b) does not apply then point (a) applies;
(2) in matters relating to tort, delict or quasi-delict, in the courts for the place where the harmful event occurred or may occur;
(3) as regards a civil claim for damages or restitution which is based on an act giving rise to criminal proceedings, in the court seised of those proceedings, to the extent that that court has jurisdiction under its own law to entertain civil proceedings;
(4) as regards a civil claim for the recovery, based on ownership, of a cultural object as defined in point 1 of Article 1 Directive 93/7/EEC initiated by the person claiming the right to recover such an object, in the courts for the place where the cultural object is situated at the time when the court is seised;
(5) as regards a dispute arising out of the operations of a branch, agency or other establishment, in the courts for the place in which, the branch, agency or other establishment is situated;
(6) as regards a dispute brought against a settlor, trustee or beneficiary of a trust created by the operation of a statute, or by a written instrument, or created orally and evidenced in writing, in the courts of the Member State in which the trust is domiciled;
(7) as regards a dispute concerning the payment of remuneration claimed in respect of the salvage of a cargo or freight, in the court under the authority of which the cargo or freight in question:
  (a) has been arrested to secure such payment; or
  (b) could have been so arrested, but bail or other security has been given;
    provided that this provision shall apply only if it is claimed that the defendant has an interest in the cargo or freight or had such an interest at the time of salvage.

Bibliography

To (1):
d'Adamo, Le Sezione Unite ritornano sull'interpretazione dell'art 5. n. 1 reg. CE 44/2001, Riv. dir. proc. 2010, 944
Adobati, Il luogo di consegna dei beni quale criterio di individuazione della competenza per tutte le obligazioni derivanti da un contratto di compravendita, Dir. scambi int. 2006, 345
Adobati, Individuazione del foro competente a diri-

mere le controversie in materia di contratti di compravendita conclusi tra operatori di Stati diversi, alle luce del regolamento CE N. 44/2001 e della Convenzione di Lugano nella versione del 30 ottobre 2007, secondo le sezione unite della Corte di Cassazione, Dir. com. sc. int. 2011, 111
Afferni, The Qualification of Pre-Contractual Liability, ERCL 2005, 97
Altmeyer, Car Trim si sta facendo strada: "contratto

di vendita" vs. "contratto di prestazione di servizi" ai fini del foro contrattuale di cui all'art. 5, n. 1, lett. b) Reg. (CE) n. 44/2001, Giur. It. 2014, 1125

Marie-Élodie Ancel, Le for du contrat: point faible du contentieux européen?, Rev. jur. comm. 2010, 245

Attal, Propriété littéraire et artistique et droit international privé dans le contexte de l'internet: logiques incompatibles ou exigences conciliables?, JCP 2015, 680

Azzi, De quelques difficultés d'application de l'article 5.1, b, du règlement Bruxelles I en matière de contrats de fourniture de marchandises à fabriquer ou à produire, D. 2010, 1837

Bach, Was ist wo Vertrag und was wo nicht?, IHR 2010, 17

Birgit Bachmann, Art. 5 Nr. 1 EuGVÜ: Wechselrechtliche Haftungsansprüche im Gerichtsstand des Erfüllungsorts?, IPRax 1997, 237

Bajons, Gerichtsstand des Erfüllungsortes, in: FS Reinhold Geimer (2002), p. 15

Bajons, Autonome Bestimmung des Erfüllungsorts und Incoterms, in: FS Daphne-Ariane Simotta (2012), p. 57

Barone, Sulla nozione di "luogo di consegna" ai sensi dell'art. 5 n. 1 lett. b del regolamento n. 44/2001 nelle giurisprudenza della Corte di cassazione, Dir. UE 2007, 888

Beaumart, Haftung in Absatzketten im französischen Recht und im europäischen Zuständigkeitsrecht (1999)

Beaumont, The Brussels Convention Becomes a Regulation: Implications for Legal Basis, External Competence and Contract Jurisdiction, in: Essays in Honour of Sir Peter North (Oxford 2002), p. 9

Behar-Touchait, La qualification européenne du contrat de concession (À propos de l'arrêt de la Cour de cassation du 29 novembre 2014), RLDA 102 (2015), 35

Bělohlávek, Law Applicable to International Carriage: EU Law and International Treaties, Czech Yb. Int. L. 6 (2015), 27

Berg, Autonome Bestimmung des Erfüllungsortes nach Art. 5 Nr. 1 EuGVVO, NJW 2006, 3035

Berlioz, La notion de fourniture de services au sens de l'article 5-1, b) du règlement Bruxelles I, Clunet 135 (2008), 675

Berlioz, Le contrat de concession est un contrat de

fourniture de services au sens du règlement Bruxelles I, JCP G 2014, 271

Bernaert, De bevoegde rechter bij een documentair krediet met aangewezen bank, TBH 2015, 205

Bertoli, Criteri di giurisdizione e legge applicabile in tema di responsabilità precontrattuale alla luce della sentenza Fonderie Meccaniche Tacconi, RDIPP 2003, 109

Di Blase, La giurisdizione competente in materia di compravendita e di prestazione di servizi nel regolamento Bruxelles I, Europa e dir. priv. 2011, 459

Blobel, Lack of International Jurisdiction for Contractual Claims in the *forum delicti*, EuLF 2005, I-67

Bonell, Responsabilità precontrattuale, Convenzione di Bruxelles sulla competenza giurisdizionale e l'esecuzione delle sentenze e ... Principi UNIDROIT, Dir. comm. int. 2003, 183

Briggs, Jurisdiction over Restitutionary Claims, [1992] LMCLQ 283

Briggs, Claims against Sea Carriers and the Brussels Convention, [1999] LMCLQ 333

Brinkmann, Der Vertragsgerichtsstand bei Klagen aus Lizenzverträgen unter der EuGVVO, IPRax 2009, 487

Brödermann, Der europäische GmbH-Gerichtsstand, ZIP 1996, 491

Broggini, Il forum solutionis: passato, presente e futuro, RDIPP 2000, 15

Campeis/de Pauli, Luogo di adempimento del contratto di compravendita come titolo di giursdizione "europea" fra convenzione di Bruxelles del 1968 e regolamento UE n. 44/2001, NGCC 2003 I 234

Carballo Piñeiro, Obligación de no hacer y competencia judicial internacional, La Ley 5534 (2002), 1

Cavalier, La notion de contrat de fourniture de service au sens de Bruxelles I, Rev. Lamy dr. aff. Juin 2009, p. 57

Cebrián Salvat, Competencia judicial internacional en defecto de pacto en los contratos de distribución europeos: el contrato de distribución come contrato de prestación de servicios en el Reglamento 44, CDT 5 (1) (2013), 125

Cebrián Salvat, Estrategia procesal y litigación internacional en la Unión Europea: distinción ente materia contractual y extracontractual, CDT 6 (2) (2014), 315

Claeys, De internationale rechtsmacht ten aanzien

van vorderingen voortspruitend uit het documentair krediet, TBH 1995, 433

Clerici, Forum solutionis e Convenzione di Roma del 19 giugno 1980 al vaglio della giurisprudenza italiana, RDIPP 1997, 873

Coester-Waltjen, Der Erfüllungsort im internationalen Zivilprozessrecht, in: FS Athanassios Kaissis (2012), p. 91

Cornette, La nécessaire modification ou suppression de l'article 7-1 du règlement Bruxelles Ibis relatif au for contractuel dans un future règlement Bruxelles I ter, in: Emmanuel Guinchard (dir.), Le nouveau règlement Bruxelles Ibis (2014), p. 335

Crespo Hernández, Delimitación entre materia contractual y extracontractual en el Convenio de Bruselas, La Ley 1998, 2178

de Cristofaro, Il foro delle obbligazioni (1999)

Dickinson, Restitution and the Conflict of Laws, [1996] LMCLQ 556

Dornis, Von Kalfelis zu Brogsitter – Künftig enge Grenzen der Annexkompetenz im europäischen Vertrags- und Deliktsgerichtsstand, GPR 2014, 352

Droz, Delendum est forum contractus?, D. 1997 Chron. 351

de Durantaye, Das Auseinanderfallen von Gerichtsstand und anwendbarem Recht bei Versendungskaufverträgen, in: FS Daphne-Ariane Simotta (2012), p. 115

Eltzschig, Art. 5 Nr. 1 b EuGVO: Ende oder Fortführung von forum actoris und Erfüllungsortbestimmung lege causae?, IPRax 2002, 491

Emde, Heimatgerichtsstand für Handelsvertreter und anderer Vertriebsmittler?, RIW 2003, 505

Espiniella Menéndez, El lugar de etrega de las mercancías en la contratación internacional, AEDIPr 2008, 283

Fach Gómez, El Reglamento 44/2001 y los contratos de agencia comcerical internacional: aspectos jurisdiccionales, Rev. der. com. eur. 14 (2003), 181

Falaschi, Obbligazioni e luogo di consegna ai sensi dell'articolo 5 n. 1 lett. B) del Regolamento n. 44/2001, Corr. giur. 2010, 967

Fernet, Application de l'article 5-1 du règlement Bruxelles I à un contrat d'agent commercial s'agissant du paiement d'indemnités de clientèle, JCP E 17 juin 2010, p. 21

Ferrari, La determinazione del foro competente in materia di compravendita internazionale: breve guida agli errori da evitare, Corr. giur. 2002, 372

Ferrari, L'interpretazione autonoma del Regolamento CE 44/2001 e, in particolare, del concetto di "luogo di adempimento dell'obbligazione" di cui all'art. 5 nr. 1 lett. b, Giur. it. 2006, 1016

Ferrari, Remarks on the Autonomous Interpretation of the Brussels I Regulation, in Particular of the Concept of "Place of Delivery" under Article 5 (1) (b), and the Vienna Sales Convention, RDAI 2007, 83

Ferrari, Zur autonomen Auslegung der EuGVVO, insbesondere des Begriffs des "Erfüllungsortes der Verpflichtung" nach Art. 5 Nr. 1 lit. b, IPRax 2007, 61

Ferrari, Ancora in materia di regolamento n. 44/2001/CE e del concetto di "luogo di consegna di beni" di cui all'art. 5, n. 1, lett. b, Giust. civ. 2007 I 1397

Ferrari, Verkäufergerichtsstand auch nach Art. 5 Nr. 1 lit. b EuGVVO?, ecolex 2007, 303

Fiorelli, Contratti telematici, strumenti di diritto internazionale privato e prospettive di armonizzazione della discplina materiale, Dir. comm. int. 2003, 427

Elisabeth Fischer/Schöfmann, Der Erfüllungsort bei internationalen Dienstleistungsverträgen, ecolex 2010, 669

Fogt, Gerichtsstand des Erfüllungsortes bei streitiger Existenz des Vertrages, Anwendbarkeit des CISG und alternative Vertragsschlussformen, IPRax 2001, 358

Font i Segura, La competencia de los Tribunales españoles en materia de contratos internacionales, RJC 2006, 79

Forsyth, Brussels Convention Jurisdiction "In Matters Relating to a Contract" When the Plaintiff Denies the Existence of a Contract, [1996] LMCLQ 329

Forsyth/Moser, The Impact of the Applicable Law of Contract on the Law of Jurisdiction under the European Conventions, (1996) 45 ICLQ 190

Foss/Bygrave, International Consumer Purchases through the Internet: Jurisdictional Issues pursuant to European Law, (2000) 8 Int. J. L. & Info. Tech. 99

de Franceschi, Compravendita internazionale di beni mobili con pluralità di luoghi di consegna, Int'l. Lis 2007, 120

de Franceschi, Il *locus destinatae solutionis* nella disciplina comunitaria della competenza giurisdizionale, Contratto e impresa/Europa 2008, 637

de Franceschi, Il foro europeo della materia contrattuale alla luce delle recenti acquisizioni della Corte di Giustizia e delle Sezioni unite, Int'l. Lis 2010, 81

Franzina, Obbligazioni di non fare e obbligazioni esigibili in più luoghi nella Convenzione di Bruxelles del 1968 e nel Regolamento (CE) n. 44/2001, Riv. dir. int. priv. proc. 2002, 391

Franzina, La responsabilità precontrattuale nello spazio giuridico europeo, Riv. dir. int. 2003, 714

Franzina, La giurisdizione in materia contrattuale (Padova 2006)

Franzina, La nuova disciplina comunitaria della giurisdizione in materia contrattuale al vaglio delle sezioni unite della Corte di Cassazione, NGCC 2007 I 537

Franzina, Interpretazione e destino del richiamo compiuto dalla legge di riforma del diritto internazionale privato ai criteri di giurisdizione della Convenzione di Bruxelles, Riv. dir. int. 2010, 817

Franzina, Struttura e funzionamento del foro europeo della materia contrattuale alla luce delle sentenze Car Trim e Wood Floor della Corte di Giustizia, RDIPP 2010, 655

Furrer/Schramm, Zuständigkeitsprobleme im europäischen Vertragsrecht, SJZ 2003, 105 and 137

Garcimartín, El fuero especial en materia de obligaciones contractuales en el Regolamento Bruselas I: El status quaestionis interpretativo, Int. J. Proced. L. 3 (2013), 22

Gardella, The ECJ in Search of Legal Certainty for Jurisdiction in Contract: The Color Drack Decision, IX (2007), 439

Gaudemet-Tallon, Quelques réflexions à propos de trois arrêts récents de la Cour de Cassation française sur l'art. 5-1 et de l'avis 1/03 de la Cour de justice des Communautes sur les compétences externes de la Communauté, in: Bonomi/Cashin Ritaine/Romano (dir.), La Convention de Lugano – passé, présent et devenir (Zürich 2007), p. 97

Gebauer, Neuer Klägergerichtsstand durch Abtretung einer dem UN-Kaufrecht unterliegenden Zahlungsforderung?, IPRax 1999, 432

Gehri, Vertrag – quasi? Abgrenzungsprobleme und Prozessplanung nach Art. 5 Nr 1 und 3 LugÜ, in: FS Ivo Schwander (St. Gallen 2011), p. 699

Giancotti, La determinazione del foro competente, in tema di compravendita internazionale di beni mobili, in caso di cumulo di domande relative ad obbligazioni da eseguirsi in Stati diversi, Giur. it. 2001, 233

Girsberger, The Internet and Jurisdiction Based on Contract, Eur. J. L. Reform 4 (2002), 165

de Götzen, La licenza d'uso di diritti di proprietà intellettuale nel regolamento Bruxelles I: il caso Falco, RDIPP 2010, 383

Gottwald, Streitiger Vertragsschluß und Gerichtsstand des Erfüllungsortes, IPRax 1983, 13

Gottwald, Internationale Vereinbarungen des Erfüllungsortes und des Gerichtsstandes nach Brüssel I und Den Haag, in: Księga Pamiątkowa ku czci Profesora Tadeusza Erecińskiego (2011) 1067

Graffi, Spunti in tema di vendita internazionale e forum shopping, Dir. comm. int. 17 (2003), 821

Gregor, Der Gerichtsstand des Erfüllungsorts beim Luftbeförderungsvertrag, IPRax 2008, 403

De Groote, Art. 5 sub 1 EEX-Verdrag: problematiek van de bepaling van de plaats waar de verbintenis die aan de eis ten grondslag ligt is uitgevoerd of moet worden uitgevoerd, R.W. 1996-97, 252

Grundmann, Gerichtsstand und Erfüllungsort bei Scheckeinlösung unter Verstoß gegen die Sicherungsabrede, IPRax 2002, 136

Grušić, Jurisdiction in Complex Contracts under the Brussels I Regulation, (2011) 7 JPrIL 321

Gsell, Autonom bestimmter Gerichtsstand am Erfüllungsort nach der Brüssel I-Verordnung, IPRax 2002, 484

Gsell, Erfüllungsort beim Versendungskauf und Abgrenzung von Kauf und Dienstleistung nach Art. 5 Nr. 1 lit. b EuGVVO, ZEuP 2011, 669

Günes/Freidinger, Gerichtsstand und anwendbares Recht bei Konsignationslagern, IPRax 2012, 48

Haas, Die zuständigkeitsrechtliche Verortung gesellschaftsrechtlicher Gläubigerschutzansprüche, NZG 2013, 1161

Haas/Amrei Keller, Die örtliche und internationale Zuständigkeit für Ansprüche nach § 128 HGB, ZZP 126 (2013), 335

Haas/Oliver Vogel, Zum Erfüllungsortsgerichtsstand nach Art. 5 Nr. 1 lit. b EuGVVO im europäischen Warenhandelsverkehr, NZG 2011, 766

Hackenberg, Der Erfüllungsort von Leistungspflichten unter Berücksichtigung des Wirkungsortes von Erklärungen im UN-Kaufrecht und der Gerichtsstand des Erfüllungsortes im deutschen und europäischen Zivilprozessrecht (2000)

Hackl, Örtliche Zuständigkeit gemäß Art. 5 (1) und (3) des Brüsseler EG-Übereinkommens vom 27.9. 1968 über die gerichtliche Zuständigkeit und die Vollstreckung gerichtlicher Entscheidungen in Zivil- und Handelssachen, ZfRV 1985, 1

Günter Hager/Bentele, Der Lieferort als Gerichtsstand – zur Auslegung des Art. 5 Nr. 1 lit. b EuGVO, IPRax 2004, 73

Hare/Hinks, Sale of Goods and the Brussels I Regulation, [2008] LMCLQ 353

Harris, Sale of Goods and the Relentless March of the Brussels I Regulation, (2007) 123 L.Q.Rev. 522

Hartley, Carriage of Goods and the Brussels Jurisdiction and Judgments Convention, (2000) 25 Eur. L. Rev. 89

Hau, Der Vertragsgerichtsstand zwischen judizieller Konsolidierung und legislativer Neukonzeption, IPRax 2000, 354

Hau, Zum Vertragsgerichtsstand für Rückforderungsklagen nach Legalzession, IPRax 2006, 507

Hau, Die Kaufpreisklage des Verkäufers im reformierten europäischen Vertragsgerichtsstand – ein Heimspiel?, JZ 2008, 974

Hau, Gerichtsstandsvertrag und Vertragsgerichtsstand beim innereuropäischen Versendungskauf, IPRax 2009, 44

Hau, Zur internationalen Zuständigkeit für Streitigkeiten über (angebliche) Vertragshändlerverträge, ZVertriebsR 2014, 79

Haubold, Internationale Zuständigkeit für gesellschaftsrechtliche und konzerngesellschaftsrechtliche Haftungsansprüche nach EuGVÜ und LugÜ, IPRax 2000, 375;

von Hein, Der europäische Gerichtsstand des Erfüllungsortes (Art. 5 Nr. 1 EuGVVO) bei einem unentgeltlichen Beratungsvertrag, IPRax 2013, 54

Hertz, Jurisdiction in Contract and Tort under the Brussels Convention (1998)

Hertz, Bruxelles-konventionens artikel 5, nr. 1, UfR 1999 B 533

Heuzé, De quelques infirmités congénitales du droit uniforme: l'exemple de l'article 5.1 de la Convention de Bruxelles du 27 septembre 1968, RCDIP 89 (2000), 595

Hill, Jurisdiction in Matters Relating to a Contract under the Brussels Convention, (1995) 44 ICLQ 591

Holl, Der Gerichtsstand des Erfüllungsortes gemäß Art. 5 Nr. 1 EuGVÜ, WiB 1995, 462

Holl, Der Gerichtsstand des Erfüllungsortes gemäß Art. 5 Nr. 1 EuGVÜ bei einem "claim for restitution based upon unjust enrichment", IPRax 1998, 120

Hollander, L'arrêt Leathertex: Shenavai revisité?, TBH 2000, 175

Huber-Mumelter/Mumelter, Mehrere Erfüllungsorte beim forum solutionis: Plädoyer für eine subsidiäre Zuständigkeit am Sitz des vertragscharakteristisch Leistenden, JBl 2008, 561

André Huet, Convention de Vienne du 11 avril 1980 sur les contrats de vente internationale de marchandises et compétence des tribunaux en droit judiciaire européen, in: Mélanges en l'honneur de Paul Lagarde (2005), p. 417

Ignatova, Art. 5 Nr. 1 EuGVVO – Chancen und Perspektiven der Reform des Gerichtsstands am Erfüllungsort (2005)

Jiménez Blanco, La aplicación del foro contractual del reglamento Bruselas I a los contratos aéreo de pasajeros, La Ley Unión Europea 7294 (30 noviembre 2009), 1

Junker, Der Gerichtsstand des Erfüllungsortes nach der Brüssel I-Verordnung im Licht der neueren EuGH-Rechtsprechung, in: FS Athanassios Kaissis (2012), p. 439

Junker, Der Gerichtsstand für internationale Verträge nach der Brüssel I-Verordnung im Licht der neueren EuGH-Rechtsprechung, in: FS Dieter Martiny (2014), p. 761

Kadner, Gerichtsstand des Erfüllungsortes im EuGVÜ, Jura 1997, 240

Christoph A. Kern, Der Gerichtsstand des Erfüllungsortes beim Kauf eines zu bebauenden und zu vermietenden Grundstücks, IPRax 2014, 503

Kessedjian, Le for contractuel en droit européen – Wood Floor, Car Trim et les autres, in: FS Ingeborg Schwenzer (2011), p. 937

Kienle, Eine ökonomische Momentaufnahme zu Art. 5 Nr. 1 lit. b EuGVVO, IPRax 2005, 113

Kienle, Der Maklervertrag im europäischen Zuständigkeitsrecht, IPRax 2006, 614

Kindler, Gesellschafterinnenhaftung in der GmbH und internationale Zuständigkeit nach der Verordnung (EG) Nr. 44/2001, in: FS Peter Ulmer (2003), p. 305

Kindler, Konzernhaftung zwischen Vertrag und Delikt – Die internationale Gerichtszuständigkeit bei

Peter Mankowski

Verstößen gegen gesetzliche Mitteilungspflichten, IPRax 2014, 486

Klemm, Erfüllungsortvereinbarungen im Europäischen Zivilverfahrensrecht (2005)

Harald Koch, Europäische Vertrags- und Deliktsgerichtsstände für Seetransportschäden ("Weiche Birnen"), IPRax 2000, 186

Kropholler/von Hinden, Die Reform des europäischen Gerichtsstands am Erfüllungsort, in: GS Alexander Lüderitz (2000), p. 401

Kubis, Gerichtspflicht durch Schweigen, Erfüllungsortvereinbarung und internationale Handelsbräuche, IPRax 1999, 10

Kubis, Internationale Zuständigkeit bei Persönlichkeits- und Immaterialgüterrechtsverletzungen (1999)

Kubis, Gerichtsstand am Erfüllungsort: Erneute Enttäuschung aus Luxemburg, ZEuP 2001, 737

Kuipers, De plaats waar een dienstenovereenkomst dient te worden verricht als grond voor rechterlijke bevoegdheid, NIPR 2010, 622

Kulms, Qualifiziert faktische GmbH-Konzerne und Außenhaftung: (k)ein Fall für Art. 5 Nr. 1 EuGVÜ?, IPRax 2000, 488

Lajolo/Stefano Rossi, Compravendite internazionali: la giurisdizione ai sensi del Regolamento (CE) n. 44/2001, Giur. mer. 2011, 1603

Leandro, Se l'acquirente non è determinante nella produzione la fornitura die beni viene assimilat alla vendita, Guida dir. 2010 n. 13 p. 104

Leandro, Agenti di commercio: la giurisdizione va individuata nel luogo con il legame più stretto contratto-foro, Guida dir. 2010 n. 16 p. 103

Leffler, Brysselförordningens artikel 5: Vad har förandrats?, SvJT 2002, 816

Matthias Lehmann, Gemeinschaftsrechtliche Zuständigkeitsregeln für GmbH-Streitigkeiten, GmbHR 2005, 978

Matthias Lehmann, Gerichtsstand bei Klagen wegen Annullierung einer Flugreise, NJW 2010, 655

Matthias Lehmann/Duczek, Zuständigkeit nach Art. 5 Nr. 1 lit. b EuGVVO – besondere Herausforderungen bei Dienstleistungsverträgen, IPRax 2011, 41

Leible, Luxemburg locuta – Gewinnzusage finita?, NJW 2005, 796

Leible, Warenversteigerungen im Internationalen Privat- und Verfahrensrecht, IPRax 2005, 424

Leible, Der Erfüllungsort i.S.v. Art. 5 Nr. 1 lit. b EuGVVO – ein Mysterium?, in: FS Ulrich Spellenberg (2010), p. 451

Leible/Sommer, Tücken bei der Bestimmung der internationalen Zuständigkeit nach der EuGVP: Rügelose Einlassung, Gerichtsstands- und Erfüllungsortvereinbarungen, Vertragsgerichtsstand, IPRax 2006, 568

Lein, La compétence en matière contractuelle: un regard critique sur l'article 5 1er de la nouvelle convention de Lugano, in: Bonomi/Cashin Ritaine/Romano (éds.), La convention de Lugano – Passé, présent et devenir (Zürich 2007), p. 41

Lein, Modern Art: The ECJ's Latest Sketches of Art. 5 No. 1 lit. b Brussels I Regulation, Yb. PIL 12 (2010), 571

Leipold, Internationale Zuständigkeit am Erfüllungsort – das Neueste aus Luxemburg und Brüssel, in: GS Alexander Lüderitz (2000), p. 431

Lheureux, La qualification du contrat de concession au sens de l'article 5, 1. du Règlement Bruxelles I, TBH 2015, 88

Lindacher, Delikt und Vertrag – Zur Zuständigkeit deutscher Wettbewerbsgerichte für Unterlassungs- und Vertragsstrafeklagen bei Zuwiderhandlungen nach internationaler Unterwerfung, in: FS Kontantinos Kerameus, vol. I (Athens/Bruxelles 2009), p. 709

Linton, The Place of Performance in the Brussels I Regulation Reconsidered, in: Festskrift Helge Johan Thue (Oslo 2007), p. 342

van Lith, International Jurisdiction and Commercial Litigation – Uniform Rules for Contract Disputes (The Hague 2009)

Lohse, Das Verhältnis von Vertrag und Delikt. Eine rechtsvergleichende Studie zur vertragsautonomen Auslegung von Art. 5 Nr. 1 und Art. 5 Nr. 3 GVÜ (1991)

López Rodríguez, El contrato de distribución exclusiva o concesión comercial ciómo contrato de prestación de servicios a efectos de la aplicación del foro contractual del RB I., La Ley UE n° 13, 2014, p. 37

Stephan Lorenz, Gewinnmitteilungen als "geschäftsähnliche Handlungen": Anwendbares Recht, internationale Zuständigkeit und Erfüllungsort, NJW 2006, 472

Lüderitz, Fremdbestimmte internationale Zuständigkeit? Versuch einer Neubestimmung von § 29

ZPO, Art. 5 Nr. 1 EuGVÜ, in: FS Konrad Zweigert (1981), p. 233

Lupoi, La competenza in materia contrattuale nella convenzione di Bruxelles del 17 settembre 1968, Riv. trim. dir. proc. civ. 1994, 1263

Lupoi, Il "nuovo" foro per le controverse contrattuali, Riv. trim. dir. proc. civ. 2007, 495

Lupoi, The "New" Forum for Contractual Disputes in Regulation (EU) 44/2001, in: FS Kontantinos Kerameus, vol. I (Athens/Bruxelles 2009), p. 733

Luzi Crivellini/Samburgaro, Quale giudice competente in caso di pluralità di luoghi di consegna?, Giur. it. 2008, 148

Lynker, Der besondere Gerichtsstand am Erfüllungsort in der Brüssel I-Verordnung (Art. 5 Nr. 1 EuGVVO) (2006)

Magnus, Das UN-Kaufrecht und die Erfüllungsortzuständigkeit in der neuen EuGVO, IHR 2002, 45

Mahinga, La compétence juridictionelle dans les contrats de distribution exclusive: la fin de l'incertitude: Petites affiches No. 27, 6 février 2015, p. 7

Mankowski, EuGVÜ-Gerichtsstand für Gesellschafterhaftungsklage des Insolvenzverwalters, NZI 1999, 56

Mankowski, Das Internet im Internationalen Vertrags- und Deliktsrecht, RabelsZ 63 (1999), 203

Mankowski, Internet und besondere Aspekte des Internationalen Vertragsrechts (I), CR 1999, 512

Mankowski, Internet und besondere Aspekte des Internationalen Vertragsrechts (II), CR 1999, 581

Mankowski, Die Qualifikation der culpa in contrahendo – Nagelprobe für den Vertragsbegriff des europäischen IZPR und IPR, IPRax 2003, 127

Mankowski, Jurisdiction and Enforcement in the Information Society, in: Ruth Nielsen/Sandfeld Jacobsen/Trzaskowski (eds.), EU Electronic Commerce Law (2004), p. 125

Mankowski, Internationale Zuständigkeit und anwendbares Recht, in: FS Andreas Heldrich (2005), p. 867

Mankowski, Der europäische Erfüllungsortsgerichtsstand bei grenzüberschreitenden Anwaltsverträgen, AnwBl 2006, 806

Mankowski, Mehrere Lieferorte beim Erfüllungsortsgerichtsstand unter Art. 5 Nr. 1 lit. b EuGVVO, IPRax 2007, 404

Mankowski, Der europäische Erfüllungsortsge-

richtsstand nach Art. 5 Nr. 1 lit. b EuGVVO und Transportverträge, TranspR 2008, 67

Mankowski, Commercial Agents under European Jurisdiction Rules, (2008) 11 Yb. PIL 19

Mankowski, Der Erfüllungsortsbegriff unter Art. 5 Nr. 1 lit. b EuGVVO, IHR 2009, 46

Mankowski, Der Erfüllungsortsbegriff unter Art. 5 Nr. 1 lit. b EuGVVO, Ausgangs- und Bestimmungsort sind Erfüllungsorte im europäischen Internationalen Zivilprozessrecht, TranspR 2009, 303

Mankowski, Der Erfüllungsortsbegriff unter Art. 5 Nr. 1 lit. b EuGVVO, Internationale Zuständigkeit am Erfüllungsort bei Softwareentwicklungsverträgen, CR 2010, 137

Mankowski, Der Erfüllungsortsbegriff unter Art. 5 Nr. 1 lit. b EuGVVO, Der Immobilienbewertungsvertrag im europäischen Internationalen Privat- und Prozessrecht, in: FS Stanisława Kalus (2010), p. 287

Mankowski, Der Erfüllungsortsbegriff unter Art. 5 Nr. 1 lit. b EuGVVO, EuGVVO/revLugÜ und CISG im Zusammenspiel – insbesondere beim Erfüllungsortsgerichtsstand, in: FS Ingeborg Schwenzer (2011), p. 1175

Mari, Equo processo e competenza in materia contrattuale, in: Liber Fausto Pocar (2009), p. 673

Markus, Der Vertragsgerichtsstand gemäss Verordnung "Brüssel I" und revidiertem LugÜ nach der EuGH-Entscheidung Color Drack, ZSR 2007 I 319

Markus, Tendenzen beim materiellrechtlichen Vertragserfüllungsort im internationalen Zivilverfahrensrecht (2009)

Markus, Vertragsgerichtsstände nach Art. 5 Ziff. 1 revLugÜ/EuGVVO – ein EuGH zwischen Klarheit und grosser Komplexität, AJP 2010, 971

Markus, Erfüllungsortsvereinbarungen und Konzentrationsprinzip beim Vertragsgerichtsstand unter dem System von Brüssel und Lugano, IPRax 2015, 277

Martiny, Internationale Zuständigkeit für "vertragliche Streitigkeiten", in: FS Reinhold Geimer (2002), p. 641

Martiny, Einseitige verpflichtende Rechtsgeschäfte und Gewinnzusagen im Internationalen Privat- und Prozessrecht, in: Księga pamiątkowa Profesora Maksymiliana Pazdana (2005), p. 189

McGrath, Kleinwort Benson v. Glasgow City Council: A Simple Point of Jurisdiction, (1999) 18 Civ. Just. Q. 41

McGuire, Internationale Zuständigkeit für "isolierte Gewinnzusagen", ecolex 2005, 489

McGuire, Der Gerichtsstand des Erfüllungsorts nach Art. 5 Nr. 1 EuGVO bei Lizenzverträgen, GPR 2010, 97

McGuire, Jurisdiction in Cases Related to a License Contract under Art. 5 (1) Brussels Regulation, Yb. PIL 11 (2009), 453

Meani, Contratto di compravendita internazionale: determinazione della giurisdizione ai sensi dell'art. 5 n. 1 lett. B) del regolamento CE n. 44/2001, Corr. giur. 2007, 1528

Meeusen/Neut, De EEX 1-Verordening en het transportrecht: aspecten van het communautarisering van het Belgisch internationaal procesrecht, in: van Hooydonk (ed.), Actualia zee- en vervoerrecht (Antwerp 2003), p. 37

de Meij, Het forum contractus in zeevervoerszaken: EE-eXit?, TVR 1999, 125

Merlin, La s.c. prende posizione sul "forum destinatae solutionis" nel Regolamento CE 44/2001, Riv. dir. proc. 2007, 1305

Merlin, Il foro speciale die contratti di "compravendita di beni" nel Reg. 44/2001 non trova una definizione univoca nell'intervento della Corte di Giustizia, Riv. dir. proc. 2011, 691

Merrett, Place of Delivery in International Sales Contracts, (2008) 67 Cambridge L.J. 244

Axel Metzger, Zum Erfüllungsortsgerichtsstand bei Kauf- und Dienstleistungsverträgen gemäß der EuGVVO, IPRax 2010, 420

Ernst Mezger, Zur Bestimmung des Erfüllungsortes im Sinne von Art. 5 Nr. 1 EuGVÜ bei einem gegenseitigen Vertrag, IPRax 1987, 346

Micha, Distance Selling – Distinction between the sale of goods and the provision of services for the purposes of Article 5 (1) (b) Brussels I Regulation and determination of the place of delivery, EuLF 2009, I-6

Michaels, Jurisdiction for contracts and torts under the Brussels I Regulation when Arts. 5 (1) and 5 (3) do not designate a place in a Member State, in: Nuyts/Watté (eds.), International Civil Litigation in Europe and Relations with Third States (Bruxelles 2005), p. 129

de Miguel Asensio, El lugar de ejecución de los contratos de prestación de servicios come criterio atri-

butivo de competencia, in: Liber amicorum Alegría Borrás (2013), p. 291

Mittmann, Difficultés d'une interprétation autonome de l'article 5, 1 b) du règlement CE du 22 décembre 2000, Gaz. Pal. 28/29 avril 2010, p. 6

Mittmann, Die Bestimmung des Lieferorts beim Versendungskauf nach Art. 5 Nr. 1 lit. b EuGVVO nach der Entscheidung "Car Trim" des EuGH, IHR 2010, 146

Mittmann, Compétence internationale en matière contractuelle, D. 2011, 834

Mörsdorf-Schulte, Autonome Qualifikation der isolierten Gewinnzusage, JZ 2005, 770

Mumelter, Der Gerichtsstand des Erfüllungsortes im Europäischen Zivilprozessrecht (Wien/Graz 2007)

Peter Arnt Nielsen, Behind and Beyond Brussels I, in: Liber Professorum College of Europe 2005, p. 245

Peter Arnt Nielsen, European Contract Jurisdiction in Need of Reform, Liber Fausto Pocar (Milano 2009), p. 773

Notdurfter/Petruzzino, Luogo di consegna e relativo accordo delle parti nell'ambito del foro comunitario del contratto, Contratto e impresa/Europa 2011, 223

Oberhammer/Slonina, Grenzüberschreitende Gewinnzusagen im europäischen Prozess- und Kollisionsrecht: Gabriel, Engler und die Folgen, in: Studia in honorem Pelayia Yessiou-Faltsi (2007), p. 419

Østergaard, Commercial Agents and Special Jurisdiction, in: Liber amicorum ole Lando (2012), p. 399

Ost, Doppelrelevante Tatsachen im internationalen Zivilverfahrensrecht. Zur Prüfung der internationalen Zuständigkeit bei den Gerichtsständen des Erfüllungsortes und der unerlaubten Handlung (2002)

Karsten Otte, Vertragspflichten nach Seefrachtrecht (Haager-Visby-Regeln) – gerichtsstandsweisende Kraft für Art. 5 Nr. 1 EuGVÜ?, IPRax 2002, 132

von Overbeck, Interprétation traditionelle de l'article 5.-1. des Conventions de Bruxelles et de Lugano: Le coup de grâce?, in: E Pluribus Unum – Liber amicorum Georges A.L. Droz (1996), p. 287

Pålsson, The Unruly Horse of the Brussels and Lugano Conventions: The Forum Solutionis, in: Festskrift til Ole Lando (1997), p. 259

Papp, The End of the Saga Surrounding Article 5 (1) (b) of the Brussels I Regulation, Eur. L. Rpter 2010, 228;

Paredes Pérez, Algunas consideraciones en torno al alcance de la noción autónoma de contrato en derecho internacional privado comunitario, REDI 2006, 319

Peel, Non-Admissibility and Restitution in the European Court of Justice, [1996] LMCLQ 8

Peel, Jurisdiction over Non-Existent Contracts, (1996) 112 L.Q.Rev. 541

Peel, Jurisdiction over Restitutionary Claims, [1998] LMCLQ 22

Peleggi, La competenza giurisdizionale nei contratti per la fornitura di beni da fabbricare o produrre e nella vendita con trasporto: a proposito di una recente pronuncia della Corte di giustizia europea, Dir. comm. int. 24 (2010), 653

Peltzer, Toepassing van art. 2 en art. 5, 1 EEX/ EVEX-Verdrag in internationaal weg- en zeevervoer, ETL 2000, 595

Perrella, Vendita internazionale (in ambito comunitario) e giurisdizione: la Cassazione cambia tutto (e precede la Corte di Giustizia), Dir. mar. 2010, 527

Pertegás, The Notion of Contractual Obligation in Brussels I and Rome I, in: Meeusen/Pertegás/ Straetmans (eds.), Enforcement of International Contracts in the European Union (2004), p. 175

Piltz, Der Gerichtsstand des Erfüllungsortes nach dem EuGVÜ, NJW 1981, 1876

Piltz, Gerichtsstand des Erfüllungsortes in UN-Kaufverträgen, IHR 2006, 53

Piltz, Gerichtsstand bei Verkauf beweglicher Sachen mit mehreren Lieferorten in einem Mitgliedstaat, NJW 2007, 1802

Piltz, Gerichtsstand des Erfüllungsortes in UN-Kaufverträgen, IHR 2008, 166

Piroddi, Incoterms e luogo di consegna dei beni nel regolamento Bruxelles I, RDIPP 2011, 939

Pitel, Jurisdiction over Restitutionary Claims, (1998) 57 Cambridge L.J. 19

Pittaluga, La nozione di "materia contrattuale" e l'ambito di applicazione dell'art. 5.1 della convenzione di Bruxelles del 1968, Dir. mar. 105 (2003), 1304

Pitton, L'article 5, 1, b dans la jurisprudence franco-britannique, ou le droit comparé au secours des compétences spéciales de règlement (CEE) n° 44/ 2001, Clunet 136 (2009), 854

Poggio, Vendita internazionale di beni e foro speziale contrattuale au sensi del Regolamento (CE) 44/2001 del Consiglio dell'Unione Europea, Giur. it. 2005, 1008

Poillot-Peruzzetto, La compétence internationale en matière de contrat d'agence commerciale, Rev. jur. comm. 2007, 48

Polak, Something old, something new, something borrowed, something blue?, Ars Aequi 2009, 400

Porcheron, La fin de la dispersion du contentieux en matière de contrat d'agence commercial, Rev. Lamy dr. aff. juillet-août 2010, 72

Quéguiner, La vente, les objectifs et le système du règlement Bruxelles I, Rev. Lamy dr. aff. juillet-août 2010, 69

Quéguiner, Le juge du contrat dans l'espace européen – Qualification et détermination d'une compétence spéciale (thèse Lyon 3-Jean Moulin 2012)

Queirolo, La forma degli accordi sul foro nella convenzione di Bruxelles del 1968: una recente pronuncia della Corte di giustizia, RDIPP 1997, 601

Ragno, Forum destinatae solutionis e regolamento (CE) n. 44 del 2001: alcuni spunti innovativi dalla giurisprudenza di merito, Giur. mer. 2006, 1413

Queirolo, Convenzione di Vienna e Diritto europeo (2008)

Queirolo, The ECJ and the Concept of "place of Delivery" for Contracts of Sale Involving Carriage of Goods: the Price of Clarity, EuLF 2010, I-121

Rauscher, Verpflichtung und Erfüllungsort in Art. 5 Nr. 1 EuGVÜ unter besonderer Berücksichtigung des Vertragshändlervertrages (1984)

Rauscher, Zuständigkeitsfragen zwischen CISG und Brüssel I, in: FS Andreas Heldrich (2005), p. 933

Rauscher, Internationaler Gerichtsstand des Erfüllungsorts – Abschied von Tessili und de Bloos, NJW 2010, 2251

Reydellet, La pluralité des contrats de distribution et l'article 5.1 du règlement Bruxelles I, RLDA 103 (2015), 46

Reiher, Der Vertragsbegriff im europäischen Internationalen Privatrecht (Frankfurt etc. 2010)

Reinstadler/Reinacher, Der Erfüllungsort bei grenzüberschreitenden Versendungskäufen und Dienstleistungen nach den EuGh-Urteilen Car Trim, Wood Floor und Electrosteel, in: FS Hansjörg Pobitzer (Milano 2012), p. 157

Requejo Isidro, Tessili y Concorde, De Bloos y Leathertex, o la determinación del lugar de la(s) obligación(es) que da(n) base a la demanda, La Ley 2000, 1549

Ribeiro Oertel, Le contrat de distribution intra-communautaire – Les modalités de règlement des litiges: questions sensibles, RJcom 2014, 397

Rochaix, Probleme der gerichtlichen Zuständigkeitsregel für vertragliche Ansprüche im europäischen Zivilprozessrecht, in: Liber discipulorum Kurt Siehr (2001), p. 187

Rodriguez, Beklagtenwohnsitz und Erfüllungsort im europäischen IZVR (Zürich 2005)

Rogerson, Plus ça change? Article 5.1 of the Regulation on Jurisdiction and the Recognition and Enforcement of Judgements, [2001] Cambridge Yb. Eur. L. 383

Romano, Le for au lieu d'exécution dans la jurisprudence récente de la Cour de Justice de l'Union européenne, in: Bonomi/Tappy/Gaulis (éds.), Nouvelle procédure civile et espace judiciaire européen (Genève 2012), p. 63

Rommelaere, De internationale bevoegdheid inzake verbintenissen uit overeenkomst, TBH 2003, 103

Herbert Roth, Der Versendungskauf bei Art. 5 Nr. 1 lit. b EuGVO, in: FS Daphne-Ariane Simotta (2012), p. 495

Wulf-Henning Roth, Persönlichkeitsschutz im Internet: Internationale Zuständigkeit und anwendbares Recht, IPRax 2013, 215

Rutten, I.P.R.-aspecten met betrekking tot de betaling van de koopprijs – Art. 5, 1° b) EEX-Verordening, R.W. 2002-2003, 666

Salerno, L'incidenza del diritto applicabile nell' accertamento del forum destinatae solutionis, Riv. dir. int. 1995, 76

Salerno, L'incidenza del diritto applicabile nell'accertamento del forum destinatae solutionis, in: Scritti degli allievi in memoria di Giuseppe Barile (1995), p. 613

Samad, Article 5 (1) of the Brussels Regulation on Jurisdiction and the Recognition and Enforcement of Judgments in Civil and Commercial Matters, 2010 ILT 233 (Part I) and 247 (Part II)

Samyn, De verhouding tussen art. 5, 1 a) en art. 5, 1 b) EEX-Verordening, R.W. 2006-2007, 872

Santori, Spunti in merito alle interpretazione dell'art. 5, punto 1, della Convenzione di Bruxelles del 27 settembre 1968, Europe e dir. priv. 2006, 333

Savini, Delocalizzazione del contratto stipulato su Internet – Problemi di giurisdizione e legge applicabile, Contratto e impresa/Europa 2002, 1131

Schack, Der Erfüllungsort im deutschen, ausländischen und internationalen Privat- und Zivilprozessrecht (1985)

Schack, Abstrakte Erfüllungsortvereinbarungen: form- oder sinnlos?, IPRax 1996, 247

Friederike Schäfer, Der Erfüllungsort nach Art. 5 EuGVVO bei Vertriebsverträgen, ecolex 2014, 605

Schlosser, Europäisch-autonome Interpretation des Begriffs "Vertrag oder Ansprüche aus einem Vertrag" im Sinne von Art. 5 Nr. 1 EuGVÜ, IPRax 1984, 65

Schoibl, Ausgewählte Zuständigkeitstatbestände in der Rechtsprechung des EuGH: Die gerichtlichen Zuständigkeiten am Erfüllungsort des Vertrages nach Art. 5 Nr. 1 und die Zuständigkeitsvereinbarung nach Art. 17 des Brüsseler und des Luganer Übereinkommens, in: Bajons/Mayr/Zeiler (eds.), Die Übereinkommen von Brüssel und Lugano (Wien 1997), p. 61

Günter Christian Schwarz, Insolvenzverwalterklagen bei eigenkapitalersetzenden Gesellschafterleistungen nach der Verordnung (EG) Nr 44/2001 (EuGVVO), NZI 2002, 290

Schwenzer, Internationaler Gerichtsstand für die Kaufpreisklage, IPRax 1989, 274

von der Seipen, Italienische Aktionäre vor deutschen Gerichten – Treuepflicht des Gesellschafters und Art. 5 Nr. 1 EuGVVO, in: FS Erik Jayme (2004), p. 859

Serranò, Cancellazione del volo e giurisdizione in materia di trasporto aereo: il caso Air Baltic, RDIPP 2010, 77

Shine, The Problem of Place of Performance in Contract under the Brussels I Regulation: Can One Size Fit All?, [2011] ICCLR 20

Silvestri, L'interpretazione del "luogo di consegna" ai sensi del novellato art. 5 n.1 lett. B Reg. 44/2001: qualche osservazione sui limiti del criterio fattuale, Int'l. Lis 2005, 132

Silvestri, Brevi note in tema di proroga i competenza e "forum contractus" nel passaggio dalaa convenzione di Bruxelles del 27 septtembre 1968 al regolamento 44/2001, Foro it. 2006 I col. 2187

Sindres, De la qualification de un contrat-cadre de distribution au regard des règles communautaires de compétence, RCDIP 97 (2008), 863

Sindres, Compétence judiciaire, reconaissance et exécution des decisions en matière civile et commerciale – Compétence, Règles ordinaires de compétence, Option de compétence en matière contractuelle, Article 7, § 1, du règlement (UE) n° 1215/2012, Jur-Cl. Dr. int. fasc. 584-130 (mars 2014)

Spellenberg, Der Gerichtsstand des Erfüllungsortes im europäischen Gerichtsstands- und Vollstreckungsübereinkommen, ZZP 91 (1978), 38

Spellenberg, Die Vereinbarung des Erfüllungsortes und Art. 5 Nr. 1 EuGVÜ, IPRax 1981, 75

Stadler, Vertraglicher und deliktischer Gerichtsstand im europäischen Zivilprozessrecht, in: FS Hans-Joachim Musielak (2004), p. 569

Ansgar Staudinger, Internet-Buchung von Reisen und Flügen, RRa 2007, 155

Ansgar Staudinger, Gemeinschaftsrechtlicher Erfüllungsortsgerichtsstand bei grenzüberschreitender Luftbeförderung, IPRax 2008, 493

Ansgar Staudinger, Streitfragen zum Erfüllungsortsgerichtsstand im Luftverkehr, IPRax 2010, 140

Stoffel, Place of Performance Jurisdiction and Plaintiff's Interests in Contemporary Societies, Eur. J. L. Reform 4 (2002), 185

Stoll, Gerichtsstand des Erfüllungsortes nach Art. 5 Nr. 1 EuGVÜ bei strittigem Vertragsschluß, IPRax 1983 252

Henri Storme, Concretisering van "plaats van levering" in art. 5, 1, b) EEX-Verordening geen sinecure, R.W. 2009-10, 409

Storp, Internationale Zuständigkeit des Erfüllungsorts bei Verträgen mit französischen Vertretern, RIW 1999, 823

Michael Stürner, Internationale Zuständigkeit bei Schadensersatzklage wegen Nichtabgabe einer Willenserklärung, IPRax 2006, 450

Sznajder-Peroń, Znaczenie koncepji świadczenia charakterystycznego w określaniu właściwości sądu i prawa, in: Księga dedykowana Profesorowi Dieterowi Martiny (2014), p. 281

Takahashi, Jurisdiction in Matters Relating to Contract: Article 5 (1) of the Brussels Convention and Regulation, (2002) 27 Eur. L. Rev. 530

Theis/Bronnen, Der Gerichtsstand des Erfüllungsortes im Europäischen Zivilprozessrecht unter besonderer Berücksichtigung des Werklieferungsvertrages, EWS 2004, 350

Clemens Thiele, Erfüllungsort und Honorarklagen österreichischer Anwälte nach Art. 5 EuGVÜ/LGVÜ, öAnwBl 2000, 258

Thole, Die internationale Zuständigkeit für Vertragsstrafe- und Unterlassungsklagen von Wettbewerbsverbänden, IPRax 2015, 65

Thorn, Gerichtsstand des Erfüllungsorts und intertemporales Zivilverfahrensrecht, IPRax 2004, 354

Tichadou, Conventions internationales unifiant le droit matériel et détermination du lieu d'exécution au sens de l'article 5-1° de la Convention de Bruxelles, RTDE 1995, 95

Tiefenthaler, LGVÜ: Gerichtsstand am "Erfüllungsort" des Bereicherungsanspruchs?, ÖJZ 1998, 544

Tuo, Gli effetti (indesiderati?) dell'interpretazione tra le norme comunitarie in materia di competenza giurisdizionale e la Convenzione di Vienna del 1980 sulla vendita internazionale, Dir. mar. 109 (2007), 1080

Ubertazzi, IP-Lizenzverträge und die EG-Zuständigkeitsverordnung, GRUR Int. 2010, 103

Vaccari, Criteri per la determinazione della giurisdizione in materia contrattuale, Dir. mar. 103 (2001), 682

Valloni, Der Gerichtsstand des Erfüllungsortes nach Luganer und Brüsseler Übereinkommen (1998)

van der Hof, Internationale on-line overeenkomsten (Tilburg 2002)

Virgo, Jurisdiction over Unjust Enrichment Claims, (1998) 114 L.Q.Rev. 386

Vlek, Forum contractus Revisited: Twee mogelijke interpretaties van Art. 5 sub 1 onder b EEX-Verordening in het licht van de arresten Car Trim en Electrosteel, in: IPR in de Spiegel van Paul Vlas (2012), p. 277

Rolf Wagner, Die Entscheidungen des EuGH zum Gerichtsstand des Erfüllungsorts nach der EuGVVO – unter besonderer Berücksichtigung der Rechtssache Rehder, IPRax 2010, 143

Hannes Wais, Die Bestimmung des Erfüllungsortes nach Art. 5 Nr. 1 lit. b 2. Spiegelstrich EuGVVO bei Dienstleistungserbringung in verschiedenen Mitgliedstaaten, GPR 2010, 256

Hannes Wais, Internationale Zuständigkeit bei gesellschaftsrechtlichen Ansprüchen aus Geschäftsführerhaftung gemäß § 64 Abs. 2 Satz 1 GmbHG a.F./§ 64 Satz 1 GmbHG n.F., IPRax 2011, 138

Hannes Wais, Der Europäische Erfüllungsortsgerichtsstand für Dienstleistungsverträge – Zur Auslegung des Art. 5 Nr. 1 lit. b 2. Spiegelstrich EuGVO (2013)

Hannes Wais, Geld oder Entgelt? Zur Entgeltlichkeit

der Dienstleistung im Sinne von Art. 5 Nr. 1 lit. b
2. Spiegelstrich EuGVO, GPR 2014, 165
Johannes Weber, Internationale Zuständigkeit und
Gläubigerschutz nach dem Wegzug von Gesell-
schaften, ZvglRWiss 107 (2008), 193
Johannes Weber, Gesellschaftsrecht und Gläubiger-
schutz im Internationalen Zivilverfahrensrecht
(2011)
Wedemann, Die internationale Zuständigkeit
für Haftungsklagen gegen Gesellschafter und
Geschäftsführer, ZEuP 2014, 861
Marc-Philippe Weller, Internationale Zuständigkeit
für mitgliedsschaftsbezogene Klagen nach der
Brüssel I-VO, ZGR 2012, 606
Wendenburg/Maximilian Schneider, Vertraglicher
Gerichtsstand für Ansprüche aus Delikt?, NJW 2014,
1633
Wipping, Der europäische Gerichtsstand des Erfül-
lungsortes – Art. 5 Nr. 1 EuGVVO (2008)
Christian Ulrich Wolf, Feststellungsklage und An-
spruchskonkurrenz im Rahmen von Art. 5 Nr. 1 und
Nr. 3 LugÜ, IPRax 1999, 82
Graf Wrangel, Der Gerichtsstand des Erfüllungsortes
im deutschen, italienischen und europäischen Recht
(1988)
Wurmnest, UN-Kaufrecht und Gerichtsstand des
Erfüllungsorts bei Nichterfüllung einer Alleinver-
triebsvereinbarung durch den Lieferanten, IHR
2005, 107
Zimmer, Ende der Konzernhaftung in "internationalen" Fällen?, IPRax 1998, 187
Zogg, Accumulation of Contractual and Tortious
Causes of Action under the Judgments Regulation,
(2013) 9 JPrIL 39.

To (2):

Marie-Élodie Ancel, Contrefaçon de marque sur un
site web: quelle compétence intracommunautaire
pour lex tribunaux français?, in: Études à la mémoire
du Xavier Linant de Bellefonds (2007), p. 1
Arenas García, Responsabilidad de accionistas y
administradores por las deudas sociales: cuestiones
de competencia judicial internacional, La Ley UE
nº 9, 2013, p. 35
García, Tribunales competentes en materia de in-
fracciones de derechos patrimoniales de autor co-
metidas a través de Internet, La Ley UE nº 11, 2014,
p. 36

Ashton/Vollrath, Choice of Court and Applicable
Law in Tortious Actions for Breach of Community
Competition Law, ZWeR 2006, 1
Azzi, Tribunal compétent et loi applicable en matière
d'atteintes aux droits de la personnalité commises
sur Internet, D. 2012, 1279
Azzi, Contrefaçon de marque sur Internet: inter-
prétation de l'article 5 § 3 du règlement Bruxelles I,
D. 2012, 1926
Azzi, Compétence juridictionelle en cas d'atteinte au
droit d'auteur commise au moyen d'un site internet:
la Cour de justice adopte le critère de l'accessibilité,
D. 2014, 411
Birgit Bachmann, Der Gerichtsstand der unerlaub-
ten Handlung im Internet, IPRax 1998, 179
Banholzer, Die internationale Gerichtszuständigkeit
bei Urheberrechtsverletzungen im Internet (2011)
Basedow, Der Handlungsort im internationalen
Kartellrecht – Ein juristisches Chamäleon auf dem
Weg vom Völkerrecht zum internationalen Zivilprozessrecht, in: Wettbewerbspolitik und Kartell-
recht in der Marktwirtschaft – 50 Jahre FIW 1960–
2010 (2010), p. 129
Moritz Becker, Kartelldeliktsrecht: § 826 BGB als
"Zuständigkeitshebel" im Anwendungsbereich der
EuGVVO?, EWS 2008, 228
Behr, Internationale Tatortzuständigkeit für vor-
beugende Unterlassungsklagen bei Wettbewerbs-
verstößen, GRUR Int. 1992, 604
Christian Berger, Die internationale Zuständigkeit
bei Urheberrechtsverletzungen in Internet-Websites
aufgrund des Gerichtsstands der unerlaubten
Handlung nach Art. 5 Nr. 3 EuGVO, GRUR Int.
2005, 465
Bettinger/Thum, Territoriales Markenrecht im Glo-
bal Village, GRUR Int. 1999, 659
Blobel, Der europäische Deliktsgerichtsstand und
reine Vermögensschäden, EuLF 2004, 187
Bogdan, Contract or Tort under Article 5 of the
Brussels I Regulation: Tertium non Datur?, in: FS
Bernd von Hoffmann (2011), p. 561
Bogdan, Defamation on the Internet, *forum* delicti
and the E-Commerce-Directive: Some Comments
on the ECJ Judgment in the eDate Case, Yb. PIL 13
(2011), 483
Bollée/Haftel, Les nouveaux (dés) équilibres de la
compétence internationale en matière de cyberdelits

après l'arrêt eDate Advertising et Martinez, D. 2012, 1285

Bossi, Le azioni di accertamento negativo della contraffazione ed il forum commissi delicti, Giur. it. 2014, 588

Braggion, Sulla giurisdizione per responsabilità extracontrattuale nei confronti di fabriccante, Dir. comm. int. 2011, 588

Brand, Persönlichkeitsrechtsverletzungen im Internet, E-Commerce und "Fliegender Gerichtsstand", NJW 2012, 127

Brenn, Rechtsverletzung im Internet, ÖJZ 2012, 493

Briggs, The Uncertainty of Special Jurisdiction, [1996] LMCLQ 27

Bukow, Verletzungsklagen aus gewerblichen Schutzrechten (2003)

Busnelli, Itinerari europei nella "terra di nessuno tra contratto e fatto illecito": la responsibilità da infomazioni inesatte, Contratto e impresa 1991, 564

Callori, Giurisdizione im materia di responsabilità extracontrattuale: l'art. 5 n. 3 della convenzione di Bruxelles del 1968 e la questione della locazione del forum damni, RDIPP 1997, 614

van Calster, ÖFAB: de niet steds heldere verhouding tussen de EEX en de insolventieverordening, TBH 2015, 64

Calvo Caravaca/Carrascosa González, Los daños financieros transfronterizos, Rev. Der. Mercantil 292 (2014), 51

Carpi, Observations on Jurisdiction in Cases of Damages for Torts, in: FS Rolf Stürner (2013), p. 1191

Cavallaro, Accertamento negativo di contraffazione e tutela cautelare, Dir. ind. 1997, 828

Cebrián Salvat, Estrategia procesal y litigación internacional en la Unión Europea: distinción ente materia contractual y extracontractual, Cuad. Der. Trans. 6 (2) (2014), 315

de Clavière, De la notion de fait dommageable en droit international privé européen et de la responsaibilité du fait des produits défectueux, Rev. Lamy dr. aff. 92 (2014), 60

Coester-Waltjen, Internationale Zuständigkeit bei Persönlichkeitsrechtsverletzungen, in: FS Rolf A. Schütze zum 65. Geb. (1999), p. 175

Cordero Álvarez, Algunos problemas de aplicación de Art. 5.3° del Reglamento 44/2001, AEDIPr 2009, 411

de Cristofaro, La Corte di Giustizia tra forum shopping e forum non conveniens per le azioni risarcatorie da illecito, Giur. it. 1997 I col. 5

Davì, Der italienische Kassationshof und der Gerichtsstand des Ortes des schädigenden Ereignisses nach Art. 5 Nr. 3 EuGVÜ bei reinen Vermögensschäden, IPRax 1999, 484

Dehnert, Der deliktische Erfolgsort bei reinen Vermögensschäden und Persönlichkeitsrechtsverletzungen (2011)

Diederichsen, Die internationale Zuständigkeit der französischen Gerichte bei wettbewerbs- und markenrechtlichen Verstößen im Internet, RIW 2008, 53

Domej, Negative Feststellungsklagen im Deliktsgerichtsstand, IPRax 2008, 550

Domej, Negative Feststellungsklagen am Deliktsgerichtsstand: Der EuGH schafft Klarheit, ecolex 2013, 123

Dornis, Von Kalfelis zu Brogsitter – Künftig enge Grenzen der Annexkompetenz im europäischen Vertrags- und Deliktsgerichtsstand, GPR 2014, 352

Duintjer Tebbens, Het "forum delicti" voor professionele produktaansprakelijdheid in het Europese Hof van Justitie: een initieel antwoort over initiële schade, NIPR 2010, 206

Dutta, Ein besonderer Gerichtsstand für die Geschäftsführung ohne Auftrag in Europa?, IPRax 2011, 134

Ebner, Markenschutz im internationalen Privat- und Zivilprozessrecht (2004)

Ehmann/Thorn, Erfolgsorte bei grenzüberschreitenden Persönlichkeitsrechtsverletzungen, AfP 1996, 20

Endrös, Gerichtsstand und Haftung europäischer Zulieferer für reine Vermögensschäden in Produkthaftungsfällen nur nach französischem Recht?, PHI 2011, 102

Fach Gómez, Acciones preventivas en supuestos de contaminación transfronteriza y aplicabilidad del articulo 5.3 Convenio de Bruselas, ZEuS 1999, 583

Fähndrich/Ibbeken, Gerichtszuständigkeit und anwendbares Recht im Falle grenzüberschreitender Verletzungen (Verletzungshandlungen) der Rechte des geistigen Eigentums, GRUR Int. 2003, 616

Fenge, Zur europäischen internationalen Zuständigkeit in Fällen der Haftung für eine Schädigung in Vertragsnähe, in: Studia in honorem Pelayia Yessiou-Faltsi (2007), p. 79

Feraci, Diffamazione internazionale a mezzo di

Internet: quale foro competente? Alcune considerazioni sull sentenze eDate, Riv. dir. int. 2012, 461

Feraci, Diffamazione internazionale emezzo intenret: Quale foro competente?, Riv. dir. int. 2012, 461

Federica Ferrari, Le torpedo e le recente giurisprudenza della Corte di giustizia, Riv. trim. dir. proc. civ. 2013, 1126

Fitchen, Allocating Jurisdiction in Private Competition Law Claims within the EU, (2006) 13 Maastricht J. Eur. & Comp. L. 381

Franzina, L'elusiva proiezione geografica del danno meramente patrimoniale: la responsabilità da informazioni inesatte tra forum commissi delicti e forum destinatae solutionis, Int'l. Lis 2004, 126

Freitag, Internationale Zuständigkeit für Schadensersatzklagen aus Insolvenzverschleppungshaftung, ZIP 2014, 302

Gabellini, La competenza giurisdizionale nel caso di lesione di un diritto della personalità attraverso internet, Riv. trim. dir. proc. civ. 2014, 271

Garavaglia, Azione di accertamento negativo e forum delicti nel Regolamento CE n. 44/2001, Riv. dir. proc. 2013, 1245

Garber, Die internationale Zuständigkeit für Klagen aufgrund einer Persönlichkeitsrechtsverletzung im Internet, ÖJZ 2012, 108

Garber, Zur internationalen Zuständigkeit bei Streitigkeiten wegen Persönlichkeits-, Immaterialgüter- und Lauterkeitsrechtsverletzungen, ÖBl 2014, 100

Gardella, Giurisdizione su illeciti senza danno – l'applicazione dell'art. 5 n. 3 convenzione di Bruxelles a le azione preventive, Int'l. Lis 2003, 22

Gehri, Vertrag – quasi? Abgrenzungsprobleme und Prozessplanung nach Art. 5 Nr 1 und 3 LugÜ, in: FS Ivo Schwander (St. Gallen 2011), p. 699

Geimer, Die Gerichtspflichtigkeit des Beklagten nach Art. 5 Nr. 1 und Nr. 3 EuGVÜ bei Anspruchskonkurrenz, IPRax 1986, 80

Gillies, Jurisdiction for cross-border breach of personality and defamation, (2012) 61 ICLQ 1007

Gioia, Sulla distribuzione della competenza internazionale nelle liti da diffamazione tramite internet, Riv. dir. proc. 2012, 1317

Girsberger, Erfolg mit dem Erfolgsort bei Vermögensdelikten?, in: Liber amicorum Kurt Siehr (2000), p. 219

Grabinski, Zur Bedeutung des EuGVÜ und des Lu-

ganerÜ in Rechtsstreitigkeiten über Patentverletzungen, GRUR Int. 2001, 199

Grannino, Italian torpedo actions can sink cross-border patent infringement proceedings, (2014) 9 J. IP Law & Practice 172

Greaves, Art. 5 (3) of the 1968 EC Convention on Jurisdiction and Enforcement of Judgments in Civil and Commerical Matters, in: FS Hilmar Fenge (1997), p. 33

Grünberger, Zuständigkeitsbegründender Erfolgsort bei Urheberrechtsverletzungen, IPRax 2015, 56

Haas, Die zuständigkeitsrechtliche Verortung gesellschaftsrechtlicher Gläubigerschutzansprüche, NZG 2013, 1161

Hackbarth, EuGH "Coty": Teilnehmerhandeln im Ausland und internationale Zuständigkeit deutscher Gemeinschaftsmarkengerichte, GRUR-Prax 2014, 320

van Haersolte-van Hof, Zeevervoer en artikel 5 (3) EEX, NIPR 2000, 386

Günter Hager/Felix Hartmann, Internationale Zuständigkeit für vorbeugende Unterlassungsklagen, IPRax 2005, 266

Hartley, Cross-border privacy injunctions: The EU dimension, (2012) 128 L.Q.Rev. 197

Hausmann, Die Verletzung gewerblicher Schutzrechte im europäischen Internationalen Privat- und Verfahrensrecht, EuLF 2003, 278

Heiderhoff, Der Erfolgsort bei der Persönlichkeitsverletzung im Internet, in: FS Dagmar Coester-Waltjen (2015), p. 413

von Hein, Internationale Zuständigkeit und anwendbares Recht bei grenzüberschreitendem Kapitalanlagebetrug, IPRax 2006, 460

von Hein, Die Produkthaftung des Zulieferers im Europäischen Internationalen Zivilprozessrecht, IPRax 2010, 330

von Hein, Verstärkung des Kapitalanlegerschutzes: Das Europäische Zivilprozessrecht auf dem Prüfstand, EuZW 2011, 369

von Hein, Finanzkrise und Internationales Privatrecht, BerDGfIR 45 (2011), 369

von Hein, Der Gerichtsstand der unerlaubten Handlung bei arbeitsteiliger Tatbegehung im europäischen Zivilprozessrecht, IPRax 2013, 505

Heinze, Der europäische Deliktsgerichtsstand bei Lauterkeitsverstößen, IPRax 2009, 231

Heinze, Surf global, sue local! Der europäische Klägergerichtsstand bei Persönlichkeitsrechtsverletzungen im Internet, EuZW 2011, 947

Hess, Der Schutz der Privatsphäre im Europäischen Zivilverfahrensrecht, JZ 2012, 189

von Hinden, Internationale Zuständigkeit und anwendbares Recht bei Persönlichkeitsrechtsverletzungen im Internet, ZEuP 2012, 940

Jochen Hoffmann, Internationale Deliktszuständigkeit bei Markenrechtsverletzungen im Internet, MarkenR 2013, 417

Hootz, Durchsetzung von Persönlichkeits- und Immaterialgüterrechten bei grenzüberschreitenden Verletzungen in Europa (2004)

Peter Huber, Persönlichkeitsschutz gegenüber Massenmedien im Rahmen des europäischen Zivilprozessrechts, ZEuP 1996, 300

Peter Huber, Haftung für Kapitalanlageprodukte: Lugano-Übereinkommen und Fragen des internationalen Insolvenzrechts, IPRax 2015, 403

Stefan Huber, Ausländische Broker vor deutschen Gerichten, IPRax 2009, 134

Hye-Knudsen, Marken-, Patent- und Urheberrechtsverletzungen im europäischen Internationalen Zivilprozessrecht (2005)

Joubert, Cyber-torts and personal jurisdiction: The Paris Court of Appeal makes a stand, (2009) 58 ICLQ 476

Junker, Der Gerichtsstand des Deliktsortes nach der Brüssel I-VO bei der Verletzung von Persönlichkeitsrechten im Internet, in: FS Helmut Rüßmann (2013), p. 811

Kerameus, Recenti sviluppi della competenza giurisdizionale in materia extracontrattuale nella convenzione di Bruxelles, Riv. dir. proc. 1995, 1161

Kernen, Persönlichkeitsrechtsverletzungen im Internet (2014)

Kernen, Persönlichkeitsrechtsverletzungen im Internet (Zürich/St. Gallen 2014)

Kessedjian, Les actions collectives en dommages et intérêts pour infraction aux règles communautaires de la concurrence et le droit international privé, in: Liber Fausto Pocar (2009), p. 533

Kieninger, Internationale Zuständigkeit bei der Verletzung ausländischer Immaterialgüterrechte, GRUR Int. 1998, 280

Kiethe, Internationale Tatortzuständigkeit bei unerlaubter Handlung – die Problematik des Vermögensschadens, NJW 1994, 222

Kindler, Konzernhaftung zwischen Vertrag und Delikt – Die internationale Gerichtszuständigkeit bei Verstößen gegen gesetzliche Mitteilungspflichten, IPRax 2014, 486

Markus Köhler, Der fliegende Gerichtsstand – Die Bestimmung des zuständigen Gerichts bei ubiquitären Rechtsverletzungen, WRP 2013, 1130

Koppenol-Laforce, De plaats waar het schadebrengende feit zich heeft voorgedaan: art. 5 sub 3 EEX, JutD 2/2000, 16

Kosmehl, Welchen Wert hat der Gerichtsstand der unerlaubten Handlung im Europäischen Zivilprozessrecht?, in: Liber amicorum Thomas Rauscher (2005), p. 79

Kreuzer/Klötgen, Die Shevill-Entscheidung des EuGH, IPRax 1997, 90

Krog, Jurisdiction pursuant to the Lugano Convention art. 5.3 applied on defamatory statements in TV broadcasting, IPRax 2004, 154

Kubis, Internationale Zuständigkeit bei Persönlichkeits- und Immaterialgüterrechtsverletzungen (1999)

Kuipers, Case note, (2012) 49 CML Rev. 1211

Kuipers, Het internet en de Brussel I Verordening: een kwestie van Luxemburgse wispelturigheid?, NIPR 2012, 390

Kurtz, Zum Inlandsbezug der Marke im Internet, IPRax 2004, 107

Lagarde, Competence juridictionelle en matière de délit commis par un organe de presse diffusé dans plusieurs Etats, RCDIP 85 (1996), 487

Lange, Der internationale Gerichtsstand der unerlaubten Handlung nach dem EuGVÜ bei Verletzungen von nationalen Kennzeichen, WRP 2000, 940

Lederer, Der "Gerichtsstand am Interessenmittelpunkt" – ein zeitgemäßer Gerichtsstand, K&R 2011, 791

Matthias Lehmann, Where does economic loss occur?, (2011) 7 JPrIL 527

Leipold, Neues zum Gerichtsstand der unerlaubten Handlung nach europäischem Zivilprozessrecht, in: Studia in honorem Németh János (2003), p. 633

Lindacher, Internationale Zuständigkeit in Wettbewerbssachen, in: FS Hideo Nakamura (Tokyo 1996), p. 323

Lindacher, Die internationale Dimension lauterkeitsrechtlicher Unterlassungsansprüche: Marktterritorialität versus Universalität, GRUR Int. 2008, 453

Lindacher, Delikt und Vertrag – Zur Zuständigkeit deutscher Wettbewerbsgerichte für Unterlassungsund Vertragsstrafeklagen bei Zuwiderhandlungen nach internationaler Unterwerfung, in: FS Kontantinos Kerameus, vol. I (Athens/Bruxelles 2009), p. 709

Lindacher, Internationales Wettbewerbsverfahrensrecht (2009)

Lorente Martínez, Daños causados pro los productos y competencia judicial internacional en el Unión Euopea, Cuad. Der Trans. 6 (2) (2014), 351

Mäsch, Vitamine für Kartellopfer – Forum shopping im europäischen Kartelldeliktsrecht, IPRax 2005, 509

Helena Isabel Maier, Marktortanknüpfung im internationalen Kartelldeliktsrecht (2011)

Mankowski, Zur Anwendbarkeit des Art. 5 Nr. 3 EuGVÜ auf vorbeugende Unterlassungsklagen, EWS 1994, 305

Mankowski, Schadensersatzklagen bei Kartelldelikten – Fragen des anwendbaren Rechts und der internationalen Zuständigkeit (2012)

Mankowski, Der europäische Gerichtsstand des Tatortes aus Art. 5 Nr. 3 EuGVVO bei Schadensersatzklagen bei Kartelldelikten, WuW 2012, 797

Mansel, Gerichtliche Prüfungsbefugnisse im forum delicti, IPRax 1989, 84

Mari, Problematica del forum damni nella Convenzione di Bruxelles del 27 settembre 1968 concernente la competenza giurisdizionale e l'esecuzione delle decisioni in materia civile e commerciale, in: Mélanges Fritz Sturm (1999), p. 1573

Marino, La violazione die diritti della personalità nella cooperazione giudiziaria civile europea, RDIPP 2012, 363

McGuire, Internationale Zuständigkeit bei Markenverletzung durch Keyword-Advertising, ZEuP 2014, 160

McLachlan/Nygh (eds.), Transnational Tort Litigation (1996)

Michaels, Jurisdiction for contracts and torts under the Brussels I Regulation when Arts. 5 (1) and 5 (3) do not designate a place in a Member State, in: Nuyts/Watté (eds.), International Civil Litigation in Europe and Relations with Third States (Bruxelles 2005), p. 129

Michailidou, Internationale Zuständigkeit bei vorbeugenden Verbandsklagen, IPRax 2003, 223

de Miguel Asensio, Cross-Border Adjudication of Intellectual Property Rights and Competition between Jurisdictions, AIDA 2007, 105

Michael Müller, Der zuständigkeitsrechtliche Handlungsort des Delikts bei mehreren Beteiligten in der EuGVVO, EuZW 2013, 130

Müller-Feldhammer, Der Deliktsgerichtsstand des Art. 5 Nr. 3 EuGVÜ im internationalen Wettbewerbsrecht, EWS 1998, 162

Muir Watt, De la localisation d'un préjudice patrimonial subi à l'occasion de placements financier à l'étranger, RCDIP 94 (2005), 334

Negri, Mero accertamento negativo dell'illecito antritrust e forum damni, Int'l. Lis 2013, 70

Wilfried Neuhaus, Das Übereinkommen über die gerichtliche Zuständigkeit und die Vollstreckung gerichtlicher Entscheidungen in Zivil- und Handelssachen vom 27.9.1968 (EuGVÜ) und das Luganer Übereinkommen vom 16.9.1988, soweit hiervon Streitigkeiten des gewerblichen Rechtsschutzes betroffen sind, MittPat 1996, 257

Sophie Neumann, Die Haftung der Intemediäre im Internationalen Immaterialgüterrecht (2014)

Nikas, Das europäische Zuständigkeitsrecht bei Persönlichkeitsrechtsverletzungen in den Massenmedien und im Internet, in: FS Peter Gottwald (2014), p. 477

Nisi, La giurisdizione in materia di responsabilità delle agenzie di rating alla luce del regolamento Bruxelles I, RDIPP 2013, 385

Oró Martínez, Las acciones déclarativas negativos y el art. 5.3° del Regolamento Bruselas I, AEDIPr 2011, 198

Ortiz Vidal, Ilícitos a distancia y bienes immateriales: la precisión del hecho causal y del concepto del "daño directo" y "daño indirecto", CDT 6 (2) (2014), 362

Karsten Otte, Internationale Zuständigkeit und Territorialitätsprinzip: Wo liegen die Grenzen der Deliktszuständigkeit bei der Verletzung eines europäischen Patents?, IPRax 2001, 315

Pansch, Der Gerichtsstand der unerlaubten Handlung bei der grenzüberschreitenden Verletzung gewerblicher Schutzrechte, EuLF 2000/01, 353

Peifer, Internationale Zuständigkeit nach Art. 5 Nr. 3

EuGVVO und anwendbares Recht bei Marken-rechtsverletzungen, IPRax 2013, 228

Clemens Rufus Pichler, Forum-Shopping für Opfer von Internet-Persönlichkeitsverletzungen, MR 2011, 365

Picht, Von eDate zu Wintersteiger – Die Ausformung des Art. 5 Nr. 3 EuGVVO für Internetdelikte durch die Rechtsprechung des EuGH, GRUR Int. 2013, 19

Pietrobon, Art. 5 note sulla giurisdizione in materia di accertamento negativo della concorrenza sleale, AIDA 1994, 244

Pironon, Dits et non-dits sur la mèthode de focalisation dans le contentieux – contractuel et delictuel – du commerce électronique, Clunet 138 (2011), 915

Rathenau, Das Brüsseler und Lugano-Übereinkommen sowie die Brüssel I-Verordnung in der portugiesischen Rechtsprechung (1992–2006): Der Einfluss eigentypischer Regelungen des nationalen Rechts, ZZP Int. 10 (2005), 195

Raymond, Jurisdiction in Case of Personality Torts Committed over the Internet: A Proposal for a Targeting Test, Yb. PIL 14 (2012/13), 205

Reed, Special Jurisdiction and the Convention: The Case of Domicrest Ltd. v. Swiss Bank Corporation, [1999] Civ. Just. Q. 218

Reed/T.P. Kennedy, International Torts and Shevill: the Ghost of Forum Shopping Yet to Come, [1996] LMCLQ 108

Reichardt, Internationale Zuständigkeit im Gerichtsstand der unerlaubten Handlung bei Verletzung europäischer Patente (2006)

Reymond, Jurisdiction in Cases of Personality Torts Committed over the Internet: A Proposal for a Targeting Test, Yb. PIL 13 (2011), 205

Risso, La responsibilità extracontrattuale della società di rating: riflessioni in tema di competenza giurisdizionale, Dir. comm. int. 2013, 849

Robak, Drei sind einer zuviel: Internationale Gerichtsstände bei Verletzung des Persönlichkeitsrechts im Internet, GRUR-Prax 2011, 257

Rolfi, Dalla competenza alla giurisdizione: le "mobili frontiere" di internet, Corr. giur. 2012, 760

Isabel Roth, Die internationale Zuständigkeit deutscher Gerichte bei Persönlichkeitsrechtsverletzungen im Internet (2007)

Wulf-Henning Roth, Persönlichkeitsschutz im Internet: Internationale Zuständigkeit und anwendbares Recht, IPRax 2013, 215

Saravalle, "Forum damni" o "fora damni"?, Foro it. 1995, 337

Schauwecker, Extraterritoriale Patentverletzungsjurisdiktion (2009)

Guus E. Schmidt, Valt de revindicatie onder artikel 5 sub 3 EEX?, NIPR 2004, 296

Matthias Schwarz, Der Gerichtsstand der unerlaubten Handlung nach deutschem und europäischem Zivilprozessrecht (1991)

Slonina, Örtliche und internationale Zuständigkeit für Patentverletzungsklagen, SZZP 2005, 313

Slonina, Erfolgsortsgerichtsstand nach Art. 5 Nr. 3 EuGVO bei Persönlichkeitsrechtsverletzungen im Internet (auch) am Mittelpunkt der Interessen des Opfers, ÖJZ 2012, 61

Slonina, Deliktsgerichtsstand für Markenrechtsverletzungen, ecolex 2012, 484

Slonina, Rechtsmissbräuchliche Wahl des Erfolgsortsgerichtsstands für Filesharing-Klagen?, ecolex 2014, 608

Joel Smith/Leriche, CJEU Ruling in *Pinckney v. Mediatech*: Jurisdiction in Online Copyright Infringement Cases Depends on the Accessibility of Website Content, [2014] EIPR 137

Spickhoff, Die Arzthaftung im Europäischen Internationalen Privat- und Prozessrecht, in: FS Gerda Müller (2009), p. 287

Spickhoff, Persönlichkeitsverletzungen im Internet: Internationale Zuständigkeit und Kollisionsrecht, IPRax 2011, 131

Spindler, Die internationale deliktsrechtliche Zuständigkeit für Informationsdelikte (unrichtige Bankauskünfte), IPRax 2001, 153

Spindler, Kollisionsrecht und internationale Zuständigkeit bei Persönlichkeitsrechtsverletzungen im Internet – die eDate-Entscheidung des EuGH, AfP 2012, 114

Stadler, Die internationale Durchsetzung von Gegendarstellungsansprüchen, JZ 1994, 642

Ansgar Staudinger/Czaplinski, Verkehrsopferschutz im Lichte der Rom I-, Rom II- sowie Brüssel I-Verordnung, NJW 2009, 2249

Steinbrück, Der Vertriebsort als Deliktsgerichtsstand für internationale Produkthaftungsklagen, in: FS Athanassios Kaissis (2012), p. 965

Stufler, Questioni sulla competenza giurisdizionale nelle azioni di accertamento negativo in materia di illeciti civili, Dir. ind. 2009, 541

Peter Mankowski

Sujecki, Persönlichkeitsrechtsverletzungen über
das Internet und gerichtliche Zuständigkeit, K&R
2011, 315

Sujecki, Torpedoklagen im europäischen Binnenmarkt, GRUR Int. 2012, 18

Sujecki, Zur Bestimmung des Erfolgsortes nach
Art. 7 Nr. 2 EuGVVO bei Internetdelikten, EWS
2015, 305

Tenenbaum, Retombées de l'affaire *Madoff* sur la
convention de Lugano, RCDIP 101 (2012), 45

Tenenbaum, La localisation du préjudice financier au
regard des règles européennes de compétence en
matière délictuelle, Bull. Joly Bourse 2014, 145

Tenenbaum, La mise en oeuvre dans l'affaire Luxal-
pha des règles de compétence européennes et de la
Convention de Lugano en matière de responsabilité
délictuelle, Bull. Joly Bourse 2014, 400

Thiede, Online Medien, Persönlichkeitsrechtsschutz
und Internationale Zuständigkeit, GPR 2011, 259

Thiede, Aktivgerichtsstand für Betroffene von Persönlichkeitsrechtverletzungen im Onlinebereich,
ecolex 2012, 131

Thiede, Bier, Shevill und eDate – Aegrescit meden-
do?, GPR 2012, 219

Thiede, Straßenverkehrsunfall mit Auslandsbezug –
Internationale Zuständigkeit und anwendbares
Recht, Zak 2013, 751

Thiede/Florian Sommer, Vorsätzliche Schädigung
von Anlegern im europaweiten arbeitsteiligen
Wertpapiervertrieb: Der internationale Gerichtsstand nach der EuGVVO, ÖBA 2015, 175

Thole, Die Durchgriffshaftung im Deliktsgerichtsstand des Art. 5 Nr. 3 EuGVVO, GPR 2014, 113

Thole, Die internationale Zuständigkeit für Ver-
tragsstrafe- und Unterlassungsklagen von Wettbewerbsverbänden, IPRax 2015, 65

Thole, Die zuständigkeitsrechtliche Zurechnung des
Handlungsortes unter § 32 ZPO und Art. 7 Nr. 2
EuGVVO n.F. (Art. 5 Nr. 3 EuGVVO a.F.), in: FS
Eberhard Schilken (2015), p. 523

Thorn, Internationale Zuständigkeit bei Persönlichkeitsrechtsverletzungen durch Massenmedien, in: FS
Bernd von Hoffmann (2011), p. 746

Die Haftung für Kartellrechtsverstöße im internationalen Rechtsverkehr (2011)

Uhl, Internationale Zuständigkeit gemäß Art. 5 Nr. 3
des Brüsseler und Lugano-Übereinkommens, aus-
geführt am Beispiel der Produktehaftung unter Be-

rücksichtigung des deutschen, englischen, schweizerischen und US-amerikanischen Rechts (2000)

Vanleenhove, European Court of Justice opens the
door further to torpedo proceedings, NIPR 2013, 25

Vanleenhove, Artikel 5, 3. Brussel I-Verordening laat
niet toe verweerder te dagen op de plaats van de
schadeverwekkende handeling van de mededader –
De terugvordering door een overheidslichaam van
een te veel betaald bedrag na een administrative
procedure valt on der de Brussel I-Verordening, TBH
2015, 53

de Vecchi Lajolo, Torpedo e diritti di personalità, Dir.
ind. 2013, 47

Veenstra, Artikel 5 EEX en afgebroken onderhan-
delingen, NTBR 2003, 138

Francesca Villata, Offerta di strumenti finanziari
esteri in Italia e art. 5, n. 3, del Regelomanto Bruxelles
I, Riv. dir. proc. 2012 II 476

Stefano Alberto Villata, Locus commissi delicti e
concorso nell'illecito nell'art. 5, n. 3 del Regolamento
Bruxelles I, Riv. dir. proc. 2014, 1229

Vinaixa i Miquel, La calificación de la responsabilidad precontractual en el marco del convenio de
Bruselas de 1968, Rev. der. com. eur. 2002, 977

Vitellino, Conflitti di leggi e di giurisdizioni in materia di azione inibitoria collettiva, in: Liber Fausto
Pocar (2009), p. 985

Wadlow, Bugs, Spies and Paparazzi: Jurisdiction over
Actions for Breach of Confidence in Private International Law, [2008] EIPR 269

Gerhard Wagner, Ehrenschutz und Pressefreiheit im
europäischen Zivilverfahrens- und Internationalen
Privatrecht, RabelsZ 62 (1998), 243

Rolf Wagner/Gess, Der Gerichtsstand der unerlaubten Handlung nach der EuGVVO bei Kapitalanla-
gedelikten, NJW 2009, 3481

Johannes Weber, Gesellschaftsrecht und Gläubigerschutz im Internationalen Zivilverfahrensrecht
(2011)

Wedemann, Die internationale Zuständigkeit für
Haftungsklagen gegen Gesellschafter und Geschäftsführer, ZEuP 2014, 861

Wefers Bettink, Het arrest Wintersteiger en de plaats
van de schadebrengende feit: het Hof van Justitie zet
de doos van Pandora verder open, NTER 2012, 288

Matthias Weller, Zur Handlungsortbestimmung im
internationalen Kapitalanlagerprozess bei arbeitsteiliger Deliktsverwirklichung, IPRax 2000, 202

To (3):

Matthias Weller, Persönlichkeitsrechtsverletzungen im Internet – Internationale Zuständigkeit am "Ort der Interessenkollision"?, in: FS Athanassios Kaissis (2012), p. 1039

Matthias Weller, Neue Grenzen der internationalen Zuständigkeit im Kapitalanlageprozess: Keine wechselseitige Zurechnung der Handlungsbeiträge nach Art. 5 Nr. 3 EuGVO, WM 2013, 1681

Wendenburg/Maximilian Schneider, Vertraglicher Gerichtsstand für Ansprüche aus Delikt?, NJW 2014, 1633

Wiesener, Der Gegendarstellungsanspruch im deutschen internationalen Privat- und Verfahrensrecht (1998)

Willems, Wettbewerbsstreitsachen am Mittelpunkt der klägerischen Interessen? Zum Verständnis des "fliegenden Gerichtsstands" in § 14 II UWG de lege ferenda sowie de lege lata, GRUR 2013, 462

Martin Winkler, Die internationale Zuständigkeit für Patentverletzungsstreitigkeiten (2011)

Matteo M. Winkler, Giurisdizione e diritto applicabile agli illeciti via web: nuovi importanti chiarimenti dalla Corte di Giustizia, Resp. civ. e prev. 2012, 806

ten Wolde/Kirsten C. Henckel, The ECJ's Interpretation of Article 5 (3) Brussels I Regulation – A Carefully Balanced System of Jurisdictional Rules?, Int. J. Proced. L. 3 (2013), 195

Wüllrich, Das Persönlichkeitsrecht des Einzelnen im Internet (2006)

Würthwein, Zur Problematik der örtlichen und internationalen Zuständigkeit aufgrund unerlaubter Handlung, ZZP 106 (1993), 51

Wurmnest, Internationale Zuständigkeit und anwendbares Recht bei grenzüberschreitenden Kartelldelikten, EuZW 2012, 933

Yeo, Constructive Trustees and the Brussels Convention, (2001) 117 L.Q.Rev. 560

Zanolini, La (in)competenza del giudice italiano ai sensi dell'art. 5.3 della convenzione di Bruxelles, Riv. dir. ind. 2005 II 166

Zigann, Entscheidungen inländischer Gerichte über ausländische gewerbliche Schutzrechte und Urheberrechte (2002)

Zogg, Accumulation of Contractual and Tortious Causes of Action under the Judgments Regulation, (2013) 9 JPrIL 39.

To (3):

Kaye, Civil Claims in Criminal Proceedings in Courts of the Common Market: Risks to English Defendants, (1988) 7 Lit. 13

Christian Kohler, Adhäsionsverfahren und Brüsseler Übereinkommen 1968, in: Will (Hrsg.) Schadensersatz im Strafverfahren (1990), p. 74

Mankowski, Zivilverfahren vor Strafgerichten und die EuGVVO, in: FG Rudolf Machacek und Franz Matscher (2008), p. 785

Schoibl, Adhäsionsverfahren und Europäisches Zivilverfahrensrecht, in: FS Rainer Sprung (2001), p. 321.

To (4):

Crespi Reghizzi, A New Special Forum for Disputes Concerning Rights in Rem over Movable Assets, in: Pocar/Viarengo/Villata (eds.), Recasting Brussels I (2012), p. 173

Crespi Reghizzi, Per una prima lettura del regolamento "Bruxelles Ibis". Il nuovo foro alternativo per le controversie in materia di beni culturali www.aldricus.com/2012/12/13/crespi

Franzina, The Proposed New Rule of Special Jurisdiction Regarding Rights in Rem in Moveable Property – A Good Option for a Reformed Brussels I Regulation?, Riv. dir. int. 2011, 789

Gebauer, A New Head of Jurisdiction in Relation to the Recovery of Cultural Objects, in: Ragno (ed.), International Litigation in Europe: The Brussels I Recast as a Panacea? (Milano 2015)

Gillies, The contribution of jurisdiction as a technique of demand side regulation in claims for the recovery of cultural objects, (2015) 11 JPrIL 295

Jayme, Ein internationaler Gerichtsstand für Rechtsstreitigkeiten um Kunstwerke, in: FS Reinhard Mußgnug (2005), p. 517

de Lambertye-Autrand, La nouvelle compétence au forum rei sitae en matière d'actions en restitution de biens culturels dans le règlement Bruxelles Ibis, in: Emmanuel Guinchard (dir.), Le nouveau règlement Bruxelles Ibis (Bruxelles 2014), p. 83

Siehr, Das Forum rei sitae in der neuen EuGVO (Art. 7 Nr. 4 EuGVO n.F.) und der internationale Kulturgüterschutz, in: FS Dieter Martiny (2014), p. 837.

To (5):
Christiane Albers, Die Begriffe der Niederlassung und der Zweigniederlassung im Internationalen Privat- und Zivilverfahrensrecht (2010)
Fawcett, Methods of Carrying on Business and Article 5 (5) of the Brussels Convention, (1984) 9 Eur. L. Rev. 326
Geimer, Die inländische Niederlassung als Anknüpfungspunkt für die internationale Zuständigkeit, WM 1976, 146
Hunnings, Agency and Jurisdiction in the EEC, [1982] JBL 244
Jaspert, Grenzüberschreitende Unternehmensverbindungen im Zuständigkeitsbereich des EuGVÜ (Diss. Bielefeld 1995)
Jayme, Subunternehmervertrag und EuGVÜ, in: FS Klemens Pleyer (1986), p. 371
Kronke, Der Gerichtsstand nach Art. 5 Nr. 5 EuGVÜ, IPRax 1989, 81
Linke, Der "klein-europäische" Niederlassungsgerichtsstand (Art. 5 Nr. 5 EuGVÜ), IPRax 1982, 46
Mankowski, Zu einigen internationalprivat- und internationalprozessrechtlichen Aspekten bei Börsentermingeschäften, RIW 1996, 1001
Mankowski, Die österreichischen Gerichtsstände der Streitgenossenschaft, des Vermögens und der inländischen Vertretung mit Blick auf das Lugano-Übereinkommen, IPRax 1998, 122
Mathias Otto, Der prozessuale Durchgriff (1993)
Andreea-Teodora Stănescu/Șerban-Alexandru Stănescu, Determinarea competenței de drept internațional privat în materia litigiilor referitoare la exploatarea de sedii secundare potrivit art. 5 pct. 5 din Regulamentul (CE) nr. 44/2001, in: In Honorem Corneliu Bîrsan (București 2013), p. 453.

To (6):
Berti, Trusts and Lugano Convention – Does it Matter?, in: Vogt (ed.), Disputes Involving Trusts (1999), p. 9
Berti, Der trust, das Lugano-Übereinkommen und das schweizerische IPR, in: Aspekte des Wirtschaftsrecht – FG zum Schweizerischen Juristentag 2004 (2004) 223

Conrad, Qualifikationsfragen des Trust im Europäischen Zivilprozessrecht (2001)
Frigessi di Rattalma, La competenza giurisdizionale in materia del trust nel regolamento comunitario n. 44/2001, RDIPP 2004, 783
Glasson, Jurisdiction, Remedies, and the Recognition and Enforcement of Foreign Judgments, in: Thomas/Alastair Hudson, The Law of Trusts (2004), ch. 42
Graue, Der Trust im internationalen Privatrecht- und Steuerrecht, in: FS Murad Ferid (1978), p. 151
Graupner, Der englische Trust im deutschen Zivilprozess, ZvglRWiss 88 (1989), 149
Jonathan Harris, Jurisdiction and the Enforcement of Foreign Judgments in Transnational Trust Litigation, in: Glasson (ed.), The International Trust (2002), p. 9
Hayton, Jurisdiction over Trust Disputes under Article 5 (6), (2008) 14 Trust & Trustees 384
Hayton, Trust Disputes within Art. 5 (6) of Brussels I, (2009) 23 Trust L.J. 3
Hayton, "Trusts" in Private International Law, RdC 366 (2013), 9
Roman Huber, Gerichtsstands- und Schiedsgerichtswahl in trustrechtlichen Angelegenheiten (Zürich/Basel/Genf 2013)
Robert Stevens, Resulting Trusts in the Conflict of Laws, in: Birks/Rose (eds.), Restitution and Equity I: Resulting Trusts and Equitable Compensation (2000), p. 147.

To (7):
Brice/Reeder, Maritime Law on Salvage (5th ed. 2011)
Pellis, Forum arresti (Zwolle 1993) p. 84–86
Pocar, La giurisdizione sulle controversie marittime nella sviluppa della Convenzione di Bruxelles del 1968, Dir. mar. 101 (1999), 183.

General:
Egler, Seerechtliche Streitigkeiten unter der EuGVVO (2011)
Vinaixa Miquel, La aplicación extracomunitaria de los foros especiales del Art. 5 del RB I, AEDIPr 2009, 391.

I. **General considerations**

I. General considerations

1. Ratio legis

Art. 7 confers jurisdiction on other courts than those of the state where the defendant has his **1**
domicile. It is for the plaintiff to choose. This freedom of choice was introduced in view of
the existence of certain well-defined cases that involved a particularly close relationship
between the dispute and the court which may most conveniently be called upon to take
cognizance of the matter.[1] The dispute and the court having jurisdiction to entertain shall be
linked by an especially close connecting factor.[2] The sound administration of justice and the
efficacious conduct of proceedings ought to be fostered and enhanced[3] as is evidenced by
Recitals (12) Brussels I Regulation and (16) Brussels I*bis* Regulation. Behind this lies the
general principle of private international law (in a wider, non technical meaning) to search
for proximity.[4] Additionally, Art. 7 attempts to strike the balance between the plaintiff's and
the defendant's interests and to put it on a more evenly balanced level whereas if only Art. 4
existed, the defendant would be overly favoured.[5] In practice, Art. 7 has proved itself to be

---

[1] *Siegfried Zelger v. Sebastiano Salinitri*, (Case 56/79) [1980] ECR 89, 96 para. 3; *SAR Schotte GmbH v.
    Parfums Rothschild SARL*, (Case 218/86) [1987] ECR 4905, 4919 para. 9; *Custom Made Commercial Ltd.
    v. Stawa Metallbau GmbH*, (Case C-288/92) [1994] ECR I-2913, I-2955 para. 12.

[2] Report *Jenard* p. 22; *Lloyd's Register of Shipping v. Société Campenon Bernard*, (Case C-439/93) [1995]
    ECR I-961, I-981 para. 21; *Color Drack GmbH v. Lexx International Vertriebs GmbH*, Case C-386/05
    [2007] ECR I-3699, I-3734 para. 22; *Peter Rehder v. Baltic Air Corporation*, (Case C-204/08) [2009] ECR
    I-6073, I-6089 para. 32; *Car Trim GmbH v. KeySafety Systems Srl*, (Case C-381/08) [2010] ECR I-1255,
    I-1284 para. 48; *Wood Floor Solutions Andreas Domberger GmbH v. Silva Trade SA*, (Case C-19/09)
    [2010] ECR I-2121, I-2170 para. 22; A-G *Trstenjak*, [2010] ECR I-2124, I-2150 paras. 70 *et seq.*

[3] *Industrie Tessili Italiana Como v. Dunlop AG*, (Case 12/76) [1976] ECR 1473, 1486 para. 13; *Martin Peters
    Bauunternehmung GmbH v. Zuid Nederlandse Aannemers Vereniging*, (Case 34/82) [1983] ECR 987,
    1002 para. 11; *Hassan Shenavai v. Klaus Kreischer*, (Case 266/85) [1987] ECR 239, 253 para. 6; *Dumez
    France SA and Tracoba SARL v. Hessische Landesbank*, (Case C-220/88) [1990] ECR I-49, I-79 para. 17;
    Mulox IBC Ltd. v. Hendrick Geels, (Case C-125/92) [1993] ECR I-4075, I-4104 para. 17; *Antonio Marinari
    v. Lloyd's Bank plc and Zubaidi Trading Co.*, (Case C-364/93) [1995] ECR I-2719, I-2738 para. 10;
    *Réunion européenne SA v. Spliethoff's Bevrachtingskantoor BV and Master of the vessel "Alblasgracht
    002"*, (Case C-51/97) [1998] ECR I-6511, I-6544 para. 27; *Besix SA v. Wasserreinigungsbau Alfred
    Kretzschmar GmbH & Co. KG (WABAG) and Planungs- und Forschungsgesellschaft Dipl. Ing. W.
    Kretzschmar GmbH & Co. KG (Plafog)*, (Case C-256/00) [2002] ECR I-1699, I-1727 para. 31; *Rudolf
    Kronhofer v. Marianne Maier*, (Case C-168/02) [2004] ECR I-6009, I-6029 para. 15.

[4] *Teixeira de Sousa/Moura Vicente* Art. 5 note 1; *Fallon*, in: Mélanges en l'honneur de Paul Lagarde (2005),
    p. 241, 243, 244. But cf. critical *Matthias Lehmann*, ZZP Int. 9 (2004), 172; *Matthias Lehmann*, in:
    Dickinson/Lein para. 4.06.

[5] See only *Ignatova*, Art. 5 Nr. 1 EuGVVO – Chancen und Perspektiven der Reform des Gerichtsstands am
    Erfüllungsort (2005) pp. 71 *et seq.*; *Matthias Lehmann*, in: Dickinson/Lein para. 4.07.

the perhaps most important Article of the entire Brussels I-Lugano regime generating more requests for preliminary rulings to the ECJ than any other Article.[6]

2   Since rules on jurisdiction require particular clarity and a clear structure in order to become workable and since the general aim of the Regulation is to the same end,[7] Art. 7 nevertheless does not employ a (or even worse *the*) close connection *per se* as a connecting factor in its own right,[8] but denominates certain more specific connecting factors. The respective list is – save for Arts. 8; 9 – exhaustive in terms of special jurisdiction besides the general jurisdiction granted by Art. 4.[9] To accept as the sole criterion of jurisdiction the mere existence of a connecting factor between the facts at issue in a dispute and a particular court would be to oblige the court to investigate other circumstances and would render the defined heads of jurisdiction in Art. 7 nugatory.[10] Above all, it would jeopardise the possibility of foreseeing, i.e. calculating in advance, which court could have jurisdiction, and would thus defy the main aim of the jurisdictional rules of the Regulation.[11] Rules on jurisdiction must not be subjected to scrutinising each and every fact in a single case. The strengthening of the legal protection of persons domiciled in the EU by enabling the claimant easy access into the court in which he may choose to sue and the defendant to reasonably foresee in which court he may be sued, stars amongst the main objectives of the entire Brussels I Regulation.[12]

3   With the exception of (6) all heads of special jurisdiction contained in Art. 7 vest jurisdiction in a certain *court*, not only in the courts of a state. Hence, Art. 7 – with the exception of (6) – does not only regulate international jurisdiction, but also local jurisdiction or venue,[13] ex-

---

6   See only *de Boer*, NJ 2005 Nr. 337 p. 2611, 2612.

7   *Custom Made Commercial Ltd. v. Stawa Metallbau GmbH*, (Case C-288/92) [1994] ECR I-2913, I-2956 para. 15.

8   See *Custom Made Commercial Ltd. v. Stawa Metallbau GmbH*, (Case C-288/92) [1994] ECR I-2913, I-2955 para. 12.

9   *Jakob Handte & Co. GmbH v. Traitements Mécano-chimiques des surfaces SA*, (Case C-26/91) [1992] ECR I-3967, I-3994 para. 13; *Custom Made Commercial Ltd. v. Stawa Metallbau GmbH*, (Case C-288/92) [1994] ECR I-2913, I-2955 para. 12; *Frahuil SA v. Assitalia SpA*, (Case C-265/02) [2004] ECR I-1543, I-1555 para. 23.

10 *Custom Made Commercial Ltd. v. Stawa Metallbau GmbH*, (Case C-288/92) [1994] ECR I-2913, I-2956 para. 19.

11 *Custom Made Commercial Ltd. v. Stawa Metallbau GmbH*, (Case C-288/92) [1994] ECR I-2913, I-2956 para. 18.

12 *Besix SA v. Wasserreinigungsbau Alfred Kretzschmar GmbH & Co. KG (WABAG) and Planungs- und Forschungsgesellschaft Dipl. Ing. W. Kretzschmar GmbH & Co. KG (Plafog)*, (Case C-256/00) [2002] ECR I-1699, I-1726 paras. 25 *et seq.*; *Fonderie Officine Meccaniche Tacconi SpA von Heinrich Wagner Sinto Maschinenfabrik GmbH*, (Case C-334/00) [2002] ECR I-7357, I-7392 para. 20; *Danmarks Rederiforening, acting on behalf of DFDS Torline AS v. LO Landsorganisationen i Sverige, acting on behalf of SEKO Sjöfolk Facket for Service och Kommunikation*, (Case C-18/02) [2004] ECR I-1417, I-1455 para. 36.

13 See only Report *Jenard* p. 22; A-G *Jääskinen*, Opinion of 29 November 2012 in Case C-228/11 para. 55; OLG Köln WM 2005, 612, 615 = AG 2005, 123, 125; Rb. Rotterdam NIPR 2000 Nr. 146 p. 233; *Leible*, in: Rauscher Art. 5 note 4; *Schurig*, in: FS Hans-Joachim Musielak (2004), p. 493, 496; *Hofmann/Kunz*, in: Basler Kommentar, Art. 5 note 32; for (1) (b) *Color Drack GmbH v. Lexx International Vertriebs GmbH*, Case C-386/05 [2007] ECR I-3699, I-3735 para. 30; *Vlas*, NJ 2008 Nr. 237 p. 2282; for (3) OGH ZfRV 2008/32, 81, 82. Erroneously *contra* Trib. Milano RDIPP 2014, 629, 632 for (1) (b).

cluding the rules of the national law of the *forum* on local jurisdiction from application.[14] These rules are rendered inoperative. They do not even serve in a supplementary role.[15] The onus to plead the facts supporting jurisdiction under Art. 7 is generally on the plaintiff,[16] but more precisely: on the party invoking a specific ground of jurisdiction under Art. 7.[17] The mere allegation, e.g. of a contract, might not be deemed sufficient to invoke (1), not even if there is a serious question calling for a trial in this regard arises.[18] Art. 7 does not distinguish between different kinds of *petita* in a formal sense.[19]

2. Legislative history

a) Drafting history from the Brussels Convention to the Brussels I Regulation
Art. 7 has always been part of the overall scheme, with a starring role ever since the original **4** Brussels Convention back in 1968. In part, predecessors in national legislation can be identified for some of the heads of jurisdiction contained in Art. 5: Belgian Arts. 41; 52 (1) loi sur la compétence du 25 mars 1876 plus Art. 624 Code judiciaire, French Arts. 59 (3); 420 cpc (ancien), Italian Art. 20 Codice di procedura civile and German § 29 ZPO provided the role models for (1) in its initial shape,[20] and the concept of (3) is derived from Belgian Arts. 41; 52 loi sur la compétence du 25 mars 1876, French Arts. 59 (12) cpc (ancien) plus Art. 21 décret du 22 decembre 1958, Italian Art. 20 Codice di procedura civile and German § 32 ZPO,[21] whereas § 21 ZPO in Germany could possibly claim ideological parentage for (5) but for the interference of a number of bilateral treaties between the original Member States.[22] Such bilateral treaties were also considered as models for (1) and (3).[23] National ancestors to (2) and (4) are not listed whilst (2) was partially modelled on the 1958 Hague Convention on the recognition and enforcement of judgments for child maintenance.[24]

On the way from the original Brussels Convention to the Brussels I Regulation, the then **5** Art. 5 has undergone a number of changes, not surprisingly as Art. 5 has always been at the very forefront of jurisdiction and has attracted many judgments both on the European and national level on the one hand and much scrutiny in academic writing on the other. The intense discussion generated the need for legislative reaction. Only the then (3), then (4) and

---

[14]   Hence, even the scenario that a lawsuit is lodged in the right state but in the wrong place within that state can occur occasionally; e.g. Rb. Zutphen NIPR 2005 Nr. 69 p. 112.

[15]   As Holbæk District Court [2014] ILPr 525, 527–528 and ØLD [2014] ILPr 528, 529 appear to believe when the combine Art. 5 (3) Brussels I Regulation with a rule of Danish national law.

[16]   See only *Hanbridge Ltd. v. British Aerospace Communications Ltd.* [1993] 3 I.R. 343, 358 (S.C., per *Finlay* C.J.).

[17]   See A-G *Jääskinen*, Opinion of 25 April 2013 in Case 9/12, para. 61.

[18]   *Tesam Distribution Ltd. v. Schuh Mode Team GmbH* [1990] I.L.Pr. 149, 158 (C.A., per *Nicholls* L.J.); *New England Reinsurance Corp. v. Messoghios Insurance Co. SA* [1992] 1 Lloyd's Rep. 251, 252 (C.A., per *Leggatt* L.J.); *Rank Film Distributors Ltd. v. Lanterna Editrice Srl* [1992] I.L.Pr. 58, 67 *et seq.* (Q.B.D., *Saville* J.); *Collins*, in: Dicey/Morris para. 11–249.

[19]   Aud. Prov. Barcelona REDI 2009, 183, 184 with note *Carballo Piñeiro* = AEDIPr 2009, 958.

[20]   Report *Jenard* p. 22 *et seq.* In detail see *Newton* p. 124–130.

[21]   Report *Jenard* p. 25.

[22]   Report *Jenard* p. 26.

[23]   Report *Jenard* p. 23 and 25 respectively.

[24]   Report *Jenard* p. 24 *et seq.*

(5) remained unaltered ever since. (6) and (7) were additions on the occasion of the first Accession Convention in 1978.

6   The present (2), then (3) has been subject to only a modest and considerate change of wording insofar as the last clause was inserted when the Brussels I Regulation was drafted, in order to make it unambiguously clear that actions for preventing tortious damage were included as well.[25] In the near future major reform might threaten the very existence of (2) since the pending Proposal for a Regulation on (i.a.) jurisdiction in matters relating to maintenance obligations[26] opts for a comprehensive code on private international law matters of maintenance in the largest sense. If such a Regulation is implemented jurisdiction in maintenance matters would not be governed by the Brussels I Regulation anymore but exclusively by the specific instrument[27] which would, to this extent, supersede the Brussels I Regulation.[28]

7   Shining prominently in many instances of international trade, (1) has seen almost constant law reform for fifteen years in the past. In 1988 the Lugano Convention added to the original text, which contained not more than the present (1) (a), two more sentences, the latter of which had been modified previously in 1989 by the Accession Convention of San Sebastian-Donostía. Both additional parts formed a reaction to the case-law from the ECJ[29] concerning labour contracts,[30] most prominently indicated by the modification in 1989, which directly and instantly mirrored the decision in *Six Humbert*,[31][32] and were later moved to Art. 19 (2) of the Regulation exerting major restructuring work. Jurisdiction in labour lawsuits is now exclusively dealt with by Arts. 18–21. (1) in general was slightly re-edited in 1978 in order to codify the then case-law of the ECJ[33] by adding "in question" after "obligation".[34]

8   During the process of drafting the Brussels I Regulation (1) was one of the main points of discussion. Traditionalists advocating in favour of the *status quo* fought against modernizers who opted for a change from a more normative to a factual approach towards ascertaining the place of performance in contract.[35] In particular, two of the grand lines in the jurispru-

---

[25]   Commission Proposal COM (1999) 348 final p. 14; A-G *Jääskinen*, Opinion of 29 November 2012 in Case C-228/11 para. 28.

[26]   Proposal for a Council Regulation on Jurisdiction, Applicable Law, Recognition and Enforcement of Decisions and Cooperation in Matters Relating to Maintenance Obligations, COM (2005) 649 final.

[27]   Arts. 3–11 Proposal for a Council Regulation on Jurisdiction, Applicable Law, Recognition and Enforcement of Decisions and Cooperation in Matters Relating to Maintenance Obligations, COM (2005) 649 final.

[28]   See Art. 48 (1) Proposal for a Council Regulation on Jurisdiction, Applicable Law, Recognition and Enforcement of Decisions and Cooperation in Matters Relating to Maintenance Obligations, COM (2005) 649 final.

[29]   Thence *Roger Ivenel v. Helmut Schwab*, (Case 133/81) [1982] ECR 1891; *Hassan Shenavai v. Klaus Kreischer*, (Case 266/85) [1987] ECR 239.

[30]   Report *Jenard/Möller* paras. 37–40; Report *Almeida Cruz/Desantes Real/Jenard* para. 23.

[31]   *Six Constructions Ltd. v. Paul Humbert*, (Case 32/88) [1989] ECR 341.

[32]   Report *Almeida Cruz/Desantes Real/Jenard* para. 23.

[33]   *A. de Bloos SPRL v. Société en commandite par actions Bouyer*, (Case 14/76) [1976] ECR 1497, 1508 paras. 8–14.

[34]   Report *Schlosser* para. 89.

dence of the ECJ were at issue, namely whether to restrict the place of performance to the very claim in question and whether to employ substantive law *via* the private international law of the *forum*. Eventually, (1) settled for a compromise[36] which in essence gives the edge to the modernisers although it complicates matters, but only in rare cases.[37]

b) Brussels I*bis* recast

aa) Implemented alterations

The recast modified special jurisdiction in some detail only. Art. 7 has not been subject to a **9** major reshuffle. Its new shape can be summarised as a renumbering leaving in place all known strengths and weaknesses.[38] Firstly, the article number has been switched from Art. 5 Brussels I Regulation to Art. 7 Brussels I*bis* Regulation. Adding two numbers and the ensuing re-numbering was necessary after the implementation of a completely new Art. 2 which had had no predecessor in the Brussels I Regulation, and after elevating the former Art. 62 Brussels I Regulation in the numerical order to Art. 3 Brussels I*bis* Regulation switching it to the front of the new Regulation.

Secondly, the internal order within Art. 7 has been partially reversed as compared to the **10** order of Art. 5 Brussels I Regulation.
– (1), (5), (6) and (7) retain their place and number, and remain unchanged as to substance.
– The former (2) which dealt with special jurisdiction in maintenance matters is deleted.
– The former (3) has now become (2), and the former (4) has now become (3) both without any changes as to substance.
– (4) is a novelty and a new entrance.

The only substantial alterations in Art. 7 are the disappearance of a head of jurisdiction **11** devoted to maintenance obligations as was to be found in Art. 5 (2) Brussels Regulation, and the introduction of the new (4).[39] Anything else remained as it stood under Art. 5 Brussels I Regulation. In particular, the two heads of jurisdiction for claims in contract and tort respectively, the two most relevant heads of special jurisdiction for practical purposes by far, remain virtually untouched.[40] (1) remains intact in spirit,[41] and contracting practice has not adapted to a different guidance. This implies a transfer of authority rendered by the ECJ

---

[35] See in more detail *Markus*, SZW 1999, 205, 210; *Christian Kohler*, in: Gottwald (ed.), Revision des EuGVÜ/Neues Schiedsverfahrensrecht (2000), p. 1, 12; *Campuzano Díaz*, AEDIPr 2001, 920, 921; *Beaumont*, in: Essays in Honour of Sir Peter North (2002), p. 9, 15–20; *Peter Arnt Nielsen*, in: Liber Professorum College of Europe 2005, p. 245, 254 *et seq.*; *Peter Arnt Nielsen*, in: Liber Fausto Pocar (2009), p. 773, 777–779; *Ignatova*, Art. 5 Nr. 1 EuGVVO – Chancen und Perspektiven der Reform des Gerichtsstands am Erfüllungsort (2005) pp. 169–182; *Rodriguez*, Beklagtenwohnsitz und Erfüllungsort im europäischen IZVR (Zürich 2005) paras. 639–643.

[36] See only A-G *Trstenjak*, [2009] ECR I-3330, I-3365 para. 94; *Peter Arnt Nielsen*, in: Liber Fausto Pocar (2009), p. 773, 776–779; *Mankowski*, JZ 2009, 958, 960.

[37] See *Campuzano Díaz*, AEDIPr 2001, 920, 921; *Tagaras*, CDE 2003, 399, 402 *et seq.*

[38] *von Hein*, RIW 2013, 97, 102.

[39] *Miriam Pohl*, IPRax 2013, 109, 110, 111; *Gaudemet-Tallon/Kessedjian*, Rev. trim. dr. eur. 2013, 435, 443.

[40] *Miriam Pohl*, IPRax 2013, 109, 111.

[41] *Sindres*, J-Cl. Dr. int. fasc. 584-130 no. 2 (mars 2014).

in particular, from the interpretation of Art. 5 Brussels I Regulation to the continuing parts of Art. 7.

12 The former (2) might not have been formally repealed under the reign of the Brussels I Regulation, but had effectively been superseded on 18 June 2011 by virtue of Art. 68 Maintenance Regulation. Brussels I*bis* only formalises this. This is of declaratory nature only, but sensible nevertheless for they avoid confusing practitioners and students alike who might else resort to the wrong Act.[42] The accompanying express exclusion of maintenance obligations arising from a family relationship, parentage, marriage or affinity from the scope of Brussels I*bis* by virtue of Art. 1 (2) (d) is to be welcomed for the same reason and puts matters finally beyond any reasonable doubt. Insofar as maintenance obligations exceptionally are still subject to the Brussels I*bis* Regulation, i.e. outside the are excluded by Art. 1 (2) (d), an own, separate head of special jurisdiction for them has not been retained. Insofar as they are based on contractual agreements they qualify as contractual obligations and profit from (1) (a).

bb) Continuity as to the *forum solutionis* and the *forum delicti commissi*

13 Despite reasoned calls for reform of (1) after practically and methodologically disappointing results gained from (1) (b)[43] and despite reasoned calls for return to an approach based on normative considerations (this time uniform ones, not ones following the *lex causae*),[44] (1) has not been substantially altered in the recast process.[45] This is deplorable for it continues the difficulties of characterisation inherent in distinguishing (1) (a) from (1) (b) and the split of approach between (1) (a) and (1) (b).[46] Apparently, the issue was too contested back when the Brussels I Regulation was negotiated to stir up matters yet again, and would thus be too hot politically.[47] On the other hand, the *forum solutionis* is needed to strike the balance and to suit the interests of potential plaintiffs since it does not allow *actor sequitur forum rei* to become overly rigid. It would be a remarkably bold step into the wrong direction[48] to restrict the *forum destinatae solutionis* to the categories of contracts now covered by (1) (b).[49] This would have been to answer severe questions about privileges and discriminating.[50] Anyway,

---

[42] *Magnus/Mankowski*, ZvglRWiss 110 (2011), 252, 299.

[43] See the evaluation e.g. by *Markus*, ZSR 2007 I 319, 324; *Kessedjian*, in: FS Ingeborg Schwenzer (2011), p. 937, 943–944; *Junker*, in: FS Athanassisos Kaissis (2012), p. 439, 440; *Hess*, in: Pocar/Viarengo/Villata (eds), Recasting Brussels I (2012), p. 91, 95.

[44] *Mankowski*, IHR 2009, 46, 60 *et seq.*; *Mankowski*, JZ 2009, 958, 961; *Mankowski*, IGKK/IACPIL 1 (2010), 31, 73–76; *Magnus/Mankowski*, ZvglRWiss 109 (2010), 1, 32 *et seq.*; *Leible*, in: FS Spellenberg (2010), p. 451, 464 *et seq.*; *Leible*, in: Rauscher, Art. 5 note 33a; see also *Mumelter*, Der Gerichtsstand des Erfüllungsortes im Europäischen Zivilprozessrecht (2007) p. 222; *Huber-Mumelter/Mumelter*, JBl 2008, 561, 577.

[45] See only *von Hein*, RIW 2013, 97, 102; *Domej*, RabelsZ 78 (2014), 508, 528; *Nordmeier*, GPR 2014, 299; *Christoph A. Kern*, IPRax 2014, 503, 505. Slight linguistic changes might raise questions as to their impact, though; *d'Avout*, D. 2013, 1014, 1020.

[46] *von Hein*, RIW 2013, 97, 102.

[47] *Mankowski*, IGKK/IACPIL 1 (2010), 31, 76; *Domej*, RabelsZ 78 (2014), 508, 528; see also *Pfeiffer*, in: Heidelberg Report paras. 189–192.

[48] *Magnus/Mankowski*, ZvglRWiss 109 (2010), 1, 33.

[49] As proposed by *Peter Arnt Nielsen*, in: Liber amicorum Fausto Pocar (2009), p. 773, 783 *et seq.*

[50] *Magnus/Mankowski*, ZvglRWiss 109 (2010), 1, 33.

provident practitioners will still be well advised to resort to agreements on the place of performance or even better, agreements on jurisdiction in order to avoid the conundrum and mystery of (1) (b).[51] In particular, sellers/exporters might be tempted so for material reasons, namely to avoid jurisdiction at the buyer/importer's place.[52] That such clauses are the rule in practice[53] must not be taken as an excuse that he who does not conclude such an agreement must be blamed for suffering from major uncertainty.[54]

Calls for reforming the then (3)[55] remained unheard singularities, and the now (2) is sub- **14** stantially unaltered. In particular, (2) has not been remoulded and reshaped in the light of the Rome II Regulation. The Rome II Regulation distinguishes between a variety of different special torts and introduces custom-made conflicts rules for each of them. (2) does not follow in the steps of this lead and retains in its wording a general rule for all kinds of torts. Recital (16) cl. 3 is an addition, but as a mere recital only a means of interpretation, certainly an important one, but not elevated to the rank of a full normatively applicable rule.

Yet a rather unfortunate and unwarranted consequence of the renumbering as part of the **15** recast is that the *forum delicti*, a most important head of jurisdiction in practice, moves one up in the numerical order. One has to get accustomed to that. Possibly it is arguable that special jurisdiction in (2) now gains the second place in the numbering which it deserves in terms of importance. Anyway, there is no proper and really convincing reason why it should not have been for the newly introduced (4) to fill in the spot vacated by the elimination of the former (2) concerning maintenance obligations, thus leaving the traditional numbering of the remaining heads of jurisdiction untouched.[56]

cc) No extension to defendants resident outside the Member States

The most substantial alteration which the Brussels I*bis* reform process aspired at, was the **16** extension of the heads of special jurisdiction to all defendants regardless whether such defendants are domiciled in the Member States or not. At least the Commission Proposal Brussels I*bis* so proposes. It set out to alter the initial phrase of Art. 5 from the present "A person domiciled in a Member State may, in another Member State, be sued" into "**The following courts shall have jurisdiction**".[57]

Extracomunitarial extension[58] was envisaged including defendants domiciled outside the

---

51 See *Mankowski*, IPRax 2007, 404, 412; *Mankowski*, TranspR 2008, 67, 74; *Mankowski*, IHR 2009, 46, 60–61; *Mankowski*, EWiR Art. 5 EuGVVO 2/09, 607, 608; *Mankowski*, JZ 2009, 958, 961; *Mankowski*, CR 2010, 137, 140; *Geimer*, LMK 2008, 266925; *Schmidt-Bendun*, Haftung der Eisenbahnverkehrsunternehmen (2006) p. 133.

52 *Moritz Becker*, EWiR Art. 5 EuGVVO 3/10, 817, 818; *Piltz*, NJW 2010, 1061, 1062.

53 See only *Tuo*, Dir. mar. 109 (2007), 1080, 1101.

54 *Mankowski*, CR 2010, 137, 141. Contra *Hau*, IPRax 2000, 354, 357.

55 *Cordero Álvarez*, AEDIPr 2009, 411.

56 *Magnus/Mankowski*, ZvglRWiss 110 (2011), 252, 299.

57 Commission Proposal Brussels I*bis* Regulation COM (2010) 748/3 p. 26.

58 Discussion of the idea e.g. by *Vinaixa Miquel*, AEDIPr 2009, 391. The wider picture is discussed i.a. by *Fallon*, in: Liber amicorum Hélène Gaudemet-Tallon (2008), p. 241; *de Vareilles-Sommières*, ibid., p. 397; *Pocar*, ibid., p. 573; *Gaudemet-Tallon*, in: mèlanges en l'honneur de Serge Guinchard (2010), p. 465; *Fentiman*, (2010–11) 3 CYELS 65.

EU. Previously the Groupe Européen de Droit International Privé (GEDIP)[59] and the officially commissioned *Nuyts* Study[60] had suggested to commence the resulting Article with "A person, whether or not domiciled in a Member State".[61] The solution proposed had considerable advantages[62] and would have overcome the most unwelcome feature that under certain circumstances defendants under the present Regulation can be better off not being domiciled in the EU.[63] A straightforward extension of the EU regime would have overcome the unfortunate split into EU rules for EU domiciliaries and national rules for non-EU domiciliaries.[64] The proposed extension would have been a wholesale one. The EU regime of rules on jurisdiction as applicable in intra-EU cases would have been extended. There would not have been any special leave when it comes down to cases with a non-EU element. In particular, not the slightest degree of additional discretion would be introduced,[65] and the grounds of jurisdiction would contain as firm a guarantee in the plaintiff's favour as they do in the intra-EU cases.[66]

17 But the issue was politically contested, proved very controversial and became the object of major debate both at the academic[67] and at the political level. The European Parliament's Committee on Legal Affairs strongly argued in favour of retaining the present wording and concept.[68] It earmarked the Commission's advance as precipitative and premature.[69] Major Member States joined in and expressed opposition in the Council's Working Group, too. Eventually, they were successful. The issue was dropped, and the approach pursued by the Proposal did not make it into the final Recast Regulation.[70] This establishes a very strong *argumentum e contrario* for future debates since it evidences an outright rejection of an extension. The main reason for the refusal appears to be that an extension was believed to tie the EU's hands in future negotiation with non-Member States for instance in the framework

---

[59] European Group for Private International Law (Bergen Session, 21 September 2008), IPRax 2009, 283 Art. 5.

[60] *Nuyts*, Study on residual jurisdiction, 3 September 2007 http:ec.europa.eu/justice_home/doc_centre/ civil/studies/doc/study_residual_jurisdiction.en paras. 147 *et seq.*

[61] Applauding *Thalia Kruger*, Civil Jurisdiction Rules of the European Union and Their Impact on Third States (2008) para. 8.11; *Magnus/Mankowski*, ZvglRWiss 109 (2010), 1, 7. But cf. rather sceptical *de Vareilles-Sommières*, in: Liber amicorum Hélène Gaudemet-Tallon, Paris 2008, p. 397, 403 *et seq.*

[62] *Magnus/Mankowski*, ZvglRWiss 109 (2010), 1, 7; *Mankowski*, IGKK/IACPIL 1 (2010), 31, 40.

[63] See only *Pataut*, in: Etudes offertes à Jacques Normand, 2003, p. 365; *Magnus/Mankowski*, ZvglRWiss 109 (2010), 1, 7; *Mankowski*, IGKK/IACPIL 1 (2010), 31, 40.

[64] *Magnus/Mankowski*, ZvglRWiss 110 (2011), 252, 263.

[65] *Briggs*, [2011] LMCLQ 157, 160 fn. 21.

[66] *Magnus/Mankowski*, ZvglRWiss 110 (2011), 252, 263–264.

[67] *Borrás*, Yb. PIL 12 (2010), 333; *Dickinson*, Yb. PIL 12 (2010), 247, 270 *et seq.*; *Kessedjian*, Rev. trim. dr. eur. 2011, 117; *Magnus/Mankowski*, ZvglRWiss 110 (2011), 252, 261 *et seq.*; *Buhr*, in: Bonomi/Schmid (eds.), Revision der Verordnung 44/2001 (Brüssel I) – Welche Folgen für das Lugano-Übereinkommen? (2011), p. 11; *Johannes Weber*, RabelsZ 75 (2011), 619; *Hau*, in: FS Bernd v. Hoffmann (2011), p. 617; *Gaudemet-Tallon*, in: Douchy-Oudot/Guinchard (éds.), La justice civile européenne en marche (2012), p. 21; *Luzzatto*, in: Pocar/Viarengo/Villata (eds.), Recasting Brussels I (2012), p. 111; *Weitz*, in: FS Daphne-Ariane Simotta (2012), p. 679; *Gillies*, (2012) 8 JPrIL 489.

[68] Draft Report *Zwiefka* p. 14.

[69] Draft Report *Zwiefka* p. 47.

[70] For details of the legislative process see *Gillies*, (2012) 8 JPrIL 489, 493 *et seq.*, 507 *et seq.*

of the Hague Conference on Private International Law.[71] There were fears that external competence would be shifted and transferred completely to the EU depriving the Member States of the remainder of competence they might have cherished.[72] Furthermore, direct proof that an extension would be economically advantageous, was lacking.[73]

dd) No comprehensive *forum rei sitae*

Art. 5 (3) Proposal Brussels I*bis* ventured, and went out, to introduce a new ground of **18** jurisdiction which should be described as *forum rei sitae*:

"[A]s regards rights in rem or possession in moveable property, the courts for the place where the property is situated,"

enjoy special jurisdiction.[74] This was believed to improve the practical functioning of the jurisdiction rules and the access to justice.[75] The proposed new forum stemmed from respective suggestion in the Heidelberg Report.[76] It was best understood when contrasted with Art. 22 (1) Proposal where the counterpart for immoveables was to be found. Of course, Art. 5 (3) Proposal only conveyed special, not exclusive jurisdiction. Else old acquaintances reappeared in a slightly different environment. The frontier between immoveables and moveables had to be drawn according to the yardsticks which have been developed for Art. 24 (1).[77] Abuse by moving chattels around for tactical purposes would have posed a considerable threat.[77a] The inclusion of incorporeal goods stirred the question as to how and where to locate them.[78] Matters of characterization generally would have gained more importance taking into account also possible inferences to be considered from Art. 5 European Insolvency Regulation, also with regard to the second issue what constitutes a right in rem. The different understanding and notions of property as to be comparatively encountered in the laws of the Member States[79] posed another severe problem.[80]

The better claim might have been the one of Art. 22 (1) Proposal, though, not the least since **19** Art. 5 (3) Proposal Brussels I*bis* in most instances deliberately copied the respective terminology.[81] Yet there was a difference between "as regards" and "have as their object" which

---

71 Discussion Paper of the Danish Presidency of January 2012 sub 4 http://eu2012.de/en/Meetings/Infor mal-Meetings/Jan/~media/Files/Informal%20ministerial%20meetings/Informal%20JHA/Discussion% 20paper%204%20-%20Brussels%20I-Regulation.pdf; *Kessedjian*, Rev. trim. dr. eur. 2011, 117, 119.

72 See *Peter Arnt Nielsen*, Nordic J. Int. L. 83 (2014), 61, 64.

73 *Dickinson*, Yb. PIL 12 (2010), 247, 272 *et seq.*; *Peter Arnt Nielsen*, in: Liber amicorum Ole Lando (2012), p. 257, 263; *Peter Arnt Nielsen*, (2013) 50 CMLRev. 503, 513 with reference to Centre for Strategy & Evaluation Services (CES), Study on Data Collection and Impact Analysis Certain Aspects of a Possible Revision of Council Regulation No. 44/2001 on Jurisdiction and the Recognition and Enforcement of Judgments in Civil and Commercial Matters (2010) p. 25.

74 Commission Proposal Brussels I*bis* Regulation COM (2010) 748/3 final p. 26.

75 Commission Proposal Brussels I*bis* Regulation COM (2010) 748/3 final p. 11.

76 Heidelberg Report para. 704.

77 *Magnus/Mankowski*, ZvglRWiss 110 (2011), 252, 298.

77a *Matthias Lehmann*, in: Dickinson/Lein para. 4.10.

78 *de Lambertye-Autrand*, in: Emmanuel Guinchard, p. 83, 88.

79 See *Gretton*, RabelsZ 71 (2007), 802; *van Erp*, in: Reiner Schulze/Schulte-Nölke (eds.), European Private Law – Current Status and Perspectives (2011), p. 226.

80 *de Lambertye-Autrand*, in: Emmanuel Guinchard, p. 83, 88.

81 *Magnus/Mankowski*, ZvglRWiss 110 (2011), 252, 298.

might have been unintended, yet substantially important.[82] The limits attached to Art. 5 (3) Proposal Brussels I*bis* appeared to keep the fine balance between over- and underinclusiveness.[83] Art. 5 (3) Proposal Brussels I*bis* had a particularly fine relation with the abolition of exequatur and the introduction of direct enforcement.[84] Claims for delivery might have been the prime candidates to qualify.[85]

20 The proposed *forum rei sitae* did not find favour in the legislative process. It was criticised for opening the floodgates for forum shopping, and for raising difficult issues of characterisation.[86] Furthermore, problems with localisation were expected.[87] Hence, the Proposal was ever more redimensionated and reduced.[88] Finally and eventually, the legislative process generated not more than the rather confined (4) restricted to cultural objects. A *forum rei sitae* has been introduced, but not in a comprehensive manner for all rights in rems in all kinds of moveable property or chattels, but limited to claims based on property in cultural objects. The intended purpose of (4) is a rather specific and idiosyncratic one and must not be generalised. Yet one could argue that it had already been the idea behind the core of Art. 5 (3) Brussels I Proposal, and that the present rule represents a precisation of the original idea.[89] To a certain extent, the very outcome returns to the beginning of the discussion.[90] The idea of a general *forum rei sitae* has been abandoned, though,[91] and (4) in particular if read in the light of its legislative history, constitutes a very strong *argumentum e contrario* to the avail that a *forum rei sitae* does not exist for other chattels than cultural objects.[92] Art. 5 (3) Brussels I Proposal was clearly more ambitious[93] but did not succeed eventually. Whether an own head of special jurisdiction for claims based on ownership of cultural objects was really necessary is not beyond any doubt. To coin its advent an *"introduction curieuse"*[94] might overstep a little bit, though. But certainly it generates the necessity to distinguish and does not do service to the idea of a generalised *forum rei sitae*.[95]

---

82 *Briggs*, [2011] LMCLQ 157, 166.

83 *Magnus/Mankowski*, ZvglRWiss 110 (2011), 252, 298.

84 *Geimer*, in: FS Gert Delle Karth (2013), p. 319, 330.

85 *Briggs*, [2011] LMCLQ 157, 165.

86 *Franzina*, Riv. dir. int. 2011, 789; *Marie-Laure Niboyet*, Note à la Commission des affaires juridiques du Parlement européen, sept. 2011, pp. 24–26; *Crespi Reghizzi*, in: Pocar/Viarengo/Villata (a cura di), Recasting Brussels I (2012), p. 173; *Nuyts*, in: Nuyts (coord.), Actualités en droit international privé (Bruxelles 2013), p. 77, 129. See also Proposal by the British and Cyprus Delegations, JUSTCIV 214 CODEC 1519 (8 June 2012).

87 *Silvestri*, Riv. trim. dir. proc. civ. 2013, 677, 691.

88 *Silvestri*, Riv. trim. dir. proc. civ. 2013, 677, 691.

89 *von Hein*, RIW 2013, 97, 102.

90 *Nuyts*, RCDIP 102 (2013), 1, 59; *Nuyts*, in: Nuyts (coord.), Actualités en droit international privé (Bruxelles 2013), p. 77, 129.

91 See *Francq*, TBH 2013, 309, 326.

92 *Crespi Reghizzi* www.aldricus.com/2012/12/13/crespi; *von Hein*, RIW 2013, 97, 103; *Nuyts*, RCDIP 102 (2013), 1, 59.

93 *Nuyts*, RCDIP 102 (2013), 1, 59; *Nuyts*, in: Nuyts (coord.), Actualités en droit international privé (Bruxelles 2013), p. 77, 128.

94 *d'Avout*, D. 2013, 1014, 1020.

95 *Matthias Weller*, GPR 2012, 328, 331; *Geimer*, in: FS Gert Delle Karth (2013), p. 319, 330.

ee) Neither *forum fortunae* nor *forum necessitatis*

The generally conservative approach taken by the transformation of Art. 5 Brussels Regu- **21**
lation into Art. 7 Brussels I Regulation is supported by two other features of the Brussels I*bis*
Proposal which did not make it in the final recast. These features would have been found in
separate articles, not in what has now become Art. 7 but would have granted special jurisdiction: the *forum fortunae* and the *forum necessitatis* as put forward by Arts. 25; 26 Brussels
I*bis* Proposal. Both of them would have applied only against defendants resident outside the
Member States. This aligned and supplemented the proposed extensions of the heads of
special jurisdiction to defendants resident outside the Member States, and shared the same
fate. The overall approach of extending and taking a rougher stance on non-EU-defendants
faltered politically. The time was evidently not ripe yet for an approach which would have
introduced autarky in the European system for jurisdiction rules and excluded any recourse
to be had to national jurisdiction rules.[96]

3. Non-exclusivity and relationship with other heads of jurisdiction

a) Relationship with general jurisdiction under Art. 4

Art. 7 does not grant exclusive jurisdiction[97] and even less a defence for a defendant sued in **22**
his domicile.[98] Conversely, Art. 7 presupposes as a prerequisite that there is general jurisdiction within the EU. Art. 7 comes only into operation if the defendant has his domicile
within the EU and not in a non-Member State,[99] i.e. when the general requirements of Art. 4
are fulfilled. The opening words of the very wording make this abundantly and unmistak-
ably clear as they emphasise the defendant's domicile in a Member State as a prerequisite. If
the defendant is not domiciled in any Member State, Art. 7 is inapplicable whereas by virtue
of Art. 6 (1) the national rules on jurisdiction of the *forum* state apply.[100] Thus special
jurisdiction under any and whichever head of Art. 7 co-exists as a matter of definition with
general jurisdiction under Art. 4 and does not render Art. 4 inoperable.[101] Conversely,
whenever Art. 7 is operable the claimant has the choice between the respective head(s) of
Art. 7 and Art. 4.[102] For instance, a claimant is not forced to sue a German, domiciled in
Germany, who is running a business in England under (5) at the place of the business in
England, but can resort to Art. 4.[103] The choice afforded by this co-existence is given to the
claimant and is not to be pre-empted by the court which is not allowed to restrict this choice
by employing a doctrine of *forum non conveniens*.[104] The appropriateness of the court must
not be justified on a full blown *forum conveniens* analysis but in a much more limited

---

[96]   *d'Avout*, D. 2013, 1014, 1018.
[97]   See only OLG Nürnberg RdTW 2014, 119, 121; Trib. Rel. Porto Col. Jur. 1995 III 237, 239.
[98]   Cass. RCDIP 94 (2005), 732, 733; D. 2005, 1332; *Mahinga*, D. 2005, 1332, 1335; *Mourre/Lahlou*, Rev. dr.
       aff. int. 2005, 509, 520; *Gaudemet-Tallon*, RCDIP 94 (2005), 733, 739 *et seq.*
[99]   See only BGE 129 III 738; OGH ZfRV 2004, 77, 79; Rb. Rotterdam NIPR 2002 Nr. 48 p. 90.
[100] See only *Carrascosa González*, in: Calvo Caravaca, Art. 5.1 CB note 3.
[101] See only *Mahinga*, D. 2005, 1332, 1335.
[102] See only *Hofmann/Kunz*, in: Basler Kommentar, Art. 5 note 8; *Cachard*, DMF 2013, 987, 989.
[103] OLG Köln IHR 2005, 167, 168.
[104] *Boss Group Ltd. v. Boss France SA* [1997] 1 WLR 351, 358 (C.A., per *Saville* L.J.); *L'Aiglon Ltd. v. Gau Shan
       & Co. Ltd.* [1993] 1 Lloyd's Rep. 164, 175 (Q.B.D., *Hirst* J.); *Mahme Trust Reg v. Lloyd's TSB Bank plc*
       [2004] 2 Lloyd's Rep. 637, 641 (Ch.D., Sir *Andrew Morritt* V.-C.); *Rogerson*, [2001] Cambridge Yb. Eur. L.
       383.

manner, Art. 7 being a much more blunt instrument.[105] The conclusion that Art. 7 jurisdiction is not discretionary should go without saying.[106]

23 Art. 7 solely establishes special, facultative, specific or optional jurisdiction. But this co-existence is restricted insofar as special jurisdiction can only be established in a Member State different from the Member State where the defendant has his domicile.[107] In this regard the wording of Art. 7 is unambiguously clear, too. The starting clause before (1) expresses the restriction perfectly clear. It is less a restriction in terms of international jurisdiction than in terms of venue or local jurisdiction determining which court in a given state shall be competent. Since all heads of jurisdiction contained in Art. 7 (with the exception of (6)) also determine venue (or local jurisdiction in this meaning) the restriction is not to be neglected. Otherwise Art. 7 would permutate to a rule on local jurisdiction or venue only which it is not intended for.[108]

24 The relation with Art. 4 raises the question as to whether the fact that there exists a head of general jurisdiction, influences the interpretation of the heads for special jurisdiction contained in Art. 7. If a decision has to be made between an extensive and a restrictive interpretation of one of the heads of jurisdiction under Art. 7, it could arguably militate against an extensive interpretation that this would narrow and diminish the weight of general jurisdiction under Art. 4.[109] The principle of *actor sequitur forum rei* as earmarked and highlighted by Art. 4 should gain its proper weight and should not be overly pierced since nonetheless it is the fundamental principle attributing jurisdiction.[110] In particular, a cautious approach has to be advocated for wherever the possibility of a *forum actoris* arises and would thus not only negate, but partially reverse the principle laid down in Art. 4.[111] Since legal certainty is one of the main aims of the Regulation, Art. 7 should be interpreted in a way as to enable a normally well-informed defendant reasonably to foresee before which courts, other than those of the state in which he is domiciled, he may be sued.[112]

25 Although to allow for special jurisdiction besides general jurisdiction does not lead to general jurisdiction being extinguished or pushed aside entirely. Insofar the model employed by Art. 7 is absolutely different from e.g. Arts. 17–19 or Arts. 20–22 which erect

---

[105] *Rogerson*, [2001] Cambridge Yb. Eur. L. 383.

[106] *Rogerson*, [2001] Cambridge Yb. Eur. L. 383.

[107] See only BGE 131 III 76, 80 = EuLF 2005, II-48, II-50; CA Paris [2000] I.L.Pr. 799, 804; OLG Brandenburg IPRspr. 2009 Nr. 195 p. 504; *Slonina*, SZZP 2005, 313, 323; *Rolf Wagner/Gess*, NJW 2009, 3481, 3482.

[108] *Slonina*, SZZP 2005, 313, 323.

[109] *Schmidt-Kessel*, ZEuP 2004, 1021, 1025.

[110] *Rudolf Kronhofer v. Marianne Maier*, (Case C-168/02) [2004] ECR I-6009, I-6029 para. 13; *AMT Futures Ltd. v. Marzillier, Dr. Meier & Dr. Guntner Rechtsanwaltsgesellschaft mbH* [2014] EWHC 1085 (Comm), [2015] 2 WLR 187 [34] (Q.B.D., *Popplewell* J.).

[111] *Antonio Marinari v. Lloyd's Bank plc and Zubaidi Trading Co.*, (Case C-364/93) [1995] ECR I-2719, I-2739 para. 13.

[112] *Jakob Handte & Co. GmbH v. Traitements Mécano-chimiques des surfaces SA*, (Case C-26/91) [1992] ECR I-3967, I-3995 para. 18; *GIE Groupe Concorde v. Master of the vessel "Suhadiwarno Panjan"*, (Case C-440/97) [1999] I-6307, I-6350 *et seq.* para. 24; *Besix SA v. Wasserreinigungsbau Alfred Kretzschmar GmbH & Co. KG (WABAG) and Planungs- und Forschungsgesellschaft Dipl. Ing. W. Kretzschmar GmbH & Co. KG (Plafog)*, (Case C-256/00) [2002] ECR I-1699, I-1726, I-1733 paras. 26, 54.

their own cosmos and exclude Art. 4 from operation. Accordingly, Art. 7 should be mainly interpreted in its own right and on its own merits, this is the more so the case since at least Art. 7 (1) and (2) bear close relationships with acts of EU law in the field of PIL where a parallel to Art. 4 does not exist. For instance, to give "contract" a narrower meaning in the context of Art. 7 (1) than under the Rome I Regulation or previously under the Rome Convention would unduly separate sister Acts from each other.[113]

The mere existence of Art. 4 should not lead to the preponderance of a narrow or even **26** restrictive interpretation.[114] Insofar a standard phrase in the jurisprudence of the ECJ should not be overestimated. The Court has a number of standard paragraphs on its word processor, and these are slotted into judgments as if to suggest that what is said immediately after one of these boilerplate clauses is consistent with or may be dictated by it, e.g. the need to construe certain provisions restrictively.[115] Art. 4 is not a principle which may be derogated from only on grounds of absolute necessity.[116] It would be particularly unfortunate if such a narrow approach would be established at the expense of overall coherence of the Regulation.[117] The mere existence of heads of special jurisdiction as such enhances the possibility that the defendant is subjected to jurisdiction abroad (i.e. in another state than the state of his domicile). Hence, this possibility is inherent in the basic decision to install heads of special jurisdiction and must not be criticised abstractly or invoked as some kind of counter-

---

[113] See *infra* Art. 7 notes 39–50 (*Mankowski*).

[114] *Contra Rudolf Kronhofer v. Marianne Maier*, (Case C-168/02) [2004] ECR I-6009, I-6029 para. 14; *Falco Privatstiftung and Thomas Rabitsch v. Gisela Weller-Lindhorst*, (Case C-533/07) [2009] ECR I-3327, I-3382 *et seq.* para. 37; *Zuid-Chemie v. Philippo's Mineralenfabriek NV/SA*, (Case C-189/08) [2009] ECR I-6917, I-6927 para. 22; *Berliner Verkehrsbetriebe (BVG) Anstalt des öffentlichen Rechts v. JP Morgan Chase Bank NV, Frankfurt Branch*, (Case C-144/10) [2011] ECR I-3961 para. 30; *Melzer v. MF Global UK Ltd.* (Case C-228/11), ECLI:EU:C:2013:305 para. 24; *ÖFAB Östergötlands Fastigheter AB v. Frank Koot and Evergreen Investments BV* (Case C-147/12), ECLI:EU:C:2013:490 para. 31; *Peter Pinckney v. KDG Mediatech AG* (Case C-170/12), ECLI:EU:C:2013:635 para. 25; *Andreas Kainz v. Pantherwerke AG* (Case C-45/13), ECLI:EU:C:2014:7 para. 22; *Hi Hotel HCF SARL v. Uwe Spoering* (Case C-387/12), ECLI:EU: C:2014:215 para. 26; *Coty Germany GmbH v. First Note Perfumes NV* (Case C-360/12), ECLI:EU: C:2014:1318 para. 45; A-G *Jääskinen*, Opinion of 19 April 2012 in Case C-133/11 para. 56; A-G *Jääskinen*, Opinion of 29 November 2012 in Case C-228/11 para. 54; BGE 130 III 285, 289; *Handbridge Ltd. v. British Aerospace Communications Ltd.* [1993] 3 I.R. 342 = [1994] 1 ILRM 39 (S.C., per *Finlay* C.J.); *Leo Laboratories Ltd. v. Crompton BV* [2005] 2 ILRM 423, 429 (S.C., per *Fennelly* J.); *Royal & Sun Alliance Insurance plc v. MK Digital FZE (Cyprus) Ltd.* [2007] I.L. Pr. 29, 55 (C.A., per *Rix* L.J.); Hof Arnhem-Leeuwarden, locatie Leeuwarden NIPR 2014 Nr. 272 p. 477; *SanDisk Corp. v. Koninklijke Philips Electronics NV* [2007] ILPr 325, 333, 341 (Ch.D., *Pumfrey* J.); *AMT Futures Ltd. v. Marzillier, Dr. Meier & Dr. Guntner Rechtsanwaltsgesellschaft mbH* [2014] EWHC 1085 (Comm), [2015] 2 WLR 187 [34] (Q.B.D., *Popplewell* J.); A-G *Vlas*, NJ 2015 Nr. 44 p. 539, 541–542 and most dangerously A-G *Jääskinen*, Opinion of 11 December 2014 in Case C-352/13, ECLI:EU:C:2014:2443 para. 50. To the same avail as here *Donzallaz* para. 4422; *Oberhammer*, in: Dasser/Oberhammer, Art. 5 note 9; *Schlosser*, Vor Art. 5 note 3; *Geimer/Schütze*, Art. 5 note 1; *Kropholler/von Hein*, Vor Art. 5 note 3; *Leible*, in: Rauscher, Art. 5 note 3; *Hofmann/Kunz*, in: Basler Kommentar, Art. 5 note 5; see also Cassaz. RDIPP 2013, 1002, 1004.

[115] *Briggs*, [2005] LMCLQ 124.

[116] *Lando*, in: ECJ (ed.), Civil Jurisdiction and Judgments in Europe (1992), p. 23, 26; *Hau*, ZZP Int. 7 (2002), 214, 215.

[117] *Peel*, [1998] LMCLQ 22, 25.

Peter Mankowski

argument in single cases.[118] Every ground of jurisdiction under Art. 7 pursues a specific objective and is thus not inferior to Art. 4.[119] The extensive range of exceptions to Art. 4 renders any grudging attitude inappropriate.[120] Whereas Art. 4 looks at the defendant, Art. 7 looks at the substance matter.[121] The heads of jurisdiction contained in Art. 7 have been clearly and forcefully recognised as justifiable and desirable in the interests of certainty.[122]

27 Accordingly, each head of jurisdiction under Art. 7 should be judged separately, on its individual merits and properly without a restrictive guideline derived from the existence of Art. 4. The *effet utile* and the effectivity of the single head of jurisdiction should be the guiding maxim.[123] That an interpretation going beyond the cases expressly envisaged by Art. 7 should be avoided[124] is nothing more than a *petitio principii* if the question at stake is which cases are envisaged. It does for instance not bar attributing a broad scope to the notion of "contract" encompassing unilateral promises[125] or even concurring claims if the conduct complained of may be considered a breach of contract.[126] Even less (2) should be narrowly confined but allow for some judicial generosity favouring the alleged victim.[127] The principle

---

[118] *Geimer*, EuZW 1992, 518; *Holl*, WiB 1995, 462, 465; *Mankowski*, Jura 1996, 145, 148; *Peter Huber*, ZZP Int. 1 (1996), 171, 173; see also *Mercury Publicity Ltd. v. Wolfgang Loerke GmbH* [1992] I.L.Pr. 142, 154 (C.A., per *Purchas* L.J.); *Gascoine v. Pyrah* [1994] I.L.Pr. 82, 94 (Q.B.D., *Hirst* J.); *Pontier/Burg* pp. 55 *et seq.*; *Hess*, in: Liber amicorum Walter F. Lindacher (2007), p. 53, 55.

[119] *Bio-Medical Research Ltd. trading as Slendertone v. Delatex SA* [2001] 2 ILRM 51, 60 (S.C., per *Fennelly* J.).

[120] *Agnew v. Länsförsäkringsbolagens AB* [2001] 1 A.C. 223, 247 (H.L., per Lord *Cooke of Thorndon*).

[121] Report *Jenard* p. 22; *Bajons*, in: FS Reinhold Geimer (2002), p. 15, 41 *et seq.*; *de Franceschi*, Contratto e impresa/Europa 2008, 637, 662.

[122] *Credit Agricole Indosuez v. Chailease Finance Corp.* [2000] 1 All ER (Comm) 399, 411 (C.A., per *Potter* L.J.).

[123] Cassaz. RDIPP 2013, 1002, 1004; *Matthias Lehmann*, in: Dickinson/Lein para. 4.25.

[124] *Anastasios Kalfelis v. Bankhaus Schröder Münchmeyer Hengst & Cie.*, (Case 189/87) [1988] ECR 5565, 5585 para. 19; *Jakob Handte & Co. GmbH v. Traitements Mécano-chimiques des surfaces SA*, (Case C-26/91) [1992] ECR I-3967, I-3994 para. 14; *Réunion europénne SA v. Spliethoff's Bevrachtingskantoor BV and Master of the vessel "Alblasgracht 002"*, (Case C-51/97) [1998] ECR I-6511, I-6541 *et seq.* para. 16; *Freistaat Bayern v. Jan Blijdenstein*, (Case C-433/01) [2004] ECR I-981, I-1000 *et seq.* para. 25; *Rudolf Kronhofer v. Marianne Maier*, (Case C-168/02) [2004] ECR I-6009, I-6029 para. 14; *Melzer v. MF Global UK Ltd.* (Case C-228/11), ECLI:EU:C:2013:305 para. 24; *Coty Germany GmbH v. First Note Perfumes NV* (Case C-360/12), ECLI:EU:C:2014:1318 para. 45; *A-G Jääskinen*, Opinion of 21 November 2013 in Case C-360/12, ECLI:EU:C:2013:764 para. 51.

[125] *Petra Engler v. Janus Versand GmbH*, (Case C-27/02) [2005] ECR I-481, I-517 para. 48; *Samad*, 2010 ILT 233, 235.

[126] *Marc Brogsitter v. Fabrication de Montres Normandes EURL and Karsten Fräßdorf* (Case C-519/12), ECLI:EU:C:2014:148 paras. 24 *et seq.*

[127] *London Helicopters Ltd. v. Helportugal LDA-INAC* [2006] 1 All ER (Comm) 595, 601 (Q.B.D., *Simon* J.); *Briggs/Rees* para. 2.156. Implicitly recognising a certain tension between the alleged maxim of a restrictive interpretation and the case law regarding (3) *Zuid-Chemie v. Philippo's Mineralenfabriek NV/SA*, (Case C-189/08) [2009] ECR I-6917, I-6927 paras. 22–24; *Melzer v. MF Global UK Ltd.* (Case C-228/11), ECLI:EU:C:2013:305 paras. 24–25; *ÖFAB Östergötlands Fastigheter AB v. Frank Koot and Evergreen Investments BV* (Case C-147/12), ECLI:EU:C:2013:490 paras. 31–32; *Peter Pinckney v. KDG Mediatech AG* (Case C-170/12), ECLI:EU:C:2013:635 paras. 25–26; *Andreas Kainz v. Pantherwerke AG* (Case C-45/13),

of ubiquity as such displays such generosity (although each of its limbs should not be given too broad an interpretation).[128] The results of the ECJ's case law show a fairly different line than the boilerplate admonition verbally favouring a restrictive interpretation.[129] Since the list of heads of special jurisdiction contained in Arts. 7–9 is exhaustive[130] an extension nevertheless remains clearly confined. Beyond that, the language employed should be given its natural meaning and should not be artificially confined so as to produce unconvincingly narrow interpretations.[131] In particular, narrowing (1) is not necessarily a social good.[132] In any event, restrictive interpretation must not become destructive interpretation which is quite another thing.[133]

b) Relationship with other heads of jurisdiction in the Regulation

Friendly co-existence is also possible with the heads of jurisdiction found in Art. 8. Arts. 7   **28** and 8 are not mutually exclusive. An accumulation is possible since Art. 6 follows a different *ratio*, namely to bundle proceedings bearing a relationship with each other. Whereas Art. 7 looks at the *ratio materiae* of each single claim in isolation, Art. 8 pursues a *ratio connexitatis*.

Adversely, if one of the special regimes designed to protect weaker parties, found in Arts. 10–   **29** 16, 17–19 and 20–22 respectively, is applicable, Art. 7 can not be invoked save for an express proviso to the contrary. Arts. 10, 17 (1) and 20 (1) only contain an express proviso in favour of Art. 7 (5). Consequentially, all other heads of jurisdiction under Art. 7 are excluded if a collision with one of the special regimes arises. But as the special protective regimes operate only in contract, (2) should not be seriously affected.

It goes without saying that Art. 7 also gives way to any kind of exclusive jurisdiction under   **30** Art. 24 or Art. 25. Art. 7 does not contain *ius cogens* and can thus be derogated from by way of a party-made agreement on jurisdiction.[134] Even the most important head of jurisdiction in contract under (1) can be seen differently in this light as a mere default or fall-back rule in the case that the parties were for whichever reason not capable to exercise their prerogative by contractual agreement on jurisdiction.[135] Whether a jurisdiction clause as contained in a

---

ECLI:EU:C:2014:7 paras. 22–23; *Coty Germany GmbH v. First Note Perfumes NV* (Case C-360/12), ECLI: EU:C:2014:1318 para. 45–46; A-G *Jääskinen*, Opinion of 21 November 2013 in Case C-360/12, ECLI:EU: C:2013:764 para. 42.

[128] *Rudolf Kronhofer v. Marianne Maier*, (Case C-168/02) [2004] ECR I-6009, I-6029 *et seq.* para. 16; A-G *Jääskinen*, Opinion of 29 November 2012 in Case C-228/11 para. 54; *Thole*, in: FS Eberhard Schilken (2015), p. 523, 530.

[129] *Guzmán Zapater*, REDI 2009, 490, 491; *von Hein*, IPRax 2013, 505, 511; *Matthias Lehmann*, in: Dickinson/Lein para. 4.25.

[130] *Custom Made Commercial Ltd. v. Stawa Metallbau GmbH*, (Case C-288/92) [1994] ECR I-2913, I-2955 para. 12; *Frahuil SA v. Assitalia SpA*, (Case C-265/02) [2004] ECR I-1543, I-1555 para. 23.

[131] *Agnew v. Länsförsäkringsbolagens AB* [2001] 1 A.C. 223, 240 (H.L., per Lord *Woolf* M.R.).

[132] *Briggs*, (2000) 71 BYIL 435, 453.

[133] *Briggs*, (1996) 67 BYIL 577, 585.

[134] See only *Mainschifffahrts-Genossenschaft eG (MSG) v. Les Gravières Rhenanes SARL*, (Case C-106/95) [1997] ECR I-911, I-939 para. 14; LG Neubrandenburg IHR 2006, 26, 28; Vzngr. Rb. Rotterdam S&S 2011 Nr. 73 p. 379; *Leible*, in: Rauscher, Art. 5 note 1; *Hofmann/Kunz*, in: Basler Kommentar, Art. 5 note 20.

[135] *Hau*, IPRax 2000, 354, 357.

contract intends, and is wide enough to also cover claims in tort, is a matter of construction of the contractual clause.[136] Likewise, Art. 7 falls victim to tacit submission on the defendant's part pursuant to Art. 26. Furthermore, Art. 7 does not guarantee the plaintiff jurisdiction if the plaintiff himself had previously consented to a jurisdiction clause in favour of a court in a non-Member State of the EU with a such jurisdiction clause by recognition of party autonomy prevailing.[137]

c) Relationship between the heads of jurisdiction under Art. 7

31 Following from the non-exclusive nature of the single heads of jurisdiction which are independent of each other[137a], a claim could also come under two or more heads. But this can only occur if such co-existence is consistent with the scopes of application of the respective heads. Since most of the heads are restricted to certain classes of claims not covered by any other head and are insofar *ratione materiae* mutually exclusive, special jurisdiction under two or more heads for the same claim is a rare event. A claim in contract simply can not be a claim in tort simultaneously.[138] A claim in maritime salvage can not be regarded as a claim arising in matters of a trust. The likeliest candidate to co-exist with another head is Art. 7 (5) since it is not restricted to a specific class of claims[139] but covers, for instance, claims in contract (which also fall under Art. 7 (1)) or tort (which also fall under Art. 7 (2)). Another possibility is Art. 7 (3). Both Art. 7 (5) and (3) do not bear a restriction to certain classes of claims but require some link with the *forum* encompassing in principle all classes of claims. Practitioners are well advised and act wisely if they do not focus exclusively on a certain ground of jurisdiction but also open their mind to taking into account other grounds, particularly so in the swamp where (1) borders on (2).[140] Opting for an alternative reasoning, at least subsidiarily, might be an elegant choice as long as argumentation as to jurisdiction and argumentation as to the merits are consistent.[141]

d) Concurring jurisdiction

32 Special jurisdiction for different claims can lead to the same jurisdiction and to joint treatment by the same court.[142] But this is a coincidence as it relates to a multiplicity of claims not to the same claim. A claim in contract can be accompanied by a claim in tort resulting in both being tried in the same *forum* competent for the claim in contract by virtue of Art. 7 (1) and for the claim in tort by virtue of Art. 7 (2), but this is by no means a necessary event. Concurring jurisdiction is possible but not mandatory.[143]

---

[136] See only *Roche Products Ltd. v. Provimi Ltd.* [2003] 2 All ER (Comm) 683 (Q.B.D., *Aikens* J.); *Briggs*, (2003) 74 BYIL 535; *Vischer*, in: FS Erik Jayme (2004), p. 993.

[137] Aud. Prov. Madrid AEDIPr 2002, 699, 703 *et seq.* with note *Bouza Vidal*.

[137a] *Matthias Lehmann*, in: Dickinson/Lein para. 4.18.

[138] *Anastasios Kalfelis v. Bankhaus Schröder Münchmeyer Hengst & Cie.*, (Case 189/87) [1988] ECR 5565, 5585 *et seq.* para. 19 *et seq.*; *Base Metal Trading Ltd. v. Shamurin* [2005] 1 All ER (Comm) 17, 28 (C.A., per *Tuckey* L.J.).

[139] See only *Anton Durbeck GmbH v. Den Norske Bank ASA* [2003] 2 WLR 1296, 1309 (C.A., per Lord *Phillips of Worth Matravers* M.R.).

[140] *Gehri*, in: FS Ivo Schwander (2011), p. 699, 709.

[141] *Gehri*, in: FS Ivo Schwander (2011), p. 699, 708, 709.

[142] See only OLG Karlsruhe NJOZ 2007, 2153, 2154 *et seq.*; Rb. Rotterdam NIPR 2010 Nr. 492 p. 805; *Vlas*, NJ 2005 Nr. 39 p. 209, 210.

[143] See only *Vlas*, NJ 2005 Nr. 39 p. 209, 210.

Where the plaintiff alleges to have a majority of claims the question arises as to whether one **33** of those should be regarded as the most important claim, and whether consequentially jurisdiction of that claim should attract jurisdiction for the other claims too although these other claims if classified on their own merits, would not fall under the same head of jurisdiction as the "governing" claim. The most prominent instance where this issue gains importance is where the claims are allegedly founded in both contract and tort. The desire to save costs by joint treatment of the different claims might provide an incentive to allow for concurring jurisdiction to be construed.[144] The technical instrument would be some kind of attractiveness whereby the jurisdiction for one claim would attract the concurring jurisdiction for the other claim, too.[145]

Such a *forum attractivitatis* is not expressly provided for in the system of the Brussels I*bis* **34** Regulation. To the contrary, it would pierce the bounds of classification ordinarily applicable to the single heads of jurisdiction.[146] A supporting *argumentum e contrario* can be derived from Art. 8 where the Regulation expressly provides for *fora connexitatis* thus honouring the desire for joint proceedings, but only insofar as listed in Art. 8. The deeper concern, however, is that it would overly favour the plaintiff as it would provide him with a *forum* otherwise not available for the concurring claim, and in turn disfavour the defendant severely.[147] The entire system of heads of jurisdiction contained in the Brussels I*bis* Regulation tries to strike a fair balance between plaintiff and defendant. Its centrepiece, Art. 4, conveys the basic decision to value the defendant over the plaintiff in case of reasonable doubt. Here a case of considerable doubt is in question.[148] Furthermore, a *forum attractivitatis* would fit ill in jurisdictions which in their own law follow the principle of *non cumul* like most prominently France does.[149] For all these reasons, the better solution is that a *forum attractivitatis* does not exist.[150] Eventually, Art. 48 might bridge the gap between the different proceedings and provide for an appropriate instrument to handle them.[151]

---

[144] Most prominently advocated for by *Geimer*, IPRax 1986, 80, 81; *Geimer*, NJW 1988, 3089.

[145] Favouring such an approach e.g. OLG Koblenz RIW 1990, 316; *Geimer*, NJW 1988, 3089; *Gottwald*, IPRax 1989, 272, 273; *Gottwald*, in: Münchener Kommentar zur ZPO Art. 5 EuGVÜ with note 8; *Kropholler/von Hein* Art. 5 note 79; *Schlosser* Vor Art. 5 note 2k.

[146] *Leible*, in: Rauscher Art. 5 note 17.

[147] See only *Thomas Pfeiffer*, Internationale Zuständigkeit und prozessuale Gerechtigkeit (1995) p. 611; *Mankowski*, IPRax 1997, 173, 178; *Mankowski*, JZ 2003, 689 et seq.; *Spickhoff*, in: GS Halûk Konuralp, vol. I (2009), p. 977, 982 et seq.; *Spickhoff*, IPRax 2009, 128, 131 et seq.

[148] See *Anastasios Kalfelis v. Bankhaus Schröder Münchmeyer Hengst & Cie.*, (Case 189/87) [1988] ECR 5565, 5586 para. 20; *Réunion europénne SA v. Spliethoff's Bevrachtingskantoor BV and Master of the vessel "Alblasgracht 002"*, (Case C-51/97) [1998] ECR I-6511, I-6549 para. 49; Cass. RCDIP 93 (2004), 652 with note *Marie-Élodie Ancel*; HG Zürich SZIER 1996, 74, 75 note *Volken*; Rb. Middelburg NIPR 1996 Nr. 133 p. 204; *Mansel*, IPRax 1989, 84, 85; *Layton/Mercer* para. 15.016.

[149] *Schlosser*, LMK 2005, 79, 80.

[150] *Anastasios Kalfelis v. Bankhaus Schröder Münchmeyer Hengst & Cie.*, (Case 189/87) [1988] ECR 5565, 5585 et seq. paras. 19 et seq.; *Réunion europénne SA v. Spliethoff's Bevrachtingskantoor BV and Master of the vessel "Alblasgracht 002"*, (Case C-51/97) [1998] ECR I-6511, I-6549 para. 49; Cass. RCDIP 93 (2004), 652 with note *Marie-Élodie Ancel*; OLG Köln WM 2006, 122, 125; HG Zürich SZIER 1996, 74, 75 note *Volken*; Rb. Middelburg NIPR 1996 Nr. 133 p. 204.

[151] *Anastasios Kalfelis v. Bankhaus Schröder Münchmeyer Hengst & Cie.*, (Case 189/87) [1988] ECR 5565, 5586 para. 20.

35 Accordingly, neither does the *forum delicti* attract concurring contractual claims,[152] nor *vice versa* does the *forum contractus* attract concurring claims in tort.[153] The former contention can be additionally supported by the argument that the tortious activity does not imprint its stamp mark and signature on the contract, but is rather fortuitous if viewed in relation to the contract.[154] Furthermore, extending and widening the scope of the *forum delicti* could possibly lead to an augmented potential for threats and the probability of inefficient compromises.[155] Unwelcome *forum shopping* for contractual claims by simply alleging a concurring tort would become too seductive an option for the claimant.[156] Neither does replacing the traditional *forum loci delicti* with an accessory connection following a governing contract form part of the *lex lata* under the Brussels I*bis* Regulation.[157] Admittedly, Art. 4 (3) cl. 2 Rome II Regulation has bolstered the opposite result.[158] Re-characterizing certain claims in tort as claims in contract if they can be said to be based on a breach of contractual obligations,[159] and the result that two claims in contract compete is an bypassing escape strategy.[160] That competing claims would be related in the sense Art. 30 employs, does not change the picture since Art. 30 is not a rule on jurisdiction and does not vest jurisdiction in any court.[161]

---

[152] *Anastasios Kalfelis v. Bankhaus Schröder Münchmeyer Hengst & Cie.*, (Case 189/87) [1988] ECR 5565, 5585 para. 19; *Réunion européenne SA v. Spliethoff's Bevrachtingskantoor BV and Master of the vessel "Alblasgracht 002"*, (Case C-51/97) [1998] ECR I-6511, I-6549 para. 49; BGHZ 132, 105, 112 *et seq.*; BGHZ 153, 173, 180; BGH WM 2005, 339, 341 *et seq.* = NJW-RR 2005, 581, 583 *et seq.*; Cass. RCDIP 93 (2004), 652 with note *Marie-Élodie Ancel*; OLG Brandenburg IPRspr. 2006 Nr. 115; OLG Dresden IPRspr. 2007 Nr. 140 = NJ 2007, 509 with note *Ochmann*; OLG Düsseldorf IPRspr. 2008 Nr. 25 p. 60; HG Zürich SZIER 1996, 74, 75 note *Volken*; Rb. Middelburg NIPR 1996 Nr. 133 p. 204; Rb. Roermond NIPR 2007 Nr. 320 p. 438; *Blobel*, EuLF 2005, I-68, I-70. *Contra Banniza von Bazan*, Der Gerichtsstand des Sachzusammenhangs im EuGVÜ, dem Lugano-Abkommen und im deutschen Recht (1995) pp. 148 *et seq.*; *Otte*, Umfassende Streitentscheidung durch Beachtung von Sachzusammenhängen (1998) pp. 520 *et seq.*; *Herbert Roth*, in: FS Ekkehard Schumann (2001), p. 355; *Geimer/Schütze* Art. 5 note 222.

[153] See only Hoge Raad NJ 2005 Nr. 39 p. 208 with note *Vlas*; *Watson v. First Choice Holidays and Flights Ltd.* [2001] 2 Lloyd's Rep. 339, 343 (C.A., per *Lloyd* J.); OLG Stuttgart OLGR Stuttgart 2009, 717; OLG München WM 2010, 1463, 1466; Protodikeio Athinai EED 1998, 227 with note *Vassilikakis*; Protodikeio Thessaloniki Arm. 2002, 1167; *Spickhoff*, in: FS Gerda Müller (2009), p. 287, 293.

[154] *Matthias Schwarz*, Der Gerichtsstand der unerlaubten Handlung nach deutschem und europäischem Zivilprozeßrecht (1991) p. 169; *Lohse*, Das Verhältnis von Vertrag und Delikt (1991) p. 26; *Mankowski*, IPRax 1997, 173, 178; *Mankowski*, JZ 2003, 689, 690; *Schlosser*, LMK 2005, 79, 80.

[155] *Mankowski*, JZ 2003, 689, 690.

[156] *Johannes Hager*, in: FS Otto Rudolf Kissel (1994), p. 237; *Mankowski*, JZ 2003, 689, 690.

[157] *Mankowski*, in: FS Andreas Heldrich (2005), p. 867, 886.

[158] *Spickhoff*, IPRax 2009, 128 132; *von Hein*, IPRax 2010, 330, 342; *Kropholler/von Hein*, Art. 5 note 79.

[159] *Marc Brogsitter v. Fabrication de Montres Normandes EURL and Karsten Fräßdorf* (Case C-519/12), ECLI:EU:C:2014:148 paras. 21–27.

[160] *Baumert*, EWiR 2014, 435, 436.

[161] See only *Burke v. UVEX Sports GmbH and Motorrad TAF GmbH* [2005] I.L.Pr. 348, 355 (High Ct. of Ireland, *Herbert* J.).

II. Special jurisdiction in contract, Art. 7 (1)

1. General considerations

a) Structure

In cross-border trade or commerce, (1) is by far the most important special head of juris-   **36**
diction contained not only in Art. 7 but in the entire Brussels I Regulation since it provides a
special *forum* in contract, i.e. in the main instrument of commerce.[162] (1) is not intended at
personally benefiting certain classes of creditors but takes into account that the creditor and
debtor in contract are linked by a voluntary bond.[163] It attains an equal balance for the
creditor preventing and avoiding the undesirable result that the debtor would be overly
favoured by an exclusive application of Art. 4.[164] In its complex structure (1) reflects a
compromise between an autonomous solution and the model which developed under its
predecessor Art. 7 (1) Brussels Convention. Without repeated recourse to both the history
and the genesis (1) can not be understood properly.[165] In particular (1) (a) disguises more
than it reveals at first glance and ought to be read in the light of the previous judgments of
the ECJ starting with two of the oldest under the Brussels Convention, namely *Tessili* and *de
Bloos*, both of 1976.[166] (b) is the modernising element as it introduces an autonomous fact-
based concept for the most important categories of contracts. Then follows (c), which comes
as some kind of surprise, as at first glance it appears to be a kind of catch-all clause[167] but in
reality only has a very limited scope.[168]

The main rule is stated in (b). (b) is *lex specialis* to (a) and thus gains prevalence over (a)   **37**
since it deals with two specific categories of contracts whereas (a) covers all types of contracts.[169] Although it treats only two categories (b) covers most contracts as the majority of
contracts in international trade can be identified either as contracts for the sale of goods or
contracts for performing services. Outside and besides these categories only a rather frac-
tional remainder of contracts exists. Insofar (a) sounds more comprehensive than it actually
turns out to be. In practice, the application of (a) is exceptional and not the rule.[170] It serves a

---

[162] See only *Mankowski*, in: FS Andreas Heldrich (2005), p. 867, 889; *Kropholler/von Hein* Art. 5 note 1.

[163] *Matthias Lehmann*, ZZP Int. 9 (2004), 172, 182 *et seq.*; see also *Manfred Wolf*, in: Liber amicorum Walter
F. Lindacher (2007), p. 201, 210 *et seq.*

[164] *Schack*, Der Erfüllungsort im deutschen, ausländischen und internationalen Privat- und Zivilprozessrecht (1985) p. 104; *Schack*, para. 256; *Matthias Lehmann*, ZZP Int. 9 (2004), 172, 183.

[165] A-G *Bot*, [2007] ECR I-3702, I-3710 para. 43.

[166] References *infra* in Art. 7 notes 198, 205; see in particular *Marie-Élodie Ancel*, RCDIP 90 (2001), 158, 159.

[167] See *Kerameus*, in: Liber amicorum Pierre Widmer (2003), p. 163, 166.

[168] Misconceived by *Falco Privatstiftung and Thomas Rabitsch v. Gisela Weller-Lindhorst*, (Case C-533/07)
[2009] ECR I-3327, I-3383 para. 40; *Corman-Collins SA v. La Maison du Whisky SA*, (Case C-9/12), ECLI:
EU:C:2013:860 para. 42; *Marc Brogsitter v. Fabrication de Montres Normandes EURL and Karsten
Fräßdorf* (Case C-519/12), ECLI:EU:C:2014:148 para. 28.

[169] Approved by Rapport *Potocki*, RCDIP 100 (2011), 139, 144–145 = DMF 2011, 231, 234–235; *Markus*,
AJP 2010, 971, 973; *Hannes Wais*, IPRax 2011, 138, 142. To the same avail Trib. Trapani Giur. mer. 2011,
1599, 1600; Rb. Rotterdam NIPR 2011 Nr. 250 p. 438; *Berlioz*, Clunet 135 (2008), 675, 677; *van Lith*,
International Jurisdiction and Commercial Litigation – Uniform Rules for Contract Disputes (The Hague
2009) p. 86; *Franzina*, RDIPP 2010, 655, 658; *García Gutiérrez*, REDI 2013–1, 305, 307.

[170] *Droz/Gaudemet-Tallon*, RCDIP 90 (2001), 601, 634; *Kropholler/von Hein* Art. 5 note 28; *Wernicke/Vera*

---

purely subsidiary function only.[171] (b) is the leading rule for practical purposes.[172] The overall structure and (c) in particular establish a strict hierarchy with (a) being intended to apply only in the alternative and by default with respect to (b).[173]

38   For practical purpose the first look should be in the contract, namely whether it contains a concrete agreement on the place of performance.[174] If this is not the case one should start with (b).[175] If the contract in question does not fall under (b) because that contract can not be classified as a contract for the sale of goods or for performing services, one has to fall back upon (a).[176] Hence, the application of (a) is essentially a matter of a negative characterisation under (b).[177] The scope of (a) effectively is a matter of subtraction: all contracts minus the contracts covered by (b).[178] If the contract comes within either of the two categories under (b), but the place of performance as determined following (b) is located outside the EU, (c) comes into operation and leads back to (a).[179] Hence, (b) ought to be asked first whether it is applicable. Insofar additional issues of characterisation beyond classifying an issue as contractual arise.[180]

b) **Characterisation**

aa) **Contractual issues**

39   (1) *in toto* requires that a contractual issue is at the core of the claim. Accordingly, a question of classification arises. The question is tricky, and answers might not be easily found in concrete cases.[181] One has to assert whether the core matter of the present claim falls under the concept of "contract" underlying (1). Two steps are necessary. Firstly, a definition of "contract" ought to be developed.[182] For the sake of uniformity an autonomous and inde-

---

Hoppe, MMR 2002, 643, 645; *Muir Watt*, RCDIP 97 (2008), 140; *Markus*, Tendenzen beim materiell-rechtlichen Vertragserfüllungsort im internationalen Zivilverfahrensrecht (Basel 2009) p. 139; *Markus*, AJP 2010, 971, 973; *Henri Storme*, R.W. 2009–2010, 409, 410; see also *Wipping*, Der europäische Gerichtsstand des Erfüllungsortes – Art. 5 Nr. 1 EuGVVO (2008) p. 133.

[171]   See only A-G *Bot*, [2007] ECR I-3702, I-3717 para. 86; *Ragno*, Convenzione di Vienna e Diritto europeo (2008) p. 212; *Kropholler/von Hein*, Art. 5 note 28.

[172]   See A-G *Bot*, [2007] ECR I-3702, I-3717 para. 86.

[173]   *Corman-Collins SA v. La Maison du Whisky SA*, (Case C-9/12), ECLI:EU:C:2013:860 para. 42; *Marc Brogsitter v. Fabrication de Montres Normandes EURL and Karsten Fräßdorf* (Case C-519/12), ECLI:EU:C:2014:148 para. 28; A-G *Jääskinen*, Opinion of 25 April 2013 in Case 9/12, para. 67; Cass. RCDIP 100 (2011), 917; *Jeremy Heymann*, Clunet 141 (2014), 888, 899.

[174]   See only Rb. Haarlem NIPR 2010 Nr. 86 p. 164; *Simotta*, in: Fasching/Konecny Art. 5 note 92.

[175]   Approved by Rapport *Potocki*, RCDIP 100 (2011), 139, 144 *et seq.* = DMF 2011, 231, 234 *et seq.*

[176]   Paradigmatically Cass. DMF 2011, 241; Rb. Rotterdam NIPR 2004 Nr. 156 p. 251; *Gehri*, Wirtschaftsrechtliche Zuständigkeiten im internationalen Zivilprozessrecht der Schweiz (2002) p. 197; see also *Layton/Mercer* para. 15.003.

[177]   Rb. Leeuwarden NIPR 2010 Nr. 484 p. 791; Rb. Leeuwarden NIPR 2010 Nr. 485 p. 793; *Marie-Élodie Ancel*, RCDIP 90 (2001), 158, 160; *Simotta*, in: Fasching/Konecny Art. 5 notes 89, 91.

[178]   See OLG Saarbrücken IPRax 2013, 74, 77.

[179]   See in more detail *infra* Art. 7 notes 141–144 (*Mankowski*).

[180]   *Tagaras*, CDE 2003, 399, 404.

[181]   *Sindres*, J-Cl. Dr. int. fasc. 584-130 no. 5 (mars 2014).

[182]   In detail *Haftel*, La notion de matière contractuelle en droit international privé (Thèse Paris II 2008);

pendent interpretation without reference to any national law in particular (be it the *lex fori* or the *lex causae)* is required.[183] The phrase "matters relating to contract" must not be taken as referring to how the legal relationship in question is classified by the relevant national law.[184] Generally, the wording of (1) should not be overrated in this detail since the versions in the different languages are sometimes wider ("en matière contractuelle", "in materia contrattuale", "matters relating to a contract"), sometimes narrower ("verbintenissen uit overeenkomst"), and sometimes in between ("vertragliche Ansprüche").[185] Secondly, the concrete matter has to undergo subsumption under that definition.[186]

The ordinary case of "contract" appears evident and obvious: a mutual consent binding **40** upon all parties under which each party has to perform obligations. Consensual transactions are contracts.[187] Obligations voluntarily assumed by agreement are contractual by their nature.[188] This is by no means restricted to commercial transactions, but covers all and every mutual agreements.[189]

But does this exhaustively and comprehensively define "contract" also with regard to less **41** obvious cases? Can there be a conclusion that anything else apart from a mutual contract with consideration (in the English legal terminology) can not be treated as a "contract" for the purposes of Art. 7 (1)? Should the seemingly obvious impression gained at first glance narrow the overall concept, or should this concept be broader? Some examples of practical importance might suffice to illustrate and emphasise the problem: How about cheques, bills of exchange or independent warranties (the latter issued by the producer not by the seller)?[190] Apart from classifying these instruments of a rather unilateral than mutual nature,

---

Reiher, Der Vertragsbegriff im europäischen Internationalen Privatrecht (2011); *Queguiner*, Qualification et d'termination de la compétence spéciale – L'exemple de la matière contractuelle (Thèse Lyon III 2012). Comparative survey including European private law *Matthias Storme*, TPR 2008, 305.

[183] *Martin Peters Bauunternehmung GmbH v. Zuid Nederlandse Aannemers Vereniging*, (Case 34/82) [1983] ECR 987, 1002 para. 10; *SPRL Arcado v. SA Haviland*, (Case 9/87) [1988] ECR 1539, 1554 *et seq.* paras. 10 *et seq.; Jakob Handte & Co. GmbH v. Traitements Mécano-chimiques des surfaces SA*, (Case C-26/91) [1992] ECR I-3967, I-3993 para. 10; *Réunion europénne SA v. Spliethoff's Bevrachtingskantoor BV and Master of the vessel "Alblasgracht 002"*, (Case C-51/97) [1998] ECR I-6511, I-6541 para. 15; *Frahuil SA v. Assitalia SpA*, (Case C-265/02) [2004] ECR I-1543, I-1554 para. 22; *Marc Brogsitter v. Fabrication de Montres Normandes EURL and Karsten Fräßdorf* (Case C-519/12), ECLI:EU:C:2014:148 para. 21; Hof Amsterdam NIPR 2009 Nr. 133 p. 232; Aud. Prov. Barcelona AEDIPr 2001, 898, 900; Trib. Padova, sez. Este RDIPP 2007, 147, 150; *Oberhammer/Slonina*, in: Studia in honorem Pelayia Yessiou-Faltsi (2007), p. 419, 428; *Sindres*, J-Cl. Dr. int. fasc. 584-130 nos. 6–7 (mars 2014).

[184] *Jakob Handte & Co. GmbH v. Traitements Mécano-chimiques des surfaces SA*, (Case C-26/91) [1992] ECR I-3967, I-3993 para. 10; Cass. January 17, 2006 – *Koogar v. AMS Neve. Stephan Lorenz/Unberath*, IPRax 2005, 516, 518 advocate that even claims between former fiancés stemming the split or breach of an engagement qualify under (1) barring Art. 1 (2) (a).

[185] *Martiny*, in: FS Reinhold Geimer (2002), p. 641, 648.

[186] See only *Falco Privatstiftung and Thomas Rabitsch v. Gisela Weller-Lindhorst*, (Case C-533/07) [2009] ECR I-3327, I-3381 *et seq.* paras. 28–41.

[187] *Agnew v. Länsförsäkringsbolagens AB* [2001] 1 A.C. 223, 264 (H.L., per Lord *Millett*).

[188] *Base Metal Trading Ltd. v. Shamurin* [2005] 1 All ER (Comm) 17, 27 (C.A., per *Tuckey* L.J.).

[189] Høyesteret [1998] I.L.Pr. 804, 806.

[190] See Art. 5 note 60.

---

questions might arise as to the classification of side issues which can occur in the vicinity of any contract, i.e. claims for terminating negotiations without a justifying reason, or claims for damage done to the goods or assets of either party in the conduct of a negotiation or of the performance of a contract concluded.

42 "Contract" should be given a broader meaning[191] adjusted to the underpinning economic issues.[192] Offer and acceptance as such are not the all-decisive elements.[193] The paramount borderline is to distinguish between contract and tort.[194] Functionally, two distinguishing features can be detected: the fortuitous character of the meeting of the parties on the one hand, and the possibility or opportunity for (self-)protection or distribution of risks by agreement on the other hand.[195] A contract is the result of strategic and co-operative inter-action between the parties searching to transform an uncooperative game into a cooperative game.[196] Its core consists of reliable commitment which is sanctioned and enforceable.[197] It aims at protecting transaction specific investments.[198] The creditor chooses deliberately to invest. He is active and not only passively subjected to the debtor's activities[199] since contract is a mechanism for planning and for reducing complexity.[200] Choice, commitment and co-operation are the keywords for contract.[201] An involuntary creditor in tort has nothing to chose. The accidental meeting is not the intentional meeting of the minds.[202] Electronization has not changed the notion of contract a bit(e).[203]

43 That the debtor voluntarily entered into it technically is the basic characteristic feature of a contractual obligation. If the obligation at stake is not freely assumed by the debtor it can not be characterised as contractual.[204] Where a sub-buyer of goods purchased from an inter-

---

[191] See only *Petra Engler v. Janus Versand GmbH*, (Case C-27/02) [2005] ECR I-481, I-517 para. 48; A-G *Szpunar*, Opinion in Case C-375/13 of 3 September 2014, ECLI:EU:C:2014:2135 para. 49; BAG AP Nr. 1 zu Art. 5 Lugano-Abkommen Bl. 5 note *Mankowski*; OLG Saarbrücken IPRax 2013, 74, 77; *Ferrari*, Giust. civ. 2007 I 1397, 1405 *et seq.*

[192] *Mankowski*, IPRax 2003, 127, 131.

[193] *Stephan Lorenz/Unberath*, IPRax 2005, 219, 222.

[194] See only OLG Hamburg WRP 2015, 87 [61]; *Hofmann/Kunz*, in: Basler Kommentar, Art. 5 note 72.

[195] *Mankowski*, IPRax 2003, 127, 131.

[196] *Urs Schweizer*, Vertragstheorie (1999) p. 5; *Brousseau/Glachant*, in: Brousseau/Glachant (eds.), The Economics of Contract (2002) p. 3; *Cooter/Ulen*, Law and Economics (4th ed. 2003) p. 196 *et seq.*

[197] See only *Masten*, in: Bouckaert/De Geest (eds.), Encyclopedia of Law and Economics, vol. III (2000), p. 25, 26.

[198] See only *Oliver E. Williamson*, 22 J. L. & Econ. 233 (1979); *Katz*, in: Newman (ed.), The New Palgrave Dictionary of Economics and the Law, vol. I: A-D (2nd ed. 1998), p. 425, 427.

[199] *Mankowski*, IPRax 2003, 127, 131.

[200] *Macaulay*, in: L. Friedman/Macaulay, Law and the Behavioral Sciences (2nd ed. 1977), p. 141; *Ripperger*, Ökonomik des Vertrauens (1998) p. 29.

[201] See only *Macneil*, The New Social Contract (1980) p. 3 *et seq.*; *Oliver E. Williamson*, in: Brousseau/Glachant (eds.), The Economics of Contract (2002), p. 49.

[202] *Ghestin*, in: Brousseau/ Glachant (eds.), The Economics of Contract (2002), p. 99, 102–104.

[203] *Marianne Roth*, in: Studia in honorem Pelayia Yessiou-Faltsi (2007), p. 531, 537 *et seq.*

[204] *Jakob Handte & Co. GmbH v. Traitements Mécano-chimiques des surfaces SA*, (Case C-26/91) [1992] ECR I-3967, I-3994 para. 15; *Réunion europénne SA v. Spliethoff's Bevrachtingskantoor BV and Master of the vessel "Alblasgracht 002"*, (Case C-51/97), [1998] ECR I-6511, I-6542 para. 17; *Fonderie Officine*

mediate seller brings an action against the manufacturer for damages on the ground that the goods are not in conformity, no contractual relationship between the sub-buyer and the manufacturer exists because the latter has not undertaken any contractual obligation against the former.[205] It is immaterial whether the substantive law of the *forum* (be it the applicable substantive law or not) qualifies product liability as contractual[206] since the meaning of "contract" under (1) must be an independent and autonomous one. Legal certainty and predictability demand that the manufacturer or any previous seller must not be confronted with a writ by a person personally unknown to him in the contractual *forum destinatae solutionis*.[207] *Pacta tertiis nec nocent nec prosunt* appears to be the appropriate adage.[208] Additionally, in a chain of contracts, the parties' contractual rights and obligations may vary from contract to contract so that the contractual rights a buyer can enforce against his immediate seller will not necessarily be identical with, and equal to, the rights which the seller can exercise against his own seller or the rights which the manufacturer will have accepted in his relationship with the first buyer/re-seller.[209] A chain of contract does not overcome the principle of privity of contract. There are contractual relations in it, but only relatively between the respective parts of the chain, not directly between all and every parts of the chain.[210]

As to the scope to which claims arising in connection with a contract can be characterised as **44** contractual, Art. 12 Rome I Regulation provides a most helpful guideline: An issue listed in Art. 12 (1) Rome I Regulation should be classified as contractual for the purposes of (1), as well.[211] Otherwise the interpretation of the sister acts would differ in a paramount issue of

---

Meccaniche Tacconi SpA von Heinrich Wagner Sinto Maschinenfabrik GmbH, (Case C-334/00) [2002] ECR I-7357, I-7393 para. 23; *Frahuil SA v. Assitalia SpA*, (Case C-265/02) [2004] ECR I-1543, I-1555 para. 24; *Petra Engler v. Janus Versand GmbH*, (Case C-27/02) [2005] ECR I-481, I-517 para. 50; *Česká spořitelna as v. Gerald Feichter*, (Case C-419/11), ECLI:EU:C:2013:165 paras. 46 *et seq.*; *ÖFAB Östergötlands Fastigheter AB v. Frank Koot and Evergreen Investments BV* (Case C-147/12), ECLI:EU:C:2013:490 para. 33; *OTP Bank Nyilvánosan Működő Részvénytársaság v. Hochtief Solution AG* (C-519/12), ECLI: EU:C:2013:674 para. 23; *Harald Kolassa v. Barclays Bank plc* (Case C-375/13), ECLI:EU:C:2015:37 para. 39; Cassaz. Foro it. 2006 col. 3388, 3394 = RDIPP 2006, 1076, 1082; BGHZ 176, 342 = NJW 2008, 2344; BGH WM 2014, 1614 [26]; OLG Saarbrücken IPRax 2013, 74, 77; OLG Hamburg WRP 2015, 87 [61]; Rb. Rotterdam NIPR 2011 Nr. 250 p. 437. *Sindres*, J-Cl. Dr. int. fasc. 584-130 no. 9 (mars 2014) complains this to leave some uncertainty.

205 *Jakob Handte & Co. GmbH v. Traitements Mécano-chimiques des surfaces SA*, (Case C-26/91) [1992] ECR I-3967, I-3994 *et seq.* para. 16; *Béraudo*, Clunet 128 (2001), 1033, 1041.

206 Wrongly decided by Cass. RCDIP 76 (1987), 612 with note *Gaudemet-Tallon*. But correctly Cass. DMF 1995, 283, 286 with note *Tassel*.

207 *Jakob Handte & Co. GmbH v. Traitements Mécano-chimiques des surfaces SA*, (Case C-26/91) [1992] ECR I-3967, I-3995 para. 19.

208 *Franzina*, Riv. dir. int. 2003, 714, 727.

209 *Jakob Handte & Co. GmbH v. Traitements Mécano-chimiques des surfaces SA*, (Case C-26/91) [1992] ECR I-3967, I-3995 para. 17.

210 A-G *Szpunar*, Opinion in Case C-375/13 of 3 September 2014, ECLI:EU:C:2014:2135 paras. 51–52.

211 Seminally still *SPRL Arcado v. SA Haviland*, (Case 9/87) [1988] ECR 1539, 1555 para. 15. See additionally Cass. RCDIP 90 (2001), 153, 154; *Kleinwort Benson Ltd. v. Glasgow City Council* [1996] 2 All ER 257 (C. A.); *Barclays Bank plc v. City of Glasgow Council* [1993] Q.B. 429, 440 (Q.B.D., *Hirst* J.); *Mankowski*, IPRax 1997, 173, 176; see also *Sindres*, J-Cl. Dr. int. fasc. 584-130 no. 17 (mars 2014).

utmost importance. At least there is not a trace of a convincing reason why such divergence should be allowed to intrude and disturb. The Brussels and Rome Conventions were designed to compliment each other.[212] The Recitals (7) of the two Rome Regulations make them and the Brussels I*bis* Regulation an interpretative threesome and tie them to some kind of united entity. Accordingly, the respective interpretation should pay mutual respect to the other acts.[213] If private international law answers the question which issues have to be characterised as contractual in an extensive (if not comprehensive) manner, the law on jurisdiction should follow this lead as closely as possible and should not deviate without proper justification or better insight, the less since historically private international law was concerned earlier with issues of classification and has developed more sophisticated answers. With the growing number of EU instruments in the area of contract law, the ambition and desire should thrive for a common und uniform understanding of "contract" throughout all European instruments.[214] Even the DCFR and its definition of contract in its Art. II – 4:101 provide interpretative guidance[215] despite its lack of official and binding character.

45 A very formal counter-argument formerly read that the Rome Convention was not binding upon the Accession States which were not signatories of the Rome Convention. The Rome I Regulation has cured this anyway (now Denmark could be the special case). Beyond that, the Accession States accepted the *acquis communautaire* as it stands including the interpretation of existing Community acts by the ECJ. Additionally, the Accession States did not raise any protest against the interpretation of the Brussels Convention being transferred to the Brussels I Regulation in particular.

46 But does the term "contract" in (1) not fulfil a function different from the role which it has to perform with regard to the Rome I Regime? Under the Rome I Regime it is the basic term whereas for the purposes of (1) it only serves as the common denominator for but one case of special jurisdiction. Special jurisdiction can be seen as a deviation from general jurisdiction and thus it could tentatively be argued that "contract" should be construed restrictively as far as (1) is concerned.[216] However, the price would be way too high: to alienate the two sister regimes.[217] There has never been something like a genuinely procedural definition of "contract", nor will there ever be.

47 The assertive look at Art. 12 Rome I Regulation has the additional advantage to stress and emphasize that rules for the breach of contract, even if they are contained in legal acts, should be qualified as contractual.[218] Contract law is underlying and supplementing contracts. It serves as the foundation for quasi-implied terms in a contract.[219] Not only those

---

[212] Report *Schlosser* para. 155.

[213] See only *SPRL Arcado v. SA Haviland*, (Case 9/87) [1988] ECR 1539, 1555 para. 15; BGHZ 123, 380, 384 *et seq.*; *Mankowski*, RIW 1994, 421, 423; *Magnus*, in: FS 75 Jahre Max-Planck-Institut für Privatrecht (2001) p. 571.

[214] *Briggs*, (2003) 119 L.Q.Rev. 352, 356.

[215] A-G *Trstenjak*, [2009] ECR I-3962, I-3985 para. 49; *Bach*, IHR 2010, 17, 25; *von Hein*, IPRax 2013, 54, 55.

[216] *Schmidt-Kessel*, ZEuP 2004, 1021, 1025.

[217] See *infra* Art. 5 note 43 (*Mankowski*) and *Pertegás*, in: Meeusen/Pertegás/Straetmans (eds.), Enforcement of International Contracts in the European Union (2004), p. 175, 181 § 5–17.

[218] *Mankowski*, IPRax 2003, 127, 132.

[219] *Agnew v. Länsförsäkringsbolagens AB* [2001] 1 A.C. 223, 253 (H.L., per Lord *Hope of Craighead*); *Mennie*,

obligations are contractual which are expressly spelled out by the parties in the contract itself, but also those contained in implied terms in English terminology[220] and in supplementary rules of contract law.[221] The perfect contract stipulating for all and every contingency does not exist as its negotiation would run into prohibitively high transaction costs.[222] Damages for a breach of contract arising *ex lege* fall under (1),[223] also if due for late performance.[224] La *rupture brutale* (as French law regulates it in Art. 442-6 (1) pt. 5 C. comm.) is contractual.[225] Every contractual remedy qualifies as exactly that: a *contractual* remedy.[226] Likewise, contractual penalties based on penalty clauses are contractual.[227]

The ECJ in *Brogsitter* supports a very broad understanding of "contract". A claim concerns **48** matters relating to a contract in the sense of (1) if the conduct complained of may be considered a breach of contract.[228] That will be *a priori* the case where the interpretation of the contract which links the defendant to the applicant is indispensable to establish the lawful or, on the contrary, unlawful nature of the conduct complained of against the former by the latter.[229] It is for the national court to determine in the concrete case whether the purpose of the claims brought is to seek damages the legal basis of which can reasonably be regarded as a breach of the rights and obligations set out in the contract which would make its taking into account indispensable in deciding the action.[230] If so the case falls under (1), if not it falls under (2).[231] Hence, the judge sitting is called upon to do a good deal of checking as to substance already at the stage of determining jurisdiction.[232] One step further, there is a slight danger that after classifying a claim as contractual for the purposes of jurisdiction, the

---

1990 SLT (News) 1, 5. But cf. *Bank of Scotland v. Investment Management Regulatory Ltd.* 1989 SLT 432, 443, 445 (Ct. Sess. Extra Div., per Lords *Morison* and *Maxwell* respectively).

[220] *Raiffeisen Zentralbank Österreich AG v. National Bank of Greece SA* [1999] 1 Lloyd's Rep. 408, 412 (Q.B. D., *Tuckey* J.).

[221] OLG Bremen RIW 1998, 63; OLG Jena ZIP 1998, 1496, 1497; OLG Koblenz NZG 2001, 759, 760 with note *Günther Christian Schwarz*; OLG Dresden VuR 2002, 187, 189; *Mankowski*, IPRax 2003, 127, 131; see also *Engdiv Ltd. v. G. Percy Trentham Ltd.* 1990 SLT 617 (O.H., Lord *Prosser*); Rb. Middelburg NIPR 2007 Nr. 51 p. 80; *Sindres*, J-Cl. Dr. int. fasc. 584-130 no. 17 (mars 2014).

[222] See only *Hans-Bernd Schäfer/Claus Ott*, Lehrbuch der ökonomischen Analyse des Zivilrechts (4th ed. 2005) p. 426; *Mankowski*, IPRax 2003, 127, 131.

[223] See only BayObLG BB 2001, 1923.

[224] LG München II IHR 2013, 72.

[225] *Sindres*, J-Cl. Dr. int. fasc. 584-130 no. 17 (mars 2014).

[226] See only *Agnew v. Länsförsäkringsbolagens AB* [2001] 1 A.C. 223, 252 (H.L., per Lord *Hope of Craighead*); BayObLG RIW 2001, 862.

[227] OLG München IPRspr. 2011 Nr. 204 p. 537.

[228] *Marc Brogsitter v. Fabrication de Montres Normandes EURL and Karsten Fräßdorf* (Case C-519/12), ECLI:EU:C:2014:148 para. 24.

[229] *Marc Brogsitter v. Fabrication de Montres Normandes EURL and Karsten Fräßdorf* (Case C-519/12), ECLI:EU:C:2014:148 para. 25.

[230] *Marc Brogsitter v. Fabrication de Montres Normandes EURL and Karsten Fräßdorf* (Case C-519/12), ECLI:EU:C:2014:148 para. 26. The first example is provided by LG Krefeld 26 August 2014 – Case 12 O 28/12 [30]-[32] in the *Brogsitter* case itself.

[231] *Marc Brogsitter v. Fabrication de Montres Normandes EURL and Karsten Fräßdorf* (Case C-519/12), ECLI:EU:C:2014:148 para. 27.

[232] *Sujecki*, EuZW 2014, 384, 385.

very same claim ought to be treated as tortious with regard to the merits.[233] But insofar as the Rome I and Rome II Regulations on the one hand and (1) on the other hand apply comparable classificatory standards, this danger will not be too imminent. Nonetheless, it is not beyond doubt that the *Brogsitter* approach will also be employed for drawing and fine-tuning the frontier between the Rome I and Rome II Regulations.[234] Yet Art. 4 (3) cl. 2 Rome II Regulation does not give rise to an argument in the context of jurisdiction.[234a]

49 By re-characterising the claim as contractual the outlined approach is different from a solution of the question whether there is jurisdiction to hear both contractual and delictual claims either in the contractual forum under (1) or in the *forum delicti* under (2).[235] This in effect overcomes the result of splitting jurisdiction which *Kalfelis*[236] generated,[237] not met favourably in all quarters of Europe.[238] All claims concerned are equally treated as contractual. Accordingly, two claims in contract are concurring, and resulting from the same contract at that. But re-characterizing can not avoid from the criticism that the solution found is hardly consistent and compatible with the negation of an *Annexkompetenz* for competing claims in contract and in tort.[239] A contractual justification for an illicit act is a mere preliminary question and should not carry the characterisation of the entity.[240] The *Brogsitter* approach opens up opportunities for the defendant to escape from jurisdiction under (2).[241]

50 In the *Brogsitter* case, the claim concerned was based on § 823 (2) BGB, one of the epitomes of tort law under German national law; however, this did not prevent it from being classified as contractual in the concrete case.[242] Whether the *Anspruchsgrundlage* is found in rules which are characterised as contract law or as tort law for the purposes of national law, does not matter, since interpretation under (1) looks at the purpose of the contract.[243] This makes mattes a bit more complicated for lawyers not versed in European law for they lose their *prima facie* orientation mark in national law and their natural starting point for characterisation.[244] Any generalisation is inhibited.[245] Any argument based simply on the *Anspruchs-*

---

[233] *Sujecki*, EuZW 2014, 384, 385.

[234] *Reydellet*, Rev. Lamy dr. aff. 95 (2014), 58, 59.

[234a] *Haftel*, RCDIP 103 (2014), 867, 869.

[235] *Baumert*, EWiR 2014, 435, 436.

[236] *Anastasios Kalfelis v. Bankhaus Schröder Münchmeyer Hengst & Cie.*, (Case 189/87) [1988] ECR 5565, 5586 para. 21.

[237] *Sindres*, J-Cl. Dr. int. fasc. 584-130 no. 19 (mars 2014); *Dornis*, GPR 2014, 352, 353; *Haftel*, RCDIP 103 (2014), 867, 869; see also *Cordero Álvarez*, REDI 2014-2, 251.

[238] See Cass. RCDIP 90 (2001), 88 with note *Lagarde* = Clunet 128 (2001), 1123 with note *André Huet* = JCP G 2001 II.10634 with note *Raynard* = RLDA février 2002 n° 2898 p. 5 with note *Kenfack*.

[239] *Slonina*, ecolex 2014, 790.

[240] *Matthias Weller*, LMK 2014, 359127; *Slonina*, ecolex 2014, 790.

[241] *Slonina*, ecolex 2014, 790.

[242] *Sujecki*, EuZW 2014, 384, 385; *Wendenburg/Maximilian Schneider*, NJW 2014, 1633, 1634.

[243] *Marc Brogsitter v. Fabrication de Montres Normandes EURL and Karsten Fräßdorf* (Case C-519/12), ECLI:EU:C:2014:148 para. 21.

[244] On the contrary, *Wendenburg/Maximilian Schneider*, NJW 2014, 1633, 1634–1635 see an augmentation of legal certainty.

[245] *Wendenburg/Maximilian Schneider*, NJW 2014, 1633, 1635.

grundlage being a rule of tort law for the purposes of national law, would be too simple. This hits home for instance with regard to *rupture brutale*, based on Art. 442-6-1-5 C. comm.[246]

bb) Unilateral promises

Unilateral promises lack mutuality of obligations, or in English legal terminology: consid- **51** eration. Yet they are binding upon the promisor, and the promisee can enforce them. The promisor issues a unilateral promise voluntarily in order to oblige and bind himself legally. In turn the promisee accepts and retains it. Insofar some kind of basic consensus exists as the promise approves of the promise and does not reject it. Likewise the paramount element of voluntariness on the side of the obliged party exists. The promisor freely decides whether to issue the promise at all and in whose favour.[247] He even takes the initiative on his very own motion having made up his own mind.[248] The main and most material elements which can be identified in the definition of "contract" are thus fulfilled. The bond between the parties is not fortuitous, nor is the obliged party subjected to its obligation by the operation of law. Accordingly, unilateral promises should be deemed to be covered by a wide notion of "contract" not specifically demanding consideration.[249] The clear expression to be bound by a legal commitment suffices.[250] A freely assumed obligation must not be equated with mutuality or any doctrine of consideration.[251] Consequentially, donations and gifts are also covered by (1)[252] (but not (b)[253]). The decisive element is that the debtor is obliged and has assumed a duty on his part.[254] Art. II – 4:101 DCFR indicates some kind of common European understanding relegating the common law doctrine of consideration to a minority position.[255]

To limit "contract" to contracts generating mutual obligations would allow the English **52** doctrine of consideration to creep in by the backdoor although "contract" remained unaltered since the original version of Art. 5 (1) Brussels Convention and none of the original Member States adhered to the concept of consideration as a prerequisite for a contract. Genetically, the case for limiting is thus quite weak. As seductive it might appear at first glance to give contract a restricted meaning and to classify only mutual contracts as genuine contracts, one should withstand this seduction. Rather one should look not at the formal

---

[246] Characterised as tort and subjected under (2) by Trib comm Paris Gaz. Pal. 13/14 août 2014, p. 25.

[247] See *Petra Engler v. Janus Versand GmbH*, (Case C-27/02) [2005] ECR I-481, I-518 para. 53.

[248] *Petra Engler v. Janus Versand GmbH*, (Case C-27/02) [2005] ECR I-481, I-518 para. 52.

[249] *Petra Engler v. Janus Versand GmbH*, (Case C-27/02) [2005] ECR I-481, I-518 paras. 52 *et seq.*; *Renate Ilsinger v. Martin Dreschers acting as administrator in the insolvency of Schlank & Schick GmbH*, (Case C-180/06), [2009] ECR I-3961, I-4016 para. 51; OGH IPRax 2006, 489; OLG Brandenburg IPRspr. 2002 Nr. 138 p. 357; OLG Celle IPRspr. 2002 Nr. 159 p. 422; OLG Nürnberg NJW 2002, 3637; *Schlosser*, IPRax 1984, 65, 66; *Reiher*, Der Vertragsbegriff im europäischen Internationalen Privatrecht (2010) pp. 71 *et seq.* In greater detail *Urlaub*, Einseitig verpflichtende Rechtsgeschäfte im Internationalen Privatrecht (2010).

[250] *Renate Ilsinger v. Martin Dreschers acting as administrator in the insolvency of Schlank & Schick GmbH*, (Case C-180/06), [2009] ECR I-3961, I-4017 para. 55.

[251] *Samad*, 2010 ILT 233, 235.

[252] Trib. Venezia RDIPP 2004, 272, 273; *Mankowski*, IPRax 1997, 173, 175 *et seq.*; *Stephan Lorenz/Unberath*, IPRax 2005, 516, 518.

[253] *Infra* Art. 5 note 77 (*Mankowski*).

[254] In more detail *von Hein*, IPRax 2013, 54, 55–56.

[255] *von Hein*, IPRax 2013, 54, 55.

---

clothing and wrapping, but at the material content: Even a mutual contract is only an instrument for commitment and self-binding promises whereas the commitment is the material core.[256] On the recipient's part some kind of acceptance might be required[257] but such minimum acceptance can be easily found in any attempt by the recipient to enforce the given promise in reliance upon its validity.[258] The absence of consideration (in English legal terminology) will not prevent an obligation from being contractual.[259] That the *travaux préparatoires* dub it an open question whether disputes arising from unilateral acts are covered by (1)[260] should not prohibit answering the question if a convincing and well-reasoned answer can be found. The notion of promise should not be (over)loaded with too much reliance on the promisor's willingness in his *forum internum* but rightly be judged by its external appearance. This external appearance can be ascertained with convenient ease.[261] Even if one felt obliged by drawing parallels to the distinction made in Art. II – 1:101 DCFR to distinguish between contracts and juridical acts, the latter would have to be treated analogous to contracts.[262]

53 Apparently a German and Austrian speciality[263] exists in the field of the so-called *Gewinn-zusagen*, i.e. prize notifications: A consumer receives a letter promising him a considerable sum of money (or a valuable prize like a holiday trip or a car, or at least the chance to win either money or a prize) which he allegedly won as a participant in a lottery (in which, in fact, the consumer had never participated and of which he had not even heard of before). In small print the offer pretending such generosity is sometimes revoked, if so, in most instances on the backside. The consumer might in some instances be left with the remainder, namely his own order for goods which he was asked to place in order to get the opportunity and to fulfil the alleged prerequisites for cashing in the prize. Now in Germany and Austria the legislator respectively seizes the offeror on his word and enforces the promise.[264] The question arises as to whether the promise constitutes a contract. The ECJ first backed out of answering the question in a general matter, but rather instrumentalised particularities of a certain constellation in order to ascertain that a consumer contract exists if the consumer orders goods or services and if such order is intrinsically linked with the foregoing promise.[265] This was a clear escape strategy avoiding a comprehensive answer.[266] When seized the second time and getting a second opportunity, the ECJ proclaimed the promise as such to be contractual.[267] It

---

[256] *Mankowski*, IPRax 2003, 127, 133.

[257] See *Petra Engler v. Janus Versand GmbH*, (Case C-27/02) [2005] ECR I-481, I-519 para. 55. But sceptical e.g. *Leible*, in: Rauscher Art. 5 note 19; *Leible*, NJW 2005, 796, 797.

[258] See only *Petra Engler v. Janus Versand GmbH*, (Case C-27/02) [2005] ECR I-481, I-519 para. 55; *Leible*, NJW 2005, 796, 797.

[259] *Layton/Mercer* para. 15.005.

[260] Report *Evrigenis/Kerameus* para. 49.

[261] *Häcker*, ZvglRWiss 103 (2004), 464, 486; *Mörsdorf-Schulte*, JZ 2005, 770, 776.

[262] *Bach*, IHR 2010, 17, 23.

[263] But cf. Cass. D. 1999 somm. 109 with note *Libchaber*; Cass. JCP G 2002 II 10104 with note *Houtcieff*; Cass. D. 2002, 2963 with note *Mazeaud* = Rép. Défrenois 2002, 1608 with note *Savaux* = ZEuP 2005, 134 with note *Claude Witz/Reinert*; Cass. RCDIP 99 (2010), 558; Cass. RCDIP 99 (2010), 560; Cass. RCDIP 99 (2010), 562 with common with note *Gaudemet-Tallon* in France.

[264] § 661 a BGB in Germany, § 5j Konsumentenschutzgesetz in Austria.

[265] *Rudolf Gabriel*, (Case C-96/00) [2002] ECR I-6367, I-6398 para. 33.

[266] *Mankowski*, EWiR Art. 13 EuGVÜ 1/02, 873, 874.

asserted that consideration is not required nor mutuality of obligations, but only a freely entered promise to perform, be it unilateral or not.[268] This was insofar confirmed on a third occasion.[269] At least one party should undertake an obligation, though.[270]

The impression of a binding promise legitimately gained by the recipient carries that clas-   **54** sification.[271] Mental reservations on the promisor's side are immaterial.[272] He who wilfully conveys the impression of an enforceable obligation must be hold to his loud word and must not be allowed to step back into small print on the back side.[273] Insofar the basic requirement of a voluntary act is complied with since the promisor is not by any means compelled to issue the *Gewinnzusage*.[274] Paradoxically, for the very case of *Gewinnzusagen* the contractual characterisation results in *Gewinnzusagen* dropping out of the realm of (1) and being transferred to the reign of Arts. 7–19: Since Arts. 7–19 cover all types of contracts pursuant to Art. 17 (1) (c) unless Art. 24 takes precedence and since the former restriction to contracts for the sale of goods and the provision of services as contained in Art. 13 (1) Brussels Convention has been deleted, even the so-called isolated *Gewinnzusage* (not combined with any contract selling goods or services)[275] has now mainly[276] emigrated into the realm of the specific rules on procedural consumer protection.[277]

cc) Validity of contract in question
A claim in contract normally implies the validity of the contract. Yet this premise is not   **55** absolute. If a positive declaratory action aims at asserting the very existence of a contract, or, *vice versa*, if a negative declarative action (as far as permitted by the national procedural law

---

[267] *Petra Engler v. Janus Versand GmbH*, (Case C-27/02) [2005] ECR I-481, I-516-I-520 paras. 44–61. Followed by BGH NJW 2006, 230, 231 *et seq.* = WRP 2006, 257, 259 = JZ 2006, 519, 520 with note *Carsten Schäfer.*

[268] *Petra Engler v. Janus Versand GmbH*, (Case C-27/02) [2005] ECR I-481, I-518 paras. 52 *et seq.*; applauded e.g. by *McGuire*, ecolex 2005, 489, 491; *Mörsdorf-Schulte*, JZ 2005, 770, 774 *et seq.*

[269] *Renate Ilsinger v. Martin Dreschers acting as administrator in the insolvency of Schlank & Schick GmbH*, (Case C-180/06), [2009] ECR I-3961, I-4016 para. 51.

[270] *Renate Ilsinger v. Martin Dreschers acting as administrator in the insolvency of Schlank & Schick GmbH*, (Case C-180/06), [2009] ECR I-3961, I-4016 *et seq.* para. 54.

[271] *Petra Engler v. Janus Versand GmbH*, (Case C-27/02) [2005] ECR I-481, I-518 *et seq.* paras. 54–57; *Martiny*, in: Księga pamiątkowa Profesora Maksymiliana Pazdana (Zakamycze 2005), p. 189, 199 *et seq.*; *Oberhammer/Slonina*, in: Studia in honorem Pelayia Yessiou-Faltsi (2007), p. 419, 429.

[272] *Petra Engler v. Janus Versand GmbH*, (Case C-27/02) [2005] ECR I-481, I-520 para. 59.

[273] *Petra Engler v. Janus Versand GmbH*, (Case C-27/02) [2005] ECR I-481, I-518 *et seq.* paras. 54, 56.

[274] Insofar overly critical *Mörsdorf-Schulte*, JZ 2005, 770, 775; *Carsten Schäfer*, JZ 2005, 981, 985; *Carsten Schäfer*, JZ 2006, 522, 523.

[275] For its treatment under Arts. 13–15 Brussels Convention see most recently BGH NJW 2006, 230, 231 *et seq.* = WRP 2006, 257, 258 *et seq.*

[276] But cf. *Renate Ilsinger v. Martin Dreschers acting as administrator in the insolvency of Schlank & Schick GmbH*, (Case C-180/06), [2009] ECR I-3961, I-4017 paras. 56–58.

[277] See only *Renate Ilsinger v. Martin Dreschers als Insolvenzverwalter im Konkurs der Schlank & Schick GmbH*, (Case C-180/06), [2009] ECR I-3961, I-4016 *et seq.* paras. 51–55; *Mörsdorf-Schulte*, ZZP Int. 8 (2003), 407, 440 *et seq.*; *Häcker*, ZVglRWiss 103 [2004], 464, 491 f; *Mankowski*, EWiR Art. 5 EuGVÜ 1/ 05, 387 *et seq.*; *McGuire*, ecolex 2005, 489, 491 *et seq.*; *Añoveros Terradas*, REDI 2005, 929, 933; *Stephan Lorenz*, NJW 2006, 472, 475; *Bach*, IHR 2010, 17, 21 *et seq.*

---

of the *forum*) seeks an assertion that a contract does not exist, these issues ought to be characterised as contractual.[278] This applies to whichever ground of vitiation including (but by no means restricted) to rescission, annulation, withdrawal, lack of agent's power or lack of consensus.[279] The applicant may invoke the jurisdiction of the courts of the place of performance even when the existence of the contract on which the claim is based is in dispute between the parties.[280] "Contract" does not require nor presuppose a *valid* contract as a necessary prerequisite.[281] Otherwise it would be too seductive an *exceptio* for the defendant to allege that a contract does not exist in order to deprive the plaintiff of the *forum contractus*.[282] (1) could be bereft all too easily of its legal effect.[283] A mere defence raised by the defendant can not influence the scenario[284] which must be clarified before the writ issued in order to give the plaintiff the required security. Furthermore, one could point to Art. 8 (1) Rome Convention where the validity of the contract is clearly included in the contractual ambit and not treated as a type of prerequisite. The existence of the elements constituting a contract is a contractual matter.[285] Additionally, it would not make all too much sense to decide in one *forum* that the contract exists and then in another *forum* which claims follow from the contract.[286] On the other hand, this undeniably opens the door for strategic and opportunistic litigation by alleging the existence of a contract.[287]

56 For the same reasons (1) covers suits which primarily aim at asserting the further existence or the future or present non-existence of a contract in particular due to a rescission, repudiation, withdrawal or another attempt by either party to liberate itself from the contractual bond.[288] Merely voidable contracts are even actual contracts.[289] The contractual nature holds

---

[278] *Effer SpA v. Hans-Joachim Kantner*, (Case 38/81) [1982] ECR 825, 834 *et seq.* para. 7; BGH IHR 2010, 212, 214; BAG RIW 1987, 465; Cassaz. RDIPP 1995, 693; Cassaz. RDIPP 2004, 278, 280 *et seq.*; Cassaz. RCDIP 93 (2004), 612, 619 with note *Petrelli*; Cassaz. Giust. civ. 2011 I 1028, 1032; OGH ÖJZ 2004, 138, 139; OGH ÖJZ 2004, 141, 142 = ZfRV 2004, 105, 107; OLG Hamm RIW 1980, 662; OLG Koblenz IPRax 1986, 105; *Tesam Distribution Ltd. v. Schuh Mode Tesam GmbH* [1990] I.L.Pr. 149 (C.A.); *Mölnlycke AB v. Procter & Gamble Ltd.* [1992] 1 WLR 1112 = [1992] 4 All ER 47 (C.A.); *Boss Group Ltd. v. Boss France SA* [1996] 4 All ER 970 = [1997] 1 WLR 351 (C.A.); CA Paris D. 2000, 1394 with note *Audit*; ØLD UfR 1998, 1092 (with note by *Fogh*, IPRax 2001, 358); OLG Saarbrücken IPRax 2013, 74, 77; LG Trier NJW-RR 2003, 287; Rb. Utrecht NIPR 2008 Nr. 316 p. 582; *Harald Koch*, ZZP Int. 3 (1998), 230, 232; *Martiny*, in: FS Reinhold Geimer (2002), p. 641, 666; *Carballo Piñeiro*, REDI 2002, 372, 374; *Audit*, Rec. des Cours 305 (2003), 9, 430 *et seq.*; *Wurmnest*, IHR 2005, 107, 109; *Samad*, 2010 ILT 233, 237.

[279] *Carrascosa González*, in: Calvo Caravaca, Art. 5.1 CB note 12.

[280] *Effer SpA v. Hans-Joachim Kantner*, (Case 38/81) [1982] ECR 825, 835 para. 8; *Krejci Lager & Umschlagbetriebs GmbH v. Olbrich Transport und Logistik GmbH*, (Case C-469/12), ECLI:EU:C:2013:788 para. 21.

[281] *Infra* Art. 5 notes 42–44 (*Mankowski*) and *Rémy-Corlay*, RCDIP 92 (2003), 673, 679.

[282] *Effer SpA v. Hans-Joachim Kantner*, (Case 38/81) [1982] ECR 825, 834 *et seq.* para. 7; *Samad*, 2010 ILT 233, 239; *Kropholler/von Hein* Art. 5 note 8.

[283] *Effer SpA v. Hans-Joachim Kantner*, (Case 38/81) [1982] ECR 825, 834 *et seq.* para. 7.

[284] See only *Effer SpA v. Hans-Joachim Kantner*, (Case 38/81) [1982] ECR 825, 834 *et seq.* para. 7; BGE 122 III 298, 299 *et seq.*; BGE 126 III 334, 336; Hoge Raad NIPR 2002 Nr. 202 p. 346; Rb. Utrecht NIPR 2002 Nr. 56 p. 100.

[285] *Lima Pinheiro* p. 82.

[286] Concurring *Carrillo Lerma*, CDT 6 (1) (2014), 349, 355.

[287] *Gehri*, in: FS Ivo Schwander (2011), p. 699, 703–704.

[288] Cassaz. RDIPP 2000, 738, 740; OLG Frankfurt RIW 1980, 585; Trib. Milano RDIPP 1995, 450; *Martiny*,

---

true for an action to annul or nullify a contract[290] as such action might be necessary e.g. pursuant to Art. 1184 or 1304 Code civil or Art. 1427 Codice civile. In the extreme consequence, since (1) is not expressly limited to the parties of the contract themselves,[291] even an action by a creditor of one of the parties to assert the invalidity of a contract *vis-à-vis* the claimant creditor if permitted by the law of the *forum* can be covered.[292]

dd) Collective agreements

In labour relations collective agreements are a common feature, be it as between trade **57** unions and employers' associations, be it between employee's local organisation or representatives and a certain employer. Generally, such collective agreements come within the notion of contract under (1). That they do not feature as *individual* employment agreements for the purposes of Arts. 20–23,[293] does not constitute any obstacle. The participants submitted to them freely and voluntarily even if indirectly *via* their membership in one of the concluding organisations. The case is different, though, where by operation of statute and constitutive declaration by the competent State body collective agreements are declared generally binding, i.e. also on non-participants. Still the collective agreement is a civil and commercial matter[294] but any obligations of non-participants are not contractual in nature.[295]

ee) Contracts coerced by law

Sometimes parties are forced or coerced by the applicable law to conclude a contract. If one **58** party benefiting from such legal rules sues the other party with the ultimate goal to coerce this other party to conclude the contract (if only the other party's actual consent is replaced with the judgment) the claim aims at a contractual issue.[296] Although the element of the second party voluntarily entering into the contract is lacking since this party is not acting upon its own free will, the result as such dominates the characterisation of the result.[297] On its face, the resulting contract does not spell out that it was formed pursuant to legal

---

in: FS Reinhold Geimer (2002), p. 641, 666. But cf. *Heuzé*, Joly (Conflits de juridiction et contrats internationaux), Livre IX no. 65; *Sindres*, J-Cl. Dr. int. fasc. 584-130 no. 13 (mars 2014). There is a referral pending from the Cassaz. to the CJEU as *Profit Investment SIM SpA v. Stefano Ossi and Commerzbank AG* (Case C-366/13).

[289] *Briggs*, (2000) 71 BYIL 435, 452.

[290] Cass. RCDIP 72 (1983), 516 with note *Gaudemet-Tallon*; Cassaz. RDIPP 2004, 278; *Pertegás*, in: Meeusen/Pertegás/Straetmans (eds.), Enforcement of International Contracts in the European Union (2004), p. 175, 187 § 5-35; *Geimer/Schütze* with notes 59–61.

[291] *Mongiò-Erdelbrock*, EuLF (D) 2004, 195, 196. But cf. critically *Petrelli*, RCDIP 93 (2004), 623, 624 *et seq.*

[292] Cassaz. RDIPP 2004, 635, 640–644 = RCDIP 93 (2004), 612, 617–622 with note *Petrelli* = EuLF 2004, 194, 195; *Mongiò-Erdelbrock*, EuLF (D) 2004, 195, 196.

[293] See only *Trenner*, Internationale Gerichtsstände in grenzüberschreitenden Arbeitsvertragsstreitigkeiten (2001) p. 93; *Junker*, NZA 2005, 199, 201; *Junker*, in: FS Peter Schlosser (2005), p. 299, 302; *Mankowski*, NZA 2009, 584, 585; *Mankowski*, in: Rauscher Art. 18 note 7.

[294] See in detail *Mankowski*, NZA 2009, 584, 585.

[295] Hessisches LAG IPRax 2008, 131, 132; *Mankowski*, NZA 2009, 584, 588.

[296] *Leible*, in: Rauscher, Art. 5 note 29; *Martiny*, in: FS Reinhold Geimer (2002), p. 641, 649; *Reiher*, Der Vertragsbegriff im europäischen Internationalen Privatrecht (2010) p. 71. Doubtful *Stadler*, in: FS Hans-Joachim Musielak (2004), p. 569, 580.

[297] *Martiny*, in: FS Reinhold Geimer (2002), p. 641, 650.

obligations. But any suit which aims at coercing the defendant into concluding such contract is not qualified by the result it goes for, but by its own ground which might be in tort e.g. if a non-cartelant sues a cartelant[298] or if someone claims for a compulsory license.[299]

ff) Pre-contract and pre-contractual instruments

59 The claim is more contractual if a party is sued due to a commitment stemming from a pre-contract[300] or a contractual option[301] or a (binding) letter of intent[302] or a (binding) memorandum (of understanding)[303] or binding heads of agreement.[304] In this situation a party's obligation (e.g. to conclude a contract) generates from its own previous consent to do so in the then future. The same applies if previously one party granted the other an option to actualise a contract and the other party enforces such option.[305] Likewise consented obligations to negotiate are contractual.[306] In all these instances the party entered voluntarily in a binding agreement. "Contract" must not be sublimated to "main contract".

gg) Claims arising out of invalid contracts

60 Claims arising due to the invalidity of a contract are also covered by the notion of contractuality. Although they are not directly based on the contract insofar as they would follow from the contract itself, they are clearly related to the contract. The parties themselves might even have provided for a regime designed for the event of invalidity of the contract. If they do not so, the rules of the applicable law step in as gap-fillers. This encompasses in particular claims based on *condictio indebiti* or *condictio ob causam finitam* as the case may be.[307] All modes of returning the performances exchanged under a contract should be treated in equal manner and be characterised as contractual *quasi* infected by their object.[308] In essence, no material difference can be detected in this regard between a contract set aside, a never existing contract and a void contract.[309] If a plaintiff claims breach of contract or return alternatively, both pleadings should be handled the same way and be covered by (1).[310] One should even widen the spectrum and classify claims based on *condictio causa data non*

---

[298]   LG Leipzig IPRspr. 2008 Nr. 96 p. 316 InstGE 9, 167.

[299]   LG Leipzig IPRspr. 2008 Nr. 96 p. 316 = InstGE 9, 167; *Leible*, in: Rauscher, Art. 5 note 29.

[300]   *Franzina*, La giurisdizione in materia contrattuale (2006) p. 316.

[301]   *Franzina*, La giurisdizione in materia contrattuale (2006) p. 316.

[302]   Trib. Bergamo RDIPP 2003, 451.

[303]   Cass. Clunet 128 (2001), 133 with note *André Huet*; CA Chambéry D. 1999, 292 with note *Bertrand Audit* = Clunet 126 (1999), 188 with note *André Huet*; *André Huet*, Clunet 130 (2003), 145; *Rémy-Corlay*, RCDIP 92 (2003), 673, 680; *Leible*, in: Rauscher Art. 5 note 29; *Kropholler/von Hein*, Art. 5 note 18.

[304]   Rb. 's-Hertogenbosch NIPR 2005 Nr. 169 p. 234.

[305]   See App. Milano RDIPP 2004, 1367, 1370.

[306]   Hof 's-Hertogenbosch NIPR 2007 Nr. 40 p. 68.

[307]   A-G *Darmon*, [1993] ECR I-157, I-178 *et seq.*; OLG Brandenburg IPRspr. 2002 Nr. 138 p. 357; *Briggs*, [1992] LMCLQ 283, 284 *et seq.*; *Robert Stevens*, (1996) L.Q.Rev. 391, 393 *et seq.*; *Dickinson*, [1996] LMCLQ 556, 563; *Pertegás*, in: Meeusen/Pertegás/Straetmans (eds.), Enforcement of International Contracts in the European Union (2004), p. 175, 188 § 5-36; *Stephan Lorenz/Unberath*, IPRax 2005, 516, 518; *Franzina*, La giurisdizione in materia contrattuale (2006) pp. 277–283; *Kropholler/von Hein*, Art. 5 note 75.

[308]   *Stadler*, in: FS Hans-Joachim Musielak (2004), p. 569, 581.

[309]   *Peel*, (1996) 112 L.Q.Rev. 541, 544.

[310]   *Briggs*, (2000) 71 BYIL 435, 452.

secuta or *condictio ob rem* as contractual although they only relate to a purpose accompanying the contract and not serving as the goal of the contract itself.

The entire matter has to be characterised as contractual.[311] Art. 12 (1) (e) Rome I Regulation **61** unambiguously demands so.[312] This rule clearly counts claims arising out of invalid contracts as contractual.[313] That unfortunately Art. 24 Rome Convention gave the Member States permission to declare a reservation against Art. 10 (1) (e) Rome Convention, and that in particular the United Kingdom had seized upon this opportunity has been overcome with the advent of the Rome I Regulation where such loophole has been deleted and erased. Nevertheless, even before the existence of such loophole had not allowed to leave the general line[314] following then Art. 10 (1) Rome Convention and now Art. 12 (1) Rome I Regulation as the basic classification. The sister rules ought to be interpreted harmoniously.[315] Hence, claims in restitution or unjust enrichment are covered by (1) insofar as they purport to involve a contractual exchange.[316] Insofar the words "in matters relating to contract" might not prove synonymous with the words "in proceedings based upon contract",[317] with the latter being slightly narrower. But the wording of (1) as such can not be taken to be decisive in this regard in the fear that the language version differ slightly from each other.[318]

In addition to the comparative argument based on Art. 12 (1) (e) Rome I Regulation, a **62** further, substantive argument militates for this result, namely that otherwise denominations would gain too much weight: Claims resulting from the termination, withdrawal or rescission of a contract would be characterised as contractual in any event[319] whereas claims resulting from the initial voidness of the same contract would not. The reason why the

---

[311] Lord *Nicholls of Birkenhead* (dissenting) in *Kleinwort Benson Ltd. v. Glasgow City Council* [1997] 3 WLR 923, 936–940 (with Lord *Mustill* concurring, ibid., 936); *Schack*, Der Erfüllungsort im deutschen, ausländischen und internationalen Privat- und Zivilprozessrecht (1985) para. 311; *Wieczorek/Schütze/ Hausmann* Art. 5 note 6; *Peel*, [1998] LMCLQ 22, 25 *et seq.*; *Virgo*, (1998) 114 L.Q.Rev. 386, 388–390; *Geimer/Schütze* Art. 5 note 64; *Franzina*, La giurisdizione in materia contrattuale (2006) pp. 277–283; *Kropholler/von Hein*, Art. 5 note 15; *Michael Stürner*, in: FS Athanassios Kaissis (2012), p. 975, 982. *Contra Kleinwort Benson Ltd. v. Glasgow City Council* [1997] 3 WLR 923, 931–935, 942–947 (H.L., per Lords *Goff of Chieveley*, *Clyde* and *Hutton* respectively); *Pitel*, (1998) 57 Cambridge L.J. 19, 21; *Samad*, 2010 ILT 233, 237 *et seq.*

[312] *Schlosser* Art. 5 note 5; *Reiher*, Der Vertragsbegriff im europäischen Internationalen Privatrecht (2011) p. 78; *Kropholler/von Hein*, Art. 5 notes 15, 75; *Michael Stürner*, in: FS Athanassios Kaissis (2012), p. 975, 982; *Crawford/Carruthers*, (2014) 63 ICLQ 1, 13.

[313] See only *Jayme*, in: In memoria Mario Giuliano (1989), p. 529; *Reiher*, Der Vertragsbegriff im europäischen Internationalen Privatrecht (2011), p. 78.

[314] As established in *SPRL Arcado v. SA Haviland*, (Case 9/87) [1988] ECR 1539, 1555 para. 15.

[315] *Briggs*, [1992] LMCLQ 283, 284 *et seq.*

[316] OLG Frankfurt RIW 1970, 204.

[317] *Contra Kleinwort Benson Ltd. v. Glasgow City Council* [1997] 3 WLR 923, 944 (H.L., per Lord *Clyde*); *Davenport v. Corinthian Motor Policies at Lloyd's* 1991 SLT 774, 778 (OH, Lord *McCluskey*).

[318] *Layton/Mercer* para. 15.014.

[319] OLG Oldenburg WM 1976, 1288 with note *Geimer*; OLG Düsseldorf IPRax 1987, 234; Aud. Prov. Vizcaya REDI 2000, 563, 564 *et seq.* with note *Marín López*; *Martiny*, in: FS Reinhold Geimer (2002), p. 641, 653; see also *Medway Packaging Ltd. v. Meurer Maschinen GmbH & Co. KG* [1990] 2 Lloyd's Rep. 112, 116 (C. A., per *Fox* L.J.).

---

contractual exchange failed should not be decisive for the characterisation of the claims aiming at the return of the already exchanged. Neither should the mere denomination with its accidentalities. Whether a national law coins a claim for the return of something exchanged under an invalid contract a claim by way of unjust enrichment or else, must not determine the outcome of the autonomous classification. The autonomous classification does not refer to any national law in particular, hence it must not be all-decisive if the substantive law of the *forum* is not familiar or, even worse, hostile to any concept of unjust enrichment or restitution. The European notion of "contract" might be wider than the respective notion under national law.[320] Even less convincing is any approach[321] that relies on a void contract as having no basis for a contractual claim. That places way too much weight on terminology and wording. Such playing with words is disreputable.[322]

63 Additionally, it would be contrary to the purpose of the Regulation to promote the efficacious conduct of proceedings and to avoid multiplicity of related proceedings, if having decided that a contract is null and void, the same court could not proceed to decide on the restitutionary consequences following directly from this.[323] Claims for consequential relief are an integral and unexceptional part of disputes to set aside contracts.[324] It would be strictly unadvisable to split jurisdiction between courts, one determing whether the contract is void and the other dealing with the consequential remedies.[325] There is no helpful dividing line between voidable and void contracts for this would deprive of jurisdiction to award an restitutionary payment a forum which had decided that the alleged contract is void.[326]

hh) Claims founded in company law

64 A quite sensitive area with regard to classification is the field of claims stemming from company law. The more sophisticated and elaborate company law became the more it departed from the basics founded in the corporate charter. The corporate charter is a contract if yet with some peculiarities.[327] (1) is not limited to mutual agreements between just and exactly two parties.[328] For the purposes of (1), the specifically procedural answer to the question as to whether a corporation is a network (or set) of contracts[329] or a collectivistic

---

[320] *Briggs*, (1996) 67 BYIL 577, 582.

[321] As undertaken by *Kleinwort Benson Ltd. v. Glasgow City Council* [1997] 3 WLR 923, 931 (H.L., per Lord *Goff of Chieveley*); *McGrath*, (1999) 18 Civ. Just. Q. 41, 48.

[322] *Briggs*, (1996) 67 BYIL 577, 582.

[323] Lord *Nicholls of Birkenhead* (dissenting) in *Kleinwort Benson Ltd. v. Glasgow City Council* [1997] 3 WLR 923, 938. *Contra McGrath*, (1999) 18 Civ. Just. Q. 41, 51 *et seq*.

[324] Lord *Nicholls of Birkenhead* (dissenting) in *Kleinwort Benson Ltd. v. Glasgow City Council* [1997] 3 WLR 923, 938.

[325] *Briggs*, (1996) 67 BYIL 577, 582; *Briggs*, (1997) 68 BYIL 331, 336; *Sindres*, J-Cl. Dr. int. fasc. 584-130 no. 14 (mars 2014).

[326] *Jonathan Hill/Chong* para. 5. 6. 17; *Crawford/Carruthers*, (2014) 63 ICLQ 1, 13–14.

[327] *Martin Peters Bauunternehmung GmbH v. Zuid Nederlandse Aannemers Vereniging*, (Case 34/82) [1983] ECR 987, 1002 para. 13; *Powell Duffryn plc v. Wolfgang Petereit*, (Case C-214/89) [1992] ECR I-1745, I-1774 *et seq*. paras. 14 *et seq*.; *Petra Engler v. Janus Versand GmbH*, (Case C-27/02) [2005] ECR I-481, I-517 para. 47; LG Mainz WM 1989, 1053; Rb. Rotterdam NIPR 2007 Nr. 322 p. 441 *et seq*.; *Johannes Weber*, Gesellschaftsrecht und Gläubigerschutz im Internationalen Zivilverfahrensrecht (2011) pp. 230–234; *Haas*, NZG 2013, 1161, 1162.

[328] See only *Atlas Shipping Agency (UK) Ltd. and United Shipping Services Ltd. v. Suisse Atlantique Société*

entity,[330] favours the former.[331] The corporate charter is binding upon persons who accede to the company be it by original accession, be it by derivative acquiring of corporate shares, and even more, it is binding even upon those who opposed in meetings but did not leave the company. Company law particularly in Germany has moved quite some way from its beginnings and developed rules finely tuning the balance between company interests, shareholders' interests, stakeholders' interests and the interests of the creditors of the company. Yet it did not abandon the contractual bond completely. At least as far as intra-corporate relations are concerned, company law, be it *ius cogens* or be it *ius dispositivum*, generates contractual claims.[332] Whether a corporate charter can under certain circumstances or at least in relation to investors for private purposes can qualify as a consumer contract thus triggering the application of Arts. 17–19 is an open question[333] the more so since it would have to surmount major difficulties in identifying any relevant professional counter-party.

The contractual classification of a corporate charter has the additional advantage that under **65** the national (substantive) law applicable the place of performance of intra-corporate obligations between the company and the shareholders or *vice versa* or between the shareholders in this specific capacity is established to be the place where the association is established.[334] Through the back-door some kind of *forum societatis* can be found which is not otherwise recognised[335] in the Brussels Ibis Regulation and denied even by Art. 24 (2), but could prove rather useful.[336]

If the corporate charter is characterised as contractual, the liability of the shareholders **66** towards the company is classified the same way.[337] The shareholders are bound by the very

---

d'Armement Maritime SA [1995] 2 Lloyd's Rep. 188, 194 = [1995] I.L.Pr. 600 (Q.B.D., *Rix* J.); *Mankowski*, NZI 1999, 56, 57.

[329] See only *Easterbrook/Fishel*, The Economic Structure of Corporate Law (1991) p. 14.

[330] See only *Karsten Schmidt*, Gesellschaftsrecht (4th ed. 2002) p. 80.

[331] See *Gerhard Wagner*, in: Lutter (ed.), Europäische Auslandsgesellschaften in Deutschland (2005), p. 223, 271.

[332] *Martin Peters Bauunternehmung GmbH v. Zuid Nederlandse Aannemers Vereniging*, (Case 34/82) [1983] ECR 987, 1002 para. 13; *Powell Duffryn plc v. Wolfgang Petereit*, (Case C-214/89) [1992] ECR I-1745, I-1774 *et seq.* paras. 14 *et seq.*; OLG Bremen RIW 1998, 63; OLG Jena NZI 1999, 81; OLG Koblenz NZG 2001, 759 with note *Günter Christian Schwarz*; OLG Köln WM 2005, 612, 614 = AG 2005, 123, 124; OLG Stuttgart NJW-RR 2005, 814; LG Essen ZIP 2011, 875, 876; Aud. Prov. Zaragoza REDI 1996, 2, 258, 259 with note *Sancho Villa*; *Brödermann*, ZIP 1996, 481, 482 *et seq.*; *Mankowski*, EWiR Art. 5 EuGVÜ 1/98, 269, 270; *Mankowski*, NZI 1999, 56, 57; *Fawcett*, in: Fawcett/Harris/Bridge para. 3.65; *Sindres*, J-Cl. Dr. int. fasc. 584-130 no. 16 (mars 2014).

[333] *Johannes Weber* Gesellschaftsrecht und Gläubigerschutz im Internationalen Zivilverfahrensrecht (2011), pp. 234–236; see also *Barta*, NJOZ 2011, 1033, 1034 *et seq.*

[334] *Martin Peters Bauunternehmung GmbH v. Zuid Nederlandse Aannemers Vereniging*, (Case 34/82) [1983] ECR 987, 1003 para. 14; OLG Köln WM 2005, 612, 614 = AG 2005, 123, 124.

[335] See *Martin Peters Bauunternehmung GmbH v. Zuid Nederlandse Aannemers Vereniging*, (Case 34/82) [1983] ECR 987, 1003 para. 14.

[336] OLG Köln WM 2005, 612, 614 = AG 2005, 123, 124; *Leible*, in: Rauscher Art. 5 note 25.

[337] OLG Rostock 4. June 2014 – Case 1 U 51/11 [32]; Rb. Rotterdam NIPR 2007 Nr. 322 p. 442; *Jaspert*, EuGVÜ-Gerichtsstände und Anspruchsdurchsetzung gegen ausländische herrschende Unternehmen (1995) p. 113; *Mankowski*, NZI 1999, 56, 57; *Martiny*, in: FS Reinhold Geimer (2002), p. 641, 659;

corporate charter whether the company itself can be regarded as a party to the charter by virtue of the applicable national law or not. The internal liability of the shareholders can in some instances be qualified as breach of contract.[338] Amongst the qualifiers are for instance claims based on §§ 32a; 32b GmbHG[339] or on § 30 GmbHG[340] or on § 11 (2) GmbHG[341] or obligations in analogy to §§ 30; 31 GmbHG.[342] The obligation to pay the promised portion of the capital to the company as enforced by the creditors of the company by virtue of § 171 (2) HGB should be located in the contractual realm,[343] *a fortiori* accessory liability towards creditor of the company's debts, for instanced pursuant to § 128 HGB.[344] The same applies to claims against the members of a property-holding community like e.g. the German *Wohnungseigentümergemeinschaft*[345] if the latter is organised as some kind of corporate body either by operation of law or by actual agreement and if and insofar as Art. 24 (1) does not come into application.[346] The obligations must not be derived directly from the corporate charter itself, but can follow from acts or decisions made by organs of the association.[347] Otherwise matters which are closely related to each other, if not practically interchangeable, would be unduly separated.[348] Functionally, those decisions by the organs crystallise the corporate charter and draw their legitimacy from it.

67 Within the intra-corporate realm, the liability of the directors and the members of the board towards the company also features,[349] but only in principle. The paramount question in this

---

Kindler, in: FS Peter Ulmer (2003), p. 305, 312 *et seq.*; *Matthias Lehmann*, GmbHR 2005, 978, 980; *Johannes Weber*, Gesellschaftsrecht und Gläubigerschutz im Internationalen Zivilverfahrensrecht (2011), pp. 359 *et seq.*

[338] *Kindler*, in: FS Peter Ulmer (2003), p. 305, 312 *et seq.*

[339] OLG Bremen RIW 1998, 63; OLG Jena NZI 1999, 81; OLG Köln WM 2005, 612, 614 = AG 2005, 123, 124; *Altmeppen*, NJW 2004, 97, 103. *Contra Haas*, NZI 2002, 457, 465 *et seq.*; *Peter Ulmer*, NJW 2004, 1201, 1207; *Peter Ulmer*, KTS 2004, 291, 299; *Weller*, IPRax 2004, 412, 414.

[340] OLG Koblenz NZG 2001, 759; *Günther Christian Schwarz*, NZG 2001, 761; *Günther Christian Schwarz*, NZG 2002, 290, 297. *Contra Haas*, DStR 2002, 144.

[341] OLG Rostock 4 June 2014 – Case 1 U 51/11 [32].

[342] OLG Jena NZI 1999, 81; OLG München GmbHR 2006, 1152, 1154; *Kranemann*, EWiR Art. 5 EuGVÜ 1/ 98, 779; *Matthias Lehmann*, GmbHR 2005, 978, 98.

[343] BGH NZG 2003, 812; OLG Stuttgart NJW-RR 2005, 814, 815; *Carsten Schneider*, BGH-Report 2003, 1007, 1008. *Contra* OLG Naumburg NZG 2000, 1218, 1219; *Matthias Lehmann*, IPRax 2005, 109, 110; *Matthias Lehmann*, GmbHR 2005, 978, 980.

[344] BGH BeckRS 2008, 21694; *Mankowski*, NZI 1999, 56, 57; *Haas/Amrei Keller*, ZZP 126 (2013), 335, 336–338; *Haas*, NZG 2013, 1161, 1164; *Wedemann*, ZEuP 2014, 861, 875–876.

[345] OLG Stuttgart NJW-RR 2005, 814; *Alexandra Schreiber*, juris-PR 2005, 86, 88.

[346] Favouring the application of Art. 24 (1) to claims for financial contributions amongst the members of a *Wohnungseigentümergemeinschaft* OLG Düsseldorf OLG-Report Düsseldorf 2004, 24. The opposite approach is preferred by BayObLG FGPRax 2003, 159; OLG Stuttgart NZM 2005, 430; LG Frankfurt/ Main NJW-RR 2014, 907, 908 = ZMR 2014, 573–574.

[347] *Martin Peters Bauunternehmung GmbH v. Zuid Nederlandse Aannemers Vereniging*, (Case 34/82) [1983] ECR 987, 1003 paras. 16–18.

[348] *Martin Peters Bauunternehmung GmbH v. Zuid Nederlandse Aannemers Vereniging*, (Case 34/82) [1983] ECR 987, 1003 para. 17.

[349] OLG München ZIP 1998, 1558 = RIW 2000, 143; OLG Celle RIW 2000, 710; OLG Düsseldorf IPRax 2011, 176; HG St. Gallen ZGGVP 1998 Nr. 48 p. 126; *Kropholler/von Hein* Art. 5 note 13; *Leible*, in: Hirte/

regard is as to whether the directors and alike are tied to the company by employment contracts or not: If the answer is affirmative, Arts. 18–21 apply and not (1); if this answer is negative, (1) is applicable.[350] The more specific corporate regime gains prevalence insofar as it demands as such. To answer the question and to find a generally contractual nature of the relationship, the law applicable to the company might provide a helping hand, without contravening the autonomous interpretation of (1).[351] Furthermore, (1) is relevant not only for the liability of organs towards the company which have been properly installed, but also of so called factual organs who act like organs without having been formally installed.[352]

One further complicating step are rules on fixed capital or alike, governing the minimum   68
funds of the company and the possible redistribution among the creditors of the company. Particularly in Germany issues regarding groups of companies are relevant in this context. The German *Konzernrecht* calls for an answer in matters of international jurisdiction, as well.[353] Insofar as the internal redress by the subsidiary, its management or (in case of bankruptcy) its receivers *(Insolvenzverwalter)* is at stake, shareholding and thus a matter intrinsically linked to the contractual bond around the subsidiary is the dominant factor and hence such internal redress should be qualified as contractual,[354] even if is clothed in such a complicated manner as the German *Existenzvernichtungshaftung*[355] (its successor[356] *Haftung wegen existenzvernichtenden Eingriffs*[357] at its core a liability for causing insolvency[358] results only in internal liability towards the company itself, but not in external liability

---

Bücker (eds.), Grenzüberschreitende Gesellschaften (2ⁿᵈ ed. 2006) § 11 with note 18; *Altmeppen*, in: FS Volker Röhricht (2005), p. 3, 22; *Matthias Lehmann*, GmbHR 2005, 978, 981; *Ignatova*, Art. 5 Nr. 1 EuGVVO – Chancen und Perspektiven der Reform des Gerichtsstands am Erfüllungsort (2005) p. 122 *et seq.*; *Hannes Wais*, IPRax 2011, 138, 141 *et seq.*; *Johannes Weber*, Gesellschaftsrecht und Gläubigerschutz im Internationalen Zivilverfahrensrecht (2011), pp. 236–239; *Haas*, NZG 2013, 1161, 1163; *Arons*, Ondernemingsrecht 2013, 563, 565–566. Rather for (2) OLG Karlsruhe IPRax 2011, 179, 180; *Haas*, NZG 2010, 495, 497.

[350] *Mankowski*, EWiR Art. 5 EuGVÜ 1/99, 949, 950; *Johannes Weber*, Gesellschaftsrecht und Gläubigerschutz im Internationalen Zivilverfahrensrecht (2011), pp. 240–242.

[351] OLG München ZIP 1998, 1558; *Mankowski*, EWiR Art. 5 EuGVÜ 1/99, 949, 950.

[352] OLG Köln NZI 2012, 52 with note *Mankowski*; *Haas*, NZG 2013, 1161, 1163.

[353] Monographically *Bruhns*, Das Verfahrensrecht der internationalen Konzernhaftung (2006).

[354] To the same result *Ignatova*, Art. 5 Nr. 1 EuGVVO – Chancen und Perspektiven der Reform des Gerichtsstands am Erfüllungsort (2005) pp. 124 *et seq.*; *Johannes Weber*, Gesellschaftsrecht und Gläubigerschutz im Internationalen Zivilverfahrensrecht (2011), pp. 366 *et seq.*; *Haas*, NZG 2013, 1161, 1163.

[355] As judicially established by BGHZ 149, 10, 16 *et seq.*; BGHZ 150, 61, 67 *et seq.*; BGHZ 151, 181, 186 *et seq.*; BGH GmbHR 2005, 225; BGH GmbHR 2005, 299, 300.

[356] The difference between the two closely related approaches consists in the extension of the latter to pseudo-foreign companies by virtue of a proper delictual qualification and application of Art. 4 Rome II Regulation; *Marc-Philippe Weller*, ZIP 2007, 1681, 1688; *Gerhard Wagner*, in: FS Claus Wilhelm Canaris, vol. II (2007), p. 473, 497 *et seq.*; *Gerhard Wagner*, in: Münchener Kommentar zum BGB, vol. V: §§ 705-823 BGB; PartGG; ProdHaftG (6ᵗʰ ed. 2013) § 826 BGB note 135; *Ansgar Staudinger*, AnwBl 2008, 316, 320 *et seq.*

[357] Judicially established by BGHZ 173, 246, 255 *et seq.* – Trihotel; BGHZ 176, 204 [10] – Gamma; BGHZ 179, 144 [15] *et seq.* – Sanitary; BGH ZIP 2012, 1071 [10] *et seq.*; BAG ZIP 2011, 1433 [35]-[36].

[358] *Gerhard Wagner*, in: Münchener Kommentar zum BGB, vol. V: §§ 705-823 BGB; PartGG; ProdHaftG (6ᵗʰ ed. 2013) § 826 BGB note 135.

---

towards the creditors of the company[359]) or previously an analogy to § 302 AktG.[360] The so called *qualifizierte faktische GmbH-Konzern* nonetheless implies a contractual element as the dominating influence is exerted based on a shareholder position.[361] To rely entirely on "faktisch"[362] would overemphasize words. The lack of a concrete *Beherrschungsvertrag* does not wrestle the contractual element away. Liability stemming from a *Vertragskonzern* with a *Beherrschungsvertrag* is contractual *a fortiori*.[363]

69 The next issue to be tried features claims by creditors of the company holding the members of the board or the directors of the company liable. Now externals who are not parties to the corporate charter enter the picture. The best approach should be to classify claims stemming from such rules as accessory to those claims which they are providing security for.[364] Compare the rules on capital and funds with the rules regarding the extent to which a human is liable. The latter are classified not by the source from which they arise (which would tentatively be a non-existing "law of persons"), but fall within the ambit of the claims to which they provide a person liable, respectively. The fact that the Brussels *Ibis* Regulation does not contain an express provision about accessoriety does not amount to a counter-argument[365] since the result can be developed without such rule. Hence the result can be summarised as follows: If the external creditor has a claim in contract against the company, his further claim to hold the shareholders liable, also qualifies in contract. If his claim against the company is in tort, the liability claim is also in tort.[366] The main argument put forward against this approach is that it might lead to multiplying the courts with jurisdiction to hear actions calling into question the same improper conduct, contrary to proximity and predictability as required by Recital (11).[367] Assisting, it is argued that piercing the corporate veil can only be

---

[359] BGHZ 173, 246, 255 *et seq.* – Trihotel; BGHZ 176, 204 [10] – Gamma, BGHZ 179, 144 [15] *et seq.* – Sanitary; *Altmeppen*, ZIP 2008, 1201, 1204–1205. Critical *Gerhard Wagner*, in: FS Claus Wilhelm Canaris, vol. II (2007), p. 473, 477 *et seq.*; *Gerhard Wagner*, in: Münchener Kommentar zum BGB, vol. V: §§ 705–823 BGB; PartGG; ProdHaftG (6ᵗʰ ed. 2013) § 826 BGB note 137; *Rubner*, DStR 2009, 1538, 1539–1540.

[360] OLG München IPRax 2000, 416, 417; *Haubold*, IPRax 2000, 375, 381; *Kulms*, IPRax 2000, 488, 492 *et seq.*; *Martiny*, in: FS Reinhold Geimer (2002), p. 641, 664; *Kindler*, in: FS Peter Ulmer (2003), p. 305, 312 *et seq.*; *Altmeppen*, in: FS Volker Röhricht (2005), p. 3, 23. Doubtful *Zimmer*, IPRax 1998, 187, 190. Apparently contra OLG München GmbHR 2006, 1152, 1155. *Contra Matthias Lehmann*, GmbHR 2005, 978, 981 *et seq.*; *Wedemann*, ZEuP 2014, 861, 877. Für a double characterisation of the *Existenzvernichtungshaftung* as contractual and tortious *Johannes Weber* Gesellschaftsrecht und Gläubigerschutz im Internationalen Zivilverfahrensrecht (2011), pp. 383–407.

[361] *Contra* OLG Düsseldorf NZG 1999, 81; OLG Stuttgart ZIP 2007, 1210 = IPRax 2008, 433; LG Kiel IPRax 2009, 164, 165; *Zimmer*, IPRax 1998, 187, 189.

[362] As OLG Stuttgart ZIP 2007, 1210 = IPRax 2008, 433 does.

[363] LG Flensburg IPRspr. 2005 Nr. 144.

[364] *Contra ÖFAB Östergötlands Fastigheter AB v. Frank Koot and Evergreen Investments BV* (Case C-147/12), ECLI:EU:C:2013:490 paras. 39 *et seq.*; *Haas*, NZG 2013, 1161, 1163; *van Calster*, TBH 2015, 64, 66.

[365] *Contra Daniel Reichert-Facilides*, in: Marxer/Fritz Reichert-Facilides/Anton K. Schnyder (Hrsg.), Gegenwartsfragen des liechtensteinischen Privat- und Wirtschaftsrechts (1998), p. 27, 31.

[366] See Hof Amsterdam NIPR 1996 Nr. 269 p. 376. For a general contractual characterisation *Johannes Weber*, Gesellschaftsrecht und Gläubigerschutz im Internationalen Zivilverfahrensrecht (2011), pp. 243–291 with extensive argument.

[367] *ÖFAB Östergötlands Fastigheter AB v. Frank Koot and Evergreen Investments BV* (Case C-147/12), ECLI:EU:C:2013:490 para. 40; *Haas*, NZG 2013, 1161, 1163.

justified by improper behaviour on the shareholders' side.[368] To recognise accessoriety is said to lead to a *forum connexitatis* which in other respects does not find a home in (2).[369]

A first alternative to the approach just outlined would be to classify the claim against the **70** parent body or the shareholders as contractual for they assented to the corporate structure.[370] This would not provide a convincing reasoning for the liability of members of the board and thus would open up a need to distinguish in reasoning. A second alternative would resort to a tortious characterisation.[371] There could possibly be a further qualification that at least some allegations could be based on tort, too,[372] depending on the applicable substantive law. The argument favouring such approach is evident: There is nothing like a *direct* contractual link based on voluntary commitment between the directors and the creditor,[373] and the respective liabilities are imposed by law (or be judge-made rules substituting for, or complementing law).[374] The more refined thoughts based on the overall structured are to a certain extent neglected or assessed as carrying less weight. In some instances, liability stemming from *Konzernvertrauen* as a sub-feature of *culpa in contrahendo* under Swiss law[375] was characterised as contractual,[376] but relying too much on the classification by national law.

Last but definitely not least and even less as some kind of coda comes the external liability of **71** shareholders, in particular of a dominant shareholder or a genuine parent body, towards creditors of the company (or even subsidiary). It can be argued that the accessory characterisation should be chosen as the appropriate device.[377] Alternatively, one could feel bound to say without differentiation that the liability is extended only by legal rules and can not be based on a contractual bond, but ought be one in tort.[378] Yet such an approach could misidentify and misdo the nature of the collective promise[379] which the shareholders issue, at least by signing the minimum capital and subjecting themselves to the applicable liability

---

368 *Thole*, GPR 2014, 113, 114.

369 *Thole*, GPR 2014, 113, 115.

370 *Möllers*, Internationale Zuständigkeit bei Durchgriffshaftung (1987) p. 86; *Kulms*, IPRax 2000, 488, 493. Contra ÖFAB Östergötlands Fastigheter AB v. *Frank Koot and Evergreen Investments BV* (Case C-147/ 12), ECLI:EU:C:2013:490 paras. 36 *et seq.*; BGH WM 2014, 1614 [25]-[28].

371 *ÖFAB Östergötlands Fastigheter AB v. Frank Koot and Evergreen Investments BV* (Case C-147/12), ECLI: EU:C:2013:490 paras. 36 *et seq.*; BGH WM 2014, 1614 [27], [28]; *Arons*, Ondernemingsrecht 2013, 563, 565.

372 OLG Köln WM 2005, 612, 614 = AG 2005, 123, 124; *Gerhard Wagner*, in: Lutter (ed.), Europäische Auslandsgesellschaften in Deutschland (2005), p. 223, 281.

373 *Gerhard Wagner*, in: Lutter (ed.), Europäische Auslandsgesellschaften in Deutschland (2005), p. 223, 281.

374 *Arons*, Ondernemingsrecht 2013, 563, 565.

375 See only BGE 120 II 331, 335.

376 BG 11 July 2000; HG Zürich ZR 99 (2000) Nr. 107.

377 To this avail BGH EuLF 2009, II-20.

378 See Cass. RCDIP 101 (2012), 639, 640 with note *Usunier* = Clunet 139 (2012), 684, 685 with note *Clavel*; OLG Düsseldorf IPRax 1998, 210; OLG Frankfurt IPRax 2000, 525; *Haubold*, IPRax 2000, 375, 381; *Ignatova*, Art. 5 Nr. 1 EuGVVO – Chancen und Perspektiven der Reform des Gerichtsstands am Erfüllungsort (2005) pp. 125 *et seq.*

379 See in particular *Wolfgang Schön*, EBOR 5 (2004), 429, 439 *et seq.*; *Wolfgang Schön*, Der Konzern 2004, 162, 166 *et seq.*

---

regime.[380] The fixed capital is the minimum chip which the shareholders put on the table. They have something to lose and commit themselves to the common cause of the company. The fixed capital defines the minimum investment. Fixed capital forces the shareholders to share in a minimum amount of the corporate risk.[381] Owning capital in the company is capital at risk.[382] The shareholders act as agents for the company creditors in any event.[383] Fixed capital deploys desirable incentives by subjecting the shareholder-agents to their own risk. As the incorporators declare *vis-à-vis* present and future creditors that they are willing to provide a certain amount of their own assets a first signal is given as to the creditworthiness of the company thus mitigating the creditors' informational disadvantage.[384]

72   A company acquiring the majority of shares on another company does not enter into direct contractual bonds with contractual creditors of its new subsidiary.[385] If company law imposes upon it certain obligations towards these creditors as a consequence of the share deal this is deemed to be outside the contractual realm[386] and the violation or breach of obligations so imposed might constitute a tort.[387]

ii) Pre-contractual dealings and liability

(1) In general

73   Before parties conclude a contract they are often involved in extensive pre-contractual negotiations. They are not total strangers to each other whilst they have not reached final agreement yet. Between these poles a realm of interdependencies emerges, and perhaps – depending on the applicable law – even obligations between the parties arise. The social contact has been established and intensified. The existence of a contract, i.e. that a contract was successfully concluded, is not a strict prerequisite for (1) to come into operation.[388] The ultimate goal of concluding a contract and the intensified contact both must not be neglected. The parties in pre-contractual dealings do not interact fortuitously, but with a common goal. They are not strangers to each other or passers-by as in the situation of an ordinary tort.[389] That *culpa in contrahendo* has been transferred into the realm of the Rome II Regu-

---

380   See *Kulms*, IPRax 2000, 488, 492 *et seq.*; *Martiny*, in: FS Reinhold Geimer (2002), p. 641, 665.

381   See *Wiedemann*, FS Karl Beusch (1993), p. 893, 909.

382   See only *Fleischer*, Finanzplankredite (1995) p. 87; *Wiedemann*, FS Karl Beusch (1993), p. 893, 909.

383   See only *Jensen/Meckling*, 3 J. Fin. Econ. 306 (1976); *Engert*, ZGR 2004, 813, 820.

384   *Mülbert/Birke*, EBOR 3 (2002), 696, 727 *et seq.*; *Wolfgang Schön*, EBOR 5 (2004), 429, 440; *Wolfgang Schön*, Der Konzern 2004, 162, 166; *Eidenmüller*, in: FS Andreas Heldrich (2005), p. 581, 593.

385   *OTP Bank Nyilvánosan Müködö Részvénytársaság v. Hochtief Solution AG* (C-519/12), ECLI:EU:C:2013:674 para. 25.

386   *OTP Bank Nyilvánosan Müködö Részvénytársaság v. Hochtief Solution AG* (C-519/12), ECLI:EU:C:2013:674 para. 24.

387   *OTP Bank Nyilvánosan Müködö Részvénytársaság v. Hochtief Solution AG* (C-519/12), ECLI:EU:C:2013:674 para. 26.

388   *Fonderie Officine Meccaniche Tacconi SpA von Heinrich Wagner Sinto Maschinenfabrik GmbH*, (Case C-334/00) [2002] ECR I-7357, I-7393 para. 22; *Petra Engler v. Janus Versand GmbH*, (Case C-27/02) [2005] ECR I-481, I-516 para. 45, I-517 para. 50.

389   But cf. for an apparently general characterisation of claims based on pre-contractual liability as tortious Cassaz. RDIPP 2004, 1008, 1009; OLG Köln WM 2005, 612, 614 =AG 2005, 123, 124; OLG Düsseldorf EuLF 2006, II-93; OLG Stuttgart ZIP 2013, 2154; Hof Arnhem NIPR 2006 Nr. 304 p. 449.

lation and has been expelled from the Rome I Regulation by virtue of its Art. 1 (2) (i) should not result in a completely tortious characterisation for the purposes of the Brussels I Regulation since in essence Art. 12 (1) Rome II Regulation relates back to the *lex contractus* and thus submits *culpa in contrahendo* to the law governing the envisaged contract.[390]

An additional element needs to be considered if the contract was eventually not concluded. **74** Although the original aim was not achieved, this does not disqualify the pre-contractual relations from the realm of (1) automatically. Parties might have found themselves bound by duties to inform and to respect the other's assets or alike. As long as they were still in the process of negotiating they were under the specific pre-contractual regime. The outcome of their negotiations can not alter this retrospectively. If there is a specific pre-contractual regime structuring negotiations and establishing specific duties of good faith tailor-made for the negotiations, such regime would be rendered nugatory if its application depended on the eventual outcome of the negotiations. The parties need their guidelines and rules of the game during the negotiations. Incentives must be actual and effective and must not be blown away later-on by the winds of misfortune.

At least pre-contractual duties to inform or to disclose information should be classified as **75** contractual.[391] This is the more appropriate if they can prompt and generate a claim to rescind a contract that is eventually concluded, with such actions being contractual by nature.[392] It would be unfortunate to split jurisdication between attempts to rescind a contract and alternatively to claim damages for misrepresentation or intimidation.[392a] *Culpa in contrahendo* must not be classified as tortious due to a mere allegation that a place of performance can not be identified, either.[393] If there is an obligation, it must as a matter of law and construction have a place of performance.[394] Nevertheless the case should be different if duties protecting the integrity of the other party's assets, as such, are at stake.[395] In this instance claims stemming from *culpa in contrahendo* should be characterised as claims in tort since *culpa in contrahendo* then tends to be a tool to short-cut deficiencies in national tort law. Functionally such claims are in tort although the parties could have contracted for a specific regime since they knew each other before the incident. Even claims in prospectus liability transmogrify into contractual ones if a contract is eventually concluded.[396]

---

[390] See tentatively in a similar direction *Spickhoff*, IPRax 2009, 128 132 *et seq.*; *Hofmann/Kunz*, in: Basler Kommentar, Art. 5 note 126. *Contra Kropholler/von Hein*, Art. 5 note 79; see also *Gehri*, in: FS Ivo Schwander (2011), p. 699, 705.

[391] LG Dortmund IPRspr. 1998 Nr. 139 p. 255; LG Potsdam VersR 2003, 378; LG Hof IPRspr. 2002 Nr. 132a p. 341; *Franzina*, Riv. dir. int. 2003, 714, 731 *et seq.*; *Dörner*, IPRax 2005, 26, 27; *Ignatova*, Art. 5 Nr. 1 EuGVVO – Chancen und Perspektiven der Reform des Gerichtsstands am Erfüllungsort (2005) p. 118; to the same result Cass. EuLF 2006, II-92 but the court does not take any account of the jurisprudence of the ECJ, *Magnier*, EuLF 2006, II-93. Further differentiating *Moura Vicente*, RabelsZ 67 (2003), 699, 711 if and insofar as such duties to disclosure simultaneously aim at guarding public interests such as the regular and transparent functioning of markets, fair competition and stability of prices.

[392] *Agnew v. Länsforskäringsbolagens AB* [2001] A.C. 223, 244 (H.L., per Lord *Woolf* M.R.); see also *Stadler*, (2005) 42 CMLRev. 1637, 1653; *Sindres*, J-Cl. Dr. int. fasc. 584-130 no. 22 (mars 2014).

[392a] *Briggs* para. 2.191.

[393] *Contra* Epheteio Athinai Arm. 2001, 1239.

[394] Similarly *Sindres*, J-Cl. Dr. int. fasc. 584-130 no. 22 (mars 2014).

[395] *Mankowski*, IPRax 2003, 127, 133 *et seq.*, *Moura Vicente*, RabelsZ 67 (2003), 699, 711.

(2) Breaking off of negotiations

76 A special and most intricate case is the breaking off or rupture of the negotiations by either party. Although the parties are generally free in their decision whether to consent to contract, and might break off negotiations even at the last moment, the rupturing party might have signalled otherwise before and might be bound by its previous dealings and behaviour.

77 In the absence of any pre-agreements the ECJ characterised a claim for the breaking off or rupture of negotiations as tortious, not as contractual.[397] The main argument on which this finding[398] was based reads that the obligation to make good the damage allegedly caused by the unjustified breaking off of negotiations could derive only from breach of rules of law, in particular the rule which requires the parties to act in good faith in negotiations with a view to the formation of a contract.[399] This argument misapprehends the function of supplementary rules of law. It can easily be falsified: One only has to remember all the rules for breach of contract which are contained in legislative acts that must undoubtedly be characterised as rules of contract law.[400] Following the ECJ, the entire body of contract law could not exist or else be classified as non-contractual – an evidently absurd result. If backing by the very text of (1) was required, the French and Italian version ("en matière contractuelle", "in materia contrattuale") would provide it.[401] Specifically with regard to duties of good faith such duties would be meaningless without their specific point of reference, namely the intended contract.[402] Even worse is a tortious characterisation of a rupture of an existing commercial relationship which has generated some contractual foundations in the past.[403]

78 If a classification as tort was preferred, in the extreme consequence parties may better be advised as to choosing the places where they negotiate, while carefully considering the respective legal risks in such a choice.[404] Yet the better approach is to opt for a characterisation as contractual.[405] The parties of negotiations are not strangers to each other who have

---

396   OLG München WM 2010, 1463, 1468.

397   *Fonderie Officine Meccaniche Tacconi SpA von Heinrich Wagner Sinto Maschinenfabrik GmbH*, (Case C-334/00) [2002] ECR I-7357, I-7393 *et seq.* paras. 24–27. To the same result OGH JBl 2007, 800, 803; Cass. RDC 2009, 197 with note *Behar-Touchais* = CCC 2009 comm. 8 with note *Mathey*; Cass. CCC 2010 comm. 179 with note *Mathey*; Cass. CCC 2011 comm. 64 with note *Mathey*; CA Rennes Bull. Joly 1993, 464 § 132 with note *Daigre*; CA Lyon CCC 2009 comm. 8 with note *Mathey*; Epheteio Athinai Arm. 2001, 1239 with note *Arvanitakis*; Rb. 's-Hertogenbosch NIPR 2005 Nr. 169 p. 234; *Gaudemet-Tallon*, RCDIP 88 (1999), 335; *André Huet*, Clunet 126 (1999), 188, 189; *André Huet*, Clunet 130 (2003), 145 *et seq.*

398   Which by some is only used as a point of reference and not a foreclusion; *André Huet*, Clunet 130 (2003), 668, 670; *Pertegás*, in: Meeusen/Pertegás/Straetmans (eds.), Enforcement of International Contracts in the European Union (2004), p. 175, 186 § 5-31.

399   *Fonderie Officine Meccaniche Tacconi SpA von Heinrich Wagner Sinto Maschinenfabrik GmbH*, (Case C-334/00) [2002] ECR I-7357, I-7393 *et seq.* para. 25.

400   See only BAG AP Nr. 1 zu Art. 5 Lugano-Abkommen Bl. 5R with note *Mankowski*; Rel. Lisboa Col. Jur. 2001 v. 124, 125; Vzngr. Rb. Arnhem NIPR 2010 Nr. 54 p. 113; *Mankowski*, IPRax 2003, 127, 131.

401   *Jaspert*, EuGVÜ-Gerichtsstände und Anspruchsdurchsetzung gegen ausländische herrschende Unternehmen (1995) p. 110; *Mankowski*, NZI 1999, 56, 57; *Briggs*, (1997) 68 BYIL 331, 333.

402   See *Collins*, in: Dicey/Morris/Collins para. 11–249.

403   *Contra* Cass. com. JCP E 2011 N°. 1179 = JCP E 3 mars 2011 p. 37 note *de Lammerville/Nicolas Aynès*.

404   *Veenstra*, NTBR 2003, 138, 142.

405   Cass. Clunet 128 (2001), 133; CA Chambéry Clunet 126 (1999), 188; Rb. Kh. Gent TBH 2003, 175, 177;

met by accident.[406] They invest at least as much commitment and reliance as to maintain the contact. They could have also established an own regime for their negotiations laid down in letters of intent and alike. If they do not so, the applicable *ius dispositivum* steps in for mere gap-filling. Functionally, this reflects contractuality and does not mirror the prerequisites of a tort.[407] It is rather accidental whether the parties structure their negotiations by instruments like a letter of intent (and would accordingly bring them clearly and unambiguously within a contractual regime),[408] and thus too much emphasis should not be placed on the absence of such a letter, but the overall bond of a unitary pre-contractual sphere should be recognised, not the least since any distinguishing differentiation of modes of conduct would be both difficult and dangerous.[409] Furthermore, the economic theory of incomplete contracts could give a helping hand in reference to low transaction costs.[410] Any approach to try to characterise the partners of the negotiations as a kind of company and to employ an analogy to (6) in order to reach jurisdiction at the place where this "company" has its seat,[411] ought to be rejected outrightly as over-construed and over-pensive.

jj) Bills of lading

Claims arising out of bills of lading are contractual by their very nature:[412] The carrier under   **79** the bill of lading voluntarily promises to deliver the goods to the bearer or the consignee as the case may be. As unilateral promises are contractual, too,[413] there is no need to ascertain whether the bill of lading is a contract of carriage or only a means of evidence for an original contract of carriage. Nevertheless, if the plaintiff relies on the bill of lading in order to sue the actual carrier, not the carrier according to the wording of the bill of lading, there a voluntary submission does not exist and the issue is a tortious one.[414] Sub-carriers in particular are not germane to the bill of lading.[415] Yet like so many instances beyond the ordinary case,[416] the characterisation as tortious generates more difficulties as to the localisation of the place where the damage occurred.[417]

Mankowski, IPRax 2003, 127, 131; *Stadler*, in: FS Hans-Joachim Musielak (2004), p. 569, 590 *et seq.*; *Broggini*, Europa e dir. priv. 2004, 1127, 1143; *Sindres*, J.-Cl. Dr. int. fasc. 584-130 no. 17 (mars 2014).

[406] *Mankowski*, IPRax 2003, 127, 131.

[407] *Mankowski*, IPRax 2003, 127, 131; see also *Kulms*, IPRax 2000, 488, 491 *et seq.*

[408] *Supra* Art. 7 note 59 (*Mankowski*).

[409] *Mankowski*, IPRax 2003, 127, 133 *et seq.*; *Rémy-Corlay*, RCDIP 92 (2003), 673, 680; see also *Afferni*, ECRL 2005, 97, 105–107.

[410] *Afferni*, ECRL 2005, 97, 107 *et seq.*

[411] See *Volken*, SZIER 2004, 637 *et seq.*

[412] See only CA Paris DMF 1999, 542 with note *Achard*; CA Aix Rev. Scapel 2008, 13, 15; *Hartley*, (2000) 25 Eur. L. Rev. 89, 92; *van Haersolte-van Hof*, NIPR 2000, 386, 388; *Mankowski*, TranspR 2008, 67, 74; *Egler*, Seerechtliche Streitigkeiten unter der EuGVVO (2011) pp. 64–67. But cf. *Réunion europénne SA v. Spliethoff's Bevrachtingskantoor BV and Master of the vessel "Alblasgracht 002"*, (Case C-51/97) [1998] ECR I-6511, I-6542 *et seq.* paras. 19, 23.

[413] *Supra* Art. 7 notes 34–36 (*Mankowski*).

[414] *Réunion europénne SA v. Spliethoff's Bevrachtingskantoor BV and Master of the vessel "Alblasgracht 002"*, (Case C-51/97) [1998] ECR I-6511, I-6543 paras. 23 *et seq.*; Hof Arnhem NIPR 2003 Nr. 279 p. 433; Aud. Prov. Barcelona AEDIPr 2001, 898, 900; *Perrella*, Dir. mar. 102 (2000), 106, 111.

[415] *Harald Koch*, IPRax 2000, 186, 187.

[416] See *Eslava Rodríguez*, AEDIPr 2000, 810, 812.

[417] *Infra* Art. 7 notes 318 *et seq.* (*Mankowski*).

kk) Bills of exchange and cheques

80   Bills of exchange and cheques also are contractual.[418] They evidence and contain a unilateral promise on the debtor's side. Claims against the person accepting and guaranteeing a bill of exchange, by the indorsee against this person and against the person signing an own solar bill of exchange qualify as contractual, too.[419] They do not share the place of performance of the original debt which to fulfil indirectly they have been issued.[420] Bills of exchange and cheques do not contain, however, a voluntary promise by the person signing them, towards the creditor. Insofar as a redress by the creditor against the person signing the cheque or bill of exchange is at stake, a contractual characterisation is subject to criticism.[421]

ll) Internal redress between jointly liable debtors in contract

81   If joint debtors are liable towards their common creditor in contract, their internal redress should also qualify as contractual.[422] Insofar an accessory classification should prevail. The voluntary act on the single debtor's side is the act establishing his contractual liability towards the creditor. Anything else would run contrary to the institution of joint and several liability.[423]

mm) Negotiorum gestio

82   Though the optimal construction of the content of claims based on *negotiorum gestio* might be explained best by adopting the model of hypothetising a contract,[424] *negotiorum gestio* lacks the element of an obligation voluntarily assumed at least on the principal's part.[425] Furthermore, *negotiorum gestio* is clearly and indubitably relegated to the realm of extra-contractual obligations by Art. 11 Rome II Regulation.[426] Accordingly, *negotiorum gestio* can not be characterised as a contractual issue,[427] even not with regard to compensation or remuneration as a consequence of a justified *negotiorum gestio*.[428]

nn) Claims by third party-beneficiaries

83   Under many national laws including German law (§ 328 BGB: *Vertrag zu Gunsten Dritter)*

---

[418]   OGH IPRax 2002, 131; BGH BGH-Report 2004, 549, 551 with note *Matthias Kilian.*

[419]   *Birgit Bachmann*, IPRax 1997, 153, 155 *et seq.*; *Martiny*, in: FS Reinhold Geimer (2002), p. 641, 659.

[420]   *Hofmann/Kunz*, in: Basler Kommentar, Art. 5 note 96.

[421]   LG Göttingen RIW 1977, 235; LG Bayreuth IPRax 1988, 230; LG Frankfurt/Main IPRax 1997, 258; *Martiny*, in: FS Reinhold Geimer (2002), p. 641, 660.

[422]   To the same avail *Kerstin Thoma*, Der interne Regress (2007) pp. 201–204.

[423]   *Engdiv Ltd. v. G. Percy Trentham Ltd.* 1990 SLT 617, 621 (O.H., Lord *Prosser*); *Kulms*, IPRax 2000, 488, 492.

[424]   Seminally *Köndgen*, in: Rechtsgeschichte und Privatrechtsdogmatik – Hans Hermann Seiler zum 24. Dezember 1999 (1999), p. 371.

[425]   *Martiny*, in: FS Reinhold Geimer (2002), p. 641, 655.

[426]   *Dutta*, IPRax 2011, 134, 136.

[427]   OLG Düsseldorf IPRax 1998, 210; OLG Köln IPRax 2011, 174, 175; *Uhl*, Internationale Zuständigkeit gemäß Art. 5 Nr. 3 des Brüsseler und Lugano-Übereinkommens (2000) p. 126; *Nagel/Gottwald* § 3 Art. 5 note 41; *Martiny*, in: FS Reinhold Geimer (2002), p. 641, 655; *Stadler*, in: FS Hans-Joachim Musielak (2004), p. 569, 581; *Gottwald*, in: Münchener Kommentar zur ZPO Art. 5 note 11; *Simotta*, in: Fasching/Konecny Art. 5 note 76; *Späth*, Die gewerbliche Erbensuche im grenzüberschreitenden Rechtsverkehr (2008) p. 259; *Leible*, in: Rauscher, Art. 5 note 21; *Dutta*, IPRax 2011, 134, 136.

[428]   BH NJW 1996, 1411, 1412; OLG Köln IPRax 2011, 174, 175; *Looschelders*, IPRax 2014, 406, 407.

and English Law (Contracts (Rights of Third Party) Act 1999)[429] contractual claims can be established in the favour of third parties who are not formal parties to the contract. Such third party beneficiaries nevertheless derive their status from the contract and from the contract exclusively. The debtor is bound and has voluntarily submitted himself to perform such an obligation in their favour. This should also be recognised by a characterisation of claims by third party-beneficiaries as contractual for the purposes of (1).[430] In addition, claims by the beneficiary against a trust also should qualify as contractual.[431]

The case is different however, if a third party is deemed by national law to be included in the **84** wider ambit of the contract insofar as this party is not able to claim for specific performance of a primary obligation, but gets protection according the contractual regime (mostly in order to overcome deficiencies in national tort law). Such a *Vertrag mit Schutzwirkung für Dritte*, in German terminology, does not establish a claim in contract, but must be submitted to the realm of tort under (3).[432]

oo) Representation and agency
Agency poses quite some problems. The starting point nevertheless is trite: If the contract **85** concluded by the agent on the principal's behalf is binding upon the principal pursuant to the agent having proper authorisation under the applicable substantive law, a contractual bond between the principal and the other party exists. The activities and declarations by the agent are held by the principal in this instant. Yet one can not judge and ascertain this without recourse to the substantive law applicable to the agency. Any attempt to try otherwise and establish autonomous rules is doomed for failure since (1) does not contain even the slightest indication to the extent of such rules. According to the respective *lex causae*, even undisclosed agency could – as under English law[433] – result in direct contractual bonds between the principal and the other party which should be duly recognised as contractual by (1).[434]

c) Assignment and subrogation
Quite often contractual claims are assigned by the original creditor, the assignor, to another **86** person, the assignee (e.g. a trading company assigns its own claims against its customers to its bank). The assignee and the debtor have never entered into a direct contractual bond between themselves. Yet originally, as between the assignor and the debtor, the claim in

---

[429] See on this Act e.g. *Nisshin Shipping Co. Ltd. v. Cleaves & Co. Ltd.* [2004] 1 Lloyd's Rep. 38 (Q.B.D., Colman J.); *Bridge*, (2001) 5 Edinburgh L. Rev. 85; *MacMillan*, (2000) 63 Mod. L. Rev. 721; *Hans-Friedrich Müller*, RabelsZ 67 (2003), 140.

[430] *Jiménez Blanco*, El contrato internacional a favor de tercero (2002) p. 95 *et seq.*; *Jiménez Blanco*, REDI 2002, 881, 885; *Hofmann/Kunz*, in: Basler Kommentar, Art. 5 note 149.

[431] *Atlas Shipping Agency (UK) Ltd. and United Shipping Services Ltd. v. Suisse Atlantique Société d'Armement Maritime SA* [1995] 2 Lloyd's Rep. 188 = [1995] I.L.Pr. 600 (Q.B.D., Rix J.); *Kulms*, IPRax 2000, 488, 492; see also *Layton/Mercer* para. 15.017.

[432] OGH JBl 2001, 185; OGH 29.1.2003 – 7 Ob 291/02y; OGH IPRax 2006, 489, 490; *Martiny*, in: FS Reinhold Geimer (2002), p. 641, 663 and with extensive reasoning *Dutta*, IPRax 2009, 293, 294–297.

[433] *Reynolds*, Bowstead and Reynolds on Agency (17th ed. 2001) Art. 78.

[434] *Stephan Lorenz/Unberath*, IPRax 2004, 298, 303; see also *Carrascosa González*, in: Calvo Caravaca, Art. 5.1 CB note 10.

question has been a contractual one. Does the claim cease to be contractual and strip off its original virtue due to the assignment?

87 The ECJ tentatively appears to restrict (1) to cases where there exists a *direct* contractual bond between plaintiff and defendant,[435] thus expelling cases from the realm of (1) in which an assignment has taken place and in which the assignee sues.[436] Apparently, special jurisdiction under (1) is measured as a grace and gift for the plaintiff and denied wherever possible. Such an interpretation of (1) nevertheless would be erroneous, though. Unlike Art. 5 (2) Brussels I Regulation (now Art. 3 (1) (b) Maintenance Regulation), Arts. 9–15, Arts. 17–19 or Arts. 20–23, (1) does not benefit or privilege the individual in a specific capacity (like a consumer or employee or insured person or claimant in maintenance),[437] but is based on a certain classification of the claim in question.[438] The very nature of the claim in question needs to be determined and ascertained *ab initio*. When the claim is generated and originates, it has a certain nature and bears a certain classification. This will not be altered by replacing the creditor with another person. A claim originating from a contract does not alter its contractual nature. It is founded in contract, and this is the relevant, all-important and all-decisive issue.[439] What is correct under Rome I, must also be correct under Brussels I.[440] (1) aims at facilitating to enforce the obligation at stake regardless who is the creditor.[441] The formula of the ECJ should not become a mantra as it is not comprehensive, but only particular, partial and specific.[442]

88 If a claim requires a bond freely assumed by one party towards another in order to be characterised as contractual this does not automatically dictate that it necessarily must originally be founded in the present plaintiff's favour.[443] No such implication exists. He who freely and voluntarily creates obligations against himself cannot complain if the obli-

---

[435] Starting with *Jakob Handte & Co. GmbH v. Traitements Mécano-chimiques des surfaces SA*, (Case C-26/91) [1992] ECR I-3967, I-3994 *et seq.* paras. 15–21.

[436] *Réunion europénne SA v. Spliethoff's Bevrachtingskantoor BV and Master of the vessel "Alblasgracht 002"*, (Case C-51/97) [1998] ECR I-6511, I-6541 para. 15; *Verein für Konsumenteninformation v. Karl-Heinz Henkel*, (Case C-167/00) [2002], I-8111, I-8140 paras. 38 *et seq.* and in particular – also in the context of Art. 1 (1) – *Frahuil SA v. Assitalia SpA*, (Case C-265/02) [2004] ECR I-1543, I-1554 para. 21; see also *Harald Kolassa v. Barclays Bank plc* (Case C-375/13), ECLI:EU:C:2015:37 para. 40 (not quite clear as *Michael Müller*, EuZW 2015, 218, 222 rightly ruminates). Bu cf. to the opposite result A-G *Szpunar*, Opinion in Case C-375/13 of 3 September 2014, ECLI:EU:C:2014:2135 para. 47.

[437] See *Shearson Lehman Hutton, Inc. v. TVB Treuhandgesellschaft mbH*, (Case C-89/91) [1993] ECR I-139, I-188 *et seq.* paras. 22–25; *Freistaat Bayern v. Jan Blijdenstein*, (Case C-433/01) [2004] ECR I-981, I-1001-I-1003 paras. 27–34.

[438] OGH IPRax 2006, 489, 490; *Mankowski*, EWiR Art. 5 EuGVÜ 1/04, 379; *Mankowski*, RIW 2004, 481, 495; *Schlosser*, JZ 2004, 408, 409; *Hau*, IPRax 2006, 507, 508; *Michael Müller*, EuZW 2015, 218, 222; in: von Hein/Rühl (eds.), Kohärenz im Internationalen Privat- und Verfahrensrecht der Europäischen Union (2015).

[439] OGH IPRax 2006, 489, 490; *Mankowski*, RIW 2004, 481, 495.

[440] Doubtful in this respect however *Pertegás*, in: Meeusen/Pertegás/Straetmans (eds.), Enforcement of International Contracts in the European Union (2004), p. 175, 179 *et seq.* § 5-12, 189 *et seq.* § 5-40.

[441] *Mankowski*, EWiR Art. 5 EuGVÜ 1/04, 379, 380; *Johannes Weber*, ZvglRWiss 107 (2008), 193, 203.

[442] *Briggs*, [1999] LMCLQ 333, 334.

[443] As wrongly assumed by *Frahuil SA v. Assitalia SpA*, (Case C-265/02) [2004] ECR I-1543, I-1555 para. 23.

gation is assigned later, all the more since this does not alter the place of performance. The place of performance remains the same since it is either linked with the factual delivery or with the original creditor, not subsequent creditors including the present plaintiff. The defendant *debitor cessus* is not unfairly treated since he faces jurisdiction only in a place which he could envisage from the outset. Otherwise the *debitor cessus* would gain an unjustified windfall profit from the assignment, and parties contemplating a transfer of the obligation from the original creditor would be advised only as to the transfer of the eventual proceeds of the obligation in advance and to order the original creditor to stay upfront and to cash in the obligation. It does not matter that the *debitor cessus* is not party to the assignment or subrogation and did not participate voluntarily in this process.[444] Nor does the fact become relevant that the assignee was previously unknown to the debtor.[445] Accordingly, assignees and subrogating persons can also sue in the court designated by (1) if only the claim assigned or subrogated has been in contract initially.[446] It may be added that in the event of another person individually succeeding to the debt by agreement the claim retains its contractual nature and can be pursued in the *forum* provided by (1).[447] For the sake of clarification, it should be asserted that the holder of a lien to a claim sort of subrogates into the claim when exercising his lien and should thus be enabled to rely on (1) if the claim is a contractual one.[448]

2. Art. 5 (1) (b)

a) Characterisation

aa) Contracts for the sale of goods
The first category covered by (b) comprises contracts for the sale of goods. This expression **89** should be given an autonomous meaning independent from the definition a contract for the sale of goods is given by the *lex fori*, the *lex causae* or any other (single) national law. Rightly it should be taken as a concept of EU law.[449] The national sales laws might provide some help, but only in their entirety and as a kind of comparative background, not with defining power. Whether national law, particularly the substantive law of the *lex fori*, would coin the concrete contract a contract for the sale of goods or else bears no relevance.[450]

(1) Contract for sale
The phrase "sale of goods" ought to be coined widely, i.e. at least interpreted regardless of **90** whether a transfer of property is automatically executed or not.[451] (1) (b) does not contain a

---

444 OGH IPRax 2006, 489, 490; *Mankowski*, EWiR Art. 5 EuGVÜ 1/04, 379.

445 *Briggs*, [1999] LMCLQ 333, 334.

446 OGH RIW 1998, 634; OLG Bremen RIW 1998, 63; OLG Celle IPRax 1999, 456; *Hartley*, (1993) 18 Eur. L. Rev. 506, 516; *Hertz* p. 74; *Donzallaz* Art. 5 note 4562; *Gebauer*, IPRax 1999, 432; *Bauerreis*, RCDIP 89 (2000), 331, 346; *Briggs/Rees* p. 123 *et seq.*; *Martiny*, in: FS Reinhold Geimer (2002), p. 641, 661; *Leible*, in: Rauscher Art. 5 note 9a; *Mankowski*, RIW 2004, 481, 495; *Schlosser*, JZ 2004, 408, 409.

447 Hoge Raad RvdW 2003 Nr. 164; *Polak*, AA 2004, 52, 54 *et seq.*

448 *Contra* Rb. Middelburg NIPR 2006 Nr. 59 p. 93.

449 OLG München CR 2010, 156, 157; Rb. Kh. Antwerpen ETL 2005, 657, 667; Rb. Arnhem NIPR 2006 Nr. 51 p. 83; *Mankowski*, CR 2010, 137, 138; *Axel Metzger*, IPRax 2010, 420, 421.

450 *Mankowski*, CR 2010, 137, 138.

451 *Béraudo*, Clunet 128 (2001), 1033, 1044. But cf. *Briggs* para. 2.174.

proper definition, though,[452] and insofar its drafting might be called opaque.[453] Otherwise contracts governed by a *lex causae*, which – like German law or even the CISG – strictly distinguishes between contractual issues and issues of property law, would be excluded. Since only contractual issues are inside (1), property law falls completely outside and does not even have indirect influence via questions of classification.[454] The basic meaning of "sale of goods" thus should read as the contractual exchange of goods against money.[455] This covers all kinds of sale contracts.[456]

91 But on the other hand the phrase "sale of goods" requires that parties contract for a transfer of property since otherwise it would be impossible to distinguish between a sale of goods and the mere hire of goods. Delivery is the physical hand-over when material and corporeal goods are concerned. Under a hire contract the goods in question are also handed over which implies that something else must serve as the distinguishing and characteristic element of a sale of goods. Hence, in solving case the first practical step is to identify the obligations which characterises the concrete contract.[457] Only contracts which have the supply of goods as their characteristic obligation, qualify as contracts for the sale of goods.[458] The supplier's responsibility can also be a factor to consider: If the supplier is responsible for the quality of the goods, even if the goods are result of activities on his part, and the compliance of the goods with the contract, that responsibility will tip the balance in favour of classification as a "contract for the sale of goods".[459] On the other hand, if the supplier is responsible only for correct implementation in accordance with the recipient's instructions, that fact indicates rather that the contract should be characterised as one for the provision of services.[460] The characteristic performance is the relevant one,[461] faithful to principle.[462]

92 Seizing upon the meaning of "sales"[463] in the CISG,[464] the most elaborate and most widely

---

[452] A-G *Mazák*, [2010] ECR I-1258, I-1262 para. 17.

[453] *Shine*, [2011] ICCLR 20, 22.

[454] But cf. *Martiny*, in: FS Reinhold Geimer (2002), p. 641, 651 *et seq.*

[455] OLG München CR 2010, 156, 157; Rb. Rotterdam NIPR 2010 Nr. 357 p. 580; *Magnus*, IHR 2002, 45, 47; *Kropholler/von Hein* Art. 5 note 32; *Magnus*, in: Staudinger, BGB, CISG (2005) Art. 1 CISG with note 13; *Lynker*, Der besondere Gerichtsstand am Erfüllungsort in der Brüssel I-Verordnung (Art. 5 Nr. 1 Eu-GVVO) (2006) p. 54; *Henri Storme*, R.W. 2009–2010, 409, 411.

[456] See only (with lists of sub-types) *Burgstaller*, in: Neumayr/Burgstaller, Art. 5 note 10 (2002); *Simotta*, in: Fasching/Konecny, Art. 5 note 161; *Leible*, in: Rauscher, Art. 5 note 46.

[457] *Car Trim GmbH v. KeySafety Systems Srl*, (Case C-381/08) [2010] ECR I-1255, I-1280 para. 32.

[458] *Car Trim GmbH v. KeySafety Systems Srl*, (Case C-381/08) [2010] ECR I-1255, I-1280 para. 32.

[459] *Car Trim GmbH v. KeySafety Systems Srl*, (Case C-381/08) [2010] ECR I-1255, I-1282 para. 40; Trib. Sant'Angelo dei Lombardi Giur. It. 2014, 1123.

[460] *Car Trim GmbH v. KeySafety Systems Srl*, (Case C-381/08) [2010] ECR I-1255, I-1282 para. 42.

[461] *Car Trim GmbH v. KeySafety Systems Srl*, (Case C-381/08) [2010] ECR I-1255, I-1280 paras. 31–32; OLG Köln IHR 2007, 164; LG Baden-Baden IPRspr. 2009 Nr. 182 p. 475; *Simotta*, in: Fasching/Konecny, Art. 5 note 165; *Franzina*, RDIPP 2010, 655, 662 *et seq.*; *Di Blase*, Europa e dir. priv. 2011, 459, 470 *et seq.*; *Gsell*, ZEuP 2011, 669, 679.

[462] *Shine*, [2011] ICCLR 20, 23 does not grasp the principle.

[463] The German wording of (b) reads "bewegliche Sachen", not "Waren" and thus employs a different terminology, but should be taken as equivalent, though; *Lynker*, Der besondere Gerichtsstand am Erfüllungsort in der Brüssel I-Verordnung (Art. 5 Nr. 1 EuGVVO) (2006) p. 53.

used international instrument in modern times,[465] worlds apart from any national particu-larities,[466] it does not matter whether the seller is called upon to manufacture or produce the goods or not as Art. 3 CISG demonstrates.[467] The understanding under Art. 1 (4) Consumer Sales Directive[468] and Art. 6 (2) UN Convention of 16 June 1974 on the Limitation Period in the International Sale of Goods amply support this.[469] If the element of activity does not become predominant the mere result that a product is handed-over and property in this product has passed, becomes the important characteristic.[470] The seller-producer and the mere re-seller are both covered by (a).[471] How the seller obtains the goods and comes into a position to transfer property in them, has no relevance if not the process of producing (as opposed to its resulting outcome) as such is the topic the parties are mainly interested in. A sales contract with a subsequent agreement on modifying the goods still is a sales contract.[472]

However, it might be an indication pointing towards activity and the production process as **93** such being the dominant element and the contract qualifying as one for the provision of services if the purchaser supplies the materials from which the goods are manufactured.[473] On the hand if the contract purports at the supply of goods to be manufactured or produced, such contract is for the sale of goods even though the purchaser has specified certain instructions and requirements with regard to the provision, fabrication and delivery of the components to be produced.[474] The place of manufacture is irrelevant when the contract is for supply of goods elsewhere, anyway.[475] If the seller is first called upon to invest sweat of

---

[464] See only *Car Trim GmbH v. KeySafety Systems Srl*, (Case C-381/08) [2010] ECR I-1255, I-1281 para. 36; Trib. Padova, sez. Este RDIPP 2007, 147, 151; *Magnus*, IHR 2002, 45, 47; *Czernich*, WBl 2002, 337, 339; *Burgstaller/Neumayr* Art. 5 note 10 (Oct. 2002); *Rauscher*, in: FS Andreas Heldrich (2005), p. 933, 944; *Ignatova*, Art. 5 Nr. 1 EuGVVO – Chancen und Perspektiven der Reform des Gerichtsstands am Erfül-lungsort (2005) p. 185; *Ferrari*, IPRax 2007, 61, 65 *et seq.*; *Ferrari*, RDAI 2007, 83, 90 *et seq.*; *García Mirete*, AEDIPr 2007, 935, 937; *Ragno*, Convenzione di Vienna e Diritto europeo (2008) pp. 215–218; *Markus*, Tendenzen beim materiellrechtlichen Vertragserfüllungsort im internationalen Zivilverfahrensrecht (Basel 2009) p. 143; *Markus*, AJP 2010, 971, 973; *Espiniella Menéndez*, AEDIPr 2010, 1024, 1026–1027.

[465] For the limited purposes of gaining interpretatory guidance it does not matter that the United Kingdom and Portugal (plus Iceland in the context of the Lugano Convention) are not Member States of the CISG; *Schlosser* Art. 5 note 10a; *Lynker*, Der besondere Gerichtsstand am Erfüllungsort in der Brüssel I-Ver-ordnung (Art. 5 Nr. 1 EuGVVO) (2006) p. 53 fn. 235.

[466] *Di Blase*, Europa e dir. priv. 2011, 459, 465.

[467] *Car Trim GmbH v. KeySafety Systems Srl*, (Case C-381/08) [2010] ECR I-1255, I-1281 para. 36; Cassaz. RDIPP 2013, 169, 171; Rb. 's-Hertogenbosch NIPR 2010 Nr. 483 p. 790. But cf. *Gsell*, IPRax 2002, 484, 486 *et seq.*

[468] Directive 1999/44/EC of the European Parliament and the Council of 25 May 1999 on certain aspects of the sale of consumer goods and associated guarantees, OJ 1999 L 171/12.

[469] *Car Trim GmbH v. KeySafety Systems Srl*, (Case C-381/08) [2010] ECR I-1255, I-1281 paras. 35, 37; Cassaz. RDIPP 2013, 169, 171; sceptical as to the methodical correctness *Axel Metzger*, IPRax 2010, 420, 421 *et seq.*

[470] *Kubis*, ZEuP 2001, 737, 750; see also *Car Trim GmbH v. KeySafety Systems Srl*, (Case C-381/08) [2010] ECR I-1255, I-1281 para. 36.

[471] Rb. Rotterdam NIPR 2010 Nr. 357 p. 580; see also OLG Stuttgart IHR 2011, 236, 238 = IHR 2012, 38, 40.

[472] Trib. Padova RDIPP 2011, 468, 473.

[473] *Car Trim GmbH v. KeySafety Systems Srl*, (Case C-381/08) [2010] ECR I-1255, I-1282 para. 40; *Axel Metzger*, IPRax 2010, 420, 422.

---

the brow and to develop concepts or construction plans this might become a dominant feature, but not necessarily so.[476]

94 Printing orders should be taken as constituting sales contracts.[477] Even an artist selling a picture to be painted, should be regarded as a seller since the buyer is interested in the result of the artist's efforts not in the painting process itself.[478] If the seller is obliged to install the goods at the buyer's place, that does not alter the nature of the contract as one for the sale of goods, either.[479] Likewise demolishing a previous good not to be substituted with the sold one will not become characteristic.[480]

95 The mere fact that after-sale services have to be provided by the seller, does not alter the nature of the contract.[481] Neither such a split, nor would regarding such services as the dominant element do justice to the over-all structure of (a) in most instances. One has only to compare this case with an event in which the seller has to perform warranties due to defective goods by repairing them (regardless as to whether such warranties are generated by contract[482] or *ex lege*). However, the picture might change if the after-sale services are not declared as such but form the subject of a separate contract for e.g. schooling staff, monitoring, maintaining and repair in case of need.[483] In this case the parties themselves have opted for a split. Different contracts can and should be treated as such: different contracts. A contract containing mixed obligations for supply, delivery, maintenance and support ought to be subjected to identifying the most important obligation, though.[484] On yet another hand, contracts providing for regular or occasional up-dates should be treated as sales contracts.

96 Complex contracts, the elements of which are the sale of goods and the provision of services at a roughly equivalent level, should not be transferred to the realm to (a) but kept within the confines of (b).[485] Although, the Joint Working Group which elaborated (1), might have held a different view.[486] But would it really make sense to allow for two elements, which if agreed

---

474 *Car Trim GmbH v. KeySafety Systems Srl*, (Case C-381/08) [2010] ECR I-1255, I-1283 para. 43; BGH IHR 2010, 216, 217; Cass. RCDIP 100 (2011), 915, 916.

475 *MBM Fabri-Clad Ltd. v. Eisen- und Hüttenwerke Thale AG* [2000] I.L.Pr. 505, 510 *et seq.*, 512 (C.A., per *Pill* and *Aldous* L.JJ. respectively).

476 See for the latter and characterising the developing process as *accessorium* in the concrete cases Rb. Rotterdam NIPR 2010 Nr. 357 p. 580; Rb. 's-Hertogenbosch NIPR 2010 Nr. 483 p. 790.

477 *Contra* Rb. Kh. Turnhout TBH 1994, 730, 733 with note *Erauw*.

478 Appraises by *Axel Metzger*, IPRax 2010, 420, 423.

479 *Burgstaller/Neumayr* Art. 5 note 10 (Oct. 2002).

480 Hof Amsterdam NIPR 2010 Nr. 328 p. 547.

481 Tentatively doubting *Peter Arnt Nielsen*, in: Liber Professorum College of Europe 2005, p. 245, 256. Tentatively as here *Axel Metzger*, IPRax 2010, 420, 423.

482 Rb. Rotterdam NIPR 2011 Nr. 250 p. 438.

483 See *Rogerson*, [2001] Cambridge Yb. Eur. L. 383.

484 See *Rogerson*, [2001] Cambridge Yb. Eur. L. 383.

485 OLG Köln EuLF 2007, II-112; Trib. Ferrara Giur. mer. 2005, 1556; Trib. Padova, sez. Este RDIPP 2007, 147, 152; *Lupoi*, Riv. trim. dir. proc. Civ. 2007, 495, 506; *de Franceschi*, Contratto e impresa/Europa 2008, 637, 688.

486 *Peter Arnt Nielsen*, in: Liber Professorum College of Europe 2005, p. 245, 256.

upon separately, would clearly fall within (b), but when being combined, drop out of (b)? Admittedly, it must be conceded that in the next step the choice for the appropriate connecting factor is a difficult issue. But perhaps a lenient tendency towards a *dépeçage* could cure the illness and provide the requisite remedy. Alternatively, the search for a relative centre of the contract would be on with the single obligations to be weighed against each other.[487] The economic value of the respective elements can be factor in this regard.[488] Yet it should be clear that distribution agreements as such do not qualify as sale contracts[489] whereas an actual contract for the transfer of goods under the umbrella of a master agreement does.[490]

Since an obligation to transfer property is the decisive element leasing contracts do not **97** feature as contracts for the sale of goods. They are effectively for the hire of goods unless either party seizes upon given options to actualise a dormant sales element contained in some leasing contracts. To effectivate such an option transforms the contract into a contract for the sale of goods, but only after the actualisation. Before the option is exercised a leasing contract is for hire and not for sale.[491]

Barter contracts are not sales contracts, either,[492] but for a different reason. As barter con- **98** tracts establish mutual obligations to transfer property, it is impossible to identify a performance by a single party which would be characteristic for the entire contract. Consequentially, it is impossible to identify any place of the delivery of *the* goods under (b) since the mutual main obligations are equivalent and bear the same relevance.

For yet another reason donations and gifts are not covered by (b): Whereas "contract" in **99** general does not require consideration to be agreed upon, it is different in the case of sale contracts.[493] Sale contracts are for remuneration and thus require consideration to be agreed upon.[494] Yet the case can be different in the event of so-called *gemischte Schenkungen* (literally to be translated as "mixed donations") where a consideration is agreed upon, but to the knowledge of both parties does not properly reflect the value of the good to be transferred. If the sales part of the transaction is the dominant one, (b) should apply, sticking to the ordinary yardstick that the preponderant part qualifies the entire transaction in the case of doubt.[495]

---

487 Favouring this *de Franceschi*, Contratto e impresa/Europa 2008, 637, 689 *et seq.*

488 *Simotta*, in: Fasching/Konecny, Art. 5 note 163.

489 Hof's-Gravenhage NIPR 2005 Nr. 51 p. 92; *Wurmnest*, IHR 2005, 107, 112 *et seq.* With regard to its case law under the CISG the Corte di Cassazione might hold otherwise; see Cassaz. Giur. it. 2000 I col. 2333 with note *Ferrari*; Cassaz. IHR 2005, 115.

490 Rb. Zwolle-Lelystad NIPR 2006 Nr. 304 p. 447.

491 *Czernich*, in: Czernich/Tiefenthaler(Kodek, Art. 5 note 30; *Leible*, in: Rauscher Art. 5 note 46c; *Geimer/ Schütze* Art. 5 note 88a; *Hofmann/Kunz*, in: Basler Kommentar, Art. 5 note 196.

492 See only *Geimer/Schütze* Art. 5 note 88; *Rodriguez*, Beklagtenwohnsitz und Erfüllungsort im europäischen IZVR (Zürich 2005) para. 664; *Lynker*, Der besondere Gerichtsstand am Erfüllungsort in der Brüssel I-Verordnung (Art. 5 Nr. 1 EuGVVO) (2006) p. 55; *Kropholler/von Hein* Art. 5 note 39.

493 See only *Hofmann/Kunz*, in: Basler Kommentar, Art. 5 note 185.

494 *Kropholler/von Hein* Art. 5 note 39; *Burgstaller/Neumayr* Art. 5 note 10 (Oct. 2002); *Geimer/Schütze* Art. 5 note 88; *Rodriguez*, Beklagtenwohnsitz und Erfüllungsort im europäischen IZVR (Zürich 2005) para. 664; *Henri Storme*, R.W. 2009–2010, 409, 412.

(2) Goods

(a) In general

100 Goods in the literal every-day meaning are tangibles, corporeal goods.[496] A more accurate and reasonably refined approximation defines goods as physically tangible objects (other than real estate) to which tradable personal property rights attach.[497] This encompasses already the majority of possible objects of a contract under which delivery shall take place and property shall be transferred. Tangibles are the evident realm of "goods". If the contract provides for the good to be produced by the seller, the contract will nevertheless be a sales contract[498] unless the buyer's specification are so exhausting that the element of services gains prevalence and the contract should be denominated as a contract essentially for the provision of services. The borderline between those two categories of contracts reflects and mirrors the similar borderline between the fundamental freedom of movement of goods under Arts. 34 *et seq.* TFEU (ex-Arts. 23 *et seq.* EC Treaty) and the fundamental freedom for the provision of services under Arts. 56 *et seq.* TFEU (ex-Arts. 49 *et seq.* EC Treaty) on the other hand.[499] Generally, the understanding of goods under (b) should follow the path cut by the respective definition in the CISG as far as possible.[500] That four Member States of the Brussels I*bis* Regulation (namely the United Kingdom, Ireland, Portugal and Malta) are not Contracting States of the CISG does not amount to an obstacle[501] for in the present context the CISG is employed solely as persuasive authority and not applied in the strict and technical sense.[502]

(b) Ships and vessels

101 Since no express exception can be found, even ships which are definitely tangibles in the natural sense, are covered.[503] Art. 2 (e) CISG is not mirrored in (b).[504] There are no (assumed) particularities of ship sales that would demand the treatment of ships as immovable

---

[495] See *Rodriguez*, Beklagtenwohnsitz und Erfüllungsort im europäischen IZVR (Zürich 2005) para. 673. *Contra Geimer/Schütze* Art. 5 note 88. More generous *Hofmann/Kunz*, in: Basler Kommentar, Art. 5 note 185: Every consideration suffices, be it only more than symbolic.

[496] See only Trib. Padova, sez. Este RDIPP 2007, 147, 152; *Franzina*, La giurisdizione in materia contrattuale (2006) p. 301.

[497] *Foss/Bygrave*, (2000) 8 Int. J. L. & Info. Tech. 99, 108.

[498] *Leipold*, in: GS Alexander Lüderitz (2000), p. 431, 446. *Contra Kubis*, ZEuP 2001, 737, 750.

[499] *Furrer/Schramm*, SJZ 2003, 137, 138; *Wipping*, Der europäische Gerichtsstand des Erfüllungsortes – Art. 5 Nr. 1 EuGVVO (2008) p. 161; see also A-G *Mazák*, [2010] ECR I-1258, I-1264 para. 25.

[500] Rb. Arnhem NIPR 2006 Nr. 51 p. 83; Trib. Padova, sez. Este RDIPP 2007, 147, 151; *Kubis*, ZEuP 2001, 742, 750; *Kropholler/von Hein*, Art. 5 note 38; *Magnus*, IHR 2002, 45, 47; *Leible*, in: Rauscher, Art. 5 note 46; *Ulrich G. Schroeter*, UN-Kaufrecht und Europäisches Gemeinschaftsrecht (2005) § 17 with note 33; *Ignatova*, Art. 5 Nr. 1 EuGVVO – Chancen und Perspektiven der Reform des Gerichtsstands am Erfüllungsort (2005) p. 185; *Franzina*, La giurisdizione in materia contrattuale (2006) p. 309; *Mankowski*, CR 2010, 137, 138; see also *Fawcett*, in: Fawcett/Harris/Bridge para. 3.149 (same general line but with express tendency to a wider definition).

[501] But cf. (yet in a slightly different context) Trib. Rovereto RDIPP 2005, 162, 165 and also Trib. Brescia Int'l. Lis 2005, 131, 132.

[502] *Mankowski*, IHR 2009, 46, 56; *Leible*, EuZW 2010, 301, 304; *Gsell*, ZEuP 2011, 669, 679.

[503] Rb. Rotterdam NIPR 2010 Nr. 322 p. 529.

[504] *Magnus*, IHR 2002, 45, 47 fn. 26.

property. That property in ships is registered in the real rights register does not affect the mere sales contract too much. The same applies to the sale of other vessels which might be registered somewhere (like aircrafts).[505]

(c) Money

On the other hand money, if taken as an instrument to measure and denominate value, is not **102** covered.[506] Not a single coin or Art. 5 note matters if currency swaps are entered in and executed, even more so since such deals today do not involve genuine coins or notes anymore but only numbers and figures in accounts. Things are different if Krugerrands, Golden Eagles or Maple Leafs are bought and the delivery of genuine coins is at stake. Then and only then a sales contract is at stake.

(d) Real estate (immovables)

Of the catalogue of exceptions to be found in Art. 2 CISG, which should serve as some **103** guideline for the interpretation of "goods" under (b), real estate (immovables) and electricity remain. Unfortunately, as for the sale of immoveable property the answer is not already found in Art. 24 (1) since this paragraph only deals with claims founded in rights *in rem* and not with contracts on acquiring such rights.[507] Hence, the sale of immovables is only excluded from (b) if one could restrict the meaning of "goods" to movables, since immovables are without the slightest doubt tangibles and corporeal. Passing possession does not pose a major problem. Delivery of an immovable takes place where this immovable is located. Effects in the books (if they are necessary under, or demanded by, the applicable legal system for the transfer of property) are of no avail since delivery as such does not refer to the transfer of property but to the change in possession.

Nevertheless, these constructive steps are only of secondary importance. The first and **104** logically paramount question that needs to be answered is whether the sale of land can be qualified as a sale of goods or whether the notion of "goods" implicitly requires that the object of the sale can be transported and moved. The German and Dutch versions unequivocally demand so for they refer to "bewegliche Sachen" or "roerende zaken" respectively thereby excluding "unbewegliche Sachen" or "onroerende zaken" by the way of *argumentum e contrario*.[508] This gains strong support from some quarters of EU law since Art. 1 (2) (b) Consumer Sales Directive expressly restricts "consumer goods" to tangible *movable* items. The interpretation of (1) (b) should not be uninfluenced by other instruments of EU law which refer to the sale of goods or the provision of services in comparable circumstances.[509] Some coordination with the understanding of "sale" under Art. 15 (1) (a) also is desirable.[510]

---

[505] Rb. Rotterdam NIPR 2011 Nr. 250 p. 438.

[506] *Magnus*, IHR 2002, 45, 47 fn. 26.

[507] See only *Mankowski*, in: Rauscher, Art. 24 notes 8 *et seq.*; *Christoph A. Kern*, IPRax 2014, 503, 504.

[508] See *Kropholler/von Hein* Art. 5 note 41; *Burgstaller/Neumayr* Art. 5 note 10 (Oct. 2002); *Mankowski*, in: FS Andreas Heldrich (2005), p. 867, 889; *Mankowski*, in: FS Ingeborg Schwenzer (2011), p. 1175, 1182; *Christoph A. Kern*, IPRax 2014, 503, 505 and also Hof 's-Hertogenbosch NIPR 2006 Nr. 46 p. 77; Hof 's-Gravenhage NIPR 2011 Nr. 233 p. 416.

[509] *Layton/Mercer* para. 15.047; see also Trib. Padova, sez. Este RDIPP 2007, 147, 152.

[510] *Hofmann/Kunz*, in: Basler Kommentar, Art. 5 note 182.

105 Distinguishing between goods and immovables gives rise to consequential questions. Firstly, according to which law the characterisation issue as to whether the tangible is deemed a movable or an immovable (the *lex fori*[511] or the *lex rei sitae*[512] or in autonomous interpretation[513]) and, secondly, how to deal with the nitty-gritty of movable tangibles which form part of land or are *accessoire* to land pursuant to the applicable national law. If under Art. 24 (1) a characterisation pursuant to the *lex rei sitae* ought to be preferred[514] there is a strong case for proceeding down the same avenue here. Yet the search for consistency might not stop with Art. 24, but also indicate a look at other attempts in EU law to deal with the problem. Art. 1 (2) (b) Consumer Sales Directive provides an example for an autonomous try.

106 But the parallel could be taken one step further and land could be treated as a "good", subjecting the German version to a teleological reduction. Insofar (1) could complement Art. 24 (1) and help filling the gaps of the latter. At least the courts at the place where the immovable is located would have jurisdiction but for the difference between exclusive jurisdiction under Art. 24 (1) and special jurisdiction here. At least treating land as a "good" would avoid any difficulties in distinguishing and would solve the case of *Zubehör* by simply not allowing it to arise. On the other hand, the price would be considerably high by deviating from the internationally common circumscription of goods in Art. 2 CISG which expressly excludes immovables, and from Art. 1 (2) (b) Consumer Sales Directive. Between Scylla and Charybdis the dice should eventually be cast in favour of the traditional approach to regard real estate to be excluded from the realm of "goods". The areas of doubt connected with it are rather minor and do eventually not amount to convincing counterarguments.

(e) Electricity and other sources for energy

107 Electricity is a virtual quantity. It is not tangible in the natural sense that one could touch it, nor has it ever been transported or produced in a tangible form. In terms of physics energy might be a function of mass ($e = mc^2$), but in terms of physics only. Thus, although electricity is not expressly excluded from the circle of goods it should fall outside this circle.[515] That one can speak of a delivery of electricity at the customer's place does not turn the tide. Oil is a tangible and does not pose any major problems. Gas as another source for energy might not be corporeal in a strict sense but could materialise if transferred into another stage physically. Accordingly, it should be regarded as a "good".[516]

(f) Software and other digitised products

108 Modern times have raised the question of whether software or information be can be regarded as "goods" for the purposes of (b). Perhaps surprisingly the better arguments can be raised in favour of an affirmative answer at least for standard software.[517] Despite

---

511 *Czernich*, in: Czernich/Tiefenthaler/Kodek, Art. 5 note 32.

512 *Hüßtege*, in: Thomas/Putzo, Art. 5 note 6.

513 *Kropholler*, Art. 5 note 34; *Leible*, in: Rauscher, Art. 5 note 48.

514 Report *Schlosser*, para. 129; *Schlosser*, in: GS Rudolf Bruns (1980), p. 45, 58–60; *Kaye*, pp. 894–898; *Mankowski*, in: Rauscher, Art. 24 with note 5.

515 *Contra Magnus*, IHR 2002, 45, 47 fn. 26.

516 Concurring OLG Brandenburg IPRspr. 2011 Nr. 212 p. 552.

517 *Klimek/Susanne Sieber*, ZUM 1998, 902, 906 *et seq.*; *Thorn*, IPRax 1999, 1, 3; *Mankowski*, RabelsZ 63 (1999), 203, 232 *et seq.*; *Mankowski*, CR 1999, 512, 515; *Mankowski*, in: Ruth Nielsen/Sandfeld Jacobsen/ Trzaskowski (eds.), EU Electronic Commerce Law (2004), p. 125, 128; *Magnus*, IHR 2002, 45, 47;

the naturalistic impression at first glance that both software and information are intangibles, the notion of "goods" ought not to be restricted to tangibles.[518] For software there is a line of argument relating back to the interpretation of the CISG. Under the CISG the almost general opinion subjects standard software (i.e. software not specifically designed to meet the customer's individual orders and requirements) to the notion of "goods" for it should not make a fundamental difference whether the software is delivered on a hard disk or on-line.[519] The mere wrapping of the hard disk does not matter, it is the content inside. The wrapping cannot determine the nature of the entity itself.[520] Historically anything started with the hard disk and software thus was believed to be covered by the CISG. Alterations based upon technological progress have been rejected. A justification to treat someone who buys standard software on a hard disk or CD more preferential insofar as an additional ground for jurisdiction is opened in his favour, compared to someone who buys the software in digitised mode can hardly be found.[521] Furthermore, parallels to the notion of sale of a copy of a program under Art. 4 (2) Directive 2009/24/EC[522] could advance helpful guidelines and arguments.[523] Arts. 5 (b); 2 (j) Proposal CESL[524] might add valuable insights for demarcating the line in the are of digitised products.[525]

Other digitised products could possibly follow an analogy to the standard/individual soft- **109**
ware divide.[526] Mostly, matters of licensing and transferring usage rights under intellectual property law could be the most imminent cause and purpose for contracting. Perhaps this

---

Mochar/Seidl, ÖJZ 2003, 241, 243; *Ganssauge*, Internationale Zuständigkeit und anwendbares Recht bei Verbraucherverträgen im Internet (2004) p. 25.

[518] *Contra Terlau*, in: Moritz/Dreier (eds.), Rechts-Handbuch zum E-Commerce (2nd. ed. 2005) Part C note 59.

[519] See only OLG Koblenz RIW 1993, 934, 936; OLG Köln RIW 1994, 970, 974; *Diedrich*, Autonome Auslegung von Internationalem Einheitsrecht (1994) pp. 174–323; *Diedrich*, RIW 1993, 441, 452; *Mankowski*, CR 1999, 581, 586; *Hans Markus Wulf*, UN-Kaufrecht und eCommerce (2003) pp. 42–51.

[520] *Mankowski*, RabelsZ 63 (1999), 203, 232 et seq.; *Ignatova*, Art. 5 Nr. 1 EuGVVO – Chancen und Perspektiven der Reform des Gerichtsstands am Erfüllungsort (2005) p. 187.

[521] *Mankowski*, in: Ruth Nielsen/Sandfeld Jacobsen/Trzaskowski (eds.), EU Electronic Commerce Law (2004), p. 125, 128. See *Terlau*, in: Moritz/Dreier (eds.), Rechts-Handbuch zum E-Commerce (2nd. ed. 2005), Part C note 235.

[522] Directive 2009/24/EC of the European Parliament and of the Council of 23 April 2009 on the legal protection of computer programs, OJ EU 2009 L 111/16.

[523] *de Miguel Asensio*, in: Liber amicorum Alegría Borrás (2013), p. 291, 300 with reference to *UsedSoft GmbH v. Oracle International Corp.* (Case C-328/11), ECLI:EU:2012:407 paras. 35–72.

[524] Proposal for a Regulation of the European Parliament and of the Council on a Common European Sales Law, submitted by the Commission on 11 October 2011, COM (2011) 635 final.

[525] *de Miguel Asensio*, in: Liber amicorum Alegría Borrás (2013), p. 291, 301.

[526] See *Mankowski*, RabelsZ 63 (1999), 203, 232; *Mochar/Seidl*, ÖJZ 2003, 241, 243.

Peter Mankowski   197

can be reflected in classification.[527] Information, however, has never had a tangible form and can thus not be treated as a "good".[528] Engaging in database research, however, would constitute a "supply of services", *a fortiori* conducting such research as a kind of shopping or research agent;[529] hence, such activity would enter the realm of (b) not by the first, but by the second door.[530]

(g) Rights and securities

110 Rights, e.g. to claims, patents, trademarks, etc. do not star amongst the goods since they are not corporeal tangibles; the sale of shares of a company (or of units of a unit trust) also falls outside the scope of application of (b).[531] Although the latter might be deemed as incorporated in some kind of corporealisation (the old idea of a share in paper), the important issue behind the sale of shares is the transfer of the right, not the transfer of some piece of paper (if such paper in the age of electronic account holding still exists). The same should apply to other securities.[532] Though substantive law might treat them differently in some respect, what matters with regard to them is the right and title, not the paper (if some substitute for paper can still be construed). In modern times securities are kept electronically, and it would fit ill if securities in printed form were treated differently. The German distinction between *Wertpapiere* and *Wertrechte* should not matter, either.[533]

bb) Contracts for the provision of services

(1) General considerations

111 The second category covered by (b) comprises contracts for services. The notion of "services"[534] bears an autonomous meaning independent from any respective notions contained in the national legal orders of the Member States.[535] Insofar the TFEU provides the most

---

[527] See *Foss/Bygrave*, (2000) 8 Int. J. L. & Info. Tech. 99, 109–112; *Mankowski*, CR 1999, 512, 516 *et seq.*; *Fawcett*, in: Fawcett/Harris/Bridge para. 10.45.

[528] *Mankowski*, CR 1999, 581, 586.

[529] *Foss/Bygrave*, (2000) 8 Int. J. L. & Info. Tech. 99, 113; *Papathoma-Baetge/Nehrenberg/Finke*, in: Kaminski/Henßler/Kolaschnik/Papathoma-Baetge (eds.), Rechtshandbuch E-Business (Neuwied/Kriftel 2002) Part 2 A with note 84; *Mochar/Seidl*, ÖJZ 2003, 241, 243; *Hans Markus Wulf*, UN-Kaufrecht und eCommerce (2003) pp. 34–37.

[530] *van der Hof*, Internationale on-line overeenkomsten (2002) p. 57; *Mankowski*, in: Ruth Nielsen/Sandfeld Jacobsen/Trzaskowski (eds.), EU Electronic Commerce Law (2004), p. 125, 129.

[531] See only Trib. Matova RDIPP 2007, 393, 398; *Czernich*, WBl 2002, 337, 340; *Magnus*, IHR 2002, 45, 47; *Burgstaller/Neumayr* Art. 5 note 10 (Oct. 2002); *Leible*, in: Rauscher, Art. 5 note 47; *Fawcett*, in: Fawcett/Harris/Bridge para. 3.147; *Ignatova*, Art. 5 Nr. 1 EuGVVO – Chancen und Perspektiven der Reform des Gerichtsstands am Erfüllungsort (2005) p. 186; *Lynker*, Der besondere Gerichtsstand am Erfüllungsort in der Brüssel I-Verordnung (Art. 5 Nr. 1 EuGVVO) (2006) pp. 56 *et seq.*; *Franzina*, La giurisdizione in materia contrattuale (2006) p. 319; *von Hein*, BerDGfIR 2011, 369, 386–387 and (with regard to the parallel question under Art. 13 (1) Brussels Convention) *Waverley Asset Management Ltd. v. Saha* 1989 SLT (Sh Ct) 87, 88 (Sheriff Court of Lothian and Borders at Edinburgh, Sheriff *Shiach*).

[532] *Contra Gehri*, Wirtschaftsrechtliche Zuständigkeiten im internationalen Zivilprozessrecht der Schweiz (2002) p. 199.

[533] *Contra Basedow*, in: FS Erik Jayme (2004), p. 3, 9.

[534] For a comparative approach see *Merchiers*, in: Études offertes au Philippe Malivaud (2007), p. 431.

[535] BGH NJW 2006, 1806; OLG Düsseldorf IHR 2004, 108, 110 with further references; OLG Köln RIW

---

valuable guidelines. As an act of EU law the Brussels I Regulation should seek conformity and parallel interpretation with the TFEU wherever possible. Hence, it appears most appropriate to adopt the meaning given to "services" under Arts. 56; 57 TFEU (ex-Arts. 49; 50 EC Treaty)[536] if and insofar as the Brussels I system itself does not demand otherwise.[537] The recourse to Arts. 56; 57 TFEU is not a slavish one and must not be mistaken as an identical interpretation of "services" in both areas.[538] Arts. 56; 57 TFEU are not dominating and absolutely determining in this regard.[539] But taking them into account prevents from inventing the wheel afresh.[540] The notion of "services" under Arts. 56; 57 TFEU is tentatively wider as these rules strive at including as many economic activities as possible whereas this *rationale* is not shared by (1) (b) 2nd lemma.[541]

On the other hand Art. 57 cl. 1 TFEU at first glance appears to limit and restrict the notion of **112** services insofar as it requires that they are normally required for remuneration. But again this does not need to be mirrored for the purposes of (1) (b) 2nd lemma.[542] Such restriction would conflict with the general assumption that contracts do not require consideration in the common law sense. Art. 57 TFEU operates in the context of the Internal Market where exclusion of non-economic activities might be sensible whereas Art. 81 TFEU (ex-Art. 65 EC Treaty) as the fundament for the Brussels Ibis Regulation does not pursue such a policy.[543] Furthermore, the "normally" in Art. 57 cl. 1 TFEU ought to be emphasised.[544] That contracts for the sale of goods as covered by (1) (b) 1st lemma are *per definitionem* contracts for remuneration, does not automatically lead to a like understanding of (1) (b) 2nd lemma[545] since a like definition with clear elements is lacking for services.

2005, 778, 779; OLG Koblenz IHR 2008, 198, 200; OLG Köln 16 December 2008 – Case 9 U 47/07 [47]; Rb. Kh. Antwerpen ETL 2005, 657, 667; *Kropholler/von Hein* Art. 5 note 42.

[536] A-G *Trstenjak*, [2009] ECR I-3330, I-3352 para. 60; OGH ÖJZ 2004, 388, 390; OLG Düsseldorf IHR 2004, 108, 110; OLG Düsseldorf NJW-RR 2008, 223; Rb. Kh. Hasselt TBH 2003, 623 with note *Kruger; Markus*, SZW 1999, 205, 211; *Bajons*, in: FS Reinhold Geimer (2002), p. 15, 55 fn. 118; *Fach Gómez*, Rev. der. com. eur. 14 (2003), 181, 207 *et seq.*; *Ignatova*, Art. 5 Nr. 1 EuGVVO – Chancen und Perspektiven der Reform des Gerichtsstands am Erfüllungsort (2005) p. 195; *Kienle*, IPRax 2006, 614, 615; *Franzina*, La giurisdizione in materia contrattuale (2006) pp. 304 *et seq.*; *Berlioz*, Clunet 135 (2008), 675, 691; *Polak*, AA 2009, 400, 406; *Mankowski*, JZ 2009, 958, 960; *Brinkmann*, IPRax 2009, 487, 490. Yet *contra Falco Privatstiftung and Thomas Rabitsch v. Gisela Weller-Lindhorst*, (Case C-533/07) [2009] ECR I-3327, I-3382 para. 34; A-G *Mazák*, [2010] ECR I-1258, I-1262 para. 18; Yb. PIL 11 (2009), 453, 466; *Franzina*, RDIPP 2010, 655, 660; *Hofmann/Kunz*, in: Basler Kommentar, Art. 5 note 199.

[537] See only A-G *Trstenjak*, [2009] ECR I-3330, I-3353 *et seq.* para. 64; *Mankowski*, JZ 2009, 958, 960 (with the main examples listed).

[538] *Mankowski*, JZ 2009, 958, 960.

[539] *Mankowski*, JZ 2009, 958, 960.

[540] *Polak*, AA 2009, 400, 406.

[541] *Falco Privatstiftung and Thomas Rabitsch v. Gisela Weller-Lindhorst*, (Case C-533/07) [2009] ECR I-3327, I-3383 para. 36; *Brinkmann*, IPRax 2009, 487, 490; see also *von Hein*, IPRax 2013, 54, 56–57.

[542] *Contra Falco Privatstiftung and Thomas Rabitsch v. Gisela Weller-Lindhorst*, (Case C-533/07) [2009] ECR I-3327, I-3383 para. 36; OLG Saarbrücken IPRax 2013, 74, 78; *Rauscher*, NJW 2010, 2251, 2253.

[543] *von Hein*, IPRax 2013, 54, 57.

[544] *Johannes Weber*, IPRax 2013, 69, 71–72.

[545] *Contra von Hein*, IPRax 2013, 54, 59.

113 Additional help for the understanding of the notion of "services" can be provided by, and recourse can be held to, the interpretation of the notion of "services" under Art. 13 Brussels Convention and under Art. 5 Rome Convention,[546] likewise now under Art. 4 (1) (b) Rome I Regulation.[547] In the latter regard particularly the carve-outs and the relegations to other litterae outside Art. 4 (1) (b) Rome I Regulation matter and provide valuable indications.[548] In other areas of EU law (e.g. the VAT Directives), different concepts and notions of "services" prevail for their respective purposes so that an import from them is rather inadmissible.[549] This might even apply to the Services Directive[550] with its very wide basic definition of services in Art. 24 although it might nonetheless provide some guidance to be gained from its more specific rules.[551]

114 Classical examples of services are provided by brokers,[552] commercial agents[553] and distributors,[554] in more modern times accompanied by franchisees.[555] Researchers, private inves-

---

[546] See only OGH ÖJZ 2004, 388, 390; OLG Düsseldorf IHR 2004, 108, 110; OLG Düsseldorf NJW-RR 2008, 223; *Leipold*, in: GS Alexander Lüderitz (2000), p. 431, 446; *Hau*, IPRax 2000, 354, 359; *Micklitz/Rott*, EuZW 2001, 325, 328; *Lima Pinheiro* p. 84 *et seq*.; *Ganssauge*, Internationale Zuständigkeit und anwendbares Recht bei Verbraucherverträgen im Internet (2004) p. 26; *Klemm*, Erfüllungsortvereinbarungen im Europäischen Zivilverfahrensrecht (2005) p. 67; *Lynker*, Der besondere Gerichtsstand am Erfüllungsort in der Brüssel I-Verordnung (Art. 5 Nr. 1 EuGVVO) (2006) p. 59; *Simotta*, in: Fasching/Konecny, Art. 5 note 170; *Markus*, AJP 2010, 971, 974; *Hofmann/Kunz*, in: Basler Kommentar, Art. 5 note 200.

[547] A-G *Trstenjak*, [2009] ECR I-3330, I-3356 para. 69; *Brinkmann*, IPRax 2009, 487, 490; *Mankowski*, JZ 2009, 958, 959; *Azzi*, D. 2010, 1840; *De Götzen*, RDIPP 2010, 383, 402 *et seq*.; *Kropholler/von Hein*, Art. 5 note 43.

[548] A-G *Trstenjak*, [2009] ECR I-3330, I-3356 para. 69.

[549] *Falco Privatstiftung and Thomas Rabitsch v. Gisela Weller-Lindhorst*, (Case C-533/07) [2009] ECR I-3327, I-3383 paras. 38–39; A-G *Trstenjak*, [2009] ECR I-3330, I-3357 *et seq*. paras. 70–73.

[550] Council Directive 2006/123/EC of 12 December 2006 on services in the internal market, OJ EU 2006 L 376/36.

[551] OLG Düsseldorf NJW-RR 2008, 223; see also *Berlioz*, Clunet 135 (2008), 675, 694; *Fernet*, JCP E 2010 N°. 24, 17 juin 2010, p. 21, 22.

[552] OGH IPRax 2006, 608, 610; OLG Zweibrücken NJOZ 2011, 1940 = IPRspr. 2010 Nr. 204; *Kienle*, IPRax 2006, 614, 616.

[553] A-G *Trstenjak*, [2010] ECR I-2124, I-2146 para. 59; Cass. JCP G 2006 IV 2789; Cass. Bull. civ. 2006 I n° 373 p. 320 = Clunet 134 (2007), 132; Cass. Bull. civ. 2006 I n° 423 p. 365; Cass. RCDIP 101 (2012), 430, 431 with note *Corneloup*; Hof Gent TBH 2005, 70; OLG Düsseldorf NJW-RR 2008, 223; Trib. Genova RDIPP 2006, 1089, 1091; Rb. Rotterdam NIPR 2010 Nr. 492 p. 805; LG Aachen IPRspr. 2012 Nr. 192 p. 436; *Hollander*, TBH 2000, 175, 178; *Gaudemet-Tallon*, RCDIP 89 (2000), 84, 88; *Micklitz/Rott*, EuZW 2001, 325, 328; *Marie-Élodie Ancel*, RCDIP 90 (2001), 158, 162; *Couwenberg/Pertegás Sender*, in: van Houtte/Pertegás Sender (eds.), Het nieuwe Europese IPR: van verdrag naar verordening (2001), p. 31, 47 § 3-28; *Ibili*, NILR 2002, 114, 115; *Emde*, RIW 2003, 505, 508; *Tagaras*, CDE 2003, 717, 745 *et seq*.; *Fach Gómez*, Rev. der. com. eur. 14 (2003), 181, 206–208; *Égéa/Martel*, Clunet 134 (2007), 133, 138; *Fernet*, JCP E 2010 N°. 24, 17 juin 2010, p. 21, 22.

[554] Protodikeio Thessaloniki 11862/2004 (quotation taken from *Vassilakakis*, IPRax 2005, 279, 280); *Bajons*, in: FS Reinhold Geimer (2002), p. 15, 55; *de Lind van Wijngaarden-Maack*, IPRax 2004, 212, 219; *Wurmnest*, IHR 2005, 107, 113; *Égéa/Martel*, Clunet 134 (2007), 133, 138. But cf. the discussion in Art. 7 note 120 (*Mankowski*) with further references.

[555] *Emde*, RIW 2003, 505, 511.

tigators,[556] builders,[557] evaluators (e.g. of real estate),[558] customs declarants,[559] freight forwarders,[560] marketing agencies and architects also accompany them,[561] likewise teachers,[562] hospitals,[563] lawyers,[564] accountants, consultants and advisors.[565] From the modern trades, e.g. *création de marquette*,[566] software development,[567] website designing and access providing feature as services.[568] Financial business adds fund administration,[569] investment banking[570] and intermediation of securities.[571] Letters of credit and confirmed letters of credit are also amongst the qualifiers.[572] Managers and board members provide services to the respective companies.[573]

The storage of goods joins in[574] as to be distinguished from the rental of premises, the latter **115** being subject to Art. 24 (1).[575] The commitment to store the goods concerned entails a specific activity, consisting, at the least, of the reception of the goods, their storage in a safe place and the return to the person who gave them in bail, in an appropriate state.[576] Surveillance, care and handling should be added.

---

556   See Rb. Utrecht NIPR 2003 Nr. 297 p. 455.

557   OLG München NZBau 2011, 560, 561–562; *Christoph A. Kern*, IPRax 2014, 503, 506.

558   *Mankowski*, in: FS Stanisława Kalus (2010), p. 287, 290.

559   See only Rb. Rotterdam S&S 2008 Nr. 102 p. 481; *Vlas*, NJ 2005 Nr. 39 p. 209, 210.

560   Rb. Rotterdam NIPR 2009 Nr. 146 p. 250; Rb. Amsterdam NIPR 2010 Nr. 76 p. 154.

561   *Béraudo*, Clunet 128 (2001), 1033, 1046.

562   See only *Simotta*, in: Fasching/Konecny, Art. 5 note 175 with further references.

563   BGH NJW 2012, 860; OLG Oldenburg NJW-RR 2008, 1592 = VersR 2010, 231; *Kropholler/von Hein*, Art. 5 note 44.

564   BGH NJW 2006, 1806; *Burgstaller/Neumayr* Art. 5 note 11 (Oct. 2002); *Kropholler/von Hein* Art. 5 note 44; *Mankowski*, AnwBl 2006, 806, 807.

565   Rb. Rotterdam NIPR 2007 Nr. 153 p. 217 (advice on EU-subsidies).

566   Cass. Bull. civ. 2007 I n° 352 p. 310 = RCDIP 97 (2008), 139 with note *Gaudemet-Tallon* = JCP G 2008 II 10035 note *Attal*.

567   OLG München CR 2010, 156, 157; *Mankowski*, CR 2010, 137, 139; *Axel Metzger*, IPRax 2010, 420, 423.

568   *Mankowski*, in: Spindler (ed.), Vertragsrecht der Internet-Provider (2nd ed. 2004) ch. III note 24; *Fawcett*, in: Fawcett/Harris/Bridge para. 10.50.

569   *Simotta*, in: Fasching/Konecny, Art. 5 note 177.

570   *Burke*, 10 Col. J. Eur. L. 527 (2004); *Simotta*, in: Fasching/Konecny, Art. 5 note 177; *von Hein*, BerDGfIR 2011, 369, 386–387; see also OLG Hamburg RIW 2004, 709 = IPRax 2005, 251; OLG Brandenburg IPRspr. 2006 Nr. 115.

571   *Burke/Ostrowsky*, EuLF 2007, II-197; *von Hein*, BerDGfIR 2011, 369, 386–387.

572   Hof Brussel TBH 2015, 198, 201; *Bernaert*, TBH 2015, 205, 206–207.

573   LG Bonn IPRax 2013, 80, 82–83; *Johannes Weber*, IPRax 2013, 69, 71–72.

574   *Krejci Lager & Umschlagbetriebs GmbH v. Olbrich Transport und Logistik GmbH*, (Case C-469/12), ECLI: EU:C:2013:788 paras. 24–30.

575   *Krejci Lager & Umschlagbetriebs GmbH v. Olbrich Transport und Logistik GmbH*, (Case C-469/12), ECLI: EU:C:2013:788-469/12 para. 29.

576   *Krejci Lager & Umschlagbetriebs GmbH v. Olbrich Transport und Logistik GmbH*, (Case C-469/12), ECLI: EU:C:2013:788 para. 27.

116 Services should be given a broad meaning.[577] The *effet utile* pursued militates against too narrow and restrictive an interpretation.[578] The notion of services encompasses every activity rendered in the interest of another person.[579] According to the ECJ, it implies, at least, that the party who provides services carries out a particular activity, in return for remuneration.[580] The remuneration might not be a necessary element, though,[581] as nothing in (1) (b) refers to a requirement of consideration or alike; only the parallel with contract of sales in the other indent might support such implication. But Art. 57 TFEU refers to services where they are *normally* provided for remuneration. Yet this can be easily explained since Art. 57 TFEU operates in the context of the Internal Market and envisages only the commercial rendering of services.[582]

117 Anyway, if remuneration is regarded as a requirement, it is not necessary that such remuneration is to be understood strictly as payment of a sum of money.[583] A like restriction is neither stipulated by the very general wording of (1) (b) 2nd lemma[584] nor consistent with the objectives of proximity and standardisation pursued by that rule.[585] Conversely, remuneration must not be understood as consideration to be paid in money.[586] An economic value to be evaluated as constituting remuneration might be represented e.g. by assistance rendered to a distributor regarding access to advertising, communicating knowhow by means of training or yet even payment facilities.[587] Competitive advantages *vis-à-vis* competitors might also qualify.[588] Remuneration must be understood as an economic function, as an exchange of services for corporeal, financial or immaterial assets which have a market value or could be acquired for a price to be expressed in money. Keeping services in line with the sale of goods, the classic exchange of goods for money, does not amount to a sufficient counterargument.[589] It is a different question whether a contract under which the remu-

---

[577] See only OGH ÖJZ 2004, 388, 390; OLG Köln RIW 2005, 778, 779; OLG München CR 2010, 156, 157; *Brenn* para. 72; *Berlioz*, Clunet 135 (2008), 675, 676; *Henri Storme*, R.W. 2009–2010, 409, 412. More cautiously *Kropholler/von Hein*, Art. 5 note 42.

[578] A-G *Jääskinen*, Opinion of 25 April 2013 in Case C-9/12, ECLI:EU:C:2013:273 para. 53.

[579] See only Vzngr. Rb. Rotterdam NIPR 2010 Nr. 486 p. 795.

[580] *Falco Privatstiftung and Thomas Rabitsch v. Gisela Weller-Lindhorst*, (Case C-533/07) [2009] ECR I-3327, I-3381 para. 29; *Corman-Collins SA v. La Maison du Whisky SA*, (Case C-9/12), ECLI:EU:C:2013:860 para. 37; *Krejci Lager & Umschlagbetriebs GmbH v. Olbrich Transport und Logistik GmbH*, (Case C-469/12), ECLI:EU:C:2013:788 para. 26; OLG Oldenburg NJW-RR 2008, 1592 = VersR 2010, 231; A-G *Trstenjak*, [2010] ECR I-2124, I-2146 para. 59.

[581] A-G *Jääskinen*, Opinion of 25 April 2013 in Case C-9/12, ECLI:EU:C:2013:273 paras. 55–56; *Geimer/Schütze*, Art. 5 note 90; *Hofmann/Kunz*, in: Basler Kommentar, Art. 5 note 205; see also *Markus*, Tendenzen beim materiellrechtlichen Vertragserfüllungsort im internationalen Zivilverfahrensrecht (Basel 2009) p. 143. But *contra Markus*, AJP 2010, 971, 974; *Dutta*, IPRax 2011, 134, 137.

[582] *Berlioz*, JCP G 2014, 271, 274.

[583] *Corman-Collins SA v. La Maison du Whisky SA*, (Case C-9/12), ECLI:EU:C:2013:860 para. 39; *Berlioz*, JCP G 2014, 271, 274.

[584] *Strikwerda*, Ned. Jur. 2014 Nr. 346 p. 4354, 4356.

[585] *Corman-Collins SA v. La Maison du Whisky SA*, (Case C-9/12), ECLI:EU:C:2013:860 para. 39.

[586] *Strikwerda*, Ned. Jur. 2014 Nr. 346 p. 4354, 4356.

[587] *Corman-Collins SA v. La Maison du Whisky SA*, (Case C-9/12), ECLI:EU:C:2013:860 para. 40.

[588] *Corman-Collins SA v. La Maison du Whisky SA*, (Case C-9/12), ECLI:EU:C:2013:860 para. 40; A-G *Jääskinen*, Opinion of 25 April 2013 in Case C-9/12, ECLI:EU:C:2013:273 para. 56.

neration consists of something else than money, can still be characterised as a contract which has providing services as its characteristic performance.[590] If services are exchanged for services it would be rather difficult to determine which services constitute the characteristic performance determing the relevant place where services are provided for the purposes of (1) (b) 2nd lemma.[591]

An obligation to refrain from doing something does not imply a service since activity is the   **118** essential element and there is nothing like a notion of "negative services".[592] The performance of positive acts is required rather than mere omissions.[593] This is a factual criterion.[594] In general this notion of services as relating to activities coincides with, and is fostered by, an economic understanding: Services are acts of production. As economic goods they are not perfected products but activities that could be the object of a demand.[595] To rule out *obligations de résultat* summarily[596] would be too rash, though.[597]

For instance, a handyman provides services.[598] Production for remuneration is a qualifier[599]   **119** as are repair or shipbuilding contracts with a shipyard[600] or contracts for installing the electric equipment and cables in a building,[601] even building contracts in general.[602] A contract for the carriage of goods also qualifies as a contact for the provision of services,[603]

---

589   *Wais*, GPR 2014, 165, 167.
590   *Wais*, GPR 2014, 165, 168.
591   *Wais*, GPR 2014, 165, 168.
592   See *Berlioz*, Clunet 135 (2008), 675, 687 *et seq.*
593   *Falco Privatstiftung and Thomas Rabitsch v. Gisela Weller-Lindhorst*, (Case C-533/07) [2009] ECR I-3327, I-3381 paras. 29–31; *Corman-Collins SA v. La Maison du Whisky SA*, (Case C-9/12), ECLI:EU: C:2013:860 para. 38; A-G *Jääskinen*, Opinion of 25 April 2013 in Case C-9/12, ECLI:EU:C:2013:273 para. 54.
594   *Strikwerda*, Ned. Jur. 2014 Nr. 346 p. 4354, 4355.
595   *Heike Wegner*, Internationaler Verbraucherschutz beim Abschluss von Timesharingverträgen: § 8 TzWrG, (1998) p. 104 with further references; *Mankowski*, in: Spindler/Wiebe (eds.), Internet-Auktionen und Elektronische Marktplätze (2nd ed. 2005), ch. 11 note 13; *Mankowski*, RIW 2006, 321, 322; *Mankowski*, AnwBl 2006, 806, 807; *Jacquet*, Clunet 135 (2008), 524, 526.
596   Tentatively so *Berlioz*, Clunet 135 (2008), 675, 684 *et seq.*
597   *Metzger*, IPRax 2010, 420, 422; *Hofmann/Kunz*, in: Basler Kommentar, Art. 5 note 189.
598   OLG Düsseldorf IHR 2004, 108, 110.
599   Vzngr. Rb. Rotterdam NIPR 2010 Nr. 486 p. 795.
600   CA Aix JCP G 2011, 102.
601   Vzngr. Rb. Rotterdam NIPR 2010 Nr. 486 p. 795.
602   OLG München NJW-RR 2011, 1169.
603   Cass. D. 2010, 2917 with applauding with note *Delpech*; Rb. Kh. Hasselt, TBH 2003, 623 with note *Kruger*; Rb. Kh. Antwerpen, ETR 2005, 657, 668 *et seq.*; *Leipold*, in: GS Alexander Lüderitz (2000), p. 431, 446; *Hau*, ZZP Int. 5 (2000), 284, 289; *Bonassies*, ETR 2002, 727, 732; *Meeusen/Neut*, in: van Hooydonk (ed.), Actualia zee- en vervoerrecht (2003), p. 37, 63; *Stephan Roland*, JPA 2003, 136; *Leible*, in: Rauscher, Art. 5 note 50; *Matthias Lehmann*, NJW 2007, 1500, 1502; *Mankowski*, TranspR 2008, 67, 68 *et seq.*; *Mankowski*, TranspR 2009, 303, 304; *Ansgar Staudinger*, RRa 2007, 155, 157; *Legros*, Clunet 134 (2007), 799, 821; *Wipping*, Der europäische Gerichtsstand des Erfüllungsortes – Art. 5 Nr. 1 EuGVVO (2008) pp. 167 *et seq.*, 200; *Schlosser*, Art. 5 note 10b; *Rolf Wagner*, TranspR 2009, 281, 283; *Reis*, MR-Int 2009, 118, 119; *Jiménez Blanco*, La aplicación del foro contractual del reglamento Bruselas I a los contratos aéreo de

likewise travel contracts and holiday arrangements.[604] Amongst the contracts for the provision of services agreements between a customer and its bank for the purpose that the bank should issue a letter of credit or a guarantee to the benefit of a third party (e.g in the event that an importing buyer asks his bank to open a letter of credit in favour of the seller exporting to this buyer) also feature.[605] Even hotel accommodation can classify as a service.[606] The required element of activity nevertheless rules out a *Gewinnzusage*, a prize notification.[607]

120 The French Cour de Cassation[608] did not regard *contrats de concession exclusive* and like distribution contracts as contracts for the provision of services for the purposes of (1) (b).[609] Yet there are enough elements of activity to prevent placing too much emphasis on the exclusivity and thus the element to refrain from something.[610] That Art. 4 (1) (f), (g) Rome I Regulation establish special rules for PIL in this area does not support the contention of the Cour de cassation, though, since these rules are formal, but not substantive carve-outs from Art. 4 (1) (b) Rome I Regulation.[611] Conversely, these rules might provide an argument in favour of the opposite result that distribution contracts are contracts for services for the purposes of (1) (b)[612] since they distinguish between distribution contracts and the sales contracts resulting from distributory activities.[613] Recital (17) Rome I Regulation adds another supportive element to the blend.[614] Rightly, the ECJ regards exclusive distribution agreements as covered by (1) (b)[615] (and the Cour de Cassation has followed suit[616] thus

---

pasajeros, La Ley Unión Europea 7294 (30 noviembre 2009), 1, 5; *Tenenbaum*, Rev. contrats 2010, 206, 208–211 and *Peter Rehder v. Baltic Air Corporation*, (Case C-204/08) [2009] ECR I-6073.

[604] *Brenn* para. 72.

[605] See *Stephan Lorenz/Unberath*, IPRax 2004, 298, 303.

[606] OGH ÖJZ 2004, 388, 390.

[607] *Martiny*, in: Księga pamiątkowa Profesora Maksymiliana Pazdana (Zakamycze 2005), p. 189, 200.

[608] For differences between the Première Chambre civile and the Chambre commerciale see *Ribeiro Oertel*, RJcom 2014, 397, 398–402.

[609] Cass. Bull. civ. 2007 I n° 30 = D. 2007, 511 with note *Chevrier* = D. 2007, 1085 note *Gallmeister* = D. 2007, 1575 note *Kenfack* = JCP G 2007 II 10074 with note *Azzi* = RDC 2007, 887 obs. *Deumier* = Clunet 135 (2008), 521 with note *Jacquet* = RCDIP 97 (2008), 661, 662; Cass. Bull. civ. 2008 I n° 61= RCDIP 97 (2008), 664, 665 = D. 2008, 1729 note *Kenfack*; Cass. Bull. civ. 2008 I n° 192. To the same avail Hof 's-Gravenhage NIPR 2010 Nr. 469 p. 777. *Contra Berlioz*, Clunet 135 (2008), 675, 710–714; *Sindres*, RCDIP 97 (2008), 864, 869 and, concurring in the result, *Bajons*, in: FS Reinhold Geimer (2002), p. 15, 53 *et seq.*; *Wurmnest*, IHR 2005, 107. Doubts are expressed also by *de Franceschi*, Contratto e impresa/Europa 2008, 637, 691.

[610] See *Sindres*, RCDIP 97 (2008), 864, 870; *Leible*, in: Rauscher, Art. 5 note 50; *de Miguel Asensio*, in: Liber amicorum Alegría Borrás (2013), p. 291, 298.

[611] See *Marie-Élodie Ancel*, RCDIP 97 (2008), 561, 576–579. *Contra Nourissat*, Procédures mai 2008, p. 18; *Jacquet*, Clunet 135 (2008), 524, 526; see also *Sindres*, RCDIP 97 (2008), 864, 871.

[612] *Lenzing*, EuZW 2014, 183, 184; see also *Lheureux*, TBH 2015, 88, 92.

[613] *Espiniella Menéndez*, REDI 2014-2, 241, 242–243.

[614] *de Miguel Asensio*, in: Liber amicorum Alegría Borrás (2013), p. 291, 298.

[615] *Corman-Collins SA v. La Maison du Whisky SA* (Case C-9/12), ECLI:EU:C:2013:860 paras. 38–41; A-G *Jääskinen*, Opinion of 25 April 2013 in Case 9/12, paras. 44, 57; *Cebrián Salvat*, CDT 5 (1) (2013), 125; *Idot*, Europe février 2014 comm. 2 p. 50; *Berlioz*, JCP G 2014, 271, 273; *Lenzing*, EuZW 2014, 183; *Berlioz*, JCP G 2014, 271; *Friederike Schäfer*, ecolex 2014, 605, 607; *López Rodríguez*, El contrato de distribución

resolving any possibly remaining uncertainty[617]). If and insofar as licensing elements form part of a distribution agreement they are not characteristic.[618] Likewise, a distribution contract does not entail the sale of goods, but only and possibly an obligation to conclude sales contracts in the future.[619] Admittedly, it is not always the easiest task to assign a concrete contract either to the first or to the second lemma of (1) (b).[620]

Nevertheless some modifications departing from the meaning derived from Art. 56 TFEU **121** (ex-Art. 49 EC Treaty) are necessary and inevitable due to particularities inside the Brussels I*bis* system: This system contains a specific and comprehensive regime for insurance contracts in Arts. 10–16 Brussels I*bis* Regulation which is why in turn (*argumentum e contrario*) insurance contracts can not be covered by the general rule of (b).[621] The same holds true with regard to labour contracts which fall under the specific and comprehensive regime of Arts. 20–23 Brussels I*bis* Regulation. Although *per definitionem* labour contracts are concerned with providing services their social function and the apparent necessity to protect the employee as the (typically) weaker party appeal for a specific regime taking into account these particularities. Accordingly, labour contracts as covered by Arts. 20–23 are excluded from the meaning of services under (b).[622]

Mixed contracts with two or more elements, from which one can be regarded as, the provi- **122** sion of services whereas the other(s) can not, are covered by (b) if the provision of services is characteristic for the contract in its entirety or else preponderant.[623] The economic purpose and the economic background of the contract might provide for some guidance.[624] The alternatives either fall short of characterising the contract as such, namely to emphasise the principal obligation on which the action is based,[625] or lead too much to (a) with its inherent drawbacks, namely to demand that all obligations must come within the ambit of (b).[626]

---

exclusiva o concesión comercial ciómo contrato de prestación de servicios a efectos de la aplicación del foro contractual del RB I., La Ley UE n° 13, 2014, p. 37; *Jeremy Heymann*, Clunet 141 (2014), 888, 895–898; *Bureau*, RCDIP 103 (2014), 666; *Ribeiro Oertel*, RJcom 2014, 397, 402.

[616] Cass. D. 2014, 2416.

[617] *d'Avout*, D. 2014, 1972; *Lardeux*, D. 2015, 51; *Mahinga*, Petites affiches No. 27, 6 février 2015, p. 7; *Behar-Touchait*, RLDA 102 (2015), 35.

[618] *Friederike Schäfer*, ecolex 2014, 605, 607.

[619] *Wurmnest*, IHR 2005, 107.

[620] *de Miguel Asensio*, in: Liber amicorum Alegría Borrás (2013), p. 291, 299.

[621] See only OGH ÖJZ 2004, 388, 390; *Hau*, IPRax 2000, 354, 359; *Furrer/Schramm*, SJZ 2003, 137; *Leible*, in: Rauscher Art. 5 note 50.

[622] OGH ÖJZ 2004, 388, 390.

[623] *Corman-Collins SA v. La Maison du Whisky SA* (Case C-9/12), ECLI:EU:C:2013:860 para. 34; OGH EuLF 2006, II-10; BGH NJW 2008, 3001, 3003; OLG Köln RIW 2005, 778, 779; OLG Düsseldorf IPRax 2014, 535, 536; *Hau*, IPRax 2000, 354, 359; *Kropholler/von Hein* Art. 5 note 44; *Leible*, in: Rauscher Art. 5 note 50; *Fawcett*, in: Fawcett/Harris/Bridge para. 3.154; *Lynker*, Der besondere Gerichtsstand am Erfüllungsort in der Brüssel I-Verordnung (Art. 5 Nr. 1 EuGVVO) (2006) pp. 67 *et seq.*; *Christoph A. Kern*, IPRax 2014, 503, 507.

[624] *Christoph A. Kern*, IPRax 2014, 503, 508.

[625] *Fawcett*, in: Fawcett/Harris/Bridge para. 3.155.

[626] *Fawcett*, in: Fawcett/Harris/Bridge para. 3.156.

Splitting the contract is simply no option[627] not the least for this might lead to the chaos of (a) being applying applied to one part and (b) to the other, employing two completely different concepts of how to determine the place of performance. The parties to the contract can establish a ranking order between the single obligations and can classify certain obligations as main obligations, others as secondary obligations.[628]

123 In a random constellation, contracts combine elements of a sale contract and elements of a distribution contract; even then one has to ask which obligation characterises the contract most.[629] To stick with a result that such contracts are within both categories of (b) at least where the distributor acquires title to the goods,[630] falls one step short. If the contract does not require consideration but defines only a gratuitous *mandatum* (b) should not be held applicable[631] in order to keep pace with both the definition of sale of goods and the general understanding of demand on markets. If the contract is for a result and rather less for the activity possibly leading to the result, it is a matter of fact and degree whether the element of activities required is important enough to qualify under services.[632]

(2) Loan agreements

124 The most difficult issue concerns loan agreements. They are definitely not covered by Art. 56 TFEU (ex-Art. 49 EC Treaty) since – *lex specialis derogat legi generali* – specific rules on the freedom of capital movement are to be found in Arts. 63 *et seq.* TFEU (ex-Arts. 56–60 EC Treaty). On the other hand the Brussels *Ibis* Regulation does not contain a specific sub-regime for loan agreements and mentions only a small variety of them briefly in Art. 17 (1) (b). Hence the maxim of *lex specialis* does not apply in this context. In this regard (b) plays host for a controversy which previously emerged under Art. 13 (1) Brussels Convention. There (some[633]) French courts opened a line of argument that loan agreements without a specific financing purpose would be covered by "contracts for services"[634] whilst the prevailing opinion – in particular in legal writing – was to the contrary.[635] Art. 17 (1) (c) now solves the case for consumer contracts, but the problem reappears under Art. 7 (1) (b).[636]

---

627 *Christoph A. Kern*, IPRax 2014, 503, 507.

628 See *Corman-Collins SA v. La Maison du Whisky SA* (Case C-9/12), ECLI:EU:C:2013:860 para. 43; *Lenzing*, EuZW 2014, 183, 184.

629 *Car Trim GmbH v. KeySafety Systems Srl*, (Case C-381/08) [2010] ECR I-1255, I-1279 para. 32; Cassaz. Giur. It. 2000 col. 2057 with note *Migliore* = Giust. Civ. 2000 I col. 2333 with note *Ferrari*; *Ferrari*, EuLF 2000-01, 7, 9; *Bajons*, in: FS Reinhold Geimer (2002), p. 15, 57–59.

630 So *Collins*, in: Dicey/Morris para. 11–257 with reference to *Print Concept GmbH v. GEW (EC) Ltd.* [2002] CLC 382 (C.A.).

631 *Leible*, in: Rauscher Art. 5 note 50.

632 See *Czernich*, WBl 2002, 337, 341; *Burgstaller/Neumayr* Art. 5 note 11 (Oct. 2002).

633 For the opposite approach see CA Poitiers 23.7.1997 – 95/3112, inédit; CA Toulouse JCP 2004 IV 1665; CA Colmar Dr. aff. 2004, 1898 with note *Avena-Robardet* (further Art. 5 note by *Attal*, Rev. jur. comm. 2005, 51); TGI Strasbourg 21.1.1998 – 95/5311, inédit.

634 CA Nancy 16.6.1998 – 97/1867, inédit; CA Colmar RCDIP 90 (2001), 135 note *Gaudemet-Tallon* = ZIP 1999, 1209 with note *Norbert Reich* (further with notes by *André Huet*, Clunet 127 [2000], 79; *Sibylle Neumann/Rosch*, IPRax 2001, 257; *Mankowski*, EWiR Art. 13 EuGVÜ 2/99, 1171); CA Versailles RIW 1999, 884.

635 OGH ÖJZ 2003, 647, 648 *et seq.*; BGH WM 2006, 373, 374 *et seq.*; *Czernich/Tiefenthaler*, ÖBA 1998, 663, 668; *Schoibl*, JBl 1998, 700, 706 *et seq.*; *Lutz/Sibylle Neumann*, RIW 1999, 827, 829; *Sibylle Neumann/*

In EU law, loan agreements feature amongst bank services, namely in the Annex to the   **125**
amended Banking Directive[637] and, insofar as they are not covered by Arts. 63 *et seq.* TFEU
(ex Arts. 56 *et seq.* EC Treaty), under Art. 57 TFEU (ex Art. 50 EC Treaty).[638] In one of the
most specific acts of Community legislation concerning banks the notion of "services" thus
comprises loan agreements. This at least increases the burden to argue in favour of the
opposite result under (1) (b).[639] Also the *argumentum e contrario* ex Art. 13 (1) pt. 2 Brussels
Convention which was the main argument for the opposite approach under Art. 13 (1) (3)
Brussels Convention can not be imported into (1) (b).[640] Political reasons which might have
made it advisable to attempt to escape the strict regime of consumer protection rules as to
jurisdiction under Art. 13 Brussels Convention, do not apply in the context of (1) (b), even
less so since banks, as they might feel burdened by (1) (b), can derogate from (1) (b) easily by
employing a jurisdiction clause. Accordingly, loan agreements should be deemed included
in (1) (b).[641] This result emerges regardless whether the loan is coupled with a fixed purpose
for spending the loan sum, i.e. whether it is for identified financing purposes or not.[642]

(3) Letting and hire
The mere letting of goods, other tangibles, immovables, or rights does not constitute a   **126**
service since it lacks the characteristic element of activity whether it is called hire, borrowing
or else.[643] To the contrary, it is rather defined by refraining from activity and emitting
something from the lessor's sphere. Accordingly, the letting of rooms or flats is not covered
although it might result in some obligations on the landlord's part to provide for activities.

Rosch, IPRax 2001, 257, 258 *et seq.*; also obiter OLG Köln RIW 2004, 866, 867. *Adde* the references in
fn. 358.

[636] For an application of (1) (a) without sensing the problem OLG Stuttgart EuLF 2010, II-134; LG Fran-
kenthal IPRspr. 2008 Nr. 131 p. 443.

[637] Annex I No. 2 Directive 2000/12/EC of the European Parliament and of the Council of 20 March 2000
relating to the taking up and pursuit of the business of creit institutions, OJ 2000 L 126/1. Fn. 1 thereto
expressly mentions inter alia consumer credit and mortgage credit to be covered.

[638] *Burgstaller/Neumayr* Art. 5 note 11 (Oct. 2002) with reference to *Peter Svensson and Lena Gustavsson v.
Ministre de Logement et de l'Urbanisme*, (Case C-484/93) [1995] ECR I-3955.

[639] To the same avail OLG München IPRspr. 2010 Nr. 202 p. 509; *Leible*, in: Rauscher, Art. 5 note 50a.

[640] *Hau*, IPRax 2000, 354, 359; *Micklitz/Rott*, EuZW 2001, 325, 328; *Lynker*, Der besondere Gerichtsstand
am Erfüllungsort in der Brüssel I-Verordnung (Art. 5 Nr. 1 EuGVVO) (2006) p. 61; *Leible*, in: Rauscher,
Art. 5 note 50a.

[641] BGH WM 2012, 747 [6]; OLG Naumburg NJOZ 2003, 2679; CA Bruxelles TBH 2015, 198, 201 (documentary credit) with note *Bernaert*; *Micklitz/Rott*, EuZW 2001, 325, 328; *Kropholler/von Hein* Art. 5
note 44; *Furrer/Schramm*, SJZ 2003, 137, 138; *Leible*, in: Rauscher Art. 5 note 50; *Ignatova*, Art. 5 Nr. 1
EuGVVO – Chancen und Perspektiven der Reform des Gerichtsstands am Erfüllungsort (2005) pp. 196–
198; *Brenn* para. 72; *Lynker*, Der besondere Gerichtsstand am Erfüllungsort in der Brüssel I-Verordnung
(Art. 5 Nr. 1 EuGVVO) (2006) p. 61; *Berlioz*, Clunet 135 (2008), 675, 692 *et seq.*; *Romy*, SZZP 2009, 317,
327; *Leible*, in: Rauscher, Art. 5 note 50a; see also BGH WM 2014, 2088 [34]; *Markus*, AJP 2010, 971, 974.
Contra Hau, IPRax 2000, 354, 359. Sceptical *Droz/Gaudemet-Tallon*, RCDIP 90 (2001), 601, 634; *Schlosser* Art. 5 note 10b.

[642] *Contra Béraudo*, Clunet 128 (2001), 1033, 1046.

[643] *Oberhammer*, in: Dasser/Oberhammer, Art. 5 note 43; *Leible*, in: Rauscher, Art. 5 note 50c; see also Hof
Amsterdam NIPR 2008 Nr. 296 p. 551.

These obligations are not the all-important characteristic performance for a lease agreement. The letting of immoveables in the EU is governed by Art. 24 (1) anyway.

b) Factual concept behind (b)

127 The genesis reveals the concept behind (b):[644] "Anti-*Tessili* and *Anti-De Bloos*" or "Anything but *Tessili* and *De Bloos*" are the maxims.[645] There must not be a continuity of interpretation in this regard.[646] Genetically, (b) follows an autonomous, factual concept,[647] particularly derived from the French model of Art. 46 ncpc[648] and from respective French insinuations.[649]

---

[644] Commission Proposal COM (1999) 348 final p. 15; see also Report *Pocar* paras. 49–51.

[645] *Color Drack GmbH v. Lexx International Vertriebs GmbH*, Case C-386/05 [2007] ECR I-3699, I-3734 para. 24, I-3737 para. 39; A-G *Jääskinen*, Opinion of 25 April 2013 in Case C-9/12, ECLI:EU:C:2013:273 para. 38; Cassaz. RDIPP 2008, 505, 510; OLG Oldenburg IHR 2008, 112, 114; *Hau*, ZZP Int. 5 (2000), 284, 286 *et seq.*; *Couwenberg/Pertegás Sender*, in: van Houtte/Pertegás Sender (eds.), Het nieuwe Europese IPR: van verdrag naar verordening (2001), p. 31, 50 § 3-33; *Gsell*, IPRax 2002, 484, 485; *Bajons*, in: FS Reinhold Geimer (2002), p. 15, 42; *Martiny*, in: FS Reinhold Geimer (2002), p. 641, 642 *et seq.*; *Leffler*, SvJT 2002, 816, 820 *et seq.*; *Rutten*, R.W. 2002–2003, 666, 668; *Newton* p. 116; *Kienle*, IPRax 2005, 113; *André Huet*, in: Mélanges en l'honneur de Paul Lagarde (2005), p. 417, 428; *Rodriguez*, Beklagtenwohnsitz und Erfüllungsort im europäischen IZVR (Zürich 2005) paras. 651–657; *Ferrari*, RDAI 2007, 83, 88 *et seq.*; *Ferrari*, Giust. civ. 2007 I 1397, 1406 *et seq.*; *Franzina*, NGCC 2007 I 537, 538; *Gardella*, Yb. PIL IX (2007), 439, 442 *et seq.*; *Hau*, JZ 2008, 974, 978; *Vlas*, NJ 2008 Nr. 237 p. 2282; *Vlek*, WPNR 6799 (2009), 407, 409; *Henri Storme*, R.W. 2009–2010, 409, 411; *Grušić*, (2011) 7 JPrIL 321, 325.

[646] Hof van Cass. R.W. 2009–2010, 408, 409; Trib. Rovereto RDIPP 2005, 162, 167 = Giur. it. 2005, 1005 note *Poggio*.

[647] See only *Color Drack GmbH v. Lexx International Vertriebs GmbH*, Case C-386/05 [2007] ECR I-3699, I-3737 para. 39; *Car Trim GmbH v. KeySafety Systems Srl*, (Case C-381/08) [2010] ECR I-1255, I-1284 para. 52, I-1285 para. 57; *Wood Floor Solutions Andreas Domberger GmbH v. Silva Trade SA*, (Case C-19/09) [2010] ECR I-2121, I-2170 para. 23; A-G *Mazák*, [2010] ECR I-1258, I-1266 paras. 36, 40; OGH ÖJZ 2004, 388, 389; OGH EuLF 2005, II-80, II-81; OGH EuLF 2006, II-10; Cassaz. RDIPP 2008, 505, 510; Cassaz. RDIPP 2008, 511, 514; Hof van Cass. R.W. 2009–2010, 408, 409; OLG Hamm IHR 2006, 84, 85; OLG München NJW-RR 2007, 1428; OLG Oldenburg IHR 2008, 112, 114; OLG Karlsruhe IHR 2008, 194, 195; OLG München CR 2010, 156, 157; OLG Düsseldorf IPRax 2014, 535, 537; Hof 's-Gravenhage NIPR 2006 Nr. 307 p. 453; Rb. Kh. Hasselt TBH 2003, 623 with note *Kruger*; Rb. Kh. Hasselt R.W. 2007–2008, 1047, 1049; *Kerameus*, in: Liber amicorum Pierre Widmer (2003), p. 163, 165; *Audit*, Rec. des Cours 305 (2003), 9, 437; *Kaster-Müller*, EuLF 2005, II-47, II-48; *Lynker*, Der besondere Gerichtsstand am Erfüllungsort in der Brüssel I-Verordnung (Art. 5 Nr. 1 EuGVVO) (2006) p. 90; *Merlin*, Riv. dir. proc. 2007, 1305, 1311; *Gardella*, Yb. PIL 9 (2007), 439, 443; *van Lith*, International Jurisdiction and Commercial Litigation – Uniform Rules for Contract Disputes (The Hague 2009) p. 87; *Kuipers*, NIPR 2010, 622, 623; *Notdurfter/Petruzzino*, Contratto e impresa/Europa 2011, 223, 226; *Herbert Roth*, in: FS Daphne-Ariane Simotta (2012), p. 495, 498–499; *de Miguel Asensio*, in: Liber amicorum Alegría Borrás (2013), p. 291, 293.

[648] Which reads: "Le demandeur peut saisir à son choix, outre la juridiction du lieu où demeure le défendeur: [...] en matière contractuelle, la juridiction du lieu de la livraison effective de la chose ou du lieu de l'exécution de la prestation de services." But cf. on divergences in details *Ignatova*, Art. 5 Nr. 1 EuGVVO – Chancen und Perspektiven der Reform des Gerichtsstands am Erfüllungsort (2005) pp. 219–223.

[649] OLG Karlsruhe IPRspr. 2009 Nr. 169 p. 444; *Kropholler/von Hinden*, in: GS Alexander Lüderitz (2000), p. 401, 405 *et seq.*; *Klemm*, Erfüllungsortvereinbarungen im Europäischen Zivilverfahrensrecht (2005) p. 61; *Simotta*, in: Fasching/Konecny Art. 5 note 158; *Kropholler/von Hein* Art. 5 note 27.

Its main purpose is to avoid recourse on normativity and in particular gap-filling by means of recourse to the applicable national law via the private international law of the *forum*[650] as *Tessili* advocated for and prescribed.[651] The previous approach was believed to have generated too much diversity and to have been marred by different handling of PIL rules in the various Member States.[652] Jurisdiction under (1) (b) thus shall be determined without having to employ private international law. PIL is deemed (overly) complicated,[653] and ascertaining jurisdiction shall not be burdened and hampered with incidental questions of substantive law if ever possible. Issues of substantive law shall be left to later stages of the proceedings and erased as far as possible from the initial and rather early stage of jurisdiction. Jurisdiction shall be ascertained following an autonomous concept with uniform solutions independent of the forum seised and without interference by different approaches in the substantive laws of the Member States. What survived from *Tessili* is redistributed to (a) and expelled from the realm of (b).[654] Pragmatism reigns.[655] The places of performance for the purposes of jurisdiction and of substantive law respectively part ways.[656] Insofar as (b) comes into operation the opponents of the *status quo* were victorious and got the better of the ensuing compromise. (b) is definitely not a presumption for ascertaining the place of performance under (a).[657]

This factual concept presents more problems in detail than might be recognised at first **128** glance. However, for the majority of cases it works and is operable without major difficulties. In the majority of cases a simple solution emerges,[658] all the better since it becomes unnecessary to ask whether the buyer's obligation to pay has its own place of performance as this question has been answered abstractly in the negative.[659] E.g. it has become unnecessary to dive too deep into the nitty-gritty of auction contracts in order to ascertain the place of performance[660] since only the delivery of the auctioned goods is relevant.[661] Without re-

---

[650] See only *Car Trim GmbH v. KeySafety Systems Srl*, (Case C-381/08) [2010] ECR I-1255, I-1284 *et seq.* paras. 52, 53, 55; Commission Proposal COM (1999) 348 final p. 15; OGH ÖJZ 2004, 388, 389; BGH NJW 2006, 1806; Hof van Cass. R.W. 2009–2010, 408, 409; OLG Koblenz IPRspr. 2001 Nr. 151 p. 307; OLG Köln RIW 2005, 778, 779; OLG Düsseldorf NJW-RR 2008, 223, 224; Rb. Kh. Hasselt R.W. 2004–2005, 833, 834; Trib. Rovereto RDIPP 2005, 162, 165 = Giur. it. 2005, 1005 note *Poggio*; LG Neubrandenburg IHR 2006, 26, 27; *Scapinello*, Dir. mar. 107 (2005), 588, 590 *et seq.*; *de Franceschi*, Contratto e impresa/Europa 2008, 637, 659 *et seq.*; *Hau*, IPRax 2009, 44 *et seq.*; *Shine*, [2011] ICCLR 20, 24; *Di Blase*, Europa e dir. priv. 2011, 459, 461 *et seq.*; *Haas/Oliver Vogel*, NZG 2011, 766, 768; *García Gutiérrez*, REDI 2013-1, 305, 308.

[651] See *Industrie Tessili Italiana Como v. Dunlop AG*, (Case 12/76) [1976] ECR 1473, 1486 para. 15.

[652] *Kuipers*, NIPR 2010, 622.

[653] See A-G *Bot*, [2007] ECR I-3702, I-3715 para. 69.

[654] Completely wrong in this regard Rb. Arnhem NIPR 2005 Nr. 56 p. 97.

[655] *Car Trim GmbH v. KeySafety Systems Srl*, (Case C-381/08), [2010] ECR I-1255 para. 52; OGH ÖJZ 2004, 388, 389.

[656] OLG Karlsruhe IPRspr. 2009 Nr. 169 p. 443.

[657] *Takahashi*, (2002) 27 Eur. L. Rev. 530, 534; *Samyn*, R.W. 2006–2007, 972; *Franzina*, NGCC 2007 I 537, 541; *Henri Storme*, R.W. 2009–2010, 409, 410. Mistakenly *contra* Hof Gent Tijdschrift@ipr.be 2006, 51; Hof Gent RABG 2008, 1107 with critical note *Samyn*.

[658] *Jacquet*, Clunet 135 (2008), 524, 530.

[659] OGH IPRax 2004, 349, 350; A-G *Ruiz-Jarabo Colomer*, [1999] ECR I-6309, 6324 para. 55.

[660] See under Art. 5 (1) Brussels Convention BGH ZIP 2003, 213.

---

course to national PIL and the diverging solutions under national substantive laws,[662] uniformity is enhanced and procedural law as the sole sovereign rules its very own realm of evaluating jurisdictional interests.[663]

129   Where goods were actually delivered or where an activity takes place and can be located is mainly a question of whether enough proof and backing can be provided for any sustainable contention. He who alleges that the goods had to be delivered, or were in fact delivered, or that the activity ought to be performed, or was in fact performed, in a certain place generally has to shoulder the burden of proof in accordance with the rules regarding such a burden in the national (procedural) law of the forum seized. Yet if an allegation is made that delivery was in fact effectuated at a certain place (e.g. the buyer's place of business) and the other party does not contest this, the issue will be solved rather easily and expeditiously.[664]

c) Principle of characteristic performance

130   Unlike the traditional approach established by *de Bloos* and still followed under (a),[665] under (b) a single, unitary and uniform place of performance under the entire contract is deemed to exist.[666] This place is deemed identical for every obligation stemming from the same contract.[667] No split or fragmentation between the different obligations occurs,[668] there is no need to distinguish between obligations to perform and other, accompanying obliga-

---

661   *Stephan Lorenz*, EWiR Art. 5 EuGVÜ 1/03, 417, 418; *Leible*, IPRax 2005, 424, 427.

662   A-G *Mazák*, [2010] ECR I-1258, I-1266 para. 40.

663   *Leipold*, in: GS Alexander Lüderitz (2000), p. 431, 438.

664   Rb. Arnhem NIPR 2003 Nr. 49 p. 100.

665   See *infra* Art. 5 notes 128 *et seq.* (*Mankowski*).

666   See only *Color Drack GmbH v. Lexx International Vertriebs GmbH*, Case C-386/05 [2007] ECR I-3699, I-3734 para. 26, I-3737 para. 39; A-G *Bot*, [2007] ECR I-3702, I-3717 *et seq.* para. 87; OGH IPRax 2004, 349, 350; OGH ZfRV 2008/29, 81; BGH NJW 2006, 1806; Cassaz. RDIPP 2010, 738; BGE 140 III 115, 120; BG 15.7.2014 – 4A_113/2014 E 3.2; OLG München NJW-RR 2007, 1428; OLG Karlsruhe IHR 2008, 194, 195; OLG München IPRax 2009, 69, 70; OLG Karlsruhe IPRspr. 2009 Nr. 169 p. 442; OLG Stuttgart IHR 2012, 163, 165; OLG Hamm IHR 2012, 216, 218; OLG Zweibrücken MDR 2013, 510; OLG Naumburg IPRspr. 2013 Nr. 194 p. 425; Hof Amsterdam NIPR 2009 Nr. 133 p. 232 *et seq.*; LG München II IPRax 2005, 143, 144; Rb. Arnhem NIPR 2006 Nr. 51 p. 83; Trib. Arezzo Dir. scambi int. 2006, 343, 344; Trib. Varese RDIPP 2013, 455, 457; Trib. Milano RDIPP 2014, 629, 631; Rb. Midden-Nederland, zittingsplaats Utrecht NIPR 2015 Nr. 70 p. 170. *Ibili*, NILR 2002, 114, 115; *Audit*, Rec. des Cours 305 (2003), 9, 434; *Kienle*, IPRax 2005, 113; *Fawcett*, in: Fawcett/Harris/Bridge para. 3.171; *Stephan Lorenz/Unberath*, IPRax 2005, 219, 222 *et seq.*; *Ignatova*, Art. 5 Nr. 1 EuGVVO – Chancen und Perspektiven der Reform des Gerichtsstands am Erfüllungsort (2005) pp. 205 *et seq.*; *Rodriguez*, Beklagtenwohnsitz und Erfüllungsort im europäischen IZVR (Zürich 2005) paras. 648–650; *Merlin*, Riv. dir. proc. 2007, 1305, 1311; *Berlioz*, Clunet 135 (2008), 675, 681; *Fernet*, JCP E 2010 N°. 24, 17 juin 2010, p. 21, 22 *et seq.*; *Leible*, in: FS Ulrich Spellenberg (2010), p. 451, 453; *Perrella*, Dir. mar. 2010, 527, 530; *Rauscher*, NJW 2010, 2251; *Grušić*, (2011) 7 JPrIL 321, 336; *Markus*, IPRax 2015, 277, 278.

667   *Color Drack GmbH v. Lexx International Vertriebs GmbH*, Case C-386/05 [2007] ECR I-3699, I-3734 para. 26. Of course, prior to such operation it has to be checked as to whether in the concrete case a majority of contracts and not one unitary contract exists; *Markus*, Tendenzen beim materiellrechtlichen Vertragserfüllungsort im internationalen Zivilverfahrensrecht (Basel 2009) p. 151.

668   See only Rb. 's-Hertogenbosch NIPR 2007 Nr. 318 p. 436; *Grušić*, (2011) 7 JPrIL 321, 336; *Markus*, IPRax 2015, 277, 278–279.

tions,[669] and cases of declaratory actions concerning the contract in its entirety are also appropriately dealt with.[670] This intends to, and aims at, focusing and concentrating (but for Art. 4) special jurisdiction in contract to a single court.[671] In principle, jurisdiction here should be determined by reference to the place with the closest linking factor between the contract and any court.[672] In order to determine such single place of performance in effect for the entire contract, the principle of characteristic performance is employed.[673] It might not be spelled out expressly in the wording like it is in Art. 4 (1) (a), (b), (2) Rome I Regulation or was in Art. 4 (2) 1, 2 Rome Convention but (b) reflects and mirrors the principle in its concrete appearance, namely by concentrating on the place of delivery of goods or of rendering services respectively. On the other hand, it would do injustice to the wording of (1) (b) which does not refer to the closest connection as such, but tries to identify typicised expressions of the closest connection without employing any escape clause (like Art. 4 (3) Rome I Regulation) to assert that the closest linking connection was the main criterion.[674]

The practical consequences of this unitary approach are eminent and of the utmost importance: The concentration of jurisdiction is warranted for.[675] All secondary obligations including claims for damages share the place of performance of the obligation characterising the contract.[676] Obligations which might be characterised as *autonomes* by national law are also covered for national law has lost its qualificatory sway.[677] A discernible place of performance with regard to declaratory actions, be they affirmative or negative, emerges.[678] But foremost and most importantly, the obligation to pay has the same place of performance as the said obligation characterising the contract.[679] Sellers and service providers, as money   **131**

---

669 See LG München II IHR 2013, 72.

670 See only *Eltzschig*, IPRax 2002, 491, 492 et seq.; *Thorn*, IPRax 2004, 354, 356.

671 *Stadler*, (2005) 42 CMLRev. 1637, 1648; *Garcimartín*, Int. J. Proced. L. 3 (2013), 22, 37.

672 *Color Drack GmbH v. Lexx International Vertriebs GmbH*, Case C-386/05 [2007] ECR I-3699, I-3738 para. 40; *Peter Rehder v. Baltic Air Corporation*, (Case C-204/08) [2009] ECR I-6073, I-6090 para. 36; A-G *Mazák*, [2010] ECR I-1258, I-1265 para. 35; A-G *Trstenjak*, [2010] ECR I-2124, I-2150 para. 71; *Lynker*, Der besondere Gerichtsstand am Erfüllungsort in der Brüssel I-Verordnung (Art. 5 Nr. 1 EuGVVO) (2006) p. 141.

673 See only OLG Köln RIW 2005, 778, 779; OLG Hamm IHR 2006, 84, 85 et seq.; OLG Köln IHR 2006, 86, 87; OLG Celle IHR 2010, 164, 166 with note *Jungemeyer*; Rb. Arnhem NIPR 2006 Nr. 52 p. 84; Trib. Verona RDIPP 2007, 367, 369; Trib. Trapani Giur. mer. 2011, 1599, 1601; Vzngr. Rb. Utrecht NIPR 2002 Nr. 215 p. 365; *Marie-Élodie Ancel*, RCDIP 90 (2001), 158, 163; *Pålsson*, SvJT 2001, 373, 379; *Marquette*, TBH 2002, 499, 500 et seq.; *Carballo Piñeiro*, REDI 2002, 856, 859; *Schoibl*, JBl 2003, 149, 157; *Romme-laere*, Rev. dr. comm. belge 2003, 103, 106 et seq.; *Kerameus*, in: Liber amicorum Pierre Widmer (2003), p. 163, 165 et seq.; *Tagaras*, CDE 2003, 717, 743, 745; *Grisay/Piccininno*, J. trib. 2005, 97, 101; *Berlioz*, Clunet 135 (2008), 675, 699; *de Franceschi*, Contratto e impresa/Europa 2008, 637, 652; *Markus*, Tendenzen beim materiellrechtlichen Vertragserfüllungsort im internationalen Zivilverfahrensrecht (Basel 2009) p. 149; *Grušić*, (2011) 7 JPrIL 321, 334.

674 As A-G *Trstenjak*, [2010] ECR I-2124, I-2150 para. 74 does.

675 See only *Vlas*, WPNR 6421 (2000), 745, 749.

676 OGH ÖJZ 2004, 388, 389.

677 *Égéa/Martel*, Clunet 134 (2007), 133, 138.

678 See LG Neubrandenburg IHR 2006, 26, 27.

679 See only A-G *Bot*, [2007] ECR I-3702, I-3718 para. 89; OGH ÖJZ 2004, 388, 389; OGH ZfRV 2008/29, 80;

---

creditors, can sue the buyers and customers at the place of performance of the obligation characterising the contract. (b) might not suit them by establishing a *forum actoris* at their respective place of business automatically.[680] But if (and only if) the place of performance can be identified at the seller's place of business a *forum actoris* emerges. Whenever the contract binds the buyer to take delivery at the seller's place of business this formation arises, likewise if the service is to be rendered at the provider's place of business. Then the seller enjoys a *forum actoris* if he sues the buyer for payment. Sellers under fob-contracts and under cif-contracts[681] also profit as the place of performance, equalling the place of delivery of the goods to the buyer, is in the port of loading[682] (which will in most instances be near, and at least in the same state as, one of the seller's places of business), not in the port of discharge. The same applies under fas (free alongside ship).[683] On the other hand, the buyer gets a *forum actoris* for actions for repayment or other remedies due to defective goods if the delivery of the goods happens at his place.[684] Yet the place of delivery need not necessarily coincide with the place of either party and can lead to jurisdiction of a court in a state where none of the parties has a place of business.[685]

d) Accordance with the contract

aa) Ambit of the reference to the contract

132 The first clouds of doubt as to the proper interpretation of the fact-oriented concept are shed by the words "under the contract".[686] Primarily, this appears at first glance to refer to express provisions in the contract explicitly spelling out the place of performance. Such express stipulations however are already dealt with on a higher level in the structure of (1): (b) and (a) alike come only into operation if the contract does not contain an express and explicit stipulation of the place of performance. Hence, the reference in (b) can not be read as to express and explicit contractual provisions.[687] Otherwise it would amount to a redundant

---

Cass. Clunet 134 (2007), 132 with note *Martel/Egéa*; Cass. D. 2007, 1756 with note *Jault-Seseke*; OLG Hamm IHR 2006, 84, 85; OLG Köln IHR 2013, 68, 70; Rb. Zutphen NIPR 2005 Nr. 69 p. 112; Rb. Zwolle-Lelystad NIPR 2006 Nr. 304 p. 447; Rb. Haarlem NIPR 2007 Nr. 145 p. 210; Vzngr. Rb. Alkmaar NIPR 2003 Nr. 281 p. 437; Trib. Padova, sez. Este RDIPP 2007, 147, 151; Trib. Varese RDIPP 2013, 455, 457; *Vlas*, WPNR 6421 (2000), 745, 749; *Couwenberg/Pertegás Sender*, in: van Houtte/Pertegás Sender (eds.), Het nieuwe Europese IPR: van verdrag naar verordening (2001), p. 31, 50 § 3-33; *Lima Pinheiro* p. 84; *Piltz*, IHR 2006, 53, 55.

[680] See highlighting this Trib. Forli RDIPP 2014, 172, 173.

[681] For cif-contracts differing *Fawcett*, in: Fawcett/Harris/Bridge para. 3.185: place of delivery ought to be equalled with delivery of the documents substituting for the goods. Unclear Cassaz. RDIPP 2006, 447, 449; Cassaz. Mass. Giust. Civ. 2005 no. 14208.

[682] BGH NJW 2009, 2606, 2608; BGH EuZW 2010, 72, 73; Protodikeio Thessaloniki 1998, 1238; *Fawcett*, in: Fawcett/Harris/Bridge para. 3.183; *Hau*, JZ 2008, 974, 978; *Merrett*, (2008) 54 Cambridge L.J. 244, 245 *et seq.*; *Leible*, in: Rauscher Art. 5 note 52; *Leible*, EuZW 2011, 604, 606.

[683] *Fawcett*, in: Fawcett/Harris/Bridge para. 3.182.

[684] *Hau*, IPRax 2000, 354, 359; *Bajons*, in: FS Reinhold Geimer (2002), p. 15, 54; *Magnus*, IHR 2002, 45, 47; *Mankowski*, in: FS Andreas Heldrich (2005), p. 867, 889.

[685] *Kropholler/von Hinden*, in: GS Alexander Lüderitz (2000), p. 401, 407.

[686] See in particular *Marie-Élodie Ancel*, RCDIP 90 (2001), 158, 162; *Droz/Gaudemet-Tallon*, RCDIP 90 (2001), 601, 635; *Béraudo*, Clunet 128 (2001), 1033, 1044; *André Huet*, Clunet 128 (2001), 1126, 1128–1130; *Eltzschig*, IPRax 2002, 491, 495 *et seq.*

duplication.[688] It would be disastrous to deprive the phrase "unless otherwise agreed" of any meaningful sense, waiting for some imaginative court to breathe meaning in it, elsewhile attributing to it only an incoherent interpretation, which the opposite approach would be bound to do.[689] The phrase requires to pay proper regard to all clauses and conditions of the contract.[690] At stake here are only clauses not identifying directly or explicitly the place of performance.[691] The ECJ alleges agreements to determine the place of delivery (but not the place of performance as such) to fit this bill, though.[692] It might be difficult to draw such fine lines of distinction.[693] Secondly, contractual provisions from which a like inference can be gained operate without any contradiction to the fundamental decision to have no recourse to the *lex causae* since they are implications from the contract, not from any rule supplementing the contract.[694] Here contractual fixations regarding the place of delivery definitely are masters of the game.[695] The most prominent examples are provided by cif- or fob-contracts.[696] Fob, as such, is concerned with the delivery of the goods,[697] albeit it is influenced by technical modalities of transport and might overemphasise the importance of the port of loading to some degree, though.[698] Furthermore, there might be modifications attaching more importance to the documents if the seller demands the bill of lading made to be out to him so that he retains control of the goods until paid on presentation of the documents.[699]

Generally, the use of one of the clauses from Incoterms clarifies the matter considerably.[700] **133** They make it easier for traders to draft contracts because, through the use of short and simple terms, they can define may aspects of their business relations.[701] Standardisation and the level of explanation by the rules which explain the details of the respective Incoterms clauses are a major advantage. As yet another example, "cash against delivery" might establish the place of performance for the buyer's obligation to pay at the place of delivery

---

[687] Bruneau, JCP 2001 I 304 no. 11; *Droz/Gaudemet-Tallon*, RCDIP 90 (2001), 601, 635. *Contra Briggs/Rees* p. 131; *Vlas*, WPNR 2000, 749, 750; *Klemm*, Erfüllungsortvereinbarungen im Europäischen Zivilverfahrensrecht (2005) p. 71; see also *Layton/Mercer* para. 15.045.

[688] See *André Huet*, Clunet 128 (2001), 1126, 1128 *et seq.*

[689] See for such an opposite approach *Briggs/Rees* p. 131; *Klemm*, Erfüllungsortvereinbarungen im Europäischen Zivilverfahrensrecht (2005) p. 71.

[690] See only Rb. Limburg, zittingsplaats Maastricht NIPR 2015 Nr. 69 p. 169.

[691] *Electrosteel Europe SA v. Edil Centro SpA*, (Case C-87/10) [2011] ECR I-4987 para. 18.

[692] *Car Trim GmbH v. KeySafety Systems Srl*, (Case C-381/08) [2010] ECR I-1255, I-1283 para. 46; see also OLG Karlsruhe NJOZ 2009, 2282, 2289 *et seq.*

[693] *Haas/Oliver Vogel*, NZG 2011, 766, 767.

[694] *Kienle*, IPRax 2005, 113, 115; see also *Electrosteel Europe SA v. Edil Centro SpA*, (Case C-87/10) [2011] ECR I-4987 para. 16.

[695] *André Huet*, Clunet 128 (2001), 1126, 1129 *et seq.*; see also *Electrosteel Europe SA v. Edil Centro SpA*, (Case C-87/10) [2011] ECR I-4987 paras. 18 *et seq.*

[696] *Magnus*, IHR 2002, 45, 48; *Rauscher*, in: FS Andreas Heldrich (2005), p. 933, 942; see also *Kruger*, TBH 2003, 623.

[697] BGH NJW 2009, 2606; *Thomas Pfeiffer*, LMK 2009, 286480; *Haas/Oliver Vogel*, NZG 2011, 766, 767.

[698] See *Piltz*, IHR 2006, 53, 55.

[699] *Merrett*, (2008) 54 Cambridge L.J. 244, 246.

[700] See only *Electrosteel Europe SA v. Edil Centro SpA*, (Case C-87/10) [2011] ECR I-4987 para. 21; *Carrascosa González*, in: Calvo Caravaca, Art. 5.1 CB note 20.

[701] *Electrosteel Europe SA v. Edil Centro SpA*, (Case C-87/10) [2011] ECR I-4987 para. 21.

---

contractually.[702] CPT (Carriage Paid To) does not indicate a place of delivery.[703] If the parties inserted "free house", "frei Haus", "frei Baustelle" or alike in their contract, it is nevertheless doubtful whether this constitutes an agreement influencing the place of delivery or whether this only bears relevance for the passing of the risk and the allocation of costs between the parties.[704] The clause does not have an unequivocal content.[705] It depends on the circumstances in which the two alternating meanings should prevail under the concrete contract.[706] If, for instance, the seller has undertaken to install the goods or to instruct the buyer's personnel the place of delivery is influenced;[707] the same applies if the seller issued a warranty or has undertaken to provide repair services for a certain period.[708] It is not necessary that the relevant clauses are genuine Incoterms clauses; stipulations borrowing some elements from Incoterms clauses can be equally helpful.[709] Art. 25 (1) (c) is cornerstone for the general contention that trade usages and established commercial practices bear major relevance.[710]

134 A most decisive feature is to distinguish between clauses which are to identify the place of delivery on the one hand and clauses which merely lay down conditions relating to the allocation of the risks connected to the carriage of the goods or the division of costs between the contracting parties.[711] Clauses dealing with costs or insurance exclusively (e.g. CPT "carriage paid to" or CIP "carriage and insurance paid") have no impact on the place of performance.[712] Particular observance must be paid to D-clauses (like DES "delivered ex ship" or DEQ "ex quay" or DDU "delivered duty unpaid" or DDP "delivered duty paid" under Incoterms 2000 and DAT "delivered at terminal", DAP "delivered at place" or DDP "delivered duty paid" under Incoterms 2010).[713] Parties cannot successfully plead that they

---

702 LG Nürnberg-Fürth IHR 2004, 20.

703 OLG Hamm IPRspr. 2012 Nr. 186 pp. 425 *et seq.*

704 See BGH CLOUT 268; OGH SZ 71/145; OLG Karlsruhe CLOUT 317; *Simotta*, in: Fasching/Konecny Art. 5 note 94. In preference of the latter, narrower scope OGH JBl 1999, 333; OGH RdW 1999, 210; OLG Köln IHR 2002, 66; OLG Koblenz IHR 2003, 66; KantonsG Zug IHR 2005, 119, 121 *et seq.*; *Fountoulakis*, IHR 2005, 122, 123.

705 See only OLG Köln IHR 2002, 66.

706 *Magnus*, IHR 2002, 45, 48.

707 See in a slighty different context in the near vicinity OLG Köln IHR 2006, 86, 87.

708 Cassaz. Giur it. 1995 I/1 col. 1480, 1484; Cassaz. Foro it. 2000 I col. 2226, 2231; *Bajons*, in: FS Reinhold Geimer (2002), p. 15, 51 *et seq.* Unclear *Fawcett*, in: Fawcett/Harris/Bridge para. 3.157.

709 See *Electrosteel Europe SA v. Edil Centro SpA*, (Case C-87/10) [2011] ECR I-4987 para. 20.

710 See *Electrosteel Europe SA v. Edil Centro SpA*, (Case C-87/10) [2011] ECR I-4987 para. 19.

711 *Electrosteel Europe SA v. Edil Centro SpA*, (Case C-87/10) [2011] ECR I-4987 para. 23; BG 15.7.2014 – 4A_113/2014 E 4. 4. 1; *Notdurfter/Petruzzino*, Contratto e impresa/Europa 2011, 223, 239; *Leible*, EuZW 2011, 305, 307; *Mankowski*, EWiR Art. 5 EuGVVO 1/11, 497, 498.

712 Cassaz. Dir. mar. 111 (2009), 469, 472 with note *Tuo* (for cif, fob, FIO, franco stabilimento, which might be one step too far); OLG Hamm IHR 2006, 84, 85; OLG München IHR 2009, 201 with note *Großkopf*; *Rauscher*, in: FS Andreas Heldrich (2005), p. 933, 942; *Piltz*, IHR 2006, 53, 57. But cf. also Rb. Leeuwarden NIPR 2010 Nr. 485 p. 793. Outside the Incoterms "Resa: Franco Partenza" was believed to be a clause solely on costs; BGH NJW 2010, 3452, 3453 = BGHZ 186, 81; OLG München IPRax 2009, 69. *Contra* Trib. Arezzo Dir. scambi int. 2006, 343, 344 for "franco destinazione sdoganato".

713 BGH ZIP 2013, 44, 46–47 (DDP); OLG Hamm IHR 2012, 216, 219; LG Siegen 7 March 2007 – Case 8 O 250/06; *Rauscher*, in: FS Andreas Heldrich (2005), p. 933, 943; *Fawcett*, in: Fawcett/Harris/Bridge

were actually ignorant of the concrete meaning of any of these clauses.[714] Inherent in In-coterms clauses is the restriction that such clauses will not directly influence the place of payment as they only deal with modalities of the delivery of the goods.[715] On the other hand, it would be rash to state that Incoterms never influence jurisdiction.[716] For instance, "free on truck" clearly indicates that delivery at the truck is agreed upon[717] whereas "ex works", "ex factory", "franco fabbrica" or "ab Werk" point towards the seller's production facilities as the place of delivery;[718] likewise do "ex warehouse" or "ex store" point to the places respectively named[719] whereas "ex ship" and "ex quay" designate the port of discharge.[720] If the seller has also to install the goods (in particular machinery) at the buyer's premises the place of delivery should be located at the buyer's premises.[721]

But doubts arise in the remaining instances where the contract itself neither contains an **135** express provision nor allows for an inference. Does "under the contract" then open the backdoor and put the construction of the contract as to the legal rules applicable, particularly the respective *ius dispositivum* of the *lex causae* or e.g. Art. 31 CISG, centerstage,[722] be it only as part of some *économie générale du contrat*?[723] At least this could be maintained due to one of the main rationales behind *ius dispositivum*: The very purpose of *ius dispositivum* is to fill gaps and *lacunae* in the contract. So, if the contract contains a gap it would be most natural for *ius dispositivum* to step in. Or, even worse, should (a) step in by virtue of (c)?[724] However,

---

para. 3.188 *et seq.*; *Hau*, JZ 2008, 974, 978; *Leible*, in: Rauscher Art. 5 note 52; *Leible*, EuZW 2011, 604, 605; see also Højesteret UfR 2001, 1039, 1043. Very affirmatively Rb. Arnhem NIPR 2006 Nr. 51 p. 83; Rb. 's-Hertogenbosch NIPR 2010 Nr. 483 p. 790.

[714] BGH NJW-RR 2013, 309; *Matusche-Beckmann*,LMK 2013, 343555.

[715] *Rauscher*, in: FS Andreas Heldrich (2005), p. 933, 942 *et seq.*

[716] Tentatively *contra* KantonsG Zürich ZGGVP 2003, 208.

[717] Rb. Rotterdam NIPR 2005 Nr. 63 p. 105; *Fawcett*, in: Fawcett/Harris/Bridge para. 3.182.

[718] Cass. D. 2011, 1024 obs. *Delpech* = D. 2010, 2434 obs. *d'Avout*; OLG Karlsruhe InVo 2007, 33, 38 = IPRapsr. 2006 Nr. 111; OLG Stuttgart IHR 2011, 236; Hof Arnhem-Leeuwarden, locatie Leeuwarden NIPR 2014 Nr. 271 p. 474; Rb. 's-Gravenhage NIPR 2005 Nr. 51 p. 90; Rb. 's-Hertogenbosch 21 July 2010 – LJN BN2826; Trib. Novara RDIPP 2013, 171, 173; LG Düsseldorf IPRspr. 2012 Nr. 195 p. 448; *Vlas*, WPNR 6421 (2000), 745, 749 *et seq.*; *Fawcett*, in: Fawcett/Harris/Bridge para. 3.180; *Notdurfter/Petruz-zino*, Contratto e impresa/Europa 2011, 223, 239; *Delpech*, D. 2011, 1694; *Leible*, EuZW 2011, 604, 605; *Vlek*, in: Der IPR in de spiegel van Paul Vlas (2012), p. 277, 282; *Sindres*, J-Cl. Dr. int. fasc. 584–130 no. 57 (mars 2014); see also A-G *Kokott*, Opinion in Case C-87/10 of 3 March 2011, [2011] ECR I-4990 para. 40. Yet more cautious OGH EuLF 2006, II-10.

[719] *Fawcett*, in: Fawcett/Harris/Bridge para. 3.180. More cautiously OLG Hamm IHR 2006, 84, 85.

[720] *Fawcett*, in: Fawcett/Harris/Bridge paras. 3.186 *et seq.*

[721] OLG Köln IHR 2006, 86, 87 with reference to OLG Celle IPRax 1985, 284, 288; OLG München RIW 2000, 712, 713.

[722] See *Béraudo*, Clunet 128 (2001), 1033, 1045; *Marie-Élodie Ancel*, RCDIP 90 (2001), 158, 162; *Claude Witz*, D. 2001, 3614; *Takahashi*, (2002) 27 Eur. L. Rev. 530, 535 *et seq.*; *Lima Pinheiro* p. 84; *Eltzschig*, IPRax 2002, 491, 495 *et seq.*; *Newton* p. 117; *Vlas*, NILR 2004, 451, 453; *Piltz*, IHR 2006, 53, 57 and tentatively *Jault*, Petites affiches, 29 mai 2002, no. 107 p. 19; *Magnus*, in: Ferrari (ed.), Quo vadis CISG? (2005), p. 211, 232; *Franzina*, NGCC 2007 I 537, 542.

[723] *André Huet*, in: Mélanges en l'honneur de Paul Lagarde (2005), p. 417, 428.

[724] See *Couwenberg/Pertegás Sender*, in: van Houtte/Pertegás Sender (eds.), Het nieuwe Europese IPR: van

---

Peter Mankowski   215

a stark contrast with the general, factual approach behind (b) would result.[725] PIL and substantive law would creep in again[726] through the backdoor to the detriment of uniform solutions independent from the forum seized and the substantive law applicable. Thus, the contention to have recourse to the *ius dispositivum* quasi automatically is unsustainable in the light of the genesis of (b).[727] Overeagerness to withdraw matters would partially lead to the approach pursued by (a) with its inherent drawbacks and rather defeat the purpose of (b).[728] Furthermore, the further aim of concentrating the contractual lawsuits in a single *forum* as pursued by (b) would be jeopardized, too.[729] Caution suggests that "according to the contract" should be read as nothing more than a decent hint that the characteristics of the contract should be taken into account.[730]

136 At least one should not hold direct recourse to either the European or the UNIDROIT Principles on Contract Law. They do not form part of EU law, nor have they ever been recognised in any way by the Community legislator. They do not have a binding force of law anywhere, and it would be way too progressive to introduce them into practice in the interpretation of the most important head of special jurisdiction. As a further hindrance it can be identified that they were not developed with an eye on procedural issues.[731] They do not constitute some kind of generally applicable rules or yardsticks in instances involving international trade, either. They call for contractual implementation and do not form part of any kind of *lex mercatoria* (if such notion was ever believed to exist at all). If parties want to introduce them into their contract they can do so. If they have not done so one should be very cautious to refer to them directly. Matters are different if they are taken into account *argumentandi causa* in a more general argument.[732] As to substance, both sets of principles would produce the rather result of a *forum actoris* favouring the seller insofar as they both[733] establish the seller's place of business as the place of performance for the obligation to pay.[734] Since the Principles have not been accepted in practice, where they are widely unknown and not even their mere existence forms part of general knowledge, it would be very impractical to let them form part of the *contractual* regime.

bb) Conflict between inference from the contract and later facts

137 Another issue might arise if the place of delivery or performance expressly or impliedly

---

verdrag naar verordening (2001), p. 31, 50 § 3-34; *Vlas*, NILR 2004, 451, 453; *Klemm*, Erfüllungsortvereinbarungen im Europäischen Zivilverfahrensrecht (2005) p. 83.

[725] See *Car Trim GmbH v. KeySafety Systems Srl*, (Case C-381/08) [2010] ECR I-1255, I-1285 paras. 56 *et seq.*; *Jonathan Harris*, (2001) 20 Civ. Just. Q. 218, 220; Note, D. 2001, 2592; *André Huet*, in: Mélanges en l'honneur de Paul Lagarde (2005), p. 417, 428; *Fawcett*, in: Fawcett/Harris/Bridge paras. 3.194-3.196.

[726] As advocated for e.g. by *Béraudo*, Clunet 128 (2001), 1033, 1045; *Rommelaere*, Rev. dr. comm. belge 2003, 103, 108.

[727] *André Huet*, in: Mélanges en l'honneur de Paul Lagarde (2005), p. 417, 428; see also *Leible*, EuZW 2011, 604, 605.

[728] *Fawcett*, in: Fawcett/Harris/Bridge para. 3.193.

[729] *Vlas*, NILR 2004, 451, 453.

[730] See *Audit*, Rec. des Cours 305 (2003), 9, 437.

[731] *Magnus*, IHR 2002, 45, 48.

[732] See Art. 7 note 150 (*Mankowski*).

[733] Art. 7:101 European Principles; Art. 6.1.6 UNIDROIT Principles.

[734] *Magnus*, IHR 2002, 45, 48.

provided for in the contract does not coincide with, and conform with, the factual place of delivery or performance. Should the latter prevail, or should one stick with the inference from the contract,[735] or should both places gain equal weight,[736] or should only the place of factual delivery matter[737] or should delivery at the "wrong" place be disregarded as not being "under the contract" with switching over to (1) (a)?[738] The sequence in (b) indicates that the first approach is the correct one.[739] The contract and its wording reign as long as the delivery or performance have not yet taken place,[740] not the least since there does not exist a feasible alternative (or, in a functional perspective, replacement). This situation is radically altered the very moment the factual developments take place.[741] A factual concept should place as much reliance on facts as possible.[742] The factual approach would lose its consistency if, in the case of a divergence between the terms of the contract and the facts, (b) should become inoperable and refuge were to be found in (a).[743]

However, this appears to open up some opportunities for the debtor if he intentionally **138** deviates from the contract and delivers (or performs) in another place than the place which can be implied from the contract as the place of performance. He gains both the opportunity and an unwelcome incentive to shift jurisdiction in his favour and to the creditor's detriment. But the picture would be incomplete if one did not take the massive counter-incentives into account: Delivering in the wrong place could make the debtor liable for damages according to the national law applicable. He would have to pay quite a high price, and in most instances too high a price, in exchange for a rather minor advantage. Simple sending the goods to the wrong place does not have consequences for jurisdiction under (b).[744] Additionally, the buyer might find himself in a position not to accept delivery in the non-contractual and thus wrong place, with the seller incurring additional expenses. Generally, the place of delivery can be shifted if the buyer voluntarily and without objections accepts delivery in a different place than originally agreed upon.[745] Parties can in any event avoid such ambiguities and calamities if they expressly stipulate for a certain place of performance since (b) gives like prevalence to such stipulation as (a) and a deviation can only be effected in mutual consent by both parties.

---

[735] Favoured by BG 15.7.2014 – 4A_113/2014 E 4.3; Trib. Padova EuLF 2006, II-16, 18; *Fawcett*, in: Fawcett/Harris/Bridge paras. 3.201 *et seq.*

[736] Tentatively favoured by *Gaudemet-Tallon* para. 199.

[737] Favoured by *Kropholler/von Hein* Art. 5 note 47; *Oberhammer*, in: Dasser/Oberhammer, Art. 5 LugÜ note 50.

[738] Favoured by *André Huet*, in: Mélanges en l'honneur de Paul Lagarde (2005), p. 417, 428.

[739] See also Rb. Utrecht NIPR 2003 Nr. 297 p. 455. Undecided Rapport *Potocki*, RCDIP 100 (2011), 139, 146 = DMF 2011, 231, 236. *Contra Vlas*, WPNR 6421 (2000), 745, 750; *Takahashi*, (2002) 27 Eur. L. Rev. 530, 535.

[740] *Kropholler/von Hein* Art. 5 note 47.

[741] *Mankowski*, TranspR 2008, 67, 71.

[742] See *Magnus*, IHR 2002, 45, 47.

[743] As advocated for by *Layton/Mercer* para. 15.048.

[744] *Eltzschig*, IPRax 2002, 491, 495; *Günter Hager/Bentele*, IPRax 2004, 73, 74; *Ulrich G. Schroeter*, UN-Kaufrecht und Europäisches Gemeinschaftsrecht (2005)§ 17 with note 39.

[745] *Kropholler/von Hein* Art. 5 note 47; *Magnus*, IHR 2002, 45, 47; *Leible*, in: Rauscher Art. 5 note 51; *Günter Hager/Bentele*, IPRax 2004, 73, 74; *Thorn*, IPRax 2004, 354, 356; *Fawcett*, in: Fawcett/Harris/Bridge para. 3.203.

Peter Mankowski   217

e) **Place of delivery of the goods**

139 At the outset, goods are delivered where they switch physical possession[746] and where the factual control passes onto the buyer (or his personnel)[747] so that he obtains actual power of disposal.[748] After-sale services like schooling the purchaser's staff or the permission to use technological components or related IP rights do not matter.[749] Any unforeseen further movement of the goods by the purchaser is irrelevant since it falls outside the execution of the sales transaction.[750] How the goods are processed once they have been handed over into the buyer's sphere is the buyer's business and none of the seller's business.[751] If defects later on are detected at a place where the goods are not discernible to be from the contract, this does not alter the place of performance which has been established prior to that detection.

140 This outset which keeps matters as simply and easily identifiable as possible,[752] perfectly matches a factual approach. It uses a factual criterion not recurring on legal connotations, like for instance, the passing of the risk.[753] The place of delivery thus need not be identical with the place where the risk passes from the seller to the buyer as a matter of the respective applicable law.[754] A simple hint to cif-contracts might serve as an illustration for this contention.[755] Neither should any conclusion be drawn from Art. 63 (1) Brussels I Regulation and the notion of *final* place of delivery contained therein.[756] Sometimes such conclusion is employed against stressing the place of the physical possession of the goods and in favour of emphasising the place where the seller exerted activities instead.[757] Placing importance on the latter place[758] is irreconcilable with the most basic understanding of delivery: "delivery"

---

[746] *Car Trim GmbH v. KeySafety Systems Srl,* (Case C-381/08) [2010] ECR I-1255, I-1286 para. 60; A-G *Mazák,* [2010] ECR I-1258, I-1266 para. 38; A-G *Kokott,* Opinion in Case C-87/10 of 3 March 2011, [2011] ECR I-4990 paras. 47, 50; OGH EuLF 2005, II-80, II-81; Cassaz. RDIPP 2010, 150, 151; BGH IHR 2010, 216, 217; OLG Hamm IHR 2006, 84, 86; OLG Köln IHR 2006, 86; OLG Köln IHR 2007, 164; OLG Oldenburg IHR 2008, 112, 114; OLG Karlsruhe OLGR Karlsruhe 2009, 485; Rb. 's-Hertogenbosch NIPR 2005 Nr. 61 p. 102; Trib. Rovereto EuLF 2005, II-46; Trib. Treviso Diritti 4/2006, 41 with note *Barel*; *Günter Hager/Bentele,* IPRax 2004, 73, 74–77; *Franzina,* La giurisdizione in materia contrattuale (2006) p. 384; *Franzina,* NGCC 2007 I 537, 539; see also TGI Périgueux EuLF 2006, II-20, II-21. See also *Dallafior/Götz-Staehelin,* SJZ 2008, 105, 107 (but with an irritating reference to the *lex causae*).

[747] OLG Köln IHR 2006, 86; *Piltz,* IHR 2006, 53, 56 *et seq.*; *Merlin,* Riv. dir. proc. 2007, 1305, 1315; *Mankowski,* IHR 2009, 46, 52; *Notdurfter/Petruzzino,* Contratto e impresa/Europa 2011, 223, 229; *Hofmann/Kunz,* in: Basler Kommentar, Art. 5 note 238.

[748] A-G *Kokott,* Opinion in Case C-87/10 of 3 March 2011, [2011] ECR I-4990 para. 47; Trib. Sant'Angelo dei Lombardi Giur. It. 2014, 1123.

[749] Tentatively *contra Franzina,* RDIPP 2010, 655, 662.

[750] A-G *Kokott,* Opinion in Case C-87/10 of 3 March 2011, [2011] ECR I-4990 para. 52.

[751] See A-G *Kokott,* Opinion in Case C-87/10 of 3 March 2011, [2011] ECR I-4990 para. 52.

[752] A-G *Mazák,* [2010] ECR I-1258, I-1266 paras. 39 *et seq.*

[753] See only Rb. Kh. Hasselt R.W. 2007–2008, 1047, 1049; *Rutten,* R.W. 2002–2003, 666, 668; *Merlin,* Riv. dir. proc. 2007, 1305, 1312 and in more detail Art. 5 note 109a (*Mankowski*).

[754] *Rutten,* R.W. 2002–2003, 666, 668; *Mankowski,* IHR 2009, 46, 52; *Markus,* AJP 2010, 971, 979 *et seq.*

[755] *Mankowski,* IHR 2009, 46, 52.

[756] A-G *Kokott,* Opinion in Case C-87/10 of 3 March 2011, [2011] ECR I-4990 para. 55; *Hau,* JZ 2008, 974, 977.

[757] *Piltz,* IHR 2006, 53, 56.

relates to the goods as such and it is absolutely vital and essential that the buyer's sphere is involved.[759] Activities merely in the seller's sphere might influence the passing of the risk but do not automatically touch the buyer's sphere. Else the seller would find himself in too strong a position to act strategically and opportunistically since his potential for manipulating internally and without control would be enhanced.

In particular it would appear unwise to hold recourse to the transfer of property.[760] Insofar   **141** the legal systems of the Member States, let alone of other possibly applicable laws, differ too wildly. One would have to deal with a variety of laws stretching from transfer by consensus already in the contract (thus before the goods were afflicted physically) to the delayed transfer flowing from the German *Eigentumsvorbehalt*.

Likewise, the passing of risks does not matter for it once again would have to be determined   **142** by the applicable substantive law with possibly differing concepts amongst various laws. Any reference to the passing of the risk[761] would put the applicable substantive law at the core of the matter since such passing could not be determined autonomously according to yardsticks from (b) itself, and such reference to substantive law (with an immense variety of possible answers to an intricate question[762]) would contravene both the genesis and the purpose of (b)[763] – not to mention that each and every Incoterm then would constitute an agreement on the place of performance.[764] Actual power of disposal on the buyer's side matters,[765] though, which is not to be equated with passing of the risk as a genuine legal and normative notion.

Where goods are delivered effectively in fact[766] and are transferred from the seller's sphere   **143** into the buyer's sphere can be ascertained by proving the facts in most instances. The ordinary case does not inflict major difficulties: Goods pass into a warehouse or into the hands of a carrier designated by the buyer. The goods are physically transferred to the

---

[758] As OLG Düsseldorf IHR 2004, 108, 110; Rb. Maastricht November 11, 2003; Rb. Kh. Kortrijk December 4, 2003; *Bajons*, in: FS Reinhold Geimer (2002), p. 15, 52; *Gsell*, IPRax 2002, 484, 491; *Leible*, in: Rauscher Art. 5 note 53; *Kienle*, IPRax 2005, 113, 116; *Piltz*, IHR 2006, 53, 56 generally do.

[759] *Wipping*, Der europäische Gerichtsstand des Erfüllungsortes – Art. 5 Nr. 1 EuGVVO (2008) p. 185; *Mankowski*, IHR 2009, 46, 53; see also OLG Düsseldorf RIW 2006, 632, 634; LG Trier IHR 2004, 115, 116.

[760] *Mankowski*, IHR 2009, 46, 52.

[761] Favouring such approach *Wipping*, Der europäische Gerichtsstand des Erfüllungsortes – Art. 5 Nr. 1 EuGVVO (2008) p. 196; *Castellanos Ruiz*, in: Calvo Caravaca/Areal Ludeña (dir.), Cuestiones actuales del derecho mercantil internacional (Madrid 2005), p. 105, 137–140; see also *Scottish & Newcastle International Ltd. v. Othon Ghalanos Ltd.* [2008] UKHL 11 [48] *et seq.*, [2008] I.L.Pr. 414, [2008] 1 Lloyd's Rep. 462 (H.L., per Lord Mance); *Scottish & Newcastle International Ltd. v. Othon Ghalanos Ltd.* [2007] EWCA Civ 1750 [48], [2007] 1 All ER (Comm) 1027 (C.A., per Rix L.J.); *Franzina*, RDIPP 2010, 655, 671.

[762] Comparative survey by *Tanja Hoffmann/Florian Linder*, JBl 2008, 623.

[763] OGH EuLF 2005, II-80, II-81; *Mankowski*, IHR 2009, 46, 51; see also *Gsell*, IPRax 2002, 484, 486 *et seq.*

[764] See *Magnus*, IHR 2002, 45, 48, 52; *Castellanos Ruiz*, in: Calvo Caravaca/Areal Ludeña (dir.), Cuestiones actuales del derecho mercantil internacional (Madrid 2005), p. 105, 134; *Rauscher*, in: FS Andreas Heldrich (2005), p. 933, 942 *et seq.*; *Hare/Hinks*, [2008] LMCLQ 353, 364; *Mankowski*, IHR 2009, 46, 51.

[765] Arts. 7:101 (1) (b) PECL; 6.1.6 (1) (b) UNIDROIT Principles; III 2:101 DCFR

[766] See OGH EuLF 2005, II-80, II-81; Rb. Kh. Hasselt R.W. 2004–2005, 833, 834; Trib. Padova, sez. Este RDIPP 2007, 147, 153 and also *Bernard Audit*, Rec. des Cours 305 (2003), 9, 439.

---

purchaser at their final destination.[767] Or the purchaser collects the goods in person at the seller's place.[768] Once physical transfer has been effectuated in most instances no relevant doubts remain.[769] Prior to that, at least a certain degree of predictability can be awarded.[770]

144 A "final destination" so defined[771] is the final destination in fact (namely the end of physical transportation by the seller) and not a previous hand-off to the first carrier only if that carrier is not designated by the buyer but by the seller.[772] If the seller has designated and hired the carrier the matter is straightforward: The truck arrives and delivers there at the end of its journey.[773] In ordinary cases the solution is painfully simple and thus has the big advantage of almost unbeatable simplicity. No serious problems arise in the event of optional or range agreements between the parties calling for the final destination to be nominated at a time when the goods are already shipped:[774] If the buyer opts for a certain destination and the goods are delivered there accordingly, this destination is the place of delivery.[775] Where the contract calls for delivery to alternative places and delivery ultimately fails at either place each place where delivery should have been effectuated, should suffice.[776] A consented delivery address matters.[777] If a conflict arises between the delivery address mentioned in invoices or other documents and the place where delivery was indeed effectuated the latter should prevail[778] but the *onus* to prove such conflict will be on the party alleging the delivery address on the face of the invoice to be incorrect.

145 An additional advantage is the appropriateness of the solution wherever defects in the goods are the core issue of the ensuing lawsuits[779] if the possibly defective goods are at the final destination and ready for inspection there.[780] This result does not conflict with the freedom

---

[767] *Car Trim GmbH v. KeySafety Systems Srl*, (Case C-381/08) [2010] ECR I-1255, I-1286 para. 60; Cassaz. RDIPP 2010, 150; Trib. Trapani Giur. mer. 2011, 1599, 1602; *Wittwer*, ZEuP 2011, 636, 639 *et seq.*; *Lajolo/ Stefan Rossi*, Giur. mer. 2011, 1603, 1609.

[768] A-G *Kokott*, Opinion in Case C-87/10 of 3 March 2011, [2011] ECR I-4990 para. 53.

[769] Commission Proposal COM (1999) 348 final p. 15; *Hager/Bentele*, IPRax 2004, 73, 74; *Ferrari*, IPRax 2007, 61, 66; *Geimer/Schütze*, Art. 5 note 86. But cf. *Markus*, AJP 2010, 971, 978; *Matthias Lehmann/ Duczek*, IPRax 2011, 41, 44; *Hofmann/Kunz*, in: Basler Kommentar, Art. 5 notes 262 *et seq.*

[770] More appraisive *Car Trim GmbH v. KeySafety Systems Srl*, (Case C-381/08) [2010] ECR I-1255, I-1286 para. 61.

[771] Doubting the wisdom of this criterion *Notdurfter/Petruzzino*, Contratto e impresa/Europa 2011, 223, 230.

[772] OGH EuLF 2005, II-80, II-81; OLG Stuttgart IPRax 2009, 64, 67; *Hau*, JZ 2008, 974, 975 *et seq.*; *Simotta*, in: Fasching/Konecny, Art. 5 note 184; *Rauscher*, NJW 2010, 2251, 2252. *Contra* e.g. OLG München IPRax 2009, 69, 70; *Bajons*, in: FS Reinhold Geimer (2002), p. 15, 64; *Junker*, RIW 2002, 569, 572; *Piltz*, NJW 2007, 1801, 1802; *Piltz*, IHR 2008, 168.

[773] Rb. Maastricht, sector kanton, locatie Heerlen NIPR 2005 Nr. 169 p. 234.

[774] Tentatively *contra Kubis*, ZEuP 2001, 737, 750.

[775] *Layton/Mercer* para. 15.048; *Fawcett*, in: Fawcett/Harris/Bridge para. 3.220; see also Rb. Rotterdam NIPR 2008 Nr. 133 p. 221.

[776] Tentatively *contra Fawcett*, in: Fawcett/Harris/Bridge para. 3.212.

[777] Hof 's-Gravenhage S&S 2007 Nr. 45 p. 229.

[778] Tentatively *contra* Rb. Rotterdam NIPR 2005 Nr. 272 p. 368.

[779] *Kropholler/von Hinden*, in: GS Alexander Lüderitz (2000), p. 401, 407; *Günter Hager/Bentele*, IPRax 2004, 73, 76.

of movement of goods.[781] It avoids that the seller gains the dreaded *forum actoris* for claims to pay.[782] The price for this is that the buyer in most instances[783] gains a rather favourable *forum actoris* if the goods are delivered to his place.[784] (1) (b) 1st indent insofar degenerates to a certain extend to "warranty jurisdiction",[785] rather complicated by the scenario that the court will have to apply the seller's law in most instances.[786] "Buyer's forum" plus "seller's law" is alleged to be harlequin style and in its conjoined effect to produce a mismatch.[787] This is a serious drawback enhancing the costs of litigation that the buyer's forum might be compelled to apply the seller's law by virtue of either parties' choice of law or Art. 4 (1) (a) Rome I Regulation.[788] Furthermore, the final destination is rather unrelated to the core issue if the condition of the goods when received by the first carrier is in dispute.[789]

Yet under the ordinary fob- or cif-contract the seller can not complain about unfairness if he **146** himself agreed to transport the goods to the buyer which he was not forced to do from the outset. The old adage of *volunti non fit iniuria* lurks around the corner. Of course, the backing by the goods being at the final destination is not given either if no delivery has taken place at all[790] or where the buyer never has had actual possession of the goods since he had re-sold them to a third party under a so-called *Streckengeschäft*[791] or where the goods have already been processed in some manufacturing process or consumed.[792] Even typisation[793] might find its limits there.[794] In the event of delivery to the original purchaser's customer under a *Streckengeschäft* or of direct delivery to any plant or store designated by the buyer, the place of such factual delivery should be the relevant one.[795] A solution which is simple in

---

[780] See *Car Trim GmbH v. KeySafety Systems Srl*, (Case C-381/08) [2010] ECR I-1255, I-1286 para. 61; *Hau*, IPRax 2009, 44, 45.

[781] *Günter Hager/Bentele*, IPRax 2004, 73, 77.

[782] *Kropholler/von Hein* Art. 5 note 49.

[783] Not in all for factual delivery can take place at other places than the buyer's seat, for instance at building sites desiganted by the buyer; OLG Karlsruhe IPRspr. 2009 Nr. 169 p. 443.

[784] *Schack*, ZEuP 1998, 931, 932 *et seq.*; *Kubis*, ZEuP 2001, 737, 749 *et seq.*; *Piltz*, NJW 2010, 1061, 1062.

[785] *Haas/Oliver Vogel*, NZG 2011, 766, 769.

[786] *Haas/Oliver Vogel*, NZG 2011, 766, 770.

[787] *Crawford/Carruthers*, (2014) 63 ICLQ 1, 9.

[788] *Micha*, EuLF 2009, I-6, I-7 *et seq.*

[789] *Gsell*, ZEuP 2011, 669, 680.

[790] *Leible*, EuZW 2010, 303, 305; *Leible*, in: FS Ulrich Spellenberg (2010), p. 451, 463; *Leible*, in: Rauscher, Art. 5 note 53c; *Henri Storme*, R.W. 2009–2010, 409, 414.

[791] *Gsell*, IPRax 2002, 484, 489; *Wipping*, Der europäische Gerichtsstand des Erfüllungsortes – Art. 5 Nr. 1 EuGVVO (2008) p. 198; *Mankowski*, EWiR Art. 5 EuGVVO 1/10, 287, 288; *Mittmann*, IHR 2010, 146, 147; *Mittmann*, D. 2010, 834, 835; see also *Henri Storme*, R.W. 2009–2010, 409, 414.

[792] *Mankowski*, IHR 2009, 46, 55; *Mankowski*, EWiR Art. 5 EuGVVO 1/10, 287, 288.

[793] On which ground *Hau*, JZ 2008, 974, 978; *Hau*, IPRax 2009, 44, 46 argues.

[794] *Leible*, in: FS Ulrich Spellenberg (2010), p. 451, 463; *Leible*, in: Rauscher, Art. 5 note 53c; see also OLG München IPRax 2009, 69, 70.

[795] OGH IHR 2006, 122, 124; *Ignatova*, Art. 5 Nr. 1 EuGVVO – Chancen und Perspektiven der Reform des Gerichtsstands am Erfüllungsort (2005) p. 234; *Wipping*, Der europäische Gerichtsstand des Erfüllungsortes – Art. 5 Nr. 1 EuGVVO (2008) pp. 197 *et seq.*; *Mankowski*, IHR 2009, 46, 54.

---

its first step must not become mechanical and rigid, and thus allow to adaption to specific cases.[796]

147 If the buyer has designated the carrier and if the carrier is acting on the buyers behalf the actual power of disposal over the goods passes to the buyer in the moment the goods are handed over to this carrier.[797] The purchaser is believed to control such carrier for he is responsible for persons he has contracted in.[798] Hence, it might be necessary to identify who, seller or buyer, has contracted with the carrier, even if this requires to employ the applicable law of agency.[799] Merely giving instructions might not suffice for this can be on special invitation by the true contracting party. The ECJ has not addressed this constellation and has not circumscribed "final" conclusively yet.[800]

148 Yet on a second level, the question arises as to whether constructive delivery could suffice[801] since factual delivery cannot solve the instances where delivery has not taken place whatsoever[802] (be it that goods have never been produced or have never even commenced their journey to the buyer, be it that the goods are perished during the carriage, be it that the goods were not accepted by the buyer and the buyer rejected hand-over). The intricate problem introduced by this question reads as to whether legal connotations should creep in by the backdoor and how to determine the law governing aspects of constructive delivery. If constructive delivery was allowed in, legal questions would arise inevitably. On the other hand the reference to accord with the contract already raises like questions.[803] The answer to the present question must be consistent with the answer previously given in the context akin. On the first level, if the parties for instance agreed that delivery should be deemed perfected when the seller transfers possession to the first carrier, this agreements prevails, and delivery is identical with the handover to the first carrier.[804] Delivery takes place where upon the terms consented by the parties the seller must present the goods in order to fulfil his obligations under the contract.[805] What suits the parties should be enforced.[806]

149 Even on a second level, one should nevertheless not switch back to a pure normative

---

[796] See *Franzina*, RDIPP 2010, 655, 676.

[797] Cass. RDIPP 2007, 1105, 1107 = Giust. civ. 2007 I 1624, 1625. For different reasons to the same result *Haas/Oliver Vogel*, NZG 2011, 766, 770.

[798] See OLG Köln IHR 2006, 86; OLG Hamm OLGR Hamm 2006, 327, 330; OLG Köln IHR 2007, 164, 166; OLG Oldenburg IHR 2008, 113, 118; Trib. Verona RDIPP 2007, 367, 369; *Piltz*, IHR 2006, 53, 56 *et seq.*

[799] *Hare/Hinks*, [2008] LMCLQ 353, 361; *Mankowski*, IHR 2009, 46, 52; see also *Scottish & Newcastle International Ltd. v. Othon Ghalanos Ltd.* [2008] UKHL 11 [34], [2008] I.L.Pr. 414, [2008] 1 Lloyd's Rep. 462 (H.L., per Lord *Mance*).

[800] A-G *Kokott*, Opinion in Case C-87/10 of 3 March 2011, [2011] ECR I-4990 para. 56 (even calling for abandoning "final" in para. 57); *Mankowski*, EWiR Art. 5 EuGVVO 3/11, 497, 498.

[801] *Fawcett*, in: Fawcett/Harris/Bridge para. 3.218.

[802] *Mankowski*, EWiR Art. 5 EuGVVO 1/10, 287, 288; *Kruisinga*, NTHR 2011, 1, 8; *Vlek*, in: Der IPR in de spiegel van Paul Vlas (2012), p. 277, 283.

[803] *Supra* Art. 5 notes 101–103 (*Mankowski*).

[804] *Magnus*, IHR 2002, 45, 47.

[805] OGH ÖJZ 2004, 140 = JBl 2004, 186, 187; *Ignatova*, Art. 5 Nr. 1 EuGVVO – Chancen und Perspektiven der Reform des Gerichtsstands am Erfüllungsort (2005) pp. 234–237.

[806] *Fawcett*, in: Fawcett/Harris/Bridge para. 3.218.

approach and even less to the *Tessili*-doctrine for a second option where actual delivery has not taken place,[807] as this would implement a major split into a uniform concept in clear contradiction to the *travaux préparatoires*. Any place of delivery envisaged in the contract should answer the question.[808] Even worse is a combination of (b) and *Tessili*[809] since (b) was designed and introduced as a genuine anti-*Tessili*-device.[810] The same applies to any normative combination of (b) and CISG as *lex causae*[811] or to any attempt to circle back to (a) *via* (c) in the event that the parties have not agreed upon any place of delivery in particular.[812] That the parties can agree so, is a prejudicious option and (b) only steps in as a gap-filler if they have not exercised this option.

A completely different idea is to employ Art. 31 CISG as an interpretatory means.[813] Then **150** this rule would not be applied in the strict sense and would not come into operation as any kind of *lex causae*, but as an auxiliary instrument only. These are two completely distinct and different notions.[814] Arts. 7:101 (1) PECL; 6.1.6 (1) UNIDROIT Principles; III 2:101 DCFR might also be possible candidates yet are only soft law or, in the case of the DCFR, a

---

[807] As proposed by *Rauscher*, in: FS Andreas Heldrich (2005), p. 933, 944; *André Huet*, in: Mélanges en l'honneur de Paul Lagarde (2005), p. 417, 429; *Henri Storme*, R.W. 2009–2010, 409, 416 and at least ventilated by *Droz/Gaudemet-Tallon*, RCDIP 90 (2001), 601, 635.

[808] *Kienle*, IPRax 2005, 113, 115.

[809] Uncunningly implemented by Rb. Almelo NIPR 2003 Nr. 206 p. 310; *Brenn* para. 71; see also OGH RdW 2004/184.

[810] *Supra* Art. 5 note 96 (*Mankowski*).

[811] Hof van Cass. R.W. 2009–2010, 408, 409; Trib. Rovereto RDIPP 2005, 162, 168 = Giur. it. 2005, 1005 note *Poggio* = EuLF 2005, II-46, II-47. See also *Kaster-Müller*, EuLF 2005, II-47, II-48. But *contra* Trib. Padova, sez. Este RDIPP 2007, 147, 153 (applying Art. 31 CISG); Trib. Padova EuLF 2006 II-16; Trib. Reggio Emilia EuLF 2005, II-177.

[812] Another time uncunningly presented by Rb. Almelo NIPR 2003 Nr. 206 p. 310; Rb. Arnhem NIPR 2003 Nr. 289 p. 445 and also by BGH RIW 2005, 776, 777 *et seq.* See in more detail *infra* Art. 5 note 143 (*Mankowski*).

[813] Cassaz. Giust. civ. 2007 I 1393 with note *Ferrari* = NGCC 2007 I 534 with note *Franzina* = RDIPP 2007, 759 = Riv. dir. proc. 2007, 1303 with note *Merlin* = ZEuP 2008, 165 note *Thomas Rüfner*; Cassaz. RDIPP 2007, 1105; Cassaz. RDIPP 2008, 221; Cassaz. RDIPP 2008, 505, 510; Cassaz. RDIPP 2008, 511, 515 *et seq.*; Trib. Padova, sez. distaccata di Este RDIPP 2007, 147, 153 *et seq.*; *Ragno*, Giur. mer. 2006, 1413; *Ragno*, Convenzione di Vienna e Diritto europeo (2008) pp. 226–231; *Ferrari*, RDAI 2007, 83; *Ferrari*, IPRax 2007, 61; *Ferrari*, Giust. civ. 2007 I 1397, 1411; *Salerno* p. 142; *Lein*, in: Bonomi/Cashin Ritaine/Romano (dir.), La Convention de Lugano – passé, présent et devenir (Zürich 2007), p. 41, 55–57; *Tuo*, Dir. mar. 109 (2007), 1080, 1099; *Wipping*, Der europäische Gerichtsstand des Erfüllungsortes – Art. 5 Nr. 1 EuGVVO (2008) pp. 196 *et seq.*; *Mankowski*, IHR 2009, 46, 59 *et seq.*; *Perrella*, Dir. mar. 2010, 527, 532; *Mittmann*, IHR 2010, 146, 149; *Mittmann*, D. 2010, 834, 837; *Di Blase*, Europa e dir. priv. 2011, 459, 476; *Haas/Oliver Vogel*, NZG 2011, 766, 770; see also Cassaz. RDIPP 2010, 150, 151 = Riv. dir. proc. 2010, 940 with critical with note *d'Adamo*; Trib. Trapani Giur. mer. 2011, 1599, 1601. *Contra Thomas Rüfner*, ZEuP 2008, 165, 175 *et seq.*; *de Franceschi*, Contratto e impresa/Europa 2008, 637, 655 *et seq.* The difference between application and use as a source of inspiration appears to be not recognised by *Henri Storme*, R.W. 2009–2010, 409, 415.

[814] See only *Ferrari*, Giust. civ. 2007 I 1397, 1411; *Tuo*, Dir. mar. 109 (2007), 1080, 1099; *Lein*, in: Bonomi/Cashin Ritaine/Romano (dir.), La Convention de Lugano – passé, présent et devenir (Zürich 2007), p. 41, 55; *Mankowski*, IHR 2009, 46, 55 and also Cassaz. RDIPP 2008, 511, 515.

---

preliminary cause.[815] Once a proper European instrument has been implemented, be it optional or not, but nevertheless a codification binding upon the Member States, such instrument would be the first address to resort to for interpretatory help.[816] Nonetheless, the ECJ has not endorsed any approach leading back to such indirect re-normativisation in *Car Trim*.[817], [818] But that should not be taken as a conclusive negative answer,[819] the more so since even *Car Trim* could not avoid some normative elements creeping in by the backdoor if delivery has not taken place in fact.[820] A truly factual approach reaches its limits faster than it would be desirable.[821] At least one should stay open-minded enough to keep an opportunity to reduce if not bridge the gap between (1) (a) and (1) (b).[822] Any general approach based on normative yardsticks would also overcome the developing sub-differentiation[823] between (1) (a) and (1) (b) or even within (1) (b).

f) Place where a service is rendered

151 Ideally, a service is rendered where the service provider performs the necessary activities and where the customer receives the respective results. If those places to do not coincide or, worse, are located in different countries a decision has to be made as to whether the activity or the result should become the dominating factor. On the one hand we have the activity and the availability of the result, on the other hand we have the mere extraction of the result. Drawing an analogy to the delivery of goods would slightly favour the completion of the service, i.e. the result passing into the customer's sphere. Playing with words would place reliance and emphasis on the wording that the services have to be "provided", as this wording does not employ "performed". "Performed" could point a little further towards the activity, whereas "provided" brings the customer's perspective into the picture more prominently. Providing services gives an eye to the customer receiving the services.[824] The natural reflection could point to the provider's place at least insofar as research or teaching efforts are at stake.[825] If the service is for designing another service and advising upon it, the relevant service should be where the sweat of the brow is invested,[826] not where its result is finally communicated to the customers.[827]

---

[815] *Gsell*, IPRax 2002, 484, 491; *de Franceschi*, Contratto e impresa/Europa 2008, 637, 653 *et seq.*; *Mankowski*, IHR 2009, 46, 58; *Axel Metzger*, IPRax 2010, 420, 423; *Franzina*, RDIPP 2010, 655, 681 *et seq.*; *Di Blase*, Europa e dir. priv. 2011, 459, 476.

[816] *Mankowski*, IHR 2009, 46, 58 *et seq.*

[817] *Car Trim GmbH v. KeySafety Systems Srl*, (Case C-381/08) [2010] ECR I-1255.

[818] *Mankowski*, EWiR Art. 5 EuGVVO 1/10, 287, 288.

[819] *Mankowski*, IHR 2009, 46, 59. To the opposite avail *Perrella*, Dir. mar. 2010, 527, 533 *et seq.*; see also Cassaz. Dir. mar. 2010, 527.

[820] *Markus*, AJP 2010, 971, 982.

[821] See in detail *Markus*, Tendenzen beim materiellrechtlichen Vertragserfüllungsort im internationalen Zivilverfahrensrecht (Basel 2009) pp. 174–183 and also *McGuire*, Yb. PIL 11 (2009), 453, 464.

[822] *Leible*, in: FS Ulrich Spellenberg (2010), p. 451, 463 *et seq.*; *Leible*, in: Rauscher, Art. 5 note 53d.

[823] Outlined by *Markus*, AJP 2010, 971, 983, 984.

[824] *Mankowski*, in: Ruth Nielsen/Sandfeld Jacobsen/Trzaskowski (eds.), EU Electronic Commerce Law (2004), p. 125, 130. See also *van der Hof*, Internationale on-line overeenkomsten (2002) p. 58.

[825] *Béraudo*, Clunet 128 (2001), 1033, 1047; *Mankowski*, in: Ruth Nielsen/Sandfeld Jacobsen/Trzaskowski (eds.), EU Electronic Commerce Law (2004), p. 125, 130; *Kuipers*, NIPR 2010, 622, 624.

[826] *Attal*, Rev. jur. comm. 2008, 29, 32 *et seq.*

[827] *Contra* Cass. Bull. civ. 2007 I n° 352 p. 310.

Particularly under short term service contracts the service can be entirely rendered in an- **152**
other country than the country where the service provider has his place of business. If for
example an expert is hired to inspect goods stored in another country, flies there, reports or
gives advice there, the service is rendered in the country where the goods are inspected.[828]
Even some period of preparation spent in the home country does not militate against this
result.[829] The case might be different if the expert performs an inspection locally but writes
and completes his report only after his return home. The service required is not the mere
inspection as such, but also, if not dominantly, the report on the quality of the goods. In the
latter case the service ordinarily should be deemed as rendered at the expert's place of
business with the inspection considered as being a vital act, but grounded in preparation.

Managers and board members render their services to their respective companies at the **153**
company's *siége réel*,[830] not at its statutory seat neither at both of them.[831] There should not
be an analogy to Art. 24 (2) cl. 2 and recourse to the notion of seat as developed in the PIL of
the forum.

g) Particular situations

aa) Delivery of goods in instalments
Sales contracts can provide for the goods to be delivered in instalments. If all instalments are **154**
to be delivered and are in fact delivered at the same place (b) does not give rise to any
particular problem as only one single place of delivery of the goods exists. This is the normal
situation of a standing relationship between an exporter and an importer in which the
importer takes delivery in a regular manner, with reduced costs due to the implementation
of standardisation procedures. Nor does a problem arise if every instalment is related to a
single and separate contract.[832]

Yet instalments might be scheduled to be delivered at different places. Imagine either a seller **155**
delivering from different warehouses, or conversely a buyer asking for delivery to different
plants. Another time for the purposes of applying (b) two sub-constellations must be distinguished. The first poses a lesser problem, or in fact no problem at all, at the level of
international jurisdiction: The places where the instalments are to be delivered, are located
in the same state. Then only the only problem is the identification of the *place* and thus
ascertaining local, not international jurisdiction. The possible solutions are the same as in
the second sub-formation.

The latter sub-formation is concerned with the rather exceptional case that delivery of **156**
instalments takes place in different states, e.g. the first instalment at Hamburg, the second
at Rotterdam etc. A variety of solutions can be sketched: (1) Every place of delivery establishes a place of performance for the entire contract even if only a single instalment was
delivered there. (2) The single place of delivery establishes a place of performance only with

---

[828] See OLG Frankfurt RIW 2004, 864.
[829] OLG Frankfurt RIW 2004, 864.
[830] *Matthias Lehmann*, GmbHR 2005, 978, 981; *Mock*, RabelsZ 72 (2008), 264, 286; *Arenas García*, FS Klaus
J. Hopt (2010), 321, 326–327.
[831] *Contra Johannes Weber*, IPRax 2013, 69, 73.
[832] *Fawcett*, in: Fawcett/Harris/Bridge para. 3.211.

regard to the respective instalment.[833] Intellectually the contract must be sliced and compartmentalised into parts belonging to the single instalments. (3) A centre of gravity needs to be identified.[834] The principal place of delivery becomes the protagonist and dominates the other ones into oblivion. This is the solution preferred by the ECJ in *Color Drack*.[835] (4) A place of performance can not be identified at all and (1) in its entirety becomes inoperable.[836] (5) Since (b) is not operable one has to fall back on (a) via (c).[837] (6) An auxiliary presumption must be developed, for instance instrumentalising the parties' places of business and more specifically falling into line with Art. 4 (1) (a) Rome I Regulation.[838]

157 Of the possible solutions the first overly favours the plaintiff[839] and dramatically increases the risk of irreconcilable judgments[840] whereas the fourth goes to the other extreme and lets the pendulum swing entirely in the defendant's favour depriving the plaintiff of the advantage of special jurisdiction. Nevertheless the fourth solution can draw some support from the judgment of the ECJ in *Besix*.[841] But *Besix*[842] should not form part of the solution or its reasoning since *Besix* should be regarded as fundamentally misconceived. *Besix* decrees that an obligation to refrain from certain behaviour in a majority of countries does not have any place of performance at all.[843] This case now would fall under (b) since the contract in question could not be characterised as one for the sale of goods or for performing services, but the judgment was decided in a way consistent with the approach prevailing under (b).[844] Even if that could be possibly set aside or else overcome,[845] its reasoning ought to be distinguished from cases concerning the delivery of goods in instalments internationally

---

[833]   *Kropholler/von Hein*, Art. 5 note 50b.

[834]   *Magnus*, IHR 2002, 45, 49; *Takahashi*, (2002) 27 Eur. L. Rev. 530, 539; *Leible*, in: Rauscher, Europäisches Zivilprozessrecht (2nd ed. 2006) Art. 5 note 55.

[835]   *Color Drack GmbH v. Lexx International Vertriebs GmbH*, Case C-386/05 [2007] ECR I-3699, I-3737 para. 40; following this e.g. LG Baden-Baden IPRspr. 2009 Nr. 182 p. 476; Trib. Novara RDIPP 2013, 171, 175.

[836]   Subsidiarily *Magnus*, IHR 2002, 45, 49.

[837]   E.g. *Marie-Élodie Ancel*, RCDIP 90 (2001), 158, 160.

[838]   *Leible*, in: Rauscher, Art. 5 note 55d.

[839]   A-G *Bot*, [2007] ECR I-3702, I-3725 para. 127; *Takahashi*, (2002) 27 Eur. L. Rev. 530, 538.

[840]   See *Besix SA v. Wasserreinigungsbau Alfred Kretzschmar GmbH & Co. KG (WABAG) and Planungs- und Forschungsgesellschaft Dipl. Ing. W. Kretzschmar GmbH & Co. KG (Plafog)*, (Case C-256/00) [2002] ECR I-1699, I-1727 para. 28.

[841]   See *Leible*, in: Rauscher, Art. 5 note 55 and also *Besix SA v. Wasserreinigungsbau Alfred Kretzschmar GmbH & Co. KG (WABAG) and Planungs- und Forschungsgesellschaft Dipl. Ing. W. Kretzschmar GmbH & Co. KG (Plafog)*, (Case C-256/00) [2002] ECR I-1699, I-1728 para. 32 *verbatim*.

[842]   *Besix SA v. Wasserreinigungsbau Alfred Kretzschmar GmbH & Co. KG (WABAG) and Planungs- und Forschungsgesellschaft Dipl. Ing. W. Kretzschmar GmbH & Co. KG (Plafog)*, (Case C-256/00) [2002] ECR I-1699, I-1728, I-1733 paras. 34, 55.

[843]   *Besix SA v. Wasserreinigungsbau Alfred Kretzschmar GmbH & Co. KG (WABAG) and Planungs- und Forschungsgesellschaft Dipl. Ing. W. Kretzschmar GmbH & Co. KG (Plafog)*, (Case C-256/00) [2002] ECR I-1699, I-1733 para. 55; followed by Rb. 's-Hertogenbosch NIPR 2005 Nr. 169 p. 234.

[844]   *Mankowski*, EWiR Art. 5 EuGVÜ 1/02, 519; *Hess*, IPRax 2002, 376; see also *Carballo Piñeiro*, La Ley 5534 (2002), 1; *Carballo Piñeiro*, REDI 2002, 372, 377 *et seq.*; *Hau*, ZZP Int. 7 (2002), 214, 216; *Layton/Mercer* para. 15.028.

[845]   Not withstanding that even the *praemissio* in *Besix* that performance should have taken place everywhere

spread.[846] Whilst with regard to obligations to refrain from something one could randomly to localise them in any way, the same can not possibly be said of obligations to deliver.[847] The fourth solution generates rather insurmountable problems by multiplying the possible number of jurisdictions and, in particular, enhances the danger of conflicting judgments.[848] To avoid conflicting judgments is one of the main goals of the entire Brussels I*bis*-system as illustrated by Arts. 29; 45 (1) (c). Accordingly, regard should be paid to it when deciding between the solutions.

The second solution, i.e. compartmentalising the contract, bears some difficulties but is **158** generally feasible. E.g. Art. 73 CISG reflects such compartmentalisation with a restriction to the instalment in question; hence, compartmentalising could be regarded as a solution with some backing in sales law.[849] In support of the respective contention one could also look at the mosaic principle[850] as it was developed by the ECJ in *Shevill* for torts with regard to the place where the material damage was sustained, under Art. 7 (2).[851] On the other hand, it could amount to an onslaught of the structure of the contract if one turns to the obligation to pay.[852] Yet in most instances it would be possible to affiliate portions of the price with the single instalments. Nevertheless, problems would arise if the seller claims the price for more than one instalment.[853] On a more general level, it appears to part with a unitary approach as should be pursued under (1) (b).[854]

Looking for a centre of gravity as the ECJ proposes[855] is generally in line with the most **159** fundamental ideas of PIL, namely centralization an the search for a unitary forum.[856] Beyond that, looking for a centre of gravity spares any recourse to *lex causae* and substantive law whilst it employs (allegedly) economic criteria.[857] Furthermore, it is very much in line with the concentrating effect which Art. 7 (1) (b) is intended to exert as contrasted to Art. 5 (1) Brussels Convention.[858] Searching for a single centre of gravity would certainly accord with

---

and worldwide was misapprehended since the obligation in question only concerned the Benelux-countries; *Verlinden*, 8 Col. J. Eur. L. 493, 496 *et seq.* (2002).

[846] A-G *Bot*, [2007] ECR I-3702, I-3723 para. 115; *de Franceschi*, Contratto e impresa/Europa 2008, 637, 667 *et seq.* Apparently *contra Fawcett*, in: Fawcett/Harris/Bridge para. 3.207.

[847] *Simotta*, in: Fasching/Konecny, Art. 5 note 197.

[848] *Leible*, in: Rauscher, Art. 5 note 55.

[849] *Mankowski*, IPRax 2007, 404, 406; *Huber-Mumelter/Mumelter*, JBl 2008, 561, 573; *Kropholler/von Hein*, Art. 5 note 50b.

[850] Taken up by *Kropholler/von Hein*, Art. 5 note 50b.

[851] See *infra* Art. 5 note 208 (*Mankowski*).

[852] *Takahashi*, (2002) 27 Eur. L. Rev. 530, 538 *et seq.*

[853] *Mankowski*, IPRax 2007, 404, 406.

[854] *de Franceschi*, Contratto e impresa/Europa 2008, 637, 673; *Simotta*, in: Fasching/Konecny, Art. 5 note 196.

[855] *Color Drack GmbH v. Lexx International Vertriebs GmbH*, Case C-386/05 [2007] ECR I-3699, I-3737 para. 40.

[856] See *Arenas García*, AEDIpr 2007, 921, 927 *et seq.*

[857] *Nadaud*, JCP E 2008 I 112, p. 25.

[858] *Wipping*, Der europäische Gerichtsstand des Erfüllungsortes – Art. 5 Nr. 1 EuGVVO (2008) p. 205.

the general tendency towards unitary jurisdiction under (1) (b).[859] Methodologically, it attempts at a *reductio ad unum*.[860]

160 Yet searching for a single centre of gravity generates intrinsic problems, not to be underestimated, though. One should not overlook or underestimate the difficulties mounting under such an approach. Imagine that – however this might be measured – 28 % of the goods are delivered in one country, 25 % each are spent in a second and third country, and the remainder of 22 % in a fourth. By sheer mathematics, 28 % are more than 25 % or 22 %. But equally by sheer mathematics 28 % is not surmounting, not even barely reaching the sum of 72 % and can thus hardly be said to dominate and to identify the very focus of the execution of the contract.[861] Anyone relying on *accessorium sequitur principale*[862] goes wrong.[863]

161 Furthermore, how shall one reach the ground for any such calculation? "Economic criteria" are invoked, but not explained in *Color Drack*.[864] Economically motivated and (on top of it) comparative relevance is not the easiest treat to handle.[865] As to goods, would it be objective value, contract price or resale price that matters?[866] Might the number of carriages to given places matter?[867] Could costs and organisational effort possibly be relevant?[868] What about volume of the goods?[869] Or is weight the decisive factor? The latter would be hardly conceivable since it would mean to compare ten tons of scrap to ten parcels with microchips, or quite literally comparing apples to pears, i.e. comparing the incomparable.[870] Quantitative yardsticks should not trump qualitative elements completely.[871] On the other hand, weight could well come into play where goods of equal consistence and quality are measured by weight units.[872] Assessing objective value has proven a task economics cannot handle prop-

---

[859] *Oberhammer*, in: Dasser/Oberhammer, Art. 5 LugÜ with note 67; see also *Leible/Reinert*, EuZW 2007, 372, 373; *de Franceschi*, Contratto e impresa/Europa 2008, 637, 677.

[860] *de Franceschi*, Contratto e impresa/Europa 2008, 637, 670.

[861] *Mankowski*, IPRax 2007, 404, 410; *Grušić*, (2011) 7 JPrIL 321, 339 with fn. 59.

[862] Like *Oberhammer*, in: Dasser/Oberhammer, Art. 5 LugÜ note 67.

[863] A-G *Bot*, [2007] ECR I-3702, I-3723 to I-3725 paras. 120–126; *Czernich*, in: Czernich/Tiefenthaler/Kodek, Art. 5 Brussels I Regulation with note 15; *Franzina*, La giurisdizione in materia contrattuale (2006) p. 409; *Mankowski*, IPRax 2007, 404, 410; see also *Franzina*, RDIPP 2010, 655, 672.

[864] *Color Drack GmbH v. Lexx International Vertriebs GmbH*, Case C-386/05 [2007] ECR I-3699, I-3737 para. 40.

[865] See *Huber-Mumelter/Mumelter*, JBl 2008, 561, 568; *de Franceschi*, Contratto e impresa/Europa 2008, 637, 671; *Kuipers*, NIPR 2010, 622, 625; *Franzina*, RDIPP 2010, 655, 671; *Notdurfter/Petruzzino*, Contratto e impresa/Europa 2011, 223, 231 *et seq.*

[866] *Harris*, (2007) 123 LQR 522, 526; *Lein*, in: Bonomi/Cashin Ritaine/Romano (dir.), La Convention de Lugano – passé, présent et devenir (Zürich 2007), p. 41, 58; *Matthias Lehmann*, ZZP Int. 12 (2007), 206, 208; *Vlas/Ibili/Zilinsky/Vlek*, NILR 2009, 245, 253.

[867] See *Mankowski*, IPRax 2007, 404, 409; *de Franceschi*, Contratto e impresa/Europa 2008, 637, 672.

[868] See *Mankowski*, IPRax 2007, 404, 409.

[869] See *Vlas*, NJ 2008 Nr. 237 p. 2282, 2283.

[870] Similarly *Espiniella Menéndez*, REDI 2007, 282, 284; *de Franceschi*, Contratto e impresa/Europa 2008, 637, 672.

[871] *Mankowski*, IPRax 2007, 404, 410 *et seq.*; *Lupoi*, Riv. trim. dir. proc. civ. 2007, 495, 510 *et seq.*; *de Franceschi*, Contratto e impresa/Europa 2008, 637, 672; *Gardella*, Yb. PIL 9 (2007), 439, 445.

erly if scrutinised. Market prices are within a range and might differ regionally or even locally,[873] on top of that graced by a time factor in particular if long-term contracts are at stake. This should rule out objective value as the proper basis. Similar objections put hurdles in the way of resale prices, the more so since resale might involve either particular business sense on the reseller's side or deductions for selling goods now second hand. Contract prices thus look like the most viable candidate.[874] In most instances, they van be easily grappled. Neither party can be surprised, and neither party can denounce them as unfair after having consented to them. Assessing them entails lesser difficulties even in the case of different goods sold under a single contract for in that instance prudent parties will have detailed prices for the single goods in the contract.

Weighing contacts has never been the easiest task as PIL amply illustrates. Legal certainty is **162** ill-served with it.[875] Since the ECJ has adopted this approach it might be also charged with answering a flurry of questions referred for preliminary rulings each related to a fact-specific situation. Some match of ping-pong between the ECJ and the national courts is very likely,[876] and even so no comprehensive code might be written, but that at considerable cost. Uncertainty is a high price. *Ex post* assessments threaten.[877] "Trial and error" must not be the prevailing "method".[878] Each case with a factual setting differing from the ordinary and simple one might pose new questions, and determining the "main place of delivery" might boil down to a very intricate matter of fact and degree. On top of this, other deliveries than the main delivery might not have a close connection with the place of the main delivery as a matter of principle.[879]

Finally, if no centre of gravity can be properly identified a default rule is badly needed. The **163** ECJ in *Color Drack* resorted to plaintiff's choice between the various factual places of delivery.[880] This default rule suffers from the same deficiencies from which a like rule would suffer as main rule: It overly favours the plaintiff. The persuasive force of the solution has been further reduced since the ECJ in *Wood Floor* did not establish a like default rule with regard to service contracts.[881] Such split in the system can be barely disguised and even less justified. If the solution suffers from incurable deficits in one branch it begs a very good and convincing explanation why this should not be the case in the other branch. Split yardsticks between the two indents of (b) are not the best advertisement for the solution in *Color Drack*.

---

872   *de Franceschi*, Contratto e impresa/Europa 2008, 637, 672.

873   *Mankowski*, IPRax 2007, 404, 411; but see *de Franceschi*, Contratto e impresa/Europa 2008, 637, 673.

874   To the same result *Kropholler/von Hein* Art. 5 note 50.

875   See only *Harris*, (2007) 123 LQR 522, 525; *Huber-Mumelter/Mumelter*, JBl 2008, 561, 568 *et seq.*; *Simotta*, in: Fasching/Konecny, Art. 5 note 195; *Leible*, in: FS Ulrich Spellenberg (2010), p. 451, 459 *et seq.*; *Looschelders*, JR 2011, 345, 347.

876   *Leible*, EuZW 2009, 571, 573; *Mankowski*, EWiR Art. 5 EuGVVO 3/11, 497, 498.

877   *Matthias Lehmann*, ZZP Int. 12 (2007), 206, 208.

878   *Leible*, EuZW 2009, 370, 372; *Leible*, EuZW 2009, 571, 573; *Mankowski*, JZ 2009, 958, 961; *Mankowski*, EWiR Art. 5 EuGVVO 3/11, 497, 498.

879   *Matthias Lehmann*, ZZP Int. 12 (2007), 206, 209.

880   *Color Drack GmbH v. Lexx International Vertriebs GmbH*, Case C-386/05 [2007] ECR I-3699, I-3737 para. 42.

881   *Wood Floor Solutions Andreas Domberger GmbH v. Silva Trade SA*, (Case C-19/09) [2010] ECR I-2121, I-2174 paras. 41–42.

On top of that, *Color Drack* expressly confined its default solution to local jurisdiction leaving open the solution for international jurisdiction[882] which for the first time was addressed in *Wood Floor* where the inherent danger of the default rule from *Color Drack* was duly recognised.[883] Preferable would be the presumption that the seller's relevant place of business should prevail. In *Wood Floor* the ECJ points towards a like solution for service contracts.[884] That should indicate second thoughts in Luxemburg the more so since *Color Drack* expressly dealt with venue and local jurisdiction only where the problems of *forum shopping* can occur only within a single State and not in a cross-border setting.

bb) Contracts for services to be rendered in multiple jurisdictions

164 For contracts regarding the performance of services the factual approach bears additional delicacies. The contractual relationship between a commercial agent and his principal might be viewed as paradigmatic: How should one ascertain the place of performance if the commercial agent is called upon to render his services in a number of countries, e.g. the three Benelux states, northern France and the west of Germany? Or think of a shipping company performing a sea carriage across the Atlantic.[885] Another example is provided by a Munich-based lawyer engaged for arbitration proceedings in London including a hearing in London and taking evidence there.[886] Not less than six alternative solutions can be proposed:[887] (1) to search for the factually most relevant part of the activities,[888] the place of the main provision of services as the ECJ coins it;[889] (2) to let every place of performance suffice to grant jurisdiction for the entire contract; (3) to call an end to the attempt to ascertain a place of performance under (b) and to fall back on (a) via (c);[890] (4) to let every place of performance suffice to grant jurisdiction but only with regard to the activity exerted in the respective state;[891] (5) to deny any place of performance; (6) to employ a subsidiary normative approach, namely a rebuttable presumption that the activity is centred on the service provider's principal place of business, akin to Art. 4 (1) (b) Rome I Regulation.

---

[882] See *Color Drack GmbH v. Lexx International Vertriebs GmbH*, Case C-386/05 [2007] ECR I-3699, I-3733 para. 16.

[883] A-G *Trstenjak*, [2010] ECR I-2124, I-2154 para. 84; *Mankowski*, EWiR Art. 5 EuGVVO 1/10, 355, 356.

[884] *Wood Floor Solutions Andreas Domberger GmbH v. Silva Trade SA*, (Case C-19/09) [2010] ECR I-2121, I-2174 para. 42.

[885] See Rb. Kh. Antwerpen ETL 2005, 657, 669.

[886] See BGH NJW 2006, 1806.

[887] *Hertz* pp. 112 *et seq.* lists the first five respectively.

[888] E.g. *Wood Floor Solutions Andreas Domberger GmbH v. Silva Trade SA*, (Case C-19/09) [2010] ECR I-2121, I-2172 para. 33; BGH NJW 2006, 1806; OGH ZfRV 2008, 173; Cass. ZvertriebsR 2014, 58, 59 with note *Bottiau*; *Magnus*, IHR 2002, 45, 49; *Gaudemet-Tallon*, RCDIP 89 (2000), 76, 88; *Fach Gómez*, Rev. der. com. eur. 14 (2003), 181, 211; *Wurmnest*, IHR 2005, 107, 114; *Kreuzer/Rolf Wagner*, in: Dauses (ed.), Handbuch des EU-Wirtschaftsrechts, München looseleaf 1993 ongoing, ch. Q with note 443 (2007); *Oberhammer*, in: Dasser/Oberhammer, Art. 5 LugÜ with note 67; *Wipping*, Der europäische Gerichtsstand des Erfüllungsortes – Art. 5 Nr. 1 EuGVVO (2008) p. 205; *Ofner*, ZfRV 2008, 173.

[889] *Wood Floor Solutions Andreas Domberger GmbH v. Silva Trade SA*, (Case C-19/09) [2010] ECR I-2121, I-2172 para. 33.

[890] *Marie-Élodie Ancel*, RCDIP 90 (2001), 159, 160; *Rommelaere*, Rev. dr. comm. belge 2003, 103, 109.

[891] *Droz*, D. 1997 chron. 351, 356; *Lynker*, Der besondere Gerichtsstand am Erfüllungsort in der Brüssel I-Verordnung (Art. 5 Nr. 1 EuGVVO) (2006) p. 115.

(1) The ECJ's favourite: the factually most relevant place

The first alternative preferred by the ECJ in *Wood Floor Solutions*, is to search for the   **165**
factually most relevant part of the activities.[892] One has to weigh the activity in quantity
according to the time spend on it and in quality according to its importance. On the one
hand this alternative may become difficult and take a lot of time to assert. It might run into
insuperable factual problems, at least in hard cases.[893] The problems are even more acerbated
compared to the problems incurred under the first indent when looking for the place of
main delivery of goods. The quality of the activity rendered should also matter, not only the
time spent which of course is the prime aspect to be considered. For instance, mere travelling
might not assume the same importance as intense negotiating or construction work. Furthermore, insofar as factual activity matters the service provider might feel enticed to forge
time sheets or alike in barely concealed self-interest. Economically speaking, a principal-
agent conflict is lurking.

On the other hand the first alternative may lead to appropriate results, at least in the cases   **166**
where the service provider acts mainly at the same place, e.g. at the place where he has his
office. If the service provider pursues his activity under the contract solely and exclusively in
a certain country the place of performance indubitably ought to be located in that country
since the lack of a sensible alternative is a very convincing reason.[894] On Counsel this puts the
task and burden to argue and prove which parts of the activity are located where and to
which percentage the respective partial activities amount as measured against the totality of
services rendered under the contract.[895] Easy handling of (1) (b) is something different,
apparently.[896]

With regard especially to commercial agents, a particularly relevant species of service pro-   **167**
viders, at least at first glance a variety of factors might appear feasible. These factors at the
first level include:[897] time spent in the single countries respectively; the time required for the
individual services; the expenditure incurred and the efforts made by the commercial agent;
the length of the negotiations with individual customers; the expenses incurred by the
commercial agent in representing the principal; the place from which the commercial agent
organized his activity; the turnover generated by the commercial agent.[898] Preparatory work
counts to the same extent as external negotiating or concluding transactions[899] as can be
derived in the specific context from Art. 1 (2) Commercial Agents Directive.[900], [901] From an

---

[892] *Wood Floor Solutions Andreas Domberger GmbH v. Silva Trade SA*, (Case C-19/09) [2010] ECR I-2121,
       I-2172 para. 33, I-2173 paras. 38–39; LG Aachen IPRspr. 2012 Nr. 192 p. 436; *Noreisch*, GWR 2011, 136.

[893] See similarly *Lynker*, Der besondere Gerichtsstand am Erfüllungsort in der Brüssel I-Verordnung (Art. 5
       Nr. 1 EuGVVO) (2006) p. 114.

[894] See only Cassaz. RDIPP 2008, 795, 799.

[895] See for a model-like and well done example OLG München CR 2010, 156, 157; *Mankowski*, CR 2010, 137,
       139 *et seq.*

[896] *Matthias Lehmann/Duczek*, IPRax 2011, 41, 46.

[897] A-G *Trstenjak*, [2010] ECR I-2124, I-2152 para. 78.

[898] See A-G *Trstenjak*, [2010] ECR I-2124, I-2152 para. 79; *Matthias Lehmann/Duczek*, IPRax 2011, 41, 43.

[899] *Wood Floor Solutions Andreas Domberger GmbH v. Silva Trade SA*, (Case C-19/09) [2010] ECR I-2121,
       I-2173 para. 38.

[900] Council Directive 86/653/EEC of 18 December 1986 on the coordination of the laws of the Member States
       relating to self-employed commercial agents, OJ EEC 1986 L 362/17.

---

economic perspective, it is less enticing that services might be evaluated which are not available separately on the market but form only part of a inseparable package.[902]

168   Other factors might join it: distribution of the agents gross earnings; distribution of the agents net earnings; distribution of the principal's gross earnings prompting from customers who were intermediated and brokered by the agent; distribution of the principal's net earnings prompting from customers who were intermediated and brokered by the agent. At least, in the internal relationship between agent and principal information problems as to the three latter figures should not occur since as one party would not have the figures the other party would be obliged to produce them. Such vital information should not be kept private eventually.

169   Time spent should be the relevant factor, though. Commercial agents provide services, and it is the service as such that should matter however important the eventual results might be. Also the parallel with the determination of the habitual place of working for employees should be kept[903] since there a service rendered (if only in a not self-employed, but economically dependent manner) is calculated by time units and the thumb rule for the habituality[904] relates to percents of time spent. To rely on external relations would give rise to incentives as to manipulate and as to collusive co-operation of either side with the external partners. Time spent might be evidenced by time-sheets and diaries with the opportunity for an accompanying check on plausibility by the results and possibly by contacting the external partners.[905] Yet such internal documents on the agent's parts as time-sheets and journals might appear suspicious. But in most instances, principals might have enough opportunities to control and counter-check with the reports the agent once had sent in.[906]

170   But any factor based on time spent raises another query:[907] How long should the period to go back in the past be? Shall it really be the entire past duration of the contract? Or shall it be, let say, the last year? Any limitation in time might appear a little arbitrary. Why the last year and not the last two years, or which reason could be fielded against the last six months? Accordingly, the entire period for which the contract has been running, is relevant.

171   Generally, the approach relying on the *principal* place of performance may work in easy cases where it is evident which is the most important and dominant amongst a number of places where services were performed and rendered. It might work where in the event of performing specific services one place of business is the dominating one and the others serve as mere auxiliaries for the purposes of the concrete contract.[908] But the approach may run

---

[901] See *Wood Floor Solutions Andreas Domberger GmbH v. Silva Trade SA*, (Case C-19/09) [2010] ECR I-2121, I-2173 paras. 37–38; *Shine*, [2011] ICCLR 20, 25.

[902] *Matthias Lehmann/Duczek*, IPRax 2011, 41, 43.

[903] See on a more general level *Wipping*, Der europäische Gerichtsstand des Erfüllungsortes – Art. 5 Nr. 1 EuGVVO (2008) p. 205.

[904] See *Mankowski*, IPRax 1999, 332 at 334 and 336; *Mankowski*, in: Rauscher Art. 18 with note 6 and A-G *Strikwerda*, NJ 1997 p. 3943, 3947; *Mankowski*, NJ 1998 Nr. 546 p. 3126.

[905] *Mankowski*, Yb. PIL 10 (2008), 19, 34.

[906] *Mankowski*, Yb. PIL 10 (2008), 19, 34.

[907] *Mankowski*, Yb. PIL 10 (2008), 19, 34; *Matthias Lehmann/Duczek*, IPRax 2011, 41, 46.

[908] *Mankowski*, AnwBl 2006, 806, 809 *et seq.*; *Huber-Mumelter/Mumelter*, JBl 2008, 561, 569.

into deep and deepening trouble wherever matters get a little more complicated (for instance where a number of places of almost equal relevance can be identified[909]), and might be prone to generate an almost intolerable level of uncertainty and insecurity in the really hard cases.[910]

It definitely needs a default rule, some kind of back up. The ECJ finally opted for the service **172** provider's domicile as the default rule[911] which might be as good as it gets.[912] At least this properly reflects the residual importance of preparatory work done at the service provider's "home".[913] To rely on the obligation at stake instead (or even instead of identifying the factually most relevant place where services are rendered)[914] would run counter to the unitary approach of ascertaining unitary jurisdiction for the entire contract under (1) (b) and would encounter insuperable difficulties if the service provider sues the customer e.g. for fees due.[915]

(2) Second alternative: plaintiff's free choice from the menu
The second alternative is to let every place of performance suffice to grant jurisdiction for the **173** entire contract.[916] But this is not convincing.[917] It means to increase the jurisdictional liability to the defendant's – and this is in the vast majority of instances concerning lawsuits involving commercial agents: the principal's – detriment.[918] Eventually it would amount to an invitation to forum shopping.[919] Furthermore one would give up the weighting and search for local connecting factors. But this is the very rationale underlying, and the core of, a head of special jurisdiction. Thus, this alternative contradicts the concept of a uniform jurisdiction. (1) (b) purports at avoiding a wealth of jurisdiction (even if the several *fora* are only applicable to a single obligation). The alternative under consideration overly favours the plaintiff and disposes of the justified interests of the defendant rashly and unfairly.[920] The level of almost total absurdity is reached if one considers the consequence that if all claims

---

[909] *Kuipers*, NIPR 2010, 622, 625.

[910] *Lynker*, Der besondere Gerichtsstand am Erfüllungsort in der Brüssel I-Verordnung (Art. 5 Nr. 1 EuGVVO) (2006) p. 71; *Mumelter*, Der Gerichtsstand des Erfüllungsortes im Europäischen Zivilprozessrecht (2007) pp. 174 *et seq.*; *Leible*, EuZW 2009, 572, 573; *Mankowski*, EWiR Art. 5 EuGVVO 2/09, 607, 608.

[911] *Wood Floor Solutions Andreas Domberger GmbH v. Silva Trade SA*, (Case C-19/09) [2010] ECR I-2121, I-2174 para. 42.

[912] *Mankowski*, EWiR Art. 5 EuGVVO 2/10, 355, 356.

[913] See *Kuipers*, NIPR 2010, 622, 625.

[914] As *Matthias Lehmann/Duczek*, IPRax 2011, 41, 48 propose.

[915] Admitted by *Matthias Lehmann/Duczek*, IPRax 2011, 41, 48.

[916] *Droz*, D. 1997 chron. 351, 356; *Takahashi*, (2002) 27 Eur. L. Rev. 530, 539; *Gottwald*, in: Münchener Kommentar zur ZPO Art. 5 note 21; *Geimer/Schütze*, Art. 5 note 87.

[917] *Fach Gómez*, Rev. der. com. eur. 14 (2003), 181, 210; *De Franceschi*, Int'l. Lis 2007, 120, 123.

[918] *Fach Gómez*, Rev. der. com. eur. 14 (2003), 181, 210; *Leible*, in: Rauscher Art. 5 Brüssel I-VO with note 55. More sympathetically *Huber-Mumelter/Mumelter*, JBl 2008, 561, 569–571.

[919] *Lynker*, Der besondere Gerichtsstand am Erfüllungsort in der Brüssel I-Verordnung (Art. 5 Nr. 1 EuGVVO) (2006) p. 114.

[920] *Markus*, ZSR 2007 I 319, 332; *Wipping*, Der europäische Gerichtsstand des Erfüllungsortes – Art. 5 Nr. 1 EuGVVO (2008) p. 202.

could be brought at all places it would be possible to commence lawsuits for one instalment at a place where only another, different instalment was to be delivered.[921]

174   In the relevant cases in particular, the suing service provider would be far better off. Imagine that 1% of the service is performed in a certain country and that 1% would be allowed to trigger jurisdiction for 100% on aggregate. That would be grossly unfair to the customer[922] the more so since the Brussels *Ibis* regime does not employ the escape devices of either a *de minimis* rule or any kind of *forum non conveniens* doctrine. Furthermore, the alternative under consideration multiplies the number of available jurisdictions contrary to some general tendencies of restricting such numbers.[923] It would do the maximum harm and damage to general jurisdiction under Art. 2 Brussels I Regulation. It would unhinge the entire system of checks and balances.

(3) Third alternative: back to the normative approach under Art. 7 (1) (a) via (c)

175   The third alternative is to call an end to the attempt to ascertain a place of performance[924] and to fall back on (1) (a) *via* (c).[925] This solution would be in accordance with Art. 5 (1) cl. 2, 3 Brussels Convention or original Lugano Convention respectively, as well as with Art. 21 (1) (a) and (b) concerning employment matters. One would always fall back on a subsidiary complementary rule, as far as considering the primary connecting factor as indeterminate. Indeed (1) (c) ordinarily means that the place of performance as determined in (b) is not situated in the area of the Community.[926] However the wording is broad enough for including a stopgap solution for other constellations. Admittedly one would give up the intended unitary jurisdiction[927] because (a) follows the *de Bloos*- and *Tessili*-doctrines of the ECJ and determines the place of performance only for the single matter in dispute, furthermore by using the applicable substantive law. Rashly reverting to (c) would foster an unwarranted tendency to stick to this method which should in general be rendered obsolete for the types of contract covered by (b).[928] A further disadvantage is threatening frictions with the yardsticks applied to venue or local jurisdiction.[929] At least the inapplicability can not be deducted from the use of the singular "place" or "Member State" instead of the plural "places" or "Member States" since (3) is similarly phrased in this regard and clearly covers a majority of places.[930]

---

[921]   *Lynker*, Der besondere Gerichtsstand am Erfüllungsort in der Brüssel I-Verordnung (Art. 5 Nr. 1 EuGVVO) (2006) p. 114; *Mankowski*, IPRax 2007, 404, 406; *Mankowski*, Yb. PIL 10 (2008), 19, 35; *Wipping*, Der europäische Gerichtsstand des Erfüllungsortes – Art. 5 Nr. 1 EuGVVO (2008) p. 202.

[922]   See only *Mankowski*, IPRax 2007, 404, 406; *Mankowski*, Yb. PIL 10 (2008), 19, 35; *Wipping*, Der europäische Gerichtsstand des Erfüllungsortes – Art. 5 Nr. 1 EuGVVO (2008) p. 202.

[923]   *Lynker*, Der besondere Gerichtsstand am Erfüllungsort in der Brüssel I-Verordnung (Art. 5 Nr. 1 EuGVVO) (2006) p. 114.

[924]   With a like tendency *Leible*, in: Rauscher Art. 5 Brüssel I-VO with note 55 in the event of duties to act not limited in geographic regards.

[925]   See *Marie-Élodie Ancel*, RCDIP 90 (2001), 135, 160; *Fach Gómez*, Rev. der. com. eur. 14 (2003), 181, 210.

[926]   See only the explanatory with note of the Commission to the Proposal for a Brussels I Regulation, BR-Drs. 534/99, p. 14.

[927]   *Huber-Mumelter/Mumelter*, JBl 2008, 561, 564 *et seq.*

[928]   *Huber-Mumelter/Mumelter*, JBl 2008, 561, 565.

[929]   *Mankowski*, IPRax 2007, 404, 407.

[930]   *Mankowski*, IPRax 2007, 404, 407; *Lein*, in: Bonomi/Cashin Ritaine/Romano (dir.), La Convention de

The decision of the ECJ in *Besix* does not provide overwhelming backing, either.[931] In *Besix* **176** the ECJ denied Art. 5 (1) Brussels Convention to become operative in the event that a duty to refrain from certain activities was not subject to geographical limitations.[932] This *Besix*-doctrine should not be applied because it is in clear contradiction with the principle underlying the notion of jurisdiction at the place of performance.[933] Technically, *Besix* is guided by peculiarities of duties to refrain from something.[934] The lack of geographical limitations and thus the ubiquity are a core element.[935] This core element is not repeated either with regard to delivery in instalments in different locations nor with regard to services to be rendered in a variety of named and certain States.[936] The problem is different and diverging: Whereas *Besix* battled with problems to locate at all now one is concerned with the task of reconciling activities which are clearly located but in a number of States.[937]

(4) Fourth alternative: denying any place of performance
At least the third solution ought to be preferred to yet another alternative, namely to deny **177** any place of performance altogether.[938] It deprives the prospective claimant of an option. But such option is in principle guaranteed by (1) (b).[939] There would be not better justification than one could not decide whether one place of performance might possibly take precedence over the others.[940] Such a non-solution contrary to the overall structure[941] is spell-bound for disaster. It resembles committing suicide for fear of death. It should give way at least to applying (1) (a) since the latter pays better regard to the internal structure of (1).[942] It is short of a very desperate attempt of *ultima ratio*.[943]

(5) Fifth alternative: the mosaic principle
The fifth alternative splits jurisdiction: A forum can be located at any place where activity is **178** displayed – but only for the part and the fraction of the activity displayed there.[944] Vaguely

---

Lugano – passé, présent et devenir (Zürich 2007), p. 41, 58; *Huber-Mumelter/Mumelter*, JBl 2008, 561, 563; see also A-G *Trstenjak*, [2010] ECR I-2124, I-2147 para. 61.

[931] Contra A-G *Bot*, [2007] ECR I-3702, I-3722 para. 115 fn. 30.

[932] Besix AG v. WABAG, Case C-256/00 [2002] ECR I-1699, I-1733 para. 55; following suit Rb. 's-Hertogenbosch NIPR 2005 Nr. 169 p. 234.

[933] See *Mankowski*, EWiR Art. 5 EuGVÜ 1/02, 519; *Hess*, IPRax 2002, 376; *De Franceschi*, Int'l. Lis 2007, 120, 122.

[934] *Mankowski*, IPRax 2007, 404, 407; *Huber-Mumelter/Mumelter*, JBl 2008, 561, 572.

[935] See *Franzina*, RDIPP 2002, 391, 402; *Franzina*, La giurisdizione in materia contrattuale (2006) pp. 409 *et seq.*

[936] *Mankowski*, IPRax 2007, 404, 407.

[937] *Mankowski*, IPRax 2007, 404, 407.

[938] Favouring this *Rodriguez*, Beklagtenwohnsitz und Erfüllungsort im europäischen IZVR (Zürich 2005) para. 676. See also tentatively as some kind of default rule of last resort *Magnus*, IHR 2002, 45, 49.

[939] *Mankowski*, Yb. PIL 10 (2008), 19, 37.

[940] *Rodriguez*, Beklagtenwohnsitz und Erfüllungsort im europäischen IZVR (Zürich 2005) para. 676.

[941] *Ignatova*, Art. 5 Nr. 1 EuGVVO – Chancen und Perspektiven der Reform des Gerichtsstands am Erfüllungsort (2005) p. 236; *Mankowski*, IPRax 2007, 404, 408.

[942] *Mankowski*, IPRax 2007, 404, 408.

[943] *Magnus*, IHR 2002, 45, 49; *Mankowski*, Yb. PIL 10 (2008), 19, 38; see also *Lynker*, Der besondere Gerichtsstand am Erfüllungsort in der Brüssel I-Verordnung (Art. 5 Nr. 1 EuGVVO) (2006) p. 117.

[944] *Czernich*, in: Czernich/Tiefenthaler/Kodek Art. 5 note 15; *Ignatova*, Art. 5 Nr. 1 EuGVVO – Chancen und

---

one could align this with the approach taken by the ECJ in *Shevill*,[945] yet then in tort.[946] In substantive law, Art. 73 CISG and Art. 9:302 PECL also give an indication in the like direction.[947] Quite some parallels with the case that obligations arise not under a single contract, but under a bunch of separable contracts might be drawn in support, too.[948] It could be wise to keep the two possible constellations which in practice are to a certain degree interchangeable as far in line as possible not the least since it might be rather fortuitous and accidental whether parties conclude a number of separable contracts or a unitary contract to an almost identical economic avail.[949] A mosaic principle, meaning that in the state of activity only the part of the contract connected with this state is relevant, can avoid neither parallel proceedings nor contradicting results in these proceedings.[950] But fairness should also take into account that fractions of the dispute being fought in different Member States are at least connected and interrelated in a manner which would suffice to trigger Art. 28 so that either Art. 27 (1) (if one feels inclined to regard such fractions as dealing with the same cause[951]) or Art. 28 might stop different results from being reached in their tracks.[952] As a matter of principle, any attempt at concentrating lawsuits would implode, though.[953] But such split can be said to be consequential, and be prompted by, the factual split between instalments to be delivered in different States.[954] Another time, the issue of a minimum requirement might arise in order to mitigate the jurisdictional risk.[955]

179 The most severe – and eventually insuperable – problems relate to remuneration and compensation.[956] The agent's claims might be deemed as providing some kind of tying bond around the entire contract. But for instance in the specific event of commercial agents, one could perhaps argue that both remuneration and compensation can be attributed to certain fractions of the agent's work and effort. The claimant agent would be left with the severe burden of either commencing several lawsuits in a number of jurisdictions in order to

---

Perspektiven der Reform des Gerichtsstands am Erfüllungsort (2005) p. 236; *Lynker*, Der besondere Gerichtsstand am Erfüllungsort in der Brüssel I-Verordnung (Art. 5 Nr. 1 EuGVVO) (2006) pp. 116 *et seq.*; *Sujecki*, EWS 2007, 398, 401; *Mumelter*, Der Gerichtsstand des Erfüllungsortes im Europäischen Zivilprozessrecht (2007) p. 175; tentatively so *Fawcett*, in: Fawcett/Harris/Bridge para. 3.207; *Hare*, [2007] LMCLQ 566, 569.

[945] *Fiona Shevill v. Presse Alliance SA*, (Case C-68/93) [1995] ECR I-415, I-461 *et seq.* paras. 28–33.

[946] See *Fach Gómez*, Rev. der. com. eur. 14 (2003), 181, 210; *Sujecki*, EWS, 2007, 398, 401; *Wipping*, Der europäische Gerichtsstand des Erfüllungsortes – Art. 5 Nr. 1 EuGVVO (2008) p. 203.

[947] *Mankowski*, IPRax 2007, 404, 406; *Huber-Mumelter/Mumelter*, JBl 2008, 561, 573.

[948] See *Huber-Mumelter/Mumelter*, JBl 2008, 561, 574.

[949] *Mankowski*, IPRax 2007, 404, 406 *et seq.*; see also *Oberhammer*, in: Dasser/Oberhammer, Art. 5 LugÜ with note 68.

[950] *Leible*, in: Rauscher, Art. 5 note 55; *Mankowski*, Yb. PIL 10 (2008), 19, 39; see also *Kuipers*, NIPR 2010, 622, 627.

[951] Contra *Lynker*, Der besondere Gerichtsstand am Erfüllungsort in der Brüssel I-Verordnung (Art. 5 Nr. 1 EuGVVO) (2006) p. 117. But cf. *Magnus*, in: Arter (ed.), Vertriebsverträge (2007), p. 221, 233.

[952] *Mankowski*, IPRax 2007, 404, 406; *Huber-Mumelter/Mumelter*, JBl 2008, 561, 573 *et seq.*

[953] *Huber-Mumelter/Mumelter*, JBl 2008, 561, 574.

[954] *Wipping*, Der europäische Gerichtsstand des Erfüllungsortes – Art. 5 Nr. 1 EuGVVO (2008) p. 204.

[955] *Huber-Mumelter/Mumelter*, JBl 2008, 561, 574.

[956] *Lynker*, Der besondere Gerichtsstand am Erfüllungsort in der Brüssel I-Verordnung (Art. 5 Nr. 1 EuGVVO) (2006) p. 116; *Mankowski*, IPRax 2007, 404, 406.

recover the entirety of compensation due or to let go part of what he believes to be earned. This would not be the most promising prospect but in the result too severe and heavy a burden to be put on the prospective claimant's shoulders.[957] In tort cases the alternative option to go for the place of activity instead of the split places where the primary damage was sustained, provides some consolation. Such means of calming the waves are missing in contract cases[958] where only general jurisdiction at the defendant's domicile is another option at hand.[959]

(6) Sixth alternative: an auxiliary presumption in favour of the service provider's principal place of business

The sixth and last alternative results in a presumption. One would presume to equate the **180** place of the service provider's performance with the service provider's principal place of business or, in case the service provider is an individual, with its habitual residence.[960] After all, for the most part the service provider probably does his organisational work (such as completing orders, registering contracts and notifying and informing his principal) at this place. The criterion of the principal place of business would create a welcome parallel and synchrony with the assessment which the PIL produces under Art. 4 (2) cl. 2 Var. 1 Rome Convention and Arts. 4 (1) (b); 19 (1) subpara. 2 Rome I Regulation.[961] If activity by a certain branch or place of business can be positively ascertained, the presumption is open enough to recognise this. Generally, by proceeding down this avenue one would translate the typical subsidiary solution into action by filling up factors based on factual approaches in case of need by the alternate use of normative elements.[962] Normative starting points are always feasible and available, whereas factual ones can result in problems with determination, therewith in factual problems. Additional backing might be provided by Art. 31 (c) CISG which indicates a like subsidiary solution in case of doubt.[963] In general, are to the same avail and give further credibility to this solution.[964] If and insofar one generally permits normativity to slip in as interpretatory means by having resort to Art. 31 CISG,[965] the approach could be reformulated as leaning on Art. 31 (c) CISG.

---

[957] *Markus*, ZSR 2007 I 319, 332.

[958] *Markus*, ZSR 2007 I 319, 332.

[959] *Mankowski*, IPRax 2007, 404, 406.

[960] *Mankowski*, in: Hopt/Tzouganatos (eds.), Europäisierung des Handels- und Wirtschaftsrechts (2006), p. 131, 141; *Huber-Mumelter/Mumelter*, JBl 2008, 561, 575 *et seq.*; tentatively also *Magnus*, in: Arter (ed.), Vertriebsverträge (2007), p. 221, 233 and joining in the result Cass. RCDIP 101 (2012), 430, 431 with note *Corneloup*; OLG Koblenz IHR 2008, 198, 200 = NJW-RR 2009, 502.

[961] *Mankowski*, IPRax 2007, 404, 408; *Huber-Mumelter/Mumelter*, JBl 2008, 561, 576.

[962] See in more detail *Mankowski*, RabelsZ 63 (1999), 203, 257 *et seq.*

[963] *Huber-Mumelter/Mumelter*, JBl 2008, 561, 576.

[964] *Huber-Mumelter/Mumelter*, JBl 2008, 561, 576; *Mankowski*, IHR 2009, 46, 59 *et seq.*; *Mankowski*, EWiR Art. 5 EuGVVO 2/09, 607, 608.

[965] Cassaz. Giust. civ. 2007 I 1393 with note *Ferrari* = NGCC 2007 I 534 with note *Franzina* = RDIPP 2007, 759 = Riv. dir. proc. 2007, 1303 with note *Merlin* = ZEuP 2008, 165 note *Thomas Rüfner*; Cassaz. RDIPP 2007, 1105; Cassaz. RDIPP 2008, 221; Cassaz. RDIPP 2008, 505, 510; Cassaz. RDIPP 2008, 511; Trib. Padova, sez. distaccata di Este RDIPP 2007, 147, 153 *et seq.*; *Ragno*, Giur. mer. 2006, 1413; *Ferrari*, RDAI 2007, 83; *Ferrari*, IPRax 2007, 61; *Salerno* p. 142; *Lein*, in: Bonomi/Cashin Ritaine/Romano (dir.), La Convention de Lugano – passé, présent et devenir (Zürich 2007), p. 41, 55–57; *Wipping*, Der europäische

181 This rescues the factual approach to the fullest extent possible, though. Firstly, it gives due weight to the factual setting of the individual case insofar as it allows for a rebuttal of the presumption. Normativity does not gain prevalence as such and does not dispose of the facts single-handedly, but serves as some kind of last resort, of *ultima ratio*.[966] Secondly, it is in conformity with a general approach to fill factual connecting points with autonomous normativity in cases of need.[967] Rather the approach chosen prioritises and accentuates – quite in accordance with the overall system – the question whether a factually ascertained place exists. Not until this question is answered to the negative the approach advocated for comes to the rescue. In doing so it is in the interest of the primarily factually orientated connecting factor in order to prevent it from being rendered nugatory. Construing a presumption opens up matters for specific and particular evaluations in individual cases and eliminates any excessive rigidity. The presumption develops in fact a certain net weight, but neither in excess or back-breaking. It consciously is conceived only as a back door, as an escape device from a dilemma. One has to accept its comparative weakness mainly because its self-perception does not extend beyond being just an escape device and some kind of *ultima ratio*.[968]

182 But being in line and compatible with the very wording of the rule requires that the respective place of business happens to coincide with a place where services are rendered.[969] The case is even more pressing and problematic in the event of a contract for the sale of goods since in that event it is necessary that the respective place of business happens to coincide with a place of delivery; merely organising delivery would possibly not suffice.[970] Hence, merely organising services might not do the trick, either. Yet it will only rarely happen that for instance commercial agents at their principal place of business can not be regarded as rendering services under the contract. Organising, re-arranging and in particular administrating contracts e.g. by keeping (electronic files) *à jour* are relevant activities under the agency contract and not mere auxiliary elements. Organisational work gets more relevance for services than the outbound delivery of goods.[971] In the rare case that such work is not undertaken at the agent's principal place of business one would feel forced to part with (1) (b) and to proceed to (1) (c), (a) as the subsidiary solution.[972]

cc) **Contracts for services rendered online**

183 To determine where services rendered online are performed, is a daunting task if one is restricted to a mere look at the facts. Certainly, the service provider executes his activity where his personnel acts or where his technical equipment electronically executing what is on demand, is located. Nevertheless, most services are not completed without the customer

---

Gerichtsstand des Erfüllungsortes – Art. 5 Nr. 1 EuGVVO (2008) pp. 196 *et seq.*; *Mankowski*, IHR 2009, 46, 59 *et seq.*

[966] *Mankowski*, Yb. PIL 10 (2008), 19, 41.

[967] *Mankowski*, Yb. PIL 10 (2008), 19, 41.

[968] *Mankowski*, in: Hopt/Tzouganatos (eds.), Europäisierung des Handels- und Wirtschaftsrechts (2006), p. 131, 141.

[969] *Mankowski*, Yb. PIL 10 (2008), 19, 41; *Hannes Wais*, GPR 2010, 256, 258. See insofar also *Matthias Lehmann/Duczek*, IPRax 2011, 41, 47.

[970] *Mankowski*, IPRax 2007, 404, 408.

[971] *Mankowski*, IPRax 2007, 404, 409.

[972] See *Mankowski*, IPRax 2007, 404, 408 *et seq.*

gaining and acquiring some result. The mere activity as such does not suffice. He who asks for research wants the results of that research. Who asks for access wants to gain this access, etc. The lawyer appears to be left with the question what should gain prevalence under (b), the activity or the result?

As nothing happens online without input either by men or by machine programmed by **184** men, any notion that the service is rendered in a legal vacuum, should be easily disposed off. Thus it comes down to the alternative of whether the uploading by the content provider[973] (literally taken: the service provider[974]), or the downloading by the customer bears more weight.[975] Applying the general approach developed above,[976] the pendulum should swing in favour of the first alternative.[977] Otherwise the additional difficulty would arise that a last step entirely controlled by the customer would determine the supplier's performance – a result which sounds quite a paradox if clad in these terms.[978] In any regard, the place of the server employed by the content provider should be ruled out as it could be arbitrarily located[979] and appears rather fortuitous. The same applies *a fortiori* to the places of inter-mediate servers.[980]

Another concept puts forward the submission that in case of doubt the place where the **185** service is performed, should be equated with the place where the person providing the service has its relevant place of business; allegedly a comparative survey is said to support such a submission.[981] This would, however, be tantamount to re-introducing normative concepts[982] through the backdoor in spite of the fact that this rule was developed as a deviation and as opposed to normative concepts (in particular like those in *Tessili*)[983] and

---

[973] *Gabellini*, Riv. trim dir. proc. civ. 2014, 271, 284.

[974] Since in an internet context ISP (Internet Service Provider) is often used invariably and as a kind of synonym for Access Provider, "content provider" as the more neutral denomination is used here deliberately in order to avoid misunderstandings.

[975] The alternative is formulated e.g. by *Savini*, Contratto e impresa/Europa 2002, 1131, 1147.

[976] *Supra* Art. 7 note 182 (*Mankowski*).

[977] *Mankowski*, CR 1999, 512, 515; *Marianne Roth*, in: Michael Gruber/Mader (eds.), Internet und e-commerce (2000), p. 157, 161. But critical *Ganssauge*, Internationale Zuständigkeit und anwendbares Recht bei Verbraucherverträgen im Internet (2004) pp. 30 *et seq. Contra Lynker*, Der besondere Gerichtsstand am Erfüllungsort in der Brüssel I-Verordnung (Art. 5 Nr. 1 EuGVVO) (2006) pp. 106 *et seq.*

[978] *Ganssauge*, Internationale Zuständigkeit und anwendbares Recht bei Verbraucherverträgen im Internet (2004) p. 30.

[979] BGH NJW 2011, 2059, 2061; *Birgit Bachmann*, IPRax 1998, 179, 183 *et seq.*; *von Hinden*, in: Basedow (ed.), Private Enforcement of EC Competition Law (2007), pp. 61 *et seq.*; *Grolimund*, ZSR NF 119 (2000) I 339, 362; *Ganssauge*, Internationale Zuständigkeit und anwendbares Recht bei Verbraucherverträgen im Internet (2004) p. 31; *Wüllrich*, Das Persönlichkeitsrecht des Einzelnen im Internet (2006) p. 229; *Rufus Pichler*, Internationale Zuständigkeit im Zeitalter globaler Vernetzung (2008) paras. 782 *et seq.*; *Spindler*, in: FS Erwin Deutsch zum 80. Geburtstag (2008), p. 925, 937.

[980] *Wüllrich*, Das Persönlichkeitsrecht des Einzelnen im Internet (2006) p. 230.

[981] *Leible*, in: Rauscher Art. 5 note 54; *de Miguel Asensio*, in: Liber amicorum Alegría Borrás (2013), p. 291, 305–307 (with reference to Arts. 6.1.6 UNIDROIT Principles; III 2:101 DCFR).

[982] As *Peter Schlosser* Art. 5 note 10b openly does.

[983] Commission Proposal COM (1999) 348 final p. 14.

---

thus is bound to revert to a factual concept.[984] Dropping any reasoning which refers to legal concepts of a specific law, namely a rebuttable presumption that the service is provided at the relevant place of business of the service provider, could offer some help.[985] In particular it could avoid difficulties which were to be encountered if one referred to the factual place of uploading.[986] European PIL provides a supporting hint fostering this answer: Art. 4 (2) cl. 2 Rome Convention elevates the service provider's relevant place of business to be the connecting factor. Hence, PIL places more reliance on the activity. No striking counter-arguments are discernible why the rules on jurisdiction should proceed down a different avenue. At least the contention to follow the approach preferred in PIL can be supported and fostered by the fact that behind the mere activity in most instances there is the organisational background. Delivery of goods is far more significant to the respective contract since it mostly involves questions of passing on property or title in the goods delivered. Rendering services does not have such implications. Accordingly, it seems appropriate to put emphasis on the activity. If further backing is required, the accepted definition of contracts on the provision of services[987] might provide it as its central and paramount element is the activity.[988] Finally, the presumption developed should enable the necessary foreseeability and thus calm calls[989] for inapplicability of (b).

dd) Contracts for the transport of goods or passengers

186 Contracts for the transport of goods or passengers come within the broad definition[990] of contracts for services.[991] There is no differentiation between either type of carriage or be-

---

984 See only *Kropholler/von Hinden*, in: GS Alexander Lüderitz (2000), p. 401, 409 *et seq.*; *Thomas Pfeiffer*, in: Gounalakis (ed.), Rechtshandbuch Electronic Business (2003), § 13 note 38; *García Gutiérrez*, REDI 2013-1, 305, 308.

985 *Mankowski*, in: Spindler/Wiebe (eds.), Internet-Auktionen und Elektronische Marktplätze (2nd ed. 2005), ch. 12 notes 31 *et seq.*; *Mankowski*, in: Ruth Nielsen/Sandfeld Jacobsen/Trzaskowski (eds.), EU Electronic Commerce Law (2004), p. 125, 130; *Calvo Caravaca/Carrascosa González*, Conflictos de leyes y conflictos de jurisdicción en Internet (2001) p. 53 *et seq.*; see also *de Miguel Asensio*, Derecho privado de Internet (3rd ed. 2002) para. 338 *in fine*; *Gsell*, IPRax 2002, 484 at 491; *Czernich*, in: Czernich/Tiefenthaler/Kodek, Art. 5 note 42.

986 As described by *Droz/Gaudemet-Tallon*, RCDIP 90 (2001), 601, 636.

987 *Supra* Art. 5 note 89 (*Mankowski*).

988 *Savini*, Contratto e impresa/Europa 2002, 1131, 1147.

989 In particular *Ganssauge*, Internationale Zuständigkeit und anwendbares Recht bei Verbraucherverträgen im Internet (2004) p. 31.

990 *Supra* Art. 7 note 111 (*Mankowski*).

991 Cass. D. 2010, 2917 with applauding note *Delpech*; OLG Hamm IPRspr. 2011 Nr. 190 p. 501; Rb. Hasselt TBH 2003, 623 with note *Kruger*; Rb. Kh. Antwerpen, ETR 2005, 657, 668 *et seq.*; *Leipold*, GS Alexander Lüderitz (2000), p. 431, 446; *Hau*, ZZP Int. 5 (2000), 284, 289; *Bonassies*, ETR 2002, 727, 732; *Meeusen/Neut*, in: van Hooydonk (ed.), Actualia zee- en vervoerrecht (2003), p. 37, 63; *Stephan Roland*, JPA 2003, 136; *Leible*, in: Rauscher, Art. 5 note 50; *Matthias Lehmann*, NJW 2007, 1500, 1502; *Mankowski*, TranspR 2008, 67, 68 *et seq.*; *Mankowski*, TranspR 2009, 303, 304; *Ansgar Staudinger*, RRa 2007, 155, 157; *Legros*, Clunet 134 (2007), 799, 821; *Wipping*, Der europäische Gerichtsstand des Erfüllungsortes – Art. 5 Nr. 1 EuGVVO (2008) pp. 167 *et seq.*, 200; *Schlosser*, Art. 5 note 10b; *Rolf Wagner*, TranspR 2009, 281, 283; *Reis*, MR-Int 2009, 118, 119; *Tenenbaum*, Rev. contrats 2010, 206, 208–211 and *Peter Rehder v. Baltic Air Corporation*, (Case C-204/08) [2009] ECR I-6073. *Contra* OLG Köln TranspR 2009, 37, 38; Rb. Kh. Antwerpen ETL 2005, 687, 700; AG Geldern NJOZ 2008, 309; AG Lübeck NJOZ 2008, 1239.

tween different modes of transportation.[992] Following the general tendency to look at Arts. 56 *et seq.* TFEU (ex Arts. 50 *et seq.* EC Treaty) for first guidance,[993] Art. 58 TFEU (ex Art. 51 EC Treaty) provides the appropriate backing.[994] Arts. 6 (4) (b) Rome I Regulation; 5 (4) (b) Rome Convention; 13 (3) Brussels Convention further support this.[995] Volume contracts or Ocean Liner Service Agreements are *a fortiori* for the provision of services.[996]

Bills of lading and analogous instruments which tend to be unilaterally issued are to be **187** treated differently, though: They constitute a claim for delivery, but not a claim for transport and thus for activities and services.[997] They are concerned with a delivery on the spot, the mere handing over of the goods and not with the act of transporting them as such. It might matter what has happened during the transportation process once the goods are not delivered or only delivered in a damaged condition but exclusively under the limited auspices of an incidental question as to whether a breach of the claim for delivery as constituted by the bill of lading, generates damages. Accordingly, bills of lading and analogous instruments do not come within (1) (b) and are subject to (1) (a).[998]

One *caveat* ought to be applied before discussing the application of (b) to such contracts in **188** detail: Many of the international conventions governing the carriage of goods or passengers contain rules on jurisdiction which in turn gain prevalence over (b) by virtue of Art. 71 so that any questions concerning (b) would not even arise. Most prominent examples are provided by Art. 33 Montreal Convention, Art. 28 Warsaw Convention (both on the carriage of passengers or goods by air) and Art. 31 CMR (on the carriage of goods by road). Nevertheless, some modes of carriage are not governed by conventions yet in force (for instance the carriage of passengers by road), and some conventions do not contain rules on jurisdiction. The latter is particularly true for carriage of goods by sea because neither the Hague nor the Hague-Visby Rules (directly) deal with jurisdiction. Only Art. 21 Hamburg Rules expressly establishes a jurisdictional regime but the Hamburg Rules are not in force for any of the Member States of the EU yet. The same applies to the jurisdictional regime of the Rotterdam Rules with its twisted and complicated nature which goes back to a respective demand by the EU.[999]

The relevant services under a contract of carriage are the carrier's one. They are performed at **189**

---

[992] *Mankowski*, TranspR 2009, 303; *Ansgar Staudinger*, IPRax 2010, 140, 141; *Roland/Insel*, JPA 2009, 320, 322 f., 324; see also *Matthias Lehmann/Duczek*, IPRax 2011, 41, 45. But cf. *Jiménez Blanco*, La Ley Unión Europea 7294 (30 noviembre 2009), 1, 6 who emphasizes passenger (i.e. consumer) protection which of course would not re-appear in the carriage of goods.

[993] *Supra* Art. 5 note 89 (*Mankowski*).

[994] Rb. Kh. Hasselt TBH 2003, 623 with note *Kruger*; *Mankowski*, TranspR 2008, 67, 68 *et seq.*; *Mankowski*, Neues aus Europa zum Internationalen Privat- und Prozessrecht der seerechtlichen Beförderungsverträge (2011) para. 15; *Egler*, Seerechtliche Streitigkeiten unter der EuGVVO (2011) pp. 32–36.

[995] *Mankowski*, Neues aus Europa zum Internationalen Privat- und Prozessrecht der seerechtlichen Beförderungsverträge (2011) para. 16; *Egler*, Seerechtliche Streitigkeiten unter der EuGVVO (2011) p. 39.

[996] Aud. Prov. Pontevedra REDI 2007-1, 270, 271; *Espiniella Menéndez*, REDI 2007-1, 273, 274.

[997] *Mankowski*, TranspR 2008, 67, 74.

[998] *Mankowski*, TranspR 2008, 67, 74. *Contra* CA Aix Rev. Scapel 2008, 13, 15; *Egler*, Seerechtliche Streitigkeiten unter der EuGVVO (2011) p. 68.

[999] See in detail *Cachard*, EJCCL 2010, 1; *Espinosa Calabuig*, Dir. mar. 2011, 18.

the place of departure *and* the place of arrival (for the carriage of passengers) or delivery (for the carriage of goods) respectively.[1000] Both the starting point and the final destination of the carriage carry equal weight. Carriage consists, by its very nature, of services provided in an indivisible and identical manner from the starting point to the final destination.[1001]

190 Each of those places has a sufficiently close link of proximity to the material elements[1002] and is predictable.[1003] If as here no (even relative) centre of activity can be identified each place where services are performed matters.[1004] Conversely, any activities undertaken at the carrier's relevant place of business are only logistical and preparatory measures whereas the transportation as such is the only service that matters under the contract.[1005] Furthermore, if the carrier's seat or place of business was relevant this would diminish the practical relevance of (1) keeping in mind the initial phrase of (1) ("in another Member State").[1006]

191 The place of (final)[1007] delivery under the contract of carriage has to its credit that it is only with the delivery that the carrier's obligations are fulfilled in their entirety.[1008] To emphasize the delivery draws a parallel to the treatment of contracts for the sale of goods.[1009] The practical interests of cargo interests strongly support the relevance of the place of delivery since there it is where they will discover damage to the goods and sue.[1010] Likewise passengers will most likely sue after returning to their home state where the carriage finally terminates.

192 The place of departure has to its credit the activities rendered by the carrier there and the cases in which the transportation is cancelled.[1011] A certain probability exists that a breach of

---

[1000] *Peter Rehder v. Baltic Air Corporation*, (Case C-204/08) [2009] ECR I-6073, I-6092 *et seq.* paras. 43–47; BGH RRa 2013, 1813, 184; BezG Schwechat RRa 2014, 204, 206; AG Königs Wusterhausen RRa 2011, 196; *Matthias Lehmann*, NJW 2007, 1500, 1502; *Mankowski*, TranspR 2008, 67, 74; *Mankowski*, TranspR 2009, 303; *Rolf Wagner*, TranspR 2009, 281, 283 *et seq.*; *Rolf Wagner*, IPRax 2010, 143, 146 *et seq.*; *Leible*, EuZW 2009, 572; *Jiménez Blanco*, REDI 2009-1, 487, 488; *Ansgar Staudinger*, IPRax 2010, 140, 141.

[1001] *Peter Rehder v. Baltic Air Corporation*, (Case C-204/08) [2009] ECR I-6073, I-6091 para. 41.

[1002] *Peter Rehder v. Baltic Air Corporation*, (Case C-204/08) [2009] ECR I-6073, I-6092 para. 44.

[1003] *Peter Rehder v. Baltic Air Corporation*, (Case C-204/08) [2009] ECR I-6073, I-6092 para. 45.

[1004] OLG Hamm IPRspr. 2011 Nr. 190 pp. 501–502; *Leible*, EuZW 2009, 572; *Mankowski*, EWiR Art. 5 EuGVVO 2/09, 607, 608; *Rauscher*, NJW 2010, 2251, 2253.

[1005] *Peter Rehder v. Baltic Air Corporation*, (Case C-204/08) [2009] ECR I-6073, I-6090 *et seq.* para. 39; *Ansgar Staudinger*, RRa 2007, 155, 158; *Mankowski*, TranspR 2008, 67, 72; *Egler*, Seerechtliche Streitigkeiten unter der EuGVVO (2011) pp. 45–47. *Contra* OLG München RRa 2007, 182, 183.

[1006] *Ansgar Staudinger*, RRa 2007, 155, 159; *Mankowski*, TranspR 2008, 67, 73; *Egler*, Seerechtliche Streitigkeiten unter der EuGVVO (2011) p. 46.

[1007] LG Hannover RRa 2012, 92 = IPRspr. 2011 Nr. 213 p. 552.

[1008] CA Rouen DMF 1998, 577, 579 with note *Nicolas*; *Hau*, ZZP Int. 5 (2000), 284, 289 *et seq.*; *Meeusen/Neut*, in: van Hooydonk (ed.), Actualia zee- en vervoerrecht (Antwerp 2003), p. 37, 63; *Stephan Roland*, JPA 2003, 136.

[1009] Rb. Kh. Antwerpen ETL 2005, 657, 669.

[1010] In more detail *Mankowski*, TranspR 2008, 67, 70 *et seq.*; also *Jiménez Blanco*, REDI 2009, 487, 489; *Roland/Insel*, JPA 2009, 320, 323; *Egler*, Seerechtliche Streitigkeiten unter der EuGVVO (2011) pp. 41–43.

[1011] In more detail *Mankowski*, TranspR 2008, 67, 71 *et seq.*; *Ansgar Staudinger*, RRA 2007, 155, 158 *et seq.* Underrated by *Egler*, Seerechtliche Streitigkeiten unter der EuGVVO (2011) pp. 47–49.

contract might happen there.[1012] To judge them, courts at the place of destination would be misplaced.[1013]

Generally (1) (b) strives for a unitary approach establishing only one place of performance **193** for a single contract; to this approach it is rather a contrast to have two different places as places where services are provided. Yet there are good reasons for the equivalence of both places in the concrete context: Firstly, a parallel to (3) can be seen where *Handlungsort* and *Erfolgsort* also peacefully co-exist[1014] despite the wording using the singular "place".[1015] Secondly, both places share equal weight in Art. 5 (1) cl. 1, (2) subpara. 1 cl. 1, (2) subpara. 2 litt. d and e Rome I Regulation. Thirdly, Arts. 31 (1) cl. 1 lit. b CMR; 21 (1) lit. c Hamburg Rules show the same pattern.[1016] Fourthly, to emphasise the success of transportation would diminish the importance of activity which would contradict the general notion that for services activity matters whereas its outcome is of secondary importance only.[1017] Otherwise characterisation and localisation would pursue different yardsticks.[1018] Fifthly, the service "carriage" consists of a number of consecutive elements[1019] and is the prime example for so called *gestreckte Erfüllung*.[1020] Sixthly, both places can claim to be on the spot for some of the elements respectively.[1021] Since the solution applies to both carriage of goods or of passengers and is not restricted to the transportation of travellers for private purposes, but also encompasses carriage of goods for professional customers it can not be accused of being specifically 'consumer-friendly'.[1022]

The place of destination is the one where the goods are discharged and released from the **194** carrier's custody. Once that has happened the factual setting prevails.[1023] But in principle the contractual determination carries its weight the more so since consensual alterations after the conclusion of the initial contract should be deemed alterations of the contract.[1024] In the

---

[1012] BGH NJW 2008, 2121, 2122; *Ansgar Staudinger*, RRa 2007, 155, 158; *Ansgar Staudinger*, IPRax 2008, 493, 495; *Mankowski*, TranspR 2009, 303, 305.

[1013] *Ansgar Staudinger*, IPRax 2008, 493, 495; *Mankowski*, TranspR 2009, 303, 305.

[1014] *Peter Rehder v. Baltic Air Corporation*, (Case C-204/08) [2009] ECR I-6073, I-6092 para. 45; *Verguts/Verhees*, ETR 2003, 403, 451 *et seq.*; *Mankowski*, TranspR 2008, 67, 74; *Mankowski*, TranspR 2009, 303, 305.

[1015] *Verguts/Verhees*, ETR 2003, 403, 451 *et seq.*; *Mankowski*, TranspR 2008, 67, 74; *Mankowski*, TranspR 2009, 303, 305.

[1016] *Mankowski*, TranspR 2008, 67, 72; *Mankowski*, TranspR 2009, 303, 305.

[1017] *Mankowski*, TranspR 2009, 303, 305.

[1018] *Mankowski*, TranspR 2009, 303, 305.

[1019] *Leible*, EuZW 2009, 571, 572; *Mankowski*, TranspR 2009, 303, 305; *Rolf Wagner*, IPRax 2010, 143, 146; see also *Rolf Wagner*, TranspR 2009, 281, 284.

[1020] *Leible*, FS Ulrich Spellenberg, 2010, p. 451, 460; *Leible*, in: Rauscher, Art. 5 Brüssel I-VO para. 55h.

[1021] See A-G *Lenz*, [1994] ECR I-2915, I-2933 para. 72; *Spellenberg*, ZZP 91 (1978), 38, 56 f; *Rauscher*, Verpflichtung und Erfüllungsort in Art. 5 Nr. 1 EuGVÜ (1984) p. 213; *Droz*, D. 1997 chron. 351, 355; *Kropholler/von Hinden*, GS Alexander Lüderitz (2000), p. 401, 407; *Mankowski*, TranspR 2008, 67, 71 for the place of destination and *Matthias Lehmann*, NJW 2007, 1500, 1502; *Ansgar Staudinger*, RRa 2007, 155, 158; *Mankowski*, TranspR 2008, 67, 72 for the place of departure.

[1022] *Contra Kuipers*, NIPR 2010, 622, 626.

[1023] *Mankowski*, TranspR 2008, 67, 71.

[1024] *Mankowski*, TranspR 2008, 67, 71.

event of a round-trip the place of destination is the final destination (equalling the starting point of the voyage).[1025] Mere intermediate landings do not matter.[1026]

3. Traditional approach, Art. 7 (1) (a)

a) General considerations

195 Since (a) is not limited to certain classes or categories of contracts it only requires the classification of the matter at stake as contractual and no further or additional refinements. If the correct order is chosen the negative issue of characterisation that the contract at stake is not governed by (b) has already been ascertained in advance as one correctly has started with (b). To proceed directly and primarily to (a) would be incorrect.[1027] (a) is clearly conceived as a rule for the remainder of contracts not caught by (b).[1028] It is the direct successor to Art. 5 (1) cl. 1 Brussels Convention continuing the approach pursued by that rule[1029] and maintaining its imprint.

196 Contractual matters still regulated by (a) are for instance: corporate matters;[1030] guarantees by third parties[1031] (which do not follow the guaranteed transaction with regard to their places of performance[1032]); agreements to negotiate;[1033] letters of comfort[1034] (since unilateral promises ought to be characterised as contractual in nature[1035]); other contracts or agreements for the purpose of contributions to a common venture[1036] or reimbursement[1037] (except insurance contracts which are subject to Arts. 10–16); sale of immovables;[1038] sale of intangibles, in particular sale of securities;[1039] share deals and asset deals for acquiring a business;[1040] bonds and certificates;[1041] licensing agreements;[1042] complex contracts (e.g.

1025 AG Geldern IPRspr. 2008 Nr. 120 p. 416.

1026 AG Düsseldorf RRa 2011, 146 = IPRspr. 2011 Nr. 189 p. 499.

1027 As it unfortunately happened e.g. in LG Gießen IHR 2003, 276.

1028 *Hau*, IPRax 2000, 354, 359; *Newton* p. 116; *Schoibl*, JBl 2003, 149, 158.

1029 *Falco Privatstiftung and Thomas Rabitsch v. Gisela Weller-Lindhorst*, (Case C-533/07) [2009] ECR I-3327 para. 56; *OTP Bank Nyilvánosan Müködö Részvénytársaság v. Hochtief Solution AG* (C-519/12), ECLI: EU:C:2013:674 para. 23.

1030 OLG Stuttgart NJW-RR 2005, 814, 815; LG Essen ZIP 2011, 875, 876; *Wehler*, EWiR Art. 5 EuGVVO 1/11, 559, 560.

1031 Cassaz. RDIPP 2013, 989; OLG Brandenburg IPRspr. 2010 Nr. 200 p. 506; *Leible*, in: Rauscher, Art. 5 note 26a.

1032 OGH SZ 71/191; *Rauscher*, in: FS Andreas Heldrich (2005), p. 933, 937; *Hofmann/Kunz*, in: Basler Kommentar, Art. 5 note 159.

1033 Hof 's-Hertogenbosch NIPR 2007 Nr. 40 p. 68.

1034 CA Paris D. 2002 somm. 1394 with note *Audit*; LG Düsseldorf RIW 2005, 629 with note *Mecklenbrauck*; *Commercial Marine & Piling Ltd. v. Pierce Contracting Ltd.* [2009] 2 Lloyd's Rep. 659 (Q.B.D.).

1035 *Mecklenbrauck*, RIW 2005, 630, 631. Generally *supra* Art. 5 notes 34–37 (*Mankowski*).

1036 See *Mora Shipping, Inc. v. Axa Corporate Solutions Assurance SA* [2005] 2 Lloyd's Rep. 769, 773 para. 19 (C.A., per *Clarke* L.J.).

1037 *Takahashi*, Claims for contribution and reimbursement in an international context (2000) pp. 27 *et seq.*; see also *Engdiv Ltd. v. G. Percy Trentham Ltd.* 1990 SLT 617 (O.H., Lord *Prosser*).

1038 See only ØLD UfR 2006, 2794, 2797; Rb. Utrecht NIPR 2007 Nr. 156 p. 221; *Matthias Lehmann*, in: Dickinson/Lein para. 4.51.

1039 *Pålsson*, SvJT 2001, 373, 380.

proxy contracts[1043]) insofar as they do not qualify as contracts for the sale of goods or the provision of services;[1044] databank contracts; cooperation agreements;[1045] agreements not to compete in certain markets; agreements to refrain from the use of certain trademarks, patents or other protected rights of intellectual property;[1046] agreements to abstain form a certain behaviour and form certain activities;[1047] contracts for the carriage of goods but only insofar as they are – incorrectly[1048] – not identified as contracts for the provision of services;[1049] letters of credit (if they are not characterised as financial services and thus fall within (b)); bills of exchange;[1050] undertakings to pay another's debts toward third parties.[1050a]

To subject claims, in particular restitutionary claims, based on the initial voidness or in- **197** validity of a contract under (a) in any event would disregard the watershed established by (b), though.[1051] If the contract in question envisaged the sale of goods or the provision of services, (b) should be master of the matter, not (a). Otherwise one would on the second level deviate from the seminal decision[1052] on the first level to assert a contractual characterisation and to stick with the approach lined out in Art. 12 (1) (e) Rome I Regulation, namely to let the law of the contract govern the *condictio indebiti* as far as possible.

b) Relevance of the single obligation
Under (a) the principle of characteristic performance does not apply,[1053] quite unlike as **198** under, and quite in contrast to, (b) but long asserted in the case law of the ECJ[1054] unter the Brussels Convention and ever confirmed[1055] against fierce challenges.[1056] Every single obli-

---

1040 *Simotta*, in: Fasching/Konecny Art. 5 note 108.

1041 See A-G *Szpunar*, Opinion in Case C-375/13 of 3 September 2014, ECLI:EU:C:2014:2135 para. 54.

1042 See only *Falco Privatstiftung and Thomas Rabitsch v. Gisela Weller-Lindhorst*, (Case C-533/07) [2009] ECR I-3327, I-3385 paras. 46 *et seq.*; A-G *Trstenjak*, [2009] ECR I-3330, I-3362 *et seq.* para. 86; *Fawcett*, in: Fawcett/Harris/Bridge para. 10.45; *Sujecki*, EWS 2009, 466, 467; *Mankowski*, JZ 2009, 958, 959; *Brinkmann*, IPRax 2009, 487, 491; *de Miguel Asensio*, REDI 2009, 200, 201; *Ubertazzi*, GRUR Int. 2010, 103, 108–111, 114 *et seq.*; *McGuire*, GPR 2010, 97, 100; *McGuire*, Yb. PIL 11 (2009), 453, 463 *et seq.*

1043 See OLG Stuttgart IPRax 2006, 472; *Michael Stürner*, IPRax 2006, 450, 452.

1044 *Leffler*, SvJT 2002, 816, 822. Questionable Cassaz. RDIPP 2006, 427, 429.

1045 OLG Hamm EuLF 2013, 23 = IPRspr. 2012 Nr. 190 p. 430 *et seq.*

1046 LG Mannheim InstGE 20, 240 paras. 7 *et seq.*; Vzngr. Rb. Arnhem NIPR 2003 Nr. 209 p. 318; *Lindacher*, in: FS Konstantinos Kerameus, vol. I (2009), p. 709, 713.

1047 OLG München IPRspr. 2011 Nr. pp. 534 *et seq.*; KG BeckRS 2014, 116810.

1048 See *supra* Art. 7 note 119 (*Mankowski*).

1049 Rb. Kh. Antwerpen ETL 2005, 687, 700.

1050 *Matthias Kilian*, BGH-Report 2004, 552, 553.

1050a *Canyan Offshore Ltd. v. GDF Suez E & P Nederland BV* [2014] EWHC 3801 (Comm), [2015] ILPr 110 [30] (Q.B.D., Judge *Mackie* QC).

1051 *Contra Bajons*, in: FS Reinhold Geimer (2002), p. 15, 63 *et seq.*

1052 *Supra* Art. 5 note 24 (*Mankowski*).

1053 See only *Falco Privatstiftung and Thomas Rabitsch v. Gisela Weller-Lindhorst*, (Case C-533/07) [2009] ECR I-3327, I-3387 para. 54; *Furrer/Schramm*, SJZ 2003, 105, 109; *Kerameus*, in: Liber amicorum Pierre Widmer (2003), p. 163, 166; *Ignatova*, Art. 5 Nr. 1 EuGVVO – Chancen und Perspektiven der Reform des Gerichtsstands am Erfüllungsort (2005) pp. 241 *et seq.*; *Rodriguez*, Beklagtenwohnsitz und Erfüllungsort im europäischen IZVR (Zürich 2005) para. 659. Apparently overlooked by Hof Amsterdam NIPR 2009 Nr. 135 p. 238.

gation carries in principle its own place of performance. It does not matter where the place of performance of the characteristic obligation can be located, nor should a principle of *priore temporis* (allocating most to the obligation first in time) weight be established.[1057] Relevant is only the obligation specifically at stake and under surveillance. The wording emphasising "the obligation" (and not "the contract") supports this contention which was established by the ECJ as early as 1976[1058] and has despite the numerous challenges mounted against it never been corrected save for the legislative intervention in (b). The splitting-the-cake solution formed part of an overall compromise with the defenders of the *status quo* as otherwise reform of (1) would not have been achievable at all.[1059] Thus if it comes down to (a) the relevant obligation at stake has to be identified.[1060] The principle of continuity between the Brussels Convention and the Brussels I Regulation safe for an express alteration, as enshrined in Recital (19), demands so.[1061] If the ECJ has established a standing jurisprudence over decades under the Brussels Convention this adds even more weight to maintaining continuity for such jurisprudence generates trust and faith.[1062]

199 Yet the principle gets some refinement: Secondary obligations, i.e. obligations arising out of the breach of another obligation, the so-called primary obligation, do not keep their own and independent place of performance, but follow the primary obligation. The breach of the contract follows the contract. *Accessorium sequitur principale.*[1063] One has to look at the

---

[1054] *A. de Bloos SPRL v. Société en commandite par actions Bouyer*, (Case 14/76) [1976] ECR 1497, 1508 paras. 8–14.

[1055] *Leathertex Divisione Sintetici SpA v. Bo"detex BVBA*, (Case C-420/97) [1999] ECR I-6747, I-6790 *et seq.* paras. 31–42; BGH NJW 1992, 2428; BGH NJW 1993, 2753; BAG AP Nr. 1 zu Art. 5 Lugano-Abkommen Bl. 5R with note *Mankowski*; BGE 124 III 188, 190 *et seq.*; Aud. Prov. Barcelona REDI 1999, 706, 707 with note *Gardeñas Santiago*.

[1056] E.g. Cassaz. RDIPP 1996, 117; Cassaz. RDIPP 1996, 529, 538; Cass RCDIP 86 (1997), 585 note *Gaudemet-Tallon* = Clunet 125 (1998), 129 with note *André Huet* = D. 1998 somm. 279 with note *Audit*; Cass. RCDIP 87 (1998), 117 rapport *Rémery*; *Droz*, D. 1997 chron. 351, 353. The story of the jurisprudence of the ECJ concerning Art. 5 (1) Brussels Convention is very aptly told by *Bajons*, in: FS Reinhold Geimer (2002), p. 15, 19–35.

[1057] *Rogerson*, [2001] Cambridge Yb. Eur. L. 383.

[1058] *A. de Bloos SPRL v. Société en commandite par actions Bouyer*, (Case 14/76) [1976] ECR 1497, 1508 paras. 8–14.

[1059] *Peter Arnt Nielsen*, in: Liber Professorum College of Europe 2005, p. 245, 255; see also *Klemm*, Erfüllungsortvereinbarungen im Europäischen Zivilverfahrensrecht (2005) p. 61; *Kropholler/von Hein* Art. 5 note 31.

[1060] E.g. *Falco Privatstiftung and Thomas Rabitsch v. Gisela Weller-Lindhorst*, (Case C-533/07) [2009] ECR I-3327, I-3387 para. 55; A-G *Trstenjak*, [2009] ECR I-3330, I-3364 *et seq.* paras. 93–100; Cass. RCDIP 100 (2011), 915, 916; Cassaz. RDIPP 2013, 989, 993; Aud. Prov. Les Illes Balears AEDIPr 2005, 664; Trib. Padova, sez. Este RDIPP 2007, 147, 153; Aud. Prov. Madrid AEDIPr 2007, 932, 933 with note *García Mirete*; LG Aachen IPRspr. 2012 Nr. 192 p. 437.

[1061] A-G *Trstenjak*, [2009] ECR I-3330, I-3363 paras. 87–89.

[1062] *Falco Privatstiftung and Thomas Rabitsch v. Gisela Weller-Lindhorst*, (Case C-533/07) [2009] ECR I-3327, I-3387 para. 53; *Polak*, Ars Aequi 2009, 400, 403; *Mankowski*, JZ 2009, 958, 961.

[1063] *Hassan Shenavai v. Klaus Kreischer*, (Case 266/85) [1987] ECR 239, 259 para. 19; *Leathertex Divisione Sintetici SpA v. Bo"detex BVBA*, (Case C-420/97) [1999] ECR I-6747, I-6791 *et seq.* para. 38; A-G *Mazák*, [2010] ECR I-1258, I-1263 para. 23; OLG Naumburg IPRspr. 2013 Nr. 190 p. 411; Epheteio Thessaloniki

obligation forming the basis of the legal proceedings,[1064] i.e. the one which corresponds to the contractual right on which the plaintiff's action is based.[1065] Insofar not the *petitum* as such but the *causa petendi* matters.[1066] As far as a right to be paid damages or the dissolution of a contract on the ground of the wrongful conduct of the other party are concerned, the obligation referred to in (a) is that which still arises under the contract and the non-performance of which is relied upon to support such claims or contentions.[1067] This also extends to claims for damages alleging and anticipating a future breach of contract.[1068] The obligation broken and the claim for damages resulting from the breach, share the same place of performance which is determined according to the primary obligation.[1069] The same applies if the breach of the contract generates contractually agreed default payments or contractual penalties (regardless whether besides or *in lieu* of damages).[1070] In essence and in the very result, it comes to every party gaining *its* place of performance against the other party for the purposes of jurisdiction.[1071]

Likewise, accompanying duties follow the main and primary duties under the contract.[1072] **200** For instance, if a right to information is pleaded in order to gain necessary data for a claim of payment, such a right is an accompanying right.[1073] On the other hand, primary duties do not follow each other, but ought to be treated separately.[1074] The equivalent rank of such primary duties is decisive, an equal weight and importance within the contractual structure

---

Arm. 1999, 1744; Rb. Kh. Gent TBH 2003, 175, 177; *Rogerson*, [2001] Cambridge Yb. Eur. L. 383; *Collins*, in: Dicey/Morris para. 11–252; *de Miguel Asensio*, in: Liber amicorum Alegría Borrás (2013), p. 291, 295; *Christoph A. Kern*, IPRax 2014, 503, 505–506.

[1064] *A. de Bloos SPRL v. Société en commandite par actions Bouyer*, (Case 14/76) [1976] ECR 1497, 1508 para. 11.

[1065] *A. de Bloos SPRL v. Société en commandite par actions Bouyer*, (Case 14/76) [1976] ECR 1497, 1508 para. 13.

[1066] Trib. Bergamo RDIPP 2003, 451, 455 *et seq.*; see also Cassaz. RDIPP 2005, 443, 446.

[1067] *A. de Bloos SPRL v. Société en commandite par actions Bouyer*, (Case 14/76) [1976] ECR 1497, 1508 para. 14; Cassaz. Dir. mar. 96 (1994), 1047, 1048; BGE 122 III 45; OGH JBl 1998, 515; OGH IPRax 2002, 131; KantonsG Zug IHR 2005, 119, 121; *Valloni* p. 105 *et seq.*, 259.

[1068] BGE 124 III 188, 192.

[1069] See only *A. de Bloos SPRL v. Société en commandite par actions Bouyer*, (Case 14/76) [1976] ECR 1497, 1508 para. 14; BGHZ 134, 201; BAG AP Nr. 1 zu Art. 5 Lugano-Abkommen Bl. 5R with note *Mankowski*; OGH ÖJZ 2004, 140 = JBl 2004, 186, 187; Cassaz. RDIPP 2003, 973, 975; Dir. mar. 106 (2004), 1336, 1337; OLG Hamm NJW-RR 1995, 188; OLG Stuttgart RIW 2004, 711, 712; Aud. Prov. Murcia REDI 2002, 371, 372 with note *Carballo Piñeiro*; Juzgado Primera Instancia n° 1 Tolosa (Guipúzcoa) REDI 1998, 1, 277, 278 with note *Jiménez Blanco*.

[1070] Trib. Bergamo RDIPP 2003, 451, 455 *et seq.*

[1071] *Schlosser*, EuGVÜ (1996) Art. 5 EuGVÜ with note 7; *Bajons*, in: FS Reinhold Geimer (2002), p. 15, 46.

[1072] See only Cassaz. Dir. mar. 2004, 1336; Cassaz. RDIPP 2007, 201, 203; BayObLG RIW 2001, 862, 863; OLG Düsseldorf IHR 2003, 121, 122; OLG Stuttgart RIW 2004, 711, 712.

[1073] *Banniza von Bazan*, Der Gerichtsstand des Sachzusammenhangs im EuGVÜ, dem Lugano-Abkommen und im deutschen Recht (1995) pp. 92 *et seq.*

[1074] See only *Leathertex Divisione Sintetici SpA v. Bo"detex BVBA*, (Case C-420/97) [1999] ECR I-6747, I-6791 *et seq.* paras. 38–40; BGH BGH-Report 2004, 549, 552 with note *Matthias Kilian*; OLG Düsseldorf IHR 2003, 121, 122.

---

is not required.[1075] Whether the duty in question is a primary or a secondary or an accompanying one is determined according to the *lex causae*, the substantive law applicable.[1076]

201 However, it must not be allowed to assume that if one party sues for payment and the defendant invokes breach of contract by the plaintiff as a defence, the claimant's obligation is the obligation in question.[1077] The writ identifies the claim at stake, and if the writ asks for payment, defenses are not to alter the qualification.[1078] If a letter of credit is still deemed to be covered by (a)[1079] and the beneficiary sues the issuing bank, the obligation in question is the obligation to pay, not any obligation to examine and take up the documents presented.[1080] The contractual nature of a letter of credit should be beyond any reasonable doubt.[1081]

202 Restitutionary claims stemming from the invalidity of contractual relationships borrow their very nature from the contractual relationship.[1082] Accordingly and consequentially, the place of performance designated for the contractual relationship should prevail,[1083] not the search for a place of performance for the restitutionary claim in its own right.[1084]

203 Concentration insofar features amongst the aims pursued by (a) not allowing for a majority of places of performance to exist for a single obligation.[1085] The risk of irreconcilable judgments contrary to Arts. 29; 45 (1) (c), (d) militates against any other approach.[1086] Courts can not get away with asserting to the contrary particularly, if they have not made the effort the obligation at stake.[1087] Yet different obligations of equal rank may have different places of performance in different states.[1088]

1075 See *Leathertex Divisione Sintetici SpA v. Bo"detex BVBA*, (Case C-420/97) [1999] ECR I-6747, I-6791 *et seq.* paras. 38–40.

1076 *A. de Bloos SPRL v. Société en commandite par actions Bouyer*, (Case 14/76) [1976] ECR 1497, 1509 para. 15/17; OLG Stuttgart RIW 2004, 711, 712; *The "Sea Maas"* [2000] 1 All ER 536, 542 = [1999] 2 Lloyd's Rep. 281, 284 (Q.B.D., *Rix* J.); *Bajons*, in: FS Reinhold Geimer (2002), p. 15, 22. *Contra Rüßmann*, IPRax 1993, 40; *Karsten Otte*, IPRax 2002, 132, 135.

1077 *Contra* ØLD UfR 1993 A 802.

1078 See *Pålsson*, in: Festskrift til Ole Lando (1997), p. 259, 272 *et seq.*; *Mankowski*, EWiR Art. 5 EuGVÜ 2/99, 1117, 1118.

1079 In favour of a characterisation bringing it under (b) *supra* Art. 7 notes 116–118 (*Mankowski*).

1080 *Credit Agricole Indosuez v. Chailease Finance Corp.* [2000] 1 All ER (Comm) 399, 406 *et seq.* (C.A., per *Potter* L.J.).

1081 See only Rb. Kh. Antwerpen TBH 1995, 429, 431; *Claeys*, TBH 1995, 433, 435 *et seq.*

1082 *Supra* Art. 5 notes 45, 130 (*Mankowski*).

1083 OGH EvBl 2002/172; *Peel*, [1996] LMCLQ 8, 13 *et seq.*; *Dickinson*, [1996] LMCLQ 556, 563; *Tiefenthaler*, ÖJZ 1998, 544, 545; *Martiny*, in: FS Reinhold Geimer (2002), p. 641, 653, 658; *Jethan*, ecolex 2003, 583, 584; *Geimer/Schütze* Art. 5 note 68.

1084 *Contra* OGH JBl 1998, 515 = ZfRV 1998, 157; OGH ZfRV 1998, 161 = RdW 1998, 552; *Bajons*, in: FS Reinhold Geimer (2002), p. 15, 53 *et seq.*

1085 *Besix SA v. Wasserreinigungsbau Alfred Kretzschmar GmbH & Co. KG (WABAG) and Planungs- und Forschungsgesellschaft Dipl. Ing. W. Kretzschmar GmbH & Co. KG (Plafog)*, (Case C-256/00) [2002] ECR I-1699, I-1727 para. 29; Hof van Cass. ETL 2006, 49, 53.

1086 *Besix SA v. Wasserreinigungsbau Alfred Kretzschmar GmbH & Co. KG (WABAG) and Planungs- und Forschungsgesellschaft Dipl. Ing. W. Kretzschmar GmbH & Co. KG (Plafog)*, (Case C-256/00) [2002] ECR I-1699, I-1727 para. 28.

Major problems occur if the law suit involves questions with regard to the contract in its **204**
entirety, not to a single obligation. The main example is provided by negative declaratory
actions that have the goal to declare the entire contract null and void, a second example by
positive declaratory actions that have the goal to assert the contract in its entirety.[1089] At least
five possible ways out of the ensuing dilemma appear feasible: (i) to identify the obligation
which is the plaintiff's primary target;[1090] (ii) to seize upon the obligation characteristic of the
contract in its entirety;[1091] (iii) to let every single obligation trigger jurisdiction;[1092] (iv) to let
every main obligation trigger jurisdiction;[1093] (v) to hold (1) (a) inapplicable[1094] if not all
obligations share a common place of performance.[1095] The third and fourth solutions might
lead to an unwarranted multiplication of jurisdiction whereas the fifth appears circular and
escapist simultaneously. The first solution is more consistent with the general approach
whereas the second attempts at introducing a concept not followed generally, through the
backdoor for a special instance.[1096] On the other hand the first solution generates the need to
identify the relevant obligation by a rather subjective criterion. The plaintiff gets some
opportunities to influence the choice, and there ought to be same safeguards preventing
the plaintiff from dominating the concrete result. He might have a most pressing obligation
in mind of which he wants to be liberated, but the writ might not expressly reflect this, e.g.
due to formalities of the national procedural law. To materialise the plaintiff's intention
might in any event prove difficult.

c) Place of performance according to the applicable substantive law

Back in 1976 the ECJ developed the so-called *Tessili*-doctrine: For the purposes of Art. 5 (1) **205**
Brussels Convention in its original version of 1968 the place of performance ought to be
determined pursuant to the substantive law applicable on the claim in question.[1097] As for the
reasoning the ECJ detected too big a divergence in the approaches followed by the national
laws of the (original) Member States as to gain an opportunity to develop a uniform solution
by comparing these national laws. Because the Member States in their national laws determined the place of performance all too differently the ECJ was not prepared to opt for an
autonomous solution.[1098] This doctrine withstood every challenge which reached the

---

[1087] Hof van Cass. ETL 2006, 49, 53. *Contra* Hof Antwerpen ETL 2003, 446; Rb. Kh. Antwerpen ETL 2005,
657, 669.

[1088] *Leathertex Divisione Sintetici SpA v. Bo"detex BVBA*, (Case C-420/97) [1999] ECR I-6747, I-6791 *et seq.*
paras. 38, 40.

[1089] See only BGHZ 185, 241; *Looschelders*, JR 2011, 345, 346.

[1090] BAG AP Nr. 1 zu Art. 5 Lugano-Abkommen Bl. 6 with note *Mankowski*; *USF Ltd. (trading as USF
Memcor) v. Aqua Technology Hanson NV/SA* [2001] 1 All ER (Comm) 856, 862 (Q.B.D., Aikens J.);
Oberhammer, in: Dasser/Oberhammer Art. 5 note 29; see also Cass. RCDIP 72 (1983), 516 with note *Gaudemet-Tallon*; Cassaz. RDIPP 1986, 981 = Nuova giurisprudenza civile commentata 1986 I 689 with
note *Campeis/Arrigo de Pauli*; OLG Frankfurt/M. RIW 1980, 585; OLG Stuttgart IPRax 1999, 103.

[1091] *André Huet*, Clunet 110 (1983), 395 at 397; *Gaudemet-Tallon*, Rev. crit. dr. int. pr. 72 (1983), 516 at 518;
Gottwald, in: Münchener Kommentar zur ZPO Art. 5 note 32; see also *Lima Pinheiro* p. 83.

[1092] LG Trier NJW-RR 2003, 287, 288.

[1093] *Simotta*, in: Fasching/Konecny Art. 5 note 123; *Geimer/Schütze* Art. 5 note 110.

[1094] BGH IHR 2010, 212, 215 = BGHZ 185, 241.

[1095] *Schlosser* Art. 5 note 9.

[1096] BGH IHR 2010, 212, 215 = BGHZ 185, 241.

[1097] *Industrie Tessili Italiana Como v. Dunlop AG*, (Case 12/76) [1976] ECR 1473, 1486 paras. 13–15.

Court,[1099] however massive these challenges were,[1100] including a frontal head-on attack by A-G *Lenz*.[1101] The ECJ even crushed[1102] a simultaneous rebellion by A-Gs *Ruiz-Jarabo Colomer*[1103] and *Léger*[1104] and thus placated even the slightest doubts as to the firmness of its holdings.[1105] Obediently the *Tessili*-approach was followed in the national courts at last.[1106] Finally, as part of the overall compromise the doctrine found refuge in (a).[1107] The *travaux*

[1098] *Industrie Tessili Italiana Como v. Dunlop AG*, (Case 12/76) [1976] ECR 1473, 1486 para. 14; *GIE Groupe Concorde v. Master of the vessel "Suhadiwarno Panjan"*, (Case C-440/97) [1999] I-6307, I-6349 para. 17.

[1099] *Custom Made Commercial Ltd. v. Stawa Metallbau GmbH*, (Case C-288/92) [1994] ECR I-2913, I-2957 *et seq.* paras. 23–29; *GIE Groupe Concorde v. Master of the vessel "Suhadiwarno Panjan"*, (Case C-440/97) [1999] ECR I-6307, I-6349-I-6352 paras. 17–30; *Leathertex Divisione Sintetici SpA v. Bodetex BVBA*, (Case C-420/97) [1999] I-6747, I-6791 para. 33.

[1100] See Cass. RCDIP 87 (1998), 117.

[1101] A-G *Lenz*, Opinion in Case C-288/92, [1994] ECR I-2915.

[1102] The story is entertainingly told by *Newton* p. 150–159.

[1103] A-G *Ruiz-Jarabo Colomer*, Opinion in Case C-440/97, [1999] ECR I-6309.

[1104] A-G *Léger*, Opinion in Case C-420/97, [1999] ECR I-6793.

[1105] *GIE Groupe Concorde v. Master of the vessel "Suhadiwarno Panjan"*, (Case C-440/97) [1999] ECR I-6307, I-6349-I-6352 paras. 17–30; *Leathertex Divisione Sintetici SpA v. Bo"detex BVBA*, (Case C-420/97) [1999] ECR I-6747, I-6791 para. 33.

[1106] E.g. BGHZ 134, 201; BGH NJW-RR 2003, 192; BAG AP Nr. 1 zu Art. 5 Lugano-Abkommen Bl. 5R with note *Mankowski*; Cassaz. RDIPP 1996, 97; Cassaz. RDIPP 1999, 319; Cassaz. RDIPP 2000, 738; Cassaz. RDIPP 2000, 773; Cassaz. RDIPP 2001, 415; Cass. RCDIP 90 (2001), 149; Cass. JCP 2000 IV 2393; Cass. RCDIP 90 (2001), 150, 151; Cass. RCDIP 90 (2001), 151, 152; Cass. RCDIP 90 (2001), 153; Cass. RCDIP 90 (2001), 153, 154; Cass. RCDIP 90 (2001), 155, 156; Cass. RCDIP 90 (2001), 156, 157; Cass. RCDIP 90 (2001), 157; HD NJA 1999, 673, 678; Hoge Raad NJ 2005 Nr. 39 p. 208 with note *Vlas*; Epheteio Thessaloniki Arm. 1992, 367; Epheteio Thessaloniki Arm. 1999, 1744; App. Milano RDIPP 2004, 1367, 1370; Hof 's-Hertogenbosch NIPR 2005 Nr. 143 p. 187; ØLD UfR 2002, 1370, 1371; OLG Brandenburg NJOZ 2008, 1677; OLG Brandenburg IPRspr. 2010 Nr. 200 p. 507; Trib. Udine RDIPP 2004, 237; Aud. Prov. Vizcaya REDI 2000, 563, 564 with note *Marín López*; Aud. Prov. Barcelona AEDIPr 2001, 901, 902; Aud. Prov. Barcelona AEDIPr 2002, 679 with note *de Miguel Asensio*; Aud. Prov. Murcia REDI 2002, 371, 372 with note *Carballo Piñeiro*; Aud. Prov. Madrid AEDIPr 2007, 932, 933 with note *García Mirete*; LG Koblenz IHR 2011, 145, 147; HG St. Gallen IHR 2011, 149, 150; LG Aachen IPRspr. 2012 Nr. 192 p. 437; Juzgado Primera Instancia n° 1 Tolosa (Guipúzcoa) REDI 1998, 1, 277, 278 with note *Jiménez Blanco*.

[1107] See only *Falco Privatstiftung and Thomas Rabitsch v. Gisela Weller-Lindhorst*, (Case C-533/07) [2009] ECR I-3327, I-3387 paras. 54–55; *Česká spořitelna as v. Gerald Feichter*, (Case C-419/11), ECLI:EU:C:2013:165 paras. 43–44; A-G *Trstenjak*, [2009] ECR I-3330, I-3362 para. 85; A-G *Jääskinen*, Opinion of 25 April 2013 in Case 9/12, para. 74; BGH RIW 2005, 776, 777; Cassaz. Mass. Giust. Civ. 2005 no. 9106; Bull. civ. 2007 I n° 30 = D. 2007, 511 with note *Chevrier* = D. 2007, 1085 note *Gallmeister* = D. 2007, 1575 note *Kenfack* = JCP G 2007 II 10074 with note *Azzi* = RDC 2007, 887 obs. *Deumier* = Clunet 135 (2008), 521 with note *Jacquet* = RCDIP 97 (2008), 661, 662; Cass. RCDIP 97 (2008), 863, 864; Cass. D. 2008, 1729 with note *Kenfack*; Cass. RCDIP 100 (2011), 139, 151; Cass. RCDIP 100 (2011), 917; Cassaz. Giust. civ. 2011 I 1028, 1031; Cassaz. RDIPP 2013, 989, 993; Hof 's-Gravenhage NIPR 2005 Nr. 51 p. 92; Hof Amsterdam NIPR 2008 Nr. 296 p. 551; *Mora Shipping, Inc. v. Axa Corporate Solutions Assurance SA* [2005] 2 Lloyd's Rep. 769, 773 para. 21 (C.A., per *Clarke* L.J.); OLG Oldenburg NJW-RR 2008, 1592 = VersR 2010, 231; OLG Köln 16 December 2008 – Case 9 U 47/07 [44]; Rb. Arnhem NIPR 2005 Nr. 56 p. 97; Rb. 's-Hertogenbosch NIPR 2005 Nr. 169 p. 234; Rb. 's-Gravenhage NIPR 2008 Nr. 305 p. 564; Rb.

préparatoires are quite clear and unambiguous in this regard.[1108] The traditional approach reasserts itself and prevails insofar.[1109] To bring (a) and (b) more in line with each other, particularly on the general line of a factual approach like under (b), might be (or have been) a desideratum for some[1110] but is a matter for a future *regulatio ferenda*, not for the present *regulatio lata*.[1111] You may not like the compromise reached by the Community legislator, but you have to accept it and can not *ex post* topple the defenders of the *status quo* insofar as they were successful.[1112] The increasing problems incremental to (b) might have further reduced the attractivity of an overall approach based on (b).[1113]

Accordingly, the interpretation of (a), which was designed to keep the judge-made *Tessili* **206**

Rotterdam NIPR 2010 Nr. 322 p. 529; Rb. Kh. Antwerpen ETL 2005, 687, 700; LG Köln IPRspr. 2013 Nr. 192 p. 422; *Tavoulareas v. Tsavliris* [2006] I.L.Pr. 314, 329 *et seq.* (Q.B.D., *Smith* J.); Trib. Padova, sez. Este RDIPP 2007, 147, 153; Rapport *Potocki*, RCDIP 100 (2011), 139, 147 *et seq.*; *Kropholler/von Hinden*, in: GS Alexander Lüderitz (2000), p. 401, 408 *et seq.*; *Leipold*, in: GS Alexander Lüderitz (2000), p. 431, 445, 451; *Hausmann*, EuLF 2000-01, 40, 44; *Karsten Otte*, ZZP Int. 5 (2000), 272, 274, *Marie-Élodie Ancel*, RCDIP 90 (2001), 158, 159; *Kropholler/von Hein* Art. 5 note 29; *Zilinsky*, NILR 2002, 110, 111; *Mankowski*, EWiR Art. 5 EuGVÜ 1/02, 519, 520; *Mankowski*, in: Spindler/Wiebe (eds.), Internet-Auktionen und Elektronische Marktplätze (2nd ed. 2005), ch. 12 note 33; *Mankowski*, JZ 2009, 958, 960; *Verlinden*, 8 Col. J. Eur. L. 493, 497 (2002); *Leffler*, SvJT 2002, 816, 822; *Schlosser* Art. 5 note 10c; *Leible*, in: Rauscher Art. 5 note 41; *von der Seipen*, in: FS Erik Jayme (2004), p. 859, 867; *Klemm*, Erfüllungsortvereinbarungen im Europäischen Zivilverfahrensrecht (2005) pp. 61, 62; *Rodriguez*, Beklagtenwohnsitz und Erfüllungsort im europäischen IZVR (Zürich 2005) para. 659; *Ballarino/Mari*, Riv. dir. int. 2006, 7, 30; *Sindres*, RCDIP 97 (2008), 864, 866; *Vlas*, NJ 2008 Nr. 237 p. 2282; *Polak*, AA 2009, 400, 403; *Brinkmann*, IPRax 2009, 487, 491; *van Lith*, International Jurisdiction and Commercial Litigation – Uniform Rules for Contract Disputes (The Hague 2009) p. 94; *McGuire*, GPR 2010, 97, 101; *Mittmann*, IHR 2010, 146, 148; *Mittmann*, D. 2010, 834, 836; *Markus*, AJP 2010, 971, 975; *Leible*, in: FS Ulrich Spellenberg (2010), p. 451, 452; *Franzina*, RDIPP 2010, 655, 656 *et seq.*; *Kropholler/von Hein*, Art. 5 note 29; *Notdurfter/Petruzzino*, Contratto e impresa/Europa 2011, 223, 225; *Hofmann/Kunz*, in: Basler Kommentar, Art. 5 notes 281, 284; *Marie-Elodie Ancel*, RCDIP 100 (2011), 917, 921; *Garau Sobrino*, AEDIPr 2013, 1053, 1054–1055 and also Cassaz. RDIPP 2006, 427, 429 *et seq.* Wrongly applying the principle of characteristic performance under (a) Hof 's-Gravenhage NIPR 2011 Nr. 233 p. 416; Rb. Rotterdam NIPR 2008 Nr. 311 p. 574; Rb. Rotterdam TvA 2011, 81, 83.

[1108] Report by the Commission COM (1999) 348 final p. 14.

[1109] A-G *Trstenjak*, [2009] ECR I-3330, I-3365 paras. 94–95; *Newton* p. 116; *Brinkmann*, IPRax 2009, 487, 491.

[1110] *Jayme/Christian Kohler*, IPRax 1999, 401, 405; *Kropholler/von Hinden*, in: GS Alexander Lüderitz (2000), p. 401, 409; *Micklitz/Rott*, EuZW 2001, 325, 329; *Junker*, RIW 2002, 569, 572; *Bajons*, in: FS Reinhold Geimer (2002), p. 15, 64 *et seq.*; *Ignatova*, Art. 5 Nr. 1 EuGVVO – Chancen und Perspektiven der Reform des Gerichtsstands am Erfüllungsort (2005) pp. 263–265; *Kropholler/von Hein* Art. 5 note 31; *Ballarino/Mari*, Riv. dir. int. 2006, 7, 30 *et seq.*; *Leible/Sommer*, IPRax 2006, 568, 570.

[1111] A-G *Trstenjak*, [2009] ECR I-3330, I-3366 para. 99; *Leipold*, in: GS Alexander Lüderitz (2000), p. 431, 451; *Karsten Otte*, ZZP Int. 5 (2000), 272, 274; *Kropholler/von Hein* Art. 5 note 31.

[1112] A-G *Trstenjak*, [2009] ECR I-3330, I-3366 para. 99.

[1113] *Reinstadler*, Giur. it. 2007, 430; *Matthias Lehmann*, ZZP Int. 12 (2007), 206; *Markus*, Tendenzen beim materiellrechtlichen Vertragserfüllungsort im internationalen Zivilverfahrensrecht (Basel 2009) pp. 178–179 et passim; *Mankowski*, JZ 2009, 958, 961; *Henri Storme*, R.W. 2009–2010, 409, 414; *Mittmann*, IHR 2010, 146, 149; *Mittmann*, D. 2010, 834, 837.

Peter Mankowski

-doctrine, should mirror the judgments of the ECJ as closely as possible. Under (a) one has still to ascertain the applicable substantive law and must ask this law where it locates the place of performance for the obligation in question.[1114] At least this gives a clear guideline how to proceed and thus gains the edge over determining the place of performance by reference to the nature of the relationship of the obligation and the circumstances of the single case.[1115] As to substance the debtor can be sued where he is obliged to perform according to substantive law.[1116] Paying due regard to the standing line of decisions of the ECJ interpreting Art. 5 (1) Brussels Convention generates the necessary guidance and thus meets the general requirements for clarity and security. The ECJ held steadily to its line,[1117] and advising the court to deviate from it would produce unwelcome insecurity and uncertainty.[1118] Admittedly, the ECJ might not be bound by the *travaux préparatoires*[1119] but would nevertheless undermine the *ratio* underlying (a) if it switched approaches. Rightly, the ECJ confirmed the applicability and persistence of the *Tessili* doctrine on the first possible occasion.[1120] Furthermore, the alternative of an autonomous approach trying to resemble (b)[1121] might result in chaos as it would have to surmount and overcome a wealth of difficulties defining the "natural" place of performance for each type of contract.[1122]

207   In order to ascertain the applicable substantive law one has to employ the private international law of the *forum*.[1123] The rules of PIL serve the very purpose to determine the applicable law on the concrete claim. There is nothing more to it. In particular nothing like a parallel between *forum* and *ius* shall be achieved by the *Tessili*-approach[1124] (and is a rather accidental result if the *locus executionis* coincides with the place of business of the party responsible for the characteristic performance[1125]). *Tessili* was not about implementing a *forum legis*. Whilst back in 1976 even the PIL rules of the Member States wildly differed, in the past the Rome Convention – but of course only for its Member States – and now the Rome I Regulation, provide uniform European conflicts rules for contracts. Thus a possible

---

[1114]   See only OLG Stuttgart RIW 2004, 711, 712 *et seq.*; Rb. Rotterdam NIPR 2004 Nr. 156 p. 251; *Kropholler/ von Hinden*, in: GS Alexander Lüderitz (2000), p. 401, 408 *et seq.*; *Vlas*, WPNR 6421 (2000), 745, 749; *Jayme/Christian Kohler*, IPRax 2000, 454, 460; *Cavalier*, Rev. Lamy dr. aff. N° 39, juin 2009, p. 57, 58; *Franzina*, RDIPP 2010, 655, 656.

[1115]   *GIE Groupe Concorde v. Master of the vessel "Suhadiwarno Panjan"*, (Case C-440/97) [1999] ECR I-6307, I-6351 para. 25.

[1116]   See only BAG AP Nr. 1 zu Art. 5 Lugano-Abkommen Bl. 5R with note *Mankowski*; *Franzina*, RDIPP 2010, 655, 657.

[1117]   See references in fn. 3.

[1118]   *Mankowski*, EWiR Art. 5 EuGVÜ 1/02, 519, 520.

[1119]   *Klemm*, Erfüllungsortvereinbarungen im Europäischen Zivilverfahrensrecht (2005) pp. 63 *et seq.*

[1120]   *Falco Privatstiftung and Thomas Rabitsch v. Gisela Weller-Lindhorst*, (Case C-533/07) [2009] ECR I-3327, I-3387 paras. 54–55.

[1121]   In such direction uncunningly Rb. Rotterdam TvA 2011, 81, 83.

[1122]   *Klemm*, Erfüllungsortvereinbarungen im Europäischen Zivilverfahrensrecht (2005) p. 64.

[1123]   See only A-G *Trstenjak*, [2009] ECR I-3330, I-3366 para. 99; OLG Frankfurt RIW 2004, 864, 865; OLG Karlsruhe NJOZ 2004, 1304; *Geimer/Schütze* Art. 5 note 92; *Hüßtege* in: Thomas/Putzo, Art. 5 note 11.

[1124]   Contra Juzgado Primera Instancia n° 3 Barcelona REDI 1998, 177 with note *Gardeñes Santiago*.

[1125]   See *Graf Wrangel*, Der Gerichtsstand des Erfüllungsortes im deutschen, italienischen und europäischen Recht (1988) pp. 173 *et seq.*; *von Overbeck*, in: Liber amicorum Georges A.L. Droz (1996), p. 287, 293; *Holl*, IPRax 1998, 120, 121.

source for diverging results has been reduced and is scheduled to vanish further.[1126] That courts apply the conflicts rules incorrectly and thereby would reach different results in cases of the same kind, does not undermine the argument based on uniformity of the conflicts rules. Judicial errors remain judicial errors and do not account for the quality of the rules the judges are bound to apply. If judges neglect their duty to apply conflict rules contained in a treaty *ex officio* and fall back on the substantive law of the *lex fori*, following a fact doctrine without remorse and without a second thought,[1127] this is a deplorable result[1128] but no inherent default of the *Tessili*-approach.[1129] Yet the adoption of the *Tessili* doctrine, combined with vacillations between national laws on the place of payment, can lead to perverse results depending on the accident of the court before which the matter is brought, since for instance English, Dutch, Italian and Greek law make it generally incumbent upon the debtor to physically seek out his creditor whilst German, French and Belgish law opted for the opposite approach favouring the debtor's residence.[1130] In summary, the detour to PIL and the *lex causae* introduces an element of capriciousness unto the proximity equation, varying according to the particular approach of determing the place of performance employed by the concrete *lex causae*.[1131]

General assertations that negative obligations (i.e. obligations to refrain from doing some- **208** thing specified) do not have any place of performance,[1132] are rash and in this generality not supported by a correct application of the normative approach namely to refer to the applicable substantive law: If the applicable law equals such place of performance with the debtor's or the creditor's domicile, a place of performance can be identified,[1133] and at the same time the danger of multiple places of performance (which indeed are not desirable[1134]) would be effectively banned.

The substantive law applicable is not bound to be of national origin. To the contrary, uni- **209** form law could play a major role. Insofar as uniform law is applicable pursuant to its own rules on its on own scope of application it also fits well into the overall scheme designed by (a). Uniform law forms a kind of substantive law and features as part of the legal orders of its member states. Accordingly, it must find proper application if a recourse on substantive law takes place. This has always been recognised under Art. 5 (1) Brussels or Lugano Convention

---

[1126] *GIE Groupe Concorde v. Master of the vessel "Suhadiwarno Panjan"*, (Case C-440/97) [1999] ECR I-6307, I-6352 para. 30; *Hau*, ZZP Int. 5 (2000), 284, 287.

[1127] Examples are provided i.a. by *Viskase Ltd. v. Paul Kiefel GmbH* [1999] 1 WLR 1305 = [1999] 3 All ER 362 = [2000] I.L.Pr. 29 (C.A.); *The "Ethniki"* [2000] I.L.Pr. 426 (C.A.); *Credit Agricole Indosuez v. Chailease Finance Corp.* [2000] 1 All ER (Comm) 399, 410 (C.A., per *Potter* L.J.); *John Charles Barry v. Kenneth Bradshaw* [2000] I.L.Pr. 706 (C.A.); Pret. Burso Arsizio Dir. comm. int. 2001, 935.

[1128] See only *Sánchez Lorenzo*, REDI 1998, 319; *Briggs*, (1999) 70 BYIL 319, 337; *Esteve González*, AEDIPr 2000, 816, 818; *Portatadino*, Dir. comm. int. 2001, 937.

[1129] Tentatively *contra Kubis*, ZEuP 2001, 737, 746.

[1130] See only *Reed*, (1999) 18 Civ. Just. Q. 218, 234 *et seq.*

[1131] *Newton* p. 122.

[1132] So namely *Agnew v. Länsförsäkringsbolagens AB* [2001] 1 A.C. 223, 241 (H.L., per Lord *Woolf* M.R.); *von der Seipen*, in: FS Erik Jayme (2004), p. 859, 870.

[1133] *Mankowski*, EWiR Art. 5 EuGVÜ 1/02, 519, 520.

[1134] See only *Forsyth*, [1996] LMCLQ 329, 332 *et seq.*

and holds true for (a), too.[1135] The main example in the past was provided by the CISG,[1136] in particular Art. 57 (1) (a) CISG with the much criticised[1137] consequence of a *forum actoris* for the seller. Today the bulk of sale of goods within Europe is dealt with under (b) without having recourse to the applicable substantive law. Thus the CISG has lost much of its impact for (1).[1138] Only under (c) can some instances can arise where Art. 57 (1) (a) CISG still comes into operation for the purposes of the European jurisdictional regime.[1139] It is definitely wrong to start with a combination of (1) and CISG.[1140]

210 The German version of (1) (a) contains an unfortunate oddity. Its wording appears to suggest that besides the place of performance as ascertained by recourse to the applicable law there is a second alternative which comes into operation if and where the obligation was effectively performed. This had led (or rather: misled) to assertions that the factual place of the performance is to be determined once performance took place.[1141] But the reduplication or better the scission appears only in the German version and few other versions. The German wording is accompanied by the Spanish ("lugar en el que se haya cumplido o deba cumplirse la obligación"), the Portuguese ("lugar onde foi ou deva ser cumprida"), the Dutch ("the plaats waar de verbintenis […] is uitgevoerd of moet worden uitgevoerd"). But the English wording for instance simply reads "place of performance", the French "lieu d'exécution", the Italian "luogo di esecuzione",, the Swedish "uppfyllelseorten" and the Romanian "locul de executare". Only one term is also used in the Polish, Czech, Slovakian, Lithuanian, Latvian and Slovenian versions.

[1135] See only *Custom Made Commercial Ltd. v. Stawa Metallbau GmbH* (Case C-288/92) [1994] ECR I-2913, I-2958 *et seq.* para. 29.

[1136] See only BGHZ 74, 136, 139; BGHZ 78, 257; BGH EuZW 1992, 518, 520; Cassaz. RDIPP 1983, 383; Cassaz. RDIPP 1986, 691; Cassaz. RDIPP 1990, 155; Cassaz. RDIPP 1991, 172; Cassaz. RDIPP 1991, 441; Cassaz. RDIPP 1992, 593; Cassaz. RDIPP 1994, 649; Cassaz. RDIPP 1999, 290; Cassaz. RDIPP 2000, 1078; Cassaz. Dir. mar. 103 (2001), 757; Cassaz. RDIPP 2003, 973, 974 *et seq.*; Cassaz. RDIPP 2005, 111, 114; Cassaz. RDIPP 2005, 443, 447; Cassaz. Mass. Foro it. 2009, 179; BGE 122 III 43, 46; Cass. RCDIP 88 (1999), 122 with note *Bertrand Ancel/Muir Watt* = Clunet 126 (1999), 196 with note *André Huet* = D. 1999, 117 with note *Claude Witz*; Cass. JCP 2002 I 144 with note *Rueda*; Cass. [2003] I.L.Pr. 203, 206; OGH ZfRV 2004, 77; Hof Antwerpen R.W. 1979–80, 1045 note *Laenens*; CA Riom JCP 1997 II 22772 with note *de Vareilles-Sommières*; CA Paris [1997] I.L.Pr. 825, 827; Hof Gent TBH 1998, 389 with note *Watté*; Hof Brussel R.W. 1998–1999, 924, 926; Hof Gent R.W. 2002–2003, 664, 665 note *Rutten*; App. Milano RDIPP 2004, 1011; App. Milano Dir. mar. 107 (2005), 588, 592 with note *Scapinello*; App. Milano RDIPP 2006, 1050; ØLD UfR 1993, 302; ØLK UfR 1996, 616; ØLK UfR 1998, 1092, 1093; Rb. Kh. Gent TBH 1998, 403, 404; Rb. Kh. Hasselt TBH 1999, 65 note *van Houtte*; Aud. Prov. Barcelona REDI 1999, 706, 707 with note *Gardeñas Santiago* = AEDIPr 2001, 901; Aud. Prov. Ciudad Real AEDIPr 2002, 572, 573; Rb. Rotterdam NIPR 2002 Nr. 130; Aud. Prov. Murcia AEDIPr 2003, 874; Aud. Prov. Valladolid AEDIPr 2005. 625 note *Esteban de la Rosa*.

[1137] See only *Schack*, IPRax 1986, 82, 84; *Schwenzer*, IPRax 1989, 274, 275; *Jayme*, IPRax 1992, 357, 358; *Jayme*, IPRax 1995, 13 *et seq.*; *Jayme/Christian Kohler*, IPRax 1994, 405, 410 *et seq.*; *Volken*, SZIER 1995, 295, 297 *et seq.*

[1138] *André Huet*, in: Mélanges en l'honneur de Paul Lagarde (2005), p. 417, 427 *et seq.*; see LG München II IPRax 2005, 143, 144.

[1139] *Magnus*, IHR 2002, 45, 47.

[1140] An example how not to proceed is provided by LG Gießen IHR 2003, 276.

[1141] OLG Saarbrücken IPRax 2013, 74, 78–79; *von Hein*, IPRax 2013, 54, 59.

4. Scope of Art. 7 (1) (c)

(c) is not the catch-all clause that it might appear at first glance. It covers only those cases **211** which drop through the net of (b). (c) at second glance may even appear redundant but on closer inspection serves a useful and unique purpose if only in limited circumstances. Certainly (c) would be redundant (or politely expressed: declaratory)[1142] if it served as a simple reminder of the very existence of (a) insofar as cases are concerned which are covered by (a) in its own right.[1143] There is, however, one variety of cases which do not fall under (a) in its own right since insofar (a) would be derogated from by (b): contracts for the sale of goods or for performing services where under (b) the place of performance would be located outside the EU. Generally, (b) would govern those cases but would not lead to special jurisdiction in contract inside the EU. Now enter (c) which, after the factual approach failed to identify a special *forum* in a Member State and pointed towards some place in a non-Member State, changes approaches and switches over to the normative approach followed by (a).[1144] This is confirmed by the *travaux préparatoires*.[1145] The plaintiff gets some kind of a second chance to establish special jurisdiction.[1146] In practice, exporting companies established in the EU might profit to the detriment of their partners in contract who are established outside the EU.[1147] This draws criticism from some quarters.[1148]

Besides this it is often argued that (c) also applies if the application of (b) leads to multiple **212** places of performance.[1149] Then, these authors submit, a place of performance under (b)

[1142] *Kropholler/von Hinden*, in: GS Alexander Lüderitz (2000), p. 401, 411.

[1143] But compare OLG Stuttgart RIW 2004, 711, 712; *Peter Arnt Nielsen*, in: Liber Fausto Pocar (2009), p. 773, 779.

[1144] OLG Düsseldorf IHR 2004, 108, 110; OLG Frankfurt RIW 2004, 864, 865; Trib. Padova EuLF 2006, II-16, 18; Vzngr. Rb. Maastricht NIPR 2008 Nr. 62 p. 104; Rapport *Potocki*, RCDIP 100 (2011), 139, 147, 148; *Kropholler/von Hinden*, in: GS Alexander Lüderitz (2000), p. 401, 411; *Leipold*, in: GS Alexander Lüderitz (2000), p. 431, 450; *Hau*, ZZP Int. 5 (2000), 284, 290; *Marie-Élodie Ancel*, RCDIP 90 (2001), 158, 160; *Zilinsky*, NILR 2002, 110, 111 *et seq.*; *Marquette*, Rev. dr. comm. belge 2002, 499, 501; *Rommelaere*, Rev. dr. comm. belge 2003, 103, 109; *Tagaras*, CDE 2003, 399, 406; *Vlas*, NILR 2004, 451, 452 *et seq.*; *André Huet*, in: Mélanges en l'honneur de Paul Lagarde (2005), p. 417, 429 *et seq.*; *Vlas/Zilinsky*, WPNR 6706 (2007), 337, 340; *Simotta*, in: Fasching/Konecny Art. 5 note 90; *Mittmann*, IHR 2010, 146, 148; *Mittmann*, D. 2010, 834, 836; *Grušić*, (2012) 61 ICLQ 91, 110; *Strikwerda*, Ned. Jur. 2014 Nr. 346 p. 4354, 4355. Openly opposing *van Lith*, International Jurisdiction and Commercial Litigation – Uniform Rules for Contract Disputes (The Hague 2009) p. 90; *Markus*, AJP 2010, 971, 985; *Rauscher*, NJW 2010, 2251, 2254. Critical *Kropholler/von Hein*, Art. 5 note 53. To the same result namely applying (a) but rather directly without employing (c) Report *Pocar* para. 51; *Hofmann/Kunz*, in: Basler Kommentar, Art. 5 note 272. Overlooked by *Di Blase*, Europa e dir. priv. 2011, 459, 477 *et seq.*

[1145] Commission Proposal COM (1999) final p. 15.

[1146] *Kubis*, ZEuP 2001, 737, 751; *Carballo Piñeiro*, REDI 2002, 372, 377; *Hau*, ZZP Int. 7 (2002), 214, 219; *Kienle*, IPRax 2005, 113, 114 *et seq.*; *Simotta*, in: Fasching/Konecny Art. 5 notes 90, 212. Critical *van Lith*, International Jurisdiction and Commercial Litigation – Uniform Rules for Contract Disputes (The Hague 2009) p. 90; *Rauscher*, NJW 2010, 2251, 2254.

[1147] *Hau*, IPRax 2000, 354, 360; *Markus*, AJP 2010, 971, 985.

[1148] *Hau*, IPRax 2000, 354, 360; *Leipold*, in: GS Alexander Lüderitz (2000), p. 431, 450 *et seq.*; *Kropholler/von Hein* Art. 5 note 53.

[1149] E.g. *Marie-Élodie Ancel*, RCDIP 90 (2001), 158, 160.

should be deemed unidentifiable.[1150] The alternative, however, should be first to look whether one amongst the place of performances is the dominating one. All and any means of properly understanding and construing (b) have to be employed before one could resort to (c) which as some kind of escape clause should insofar be treated as a last resort or *ultima ratio*. It depends on the yardsticks applied, and the answers provided, under (b) as to whether (c) is triggered where at least one of a number of places of performance is located outside the EU.[1151] For instance, if a contract is for the carriage of persons by air from Frankfurt/Main to a destination outside the EU, (b) is applicable since after *Rehder* the place of departure and the place of destination are both full-fledged places[1152] where services are provided according to the contract.[1153]

213   If the place of performance under (b) is located outside any State (e.g. on the High Seas) and not to be attributed to any State even by auxiliary means (like the flag of a seagoing ocean vessel), (c) will become operable, too.[1154]

5. Agreements on the place of performance

214   Determining jurisdiction under (1) leaves quite some room for doubt and insecurity. Parties and their advisers might want to strike out or at least reduce the remaining potential for insecurity. Provident practitioners are well advised to resort to agreements on the place of performance or even better, agreements on jurisdiction in order to avoid the conundrum and mystery of (1) (b) in particular.[1155] For evidential reasons and purposes every agreement should best be in writing or else well documented. Furthermore, such agreement might help to steer their client's cause through heavy sea.[1156] Their ingenuity can result in an agreement on the place of performance in the contract itself (which might the regular appearance in practice[1157]). The words "unless otherwise agreed" in (1) (b) evidence that the jurisdictional rule gives way and cedes if such clause is legally recognised.[1158] The parties enjoy a certain freedom and autonomy to define the place of performance.[1159] Party autonomy takes precedence in this regard.[1160]

[1150] Same references as in the penultimate fn.

[1151] See *Ansgar Staudinger*, IPRax 2010, 140, 141; *Rauscher*, NJW 2010, 2251, 2253; *Kropholler/von Hein*, Art. 5 note 53a.

[1152] *Supra* Art. 7 notes 189–194 (*Mankowski*).

[1153] Comp. LG Frankfurt/Main 6 June 2014 – 2-24 S 152/13 [17]-[18].

[1154] *Michaels*, in: Nuyts/Watté (eds.), International Civil Litigation in Europe and Relations with Third States (Bruxelles 2005), p. 129, 134 *et seq.*; *Gaudemet-Tallon* para. 200; *Kropholler/von Hein*, Art. 5 note 53b.

[1155] See *Mankowski*, IPRax 2007, 404, 412; *Mankowski*, TranspR 2008, 67, 74; *Mankowski*, IHR 2009, 46, 60–61; *Mankowski*, EWiR Art. 5 EuGVVO 2/09, 607, 608; *Mankowski*, JZ 2009, 958, 961; *Mankowski*, CR 2010, 137, 140; *Geimer*, LMK 2008, 266925; *Schmidt-Bendun*, Haftung der Eisenbahnverkehrsunternehmen (2006) p. 133.

[1156] *Moritz Becker*, EWiR Art. 5 EuGVVO 3/10, 817, 818.

[1157] *Tuo*, Dir. mar. 109 (2007), 1080, 1101.

[1158] See only *Car Trim GmbH v. KeySafety Systems Srl*, (Case C-381/08) [2010] ECR I-1255, I-1283 para. 46; OLG Zweibrücken MDR 2013, 510; Rb. 's-Hertogenbosch S&S 2011 Nr. 43 p. 193; *Notdurfter/Petruzzino*, Contratto e impresa/Europa 2011, 223, 224–236. Overly thoughtful *Eltzschig*, IPRax 2002, 491, 493.

[1159] *Car Trim GmbH v. KeySafety Systems Srl*, (Case C-381/08) [2010] ECR I-1255, I-1283 para. 45; Rb. 's-

Although (1) (a) does not contain alike or similar words expressly the prevalence of recog-   **215**
nised clauses is upheld.[1161] It is clearly wrong to restrict such precedence of party autonomy[1162] to (b) – with the consequence that in the event of a contractual agreement one had to
leave only (b) and had to fall back on (a).[1163] (a) is equally subjected under the reign of party
autonomy; otherwise one would substantially change the approach generally accepted under
Art. 5 (1) Brussels Convention[1164] and would separate (a) from its predecessor whilst the
opposite approach should prevail.[1165] Equally wrong would be the opposite approach[1166] to
have recourse to (a) every time an agreement on the place of performance is in question.[1167]
Proposals to dispose of the possibility to agree on the place of performance and to refer the
parties exclusively to the possibility to conclude agreements on jurisdiction[1168] did not
succeed, either. Yet if an agreement on the place of performance conflicts with a jurisdiction
clause in the same contract (a rare event to be observed only if draftsmanship has completely
failed) the latter must prevail since the jurisdiction clause principally generates exclusive
jurisdiction.[1169] Likewise, different clauses in the respective Standard Terms and Conditions
of either party might result in the lack of an agreement on a place of performance.[1170]

There is a sharp distinction between two types of agreements on the place of performance: **216**
The first designs a place which bears some factual relationship with the performance of the
contract. It is fully recognised without a need to pay observance to particular formalities.[1171]

Hertogenbosch S&S 2011 Nr. 43 p. 193. Crticial already *de lege lata Herbert Roth*, in: FS Daphne-Ariane
Simotta (2012), p. 495, 501.

[1160] See only BG IHR 2014, 251, 252; *Vlek*, in: IPR in de spiegel van Paul Vlas (2012), p. 277, 281–282.

[1161] Trib. Rel. Porto Coll. Jr. 2014, II-181, II-183; *Micklitz/Rott*, EuZW 2001, 325, 329; *André Huet*, Clunet 128
(2001), 1126, 1129; *Kropholler/von Hein* Art. 5 note 35; *Wernicke/Vera Hoppe*, MMR 2002, 643, 645;
Rommelaere, Rev. dr. comm. belge 2003, 103, 105; *Ganssauge*, Internationale Zuständigkeit und anwend-
bares Recht bei Verbraucherverträgen im Internet (2004) p. 23; *Mankowski*, LMK 2005 Nr. 155248;
Simotta, in: Fasching/Konecny Art. 5 note 97; *Matthias Lehmann*, in: Dickinson/Lein para. 4.54; see also
BGH RIW 2005, 776, 777. Doubting *Hau*, IPRax 2000, 354, 360.

[1162] The precedence of party autonomy is emphasised e.g. by OLG München IHR 2009, 201 with note *Großkopf*; LG Landshut IHR 2008, 184, 187.

[1163] As *Takahashi*, (2002) 27 Eur. L. Rev. 530, 537 erroneously assumes.

[1164] *Siegfried Zelger v. Sebastiano Salinitri*, (Case 56/79) [1980] ECR 89, 97 para. 5; *Mainschifffahrts-Genos-
senschaft eG (MSG) v. Les Gravières Rhénanes SARL*, (Case C-106/95) [1997] I-911, I-943 para. 30; *GIE
Groupe Concorde v. Master of the vessel "Suhadiwarno Panjan"*, (Case C-440/97) [1999] ECR I-6307,
I-6351 et seq. para. 28; BGH, RIW 1980, 725.

[1165] *Klemm*, Erfüllungsortvereinbarungen im Europäischen Zivilverfahrensrecht (2005) pp. 65 *et seq.*

[1166] As uncunningly implemented by BGH RIW 2005, 776, 777 *et seq.*

[1167] *Mankowski*, LMK 2005 Nr. 155248.

[1168] *Harald Koch*, JZ 1997, 841, 843; *Schack*, ZEuP 1998, 931, 939, *Leipold*, in: GS Alexander Lüderitz (2000),
p. 431, 449.

[1169] *Klemm*, Erfüllungsortvereinbarungen im Europäischen Zivilverfahrensrecht (2005) pp. 114 *et seq.*

[1170] OLG Stuttgart IHR 2011, 236, 238 = IHR 2012, 38, 40 ("ex works" vs. "foc"/"Free of charge").

[1171] *Siegfried Zelger v. Sebastiano Salinitri*, (Case 56/79) [1980] ECR 89, 97 para. 5; *Mainschifffahrts-Genossenschaft eG (MSG) v. Les Gravières Rhénanes SARL*, (Case C-106/95) [1997] I-911, I-943 para. 30; *GIE
Groupe Concorde v. Master of the vessel "Suhadiwarno Panjan"*, (Case C-440/97) [1999] ECR I-6307,
I-6351 et seq. para. 28; *Česká spořitelna as v. Gerald Feichter*, (Case C-419/11), ECLI:EU:C:2013:165
para. 56; BGH, RIW 1980, 725; BGH NJW 1994, 2699, 2700; OLG Celle NJW-RR 2010 136, 138; OLG

That the parties had at the back of their minds to influence jurisdiction, is neither required nor necessary.[1172] It does not even prove detrimental if the contract confers an option upon one of the parties to choose the relevant place, e.g. the place of payment under a letter of credit or any other contract.[1173] Insofar the other party arguably can be said to have waived their right to certainty putting itself at the mercy of the claimant.[1174] In addition, it should not be stated as a prerequisite that parties intended to deviate from the place of performance to be established *ex lege* lacking any agreement.[1175] Even a declaratory agreement in substance confirming such place of performance still serves clarity and simplifies matters.

217   The second kind of agreement on the place of performance is inserted in the contract for the sole purpose of ascertaining and distributing jurisdiction; it designs a place which does not bear a factual relationship with the performance of the contract. Looking not at the words of the clauses but at their purpose the latter type aims solely at influencing jurisdiction and should thus be treated as a jurisdiction clause. It should be measured against Art. 25 and must fulfil the formal requirements spelled out there.[1176] Furthermore it can fall victim to the restrictions in Arts. 15; 19; 23 if they are applicable.[1177] Compared to, and contrasted with, Art. 5 (1) Brussels Convention the latter emphasis is even strengthened as (b) establishes a fact-oriented notion of "place of performance".[1178] A place of "performance" without an actual connection with the subject-matter can be regarded as fictitious.[1179] (1) in its entirety follows an effective and objective approach, not one relying on fictivities, hence, a deviation should pay due regard to this basic feature.[1180] On the over hand, not every deviation from the place of performance as ascertained under (a) in particular qualifies the agreement as an abstract one.[1181] In any event, an abstract agreement is identified if performance is not at all possible at the agreed place.[1182] This circumscribes the necessity that the place of perform-

---

Hamm ZVertriebsR 2015, 435, 437; *Kropholler/von Hein* paras. 28 *et seq.* But cf. critically e.g. *Peter Huber*, ZZP Int. 1 (1996), 171, 178 *et seq.*

[1172] *Rauscher*, in: FS Andreas Heldrich (2005), p. 933, 939. But cf. unclear OGH SZ 71/145.

[1173] *Credit Agricole Indosuez v. Chailease Finance Corp.* [2000] 1 All ER (Comm) 399, 411 *et seq.* (C.A., per *Potter* L.J.).

[1174] See *Rogerson*, [2001] Cambridge Yb. Eur. L. 383.

[1175] *Contra* OLG Köln IHR 2006, 86, 87.

[1176] *Mainschifffahrts-Genossenschaft eG (MSG) v. Les Gravières Rhénanes SARL*, (Case C-106/95) [1997] I-911, I-943 *et seq.* paras. 31–35; *GIE Groupe Concorde v. Captain of the vessel "Suhadiwarno Panjan"*, (Case C-440/97) [1999] ECR I-6307, I-6351 *et seq.* para. 28; BGH NJW-RR 1998, 755; BG IHR 2014, 251, 252; OLG Köln IHR 2006, 86, 87; *7E Commuciations Ltd. v. Vertex Antennentechnik GmbH* [2007] I.L.Pr. 278, 291 *et seq.* (C.A., ct. Judgm. Per Sir *Anthony Clarke* M.R.); LG Trier IHR 2004, 115, 116; LG Landshut IHR 2008, 184, 187; *Schack*, IPRax 1996, 247; *Mittmann*, IHR 2010, 146, 148; *Mittmann*, D. 2010, 834, 836; *Kropholler/von Hein* Art. 5 note 36. Tentatively otherwise *Geimer*, LMK 2010, 301816.

[1177] *Kropholler/von Hein* Art. 5 note 36.

[1178] LG Trier IHR 2004, 115, 117.

[1179] *Mainschifffahrts-Genossenschaft eG (MSG) v. Les Gravières Rhenanes SARL*, (Case C-106/95) [1997] ECR I-911, I-943 para. 33.

[1180] *Rodríguez Benot*, REDI 1997, 1, 211, 215.

[1181] *Mainschifffahrts-Genossenschaft eG (MSG) v. Les Gravières Rhénanes SARL*, (Case C-106/95) [1997] I-911, I-943 para. 31; *Peter Huber*, ZZP Int. 2 (1997), 168, 177.

[1182] *Mainschifffahrts-Genossenschaft eG (MSG) v. Les Gravières Rhénanes SARL*, (Case C-106/95) [1997] I-911, I-943 para. 31; *Peter Huber*, ZZP Int. 2 (1997), 168, 178.

ance agreed upon must bear some relation to the reality of the contractual exchange and does not refer to concepts of factual impossibility as they might be contained in national laws.[1183]

It should be borne in mind that performance is not solely related to the delivery of the goods   **218** or the provision of the services, but that payment constitutes also part of the performance of an contractual obligation. Hence, the seller's place of business is not ruled out *per se* from factual connections with any obligation under the contract.[1184] A place of performance happening to coincide with the place where payment under the contract is to be effected carries quite some factual connection with the contract. Matters would only be different if the seller's seat is named as place of performance whilst delivery is to take place at the buyer's seat and payment ought to be effected somewhere else than at the seller's place of business, for instance on a certain bank account held with a certain intermediary. The principle of characteristic performance certainly is dominant when it comes down to determining an objective place of performance under (1) (b). But it is not likewise dominant when an agreement by the parties is at stake. The parties have the liberty to chose within a range the outer limits of which are defined by factual connections. A parallel idea would be a limited choice of law as Art. 5 (2) Rome I Regulation offers it prominently.

Whether the parties have reached an agreement as to the place of performance (or only   **219** consented as to a mere address of delivery[1185]), whether the necessary consensus exists,[1186] whether mistake, duress or fraud persist, whether General Terms and Conditions are included in a contract and whether an agreement might have been terminated, rescinded or revoked afterwards, has to be determined in accordance with the applicable substantive law.[1187] Matters of construction and interpretation are also subjected to the *lex causae*[1188] (and not *per se* to the law of the place of performance possibly agreed upon[1189]). The parties

---

[1183] *Klemm*, Erfüllungsortvereinbarungen im Europäischen Zivilverfahrensrecht (2005) p. 104–106.

[1184] *Contra* BG IHR 2014, 251, 252–253; *Markus*, Tendenzen beim materiellrechtlichen Vertragserfüllungsort im internationalen Zivilverfahrensrecht (Basel 2009) pp. 171–173.

[1185] See KantonsG Zürich ZGGVP 2003, 208.

[1186] See OGH ZfRV 2002/49: Unilateral request to perform at a certain place does not suffice.

[1187] *Siegfried Zelger v. Sebastiano Salinitri*, (Case 56/79) [1980] ECR 89, 97 paras. 5 *et seq.*; BGE 122 III 249, 251; BGH RIW 2005, 776, 777 *et seq.*; OLG Karlsruhe RIW 1994, 1046, 1047; OLG Düsseldorf IHR 2004, 108, 113; OLG Köln IPRspr. 2011 Nr. 215 pp. 541–542; Hof Arnhem NIPR 2006 Nr. 304 p. 447; HG Zürich ZR 98 (1999) Nr. 34 p. 136; Rb. Kh. Brussel R. W. 2006–2007, 969, 970 with note *Samyn*; Rb. Zwolle-Lelystad NIPR 2006 Nr. 304 p. 447; *Kropholler/von Hinden*, in: GS Alexander Lüderitz (2000), p. 401, 409; *Eltzschig*, IPRax 2002, 491, 494; *Leible*, in: Rauscher Art. 5 note 44; *Layton/Mercer* para. 15.045; *Rauscher*, in: FS Andreas Heldrich (2005), p. 933, 938; *Mankowski*, LMK 2005 Nr. 155248; *Magnus*, WuB VII B. Art. 5 EuGVÜ 1.06, 342; *Markus*, Tendenzen beim materiellrechtlichen Vertragserfüllungsort im internationalen Zivilverfahrensrecht (2009) pp. 167–170; *Markus*, AJP 2010, 971, 978, 982; *Oberhammer*, in: Dasser/Oberhammer, Art. 5 LugÜ note 52; *Acocella*, in: Schnyder, Art. 5 LugÜ notes 122, 127; *Bonomi*, in: Commentaire romand, Art. 5 LugÜ note 66; *Haas/Oliver Vogel*, NZG 2011, 766, 768. Expressly leaving open the answer BGE 140 III 115, 120; BG 15.7.2014 – 4A_113/2014 E. 4.1.

[1188] ØLD [2001] I.L.Pr. 22; *Klemm*, Erfüllungsortvereinbarungen im Europäischen Zivilverfahrensrecht (2005) p. 127.

[1189] As proposed by *Christian Kohler*, IPRax 1983, 265, 268.

---

enjoy autonomy even if their agreement is ambiguous and thus needs clarifying interpretation.[1190] The *lex causae* is even called upon to decide whether such an agreement is permissible at all[1191] or whether an implied agreement would suffice.[1192] (1) does not contain
appropriate yardsticks for answering these questions autonomously.[1193] To the contrary,
since even Art. 25 (the most appropriate place where to find something about consensus
in the entire Brussels I Regulation and the hypothetical place where to look to in this respect)
does not contain respective answers,[1194] the parallel with Art. 25 is a supporting reason for
referring to the applicable substantive law. If the private international law of the *forum*
permits so, the parties are free to choose another applicable law for the agreement on the
place of performance than for the remainder of the contract.[1195] Such *dépeçage* by choice of
law will, however, only randomly appear in practice as it complicates matters without a
discernible gain. Yet it should be stressed and emphasised that the requirements of the *lex
causae* for the validity of such agreements on the place of performance are *additional* to the
autonomous requirement of a factual relationship between the agreed place and the exchange of performances.[1196]

220 Generally, it should be called into recollection that the nomination of a place of performance
or the inclusion of Incoterms merely in invoices or alike, e.g. documents issued subsequently
to the conclusion of the contract as such, regularly does not amount to any kind of agreement subject to the *lex causae* and can thus not carry an agreement on the place of the
performance, either.[1197] The consensus required is lacking.[1198] The case might be different if
the other party has agreed to the nomination in the past. Even if the other party did not reject
such nomination repeatedly in the past, consensus can be deemed to exist at least if one is
prepared to apply Art. 25 (1) cl. 3 lit. c by way of analogy. Nevertheless, the mere inclusion of
an Incoterm might not amount to a proper agreement on the place of performance.[1199]

221 In practice, it would go way too far to assume that agreements on the place of performance
are generally invalid if they determine the seller's place of business as the place of perform-

---

[1190] Report *Pocar* para. 51; *Markus*, AJP 2010, 971, 981 *et seq.*; *Gsell*, ZEuP 2011, 669, 681. But cf. *Car Trim
GmbH v. KeySafety Systems Srl*, (Case C-381/08) [2010] ECR I-1255, I-1285 paras. 54–56.

[1191] *Siegfried Zelger v. Sebastiano Salinitri*, (Case 56/79) [1980] ECR 89, 97 para. 6; BGE 122 III 249, 251; Hof
Antwerpen TBH 1995, 387, 388 with note *Erauw*; Hof Antwerpen TBH 2003, 150, 151 with note *Stuer*;
OLG Hamm ZVertriebsR 2015, 435, 437; HG Zürich ZR 98 (1999) Nr. 34 p. 136; Rb. Kh. Hasselt R.W.
2000–2001, 1244, 1247; *Pålsson*, SvJT 2001, 373, 380; *Furrer/Schramm*, SJZ 2003, 105, 113; *Tagaras*, CDE
2003, 399, 405; *Arenas García*, AEDIpr 2007, 921, 924; *Simotta*, in: Fasching/Konecny Art. 5 note 96;
Gsell, ZEuP 2011, 669, 683.

[1192] Differently *Notdurfter/Petruzzino*, Contratto e impresa/Europa 2011, 223, 242. See also *Franzina*, RDIPP
2010, 655, 679. Ruling out implied agreements altogether *Herbert Roth*, in: FS Daphne-Ariane Simotta
(2012), p. 495, 496, 501.

[1193] *Eltzschig*, IPRax 2002, 491, 494.

[1194] See Art. 25 note 80 *(Magnus)*.

[1195] *Siegfried Zelger/Sebastiano Salinitri*, (Case 56/79) [1980] ECR 89, 97 para. 6; *Leible*, in: Rauscher Art. 5
note 44.

[1196] *Wautelet*, 3 Col. J. Eur. L. 465, 472 (1998).

[1197] OGH EuLF 2005, II-80, II-81; KantonsG Zug IHR 2005, 119, 121; Rb. Kh. Hasselt IHR 2005, 114, 115.

[1198] OGH EuLF 2005, II-80, II-81; *Slevogt*, EuLF 2005, II-81.

[1199] *Poggio*, Giur. it. 2005, 1008, 1009.

ance. Firstly, under most contracts (and not only under those featuring "ex works" or similar provisions) the seller's place of performance bears some relation with the actual exchange of performances.[1200] Delivery is not the only performance that matters. Payment must not be totally disregarded. In most instances, the payment in one or the other kind is related to the seller's seat if the latter is not outrightly the final destination of the price.[1201] Secondly and conceptionally even more importantly, it is by no means equivalent to invalidity that an agreement falls within the second category. If and insofar as such agreement fulfils the requirements of Art. 25, it is valid, however remote the agreed place might be from the actual exchange of performances. Agreements on places of performance will mainly appear in pre-printed form as part of General Terms and Conditions.[1202] Thus they will in most instances comply with Art. 25 (1) (a).[1203]

An agreement on the place of performance might not withhold and might not stand in the **222** light of the later performance of the contract. The parties might have agreed on X as the place of delivery of the goods whereas later-on delivery is effected by the seller in Y and accepted by the buyer. Then the parties in their autonomy lifted and waived the original agreement and entered into a replacing agreement tacitly.[1204]

In any event, an agreement on the place of *performance* needs to be distinguished from a **223** mere agreement on the place of *payment*[1205] or the place of *delivery* of the goods.[1206] Those kinds of agreements do not provide the necessary width to indirectly determine the *forum* for the entire contract but is expressly related to only one of the obligations. A concentration of disputes is not accomplished since the court of the place of payment will have only jurisdiction to entertain suits for payment[1207] whereas disputes regarding the delivery of the goods are not covered,[1208] and *vice versa*. Nevertheless, in this limited capacity it ought to be recognised[1209] since party autonomy is granted and an agreement for the place of payment is only a *minus* to an agreement on the place of performance for all contractual obliga-

---

[1200] *Herber*, IHR 2004, 117, 118.

[1201] *Supra* Art. 7 note 218 (*Mankowski*).

[1202] On the respective questions of consensus and validity under German, Austrian and English law comprehensively *Klemm*, Erfüllungsortvereinbarungen im Europäischen Zivilverfahrensrecht (2005) p. 153–195.

[1203] *Herber*, IHR 2004, 117, 118.

[1204] *Magnus*, IHR 2002, 45, 47.

[1205] Such an agreement on the place of payment may not follow from a simple indication on a contractual document or the invoice about a SWIFT code; ØLD [2001] I.L.Pr. 314, 319. Even less the mere nomination of an account to which to pay, should suffice; see *Kruger*, TBH 2003, 352.

[1206] *Herbert Roth*, in: FS Daphne-Ariane Simotta (2012), p. 495, 501.

[1207] See Rb. Rotterdam NIPR 2002 Nr. 50 p. 93; Rb. Kh. Hasselt R.W. 2004–2005, 833, 834; *Vlas*, WPNR 6421 (2000), 745, 749.

[1208] *Vlas*, NILR 2004, 451, 452.

[1209] *Markus*, Tendenzen beim materiellrechtlichen Vertragserfüllungsort im internationalen Zivilverfahrensrecht (Basel 2009) pp. 171–173. Tentatively *contra Vlas*, WPNR 2000, 745, 749; *Koppenol-Laforce/van Rooij*, AdvBl 2002, 418, 421; *Broeckx*, Nieuw Juridisch Weekblad 2003, 186, 193; *Kruger*, TBH 2003, 352; *Rauscher*, in: FS Andreas Heldrich (2005), p. 933, 947; *Markus*, IPRax 2015, 277, 278; see also BGE 140 III 170.

tions.[1210] That this results in a split between the places of performance of the single obligations contrary to the concept followed by (b) has to be accepted, although it is unwelcome.[1211] Under systematic auspices the precedence given to party autonomy under (b) is derived from ideas time-tested under Art. 5 (1) cl. 1 Brussels Convention which has now become (a).[1212]

224 At least it should not be caused to switch over to (a) by operation of law.[1213] The concept underlying (b) cedes if an agreement by the parties is made however restricted in scope it might be. Likewise it should be recognised if parties opted to depart from (b) in favour of adopting the *Tessili*-approach[1214] – *volenti non fit iniuria*. Whether an agreement upon the place of *delivery* constitutes an agreement on the place of *performance* is a matter of interpretation of the respective contract term.[1215] It is not required that an agreement on the place of performance must be made out strictly as such and named as such; a like agreement can be derived by interpretation of the terms of the contract, too,[1216] for instance of Incoterms clauses used.[1217]

225 If the parties only agree upon a place of performance for the main and characteristic obligation, the place of payment should be determined according to (b) and thus by operation of law follow this agreed place of performance.[1218] The parties might not have considered this consequence when drafting their agreement, but the concentration effect aimed at by (b)[1219] demands such consequence unless the parties have expressly or impliedly agreed upon a differing place of payment.[1220]

III. Special jurisdiction in tort, Art. 7 (2)

1. General remarks

a) Generalities

226 The second most important among the heads of special jurisdiction contained in Art. 7 is (2) conferring jurisdiction in matters of tort, delict or quasi-delict on the courts of the place

---

[1210] *Klemm*, Erfüllungsortvereinbarungen im Europäischen Zivilverfahrensrecht (2005) pp. 205 *et seq.*; *Henri Storme*, R.W. 2009–2010, 409, 412. See also *Rogerson*, [2001] Cambridge Yb. Eur. L. 383; *Mäsch*, IHR 2014, 253, 254.

[1211] *Contra* BG IHR 2014, 251, 253; *Rauscher*, in: FS Andreas Heldrich (2005), p. 933, 946 *et seq.*; *Markus* p. 173.

[1212] *Mäsch*, IHR 2014, 253, 254. But cf. *Herbert Roth*, in: FS Daphne-Ariane Simotta (2012), p. 495, 500–501.

[1213] Tentatively *contra* Rb. Kh. Hasselt TBH 2002, 595; *van Houtte*, TBH 2002, 595, 596; *Stuer*, TBH 2003, 152, 153.

[1214] *Heuzé*, RCDIP 89 (2000), 595, 625; *André Huet*, Clunet 128 (2001), 1126, 1127; *André Huet*, in: Mélanges en l'honneur de Paul Lagarde (2005), p. 417, 429.

[1215] OGH EuLF 2005, II-82.

[1216] BG 15.7.2014 – 4A_113/2014 E 4.4.2; *Gaudemet-Tallon* para. 202; *Acocella*, in: Schnyder, Art. 5 LugÜ note 121; *Bonomi*, in: Commentaire romand, Art. 5 LugÜ note 69.

[1217] BG 15.7.2014 – 4A_113/2014 E 4. 4. 1.

[1218] *Klemm*, Erfüllungsortvereinbarungen im Europäischen Zivilverfahrensrecht (2005) pp. 204 *et seq.*

[1219] *Supra* Art. 7 note 130 (*Mankowski*).

[1220] *Klemm*, Erfüllungsortvereinbarungen im Europäischen Zivilverfahrensrecht (2005) p. 205.

where the harmful event occurred or may occur. It provides for special jurisdiction in the case of extra-contractual obligations based upon the debtor's liability towards the creditor. Drawing upon experience gained from rules in the legal orders of some Member States and in bilateral conventions special jurisdiction was established particularly with traffic accidents in mind.[1221] Later experience proved that other instances provided for more substantial mattering cases.

There are three core arguments and considerations for the interpretation and application of (2) at the general level. They are indicated in Recital (11) Brussels I Regulation and Recital (16). Firstly, grounds of special jurisdiction are based on a close connection between the court and the action or in order to facilitate the sound administration of justice.[1222] The existence of a close connection should ensure legal certainty and avoid the possibility of the defendant being sued in a court of a Member State which he could hot have reasonably foreseen.[1223] Secondly, easy access, and local vicinity, to means of evidence is of relevance.[1224] Thirdly, there can be a particularly close connection with the applicable substantive law. Yet there are limits to this reasoning since a strict *Gleichlauf* has not been realised.[1225] Nowhere is something discernible even remotely resembling a genuine *forum legis*.   227

Courts should not adopt a two-tier test first asking whether the requirements of (2) are met and then, guided by a presumption favouring the affirmative result, whether it is justified to attribute jurisdiction to the courts so designated,[1226] but a total one-tier assessment.[1227] The party alleging a claim in tort has to plead accordingly and has in particular to plead supporting facts in accordance with the standards as established by the procedural law of the *forum*.[1228] The *lex fori* has to decide whether it employs a doctrine of *doppelrelevante Tatsachen* for which full proof is not to appear at the stage of jurisdiction and admissibility in general, but left to the later stage when one comes to the merits.[1229] Positive declaratory actions are clearly within the concept.[1230]   228

b) Negative declaratory actions

Under (2) the court also has the jurisdiction to entertain negative declaratory actions with which an alleged tortfeasor tries to ascertain that he does not commit or has not committed a   229

[1221] Report *Jenard* p. 26.

[1222] Recital (16) cl. 1.

[1223] Recital (16) cl. 2.

[1224] See only Hoge Raad NIPR 2015 Nr. 51 p. 140.

[1225] *Michael Müller*, EuZW 2014, 434.

[1226] *Contra* Norsk Högsterett Rt. 2001, 1322.

[1227] *Krog*, IPRax 2004, 154, 156.

[1228] See only *Fiona Shevill v. Presse Alliance SA* (Case C-68/93), [1995] ECR I-415 paras. 35 *et seq.*; *Wintersteiger AG v. Products 4U Sondermaschinenbau* (Case C-523/10), ECLI:EU:C:2012:220 para. 26; *Folien Fischer AG and Fofitec AG v. Ritrama SpA* (Case C-133/11), ECLI:EU:C:2012:664 para. 50; BGH WRP 2015, 735 [25] – *Parfümflakon III*; Hof Amsterdam NIPR 2006 Nr. 32 p. 61; OLG Frankfurt ZIP 2006, 769; *SanDisk Corp. v. Koninklijke Philips Electronics NV* [2007] ILPr 325, 335 (Ch.D., *Pumfrey* J.).

[1229] *von Hein*, IPRax 2013, 505, 509; see also *Melzer v. MF Global UK Ltd.* (Case C-228/11), ECLI:EU: C:2013:305 para. 31; BGHZ 176, 342 [11]; BGH WM 2008, 479 [14]; BGH ZIP 2010, 2004 [19]; BGH WM 2010, 2214 [21]; BGH WM 2014, 1400 [17]; BGH WM 2014, 1614 [19].

[1230] LG Kiel IPRax 2009, 164, 167.

tort, e.g. an infringement.[1231] The negation is governed by the same jurisdictional rules as the claim for damages. It mirrors the positive action by the victim.[1232] It entails a reversal of normal roles for the alleged perpetrator is the claimant and the presumptive victim is the defendant.[1233] It gives the alleged tortfeasor the weapon for a preventive counterstrike against manoeuvres by the alleged victim.[1234] Furthermore, the negative declaratory action falls on its merits under the definition of tort.[1235] The same objective rationales guiding purposive interpretation apply as in the ordinary case of an action in tort, and the reversal of party roles is not such as to exclude negative declaratory actions from the realm of (2).[1236]

230 (2) is not designed as special protective jurisdiction for a weaker party; in this regard it differs conceptually, structurally and fundamentally from jurisdiction under Arts. 10–16, 17–19 or

---

[1231] *Folien Fischer AG and Fofitec AG v. Ritrama SpA* (Case C-133/11), ECLI:EU:C:2012:664 paras. 41–54; BGE 125 III 346, 349; BGE 129 III 295; BG 24 April 2007 – Case 4C.40/2007; BG IPRax 2008, 544, 546; BGE 133 III 282; BGH ZIP 2011, 975, 976 *et seq.* = GRUR 2011, 554, 555 *et seq.* – Trägermaterial für Kartenformulare; BGH GRUR-RR 2013, 228; Cassaz. RDIPP 2014, 647. 650–652; *Messier-Dowty Ltd. v. Sabena SA* [2000] 1 WLR 2040, 2046 = [2000] 1 Lloyd's Rep. 428, 433 *et seq.* (C.A., per Lord *Woolf* M.R.); Hof Arnhem NIPR 2003 Nr. 279 p. 433; OLG Bamberg IPRax 2015, 154 = IHR 2013, 253 with note *Smytek*; Trib. Brescia Riv. dir. ind. 2000 II 236 with note *Jandoli*; Rb. Utrecht NIPR 2003 Nr. 297 p. 457; *Equitas Ltd. v. Wave City Shipping Co. Ltd.* [2005] 2 All ER (Comm) 301, 306–308 (Q.B.D., *Christopher Clarke* J.); LG Wien 9 January 2009 – Case 92 Hv 110/08g; LG Frankfurt/Main AfP 2010, 509 = IPRspr. 2010 Nr. 220 p. 563; Aud. Prov. Lleida REDI 2013-2, 308 with note *Fontanellas Morell*; *Pietrobon*, AIDA 1994, 244; *Bell*, (1995) 111 L.Q.Rev. 674, 695; *Donzallaz* vol. III para. 5121; *de Cristofaro*, Resp. civ. prel. 2000, 756; *Knut Werner Lange*, WRP 2000, 940, 946; *Lundstedt*, GRUR Int. 2001, 103, 110; *Grabinski*, GRUR Int. 2001, 199, 203; *Ullmann*, GRUR Int. 2001, 1027, 1031; *von Hoffmann*, in: Staudinger, BGB, Artt. 38–42 EGBGB (14th ed. 2001) Vor Art. 40 EGBGB Art. 5 note 92; *Kropholler/von Hein* Art. 5 note 78; *Schack*, para. 295; *Franzosi*, IIC 2002, 154, 156–159; *Gottwald*, in: FS Reinhold Geimer (2002), p. 231, 248; *Gardella*, Int. lis 2003, 22; *Czernich*, in: Czernich/Tiefenthaler/Kodek Art. 5 note 78; *Leible*, in: Rauscher Art. 5 note 82; *Hootz* p. 186; *Wurmnest*, GRUR Int. 2005, 265, 267 *et seq.*; *Hye-Knudsen*, Marken-, Patent- und Urheberrechtsverletzungen im europäischen internationalen Zivilprozessrecht (2005) pp. 115 *et seq.*; *Domej*, IPRax 2008, 550; *Wukoschitz*, AfP 2009, 127; *Leible*, in: Rauscher, Art. 5 note 83; *Matthias Weller*, LMK 2011, 318709; *Mankowski*, EWiR Art. 5 EuGVVO 2/11, 253; *Kropholler/von Hein*, Art. 5 note 78; *Hofmann/Kunz*, in: Basler Kommentar, Art. 5 note 531; *Oró Martínez*, AEDIPr 2011, 198; *Sujecki*, GRUR Int. 2012, 18, 21–23. *Contra* Cassaz. Foro it. 1990 I 117; Cassaz. AIDA 1994, 237; Cassaz. RDIPP 2004, 245, 250; Cassaz. RDIPP 2004, 1372, 1375 *et seq.*; HD NJA 2000, 273, 277 *et seq.* = GRUR Int. 2001, 178, 179; Hof 's-Gravenhage NIPR 1998 Nr. 221; OLG Dresden InstGE 11, 163; Rb. 's-Gravenhage NIPR 2002 Nr. 279; LG Leipzig IPRspr. 2008 Nr. 96 p. 315; LG München I InstGE 10, 178; *Foerste*, in: FS Helmut Kollhosser, vol. II (2004), p. 141; *Schlosser* Art. 5 note 15; *Lindacher*, Internationales Wettbewerbsverfahrensrecht (2009) § 9 note 26; *Vanleenhove*, NIPR 2013, 25, 28 and Trib. Bologna Resp. civ. prel. 2000, 754 = GRUR Int. 2000, 1021 with note *Dieter Stauder*; Trib. Bruxelles GRUR Int. 2001, 170, 172 *et seq.* (the latters being in fact overruled by the last clause of (2)).

[1232] See only *Sujecki*, GRUR Int. 2012, 18, 22.

[1233] *Folien Fischer AG and Fofitec AG v. Ritrama SpA* (Case C-133/11), ECLI:EU:C:2012:664 para. 43; A-G *Jääskinen*, Opinion of 19 April 2012 in Case C-133/11 ECLI:EU:C:2012:226 para. 46.

[1234] *Muir Watt*, RCDIP 102 (2013), 506, 509.

[1235] Rb. Utrecht NIPR 2003 Nr. 297 p. 457; *Sujecki*, EWS 2012, 952. Tentatively *Folien Fischer AG and Fofitec AG v. Ritrama SpA* (Case C-133/11), ECLI:EU:C:2012:664 para. 36.

[1236] *Folien Fischer AG and Fofitec AG v. Ritrama SpA* (Case C-133/11), ECLI:EU:C:2012:664 paras. 44–45.

20–23.[1237] In consequence, the application of (2) is not contingent upon the potential victim initiating proceedings.[1238]

At their core the proceedings are about liability and nothing else.[1239] That it is not in itself an **231** action for damages, does not militate against the result,[1240] nor does the general approach that special jurisdiction as a deviation from the fundamental rule in Art. 4 (1) should be construed strictly and rather narrowly.[1241] What is correct in contract[1242] should also be correct in tort. With the introduction of the last clause of (2), any attempt of arguing that the negative declaratory action seeking permittance *ex ante* and not dealing with events *ex post* is incorrect as it is not concerned with liability[1243] since the concept of liability does not require actual damage to be sustained.

Any other result would conflict with the fundamental line of reasoning under the notion of **232** *lis alibi pendens* as contained in Art. 29 since there the positive action for damages and the negative declaratory action aiming at non-liability are deemed to cover the same cause of action.[1244] Negative declaratory actions are mirror-image actions.[1245] Furthermore, an unexplainable split between jurisdiction for positive and negative declaratory relief would emerge.[1246] The creditor (and in particular if suing for damages) would be treated more favourably without justification for such privilege being readily discernible.[1247] To the contrary, the creditor's and the prospective debtor's (or alleged non-debtor's) array of weaponry should carry equal weight.[1248] Equality of arms is desirable and a *petitum*.[1249] Special jurisdiction is neutral to the parties.[1250] Positive and negative declaratory actions should be

---

[1237] *Folien Fischer AG and Fofitec AG v. Ritrama SpA* (Case C-133/11), ECLI:EU:C:2012:664 para. 46; *Domej*, ecolex 2013, 123; *Nisi*, RDIPP 2013, 385, 395 *et seq.*; see also *Verein für Konsumenteninformation v. Karl-Heinz Henkel*, (Case C-167/00) [2002], I-8111 para. 46; *Zuid-Chemie v. Philippo's Mineralenfabriek NV/SA*, (Case C-189/08) [2009] ECR I-6917 para. 24; *Andreas Kainz v. Pantherwerke AG* (Case C-45/13), ECLI:EU:C:2014:7 para. 31; *de Clavière*, Rev. Lamy dr. aff. 92 (2014), 60, 61–62.

[1238] *Folien Fischer AG and Fofitec AG v. Ritrama SpA* (Case C-133/11), ECLI:EU:C:2012:664 para. 47.

[1239] *Wurmnest*, GRUR Int. 2005, 265, 267; *Matthias Weller*, LMK 2011, 318709.

[1240] *Hofmann/Kunz*, in: Basler Kommentar, Art. 5 note 532. *Contra* Högsta Domstolen GRUR 2001, 178, 179; Hof's-Gravenhage [1998] EIPR 61, 62; Trib. Bologna GRUR Int. 2000, 1021 with noted by *Stauder*; more Italian judgments are listed by *Jandoli*, IIC 2000, 783, 789; *Franzosi*, IIC 2002, 154, 156. See also A-G *Jääskinen*, Opinion of 19 April 2012 in Case C-133/11, ECLI:EU:C:2012:226 para. 47.

[1241] *Contra* Högsta Domstolen NJA 2000, 272, 277 *et seq.* = GRUR 2001, 178, 179; Hof's-Gravenhage [1998] EIPR 61, 62; Trib. Bologna GRUR Int. 2000, 1021 with note *Stauder*; Trib. Bruxelles GRUR Int. 2001, 170, 172.

[1242] *Supra* Art. 5 note 11 (*Mankowski*).

[1243] As put forward by Cassaz. RDIPP 2004, 1372, 1376.

[1244] *The owners of cargo lately laden on board of the ship "Tatry" v. Owners of the ship "Maciej Rataj"*, (Case C-406/92) [1994] ECR I-5460, I-5476 para. 45.

[1245] *ten Wolde/Kirsten C. Henckel*, Int. J. Proced. L. 3 (2013), 195, 205.

[1246] *Wurmnest*, GRUR Int. 2005, 265, 267 *et seq.*

[1247] *Lundstedt*, GRUR Int. 2001, 103, 107; *Wurmnest*, GRUR Int. 2005, 265, 268.

[1248] *Wurmnest*, GRUR Int. 2005, 265, 268.

[1249] *Pålsson*, SvJT 2001, 578, 581; *Wurmnest*, GRUR Int. 2005, 265, 268; *Vanleenhove*, NIPR 2013, 25, 28.

[1250] *Muir Watt*, RCDIP 102 (2013), 506, 508.

Peter Mankowski

treated alike.[1251] It would be not advisable to estrange and alienate the positive and the negative declaratory actions, sisters in mind, from each other.[1252] Furthermore, evidential means like witnesses do not shift their location depending upon whether the action is for positive or for negatory relief.[1253]

233   Additional support can be gained from the fact that (2) also covers future torts as must be deducted from its last clause[1254] (although it ought to be admitted that a successful negative declaratory action tends to wipe out the very connecting factor it uses[1255]). *Folien Fischer*[1256] is perfectly in the logic of *Henkel*[1257] and *The "Tatry"*.[1258][1259] A risk of error where the future tort might be staged, remains indubitably[1260] but must not carry more weight in the present context than in the context of (2) last clause. Art. 93 (5) Regulation (EC) No. 40/94 does not give rise to an argument to the contrary, but should be restricted to its own ambit and scope of application.[1261]

234   The negative answer is mainly caused by fear of just another overboarding torpedo-problem.[1262] Yet the appropriate – and in fact the only – place to deal with torpedoes must be Art. 29, not the interpretation of (2).[1263] The decent way out of the *impasse* would be to give courts second seised discretion to disregard prior negative declaratory actions,[1264] but the reform for Brussels I*bis* would not have this.[1265] Lastly, it is too broad a statement that the alleged tortfeasor cannot avail himself of (2)[1266] since in the event of a negative declaratory action he can. He can launch a preventive counterstrike even against a private attorney general.[1267][1268] Good faith litigants deserve acceptance.[1269] Whether the claimant has an

---

[1251] *Sujecki*, EWS 2012, 952, 953.

[1252] But cf. the ruminations by A-G *Jääskinen*, Opinion of 19 April 2012 in Case C-133/11, ECLI:EU:C:2012:226 paras. 40–41.

[1253] See OLG Celle IPRspr. 2012 Nr. 236 p. 546.

[1254] *Véron*, Clunet 128 (2001), 805, 827.

[1255] A-G *Jääskinen*, Opinion of 19 April 2012 in Case C-133/11, ECLI:EU:C:2012:226 paras. 49–50.

[1256] *Folien Fischer AG and Fofitec AG v. Ritrama SpA* (Case C-133/11), ECLI:EU:C:2012:664.

[1257] *Verein für Konsumenteninformation v. Karl-Heinz Henkel*, (Case C-167/00) [2002], I-8111.

[1258] *The owners of cargo lately laden on board of the ship "Tatry" v. Owners of the ship "Maciej Rataj"*, (Case C-406/92) [1994] ECR I-5460.

[1259] *Treppoz*, RCDIP 102 (2013), 479, 486.

[1260] A-G *Jääskinen*, Opinion of 19 April 2012 in Case C-133/11, ECLI:EU:C:2012:226 para. 58. Art. 93 (5) Regulation (EC) No. 49/94 is to be interpreted independently from (2); *Coty Germany GmbH v. First Note Perfumes NV* (Case C-360/12), ECLI:EU:C:2014:1318 paras. 31–38; A-G *Jääskinen*, Opinion of 21 November 2013 in Case C-360/12, ECLI:EU:C:2013:764 paras. 25–31; *Hackbarth*, GRUR-Prax 2014, 320, 321; but see critical *von Hein*, EuZW 2014, 667. The same should be true *vice versa*.

[1261] *Contra Christian Kohler*, in: Gottwald (ed.), Revision des EuGVÜ/Neues Schiedsverfahrensrecht (2000), p. 1, 28; *Burgstaller/Neumayr* Art. 5 note 48 (Oct. 2002).

[1262] *Dieter Stauder*, GRUR Int. 2000, 1022 *et seq*.

[1263] *Czernich*, in: Czernich/Tiefenthaler/Kodek Art. 5 note 78; *Hootz* p. 188; *Mankowski*, EWiR Art. 5 EuGVVO 2/11, 253, 254. See also Cassaz. Foro it. 2004 I col. 2464; *Franzosi*, Dir. ind. 2004, 429; *Zanolini*, Riv. dir. ind. 2005 II 166; *de Jong*, [2005] EIPR 75.

[1264] *Delebecque*, DMF 2009, 815, 817; *Mankowski*, IGKK/IACPIL 1 (2010), 31, 55 *et seq*.

[1265] See Arts. 29; 32 (2) Commission Proposal Brussels I*bis*, COM (2010) 748 final.

[1266] See Trib. Siracusa Dir. Mar. 2006, 906, 915 *et seq*.

acceptable interest in bringing proceedings, is a matter to be judged in accordance with national procedural rules on admissibility, but appears only at a later stage after international jurisdiction has been ascertained.[1270] Any kind of implicit or hidden presumption that a negative declaratory action would be a torpedo action, would be misplaced[1271] and would disregard the legitimate interests of *bona fide* plaintiffs. (2) is not the right instrument to remedy shortcomings in the judicial systems of certain Member States.[1272]

An exception ought to be made for negative declaratory actions in the context of infringe-   **235** ment of registered IP rights. Here, *GAT v. LuK*[1273] and the ensuing codification first in Art. 22 (4) Lugano Convention 2007 and subsequently in Art. 24 (4) for practical purposes demand exclusive jurisdiction to be vested in the courts at the place where the respective IP right is registered.[1274]

c) **Assignment and subrogation**
Assignment or subrogation of a claim in tort, delict or quasi-delict does not alter the nature   **236** of this claim and does not deprive of the jurisdictional privilege of special jurisdiction under (2).[1275] Special jurisdiction under (2) is not a personal privilege exclusively favouring the initial creditor but attached to, and engraved in the DNA of, the claim. It stems from the tort, and jurisdiction is based on the facts of the tort which remain unchanged whoever is the current creditor of the claim. (2) reflects the aim of proximity and is based on a particularly close connecting factor between the dispute and the courts of the place where the harmful event occurred.[1276] A dispute concerning claims in tort continues to be closely connected with the place where the harmful event occurred even if the claim is transferred.[1277] Evidence is still located where it has ever been, and the factual sequence on which the tort is based, remains unaltered, too. The event and the facts fixed in time are the dominant element not any kind of obligatory bond.

Yet a conflict with predictability could not possibly arise.[1278] The alternative would not be   **237** that the *forum delicti* wandered with the creditorship to the assignee's domicile or habitual residence. The alternative would rather consist to wipe out and erase the *forum delicti* once

---

1267 On the concept of private attorney general e.g. *Hannah Buxbaum*, 26 Yale J. Int'l. L. 219 (2001).

1268 *Muir Watt*, RCDIP 102 (2013), 506, 509.

1269 Admitted by *Vanleenhove*, NIPR 2013, 25, 28.

1270 A-G *Jääskinen*, Opinion of 19 April 2012 in Case C-133/11, ECLI:EU:C:2012:226 paras. 29, 35.

1271 *Domej*, ecolex 2013, 123 *et seq.*

1272 *Domej*, ecolex 2013, 123, 124.

1273 GAT v. LuK, (Case C-4/03) [2006] ECR I-6509.

1274 OLG Dresden IPRspr. 2009 Nr. 196 pp. 505 *et seq.*; *Hofmann/Kunz*, in: Basler Kommentar, Art. 5 notes 508–512.

1275 *ÖFAB Östergötlands Fastigheter AB v. Frank Koot and Evergreen Investments BV* (Case C-147/12), ECLI:EU:C:2013:490 para. 59.

1276 *ÖFAB Östergötlands Fastigheter AB v. Frank Koot and Evergreen Investments BV* (Case C-147/12), ECLI:EU:C:2013:490 para. 57.

1277 *ÖFAB Östergötlands Fastigheter AB v. Frank Koot and Evergreen Investments BV* (Case C-147/12), ECLI:EU:C:2013:490 para. 57.

1278 Insofar *contra* *ÖFAB Östergötlands Fastigheter AB v. Frank Koot and Evergreen Investments BV* (Case C-147/12), ECLI:EU:C:2013:490 para. 58.

the claim is transferred. Predictability would be preserved for the debtor, and the assignee would also know where to stand if such a rule was implemented.

2. Characterisation

a) Non-contractual liability

238   For the purposes of characterisation the ECJ employs a negative and autonomous,[1279] non-national[1280] definition: Tort, quasi-tort and delict cover all actions which seek to establish liability of a defendant and which are not related to a contract within the meaning of (1).[1281] Tort is primarily defined as a non-contractual issue. Accordingly, contract and tort (= non-contract) are construed as strict alternatives. A contractual issue can not qualify as tortious and *vice versa*. There is no overlap between (1) and (2).[1282] The principle of mutual exclusivity with regard to the single claim[1283] reigns.[1284] (2) to a certain extent serves a residual function to (1) and is subsidiary to (1) in terms of characterisation.[1285] Accordingly, the first step for practical purposes must be to ascertain that the issue in question is *not* contractual.[1286] This has to be tested against the definition of contract under (1) (and under Art. 17[1287]). Hence, to assert that the breach of a fiduciary duty could come within (2)[1288]

[1279] See only *Anastasios Kalfelis v. Bankhaus Schröder Münchmeyer Hengst & Cie.*, (Case 189/87) [1988] ECR 5565, 5585 para. 18; OLG Düsseldorf DB 2004, 128; *SanDisk Corp. v. Koninklijke Philips Electronics NV* [2007] ILPr 325, 333 (Ch.D., *Pumfrey* J.); *Hewden Tower Cranes Ltd. v. Wolffkran GmbH*, [2007] EWHC 857 (TCC), [2007] 2 Lloyd's Rep. 138, 143 (Q.B.D., *Jackson* J.).

[1280] BGH WM 2014, 1614 [19].

[1281] *Anastasios Kalfelis v. Bankhaus Schröder Münchmeyer Hengst & Cie.*, (Case 189/87) [1988] ECR 5565, 5585 para. 18; *Mario Reichert et al. v. Dresdner Bank AG*, (Case C-261/90) [1992] ECR I-2149, I-2180 para. 16; *Réunion europénne SA v. Spliethoff's Bevrachtingskantoor BV and Master of the vessel "Alblasgracht 002"*, (Case C-51/97) [1998] ECR I-6511, I-6543 para. 22; *Rudolf Gabriel*, (Case C-96/00) [2002] I-6367, I-6398 para. 33; *Verein für Konsumenteninformation v. Karl-Heinz Henkel*, (Case C-167/00) [2002], I-8111, I-8139 para. 36; *ÖFAB Östergötlands Fastigheter AB v. Frank Koot and Evergreen Investments BV* (Case C-147/12), ECLI:EU:C:2013:490 para. 32; *OTP Bank Nyilvánosan Müködö Részvénytársaság v. Hochtief Solution AG* (C-519/12), ECLI:EU:C:2013:674 para. 26; *Marc Brogsitter v. Fabrication de Montres Normandes EURL and Karsten Fräßdorf* (Case C-548/12), ECLI:EU:C:2014:148 para. 20; *Harald Kolassa v. Barclays Bank plc* (Case C-375/13), ECLI:EU:C:2015:37 para. 44. Followed e.g. in BGHZ 176, 342 = NJW 2008, 2344; BGH WM 2014, 1614 [20]; *Source Ltd. v. TÜV Rheinland Holding AG* [1997] 3 WLR 365, 371 (C.A., per *Staughton* L.J.); OLG Stuttgart IPRax 1999, 103, 104; *Con"stance Short and others v. Ireland, The Attorney General and British Nuclear Fuels plc* [1996] 2 I.R. 188, 202 (H. C., *O'Hanlon* J.); HG Zürich SZIER 1996, 74, 75 note *Volken*; LAG Rheinland-Pfalz IPRspr. 2008 Nr. 160 p. 515; LG Kiel IPRax 2009, 164, 165; AG Frankfurt/Main AG 2006, 859 *et seq.*

[1282] *Raiffeisen Zentralbank Österreich AG v. National Bank of Greece SA* [1999] 1 Lloyd's Rep. 408, 411 (Q.B. D., *Tuckey* J.).

[1283] A claim in contract and a claim in tort can concur, but then there are *two* claims at stake, not only a single one.

[1284] See *Burke v. UVEX Sports GmbH and Motorrad TAF GmbH* [2005] I.L.Pr. 348, 353 (High Ct. of Ireland, *Herbert* J.).

[1285] Arenas García, AEDIPr 2013, 1021.

[1286] *Verein für Konsumenteninformation v. Karl-Heinz Henkel*, (Case C-167/00) [2002], I-8111, I-8140 para. 37; *Source Ltd. v. TÜV Rheinland Holding AG* [1997] 3 WLR 365, 371 (C.A., per *Staughton* L.J.); Protodikeio Herakleion Archeio Nomologias 2001, 240; Aud. Prov. Madrid AEDIPr 2008, 892, 894 with

holds true only insofar as such duty can not be characterised as contractual. The notion of contract evidently encompasses gap-filling rules of contract law and is not restricted to claims verbally spelt out in the text of the contract itself.[1289] In the event of an agreement on excluding or limiting liability, even if such liability is arising from a tort, nevertheless not the contractual character of the agreement, but the matter regulated by agreement and not changing its character, should gain the advantage.[1290] Breach of a contract might be unlawful but is nevertheless contractual and not in tort.[1291]

In other regards, the concept of tort obviously needs refinement without which it would bear **239** considerable imprecision and uncertainty.[1292] A purely negative definition in the strict sense would be rather problematic.[1293] Without further refinement and restriction e.g. maintenance claims could be regarded as claims in tort insofar as one stretches the natural meaning of "liability" – an obviously absurd result. Not every claim which can not be qualified as contractual, automatically classifies as tortious.[1294] Extra-contractual or non-contractual on the one hand and tortious on the other hand are not synonymous as is evidenced by Art. 2 Rome II Regulation. In this regard the wording of (2) in some languages (Danish: "i sager om erstatning uden for kontrakt"; Portuguese: "en matéria extracontractual") is too wide.[1295] Some obligations simply are not covered by (1) *and* (2).[1296] Suffice it to point to maintenance claims as the most striking example. Insofar the dividing line between (1) and (2) is different from the dividing line between Rome I and Non-Rome I, where it suffices to classify something as non-contractual to keep it out negatively,[1297] whereas here a positive inclusion in (2) is at stake (and the correct counterpart in PIL should be the outside frontier of Rome II). Furthermore, the mere existence of Arts. 10; 11 Rome II Regulation besides Arts. 4–9 Rome II Regulation is a clear indication that there are categories between contract and tort which

---

note *de Miguel Asensio*; *Braggion*, Dir. comm. int. 2011, 588, 591; in more detail *Arenas García*, AEDIPr 2006, 393.

[1287] See BGHZ 187, 156 = NJW 2011, 532 where a very wide notion of claims arising out of a (consumer) contract is employed; applauding *Baumert*, EWiR Art. 13 LugÜ 1/10, 795, 796; *Renate Schaub*, LMK 2011, 313318; *Michael Stürner*, jurisPR-ZivilR 7/2011 Anm. 4 sub D; *Ultsch*, WuB VII C 3. Art. 13 LugÜ 1.11.

[1288] *Casio Computer Co. Ltd. v. Sayo* [2001] I.L.Pr. 694, 701 (C.A., per *Tuckey* L.J.).

[1289] Hoge Raad NJ 2005 Nr. 39 p. 208 with note *Vlas*.

[1290] *Kaye* p. 510. *Contra Burke v. UVEX Sports GmbH and Motorrad TAF GmbH* [2005] I.L.Pr. 348, 354 *et seq.* (High Ct. of Ireland, *Herbert* J.)

[1291] Overlooked by Rb. Utrecht as cited in Hof Amsterdam, nevenzittingsplaats Arnhem NIPR 2010 Nr. 466 p. 772.

[1292] See *Vinaixa i Miquel*, Rev. der. com. eur. 2002, 977, 992.

[1293] *Vlas*, NILR 2002, 118, 119.

[1294] Cassaz. RDIPP 2005, 435, 440; Hessisches LAG IPRax 2008, 131, 132; *Gothot/Holleaux* para. 85; *Gaudemet-Tallon*, RCDIP 78 (1989), 121; *Blanco-Morales Limones*, in: Calvo Caravaca, Art. 5.3 CB note 7; *Libchaber*, Rép. Defrénois 2003, 254, 257 *et seq.*; *Veenstra*, NTBR 2003, 138, 141; *Leclerc*, Clunet 131 (2004), 911, 915.

[1295] *Guus E. Schmidt*, NIPR 2004, 296, 297.

[1296] *Briggs*, [1992] LMCLQ 283, 285 *et seq.*; *Bertrand Ancel*, RCDIP 81 (1992), 721, 725; *Robert Stevens*, (1996) L.Q.Rev. 391, 396. *Contra Delebecque*, DMF 1999, 33, 34.

[1297] See *Pertegás*, in: Meeusen/Pertegás/Straetmans (eds.), Enforcement of International Contracts in the European Union (2004), p. 175, 184 § 5–26.

Peter Mankowski   269

are neither contract nor tort.[1298] As to the consequences of liability, not only damages are sufficient to qualify, but also claims for removal or for refraining from doing something.[1299]

240 Generally, (2) nevertheless pursues a broad concept of tort.[1300] Liability of the defendant must not be equated with, and confined to, an action for damages. Injunctions are equally covered.[1301] If any proof for this was required (2) *in fine* covering preventive actions would provide it in the most evident fashion.

241 In particular, it covers not only situations where an individual has personally sustained damage but also the undermining of legal stability for instance by the use of unfair contract terms.[1302] Quasi-collective actions by associations or institutions seeking the prevention of such damage to the general good are included[1303] not the least since in the specific case of unfair contract terms Art. 7 Directive 93/13/EC[1304] demands efficacy of such actions[1305] as does, in the wider context, Directive 98/27/EC.[1306] Although a Swedish proposal[1307] to include a new paragraph in then Art. 5 expressly dealing with collective actions by consumer protection associations or official bodies, was rejected (mainly because actions by official bodies could fall outside the notion of "civil and commercial matters"), leaving collective actions covered by (2).[1308] A certain concentration could be effected if jurisdiction was established at the seat of the respective organisation.[1309]

241a If an allegedly tortious activity took place in the past the fact that it was suspended by the

---

[1298] *Strikwerda*, Ned. Jur. 2015 Nr. 1 p. 3, 5.

[1299] *Verein für Konsumenteninformation v. Karl-Heinz Henkel*, (Case C-167/00) [2002], I-8111, I-8139 paras. 35–36; BGH NJW 2005, 1435 – Hotel Maritim; BGH NJW 2006, 689; BGH NJW 2012, 2197 [13]; BGH GRUR-RR 2013, 228 [12] – Trägermaterial für Kartenformulare.

[1300] *Handelskwekerij G.J. Bier BV v. Mines de Potasse d'Alsace SA*, (Case 21/76) [1976] ECR 1735, 1746 *et seq.* para. 15/19; *Verein für Konsumenteninformation v. Karl-Heinz Henkel*, (Case C-167/00) [2002], I-8111, I-8141 para. 42; BGH WM 2006, 350.

[1301] See only *Verein für Konsumenteninformation v. Karl-Heinz Henkel*, (Case C-167/00) [2002], I-8111, I-8141 *et seq.* para. 42–44; BGH NJW 2005, 1435 – Hotel Maritime; BGH NJW 2006, 689; BGH RIW 2011, 564, 565; BGH NJW 2012, 2197.

[1302] *Verein für Konsumenteninformation v. Karl-Heinz Henkel*, (Case C-167/00) [2002], I-8111, I-8141 para. 42.

[1303] *Verein für Konsumenteninformation v. Karl-Heinz Henkel*, (Case C-167/00) [2002], I-8111, I-8141 para. 42; OGH RdW 2003/124; BGHZ 182, 24; BGH NJW 2010, 1958; BGH NJW 2010, 2719; OLG Frankfurt VuR 2009, 72, 73; KG K&R 2009, 498; LG Frankfurt/Main WM 2008, 501; *Purnhagen*, VuR 2009, 75; *Vitellino*, in: Liber Fausto Pocar (2009), p. 985, 992 *et seq.*; *Ansgar Staudinger/Czaplinski*, NJW 2009, 3395; *Stadler*, VuR 2010, 83; *Paredes Pérez*, AEDIPr 2009, 355, 357 *et seq.* Sceptical *Muir Watt*, IPRax 2010, 111, 113; *Hess*, IPRax 2010, 116, 118.

[1304] Council Directive 93/13/EEC of 5 April 1993 on unfair terms in consumer contracts, OJ 1993 L 95/29.

[1305] *Verein für Konsumenteninformation v. Karl-Heinz Henkel*, (Case C-167/00) [2002], I-8111, I-8141 para. 43.

[1306] Council Directive 98/27/EC of 7 May 1998 on harmonisation of the main provisions concerning export credit insurance for transactions with medium and long-term cover, OJ 1998 L 148/22.

[1307] Exposé by the Swedish delegation, Doc. 6248/98 JUSTCIV 12 (February 27, 1998).

[1308] *Christian Kohler*, in: Gottwald (ed.), Revision des EuGVÜ/Neues Schiedsverfahrensrecht (2000), p. 1, 21.

[1309] *Leclerc*, Clunet 131 (2004), 911, 916.

alleged tortfeasor does not deprive the claimant of the opportunities (2) offers, the more so if a ruling on the legality of such activity is already pending.[1310] Insofar a *perpetuatio fori* must prevail, and the plaintiff can avail himself of (2).

Class actions or group actions are a different matter, but might also avail themselves of (2) in   **242** the proper setting.[1311] Yet unlike for collective actions it is more difficult to argue that such actions serve market-related purposes. Eventually, class actions might still be regarded as regulation through litigation, and lead plaintiffs and class actions lawyers as some kind of private attorney-generals. But this is rather remote from the typical case of (2) that individuals seek compensation for individual damage suffered.

That the tortfeasor's activity might be possibly justified is a matter of the merits and cannot   **243** wrestle away the characterisation for jurisdictional purposes.[1312]

b) Tort, delict and quasi-delict

That the wording lists tort, delict and quasi-delict side by side each other does not add   **244** significantly to the classification. The inclusion of both tort and delict is a concession to differing linguistic denominations in the English-speaking legal community, namely the use of "delict" in Scotland. The doubling does not appear in the other versions, for instance in French or German.[1313] Another reverence to, and bowing before, a certain national tradition in substantive law is the addition of quasi-delict. It is due to particularities of French law reflecting and distinguishing strict and fault-based liability.[1314] The only conclusion gained should be that (2) covers torts regardless whether they establish strict or fault-based liability.[1315] Fault or non-fault does not feature as an excluding factor. A causal link between the damage and the event in which that damage originates is required,[1316] though, but should not pose too big an obstacle. A denomination in some languages which expressly refers to the illeceity of the act committed must not be taken as an order to prove such legality or illeceity already at the stage of ascertaining jurisdiction.[1317] Such task should be left to later stages whereas it should be sufficient for the purposes of (2) that the plaintiff alleges a tort to have happened. Hence, compensation for lawful acts can also be covered by (2).[1318]

[1310] *Danmarks Rederiforeniging, acting on behalf of DFDS Torline AS v. LO Landsorganisationen i Sverige, acting on behalf of SEKO Sjöfolk Facket for Service och Kommunikation,* (Case C-18/02) [2004] ECR I-1417, I-1455 paras. 37 *et seq.*

[1311] *Danov,* (2010) 6 JPrIL 359, 367 *et seq.*

[1312] BGH NJW-RR 2010, 1546; see also OLG Köln TranspR 2009, 37, 38.

[1313] In particular the Italian version has been reformulated on the occasion of drafting the Brussels I Regulation; see Cassaz. RDIPP 2005, 435, 439.

[1314] *Schlosser* Art. 5 note 15; *Mörsdorf-Schulte,* ZZP Int. 8 (2003), 407, 430.

[1315] See only OLG Karlsruhe IPRax 2011, 179, 180; *Mankowski,* EWiR Art. 5 EuGVÜ 1/98, 269, 270; *Kindler,* in: FS Peter Ulmer (2003), p. 305, 317; *Gehri,* in: FS Ivo Schwander (2011), p. 699, 707. Erroneously to the contrary *Götte,* DStR 1997, 503, 505.

[1316] *Handelskwekerij G.J. Bier BV v. Mines de Potasse d'Alsace SA,* (Case 21/76) [1976] ECR 1735, 1746 *et seq.* para. 15/19; *Danmarks Rederiforeniging, acting on behalf of DFDS Torline AS v. LO Landsorganisationen i Sverige, acting on behalf of SEKO Sjöfolk Facket for Service och Kommunikation,* (Case C-18/02) [2004] ECR I-1417, I-1453 *et seq.* para. 32.

[1317] Apparently *contra* Trib. Siracusa Dir. Mar. 2006, 906, 915.

[1318] *Geimer/Schütze,* Art. 5 note 206; *Gehri,* in: FS Ivo Schwander (2011), p. 699, 707.

245 On the other hand, the phrase "quasi-delict" should not be overly extended and should thus not be taken as a *per se* inclusion of unjust enrichment, restitution or *negotiorum gestio*.[1319] Nevertheless, restitutionary claims based on wrongdoing are covered although their denomination does not refer to torts expressly.[1320] If *Kalfelis* is invoked to the contrary,[1321] the invocation is unjustified since *Kalfelis* does not express anything on restitutionary claims directly.[1322] Nothing in (2) restricts claims covered by those claims for damages,[1323] the material point being the enforcement of liability by whichever means are instrumentalised for this purpose. Perhaps some notion of "restitution in wrong" could help terminologically, if it is not burdened with particularities.[1324] (2) also applies to claims founded in *negotiorum gestio* since it can be said that either the principal or the *gestor* suffers disadvantages.[1325] Claims for damages under this heading thus would be covered whereas claims for compensation or remuneration would not.[1326]

246 Even vindicatory claims, the *vindicatio rei*, can be said to fall in the scope of (2).[1327] Whether the substantive law of the *lex fori* or the *lex causae* or the *lex rei sitae* classifies a matter as an issue of the law of property, is not all-decisive for the purposes of (2) due to the general necessity of an autonomous interpretation. Accordingly, claims for removal flowing from the ownership of a good can in some instances be characterised as tortious under (2).[1328]

247 Tortious liability must not be held to be synonymous with damages. Other possible consequences and the actions pursuing them are also covered. The last clause of (2) should make this clear since it unambiguously grants jurisdiction for actions to interdict future activities.[1329] Accordingly, e.g. actions against the press and other media enterprises for publish-

---

[1319] See *Werner Lorenz*, IPRax 1993, 44; *Blanco-Morales Limones*, in: Calvo Caravaca, Art. 5.3 CB note 15; *Hootz* p. 185; *Dutta*, IPRax 2011, 134, 137; *ten Wolde/Kirsten C. Henckel*, Int. J. Proced. L. 3 (2013), 195, 206. But cf. also Cassaz. RDIPP 1991, 772. *Contra Hartley*, (1989) 14 Eur. L. Rev. 169, 174.

[1320] *Peel*, [1998] LMCLQ 22, 26 *et seq.*; *Virgo*, (1998) 114 L.Q.Rev. 386, 389; *Briggs*, (2001) 72 BYIL 437, 473; *Guus E. Schmidt*, NIPR 2004, 296, 297 *et seq.*; *Isabel Roth*, Die internationale Zuständigkeit deutscher Gerichte bei Persönlichkeitsrechtsverletzungen im Internet (2007) pp. 137–143; *Dutta*, IPRax 2011, 134, 137; *Hofmann/Kunz*, in: Basler Kommentar, Art. 5 notes 491–494. See also *Kleinwort Benson Ltd. v. Glasgow City Council* [1997] 3 WLR 923, 935 (H.L., per Lord *Goff of Chieveley*); OGH EvBl 2002/3; Hof 's-Hertogenbosch NIPR 2005 Nr. 159 p. 219 *et seq. Contra* OGH ZfRV 2001, 70; *Blanco-Morales Limones*, in: Calvo Caravaca, Art. 5.3 CB note 14; *Uhl* pp. 125 *et seq.*; *Kropholler/von Hein* Art. 5 note 75; *Olaf Weber*, MMR 2012, 48, 49 (since restitution is not for damages). Doubtful *Yeo*, (2001) 117 L.Q.Rev. 560, 564 *et seq.*; *Hootz* p. 185.

[1321] As e.g. by *Leible*, in: Rauscher Art. 5 note 83.

[1322] See *Anastasios Kalfelis v. Bankhaus Schröder Münchmeyer Hengst & Cie.*, (Case 189/87) [1988] ECR 5565, 5586 para. 21.

[1323] Erroneously *contra* Trib. Bergamo RDIPP 2003, 451, 460; similar as here *Lein*, in: Dickinson/Lein paras. 4.80–4.81.

[1324] As in English law; see *Birks*, in: Essays in Honour of Gareth Jones (1998), p. 1; *Birks*, Unjust Enrichment (2003); *Tettenborn*, in: Essays in Honour of Gareth Jones (1998), p. 31; *Virgo*, ibid., p. 307; *Swadling*, ibid., p. 331.

[1325] See in more detail *Uhl* pp. 126 *et seq.*

[1326] OLG Köln IPRax 2011, 174, 175; *Dutta*, IPRax 2011, 134, 137; *Looschelders*, IPRax 2014, 406, 407.

[1327] *Guus E. Schmidt*, NIPR 2004, 296, 298. *Contra* Rb. Breda NIPR 1991 Nr. 158.

[1328] *Kindler*, in: FS Peter Ulmer (2003), p. 305, 318; *Hüßtege*, in: Thomas/Putzo Art. 5 note 10.

ing statements denouncing previous publications should not drop outside the ambit of torts.[1330] Also, (2) is open for actions which aim at local inspections or at gaining information in order to prepare the main strike in damages or interdiction.[1331] Furthermore, (2) covers (auxiliary) claims for information, too.[1331a]

c) Torts covered

Amongst the torts encompassed feature *inter alia*:[1332] car and other traffic accidents;[1333] **248** medical maltreatment;[1334] infringement of personality rights;[1335] breach of constitutional rights if granted also by EC law like the right of free movement;[1336] conspiracy;[1337] antitrust matters,[1338] also if concerned with European law like in particular Art. 101 TFEU (ex-Art. 81 EC Treaty);[1339] unfair commercial practices;[1340] copyright, patent or trademark infringe-

---

[1329] OLG München AfP 2008, 394, 395; see also BGH GRUR-RR 2013, 228 [12]; BGH WRP 2015, 735 [26] – *Parfümflakon III.*

[1330] *Stadler*, JZ 1994, 642, 648 *et seq. Contra* tentatively *Kubis*, Internationale Zuständigkeit bei Persönlichkeits- und Immaterialgüterrechtsverletzungen (1999) pp. 116 *et seq.*

[1331] *Hye-Knudsen*, Marken-, Patent- und Urheberrechtsverletzungen im europäischen Internationalen Zivilprozessrecht (2005) p. 64.

[1331a] BGH WRP 2015, 735 [26] – *Parfümflakon III*; BGH GRUR 2015, 264 [15] – *Hi Hotel II.*

[1332] See OLG Saarbrücken IPRax 2013, 74, 79; *ten Wolde/Kirsten C. Henckel*, Int. J. Proced. L. 3 (2013), 195, 203–204.

[1333] See only Report *Jenard* p. 26; Areios Pagos Ell. D. 2004, 421; *Blanco-Morales Limones*, in: Calvo Caravaca, Art. 5.3 CB note 13.

[1334] See only *Kropholler/von Hein*, Art. 5 note 74.

[1335] See only Areios Pagos Ell. D. 2004, 421; AP Madrid REDI 2011-2, 260 with note *Cordero Álvarez.*

[1336] *Norbert Schmidt v. Home Secretary of the Government of the United Kingdom* [1995] ILRM 301 (High Ct. of Ireland).

[1337] *Sunderland Marine Mutual Insurance Co. Ltd. v. Wiseman (The "Seaward Quest")*, [2007] EWHC 1460 (Comm), [2007] 2 Lloyd's Rep. 308, 313 (Q.B.D., *Langley* J.).

[1338] See only OGH ZfRV 2008/32, 81, 82; Cass. RCDIP 102 (2013), 464, 465–466 with note *Pironon*; BGH GRUR-RR 2013, 228 = NZKart 2013, 202 – Trägermaterial für Kartenformulare; Protodikeio Thessaloniki [2003] I.L.Pr. 39; LG Dortmund IPRax 2005, 542 = EWS 2004, 434; *Zimmer/Leopold*, EWS 2005, 149, 150; *Ashton/Vollrath*, ZWeR 2006, 1, 7; *Moritz Becker*, EWS 2008, 228, 229; *Basedow*, in: Wettbewerbspolitik und Kartellrecht in der Marktwirtschaft – 50 Jahre FIW 1960–2010 (2010), p. 129, 131; *Helena Isabel Maier*, Marktortanknüpfung im internationalen Kartelldeliktsrecht (2011) p. 124.

[1339] *Roche Products Ltd. v. Provimi Ltd.* [2003] 2 All ER (Comm) 683 (Q.B.D., *Aikens* J.).

[1340] *Coty Germany GmbH v. First Note Perfumes NV* (Case C-360/12), ECLI:EU:C:2014:1318 para. 42; BGH GRUR 1988, 483, 485 – AGIAV = NJW 1988, 1466; BGH GRUR 1998, 419 – Gewinnspiel im Ausland; BGH GRUR 1998, 945 – Co-Verlagsvereinbarung; BGHZ 153, 82, 91; BGH GRUR 2006, 513 – Arzneimittelwerbung im Internet; Cassaz. RDIPP 1994, 344; Cassaz. RDIPP 1996, 529, 538 *et seq.*; Cass. RCDIP 93 (2004), 652 with note *Marie-Élodie Ancel*; Cass. JCP G 2007 II 10088 with note *Marie-Éldoie Ancel* = RCDIP 97 (2008), 322 with note *Treppoz*; OGH WBl 2011, 279; OLG München NJW-RR 1994, 190 = EuZW 1994, 190; KG WRP 1994, 868, 870; OLG Frankfurt/M. OLG-Report Frankfurt 1996, 259, 260 f; OLG Stuttgart IPRax 1999, 103, 104; OLG Hamm RIW 2000, 58; KG NJW-RR 2002, 113 = MMR 2001, 759 – DocMorris; OLG Dresden RIW 2002, 959, 960 = IPRax 2002, 421, 422; OLG Stuttgart MDR 2003, 350 with note *Stefan Braun*; KG ZLR 2003, 604 with note *Meisterernst*; OLG München IPRspr. 2003 Nr. 102 p. 306; OLG München IPRspr. 2009 Nr. 125b p. 307; OLG München IPRspr. 2009 Nr. 138 p. 349; OLG Hamburg WRP 2009, 1305 = MMR 2010, 185; OLG Stuttgart K&R 2010, 40; OLG Karlsruhe IPRax

---

Peter Mankowski

ment;[1341] infringement of domain names;[1342] infringement of IP rights related to songs and other kinds of music;[1342a] unjustified allegations of infringing IP rights;[1342b] rape and bodily or physical violence;[1343] industrial action and strike;[1344] product liability or non-contractual liability from defective goods;[1345] environmental damage insofar as it is not (wrongly)[1346] deemed covered by Art. 24 (1);[1347] unjustified execution of judgments judicially squashed later-on insofar as this is not deemed to be covered by Art. 24 (5);[1348] fraud;[1349] deception; torts committed on the capital markets;[1350] prospectus liability;[1351] actions challenging the

---

2011, 179, 180; CA Orléans RCDIP 93 (2004), 139 with note *Gaudemet-Tallon* = Clunet 131 (2004), 193 with note *André Huet*; Rb. Kh. Dendermonde TBH 2000, 242, 244 with note *Wautelet*; Rb. Kh. Veurne [2006] I.L.Pr. 336, 344; LG München I MMR 2008, 782; LG Stuttgart VuR 2009, 196; LG Hamburg CR 2011, 756; Juzgado de Mercantil Bilbao AEDIPr 2008, 885.

[1341] See only *Peter Pinckney v. KDG Mediatech AG* (Case C-170/12), ECLI:EU:C:2013:635 para. 45; *Hi Hotel HCF SARL v. Uwe Spoering* (Case C-387/12), ECLI:EU:C:2014:215 para. 38; Cass. RCDIP 93 (2004), 632 with note *Cachard*; BGH GRUR 1994, 530, 531 – Beta; OGH EvBl 2001/194; OGH WBl 2001, 231 with note *Thiele*; OGH ÖJZ-LSK 2002/54; BGH GRUR 2005, 431, 432 – Hotel Maritime= WRP 2005, 493, 494 = JZ 2005, 736 with note *Ohly*; BGH GRUR 2012, 621 [18] – OSCAR; BG sic! 2007, 279, 281; *Mölnlycke AB v. Procter & Gamble Ltd.* [1992] 4 All ER 47 (C.A.); KG RIW 2001, 611, 613 = GRUR Int. 2002, 327, 328 – Euro-Paletten; OLG Nürnberg GRUR 2009, 786; OLG München GRUR-RR 2010, 157; ObG Zürich sic! 2004, 793, 794; Rb. 's-Gravenhage NIPR 1999 Nr. 83 p. 130; LG Düsseldorf GRUR Int. 1999, 455, 457 – Schussfadengreifer; LG Düsseldorf GRUR Int. 1999, 775, 776 – Impfstoff II; LG Hamburg GRUR Int. 2002, 163 – hotel-maritime.dk with note *Pellens/Pietsch*; LG Mannheim IPRspr. 2009 Nr. 144 p. 364; Trib. Bruxelles J. trib. 2003, 234, 235; Aud. Prov. Madrid AEDIPr 2008, 892, 893 *et seq.* with note *de Miguel Asensio*; *Kieninger*, GRUR Int. 1998, 280, 282; *Glöckner*, WRP 2005, 795, 798; *Ahrens*, in: Ahrens (ed.), Der Wettbewerbsprozess (5th ed. 2005) ch. 16 with note 11; *Hye-Knudsen*, Marken-, Patent- und Urheberrechtsverletzungen im europäischen internationalen Zivilprozessrecht (2005) p. 63; *McGuire*, ZEuP 2014, 160 at 160.

[1342] BG 6 March 2007 – Case 4C.341/2005.

[1342a] BGH NJW 2013, 2345.

[1342b] LG Hamburg CR 2014, 341 = MMR 2014, 267 with note *Carl Christian Müller/Rößner*.

[1343] Hoge Raad NJ 2002 Nr. 539 = NIPR 2002 Nr. 35.

[1344] See only *Danmarks Rederiforeniging, acting on behalf of DFDS Torline AS v. LO Landsorganisationen i Sverige, acting on behalf of SEKO Sjöfolk Facket for Service och Kommunikation*, (Case C-18/02) [2004] ECR I-1417; *Kropholler/von Hein*, Art. 5 note 74.

[1345] OGH JBl 2001, 185; OGH JBl 2014, 400; Areios Pagos Ell. D. 2004, 421; ØLD UfR 1994, 342; Leo Laboratories Ltd. v. Crompton BV [2005] 2 IR 225, 233 *et seq.* (S.C., per *Fennelly* J.); Hof Antwerpen R.W. 2007–2008, 989, 992; Rb. Dordrecht NIPR 2008 Nr. 55 p. 96.

[1346] See only *Zuid-Chemie v. Philippo's Mineralenfabriek NV/SA*, (Case C-189/08) [2009] ECR I-6917. But cf. in favour of applying Art. 24 (1) if environmental damage to real estate is at stake, OGH ÖJZ 2004, 77, 80 = JBl 2004, 105 note *Rotter*; further with noted by *Tiefenthaler/Hanusch*, ecolex 2004, 330; *Wehdeking*, DZWIR 2004, 323; *Hadeyer*, ecolex 2004, 828. See also the reference for a premiliary ruling in OGH ecolex 2004, 859 with note *Mayr*.

[1347] *Blanco-Morales Limones*, in: Calvo Caravaca, Art. 5.3 CB note 13; *Schack*, IPRax 2005, 262, 265; *Günter Hager/Felix Hartmann*, IPRax 2005, 266, 268 *et seq.*

[1348] Rb. Rotterdam NIPR 2006 Nr. 319 p. 468 = S&S 2007 Nr. 39 p. 212; *Kindler*, in: FS Peter Ulmer (2003), p. 305, 318; *Hüßtege*, in: Thomas/Putzo Art. 5 note 10.

[1349] BGH WM 2008, 479; OLG Köln WM 2006, 122, 124 *et seq.* = IPRax 2006, 479; *von Hein*, IPRax 2006, 460.

[1350] *Harald Kolassa v. Barclays Bank plc* (Case C-375/13), ECLI:EU:C:2015:37 para. 53; OLG Bremen IPRax

financial integrity of a company even if concurring with contractual claims to the same avail.[1352] The *action directe en responsabilité* within a chain of contracts qualifies as tort at least insofar as the product damages other assets,[1353] and must not be deemed to fall outside (1) *and* (2) entirely.[1354] Cargo claims by cargo owners against someone else than their contractual carrier are within (2), too;[1355] who is the contractual carrier is an incidental question to be answered *via* private international law and applicable substantive law.[1356]

It is not necessary that damage was actually sustained in the past. This follows at least from **249** the last clause of (2),[1357] but could be derived even without it. Actions for preventing future damage must be treated equivalent to actions for compensatory damages.[1358] Otherwise the paradox result would appear that the most proficient and efficient way to deal with torts (namely to prevent them and to spare the accompanying financial and social costs of a wrongdoing) would find limits and would have to overcome high stakes and hurdles.

That the claim is one for damages is not required. Generally, the claim must not be for **250** damages, but can pursue any possible goal if such goal is based on non-contractual liability.[1359] Accordingly a declarative action ascertaining tortious liability triggers off the application of (2) as well.[1360] Whether the court seised has jurisdiction under national procedural rules to entertain claims for damages or is restricted to hear actions for ascertaining liability only, resulting in a special nature of the court under national law, is immaterial.[1361] Since (2) does not require a damage already sustained, redress claims between jointly liable tortfeasors

2000, 226, 228; OLG Köln WM 2006, 122, 124; OLG Fankfurt ZIP 2010, 2217; Protodikeio Athinai EED 2001, 268; Protodikeio Peiraios CID 2001, 322 and comprehensively *Christian Schmitt*, Die Haftung wegen fehlerhafter oder pflichtwidrig unterlassener Kapitalmarktinformation (2009).

[1351] *Harald Kolassa v. Barclays Bank plc* (Case C-375/13), ECLI:EU:C:2015:37 para. 44; A-G *Szpunar*, Opinion in Case C-375/13 of 3 September 2014, ECLI:EU:C:2014:2135 para. 58; *von Hein*, RIW 2004, 602, 604 *et seq.*; *von Hein*, BerDGfIR 45 (2011), 369, 3894–395; *Reuschle*, WM 2004, 966, 975 *et seq.*; *Gregor Bachmann*, IPRax 2007, 77, 81 *et seq.*; *Christian Schmitt*, Die Haftung wegen fehlerhafter oder pflichtwidrig unterlassener Kapitalmarktinformation (2009) p. 228; *Michael Müller*, EuZW 2015, 218, 222.

[1352] OLG München GmbHR 2006, 1152, 1155.

[1353] *Bauerreis*, RCDIP 89 (2000), 331, 346 *et seq.*; *Bauerreis*, Das französische Rechtsinstitut der action directe und seine Bedeutung in internationalen Vertragsketten (2000) pp. 224 *et seq.*

[1354] *Bauerreis*, Das französische Rechtsinstitut der action directe und seine Bedeutung in internationalen Vertragsketten (2000) pp. 222 *et seq.* Contra *Gaudemet-Tallon*, RCDIP 81 (1992), 726, 737; *Bauerreis*, RCDIP 82 (1993), 485, 489.

[1355] See only *Réunion europénne SA v. Spliethoff's Bevrachtingskantoor BV and Master of the vessel "Alblasgracht 002"*, (Case C-51/97) [1998] ECR I-6511; Rb. Rotterdam S&S 2007 Nr. 51 p. 264.

[1356] Rb. Rotterdam S&S 2007 Nr. 51 p. 264.

[1357] *Verein für Konsumenteninformation v. Karl-Heinz Henkel*, (Case C-167/00) [2002] ECR I-8111, I-8143 para. 49.

[1358] *Verein für Konsumenteninformation v. Karl-Heinz Henkel*, (Case C-167/00) [2002] ECR I-8111, I-8142 para. 47.

[1359] *Leible*, IPRax 2003, 28, 31.

[1360] *Danmarks Rederiforeniging, acting on behalf of DFDS Torline AS v. LO Landsorganisationen i Sverige, acting on behalf of SEKO Sjöfolk Facket for Service och Kommunikation*, (Case C-18/02) [2004] ECR I-1417, I-1451 *et seq.* paras. 22–28.

[1361] *Danmarks Rederiforeniging, acting on behalf of DFDS Torline AS v. LO Landsorganisationen i Sverige,*

are also covered by (2).[1362] Any notion restricting liability to damages in the strict sense would be irreconcilable with the last clause of (2) at least and would unnecessarily narrow the proper ambit of (2). (2) should be deemed to also cover the *actio quasi-negatoria*.[1363]

3. Place where the harmful event occurred

a) Principle of ubiquity

aa) The principle

251 The place where the harmful event occurred is not defined expressly in (2). In a long and standing line of decisions dating back to 1976 and confirmed ever since the ECJ has established that this place can be understood twofold: on the one hand as the place where the harmful event giving rise to the damage occurred, and on the other hand as the place where the damage occurred;[1364] both are in principle[1365] equivalent and on equal footing. The choice between them is for the plaintiff.[1366] To place reliance exclusively on the place of

---

acting on behalf of SEKO Sjöfolk Facket for Service och Kommunikation, (Case C-18/02) [2004] ECR I-1417, I-1451 *et seq.* paras. 22–28.

1362 *Hewden Tower Cranes Ltd. v. Wolffkran GmbH*, [2007] EWHC 857 (TCC), [2007] 2 Lloyd's Rep. 138, 143 (Q.B.D., *Jackson* J.); *Kropholler/von Hein* Art. 5 note 74; *Burgstaller/Neumayr* Art. 5 note 51 (Oct. 2002); *Schlosser* Art. 5 note 15; *Spickhoff*, VersR 2003, 665, 666; *Leible*, in: Rauscher Art. 5 note 81; *Ansgar Staudinger*, ZEuP 2004, 767, 777; *Kerstin Thoma* pp. 206–208, 211.

1363 See only BGH WM 2006, 350; *Glöckner*, WRP 2005, 795, 799.

1364 *Handelskwekerij G.J. Bier BV v. Mines de Potasse d'Alsace SA*, (Case 21/76) [1976] ECR 1735, 1746 *et seq.* paras. 15/19-24/25; *Dumez France SA and Tracoba SARL v. Hessische Landesbank*, (Case C-220/88) [1990] ECR I-49, I-78 para. 10; *Fiona Shevill v. Presse Alliance SA*, (Case C-68/93) [1995] ECR I-415, I-460 para. 20; *Antonio Marinari v. Lloyd's Bank plc and Zubaidi Trading Co.*, (Case C-364/93) [1995] ECR I-2719, I-2738 *et seq.* para. 11; *Réunion européenne SA v. Spliethoff's Bevrachtingskantoor BV*, (Case C-51/97) [1998] ECR I-6511, I-6544 para. 28; *Verein für Konsumenteninformation v. Karl-Heinz Henkel*, (Case C-167/00) [2002] ECR I-8111, I-8141 para. 44; *Danmarks Rederiforeniging, acting on behalf of DFDS Torline AS v. LO Landsorganisationen i Sverige, acting on behalf of SEKO Sjöfolk Facket for Service och Kommunikation*, (Case C-18/02) [2004] ECR I-1417, I-1456 para. 40; *Rudolf Kronhofer v. Marianne Maier*, (Case C-168/02) [2004] ECR I-6009, I-6029 *et seq.* para. 16; *Zuid-Chemie v. Philippo's Mineralenfabriek NV/SA*, (Case C-189/08) [2009] ECR I-6917, I-6927 para. 24; *eDate Advertising v. X and Olivier Martinez and Robert Martinez v. MGN Ltd.* (Joined Cases C-509/09 and C-161/10), [2011] ECR I-10269 paras. 40–41; *Wintersteiger AG v. Products 4U Sondermaschinenbau GmbH* (Case C-523/10), paras. 19–20; *Melzer v. MF Global UK Ltd.* (Case C-228/11), para. 25; *ÖFAB Östergötlands Fastigheter AB v. Frank Koot and Evergreen Investments BV* (Case C-147/12), ECLI:EU:C:2013:490 para. 51; *Peter Pinckney v. KDG Mediatech AG* (Case C-170/12), ECLI:EU:C:2013:635 para. 26; *Andreas Kainz v. Pantherwerke AG* (Case C-45/13), ECLI:EU:C:2014:7 para. 23; *Hi Hotel HCF SARL v. Uwe Spoering* (Case C-387/12), ECLI:EU:C:2014:215 para. 27; *Coty Germany GmbH v. First Note Perfumes NV* (Case C-360/12), ECLI:EU:C:2014:1318 para. 46; *Pez Hejduk v. EnergieAgentur.NRW GmbH* (Case C-441/13), ECLI:EU:C:2015:28 para. 18; *Harald Kolassa v. Barclays Bank plc* (Case C-375/13), ECLI:EU:C:2015:37 para. 45; from national supreme courts see only *pars pro toto* BGH WM 2014, 1614; Cassaz. RDIPP 2013, 1002, 1003.

1365 But cf. on the restriction of the second option Art. 7 notes 256–262 (*Mankowski*).

1366 See only *Handelskwekerij G.J. Bier BV v. Mines de Potasse d'Alsace SA*, (Case 21/76) [1976] ECR 1735, 1747 para. 24/25; Hof Arnhem NIPR 1999 Nr. 272 p. 364.

the event giving rise to the damage would allegedly make (2) lose most of its effectiveness since ordinarily a person acts where that person has his domicile and thus Art. 4 would come into play to the detriment of (2).[1367]

This so-called principle of ubiquity avoids choosing between the alleged tortfeasor's activity **252** and its results by attributing the same weight to both, and thereby favours the plaintiff, the alleged victim. Being undecided between activity and damage does not lead to tossing a coin but to using sympathy for the victim as the tie-breaker. This approach allows the victim-claimant a certain amount of decision-making discretion which, in addition, ensures the proximity of the court seised to the relevant facts of the dispute.[1368] An escape strategy produces a quite remarkable *favor actoris*.[1369] It simply doubles the opportunity for the plaintiff. The justification of the principle is not beyond doubt, but on the contrary rather dubious.[1370]

In practice, the principle does not produce too many results differing from those which **253** would be reached if only the place where the damage was sustained was used as the sole connecting factor: Usually the plaintiff is interested in the *forum actoris* and will sue in this place anyway or at least in case of doubt.[1371] If the defendant acted in the same state there is no difference between both connecting factors employed, but congruence and coincidence. A differing place of activity becomes only relevant in the rare instances where it is located neither in the state where the defendant has his domicile (covered by Art. 2, not by Art. 7 (2)),[1372] nor in the state where the damage was sustained.[1373]

(2) does not contain any escape clause, for instance, in favour of the courts of the state of the **254** common habitual residence,[1374] quite unlike Art. 4 (2) Rome II Regulation in conflicts law. If the relevant facts are located abroad, (2) does not lead the parties back home.[1375] On closer inspection there does not exist the slightest necessity to introduce such an escape device, in particular, bearing in mind that Art. 2 points to the defendant's domicile anyway. On the other hand, (2) must under no circumstances be interpreted as containing a principle of territoriality that the localisation of one element of the case within the forum state already suffices however strong such principle might be in the national law of the forum state.[1376]

[1367] *Handelskwekerij G.J. Bier BV v. Mines de Potasse d'Alsace SA*, (Case 21/76) [1976] ECR 1735, 1747 para. 20/23; *Fiona Shevill v. Presse Alliance SA*, (Case C-68/93) [1995] ECR I-415, I-460 para. 22; *Antonio Marinari v. Lloyd's Bank plc and Zubaidi Trading Co.*, (Case C-364/93) [1995] ECR I-2719, I-2739 para. 12; *ten Wolde/Kirsten C. Henckel*, Int. J. Proced. L. 3 (2013), 195, 199.

[1368] A-G *Cruz Villalón*, Opinion of 16 February 2012 in Case C-523/10, ECLI:EU:C:2012:90 para. 17.

[1369] But cf. *Gabellini*, Riv. trim dir. proc. civ. 2014, 271, 276.

[1370] See only *von Hein*, Das Günstigkeitsprinzip im Internationalen Deliktsrecht (1999) p. 97–102; *Mankowski*, in: FS Andreas Heldrich (2005), p. 867, 884 *et seq.*

[1371] *Schurig*, in: GS Alexander Lüderitz (2000), p. 699, 706.

[1372] *Handelskwekerij G.J. Bier BV v. Mines de Potasse d'Alsace SA*, (Case 21/76) [1976] ECR 1735, 1747 para. 20/23; *Fiona Shevill v. Presse Alliance SA*, (Case C-68/93) [1995] ECR I-415, I-461 para. 26.

[1373] *Mankowski*, in: FS Andreas Heldrich (2005), p. 867, 885.

[1374] See Hoge Raad NJ 2002 Nr. 539 = NIPR 2002 Nr. 35.

[1375] Hoge Raad NJ 2002 Nr. 539 = NIPR 2002 Nr. 35.

[1376] *Rathenau*, ZZP Int. 10 (2005), 195, 213–217 with full force and rightly so criticising the idiosyncratic approach apparently employed by the Portuguese courts, e.g. STJ Doc. Dir. Comp. 469 (1997), 445; Rel.

Furthermore, the connecting factors are defined on an abstract level, and there must not be an additional element of close connection with the forum state.[1377] (2) does not acknowledge a European concept of *forum conveniens* nor does (2) negate minimum contacts.[1378]

255   On the other hand, the principle of ubiquity also applies if both relevant places are in the same Member State (different from the Member State where the defendant is domiciled) so that to chose either of them is only a matter of local jurisdiction or venue.[1379]

bb) The so-called "mosaic principle" as a restriction to the second option

256   The principle of ubiquity privileges and favours the plaintiff. From the other angle it disfavours the defendant. Particularly detrimental, dangerous and burdensome for the defendant is the jurisdiction at the place where the damage was sustained. The nightmare opposite, if not presenting the victim with a proper forum, is inviting the alleged victim to sue for the entire damage wherever he holds even part of the intangible allegedly affected. This would jeopardise the alleged wrongdoer's prospects severely as it would result in world-wide or at least Europe-wide forum shopping. The mere possibility to sue here or there offers the plaintiff a bargaining chip not to be underestimated. Hold-up games become feasible. In order not to give the edge to the plaintiff *a priori*, but to get something akin to a level-playing field with roughly equal chances for plaintiff and defendant, some counter-balance must be introduced. (2) must not become a full-swing *forum actoris*.[1380]

257   In *Shevill* the ECJ developed the so-called mosaic principle: At the place where the damage was sustained, a claim can only be brought for the damage sustained in the forum state, not for the world-wide damage.[1381] The advantage of having a *forum actoris* is combined with (and simultaneously poisoned by) a restriction. The mosaic principle should be regarded as a structural element in (2).[1382] It should be recognised as a much-welcome obstacle to ex-

---

Coimbra Cases 2581/03, 36131/04 and 1481/04; Rel. Guimarães Case 38/03-2; but see also STJ Case 04A4283 (all available at <http://www.dgsi.pt>).

[1377] BG sic! 2007, 279, 281; *Grabinski*, GRUR Int. 2001, 199, 204 *et seq.*; *Véron*, Clunet 128 (2001), 805, 826 *et seq.*

[1378] *Braggion*, Dir. comm. int. 2011, 588, 593.

[1379] *Geimer/Schütze*, Art. 5 notes 241 *et seq. Hofmann/Kunz*, in: Basler Kommentar, Art. 5 note 556.

[1380] Areopagos CID 2004, 350; Epheteio Peiraios CID 2001, 61 with note *Stamatopoulos*.

[1381] *Fiona Shevill v. Presse Alliance SA*, (Case C-68/93) [1995] ECR I-415, I-461 *et seq.* paras. 28–33.

[1382] Cass. Clunet 125 (1998), 136, 137 with note *Huet*; OGH RdW 2002, 603; OGH RdW 2002, 664; Cass. RCDIP 93 (2004), 632 with note *Cachard*; OLG Hamburg AfP 1996, 69, 71; OLG München MMR 2000, 277; Hof's-Gravenhage [1999] FSR 352, 359; Trib. Bruxelles J. trib. 2003, 234, 235; Hof Amsterdam NIPR 2007 Nr. 297 p. 424; *Ehmann/Thorn*, AfP 1996, 20, 23; *Birgit Bachmann*, IPRax 1997, 179, 187; *Gerhard Wagner*, RabelsZ 62 (1998), 243, 283 *et seq.*; *Stauder*, IPRax 1998, 317, 321; *Mankowski*, RabelsZ 63 (1999), 203, 274–276; *Mankowski*, MMR 2002, 817, 819; *Perret*, in: Mélanges en l'honneur de Jean-François Poudret (1999), p. 125, 132; *Brinkhof*, IIC 2000, 706, 713; *Pansch*, EuLF 2000/01, 353, 357 *et seq.*; *Véron*, Clunet 128 (2001), 805, 820; *Hausmann*, EuLF 2003, 278, 279 *et seq.*; *Schlosser* Art. 5 note 20; *Thomas Pfeiffer*, in: Gounalakis (ed.), Rechtshandbuch Electronic Business (2003), § 13 note 60; *Pataut*, RCDIP 93 (2004), 800, 807 *et seq.*; *Hausmann/Obergfell*, in: Fezer, UWG (2nd ed. 2010) Einl. I note 404; *Christian Berger*, GRUR Int. 2005, 465, 469; *Junker*, ZZP Int. 9 (2004), 200, 203; *Kessedjian*, in: Liber Fausto Pocar (2009), p. 533, 538. But *contra* e.g. ObG Zürich sic! 2004, 793, 795; *Kreuzer/Klötgen*, IPRax 1997, 90, 96; *Rauscher*, ZZP Int. 1 (1996), 145; *Kaufmann-Christian Kohler*, in: Katharina Boele-Woelki/

cessive forum shopping.[1383] Its scope of application should not be confined to infringement of personality rights, defamation, libel or slander,[1384] although *Shevill* was a judgment against a newspaper corporation.[1385] In a first step the ECJ multiplicated jurisdiction by introducing the principle of ubiquity, in a second step it reverses this multiplication in part.[1386] This is not germane to any specific tort, but a matter of general construction. The restriction does not torpedo the purpose of (2), but only strikes the necessary right balance. To favour the plaintiff overly would constitute a windfall profit for the plaintiff and would deny, or at least neglect, the defendant's legitimate interests. The equality between the two options has to give way to procedural justice. The option to sue wherever damage was sustained still plays enough into the plaintiff's hands and is favourable enough. Almost unlimited or universal jurisdiction by virtue of the places where damage was sustained, spread out would not serve the purpose of (2).[1387] Sympathy with the alleged victim leads quite some miles but not everywhere. One has to bear at least at the back of one's mind that the general principle as laid down in Art. 2 reads *actor sequitur forum rei* and that thus every special jurisdiction widening the defendant's jurisdictional liability must find a justification. Furthermore, if the purpose of the second option is to attribute jurisdiction to the courts of the place which are territorially best suited and most appropriate to assess the local damage due to their vicinity to the evidence and the victim's assets damaged assets, this *rationale* is the less convincing the further away the damage are sustained.[1388]

The fragmentation of jurisdiction carries the danger that different courts in different states **258** where different parts of the damage occurred, reach different results and in the most unfortunate event reach irreconcilable judgments.[1389] Yet this will only happen if the damage is spread in a way that it is worthwhile for the victim to pursue his aims in different jurisdictions. In most instances, however, the bulk of the damage will occur in one jurisdiction, whereas in another jurisdiction no damage or only minor portions can be identified, which do not make it worth the effort to bring an action for liability. That the victim would have to commence litigation in every state concerned in order to collect part of the damage, is too expensive, too costly and thus not too attractive for the alleged victim.[1390] Imagine the

---

Catherine Kessedjian (eds.), Internet – Which Court Decides? Which Law Applies? Quel tribunal décide? Quel droit s'applique? (1998), p. 89, 113 *et seq.*; *Coester-Waltjen*, in: FS Rolf A. Schütze (1999), p. 175; *Briggs*, (2001) 72 BYIL 437, 471; *Furrer/Schramm*, SJZ 2005, 91, 92. See also *Kubis*, Internationale Zuständigkeit bei Persönlichkeits- und Immaterialgüterrechtsverletzungen (1999) pp. 130 *et seq.*, pp. 199 *et seq.*

[1383] *Peter Huber*, ZEuP 1996, 300, 305 *et seq.*; *Mankowski*, in: FS Andreas Heldrich (2005), p. 867, 884; *Slonina*, ecolex 2014, 608, 609 *et seq.*

[1384] See *Peter Pinckney v. KDG Mediatech AG* (Case C-170/12), ECLI:EU:C:2013:635 para. 45; *Hi Hotel HCF SARL v. Uwe Spoering* (Case C-387/12), ECLI:EU:C:2014:215 para. 38 for application with regard to copyright infringements; A-G *Szpunar*, Opinion in Case C-375/13 of 3 September 2014, ECLI:EU: C:2014:2135 para. 66.

[1385] E.g. *Christian Berger*, GRUR Int. 2005, 465, 469. *Contra Kreuzer/Klötgen*, IPRax 1997, 90, 95 *et seq.*; *Kurtz*, IPRax 2004, 107, 108 *et seq.*

[1386] *Kessedjian*, in: Liber Fausto Pocar (2009), p. 533, 537.

[1387] *Pataut*, RCDIP 93 (2004), 800, 807.

[1388] See *Fiona Shevill v. Presse Alliance SA*, (Case C-68/93) [1995] ECR I-415, I-462 para. 31.

[1389] *Fiona Shevill v. Presse Alliance SA*, (Case C-68/93) [1995] ECR I-415, I-462 para. 32.

[1390] *Rufus Pichler*, in: Hoeren/Ulrich Sieber (eds.), Handbuch Multimedia-Recht (looseleaf 1999 *et seq.*) Part

---

alternative: Without restricting the competence of the courts, every court seized would rule over the global damage. It could not be said that this concerns a different cause and action, but instead a perfect collision occurs. Hence, absolutely contrary to the apparent point of criticism, the mosaic principle does not augment, but reduce the danger of irreconcilable judgments.

259 Yet this solution is not unfair to the victim since the victim has an option to sue the alleged tortfeasor for the global damage sustained either at the latter's domicile or at the place where the relevant activity can be located.[1391] Fairness is safeguarded and guaranteed by the two other elements of the over-all system: The alleged victim still has any opportunity to recover his global damage, if only elsewhere: at the alleged perpetrator's domicile and, if differing from this domicile, at the place where the alleged perpetrator displayed his activities.[1392] The victim is not without protection and not without a forum where he can claim all in one.

260 The mosaic principle provides a very effective counter-incentive against forum shopping by supposed or alleged victims and thus effectively safeguards the legitimate jurisdictional interests on the alleged wrongdoer's side.[1393] Even a step further, a kind of escape clause has been proposed for infringement lawsuits in particular in order to avoid that the defendant has to pursue the case substantially in potentially multiple jurisdictions for seeing it dismissed and to get rid of cases where the effect in a certain jurisdiction would be minimal or purely accidental:[1394] "In disputes concerned with infringement of an intellectual property right, a person may be sued in the courts of the State where the alleged infringement occurs or may occur, unless the alleged infringer has not acted in that State to initiate or further the infringement and her/his activity cannot reasonably be see as having been directed to that State."[1395]

261 There is nothing specific and special about defamation[1396] that warrants confining the mosaic principle to it;[1397] to the contrary it should be recognised as a principle of general applicability.[1398] That the probability of harmful effects occurring in a multiplicity of juris-

---

31 Art. 5 note 189 (December 1998); *Mankowski*, in: Ruth Nielsen/Sandfeld Jacobsen/Trzaskowski (eds.), EU Electronic Commerce Law (2004), p. 125, 151 *et seq.*

[1391] *Fiona Shevill v. Presse Alliance SA*, (Case C-68/93) [1995] ECR I-415, I-462 para. 32.

[1392] *Fiona Shevill v. Presse Alliance SA*, (Case C-68/93) [1995] ECR I-415, I-462 para. 32.

[1393] *Mankowski*, RabelsZ 63 (1999), 203, 276; *Mankowski*, in: Ruth Nielsen/Sandfeld Jacobsen/Trzaskowski (eds.), EU Electronic Commerce Law (2004), p. 125, 151.

[1394] *Torremans*, in: Torremans (ed.), Research Handbook on Cross-Border Enforcement of Intellectual Property (2014), p. 381, 387.

[1395] Art. 2:2:202 CLIP Principles.

[1396] For another application of the mosaique principle in a case of libel and slander see *Dow Jones & Co., Inc. v. Yousef Abdul Latif Jameel* [2005] EWCA Civ 75 (C.A., per Lord *Philipps of Worth Matravers* M.R.).

[1397] Conversely, it is even argued that the mosaic principle fits ill for defamation in particular since damage to reputation and personal insult are alleged not to be mathematically quantifiable and the possibility to subdivide insult in territorial units is challenged; *P. Rufus Pichler*, MR 2011, 367; *Garber*, ÖBl 2014, 100, 103.

[1398] *Mankowski*, RabelsZ 63 (1999), 203, 274–276; *Thomas Pfeiffer*, in: Gounalakis (ed.), Rechtshandbuch Electronic Business (2003), § 13 note 60 and the references in fn. 1375. But *contra* e.g. *Kreuzer/Klötgen*, IPRax 1996, 90, 96; *Kaufmann-Christian Kohler*, in: Katharina Boele-Woelki/Catherine Kessedjian (eds.), Internet – Which Court Decides? Which Law Applies? Quel tribunal décide? Quel droit s'applique? (1998), p. 89, 113 *et seq.*

dictions is higher in the event of a defamatory article in a newspaper in comparison to a shot by a gun does not justify different treatment. To the contrary, that the restriction was introduced in an instance where it matters most, is only confirmation for the generality of the approach. In support one could for instance imagine the case of a mass pollution by an industrial plant near a border.

It has been argued that the mosaic principle does not fit too well with actions not for **262** damages but for prohibiting certain activities.[1399] In this regard prohibiting the activity for one country could lead to its total prohibition if the activity can not be nationally split, e.g. due to technical means in the case of an advertisement or a website on the World Wide Web.[1400] But this argument falls short if one looks at the alternative: The mosaic principle is a restriction on jurisdiction at the place where the damage occurred. Without such jurisdiction the courts at this place would have unrestricted, in principle "universal" jurisdiction – with the same result that a prohibition would produce global effects.[1401]

b) Place where the harmful event giving rise to the damage occurs

aa) General notion
Where the harmful event giving rise to the damage occurs appears to be a concept simple to **263** grasp.[1402] It may constitute a significant connecting factor in jurisdiction since it could be particularly helpful in relation to the evidence and the conduct of proceedings.[1403] The advantage it presents includes the ease with which the court may gather evidence relating to that event.[1404]

In general terms, the harmful event relates to the tortfeasor's conduct and activities[1404a] or, in **264** the event of a material inactivity, inactivities or omissions. In principle this comes down to physicalities. One needs to identify and localise the consciously conducted activity on the potential tortfeasor's side which amounts to a relevant cause for the resulting damage.[1405] The notion is a rather factual one and cannot depend on criteria which are specific to the

---

[1399] See *Kubis*, Internationale Zuständigkeit bei Persönlichkeits- und Immaterialgüterrechtsverletzungen (1999) pp. 139 *et seq.*; *Kurtz*, IPRax 2004, 107, 109.

[1400] E.g. *Leible*, in: Rauscher Art. 5 note 92.

[1401] See to this alternative result *Kreuzer/Klötgen*, IPRax 1997, 90, 95; *Schack*, ZEuP 1998, 931, 951; *Schack*, MMR 2000, 135, 139; *Kurtz*, IPRax 2004, 107, 109; *Hausmann/Obergfell*, in: Fezer, UWG (2nd ed. 2010), Einl. I note 403.

[1402] A-G *Vlas*, NJ 2015 Nr. 44 p. 539, 542.

[1403] *Wintersteiger AG v. Products 4U Sondermaschinenbau* (Case C-523/10), ECLI:EU:C:2012:220 para. 32; *Wulf-Henning Roth*, in: FS Eberhard Schilken (2015), p. 427, 430.

[1404] *Wintersteiger AG v. Products 4U Sondermaschinenbau* (Case C-523/10), ECLI:EU:C:2012:220 para. 33.

[1404a] See only *Lein*, in: Dickinson/Lein para. 4.73.

[1405] *Zuid-Chemie v. Philippo's Mineralenfabriek NV/SA*, (Case C-189/08) [2009] ECR I-6917, I-6929 para. 27; BGE 125 III 346, 350; BGE 131 III 153; OLG Düsseldorf IPRspr. 2011 Nr. 234 p. 607; *Chronos Containers NV v. Palatin* [2003] I.L.Pr. 283, 293 *et seq.* (Q.B.D., *Morrison* J.); LG Frankfurt/Main AfP 2010, 512; *Hohloch*, Das Deliktsstatut (1984) p. 104; *Ulrike Wolf*, Deliktsstatut und internationales Umweltrecht (1995) p. 163; *Mankowski*, RabelsZ 63 (1999), 203, 257; *Mankowski*, in: Spindler/Wiebe (eds.), Internet-Auktionen und Elektronische Marktplätze (2nd ed. 2005), ch. 12 note 63; *von Hinden*, Persönlichkeits-verletzungen im Internet (1999) p. 54.

examination of the substance.[1406] But a basic restriction remains: The alleged tortfeasor's actions or omissions must constitute a necessary precondition for the loss suffered by the victim.[1407] The event giving rise to the damage can be denominated and circumscribed as the causal event.[1408]

265 In contrast to Art. 17 (1) (c), generally it is not required that the activity is purposefully directed at a certain State.[1409] At the least, activities fulfilling part of the tort in question and emanating from the tortfeasor's sphere to the external world are covered.[1410] For instance, if a fraudulent intermediate acquires securities with the monies extracted from the investors this constitutes activity.[1411] Any relevant activity matters if the tortious conduct consists of a majority of elements.[1412] Directly and indirectly causal activities are on equal footing.[1413]

266 To strip the rule to the low level, in which only the last event would be covered,[1414] would not do justice.[1415] Neither would relying only on the origin of a chain of events which eventually to the damage.[1415a] Other activities are still causal in the ordinary sense[1416] of the outcome and are not prevented by the very last event which then would have to be thought as hypothetically interrupting causality and negating its own history. To require "direct" causality[1417] introduces an element of uncertainty for the borderline between "direct" and "indirect" would lack the necessary precision and would leave to much leeway for argument.

267 If activities are first announced and later-on implemented and if the announcement itself already contains a tortious element, the announcement is a relevant activity,[1418] along with proceeding implementation.[1419]

[1406] *Peter Pinckney v. KDG Mediatech AG* (Case C-170/12), ECLI:EU:C:2013:635 para. 41.

[1407] *Danmarks Rederiforeniging, acting on behalf of DFDS Torline AS v. LO Landsorganisationen i Sverige, acting on behalf of SEKO Sjöfolk Facket for Service och Kommunikation*, (Case C-18/02) [2004] ECR I-1417, I-1454 para. 34; *Harald Kolassa v. Barclays Bank plc* (Case C-375/13), ECLI:EU:C:2015:37 para. 52.

[1408] *Zuid-Chemie v. Philippo's Mineralenfabriek NV/SA*, (Case C-189/08) [2009] ECR I-6917, I-6929 para. 28; *Pez Hejduk v. EnergieAgentur.NRW GmbH* (Case C-441/13), ECLI:EU:C:2015:28 para. 23.

[1409] *Peter Pinckney v. KDG Mediatech AG* (Case C-170/12), ECLI:EU:C:2013:635 para. 42.

[1410] BGH IPRspr. 2002 Nr. 107 p. 108; LG Kiel IPRax 2009, 164, 167.

[1411] *Corneloup*, RDCIP 103 (2014), 438, 440.

[1412] BGE 125 III 346; BG 5 May 2006 – Case 4C.329/2005; *Hofmann/Kunz*, in: Basler Kommentar, Art. 5 note 562.

[1413] *de Clavière*, Rev. Lamy dr. aff. 92 (2014), 60, 63.

[1414] See *Leible*, in: Rauscher Art. 5 note 88; further references are to be found in *Mari*, in: Mélanges Fritz Sturm (1999), p. 1573, 1580.

[1415] Assenting *von Hein*, IPRax 2010, 330, 339.

[1415a] But cf. *Lein*, in: Dickinson/Lein para. 4.89.

[1416] See *Mari*, in: Mélanges Fritz Sturm (1999), p. 1573, 1577.

[1417] To this avail *Zuid Chemie v. Philippo's Mineralenfabriek NV/SA* (Case C-189/08), [2009] ECR I-6917 para. 31; *Calvo Caravaca/Carrascosa González*, Rev. Der. Mercantil 292 (2014), 51, 59.

[1418] See *Danmarks Rederiforeniging, acting on behalf of DFDS Torline AS v. LO Landsorganisationen i Sverige, acting on behalf of SEKO Sjöfolk Facket for Service och Kommunikation*, (Case C-18/02) [2004] ECR I-1417, I-1456 para. 41.

[1419] In the present writer's opinion neglected by *Danmarks Rederiforeniging, acting on behalf of DFDS Torline*

According to the prevailing opinion, particularly in legal writing, mere acts of preparation **268** are not covered.[1420] For instance, the technical uploading are said not to constitute relevant activity in the event of infringements *via* the WWW.[1421] Although this might sound appreciable in principle, the following tricky question needs to be answered: What are mere acts of preparation? Three alternative concepts appear feasible: first to let any activity suffice (at least such activity which gains a certain level of factual relevance), or second, to declare only the very last act completing the tort in question relevant,[1422] or third, to have recourse to the law of the state where the activity in question can be located, and to ask it (i.e. the *"lex causae"* and not the *lex fori*[1423]) whether it regards such activity already to be a tortious activity. Given the necessary precondition that a relevant damage ultimately occurred,[1424] the latter concept is the most convincing and by far the most satisfying.[1425] In the last consequence, it is for the law at the place of activity to decide whether and to which extent it is willing to protect which values and how low or how high it sets the threshold.[1426] The alternative, when it comes down to distinguishing such concepts, would have to fall back to a certain degree at least on either the impression gained by others or on the tortfeasor's subjective intention (i.e. insofar as the tortfeasor believed that he had done everything he could do, the stadium of preparation would be left,[1427] whereas preparation would be at stake if the tortfeasor believed his previous activities would not to have generated external effects as yet[1428]). The first of the three alternatives would lead to imprevisibility and uncertainty potentially generating jurisdiction based on only spurious connections.[1429]

AS v. LO Landsorganisationen i Sverige, acting on behalf of SEKO Sjöfolk Facket for Service och Kommunikation, (Case C-18/02) [2004] ECR I-1417, I-1456 para. 41.

[1420] BGE 125 III 346, 350; BGE 131 III 153, 161; BGH IPRspr. 2002 Nr. 107 p. 108; AG Hamburg RIW 1990, 319, 320; *Hohloch,* Das Deliktsstatut (1984) p. 104; *Birgit Bachmann,* IPRax 1997, 179, 182; *Coester-Waltjen,* in: FS Rolf A. Schütze (1999), p. 175, 177; *Kubis,* Internationale Zuständigkeit bei Persönlichkeits- und Immaterialgüterrechtsverletzungen (1999) pp. 148 *et seq.; Schack* para. 300; *Leible,* in: Rauscher Art. 5 note 87; *Ebner,* Markenschutz im internationalen Privat- und Zivilprozessrecht (2004) pp. 189 *et seq.; Lindacher,* Internationales Wettbewerbsverfahrensrecht (2009) § 9 note 18; *Geimer/Schütze* Art. 5 note 250; *Wulf-Henning Roth,* in: FS Eberhard Schilken (2015), p. 427, 431.

[1421] See *Wintersteiger AG v. Products 4U Sondermaschinenbau* (Case C-523/10), ECLI:EU:C:2012:220 paras. 34–35; *Pez Hejduk v. EnergieAgentur.NRW GmbH* (Case C-441/13), ECLI:EU:C:2015:28 para. 24.

[1422] *Bukow,* Verletzungsklagen aus gewerblichen Schutzrechten (2003) p. 57.

[1423] But cf. BGE 131 III 151, 161.

[1424] *Sophie Neumann,* Die Haftung der Intemediäre im Internationalen Immaterialgüterrecht (2014) pp. 496–497.

[1425] *Mankowski,* RabelsZ 63 (1999), 203, 263 *et seq.; Schack,* MMR 2000, 135, 137; *Schack,* para. 299; *Isabel Roth,* Die internationale Zuständigkeit deutscher Gerichte bei Persönlichkeitsrechtsverletzungen im Internet (2007) pp. 192 *et seq.;* see also *Kernen,* Persönlichkeitsrechtsverletzungen im Internet (2014) para. 372.

[1426] *Mankowski,* RabelsZ 63 (1999), 203, 263.

[1427] *Kubis,* Internationale Zuständigkeit bei Persönlichkeits- und Immaterialgüterrechtsverletzungen (1999) p. 148.

[1428] *Kubis,* Internationale Zuständigkeit bei Persönlichkeits- und Immaterialgüterrechtsverletzungen (1999) p. 149.

[1429] *Kernen,* Persönlichkeitsrechtsverletzungen im Internet (2014) para. 369.

269   An example used for purposes of illustration is the case of a photograph taken and later-on distributed. According to the prevailing opinion, only the distribution should matter.[1430] But how about the variation that is was illegal to take the photograph at all at the place where the photograph was taken? Why shall the protection of privacy granted there give way – to which avail or for which general good? Could there be a more obvious activity than taking the photograph itself?[1431] Or secondly, an even more famous example: A defamatory letter is written and conceived in one country, but eventually posted in another one. Why should the concept be neglected? Is the incriminating element really sufficiently and exhaustively described by the emanation to externals – with the consequence that the content, the most incriminating element, is pushed aside? The case is even clearer in the event of a conspiracy where the collusive agreement was concluded in one country and executed in another: No-one would doubt that the central element of a conspiracy is the collusive agreement.[1432] The CJEU has tentatively accepted a similar approach: It relies on the activation of the process for the technical display of the incriminated content.[1433] But it goes a decisive step too far, particularly in the light of Art. 7 pr., to rule that the acts or omissions liable to constitute a violation of the claimant's rights can *only* be located at the place where the defendant is domiciled.[1434]

270   To seize upon the conception closely mirrors the reason why the tortfeasor's activity generally is apt to carry jurisdiction:[1435] because activity is what is at the core of the matter and in substance founds the tort.[1436] He who wants to enjoy the benefits and privileges of a liability haven should at least be forced to move more than the mere posting into this haven, namely the production.[1437] To the contrary, he who deliberately splits the conception and the emanation over a border should bear the risk: Without his crossing, the border a reduplication of places of activity would be out of question.[1438] The place where something was planned and contrived might not be evidently clear to the external observer, in particular the victim. A presumption that a person locates his main activities where he is resident, could help at least for the purposes of PIL[1439] and would on the other hand limit the jurisdictional risk in the light of the relationship between (2) and Art. 4.[1440] Any alternative relying on the emanation only, the last activity the tortfeasor exerts,[1441] or more drastically: the act with which the

---

[1430]   OLG Bremen IPRax 2000, 226; *Leible*, in: Rauscher Art. 5 note 87.

[1431]   See AG Hamburg RIW 1988, 319; *Kubis*, Internationale Zuständigkeit bei Persönlichkeits- und Immaterialgüterrechtsverletzungen (1999) p. 144.

[1432]   See *Sunderland Marine Mutual Insurance Co. Ltd. v. Wiseman (The "Seaward Quest")*, [2007] EWHC 1460 (Comm), [2007] 2 Lloyd's Rep. 308, 313 (Q.B.D., *Langley* J.).

[1433]   *Wintersteiger AG v. Products 4U Sondermaschinenbau* (Case C-523/10), ECLI:EU:C:2012:220 paras. 34–35; *Pez Hejduk v. EnergieAgentur.NRW GmbH* (Case C-441/13), ECLI:EU:C:2015:28 para. 24.

[1434]   As *Pez Hejduk v. EnergieAgentur.NRW GmbH* (Case C-441/13), ECLI:EU:C:2015:28 para. 25 does.

[1435]   *Mankowski*, RabelsZ 63 (1999), 203, 262; *Isabel Roth*, Die internationale Zuständigkeit deutscher Gerichte bei Persönlichkeitsrechtsverletzungen im Internet (2007) pp. 197 *et seq.*

[1436]   See *Minster Investments Ltd. v. Hyundai Precision and Industry Co. Ltd.* [1988] 2 Lloyd's Rep. 621, 624 (Q.B.D., *Steyn* J.); *Modus Vivendi Ltd. v. The British Products Sammex Co. Ltd.* [1997] I.L.Pr. 654, 668 (Ch.D., *Knox* J.).

[1437]   *Mankowski*, RabelsZ 63 (1999), 203, 263.

[1438]   *Mankowski*, RabelsZ 63 (1999), 203, 264.

[1439]   *Mankowski*, RabelsZ 63 (1999), 203, 265 *et seq.*

[1440]   But cf. *Matthias Lehmann/Stieper*, JZ 2012, 1016, 1019.

perpetrator gives the further process out of his hand,[1442] implicitly depends heavily on categories of the applicable law without admitting, else it could not cope properly with so called *abstrakten Gefährdungsdelikten*.[1443]

bb) Special cases of areas under sovereignty and jurisdiction of a State
If the relevant activity took place aboard an ocean going vessel outside territorial waters, the   271
vessel has to be attributed to the state of the flag which she is flying.[1444] Flag state sovereignty
is a kind of sovereignty recognised by international law.[1445] It is for international law to
answer the incidental question posed to it as to whether a vessel is deemed to be subjected to
jurisdiction to legislate or adjudicate of a certain state. Generally, such incidental questions
as to whether a certain state can claim sovereignty or jurisdiction over a certain area, is
submitted to international law as well.[1446]

Accordingly, the territorial waters, the Exclusive Economic Zone (EEZ) and the continental   272
shelf are subject to the jurisdiction of the coastal state also for the purposes of (2). This is
recognised and generally accepted for Arts. 20–23.[1447] It would require justification if one
was not prepared to follow international law in the same vain for other subjects,[1448] in
particular for torts.

While the proposed extension to (2) might be a rough assumption, it gains quite some   273
support for oil rigs, drilling platforms and other fixed installations,[1449] and the alternative is

---

[1441] *Kubis*, Internationale Zuständigkeit bei Persönlichkeits- und Immaterialgüterrechtsverletzungen (1999) pp. 148, 153–155.

[1442] *Rufus Pichler*, Internationale Zuständigkeit im Zeitalter globaler Vernetzung (2008) para. 766; see also *Hootz*, Durchsetzung von Persönlichkeits- und Immaterialgüterrechten bei grenzüberschreitenden Verletzungen in Europa (2004) pp. 323–324.

[1443] See *Kernen*, Persönlichkeitsrechtsverletzungen im Internet (2014) para. 370.

[1444] *Danmarks Rederiforeniging, acting on behalf of DFDS Torline AS v. LO Landsorganisationen i Sverige, acting on behalf of SEKO Sjöfolk Facket for Service och Kommunikation*, (Case C-18/02) [2004] ECR I-1417, I-1457 paras. 44 *et seq.*; *Hofmann/Kunz*, in: Basler Kommentar, Art. 5 note 613; *Basedow*, in: Liber amicorum Rüdiger Wolfrum (2012), p. 1869, 1887–1888.

[1445] See only *Mankowski*, RabelsZ 53 (1989), 487, 501; *Mankowski*, Seerechtliche Vertragsverhältnisse im Internationalen Privatrecht (1995) pp. 477 *et seq.*; *Mankowski*, IPRax 2003, 21, 26 *et seq.*

[1446] *Mankowski*, IPRax 2003, 21, 26; *Junker*, in: FS 50 Jahre BAG (2004), p. 1193, 1204; *Junker*, in: FS Andreas Heldrich (2005), p. 719, 730.

[1447] *Herbert Weber v. Universal Ogden Services Ltd.*, (Case C-37/00) [2002] ECR I-2013, I-2044 para. 36; Hoge Raad NIPR 2003 Nr. 108; Hoge Raad NJ 2003 Nr. 344; Pres. Rb. Leeuwarden NIPR 1998 Nr. 301 p. 365; *Roelvink*, in: Bundel opstellen aangeboden aan A.V.M. Struycken (1996), p. 273, 282; *Mankowski*, IPRax 2003, 21 *et seq.*, 26; *Mankowski*, IPRax 2005, 58, 59 *et seq.*; *Mankowski*, in: Ferrari/Leible (eds.) Rome I Regulation (München 2009), p. 171, 199; *Wurmnest*, in: Basedow/Magnus/Wolfrum (eds.), The Hamburg Lectures on Maritime Affairs 2009 & 2010 (2012), p. 113, 124–125; see also *González Vega*, AEDIPr 2000, 818, 820; *Wurmnest*, Ocean Yb. 25 (2011), 311, 337–338.

[1448] See *Wurmnest*, RabelsZ 72 (2008), 236, 247–248; *Basedow*, in: Liber amicorum Rüdiger Wolfrum (2012), p. 1869, 1884–1885; *Dickinson*, [2013] LMCLQ 86, 126.

[1449] See Cass. RCDIP 89 (2000), 200; CA Paris Clunet 124 (1997), 990; *Dahm/Delbrück/Wolfrum*, Völkerrecht, vol. I/1 (3rd ed. 1989) p. 506; *Jenisch*, in: Peter Ehlers/Erbguth (eds.), Neue Entwicklungen im Seerecht (2000), p. 21, 27; *Junker/Dorothee Schramm*, IPRax 2001, 482, 483; *Lagoni*, NuR 2002, 121, 124;

---

unconvincing and unpromising, in particular for "external" torts concerning ships in transit. Imagine the collision of two ships flying different flags in the EEZ of a certain State. If is true that the UN Convention of the Law of the Sea[1450] does not attribute comprehensive jurisdiction for each and every purpose to the Coastal State to which the EEZ belongs, and that jurisdiction is mainly restricted to economic exploitation. But this should not lead to an approach that "external" torts involving the ship and its respective surroundings or other ships cannot be regulated by the Coastal State.[1451] The Coastal State has at least to some extent sovereignty and jurisdiction as granted to it pursuant to Art. 56 (1) *iuncto* Arts. 80; 60 UNCLOS, and that should be the basis from which to proceed.[1452]

274 It might be a long shot to assert that regulation in tort forms an integral part of economic exploitation,[1453] but still applying the tort law of the Coastal State is vastly superior and a relative optimum compared to third-best solutions relying on the flag of only one of the ships concerned. In any event, there are some cases where jurisdiction of thee Coastal State is admitted even by general critics of the proposed solution, namely collisions between ships and fixed installations, and oil or chemical pollution by ships in transit.[1454]

275 A supportive argument can be advanced based on Art. 18 (a) Proposal Rome II Regulation.[1455] [1456] It tried to re-define the notion of territory[1457] and asserted that for the purposes off the proposed Rome II Regulation installations and other facilities for the exploration and exploitation of natural resources in, on or below the part of the seabed situated outside the State's territorial waters if the State, under international law, enjoys sovereign rights to explore and exploit natural resources there, shall be treated as being the territory of that State. That this was not promulgated in an Article of the eventual Rome II Regulation does not give rise to an *argumentum e contrario*.[1458]

276 Matters are different with regard to internal affairs happening entirely onboard the ship: They are regulated by the flag state. Ships might be only passing the EEZ. But that does not liberate them entirely from the jurisdiction of the Coastal State. In harbours and ports, ships are visitors in a like manner, but they are subjected to the jurisdiction of the port state, though. The port state does only refrain from exercising its jurisdiction with regard to internal affairs onboard the ship, for pragmatic reasons and due to international custom. Accordingly, (2) leads primarily to the flag state, subsidiarily to the Coastal State.[1459] To determine local jurisdiction or venue poses yet another problem in the next step.

Risch, Windenergieanlagen in der Ausschließlichen Wirtschaftszone (2006) p. 43; *Egler*, Seerechtliche Streitigkeiten unter der EuGVVO (2011) pp. 296–297.

[1450] UN Convention on the Law of the Sea, Concluded at Montego Bay on 10 December 1982, UNTS 1833, I-31363.

[1451] See *Dickinson*, [2013] LMCLQ 86, 126.

[1452] *Wurmnest*, RabelsZ 72 (2008), 236, 247; *Leif Böttcher*, RNotZ 2011, 589, 593.

[1453] See *Egler*, Seerechtliche Streitigkeiten unter der EuGVVO (2011) p. 296.

[1454] *Basedow*, in: Liber amicorum Rüdiger Wolfrum (2012), p. 1869, 1889–1890.

[1455] Proposal for a Regulation of the European Parliament and the Council on the law applicable to non-contractual obligations, submitted by the Commission on 22 July 2003, COM (2003) 427 final.

[1456] *Leif Böttcher*, RNotZ 2011, 589, 595.

[1457] Explanatory memorandum COM (2003) 427 final p. 27.

[1458] See *Dickinson*, [2013] LMCLQ 86, 126.

cc) Omissions

A rather tricky case is the case of omissions, i.e. the instance that the wrongdoer should have **277**
acted but did not meet his duties and remained inactive and passive. Omissions are clearly
included in the definition of tort.[1460] Thus, there must be a solution. Firstly, one can not avoid
having recourse to the applicable substantive law in order to define which duties existed and
which obligations the prospective tortfeasor had to obey. Secondly, the place of the relevant
inactivity has to be identified. If inactivity is the tortious conduct alleged the place where
activity ought to have taken place becomes relevant.[1461] Another time the relevant duty, and
for this purpose the applicable substantive law, must answer the question as to where he who
was under this or that duty, was obliged to act.[1462]

If a statement had to be issued and the debtor failed to so, the relevant place might tentatively **278**
be the place where the statement was due to be received for only the receipt will complete the
goal to inform the recipient-creditor.[1463] This would be in line with the reasoning for cases in
which statements due have been issued, but are false or misleading.[1464]

To identify the relevant place of an "activity by way of omission" as the tortfeasor's domi- **279**
cile[1465] would be too simplistic and would deprive (2) of any applicability since Art. 7 in its
entirety only comes into operation where the defendant is domiciled in another Member
State than that of the relevant place.

dd) Scope of jurisdiction

There is no restriction as to the jurisdiction of the court at the place where the harmful act, **280**
i.e. the harmful event giving rise to the damage, occurred. This court has jurisdiction to
entertain claims concerning the entire global damage inflicted. Such a jurisdiction does not
do injustice to the defendant tortfeasor since he had had every opportunity to choose the
place where he himself exerted activity. If he chooses imprudently (insofar as he neglects his
own interests and acts in a country with a high liability standard), he has to internalise the
negative consequences of his own unfortunate decision regardless of whether this decision
was made on purpose or rather accidentally. Where he acts he can be held responsible. For
instance, the parties to an agreement that purportedly restrict competition both act where
they reach such agreement (however spurious and accidental that location might be) and
where they act upon the agreement implementing its term and transforming them into

---

[1459] See *Basedow*, in: Liber amicorum Rüdiger Wolfrum (2012), p. 1869, 1887–1888.

[1460] *Duintjer Tebbens*, in: ECJ (ed.), Civil Jurisdiction and Judgments in Europe (1992), p. 97, 101; *Requejo Isidro*, REDI 2002, 878, 880.

[1461] See only OLG Düsseldorf EuLF 2006, II-93, 94; *Rott/Glinski*, ZeuP 2015, 192, 201; *van Calster*, TBH 2015, 64, 66.

[1462] See Hof 's-Hertogenbosch NIPR 2005 Nr. 159 p. 219; OLG Düsseldorf SchiedsVZ 2006, 331, 334 = IPRspr. 2006 Nr. 211; LG Kiel IPRax 2009, 164, 167. For an entirely autonomous approach *Wedemann*, ZEuP 2014, 861, 878.

[1463] See Hoge Raad Ned. Jur. 2002 Nr. 255 with note *de Boer; ten Wolde/Kirsten C. Henckel*, Int. J. Proced. L. 3 (2013), 195, 216.

[1464] *Infra* Art. 7 note 296 (*Mankowski*).

[1465] To this avail LG Kiel IPRax 2009, 164, 167.

concrete practice.[1466] Admittedly, the ECJ held that in the event of a negligent publication the editor's domicile should be deemed to be the place of relevant activity,[1467] thus implicitly striking out, e.g. the printing process, the release as such and the actual distribution process. Yet this can be explained as adding another dimension to the place of actual release.[1468] In an internet context the notion of edition ought to be understood as "content provider".[1469]

281   The risk resulting from this "global" jurisdiction is the more sustainable for the defendant tortfeasor as in the majority of cases the place where he acted is identical with the place of his habitual residence or at least a place where he has a place of business. If the place of the action happens to coincide with the tortfeasor's habitual residence and with the tortfeasor's domicile, (2) will not even be operable since in this event the pre-condition of Art. 5 *in toto* is not met, being that the place which is designed by the head of special jurisdiction, must not be located in the country where the defendant has his domicile.[1470]

ee) Multiple tortfeasors

282   Another tricky issue arises if the victim faces a multiple tortfeasors: Can he hold all of them of them liable at the place where only one of them acted? Does a joint and commonly planned activity make them join as accomplices under the auspices of jurisdiction, too? Contrary to the approach taken by the CJEU in *Melzer*,[1471] *Hi Hotel*[1472] and *Coty Germany*,[1473] but not in *CDC*,[1473a] the answer should be affirmative.[1474] (2) is not confined to acts of

---

[1466] See Rb. Kh. Veurne [2006] I.L.Pr. 336, 344; LG Kiel IPRax 2009, 164, 167; *Moritz Becker*, EWS 2008, 228, 230. *Contra Beust*, EWS 2004, 403, 405; *Mäsch*, IPRax 2005, 509, 515.

[1467] *Fiona Shevill v. Presse Alliance SA*, (Case C-68/93) [1995] ECR I-415, I-460 *et seq.* para. 24.

[1468] See in more detail *infra* Art. 7 note 225 (*Mankowski*).

[1469] *Guiziou*, Clunet 139 (2012), 201, 204.

[1470] References in footnotes to Art. 7 note 9 (*Mankowski*).

[1471] *Melzer v. MF Global UK Ltd.* (Case C-228/11), ECLI:EU:C:2013:305 paras. 25–41. Followed by A-G *Jääskinen*, Opinion of 13 June 2013 in Case C-170/12 para. 38.

[1472] *Hi Hotel HCF SARL v. Uwe Spoering* (Case C-387/12), ECLI:EU:C:2014:215 paras. 27–40.

[1473] *Coty Germany GmbH v. First Note Perfumes NV* (Case C-360/12), ECLI:EU:C:2014:1318 para. 50; A-G *Jääskinen*, Opinion of 21 November 2013 in Case C-360/12, ECLI:EU:C:2013:764 para. 53.

[1473a] *CDC Hydrogen Peroxide SA v. Akzo Nobel NV* (Case C-352/13), ECLI:EU:C:2015:335 paras. 48–49.

[1474] BGH WM 1999, 540, 541; BGH RIW 2008, 399, 401 *et seq.*; BGHZ 184, 365; BGH 12 April 2011 – Case XI ZR 101/09; BGH GRUR 2012, 1065, 1068 – Parfümflacon II; OLG Düsseldorf WM 1996, 1489, 1491; OLG Düsseldorf NJW-RR 2011, 572; OLG Bremen IPRax 2000, 228; *Vollkommer*, IPRax 1992, 207, 211; *Geimer/Schütze* Art. 5 note 250; *von Hein*, IPRax 2006, 460, 461; *von Hein*, LMK 2010, 308395; *von Hein*, EuZW 2011, 369, 370; *von Hein*, BerDGfIR 2011, 369, 396; *von Hein*, LMK 2012, 338414; *Geimer*, WuB VII C. Art. 5 LugÜ 1.08; *Simotta*, in: Fasching/Konecny Art. 5 note 297; *Rolf Wagner/Gess*, NJW 2009, 3481, 3484 *et seq.*; *Kropholler/von Hein*, Art. 5 note 83b; *Michael Müller*, EuZW 2013, 130; *Michael Müller*, NJW 2013, 2101, 2102; *Michael Müller*, EuZW 2014, 434; *Rolf Wagner*, EuZW 2013, 546; *Sophie Neumann*, Die Haftung der Intermediäre im Internationalen Immaterialgüterrecht (2014) pp. 501–502; *Thole*, in: FS Eberhard Schilken (2015), p. 523, 533; see also OLG Düsseldorf IPRax 2009, 158, 160. Tentatively more cautious *Stefan Huber*, IPRax 2009, 134, 139. *Contra* LG Mönchengladbach 5 February 2009 – Case 10 O 422/07; *Schlosser*, Art. 5 note 20a; *Leible*, in: Rauscher, Art. 5 note 88c; *Hofmann/Kunz*, in: Basler Kommentar, Art. 5 note 626; *Idot*, Europe 2013 comm. 329; *Stefano Alberto Villata*, Riv. dir. proc. 2014, 1229, 1237; *Vanleenhove*, TBH 2015, 53, 54. Open BGH WM 2010, 1590, 1593; BGH ZIP 2010, 2004, 2007; BGH WM 2010, 2214, 2217 = RIW 2011, 77, 80.

the principal himself,[1475] but requires acts by the defendant or those for which he is in law responsible.[1476] Composite activities demand for plurilocalisation.[1477] Else one would deny their composite character. The wording might not imply this, but on the other hand it does definitely not rule it out.[1478] Factual relations between the activities by the different actors provide a sufficient bond tying these activities together to form an *ensemble*.[1479]

The very existence of Art. 8 (1) does not give rise to an *argumentum e contrario*.[1480] By not   **283** opting for jurisdiction under Art. 8 (1) (if such jurisdiction existed) the applicant might not forfeit the opportunity to avail himself of the extension of jurisdiction based on the domicile of a third party[1481] – but he does not forfeit jurisdiction based on activity of a third party acting in concert with the defendant for this is another, distinct element.[1482] Just consider that the third party might not have acted at the place of its domicile but somewhere else. By picking one amongst the several perpetrators the applicant exercises a right to choose; he is by no means obliged to sue all perpetrators or none.[1483] Art. 8 (1) is structured differently, pursues different goals and has different prequisites.[1484]

Composite activities and acting in concert are different from activities by single perpetrators   **284** and call for other considerations in order to pursue the sound administration of justice.[1485] Predictability is complied with for it is the single perpetrator who chose his accomplices and partners in torts.[1486] He who decides to split activities working in concert with others cannot be heard if he claims afterwards that he could nor foresee where the others would act. But for instance a parent company might instrumentalise one or more of its subsidiaries to violate rules of competition law; the parent company must not be allowed to hide behind the corporate veil.[1487] The regress in the purported chain of causality is not infinite,[1488] but limited by the precondition that the perpetrators must have acted in concert. If a third party

---

[1475] *Casio Computer Co. Ltd. v. Sayo* [2001] I.L.Pr. 694, 709 (C.A., per *Pill* L.J.).

[1476] *Dexter Ltd. v. Harley* The Times 2 April 2001 (Q.B.D., *Lloyd* J.).

[1477] *Bureau/Muir Watt*, Droit international privé, vol. II (2007) p. 372 n° 971; *Bernard Audit/d'Avout*, Droit international privé (6th ed. 2010) p. 466 n° 534.

[1478] *Michael Müller*, EuZW 2013, 130, 131.

[1479] *Berlioz*, Rev. jur. comm. 2014, 266, 278.

[1480] *Michael Müller*, EuZW 2013, 130, 131–132. But cf. A-G *Jääskinen*, Opinion of 29 November 2012 in Case C-228/11, ECLI:EU:C:2012:766 para. 53; A-G *Jääskinen*, Opinion of 21 November 2013 in Case C-360/12, ECLI:EU:C:2013:764 para. 63.

[1481] *Melzer v. MF Global UK Ltd.* (Case C-228/11), ECLI:EU:C:2013:305 para. 39; A-G *Jääskinen*, Opinion of 29 November 2012 in Case C-228/11, ECLI:EU:C:2012:766 para. 53.

[1482] To a similar avail *von Hein*, IPRax 2013, 505, 513.

[1483] *Contra* A-G *Jääskinen*, Opinion of 29 November 2012 in Case C-228/11, ECLI:EU:C:2012:766 para. 59.

[1484] *Michael Müller*, EuZW 2013, 130, 132.

[1485] Overlooked by A-G *Jääskinen*, Opinion of 29 November 2012 in Case C-228/11, ECLI:EU:C:2012:766 para. 59.

[1486] *von Hein*, IPRax 2013, 505, 509. But cf. A-G *Jääskinen*, Opinion of 29 November 2012 in Case C-228/11, ECLI:EU:C:2012:766 para. 62.

[1487] Tentatively contra *Wulf-Henning Roth*, in: FS Eberhard Schilken (2015), p. 427, 435.

[1488] As A-G *Jääskinen*, Opinion of 21 November 2013 in Case C-360/12, ECLI:EU:C:2013:764 para. 64 fears.

intervened on its own motion in the action, its activity can not be also attributed to the first perpetrator.[1489]

285 Nor would a concentration of jurisdiction at the place where the main perpetrator displayed his activity or in the event of a majority of equivalent perpetrators a limitation of the scope of jurisdiction to each one's personal activity be convincing.[1490] Identifying a centre would generate uncertainty and would in many instances rely on information to which the plaintiff is not privy.[1491]

286 This can be implemented by a truly and uniform European understanding. Otherwise the European regime would be woefully incomplete.[1492] Any recourse to a particular national law is not necessary. § 830 BGB might be a particular rule of German law, not expressly shared in other Member States,[1493] but its logic or at least one decisive part of the logic behind it can be imported and transferred to the European stage.[1494] The victim shall be protected against running in trouble of proving causality. However, it might be doubted that like structural deficits occur under (2).[1495] But there should and con not be serious doubts that working in concert and distributing activity amongst several perpetrators must not be privileged.[1496] Scrutinizing attribution of activities for the purposes of jurisdiction would not overly burden this stage of the proceedings with elements which should be reserved for the merits of the case.[1497] On the contrary, to deny mutual attribution of activities between multiple perpetrators would give unwanted incentives for the victim to invest in arguing the relevance of acts by single perpetrators.[1497a] Furthermore, it would have to explain where the line should be drawn to the evident necessity of attributing the acts done by employees in the realm of their jobs to their employer.[1497b]

287 Any allegation of national particularism[1498] would cede if the underlying concept was made an autonomous European concept.[1499] Art. 9:101 (1) Principles of European Tort Law is a valuable hint that the said idea could be shared in Europe.[1500] Art. VI – 4:102 DCFR is in the same vein.[1501] Legal certainty would be enhanced and not endangered.[1502] *Lacunae* in the

---

[1489] *Michael Müller*, EuZW 2014, 434.

[1490] *Contra Matthias Weller*, IPRax 2000, 202, 208; *Stefano Alberto Villata*, Riv. dir. proc. 2014, 1229, 1240–1241.

[1491] *Kessedjian*, in: Liber Fausto Pocar (2009), p. 533, 538 *et seq.*

[1492] *Chacornac*, RCDIP 102 (2013), 938, 945.

[1493] *Melzer v. MF Global UK Ltd.* (Case C-228/11), ECLI:EU:C:2013:305 paras. 32–35; *Chacornac*, RCDIP 102 (2013), 938, 945.

[1494] To the same avail *Thiede/Florian Sommer*, ÖBA 2015, 175, 185. But cf. (raising doubts whether the logic behind § 830 BGB might not be a logic only appropriate for the purposes of substantive law) *Matthias Weller*, IPRax 2000, 202, 206–207; *Michael Müller*, EuZW 2013, 130, 132.

[1495] *Matthias Weller*, WM 2013, 1681, 1684.

[1496] *Matthias Weller*, WM 2013, 1681, 1684.

[1497] *Rolf Wagner*, EuZW 2013, 546, 547.

[1497b] *Thole*, in: FS Eberhard Schilken (2015), p. 523, 536.

[1497b] *Thole*, in: FS Eberhard Schilken (2015), p. 523, 536.

[1498] As it is raised by *Melzer v. MF Global UK Ltd.* (Case C-228/11), ECLI:EU:C:2013:305 paras. 32–34.

[1499] Similarly *von Hein*, IPRax 2013, 505, 508; *Thole*, in: FS Eberhard Schilken (2015), p. 523, 532.

[1500] *von Hein*, IPRax 2013, 505, 508.

Brussels I*bis* Regulation must be filled, and it is not conceivable to deny jurisdiction for the only reason that something is not expressly prescribed in its wording as might be best illustrated by a company being held liable for activities of its organs.[1503] That the defendant did not act personally in the district of the forum is not a counter-argument[1504] but way too naturalistic (and once again not fitting for companies)[1505] and a mere *petitio principii.* Still an interpretation of the first limb of the principle of ubiquity under (2) is asked for, not the implementation of a new ground of jurisdiction.[1506] Proximity and ease of taking evidence might be best served if jurisdiction is founded where the evidence, not where the defendant is, for not the defendant, but another accomplice might be the central figure of the events.[1507] Previsibility and predictability of jurisdiction are preserved if the perpetrators act in concert and thus have at least a basic knowledge of the others' activities,[1508] if not an outright voluntary coordination.

Alternatively, recourse might be held to the applicable law for a complicated issue not **288** expressly regulated by European yardsticks. To derive an *argumentum e contrario* namely that attribution ought to be ruled out as it is not expressly provided for, would be precipitative. Conversely, Art. 15 (1) (g) Rome II Regulation could come into operation.

A real and genuine danger of unjustified *forum shopping* by the plaintiff is not discernible: **289** He only holds the co-actors liable where their chosen accomplices acted. Furthermore, the Rome II Regulation fashions a uniform PIL of torts in all Member States which diminishes the danger of different results being reached in different jurisdictions.[1509] Claimants shop forum but only to the extent that this is allowed by (2) not extending (2) to a general *forum actoris* and not overly fostering litigious strategies.[1510] Dividing activity must not lead to results different from those which would be found if a single tortfeasor had exerted all necessary activities. The *effet utile* of special jurisdiction under (2) would be challenged if in all likelihood such special jurisdiction would not exist because the place of activity was to be identified with the defendant's domicile for then Art. 4 would displace (2).[1511]

To correct too narrow an approach with regard to identifying the relevant activity where a **290** majority of perpetrators has acted, by generously opening the backdoor of the second prong

---

1501 *Thole,* in: FS Eberhard Schilken (2015), p. 523, 532. But cf. for substantive reasons *Matthias Weller,* WM 2013, 1681, 1684.

1502 As *Melzer v. MF Global UK Ltd.* (Case C-228/11), ECLI:EU:C:2013:305 para. 35 fears.

1503 *von Hein,* IPRax 2013, 505, 507 *et seq.*

1504 But cf. *Melzer v. MF Global UK Ltd.* (Case C-228/11), ECLI:EU:C:2013:305 para. 36.

1505 *von Hein,* IPRax 2013, 505, 510.

1506 As A-G *Jääskinen,* Opinion of 29 November 2012 in Case C-228/11, ECLI:EU:C:2012:766 para. 57 wrongly suggests.

1507 *von Hein,* IPRax 2013, 505, 510.

1508 *Michael Müller,* EuZW 2013, 130, 133.

1509 *von Hein,* IPRax 2013, 505, 511.

1510 But cf. A-G *Jääskinen,* Opinion of 21 November 2013 in Case C-360/12, ECLI:EU:C:2013:764 paras. 62–63.

1511 *von Hein,* IPRax 2013, 505, 511 with reference to *Zuid Chemie v. Philippo's Mineralenfabriek NV/SA* (Case C-189/08), [2009] ECR I-6917 para. 31.

of (2), namely the place where the relevant damage occurred,[1512] is only a second best solution and more than only slightly self-contradictory.[1513] The CJEU argues that the damage was caused by the act committed by another tortfeasor in another Member State.[1514] But recognising and acknowledging causality implies that the activity was relevant. This is at odds with not ascertaining the very same activity as one giving rise to the damage.[1515] The activity *is* the cause and is causing the result produced by this very activity. Causality alone might provide only a rather weak justification for attributing the others' contribution.[1516] Predictability and previsibility of jurisdiction are not served optimally.[1517] Furthermore, the second prong of (2) is subject to the mosaic principle, and jurisdiction is found only for the damage which occurred in the forum State. In cases of infringement of IP rights or copyright which are by their very nature limited by the principle of territoriality, the difference does not matter,[1518] but in other cases it would.

291 The dishonest assistant is at home in (2) and could face a lawsuit where he acted,[1519] even if the main co-actor is not sued (for instance because he was declared insolvent or wound up after the events were staged).[1520] A matter of characterisation arises as to who can be regarded as an accomplice, and has to be answered sticking to a European concept[1521] (which must not necessarily be shared by each and every of the 27 legal orders of the Member States[1522]). Since the main actor's activity is the main activity and the centre of the entire activity on which all other part activities are focused and to which all other part activities contribute, it appears justified to open up jurisdiction there also against the accomplice; there could not be any court more apt or in a better position to gather or hear evidence.[1523] Any allegation that attributing activity under (2) would possibly lead to for a which are distant from the case and the evidence,[1524] ist not convincing. Conversely, any court limiting its cognizance and perspective to the part of activity which occurred in the concrete forum state, would miss out badly on the overall picture and would not grasp most pieces in the jigsaw. Activities in concert gain their character only if viewed not together, not if viewed in isolation. Could one really talk of assistance without considering the main activity?[1525]

[1512] As the CJEU effectively does in *Peter Pinckney v. KDG Mediatech AG* (Case C-170/12), ECLI:EU:C:2013:635 para. 43; *Coty Germany GmbH v. First Note Perfumes NV* (Case C-360/12), ECLI:EU:C:2014:1318 paras. 57, 59. See *Oró Martínez*, REDI 2014-2, 253, 255.

[1513] *Strikwerda*, Ned. Jur. 2015 Nr. 67 p. 795, 797.

[1514] *Coty Germany GmbH v. First Note Perfumes NV* (Case C-360/12), ECLI:EU:C:2014:1318 paras. 57, 59.

[1515] To a similar resulting argument, but with different reasoning A-G *Jääskinen*, Opinion of 21 November 2013 in Case C-360/12, ECLI:EU:C:2013:764 paras. 58–59, 64, 66–70.

[1516] *Michael Müller*, EuZW 2014, 434.

[1517] *Michael Müller*, EuZW 2014, 434.

[1518] See *Peter Pinckney v. KDG Mediatech AG* (Case C-170/12), ECLI:EU:C:2013:635 para. 45; *Sujecki*, EuZW 2013, 866, 867.

[1519] *Briggs*, (2001) 72 BYIL 437, 471; *Stefan Huber*, IPRax 2009, 134, 135; *Rolf Wagner*, EuZW 2013, 546.

[1520] *von Hein*, IPRax 2013, 505, 510.

[1521] *von Hein*, IPRax 2006, 460, 461 *et seq.*; *Michael Müller*, EuZW 2013, 130, 133.

[1522] *Rolf Wagner*, EuZW 2013, 546, 547.

[1523] *Michael Müller*, EuZW 2013, 130, 133; *von Hein*, EuZW 2014, 667.

[1524] *Matthias Weller*, WM 2013, 1681, 1685.

[1525] *Rolf Wagner*, EuZW 2013, 546 at 546.

The internal redress for reimbursement or contribution between tortfeasors should be **292**
characterised as a matter of tort as well.[1526]

But if two or more perpetrators are not acting willingly in concert, not coordinated with each **293**
other, every perpetrator's activity ought to be singled out and looked at in isolation.[1527]

(2) is not designed as a rule of specific consumer or investor protection. It does not amount **294**
to a general instrument of piercing veils or circumventing bankruptcy by the primary
tortfeasor.[1528] Accordingly, it does not *per se* allow for jurisdiction against the managers
or employees of a company (standing or in distress) which has committed a tort. Only if
these managers or employees can be said to have acted collusively in joined concert with the
tortfeasing company or have themselves committed torts, (2) will become operative against
them.

ff) Single torts

(1) Traffic accidents
The judge and the lawyer are invited to distinguish between the single classes of tort in order **295**
to identify the proper *forum* respectively.[1529] Traffic accidents do not pose any major problems. They are *per definitionem* a local affair, and the wrongdoing can be easily identified.[1530] Car crashes materialise somewhere on real streets just like accidents inflicting personal and physical injury to pedestrians or bikers do. Of course, the matter is no different if it
is not a car but a motorbike or a truck is involved. The vehicle operated is not any kind of
distinguishing factor. The mere fact is the same: To identify the place of an accident does not
give rise to legal, but only to factual problems.

(2) Torts via statements
If the material tort is one set in motion by statements by the tortfeasor, the place where the **296**
statement leaves the tortfeasor's *forum internum* is the place of the harmful act,[1531] e.g. the
place where a union issued a call for industrial action or strike[1532] or where a financial adviser
gave a specific advice[1533] e.g. during a meeting[1534] or where wrong (or even worse, forged)

[1526] See *Takahashi*, Claims for contribution and reimbursement in an international context (2000) pp. 31 *et
seq.* with reference to *Santa Fe v. Gates* LMLN 23 February 1991 (Q.B.D., *Ognall* J.).

[1527] See *Engert/Groh*, IPRax 2011, 458, 461; *Maseda Rodríguez*, REDI 2013-2, 296, 299; *Michael Müller*,
EuZW 2014, 434; *Thole*, in: FS Eberhard Schilken (2015), p. 523, 533–534.

[1528] *Blobel*, EuLF 2004, 187, 188; *von Hein*, BerDGfIR 45 (2011), 369, 394.

[1529] See only *Muir Watt*, RCDIP 94 (2005), 330, 333 *et seq.*

[1530] See only Rel. Lisboa Col. Jur. 1998 v. 86, 87; Aud. Prov. Salamanca AEDIPr 2003, 845; Juzgado Primera
Instancia de Oviedo (n° 4) AEDIPr 2003, 843, 844.

[1531] *ABCI v. Banque Franco-Tunisienne* [2003] Lloyd's Rep. 146, 160 (C.A., per *Mance* L.J.); *Domicrest Ltd. v.
Swiss Bank Corporation* [1999] QB 548, 567 (Q.B.D., *Rix* J.); *Alfred Dunhill Ltd. v. Diffusion Internatio-
nale de Maroquinerie de Prestige SARL* [2002] 1 All ER (Comm) 950, 957 (Q.B.D., Judge *Kenneth Rokison*
Q.C.); *London Helicopters Ltd. v. Helportugal LDA-INAC* [2006] 1 All ER (Comm) 595, 604 *et seq.* (Q.B.
D., *Simon* J.); *Newsat Holdings Ltd. v. Zani* [2006] 1 All ER (Comm) 607, 617–619 (Q.B.D., *David Steel* J.);
Wulf-Henning Roth, in: FS Eberhard Schilken (2015), p. 427, 431.

[1532] *Hergenröder*, GPR 2005, 33, 35.

[1533] Rb. Rotterdam NIPR 2007 Nr. 153 p. 218.

---

certificates are issued.[1534] Where the victim or other persons receive the message or statement on the other hand, should not be considered.[1535] Yet for the opposite result the following argument can be put forward: The act consists of two elements, only the first of which is issuing the statement. But the second element is the reception by another person. Unless another person receives the statement, the act could be deemed incomplete with the second element missing. The most appreciable approach nevertheless appears to be even wider: to identify two places of harm-inducing activities, namely issuing the statement and even before that conceiving the statement.[1537]

(3) Informational torts

297 Informational torts are based on the distribution of the incriminated information. Thus this distribution is the material act. Fraud and deception are executed where the malfeasor gives the misleading information or refrains from informing properly and dutifully.[1538] If a market is misinformed (be it negligently, be it deliberately) spreading the information on the market concerned is the activity that matters.[1539] For the purposes of the first alternative under (2) this holds true even if reliance is placed on such a statement elsewhere.[1540] The victim acting in reliance on the negligent misstatement might become relevant only in the context of the place where the damage occurred. On the other hand, issuing or publishing the information is a relevant activity[1541] even if the decisions regarding the information and the content of the information were made elsewhere or if the information (for instance a prospectus) was drafted somewhere else.[1542]

298 **Rating** provides an interesting and economically important example for potentially misleading and defective information.[1543] The alternatives ventilated are the place where the rating was issued or the place where the rating was received by the investor or the place where the investor decided to act upon the information relayed.[1544] Activity on the rating agency's side is only the publication of the rating. If the rating is publicly announced in particular *via* the Internet this has to be judged accordingly. If the rating is issued personally to specific investors the place where the external communication to the investors is staged, is the relevant one[1545] (if in such cases one is content with a non contractual characterisation at

---

[1534] OLG Düsseldorf IPRspr. 2008 Nr. 25 p. 61.

[1535] Rb. Rotterdam NIPR 2008 Nr. 65 p. 109.

[1536] *Contra* OLG Koblenz NJW-RR 2008, 148, 149; OLG Düsseldorf IPRspr. 2011 Nr. 234 p. 607; OLG Hamm IPRspr. 2011 Nr. 242 p. 622.

[1537] *Infra* Art. 7 notes 268–270 (*Mankowski*).

[1538] See only BGH WM 2008, 489; *Mankowski*, EWiR Art. 5 LugÜ 1/09, 215, 216.

[1539] *van Houtte*, in: McLachlan/Nygh (eds.), Transnational Tort Litigation (1996), p. 155, 169; *von Hein*, RabelsZ 64 (2000), 194, 198; *von Hein*, RIW 2004, 602, 604.

[1540] *Domicrest Ltd. v. Swiss Bank Corp.* [1999] QB 548, 567 *et seq.* (Q.B.D., *Rix* J.); *Alfred Dunhill Ltd. v. Diffusion Internationale de Maroquinerie de Prestige SARL* [2002] 1 All ER (Comm) 950, 957 (Q.B.D., Judge *Kenneth Rokison* Q.C.); *London Helicopters Ltd. v. Helportugal LDA-INAC* [2006] 1 All ER (Comm) 595, 604 *et seq.* (Q.B.D., *Simon* J.); *Newsat Holdings Ltd. v. Zani* [2006] 1 All ER (Comm) 607, 617–619 (Q.B.D., *David Steel* J.).

[1541] *Mankowski*, LMK 2015,

[1542] *Contra Harald Kolassa v. Barclays Bank plc* (Case C-375/13), ECLI:EU:C:2015:37 para. 53.

[1543] See *Nisi*, RDIPP 2013, 385, 399.

[1544] See *Nisi*, RDIPP 2013, 385, 399.

all where the investors have ordered a rating and have thus entered into contractual relations with the rating agency). To fall back on the rating agency's seat would lead to the State in which general jurisdiction is founded by virtue of Art. 4 (1) and thus would render (2) nugatory in the concrete case. Analogies to the publisher's domicile[1546] in the wake of *Shevill* are thus unwelcome.

(4) Torts via media

Torts by way of media are committed where the respective media is published.[1547] Never- **299** theless the publishers' or editors' seat bears equal relevance[1548] yet it is best to explain these places as presumably being the places where the tortious content is conceived. The publisher ist the person responsible for the decision to publish the incriminated content so that neither the statutory seat nor the *siége réel* of the publishing house ought to be inspected.[1549]

If a tort is committed *via* television, the place of broadcasting defines at least a relevant **300** activity[1550] if not the most relevant activity. In the event of a publication uploaded on satellite TV the country-of-origin principle as endorsed in Art. 1 (2) (b) Directive 93/83/EC[1551] expressly nominates the place of broadcasting, also for the purposes of identifying the relevant activity under (2).[1552] But it would be a fallacy to deduct from Art. 1 (2) (b) Satellite Directive that the courts of the country where the TV program was broadcasted, had *exclusive* jurisdiction.[1553]

(5) Torts via Internet

Torts committed *via* the Internet display their most relevant activity with the uploading of **301** the incriminated content.[1554] The activation by the advertiser of the technical process displaying, according to pre-defined parameters, the potentially incriminated advertisement

---

[1545] Compare *Wildmoser/Schiffer/Langoth*, RIW 2009, 657, 662; *Mathias Audit*, RCDIP 100 (2011), 591; *Dutta*, IPRax 2014, 33, 37.

[1546] *Nisi*, RDIPP 2013, 385, 401–403.

[1547] OLG München AfP 2008, 394, 395; Aud. Prov. Marcia AEDIPr 2007, 890 with note *Cordero Álvarez*; Juzgado Primera Instancia n° 7 Murcia AEDIPr 2007, 889; *Coester-Waltjen*, in: FS Rolf A. Schütze (1999), p. 175, 179; *Leible*, in: Rauscher Art. 5 note 92; *André Huet*, Clunet 131 (2004), 873, 874; *Cordero Álvarez*, AEDIPr 2009, 411, 417.

[1548] *Fiona Shevill v. Presse Alliance SA*, (Case C-68/93) [1995] ECR I-415, I-460 *et seq.* para. 24.

[1549] *Garber*, ÖBl 2014, 100, 101.

[1550] OLG München OLGZ 1987, 216, 218; *Coester-Waltjen*, in: FS Rolf A. Schütze (1999), p. 175, 179.

[1551] Council Directive 93/83/EEC of 27 September 1993 on the coordination of certain rules concerning copyright applicable to satellite broadcasting and cable retransmission, OJ 1993 L 248/15.

[1552] *Reindl*, in: Koppensteiner (ed.), Österreichisches und europäisches Wirtschaftsprivatrecht, Vol. II (1996), p. 249, 350 fn. 228; *Thomas Dreier*, in: Michael Walter (ed.), Europäisches Urheberrecht (2001) Art. 1 Satelliten- und KabelRL Art. 5 note 11.

[1553] BGH GRUR 2012, 621 [22]-[27] – OSCAR.

[1554] See only *Wintersteiger AG v. Products 4U Sondermaschinenbau* (Case C-523/10), ECLI:EU:C:2012:220 para. 34; A-G *Jääskinen*, Opinion of 13 June 2013 in Case C-170/12 para. 29; *Birgit Bachmann*, IPRax 1997, 179, 182; *Mankowski*, RabelsZ 63 (1999), 203, 269 *et seq.*; *Christian Berger*, GRUR Int. 2005, 465, 467; *Spickhoff*, IPRax 2011, 131, 132; *Sujecki*, EWS 2015, 305. But cf. also *Feraci*, Riv. dir. int. 2012, 461, 466; *Garber*, ÖBl 2014, 100, 102.

---

which is created for its own commercial purposes should be considered central and relevant.[1555]

302 But the decision to upload the content is relevant, too. Generally, the decision of the interested person matters not the decisions made by the persons managing technical equipment. The decision making process is not focussed on mere auxiliary personnel but follows the personal or economic interest. Accordingly, the operator on Internet search engine is not the relevant person for the decision whether an advertisement potentially infringing IP rights is uploaded, but the business who decides to advertise.[1556] The advertises selects and chooses for instance a keyword identical to another person's trademark, and not the provider of the respective referencing service.[1557] That consequentially the service provider activates the technical display process and his servers is not the relevant decision.[1558] Commercial content matters in this regard, not mere technicalities. The search engine is a mere auxiliary instrument. Technical accidentalities must not become all-decisive.[1559] This is perfectly in line with Recital (18) e-commerce-Directive[1560] which highlights the relevance of the economic over the technical case.[1561] Cloud computing provides such another justification that this approach is correct.[1562]

303 The mere accessibility as such does not constitute an activity.[1563] Accessibility is on the receiving end and is the result of the activity, but not part of the activity itself. The display of an advertisement is not a relevant activity.[1564] Even less the actual access by the user is an activity by the tortfeasor. Neither are the places where the technical equipment employed for transmitting – like gateways, routers or intermediate servers – is located, places of relevant activity.[1565] The place of the server is almost fortuitous and open to opportunistic manipulation.[1566]

[1555] *Wintersteiger AG v. Products 4U Sondermaschinenbau* (Case C-523/10), ECLI:EU:C:2012:220 para. 34.

[1556] *Wintersteiger AG v. Products 4U Sondermaschinenbau* (Case C-523/10), ECLI:EU:C:2012:220 paras. 35, 37.

[1557] *Wintersteiger AG v. Products 4U Sondermaschinenbau* (Case C-523/10), ECLI:EU:C:2012:220 para. 35.

[1558] See *Wintersteiger AG v. Products 4U Sondermaschinenbau* (Case C-523/10), ECLI:EU:C:2012:220 para. 36.

[1559] *McGuire*, ZEuP 2014, 160, 165.

[1560] Directive 2000/31/EC of the European Parliament and of the Council of 8 June 2000 on certain aspects of information society services, in particular electronic commerce, in the Internal Market (Directive on electronic commerce), OJ EC 2000 L 178/1.

[1561] *McGuire*, ZEuP 2014, 160, 165.

[1562] *Mc Guire*, in: Leible (ed.), Der Schutz des Geistigen Eigentums im Internet (2012), p. 143.

[1563] *Bonnier Media Ltd. v. Lloyd, Smith and Kestel Trading Corp.* [2003] SC 36 (S.C.); *Birgit Bachmann*, IPRax 1997, 179, 184; *Mankowski*, RabelsZ 63 (1999), 203, 269; *Wüllrich*, Das Persönlichkeitsrecht des Einzelnen im Internet (2006) p. 235; *Marie-Élodie Ancel*, in: Études à la mémoire du Xavier Linant de Bellefonds (2007), p. 1, 10–15; *Spickhoff*, IPRax 2011, 131, 132; see also A-G *Cruz Villalón*, Opinion of 16 February 2012 in Case C-523/10, ECLI:EU:C:2012:90 para. 23.

[1564] *Wintersteiger AG v. Products 4U Sondermaschinenbau* (Case C-523/10), ECLI:EU:C:2012:220 para. 34.

[1565] *Christian Berger*, GRUR Int. 2005, 465, 467; *Hye-Knudsen*, Marken-, Patent- und Urheberrechtsverletzungen im europäischen internationalen Zivilprozessrecht (2005) pp. 97 *et seq.*; *Garber*, ÖBl 2014, 100, 102.

[1566] *Wintersteiger AG v. Products 4U Sondermaschinenbau* (Case C-523/10), ECLI:EU:C:2012:220 para. 37.

(6) Infringement of IP rights or copyright
In the event of a copyright or trademark infringement the delivery of the potentially in- **304**
criminating goods or publications is at least a relevant activity.[1567] Where an incriminating
advertisement is published and distributed to the public, relevant activities are exerted.[1568]
Yet it is argued that the principle of territoriality, still prevailing in matters of intellectual
property, prohibits and prevents that a place of relevant activity exists outside the state
where the copyright is allegedly infringed.[1569] But this approach lacks convincing power. The
infringement as such is the result of the activity whereas activity is directed to, and related to,
but not identical with its eventual object. Hence, a place of relevant activity outside the state
where the copyright can be normatively located, is possible.[1570] That such activity aims at
infringing an IP right registered and protected only in another state does not erase relevance
or causality and even less the fact of the activity. The activity might not be prohibited in the
State where it takes place[1571] but is nonetheless an activity leading to a legally inhibited
result.[1572]

It is right that where a protected right is used, activity takes place.[1573] But this does not rule **305**
out that relevant activity is exerted elsewhere, too. The principle of territoriality is concerned
only with the protected asset whereas it is not deemed to restrict jurisdiction;[1574] otherwise it
would imply that not even general jurisdiction under Art. 4 (1) would lay – a result evidently
not envisaged and not tenable. Accordingly, the production of the goods the labels of which
amount to the infringement, should be regarded as a relevant activity,[1575] and a restriction
following an alleged "last event rule"[1576] should not be recognised. Even from the opposite
view, an exception to the principle of territoriality is conceded when a majority of parallel
rights in several states is infringed allowing a uniform activity to take place[1577] (if there are
not several distinct infringers[1578]).

[1567] LG Mannheim NJW 2002, 624; *Matthias Lehmann/Stieper*, JZ 2012, 1016, 1019.

[1568] OLG Düsseldorf IPRspr. 2011 Nr. 234 p. 607.

[1569] To this avail A-G *Jääskinen*, Opinion of 13 June 2013 in Case C-170/12 para. 53; *Dieter Stauder*, GRUR
Int. 1976, 465, 474; *Wilfried Neuhaus*, MittPat 1996, 257, 264; *Bettinger/Thum*, GRUR Int. 1999, 659, 664;
Sack, WRP 2000, 269, 271; *Grabinski*, GRUR Int. 2001, 199, 204; *Treichel*, Die Sanktionen der Patent-
verletzung und ihre gerichtliche Durchsetzung im deutschen und französischen Recht (2001) p. 22;
Schack para. 306a; *Bukow* Verletzungsklagen aus gewerblichen Schutzrechten (2003) pp. 74, 91; *Matthias
Lehmann/Stieper*, JZ 2012, 1016, 1017.

[1570] *Wintersteiger AG v. Products 4U Sondermaschinenbau* (Case C-523/10), ECLI:EU:C:2012:220 paras. 34–
39; *Pansch*, EuLF 2000, 353, 355; *Nagel/Gottwald* § 3 note 66; *Hausmann*, EuLF 2003, 278, 280 *et seq.*;
Garber, ÖBl 2014, 100, 105.

[1571] *Schack*, MMR 2000, 135, 137; *Leible*, in: Rauscher, Art. 5 note 85a; *Hopf*, MarkenR 2012, 229, 234;
Matthias Lehmann/Stieper, JZ 2012, 1016, 1017.

[1572] See *McGuire*, ZEuP 2014, 160, 166.

[1573] See only *Matthias Lehmann/Stieper*, JZ 2012, 1016, 1017.

[1574] *Wilfried Neuhaus*, MittPat 1996, 257, 261; *Karsten Otte*, IPRax 2001, 315, 317. *Contra Ebner*, Markenschutz im internationalen Privat- und Zivilprozessrecht (2004) pp. 186 *et seq.*

[1575] *Pansch*, EuLF 2000/01, 353, 355; *Hye-Knudsen*, Marken-, Patent- und Urheberrechtsverletzungen im
europäischen internationalen Zivilprozessrecht (2005) p. 73.

[1576] As advocated for by *Wilfried Neuhaus*, MittPat 1996, 257, 264; *Grabinski*, GRUR Int. 2001, 199, 204.

[1577] *Dieter Stauder*, GRUR Int. 1976, 465, 477; *Ebner*, Markenschutz im internationalen Privat- und Zivilprozessrecht (2004) p. 187.

306 The relevant activity should be located based on the facts of the concrete case and not schematically at the perpetrator's seat or domicile.[1578] Such a strict approach would make the first prong of (2) irrelevant besides general jurisdiction under Art. 4 (1) since Art. 7 pr. establishes special jurisdiction only in states different from that of the tortfeasor's domicile.[1580] Furthermore, it would possibly negate the relevance of activities elsewhere. For instance, the transit of wrongfully labelled goods can constitute relevant supporting activity for the infringement of a trademark registered in another state.[1581]

(7) Product liability

307 As to product liability, at least the place where the respective goods are manufactured or produced (physically where appropriate[1582]) is a place of relevant activity.[1583] There is at least a presumption to this avail which can be rebutted by positively locating the source of the damage elsewhere and referring it back to another activity.[1584] The place of manufacture is in almost any instance also the place of despatch from the manufacturer's factory.[1585] Yet there are scenarios and cases which raise additional questions when the goods are manufactured by a number of manufacturers or when components are produced in different place whereas they are finally assembled in another place.[1586] Another problem raises where the goods are manufactured outside the EU which happens so often in modern times. If the relevant activity was restricted to production and manufacturing, the first prong of (2) could not apply in this instance.[1587] Thirdly, Art. 3 (1), (2) Product Liability Directive[1588] employs a wider notion of "producer" extending it far beyond the mere manufacturer. Should consistency with the Product Liability Directive prevail over strictly referring to the place of manufacturing?[1589]

308 To the place of manufacture the places where the goods are purposefully marketed by the

---

[1578] *Dieter Stauder/Kur*, in: Schricker/Dreier/Kur (eds.), Geistiges Eigentum im Dienst der Innovation (2001), p. 151, 155; *Ebner*, Markenschutz im internationalen Privat- und Zivilprozessrecht (2004) p. 187.

[1579] But cf. to this avail *Garber*, ÖBl 2014, 100, 105.

[1580] See *McGuire*, ZEuP 2014, 160, 167.

[1581] BGH GRUR 2012, 1263; *Geimer/Schütze* Art. 5 note 250; *McGuire*, ZEuP 2014, 160, 166. *Contra Grabinski*, GRUR Int. 2001, 199, 204; *Hye-Knudsen*, Marken-, Patent- und Urheberrechtsverletzungen im europäischen internationalen Zivilprozessrecht (2005) p. 74.

[1582] *de Clavière*, Rev. Lamy dr. aff. 92 (2014), 60, 62.

[1583] *Zuid-Chemie v. Philippo's Mineralenfabriek NV/SA*, (Case C-189/08) [2009] ECR I-6917, I-6928 para. 25; *Andreas Kainz v. Pantherwerke AG* (Case C-45/13), ECLI:EU:C:2014:7 paras. 26–29; Hoge Raad NJ 2011 Nr. 350 p. 3531; OGH ÖJZ 2014, 660 with notes *Hoch* and *Garber* = JBl 2014, 400; Hof Arnhem-Leeuwarden, locatie Leeuwarden NIPR 2014 Nr. 272 p. 477; Rb. Dordrecht NIPR 2008 Nr. 55 p. 96; *Sujecki*, EWS 2014, 94; *Dietze*, EuZW 2014, 234; *Schmon*, ecolex 2014, 334.

[1584] *de Clavière*, Rev. Lamy dr. aff. 92 (2014), 60, 62.

[1585] See *Allen v. Depuy International Ltd.* [201] EWHC 753 (QB), [2015] 2 WLR 442 [13 (iii)] (Q.B.D., *Stewart* J.).

[1586] *Freitag*, LMK 2014, 355576; *Sujecki*, EWS 2014, 94, 95; *Garber*, ÖJZ 2014, 661, 662.

[1587] *Freitag*, LMK 2014, 355576; *Sujecki*, EWS 2014, 94, 95.

[1588] Council Directive 85/374/EEC of 25 July 1985 on the approximation of the laws, regulations and administrative provisions of the Member States concerning liability for defective products, OJ EEC 1985 L 29/33 as amended by Directive 1999/34/EC of 10 May 1999, OJ EC 1999 L 141/20.

[1589] *Freitag*, LMK 2014, 355576; *Sujecki*, EWS 2014, 94, 95.

manufacturer should be added.[1590] The definition where the marketing of goods takes place should be borrowed from Arts. 7 litt. a, b; 11 Product Liability Directive,[1591] at least with regard to damage sustained by the manufacturer or assembler of any final product using the defective component as an educt.[1592] Marketing in this restricted sense requires the (where appropriate: physical) release of the goods and does not include mere advertising; it must not be extended to a meaning resembling the directing of commercial activity under Art. 15 (1) (c).[1593] At least the conclusion of external sales contracts is in demand.[1594] As a rule of thumb, marketing takes place everywhere where the goods are on sale (or *commercialisée* in French).[1595] This relieves of the place of production often coinciding with the manufacturer's domicile and thus general jurisdiction under Art. 4 (1).[1596] Factually ascertaining where marketing takes place should not pose insurmountable difficulties.[1597] For the limited purposes of ascertaining the place of the event giving rise to the damage it should be irrelevant whether the eventual victim acquired the defective goods in one of those places or elsewhere. Art. 5 Rome II Regulation does not indicate otherwise for it is in this context primarily concerned with identifying an place where the damage occurred and not with ascertaining a place of the event giving rise to the damage which concept does generally not bear major importance under the Rome II Regulation.

Kainz firmly rejected to have recourse to Art. 5 Rome II Regulation[1598] and did not import **309** the very elaborate (and overly complicated[1599]) rule contained in this article to (2). It clinged to the yardsticks previously developed in the case law of the ECJ.[1600] One can only speculate that the true rationale underlying this was a disbelief in the structure and content of Art. 5 Rome II Regulation. In support it is argued that (2) and Art. 5 Rome II Regulation pursue different aims as underlined by Recital (20) Rome II Regulation.[1601] Generally, Recitals (7) of both the Rome I and Rome II Regulations would have advocated in favour of a harmonising,

---

[1590] OGH EvBl-LS 201367 with note *Hoch*; Rb. Rotterdam NIPR 1996 p. 587; *Buchner*, Kläger und Beklagtenschutz im Recht der internationalen Zuständigkeit (1998) p. 134; *Uhl*, Internationale Zuständigkeit gemäß Art. 5 Nr. 3 des Brüsseler und Lugano-Übereinkommens (2000) p. 183; *von Hein*, IPRax 2010, 330, 339; *Steinbrück*, in: FS Athanassios Kaissis (2012), p. 965, 971; *Lüttringhaus*, RabelsZ 77 (2013), 31, 60–61; *Eric Wagner*, BB 2014, 661; *Garber*, ÖJZ 2014, 661; *Paradela Aréan*, REDI 2014-2, 244, 245; see also OLG Stuttgart NJW-RR 2006, 1362. Not mentioned, but for para. 31 in a specific context, and thus implicitly rejected (*Schmon*, ecolex 2014, 334; *de Clavière*, Rev. Lamy dr. aff. 92 [2014], 60, 62) in *Andreas Kainz v. Pantherwerke AG* (Case C-45/13), ECLI:EU:C:2014:7.

[1591] *Garber*, ÖJZ 2014, 661.

[1592] *von Hein*, RIW 2000, 820, 826; *von Hein*, IPRax 2010, 330, 334; *Kropholler/von Hein*, Art. 5 note 83c.

[1593] *Kropholler/von Hein*, Art. 5 note 83c.

[1594] See *Hartley*, (2008) 57 ICLQ 899, 904.

[1595] *Dietze*, EuZW 2014, 234.

[1596] *Paradela Aréan*, REDI 2014-2, 244, 245.

[1597] *Garber*, ÖJZ 2014, 661. Tentatively *contra Dietze*, EuZW 2014, 234.

[1598] *Andreas Kainz v. Pantherwerke AG* (Case C-45/13), ECLI:EU:C:2014:7 para. 20.

[1599] See the criticisms by *Peter Huber/Illmer*, (2007) 9 Yb. PIL 31; *Stone*, Ankara L. Rev. 4 (2007), 95, 118–123; *Kozyris*, 56 Am. J. Comp. L. 471, 485–495 (2008); *Hartley*, (2008) 57 ICLQ 899; *Spickhoff*, in: FS Jan Kropholler (2008), p. 671; *Schwartze*, NIPR 2008, 430; *Illmer*, RabelsZ 73 (2009), 269; *Rudolf*, wbl 2009, 525; *Junker*, in: Liber amicorum Klaus Schurig (2012), p. 81.

[1600] *Andreas Kainz v. Pantherwerke AG* (Case C-45/13), ECLI:EU:C:2014:7 paras. 26–28.

[1601] *Berlioz*, Rev. jur. comm. 2014, 266, 269.

---

triangulating interpretation[1602] if one was not prepared to judge Art. 5 Rome II Regulation as being only concerned with the second prong of (2) whereas the question referred to the ECJ in *Kainz* was solely related to the place of the event giving rise to the damage. The place of manufacture does not feature in Art. 5 Rome II Regulation, anyway.[1603] But the place of marketing does, and Art. 17 Rome II Regulation adds to its strength.[1604]

(8) Wrongful birth

310   If wrongful birth is qualified as tortious, the tortfeasor's activity is not the birth of the child,[1605] but his negligent mistreatment leading to the misinformation about the pregnancy or the health of the future child.

(9) Unfair competition

311   Under the auspices of competition law, categories of activities have to be distinguished.[1606] Unilateral acts by single enterprises are located also for the purposes of competition law where they are staged, in many instances at the respective enterprise's seat.[1607] Agreements which are incriminated by antitrust law, are staged where they are concluded.[1608] The places of meetings might be fortuitous[1609] or even expertly selected by the cartelants,[1610] but undeniably relevant activities take place there.[1611] It does not rule these places out *a limine* that it might not be possible due to the secrete nature of the concrete cartel.[1612] Yet the characteristics of different types of cartels might generate the need to refine the notion of the place where the cartel was agreed, particularly so if the cartel is long-running and kind of standing order and if the participants meet in various places in different States over the time.[1613] If the cartelants meet only once or if they meet repeatedly, but every time in the same place the respective place is a relevant place of activity.[1614]

[1602] Admitted in *Andreas Kainz v. Pantherwerke AG* (Case C-45/13), ECLI:EU:C:2014:7 para. 20.

[1603] *Dietze*, EuZW 2014, 234.

[1604] *Eric Wagner*, BB 2014, 661.

[1605] *Contra* Rb. Middelburg NIPR 2003 Nr. 53 p. 104.

[1606] *Wurmnest*, EuZW 2012, 933, 934; *Wulf-Henning Roth*, in: FS Eberhard Schilken (2015), p. 427, 431.

[1607] *Wulf-Henning Roth*, in: FS Eberhard Schilken (2015), p. 427, 431.

[1608] *Cartel Damage Claims (CDC) Hydrogen Peroxide SA v. Akzo Nobel NV* Case C-352/13), ECLI:EU:C:2015:335 para. 44; *Ashton/Vollrath*, ZWeR 2006, 1, 8; *Basedow*, in: Basedow (ed.), Private Enforcement of EC Competition Law (2007), p. 229, 250; *Basedow*, in: Wettbewerbspolitik und Kartellrecht in der Marktwirtschaft – 50 Jahre FIW 1960–2010 (2010), p. 129, 136; *Mankowski*, RIW 2008, 177, 181; *Mankowski*, WuW 2012, 797, 801; *Moritz Becker*, EWS 2008, 228, 229; *Helena Isabel Maier*, Marktortanknüpfung im internationalen Kartelldeliktsrecht (2011) p. 129; *Wurmnest*, EuZW 2012, 933, 934. *Contra Tzakas*, Die Haftung für Kartellrechtsverstöße im internationalen Rechtsverkehr (2011) p. 110; *Schnyder/Acocella*, Art. 5 LugÜ Nr. 1 bis 3 note 242.

[1609] *Wulf-Henning Roth*, in: FS Eberhard Schilken (2015), p. 427, 432.

[1610] *Helena Isabel Maier*, Marktortanknüpfung im internationalen Kartelldeliktsrecht (2011) p. 130; *Tzakas*, Die Haftung für Kartellrechtsverstöße im internationalen Rechtsverkehr (2011) p. 110.

[1611] *Mankowski*, WuW 2012, 797, 801.

[1612] But cf. A-G *Jääskinen*, Opinion of 11 December 2014 in Case C-352/13, ECLI:EU:C:2014:2443 para. 49.

[1613] *Cooper Tire & Rubber Co. v. Shell Chemicals UK Ltd.* [2009] EHC 2609 (Comm) [65] (Q.B.D., *Teare* J.); *Wurmnest*, EuZW 2012, 933, 934. In detail *Basedow*. in: Wettbewerbspolitik und Kartellrecht in der Marktwirtschaft – 50 Jahre FIW 1960–2010 (2010), p. 129, 138–142.

If the cartelants meet at different places over the time the specific weight of the single place **312** might be reduced (the more so if the meeting places are chosen for touristic values, convenience of travelling there or without any discernible pattern).[1615] Long running cartels where the members met in different places over the time pose another problem, too.[1616] To give relevance to single meeting places might be regarded as over-generous, too diffuse and fortuitous.[1617] But each meeting place is a place of relevant activity, though. This is not unfair to the cartelants for they can freely chose where they want to meet.[1618] If cartelants want to avoid being held liable at each and every meeting place they must refrain from meeting in different places, but ought to be so consequent as to meet only in a single place. Yet there might be a need to distinguish whether at certain places only the cartelants' trading on certain markets is agreed upon and hence only unfair competition on those markets is causally influenced.[1619] If a specific agreement can be singled out as the sole causal event giving rise to the loss allegedly inflicted on a buyer, the place where this agreement was concluded, would attract jurisdiction.[1619a] But there should be some second level consideration taking into account possible basic effects continuing from previous understandings between the cartelants.[1620] Sceptics ruminate that this might be hard to prove.[1621] But it would be a step too far to give in *a priori* for fear of lack of proof and the respective costs of eventually futile attempts to prove.[1622] To deny any place of activity to exist[1623] would be a fallacy in any event.[1624] To identify the place of activity with the seats of the participating enterprises[1625] would diminish the applicability of (2) in the light of Art. 7 pr., and would leave put Art. 8 (1) to the forefront.

If the cartelants do not meet at all, but coordinate their market conduct by means of distance **313** communication, Art. 11 (2) Rome I Regulation could possibly serve as a tool for the solution.[1626] This rule refers to either of the countries where either of the parties or its agent is

---

[1614] *Basedow*, in: Wettbewerbspolitik und Kartellrecht in der Marktwirtschaft – 50 Jahre FIW 1960–2010 (2010), p. 129, 140; *Mankowski*, WuW 2012, 797, 801; *Wurmnest*, EuZW 2012, 933, 934.

[1615] *Cartel Damage Claims (CDC) Hydrogen Peroxide SA v. Akzo Nobel NV* Case C-352/13), ECLI:EU:C:2015:335 para. 45. *Cooper Tire & Rubber Co. v. Shell Chemicals UK Ltd.* [2009] EWHC 2609 (Comm) [65] (Q.B.D., *Teare J.*).

[1616] *Wulf-Henning Roth*, in: FS Eberhard Schilken (2015), p. 427, 433.

[1617] *A-G Jääskinen*, Opinion of 11 December 2014 in Case C-352/13, ECLI:EU:C:2014:2443 para. 49.

[1618] *Mankowski*, WuW 2012, 797, 801.

[1619] *Basedow*, in: Wettbewerbspolitik und Kartellrecht in der Marktwirtschaft – 50 Jahre FIW 1960–2010 (2010), p. 129, 140; *Wurmnest*, EuZW 2012, 933, 934.

[1619a] *Cartel Damage Claims (CDC) Hydrogen Peroxide SA v. Akzo Nobel NV* (Case C-352/13), ECLI:EU:C:2015:335 para. 46.

[1620] *Basedow*, in: Wettbewerbspolitik und Kartellrecht in der Marktwirtschaft – 50 Jahre FIW 1960–2010 (2010), p. 129, 140; *Wurmnest*, EuZW 2012, 933, 934.

[1621] *Wurmnest*, EuZW 2012, 933, 934–935; see also *Matthias Weller/Wäschle*, RIW 2015, 603, 604.

[1622] But cf. to this avail *Wurmnest*, EuZW 2012, 933, 935.

[1623] *Contra Cooper Tire & Rubber Co. v. Shell Chemicals UK Ltd.* [2009] EWHC 2609 (Comm) [65] (Q.B.D., *Teare J.*).

[1624] *Mankowski*, WuW 2012, 797, 801.

[1625] As *Wulf-Henning Roth*, in: FS Eberhard Schilken (2015), p. 427, 433 proposes.

[1626] *Mankowski*, WuW 2012, 797, 801. But cf. *Wulf-Henning Roth*, in: FS Eberhard Schilken (2015), p. 427, 433.

---

present at the time when the agreement is concluded. But against a transfer of this approach to antitrust matters it can be said that Art. 11 (2) Rome I Regulation pursues a *favor validitatis* trying to avoid formal invalidity of the contract in favour of upholding the parties' bargain whereas antitrust law meets the reverse goal.[1627]

314 The place of implementation and performance of the cartel is *also* a place of relevant activity.[1628] Without implementation the incriminated agreement would not be filled with life. Such implementation could consist in coordination and governance by a central institution[1629] as it will be found in the case of institutionally organised cartels, consortia, networks or liner conferences.[1630] It is not a counter-argument that the place of implementation coincides with the place where the damage occurred[1631] since the latter, the *Erfolgsort*, is subject to the mosaic principle whereas the *Handlungsort* is not. Mutual information about trade volumes, prices, contractual conditions between the cartelants gains like relevance,[1632] be it on a regular basis, be it where appropriate or in case of need.[1633] Relevant activity takes also place where cartelants act in accordance and in execution of the agreement.[1634] A dominant business acts where it breaks down its dominance into single activities, e.g. by offering customers certain conditions.[1635]

315 If the agreement entails a distribution of markets that only single cartelants shall act on certain markets, the other cartelants exert relevant activities if they comply with the agreement and do not act on the market reserved for the one beneficiary.[1636] Inactivity agreed upon is performance of the cartel. *A fortiori* this applies to mere sham offers.[1637]

316 Furthermore, relevant activities are staged where a cartelant makes ist strategic decisions in accordance with the agreement.[1638] Typically this happens at the *siége réel* or at the place of business concerned. For jurisdictional purposes, the *siége réel* is already focussed on under the auspices of Art. 4 (1) *iuncto* Art. 63 (b). But still it could matter for the other cartelants

---

[1627] See *Mankowski*, WuW 2012, 797, 801.

[1628] *Withers*, [2002] JBL 250; *Basedow*, in: Basedow (ed.), Private Enforcement of EC Competition Law (2007), p. 229, 250; *Basedow*, in: Wettbewerbspolitik und Kartellrecht in der Marktwirtschaft – 50 Jahre FIW 1960–2010 (2010), p. 129, 136 *et seq.*, 141; *Moritz Becker*, EWS 2008, 228, 229; *Helena Isabel Maier*, Marktortanknüpfung im internationalen Kartelldeliktsrecht (2011) pp. 131–137. See also A-G *Jääskinen*, Opinion of 11 December 2014 in Case C-352/13, ECLI:EU:C:2014:2443 para. 49.

[1629] *Basedow*, in: Wettbewerbspolitik und Kartellrecht in der Marktwirtschaft – 50 Jahre FIW 1960–2010 (2010), p. 129, 141; *Mankowski*, WuW 2012, 797, 802; *Wurmnest*, EuZW 2012, 933, 935.

[1630] *Basedow*, in: Wettbewerbspolitik und Kartellrecht in der Marktwirtschaft – 50 Jahre FIW 1960–2010 (2010), p. 129, 138–139.

[1631] As *Wulf-Henning Roth*, in: FS Eberhard Schilken (2015), p. 427, 433 puts forward.

[1632] *Basedow*, in: Wettbewerbspolitik und Kartellrecht in der Marktwirtschaft – 50 Jahre FIW 1960–2010 (2010), p. 129, 141.

[1633] *Mankowski*, WuW 2012, 797, 802.

[1634] *Withers*, 2002 JBL 261; *Wurmnest*, EuZW 2012, 933, 935.

[1635] *Mankowski*, WuW 2012, 797, 802; *Wurmnest*, EuZW 2012, 933, 934; see also OLG Hamburg EuLF 2007, II-133 = GRUR-RR 2008, 31 – Exklusivitätsklausel.

[1636] *Mankowski*, WuW 2012, 797, 802.

[1637] *Mankowski*, WuW 2012, 797, 802.

[1638] *Geimer/Schütze* Art. 5 EuGVVO note 260a.

insofar as the strategic decisions of their accomplice are attributed also to them.[1639] But to assume that the single cartelants each act solely at their respective seats[1640] would unduly diminish (2) in the face of Art. 4 (1)[1641] and Art. 8 (1). This would be an unjustified privilege for cartelants compared to other tortfeasors.[1642] Furthermore, it would fit ill with the character of unfair competition as a tort directed at markets.[1643]

(10) Breaking off of negotiations

Breaking off negotiations, if characterised as tortious, ought to be located where the break **317** was communicated in order to have effect. If a letter is sent terminating negotiations the relevant activity is where it is issued and sent, not where it is received.[1644] Hence, the place of relevant activity where the harmful event originates will often coincide with the alleged tortfeasor's domicile or place of business.[1645]

c) Place where the damage occurred

aa) Harmful effects on the victim

The damage occurs where the event giving rise to the damage produces and inflicts its **318** harmful effects on the victim[1646] or, more precisely, on the primarily protected assets or values of the victim.[1647] In principle, the place of damage connotes the place where the physical damage is done or where the recoverable economic loss is actually suffered.[1648] A causal connection between the damage and the event giving rise to it is required.[1649] It is irrelevant whether the victim or any *agrent provocateur* provoked the damage.[1650] As far as possible and conceivable the task is to identify a single place for the occurrence of damage since the search is for the place where *the* damage occurred.[1651]

[1639] See generally Art. 7 notes 282–291 (*Mankowski*).

[1640] *Bulst* EWS 2004, 403, 405; *Mäsch*, IPRax 2005, 509, 512 *et seq.*; *Gebauer/Ansgar Staudinger*, in: Terhechte (ed.), Internationales Kartell- und Fusionskontrollverfahrensrecht (2008) para. 7.44; *Leible*, in: Rauscher, Art. 5 note 88d; *Helena Isabel Maier*, Marktortanknüpfung im internationalen Kartelldeliktsrecht (2011) pp. 137–142; *Acocella*, in: Schnyder, Art. 5 Nr. 1 bis 3 LugÜ note 242.

[1641] *Basedow*, in: Wettbewerbspolitik und Kartellrecht in der Marktwirtschaft – 50 Jahre FIW 1960–2010 (2010), p. 129, 137; *Wurmnest*, EuZW 2012, 933, 935.

[1642] *Mankowski*, WuW 2012, 797, 803; see also *Basedow*, in: Wettbewerbspolitik und Kartellrecht in der Marktwirtschaft – 50 Jahre FIW 1960–2010 (2010), p. 129, 137–138.

[1643] *Tzakas*, Die Haftung für Kartellrechtsverstöße im internationalen Rechtsverkehr (2011) p. 113; *Mankowski*, WuW 2012, 797, 803.

[1644] *Contra* Hoge Raad Ned. Jur. 2002 Nr. 254 with note *de Boer*.

[1645] *ten Wolde/Kirsten C. Henckel*, Int. J. Proced. L. 3 (2013), 195, 217.

[1646] See only *Leible*, in: Rauscher Art. 5 note 86; *Bank of Tokyo-Mitsubishi Ltd. v. Baskan Gida Sanayi* [2004] 2 Lloyd's Rep. 395, 418 (Ch.D., *Lawrence Collins* J.).

[1647] See only *Mari*, in: Mélanges Fritz Sturm (1999), p. 1573, 1583 *et passim*.

[1648] *Collins*, in: Dicey/Morris para. 11–262.

[1649] *Dexter Ltd. v. Harley* The Times 2 April 2001 (Q.B.D., *Lloyd* J.); *Mari*, in: Mélanges Fritz Sturm (1999), p. 1573, 1577, 1583.

[1650] Cass. Bull. Civ. 2009 I n° 64; *Reinmüller/Bücken*, IPRax 2013, 185, 187.

[1651] *AMT Futures Ltd. v. Marzillier, Dr. Meier & Dr. Guntner Rechtsanwaltsgesellschaft mbH* [2014] EWHC 1085 (Comm), [2015] 2 WLR 187 [34] (Q.B.D., *Popplewell* J.).

319 The ECJ condemns any approach to imply a reference to the applicable substantive law and to its pre-requisites for liability.[1652] Allegedly this would overload the jurisdictional rule with too many normative and legal implications[1653] (besides the fact that the modern PIL of torts itself uses the place where the damage occurred, as one of its main connecting factors and some kind of vicious circle appears to be threatening). At least such a normative approach would be accompanied by unwelcome uncertainty.[1654] A causal link between activity and damage should suffice.[1655] In the event that two or more perpetrators acted in concert (as co-actors or as main actors and accomplices) the primary damage caused by one shall be attributed also to the other,[1656] without having recourse to national law, e.g. § 830 BGB.[1657] This ist not easily accomplished, given the lack of proper criteria in (2) itself.[1658] As a s disadvantage of attributing damages to other perpetrators it is alleged that such a concept diminishes the opportunity and the chance to conclude settlements with single tortfeasors without having to sue them under Art. 8 (1) first.[1659]

320 Yet this approach fits rather ill with the emphasis[1660] placed on the primary damage afflicted to the primarily protected asset or value. How could one possibly determine which protection, to which extent, is allegedly granted to which asset or value without having recourse to a national law? In substance, (2) does not grant such protection. Intuition might lead quite some way as to which value or asset is protected, but can not defy entirely the grave doubts. And that the intuition can differ where different individuals are invited to become intuitive (just to avoid the term "inventive") is commonplace and trite.

321 A task left for national law, yet not for the applicable substantive law but for the procedural law of the *forum*, is to ascertain to which extent the court may scrutinize the plaintiff's allegations as to the facts.[1661] If recourse on the applicable substantive law is not be had for the definition of the tort at stake, the plaintiff is not required to plead such tort fully, but only

---

[1652] *Antonio Marinari v. Lloyd's Bank plc and Zubaidi Trading Co.*, (Case C-364/93) [1995] ECR I-2719, I-2740 *et seq.* paras. 18 *et seq.*; Cassaz. RDIPP 2004, 1372, 1374; *Alfred Dunhill Ltd. v. Diffusion Internationale de Maroquinerie de Prestige SARL* [2002] 1 All ER (Comm) 950, 961 (Q.B.D., Judge *Kenneth Rokison* Q.C.); *Holl*, EuZW 1995, 766, 767; *Volken*, SZIER 1996, 137; *Rauscher*, ZZP Int. 1 (1996), 151, 165 *et seq.*; *Kubis*, Internationale Zuständigkeit bei Persönlichkeits- und Immaterialgüterrechtsverletzungen (1999) p. 105; *Briggs*, (2001) 72 BYIL 437, 471; *Kropholler/von Hein* Art. 5 note 88; *Schlosser* Art. 5 note 19; *Hootz* p. 179. *Contra Bischoff*, Clunet 109 (1982), 463, 468; *Kaye* p. 567; *Geimer*, JZ 1995, 1108; *Nerlich*, WiB 1995, 972; *Mansel*, RabelsZ 61 (1997), 756, 757 *et seq.*; *Schack* para. 299.

[1653] *Antonio Marinari v. Lloyd's Bank plc and Zubaidi Trading Co.*, (Case C-364/93) [1995] ECR I-2719, I-2740 *et seq.* paras. 18 *et seq.*; *Hootz* p. 179.

[1654] *Antonio Marinari v. Lloyd's Bank plc and Zubaidi Trading Co.*, (Case C-364/93) [1995] ECR I-2719, I-2741 para. 19.

[1655] *Handelskwekerij Bier BV v. Mines de Potasse d'Alsace SA*, (Case 21/76) [1976] ECR 1735, 1746 *et seq.* para. 15/19; *Danmarks Rederiforening, acting on behalf of DFDS Torline AS v. LO Landsorganisationen i Sverige, acting on behalf of SEKO Sjöfolk Facket for Service och Kommunikation*, (Case C-18/02) [2004] ECR I-1417, I-1453 *et seq.* paras. 31–34.

[1656] *Coty Germany GmbH v. First Note Perfumes NV* (Case C-360/12), ECLI:EU:C:2014:1318 paras. 52 *et seq.*

[1657] *von Hein*, EuZW 2014, 667, 668.

[1658] *von Hein*, EuZW 2014, 667, 668.

[1659] *von Hein*, EuZW 2014, 667, 668.

[1660] See *infra* Art. 5 note 233 (*Mankowski*) and *Rauscher*, ZZP Int. 1 (1996), 151, 162.

to establish some kind of arguable case coming within the autonomous definition of tort under (2).[1662]

bb) Primary damage and consequential damage

Only the primary or immediate damage is relevant for the purposes of (2). Primary damage **322** is the damage to the asset originally protected. The search is for the place where the original damage is manifested,[1663] where the original injury can be located.[1664] This might vary depending on the nature of the right allegedly infringed.[1665] It is a necessary and basic precondition that the right of which infringement the is alleged is protected in the Member State of the forum.[1666] Which asset is protected, must be determined pursuant to the tort in question. Specific torts are designed to protect certain assets or values. Since the tort at stake must provide the answer to the question, an autonomous and uniform approach which would be entirely fact-based, is not feasible. It might be not the easiest task to identify for instance if protection against a certain kind of misinformation on the market aims at protecting the market or even a specific exchange on the institutional level or (also?) the fortune of investors relying on such information.[1667] The liability of rating agencies provides a modern example.[1668]

Indirect financial damage or adverse consequences of an event which has already caused **323** damage elsewhere do not establish jurisdiction. It would be too extensive to encompass any place where the adverse consequences of an event can be felt which has already caused damage actually arising elsewhere.[1669] Otherwise that would give too much weight to the plaintiff's domicile and enable a plaintiff to determine the competent court by his choice of

---

[1661] Høgsteret Rt. 2015, 129, 133; *Peter Huber*, ZEuP 1996, 300, 311 *et seq.*; *Rauscher*, ZZP Int. 1 (1996), 151, 166; *von Hein*, IPRax 2005, 17, 22.

[1662] Høgsteret Rt. 2015, 129, 133; *Rauscher*, ZZP Int. 1 (1996), 151, 166.

[1663] *AMT Futures Ltd. v. Marzillier, Dr. Meier & Dr. Guntner Rechtsanwaltsgesellschaft mbH* [2014] EWHC 1085 (Comm), [2015] 2 WLR 187 [34] (Q.B.D., *Popplewell* J.).

[1664] *Carpi*, in: FS Rolf Stürner (2013), p. 1191, 1193.

[1665] *Peter Pinckney v. KDG Mediatech AG* (Case C-170/12), ECLI:EU:C:2013:635 paras. 32–33; *Pez Hejduk v. EnergieAgentur.NRW GmbH* (Case C-441/13), ECLI:EU:C:2015:28 para. 29. An illustrative example: If a horse suffers from veterinary malpractice the primary demage is inflicted on the health of the horse where the veterinary treatment took place; OGH JBl 2015, 522, 524.

[1666] *Peter Pinckney v. KDG Mediatech AG* (Case C-170/12), ECLI:EU:C:2013:635 paras. 32–33; *Pez Hejduk v. EnergieAgentur.NRW GmbH* (Case C-441/13), ECLI:EU:C:2015:28 para. 29.

[1667] See OLG Frankfurt ZIP 2010, 2217, 2218 = EuZW 2010, 918; *Mankowski*, EWiR § 37b WpHG 1/10, 725; *von Hein*, EuZW 2011, 369, 371; *von Hein*, BerDGfIR 2011, 369, 400–401.

[1668] Cassaz. RDIPP 2013, 431, 432.

[1669] *Antonio Marinari v. Lloyd's Bank plc and Zubaidi Trading Co.*, (Case C-364/93) [1995] ECR I-2719, I-2739 para. 14; *Rudolf Kronhofer v. Marianne Maier*, (Case C-168/02) [2004] ECR I-6009, I-6030 para. 19; *Harald Kolassa v. Barclays Bank plc* (Case C-375/13), ECLI:EU:C:2015:37 paras. 48–49; Cassaz. RDIPP 1997, 729, 733 *et seq.*; Cassaz. RDIPP 2006, 1059, 1061; Cassaz. RDIPP 2013, 431, 432; OGH SZ 71/31; Hof van Cass. R.W. 2003–2004, 457; OGH ÖJZ 2005, 111, 112; OGH SZ 208/122; OGH WBl 2011, 279, 280; OGH JBl 2015, 522, 523; BGH WM 2014, 1614 [32]; Hoge Raad NIPR 2015 Nr. 51 p. 140; Høgsteret Rt. 2015, 129, 135; OLG Frankfurt IPRspr. 2013 Nr. 180 p. 391; Rb. Kh. Dendermonde TBH 2000, 242, 244 with note *Wautelet*; Rb. Dordrecht NIPR 2008 Nr. 55 p. 96; Rb. Rotterdam NIPR 2008 Nr. 65 p. 109.

domicile.[1670] An almost complete *forum actoris* is undesirable.[1671] The expenses and losses of profit incurred as a consequence of the initial harmful event might be incurred elsewhere so that, as far as the efficiency of proof is concerned, the court of the place where consequential damage was sustained, would be inappropriate.[1672] No "money pocket rule" (along the line "the damage was suffered in my pocket") applies.[1673] That it would be easier for the victim to hold redress if he could do so at the centre of his financial interests, is conceded, but does not overcome the tortfeasor's legitimate interests.[1674] The fundamental objective of the Brussels *Ibis* Regulation militates against an interpretation which as some kind of rule might lead to jurisdiction at the claimant's domicile and thus would generally enable the claimant to determine the competent court by his choice of domicile.[1675] Any approach fostering forum shopping and stirring an inextricable tangle of conflicts over jurisdiction ought to be rejected, too.[1676] On the other hand, it must be conceded that distinguishing the economic consequences of the damage from the immediate damage may not be easy, particularly in cases of economic torts.[1677] There could be something like an "also-primary" financial damage.[1678] To assert a general precedence of physical damage over financial damage[1679] would be precipitative.

324 The case is different, though, if the victim after the initial damage sustains further damage to the primarily protected asset or good. Imagine for instance a medical maltreatment where the maltreatment caused the initial damage in one state but the victim suffers additional damage later-on after his return in his home country. Then the consequential damage affects the primarily protected asset or value and can not be regarded as irrelevant. Accordingly, as far as the additional damage is at stake, (2) establishes jurisdiction in the victim's favour where the victim sustained the additional damage.[1680] Aggravation and deterioration of

---

[1670] *Dumez France SA and Tracoba SARL v. Hessische Landesbank*, (Case C-220/88) [1990] ECR I-49, I-80 para. 19; *Antonio Marinari v. Lloyd's Bank plc and Zubaidi Trading Co.*, (Case C-364/93) [1995] ECR I-2719, I-2739 *et seq.* paras. 13–15; Cassaz. RDIPP 2006, 1059, 1061; *Mazur Media Ltd. v. Mazur Media GmbH* [2004] 1 WLR 2966, 2973 (Ch.D., *Lawrence Collins* J.); OLG Köln IPRspr. 2010 Nr. 219 p. 556; OLG Frankfurt ZIP 2010, 2217; see also *Réunion europénne SA v. Spliethoff's Bevrachtingskantoor BV and Master of the vessel "Alblasgracht 002"*, (Case C-51/97) [1998] ECR I-6511, I-6544 *et seq.* para. 29.

[1671] *Antonio Marinari v. Lloyd's Bank plc and Zubaidi Trading Co.*, (Case C-364/93) [1995] ECR I-2719, I-2739 para. 13; *Rudolf Kronhofer v. Marianne Maier*, (Case C-168/02) [2004] ECR I-6009, I-6031 para. 20; Rb. Almelo NIPR 2003 Nr. 47 p. 97 *et seq.*

[1672] *Antonio Marinari v. Lloyd's Bank plc and Zubaidi Trading Co.*, (Case C-364/93) [1995] ECR I-2719, I-2741 para. 20.

[1673] See only *Hans-Jürgen Ahrens*, IPRax 1990, 129, 132; *Geimer*, JZ 1995, 1108; *Nisi*, RDIPP 2013, 385, 409 with fn. 118.

[1674] See *Antonio Marinari v. Lloyd's Bank plc and Zubaidi Trading Co.*, (Case C-364/93) [1995] ECR I-2719, I-2741 para. 20.

[1675] *Dolphin Maritime & Aviation Services Ltd. v. Sveriges Angartyggs Assurans Forening* [2009] EWHC 716 (Comm), [2010] 1 All ER (Comm) 473, 483 [29] (Q.B.D., *Christopher Clarke* J.); *AMT Futures Ltd. v. Marzillier, Dr. Meier & Dr. Guntner Rechtsanwaltsgesellschaft mbH* [2014] EWHC 1085 (Comm), [2015] 2 WLR 187 [34] (Q.B.D., *Popplewell* J.).

[1676] *Carpi*, in: FS Rolf Stürner (2013), p. 1191, 1194.

[1677] *Collier*, (1996) 55 Cambridge L.J. 216, 218.

[1678] *Kosmehl*, in: Liber amicorum Thomas Rauscher (2005), p. 79, 88.

[1679] Tentatively so *de Boer*, NJ 2011 Nr. 349 p. 3526.

condition might not be a fresh cause of action or a fresh wrong.[1681] But nevertheless they are a further detriment to the protected value. This is latent damage directly deriving from the original wrong and thus causally and immediately linked with the initial wrongdoing, not in any way derived from some intermediate step.[1682]

Securities fraud implies activities on capital markets, as does wrong information of capital   **325** markets. Insofar as market values are identified as the primary damage, questions arise as to how to determine the relevant market. Particular difficulties arise if the shares or securities are cross-listed with a number of exchanges[1683] or if the customer gave an order for best execution only, leaving it to the tortfeasor where eventually to execute the order.[1684]

cc) Damage to the assets of third parties
Generally, indirect victims of a tort can not avail them of the jurisdiction of the place where   **326** they themselves suffer financial consequences from the tort, but can only sue at the place where the primary damage was inflicted to the primary and direct victim.[1685] Only the immediate victim matters.[1686] This holds particularly true for parent companies who allege that they have been detrimentally affected by actions upon their subsidiaries.[1687] Other shareholders can not successfully argue otherwise, either. The case is different, though, where the tortfeasor himself is a shareholder intentionally acting to his companions' detriment insofar as the claim is one in tort and not in contract.[1688]

Yet the other party might be not the primary victim, but a victim of its own and in its own   **327** right. Whether this can hold true must be determined pursuant to the ambit of the tort in question. If according to the applicable national law the tort in question can be deemed also against the other party as a second victim, this party can claim damages in its own right. It can join the proceedings as a second plaintiff. To exclude it from the proceedings would negate the protection granted to the second victim; protection of financial interests must also be recognised in the administration of justice. What remains not feasible, however, is that the first victim can seize upon the damage inflicted to the second victim and profit from

---

[1680] Cassaz. RDIPP 1999, 966, 972–975. *Contra* Hoge Raad NJ 2002 Nr. 539 with note *Vlas*; *Henderson v. Jaouen* [2002] 1 WLR 2971, 2976 (C.A., per *Wall* J.); *Briggs*, (2002) 73 BYIL 453, 459; *Gaudemet-Tallon* para. 216; *Schlosser*, Art. 5 note 19; *Leible*, in: Rauscher, Art. 5 note 86; *Kropholler/von Hein*, Art. 5 note 83d.

[1681] *Henderson v. Jaouen* [2002] 1 WLR 2971, 2976 (C.A., per *Wall* J.).

[1682] Not properly evaluated by Henderson v. Jaouen [2002] 1 WLR 2971, 2976 (C.A., per *Wall* J.).

[1683] *von Hein*, BerDGfIR 2011, 369, 400–401.

[1684] *van Houtte*, in: McLachlan/Nygh (eds.), Transnational Tort Litigation (1996), p. 155, 162; *von Hein*, BerDGfIR 2011, 369, 400–401.

[1685] *Dumez France SA and Tracoba SARL v. Hessische Landesbank*, (Case C-220/88) [1990] ECR I-49, I-80 para. 22; *Réunion européenne SA v. Spliethoff's Bevrachtingskantoor BV and Master of the vessel "Alblasgracht 002"*, (Case C-51/97) [1998] ECR I-6511, I-6545 para. 31.

[1686] *AMT Futures Ltd. v. Marzillier, Dr. Meier & Dr. Guntner Rechtsanwaltsgesellschaft mbH* [2014] EWHC 1085 (Comm), [2015] 2 WLR 187 [34] (Q.B.D., *Popplewell* J.).

[1687] *Dumez France SA and Tracoba SARL v. Hessische Landesbank*, (Case C-220/88) [1990] ECR I-49, I-80 para. 20; Cass. D.S. 1990 IR 158.

[1688] OLG Stuttgart ZIP 2007, 1210; OLG Schleswig NZG 2008, 868; LG Kiel IPRax 2009, 164, 166; *Gregor Bachmann*, IPRax 2009, 140, 143 *et seq.*

the other's damage in matters of jurisdiction directly. Not even Art. 8 (1) might lend a helping hand to the first victim insofar since it seizes upon a majority of defendants, not of plaintiffs. In the event of damage inflicted upon a subsidiary, however, the parent company might prove that this also damaged her own assets *via* the subsidiary and thus obtain a *forum* at the place where the damage was sustained by the subsidiary.[1689]

dd) Relevant damage to the fortune as such (patrimonial loss)

328 If the tort committed was a tort designed to protect the victim's fortune as such the damage to the fortune (or synonymous, the patrimonial loss) is the relevant damage.[1690] In this exceptional formation the damage to the fortune is the primary damage. However, the difficulty to locate a fortune does not vanish. Yet this should pave the way for entirely striking out a jurisdiction alternative to the jurisdiction of the courts of the place where the tortfeasor displayed his activities.[1691] If a particular asset has been lost or damaged, such as a physical object, a number of financial instruments or a certain, identifiable amount of money, its location should be considered where the damaged occurred.[1692] Distinguishable and locatable assets get located.[1693]

329 If the victim only has one body of fortune the answer where to locate the patrimonial loss is also an easy one. Yet it would be fallible to identify the location of this fortune *tel quel* with the victim's domicile. This would man to generalise too much and to take the most common answer as an absolute answer. The ordinary person will have its only body of fortune at its domicile in over to have it at hand and to have ready access to it in case of need. In particular, any bank account might be held there. But this is only the ordinary case. At best it supports a presumption to be established. But such presumption must be rebuttable. It must not be construed as irrefutable and irrebuttable. The connecting factor is not the victim's domicile as such, but the place where the victim's sole body of fortune is held.[1694]

330 But the problem increases if the victim holds several masses or parts of fortune. If a certain and identifiable account is exclusively affected, i.e. transfer was made from this account to another person than the victim (be it the tortfeasor himself, be it an accomplice, be it someone else) and an internal transfer was made to this account this account appears at first glance to be the relevant one.[1695] The material point is the exit transfer to the external

---

[1689] *André Huet*, Clunet 117 (1990), 497, 502; *Gaudemet-Tallon*, RCDIP 79 (1990), 368, 376; *Kropholler/von Hein* Art. 5 note 90; *Hausmann*, EuLF 2003, 278, 280; *Hausmann/Obergfell*, in: Fezer, UWG (2nd ed. 2010), Einl. I note 396.

[1690] See only Hoge Raad NJ 2015 Nr. 44 pp. 548–549; LG Dortmund IPRax 2005, 542, 544.

[1691] Contra Trib. Roma RDIPP 1979, 96; Trib. Monza RDIPP 1980, 229; see also Hof Arnhem NIPR 1999 Nr. 272 p. 364.

[1692] *Matthias Lehmann*, (2011) 7 JPrIL 527, 543.

[1693] See *Matthias Lehmann*, (2011) 7 JPrIL 527, 543.

[1694] Not properly differentiating this in a case of prospectus liability *Harald Kolassa v. Barclays Bank plc* (Case C-375/13), ECLI:EU:C:2015:37 para. 53; A-G *Szpunar*, Opinion of 3 September 2014 in Case C-375/13, ECLI:EU:C:2014:2135 para. 67.

[1695] *Rudolf Kronhofer v. Marianne Maier*, (Case C-168/02) [2004] ECR I-6009, I-6031 para. 20; A-G *Jääskinen*, Opinion of 29 November 2012 in Case C-228/11 para. 32; BGH ZIP 2010, 1998, 2004; OLG Köln IPRspr. 2010 Nr. 219 p. 557; OLG Karlsruhe IPRspr. 2011 Nr. 199 p. 529; *Tenenbaum*, Bull. Joly Bourse 2014, 400, 402.

party:[1696] it releases the asset out of the victim's fortune, and the lack of a transaction related transfer or reorganisation within the victim's sphere. An additional advantage is that this is foreseeable and predictable[1697] (if only where the internal transfer was made intentionally and consciously by the victim, untainted by fraud or deception[1698]). On the other hand, accounts through which the money only passes or which are used for channelling for technical reasons only ought to be disregarded.[1699] Legal uncertainty would be generated to an intolerable degree if even indirect or remote consequences ought to be taken into account.[1700]

Localising accounts does not fall into a linguistical trap to treat patrimony as a quasi-   **331** ontological category; it refers to specific items, assets and monies not to an ominous sum of rights or obligations.[1701] A little simplified, book money is the balance in a bank account, the customer's claim against the bank, and thus accounts matter.[1702] If a transfer is effected from several bank accounts,[1703] each bank account is a relevant place but only for such transfer as has been made from particularly this bank account.

To regard the last of the victim's accounts, which was active before the ultimate exit transfer   **332** or where the money was finally taken from the victim's (nominal) control,[1704] as the relevant account under every possible circumstances[1705] would open unwanted and undesirable potential for manipulation firstly on the tortfeasor's side, though.[1706] Just imagine a transaction induced by fraud which involves setting up a new account: Is the damage sustained where the new account is established[1707] or where the account from which the transfer to the new account was made, can be located? The fraudulent tortfeasor could easily advise as part of his fraud scheme where the new account shall be drawn up and thus diminish the victim's possibilities. Accordingly, the account from which the transfer to the newly established account was perfected should serve as the connecting factor in initial fraud cases[1708] includ-

---

[1696] *Corneloup*, RCDIP 103 (2014), 438, 441; *Michael Müller*, EuZW 2015, 218, 223, 224; *Mankowski*, LMK 2015,

[1697] *Matthias Lehmann*, (2011) 7 JPrIL 527, 544.

[1698] *Matthias Lehmann*, (2011) 7 JPrIL 527, 545.

[1699] *Matthias Lehmann*, (2011) 7 JPrIL 527, 545.

[1700] *Calvo Caravaca/Carrascosa González*, Rev. Der. Mercantil 292 (2014), 51, 60.

[1701] See *Matthias Lehmann*, (2011) 7 JPrIL 527, 532.

[1702] See *Matthias Lehmann*, (2011) 7 JPrIL 527, 535.

[1703] See A-G *Vlas*, NJ 2015 Nr. 44 p. 539, 544.

[1704] See *Casio Computer Co. Ltd. v. Sayo* [2001] I.L.Pr. 694, 703 (C.A., per *Tuckey* L.J.); OLG Düsseldorf EuLF 2006, II-93, 94.

[1705] Tentatively so *Rudolf Kronhofer v. Marianne Maier*, (Case C-168/02) [2004] ECR I-6009, I-6031 para. 20; Cassaz. RDIPP 2011, 1103; Cassaz. RDIPP 2012, 432; *Calvo Caravaca/Carrascosa González*, Rev. Der. Mercantil 292 (2014), 51, 62–63. But cf. also *Harald Kolassa v. Barclays Bank plc* (Case C-375/13), ECLI: EU:C:2015:37 para. 55.

[1706] A-G *Vlas*, NJ 2015 Nr. 44 p. 539, 544; *Mankowski*, RIW 2005, 561, 562; *Mankowski*, LMK 2015, 367447; *Matthias Lehmann*, (2011) 7 JPrIL 527, 545; *von Hein*, BerDGfIR 2011, 369, 397–398.

[1707] To this avail A-G *Jääskinen*, Opinion of 29 November 2012 in Case C-228/11, ECLI:EU:C:2012:766 para. 32.

[1708] BGH WM 2010, 1590, 1593; BGH ZIP 2010, 2010, 2004, 2007; BGH WM 2010, 2214, 2217; BGH IPRspr. 2011 Nr. 245 pp. 629–630; BGH BKR 2012, 78 [32]; BGH WM 2014, 1614 [34]; OLG München IPRspr.

---

ing cases of intended churning.[1709] The fraudulent advisor is not hampered and can foresee and identify quite easily where the victim shall draw upon: He himself lures the victim into the internal transaction.[1710] That the transfer is completed and that the monies arrive untarnished does not alter matters.[1711] Hence, difficult issues of causality possibly obscuring and clouding the picture should not occur.[1712] That this would emasculate the basic rule and provide a charter for claimants to select a jurisdiction of their choice can hardly be said:[1713] The fraudster picks his victim, but has to take his victim as it is and where it has its accounts. The market where eventual placements are made, is irrelevant anyway.[1714]

333 Embezzlement is a different issue for it clearly affects moneys already received by, or entrusted to, the tortfeasor; there the account from which the unlawful fees are taken is the relevant one.[1715] These monies are already separated from the remainder of the victim's fortune when the relevant tort occurs. Insofar the manipulation was undeniably insofar successful as it secured the application of a law factually chosen by the tortfeasor. A further consequence might be that (2) is inapplicable at all where the tortfeasor established his client's account in the very State of his, the tortfeasor's, own domicile.[1716]

334 On the other hand a general rule that the victim is deemed to hold his fortune at the place where his habitual residence is located, can not be sanctioned, at least not as a strict rule.[1717] Modern times with the increasing number of cross-border investments and the ever growing numbers of migrants have enhanced the possibility and likelihood that there are different accounts in different states. A cautious approach phrased in general terms could resort to the place where the money was first abstracted from the victim.[1718] However, a rebuttable presumption that the victim's fortune is to be regarded as located at the victim's habitual residence can serve as a useful line of last resort. The presumption is rather weak but helps to answer the case in which no other solution is reasonably available. Given the alternative,

---

2009 Nr. 200 p. 516; *Girsberger*, AJP 2000, 177; *Schwander*, SZIER 2000, 354, 355 *et seq.*; *Junker*, ZZP Int. 9 (2004), 200, 206; *Mankowski*, RIW 2005, 561, 562; *Mankowski*, EWiR Art. 5 LugÜ 1/09, 215, 216; *Mankowski*, in: Gerner-Beuerle/Pietrancosta/Mankowski/Lee Neumann, RTDF 2011, 66, 75; *Rolf Wagner/Gess*, NJW 2009, 3481, 3484; *Leible*, in: Rauscher, Art. 5 note 86b; *Kiesselbach*, [2011] JIBFL 25, 27; *von Hein*, LMK 2010, 308395; *von Hein*, EuZW 2011, 369, 371; *von Hein*, BerDGfIR 2011, 369, 397–398.

[1709] LG Regensburg WM 2009, 847; *Mankowski*,LMK 2015,

[1710] BGH WM 2010, 1590, 1593; *Muir Watt*, RCDIP 94 (2005), 330, 334. Not properly recognised by *Rudolf Kronhofer v. Marianne Maier*, (Case C-168/02) [2004] ECR I-6009, I-6031 para. 20.

[1711] But cf. OLG München WM 2010, 1463, 1466.

[1712] But cf. generally *Muir Watt*, RCDIP 94 (2005), 330, 332 *et seq.*

[1713] *Contra Sunderland Marine Mutual Insurance Co. Ltd. v. Wiseman (The "Seaward Quest")*, [2007] EWHC 1460 (Comm), [2007] 2 Lloyd's Rep. 308, 313 (Q.B.D., *Langley* J.).

[1714] *Pietrancosta*, in: Gerner-Beuerle/Pietrancosta/Mankowski/Lee Neumann, RTDF 2011, 66, 73.

[1715] BGH WM 2010, 1590, 1593; BGH ZIP 2010, 2010, 2004, 2007; BGH WM 2010, 2214, 2217; OLG Stuttgart NJW-RR 1999, 318; *Mankowski*, EWiR Art. 5 LugÜ 1/09, 215, 216; *Rolf Wagner/Gess*, NJW 2009, 3481, 3482; *von Hein*, BerDGfIR 2011, 369, 397–398; *Matthias Lehmann*, (2011) 7 JPrIL 527, 544; *Engert/Groh*, IPRax 2011, 458, 463–464; *Peter Huber*, IPRax 2015, 403, 404–405.

[1716] *Mankowski*, EWiR Art. 5 LugÜ 1/09, 215, 216.

[1717] See only OGH ÖJZ 2005, 271, 272.

[1718] *Casio Computer Co. Ltd. v. Sayo* [2001] I.L:Pr. 694, 703 (C.A., per *Tuckey* L.J.); see also *Mäsch*, IPRax 2005, 509, 515.

namely to deprive the victim of an opportunity to invoke the second option ordinarily granted under (2), the presumption mirrors the remaining sympathy for the victim. As a matter of fact it is backed by the observation that the majority of people hold at least their main account at their home place. Where the money is eventually spent should not weigh too heavily.[1719] Furthermore, as a subsidiary solution recourse might be held to the victim's habitual residence where economic loss can be proven mathematically or statistically.[1720] Any *horror fori actoris* should not be overdone. If no other solution is convincing in the concrete case the victim's habitual residence is the relatively best offer among the bad ones particularly so if the main alternative was to hold the second prong of (2) inapplicable.

There is a difference between a loss of money or goods which the victim owned before the   **335** tort, and not receiving a sum due.[1721] In the latter case the loss is sustained where the non-receipt is staged, i.e. where the money should have been received.[1722] If the victim designated a certain account it is the place where this particular account is held. A major *caveat* applies, though: If the money is due to a contract the secondary claim for damages is also in contract and not in tort rendering (2) inapplicable altogether.

If an incorrect rating entices investors to invest monies and funds in a certain asset this will   **336** happen at the market where the victims acquire the said asset. The devaluation and paying a higher price than justified since they rely on the rating, takes place at the respective exchange.[1723] This might not display strong connections and might be a trifle fortuitous, though.[1724]

Securities suffer the decisive loss in value at the place where the account is held with which   **337** they (or the representing jumbo certificates, *Globalurkunden)*[1725] are registered.[1726] This place might differ from the investor's habitual residence.[1727] The loss in value is equivalent to a loss of substance.[1728] It has been argued though that the relevant loss occurs with the loss

---

[1719] But cf. *Alfred Dunhill Ltd. v. Diffusion Internationale de Maroquinerie de Prestige SARL* [2002] 1 All ER (Comm) 950, 962 (Q.B.D., Judge *Kenneth Rokison* Q.C.).

[1720] See *Matthias Lehmann*, (2011) 7 JPrIL 527, 537.

[1721] *Dolphin Maritime & Aviation Services Ltd. v. Sveriges Angartyggs Assurans Forening* [2009] EWHC 716 (Comm), [2010] 1 All ER (Comm) 473, 491 [90] (Q.B.D., *Christopher Clarke* J.); *AMT Futures Ltd. v. Marzillier, Dr. Meier & Dr. Guntner Rechtsanwaltsgesellschaft mbH* [2014] EWHC 1085 (Comm), [2015] 2 WLR 187 [34] (Q.B.D., *Popplewell* J.).

[1722] *Dolphin Maritime & Aviation Services Ltd. v. Sveriges Angartyggs Assurans Forening* [2009] EWHC 716 (Comm), [2010] 1 All ER (Comm) 473, 492 [90] (Q.B.D., *Christopher Clarke* J.); *AMT Futures Ltd. v. Marzillier, Dr. Meier & Dr. Guntner Rechtsanwaltsgesellschaft mbH* [2014] EWHC 1085 (Comm), [2015] 2 WLR 187 [34] (Q.B.D., *Popplewell* J.).

[1723] Cassaz. RDIPP 2013, 431, 432–433; see also *Risso*, Dir. comm. int. 2013, 849, 857–859.

[1724] *Nisi*, RDIPP 2013, 385, 411.

[1725] See *Matthias Lehmann*, (2011) 7 JPrIL 527, 533.

[1726] Cass. RCDIP 103 (2014), 432, 434 with note *Corneloup*; *Matthias Lehmann*, (2011) 7 JPrIL 527, 543. Contra *Calvo Caravaca/Carrascosa González*, Rev. Der. Mercantil 292 (2014), 51, 61–62.

[1727] *Corneloup*, RCDIP 103 (2014), 438, 441.

[1728] *Berlioz*, Rev. jur. comm. 2014, 266, 271.

in value of the company into which the investment was made and that the loss in value of the securities would be only an indirect and consequential damage.[1729]

338 Loss stemming from an unfavourable contract is at its core financial loss. It might be generated by the contract, but the contract is only the means causing the loss and thus the cause for the loss, but not the loss *per se*. Consequentially, one should not try to localise the contract or resort to the place where the contract was concluded, or to the place where the contract was performed.[1730] Even where investments on financial markets are at stake, the places of negotiation or acquisition should not become dominant.[1731]

339 An approach relying on the so called *Handlungswirkungsort* has gained some support.[1732] But this attaches only a tag and a label which in turn needs concretisation. Furthermore, it is prone to confuse terminology. As there ought to be causality between the activity causing the damage and the damage every effect is caused by an activity.

ee) Damage to goods on transport (res in transitu)

340 Damage to goods *in transitu*, i.e. in a transport operation onboard a ship or aircraft raises the problem as to locating the place where the goods were damaged. Particularly in the age of containers it can become practically impossible to identify and even more to prove the place where the goods were actually damaged. Accordingly, some more normative solutions must provide for the tie-breaker otherwise the consignee would be deprived of the benefits of (2). The ECJ has ruled out both the place of actual final delivery and the place where the damage to the goods was finally ascertained.[1733] Firstly, the ECJ sensed some danger in an exaggerated *forum actoris*.[1734] Secondly, the place of final delivery was held to be subject to change during the voyage and thus did not fulfil the necessary criteria for foreseeability to protect the prospective perpetrator.[1735] This holds even truer for the place where the victim finally discovered the damage.[1736]

341 Instead the ECJ championed the place where the carrier was to deliver the goods.[1737] This in substance is a fictitious[1738] approach that forces recourse to contractual documents and can

---

[1729] *Berlioz*, Rev. jur. comm. 2014, 266, 271.

[1730] But cf. *Matthias Lehmann*, (2011) 7 JPrIL 527, 548; *Thiede/Florian Sommer*, ÖBA 2015, 175, 180.

[1731] *Calvo Caravaca/Carrascosa González*, Rev. Der. Mercantil 292 (2014), 51, 61. But cf. *Sánchez Fernández*, AEDIPr 2011, 335; *Sánchez Fernández*, REDI 2013-1, 304; *Matthias Lehmann*, IPRax 2012, 399; *Matthias Lehmann*, RCDIP 101 (2012), 485.

[1732] BGH WM 2014, 1614 [35]; *Stefan Huber*, IPRax 2009, 134, 137; *ten Wolde/Knot/Matthias Weller*, in: unalex Kommentar Art. 5 Nr. 3 note 50.

[1733] *Réunion europénne SA v. Spliethoff's Bevrachtingskantoor BV and Master of the vessel "Alblasgracht 002"*, (Case C-51/97) [1998] ECR I-6511, I-6546 para. 34.

[1734] *Réunion europénne SA v. Spliethoff's Bevrachtingskantoor BV and Master of the vessel "Alblasgracht 002"*, (Case C-51/97) [1998] ECR I-6511, I-6546 para. 34.

[1735] *Réunion europénne SA v. Spliethoff's Bevrachtingskantoor BV and Master of the vessel "Alblasgracht 002"*, (Case C-51/97) [1998] ECR I-6511, I-6546 para. 34; *Vlas*, NILR 2002, 118, 119 *et seq.*

[1736] *Réunion europénne SA v. Spliethoff's Bevrachtingskantoor BV and Master of the vessel "Alblasgracht 002"*, (Case C-51/97) [1998] ECR I-6511, I-6546 para. 34; Cass. ETL 1999, 675; Hof 's-Hertogenbosch NIPR 2000 Nr. 210 p. 348; *Kropholler/von Hein* Art. 5 note 89; *Hausmann/Obergfell*, in: Fezer, UWG (2nd ed. 2010), Einl. I note 401; *ten Wolde/Kirsten C. Henckel*, Int. J. Proced. L. 3 (2013), 195, 218.

lead to a split if the actual carrier is responsible only for one part of a combined transport, in that his liability terminates at the place where he hands over the goods to the next actual carrier.[1739] That the goods transported are not unpacked at the place of delivery does not provide a counter-argument[1740] since this would be tantamount to switching back to the place where the damage was discovered, the latter being unsustainable from the angle of foreseeability for the carrier. That in practice the place of delivery will in most instances coincide with the place where the damages was discovered,[1741] is fortuitous.[1742]

ff) Single torts

Once again one must look at each class of torts separately in order to properly identify the place where the relevant damage was sustained.[1743] If the relevant damage can be equalled with physical or bodily harm and injury, such damage can be located quite easily, namely where the victim was hurt, i.e. where the victim's body was injured. Neither the places where consequential damages is discovered or unearthed later-on are relevant, nor the places from which the victim must draw on his assets in order to cover the ensuing medical costs. Where the victim was injured by the hit, the bullet, the accident or else, is the only material place. For the purpose of ascertaining jurisdiction, it does not matter whether the tortfeasor acted intentionally or negligently or without personal fault. Medical maltreatment affects the victim's health wherever its consequences hit the victim. If a doctor does not provide proper information and a prescribed medicine or drug proves detrimental, the place where the harmful event occurred primarily is the one where that medicine or drug was administered.[1744] Where the tort relates to identifiable single assets (e.g. a car or estate) the relevant place is the place where this asset was located at the time of the affliction.[1745]

(1) Negligent misstatements, fraud or misrepresentation, in particular in a financial market context

In the event of negligent misstatements the place of receipt and reliance becomes material.[1746] However, if the place of mere receipt differs from the place where the victim acted upon the misstatement to the detriment of his own fortune, the place of the latter action should prevail.[1747] The simple receipt of the misstatement does not automatically harm the potential victim's assets. Only the victim's action in reliance on the misstatement triggers off

342

343

[1737] *Réunion europénne SA v. Spliethoff's Bevrachtingskantoor BV and Master of the vessel "Alblasgracht 002"*, (Case C-51/97) [1998] ECR I-6511, I-6546 para. 35.

[1738] *van Haersolte-van Hof*, NIPR 2000, 386, 389.

[1739] See *Harald Koch*, IPRax 2000, 186, 188.

[1740] *Contra Gaudemet-Tallon*, RCDIP 88 (1999), 331, 337 *et seq.*; *Vlas*, NILR 2002, 118, 120.

[1741] *de Meij*, TVR 1999, 125, 129 *et seq.*; *Vlas*, NJ 2000 Nr. 156.

[1742] See *van Haersolte-van Hof*, NIPR 2000, 386, 389.

[1743] See only *Muir Watt*, RCDIP 94 (2005), 330, 333 *et seq.*

[1744] BGHZ 176, 342 = BGH NJW 2008, 3244; OLG Karlsruhe OLGR Karlsruhe/Stuttgart 2007, 458; *Spickhoff*, in: FS Gerda Müller (2009), p. 287, 294; *Spickhoff*, IPRax 2009, 128, 129; *Kropholler/von Hein*, Art. 5 note 83 f.

[1745] See as an example Vzngr. Rb. Breda NIPR 2007 Nr. 38.

[1746] *Domicrest Ltd. v. Swiss Bank Corporation* [1999] QB 548, 567 (Q.B.D., *Rix* J.) and also, albeit not followed *Minster Investments Ltd. v. Hyundai Precision and Industry Co. Ltd.* [1988] 2 Lloyd's Rep. 621 (Q.B.D., *Steyn* J.).

[1747] *Girsberger*, in: Liber amicorum Kurt Siehr (2000), p. 219, 228 *et seq.*; *Spindler*, IPRax 2001, 153, 155;

the consequences. Unlike defamation, libel and slander, misstatements are not concerned with the protection of personal values. The different direction of protection asks for a different treatment as to the material place.[1748]

344 Fraud and misrepresentation inflict their damage at the place where they trigger off financial transactions on the victim's side.[1749] If a statement, allegedly fraudulent or involving misrepresentation, is made to the victim in one place, but the victim acts on this statement in another place (e.g. by arranging credit facilities), the latter place is the relevant one.[1750] If the place where the detrimental decision was made by the victim does not coincide with the location of any assets with which the victim passes over as a result of his decision, the latter location should prevail.[1751] The place of the decision can be fortuitous and could all too easily be subject to carefully and cunningly planned manipulation by the tortfeasor.[1752] The protection is granted to the assets and the fortune, whereas protection of the free will of the person is only instrumental and a kind of vehicle.

(2) Strikes or industrial action

345 Financial loss caused by strike, industrial action or sympathy actions by trade unions ordinarily arise at the place where the respective enterprise is established.[1753] That single assets of this enterprise are the primary objects of the strike etc. should not be held decisive since these assets are only instrumentalised whereas the main object is to detrimentally affect the fortune and the earnings of the enterprise.[1754] Yet if a specific plant or office is targeted the loss is felt there primarily.[1755] If the financial loss consisted from the withdrawal of one ship from its normal route and the hire of another ship to serve the same route, the damage should not be said to have occurred onboard the first ship.[1756] Art. 9 Rome II Regulation does not provide additional guidance for identifying the place where the relevant damage was sustained as it deliberately refrains from seizing upon this place as a connecting factor.

(3) Infringement of personality rights, particularly defamation, libel or slander

(a) In general

346 If the tort does harm to the victim's reputation, that reputation needs to be localised.[1757]

---

comp. Domicrest Ltd. v. Swiss Bank Corporation [1999] QB 548, 567 (Q.B.D., *Rix* J.); *Layton/Mercer* para. 15.095.

[1748] See *Spindler*, IPRax 2001, 153, 155.

[1749] *Supra* Art. 5 note 239 (*Mankowski*).

[1750] *Raiffeisen Zentralbank v. Tranos* [2001] I.L.Pr. 85 (Q.B.D., *Longmore* J.); see also London Helicopters Ltd. v. Helportugal LDA-INAC [2006] 1 All ER (Comm) 595, 604 (Q.B.D., *Simon* J.).

[1751] *Girsberger*, in: Liber amicorum Kurt Siehr (2000), p. 219, 229 *et seq.*

[1752] *Girsberger*, in: Liber amicorum Kurt Siehr (2000), p. 219, 229 *et seq.*

[1753] See Danmarks Rederiforeniging, acting on behalf of DFDS Torline AS v. LO Landsorganisationen i Sverige, acting on behalf of SEKO Sjöfolk Facket for Service och Kommunikation, (Case C-18/02) [2004] ECR I-1417, I-1457 para. 43; *Palao Moreno*, REDI 2004, 848, 852.

[1754] *Mankowski*, RIW 2004, 481, 495.

[1755] *Heinze*, RabelsZ 73 (2009), 770, 775 *et seq.*; *Kropholler/von Hein*, Art. 5 note 86a.

[1756] But cf. *Danmarks Rederiforeniging, acting on behalf of DFDS Torline AS v. LO Landsorganisationen i Sverige, acting on behalf of SEKO Sjöfolk Facket for Service och Kommunikation,* (Case C-18/02) [2004] ECR I-1417, I-1457 paras. 44 *et seq.*

Where a person is not known, this person does not have a reputation. It is not the place of the publication of a defamatory or libellous statement which qualifies as the place where the damage was sustained,[1758] but the place where the victim's reputation allegedly is ruined. In the event of defamatory letters sent to individual recipients, the place(s) where these letters are received and read by the addressees will regularly coincide with that latter place.[1759] A publication *via* mass media inflicts its harm to the victim's reputation where it reaches its audience, viewers or readers (as the case may be) if the victim has a defendable reputation there.[1760] The damage to reputation is not to be localised automatically at the victim's domicile.[1761] Where the victim enjoys goodwill and the detrimental affect to their reputation is felt locally, the damage occurs there.[1762]

Insofar as torts are committed by means of mass media or publication, a restriction on **347** jurisdiction is required to strike the right balance. Therefore a mere spill-over, i.e. an accidental distribution of a publication in a country where it is not intended to be distributed, ought to be ruled out.[1763] The single copy of a Finnish newspaper taken by a traveller from his plane and imported into his home country Malta does not trigger off the jurisdiction of the Maltese courts. Unlike the search for the applicable law which is politically contaminated[1764] – as evidenced by the exclusion in Art. 1 (2) (g) Rome II Regulation – the search for jurisdiction is not burdened with striking the difficult balance between protecting potential victims on the one hand and the freedom of speech and the freedom of the press on the other hand.

(b) In particular via the Internet

Torts committed *via* the Internet do not enjoy specific rules on jurisdiction tailor-made to **348** their scope. In particular, the E-Commerce-Directive[1765] does not contain any such rules nor alterations of the rules of the Brussels I Regulation including (2); insofar Art. 1 (4) E-Com-

---

[1757] E.g. *Reed/T.P. Kennedy*, [1996] LMCLQ 108, 119 *et seq.*

[1758] But cf. CA Paris D. 1999 I.R. 270; Vzngr. Rb. Almelo NIPR 2005 Nr. 52 p. 94.

[1759] See Cassaz. Foro it. 2006 col. 3388, 3398 = RDIPP 2006, 1076, 1088; OLG Saarbrücken NJW-RR 2003, 176.

[1760] See only LG Köln IPRspr. 2010 Nr. 230 p. 580; *Bogdan*, in: Beater/Habermeier (eds.), Verletzungen von Persönlichkeitsrechten durch die Medien (2005), p. 138, 141.

[1761] OGH ÖJZ 2005, 111, 112.

[1762] *Modus Vivendi Ltd. v. Procter & Gamble, Inc.* [1996] F.S.R. 790, 802 (Ch.D., *Knox* J.); *Mecklermedia Corp. v. D.C. Congress GmbH* [1997] I.L.Pr. 629, 637 *et seq.* (Ch.D., *Jacob* J.).

[1763] BGH GRUR 2005, 431, 433 – Hotel Maritime; OLG München NJW-RR 1994, 190; OLG München IPRax 2009, 256, 257; *Coester-Waltjen*, in: FS Rolf A. Schütze (1999), p. 175, 183 *et seq.*

[1764] See in particular recently *Wallis*, Working Document on the Amendment of Regulation No. (EC) 864/2007 on the Law Applicable to Non-Contractual Obligations of June 13, 2010, PE443.025v01-00; Comparative Study on the Situation in the 27 Member States As Regards the Law Applicable to Non-Contractual Obligations Arising Out of Violations of Privacy and Rights Relating to Personality, JLS/ 2007/ C4/028 and the online symposion on conflict-of-laws.net http://conflictoflaws.net/2010/rome-ii-and-defamation-online-symposium with contributions by *von Hein, Hartley, Dickinson, Boskovic, Heiderhoff, Magallón, Perreau-Saussine, Mills Wade, Wallis.*

[1765] Directive 2000/31/EC of the European Parliament and of the Council of 8 June 2000 on certain legal aspects of information society service, in particular electronic commerce, in the Internal Market (Directive on electronic commerce), OJ 2000 L 178/1.

---

merce-Directive can be seized at its word and taken at face value.[1766] Infringement of trademarks, patents or copyrights taking place over the Internet produces a violation of a protected right where it produces, but only its effects if the respective right is protected there. The World Intellectual Property Organisation (WIPO) has drafted some recommendations in this regard[1767] which can aptly be summarised as attempting to establish some kind of commercial effects doctrine.[1768] Yet caution should be applied since the WIPO Recommendation does by no means form anything like a binding rule, nor has it gained approval by courts yet.[1769] Generally, the same approach, but for the specialities of intellectual property law, should prevail as in matters of unfair commercial practices.[1770]

349 The mere accessibility of a website via the World Wide Web does not suffice.[1771] To establish jurisdiction at every place where a website could be accessed would not be compatible with the rationes underpinning the place where the damage occurred. Even possibilities of restricting access by means of geolocalising users willing to access lead to a different result.[1772] Neither would there be a particularly close connection, nor would there be a particularly

---

[1766] See only KG ZLR 2003, 604 with note *Meisterernst*; *Mankowski*, ZvglRWiss 100 (2001), 137, 175 *et seq.*

[1767] Standing Committee on Trademarks of the WIPO, Joint Recommendation Concerning the Protection of Marks and Other Industrial Property Rights in Signs on the Internet (2001), http://www.wipo.int/sct/en/documents/session_6/pdf/sct6_7p.pdf with explanatory remarks under http://www.wipo.int/sct/en/documents/session_6/pdf/sct6_with notesrev.pdf; re-printed i.a. in WRP 2001, 833; on these Recommendation see only *Bettinger*, WRP 2001, 789; *Kur*, GRUR Int. 2001, 861.

[1768] *Ohly*, JZ 2005, 738, 739.

[1769] *Mankowski*, CR 2005, 758, 762.

[1770] See *infra* Art. 7 notes 350 *et seq.* (*Mankowski*) and *Hye-Knudsen*, Marken-, Patent- und Urheberrechtsverletzungen im europäischen internationalen Zivilprozessrecht (2005) pp. 104 *et seq.*

[1771] A-G *Cruz Villalón*, Opinion of 16 February 2012 in Case C-523/10, ECLI:EU:C:2012:90 para. 25; A-G *Jääskinen*, Opinion of 13 June 2013 in Case C-170/12 para. 68; BGH GRUR 2005, 431, 432 – Hotel Maritime; BGH GRUR Int. 2006, 605, 606 *et seq.*; BGH RIW 2010, 67 = EuZW 2010, 313; BGHZ 184, 313 = NJW 2010, 1752; BGH GRUR 2012, 621 [34] – OSCAR; Cass. Bull. Cib. 2010 IV n° 66 = D. 2010, 1183 with note *Lardeux*; Cass D. 2011, 806 obs. *Durrande* = RTDcom 2011, 329 obs. *Azéma* = RTDcom 2013, 404 obs. *Bouloc*; Cass. D. 2011, 2363 obs. *Larrieu/Le Stanc/Tréfigny-Goy* = D. 2011, 2434 obs. *D'Avout/Bollée* = D. 2012, 1228 obs. *Gaudemet-Tallon/Jault-Seseke*; Cass. Clunet 139 (2012), 991, 992; Cass. D. 203, 1503 obs. *Jault-Seseke* = D. 2013, 2331 obs. *d'Avout/Bollée* = D. 2013, 2836 obs. *Sirinelli*; Hof Brussels TBH 2005, 694; OLG München IPRax 2009, 256, 257; CA Paris Clunet 139 (2012), 992, 994; LG Köln IPRspr. 2010 Nr. 230 p. 579–580; *Mankowski*, CR 2002, 450 *et seq.*; *Mankowski*, MMR 2002, 817 *et seq.*; *Mankowski*, GRUR Int. 2006, 609; *Mourre/Lahlou*, RDAI 2005, 509, 523; *Joubert*, (2009) 58 ICLQ 476, 477 *et seq.*; *Sujecki*, K&R 2011, 315, 317; *Robak*, GRUR-Prax 2011, 257, 259; *Lederer*, K&R 2011, 791, 792; *Brand*, NJW 2012, 127, 129–130; *Pironon*, Clunet 139 (2012), 996, 998 *et seq.*; *Picht*, GRUR Int 2013, 19, 23; *Markus Köhler*, WRP 2013, 1130, 1132; *Reymond*, Yb. PIL 14 (2012/13), 205, 217–221. *Contra* Pez Hejduk v. EnergieAgentur.NRW GmbH (Case C-441/13), ECLI:EU:C:2015:28 para. 34; Cass. RCDIP 93 (2004), 632 with note *Cachard* = Clunet 131 (2004), 872 with note *André Huet* = D. 2004, 276 with note *Manara* = JCP 2004 II 10055 note *Chabert*; OLG München NJW 2002, 611 – literaturhaus.de; OLG Karlsruhe MMR 2002, 814, 815 – intel; OLG Hamburg MMR 2002, 822, 823 – hotel-maritime.dk; CA Paris Clunet 131 (2004), 492 with note *Bergé*; TGI Nanterre JCP, éd. E, 1999, 954 with note *Vivant/Le Stanc*; *Spindler*, ZUM 1996, 533, 562; *Schack*, MMR 2000, 135, 138 *et seq.*; *André Huet*, Clunet 131 (2004), 873, 878; *Azzi*, D. 2014, 411, 414; *McGuire*, ZEuP 2014, 160, 168.

[1772] *Arenas García*, AEDIPr 2013, 1024, 1025. But cf. *Reymond*, Yb. PIL 14 (2012/13), 205, 227–237.

privileged access to evidence. On-site inspection does not matter[1773] in the age of screen shots and could not reliably reveal any status of the website at the relevant point of time in the past. Witnesses are available rather there where the alleged victim lives, is known or carries out activities, and it would be fortuitous and accidental if witnesses were found elsewhere.[1774]

Hence, in addition to accessibility it is at least required that the website provider purpose- **350** fully availed and directed his website to the country in question and its market.[1775] "Foca- lisation"[1776] and purposeful availment provide the necessary previsibility[1777] and avoid es- tablishing a virtually union-wide responsibility. That "focalisation" ist not expressly men- tioned in the wording of (2) and that (2) does – unlike Art. 17 (1) (c) – not require a targeted or directed activity does not amount to an insuperable obstacle.[1778] The principle of ubiquity and thus the most fundamental understanding of (2) does not appear in the wording, either. "Focalisation" is not an approach confined to the realm of contracts, but ought to be established as a general approach, also extending to torts, without an *argumentum e contra- rio* to be drawn from Art. 17 (1) (c).[1779] At least it provides an appropriate approach in all fields of economic activity striving for financial gain and directed at the penetration of markets.[1780] It provides for a restrictive criterion closing the floodgates for any misuse of (7), for instance by excessive negative declaratory actions.[1781] Its subjective elements and its implied recourse to the potential perpetrator's intentions are acceptable if compared to the structure of criminal rules of penal law.[1782]

[1773] *Markus Köhler*, WRP 2013, 1130, 1132.

[1774] *Markus Köhler*, WRP 2013, 1130, 1132.

[1775] A-G *Jääskinen*, Opinion of 13 June 2013 in Case C-170/12 para. 67; BGH GRUR 2005, 431, 432 – Hotel Maritime; BGH GRUR 2006, 513, 514; BGH GRUR 2007, 884, 886; KG NJW 1997, 3321; OLG Düsseldorf AfP 2009, 159 = IPRspr. 2008 Nr. 115; OLG München IPRspr. 2009 Nr. 203; OLG Köln IPRspr. 2011 Nr. 222a p. 583; OLG München WRP 2012, 850; *Mankowski*, MMR 2002, 817, 818; *Mankowski*, GRUR Int. 2006, 609, 610; *Kurtz*, IPRax 2004, 107; *Cachard*, RCDIP 93 (2004), 634, 641–644; *Spindler*, AfP 2012, 114, 117; see also BGH GRUR 2005, 431, 432– Hotel Maritime= WRP 2005, 493, 494 = JZ 2005, 736 with note *Ohly*.

[1776] The phrase is coined, and the concept of "focalisation" is developed, by *Cachard*, La régulation interna- tionale du marché électronique (2002) pp. 193–217 et passim. For an elaborate criticism see *Pironon*, Clunet 138 (2011), 915.

[1777] Conversely, *Garber*, jusIT 2011, 129; *Garber*, ÖBl 2014, 100, 106; *Slonina*, ecolex 2012, 485 *et seq.*; *Azzi*, D. 2014, 411, 414 allege it to generate uncertainty.

[1778] See A-G *Jääskinen*, Opinion of 13 June 2013 in Case C-170/12, ECLI:EU:C:2013:400 paras. 61–66. Contra Peter Pinckney v. KDG Mediatech AG (Case C-170/12), ECLI:EU:C:2013:635 paras. 41–42; A-G *Cruz Villalón*, Opinion of 29 March 2011 in Joined Cases C-509/09 and C-161/10, [2011] ECR I-10272 para. 62; *Azzi*, D. 2014, 411, 414; *Pollaud-Dulian*, RTDcom 2013, 731, 733–734.

[1779] *Contra Pollaud-Dulian*, RTDcom 2013, 731, 736.

[1780] A-G *Cruz Villalón*, Opinion in Case C-441/13 of 11 September 2014 para. 31.

[1781] *Banholzer* p. 69.

[1782] *Banholzer* p. 68.

351 Unfortunately, the ECJ has lowered the threshold in *eDate*,[1783] *Wintersteiger*,[1784] *Pinckney*[1785] and *Hejduk*[1786] plus – in another area of the law – in *Football Dataco*.[1787] This oversteps even the outer borders of the *rationale* underpinning (2).[1788] Previsibility suffers badly[1789] (unless one is prepared to argue cynically that the alleged tortfeasor can forecast that he could be sued virtually everywhere at the victim's liberty[1790]). The specific context of IP rights in the close vicinity of Art. 24 (4) in particular in the light of the (misconceived) judgment in *GAT v. LuK*[1791] and its codification in Art. 24 (4) subpara. 1 might cure the worst excesses of forum shopping,[1792] but only in that context.

352 The Top Level Domain (TLD) could provide an indication that the website aims at certain countries.[1793] It ceases to extend a helpful hand in the event of a generic TLD like.com, .org or.eur.[1794] In particular, it cannot provide an indication to the negative that the website might not aim at other countries than the one displayed by the TLD. This would entice opportunistic behaviour like operating under TLDs like .tv (for Tuvalu) or.tk (for Tokelaw) whilst penetrating the market of a different country.[1795]

353 The language used might be an important indication[1796] but not the sole and *per se* decisive factor.[1797] For instance, German might attract users resident in Austria and Germany[1798] (or the other way round, users resident in Germany are attracted by a website entertained by a Swiss enterprise[1799]). There might be supporting factors adding weight like the name of the

---

[1783] *eDate Advertising GmbH v. X; Olivier and Robert Martinez v. MGN Ltd.*, (Joined Cases C-509/09 and C-161/10) [2011] ECR I-10269 para. 44.

[1784] *Wintersteiger AG v. Products 4U Sondermaschinenbau* (Case C-523/10), ECLI:EU:C:2012:220 para. 21–29.

[1785] *Peter Pinckney v. KDG Mediatech AG* (Case C-170/12), ECLI:EU:C:2013:635 para. 42. Duly followed by Cass. JurisData n° 2014-000774; *Marie-Élodie Ancel*, JCP G 2014, 188.

[1786] *Pez Hejduk v. EnergieAgentur.NRW GmbH* (Case C-441/13), ECLI:EU:C:2015:28 para. 32–33.

[1787] *Football Dataco Ltd. v. Sportradar GmbH* (Case C-173/11), nyr. paras. 35, 37. Commented upon by *Costes*, Dr. imm. 2012 n° 87 p. 22; *Varet*, Dr. imm. 2012 n° 88 p. 11; *Treppoz*, RTDeur 2012, 947; *Cohen Jehoram*, BIE 2013, 26; *Jault-Seseke*, D. 2013, 1503; *Josel Smith/Montagnan*, [2013] EIPR 111; *d'Avout/ Bollée*, D. 2013, 2293; *Larrieu/Le Stanc/Tréfigny*, D. 2013, 2487; *Pollaud-Dulian*, RTDcom 2013, 309; *García Mirete*, AEDIPr 2012, 970.

[1788] *Picht*, GRUR Int 2013, 19, 23.

[1789] *Lederer*, K&R 2011, 791, 792; *Picht*, GRUR Int 2013, 19, 23.

[1790] *Joel Smith/Leriche*, [2014] EIPR 137, 138 consequentially herald and welcome *Pinckney* as good news for copyright owners which are no longer urged upon to show that a website's acitivity is targeted at internet users in a certain forum State. Conversely, A-G *Cruz Villalón*, Opinion in Case C-441/13 of 11 September 2014 paras. 28–32 tries to find a way around *Pinckney* wherever feasible.

[1791] *GAT v. LuK* (C-4/03), [2006] ECR I-6509.

[1792] *McGuire*, ZEuP 2014, 160, 169.

[1793] See only *Reymond*, Yb. PIL 14 (2012/13), 205, 225–227.

[1794] *McGuire*, ZEuP 2014, 160, 167.

[1795] *McGuire*, ZEuP 2014, 160, 167.

[1796] See only Cass. Clunet 137 (2010), 870, 871 *et seq.* = D. 2010, 1183 with note *Lardeux*; LG Köln MMR 2007, 610; *Reymond*, Yb. PIL 14 (2012/13), 205, 223–224.

[1797] See only *Treppoz*, RCDIP 97 (2008), 332, 336; *Joubert*, (2009) 58 ICLQ 476, 483.

[1798] OLG München IPRspr. 2009 Nr. 203; OLG München WRP 2012, 850.

perpetrator (e.g. German language by a name commencing with "Deutsche", "Deutscher" or "Deutsches").[1800]

On the other hand, language might be used as a limiting factor. But English is quite inap-   **354**
propriate in this vein for safely excluding focalisation on non English speaking countries.[1801]
There is an ever growing number of people who have English not as their native language
but as their second language or at least as a further language.[1802] It might not constitute the
majority of the population in the non English speaking countries, but it is a relevant minority, and a commercially very interesting minority at that since it consists of more educated
people who have acquired the knowledge of a further language beyond their native tongue.
To those who already master English as their second language those might be added who are
actually learning English[1803] (whereas mere willingness and intentions to learn English in the
future do not qualify). Furthermore, English has permeated today's live in the Western
world. English has become the almost universal language of advertising and the more so
of advertising slogans even in genuinely domestic campaigns for instance in Germany. In
particular, English is *the* language of the Internet. Online users are – if playing with words
might be permitted for a second – used to read English. If users from a certain country are
specifically invited to submit comments in a separate column of the website, this carries
some weight, too.[1804] English used with a certain website is not excluding if a menu offers the
choice between different language versions; in this regard the intended range of the other
languages adds to the range of the English version, and the ensemble so constituted matters.[1805]

Yet it should be recalled and reiterated time and again that "focalisation" alone does not   **355**
suffice for the purposes of the second limb of (2), but that a relevant damage is required to
establish jurisdiction under the second limb of (2).[1806] (2) is not content with a professional
activity being directed at a certain State.[1807] Focalisation not accompanied by, and not generating, any damage would not do.

Other factors in a meaningful targeting test might comprise page views, search engine   **356**
ranking and visibility, the character of the website, the display of paid advertisements aiming
at a certain market, and the conduct and direction of offline activity on the perpetrator's
side.[1808] To rely on page views might come as close to actual metric of a multistate contribu-

---

[1799] LG Köln IPRspr. 2010 Nr. 222 p. 565.

[1800] OLG Köln MMR 2013, 403.

[1801] See BGH NJW 2014, 2504 = GRUR 2014, 601 – Englischsprachige Pressemitteilung. *Contra* OLG
Frankfurt GRUR-RR 2012, 392.

[1802] *Banholzer* p. 74.

[1803] *Banholzer* p. 73.

[1804] Cass. Clunet 137 (2010), 870, 871 *et seq.* = D. 2010, 1183 with note *Lardeux.*

[1805] BGH NJW 2014, 2504 = GRUR 2014, 601 – Englischsprachige Pressemitteilung (English press release);
Mankowski, EWiR 2014, 403, 404.

[1806] *Usunier*, Clunet 137 (2010), 874, 875 *et seq.*

[1807] See Peter Pinckney v. KDG Mediatech AG (Case C-170/12), ECLI:EU:C:2013:635 para. 42 and also Pez
Hejduk v. EnergieAgentur.NRW GmbH (Case C-441/13), ECLI:EU:C:2015:28 para. 32.

[1808] See in more detail *Reymond*, Yb. PIL 14 (2012/13), 205, 222–225, 237–240.

tion as it gets[1809] – if one succeeds in it. But this criterion creates severe problems of availability and correctness since the respective data are in the perpetrator's possession and website usage statistics are diverse in both reliability and implementation.[1810] Theoretically meta-tag coverage might be an alternative,[1811] but practically it suffers from the lacking availability of the necessary data to the victim, too.

357 For instance, it has been taken as a factor that calls for personal interviews were invited; this was believed to indicate that the website at stake at least addressed such public as was located in a range which made travelling for like interviews feasible.[1812] If a menu of phone or fax numbers with national pre-dial codes is offered this relays that the website intends to attract traffic and interest from at least the countries covered by the respective national codes. If only a single national code aims at identifying the advertising enterprise and at complying with requirements of European e-commerce or distance selling rules is displayed this can not be taken as a positive indication that calls from abroad are invited.[1813]

358 A rather wide shot would be to have a look at the use of geolocation technologies like GPS, too.[1814] Care must be taken that purposeful availment does not degenerate to a catch-all notion little if any better than mere accessibility. But to replace it with commercial effect[1815] would not fit for torts which do not have an underlying economic purpose. The splinter of truth is that commercial effect can serve as an indication of purposeful availment for torts which do have an economic background. Geolocation services have become more reliable and advanced by the time.[1816] Constant enhancement of Internet Protocols (for instance the step from IPv4 to IPv6) might add to the development.[1817] Geolocation services might be circumvented (for instance by dial-up techniques using another's IP address), but countermeasures are aiming to catch up.[1818] Java-applets or analysing answers with the help of HTTP-refreshments are a first step.[1819] The main practical argument against geolocation technologies might be the organisational and financial effort necessary to implement them.[1820]

359 Generally, it appears unadvisable to distinguish between so-called active, interactive and so-called passive websites.[1821] For the purposes of (2) either notion does not carry relevance since such (inter)activity would relate to the recipient's activity whereas the original website

---

[1809] *Reymond*, Yb. PIL 14 (2012/13), 205, 222.

[1810] *Reymond*, Yb. PIL 14 (2012/13), 205, 222 with reference to *Clifton*, Advanced Web Metrics with Google Analytics (2012) pp. 27–52.

[1811] *Banholzer* pp. 100–101.

[1812] OLG München WRP 2012, 850, 851.

[1813] OLG München WRP 2012, 850, 852.

[1814] In favour of such an approach *Reymond*, Yb. PIL 14 (2012/13), 205, 227–237.

[1815] As proposed by *Markus Köhler*, WRP 2013, 1130, 1136.

[1816] *Banholzer* pp. 90–92.

[1817] *Banholzer* pp. 96–98.

[1818] *Banholzer* pp. 92–93.

[1819] *Banholzer* p. 93.

[1820] *Banholzer* pp. 93–94.

[1821] *André Huet*, Clunet 131 (2004), 873, 879; *Malaurie-Vignal*, CCC 2011 n° 59 p. 21; *Reymond*, Yb. PIL 14 (2012/13), 205, 240–242. But cf. CA Paris D. 2008, 1515 with note *Jault-Seseke*; CA Paris JCP G 2008 II

could do its wrong anyway even if it was only a so-called passive one. The website as such is not the object of scrutiny, but only the relevant statement as such[1822] (even though it has to be seen in its context).

Potentially libellous statements on websites have attracted major attention..[1823] Deducting **360** from basic standards of construing (2), the victim can be harmed only where he had previously built a reputation. If the victim is completely unknown by diligent standards in a certain country, his reputation will not be harmed there in a relevant manner for he did not have a discernible one which could have been diminished by the respective statement. Simple recourse to accessibility or intentional distribution[1824] is in this context insufficient insofar as it would either way not relate to the value possibly harmed. Harm is inflicted if recipients recognise, digest or peruse the content.[1825]

In order to avoid fortuitous jurisdiction, the yardsticks for such reputation should be rather **361** severe and strict establishing a firm and unambiguous connection with the respective State.[1826] Yet confined communities and minorities within a country matter in this regard: If, for instance, a website in Russian language and Kyrillic letters contains some statement about an emigrant Russian now living in Germany that statement might do harm to this Russian's reputation within the Russian or emigrant-Russian circles in Germany although it is incomprehensible and unintelligible to the general public in Germany.[1827] Unlike online torts in a commercial and market-related context, it does not matter whether the potential defamator directed his statement purposefully at a certain country[1828] if only the potentially defamed person had build a reputation there which could be harmed. The victim indirectly defines the localisation, and there is no additional minimum threshold of this kind once a reputation has been ascertained and acknowledged for a certain country.

An intentional attack by the tortfeasor specifically for a certain State is a most valuable **362** indication if proven, but is not required[1829] (the more so as it is not required for print media

---

10016 with note *Chabert*; CA Paris JCP G 2008 II 10080 with note *Chabert*; CA Paris D. 2008, 2284 with note *Manara*.

[1822] *Nordmeier*, LMK 2010, 296245.

[1823] For the application of (3) on potentially libellous statements so far see e.g. KG AfP 2006, 258, 259; *Hernández Rodríguez*, AEDIPr 2005, 642, 644.

[1824] See the references in BGH RIW 2010, 67 = EuZW 2010, 313 and KG MMR 2007, 653; OLG München IPRspr. 2009 Nr. 203 p. 520; OLG München IPRspr. 2009 Nr. 125b p. 307; OLG München IPRspr. 2009 Nr. 138 p. 349; OLG Hamburg WRP 2009, 1305 = MMR 2010, 185; OLG Stuttgart K&R 2010, 40; LG München I IPRspr. 2009 Nr. 197 p. 507 *et seq.*; *Wüllrich*, Das Persönlichkeitsrecht des Einzelnen im Internet (2006) pp. 235–242; *Adena*, RIW 2010, 868, 869.

[1825] *Wüllrich*, Das Persönlichkeitsrecht des Einzelnen im Internet (2006) p. 235.

[1826] See BGHZ 184, 313 – New York Times = NJW 2010, 1752; BGH NJW 2011, 2059 – Sieben Tage in Moskau.

[1827] See BGH NJW 2011, 2059 – Sieben Tage in Moskau (not quite taking the point) with disapproving note *Peter-Andreas Brand*.

[1828] BGH RIW 2010, 67 = EuZW 2010, 313; BGHZ 184, 313 – New York Times = NJW 2010, 1752; *von Hinden*, Persönlichkeitsrechtsverletzungen im Internet (1999) p. 83; *Musiol*, GRUR-Prax 2010, 67; *Nordmeier*, LMK 2010, 296245.

[1829] See BGHZ 184, 313 = NJW 2010, 1752; A-G *Cruz Villalón*, Opinion of 29 March 2011 in Joined Cases

---

or TV and could thus become discriminatory against such media).[1830] Furthermore, redu-plication by, or discussion in, secondary websites like blogs or caches could enhance the reach of a given website, and the content provider of the original website does implicitly consent to this by posting the content without restrictions.[1831] Only the violation of the reputation attacked might resort to such auxiliary criteria like language, content or mini-mum number (or better: likelihood) of hits[1832] from that State.[1833] One should be very cautious not to let slip the overall assessment into some kind of *forum non conveniens* doctrine.[1834] A clash of interests between the one posting the statement and the stake and the potential victim should not be relevant, either,[1835] since the potential tortfeasor's interests should not feature where the issue at stake boils down to localising the victim's reputa-tion.[1836] Any *commercial* effects doctrine would be misplaced in this context.[1837] That the party posting content might in the future refrain from posting such content or block users from certain countries if attributed to a certain State by their IP numbers,[1838] should not be a relevant concern, either.[1839]

363 The main task is to ascertain in a concrete case where the victim has built a reputation. Starting point is the victim's habitual residence,[1840] but this should not imply any conclusive or comprehensive approach. In particular, celebrities might have a reputation in many other countries apart from that where they are living. Carla Bruni, Christiano Ronaldo, Silvio Berlusconi or Umberto Eco enjoy a reputation almost worldwide.[1841] This relieves to a certain extent from the sometimes devious task to identify their habitual residence (which might be very difficult if confronted with formal domiciles established for tax purposes or with multiple homes virtually all over the world). Information about them is news and thus material.[1842] He who writes about them online feeds on exactly this and can thus not com-

---

C-509/09 and C-161/10, [2011] ECR I-10272 para. 62; *Adena*, RIW 2010, 868, 871. *Contra Oliver Schlüter*, AfP 2010, 340, 346 *et seq.*

[1830] *Feldmann*, jurisPR-ITR 8/2010 Anm. 2 sub C; *Matthias Weller*, LMK 2010, 305128; *Ole Damm*, GRUR 2010, 891, 893.

[1831] See *Feldmann*, jurisPR-ITR 8/2010 Anm. 2 sub C.

[1832] To rely on the actual number of hits (tentatively so *Oliver Schlüter*, AfP 2010, 340, 347 *et seq.*) would burden the plaintiff with a probatio diabolica as he would be hardly in a position to prove such number; BGH RIW 2010, 67 = EuZW 2010, 313; *Isabel Roth*, Die internationale Zuständigkeit deutscher Gerichte bei Persönlichkeitsrechtsverletzungen im Internet (2007) pp. 232 *et seq.* Additionally, it would conflict with data protection rules; BGH RIW 2010, 67 = EuZW 2010, 313; BGHZ 184, 313 – New York Times = NJW 2010, 1752; *Sujecki*, K&R 2011, 315, 317.

[1833] BGH RIW 2010, 67 = EuZW 2010, 313; *Spickhoff*, IPRax 2011, 131, 132.

[1834] See *Spickhoff*, IPRax 2011, 131, 132.

[1835] Critical for other reasons *Ansgar Staudinger*, NJW 2010, 1754, 1755; *Feldmann*, jurisPR-ITR 8/2010 Anm. 2 sub D; *Ole Damm*, GRUR 2010, 891, 893; *Oliver Schlüter*, AfP 2010, 340, 347.

[1836] Tentatively contra BGH RIW 2010, 67 = EuZW 2010, 313; *Klinger*, jurisPR-ITR 4/2010 Anm. 2 sub D.

[1837] Apparently *contra Matthias Weller*, LMK 2010, 305128.

[1838] As *Feldmann*, jurisPR-ITR 8/2010 Anm. 2 sub D surmises.

[1839] *Matthias Weller*, LMK 2010, 305128.

[1840] See only *Ehmann/Thorn*, AfP 1996, 20, 23; *Adena*, RIW 2010, 868, 872.

[1841] See only *Lütcke*, Persönlichkeitsrechtverletzungen im Internet (2000) p. 136; *Adena*, RIW 2010, 868, 872.

[1842] See the criteria introduced by A-G *Cruz Villalón*, Opinion of 29 March 2011 in Joined Cases C-509/09 and C-161/10, [2011] ECR I-10272 para. 60; *Sujecki*, K&R 2011, 315, 318.

plain that he triggers exactly the kind of geographically unlimited interest he is striving for.[1843] On the other hand, John Doe or Otto Normalverbraucher or the man on the Clapham omnibus is not a VIP known almost everywhere,[1843a] but John Doe or Otto Normalverbraucher or the man on the Clapham omnibus cannot be denied a reputation hard-fought for, at least in their local surroundings.[1844]

(c) The eDate approach

In *eDate* the ECJ deviates from the traditional concept. The ECJ adds more than a mere   **364**
variation, but a third ground of jurisdiction[1845] *besides*, and really in addition to, the place of activity and the place where the harmful event occurred, the latter restricted by the mosaic principle.[1846] The clue: Under this new ground of jurisdiction the respective court is competent to decide about the world-wide damage. The mosaic principle does not apply. This new unrestricted jurisdiction is an additional option.[1847] It amplifies the claimant's array. It further benefits the plaintiff-victim and deliberately so in order to balance the gravity of the harm inflicted[1848] in Internet cases and to avoid possible disadvantages stemming from the mosaic principle.[1849] The ECJ aims at re-balancing the globality of the medium Internet.[1850] To this avail it establishes a true ground of special jurisdiction with full competence.[1851] The declared goal of this so called "adaptation" is to allow a person who has suffered an infringement of a personality right by means of the internet to bring an action in one forum in respect of all the damage caused.[1852] This enhances the protection granted to personality rights.[1853]

[1843] *Contra Heiderhoff*, EuZW 2007, 428, 430.

[1843a] *Thorn*, in: FS Bernd von Hoffmann (2011), p. 746, 751; *Heiderhoff*, in: FS Dagmar Coester-Waltjen (2015), p. 413, 423.

[1844] See only *Benedikt Buchner*, Kläger- und Beklagtenschutz im Recht der internationalen Zuständigkeit (1998) p. 142; *Adena*, RIW 2010, 868, 872.

[1845] *eDate Advertising GmbH v. X; Olivier and Robert Martinez v. MGN Ltd.*, (Joined Cases C-509/09 and C-161/10) [2011] ECR I-10269 para. 51; A-G *Cruz Villalón*, Opinion of 29 March 2011 in Joined Cases C-509/09 and C-161/10, [2011] ECR I-10272 para. 57; *Olaf Weber*, MMR 2012, 48, 49; *Slonina*, ÖJZ 2012, 61, 63.

[1846] *Lederer*, K&R 2011, 791, 792–793 critices it as illogical to retain the traditional place where the harm occurred. To a different avail, analysing the plaintiff's interests, *Slonina*, ÖJZ 2012, 61, 63.

[1847] See only *von Welser*, GRUR-Prax 2011, 513.

[1848] This is a criterion which should become relevant only if it comes to the merits; *Lederer*, K&R 2011, 791, 792.

[1849] *eDate Advertising GmbH v. X; Olivier and Robert Martinez v. MGN Ltd.*, (Joined Cases C-509/09 and C-161/10) [2011] ECR I-10269 para. 47.

[1850] *eDate Advertising GmbH v. X; Olivier and Robert Martinez v. MGN Ltd.*, (Joined Cases C-509/09 and C-161/10) [2011] ECR I-10269 para. 47; even more explicit A-G *Cruz Villalón*, Opinion of 29 March 2011 in Joined Cases C-509/09 and C-161/10, [2011] ECR I-10272 para. 57. Supported by *Hans-Peter Roth*, CR 2011, 811, 812; *Picht*, GRUR Int. 2013, 19, 21; *Gabellini*, Riv. trim dir. proc. civ. 2014, 271, 279. Critical *Christian Heinze*, EuZW 2011, 947, 948.

[1851] *Lederer*, K&R 2011, 791, 792.

[1852] *eDate Advertising GmbH v. X; Olivier and Robert Martinez v. MGN Ltd.*, (Joined Cases C-509/09 and C-161/10) [2011] ECR I-10269 para. 48.

[1853] *Rolf Stürner*, JZ 2012, 10, 24.

365 To a certain extent this is some correction of *Shevill* and the mosaic principle.[1854] Less politely, one could say that *eDate* disturbs the traditional *Shevill* formula.[1855] But erecting a special protective sub-regime also establishes a *forum actoris*,[1856] which is not consistent with the general line[1857] not to seek for such forum under (2). *Shevill* has established some kind of equilibrium, and *eDate* stirs this up wilfully.[1858] *eDate* multiplies the possible *fora*.[1859] In fact, it duplicates the sub-headings for the place where the damage occurred.[1860] It adds a third sub-head of jurisdiction to the two already existing.[1861] This does not restore any balance but shifts it too much in the victim's favour.[1862] One has to bear in mind that at the stage of ascertaining jurisdiction the tort at stake is only an alleged and that it is by not means certain that the alleged victim is really a victim and that the alleged perpetrator is really a perpetrator for this has only to be established when judging the merits.[1863] Sympathy with the alleged victim carries some way, but only some way. The floodgates for forum shopping are opened wide.[1864]

366 The relevant connecting factor for the third prong of the *eDate* approach is the centre of the victim's interests.[1865] The ECJ believes that the courts of this place are best suited to assess the impact which material placed online is liable to have on an individual's personality rights.[1866] The attribution of jurisdiction to those courts thus is said to correspond to the objective of the sound administration of justice.[1867] Predictability is alleged to be preserved also with regard to the defendants since the publisher of harmful content is, at the time when the content is published online, in a position to know the centres of interests of the persons who are the subject of that content.[1868]

[1854] *Matthias Lehmann/Stieper*, JZ 2012, 1016, 1017; *Wulf-Henning Roth*, IPRax 2013, 215, 219; *Garber*, ÖBl 2014, 100, 104.

[1855] *Reymond*, Yb. PIL 14 (2012/13), 205, 243.

[1856] *Guiziou*, Clunet 139 (2012), 201, 205; *Gioia*, Riv. dir. proc. 2012, 1317, 1321; *Markus Köhler*, WRP 2013, 1130, 1133; *Gabellini*, Riv. trim dir. proc. civ. 2014, 271, 282, 286. For further discussion *Bollée/Haftel*, DN 2012, 1285.

[1857] *Folien Fischer AG and Fofitec AG v. Ritrama SpA* (Case C-133/11), ECLI:EU:C:2012:664 para. 46; *Andreas Kainz v. Pantherwerke AG* (Case C-45/13), ECLI:EU:C:2014:7 para. 31; *de Clavière*, Rev. Lamy dr. aff. 92 (2014), 60, 61–62.

[1858] *Feraci*, Riv. dir. int. 2012, 461, 465.

[1859] *Feraci*, Riv. dir. int. 2012, 461, 462.

[1860] *Heinze*, EuZW 2011, 947, 949; *Junker*, in: FS Helmut Rüßmann (2013), p. 811, 818.

[1861] *Nikas*, in: FS Peter Gottwald (2014), p. 477, 482.

[1862] *Markus Köhler*, WRP 2013, 1130, 1133. *Contra Nikas*, in: FS Peter Gottwald (2014), p. 477, 482.

[1863] *Markus Köhler*, WRP 2013, 1130, 1133.

[1864] *Gabellini*, Riv. trim dir. proc. civ. 2014, 271, 281.

[1865] *eDate Advertising GmbH v. X; Olivier and Robert Martinez v. MGN Ltd.*, (Joined Cases C-509/09 and C-161/10) [2011] ECR I-10269 para. 48; see also A-G *Cruz Villalón*, Opinion of 29 March 2011 in Joined Cases C-509/09 and C-161/10, [2011] ECR I-10272 para. 66.

[1866] *eDate Advertising GmbH v. X; Olivier and Robert Martinez v. MGN Ltd.*, (Joined Cases C-509/09 and C-161/10) [2011] ECR I-10269 para. 48. Applauded by *Hans-Peter Roth*, CR 2011, 811, 812.

[1867] *eDate Advertising GmbH v. X; Olivier and Robert Martinez v. MGN Ltd.*, (Joined Cases C-509/09 and C-161/10) [2011] ECR I-10269 para. 48.

[1868] *eDate Advertising GmbH v. X; Olivier and Robert Martinez v. MGN Ltd.*, (Joined Cases C-509/09 and C-161/10) [2011] ECR I-10269 para. 50; *Garber*, ÖJZ 2012, 108, 117.

In the next step it is necessary to identify the centre of the victim's interests. Generally and   367
regularly, it is to be identified, and corresponds, with the victim's habitual residence.[1869] That
is where the individual concerned, in the enjoyment of his personality rights, carries out his
life plan if such plan exists.[1870] That is also where regularly the victim's reputation and the
circumstances of his life can be assessed best.[1871] With the relatively highest probability
negative reactions by the victim's family, acquaintances and general public will show there
and not somewhere else.[1872] Furthermore, habitual residence is not prone to manipula-
tions.[1873] Even an Art. 2b reflecting this was proposed in the course of the negotiations with
the Parliament,[1874] but has not made it into the eventual Regulation.[1875] Generally, relying on
the victim's habitual residence enhances previsibility[1876] since the perpetrator regularly can
identify and ascertain *ex ante* where his prospective victim lives. But on the other hand it
gives a license to the victim to cash in at its own habitual residence.[1877] This is hardly
justifiable if one takes into account that it has become standard for professional media to
publish the same content offline and online.[1878]

However, a person may have the centre of his interests in a Member State in which he does   368
not habitually reside, insofar as other factors, such as the pursuit of a professional activity,
may establish the existence of a particularly close link with that State.[1879] This "escape clause"
has the advantage that employing the habitual residence is not rigid and fixed, and a degree
of openness is maintained.[1880] Furthermore, this slight escape device avoids importing the
whole ballast surrounding the notion of habitual residence *tel quel*.[1881] Nevertheless, it generates a good deal of uncertainty and calls for concretisation.[1882] A mere minimum contact
threshold will probably not do.[1883]

The term "centre of interests" resembles the centre of main interests (COMI), the connect-   369
ing factor employed by Art. 3 (1) Insolvency Regulation (both 2000 and 2015).[1884] This

---

[1869] *eDate Advertising GmbH v. X; Olivier and Robert Martinez v. MGN Ltd.*, (Joined Cases C-509/09 and
C-161/10) [2011] ECR I-10269 para. 49; LG Köln IPRspr. 2012 Nr. 238 p. 547.

[1870] A-G *Cruz Villalón*, Opinion of 29 March 2011 in Joined Cases C-509/09 and C-161/10, [2011] ECR
I-10272 para. 59. Criticising a subjective understanding of the life plan *Thiede*, GPR 2011, 261, 263.

[1871] *Hans-Peter Roth*, CR 2011, 812.

[1872] *Matthias Weller*, in: FS Athanassios Kaissis (2012), p. 1039, 1047; *Picht*, GRUR Int. 2013, 19, 22.

[1873] *Slonina*, ÖJZ 2012, 61, 63–64.

[1874] Art. 2bis by the Legal Committee of the European Parliament, proposed Amendment of 19 October 2011.

[1875] *Silvestri*, Riv. trim. dir. proc. civ. 2013, 677, 691.

[1876] *Muir Watt*, RCDIP 101 (2012), 401, 404; *Lein*, REDI 2012-1, 194, 196.

[1877] *Matthias Lehmann/Stieper*, JZ 2012, 1016, 1017.

[1878] *Thiede*, ecolex 2012, 131, 133; see also *Junker*, in: FS Helmut Rüßmann (2013), p. 811, 821.

[1879] *eDate Advertising GmbH v. X; Olivier and Robert Martinez v. MGN Ltd.*, (Joined Cases C-509/09 and
C-161/10) [2011] ECR I-10269 para. 49.

[1880] *Matthias Weller*, in: FS Athanassios Kaissis (2012), p. 1039, 1047.

[1881] *Muir Watt*, RCDIP 101 (2012), 401, 403.

[1882] *Hess*, JZ 2012, 189, 192; *Leible*, LMK 2012, 329468; *Picht*, GRUR Int. 2013, 19, 22–23.

[1883] But cf. *Spindler*, AfP 2012, 114, 116; *Picht*, GRUR Int. 2013, 19, 23 fn. 42.

[1884] *Bogdan*, Yb. PIL 13 (2011), 483, 486; *Lein*, REDI 2012-1, 194, 196; *Junker*, in: FS Helmut Rüßmann
(2013), p. 811, 820; *Gabellini*, Riv. trim dir. proc. civ. 2014, 271, 283.

---

would not be by chance.[1885] For private persons, the COMI has to be equated, and corresponds, with their habitual residence, too, and permits variations for commercially acting or self-employed persons.[1886] That is where the holder of personality rights will suffer the most extensive and serious harm,[1887] even if the centre of gravity of the dispute is less at stake, a criterion which would look also at the perpetrator and the content of the incriminated online publication.[1888] A particular relevance of the harm inflicted to the victim's interests is not called for, though.[1889] Overly concentrating and focussing on the publisher's seat is avoided[1890] (if that was ever admitted given the emphasis the place where the damage occurred puts on the rights and positions injured). At its core, the third option is a *forum actoris*.[1891] Naturally, it bears particular attractivity to the claimant-victim.[1892] But the victim's disgust or chagrin does as such not make for objective closeness and proximity to the cause of action.[1893]

370 The quest for justice, balancing and relative equality of arms[1894] as between the parties[1895] plus the introduction of a dynamic element[1896] comes at quite some price for the overall system.[1897] It raises a lot of consequential issues under (2):[1898] Which other torts than infringement of personality rights are opened up for the addition of a third option besides the place where the damage occurred?[1899] Can only natural persons avail themselves of *eDate*?[1899a] How far does a "materialisation" of jurisdiction reach?[1900] Infringement of IP rights in the Internet put it to the test[1901] (which it did not pass[1902]), and unfair commercial practices might do so, too.[1903] It is not by chance that the ECJ in *Wintersteiger* adopted a deliberately[1904] different approach from that in *eDate*. *Pinckney*[1905] did not even mention the

---

[1885] *Mankowski*, EWiR Art. 5 EuGVVO 5/11, 743, 744; see also *Slonina*, ÖJZ 2012, 61, 66.

[1886] In more detail *Mankowski*, NZI 2005, 368.

[1887] A-G *Cruz Villalón*, Opinion of 29 March 2011 in Joined Cases C-509/09 and C-161/10, [2011] ECR I-10272 para. 58.

[1888] See A-G *Cruz Villalón*, Opinion of 29 March 2011 in Joined Cases C-509/09 and C-161/10, [2011] ECR I-10272 paras. 58–66; *Cordero Álvarez*, REDI 2011-2, 261, 262.

[1889] *Lederer*, K&R 2011, 791, 792.

[1890] *Hess*, JZ 2012, 189, 191.

[1891] *Thiede*, ecolex 2012, 131, 132; *Hess*, JZ 2012, 189, 192; *Muir Watt*, RCDIP 101 (2012), 401, 402; *Junker*, in: FS Helmut Rüßmann (2013), p. 811, 818.

[1892] *von Welser*, GRUR-Prax 2011, 513.

[1893] *Thiede*, ecolex 2012, 131, 132.

[1894] *Thiede*, ecolex 2012, 131, 132 castigates the ECJ's quest for such alleged re-balancing in the plaintiff's favour as mistaken since the palintiff already enjoys a massive starting advantage.

[1895] *Hess*, JZ 2012, 189, 191.

[1896] *Thiede*, GPR 2011, 261, 263.

[1897] *Mankowski*, EWiR Art. 5 EuGVVO 5/11, 743, 744.

[1898] *Mankowski*, EWiR Art. 5 EuGVVO 5/11, 743, 744; *Leible*, LMK 2012, 329468.

[1899] *Junker*, in: FS Helmut Rüßmann (2013), p. 811, 822.

[1899a] *Briggs* para. 2.204.

[1900] *Christian Heinze*, EuZW 2011, 947, 950.

[1901] *Wintersteiger AG v. Products 4U Sondermaschinenbau* (Case C-523/10), ECLI:EU:C:2012:220 paras. 24–29; *Heinze*, EuZW 2011, 947, 948; *Spindler*, AfP 2012, 114, 118.

[1902] *Boskovic*, RCDIP 101 (2012), 912, 914.

[1903] *Kruger*, DCCR 92–93 (2011), 59, 65; *Markus Köhler*, WRP 2013, 1130, 1135. But cf. OGH ecolex 2012/

eDate approach, when relaying in the field of infringement of copyrights,[1906] and A-G *Cruz Villalón* castigates it in the same area as generating insecurity and generating intolerable risks.[1907] In fact, in the outset and in its structure the reasoning in *Wintersteiger* could not possibly be more different from that in *eDate*: In *eDate* it is all important that the infringement was staged in the Internet,[1908] whereas in *Wintersteiger*[1909] the right to which the damage is inflicted is the decisive element.[1910] The approaches are thus partially conflicting and display a certain degree of eclecticism.[1911] Pandora's box is opened rather wide,[1912] and uncertainty as to the correct reasoning raises its head.

The *eDate* approach undermines the mosaic principle by introducing a *forum actoris* and **371** opens a case for forum shopping. To which extent? A special treatment for internet torts is not consistent with the call for a technologically neutral approach.[1913] Only he who has always mistrusted and disliked the mosaic principle will rejoice over the *eDate* approach.[1914] One step ahead would be to replace the mosaic principle entirely with the centre of the victim's interest at least for online infringement of personality rights.[1915] Another logical extension would be to infringement of personality rights by mass media or offline media with an undetermined and uncontrollable receivership.[1916]

Which exceptions, based on which reasoning, are to be made from the newly introduced rule that the victim's habitual residence is the regular connecting factor? Should a *de minimis* clause be introduced,[1917] or even a presumption that in cases of doubt the incriminating content would be recognised at the victim's habitual residence with the greatest likeli-

---

450 with note *Horak*, tentatively leaning towards the eDate approach, and clearly so *Willems*, GRUR 2013, 462, 466.

[1904] *Wintersteiger AG v. Products 4U Sondermaschinenbau* (Case C-523/10), ECLI:EU:C:2012:220 para. 25.

[1905] *Peter Pinckney v. KDG Mediatech AG* (Case C-170/12), ECLI:EU:C:2013:635 paras.38–47.

[1906] *Azzi*, D. 2014, 411, 412–413.

[1907] A-G *Cruz Villalón*, Opinion in Case C-441/13 of 11 September 2014 paras. 26–27.

[1908] *eDate Advertising GmbH v. X; Olivier and Robert Martinez v. MGN Ltd.*, (Joined Cases C-509/09 and C-161/10) [2011] ECR I-10269 para. 47; even more explicit A-G *Cruz Villalón*, Opinion of 29 March 2011 in Joined Cases C-509/09 and C-161/10, [2011] ECR I-10272 para. 57.

[1909] *Wintersteiger AG v. Products 4U Sondermaschinenbau* (Case C-523/10), ECLI:EU:C:2012:220 paras. 24–29.

[1910] *Kuipers*, NIPR 2012, 390, 394; see also A-G *Cruz Villalón*, Opinion of 16 February 2012 in Case C-523/10, ECLI:EU:C:2012:90 paras. 20, 26. Differently *McGuire*, ZEuP 2014, 160, 163.

[1911] *Pollaud-Dulian*, RTDcom 2013, 731, 735.

[1912] *Wefers Bettink*, NTER 2012, 288.

[1913] See A-G *Cruz Villalón*, Opinion of 29 March 2011 in Joined Cases C-509/09 and C-161/10, [2011] ECR I-10272 paras. 53 *et seq.*; *Thiede*, GPR 2011, 261, 263; *Christian Heinze*, EuZW 2011, 947, 949–950; *Kuipers*, NIPR 2012, 390, 395 and *Thorn*, in: FS Bernd von Hoffmann (2011), p. 746, 757. Acknowledged by A-G *Cruz Villalón*, Opinion of 29 March 2011 in Joined Cases C-509/09 and C-161/10, [2011] ECR I-10272 paras. 50, 53.

[1914] *Wulf-Henning Roth*, IPRax 2013, 215, 219.

[1915] Favouring this *Gabellini*, Riv. trim dir. proc. civ. 2014, 271, 286.

[1916] *Bogdan*, Yb. PIL 13 (2011), 483, 485.

[1917] To this avail *Matthias Weller*, in: FS Athanassios Kaissis (2012), p. 1039, 1048.

hood?[1918] Should there be special sub-rules for celebrities and jetsetters?[1919] If so, which ones? How about the victim not being a natural person but a corporation or a club?[1920]

372   The basic assumption that the mosaic principle is not fitting for the internet is by no means evident.[1921] In the ordinary case, the main damage to reputation is inflicted where the victim lives or has professional contacts. The damages in other States where the victim is not known and does not have a reputation are generally negligible (and even in substantive law severe problems arise with regard to assessing and measuring them). That the victim's soul is indivisible[1922] is not more than a catch-phrase, either. The victim's soul is only touched and affected if the victim knows about the infringement, and a personality right with its objective foundation is something different from a subjectively understood "soul".

372a Why are place of activity and the defendant's domicile not sufficient for recovering the world-wide damage? The general tendency for torts committed *via* the internet is to introduce restrictions in order to avoid holding the publishers liable and responsible in total Europe.[1923] The *eDate* approach catapults the claimant in the most favourable of all conceivable worlds,[1924] the more so since the new ground of jurisdiction is established as an addition to the traditional place where the damage occurred, the latter subject to the mosaic principle.[1925] Partial claims employing the mosaic principle are feasible[1926] and retain some opportunity for threats and hold-up games. It is conceded that in practice they will occur only rarely.[1927]

372b Would it not be preferable to adapt the understanding of place of activity if one is inclined to open up potentially world-wide jurisdiction not territorially restricted?

373   To develop a special sub-rule which would add the centre of the conflict as a third, independent head of jurisdiction under (2) for defamatory statements made over the WWW[1928] is rather ill advised the more so if such advice is given in order to avoid problems in localising the place where the damage was sustained. Since one cannot erase this second alternative from the principle of ubiquity it would stay, and what was introduced in order to limit jurisdiction[1929] would conversely and paradoxically amplify and extend jurisdiction by adding the sketched third alternative.[1930] Additionally, legal certainty would be undermined if

---

[1918] Preferring this *Matthias Weller*, in: FS Athanassios Kaissis (2012), p. 1039, 1048.

[1919] *Hess*, JZ 2012, 189, 192.

[1920] *Christian Heinze*, EuZW 2011, 947, 950.

[1921] Similarly *Christian Heinze*, EuZW 2011, 947, 949. But cf. *contra Markus Köhler*, WRP 2013, 1130, 1133.

[1922] *Thiede*, GPR 2011, 261, 263.

[1923] E.g. *Sujecki*, EWS 2011, 315, 317 with further references; *Kruger*, DCCR 92–93 (2011), 59, 65.

[1924] *Christian Heinze*, EuZW 2011, 947, 949.

[1925] *Thorn*, in: FS Bernd von Hoffmann (2011), p. 746, 757.

[1926] *Brandes*, NJW 2012, 127, 128–129. Critical *Garber*, ÖJZ 2012, 108, 117.

[1927] *Hess*, JZ 2012, 189, 191.

[1928] As A-G *Cruz Villalón*, Opinion of 29 March 2011 in Joined Cases C-509/09 and C-161/10, [2011] ECR I-10272 paras. 57–61 does.

[1929] See A-G *Cruz Villalón*, Opinion of 29 March 2011 in Joined Cases C-509/09 and C-161/10, [2011] ECR I-10272 para. 56.

[1930] See *Robak*, GRUR-Prax 2011, 257, 259.

such an open criterion calling for refinement[1931] was introduced as the closest connection.[1932] Apparently, jurisdiction was taken as the place to get a fair balance between freedom of information and protection of personality rights,[1933] disregarding that the former is an aspect of justification and thus of substantive law.

(4) Pre-contractual liability
Insofar as pre-contractual liability qualifies as tortious[1934] it will in most instances only   **374** generate financial and economic loss. The creditor's domicile or habitual residence should generally be regarded as the place where the respective damage was sustained.[1935]

(5) Wrongful birth
In the event of wrongful birth qualifying as a tortious event, the damage sustained consists of   **375** the maintenance due to the child, the loss of earnings etc.[1936] The primary damage is pure economic loss. It occurs where the respective moneys can originally be located in the parents' accounts.[1937] Thus it appears misapprehended to define the conception of the child as the damage.[1938]

(6) Tricking into lost lawsuits with third parties
If the damage is the result of a lawsuit brought by a third party (i.e. the victim was tricked   **376** into behaving in a way that he could be successfully sued by this third party), the place where the damage occurred is not necessarily identical with the place where the *forum* of the suit by the third party is located.[1939] To hold otherwise raises the danger of a *forum actoris* since the result would be to entitle the claimant to sue in his domicile for contribution or reimbursement whenever he was sued there by virtue of Art. 4.[1940]

(7) Unfair commercial practices
In matters of unfair commercial practices the threshold can be higher. Taking (2) literally,   **377** this rule does not contain a sub-rule specifically designed for unfair commercial practices. Hence, the question as to the appropriate connecting factor appears to be answered once it is raised: (2) applies, as clad in its usual terms, without modification or adaptation.[1941] But learned conflicts lawyers might hesitate before concluding this as the final result. At the back of their minds they have the traditional rule in private international law specifically designed

---

[1931] Attempting at such refinement A-G *Cruz Villalón*, Opinion of 29 March 2011 in Joined Cases C-509/09 and C-161/10, [2011] ECR I-10272 paras. 58–60.

[1932] *Robak*, GRUR-Prax 2011, 257, 259.

[1933] A-G *Cruz Villalón*, Opinion of 29 March 2011 in Joined Cases C-509/09 and C-161/10, [2011] ECR I-10272 para. 58.

[1934] *Supra* Art. 7 notes 73–78 (*Mankowski*).

[1935] Cassaz. RDIPP 2004, 674, 678; Cassaz. RDIPP 2004, 1008, 1010.

[1936] Rb. Middelburg NIPR 2003 Nr. 53 p. 104.

[1937] Rb. Middelburg NIPR 2003 Nr. 53 p. 104.

[1938] *Contra* Hof 's-Gravenhage NIPR 2005 Nr. 50 p. 89.

[1939] *Waterford Wedgwood plc v. David Nagli Ltd.* [1999] I.L.Pr. 9, 22 (Q.B.D., Judge *Charles Aldous* Q.C.).

[1940] *Waterford Wedgwood plc v. David Nagli Ltd.* [1999] I.L.Pr. 9, 22 (Q.B.D., Judge *Charles Aldous* Q.C.); *Takahashi*, Claims for contribution and reimbursement in an international context (2000) p. 30.

[1941] See only Cassaz. RDIPP 1994, 344; OLG Hamm RIW 2000, 58; Rb. Amsterdam NJ 1979 Nr. 146 with note *Schultsz*; Trib. Monza RDIPP 1980, 429; Trib. comm. Liège J. trib. 1983, 556.

for unfair commercial practices, namely the so-called marketplace rule as embodied in Art. 6 (1) Rome II Regulation. The PIL of unfair commercial practices does not follow the principle of ubiquity, but developed it's own rule. Applying the ordinary principle of ubiquity when jurisdiction in unfair commercial practices has to be judged, does not therefore coincide with the revered PIL rule. One could argue that the jurisdictional rule is still inchoate and needs refinement in order to reach the higher echelon and more elevated level the PIL has already reached. To reconcile PIL and jurisdiction, one could feel tempted to instrumentalise a purposive interpretation of (2) in order to establish the marketplace rule insofar as unfair commercial practices are committed on the market.[1942]

378 Insofar as Art. 6 (2) Rome II Regulation reigns and thus insofar as the marketplace rule would be not applicable in PIL, (2) should equally follow suit and should insofar not adopt a marketplace rules for torts directed against competitors not *via* the market, but by immediately attacking their assets or interests.[1943]

379 The parallelisation should go even farther insofar as for market-related unfair commercial practices any minimum threshold prevailing under Art. 6 (1) Rome II Regulation[1944] should be imported into (2), too.[1945] This can very well be justified since (2) sanctions the violation of the primarily protected assets or values of the victim.[1946] If a market is not affected in a relevant manner for the respective conduct does not reach a given threshold there is no such violation.

380 Nevertheless practitioners should be warned that this has not been affirmed by reliable authority yet.[1947] The likelihood of differing results using the different approaches is not all too high in any event. The marketplace can be described as the place where the incriminated action took place,[1948] or the place where the protected interested, namely fair

---

[1942] In favour of such an approach *Kessedjian*, in: *McLachlan/Nygh* (eds.), Transnational Tort Litigation – Jurisdictional Prin"ciples (1996), p. 171, 184–187; *Bernd Schauer*, Electronic Commerce in der EU (1999) p. 257; *Schack*, MMR 2000, 135, 137; *von Hein*, RabelsZ 64 (2000), 194, 198; *Thomas Pfeiffer*, in: Gounalakis (ed.), Rechtshandbuch Electronic Business (2003), § 13 note 60; *Mankowski*, in: Münchener Kommentar zum Lauterkeitsrecht (2nd ed. 2014) IntWettbR with notes 385 *et seq.*; *Glöckner*, in: Harte-Bavendamm/Henning-Bodewig (eds.), UWG (2nd ed. 2008) Einl. D Art. 5 note 16; *Christian Heinze*, IPRax 2009, 231, 233 *et seq.*; *Lindacher*, Internationales Wettbewerbsverfahrensrecht (2009) § 9 notes 7, 12; *Ohly*, in: Piper/Ohly/Sosnitza, UWG (5th ed. 2010) Einf. B with note 8; *Hausmann/Obergfell*, in: Fezer, UWG (2n ed. 2010), Einl. I note 405; *Fezer/Koos*, in: Staudinger, BGB, Internationales Wirtschaftsrecht (15th ed. 2010) note 804. But sceptical e.g. *Helmut Rüßmann*, K & R 1998, 422, 424; *Fitchen*, (2006) 13 Maastricht J. Eur. & Comp. L. 391, 393–399.

[1943] *Christian Heinze*, IPRax 2009, 231, 233, 236.

[1944] Extensively explained by *Mankowski*, in: Münchener Kommentar zum Lauterkeitsrecht (2nd ed. 2014) IntWettbR notes 210–221.

[1945] To a similar avail *Christian Heinze*, IPRax 2009, 231, 234 *et seq.* See also *Mankowski*, in: Münchener Kommentar zum Lauterkeitsrecht (2nd ed. 2014) IntWettbR note 394; *Mankowski*, EWiR 2014, 403, 404.

[1946] *Supra* Art. 7 note 318 (*Mankowski*).

[1947] *Thomas Pfeiffer*, in: Gounalakis (ed.), Rechtshandbuch Electronic Business (2003), § 13 Art. 5 note 60; *Mankowski*, in: Ruth Nielsen/Sandfeld Jacobsen/Trzaskowski (eds.), EU Electronic Commerce Law (2004), p. 125, 154.

[1948] So e.g. *Rolf Sack*, WRP 2000, 269, 272; *Veelken*, in: FS 75 Jahre Max-Planck-Institut für Privatrecht,

competition with regard to consumers or customers, is affected.[1949] To operate either of both these approaches properly an additional requirement of minimum market relevance has to be introduced[1950] depending whichever approach is preferred. The activity should have some measurable impact on the targeted market.

For instance, the mere receivability of an electronic advertisement in a country where the **381** advertising company does not sell or market its products (or at least under a different name), should not trigger off jurisdiction.[1951] The mere accessibility of a website via the World Wide Web does not suffice.[1952] Additionally, it is at least required that the marketer purposefully availed and directed his website at the country in question.[1953] The marketer should be intended to be of significant interest in the country at stake.[1954] The language employed,[1955] the marketer's entrepreneurial structure,[1956] the nature of the product marketed, the transport cost sensitivity and the ensuing logistic abilities to distribute can provide valuable indications.[1957] Proper measures by the marketer to minimise his jurisdictional risk may be recognised.[1958] If the website displays national symbols like flags or offers national contact lines, it is directed at the respective countries.[1959] This holds true where a menu offers several options for the user to choose between different languages and different versions each

---

(2001), p. 293, 315 *et seq.*; *Mankowski*, in: von Bar/Mankowski, Internationales Privatrecht, Vol. I: Allgemeine Lehren (2nd ed. 2003) § 7 with note 61.

[1949] So e.g. *Lindacher*, WRP 1996, 645, 648; *Rufus Pichler*, Jahrbuch Junger Zivilrechtswissenschaftler 1998, 229, 249; *Hausmann/Obergfell*, in: Fezer, UWG (2nd ed. 2010), Einl. I note 409.

[1950] Guidelines for, and elements of, designing such restrictions are provided by *Mankowski*, GRUR Int. 1999, 909, 916–918; *Mankowski*, CR 2000, 763; *Hausmann/Obergfell*, in: Fezer, UWG (2nd ed. 2010), Einl. I note 409.

[1951] Cass. RCDIP 97 (2008), 322 with note *Treppoz*; CA Orléans RCDIP 93 (2004), 139, 145 with note *Gaudemet-Tallon* = Clunet 131 (2004), 193 with note *André Huet*.

[1952] Hof Brussels TBH 2005, 694; *Mankowski*, CR 2002, 450 *et seq.*; *Mankowski*, MMR 2002, 817 *et seq.*; *Mourre/Lahlou*, RDAI 2005, 509, 523. *Contra* Cass. RCDIP 93 (2004), 632 with note *Cachard* = Clunet 131 (2004), 872 with note *André Huet* = D. 2004, 276 with note *Manara* = JCP 2004 II 10055 note *Chabert* = RTDcom 2004, 281 with note *Pollaud-Dulian*; OLG München NJW 2002, 611 – literaturhaus.de; OLG Karlsruhe MMR 2002, 814, 815 – intel; OLG Hamburg MMR 2002, 822, 823 – hotel-maritime.dk; CA Paris Clunet 131 (2004), 492 with note *Bergé*; TGI Nanterre JCP, éd. E, 1999, 954 with note *Vivant/Le Stanc*; *André Huet*, Clunet 131 (2004), 873, 878; *Garber*, ÖBl 2014, 100, 108.

[1953] KG NJW 1997, 3321; *Mankowski*, MMR 2002, 817, 818; *Kurtz*, IPRax 2004, 107; *Cachard*, RCDIP 93 (2004), 634, 641–644; see also BGH GRUR 2005, 431, 432 – Hotel Maritime= WRP 2005, 493, 494 = JZ 2005, 736 with note *Ohly*.

[1954] See 1–800 Flowers, Inc. v. Phonename Ltd. [2002] F.S.R. 191, 212, 221 (C.A., per *Jonathan Parker* and *Buxton* L.JJ. respectively), ~ [2000] F.S.R. 697 (Ch.D., *Jakob* J.); Euromarket Designs, Inc. v. Peters and Trade and Barrel Ltd. [2001] F.S.R. 288, 295 *et seq.* (Ch.D., *Jakob* J.); Bonnier Media Ltd. v. Greg Lloyd Smith and Kestrel Trading Corp. The Times July 10, 2002, paras. 14–20 (O.H., Lord *Drummond Young*) http://www.scotcourts.gov.uk/opinions/dru2606.html; Vzngr. Rb. 's-Gravenhage NIPR 2005 Nr. 168 p. 233.

[1955] See TGI Paris Clunet 131 (2004), 491, 493 with note *Bergé*. Overly cautious OLG Köln NJW-RR 2008, 359.

[1956] LG München I IPRspr. 2009 Nr. 197 p. 508; *Banholzer* p. 83.

[1957] See in more detail *Mankowski*, CR 2000, 763, 765–767.

[1958] *Mankowski*, MMR 2002, 817, 818.

aiming at a certain country.[1960] Sub-sites specifically addressing a single selected country each are a clear indication of targeting the respective countries.[1961]

382　The list of indicators which the ECJ detailed in *Pammer*[1962] for the purposes of Art. 15 (1) (c) Brussels I Regulation can be imported here as it can be imported into Art. 6 (1) Rome II Regulation.[1963] It encompasses: offering of services or goods in States designated by name;[1964] disbursement of expenditure on an Internet referencing service to the operator of a search engine in order to facilitate access to the trader's site by customers domiciled in various States;[1965] language; currency; international nature of services or goods advertised; mention of telephone numbers with an international code; use of a top-level domain other than that of the Member State in which the trader is established, or use of neutral top-level domains such as.com or .eu;[1966] description of itineraries from one or more other Member States to the place where the service is provided or where the goods are sold; mention of an international clientele composed of customers in various states.[1967]

383　If marketing takes place at the market in one country whereas the final supply is executed in another country, the relevant place either as the marketplace or the place where the damage was sustained, is in the former country of marketing.[1968]

384　In the field of unfair commercial practices disclaimers might serve a useful purpose. In unfair commercial practices a generalisation has to be implemented. Disclaimers indicate the spatial ambit in particular of a web-site[1969] but only insofar as the advertising person himself generally pays due regard to his own disclaimer and complies with it.[1970] That a handful of contracts is concluded with consumers from an "unwanted" or "undesired"

[1959] KG GRUR Int. 2002, 448, 450; *Mankowski*, GRUR Int. 1999, 909, 917; *Hausmann/Obergfell*, in: Fezer, UWG (2n ed. 2010), Einl. I note 409.

[1960] BGH WRP 2014, 548 – Englischsprachige Pressemitteilung; *Mankowski*, EWiR 2014, 403, 404.

[1961] *Banholzer* pp. 86–87.

[1962] *Peter Pammer v. Reederei Karl Schlüter GmbH & Co. KG; Hotel Alpenhof GmbH v. Oliver Heller* (joined Cases C-585/08 and C-144/09), nyr. paras. 81, 83 *et seq.*; even more extensive A-G *Trstenjak*, Opinion of 18 May 2010 in joined Cases C-585/08 and C-144/09, nyr. paras. 76 *et seq.* Discussed in detail by *Mankowski*, IPRax 2011 issue 5 sub III.

[1963] For the latter *Mankowski*, IPRax 2012, 144, 156; *Mankowski*, EWiR 2014, 403, 404; see also *Usunier*, RDCIP 103 (2014), 195, 200.

[1964] *Peter Pammer v. Reederei Karl Schlüter GmbH & Co. KG; Hotel Alpenhof GmbH v. Oliver Heller* (joined Cases C-585/08 and C-144/09), nyr. para. 81.

[1965] *Peter Pammer v. Reederei Karl Schlüter GmbH & Co. KG; Hotel Alpenhof GmbH v. Oliver Heller* (joined Cases C-585/08 and C-144/09), nyr. para. 81. Discussed by *Mankowski*, IPRax 2011 issue 5 sub III 6.

[1966] See also *Banholzer* pp. 77–78.

[1967] All Peter Pammer v. Reederei Karl Schlüter GmbH & Co. KG; Hotel Alpenhof GmbH v. Oliver Heller (joined Cases C-585/08 and C-144/09), nyr. para. 83.

[1968] *Hausmann/Obergfell*, in: Fezer, UWG (2n ed. 2010), Einl. I notes 400, 405; compare for the purposes of PIL BGHZ 113, 115, 15 *et seq.* – Kauf im Ausland; BGH GRUR 1998, 419, 420 – Gewinnspiel im Ausland.

[1969] OLG Frankfurt MMR 2001, 751, 752 with note *Mankowski*; LG Frankfurt/Main, CR 2002, 222 with note *Dieselhorst*.

[1970] BGH GRUR Int. 2006, 605, 607 – Arzneimittelwerbung im Internet; OLG Frankfurt MMR 2001, 751, 752 with note *Mankowski*; KG ZLR 2003, 604 with note *Meisterernst*; *Mankowski*, GRUR Int. 1999, 909, 919

country over a longer period does not render the disclaimer ineffective as such an indica-tion.[1971] To apply the law of the place where it is issued, to the disclaimer[1972] appears to be an unnecessary complication and divides closely related issues. More precisely, it would elevate the disclaimer beyond its proper rank making the disclaimer an issue of its own. But since the disclaimer only provides nothing more than a mere indication, its validity is not an issue at stake.[1973]

(8) Unfair competition (anti-competitive practices and cartels)

Anti-competitive practices and cartels inflict harm on the victim where market access is **385** denied in the event that the victim is a prospective competitor, or where the overcharged prices had to be paid on acquiring goods or services in the event that the victim is a customer.[1974] The effects doctrine can be imported from Art. 6 (3) Rome II Regulation.[1975] Loss corsisting in additional costs incured because of a trificially high prices, might be infricted on each alleged victim where identifiable, generally at that victim's registered office.[1975a] This holds true equally for follow-on actions after the competent public autho-rities have issued a binding finding upon the illegality of the cartel,[1975b] and for stand-alone actions.[1975c] Referring to each viction's seat respectively the opportunity to on solidate ac-tions several undertakings' potential claims for damages woiding the need to bring separate actions.[1975d] A threshold of substantive effects should be implemented[1976] since otherwise the relevant rules of antitrust law would not violated. But the market affected can be located elsewhere from the *instrumenta sceleris*. Even under Art. 101 TFEU it is not true that a

---

et seq.; *Mankowski*, GRUR Int. 2006, 609, 610; *Hausmann/Obergfell*, in: Fezer, UWG (2n ed. 2010), Einl. I note 409; *Sebastian Köhler*, JR 2007, 284, 285; *Banholzer* pp. 75–76.

1971 *Mankowski*, in: Ruth Nielsen/Sandfeld Jacobsen/Trzaskowski (eds.), EU Electronic Commerce Law (2004), p. 125, 155; *Mankowski*, GRUR Int. 2006, 609, 610.

1972 As proposed e.g. by *Radicati di Brozolo*, in: Ferrarini/Hopt/Wymeersch (eds.), Capital Markets in the Age of the Euro (2002), p. 165, 167.

1973 *Mankowski*, in: Ruth Nielsen/Sandfeld Jacobsen/Trzaskowski (eds.), EU Electronic Commerce Law (2004), p. 125, 155.

1974 *Ashton/Vollrath*, ZWeR 2006, 1, 8; see also *Bulst*, EWS 2004, 403, 406; *Moritz Becker*, EWS 2008, 228, 230; *Kropholler/von Hein*, Art. 5 note 84a; *Helena Isabel Maier*, Marktortanknüpfung im internationalen Kartelldeliktsrecht (2011) pp. 142–156; *Mankowski*, WuW 2012, 797, 804–805; *Wulf-Henning Roth*, in: FS Eberhard Schilken (2015), p. 427, 437.

1975 *Mankowski*, WuW 2012, 797, 805–807; *Kropholler/von Hein* Art. 5 EuGVO note 84a; *Wurmnest*, EuZW 2012, 933, 935; see also OGH SZ 2008/102 E. 3.22; *Tzakas*, Die Haftung für Kartellrechtsverstöße im internationalen Rechtsverkehr (2011) pp. 119–122; *Helena Isabel Maier*, Marktortanknüpfung im inter-nationalen Kartelldeliktsrecht (2011) pp. 146–148, 152–154. But of. *Matthias Weller/Wäschle*, RIW 2015, 603, 604.

1975a *Cartel Damage Claims (CDC) Hydrogen Peroxide SA v. Akzo Nobel NV* (Case C-352/13), ECLI:EU:C:2015:335 para. 52.

1975b *Cartel Damage Claims (CDC) Hydrogen Peroxide SA v. Akzo Nobel NV* (Case C-352/13), ECLI:EU:C:2015:335 para. 53.

1975c *Mankowski*, EWiR 2015 (Forth Loming, note on CDC).

1975d *Cartel Damage Claims (CDC) Hydrogen Peroxide SA v. Akzo Nobel NV* (Case C-352/13), ECLI:EU:C:2015:335 para. 55.

1976 *Mankowski*, WuW 2012, 797, 807. *Contra Wulf-Henning Roth*, in: FS Eberhard Schilken (2015), p. 427, 438.

violation of this rule (which has undeniably the force of law in all Member States) automatically affects the markets of all Member States.[1977] For each national market it has to be judged, measured and evaluated separately whether this particular market is affected. But if a certain market is affected in a relevant manner, jurisdiction should lay there, irrespective how many other markets might be affected besides that.[1978] For the sake of illustration, an anti-competitive agreement fixing hotel prices in Spain will exert its effects in Germany where the vast majority of travellers and guests books rooms or accommodation in the hotels at stake.[1979] If a commercial agent is denied of professional activity in a certain State due to a respective verdict by a monopolist[1980] the relevant damage occurs in that State.[1981] If a victim's fortune is identified as an (additional?) value to be protected it also matters where such fortune is affected, with a presumption that this might in case of doubt be at the victim's domicile as the centre of its fortune becoming attractive again.[1982] Passing-on defences and damages passed on by the immediate victims of the cartel to their customers do not compose direct, but only indirect damages and are thus not relevant for the purposes of (2).[1983] If a multiplicity of enterprises (be it as cartelants, bei it within a group of companies or an economic entity) it suffices that either of them causes the damage.[1984]

(9) Product liability

386 As to product liability, according to *Zuid-Chemie* the place where the harmful event occurred designates the place where the initial damage occurred as a result of the normal use of the purpose for which it was intended.[1985] This solves the simple and easy cases, and it makes clear that the eventual use and not the delivery matters, the latter bearing relevance only for ascertaining the *Handlungsort*.[1986] Even less the mere delivery to a warehouse where no damage was actually inflicted, does not constitute jurisdiction.[1987]

387 The place where the damage occurred must not be confused with the place which damaged the product itself occurred, but must be identified where the defect to the goods produces its harmful effects, i.e. the place where the damage caused by the defective product actually manifests itself.[1988] The damage to the goods and the defect as such affect only the goods which are handed over in the defective state whereas product liability deals with damage to the victim's other assets. Hence the damage to the defective product as such does not matter

---

[1977] This is the first fallacy in A-G *Jääskinen*, Opinion of 11 December 2014 in Case C-352/13, ECLI:EU:C:2014:2443 para. 50.

[1978] But cf. the second fallacy in A-G *Jääskinen*, Opinion of 11 December 2014 in Case C-352/13, ECLI:EU:C:2014:2443 paras. 50–51.

[1979] OLG Hamburg EuLF 2007, II-133; *Kropholler/von Hein*, Art. 5 note 84a.

[1980] In the concrete case, the FIFA was this monopolist.

[1981] Cass. Clunet 139 (2012), 980, 981; *Guillaumé*, Clunet 139 (2012), 982, 986 *et seq.*

[1982] *Moritz Becker*, EWS 2008, 228, 233.

[1983] *Wulf-Henning Roth*, in: FS Eberhard Schilken (2015), p. 427, 438.

[1984] *Wulf-Henning Roth*, in: FS Eberhard Schilken (2015), p. 427, 438.

[1985] *Zuid-Chemie v. Philippo's Mineralenfabriek NV/SA*, (Case C-189/08) [2009] ECR I-6917, I-6929 para. 32; following this Hoge Raad NJ 2011 Nr. 350 p. 3531; A-G *Strikwerda*, NJ 2011 Nr. 350 p. 3530; OLG Saarbrücken IPRax 2013, 74, 80.

[1986] *Mankowski*, EWiR Art. 5 EuGVVO 1/09, 569, 570; *Kropholler/von Hein* Art. 5 note 83e.

[1987] LG Dessau-Roßlau IPRspr. 2011 Nr. 223.

[1988] *Zuid-Chemie v. Philippo's Mineralenfabriek NV/SA*, (Case C-189/08) [2009] ECR I-6917, I-6928 para. 27.

here[1989] but possibly for contractual purposes which are quite another context subject to (1). Defective goods might thus not inflict damage to the buyer in negligence where they are delivered to the buyer[1990] the more so since this would reduce the applicability of (2) if the victim is taking delivery at the manufacturer's seat.[1991]

The defective product causes relevant harm where it (as an educt) is processed into further **388** products[1992] regardless whether out together with other components or blended with other elements. Mere financial loss without physical damage to, or contamination of other tangibles on the victim's side should also suffice[1993] if the protective purpose of product liability is rightly believed to encompass protection against financial losses for instance where the victim resells the goods infested by the defective product to a third party and encumbers liability (be in contractual or tortious one) towards that third party. Loss of business in the market due to a loss of reputation caused by the customer marketing the defective good he had received is also recoverable under (2).[1994] Likewise, bodily harm inflicted to the health of the customer's employees by the defective goods constitutes a primary damage.[1995]

Yet to rely on the place where the initial damage occurred as a result of the normal use of the **389** purpose for which it was intended runs into problems where the goods have been marketed without, or even against, the manufacturer's intention. In particular, Art. 5 Rome II Regulation[1996] should be taken into account[1997] (but not followed in the strict sense[1998] since it erects an overly complicated system[1999] with not less than seven steps[2000]). It ostentatiously indicates that previsibility for the manufacturer is a major issue. *Zuid-Chemie* does not provide a conclusive answer and can only serve at a starting point.[2001]

(10) Infringement of intellectual property
Intellectual property (IP) including i.a. copyright, patents, trademarks, is governed by the **390** principle of territoriality or *lex loci protectionis*. Any national IP right guarantees protection

---

[1989] *Zuid-Chemie v. Philippo's Mineralenfabriek NV/SA*, (Case C-189/08) [2009] ECR I-6917, I-6928 para. 29.

[1990] *Kropholler/von Hein* Art. 5 note 83e. Contra *Leo Laboratories Ltd. v. Crompton BV [2005] 2 IR 225*, 233 et seq. (S.C., per *Fennelly* J.).

[1991] *Zuid-Chemie v. Philippo's Mineralenfabriek NV/SA*, (Case C-189/08) [2009] ECR I-6917, I-6929 para. 31; *Kropholler/von Hein* Art. 5 note 83e.

[1992] *Zuid-Chemie v. Philippo's Mineralenfabriek NV/SA*, (Case C-189/08) [2009] ECR I-6917, I-6928 para. 29; OLG Koblenz NJW-RR 2008, 148, 149; OLG Saarbrücken IPRax 2013, 74, 80.

[1993] See OLG Koblenz NJW-RR 2008, 148, 149. *Leaving this point open in the concrete case Zuid-Chemie v. Philippo's Mineralenfabriek NV/SA*, (Case C-189/08) [2009] ECR I-6917, I-6929 et seq. paras. 33–36. Too strict *Duintjer Tebbens*, NIPR 2010, 206.

[1994] Rb. Dordrecht NIPR 2008 Nr. 55 p. 96.

[1995] Rb. Dordrecht NIPR 2008 Nr. 55 p. 96.

[1996] On this rule in particular *Illmer*, RabelsZ 73 (2009), 269.

[1997] *Spickhoff*, in: FS Jan Kropholler (2008), p. 671, 678; *Mankowski*, EWiR Art. 5 EuGVVO 1/09, 569, 570; *Leible*, in: Rauscher, Art. 5 notes 86 et seq.; *Sujecki*, EWS 2014, 94.

[1998] *von Hein*, IPRax 2010, 330, 340–343; *Kropholler/von Hein* Art. 5 note 83e.

[1999] See only *Stone*, Ankara L. Rev. 4 (2007), 95, 118; *Hartley*, (2008) 57 ICLQ 899, 908; *von Hein*, ZEuP 2009, 6, 26.

[2000] *Kadner Graziano*, RabelsZ 73 (2009), 1, 38; *Thorn*, in: FS Karsten Schmidt (2009), p. 1561, 1574.

[2001] *Duintjer Tebbens*, NIPR 2010, 206.

only for the territory of the State granting it.[2002] Hence, some doubts are ventilated whether there can be any place where the harmful event occurs different from a relevant place of activity.[2003] However, this can be overcome: With regard to damage resulting from infringements of an intellectual and commercial property right, the occurrence of damage in a particular Member State is subject to the protection, in that State, of the IP right in respect of which infringement is alleged[2004] whereas the courts of other Member States in principle retain jurisdiction to rule on the damage to IP rights caused in their respective Member States for they are best placed, first, to ascertain whether those rights guaranteed by the Member State concerned have in fact been infringed and, secondly, to determine the nature of the damage caused.[2005] Under this premise there can be little if any doubt that infringement of IP rights enjoys a place where the harmful event occurs.[2006] The opposite premise that there is not a place where the harmful event occurs different from the place of activity since the principle of territoriality as prevailing in IP matters grants protection only against activity in the State of the *lex protectionis*[2007] is not convincing. The place where the harmful event occurs might in many instances happen to coincide and concur with a place of activity, but operates nonetheless under a different concept. The relevance of the distinction is evident insofar as the mosaic principle limiting jurisdiction applies only to the second prong, but not to the se first prong of (2). Hence, conversely, if one of the two prongs of (2) were to be eliminated it would be the first, not the second one. The first one needs specific explanation in an IP context whereas the second one is a natural.

391 Jurisdiction for infringement of IP rights based on the second prong of (2) follows the territoriality of IP rights.[2008] It thus leads to a re-territorialisation.[2009] This amounts to a welcome restriction, and hindrance in the way of, potentially excessive forum shopping.[2010] It is correct parlance t talk about the infringement of the German part of a bundle patent.[2011] Unlike the infringement of personality rights, the infringement of IP rights typically does

---

[2002] See only *Peter Pinckney v. KDG Mediatech AG* (Case C-170/12), ECLI:EU:C:2013:635 para. 46; *Pez Hejduk v. EnergieAgentur.NRW GmbH* (Case C-441/13), ECLI:EU:C:2015:28 para. 36; BGH GRUR 2012, 621 [34] – OSCAR; *Matthias Lehmann/Stieper*, JZ 2012, 1016, 1017.

[2003] *Schack*, NJW 2013, 3629; *Michael Müller*, EuZW 2014, 434.

[2004] *Wintersteiger AG v. Products 4U Sondermaschinenbau* (Case C-523/10), ECLI:EU:C:2012:220 para. 25; *Peter Pinckney v. KDG Mediatech AG* (Case C-170/12), ECLI:EU:C:2013:635 paras. 33, 39; *Coty Germany GmbH v. First Note Perfumes NV* (Case C-360/12), ECLI:EU:C:2014:1318 para. 55.

[2005] *Pez Hejduk v. EnergieAgentur.NRW GmbH* (Case C-441/13), ECLI:EU:C:2015:28 para. 37; see also *Peter Pinckney v. KDG Mediatech AG* (Case C-170/12), ECLI:EU:C:2013:635 para. 46.

[2006] See *Coty Germany GmbH v. First Note Perfumes NV* (Case C-360/12), ECLI:EU:C:2014:1318 para. 53; *Matthias Lehmann/Stieper*, JZ 2012, 1016, 1017.

[2007] *Schack*, NJW 2013, 3629, 3630; *Schack*, para. 343; *Hopf*, MarkenR 2012, 229, 234.

[2008] *Wintersteiger AG v. Products 4U Sondermaschinenbau* (Case C-523/10), ECLI:EU:C:2012:220 para. 25; *Peter Pinckney v. KDG Mediatech AG* (Case C-170/12), ECLI:EU:C:2013:635 para. 33; *Coty Germany GmbH v. First Note Perfumes NV* (Case C-360/12), ECLI:EU:C:2014:1318 para. 55; A-G *Jääskinen*, Opinion of 13 June 2013 in Case C-170/12 para. 46; A-G *Cruz Villalón*, Opinion of 16 February 2012 in Case C-523/10, ECLI:EU:C:2012:90 para. 25; *Matthias Lehmann/Stieper*, JZ 2012, 1016, 1017–1018; *McGuire*, ZEuP 2014, 160, 167; *Usunier*, RDCIP 103 (2014), 195, 201.

[2009] *Treppoz*, RCDIP 98 (2009), 582, 584; *Boskovic*, RCDIP 101 (2012), 912, 913.

[2010] *Slonina*, ecolex 2014, 608, 610.

[2011] See OLG Düsseldorf NJOZ 2010, 1781 = IPRspr. 2010 Nr. 211.

not require any recourse to protected interests which need further circumscription or localisation.[2012] The *forum protectionis* prevails, and foreseeability and sound administration of justice militate in favour of conferring jurisdiction, in respect of the damage occurred, on the courts of the Member State in which the right at issue is protected.[2013] The courts of the Member State where an IP right is registered are in the best position to assess, taking into account the judicial interpretation[2014] of Directive 2008/95/EU,[2015] whether a concrete situation actually infringes the protected IP right.[2016] Those courts have the power to determine all the damage allegedly caused to the proprietor of the protected right because of the infringement and to hear an application seeking cessation of all infringements of the IP right at stake.[2017] But the principle of territoriality limits the protective ambit to the protection of particularly the right registered in the forum state.[2018] The forum is not entitled to decide about the protection of IP rights not registered on the forum state since such IP rights cannot be infringed in the forum state where they do not have an existence in their own right.[2019] Forum shopping[2020] is opened only insofar as the same activity leads to infringement of different, but parallel IP rights protected under the laws of different states.

The mere risk of an infringement is not an infringement in itself, and genuine impact is **392** required.[2021] Yet the infringement potential of particular conduct indicates that the respective means are necessary to commit an infringement.[2022] But where the mere use of a protected right already constitutes an infringement it is not necessary that, for instance, something was actually downloaded from the internet if the opportunity to download was offered.[2023] An exception has been proposed in order to deal with the scenario where the infringement is truly global in scope or rather where it involves ubiquitous media which give it unavoidably a global scope:[2024] "In disputes concerned with infringement carried out through ubiquitous media such as the Internet, the court [...] shall also have jurisdiction in respect of infringements that occur or may occur within the territory of any other State provided that the activities giving rise to the infringement have no substantial effect in the State, or any of the States, where the infringer is habitually resident and

---

[2012] *Peifer*, IPRax 2013, 228, 229.

[2013] *Wintersteiger AG v. Products 4U Sondermaschinenbau* (Case C-523/10), ECLI:EU:C:2012:220 para. 27.

[2014] *Google France SARL and Google, Inc. v. Louis Vuitton Malletier SA; Google France SARL v. Viaticum SA and Luteicel SARL; Google France SARL v. Centre national de recherche en relations humaines (CNRRH)* (Joined Cases C-236/08 to C-238/08), [2010] ECR I-2417; *L'Oréal SA v. eBay International AG* (Case C-324/09) [2011] ECR I-6011.

[2015] Directive 2008/95/EU of the European Parliament and of the Council of 22 Octover 2008 to approximate the laws of the Member States relating to trade marks, OJ EU 2008 C 229/25.

[2016] *Wintersteiger AG v. Products 4U Sondermaschinenbau* (Case C-523/10), ECLI:EU:C:2012:220 para. 28.

[2017] *Wintersteiger AG v. Products 4U Sondermaschinenbau* (Case C-523/10), ECLI:EU:C:2012:220 para. 28.

[2018] *Matthias Lehmann/Stieper*, JZ 2012, 1016, 1018.

[2019] *Matthias Lehmann/Stieper*, JZ 2012, 1016, 1019.

[2020] As it is welcomed from the perspective of victims' lawyers by *Sylvia Lorenz*, jurisPR-ITR 2012 Anm. 5.

[2021] A-G *Cruz Villalón*, Opinion of 16 February 2012 in Case C-523/10, ECLI:EU:C:2012:90 para. 28.

[2022] A-G *Cruz Villalón*, Opinion of 16 February 2012 in Case C-523/10, ECLI:EU:C:2012:90 paras. 30–31.

[2023] See LG Hamburg ZUM-RD 2011, 494 = IPRspr. 2011 Nr. 236.

[2024] *Torremans*, in: Torremans (ed.), Research Handbook on Cross-Border Enforcement of Intellectual Property (2014), p. 381, 388.

(a) substantial activities in furtherance of the infringement in its entirety have been carried out within the territory of the State in which the court is situated, or

(b) the harm causes by the infringement in the State where the court is situated is substantial in relation to the infringement in its entirety."[2025]

393 The ECJ reiterated and exemplified this approach with regard to **copyright**, thus indicating that registration of the IP right protected is not the all-decisive factor: In so far as the protection of copyright afforded by the Member State of the court seised applies only in that Member State the court seised on the basis of the place where the damage occurs has jurisdiction only to determine the damage caused in the territory of that Member State.[2026] Since copyright in most states does not require registration, registration can not provide an appropriate connecting factor here, in contrast to the infringement of registered IP rights.[2027] The courts of other Member States in principle retain jurisdiction, in the light of (2) and the principle of territoriality, to rule on the damage caused to copyright caused in their respective Member States, given that they are best placed, first, to ascertain whether the rights of copyright guaranteed by the Member State concerned have in fact been infringed and, secondly, to determine the nature of the damage caused.[2028] The principles of territoriality and the mosaic principle are a good match. To establish jurisdiction and cognisance for the world-wide damage in the *forum protectionis*[2029] would have to overcome both of them. By necessity jurisdiction for infringement of unregistered rights can not be based on the place of registration.[2030] This leads to a rather unwelcome dogmatic split and much distinguishing and differentiation.[2031]

394 The case is different with regard to IP rights of a non-national character, in particular Community patents, Uniform Patents or Community trademarks.[2032] Community trademarks, however, are subject to the special rules on jurisdiction as contained in Arts. 91; 92; 93 (5) Regulation (EC) No. 40/94 which expressly preclude the application of (2).[2033]

4. Place where the harmful event may occur

395 The second alternative found in (2) vests jurisdiction in the courts of the place where the harmful event *may* occur. It is entirely related to future torts and is specifically designed to cover preventive actions.[2034] Thus it does not bear relevance to torts which have already

---

[2025] Art. 2:203 (2) CLIP Principles.

[2026] *Peter Pinckney v. KDG Mediatech AG* (Case C-170/12), ECLI:EU:C:2013:635 para. 45; *Hi Hotel HCF SARL v. Uwe Spoering* (Case C-387/12), ECLI:EU:C:2014:215 para. 38; A-G *Jääskinen*, Opinion of 13 June 2013 in Case C-170/12 para. 48.

[2027] *Azzi*, D. 2014, 411, 412.

[2028] *Peter Pinckney v. KDG Mediatech AG* (Case C-170/12), ECLI:EU:C:2013:635 para. 46; *Hi Hotel HCF SARL v. Uwe Spoering* (Case C-387/12), ECLI:EU:C:2014:215 para. 39.

[2029] As advocated for by *Garber*, ÖBl 2014, 46; eod., ÖBl 2014, 100, 107–108; *Sujecki*, EuZW 2013, 866.

[2030] *Höller*, ÖJZ 2013, 1024 at 1024.

[2031] *Höller*, ÖJZ 2013, 1024, 1025.

[2032] *Michael Müller*, EuZW 2014, 434, 435.

[2033] *Coty Germany GmbH v. First Note Perfumes NV* (Case C-360/12), ECLI:EU:C:2014:1318 para. 28. For an understanding parallel with (2), though, BGH GRUR 2012, 925 – Parfumflakon II; *Picht*, GRUR Int 2013, 19, 26.

happened and have been perfected in the past. Accordingly, claims for damages can not be brought there since damages require an event in the past and negative consequences inflicted upon the victim's assets or fortune. Harm not yet materialised but only pending in the dark clouds and the insecurity of the future, does not trigger damages in whichever substantive law. Generally, the principle of ubiquity also applies,[2035] and accordingly both the courts of the place where the future activity will happen, and of the place where the future damage will be sustained, have jurisdiction. The latter was hotly debated (and mostly[2036] denied[2037]) under Art. 5 (2) Brussels or Lugano Convention, but now contemplates and reflects the protective aspects at issue and the legislative developments, particularly in environmental matters.[2038]

Two scenarios must be distinguished: the first where in the past a harmful event already has **396** taken place, and the second where this was not the case. The first scenario provides an evident solution for localising the future tort tentatively: Under the assumption that the future tort roughly mirrors, and coincides with, the particulars of the past tort at least a presumption should be formulated that the future tort will take place where the tort in the past has happened.[2039] In order to trigger this presumption the similarity between the past and the future tort is required, but there need not be total correspondence between the two of them. The main features have to bear this similarity.

More problematic (but nevertheless firmly encompassed by the second alternative of (2)[2040]) **397** is the second scenario since here the past does not provide a helping hand regularly or on a

---

[2034] See only Commission Proposal COM (1999) 348 final p. 15; *Verein für Konsumenteninformation v. Karl Heinz Henkel* (Case C-167/00), [2002] ECR I-8111, I-8142 para. 48; BGH WM 2006, 350, 351; *Markus*, SZW 1999, 205, 207; *Christian Kohler*, in: Gottwald (ed.), Revision des EuGVÜ/Neues Schiedsverfahrensrecht (2000), p. 1, 21; *Hausmann*, EuLF 2000-01, 40, 48; *Micklitz/Rott*, EuZW 2001, 325, 329; *Piltz*, NJW 2002, 789, 792; *Michailidou* IPRax 2003, 223, 225; *Kropholler/von Hein* Art. 5 note 68; *Rauscher/ Leible* Art. 5 note 81.

[2035] *Niboyet*, Gaz. Pal. 2001, 1, 943, 946; *Droz/Gaudemet-Tallon*, RCDIP 90 (2001), 601, 637; *André Huet*, Clunet 131 (2004), 193, 195.

[2036] But cf. for an affirmative answer *Geimer/Schütze* Internationale Urteilsanerkennung I/1 p. 621 *et seq.*; *Jürgen Heinrichs*, Die Bestimmung der gerichtlichen Zuständigkeit nach dem Begehungsort im nationalen und internationalen Zivilprozessrecht (1984) p. 50; *Behr*, GRUR Int. 1992, 605, 607; *Mankowski*, EWS 1994, 305, 307 and tentatively WAC Ltd. v. Wilcock 1990 SLT 213, 215 (O.H., Lord *Cameron of Lochbroom*).

[2037] Cassaz. RDIPP 1990, 685, 687; OLG Bremen RIW 1992, 231, 233; LG Bremen RIW 1991, 416; Trib. Lodi RDIPP 1992, 332, 336 *et seq.*; Pres. Rb. Middelburg NJ 1989n Nr. 744 p. 2891 = [1990] I.L.Pr. 249; *Desantes Real*, La competencia judicial en la Comunidad Europea (1986) p. 317.

[2038] See *Betlem*, Civil Liability for Transfrontier Pollution (1993) p. 108–112; *Fach Goméz*, ZEuS 1999, 583, 603 *et seq.*

[2039] Rb. Arnhem 3 July 1975 – Forge et Coutellerie Dubois NV and Wolpa Plastics v. Fantu Food BV, in: Digest I-5.3 B 1; WAC Ltd. v. Wilcock 1990 SLT 213, 215 (O.H., Lord *Cameron of Lochbroom*); *Mankowski*, EWS 1994, 305, 307.

[2040] Convincing arguments may be found in *Hye-Knudsen*, Marken-, Patent- und Urheberrechtsverletzungen im europäischen internationalen Zivilprozessrecht (2005) p. 113.

Peter Mankowski

reliable basis with the possibility that the tort might be staged for the first time.[2041] Even now some cases can be solved fairly easily: If the potential tortfeasor announces to strike at a certain place or against certain parts of the potential victim's assets which can be located at a certain place the victim can seize the tortfeasor upon his own word. The tortfeasor can not duck away, and the victim can rely on the threat in order to determine where to launch his pre-emptive counter-strike. Insofar the threatening announcement turns against its own master.

398 If no act or announcement by the prospective tortfeasor directly indicates where the tort will occur one has to look at the facts of the particular case.[2042] There might at least be some indications which kind of tort is lurking around the corner. The kind of future tort at stake heavily influences the possible target, i.e. the kind of assets held by the victim which are threatened and might be affected. The target of the projected attack is vital for defining the attack. If for instance a copyright infringement ought to be discussed it is immaterial where the victim holds his main account since it is not the money in the books which is threatened. If bodily harm and injury is in question the location of other assets would not matter either. If unfair competition is at stake the relevant market targeted at by the attack is the decisive factor. The same approach applies if pollution of the environment is at stake: The relevant place is where the harm to the environment of the claimant's property materialises.[2043] If an infringement is threatened, the starting point of the production of the products infringing the victim's intellectual property rights or trademarks should suffice.[2044] In any event, there must be a serious danger of a damaging act, not a mere theoretical possibility.[2045] Localisation might be based on some kind of guessing and speculative thinking but needs to be backed by some factual indications at least.[2046]

IV. Special jurisdiction in connection with criminal proceedings, Art. 7 (3)

1. Annex jurisdiction

399 Civil claims can be handled as annexed matters in criminal proceedings by criminal courts[2047] if the applicable national law on criminal procedure permits so. For the purposes of (3) jurisdiction in such annexed civil matters is established before the court hearing the respective criminal proceedings. Eventually this is only a kind of consequence flowing from legislative decisions made in Art. 1: For the purposes of its applicability the Brussels I Regulation does not distinguish between different kinds of courts, but only between the

---

[2041] See OLG Bremen RIW 1992, 231, 233; *Kubis*, Internationale Zuständigkeit bei Persönlichkeits- und Immaterialgüterrechtsverletzungen (1999) p. 113.

[2042] See *Kaye* p. 571.

[2043] *Fach Goméz*, ZEuS 1999, 583, 604 *et seq.*

[2044] *Ebner*, Markenschutz im internationalen Privat- und Zivilprozessrecht (2004) p. 190.

[2045] CA Orléans RCDIP 93 (2004), 139, 146 with note *Gaudemet-Tallon* = Clunet 131 (2004), 193 with note *André Huet*; *Gaudemet-Tallon*, RCDIP 93 (2004), 147, 150 *et seq.*

[2046] See OLG Düsseldorf WRP 1994, 877, 879; *Lindacher*, in: FS Hideo Nakamura (Tokyo 1996), p. 321, 328; *Lindacher*, Internationales Wettbewerbsverfahrensrecht (2009) § 9 note 1.

[2047] On the underpinning ratio of such civil proceedings *Mankowski(/Bock)*, in: FG Rudolf Machacek and Franz Matscher (2008), p. 785, 787 *et seq.*

matters at stake. Accordingly, a civil matter[2048] tried in a criminal court is covered.[2049] Ancillary civil proceedings are not criminal proceedings and thus they are not by virtue simply of their links with criminal matters excluded from the scope of application of the Brussels Ibis Regulation.[2050] The plaintiff gets some kind of *forum connexitatis* by virtue of (3).[2051] He might gain a major advantage from a participation in the criminal proceedings: he may profit and benefit from the inquiries and inquisitions official bodies execute, and will thus run less into lack of evidence.[2052] From a higher level of abstraction, (3) serves purposes of procedural economy and of maintaining the unity of the proceedings.[2053] In practice ancillary proceedings trying civil claims bear a very differing relevance in the Member States; they are rather important in Belgium, the Scandinavian countries, France (*action civile*), and Italy whereas they only seldom are staged in Germany (*Adhäsionsverfahren*) or in Austria.[2054] The main relevance of (3) might be with regard to traffic accidents.[2055]

2. Reference to national law for criminal proceedings as such

On the other hand criminal proceedings follow different rules apart from those for genuine **400** civil proceedings. Taking this into account the jurisdictional regime has to pay quite some respect. (3) features as a peculiarity among the heads of jurisdiction in Art. 7: In contrast to the other heads (with the exception of the second prong of (2)) it does not define itself as being the connecting factor employed for establishing jurisdiction but makes jurisdiction indirectly dependent upon the heads of jurisdiction, and of *criminal* jurisdiction at that, in the national law of the *forum*.[2056] Whichever link the national law deems sufficient to grant criminal jurisdiction is indirectly accepted by (3). Apparently Brussels I did not want to intervene in criminal procedural law (which generally is outside the scope of application of Brussels I) and did not deem it worthwhile to circumscribe factors eventually restricting excessive jurisdiction with regard to annexed civil matters.[2057] If national law on criminal procedure e.g. vests jurisdiction in the courts where the accused was apprehended this will

---

[2048] But characterisation must come first; *Burgstaller/Neumayr* Art. 5 note 61 (Oct. 2002).

[2049] Art. 1 note 15 (*Rogerson*).

[2050] *Davenport v. Corinthian Motor Policies at Lloyd's* 1991 SLT 774 (OH, Lord *McCluskey*); *Layton/Mercer* para. 15.100.

[2051] *Schoibl*, in: FS Rainer Sprung (2001), p. 321, 323; *Mankowski*, in: FG Rudolf Machacek and Franz Matscher (2008), p. 785, 789.

[2052] *Christian Kohler*, in: Will (ed.), Schadensersatz im Strafverfahren (1990), p. 74, 75; *Schoibl*, in: FS Rainer Sprung (2001), p. 321, 325; *Leible*, in: Rauscher Art. 5 note 93; *Mankowski*, in: FG Rudolf Machacek and Franz Matscher (2008), p. 785, 789.

[2053] *Teixeira de Sousa/Moura Vicente* Art. 5 note 7.

[2054] *Schoibl*, in: FS Rainer Sprung (2001), p. 321, 323. Comparative survey by *Zander*, Das Adhösionsverfahren im neuen Gewand (2011).

[2055] *Droz* para. 36; *Weser* para. 199; *Collins* p. 61; *Layton/Mercer* para. 15.100.

[2056] See only *Blanco-Morales Limones*, in: Calvo Caravaca, Art. 5.4 CB note 10; *Piekenbrock*, IPRax 1998, 177 *et seq.*; *Prinz von Sachsen Gessaphe*, ZZP Int. 5 (2000), 225, 231; *Burgstaller/Neumayr* Art. 5 note 60 (Oct. 2002); *Mankowski*, in: FG Rudolf Machacek and Franz Matscher (2008), p. 785, 789; *Matthias Lehmann*, in: Dickinson/Lein para. 4.125.

[2057] *Hausmann*, in: Wieczorek/Schütze Art. 5 EuGVÜ with notes 65, 68; *Schoibl*, in: FS Rainer Sprung (2001), p. 321, 327.

---

suffice.[2058] Even heads of jurisdiction which would be unsustainable in mere civil proceedings in the light of Art. 5 (2) like the victim's nationality gain access through the backdoor.[2059] (3) does not employ it's own restrictive approach like e.g. Art. 5 (2) Brussels I Regulation did for maintenance matters.[2060]

3. Bringing ancillary civil claims in criminal proceedings must be allowed by national law

401 A precondition may require that the national law of the *forum* allows to bring civil claims to be brought in criminal proceedings. If the national law does not permit this, (3) is not applicable as the final clause of (3) demonstrates with ultimate clarity.[2061] (3) does not guarantee the possibility to bring civil claims in criminal proceedings independent from, and the less overriding, national law.[2062] Also (3) accepts any restrictions or conditions with which the national law qualifies such annexed civil claims before permitting them.[2063] (3) generally does not intervene with the national code on proceedings before criminal courts. Accordingly, collective actions, like for instance the action civile under French law, are included.[2064] The wording of (3) would even cover civil claims brought against another defendant other than the defendant in the criminal proceedings,[2065] but this should be restricted to cases where the defendant is identical in both sets of proceedings.[2066]

402 Orders by the criminal court for recompensation of the victim and other restitution orders do not fall under (3)[2067] if and insofar as they are prompted either on the own motion of the court or an application by the public prosecutor. They lack the nature of a civil matter by virtue of Art. 1,[2068] since they are not pursued by a person in a private capacity. Deprivation orders and confiscation orders are definitely not covered.[2069]

[2058] Report *Jenard* p. 26. See *Christian Kohler*, in: Will (ed.), Schadensersatz im Strafverfahren (1990), p. 74, 76; *Schoibl*, in: FS Rainer Sprung (2001), p. 321, 328.

[2059] See *Prinz von Sachsen Gessaphe*, ZZP Int. 5 (2000), 225, 231 *et seq.*, 234 *et seq.*; *Geimer*, in: Studia in honorem János Németh (2003), p. 229, 231 *et seq.*; *Geimer/Schütze* Art. 5 note 284 and also *Idot*, Europe 157 (2000), 22.

[2060] *Schoibl*, in: FS Rainer Sprung (2001), p. 321, 324.

[2061] *Mankowski*, in: FG Rudolf Machacek and Franz Matscher (2008), p. 785, 790.

[2062] See only *Schoibl*, in: FS Rainer Sprung (2001), p. 321, 327 *et seq.*; *Mankowski*, in: FG Rudolf Machacek and Franz Matscher (2008), p. 785, 790; *Simotta*, in: Fasching/Konecny Art. 5 note 353 with further references.

[2063] *Mankowski*, in: FG Rudolf Machacek and Franz Matscher (2008), p. 785, 790; *Hofmann/Kunz*, in: Basler Kommentar, Art. 5 note 656.

[2064] *Michailidou*, IPRax 2003, 223, 226.

[2065] *Ras*, TPR 1975, 851, 872 *et seq.*; *Leible*, in: Rauscher, Art. 5 note 97; *Kropholler/von Hein*, Art. 5 note 98.

[2066] *Schoibl*, in: FS Rainer Sprung (2001), p. 321, 328 *et seq.*; *Burgstaller/Neumayr* Art. 5 note 60 (Oct. 2002); *Hess*, § 6 note 75; *Geimer/Schütze* Art. 5 note 290; *Matthias Lehmann*, in: Dickinson/Lein para. 4.123.

[2067] *Schoibl*, in: FS Rainer Sprung (2001), p. 321, 326; *Burgstaller/Neumayr* Art. 5 note 61 (Oct. 2002). Against the inclusion of orders under (then) sec. 35 Powers of Criminal Courts Act 1973, today sec. 130; 148; 149 Powers of Criminal Courts (Sentencing) Act 2000 and sec. 58 Criminal Justice (Scotland) Act 1980 *Kaye* p. 589; *Christian Kohler*, in: Will (ed.), Schadensersatz im Strafverfahren (1990), p. 74; but see also *Layton/Mercer* para. 15.100.

[2068] *Kaye* p. 589.

4. Criminal court seised

Jurisdiction under (3) is only granted if the criminal court is seised, i.e. if the criminal court is **403** entertaining the criminal proceedings. (3) acknowledges that according to national law on criminal procedure the civil matter might be annexed to the criminal proceedings but demands that the criminal proceedings established take the lead for the civil matter.[2070] In this regard it is not detrimental if the writ for the annexed civil proceedings is issued simultaneously with the opening step in the criminal proceedings. It is not necessary that the criminal proceedings are initiated first and that there must be some space of time between this and issuing the writ for the annexed civil matter.[2071] The point of time when the criminal court becomes seised with the criminal proceedings must be determined pursuant to the national law of the *forum*. It defines "seisin" and the respective prerequisites (whether in a system employing judges for exploring the initial case actions by this judge are relevant, whether issuing the summons matters, whether service on the accused/defendant is necessary, whether only a formal initiation and opening of the proceedings by the court suffices etc.). Mere preliminary investigations do not seise a criminal court.[2072] If the criminal investigation is not under way at all, (3) is wholesale inoperable.[2073]

If on the other hand any national procedural law should go so far as to allow isolated civil **404** matters in criminal courts, (3) would not come into operation and jurisdiction for such an isolated claim could only be based on other heads of jurisdiction.[2074] The idea behind (3) is to acknowledge annex competence. Accordingly, if there is nothing to which the civil matter is or could be annexed this idea can not be validly invoked.[2075] Even less (3) can vest jurisdiction in civil courts.[2076]

Likewise the mere possibility that criminal proceedings could possibly be established does **405** not suffice, nor does any only hypothetical, but not actual criminal proceedings.[2077] (3) does not come into operation either if criminal proceedings take place in the state where the accused has its domicile, by virtue of the opening words of Art. 7 pr.[2078] But under the general notion of *perpetuatio fori* the *forum* provided by (3) should be retained if *in concreto* the criminal proceedings were terminated with the accused being acquitted whereas the civil proceedings of adhesion are pursued further by the plaintiff.[2079] Accordingly, the actual

---

[2069] *Layton/Mercer* paras. 12.023, 15.100; *Mankowski*, in: FG Rudolf Machacek and Franz Matscher (2008), p. 785, 791.

[2070] *Mankowski*, in: FG Rudolf Machacek and Franz Matscher (2008), p. 785, 791.

[2071] *Mankowski*, in: FG Rudolf Machacek and Franz Matscher (2008), p. 785, 791.

[2072] *Layton/Mercer* para. 15.100; *Mankowski*, in: FG Rudolf Machacek and Franz Matscher (2008), p. 785, 791.

[2073] Protodikeio Thessaloniki Arm. 1994, 308 with note *Vassilikakis*.

[2074] *Mankowski*, in: FG Rudolf Machacek and Franz Matscher (2008), p. 785, 791.

[2075] Cassaz. RDIPP 1997, 729, 734.

[2076] *Vassilikakis*, Arm. 1994, 310; *Vassilikakis*, IPRax 2005, 279, 281.

[2077] Cassaz. RDIPP 1997, 729, 734; Trib. Varese DRIPP 1998, 425, 428.

[2078] Cassaz. RDIPP 2003, 547, 553.

[2079] *Mankowski*, in: FG Rudolf Machacek and Franz Matscher (2008), p. 785, 792; *Hofmann/Kunz*, in: Basler Kommentar, Art. 5 note 668. See BGE 124 IV 13, 20.

pending of the criminal proceedings at the time when judgment is given in the ancillary civil proceedings, is not required.[2080]

5. Special rule in Art. 64

406 Without prejudice to any more favourable provisions of national laws, persons domiciled in a Member State who are being prosecuted in the criminal courts of another Member State of which they are not nationals for an offence which was not intentionally committed, may be defended by persons qualified to do so, even if they do not appear in person, pursuant to Art. 64. Yet likewise by virtue of Art. 64, the court seised of the matter may order an appearance in person; in the case of a failure to appear, a judgment given in the civil action without the person concerned having had the opportunity to arrange for his defence need not be recognised or enforced in the other Member States.

V. Special jurisdiction based on ownership of cultural objects, Art. 7 (4)

407 As the remainder and remnant of a more ambitious approach[2081] pursued by Art. 5 (3) Brussels I*bis* Proposal, namely to introduce a general head of special jurisdiction for all rights in rem in any kind of moveable ownership,[2082] (4) is an innovative outcome of the recasting process.[2083] It establishes special jurisdiction for claims based on ownership of cultural objects, in the courts of the place where the respective cultural object is located. Its genesis explains why ownership of cultural objects is the only cause of action for which (4) is opened; insofar (4) at its core remains a *forum rei sitae* for a *rei vindicatio*.[2084] Cyprus was particularly interested in a head of special jurisdiction for cultural objects and urged to implement it.[2085] (4) cannot be said to be exorbitant[2086] but is rather related to the physical object at the core of the matter.

408 A possible example for a case which now would be covered by (4) might be provided by the *Halphen* case before French courts[2087] in the 1970s:[2088] A table was looted in France during the German occupation. The former owner re-claimed it from the then present possessor. He invoked Art. 5 (3) Brussels Convention for establishing a forum in France. The French courts denied such forum since although it clearly was an extra-contractual matter, Art. 5 (3) Brussels Convention had as its sole object dealing with the defendant's responsibility in damages.[2089] A *forum rei sitae* permitting special jurisdiction for a *rei vindicatio* of chattels

---

[2080] *Mankowski*, in: FG Rudolf Machacek and Franz Matscher (2008), p. 785, 792. Tentatively *contra Layton/ Mercer* para. 15.100.

[2081] *Nuyts*, in: Nuyts (coord.), Actualités en droit international privé (Bruxelles 2013), p. 77, 128; *de Lambertye-Autrand*, in: Emmanuel Guinchard, p. 83, 92.

[2082] *Supra* Art. 7 notes 18–20 (*Mankowski*).

[2083] *Crespi Reghizzi* www.aldricus.com/2012/12/13/crespi; *Cadet*, Clunet 140 (2013), 765, 775.

[2084] *Leandro*, Giust. proc. civ. 2013, 583, 595; *Rogerson*, in: Dickinson/Lein para. 4.130; see also *Beraudo*, Clunet 140 (2013), 741, 746.

[2085] *Mansel/Thorn/Rolf Wagner*, IPRax 2013, 1, 9.

[2086] *Matthias Weller*, GPR 2013, 329; *Pfeiffer*, ZZP 127 (2014) 409, 419.

[2087] TGI Paris RCDIP 63 (1974), 696 with note *Lagarde* = Clunet 102 (1975), 82 with note *Holleaux* = D. 1975, 638 with note *Droz*; CA Paris Clunet 103 (1976), 146 with note *Holleaux*.

[2088] *Nuyts*, RCDIP 102 (2013), 1, 59.

thus was in some demand since the *forum delicti* did not provide a remedy in all instances.[2090] Looted property was the prime example, and the most prominent instances were cultural objects looted in occupied territories by forces or single soldiers of belligerent forces (barring the sometimes very peculiar and fact-specific historic backgrounds and circumstances). But if the present occupier is not domiciled in a Member State (4) will not be applicable.[2091]

The protection of cultural objects has advanced and progressed substantively in internatio- **409** nal law[2092] and in EU law over the last decades.[2093] EU law alone promulgated the Directive 93/7/EEC[2094] and first the Regulation (EEC) No. 3911/92,[2095] now the Regulation (EU) No. 116/2009.[2096] Yet there was not an accompanying move as to jurisdiction which would take precedence over the Brussels I Regulation pursuant to Art. 67 Brussels I Regulation.[2097] (4) is set to fill this presumed *lacuna*. It is to supplement Directive 93/7/EEC in order to accomplish the goals pursued by that Directive. (4) is closely interrelated and connected with Directive 93/7/EEC. It provides a missing piece in the jigsaw, namely the jurisdictional occasion for original owners to go after, and relinquish, their ownership. Cultural objects indirectly gain better and enhanced protection as their owners get special jurisdiction in a forum where the goods can be effectively returned, and do not have to sue the present holder in the state of his domicile under Art. 4 (1).[2098] (4) liberates the claimant-owner from the restriction that he ought to sue in the State of the defendant's domicile pursuant to Art. 4 (1).[2099] The *effet utile* of a return policy for cultural objects is fostered. It adds another piece to the array of weaponry in the fight against illicit export and import of cultural objects, this piece being based on the very personal interests of the legitimate owners.[2100] Art. 36 TFEU

[2089] TGI Paris RCDIP 63 (1974), 696 with note *Lagarde* = Clunet 102 (1975), 82 with note *Holleaux* = D. 1975, 638 with note *Droz*; CA Paris Clunet 103 (1976), 146 with note *Holleaux*.

[2090] *Franzina*, Riv. dir. int. 2011, 789; *Nuyts*, in: Nuyts (coord.), Actualités en droit international privé (Bruxelles 2013), p. 77, 128–129; *Pfeiffer*, ZZP 127 (2014), 409, 419.

[2091] *de Lambertye-Autrand*, in: Emmanuel Guinchard, p. 83, 98.

[2092] Most prominently UNESCO Convention on the Means of Prohibiting and Preventing the Illicit Import, Export and Transfer of Ownership of Cultural Property of 14 November 1970, 823 UNTS 231; UNI-DROIT Convention on Stolen or Illegally Exported Cultural Objects of 24 June 1995, (1995) 34 ILM 1322. For more detailed discussion e.g. Nafziger (ed.), Cultural Heritage Law (2012); Francioni/Gordley (eds.), Enforcing International Cultural Heritage Law (2013).

[2093] See in particular the respective Acts discussed in *Radloff*, Kulturgüterrecht (2013) pp. 230–316; *Krenz*, Rechtliche Probleme des internationalen Kulturgüterschutzes (2013).

[2094] Council Directive 93/7/EEC of 15 March 1993 on the return of cultural objects unlawfully removed from the territory of a Member State, OJ EEC 1993 L 74/74.

[2095] Council Regulation (EEC) No. 3911/92 of 9 December on the export of cultural objects, OJ EEC 1992 L 395/1.

[2096] Council Regulation (EU) No. 116/2009 of 18 December 2008 on the export of cultural objects, OJ EU 2009 L 39/1.

[2097] See *d'Avout*, D. 2013, 1014, 1020 fn. 32.

[2098] *Alio*, NJW 2014, 2395, 2399.

[2099] *Alio*, NJW 2014, 2397, 2399.

[2100] *de Lambertye-Autrand*, in: Emmanuel Guinchard, p. 83, 84.

gives legitimacy to respective measures,[2101] and Art. 8 of the relevant UNIDROIT Convention[2102] provides cover in the quarters of international law.[2103]

410 Consequentially, (4) does not provide jurisdiction for claims by States based on Directive 93/7/EEC since these claims would not be based on ownership of the private law sense, but on indictions inflicted by public law.[2104] Recital (17) cl. 2[2105] underlines that proceedings under Directive 93/7/EEC do not fall under (4) and that proceedings under (4) should be without prejudice to proceedings initiated under Directive 93/7/EEC. Proceedings under Directive 93/7/EEC are thus not prejudiced by proceedings under (4),[2106] neither in terms of *lis pendens* nor in any ban on different outcomes in different sets of proceedings. (4) is analogous, and a parallel, for claims by private parties to Art. 5 Directive 93/7/EEC for claims by Member States.[2107] The latter are not civil and commercial matters and thus are outside the scope of application of the Brussels *Ibis* Regulation by virtue of Art. 1 (1).[2108]

411 As for the definition of cultural object, (4) expressly turns to the respective definition as contained in Art. 1 (1) Directive 93/7/EEC. The definition substantially covers national treasures to which this tag and label is attached by the State from which they were removed later-on.[2109] In fact the reference is a multi-tier one with two prongs on the second tier for Art. 1 (1) Directive 93/7/EEC refers firstly to Art. 36 EEC Treaty (which has become first Art. 30 EC Treaty and now Art. 36 TFEU) which in turn refers to national legislative and administrative rules, and secondly to the Annex of Directive 93/7/EEC making (4) a little bit more complicated to handle (4).[2110] Furthermore, Directive 93/7/EEC is subject to a reform process,[2111] and the reference will have to be adopted accordingly[2112] (but this will be done automatically by a rule like Art. 19 subpara. 2 Proposal COM [2013] 311 final).

412 The wording of (4) is not restricted to cases where the cultural object was removed from the territory of a Member State.[2113] Insofar (4) does not resemble Directive 93/7/EEC, but at first glance appears to go beyond it. Yet second thoughts might overturn this preliminary result. As to the definition of "cultural object", (4) expressly turns to Art. 1 (1) Directive 93/7/EEC.

[2101] *de Lambertye-Autrand*, in: Emmanuel Guinchard, p. 83, 85, 93.

[2102] UNIDROIT Convention on Stolen or Illegally Exported Cultural Objects of 24 June 1995, (1995) 34 ILM 1322.

[2103] *de Lambertye-Autrand*, in: Emmanuel Guinchard, p. 83, 105.

[2104] See *Francq*, TBH 2013, 309, 327; *Rogerson*, in: Dickinson/Lein para. 4.129.

[2105] In other respects Recital (17) does not add anything substantial to Art. 7 (4); *Emmanuel Guinchard*, Rev. trim. dr. eur. 49 (2013), 319, 331.

[2106] *Nuyts*, RCDIP 102 (2013), 1, 59; *Zilinsky*, NIPR 2014, 3, 6.

[2107] *Leandro*, Giust. proc. civ. 2013, 583, 594.

[2108] *Siehr*, in: FS Dieter Martiny (2014), p. 837, 842–843; *de Lambertye-Autrand*, in: Emmanuel Guinchard, p. 83, 100–101.

[2109] *Beraudo*, Clunet 140 (2013), 741, 746.

[2110] *de Lambertye-Autrand*, in: Emmanuel Guinchard, p. 83, 95; *Pfeiffer*, ZZP 127 (2014), 409, 419.

[2111] Proposal for a Directive of the European Parliament and of the Council on the return of cultural objects unlawfully removed from the territory of a Member State (recast), submitted by the Commission on 30 May 2013, COM (2013) 311 final.

[2112] See *de Lambertye-Autrand*, in: Emmanuel Guinchard, p. 83, 96.

[2113] See *Gaudemet-Tallon/Kessedjian*, Rev. trim. dr. eur. 2013, 435, 443.

Art. 1 (1) Directive 93/7/EEC contains a restriction to cultural objects unlawfully removed from the territory of a Member State (and so does the very heading of Directive 93/7/EEC). If this definition is to be imported verbally and *tel quel* it contains the restriction missing in the remainder of the wording of (4). Such understanding would leave owners of cultural objects removed from a non-Member-State without special protection and privilege in terms of jurisdiction. The reason why Directive 93/7/EEC is restricted to cultural objects removed form Member States, namely that EU law can, and is willing to, vest privileges only in Member States when it comes down to State actors, does not apply equally with regard to private persons.[2114] Claims by States, based on public law, are a fundamentally different treat from claims by private persons, based on private law. Thus, a different understanding is feasible and preferable.[2115] The referral is restricted to the definition of cultural object as contained in Art. 1 (1) Directive 93/7/EEC, i.e. the definition as such, *stricto sensu*, and does not comprise the spatial or temporal dimensions of Directive 93/7/EEC.[2116] More generally, Directive 93/7/EC and (4) pursue different aims and approach the matter from different angles.[2117]

(4) does not alter the concept of defendant. It might establish a *forum rei sitae* in limited **413** instances, but it does not establish a proper action *in rem* which would be directed not against a person but against the chattel at stake itself. The action covered is an action based on ownership, but remains an action *in personam* against a named defendant.

The proper defendant is the possessor of the cultural object at the time when the lawsuit **414** becomes pending. It is irrelevant whether this person happens to be the same person who initially removed, detained or looted the cultural object. This is of particular importance if the cultural object has changed hands after its initial removal. (4) allows to directly attack that member of the art market who has become possessor of the cultural object.[2118] The debtor in possession might be a thief, innocent bailee, custodian, third party holder, or buyer.[2118a] (4) amounts to regulating the demand side of the international art market, too.[2118b] Auction houses, galleries, museums, and collectors are the intended targets.[2118c]

(4) covers claims based on ownership. It is irrelevant whether the claim is based directly on **415** ownership, i.e. whether a genuine *rei vindicatio* is at stake, or whether the claim is based on some kind of tort for the violation of property.[2119] "Actions based on property" is a wider and more functional notion than a hypothetical "actions in property" would be. Ownership could be understood as an autonomous European concept, but alternatively there could be a recourse to the *lex rei sitae* or the *lex fori* respectively, in some parallel to the approach

---

[2114] See *Siehr*, in: FS Dieter Martiny (2014), p. 837, 843–844.

[2115] To the same avail *Siehr*, in: FS Dieter Martiny (2014), p. 837, 843–844.

[2116] *Siehr*, in: FS Dieter Martiny (2014), p. 837, 843–844.

[2117] *de Lambertye-Autrand*, in: Emmanuel Guinchard, p. 83, 95.

[2118] See *Cadet*, Clunet 140 (2013), 765, 775.

[2118a] *Gillies*, (2015) 11 JPrIL 297, 309.

[2118b] *Gillies*, (2015) 11 JPrIL 297, 315.

[2118c] *Briggs* para. 2.212.

[2119] *Siehr*, in: FS Dieter Martiny (2014), p. 837, 843–844; *Gebauer*, in: Ragno (ed.), International Litigation in Europe: The Brussels I Recast as a Panacea? (Milano 2015).

prevailing under Art. 24 (1) subpara. 1 1st option.[2120] *Usufructus* or any kind of security right do not qualify as property for the purposes of (4),[2121] though. To open (4) to claims in tort might have the additional advantage to lead to concurring results of different, but concurring heads of special jurisdiction, in this case (4) and (2).[2122] Actions in contract might be concurring but are not covered by (4).[2123]

416 "Recovery", "récuperation", "Wiedererlangung" (as the term is also used in Recital [17]) might not be the most common notion, but it provides a clear enough indication of the ultimate goal to be pursued, though.[2124] The initial "re" must not be understood in the sense that the present claimant-owner must also be the owner at the time when the cultural object at stake was looted or detained. Transfer of legitimate property or property claims have to be duly recognised and followed. On the other hand, it is not necessary that the owner aims at the restitution of the cultural good to him personally; the restitution to a third person on the owner's demand suffices which covers the case of a revendication against und acquirer *a non domino*.[2125] The action must be for return of the cultural good, not merely for demages, however.[2125a]

417 Furthermore, declaratory actions aiming at a declaration that the plaintiff is the owner of the respective cultural object whereas another person alleging ownership is not the proper owner, are also covered.[2126] The case is a trifle more complicated with regard to negative declaratory actions aiming at a declaration that the possessor is not obliged to return the cultural object.[2127] (4) might cover them only insofar as the possessor can avail himself of ownership since otherwise the prerequisite that the claim must be based on ownership, would not be fulfilled.

418 Whether the claimant really is the present owner of the cultural object at stake is a matter of the applicable law as to substance.[2128] For the limited purposes of (4) it suffices that the claimants alleges to be the owner. It is then for the proceedings to come, to establish as to whether his claim is right.

419 (4) does not contain an evident restriction to claims by private persons. It might be applicable even if a State proceeds against a present possessor and bases its claims on (public) property. Public property making the respective cultural objects state-owned, might be of

---

[2120] *Gebauer*, in: Ragno (ed.), International Litigation in Europe: The Brussels I Recast as a Panacea? (Milano 2015). Different suggestions by *Gillies*, (2015) 11 JPrIL 297, 311.

[2121] *de Lambertye-Autrand*, in: Emmanuel Guinchard, p. 83, 100.

[2122] *Gebauer*, in: Ragno (ed.), International Litigation in Europe: The Brussels I Recast as a Panacea? (Milano 2015).

[2123] But cf. *de Lambertye-Autrand*, in: Emmanuel Guinchard, p. 83, 101–103.

[2124] Tentatively *contra de Lambertye-Autrand*, in: Emmanuel Guinchard, p. 83, 99; see also *Gillies*, (2015) 11 JPrIL 297, 312.

[2125] *de Lambertye-Autrand*, in: Emmanuel Guinchard, p. 83, 101.

[2125a] *Rogerson*, in: Dickinson/Lein para. 4.131.

[2126] *Siehr*, in: FS Dieter Martiny (2014), p. 837, 843–844. With some doubts *Gebauer*, in: Ragno (ed.), International Litigation in Europe: The Brussels I Recast as a Panacea? (Milano 2015).

[2127] See *Siehr*, in: FS Dieter Martiny (2014), p. 837, 843–844.

[2128] See *Francq*, TBH 2013, 309, 327.

particular relevance with regard to archaeological cultural objects.[2129] Yet the restriction to "civil claims" has to be observed.[2130]

As its connecting factor, (4) employs the location of the cultural object at the time when the **420** court is seised. Seen in a wider context, this might appear a little bit at odds with the eventual rejection of a *forum fortunae* as it was tabled by the Commission in Art. 25 Brussels I*bis* Proposal.[2131] But in the narrower context, it is the proper connecting factor given that (4) covers only actions for return of the cultural object. The cultural object is the prospective object of future enforcement of the decision rendered, and relying on its *situs* establishes a connection between court proceedings generating a judicial title and enforcement. (4) has the additional benefit that it vests jurisdiction in the courts of the place where the cultural object actually is, for issuing preliminary measures and in particular effectively arresting the cultural object under the auspices of Art. 35. When a court is seised should be ascertained in accordance with Art. 32 not with the national procedural laws of the respective *lex fori* despite Art. 32 restricting its direct ambit to Section 9.[2132] With regard to negative declaratory actions, the connecting factor, *situs rei*, might be open to manipulation by the possessor and risks abusive control of choice of forum in the possessor's favour (for instance if the possessor carries the cultural object to the intended forum in his luggage).[2133]

It is equally important and noteworthy that (4) does not establish a forum in the Member **421** State from which the cultural object was removed. Despite considerations to the contrary,[2134] a *forum originis* has not been promulgated. To determine the "origin" of a cultural object could become fairly difficult, in particular if more than one State claims the respective object to be a "national treasure". Referring to the removal ob the cultural object does not help all too much further but only shifts the basic problem to another level. For the purposes of jurisdiction, the *situs* is the more appropriate connecting factor, and the arguments advanced in favour of applying the *lex originis* in private international law,[2135] are of lesser

---

[2129] See in detail *Siehr*, in: Liber amicorum Paolo Picone (2011), p. 983.

[2130] *Gebauer*, in: Ragno (ed.), International Litigation in Europe: The Brussels I Recast as a Panacea? (Milano 2015).

[2131] *Cadet*, Clunet 140 (2013), 765, 775.

[2132] *Contra de Lambertye-Autrand*, in: Emmanuel Guinchard, p. 83, 99.

[2133] *Gebauer*, in: Ragno (ed.), International Litigation in Europe: The Brussels I Recast as a Panacea? (Milano 2015).

[2134] *Jayme*, in: FS Reinhard Mußgnug (2005), p. 517, 524.

[2135] Art. 2 Resolution La vente internationale d'objets d'art sous l'angle de la protection du patrimoine culturel, (Session Bâle 1991), Ann. Inst. Dr. Int. 64 (1992), 402; *Jayme*, in: Dolzer/Jayme/Mußgnug (Hrsg.), Rechtsfragen des internationalen Kulturgüterschutzes, 1994, S. 35, 42 *et seq.*; *Jayme*, Nationales Kunstwerk und Internationales Privatrecht (1999), p. 49, 54 *et seq.* and p. 95, 100 *et seq.*; *Jayme*, in: FS Reinhard Mußgnug (2005), p. 517, 518 *et seq.*; *Jayme/Christian Kohler*, IPRax 1993, 357, 360; *Müller-Katzenburg*, Internationale Standards im Kulturgüterverkehr und ihre Bedeutung für das Sach- und Kollisionsrecht (1996) pp. 225 *et seq.*; *Armbrüster*, NJW 2011, 3581, 3582–3583; *Marc Weber*, Unveräußerliches Kulturgut im nationalen und internationalen Rechtsverkehr (2002) p. 410; *Kienle/Marc-Philippe Weller*, IPRax 2004, 290, 291; *Symeonides*, 38 Vand. J. Trans. L. 1177, 1186 (2005); *Fincham*, 32 Columb. J. L. & Arts 111, 146–149 (2008); *Siehr*, in: Liber Fausto Pocar, vol. II (2009), p. 879; *Michael Anton*, Internationales Kulturgüterprivat- und -zivilverfahrensrecht (2010) pp. 803–1009 and *Kurpiers*, Die lex originis-Regel im Internationalen Sachenrecht (2005).

significance. This might lead to a divergence between the actual situs and the historical lex situs, however, the latter necessarily to be refered to for assessing original title to the cultural good.[2135a]

VI. Special jurisdiction based on an establishment, Art. 7 (5)

1. General remarks

422   (5) grants special jurisdiction in favour of the courts of the place where the defendant has an establishment if and insofar as the claim bears a relation to this establishment. It is funded on the *ratio* that the defendant should be held liable where he himself voluntarily founded an establishment and thus enhanced the local reach of his own activities. Where you seek your advantage you must face the consequences even if they are adversarial. Anything else would amount to a *venire contra factum proprium*.[2136] The underlying *ratio* is akin to, but not identical with, the American concept of doing business.[2137] Playing with words, one could feel tempted to call (5) a "small (or miniaturised) general jurisdiction"[2138] or "quasi-general jurisdiction"[2139] since it is neither restricted nor related to certain classes of claims but requires a connecting factor derived from the defendant. Only the factor chosen differs from Art. 4 and justifiedly restricts which claims can be brought in this special forum.[2140] Alternatively, (5) could be called a quasi defendant's domicile for the purposes of jurisdiction.[2141] On the other hand, the underpinning rationales are different.[2142] In any event, as with all heads of special jurisdiction contained in Art. 7, an establishment only matters if it is located outside the state where the defendant is domiciled.[2143]

423   (5) only provides a *forum* against the owner of the establishment but not a *forum actoris* in his favour. It does not augment his possibilities but only extends jurisdiction against him. The owner of the establishment can only rely on other heads of jurisdiction if he actively brings claims stemming from the activity of the establishment (for instance the proprietor of an agency business against the principal hiring his services).[2144] This applies even if the owner of a legally independent entity regarded as the establishment of another entity, sues this other entity as his principal.[2145]

[2135a] *Rogerson*, in: Dickinson/Lein para. 4.130.

[2136] *Johannes Weber*, ZvglRWiss 107 (2008), 193, 205 *et seq.*

[2137] See for an extensive and in depth comparison between the two concepts and their respective particularities *Mathias Otto*, Der prozessuale Durchgriff (1993).

[2138] *Gottwald*, in: Münchener Kommentar Art. 5 note 49; *Leible*, in: Rauscher Art. 5 note 99; *Mankowski*, in: FS Andreas Heldrich (2005), p. 867, 887.

[2139] *Virgós Soriano/Garcimartín Alférez*, Derecho procesal civil internacional (2000) para. 102.

[2140] *Kessedjian*, in: Liber Fausto Pocar (2009), p. 533, 539.

[2141] *Anton Durbeck GmbH v. Den Norske Bank ASA* [2003] 2 WLR 1296, 1309 (C.A., per Lord *Phillips of Worth Matravers* M.R.).

[2142] *Löser*, Zuständigkeitsbestimmender Zeitpunkt und perpetuatio fori im internationalen Zivilprozess (2009) p. 155; *Leible*, in: Rauscher, Art. 5 note 99.

[2143] *Mankowski*, in: FS Andreas Heldrich (2005), p. 867, 887.

[2144] See only *Fach Gómez*, Rev. der. com. eur. 14 (2003), 181, 215.

[2145] Cassaz. RDIPP 1998, 160, 162; *Linke*, IPRax 1982, 46, 48 *et seq.*; *Kindler*, in: FS Peter Ulmer (2003), p. 305, 321.

On the other hand, (5) is concerned with jurisdiction for suits against the owner of the **424** establishment, the principal, only. It is not related to jurisdiction for suits against the establishment if the latter is a legal entity in its own right, e.g. a subsidiary. Jurisdiction for such suits has to be ascertained independently. Nevertheless jurisdiction for joined suits against the principal and the legally independent establishment might coincide by virtue of (5) against the former and Art. 4 (1) (plus national rules on local jurisdiction or venue) against the latter (or by a combination involving Art. 8 (1)).

2. Establishment

a) General definition

An establishment is defined as a place of business which has the appearance of permanency, **425** such as the extension of a parent body, has a management and is materially equipped to negotiate business with third parties so that the latter, although knowing that there will if necessary be a legal link with the parent body, the head office of which is abroad, do not have to deal directly with such parent body but may transact business at the place of business constituting the extension.[2146] An establishment is therefore an entity capable of being the primary, or even exclusive, interlocutor for third parties e.g. in the negotiation of contracts.[2147] The establishment acts as the decentralised and prolonged arm of the principal.[2148] Yet a minimum degree of independence going beyond the fact that the establishment covers a certain area, should not be recognised.[2149] The definition is autonomous and excludes any reference to national law.[2150] Its shorthand version reads that every stable structure of an undertaking is covered.[2151] A degree of permanence is required, and a mere transitory presence does not suffice.[2152]

This definition implies that an establishment needs at least a basic and minimum amount of **426** equipment and some personnel.[2153] The personnel should not be identical with the entre-

---

[2146] *Somafer SA v. Saar-Ferngas AG*, (Case 33/78) [1978] ECR 2183, 2193 para. 12; *Blanckaert & Willems PVBA v. Luise Trost*, (Case 139/80) [1981] ECR 819, 828 *et seq.* para. 11; *SAR Schotte GmbH v. Parfums Rothschild SARL*, (Case 218/86) [1987] ECR 4905, 4919 para. 10; *Lloyd's Register of Shipping v. Société Campenon Bernard*, (Case C-439/93) [1995] ECR I-961, I-980 para. 18; *Ahmed Mahamdia v. People's Democratic Republic of Algeria*, (Case C-154/11), nyr. para. 48; Cassaz. RDIPP 2013, 459, 464.

[2147] *Lloyd's Register of Shipping v. Société Campenon Bernard*, (Case C-439/93) [1995] ECR I-961, I-980 para. 19.

[2148] *Marie-Élodie Ancel*, RCDIP 89 (2000), 464, 466.

[2149] *Bogdan*, SvJT 1998, 825, 833; *Foss/Bygrave*, (2000) 8 Int. J. L. & Info. Tech. 99, 126. Tentatively stricter OLG Naumburg IPRspr. 2013 Nr. 190 p. 413.

[2150] See only BGH RIW 2007, 873, 874; Cassaz. RIW 1999, 291; CA Paris D. 1996, 167; OLG Düsseldorf IPRax 1997, 115, 116; OLG München RIW 1999, 872; OLG Düsseldorf NJW-RR 2004, 1720, 1721; OLG Rostock NJW-RR 2006, 209; *Marie-Élodie Ancel*, RCDIP 89 (2000), 464, 466; *Collins*, in: Dicey/Morris para. 11-271.

[2151] *Jan Voogsgeerd v. Navimer SA*, (Case C-384/10) [2011] ECR I-13275 para. 54.

[2152] *Jan Voogsgeerd v. Navimer SA*, (Case C-384/10) [2011] ECR I-13275 para. 55; A-G *Trstenjak*, Opinion of 8 September 2011 in Case C-384/10, [2011] ECR I-13278 para. 81.

[2153] See e.g. Aud. Prov. Valencia AEDIPr 2002, 540, 541; *Christiane Albers*, Die Begriffe der Niederlassung und der Hauptniederlassung im Internationalen Privat- und Zivilverfahrensrecht (2010) p. 82.

preneur himself.[2154] Thus, if the only person employed is the entrepreneur, only in rare circumstances an establishment can be said to exist. Such rare circumstances might occur if the entrepreneur has a branch office in another state than that where he is domiciled, and if he visits this second office on regular basis or at least to such an extent that it can be said to have been established permanently.[2155] The presence at a temporary fair for a few days lacks the element of permanency, too, even if it is repeated every year.[2156] On the other hand, personnel needs not to be own personnel, but employing external office services can do.[2157]

427 The necessary requirements are also lacking in the event of services offered online: A website and its accessibility do not account for equipment.[2158] Otherwise the grim and undesirable result would emerge that the entrepreneur would avail himself by means of (5) almost everywhere in the EU. Yet in some instances and under particular circumstances the website might generate the impression to prospective customers that the entrepreneur entertains an establishment in a certain country.[2159] But any concept of a "virtual branch"[2160] should be recognised as futile and doomed.[2161] The *coup de grâce* is delivered by Recital (19) of the E-Commerce-Directive[2162].[2163]

428 Also the establishment must be used for external business on the market. A mere production facility without an outlet does not fit the definition. Neither does a pure storage facility or an office without contact to the external world, with only lines of communications within the enterprise. A mere accountancy office does not constitute an establishment and place of business, either. The less, mere technical equipment and machinery could gain relevance. In particular, mere servers can not amount to something remotely akin to an establishment.[2164] Even a foreign office without external business does not suffice, either.[2165] The case could

---

[2154] OLG Naumburg IPRspr. 2013 Nr. 190 pp. 413–414; *Christiane Albers*, Die Begriffe der Niederlassung und der Hauptniederlassung im Internationalen Privat- und Zivilverfahrensrecht (2010) p. 82.

[2155] *Christiane Albers*, Die Begriffe der Niederlassung und der Hauptniederlassung im Internationalen Privat- und Zivilverfahrensrecht (2010) p. 82.

[2156] OLG Düsseldorf IPRax 1998, 210, 211.

[2157] *Trenner*, Internationale Gerichtsstände in grenzüberschreitenden Arbeitsvertragsstreitigkeiten (2001) p. 166; *Christiane Albers*, Die Begriffe der Niederlassung und der Hauptniederlassung im Internationalen Privat- und Zivilverfahrensrecht (2010) p. 82.

[2158] *Bogdan*, SvJT 1998, 825, 832–834.

[2159] *Grolimund*, ZSR NF 119 (2000) I 339, 359.

[2160] As proposed in particular by *Ganssauge*, Internationale Zuständigkeit und anwendbares Recht bei Verbraucherverträgen im Internet (2004) pp. 37–39; see also *Calvo Caravaca/Carrascosa González*, Conflictos de leyes y conflictos de jurisdicción en Internet (2001) para. 38.

[2161] *Schu*, (1997) 5 Int. J. L. & Info. Tech. 192, 221 *et seq*.; *Grolimund*, ZSR NF 119 (2000) I 339, 360; *Zanobetti*, Rev. dr. aff. int. 2000, 545; *Fiorelli*, Dir. comm. int. 2003, 427, 432–434; see also *Foss/Bygrave*, (2000) 8 Int. J. L. & Info. Tech. 99, 131–133.

[2162] Directive 2000/31/EC of the European Parliament and of the Council of 8 June 2000 on certain legal aspects of information society service, in particular electronic commerce, in the Internal Market (Directive on electronic commerce), OJ 2000 L 178/1.

[2163] *Contra Ganssauge*, Internationale Zuständigkeit und anwendbares Recht bei Verbraucherverträgen im Internet (2004) pp. 38 *et seq*.

[2164] *Trzaskowski*, UfR 1998 B 285, 288; *Mankowski*, RabelsZ 63 (1999), 203, 227; see also *Boele-Woelki*, Molengrafica 1997, 139, 145 *et seq*.

possibly be different with sales offices yet they require their own management.[2166] A ship does not amount to an establishment, nevertheless.[2167] A letterhead address with an office open for external business would suffice, on the other hand.[2168]

On the other hand an establishment does not require any formalities. In particular, it does **429** not need to be registered in any national register or list by public authorities,[2169] if only for the simple reason that registers do not exist in every Member State. Many instances are possible where, even if a company register or alike existed, an enlistment or registration would not even be feasible, e.g. if the principal is not a company. A legal personality is not required so that a mere office might suffice.[2170] Generally, it is irrelevant whether the defendant is a company, an association, a commercial man or else.[2171] Even the embassy, a consulate or a permanent diplomatic mission of a foreign State is an establishment for the purposes of (5) and consequentially for the purposes of Art. 18 (2) or Art. 19 (1) (b) ii) following the prevailing interpretation.[2172]

Establishment and place of business are synonyms. It is not required that the establishment **430** constitutes the *principal* place of business. Every place of business suffices if it satisfies the elements of the definition. Surprisingly, to the contrary, the principal place of business is excluded if the defendant is a company. Although the principal place of business is a place of business in every respect, the answer follows inevitably from Art. 63 (1) (c): The principal place of business of a company already constitutes a general jurisdiction and can thus, by the very logic and the opening words of Art. 5, not be used in order to establish special jurisdiction. Insofar the change in the way how to determine the seat, from Art. 53 Brussels Convention first to Art. 60 Brussels I Regulation and subsequently to Art. 63 (1) has some slight consequences. If the defendant, however, is not a company but a genuine person (a simple human being), Art. 63 (1) (c) does not apply, and the principal place of business remains a place of business within the meaning of (5).

Yet the degree of independence of an agent could become too high in order to convey the **431** impression to externals that he acts under a principal's direction.[2173] If the agent is basically free to organise his own work or hours of work (as the German *Handelsvertreter* pursuant to § 84 (1) 2 HGB) this indicates such independence.[2174] In particular, an agent is not acting under a specific principal's direction and instructions if he is free to represent at the same

---

[2165] OLG Düsseldorf IPRax 1998, 210, 211.

[2166] See OLG Düsseldorf IPRax 1998, 210, 211.

[2167] Protodikeio Peiraios Arm. 1998, 1515 note *Vassilakakis*.

[2168] OLG Rostock IPRspr. 2009 Nr. 174 p. 453.

[2169] OLG Düsseldorf NJW-RR 2004, 1720, 1721; *Jeantet*, Cah. dr. eur. 1972, 375, 400; *Christiane Albers*, Die Begriffe der Niederlassung und der Hauptniederlassung im Internationalen Privat- und Zivilverfahrensrecht (2010) p. 67; *Kropholler/von Hein* Art. 5 note 109; *Geimer/Schütze* Art. 5 note 311.

[2170] *Jan Voogsgeerd v. Navimer SA*, (Case C-384/10) [2011] ECR I-13275 para. 54.

[2171] See only *Simotta*, in: Fasching/Konecny Art. 5 note 365 with further references.

[2172] *Ahmed Mahamdia v. People's Democratic Republic of Algeria*, (Case C-154/11), nyr. paras. 50–52; Cassaz. RDIPP 2011, 431, 434; *Junker*, EuZA 2013, 83, 93; *Pataut*, RCDIP 102 (2013), 223, 231; *Nino*, Giur. it. 2013, 1841, 1844; *de Boer*, Ned. Jur. 2013 Nr. 334 p. 3723, 3724; *Martiny*, IPRax 2013, 536, 541–542.

[2173] See in more detail *infra* Art. 5 notes 292–294 (*Mankowski*).

[2174] *Blanckaert & Willems PVBA v. Luise Trost*, (Case 139/80) [1981] ECR 819, 829 para. 12.

time several rival firms producing or marketing similar products or services.[2175] Only under very special circumstances external specialists and service providers like lawyers would qualify as someone else's establishment pursuant to (5).[2176] The general test is that of direction and control,[2177] if only to be met with regard to the concrete matter at hand.

432 Since (5) is aiming at suiting externals, it is not applicable in the event that the owner of an legally and formally separated legal entity serving as an establishment for a principal, sues this very principal for matters concerning the internal relationship between the said legal entity and the principal;[2178] neither does it apply if such an owner sues third parties.[2179] Purely internal functionalities and relationships are not within (5).[2180] Furthermore, even some important external relationships are governed by special rules of jurisdiction, namely tenancy contracts (Art. 24 (1) subpara. 1) and employment agreements (Arts. 20–23).[2181] Those comprehensive regimes prevail over (5).

b) Irrelevance of links under company law

433 Whether the establishment is a subsidiary (and thus a company as an own legal entity) or a dependent branch does not matter. Both are equally covered.[2182] The autonomous concept of interpretation indirectly prevents (5) to be made an accomplice to the purposes of national company laws.[2183] The establishment without the additional element of a legal entity is the main example, but the main example only, for the notion of establishment.[2184] This main example serves as an illustration only and should by no means be treated as conclusive.

434 If subsidiaries and formally separated legal entities were excluded from the realm of (5), disaster would dawn and the floodgates for strategic and opportunistic behaviour would be opened.[2185] Substance over form should prevail as the leading maxim if a formally independent entity is in fact functionally operated like a dependent branch.[2186] Equally immaterial is the degree of dependency of the establishment on the principal pursuant to company law,[2187] and *vice versa*. The principal must not exert legal control over the establishment in the sense that it must be owner or at least majority shareholder of a subsidiary. The plaintiff must not be held to invest in information about the internal relationship between the establishment and the principal. He has not to enquire whether the principal is a parent company. He has

---

[2175] *Blanckaert & Willems PVBA v. Luise Trost*, (Case 139/80) [1981] ECR 819, 829 para. 12.

[2176] More generously *Nagel/Gottwald* § 3 Art. 5 note 74; *Burgstaller/Neumayr* Art. 5 note 67 (Oct. 2002).

[2177] *Collins*, in: Dicey/Morris para. 11–272.

[2178] *Fach Gómez*, REDI 2008, 224, 225; *Garriga Suau*, AEDIPr 2008, 876, 879. Overlooked by Aud. Prov. Barcelona AEDIPr 2008, 875, 876.

[2179] A-G *Reischl*, [1976] ECR 1511, 1518; A-G *Reischl*, [1981] ECR 831, 838, *Bischoff*, Clunet 104 (1977), 719, 727; *Linke*, IPRax 1982, 46, 48 *et seq.*; *Kropholler/von Hein* Art. 5 note 101.

[2180] See *Marie-Élodie Ancel*, RCDIP 89 (2000), 464, 465.

[2181] *Marie-Élodie Ancel*, RCDIP 89 (2000), 464, 465.

[2182] See only SAR Schotte GmbH v. Parfums Rothschild SARL, (Case 218/86) [1987] ECR 4905, 4920 para. 16; OLG Düsseldorf GRUR-RR 2012, 200; LG Düsseldorf GRUR-RR 2011, 361, 362.

[2183] *Kulms*, IPRax 2000, 488, 489.

[2184] Report *Jenard/Möller* para. 43.

[2185] OLG Düsseldorf IPRspr. 1986 Nr. 137 p. 328; *Mankowski*, RIW 1996, 1001, 1004.

[2186] *Zimmer*, IPRax 1998, 187, 191.

[2187] OLG Düsseldorf EuLF 2006, II-93, 94.

not to pierce the artful and wilful obscuration of links *via* multiple tier stake holding or *via* holding companies which so often takes place.

In fact it is not even required that the principal owns a single share of the legal entity or company owning the establishment. Even companies which are entirely independent and unrelated in terms of company law (for instance commercial agents), can serve as establishments under (5) insofar as they do not exceed the degree of concrete independence permitted by the general definition.[2188] Economically the principal can choose between three ways of distribution and working a market: a branch, a subsidiary or a network of agents. These three options are of generally equal value, and should thus be treated in an equal manner as far as possible.[2189]   **435**

As the concept is a factual one, only factual sub-ordination by the establishment under the purposes pursued by the principal matters. Under extreme circumstances the ordinary "chain of command" might even be reversed with the result that a parent company becomes an establishment of an own subsidiary for the limited purposes of (5).[2190] The *concrete* subordination is the key element. At first glance this result might appear astonishing, surprising and not easily deducted from the wording of (5),[2191] but as a matter of concept it becomes fully justified.[2192]   **436**

Yet care and caution have to be exercised. In contractual matters in particular, it is necessary first to ascertain which of the companies involved should become partner to the contract. If the plaintiff contracted with the subsidiary, not with the parent company, he generally can not sue the parent company under the contract, and the consequential issue whether the subsidiary constitutes an establishment of the parent company does not even arise.[2193] Accordingly, the mere existence of a subsidiary does not *per se* guarantee the existence of an establishment.[2194] If the subsidiary has not performed a role in, or taken part in, either the formation or the execution of the contract in question, the corporate link is irrelevant. The mere existence of a group of companies does not indicate that one does serve as the establishment of the others, either.[2195] Only if the subsidiary has acted on behalf of the parent company (e.g. taken over part of the performance of a contract concluded by the parent company), will the subsidiary serve as an establishment of the parent company.[2196] The same applies amongst sister companies.   **437**

[2188] *Infra* Art. 7 notes 444–448 (*Mankowski*).

[2189] *Mankowski*, RIW 1996, 1001, 1004.

[2190] *SAR Schotte GmbH v. Parfums Rothschild SARL*, (Case 218/86) [1987] ECR 4905, 4920 para. 16.

[2191] See the – sometimes harsh and severe – criticism by *Bischoff*, Clunet 115 (1988), 544; *Droz*, RCDIP 77 (1988), 737; *Schultsz*, NJ 1989 Nr. 750.

[2192] *Kropholler/von Hein* Art. 5 note 108.

[2193] *Leible*, in: Rauscher Art. 5 note 107.

[2194] *Kropholler/von Hein* Art. 5 note 107; *Gottwald* in: Münchener Kommentar Art. 5 note 54; *Leible*, in: Rauscher Art. 5 note 107.

[2195] *Kulms*, IPRax 2000, 488, 490; *Schack*, in: GS Jürgen Sonnenschein (2003), p. 705, 707; see Rb. Roermond NIPR 2004 Nr. 52 p. 109.

[2196] OGH ZfRV 2000, 79; OLG München RIW 1999, 873.

c) **Paramount importance of the external perception and appearance**

438 Paramount and decisive is the external perception and appearance measured by reasonable standards.[2197] Internal structures which are not perceivable to externals and to the public must not constitute excuses for the holder of the establishment. An *exceptio ex iure proprio*, in the worst and most malign case stemming from an own manipulation, must not be permitted. The impression that externals receive of the establishment carries weight and in fact is the only thing that matters. Hiding behind a home-made construction must not lead to successfully luring the externals into losing suits brought under (5).[2198] To the contrary, the plaintiff's reliance on the impression which he gained justifiedly, merits protection. The more generous interpretation of (5) is the price enterprises have to pay for mobility and penetration of foreign markets.[2199] If for instance, a parent company deliberately develops its subsidiary as the central market player, both in its advertising measures and in the terms of the contracts eventually concluded with the customers, and the parent company acts in a subordinated and auxiliary position, the principal (or other relevant) place of business parent company must be regarded as an establishment of the subsidiary.[2200]

439 A c/o address used in correspondence has been held not to constitute an establishment.[2201] The holding appears doubtful, though. A c/o address channels communication and makes direct contact with the principal unnecessary. That the principal can be perceived as a legal entity different from the one established at the address named, does not exclude anything, but simply clarifies the ordinary case that the contractual partner is the principal, not the c/o address, a basic requirement for raising the question whether there is an establishment.

440 If an establishment or branch is still registered with the local authorities, the external plaintiff can rely on the impression conveyed by the registration even if the establishment has already ceased to exist.[2202] An excuse based on the practical inexistence of the registered establishment will not be permitted.

441 If the establishment has never existed and has never been active on the market, it will not constitute the necessary links. An establishment without activities has not contacted anyone, nor participated in the performance of anything. In such instances, the necessary bond between the claim in question and the establishment[2203] will most certainly be lacking.[2204] Also an establishment founded only after the claim had come into existence, be it before or after the writ was issued, will not have the necessary links with that claim.[2205]

[2197] *SAR Schotte GmbH v. Parfums Rothschild SARL*, (Case 218/86) [1987] ECR 4905, 4920 para. 15; *Geimer*, EWiR Art. 5 EuGVÜ 1/88, 63, 64; *Pocar*, in: ECJ (ed.), Jurisdiction and Enforcement of Judgments in Europe (1992), p. 99, 104; *Wieczorek/Schütze/Hausmann* Art. 5 EuGVÜ with note 78.

[2198] *Duintjer Tebbens*, in: ECJ (ed.), Jurisdiction and Enforcement of Judgments in Europe (1992), p. 84; *Mankowski*, RIW 1996, 1001, 1004; *Geimer/Schütze* Art. 5 note 314.

[2199] *Chaput*, Dr. sociétés 6/2000, 23.

[2200] *Mankowski*, EWiR Art. 15 EuGVVO 1/05, 251 *et seq.*

[2201] LG Wuppertal NJW-RR 1994, 181; LG Koblenz IHR 2011, 145, 147; *Leible*, in: Rauscher Art. 5 note 105.

[2202] *Geimer/Schütze* Art. 5 note 311.

[2203] *Infra* Art. 7 notes 448–453 (*Mankowski*).

[2204] Less cautionary *Geimer/Schütze* Art. 5 note 311.

[2205] *Löser*, Zuständigkeitsbestimmender Zeitpunkt und perpetuatio fori im internationalen Zivilprozess (2009) p. 158; *Leible*, in: Rauscher, Art. 5 note 108a.

If an agent serves as a mere transmitter of messages, passing incoming ones on to the **442** undertaking he represents, the external perception could fall into doubt as to whether he reaches a sufficient degree of (managerial) competence to have direct recourse to that undertaking unnecessary.[2206]

3. Branch or agency

The terms "branch" or "agency"[2207] do not have much relevance nor an independent mean- **443** ing worth discussing at length. They serve as illustrations for the over-all (and catch all) notion of establishment.[2208] Their inclusion indicates some kind of *eiusdem generis* rule for the interpretation of the notion of establishment that the general notion has to be construed in analogy to the (natural) understanding of the examples given. Accordingly it would be futile to attempt individual in-depth definitions for anyone of these illustrating terms in order to develop something apart from the general notion. Tentatively one could argue that the inclusion of an agency supports, and lends additional force to, the contention that it does not matter whether the establishment is a legal entity in its own right or not,[2209] since agencies are mostly legal entities of their own.

4. Commercial agents and other intermediaries

Commercial agents, distributors, brokers and other intermediaries pose another problem. If **444** and insofar as they carry out their own decisions, it can hardly be said that they are con- cretely subjecting themselves under another person's orders. Insofar as this perception prevails, they do not constitute establishments of the companies or persons they are acting for or the products or services of which they are distributing.[2210] The mere fact that agents represent principals in certain affairs does not *per se* elevate them to the status of an estab- lishment of such principal.[2211]

In particular, if the intermediary acts for a number of companies, it becomes even less **445** possible to denominate him as an establishment of either of these companies.[2212] The case can be settled more simply and for an obvious reason, though, at least in contractual matters: An intermediary sporting such a degree of independence will almost inevitably contract in his own name and on his own behalf, not on the behalf of any principal. To use the extreme

---

[2206] See Blanckaert & Willems PVBA v. Luise Trost, (Case 139/80) [1981] ECR 819, 829 para. 12.

[2207] See Højesteret UfR 2004, 2710, 2713.

[2208] OLG Rostock IPRspr. 2009 Nr. 174 p. 453; *Christiane Albers*, Die Begriffe der Niederlassung und der Hauptniederlassung im Internationalen Privat- und Zivilverfahrensrecht (2010) p. 67; see A. de Bloos SPRL v. Société en commandite par actions Bouyer, (Case 14/76) [1976] ECR 1497, 1509 *et seq.* para. 21 and also Report *Jenard/Möller* para. 43; *Blanco-Morales Limones*, in: Calvo Caravaca, Art. 5.5 CB note 7 *et seq.*

[2209] *Supra* Art. 7 notes 435, 438 (*Mankowski*).

[2210] *Blanckaert & Willems BVBA v. Luise Trost*, (Case 139/80) [1981] ECR 819, 829 para. 12 (commercial agent); LG Hamburg IPRspr. 1974 Nr. 154 p. 407 (broker).

[2211] A little rash for instance Aud. Prov. Barcelona AEDIPr 2003, 875, 876 but apparently in a case not bearing any major problems.

[2212] *Blanckaert & Willems PVBA v. Luise Trost*, (Case 139/80) [1981] ECR 819, 829 para. 12.

case as an illustrating and telling example: The wholesale store is not an establishment of any manufacturer and definitely contracts with its customers in its own name and on its own behalf.

446 If the intermediary, nevertheless, does not act in his own name, but serves as a place where the customers of the principal can turn to, e.g. for cashing in warranties, he concretely subordinates himself under the purposes pursued by the principal and thus acts as an establishment however he might be at the level of making entrepreneurial decisions in general.[2213] In these instances he is simply a substitute for an individual branch run by the principal directly. Functionally he will be perceived by the customers as part of the distributional system of this particular principal with regard to the goods or services in question.[2214] This applies in particular if the agent throughout his entire trade and business acts on the behalf of the principal in question exclusively.[2215]

447 If the external perception is to this avail and if the agent has already acted in external reception it should not matter as to whether internally the agency agreement was finalised or whether only a pre-contract existed.[2216] Yet such an external perception should not possibly be generated where the agent has not commenced his activity on the principal's behalf.[2217]

5. Connection or nexus between claim and establishment

448 In order to entertain jurisdiction at the place of an establishment, a specific connection between the claim and specifically this establishment must be ascertained. The establishment does not substitute for the domicile or the seat as it would if it attracted all claims against the defendant. In balancing the legitimate interests of both parties the additional *forum* for the plaintiff is opened and available only insofar as the defendant availed himself there through activities of his own. In order to distinguish special jurisdiction under (5) from general jurisdiction under Art. 4 and to deny (5) any power of gravitational attraction or an anchoring function as Art. 4 has,[2217a] activities of the branch must carry a nexus with the dispute.[2218] This nexus can be either of a contractual or of a tortious or delictual nature; either suffices[2219] and it is not required that the nexus itself come within certain categories.[2219a]

449 If a contractual claim is at stake the establishment must have played a role either in the formation or in the performance of the contract. Either suffices. Likewise some activity on

---

[2213] *Mankowski*, RIW 1996, 1001, 1005.

[2214] *Mankowski*, RIW 1996, 1001, 1005; *Leible*, in: Rauscher Art. 5 note 106.

[2215] See only *Lima Pinheiro* p. 91.

[2216] But cf. Aud. Prov. Islas Baleares AEDIPr 2003, 871, 872.

[2217] Aud. Prov. Islas Baleares AEDIPr 2003, 871, 872.

[2217a] *Briggs* para. 2.214.

[2218] Anton Durbeck GmbH v. Den Norske Bank ASA [2003] 2 WLR 1296, 1309 (C.A., per Lord *Phillips of Worth Matravers* M.R.).

[2219] See only Cass. RCDIP 89 (2000), 462, 463 with note *Marie-Élodie Ancel*; Cass. RCDIP 90 (2001), 157, 158 with note *Marie-Élodie Ancel*.

[2219a] But cf. the peculiar case of OLG Karlsruhe IPRspr. 2013 Nr. 174b p. 380; LG Baden-Baden IPRspr. 2013 Nr. 174a p. 378.

account of the parent body can suffice.[2220] Even some brokering might do. Otherwise there would be too much of an incentive for the holder of the establishment to allow the establishment do all the advertising, the hooking and poking, letting the establishment get the customer on the hook, but finally allowing his principal place of business step in to conclude the contract. Formalities and formal positions are not required as (5) follows an entirely factual approach. But it might prove extremely difficult to sue the parent company successfully if a subsidiary as an own legal entity entered into the contract.[2221] Then the burden is to prove the involvement of the parent company in the contract. If the contract is concluded in the name, and on behalf, of the parent body matters are far easier and almost obvious.[2222] Yet a contract entered in the name of the agent, but materially clearly on behalf of the identified principal should suffice.[2223] Where the contract is concluded does not matter, regardless whether the contract was signed at the place of the establishment or whether the manager of the establishment entered into it in his capacity as branch manager while away from the place of business.[2224] If the establishment participates in the performance of the contract, it should not matter whether the establishment already existed at the time when the contract was concluded.[2225]

A claim in tort must also bear some relationship with the activity of the establishment, be it **450** that it results from commercial contracts concluded or performed by personnel of the establishment or be it that it results from factual activities of the establishment, e.g. such activity as doing harm to neighbourhood or environment or customers. In the majority of instances, the place of the establishment will also constitute the place where the harmful act giving rise to the damage occurred, and accordingly in most instances jurisdiction can be based on (2) as well.[2226] Where the damage is eventually sustained does not matter for the purposes of (5).[2227]

Rather difficult to answer is whether (5) is available for claims against the parent body **451** allegedly based on piercing the corporate veil. If and insofar as the establishment exerted external activities, but was not equipped with the necessary funding, a harmful activity set into motion through the establishment can be said to exist. Insofar at first glance it appears not justified to attribute the activity not also to the establishment, but only to the parent body. Yet the main allegation could be identified as not equipping the establishment with the necessary funding or draining it out or putting a "bad company" forefront. These allegations relate to (in)activities on the part of the parent body.[2228] Tossing the coin nevertheless should lead to jurisdiction under (5) being established since without the activity by the establish-

---

[2220] LG Bremen VersR 2001, 782, 783 with note *Schuler*.

[2221] *Supra* Art. 7 notes 435–438 (*Mankowski*).

[2222] See Cass. RCDIP 90 (2001), 157, 158 with note *Marie-Élodie Ancel* = Dr. sociétés 6/2000, 22.

[2223] *Layton/Mercer* para. 15.108.

[2224] See *Layton/Mercer* para. 15.108.

[2225] Contra OLG Celle IPRspr. 2001 Nr. 155 p. 315 = OLG-Report Celle/Braunschweig/Oldenburg 2002, 59.

[2226] See only *Leible*, in: Rauscher Art. 5 note 108; *Pulkowski*, IPRax 2004, 543, 545.

[2227] *Anton Durbeck GmbH v. Den Norske Bank ASA* [2003] 2 WLR 1296, 1308 (C.A., per Lord *Phillips of Worth Matravers* M.R.)

[2228] Tentatively so *Gerhard Wagner*, in: Lutter (ed.), Europäische Auslandsgesellschaften in Deutschland (2005), p. 223, 258 *et seq.*

ment no claims would have arisen which now indirectly qualify for piercing the corporate veil.[2229]

452 (5) does not require that the claim has to be fulfilled at the respective place of performance.[2230] To restrict (5) in such a manner would deprive it of almost all its effect.[2231] In the contractual context (5) would be thwart and would only duplicate (1).[2232] Furthermore, the establishment can be involved in the negotiation process only whereas other branches carry out the later execution of the contract, and it still would be beyond doubt that the contract in question is sufficiently closely linked with the first establishment.[2233] Shifting to a higher and more abstract level, the lack of a restricting requirement is a general statement, equally applying to claims in tort.[2234] But the mere attempt to hold the parent body liable at the place of the establishment does not constitute the necessary nexus.[2235]

453 The establishment must still exist at the time when the writ is issued and the lawsuit becomes pending.[2236] If it has been dissolved earlier, there is no appropriate connecting factor left. If the establishment has been abandoned (and in the case that a previously registered establishment has fallen out of the register)[2237] before the writ was issued and the proceedings were instituted, this instance, the plaintiff can not rely on his impression since the basis for it has been destroyed. The past is irrelevant, and only this point in time when the lawsuit becomes pending matters. A former establishment does not suffice. If, however, the establishment gets dissolved only after the lawsuit had become pending, the general principle of *perpetuatio fori* prevails, and jurisdiction is retained. On the other hand, the establishment must have existed at the time when the relevant event happened;[2238] this can be deducted from the prerequisite of a connection between the claim and the establishment which can not be effected simply by the fact that the establishment later-on acted as agent for the principal. The concept of establishment relates to relevant operations, and this must be taken into account appropriately. Nevertheless, it does not overcome any scenario that the establishment does not exist anymore at the commencement of proceedings.[2239]

[2229] To the opposite result *Gerhard Wagner*, in: Lutter (ed.), Europäische Auslandsgesellschaften in Deutschland (2005), p. 223, 258 *et seq.*

[2230] *Lloyd's Register of Shipping v. Société Campenon Bernard*, (Case C-439/93) [1995] ECR I-961, I-980 para. 16.

[2231] *Lloyd's Register of Shipping v. Société Campenon Bernard*, (Case C-439/93) [1995] ECR I-961, I-980 para. 17; *Kropholler/von Hein* Art. 5 note 111.

[2232] *Lloyd's Register of Shipping v. Société Campenon Bernard*, (Case C-439/93) [1995] ECR I-961, I-980 para. 17.

[2233] *See Lloyd's Register of Shipping v. Société Campenon Bernard*, (Case C-439/93) [1995] ECR I-961, I-981 para. 20.

[2234] *Anton Durbeck GmbH v. Den Norske Bank ASA* [2003] 2 WLR 1296, 1308 (C.A., per Lord *Phillips of Worth Matravers* M.R.)

[2235] LG Bremen VersR 2001, 782, 783 with note *Schuler*.

[2236] BGH RIW 2007, 873 = IPRax 2008, 128; OLG Saarbrücken RIW 1980, 796, 799; OLG Düsseldorf NJW-RR 1994, 1720, 1721; OLG Düsseldorf IPRax 1998, 210, 211; OLG Frankfurt NJW-RR 2009, 645, 647; *Kulms*, IPRax 2000, 488, 489. *Contra Kaye* p. 591.

[2237] See *supra* Art. 7 note 440 (*Mankowski*).

[2238] *Schlosser* Art. 5 note 24; *Leible*, in: Rauscher Art. 5 note 109 fn. 381; see also OGH ZfRV 2000, 79.

[2239] *Contra Kaye* p. 591.

VII. Special jurisdiction in matters of trusts, Art. 7 (6)

Pursuant to (6), a person can be sued outside the state of his domicile as settlor, trustee or   **454**
beneficiary of a trust created by the operation of a statute, or by a written instrument, or
created orally and evidenced in writing, in the courts of the Member State in which the trust
is domiciled. Genetically, (6) was a concession on the occasion of the accession of the United
Kingdom and Ireland to the Brussels Convention since the concept of trust was then unknown to the legal orders of the continental Member States.[2240] A trust does not constitute a
legal entity in its own right. Therefore it can not be sued as such,[2241] but the proper defendant
is the trustee. Without (6) it would be necessary to rely on Art. 4 (1) and to sue the trustee in
the state of his personal domicile[2242] notwithstanding special jurisdiction for instance under
(2). (6) widens the spectre and grants additional jurisdiction favouring the claiming creditors. (6) was introduced in order to remedy presumed shortcomings of the other heads of
jurisdiction.[2243] It is unnecessary to ascertain that a claim is in contract or in tort.[2244] Insofar
(6) resembles (6) and establishes some kind of "small general jurisdiction".

Bearing the history of the legal institution and the genesis of (6) in mind, the definition of   **455**
trust should take into consideration the English understanding foremost.[2245] Scottish and
Irish concepts might provide additional value,[2246] theoretically also Maltese concepts.[2247] The
common law provided the problem to be dealt with, and accordingly, it would be the first
haven for the answers.[2248] An autonomous European notion of trust is hardly conceivable.[2249]
Yet the most elegant solution is to hold recourse to the definition in the 1985 Hague Trusts
Convention[2250].[2251] The justification for such a recourse becomes better by the time the more
civil law countries introduce the legal institution of trust in their national law after ratifying,
or acceding to, the 1985 Hague Trusts Convention. The most prominent entries in that list of

---

[2240] In recent times matters have changed considerably, and the trust has successfully permeated for instance
to Italy or the Netherlands; see e.g. Trib. Parma Dir. e giur. 2004, 655; Trib. Milano Riv. not. 2005, 850;
Trib. Parma Riv. not. 2005, 851; Trib. Velletri Europa e dir. priv. 2005, 785; Trib. Reggio di Emilia Giur. it.
2008 I 629 with note *Monteleone; Giuliani*, Contratto e impresa 19 (2003) 433; *Carro*, Dir. e. giur. 2004,
656; *Barla de Guglielmi*, Riv. not. 2005, 858; *Monegat*, Riv. not. 2005, 868; *Mazzamuto*, Europa e dir. priv.
2005, 803; *Neri*, Il trust e la tutela del beneficiario (2005). See in the Netherlands *Aertsen*, De trust –
Beschouwingen over invoering van de trust in het Nederlandse recht (2004) pp. 103–281. Comparative
sketch by *Mankowski*, in: FS Gunther Kühne (2009), p. 795, 796 *et seq.*

[2241] See only Report *Schlosser* para. 113; *Leible*, in: Rauscher Art. 5 note 111; *Geimer/Schütze* Art. 5 note 325.

[2242] See only *Roman Huber* para. 112.

[2243] *Roman Huber* para. 114.

[2244] *Roman Huber* para. 114.

[2245] *Leible*, in: Rauscher Art. 5 note 112; *Layton/Mercer* para. 15.117. See *Conrad* pp. 278 *et seq.*

[2246] *Layton/Mercer* para. 15.117.

[2247] See in particular *Berti-Riboli/Ganado*, La legge di Malta sul trust (Milano 2007).

[2248] See *Gardella/Radicati di Brozolo*, 51 Am. J. Comp. L. 611, 619 *et seq.* (2003).

[2249] *Roman Huber* para. 118.

[2250] Hague Convention on the Law Applicable to Trusts and Their Recognition, July 1, 1985, published i.a. in:
RabelsZ 50 (1986), 698.

[2251] To the same avail *Roman Huber* para. 118; see also *Conrad* p. 292.

civil law countries entail the Netherlands,[2252] France,[2253] Italy[2254] and Luxemburg[2255] plus to some degree (and under the auspices of the Lugano Convention) Switzerland.[2256] Overall, an autonomous understanding is called for which might get some guidance from national concepts, but is not determined by them.[2257] Generally (6) indicates – like Art. 63 (3) – that the Brussels I*bis* Regulation regards trusts *inter vivos* as something akin to, or in the vicinity of, corporations, a view which will conflict with the English understanding to a certain degree.[2258]

456 In order to restrain the scope of (6) it is necessary that the defendant is sued in his specific function related to the trust. (6) does not constitute another general jurisdiction to the detriment of representatives or beneficiaries[2259] of a trust. Only settlors, beneficiaries and trustees *as such*, in this specific function, are proper defendants for the purposes of (6). A beneficiary may be sued under (6) for the return of undue monies paid to him by the trustee.[2260] A beneficiary being overpaid more than he can justifiedly claim, might be a problematic case, though.[2260a]

457 The wording of (6) is slightly different from that of Art. 5 (6) Brussels I Regulation. Whereas the latter allowed a person to be sued "as settlor, trustee or beneficiary", the current wording allows a person to be sued "as regards a dispute brought against a settlor, trustee or beneficiary". Even bearing in mind the emphasis which common law jurisdictions, the motherlands of trusts, place on words this should not amount to a substantial difference.[2261] The

---

[2252] *Diederik Walahfrid Aertsen*, De Trust – Beschouwingen over invoering van de Trust in het Nederlandse recht (Deventer 2004) pp. 103–281 with further references.

[2253] Loi n° 2007-211 du 19 février 2007 instituant la fiducie, JO 2007, 3052. On this e.g. *Barrière*, (2013) 58 McGill L.J. 869.

[2254] Cassaz. NGCC 2009 I 78 with note *Martone*; Trib. Belluno NGCC 2003 I 329; Trib. Bologna NGCC 2004 I 844 m. Anm. *Renda*; Trib. Parma Dir. e Giur. 2004, 655; Trib. Milano Riv. not. 2005, 850; Trib. Parma Riv. not. 2005, 851; Trib. Velletri Europa e dir. priv. 2005, 785; Trib. Reggio di Emilia Giur. it. 2008 I 629 with note *Monteleone*; *Federico Maria Giuliani*, Contratto e impresa 19 (2003) 433; *Carro*, Dir. e. Giur. 2004, 656; *de Guglielmi*, Riv. not. 2005, 858; *Monegat*, Riv. not. 2005, 868; *Mazzamuto*, Europa e dir. priv. 2005, 803; *Arianna Neri*, Il Trust e la tutela del beneficiario (2005); *Bartoli*, Trust e atto di destinazione nel diritto di famiglia e delle persone (2011); *Maurizio Lupoi*, Vita not. 2013, 1049. A popular denomination for the trust Italian style is "trust tricolore"; *Fusaro*, Riv. not. 2013, 859, 863.

[2255] Loi du 27 juillet 2003 relative au trust et aux contrats fiduciaires, Mémoire n° 124 du 3 septembre 2003, p. 2620.

[2256] See only *Matthias Seiler*, Trust und Treuhand im schweizerischen Recht (Zürich etc. 2005); *Stephan Wolf/ Jordi*, Trust und schweizerisches Zivilrecht, insbesondere Ehegüter-, Erb- und Immobiliarsachenrecht, in: Der Trust (Bern 2008), p. 29.

[2257] *Donzallaz* para. 5374 with fn. 17; *Geimer/Schütze*, Art. 5 note 326; *Hofmann/Kunz*, in: Basler Kommentar, Art. 5 note 758.

[2258] *Aubrey L. Diamond*, RDIPP 1981, 289, 303; *Wittuhn*, Das Internationale Privatrecht des trust (1987) pp. 112 *et seq.*, 117 *et seq.*

[2259] The position as beneficiary was examined in the concrete case by *Gomez v. Gomez Monche Vives* [2008] EWHC 259 (Ch), [2008] I.L.Pr. 461, [2008] 3 WLR 309, [2008] 1 All ER (Comm) 973 [87]-[88] (Ch.D., *Morgan* J.).

[2260] *Gomez v. Gomez Monche Vives* [2009] 2 WLR 950, 969 (C.A.); *Hayton*, (2009) 23 Trust L.J. 3.

[2260a] *Briggs*, PIL para. 4.283.

slight alteration appears to aim at bringing (6) in line with Art. 25 (3) and Art. 23 (4) Brussels I Regulation.[2262]

Appointors, protectors, guardians or other persons with a power to intervene are believed **458** not to be covered, though.[2263] Since these positions in the structure of trusts have been developed and have emerged mainly after Art. 5 (6) 1978 Brussels Convention introduced trusts into the Brussels system for the first time, they are not reflected in the wording of (6) which has remained without major amendments over the times and ever since. If (6) pursues to cover all internal relations within a trust it would be sensible to include the relations with appointers, protectors and other possible interveners.[2264] If persons other than trustees hold significant powers affecting the internal governance of a trust and are sued for alleged improper use of such powers, it is best if the claimant is able to sue them in the jurisdiction of the trust's domicile just as trustees can so be sued.[2265] Further support for the most important cases might be gained from the modification of (6), bringing in line (6) with the wording of Art. 25 (3): Now it relates to actions brought against a settlor, trustee or beneficiary whereas Art. 5 (6) Brussels I Regulation referred to the defendant being sued as settlor, trustee or beneficiary, i.e. against a person in his specific capacity as settlor, trustee or beneficiary. If a beneficiary happens to be also a protector an action against him for misconduct as a protector still is an action against some one who is a beneficiary even if not in that specific capacity.[2266]

(6) is designed solely for internal struggles[2267] and does not generally benefit external credi- **459** tors[2268] or other outsiders.[2269] Only persons personally benefited by the trust may sue in the additional *forum* established by (6).[2270] Accordingly, external creditors are still bound to sue the trustee at his domicile or in the courts of the place in which special jurisdiction is vested pursuant to one of the other heads of Art. 7[2271] or 8 or for which exclusive jurisdiction exists for instance under Art. 24 (1).[2272] In many instances, lawsuits against the trustee concerning immovables are in fact battles about land so that Art. 24 (1) will apply.[2273]

[2261] But cf. *Hayton*, RdC 366 (2013), 9, 44 (slight change in a way which is capable of being significant).

[2262] *Hayton*, RdC 366 (2013), 9, 44.

[2263] *Gomez v. Gomez Monche Vives* [2009] 2 WLR 950, 971 (C.A.).

[2264] *Hayton*, (2008) 14 Trusts & Trustees 384; *Hayton*, (2009) 23 Trust L.J. 3; *Hayton*, RdC 366 (2013), 9, 43–44; *Thévenoz*, in: Journée 2006 de droit bancaire et financier (2006), p. 51, 57; *Roman Huber* paras. 138–139.

[2265] *Hayton*, RdC 366 (2013), 9, 43.

[2266] *Hayton*, RdC 366 (2013), 9, 44–45.

[2267] *Jonathan Harris*, in: Essays in Honour of Sir Peter North (2002), p. 187, 206; *Matthias Lehmann*, in: Dickinson/Lein para. 4.145.

[2268] See only *Teixeira de Sousa/Moura Vicente* Art. 5 note 9; *Frigessi di Rattalma*, RDIPP 2003, 783, 787–789; *Collins*, in: Dicey/Morris para. 11–277. Contra *Contaldi*, Il trust nel diritto internazionale privato (2001) p. 305; *Roman Huber* paras. 125–129.

[2269] Tentatively *contra* Layton/Mercer para. 15.116.

[2270] Report *Schlosser* para. 110; *Geimer/Schütze* Art. 5 note 327; *Glasson*, in: Thomas/Alastair Hudson (eds.), The Law of Trusts (2004) para. 42.19.

[2271] *Conrad* p. 277, 299–308.

[2272] Report *Schlosser* para. 110; *Leible*, in: Rauscher Art. 5 note 111; comprehensively *Conrad* p. 223–274.

[2273] *Basedow*, in: Handbuch des Internationalen Zivilverfahrensrechts, Vol. I (1982), Ch. II with note 42; see

460 In common law jurisdictions the trustee may apply for so called construction or direction summonses. These summonses are judicial ascertainments of the content of the trust conditions. It is argued that it would be davisable to resort to Art. 8 (2) (a)-(j) Hague Trust Convention and to characterise anything what qualifies as a matter related to trusts under these rules, as matters related to trusts under (7), too.[2274] This is not compatible with the wording and the direction of (7): (7) covers only lawsuits against the trustee as defendant, not lawsuits initiated by the trustee.[2275]

461 Even (6) does not establish a comprehensive *forum societatis* in trust matters since it only grants jurisdiction if a claim against the mentioned persons is brought, but not a *forum actoris* for either the mentioned persons or the trust itself.[2276] It does not cure the generally missing *forum societatis* the less since trusts are a far more impersonal concept than companies. Yet it does not matter if the defendant raises the objection that the trust does not exist or is legally invalid.[2277] Otherwise jurisdiction would depend on defences possibly raised contrary to the approach pursued under (1).[2278]

462 With the restriction to trusts created by the operation of a statute,[2279] written act or act confirmed in writing, (6) excludes simple oral trusts. There must be some evidence of the founding of the trust if they trust is not construed as a matter of law, but based on party autonomy. The writing requirement serves evidentiary purposes.[2280] (6) is silent as to whom has to have confirmed.[2281] It should suffice if the trustee confirms that he has been installed as trustee for the respective trust.[2282] A statutory trust need not be a trust expressly and specifically established by statute, but it suffices that it is created by the operation of statute.[2283]

463 Matters are more complicated with legal trusts. If it strived to remain consistent in every possible respect the law would have to recognise them. In the last consequence this wide notion even would include constructive trusts if they are established by law and even if the law instrumentalises acts by parties to imply the existence of a trust. The requirement that a legal trust must be created by the operation of a statute, is stricter and narrower. In particular it does not comprise constructive trusts,[2284] resulting trusts[2285] or implied trusts created by

---

[2274] also *Re Hayward (Deceased)* [1997] Ch. 45 (Ch.D., *Rattee* J.); *Jonathan Harris*, (1997) 22 Eur. L. Rev. 179; *Jonathan Harris*, in: Glasson (ed.), The International Trust (2002), p. 9, 18 *et seq.*

[2274] *Guillaume*, in: Commentaire romand, Art. 5 LugÜ note 170.

[2275] *Roman Huber* para. 133.

[2276] Report *Schlosser* para. 112; *Wieczorek/Schütze/Hausmann* Art. 5 note 87; *Leible*, in: Rauscher Art. 5 note 112; *Geimer/Schütze* Art. 5 note 332.

[2277] *Conrad* p. 277.

[2278] *Conrad* p. 277.

[2279] See the non-exhaustive list of statutes concerned as compiled by *Conrad* p. 278, in particular sec. 19; 34; 104 Law of Property Act 1925; sec. 2 sched. 1 (1) Trusts of Land and Appointment of Trustees Act 1996.

[2280] *Roman Huber* para. 119.

[2281] *Roman Huber* para. 119.

[2282] *Siehr*, in: Schnyder, Art. 5 Nr. 6 LugÜ note 6.

[2283] *Hayton*, RdC 366 (2013), 9, 47–48.

[2284] *Chellaram v. Chellaram (No. 2)* [2002] 3 All ER 17, 44 (Ch.D., *Lawrence Collins* J.); *Gomez v. Gomez Monche Vives* [2008] EWHC 259 (Ch), [2008] I.L.Pr. 461, [2008] 3 WLR 309, [2008] 1 All ER (Comm)

common law rules.[2286] Yet an exception should be made for resulting trusts which arise upon the failure or exhaustion of an express trust which was created by a written instrument, orally or evidenced in writing.[2287] Furthermore, trusts created by a contract for the sale of land are excluded from (6).[2288] Testamentary trusts, trusts arising under wills or trusts in bankruptcy are already exempt by virtue of Art. 1 (2) (f) and (b) respectively.[2289]

Pursuant to (6) the courts of the Member State where the trust has its seat gain jurisdiction to **464** entertain lawsuits against the mentioned persons. The general idea behind this approach reads that the defendant in question is sued as a kind of representative of the trust, hence *in lieu* of the trust. If the trust itself was sued, Art. 4 (1) would lead to international jurisdiction of the courts of the state where the trust has its domicile as defined in Art. 63 (3). (6) constructively extends this approach to suits against the persons representing the trust. Accordingly, the connecting factor is the domicile of the trust. The definition for domicile of the trust is provided by Art. 63 (3) although, strictly speaking, a trust is neither a company nor any other kind of legal entity nor an association of natural or legal persons.

The connecting factor employed by (6) is the domicile or seat of the trust. It has to be **465** ascertained pursuant to Art. 63 (3)[2290] and consequentially the private international of the forum. Art. 63 (3) is specifically designed for accomplishing this feat. The relevant point of time for ascertaining whether someone had his domicile in the forum state is the same as under Art. 4 in conjunction with Art. 63.[2291] According to English authority the relevant point of time under English law (in order to answer the question as to whether the defendant

---

973 [59] (Ch.D., *Morgan* J.); *Leible*, in: Rauscher, Art. 5 note 112a. On the concept of constructive trust under English law *Hudson*, Equity and Trusts (8th ed. 2015) pp. 546–650 with extensive references.

2285 But differenciating *Conrad* pp. 281–283; *Leible*, in: Rauscher, Art. 5 note 112a; *Roman Huber* para. 121. On resulting trusts in the conflict of laws *Robert Stevens*, in: Birks/Rose (eds.), Restitution and Equity I: Resulting Trusts and Equitable Compensation (2000), p. 147. On the concept of resulting trust under English law *Alastair Hudson*, Equity and Trusts (8th ed. 2015) pp. 499–545 with extensive references.

2286 Report *Schlosser* para. 117; *Kropholler*, in: Handbuch des Internationalen Zivilverfahrensrechts, Vol. I (1982), Ch. III Art. 5 note 709; *Hartley* p. 55; *Iriarte Angel*, in: Calvo Caravaca, Art. 5.6 CB note 7; *Broggini*, in: Beneventi (ed.), I trusts in Italia oggi (1996), p. 11, 17; *Robert Stevens*, in: Birks/Rose (eds.), Restitution and Equity I: Resulting Trusts and Equitable Compensation (2000), p. 147, 150; *Frigessi di Rattalma*, RDIPP 2003, 783, 801; *Geimer/Schütze* Art. 5 note 329; *Collins*, in: Dicey/Morris/Collins para. 11–277; *Layton/Mercer* para. 15.117; *Leible*, in: Rauscher, Art. 5 note 112a. But cf. *Conrad* p. 279–283.

2287 *Gomez v. Gomez Monche Vives* [2009] 2 WLR 950, 969 (C.A.); *Gomez v. Gomez Monche Vives* [2008] EWHC 259 (Ch), [2008] I.L.Pr. 461, [2008] 3 WLR 309, [2008] 1 All ER (Comm) 973 [57] (Ch.D., *Morgan* J.); *Robert Stevens*, in: Birks/Rose (eds.), Restitution and Equity I: Resulting Trusts and Equitable Compensation (2000), p. 147, 150; *Hayton*, (2009) 23 Trust L.J. 3; *Leible*, in: Rauscher, Art. 5 note 112a.

2288 Report *Schlosser* paras. 117, 172; *Jonathan Harris*, in: Glasson Glasson (ed.), The International Trust (2002), p. 9, 25.

2289 Report *Schlosser* para. 52; *Lima Pinheiro* p. 92; *Collins*, in: Dicey/Morris para. 11–277; *Leible*, in: Rauscher, Art. 5 note 112a. But cf. sceptical *Glasson*, in: Thomas/Alastair Hudson (eds.), The Law of Trusts (2004) para. 42.19.

2290 *Conrad* p. 284; *Jonathan Harris*, in: Glasson Glasson (ed.), The International Trust (2002), p. 9, 25; *Frigessi di Rattalma*, RDIPP 2003, 783, 792; *Layton/Mercer* para. 15.118.

2291 See *Chellaram v. Chellaram (No. 2)* [2002] 3 All ER 17, 47 (Ch.D., *Lawrence Collins* J.).

has his domicile in England) is the date when the proceedings are instituted and not when they were served.[2292] The technique employed by Art. 63 (3) is in principle akin to that used by Art. 24 (2) cl. 2, but Art. 63 (3) poses only a closed not an open question. It does not ask where the seat of the trust is but only whether the trust has its seat in the forum state. It extracts a "yes/no" answer. Insofar Art. 4 (1) serves as the role model.

466 (6) establishes only international jurisdiction and leaves it to the national law of the state to answer where the trust has its seat, and thus to clarify the matters of local jurisdiction or venue.[2293] In principle, this mirrors the approach followed in Art. 4 (1). Comparing the heads of jurisdiction contained in Art. 7 to each other, (6) is an exception in this regard.

467 The practical relevance of (6) is rather limited: From the point of view of the continental Member State which have not imported the trust into their domestic law, it can become rarely operative since trusts with their seat on the continent in a hostile legal environment not recognising the institution internally, are *rarae aves*.[2294] And from the perspective of the Member States which recognise the trust as an institution of their domestic law, it will only rarely occur that settlor, trustees or beneficiaries are domiciled abroad and not in the *forum* state.[2294a] Only if such divergence between the domicile of the defendant and the seat of the trust can be detected, (6) provides an additional *forum* – and even then only in those instances covered by Art. 1, i.e. with the important exception of testamentary trusts *post mortem*,[2295] matrimonial trusts and trusts generated by insolvency proceedings.

VIII. Special jurisdiction in maritime salvage, Art. 7 (7)

468 Like (6), (7) was added to the original Brussels Convention on the occasion of the accession of the United Kingdom and Ireland in 1978. The maritime community in the city of London required its inclusion just for the sake of acknowledging the established practice with maritime disputes, especially in salvage, centred in London.[2296] Yet the rule was not tailor-made for accommodating English rules of jurisdiction *in rem* in maritime matters in particular[2297] for it operates only *in personam*.[2298] The more dogmatic *rationale* reads that the salvor saved the ship, the cargo and the respective interests which possibly would have been extinguished but for his activity. Whereas substantive law grants a privilege to the salvor, in most instances materialising as a maritime lien, procedural law must provide for the means for

---

[2292] *Chellaram v. Chellaram (No. 2)* [2002] 3 All ER 17, 47 (Ch.D., *Lawrence Collins* J.) relying on *Canada Trust Co. v. Stolzenberg (No. 2)* [2002] 1 A.C. 1 (H.L.).

[2293] *O'Malley/Layton* para. 17.67; *Geimer/Schütze* Art. 5 note 339; *Oberhammer*, in: Dasser/Oberhammer, Art. 5 LugÜ note 145; *Hofmann/Kunz*, in: Basler Kommentar, Art. 5 LugÜ note 778; *Roman Huber* para. 107.

[2294] But cf. the case of Trib. Milano RDIPP 2003, 539.

[2294a] (6) does not constitute a *forum legis*, though. Tentatively *contra Briggs*, PIL para. 4.281.

[2295] Report *Schlosser* paras. 52, 112; *Conrad* pp. 107–159; *Kropholler/von Hein*, Art. 1 note 29; *Siehr*, in: Schnyder, Art. 5 Nr. 6 LugÜ note 4. *Contra Hofmann/Kunz*, in: Basler Kommentar, Art. 5 note 759; *Roman Huber* para. 120 and *Geimer/Schütze* Art. 5 note 330; *Oberhammer*, in: Dasser/Oberhammer, Art. 5 LugÜ note 144.

[2296] See Report *Schlosser* para. 121; *Geimer/Schütze* Art. 5 note 346.

[2297] *Contra Layton/Mercer* para. 15.120.

[2298] *Infra* Art. 7 note 473 (*Mankowski*).

effective enforcement.[2299] Claims secured by maritime liens were in the draftsmen's mind[2300] but the wording does not contain a respective restriction. Taking the goal of protecting the salvor seriously negative declaratory actions against the salvor would not be included in (7).[2301] Nonetheless, so restrictive an approach would be contrary to the general line to be pursued with regard to all heads of jurisdiction contained in Art. 7 and would single (7) out amongst them.[2302] However, salvage disputes only rarely come to court since arbitration clauses are commonplace in salvage contracts, and the salvage arbitration falls outside the Brussels I*bis* Regulation by virtue of Art. 1 (2) (d).[2303] Furthermore it might be justified that (7) does not provide a special *forum* for all and any maritime claims but only for a rather limited class of them.[2304]

(7) establishes a *forum arresti*.[2305] It grants jurisdiction where arrested assets of the defendant **469** or assets of the defendant bailing other assets outs, are, and thus aims at ensuring great effectiveness. Since cargo and freight are volatile, this helps both sides, plaintiff and defendant, although there is only such relationship between the arrest and the main procedure as the national law allows. Generally, the *forum arresti* benefits the arresting salvor who is not bound to follow the rule of *actor sequitur forum rei*, but is privileged by getting another head of jurisdiction the location of which he can influence heavily.[2306] He who has helped fast shall get his remuneration as expeditiously as possible.[2307] On the other hand, cargo interests might sue a would-be salvor under (3) for negligence.[2308]

Where freight or cargo can be arrested, or in other words: which court has jurisdiction to **470** entertain arresting proceedings, is not for (7) to determine. (7) is only concerned with ensuing main proceedings and co-ordinates the follow-up. Jurisdiction in the arresting proceedings ought to be determined according to national law, pursuant to Art. 31. In maritime matters the 1952 Arrest Convention takes the lead in those states which are Member States to this treaty. Otherwise the courts have to have recourse to their very national law. (a) however is modelled on Art. 7 of the 1952 Arrest Convention,[2309] and in particular on Art. 7 (1) (2) (e) of that Convention.[2310]

An actual arrest is not required but can be substituted under certain circumstances. (b) **471** reflects this in dealing with the case that freight or cargo could have been arrested, but the prospective applicant refrained from commencing arresting proceedings because bail or

---

[2299] Report *Schlosser* para. 123; *Kropholler*, RIW 1986, 929, 931; *Pellis*, Forum arresti (1993) p. 86; *Niegisch*, Die Doktrin forum non conveniens und das EuGVÜ im Vereinigten Königreich (1996) pp. 140 *et seq.*; *Geimer/Schütze* Art. 5 note 348.

[2300] Report *Schlosser* para. 123.

[2301] *Pellis*, Forum arresti (1993) p. 86; *Gottwald*, in: Münchener Kommentar zur ZPO Art. 5 note 92.

[2302] See *Kropholler/von Hein* Art. 5 note 126.

[2303] *David C. Jackson*, Enforcement of Maritime Claims (3rd ed. 2000) para. 6.143.

[2304] *Iriarte Angel*, in: Calvo Caravaca, Art. 5.7 CB note 7.

[2305] *Pellis*, Forum arresti (1993) p. 84; *Matthias Lehmann*, in: Dickinson/Lein para. 4.150.

[2306] *Geimer/Schütze* Art. 5 note 348.

[2307] *Niegisch*, Die Doktrin forum non conveniens und das EuGVÜ im Vereinigten Königreich (1996) p. 141.

[2308] *Brice/Reeder*, Maritime Law on Salvage (5th ed. 2011) para. 2.61.

[2309] *Pocar*, Dir. mar. 101 (1999), 183, 188 *et seq.*

[2310] *Iriarte Angel*, in: Calvo Caravaca, Art. 5.7 CB note 6.

other security had been given. Insofar (7) goes beyond the ideas of the 1952 Arrest Convention.[2311] It is not necessary that the other security was given by cargo interests or persons interested in the freight or expressly on behalf of such persons.[2312] A guarantee bond issued by the P & I club of the ship suffices. For the purposes of (b) it is irrelevant where the security was given; material is only the hypothetical *forum* of the arrest.[2313] Yet (7) does not come into operation if neither an arrest took place nor security was put up.[2314]

472   "Freight" has not to be taken literally (which would restrict it mainly to freight under voyage charters or individual contracts of carriage) and should include hire under time charters.[2315] In (7) the term "freight" has an untechnical meaning not derived from the terminological technicalities of English maritime law. It covers both freight under contracts of carriage and voyage charters on the one hand and hire under a time charter on the other hand. The inclusion of freight is to cater in particular for cases in which the freight is payable conditionally upon the safe arrival of the cargo at its destination; if it had not been salvaged, no freight would have been payable and it is appropriate that the salvor should have a prior right to be satisfied out of the freight.[2316]

473   The *forum arresti* exists only against the persons interested in freight or cargo but not against the ship nor against the shipowner.[2317] (7) does not recognise any concept of an action *in rem*.[2318] The shipowner enters the picture only insofar as he is interested in the freight possibly earned. Thus, (7) might be of particular interest in states which do not recognise a joint and several or common liability on the shipowner's behalf for the salvage quota of cargo and freight.[2319] But on the other hand interest in the freight does not require the interested person to be owner of the ship earning the freight. Interests in the freight include every creditor of the freight claim be it the shipowner, be it a charterer, be it an assignee (e.g. a bank). Bunkers are yet again outside (7).[2320]

474   (7) *in fine* gives two points of time at which the interest in freight or cargo can be properly ascertained: first the time when the suit commences (i.e. dependent on the national law, when the writ is issued or served on the defendant or the suit is enlisted with the court), and second the time of the salvage. Thus (7) grants jurisdiction against former cargo interests which now have ceded with their interest, but possessed it at the time of the salvage. Time of the salvage means the entire duration of the salvage operation. He who had an interest in

---

[2311]   *Pocar*, Dir. mar. 101 (1999), 183, 189.

[2312]   Appraised by *Egler*, Seerechtliche Streitigkeiten unter der EuGVVO (2011) p. 269.

[2313]   Appraised by *Egler*, Seerechtliche Streitigkeiten unter der EuGVVO (2011) p. 269.

[2314]   Trib. comm. Liège Rev. dr. comm. belge 1996, 837.

[2315]   Insofar suggestions that interpretation should reflect the meanings given to the various expressions in international maritime law generally (*Layton/Mercer* para. 15.121) is dangerous even if one is not contemplating the fact that there is nothing like an established body of general maritime law worldwide.

[2316]   Report *Schlosser* para. 122; *Layton/Mercer* para. 15.120.

[2317]   *Brice/Reeder*, Maritime Law on Salvage (5th ed. 2011) para. 2.61; *Matthias Lehmann*, in: Dickinson/Lein para. 4.149; see also *Pocar*, Dir. mar. 101 (1999), 183, 188.

[2318]   *Egler*, Seerechtliche Streitigkeiten unter der EuGVVO (2011) p. 266.

[2319]   *Berlingieri*, Dir. mar. 89 (1987), 166.

[2320]   *Brice/Reeder*, Maritime Law on Salvage (5th ed. 2011) para. 2.61; see also *Iriarte Angel*, in: Calvo Caravaca, Art. 5.7 CB note 7.

cargo or freight at any point of time between the beginning and the end of the salvage operation is a proper defendant.

The relevance of (7) appears to be further restricted if one limits (7) to non-contractual **475** salvage claims and lets (1) govern contractual claims in salvage.[2321] Since the overwhelming majority of salvage claims nowadays is in contract, this would appear to render (7) almost nugatory. At least professional salvors only become active if a salvage contract is entered into, sometimes playing even hold-up games on the High Seas with ships in need. However, the first impression is slightly deceptive since jurisdiction under (7) is not founded against the shipowner, but against persons who are interested in freight or cargo. Salvage contracts ordinarily are entered into between the salvor and the shipowner. Not too frequently cargo interests join in. Hence, (7) gives way to the contractual regime only in the event that either the shipowner who previously entered into a salvage agreement, is sued or cargo interests which became parties to a like agreement, are defendants.[2322]

Article 8

A person domiciled in a Member State may also be sued:
(1) where he is one of a number of defendants, in the courts for the place where any one of them is domiciled, provided the claims are so closely connected that it is expedient to hear and determine them together to avoid the risk of irreconcilable judgments resulting from separate proceedings;
(2) as a third party in an action on a warranty or guarantee or in any other third-party proceedings, in the court seised of the original proceedings, unless these were instituted solely with the object of removing him from the jurisdiction of the court which would be competent in his case;
(3) on a counter-claim arising from the same contract or facts on which the original claim was based, in the court in which the original claim is pending;
(4) in matters relating to a contract, if the action may be combined with an action against the same defendant in matters relating to rights in rem in immovable property, in the court of the Member State in which the property is situated.

Bibliography

Albicker, Der Gerichtsstand der Streitgenossenschaft (1996)

d'Alessandro, La connessione tra controversie transnazionali (2nd ed. 2009)

Auer, Die internationale Zuständigkeit des Sachzu- sammenhangs im erweiterten EuGVÜ-System nach Artikel 6 EuGVÜ (1996)

Banniza von Bazan, Der Gerichtsstand des Sachzu- sammenhangs im EuGVÜ, dem Lugano-Überein- kommen und im deutschen Recht (1995)

[2321] Like *Kropholler*, RIW 1986, 929, 931; *Kropholler/von Hein*, Art. 5 note 125; *Niegisch*, Die Doktrin forum non conveniens und das EuGVÜ im Vereinigten Königreich (1996) p. 141; *Leible*, in: Rauscher, Art. 5 note 116; *Hofmann/Kunz*, in: Basler Kommentar, Art. 5 note 797; *Egler*, Seerechtliche Streitigkeiten unter der EuGVVO (2011) p. 267 do. See also Report *Schlosser* para. 123; *Hausmann*, in: Wieczorek/Schütze, Art. 5 EuGVÜ note 96; *Geimer/Schütze* Art. 5 note 350.

[2322] *Egler*, Seerechtliche Streitigkeiten unter der EuGVVO (2011) p. 268 supports this.

Brandes, Der gemeinsame Gerichtsstand: Die
Zuständigkeit im europäischen Mehrparteien-
prozess nach Art. 6 Nr. 1 EuGVÜ/LÜ (1998)
Coester-Waltjen, Die Bedeutung des Art. 6 Nr. 2
EuGVÜ, IPRax 1992, 290
Coester-Waltjen, Konnexität und Rechtsmissbrauch
– zu Art. 6 Nr. 1 EuGVVO, in: FS Jan Kropholler
(2008), p. 747
Eickhoff, Inländische Gerichtsbarkeit und internationale Zuständigkeit für Aufrechnung und Wider-
klage unter besonderer Berücksichtigung des Euro-
päischen Gerichtsstands- und Vollstreckungsüber-
einkommens (1985)
Geier, Die Streitgenossenschaft im internationalen
Verhältnis (2005)
Geimer, Fora connexitatis – Der Sachzusammen-
hang als Grundlage der internationalen Zuständig-
keit, Bemerkungen zu Art. 6 des EWG-Überein-
kommens vom 27. September 1968, WM 1979, 350
Geimer, Härtetest für deutsche Dienstleister im
Ausland, IPRax 1998, 175
Geimer, Forum Condefensoris, in: FS Jan Kropholler
(2008), p. 777
Gottwald, Europäische Gerichtspflichtigkeit kraft
Sachzusammenhangs, IPRax 1989, 272
Grolimund, Drittstaatenproblematik des euro-
päischen Zivilverfahrensrechts (2002)
Grothe, Die Streitgenossenzuständigkeit gemäß
Art. 6 Nr. 1 EuGVO und das Schicksal der Wohn-
sitzklage, in: FS Konstantinos Kerameus (Athinai
2009), p. 459
Guillaume, Les fors de la connexité en droit inter-
national privé, in: Nouvelle procédure civile et espace
judiciaire européen (Genève 2012), p. 227
von Hoffmann/Hau, Probleme der abredewidrigen
Streitverkündung im Europäischen Zivilrechtsver-
kehr, RIW 1997, 89
Kannengießer, Die Aufrechnung im internationalen
Privat- und Verfahrensrecht (1998)
Knöfel, Gerichtsstand der prozessübergreifenden
Streitgenossenschaft gemäß Art. 6 Nr. 1 EuGVVO?,
IPRax 2006, 503
Köckert, Die Beteiligung Dritter im internationalen
Zivilverfahrensrecht (2010)
Kraft, Grenzüberschreitende Streitverkündung und
Third Party Notice (1997)
Lemaire, La connexité internationale, Trav. com. fr.
dip 2008 (2)010, 95

Mankowski, Die österreichischen Gerichtsstände der
Streitgenossenschaft, des Vermögens und der inländischen Vertretung mit Blick auf das Lugano-
Übereinkommen, IPRax 1998, 122
Mankowski, Verdrängt das europäische Internatio-
nale Arbeitsprozessrecht (Artt. 18 (2)1 EuGVVO)
auch den Gerichtsstand der Streitgenossenschaft aus
Art. 6 Nr. 1 EuGVVO?, EuZA 2008, 104
Mansel, Streitverkündung und Interventionsklage
im Europäischen internationalen Zivilprozessrecht
(EuGVÜ/Lugano-Übereinkommen), in: Hommel-
hoff/Jayme/Mangold (eds.), Europäischer Binnen-
markt: IPR und Rechtsangleichung (1995), p. 161
Mansel, Gerichtspflichtigkeit von Dritten: Streitverkündung und Interventionsklage (Deutschland), in:
Bajons/Mayr/Zeiler (eds.), Die Übereinkommen von
Brüssel und Lugano (1997), p. 177
Marongiu Buonaiuti, Litispendenza e connessione
internazionale, Strumenti di coordinamento tra
giurisdizioni statali in materia civile (2008)
Moissinac, Les *conflits de* décisions et de procédures
en droit international privé (2004)
Müller-Chen/R. M. Keller, Wirksamkeit der Rechts-
hängigkeitssperre im transatlantischen Verhältnis,
in: FS Ivo Schwander (2011), p. 769
Norrgård, A Spider without a Web? Multiple
Defendants in IP Litigation, in: Leible/Ohly (eds.),
Intellectual Property and Private International Law
(Tübingen 2009), p. 211
Nuyts, L'exception de *forum non conveniens* (2003)
Otte, Umfassende Streitentscheidung durch Beach-
tung von Sachzusammenhängen – Gerechtigkeit
durch Verfahrensabstimmung? (1998)
Polak, "Als u begrijpt wat ik bedoel": het Hof van
Justitie herinterpreteert zijn rechtspraak over
rechterlijke bevoegdheid bij pluraliteit van verweer-
ders, Ars aequi 2007, 990
Herbert Roth, Aufrechnung und internationale
Zuständigkeit nach deutschem und europäischem
Prozessrecht, RIW 1999, 819
Herbert Roth, Das Konnexitätserfordernis im
Mehrparteiengerichtsstand des Art. 6 Nr. 1 EuGVO,
in: FS Jan Kropholler (2008), p. 869
Rüssmann, Die internationale Zuständigkeit für
Widerklage und Prozessaufrechnung, in: FS Akira
Ishikawa (2001) 455
Schurig, Der Konnexitätsgerichtsstand nach Art. 6
Nr. 1 EuGVVO und die Verschleifung von örtlicher

und internationaler Zuständigkeit im europäischen Zivilverfahrensrecht, in: FS Hans-Joachim Musielak (2004), p. 493

Scott, Réunion Revisited?, (2008) LMCLQ 113

Slonina, Aufrechnung nur bei internatinaler Zuständigkeit oder Liquidität, IPRax 2009, 399

Michael Stürner, Zur Reichweite des Gerichtsstandes der Widerklage nach Art. 6 Nr. 3 EuGVVO, IPRax 2007, 21

Rolf Stürner, Die erzwungene Intervention Dritter im europäischen Zivilprozess, in FS Rolf A. Schütze (2002), p. 1307

Trunk, Die Erweiterung des EuGVÜ-Systems am Vorabend des Europäischen Binnenmarktes: das Lugano-Übereinkommen und das EuGVÜ-Beitrittsübereinkommen von San Sebastian (1991)

Usunier, La régulation de la compétence juridictionnelle en droit international privé (2008)

Rolf Wagner, Die Aufrechnung im Europäischen Zivilprozessrecht, IPRax 1999, 65

Werner, Widerklage auf nationaler und internationaler Ebene (2002)

Wolfgang Winter, Ineinandergreifen von EuGVVO und nationalem Zivilverfahrensrecht am Beispiel des Gerichtsstands des Sachzusammenhangs, Art. 6 EuGVVO (2007).

I. General considerations

1   An apparently modest device within the overall scheme of the Regulation, Art. 8 differs from the other provisions on "special jurisdiction" comprised within Chapter II, Section 2, insofar as it provides for a forum by not reference to any specific subject-matter, but by reason of connection between existing claims. As such, it creates a head of "derived" jurisdiction, conferring jurisdiction upon an otherwise incompetent court seized of the initial or "anchor" claim. If the requisite connection raises difficult definitional issues, it is easy to see that these are linked to the particular function of this forum and the ways in which it impacts upon the various balances struck within the other provisions of the Regulation, from which it derogates. Such difficulties have appeared with peculiar frequency in recent years, in the field of multi-jurisdictional intellectual property, or in cases involving the conduct of corporate groups. This evolution of litigation practice suggests, first of all, that Art. 8 may be fulfilling an increasingly significant role in adjusting the fora of the common judicial area to new needs generated by networks of activities or actors within the internal market. Disputes tend still to be allocated by Regulation Brussels I (recast) on the assumption that they are discrete, unlinked and non-repetitive; reconnecting claims is one way of taking account of the more complex structure of market relationships. Secondly, derived jurisdiction also represents a potentially important contribution to the reduction of opportunistic forum shopping through multiple claims, and the attendant waste of judicial resources, which has also increased exponentially in recent decades. In order to understand both these aspects, it is helpful to begin with a general picture of both the internal economy of Art. 8 and the place it occupies in relation to other procedural mechanisms inspired by similar, or indeed conflicting, objectives.

1. Jurisdiction by reason of connected claims: internal economy

a) Derived jurisdiction

2   Similarly to Art. 7 and 9, also rules of "special jurisdiction" comprised within Chapter II, Section 2, of the Regulation, Art. 8 operates by exception to Art. 2 and the general rule conferring jurisdiction on the courts of the Member State of the place in which the defendant is domiciled. However, unlike these provisions, the exceptions it creates do not depend upon the subject-matter of the claim. On the other hand, the specific function of Art. 8, which it shares on this point with Art. 9, is to allow for the joining before a single court of closely connected claims over which several different courts would otherwise respectively have jurisdiction, so that the jurisdiction of a court originally seised of a given claim extends, if the claimant bringing the connected claim so chooses, to other closely related claims *solely by virtue of the connection between them*. A close connection between claims thus becomes a specific ground for exercising jurisdiction. In this sense, it is a case of *derived* jurisdiction, in the sense that the jurisdiction of that court over the related claim would not exist but for the close connection which it entertains with the original claim; a court which is not otherwise competent to hear a particular claim can nevertheless become so by sole virtue of the fact that this claim is closely related to, or derives from, another, which it is competent to hear. Several other provisions of the Regulation similarly provide for instances of derived jurisdiction (Art. 11 (1) (c), co-insurers sued before the court seised of proceedings against the leading insurer; Art. 18 (3), counterclaims arising from consumer contracts; 22 (2), counterclaims arising from employment contracts; Art. 7 (3), civil claims for damages in criminal proceedings).

b) Rationale

The rationale of the whole provision now appears in the text of Art. 8 (1), whose wording **3** borrows on this point from the ruling of the Court of Justice in *Kalfelis* v. *Bankhaus Schrö-der*:[1] Related claims may be brought before a single court when they are "so closely connected that it is expedient to hear and determine them together to avoid the risk of irreconcilable judgments resulting from separate proceedings". Such considerations are important enough to warrant an exception to the rules determining the jurisdiction of the courts which are otherwise competent to hear the connected claims. Despite considerable uncertainties in ascertaining the determination and requisite degree of connectedness between claims, it is indisputable that if narrowly related or interdependent issues are decided separately in different courts, the result may well be incoherent. It can of course be argued that the diversity of judicial outcomes is merely the price to be paid for maintaining pluralism within the European Union; this may indeed explain why the joining of connected claims is allowed, but not imposed, by the Regulation. However, avoiding multiple or contradictory outcomes is not merely an esthetic concern, or indeed a more political aspiration towards uniformity; incoherence might lead to unfairness in many cases. Thus, more specific drawbacks of the availability of multiple fora for connected claims may take the form either of an unreasonable burden for one of the parties (serial claims against a given defendant; claimant obliged to bring claims before several fora) or of avoidable social costs in the administration of justice (excessive transaction costs linked to repetitive litigation; strategic manipulation of multiple available fora in complex legal relationships). Often emphasized by the European Court of justice in this context, the importance of procedural economy within the scheme of the Regulation/Convention must therefore be understood in relation both to good administration of justice in the general interest and the threshold of individual acceptability of potentially diverse outcomes. In this respect, the four paragraphs of Art. 8 illustrate the various risks associated with separate jurisdictional allocation of connected claims. Thus, if connected claims against several defendants are heard by different courts, co-debtors' obligations or the liability of multiple tortfeasors could be determined differently (Art. 8 (1)); a claim for indemnity could be successfully pursued against a third party even when no initial liability or obligation is established in respect of the litigant who brings the claim in indemnity (Art. 8 (2)); an action might be heard without regard for a reciprocal claim brought elsewhere by the defendant, and issuing from the same events (Art. 8 (3)); issues relating to rights *in rem* in immovable property which were designed to secure a contractual debt could be solved independently of litigation relating to rights arising under the contract (Art. 8(4)).

c) Defining connection

While the demands of expediency and coherence might appear to be uncontroversial, the **4** application of Art. 8 has proved difficult in practice. This is so, in particular, in relation to the definition of connection. This is due not only to the place of this provision within the general scheme of the Regulation and its relationship to other mechanisms designed to facilitate the joining of connected claims (specifically Art. 30 (ex-28) of the Regulation recast; the new provision Art. 34 relating to proceedings in third States); Art. 45 (d) designed to eradicate conflicts of irreconcilable judgments), but also to the more general difficulty, within the purview of Art. 8 itself, of ascertaining the extent to which requirements contained or construed within the context of one paragraph of Art. 8 are equally valid for the others.

---

[1] *Athanasios Kalfelis v. Bankhaus Schröder Münchmeyer Hengst and Co. and others*, (Case 189/87) [1988] ECR 5565.

Although variations in the structure and wording of the four paragraphs of Art. 8 have fuelled discussion on this point, it would appear from the European Court's decisions both in *Kalfelis*[2] and in *Kongress Agentur Hagen v. Zeehaghe*[3] concerning ex-Artt. 6 (1) and 6 (2) respectively, that a close connection between the claims to be joined is required throughout the provision, even when not expressly stated. Furthermore, as far as the very definition of the requisite connection is concerned, certain types of disputes, such as in the field of intellectual property or financial markets, tend intrinsically to trigger multiple claims and moreover bear stakes high enough for subsequent jurisdictional issues to be litigated intensively. Interpretations by the Court of justice tend therefore to bear the distinct imprint of the specific characteristics of these disputes and are not necessarily adapted to other situations involving risks linked to the availability of multiple fora for related issues. For instance, the requirement that the connected claims arise from "the same situation of fact or law" (see *Roche Nederland BV v. Frederick Primus, Milton Goldenberg)* appeared and has been applied and refined in a line of cases relating to patent infringements in the context of ex-Art. 6 (1) (see *Freeport, Painer, Solvay, Melzer*),[4] but has proved unsuitable in other contexts.

d) Close connection and risk of abuse

5 However, the real difficulty lies in the relationship between the condition and the concern that the joining of connected claims might be used solely to oust the jurisdiction of the "natural forum" of a claim. Such a concern is undoubtedly gaining in significance within the general scheme of the Regulation, as strategic litigation increases. Art. 8 (2) provides expressly that third party proceedings cannot be brought before the court seised of the original claim if they "were instituted solely with the object of removing (the defendant) from the jurisdiction of the court which would be competent in his case". Thus, on the one hand, the Court of Justice has made it clear in the context of this provision that there must a connection between the claims "sufficient to establish that the claimant's choice of forum does not amount to abuse".[5] This is entirely understandable. The grouping of claims in the name of procedural expediency comes with the risk that the balance otherwise deemed appropriate in the allocation of disputes between the different interests involved, may be skewed in favour of one or the other. Moreover, although Art. 8 is presented formally as an exception to Art. 4, nevertheless, the joining of connected claims can also in effect deprive other courts competent under the Regulation, such as those designated by Art. 7, of their jurisdiction over a connected claim. This is why, in the context of Art. 8 (2) (ex 6(2)), the Court has adopted a functional definition of the requisite link between claims, requiring of the national court in every case to satisfy itself that the connection invoked is such that it excludes abuse. However, on the other hand, in the context of Art. 8 (1) (ex 6 (2)), the Court has also ruled that the risk of abuse, depriving a co-defendant of her natural forum, cannot give rise to any *separate* argument once the claims are established as connected.[6] In other words, *either* there is a

---

2   *Athanasios Kalfelis* v. *Bankhaus Schröder Münchmeyer Hengst and Co. and others*, (Case 189/87) [1988] ECR 5565.

3   *Kongress Agentur Hagen GmbH* v. *Zeehaghe BV*, (Case C-365/88) [1990] ECR I-1845, I-1864 para. 11.

4   *Freeport plc v. Olle Arnoldsson* (Case C-98/06), [2007] ECR I-8319; *Eva-Maria Painer v. Standard Verlags GmbH and others* (Case C-145/10)[2011]; *Solvay v. Honeywell* (C-616/10) [2012]; *Melzer v. MF Global UK Ltd* (Case C-228/11) [2013].

5   See *Groupement d'intérêt économique* (GIE) *Réunion européenne et al.* v. *Zurich España, Société pyrénéenne de transit d'automobiles (Soptrans)*, (Case C-77/04) [2005] ECR I-4509.

6   *Freeport plc v. Olle Arnoldsson* (Case C-98/06), [2007] ECR I-8319.

connection, *or* an abuse, but each is functionally exclusive of the other. While this might seem somewhat tautological, it is fair to say that similar difficulties attach to the articulation between the requirement of close connection and the exclusion of abuse or fraud in various other contexts of private international law (such as the jurisdictional link required for the recognition of foreign judgments, or the component of integration in the definition of domicile). The Court's position on this point may also be designed to avoid sticky issues of proof of intentional manipulation of available fora.

e) Narrow construction of Art. 8

The risk left open by *Freeport*, that a close connection is not necessarily exclusive of strategic forum shopping, may explain, too, why the Court has consistently held that Art. 8 is to be construed narrowly, and why indeed additional requirements to bare connectedness, or further restrictions to the availability of the derived forum, are imposed in some instances by the text of the provision itself. Indeed, Art. 8 does not make bare connectedness – defined so as to exclude abuse – a sufficient basis for the joining of several claims. Unlike Art. 30 (ex 28), the extension of the jurisdiction of the court originally seised of a claim is subordinated to further, stricter, requirements. Thus, under Art. 8 (1), connected claims against multiple defendants can be heard only by the court for the place of the domicile of any of them; apparently more flexible, Art. 8 (2) allows for a claim against a third party to be heard by the court seised of the initial litigation, but the claim itself, which will usually be framed as a claim for indemnity, must present the technical characteristics of third party proceedings; according to Art. 8 (3), the court seised of a claim can also hear a counterclaim, provided however that it arises from same contract or event as the initial action; Art. 8 (4) deals with the very specific case of actions to recover secured debt and enforce a security on immovable property. **6**

The Court of Justice has construed the four cases in Art. 8 so as to prevent the extension of a given court's jurisdiction in cases which do not fit the requirements in those paragraphs. Thus, in *La Réunion européenne*,[7] it considered that Art. 8 (1) did not allow the extension of the jurisdiction of the court of a Member State when that court was not the court of the domicile of one of the defendants. The explanation for the more restrictive conditions of Art. 8, as compared with those of Art. 30, would appear to lie in the fact that the former provides for derived jurisdiction, whereas the latter operates merely by way of an exception raised before the court second seised.[8] Indeed, as seen above, the risk of fraud or abuse may be greater in respect of this particular head of jurisdiction, which could be used solely to justify the jurisdiction of a court which is not competent over the related claim, correlatively ousting that of the natural forum. It may well be, too, that the risk of transforming jurisdiction over connected claims into a *forum actoris* is more particularly present in the cases which fall under Art. 8. Thus, for instance, in the case of Art. 8 (3), the counterclaimant will be allowed to sue before the courts of his own domicile, at least to the extent that the court seised of the initial claim is competent under Art. 2. As will be seen below, the corollary to the more liberal requirements of Art. 30 is the discretion to decline or retain jurisdiction invested in the court second seised under its paragraph 2; conversely, once the conditions for **7**

---

7   *Réunion europénne SA v. Spliethoff's Bevrachtingskantoor BV and Master of the vessel "Alblasgracht 002"*,
    (Case C-51/97) [1998] ECR I-6511.
8   *Athanasios Kalfelis v. Bankhaus Schröder Münchmeyer Hengst and Co. and others*, (Case 189/87) [1988]
    ECR 5565.

any derived jurisdiction under Article 8 are met, the court has no discretion to refuse to join the claims.

f) Scope

8   Previous versions of this provision were understood to apply only to claims subject to the jurisdiction of courts of Member States by virtue of the Regulation; in *La Réunion européenne v. Spliethoff's Bevrachtingskantoor e.a.*, the ECJ ruled that ex-Art. 6 (1) of the Convention did not operate to confer derived jurisdiction on the Court of a Contracting State when the defendant to the claim of which it was seised was domiciled in a non-Contracting State and jurisdiction was thereby determined under national rules of private international law. The inapplicability of Article 6 in respect of claims brought against defendants who are domiciled in third countries has been re-affirmed recently in *Land Berlin v. Ellen Mirjam and Others*.[9] However, as will be seen below, changes concerning the scope of the closely related provision on connexity in Art. 34 of Regulation Brussels I recast, encouraging deference towards proceedings in third countries, raises the converse question of whether Art. 8 might now encourage similar deference in cases where the initial claim is to be brought in the court of a third state. Moreover, the European Court has not yet determined whether, in cases (other than Art. 8 (1)) in which Art. 8 does not identify the court seised of the original claim, so that the basis on which it is exercising jurisdiction is indifferent, it allows for the joining of connected claims before the court of a Member State competent over a claim brought against a defendant domiciled in a third State, on the basis of the national private international law rules of that Member State, which could include rules of exorbitant jurisdiction (now mentioned in Art. 5(2)). Art. 8 (4) is not concerned with this issue, since it provides exclusively for the extension of the jurisdiction of the court competent under Art. 24 (1), that is, the court of the Member State where immoveable property is situated.

2. Derived jurisdiction within the general scheme of the Regulation

a) Variable geometry of connectedness

9   Avoiding connected claims from being heard by different courts could simply be seen as an issue of costs incurred by serial litigation. However, further risks of legal incoherence and practical unfairness attach to the fact that parallel proceedings to which connected claims give rise may also generate potentially separate and conflicting decisions, which in turn are able to move freely throughout the European Union. In order to avert the disorder, contradictions and embarrassment which would arise if irreconcilable judgments were handed down in different Member States, the Regulation provides for three distinct preventive mechanisms, each designed to come into play at successive stages in the procedural treatment of the connected claims. While Art. 8 provides a preventive remedy at the prior, jurisdictional stage, Art. 30 allows for (without imposing) the joining of related actions already pending before the courts of different Member States on the basis of bare connectedness. If neither has led to a joining of the connected claims, as a last resort, Art. 45 (1) (d) solves the ultimate conflict of judgments when these "cannot logically be executed simultaneously". This progressive approach must be correlated to the circumstance that neither derived jurisdiction over connected claims, nor the stay of related proceedings is compulsory, nor designed to be watertight; in other words, they are framed in such a way as to leave

---

[9]   *Land Berlin v. Ellen Mirjam Sapir* (Case C-645/11), nyr.

room for both individual choice and judicial discretion, and do not purport to eliminate every instance in which different courts may be seized simultaneously of connected claims, nor indeed does the pursuit of coherence necessarily prevail over the risk of disorder, unless it leads ultimately to contradictory judicial rulings in a specific case. This explains why, on the one hand, the threshold of connectedness varies throughout the Regulation and, on the other, why the concept of derived jurisdiction is specific to Article 8.

Although it is sometimes argued that the same definition of connectedness should apply in **10** the various contexts in which it is used (see concl. ad. gen. Léger, in the *Roche Nederland* case),[10] the pattern which emerges from the case-law of the European Court is one of a progressively more restrictive threshold of potential contradiction, required respectively in order to justify joining the claims, staying a parallel procedure and, ultimately, subordinating one judgment to the other. Indeed, although the court seised of an original claim has no discretion to refuse to hear a connected claim brought before it, if such a claim fulfills the requirements laid down by one or other of the paragraphs of Art. 8, the claimant is in no way obliged to bring the connected claim before the court seised of the original claim. For instance, a counterclaimant may well choose to bring the counterclaim elsewhere. At a later date, in a case where parallel proceedings have been engaged, the court seised of the counterclaim may under Art. 30, on the request of the defendant, stay proceedings in order that the claims should be joined if they are connected in such a way that it is expedient to join them; however, it is not obliged to do so. If, lastly, both courts give judgment, with differing content, it is still conceivable that, however disorderly such an outcome may seem, both decisions may still be enforced simultaneously. It is only in cases of "irreconcilable judgments resulting from separate proceedings", defined by the Court in *Hoffmann* as involving "mutually exclusive consequences", that Art. 45 (1) (d) provides for the primacy of one over the other. This is however a far narrower concept than mere inconsistency, and appears to be designed more as a remedy *ex post* to the failure of *lis pendens* than with connexity in mind.

There are also other differences between these various procedural devices in structure and **11** function. Thus, like the *lis pendens* provisions in Art. 29, Art. 30 envisages two related actions which are each *already pending* before the courts of different Member States. It provides that the court second seised has discretion to stay proceedings, or indeed decline jurisdiction under certain conditions, when the claim of which it is seised is related to an action already pending in the courts of another Member State (while not identical, since in such a case the *lis pendens* provisions of Art. 27 would be applicable). By contrast, under Art. 8, the court originally seised of a claim extends its jurisdiction to the connected claim brought before it immediately, *regardless of whether another court is subsequently seised* (if this is the case, Art. 29 is there to ensure its priority in respect of the connected claim). More importantly still, pursuant to Art. 30 (2), the court first seised must be *competent over the related claim* in order for the second court to decline jurisdiction; the required connection between that claim and the action which is already pending before the first court is insufficient. This means that Art. 30 operates merely to join proceedings pending before competent courts through the use of an exception, whereas Art. 8 invests an otherwise incompetent court with derived jurisdiction over the connected claim, by sole virtue of the connection between that claim and another of which it is competently seised. For instance, in the case of Art. 8 (1), the court seised of the initial claim, being the court of the defendant's domicile, is

---

10   *Roche Nederland BV v. Frederick Primus and Milton Goldenberg* (Case C-539/03), [2006] ECR I-6535.

not otherwise competent, at least on the basis of that particular provision, in respect of the claim brought against a co-defendant whose domicile is in another Member State. Similarly, Art. 8 (4) expressly provides that a claim in contract may be brought before the court with exclusive jurisdiction under Art. 24 (1) over proceedings concerning rights *in rem* in immovable property. This is a clear exception to the principle that jurisdiction under Art. 22 exists only for the purposes of the specific proceedings whose object justifies an exception to Art. 4, so that Art. 8 (4) extends the jurisdiction of a court not otherwise competent under the Regulation. In cases of third party proceedings (Art. 8 (2)) or counterclaims arising from the same contract or facts (Art. 8 (3)), the court originally seised may or may not be otherwise competent over the connected claim under Artt. 4 or 7.

b) Close connection as a general ground for derived jurisdiction?

12 Despite differences between the three provisions designed to avert the risk of conflicting judgments, a similar functionality appears in all these contexts. Thus, it has been argued that there is a wider principle, deriving inductively from the four cases set out in Art. 8, under which a close connection between claims might be made into a general, subsidiary, head of jurisdiction, allowing the joining of claims before a court initially seised in every case in which there would otherwise be a risk of irreconcilable judgments, beyond the restrictive conditions laid down in Art. 8. Indeed, some cases in which it would nevertheless be expedient to allow claims to be grouped together fall outside the requirements of Art. 8, while Art. 30 does not necessarily ensure that they will be joined at a later stage. However, given the pattern of progressively more restrictive requirements contained within the various provisions outlined above, the Court of Justice has refused to include connectedness as a general basis for jurisdiction outside the instances in which the grouping of related or derived claims is expressly provided for. Thus, in *Elefanten Schuh v. Jacquemain*,[11] it refused to consider that Art. 22 of the Convention (now Art. 30 Regulation recast) could operate otherwise than by way of exception to an action already pending before a court of competent jurisdiction. Furthermore, in *La Réunion européenne*,[12] it rejected the argument according to which, when the connection between two claims is so close as to make them indivisible, the requirements of Art. 8 might be redundant, and emphasized that the concept of indivisibility (borrowed here from French civil procedure) understood as a connection strong enough to justify derived jurisdiction unconditionally, had no place within the scheme of the Convention.

c) Ordering competing objectives

13 In order to understand the Court's reluctance to allow a more extensive reading of Art. 8, it must also be remembered that the pursuit of procedural expediency has to be weighed against other conflicting values. Indeed, one of the particular interests of Art. 8 is that it serves to reveal a certain hierarchy among the various objectives pursued by the Regulation. Thus, while considerations of procedural expediency such as joining connected claims to avoid incoherent decisions or reduce costs involved in multiple proceedings are certainly important, they are not exclusive. Indeed, it can be seen from the restrictive content of Art. 8 (1), which operates solely in favour of the courts of the domicile of one of the co-defendants, or indeed from the wording of Art. 8 (2), which expresses concern to avoid the ousting of the

---

11 *Elefanten Schuh GmbH v. Jacquemain*, (Case 150/80) [1981] ECR 1671.

12 *Réunion europénne SA v. Spliethoff's Bevrachtingskantoor BV and Master of the vessel "Alblasgracht 002"*, (Case C-51/97) [1998] ECR I-6511.

jurisdiction of an otherwise competent court, that procedural expediency must be weighed against the protection of the natural forum of the claim. They may therefore have to give way before stronger bases of jurisdiction. Thus, the Court has ruled out recourse to Art. 8 within the scope of the protective rules of sections 3–5 (or at least in the context of section 5 which deals with the individual employment contract) thereby preventing the extension of the existing rules to connected claims from working in favour of any stronger party to the detriment of the weaker *(Glaxosmithkline)*.[13] Furthermore, the Court has also given priority to party choice of forum, so that 8 (1) cannot paralyze an explicit agreement on jurisdiction, as will be seen below in the various instances where a conflict is conceivable.

d) Jurisdiction over connected claims and national rules of procedure

The specific nature of derived jurisdiction over connected claims raises the issue of the **14** relationship between the rules of jurisdiction under the Regulation, and the national rules of procedure of the *forum*. The *forum* seised of a claim may have jurisdiction under the Regulation to hear a connected claim, but its rules of procedure may not allow the joinder of the claims. In *Kongress Agentur*,[14] the Court of justice considered that the court seised of the original claim may apply its national procedural rules, but in doing so must not deprive Art. 8 of its effectiveness. Thus, a court seised on the basis of Art. 8 (2) can apply its procedural law to determine whether an action on a guarantee may be brought, but it could not base a refusal on the fact that the guarantor is domiciled in another Member State and that the joining of the claims would cause extra delay. The question arises as to whether there is an obstacle to national procedural law imposing specific, additional, requirements as to the sufficiency of the connection between claims; the concern might be that too high a threshold could upset the delicate balance between the protection afforded to the natural forum by preventing artificial claims and the freedom of choice open to the claimant when several courts are simultaneously available under the Regulation.

The weight to be given respectively to these considerations is not always very clear, however. **15** Thus, as will be seen below, it appears for instance that a Member State can require that there be a "real issue" to be tried against a co-defendant in the case of Art. 8 (1). Similarly, in *Cie Réunion Européenne v. Zurich Espana*,[15] the Court specifically directed the national court to satisfy itself that third-party proceedings within the ambit of Art. 8 (2) do not seek to remove the defendant from the jurisdiction of the court which would otherwise be competent. However, in *Reisch Montage v. Kiesel Baumaschinen Handels GmbH*[16] the Court held that the fact that the claim brought against a particular defendant was inadmissible from the start under the procedural rules of the court for the domicile of that defendant, did not preclude the joining of the claims before that court in respect of a co-defendant domiciled elsewhere. This position is debatable in the light of the purpose of Art. 8. If this provision is indeed designed to ensure that connected claims do not give rise to irreconcilable decisions (or indeed if it pursues wider considerations of procedural expediency), it can hardly justify that

---

[13] *Glaxosmithkline Laboratoires v. Rouard* (Case C-462/06), [2008] ECR I-3965.

[14] *Kongress Agentur Hagen GmbH v. Zeehaghe BV*, (Case C-365/88) [1990] ECR I-1845. See, too, *Groupement d'intérêt économique (GIE) Réunion européenne et al. v. Zurich España, Société pyrénéenne de transit d'automobiles (Soptrans)*, (Case C-77/04) [2005] ECR I-4509.

[15] *Groupement d'intérêt économique (GIE) Réunion européenne et al. v. Zurich España, Société pyrénéenne de transit d'automobiles (Soptrans)*, (Case C-77/04) [2005] ECR I-4509.

[16] In *Reisch Montage v. Kiesel Baumaschinen Handels GmbH* (Case C-103/05) (2006)

a co-defendant be hailed before a court other than that of his domicile when there is no such risk from the start. Under the facts of *Reisch Montage*, the German guarantor who stood security for an Austrian businessman, would have to defend his case before an Austrian court, in the absence of any suit against the German principal who had been declared insolvent before the claim was brought. Here, the Court's concern that national procedural rules should not frustrate the purposes of the uniform jurisdictional rules is understandable; however, the Regulation itself does actually subordinate the joining of claims to the procedural rules of the forum on the threshold issue of the possibility of a claim being brought, in the arguably similar case where the court seised of a claim against an insured tortfeasor may also hear the claim against the insurer (Art. 13-1) and, in the case of a direct action, the insured or the insurance policy holder (Art. 13-3). A particular case is Art. 8 (4), which expressly subordinates the derived jurisdiction (in matters of contract) of the court competent under Art. 24 (1) over immovable property, to the condition that the action in contract "may be combined", presumably under the law of the forum, with an action concerning rights *in rem* against the same defendant.

e) Derived jurisdiction and claims involving Third States

16 For the first time in the history of the common judicial area, Regulation Brussels I (recast) has addressed its relationship with the courts of third states. According to Recital (23), which is clearly designed to qualify the exclusive nature of Art. 4 resulting from the Court's *Owusu* judgment,[17] the innovation consists in "a flexible mechanism allowing the courts of the Member States to take into account proceedings pending before the courts of third States, considering in particular whether a judgment of a third State will be capable of recognition and enforcement in the Member State concerned under the law of that Member State and the proper administration of justice". Under Recital 24, the latter involves assessing "all the circumstances of the case before it. Such circumstances may include connections between the facts of the case and the parties and the third State concerned, the stage to which the proceedings in the third State have progressed by the time proceedings are initiated in the court of the Member State and whether or not the court of the third State can be expected to give a judgment within a reasonable time". These considerations go to the heart of the rationale of the various procedural mechanisms designed to coordinate the allocation of connected claims, including Art. 8 as applicable to claims before the courts of Member States.

17 However, the subsequent amendments to the provisions of the Regulation affect only connected proceedings already pending, or judgments already rendered. On the first point, under Art. 45 (1) (a), in cases where the court of a Member State exercises jurisdiction based on Art. 4 or on Arts 7, 8 or 9, it may stay the proceedings in favour an action pending before a court of a third State, if "it is expedient to hear and determine the related actions together to avoid the risk of irreconcilable judgments resulting from separate proceedings". On the second point, under § 3, the court of the Member State may dismiss the proceedings before it if the proceedings in the court of the third State are concluded and have resulted in a judgment capable of recognition and, where applicable, of enforcement in that Member State. This expands the cause of refusal or recognition of the judgment of another Member State under Art. 45 (1) (d), which provides for such refusal only "if the judgment is irreconcilable with an earlier judgment given … in a third State involving the same cause of

---

17 *Owusu v. Jackson* (Case-C 128/02), [2005] QB 801.

action and between the same parties, provided that the earlier judgment fulfills the conditions necessary for its recognition in the Member State addressed".

The extent to which Art. 8 may allow a similar result, in cases where connected claims fall **18** respectively within and outside the scope of the jurisdiction of the courts of Member states, is not addressed. The possibility for the court of a Member State to hear a connected claim which would otherwise not fall within its jurisdiction in such a case under the Regulation will no doubt continue to depend upon its national private international law. Conversely, however, to enable the courts of Member States to refuse to hear a claim on the grounds that proceedings are already pending (or indeed might be more appropriately be instituted) in a third state, would be to allow for *forum non conveniens*; this would expand upon the possibility already provided for under Art. 34 § 1 and would contradict more directly the Court's ruling in *Owusu*.[18] The latter provision might inspire an analogical reading of Art. 8; on the contrary, it could be taken to signify that the only case in which a court may decline jurisdiction over a claim within the scope of the Regulation is when such permission is conferred specifically – that is, when it is second seised, or when a judgment has already been given in a third state. Which of these readings is correct remains to be seen.

II. Multiple defendants – Art. 8 (1)

1. General function and content

In cases in which a claimant pursues connected claims against multiple defendants domi- **19** ciled in different Member States, this provision allows for the claims to be brought before a single court, that is the court for the domicile of any one of the defendants. Typically, it allows for the grouping of similar claims against joint tortfeasors or co-debtors. It is the only one out of the four paragraphs of Art. 8 to provide for the grouping of independent claims which do not have some specific procedural link between them (such as third party proceedings, counterclaims, or claims which aim to recover secured debt and enforce the security on immovable property). As such, exemplifying derived jurisdiction based on a connection between claims, it contains a general definition of the connection requirement, which is in fact applicable throughout Art. 8. It is also a rule of special jurisdiction, in that the grouping of the litigation takes place before a specific court; this means that it invests jurisdiction over the connected claim in the court for the place of domicile of one of the defendants, and not in the courts of the Member State where the defendant is domiciled, in general. Therefore, for the provision to operate, it is not enough for the initial claim to have been brought before any court of the Member State in which the defendant is domiciled, other than the court for the place of his domicile – although in some systems, the jurisdiction of the competent court may not be local, as in the case of the High Court of England.

The grouping of multiple claims is a faculty for the claimant, who may continue to pursue **20** the defendants severally, before the courts of their respective domiciles under Art. 4, despite the importance, within the scheme of the Regulation, of avoiding irreconcilable decisions; thus, the defendant to the connected claim has no means of obliging the claimant to make use of Art. 8 (1), although he may subsequently raise an exception to the jurisdiction of the court second seised under Art. 30 (2) once the action is pending before the court of another

---

[18] *Owusu v. Jackson* (Case C-128/02), [2005] QB 801.

Member State. On the other hand, the court seised of a connected claim has no discretion, as it does under Art. 30 (2), to decide whether expediency requires the claims to be heard together. Practically, however, since it is up to the court to decide whether the claims are connected within the meaning of Art. 8 (1), it is unclear whether there is any real difference in this respect between the two texts.

2. Court for the place of domicile of a defendant

21 The text makes it clear that jurisdiction over a connected claim against a defendant domiciled in another Member State belongs exclusively to the courts for the place of the domicile of one of the other defendants.[19] Domicile is no doubt to be ascertained at the date of issue of proceedings, following the principle which applies more generally for the determining of jurisdiction, although it is not made explicit even under Art. 4. This means that connected claims can be concentrated before a court which is initially that of the place of domicile of one defendant, even if that defendant later moves to another Member State, including that of a co-defendant, or even to a non Member State. When one or more of the several defendants are domiciled in non Member States, the effect of the connection between the claims on the jurisdiction of the court of a Member State seised on the basis of Art. 4 in respect of those defendants, will be determined by the national private international law of the forum. On the other hand, the domicile of a co-defendant in a non Member State cannot serve to attract the other claims under Art. 8 (1).[20] Under Art. 8 (1), a court whose jurisdiction is based on any grounds other than domicile is not empowered to hear the connected claim. This is true whether such a court is competent by virtue of one the special heads of jurisdiction of Art. 7 (1) or 7 (3), or indeed even pursuant to a choice of forum clause under Art. 25.

22 This is often considered to mean that outside the specific instances of indemnity, counterclaim, or recovery of secured debt dealt with in the subsequent paragraphs, in which the claims are naturally interdependent, only jurisdiction based on the domicile of a defendant under Art. 4 is "strong" enough to justify its extension to related but independent claims which would ordinarily be brought before the courts of the domicile of the other defendants. However, while plausible, this reasoning is also subject to caution. It is true that both the *Jenard* Report[21] and the Court of justice in *Kalfelis*[22] reflect concern that the provision might be invoked abusively to oust the jurisdiction of the courts of the Member States where the other defendants are domiciled. Clearly, the joining of claims, which will deprive the co-defendants of their right under Art. 4 to be sued in the courts of the Member States of their own domicile, must be allowed only on serious grounds – grounds which are now expressed in the codified definition of connection requirement in Art. 8 (1) itself. Arguably, if such good reasons do indeed exist, and expediency requires that a defendant be deprived of the right to be sued before the courts of the Member State of his domicile, it is not clear why the exception should operate exclusively in favour of a court exercising jurisdiction under Art. 4.

---

[19] For instance see Cour d'Appel Amiens, 15th May 2012, 11/02752.

[20] See *Réunion europénne SA v. Spliethoff's Bevrachtingskantoor BV and Master of the vessel "Alblasgracht 002"*, (Case C-51/97) [1998] ECR I-6511. Again, recently, *Land Berlin v. Ellen Mirjam Sapir* (Case C-645/11), nyr.

[21] Report *Jenard* p. 26.

[22] *Athanasios Kalfelis* v. *Bankhaus Schröder Münchmeyer Hengst & Co.*, (Case 189/87) [1988] ECR 5565.

A similar point was put to the European Court in *La Réunion Européenne*,[23] in a case where **23** the national court was originally seised of claim against a defendant who was not domiciled in a Contracting State, and its jurisdiction based on the national rules of the forum. It was argued that in circumstances in which there was a particularly close link between claims so as to make them indivisible, a court seised on grounds other than ex Art. 2 of the Convention (Art. 4 Regulation recast) should also be able to extend its jurisdiction to related claims against co-defendants domiciled in Contracting States. In rejecting this argument, the Court pointed out that "the objective of legal certainty pursued by the Convention would not be attained if the fact that a court in a Contracting State had accepted jurisdiction as regards one of the defendants not domiciled in a Contracting State made it possible to bring another defendant, domiciled in a Contracting State, before that same court in cases other than those envisaged by the Convention, thereby depriving him of the benefit of the protective rules laid down by it". This reasoning rests more on the need to ensure the effectiveness of the Convention/Regulation, particularly insofar as it aims to protect defendants from unfair surprise, than on the specific architecture of ex-Art. 6, now Art. 8 (1). If the court originally seised has jurisdiction under the Regulation, in cases where the Convention/Regulation itself allows an exception to Art. 4, then the particular objections voiced by the Court would seem to lose their relevance. However, the restriction has been reiterated unerringly.[24]

3. The court for the place of domicile of any defendant

The provision allows the claims to be joined before the court for the place of the domicile of **24** any one of the multiple defendants. Since the claims envisaged by Art. 8 (1) are independent in the sense that there is no specific procedural link between them, any one of the claims can determine the jurisdiction of the court which will hear them all; there is no requirement that that claim be more important or central than the others or that the defendant be in some way "principal". In an interesting Dutch case[25] involving multiple claims for concerted violation of industrial property rights, it was considered that only the court of the seat of the principal defendant ("the spider at the centre of the web") is empowered to hear the multiple connected claims. However, no such hierarchy between the various courts of the respective domiciles of the defendants appears in the text of Art. 8 (1), which would seem to indicate that jurisdiction over the whole set of claims can invest in any one of them, however small the claim or secondary the part played by that particular defendant. This aggravates the risk of fraud, since it might provide an incentive to frame an insignificant claim in order to determine jurisdiction. This is why some national systems therefore require, additionally to the connection requirement, that there be a serious claim against the defendant whose domicile is used to attract jurisdiction. The same lack of hierarchy between the claims can also lead to difficulties concerning the definition of the respective scope of Art. 8 (1) and the subsequent paragraph, Art. 8 (2), which concerns third party claims.

4. Requirement of close connection

This is no doubt the most difficult issue of interpretation in respect of the text of Art. 8 (1). **25**

---

[23]   *Réunion europénne SA v. Spliethoff's Bevrachtingskantoor BV and Master of the vessel "Alblasgracht 002"*, (Case C-51/97) [1998] ECR I-6511.

[24]   *Land Berlin v. Ellen Mirjam Sapir* (Case C-645/11), nyr.

[25]   Hof 's-Gravenhage [1999] FSR 352.

The initial version of the text (in the Convention) contained no requirement as to the connection between the claim of which the court was originally seised and the claim brought against another defendant to which it could extend its jurisdiction. The provision merely read: "A person domiciled in a Member State may also be sued: 1) where he is one of a number of defendants, in the courts for the place where any one of them is domiciled". This is still the wording of Art. 6 (1) Lugano Convention. However, legal doctrine and national case-law soon read into this Art the requirement that, to justify that claims against various defendants domiciled in different Contracting States be heard and determined by a single court, there should be a close connection between such claims. Indeed, the *Jenard* Report had already pointed out the risk of abuse inherent in derived jurisdiction, which could lead a claimant to make entirely unrelated claims against several defendants solely in order to oust the jurisdiction of the courts of their respective domiciles.[26] Clearly, Art. 8 (1) is designed to enhance the interests of coherent administration of justice within Europe, and in no way to turn the objectives of the Regulation on their head. This appears to be the reason for which, in *Glaxosmithkline v. Rouard*,[27] the Court refused to allow ex-Art. 6 (1) to work in conjunction with the special protective rules of section 5, for fear of upsetting the economy of these special fora in the field of employment contracts. It is also why, in *Kalfelis*,[28] the European Court of Justice ruled that a close connection between claims is required, and that it must receive a uniform definition, "in order to ensure, as far as possible, the equality and uniformity of the rights and obligations under the Convention of the Contracting States and of the persons concerned". This definition, which also finds expression in Art. 30 (3) Regulation (22 (3) Convention), was in turn codified in Art. 8 (1) of the Regulation, which now requires that the claims be "so closely connected that it is expedient to hear and determine them together to avoid the risk of irreconcilable judgments resulting from separate proceedings". Such a connection might typically exist in cases where the several claims involve a company and its shareholders, the main debtor and the guarantor, or several participants in a chain of contracts.

26   The need for a uniform definition under Art. 8 (1) stemmed from various factors generating uncertainty. Some of these are linked to the content of the various national laws. Thus, the very concept of derived jurisdiction in cases of connected claims, outside third party proceedings or counterclaims, is not familiar to all national systems. Moreover, in all events, connexity as a procedural concept does not necessarily coincide with categories of substantive law which may nevertheless be relevant in situations comprised within the scope of Art. 8 (1), in particular the concept of joint and several liability. But the source of uncertainty also lies within the Regulation itself, where there are multiple applications of the connection requirement which do not always rest on the same degree of connectedness. Thus, as explained in the *The Owners of the Cargo Lately Laden on Board the Ship "Tatry" v. The Owners of the Ship "Maciej Rataj"*[29] a sufficient connection exists for the needs of Art. 22 (now 30 Regulation recast) of the Convention when there is a risk that, if decided separately, the various claims could give rise to decisions which are contradictory – even if they can be

---

26   Report *Jenard*, p. 26.

27   *Glaxosmithkline Laboratoires v. Rouard* (Case C-462/06), [2008] ECR I-3965.

28   *Athanasios Kalfelis v. Bankhaus Schröder Münchmeyer Hengst and Co. and others*, (Case 189/87) [1988] ECR 5565.

29   *The Owners of the Cargo Lately Laden on Board the Ship "Tatry" v. The Owners of the Ship "Maciej Rataj"*, (Case C-406/92) [1994] ECR I-5439.

executed separately and their legal consequences are not mutually exclusive. For instance, calling on a third party's guarantee or indemnity, while rejecting the initial claim in liability against the defendant who has initiated the third party claim, is not technically impossible, although it is clearly incoherent and no doubt incomprehensible to the parties concerned. On the other hand, mutually exclusive consequences are required by Art. 45 (1) (d), whose stricter conditions can be explained by the fact that it serves to impede free movement of judgments. When providing a uniform definition in *Kalfelis*,[30] the court opted for the wider concept in Art. 22 (3) of the Convention. In *La Réunion européenne*,[31] it confirmed that such a definition was the only operational one under Art. 8 (1), and that the narrower concept of indivisibility, known to the civil procedure of some national systems, had no place in the scheme of the Convention.

However, by far the most sensitive issue, which has given rise to a recent series of high- **27** profile cases largely involving disputes in the area of intellectual property, concerns the impact of diverse legal grounds, including differences induced by a conflict of laws, on the framing of different claims. Is the connectedness requirement under Art. 8 (1) still satisfied if the claims are governed by different laws or, even if comprised within one legal system, when they have different legal foundations (such as contract and tort, or tort and restitution, etc). The initial uncertainty arose in *Roche Nederland BV v. Frederick Primus, Milton Goldenberg*,[32] concerning concerted violation of industrial property rights by legally distinct defendants belonging to the same corporate group. While the specific characteristics of patents, each subject to a distinct territorial law, was no doubt decisive here, the ruling was read to have more far-reaching consequences both for other instances of claims involving intellectual property, or for connected claims in other areas; however these consequences were not necessarily appropriate in other contexts. In this case, a connection within the meaning of that provision was judged not to exist, in respect of multiple claims for the concerted violation of property rights in different Member States against various defendants belonging to the same corporate group. Despite the apparent links between the claims brought against the various defendants, which were based on identical violations of a European patent, the Court maintained that since different national laws would be applied in the various Member States, each applying its own rules in respect of acts occurring within its own territory, there was no risk that the resulting decisions would be irreconcilable. This construction of connection under Art. 8 (1) might suggest that whenever claims – in tort for example – against several defendants, albeit having an identical object and based on parallel sets of facts, are governed by different laws, then the irreconcilability requirement is not fulfilled. However, such a consequence would be overly dogmatic. Inconsistency justifying the joining of claims can obviously exist even when different laws are applicable to different claims, in the same way that under the same governing law, various claims grounded in different legal provisions or categories can equally give rise to contradictory results;[33] moreover, the content of

---

[30] *Athanasios Kalfelis v. Bankhaus Schröder Münchmeyer Hengst and Co. and others*, (Case 189/87) [1988] ECR 5565.

[31] *Réunion europénne SA v. Spliethoff's Bevrachtingskantoor BV and Master of the vessel "Alblasgracht 002"*, (Case C-51/97) [1998] ECR I-6511.

[32] *Roche Nederland BV v. Primus NV and Milton Goldberg* (Case C-539/03), [2006] ECR I-6535.

[33] See for various cases of overly restrictive determinations of connexity (or the lack of it), Cass. RCDIP 96 (2007), 622 with note *Marie-Élodie Ancel* (where claims had different legal grounds but being interdependent could clearly lead to inconsistent results (without remedy under Art. 34 as concerning different

different laws could be similar, whereas analogous legal provisions can of course be interpreted in different ways by different courts.

28   To a large extent, subsequent case-law of the European Court bears witness to an attempt to mitigate the consequences of a reading of *Roche Nederland*.[34] On the one hand, there have been instances involving simultaneous violations of other intellectual or industrial property rights, or diverse combinations of claims involving such violations and claims on other grounds such as tort. On the other hand, cases have arisen involving claims connected either by the fact that the various defendants are part of common corporate group (as in *Roche Nederland*; see too *Solvay*), or by reason of complex transactions such as those which take place within financial markets. In such circumstances, in a series of cases *(Freeport, Painer, Solvay, Melzer)*,[35] the Court has seems to have attenuated the rigid exclusion of claims governed by different laws, accepting connectedness in certain instances where different claims are, additionally, framed on the basis of different legal grounds or in different legal terms. Moreover, in *Land Berlin v. Ellen Mirjam Sapir*, which concerned claims for the payment of a sum of money on two distinct legal grounds (unjust enrichment and tort), it ruled that such a difference is immaterial as long as the same cause (here, the repayment of sums unduly paid) is served by the two claims.[36] Thus, only the requirement that the claims arise from the same set of facts has not been challenged to date. One important way in which the softening of the initial connection requirement has taken place has been through the concrete assessment by national courts in each case as to whether a variable outcome under respectively applicable national laws is or not reasonably intelligible from the point of view of the parties concerned. Furthermore, it results from the structure of the provisions of the Regulation that the national court seized of the anchor claim is dispensed from determining, as a separate matter, whether irreconcilable judgments are likely to follow in the absence of joinder. National courts have indeed largely followed this lead and have considered as connected various situations in which claims governed by different national laws or based on different legal grounds nevertheless create a risk of unintelligible legal outcomes.[37]

29   Thus, in *Freeport plc v. Olle Arnoldsson*,[38] the Court ruled that different applicable laws are not *per se* an obstacle to connectedness. Moreover, it is left to the national court "to assess whether there is a connection between the different claims brought before it, that is to say, a

---

parties). The English courts appear to be similarly baffled: see for example, *Watson v. First Choice Holidays and Flights Ltd.*, [2001] 2 Lloyd's Rep. 339 (C.A.), *Andrew Weir Shipping v. Wartsila UK* [2004] 2 Lloyd's Rep.377.

[34]   *Roche Nederland BV v. Frederick Primus and Milton Goldenberg* (Case C-539/03), [2006] ECR I-6535.

[35]   *Freeport plc v. Olle Arnoldsson* (Case C-98/06), [2007] ECR I-8319; *Eva-Maria Painer v. Standard VerlagsGmbH* (Case C-145/10), [2011] ECR I-12533; *Solvay v. Honeywell* (Case C-616/10), nyr.; *Melzer v. MF Global UK Ltd* (Case C-228/11), nyr.

[36]   *Land Berlin v. Ellen Mirjam Sapir* (Case C-645/11), nyr.

[37]   For instance, the French Court of Cassation decided, in a case where a claimant, owner of a bank account operated by a French financial company and a Luxemburg bank, sued these two entities in French courts for loss of profits, that "*even though the two claims against the two companies are founded on different national laws, there is an interest in judging them together in front of the same court in order to avoid irreconcilable decisions*" (v. Cass. 1ère civ, 26th September 2012, 11–26.022).

[38]   *Freeport plc v. Olle Arnoldsson*, Case C-98/06, para. 41. *This was also the suggestion in the first edition of this Art. See too, Watson* v. *First Choice Holidays and Flights Ltd.*, [2001] 2 Lloyd's Rep. 339 (C.A.).

risk of irreconcilable judgments if those claims were determined separately and, in that regard, to take account of all the necessary factors in the case-file, which may, if appropriate yet without its being necessary for the assessment, lead it to take into consideration the legal bases of the actions brought before that court". Then, in *Eva-Maria Painer*,[39] the Court ruled that several claims brought under different laws in violation of copyright were nevertheless connected. At this point, the conclusions of A-G *Trstenjak*[40] in this case provides an instructive overview of the case-law, suggesting that while it is essential for the purposes of ex-Art. 6 (1), now Art. 8 (1), that the various claims against different defendants arise out of the same situation of fact (which therefore naturally excludes unconnected parallel conduct in copyright infringement cases), the requirement of a sufficient legal connection does not necessarily imply that the same law must govern all the claims. Furthermore, in *Solvay*,[41] the Court continued along this avenue in a situation which bore a strong resemblance, *prima facie*, to the one which gave rise to *Roche Nederland*. Here, claims for patent infringement arising out of the same facts were brought against several defendants belonging to the same corporate group, Honeywell. However, the claims were not brought respectively for distinct infringements by each of the several defendants in different countries under separate territorial laws (as in *Roche Nederland*), but for infringements by each of the defendants in other countries ("each separately accused of committing an infringement of the same national part of a European patent which is in force in yet another Member State"). There was therefore a risk of directly conflicting decisions regarding different claims arising from what were in essence mixed facts brought in different courts. National courts have followed this more flexible turn in the field of intellectual and industrial property, taking it further on occasion and judging for instance that claims for violation of copyright and unfair competition arising out of the same facts are connected despite the differences *both* in legal basis and applicable law.[42]

Beyond disputes involving intellectual and industrial property, the Court appears to adopts a   **30** generally more flexible approach to connectedness. In *Melzer*,[43] the equally sensitive area of financial markets illustrates a possibly novel function for derived jurisdiction within the overall scheme of the Regulation. Typically here, whether claims are framed in tort or contract – a choice which is likely to be mandated by the structure of the law of obligations in national legal systems –, the various defendants have participated in a complex chain of financial transactions. In such cases, it is notoriously difficult to locate the various elements (place of conduct, harm, performance, etc) which constitute the special jurisdictional connecting factors in the context of Article 7; in particular, in *Kronhofer*,[44] the Court disqualified the claimant's domicile as place of the loss, while it has emphasized elsewhere, where cybertorts are concerned, that the identification of the requisite connecting factors is highly dependent upon the content of the right allegedly violated.[45] However, by allowing for connectedness within the meaning of ex-Art. 6 (1) now Art. 8 (1) in a case involving tort

---

39   A-G *Trstenjak*, Opinion in Case C-145/10 *(Eva-Maria Peiner)* of 12 April 2011, nyr.

40   A-G *Trstenjak*, Opinion in Case C-145/10 *(Eva-Maria Peiner)* of 12 April 2011, nyr.

41   *Solvay v. Honeywell* (C-616/10) [2012].

42   Cass Com 26 février 2013, *Pucci*, Rev crit DIP 2013.922, note *T Azzi*.

43   *Melzer v. MF Global UK Ltd* (Case C-228/11) [2013].

44   *Kronhofer v. Maier c.s.* (Case C-168/02) ECR [2004].

45   See ECJ *Wintersteiger* v. Products 4U Sondermaschinenbau GmbH, Case C-523/10, pts 21 à 24; *Peter Pinckney v. KDG Mediatech AG*, Case C-170/12, pt. 32.

claims by an investor, Melzer, against two different market actors (a German intermediary, WWH, and a UK brokerage company, MF Global, which traded in futures and lost a great deal of the financial investment), the Court compensates to a certain extent for its refusal to use the special fora of Article 7 as a tool of investor protection, by allowing for concentration of claims. While the policy issues can surely be debated, in relation to the protection due to private investment and indeed the balance to be struck between the interests of the various actors operating financial markets, one can nevertheless begin to see here how derived jurisdiction may be able to play a role in adapting the content of the Brussels Regulation to the newer economic reality of networks, whether comprising corporate groups or complex market transactions. National courts, here again, have followed the European Court's recent lead in cases involving networked defendants, despite diverse applicable laws, in an abundant range of cases involving, for example, both insolvency proceedings and an enforcement procedure on immoveable property[46] or the liability of shareholders and corporate officers[47] or multiple connected contract claims. Several difficulties in relation to the connection remain outstanding, however; but they are due to the perturbation caused by the introduction of derived jurisdiction within the delicate balance of dispute allocation pursued by the Regulation and will be addressed distinctly below. The most severe is no doubt the relationship between tort and contract claims.

31 Finally, in a recent decision *(Land Berlin v. Ellen Mirjam and Others)* involving claims in both unjust enrichment and tort, the ECJ ruled that such claims were connected within the meaning of Art. 6 (1) since they "have their origin in a single situation of law and fact, namely the right to compensation".[48] The case involved proceedings against parties domiciled in various countries (Germany, United-Kingdom, Spain and Israel) by the Land of Berlin to recover a sum of money unintentionally paid to the heirs of the owner of a plot of land in reparation for expropriation. Additionally, a tort claim was brought against their lawyer. Here, both sets of claims "relied on rights to additional compensation which it is necessary to determine on a uniform basis". The decisive consideration seems to have been that the very existence of an unjust enrichment, which determined the claimant Land's right to restitution, was a condition for the conduct of the defendant lawyer to be qualified as tortious. Despite the difference of legal grounds, there was therefore a question common to all the defendants, which mandated a single answer.

5. Connected claims in contract and tort

32 Whether claims brought respectively in contract and tort may be connected within the meaning of Article 8 (1) gave rise to a considerable amount of uncertainty, prior to the series of cases discussed above, but which appears now to have been dissipated in favour of an affirmative answer in *Freeport v. Olle Arnoldsson*.[49] The origin of the difficulty can be traced back to *La Réunion européenne*, in which the European Court ruled that that claims brought respectively in contract and in tort against different defendants could not be joined.[50] This ruling was understood to mean that Art. 6 (1) – although disqualified in this

---

[46] See for a recent application a French case, Cass. Com 12 mars 2013, *Rev crit* DIP 2013.649, note Rémery.

[47] See ECJ C-147/12, *Koot*, accepting that ex-Art. 5-3 applies in cases of joint liability of corporate officer and shareholder for financial loss by the company in liquidation

[48] *Land Berlin v. Ellen Mirjam Sapir* (Case C-645/11), nyr.

[49] *Freeport plc v. Olle Arnoldsson* (Case C-98/06), [2007] ECR I-8319.

particular case however because the court seised of the original claim was not the court of the place of domicile of one of the defendants – would not in any event allow such claims to be joined, even when the court seised of the original claim considers the two claims to be otherwise so closely related as to give rise to the risk of irreconcilable decisions if determined separately by different courts. In its ruling in *La Réunion européenne*,[51] the Court had referred to its prior position in *Kalfelis*.[52] However, the latter decision was in fact addressing a different issue, concerning the extent of the respective jurisdiction of courts under ex-Artt. 5 (1) and 5 (3). The question was whether the court which had jurisdiction in matters of tort could decide an issue in contract.[53] But in deciding that the jurisdiction of the court seised on the basis of ex-Art. 5 (3) did not extend to issues in contract, *Kalfelis*[54] did not exclude the existence of a connection between claims brought in contract and tort respectively, within the meaning of ex-Art. 6 (1). On the contrary, it seemed clear under the ruling in *Kalfelis* that subject to the conditions defined by any of the four paragraphs of ex-Art. 6, it was up to the national court seised of several claims to decide in each case whether these claims were connected in such a way as to justify their being heard by a single court. Indeed, since this provision operates to confer jurisdiction on a court which is otherwise incompetent to hear the claim, the fact that the court seised of the original claim has no jurisdiction over the connected claim is hardly a convincing argument (on this point, see the argument which can be drawn from the content of ex-Art. 6 (4)).This means that the delimitation in *Kalfelis* of the jurisdiction of the courts respectively competent in matters of contract and tort under the relevant provisions of ex-Art. 6 did not necessarily mean that there could not be a close connection between the two claims.

This has been confirmed by the European Court, subsequently distinguishing *La Réunion*   **33** *européenne*,[55] in *Freeport plc v. Olle Arnoldsson*,[56] where different claims sounding potentially in contract and tort were brought against co-defendants before the courts of the domicile of one of them. Here the Court indicated clearly that *La Réunion Européenne*, which concerned the case in which the anchor proceedings were brought before the forum of Art. 5-3 and not Art. 2, did not exclude the operation of ex-Art. 6 (1) so as to join two claims

---

50   *Réunion europénne SA v. Spliethoff's Bevrachtingskantoor BV and Master of the vessel "Alblasgracht 002"* (Case C-51/97) [1998] ECR I-6511, I-6549, para. 50.

51   *Réunion europénne SA v. Spliethoff's Bevrachtingskantoor BV and Master of the vessel "Alblasgracht 002"*, (Case C-51/97) [1998] ECR I-6511.

52   *Athanasios Kalfelis v. Bankhaus Schröder Münchmeyer Hengst and Co. and others*, (Case 189/87) [1988] ECR 5565.

53   Compare *Roche Nederland v. Frederick Primus and Milton Goldberg* (Case C-539/03), [2006] ECR I-6535 and *Freeport plc v. Olle Arnoldsson* (Case C-98/06), [2007] ECR I-8319. Comp. the critical observations of A-G *Trstenjak* of 12 April 2011 in Case C-145/10, *Eva-Maria Painer*. For the hesitations of national courts, see for instance, the various French decisions in Rev crit DIP 2008, 618, annotated by *M. E Ancel*, illustrating difficulties affecting the requirement of connected claims under Art. 6 (1) when these are variously in contract and tort, or based on different contracts, or governed by different laws, even when there is a clear risk of inconsistency between the various decisions. See below para. 9.

54   *Athanasios Kalfelis v. Bankhaus Schröder Münchmeyer Hengst and Co. and others*, (Case 189/87) [1988] ECR 5565.

55   *Réunion europénne SA v. Spliethoff's Bevrachtingskantoor BV and Master of the vessel "Alblasgracht 002"* (Case C-51/97) [1998] ECR I-6511, I-6549, para. 50.

56   *Freeport plc v. Olle Arnoldsson* (Case C-98/06), [2007] ECR I-8319.

---

with potentially different legal foundations before the courts of the domicile of one of the several defendants. Claims sounding in tort and contract may therefore be joined. However, in order to dispel any impression that La Réunion Européenne and Freeport are internally inconsistent, the Court added that the national court assessing the connection will "take account of all the necessary factors in the case-file, which may be, if appropriate yet without its being necessary for the assessment, lead it to take into consideration the legal bases brought before that court". This appears to leave room for the national court to factor in the risk of inconsistency arising despite differences not only in legal grounds (as between tort or contract), but in legal categories (such as between intentional tort and fraud under a specific legal regime such as securities).

6. Impact of contractual choice of forum

34 To what extent does Art. 8 interfere with the effects of contractual choice of forum? For instance, one of the co-defendants to connected claims brought before a single court under Art. 8 (1), might be bound individually to the claimant by such a clause. The first issue is whether a close connection between the various claims can override the clause and deprive the defendant to the connected claim of access to the contractually designated court. The Court of Justice has ruled on several occasions that the contractually chosen forum has priority, thus preventing the court seised of an initial claim from determining related claims, even when the claims are closely connected.[57] Party autonomy, unsurprisingly, prevails (see Recital 19). Indeed, Art. 25 does not reserve the case of connected claims; moreover, neutralizing the parties' choice of forum for reasons of expediency would go against one of the fundamental policies of the Regulation, which takes party choice to be central. It could of course be argued that the parties can be presumed not to have intended the clause to operate so as to separate a claim covered by the clause from another so closely related as to be indivisible. However, in La Réunion européenne,[58] the Court ruled that indivisibility, as distinct from mere connection, had no place in the Convention (in the different context of allowing such a concept to overcome the restrictions inherent in ex-Art. 6 (1)). It is indeed doubtful that the parties could be assumed to have wanted the clause to give way to the jurisdiction of another court, even when the claim covered by the clause is perceived to be indivisible from a claim against a different defendant that falls outside its scope. The remedy to possible inconsistency lies in the possibility under Art. 30 (1)for the court second seised to stay proceedings, whether or not it is the chosen forum. A second, related, issue arises in the converse situation, when the choice of forum clause designates the courts of a non Member State, while the connected claim belongs to the jurisdiction of the courts of a Member State under the Regulation. Here, it is up to the national private international law of the forum seised of the connected claim to determine the effect of the connection between claims on the application of the clause, subject however (as seen above) to the new provisions of Art. 34 (1) in a case where the court of a third country is first seised.

---

[57] *Estasis Salotti di Colzani Aimo and Gianmario Colzani v. RÜWA Polstereimaschinen GmbH*, (Case 24/76) [1976] ECR 1831; Nikolaus Meeth v. Glacetal, (Case 23/78) [1978] ECR 2133.

[58] *Réunion europénne SA v. Spliethoff's Bevrachtingskantoor BV and Master of the vessel "Alblasgracht 002"* (Case C-51/97) [1998] ECR I-6511, I-6549, para. 50.

7. Jurisdiction if initial claim is inadmissible under national law

A particular difficulty arose in *Reisch Montage AG v. Kiesel Baumaschinen Handels GmbH*,[59] **35**
as to whether jurisdiction over a connected claim still exists when the initial claim is inadmissible from the very time it is brought, under the national procedural rules of the forum.
In this case, the initial claim against a defendant domiciled in the forum state was inadmissible due to the fact that bankruptcy proceedings against that defendant's assets were still
pending. The reason given was that ex-Art. 6 (1) "does not include any express reference to
the application of domestic rules or any requirement that an action brought against a
number of defendants should be admissible, at the time it is brought, in relation to each
of those defendants under national law". Although it is quite true that the text does not make
this explicit, it is certainly arguable that an inadmissible claim is an overly flimsy basis to
anchor another claim under Art. 8 (1)! If the purpose of Art. 8 (1) is to promote procedural
expediency and avoid irreconcilable judgments, neither of these objectives would be promoted in a case where in any event, the initial claim cannot go ahead. Moreover, there is a
particular risk in such circumstances that any artificial – and ultimately inadmissible – claim
might be used to establish the jurisdiction of a given court, with the sole purpose of ousting
the jurisdiction of the court of the (real) remaining defendant's domicile, thereby contradicting the provision's specific requirements. The result is particularly unfortunate when the
reason for which the anchor claim is inadmissible existed already and was clearly ascertain-
able, before the court was seised. This was the case under the facts in *Reisch Montage*, where
the first defendant was clearly immune from suit under insolvency provisions before the
claim was brought, the insolvency being the very reason for the claim. Furthermore, the
exclusion of the role of national procedural rules here does not appear to be entirely compatible with the margin left to national law in the context of ex-Art. 6 (2) by *Kongress
Agentur Hagen*.[60]

8. Disputes involving protective or otherwise imperative jurisdictional rules

In *Glaxosmithkline v. Rouard*,[61] the ECJ ruled that ex-Art. 6 (1) does not apply when the **36**
dispute involving several co-defendants domiciled in different Member States falls under the
special protective rules relative to individual employment contracts. It is likely that this
ruling is valid more generally for disputes involving unequal relationships *(Chapter II,
sections 3–5)*. The concern voiced here by the Court is that the employee might be deprived
of the jurisdictional protection afforded by Section 5 if, as would be logical, the benefit of
derived jurisdiction were to be extended bilaterally to both parties to the employment
contract. This approach has been extended by the national courts beyond the workplace.
Thus, for example, the benefit of the (derived) jurisdiction of the court competent on the
basis of Art. 14 (1) (ex-Art. 12 (1)) has been refused to an insurer claiming against the injured
policy holder (in an attempt to obtain judicial homologation of an expert's report).[62] However, while the concern that the stronger party might use Art. 8 (1) to circumvent protective
rules is understandable, there are other sides to the question. Firstly, another approach
would have been to consider that derived jurisdiction as defined under Art. 8 (1) must

---

[59]   *Reisch Montage AG v. Kiesel Baumaschinen Handels GmbH* (C-103/05).
[60]   *Kongress Agentur Hagen GmbH v. Zeehaghe BV* (Case C-365/88) and see below para. 39.
[61]   *Glaxosmithkline Laboratoires v. Rouard* (Case C-462/06), [2008] ECR I-3965.
[62]   See for ex. Cass Civ. 1re – 27 février 2013, *Rev crit DIP*, 2013. 731, note *Corneloup*.

pursue the purposes of the fora it extends, and to allow it to operate exclusively in favour of the protected party, who could choose (or not) to join claims. While it is true that Art. 8 (1) is drafted in neutral terms, apparently exclusive of any differentiation as to the party by whom it may be invoked, it may be remembered that the same could have be said of the initial text of Art. 5-1 of the Convention (now 7-1 of the Regulation recast), which the Court itself gradually transformed into the one-way protective rule now consecrated in section 5. Such a reading would be all the more plausible in the case of Art. 8(1), moreover, that derived jurisdiction could be seen to be the auxiliary, as it were, to jurisdiction over the anchor claim. Thus, if the latter is designed to protect one of the parties, this policy should be prolonged through, or at least not frustrated by, the existence of the derived forum.

37 Moreover, under the facts of *Glaxosmithkline*, it is easy to see that, beyond the concern that the employer might use derived jurisdiction to her own advantage, the neutralization of Art. 8 (1) in cases of claims brought against joint employers is likely to work to the detriment of the employee. Indeed, while the employee can often bring connected claims before the court at the place of employment (Art. 21(1) (b)(i)), this is hardly helpful when this place is splintered, and the place of engagement not within a Member State (Art. 21 (1) (b) (ii)). Therefore, beyond the additional costs to the employee obliged to bring two different claims in different fora, the result works to subvert the very purpose of the doctrine of joint employers, which is designed to improve the protection of mobile employees (as recognized in the *Pugliese* case[63]). The risk of a more general undermining of the economy of the Regulation, which the Court seems to fear, is hardly plausible here, since the usefulness of Art. 8 (1) would be limited in practice to cases in which the employee was working outside the EU and thus unable to invoke the provisions of Art. 21 (1). Indeed, the other protective provisions (insurance and consumer disputes: sections 3 and 4) do not appear to be at risk, since claims brought by the protected party can be brought against all defendants before the court of the country of his own domicile – a possibility not open to the employee under section 5. Indeed, a French case has allowed the operation of Art. 6 (1) in a conflict within the workplace, in which the dispute fell outside the scope of section 5. It involved attempts by the liquidator to establish the validity of a redundancy plan and obtain information from various corporate entities considered to be the joint employers. The Cour de cassation allowed all these actions to be joined before the French court insofar as they were all "part of a sole framework of fact and law".[64]

38 For slightly different reasons, it is likely that 8 (1) cannot be used to derogate from heads of jurisdiction deriving from international treaties and considered as imperative. Thus, in a case before the French courts, it was judged that derived jurisdiction could not work to substract a claim from the forum designated by the Warsaw Convention.[65]

III. Third party proceedings – Art. 8 (2).

1. Determination of third party claims

39 The concepts of warranty and guarantee are not defined by this provision, although the

---

[63]   ECJ 10.04.2003 – C-437/00 – *Giulia Pugliese/Finmeccanica SpA, Betriebsteil Alenia Aerospazio.*

[64]   Cass. soc., Rev. dr. trav. 2008, 767 with note *Pataut.*

[65]   Civ. 1re, 12 nov. 2009, n° 08 (1)5.269, *Rev crit DIP* 2010.372, note *H. Muir Watt.*

additional reference to "any other third party proceedings" in the English language text tends to confirm the idea, generally upheld in continental legal doctrine, that they should be interpreted sufficiently flexibly so as to include any procedural mechanism by which initial proceedings are made to extend to a third party. Voluntary interventions of third parties would seem to be included, in the same way as compulsory joinder. The third party claim, which may have its legal basis in a contract, as in a claim on a guarantee, or which may be an action for indemnity in a tort case, will be incidental to, or conditional on, the original claim, in the sense that it is brought in the event that the claimant succeeds in his action against the defendant, at which point the third party is called upon to contribute in whole or in part to the debt. In an important case, *GIE Groupe européen v. Zurich España*,[66] the Court of justice decided that proceedings whereby an insurer, defendant to action in indemnification, seeks contribution from another insurer considered to have provided cover for the same event, are third party proceedings which come within the ambit of ex-Art. 6 (2).[67] Clearly, there may be significant definitional and procedural disparities between national systems here. In the case of Germany and Austria, these differences are sufficient to warrant a specific provision in order to accommodate procedural specificities (as will be seen below).

There is debate, however, as to whether third party proceedings within the meaning of Art. 8 **40** (2) require that the initial proceedings should have been initiated already when the third party is joined. Does the provision still apply if the initial claim is addressed to the main defendant and the third party simultaneously? There seems to be no reason why it should not, as long as the claim against the third party is relevant only in the event that judgment is given against the main defendant; otherwise, the case would seem to fall naturally under the stricter conditions of Art. 8 (1). However, some situations may be problematic in this respect, and the lack of a general head of jurisdiction based on the connection between claims, or alternatively, the excessively narrow conditions in which the instances of derived jurisdiction allowed under Art. 8 are framed, may be regrettable. For instance, it could happen that a third party to a claim in guarantee or indemnity counter-attacks in turn by bringing an action against both the initial claimant and the defendant to the original action (who in turn makes the claim against the third party in guarantee). In respect of the defendant to the original claim, the claim brought by the third party is a counterclaim and may be joined pursuant to Art. 8 (3). But in absence of reciprocity, the claim brought by the third party against the original claimant is not, and must be either a third party claim or a claim against several defendants. However, Art. 8 (2) is disqualified if third party claims are strictly defined as joining a party who is not involved in the initial proceedings. But if this is a claim against multiple defendants, then Art. 8 (1) will not allow it to be brought before the court originally seised unless this is the court of the domicile of the defendant (both to the original claim and to the third party's counterclaim). This contrasts with the position under Art. 8

---

[66]   *Groupement d'intérêt économique (GIE) Réunion européenne et al. v. Zurich España, Société pyrénéenne de transit d'automobiles (Soptrans)*, (Case C-77/04) [2005] ECR I-4509.

[67]   *Groupement d'intérêt économique (GIE) Réunion européenne et al. v. Zurich España, Société pyrénéenne de transit d'automobiles (Soptrans)* (Case C-77/04), [2005] ECR I-4509. This case also decided that the special provisions of Section 3, Title II of the Convention, which concern relations characterised by an imbalance between the parties and establish for that reason a body of rules on special jurisdiction which favours the party regarded as economically weaker and less experienced in legal matters, are not applicable in cases involving claims among insurers.

(2), which comes into play even if the original claim has not been brought before the courts in the Member State where the defendant is domiciled.

2. Basis of the court's jurisdiction indifferent

41   Indeed, the requirements relating to the jurisdiction of the court seised of the initial claim are far more flexible under Art. 8 (2) than under Art. 8 (1). While the latter does not allow the grouping of connected claims before any court other than that for the place of domicile of one of the defendants, the former is indifferent to the grounds on which the court seised of the main claim is exercising its jurisdiction. This point was made clearly by the Court in *Kongress Agentur Hagen*,[68] where the court was seised of the original claim on the basis of ex-Art. 5 (1): "To enable the entire dispute to be heard by a single court, Art. 6 (2) (now 8 (2)) simply requires there to be a connecting factor between the main action and the action on a warranty or guarantee, irrespective of the basis on which the court has jurisdiction in the original proceedings". Thus, a court originally seised on the basis of any other provision of Art. 7, or indeed on that of Art. 25 of the Regulation, could equally hear and determine a connected third party claim. This flexible interpretation of Art. 8 (2) is in conformity with policies of procedural economy and expediency. It may be wondered why similar flexibility does not exist in the case of independent but closely connected claims against several co-defendants, where analogous policy considerations would be equally relevant.

3. Exorbitant fora

42   However, it still has to be determined whether considerations of procedural economy and expediency are sufficiently strong to justify the extension of the jurisdiction of a court seised on the basis of an exorbitant head of jurisdiction under its own national private international law, to a connected claim which would itself belong to the court of another Member State under the Regulation. Indeed, while it is perfectly conceivable that the grounds for the jurisdiction of the court seised of the initial claim should be indifferent when they result from the Regulation or Convention itself, as in *Kongress Agentur Hagen*,[69] a more difficult issue arises when the jurisdiction of that court is based on its own private international law, in cases where the defendant is not domiciled in a Member State.[70] This may mean that the grounds are exorbitant and that the court has been seised on the basis of one of the "disapproved" national heads of jurisdiction now mentioned in Art. 5 (1). For instance, a French court seised by virtue of the claimant's French nationality under Art. 14 of the French Civil Code has been considered by the French courts as competent under ex-Art. 6 (2) over connected claims for which the courts of another Member State were otherwise competent under the Regulation/Convention. Similarly, jurisdiction over provisional measures (Art. 33 of the Regulation), which refers back to national jurisdictional rules, has been extended to connected claims on the basis of ex-Art. 6 (2).[71]

43   At first glance, it may seem undesirable that an exorbitant forum competent under national rules could serve as a magnet to claims which would otherwise be allocated according to the

---

[68]   *Kongress Agentur Hagen GmbH v. Zeehaghe BV*, (Case C-365/88) [1990] ECR I-1845.

[69]   *Kongress Agentur Hagen GmbH v. Zeehaghe BV*, (Case C-365/88) [1990] ECR I-1845.

[70]   See opinion of A-G *Lenz*, (Case C-365/88) [1990] ECR I-1845.

[71]   In the *Mont Blanc Tunnel* case: Cass. civ I, 19 juin 2007, Rev crit DIP 2007, 846 note *E. Pataut*.

Regulation. Indeed, *La Réunion européenne*[72] might well provide authority for the contrary view, since it refused to allow a court seised of a claim against a defendant domiciled in a non Member State on the basis of national rules, to extend its jurisdiction to connected claims under ex-Art. 6 (1). However, expediency might appear, on the other hand, to support a flexible reading of 8 (2) on this point.

Indeed, whatever the grounds on which a court of a Member State was actually seised, once **44** proceedings have been instituted, the only practical issue is to reduce the risk of waste and incoherence inherent in any dispersion of connected proceedings. It is true that the third party might then be subjected to an exorbitant forum. But it can be argued that, from the point of view of that third party, the effect of Art. 8 (2) is, in any event, to remove him from the forum ordinarily competent under the Regulation; moreover such a forum is exorbitant in respect of the defendant to the original claim, but as regards the third party, there is little difference between the situation in which he is joined in proceedings before the court of the domicile of the defendant to initial claim, and the one in which he is hailed before the court of the claimant's nationality or domicile. Moreover, the considerations put forward by the European Court in *La Réunion européenne*[73] in order to justify why a court seised on the basis of its national jurisdictional rules is not empowered under ex-Art. 6 (1) to hear connected claims against defendants domiciled in Member States, and principally the concern to ensure the effective protection of such defendants,[74] are not necessarily relevant in the case of Art. 8 (2), which is otherwise indifferent to the basis on which the court is seised of the original claim under the Regulation.

4. Initial claim outside the substantive scope of the Regulation

A similar, but not identical, problem arises when the initial claim is not comprised within the **45** subject-matter scope of the Regulation, whereas the third party proceedings are. For instance, the defendant might be involved in the Member State of her domicile in an administrative procedure related to import duties on mislabeled products (excluded from the scope of the Regulation under Art. 1 (1)), and could wish to join the supplier, domiciled in another Member State and responsible for the mislabeling. There is debate as to whether the indifference of Art. 8 (2) in respect of the basis of the jurisdiction of the court seised of the original claim goes as far as allowing the joining of the claims when the original claim is outside the scope of the Regulation (subject to the national procedural provisions of the forum, which of course may not allow the joining of an administrative procedure and a civil claim for indemnity). It has been said that Art. 8 (2) is too weak a ground on which to bring within the Regulation claims which would ordinarily fall outside it. However, the distinction between "strong" and "weak" *fora* within Art. 8 is hardly convincing in this respect, since they all pursue an identical goal of procedural efficiency. A more plausible reading would be that Art. 8 (2) is inapplicable when the original claim falls outside the scope of the Regu-

---

[72] *Réunion europénne SA v. Spliethoff's Bevrachtingskantoor BV and Master of the vessel "Alblasgracht 002"*, (Case C-51/97) [1998] ECR I-6511.

[73] *Réunion europénne SA v. Spliethoff's Bevrachtingskantoor BV and Master of the vessel "Alblasgracht 002"*, (Case C-51/97) [1998] ECR I-6511.

[74] *Réunion europénne SA v. Spliethoff's Bevrachtingskantoor BV and Master of the vessel "Alblasgracht 002"*, (Case C-51/97) [1998] ECR I-6511; I-6548 paras. 46 seq.

Horatia Muir Watt

lation, so that it is up to the law of the forum of that court to determine whether a third party claim can be joined, even when that claim falls within the scope of the Regulation.[75]

46 In cases of complex claims, in which the main issue falls outside the Regulation and an ancillary question within, it is frequent to distinguish according to whether the solution to the main question depends on the answer to the ancillary question (for instance, the main claim relating to the payment of social security may be dependent upon the existence of an employment contract) or can be solved independently of it (which would be the case in the import duty example cited above, since the civil claim is merely a claim for indemnity, whose very cause lies in the existence of the main proceedings). In the first case, the ancillary question would be absorbed by the regime of the main question, and so excluded from the Regulation. In the second case, the independent ancillary claim would remain within its scope. Even in the latter case, it would appear to be up to the law of the forum to determine whether the claims can be joined. Exceptionally, however, in cases of civil claim for indemnity dependent upon criminal proceedings, Art. 7 (3) contains rules of derived jurisdiction which allow the joining of the ancillary claim before the court competent to decide the main question, even if it falls outside the scope of the Regulation (and which constitutes, in conflict of laws terminology, an "incidental question"). The law of the forum of a court seised of the original claim under the Regulation should equally determine under its own procedural law whether a connected claim may be brought before it, when that claim does not fall within the scope of the Regulation.

5. Implied close connection requirement?

47 Although the text of Art. 8 (2) does not expressly require that there be a close connection between the main claim and the third party proceedings, so that such a requirement has sometimes been considered not to exist, it seems difficult to conceive that it is not implied. If any, unconnected, claim could be made against a third party, there would be a risk, similar to the one addressed in *Kalfelis*[76] in the context of ex-Art. 6 (1), that derived jurisdiction be used to oust the jurisdiction of the court of the domicile of the third party. That the requirement of a close connection exists implicitly in Art. 6 (2) was first suggested by the ECJ in *Kongress Agentur Hagen*,[77] when it ruled that, to enable the entire dispute to be heard by a single court, Art. 6 (2) (now 8 (2)) "simply requires there to be a connecting factor between the main action and the action on a warranty or guarantee, irrespective of the basis on which the court has jurisdiction in the original proceedings". Indeed, the existence of a close connection between the claims is the very reason for all the instances of derived jurisdiction in Art. 8, and the codified definition in Art. 8 (1) of the Regulation would seem to be relevant to the whole provision. That the requirement of a close connection exists in respect of Art. 8 (2) was expressly confirmed (in respect of ex-Art. 6 (2)) by *GIE Groupe européen v. Zurich España*,[78] in which the Court states that the "applicability [...] of Art. 6 (2) of the Convention

---

75 For the case where the connected claim relates to an issue which is ancillary to the main proceedings see opinion of A-G *Darmon* (C-190/98) [1991] ECR I-3855.

76 *Athanasios Kalfelis v. Bankhaus Schröder Münchmeyer Hengst and Co. and others*, (Case 189/87) [1988] ECR 5565.

77 *Kongress Agentur Hagen GmbH v. Zeehaghe BV*, (Case C-365/88) [1990] ECR I-1845.

78 *Groupement d'intérêt économique (GIE) Réunion européenne et al. v. Zurich España, Société pyrénéenne de transit d'automobiles (Soptrans)*, (Case C-77/04), [2005] ECR I-4509. This case also decided that the

remains subject to compliance with the condition requiring that the third-party proceedings should not have been instituted with the sole object of removing the party sued from the jurisdiction of the court which would be competent in the case. [...] The existence of a connection between the two sets of proceedings before the courts is inherent in the very concept of third-party proceedings. [...] There is an inherent relation between an action brought against an insurer seeking indemnification for the consequences of an insured event and proceedings whereby that insurer seeks contribution from another insurer considered to have provided cover for the same event. [...] It is for the national court seised of the original claim to verify the existence of such a connection, in the sense that it must satisfy itself that the third-party proceedings do not seek to remove the defendant from the jurisdiction of the court which would be competent in the case". However, the Court then took pains to emphasize that the close connection required here is purely functional, insofar that "Art. 6 (2) of the Convention does not require the existence of any connection other than that which is sufficient to establish that the choice of forum does not amount to an abuse".[79] This essentially displaces the difficulty, however, so that it is ultimately up to the national court to determine the reasonableness of joining the claims, as seen above.

In the case of third party claims on warranties or actions for indemnity, Art. 8 (2) is designed **48** to allow the joining of a third party claim which is causally linked to the main claim, in the sense that the third party is joined in indemnity or guarantee only in the event the main defendant is liable or called upon to pay. It is not designed to allow a party to the main claim to secure a favourable forum for any, unconnected claim against a third party. The requirement might arguably be even more useful here than in the context of Art. 8 (1), since Art. 8 (2) works to extend the jurisdiction of *fora* other than that of the defendant's domicile; the wider choice might arguably present a greater danger of manipulation. In fact, the connection requirement appears negatively in the text of Art. 8 (2), which reserves the case in which the provision is used to remove a third party from an otherwise competent court.

6. Abuse of derived jurisdiction

While Art. 8 (2) does not expressly require a close connection, it does on the other hand **49** reserve the case where it is invoked with the sole aim of removing the third party from the jurisdiction of the court which would otherwise be competent under the Regulation. Arguably, this is one and the same requirement, as if the lack of abuse were merely the flip-side of the connectedness requirement under Art. 8 (1).[80] This is indeed confirmed by the Court of justice's decision in *GIE Groupe européen v. Zurich España*[81] and may entail important

---

special provisions of Section 3, Title II of the Convention, which concern relations characterised by an imbalance between the parties and establish for that reason a body of rules on special jurisdiction which favours the party regarded as economically weaker and less experienced in legal matters, are not applicable in cases involving claims among insurers.

79   *Groupement d'intérêt économique (GIE) Réunion européenne et al. v. Zurich España, Société pyrénéenne de transit d'automobiles (Soptrans)*, (Case C-77/04) [2005] ECR I-4509.

80   This appears to be the view of the Cour de cassation in the Mont Blanc Tunnel case: Cass. civ., RCDIP 96 (2007), 847 with note *Pataut*.

81   *Groupement d'intérêt économique (GIE) Réunion européenne et al. v. Zurich España, Société pyrénéenne de transit d'automobiles (Soptrans)*, (Case C-77/04) [2005] ECR I-4509. This case also decided that the special provisions of Section 3, Title II of the Convention, which concern relations characterised by an

---

Horatia Muir Watt

consequences in respect of the allocation of the burden of proof. Discussion on this point tends to underline the fact that the requirement of a close connection is actually implied by the very existence of the derived forum, so that a showing of such connection must be made by the claimant (or verified by the court of its own motion); but once the connection is established, the defendant would have the burden of proving that it is being used nevertheless for the sole purpose of ousting the jurisdiction of another court. This is no doubt a very demanding task, since when a connection is established within the meaning of Art. 8 (1), so close that the court is satisfied that expediency justifies joining the claims, it will be difficult to prove abuse. However, in *GIE Groupe européen v. Zurich España*,[82] the Court placed a heavy burden on the national court seised of the original claim, which must "verify the existence of such a connection, in the sense that it must satisfy itself that the third-party proceedings do not seek to remove the defendant from the jurisdiction of the court which would be competent in the case". This reserve, which has been taken seriously by national courts,[83] is of obvious service in systems which do not have any more general means of preventing procedural fraud. There could therefore be an additional requirement that the connected claim be a serious one (or a "good arguable case").

7. Forum selection clause

50 The third party called upon in warranty or guarantee, for instance a manufacturer in a products liability claim against the retailer, may be able to oppose a contractual choice of forum to the defendant to the main claim. How far should this clause paralyze the derived jurisdiction of the court seised of the original claim? In various early rulings (emblematically, *Meeth)*,[84] the Court of justice affirmed the priority of ex Art. 23 (now 25) over the "derived" fora.[85] Moreover, as seen above, it does not appear to leave any room for an exception in the case where the claims are perceived to be indivisible, as some national systems do, when assuming that parties themselves would not have intended the claims to be separated in such a case. In the converse situation however, where the anchor claim has been brought before the court designated by a forum selection clause, there does not seem to be any reason why the chosen court should not be called upon to hear a connected action indemnity or on a warranty or guarantee. Indeed, under Art. 8 (2), there is no requirement concerning the identity of the court seised of the original claim.

8. Additional requirements under national procedural law

51 In *Kongress Agentur Hagen*,[86] the Court made it plain that in authorizing the joining of a

---

imbalance between the parties and establish for that reason a body of rules on special jurisdiction which favours the party regarded as economically weaker and less experienced in legal matters, are not applicable in cases involving claims among insurers.

[82] *Groupement d'intérêt économique (GIE) Réunion européenne et al. v. Zurich España, Société pyrénéenne de transit d'automobiles (Soptrans)*, (Case C-77/04) [2005] ECR I-4509.

[83] See again, the Cour de cassation in the *Mont Blanc Tunnel* case: Cass. civ., RCDIP 96 (2007), 847 with note *Pataut*.

[84] *Nikolaus Meeth v. Glacetal*, (Case 23/78) [1978] ECR 2133.

[85] *Estasis Salotti di Colzani Aimo and Gianmario Colzani v. RÜWA Polstereimaschinen GmbH*, (Case 24/76) [1976] ECR 1831; *Nikolaus Meeth v. Glacetal*, (Case 23/78) [1978] ECR 2133.

[86] *Kongress Agentur Hagen GmbH v. Zeehaghe BV*, (Case C-365/88) [1990] ECR I-1845.

third party claim, ex-Art. 6 (2) does not prevent the court seised of the original claim from applying its own rules of procedure to determine the conditions in which leave to bring the third party claim can be granted, and whether the joinder is possible. However, this ruling also implies that derived jurisdiction must not interfere unduly with the operation of the Regulation and, in particular, a court cannot, by reference to its own procedural rules, refuse such leave for the sole reason that the third party is domiciled in another Member State and that the joinder of the connected proceedings would thereby cause delay. This principle strikes a balance between the procedural autonomy of Member States, and the effectiveness of the Regulation.

9. Special rules for Member States of which the law does not allow certain third party claims

Art. 65 of the Regulation contains special rules designed to take account of the procedural **52** specificity of third party proceedings in certain national laws. It provides:
1. The jurisdiction specified in point 2 of Art. 8 and Art. 13 in actions on a warranty or guarantee or in any other third-party proceedings may be resorted to in the Member States included in the list established by the Commission pursuant to point (b) of Art. 76 (1) and Art. 76 (2) only in so far as permitted under national law. A person domiciled in another Member State may be invited to join the proceedings before the courts of those Member States pursuant to the rules on third-party notice referred to in that list.

2. Judgments given in a Member State by virtue of point 2 of Art. 8 or Art. 13 shall be **53** recognized and enforced in accordance with Chapter III in any other Member State. Any effects which judgments given in the Member States included in the list referred to in paragraph 1 may have, in accordance with the law of those Member States, on third parties by application of paragraph 1 shall be recognized in all Member States.

3. The Member States included in the list referred to in paragraph 1 shall, within the **54** framework of the European Judicial Network in civil and commercial matters established by Council Decision 2001/470/EC (1) ('the European Judicial Network') provide information on how to determine, in accordance with their national law, the effects of the judgments referred to in the second sentence of paragraph 2.

Illustrating the occasionally difficult encounter between common European rules of jurisdiction and national rules of procedure, this provision addresses the problem which arises in connection with Art. 8 (2) specifically under German and Austrian law, which do not recognize any procedural mechanism by which judgment can be given against a third party as such. Art. 65 therefore renders Art. 8 (2) inapplicable before German and Austrian courts, but allows for the application of rules of civil procedure of the forum, according to which a judgment on a main claim can be made "opposable" to a third party under a notice procedure *(litis denuntiatio)*. Under these provisions, a third party domiciled in another Member State may be subject to such notice before the German and Austrian courts. The second paragraph of the same provision ensures that despite these differences, judgments handed down in other Member States in respect of third party claims by virtue of Art. 8 (2) will be recognized and enforced in Germany and Austria in accordance with Chapter III, while reciprocally, other Member States will recognize the effects that judgments handed down in Germany and Austria may have on third parties, under their procedural rules.

IV. Counterclaims – Art. 8 (3)

1. Definition of counterclaim

55 Although bringing a claim by way of defense might seem to be a widely shared institution of civil procedure, Art. 8 (3) has raised some very difficult issues due to technical differences on this point between the various legal systems. Thus the definition of a counterclaim varies considerably.[87] According to the *Jenard* Report, ex-Art. 6 (3) was inspired from Belgian law, and envisages a claim which could have been the object of distinct proceedings, while its object does not disappear if the initial claimant desists from the claim.[88] In its important ruling in *Danvaern Production*,[89] the Court of Justice distinguished the counterclaim within the meaning of ex-Art. 6 (3), and a claim raised as a pure defense, which can always be brought before the court seised of the original claim. The latter is "where the defendant pleads, as a defense, the existence of a claim he allegedly has against the plaintiff, which would have the effect of wholly or partially extinguishing the plaintiff's claim". The former is "where the defendant, by a separate claim made in the context of the same proceedings, seeks a judgment or decree ordering the plaintiff to pay him a debt". For the provision to have any significance, the counterclaim must of necessity be a distinct claim, that is, a claim aiming to obtain the pronouncement of a separate judgment or decree. In the same decision, the Court said it was up to the law of the forum to determine what constitutes a defense and in what circumstances such a defense may be raised. As seen below, the distinction between a pure defense and counterclaim under Art. 8 (3) raises persistent difficulties as far as set-off is concerned.

2. Reciprocal claim between identical parties

56 A counterclaim within the meaning of this text involves the same parties as the original claim and does not comprise any action which aims at joining an additional party (which would come under Art. 8 (2) or even 8 (1)). The strict requirements of the text may lead to unfortunate consequences, given that close connection between claims is not a head of jurisdiction under the Regulation. For instance, in a case where a French driver (or his insurer), who was sued in the French court of his domicile by a passenger harmed in an car accident in Italy, raises two claims in the course of the same proceedings against the Italian domiciled driver (or his insurer) of the other vehicle involved in the accident, one in indemnity for any payment to be made to the passenger, the other in compensation of his own harm, only the former can be brought before the court seised of the original action brought by the passenger: while Art. 8 (2) can justify the extension of its jurisdiction to the third party claim in indemnity, the tort claim, which clearly does not count as a third party action, will have to be severed from the others despite the close links they entertain and the equally obvious reasons of expediency which would make the jurisdiction of a single court desirable. Indeed, it is not a counterclaim under Art. 8 (3) since it is not reciprocal.

---

[87] For comparative aspects, see opinion A-G *Léger*, (Case C-341/93) [1995] ECR I-2053; for instance, the counterclaim known to English law does not correspond exactly to the civil reconvention procedure.

[88] Report *Jenard*, p. 28.

[89] *Danværn Production A/S v. Schuhfabriken Otterbeck GmbH & Co.*, (Case C-341/93) [1995] ECR I-2053.

3. Claim deriving from same contract or facts as the original claim

Furthermore, the counterclaim within the meaning of Art. 8 (3) must, according to the **57**
wording of the text, derive from the same contract or facts as the original claim. On this
point, it is far more restrictive than the positions generally adopted by national legal systems,
and goes far beyond the requirement of a close connection. The *Jenard* Report seems however to suggest that a more flexible approach was in fact envisaged, and that the present
wording can in fact be explained by the difficulty encountered by the drafters of the initial
Brussels Convention of 1968, in finding a single concept expressing the relatedness of two
claims which was recognized by the law of all the Contracting States.[90] However, it would
have sufficed to introduce a functional definition such as the one to be found in *Kalfelis*[91] and
now codified in Art. 8 (1) of the Regulation.

Indeed, it is hard to find a convincing reason for which the connection required between the **58**
two claims should answer to a more restrictive definition under Art. 8 (3) than under Art. 8
(1),[92] even as the latter evolves after a period of uncertainty towards more flexibility. It is true
that, contemplating reciprocal claims, Art. 8 (3) naturally creates a greater risk of introducing a *forum actoris*, since, in cases where the original claim was brought before the court for
the place of the defendant's domicile under Art. 4, the forum of the counterclaim will
necessarily be the court of the counterclaimant's domicile. However, under Art. 8 (3), the
original claim may be brought before any court competent under the Regulation, so that the
fear of encouraging a *forum actoris* can hardly justify the condition more generally. Moreover, when the counterclaim arises from a different contract or set of events, the counterclaimant who cannot successfully bring his action before the court seised of the original
claim will take his action elsewhere; by definition, the claim is independent and can be the
object of separate proceedings, and the counterclaimant is under no obligation in any event
to bring the claim before the same court. If she brings it before the courts of another Member
State, then either party can raise an exception under Art. 30 before the court second seised. It
may well be that the claim is finally brought back before the court originally seised, after a
considerable loss of time and expense.

4. Defining the "same contract"

The requirement, particularly of the "same contract" is itself source of considerable diffi- **59**
culties, since it can be read either restrictively or more extensively, the two trends being
present in national case-law. Here again, a flexible reading seems desirable, so as not to leave
out situations where expediency clearly requires the joining of distinct claims which are not
otherwise caught by the other paragraphs of Art. 8. A typical example would include claims
arising from contracts which are part of a group, comprising for instance, a frame contract
and successive sales. The main claim might be based on the violation of an exclusive distribution agreement, while the counterclaim might concern the payment of the price of

---

[90]   Report *Jenard*, p. 28.
[91]   *Athanasios Kalfelis v. Bankhaus Schröder Münchmeyer Hengst and Co. and others*, (Case 189/87) [1988]
      ECR 5565.
[92]   See however, opinion A-G *Léger*, (Case C-341/93) [1995] ECR I-2053, who considers that the functional
      difference between Artt. 6 (3) and 22 of the Convention justifies a more restrictive definition of the
      required connection under the former text.

successive sales which took place in accordance with that agreement; if too strict a definition of the "same contract" is retained, these claims which are clearly closely connected, cannot be joined. In *Danvaern Production*[93] a similar situation arose in connection with an agency contract, in which the respective claims derived from the ending of the agency agreement on the one hand and the non payment of goods on the other (though in this case the claimant later desisted from the agency claim).

5. Compensation or set-off

60 The most difficult issue which arises under Art. 8 (3) concerns the treatment to be given to set-off. It has been controversial whether set-off is included naturally within the scope of the jurisdiction of the court deciding the main claim. In *Danvaern Production*[94] the European Court excluded from the scope of ex-Art. 6 (3) "the situation where a defendant raises, as a pure defense, a claim which he allegedly has against the plaintiff". This would seem to indicate that set-off or compensation raised by way of defense does indeed come within the jurisdiction of the court seised of the main claim. Indeed, in *Meeth*,[95] it was said, without any reference to Art. 8 (3), that the court seised on the basis of a choice of forum clause can take account of set-off, thus appearing to exclude set-off from the definition of a counter-claim under that text. However, in *Danvaern Production*, the Court then decided that it was up to the law of the forum to characterize set-off either as a defense or "a claim aiming to obtain the pronouncement of a separate judgment or decree". In the latter case, it will be subject to the strict requirements of Art. 8 (3), which will not allow reciprocal claims to be joined unless they derive from the same contract or facts. This of course assumes that set-off in such a case is not naturally included within the scope of the jurisdiction of the court seised of the main claim.

61 One of the difficulties of this distinction is that it may cut across the categories of national law, creating confusion. For instance, in many civil law systems, compensation or set-off between two debts which are liquidated and immediately enforceable takes place by operation of law and is always considered as set-off by way of defense, whereas compensation involving a claim which requires to be judicially determined is always a reconvention or counterclaim. But this does not necessarily coincide with the distinction laid down by the Court of justice. Indeed, supposing there were plausible stakes, a defendant might, circumventing this distinction, ensure that the court seised of the initial claim could also deal with the set-off, by making a claim for a sum not exceeding that of the claim brought by the other party. Even if that claim had to be judicially determined, and would be characterized as a counterclaim by some national laws, it would nevertheless be considered as a set-off by way of defense according to the definition in *Danvaern Production*.[95a]

6. Forum selection clauses, counterclaim and set-off

62 In *Meeth*, it was said that the court of the defendant's domicile, seised by virtue of a forum selection clause, could take account of set-off. The issue arose here because the clause was

---

[93] *Danværn Production A/S v. Schuhfabriken Otterbeck GmbH & Co.*, (Case C-341/93) [1995] ECR I-2053.
[94] *Danværn Production A/S v. Schuhfabriken Otterbeck GmbH & Co.*, (Case C-341/93) [1995] ECR I-2053.
[95] *Nikolaus Meeth v. Glacetal*, (Case 23/78) [1978] ECR 2133.
[95a] *Danværn Production A/S v. Schuhfabriken Otterbeck GmbH & Co.*, (Case C-341/93) [1995] ECR I-2053.

reciprocal, so that independent claims raised by the defendant to the main claim would have been allocated to the court of the domicile of the initial claimant, defendant to the counterclaim. However, the Court of Justice referred exclusively to Art. 17 of the Convention (now Art. 25 of the Regulation recast) without mentioning ex-Art. 6 (3) nor the distinction subsequently outlined in *Danvaern Production* between independent claims and set-off by way of defense. However, if, following that distinction, the set-off is considered as an independent claim, there is no reason why the jurisdiction of the court seised on the basis of a clause should not extend to a counterclaim which fulfills the requirements of Art. 8 (3). There is no restriction in that provision as to the grounds on which the court seised of the original claim is exercising its jurisdiction.

By contrast, the requirement that the counterclaim issue from the same contract may be **63** problematic, if as in the examples cited above, the two claims derive not from the same agreement but from two closely connected contracts. On the different question of whether Art. 8 (3) could paralyze a contractual choice of forum, the issue would only arise in the case of a reciprocal clause, as in *Meeth*.[96] In such as case, the question would be whether the distinct counterclaim, which should otherwise be brought before a different court (the court of the domicile of the defendant to the counterclaim, while the main claim has been brought before the court of the domicile of the initial defendant, now counterclaimant) could nevertheless be brought before the court seised of the initial claim. But the relationship between Art. 8 (3) and Art. 25 of the Regulation is certainly the same as for the other provisions of Art. 8. Only by re-characterizing the set-off as a defense rather than a counterclaim, as in *Meeth*, could the joining of the claims be obtained. A distinct, although related, issue in the light of *Meeth*, is whether the chosen court can extend its jurisdiction to connected claims involving third parties. There seems to be no reason to exclude this possibility, although care should be taken to distinguish this situation from that which would consist in extending the effect of the clause itself to parties who had not consented to it.

V. Secured debts – Art. 8 (4)

1. Function and content

The court of the place where immovable property is situated has exclusive jurisdiction under **64** Art. 24 of the Regulation over proceedings which have as their object rights *in rem* in that property. Art. 8 (4) provides an exception to the general rule, recalled in *Rösler v. Rottwinkel*,[97] that the courts with exclusive jurisdiction under Art. 24 (ex-Art. 22) of the Regulation are not competent to hear other issues, be they ancillary to those for which the court has exclusive jurisdiction. Conversely, courts which are not invested with exclusive jurisdiction may not decide claims which come under such jurisdiction. This is however a sensitive topic.[98]

In turn, Art. 8(4) raises its own difficulties. The concept of rights *in rem* does not necessarily **65** coincide with existing categories of property law in the various Member States; it appears to

---

[96] *Nikolaus Meeth v. Glacetal*, (Case 23/78) [1978] ECR 2133.
[97] *Erich Rösler v. Horst Rottwinkel*, (C 241/83) [1985] ECR I-99.
[98] GAT *(Case C-4/03) [2006] ECR I-6509; Berliner Verkehrsbetriebe (BVG), Anstalt des öffentlichen Rechts v. JPMorgan Chase Bank NA, Frankfurt* Branch (Case C-144/10).

have been inspired by the French civil law category of "droits réels immobiliers" and essentially covers claims involving title to immoveable and tenancies in immoveable property, exclusive of actions of a contractual nature even if they involve title to land. Under Art. 8 (4), the jurisdiction of the court of the place where the immoveable property is situated extends to contractual claims connected to those rights. Such extended jurisdiction operates solely in favour of that court; issues relating to rights *in rem* in the property may not be joined with a contractual claim before the forum competent to decide on issues of contract. This provision, which first appeared in the Lugano Convention, was later introduced into the Brussels Convention by the Convention of San Sebastien. Contractual debts being frequently secured on immovable property, it aims essentially to join actions to recover the secured debt and enforce the security *(actio hypothecaria)*. Indeed, when the creditor is not paid, it is clearly expedient that the litigation be joined before the court at the place where the security will be enforced. While the text indicates that the proceedings, in contract and *in rem*, must be brought against the same defendant, it presumably also requires that the claimant be also the same in both cases. The identification of the defendant to a claim *in rem* is problematic, but may be assumed to be the owner or any person whose interest in the property would be affected by the claim.[99] This is a particular illustration, in the field of immovable property, of a derived forum that can be found in some national systems, according to which an action on the merits can be brought before the court of the place of enforcement of a security, for reasons of procedural expediency.

2. The law of the forum must allow the claims to be joined

66 Art. 8 (4) expressly subordinates the joining of the claims in contract and *in rem* to the condition that "the action [in contract] may be combined with an action [*in rem*] against the same defendant". This is presumably a reference to the national procedural law of the forum. It makes the provision unequally applicable in different Member States, since some national rules are more restrictive on this point. However, in *Kongress Agentur Hagen*,[100] in the context of ex-Art. 6 (2), the Court of justice considered that the court seised of the original claim may apply its national procedural rules, but in doing so must not deprive the jurisdictional provision of its effectiveness. In that case, a court seised on the basis of ex-Art. 6 (2) could apply its procedural law to determine whether an action on a guarantee could be brought, but it could not base a refusal on the fact that the guarantor is domiciled in another Contracting State and that the joining of the claims would cause extra delay. Presumably, similar considerations apply here. A restrictive national rule on the joinder of different claims is acceptable if it applies in the same way to purely domestic cases, but it must not be used to prevent the operation of Art. 8 (4) for the sole reason that the defendant is domiciled in another Member State.

3. Contractual choice of forum

67 If the action in contract falls under a choice of forum clause in favour of a different court, the clause must prevail over the derived forum of Art. 8 (4). The fact that the court of the place of the property has exclusive jurisdiction over the connected action *in rem* should not make any difference to the solution accepted in the case of the other provisions of Art. 8 (see

---

[99] See *Collins*, in: Dicey/Morris para. S 1 3-024.

[100] *Kongress Agentur Hagen GmbH v. Zeehaghe BV*, (Case C-365/88) [1990] ECR I-1845.

above). The same fact explains why, in the reverse situation, the court seised of the contractual claim would not be empowered in any event, for instance under Art. 8 (3), to hear the connected claim *in rem*. Indeed, subject to the qualifications in the area of intellectual property encountered above, courts other than those with exclusive jurisdiction under Art. 24 of the Regulation may not determine an issue which falls within the scope of such jurisdiction unless it arises as a purely ancillary issue.[101]

Article 9

Where by virtue of this Regulation a court of a Member State has jurisdiction in actions relating to liability from the use or operation of a ship, that court, or any other court substituted for this purpose by the internal law of that Member State, shall also have jurisdiction over claims for limitation of such liability.

I. Function and structure

This provision determines jurisdiction over actions for negative declarations concerning **1** liability which might be incurred in connection with the use or operation of a ship. The presence of this rule can be explained by the fact that international conventions to which Member States may be party and which allow for limitations of liability in connection with the use or operation of ships, do not provide jurisdictional rules. Such an action, which will typically seek for a judicial declaration to the effect that the liability will not exceed a certain value based on the tonnage of the ship, can be brought by the beneficiary of a limitation of liability (shipowner, captain, charterer) against a potential claimant before the court which would be competent under the Regulation to hear and determine the main action, usually in tort. This forum, which is, like the fora of Art. 8, a case of derived jurisdiction, supposes that the shipowner (or other), defendant to a potential action in tort and claimant for the purpose of the negative declaration, is domiciled in a Member State. The competent court might then be the domicile of the shipowner, or the place of the harmful event by virtue of Art. 7 (2), or the place of arrest of the ship or sister ship.[1]

II. Forum actoris and first mover advantage

This provision does not appear to have given rise to much national case-law, and the **2** European Court has not yet been called upon to interpret it. However, it is not unproblematic. Insofar as it allows the claimant to bring the action before the courts of his own domicile, this provision introduces, in effect, a *forum actoris*. Moreover, it provides the same claimant, potential defendant to a tort claim, with a considerable first mover advantage, since he is able to determine the competent forum. This forum could be used to oust the jurisdiction of the court before which the victim would have wished to bring his action. If the victim chose to bring an independent action elsewhere, the defendant to that action, counterclaimant to the negative action, could raise the exception of *lis pendens* under Art. 29. This was accepted by the European Court in *The Ship Tatry*: "An action seeking to have the

---

[101] See Art. 25 Regulation, 19 Convention; Report *Jenard*, p. 34.
[1] See *Dicey & Morris*, para. 11–285.

defendant held liable for causing loss and ordered to pay damages has the same cause of action and the same object within the meaning of that Article as earlier proceedings brought by that defendant seeking a declaration that he is not liable for that loss".[2] This is why it is suggested by some authors that *lis pendens* should not be able to operate in cases where the prior action is an action for a negative declaration. However, the provision only guarantees the advantage of choosing the forum to the shipowner (or other person bringing the claim for a limitation of liability) when he initiates the proceedings. If the tort victim brings the initial action, the negative claim has to be brought before the same court by way of a counterclaim.

3 An illustration is provided by the *Darfur* case before the Court of Appeal of Rouen (France).[3] In this case, two ships – the *Darfur* and the *Happy Fellow* –collided in the estuary of the Seine because of a mechanical breakdown of the *Darfur*. The owners of the *Happy Fellow* initiated proceedings against the owners of the *Darfur* in the Commercial Court of Le Havre (France, within the jurisdiction of the Court of Appeal of Rouen). At the same time, the time charterers of the *Darfur* launched proceedings in the London Admiralty Court against the owner of the *Darfur* claiming damages and other relief. The latter (owner of the *Darfur*) obtained from the English court the constitution of a limitation fund. The question arose as to whether the matter should be judged in London where the limitation fund was constituted or in France where the Commercial Court was first seized of the liability issue.

4 Because of the connexity between the general liability question and the limitation fund, the English court decided to stay its proceedings until the Commercial Court of Le Havre rendered its judgment. The French court accepted jurisdiction and the owners of the *Darfur* appealed. The Court of Appeal of Rouen ruled that under Art. 7 (now Art. 9) of the Regulation, the court competent to decide the general liability issue (the Commercial Court of Le Havre) was also the competent forum to appreciate the limitation of liability of the shipowner (*"the Article does not establish any rule according to which the appreciation of the liability limitation of the shipowner of the Darfur is within the jurisdiction of the Court in which the fund of limitation was constituted"*). According to the French courts, Article 9 requires that once the jurisdiction of the judge adjudicating the merits of the claim is established, that judge would remain competent to deal with the liability limitation issue.

5 In the same way, if the shipowner moves first, the victim may decide to bring a counterclaim before the same court under Art. 8 (3), which would allow the two reciprocal claims to be joined as they would derive from the same events.

III. Any court substituted for that purpose

6 It may be that under its rules of venue or special jurisdiction, a Member State would allocate the action to a court other than the one which would ordinarily be competent to hear the initial claim, particularly if it is the court of the domicile of the claimant. Jurisdiction will remain with the courts of the Member State whose court is competent to hear the main claim, but special jurisdiction may be reallocated among its courts. This is the usual situation

---

[2] *The Owners of the Cargo Lately Laden on Board the Ship "Tatry" v. The Owners of the Ship "Maciej Rataj"*, (Case C-406/92) [1994] ECR I-5439.

[3] CA Rouen DMF 2001, 109 – *Darfur v. Happy Fellow*.

under rules of general jurisdiction such as Art. 4, but exceptional in cases of derived jurisdiction, where such jurisdiction is generally invested in a specific court, as in Art. 8. However, the forum of Art. 9 is designed to provide a procedural advantage to the shipowner, and
does not pursue considerations of expediency as in the case of Art. 8.

Section 3: Jurisdiction in matters relating to insurance

Bibliography

Calvo Caravaca/Carrascosa González, Práctica procesal civil internacional (Granada 2001)
Csach, Rozsudok "Bilas", Výber z rozhodnutí Súdne-
ho dvora Európskych spoločenstiev 2010 n° 3
p. 57–60
Fricke, Internationale Zuständigkeit und Anerkennungszuständigkeit in Versicherungssachen nach
europäischem und deutschem Recht, VersR 1997, 399
Fricke, Europäisches Gerichtsstands- und Vollstre-
ckungsübereinkommen revidiert – Was bringt die
Neufassung der Versicherungswirtschaft?,
VersR 1999, 1055
Fuchs, Gerichtsstand für die Direktklage am Wohn-
sitz des Verkehrsunfallopfers?, IPRax 2007, 302
Fuchs, Internationale Zuständigkeit für Direktkla-
gen, IPRax 2008, 104–107
Fuentes Camacho, Los contratos de seguro y el
derecho internacional privado en la Unión Europea
(Madrid 1999)
Heiss, Gerichtsstandsfragen in Versicherungssachen
nach europäischem Recht, in: Reichert-Facilides/
Schnyder (eds.), Versicherungsrecht in Europa –
Kernperspektiven am Ende des 20. Jahrhunderts,
ZSR 2000 Beiheft 34, 105
Heiss, Gerichtsstandsvereinbarungen zu Lasten
Dritter, insbesondere in Versicherungsverträgen zu
ihren Gunsten, IPRax 2005, 497
Heiss, Die Direktklage vor dem EuGH: 6 Antithesen
zu BGH 29.9.2006 (VI ZR 200/05), VersR 2007, 327–
331
Heiss, Das Direktklagerecht des Geschädigten:
Welche Folgen hat die Entscheidung des EuGH vom
13.12.2007 – Rs C-463/06 FBTO Schadeverzekerin-
gen?, HAVE 2009, 72–75
Heiss/Kosma, Die Direktklage des Geschädigten im
Europäischen Versicherungsrecht, in: van Tiggele/
van der Velde/Kamphuisen/Lauwerier (Hrsg), van

draden en daden – Liber Amicorum für Prof. J.H.
Wansink (2006) 279–294
Heiss/Loacker, Die Vergemeinschaftung des Kollisionsrechts der außervertraglichen Schuldverhältnisse
durch Rom II, JBl 2007, 613
Heiss/Loacker, Verkehrsopferschutz und Staatshaf-
tung (Entscheidung des EFTA-Gerichtshofs vom
20. Juni 2008, Rs. E-8/07), ZEuP 2011, 684 – 705
D. Herrmann, Gerichtsstand am Wohnsitz des Klä-
gers bei einer Direktklage des Geschädigten gegen
den Versicherer gem Art. 11 Abs. 2 iVm Art. 9 Abs 1
lit. b EuGVO?, VersR 2007, 1470–1475
Hertz, Jurisdiction in Contract and Tort under the
Brussels Convention (København 1998)
Hub, Internationale Zuständigkeit in Versiche-
rungssachen nach der VO 44/01/EG (EuGVVO)
(Berlin 2005)
Hübner, Der Umfang des Schriftformerfordernisses
des Art. 17 EuGVÜ bei (Versicherungs-)Verträgen
zugunsten Dritter und die Folgen der hilfsweisen
Einlassung nach Rüge der Zuständigkeit im Hinblick
auf Art. 18 EuGVÜ, IPRax 1984, 237
Idot, Prorogation de compétence, Europe 2010 Juillet
Comm. n° 261 p. 35
Leandro, Lecito anche nelle controversie assicurative
accettare la giurisdizione in modo tacito, Guida al
Diritto 2010 n° 23 p. 100–102
Looschelders, Der Klägergerichtsstand am Wohnsitz
des Versicherungsnehmers nach Art. 8 Abs. 1 Nr. 2
EuGVÜ, IPRax 1998, 86
Mankowski, Versicherungsverträge zu Gunsten
Dritter: Internationales Privatrecht und Art. 17
EuGVÜ, IPRax 1996, 427
Mankowski, Besteht der europäische Gerichtsstand
der rügelosen Einlassung auch gegen von Schutzre-
gimes besonders geschützte Personen?, Recht der
internationalen Wirtschaft 2010 p. 667–672

Helmut Heiss   407

Mankowski, Internationales Versicherungsprozess-recht: Professioneller Leasinggeber als Geschädigter und Typisierung statt konkreter Prüfung der Schutzbedürftigkeit, IPRax 2015, 115–119

Micha, Der Klägergerichtsstand des Geschädigten bei versicherungsrechtlichen Direktklagen in der Revision der EuGVVO, IPRax 2011, 121–124

Micha, Der Direktanspruch im europäischen Internationalen Privatrecht, 2010

Michailidou, Epitrepto parektasis diethnous dikaiodosias, Efarmoges Astikou Dikaiou 2010 p. 1009–1010

Reichert-Facilides, Internationale Versicherungsverträge und Verbraucherschutz: Gerichtliche Zuständigkeit und anwendbares Recht, in: Basedow/Hans-Dieter Meyer/Schwintowski (eds.), Lebensversicherung, internationale Versicherungsverträge und Verbraucherschutz, Versicherungsvertrieb – Versicherungswissenschaftliche Studien, Band 4 (Baden-Baden 1996), 77

Achim Richter, Das EWG-Übereinkommen über die gerichtliche Zuständigkeit und die Vollstreckung in Zivil- und Handelssachen aus versicherungsrechtlicher Sicht, VersR 1978, 801

J. Richter J, Internationales Versicherungsvertragsrecht (Frankfurt a.M. 1980)

Riedmeyer, Gerichtliche Zuständigkeit und anwendbares Recht bei Unfällen im Ausland, zfs 2008, 602

Rodriguez, Direktklage gegen den Haftpflichtversicherer unter dem revidierten Lugano-Übereinkommen: "Odenbreit" vor der Einbürgerung und die Folgen, HAVE 2011, 12

Rudisch, Das sogenannte Lugano-Übereinkommen und seine Bedeutung für die österreichische Versicherungswirtschaft, VR 1997, 201

Sánchez Lorenzo, Competencia judicial y reconocimiento y ejecución de decisiones en materia civil y mercantil: del convenio de Bruselas al reglamento "Bruselas I", in: Borrás (ed.), Cooperación Jurídica Internacional en Materia Civil: El Convenio de Bruselas (Madrid 2001), p. 181

Seatzu, Insurance in Private International Law (Oxford 2003)

Sperlich/Wolf, Internationale Zuständigkeit für Versicherungssachen aufgrund rügeloser Einlassung, Versicherungsrecht 2010, p. 1101–1102

Staudinger/Czaplinski, Verkehrsopferschutz im Lichte der Rom I-, Rom II- sowie Brüssel I-Verordnung, NJW 2009, 2249

Tomson, Der Verkehrsunfall im Ausland vor deutschen Gerichten – Alle Wege führen nach Rom, EuZW 2009, 204

Vassilakakis, International Jurisdiction in Insurance Matters under Regulation Brussels I, in: Essays in honour of Spyridon Vl. Vrellis (Athens 2014), p. 1079 – 1096

Wasserer, Paradigmenwechsel in der internationalen Zuständigkeit für Direktklagen: Wohnsitzgerichtsstand des Geschädigten bei Klagen gegen ausländische Kfz-Haftpflichtversicherungen, ELR 2008, 143 – 147

Wasserer, Kein Klägergerichtsstand für die Regressklage eines Sozialversicherungsträgers, ELR 2010, 14 – 19

Wittmann, Kann eine durch einen Verkehrsunfall geschädigte juristische Person gegen den Kfz-Haftpflichtversicherer aus einem Mitgliedsstaat der EU an ihrem Sitz klagen? r+s 2011, 145

Wittwer, Direktklage im Inland gegen ausländische Kfz-Haftpflichtversicherung, ZVR 2006/142

Wittwer, Auswirkungen des EuGH-Urteils Odenbreit auf die internationale Schadensregulierung ZVR 2008/260.

Introduction to Articles 10–16

1 Section 3 (Art. 10–16) contains rules dealing specifically with insurance contracts. This section's regulatory aim is to protect the policyholder and certain third parties (the insured, the beneficiary and the injured party).[1] In its aim to protect the weaker party[2] Section 3 is in line with Section 4 (consumer contracts) and Section 5 (contracts of employment). It is meant to protect the policyholder against the risks of cross border insurance contracts and to

enable him/her to efficiently participate in the internal market. Thereby, protection of the weaker party helps the proper functioning of the internal market.[3]

On the other hand, it should be taken into consideration that insurance is a somewhat **2** special product. Not only is the policyholder regularly the economically and professionally weaker party, he is also the recipient of a complex product which is intensively influenced by the law applicable to it (insurance as a "legal product"). Therefore, protection of the policy-holder goes further than general consumer protection.

Whereas Section 4 only covers consumer contracts, i.e. contracts concluded by the consu- **3** mer for a purpose which can be regarded as being outside his trade or profession,[4] Section 3 grants its protection to nearly all policyholders, including those that conclude the insurance contract within their trade or profession.[5] Only insurance companies as policyholders of reinsurance contracts are completely exempted from the protection of Section 3.[6] Policy-holders taking insurance for *large risks*[7] are protected by Section 3. They may, however, enter freely into agreements on jurisdiction.[8]

Whereas Section 4, at least in most cases,[9] affords protection to the consumer only if he/she **4** acts as a passive consumer, policyholders are protected regardless of whether they stay passive or shop actively for insurance cover abroad. Section 3 does not establish a criterion of passiveness as does Art. 17 (1) (c), depriving the consumer of his/her protection if the contract is concluded with a foreign entrepreneur not engaging in business in the Member State of the consumer's domicile. It follows, that the policyholder enjoys protection of Section 3 even if he actively shops for insurance coverage abroad.

In substance, Section 3 provides the policyholder with a menu of jurisdictions in which he **5** may bring an action according to his choice,[10] whereas such choice is limited for the insurer. Above all, the rules on jurisdiction are mostly mandatory. Parties may not deviate from the

---

[1]   See also *Blanco-Morales Limones*, in: Calvo Caravaca Art. 7 CB notes 4–13; *Vassilakakis* in: Essays in honour of Spyridon Vl. Vrellis, p. 1081 ff.

[2]   See *Gerling and Others v. Amministrazione del Tesoro dello Stato*, (Case 201/82) [1983] ECR 2503, 2516 para. 17; in general *Seatzu*, Insurance in Private International Law (2003) p. 51 with further references.

[3]   As to the legal policy behind Section 3 see Report *Jenard*, p. 13; for a discussion see *Heiss*, in: Reichert-Facilides/Schnyder, p. 108 *et seq.*

[4]   See Art. 17 (1).

[5]   See also *New Hampshire Insurance Co. v. Strabag Bau AG*, [1992] 1 Lloyd's Rep. 361 (C. A.); as to this decision see *Collins*, in: Dicey/Morris/Collins para. 11-339; see also OLG Frankfurt 23.6.2014 (16 U 224/13) IPRax 2015, 148; as to this decision *Mankowski* IPRax 2015, 115.

[6]   As to the exception of reinsurance contract from the scope of application of Section 3 *infra* Art. 10 note 6.

[7]   In more detail *infra* Art. 15 (5) in connection with Art. 16.

[8]   As to party autonomy of policyholders taking insurance for large risks, *infra* Art. 16 note 6.

[9]   This is not true for consumer contracts for the sale of goods on instalment contract terms and consumer loans financing such sale; see Art. 17 (1) (a) and (b).

[10] As to the risk to encourage forum shopping see *Heiss*, in: Reichert-Facilides/Schnyder, p. 135 *et seq.* referring to the US-American case *Allstate Ins. Co. v. Hague, Personal Representative of Hague's Estate* 449 US 302 (S.Ct. 1980) and further cases.

rules on jurisdiction to the detriment of the policyholder.[11] Consequently, courts in the Member State of the policyholder's domicile will not recognize or enforce a judgement of another court that took jurisdiction in violation of Section 3.[12] For this reason, the German BGH has even refused to recognise a "Scheme of Arrangement" under s. 425 British Companies Act 1985 concerning an English insurer and a German policyholder.[13]

Section 3: **Jurisdiction in matters relating to insurance**

Article 10

In matters relating to insurance, jurisdiction shall be determined by this Section, without prejudice to Article 6 and point 5 of Article 7.

I. Comprehensive regulation of jurisdiction

1 Section 3 (Art. 10–16) contains a comprehensive regulation of jurisdiction in matters relating to insurance. Art. 10 prevents recourse to provisions on jurisdiction other than those of Section 3, unless they are specifically mentioned in Section 3 (exclusionary nature of Section 3).[1] The latter is the case with Art. 6 and point 5 of Art. 7. Furthermore, Art. 14 (2) implicitly refers to point 8 of Art. 8.[2]

II. Applicability of Section 3

1. Defendant domiciled in a Member State

2 Since Art. 10 refers to Art. 6, the rules on jurisdiction in matters relating to insurance are

---

[11] See in detail Arts. 15 and 16.

[12] See Art. 45 (1) lit. e (recognition) and Art. 46 i.c.w. Art. 45 (l) lit. e (enforcement).

[13] BGH 15.2.2012 (IV ZR 194/09) NJW 2012, 2113 = RIW 2012, 397 = IPrax 2013, 264 at no. 27; see also BGH 18.4.2012 (IV ZR 147/10 and IV ZR 193/10) NJW 2012, 2352 = VersR 2012, 1110.

[1] See *Kaye* p. 807; see also *Jordan Grand Prix Ltd. and others v. Baltic Insurance Group*, [1999] 2 W. L. R. 134, 138 (H. L., per Lord *Steyn*): "... Section 3 is a self contained and exclusive code governing insurance"; *Fuentes Camacho*, p. 45; furthermore LG Bremen VersR 2001, 782 with note *Schüler*; *Fricke*, VersR 1997, 399, 401; critically as to this exclusionary nature *Geimer/Schütze* Art. 8 note 1.

[2] As to differences of the two provisions *Blanco-Morales Limones*, in: Calvo Caravaca, Art. 11 CB notes 24–26.

applied if the defendant is domiciled in a Member State.[3] Thus, for instance, Art. 13 para. 2 will only provide the injured party with a *forum actoris*, when the defendant insurer is domiciled in a Member State.[4] Up to this point the provisions on insurance are in line with general principles.

2. Defendant third country insurer established in a Member State

If a defendant insurer is not domiciled within a Member State but has a branch, agency or **3** other establishment[5] in a Member State, such insurer is deemed to be domiciled in that Member States according to Art. 11 (2). Thereby, such insurer is subjected to the rules on jurisdiction of the regulation. Consequently, he also enjoys the protection provided by Art. 5 (2) (exorbitant jurisdiction).[6]

Art. 11 (2) does not apply to policyholders domiciled in a third country and having a branch, **4** agency or other establishment in a Member State.

III. Scope of application: "matters relating to insurance"

1. Private insurance

The scope of application of Section 3 covers all matters relating to insurance.[7] This, however, **5** refers only to private insurance, whereas Art. 1 (2) (c) expressly excludes *social security* from the scope of application of the Regulation and, thereby, also from Section 3.

2. Reinsurance

From a substantive point of view, actions brought under a contract of *reinsurance* would **6** constitute a matter relating to (private) insurance. Nevertheless, it was held by the ECJ in *Group Josi* that Section 3 may not be regarded as applying to the relationship between a reinsured and his reinsurer in connection with a reinsurance contract.[8] This view would be

---

[3]   See Art. 4 par 1; as to the definition of domicile according to the Regulation see Art. 62, 63; as to the reference to Art. 4 see *Blanco-Morales Limones*, in: Calvo Caravaca Art. 7 CB notes 37–39.

[4]   OLG Zweibrücken 29.9.2009 and 10.11.2009 (1 U 119/09) NZV 2010, 198 holding also that the law applicable and the place where the accident occurred plaid no role insofar.

[5]   As to the criteria of a branch, agency or other establishment *infra* Art. 11 note 18 *et seq*.

[6]   *Kropholler/von Hein* Art. 9 note 5.

[7]   The Regulation explicitly refers to insurances such as compulsory insurance, liability insurance, insurance of immovable property, marine insurance, aviation insurance; this is mentioned by the ECJ in *Group Josi Reinsurance Company SA v. Universal General Insurance Company (UGIC)*, (Case C-412/98) [2000] ECR I-5925; for a more detailed analysis of the term "insurance" see *Blanco-Morales Limones*, in: Calvo Caravaca, Art. 7 CB notes 16–20 and *Hertz*, p. 187 *et seq*.

[8]   *Group Josi Reinsurance Company SA v. Universal General Insurance Company (UGIC)*, (Case C-412/98) [2000] ECR I-5925, I-5961 paras. 73 and 76 referring to the *Schlosser* Report; see also *Agnew and others v. Lansforsakringsbolagens AB* [1997] 4 All ER 937 (C. A.), affirmed by *Agnew and others v. Lansforsakringsbolagens AB* [2000] 1 All ER 737 (H. L.); the question was left unanswered in *Overseas Union Ins. Ltd., Deutsche Rück UK Reinsurance Co Ltd. and Pine Top Insurance Co Ltd. v. New Hampshire Ins. Co* (Case C-351/89) [1991] ECR I-3317.

in line with the letter and the spirit and purpose of Section 3.[9] However, the ECJ has expressly stated that Section 3 will apply to actions brought directly against a re-insurer by a policyholder, insured or beneficiary of an insurer.[10] The same must be true regarding direct actions brought by an injured party. A right of the policyholder or third party to bring direct action against the reinsurer is sometimes granted by national law, e.g. in cases of bankruptcy or liquidation of the insurer.[11]

3. Actions of an insurer against another insurer

7 For the same teleological reasons mentioned above for reinsurance, Section 3 does not apply in cases where an action is brought by an insurer against another insurer.[12] This view is also supported by the wording of the Regulation regarding actions brought by the policyholder, insured or beneficiary against the insurer or vice versa. It does not mention actions brought by an insurer against another insurer.[13] Such actions arise e.g. in cases of double insurance, when the company that has paid the insurance money to the insured seeks recovery of a pro rata share from the other insurer.[14] It may as well occur when a (social or indemnity) insurer takes a recourse direct action against the liability insurer of the tortfeasor.[15] As a result, the insurer may invoke jurisdiction under Art. 8 (2) which is not applicable in matters relating to insurance within the scope of Section 3.[16]

4. Insurance of large risks

8 Section 3 applies to matters relating to insurance contracts covering large risks.[17] Insofar even the policyholders of large risk insurance enjoy the protection that Section 3 offers. However, since they are less worthy of protection,[18] Section 3 is non-mandatory in the field

---

9   *Group Josi Reinsurance Company SA v. Universal General Insurance Company (UGIC)*, (Case C-412/98) [2000] ECR I-5925, I-5959 para. 67; see also *Gaudemet-Tallon*, p. 216; *Hub*, p. 63 *et seq.*

10 *Group Josi Reinsurance Company SA v. Universal General Insurance Company (UGIC)*, (Case C-412/98) [2000] ECR I-5925, I-5961 para. 75; the rationale of this counter-exception must also apply to the injured party.

11 See *Group Josi Reinsurance Company SA v. Universal General Insurance Company (UGIC)*, (Case C-412/98) [2000] ECR I-5925, I-5961 para. 75.

12 See *Groupement d'intérêt économique (GIE) Réunion européenne et al. Zurich España, Société pyrénéenne de transit d'automobiles (Soptrans)*, (Case C-77/04) [2005] ECR I-4509 = VersR 2005, 1001 with note *Heiss*; see also LG Bremen VersR 2001, 782 with note *Schüler*.

13 See *Groupement d'intérêt économique (GIE) Réunion européenne et al. Zurich España, Société pyrénéenne de transit d'automobiles (Soptrans)*, (Case C-77/04) [2005] ECR I-4509 para. 21 = VersR 2005, 1001 with note *Heiss*.

14 This was the situation in *Groupement d'intérêt économique (GIE) Réunion européenne et al. Zurich España, Société pyrénéenne de transit d'automobiles (Soptrans)*, (Case C-77/04) [2005] ECR I-4509 = VersR 2005, 1001 with note *Heiss*; see also Cass. Civ. I, 10 mai 2006, 01–11.229; Bulletin 2006 I N° 222 S 195.

15 *Vorarlberger Gebietskrankenkasse v. WGV-Schwäbische Allgemeine Versicherungs AG* (Case C-347/08) [2009] ECR I-8661.

16 In more detail *Heiss*, in: Reichert-Facilides/Schnyder, p. 105, 118.

17 As to the definition of large risks *infra* Art. 16.

18 In more detail and with examples *Heiss*, in: Reichert-Facilides/Schnyder, p. 105, 113 *et seq.*

of large risk insurance and parties may deviate from the Regulation by agreement.[19] Thereby, large risks are treated in the context of jurisdiction in the same way as they are in the conflict of law rules in the insurance directives.[20]

5. Rights to subrogation

If an indemnity insurer pays the insurance money to the insured for an event caused by a   **9** third party, the insurer may recover the payment from the tortfeasor according to the rules on subrogation.[21] In this case the insurer files the claim in tort to which the policyholder was originally entitled. Such action remains an action in tort and is not covered by Section 3.[22] The insurer is not bound by a jurisdiction clause contained in the insurance contract concluded with the policyholder.[23]

If several insurers are jointly liable and one of them pays the policyholder, this insurer may   **10** seek pro-rata-indemnification from the others.[24] Although this would constitute a matter relating to insurance under substantive law, it is not covered by Section 3 because the underlying protective purposes are not considered.[25]

If a liability insurer has to indemnify an injured person even though he was freed from   **11** liability as against the policyholder, e.g. due to non-payment of premium, he may sue the policyholder for reimbursement later on.[26] In this case, the action concerns the contractual relationship of the insurer and the policyholder, because its success depends on whether or not there was insurance cover. Thereby, such an action constitutes a matter relating to insurance and jurisdiction is regulated by Section 3.[27]

6. Actions against an insurance broker

Section III only covers matters related to an insurance contract. This does not include   **12** matters related to a contract of brokerage concluded between a policyholder and his/her broker. Thus, jurisdiction for an action brought by a customer against his/her insurance broker will fall outside the scope of Section 3.[28]

---

[19] See Art. 15 in connection with Art. 16; as a result, doubts and criticism put forward by *Staudinger*, in: Rauscher, Art. 8 note 15 are not convincing.

[20] In more detail *infra* Art. 14 note 6.

[21] See e.g. § 86 German VVG (Insurance Coutract Act).

[22] See also *Blanco-Morales Limones*, in: Calvo Caravaca Art. 7 CB note 33; *Staudinger*, in: Rauscher Art. 8 note 17.

[23] Cass. Civ. I, 14. November 2007, 06–20.704 (unpublished).

[24] See e.g. the right to subrogation under § 78 (2) German VVG (Insurance Coutract Act).

[25] See *supra* Art. 10 note 6 (*Heiss*).

[26] See e.g. the right to subrogation granted by § 117 (5) German VVG (Insurance Coutract Act).

[27] See also *Geimer/Schütze*, Art. 8 note 15: *Heiss*, in: Czernich/Tiefenthaler/Kodek, Art. 10 note 6.

[28] See *Vassilakakis* in: Essays in honour of Spyridon Vl. Vrellis, p. 1081 with reference to Court of Appeals of Piraeus, judgment no. 546/2006, Harmenopoulos 2008, 437.

IV. Reference to point 5 of Art. 7

13 Art. 7 point 5 also applies to matters relating to insurance.[29] Jurisdiction granted by Art. 7 point 5 may be invoked not only by a plaintiff policyholder[30] but also by a plaintiff insurer.[31]

Article 11

1. An insurer domiciled in a Member State may be sued:
   (a) in the courts of the Member State in which he is domiciled;
   (b) in another Member State, in the case of actions brought by the policyholder, the insured or a beneficiary, in the courts for the place where the claimant is domiciled; or
   (c) if he is a co-insurer, in the courts of a Member State in which proceedings are brought against the leading insurer.
2. An insurer who is not domiciled in a Member State but has a branch, agency or other establishment in one of the Member States shall, in disputes arising out of the operations of the branch, agency or establishment, be deemed to be domiciled in that Member State.

I. Choice of jurisdiction by the policyholder and third party beneficiaries

1. Forum rei, Art. 11 (1) (a)

1 Art. 11 (1) (a) grants jurisdiction to the courts of the Member State in which the defendant insurer is domiciled.[1] The provision refers to international but does not determine local jurisdiction.

2 Art. 11 (1) (a) in a way repeats Art. 4 (1) *(forum rei)*. This happens for two reasons: Section 3 is, first of all, a comprehensive regulation of jurisdiction in matters relating to insurance,[2] rendering Art. 4 (1) inapplicable in this field. Secondly, Section 3 contains mandatory[3] rules

---

[29] See the explicit reference in Art. 10; as to the question whether the reference is mandatory or may be derogated from by parties agreement see *infra* Art. 15 note 4 (*Heiss*).

[30] Details in Art. 11 notes 16 *et seq.* (*Heiss*).

[31] Details in Art. 14 note 7 (*Heiss*).

[1] As to the domicile of an insurer see Art. 63; see also *Fricke*, VersR 1999, 1055, 1056.

[2] *Supra* Art. 10 note 1 (*Heiss*).

protecting the policyholder, whereas Art. 4 (1) is non-mandatory and may be derogated by a choice of jurisdiction of the parties under Art. 15.

According to Art. 11 (2) an insurer domiciled in a third country but established in a Member **3**
State shall be deemed to be domiciled in that Member State.[4] As a result, the domicile mentioned in Art. 11 (1) (a) includes the branch office of a third country insurer. However, the rule only applies to claims arising out of insurance contracts concluded by this branch.[5]

2. Forum actoris, Art. 11 (1) (b)

a) Forum of the policyholder
Art. 11 (1) (b) establishes an exception to the general principle of *actor sequitur forum rei*[6] **4**
and provides the plaintiff policyholder[7] with an alternative forum in the place of his/her domicile.[8] Instead of bringing an action in the courts of the Member State, where the defendant insurer is domiciled, the policyholder may freely choose to sue the insurer in the courts for his own domicile.[9]

If the policyholder is a company or other legal person or association of natural or legal **5**
persons, its domicile is determined by Art. 63 (1). Therefore, Art. 11 (1) (b) applies if a plaintiff corporation having its statutory seat in a third country but its central administration in a Member State. The plaintiff corporation may sue in the courts for the place of its central administration.[10]

The provision determines international and, simultaneously, local jurisdiction.[11] Jurisdic- **6**
tion depends upon the domicile of the policyholder at the time when he/she files the action.[12]

b) Forum of third party beneficiaries
Frequently, insurance is taken for the benefit of a third party. Whereas the policyholder is **7**

---

[3]   As to the limits of party autonomy in matters relating to insurance see Art. 15 and 16; see e.g. Cass. Civ. 1, vom 14 November 2006, 04–15.276, Bulletin 2006 I N° 470 S 404.

[4]   See also *supra* Art. 10 note 3 (*Heiss*).

[5]   Similarly Cassaz. Giust. Civ. 1994 I 2975; Cassaz. 13 February 1993 as reported in *Kaye*, Case Law, p. 663; Cass. JCP éd. G 1994 IV 205; to the contrary Trib. Tournai J. trib. 1980, 391 = *Kaye*, Case Law, p. 21 (see also the criticism of this decision in the Comment by *Kaye*).

[6]   See also *Hertz*, p. 187: "… an exception to the Convention's otherwise hostile attitude towards a *forum actoris*"; as to the rule "actor sequitur forum rei" see Art. 4 (1).

[7]   "Policyholder" is the party who entered into the insurance contract with the insurer; see Polymeles Protodikeio Piraia DEE 1995, 82 = *Kaye*, Case Law, p. 599.

[8]   See e.g. BGE 124 III 436, 441; see also Cass. Civ. 1, vom 14 November 2006, 04–15.276, Bulletin 2006 I N° 470 S 404.

[9]   This choice must not be infringed by national legislation; see Högsta domstolen 3 January 2000 – Ö 1122-98; according to OLG Saarbrücken 27.3.2013 (5 U 463/11-63) a policyholder may have more than one domicile and, thus, more than one *forum actoris*.

[10]   Areios Pagos Diki 2000, 210 = NB 1999, 1113.

[11]   KG Berlin Neue Justiz 2007, 79 (*Gebauer*).

[12]   See also *Blanco-Morales Limones*, in: Calvo Caravaca Art. 8 CB note 17; critically *Geimer/Schütze* Art. 9 note 9 s.

the person concluding the contract and owing the premium to the insurer, the third party beneficiary is the person entitled to the insurance money. In insurance against damages, the third party beneficiary is called the "insured" (e.g. liability policies frequently cover the children of the policyholder).[13] In insurance for fixed sums the third party beneficiary is called the "beneficiary" (e.g. spouses named as beneficiaries by the holder of a life assurance policy).

8 The Regulation provides third parties, i.e. insured persons and beneficiaries, with their own *forum actoris*.[14] According to Art. 11 (1) (b), an insured or beneficiary may sue the insurer based on an insurance contract in the courts for the place where the plaintiff insured or beneficiary is domiciled.[15] There is some harshness to the insurer in this rule because the domicile of a third party beneficiary cannot always be determined upfront.[16] Indeed, quite often not even the identity of the third party is determined at the time the contract is made (insurances "for whom it may concern"). Furthermore, the number of insured parties or beneficiaries may be very high.

9 The provision determines international and, simultaneously, local jurisdiction. Jurisdiction depends upon the domicile of the insured or beneficiary at the time when he/she files the action.

3. Forum of co-insurers

10 Co-insurance is a technique by which an interest is insured by two or more insurers together. According to common practice, co-insurers do not commit themselves to a joint liability. Instead, each insurer only assumes liability for a specified part of the insured sum. Nevertheless, it is also common practice to name one insurer as the leading insurer. Such leadership clauses usually grant power to the leading insurer to represent all co-insurers in private negotiations as well as in court procedures with the policyholder. As a consequence, the policyholder may bring an action for the overall insurance money against the leading insurer who will be the defendant himself and at the same time represent the other defendant insurers.

11 Usually, the policyholder is interested in suing co-insurers jointly. In the absence of Art. 11 (1) (c) the possibility to bring a joint action against all co-insurers would depend on whether a specific court would hold jurisdiction over all co-insurers. This is the case whenever the plaintiff policyholder decides to use the *forum actoris* provided by Art. 11 (1) (b). It is not the case, however, when the plaintiff policyholder wants to use the *forum rei* provided by Art. 11

---

[13] See also *Société financière et industrielle du Peloux v. Axa Belgium et al.*, (Case C-112/03) [2005] ECR I-3707 = IPRax 2005, 531; as to this decision see *Heiss*, IPRax 2005, 497, concerning an insurance contract concluded by a mother company in favour of several daughter companies.

[14] As to this shift in policy see e.g. *Sánchez Lorenzo*, in: Borrás (ed.) Cooperación Jurídica Internacional en Materia Civil: El Convenio de Bruselas (2001), p. 201, 204; and *Calvo Caravaca/Carrascosa González*, p. 169.

[15] See *Fricke*, VersR 1999, 1055, 1058.

[16] As to group insurances *Fricke*, VersR 1999, 1055, 1058.

(1) (a) when the co-insurers are domiciled in different Member States. The plaintiff policy-holder may not rely on Art. 8 point 1 because it is inapplicable in matters relating to insurance.[17] Section 3 does not contain a parallel rule.[18]

In order to make it possible[19] for the policyholder to bring a joint action in the *forum rei*,   **12** Art. 11 (1) (c) allows the policyholder to bring the action against all defendant co-insurers in the courts of the Member State in which proceedings are brought against the leading in-surer.[20]

Art. 11 (1) (c) only covers situations where parties intend to create co-insurance and de-   **13** termine a leading insurer.[21] However, similar situations may occur whenever a policyholder takes two or more insurances on the same insurable interest either unintentionally or at least without notifying each insurer about the existence of further insurances. National insurance contract laws sometimes provide for a joint liability of the insurers involved.[22] Art. 11 (1) (c) does not apply to these situations and the policyholder cannot rely on Art. 8 point 1.[23] As a consequence, the policyholder can only bring a joint action in the courts of his own domicile (*forum actoris*). If the policyholder decides to sue the insurers in the *forum rei*, separate actions must be brought.

If one of the insurers, who are jointly liable under the rules of the applicable law, is sued by   **14** the policyholder in a particular court, he may want to bring an action against the other insurers for recovery of an adequate share under the rules on joint liability. Such a claim is not considered a matter relating to insurance.[24] Therefore, Section 3 does not apply to such cases and the plaintiff insurer may avail himself of the jurisdiction granted by Art. 8 point 2. As a consequence, an insurer sued by the policyholder in a particular court may sue all other insurers that are jointly liable as third parties in the same court.[25] If the insurer pays the insurance money to the policyholder and wants to recover an adequate share from the other insurers under the rules on joint liability, he may furthermore rely on Art. 8 point 1.

---

[17]   As to the comprehensiveness of Section 3 *supra* Art. 10 note 1.

[18]   See *Heiss*, in Czernich/Tiefenthaler/Kodek Art. 11 note 6.

[19]   Art. 11 (1) (c) does not impose an obligation of the policyholder to concentrate proceedings in one court; see *Collins*, in: Dicey/Morris/Collins para. 11–343.

[20]   See *Tradigrain SA v. SIAT SpA and others* [2002] 2 Lloyd's Rep. 553 paras. 63 and 64 (Q. B. D., *Colman* J.).

[21]   And the co-insurance is openly agreed upon with the policyholder; see *Blanco-Morales Limones*, in: Calvo Caravaca, Art. 8 CB note 23.

[22]   See e.g. § 78 German VVG (Insurance Contract Act).

[23]   *Heiss*, in: Reichert-Facilides/Schnyder, p. 105, 118.

[24]   See *supra* Art. 10 note 10 (*Heiss*).

[25]   See *Heiss*, in: Czernich/Tiefenthaler/Kodek Art. 11 note 7; as to the modification of Art. 8 (2) if actions are brought in Austria or Germany, see Art. 67; *Heiss*, in: Reichert-Facilides/Schnyder, p. 105, 118.

Helmut Heiss   417

II. Further choices

1. Art. 7 point 5

a) General remarks

15 The options of the policyholder granted by Art. 11 (1) are supplemented[26] by Art. 7 point 5 which, according to Art. 10, remains applicable to matters relating to insurance. Art. 7 point 5 provides the policyholder with yet another option and does not derogate other provisions, e.g. Art. 11.

16 The reference to Art. 7 point 5, as contained in Art. 10, is a consequential change to the abolishment of a specific rule on jurisdiction of the courts for the place where the intermediary is domiciled in the original version of the Brussels Convention.[27] Such a special provision was held to be superfluous in the light of 7 point 5.[28]

17 According to Art. 7 point 5, a policyholder may sue an insurer domiciled in a Member State in the courts for the place in which the insurer maintains a branch, agency or other establishment if the dispute arises out of its operation. Art. 7 point 5 grants international jurisdiction and determines local jurisdiction *uno actu*.[29]

b) Branch, agency or other establishment

18 It is subject to dispute what constitutes a branch, agency or other establishment.[30] For insurance matters it seems sufficient to point out that marketing of insurance contracts through an independent broker does not constitute a branch, agency or other establishment. Support for this view can be drawn from the legislative history. Former Art. 8 (2) Brussels Convention was abolished because it included cases where the intermediary was in fact an independent broker.[31] On the other hand, it was held that a special rule, providing for jurisdiction of the courts at the place where the insurance agent is domiciled, would be superfluous because the case would be covered by Art. 7 point 5.[32] As a consequence, marketing of insurance contracts through an insurance agent fulfils the criteria of a branch, agency or other establishment. The same must be true for so called pseudo brokers. Such brokers appear to be independent but are in fact tied to a particular insurer in a way that makes them agents in fact.

c) Apparent branch, agency or other establishment

19 The ECJ has held that jurisdiction under Art. 7 point 5 applies also to cases where the defendant has created the appearance of a branch, agency or other establishment.[33] This

---

[26] The reference of Art. 10 to Art. 7 point 5 does, of course, not exclude the choices of the policyholder granted by Art. 11; see LG Stuttgart IPRax 1998, 100, 101 with note *Looschelders*, IPRax 1998, 86.

[27] Art. 8 (2) Brussels Convention.

[28] However, the legislator might have overlooked the fact that Art. 7 point 5 is non-mandatory as opposed to former Art. 8 (2) Brussels Convention; see *infra* Art. 13 note 4 (*Heiss*).

[29] In more detail *supra* Art. 7 note 3 (*Mankowski*).

[30] In general see *supra* Art. 7 note 425 *et seq.* (*Mankowski*); for "Lloyd's of London" in particular see Cassaz., Mass. Foro it. 1999 col. 1170.

[31] *Heiss*, in: Czernich/Tiefenthaler/Kodek Art. 10 note 8.

[32] *Heiss*, in: Czernich/Tiefenthaler/Kodek Art. 10 note 8.

decision by the ECJ might be of particular importance for insurance cases because the status of an intermediary as an agent or broker is sometimes hard to figure out as hybrid types of intermediaries can be found in the markets.[34]

It must be noted in the context that the directive on insurance mediation[35] acknowledges the **20** fact that it is essential for the customer to know whether he is dealing with an intermediary who is advising him on products from broad range of insurance undertakings or on products provided by a specific number of insurance undertakings.[36] The directive also provides a definition for what it calls a tied insurance intermediary.[37] Finally, it intends to create transparency by obliging the intermediary to give information on his status of independence.[38] However, hybrid types of intermediaries are still not ruled out completely.

d) Disputes arising out of the operation of the establishment

Art. 7 point 5 only grants jurisdiction if the dispute arises out of the operation of the branch, **21** agency or other establishment.[39] This is the case if the contract under dispute was *negotiated* by the branch, agency or other establishment. However, if the establishment did not negotiate the contract and only represents the insurer for purposes of its fulfilment (claims settlement) a dispute out of the insurance contract will not be held to be a dispute arising out of the operation of an establishment.[40] For the same reason, a claims representative established according to Art. 4 fourth motor insurance Directive[41] in the country where the injured party is domiciled, is not a branch, agency or other establishment within the meaning of Art. 7 point 5.[42]

---

[33] *SAR Schotte GmbH v. Parfums Rothschild SARL*, (Case 218/86) [1987] ECR 4905, 4928 para. 15.

[34] As to this problem *Heiss*, in: Reichert-Facilides/Schnyder, p. 105, 122.

[35] Directive 2002/92/EC of the European Parliament and the Council of 9 December 2002 on insurance mediation, OJ 2003 L 9/3.

[36] Comment 18 Directive 2002/92/EC of the European Parliament and the Council of 9 December 2002 on insurance mediation, OJ 2003 L 9/3.

[37] See Art. 2 (7) Directive 2002/92/EC of the European Parliament and the Council of 9 December 2002 on insurance mediation, OJ 2003 L 9/3.

[38] See Art. 12 (1) (e) Directive 2002/92/EC of the European Parliament and the Council of 9 December 2002 on insurance mediation, OJ 2003 L 9/3.

[39] As to this criterion in general see *supra* Art. 7 notes 425 *et seq.* (*Mankowski*).

[40] This follows from *Lloyd's Register of Shipping v. Société Campenon Bernard*, (Case C-439/93) [1995] ECR I-961.

[41] Directive 2000/26/EC of the European Parliament and of the Council of 16 May 2000 on the approximation of the laws of the Member States relating to insurance against civil liability in respect of the use of motor vehicles and amending Council Directives 73/239/EEC and 88/357/EEC (Fourth Motor Insurance Directive), OJ 2000 L 181/65.

[42] See also the position of the EC legislator in Comments 13 and 16 Directive 2000/26/EC of the European Parliament and of the Council of 16 May 2000 on the approximation of the laws of the Member States relating to insurance against civil liability in respect of the use of motor vehicles and amending Council Directives 73/239/EEC and 88/357/EEC (Fourth Motor Insurance Directive), OJ 2000 L 181/65; see also *Heiss*, in: Reichert-Facilides/Schnyder, p. 146; *Hub* p. 87.

2. Other options of the policyholder and third parties

22 The policyholder and specified third parties are provided with further options in Art. 12 and 13. Again, these rules provide for alternatives to and do not derogate Art. 11.

Article 12

In respect of liability insurance or insurance of immovable property, the insurer may in addition be sued in the courts for the place where the harmful event occurred. The same applies if movable and immovable property are covered by the same insurance policy and both are adversely affected by the same contingency.

I. Liability insurance

1 Art. 12 clause one applies first of all to liability insurance.[1] This means any kind of insurance providing indemnification of the insured in the event that he becomes liable (*ex delicto* or *ex contractu*)[2] to third parties.

2 Art. 12 clause one broadens the choice of the policyholder of a liability insurance by granting jurisdiction to the courts for the place where the harmful event occurred (*locus delicti commissi*).[3] Sometimes the occurrence of a harmful event stretches over two or more countries. This is the case whenever the place of the happening of the event which gives rise to liability in tort and the place where the event results in damage are not identical. The same situation arises in tort cases under Art. 7 point 3. The ECJ has held that the *locus delicti commissi* covers both places.[4] As a result, the plaintiff may choose to bring his action in the courts of either one of the places.[5] The same applies to Art. 12.[6]

---

[1] And (see *infra* Art. 10 note 2 [*Heiss*]) of an insurance of immovable property; the provision does, however, not apply to other insurances, see Cassaz. RDIPP 1977, 605.

[2] Art. 12 is not restricted to liability in tort, see Cass. civ. 1, 10 Mai 2006 02-20272 und 02-20273, Bulletin 2006 I N° 221 S 194.

[3] See e.g. Høyesterett NRe 2002, 180.

[4] See *Handelskwekerij G. J. Bier BV v. Mines de potasse d'Alsace SA*, (Case 21-76) [1976] ECR 1735; Cass. civ. 1, 10 Mai 2006 02-20272 und 02-20273; Bulletin 2006 I N° 221 S 194; Cass. civ. 1, du 30 octobre 2006, 04–19.859, Bulletin 2006 I N° 448 p. 384.

[5] See *Handelskwekerij G. J. Bier BV v. Mines de potasse d'Alsace SA*, (Case 21-76) [1976] ECR 1735; Cass. civ. 1, 10 Mai 2006 02-20272 und 02-20273; Bulletin 2006 I N° 221 S 194; Cass. civ. 1, du 30 octobre 2006, 04–19.859, Bulletin 2006 I N° 448 p. 384.

[6] See e.g. *Fuentes Camacho*, p. 52; Cour de cassation, chambre civile, Bull. civ. 2006 I, n° 448, p. 384; as to the meaning of the "place where the harmful event occurred" see *Vassilakakis* in: Essays in honour of Spyridon Vl. Vrellis, p. 1084 f.

II. Insurance of immovable property and combined cover for movable property

1. Insurance of immovable property

Art. 12 clause one also applies to insurances of immovable property. Legal literature repeat- **3**
edly states that this should also hold true to cover a harmful event that stretches over two or
more countries. The policyholder would have the choice to either bring the action in the
courts at the place of the happening of the event, which gave rise to the damage, or in the
courts at the place where the event resulted in damage (which is the *locus sitae* of the
immovable property).[7] It is, however, doubtful whether this was intended by the legislator.
It is quite probable that the legislator wanted to confer jurisdiction only upon the courts at
the place where the immovable property is located.[8] As a consequence, Art. 12 should be
interpreted narrowly as far as insurances of immovable property are concerned.[9]

2. Combined cover for movable property

The alternative forum provided by Art. 12 clause one for insurances of immovable property **4**
also applies to *movables* if the policyholder is insured under the same policy and affected by
the same contingency.[10] In such cases, the policyholder can sue for damages to or loss of
movable property together with the action for damages to the immovable property.

III. Local jurisdiction

Art. 12 determines international and, simultaneously, local jurisdiction.   **5**

IV. Party autonomy

Under certain circumstances parties may derogate Art. 12 by agreement. Validity of such an **6**
agreement on jurisdiction requires that the insurer as well as the policyholder have their
domicile or habitual residence in the same Member State, the parties agree to confer jurisdiction on the courts of that State and the State law allows such an agreement.[11]

Article 13

1. In respect of liability insurance, the insurer may also, if the law of the court permits it, be
   joined in proceedings which the injured party has brought against the insured.
2. Articles 10, 11 and 12 shall apply to actions brought by the injured party directly against the
   insurer, where such direct actions are permitted.
3. If the law governing such direct actions provides that the policyholder or the insured may be
   joined as a party to the action, the same court shall have jurisdiction over them.

---

[7] See *Heiss* in: Czernich/Tiefenthaler/Kodek, Art. 12 note 1.
[8] In more detail see *Heiss*, in: Reichert-Facilides/Schnyder, p. 120.
[9] See also *Blanco-Morales Limones*, in: Calvo Caravaca, Art. 9 CB note 22; *Hub* p. 109.
[10] Art. 12 clause two.
[11] See *infra* Art. 15 note 11 (*Heiss*).

I. Art. 13 (1)

1   Art. 13 (1) is a provision similar to Art. 8 point 2 (action on a warranty or guarantee or other third party proceedings). If the insured is sued in tort in a competent[1] court, the insured may bring an action against his liability insurer in the same court.[2] However, such a right to bring an action in the forum of the tort procedure depends on whether the *lex fori* allows such action.[3]

2   A judgement given by a court of a Member State assuming jurisdiction based on Art. 13 (1) is recognised and will be enforced in all other Member States including those that do not provide for an action on a warranty or guarantee.

3   Under regular circumstances Art. 13 (1) does not provide the policyholder with a further choice of jurisdiction. The injured party may sue the insured either in the courts of the Member State where the insured is domiciled[4] or in the courts for the place where the harmful event occurred.[5] However, Art. 11 (1) (b) and 12 provide the policyholder and/or the insured with a forum in both places anyway. It is the function of Art. 13 (1) to give the policyholder access to an action on a warranty or guarantee where the *lex loci* provides for such it.

4   According to Art. 65, Art. 13 (1) does not apply in the courts of Austria, Germany and Hungary. Defendants domiciled in these countries are, however, subject to jurisdiction under Art. 13 (1) in other countries. Furthermore, decisions rendered by a foreign court holding jurisdiction based on Art. 13 (1) must be recognised and enforced also in those countries.[6]

II. Direct action of the injured party

1. Direct action

5   Art. 13 (2) of the Brussels I Regulation contains rules of jurisdiction for cases in which an injured party brings a **direct action** against an insurer.[7] Under general liability (insurance) law, the injured party would first have to sue the tortfeasor for damages and – if that action were successful – later assume the tortfeasor's right of indemnity and enforce it against the insurer.[8] A direct action, on the other hand, enables an injured party to consolidate an action for establishing liability and an action for indemnity into one set of proceedings. Pursuant to Art. 3 of the Consolidated Motor Insurance Directive such a right of direct action exists in

---

[1]   As to this criterion see *Kropholler/von Hein* Art. 11 note 3.

[2]   Cass. civ. 1, 10 Mai 2006 02-20272 und 02-20273; Bulletin 2006 I N° 221 S 194.

[3]   For Austria and Germany see Art. 65.

[4]   Art. 4 (1).

[5]   Art. 7 point 3.

[6]   See e.g. OLG Celle 27.10.2010 (8 W 15/10) (final, see BGH 14.6.2012 (IX ZB 245/10) openJur 2012, 69405).

[7]   As to the meaning of "direct action" see *Micha* 7 ff; see also *Heiss/Kosma* 275 ff.

[8]   As to the relationship between tort and insurance law in European directives' law see *Heiss/Loacker*, ZEuP 2011, 684–705.

relation to motor vehicle liability insurance.[9] In other European countries, direct action has become a fundamental principle – either with respect to compulsory insurance only or with respect to all types of liability insurance generally.[10]

A direct action can only be brought in the proper jurisdiction "if the law of the court **6** **permits**" such an action. According to prevailing opinion, this is taken as a reference to the law governing the determination of the existence of a direct action in accordance with the conflict rules of the *lex fori*.[11] The proper law must be determined pursuant to **rules of conflict of laws**. The right of direct action is governed by Art. 18 of the Rome II Regulation.[12] According to Art. 18 Rome II the injured will enjoy a direct action against the insurer, "if the law applicable to the non-contractual obligation or the law applicable to the insurance contract so provides".[13] An exception is made e.g. with regard to the right of direct action in the case of civil nuclear liability, where the right continues to be determined in accordance with national conflict-of-law provisions. This is because "non-contractual obligations arising out of nuclear damage" are excluded by Art. 1 (2) (f) of the Rome II Regulation[14] from its scope.[15] Another exception exists in the context of traffic accidents where the direct action is dealt with specifically in Art. 9 of the Hague Convention on the Law applicable to Traffic Accidents.[16] This convention takes priority over Rome II (see its art 28 para. 1) in those Member States which have ratified the convention (Austria, Belgium, Czech Republic, France, Latvia, Lithuania, Luxembourg, Netherlands, Poland, Slovakia, Spain).

2. Jurisdiction

Art. 13 (2) grants the injured party a position similar to the policyholder and to third party **7** beneficiaries. The injured party may bring his action in any one of the courts holding jurisdiction under Art. 10, 11[17] and 12.[18]

According to the decision in *Odenbreit*,[19] the reference in Art. 13 (2) to Art. 11 (1) (b) grants **8** an injured party **home jurisdiction**.[20] It is held that this would apply even if the tort was

---

9   [2009] OJ L 263/11 as amended.

10   See *Heiss/Kosma* 275 ff; *Heiss/Loacker*, JBl 2007, 613, 637 f.

11   See *Kropholler/von Hein* Art. 11 note 4.

12   [2007] OJ L199/40, see *Heiss/Loacker*, JBl 2007, 613, 637 f; in detail *Micha* 88 ff.

13   See *Vassilakakis* in: Essays in honour of Spyridon Vl. Vrellis, p. 1087 f.

14   [2007] OJ L199/40.

15   See *Heiss/Loacker* JBl 2007, 613, 638.

16   Concluded on 4 May 1971. See the exception made for international conventions under Art. 28 (1) of Rome II, [2007] OJ L199/40; *Heiss/Loacker*, JBl 2007, 613, 617 and 638; *Wittwer*, ZVR 2006/142, 407.

17   As to Art. 11 (1) (a) see Aud. Prov. de Castellón R. G. D. 608 (1995), 6127 *et seq.* = *Kaye*, Case Law, p. 842.

18   See also *Collins*, in: Dicey/Morris/Collins para. 11–347; and Efeteio Athina 7455/1993 Elliniki Dikaiosyni 1995, 389 = *Kaye*, Case Law, p. 601.

19   *FBTO Schadeverzekeringen NV v. Jack Odenbreit*, (Case C-463/06) [2007] ECR I-11321 in this context and with regard to the decisions in OLG Karlsruhe IPRax 2008, 125 and AG Bremen, IPRax 2008, 126, see *Fuchs*, IPRax 2008, 104; see also *Wasserer* ELR 2008, 143.

20   See, e.g., also the decision in OLG Wien AnwBl 2007/8112 [commentary by *Wittwer*]; there was no home jurisdiction of the injured party under the Brussels Convention, see e.g. OGH 29 March 2001 – 2Ob71/01g ZfRV 2001, 230.

Helmut Heiss

committed outside the Member States, as long as Section 3 is applicable.[21] This of course is also the case where the injured party concerned is a legal entity.[22] It does not apply if a social[23] or indemnity[24] insurer takes a recourse direct action against the liability insurer of the tortfeasor, because actions brought by an insurer against another insurer do not fall within the scope of application of Section III and, thus, Art. 13 (2) is inapplicable in such cases. It does not apply as well to an **assignee** of the direct claim.[25]

9   By this means, injured parties are treated in a manner similar to policyholders and insureds and can bring an action before the courts of the place where they are **domiciled**. This jurisdictional competence does **not** however extent to tortious claims made by an injured party **against a tortfeasor**.[26] Thus, notwithstanding point 1 of Art. 8, an injured party is not able to inextricably establish the place of his domicile as the proper jurisdiction for proceedings on all matters of law.[27]

10   The justification for allowing injured parties to sue in their home countries is based on two grounds: 1) the wording of Art. 13 (2), which pursuant to the teleology of section 3 should serve to protect the weaker party;[28] and 2) Recital 16a (a non-binding recital inserted long after the enactment of the Brussels I Regulation) to the Fourth Motor Insurance Directive,

---

21   See *Vassilakakis* in: Essays in honour of Spyridon Vl. Vrellis, p. 1090 f.

22   See OLG Celle VersR 2009, 61 [with commentary by *Tomson*, who correctly points out that the proper jurisdiction is elsewhere when action for recourse is brought by, for example, an injured party's hull underwriter against the tortfeasor's liability insurer. In such cases, an insurance matter as defined under section 3 is not concerned; see *Heiss* in: Czernich/Tiefenthaler/Kodek Art. 8 note 6]; OLG Frankfurt am Main 23.6.2014 (16 U 224/13), IPRax 2015, 148; as to this decission *Mankowski* IPRax 2015, 115; see, however, the – incorrect – approach taken by OLG Köln 11.1.2010 (13 U 119/09) DAR 2010, 582 trying to decide whether a legal entity diserves protection under Section 3 on a case by case basis; see also *Wittmann*, r+s 2011, 145 with reference to German case law; it is held, however, by OLG Koblenz 15.10.2012 (12 U 1528/11) DAR 2013, 30 that a State within Germany would be comparable to a social insurer and, thus, Art. 13 para. 2 would not apply.

23   *Vorarlberger Gebietskrankenkasse v. WGV-Schwäbische Allgemeine Versicherungs AG* (Case C-347/08) [2009] ECR I-8661; *Wasserer* ELR 2010, 14; this leads to the question whether Art. 12 may be applied; this question was left unanswered by the Austrian OGH 19.1.2012 (2 Ob 210/11p) ecolex 2012, 614 = IPRax 2013/32 due to fact that the same result could be reached by applying Art. 7 point 3.

24   LG Hamburg 8.7.2011 (306 O 349/10) (hull insurance) VersR 2012, 562; see in contrast LG Hanau 9.6. 2011 (4 O 28/09) where the direct action was, however, not brought by the hull insurer but by the insured victim himself.

25   KG Berlin 19.7.2013 (6 U 103/11) VersR 2014, 1020; AG Bergisch Gladbach 2.2.2012 (60 C 241/11) VersR 2012, 1027.

26   *Heiss* VersR 2007, 327, 330 f; see also *Riedmeyer* zfs 2008, 602, 604; LG Dortmund 18.6.2014 (4 S 110/13) EuZW 2014, 680; LG Konstanz 27.8.2010 (2 O 21/09 D; final; see BGH 19.2.2013 (VI ZR 45/12)); this appears to have been overlooked in OLG München 14.3.2008 (10 U 5007/06); see in context OLG Nürnberg 10.4.2012 (3 U 2318/11) r+s 2013, 260.

27   With regard to a policyholder's 'indirect submission' to the same jurisdiction under Art. 13 (3), see *infra* note 15.

28   See *Looschelder* in his commentary on the decision in OLG Köln VersR 2005, 1721, 1723; *Herrmann*, VersR 2007, 1470, 1474 f; *Staudinger*, in *Rauscher* Art. 11 Brüssler I-VO note 6; *Wittwer*, ZVR 2006/142, 406 f; critical of this approach, *Wasserer*, ELR 2008, 143, 145.

which asserts that home jurisdiction for injured parties exists under the Brussels I Regulation.[29]

The ECJ did not tackle the various consequences which arise from its decision: First, by **11** granting home jurisdiction to injured parties, any policyholders and insureds joined to the proceedings (also protected under the section 3) will be **indirectly submitted to the same jurisdiction**, i.e. at the place where the respective injured party is domiciled. This is due to the fact that, pursuant to Art. 14 (1) read together with Art. 13 (3), the insurer can issue a third party notice at that place.[30] Second, the ECJ's decision dealt with a case of **motor vehicle liability insurance** and is tailored to this sector – not least because of the systematic arguments stemming from Recital 16a to the Fourth Motor Insurance Directive.[31] However, as illustrated in note 3 above, in other European countries, a right of direct action exists either for **all types of liability insurance** or for **all types of compulsory insurance**.[32] On the ECJ's construction, home jurisdiction will be granted to an injured party even in such cases.[33] Third, the decision has the *de facto* effect of undermining the **intended effect of Art. 4 (8) of the Fourth Motor Insurance Directive**.[34] According to this provision, jurisdiction at the place of establishment – as determined by Art. 10 in conjunction with point 5 of Art. 7 – is not constituted when a claims representative processes a claim in the country of the injured party's domicile as required by the directives.[35]

The ECJ decision also has significant **practical** consequences.[36] An injured party is namely **12** granted home jurisdiction even in cases where the domicile of the policyholder or insured causing the harm, the liability insurer's domicile and the place at which the accident occurred are all located in one and the same Member State. Under these circumstances, if a claimant domiciled in Austria brings an action based on an accident which occurred abroad, the competent Austrian court at the place of the claimant's domicile will, pursuant to Art. 13 (2) together with Art. 11 (1) (b), almost always have to decide the case on the basis of **foreign liability** and **foreign insurance laws**. Most of the **evidence** will be located in **another country**; foreign and often foreign-language documents, such as police reports, will have to be inspected; and **foreign** and often foreign-language **witnesses** will have to be heard. These problems cannot be overcome by the existence of a few lawyers who are well-versed in foreign laws. Furthermore, citing the reference made to a consumer's jurisdiction as deter-

---

[29] Critical of this line of argumentation on the reference for a preliminary ruling in BGH, VersR 2006, 1677, *Heiss*, VersR 2007, 327; similarly *Wasserer*, ELR 2008, 143, 146; even the historical background of Art. 9 (1) (b) contradicts the reasoning of the ECJ; in this respect, see *Fuchs*, IPRax 2008, 104, 106 and in more detail *Fuchs*, IPRax 2007, 302, 303 f; see also *Wasserer*, ELR 2008, 143, 145; in LG Hamburg NJW-RR 2006, 1655, the court rightly raised the issue of the cited recital's role and made reference to a 'retrospective change of opinion'; from a methodical perspective, see the commentary by *Looschelders* on the decision in OLG Köln VersR 2005, 1721, 1723.

[30] See *Heiss*, VersR 2007, 327, 330; *Fuchs*, IPRax 2008, 104, 107.

[31] [2000] OJ L181/65.

[32] See *Heiss*, VersR 2007, 327, 329 f.

[33] See the criticisms made by *Fuchs*, IPRax 2008, 104, 107.

[34] [2000] OJ L181/65.

[35] See *Heiss*, in: Czernich/Tiefenthaler/Kodek Art. 10 note 9; *Heiss*, VersR 2007, 327, 328; *Fuchs*, IPRax 2008, 104, 106.

[36] See e.g. *Heiss*, HAVE 2009, 72; *Rodriguez*, HAVE 2011, 12.

Helmut Heiss

mined pursuant to the second alternative in Art. 18 (1) as a means of comparison is also not convincing. This is because in most cases the law of the Member State in which the consumer has his habitual residence will also apply in accordance with Art. 6 of the Rome I Regulation;[37] leading in turn to a congruity between international jurisdiction and applicable law.

13 A(nother) *forum actoris* of the injured party is not created by virtue of Art. 7 point 5 even if the insurer provides for a claims representative in the country where the injured party is domiciled.[38] However, frequently the harmful event will occur in the country in which the injured party is domiciled and, therefore, jurisdiction is granted to the courts of this country by virtue of Art. 12 clause one.[39]

14 According to the *Schlosser* Report,[40] an agreement on jurisdiction validly[41] entered into by the parties to the insurance contract (i. e. the insurer and the policyholder) shall not bind the injured party.[42]

3. Third Party Notice for Direct Actions

15 In the event of a direct action being brought, Art. 13 (3) – read together with Art. 14 (1) – provides the insurer with the option of issuing the policyholder with a third party notice. The purpose of this provision is to prevent incompatible decisions from being made by different courts and, as a result, to hinder any fraudulent schemes devised to profit from the vast number of proceedings.[43] Under Art. 13 (3), such third party notice must be issued in the same jurisdiction in which the direct action is brought.[44] Thus, if an action is brought before a court at the place of an injured party's domicile, the insurer can issue a third party notice to the policyholder concerned at that place.[45]

Article 14

1. **Without prejudice to Article 13(3), an insurer may bring proceedings only in the courts of the Member State in which the defendant is domiciled, irrespective of whether he is the policyholder, the insured or a beneficiary.**
2. **The provisions of this Section shall not affect the right to bring a counter-claim in the court in which, in accordance with this Section, the original claim is pending.**

---

[37] [2008] OJ L177/6.

[38] Insurers are obliged to install a claims representative according to Art. 4 (1) of the Fourth Motor Insurance Directive (see fn. 102); see *Heiss*, in: Reichert-Facilides/Schnyder, p. 105, 145 *et seq.*; *Staudinger*, in: Rauscher Art. 11 note 7b.

[39] See Art. 12 note 1 (*Heiss*).

[40] Report *Schlosser* para. 116.

[41] See e.g. the prorogation allowed by Art. 15 (3).

[42] See also Cass. civ. 1, 19 mars 2008, 07–10.216 (unpublished); CA Paris D. 1991 Somm 285 = *Kaye*, Case Law, 434.

[43] See the *Jenard* Report on Art. 10 of the Brussels Convention.

[44] See *supra* note 11.

[45] Aspects of legal policy *supra* note 11.

I. Restricted choice of forum by the insurer

1. Aim and scope of (1)

Art. 14 aims at protecting the defendant policyholder (as well as defendant third party **1** beneficiaries) by restricting the choice of the forum on the side of the insurer. The reference to Art. 6 given by Art. 10 makes clear that this protection is only afforded to policyholders domiciled in a Member State. On the other hand, the domicile of the insurer is irrelevant in the context of Art. 14 (1).[1]

2. Restriction to the forum rei

In principle, the insurer may bring his action only in the courts of the Member State in which **2** the defendant policyholder or defendant third party beneficiary is domiciled.[2] Jurisdiction depends on the domicile of the defendant at the time when the action is filed. This rule corresponds with Art. 4 (1). However, at least two peculiarities of Art. 14 (1) have to be mentioned: Art. 14 (1) is, first of all, mandatory as far as Art. 15 and Art. 16 do not allow deviations to the detriment of the policyholder. Secondly, the insurer cannot avail himself of special jurisdictions, e.g. those granted by Art. 7 and Art. 8.[3]

3. Joint policyholders

If there are two or more policyholders to an insurance contract, the insurer must sue every **3** individual policyholder in the courts of the Member State where he is domiciled even if all defendants are jointly liable for the claim of the insurer (e.g. premiums due[4]).[5] The insurer cannot rely on Art. 8 (1).[6]

If, on the other hand, one policyholder pays the insurer the amount jointly owed by all **4** policyholders, he may sue the other policyholders for reimbursement of an adequate share. Such a claim is not considered a "matter relating to insurance" and, therefore, not subject to Section 3. As a consequence, the policyholder may rely on all *fora* granted by Art. 4, Art. 7 and Art. 8, where applicable. When he is sued by the insurer for payment of the premium, he may also invoke Art. 8 (2) (action on a warranty or guarantee).

---

[1]   Lord *Steyn* in *Jordan Grand Prix Ltd. and others v. Baltic Insurance Group*, [1999] 2 W. L. R. 134 [138] (H. L.).

[2]   See e.g. *Fuentes Camacho*, p. 53.

[3]   Note, however, the exceptions presented *infra* Art. 14 notes 5 *et seq.* (*Heiss*).

[4]   Joint liability of all policyholders for payment of premium is established e.g. by the OGH WBl 1989, 338.

[5]   See the critical analysis by *Blanco-Morales Limones*, in: Calvo Caravaca Art. 11 CB note 9.

[6]   See Lord *Steyn* in *Jordan Grand Prix Ltd., and others v. Baltic Insurance Group*, [1999] 2 W. L. R. 134 [138] (H. L.).

II. Exceptions

1. Counter-claim (Art. 14 (2))

5 If the policyholder sues the insurer and chooses a forum granted by Section 3, there is no reason any more to prevent an insurer from suing on a counter-claim in the same court. This is why Art. 14 (2) provides the insurer with the same forum for its counter-claim.[7]

6 The right to bring a counter-claim under Art. 14 (2) depends upon the fulfilment of the criteria of Art. 8 par 3. Accordingly, the counter-claim of the insurer must arise out of the same contract or facts on which the original claim of the policyholder or third party beneficiary is based.[8] It must also arise between the same parties, because the policy of non-fragmentation of legal proceedings has been trumped in Section 3 by giving primacy to the protection of the insured.[9]

2. Art. 7 point 5

7 Art. 7 point 5 remains applicable also in matters relating to insurance (Section 3) according to Art. 10. Art. 7 point 5 does not only apply to establishments of the insurer but also of the policyholder.[10] It follows, that an insurer may rely on Art. 7 point 5 if the criteria of this provision are fulfilled. One prerequisite is that the defendant policyholder is domiciled in a Member State.[11]

3. Art. 13 (3)

8 Art. 14 (1) also refers to Art. 13 (3) making clear that it does not derogate this provision.[12]

Article 15

The provisions of this Section may be departed from only by an agreement:
(1) which is entered into after the dispute has arisen;
(2) which allows the policyholder, the insured or a beneficiary to bring proceedings in courts other than those indicated in this Section;
(3) which is concluded between a policyholder and an insurer, both of whom are at the time of conclusion of the contract domiciled or habitually resident in the same Member State, and which has the effect of conferring jurisdiction on the courts of that Member State even if the harmful event were to occur abroad, provided that such an agreement is not contrary to the law of that Member State;

---

[7]   As to Art. 14 (2) in comparison with Art. 8 (3) *Blanco-Morales Limones*, in: Calvo Caravaca Art. 11 CB notes 24–26; also *Kropholler/von Hein* Art. 12 note 3.

[8]   In more detail see Art. 8 notes 43–45 (*Muir Watt*).

[9]   *Jordan Grand Prix Ltd. and others v. Baltic Insurance Group* [1999] 2 W. L. R. 134, 140 (H. L., per Lord Steyn).

[10]   *Gaudemet-Tallon* p. 217.

[11]   There is no provision in Section 3 parallel to Art. 11 (2) applying only to third country insurers.

[12]   As to Art. 13 (3) see *supra* Art. 13 note 7 (*Heiss*).

(4) which is concluded with a policyholder who is not domiciled in a Member State, except in so
   far as the insurance is compulsory or relates to immovable property in a Member State;
(5) which relates to a contract of insurance in so far as it covers one or more of the risks set out in
   Article 16.

I. Semi-mandatory Character of Section 3, Art. 15 point 2

1. Agreements to the benefit of the policyholder or third party beneficiary

The basic rule contained in Art. 15 point 2 allows prorogation agreements to the benefit of   **1**
the policyholder and third party beneficiaries, i.e. agreements that allow the policyholder or
the third party beneficiary to bring proceedings in courts other than those indicated in
Section 3. In turn, the choice of forum of the policyholder or the third party beneficiary may
not be restricted and the choice of forum of the insurer may not be broadened by an
agreement on jurisdiction.[1]

2. Agreements violating Art. 15

Agreements on jurisdiction which are contrary to Art. 15 are void according to Art. 25 (5).[2]   **2**

3. The impact of Art. 45 (1) (e) i) and Art. 46 (1) i.c.w. Art. 45 (1) (e) i)

If a court of a Member State assumes jurisdiction based on an invalid agreement on juris-   **3**
diction, a judgment of this court will not be recognised (Art. 45 (1) lit. e)i)) and enforced
(Art. 46 i.c.w. Art. 45 (1) lit. e)i) in other Member States.[3] This will only apply if the

---

[1] See also *Gaudemet-Tallon*, p. 220 talking about a "principe d'interdiction des prorogations de compe-
    tences".
[2] Art. 25 (5) reads: "… shall have no legal force …"; see BGE 124 III 436, 441 and 443.
[3] See e.g. BGHZ 74, 248; see also Aud. Prov. Madrid núm. 26/2001 (Sección 12ª) of 22 January 2001;
    Fuentes Camacho, Los contratos de seguro y el derecho intenacional privado en la Unión Europea (1999),
    p. 45.

defendant is a person protected by Section 3 (policyholder, insured, beneficiary or third party victim) but not when the defendant is an insurer (see Art. 45 (1) lit. 3)i)). Thereby, the protection of the policyholder and third party beneficiaries is further improved. However, this rule only applies if the policyholder has contested jurisdiction of the incompetent court. Otherwise the court shall have jurisdiction in accordance with Art. 26.[4]

4. Art. 7 point 5 as an exception?

4 Art. 10 reserves the applicability of Art. 7 point 5 also in matters relating to insurance. In general, Art. 7 point 5 may be derogated by an agreement on jurisdiction. From a systematic point of view this should also be the case in matters relating to insurance. Art. 10 does not incorporate Art. 7 point 5 into Section 3, which would make the provision mandatory. Instead, Art. 10 only preserves the applicability of Art. 7 point 5 to matters relating to insurance. As a result, Art. 7 point 5 should be non-mandatory even in matters relating to insurance. However, this result is contrary to the purpose of Section 3. It is probably also not in line with what the intention of the legislator was. The reference to Art. 7 point 5 was introduced to replace former Art. 8 (2) Brussels Convention of 1968 which granted jurisdiction to the courts at the place where the insurance intermediary had its domicile. Probably the legislator did not realise that a mandatory rule was replaced by a non-mandatory rule. Since the matter requires clarification, courts dealing with it should refer the case to the ECJ for a preliminary ruling.

5. Arbitration

5 Art. 1 (2) (d) makes clear that the Regulation does not apply to arbitration. This also applies to matters relating to insurance. As a consequence, parties to an insurance contract can opt out of the regime of the Regulation by an arbitration agreement.[5]

6 Arbitration as mentioned in Art. 1 (2) (d) only covers private procedures that lead to a decision in law. In my view, an agreement calling for experts to decide on certain matters of fact which are prejudicial to a claim of an insured[6] (such as the degree of invalidity of the insured in accident insurance) do not constitute arbitration procedures within the meaning of Art. 1 (2) (d).[7] This should hold true even if the court should be bound by the findings of the experts. The court, competent under Section 3, would retain jurisdiction over these issues and determine by the law applicable whether it is bound by the findings of the experts.

---

4 *Česká podnikatelská pojišťovna as, Vienna Insurance Group v. Michal Bilas*, (Case C-111/09) [2010] ECR I-4545; as to this decision see *Csach*, p. 57–60; *Idot* Europe 2010 Juillet Comm. n° 261 p. 35; *Leandro*, Guida al Diritto 2010 n° 23 p. 100–102; *Mankowski*, Recht der internationalen Wirtschaft 2010 p. 667–672; *Marino*, Rivista di diritto internazionale privato e processuale 2010 p. 915–924; *Michailidou* Efarmoges Astikou Dikaiou 2010 p. 1009–1010; *Sperlich/Wolf*, Versicherungsrecht (2010) p. 1101–1102.

5 See also *Collins*, in: Dicey/Morris/Collins para. 11–350; *Seatzu*, p. 57; an arbitration clause may, however, be abusive and thereby void: see *Elisa María Mostaza Claw v. Centro Móvíl Milenium SL*, (Case C-168/05) [2006] ECR I-10421.

6 See e.g. § 64 Austrian VersVG (Insurance Contract Act); § 84 German VVG (Insurance Contract Act).

7 Apparently another view is taken in *News Hampshire Insurance Co. and others v. Strabag Bau AG and others*, [1992] 1 Lloyd's Rep. 361 [C. A.].

II. Limited party autonomy

1. Special and large risks (Art. 15 point 5)

No protection of the policyholder is needed in branches of insurance in which policyholders **7** usually appear to be economically as well as professionally strong.[8] This is the case with insurances taken by policyholders for special or large risks as listed in Art. 16. This is why in these cases Art. 15 point 5 grants full party autonomy to the parties.[9]

2. Ex post agreements on jurisdiction (Art. 15 point 1)

Agreements on jurisdiction which are detrimental to the policyholder are valid as long as **8** they are concluded after the dispute has arisen.[10] The legislator assumes that the policyholder knows about the risks of agreements on jurisdiction once the dispute has arisen. As a result, he will be hesitant to conclude such an agreement. The need to protect the policyholder lapses once matters have come that far.[11]

3. Third country policyholders (Art. 15 point 4)

Even though policyholders domiciled in a third country are in need of protection, they are **9** not granted such protection under Section 3. Therefore, insurers may freely conclude agreements on jurisdiction with third country policyholders.

There are, however, two exceptions to this rule.[12] The first one relates to the insurance of **10** immovable property situated in a Member State, while the second one concerns mandatory insurance imposed on the third country policyholder by the law of a Member State. In these two cases an agreement on jurisdiction concluded with a third country policyholder may not depart from the provisions of Section 3. This restriction can only be of relevance to clauses applying to actions of the third country policyholder brought against an insurer domiciled or established (Art. 11 (2)) in a Member State. An agreement on jurisdiction for actions brought against the third country policyholder would not depart from Section 3, because its provisions, i. p. Art. 14, do not apply in such a situation. The same is true if the prorogation agreement applies to actions brought by a third country policyholder against a third country insurer who is neither domiciled nor established (Art. 11 (2)) in a Member State.

4. Derogation of Art. 12 and Art. 13 (1) (Art. 15 point 3)

Finally, parties may derogate Art. 12 and Art. 13 (1) by an agreement on jurisdiction. Such **11** agreement is permitted by Art. 15 point 3 if three conditions are met. Firstly, the insurer and the policyholder must be domiciled or habitually resident in the same Member State. Secondly, the law of that Member State must permit the prorogation agreement. Thirdly, the agreement must confer jurisdiction on the courts of that State.

---

[8]   See *Tradigrain SA v. SIAT SpA and others*, [2002] 2 Lloyd's Rep. 553 para. 4.

[9]   Critical as to the legislative approach *Hub* p. 175.

[10]   See Art. 15 (1).

[11]   As to Art. 15 (1) see *Fricke*, VersR 1997, 399, 403.

[12]   Critical as to these exceptions *Hub*, p. 167 *et seq.*

III. Validity and effects of an agreement on jurisdiction

1. Formation of the agreement on jurisdiction

12 Section 3 does not provide any rules governing the formation of an agreement on jurisdiction. It also does not directly refer to Art. 25. Nevertheless, there can be no doubt that Art. 25 also applies in matters relating to insurance.[13] Further more, Art. 25 (4) directly refers to Art. 15 indicating that an agreement on jurisdiction in matters relating to insurance is governed by Art. 25.[14] Thereby, parties are protected by the requirements as to consensus and form in Art. 25.[15]

2. Parties affected by an agreement on jurisdiction

a) Policyholder, insured and beneficiary

13 A valid agreement on jurisdiction is binding upon the insurer and the policyholder. The ECJ has held that a valid agreement also has an effect on the insured or the beneficiary, at least in their own favour.[16]

14 It is subject to dispute, whether an agreement on jurisdiction validly entered into under Art. 15 may also be detrimental to the third party beneficiary. In general, agreements to the detriment of third parties have no effect on them. A detrimental effect of an agreement on jurisdiction arises whenever the defendant third party is subjected to other jurisdictions than those provided for by the Regulation. Therefore, such agreements do not bind the third party. To the contrary, it is at least doubtful whether an agreement on jurisdiction is detrimental to a plaintiff third party if it restricts access to the courts that hold international jurisdiction under the Regulation.[17] The right, on which the claim of the plaintiff third party beneficiary is based, was created by the parties to the contract. It is commonly held in substantive insurance law that the insurer and the policyholder are free to limit the right of the beneficiary or to burden the third party beneficiary with warranties.[18] It is held in international insurance contract law that a choice of law clause agreed upon by the insurer and the policyholder is binding on the third party beneficiary.[19] Finally, an arbitration clause binds the beneficiary of a contract.[20] As a consequence, an agreement on jurisdiction should

---

[13]   *Gerling and Others v. Amministrazione del Tesore dello Stato*, (Case 201/82) [1983] ECR 2503, 2516 para. 17; *Tradigrain SA v. SIAT SpA and others* [2002] EWHC 106 (Comm), [2002] 2 Lloyd's Rep. 553 [in no. 34]; see also *Collins*, in: Dicey/Morris/Collins para. 11–350 (formal requirements); *Blanco-Morales Limones*, in: Calvo Caravaca Art. 12 CB note 13; *Fuentes Camacho*, p. 60; *Gaudemet-Tallon*, p. 220; *Kaye*, p. 817; *Seatzu*, p. 55.

[14]   See also BGE 124 III 436, 441 and 443.

[15]   See Cass. Bull. Arr. 1997 IV no. 66: an agreement on jurisdiction lacking the form prescribed by Art. 17 Brussels Convention (now Art. 25 of the Regulation) was held invalid.

[16]   *Gerling and Others v. Amministrazione del Tesore dello Stato*, (Case 201/82) [1983] ECR 2503; see also *Hübner*, IPRax 1984, 237.

[17]   With a view to the Brussels and the Lugano Convention see e.g. CA Aix-en-Provence IPRax 1996, 427 with note *Mankowski*; *Kropholler/von Hein* Art. 23 note 65; in more detail *Heiss*, in: Reichert-Facilides/ Schnyder, p. 105, 142.

[18]   See *Heiss*, IPRax 2005, 497.

[19]   See *Heiss*, IPRax 2005, 497.

equally bind the third party beneficiary.[21] However, the agreement on jurisdiction must be entered, at the latest, together with the insurance contract granting rights to the third party beneficiary. An ex post agreement[22] would infringe an already vested right of the third party.

However, the Regulation has granted the third party beneficiary his own *forum actoris* in **15** Art. 11 (1) (b) and made this forum mandatory for mass risk insurances.[23] Therefore, as far as the *forum actoris* under Art. 11 (1) (b) is concerned, an agreement on jurisdiction concluded between the insurer and the policyholder (and, by the same token, an agreement on jurisdiction concluded by the insurer and the third party) cannot bind the third party beneficiary. The only exception is the insurance of large and special risks, where party autonomy is granted by Art. 15 point 5 in connection with Art. 16.

Within mass risk insurances the remaining party autonomy is described by Art. 15 point 3 **16** and 4. These provisions create a problem because they mention only the policyholder and remain silent as to the third party beneficiary. Following a recent ruling of the ECJ,[24] the provisions may be applied to the third party if it fulfils the relevant criteria. In such case, the policyholder may agree on jurisdiction with the insurer and thereby bind the third party within the limits of Art. 15 point 3 and 4. As far as Art. 15 point 3 is concerned, the third party must have his domicile or habitual residence in the same Member State as the insurer when the insurance contract is formed. As far as Art. 15 point 4 is concerned, the third party must have his domicile in a third country.

b) Injured party

It is commonly held, that the *fora* granted for a direct action of an injured party under Art. 13 **17** (2) may not be derogated by an agreement on jurisdiction between the insurer and the policyholder (e.g. an agreement in accordance with Art. 15 point 3).[25] An agreement on jurisdiction restricting the choices offered by the Regulation is held to be a contract to the detriment of a third party, i.e. the injured party. An agreement on jurisdiction would, therefore, require the consent of the injured party. Indeed, there are cases where it may be possible to obtain such consent. D & O; liability insurances are commonly concluded by companies in favour of their Directors and Officers. The company taking out the insurance will also be the (or at least: one) injured party. Thus, it would be possible for the insurer to obtain consent of the injured party in D & O; insurance.

---

[20]   See *Heiss*, IPRax 2005, 497.

[21]   See CA Aix-en-Provence IPRax 1996, 427 with note *Mankowski*; *Kropholler/von Hein* Art. 23 note 65; in more detail *Heiss*, in: Reichert-Facilides/Schnyder, p. 105, 142.

[22]   See Art. 15 (1).

[23]   See Art. 15 (2) which does not allow restrictions of Art. 11 (1) (b).

[24]   *Société financière et industrielle du Peloux v. Axa Belgium et al.*, (Case C-112/03) [2005] ECR I-3707 = IPRax 2005, 531; see note of *Heiss*, IPRax 2005, 497.

[25]   Report *Schlosser* para. 116; *Kropholler/von Hein* Art. 13 note 4; CA Paris D. 1991 Somm. 285 = *Kaye*, Case Law, p. 434.

Article 16

The following are the risks referred to in point 5 of Article 15:

(1) any loss of or damage to:
    (a) seagoing ships, installations situated offshore or on the high seas, or aircraft, arising from perils which relate to their use for commercial purposes;
    (b) goods in transit other than passengers' baggage where the transit consists of or includes carriage by such ships or aircraft;

(2) any liability, other than for bodily injury to passengers or loss of or damage to their baggage:
    (a) arising out of the use or operation of ships, installations or aircraft as referred to in point 1 (a) in so far as, in respect of the latter, the law of the Member State in which such aircraft are registered does not prohibit agreements on jurisdiction regarding insurance of such risks;
    (b) for loss or damage caused by goods in transit as described in point 1(b);

(3) any financial loss connected with the use or operation of ships, installations or aircraft as referred to in point 1(a), in particular loss of freight or charter-hire;

(4) any risk or interest connected with any of those referred to in points 1 to 3;

(5) notwithstanding points 1 to 4, all 'large risks' as defined in Directive 2009/138/EC of the European Parliament and of the Council of 25 November 2009 on the taking-up and pursuit of the business of Insurance and Reinsurance (Solvency II).[*]

I. Special risks

1   Art. 16 point 1–4 relate to marine and aviation insurance.[1] The list of risks given by Art. 16 point 1–4 partly overlaps with Art. 16 point 5 in connection with Art. 13 point 27 Directive 2009/138/EC (Solvency II).[2] The exemptions were introduced to serve the needs of the English insurance market.[3]

2   Art. 16 point 1 relates to casco insurances of seagoing ships and installations as well as aircrafts which are commercially used. It also relates to transport insurance of goods in transit (other than luggage of passengers) carried by such ship or aircraft.

3   Art. 16 point 2 relates to liability insurance. Such liability may, first of all, arise out of the use or operation of ships, installations or aircrafts mentioned in Art. 16 point 1. As far as liability arising out of the use or operation of an aircraft is concerned, the Member State, in which the aircraft is registered, may prohibit agreements on jurisdiction.[4] Secondly, liability may arise out of loss caused by the goods in transit.[5]

4   Art. 16 point 3 refers to any financial loss arising out of the use or operation of ships,

---

[*]   OJ L 335, 17.12.2009, p. 1.
[1]   As to problems of delimitation see Report *Schlosser*, para. 144; *Kropholler/von Hein* Art. 13 note 9; *Geimer/Schütze* Art. 14 note 3; see also *Carbone*, Lo spazio giudiziario europeo (3ʳᵈ ed. 2000) p. 112 *et seq.*
[2]   See *infra* Art. 14 notes 6 *et seq.* (*Heiss*).
[3]   In more detail *Collins*, in: Dicey/Morris/Collins para. 11–336; see also *Kropholler/von Hein* Art. 13 note 9.
[4]   Art. 16 (2) (a).
[5]   Art. 16 (2) (b).

installations or aircrafts. Art. 16 point 3 mentions loss of freight and loss of charter-hire as examples.

Art. 16 point 4 grants party autonomy to the insurance of any other risk connected with any **5**
of the risks mentioned in Art. 16 point 1–3. Even though such connected risks must not be covered within the same policy[6] there must be some link to the risks mentioned in Art. 16 point 1–3.[7]

II. Large risks

Like its predecessor, Art. 14 point 5 Regulation 44/2001, Art. 16 point 5[8] aims at bringing the **6**
scope of party autonomy for large risks in international procedural law in line with Directives' law on insurance by referring to Art. 13 point 27 (definition of "large risk") and Part A
of Annex I (classes of insurance) Directive 2009/138/EC of the European Parliament and of
the Council of 25 November 2009 on the taking-up and pursuit of the business of Insurance
and Reinsurance (Solvency II)[9] in order to define "large risks".[10] Art. 13 point 27 Directive
2009/138/EC follows in substance the former definition of "large risks" as provided by
Directive 73/239/EEC, as amended by Directives 88/357/EEC and 90/618/EEC.

The relevant provisions in the Directives' law as referred to by Art. 16 point 5 read as follows: **7**

Art. 13 (27) Directive 2009/138/EC (Solvency II) [Excerpt]:

(27) 'large risks' means:
  (a) risks classified under classes 4, 5, 6, 7, 11 and 12 in Part A of Annex I;
  (b) risks classified under classes 14 and 15 in Part A of Annex I, where the policy holder is engaged
      professionally in an industrial or commercial activity or in one of the liberal professions and
      the risks relate to such activity;
  (c) risks classified under classes 3, 8, 9, 10, 13 and 16 in Part A of Annex I in so far as the policy
      holder exceeds the limits of at least two of the following criteria:
      (i) a balance-sheet total of EUR 6,2 million;
      (ii) a net turnover, within the meaning of Fourth Council Directive 78/660/EEC of 25 July 1978
           based on Article 54(3)(g) of the Treaty on the annual accounts of certain types of com-
           panies of EUR 12,8 million;
      (iii)an average number of 250 employees during the financial year.

---

6   *Blanco-Morales Limones*, in: Calvo Caravaca Art. 12bis CB note 22.
7   See, however, *Charman and another v. WOC Offshore BV* [1993] 2 Lloyd's Rep. 551 (C. A., per *Staughton*
    L. J.); the judgment of *Staughton* L. J., is quoted in *Tradigrain SA v. SIAT SpA and others*, [2002] 2 Lloyd's
    Rep. 553 para. 41 (Q. B. D., *Colman* J.); a critical analysis is given by *Heiss*, in: Reichert-Facilides/
    Schnyder, p. 127; see also *Minister of Agriculture, Food and Forestry v. Alte Leipziger Versicherung AG*,
    [2000] 4 I. R. 32 (S. C.).
8   An overview of the changes is given by *Fricke*, VersR 1999, 1055, 1059.
9   OJ 2009 no L 335/1.
10 As to this change see also *Sánchez Lorenzo*, in: Borrás (ed.), Cooperación Jurídica Internacional en
    Materia Civil: El Convenio de Bruselas (2001), p. 201, 205; critically as to the reference to Directives
    law in the regulation *Gaudemet-Tallon* p. 224.

If the policy holder belongs to a group of undertakings for which consolidated accounts within the meaning of Directive 83/349/EEC are drawn up, the criteria set out in point (c) of the first subpara-graph shall be applied on the basis of the consolidated accounts.

Member States may add to the category referred to in point (c) of the first subparagraph the risks insured by professional associations, joint ventures or temporary groupings;

Point A of the Annex to the First Non-Life Directive [Excerpt]:

"A. Classification of risks according to classes of insurance
1. [...]
2. [...]
3. *Land vehicles* (other than railway rolling stock)
   All damage to or loss of
   - land motor vehicles,
   - land vehicles other than motor vehicles,
4. *Railway rolling stock*
   All damage to or loss of railway rolling stock.
5. *Aircraft*
   All damage to or loss of aircraft.
6. *Ships (sea, lake and river and canal vessels)*
   All damage to or loss of
   - river and canal vessels,
   - lake vessels,
   - sea vessels,
7. *Goods in transit* (including merchandise, baggage, and all other goods)
   All damage to or loss of goods in transit or baggage, irrespective of the form of transport.
8. *Fire and natural forces*
   All damage to or loss of property (other than property included in classes 3, 4, 5, 6 and 7) due to
   - fire,
   - explosion,
   - storm,
   - natural forces other than storm,
   - nuclear energy,
   - land subsidence,
9. *Other damage to property*
   All damage to or loss of property (other than property included in classes 3, 4, 5, 6 and 7) due to hail or frost, and any event such as theft, other than that included in class 8.
10. *Motor vehicle liability*
    All liability arising out of the use of motor vehicles operating on the land (including carrier's liability).
11. *Aircraft liability*
    All liability arising out of the use of aircraft (including carrier's liability).
12. *Liability for ships (sea, lake and river and canal vessels)*
    All liability arising out of the use of ships, vessels or boats on the sea, lakes, rivers or canals (including carrier's liability).

13. General liability
All liability other than those referred to in classes 10, 11 and 12.
14. Credit
 – insolvency (general),
 – export credit,
 – instalment credit,
 – mortgages,
 – agricultural credit,
15. Suretyship
 – suretyship (direct),
 – suretyship (indirect),
16. Miscellaneous financial loss
 – employment risks,
 – insufficiency of income (general),
 – bad weather,
 – loss of benefits,
 – continuing general expenses,
 – unforeseen trading expenses,
 – loss of market value,
 – loss of rent or revenue,
 – other indirect trading loss,
 – other non-trading financial loss,
 – other forms of financial loss,
17. [...]
18. [...]"

Section 4: **Jurisdiction over consumer contracts**

Bibliography

van den Aardberg, De gerichte activiteit van artikel 15 lid 1, onderdeel c, Brussel I: meer duidelijkheid door Luxemburgse gezichtspunkten, NIPR 2011, 473
Álvarez Armas/Dechamps, Arrêt Pammer et Hotel Alpenhof: L'équilibre entre consommateurs et professionales dans l'e-commerce, Rev. eur. dr. consomm. 2011, 447
Añoveros, Restriction on Jurisdiction Clauses in Consumer Contracts within the European Union, Rev. eur. dr. consomm. 2004, 77
Stefan Arnold, Zur Reichweite des verfahrensrechtlichen Verbraucherschutzes und zur Qualifikation der Ansprüche aus culpa in contrahendo und § 823 Abs. 2 BGB i.V.m. § 32 KWG, IPRax 2013, 141
Stefan Arnold, Kollisionsrechtliche und internatio-

nal-verfahrensrechtliche Aspekte bei Schadensersatzansprüchen privater Auslandsfonds-Anleger, IPRax 2013, 525
Awnrumpa Waiyamuk, La protection du consommateur en droit privé européen (thèse Paris 2 – Panthéon-Assas 2013)
Bariatti, Le azioni collettive dell'art. 140-bis del Codice del Consumo: Aspetti di diritto internazionale privato e processuale, RDIPP 2011, 19
Barta, Der Gerichtsstand für Klagen gegen Anleger als Gesellschafter von Fondsgesellschaften, NJOZ 2011, 1033
Batalla Trilla, El concepto de actividades dirigadas en el R. 44/2011 (2002)
Benicke, Internationale Zuständigkeit deutscher

Gerichte nach Art. 13, 14 EuGVÜ für Schadensersatzklagen geschädigter Anleger, WM 1997, 945

Boele-Woelki, Internet und IPR: Wo geht jemand ins Netz?, BerDGesVR 39 (2000), 307

Bogdan, Website Accessibility as a Basis for Jurisdiction under Art. 15 (1) (c) of Brussels I Regulation: Case Note on the ECJ Judgments Pammer and Alpenhof, Yb. PIL 12 (2010), 565

Borges, Die AGB-Klauselrichtlinie und der deutsche Zivilprozess, RIW 2000, 933

de Bra, Verbraucherschutz durch Gerichtsstandsregelungen im deutschen und europäischen Zivilprozessrecht (1992)

Brkan, Arrêt Mühlleitner: vers une protection renforcée des consommateurs dans l'UE, Rev. eur. dr. consomm. 2013, 113

Neil Brown, Law Jurisdiction and the Digital Nomad, CRi 2015, 38

Brugnara/Reinalter, La sentenza Emrek: verso l'assolutezza del foro speciale del consumatore, Giur. it. 2014, 578

Benedikt Buchner, E-Commerce und effektiver Rechtsschutz – oder: Wer folgt wem wohin?, EWS 2000, 147

Cachia, Consumer contracts in European private international law: The sphere of application of the consumer contract rules in the Brussels I and Rome I Regulations, (2009) 34 Eur. L. Rev. 476

Calais-Auloy, La communauté européenne et les consommateurs, in: Mélanges offerts à André Colomer (1993), p. 119

Caprioli, Règlement des litiges internationaux et droit applicable dans le commerce électronique (2002)

Castellaneta, Il risarcimento del danno per un pacchetto di viaggio va richiesto davanti al giudice dove risiede al turista, Guida 2013 n. 40/50 p. 83

de Clavière, Confirmation de la protection du consommateur actif par les règles de compétence spéciales issues du règlement 44/2001, RLDA 77 (2013), 48

de Clavière, De l'interprétation de la condition de direction de l'activité au sens de l'article 15, paragraphe 1, sous c), du règlement n° 44/2001/CE et de la notion de volonté, RLDA 89 (2014), 53

Castellaños Ruiz, El concepto de activida profesional "dirigada" al Estado miembro del consumidor: stream-of-commerce, CDT 4 (2) (2012), 70

Danov, The Brussels I Regulation: Cross-Border Collective Redress Proceedings and Judgments, (2010) 6 JPrIL 359

Debusseré, International Jurisdiction over Consumer Contracts in the European Union: *Quid Novi sub Sole?*, (2002) 10 Int. J. L. & Info. Tech. 344

Deumier, La protection des consommateurs dans les relations internationales, Rev contrats 2010, 273

de la Durantaye/Garber, Zum Erfordernis der Kausalität zwischen ausgerichteter Tätigkeit und konkretem Vertragsschluss, jusIT 2011, 203

Esteban de la Rosa, El pale del nexo de causalidad en el sistema europeo de competencia internacional de los contratos de consumo: ¿una condición para el olvido?, La Ley UE n° 11, 2014, p. 5

Esteban de la Rosa, Relación de causalidad entre la actividad comercial o profesional en las ventas transfronterizas, AEDIPr 2013, 1031

Farah, Allocation of Jurisdiction and the Internet in EU Law, (2008) 33 Eur. L. Rev. 257

Foss/Bygrave, International Consumer Purchases through the Internet: Jurisdictional Issues pursuant to European Law, (2000) 8 Int. J. L. & Info. Tech. 99

Frei, Der Abschluss von Konsumentenverträgen im Internet (Zürich 2001)

Mario Frick, Chancen und Risiken eines Beitritts Liechtensteins zum Lugano-Übereinkommen – Kritik an dem Konsumentengerichtsstand, ZvglRWiss 111 (2012), 442

Ganssauge, Internationale Zuständigkeit und anwendbares Recht bei Verbraucherverträgen im Internet (2004)

Garber, Gerichtspflicht infolge Internetpräsenz bei Streitigkeiten aus Verträgen zwischen Verbrauchern und Unternehmern im Anwendungsbereich der EuGVVO, jusIT 2011, 82 and 125

Geimer, Forum actoris für Kapitalanlegerklagen, in: FS Dieter Martiny (2014) 711

Gillies, Electronic Commerce and International Private Law – A Study of Electronic Consumer Contracts (2008)

Gillies, Clarifying the "Philosophy of Article 15" in the Brussels I Regulation, (2011) 60 ICLQ 557

Gottenberg, Internet et la protection du consommateur dans la résolution des litiges contractuels, Rev. dr. UE 2002, 513

Grušić, Submission and Protective Jurisdiction under the Brussels I Regulation, (2011) 48 C.M.L.Rev. 947

Gsell, Entwicklungen im Europäischen Verbraucherzuständigkeitsrecht, ZZP 127 (2014) 431

Heiderhoff, Zum Verbraucherbegriff der EuGVVO und des LugÜ, IPRax 2005, 320

Heiderhoff, Nationaler Verbrauchergerichtsstand nach der Brüssel I-VO?, IPRax 2006, 612

von Hein, Kapitalanlegerschutz im Verbrauchergerichtsstand zwischen Fernabsatz und konventionellem Vertrieb: Zur Konkretisierung der "Ausrichtung" in Art. 15 Abs. 1 lit. c EuGVO, IPRax 2006, 16

von Hein, Finanzkrise und Internationales Privatrecht, BerDGfIR 45 (2011), 369

Jonathan Hill, Cross-Border Consumer Contracts (2008)

van Hoek, CJEU Pammer and Hotel Alpenhof, ERCL 2012, 93

van Husen, Gerichtsstand in Verbraucherangelegenheiten im Österreichischen und Europäischen Zivilprozessrecht (Diss. Wien 2009)

di Iorio, Latest Developments in ECS Case Law on Jurisdiction Concerning Consumer Matters, Yb. PIL 15 (2013/14), 529

Jeandin, Banques suisses, droit élu et for prorogé, in: FS Ivo Schwander (St. Gallen 2011), p. 711

Kaufmann-Kohler, Choice of Court and Choice of Law Clauses in Electronic Contracts, in: Jeanneret (ed.), Aspects juridiques du commerce électronique (2001), p. 11

Keiler/Kathrin Binder, Reisen nach Brüssel, Rom und Luxemburg, RRa 2009, 210

Keiler/Kathrin Binder, Der EuGH lässt ausrichten: kein Zusammenhang von Ursache und Wirkung beim Verbrauchergerichtsstand, euvr 2013, 230

Kieninger, Grenzenloser Verbraucherschutz?, in: FS Ulrich Magnus (2014), p. 449

Kleinknecht, Die verbraucherschützenden Gerichtsstände im deutschen und europäischen Zivilprozessrecht, 2007

Klöpfer/Ramić, Der Europäische Vollstreckungstitel in C2C-Streitigkeiten, GPR 2014, 107

David Kluth, Die Grenzen des kollisionsrechtlichen Verbraucherschutzes (2009)

Harald Koch, Internationale Zuständigkeit und Auslandsbezug, RRa 2013, 173

Harald Koch, Kollisionsrecht und Auslandsbezug: Wie international ist das IPR?, in: FS Ulrich Magnus (2014), p. 475

Christian Koller/Slonina/Steinhardt, Kein Ausrichten von Finanzdienstleistungen auf künftigen Verbraucherwohnsitzstaat, ecolex 2013, 534

Lagarde, Heurs et malheurs de la protection internationale du consommateur dans l'Union européenne, in: Études en l'honneur de Jacques Ghestin (2001), p. 511

Dirk Langer, Vertragsanbahnung und Vertragsschluss im Internet, Forum Int. 1999, 1

Leandro, Trasporti marittimi: nella formula tutto compreso non basta un sito per dirigere l'attività all'estero, Guida dir 2011 n° 2 S 111

Leible, Gerichtsstandsklauseln und EG-Klauselrichtlinie, RIW 2001, 422

Leible/Michael Müller, Die Bedeutung von Websites für die internationale Zuständigkeit in Verbrauchersachen, NJW 2011, 495

Loacker, Der Vebrrauchervertrag im internationalen Privatrecht (2006)

Loacker, Verbraucherverträge mit gemischter Zwecksetzung, JZ 2013, 234

de Lousanoff, Die Anwendung des EuGVÜ in Verbrauchersachen mit Drittstaatenbezug, in: FS Peter Arens (1993) 251

Lubrich, Anmerkung zu EuGH, Urt. v. 17.10.2013, Rs. C-218/12 Emrek/Sabranovic, GPR 2014, 116

Manara, Vendre en ligne dans un pays étranger sans y être poursuivi, D. 2011, 5

Mankowski, Zur Auslegung des Art. 13 EuGVÜ, RIW 1997, 990

Mankowski, Das Internet im Internationalen Vertrags- und Deliktsrecht, RabelsZ 63 (1999), 203

Mankowski, e-commerce und Internationales Verbraucherschutzrecht, Beilage zu MMR 7/2000, 22

Mankowski, Keine örtliche Ersatzzuständigkeit der Hauptstadtgerichte für Verbrauchersachen unter dem EuGVÜ – oder: Tod einer Theorie in Berlin: IPRax 2001, 33

Mankowski, Gerichtsstand der rügelosen Einlassung in europäischen Verbrauchersachen?, IPRax 2001, 310

Mankowski, Internationales Verbraucherschutzrecht und Internet, in Studiengesellschaft für Wirtschaft und Recht (ed.), Internet und Recht (Wien 2002), p. 191

Mankowski, Jurisdiction and Enforcement in the

Information Society, in: Ruth Nielsen/Sandford Jacobsen/Trzaskowski (eds.), EU Electronic Commerce Law (København 2004), p. 125

Mankowski, Deutsches Recht im türkischen Basar? – Oder: Grundsatzfragen des internationalen Verbraucherschutzes in der Bewährung am konkreten Fall, in: FS Tuğrul Ansay (Alphen aan den Rijn 2006) 189

Mankowski, Zum Begriff des "Ausrichtens" auf den Wohnsitzstaat des Verbrauchers unter Art. 15 Abs. 1 lit. c EuGVVO, VuR 2006, 289

Mankowski, Entwicklung und Stand des europäischen Internationalen Verbraucherschutzrechts, in: Alice Wagner/Wedl (eds.), Bilanz und Perspektiven zum europäischen Recht (Wien 2007), p. 325

Mankowski, Muss zwischen ausgerichteter Tätigkeit und konkretem Vertrag bei Art. 15 Abs. 1 lit. c EuGVVO ein Zusammenhang bestehen?, IPRax 2008, 333

Mankowski, Consumer Contracts under Art. 8 of the Rome I Regulation, in: Eleanor Cashin Ritaine/Andrea Bonomi (eds.), Le nouveau règlement européen "Rome I" relatif à la loi applicable aux obligations contractuelles (Zürich 2008), p. 121

Mankowski, Neues zum "Ausrichten" unternehmerischer Tätigkeit unter Art. 15 Abs. 1 lit. c EuGVVO, IPRax 2009, 238

Mankowski, Die Darlegungs- und Beweislast für die Tatbestände des Internationalen Verbraucherprozess- und Verbrauchervertragsrechts, IPRax 2009, 474

Mankowski, Besteht der Gerichtsstand der rügelosen Einlassung auch gegen von Schutzregimes besonders geschützte Personen?, RIW 2010, 667

Mankowski, Pauschalreisen und europäisches Internationales Verbraucherschutzrecht, TranspR 2011, 70

Mankowski, EuGVVO/revLugÜ und CISG im Zusammenspiel – insbesondere beim Erfüllungsortsgerichtsstand, in: FS Ingeborg Schwenzer (2011), p. 1175

Mankowski, Autoritatives zum "Ausrichten" unternehmerischer Tätigkeit unter Art. 15 Abs. 1 lit. c EuGVVO, IPRax 2012, 144

Mankowski, Änderungen im Internationalen Verbraucherprozessrecht durch die Neufassung der EuGVVO, RIW 2014, 625

Mankowski, Internationales Versicherungsprozessrecht: Professioneller Leasinggeber als Geschädigter und Typisierung statt konkreter Prüfung der Schutzbedürftigkeit, IPRax 2015, 115

Marenghi, Contratti conclusi da consumatori e giurisdizione nell'applicazione del regolamento "Bruxelles I": il caso Emrek, Dir. comm. int. 2014, 214

Marino, I contratti di consumo online e la competenza giurisdizionale in ambito comunitario, Contratto e impresa/Europa 2011, 247

Markus, Die Konsumentenzuständigkeiten der EuGVO und des revidierten LugÜ, insbesondere im E-Commerce, ZZZ 2004, 181

Matias Fernandes, O conceito de "Actividade dirigida" inscrito no Artigo 15°, número 1, alínea c), du Regulamento "Bruxelas I" e a Internet: Subsídios do Tribunal da Justiça por ocasião do acórdão Pammer/Alpenhof, CDT 4 (1) (2012), 302

De Meyer, International jurisdiction and conflict of law rules for consumer claims: a survey of European legislation, Rev. eur. dr. consomm. 2009, 631

Mronz, Rechtsverfolgung im weltweiten E-Commerce (2004)

Nuyts, Compétence internationale et litiges en matière de consommation, J. trib. 2012, 844

Øren, International Jurisdiction over Consumer Contracts in E-Europe, (2003) 52 ICLQ 665

Ortiz Vidal, Contratos electrónicos internacionales B2C y proteccion del pequeño empresario, CDT 6 (1) (2014), 387

Paredes Pérez, Contrato de viaje celebrado entre un consumidor domiciliado en un Estado Membro y una ganecia de viajes domiciliada en otro Estado Membro, AEDIPr 2013, 1039

Pesce, La tutela del cd. Contraenti debli nel nuovo regolamento UE n. 1215/2012 (Bruxelles I*bis*), Dir. comm. int. 2014, 579

Pfeiffer, Gerichtsstandsklauseln und EG-Klauselrichtlinie, in: FS Rolf A. Schütze zum 65. Geb. (1999), p. 671

Pfeiffer, Die Unwirksamkeit von Gerichtsstandsklauseln nach der Klauselrichtlinie, ZEuP 2003, 141

Pichler, Internationale Zuständigkeit im Zeitalter globaler Vernetzung (2008)

Pironon, Les nouveaux défis du droit international privé: site actif, site passif, activitée dirigée?, in: Rochfeld (dir.), Les nouveaux défis du commerce électronique (2010), p. 93

Pironon, Dits et non-dits sur la mèthode de focalisation dans le contentieux – contractuel et delictuel – du commerce électronique, Clunet 138 (2011), 915

Piroutek/Reinhold, Wrong Direction? – Causality between Commercial Activity and Conclusion of Contract in Art. 15 para. 1 lit. c Brussels I Regulation, euvr 2014, 41

Posnow Wurm, La protection des consommateurs en droit international privé européen suite aux arrêts Pammer – Hotel Alpenhof: la notion d'"activité dirigée", Tijdschrift@ipr.be 2011, 162

Prieur, Compétence judiciaire internationale et contrat de forfait touristique conclu sur Internet, Gaz Pal 8-9 janvier 2014, 9

Ragno, Il foro del consumatore: dalla Convenzione di Bruxelles del 1968 al Regolamento CE n. 44/2001, Contratto e impresa/Europa 2009, 230

Ragno, The Law Applicable to Consumer Contracts under the Rome I Regulation, in: Ferrari/Leible (eds.), Rome I Regulation (München 2009), p. 129

Norbert Reich/Gambogi Carvalho, Gerichtsstand bei internationalen Verbraucherstreitigkeiten im e-commerce, VuR 2001, 169

Herbert Roth, Wer ist im Europäischen Zivilprozessrecht ein Verbraucher?, in: FS Bernd von Hoffmann (2011), p. 715

Herbert Roth, Schadenshaftung und erforderliche Vertragsanknüpfung bei Art. 15 EuGVO (LugÜ), in: FS Athanassios Kaissis (2012), p. 819

Marianne Roth, Gerichtsstand und Kollisionsrecht bei Internetgeschäften, in: Peter Gruber/Mader (eds.), Internet und e-commerce (2000), p. 157

Wulf-Henning Roth, Informationspflichten über das anwendbare Recht, FS Dieter Martiny (2014) 543

Rühl, Die rechtsaktübergreifende Auslegung im europäischen Internationalen Privatrecht: Art. 6 der Rom I-VO und die Rechtsprechung des EuGH zu Art. 15 der Brüssel I-VO, GPR 2013, 122

Rühl, Die Richtlinie über alternative Streitbeilegung und die Verordnung über Online-Streitbeilegung: Effektiver Rechtsschutz bei grenzüberschreitenden Verbraucherstreitigkeiten?, RIW 2013, 737

Rühl, Kausalität zwischen ausgerichteter Tätigkeit und Vertragsschluss: Neues zum situativen Anwendungsbereich der Art. 15 ff. EuGVVO, IPRax 2014, 41

Rühl, Grenzüberschreitender Verbraucherschutz:

(Nichts) Neues aus Brüssel und Luxemburg?, in: FS Dagmar Coester-Waltjen (2015), p. 697

Sachse, Der Verbrauchervertrag im Internationalen Privat- und Prozessrecht (2006)

Schaltinat, Internationales Verbraucherprozessrecht (1998)

Scheuermann, Internationales Zivilverfahrensrecht bei Verträgen im Internet (2004)

Anton K. Schnyder/Paczoska Kottmann, Zulässige Gerichtsstandsvereinbarungen in Verbrauchersachen nach Art. 17 Nr. 3 LugÜ?, in: FS Ivo Schwander (St. Gallen 2011), p. 789

Schoibl, Zuständigkeit für Verbrauchersachen nach europäischem Zivilverfahrensrecht des Brüsseler und des Luganer Übereinkommens, JBl 1998, 700 and JBl 1998, 767

Schütze, Der Verbraucher im europäischen Justizraum oder: die Zweiklassenjustiz des Europäischen Zivilprozessrechts, in: FS Friedrich Graf von Westphalen (2010), p. 621

Seibl, Verbrauchergerichtsstände, vorprozessuale Dispositionen und Zuständigkeitsprobleme bei Ansprüchen aus c.i.c., IPRax 2011, 234

Senff, Wer ist Verbraucher im internationalen Zivilprozeß? (2001)

Spindler, Internationales Verbraucherschutzrecht und Internet, MMR 2000, 18

Ansgar Staudinger, Internet-Buchung von Reisen und Flügen, RRa 2007, 98

Ansgar Staudinger, Reichweite des Verbraucherschutzgerichtsstandes nach Art. 15 Abs. 2 EuGVVO, IPRax 2008, 107

Ansgar Staudinger, Der Schutzgerichtsstand im Sinne des Art. 15 Abs. 1 lit. c Brüssel-VO bei Klagen gegen Reiseveranstalter und Vermittler, RRa 2014, 10

Ansgar Staudinger, Verbraucherverträge im Lichte der Rechtssache Emrek – Schutzgerichtsstand und anwendbares Recht, jM 2014, 229

Ansgar Staudinger, Gerichtsstände hiesiger Kunden gegenüber Veranstaltern im Inland bei Pauschalreisen mit Auslandsbezug nach der Brüssel Ia-VO – pars pro toto für eine überschätzte ZPO, jM 2015, 46

Staudinger/Steinrötter, Verfahrens- sowie kollisionsrechtlicher Verbraucherschutz bei Online-Geschäften, EWS 2011, 70

Steennot, Hof van Justitie verduidelijkt toepassings-

voorwaarde bijzondere IPR-regelen consumenteno-
vereenkomsten, Tijdschrift@ipr.be 2011, 152
Steiner/Wasserer, Zur Konkretisierung des "Ausrichtens" in Art. 15 Abs. 1 lit. c EuGVVO bei Anle-
gerklagen, ÖBA 2011, 30
Sujecki, Zum Umfang des "Ausrichtens" einer gewerblichen Tätigkeit im Internet, K&R; 2011, 181
Tang, Exclusive Choice of Forum Clauses and Consumer Contracts in E-Commerce, (2005) 1 JPrIL 237
Tang, Electronic Consumer Contracts in the Conflict
of Laws (2009)
Tang, Private International Law in Consumer Contracts: A European Perspective, (2010) 6 JPrIL 225
Tang, Consumer Collective Redress in European
Private International Law, (2011) 7 JPrIL 101
Tassone, Il regolamento Bruxelles I e l'interpreta-
zione del suo ambito di applicazione: un altro passo
della Corte di Giustizia sul cammino della tutela dei
diritti del consumatore, Giur. mer. 2013, 104
Tenreiro, La compétence internationale des tribu-
naux en matière de consommation, in: Mélanges
Jean Calais-Auloy (2004), p. 1093
Teuber, Die internationale Zuständigkeit bei Ver-
braucherstreitigkeiten (2003)
Thiede, Passkontrolle bei Vertragsabschluss,
ecolex 2014, 35
Thiede, Achtung – Verbrauchergerichtsstand im
Ausland!, Zak 2014, 63
Thiede/Florian Sommer, Vorsätzliche Schädigung
von Anlegern im europaweiten arbeitsteiligen
Wertpapiervertrieb: Der internationale Gerichts-
stand nach der EuGVVO, ÖBA 2015, 175

Thole, Klagen geschädigter Privatanleger gegen
Griechenland vor deutschen Gerichten?, WM 2012,
1793
Thole, Verbrauchergerichtsstand aufgrund schlüssi-
ger Behauptung für eine Kapitalanlegerklage gegen
die Hausbank des Anlagefonds?, IPRax 2013, 136
Thole, Gerichtsstandsklauseln in Anleihebedingun-
gen und Verbrauchergerichtsstand, WM 2014, 1205
Toro, Le règlement "Bruxelles I*bis*" et son impact
(très limité) au plan des consommateurs, Rev. eur.
dr. consomm. 2014, 81
Vasiljeva, 1968 Brussels Convention and EU Council
Regulation No. 44/2001 – Jurisdiction in Consumer
Contracts Concluded Online, (2004) 10 Eur. L. J. 123
Weber-Stecher, Internationales Konsumentenver-
tragsrecht (1995)
Wefers Bettink, Pammer en Alpenhof: het richten
van een website, NTER 2011, 164
Wilderspin, Le règlement 44/2001 du Conseil: con-
séquences pour les contrats conclus par les con-
sommateurs, Rev. eur. dr. consomm. 2002, 23
Wilke, Verbraucherschutz im internationalen
Zuständigkeitsrecht der EU – Status quo und
Zukunftsprobleme, EuZW 2015, 13
Wittwer, Das "Ausrichten" der Geschäftätigkeit des
Unternehmers auf den Wohnsitzstaat des Verbrau-
chers i.S. des Art. 15 EuGVVO, Eur. L. Rpter 2011, 2
Markus Würdinger, Europäisches Verbraucherpro-
zessrecht im Visier der Juristischen Methodenlehre,
in: FS Peter Gottwald (2014), p. 693.

Introduction to Articles 17–19

I. Introduction

1 The Brussels *Ibis* Regulation contains in Section 4 three provisions on jurisdiction over
consumer contracts (Arts. 17–19). Art. 17 determines the scope of application of the provi-

sions, and the Article contains a definition of "a consumer". The rules of jurisdiction are set forth in Art. 18 and Art. 19 determines to what extent the rules may be departed from by agreement. The ECJ has emphasised that as an exception to the general rules of *actor sequitur forum rei* as enshrined in Art. 4 (1), Arts. 17–19 should be interpreted rather strictly and restrictively.[1] But the interpretative practice of the ECJ displays quite opposite tendencies towards extending consumer protection based on its rationale, increasingly so in recent times.[2] The pleas for a restrictive interpretation are mere lip service and camouflage.[3] They are boilerplate stuff from the word processor of the ECJ and do not provide genuine and reliable guidance. Politically, there is an eternal struggle as to just how much consumer protection is just and when the consumers' case is overstated. Eruptions in either direction will emanate time and again, and the flux of time will generate different fashions with periods more generous to consumers alternating with periods more emphasising the interests of businesses.

Section 4 of the Brussels I*bis* Regulation is a comprehensive regime for consumer contracts.   **2** Thus, the Section has priority over the general and special rules of jurisdiction in Sections 1 and 2. As a consequence, Arts. 4–9 are inapplicable where the contract is covered by Section 4. On the other hand, Section 3 has priority over Section 4,[4] as has Art. 24 (Section 6). Consequently, insurance contracts with consumers are regulated exclusively by Section 3 whereas consumer contracts concerning matters where exclusive jurisdiction is granted to the courts of a Member State are regulated exclusively by Art. 24 (Section 6). For instance, a contract concluded with a consumer concerning a tenancy over immoveable property is covered exclusively by Art. 24 (1). Arts. 25 and 26 are special cases: They both apply in principle also to consumer contracts, but subject to major modifications and restrictions; those for Art. 25 are spelled out in Art. 19, those for Art. 26 in Art. 26 (2).

II. Ratio legis

The purpose of Section 4 of the Brussels I*bis* Regulation is to protect the weaker party, here   **3** the consumer, by rules of jurisdiction more favourable to his interests than provided for by the general rules. Recital (13) Brussels I Regulation underlines this. The special rules introduced by the provisions over consumer contracts serve to ensure adequate protection for the consumer, as the party deemed economically weaker and less experienced that the other, commercial, party to the contract.[5] They aim at rebalancing, at the level of international

---

[1]   *Daniela Mühlleitner v. Ahmad Yusufi and Wadat Yusufi* (Case C-190/11), ECLI:EU:C:2012:542 para. 27; *Česká spořitelna as v. Gerald Feichter*, (Case C-419/11), ECLI:EU:C:2013:165 para. 26; *Harald Kolassa v. Barclays Bank plc* (Case C-375/13), ECLI:EU:C:2015:37 para. 28; BGH NJW 2009, 298.

[2]   See *Lokman Emrek v. Vlado Sabranovic* (Case C-218/12), ECLI:EU:C:2013:666; *Armin Maletic and Marianne Maletic v. lastminute.com GmbH and TUI Österreich GmbH* (Case C-478/12), ECLI:EU: C:2013:735.

[3]   *Kieninger*, in: FS Ulrich Magnus (2014), p. 449, 454; *von Hein*, LMK 2014, 360325.

[4]   See only *Schlosser* Art. 15 note 7; *Kropholler/von Hein*, Art. 15 note 20; *Wulf-Henning Roth*, IPRax 2014, 499, 501.

[5]   *Johann Gruber v. BayWa AG*, (Case C-464/01) [2005] ECR I-439 para. 34; *Petra Engler v. Janus Versand GmbH*, (Case C-27/02) [2005] ECR I-481 para. 39; *Česká spořitelna as v. Gerald Feichter*, (Case C-419/ 11), ECLI:EU:C:2013:165 para. 33.

jurisdiction, a contractual relationship that is unequal in principle.[6] Tilting the jurisdictional balance in the consumers' favour is not to discourage consumer from enforcing their rights[7] and thus to strive (as far as it goes) for a not suboptimal level of regulation. Furthermore, in consumer contracts, only limited party autonomy is accepted.[8]

4 In brief, provided the contract falls within the scope of application of Section 4, the other party to the contract can only sue the consumer in the Member State where the consumer is domiciled. On the other hand, the consumer can institute proceedings against the other party to the contract either in the Member State, where the consumer is domiciled, or in the Member State where the other party is domiciled. Finally, Section 4 limits the effects of jurisdiction clauses because, generally, such clauses can only be entered into after the dispute has arisen. However, such clauses are also permitted if they allow the consumer to bring proceedings in other courts than those prescribed by Section 4.

5 The importance of the protective character of Section 4 of the Brussels *Ibis* Regulation is emphasized at the stage of recognition and enforcement. Although the general rule is that the jurisdiction of the foreign court may not be reviewed, an exception is made, inter alia, for cases covered by Section 4.[9] According to Art. 45 (1) (e) i), a judgment shall be denied recognition and enforcement if it conflicts with Section 4 and if the consumer has been the defendant. Consequently, a judgment from a court that took jurisdiction over a consumer domiciled in another Member State and whose contract falls within Section 4 can be denied recognition and enforcement.

6 The ECJ has emphasized that the objectives, as comprised in Arts. 15; 16 Brussels I Regulation (Arts. 13; 14 Brussels Convention), were inspired solely by a desire to protect certain categories of buyers. Thus, the buyers covered are only buyers in need of protection, their financial position being one of weakness in comparison with sellers because they are private final consumers and are not engaged in trade or professional activities when buying the product acquired. Consequently, the compulsory jurisdiction of Art. 18 (2) must be strictly limited to the objectives proper to Section 4. According to the ECJ, this interpretation is justified because the jurisdictional provisions of Section 4 derogate from the general principles of the system laid down by the Regulation in matters concerning contracts, such as Arts. 4; 7 (1).[10] Finally, the ECJ has stated that the protective role fulfilled by Section 4 implies

---

6   A-G *Cruz Villalón*, Opinion of 18 July 2013 in case C-218/12, ECLI:EU:C:2013:494 para. 23; *de Clavière*, Rev. Lamy dr. aff. 77 (2012), 48 *et seq.*; *Tassone*, Giur. mer. 2013, 104 *et seq.*; *Brkan*, Rev. eur. dr. consomm. 2013, 113 *et seq.*

7   *Jonathan Hill* para. 3.42.

8   See Recitals (13) and (14).

9   See Art. 45 (1) (e) i).

10   *Société Bertrand v. Paul Ott KG*, (Case 150/77) [1978] ECR 1431, 1445 *et seq.* paras. 17, 18, 1446 para. 21; *Shearson Lehman Hutton, Inc. v. TVB Treuhandgesellschaft für Vermögensverwaltung und Beteiligungen mbh*, (Case C-89/91) [1993] ECR I-139, I-187 paras. 14–16; *Francesco Benincasa v. Dentalkit Srl*, (Case C-269/95) [1997] ECR I-3767, I-3794 *et seq.* paras. 13 and 14; *Hans-Herman Mietz v. Intership Yachting Sneek BV*, (Case C-99/96) [1999] ECR I-2277, I-2310 para. 27; *Johann Gruber v. BayWa AG*, (Case C-464/01) [2005] ECR I-439 para. 32 and *Renate Ilsinger v. Martin Dreschers, acting as administrator in the insolvency of Schlank & Schick GmbH*, (Case C-180/06) [2009] ECR I-3961, I-4013 para. 41, I-4015 para. 47.

that the application of the rules of special jurisdiction laid down to that end should not be extended to persons for whom that protection is not justified.[11] But the case law of the ECJ displays a rather firm tendency towards consumer friendliness.[12] On the other hand, a maxim *in dubio pro consumatore*[13] (or rather *in dubio pro consumptore)*[14] has not been established as such.

All concepts in Section 4 of the Brussels I*bis* Regulation should be subject to a uniform **7** interpretation independent of national laws of the Member States in order to ensure the harmonious and efficient operation of the provisions.[15] Furthermore, the interpretation given by the ECJ as regards the Brussels Convention also applies to Brussels I*bis*, where its provisions and those of the Brussels Convention may be treated as equivalent. In addition, the system established by Art. 17 (1) (c) occupies, as it is clear from Recital (13) Brussels I Regulation with regard to its predecessor Art. 15 (1) (c) Brussels I Regulation, the same place and fulfils the same function of protecting the weaker party as did Art. 13 (1) (3) Brussels Convention.[16]

III. Legislative history

Section 4 of the Brussels I*bis* Regulation has been taken over from the Brussels Convention **8** *via* the Brussels I Regulation. At the time, Arts. 13–15 Brussels Convention were major innovations if not outrightly revolutionary. They for the first time introduced consumer protection as an important goal in PIL. However, over the years certain amendments have been made, partly due to political considerations based on an increased need for consumer protection, partly due to new technologies.

Originally, Section 4 Brussels Convention was only applicable to sale of goods on instalment **9** credit terms and contracts for loans repayable by instalments.[17] At that time, the provisions were inspired by national law in some of the original Contracting States to the Brussels Convention. Based on social considerations, the policy behind Section 4 was to offer jurisdictional protection to the buyer in contracts for sale of goods on instalment credit terms.[18]

---

[11] *Shearson Lehman Hutton, Inc. v. TVB Treuhandgesellschaft für Vermögensverwaltung und Beteiligungen mbh,* (Case C-89/91) [1993] ECR I-139, I-188 para. 19; *Johann Gruber v. BayWa AG,* (Case C-464/01) [2005] ECR I-439 para. 32.

[12] See only *Bob Schmitz,* DCCR 105 (2014), 38, 39; *Boskovic,* RDCIP 103 (2014), 633, 636.

[13] See in particular *Riesenhuber,* JZ 2005, 289.

[14] *Markus Würdinger,* in: FS Peter Gottwald (2014), p. 693, 698.

[15] *Société Betrand v. Paul Ott KG,* (Case 150/77) [1978] ECR 1431, 1445 paras. 14–16, 1446 para. 19; *Shearson Lehman Hutton, Inc. v. TVB Treuhandgesellschaft für Vermögensverwaltung und Beteiligungen mbh,* (Case C-89/91) [1993] ECR I-139, I-186 para. 13; *Francesco Benincasa v. Dentalkit Srl,* (Case C-269/95) [1997] ECR I-3767, I-3794 para. 12; *Hans-Herman Mietz v. Intership Yachting Sneek BV* (Case C-99/96) [1999] ECR I-2277, I-2310 para. 26; *Rudolf Gabriel* (Case C-96/00) [2002] ECR I-6367, I-6399 para. 37; *Johann Gruber v. BayWa AG,* (Case C-464/01) [2005] ECR I-439 para. 31; *Petra Engler v. Janus Versand GmbH,* (Case C-27/02) [2005] ECR I-481 para. 33.

[16] *Renate Ilsinger v. Martin Dreschers, acting as administrator in the insolvency of Schlank & Schick GmbH,* (Case C-180/06) [2009] ECR I-3961, I-4013 para. 41.

[17] See Art. 13 Brussels Convention 1968.

[18] Report *Jenard* p. 33.

10   Following the accession of the United Kingdom, Ireland and Denmark to the EEC and in the process of extending the Brussels Convention to include these Member States, Section 4 Brussels Convention was amended in 1978 in three ways.

11   Firstly, it was decided to expand the scope of Section 4 to cover consumer contracts and not just, as had previously been the case, sale of goods on instalment credit terms and loans repayable by instalments. Consequently, a definition of a "consumer" was added. These amendments to the Brussels Convention made it clear that the common trend to focus on and increase consumer protection in national law in the Member States at that time had become official policy of the EEC in the context of international litigation. Furthermore, according to the Report *Schlosser*, an unacceptable situation would arise if consumers were deprived of their national rights to protection when acting across European borders. Consequently, it was essential to offer consumers a fair base of jurisdiction in intra-European trade. By making these amendments, the drafters of the revised Brussels Convention, 1978 also codified the interpretation of Art. 13 Brussels Convention made by the ECJ in *Société Bertrand v. Paul Ott KG*.[19] In this judgment, the ECJ held that the concept of sale of goods on instalment credit terms did not cover sales and loans between parties acting in the course of business.

12   Secondly, it was decided that in addition to loans repayable by instalments, Section 4 should also cover any other form of credit granted to finance the sale of goods.

13   Thirdly, a new group of contracts should be covered by Section 4, *viz.* contracts with a certain specified connection to the Member State where the consumer is domiciled. According to Art. 13 (1) (3) Brussels Convention, any other contract for the supply of goods or services would be covered by Section 4, provided that in the consumer's country of domicile, the conclusion of the contract was preceded by a specific invitation addressed to the consumer directly or by advertising, and the consumer took, in that State, the steps necessary for the conclusion of the contract. These conditions should ensure procedural consumer protection in cases where the circumstances surrounding the consumer contract had sufficient connection to the Member State where the consumer is domiciled.[20] In broad terms, this provision rests on the idea that the commercial party is "fishing" for consumers by either targeting them in their home country or by advertising in that country, and in that way, reaching out for them in order to do business with them.

14   During the revision of the Brussels and Lugano Conventions in 1998-99, the Working Party composed of delegates from all EU and EFTA Member States discussed the application of the provisions of Section 4 of the Brussels and 1988 Lugano Conventions in respect to new technologies. In particular, the growing use of e-commerce was at the core of the discussions.[21] The Working Party examined three issues in this context.

15   The first issue was whether Section 4, if untouched, would cover consumer contracts con-

---

[19]   Report *Schlosser* para. 153; *Société Bertrand v. Paul Ott KG*, (Case 150/77) [1978] ECR 1431.

[20]   Report *Schlosser* para. 158.

[21]   The revision work was the basis for the Brussels I Regulation, see Proposal for a Council Regulation on Jurisdiction and the Recognition and Enforcement of Judgments in Civil and Commercial Matters, OJ C 376 (1999) 19.

cluded over the Internet. It was the general understanding of the Working Party that Art. 13 (1) (3) Brussels Convention did indeed cover such contracts, provided that the setup of the seller's e-business could be regarded as either a specific invitation addressed to the consumer in his state or as advertising in the consumer's state, and provided that the consumer took the steps necessary for the conclusion of the contract (the click) in his own State.[22]

The second issue was whether Art. 13 (1) (3) Brussels Convention should be clarified in order to explicate that e-commerce is covered by the provision while maintaining the principle the provision is based on. There was unanimous agreement that this should be the case. **16**

The third issue was whether this solution was a sound one from a political perspective. Once again, there was general agreement that the continuous need for consumer protection justified the solution. The Working Party found that the consumer is in a very weak position when shopping over the Internet because the consumer in most, if not all, cases pay in advance of delivery. Consequently, the seller is hardly going to institute proceedings against the consumer. **17**

The Working Party also found that maintaining procedural consumer protection in a European context would in fact improve e-business because consumers will be more willing to buy products and services over the Internet when they have sound legal protection.[23] In view of these considerations, the Working Party redrafted Art. 13 (1) (3) Brussels Convention. The new provision appeared as Art. 15 (1) (c) Brussels I Regulation. **18**

Another difference between the Brussels Convention and the Brussels I Regulation was that Art. 13 (1) pt. 3 Brussels Convention only covered contracts for the supply of goods or services, whereas Art. 15 (1) (c) Brussels I Regulation was not limited to such contracts, but also covered all other cases of consumer contracts whether they concerned goods, services or other subjects. **19**

Finally, under the Brussels Convention Section 4 did not apply to contracts for transport by virtue of Art. 13 (3) Brussels Convention.[24] However, under the Brussels I Regulation, this exception had been re-defined in its Art. 15 (3) so that the exception does not include package tours. Art. 17 (3) continues on this path without alterations and without adopting the more precise wording of Art. 6 (4) (b) Rome I Regulation. The Recast Regulation (fortunately) did not seize upon the opportunity to import the other instances as listed in Art. 6 (4) Rome I Regulation. **20**

Section 4 made the transfer from the Brussels I Regulation to the Brussels Ibis Regulation almost unscathed and with only one major alteration: In Art. 18 (1) 2nd option, the phrase "regardless of the domicile of the other party" was added. This extends the consumer's *forum actoris* where the other party is not domiciled in Member State and does even have a place of business in any Member State which would be elevated to the status of a domicile by virtue of **21**

---

[22] See also on the applicability of Section 4 Brussels Convention to consumer contracts concluded over the Internet the analysis by *Foss/Bygrave*, (2000) 8 Int. J. L. & Info. Tech. 99–135.

[23] *Peter Arnt Nielsen*, in: Démaret/Govaere/Hanf (eds.), European Legal Dynamics (2007), p. 241, 257.

[24] See Art. 13 (3) Brussels Convention.

Art. 17 (2). Such extension (an extension of the subjective scope of application *ratione personae)*[25] is perfectly in line with, and another expression of, the general policy to protect European consumers.[26]

22 Other changes are of an editorial nature only, paying due regard to the renumbering of other Articles: The reference by Art. 15 (1) Brussels I Regulation to Arts. 4; 5 (5) Brussels I Regulation has been adapted to become a reference to Arts. 6; 7 (5) accordingly.

IV. Internationality required

23 Arts. 17–19 presuppose internationality and a cross-border element.[27] They are not designed and intended for purely domestic cases. Internationality and extraneity should be measured by the same yardsticks as have been developed for the general scope of application of the Brussels I/*Ibis* regime. Hence, the international element might be generated by any relation to a Third State, and it is not necessary that a relation to another Member State besides the forum state exists.[28] It is not required that the parties must be domiciled in different States, either.[29] Howsoever, a sufficient cross-border element is present where either party moved abroad after the conclusion of the contract[30] as Art. 19 (3) puts beyond any doubt.[31]

24 A place of performance in a country different from the parties' common home state suffices. For instance, if a holiday package tour leads to a destination abroad internationality is given although both parties to the contract might be domiciled in the same country (in reality this is the common scenario where the trip was traditionally booked with a local travel agency[32]). If the case raises serious questions of international jurisdiction a sufficient cross-border element is given.[33] One could possible call this "juridicial internationality" as compared to "factual internationality".[34]

25 Other factors might also weigh in. In particular, a third party cooperating with the entre-

---

25 *Pesce*, Dir. comm. int. 2014, 579, 593.

26 See *Mankowski*, RIW 2014, 625, 626.

27 *Hypoteční banka a.s. v. Udo Mike Lindner* (Case C-327/10), [2011] ECR I-11543 para. 29; *Armin Maletic and Marianne Maletic v. lastminute.com GmbH and TUI Österreich GmbH* (Case C-478/12), ECLI:EU:C:2013:735 para. 25; OLG München RIW 2012, 635; *Prieur*, Gaz. Pal. 8-9 janvier 2014, 9, 11; *Mankowski*, EWiR 2014, 231, 232; *Strikwerda*, NJ 2014 Nr. 234 p. 2992, 2993; *Paredes Pérez*, AEDIPr 2013, 1039; see also *Harald Koch*, Internationale Zuständigkeit und Auslandsbezug, RRa 2013, 173; *Harald Koch*, in: FS Ulrich Magnus (2014), p. 475.

28 *Armin Maletic and Marianne Maletic v. lastminute.com GmbH and TUI Österreich GmbH* (Case C-478/12), ECLI:EU:C:2013:735 paras. 26, 28 with reference to *Andrew Owusu v. Nugent B. Jackson* (Case C-281/02), [2005] ECR I-1383 paras. 25–26; to the same avail e.g. *Ansgar Staudinger*, jM 2015, 46, 48.

29 *Prieur*, Gaz. Pal. 8-9 janvier 2014, 9, 10; *Ansgar Staudinger*, RRa 2014, 10 (10); *Ansgar Staudinger*, jM 2015, 46, 49.

30 OLG München RIW 2012, 635.

31 *Ansgar Staudinger*, jM 2015, 46, 49.

32 See *Ansgar Staudinger*, jM 2015, 46, 48.

33 *Hypoteční banka a.s. v. Udo Mike Lindner* (Case C-327/10), [2011] ECR I-11543 para. 30; OLG München RIW 2012, 635.

34 *Strikwerda*, NJ 2014 Nr 234 p. 2992, 2993.

preneur might be domiciled abroad. The necessary element and degree of internationality (or else: the necessary cross-border element) might stem from another contract within the overall transaction. Even if a single transaction is divided in several contractual relationships which the consumer concluded with different partners in contract (for instance a travel agency and a travel operator) none of those contractual relationships can be classified as purely domestic since it is inseparably linked with the other ones where it was concluded via the partner of the other relationship acting as an intermediary in this regard.[35]

Proper attention must also be paid to the objectives pursued by Recitals (13) and (15), **26** namely the protection of the consumer as the weaker party to the contract and minimising the possibility of concurring proceedings in order to ensure that irreconcilable judgments will not be given in two or more Member States.[36] Those objectives preclude any solution which allows either party (even the consumer) to pursue parallel proceedings in different States or places against parties involved in the same overall transaction, for instance against two operators involved in the bookings or the arrangements for the package holiday at issue in the main proceedings.[37]

The party who alleges Arts. 17–19 to be applicable has to argue and to prove that such cross- **27** border element exists. National yardsticks levying the burden like the theory of the so called *doppelrelevante Tatsachen* (if it is to be recognised at all[38]) do not come to his rescue for this internationality is a matter occurring only in the field of admissibility of actions and not with regard to the merits.[39] It cannot be relegated to the later stages of the lawsuit.

V. Material scope of application

1. Restriction to individual claims in contract

The protective regime established by Arts. 17–19 deals solely and exclusively with individual **28** claims in contract.[40] The notion of contract employed here takes the one employed in Art. 5 (1) as its starting point. But a purposive interpretation rather urges that it goes beyond the general notion and is wider than the general notion.[41] On the other, it requires the conclusion of a contract, conclusion understood in a technical sense.[42] The consumer has to allege the existence of a claim in contract, but has only to state a good arguable case in accordance with the respective rules of the *lex fori*.[43]

---

[35] *Armin Maletic and Marianne Maletic v. lastminute.com GmbH and TUI Österreich GmbH* (Case C-478/12), ECLI:EU:C:2013:735 para. 29; see also *Chalas*, RCDIP 103 (2014), 642, 647.

[36] *Armin Maletic and Marianne Maletic v. lastminute.com GmbH and TUI Österreich GmbH* (Case C-478/12), ECLI:EU:C:2013:735 para. 30.

[37] *Armin Maletic and Marianne Maletic v. lastminute.com GmbH and TUI Österreich GmbH* (Case C-478/12), ECLI:EU:C:2013:735 para. 31.

[38] Counter-arguments are to be found in *Mankowski*, IPRax 2006, 454.

[39] OLG Karlsruhe IPRspr. 2011 Nr 199 p. 528–529.

[40] *Rudolf Gabriel* (Case C-96/00), [2002] ECR I-6367, I-6403 paras. 36–38; *Renate Ilsinger v. Martin Dreschers, acting as administrator in the insolvency of Schlank & Schick GmbH*, (Case C-180/06) [2009] ECR I-3961, I-3998 para. 54; *Thole*, WM 2012, 1793, 1795.

[41] *Rudolf Gabriel* (Case C-96/00), [2002] ECR I-6367, I-6403 paras. 56–57.

[42] *Harald Kolassa v. Barclays Bank plc* (Case C-375/13), ECLI:EU:C:2015:37 para. 38.

29   Bonds are a common instrument for private investments. Generally, non-professional investors do not contract directly with the issuer of the bond, but with their bank. Hence, Arts. 17–19 will then not apply in the relation between private investor and issuer.[44] If the bonds are held by a fund and the private investor only acquires shares of this fund, the question at stake is as to whether the acquisition of these shares fulfils the requirements of Art. 17 (1).

30   Third parties are a special treat.[45] Insofar as a consumer benefits as the third party from a contract concluded between others Arts. 17–19 do not become operative for this consumer is not involved in the process of contracting. He has to take the contract as it stands, and the *lex causae* may only entitle him to refuse the position of a beneficiary. Arts. 17–19 might only apply if the customer concluding the contract himself is acting in a private capacity and can be regarded as a consumer (for instance the grandmother contracting with a bank for her granddaughter's benefit).

2. Exclusion of collective redress

31   Arts. 17–19 are not concerned with collective redress.[46] Collective redress has not obtained the blessing of a special rule.[47] Collective redress indicates collected strength and does not feature a typically weaker party[48] in a natural person's individual capacity. It overcomes collective action problems and is attractive for specialised lawyers to engage in. On the contracting stages consumers might have fought each one alone and have suffered inequality of bargaining power,[49] but afterwards they bundled their force. Furthermore, not even this tentative argument prevails where the claims are not based on congruent contracts concluded by a mass of consumers, but on mass or market torts.[50] Group actions are not structurally different in this regard from US style class actions.[51]

32   If a collective waiver clause is inserted in an individual contract and complied with, no questions of collective redress will arise in the ordinary course of things provided that such clause withstands scrutiny under the *lex fori* if the latter grants a *locus standi* in collective actions.

33   Even if under Art. 17 two approaches, a material one and a procedural, might be believed to compete[52] Art. 18 (1) 2nd option cannot be sensibly applied:[53] If a plethora of consumers sues,

---

43   OLG Stuttgart 18 August 2014 – Case 5 U 58/14 [9].

44   *Thole*, WM 2012, 1793, 1795.

45   See in substantive law *Mankowski*, VuR 2002, 269.

46   *Verein für Konsumenteninformation v. Karl-Heinz Henkel* (Case C-167/00), [2002] ECR I-8111 para. 33; *Carballo Piñeiro*, Las acciónes colectivas y su eficacia extraterritorial (2002) pp. 105–113. *Contra Bariatti*, RDIPP 2011, 19.

47   *Tang*, (2011) 7 JPrIL 101, 107.

48   *Tang*, (2011) 7 JPrIL 101, 112.

49   *Tang*, (2011) 7 JPrIL 101, 113.

50   Cf. *Tzakas*, (2011) 48 CML Rev. 1125, 1165.

51   But cf. *Michailidou*, Prozessuale Fragen des Kollektivrechtsschutzes im europäischen Justizraum (2007) pp. 311–313.

52   *Tang*, (2011) 7 JPrIL 101, 107–111.

which consumer's domicile should be relevant?[54] But already with regard to Art. 17 (1) (c) it might become necessary to identify the relevant consumer's domicile. Thus, Art. 18 (1) 1st option, too, would have severe problems to apply.[55] Regardless whether consumers in a mass harm situation are spread over one single or various Member States, it is practically ruled out that they all reside in the same place.[56] Difficulties abound even more where the class or group comprises members from Member States on the one hand and from Third States on the other hand.

Consumer associations suing in their own right and with own *locus standi* are not natural **34** persons.[57] They might be representatives of consumers only in a social or economic sense. But they do not sue as legal representatives in the proper sense of "the consumers" in general or of their members. The consumer fora are not open to them.[58] This hits home e.g. for the French *action en répresentation conjointe* where the action is brought on behalf of the consumer who has given a mandate to the organisation in question.[59]

Even if consumer associations become assignees of previously and original individual claims **35** in contract, assigned by consumers as the original creditors, this falls outside Arts. 17–19 since such assignees cannot avail themselves of the protection personally and individually granted to single consumers.[60]

Representative actions present a particular problem. They serve some kind of intermediate **36** role between truly individual claims and collective redress. To a representative consumer claimant, the protection provided for in Arts. 17–19 can hardly be denied, though, at least where the other consumers on whose behalf the representative is acting, are identified or at identifiable.[61] Whether a decision rendered as a result of such representative action (e.g. under the German *Kapitalanlagenmusterverfahrensgesetz)*[62] is binding upon the other claimants should technically be a matter of the *lex fori* which is called upon to rule about the extent to which the decision marks the other claims as *res iudicata*. At the stage of recognition and enforcement in another Member State, Art. 54 might enter the frame. If representative action is in the public interest, particularly so if it is pursued by state officials like the *Procurateur de la République*, Section 4 is not applicable.[63]

---

53 Art. 18 (2) is not applicable if the entrepreneur is the defendant.
54 See *Arenas García*, REDI 1996, 39, 64–67.
55 But cf. CA Colmar Clunet 127 (2000), 79 obs. *Huet* = IPRax 2001, 253 (comment by *Sibylle Neumann/ Rosch*, IPRax 2001, 257).
56 *Fuxa*, euvr 2014, 90, 98.
57 *Lüttringhaus*, RabelsZ 77 (2013), 31, 57.
58 *Verein für Konsumenteninformation v. Karl-Heinz Henkel* (Case C-167/00), [2002] ECR I-8111 para. 33; *Fuxa*, euvr 2014, 90, 97.
59 *Kessedjian*, RDIPP 1997, 281, 287–288; *Añoveros*, Rev. eur. dr. consomm. 2004, 77, 97.
60 Art. 17 note (*Nielsen/Mankowski*); *Thole*, WM 2012, 1793, 1796.
61 *Danov*, (2010) 6 JPrIL 359, 376–377; see also *Tang*, (2011) 7 JPrIL 101, 115.
62 Comprehensively *Prusseit*, Die Bindungswirkung des Musterentscheids nach dem KapMuG – Zu ihrem institutionellen Verständnis als Form der Interventionswirkung (2008); *Christoph Leser*, Die Bindungswirkung des Musterentscheids nach dem Kapitalanlegermusterverfahrensgesetz (2014).
63 *Danov*, (2010) 6 JPrIL 359, 376.

VI. Claims in torts or other non-contractual obligations

37 Likewise, Arts. 17–19 are not applicable where claims in tort or other non-contractual obligations are at stake.[64] The consumer is not privileged with regard to his claims in tort,[65] nor does he gain particular protection against claims in tort by the other party. This holds true even if such non-contractual obligations happen to concur with contractual obligations stemming from a consumer contract in the sense of Art. 17 (1). The split between contractual claims which are covered and non-contractual claims which are not, resembles the split between Art. 7 (1) and (2). If an issue can not be characterised as contractual and falling under the common notions of contract[66] but must e classified as tortious or delictual, it falls in a different category.

38 Not even a purposive interpretation in order to protect consumer can overcome this.[67] It might be desirable to open up a contractual forum at the place where the private investor's fortune is reduced (i.e. where the private investor held his relevant account) instead of submitting him to the restrictions implied in Art. 7 (2),[68] but such desire alone does not stretch the outer borders of the notion of "contract".[69] *De lege ferenda* things might be judged differently,[70] but the European legislator did not seize even upon the occasion of the transmogrification of the Brussels I Regulation into the Brussels *Ibis* Regulation to reverse and extend the scope of now Arts. 17–19.

39 Connectivity and concurrence of claims cannot generally overcome this, either.[71] An *Annexkompetenz* for tortious claim in the contractual forum would extend the limits of the latter and disregard the diverging characterisations. Yet there are some hints in *Gabriel* and *Ilsinger* that the result that certain claims under a contract concluded by a consumer would all under Arts. 17–19 whereas other actions that are linked so closely as to be indissociable are subject to other rules would not be accepted by the ECJ and that a situation in which several courts have jurisdiction in respect of one and the same contract ought to avoided.[72] These could be possibly read not a re-characterising the respective claims as contractual but establishing an *Annexkompetenz*.[73]

40 *Culpa in contrahendo* is excluded from the Rome I Regulation by virtue of its Art. 1 (2) I, supported by Recital (30) Rome I Regulation, and submitted to the realm of the Rome II

---

64 OLG Stuttgart IPRspr. 2010 Nr 184a p. 460; *David Kluth* pp. 143–151.

65 *Matthias Weller*, WM 2013, 1681, 1687.

66 See in more detail Art. 17 notes 6–18 (*Mankowski*).

67 *Contra* BGH NJW 2011, 532 = ZIP 2010, 2264 = WM 2010, 2163; BGH NJW 2011, 2809 = BGH IPRax 2013, 168, 171; BGH WM 2012, 646; *Geimer*, in: FS Dieter Martiny (2014), p. 711, 725.

68 *Renate Schaub*, LMK 2011, 313318; *Geimer*, in: FS Dieter Martiny (2014), p. 711, 725.

69 See *Thole*, IPRax 2013, 136, 137.

70 *von Hein*, EuZW 2011, 369, 372.

71 *Gebauer*, in: Gebauer/Wiedmann, Ch. 27 note 84; *Kropholler/von Hein*, Art. 15 note 3; *Thole*, IPRax 2013, 136, 137. Tentatively *contra Ansgar Staudinger*, in: Rauscher, Vor Art. 15 note 4.

72 *Rudolf Gabriel* (Case C-96/00), [2002] ECR I-6367, I-6403 paras. 56–57; *Renate Ilsinger v. Martin Dreschers, acting as administrator in the insolvency of Schlank & Schick GmbH*, (Case C-180/06) [2009] ECR I-3961, I-3998 para. 44.

73 *Engert/Groh*, IPRax 2011, 458, 466.

Regulation. Art. 12 Rome II Regulation even specifically addresses *culpa in contrahendo*. But this is not a clear-cut case for a non-contractual characterisation[74] since Art. 12 (1) Rome II Regulation refers for many instances back to applying the rules of the Rome I Regulation. Art. 12 (1) Rome II Regulation reflects a political compromise intended not to hurt in particular Germany where a contractual classification prevailed. It indicates that there might be a close enough connection between at least certain kinds of *culpa in contrahendo* and an ensuing contract.[75] The trichotomy in PIL (three possibles: contract, delict, culpa) ought to be reflected in a mere dichotomy (contract or not contract) for the purposes of Arts. 17–19.[76]

Restitutionary claims in unjust enrichment are covered by Arts. 17–19 insofar as Art. 12 (1) **41** (e) Rome I Regulation characterizes them as contractual, but not further.[77] Else, the opposite characterisation in Arts. 2; 10 Rome II Regulation as non-contractual prevails.

VII. Burden of proof

Generally, the burden of proof is incumbent on the party claiming certain rules of the pro- **42** tective regime of Art. 17–19 to be applicable instead of the general jurisdiction regime.[78] The fundamental maxim is that the party who alleges that a certain rule is applicable bears the burden of stating and proving that its conditions are met. Hence, generally it is for the consumer to show that the facts required to bring the protective regime of international consumer law into effect are present since ordinarily the consumer will allege its applicability.

The burden of proof for the international scope of application of these articles to the case at **43** hand falls upon the consumer. This is because the application of the consumer regime is favourable to the consumer. Therefore, the consumer needs to prove that (i) the (actual or hypothetical) other party contracting for a professional purpose is domiciled in a Member State, or that (ii) the (actual or hypothetical) other party not domiciled in the Member State has a branch, agency or other establishment in one of the Member States and that the dispute is arising out of the operations of the branch, agency or establishment, and (iii) that the matter relates to a second Member State thus establishing the required international element.[79]

The burden of proof for the personal scope of application of these articles also falls upon the **44** consumer. As noted above, this is because of the consumer regime's favourability to the consumer. Therefore, the consumer needs to demonstrate[80] that he or she is (i) a natural person (ii) concluding the contract for a purpose outside of his or her trade or profession[81]

---

[74] As e.g. *Engert/Groh*, IPRax 2011, 458, 465 imply.

[75] Concurring in the result BGH IPRax 2013, 168, 171 = BGHZ 190, 28; *Stefan Arnold*, IPRax 2013, 141, 145; *Stefan Arnold*, IPRax 2013, 525, 526.

[76] See *Seibl*, IPRax 2011, 234, 240.

[77] More generous *Geimer/Schütze*, Art. 15 note 25 b; *Geimer*, in: FS Dieter Martiny (2014), p. 711, 727.

[78] OLG Karlsruhe IPRspr. 2011 Nr 199 p. 529.

[79] *Mankowski*, IPRax 2009, 474, 478.

[80] A respective offer of proof – if suitable and relevant – must be followed by a taking of evidence according to the standards of the *lex fori*; BGE 133 III 295, 300–301.

[81] *Johann Gruber v. BayWa AG*, (Case C-464/01) [2005] ECR I-439, I-475 para. 46 (commented upon by *Mankowski*, IPRax 2005, 503); *Ansgar Staudinger*, in: Rauscher, Art. 15 Brüssel I-VO note 3 as well as BGE 133 III 295, 300–301.

and (iii) that the other party concluded the contract for a professional purpose.[82] The extent of this particular aspect of the consumer's burden of proof is open to debate. Is the consumer *always* forced to argue that the contract at hand is missing characteristic professional elements and therefore not a dual contract in order to satisfy the judicature[83] of the ECJ?[84] Does the consumer *always* need to demonstrate that the contract does not relate to future professional experience or setting up a business which would also exclude the dispute from the Brussels *Ibis* consumer regime?[85]

45 Exceptions to the scope of the consumer regime fall within the other party's burden of proof because a lack of applicability of the Brussels *Ibis* consumer regime is beneficial to the party contracting for a professional purpose. While the consumer needs to demonstrate the rule, the other party needs to prove the exception. Therefore, the other party is responsible for proving that (i) one of the exceptions in Art. 17 (3) Brussels *Ibis* Regulation or Art. 6 (4) Rome I Regulation is applicable or (ii) that the contract's object is in fact tenancy of immovable property as defined by Art. 24 (1) subpara. 1 2nd option Brussels *Ibis* Regulation or (iii) that another criterion of Art. 24 Brussels *Ibis* Regulation is met.[86]

46 Naturally, the burden of proof for counter-exceptions to the exceptions is incumbent on the consumer because a "return" to the consumer regime would be favourable to the consumer. In this way, the consumer would need to demonstrate that a contract of transport provides for a combination of travel and accommodation for an inclusive price (Art. 17 (3) *in fine* Brussels *Ibis* Regulation) or falls within the scope of the Package Travel Directive.[87,88]

47 Matters of the situational scope of application of the consumer regime fall within the consumer's burden of proof. As noted above, this is because the consumer profits from the jurisdiction clauses of the regulation's consumer regime. Therefore, the consumer needs to put forth that (i) the other party pursues commercial or professional activities in the Member State of the consumer's domicile (Art. 17 (1) (c) 1st option) or (ii) that the other party directs such activities to that Member State or to several states including that Member State (Art. 17 (1) (c) 2nd option Var.2) and (iii) that the contract at hand falls within the scope of such activities (Art. 17 (1) (c)).[89]

48 In addition to these general principles certain exceptional circumstances seem conceivable reversing the roles of consumer and the other party. Then, the consumer is not interested in the application of the consumer regime whereas the other party seeks to demonstrate its applicability. One example might be a consumer's action for a declaratory judgement filed in the "wrong" forum, e.g. (according to the ECJ's interpretation[90]) that of Art. 8 (1) Brussels

---

82 *Mankowski*, IPRax 2009, 474, 478–479.

83 *Johann Gruber v. BayWa AG*, (Case C-464/01) [2005] ECR I-439 paras. 31–45.

84 Affirmative *Simotta*, in: Fasching/Konecny, Art. 15 EuGVO note 31.

85 See also *Francesco Benincasa v. Dentalkit Srl*, (Case C-269/95) [1997] ECR I-3767 (commented upon by *Mankowski*, JZ 1998, 898).

86 *Mankowski*, IPRax 2009, 474, 480.

87 Council Directive 90/314/EEC of 13 June 1990 on package travel, package holidays and package tours, OJ EEC L 158/59.

88 Rb. Den Haag (Kantoonrechter) S&S 2014 Nr 58 p. 406; *Mankowski*, IPRax 2009, 474, 480.

89 *Mankowski*, IPRax 2009, 474, 480.

I*bis* Regulation,[91] against which the defendant raises a jurisdictional defense based on the fact that Art. 17 (1) as *lex specialis* does not include this particular forum in the (exhaustive) consumer regime. On a second note, the other party might claim that a consumer commuting between Member States is domiciled in a different Member State than previously claimed by the consumer. Thirdly, a consumer might argue jurisdiction of the Member State the other party is domiciled in or the other party's branch or agency is situated in because its substantive law is more favourable to the consumer than that of the Member State the consumer is domiciled in. In these cases the parties' roles would be reversed insofar as the other party would seek to undermine the consumers "attack". A tactical agenda would outweigh more general, strategic considerations. Therefore, in cases such as these where the traditional roles of the parties to the dispute are reversed the burden of proof is also reversed. Then, it is the other party, not the consumer, who is responsible for proving the elements leading to applicability of the consumer regime.[92]

A valid jurisdiction clause would supersede objective jurisdiction under the consumer re- **49** gime if it is exclusive and therefore not widening the consumer's choices. In this regard the question of the existence of a jurisdiction clause is to be viewed separately from the question whether the criteria of Art. 19 have been met. However, the general rule applies to both questions: The party claiming rules to be applicable bears the burden of proving that their criteria are met. Therefore, the party claiming the validity of a jurisdiction clause[93] needs to prove its existence, that the requirements of Art. 25 have in fact been fulfilled,[94] or that there is consensus between the parties.[95]

If a party claims that a jurisdiction clause is invalid according to Arts. 15; 19 or 21 Brussels **50** I*bis* Regulation then this party accordingly bears the burden of proving that the corresponding protective regime is in fact applicable.[96] Naturally, the burden of proving that in spite of the regime's general applicability the criteria of an exception to this applicability are met then falls upon the party benefitting from this claim. Generally, this will be the party contracting for a professional purpose.[97] Under certain circumstances, however, the consumer could be equally interested in claiming the derogation of a certain forum to undermine a suit

---

[90] *SmithGlaxoKline v. Pierre Rouard*, (Case C-462/06) [2008], ECJ I-3965 (commented upon by *Mankowski*, EWiR Art. 18 EuGVVO 1/08, 435; *Franzina*, NGCC 2008 I 1093; *Harris*, [2008] 124 LQR 523).

[91] Discussing the many aspects of the concurring problem with regard to contracts of employment, *Mankowski*, EuZA 2008, 104.

[92] *Mankowski*, IPRax 2009, 474, 481–482.

[93] OGH JBl 2001, 327; OGH ZfRV 2006, 70, 71; *Hewden Tower Cranes Ltd. v. Wolffkran GmbH* [2007] 2 Lloyd's Rep. 138, 145 (Q.B.D., *Jackson* J.); *Boglione*, Assicurazioni 2008 II/2, 41, 46.

[94] See only OGH ZfRV 2006, 70, 71; Hof 's-Hertogenbosch NIPR 2001 Nr 289 p. 480; Hof Arnhem NIPR 2008 Nr 297 p. 553; Rb. Rotterdam NIPR 2003 Nr 119 p. 212; Rb. Rotterdam NIPR 2003 Nr 215 p. 327; *Hewden Tower Cranes Ltd. v. Wolffkran GmbH* [2007] 2 Lloyd's Rep. 138, 145 (Q.B.D., *Jackson* J.); *Mankowski*, in: Rauscher, Art. 25 Brussels I*bis* Regulation note 1; Art. 25 Brussels I Regulation note 173 (*Magnus*).

[95] *Bols Distilleries BV v. Superior Yacht Services* [2007] 1 WLR 16, 20 (P.C., opinion delivered by Lord *Rodger of Earlsferry*); Cassaz. Assicurazioni 2008 II/2, 40, 57 f; *Deutsche Bank AG v. Asia Pacific Broadband Wireless Communications Inc.* [2008] 2 Lloyd's Rep. 177, 180 (Q.B.D., *Flaux* J.).

[96] *WPP Holdings Italy srl v. Benatti* [2006] 2 Lloyd's Rep. 610, 620 (Q.B.D., *Field* J.).

[97] *Mankowski*, IPRax 2009, 474, 482.

filed by the other party in that very forum. Moreover, the consumer will argue the validity of a jurisdiction clause if he is filing a suit in a forum other than those of Art. 18 (1). In particular, it will be the consumer claiming the exception according to Art. 19 (2), namely that a jurisdiction clause is not exclusive but widening the consumer's choice of fora.[98]

Article 17

1. In matters relating to a contract concluded by a person, the consumer, for a purpose which can be regarded as being outside his trade or profession, jurisdiction shall be determined by this Section, without prejudice to Article 6 and point 5 of Article 7, if:
   (a) it is a contract for the sale of goods on instalment credit terms; or
   (b) it is a contract for a loan repayable by instalments, or for any other form of credit, made to finance the sale of goods; or
   (c) in all other cases, the contract has been concluded with a person who pursues commercial or professional activities in the Member State of the consumer's domicile or, by any means, directs such activities to that Member State or to several States including that Member State, and the contract falls within the scope of such activities.
2. Where a consumer enters into a contract with a party who is not domiciled in a Member State but has a branch, agency or other establishment in one of the Member States, that party shall, in disputes arising out of the operations of the branch, agency or establishment, be deemed to be domiciled in that Member State.
3. This Section shall not apply to a contract of transport other than a contract which, for an inclusive price, provides for a combination of travel and accommodation.

---

[98] *Mankowski*, IPRax 2009, 474, 482.

I. Generalities

Art. 17 determines the scope of application of the provisions on jurisdiction for consumer **1**
contracts.

According to Art. 17 (1) in order to be covered by Section 4, there must a dispute relating to a **2**
contract concluded by a consumer. Furthermore, the contract must be one of three types of
contracts listed in Art. 17 (1) (a)-(c). However, Art. 17 (3) contains a general exception to the
scope of the application of Section 4. Finally, Art. 17 (2) sets up a technical rule concerning
contracts entered into by the consumer with a party not domiciled in a Member State.

The provisions of Section 4 of the Brussels I*bis* Regulation are independent of the general **3**
scheme of the Regulation.[1] Consequently, if Art. 17 covers the consumer contract, jurisdiction can only be determined by Arts. 16 and 17 and not, for instance, Arts. 4 and 7. However,
if the consumer contract does not fall within Art. 17, the general scheme of the Regulation
applies, e.g. Arts. 4, 7 and 8.

Jurisdiction determined by Section 4 is without prejudice to Art. 6 and Art. 7 (5). An **4**
identical reservation was contained in Art. 8 Brussels I Regulation as a proviso in favour
of Art. 4 and Art. 5 (5) Brussels I Regulation. The reference to Art. 6 means that the
provisions of jurisdiction of Arts. 16 and 17 generally only apply in respect of defendants
domiciled in a Member State. The reference also means that Member States can apply their
own rules on international jurisdiction against defendants domiciled in non-Member States.
However, as mentioned earlier, Art. 17 (2) contains an exception from the reservation.
Furthermore, the reference to Art. 6 must be read subject to Art. 18 (1) 2nd option where

---

[1] Report *Jenard* p. 33.

the consumer is granted a forum at his domicile regardless of the defendant's domicile,[2] and thus even if the defendant is domiciled outside the EU and does not have a place of business in the EU and without reference to any jurisdictional rules of the national law of the forum under Art. 6.

5 The reference to Art. 7 (5) means that branch jurisdiction under this provision can be applied even if the contract falls within the scope of Section 4. Since consumers do not happen to develop branches or other places of business the reference to Art. 7 (5) enhances and widens only jurisdiction for claims by the consumer against the other party. The really important aspect of the reference to Art. 7 (5) and solely to Art. 7 (5) that is, is that this reference serves as the basis for an *argumentum e contrario*: All other grounds of special jurisdiction are excluded for they are not expressly referred to.[3] In particular, neither party can avail itself of Art. 8 (1).[4] The regime established by Arts. 17–19 is exhaustive and conclusive[5] but for such exceptions as are expressly made. This is not necessarily to the benefit of the consumer as the party the protection of which is intended. Assume that the consumer commenced a lawsuit and invokes a "wrong" ground of jurisdiction which the other party can successfully contest. It would be helpful for the consumer if he could rely on Art. 8 (1), particularly in the instance that he wants to sue both his supplier and a producer, the latter under a warranty given or in product liability. But this appears to be hardly feasible,[6] the more so since Art. 20 (1) *in fine* remedied the parallel case of the plaintiff-employee correcting the untenable holding of the ECJ in *SmithGlaxoKline*[7] and Art. 17 (1) has not been amended in the same manner. The European legislator missed an opportunity to rectify a shortcoming and caused an unjustifiable divergence in detail between the protective regimes.[8] A bold way to overcome this would be an analogy to Art. 20 (1) *in fine*. Another idea would be that the consumer could dispose of the protection afforded to him by Arts. 17–19 in order to avail himself of Art. 8 (1).[9]

II. Matters relating to a contract

6 According to Art. 17 (1), Section 4 applies to disputes relating to a contract concluded by a consumer. The existence of a c contrat is thus the basic requirement.[10] The concept of a contract should be interpreted in basically the same manner as under Art. 7 (1) since Art. 17

---

[2] *Mankowski*, RIW 2014, 625, 627–628.

[3] See only OLG München ZIP 2013, 435. Basically wrong thus BezG Schwechat RRa 2014, 204, 206 relying on "Art. 15 (2) in conjunction with Art. 5 (1) Brussels I Regulation".

[4] BGH NJW 2013, 1399 [14]; OLG Frankfurt IPRspr. 2012 Nr 204 p. 472; OLG Frankfurt IPRspr. 2012 Nr 207 p. 481; OLG München IPRspr. 2012 Nr 212 p. 491.

[5] See only *SmithGlaxoKline v. Pierre Rouard*, (Case C-462/06) [2008] ECR I-3965; *Brugnera/Reinalter*, Giur. it. 2014, 578, 579.

[6] BGH NJW 2013, 1399 [14]; OLG Frankfurt ZIP 2013, 387, 388 with further references; OLG München ZIP 2013, 435; *Mankowski*, IPRax 2009, 474, 481.

[7] *SmithGlaxoKline v. Pierre Rouard*, (Case C-462/06) [2008] ECR I-3965. Criticised by *Mankowski*, EWiR Art. 18 EuGVVO 1/08, 435; *Franzina*, NGCC 2008 I 1093; *Harris*, (2008) 124 LQRev 523.

[8] *Magnus/Mankowski*, ZvglRWiss 110 (2011), 252, 297; *von Hein*, RIW 2013, 97, 103; *von Hein*, LMK 2014, 36025; *Domej*, RabelsZ 78 (2014), 508, 529.

[9] See OLG München IPRspr. 2012 Nr 212 p. 491.

[10] BGH MDR 2014, 918 [10].

is a *lex specialis* to Art. 7 (1).[11] In particular, this will also cover claims relating to void contracts. Furthermore, at least in the Commission's opinion, the concept of contract includes timeshare agreements concerning immoveable property.[12] However, so far such contracts have been regarded as covered by Art. 24 (1) concerning exclusive jurisdiction.

The concept of a contract has caused some difficulties with respect to Section 4 of the 7
Brussels I Regulation.[13] The ECJ has been faced with three requests for interpretation of the concept in *Gabriel*, in *Engler* and *Ilsinger*.[14]

In *Gabriel*, a German company sold goods by mail order, inter alia, in Germany and Austria. 8
An Austrian consumer received several personalised letters at his private address from the German company, which led him to believe that he was the winner of a prize being a sum of money provided he ordered goods of a certain minimum value from the German company. It appeared from various letters sent to the consumer that the indicated prize was not a firm promise to pay the prize. The consumer ordered the goods, but did not receive the prize. Consequently, the consumer instituted proceedings in Austria according to Art. 14 (1) Brussels Convention (Art. 18 (1) of the Brussels I Regulation).

The issue at stake was whether or not the proceedings instituted by the consumer where 9
contractual in nature and thus covered by Section 4. The ECJ found that the consumer and the company were linked to each other by virtue of the contract for the sale of goods, and that the contract was of the type listed in Art. 13 (1) (3) Brussels Convention (Art. 17 (1) (a) of the Brussels I Regulation). Furthermore, the ECJ found that the correspondence sent by the German company to the Austrian consumer established an in dissociable relationship between the promise of financial benefit and the order for goods, that order being presented by the seller as a prerequisite for the grant of the promised financial benefit in order to persuade the consumer to enter into a contract. As the consumer concluded the contract for the sale of goods essentially, if not exclusively, by reason of the seller's promise of financial benefit, which was substantially higher than the minimum amount required for the order, the ECJ concluded that the consumer's claim was contractual in nature. Consequently, the court competent to deal with a consumer contract also has jurisdiction in respect of the claim concerning the proposed prize.[15] In reaching this result, the ECJ emphasized the need for a court to have jurisdiction in respect of actions that are linked so closely to the contract as to be in dissociable. The ECJ also stressed the need to avoid, as far as possible, a situation in which several courts have jurisdiction in respect of one and the same contract.[16]

---

[11] *Rudolf Gabriel*, (Case C-96/00) [2002] ECR I-6367, I-6399 para. 36.

[12] Commission Proposal COM (1999) 348 final p. 14.

[13] Summarizingly *Bach*, IHR 2010, 17.

[14] *Rudolf Gabriel*, (Case C-96/00) [2002] ECR I-6367; *Petra Engler v. Janus Versand GmbH*, (Case C-27/02) [2005] ECR I-481; *Renate Ilsinger v. Martin Dreschers, acting as administrator in the insolvency of Schlank & Schick GmbH*, (Case C-180/06) [2009] ECR I-3961.

[15] *Rudolf Gabriel*, (Case C-96/00) [2002] ECR I-6367, I-6401 *et seq.* paras. 48–55.

[16] *Rudolf Gabriel*, (Case C-96/00) [2002] ECR I-6367, I-6403 *et seq.* paras. 56–57. In this context, the ECJ referred to *Besix SA v. Wasserreinigungsbau Alfred Kretzschmar GmbH & Co. KG (WABAG) and Planungs- und Forschungsgesellschaft Dipl. Ing. W. Kretzschmar GmbH & Co. KG (Plafog)*, (Case C-256/00) [2002] ECR I-1699, I-1726 para. 27.

10 A similar, yet distinct, issue arose in *Engler*. An Austrian national domiciled in Austria received a letter personally addressed to her at her domicile from a German mail order company. The letter contained a "payment notice" that led her to believe that she had won a prize of money in a lottery organised by the mail order company. The Austrian national also received a catalogue of goods marketed by the German company intended to induce her to conclude a contract for the purchase of goods offered by the German company. The payment notice contained the name and address of the Austrian national as well as the conditions for receiving the prize. The conditions were in small print. The Austrian national was instructed in the notice to sign and return the notice immediately to the German company which she did. The Austrian then believed that that was sufficient to obtain the promised prize. However, the German company refused to pay the prize to the Austrian. Consequently, the Austrian national brought proceedings in Austria under national law claiming the prize.

11 The ECJ was asked, inter alia, whether the claim constituted a claim in contract under the Brussels Convention. The ECJ first examined whether the claim was contractual in nature in respect of Art. 13 Brussels Convention (Art. 17 of the Brussels I Regulation) since this provision constitutes a *lex specialis* in relation to Art. 5 (1). The ECJ stated that Art. 13 (1) (3) is only applicable insofar that the claimant is a private final consumer not engaged in trade or professional activities, that the legal proceedings relate to a contract between that consumer and the professional vendor for the sale of goods or services which has given rise to reciprocal and interdependent obligations between the two parties, and that the conditions set out in Art. 13 (3) (a) and (b) Brussels Convention, which require a contract to be concluded, are fulfilled. The ECJ found that the present situation was not covered by Art. 13 Brussels Convention because the vendor's initiative was not followed by the conclusion of a contract between the consumer and the vendor. The Court stressed that the Austrian national did not assume any obligations towards the German company by claiming the award of the prize. In conclusion, the claim was not contractual in nature in the context of Art. 13 Brussels Convention (Art. 17 Brussels I Regulation).[17] On the other hand, the ECJ found that the claim, subject to certain conditions, was covered by Art. 5 (1) Brussels Convention because that provision does not require the conclusion of a contract.[18]

12 In *Ilsinger*, an Austrian domiciliary received, at her home address and in a sealed envelope, a letter addressed to her personally from a German mail-order company.[19] The envelope, on which the words "Important documents!", "Please open immediately" and "Private" were written, contained, inter alia, a message addressed to the Austrian domiciliary personally which gave the impression that she had won a prize of EUR 20 000. The next day, in order to obtain payment of the financial benefit promised, the Austrian domiciliary tore off a coupon containing an identification number attached to an envelope included in the letter, attached the coupon, as requested to do in the letter, to the 'prize claim certificate' and returned it to the German mail-order company. The Austrian domiciliary stated that at the same time she placed a trial order. That assertion was challenged by the mail-order company, which submitted to the contrary that no goods were ordered by the applicant. However, it is common

---

17 *Petra Engler v. Janus Versand GmbH*, (Case C-27/02) [2005] ECR I-481 paras. 34–38.

18 *Petra Engler v. Janus Versand GmbH*, (Case C-27/02) [2005] ECR I-481 paras. 45 and 61.

19 *Renate Ilsinger v. Martin Dreschers, acting as administrator in the insolvency of Schlank & Schick GmbH*, (Case C-180/06) [2009] ECR I-3961.

ground that the award of the prize supposedly won by the Austrian domiciliary did not depend on such an order. As the Austrian domiciliary had still not obtained payment of the financial benefit claimed, she brought an action for that purpose before an Austrian court. She argued that the court had jurisdiction under Art. 16 (1) Brussels I Regulation. The mail-order company argued that the court lacked jurisdiction, arguing essentially that Arts. 15; 16 Brussels I Regulation were inapplicable to the dispute since they presuppose the existence of a contract for valuable consideration, which was, however, lacking in this case. Participation in the promotional game was not subject to the placing of an order, even on a trial basis without obligation and with the right to return the goods. Furthermore, the Austrian domiciliary had not ordered goods and was not therefore entitled to protection as a consumer.

The ECJ was essentially asked whether the legal proceedings by which a consumer seeks an   **13** order requiring a mail-order company to award a prize apparently won by him, without the award of that prize depending on an order of goods offered for sale by that company, are contractual in nature within the meaning of (1) (c), if necessary, on condition that the consumer has none the less placed such an order. The ECJ noted that (1) (c) is drafted in more general and broader terms than Art. 13 (1) Brussels Convention. Whereas the latter only applies to "any other contract for the supply of goods or a contract for the supply of services", the former applies to "all other contracts". Furthermore, although the Court has held that the application of Art. 13 (1) Brussels Convention is limited to contracts which give rise to reciprocal and interdependent obligations between the parties, basing itself, moreover, expressly on the wording of that provision referring to a "contract for the supply of goods or a contract for the supply of services", the scope of (1) (c) appears, by contrast, to be no longer being limited to those situations in which the parties have assumed reciprocal obligations.[20]

On the other hand, the ECJ emphasized that Art. 17 is applicable only if the legal proceedings   **14** concerned relate to a contract which has been concluded between a consumer and a professional. The Court added that as regards that condition, it is, of course, conceivable, in the context of (1) (c), that one of the parties merely indicates its acceptance, without assuming itself any legal obligation to the other party to the contract. However, it is necessary, for a contract to exist within the meaning of that provision, that the latter party should assume such a legal obligation by submitting a firm offer which is sufficiently clear and precise with regard to its object and scope as to give rise to a link of a contractual nature as referred to by that provision. The ECJ furthermore stated that that latter requirement may be regarded as being satisfied only where, in the context of a prize notification, such as that at issue in the main proceedings, there has been a legal commitment contracted by the mail-order company. In other words, the latter must have expressed clearly its intention to be bound by such a commitment, if it is accepted by the other party, by declaring itself to be unconditionally willing to pay the prize at issue to consumers who so request. It is for the national court to determine whether that requirement is fulfilled in the dispute before it.[21] Consequently, the ECJ concluded that (1) (c) does not apply to legal proceedings such as those at issue in the

---

[20]   *Renate Ilsinger v. Martin Dreschers, acting as administrator in the insolvency of Schlank & Schick GmbH,* (Case C-180/06) [2009] ECR I-3961, I-4015 para. 48, I-4016 para. 51; *von Hein,* BerDGfIR 45 (2011), 369, 376; *Thole,* IPRax 2013, 136 (136).

[21]   *Renate Ilsinger v. Martin Dreschers, acting as administrator in the insolvency of Schlank & Schick GmbH,* (Case C-180/06) [2009] ECR I-3961, I-4016 *et seq.* para. 52, 54 and 55.

main proceedings if the professional did not undertake contractually to pay the prize promised to the consumer who requests its payment. In that case, (1) (c) is applicable to such legal proceedings only on condition that the misleading prize notification was followed by the conclusion of a contract by the consumer with the mail-order company evidenced by an order placed with the latter.[22]

15   For the sake of protecting private investors on the capital markets, the German BGH has felt inclined to interpret the concept of "contract" very broadly and extensively. The BGH emphasizes that (1) does not require "claims arising out of a contract", but only "matters relating to a contract". Consequentially, it applied (1) to claims stemming from a German Act (§ 32 (1) cl. 1 KWG) which protects investors in an indirect manner whilst it does not feature as contract law in the strict sense, but forms part of the realm of regulatory law, principally enforced by supervising and controlling official bodies.[23] Matters got ever further obscured since the BGH extended Art. 15 Brussels I Regulation even to claims covered by § 823 (2) BGB, a centrepiece of German *tort* law.[24] But in the light of the approach taken by the CJEU in *Brogsitter* to re-characterise contract-related claims as contractual if they are as a matter of interpretation of the contract to be qualified as breach of the rights and obligations set out in the contract even if there are based on rules which are characterised as delictual under national law,[25] this might be upheld.[26] Another supporting reasoning could be to invoke jurisdiction based on connectivity.[27] *Brogsitter*[28] might have opened the floodgates in this regard, too.[29] Whether it is necessary to introduce a specific understanding of cause and action[30] is doubtful. On the other hand, a more "economic" understanding of contract tends to stretch the limits imposed by the wording and the common understanding of "contract", particularly so if it extends to include third parties (which are not formal parties of a contract in the traditional sense) in the contractual realm.[31] But judged by traditional yardsticks, for instance a private investor's claim against the issuer of a bond would be rather framed in trot than in contract.[32]

16   Section 4 does not cover all consumer contracts. The Section only covers the contracts listed

---

[22]   *Renate Ilsinger v. Martin Dreschers, acting as administrator in the insolvency of Schlank & Schick GmbH*, (Case C-180/06) [2009] ECR I-3961, I-4018 para. 59.

[23]   BGH NJW 2011, 532 = ZIP 2010, 2264 = WM 2010, 2163; BGH NJW 2011, 2809 = BGH IPRax 2013, 168, 171; BGH WM 2012, 646; applauded by *Herbert Roth*, in: FS Athanassios Kaissis (2012), p. 819, 821; *Geimer*, in: FS Dieter Martiny (2014), p. 711, 725. *De lege ferenda* endorsing, *de lege lata* critical *von Hein*, EuZW 2011, 369, 370; *von Hein*, BerDGfIR 45 (2011), 369, 379–380.

[24]   BGH NJW 2011, 532.

[25]   *Marc Brogsitter v. Fabrication de Montres Normandes EURL and Karsten Fräßdorf* (Case C-548/12), ECLI:EU:C:2014:148 paras. 21–27.

[26]   *Baumert* EWiR 2014, 435, 436; *Ansgar Staudinger/Steinrötter*, JuS 2015, 1, 5; *Hüßtege*, in: Thomas/Putzo, Art. 17 EuGVVO note 2; *Peter Huber*, IPRax 2015, 403, 404.

[27]   See *Herbert Roth*, in: FS Athanassios Kaissis (2012), p. 819, 822–823, 826–831.

[28]   *Marc Brogsitter v. Fabrication de Montres Normandes EURL and Karsten Fräßdorf* (Case C-548/12), ECLI:EU:C:2014:148 paras. 21–27.

[29]   *Ansgar Staudinger*, jM 2015, 46, 52–53.

[30]   *Herbert Roth*, in: FS Athanassios Kaissis (2012), p. 819, 832–835.

[31]   A-G *Szpunar*, Opinion in Case C-375/13 of 3 September 2014, ECLI:EU:C:2014:2135, paras. 39–44.

[32]   *von Hein*, BerDGfIR 45 (2011), 369, 377–378.

in Art. 17. Furthermore, Section 4 does not cover insurance contracts with consumers since Section 3 (Arts. 10–16) regulates such contracts. Consequently, Section 3 governs an insurance contract with a consumer.[33] Finally, consumer contracts falling within the ambit of Section 6 concerning exclusive jurisdiction are not regulated by Section 4, but by Section 6. As a result, the ordinary rules on jurisdiction in Sections 1 and 2 regulate consumer contracts not governed by Section 3, Section 4 or Section 6.

Difficult issues arise where a contract is not a traditional bipartite agreement. This is not yet **17** the case if two or more persons are on one side of a contract. Two sellers might make matters a little more complicated but the contract at stake would still be a sales contract. The same holds true if there are two or more buyers. Even the combination of two or more sellers with two or more buyers does not alter the basic structure of a sales contract. Multi-partite contracts are more complex. The first example are company agreements or articles of association. Since they are contracts for the purposes of Art. 7 (1) it ought to be presumed that they also have a contractual nature for the purposes of (1).

The second example are bonds. Bonds are characterised by an accession of the investors by **18** whichever mode to a bunch of preselected Terms and Conditions establishing a level playing field. Modification or alteration of these Terms and Conditions might be subject to majority voting or other kinds of cram down. Recital (28) and Art. 6 (4) (d) Rome I Regulation might point towards an exemption of bonds from the consumer regime.[34] But given the unconvincing ratio of the latter rule which is a result of fiercest lobbying[35] it would be a bold step to transfer this rule to the realm of the Brussels I*bis* Regulation. There is reason in the Brussels I*bis* Regulation not providing for a parallel rule. The protection of private investors has starred under the Brussels I Regulation.

III. The consumer

1. Concept: Role in the concrete contract, not permanent status

Section 4 of the Brussels I Regulation only applies to consumer contracts. According to **19** Art. 17 (1), a consumer contract is defined as a contract concluded by a person for a purpose which can be regarded as being outside his trade or profession. This definition is a codification of the ECJ's judgment in *Société Bertrand v. Paul Ott KG.*[36] Furthermore, the definition is adopted from Art. 5 Rome Convention. Consequently, the Explanatory Report *Giuliano/Lagarde*[37] to the Rome Convention is of importance when interpreting the consumer concept of the Brussels I*bis* Regulation.[38] The concept of a consumer is a uniform concept. The ECJ has emphasized this point stating that the concept of a consumer is the principal factor in the determination of rules governing jurisdiction.[39] Intellectual or economic superiority

---

[33] Report *Schlosser*, para. 156.

[34] Tentatively so *Thole*, WM 2014, 1205, 1212.

[35] *Mankowski*, RIW 2009, 98.

[36] Report *Schlosser* para. 153; *Société Bertrand v. Paul Ott KG*, (Case 150/77) [1978] ECR 1431.

[37] OJ EEC 1980 C 282/1.

[38] Report *Giuliano/Lagarde* OJ EEC 1980 C 282/1, 24.

[39] *Shearson Lehman Hutton, Inc. v. TVB Treuhandgesellschaft für Vermögensverwaltung und Beteiligungen mbh*, (Case C-89/91) [1993] ECR I-139, I-188 para. 19.

on the professional's side is not required.[40] This is an autonomous European concept not having recourse to any *lex causae*.[41] The relevant point of time for judging in which capacity a person is acting, is the time when the contract is concluded not the time when the writ is issued or when the lawsuit becomes pending; an *ex ante* perspective is called for.[42] The parties are not at liberty to ascertain such capacity contractually for this would the other party enable to exploit any bargaining power it has. If the consumer employs auxiliary personnel or intermediaries (like lawyers or brokers) not becoming a proper party to the contract this is irrelevant for the contractual purpose relates only to the parties of the contract in the strict sense.[43] This implies also the solution in the event of a contract to the benefit of a third party,[44] the more so since the obligations arising under such contract and thus the risks to be carried are the contracting parties' ones.

20 Consumer is not an abstract and permanent status but has to be judged with regard to the concrete contract and the capacity in which a person is contracting in the concrete case.[45] A role is asked for concretely.[46] One and the same person may conclude a contract in his private capacity and the next contract in his professional capacity.[47] Seemingly identical contracts might turn out to be just that: only seemingly identical.[48] The decisive phrase is that a person concludes a consumer contract for a purpose which can be regarded as being outside his trade or profession. The lawyer who orders copy paper for his office acts in his professional capacity whereas the same person is acting in his private capacity if he orders toys as presents for his children. Or a person who is in his day-work involved in future trades purchases some furniture for his family home. Or that person invests his private money.[48a] Of course, both of them have some legal or professionals skills and have received some training which they will not rip-off once they act in the confines of their private lives.[49] But it would be way too complicated and would leave too much leeway to argue if it was necessary to assert the personal qualities and skills of every single customer (just imagine the plumber who is experienced and knows how to bargain, but in his specific profession only whereas he will not be equally experienced for instance with regard to paintwork[50]). Acting on the other side of the market is different. He who is used to act on the supply side is not automatically versed to the same level at the demand side the more so since as a mere customer he will conclude contracts only over lesser amounts.[51] Furthermore, the lawyer buying cloths for his

---

[40]   *Herbert Roth*, in: FS Bernd von Hoffmann (2011), p. 715, 722.

[41]   Incorrect OLG München IPRspr. 2012 Nr 212 p. 490.

[42]   *Sachse* pp. 110–111. Overlooked by *Neil Brown*, CRi 2015, 38, 41.

[43]   CA Colmar RCDIP 90 (2001), 135 with note *Gaudemet-Tallon*; *Mankowski*, EWiR Art. 13 EuGVÜ 2/99, 1171, 1172; *Sachse* p. 123. *Contra Sibylle Neumann/Rosch*, IPRax 2001, 257, 259.

[44]   *Sachse* pp. 128–129; see also (at the level of substantive law) *Mankowski*, VuR 2002, 269.

[45]   See only Rb. Rotterdam NIPR 2015 Nr 78 p. 179; *Kemper*, Verbraucherschutzinstrumente (1994) p. 25; *Harald Koch*, Verbraucherprozessrecht (1990) p. 3; *Markus Würdinger*, in: FS Peter Gottwald (2014), p. 693, 695.

[46]   See *Martin Engel/Stark*, ZEuP 2015, 32, 34–37 with further references.

[47]   OLG München RIW 2012, 635, 636 = WM 2012, 1863, 1864; Rb. Rotterdam NIPR 2015 Nr. 78 p. 179.

[48]   *Jonathan Hill* para. 3.46.

[48a] OLG Stuttgart 27 April 2015 – Case 5 U 120/14, forthcoming in RIW 2015 with note *Mankowski*.

[49]   *Añoveros*, Rev. eur. dr. consomm. 2004, 77, 92.

[50]   See *Senff* p. 241.

[51]   *Sachse* p. 102.

baby daughter acts in an evidently and obviously private capacity. Any genuine holiday trip is for private purposes[52] even if the traveller in his professional capacity works self-employed. The outer limits of a business run by a certain person have to be respected, and transactions in other areas are not within the confines of such business.[53] But that does not necessarily imply that they are for private purposes.[54] If a concrete contract can be attributed to a person's business or professional sphere there should not a distinction between "normal" acts and acts of an "exceptional" nature.[55] Secondary trades and professions are trades and professions although it might be difficult to draw a proper borderline between someone running two different businesses simultaneously and someone running a business and fashioning a mere hobby.[56] Circumstances preceding the conclusion of the contracts ought to be taken into account when judging the private or professional capacity of a party.[57]

Yet it would be wrong to fall victim to the fallacy to equate the concrete quality of being a **21** consumer with the every-day notion of consumer. A "consumer" is not necessarily required to consume in the technical sense, i.e. use up goods or services acquired. To circumscribe the sole purpose as satisfying an individual's own needs in terms of private consumption[58] comes dangerously close to such equation (if it is not a mere *petitio principii* employing the *definiendum* in a modified form as part of the *definiens*). Any discussion whether buying a birthday present for a family member or a personal friend might fall outside (1)[59] is misconceived.[60] It is not convincing to rely on a concept of "needs",[60a] to this term being attributed an every-day meaning (and impliedly associating it with catering for bare necessities of life).[60b] Puritan or socialist zeal would be even more misplaced.[60c] To differentiate between "needy" and "wanty", and in the consequence to exclude the wealthy or greedy would be a no go.[60d]

---

52   OLG Köln NZM 2010, 495.

53   *Chris Hart (Business Sales) Ltd. v. Niven* 1992 SLT (Sh Ct) 53 (Sh. Ct. Glasgow); *B.J. Mann (Advertising) Ltd. v. ACE Welding and Fabrications Ltd.* 1994 Sh. Ct. L. Rev. 763 (Sh. Ct. Glasgow)

54   *Semple Fraser WS v. Quayle* 2002 SLT (Sh Ct) 33 (Sh. Ct. Glasgow, Sheriff *James A. Taylor*); 2003 SLT (Sh Ct) 1 (Glasgow Sh. Ct., Sheriff *Mason*); *Sachse* p. 107 with reference to *Criminal proceedings against Patrice Di Pinto* (Case C-361/89), [1991] ECR I-1189 paras. 15–16.

55   *Criminal proceedings against Patrice Di Pinto* (Case C-361/89), [1991] ECR I-1189 paras. 15–16; *Jonathan Hill* paras. 3.52 *et seq.*

56   *Jonathan Hill* paras. 3.54 *et seq.*; *Briggs* para. 2.150.

57   Rb. Rotterdam NIPR 2015 Nr 78 p. 179.

58   *Francesco Benincasa v. Dentalkit SrL*, (Case C-269/95) [1997] ECR I-3767, I-3795 paras. 16, 17; *Česká spořitelna as v. Gerald Feichter*, (Case C-419/11), ECLI:EU:C:2013:165 para. 34; *AMT Futures Ltd. v. Marzillier, Dr. Meier & Dr. Guntner Rechtsanwaltsgesellschaft mbH* [2014] EWHC 1085 (Comm), [2015] 2 WLR 187 [56]-[59] (Q.B.D., *Popplewell* J.).

59   E.g. *Gehri*, in: Basler Kommentar Art. 15 LugÜ note 20.

60   *Geimer*, in: FS Dieter Martiny (2014), p. 711, 719.

60a See *Francesco Benincasa v. Dentalkit SrL*, (Case C-269/95) [1997] I-3767.

60b But cf. *Briggs* para. 2.101; *id.*, PIL para. 4.156.

60c *Briggs* para. 2.101.

60d *Briggs* para. 2.101.

2. No upper limit of volume involved

22 Investing privately held moneys or assets in any kind of investment is a private matter.[61] Private wealth is invested in, and exchanged for, the hope of profit.[62] For instance, reinvesting the gains from selling an estate in order to secure one's income in old age belongs to the investor's private sphere.[63] It does not do any harm if the private investors wants to get some return and even some earnings on his investment.[64] Administrating one's own private fortune is within the private realm unless transactions become so complex or manifold that the respective activity amounts to a professional one.[65] An investment in a real estate trust for the acquisition of shares of that trust for instance generally is in the investor's private sphere.[66] Whether the consumer invests his own money or money loaned out by some bank or other institution to him *via* a loan agreement is irrelevant.[67] Private investment via banks, brokers or funds is an area where customers and their vulnerability are chronically exploited, and thus protection is the more required,[67a] particularly considering the amounts at stake and relevance to the customers.

23 There is no cap on the amount involved.[67b] Consumer cases are not limited to small amounts. Acquiring luxury goods and spending lavish amounts of money for them is covered, and there is no restriction to the protection of "small people".[68] What will be commonly denominated as "luxurious" is highly depended on the time and the place.[69] Circumstances have changed over the ages, and what is luxurious in a "poor" Member State can be standard or even low standard in "rich" Member States.[70] If a person invests a zillion of his privately held own money this person still acts in a private capacity and thus a consumer.[70a] There is no upper limit.[71] All-decisive is only that it is private money.[72] The billionaire who orders a leisure yacht worth 150 million € is a consumer[72a] even if he is heavily shielded and guarded by an army of trained lawyers (and becomes a true nightmare

---

61 BGE 121 III 336, 343; *Standard Bank London Ltd. v. Dimitrios Apostolakis* [2000] ILPr 766 (Q.B.D., Longmore J.); Sachse pp. 98–100. *Contra Briggs/Rees* para. 2.94; see also *Maple Leaf Macro Volatility Master Fund v. Rouvroy* [2009] 2 All ER (Comm) 287 [209] (Q.B.D., *Andrew Smith* J.).

62 *Standard Bank London Ltd. v. Dimitrios Apostolakis* [2000] ILPr 766 (Q.B.D., *Longmore* J.).

63 OGH ZfRV-LS 2009/14 = ZfRV 2009, 30.

64 See only OLG Frankfurt WM 2009, 718; *Mankowski*, in: Heiss/Schnyder (eds.), Aspekte des internationalen Immobilienrechts (2011), p. 9, 30.

65 OLG Frankfurt EuZW 2009, 309, 311; *Geimer*, in: FS Dieter Martiny (2014), p. 711, 720–721.

66 *Mankowski*, in: Heiss/Schnyder (eds.), Aspekte des internationalen Immobilienrechts (2011), p. 9, 30.

67 *Geimer*, in: FS Dieter Martiny (2014), p. 711, 721.

67a *Briggs*, PIL para. 4.156.

67b OLG Hamburg IPRax 2005, 251; *Standard Bank London Ltd. v. Dimitrios Apostolakis* [2000] ILPr 766 (Q.B.D., *Longmore* J.). But cf. OLG Hamm IPRspr. 2004 Nr. 98a.

68 *Herbert Roth*, in: FS Bernd von Hoffmann (2011), p. 715, 719–720.

69 *David Kluth* pp. 197–198.

70 *Mankowski*, EWiR Art. 13 EuGVÜ 1/99, 743, 744.

70a OLG Stuttgart 27 April 2015 – Case 5 U 120/14, forthcoming in RIW 2015 with note *Mankowski*: investment of 50 million €.

71 *Mankowski*, EWiR Art. 13 EuGVÜ 1/99, 743, 744; *Gerhard Wagner*, in: Stein/Jonas, Art. 15 note 18; *Geimer*, in: FS Dieter Martiny (2014), p. 711, 719–720.

72 *Mankowski*, RIW 2009, 98, 99.

for the shipyard and the financing banks). Certainly, these are not the cases for which Arts. 17–19 were made and designed.[73] But there must not be an examination staged as to whether someone acting in his private capacity truly needs protection in the concrete case.[74] To admit such examination would give too much leeway and allow too much argument in the event leading to enhanced transaction costs and to too much compromise. To make the issue fact specific[75] means to confuse it. The formalisation of the notion of consumer, the generalisation of the typical situation, generates legal certainty in mass business with consumers.[76] An abstract approach even benefits the businesses contracting with private persons for they can react in advance and adopt their conduct to the possibility (if not likelihood) of facing a consumer as their counterparty.[77] The European legislator has had ample opportunity to impose restrictions on what has now become Arts. 17–19, and such restrictions have in deed been called for.[78] But they have never been legislatively implemented, this is telling.[79] The volume at stake is a quantitative moment (as to be contrasted to the qualitative notion of luxury) which could be easily measured. Equally easily the legislator could have implemented upper limits as it has done in substantive EU consumer contract law.[80] That it has not done so gives rise to a strong *argumentum e contrario*.[81]

But if moneys collected are held by a trust or other investment body the investment trans- **24** actions of such body are not covered by (1) for the simple reason that such bodies are not natural persons. On the other hand, a natural person acquiring shares of an investment fund in order to invest his private assets is a consumer with regard to the act of acquisition.[82]

3. Start-ups

In *Francesco Benincasa v. Dentalkit SrL*, an Italian national concluded a franchise contract **25** with an Italian firm with a view to setting up and operating a shop in Germany. Subsequently, the Italian national instituted proceedings in Germany in accordance with Section 4 Brussels Convention, arguing, inter alia, that he was entitled to do so as a consumer given that he had not yet started trading in Germany. The ECJ found that the concept of a consumer must be strictly construed and referred to earlier case law. Furthermore, reference must be made to the position of the person concerned in a particular contract, having regard to the nature and aim of that contract and not to the subjective situation of the person

---

[72a] See *Hans-Hermann Mietz v. Intership Yachting Sneek BV*, (Case C-99/96) [1999] ECR I-2277, I-2311 para. 32.

[73] *Schütze*, in: FS Friedrich Graf von Westphalen (2010), p. 621, 625.

[74] But cf. in this direction *AMT Futures Ltd. v. Marzillier, Dr. Meier & Dr. Guntner Rechtsanwaltsgesellschaft mbH* [2014] EWHC 1085 (Comm), [2015] 2 WLR 187 [58]-[60] (Q.B.D., *Popplewell J.*).

[75] As *AMT Futures Ltd. v. Marzillier, Dr. Meier & Dr. Guntner Rechtsanwaltsgesellschaft mbH* [2014] EWHC 1085 (Comm), [2015] 2 WLR 187 [58] (Q.B.D., *Popplewell J.*) does.

[76] *Stefan Arnold*, IPRax 2013, 141, 145 and in more detail *Mankowski*, IPRax 2015, 115, 116–118 with ample references.

[77] *Mankowski*, IPRax 2015, 115, 117–118.

[78] *Schlosser*, in: FS Ernst Steindorff (1990), p. 1379, 1382.

[79] *Geimer*, in: FS Dieter Martiny (2014), p. 711, 723.

[80] References in *Sachse* p. 218.

[81] In detail *Sachse* pp. 217–223.

[82] OLG Frankfurt ZIP 2013, 387, 388.

concerned. The ECJ added that the same person may be regarded as a consumer in certain transactions and as an economic operator in others. Furthermore, according to the ECJ, only contracts concluded for the purpose of satisfying an individual's own needs in terms of private consumption fall under the provisions designed to protect the consumer as the party deemed to be the weaker party financially. Consequently, the ECJ found that the consumer concept does not cover contracts for the purpose of trade or professional activity, even if that activity is only planned for the future, since the fact that an activity is a future activity in nature does not divest it in any way of its trade or professional character.[83]

26 If a natural person is in the process of setting up a business his activity on behalf of his future business will take him out of the protection granted to consumer.[84] Business starters have decided to swim with the sharks, and they have to learn swimming the very moment they jump into the shark pool.[85] They are extending the circle of their activities and have decided to undertake entrepreneurial risks.[86] Building-up activities are attributed to the business to be build up. Only an express reservation to the contrary would carry the opposite result but such reservation does not exist. To submit start-ups to the sharper treatment from the very start avoids a number of anomalies:[87] Firstly, it puts out of any question that start-ups might even possibly get consumer protection for a relaunch and second start.[88] Secondly, it relives of any necessity to distinguish between a re-start and the mere extension of an existing business. Thirdly, it avoids the awkward answer to the awkward question from which contracts onwards the protected sphere would be left alternatively if not from the start. Somewhen there ought to be a first contract outside the protected sphere, and any alternative answer would be less convincing. Any inquiry into this issue threatens to become complicated and both time and cost consuming.[89]

27 A business in the course of being built up might not generate any earnings and even less any revenue yet, and its founders might personally still be inexperienced for they will only have to gather experience and know-how in the future. But this does not matter for the purposes of Art. 17 (1).[90] Baby sharks are regarded as sharks, and SMEs do not get a different treatment than "grown-up" enterprises or MNEs. Small-scale profit generation is relevant if it is professional,[90a] even if only as a secondary profession. This follows the general line of abstract typisation, and reduces transaction costs for the contracting partners are not held to invest costs for cautionary measures.[91]

---

[83] *Francesco Benincasa v. Dentalkit SrL*, (Case C-269/95) [1997] ECR I-3767, I-3795 paras. 15, 16 and 17.

[84] *Francesco Benincasa v. Dentalkit SrL*, (Case C-269/95) [1997] ECR I-3767, I-3795 paras. 15, 16, 17; *Rinaldi*, NGCC 1998 I 346; *Corea*, Giust. civ. 1999 I 13; *Toro*, Rev. dr. eur. consomm. 2014, 81, 85.

[85] *Mankowski*, JZ 1998, 898 (898).

[86] *Mankowski*, JZ 1998, 898 (898).

[87] *Mankowski*, JZ 1998, 898 (898).

[88] Applauded by *Sachse* p. 94.

[89] *Sachse* p. 94.

[90] Further considerations by *Mankowski*, JZ 1998, 898 (898).

[90a] *Briggs* para. 2.100.

[91] *Mankowski*, JZ 1998, 898 (898).

4. Employees acquiring means for performing their jobs

The tricky borderline case is the employee who acquires equipment, clothes or other means   **28**
for performing his job from someone else than his employer. He is not acting in any trade of
his own.[92] But is he acting inside or outside his profession? If he acquires the said equipment
from his employer that could be said to be within the confines of the employment relationship and thus should be governed by Art. 21, not Art. 17.[93] If the vendor is a third party
different from the party in the first place it ought to be ascertained who is the acquirer: the
employee or the employer, with the employee acting as his agent? Even if the employee is the
acquirer it might matter to which extent he is internally reimbursed by his employer and
whether this is known to the other party. Section 4 probably does not offer protection to an
employee who purchases goods necessary for carrying out his job, if the employer reim-
burses the employee because the goods cannot be said to be acquired for a genuinely private
purpose under these circumstances.[94] On the other hand, if the employee purchases on his
own means, he should be considered to act as a consumer.[95] Arts. 20–23 cannot serve as an
argument supporting the contention that he is the weaker party since they only operate in
the relation to the employer not in the relation to a third party.[96]

5. Other instances

The number of conceivable scenarios is legion. The retired person holding himself out as   **29**
non-executive director to companies offers professional services, anything supporting the
execution of these services will be inside his trade and profession.[97] The professional football
player hiring management services acts in his professional capacity although he does not
kick a single ball in this instance.[98] The managing director, executive, or majority shareholder of a company does not act in a private capacity if he guarantees obligations of that
company.[98a]

6. *Bona fide* ignorance of the consumer acting in a private capacity on the other party's side

In contrast to Art. 2 lit. a *in fine* CISG,[99] the wording of (1) does not contain any exception   **30**
that the other party, at any time before or at the conclusion of the contract, neither knew nor
ought to have known that the buyer contracted in his private capacity. But such exception
ought to be read in (1), though.[100] Otherwise the negligent seller would be better off than the

---

[92] *Senff* p. 237.

[93] *Egon Lorenz*, RIW 1987, 569, 576; *Senff* p. 237.

[94] Concurring *García Mirete*, REDI 2013-2, 290, 291.

[95] To the same avail *Sachse* pp. 95–97.

[96] Overlooked by *Senff* p. 237.

[97] See *Semple Fraser WS v. Ian Quayle* 2002 SLT (Sh Ct) 33 (Glasgow Sh. Ct., Sheriff *James A. Taylor*).

[98] See *Popstar Management Ltd. v. Twaddle* 2003 SLT (Sh Ct) 1 (Glasgow Sh. Ct., Sheriff *Mason*).

[98a] *Česká spořitelna as v. Gerald Feichter*, (Case C-419/11), ECLI:EU:C:2013:165 para. 37.

[99] For an example under the CISG OLG Hamm IHR 2010, 59 = NJW-RR 2010, 708; *Magnus*, in: Liber
      amicorum Kurt Siehr (2010), p. 405, 413–414.

[100] *Mankowski*, RabelsZ 63 (1999), 203, 231; *Mankowski*, ZvglRWiss 105 (2006), 120, 138; *Mankowski*,
       IPRax 2009, 474, 479; *Mankowski*, in: FS Ingeborg Schwenzer (2011), p. 1175, 1192; *Justus Meyer*, in:

---

circumspect one.[101] Entrepreneurs deserve protection if they justifiedly trust in their counter-party acting for professional purposes.[102] The Report *Giuliano/Lagarde* is to the same avail.[103] The lawyer ordering a computer for use exclusively at his private home by correspondence on his professional stationery or under his professional e-mail address conveys an impression to which he can be held[104] (and he could have avoided at negligible costs). If the business asks its customer to clarify the capacity he is acting in (private or professional?) and the customer (mis)represents himself as acting in a professional capacity the business must be allowed to confide in the answer given by the customer, the latter bearing the risk of misassessing his own capacity.[104a] If the seller erroneously assumed that the buyer was acting in a professional capacity, this would only matter if one refused to correct the wording of (1) along the said lines.[105] To ascertain jurisdiction speedily and easily is not such an overarching objective that enforcing good faith and protecting worthy trust would have to bend to it necessarily.[106]

31   Art. 2 lit. a CISG excepts goods bought for personal, family or household use from the CISG, a regime specifically devoted for mutually commercial contracts between professionals. (1) does not mention either family or household use. But that does not inflict any harm: Family use and use in a private household are both sub-cases and examples for private use.[107] But it ought to be stressed that only the consumer himself, the party to the consumer contract, is protected an not members of his family even if the consumer purchased goods or services which later-on solely family-members are going to use.[108]

7. Consumer as a natural person

32   The ECJ has continuously and consistently emphasised that the concept of a consumer only covers a private and final consumer not engaged in trade or professional activities.[109] Therefore, it seems clear that only parties who are physical, natural persons are entitled to the benefit of the provisions of Section 4. This interpretation is also supported by the wording of

---

Liber amicorum Peter Hay (2005), p. 297, 316–317; *Ragno*, in: Ferrari/Leible (eds.), Rome I Regulation (2009), p. 129, 134–135; *Ansgar Staudinger*, in: Rauscher, Art. 15 Brüssel I-VO note 3; see also *Sachse* pp. 113–118. *Contra Lüderitz*, in: FS Stefan Riesenfeld (1983), p. 148, 156–157; *Senff* p. 243.

[101]   See *von Hoffmann*, in: Soergel, BGB, vol. 10: EGBGB; IPR (12th ed 1996) Art. 29 EGBGB note 14; *Heiss*, in: Czernich/Heiss, EVÜ (1999) Art. 5 EVÜ note 8.

[102]   *Mankowski*, in: FS Ingeborg Schwenzer (2011), p. 1175, 1192; see *Johann Gruber/BayWa AG* (Case C-464/01), [2005] ECR I-439, I-476 para. 52.

[103]   Report *Giuliano/Lagarde*, OJ EEC 1980 C 282/23.

[104]   *Jonathan Hill* para. 3.47.

[104a]   Compare *Neil Brown*, CRi 2015, 38, 41.

[105]   *Mankowski*, in: FS Ingeborg Schwenzer (2011), p. 1175, 1193.

[106]   *Contra Lüderitz*, in: FS Stefan Riesenfeld (1983), p. 147, 157; *de Bra* p. 148; *Senff* p. 243.

[107]   *Mankowski*, in: FS Ingeborg Schwenzer (2011), p. 1175, 1194.

[108]   See KG VersR 2014, 1020, 1023.

[109]   *Shearson Lehman Hutton, Inc. v. TVB Treuhandgesellschaft für Vermögensverwaltung und Beteiligungen mbh*, (Case C-89/91) [1993] ECR I-139 paras. 20 and 22; *Francesco Benincasa v. Dentalkit Srl*, (Case C-269/95) [1997] ECR I-3767 para. 15; *Johann Gruber v. BayWa AG*, (Case C-464/01) [2005] ECR I-439 para. 35; *Petra Engler v. Janus Versand GmbH*, (Case C-27/02) [2005] ECR I-481 para. 34; *Česká spořitelna as v. Gerald Feichter*, (Case C-419/11), ECLI:EU:C:2013:165 para. 32.

(1), because of the use of the word "a person". Consequently, legal persons, for instance small and medium sized enterprises, associations in general and even associations of consumers are not entitled to the procedural protection that consumers have under Section 4. Nobody but a natural person can have a private live.[110]

In principle, thus only natural persons can be consumers.[111] This principle has been upheld   **33** throughout all varieties of European consumer law[112] which has some significance and impact for the interpretation of (1), too.[113] In particular Art. 6 (1) Rome I Regulation employs it. Rather astonishingly (1) does not expressly add a "natural" before "person" in somewhat striking contrast to Art. 6 (1) Rome I Regulation.[114] Yet there are cases where good reasons can be put forward in favour of extending the notion of consumer to a limited extent.[115] Assume an association of consumers catering for their supply as an *ad hoc* company or as a club. Imagine the small amateur football club contracting for its equipment, e.g. jerseys or trunks.

8. Dual purpose contracts

In *Johann Gruber v. BayWa AG* the ECJ was faced with the question of whether Section 4   **34** Brussels Convention covers so-called dual purpose contracts.[116] A dual purpose contract is a contract related to activities of partly professional and partly private nature. In this case, an Austrian farmer entered into a contract with a German firm concerning delivery of tiles. The farmer wanted to replace the roof tiles of his farm building. The area of the farm building used for residential purposes was slightly more than 60 % of the total floor area of the building. In the course of the negotiations, the farmer informed the firm that he wanted to use the tiles for the farm building and that he had ancillary buildings too. However, he did not expressly state whether the building to be tiled was used mainly for business or private purposes. After delivery, the farmer considered the tiles to be defective, and he instituted proceedings against the German firm in Austria under Art. 13 (1) Brussels Convention (Art. 18 (1) of the Brussels I Regulation). The German firm contested the jurisdiction of the Austrian court.

The ECJ stated that the benefit of Arts. 13–15 Brussels Convention (now Arts. 17–19)   **35** cannot, as matter of principle, be relied on by a person who concludes a contract for a purpose which is partly concerned with his trade or profession and is therefore partly outside it. The ECJ added that it would be otherwise only if the link between the contract and the trade or profession of the person concerned was so slight as to be marginal and, therefore, had only a negligible role in the context of the supply in respect of which the contract was concluded, when considered in its entirety. The ECJ also added that the fact that the private element is predominant is irrelevant in this respect. The ECJ stressed that this interpretation

---

110   *Mankowski*, in: Heiss/Schnyder (eds.), Aspekte des internationalen Immobilienrechts (2011), p. 9, 19.
111   See only *Ragno*, in: Ferrari/Leible (eds.), Rome I Regulation (2009), p. 129, 133; *Jonathan Hill* para. 3.44;
        Lüttringhaus, RabelsZ 77 (2013), 31, 56; *Toro*, Rev. dr. eur. consomm. 2014, 81, 84.
112   *Jonathan Hill* para. 3.45; *Jonathan Hill/Chang*, para. 5.8.25; *Bisping*, ERPL 2014, 513, 522.
113   A-G *Mischo*, [2001] ECR I-9049, I-9064 paras. 17–18.
114   *Bisping*, ERPL 2014, 513, 522.
115   *Sachse* pp. 230–232.
116   *Johann Gruber v. BayWa AG*, (Case C-464/01) [2005] ECR I-439.

was supported by the restrictive definition of a consumer in Art. 13 (1) Brussels Convention; the strict interpretation of the concept of a consumer contract; the need for avoiding a multiplication of bases of jurisdiction as regards the same legal relationship and the principle of legal certainty in so far as a potential defendant should be able to know in advance where he can risk to be sued.[117] According to this concept, dual purposes contracts were deemed to be outside the ambit of the protective regime.[118] Whether the contract at stake contains a relevant private element and in fact is a dual purpose contract is for the judge at first instance to assess.[119]

36   In *Gruber v. BayWa AG* the ECJ also determined the factors a court must take into consideration when deciding whether a contract was concluded to satisfy, to a non-negligible extent, needs of the business of the person concerned or whether, on the contrary, the trade or professional purpose was negligible. Thus, a court must take into account all the relevant factual evidence objectively contained in the file. On the other hand, it must not take into account facts or circumstances of which the other party to the contract may have been aware of when the contract was concluded, unless the person who claims to be a consumer behaved in such a way as to give the other party to the contract the legitimate impression that he was acting for the purpose of his business.

37   In the general course of European consumer law, Art. 2 (1) and Recital (17) Consumer Rights Directive[120] employ a different concept of consumer namely that a person qualifies as consumer if the professional element is not dominant (which is less than demanding that the private element ought to be dominant). If one takes this as a general statement of policy and principle,[121] *Gruber v. BayWa AG* is reversed and legislatively overruled although this was not done in the specific context of jurisdiction or the Brussels I recast process.[122]

38   Admittedly, to ascertain the dominance or non-dominance of a certain purposes generates a certain level of uncertainty.[123] The entrepreneur might not detect it before or whilst concluding the contract.[124] Furthermore, it leaves quite some leeway for ex post opportunism and puts a potentially voluminous programme on parties and judges to inquire,[125] with respective tertiary costs. Nonetheless, it appears to be the fairest and most appropriate concept conceivable avoiding any kind of radicalism or giving short shrift to legitimate

---

[117]   *Johann Gruber v. BayWa AG*, (Case C-464/01) [2005] ECR I-439 paras. 39–44.

[118]   Following the ECJ BGHZ 167, 83 [18] *et seq.*; BGH NJW 2012, 1817, 1819; to the same avail earlier *de Bra* p. 144; *Senff* p. 240.

[119]   BGH NJW 2012, 455 [14]; BGH NJW 2012, 1817, 1819.

[120]   Directive 2011/83/EU of the European Parliament and of the Council of 25 October 2011 on consumer rights, amending Council Directive 93/13/EEC and Directive 1999/44/EC of the European Parliament and of the Council and repealing Council Directive 85/577/EEC and Directive 97/7/EC of the European Parliament and of the Council, OJ EU 2011 L 304/64.

[121]   Doubting that this premise is fulfilled *Patrick Meier*, JuS 2014, 777, 778–779.

[122]   Tentatively to the same avail *Herbert Roth*, in: FS Bernd von Hoffmann (2011), p. 715, 720. *Contra* Loacker, JZ 2013, 234, 238–241.

[123]   *Jude*, RCDIP 94 (2005), 505, 512.

[124]   *David Kluth* p. 48.

[125]   *Rösler/Siepmann*, EWS 2006, 497, 498–499.

interests. Radical concepts can claim the advantage of simplicity,[126] but suffer from their one-sided approaches.

9. Assignment

In *Shearson Lehman Hutton v. TVB Treuhandgesellschaft für Vermögensverwaltung und* **39** *Beteiligungen mbh* the ECJ was asked to decide whether the protection granted under Section 4 can be assigned to others. In this case, a German judge had invested through an American firm, which had offered its services in Germany through press advertisements. However, the judge lost nearly all of his investments. Subsequently, he assigned his rights to a German firm, which in turn sued the American firm in Germany under the provisions of Section 4 Brussels Convention claiming return of the sum lost by the assignor. The ECJ emphasized that the concept of a consumer only covers a private and final consumer not engaged in trade or professional activities, and that Section 4 only protects the consumer as far as he is personally the plaintiff or defendant in proceedings. Consequently, a claimant, as in the present case, who is acting in pursuance of his trade or professional activity and who is not, therefore, himself a consumer party to the contract may not enjoy the benefit of the special rules of jurisdiction in Section 4.[127] The application of the rules on special jurisdiction should not be extended to persons for whom that protection is not justified.[128]

Even if the assignee was acting in a private capacity (be it that he acts as some kind of agent – **40** in the economic sense – for the assignor-consumer, be it that he invested private assets in the acquisition of claims), Art. 16 should not be opened to the assignor.[129]

10. Avals

In *Česká spořitelna as v. Gerald Feichter* the CJEU decreed that the aval of a natural person **41** given on a promissory note issued in order to guarantee the obligations of a commercial company, cannot be regarded as having been given outside and independently of any trade or professional activity or purpose while that individual has close links with that company, such as being its managing director or majority shareholder.[130] The mere fact that the giver of the aval is a natural person is not sufficient to establish that he is a consumer.[131]

IV. The other party

Art. 17 does not in general contain requirements concerning the status of the other party to **42** the consumer contract. Nor does the Rome Convention contain such requirements. Therefore, it could be concluded that Section 4 can be invoked against parties acting in their private capacity or against a consumer in a contract between two consumers. On the other hand, this interpretation would run counter to the aim and purpose of Section 4, *viz.* to

---

[126] See *Loacker* pp. 58–59.

[127] *Shearson Lehman Hutton, Inc. v. TVB Treuhandgesellschaft für Vermögensverwaltung und Beteiligungen mbh*, (Case C-89/91) [1993] ECR I-139, I-188 *et seq.* paras. 23 and 24.

[128] *Česká spořitelna as v. Gerald Feichter*, (Case C-419/11), ECLI:EU:C:2013:165 para. 33.

[129] OLG München ZIP 2013, 435–436.

[130] *Česká spořitelna as v. Gerald Feichter*, (Case C-419/11), ECLI:EU:C:2013:165 para. 37.

[131] *Česká spořitelna as v. Gerald Feichter*, (Case C-419/11), ECLI:EU:C:2013:165 para. 38.

provide protection only to buyers in need of protection, their economic position being one of weakness in comparison with sellers because they are actin in a private capacity and eventually as consumers and are not, when buying the product acquired, engaged in trade or professional activities. Furthermore, the consumer protection directives all contain requirements concerning the status of the other party to the contract. In these directives, the other party to the contract must be a natural or legal person acting for purposes relating to his trade, business or profession.[132] Finally, Art. 17 (1) (c) presupposes that the other party to the contract is pursuing commercial or professional activities in the Member State where the consumer is domiciled. On that basis, it seems justified to require that the other party to the consumer contract must be acting for purposes relating to its trade, business or profession. The latter must be of a potentially permanent, persistent character of acting on the supply side of a market.[133] It is not necessary that such activity on the market must be with the intention of being profitable overall, but it ought to result in transactions for a remuneration.[134] The business run is not required to be the entrepreneur's main occupation but can be a side-show besides a main occupation with a job or a more important other business.[135] The entrepreneur needs not be a company but can also be a physical, natural person.[136] For instance, a lawyer contracting in his profession with a client, is an entrepreneur (and the contract is a B2C contract if legal services are to be rendered in the client's private affairs, e.g. divorce, maintenance, child care).[137]

43 In conclusion, Section 4 is inapplicable to contracts between private parties, contracts between consumers and contracts between a private party and a consumer. In modern parlance, Section 4 is restricted to Business-to-Consumer (B2C) contracts whilst it does not cover B2B, C2C or C2B contracts. Generally, European consumer contract law can be circumscribed as a law of (qualified) unilateral business contracts.[138] In *Société Bertrand v. Paul Ott KG*, a dispute arose between two commercial parties concerning a sale of a machine where payment was to be made by way of bills of exchange spread over a period of time. The ECJ emphasized that Art. 13 (2) Brussels Convention (Art. 17 (2) of the Brussels I Regulation) should be given a restrictive interpretation in conformity with the objectives pursued by Section 4. Consequently, the jurisdictional advantages entailed in Section 4

---

132 See Art. 2 Council Directive No. 85/577/EEC of 20 December 1985 to protect the consumer in respect of contracts negotiated away from business premises, OJ 1986 L 372/31; Art. 1 (2) Council Directive 87/102/EEC of 22 December 1986 for the approximation of the laws, regulations and administrative provisions of the Member States concerning consumer credit, OJ 1987 L 42/48; Art. 2 Council Directive 93/13/EEC of 5 April 1993 on unfair terms in consumer contract, OJ 1993 L 95/29; Art. 2 Council Directive 94/47/EC of 26 October 1994 on the protection of purchasers in respect of certain aspects of contracts relating to the purchase of the right to use immovable properties on a timeshare basis, OJ 1995 L 280/3; Art. 2 Council Directive 97/7/EC of 20 May 1997 on the protection of consumers in respect of distance contracts, OJ 1997 L 144/19; Art. 1 (2) Council Directive 99/44/EC of 25 May 1999 on certain aspects of the sale of consumer goods and associated guarantees, OJ 1999 L 171/12.

133 *Sachse* p. 92.

134 *Sachse* p. 92; *David Kluth* pp. 151–160.

135 *Sachse* pp. 97–98; see also *Heiderhoff*, IPRax 2005, 230, 231.

136 *Timpano*, Riv. dir. priv. 2014, 577, 593.

137 *Birute Šiba v. Arūnas Devėnas*, (Case C-537/13) paras. 23–34.

138 *Grundmann*, Europäisches Schuldvertragsrecht (1999) pp. 141, 196; *Grundmann*, ZHR 163 (1999), 635, 665; *Grundmann*, NJW 2000, 14, 16; *Mankowski*, EWiR 2014, 371, 372.

should only be granted to buyers who are in need of protection, their economic position being one of weakness in comparison with sellers, due to the fact that they are private final[139] consumers and are not engaged, when buying the product acquired on instalment credit terms, in trade or professional activities.[140] As a result, Art. 13 (now Art. 17) did not cover the contract in question between two commercial parties.

Businesses do not need protection if they contract with each other or if they acquire goods **44** from a privately acting seller. B2B contracts fall outside Arts. 17–19[141] in every possible respect. It would be almost impossible to assess in a concrete case to which degree one contracting party is intellectually or economically superior to the other.[142] In C2C contracts consumers amongst each other are on equal footing, and neither of them ought to be protected.[143] The consumer buyer must not be preferred over the consumer seller. It would be virtually impossible to protect both contracting parties simultaneously: Whereas Art. 18 (1) 2nd option would give a *forum actoris* to the buyer, Art. 18 (2) for the very same action would guarantee exclusive jurisdiction of the courts at his own domicile to the seller.[144] Teleologically it would be misconceived to equalise a non existing misbalance.[145] Finally, C2B contracts (for instance selling second hand goods or offering small services to businesses) do not feature the consumer on the demand side but as the supplier.[146] Arts. 17–19 are designed for the consumer on the demand side of a contract.[147]

On the other hand, it does not distinguish between different types or classes of businesses. In **45** particular, it does not make special provision for small and medium enterprises (SME).[148] To foster the business of SMEs does not feature amongst the aims and purposes pursued by Section 4. Thus, to give it one more terminological twist, MNE2C contracts are covered whereas B2SME contracts are not. If SMEs should be privileged as compared to MNEs[149] that would require a change of policy and a clear signal of such turning the tide.

---

[139] The meaning of "final" is not perfectly clear and generates the need for some explanation; *Añoveros*, Rev. eur. dr. consomm. 2004, 77, 93. Most likely the "final consumer" in the present context is to be equated with the "ultimate consumer" or the "end-consumer" and describes the bottom end of the chain of supply.

[140] *Société Bertrand v. Paul Ott KG*, (Case 150/77) [1978] ECR 1431, 1446 para. 21.

[141] *Walter Vapenik v. Josef Thurner* (Case C-508/12), ECLI:EU:C:2013:790 para. 32 = RCDIP 103 (2014), 648 with note *Knetsch* with – incorrect (*Matthias Klöpfer/Ramić*, GPR 2014, 107, 113) – reference to *Shearson Lehman Hutton, Inc. v. TVB Treuhandgesellschaft für Vermögensverwaltung und Beteiligungen mbh*, (Case C-89/91) [1993] ECR I-139 paras. 11, 24.

[142] *Loacker* p. 66.

[143] *Kaye* pp. 830–831; *Sachse* pp. 120–122; *Jonathan Hill* para. 3.49; *Ansgar Staudinger/Steinrötter*, JuS 2015, 1, 6; *Hüßtege*, in: Thomas/Putzo, Art. 17 EuGVVO note 2; see also *David Kluth* pp. 51–61.

[144] *Schlosser*, Art. 15 EuGVVO note 3; *Mankowski*, ZvglRWiss 105 (2006), 120, 142; *Mankowski*, VuR 2010, 16, 20; *Mankowski*, EWiR 2014, 371, 372; *Matthias Klöpfer/Ramić*, GPR 2014, 107, 111; *Bisping*, ERPL 2014, 513, 523.

[145] *de Bra* p. 142; *Senff* p. 246; *Mankowski*, VuR 2010, 16, 20.

[146] *Mankowski*, EWiR 2014, 371, 372; see also *Mankowski*, Beseitigungsrechte (2003) p. 259; *Mankowski*, SAE 2005, 70, 71.

[147] Extending Arts. 17–19 to C2B contracts also *Ansgar Staudinger*, in: Rauscher Vor Art. 15–17 note 2; *Herbert Roth*, in: FS Bernd von Hoffmann (2011), p. 715, 725–726.

[148] *Reinhart*, in: FS Reinhold Trinkner (1995), p. 657, 667; *Sachse* pp. 100–102.

46 Division of labour ought to be attributed under the auspices of the applicability of Arts. 17–19. This is not expressly spelled out anywhere in Arts. 17–19, nor has it been expressly recognised in the ECJ's case law, but it is necessary and the only feasible and justifiable approach, though. Dividing labour between different persons or enterprises must be countered by regarding them in their ensemble as an entity and by attributing their activity to the consumer's formal partner in contract.[150] Otherwise it would be a child's play to circumvent and evade protective regulation by simply employing an intermediary for the conclusion of the contract.[151] It is functionally and economically equivalent whether the entrepreneur in person generates business or whether an agent or intermediary generates business for the entrepreneur on the latter's behalf.[152] These are only two modes of acquisition pursuing the same goal and aim.

47 Attributing another person's activity to the entrepreneur operates with regard to internationality and applicability of the European regime on the one hand and with regard to directing activity at a certain State under Art. 17 (1) (c) on the other hand.[153] To make the European regime applicable is of the utmost importance since at the level of national laws consumer protection does often not exist and in particular jurisdiction at the consumer's domicile does not exist, in contrats to Art. 18 (1) 2nd option.[154] If only two contracting parties domiciled in the same State are entangled in a lawsuit primarily local jurisdiction or venue is at stake, nonetheless regulated by Art. 18 (1) 2nd option.[155]

48 Whether the term "the other party to the contract" is the correct entry for such reasoning might be questioned for technical reasons, though.[156] Firstly, it is not ruled out that an express inclusion of third parties might be required if this is really envisaged. Arts. 11 (1) (b); 14 (1) expressly puts the insured and the beneficiary (third parties) side to side with the policy holder, the contracting party. But this is not related to the entrepreneurial side of the insurance contract.[157]

49 Secondly, it can be argued that "the other party to the contract" should be understood in the formal sense with regard to jurisdiction under Art. 18. Otherwise contractual jurisdiction, in particular the consumer's *forum actoris* emanating form Art. 18 (1) 2nd option would be opened against genuine third parties not privy to the contract while in turn contractual jurisdiction would be opened in favour of third parties. This makes it necessary to distin-

---

[149] As plausibly is ventilated by *Kieninger*, in: FS Ulrich Magnus (2014), p. 449, 455.

[150] BGH IPRax 2009, 258, 259; *Mankowski*, IPRax 2009, 238, 243–244; *Fasching/Konecny/Simotta*, Art. 15 EuGVVO para. 56; *Ansgar Staudinger*, RRa 2014, 10, 11–12.

[151] *Mankowski*, IPRax 2009, 238, 243–244.

[152] *Ansgar Staudinger*, RRa 2014, 10, 11–12.

[153] BGH IPRax 2009, 258, 259; *Mankowski*, IPRax 2009, 238, 243–244.

[154] Like e.g. German law but for § 29c ZPO; in more detail BGHZ 153, 173; *Mankowski*, JZ 2003, 689.

[155] *Mankowski*, EWiR 2014, 231, 232; *Ansgar Staudinger*, jM 2015, 46, 51; see also *Michael Müller*, EuZW 2014, 34, 35.

[156] To a similar avail *Harald Kolassa v. Barclays Bank plc* (Case C-375/13), ECLI:EU:C:2015:37 para. 33 retreating from the broad interpretation advanced in *Maletic* which is alleged to rest on specific circumstances in which the consumer was linked contractually from the outset, inseparably, to two contracting partners.

[157] *Mankowski*, EWiR 2014, 231, 232.

guish between the requirement of internationality on the one hand and jurisdiction on the other hand. Such distinguishing might appear odd at first sight, but it is inevitable. In most cases it will not be become all too practical, anyway, as internationality and the necessary cross-border element might be established by other means, for instance by the place of performance being located outside the forum state.[158] The *Maletic* case provides ample evidence for such contention since the couple in question travelled from Austria to Egypt.[159] The places of performance – in an untechnical sense not limited to the meaning "place of performance has under Art. 7 (1) – can constitute the necessary cross-border element". So called *unechte Inlandsfälle* ("false" domestic conflicts) are commonplace and abound, in particular with regard to travelling trips abroad booked *via* local travel agencies.[160] Third parties can be sued only if jurisdiction is founded upon Arts. 25; 4; 7; 8 with a particular edge for Art. 8 (1).[161] The legal relations between the different parties must be judged in isolation from each other in this regard.[162]

Thirdly, the German wording of Arts. 17–19 always speaks of "Vertragspartner", be it "der **50** andere Vertragspartner" or be it "Vertragspartner des Verbrauchers".[163] Relativity of contracts and privity of contract are concepts known in the substantive laws of all Member States, which thus should by way of a comparative reasoning also be read into the Brussels I*bis* Regulation.[164] Sometimes, cases looking very similar or even not distinguishable to the layman's eye have to be treated differently depending e.g. upon whether a franchisee acted or whether the franchisor traded in his own name.[165] The requirement that the contract must be concluded with the professional concerned himself does not lend itself to an interpretation to the effect that such a requirement is satisfied when there is a chain of contracts through which certain rights and obligations of the professional in question are transferred to the consumer.[166]

V. Contracts covered

Section 4 of the Brussels I Regulation does not apply to all consumer contracts, but only to **51** the contracts expressly listed in Art. 17 (1). The list contains three kinds of contracts; the first two, (a) and (b), are characterised by the type of contract, the third, (c), is characterised by the circumstances connected to the contract. The list is exhaustive. (a) and (b) follow a different concept and have different roots in the legislative history of the original Art. 13 Brussels Convention 1968. They should not be understood as establishing an irrebuttable presumption that the entrepreneur directed his activity at the consumer's home state,[167] for that would intermingle the old approach with the newer concept employed by (c).

---

158 See COM (2013) 794 final p. 6; *Nourissat*, Procédures janvier 2014, p. 14, 15.
159 *Michael Müller*, EuZW 2014, 34, 35.
160 *Ansgar Staudinger*, jM 2015, 46, 47 *et seq.*
161 *Michael Müller*, EuZW 2014, 34, 35; *Sujecki*, NJW 2014, 531.
162 *Ansgar Staudinger*, RRa 2014, 10, 11.
163 See *Harald Kolassa v. Barclays Bank plc* (Case C-375/13), ECLI:EU:C:2015:37 para. 32.
164 *Mankowski*, EWiR 2014, 231, 232; see also *Michael Müller*, EuZW 2014, 34, 35.
165 *Gsell*, as reported by *Julia Caroline Scherpe*, ZZP 127 (2014), 483, 487. Doubtful *Thole*, as reported by *Julia Caroline Scherpe*, ZZP 127 (2014), 483, 486–487.
166 *Harald Kolassa v. Barclays Bank plc* (Case C-375/13), ECLI:EU:C:2015:37 para. 30.
167 *Contra Toro*, Rev. dr. eur. consomm. 2014, 81, 84.

52 Section 4 applies regardless of the value of the goods or services provided under the contract since no upper or lower limit in terms of money has been prescribed by Section 4. Consequently, the provisions can be invoked with respect to both small and large claims.[168] Furthermore, Section 4 does not require that the goods concerned are of a kind that consumers usually buy. Purchase of rare, sophisticated, fancy as well as ordinary goods is covered by the protective provisions. Finally, Section 4 does not require that the goods concerned are consumable.

1. Sale of goods on instalment credit terms and credit contracts financing sale of goods

a) Sale of goods on instalment credit terms

53 According to (1) (a), Section 4 applies to contracts for the sale of goods on instalment credit terms. Originally, such contracts have been given special attention under the Brussels Convention due to social considerations given that buyers are in need of protection, their economic position being one of weakness in comparison with sellers, when buying on instalment credit terms.[169] The provision only applies to sale of goods. Consequently, contracts for hire or lease of goods, contracts for sale of shares, bonds[170] or certificates[171] as well as contracts for sale of immoveable property fall outside the scope of the provision. More importantly, contracts whereby a consumer buys services on credit are not covered.[172]

54 The concept of a sale of goods on instalment credit terms is a uniform concept. The ECJ has defined the concept as a transaction in which the price is discharged by ways of several payments or which is linked to a financing contract.[173] Consequently, it does not cover a contract for the sale of a machine where payment was to be made by way of bills of exchange spread over a period of time.[174] On the other hand, the hire-purchase contract under English law, which in England is not regarded as a sale, is likely to be classified as a sale on instalment credit terms under Section 4 of the Brussels I Regulation.[175]

55 In *Hans-Hermann Mietz v. Intership Yachting Sneek BV* the ECJ was presented with a contract where a German national had bought a vessel from a Dutch company. The contract was characterised by the seller manufacturing goods corresponding to a standard model to which certain alterations had been made; the seller undertaking to transfer the property in these goods to the buyer, who had undertaken, by way of consideration, to pay the price in several instalments; and the final instalment to be paid before possession of the goods was

---

[168] For instance, *Hans-Hermann Mietz v. Intership Yachting Sneek BV*, (Case C-99/96) [1999] ECR I-2277 concerned an expensive yacht, whereas *Océano Grupo Editorial SA v. Roció Murciano Quintero* and *Salvat Editores SA v. José M. Sánchez Alcón Prades, José Luis Copano Badillo, Mohammed Berroane and Emilio Viñas Feliú*, (Joined Cases C-240/98 to C-244/98) [2000] ECR I-4941 concerned small claims.

[169] Report *Jenard* p. 29.

[170] OGH ÖBA 2010, 185; *Mankowski*, EWiR Art. 17 EuGVVO 1/10, 323; *von Hein*, BerDGfIR 45 (2011), 369, 382–383. *Contra Barta*, NJOZ 2011, 1033, 1035 with reference to *E. Friz GmbH v. Carsten von der Heyden* (Case C-215/08), [2010] ECR I-2947.

[171] A-G *Szpunar*, Opinion in Case C-375/13 of 3 September 2014, ECLI:EU:C:2014:2135, para. 27.

[172] *Jonathan Hill* para. 3.107.

[173] *Société Betrand v. Paul Ott KG*, (Case 150/77) [1978] ECR 1431, 1446 para. 19, 1447 para. 22.

[174] *Société Betrand v. Paul Ott KG*, (Case 150/77) [1978] ECR 1431, 1446 para. 20.

[175] Report *Schlosser*, para. 157.

transferred definitively to the buyer. The German buyer argued that the contract was covered by the concept of contract for the sale of goods on instalment credit terms in (1) (a).
However, the ECJ found that the provision did not cover a contract with these characteristics, because the concept is intended to cover only contracts where the seller has granted
the buyer credit, that is where the seller has transferred to the buyer possession of the goods
in question before the buyer has paid the full price.[176] Consequently, (1) (a) does not cover
contracts where the price is to be paid in several instalments and in full before transfer of
possession takes place.[177] (1) (a) does not extend to contracts where the buyer only makes an
initial payment and pays the full remainder of the price later on at once.[178]

b) Credit contracts financing sale of goods

Section 4 covers a contract for a loan repayable by instalments, or for any other form of **56**
credit, made to finance a sale of goods as (1) (b) unambiguously evidences. Like (1) (a), this
provision only covers contracts for the financial cover of sale of goods but not of the
provision of services or the sale of intangibles. The private person taking a loan for acquiring
real estate is not protected by (1) (b).[179] The ambit of credit contracts covered is very limited
and must not be extended.[180] Only credit contracts for the limited purposes listed are covered, and the specific purpose pursued must be evident from the terms of the contract.[181] The
purpose must be recognisable for the lender, and the lone, but unrevealed intention on the
consumer's side to use the money to be received for financing a certain sale does not
suffice.[182] The distinguishing feature is whether the consumer-borrower is free for which
means to use the money received, according to the contract.[183] On the other hand, it is not
required that seller and lender must be identical or, if not identical, must cooperate on an
institutional level. A certain link between seller and lender is not necessary (but in the other
hand of course not detrimental or exclusionary if such link really exists). The main examples
envisaged incur the seller himself giving credit to the consumer-buyer[184] or a specialised
financial institution financing the consumer-buyer's acquisition like for instance the Fiat
Bank financing the acquisition of a Fiat. Almost all major car manufacturers have set up
such specialised financial institutions.

The first part of (1) (b) covers a loan repayable by instalments, whereas the second part of the **57**
provision is applicable, even if the loan or credit is not based on instalment credit terms.[185] In
both cases, the loan or credit must be made to finance the sale of goods. A general loan
contract without mentioning a specific purpose for which the money ought top be used, does

---

[176] *Hans-Hermann Mietz v. Intership Yachting Sneek BV*, (Case C-99/96) [1999] ECR I-2277, I-2311 para. 31;
       Brenn, ÖJZ 2015, 280.
[177] *Hans-Hermann Mietz v. Intership Yachting Sneek BV*, (Case C-99/96) [1999] ECR I-2277, I-2311 paras. 30
       and 31.
[178] *Senff* p. 253.
[179] *Andreeva Andreeva*, REDI 2011-2, 263, 265.
[180] See BGH WM 2014, 2088 [33]; OLG Frankfurt WM 2014, 255, 259.
[181] *Senff* p. 254.
[182] *Senff* p. 254.
[183] *de Bra* p. 155; *Senff* p. 254.
[184] *Jonathan Hill* para. 3.112.
[185] Report *Schlosser* para. 157; *Senff* p. 254.

not come within the confines of (b).[186] If the consumer-borrower is at liberty how to use the money and for which purpose to spend it the necessary degree of linkage between the sale of goods and the "related" loan ist not reached. The loan is rather "unrelated".

c) No additional requirement of professional activity targeted at the consumer's home State

58 Unlike (1) (c), for the types of contracts there is not an additional requirement that the entrepreneur must have directed his professional activity at the State of the consumer's domicile.[187] The contracts covered by (1) (a) and (b) are automatic qualifiers for the application of the protective regime without further presuppositions. Read literally, (1) (a) and (b) do not even require that the contractual counter-party to the consumer is a professional, but such requirement is re-introduced by general consensus on the respective interpretation.[188]

59 (1) (a) and (b) are curiosities and have become (if they not have ever been already) oddities. Their very existence can only be explained by some historical and genetic misgivings. Back in the late 1960s (really the *Sixties)* consumer law was not as developed as it is today. It lacks reason why of all contracts instalment sales and their respective financing agreements are exempt from the necessity to establish a link to the consumer's home state.[189] In the early days of European consumer protection law one might have been prone to an approach looking at the substance of the contract.[190] But it has not proved itself as a success story for it raised question as to characterisation and was barely capable of grappling complex contracts.[191] At latest with the extension of the protective regime to in principle all kinds of contracts by (1) (c), litterae a and b have seen their day. In practice, they are very rarely applied if ever (perhaps because they are so unambiguous that their interpretation appears not worth a fight). The time would have been ripe to abandon them altogether and to make the current (1) (c) a comprehensive and the sole rule.[192] Even a discriminatory potential is lurking in the current lack of situational requirements under (1) (a) and (b).[193]

2. All other contracts

60 According to (1) (c) of the Brussels I Regulation, Section 4 applies in principally all cases other than those listed in (a) and (b) of the provision, to contracts concluded with a person who pursues commercial or professional activities in the Member State of the consumer's domicile or, by any means, directs such activities to that Member State or to several States including that Member State, provided the contract falls within the scope of such activities. Unlike (1) (a) and (b) which apply unconditionally without further prerequisites, (1) (c)

---

186 *Jonathan Hill* para. 3.113.

187 *Hans-Hermann Mietz v. Intership Yachting Sneek BV*, (Case C-99/96) [1999] ECR I-2277, I-2311 para. 33; *Mankowski*, in: FS Tuğrul Ansay (Alphen 2006), p. 189, 199–200; *Ansgar Staudinger*, in: Rauscher, Art. 15 note 5; *Bisping*, ERPL 2014, 513, 523.

188 See only *Bisping*, ERPL 2014, 513, 523.

189 *Magnus/Mankowski*, ZvglRWiss 109 (2010), 1, 34.

190 *Sachse* pp. 75–77.

191 *Sachse* pp. 78–79.

192 *Magnus/Mankowski*, ZvglRWiss 109 (2010), 1, 34.

193 Comp. *Bisping*, ERPL 2014, 513, 524.

establishes an all-important additional requirement: that the business has penetrated the market in the consumer's home state by targeting activity at this State or at a number of States including this State. This inevitably leads to a privilege for consumer domiciled in the respective and excludes protection for consumer domiciled in other states however private their contractual purposes might be.[194] A restrictive approach advocates to introduce an additional prerequisite that the contract at stake must be one for consideration, thus reducing (1) (c) to synallagmatic or mutual contracts.[195] But this is irreconcilable with the wording which does not contain a like prerequisite. Section 4 is not limited to cases in which the parties have assumed reciprocal obligations.[196] (1) (c) covers virtually all other types of contracts (but for those excluded by (3) or Art. 24), even extending e.g. to an agreement rescinding the sale of real estate, concluded before a notary.[196a]

VI. Targeting activity

1. General scope of application

(1) (c) has replaced Art. 13 (1) pt. (3) Brussels Convention. Under the similar provision in the　**61** Convention, Section 4 would apply to any other contract for the supply of goods or services, provided that, in the State of the consumer's domicile, the conclusion of the contract was preceded by a specific invitation addressed to him directly or by advertising, and the consumer took, in that State, the steps necessary for the conclusion of the contract. The provision in the Convention was based on the fact that the circumstances surrounding the consumer contract had sufficient connection to the Member State where the consumer is domiciled.[197] In broad terms, this provision was based on the idea that the commercial party is "fishing" for consumers by either targeting them directly in their home country or advertising in that country and as such reaching out for them in order to do business with them. The concept as introduced in Art. 15 (1) (c) Brussels I regulation in order to adjust the law to the enormous growth of communication technologies and distance selling.[198] The construction clearly implies that absolute and unlimited consumer protection is not aimed at.[199]

In terms of policy, no changes were intended when the provision was drafted as it appeared　**62** first in Art. 15 (1) (c) Brussels I Regulation. The purpose of the then renewed formulation was only to clarify that contracts concluded through new means of technology, in particular the Internet, were to be covered by Section 4. No major substantive changes were intended to be made with the new formulation. The only difference between the provision in the Convention and the one in the Regulation is that it is not required under the Regulation that the consumer must take the steps necessary for the conclusion in the Member State where he is domiciled. Nevertheless, the new wording was strongly opposed by the European e-com-

---

[194] Politically critical e.g. *Senff* pp. 264–271.

[195] BGH WM 2010, 2163; BGH IPRax 2013, 168, 170; *Briggs*, PIL para. 4.158.

[196] *Renate Ilsinger v. Martin Dreschers, acting as administrator in the insolvency of Schlank & Schick GmbH*, (Case C-180/06) [2009] ECR I-3961 para. 51.

[196a] LG Saarbrücken IPRspr. 2013 Nr. 212 pp. 458–459.

[197] Report *Schlosser* para. 158.

[198] *Ragno*, in: Ferrari/Leible (eds.), Rome I Regulation (2009), p. 129, 147.

[199] *Daniela Mühlleitner v. Ahmad Yusufi and Wadat Yusufi* (Case C-190/11), ECLI:EU:C:2012:542 para. 33; *Boskovic*, RDCIP 103 (2014), 633, 636.

merce sector, which argued that the provision was utterly unfair, and that it would set the sector back, blocking the evolution of e-commerce in Europe.[200] However, from a political perspective, the need for consumer protection in e-commerce is evident when it is realised that in such contracts, in most, if not all, cases, the consumer pays in advance of delivery. As a result, the commercial party is unlikely to institute proceedings against the consumer. A benefit of procedural consumer protection in e-commerce, apparently partly ignored by the e-commerce sector, is that in general consumers will be more willing to shop over the Internet when they have reasonable procedural protection. Conclusively, it may even be argued that Art. 15 (1) (c) Brussels I Regulation has contributed to the continuous growth of e-commerce in Europe.

63 (1) (c) is not restricted to sale of goods. It applies to all types of contracts, whether they concern delivery of goods, provision of services or other subjects, such as a license to use software. However, the provision does not apply to insurance contracts covered by Section 3 or contracts covered by Section 6 on exclusive jurisdiction; for instance a tenancy of immoveable property. The extension of the material scope by virtue of (1) (c) gains the utmost importance for it forecloses the application of the general regime in turn,[201] in particular of Arts. 4 and 7 (1). The aggressive "all out"-approach employed by (1) (c) thankfully renders any necessity to distinguish in the negative on a case-by-case basis obsolete.[202]

64 This gladly and thankfully rings the final bell[203] for any discussions as to whether loan agreements which are not restricted to a defined financing purpose, so called independent loans,[204] or which are purporting at financing the acquisition of immovables could be classified as contracts for "services"[205] or not.[206, 207] They are covered by (1) (c) either way, and

---

[200] *Briggs*, The Conflict of Laws (2002), p. 68. *Briggs* finds the scepticism of the e-commerce sector absurd. See also *Øren*, (2003) 52 ICLQ 665, 670 pointing out that business launched a "country-of-origin" principle and consumer organisations a "country-of destination" principle.

[201] *Brugnera/Reinalter*, Giur. it. 2014, 578, 579.

[202] *Marenghi*, Dir. comm. int. 2014, 214, 220.

[203] *Hans Stoll*, in: Aufbruch nach Europa – FS 75 Jahre Max-Planck-Institut für Privatrecht (2001), p. 463, p. 468; *Magnus/Mankowski*, ZvglRWiss 103 (2004), 131, 166 *et seq.*; *Sinay-Cytermann*, in: Mélanges en l'honneur de Paul Lagarde (2005), p. 737, 747; *Mankowski*, IPRax 2006, 101, 105; *Mankowski*, RIW 2006, 321, 330; *Jochen Hoffmann/Primaczenko*, WM 2007, 189, 190–192.

[204] *Basedow*, in: Meeusen/Pertegás/Straetmans (eds.), Enforcement of International Contracts in the European Union (Antwerpen/Oxford/New York 2004), p. 269, 271 para. 10/4.

[205] To this avail in particular many French courts: CA Nancy 16 June 1998 – 97/1867; CA Colmar 24 February 1999, RCDIP 90 (2001), 135 with note *Gaudemet-Tallon* = ZIP 1999, 1209 with note *Reich* (further notes: *Huet*, Clunet 127 [2000], 79; *Sibylle Neumann/Rosch* IPRax 2001, 257; *Mankowski*, EWiR Art. 13 EuGVÜ 2/99, 1171); CA Versailles RIW 1999, 884.

[206] To this avail BGHZ 165, 248, 250 *et seq.* (critically annotated by *Mankowski*, RIW 2006, 321); OGH ÖJZ 2003, 647, 648; CA Poitiers 23 July 1997 – 95/3112; CA Toulouse JCP G 2004 IV.1665; CA Colmar Dr. aff. 2004, 1898 with note *Avena-Robardet* (noted *Attal*, Rev. jur. comm. 2005, 51); Hof Amsterdam NIPR 2008 Nr 111 p. 191; TGI Strasbourg 21.1.1998 – 95/5311; *Czernich/Tiefenthaler*, ÖBA 1998, 663, 668; *Schoibl*, JBl 1998, 700, 706 *et seq.*; *Lutz/Sibylle Neumann*, RIW 1999, 827, 829; *Bureau*, Le droit de la consommation transfrontière (2000) para. 135; *Sibylle Neumann/Rosch*, IPRax 2001, 257, 258 *et seq.*; *Larsson*, Konsumentenskyddet over gränserna – Särskilt inom EU (2002) p. 116 and obiter OLG Köln RIW 2004, 866, 867.

even the question becomes futile.[208] This brings Art. 17 in line with the Consumer Credit Directive eventually. Any contracts on savings accompany loan contracts.[209] Contracts on the transfer of rights, including property rights, to a consumer should be equally covered by (1) (c).[210] Furthermore any queries[211] about licensing of intellectual property rights (not the smallest issue in the age of everyday software use, database research and online downloads of information. songs or movies) are settled likewise.[212]

2. Idea and concept

In order to be covered by Section 4, the consumer contract must be concluded with a party **65** who pursues commercial or professional activities in the Member State of the consumer's domicile or, by any means, directs such activities to that Member State or to several States including that Member State. This is to assert the entrepreneur's responsibility for his own activities and that activities for which he is held liable jurisdictionally can be attributed to him.[213] The interpretation of what constitutes pursuit of commercial or professional activities in the Member State of the consumer's domicile or, by any means, directs such activities to that Member State or to several States including that Member State, should be made on basis of the purpose and legislative history of the provision. From this, two consequences seem to follow.

The provision is founded on the principle that a certain specified connection to the Member **66** State where the consumer is domiciled shall exist. As such, the idea behind the provision is still that the commercial party to the contract is "fishing" for consumers by pursuing commercial or professional activities in the Member State where the consumer is domiciled. This can still be done either by targeting the consumers directly in their home country or advertising in that country. Consequently, as has so far been the case, the provision covers situations where the commercial party has taken steps to market his goods or services in the Member State where the consumer is domiciled. Thus, the provision still applies to cross-border mail-order sales and doorstep selling.[214] According to the ECJ in *Gabriel*, the concepts of advertising and specific invitation addressed directly to the consumer appearing in the Brussels Convention, Art. 13 (1) pt. (3). Art. 17 (1) (c) covers all forms of advertising carried out in the Member State in which the consumer is domiciled, whether disseminated generally by the press, radio, television, cinema or any other medium, or addressed directly,

---

[207] Cf. only *Mankowski*, IHR 2008, 133, 141; *Leible/Matthias Lehmann*, RIW 2008, 528, 537.

[208] But it should be added that the question is still a valid one with regard to Art. 7 (1) (b).

[209] *Leible*, IPRax 2006, 365, 367; *Mankowski*, IHR 2008, 133, 141.

[210] See only *Sachse*, pp. 192–194.

[211] Cf. e.g. *Klimek/Stefanie Sieber*, ZUM 1998, 902, 906 *et seq.*; *Thorn*, IPRax 1999, 1, 3; *Mankowski*, RabelsZ 63 (1999), 203, 232 *et seq.*; *Mankowski*, CR 1999, 512, 515; *Dieter Schmitz*, Die vertraglichen Pflichten und die Haftung der Informationsanbieter im Internet, München, 2000, pp. 164–165; *Pfeiffer*, in: Gounalakis (ed.), Rechtshandbuch Electronic Business (2003), § 12 note 68; see also OGH ZfRV 2008/15, 27 = [2008] I.L.Pr. 287 with regard to Art. 5 (1) (b) Brussels I Regulation.

[212] *Magnus/Mankowski*, ZvglRWiss 103 (2004), 131, 167; *Marianne Roth*, in: FS Walter H. Rechberger (2006), p. 471, 477; *Mankowski*, IHR 2008, 133, 141; *Leible/Matthias Lehmann*, RIW 2008, 528, 537.

[213] *Maultzsch*, as reported by *Julia Caroline Scherpe*, ZZP 127 (2014), 483, 489.

[214] Report *Schlosser* para. 158, referring to the similar provision of the Rome Convention (Art. 5). See in this respect Report *Giuliano/Lagarde*, OJ EEC 1980 C 282/1, 23, 24.

---

for example by means of catalogues sent specifically to that State, as well as commercial offers made to the consumer in person, in particular by an agent or door-to-door sales-man.[215] Yet targeting is not identical with, and ought not be restricted to, "advertising" since the present regime was intended and conceived to go beyond the *status quo*.[216] But *a maiore ad minus* it encompasses and covers everything that was already covered by the regime Brussels Convention, namely all kinds of advertising measures.[217] But even an invited tour for potential future cooperation partners can be an activity directed at penetrating the market in the State in which the intended cooperation would be staged.[218]

67 In any event, "directing" and the underlying concept is technologically neutral and applies to all kinds and modes of technology employed,[219] be it currently, be it in the past or be it in the future. Websites are but an example.[220] Old-fashioned market penetration by agents for instance is a qualifier.[221] Furthermore, it is related solely and exclusively to the entrepreneur's activities and does not depend on anything the consumer might do.[222] "Pursuing" activities is not a special notion with an own, independent content, but simply a special case of "directing" activities.[223] "Pursuing" relates not to marketing, but to actually exercising activities.[224] Hence, "directing" poses lesser preconditions as "pursuing".[225] It serves as some kind of default rule once "pursuing" is not given in the concrete case.[226] Both "pursuing" and "directing" apply fully with regard to the first contract concluded and do not require any repeat business to be involved.[227]

3. No restriction to contracts concluded at a distance

68 (1) (c) does not require the contract to be concluded at a distance.[228] Its wording does not make expressly its application conditional on the contract falling within its scope having

---

215 *Rudolf Gabriel*, (Case C-96/00) [2002] ECR I-6367, I-6401 para. 44; OGH ÖJZ 2015, 165, 166 with notes *Hoch* and *Loacker*.

216 BGHZ 167, 83; OGH ÖJZ 2015, 165, 166 with notes *Hoch* and *Loacker*; OLG Stuttgart 18 August 2014 – Case 5 U 58/14 [11]; *Mankowski*, VuR 2006, 289, 292; *Mankowski*, IHR 2008, 133, 142; *Mankowski*, IPRax 2009, 238; see also *Øren*, (2003) 52 ICLQ 665, 673.

217 OGH 28 February 2003 – 7 Nc 4/03b; OGH ÖJZ 2015, 165, 166 with notes *Hoch* and *Loacker*; BGHZ 167, 83 [28]; *Jonathan Hill* para. 3.117; *Mankowski*, IPRax 2009, 238, 239 with further references.

218 OLG Stuttgart 18 August 2014 – Case 5 U 58/14 [13].

219 *Mankowski*, IPRax 2009, 238, 239.

220 BGHZ 167, 83; BGH WM 2012, 36.

221 *Killias*, SZIER 2011, 691, 727.

222 *Mankowski*, IPRax 2009, 238, 239.

223 *Mankowski*, IPRax 2009, 238, 239; *Mankowski*, WuB VII B. Art. 15 EuGVVO 1.12, 255, 256.

224 *Mankowski*, WuB VII B. Art. 15 EuGVVO 1.12, 255, 256.

225 *Øren*, (2003) 52 ICLQ 665, 676; *Jonathan Hill* para. 4.27; *Mankowski*, WuB VII B. Art. 15 EuGVVO 1.12, 255, 256.

226 OGH ÖJZ 2015, 165, 167 with notes *Hoch* and *Loacker*.

227 OGH ÖJZ 2005, 307; OGH ÖJZ 2015, 165, 167 with notes *Hoch* and *Loacker*.

228 *Daniela Mühlleitner v. Ahmad Yusufi and Wadat Yusufi* (Case C-190/11), ECLI:EU:C:2012:542 para. 44; *Lokman Emrek v. Vlado Sabranovic* (Case C-218/12), ECLI:EU:C:2013:666 para. 19; A-G *Cruz Villalón*, Opinion of 18 July 2013 in case C-218/12, ECLI:EU:C:2013:494 para.12; BGH RIW 2013, 563, 565; BGH MDR 2014, 918 [13]; *Ansgar Staudinger/Steinrötter*, NJW 2012, 3227; *Kieninger*, in: FS Ulrich Magnus

been concluded at a distance.[229] Even the previous precondition as it was contained in Art. 13 (1) pt. (3) Brussels Convention that the consumer must have taken the necessary steps to concluding the contract on his side in his State has been removed.[230] The legal development followed the development in marketing techniques, but that must not be equated with letting the grip on traditional marketing techniques slip.[231] The amendment was to cure proven deficiencies in the event that the consumer had been induced, at the co-contractor's instigation, to leave his home State to conclude the contract,[232] not to open up and introduce new deficiencies where previously none had been. The protection of the consumer does not depend on the place where the contract was concluded anymore.[233] The wording became broader and more general.[234] To introduce a criterion which was not to be found even under the Brussels Convention thus would be paradox. Any restrictive interpretation would be based on a factor which, far from leaving consumers unprotected, should in fact strengthen their protection.[235]

Genetically, the European Parliament's Committee on Legal Affairs and the Internal Mar- **69** ket[236] deliberately refrained from establishing a criterion that the contract must be concluded at a distance.[237] The Joint Declaration of the Council and the Commission on Articles 15 and 73 mentions contracts concluded at a distance as but an example, one amongst a number of marketing methods covered. Under no circumstances it rules out the possibility of other modes of contracting being included.[238] On the contrary, the legislative history of (1) (c) amply underlines and confirms that this rule also encompasses situations in which the trader or the consumer travels to the other party's address to conclude the contract.[239] Distance selling ist but one factor among many possibles.[240]

Art. 15 (1) Brussels I Regulation purposefully lowered the threshold compared to Art. 13 (1) **70** Brussels Convention in order to ensure better protection of consumers.[241] (1) (c) covers not only in principle all types of contracts, but also all modes of contracting. Like its applicability does not depend on the type of contract (save for the existence of an express exception), it

---

(2014), p. 449, 453. *Contra* OLG Köln NZM 2010, 495, 496; *Kropholler/von Hein*, Art. 15 note 27; *von Hein*, JZ 2011, 954, 957.

[229] *Daniela Mühlleitner v. Ahmad Yusufi and Wadat Yusufi* (Case C-190/11), ECLI:EU:C:2012:542 para. 33.

[230] *Daniela Mühlleitner v. Ahmad Yusufi and Wadat Yusufi* (Case C-190/11), ECLI:EU:C:2012:542 para. 35.

[231] See A-G *Cruz Villalón*, Opinion of 24 May 2012 in case C-190/11, ECLI:EU:C:2012:313 para. 16.

[232] COM (1999) 348 final p. 16; A-G *Cruz Villalón*, Opinion of 24 May 2012 in case C-190/11, ECLI:EU:C:2012:313 para. 16.

[233] Report *Pocar* para. 83; A-G *Cruz Villalón*, Opinion of 24 May 2012 in case C-190/11, ECLI:EU:C:2012:313 para. 17.

[234] A-G *Cruz Villalón*, Opinion of 24 May 2012 in case C-190/11, ECLI:EU:C:2012:313 paras. 18–19.

[235] A-G *Cruz Villalón*, Opinion of 24 May 2012 in case C-190/11, ECLI:EU:C:2012:313 para. 29.

[236] Doc. A5-0253/2000 Amendment 23 and the explanations thereon.

[237] *Daniela Mühlleitner v. Ahmad Yusufi and Wadat Yusufi* (Case C-190/11), ECLI:EU:C:2012:542 para. 38.

[238] A-G *Cruz Villalón*, Opinion of 24 May 2012 in case C-190/11, ECLI:EU:C:2012:313 para. 20.

[239] A-G *Cruz Villalón*, Opinion of 24 May 2012 in case C-190/11, ECLI:EU:C:2012:313 para. 26; *Mankowski*, IPRax 2009, 238, 242–243; *Leible/Michael Müller*, NJW 2011, 495, 497.

[240] *Wilke*, EuZW 2015, 13, 15.

[241] *Daniela Mühlleitner v. Ahmad Yusufi and Wadat Yusufi* (Case C-190/11), ECLI:EU:C:2012:542 paras. 36–37.

does not depend on the way in which the contract was concluded and the circumstances of such conclusion. This clarification is a welcome addition to precisions on the notion of "targeted activity".[242] Not the least the overall purpose and aim of Arts. 17–19, namely to protect consumers, demand so.[243] That the contract was concluded at a distance might only serve as an indication that the commercial or professional activity at stake was directed to the State of the consumer's domicile and that *a fortiori* the conclusion of the contract was connected with such activity.[244] It might help to ascertain the essential conditions of (1) (c) but it is not in itself an essential condition.[245] Referring to the mode how the contract was concluded would introduce a distribution-related approach alien to Art. 17.[246] All modes are to be treated in the same manner since different treatment would lack justification,[247] and Art. 17 is not the Distance Selling Directive.[248]

4. Temporal aspects

71 The targeted activity is not required to continue and persist at the time when the lawsuit becomes pending. It suffices that it induced the consumer to conclude the contract. Necessarily and naturally, a successful triggering of the contract precedes the conclusion of the contract in time. The relevant point in time for (1) (c) is solely and exclusively the conclusion of the contract regardless of any present time that might be used in the word and might possibly be understood as pointing to the time when the lawsuit commences and becomes pending.[249] Hence, it is irrelevant whether the other party abandoned the targeted activity between the conclusion of the contract and the commencement of the lawsuit.[250] Targeted activity does not serve as the connecting factor on which jurisdiction is grounded (this is the other party's or the consumer's domicile) but as an additional element. This is different from establishment under (2) and Art. 7 (5).[251] On the other hand, it is relevant if the activity is directed only at a State in which the consumer is not yet resident; an only future residence on the consumer's side does not suffice.[252]

5. Outlines of "targeted activity"

72 In substance, targeted activity[253] is a relative optimum. Targeted activity relates to the pro-

---

242 *Sinay-Cytermann*, RCDIP 102 (2013), 491, 492–495.

243 *Daniela Mühlleitner v. Ahmad Yusufi and Wadat Yusufi* (Case C-190/11), ECLI:EU:C:2012:542 para. 40; *Sinay-Cytermann*, RCDIP 102 (2013), 491, 497, 501–502.

244 *Daniela Mühlleitner v. Ahmad Yusufi and Wadat Yusufi* (Case C-190/11), ECLI:EU:C:2012:542 para. 42.

245 See *Daniela Mühlleitner v. Ahmad Yusufi and Wadat Yusufi* (Case C-190/11), ECLI:EU:C:2012:542 para. 42.

246 Comp. *Sachse* pp. 83–86.

247 *Ansgar Staudinger/Steinrötter*, EWS 2011, 70, 73 *et seq.*; *Ansgar Staudinger/Steinrötter*, NJW 2012, 3227.

248 *Markus Würdinger*, in: FS Peter Gottwald (2014), p. 693, 702.

249 OLG Frankfurt IPRax 2011, 258, 261; LG Traunstein IPRspr. 2012 Nr 202 pp. 462–463.

250 To the same avail OLG Frankfurt IPRax 2011, 258, 261; *Seibl*, IPRax 2011, 234, 236–237.

251 See OLG Frankfurt IPRax 2011, 258, 261–262; *Seibl*, IPRax 2011, 234, 236–237.

252 *Christian Koller/Slonina/Steinhardt*, ecolex 2013, 534.

253 A thorough discussion may be found in *Øren*, (2003) 52 ICLQ 665, 673–692; *Markus*, ZZZ 2004, 181, 189–198; *Mankowski*, VuR 2006, 289; *Mankowski*, IPRax 2009, 238; *Mankowski*, IPRax 2012, 144; *Gillies*, (2007) 3 JPrIL 89; *Farah*, (2008) 33 E. L. Rev. 257, 263–269. Cf. also *Motion*, [2001] CTLR 209.

fessional's very own marketing strategy and the tools employed to this avail.[254] A proper full-scale definition of "targeted activity" is certainly desirable,[255] but is still lacking and can perhaps not be achieved anyway at all, at least not without dropping the advantages which stem from the open-mindedness[256] and abstract functionality of the concept. However, "targeted activity" must not be equated with advertising[257] but encompasses a greater number of varieties.[258] Furthermore, in contrast to Art. 2 (a) Distance Selling Directive[259] "targeted activity" does not require an organised distance sale or service-provision scheme.[260] On the other hand, "directs" demands only less than "pursues" with regard to the level of substance in business arrangements, resources and accomplished transactions.[261] Some efforts are the minimum requirement, and e-mails might provide the prime example.[262] The relevant point of time is the period immediately preceding the conclusion of the contract. If the consumer afterwards changed his habitual residence this does not bear any relevance in either direction.[263]

A Joint Declaration of Council and Commission[264] accompanies Art. 15 (1) (c) Brussels I   **73** Regulation (and is referred to in Recital (24) Rome I Regulation). It states that "for Article 15 (1) (c) to be applicable it is not sufficient for an undertaking to target its activities at the Member State of the consumer's residence, or at a number of Member States including that Member State; a contract must also be concluded within the framework of its activities" and that "the mere fact that an Internet site is accessible is not sufficient for Article 15 to be applicable, although a factor will be that this Internet site solicits the conclusion of distance contracts and that a contract has actually been concluded at a distance, by whatever means. In this respect, the language or currency which a website uses does not constitute a relevant factor." Such declarations ordinarily are in no way binding in particular on the ECJ.[265] The ECJ in *Pammer* disapproved of the Joint Declaration of Commission and Council[266] as a

---

254 OLG Stuttgart 18 August 2014 – Case 5 U 58/14 [12]; *Wulf-Henning Roth*, in: FS Hans Jürgen Sonnenberger (2004), p. 591, 609; *Mankowski*, IPRax 2009, 238, 239.

255 *Sinay-Cytermann*, in: Mélanges en l'honneur de Paul Lagarde (2005), p. 737, 748.

256 More critical *Rühl*, GPR 2006, 196, 197 ("deliberately vague"); *Ragno*, in: Ferrari/Leible (eds.), Rome I Regulation (2009), p. 129, 147.

257 As *Nassall*, JurisPR BGH-ZivilR 19/2006 note 4 suggests.

258 BGH NJW 2006, 1672; *Mankowski*, VuR 2006, 289, 292; *Mankowski*, IHR 2008, 133, 142; cf. also *Øren*, (2003) 52 ICLQ 665, 673.

259 Directive 97/7/EC of the European Parliament and the Council of 20 May 1997 on the protection of consumers in respect of distance contracts, OJ EC 1997 L 144/19.

260 *Mankowski*, VuR 2006, 289, 291.

261 *Øren*, (2003) 52 ICLQ 665, 676.

262 *Øren*, (2003) 52 ICLQ 665, 687.

263 Cf. Hof Amsterdam NIPR 2008 No. 111 p. 191.

264 Joint Declaration of Council and Commission, Statement on Articles 15 and 73, Annex II to the Note of the General Secretariat of the Council for the Committee of Permament Representatives of 14 December 2000, 14139/00 and 14139/00 COR2(en) JUSTCIV 137 http://ec.europa.eu/civiljustice/homepage/home page_ec_en_declaration.pdf, reprinted i.a. in: IPRax 2001, 259, 261 *sub* 1 and essentially repeated in Recital (24) Rome I Regulation.

265 Cf. for the latter e.g. *Ansgar Staudinger*, RRa 2007, 98, 101; *Knöfel*, EWiR 2012, 695, 696; *Rühl*, in: FS Dagmar Coester-Waltjen (2015), p. 697, 703.

266 Joint Declaration of Commission and Council, Statement on Articles 15 and 73, Annex II to the Note of

---

helpful means of interpretation and implicitly denied any binding or semi-binding force to it, even not inviting it in as persuasive authority.[267] Insofar the ECJ begs to differ at least formally from the Joint Declaration.[268] Whether this amounts to a material difference as to substance, too, is a different question. The purpose of the rule prevails over its genesis,[269] and the legislating institutions have lost their sway once they have done their legislative work. There is nothing like an authentic interpretation as an acknowledged method of interpreting EU law.

74   The said Joint Declaration focuses on contracts concluded online and gives some guidance as to how to handle websites. The mere accessibility of a website shall not trigger consumer protection. There must be some intention to address the country where the consumer is resident, at least as one amongst others. Mere accessibility shall not suffice. Yet the fact that a contract has been concluded afterwards is a very strong indication that the professional intended to direct activity at the said country. The Joint Declaration conforms to that and supports this contention. Else the professional should have turned down any offer he had received from the consumer.

75   (1) (c) certainly also applies to commercial or professional activities carried out through or by means of the Internet. The decisive factor is whether the activity can be regarded as being directed to the Member State where the consumer is domiciled. Whether this is the case or not depends on a broad discretion, taking into consideration the aim and purpose of the technical device used by the commercial party and other factors such as the language used on the homepage and to what extent, if any, the other party to the contract has tried to ring-fence his activities to one or certain Member States.[270]

6. Websites in particular

76   A website may thus be regarded as advertising in the consumer's country. For instance, a website written in, say Swedish, is directed to Sweden, not Spain. On the other hand, a website written in English may very well be directed to all states given the global acceptance of English as the international language of the Internet. In such a case, a commercial party wishing to avoid doing business with consumers in a certain State must take steps to ensure that contracts are not entered into with consumers from that State, or that the homepage

---

the General Secretariat of the Council for the Committee of Permament Representatives of 14 December 2000, 14139/00 and 14139/00 COR2(en) JUSTCIV 137 http://ec.europa.eu/civiljustice/homepage/homepage_ec_en_declaration.pdf, reprinted i.a. in: IPRax 2001, 259, 261 *sub* 1.

[267] *Peter Pammer v. Reederei Karl Schlüter GmbH & Co. KG; Hotel Alpenhof GmbH v. Oliver Heller*, (joined Cases C-585/08 and C-144/09) [2010] ECR 12527; to the same avail *Mankowski*, IPRax 2012, 144, 147; *Gsell*, ZZP 127 (2014), 431, 459.

[268] See *Nioche*, Gaz. Pal. N°s. 68 à 70, 9 au 11 mars 2014, p. 34, 35.

[269] *Gsell*, ZZP 127 (2014), 431, 459.

[270] The question of which criteria are relevant under (1) (c) in respect of business carried out through the Internet is controversial, see for instance *Peter Pammer v. Reederei Karl Schlüter GmbH & Co. KG; Hotel Alpenhof GmbH v. Oliver Heller*, (joined Cases C-585/08 and C-144/09) [2010] ECR I-12527 paras. 81, 83 *et seq.*; LG Saarbrücken IPRspr. 2013 Nr. 212 p. 460; *Vasiljeva*, (2004) 10 Eur. L.J. 123; *Debusseré*, (2002) 10 Int. J. L. & Info. Tech. 344; *Øren*, (2003) 52 ICLQ 665, especially at pp. 678–694; *Foss/Bygrave*, (2000) 8 Int. J. L. & Info. Tech. 99; *Mankowski*, IPRax 2009, 238.

cannot be reached in that State. It is irrelevant whether the entrepreneur skips his website or virtually pulls the plug after the contract at stake has been concluded.[271] In the opposite scenario, it does not suffice if the entrepreneur goes online only after the conclusion of the contract.[272]

In this context, the Commission believes that it is important whether the homepage is active **77** or passive, an active site being one through which contracts can be entered into.[273] In this regard, the Commission seems to have been inspired by American case law on jurisdiction in matters concerning the Internet.[274] However, the wording of (1) (c) does not support this interpretation. Furthermore, the Commission's interpretation wrongly focused on technicalities. Finally, the interpretation is not in conformity with the aim and purpose of Section 4.[275] It relates too much on technology and technicalities, it does not focus on commercial features, it would be prone to difficulties in distinguishing.[276] Consequently, depending on the circumstances of the case, a passive website may be tantamount to directing commercial or professional activities towards a given Member State.[277] The mode of the website, be it "interactive", "active", "passive"[278] is irrelevant and not the ground to distinguish one from the other.[279] Any sliding scale approach as it is employed in the USA ought to be dismissed.[280] Even a so called "passive" website is an *offerta ad incertas personas* and is intended to attract business.[281] The notion of a "passive website" is a *contradiction in adiecto* in commercial terms and especially in marketing terms.[282] Commercial intentions not technical standards should be the yardsticks the more so since the latter are bound to their respective time.[283] One must not confuse interactivity in technical parlance of modern communication with activity on the consumer's side in the legally relevant sense.[284] The only assertion which can be deducted safely is that the mere accessibility of a website is not enough.[285]

---

271 *Ansgar Staudinger*, jM 2014, 229, 232.

272 *Ansgar Staudinger*, jM 2014, 229, 232. But cf. *Keiler/Katrin Binder*, euvr 2013, 230, 233–234.

273 Proposal of the Commission for a Council Regulation on civil jurisdiction and the recognition and enforcement of judgments in civil and commercial matters, OJ 1999 L 376/17.

274 For instance, *Zippo Manufacturing Co v. Zippo Dot Com, Inc.* 952 F. Supp. 1119 (1997) and *Cybersell, Inc. v. Cybersell, Inc.* 130 F. 3d 414 (1997).

275 *Mankowski*, in Studiengesellschaft für Wirtschaft und Recht (ed.), Internet und Recht (2002), p. 191, 200; *Béraudo*, Clunet 128 (2001), 1056; *Droz/Gaudemet-Tallon*, RCDIP 90 (2001), 638.

276 Cf. the in-depth discussion by *Mankowski*, in: Cashin Ritaine/Bonomi (éds.), Le nouveau règlement européen "Rome I" relatif à la loi applicable aux obligations contractuelles (Zürich 2008), p. 121, 130–134; *Mankowski*, IPRax 2009, 238, 239–242.

277 This point of view seems to be supported by the ECJ in *Rudolf Gabriel*, (Case C-96/00) [2002] ECR I-6367, I-6401 para. 44, where the Court referred to technical means like "the press, radio, television, cinema or any other medium". See also *Øren*, (2003) 52 ICLQ 665, 685; *Debusseré*, (2002) 10 Int. J. L. & Info. Tech. 344, 359; *Foss/Bygrave*, (2000) 8 Int. J. L. & Info. Tech. 99, 114.

278 On those notions e.g. *Pironon*, in: Rochfeld (dir.), Les nouveaux défis du commerce électronique (2010), p. 93.

279 *Mankowski*, IPRax 2012, 144, 147–148. But cf. OLG Köln NZM 2010, 495.

280 *Marenghi*, Dir. comm. int. 2014, 214, 223.

281 *Ansgar Staudinger/Czaplinski*, NZM 2010, 461, 463.

282 *Gsell*, ZZP 127 (2014), 431, 455.

283 *Mankowski*, IPRax 2012, 144, 147; *Gsell*, ZZP 127 (2014), 431, 455.

284 *Mankowski*, IPRax 2009, 238, 240; *Mankowski*, IPRax 2012, 144, 148.

7. Indications for targeting: focalisation

a) List of indications

78 In *Pammer*,[286] the ECJ details a list of positive indications encompassing:[287] offering of services or goods in States designated by name;[288] disbursement of expenditure on an Internet referencing service to the operator of a search engine in order to facilitate access to the trader's site by customers domiciled in various States;[289] language; currency; international nature of services or goods advertised; mention of telephone numbers with an international code; use of a top-level domain other than that of the Member State in which the trader is established, or use of neutral top-level domains such as .com or .eu; description of itineraries from one or more other Member States to the place where the service is provided or where the goods are sold;[290] mention of an international clientele composed of customers in various states.[291] An example for the latter is a website addressed to customers in the German speaking countries (thus including at least Austria besides Germany)[292] or offering different options for versions in different languages to be reached *via* a menu.[293] But caution demands that not every positive indication is *per se* sufficient.[294] Grouping of contacts and careful weighing is required.[295]

79 Language and currency are not relevant factors when they correspond to the languages generally used in the Member State from which the trader pursues its activity and to the currency of that Member State. If, on the other hand, the website permits the consumers to use a different language or a different currency, the language or currency can be taken into consideration and can constitute evidence from which it may be concluded that the trader's activity is directed to other Member States.[296]

---

[285] *Peter Pammer v. Reederei Karl Schlüter GmbH & Co. KG; Hotel Alpenhof GmbH v. Oliver Heller*, (joined Cases C-585/08 and C-144/09) [2010] ECR I-12527 para. 94; OGH ÖJZ 2015, 280 with note *Brenn*.

[286] *Peter Pammer v. Reederei Karl Schlüter GmbH & Co. KG; Hotel Alpenhof GmbH v. Oliver Heller*, (joined Cases C-585/08 and C-144/09) [2010] ECR I-12527 paras. 81, 83 *et seq.*; even more extensively A-G *Trstenjak*, Opinion of 18 May 2010 in joined Cases C-585/08 and C-144/09, [2010] ECR I-12530 paras. 76 *et seq.* Discussed in detail by *Mankowski*, IPRax 2012, 144, sub III.

[287] Supported e.g. by *Brugnera/Reinalter*, Giur. it. 2014, 578, 582–583.

[288] *Peter Pammer v. Reederei Karl Schlüter GmbH & Co. KG; Hotel Alpenhof GmbH v. Oliver Heller*, (joined Cases C-585/08 and C-144/09) [2010] ECR I-12527 para. 81.

[289] *Peter Pammer v. Reederei Karl Schlüter GmbH & Co. KG; Hotel Alpenhof GmbH v. Oliver Heller*, (joined Cases C-585/08 and C-144/09) [2010] ECR I-12527 para. 81.

[290] *Wilke*, EuZW 2015, 13, 14 rightly points out that this will rather be of regional importance in areas near border between two States and rather not for a Portuguese dealer in principle willing to sell also to Estonians.

[291] All *Peter Pammer v. Reederei Karl Schlüter GmbH & Co. KG; Hotel Alpenhof GmbH v. Oliver Heller*, (joined Cases C-585/08 and C-144/09) [2010] ECR I-12527 para. 83.

[292] OGH RdW 2014/505 p. 458, 459.

[293] BGH WRP 2014, 548 – Englischsprachige Pressemitteilung.

[294] *Kieninger*, in: FS Ulrich Magnus (2014), p. 449, 453.

[295] *Mankowski*, IPRax 2012, 144, 146.

[296] *Peter Pammer v. Reederei Karl Schlüter GmbH & Co. KG; Hotel Alpenhof GmbH v. Oliver Heller*, (joined Cases C-585/08 and C-144/09) [2010] ECR I-12527 para. 84.

b) Single indicative factors

aa) Language

As to language, a menu from which the consumer can chose the language appropriate for his **80** personal comfort decorated with flags pointing towards certain States, is a clear indication that activity is directed at the States "flagged".[297] He who makes a step towards his prospective customers (for instance by signalling "Wij spreken Nederlands" in the German-Dutch border region) must stand by his word.[298] Besides that, single language advertisements might be treated along the following lines: Almost any language has a regional core area, but its community also comprises members from other states.[299] Hence, it is only a weak negative indication if a regionally concentrated language is used. Turkish might be an example. Its core area is Turkey. But there are strong and relevant Turkish communities in Germany and Austria. There could even be targeting specifically at immigrant communities abroad.[300] Furthermore, even regional concentration fails as a negative criterion in border areas where knowledge of the languages of both neighbouring states can be presumed (for instance Danish and the German-Danish border region).[301] Another example is provided by a foreign language enclave like the German speaking Eupen-Malmedy in Belgium.[302] If the language used is widely spoken or even official language in the country where the entrepreneur has his place of business that weakens its indicative weight.[302a]

A language spoken world-wide ist of course a different case, with English spearheading. It is **81** not apt to indicate a restriction in the negative.[303] Yet it rather tends towards a positive indication, particularly given the predominance of English not only in the World wide Web, but also as a second language. It is not a counter-argument that many people are not addressed by English-language content. There are enough who feel addressed. Even East Asian logograms[304] are understood potentially worldwide given the large and wide spread number of emigrants from East Asia. Additionally, translation mechanisms generate the danger of an unwarranted second hand readership in another language than the original one.[305]

bb) Currency

As to currency, today most offers in Europe will be made in Euro, the common currency of **82** the entire Euro-zone and not related to a single State. An offer in Euro can only indicate that the offer is also directed at the Euro-zone.[306] If the trader insists on payment in the currency of its home state, the indication fails.[307] But if on the other hand the trader makes a step

---

[297] *Marino*, Contratto e impresa/Europa 2011, 247, 258–259.

[298] *Kieninger*, in: FS Ulrich Magnus (2014), p. 449, 456.

[299] *Mankowski*, RabelsZ 63 (1999), 203, 247; *Sachse* p. 258.

[300] *Mankowski*, IPRax 2012, 144, 150.

[301] *Mankowski*, IPRax 2012, 144, 149.

[302] *Mankowski*, IPRax 2012, 144, 149.

[302a] *Rühl*, in: FS Dagmar Coester-Waltjen (2015), p. 697, 701.

[303] To the same avail *Reymond*, Yb. PIL 14 (2012/13), 205, 223.

[304] Example by *Reymond*, Yb. PIL 14 (2012/13), 205, 223.

[305] *Geist*, 16 Berkeley Tech. L.J. 1361, 1384–1385 (2001); *Reymond*, Yb. PIL 14 (2012/13), 205, 224.

[306] *Mankowski*, IPRax 2012, 144, 150.

[307] *Mankowski*, IPRax 2012, 144, 150.

towards his customers by offering them payment in their home currency that is a relatively clear indication that he intends to do business in the countries of the listed currencies.[308]

cc) International nature of services or goods advertised

83 The nature of the services or goods advertised can be a very indicative factor. Some offers are by their very nature only of local interest, e.g. the menu of an ordinary restaurant or the timetable of a local cinema,[309] *a priori* the menu of a pizza service.[310] But matters should be different with regard to a restaurant excelling with a *Michelin* star or with restaurants presenting their advertisements on the website of their local tourist office.[311] The decisive element is not the generally local character of the supply side, but the range of appeal on the demand side. Hence, a "local" character does not automatically imply that an international appeal and cross-border targeting are excluded.[312]

84 The nature of the goods or services is limiting in particular if these services or goods are serviceable only under certain climatic or geographic conditions.[313] Furthermore, habits on the public's side might put severe hindrances in the way of importing goods or services which are regarded as extraordinary in a certain community.[314] If, conversely, the services or goods can be used virtually world-wide, this is not limiting.[315] Prohibitively high costs of transportation for a cross-border transport might also limit the appeal of the offer; services or virtual goods which can be transmitted online or at a distance at zero cost are on the other hand not limited by this factor.[316] But the handyman or plumber will only travel locally or regionally at best. Transportability of goods will pay proper regard not only to the costs of transportation, but also to the danger of the goods not withstanding or surviving transportation.[317]

dd) Mention of telephone numbers with an international code

85 Mentioning telephone numbers with an international code might provide an indication that the respective offers reaches out beyond the borders of the trader's home state. The pretension of (pseudo-)internationality might backfire in this regard.[318] If a phone number for a so called back office under a national phone number in a certain State is given, ordinarily activity will be pursued in that very State.[319]

ee) Use of a top-level domain other than that of trader's home state or of a neutral top-level domain

86 If the ccTLD[320] of the trader's website happens to coincide with that of the trader's home

---

[308] *Mankowski*, IPRax 2012, 144, 150.

[309] *Wegner*, CR 1998, 676, 681.

[310] *Glöckner*, in: Harte-Bavendamm/Henning-Bodewig, UWG (3rd ed. 2013) Einleitung C note 90.

[311] *Mankowski*, IPRax 2012, 144, 150.

[312] *Mankowski*, IPRax 2012, 144, 151.

[313] *Mankowski*, EWiR § 1 UWG 7/99, 471, 472; *Mankowski*, IPRax 2012, 144, 150.

[314] *Mankowski*, IPRax 2012, 144, 151.

[315] OLG Frankfurt K&R; 1999, 138 with note *Kotthoff*.

[316] *Mankowski*, GRUR Int. 1999, 909, 918.

[317] *Mankowski*, GRUR Int. 1999, 909, 918; *Mankowski*, IPRax 2012, 144, 151.

[318] *Mankowski*, IPRax 2012, 144, 151.

[319] See BGH WM 2014, 2133 [14].

state this is not a positive indication for an international ambition. But matters are different where this is not the case e.g. where the ccTLD was chosen for aesthetic reasons or for some pun only (e.g. YouTube operated for a while under youtu.be and the ccTLD of Belgium).[321] If the ccTLD used differs from the one commonly used in the trader's home state this indicates at least that the entrepreneur is willing to trade abroad, particularly so if he operates under the ccTLD commonly employed in the consumer's home state.[322] Such operative approach implies enhanced dangers for the consumer for it might tend to conceal the international cross-border dimension of the contract.[323] Some ccTLD open for registration from abroad are particular prone to such practices.[324]

.eu and .com are by their very nature international TLDs not restricted to any particular **87** country.[325] They are not ccTLDs but gTLDs.[326] .org and .net should align with them as they are also gTLDs.[327] The character as an indication allows for taking into consideration if the entrepreneur is able to prove that he opted for a gTLD for other reasons different from internationalising his business,[328] for instance for budgetary or availability considerations[329] with the choice of a gTLD side-stepping that the initially wanted ccTLD was not available anymore.

ff) Disbursement of expenditure on an Internet referencing service

Disbursement of expenditure on an Internet referencing service to the operator of a search **88** engine in order to facilitate access to the trader's site by customers domiciled in various States is a rather novel entry in the list of possible indications.[330] Whereas it was imprudent to refer to a criterion stemming from internal relation between the entrepreneur and the operator of the referencing service, AdWords and keyword advertising are the phenomena envisaged.[331] Beyond this any kind of search engine marketing and search engine optimising ought to be covered.[332] However, one step later the question resurges how to identify at which countries a search engine directs its activities.[333] Search engine ranking and visibility can provide some auxiliary data in this regard.[334]

---

320 Country-Code Top Level Domain.

321 *Reymond*, Yb. PIL 14 (2012/13), 205, 226.

322 *Tang* p. 54; *Clausnitzer*, EuZW 2010, 274, 377.

323 *Clausnitzer*, EuZW 2010, 374, 377; *Clausnitzer*, EuZW 2010, 446; *Leible/Michael Müller*, NJW 2011, 495, 497.

324 *Tang* p. 54.

325 *Peter Pammer v. Reederei Karl Schlüter GmbH & Co. KG; Hotel Alpenhof GmbH v. Oliver Heller*, (joined Cases C-585/08 and C-144/09) [2010] ECR I-12527 para. 83; BGH WM 2014, 2133 [14].

326 Generic Top Level Domains.

327 A-G *Trstenjak* Opinion in joined Cases C-585/08 and C-144/09, [2010] ECR I-12530 para. 86; *Mankowski*, IPRax 2012, 144, 152.

328 *Mankowski*, IPRax 2012, 144, 152; see also *Manara*, D. 2011, 5; *Leible/Michael Müller*, NJW 2011, 495, 497.

329 *Reymond*, Yb. PIL 14 (2012/13), 205, 226; *Wilke*, EuZW 2015, 13, 14.

330 *Peter Pammer v. Reederei Karl Schlüter GmbH & Co. KG; Hotel Alpenhof GmbH v. Oliver Heller*, (joined Cases C-585/08 and C-144/09) [2010] ECR I-12527 para. 81.

331 *Mankowski*, IPRax 2012, 144, 152 with reference to *Stefan Ernst*, jurisPR-WettbR 6/2010 Anm. 1 sub C.

332 *Mankowski*, IPRax 2012, 144, 152.

333 *Mankowski*, IPRax 2012, 144, 152–153.

gg) Mention of an international clientele composed of customers in various states

89 Mention of an international clientele composed of customers in various states ist the last criterion of the list in *Pammer*.[335] Another time this does not clearly distinguish between internationality as such and a direction specifically at the consumer's home state. The criterion should be refined with a connection to the consumer's home state being added.[336] If the entrepreneur alleges to have customers in the consumer's home state he cannot bail himself out later on. Entrepreneurs are at liberty to decide whether they use such credentials.[337]

hh) Mandatory information

90 Information which the entrepreneur is mandatorily coerced to provide, does not express any particular intention other than to comply with legal requirements. Hence, it must not be taken as a positive indication. Such mandatorily required information might spring from Art. 5 (1) E-Commerce Directive,[338, 339] but also from Art. 6 Consumer Rights Directive.[340, 341] But there are cases in which the rule that mandatorily required information is not to be taken into account suffers exceptions: firstly, where entrepreneurs domiciled in Third States comply with such requirements as imposed by EU law since they are not subjected to these in their home states so that complying with them indicates they intend to do business with consumers resident in the EU; secondly, where Art. 4 (3) Timeshare Directive[342] demands the use of a certain language at the consumer's choice[343] since the chosen language might indicate that the professional activity is directed at the countries where this particular language is spoken.

ii) Size and characteristics of the enterprise

91 Another possible indication are the size and the characteristics of the enterprise. The more market relevance an enterprise has gained the more likely it is that it act internationally. If, conversely, an enterprise has only acted locally in the past, for instance running an outlet or a traditional shop, the less likely it is that it extends its activities cross-border.[344] On the other

---

[334] See *Reymond*, Yb. PIL 14 (2012/13), 205, 224–225.

[335] *Peter Pammer v. Reederei Karl Schlüter GmbH & Co. KG; Hotel Alpenhof GmbH v. Oliver Heller*, (joined Cases C-585/08 and C-144/09) [2010] ECR I-12527 para. 83.

[336] *Mankowski*, IPRax 2012, 144, 153.

[337] *Breckheimer*, BB 2011, 203, 204.

[338] Directive 2000/31/EC of the European Parliament and of the Council of 8 June 2000 on certain legal aspects of information society services, in particular electronic commerce, in the Internal Market, OJ EC 2000 L 178/1.

[339] *Peter Pammer v. Reederei Karl Schlüter GmbH & Co. KG; Hotel Alpenhof GmbH v. Oliver Heller*, (joined Cases C-585/08 and C-144/09) [2010] ECR I-12527 para. 78.

[340] Directive 2011/83/EU of the European Parliament and of the Council of 25 October 2011 on consumer rights, amending Council Directive 93/13/EEC and Directive 1999/44/EC of the European Parliament and of the Council and repealing Council Directive 85/577/EEC and Directive 97/7/EC of the European Parliament and of the Council, OJ EU 2011 L 304/64.

[341] See *van den Aardweg*, NIPR 2011, 473, 475.

[342] Directive 2008/12/EC of the European Parliament and of the Council of 14 January 2009 on the protection of consumers in respect of certain aspects of timeshare, long-term holiday product, resale and exchange contracts, OJ EU 2009 L 33/10.

[343] *van den Aardweg*, NIPR 2011, 473, 475.

hand, delivery on demand or a dispense of real world storage can point towards interna-
tionalisation of the respective business.[345] Local retailers are most likely not going international. The place where after sales services are provided or where advice can be obtained, also
become relevant.[346]

jj) Modalities of delivery or pricing

Modalities of delivery or pricing can provide an indication, particularly so if the goods or   92
services are price sensitive. A differentiation between different zones with extra costs added
for delivery outside a certain range or a bonus for delivery inside a certain range is a
candidate in this regard.[347] If customers in certain states will not be delivered effectively
this is a relatively clear cut case for arguing that the entrepreneur does not direct activity at
these states.[348]

kk) Reference to rules of certain law

If the entrepreneur in his advertisements refers to rules of a certain law this might serve as an   93
indication that his activity is directed also at the State beyond this law.[349] If for instance
reference is made to a right of withdrawal under German §§ 312g; 355 BGB the entrepreneur
can hardly argue that his activity is not directed at Germany.[350] Likewise, if a certificate
obtained in a certain state is used as an advertising tool activity ist at least also targeting this
very State.[351]

ll) Content of advertisements

The content, the information conveyed, might be of interest only in some States whereas it   94
might be completely devoid of interest in others.[352] If an advertisement employs persons
who are popular in particular States this indicates that the advertised activity is also directed
at these States. However, it might sometimes be difficult to make this operable. For instance,
stars of the NFL certainly have their major fan base and their highest appeal in the USA but
undeniably the NFL has strong fan bases also in European states, especially in the UK and
Germany.[353] Whereas celebrities might not be know to the general public in certain States
they can be very well known to selected parts of the populace in the very same States which
can serve as targeted part markets.[354]

---

[344] *Mankowski*, GRUR Int. 1999, 909, 918; *Mankowski*, IPRax 2012, 144, 153.

[345] *Mankowski*, GRUR Int. 1999, 909, 918; *Mankowski*, IPRax 2012, 144, 153.

[346] *Mankowski*, GRUR Int. 1999, 909, 918; *Mankowski*, IPRax 2012, 144, 153.

[347] *Höder*, Die kollisionsrechtliche Behandlung unteilbarer Multistate-Verstöße (2002) p. 76; *Schrimbacher/
Bühlmann*, ITRB 2010, 188, 189.

[348] *Dethloff*, Europäisierung des Wettbewerbsrechts (2001) p. 91; *Höder*, Die kollisionsrechtliche Behandlung unteilbarer Multistate-Verstöße (2002) p. 76; *Steennot*, Tijdschrift@ipr.be 2011, 152, 160.

[349] *Höder*, Die kollisionsrechtliche Behandlung unteilbarer Multistate-Verstöße (2002) p. 76.

[350] *Mankowski*, IPRax 2012, 144, 153.

[351] *Clausnitzer*, EuZW 2010, 374, 377.

[352] A-G *Cruz Villalón*, Opinion of 29 March 2011 in Joined Cases C-509/09 and C-161/10, [2011] ECR
I-10272 para. 64; *Reymond*, Yb. PIL 14 (2012/13), 205, 244–245.

[353] *Mankowski*, MMR 2002, 61–62.

[354] *Mankowski*, IPRax 2012, 144, 154.

c) Entrepreneur's self protection at the contractual level by respected disclaimers

95 He who does business with a certain country as evidenced by his contractual activities cannot claim that he does not any business with the very same country. Professionals have to adopt a consistent mode of conduct and behaviour. Otherwise a *protestatio facto contraria* will be simply disregarded.[355] This holds particular true with regard to disclaimers on websites which announce that the professional does not intend to contract with customers from particular countries if in fact the professional concludes contracts with customers from there and does accept offers from there. If the disclaimer itself displays elements clearly pointing towards a State allegedly excluded (language, postal address, phone number etc.) this renders the disclaimer nugatory, too.[356] Penetrating a certain national market and soliciting contracts from it, but hiding behind an allegation to the contrary must not be a valid approach.

96 Self-protection is the key for the enterprise in contractual matters.[357] Simply inserting a disclaimer in its web-site on the other hand does not in itself protect the enterprise. Who loudly brags around that he will not do business with certain countries but secretly concludes contracts with customers from those countries, commits self-contradiction and cannot claim legal recognition of his tactics.[358] In the majority of cases no informational problem as to where the customer is located will arise. If delivery of ordered goods has to take place in the real world, the enterprise has generally all necessary information about its customer's address.[359] Enterprises are bound to ask their respected customers about their whereabouts. The higher the earnings, the more this is a simple matter of commercial self-protection. Otherwise the enterprise singlehandedly would deprive itself of any opportunity to check its customer's standing or liquidity and to rate this particular customer.[360] If on the other hand consumers fraudulently disguise their whereabouts by giving a false address they cannot claim legal protection afterwards, but are for good reason deprived of such protection.[361]

97 He who disregards his own disclaimer cannot rely on others giving more relevance to the disclaimer. He has torn his own disclaimer and the veil intended to protect him by his very own conduct. Only he who honours his own disclaimer can make others believe in the disclaimer. Ring-fence mechanisms bear quite some relevance[362] but the first to pay attention is the fence-keeper himself. They are affordable even for SMEs since the costs incurred generally are one time costs when a certain measure is established, and such mechanisms

---

[355] See only OLG Frankfurt MMR 2001, 751, 752; *Schack*, MMR 2000, 135, 138; *Mankowski*, CR 2000, 763, 767; *Morshäuser*, Internet-Werbung im europäischen Binnenmarkt (2003) pp. 45–46; *Pichler*, Internationale Zuständigkeit im Zeitalter globaler Vernetzung (2008) para. 600.

[356] KG GRUR Int. 2002, 448, 450 – Knoblauch Kapseln; LG Frankfurt/Main GRUR-RR 2002, 81, 82 – DocMorris; *Pichler*, Internationale Zuständigkeit im Zeitalter globaler Vernetzung (2008) para. 600; *Mankowski*, IPRax 2012, 144, 154.

[357] *Mankowski*, RabelsZ 63 (1999), 203, 248 *et seq.*; *Mankowski*, MMR Beilage 7/2000, 22, 25.

[358] *Magnus/Mankowski*, ZvglRWiss 103 (2004), 131, 168.

[359] *Mankowski*, MMR Beilage 7/2000, 22, 26.

[360] *Mankowski*, MMR Beilage 7/2000, 22, 26.

[361] *Mankowski*, RabelsZ 63 (1999), 203, 249 *et seq.*; *Mankowski*, MMR Beilage 7/2000, 22, 26–27.

[362] See *Øren*, (2003) 52 ICLQ 665, 691–694.

can be implemented easily.[363] For instance, in the media and information business paid
subscriber systems might serve as "paywalls".[364]

If an entrepreneur brags that he will deliver Europe-wide or that he has customers all over   **98**
Europe this is even a positive indication that the respective commercial activity is directed at
total Europe.[365]

d) Focalisation as a concept

Pammer uses a technique aptly if not ingeniously coined *focalisation*[366] in French.[367] It does   **99**
not relate to the entrepreneur's subjective intentions, but to objective elements and indications.[368] The ECJ's list is non-exhaustive[369] and deliberately so.[370] Other positive indications
not appearing on this list might be: the direction of advertisements on the entrepreneur's
website;[371] the address of a back office mentioned on the website;[372] mention of e-mail-
addresses with a country-specific ending;[373] establishment of contact at a distance;[374] conclusion of a consumer contract at a distance;[375] a causal link between activity and contract.[376]
Further additions might evolve and unearth in the future. Of course, some degree of sub-
jectivity or hidden discretion on the deciding judges' part can not be entirely avoided and
excluded.[377] Furthermore, a casuistic approach develops which cannot guarantee one-hun-
dred percent certainty.[378] In summary, the general idea is that every factual element accompanying or preceding the conclusion of the contract might be an indication if it entails a
minimum degree, and overcomes a threshold, of connection with the consumer's home

---

[363] *Mankowski*, IPRax 2012, 144, 154.

[364] *Reymond*, Yb. PIL 14 (2012/13), 205, 238.

[365] *Mankowski*, IPRax 2012, 144, 154.

[366] The authorship of the term is attributed to *Cachard*, La régulation internationale du marché électronique
(Paris 2002) pp. 193–217 et passim; see also *Cachard*, RCDIP 93 (2004), 641. See in more detail *Pironon*,
Clunet 138 (2011), 915.

[367] *Quiñones Escámez*, REDI 2010-2, 255, 256; *Cachard*, RCDIP 100 (2011), 429, 432; *Muir Watt*, RCDIP 101
(2012), 401, 404; *Legrand*, Petites affiches N° 239, 29 novembre 2013, p. 18, 20–21.

[368] *Cachard*, RCDIP 100 (2011), 429, 433.

[369] *Daniela Mühlleitner v. Ahmad Yusufi and Wadat Yusufi* (Case C-190/11), ECLI:EU:C:2012:542 para. 44;
Lokman Emrek v. Vlado Sabranovic (Case C-218/12), ECLI:EU:C:2013:666 para. 27, 31; BGH WM 2014,
2133 [15]; OGH ÖJZ 2015, 280 with note *Brenn*.

[370] *Brugnera/Reinalter*, Giur. it. 2014, 578, 581; *Markus Würdinger*, in: FS Peter Gottwald (2014), p. 693, 700.

[371] *Pironon*, Clunet 139 (2012), 996, 1002.

[372] BGH MDR 2014, 918 [14].

[373] BGH MDR 2014, 918 [14].

[374] *Daniela Mühlleitner v. Ahmad Yusufi and Wadat Yusufi* (Case C-190/11), ECLI:EU:C:2012:542 para. 44;
Lokman Emrek v. Vlado Sabranovic (Case C-218/12), ECLI:EU:C:2013:666 para. 28.

[375] *Daniela Mühlleitner v. Ahmad Yusufi and Wadat Yusufi* (Case C-190/11), ECLI:EU:C:2012:542 para. 44;
Lokman Emrek v. Vlado Sabranovic (Case C-218/12), ECLI:EU:C:2013:666 para. 28.

[376] *Lokman Emrek v. Vlado Sabranovic* (Case C-218/12), ECLI:EU:C:2013:666 para. 29; *Legrand*, Petites
affiches N° 239, 29 novembre 2013, p. 18, 20.

[377] *Legrand*, Petites affiches N° 239, 29 novembre 2013, p. 18, 21.

[378] *Markus Würdinger*, in: FS Peter Gottwald (2014), p. 693, 700.

state.[379] A hierarchisation amongst the indications is sometimes advocated for,[380] but at its core it is nothing more than a mere relevance test.

100 The test of *focalisation* as established by *Pammer* has been criticised as hampering SMEs which are said not to be able to afford precautionary costs of safeguarding against risks to lack of financial or personal resources.[381]

101 The Joint Declaration, Recital (24) Rome I Regulation and academic debate almost exclusively and in any event overly focus on websites and online selling. Likewise does the majority of reported cases.[382] But "targeted activity" goes beyond that,[383] and rightly so. It is not limited and restricted to operating in an online environment. It even goes beyond distance selling by means of distance communication.[384] It is deliberately phrased in rather open words which do not exclude any marketing strategies whatsoever. It employs technical neutrality towards the media used.[385] One should not underestimate the ingenuity of professionals marketing their goods or services. One should readily admit that one cannot possibly predict which marketing strategies will prevail in twenty years. Hence, one should define an open enough frame for consumer protection which allows for a flexible response to changing and developing marketing strategies. This lesson can be clearly learned from Art. 5 (2) 3rd lemma Rome Convention. This rule was dated and out of fashion even before it entered into force since the marketing strategy it intended to regulate had vanished already then. Such legislative mistakes must not be repeated. A functional approach covers future developments whereas an enumerative approach relying on exemplifications would not[386] the more so if there are too few exemplifications. The more abstract level of a functional approach definitely pays off.

102 One *caveat* appears to be necessary, howsoever: That a certain activity on the entrepreneur's side is not limited to the State where the entrepreneur has his domicile is not equivalent with an activity directed at the State where the consumer at stake is resident.[387] A simple illustration: If an entrepreneur domiciled in Germany extends his activities beyond his home state Germany to Austria this does not necessarily mean that he also directs activity at Belgium or France. Directed activity has a different target area and requires a positive indication that a certain State is included whereas activity going beyond the borders of

---

379 *Steennot*, Tijdschrift@ipr.be 2011, 152, 158; *van den Aardweg*, NIPR 2011, 473, 475; *de Clavière*, RLDA 89 (2014), 53, 54 with reference to *Peter Pammer v. Reederei Karl Schlüter GmbH & Co. KG; Hotel Alpenhof GesmbH v. Oliver Heller*, (Joined Cases C-585/08 and C-144/09) [2010] ECR I-12527 paras. 81–83.

380 *de Clavière*, RLDA 89 (2014), 53, 62–63.

381 *Clausnitzer*, EuZW 2011, 98, 105; *Schultheiß*, EuZW 2013, 944, 945; *Kieninger*, in: FS Ulrich Magnus (2014), p. 449, 455.

382 For instance in Germany BGH NJW 2006, 1672; OLG Dresden IPRax 2006, 44; LG München I 18 July 2007 – Case 9 O 16842/06 and in Austria LandesG Feldkirch EuLF 2008, II-23 = ZfRV-LS 2008/27, p. 79 with note *Ofner*.

383 Rightly emphasised by OLG Dresden IPRax 2006, 44, 45.

384 Thus the *obiter dictum* in LandesG Feldkirch EuLF 2008, II-23, II-25 is rather unfortunate.

385 *Mankowski*, VuR 2006, 289, 290.

386 Amended Proposal for a Regulation on jurisdiction and recognition and enforcement of judgments in civil and commercial matters, COM (2000) 689 final p. 6; *Mankowski*, ZvglRWiss 105 (2006), 120 140.

387 *Mankowski*, IPRax 2012, 144, 148.

the entrepreneur's home state only indicates negatively that activities are not restricted to the entrepreneur's home state.[388] These are more than only differing perspectives.

e) Attribution of activities exerted by others to the entrepreneur

Advertising or marketing activities exerted by others which are either contractors of the   **103** entrepreneur (like agencies) or do so with the entrepreneur consenting, are attributed to the entrepreneur and treated as if the entrepreneur had exerted these activities *in persona*.[389] But since (1) is restricted to claims in contract one has first to identify who is the consumer's partner in contract. It might be the case that re-sellers have to be held accountable for the producer's advertisements.[390] If the entrepreneur is only listed somewhere and this list is referenced to, or linked with, by others it becomes relevant as to whether the entrepreneur had strived for the respective listing since then there would be marketing activity on his side.[391]

8. Contract must fall in scope of activity

Besides exporting "targeted activity", (1) (c) provides for a second prerequisite namely that   **104** the contract must fall in the scope of the activity targeted at the consumer's state. This part of the provision shall ensure a proper connection between the contract entered into and activities of the other party to the contract. If, for example, the professional party directs advertisements for TV sets to the Member States, a consumer who has bought such a TV set is covered by (1) (c). On the other hand, if the consumer from the same seller buys a radio, for which no advertisements have been directed to the Member State where the consumer is domiciled, the consumer cannot rely on (1) (c). If the seller is not the same entrepreneur as under a previous, related and connected contract, it might be arguable whether a later contract helping to achieve the commercial goal pursued by the first contract, can be regarded as falling in the scope of activity of the first contract.[392] (1) (b) might possibly convey an argument for such contention if it could be evaluated as containing a generalising statement.

The criterion is better explained by Recital (25) Rome I Regulation than it ever was in the   **105** context of the Brussels I Regulation: Recital (25) *in fine* Rome I Regulation asserts that the contract must be concluded as the result of the professional's activities. This introduces the need for some specific nexus between the activities and the contract.[393] The Spanish delegation in the Rome I negotiations illustrated it by the so called Corte Inglés case:[394] El Corte Inglés is a well known chain of stores in Spain also operating a store in Lisbon. If a Spanish tourist visiting Lisbon decides to buy something at the Lisbon store he cannot avail him of either that El Corte Inglés is operating stores in Spain or that there might be a website accessible from Spain.[395]

---

[388] *Mankowski*, IPRax 2012, 144, 148.

[389] OGH ÖJZ 2015, 165, 167–168; *Mankowski*, IPRax 2009, 238, 243; *Hoch*, ÖJZ 2015, 168–169; *Loacker*, ÖJZ 2015, 169.

[390] *Mankowski*, IPRax 2009, 238, 243.

[391] *Mankowski*, IPRax 2009, 238, 243 *et seq.*; see also BGHZ 167, 83.

[392] See the reference to the ECJ in BGH WM 2014, 2133 [16]-[22].

[393] See in more detail *Mankowski*, IPRax 2008, 333 with numerous references.

[394] Many thanks to *Francisco Garcimartín Alférez* for making me privy to this knowledge.

[395] *Mankowski*, IHR 2008, 133, 142. But cf. AG Braunschweig 8 January 2014 – Case 118 C-3557/13.

106 Another practical example might be provided by the facts of a German case[396] (which was decided though) where a German resident in Spain made contact with a lawyer based in Germany after he had availed him to a list of lawyers which he had requested from the local Bar Association for the respective district; later-on he claimed in Spain allegedly because of the website operated by the lawyer – unfortunately, it was easily proven that he had concluded the client agreement with the lawyer entirely without any knowledge of the existence of that very website.[397] Other examples might be provided by a business selling office furniture[398] or used staff or company cars.[399]

9. Causal link between targeted activity and conclusion of the contract

107 The wording of (1) (c) does not expressly require a causal link between the entrepreneur's targeted activity and the conclusion of the contract.[400] To introduce such a requirement thus would be a further and implicit condition.[401] Under Art. 13 (1) pt. (3) Brussels Convention a causal link was denied.[402] But all this would only be an obstacle if the conditions expressly set out in (1) (c) are to be regarded as exhaustive and conclusive.[403] To attribute an exhaustive nature to these conditions would be based on a conviction that any unwritten, additional condition would significantly upset an already delicate balance put in place by the EU legislature,[404] as well as departing from the relevant case law of the ECJ[405] whereas refraining from adding an unwritten condition would enhance consumer protection,[406] perhaps overdo it[407] and tip the scale in an overly purposive manner. Yet these arguments are less strong with regard to requiring a causal link.[408] Causal links are seldom and rarely if ever expressly required in the wording of the respective rules.[409] But implicitly they are presupposed.[410] In Art. 17 (1) (c) in particular, the term "the contract falls within the scope of such activities"

---

[396] OLG Karlsruhe NJW 2008, 85 = IPRax 2008, 348 (noted by *Mankowski*, AnwBl 2008, 358; *eod.*, IPRax 2008, 333).

[397] Cf. with the same illustration *Leible/Lehmann*, RIW 2008, 528, 538.

[398] *Kropholler/von Hein*, Art. 15 note 26.

[399] *von Hein*, LMK 2014, 36025 (with some doubts since such transactions have been made subject at least to German consumer sales law by virtue of BGH NJW 2011, 3435).

[400] *Lokman Emrek v. Vlado Sabranovic* (Case C-218/12), ECLI:EU:C:2013:666 para. 21; *Legrand*, Petites affiches N° 239, 29 novembre 2013, p. 18, 19; *Ansgar Staudinger/Steinrötter*, NJW 2013, 3505; *Schultheiß*, EuZW 2013, 944, 945; *de Clavière*, RLDA 89 (2014), 53, 56.

[401] A-G *Cruz Villalón*, Opinion of 18 July 2013 in Case C-218/12, ECLI:EU:C:2013:494 para. 22; *de Clavière*, RLDA 89 (2014), 53, 55.

[402] A-G *Darmon*, Opinion of 27 October 1992 in Case C-89/91, [1993] ECR I-164, I-175 para. 83.

[403] To this avail in particular A-G *Cruz Villalón*, Opinion of 18 July 2013 in Case C-218/12), ECLI:EU:C:2013:494 para. 23.

[404] See *Lokman Emrek v. Vlado Sabranovic* (Case C-218/12), ECLI:EU:C:2013:666 para. 24; BGH WM 2014, 2133 [17]; *Clavora*, ÖJZ 2009, 917, 918.

[405] A-G *Cruz Villalón*, Opinion of 18 July 2013 in Case C-218/12, ECLI:EU:C:2013:494 para. 24.

[406] *Lokman Emrek v. Vlado Sabranovic* (Case C-218/12), ECLI:EU:C:2013:666 para. 24.

[407] *Rühl*, IPRax 2014, 41, 43–44; *Piroutek/Reinhold*, euvr 2014, 41, 43.

[408] See *Schultheiß*, EuZW 2013, 944, 945.

[409] Comp. *Wilke*, EuZW 2015, 13, 15.

[410] *Mankowski*, EWiR Art. 15 EuGVVO 1/13, 717, 718; see also *Legrand*, Petites affiches N° 239, 29 novembre 2013, p. 18, 19–20.

could provide quite some backing for a causal link being required.[411] The German ("Tätig-keit"), Portuguese ("actividade") and Polish ("działalność") versions using the singular are even more unambiguous.[412] An alternative approach would be to understand this criterion as being related to branches of activities or even to single products.[413]

Furthermore, to require a causal link is said to generate certain evidential issues and diffi- **108** culties,[414] *in extremis* to a veritable *probatio diabolica*,[415] possibly contrary to the *effet utile* of Section 4.[416] In particular, the question might be raised as to whether it is enough for consumers simply to make a statement or to provide evidence of having taken consultations if the consumer's assertion that the decision to enter into the contract was taken on the basis of consulting an website, together with making some individual contract with the entrepre-neur.[417] In the former case, jurisdiction would be up to the consumer who would only have to assert that the decision to conclude the contract was based on the trader's activity; in the latter case, the decision-making process on the consumer's side would be virtually impos-sible to prove[418] since consumers regularly do not keep a respective documentation of the steps to leading them into concluding a contract.[419] But evidential difficulties are not ger-mane to causal links; they could also stem from other requirements which surely exist, like the nature of the contract without those requirements being negated for evidential rea-sons.[420] The requirement of targeted activity could be even more problematic and could possibly throw the consumer in severe evidential difficulties.[421]

Howsoever, consumers could be bailed out of such difficulties if their burden of pleading **109** and proof, their onus, was levied.[422] The appropriate instrument is a rebuttable presump-tion[423] that the entrepreneur's marketing strategy induced the consumer to enter into the contract, particular so if the entrepreneur entertained a website; in order to rebut the pre-sumption, the entrepreneur would have to present evidence that in the concrete case his website did not trigger the consumer's interest.[424] This overcomes any difficulties on the

---

[411] See only BGH NJW 2009, 298; OLG Karlsruhe IPRax 2008, 348; *Mankowski*, IHR 2008, 133, 142; *Mankowski*, IPRax 2009, 238, 245; *Kieninger*, in: FS Jan Kropholler (2008), p. 499, 501–502; *Leible*, JZ 2010, 272, 277; *Rühl*, IPRax 2014, 41, 42–43; *Piroutek/Reinhold*, euvr 2014, 41, 43; *Matthias Klöpfer/ Wendelstein*, JZ 2014, 298, 299.

[412] But cf. *Wilke*, EuZW 2015, 13, 15.

[413] *Wilke*, EuZW 2015, 13, 15–16, 17.

[414] But cf. *de Clavière*, RLDA 89 (2014), 53, 57.

[415] *Boskovic*, RDCIP 103 (2014), 633, 635.

[416] *Ansgar Staudinger*, jM 2014, 229 (229).

[417] *Lokman Emrek v. Vlado Sabranovic* (Case C-218/12), ECLI:EU:C:2013:666 para. 25; A-G *Cruz Villalón*, Opinion of 18 July 2013 in Case C-218/12, ECLI:EU:C:2013:494 para. 25.

[418] A-G *Cruz Villalón*, Opinion of 18 July 2013 in Case C-218/12, ECLI:EU:C:2013:494 para. 25.

[419] *Leible/Michael Müller*, EuZW 2009, 29.

[420] *Rühl*, IPRax 2014, 41, 44; *Piroutek/Reinhold*, euvr 2014, 41, 44.

[421] *Keiler/Katrin Binder*, euvr 2013, 230, 236.

[422] *Mankowski*, IPRax 2009, 474, 483.

[423] *Schultheiß*, EuZW 2013, 944, 945 prefers establishing a case of *prima facie* proof.

[424] *Mankowski*, IPRax 2008, 333, 335; *Mankowski*, IPRax 2009, 474, 483; *Mankowski*, EWiR Art. 15 Eu-GVVO 1/13, 717, 718; *Legrand*, Petites affiches N° 239, 29 novembre 2013, p. 18, 20; see also *Schultheiß*, EuZW 2013, 944, 945. But *contra Matthias Klöpfer/Wendelstein*, JZ 2014, 298, 301–302.

consumer's side that he does not keep any substantial documentation.[425] As a European solution this would be an uniform approach that could not be accused of destroying uniformity and effectivity by having recourse to the respective *lex fori*.[426] Of course, the entrepreneur will only rarely be in a position to counter this, and that could severely disturb his economic calculation.[427] But it was his decision to entertain a website which can be consulted europe-wide, and it was his decision to conclude contracts with consumer domiciled abroad. If the entrepreneur is able to prove that the consumer's interest was induced by acquaintances who told him about the supply opportunities offered by the entrepreneur, he will succeed, though.[428] On the other hand, the consumer could almost always plead that he was induced by the entrepreneur's website or by some third parties hinting at this website.[429] But it is hardly conceivable that the consumer's knowledge of the entrepreneur's activities can be taken to prove the latter's activities, though.[430]

110 Putting the focus on the consumer's evidential difficulties must not lead to neglecting the entrepreneur's evidential difficulties which might arise *vice versa*. To refrain from requiring a causal link puts the entrepreneur in a rather awkward position. It generates a need to guess and jeopardises any strategic planning which could lead to legitimately avoiding becoming liable jurisdictionally.[431] To disregard the consumer's activities as irrelevant[432] stretches the protective regime potentially beyond its core ambition to protect passive and semi-passive[433] (or semi-active, from another perspective) consumers.[434] It is conceded that consumers are deterred by, or suffer from, the prospect of court proceedings facing a defendant abroad necessitating an extra effort in time and possibly cost irrespective of whether they consulted for instance a website run by the entrepreneur-defendant or not. But focussing entirely, and judicially acting upon, such protective approach[435] would render (1) (c) nugatory and futile. To entice cross-border consumer activity might be a political goal[436] but has its limits as justification when effectively defining (1) (c) away. Deterring effects on the supply side, in particular to SMEs, might more than outweigh the surplus of demand so generated.[437]

111 But the main argument why a causal link should be required is Recital (25) Rome I Regulation.[438] It reads: "(25) Consumers should be protected by such rules of the country of their

---

[425] *Mankowski*, IPRax 2008, 333, 335; *Wulf-Henning Roth*, Internationales Versicherungsvertragsrecht (1985) pp. 414 *et seq.*; *Nassall*, WM 1993, 1950, 1952; *Benicke*, WM 1997, 945, 951.

[426] See the criticism by *Lubrich*, GPR 2014, 116, 119.

[427] *Matthias Klöpfer/Wendelstein*, JZ 2014, 298, 302; see also *Lubrich*, GPR 2014, 116, 119.

[428] *Mankowski*, IPRax 2008, 333, 335; *Mankowski*, IPRax 2009, 474, 483–484; *Mankowski*, EWiR Art. 15 EuGVVO 1/13, 717, 718; *Matthias Klöpfer/Wendelstein*, JZ 2014, 298, 302.

[429] *Mankowski*, IPRax 2009, 474, 484; *Ansgar Staudinger/Steinrötter*, NJW 2013, 3505, 3506.

[430] *Bisping*, ERPL 2014, 513, 530.

[431] *de Clavière*, RLDA 89 (2014), 53, 54–55.

[432] *Peter Pammer v. Reederei Karl Schlüter GmbH & Co. KG; Hotel Alpenhof GesmbH v. Oliver Heller*, (Joined Cases C-585/08 and C-144/09) [2010] ECR I-12527 para. 60; *Daniela Mühlleitner v. Ahmad Yusufi and Wadat Yusufi* (Case C-190/11), ECLI:EU:C:2012:542 para. 30.

[433] *Fallon/Meeusen*, RCDIP 91 (2002), 435; *Boskovic*, RDCIP 103 (2014), 633, 636.

[434] *Mankowski*, EWiR Art. 15 EuGVVO 1/13, 717, 718; *Bisping*, ERPL 2014, 513, 530.

[435] As *Gsell*, ZZP 127 (2014), 431, 456–458 advocates.

[436] *Gsell*, ZZP 127 (2014), 431, 456–457.

[437] *Markus Würdinger*, in: FS Peter Gottwald (2014), p. 693, 696–697, 700–701.

habitual residence that cannot be derogated from by agreement, provided that the consumer contract has been concluded as a result of the professional pursuing his commercial or professional activities in that particular country. The same protection should be guaranteed if the professional, while not pursuing his commercial or professional activities in the country where the consumer has his habitual residence, directs his activities by any means to that country or to several countries, including that country, *and the contract is concluded as a result of such activities.*"[439]

Art. 6 (1) (b) Rome I Regulation requires a causal link and not a mere coincidence.[440] It **112** would demand a very good explanation and justification if one was prepared to deviate from the interpretation of Art. 6 (1) (b) Rome I Regulation in the interpretation of its sister rule, (1) (c).[441] To introduce different standards would generate a split between consumer protection as to jurisdiction on the one hand and conflict of laws on the other hand.[442] Furthermore, Recital (25) Rome I Regulation makes it clear that the relevant requirement is not "targeted activity" alone, but that the concrete contract results from such activity. The result of an activity must not be equated with the very same activity. Teleologically and purposively, one would grant protection to consumers who have taken the initiative cross-border if one disposed of a requirement of causality, and thus could go beyond protecting semi-passive consumers.[443] Furthermore, it appears rather odd to privilege a consumer who did not know about the entrepreneur's targeted activity before the conclusion of the contract.[444] And finally, the sequence in time between the different elements in (1) would be obscured (but admittedly this does not conflict entirely with the grammatical structure of (1) using different tenses for the different verbs).[445]

Even if a causal link was not regarded as a necessary condition it would constitute strong **113** evidence which may be taken into consideration when determining whether the entrepreneur's activity was in fact directed (also) at the consumer's home state.[446] This can be criticised as circular for causality would be between the targeted activity and the conclusion

---

[438] *Mankowski*, IPRax 2008, 333, 337; *Mankowski*, EWiR Art. 15 EuGVVO 1/13, 717, 718; *Ansgar Staudinger/Steinrötter*, NJW 2013, 3505–3506; *Piroutek/Reinhold*, euvr 2014, 41, 43–44; *Matthias Klöpfer/Wendelstein*, JZ 2014, 298, 299; *Marenghi*, Dir. comm. int. 2014, 214, 227–228, 230–231; *Ansgar Staudinger*, jM 2014, 229, 230–231; *Rühl*, in: FS Dagmar Coester-Waltjen (2015), p. 697, 705.

[439] Emphasis added.

[440] *Mankowski*, IPRax 2008, 333, 337.

[441] *Mankowski*, IPRax 2008, 333, 335; *Mankowski*, EWiR Art. 15 EuGVVO 1/13, 717, 718; *Rühl*, IPRax 2014, 41, 43.

[442] *Ansgar Staudinger/Steinrötter*, NJW 2013, 3505, 3506; but cf. *Matthias Klöpfer/Wendelstein*, JZ 2014, 298, 300.

[443] *Mankowski*, IPRax 2008, 333, 338; *Mankowski*, EWiR Art. 15 EuGVVO 1/13, 717, 718; *Ansgar Staudinger/Steinrötter*, NJW 2013, 3505, 3506; *Matthias Klöpfer/Wendelstein*, JZ 2014, 298, 302; see also *Piroutek/Reinhold*, euvr 2014, 41, 44–45.

[444] BGH EuZW 2012, 236 with note *Sujecki*.

[445] *Keiler/Katrin Binder*, euvr 2013, 230, 234; but cf. *Wilke*, EuZW 2015, 13, 17–18.

[446] *Lokman Emrek v. Vlado Sabranovic* (Case C-218/12), ECLI:EU:C:2013:666 para. 26; A-G *Cruz Villalón*, Opinion of 18 July 2013 in Case C-218/12, ECLI:EU:C:2013:494 para. 26.

of the contract so that it cannot be an indication for targeting at the same time.[447] Even leaving such criticism aside, a consequential issue arises as to whether it is sufficient that not the contract at stake is caused by the targeted activity, but another contract with which the contract at stake is intrinsically linked and without which the contract at stake would probably not exist.[448] For instance, targeted activity for the acquisition of real estate might trigger the accompanying conclusion of an agency contract.[449] *A fortiori*, an indirect causation suffices if a causal link is not regarded as a basic requirement.[450] But nonetheless a question is left open as to which weight a causal link carries as a mere indication in relation to other indications.[451]

10. No "awareness clause" on the entrepreneur's part

114 Neither kind of "awareness clause" as a restricting element has been adopted. Art. 5 (1) *in fine* Proposal Rome I Regulation contained such a clause relating to knowledge or negligence on the professional's part. The general idea underpinning this does not lack justification but it is served by a suitable interpretation of the basic criterion of "targeted activity". A combination of "targeted activity" as the rule and lack of awareness as the exception would spell havoc if there is any meaningful case left for the exception.[452] If an awareness clause was employed to discourage consumers from cheating by misstating their habitual residence this purpose can also be fulfilled by other means. Dishonest consumers who fraudulently misstate their habitual residence and so lure uncunning professionals into contracts which the professionals would not have concluded else, must be deprived of any protection.[453] The consequential niceties and problems generated by an extra awareness clause are too numerous and too burdening than to recommend its implementation.[454]

VII. Exception for contracts of carriage, (3)

1. Exception for contracts of carriage and its alleged rationes

115 (3) excludes from the scope of Section 4 contracts of transport other than a contract which, at an all-inclusive price, provides for a combination of travel and accommodation. The exception covers all kind of transport contracts, e.g. transport by ferry, aircraft, train and coaches, to the extent that such means of transport are not governed by other international

---

[447] *Schultheiß*, EuZW 2013, 944, 945; *Wilke*, EuZW 2015, 13, 17; see also *Keiler/Katrin Binder*, euvr 2013, 230, 233; *Matthias Klöpfer/Wendelstein*, JZ 2014, 298, 300.

[448] BGH MDR 2014, 918 [13]–[18].

[449] BGH MDR 2014, 918 [18.]

[450] *von Hein*, LMK 2014, 36025.

[451] *Esteban de la Rosa*, AEDIPr 2013, 1031, 1033.

[452] Max Planck Institute for Comparative and Private International Law, "Comments on the European Commission's Proposal for a Regulation of the European Parliament and the Council on the Law Applicable to Contractual Obligations into a Community Instrument and Its Modernisation", *RabelsZ* 71 (2007), p. 225 at 274.

[453] *Mankowski*, ZvglRWiss 105 (2006), 120, 137–138 with further references.

[454] *Mankowski*, ZvglRWiss 105 (2006), 120, 136–139.

instruments. For these contracts of transport, the ordinary provisions of the Brussels I Regulation apply, e.g. for a simple contrat for the carriage of passengers by air.[455]

Ratione materiae the exception covers both contracts of carriage of passengers as well as   **116** contracts of carriage of goods. The latter will seldom be entered into by private persons, but one could imagine for instance a consumer moving cross-border for the sake of working in another state and despatching some of his furniture and at least part of his previous household. Genuine cross-border moving arrangements with specialised moving companies might be questioned as to their characterisation, i.e. as to whether they constitute "simple" contracts of carriage or as to whether they consist of a variety of services exceeding the borders of what could be described as a contract of *carriage*. Art. 1 (4) (c) CMR exempts moving arrangements from the scope of application of the CMR. This might serve as an indication.

The rationale underpinning the exception is weak and does not hold if scrutinised. The first   **117** rationale ordinarily put forward is the number of international conventions in the area of international transport law, for instance, the Montreal Convention for air travel or the UR/ CIV or UR/CIM for European rail travelling.[456] But a split second should suffice to detect the weakness of this argument: Such conventions will prevail over the Brussels I*bis* Regulation already by virtue of Art. 71 (1) insofar as they contain rules on jurisdiction, *lis pendens* or recognition and enforcement.[457] There simply is no need to pay special respect to them since Art. 71 (1) already takes care in a very appropriate and absolutely suitable manner. And of course, the arguments fails miserably and falls flat insofar as no particular convention exists for a specific area which is the case for instance with regard to multimodal transport or to travelling via bus or coach. Insofar even a teleologic reduction of (3) could be imagined as a possibility not too far off.[458]

Else one should not confuse mobility (in the factual everyday sense) with "activity" in the   **118** specific sense which has become standard in the PIL of consumer contracts.[459] "Passive" consumers have gained protection while "active" consumers "actively" seeking out their partner in contact cross-border have not. Travelling consumers are mobile but not necessarily "actively".

The second reason put forward in order to justify the exemption of contracts of carriage is   **119** that carriers should not be burdened with a variety of home laws of different consumers since carriage is a mass market.[460] If such reasoning was valid it would apply to almost any kind of consumer contracts. Consumer business is mass dealing and related to mass mar-

---

[455] See only LG Lübeck IPRspr. 2010 Nr 193 p. 485.

[456] See e.g. OGH ÖJZ 2004, 390; Heiss, H., in: Czernich, D./Heiss, H., EVÜ, (Wien 1999), Art. 5 EVÜ note 10.

[457] See OGH ÖJZ 2004, 388, 390; *Mankowski*, Seerechtliche Vertragsverhältnisse im Internationalen Privatrecht (1995) p. 395; *Magnus/Mankowski*, ZvglRWiss 103 (2004), 131, 163; *Sachse*, p. 217; *Ragno*, in: Ferrari/Leible (eds.), Rome I Regulation (2009), p. 129, 141; *Geimer/Schütze*, Art. 15 EuGVVO note 58.

[458] *Beraudo*, Clunet 128 (2001), 1033, 1050; *Schlosser*, Art. 15 EuGVVO note 10.

[459] As it happened to *Basedow*, in: FS Erik Jayme (2004), p. 3, 10.

[460] But to this avail cf. *Looschelders*, Internationales Privatrecht (2004) Art. 29 EGBGB note 37; *Basedow*, in: FS Erik Jayme (2004), p. 3, 10; Max Planck Institute for Comparative and Private International Law, RabelsZ 71 (2007), 225, 276.

kets, and it is so *per definitionem*. There is nothing particular and specific about contracts of carriage in this regard. Hence, if the mentioned reasoning was upheld it would severely undermine the very existence of Art. 17 in its entirety.[461] It is fundamentally inconsistent with the approach generally pursued. Furthermore, the alleged unfairness to carriers does not withstand scrutiny.

120 The argument neglects the criterion of activity on the professional's side which is targeted at the state where the consumer has his habitual residence. Local carriers for instance operating ferryboats from the coast to an island will only rarely fulfil this.[462] And wherever carriers offer their services *via* the WWW they quite willingly open up the opportunity to approach them from all over the world – and even then they would be in a position to turn down concluding a contract just like they would deny actual carriage if the customer fails to pay in advance or to have his credit card available. The carrier marketing through local travel agencies could not possibly allege any unfairness if he held by his own activity.

2. Re-exception for package travel

121 A re-exception is made for package travel. Classificatory difficulties with regard to the notion of package travel[463] are clarified by an express reference to the Package Travel Directive,[464] more precisely, to Art. 2 (1) Package Travel Directive. Apparently, even those supporting an exception for contracts of carriage felt not prepared to skip consumer protection in an area where it is expressly provided by other Acts of EU law. Yet it should be noted that the re-exception is not restricted to cases where the Package Travel Directive or their national transpositions are applicable in the technical sense but is framed in a more general manner and couched in more general terms. The re-exception is the more fully justified as typically a packet travel arrangement is made, and contracted for, not by carriers as such, but by specialised package travel enterprises like TUI, Thomas Cook or Globetrotter (subsidiarily in rare cases by travel agencies). British Airways, Air France, Lufthansa, Delta, United Emirates, Turkish Airlines, Alitalia, Ryanair, Easyjet, Etihad, Eurowings and their likes do not enter in package travel contracts. Package travel does not consist of simple carriage.[465] The markets are typically national markets,[466] and travel agencies providing documentation and advice locally are the best indication. Admittedly, travel arrangements are often concluded *via* the WWW in modern times but this statistically rather relates to the simpler contingencies of hotel or flight bookings and not to the more complex package travel arrangements. On the Net, many customers opt for making their own arrangements and assembling their individual trip instead of booking some package pre-packed by someone else.

---

[461] *Mankowski*, ZvglRWiss 105 (2006), 120, 124; *Ragno*, in: Ferrari/Leible (eds.), Rome I Regulation (2009), p. 129, 141.

[462] *Mankowski*, ZvglRWiss 105 (2006), 120, 124.

[463] See in more detail *Mankowski*, Seerechtliche Vertragsverhältnisse im Internationalen Privatrecht (1995) pp. 401–403; *Mankowski*, in: Reithmann/Martiny, Internationales Vertragsrecht (7th ed. 2010) paras. 2673–2677.

[464] Council Directive 90/314/EEC of 13 June 1990 on package travel, OJ EC 1990 L 158/59.

[465] BezG Schwechat RRa 2014, 204, 206.

[466] See in more detail *Mankowski*, Seerechtliche Vertragsverhältnisse im Internationalen Privatrecht (1995) pp. 398–400; *Reithmann/Martiny/Mankowski*, Internationales Vertragsrecht (6th ed. 2004) para. 1714.

Originally, the provision only excluded contracts of transport. This caused uncertainty as to   **122**
whether or not package tours were covered by Section 4. However, in the Regulation, this
question has been clarified, and Section 4 now covers contracts concerning package tours,
provided the contract is covered by (1) (c). The concept of package tours is to be interpreted
in accordance with Art. 2 Package Tour Directive.[467,468] For instance, a voyage by freighter
fulfils the relevant criteria.[469] Secondary claims for non-performance are covered, too.[469a]

VIII. Other party not domiciled, but with establishment in a Member State

(2) states that where a consumer enters into a contract with a party who is not domiciled in   **123**
the Member State, but has a branch, agency or other establishment in one of the Member
States, that party shall, in disputes arising out of the operations of the branch, agency or
establishment, be deemed to be domiciled in that State. This has gained particular importance in cases where private investors deal with companies domiciled for instance on the
Virgin Islands, but with a European head office in London.[470] (2) is identical to Art. 9 (2).
Consequently, it should be construed in the same manner as the latter provision.

The notion of establishment is the same as in Art. 7 (5).[471] A doing business approach   **124**
referring to any professional activity exerted by the entrepreneur even if it did not materialise in a permanent establishment[472] does not suffice for this would stretch the borders of
the notion of establishment[473] and would tend to confuse (1) (c) with (2) although they
pursue different concepts. The interpretation of Art. 7 (5) thus is the leading guideline.
Accordingly, an establishment is defined as a place of business which has the appearance of
permanency, such as the extension of a parent body, has a management and is materially
equipped to negotiate business with third parties so that the latter, although knowing that
there will if necessary be a legal link with the parent body, the head office of which is abroad,
do not have to deal directly with such parent body but may transact business at the place of
business constituting the extension.[474] An establishment is therefore an entity capable of

---

467   Council Directive 90/314/EEC of 13 June 1990 on package travel, package holidays and package tours, OJ
       1990 L 158/59.
468   *Peter Pammer v. Reederei Karl Schlüter GmbH & Co. KG; Hotel Alpenhof GesmbH v. Oliver Heller*, (Joined
       Cases C-585/08 and C-144/09) [2010] ECR I-12527 paras. 38–43.
469   *Peter Pammer v. Reederei Karl Schlüter GmbH & Co. KG; Hotel Alpenhof GesmbH v. Oliver Heller*, (Joined
       Cases C-585/08 and C-144/09) [2010] ECR I-12527 paras. 44–46.
469a   AG Gießen NJW-RR 2013, 1073.
470   OLG Dresden IPRax 2006, 44; *von Hein*, BerDGfIR 45 (2011), 369, 375.
471   See only *Gaudemet-Tallon*, RCDIP 82 (1993), 325, 332; *de Lousanoff*, GS Peter Arens (1993), p. 251, 265;
       Hausmann, in: Wieczorek/Schütze, Art. 13 EuGVÜ note 27; *Benicke*, WM 1997, 945, 950; *Mankowski*, in:
       FS Tuğrul Ansay (Alphen 2006), p. 189, 197. *Contra* (favouring a more extensive approach) *Senff* pp. 297–
       298.
472   As advocated for by *Geimer*, NJW 1986, 2991, 2992; *Geimer*, EuZW 1993, 564, 565; *Geimer*, RIW 1994,
       59; *Nassall*, WM 1993, 1950, 1954; *Rauscher*, IPRax 1995, 289, 290–291;
473   To a similar avail *Senff* pp. 296–297.
474   *Somafer SA v. Saar-Ferngas AG*, (Case 33/78) [1978] ECR 2183, 2193 para. 12; *Blanckaert & Willems
       PVBA v. Luise Trost*, (Case 139/80) [1981] ECR 819, 828 *et seq.* para. 11; *SAR Schotte GmbH v. Parfums
       Rothschild SARL*, (Case 218/86) [1987] ECR 4905, 4919 para. 10; *Lloyd's Register of Shipping v. Société
       Campenon Bernard*, (Case C-439/93) [1995] ECR I-961, I-980 para. 18.

---

being the primary, or even exclusive, interlocutor for third parties e.g. in the negotiation of contracts.[475]

125 As the concept is a factual one, only factual sub-ordination by the establishment under the purposes pursued by the principal matters. Under extreme circumstances the ordinary "chain of command" might even be reversed with the result that a parent company becomes an establishment of an own subsidiary for the limited purposes of Art. 7 (5).[476] The *concrete* subordination is the key element. At first glance this result might appear astonishing, surprising and not easily deducted from the wording of Art. 7 (5),[477] but as a matter of concept it becomes fully justified.[478]

126 Any links under company law are irrelevant. Even totally unrelated companies of which the principal does not hold a single share can become establishments for the purposes of (2).[479] Cooperation partners, even if upstream or downstream the stream of commerce, can be establishments for the purposes of the concrete contract.[480]

127 The establishment can be anywhere in any Member State. It is not required to be located in the forum state.[481] Hence, for instance an establishment in Spain might help to open out jurisdiction in Germany. But the establishment must exist at the time when the lawsuit becomes pending.[482] Since it helps to establish and trigger jurisdiction this is the relevant point of time in this regard. If the establishment existed at the time when the consumer contract was concluded but ceased to exist between this time and the writ being issued consumers are not protected in their reliance upon what they see from the contract and the circumstances surrounding the conclusion of the contract.[483]

128 If the principal employs freight forwarders for organising delivery of goods the necessary permanence of a local presence is lacking.[484]

129 The ECJ has given one ruling on Art. 13 (2) Brussels Convention (resembling the current Art. 17 (2)). In *Wolfgang Brenner and Peter Noller v. Dean Witter Reynolds Inc.*, two German nationals instituted proceedings in Germany against an American investment company under Section 4 Brussels Convention. They had commissioned the defendant with the implementation of commodity futures transactions on a commission basis. The claimants, who had provided large sums of money, lost all the sums invested and claimed damages

---

[475] *Lloyd's Register of Shipping v. Société Campenon Bernard*, (Case C-439/93) [1995] ECR I-961, I-980 para. 19.

[476] *SAR Schotte GmbH v. Parfums Rothschild SARL*, (Case 218/86) [1987] ECR 4905, 4920 para. 16.

[477] Cf. the – sometimes harsh and severe – criticism by *Bischoff*, Clunet 115 (1988), 544; *Droz*, RCDIP 77 (1988), 737; *Schultsz*, NJ 1989 Nr 750.

[478] *Kropholler/von Hein* Art. 5 note 108.

[479] *Mankowski*, in: FS Tuğrul Ansay (Alphen 2006), p. 189, 197.

[480] *Mankowski*, in: FS Tuğrul Ansay (Alphen 2006), p. 189, 198.

[481] *von Hein*, BerDGfIR 45 (2011), 369, 375.

[482] BGH IPRax 2008, 128, 129; *Ansgar Staudinger*, IPRax 2008, 107, 108; *Seibl*, IPRax 2011, 234, 236; *von Hein*, BerDGfIR 45 (2011), 369, 375.

[483] BGH IPRax 2008, 128, 129–130.

[484] *Mankowski*, in: FS Tuğrul Ansay (Alphen 2006), p. 189, 198.

from the defendant. Although the defendant advertised in Germany, contact between the parties was mediated exclusively through a German firm independent of the defendant. The ECJ found that no branch, agency or other establishment within the meaning of Art. 13 (2) Brussels Convention acted as an intermediary in the conclusion or the performance of the contract between the parties. Therefore, this provision could not lead to jurisdiction in Germany.[485]

(2) requires additionally that the concrete dispute must arise out of the operations of the **130** branch, agency or establishment. This is in particular complied with if contractual obligations are performed by the establishment.[486] Likewise, mere sub-contractors do not qualify regularly.

Article 18

1. A consumer may bring proceedings against the other party to a contract either in the courts of the Member State in which that party is domiciled or, regardless of the domicile of the other party, in the courts for the place in which the consumer is domiciled.
2. Proceedings may be brought against a consumer by the other party to the contract only in the courts of the Member State where the consumer is domiciled.
3. This Article shall not affect the right to bring a counter-claim in the court in which, in accordance with this Section, the original claim is pending.

I. Generalities

Art. 18 governs jurisdiction in consumer contracts covered by Art. 17. (1) regulates juris- **1** diction for claims actively pursued by the consumer, (2) jurisdiction for claims against the consumer. (3) covers the special case of counterclaims. Solely and exclusively Art. 18 rules on the grounds of jurisdiction whereas Art. 17 only deals with the scope of application thus establishing prequisites for the grounds of jurisdiction, but not the grounds of jurisdictions as such. Hence, the starting point must be Art. 18, and Art. 17 ought to be checked only incidentally.[1]

The provisions of the Brussels I Regulation on jurisdiction for consumer contracts are **2** simple and efficient in the sense that the consumer has a choice whereas the other party to the contract does not have a choice. The consumer can choose between instituting proceedings either in the Member State where the other party to the contract is domiciled, or in the Member State where the consumer is domiciled. The consumer is at liberty and can choose freely without being tied in either way. In practice, the vast majority of consumers will prefer the home game offered by (1) 2nd option. The consumer who sues the other party in the Member State of the other party's domicile will be a rare bird. Yet this does not rule out this option by law. Consumers shall have that avenue open to them if they deem it more appropriate to sue where later enforcement is likely. But after the abolition of the exequatur

---

485   *Wolfgang Brenner and Peter Noller v. Dean Witter Reynolds Inc.*, (Case C-318/93) [1994] ECR I-4275.
486   *Mankowski*, in: FS Tuğrul Ansay (Alphen 2006), p. 189, 197.
1   See only *Michael Müller*, EuZW 2015, 218, 219.

and the advent of direct enforcement by virtue of Arts. 38 *et seq.* such considerations have lost even more weight.

3 The concept of domicile[2] for the consumer is determined in accordance with Art. 62.[3] As far as the other party to the contract is concerned, the concept of domicile is also determined by Art. 62 if that party is a natural person and Art. 63 if that party is a company or other legal person or association of natural or legal persons.[3a] However, the domicile of the other party has to be read in the light of Art. 17 (2): There a branch or place of business is equated with a domicile if the other party does not have a proper domicile in the strict sense in a Member State.

II. Jurisdictions for claims by the consumer, (1)

4 Under (1), the first option corresponds to Art. 4 and its extension by Art. 17 (2), whereas the second option is an example of claimant jurisdiction justified by the need for procedural consumer protection. If the other party to the contract is domiciled in Member State A and has a branch in Member State B, and the dispute arises out of the operation of that branch, the consumer can choose between instituting proceedings in these two Member States in addition to his own Member State for Art. 17 (1) explicitly reserves special jurisdiction under Art. 7 (5). This option entails an away game, and might thus not appear all too attractive to the consumer. But the consumer might gain the advantage of a domestic enforcement of a judgment against the entrepreneur's assets in the forum State without the difficulties of a cross-border enforcement (although such advantage might have been reduced with the advent of Arts. 38 *et seq.* in the Recast.[3b]

5 The second option of (1) provides the consumer with a *forum actoris* and thus with a sharp sword. It deviates from the basic principle of the jurisdiction rules of the Brussels *Ibis* Regulation generally to favour the defendant over the plaintiff and to avoid explicit *fora actoris*. (1) 2nd option is the very rule businesses have to account for. In practice, (1) 2nd option is all dominant whereas (1) 1st option has gained almost no relevance. Consumers are particularly fond of the *forum actoris* granted to them and appreciate home games. The relevant point in time for localising the consumer's domicile for jurisdictional purposes is when the lawsuit becomes pending; afterwards the maxim of *perpetuatio fori* applies.[4]

6 Under the Brussels I Regulation, the consumer could only rely on Art. 16 (1) Brussels I Regulation if the other party to the contract was domiciled in a Member State or deemed to be so under Art. 15 (2) Brussels I Regulation.[5] Consequently, national provisions of international jurisdiction applied to situations where the other party to the contract was domi-

---

[2] See additionally Art. 18 note 12 (*Mankowski/Nielsen*).

[3] *Hypoteční banka a.s v. Udo Mike Lindner*, (Case C-327/10) [2011] ECR I-11543 paras. 40–41.

[3a] See only Rb. Rotterdam NIPR 2015 Nr. 78 p. 179.

[3b] *Bonomi*, in: Dickinson/Lein para. 6.61.

[4] *Auer*, in: Geimer/Schütze, Internationaler Rechtsverkehr Art. 16 EuGVVO note 5; *Gottwald*, in: Münchener Kommentar zur ZPO, Art. 16 EuGVVO note 5; *Ansgar Staudinger*, jM 2014, 229, 231.

[5] *Wolfgang Brenner and Peter Noller v. Dean Witter Reynolds Inc.*, (Case C-318/93) [1994] ECR I-4275; *Toro*, Rev. dr. eur. consomm. 2014, 81, 91.

ciled outside the EU and did not have a branch, agency or other establishment in one of the Member States through the operations of which the dispute arises out of.

(1) 2nd option radically and substantially alters this situation. The consumer can avail him- **7** self of the *forum actoris* at his domicile whenever the prerequisites of Art. 17 (1) are met since the European legislator added "regardless of the domicile of the other party" to the wording of this option.[6] Recital (14) para. 2 seconds and supports:
"However, in order to ensure the protection of consumers and employees, to safeguard the jurisdiction of the courts of the Member States in situations where they have exclusive jurisdiction and to respect the autonomy of the parties, certain rules of jurisdiction in this Regulation should apply regardless of the defendant's domicile."

(1) 2nd option is a significant change[7] and indicates an important step towards unilateral **8** universality.[8] It subjects enterprises resident in Third States and not having a place of business in the EU[9] to the most aggressive and most fundamental protective device in the array of European consumer protection. In particular US enterprises engaged in direct trade cannot escape European jurisdiction anymore.[10] The escape strategy direct trade does not work anymore.[11] A qualifying Internet presence might subject US enterprises and their other Third State consorts to European jurisdiction rules.[12] "Hells Bells" (AC/DC) for them, Xmas for consumers.[13] The provision enhances consumer protection but it may be unattractive for businesses located outside the EU who might find themselves vulnerable to being sued across the EU and unable to negate that risk by a jurisdiction clause.[14] (1) 2nd option stars among the remnants[15] of the bigger plan[16] to extend jurisdiction to defendants resident in third States in a wholesale manner as – after intensive preparation[17] – the Proposal Brussels

---

[6]   See only *Gsell*, ZZP 127 (2014), 431, 433–434.

[7]   *Crawford/Carruthers*, (2014) 63 ICLQ 1, 5; *Toro*, Rev. dr. eur. consomm. 2014, 81, 91; *Bonomi*, in: Dickinson/Lein para. 6.68.

[8]   *Fallon/Kruger*, Yb. PIL 14 (2012/13), 1, 19–20; *Mankowski*, RIW 2014, 625, 626–627.

[9]   For if they had a place of business in the EU, Art. 17 (2) would be triggered.

[10] *Pohl*, IPRax 2013, 109, 111; *Gaudemet-Tallon/Kessedjian*, RTDeur 49 (2013), 435, 440; *Markus*, AJP 2014, 800, 809; *Mankowski*, RIW 2014, 625, 626.

[11] *Mankowski*, RIW 2014, 625, 626.

[12] *Ansgar Staudinger*, RRa 2014, 265.

[13] *Ansgar Staudinger*, RRa 2014, 265.

[14] *Harris*, [2014] JIBFL 709, 712.

[15] *von Hein*, RIW 2013, 97, 100–101; *Peter Arnt Nielsen*, (2013) 50 CML Rev. 503, 513; *Mankowski*, RIW 2014, 625, 626–627.

[16] Discussed by *Magnus/Mankowski*, ZvglRWiss 110 (2011), 252, 261–270; *Johannes Weber*, RabelsZ 75 (2011), 619; *Borrás*, in: Lein (eds.), The Brussels I Review Proposal uncovered (2012), p. 57; *Weitz*, in: FS Daphne-Ariane Simotta (2012), p. 679; *Gilles*, (2012) 8 JPrIL 489; *Luzzatto*, in: Pocar/Viarengo/Villata (eds.), Recasting Brussels I (Padova 2012), p. 111; *Markus*, in: Pocar/Viarengo/Villata (eds.), Recasting Brussels I (Padova 2012), p. 123; *Cafari Panico*, in: Pocar/Viarengo/Villata (eds.), Recasting Brussels I (Padova 2012), p. 127; *Fallon/Kruger*, Yb. PIL 14 (2012/13), 1.

[17] European Group for Private International Law (Bergen Session, 21 September 2008), IPRax 2009, 283 and *Nuyts*, Study on residual jurisdiction, 3 September 2007, http:ec.europa.eu/justice_home/doc_centre/civil/studies/doc/study_residual_jurisdiction.en; *Fallon*, in: Liber amicorum Hélène Gaudemet-Tallon (2008), p. 241; *Gaudemet-Tallon*, in: Mélanges en l'honneur de Serge Guinchard (2010), p. 465;

Ibis Regulation pursued it by abandoning the previous Art. 4 Brussels I Regulation and skipping the prequisite of a domicile within the Member States under Art. 5 Proposal plus introducing a *forum fortunae* and a *forum necessitatis* in Arts. 25; 26 Proposal. The extension operates only in the context of (1) 2nd option and does not guarantee the consumer a forum in any Third State where a business might be domiciled, under (1) 1st option.[18]

9 If after the contract has been concluded, the consumer moves to another Member State, the question arises whether he can choose between instituting proceedings in the old and new Member State or only one of them. It was assumed under the Brussels Convention that the consumer had a choice for contracts listed in Art. 13 (1) pts. 1 and 2, but not pt. 3 Brussels Convention, since the steps necessary for the conclusion of the contract would have been taken in the old Member State.[19] Since Art. 17 (1) (a) and (b) are identical to Art. 13 (1) pts. 1 and 2 Brussels Convention, the consumer clearly has a right to choose between his old and new Member State under the Regulation in cases covered by Art. 17 (1) (a) and (b). As far as the third category of contracts is concerned, under Art. 17 (1) (c), the decisive factor is no longer the place where the consumer took the steps necessary for the conclusion of the contract, but whether the other party to the contract pursues commercial or professional activities or not in the Member State where the consumer is domiciled. Consequently, it seems that in cases covered by Art. 17 (1) (c), the consumer should have the right to choose between the old and the new Member State,[20] provided the other party to the contract pursues commercial or professional activities in both Member States and the contract falls within the scope of these activities in both States. If the consumer moves cross-border only after he has commenced the lawsuit, only his former domicile matters.[21] If the consumer moves only domestically this is irrelevant for the purposes of Art. 17 (1) (c) since the business directed its activities not a certain place but at the respective State.[22]

10 (1) 2nd option varies in an important respect from (1) 1st option and (2): Whereas the latters are only concerned with regulating *international* jurisdiction (1) 2nd option also regulates *local* jurisdiction or venue.[23] Its wording is pretty clear vesting jurisdiction in the courts *of the place* of the consumer's domicile. The reason for this ingression is clear cut and politi-

---

Grolimund, Drittstaatenproblematik des europäischen Zivilverfahrensrechts (2000); *Grolimund*, ZVR-Jb 2010, 79; *Kropholler*, in: FS Murad Ferid zum 80. Geb. (1988), p. 239; *Kruger*, Civil Jurisdiction Rules of the European Union and Their Impact on Third States (2008); *Pataut*, in: Leroyer/Jeuland (dir.), Quelle cohérence pour l'espace judiciaire européen? (2004), p. 31; *Pocar*, in: Liber amicorum Hélène Gaudemet-Tallon (2008), p. 573; *Schlosser*, in: FS Andreas Heldrich (2005), p. 1007; *de Vareilles-Sommières*, in: Liber amicorum Hélène Gaudemet-Tallon (2008), p. 397.

[18] *Gsell*, ZZP 127 (2014), 431, 440.

[19] Report *Schlosser* para. 161.

[20] *Contra* OLG München WM 2012, 1863; *Keiler/Katrin Binder*, euvr 2013, 230, 236: only the new domicile matters for only this is a current domicile at the time when the lawsuit becomes pending. *Contra Wilke*, EuZW 2015, 13, 18: option for consumer irreconcilable with the wording. But the wording is ambiguous, and an option to chose for the claimant has also been established under Art. 5 (3) Brussels Convention/ Brussels I Regulation, now Art. 7 (2) Brussels *Ibis* Regulation, without the wording indicating or even less expressly admitting so.

[21] *Ansgar Staudinger*, jM 2014, 229, 232.

[22] *Ansgar Staudinger*, jM 2014, 229, 232.

[23] *Ansgar Staudinger*, jM 2015, 46, 51. Imprecisely OLG Frankfurt ZIP 2013, 387.

cally evident: The *forum actoris* for the consumer still is a progressive solution. Many Member States (including for instance Germany[24]) have not established like rules on jurisdiction in consumer matters at the domestic level. Hence it would be odd to refer to the national law of the State where the consumer has his domicile. Either this runs the danger to trip upon a gap in national regulation or, even worse, it hits a national policy adverse to jurisdictional protection of consumers and thus opposite to the policy pursued by (1) 2nd option.

III. Jurisdiction for claims against the consumer, (2)

The other party to the contract can institute proceedings against the consumer solely and **11** exclusively in the Member State where the consumer is domiciled. (2) is unambiguous in this regard. It employs the same connecting factor as Art. 4. However, its importance lies in the fact that no alternative bases of jurisdiction are available to the other party to the contract. Consequently, the only place where proceedings can be brought against a consumer whose contract falls within the scope of Section 4 is in the Member State where the consumer is domiciled. The consumer is guaranteed a home game and reliably avoids an away game if he is attacked.[25] This procedurally safe situation for consumers combined with the choice available to consumers under (1) constitutes the key factors of consumer protection in respect of jurisdiction under the Brussels I*bis* Regulation.

(2) vests in principle exclusive jurisdiction in the courts of the State where the consumer is **12** domiciled if the consumer is sued by the other party and thus is the defendant. Consumers can in principle confide and be assured that they have a home game if they are on the defence. They must in principle not be aware to be sued elsewhere than in their home state. "Their" language, "their" procedural law (of which consumers in practice do not have sufficient knowledge, though) and in most instances "their" law (by virtue of Art. 6 Rome I Regulation) come to their benefit. There are only few exceptions to the rule that (2) is exclusive: firstly, (3) for counter-claims; secondly, jurisdiction agreements as far as permitted by Art. 19; thirdly, exclusive jurisdiction under Art. 24 which rule takes precedence over Arts. 17–19 as far as it is applicable.

If after the conclusion of the contract, the consumer moves to another Member State, his **13** new domicile is decisive for jurisdiction under (2) given the protective character of Section 4.[26]

For the purposes of (2) the CJEU has ruled that where the court is unable to identify the **14** consumer's place of domicile but also has no firm evidence to support the conclusion that the defendant consumer is in fact domiciled outside the EU, the consumer's last known

---

[24]   See BGHZ 153, 173; *Max Vollkommer/Gregor Vollkommer*, in: FS Reinhold Geimer (2002), p. 1367; *Mankowski*, JZ 2003, 689.

[25]   In reality (2) might be overlooked, misapplied or outrightly disregarded by a court seised by the business in spite of (2) in particular so if the defendant-consumer does not enter an appearance and does not object to the jurisdiction of that court. The second line of consumer protection is then provided by Art. 45 (1) (e) at the level of recognition and enforcement.

[26]   Report *Jenard* p. 33.

domicile is to step in.[27] Main purpose of this operation is to avoid a denial of justice and to avoid the applicant to be deprived of all possibility of recourse.[28] A like ratio should apply under (1) 1st option *mutatis mutandis*. But it cannot find application under (1) 2nd option for then the plaintiff-consumer's domicile is the relevant connecting factor. Matters will be solved since the plaintiff-consumer has to allege and, if necessary, to prove that he has his domicile at the place where the forum seised is.[29]

15 (2) does not apply if the consumer is domiciled in a Third State. Like all other rules in Arts. 17–19, (2) does not protect such consumers.[30] The extension of (1) 2nd option in the international arena does not find a counterpart in (2).[31] Consumers domiciled in Member States gain better options for suing businesses resident in Third States but consumers resident in Third States are not protected at all. In particular, they are not guaranteed that they could be only and exclusively sued in their home State. This cannot be done for the simple reason that the EU legislator cannot prescribe courts in Third States when to assume and exercise international jurisdiction. (2) does not exert any kind of *effet réflexe*, either.[32] Likewise, an alleged parallelism with the universal application of European conflict of law rules (Arts. 2 Rome I Regulation; 3 Rome II Regulation etc.) cannot be taken as justification[33] since every court in a Third State would not apply EU PIL, but the PIL of its own *lex fori* (vene though concrete results might happen to coincide).[34] To extend (2) in favour of consumer-defendants resident in a Third State would be tantamount to excluding access to justice in the EU for business-claimants resident in the EU and would thus be at odds with the overall policy to enhance access to justice.[35] An extension of (2) should not be regarded as a preferable option even *de lege ferenda*.[36]

IV. Counter-claims, (3)

16 Art. 18 does not affect the right to bring counter-claims in the court in which the original claim is pending in accordance with Section 4. (3) expressly preserves this right to either party. In particular, the enterprise business or professional is entitled to it. Systematically, (3) is an exception to (1) and in particular to (2). (3) makes a reservation and thus prohibits any *argumentum e contrario*. The phraseology used in (3) is identical to Art. 8 (3), and it should be construed in the same manner as Art. 8 (3).[37] In particular, the term "counter-claim" has the same meaning in both rules and does not comprise set-off or recoupment for which international jurisdiction is not required at all.

---

[27] *Hypoteční banka a.s v. Udo Mike Lindner*, (Case C-327/10) [2011] ECR I-11543 paras. 42–54.

[28] *Hypoteční banka a.s v. Udo Mike Lindner*, (Case C-327/10) [2011] ECR I-11543 paras. 51, 54.

[29] *Mankowski*, IPRax 2009, 474, 480.

[30] *von Hein*, RIW 2013, 97, 101; *Hay*, EuLF 2013, 1, 5; *Gsell*, ZZP 127 (2014), 431, 434.

[31] *Gsell*, ZZP 127 (2014), 431, 434–435.

[32] *Gsell*, ZZP 127 (2014), 431, 436–437.

[33] *Contra Gsell*, ZZP 127 (2014), 431, 460.

[34] *Althammer*, as reported by *Julia Caroline Scherpe*, ZZP 127 (2014), 483, 489.

[35] *Gsell*, ZZP 127 (2014), 431, 444.

[36] *Alexander Bruns*, as reported by *Julia Caroline Scherpe*, ZZP 127 (2014), 483, 485. *Contra Gsell*, ZZP 127 (2014), 431, 447.

[37] Report *Jenard* p. 33.

Article 19

The provisions of this Section may be departed from only by an agreement:
(1) which is entered into after the dispute has arisen; or
(2) which allows the consumer to bring proceedings in courts other than those indicated in this Section; or
(3) which is entered into by the consumer and the other party to the contract, both of whom are at the time of conclusion of the contract domiciled or habitually resident in the same Member State, and which confers jurisdiction on the courts of that Member State, provided that such an agreement is not contrary to the law of that Member State.

Bibliography

Añoveros, Restrictions on Jurisdiction Clauses in Consumer Clauses within the European Union, Rev. eur. dr. consomm. 2004, 77

Heinig, Grenzen von Gerichtsstandsvereinbarungen im Europäischen Zivilprozessrecht (2010).

I. Ratio legis

Art. 19 regulates the extent to which jurisdiction clauses are accepted under Section 4 of the **1** Regulation. The starting point is that the provisions of jurisdiction in Art. 18 are mandatory. It is important to have this in mind. The basic decision against jurisdictional party autonomy in consumer contracts must neither be overlooked nor forgotten. The protection granted to consumers by Arts. 18 would be rendered nugatory and worthless in a split second if jurisdiction agreements and procedural party autonomy were admitted in large scale.[1] However, jurisdiction clauses are permitted under certain yet rather limited circumstances. The structure of Art. 19 is identical to the structure of Art. 15 (1)-(3) concerning insurance contracts. Art. 19 establishes a control mechanism based on autonomous yardsticks already on the European level negating any recourse to national law.[2]

The idea underlying Art. 19 is to deter businesses from inserting jurisdiction clauses in **2** consumer contracts. However, at their own peril businesses might insert such clauses, though. Most consumers will not be aware of the protection granted to them by Arts. 17–

---

[1]   *Galič/Schwartze*, in: unalex Kommentar, Art. 17 note 1.
[2]   *Ansgar Staudinger*, jM 2015, 46, 53.

19 and will not be prepared to invest in taking respective advice. Hence, they in turn will be intimidated by written clauses in the small print of the supplier's General Terms and Conditions. "It's written in the contract" will appeal to the mind of the uninformed consumer. Most consumer contracts have a contract volume not worth the effort to fight the issue.

II. Formal and material validity

3   None of the provisions in Section 4 of the Brussels *Ibis* Regulation sets up formal or material requirements for a jurisdiction clause. Furthermore, it is not prescribed in Art. 19 that a jurisdiction clause in a consumer contract is subject to compliance with Art. 25. Nevertheless, it is beyond doubt and should go without saying as no-brainer that a jurisdiction clause covered by Section 4, to the extent such clause is permissible under Art. 19, must meet the formal requirements imposed by Art. 25.[3] Material validity of the jurisdiction clause, to the extent that this question is not regulated indirectly by Art. 25, is governed by the *lex fori prorogati* including its rules of private international law, pursuant to Art. 25 (1) cl. 1 *in fine* and Recital (20). Generally, Art. 19 builds upon the general regime for jurisdiction agreements as contained in Art. 25.[4] But Art. 19 takes precedence as *lex specialis* wherever it and Art. 25 do not coincide. Insofar as Art. 19 rules on a certain point either explicitly or impliedly it has the sway as a matter of ranking and hierarchy.[5] Art. 25 serves as default rule for issues not dealt with in Art. 19. A jurisdiction agreement between a business and a consumer will only withstand scrutiny if it complies with the requirements of both Art. 19 and Art. 25.[6]

III. Permissible jurisdiction clauses

1. General considerations

4   According to Art. 19, the provisions of Section 4 may be departed from only by agreement in three situations listed in the provision. Art. 19 is a straightjacket.[7] The use of "only" clarifies that the list is exhaustive. However, Art. 19 does not deal with the relationship between Section 4 and Art. 26.[8]

5   Jurisdiction clauses in consumer contract clauses are generally unenforceable.[9] This holds the more true where they attempt at conferring exclusive jurisdiction in the courts at the supplier's seat or place of business.[10] The conclusion applies irrespective of whether a jurisdiction clause is individually negotiated or forms part of a set of Standard Terms and Conditions.[11] That reports[12] and surveys of national case law have not unearthed and revealed

---

3   Report *Schlosser* para. 161a; *Schaltinat* p. 102; *Ganssauge* p. 68; *Gehri*, in: Basler Kommentar, Art. 17 LugÜ note 5 with further references; *Gottwald*, in: Münchener Kommentar ZPO, Art. 17 note 1.

4   See only *Schoibl*, JBl 1998, 767, 773; *Simotta*, in: Fasching/Konecny, Art. 17 note 3 with further references.

5   *de Bra* p. 189; *Senff* p. 306; *Crawford/Carruthers*, (2014) 63 ICLQ 1, 10.

6   Nejvyšší soud unalex CZ-19; *Galič/Schwartze*, in: unalex Kommentar, Art. 17 note 2.

7   See *Briggs/Rees* para. 2.89.

8   See *Infra* Art. 19 notes 45–49.

9   *Jonathan Hill* para. 7.14. See only AP Sevilla REDI 2011-2, 263; *Andreeva Andreeva*, REDI 2011-2, 263, 265.

10   See *Jonathan Hill* para. 7.15.

many cases explicitly dealing with Art. 17 Brussels I Regulation or Art. 15 Brussels Convention, the predecessors to Art. 19, does not come as a surprise on the one hand but does not evidence the irrelevance of the rule hidden behind Art. 19 on the one hand.[13] Conversely, the case against jurisdiction clauses in consumer contracts is so clear cut that enterprises evidently found not it worthwhile to argue against it in concrete court cases. The advent of e-commerce has not altered the picture dramatically.[14] It does not justify a complete reversal of consumer policy. Wisely and on the contrary, the EU has adopted specific regimes for consumer protection particularly in e-commerce, namely the original Distance Selling Directives[15] and nowadays the Consumer Rights Directive[16] which clearly indicate that e-consumers are not regarded as less worthy and serving of protection than "traditional" consumers.

In policy terms, Art. 19 protects consumers from being deprived of their procedural rights **6** under Art. 18, and as such, Art. 19 is a key provision in the context of consumer protection. However, the Unfair Contract Terms Directive,[17] which has priority over the Brussels I Regulation according to Art. 67,[18] supplements Art. 19. According to Arts. 3; 6; Annex (1) (q) Unfair Contract Terms Directive, a clause in a consumer contract which has the purpose or the effect of depriving the consumer of his right to go to court may be set aside as invalid. This Directive covers all consumer contracts and also contracts covered by Section 4 of the Brussels I*bis* Regulation. Consequently, a jurisdiction agreement permissible under Art. 19 may nevertheless be set aside under the Unfair Contract Terms Directive.[19]

In *Océano Grupo Editorial SA and Salvat Editores*,[20] the ECJ was faced with a situation where **7** two Spanish companies had entered into contracts with a number of consumers domiciled in Spain for the purchase by instalments of encyclopaedias. As the case was purely national in nature, the Brussels Convention was inapplicable. However, the considerations of the ECJ in this judgment are very important for the understanding of European consumer protection in general, which Section 4 of the Brussels Regulation forms part of. The contracts

---

[11]   *Ansgar Staudinger*, jM 2014, 229, 231.

[12]   In particular the Heidelberg Report and its underlying national reports.

[13]   But cf. *Jonathan Hill* para. 7.14.

[14]   Tentatively *contra* Hague Conference of Private International Law, Electronic Commerce and International Jurisdiction, Ottawa 28 February to 1 March 2000, Prel. Doc. No. 12 p. 7; *Tang* p. 133–134.

[15]   Council Directive 97/7/EC of 20 May 1997 on the protection of consumers in respect of distance contracts, OJ 1997 L 144/19; Directive 2002/65/EC of the European Parliament and of the Council of 23 September 2002 concerning the distance marketing of consumer financial services and amending Council Directives 90/619/EEC, 97/7EC and 98/27/EC, OJ 2002 L 271/16.

[16]   Directive 2011/83/EU of the European Parliament and of the Council of 25 October 2011 on consumer rights, amending Council Directive 93/13/EEC and Directive 1999/44/EC of the European Parliament and of the Council and repealing Council Directive 85/577/EEC and Directive 97/7/EC of the European Parliament and of the Council, OJ EU 2011 L 304/64.

[17]   Council Directive 93/13/EEC of 5 April 1993 on unfair terms in consumer contracts, OJ 1993 L 95/29.

[18]   Art. 67 note 5 (*Mankowski*) with references.

[19]   In detail *Simotta*, in: Fasching/Konecny, Art. 17 notes 19–34.

[20]   *Océano Grupo Editorial SA v. Roció Murciano Quintero* and *Salvat Editores SA v. José M. Sánchez Alcón Prades, José Luis Copano Badillo, Mohammed Berroane and Emilio Viñas Feliú*, (Joined Cases C-240/98 to C-244/98) [2000] ECR I-4941.

contained a term conferring exclusive jurisdiction on the courts in a Spanish city in which none of the consumers was domiciled, but where the sellers had their principal places of business. The contracts concerned small claims. When the consumers did not pay the sums due on the agreed dates, the companies instituted proceedings in the city designated in the jurisdiction clauses. Before the claims were served on the defendants, the national court had doubts as to whether or not it had jurisdiction over the claims in question. Consequently, the national court asked the ECJ for a preliminary ruling on whether the court of its own motion could determine whether an unfair term is void under the Unfair Contract Terms Directive.

8   The ECJ emphasised the unfairness of jurisdiction clauses because they oblige the consumer to submit to the jurisdiction of a court that may be a long distance away from the consumer's domicile. Furthermore, the ECJ stressed that in cases concerning small claims the costs relating to the consumer's entering an appearance could be a deterrent and cause the consumer to forgo any legal remedy or defence. The ECJ found that where a jurisdiction clause is included, without being individually negotiated, in a contract between a consumer and a seller or supplier within the meaning of the Unfair Contract Terms Directive, and where the clause confers exclusive jurisdiction on a court in the territorial jurisdiction of which the seller or supplier has his principal place of business, the jurisdiction clause must be regarded as unfair within the meaning of Art. 3 Unfair Contract Terms Directive in so far as it causes, contrary to the requirement of good faith, a significant imbalance in the parties' rights and obligations arsing under the contract, to the detriment of the consumer.[21]

9   In regard of the question submitted to the ECJ, the ECJ noted that the system of protection introduced by the Unfair Contract Terms Directive is based on the idea that the consumer is in a weak position vis-à-vis the seller or supplier, in terms of both bargaining power and level of knowledge, and that this leads to the consumer agreeing to terms drawn up in advance by the seller or supplier without being able to influence the content of the terms. The ECJ also stated that the aim of the Directive would not be achieved if the consumer were obliged to raise the unfair nature of such terms, and that there would be a real risk that the consumer, particularly because of ignorance of the law, would not challenge the term pleaded against him on the ground that it is unfair.[22] Consequently, the ECJ ruled that the protection provided for consumers by the Unfair Contract Terms Directive entails the national court being able to determine, of its own motion, whether a term of a contract before it is unfair when making its preliminary assessment as to whether a claim should be allowed to proceed before the national courts.

10 The relation between the Unfair Contract Terms Directive, in particular (1) (q) of its Annex,

---

[21]   *Océano Grupo Editorial SA v. Roció Murciano Quintero* and *Salvat Editores SA v. José M. Sánchez Alcón Prades, José Luis Copano Badillo, Mohammed Berroane and Emilio Viñas Feliú*, (Joined Cases C-240/98 to C-244/98) [2000] ECR I-4941, I-4971 para. 22, I-4973 para. 24.

[22]   *Océano Grupo Editorial SA v. Roció Murciano Quintero* and *Salvat Editores SA v. José M. Sánchez Alcón Prades, José Luis Copano Badillo, Mohammed Berroane and Emilio Viñas Feliú*, (Joined Cases C-240/98 to C-244/98) [2000] ECR I-4941, I-4973 paras. 25 and 26. In this case, the ECJ also ruled in accordance with settled case law concerning the position where a directive has not been transposed, that a national court must, when applying national law, whether adopted before or after the directive, interpret national law as far as possible in the light of the wording and purpose of the directive so as to achieve the result pursued by the directive.

expressly addressing jurisdiction clauses, and the Brussels I*bis* Regulation, in particular Art. 19, is to be judged in accordance with Art. 67.

2. Subsequent jurisdiction clauses

A jurisdiction clause in a consumer contract covered by Section 4 of the Brussels I Regu- **11**
lation is valid provided it has been entered into after the dispute has arisen.[23] Consequently, jurisdiction agreements entered into prior to the point in time when the dispute has arisen, which in practice seems to be the most common situation since such clauses usually appear in the consumer contract from the outset or as a standard term, have no effect. (1) will ensure that such clauses are only valid if the consumer ratifies the clause after the dispute has arisen. But mere conduct in judicial proceedings should not amount to any kind of implied or tacit consent.[24]

The policy underlying (1) is that the consumer is only capable of fully understanding the **12**
effect of an agreement on jurisdiction when he knows exactly what the dispute is about and on this basis is able to conclude whether or not it would be reasonable of him to accept a jurisdiction agreement.[25] The consumer will be in a better situation to understand the implications and possible consequences of agreeing.[26]

Hence, the most important function of (1) thus is that (1) serves as the basis for an *argu-* **13**
mentum e contrario: (1) makes it clear that a jurisdiction clause which is inserted and to be found already in the original consumer contract is invalid in principle.[27] The original contract is concluded before any actual dispute springing from it can possibly have arisen. To does not matter whether the jurisdiction clause war individually negotiated (hardly conceivable in the practice of B2C business but for Roman Abramovich ordering a yacht and such likes) or a boilerplate clause. Boilerplate clauses are the more prone to a verdict,[28] but the clause being a boilerplate one is not a prerequisite. To make the jurisdiction agreement which is already contained in the original contract, dependent on a precondition that a dispute arises would be a circumvention and should be denied effect.[29] Jurisdiction clauses only become effectively operative when a dispute arises.

It might be that the cause for a subsequent dispute is laid already before the contract was **14**
concluded (e.g. that the other party did not comply with duties to inform the consumer as imposed by the Directives of EU consumer law and their national transpositions). But this is

---

[23]   See Art. 19 (1).

[24]   But cf. *Andreeva Andreeva*, REDI 2011-2, 263, 265–266.

[25]   See only *de Bra* p. 184; *Añoveros*, Rev. eur. dr. consomm. 2004, 77, 115; *Ganssauge* p. 70; *Sachse* p. 47; *Heinig* p. 277.

[26]   *Jonathan Hill* para. 7.14.

[27]   See only BGH RIW 2013, 563, 565; *Layton/Mercer* para. 17.050; *Geimer/Schütze* Art. 13 EuGVO note 4; *Gehri*, in: Basler Kommentar, Art. 17 LugÜ note 9.

[28]   *Gehri*, in: Basler Kommentar, Art. 17 LugÜ note 9.

[29]   *Geimer/Schütze* Art. 13 EuGVO note 4; *Gehri*, in: Basler Kommentar, Art. 17 LugÜ note 1; *Ansgar Staudinger*, in: Rauscher, Art. 13 Brüssel I-VO note 4; *Furrer/Glarner*, in: Dasser/Oberhammer, Art. 17 LugÜ note 5.

not decisive. It solely matters whether the dispute arises before or after the conclusion of the consumer contract.

15 The point of time when a consumer contract is eventually concluded is to be judged according to the law applicable to this consumer contract. Issues of conclusion of a contract are governed by the *lex causae* of this very contract by virtue of Art. 10 (1) Rome I Regulation. The *lex causae* determines for instance as to whether a distance selling contract is only concluded after the supplier has sent a confirmation of the order to the consumer and the consumer has received this confirmation. An independent and autonomous European concept should not be called for[30] since it would lead to severe differences with the approach taken in the Rome I Regulation and conflict with the desire of Recitals (7) of the Rome I and II Regulations for a harmonising interpretation.

16 A dispute has arisen if the parties disagree on at least one specific point and legal proceedings are imminent or contemplated.[31] Legal proceedings should be immediately threatening or should have some likelihood in due course.[32] A mere difference of opinion and a simple exchange of polite letters should not be deemed sufficient.[33] Even less, the consumer exercising his rights under the contract as such should not suffice for no dispute will arise if the business is to accept the consumer's demand. A simple complaint by the consumer will as such not do either for again the business might accept it and act accordingly (for whichever reasons, even be it in order to keep the consumer as customer or to avoid bad publicity). If it is first time under the concrete contract that the consumer has filed a complaint a dispute cannot arise before the business's response.[34] If the consumer receives an unsatisfactory answer by the business the difference of opinion is evident and a dispute has arisen.[35] If matters are threatening to court, the consumer is deemed to be aware that he has to stand up to save, and fight for, his own cause.[36]

17 But the legal proceedings threatening need not necessarily be court proceedings in a court of justice.[37] Any other kind of dispute solution mechanism equally qualifies, for instance arbitration, conciliation, mediation or an ombudsman procedure. Alternative Dispute Resolution is on equal footing with litigation in this regard. Particularly the consumer must be aware that a need for dispute resolution is imminent.[38] The time when a dispute has arisen indicates an event when the consumer is able to expect the dispute could go beyond any kind of self-help communication[39] and third party adjudicators might be called to the front.

---

[30]   *Contra Tang* p. 132.
[31]   Report *Jenard* p. 33; LG Saarbrücken IPRspr. 2013 Nr. 212 p. 462.
[32]   See Report *Jenard/Möller* p. 57; Rb. Breda NIPR 2009 Nr 21 p. 65; *Junker*, in: FS Peter Schlosser (2005), p. 299, 318; *Junker*, in: FS Gunther Kühne (2009), p. 735, 740; *Simotta*, in: Fasching/Konecny, Art. 21 EuGVVO note 10; *Mankowski*, in: Rauscher, Art. 21 Brüssel I-VO note 3.
[33]   *Auer*, in: Geimer/Schütze, Internationaler Rechtsverkehr in Zivil- und Handelssachen, Art. 21 EuGVVO note 5 (2005); *Mankowski*, AP issue 8/2012 Nr 23 zu § 38 ZPO Internationale Zuständigkeit Bl. 7R, 9R.
[34]   *Tang* p. 131.
[35]   *Tang* p. 132.
[36]   *Senff* p. 220; *Gehri*, in: Basler Kommentar, Art. 17 LugÜ note 12.
[37]   *Senff* p. 220.
[38]   *Czernich*, in: Czernich/Tiefenthaler/Kodek Art. 21 EuGVVO note 2.
[39]   *Tang* p. 131; see also *Gehri*, in: Basler Kommentar, Art. 17 LugÜ note 13. But cf. *Senff* p. 220.

Furthermore, at this stage of the dispute, where the controversy has arisen and the consumer **18** thus regards the other party to the contract as an opponent, it seems unlikely that the commercial party will succeed in obtaining the consumer's acceptance of a jurisdiction clause submitted to the consumer in small print because now the consumer is far more on the alert than he was when he entered the contract. Disinterest or apathy is not a valid option and a preferred strategy anymore[40] for it is not regarded and evaluated as rational anymore. After a dispute has arisen the offer to conclude a choice of court agreement will in all likelihood be an isolated offer and will not be hidden in a multi-fold variety and catalogue of General Terms and Conditions.[41] The consumer must not feel forced to consent for fear of else losing the contract. Evidently, the conclusion of the contract cannot be any *quid pro quo* for accepting the jurisdiction agreement anymore since the main contract is already concluded. The probability that the consumer will be overwhelmed and coerced is lessened. The jurisdiction agreement is not unilaterally imposed.[42] The likelihood that the consumer has legal representation is increased.[42a] The business has less space to play tricks on the consumer and to lure the consumer into a near unconscious acceptance. The consumer can easily detect that he simply has to say "No" and is offered every proper opportunity to do so. (1) is not objectionable on the basis that consumers do not become more equal with suppliers just because a dispute has arisen,[43] since a perfect level playing field is not required.

After a dispute has arisen, the consumer will suspect that every offer by the business will be **19** submitted in the own interest of the business and thus that it will presumably not happen to coincide with the consumer's best interests.[44] His resistance will be enhanced even more if he has already taken advice at this point of time.[45] After a dispute has arisen, consumers are presumed to be cautious to reach any agreement.[46] They can contemplate and reconsider the current offer, and can take their time without time pressure being applied[47] (but for negotiation tactics by the supplier).

(1) applies to exclusive and non-exclusive jurisdiction agreements likewise.[48] But subsequent **20** jurisdiction clauses are subject to the presumption of exclusivity as formulated in Art. 25 (1) cl. 2.

At first glance, a consumer has small if any incentives to agree intentionally to the jurisdic- **21**

---

[40]   See *Galič/Schwartze*, in: unalex Kommentar, Art. 17 note 4.

[41]   LG Saarbrücken IPRspr. 2013 Nr. 212 p. 463; *Mankowski*, IPRax 2001, 310, 312; *Mankowski*, AP issue 8/2012 Nr 23 zu § 38 ZPO Internationale Zuständigkeit Bl. 7R, 9; *Senff* pp. 220–221; *Jonathan Hill* para. 7.14; *Heinig* p. 245.

[42]   *Vassilakakis*, RHDI 66 (2013), 273, 291.

[42a] *Bonomi*, in: Dickinson/Lein para. 6.84.

[43]   *Contra Dahl*, NTIR 46 (1977), 104, 107; *Jonathan Hill* para. 7.14.

[44]   *Mankowski*, in: Rauscher, Art. 21 Brüssel I-VO note 3; *Mankowski*, AP issue 8/2012 Nr 23 zu § 38 ZPO Internationale Zuständigkeit Bl. 7R, 9; *Junker*, NZA 2005, 199, 201; *Bosse*, Probleme des europäischen Internationalen Arbeitsprozessrechts (2007) p. 287; *Heinig* pp. 245, 294.

[45]   See only *Franzen*, RIW 2000, 81, 82; *Cornelia Müller*, Die internationale Zuständigkeit deutscher Arbeitsgerichte und das auf den Arbeitsvertrag anwendbare Recht (2004) p. 89.

[46]   *Tang* p. 131.

[47]   *Geimer/Schütze* Art. 13 EuGVO note 4; *Gehri*, in: Basler Kommentar, Art. 17 LugÜ note 11.

[48]   *Tang* p. 134.

tion of a court which is not in his home state, after the emergence of a dispute between the parties.[49] That diminishes and reduces the practical significance of (1).[50] But its does not extinguish such significance entirely. There can be cases where a consumer does so agree for instance in order to obtain some compensating benefit or to retain the relation with the business particularly so if the contractual relationship between the parties is about necessities.

3. Jurisdiction clauses widening the consumer's choice, (2)

22   Following the general policy to protect consumers, an agreement on jurisdiction that allows the consumer to bring proceedings in courts other than those indicated in Section 4 is permissible according to (2). If the other party is prepared to give the consumer more (and more protection at that) contractually than the consumer would have solely *ex lege* the law will not put hindrances and obstacles in the other party's way.[51] To protect someone to his own detriment would not only be hypertrophy,[52] but highly paradox. There is no reason to protect someone against acquiring a better position.[53] Arts. 17–19 establish a minimum standard, and of course the other party can voluntarily concede a higher level of protection even more favourable to the consumer. (2) envisages optional, non-exclusive jurisdiction clauses which can only be unilaterally applied and enforced in the consumer's favour.[54] It does not matter when the agreement was concluded; (2) becomes operative even if the clause was already contained in the original consumer contract and does, unlike (1) not require that a dispute has arisen.[55]

23   The regime established by Arts. 17–19 is only semi-mandatory, strictly speaking. Art. 19 ensures that the consumer must not be deprived of the protection granted to him by Art. 18. It inhibits any derogatory effect of jurisdiction clauses to the consumer's detriment, but permits prorogatory effects to the consumer's favour. But it should be emphasised that even under (2) jurisdiction clauses can only open up *additional* options (or to employ utmost precision: at least one additional option)[56] for the consumer[57] and must not derogate from Art. 18 (1). An agreement concluded before a dispute arose must allow the consumer to bring proceedings before courts other than those on which Art. 18 confers jurisdiction.[58] Merely to refer to given jurisdiction does not suffice.[59] The effect of the agreement is not to exclude the jurisdiction vested into courts by virtue of Art. 18, but to extend the consumer's

---

[49] *Jonathan Hill* para. 7.14.

[50] *Jonathan Hill* para. 7.14.

[51] See only *Geimer/Schütze* Art. 17 note 6; *Simotta*, in: Fasching/Konecny, Art. 17 note 7.

[52] *Geimer/Schütze* Art. 13 EuGVO note 6; *Ansgar Staudinger*, in: Rauscher, Art. 13 Brüssel I-VO note 5.

[53] KG VersR 2014, 1020, 1021.

[54] *Société financière et industrielle du Peloux v. Axa Belgium* (Case C-112/03), [2005] ECR I-3707 para. 42; *Tang* p. 134; *Toro*, Rev. dr. eur. consomm. 2014, 81, 89.

[55] *Layton/Mercer* para. 17.051; *Gehri*, in: Basler Kommentar, Art. 17 LugÜ notes 14–15.

[56] KG VersR 2014, 1020, 1021; LG Saarbrücken IPRspr. 2013 Nr. 212 p. 464.

[57] See *Ahmed Mahamdia v. People's Democratic Republic of Algeria* (Case C-154/11), ECLI:EU:C:2012:491 para. 61; *Junker*, EuZA 2013, 83, 94; *Martiny*, IPRax 2013, 536, 541.

[58] See *Ahmed Mahamdia v. People's Democratic Republic of Algeria* (Case C-154/11), ECLI:EU:C:2012:491 para. 61.

[59] KG VersR 2014, 1020, 1022.

possibility of choosing between several courts with jurisdiction,[60] be such jurisdiction *ex lege* or contractually granted. As the agreement may *allow* the consumer to bring proceedings in courts other than indicated in Art. 18, (2) cannot be interpreted as meaning that the agreement could apply exclusively and thus prohibit the consumer from bringing proceedings before the courts which have jurisdiction pursuant to Art. 18.[61] The objective of protecting the consumer as the weaker party would not be attained if the jurisdiction provided for in Art. 18 could be ousted by an agreement on jurisdiction concluded before any dispute arose.[62]

Hence, as a starting point the consumer has *ex lege* the most favourable option conceivable,   **24** namely the *forum actoris* at his domicile designed by Art. 18 (1) 2nd option. This diminishes his interest in every other *forum*.[63] Any additional option offered by contract might be theoretically fine but has only limited value to him. Every other forum would mean an away game to him and would confront him with the difficulties of cross-border litigation. Accordingly, it would not be really attractive to the consumer.[64] But there might be specially favourable procedural rules or advantages in the substantive law applied (like e.g. exemplary or punitive damages) which might entice the consumer to sue in the forum contracted for.[65] Or certain means of proof might be more readily available there.[66]

On the other hand, it does not follow either from the wording or the purpose of Art. 19 that   **25** an agreement on jurisdiction may not confer jurisdiction on the courts of a Third State provided that it does not exclude the jurisdiction conferred on the basis of Art. 19.[67] The additional options opened up to the consumer by agreement, may include courts outside the EU.[68] Insofar (2) goes beyond Art. 25 which rule requires the *forum prorogatum* to be in a Member State. But Art. 25 has to deal with the prorogatory element, too, whereas (2) is solely concerned with the derogatory element (which does not exist if the jurisdiction agreement only offers an additional option to the consumer).

Only the consumer, not the other party to the contract, can rely on (2). Clauses upheld by (2)   **26** are to the sole benefit of the consumer.[69] Consequently, a clause giving both the consumer

---

[60] See *Ahmed Mahamdia v. People's Democratic Republic of Algeria* (Case C-154/11), ECLI:EU:C:2012:491 para. 62.

[61] See *Ahmed Mahamdia v. People's Democratic Republic of Algeria* (Case C-154/11), ECLI:EU:C:2012:491 para. 63.

[62] See *Ahmed Mahamdia v. People's Democratic Republic of Algeria* (Case C-154/11), ECLI:EU:C:2012:491 para. 64.

[63] See only *Senff* p. 222; *Añoveros*, Rev. eur. dr. consomm. 2004, 77, 117; *Heinig* p. 278 with further references.

[64] *Jonathan Hill* para. 7.14.

[65] *Heinig* p. 278.

[66] *Heinig* p. 278.

[67] See *Ahmed Mahamdia v. People's Democratic Republic of Algeria* (Case C-154/11), ECLI:EU:C:2012:491 para. 65.

[68] See *Ahmed Mahamdia v. People's Democratic Republic of Algeria* (Case C-154/11), ECLI:EU:C:2012:491 para. 66; *Junker*, EuZA 2013, 83, 94; *Martiny*, IPRax 2013, 536, 541.

[69] See *Société financière et industrielle du Peloux v. Axa Belgium* (Case C-112/03), [2005] ECR I-3707 para. 42.

---

and the other party to the contract a wider range of possibilities than Art. 18 prescribes will only be upheld if the consumer institutes proceedings in accordance with the jurisdictional agreement, not if the other party to the contract does so. The additional options in the other party's favour are virtually deleted.[70]

27   If the other party to the contract has instituted proceedings against the consumer in the Member State where the consumer is domiciled, the consumer cannot rely on a jurisdiction clause allowing him to sue in another Member State in order to have the proceedings in his Member State dismissed. Art. 31 (2) does not come to the consumer's help in this regard for it is only concerned with exclusive jurisdiction clauses, and the other party is not in breach of an exclusive jurisdiction clause if it sues the consumer in the Member State of his domicile in strict compliance with Art. 18 (2) which takes precedence over any jurisdiction clause by virtue of Art. 19.[71]

28   In order to decide as to whether the jurisdiction clause at stake is a unilaterally optional one or an exclusive one the presumption established by Art. 25 (1) cl. 2 ought to be applied.[72] Hence, whenever the character of the jurisdiction clause is unclear the presumption comes into operation and militates in favour on an exclusive character.[73]

29   (2) has a sound theoretical idea backing it. But in practice examples might be rare since standard-form contracts as they are so common in B2C business, and their jurisdiction clauses are drafted by suppliers and suppliers have scarce incentive to open out additional jurisdictional options in their customers' favour.[74] It seems highly unlikely that businesses accept to grant such an additional option to their customers' benefit.[75] Not even competition amongst suppliers will generate such incentive for competition in consumer markets is mainly about price and not about the nitty-gritty of condition in small print. It is barely conceivable to assume a supplier advertising that his jurisdiction clause, of all clauses, is more favourable to his customers than required by law and more favourable than what his competitors offer. The obvious bias effect makes it unusual for a business and thus unlikely to conclude a non-exclusive jurisdiction clause of the kind envisaged by (2) with its consumer-customer.[76]

4. Valid jurisdiction clauses under national law in originally domestic cases, (3)

30   The third kind of jurisdiction clauses permissible under Art. 19 are those described in (3). This provision deals with a special situation where it was considered unfair to the other party to the contract if the jurisdiction clause were to be set aside. The provision concerns a case where both parties to the contract were domiciled or habitually resident in the same Member

---

[70]   Similarly *Simotta*, in: Fasching/Konecny, Art. 17 note 18. *Contra Galič/Schwartze*, in: unalex Kommentar, Art. 17 note 5: The choice of court agreement is invalid in its entirety.

[71]   Bur cf. *Sherdley v. Nordea Life and Pension SA* [2012] EWCA Civ 88, [2012] 2 All ER Comm 725 [66] (C. A., per *Rix* L.J.).

[72]   LG Potsdam NJW-RR 2012, 956; Nejvyšší soud unalex CZ-19.

[73]   Confusing *Gehri*, in: Basler Kommentar, Art. 17 LugÜ note 8.

[74]   *Jonathan Hill* para. 7.14; *Heinig* p. 278; *Furrer/Glarner*, in: Dasser/Oberhammer, Art. 17 LugÜ note 6.

[75]   *Seatzu*, Insurance in Private International Law (2003) p. 120; *Vassilakakis*, RHDI 66 (2013), 273, 291.

[76]   *Tang* p. 134.

State when the contract was entered into, and either party (but in particular the consumer) subsequently moves to another Member State.[77] The jurisdiction clause originally was a domestic one, and only afterwards the case became internationalised, and a cross-border context opened up only subsequently. Suppliers who operate and are active only on a certain market, in particular local dealers or services providers, shall not be surprised by the subsequent international dimension opening up entirely different jurisdictional regimes.[78] Exceptionally, (3) is also applicable if the consumer leaves his previous home state for an unknown destination.[79]

According to (3), a jurisdiction clause entered into between the consumer and the other **31** party to the contract will be accepted provided three conditions are satisfied. Firstly, the consumer and the other party to the contract must be domiciled or habitually resident in the same Member State at the time when the contract was entered into. Secondly, the contract must confer jurisdiction on the courts of that same Member State. Thirdly, the jurisdiction clause must not be contrary to the law of that same Member State.

Domicile and habitual residence are on equal footing, and either of them qualifies. Domicile **32** is subject to Arts. 62; 63.[80] It has been suggested that habitual residence should have the meaning which it has under the *lex fori prorogati* applying Art. 62 *per analogiam*.[81] But the alternative approach to give habitual residence an autonomous meaning is far more convincing. It would run on parallel lines with Art. 6 Rome I Regulation. Thus it would be sensible in order to preserve the same standards for *ius* and forum where possible. Another parallel to be appreciated would be to the former Art. 5 (2) Brussels I Regulation[82] and to its successor, Art. 3 Maintenance Regulation. Furthermore, habitual residence has become the dominant connecting factor in International Family Law[83] and in the Brussels II*bis* Regulation. On the entrepreneur's side Art. 17 (2) is operative for helping to explain the notion of domicile.[84] Generally, a place of business in the respective Member State suffices.[85] The reference to Art. 7 (5) as contained in Art. 17 (1) justifies his extension and partial correction of the wording which is narrower on a literal reading.

Preserving invalidity under the national law of the formerly common home state at first **33** glance appears as a particularity.[86] Yet it can be justified by the ratio underlying (3). (3) is

---

[77]   Report *Jenard* p. 33; *Jonathan Hill* para. 7.14; *Heinig* p. 279 with further references; *Gerhard Wagner*, in: Stein/Jonas, Art. 17 note 6.

[78]   *Schnyder/Paczoska Kottmann*, in: FS Ivo Schwander (2011), p. 789, 794; *Ansgar Staudinger*, jM 2015, 46, 54.

[79]   *Gerhard Wagner*, in: Stein/Jonas, Art. 17 note 7.

[80]   *Dörner*, in: Saenger, Art. 17 note 3.

[81]   *Geimer/Schütze* Art. 17 note 11; *Hausmann*, in: Wieczorek/Schütze, Art. 15 EuGVÜ note 6; *Simotta*, in: Fasching/Konecny, Art. 17 note 10.

[82]   *Dörner*, in: Saenger, Art. 17 note 3.

[83]   On the respective notion e.g. *Mellone*, RDIPP 2010, 685; *Hilbig-Lugani*, in: FS Gerd Brudermüller (2014), p. 323; *Hilbig-Lugani*, in: Boele-Woelki/Dethloff/Gephart (eds.), Family Law and Culture in Europe (Cambridge/Antwerpen/Portland, Oreg. 2014), p. 249.

[84]   *Simotta*, in: Fasching/Konecny, Art. 17 note 11; *Heinig* p. 281.

[85]   *Geimer/Schütze* Art. 17 note 12; *Teuber* p. 63; *Gehri*, in: Basler Kommentar, Art. 17 LugÜ note 20.

[86]   *Senff* p. 223; *Gehri*, in: Basler Kommentar, Art. 17 LugÜ note 16; cf. also *Galič/Schwartze*, in: unalex

---

designed to protect the justified trust primarily on the supplier's side. But trust worth of protection cannot come to existence if the jurisdiction agreement was invalid *ab ovo*. You cannot and must not trust in the validity of something invalid. There is nothing mysterious behind that. It is not necessary to ruminate that the European legislator might perhaps leave the national laws of the Member States unrestricted for they could be more progressive than previously Arts. 15–17 Brussels I Regulation, today Arts. 17–19.[87] But (3) is simply based on the thought that the law of the initially common home state would have to be applied if the consumer had not moved cross-border and the contract had remained a domestic one. Without the subsequent international element no-one would doubt that this particular national law would apply. Art. 25 is derogated insofar as (3) serves as *lex specialis*.[88]

34 Some Member States are very restrictive in admitting choice of court clauses in domestic consumer contracts.[89] They might distinguish as to whether entrepreneur and consumer had their respective domiciles at the same *place* when the contract was concluded or not.[90] In Austria § 14 KSchG has to be complied with,[91] in Germany § 38 (3) pt. 2 ZPO.[92] If the law inhibits the parties from making a contractual choice for venue in a consumer contract this should invalidate any jurisdiction agreement contravening such verdict.[93] It could be argued that an isolated agreement on venue might be controlled on the basis of national law alone since Art. 18 (1) 1st option and accordingly Art. 19 83) are only concerned with international jurisdiction.[94] Insofar the national implementation of the Directive on Unfair Contract Terms in Consumer Contracts and in particular of (1) (q) of the Annex to this Directive could come to the fore.[95] The ECJ is very critical on choice-of-court agreements altering venue.[96] One means of solving the consequential differences within EU law and their diverging rationes could possibly be to interpret Directive 93/13/EEC in the light of the Brussels *Ibis* Regulation.[97] Another one would be to establish a standard of double control first under Art. 17–19, second under Directive 93/13/EEC. But one could doubt whether there can really be anything left for this second step once the filter of Arts. 17–19 has been passed.[98]

Kommentar, Art. 17 note 9. Critical for policy reasons *Bonomi*, in: Dickinson/Lein para. 6.87; *Gaudemet-Tallon* (5th ed.) para. 292.

[87] To this avail *Senff* p. 224; *Gehri*, in: Basler Kommentar, Art. 17 LugÜ note 16.

[88] Similarly *Simotta*, in: Fasching/Konecny, Art. 17 note 12.

[89] See *Schnyder*, in: Schnyder, Art. 17 LugÜ note 7.

[90] See *Schnyder*, in: Schnyder, Art. 17 LugÜ note 8.

[91] *Simotta*, in: Fasching/Konecny, Art. 17 notes 12, 14, 15; *Tiefenthaler*, in: Czernich/Tiefenthaler/Kodek, Art. 17 note 2.

[92] *Kropholler/von Hein*, Art. 17 note 3; *Gerhard Wagner*, in: Stein/Jonas, Art. 17 note 8; *Gottwald*, in: Münchener Kommentar ZPO, Art. 17 note 2; *Dörner*, in: Saenger, Art. 17 note 3; see also *Ansgar Staudinger*, jM 2015, 46, 54.

[93] See *Simotta*, in: Fasching/Konecny, Art. 17 note 14.

[94] *Ansgar Staudinger*, jM 2015, 46, 54.

[95] *Galič/Schwartze*, in: unalex Kommentar, Art. 17 note 7.

[96] *Océano Grupo Editorial SA v. Roció Murciano Quintero* and *Salvat Editores SA v. José M. Sánchez Alcón Prades, José Luis Copano Badillo, Mohammed Berroane and Emilio Viñas Feliú*, (Joined Cases C-240/98 to C-244/98) [2000] ECR I-4941.

[97] *Pfeiffer*, ZEuP 2003, 141; *Pfeiffer*, in: Prütting/Gehrlein, Art. 17 note 7.

[98] See *Schnyder/Paczoska Kottmann*, in: FS Ivo Schwander (2011), p. 789, 801, 803–804.

Jurisdictional regimes specifically devoted to regulating cross-border cases cannot apply for **35** the jurisdiction agreement was a domestic one at the relevant point of time.[99] Accordingly, the relevant element of internationality, necessary for the Brussels I*bis* Regulation and Art. 19 to be applicable,[100] arises only subsequently. It must and cannot exist at the time when the jurisdiction agreement is concluded. The less it is required that the jurisdiction agreement must be one providing for the contingency that either party shifts its domicile to another Member State.[101]

The relevant point of time is when the jurisdiction agreement is concluded, may that concur **36** with the conclusion of the main contract, may that be subsequently, and regardless as to whether a dispute has arisen.[102] Either party shifts its domicile to another State only after this point of time. Whether an entrepreneur who is not a natural person but a company can shift its domicile cross-border is an incidental question.

If one or more of the required conditions are not meet, the jurisdiction clause will be invalid. **37** However, if the clause meets all three conditions, the consumer will be barred from instituting proceedings against the other party to the contract in the Member State where the consumer has his new domicile. On the other hand, the other party may institute proceedings in the Member State where the consumer had his former domicile. (3) protects the supplier's reasonable expectations since at the time when it is concluded the contract is like any other domestic consumer contract and the supplier has no reason to think that cross-border issues are relevant.[103] It is a case of forum fixing,[104] conservating the original forum.[105]

Systematically, (3) operates primarily in the context of Art. 18 (2) and Art. 18 (1) 1st option. If **38** (3) did not exist the entrepreneur would be given opportunity to enforce his contractual rights solely in the courts of the Member State where the consumer has his domicile at the time the lawsuit commences (this point of time to be measured in accordance with the yardsticks established by Art. 32).[106] He would be subject to an away game and would be detrimentally affected by the consumer moving cross-border after the contract was concluded; that hardly complies with basic principles of fairness when the contract was origin-

---

[99] *Schnyder*, in: Schnyder, Art. 17 LugÜ note 7; *Furrer/Glarner*, in: Dasser/Oberhammer, Art. 17 LugÜ note 10. *Schnyder/Paczoska Kottmann*, in: FS Ivo Schwander (2011), p. 789, 795–798 check the Polish regime for *international* choice of court agreements and 804–806 the like Swiss regime. This appears to be misconceived. After asserting that the Polish law does not know any particular limits for jurisdiction agreements in domestic consumer cases the train should have stopped simply as the final note of Swisse law focuses on § 35 (1) Swiss ZPO (*Schnyder/Paczoska Kottmann*, in: FS Ivo Schwander [2011], p. 789, 807).

[100] Correct insofar *Hausmann*, in: Wieczorek/Schütze, Art. 15 EuGVÜ note 7.

[101] But cf. to this avail *Linke*, in: Bülow/Böckstiegel, Internationaler Rechtsverkehr in Zivil- und Handelssachen (looseleaf), Art. 15 EuGVÜ note (1977); *Hausmann*, in: Wieczorek/Schütze, Art. 15 EuGVÜ note 7.

[102] *Lutz/Sibylle Neumann*, RIW 1999, 827, 830; *Gehri*, in: Basler Kommentar, Art. 17 LugÜ notes 17, 20.

[103] *Jonathan Hill* para. 7.14.

[104] See *Gerhard Wagner*, in: Stein/Jonas, Art. 17 note 6.

[105] *Schnyder/Paczoska Kottmann*, in: FS Ivo Schwander (2011), p. 789, 793.

[106] *Furrer/Glarner*, in: Dasser/Oberhammer, Art. 17 LugÜ note 8.

ally a domestic contract.[107] Even worse, at the time he enters into the contract the entrepreneur could not foresee and reliably predict where he might be sued by the consumer under Art. 18 (1) 2nd option.[108] (3) enhances legal certainty.[109] Insofar, (3) is some kind of contingency planning clad in legislative terms.[110]

39 But holding up the jurisdiction clause tel quel would poses a different problem to the supplier: If and insofar as the jurisdiction clause is deemed to vest exclusive jurisdiction in the court(s) designated this would deprive the supplier of the opportunity to sue the consumer at the consumer's new domicile. The supplier might be interested to have that option having regard to effective means of enforcing a judgment in his favour in the State where judgment was given without any need of cross-border enforcement. One might assume that a consumer as a private person takes his main assets with him when he shifts his domicile to another State (for instance, selling his old home and acquiring a new one in the State of his new domicile or moving his bank account to his new home state, too).

40 Quite the same problem arises *vice versa* if the supplier moves to another State after the jurisdiction was concluded.[111] To enforce the jurisdiction agreement to the letter would take away from the consumer the option which would be offered to him by virtue of Art. 18 (1) 1st option to sue the supplier in the State of the supplier's new domicile.[112]

41 The rare case where both the consumer and the other party to the contract have moved to other Member States after the conclusion of the contract seems to be covered by the wording of (3). However, the policy behind the provision and the overall purpose of Section 4 suggest that a jurisdiction clause giving jurisdiction to the Member State that both parties have left should be set aside provided the clause is contrary either to the law of the Member State in which the consumer has his new domicile or the law of the Member State where the other party to the contract has his new domicile. In the unlikely event that both parties have moved to the same Member State it might be doubted as to whether the case has sufficient internationality at the time when a lawsuit commences;[113] yet internationality is sufficiently provided by the past of the contract and its very origins.

42 An intricate question arises if either party moves its domicile to a Third State outside the EU after the jurisdiction agreement has been concluded. Does this render (3) inapplicable, and is the jurisdiction agreement to be judged pursuant to the national law of the forum state by virtue of Art. 6?[114] Or is (3) binding upon any courts in Member State whereas only courts of

---

[107] *Hausmann*, in: Wieczorek/Schütze, Art. 15 EuGVÜ note 5; *Furrer/Glarner*, in: Dasser/Oberhammer, Art. 17 LugÜ note 8; *Gehri*, in: Basler Kommentar, Art. 17 LugÜ note 16; *Schnyder/Paczoska Kottmann*, in: FS Ivo Schwander (2011), p. 789, 793; *Gottwald*, in: Münchener Kommentar ZPO, Art. 17 note 2; *Stadler*, in: Musielak, Art. 17 note 2; *Dörner*, in: Saenger, Art. 17 note 3.

[108] *Galič/Schwartze*, in: unalex Kommentar, Art. 17 note 6.

[109] *Schnyder/Paczoska Kottmann*, in: FS Ivo Schwander (2011), p. 789, 793.

[110] See *Schnyder/Paczoska Kottmann*, in: FS Ivo Schwander (2011), p. 789, 793.

[111] See *Furrer/Glarner*, in: Dasser/Oberhammer, Art. 17 LugÜ note 8.

[112] *de Bra* p. 185; *Teuber* p. 64; *Gehri*, in: Basler Kommentar, Art. 17 LugÜ note 18.

[113] *Gehri*, Wirtschaftsrechtliche Streitigkeiten im Internationalen Zivilprozessrecht der Schweiz (2002) p. 140; *Heinig* p. 285; *Furrer/Glarner*, in: Dasser/Oberhammer, Art. 17 LugÜ note 11.

[114] Preferring this solution *Schoibl*, JBl 1998, 767, 775; *Simotta*, in: Fasching/Konecny, Art. 17 note 17;

Third States may be free to decide in accordance with their national law?[115] A partial answer now is provided by Art. 18 (1) 2ⁿᵈ option partially extending the protective regime to entrepreneurs domiciled in Third States. Insofar as this extension reaches (3) has to follow suit, and its interpretation has to draw the appropriate consequences.

IV. Choice of court agreement in favour of court(s) in a Third State

Art. 19 does not distinguish as to whether the court chosen is that of a Member State or of a   **43** Third State. It applies to both kinds of choice of court agreements indiscriminately. The decisive element is the attempt to derogate and deviate contractually from the jurisdictional regime as established in Art. 18. The consumer must not be deprived of his jurisdictional privileges as granted to him by Art. 18. Any attempt at a derogation must be bound for failure as a matter of general policy. Accordingly, a jurisdiction clause in the consumer contract designating a court in a Third State is invalid. For.instance, if an Italian consumer enters into an agreement providing for the jurisdiction of the courts of San Marino, the respective jurisdiction clause does not withstand scrutiny.[116]

A derogatory effect of jurisdiction clauses in favour of courts in other Member States is ruled   **44** out although in other Member States the substantive law is up to EU standards and thus, combined with Art. 8 Rome I Regulation, would safeguard an above average level of consumer protection. *A fortiori*, a derogatory effect of jurisdiction clauses in favour of courts in Third States must be ruled out since in a Third State neither the conflictual protection of consumers as it is guaranteed by Art. 8 Rome I Regulation, nor an appreciable level of consumer protection in substantive law is safeguarded. There would be any reason to believe and to fear that in a Third State the consumer would be treated less favourably than before a *forum* in a Member State.

V. Submission

It follows from Art. 26 (1) that a court of a Member State before which a defendant enters an   **45** appearance shall have jurisdiction, unless appearance was entered to contest the jurisdiction, or where a court has exclusive jurisdiction by virtue of Art. 22. This provision applies to consumer contracts covered by Section 4 of the Regulation. Art. 26 (2) is unambiguous in this regard. It reads: "In matters referred to in Sections 3, 4, and 5 of this Chapter, the document instituting proceedings or the equivalent document must contain information for the defendant on his right to contest the jurisdiction of the court and the consequences of entering an appearance. Before assuming jurisdiction on the basis of this Article, the court shall ensure that such information was provided to the defendant."

A literal interpretation of Art. 26 suggests that this would be the case given that the only   **46** exception mentioned, apart from appearance to contest jurisdiction, is Art. 24. Furthermore, Art. 19 (1) supports this interpretation because the provision accepts agreements on juris-

---

Staudinger, in: Rauscher, Art. 17 note 3; *Gehri*, in: Basler Kommentar, Art. 17 LugÜ note 19; *Gerhard Wagner*, in: Stein/Jonas, Art. 17 note 7; *Furrer/Glarner*, in: Dasser/Oberhammer, Art. 17 LugÜ note 9; *Dörner*, in: Saenger, Art. 17 note 4; *Stadler*, in: Musielak, Art. 17 note 2.

[115] To this avail *Teuber* p. 67.
[116] Cassaz. RDIPP 2013, 482, 484.

diction in consumer contracts, provided they have been entered into after the dispute has arisen, which is also the case with tacit agreements on jurisdiction under Art. 26.

47 On the other hand, it is presupposed that a jurisdiction clause under Art. 19 must conform to the formal requirements imposed by Art. 25. This indicates the existence of some degree of awareness of the effect of the jurisdiction clause, which may be absent in cases covered by Art. 26, at least if the consumer is not informed by the court about his rights under Section 4. Furthermore, the general policy behind Section 4 to protect consumers and only allow derogations from Art. 19 in a limited number of situations supports the interpretation that Art. 26 should not be applicable to consumer contracts covered by Section 4.

48 The ECJ has decided upon the question to the opposite avail,[117] although the latter interpretation was way more favourable from a consumer policy perspective.[118] The ECJ generally gave prevalence to Art. 24 Brussels I Regulation,[119] though, yet the ECJ has established important safeguards by stressing that it is always open to the court seised to ensure that the defendant sued before it in those circumstances is fully aware of the consequences of his agreement to enter an appearance but without imposing a like strict obligation on the court from Art. 17.[120] This is reflected in Art. 26 (2).

49 After Art. 26 (2) has been finally implemented, the contentious issue is decided authoritatively: Art. 26 (1) can operate as against protected parties, but such parties gain some residual protection by a duty to ensure that they are informed about the consequences of entering an appearance without contesting jurisdiction. Such obligation is imposed upon the court. Which consequences follow from a breach of such obligation by the court is not provided for in Art. 26 (2), neither expressly nor impliedly.[121] Whether the entrepreneur is under any duty to provide information and thus employed in order to overcome the informational asymmetry on the consumer's side is even more unclear, particularly so since Art. 24 (2) Proposal Brussels *Ibis* Regulation which sought to establish an obligation to this avail, has not been implemented eventually.[122]

VI. Jurisdiction agreements and claims in tort

50 As the whole bunch of Arts. 17–19, Art. 19 is limited to claims in contracts. If a jurisdiction

---

[117] *Česká podnikatelská pojišťovna as and Vienna Insurance Group v. Michal Bílas*, (Case C-111/09) [2010] ECR I-4545 para. 36. Likewise OGH ZfRV 2003, 190; Cassaz. RDIPP 2012, 409, 410; OLG Koblenz, RIW 2000, 636, 637 = IPRax 2001, 334, 335; OLG Köln, RIW 2004, 866; OLG Rostock OLG-Report 2006, 271, 272; *Grušić*, (2011) 48 C.M.L.Rev. 947, 951–953 and BAG AP Nr 1 zu Art. 18 EuGVVO with critical note *Mankowski*; previous edition Art. 24 Brussels I Regulation note 24 (*Calvo Caravaca/Carrascosa González*).

[118] *Mankowski*, IPRax 2001, 310; *Mankowski*, RIW 2010, 667; *Richter*, RIW 2006, 568. Cf. also *Pataut*, RCDIP 99 (2010), 580.

[119] *Česká podnikatelská pojišťovna as and Vienna Insurance Group v. Michal Bílas*, (Case C-111/09) [2010] ECR I-4545, para. 36.

[120] *Česká podnikatelská pojišťovna as and Vienna Insurance Group v. Michal Bílas*, (Case C-111/09) [2010] ECR I-4545, para. 32.

[121] *Mankowski*, RIW 2014, 625, 631.

[122] *Mankowski*, RIW 2014, 625, 631.

agreement happens to cover claims in tort, too, for instance by employing the formulation that it covers "any controversy arising out or in connection with this Contract", Art. 19 does not come into operation for claims in tort directly. But if it vitiates and nullifies the part of the jurisdiction clause covering claims in contract, the other part, the one covering claims in tort, will also fall for it can not be upheld without the central contractual part surviving scrutiny. Any teleological reduction rescuing the part of the jurisdiction clause related to claims in tort would counter to Art. 6 (1) Unfair Contract Terms Directive.[123]

VII. Arbitration clauses and other modes of ADR

Art. 19 is concerned only with jurisdiction clauses. It does not say anything directly on **51** arbitration clauses, other types of ADR clauses or other dispute resolution clauses. Hence, it ought not be applied directly to arbitration clauses and other ADR clauses.[124] Yet the idea underlying it might be extended, be it by way of a (very) extensive and purposive interpretation,[125] be it by way of an analogy.[126] Consumers are not less in need, and not less worthy, of protection when they sign ADR agreements than they are when they sign jurisdiction agreements. Since Art. 19 aims at protecting against derogation of the jurisdictional rules as contained in Arts. 17; 18 a good case can be stated that it should be applied also *a minore ad maius* against derogation by arbitration and other ADR clauses.[127] In some respect, an arbitration or other ADR clause can be regarded as some kind of circumvention of Arts. 17–19[128] (if circumvention is not believed to imply some degree of malice necessarily). It disposes of the regulatory power of state courts. Art. 19 is concerned with the distribution of jurisdiction between courts in different states. Avoiding state courts at all also touches upon that state courts being competent and having jurisdiction.[129] Limited to judging the derogatory aspect, Art. 19 can be said to fight every kind of agreement that effectuates derogation of jurisdiction vested in the courts which would have jurisdiction absent this agreement.[130] Taking into account the aim of protecting the consumer as the typically weaker party, it appears sound to extend Art. 19 to the derogatory aspect of arbitration agreements.[131]

Yet with regard to arbitration agreements in particular, the arguments fielded against such **52** an approach are numerous and not lightly to be dismissed. Firstly, arbitration is excepted and exempt from the Brussels I*bis* Regulation by virtue of Art. 1 (2) (d).[132] But this comprises

---

[123]   *Matthias Weller*, WM 2013, 1681, 1682.

[124]   *Samtleben*, ZEuP 1999, 974, 977; *Samtleben*, ZBB 2003, 69, 76; *Mäsch*, in: FS Peter Schlosser (2005), p. 529, 541–542; *van Husen* p. 115; *Simotta*, in: Fasching/Konecny, Art. 17 notes 3–4; *Tiefenthaler*, in: Czernich/Tiefenthaler/Kodek, Art. 17 note 1; *Joseph*, Jurisdiction and Arbitrationa Agreements and Their Enforcem3ent (2nd ed. 2010) para. 2.101; *Ansgar Staudinger*, in: Rauscher, Art. 17 note 4; *Gottwald*, in: Münchener Kommentar ZPO, Art. 17 note 3.

[125]   *Wach/Weberpals*, AG 1989, 193, 200; *Kiel*, Internationales Kapitalanlegerschutzrecht (1994) p. 321; *Reich*, ZEuP 1999, 982; *Pfeiffer*, NJW 1999, 3674, 3685; *Senff* pp. 398–399.

[126]   *Reich*, ZEuP 1998, 981, 991.

[127]   *Reich*, ZEuP 1998, 981, 990–991; *Reich*, ZEuP 1999, 982.

[128]   *Reich*, ZEuP 1998, 981, 990.

[129]   *Reich*, ZEuP 1998, 981, 991.

[130]   *Reich*, ZEuP 1999, 982.

[131]   *Mäsch*, in: FS Peter Schlosser (2005), p. 529, 542.

[132]   *Samtleben*, ZEuP 1999, 974, 977; *Samtleben*, ZBB 2003, 69, 76; *van Husen* p. 115.

---

arbitration proceedings before arbitral tribunals and auxiliary or ancillary proceedings before municipal state courts in support of arbitration proceedings. It does not necessarily relate to arbitration agreements. Art. 1 (2) (e) 1ˢᵗ option Rome I Regulation expressly excepts arbitration agreements from the scope of the Rome I Regulation. "Arbitration" is something different and does not necessarily comprise "arbitration agreements", too. Art. 1 (2) (e) 2ⁿᵈ option Rome I Regulation states an exception for choice of court agreements. This type of agreement is definitely regulated by the Brussels *Ibis* Regulation. Surely, it cannot be said that the Brussels *Ibis* Regulation would contain any rules specifically addressing arbitration agreements and the less it contains a counterpart to Art. 25 dealing with arbitration agreements. Recital (12) para. 1 states that nothing in the Brussels *Ibis* Regulation should prevent the courts of a Member States when seised of a matter in respect of which the parties have entered into an arbitration agreement, i.a. from examining whether the arbitration agreement is null and void, inoperative or incapable of being performed, in accordance with their national law. The arbitration exception shall thus not amount to an immunisation of the arbitration agreement and to a guarantee that the arbitration agreement will be upheld under all and every circumstances.

53 Secondly, the 1958 New York Convention on the Recognition and Enforcement of Arbitral Awards shall take precedence over the Brussels *Ibis* Regulation. Art. 73 (2) is unambiguous in this regard, and even if this rule did not exist, Art. 71 would be to the same avail. Precedence and prevalence of the 1958 New York Convention should include and entail its Art. II addressing arbitration agreements specifically.[133] The 1958 New York Convention is – unlike the 1961 Geneva Convention – not restricted to international commercial arbitration. Contracting States have only an opportunity to opt-out to this avail by virtue of Art. I (3) cl. 2 1958 New York Convention. Accordingly, without the respective Contracting State having opted out, the 1958 New York Convention applies to B2C arbitration.[134] Art. II 1958 New York Convention is the only rule in that Convention directly dealing with arbitration agreements as such. It serves as a uniform rule of substantive law insofar as formal requirements are concerned. The case is a little different if the validity of arbitration agreements is concerned. Then, at least when it comes to recognition and enforcement of arbitral awards, Art. V (1) (a) 1958 New York Convention steps to the fore.

54 Thirdly, methodologically an analogy needs an unwarranted gap to be filled (even apart from the general difficulty of an analogous extension of EU law which would necessarily and invariably invade into territory held by national law[135]). It is hard to argue that such a *lacunae* exists with Art. 19 following the general scope of application of the Brussels *Ibis* Regulation and thus being subject to the arbitration exception in Art. 1 (2) (d).[136] But this depends yet again on the understanding and the scope of the arbitration exception: If the arbitration exception does not cover arbitration agreements, there would be ample space to regulate on arbitration agreements.

55 Fourthly, many international conventions some of them older than even the Brussels Convention, contain rules specifically devoted to restrict or invalidate arbitration agreements

---

[133] *Samtleben*, ZEuP 1999, 974, 977.

[134] *Mäsch*, in: FS Peter Schlosser (2005), p. 529, 538.

[135] *Mankowski*, IPRax 1991, 305.

[136] *Mäsch*, in: FS Peter Schlosser (2005), p. 529, 542.

deviating from the system of state court jurisdiction erected in the respective convention.[137] With differences as to the their content in detail, the main examples are Arts. 33 CMR; 34 Montreal Convention. If Art. 19 does not specifically mention arbitration agreements this could amount to an *argumentum e contrario*.[138] But on the next level such argument would be at odds with the arbitration exception in Art. 1 (2) (d): If arbitration is totally excluded from the realm of the Brussels I*bis* Regulation in its entirety, there is no necessity to mention it specifically in single rules of the Brussels I*bis* Regulation. Looking at content, Art. 34 (2) Montreal Convention would rather support the case for applying Art. 19 to arbitration clauses. It states that the arbitration proceedings shall, at the option of the claimant, take place within one of the jurisdictions referred to in Art. 33 Montreal Convention. The Montreal Convention is the most interesting amongst the international conventions addressing arbitration agreements for it forms part of EU law[139] since the EU has ratified it, and it is vastly concerned with B2C cases.

The case is even more complicated with regard to other ADR clauses than arbitration **56** agreements. In recent years the EU has adopted a policy of fostering ADR in consumer cases[140] and besides that especially Online Dispute Resolution (ODR)[141].[142] But then there is (1) (q) Annex Directive 93/13/EEC and the rather consumer-friendly handling of that rule by the ECJ, in particular in *Océano Grupo*,[143] *Pannon*,[144] *Mostaza Claro*[145] and *Asturcom*,[146] the last two devoted to arbitration clauses.[147] This can gain relevance in the context of the

---

137 *Samtleben*, RabelsZ 46 (1982), 716, 725.

138 Tentatively to this avail *Samtleben*, ZEuP 1999, 974, 977.

139 See OJ EU 2001 L 194/39.

140 Directive 2013/11/EU of the European Parliament and the Council of 21 May 2013 on alternative dispute resolution for consumer disputes and amending Regulation (EC) No. 2006/2004 and Directive 2009/22/ EC (Directive on consumer ADR), OJ EU 2013 L 165/63. The *status quo ante* is described in *Hodges/Iris Benöhr/Creutzfeldt-Banda*, Consumer ADR in Europe (2012).

141 Regulation (EU) No. 524/2013 of the European Parliament and the Council of 21 May 2013 on alternative dispute resolution for consumer disputes and amending Regulation (EC) No. 2006/2004 and Directive 2009/22/EC (Regulation on consumer ODR), OJ EU 2013 L 165/1.

142 The two legislative measures are discussed e.g. by *Herbert Roth*, JZ 2013, 637; *Bernheim-Desvaux*, JCP E 2013.1402 = JCP E N°. 27–28, 4 juillet 2013, p. 25; *dies.*, CCC août-septembre 2013, p. 11; *Martin Engel*, AnwBl 2013, 478; *Rühl*, RIW 2013, 737; *Rühl*, ZRP 2014, 8; *Owsiany-Hornung*, Rev. dr. UE 2014, 87; *Norbert Reich*, ECRL 2014, 258.

143 *Océano Grupo Editorial SA v. Rocló Murciano Quintero* (Joined Cases C-240/98 to C-244/98), [2000] ECR I-4941 para. 22.

144 *Pannon GSM Zrt. v. Erszébet Sustikné Györfi* (Case C-243/08), [2009] ECR I-4713 paras. 40–41.

145 *Elisa María Mostaza Claro v. Centro Móvil Milenium SpA* (Case C-168/05), [2006] ECR I-10421 paras. 35–39; commented upon i.a. by *d'Alessandro*, Riv. arb. 2006, 679; *Reich*, ERCL 2007, 41; *Jordans*, GPR 2007, 48; *Idot*, Rev. arb. 2007, 115; *Pavillon*, NTBR 2007, 149; *Legros*, Les petites affiches 2007 n° 152 p. 9; *Celeste Pesce*, Dir. pubbl. comp. eur. 2007, 430; *Mourre*, Clunet 134 (2007), 583; *Poissonnier/Tricoit*, Les petites affiches 2007 n° 189 p. 13; *Liebscher*, (2008) 45 CMLRev. 545.

146 *Asturcom Telecomunicaciones SL v. Cristina Rodríguez Nogueira* (Case C-40/08), [2009] ECR I-9579 paras. 37–59; commented upon i.a. by *Jarrosson*, Rev. arb. 2009, 822; *Mankowski*, EWiR Art. 6 RL 93/13/ EWG 1/10, 91; *Cheneviere*, Rev. eur. dr. consomm. 2010, 351; *Stuyck*, (2010) 47 CMLRev. 879; *Ebers*, ERPL 2010, 823.

147 On arbitration clauses in consumer contracts and Directive 93/13/EEC e.g. Trib. Roma Foro it. 1998 I

Brussels I*bis* Regulation *via* Art. 67.[148] Over the times the EU has adopted different policies, mostly depending on which Directorate General had the upper hand in the respective legislative process. That both the Directive on Consumer ADR and the Regulation on Consumer ODR cannot be expected to change the picture dramatically in the reality of legal relationships for they will not overcome the concerns of business and consumers,[149] is one aspect. But it is not the normative aspect for which Art. 67 cares. Cross-border consumer ADR faces many problems and question, and the most burning one relates to "jurisdiction", i.e. where the ADR ought to be staged and whether the consumer has to travel cross-border or, alternatively, seek legal advice in country other than the state where he lives.[150]

Section 5: Jurisdiction over individual contracts of employment

Article 20

1. In matters relating to individual contracts of employment, jurisdiction shall be determined by this Section, without prejudice to Article 6, point 5 of Article 7 and, in the case of proceedings brought against an employer, point 1 of Article 8.
2. Where an employee enters into an individual contract of employment with an employer who is not domiciled in a Member State but has a branch, agency or other establishment in one of the Member States, the employer shall, in disputes arising out of the operations of the branch, agency or establishment, be deemed to be domiciled in that Member State.

Bibliography

Amici, Forum loci executionis e contratto internazionale di lavoro, Riv. it. dir. lav. 2010, 655

Antonmattei, Conflits de jurisdictions en droit de travail, J-Cl. dr.int. fasc. 573-20 (1994), 8

Borrás Rodríguez, Note to *Herbert Weber v. Universal Ogden Services Ltd.* (Case 37/00), Rev. jur. Catalunya 2002, 1211

Bosse, Probleme des europäischen Internationalen Arbeitsprozessrechts (Frankfurt am Main 2007).

Buy, Compétence juridictionnelle et pluralité de lieux de travail, CJCE 27 février 2002, Droit social 11 (2002), 967

Casado Abarquero, La autonomía de la voluntad en el contrato de trabajo internacional (Cizur Menor, Navarra 2008)

Deinert, Internationales Arbeitsrecht (2013)

Droz, La Convention de San Sebastián alignant la Convention de Bruxelles sur la Convention de Lugano, RCDIP 79 (1990), 1

Esteban de la Rosa/Molina-Navarrete, La movilidad transnacional de trabajadores: reglas y prácticas (Granada 2002)

1989; Trib. Roma Banca, borrsa, tit. cred. 2008 I 110; *Gabrielli*, Riv. dir. civ. 1993, 1555; *Galletto*, Riv. arb. 2011, 127, 131–134; very arbitration-friendly (*Kröll*, SchiedsVZ 2012, 138, 140) and lenient OLG Brandenburg MDR 2011, 941 = BauR 2011, 1533.

[148] See (Art. 67 and Directive 93/13/EEC and its national implementations) Art. 67 note 5 (*Mankowski*); Aud. Prov. Santa Cruz de Tenerife REDI 2002, 378 with note *Jiménez Blanco*; *Heinig*, GPR 2010, 36, 41.

[149] In detail *Rühl*, RIW 2013, 737, 739–744.

[150] *Gascón Inchausti*, GPR 2014, 197, 201.

Franzen, Arbeitskollisionsrecht und sekundäres Gemeinschaftsrecht: Die EG-Entsende-Richtlinie, ZEuP 1997, 1055

Franzen, Internationale Gerichtsstandsvereinbarungen in Arbeitsverträgen zwischen EuGVÜ und autonomen internationalem Zivilprozessrecht, RIW 2000, 81

Gaudemet-Tallon, Compétence et exécution des jugements en Europe (Paris 2010)

Grušić, Jurisdiction in employment matters under Brussels I: a reassessment, (2012) 61 ICLQ 91

Grušić, Should the connecting factor of the "engaging place of business" be abolished in European Private International Law?, (2013) 62 ICLQ 173

Gulotta, L'estensione della giurisdizione nei confronti dei datori di lavoro domiciliati all'estero: il caso *Mahamdia* en il nuovo regime del regolamento Bruxelles I-*bis*, RDIPP 2013, 619

Harris, The Brussels I Regulation, the ECJ and the rulebook, (2008) 124 LQR 523

Huet, Note to *Mulox IBC Ltd. v. Hendrick Geels*, Clunet 121 (1994), 539

Juárez-Pérez, Orden social y litigios internacionales: competencia judicial (Granada 2002)

Junker, Die internationale Zuständigkeit deutscher Gerichte in Arbeitssachen, ZZP Int. 3 (1998), 179

Junker, Internationale Zuständigkeit für Arbeitssachen nach der Brüssel I-Verordnung, in: Festschrift für Peter Schlosser (2005), p. 299

Knöfel, *Navigare necesse est* – Zur Anknüpfung an die einstellende Niederlassung im Europäischen Internationalen Arbeitsrecht der See, IPRax 2014, 130

Krebber, Gerichtsstand des Erfüllungsortes bei mehreren, aber aufeinander abgestimmten Arbeitsverhältnissen, IPRax 2004, 309

Lagarde, Note to *Mulox IBC Ltd. v. Hendrick Geels* (Case 125/92), RCDIP 83 (1994), 573

Lajolo di Cossano, La giurisprudenza della Corte di Giustizia delle Comunita Europee e il regolamento 44/2001/CE: i contrati di lavoro subordinato, Dir. comm.int. 2002, 901

Maestre Casas, El contrato de trabajo de marinos a bordo de buques mercantes, Cuad. Der. Trans. 4 (1) (2012), 322

Mankowski, Der gewöhnliche Arbeitsort im Internationalen Prozess- und Privatrecht, IPRax 1999, 332

Mankowski, Europäisches Internationales Arbeit-

prozessrecht – Weiteres zum gewöhnlichen Arbeitsort, IPRax 2003, 21

Mankowski, Grenzüberschreitender Arbeitsvertrag, Gerichtsstand der Streitgenossenschaft ("Glaxosmithkline/Rouard"), EWIR 2008, 435

Mankowski, Zur Abgrenzung des Individual- vom Kollektivarbeitsrecht im europäischen Internationalen Zivilverfahrensrecht, IPRax 2011, 93

Mankowski, Stillschweigende Rechtswahl, Günstigkeitsvergleich und Anknüpfung von Kündigungsschutzrecht im Internationalen Arbeitsvertragsrecht, IPRax 2015, 309

Mankowski/Knöfel, On the Road Again oder: Wo arbeitet ein Fernfahrer? Neues von europäischen Internationalen Arbeitsvertragsrecht, EuZA 2011, 521

Merret, Employment contracts in Private International Law (Oxford 2011)

Molina-Navarrete/Esteban de la Rosa, Revista de Trabajo y Seguridad Social 239 (2003), 91

Mosconi, La giurisdizione in materia di lavoro nel regolamento (CE) n 44/2001, RDIPP 2003, 5

Moureau-Borlès, Le détachement des travailleurs effectuant une prestation des services dans l'Union européenne, Clunet 123 (1996), 889

Nuyts, Study on residual jurisdiction (Review of the Member States' Rules concerning the "Residual Jurisdiction" of their courts in Civil and Commercial Matters pursuant to the Brussels I and II Regulation), final version dater 3 September 2007 http://ec.europa.eu/civiljustice/news/docs/study_residual_jurisdiction_en.pdf

Palao Moreno, Los Grupos de Empresas Multinacionales y el contrato individual de trabajo (2000)

Palao Moreno, Note to *Herbert Weber v. Universal Ogden Services Ltd.* (Case 37/00), REDI 2002, 861

Palao Moreno, Multinational Groups of Companies and Individual Employment Contracts in Spanish and European Private International Law, Yb. PIL 4 (2002), 303

Palao Moreno, La competencia judicial internacional en materia de contrato de trabajo en la Comunidad Europea, Derecho internacional y de la integración 2 (2003), 7

Pataut, Note to *Jan Voogsgeerd v. Navimer SA* (Case C-384/10), RCDIP 101 (2012), 649

Pataut, Note to *Ahmed Mahamdia c. Popular and*

Democratic Republic of Algeria (Case C-154/11), RCDIP 102 (2013), 217

Polak, "Laborum dulce lenimen"? Jurisdiction and choice of law aspects of employment contracts, in: Enforcement of International Contracts in the European Union (Antwerp, 2004)

Queirolo, Prorogation of Jurisdiction in the Proposal for a Recast of the Brussels I Regulation, in: Recasting Brussels I (Milan 2012), p. 183

Sabido Rodriguez, La protección del trabajador en sucesiones internacionales de empresas (2009)

Sinay-Cyterman, La protection de la partie faible en droit international privé, in: Mélanges en l'honneur de Paul Lagarde (2005), p. 737

Sinay-Cyterman, Les clauses compromissoires dans le contrat de travail international et dans le contrat de consommation international, RCDIP 98 (2009), 427

Winterling, Die Entscheidungszuständigkeit in Arbeitssachen im europäischen Zivilverfahrensrecht (2005)

Zabalo-Escudero, Note to *Mulox IBC Ltd. v. Hendrick Geels* (Case 125/92), REDI 1993, 470

Zabalo-Escudero, Sucesión de lugares de trabajo y competencia judicial internacional: nuevos problemas planteados ante el TJCE, Rev. der. com. eur. 14 (2003), 225.

I. Preliminary remarks

1   Unlike what occurred in relation to consumer and insurance contracts, the original version of the Brussels Convention of 1968 did not include any specifically designed provision in relation to individual contracts of employment. In spite of the fact that setting up an exclusive *forum* for this matter was considered during negotiation of the Convention, the truth is that the idea was eventually rejected for several reasons.[1] In time, this void was filled by the Court of Justice of the European Communities by means of its jurisprudential practice. In line with existing solutions in relation to consumer and insurance contracts, the Court reinterpreted Art. 5 (1) of the original version of the Brussels Convention, and provided a solution specifically tailored to this type of contract, specifically different any application of Art. 5(1) to a general contractual agreement. And which guaranteed both the existence of a clear connection between the dispute put forward and the court chosen and a high degree of protection for the employee. This jurisprudential approach was later included in Art. 5 (1) of the Brussels Convention in its San Sebastián version, dated 1989, and has thenceforth been maintained in the conventional text. In the said 1989 version, furthermore, inspired to a certain extent on the solutions contemplated in the Lugano Convention,[2] a rule about freedom of choice in relation to this type of contract was incorporated in Art. 17.

2   The Brussels I Regulation altered this former situation, which also remains in relation to the Brussels *Ibis* Regulation. Thus, from a formal viewpoint, and in line with what was already happening in the Rome Convention of 1980 on the law applicable to contractual obligations – and afterwards in the Rome I Regulation –, a Section specifically dedicated to the regulation of "jurisdiction over individual contracts of employment" was incorporated, wherein a separate rule independent from the general provisions regarding contracts was included, articulating all these rules protecting the worker in a more structured and organic manner.[3] From a structural point of view, the solutions included in this Section are generally

---

[1]   Report *Jenard* p. 24; *Roger Ivenel v. Helmut Schwab*, (Case 133/81) [1982] ECR 1891, 1990; *Mosconi*, RDIPP 2003, 5, 17.

[2]   *Gaudemet-Tallon*, 296.

[3]   *Salerno*, 222.

parallel to those included in Artt. 17–19 as regards "jurisdiction over consumer contracts" and borrow much of their overall structure from there. For their part, in relation with the specific solutions incorporated, those included in Arts. 5 (1) and 17 (5) Brussels Convention were reproduced in broad outlines, albeit with the inclusion of some provisos.[4]

II. Meaning of Art. 20 (1)

Art. 20 (1), the first in this Section 5 of Chapter II, dedicated to jurisdiction "in matters **3** relating to individual contracts of employment"[5] – let us point out not in relation with collective-type labour disputes or with other contracts dependent upon individual contracts[6] – configures an exception to the rules of international jurisdiction provided in the Regulation itself. In this sense, the precept specifies that in matters "relating to individual contracts of employment", determination of competent jurisdiction shall be carried out on the exclusive basis of the international jurisdiction included in the above mentioned Section 5 Chapter II.

1. Concept of "individual contract of employment"

Significantly, Art. 20 does not include a definition or description of what is meant by **4** "individual contract of employment". A concept that is diversely qualified in the different Member States.[7] This silence, nevertheless, is broken in a way by the jurisprudence of the ECJ, which does contribute certain keys that facilitate its understanding.[8] In this sense, the Court chooses to favour an independent interpretation of the concept, considering that this option is the only one capable of ensuring uniform application of the Convention.[9] On the basis of this premise, it considers that "contracts of employment, like other contracts for work other than on a self-employed basis, differ from other contracts – even those for the provision of services – by virtue of certain peculiarities: they create a lasting bond which brings the worker to some extent within the organisational framework of the business of the undertaking or employer".[10]

---

[4] *Palao Moreno*, Derecho internacional y de la integración 2 (2003), 7, 16.

[5] Some national courts have opted for an extensive interpretation of this provision, covering also claims for discrimination or even claims in tort committed in the context of the performance of that type of contract. *Heidelberg Report* p. 87–88.

[6] As appeared in the judgment given in the case of *Hassan Shenavai v. Klaus Kreischer*, (Case 266/85) [1987] ECR 239. Situations covered elsewhere by the Brussels I Regulation. In relation to collective disputes, *Winterling*, 11–16.

[7] *Heidelberg Report* p. 88.

[8] *Mankowski*, in: Rauscher, Art. 18 notes 3–8h; *Bosse* pp. 66 *et seq.*

[9] See *Heidelberg Report* p. 88; *Mankowski*, IPRax 2011, 93.

[10] *Hassan Shenavai v. Klaus Kreischer*, (Case 266/85) [1987] ECR 239, 255–256; *Mulox IBC Ltd. v. Hendrick Geels*, (Case C-125/92) [1993] ECR I-4075, I-4103 *et seq.*; *Holterman Ferno Exploitatie BV*, (Case C-47/14) [2015] 41–47. For instance, relations between an independent commercial agent and the principal should be excluded, as estated by OGH JBl 1999, 745.

2. Exception to the general regime of the Brussels *Ibis* Regulation

5 The special characteristics of the individual contract of employment, where there is one contracting party that is clearly weaker than the other, are projected in the sphere of international jurisdiction, which requires the drawing up of rules that guarantee adequate protection for the worker and that, therefore, are "more favourable to his interests than the general rules provide for". This requirement is combined, furthermore, with the necessary compliance with the objectives that accompanied the Brussels Convention at the time and shared today by the Brussels *Ibis* Regulation: the need to "avoid as far as possible the multiplication of the bases of jurisdiction in relation to one and the same legal relationship and to reinforce the legal protection available to persons established in the EU by, at the same time, allowing the plaintiff easily to identify the court before which he may bring an action and the defendant reasonably to foresee the court before which he may be sued", ensuring at the same time the "existence of a particularly close relationship between a dispute and the court best placed, in order to ensure the proper administration of justice and effective organisation of the proceedings".[11]

6 All these principles and objectives underlie the rules about international jurisdiction contemplated in Artt. 20 to 23 and explain, under Art. 20 (1) thereof, that the rules of international jurisdiction included therein are the only ones applicable to an individual contract of employment;[12] excluding the application of the general regime contemplated in the Regulation, with the exception, pointed out above, of the provisions of Artt. 6 and 7 (5) and, in the case of proceedings brought against an employer, point 1 of Art. 8.

7 Firstly, the reference to Art. 6 made in Art. 20 (1) implies the acceptance of the existence of certain circumstances where the defendant – usually the employer – is not domiciled within the territory of the EU.[13] For these cases, Art. 6 admits that international jurisdiction shall be determined in each State of the EU in accordance with the provisions of their respective national rules, even admitting on occasions the invocation of exorbitant jurisdictions contemplated in the Schedule. This mention of Art. 6, however, is perceptibly restricted and has suffered and important change if the versions of both Brussels I Regulation and the current Brussels *Ibis* Regulation are compared.

8 In this respect and on the one hand, the first restriction can be observed in view of section 2 of this Art. 20, which will be analysed below in marginal note 9 ff. On the other hand, Brussels *Ibis* Regulation brings a major changes which affect to this provision, as it will be analysed below when analysing Art. 21 (2), relating to the exception that this Article creates to Art. 6, when enabling the application of the special *forum* established in Art. 21(2) when the employee sues an employer non-domiciled in a Member State.

9 Secondly and for its part, mention of Art. 7 (5), already present in the system of the Brussels Convention,[14] implies admitting that every employer domiciled in a Member State of the

---

11   *Petrus Wilhelmus Rutten v. Cross Medical Ltd.*, (Case C-383/95) [1997] ECR I-57, I-75; *Herbert Weber v. Universal Ogden Services Ltd.*, (Case C-37/0) [2002] ECR I-2013, I-2044–2045; *Giulia Pugliese v. Finmeccanica SpA, Betriebsteil Alenia Aerospazio*, (Case C-437/00) [2003] ECR I-3573, I-3601.

12   *Béraudo*, Clunet 128 (2001), 1033, 1057.

13   *Mankowski*, in: Rauscher Art. 18 note 10.

Union who has a branch, agency or other establishment in another Member State may be sued before the courts of the Member State where they are located with respect to disputes arising out of the activities carried out by them; in this case, logically, in relation to the "engagement of staff to work there".[15] There arises, therefore, a new alternative for the plaintiff.[16]

Thirdly, a new significant exception has been incorporated in the current Regulation, when **10** allowing the employee to make use of Art. 8 (1), in the case of proceedings brought against an employer. In this respect, it should be pointed out that ECJ in *GlaxoSmithKline v. Rouard*, stated that Art. 6 (1) Brussels I Regulation – the predecessor to the current Art. 8 (1)- could not be applied to a dispute falling under Section 5 of Chapter II of that Regulation; in relation to proceedings brought by an employee against two companies belonging to the same group, one of which (the one which engaged the employee and refused to re-employ him/her, is domiciled in a Member State and the other (for which the employee last worked in non-Member States and dismissed him/her) was not domiciled in a Member State, when the two defendants were his co-employers from whom he claims compensation for dismissal.[17] Thus, contrary to previous decisions taken by some national jurisdictions interpreting the Brussels Convention 1968 ad the Lugano Convention 1988 (accepting the application of Art. 6 (1) in relation to proceedings related to individual contracts of employment),[18] the European Court of Justice opted for a rigid interpretation of the analysed provision.[19] Therefore, with this new exception, the rigidity of the Case law of the Court of Justice of European Communities is corrected by the new wording of this paragraph and, as a result, it is also aligned to the jurisprudence of some Member States, improving the position of the employee when he/she pretend to sue several employees before the court of the place where one of them is domiciled[20] – especially when one of the employer is domiciled in a Member State-.[21]

III. Extensive interpretation of the concept of domicile present in (2)

The reality of international trade reflects the increasing existence of situations where the **11** employer is located outside the territory of the European Union. A situation of these characteristics brings us back to the above mentioned Art. 6 and, through it, to the different national rules about international jurisdiction regarding individual employment contracts. Resorting to national solutions, however, may be to the disadvantage of the worker, by preventing the presence of predictable, uniform jurisdictional worker protection mechanisms and therefore favouring forum shopping situations.[22]

---

14 *Palao Moreno*, Derecho internacional y de la integración 2 (2003), 7, 13.

15 *Somafer SA v. Saar-Ferngas AG*, (Case 33/78) [1978] ECR 2183. See *Grusic*, (2012) 61 ICLQ 91, 116–117.

16 *Mosconi*, RDIPP 2003, 5, 6 *et seq.*; *Molina-Navarrete/Esteban de la Rosa*, Revista de Trabajo y Seguridad Social 239 (2003), 91, 104.

17 OJ C 171/7 (5 July 2008). See *Harris*, (2008) 124 LQR 523; *Mankowski*, EWIR 2008, 435.

18 Cass. JCP E 1998, 353; Arbeidshof Antwerpen JPA 2004, 215; Trib. Superior de Justicia de Castilla-La Mancha Aranzadi 2005, 2583.

19 Favouring a more flexible approach, *Heidelberg Report* p. 88; *Sabido Rodriguez*, pp. 183 *et seq.*

20 *Gulotta*, RDIPP (2013), 619, 621.

21 *Cadet*, Clunet 140 (2013), 765, 773–787.

22 *Palao Moreno*, Derecho internacional y de la integración 2 (2003), 7, 19.

12   Those drawing up the Regulation, aware of this fact, introduced a rule in (2) – in line with the Arts. 11 (2); 17 (2) – that makes it possible to limit this negative situation that we mentioned above by pointing out that on those occasions where a worker enters into an individual contract of employment with an employer who is not domiciled in a Member State of the EU but who has a branch, agency or other establishment in one of the Member States, the employer shall, in disputes arising out of the operations of the branch, agency or establishment, be deemed to be domiciled in that Member State. This extends the meaning of the jurisdiction of the defendant contemplated in Art. 21, permitting the worker to bring an action in the European Union against an employer domiciled outside community territory, in accordance with the community rules regarding international judicial competence.[23]

13   The location of the rule contained in (2) and its purport prevent it from being linked to Art. 7 (5). Both these precepts cover different situations.[24] Art. 7 (5) refers to occasions where the sued employer domiciled in the EU also possesses other centres in EU territory that terminate a contract of employment with one particular worker in the performance of their duties. The situation contemplated by (2), on the other hand, is quite different: the employer is not domiciled in EU territory but does, however, have a branch, agency or establishment within a Member State, and the legislator proceeds to assimilate both situations for the purposes of applying the rules regarding international judicial competence with regard to individual employment contracts. In this way, for disputes arising from the operation of this branch, agency or establishment, including, logically, those related to employment contracts, he will be deemed to be domiciled in the Member State where the said branch, agency or establishment is located.[25] This connection, then, is presented in the last resort with Art. 6 drastically limiting its applicability: in accordance with (2), with regard to individual contracts of employment, Art. 6 refers only to those defendants who are not domiciled in the European Union and do not have a branch, agency or establishment therein.[26] Only in these cases will it be feasible to revert to national rules of international jurisdiction, with all the disadvantages involved therein.

14   The rule in (2) verifies the material scope of the article. In other words, verifying whether all types of dispute can be contemplated, that is, those related with the operation of the said branch, agency or establishment and the parent company established outside Community territory or whether, on the contrary, only the former can be contemplated. Although on the basis of a strict interpretation of the meaning of the Article only the former may be considered included, since the parent company is located outside EU territory and the work relationship with the same has not been specifically concluded.[27] While a finalist interpretation thereof emphasising the desire to protect the worker present in the system of international jurisdiction designed by the Regulation should permit the exercise of them all, especially if the working activity has been carried out inside the territory of the EU. The presence of these centres in the EU shows the connection of the employer with the European

---

[23]   Also, *Casado Abarquero*, p. 111.

[24]   *Bosse*, pp. 79 *et seq.*

[25]   *Mosconi*, RDIPP 2003, 5, 16–17; *Molina-Navarrete/Esteban de la Rosa*, Revista de Trabajo y Seguridad Social 239 (2003), 91, 104.

[26]   *Kropholler/von Hein*, Art. 18 note 5; *Palao Moreno*, Derecho internacional y de la integración 2 (2003), 7, 21.

[27]   *Palao Moreno*, Derecho internacional y de la integración 2 (2003), 7, 20.

employment market, thence the need to allow the worker to bring his actions before the courts of these countries, safeguarding his expectations.

The CJEU has interpreted this Article – *rectius* Art. 18 (2) Brussels I Regulation – in *Ma-* **15** *hamdia*,[28] in relation to an action brought by an employee of Algerian nationality –domiciled in Germany –, against the Ministry of Foreign Affairs of the Popular and Democratic Republic of Algeria – as the employee, for the services provided to the Embassy of that country in Berlin –, that "an embassy of a third State situated in a Member State is an 'establishment' within the meaning of that provision, in a dispute concerning a contract of employment concluded by the embassy on behalf of the sending State, where the functions carried out by the employee do not fall within the exercise of public powers". With this judgment a formal and flexible approach to the concept of establishment was implemented,[29] favouring the employee when the employer was domiciled outside the EU. Besides, with this decision the CJEU has favoured a strict and non-extensive interpretation of the doctrine of State immunity, in relation to cases dealing with individual contracts of employment.[30]

Article 21

1. An employer domiciled in a Member State may be sued:
    (a) in the courts of the Member State in which he is domiciled; or
    (b) in another Member State:
        (i) in the courts for the place where or from where the employee habitually carries out his work or in the courts for the last place where he did so; or
        (ii) if the employee does not or did not habitually carry out his work in any one country, in the courts for the place where the business which engaged the employee is or was situated.
2. An employer not domiciled in a Member State may be sued in a court of a Member State in accordance with point (b) of paragraph 1.

---

[28] *Ahmed Mahamdia v. Popular and Democratic Republic of Algeria*, (Case C-154/11) nyr. Also Cassaz. RDIPP 2011, 431.
[29] *Gulotta*, RDIPP 2013, 619, 633; *Pataut*, RCDIP 102 (2013), 217, 225.
[30] *Gulotta*, RDIPP 2013, 619, 633.

I. Preliminary remarks

1 When specifying the concrete jurisdictions before which actions related to individual contracts of employment may be brought, the Brussels *Ibis* Regulation distinguishes between possible disputes where the employee is the plaintiff (Art. 21) – practice shows that the majority of labour lawsuits are commenced by employees, in particular in matters of dismissals – and those where the employer is the plaintiff (Art. 22).[1] The treatment given to each special case varies according to the position occupied by each one in their work relationship. An analysis of this reveals the fact that the employer holds a strong position, whereas the employee is in a weaker position in this type of contract. This relational scheme involves the design containing a set of laws regarding competent jurisdictions in which there is an underlying intention to favour and protect the worker from the employer. Thus, as well as it happens Art. 8 of the Rome I Regulation, the *favor laboratoris* becomes the guideline for concrete solutions related to this matter incorporated in the Regulation.

2 Therefore, Art. 21 – which will be now analysed – refers to those cases where the employee is the plaintiff. This provision has suffered a dramatic change in the current Brussels *Ibis* Regulation – as it will be analysed below, as long as this provision not only covers situations where the employer is domiciled in a Member State, but it also operates for cases where the employer is domiciled in a third State outside the EU.

II. The general rule of jurisdiction of the defendant's domicile and situations of employers not domiciled in a Member State

3 Art. 21 of the Brussels *Ibis* Regulation brings an important improvement if compared to its predecessor, as it covers both situations where the employer who has been sued is domiciled inside or outside the EU. In this respect, in its paragraph 2 it is establishes that employers – regardless of his/her domicile- can be sued using those *fora* contemplated in paragraph (1) (b) for both situations. This novelty imply an extension of the jurisdictional protection recognized to the employee, in relation to situations connected to third countries, for those cases in which the employer is domiciled in a third country. A possibility which was not guaranteed in relation to the previous Brussels I Regulation, as long as the autonomous Private International Law systems of some of the Member States did not contemplated such a possibility, when the employer was domiciled outside of the EU.[2]

4 With this improvement, the new Regulation aims at protecting the interest of the employee by favouring the convergence of *forum* and *ius* and the application of the mandatory rules of the *forum*.[3] In particular, it provides a protection in terms of access to justice, when the employee habitually works in -or from- a Member State, or when he/she was engaged in a Member State.[4] Besides it could not be considered that this improvement lead to an exorbitant *forum*, as long as the connecting factors present in letter (b) guarantee the connection between the case and the courts of the Member State.[5] However, it has also been stressed that

---

[1] Also *Grusic*, (2012) 61 ICLQ 91, 100–101.

[2] See *Nuyts*, pp. 43–45.

[3] Recital (14). See *Gulotta*, RDIPP 2013, 619, 626–627.

[4] *Cadet*, Clunet 140 (2013), 765, 773–774, *Grusic*, (2012) 61 ICLQ 91, 119.

[5] *Gulotta*, RDIPP 2013, 619, 625.

this extension might create problems in relation to the recognition and enforcement of the judgments rendered in a Member State outside of the EU.[6]

Therefore, according to the new wording of this provision, while the general rule of juris- 5
diction of the defendant's domicile – present in paragraph (1) (a) – only covers situations of employers domiciled in a Member State, those protective alternatives present in letter (b) can be used in all cases, regardless where the employer is domiciled inside or outside a Member State of the EU.

In this respect, Art. 21 begins by reproducing in paragraph (1) (a) the general rule about the 6
jurisdiction of the defendant's domicile in Art. 4.[7] In this way, an employer domiciled in a Member State of the European Union may be sued by an employee before the courts of the Member State where the former is domiciled. According to the provisions of Art. 20 (2), if his domicile is outside the European Union but the employer has a branch, agency or other establishment in Community territory, this business centre shall be considered a domicile for these purposes.[8] Correlatively, if the worker has carried out all his activity within the European Union but the sued employer is not domiciled nor has a branch, agency or establishment in the European Union, the provisions of Art. 21 (1) (a) shall be inapplicable and it will be necessary to apply the alternatives present in its letter (b).

From the point of view of the sued employer, the jurisdiction of the defendant's domicile has 7
the positive element of guaranteeing his expectations of defence, since this is his natural jurisdiction. For its part, the criterion of the defendant's domicile offers the worker a juris-
diction within the Union that may be relevant in situations, most notably in today's global market place, where it is not unusual for an employee to carry out his work outside European Union territory.[9] The option favouring jurisdiction in the domicile, nonetheless, situates within the scope of an individual employment contract a series of consubstantial problems, linked to the fact that the Regulation does not include a unitary concept of the juridical term "domicile".[10] In this way, as far as natural persons are concerned, Art. 62 refers the determination of domicile to the provisions of the internal law of the different Member States, which, logically, may lead to a person being "domiciled" in more than one Member State in accordance with national laws.[11] Article 63, on the other hand, sets out a triple way of determining the domicile of companies and other corporate persons. In this sense the domicile will be understood to be either in the place where they have their head office[12] or where they have their central administration or their main business centre.

---

[6] *Gulotta*, RDIPP 2013, 619, 643–644.

[7] Trib. Sup. Aranzadi 8554; *Béraudo*, Clunet 128 (2001), 1033, 1058.

[8] Take into consideration, in situations where the workplace is situated in a third country, *Group Josi Reinsurance Company SA v. Universal General Insurance Company* (UGIC) (Case C-412/98) [2000] ECR I-5925; *Andrew Owusu v. N.B. Jackson and others* (Case C.281/02) [2005] ECR I-1383.

[9] Trib. Sup. Aranzadi 8554; LAG Bremen IPRspr. 1996, 109; Cass. Clunet 122 (1995), 134; Cass. RCDIP 83 (1994), 323; *Palao Moreno*, Derecho internacional y de la integración 2 (2003), 7, 22. See *Grusic*, (2012) 61 ICLQ 91, 103–104.

[10] A concept which needs an autonomous interpretation, *Bosse*, 119 *et seq.* See *Merret*, 88–90.

[11] *Mosconi*, RDIPP 2003, 5, 14.

[12] Cf. Art. 60 (2) regarding the meaning of this concept in the United Kingdom and Ireland.

8 Logically, the moment to verify the existence of a domicile in the European Union is when the claim is served.[13]

III. Exceptions to rule of the jurisdiction of domicile

9 Together with the possibility of resorting to the courts of the Member State where the sued employer is domiciled, Art. 21 (1) (b) designs a series of special privileges that acknowledge the worker's right to take action before the jurisdictional authorities of other states in the Union. Those alternatives are available to the employee when the employer is domiciled both inside and outside a Member State of the EU – as underlined in its paragraph (2). It depends entirely on the will of the plaintiff whether or not to have resort to these special jurisdictions and he shall decide in accordance with his interests and the particular circumstances of the case.[14]

10 The rights designed in the precept distinguish a situation where the worker has habitually carried out his work in one particular place in the European Union from a second one, contemplating other cases where has not habitually been so. In the first case, the worker may bring his action in the courts of the place where or from where the employee habitually carries out his work in the European Union, or in the courts of the last place where he did so. Should the worker not have a habitual place of work, he may bring his action before the courts of the place where the business which engaged the employee is or was situated.[15]

1. Cases of habitual workplace of the employee in a given country

a) The rule of the place where or from where the employee habitually carries out his work

aa) Introduction

11 The rule contemplated in Art. 21 (1) (b) (i) that attributes jurisdiction to the courts of the place where or from where the employee habitually carries out his work in the European Union was already envisaged in Art. 5 (1) of the San Sebastián Convention of 1989, traditionally playing an important role, furthermore, in national systems of international judicial competence.[16] The direct antecedent of the rule is to be found in the judgment of the Court of Justice of the European Communities of 26 May 1982, in the *Ivenel* case,[17] where, in relation with a dispute about a breach of an agency contract, the Court of Justice ignores the doctrine laid out in the *De Bloos* decision,[18] stating that individual employment contracts, as contracts with a specific set of problems related both to their social transcendence and the obligations involved in them, require a differentiated solution that takes their particular characteristics into account. In this sense, it states that "in the case of a contract of employment the connection lies particularly in the law applicable to the contract; and that according to the trend in the conflict rules in regard to this matter that law is determined by the obligation

---

[13] *Bosse*, 142.

[14] *Mankowski*, in: Rauscher Art. 19 note 1.

[15] *Buy*, Dr. soc. 11 (2002), 967, 968.

[16] *Palao Moreno*, Derecho internacional y de la integración 2 (2003), 7, 23.

[17] *Roger Ivenel v. Helmut Schwab*, (Case 133/81) [1982] ECR 1891. Solution confirmed in the case *Hassan Shenavai v. Klaus Kreischer*, (Case 266/85) [1987] ECR 239, 255–256.

[18] *A. de Bloos, SPRL v. Société en commandite par actions Bouyer*, (Case 14/76) [1976] ECR 1497.

characterizing the contract in question and is normally the obligation to carry out work".[19] Making it clear, in short, that the courts of the place where the employee discharges his obligations towards his employer will be the ones competent to judge any dispute that may arise.[20]

The new wording of this provision has brought a significant change, as this Article does not **12** only refer to situations in which the activity was performed in a specific place, but also those situations "*from where*" the work was carried out – not present in the former Regulation-. This modification implies an alignment of Art. 21 to Art. 8 (2) Rome I Regulation, and enables a coincidence of *forum* and *ius* for those cases.

In accordance with the then ECJ, the solution reached is that which best protects the worker **13** as the weaker party in an individual employment contract, since it is "the place where it is least expensive for the employee to commence, or defend himself against, court proceedings".[21] In this respect, some authors even consider that this could lead to a *forum actoris*.[22] Furthermore, it is a correct solution from the employer's point of view since, as it is he who determines as a last resort the place where the employee shall carry out his work, it is reasonable and predictable that he should be sued in that place.[23] Besides, as mentioned before, the doctrine gives a positive value to the fact that the rule of the habitual workplace favours the convergence between the *forum* and the *ius*, thus permitting the law of the State where the employee carries out his work to be applied by the jurisdictional authorities of the said State.[24] For those reasons *inter alia* the ECJ affirmed that this connecting factor takes priority over the others.[25]

Logically, in order for the rule to be applied, it must be a place located in a Member State of **14** the European Union. As the ECJ provided in its judgment in *Six Constructions*,[26] on occasions where the habitual workplace is found to be outside the European Union, that place may not be the basis for the application of the rule contemplated in Art. 21 (1) (b) (i). As the Court itself stated, this does not give rise to special problems in a system like that of the Brussels Convention, now the Brussels I*bis* Regulation, where the plaintiff always has the option of resorting to the general jurisdiction of the place where the defendant is domiciled – contemplated in Art. 21 (1) (a) – or to one of the special fora provided for in Art. 21 (1) (b).

---

[19] *Roger Ivenel v. Helmut Schwab*, (Case 133/81) [1982] ECR 1891, 1900; Cassaz. RDIPP 1996, 325.

[20] See BAG 27.1.2011 AP H. 4/2012, 673, with note *Mankowski*.

[21] *Mulox IBC Ltd. v. Hendrick Geels*, (Case C-125/92) [1993] ECR I-4075, I-4104; *Kropholler/von Hein* Art. 18 note 1; *Mosconi*, RDIPP 2003, 5, 1. Also, in relation to Art. 6 (2) (a) of the Convention on the law applicable to contractual obligations, *Heiko Koelzsch v. État du Grand-Duché du Luxembourg* (Case C-29/10) [2011] I-01595.

[22] *Salerno*, 223; *Casado Abarquero*, 141.

[23] Even if this subject may not refer to this forum, as we shall see in the commentary on Art. 20. Cf. *Zábalo-Escudero*, Rev. der. com. eur. 14 (2003), 225, 237.

[24] *Mankowski*, in: Rauscher Art. 19 note 4; *Palao Moreno*, Derecho internacional y de la integración 2 (2003), 7, 23.

[25] In relation to Art. 6 (2) (a) of the Convention on the law applicable to contractual obligations, *Heiko Koelzsch v. État du Grand-Duché du Luxembourg* (Case C-29/10) [2011] I-01595, at 39.

[26] *Six Constructions Ltd. v. Paul Humber*, (Case 32/88) [1989] ECR 341, 364.

Carlos Esplugues Mota/Guillermo Palao Moreno

The existence of three special jurisdictions, furthermore, increases the possibilities of resorting to one of them in practice.

bb) Determination of the habitual workplace

15 In short, a close relationship is presumed to exist between the employment contract and the place where or from where the working activity is carried out. Even though the employer ceased that activity or was transferred to third country.[27] A relationship that is even reflected in the application of that Member State's mandatory rules and collective agreements.[28] The rule, then, is based on the principle that all work is carried out in or from a particular place and that, therefore, the worker is linked to that place, and the courts of the said place are the best prepared to hear the dispute and satisfy the worker's legitimate expectations. Logically, the application of the rule requires that the said place be located in a Member State of the European Union.

16 The functioning of the rule does not give rise to any particular problems on occasions where the work is carried out by the employee in or from a single place,[29] where there are several places but one of them is the habitual place for the parties,[30] or where the work is performed in several places, although only one of them is inside the European Union. Besides, this provision could also be considered applicable, when the worker lives nearby but across the border,[31] as well as for some other specific "mobile" labour relationships when they enjoy an international character (i.e. seamen, aircraft personnel or professional drivers).[32] Greater problems arise, however, in cases where the work is carried out by the employee in more than one place.[33] In these cases, the application involves defining the place where the work is "habitually" carried out. This has been determined in the jurisprudence of the Court of Justice of the Communities by means of different hypotheses concerning the location of the *locus laboris*.

17 The question arose for the first time in *Mulox*.[34] The case was about an ex-employee who had carried out his work in different countries and brought an action against his ex-employer. The Court, when determining the habitual workplace in a case where the work was carried out in different places, underlined the need to interpret the old Art. 5 (1) of the Brussels Convention – currently Art. 21 of the Brussels I Regulation – in such a way "as to avoid any multiplication of courts having jurisdiction, thereby precluding the risk of irreconcilable decisions and facilitating the recognition and enforcement of judgments in States other than those in which they were delivered".[35] This points directly to the fact that it is impossible to

---

[27] *Casado Abarquero*, 140.

[28] *Hassan Shenavai v. Klaus Kreischer*, (Case 266/85) [1987] ECR 239, 255–256; *Mulox IBC Ltd. v. Hendrick Geels*, (Case C-125/92) [1993] ECR I-4075, I-4103-4104.

[29] For example, *Commission of the European Communities v. Italian Republic*, (Case C-279/00) [2002] ECR I-1425. Also BAG IPRspr. 1988 Nr. 50, 97.

[30] Cassaz. RDIPP 2004, 661.

[31] *Heidelberg Report* 87.

[32] *Bosse*, 184 *et seq.* In relation to seamen, BAG 24.9.2009, AP H. 6/2010, 881, note *Mankowski*. In relation to aircraft personnel, Cassaz. RDIPP 2011, 162.

[33] A connecting factor which refers to both international and territorial jurisdiction, that must be autonomously interpreted. *Winterling*, 59–60. Contra *Salerno*, 223–224.

[34] *Mulox IBC Ltd. v. Hendrick Geels*, (Case C-125/92) [1993] ECR I-4075.

grant jurisdiction to the courts of all the countries where the employee has carried out his work and the subsequent need to specify one place where he is presumed to have carried out is work habitually. Correlatively, this desire not to multiply jurisdictions implies that on occasions where the habitual place of work cannot be determined, either because there are two or more places of equal importance or because none of the places where the employee carries out his work is relevant enough to be considered competent, it will have to be accepted that the jurisdiction contemplated in Art. 21 (1) (b)[36] is inapplicable and resort to the following criteria of international jurisdiction set out in Art. 21.

On the basis of these premises, the Court of Justice of the Communities chooses to consider **18** that the place where the work is carried out is that place "where or from which the employee principally discharges his obligations towards his employer".[37] This reference to "principal" was changed in Art. 5 (1) of the San Sebastián Convention and later in Art. 19 (1) (a) of the Brussels I Regulation, of which we are now analysing "habitual".[38] A change which -as we shall point out below-, has a direct influence on the effectiveness of the criterion of international jurisdiction available to the employer, which are currently contemplated in Art. 21 (1) (b) (ii).

Specifically the employee is understood to carry out his work habitually in or from where the **19** place where he "has established the effective centre of his working activities and where, or from which, he in fact performs the essential part of his duties vis-à-vis his employer".[39] It is, in short, a presumption *iuris tantum*, for whose concretion, as the Luxembourg Court points out, the national court responsible for applying the Regulation must take into account the factual background of the case:[40] circumstances such as whether or not the worker carried out his work from one particular office, whether he organised his professional activities from that office, whether he had his residence in that place, how long he stayed there, whether he went back there after every business trip ... make it possible to verify the location of the effective centre of the employee's working activities.[41]

The position sustained by the Court of Justice assumes that the employee has an office or **20** "effective centre" from which he carries out his working activities.[42] In practice, nevertheless, it is clear that there is a possibility that this office may not exist.

---

[35]   *Mulox IBC Ltd. v. Hendrick Geels*, (Case C-125/92) [1993] ECR I-4075, I-4105.

[36]   *Herbert Weber v. Universal Ogden Services Ltd.*, (Case C-37/00) [2002] ECR I-2013, I-2049.

[37]   *Mulox IBC Ltd. v. Hendrick Geels*, (Case C-125/92) [1993] ECR I-4075, I-4105. The differences that exist between "the habitual workplace" and "the principal workplace" have been approached by *Mankowski*, IPRax 1999, 332 *et seq.*

[38]   About this point, see *Mulox IBC Ltd. v. Hendrick Geels*, (Case C-125/92) [1993] ECR I-4075 = RCDIP 83 (1994), 574, 577 with note *Lagarde*.

[39]   *Petrus Wilhelmus Rutten v. Cross Medical Ltd.*, (Case C-383/95) [1997] ECR I-57, I-77.

[40]   *Mulox IBC Ltd. v. Hendrick Geels*, (Case C-125/92), [1993] ECR I-4075, I-4105-4106; *Petrus Wilhelmus Rutten v. Cross Medical Ltd.*, (Case C-383/95) [1997] ECR I-57, I-78.

[41]   *Mankowski*, IPRax 1999, 332, 336.

[42]   *Petrus Wilhelmus Rutten v. Cross Medical Ltd.*, (Case C-383/95) [1997] ECR I-57 = CDE 1999, 172, 181 with note *Tagaras*.

---

21   This is the underlying situation in the *Weber* case,[43] referring to the work as a cook carried out by a certain person on several platforms located in the sea. In this case, the Luxembourg Court understood that, on those occasions where a person performs the same work in several places, any qualitative criteria relating to the nature and importance of work done in various places within the Contracting States are irrelevant. Therefore, "the relevant criterion for establishing an employee's habitual place of work, for the purposes of Article 5 (1) of the Brussels Convention is, in principle, the place where he spends most of his working time engaged on his employer's business",[44] independently of what was established in the individual contract of employment,[45] or where the employer carried out the first part of the activity.[46] To sum up, when taking into account the total working relationship, the duration of the different work periods carried out in the different Member States of the Union must be considered, presuming that the place where most time is spent will be considered the habitual workplace,[47] If this place could be considered suitable enough to determine an habitual workplace in relation to the other ones.[48]

22   In relation to those situations where the work is carried out in several member states, the *Koelzsch* case is worth mentioning. This Case related to a preliminary ruling concerned the application of Art. 6 (2) (a) of the Convention on the law applicable to contractual obligations. The *Koelzsch* case referred to a heavy goods vehicle driver, domiciled in Germany (and covered by Luxembourg social security), who was engaged as an international driver by a subsidiary of a Danish company, to transport goods to destinations situated mostly in Germany, as well as to other European countries, by means of lorries registered in Luxembourg, which were stationed in Germany.[49] In this case the Court of Justice ruled that this provision must be interpreted in relation to this kind of situations, as referring to country "*in which or from which, in the light of all factors which characterised that activity, the employee performs the greater part of his obligations towards his employed*". In that respect, following the opinion of Advocate General Trstenjak, the Court of Justice affirmed that attention has to be paid to the state "from which the employee carries out his transport tasks, receives instructions concerning his tasks and organises his work, and the place where his work tools are situated. It must also determine the place where the transport is principally carried out, where the goods are unloaded and the place to which the employee returns after completion of his tasks".[50] Therefore, the court has provided a specialised interpretation of this provision, in connection with transport workers, based on the "significant connection"[51] of the elements and circumstances of the activity ("the greater part of the obligations"). A quali-

---

43   *Herbert Weber v. Universal Ogden Services Ltd.*, (Case C-37/00) [2002] ECR I-2013.

44   *Herbert Weber v. Universal Ogden Services Ltd.*, (Case C-37/00) [2002] ECR I-2013, I-2048. Similarly, in relation to the application of the Lugano Convention 1988, Høyesterett, 11.4.2002 (Court of Justice of the European Communities, Information pursuant to Protocol 2 annexed to the Lugano Conventio, Case n° 2003/42).

45   *Salerno*, 226–227. Cassaz. RDIPP 2004, 664.

46   Cassaz. RDIPP 2004, 661.

47   *Mankowski*, IPRax 2003, 21, 23–24. See Cassaz. RDIPP 2008, 1081.

48   *Carbone*, 148.

49   *Heiko Koelzsch v. État du Grand-Duché du Luxembourg*, (Case C-29/10) [2011] I-01595. See *Mankowski/Knöfel*, EuZA 4 (2011) 521.

50   At 49.

51   At 44. See *Grusic*, (2012) 61 ICLQ 91, 108.

tative approach which can also be considered when interpreting Art. 21 (1) (a) (i) of the Brussels I*bis* Regulation.[52]

The time rule used in the *Weber* Case is based on a presumption that may be rebutted,   23 however, only on occasions where the factual background of a case shows that there is a greater relationship with one particular Member State. Circumstances such as the fact that an employee, having carried out his work in one particular Member State goes to work permanently in another country, and that reflect the desire that this latter place should become a new habitual place of work within the meaning of Art. 21 (1) (a) (i).[53] All of this may affect to a certain extent the predictability of the international jurisdiction of a Court, since the interpretation of all these issues depends on the judge.[54]

2. Jurisdiction of the last place where the employee has carried out his work

Together with the rule about the place where the employee habitually carries out his work,   24 Art. 21 (1) (b) (i) extends the range of options offered to the employee when bringing an action against his employer by incorporating a reference to the court of the last place he worked. This is a criterion that is not contemplated in the Brussels Convention.[55]

The location of the rule in Art. 21 (1) (b) (i) and its relationship with the first of the   25 hypotheses contemplated by the legislator – where the employee habitually carries out his work in a specific place – would lead to it being considered as a "closing" clause endowed with a plural function: Thus, in the first place, it would cover those cases where it is not very easy to specify which is the habitual workplace as the employee has carried out his work for a company in more than one State.[56] In this way, in relation with the time criterion present in the *Weber* case – a judgment issued 2 days before the Brussels I Regulation came into force – the decision would be not to take into consideration the longest period of work, as in this case, but the last one.[57] Furthermore, the criterion made it possible, in the second place, to deal with situations where the dispute arises after the work relationship has concluded, so that theoretically there would no longer exist a habitual workplace. In this case, the place chosen would be the last place where the employee habitually carried out his work.[58]

Finally, it even goes so far as to mention that it refers to situations where the employee did   26 not carry out his work in one specific country, so that the place would be the last one where he had carried out his working activities.[59] Otherwise, it states, there would be no point in introducing the criterion of the last workplace, since it would already be known as it would

---

[52]   Italian courts also favor a similar approach in relation to the Brussels I Regulation, see *Amici*, RIDL 2010, 655.

[53]   *Carbone*, 125. In relation to the different elements and criteria which could be taken into account to determine the habitual workplace, *Winterling*, 62 *et seq.*; *Bosse*, 166 *et seq.*

[54]   *Salerno*, 227; *Heidelberg Report* 86.

[55]   *Palao Moreno*, (2002) 4 Yb. PIL 303, 313.

[56]   *Mankowski*, in: Rauscher Art. 19 note 13; *Béraudo*, Clunet 128 (2001), 1033, 1058.

[57]   *Buy*, Dr. soc. 11 (2002), 967, 970.

[58]   *Gaudemet-Tallon*, 298. Also, *Herbert Weber v. Universal Ogden Services Ltd.*, (Case C-37/00) [2002] ECR I-2013 = Revista Jurídica de Catalunya (2002), 1211, 1214 with note *Borrás-Rodríguez*.

[59]   *Béraudo*, Clunet 128 (2001) 1033, 1058.

be the habitual one.[60] This option, nevertheless, would seem to be as far away from the meaning of the precept as from the location of the rule within Art. 21 (1) (b) (i): cases where the employee did not carry out his work habitually in one specific country should refer to the provisions of Art. 21 (1) (b) (ii).

IV. Cases where the employee does not carry out his working activities in one specific place

1. Generalities

27 On occasions where he does not carry out his habitual work in one specific State of the Union, the employee may resort to the courts of the place where the business which engaged the employee is or was situated.[61] This rule, included in Art. 5 (1) of the Brussels Convention, is now introduced in Art. 21 (1) (b) (ii). It is a criterion of a subsidiary character which must receive a strict interpretation – according to the Court of Justice[62]–, that has had different appraisements by the doctrine, where it has been considered a criterion both favourable and unfavourable to the employee's interests and expectations.[63]

28 The rule refers to the present or past location of the business that engaged the employee. This temporal option has the advantage that, even if the business has disappeared, the courts of the place where it was located shall be competent to hear the possible dispute.[64] Correlatively, this connecting factor has been severely criticized, *inter alia*, as its greatest disadvantage resides in the possible lack of a rational connection between the courts selected and the dispute that may arise before them.[65]

29 The jurisdiction of the location of the business that engaged the worker at first sight seems to be a predictable criterion easy to apply. Its greater complexity stems from the need to specify the meaning of employing company, adapting it to a complex practice where certain formulas of business interposition are common – see the flexible approach favoured by Judgment of the ECJ in *Pugliese*[66]– international circulation within a Multinational Business

---

60 *Palao Moreno*, Derecho internacional y de la integración 2 (2003), 7, 25.

61 Concerning the possible hypotheses that will give rise to its application, *Mankowski*, in: Rauscher Art. 18 note 15.

62 *Heiko Koelzsch v. État du Grand-Duché du Luxembourg*, (Case C-29/10) [2011] I-01595, at 44; *Jan Voogsgeerd v. Navimer SA*, (Case C-384/10) [2011] ECR I-13275, at 47. See *Maestre Casas*, Cuadernos de Derecho Transnacional 4 (2012), 322.

63 Considered favourable by: *Antonmattei*, J-Cl. dr.int. fasc. 573-20 (1994) 8-9; *Mulox IBC Ltd. v. Hendrick Geels*, (Case C-125/92) [1993] ECR I-4075 = REDI 1993, 470, 473 with note *Zabalo-Escudero*. Considered unfavourable by: *Mari*, Il diritto processuale civile della Convenzione di Bruxelles, 1999, 361; *Merret*, 119–123; *Mulox IBC Ltd. v. Hendrick Geels*, (Case C-125/92), [1993] ECR I-4075 = RCDIP 83 (1994) 573, 576 with note *Lagarde*.

64 *Béraudo*, Clunet 128 (2001), 1033, 1058.

65 *Béraudo*, Clunet 128 (2001), 1033, 1058; *Grusic*, (2013) 62 ICLQ 173, 191–192, *Mosconi*, RDIPP 2003, 5, 19; *Lajolo di Cossano*, Dir. comm. int. 2002, 901, 916.

66 *Giulia Pugliese v. Finmeccanica SpA, Betriebsteil Alenia Aerospazio*, (Case C-437/00) [2003] ECR I-3573. See Krebber, IPRax 2004, 309, 315.

Group,[67] or the presence of secondary companies that act as mere hiring agencies.[68] A broad interpretation of the concept is required here.[69]

The effectiveness of this rule has been seriously affected by the jurisprudential practice of the **30** ECJ regarding employment contracts, and it has acquired a strong residual character.[70] The jurisprudence of the Court reveals a clear tendency to "reinterpret" extensively the terms of Art. 5 (1) of the Brussels Convention in its San Sebastián version – now Art. 21 (1) (b) (i) of the Brussels I*bis* Regulation – endowing in it a character of priority in the international jurisdiction system as regards to individual employment contracts previously contemplated in the Convention and now governed by the Regulation.[71]

In cases where the employee has not carried out his working activities in a single State, this **31** leads to the court deciding to apply the concept of habituality from different angles, considering it to be one place or another by virtue of different hypotheses. The above mentioned judgments in the *Mulox* cases – pronounced before the San Sebastián Convention came into force – the *Rutten* case or the *Weber* case are a clear token of this.[72] A rationale which can also be found at the *Koelzsch* Case, interpreting Art. 6 (2) (a) of the Convention on the law applicable to contractual obligations, guided by the objective of protecting the weaker party of the contractual relationship.[73] All of this regardless of the facts, mentioned above, that this can affect the predictability of international jurisdiction.

However, the possibility of make use of this connecting factor has been supported by the **32** judgment of the European Court of Justice of 15 December 2001 in Case *Voogsgeerd*,[74] in relation to Art. 6 (2) (b) of the Rome Convention of 1980, where it stated that this connecting factor should be interpreted as follows: "the place of business through which the employee was engaged' must be understood as referring exclusively to the place of business which engaged the employee and not to that with which the employee is connected by his actual employment; the possession of legal personality does not constitute a requirement that must be met by the place of business of the employer within the meaning of that provision; the place of business of an undertaking other than that which is formally referred to as the employer, with which that undertaking has connections, may be classified as a 'place of business' within the meaning of Article 6 (2) (b) of that convention if objective factors make

---

[67]   *Palao Moreno*, Los Grupos de Empresas Multinacionales y el contrato individual de trabajo, 2000, 235–248.

[68]   However, *Grusic*, (2012) 61 ICLQ 91, 113.

[69]   *Mankowski*, in: Rauscher Art. 18 note 18; *Palao Moreno*, Derecho internacional y de la integración 2 (2003), 7, 26.

[70]   Because it was marginalised by *loci laboris*. Cf. *Mankowski*, in: Rauscher Art. 18 note 5; *Buy*, Droit social 11 (2002), 967, 968. Also Grusic, (2012) 61 ICLQ 91, 114.

[71]   *Herbert Weber v. Universal Ogden Services Ltd.*, (Case C-37/0) [2002] ECR I-2013 = REDI 2002 861, 863 with note *Palao Moreno*.

[72]   *Salerno*, 225; *Mulox IBC Ltd. v. Hendrick Geels*, (Case C-125/92) [1993] ECR I-4075 = Clunet 121 (1994), 539, 544 with note *Huet*.

[73]   At 40.

[74]   *Jan Voogsgeerd v. Navimer SA*, (Case C-384/10) [2011] ECR I-13275. Critics, *Knöfel*, IPRax 2 (2014) 130, 136; *Pataut*, Note to *Jan Voogsgeerd v. Navimer SA*, (Case C-384/10) [2011] ECR I-13275, RCDIP 3 (2012) 649, 666.

Carlos Esplugues Mota/Guillermo Palao Moreno   551

it possible to establish that there exists a real situation different from that which appears from the terms of the contract, even though the authority of the employer has not been formally transferred to that other undertaking".

33 Furthermore, the virtuality of the jurisdiction is affected, according to the doctrine, by the fact that Art. 5 (1) of the San Sebastián Convention of 1989 was replaced by the qualitative criterion of "principal" workplace, as mentioned in the *Mulox* judgment, which practically annuls the viability of the criterion of the business that engaged the employee.[75] The introduction in Art. 19 (1) (a) (ii) of the criterion of the last place where the employee carried out his working activities, also involves an additional limitation in resorting to it.[76]

2. Special cases concerning the temporary posting of workers

34 Article 21 of the Brussels I Regulation must not make us forget the validity of Directive 96/71/EC of the European Parliament and of the Council of 16 December concerning the posting of workers in the framework of the provision of services,[77] where a whole set of provisions is included with a view to guaranteeing a minimum level of rights for workers in respect of temporary posting; a different situation from the case of "shifting" a worker from one place to another.[78] Among other provisions, the Directive incorporates a norm of international jurisdiction that tends to determine competent Courts in relation to this type of situation, which prevails over the rules in the Brussels *Ibis* Regulation by virtue of its speciality, at the same time as it completes and extends the jurisdictions contemplated in the Regulation for these cases.[79]

35 With all the difficulties that its description may entail,[80] the temporary posting of a worker from the country where he habitually carries out his working activities to another State is somewhat exceptional according to Art. 2 of the Directive. In short, it is a provisional posting; limited to a specific period of time.[81] In this sense, the employee is considered to continue habitually carrying out his working activity in the country from which he was moved. All the circumstances involved in a temporary posting can have a direct influence on the determination of the competent Courts, insofar as according to Art. 21 of the Brussels *Ibis* Regulation the worker would not be entitled to sue his employer before the courts of the country where he is now carrying out his working activities. Unless, logically, there is an agreement to resort to the courts of another country on the basis of Art. 23. This situation may be to the worker's disadvantage, because it prevents him/her from resorting to the

---

[75] *Gaudemet-Tallon*, 298.

[76] *Gaudemet-Tallon*, 298.

[77] OJ 1997 L 18/1. This Directive is under re-consideration –although not directly affecting jurisdiction and conflict-of-law rules- and it has been published a Proposal for a Directive of the European Parliament and of the Council on the enforcement of Directive 96/71/EC concerning the posting of workers in the framework of the provision of services (COM (2012) 131 final).

[78] *Palao Moreno*, Derecho internacional y de la integración 2 (2003), 7, 29.

[79] *Mankowski*, in: Rauscher Art. 18 note 16; *Palao Moreno*, (2002) 4 Yb. PIL 303, 329; *Lajolo di Cossano*, Dir. comm.int. 2002, 901, 923.

[80] *Gaudemet-Tallon*, 304.

[81] Some authors consider a temporary posting, when the worker carries out less than the 40% of his work in a country. *Bosse*, 220.

courts of the country where he is carrying out his work, which at the present time are those most closely related to him/her and those that therefore facilitate concordance between the *forum* and the *ius*.[82]

In order to solve this negative situation, Art. 6 of Directive 96/71/EC incorporates a rule **36** about international jurisdiction, limited in its scope of application to cases of enforcement of the right to the terms and conditions of employment guaranteed in Art. 3 with respect to the activities stipulated in Art. 1 of the Directive. The said Art. 6 acknowledges that the worker temporarily posted to another country within the European Union is entitled to resort to the courts of the Member State in whose territory he is posted at the present time or was posted in the past. Apart from this option, he may also sue his employer before the courts of another State, in accordance with the provisions present in the existing Convention on Jurisdiction: that is, the Brussels Convention of 1968, currently the Brussels I Regulation. In this way, an alternative option is established in favour of the worker posted away from his habitual place of residence, who may choose the jurisdiction in which to serve his claim according to his specific interests.[83]

Article 22

1. **An employer may bring proceedings only in the courts of the Member State in which the employee is domiciled.**
2. **The provisions of this Section shall not affect the right to bring a counter-claim in the court in which, in accordance with this Section, the original claim is pending.**

I. Jurisdiction according to the employee's domicile

The policy of protecting the weaker party in an individual employment contract is clearly **1** reflected in Art. 22 (1), where it is plainly stated that the employer may only sue the employee in the courts of the Member State where the employee is domiciled, thus invalidating the possibilities afforded by Art. 5 (1) of the Brussels Convention with respect to bringing the proceedings against the employee in his habitual workplace.[1] Unlike what occurs with the employee, Art. 20 does not provide the employer with any alternative jurisdiction.[2] His only option is to resort to the jurisdiction where the sued employee is domiciled. In short, this is a new rule, not contemplated in Art. 5 (1) of the Brussels Convention.

Article 22 (1) basically reproduces the rule of Art. 4, whose application regarding individual **2** employment contracts is demurred by Art. 20 (1). In the case of a suit against the employee, the jurisdiction based on the employee's domicile implies referring to a place that habitually

---

82 *Moureau Borlés*, Clunet 123 (1996), 889, 903; *Franzen*, ZEuP 1997, 1055, 1071; *Palao Moreno*, Derecho internacional y de la integración 2 (2003), 7, 29.

83 *Moureau Borlés*, Clunet 123 (1996), 889, 903; *Franzen*, ZEuP 1997, 1055, 1071 *et seq*. See BAG 15.2.2012, 10 AZR 711/10.

1 *Mankowski*, in: Rauscher Art. 20 note 2. *Contra Lajolo di Cossano*, Dir.comm.int. 2002, 901, 914; *Bosse*, 270; *Polak*, 341.

2 *Kropholler/von Hein*, Art. 20 note 1.

coincides with the place where the employee carries out his working activities.[3] A place that usually depends on the employer's will.[4] The greatest problems arising from this criterion logically stem from the above mentioned lack of a unitary criterion regarding domicile, which can lead, according to Art. 62, to the fact that the worker may be considered to be domiciled in several different States.[5]

3 The reference to the domicile of the sued employee seems to incorporate a mention of the place where the employee carries out his work, a place that may or may not coincide with the place where the employer has his business.[6] In any case, neither these hypotheses will necessarily arise in practice, nor this rule will guarantee that disputes will be heard by the courts for the place where the employee is domiciled.[7]

II. Right to counter-claim

4 The above limitation does not, however, prevent the employer from serving a counter-claim before the court hearing an incidental suit contemplated in the rule regarding jurisdiction included in Section 5 of Chapter II of the Brussels I Regulation. This rule is in the same line as the provisions of Artt. 14 (1) and 18 (3). Whereas the general rule of Art. 20 was incorporated in paragraph 1 of Art. 22, in paragraph 2 the rule of Art. 8 (3) is reproduced, a provision whose application of which would otherwise be excluded by virtue of Art. 20 (1).

5 The rule is formulated in generic terms and does not refer to the employer as the person entitled to serve a counter-claim.[8] Nevertheless, the fact that the rule is physically located in Art. 22, together with the fact that the jurisdiction of the Courts of the sued employer's domicile is one of the options open to the employee by virtue of Art. 21 (1), makes the employer the person most likely to make use of this possibility.[9] An alternative, on the other hand, foreseeable for the employee and which responds to the principle of procedural economy,[10] which should be autonomously interpreted in the light of the protection of the employee.[11]

Article 23

The provisions of this Section may be departed from only by an agreement:
(1) which is entered into after the dispute has arisen; or

---

[3] *Mankowski*, in: Rauscher Art. 20 note 2.
[4] *Palao Moreno*, Derecho internacional y de la integración 2 (2003), 7, 27.
[5] *Mosconi*, RDIPP 2003, 5, 22.
[6] Although it may also be understood as a guarantee of continuity as regards jurisdiction in cases of international mobility. Cf. *Esteban de la Rosa/Molina-Navarrete*, La movilidad transnacional de trabajadores: reglas y prácticas (2002), 71–72.
[7] *Béraudo*, Clunet 128 (2001), 1033, 1059.
[8] *Gaudemet-Tallon*, 303.
[9] *Juárez-Pérez*, Orden social y litigios internacionales: competencia judicial (2002), 115; *Mosconi*, RDIPP 2003, 5, 23.
[10] *Mankowski*, in: Rauscher Art. 20 notes 3–4.
[11] *Bosse*, 284.

(2) which allows the employee to bring proceedings in courts other than those indicated in this Section.

I. Freedom of choice in individual contracts of employment

Article 23 of the Brussels I Regulation admits freedom of choice with respect to the deter- **1** mination of competent Courts in matters of individual employment contracts.[1] Just as occurs with the system of international jurisdiction contemplated in a general sense in the Brussels I*bis* Regulation, the choice to be made by the parties by virtue of Art. 21 shall prevail over the solutions contemplated in Artt. 21 and 22 thereof. However, acceptance of freedom of choice in this matter is not absolute. It is a doubly limited acceptance, both regarding the form of expressing it and regarding the scope of its application. This has a direct influence on the understanding of the role played by the principle of freedom of choice in the international jurisdiction system designed by the Brussels I*bis* Regulation in relation with individual employment contracts. Thus, contrary to the provisions of the general regime, the impossibility to derogate the special fora contemplated in Artt. 21 and 22 would constitute the general rule, whereas the possibility of derogating them by means of the parties' exercise of their freedom of choice would acquire a somewhat exceptional nature, given the limitations that accompany the exercising of this freedom of choice.[2]

The importance of the *fora* contemplated in Art. 21 and 22 has been stressed by the new **2** wording of Art. 31 (4) of the Brussels I*bis* Regulation, with the aim to protect the interest of the employee as the weak party of the contract. In this respect, this paragraph determines the prominence of the solutions present in those provisions in relation to the possible *prorogatio fori*, in order to make sure that the employed is informed of the consequences of the agreement and the alternatives at stake.[3] Besides, the non-fulfilment of this obligation would even imply the non-recognition of the judgment, according to Art. 45 (1) (e) (i).[4]

II. First limitation: Non-acceptance of tacit submission

The first of these two limitations is manifested in the fact that the use of freedom of choice **3** seems to be accepted in the precept exclusively in its express dimension and not in relation to tacit submission. Independently of the existence of some doctrinal opinions that find this

---

[1] With respect to the virtuality of express submission in this matter, cf. Cassaz. RDIPP 1982, 337.
[2] *Mosconi*, RDIPP 2003, 5, 23; *Sinay-Cytermann*, in: Mélanges en l'honneur de Paul Lagarde (2005), 737, 740; ID., RCDIP 3 (2009), 427, 440.
[3] *Beraudo*, Clunet 3 (2013), 741, 751–752, *Queirolo*, in: Recasting Brussels I (2012), 196.
[4] *Gulotta*, RDIPP 2013, 619, 622.

possibility feasible,[5] the fact that Art. 20 (1) constricts the determination of international jurisdiction in regards to individual employment contracts to the provisions of Artt. 6, 7 (5) and 20 to 23 would support this position contrary to tacit submission regarding individual employment contracts.[6]

III. Second limitation: Conditions for the exercise of express freedom of choice

4 Furthermore, as a second limitation, freedom of choice is restricted insofar as that the parties are not entirely free to choose the competent Court to hear the dispute. This is a solution already present in Art. 17 (2) 2 Brussels Convention of 1968, in its San Sebastián version of 1989, which, rejecting the underlying philosophy of the *Sanicentral* Judgment,[7] responds to a desire to protect the worker – the weaker party in the contract – rather than the employer – the stronger party – by preventing the latter from taking advantage of his strong position to limit the selection of competent Tribunals that the Regulation offers the employee or to increase the possible jurisdictions contemplated for the employer.[8] It is presumed, then, that the principle of freedom functions normally when the parties that use it occupy similar juridical positions. However, in a contract like an individual employment contract, where the position of the parties is clearly unequal, as one party is strong and the other is weak, fully accepting freedom of choice could prejudice the weak party insofar as the strong party would tend to impose his solutions on the weaker one. In this way, the underlying policy of protecting the worker in the Regulation leads the legislator to limit, although not to prevent, the use of freedom of choice, only allowing it on occasions where it is of benefit to the worker.[9]

5 On the basis of these points, Art. 23 lays down two conditions in order to exercise freedom of choice. In this sense, and on the one hand, it is surprising that Art. 23 omits all reference to the possibility of submission to the courts of the State where the parties have their domicile or habitual residence, provided that such an agreement is not contrary to the law of that Member State. This possibility is, however, contemplated in Art. 15 (3), with relation to insurance contracts, and 19 (3), concerning consumer contracts. In the case of disputes arising from individual employment contracts, this possibility, therefore, if it is carried out pursuant to Art. 23, would not be affected by what the provisions of the legal system of the Member State to whose courts the parties have resorted have to say against it.[10] On the other hand, it must be underline that the provision does not state clearly that the parties should choose a court of Member State. However, a prorogation in favour of a court of a third country should not be admitted.[11]

---

[5] *Mosconi*, RDIPP 2003, 5, 26–27. Prior to the Brussels I Regulation, Cassaz. RDIPP 1992, 327.

[6] *Palao Moreno*, Derecho internacional y de la integración 2 (2003), 7, 27, fn. 49. See BAG 2.7.2008 AP H. 1/ 2009, 111, with note *Mankowski*. Also *Mankowski*, IPRax 2015, 309.

[7] *Sanicentral GmbH v. René Collin*, (Case 25/79) [1979] ECR 3423.

[8] *Mosconi*, RDIPP 2003, 5, 23; *Franzen*, RIW 2000, 81, 81; *Junker*, ZZP Int. 3 (1998), 179, 197.

[9] *Palao Moreno*, Derecho internacional y de la integración 2 (2003), 7, 27; *Droz*, RCDIP 79 (1990), 1, 11.

[10] *Mosconi*, RDIPP 2003, 5, 24.

[11] *Winterling*, 136; *Bosse*, 298.

1. First condition

The first of the determinants contemplated in Art. 23 (1) refers to the fact that the express **6** submission to the courts of one particular country that the parties may agree upon must take place after the specific dispute in question has arisen.[12] In that case, the choice made shall prevail over the jurisdictions contemplated in Artt. 20 and 21. In short, it is assumed that just as in an agreement about competence concluded before the dispute, the stronger party will always have the temptation and the possibility to deprive the worker of the benefits concerning jurisdiction offered by Artt. 21 and 22, at this particular stage of the working relationship, after the dispute has arisen, it is very unlikely – and difficult – that the employer should abuse the position of force he has in the contract.

2. Second condition

The concise wording of the rule contemplated in Art. 23 (1) raises the question of absolute **7** invalidity of the agreements about the choice of jurisdiction agreed upon by the employee and the employer before the dispute arose. The second condition contemplated in Art. 23 addresses precisely this matter, specifically in paragraph (2). In this sense, the provision clearly states that express agreements regarding submission to any jurisdiction agreed upon before the dispute arises which permit the employee to bring actions before courts other than those contemplated in Arts. 20–22 shall be valid.[13] The extension of the choice of jurisdictions laid before the employee in itself and without going into whether they are jurisdictions linked to the employee or not is assumed to be to the employee's advantage, justifying the acceptance of a clause of submission agreed upon before the disputes arises. Otherwise, the choice of jurisdiction would be considered invalid because it would not be understood to safeguard the employee's interests.[14]

Even under (2) jurisdiction clauses can only open up *additional* options for the employee[15] **8** and must not derogate from Art. 21. An agreement concluded beforehand must allow the employee to bring proceedings before courts other than those on which Art. 18 confers jurisdiction.[16] The effect of the agreement is not to exclude the jurisdiction vested into courts by virtue of Art. 21, but to extend the employee's possibility of choosing between several courts with jurisdiction,[17] be such jurisdiction *ex lege* or contractually granted. As the agreement may *allow* the employee to bring proceedings in courts other than indicated in Art. 21, (2) cannot be interpreted as meaning that the agreement could apply exclusively and thus prohibit the employee from bringing proceedings before the courts which have jurisdiction pursuant to Art. 21.[18] The objective of protecting the employee as the weaker party would not

---

[12] Cass, RCDIP 88 (1999), 745. A similar approach can be found, in relation to an arbitration agreement in: Cass, Rev. arb. 1999, 292.

[13] *Mankowski*, in: Rauscher, Art. 21 note 3; Cassaz. RDIPP 2013, 745 and in relation to the Lugano Convention, BAG AP H. 8/2012 § 38 ZPO Internationale Zuständigkeit Nr 23 with note *Mankowski*.

[14] *Palao Moreno*, Derecho internacional y de la integración 2 (2003), 7, 28.

[15] *Ahmed Mahamdia v. People's Republic of Algeria* (Case C-154/11), nyr. para. 62; *Junker*, EuZA 2013, 83, 94; *Martiny*, IPRax 2013, 536, 541.

[16] *Ahmed Mahamdia v. People's Republic of Algeria* (Case C-154/11), nyr. para. 62.

[17] *Ahmed Mahamdia v. People's Republic of Algeria* (Case C-154/11), nyr. para. 62.

[18] *Ahmed Mahamdia v. People's Republic of Algeria* (Case C-154/11), nyr. para. 63.

be attained if the jurisdiction provided for in Art. 21 could be ousted by an agreement on jurisdiction concluded before any dispute arose.[19]

9 This possibility has been confirmed by the CJEU in *Mahamdia*, also covering the jurisdiction of third countries, when stating that: "an agreement on jurisdiction concluded before a dispute arises falls within that provision in so far as it gives the employee the possibility of bringing proceedings, not only before the courts ordinarily having jurisdiction under the special rules in Arts. 18 and 19 of that regulation, but also before other courts, which may include courts outside the European Union".[20]

IV. Exercise of freedom of choice in practice of law

10 Article 23 is limited to pointing out on what occasion and under what conditions the principle of freedom of choice can be exercised in relation to the determination of jurisdiction in matters concerning individual employment contracts. The rule, however, makes no mention of the formal requisites that must accompany its exercise in practice. In this sense, and in spite of the provisions of Art. 20 (1) about its inapplicability to individual employment contracts, everything suggests that, in line with the provisions of Art. 23 (1), it must be presented in writing or verbally with written confirmation.[21]

Section 6: Exclusive jurisdiction

Article 24

The following courts of a Member State shall have exclusive jurisdiction, regardless of the domicile of the parties:

(1) in proceedings which have as their object rights *in rem* in immovable property or tenancies of immovable property, the courts of the Member State in which the property is situated.
However, in proceedings which have as their object tenancies of immovable property concluded for temporary private use for a maximum period of six consecutive months, the courts of the Member State in which the defendant is domiciled shall also have jurisdiction, provided that the tenant is a natural person and that the landlord and the tenant are domiciled in the same Member State;

(2) in proceedings which have as their object the validity of the constitution, the nullity or the dissolution of companies or other legal persons or associations of natural or legal persons, or the validity of the decisions of their organs, the courts of the Member State in which the company, legal person or association has its seat. In order to determine that seat, the court shall apply its rules of private international law;

---

[19] *Ahmed Mahamdia v. People's Republic of Algeria* (Case C-154/11), nyr. para. 64.

[20] *Ahmed Mahamdia v. People's Democratic Republic of Algeria* (Case C-154/11), nyr. para. 66; *Junker*, EuZA 2013, 83, 94; *Martiny*, IPRax 2013, 536, 541.

[21] Without taking into consideration the reference to the habits of international trade contemplated in Art. 23 (1) (b) and (c). About this point, see *Mosconi*, RDIPP 2003, 5, 24.

(3) in proceedings which have as their object the validity of entries in public registers, the courts of the Member State in which the register is kept;

(4) in proceedings concerned with the registration or validity of patents, trade marks, designs, or other similar rights required to be deposited or registered, irrespective of whether the issue is raised by way of an action or as a defence, the courts of the Member State in which the deposit or registration has been applied for, has taken place or is under the terms of an instrument of the Union or an international convention deemed to have taken place.

Without prejudice to the jurisdiction of the European Patent Office under the Convention on the Grant of European Patents, signed at Munich on 5 October 1973, the courts of each Member State shall have exclusive jurisdiction in proceedings concerned with the registration or validity of any European patent granted for that Member State;

(5) in proceedings concerned with the enforcement of judgments, the courts of the Member State in which the judgment has been or is to be enforced.

Bibliography

Batiffol/Lagarde, Droit international privé, Vol. II (8th ed 1993)

Calvo Caravaca/Carrascosa González, Derecho Internacional Privado, Vol. I (15th ed. 2014)

Fawcett/Carruthers/North, Cheshire, North& Fawcett Private International Law (14th ed. 2008)

Fawcett/Torremans, Intellectual Property and Private International Law (2nd ed. 2011)

Fernández Arroyo, Exorbitant and Exclusive Grounds of Jurisdiction in European Private International Law: Will They Ever Survive?, in: FS Erik Jayme (2004), Vol. I, p. 169

Galvão Teles, Reconhecimento de sentenças estrangeiras: o controle de competência do tribunal de origem pelo tribunal requerido na Convenção de Bruxelas de 27 de Setembro de 1968, Rev. Fac. Dir. Univ. Lisboa 37 (1996) p. 119

Gaudemet-Tallon, Les frontières extérieures de l'espace judiciaire européen: quelques repères, in: E Pluribus Unum – Liber Amicorum Georges A. L. Droz (1996), p. 85

Hartley, Cyprus Land Rights: Conflict of Laws Meets International Politics, International and Comparative Law Quarterly, 58 (2009) p. 1013

Huet, La marque communautaire: la compétence des juridictions des États membres pour connaître de sa validité et de sa contrefaçon, Clunet 121 (1994) p. 623

Jayme, Das europäische Gerichtsstands- und Vollstreckungsübereinkommen und die Drittländer – das Beispiel Österreich, in: Schwind (ed.), Europarecht, IPR, Rechtsvergleichung (Wien 1988), p. 97

Kohler, Kollisionsrechtliche Anmerkungen zur Verordnung über die Gemeinschaftsmarke, in: FS Ulrich Everling (1995) p. 651

Kropholler, Internationales Privatrecht (6th ed. 2006)

Lehmann, Exclusive Jurisdiction under Art. 22(2) of the Brussels I Regulation: the ECJ Decision *Berliner Verkehrsbetriebe v. Jpmorgan Chase Bank* (C-144/10), Yearbook of Private International Law 13 (2011) 507

Lima Pinheiro, Direito Internacional Privado, Vol. II, Direito de Conflitos. Parte Especial (3rd ed. 2009)

Lima Pinheiro, Direito Internacional Privado, Vol. III, Competência Internacional e Reconhecimento de Decisões Estrangeiras (2nd ed. 2012)

Lima Pinheiro, O Direito de Conflitos e as liberdades comunitárias de estabelecimento e de prestação de serviços, in: Lima Pinheiro (ed.), Seminário Internacional sobre a Comunitarização do Direito Internacional Privado (2005), p. 79

Mayer/Heuzé, Droit international privé (11th ed. 2014)

Mota de Campos, Um instrumento jurídico de integração europeia. A Convenção de Bruxelas de 27 de Setembro de 1968 sobre Competência Judiciária, Reconhecimento e Execução das Sentenças, Doc. Dir. Comp. 22 (1985) p. 73

Moura Vicente, A Tutela Internacional da Propriedade Intelectual (2008)

Teixeira de Sousa, Der Anwendungsbereich von Art. 22 Nr. 1 S. 2 EuGVVO, IPRax (2003)p. 320
Teixeira de Sousa, Direito Processual Civil Europeu (photocopied Report 2003), p. 88–90
Teixeira de Sousa, A competência internacional executiva dos tribunais portugueses: alguns equívocos, Cadernos de Direito Privado (2004) no. 5, p. 49
Torremans, The Widening Reach of Exclusive Jurisdiction: Where Can You Litigate IP Rights after GAT, in: Arnaud Nuyts (ed.), International Litigation in Intellectual Property and Information Technology (2008) p. 61

Torremans, Exclusive Jurisdiction, in: European Max Planck Group on Conflict of Laws in Intellectual Property (CLIP), Conflict of Laws in Intellectual Property. The CLIP Principles and Commentary (2013), p. 138–153
Ubertazzi, Exclusive Jurisdiction in Intellectual Property (2012)
Wilderspin, La compétence juridictionnelle en matière de litiges concernant la violation des droit de propriété intellectuelle – Les arrêts de la Cour de justice dans les affaires C-04/03, GAT c. LUK et C-539/03, Roche Nederland c. Primus et Goldberg, R. crit.95 (2006) p. 777.

I. General purpose

1   The provisions on exclusive jurisdiction are contained in the Section 6 of the Chapter II of the Regulation, which comprises just one Article (24).

2   This Article refers always to "courts of a Member State" or "courts of the Member State"; this wording makes it clear that the Article regulates only the international jurisdiction. Territorial jurisdiction is regulated by the domestic law of Member States. If the domestic law of the State with exclusive jurisdiction does not provide for the territorial jurisdiction of a local court, there is a gap in the jurisdiction system; this gap shall be filled according to the criteria in force in the respective legal order. In general these criteria will lead to the same outcomes that would result from the application of the rules on international jurisdiction contained in Art. 24 to the determination of territorial jurisdiction.[1]

3   The exclusive jurisdiction of the courts of a Member State displaces the general rule of the defendant's domicile and the special rules on legal jurisdiction. The exclusive jurisdiction may also not be overridden by an agreement on jurisdiction neither by the defendant's voluntary submission to the forum (Arts. 25 (4) and 26 (1)). The court of a Member State, seized of a claim which is principally concerned with a matter over which the courts of another Member State have exclusive jurisdiction, shall declare of its own motion that it has

---

[1]   See also *Kropholler/von Hein* Art. 22 note 1; *Schlosser* Vorbem. Art. 22 note 2; and *Peter Gottwald*, in: Münchener Kommentar zur ZPO Art. 16 EuGVÜ note 2; *Peter Gottwald*, in: Münchener Kommentar zur ZPO Art. 22 note 3. Compare *Geimer/Schütze* Art. 22 note 22, in favour of a uniform rule providing for territorial jurisdiction of the court seating in the capital of the State whose courts the Art. 22 (of the Brussels I Regulation) allocates international jurisdiction. See further the criticism of *Mankowski*, in: Rauscher Art. 22 note 3.

no jurisdiction (Art. 27). Otherwise there is a defence to recognition or enforcement, in the other Member States, of the judgment given (Arts. 45 (1) (e) (ii) and 46).

Although not often, an action may come within the exclusive jurisdiction of several courts. **4** In this case, any court other than the court first seized shall decline jurisdiction in favour of that court (Art. 31 (1)).

The heads of exclusive jurisdiction contained in Art. 24 are directly applicable whenever the **5** respective connecting factor points to a Member State bound by the Regulation and the dispute arises from a transnational relationship. The exclusive jurisdiction of a Member State's courts applies regardless of defendant being domiciled in the territory of a Member State (cf. Art. 24 main sentence) and regardless of any connection with another Member State.[2]

This is related with the general reason for the exclusive legal jurisdiction stated by the ECJ: **6** "the existence of a particularly close connection between the dispute and a Contracting State, irrespective of the domicile both of the defendant and of the plaintiff".[3]

Nonetheless, strictly speaking it seems that the reason for these exclusive jurisdictions is not **7** only the intensity of the connection but also the matters that are involved. In these matters mandatory rules are in force in the whole of the Member States, the application of which shall be assured whenever there is a given connection with their State of origin. As a matter of fact, the criteria of exclusive jurisdiction tend to coincide with the connecting factors relevant for the application of these mandatory rules.[4]

II. Legislative history

Art. 24 has statutory precedents in the Art. 16 of Brussels Convention and in the Art. 22 of **8** Brussels I Regulation.

Art. 22 of Brussels I Regulation is based almost entirely in the Art. 16 of Brussels Convention. The substantial differences, of short reach, concern only two situations:
– in the § 2 of heading (1) (added to the Brussels Convention by the Accession Convention of Portugal and Spain), on the subject of tenancies of immovables, with respect to the prerequisites to the jurisdiction of the courts of the Member State where the defendant is domiciled;
– in the heading (4), on the subject of registration or of validity of intellectual property rights, with respect to rights governed by a Community act or by the Convention on European patent.

These differences will be scrutinised when dealing with those issues.

---

[2] Cf. *Gothot/Holleaux* p. 21; *Geimer/Schütze* Art. 22 notes 7–11; *Kropholler/von Hein* Art. 22 note 6; and *Mankowski*, in: Rauscher Art. 22 note 2a.

[3] Cf. *Group Josi Reinsurance Company SA v. Universal General Insurance Company (UGIC)*, (Case C-412/ 98) [2000] ECR I-5925, I-5954 para. 46.

[4] See also *Gaudemet-Tallon* para. 98; *Lima Pinheiro* p. 166; *Calvo Caravaca/Carrascosa González* p. 212; and *Mankowski*, in: Rauscher Art. 22 note 2.

In relation to Art. 22 of Brussels I Regulation, the only substantial difference is the insertion of the sentence "irrespective of whether the issue is raised by way of an action or as a defence", in the heading (4), regarding the validity of intellectual property rights, which is aimed at aligning the wording with the interpretation of Art. 16 of the Brussels Convention adopted by the ECJ.

III. Exclusive jurisdiction of third States

9 Where the connecting factor employed by the rule of exclusive legal jurisdiction points to a third State (i.e., a State that is not a Member State), and the defendant is not domiciled in a Member State, the jurisdiction is governed by the domestic law (Art. 6 (1)). Where the defendant is domiciled in a Member State the opinions, regarding Brussels I Regulation, are divided: the Reporters,[5] followed by part of the authors,[6] deem applicable the other rules of the Regulation (or of the Brussels and Lugano Conventions as the case may be), namely Art. 2 (Art. 4 of Brussels I*bis* Regulation); some authors hold that according to the spirit of the Regulation in these matters only the connecting factors contained in Art. 22 (Art. 24 of Brussels I*bis* Regulation) are suitable, and therefore the Member States' courts may decline jurisdiction.[7]

10 This second doctrine deserves preference when the third State's courts claim exclusive jurisdiction,[8] for two reasons:[9] On the one hand, this doctrine is coherent with the evaluation underlying Art. 24. That is, if the Member States claim a given exclusive jurisdiction sphere they shall also recognise the same sphere of exclusive jurisdiction to third States. On the other hand, this doctrine contributes to a harmonious allocation of jurisdiction. The opposite doctrine leads the courts of a Member State to claim jurisdiction at the same time that the courts of a third State reasonably claim exclusive jurisdiction.

---

5   Cf. Report *Jenard/Möller* para. 54; Report *Almeida Cruz/Desantes Real/Jenard* para. 25; and Report *Pocar* para. 93.

6   See namely *Mota de Campos*, Doc. Dir. Comp. 22 (1985) 73, p. 121; *Teixeira de Sousa/Moura Vicente* p. 113–114 (but compare p. 35); *Teixeira de Sousa*, IPRax (2003) 320, p. 322–323; *Geimer/Schütze* Art. 22 note 13; and *Mankowski*, in: Rauscher Art. 22 notes 2b-2e. See also ECJ Opinion 1/03 [2006] ECR I-1145.

7   Cf., namely, *Droz* p. 14–15 and *Gothot/Holleaux* p. 84, but only when the domestic law of the forum authorises it; *Gaudemet-Tallon* para. 100; *Gaudemet-Tallon*, in: E Pluribus Unum – Liber Amicorum Georges A. L. Droz (1996), p. 85, 95 *et seq.*; *Kropholler/von Hein* Art. 22 note 7; *Peter Gottwald*, in: Münchener Kommentar zur ZPO Art. 16 EuGVÜ note 6; *Schack* para. 359, with the additional prerequisite that the State of the defendant's domicile also recognises this exclusive jurisdiction; *Fernández Arroyo*, in: FS Erik Jayme (2004), p. 169, 178, 186; and *Layton/Mercer* para. 19.010.

8   Cf. *Jayme*, in: Schwind (ed.), Europarecht, IPR, Rechtsvergleichung (1988), p. 97, 110 *et seq. Calvo Caravaca/Carrascosa González* p. 216–217, show preference for a mixed doctrine asserting that the international jurisdiction of Member States's courts based upon other provisions of the Regulation only should be displaced where the judgment can only be enforced in the third State; however, since Article 24 provides for exclusive jurisdiction of Member States's courts independently from the possible need of enforcement in a third State, it also makes sense to honour the exclusive jurisdiction of a third State even if the judgment could be enforced in a Member State.

9   In favour of a general principle of relevance of foreign courts's exclusive jurisdiction based upon criteria accepted by the forum see *Lima Pinheiro* § 88 E.

The Regulation requires a Member State's court to declare it has no jurisdiction where the   **11**
court of another Member State has exclusive jurisdiction (Art. 27), but it does not preclude a
Member State's court of declaring it has no jurisdiction in other situations where this is in
accordance with the spirit of the Regulation.

Certainly the Regulation does not mandate either the Member State's court to declare it has   **12**
no jurisdiction where the connecting factor employed by one of the headings of Art. 24
points to a third State whose courts claim exclusive jurisdiction. Therefore, in these circumstances, if the court of a Member State declares it has jurisdiction, this does not amount to a
defence of recognition or enforcement of the judgment given by this court in other Member
States.[10]

IV. Interpretation

From the wording of Art. 24, as well as from its *ratio*, it is unequivocal that the list of matters   **13**
therein contained is exhaustive.[11] The Regulation does not allow the enlargement of exclusive jurisdiction's matters by way of analogy or based upon any other technique.

The concepts used in the headings of Art. 24 shall be subject to autonomous interpretation.[12]   **14**
The ECJ has been stressing that the headings of Art. 16 of Brussels Convention and of Art. 22
of Brussels I Regulation – which as aforementioned are the statutory precedents of Art. 24 of
the Regulation – must not be given a wider interpretation than is required by their objective,
since the allocation of exclusive jurisdiction results in deprivation of the freedom to choose
the forum and, in certain cases, in the submission of the parties to a jurisdiction which is not
that of the domicile of any of them.[13]

As a rule, Art. 24 applies only where the claim is principally concerned with one of the   **15**
matters listed (and not where the claim raises only one of these matters as a preliminary
question – cf. Art. 27).[14] Nevertheless, the ECJ has accepted a deviation from this rule
regarding the issue of validity of intellectual property rights and this understanding has
been incorporated in the wording of heading (4) (see *infra* note 67).

---

[10] See also *Galvão Teles*, Rev. Fac. Dir. Univ. Lisboa 37 (1996) 119, p. 152–153.
[11] Cf. *Kropholler/von Hein* Art. 22 note 1; *Gaudemet-Tallon* para. 98; *CalvoCaravaca/Carrascosa González*
        p. 212.
[12] Compare Report *Schlosser* para. 168, who seems to prefer a characterisation *lege causae* regarding the
        concept of right *in rem* in immovable property, i.e., a characterisation based upon the law of the situs. The
        ECJ, however, opted for an autonomous interpretation of this concept, cf. *Mario P. A. Reichert, Hans-*
        Heinz Reichert and Ingeborg Kockler v. Dresdner Bank, (Case 115/88) [1990] ECR I-27, I-41 para. 8.
[13] Cf. *Theodorus Engelbertus Sanders v. Ronald van der Putte* (Case 73/77), [1977] ECR 2383, 2390 *et seq.*
        paras. 17/18, restated by several decisions referred in *Dansommer A/S v. Andreas Götz*, (Case C-8/98),
        [2000] ECR I-393, I-411 para. 21. Cf. further *Berliner Verkehrsbetriebe v. JPMorgan Chase Bank NA*,
        (Case C-144/10) [2011] ECR I-03961, para. 30.
[14] Cf. Report *Jenard* p. 152.

In principle, the exclusive jurisdiction as to the substance of the matter under Art. 24 does not exclude the ordering of provisional measures by the court of another Member State under Art. 35.[15]

V. Rights in immovable property

16 In proceedings which have as their object rights in rem in immovable property or tenancies of immovable property, the courts of the Member State in which the property is situated have exclusive jurisdiction ((1) § 1).

This exclusive jurisdiction applies even regarding land situated in an area of a Member State over which its Government does not exercise effective control.[16]

However, in proceedings that have as their object tenancies of immovable property concluded for temporary private use for a maximum period of six consecutive months, the courts of the Member State in which the defendant is domiciled shall also have jurisdiction, provided that the tenant is a natural person and that the landlord and the tenant are domiciled in the same Member State ((1) § 2).

17 This exclusive jurisdiction is also provided for in the Brussels and Lugano (1988) Conventions (Art. 16 (1)), although there is a divergence between these Conventions regarding the prerequisites of the jurisdiction of the defendant's domicile courts. The Brussels Convention requires that both the landlord and the tenant are natural persons and are domiciled in the same Contracting State. Under the 1988 Lugano Convention it is sufficient that the tenant is a natural person and that none of the parties is domiciled in the Contracting State where the immovable is situated.

18 The Brussels I and *Ibis* Regulations have followed to some extent an intermediate path: it is sufficient that the tenant is a natural person, but it is required that both parties have domicile in the same Member State. The landlord can be either a natural person or a legal person.[17] The same solution has been adopted by the 2007 Lugano Convention (Art. 22 (1)). This seems to be, in the light of the provision's *ratio*, the best solution.[18] As a matter of fact, the possibility of entering a suit in the forum of the common domicile of the landlord and of the tenant is justified even if the landlord is, as frequently happens, a legal person.[19]

19 It is further required that the tenancy is concluded for temporary private use for a maximum period of six consecutive months. The concept of "private use" shall be understood in the same light as the concept of consumer contract resulting from Art. 17(1). Therefore, the

---

[15]   Cf. *Solvay SA v. Honeywell Fluorine Products Europe BV and Others* (Case C-616/10) [2012] in curia. europa.eu para. 40.

[16]   Cf. *Meletis Apostolides v. David Charles Orams and Linda Elizabeth Orams* (Case C-420/07) [2009] ECR I-03571, paras. 51–52. Compare the critical remarks of *Hartley*, Cyprus Land Rights: Conflict of Laws Meets International Politics, International and Comparative Law Quarterly, 58 (2009) p. 1013, ps. 1017 *et seq.*

[17]   Cf. Explanatory Memorandum of the Commission's Proposal (COM [1999] 348 final) p. 18.

[18]   Compare *Mankowski*, in: Rauscher, Art. 22 note 25.

[19]   See also *Gaudemet-Tallon* para. 107–108.

tenancy shall not be deemed for private use where it is concluded for the exercise of an independent economic activity.[20]

These prerequisites fulfilled, the claimant may choose between suing in the courts of the   **20**
Member State where the immovable is situated or in the courts of the Member State where the defendant is domiciled. According to the *Jenard/Möller* Report (concerning the 1988 Lugano Convention) we are in presence of "two exclusive jurisdictions", which may be considered "alternative exclusive jurisdictions".[21]

This deviation from the exclusive jurisdiction of the *forum rei sitae* is normally sufficient to   **21**
avoid that two persons domiciled in the same Member State, who are parties in a short term tenancy of an immovable situated in another Member State, are forced to discuss the disputes arising therefrom in the courts of this Member State, which will be, as a rule, an inconvenient forum for both parties. This situation arises often with respect to leasing of holiday accommodations.

The Proposal for the Brussels I*bis* Regulation added that this deviation applies when the landlord and the tenant are domiciled in the same Member State "either at the moment of conclusion of the agreement or at the moment of the institution of proceedings". Since this addition has not been adopted, it seems that the time relevant for the determination of the common domicile should be in line with the time relevant for the determination of the domicile of the defendant under Art. 4 (1). Therefore, it should be sufficient the common domicile either at the moment of the institution of the proceedings or at the moment of the judgment.[22]

An additional deviation, regarding agreements concerning tenancies of premises for professional use, has also not been adopted.

The autonomous concept of right *in rem* is characterised by the "power of its holder to claim   **22**
the property that is subject to this right against any person who does not hold a prevailing right in rem".[23]

In examining the delimitation of the actions comprised by the exclusive jurisdiction, the ECJ   **23**
has stressed the ground for this jurisdiction: "the essential reason for conferring exclusive jurisdiction on the courts of the Contracting State in which the property is situated is that the courts of the locus rei sitae are the best placed, for reasons of proximity, to ascertain the facts satisfactorily and to apply the rules and practices which are generally those of the State in which the property is situated".[24]

---

[20]   See also *Mankowski*, in: Rauscher Art. 22 note 26.
[21]   Report *Jenard/Möller* para. 52. See also *Fawcett/Carruthers/North*, Cheshire, North & Fawcett Private International Law (14th ed. 2008) p. 281, and *Kropholler/von Hein* Art. 22 note 32.
[22]   Cf., regarding Art. 2 (1) of Brussels I Regulation, *Kropholler/von Hein* Art. 2 notes 12 *et seq.*, and *Lima Pinheiro* p. 103.
[23]   Cf. Report *Schlosser* para. 166.
[24]   Cf. *Mario P. A. Reichert, Hans-Heinz Reichert and Ingeborg Kockler v. Dresdner Bank*, (Case 115/88) [1990] ECR I-27, I-41 para. 10.

24 It shall be added that the rights on immovables are generally governed by the *lex situs* and that most of the applicable rules has mandatory character and a close link with the economic Constitution, so that the exclusive jurisdiction of the *forum rei sitae* assures the application of these mandatory rules.[25]

25 It has been discussed if the concept of immovable property shall be defined autonomously or according to the law of the *situs*.[26] In favour of the last interpretation it has been argued that the provision takes into account the connection between the jurisdiction of the *forum rei sitae* and the applicability of the *lex situs*. Actually, we have just pointed out that the applicability of the *lex situs* in this matter is one of the reasons that justify the exclusive jurisdiction. Nevertheless, the argument derived therefrom to the definition of the immovable property's concept is inconclusive, since the *lex situs* rule is generally applicable irrespective of the movable or immovable nature of the property.

26 The exclusive jurisdiction comprises only an action based upon a right *in rem* and not an action having as object a right *in personam* or both a right *in rem* and a right *in personam*.[27] Thus, it excludes an action for rescission and/or damages for the loss resulting from the breach of a contract for the sale of immovable property;[28] an action based on tort for breach of right in immovable property;[29] an action to enforce the obligations of the seller regarding the transfer of title, in those systems in which this transfer is not an automatic effect of the contract for sale;[30] an action for restitution of property raised by a party where the other party to the contract is not performing his obligations under the contract for sale of the property;[31] an action for annulment of the contract for sale;[32] an action for a declaration that the son holds an apartment on trust for the father and for an order requiring him to execute documents vesting legal title in the father;[33] an action where a creditor seeks to set aside a gift of the legal ownership of immovable property alleged made by the debtor to defraud his creditors *(action paulienne)*;[34] and an action for compensation for the use of a flat following the annulment of the respective transfer of title.[35] Albeit the point being debatable, the ECJ

---

[25] See also *Dicey/Morris/Collins* para. 11–377, and *Gaudemet-Tallon* para.101. Compare the critical comments of *Geimer/Schütze* Art. 22 note 38 *et seq.*, and of *Fernández Arroyo*, in: FS Erik Jayme (2004), Vol. I, p. 169, 177–178.

[26] For the first understanding see *Mario P. A. Reichert, Hans-Heinz Reichert and Ingeborg Kockler v. Dresdner Bank*, (Case 115/88) [1990] ECR I-27, I-41, para. 8, and *Land Oberösterreich v. ČEZ, as*, (Case C-343/04) [2006] ECRI-04557, para. 25, as well as *Peter Gottwald* in: Münchener Kommentar zur ZPO Art. 16 EuGVÜ note 8, and *Geimer/Schütze* Art. 22 note 42; in favour of the second understanding see *Kropholler/von Hein* Art. 22 note 11; and *Peter Schlosser* Art. 22 note 2, who speaks in this context of a "characterization according to the lex situs"; *Mankowski*, in: Rauscher Art. 22 note 5.

[27] Cf. Report *Schlosser* paras. 171–172, *Kropholler/von Hein* Art. 22 note 21, and *Gaudemet-Tallon* para. 101. Compare *Geimer/Schütze* Art. 22 notes 55 *et seq.*, and Mankowski, in: Rauscher, Art. 22 note 8.

[28] Cf. *Richard Gaillard v. Alaya Chekili*, (Case C-518/99) [2001] ECR I-2771, I-2781 paras. 18 *et seq.*

[29] Cf. Report *Schlosser* para. 163.

[30] Cf. Report *Schlosser* para. 170.

[31] Cf. Report *Schlosser* para. 171, and *Richard Gaillard v. Alaya Chekili*, (Case C-518/99) [2001] ECR I-2771, I-2782 para. 21.

[32] Cf. *Gothot/Holleaux* p. 84–85, and *Gaudemet-Tallon* para. 101.

[33] Cf. *George Lawrence Webb v. Lawrence Desmond Webb*, (Case C-294/92) [1994] ECR I-1717, I-1738 para. 15.

has also deemed excluded an action which seeks to prevent a nuisance affecting or likely to affect land belonging to the applicant, caused by ionising radiation emanating from a nuclear power station situated on the territory of a neighbouring State.[36]

The exclusive jurisdiction does not extend to the whole of the actions concerning rights in **27** immovable property, but just to those that, simultaneously, fall within the scope of application of the Regulation and which seek to determine the extent, content, ownership or possession of immovable property or the existence of other rights *in rem* therein and to provide the holders of those rights with protection for the powers which attach to their interest.[37]

This includes an action seeking a declaration of invalidity of the exercise of a right of pre-emption attaching to that property and which produces effects *erga omnes*.[38] On the contrary, non-contentious proceedings by which a person who has been declared to be lacking full legal capacity and placed under guardianship applies to for authorisation to sell his share of a property are excluded, in view of the fact that such matter falls outside the material scope of the Regulation (Art. 1(2)(a)).[39]

The extension of this exclusive jurisdiction to tenancies is justified by two reasons: the close **28** link that often occurs between the rules applicable to tenancies and the rules on immovable property and the fact that, in general, some of the rules applicable to tenancies are mandatory and designed to protect the tenant.[40]

By "tenancies of immovable property" it is understood any type of tenancy: residential **29** tenancy, tenancy for independent professional activities, commercial tenancy and land tenancy;[41] including short term lets, namely of holiday accommodations.[42] In this last case, the circumstance of a contract for the use of a holiday accommodation being concluded between a professional tour operator (who acts as "intermediary" between the landlord and the tenant) and a client, which contains ancillary clauses relating to insurance in the event of cancellation and to guarantee of repayment of the price paid by the client, do not affect the nature of the tenancy as a tenancy of immovable property.[43]

---

[34] Cf. *Mario P. A. Reichert, Hans-Heinz Reichert and Ingeborg Kockler v. Dresdner Bank*, (Case 115/88) [1990] ECR I-27, I-42 para. 12.

[35] Cf. *Norbert Lieber v. Willi S. Göbel and Siegrid Göbel*, (Case C-292/93) [1994] ECR I-2535, I-2550 paras. 13 *et seq.*

[36] Cf. *Land Oberösterreich v. ČEZ, as*, (Case C-343/04) [2006] ECRI-04557. See *Mankowski*, in: Rauscher, Art. 22 notes 12b-12c. Compare Opinion of A-G *Poiares Maduro*.

[37] Cf. *Mario P. A. Reichert, Hans-Heinz Reichert and Ingeborg Kockler v. Dresdner Bank*, (Case 115/88) [1990] ECR I-27, I-41et seq. para. 11; *Siegfried János Schneider* (Case C-386/12) [2013] nyr. para. 21, and *Irmengard Weber v. Metchthilde Weber* (Case C-438/12) [2014] nyr. para. 42.

[38] Cf. *Irmengard Weber v. Metchthilde Weber* (Case C-438/12) [2014] nyr. paras. 44 and 47.

[39] Cf. *Siegfried János Schneider* (Case C-386/12) [2013] nyr. paras. 22 and 31.

[40] See also Report *Jenard* p. 153; *Gaudemet-Tallon* para. 103; *Fawcett/Carruthers/North* (fn. 21) p. 280; and *Peter Schlosser* Art. 22 note 1. Compare *Geimer/Schütze* Art. 22 notes 105 *et seq.*

[41] Cf. Report *Jenard* p. 153.

[42] Cf. *Erich Rösler v. Horst Rottwinkel*, (Case 241/83) [1985] ECR 99, 127 paras. 23 *et seq.*

[43] Cf. *Dansommer A/S v. Andreas Götz*, (Case C-8/98), [2000] ECR I-393, I-415 *et seq.* para. 38. Compare the critical annotation of *Huet*, Clunet 127 (2000) 551, 553.

Luís de Lima Pinheiro

30   The principal aim of the contract shall be the use of an immovable. Contracts that have other principal aim are excluded.[44] Thus, an agreement to rent a retail business is not deemed to be a "tenancy of immovable property".[45] The same applies to a contract in which the provision of services is the prevailing element, such as an agreement concluded by a travel organiser who, besides undertaking to procure for the customer the use of short-term holiday accommodation, of which he is not the owner, undertakes also to provide a set of services – such as information and advice, where the travel organiser proposes a range of holiday offers, the reservation of accommodation during the period chosen by the customer, the reservation of seats in connection with travel arrangements, the reception at the destination and, possibly, travel cancellation insurance – for an inclusive price.[46] In this case, the agreement will normally be a consumer contract within paragraph (c) of Art. 17 (1) and, occasionally, within the second sentence of Art. 17 (3) of the Regulation.

31   Regarding the nature of the dispute, this heading comprises not only the disputes concerning the existence or the interpretation of the contract, the compensation for damage caused by the tenant and the giving up possession of the premises,[47] but also the generality of the disputes concerning the obligations under the contract, including, therefore, those relating to the payment of the rent.[48] Excluded are, by way of contrast, the disputes that only indirectly concern the use of the property, such as a claim by a landlord for damages for the lost enjoyment of a holiday in the property let and for the travel expenses.[49]

32   The application of this head of jurisdiction to contracts for use of immovable property on a timeshare basis (often called "timesharing contracts") has been causing some difficulties in the Member States courts. These difficulties are to a large extent due to the differences between the laws of the Member States regarding the characterisation of the right of use conferred by these contracts. Such differences have been acknowledge by Recital (3) of the 1994 Timesharing Directive,[50] which only aimed at establishing a minimum basis of common rules on time-share arrangements so as to ensure "proper operation of the internal market" and to protect purchasers.[51] This directive was repealed by the 2008 Timesharing Directive,[52] which goes forward in the harmonization, but it is focused on the marketing, sale

---

[44]   Cf. *Theodorus Engelbertus Sanders v. Ronald van der Putte*, (Case 73/77) [1977] ECR 2383, 2390 para. 16, and *Mankowski*, in: Rauscher, Art. 22 note 15.

[45]   Cf. *Theodorus Engelbertus Sanders v. Ronald van der Putte*, (Case 73/77) [1977] ECR 2383, 2391 para. 19.

[46]   Cf. *Elisabeth Hacker v. Euro-Relais GmbH*, (Case 280/90) [1992] ECR I-1111, I-1132 paras. 14 *et seq.* See further *Mankowski*, in: Rauscher Art. 22 notes 22–23.

[47]   Cf. Report *Jenard* p. 153, followed by the ECJ in *Theodorus Engelbertus Sanders v. Ronald van der Putte*, (Case 73/77) [1977] ECR 2383, 2390 paras. 12/15.

[48]   Cf. *Erich Rösler v. Horst Rottwinkel*, (Case 241/83) [1985] ECR 99, 127 *et seq.* paras. 28–29; *Schlosser* Art. 22 notes 7 and 12; *Gaudemet-Tallon* para. 103; and *Mankowski*, in: Rauscher, Art. 22 note 20. Compare, for the contrary view, Report *Jenard* p. 153 and *Geimer/Schütze* Art. 22 note 120. See further Report *Schlosser* para. 164.

[49]   Cf. *Erich Rösler v. Horst Rottwinkel*, (Case 241/83) [1985] ECR 99, 127 *et seq.* para. 28.

[50]   Directive 94/47/EC of the European Parliament and the Council of 26 October 1994 on the protection of purchasers in respect of certain aspects of contracts relating to the purchase of the right to use immovable properties on a timeshare basis, OJ 1994 L 280/83.

[51]   Recitals (2) and (9) Timesharing Directive.

[52]   Directive 2008/122/EC of the European Parliament and of the Council of 14 January 2009 on the

and resale of timeshares and long-term holiday products, as well as on the exchange of rights deriving from timeshare contracts, and does not prejudice the national legislation regarding the determination of the "legal nature" of the rights which are the subject of the contracts (Art. 1 (2) § 2 (d)). Another difficulty results from the difference between "traditional" tenancies and timesharing contracts with respect to the means of payment.[53]

In general terms, it may be said that each timesharing contract has to be characterised in the   **33** light of its effects under the law or laws which are applicable by operation of the conflict rules of Member States.

Proceedings concerning rights *in rem* conferred by timesharing contracts are undoubtfully subject to Art. 24 (1) of the Regulation.[54]

It is controversial whether, regarding other issues, these contracts shall, in principle, be subject to the exclusive jurisdiction of Art. 24 (1) or to the jurisdiction over consumer contracts.[55] In favour of this later understanding can be invoked the Explanatory Memorandum of the Commission's Proposal (Brussels I Regulation),[56] as well as the parallel with Rome I Regulation that, for the determination of the applicable law, subjects timesharing contracts to the regime of consumer contracts (Art. 6 (4) (c)). To the contrary view, however, points the purpose of Art. 24 (1) (proximity with the State of facts, connection with the general regime of property and the frequent applicability of mandatory rules aimed, in first line, to protect the rights of timesharing holders over immovable property located in the territory of the enacting State), as well as the Timesharing Directives of 1994 and 2008 which, concerning the scope of applicability of the rules protecting the right holder, are mainly based upon the situation of the immovable property in the territory of a Member State (Art. 9 of the 1994 Directive and Art. 12 (2) of the 2008 Directive). The clarification of this issue by the ECJ would be welcome.

The mere fact that the contract provides for a service of exchange of holiday accommodations does not justify another characterisation.[57] A different situation may arise where the contract provides for the affiliation in a "holiday club" that, albeit giving a right of use, does not refer to a specific immovable. In this case it is sustained that the jurisdiction cannot be based upon the location of the immovable.[58] This understanding seems acceptable where the "holiday club" allows a right of use of immovables located in different countries.[59]

---

protection of consumers in respect of certain aspects of timeshare, long-term holiday product, resale and exchange contracts, OJ 2009 L 33/10.

53   Recital (5) 1994 Timesharing Directive.

54   Cf. *Mankowski*, in: Rauscher Art. 22 note 7, and *Kropholler/von Hein* Art. 22 note 17.

55   For the first view, regarding obligational timesharing, *Mankowski*, in: Rauscher Art. 22 notes 17–17a and 18–18a, and *Kropholler/von Hein* Art. 22 note 17; for the second view, *Gaudemet-Tallon* para. 103 and Report *Pocar* para. 81.

56   P. 16.

57   Cf. *Mankowski*, in: Rauscher Art. 22 note 17b. Compare *Brigitte and Marcus Klein v. Rhodos Management Ltd.*, (Case C-73/04) [2005] ECR I-8667, para. 25.

58   See *Mankowski*, in: Rauscher Art. 22 note 17b, and *Brigitte and Marcus Klein v. Rhodos Management Ltd.*, (Case C-73/04) [2005] ECR I-8667, paras. 24–26.

59   The same can be sustained regarding contracts that estipulate provision of services exceeding the value of

The same approach has been suggested with respect to timesharing relationships that, although formally shaped as being of "corporate" or "association" nature, are substantially equivalent to contractual relationships for use of property.[60] Nonetheless, the ECJ held in the *Klein* case that Article 16 (1) (a) of the Brussels Convention does not apply to a "club membership contract" which, in return for a membership fee which represents the major part of the total price, allows members to acquire a right to use on a time-share basis immoveable property of a specified type in a specified location and provides for the affiliation of members to a service which enables them to exchange their right of use.[61]

Disputes concerning the obligations under timesharing contracts shall be embraced by this exclusive jurisdiction, even if they confer a right *in rem* to the purchaser. As a matter of fact, it makes little sense that those disputes fall within the scope of the exclusive jurisdiction when arising from mere contractual tenancies, but not when resulting from contracts for use of immovable property that also confer a right *in rem*.[62]

34 In the case of immovable property being situated in two Contracting States, exclusive jurisdiction over the immovable property situated in each contracting State is, in principle, held by the courts of that State.[63] Nevertheless, if the immovable property situated in one Contracting State is adjacent to the property in another State and the property is situated almost entirely in one of those States, it might be appropriate to regard the property as a single unit and deem it to be entirely situated in one of those States for the purposes of conferring on the courts of that State exclusive jurisdiction.[64]

35 It is understood that these principles, enunciated by the ECJ with respect to tenancies of immovable property, are also applicable to rights *in rem* in such property.[65]

VI. Companies and other legal persons

36 In proceedings which have as their object the validity of the constitution, the nullity or the dissolution of companies or other legal persons or associations of natural or legal persons, or of the validity of the decisions of their organs, have exclusive jurisdiction the courts of the

---

the right of use of the immovable property – see *Brigitte and Marcus Klein v. Rhodos Management Ltd.*, (Case C-73/04) [2005] ECR I-8667, paras. 21–22.

[60] See also *Mankowski*, in: Rauscher Art. 22 notes 18c-18d. Compare *Kropholler/von Hein* Art. 22 note 17, *Peter Schlosser* Art. 22 note 10, and *Geimer/Schütze* Art. 22 note 112.

[61] *Brigitte and Marcus Klein v. Rhodos Management Ltd.*, (Case C-73/04) [2005] ECR I-8667. Compare the Opinion of the A-G *Leendert Geelhoed* in the same Case, paras. 27–31.

[62] On the contrary, it shall be excluded a dispute concerning the right to reimbursement of a sum erroneously paid in excess of the amount demanded in consideration for use of an apartment, which is not based on a right or obligation arising under the time-share agreement but on unjust enrichment – see aforementioned Opinion of A-G *Leendert Geelhoed* in *Brigitte and Marcus Klein v. Rhodos Management Ltd*, (Case C-73/04) para. 39.

[63] Cf. *R. O. E. Scherrens v. M. G. Maenhout, R. A. M. van Poucke and L. M. L. van Poucke*, (Case 158/87) [1988] ECR 3791, 3805 para. 13.

[64] *R. O. E. Scherrens v. M. G. Maenhout, R. A. M. van Poucke and L. M. L. van Poucke*, (Case 158/87) [1988] ECR 3791, 3805 para. 14. See further *Mankowski*, in: Rauscher Art. 22 note 14.

[65] Cf. *Gaudemet-Tallon* para. 104.

Member State in which the company, legal person or association has its seat ((2) first sentence).

In order to determine that seat, the court shall apply its rules of Private International Law **37** ((2) second sentence). The reason why the autonomous concept of domicile, defined in Art. 63, does not operate here lies in the need of assigning exclusive jurisdiction to the courts of just one State.[66]

Concerning the ground for this exclusive jurisdiction, *Jenard* states three reasons.[67] First, in **38** the interest of legal certainty one shall avoid contradictory judgments regarding the existence of legal persons and the validity of decisions of their organs. Second, it is in the seat State that the formalities of publicity of the legal person are accomplished, reason that justifies the centralisation of the proceedings in the courts of this State. Third, this rule will often lead to allocate jurisdiction to the court of the defendant's domicile.

To these reasons two more shall be added.[68]

On the one hand, this head of jurisdiction will often lead to a concurrence between forum **39** and applicable law, since the law applicable to internal affairs *(statut personnel)* of the legal person is, in most cases, the law in force at the seat's location.[69] This is true even for systems that adopt the incorporation's theory, because normally the legal person has the formal seat (seat stipulated in the Articles of Association and registered) in the country where it was incorporated.

In view of this consideration, and lacking interpretative elements that point in a different **40** direction, the second sentence of Art. 22 (2) shall be interpreted in a way that the seat relevant to the allocation of jurisdiction is the same that counts to the determination of the law applicable to the internal affairs *(statut personnel).*[70]

Consequently, in the countries that adopt the seat theory, it is the seat of the administration **41** that matters. The seat theory prevails traditionally in Germany and Austria but, due to the case law of the ECJ regarding the right of establishment, it has lost ground in favour of the incorporation theory at least with respect to "EU companies".[71] The systems that follow the

---

[66] Cf. *Droz/Gaudemet-Tallon*, RCDIP 90 (2001) 601–652, p. 641.

[67] Report *Jenard* p. 154.

[68] Cf. *Kropholler/von Hein* Art. 22 note 33. Compare the critical comments made by *Geimer/Schütze* Art. 22 notes 141 *et seq.*

[69] See Report *Pocar* para. 97, *Peter Schlosser* Art. 22 note 16, and *Lima Pinheiro*, Direito Internacional Privado, Vol. II, Direito de Conflitos/Parte Especial (3rd ed. 2009) § 59 D, with more references.

[70] This doctrine is coherent with the best understanding of Art. 53 of Brussels and Lugano (1988) Conventions – see *Lima Pinheiro* p. 77–78, with more references. For a convergent view, see *Mankowski*, in: Rauscher, Art. 22 notes 29–30.

[71] See *Kropholler*, Internationales Privatrecht, (6th ed. 2006) p. 577–581, with more references. On the ECJ case law in this matter, see *Centros Ltd v. Erhvervs- og Selskabsstyrelsen*, (Case C-212/97)[1999] ECR I-01459, *Überseering BV v. Nordic Construction Company Baumanagement GmbH (NCC) Überseering*, (Case C- 208/00) [2002] ECR I-09919, *Kamer van Koophandel en Fabrieken voor Amsterdam v. Inspire Art Ltd.*(Case 167/01) [2003] ECR I-10155, *CartesioOktató és Szolgáltató bt*, (Case 210/06) [2008] ECR

Luís de Lima Pinheiro   571

theory of incorporation (such as the English and the Dutch) submit the legal persons to the law according to which they were incorporated. As a rule, the legal persons are formally seated in the country where they were incorporated and, therefore, it could be thought that in these systems only the formal seat would matter. According to the English law, however, the legal persons are to this purpose deemed to be seated in England whether they have been incorporated in England or they have the administration's seat in its territory, unless, in this second case, the Member State where the legal person has been incorporated regards it as having seat in its territory (Sch. 1 para. 10 of the Civil Jurisdiction and Judgments Order 2001).[72]

42 Other difficulties may arise in systems like the French and the Portuguese, which in matter of companies combine the theory of the seat (of the administration) with the relevance of the formal seat towards third parties.[73] Where the company has only the formal seat or the administration seat in Portugal, it is held that for the establishment of the Portuguese courts' jurisdiction one must pay attention to the seat that forms the connecting factor used to determinate the law applicable to the issue at stake. The relevance of the formal seat or of the administration seat depends, therefore, on the nature of the issue.

43 The determination of the relevant seat shall not depend on its location in a Member State or in a third State.[74] Where the location of the formal seat in a Member State is relevant, its courts shall have jurisdiction even if the administration seat is located in a third State whose courts claim the same jurisdiction. The same can be said vice versa.

44 On the other hand, in matters of internal affairs *(statut personnel)* of legal persons there are mandatory rules of the seat's State, whose application must be assured by the exclusive jurisdiction of the respective courts.

45 Regarding this heading, there are some discrepancies in the different linguistic versions of the Regulations Brussels I and Brussels *Ibis* that are worth notice. The English versions refer to "companies or other legal persons or associations of natural or legal persons". The French, German and Italian versions speak of "companies or legal persons" *(sociétés ou personnes morales/Gesellschaft oder juristischen Person/società o persone giuridiche)*. The Spanish versions states "companies and legal persons" *(sociedades y personas jurídicas)*. The Portuguese versions seem to restrict the heading to legal persons, by referring to "companies and other legal persons" *(sociedades ou outras pessoas colectivas)*. Most of the versions make clear that this heading is not restricted to legal persons in technical sense. The authors have in general understood the Brussels and Lugano Conventions, which employ similar terms, as well as the Brussels I Regulation, where they refer to "companies", as including organisations without legal personality, such as the *Offene Handelsgesellschaft* of German law and the *partnership* of Common Law systems.[75]

      I-09641, and *Vale Építési kft.*, (Case C-378/10) [2012] in curia.europa.eu and comments of *Lima Pinheiro* p. 140–151.

[72] Compare *Dicey/Morris/Collins* para. 11–384.

[73] See *Batiffol/Lagarde* para. 1089 p. 338; *Mayer/Heuzé* p. 757–758; and *Lima Pinheiro* (fn. 69) § 59 D.

[74] Compare the different view of *Gaudemet-Tallon* para. 110.

[75] See, in respect of Art. 16 (2) of Brussels Convention, Report *Schlosser* para. 162; and, regarding the Regulation, *Kropholler/von Hein* Art. 22 note 35; *Gaudemet-Tallon* para. 110; *Lima Pinheiro* p. 125;

This exclusive jurisdiction comprises only the actions concerning the validity, the nullity or **46** the dissolution of legal persons and other organisations, or the validity of the decisions of their organs. Other matters related with the internal affairs *(statut personnel)* are excluded.[76]

As actions concerning the validity of the decisions of the organs of a company shall be understood only those in which a party is challenging the validity of the decision under the applicable company law or under the provisions governing the functioning of its organs, as laid down in its Articles of Association.[77]

There is another divergence among the various language versions of Article 24 (2). According to some of the language versions (namely French, Italian, Portuguese and Spanish), there is exclusive jurisdiction "in the matter of" the validity of constitution, nullity or dissolution of legal persons and other organizations or of the validity of the decisions of its organs (en *matière de, in materia di, em matéria de, en materia de*). By contrast, other language versions (namely English and German), provide for such jurisdiction where proceedings have such a question as their "object" or "subject-matter" *(object, Gegenstand)*. In the judgment in the case *Berliner Verkehrsbetriebe*, the ECJ held that this divergence is to be resolved by interpreting the provision as covering only proceedings whose principal subject-matter comprises the validity of the constitution, the nullity or the dissolution of the company, legal person or association or the validity of the decisions of its organs.[78] Therefore, it is not applicable to proceedings in which the validity of the decision is raised by the defendant as a preliminary question, for instance where a legal person pleads that a contract cannot be relied upon against it because the decision of its organs which led to the conclusion of the contract is supposedly invalid on account of infringement of its statutes.[79]

The term "dissolution" shall not be interpreted in the restrict technical sense given to it by **47** the Civil Law legal systems. This term embraces also the proceedings that relate to the liquidation after the "dissolution" of the company. Among these proceedings are the disputes regarding the distribution of assets to shareholders.[80]

There are conceivable difficulties in the distinction between actions concerning the "dis- **48** solution" and those relating to bankruptcy or analogous proceedings that are excluded of the material scope of the Regulation according to Art. 1 (2) (b).

Mankowski, in: Rauscher Art. 22 note 28a; *Geimer/Schütze* Art. 22 note 146 *et seq.*; *Calvo Caravaca/Carrascosa González* p. 214; and *Dicey/Morris/Collins* para. 11–379.

[76] Cf. *Peter Schlosser* Art. 22 note 19; *Kropholler/von Hein* Art. 22 note 40; *Mankowski*, in: Rauscher Art. 22 notes 35–37b, with further remarks.

[77] Cf. *Nicole Hassett v. South Eastern Health Board* and *Cheryl Doherty v. North Western Health Board* (Case 372/07) [2008] ECR I-07403, para. 26, confirmed by *flyLAL-Lithuanian Airlines AS v. Starptautiskā lidosta Rīga VAS and Air Baltic corporation AS* (Case 302/13) [2014] nyr, para. 40.

[78] Cf. *Berliner Verkehrsbetriebe v. JPMorgan Chase Bank NA*, (Case C-144/10) [2011] ECR I-03961, para. 44. See, on this case, *Lehmann*, Exclusive Jurisdiction under Art. 22(2) of the Brussels I Regulation: the ECJ Decision *Berliner Verkehrsbetriebe v. Jpmorgan Chase Bank* (C-144/10), Yearbook of Private International Law 13 (2011) p. 507.

[79] Para. 47. See further *Mankowski*, in: Rauscher, Art. 22 note 32.

[80] Cf. Report *Schlosser* para. 58, *Schlosser* Art. 22 note 17, and *Kropholler/von Hein* Art. 22 note 37.

The *Schlosser* Report states, in regard to the Brussels Convention, that this jurisdiction may comprise certain winding-up proceedings (of English and Irish laws) that, contrary to most cases, are not based upon the bankruptcy of the company.[81] The same Report clarifies that, where a company belongs to the "continental legal system", the proceedings discussing the admissibility of bankruptcy or the forms of its enforcement are not embraced by the Convention. "On the contrary, all the other proceedings that are designed to verify or to trigger the dissolution of the company do not depend on the Law of Bankruptcy. It is irrelevant whether the company is solvent or insolvent. The existence of preliminary questions subject to the Law of Bankruptcy does not change the situation either. For example, a dispute relating to the possible dissolution of a company based upon the bankruptcy of a shareholder is not subject to the Law of Bankruptcy, falling, consequently, within the scope of the Convention. The Convention is also applicable where, in the context of non-judicial dissolution of a company, third parties invoke in the courts their quality of creditors and have thereby a claim for payment against the company's assets".[82]

49 The courts of two Member States may have jurisdiction based upon Article 24 (2) where, according to their choice of law systems, the legal person has its seat in both States. This may happen because of two different reasons:
 – First, the applicable law or laws may allow the legal person to have two seats. In this case, the plaintiff is free to bring the suit in any of the States in which the legal person has a seat.[83] Although, it is not likely, that the main choice of law systems could be understood in such a way.
 – Second, the jurisdiction of the courts of two Member States may derive from a divergence regarding the concept of seat that is adopted by the respective choice of law systems. For example, where a company has a formal seat in England (because it has been incorporated in England) and an administration seat in Germany (which follows, in principle, the rule of the administration seat). Here again the plaintiff is free to bring the suit in any of these States.

50 Where the courts of two Member States, having both exclusive jurisdiction, are seized with the same action, Art. 31 (1) is applicable.

VII. Validity of entries in public registers

51 In "proceedings which have as their object the validity of entries in public registers", the courts of the Member State in which the register is kept have exclusive jurisdiction (3).

52 The justification for this exclusive jurisdiction is evident: the courts of a given State are not allowed to interfere in the operation of the public register of another State.

53 Falling within the scope of this heading, for example, are the inscriptions in the immovable property register and in the commercial and/or corporate register. The validity of the inscriptions in the "civil register" *(registre de l'état civil)* is, in principle, excluded from the scope of the Regulation (Art. 1 (2) (a)).[84]

---

[81] Report *Schlosser* para. 57.
[82] Report *Schlosser* para. 59.
[83] For a convergent view, see Report *Schlosser* para. 162.

Nonetheless, this exclusive jurisdiction comprises only the validity of inscriptions in public   **54**
registers and not the effects of these inscriptions.[85]

VIII. Registration or validity of intellectual property rights

In "proceedings concerned with the registration or validity of patents, trade marks, designs,   **55**
or other similar rights required to be deposited or registered, irrespective of whether the
issue is raised by way of an action or as a defence, the courts of the Member State in which
the deposit or registration has been applied for, has taken place or is under the terms of
instrument of the Union or an international convention deemed to have taken place" have
exclusive jurisdiction (Art. 24 (4) § 1).

"Without prejudice to the jurisdiction of the European Patent Office under the Convention   **56**
on the Grant of European Patents, signed at Munich on 5 October 1973, the courts of each
Member State shall have exclusive jurisdiction in proceedings concerned with the registration or the validity of any European patent granted for that Member State" ((4) § 2).

This exclusive jurisdiction was already provided for in the Art. 16 (4) of Brussels and Lugano   **57**
(1988) Conventions, but the new formulation given by the Brussels I Regulation and by the
2007 Lugano Convention embraced the rights of intellectual property whose register is
regulated by an European Union instrument.

Furthermore, the second paragraph of Art. 24 (4) of the Regulation makes clear that, without   **58**
prejudice to the jurisdiction of the European Patent Office under the Convention on the
European Patent, the exclusive jurisdiction extends to the European patent. This paragraph
incorporates Art. V-D of the Protocol Annexed to the Brussels Convention, except in regard
to Luxembourg Convention for the European Patent for the Common Market (1975), which
never came into force.[86]

The Convention on the European Patent (1973, revised in 1978 and 2000) establishes a
unified procedure for the granting of a patent for one or for several Contracting States
(Art. 3). In each of the Contracting States for which the European patent is granted it has the
same effects than a national patent granted in that State (Art. 2 (2)). Therefore, where the
European patent is granted for several States, there are several independent rights of intellectual property. In order to avoid that proceedings concerned with the registration or the
validity of the patent granted for one State have to be entered in a different State of regis-

---

[84]   See also *Geimer/Schütze* Art. 22 note 215, *Mankowski*, in: Rauscher Art. 22 note 38, and *Calvo Caravaca/*
       Carrascosa González p. 218. Compare *Gaudemet-Tallon* para. 112.

[85]   Cf. *Kropholler/von Hein* Art. 22 note 42; *Bülow/Böckstiegel/Safferling*, B I 1e, Art. 16 EuGVÜ note 22;
       Peter Gottwald, in: Münchener Kommentar zur ZPO Art. 22 note 31; and *Mankowski*, in: Rauscher
       Art. 22 note 39. Compare Report *Jenard* p. 154 where the reference to the "validity or the effects of the
       inscriptions" is likely due to a slip.

[86]   By operation of Art. 57 (1) of Brussels Convention the applicability of special rules on international
       jurisdiction contained in Conventions on patents is not affected. Art. V-D of the Protocol Annexed to the
       Brussels Convention assigns exclusive jurisdiction, in matters relating the registration or the validity of a
       European patent, to the courts of the State for which the patent was granted.

Luís de Lima Pinheiro

tration, Art. 24 (4) § 2 assigns exclusive jurisdiction to the courts of the State for which the patent has been granted.[87]

By virtue of the European Parliament and Council Regulation No. 1257/2012, of 17 December 2012, Implementing Enhanced Cooperation in the Area of the Creation of Unitary Patent Protection,[88] the patent proprietor may request that a European patent granted by the European Patent Office benefit from unitary effect in the participating Member States. This European patent with unitary effect provides uniform protection and shall have equal effect in all the participating Member States (Art. 3 (2)).[89] This Regulation will be applicable from the date of entry into force of the Agreement on a Unified Patent Court (Art. 18 (2) § 1), and the patent has unitary effect only in the Member States bound by this Agreement at the date of the register (Art. 18 (2) § 2).

The Agreement on a Unified Patent Court (2013), which is not yet in force, set up a Unified Patent Court, which should be a court common to the Contracting Member States and thus part of their judicial system, with jurisdiction for litigation relating to the infringement and validity of European patents and European patents with unitary effect (Arts. 1 and 32). The international jurisdiction of the Court shall be established in accordance with Brussels *Ibis* Regulation or, where applicable, on the basis of the 2007 Lugano Convention (Art. 31). Regarding European patents and European patents with unitary effect granted for the Contracting Member States, it seems that the Court will have jurisdiction under Art. 24 (4) § 2 of Brussels *Ibis* Regulation in matters that are simultaneously embraced by this provision and by Art. 32 (1) of the Agreement on a Unified Patent Court.

59 Art. 16 (4) Brussels Convention, when referring to "the Contracting State in which the deposit or registration (…) is under the terms of an international convention deemed to have taken place", had mainly in mind the system established by the Madrid Agreement Concerning the International Registration of Marks (1891, with some revisions and with a Protocol of 1989), and the Hague Agreement Concerning the International Deposit of Industrial Designs (1925, last revision in 1999).[90] According to this system, the registration or deposit made in the International Bureau, through the intermediary of the Office of the country of origin, has the same effects in the other Contracting States as the direct registration or deposit of marks or industrial designs in these States. The Patent Cooperation Treaty (Washington, 1970, amended in 1979, and modified in 1984 and 2001) establishes a similar system.

60 Art. 22 (4) of the Brussels I Regulation extended this provision to the "Member State in which deposit or registration (…) is under the terms of a Community instrument (…) deemed to have taken place". Art. 24 (4) of the Brussels *Ibis* Regulation updated this wording

---

[87]   Cf. *Kropholler/von Hein* Art. 22 note 56 and *Mankowski*, in: Rauscher Art. 22 note 49.

[88]   Based upon Council Decision 2011/167/EU, of 10 March 2011, authorising enhanced cooperation between Belgium, Bulgaria, the Czech Republic, Denmark, Germany, Estonia, Ireland, Greece, France, Cyprus, Latvia, Lithuania, Luxembourg, Hungary, Malta, the Netherlands, Austria, Poland, Portugal, Romania, Slovenia, Slovakia, Finland, Sweden and the United Kingdom.

[89]   But see Arts. 5 and 7 regarding the acts against which the patent provides protection and the applicable limitations.

[90]   Cf. Report *Jenard* p. 154. See further *Mankowski*, in: Rauscher Art. 22 note 48a.

by referring to "the terms of an instrument of the Union". It could be thought that this extension has especially in mind Council Regulation on the Community trade mark (then Regulation No. 40/94 of 20 December 1993, meanwhile replaced by Regulation No.207/ 2009).[91] Although, when considering the regulatory system established by this Council Regulation, it is quite doubtful that the provision is applicable to the Community trade mark.[92] The same may be said in respect of Council Regulation no. 6/2002, of 12 December 2001, on the Community designs.[93]

The ground for this exclusive jurisdiction lies, first of all, in the connection of certain actions **61** with the proceedings for granting the right and with the organisation of the register.[94] Furthermore, since the right of intellectual property is only protected, in principle, in the territory of the State where the deposit or registration has been made, this jurisdiction leads generally to concurrence of the forum with the applicable law.[95]

The concept of "proceedings" concerned with the registration or validity of patents, trade **62** marks, designs, or other similar rights required to be "deposited or registered" shall be interpreted autonomously regarding the laws of the Member States and in a narrow way.[96]

Thus, the disputes on regularity of the registration concern the *registration* and the disputes **63** on validity of the right or on the actual existence of the deposit or of the register concern the *validity*.

On the contrary, the exclusive jurisdiction does not embrace disputes concerning the right to **64** protection of intellectual property, or arising from contracts that have as object rights in intellectual property.[97] In this way, the ECJ held that Art. 16 (4) of Brussels Convention is not applicable to "a dispute between an employee for whose invention a patent has been applied for or obtained and his employer, where the dispute relates to their respective rights in that patent arising out of the contract of employment".[98]

Excluded from this exclusive jurisdiction are also, in principle, the actions for infringement **65** of rights of intellectual property and the actions for abstention of tortious conduct,[99] as well as the actions concerning granting, revocation or remuneration of compulsory licenses,

---

[91] OJ 1994 L 11/1. Cf. *Kropholler/von Hein* Art. 22 note 54.

[92] See *Christian Kohler*, in: FS Ulrich Everling (1995), p. 656–657, and *Mankowski*, in: Rauscher Art. 22 note 52.

[93] See *Mankowski*, in: Rauscher Art. 22 note 52.

[94] Compare the critical remarks of *Ubertazzi*, Exclusive Jurisdiction in Intellectual Property (2012), p. 108 *et seq.*, 137 *et seq.*, 206 *et seq.*, and 295 *et seq.*

[95] See, on the applicable law, *Lima Pinheiro* (fn. 69) § 70 C, with more references.

[96] See *Ferdinand M. J. J. Duijnstee v. Lodewijk Goderbauer*, (Case 288/82) [1983] ECR 3663, 3676 para. 19.

[97] Cf. *Kropholler/von Hein* Art. 22 note 48; *Gaudemet-Tallon* para. 114; *Teixeira de Sousa/Moura Vicente* p. 116; and *Fawcett/Torremans* paras. 1.40 and 3.73 *et seq.*, but sustaining that the solutions that apply in infringement cases where the defence of validity is raised, should be applied, by way of analogy, in cases where there is a claim for the payment of royalties.

[98] *Ferdinand M. J. J. Duijnstee v. Lodewijk Goderbauer*, (Case 288/82) [1983] ECR 3663, 3678 para. 28.

[99] Cf. *Kropholler/von Hein* Art. 22 note 50; *Dicey/Morris/Collins* para. 11–391, and *Peter Schlosser* Art. 22 note 22.

---

because they do not regard the registration or the validity of the right, but a public intervention that limits the exclusive power of use of the intellectual property by its holder.[100]

66 A question that has been object of some controversy regards the possibility of extending the exclusive jurisdiction of Art. 24 (4) of the Regulation (or of Art. 16 (4) of the Brussels Convention and of Art. 22 (4) of the Brussels I Regulation) to the actions for infringement of rights of intellectual property where the defendant raises invalidity as a defence, as well as to actions for a declaration of non-infringement where the author alleges invalidity of the right.[101]

67 In the *GAT* case, the Conclusions of A-G *Leendert Geelhoed*,[102] give account of three different understandings sustained by each one of the parties, the Governments concerned and the Commission:
– The first opinion, relying on a "strict interpretation" of Art. 16 (4) of Brussels Convention, held that this provision is only applicable to a dispute on the patent's validity where this dispute is the main cause of action.[103]
– The opposite understanding, grounded on an "extensive interpretation" of the same provision, asserted its application to the actions for infringement of patents.
– Finally, according to an intermediate opinion, held by the Advocate General, there is exclusive jurisdiction whenever the question of the validity or of the nullity of a patent or of other intellectual property right referred in this provision is raised; therefore, the Art. 16 (4) of the Brussels Conventions shall be applied where the defendant in an action for infringement of patent or the claimant in an action for declaration of non-infringement of patent raise the invalidity of this patent. Where an action for infringement is brought in another court and the defendant raises this defence, the court "may transfer the whole proceeding (to the court with exclusive jurisdiction), may stay the proceeding until the court with jurisdiction of other Member State, in the terms of Art. 16 no. 4, decides the validity of the patent, and may accept itself the validity in case of defendant's bad faith".

The ECJ's judgment in the above mentioned case followed to a large extent this third understanding.[104] As a matter of fact the court held that this exclusive jurisdiction should

---

100 Cf. *Kropholler/von Hein* Art. 22 note 49. According to these authors, these actions are even excluded from the Regulation scope, because they are not a "civil and commercial matter". Cf. also *Peter Schlosser* Art. 22 note 22, and *Mankowski*, in: Rauscher, Art. 22 note 44.

101 For a general view on this question see *Fawcett/Torremans* paras. 7.01 *et seq.*, and *Mankowski*, in: Rauscher Art. 22 notes 46 *et seq.*

102 *GAT Gesellschaft für Antriebstechnik mbH & Co. KG v. Luk Lamellen- und Kupplungsbau Beteiligungs KG*, (Case C-4/03) [2006] ECR I-6509.

103 See also *Fawcett/Torremans* paras. 7.30 *et seq.*; *Kropholler/von Hein* Art. 22 note 50; and *Geimer/Schütze* Art. 22 notes 19, 231 and 237–238, remarking that some systems do not allow raising the patent's nullity as a defence to the action for infringement; *Mankowski*, in: Rauscher, Art. 22 notes 47 *et seq.*, but putting forward a distinction if, according to the procedural law of the forum, the res judicata effect is extended to the incidental question of the patent validity.

104 *GAT Gesellschaft für Antriebstechnik mbH & Co. KG v. Luk Lamellen- und Kupplungsbau Beteiligungs KG*, (Case C-4/03) [2006] ECR I-6509. See also *Roche Nederland BV and Othena v. Frederick Primus, Milton Goldenberg* (Case C-539/03) [2006] ECR I-06535, para. 40.

apply whatever the form of proceedings in which the issue of a patent's validity is raised, be it by way of an action or a plea in objection, at the time the case is brought or at a later stage in the proceedings.[105]

On the other hand, the judgment does not offer guidance on whether the first court seized shall decline jurisdiction or shall stay the proceedings until the court with exclusive jurisdiction has decided the validity issue or the defendant has failed to start proceedings in this court within a reasonable time period.[106] *De lege lata* the second solution shall be preferred.[107]

The 2007 Lugano Convention incorporated this understanding providing that the exclusive jurisdiction applies irrespective of whether the issue is raised by way of an action or as a defence (Art. 22 (4)).[108] The same may be said of the Brussels I*bis* Regulation (Art. 24 (4)).

This understanding, however, is subject to the criticism of some authors, who stress that Art. 27 only imposes the duty to decline jurisdiction if the case is principally concerned with one of the grounds of exclusive jurisdiction of the court of other Member State.[109] In case of an European patent awarded for several States, in which it is discussed the infringement of parallel patents by the same party, it would not be possible to concentrate the actions before the court of a Member State (for instance the court of the domicile of the defendant); insofar as the issue of the patents validity is raised, the courts of all the Member States for which the patents at stake have been granted must deal with the issue.

It is advocated that the court of the country of register shall have exclusive jurisdiction to decide on the validity of the right with *erga omnes* effect, without prejudice to the jurisdiction of the court where the infringement action is brought to deal with the issue of validity, raised incidentally, with *inter partes* effect. Given the diversity of solutions in force in the Member States regarding the effect of this incidental decision, it is proposed to inscribe the solution in the Regulation itself.[110] The same approach has been adopted by the European Max Planck Group Principles on Conflict of Laws in Intellectual Property (CLIP Principles – Article 2:401) and by the American Law Institute Intellectual Property: Principles Gov-

---

[105] Para. 25.

[106] Compare *Torremans*, The Widening Reach of Exclusive Jurisdiction: Where Can You Litigate IP Rights-after GAT, in: Arnaud Nuyts (ed.), International Litigation in IntellectualProperty and Information Technology (2008) 61, 71, and *Wilderspin*, La compétence juridictionnelle en matière de litiges concernant la violation des droit de propriété intellectuelle – Les arrêts de la Cour de justice dans les affaires C-04/03, GAT c. LUK et C-539/03, Roche Nederland c. Primus et Goldberg, R. crit.95 (2006) ps. 787–788.

[107] See *Torremans*, Exclusive Jurisdiction, in: European Max Planck Group on Conflict of Laws in Intellectual Property (CLIP), Conflict of Laws in Intellectual Property. The CLIP Principles and Commentary (2013), Article 2:401.N09.

[108] See Report *Pocar* para. 102.

[109] See*Torremans* (fn. 106) 67 and (fn. 107) Article 2:401.N05-N08, and *Moura Vicente*, A Tutela Internacional da Propriedade Intelectual (2008) 390. See further *Geimer/Schütze* Art. 22 notes 237–238, and *Gaudemet-Tallon* para. 116.

[110] See the proposal of a Working Group of the Max-Planck-Institute for Foreign and International Private Law (2006) in *Mankowski*, in: Rauscher Art. 22 note 47j, and *Torremans* (fn. 106) p. 76–77. Compare *Magnus/Mankowski* – "Brussels I on the Verge of Reform – A Response to the Green Paper on the Review of the Brussels I Regulation", ZVgl RW 109 (2010) 1–41, p. 17.

erning Jurisdiction, Choice of Law, and Judgments in Transnational Disputes (ALI Principles 2008 – Articles 211(2), 212(4) and 213(2)).[111]

This solution shall be coupled with the grant of a discretion to the court first seized with the infringement action to stay its proceedings waiting for a decision on validity by the court with exclusive jurisdiction within a reasonable time, as provided by Article 2:703 of the CLIP Principles[112]

It shall be remarked that the court of a Member State, which does not have jurisdiction under Art. 24 (4), is not precluded of ordering a provisional cross-border prohibition against infringement under Art. 35, even if the issue of the patent's invalidity is raised in the main proceedings. In effect, since this court does not make a final decision on the validity of the patent invoked, there is no risk of conflicting decisions.[113]

68 The "*similar rights required to be deposited or registered*" are other rights on intellectual property whose acquisition depend on deposit or registration, such as plant variety rights.[114]

69 The general rules on jurisdiction contained in the Regulation are applicable to the actions in civil and commercial matters related to rights on intellectual property which do not fall within the scope of this exclusive jurisdiction.[115]

70 As in general, the rules of the Regulation are displaced by special rules contained in instruments of the Union or in national legislation harmonised pursuant to such instruments (Art. 67) or in international conventions to which Member States were parties at the time the Regulation has entered in force (Art. 71).

71 Therefore, the special rules on jurisdiction contained in the Council Regulation No. 207/2009, of 26 February 2009, on the Community trade mark (for instance in the Arts. 96 to 98), in the Council Regulation No. 2100/94, of 27 July 1994, on Community plant variety rights (Arts. 101–102),[116] and in the Council Regulation no. 6/2002, of 12 December 2001, on Community designs (Arts. 81 *et seq.*) shall be taken into account.

---

111   See the comments of *Torremans* (fn. 107) Article 2:401.C03, C10 and C12, and note Article 2:401.N14.

112   See the comments of *Torremans* (fn. 107) Article 2:401.C10, and of *van Eechoud/Peukert*, in: European Max Planck Group on Conflict of Laws in Intellectual Property (CLIP), Conflict of Laws in Intellectual Property. The CLIP Principles and Commentary (2013), Article 2:703.C01-C04. See further Article 4:202 of the CLIP Principles, providing that the recognition and enforcement of a foreign judgment may not be refused on the ground that the validity or registration of an intellectual property right which is not registered in the State of origin has been challenged, provided that the judgment only produces *inter partes* effects.

113   Cf. *Solvay SA v. Honeywell Fluorine Products Europe BV and Others* (Case C-616/10) [2012] in curia. europa.eu paras. 31 and 49–51.

114   Cf. Report *Jenard* p. 154, *Geimer/Schütze* Art. 22 notes 240 *et seq.*, *Kropholler/von Hein* Art. 22 note 52, *Layton/Mercer* p. 657, and *Mankowski*, in: Rauscher Art. 22 notes 45–45a.

115   Cf. Report *Jenard* p. 154.

116   Amended by Council Regulations No. 2506/95, of 25 October 1995, No. 807/2003, of 14 April 2003, No. 1650/2003, of 18 June 2003, and No. 873/2004, of 29 April 2004.

As to international conventions, the rules on jurisdiction (as well as the rules on recognition   72
of judgments) contained in the Protocol on Recognition (1973), which is part of the European Patent Convention (Art. 164 (1)), prevail over the Regulation.[117] This Protocol contains
jurisdiction rules in respect to claims, against the applicant, regarding the right to the grant
of a European patent.[118]

IX. Enforcement of judgments

In "proceedings concerned with the enforcement of judgments", the courts of the Member   73
State in which the judgment has been or is to be enforced have exclusive jurisdiction (5).[119]

This heading establishes a true exclusive jurisdiction: acts of enforcement in the territory of a   74
State may only be carried out by the courts of this State (notwithstanding the possibility of
delegation of this power to private persons).[120] This exclusive jurisdiction has its roots in
Public International Law:[121] the courts of a State have only jurisdiction to enforce (power to
carry out acts of force) in its territory. Since, in principle, it is not possible to order the acts of
enforcement in one State and carry them out in other State ([122]), one may infer that the
courts of the State where the enforcement shall take place have exclusive jurisdiction for the
enforcement proceedings ([123]).Nevertheless, doubt could arise with respect to certain remedies related to the enforcement, such as applications to oppose enforcement by the debtor or
by a third party.

According to the *Jenard* Report, "proceedings concerned with the enforcement of judg-   75
ments" are "disputes that may arise from 'the use of force, of coercion or of dispossession of
movable and immovable property to assure the material enforcement of judgments and
acts'".[124] This passage is generally understood in the sense of comprising the adversary
proceedings that have a close link with the enforcement, such as the applications to oppose
enforcement made by the debtor[125] or by a third party.[126]

---

[117]   See *Kropholler* Art. 22 note 56, and *Geimer/Schütze* Art. 22 note 250 *et seq.* Compare *Mankowski*, in:
        Rauscher Art. 22 note 49.
[118]   Arts. 2–6.
[119]   Regarding the attachment of international contractual rights see Report *Schlosser* para. 207, and *Man-
        kowski*, in: Rauscher Art. 22 note 62. See further *Teixeira de Sousa*, Direito Processual Civil Europeu
        (photocopied Report 2003) p. 170.
[120]   Cf. *Kropholler/von Hein* Art. 22 notes 59 *et seq.*; *Gaudemet-Tallon* para. 120; *Peter Schlosser* Art. 22
        note 24; and *Geimer/Schütze* Art. 22 note 262. Compare *Teixeira de Sousa*, Cadernos de Direito Privado
        (2004) no. 5, ps. 49–57, ps. 53 *et seq.*
[121]   See also *Geimer/Schütze* Art. 22 notes 4 and 264, and *Lima Pinheiro*, p. 22.
[122]   Cf. *Schack* para. 1061; *Teixeira de Sousa* "A competência internacional executiva dos tribunais portugu-
        eses: alguns equívocos", Cadernos de Direito Privado(5/2004) ps. 49–57, p. 55. Naturally, special regimes
        may be laid down by international conventions or European regulations.
[123]   See *Lima Pinheiro*, p. 22. See also *Kropholler/von Hein* Art. 22 note 59. Compare *Gaudemet-Tallon*
        para. 120; *Teixeira de Sousa* (fn. 119) 53–54; and *Moura Vicente* "Comércio electrónico e competência
        internacional", *in* Direito Internacional Privado. Ensaios, vol. II (2005), 263–277, 288.
[124]   Report *Jenard* p. 154.
[125]   Cf. *AS-Autoteile Service GmbH v. Pierre Malhé*, (Case 220/84) [1985] ECR 2267, 2277 para. 12. Com-
        pare *Peter Schlosser* Art. 22 note 25.

76 Excluded is the action where a creditor seeks to set aside a gift of the legal ownership of immovable property alleged made by the debtor to defraud his creditors *(action paulienne)*, which is not designed to settle a dispute relating to the enforcement.[127] The same position shall be taken with respect to actions for compensation of damages caused by undue enforcement, in which the legal foundation of the enforcement arises only as preliminary question, as well as to actions for reimbursement of unjust enrichment obtained through enforcement.[128]

77 The EU case law suggests also the exclusion of provisional or protective measures, even if they authorise or order acts of enforcement. First, because this case law allows generically that those measures may be ordered by the court vested with jurisdiction as to the substance of the matter,[129] as well as by another court that has "a real connecting link between the subject-matter of the measures sought and the territorial jurisdiction of the Contracting State of the court before which those measures are sought".[130] Second, the courts of other Member States (namely those where the acts of enforcement are sought) are, in principle, obliged to recognise and enforce, in the terms of Arts. 36 *et seq.* and 39 *et seq.*, the provisional measures ordered by the courts having jurisdiction by operation of the jurisdiction provisions of the Regulation (Art. 2 (a) § 2).[131]

78 The inclusion of a proceeding of opposition to enforcement by the debtor within the scope of this exclusive jurisdiction does not mean that in the courts of the place of enforcement all the defences allowed by the law of the forum may be raised. The ECJ has already held that Art. 16 (5) of Brussels Convention does not authorise the pleading in the courts of the place of

---

126 Cf. *Kropholler/von Hein* Art. 22 note 61; *Teixeira de Sousa/Moura Vicente* p. 118; and *Peter Schlosser* Art. 22 note 25.

127 Cf. *Mario P. A. Reichert, Hans-Heinz Reichert and Ingeborg Kockler v. Dresdner Bank*, (Case 115/88) [1990] ECR I-27, I-41 para. 28.

128 Cf. *Geimer/Schütze* Art. 22 note 272, *Kropholler/von Hein* Art. 22 note 62, and *Mankowski*, in: Rauscher Art. 22 note 59.

129 *van Uden Maritime BV, trading as van Uden Africa Line v. Kommanditgesellschaft in Firma Deco-Line et al.*, (Case C-391/95) [1998] ECR I-7091, I-7130 para. 19. See also Recital no. 33; and *Calvo Caravaca/Carrascoza González* p. 214 and 262 *et seq.*

130 *van Uden Maritime BV, trading as van Uden Africa Line v. Kommanditgesellschaft in Firma Deco-Line et al.*, (Case C-391/95) [1998] ECR I-7091, I-7135 para. 40. On the doubts arising from this wording, see *Gaudemet-Tallon* paras. 306 and 311. See also *Bernard Denilauler v. SNC Couchet Frères*, (Case 125/79) [1980] ECR 1553, 1570 *et seq.* paras. 15–16.

131 Under the Brussels Convention and the Brussels I Regulation was not settled whether there is an obligation to recognize and enforce the measures ordered under the provision now contained in Art. 35 of Brussels *Ibis* Regulation. In a negative sense, *Kropholler/von Hein* Art. 31 note 24, with more references. Compare *Andrea Schulz*, ZEuP 2001, 805, p. 824 *et seq.* See further *Gaudemet-Tallon* para. 367 and *infra* Art. 35 paras. 26–28. In the judgment *Italian Leather SpA v. WECO Polstermöbel GmbH & Co.* (Case C-80/00) [2002] ECR I-04995, the ECJ seemed to accept the application of the recognition and enforcement rules of the Brussels Convention to provisional or protective measures ordered under Art. 24 of the Convention (which corresponds to Art. 35 of the Brussels *Ibis* Regulation). Recital no. 33 of the Brussels *Ibis* Regulation states explicitly that those measures only have effect, under the Regulation, on the territory of the ordering State.

enforcement of set-off between the right whose enforcement is being sought and a claim over which these courts would not have jurisdiction if it was raised independently.[132]

It would seem obvious that this exclusive jurisdiction does not concern the order for en- **79** forcement of foreign judgments *(exequatur)*, regarding which the word "enforcement" is used in another sense.[133] The enforcement of judgements given in another Member State, within the scope of the Regulation, no more depend on an order for enforcement (Arts. 39 *et seq.*), and Art. 24 (5) is not applicable to the proceedings designed to obtain an order for enforcement of judgments given in civil and commercial matters in a third State.[134]

Section 7: **Prorogation of jurisdiction**

Introduction to Articles 25–26

Art. 25 and 26 form their own – the 7th – section of Chapter II of the Regulation dealing with **1** the prorogation of jurisdiction. The section has great practical importance and grants the parties of a legal relationship – and also the settlor of a trust instrument – a wide freedom to determine for themselves the internationally competent forum for any present or future dispute and recognises thereby the parties' autonomy to dispose over procedural matters. Though the term 'prorogation' seems only to refer to a positive designation of the competent court it is common ground that the section also covers a mere 'derogation' where the parties exclude the jurisdiction of a particular court without specifying positively the competent court.[1]

Art. 25 concerns the choice of jurisdiction through agreement between the parties or trust **2** settlement while Art. 26 regulates the choice by submission. Choice of court agreements will be regularly but not necessarily made before court proceedings started and – save the one-sided determination of the competent court by a trust settlement – require the consent of both parties. A choice by submission requires that proceedings must have already begun and that then the defendant has one-sidedly and implicitly accepted the jurisdiction of a court which originally had no jurisdiction over him or her.

However, as in substantive law the parties' autonomy is not unrestricted. Neither by agree- **3** ment nor by submission can the parties oust a court's exclusive jurisdiction under Art. 24. Nor can they do so by agreement in advance with respect to the protective jurisdiction under Art. 15, 19 and 23 (see Art. 25 (4)).

---

[132] Cf. *AS-Autoteile Service GmbH v. Pierre Malhé,* (Case 220/84) [1985] ECR 2267, 2277 para. 12 and 19. See, on the correctness of this decision, *Gaudemet-Tallon* para. 121, with more references.

[133] In fact, it is used improperly in this context, see *Lima Pinheiro* p. 232.

[134] Cf. *Owens Bank Ltd. v. Fulvio Bracco and Bracco Industria Chimica SpA,* (Case 129/92) [1994] ECR I-117, I-153 paras. 24–25.

[1] For details see *infra* Art. 25 note 38 (*Magnus*).

Article 25

1. If the parties, regardless of their domicile, have agreed that a court or the courts of a Member State are to have jurisdiction to settle any disputes which have arisen or which may arise in connection with a particular legal relationship, that court or those courts shall have jurisdiction, unless the agreement is null and void as to its substantive validity under the law of that Member State. Such jurisdiction shall be exclusive unless the parties have agreed otherwise. The agreement conferring jurisdiction shall be either:
   (a) in writing or evidenced in writing; or
   (b) in a form which accords with practices which the parties have established between themselves;
   (c) in international trade or commerce, in a form which accords with a usage of which the parties are or ought to have been aware and which in such trade or commerce is widely known to, and regularly observed by, parties to contracts of the type involved in the particular trade or commerce concerned.
2. Any communication by electronic means which provides a durable record of the agreement shall be equivalent to 'writing'.
3. The court or courts of a Member State on which a trust instrument has conferred jurisdiction shall have exclusive jurisdiction in any proceedings brought against a settlor, trustee or beneficiary, if relations between those persons or their rights or obligations under the trust are involved.
4. Agreements or provisions of a trust instrument conferring jurisdiction shall have no legal force if they are contrary to Articles 15, 19 or 23, or if the courts whose jurisdiction they purport to exclude have exclusive jurisdiction by virtue of Article 24.
5. An agreement conferring jurisdiction which forms part of a contract shall be treated as an agreement independent of the other terms of the contract.
   The validity of the agreement conferring jurisdiction cannot be contested solely on the ground that the contract is not valid.

Bibliography

1. On the new law and the reform:
Basedow, Exclusive Choice-of-Court Agreements as a Derogation from Imperative Norms, in: Essays in honour of Michael Bogdan (2013), p. 15
Basedow, Zuständigkeitsderogation, Eingriffsnormen und ordre public, in: FS Ulrich Magnus (2014), p. 337
Borrás, The Application of the Brussels I Regulation to Defendants Domiciled in Third States: From the EGPIL to the Commission Proposal, in: Lein (ed.), The Brussels I Review Proposal Uncovered (2012), p. 57
Briggs, What Should Be Done about Jurisdiction Agreements?, Yb. PIL 12 (2010), 311
Bríza, Choice-of-Court Agreements: Could the Hague Choice of Court Agreements Convention and the Reform of the Brussels I Regulation Be the Way Out of the *Gasser-Owusu* Disillusion?, (2009) 5 JPrIL 537
Camilleri, Article 23: Formal Validity, Material Validity or Both?, (2011) 7 JPrIL 297
Cook, Pragmatism in the European Union: Recasting the Brussels I Regulation to Ensure Effectiveness of Exclusive Choice-of-Court Agreements, www.abdn.ac.uk/law/documents/Pragmatism_in_the_European_Union.pdf
Dickinson, Surveying the Proposed Brussels Ibis Regulation: Solid Foundations but Renovation Needed, Yb. PIL 12 (2010), 247
Freitag, Halbseitig ausschließliche Gerichtsstandsvereinbarungen unter der Brüssel I-VO, in: FS Ulrich Magnus (2014), p. 419

Gebauer, Das Prorogationsstatut im Europäischen Zivilprozessrecht, in: FS Bernd von Hoffmann (2011), p. 577

Gebauer, Gerichtsstandsvereinbarung und Pflichtverletzung, in: FS Athanassios Kaissis (2012), p. 267

Gebauer, Zur subjektiven Reichweite von Schieds- und Gerichtsstandsvereinbarungen – Maßstab und anwendbares Recht, in: FS Rolf A. Schütze (2015), p. 95

Goodwin, Reflexive Effect and the Brussels I Regulation, (2013) 129 L.Q.Rev. 317

Gottwald, Internationale Vereinbarungen des Erfüllungsortes und des Gerichtsstandes nach Brüssel I und Den Haag, in: FS Tadeusz Erecinski (2011), p. 1067

Hartley, The International Scope of Choice-of-Court Agreements under the Brussels I Regulation, the Lugano Convention and the Hague Convention, in: Liber amicorum Ole Lando (2012), p. 197

Hartley, Choice-of-Court Agreements and the New Brussels I Regulation, (2013) 129 LQR 309

Hartley, The "Italian Torpedo" and Choice-of-Court Agreements: Sunk At Last?, in: Essays in honour of Michael Bogdan (2013), p. 95

von Hein, Die Neufassung der europäischen Gerichtsstands- und Vollstreckungsverordnung (EuGVVO), RIW 2013, 97

Heinze, Choice of Court Agreements, Coordination of Proceedings and Provisional Measures in the Reform of the Brussel I Regulation, RabelsZ 75 (2011), 581

Kohler, Agreements Conferring Jurisdiction on Courts of Third States, in: Pocar/Viarengo/Villata (eds.), Recasting Brussels I (2012), p. 199

Matthias Lehmann/Grimm, Zulässigkeit asymmetrischer Gerichtsstandsvereinbarungen nach Artikel 23 Brüssel I-VO, ZEuP 2013, 890

Lenaerts/Stapper, Die Entwicklung der Brüssel I-Verordnung im Dialog des Europäischen Gerichtshofs mit dem Gesetzgeber, RabelsZ 78 (2014), 252

Magnus, Gerichtsstandsvereinbarungen im Vorschlag zur Reform der EuGVO, in: FS Bernd von Hoffmann (2011), p. 664

Magnus, Choice of Court Agreements in the Review Proposal for the Brussels I Regulation, in: Lein (ed.), The Brussels I Review Proposal Uncovered (2012), p. 83

Magnus, Gerichtsstandsvereinbarungen in der reformierten EuGVO, in: FS Dieter Martiny (2014), p. 785

Peifer, Schutz gegen Klagen im forum derogatum (2013)

Pertegas, The Revision of the Brussels I Regulation: A View from the Hague Conference, in: Lein (ed.), The Brussels I Review Proposal Uncovered (2012), p. 193

Pocar, On the Substantive Validity of Choice-of-Court Agreements under the EU Brussels I Regulation Recast, in: Essays in honour of Michael Bogdan (2013), p. 471

Pohl, Die Neufassung der EuGVVO – im Spannungsfeld zwischen Vertrauen und Kontrolle, IPRax 2013, 109

Queirolo, Prorogation of Jurisdiction in the Proposal for a Recast of the Brussel I Regulation, in: Pocar/Viarengo/Villata (eds.), Recasting Brussels I (2012), p. 183

Queirolo/de Maestri, The effects of the proposal for a recast of the Brussels I Regulation on rules concerning prorogation of jurisdiction, EuLF 2011, 61

Radicati di Brozolo, Choice of Court and Arbitration Agreements and the Review of the Brussels I Regulation, IPRax 2010, 121

Ratkovic/Zgrabljicrotar, Choice-of-Court Agreements under the Brussels I Regulation (Recast), (2013) 9 JPrIL 245

Sánchez Fernández, Choice-of-Court Agreements: Breach and Damages Within the Brussels I Regime, Yb. PIL 12 (2010), 377

Sancho Villa, Jurisdiction over Jurisdiction and Choice of Court Agreements: Views on the Hague Convention of 2005 and Implications for the European Regime, Yb. PIL 12 (2010), 399

Schaper/Eberlein, Die Behandlung von Drittstaaten – Gerichtsstandsvereinbarungen vor europäischen Gerichten, RIW 2012, 43

Steinle/Vasiliades, The Enforcement of Jurisdiction Agreements Under the Brussels I Regulation: Reconsidering the Principle of Party Autonomy, (2010) 6 JPrIL 565

Villata, Choice-of-Court Agreements in Favour of Third States Jurisdiction in Light of the Suggestions by Members of the European Parliament, in: Pocar/Viarengo/Villata (eds.), Recasting Brussels I (2012), p. 219

Weitz, Internationale Gerichtsstandsvereinbarungen

Ulrich Magnus

und positive internationale Kompetenzkonflikte –
Ein Beitrag zum Änderungsentwurf der Brüssel
I-Verordnung, Int. J. Proc. L. 1 (2011), 337
Matthias Weller, Der Kommissionsentwurf zur
Reform der Brüssel I-VO, GPR 2012, 34
Wurmnest, Die Einbeziehung kartellrechtlicher An-
sprüche in Gerichtsstandsvereinbarungen, in: FS
Ulrich Magnus (2014), p. 567.

2. On the old law:
Addis, La conferma per iscritto delle proroga verbale
di competenza (art. 17 della convenzione di Bruxelles), Riv. trim dir. proc. civ. 1998, 831
Álvarez González, The Spanish Tribunal Supremo
grants damages for breach of a Choice-of-Court
agreement, IPRax 2009, 529
Bertrand Ancel, La clause attributive de juridiction
selon l'art. 17 de la Convention de Bruxelles, Riv. dir.
int. 1990, 263
Aull, Der Geltungsanspruch des EuGVÜ: "Binnensachverhalte" und Internationales Zivilverfahrens-
recht in der Europäischen Union, Zur Auslegung
von Art. 17 Abs. 1 S. 1 EuGVÜ (1996)
Aull, Zur isolierten Prorogation nach Art. 17 Abs. 1
LugÜ, IPRax 1999, 226
Beaumart, Haftung in Absatzketten im französi-
schen Recht und im europäischen Zuständigkeits-
recht (1999)
Beaumont, Hague Choice of Court Agreements
Convention 2005, (2009) 6 JprIL 125
Beaumont/Yüksel, The Validity of Choice of Court
Agreements under the Brussels I Regulation and the
Hague Choice of Court Agreements Convention, in:
Liber amicorum Kurt Siehr (2010), p. 563
Benecke, Die teleologische Reduktion des räumlich-
persönlichen Anwendungsbereichs von Art. 2 ff. und
Art. 17 EuGVÜ (1993)
Bernard, Les clauses attributives de juridiction dans
les conventions judiciaires européennes (2000)
Bläsi, Das Haager Übereinkommen über Gerichts-
standsvereinbarungen. Unter besonderer Berück-
sichtigung seiner zu erwartenden Auswirkungen auf
den deutsch-amerikanischen Rechtsverkehr (2010)
Boccafoschi, Zuständigkeits- und Gerichtsstandsvereinbarungen im deutschen und italienischen
Recht (2005)
Bogdan, The Brussels/Lugano Lis Pendens Rule and
the 'Italian Torpedo', Scand. Stud. L. 2007, 89

Born, Le régime général des clauses attributives de
juridiction dans la Convention de Bruxelles, J. trib.
1995, 353
Brand/Herrup, The 2005 Hague Convention on
Choice of Court Agreements (2008)
Briggs, Agreements on Jurisdiction and Choice of
Law (2008)
Burgstaller, Probleme der Prorogation nach dem
Lugano-Übereinkommen, JBl 1998, 691
Calvo Caravaca/Carrascosa González, Derecho In-
ternacional Privado I (14th ed. 2013)
Coester-Waltjen, Parteiautonomie in der internatio-
nalen Zuständigkeit, in: FS Andreas Heldrich (2005),
p. 549
Conrad, Qualifikationsfragen des Trust im Europä-
ischen Zivilprozeßrecht (2001)
Contaldi, Le clausole di proroga della giurisdizione
contenute in polizze di carico ed il nuovo testo dell'
Art. 17 della Convenzione di Bruxelles del 1968, Riv.
dir. int. 1998, 79
Contaldi, L'art. 17 della Convenzione di Bruxelles del
1968 e l'opponibilità al terzo portatore delle clausole
di proroga della giurisdizione contenute in polizze di
carico, Riv. dir. int. 1999, 889
Deli, Gli usi del commercio internazionale nel nuovo
testo dell'art. 17 della Convenzione di Bruxelles del
1968, Riv. dir. int. 1989, p. 27
Domej, Effet utile der EuGVVO und Vorrang von
Spezialübereinkommen, in: FS Heinz Mayer (2011)
41
Eichel, Das Haager Übereinkommen über Gerichtsstandsvereinbarungen vom 30.6.2005, RIW 2009,
289
Fawcett, The Impact of Art. 6 (1) of the ECHR on
Private International Law, (2007) 56 ICLQ 1
Fentiman, Exclusive Jurisdiction and Article 17, in:
Fentiman/Nuyts/Tagaras/Watté (eds.), L'espace ju-
diciaire européen en matières civiles et commerciales
(1999), p. 127
Fentiman, International Commercial Litigation
(2010)
Ferrari, Trade usage and practices established be-
tween the parties, in: Ferrari/Flechtner/Brand (eds.),
The Draft UNCITRAL Digest and Beyond: Cases,
Analysis and Unresolved Issues in the U. N. Sales
Convention (2004), p. 191
Frauenberger-Pfeiler, Der "reine Binnensachver-

halt", Art. 23 EuGVVO und der öOGH, in: FS
Rechberger (2005), p. 125

Gebauer, Die Drittwirkung von Gerichtsstandsvereinbarungen bei Vertragsketten, IPRax 2001, 471

Geimer, Zuständigkeitsvereinbarungen zugunsten und zu Lasten Dritter, NJW 1985, 533

Girsberger, Gerichtsstandsklausel im Konnossement: Der EuGH und der internationale Handelsbrauch, IPRax 2000, 87

Gottschalk/Breßler, Missbrauchskontrolle von Gerichtsstandsvereinbarungen im Europäischen Zivilprozessrecht, ZEuP 2007, 56

Gottwald, Grenzen internationaler Gerichtsstandsvereinbarungen, in: FS Karl Firsching (1985), p. 89

Gottwald, Internationale Gerichtsstandsvereinbarungen – Verträge zwischen Prozessrecht und materiellem Recht, in: FS Wolfram Henckel (1995), p. 295

Grothe, Zwei Einschränkungen des Prioritätsprinzips im europäischen Zuständigkeitsrecht: ausschließliche Gerichtsstände und Prozessverschleppung, IPRax 2004, 205

Harris, Jurisdiction Clauses and Void Contracts, (1998) 23 Eur. L. Rev. 279

Hartley, Jurisdiction Agreements under the Brussels Jurisdiction and Judgments Convention, (2000) 25 Eur. L. Rev. 279

Hartley/Dogauchi, Explanatory Report on the 2005 Hague Choice of Court Agreements Convention (2007)

Hau, Zur schriftlichen Bestätigung mündlicher Gerichtsstandsvereinbarungen, IPRax 1999, 24

Hau, Zu den Voraussetzungen gepflogenheitsgemäßer Einbeziehung von AGB-Gerichtsstandsklauseln, IPRax 2005, 301

Hau, Gerichtsstandsvertrag und Vertragsgerichtstand beim innereuropäischen Versendungskauf, IPRax 2009, 44

Hausmann, in: Reithmann/Martiny (ed.), Internationales Vertragsrecht (7th ed. 2010) paras. 2928 *et seq.*

Hau, in: Staudinger, Kommentar zum Bürgerlichen Gesetzbuch mit Einführungsgesetz und Nebengesetzen, Rom I-Verordnung Bd. 2 (2011) IntVertrVerf notes 228 *et seq.*

Heinig, Grenzen von Gerichtsstandsvereinbarungen im Europäischen Zivilprozessrecht (2010)

Heinze/Dutta, Ungeschriebene Grenzen für euro-

päische Zuständigkeiten bei Streitigkeiten mit Drittstaatenbezug, IPRax 2005, 224

Heiss, Die Form internationaler Gerichtsstandsvereinbarungen, ZfRV 2000, 202

Heiss, Gerichtsstandsvereinbarungen zulasten Dritter, insbesondere in Versicherungsverträgen zu ihren Gunsten, IPRax 2005, 497

Hernández-Breton, Internationale Gerichtsstandsklauseln in Allgemeinen Geschäftsbedingungen (1993)

Hess, Gerichtsstandsvereinbarungen zwischen EuGVÜ und ZPO, IPRax 1992, 358

Hill/Chong, International Commercial Disputes. Commercial Conflict of Laws in English Courts (4th ed. 2010) para. 5. 3. 1

von Hoffmann/Hau, Probleme der abredewidrigen Streitverkündung im Europäischen Zivilrechtsverkehr, RIW 1997, 89

Horn, Einwand des Rechtsmissbrauchs gegen eine Gerichtsstandsvereinbarung i. S. d. Art. 23 EuGVO?, IPRax 2006, 2

Huet, Relations habituelles d'affaires et acceptation tacite d'une clause attributive de juridiction en droit international privé, in: Ètudes à la Mémoire du Professeur A. Rieg (2000), p. 501

Jayme, Gerichtsstandsvereinbarung und abgelaufener Hauptvertrag in Art. 17 EuGVÜ, IPRax 1989, 361

Jayme/Aull, Zur Anwendbarkeit des Art. 17 EuGVÜ bei Wohnsitz beider Parteien in demselben Vertragsstaat, IPRax 1989, 80

Jayme/Haack, Reziproke Gerichtsstandsklauseln – EuGVÜ und Drittstaaten, IPRax 1985, 323

Joseph, Jurisdiction and Arbitration Agreements and their Enforcement (2nd ed. 2010)

Jung, Vereinbarungen über die internationale Zuständigkeit nach dem EWG-Gerichtsstands- und Vollstreckungsübereinkommen und nach § 38 Abs. 2 ZPO (1980)

Jungermann, Die Drittwirkung internationaler Gerichtsstandsvereinbarungen nach EuGVÜ/EuGVO und LugÜ (2006)

Kaufmann-Kohler, Les clauses d'élection de for dans les contrats internationaux (1980)

Killias, Die Gerichtsstandsvereinbarung nach dem Lugano-Übereinkommen (1993)

Killias, Internationale Gerichtsstandsvereinbarung mittels Schweigen auf kaufmännisches Bestätigungsschreiben?, in: Liber discipulorum Kurt Siehr (2001), p. 65

Kim, Internationale Gerichtsstandsvereinbarungen (1995)

Kindler/Huneke, Gerichtsstandsvereinbarungen in Rahmenverträgen, IPRax 1999, 435

Kohler, Internationale Gerichtsstandsvereinbarungen: Liberalität und Rigorismus im EuGVÜ, IPRax 1983, 265

Kohler, Rigueur et souplesse en droit international privé: les formes prescrites pour une convention attributive de juridiction "dans le commerce international" par l'art. 17 de la Convention de Bruxelles dans sa nouvelle rédaction, Dir. comm. int. 1990, 611

Kohler, Pathologisches im EuGVÜ: Hinkende Gerichtsstandsvereinbarungen nach Art. 17 Abs. 3, IPRax 1986, 340

Kröll, Gerichtsstandsvereinbarungen aufgrund Handelsbrauchs im Rahmen des EuGVÜ, ZZP 113 (2000), 135

Kröll, Das Formerfordernis bei Gerichtsstandsvereinbarungen nach Art. 17 LugÜ – Unwirksamkeit trotz materieller Einigung?, IPRax 2002, 113

Kropholler/Pfeifer, Das neue europäische Recht der Zuständigkeitsvereinbarung, in: FS Heinrich Nagel (1987), p. 157

Lando/Beale, Principles of European Contract Law, Parts I and II (2000)

Lehmann, Anti-suit injunctions zum Schutz internationaler Schiedsvereinbarungen und EuGVVO, NJW 2009, 1645

Leible, Gerichtsstandsvereinbarungen und Klauselrichtlinie, RIW 2001, 422

Leible/Röder, Missbrauchskontrolle von Gerichtsstandsvereinbarungen im Europäischen Zivilprozessrecht, RIW 2007, 481

Leipold, Zuständigkeitsvereinbarungen in Europa, in: Gottwald/Greger/Prütting (ed.), Dogmatische Grundfragen des Zivilprozesses im geeinten Europa (2000), p. 51

Lindacher, Internationale Gerichtsstandsklauseln in AGB unter dem Geltungsregime von Brüssel I, in: FS Peter Schlosser (2005), p. 491

Lindenmayr, Vereinbarung über die internationale Zuständigkeit und das anwendbare Recht (2002)

Magnus, Internationale Aufrechnung, in: Leible (ed.), Das Grünbuch zum Internationalen Vertragsrecht (2004), p. 209

Mance, Exclusive Jurisdiction Agreements and European Ideals, (2004) 120 LQR 357

Mankowski, Seerechtliche Vertragsverhältnisse im Internationalen Privatrecht (1995), p. 233–299

Mankowski, Versicherungsverträge zugunsten Dritter, Internationales Privatrecht und Art. 17 EuGVÜ, IPRax 1996, 427

Mankowski, Entwicklungen im Internationalen Privat- und Prozessrecht 2004/2005 (Teil 2), RIW 2005, 561

Mankowski, Ist eine vertragliche Absicherung von Gerichtsstandsvereinbarungen möglich?, IPRax 2009, 23

Mankowski, Gerichtsstandsvereinbarungen in Tarifverträgen und Art. 23 EuGVVO, NZA 2009, 584

Mark/Gärtner, Gerichtsstandsvereinbarungen zwischen Kaufleuten im internationalen Rechtsverkehr, MDR 2009, 837

Markus/Arnet, Gerichtsstandsvereinbarung in einem Konnossement, IPRax 2011, 283

McClellan, Choice of Jurisdiction Clauses under the EEC Judgments Convention, (1984) JBL 445

Merrett, The enforcement of jurisdiction agreements within the Brussels Regime, (2006) 55 ICLQ 315

Merrett, Article 23 of the Brussels I Regulation: A comprehensive code for jurisdiction agreements?, (2009) 58 ICLQ 545

Mohs, Drittwirkung von Schieds- und Gerichtsstandsvereinbarungen (2006)

Morse, Forum-Selection Clauses – EEC Style, 1989 Afr. J. Int. Comp. L. 551

Myass/Reed, European Business Litigation (1998)

Niggemann, Eine Entscheidung der Cour de cassation zu Art. 23 EuGVVO – Fehlende Einigung, fehlende Bestimmbarkeit des vereinbarten Gerichts oder Inhaltskontrolle?, IPRax 2014, 194

Oberhammer, Group Josi, Coreck – Roma locuta, causa non finita?, IPRax 2004, 264

Pataut, Clauses attributives de juridiction et clauses abusives, in: Mélanges Jean Calais-Aulois (2004) 807

Peel, Exclusive Jurisdiction Agreements: Purity and Pragmatism in the Conflict of Laws, [1998] LMCLQ 182

Thomas Pfeiffer, Halbseitig fakultative Gerichtsstandsvereinbarungen in stillschweigend vereinbarten AGB?, IPRax 1998, 17

Thomas Pfeiffer, Die Unwirksamkeit von Gerichtsstandsvereinbarungen nach der Klauselrichtlinie, ZEuP 2003, 141

Plender/Wilderspin, The European Contracts Convention. The Rome Convention on the Law Applicable to Contractual Obligations (3ʳᵈ ed. 2009)

Queirolo, Gli accordi sulla competenza giurisdizionali (2000)

Dieter Rabe, Drittwirkung von Gerichtsstandsvereinbarungen nach Art. 17 EuGVÜ, TranspR 2000, 389

Rauscher, Gerichtsstandsbeeinflussende AGB im Geltungsbereich des EuGVÜ, ZZP 104 (1991), 271

Redmann, Ordre public-Kontrolle von Gerichtsstandsvereinbarungen (2005)

Renna, Prozessvergleich und internationale Zuständigkeit, Jura 2009, 119

Rüfner, Inkrafttreten der EuGVVO, Zuständigkeitsvereinbarung und Zuständigkeit am Erfüllungsort, ZEuP 2008, 165

Rühl, Das Haager Übereinkommen über die Vereinbarung gerichtlicher Zuständigkeiten: Rückschritt oder Fortschritt, IPRax 2005, 410

Rühl, Die Wirksamkeit von Gerichtsstands- und Schiedsgerichtsvereinbarungen im Lichte der Ingmar-Entscheidung, IPRax 2007, 294

Saenger, Internationale Gerichtsstandsvereinbarungen nach EuGVÜ und LugÜ, ZZP 110 (1997), 477

Saenger, Wirksamkeit internationaler Gerichtsstandsvereinbarungen, in: FS Otto Sandrock (2000), p. 807

Saenger, Gerichtsstandsvereinbarungen nach EuGVÜ in international handelsgebräuchlicher Form, ZEuP 2000, 656

Samtleben, Internationale Gerichtsstandsvereinbarungen nach dem EWG-Übereinkommen und nach der Gerichtsstandsnovelle, NJW 1974, 1590

Samtleben, Europäische Gerichtsstandsvereinbarungen und Drittstaaten – viel Lärm um nichts?, RabelsZ 59 (1995), 670

Samtleben, Der Art. 23 EuGVVO als einheitlicher Maßstab für internationale Gerichtsstandsvereinbarungen, in: FS Ansay (2006), p. 343

Schockweiler, Les conflits de lois et les conflits de juridictions en droit international privé luxembourgeois (2ⁿᵈ ed by *Wiwinius*, 1996)

Schulz, A., The Hague Convention of 30 June 2005 on Choice of Court Agreements, JPIL 2006, 243

Simotta, Wie "international" muss eine Gerichts-

standsvereinbarung nach Art. 23 EuGVVO bzw. Art. 17 EuGVÜ/LGVÜ sein?, in: Studia in Honorem Yessiou-Faltsi (2007), p. 633

Simotta, Zur restriktiven Auslegung von Art. 17 EuGVÜ/LgVÜ und Art. 23 EuGVVO durch den österreichischen OGH, ZZP Int 2009, p. 43

Sparka, Jurisdiction and Arbitration Clauses in Maritime Transport Documents. A Comparative Analysis (2009)

Spellenberg, Doppelter Gerichtsstand in fremdsprachigen AGB, IPRax 2007, 98

Spellenberg, Der Konsens in Art. 23 EuGVVO – Der kassierte Kater –, IPRax 2010, 264

Staehelin, Gerichtsstandsvereinbarungen im internationalen Handelsverkehr Europas: Form und Willenseinigung nach Art. 17 EuGVÜ/LugÜ (Basel 1994)

Stöve, Gerichtsstandsvereinbarungen nach Handelsbrauch, Art. 17 EuGVÜ und § 38 ZPO (1993)

Michael Stürner, Gerichtsstandsvereinbarungen und Europäisches Insolvenzrecht – Zugleich ein Beitrag zur internationalen Zuständigkeit bei insolvenzrechtlichen Annexverfahren, IPRax 2005, 416

Takahashi, Damages for Breach of a Choice-of-Court Agreement, Yb. PIL 10 (2008), p. 57

Takahashi, Damages for Breach of a Choice-of-Court Agreement: Remaining Issues, Yb. PIL 11 (2009), p. 73

Tham, Damages for breach of English jurisdiction clauses: more than meets the eye, (2004) LMCLQ, 46

Vassilakis, Die Anwendung des EuGVÜ und der EuGVO in der griechischen Rechtsprechung, IPRax 2005, 279

Vischer, Der Einbezug deliktischer Ansprüche in die Gerichtsstandsvereinbarung für den Vertrag, in: FS Erik Jayme, vol. I (2004), p. 993

Vrellis, The Validity of a Choice of Court Agreement Under the Hague Convention of 2005, in: FS Siehr (2010), p. 763

Wagner, R., Das Haager Übereinkommen vom 30.6. 2005 über Gerichtsstandsvereinbarungen, RabelsZ 73 (2009) 100

Weigel/Blankenheim, Europäische Gerichtsstandsklauseln – Missbrauchskontrolle und Vermeidung von Unklarheiten bei der Auslegung widersprechender Vereinbarungen, WM 2006, 664

Matthias Weller, Auslegung internationaler Gerichtsstandsvereinbarungen als ausschließlich und

Wirkungserstreckung auf die Klage des anderen Teils
gegen den *falsus procurator*, IPRax 2006, 444
Matthias Weller, Ordre public-Kontrolle internationaler Gerichtsstandsvereinbarungen im autonomen
Zuständigkeitsrecht (2005)

Yeo/Tan, Damages for Breach of Exclusive Jurisdiction Clauses, in: Worthington (Hrsg.), Commercial
Law and Commercial Practice (2003), p. 403.

I. Contents and purpose

The Article is one of the most important provisions of the Regulation and is also the more **1** important one of the two articles which form the Regulation's section dealing with the prorogation of jurisdiction. Through the Recast of the Brussels I Regulation the provision has gained even further importance because an exclusive jurisdiction agreement is now a means, the only one, to counter "Torpedo" tactics.[1] In principle the Regulation acknowledges the parties' autonomy to select the internationally competent forum. Art. 25 concerns the choice of jurisdiction through agreement or trust settlement while Art. 26 regulates the choice by submission. The purpose of Art. 25 is twofold: on the one hand to ensure that the parties can choose the court where their disputes shall be litigated; on the other hand to give this freedom reasonable limits.

The provision allows the parties – within the boundaries of the Regulation – to agree freely **2** which court or courts of a Member State shall have jurisdiction over disputes arising between the parties.[2] The provision accepts that by their choice the parties can oust the jurisdiction of the originally competent court so that another court – in a Member State – becomes competent to determine the dispute. The parties can do so even if neither of them is

---

[1] See thereto *Hartley*, in: Essays in honour of Michael Bogdan 95 *et seq.*
[2] See Recital (14).

domiciled in an EU Member State as Art. 25 (1) now expressly indicates. Unless otherwise agreed a valid jurisdiction clause founds the exclusive jurisdiction of the designated court. This serves the parties' interest to know in advance which country's courts are to decide any later dispute between the parties while absent the jurisdiction agreement it always remains uncertain which party it will be who sues and which courts will then be competent. Jurisdiction agreements therefore promote considerably the foreseeability and certainty of the legal administration of possible future conflicts between the parties. Before the Recast of the Regulation a jurisdiction agreement did not hinder a court to examine its jurisdiction when a party approached this court in breach of the jurisdiction agreement.[3] This allowed the ill-famed "Torpedo" tactics to start rashly proceedings in a notoriously slow jurisdiction mainly by applying for a declaratory judgment not to owe a sum in order to delay a judgment (and payment) for years.[4] Now, the new Art. 31 (2) provides that any seised and derogated court (in a Member State) has to "stay the proceedings until such time as the court seised on the basis of the *jurisdiction* agreement declares that it has no jurisdiction under the agreement." This ensures that parties can rely on the priority of the prorogated court.

3   Art. 25 deals with the formal and now also with a number of material requirements of a jurisdiction agreement. The Recast added the formulation "unless the agreement is null and void as to its substantive validity under the law of that Member State." Some questions of the material validity[5] are thus governed by the law (including the conflict of law rules)[6] of the prorogated forum. The Article also orders that a jurisdiction clause in a trust instrument is treated in the same way as a jurisdiction agreement. The boundaries of a jurisdiction agreement are reminded by para. 3: Neither an otherwise exclusive jurisdiction (Art. 24) nor the specific protection of a weaker party (Arts. 15, 19, 23) can be overthrown by the parties' express designation of another competent court. Thus, jurisdiction agreements can in fact merely oust the jurisdiction under Arts. 4, 7 and 8.

4   If the parties have agreed on the jurisdiction of a court outside the Member States of the Regulation it depends on the rules applicable there whether and which prorogatory effect such a choice of forum has;[7] however their derogatory effect may affect the jurisdiction of the courts of Member States; it is disputed whether Art. 25 covers this situation.[8]

5   For disputes over international commercial contracts Art. 25 has gained particular importance since almost always in such cases each party tries to incorporate a jurisdiction clause into the contract that usually designates the jurisdiction of the courts of the own country. No question, it is a considerable advantage if a party can sue the other before the courts of their own country ('at home') because of the familiarity of language, the better knowledge of the necessary formalities, the easier access to, and lower costs of, legal advice and representation before court and because at the same time all these aspects are more difficult for the other

---

[3]   This has been so decided by the ECJ: *Erich Gasser GmbH v. MISAT Srl* (Case C-116/02) (2003) ECR I-14693; also for arbitration agreements: *Allianz SpA, Generali Assicurazioni General SpA v. West Tankers Inc.* (Case C-185/07) (2009) ECR I-663).

[4]   See the facts in *Erich Gasser GmbH v. MISAT Srl* (Case C-116/02) (2003) ECR I-14693.

[5]   See *infra* notes 77 *et seq.*

[6]   See Recital 20.

[7]   *von Hein*, RIW 2013, 104; *Magnus/Mankowski*, ZvglRWiss 110 (2011) 270; *M. Weller*, GPR 2012, 38.

[8]   See *infra* notes 36 *et seq.*

party and increase its willingness to settle. Art. 25 aims at a wide recognition of choice of court agreements;[9] party autonomy in the area of jurisdiction is subject only to few restrictions. Thus, Art. 25 entitles private persons to a rather wide extent to dispose in international cases over which Member States' courts are to decide disputes.[10] This is justified, however, only if the choice of a specific forum which otherwise would not be competent represents the unimpeded will of both parties.[11] The consensus of the parties is the core element and must therefore be clearly and precisely demonstrated.[12] Art. 25 and in particular its form requirements in (1) (a)-(c) try to ensure that this aim is achieved though in principle the Article is generous with formal requirements necessary for choice of court clauses, especially in connection with international commercial transactions. In this context the ECJ developed a full set of principles on when jurisdiction clauses are validly agreed upon and incorporated into the main contract. These principles form now a model for Europe how and when in general contracts on the basis of general conditions are validly concluded.

Though Art. 25 serves a very useful purpose it was unfortunate that the preceding text **6** version (Art. 23) gave rise to many disputed and unsettled questions.[13] In particular, the borderline between questions falling within the autonomous scope of Art. 23 and those which are regulated by the applicable national law was far from clear.[14] This impeded seriously the central aim of the Article and of jurisdiction agreements to remove any uncertainty as to the place where future disputes between the parties have to be litigated. It was one of the central objectives of the Commission's Reform Proposal for the Brussels I Regulation to reduce these uncertainties and to enhance the efficiency of choice-of-court agreements.[15] Though the added formulation on the applicable law on the validity of choice-of-court agreements (para. (1) sent. 1) removes certain problems it creates others.

II. History of the Article

Art. 25 Brussels Ibis had its predecessor in Art. 23 Brussels I which in turn followed on **7** Art. 17 Brussels Convention. It was one of the central aims of the Recast of the Brussels I Regulation to enhance the effectiveness of jurisdiction agreements.[16] Although the text of the former Art. 23 has been retained in essence a number of modifications has been made: (1) Art. 25 does no longer require that one of the parties is domiciled in a Member State; (2) the

---

[9] See also Recital (14).

[10] See also *Gaudemet-Tallon* para. 122.

[11] See *Estasis Salotti di Colzani Aimo and Gianmario Colzani v. RÜWA Polstereimaschinen GmbH*, (Case 24/76) (1976) ECR 1831 (1ˢᵗ sentence of the summary of the decision); see also *Layton/Mercer* para. 20.002.

[12] See *Estasis Salotti di Colzani Aimo and Gianmario Colzani v. RÜWA Polstereimaschinen GmbH*, (Case 24/76) (1976) ECR 1831, 1841 para. 7; *Coreck Maritime GmbH v. Handelsveem BV*, (Case C-387/98) (2000) ECR 9337, 9371 para. 13 with references to prior judgments.

[13] In the same sense *Kropholler/von Hein* Art. 23 note 10; *Schack* para. 468: scope of application unnecessarily complicated.

[14] In this sense also *Layton/Mercer* para. 20.035.

[15] See the Memorandum to the Proposal for a Regulation of the European Parliament and of the Council on jurisdiction and the recognition and enforcement of judgments in civil and commercial matters of 14 December 2010 (COM(2010) 748 final) p. 4 and now Recital 22 Brussels Ibis.

[16] See Explanatory Report to the Proposal COM (2010) 748 fin. P. 4 and Recital 22 to Brussels Ibis.

substantive validity of the jurisdiction agreement has to be determined in accordance with the law of the chosen court; (3) the former para. 3 which dealt with jurisdiction agreements of parties from third states has been deleted; (4) in the new para. 4 only the numbering has been adapted to the present Regulation; (5) the present para. 5 that states the independence of the jurisdiction agreement from the main contract is entirely new though it corresponds to the former practice.

A further change relevant for jurisdiction agreements concerns the priority rule in cases where actions on the same issue and between the same parties are brought in different courts. The new Art. 31 (2) Brussels I*bis* grants priority to the chosen court.[17] Also, the new Arts. 33 and 34 have some relevance for jurisdiction agreements. If a Member State court is seised and proceedings on the same or related matters are already pending in a third state – even on the basis of a respective jurisdiction agreement – the Member State court has certain discretion to stay the own proceedings and thereby to indirectly honour the jurisdiction agreement.

In general, the changes are moderate and useful. However, in particular with respect to the new conflicts rule they do not relieve all uncertainties. The precise scope of this new rule must still be specified by the ECJ.

8   Almost all considerations on which Art. 17 Brussels Convention and Art. 23 old Brussels I Regulation were based apply as well to Art. 25 of the recasted Regulation. In particular, the *Jenard* Report and the *Schlosser* Report are still useful. The same is true for the *Kerameus/Evrigenis* Report on the occasion of the accession of Greece. Moreover, the ECJ judgments on Art. 23 old Regulation as well as on Art. 17 Brussels Convention remain valid for the interpretation of Art. 25 Brussels I*bis* except where the new text has explicitly changed the basis for the former decision as in particular is the case with the *Gasser v. MISAT* decision of the ECJ.[18]

9   Art. 23 old Regulation, was also the model for the identical Art. 23 Lugano Convention whose revision of 2007 adapted its Art. 23 fully to the text of Art. 23 of the old Regulation. Art. 25 Brussels I*bis* now distorts this identity with the Lugano Convention until again an eventual adaptation can be concluded.[19]

III. Global regulation of jurisdiction agreements: the Hague Convention of 2005

10   After efforts to achieve a global Brussels I Convention failed, the Hague Conference on Private International Law prepared a more limited project, namely a worldwide Convention on Choice of Court Agreements. It was finally concluded on 30 June 2005 on a diplomatic conference,[20] and entered into force on 1 October 2015 in the EU and all its Member States as

---

17   See the comments to Art. 31 (*Fentiman*).
18   *Erich Gasser v. MISAT Srl.*, (Case C-116/02) (2003) ECR I-14693.
19   It remains to be seen whether, and if so, in which way the Lugano Convention will be adapted to Brussels I*bis*.
20   The text is available under www.hcch.net/index_en.php?act=conventions.text&cid=98; on this Convention see in particular *Hartley/Dogauchi*, Explanatory Report on the 2005 Hague Choice of Court Agreements Convention (Hague Conference on Private International Law 2007, http://www.hcch.net); further

well as in Mexico. The Convention defines the requirements necessary for a valid jurisdiction agreement;[21] it regulates which consequences follow from a jurisdiction agreement with respect to the jurisdiction of the designated court and of other – derogated – courts;[22] and it deals with the recognition and enforcement of judgments rendered by a court designated by a jurisdiction agreement.[23] Concerning the conclusion of a jurisdiction agreement the Convention follows to some extent the lines of Art. 25 of the Regulation but requires a stricter form of jurisdiction agreements (writing or other means of communication which renders information accessible).[24] In contrast to the Convention the Regulation does only partly address the consequences of such agreements on jurisdiction.[25] Moreover, the Convention's grounds to refuse recognition and enforcement are wider than those provided for by the Regulation.[26] The relationship between the Convention and the Regulation is regulated by Art. 26 (6) of the Convention in a rather complicated way.[27] With respect to jurisdiction the provision gives precedence to "the rules of a Regional Economic Integration Organisation" (like the EU)[28] where "none of the parties is resident[29] in a Contracting State < sc. *of the Hague Convention* > that is not a Member State of the Regional Economic Integration Organisation." Thus, Art. 25 of the Regulation prevails over the Hague Convention where both parties reside either in different EU states or outside the EU in states that are Non-Contracting States of the Hague Convention.[30] On the other hand is the Hague Convention applicable in cases where both parties are domiciled outside the EU. If then one of the parties is resident in a Hague Convention State this Convention and not Art. 25 Brussels I*bis* would apply even if a court in the EU is chosen.[31] Even if one of the parties is domiciled in the EU and the other in a Hague Convention State outside the EU the Hague provisions can apply.[32] This can reduce the ambit of the present Art. 25 Brussels I*bis* Regulation. In the case that parties, who are not domiciled in Member States of the Regulation but who are resident in Member States of the Hague Convention, agree on the jurisdiction of the courts in a Regulation State, these courts have to apply the Convention, even if its stricter form requirements

---

Bläsi, Das Haager Übereinkommen über Gerichtsstandsvereinbarungen (2010); *Brand/Herrup*, The 2005 Hague Convention on Choice of Court Agreements (2008); *Wagner*, RabelsZ 73 (2009), 100 *et seq.*; for a survey see *Rühl*, IPRax 2005, 410 *et seq.* A prior Draft of the Convention was published in 2004 (Work. Doc. No. 110 E of May 2004, also available under www.hcch.net).

21   See Art. 3 (c) HCCA; see thereto *Beaumont/Yüksel*, in: FS Kurt Siehr (2010), 563, 575 *et seq.*); *Vrellis*, in: FS Kurt Siehr (2010), 763 *et seq.*

22   See Arts. 5; 6 HCCA.

23   Arts. 8–15 HCCA.

24   See Art. 3 (c) HCCA.

25   The Regulation is silent on the derogation effect of jurisdiction agreements.

26   See in particular Art. 11 HCCA according to which judgments which grant non-compensatory damages *(punitive damages)* may not be recognised. The Regulation does not contain a parallel provision.

27   See thereto *Hartley/Dogauchi*, Explanatory Report paras. 291 *et seq.*

28   See *Hartley/Dogauchi*, Explanatory Report para. 295.

29   The Convention defines the term for other than natural persons in its Art. 4(2). The residence of natural persons is not defined; however, it is evidently their habitual residence.

30   See the explanations and examples given by *Hartley/Dogauchi*, Explanatory Report paras. 291 *et seq.*

31   See the respective example given by *Hartley/Dogauchi*, Explanatory Report para. 299.

32   See the examples of *Hartley/Dogauchi*, Explanatory Report para. 299 *et seq.* However, where there is no conflict in substance between the Hague Convention and the Brussels Regime, according to the Report, the Hague Convention evidently accepts the solution under Brussels I*(bis)*; see *Hartley/Dogauchi*, ibid.

may lead to the invalidity of the jurisdiction agreement. In order to avoid discrepancies of this kind, the Hague Convention has to be interpreted as far as possible to be compatible with rival instruments (Art. 26 (1) Hague Convention). In the same way, Art. 25 Brussels I*bis* Regulation should be construed. Anyway, the Recast has considerably narrowed the gap between the Brussels I Regulation and the Hague Convention; the remaining differences make the priority problem less important.[33]

Almost the same solutions and considerations apply with respect to the Lugano Convention – although it still requires that one of the parties is domiciled in a Lugano State[34] – since the Hague Convention gives in a similar way precedence to already existing treaties (Art. 26 (2)-(4) Hague Convention).[35]

IV. Relationship to other sources of law dealing with jurisdiction agreements

1. Relationship to further international conventions

11 International conventions which regulate "particular matters", which are in force in the involved EU Member State and which also govern international jurisdiction agreements take precedence over Art. 25 (see also Art. 71 and the comments thereto).[36] However, "their application cannot compromise the principles which underlie judicial cooperation in civil and commercial matters in the European Union such as the principles, recalled in recitals 6, 11, 12 and 15 to 17 in the preamble to Regulation No. 44/2001, free movement of judgments in civil and commercial matters, predictability as to the courts having jurisdiction and therefore legal certainty for litigants, sound administration of justice, minimisation of the risk of concurrent proceedings, and mutual trust in the administration of justice in the European Union."[37]

12 This principal precedence of special international conventions is of particular relevance with respect to the CMR. Art. 31 (1) CMR deals also with jurisdiction agreements but does not provide any form for them. It is the general view that Art. 31 CMR prevails over Art. 25 Regulation as far as Art. 31 CMR extends since the CMR is the more specific of the two conventions.[38] But it is very much disputed whether Art. 31 CMR has any meaning with respect to the form of a jurisdiction agreement concerning a contract which falls under the

---

[33] As to the relationship between the Hague Convention and the Brussels Regime see also *Beaumont*, (2009) 6 JPrIL 142 *et seq.*; *Kohler*, in: Pocar/Viarengo/Villata pp. 201 *et seq.*

[34] In this context all EU States and Iceland, Norway and Switzerland are Lugano States.

[35] See thereto *Hartley/Dogauchi*, Explanatory Report paras. 271 *et seq.*

[36] See *Nürnberger Allgemeine Versicherungs AG v. Portbridge Transport International BV*, (Case C-148/03), (2004) ECR I-10327.; *TNT Nederland Express BV v. AXA Versicherung AG*, (Case C-533/08) (2010) ECR I-4107 paras. 38 *et seq.*; *"The Bergen"* (1997) 1 Lloyd's Rep. 380 (with respect to the Arrest Convention of 1952); *Anton* p. 116; *Kropholler/von Hein* Art. 71 note 5; *Layton/Mercer* para. 20.004; *Mankowski*, in: Rauscher Art. 71 note 14; see also *Domej*, in: FS Heinz Mayer 41 *et seq.* and for the Lugano Convention *Domej*, in: Dasser/Oberhammer Art. 67 note 8.

[37] *TNT Nederland Express BV./. AXA Versicherung AG*, (Case C-533/08) (2010) ECR I-4107 para. 49.

[38] *Nürnberger Allgemeine Versicherungs AG v. Portbridge Transport International BV*, (Case C-148/03), (2004) ECR I-10327; *TNT Nederland Express BV./. AXA Versicherung AG*, (Case C-533/08) (2010) ECR I-4107 para. 38 s.; *Kropholler/von Hein* Art. 71 note 5; *Jesser-Huß* in: Münchener Kommentar zum

scope of the CMR. Three different views have been advanced: either that Art. 31 CMR itself firmly though implicitly provides that no form is required;[39] or that the national law designated by conflicts rules decides the form question;[40] or that Art. 25 Regulation has to be applied.[41] Since Art. 31 CMR on the one hand regulates jurisdiction agreements but on the other hand does not prescribe a certain form, the preferable view appears to be that this provision covers the question and requires no form.[42] This view is also supported by the fact that Art. 31 (1) CMR allows jurisdiction agreements only in the form that a non-exclusive additional jurisdiction is agreed upon, which cannot displace the jurisdiction provided for by the CMR. Given this restricted effect of jurisdiction agreements under the CMR the complete informality of their conclusion is acceptable.[43] As well, such interpretation does not compromise in any way the principles underlying the Brussels I*bis* Regulation.

A further prevailing regulation of the form of a jurisdiction agreement is Art. 2 (b) of the **13** Basle European Convention on State Immunity of 16 May 1972, which requires that a contractual provision by which a state waives its immunity must be express and in writing in order to be effective.

The relationship between the Brussels I*bis* Regulation and the (parallel) Lugano Convention **13a** is addressed in Art. 73 (1) Brussels I*bis*:[44] The Brussels I*bis* Regulation does not affect the application of the Lugano Convention. This means where the parties choose a court in a Lugano State (being not an EU State) Art. 23 Lugano Convention applies if also one of the parties is domiciled there.[45] If a court in an EU State is chosen Art. 25 Brussels I*bis* applies no matter where the parties are domiciled.

2. Relationship to national law

As far as Art. 25 is applicable it takes precedence over any national law which an EU Member **14** State has enacted on the same subject even if this national law is mandatory. The Regulation is directly applicable Community law for those States who have adopted Title IV of the Lisbon Treaty (see Art. 288 TFEU). But precedence of the Brussels regime over national law was already common ground under Art. 17 Brussels Convention.[46] The precedence is necessary in the interest of a uniform and foreseeable application of Art. 25 under the super-

---

Handelsgesetzbuch, vol. VII (2nd ed. 2009) Art. 31 CMR note 24 s.; *Mankowski*, in: Rauscher Art. 71 note 14; similarly *Auer* in: Bülow/Böckstiegel/Geimer/Schütze Art. 23 note 2 *et seq.*

[39]   In this sense for instance *Jesser-Huß* (preceding fn.), Art. 31 CMR note 25; *Mankowski*, in: Rauscher Art. 71 note 14; generally in the same sense *O'Malley/Layton* para. 33.14.

[40]   In this sense for instance *Thume*, in: Fremuth/Thume, Kommentar zum Transportrecht (2000), Art. 31 CMR note 11.

[41]   In this sense for instance *Tiefenthaler*, in: Czernich/Tiefenthaler/Kodek Art. 71 note 2; *Kropholler/von Hein* Art. 71 note 5; *Hausmann*, in: Simons/Hausmann Art. 23 note 19; apparently also *Merkt*, in: Hopt/Baumbach, Handelsgesetzbuch (36th ed. 20140, Art. 31 CMR note 1 (but in essence favouring that no form is required at all).

[42]   See *Jesser-Huß* (fn. 28), Art. 31 CMR note 25; *Mankowski*, in: Rauscher Art. 71 note 14.

[43]   See also *Jesser-Huß* (fn. 28), Art. 31 CMR note 25.

[44]   See the comment on Art. 73 (*Mankowski*).

[45]   See Art. 64 (2) (a) Lugano Convention.

[46]   See for instance OGH ZfRV 2001, 113; *O'Malley/Layton* para. 21.04.

vision of the ECJ. As far as the scope of Art. 25 extends, it therefore regulates finally and conclusively questions of international jurisdiction agreements.[47] The national control of such agreements according to the standards applicable to unfair contract terms is in principle inadmissible even if a jurisdiction agreement was contained in standard contract terms.[48] Nor does the validity of jurisdiction agreements depend on any objective connection between the chosen court and the dispute even where national law may request such connection.[49]

3. Relationship to other provisions of the Regulation

15 With few exceptions Art. 25 takes precedence also over the other provisions of the Regulation which concern jurisdiction, in particular over Arts. 4 and 7. Art. 25 is however overturned by an exclusive jurisdiction under Art. 24 and also if a jurisdiction agreement contradicts Arts. 15, 19 and 23. Neither the exclusive nor the protective jurisdiction provisions of the Regulation are posed at the parties' disposal. Otherwise their specific purpose could not be safeguarded. Also where a defendant submits under Art. 26 to a jurisdiction other than agreed upon she/he can no longer rely on the preceding jurisdiction agreement.[50]

16 Under the preceding Brussels I Regulation Art. 23, the predecessor of the present Art. 25, could also not overrule the former Arts. 27 and 28 (now Arts. 29 and 30 Brussels *Ibis*).[51] In particular English courts took the view that a valid jurisdiction agreement enabled them to disregard the former Art. 27 which gave the court first seised priority to decide on jurisdiction.[52] Jurisdiction agreements had even served as a basis for English courts in granting anti-suit injunctions in order to restrain prior foreign proceedings.[53] Under the old Regulation this disputed practice[54] had been refused by the ECJ:[55] The second court seised was obliged to

---

[47] See *Layton/Mercer* para. 20.004; *Mankowski*, in: Rauscher Art. 23 note 10; *Hausmann*, in: Simons/Hausmann Art. 23 n. 24.

[48] *Trasporti Castelletti Spedizioni Internazionali SpA v. Hugo Trumpy SpA*, (Case C-159/97) (1999) ECR I-1597, I-1656 para. 56; *Kröll*, ZZP 113 (2000), 135, 149 *et seq.*; *Gottwald*, in: Münchener Kommentar zur ZPO Art. 23 EuGVO note 79; *Mankowski*, in: Rauscher Art. 23 note 12. See *infra* Art. 25 notes 86, 96–98; also for Art. 23 Lugano Convention *Killias*, in: Dasser/Oberhammer Art. 23 note 196.

[49] *Trasporti Castelletti Spedizioni Internazionali SpA v. Hugo Trumpy SpA*, (Case C-159/97) (1999) ECR I-1597, I-1656 para. 50; *Mainschiffahrts-Genossenschaft eG (MSG) v. Les Gravières Rhénanes SARL*, (Case C-106/95) (1997) ECR I-911, I-944 para. 34; *Francesco Benincasa v. Dentalkit Srl*, (Case C-269/95) (1997) ECR I-3767, I-3798 para. 28; *Siegfried Zelger v. Sebastiano Salinitri*, (Case 56/79) (1980) ECR 89, 97 para. 4.

[50] See further Art. 26 note 29 (*Calvo Caravaca/Carrascosa González*).

[51] *Erich Gasser GmbH v. MISAT Srl*, (Case C-116/02), (2003) ECR I-14693, I-14740 para. 51; *Kropholler/von Hein* Art. 27 note 19; *Layton/Mercer* para. 20.004; *Leible*, in: Rauscher Art. 27 Rn 16.

[52] See *Continental Bank v. Aeakos Compania Naviera* (1994) 1 WLR 588 (C.A.); *Lexmar Corp. v. Nordisk Skibsrederforening* (1997) 1 Lloyd's Rep. 289 (Q.B.D.); *Glencore International AG v. Metro Trading International Inc.* (1999) 2 Lloyd's Rep. 632 (Q.B.D.); *OT Africa Line Ltd. v. Hijazy (2001)* 1 Lloyd's Rep. 76 (Q.B.D.).

[53] See for instance *Continental Bank NA v. Aeakos Compania Naviera SA* (1994) 1 WLR 588 (C.A.); *The "Angelic Grace"* (1995) 2 Lloyd's Rep. 87 (C.A.); *Phillip Alexander Futures & Securities Ltd. v. Bamberger Toepfer* (1996) CLC 1757 (C.A.); *International GmbH v. Société Cargill France* (1998) 1 Lloyd's Rep. 379 (C.A.); *OT Africa Line Ltd. v. Fayad Hijazy (2002)* ILPr 189 (Q.B.D., Aikens J).

stay proceedings until the court first seised had decided on jurisdiction even if a jurisdiction agreement accorded the second court exclusive jurisdiction. Now, Art. 31 (2) Brussels I*bis* gives the chosen court priority over other courts even when they were seised first.[56]

V. Survey over the requirements of a valid jurisdiction agreement

To be valid a jurisdiction agreement must meet the following conditions which are discussed **17** below in detail:
– The transaction to which the jurisdiction agreement refers must fall within the scope of application of the Regulation;[57]
– the jurisdiction of a court or courts in a Member State must be agreed upon;[58]
– no longer must one of the parties be domiciled in a Member State;[59]
– the jurisdiction agreement must be connected with "a particular legal relationship";[60]
– the jurisdiction agreement must be validly concluded;[61]
– the jurisdiction agreement must satisfy a specific form varying slightly whether transactions in international trade and commerce or in other civil matters are concerned;[62]
– the jurisdiction agreement must not contradict Art. 24 or Art. 15, 19, 23.[63]

VI. General scope of application of the Article

In general the scope of application of Art. 25 corresponds to that of the Regulation as such. **18** Only in territorial respect Art. 25 is of wider application than most other provisions of the Regulation. The only territorial connection with an EU Member State a forum selection agreement must have is the prorogation of a forum in a Member State – then the Article is applicable. It is no longer required that the domicile of one of the parties, let alone the domicile of the defendant lies in a Member State. Although Denmark has not adopted the Regulation as such (but ratified a separate treaty with the EU making the Regulation applicable in Denmark and has notified the Commission of its decision to implement also the Brussels I Recast) this country does also count as Member State of the Regulation (as to the specific situation of Denmark see below).[64]

---

54   *Contra Briggs*, (1994) LMCLQ 158; *Hill*, p. 145.
55   *Erich Gasser GmbH v. MISAT Srl*, (Case C-116/02) (2003) ECR I-14693; see thereto *Bogdan*, Scand. Stud. L. 2007, 89 *et seq.*; *Fawcett*, Int. Comp L.Q. 2007, 1 *et seq.*; *Grothe*, IPRax 2004, 205; *Merrett*, Int. Comp. L. Q. 2006, 315.
56   See thereto *Hartley*, in: Essays in honour of Michael Bogdan 95 *et seq.*; *von Hein* RIW 2013, 104; *Magnus*, in FS Dieter Martiny (2014), p. 785, 796 *et seq.*; also Recital 22.
57   See *infra* Art. 25 notes 18–23 (*Magnus*).
58   See *infra* Art. 25 notes 75–87 (*Magnus*).
59   See *infra* Art. 25 notes 48–51 (*Magnus*).
60   See *infra* Art. 25 notes 66–68 (*Magnus*).
61   See *infra* Art. 25 notes 77–87 (*Magnus*).
62   See *infra* Art. 25 notes 88–131 (*Magnus*).
63   See *infra* Art. 25 note 132 (*Magnus*).
64   See *infra* Art. 25 note 21 (*Magnus*).

1. Material scope of application

19 Art. 25 requires that the jurisdiction agreement concerns matters which fall within the general material scope of application of the Regulation, namely civil and commercial matters unless they are expressly excluded by Art. 1 (1) sent. 2 and (2).[65] The parties cannot expand the material scope of the Regulation by their mere agreement. Forum selection agreements on disputes not covered by the Regulation have to be dealt with according to the rules provided for either by other international instruments or by the autonomous national procedural law. In particular, Art. 25 does not extend to arbitration agreements (Art. 1 (2) (d)).[66] But as far as the Regulation covers non-commercial (civil) matters Art. 25 entitles the parties to also designate the competent court(s) for such matters.[67] Until 18 June 2011 when the Maintenance Regulation[68] came into force this had been relevant for jurisdiction clauses in maintenance agreements while agreements on matrimonial property did never fall under the Regulation.[69] The Regulation does not cover insolvency proceedings as well (Art. 1 (2) (b)); they are regulated by the Insolvency Regulation of 29 May 2000.[70] As far as the Insolvency Regulation is applicable, its jurisdiction provisions[71] take precedence over any inconsistent choice of court agreement which becomes ineffective when insolvency proceedings are instituted.[72] Whether the Insolvency Regulation is applicable depends on the true nature of the respective proceedings; only if they are strictly concerned with insolvency matters – the forced liquidation or administration of the debtor's property in the interest, and with a view to an equal treatment, of all creditors – the mandatory insolvency jurisdiction under Art. 3 Insolvency Regulation prevails over any jurisdiction agreement.[73]

2. Territorial scope of application

20 In general, the Regulation requires in respect to territory that the defendant must be domiciled within the territory of an EU Member State (Art. 4). But the Regulation knows of certain exceptions to this rule. Art. 25 introduces a rather far-reaching one: It is sufficient that a court or courts in a Member State are prorogated; neither the plaintiff nor the defendant need to be domiciled in a Member State (Art. 23 (1)). This is in sharp contrast to the prior Regulation which required one party's domicile within the EU. The details are discussed below.[74]

---

[65]   *Kropholler/von Hein* Art. 23 note 1; probably also *Ansgar Staudinger*, in: Rauscher Art. 59 note 7.

[66]   See Art. 1 notes 36 *et seq.* (*Rogerson*).

[67]   *Geimer/Schütze* Art. 23 note 61.

[68]   Regulation (EC) No. 4/2009 of 18 December 2008, OJ 2009 No. L 7, p. 1.

[69]   See Art. 1 notes 24 *et seq.* (*Rogerson*).

[70]   See also Art. 1 note 29 *et seq.* (*Rogerson*).

[71]   Art. 3 Insolvency Regulation.

[72]   Cf. *Michael Stürner*, IPRax 2005, 419.

[73]   For the distinction between insolvency proceedings and 'normal' civil or commercial proceedings where jurisdiction agreements which conform to Art. 25 Brussels *Ibis* Regulation remain effective, cf. *Mankowski*, in: Rauscher Art. 1 note 18 *et seq.*; *Michael Stürner*, IPRax 2005, 419 *et seq.*; see also the comments to Art. 1 note 34 (*Rogerson*).

[74]   See *infra* Art. 25 note 25 (*Magnus*).

3. Temporal scope of application

For its temporal application Art. 25 requires that the Regulation must have entered into **21** force in the country where and when a court is seised with the dispute concerning Art. 25 (see thereto Art. 66). For the present 28 Member States this date was 10 January 2015. Art. 25 applies if the suit is instituted on or after that day. This is even true for Denmark. This country which has a special treaty with the EU[75] extending the Regulation to Denmark on July 1, 2007 has declared in time that it also adopted the modifications of the new Brussels I*bis* Regulation.[76]

It is not necessary that the jurisdiction agreement must have been concluded on or after the mentioned date. Art. 25 applies also to jurisdiction agreements which were concluded before.[77] In the same sense the ECJ had decided the intertemporal question when the Brussels Convention had been introduced.[78] This can have the effect that a jurisdiction agreement of parties who both have their domicile in third states but have chosen a court in the EU loses its (formal or even material[79]) validity from 10 January 2015 on although under the formerly applicable law the agreement was valid.[80] Whether contrary to this result the parties' trust in the original validity of a jurisdiction agreement must be protected is open to debate.[81] Vice versa a formerly invalid agreement may become valid.[82]

4. Personal scope of application

Like the Regulation as a whole, Art. 25 also does not require specific qualifications with **22** respect to the personal scope of application. Although Art. 25 (1) (c) addresses international trade and commerce, the parties do not have to be merchants in a specific technical sense as prescribed in some legal systems.[83] Nor does the nationality of the parties of a jurisdiction agreement matter (Art. 4).

---

[75] See OJ 2005 No. L 299, p. 62.

[76] Denmark notified the EU Commission by a letter of 20 December 2012 of its decision to implement the Brussels I*bis* Regulation. According to Art. 3 (2) of the Agreement of 19 October 2005 between Denmark and the EU (see preceding fn.) Denmark must notify the EU Commission within 30 days after an amendment of the Brussels I Reguation has been adopted whether it will implement the amendment. Since the Brussels I*bis* Regulation was adopted on 12 December 2012 Denmark's notification was in time.

[77] *von Hein*, RIW 2013, 101; in the same sense for the old Regulation: LG Berlin IPRax 2005, 261 with note *Jayme*; *Kropholler/von Hein* Art. 66 note 3.

[78] *Sanicentral GmbH v. René Collin*, (Case 25/79) (1979) ECR 3423. As to the relevant point of time when the jurisdiction agreement must meet the requirements of the Regulation see however *infra* Art. 25 notes 57–64 (*Magnus*).

[79] Depending on the law that is now applicable to jurisdiction agreements under Art. 25 (1) sent. 1 Brussels I*bis* Regulation

[80] See *von Hein* RIW 2013, 101; *Burgstaller/Neumayr* Art. 23 note 9; for application of the national law *Ratkovic/Zgrabljicrotar* J.P.I.L.9 (2013) 252.

[81] Against such trust in the former validity: LG München I, IPRax 1996, 266 with review by *Trunk* IPRax 1996, 249; for the protection of this trust: *Czernich/Tiefenthaler/Kodek/Tiefenthaler* Art. 23 note 19; *Kropholler/von Hein* Art. 23 note 11.

[82] *Burgstaller/Neumayr* Art. 23 note 9; OLG Hamm RIW 2000, 382 (under the former law).

[83] E.g., Cass. civ. JCP éd. G 1997 IV 747; *Kropholler/von Hein* Art. 23 note 54.

5. Internationality

23　Since the Regulation intends to unify "the rules of conflict of jurisdiction"[84] it is clear from decisions of the ECJ that the provisions of the Regulation apply only where the case possesses a certain internationality.[85] Under the old Brussels I Regulation the precise requirements of internationality with respect to the former Art. 23 were disputed. Partly it was argued that the unification aim of the Regulation was confined to the Member States and that therefore the necessary internationality required links to more than one Member State.[86] On the other hand, a broader view was taken and it was argued that neither the text of the old Art. 23 nor its underlying policy required contacts to at least two different Member States.[87] The same discussion may arise again under Art. 25 Brussels I*bis* although the waiver of at least one party's EU domicile evidently favours the wider view. Three different aspects of the question have to be distinguished: first, whether Art. 25 applies to cases which are merely internal except that the parties have conferred jurisdiction on the courts of another Member State; secondly, whether Art. 25 requires links to at least two different Member States; and thirdly, whether Art. 25 extends to cases where only a link to a third country constitutes the international element. On all three aspects the views may still vary in the sense just mentioned.

24　In a considerable number, if not in the majority of practical cases, the differing views on the necessary international element led in the past nonetheless to the same result: The mentioned differing views concurred in applying Art. 23 old Regulation where the case had links to two or more Member States, for instance where the parties of an agreement on the jurisdiction of a Member State's court had their domiciles in different Member States[88] or where they had their domiciles in the same state but conferred jurisdiction on the courts of another Member State provided that the subject matter as such was international in character as for instance a transboundary delivery etc.[89] These results are also valid under Brussels I*bis*. The views reached, however, differing results where there were 'true' links

---

84　Recital (2).

85　*Hypotecni banka* (Case C-327/10) (2011) ECR I-11543 para. 29; *Corman-Collins SA v. La Maison du Whisky SA* (Case C-9/12) (2014) nyr. para. 18; with respect to jurisdiction agreements see Report *Jenard* to Art. 17; Report *Schlosser* para. 174; see also *Burgstaller/Neumayr* Art. 23 note 11; *Gaudemet-Tallon* paras. 133 *et seq.*; *Gottwald*, in: Münchener Kommentar zur ZPO Art. 23 note 4; *Mankowski*, RIW 2005, 561, 567.

86　See BGH NJW 1986, 1438; BGH NJW 1989, 1431; BGHZ 116, 77; in the same sense for Austria: OGH JBl 1998, 726; see further *Samtleben*, RabelsZ 59 (1995), 691.

87　See OLG München RIW 1989, 901; HG Zürich SZIER 1997, 373; *Geimer/Schütze* Art. 23 note 29; *Dutta/ Heinze*, IPRax 2005, 224, 225, 228; *Kropholler/von Hein* Art. 23 note 3; *Layton/Mercer* para. 20.006; *Mankowski*, in: Rauscher Art. 23 note 5; *Oberhammer*, IPRax 2004, 265; also incidentally but rather clearly *Andrew Owusu v. Nugent B. Jackson, trading as "Villa Holidays Bal-Inn Villas", Mammee Bay Resorts Ltd., Mammee Bay Club Ltd., The Enchanted Garden Resorts & Spa Ltd., Consulting Services Ltd., Town & Country Resorts Ltd.*, (Case C-281/02) (2005) ECR I-1383 para. 28.

88　See, e.g., BGE 125 III 108 (under Lugano Convention); OLG München IPRspr. 1985 No. 133 A; *Gottwald*, in: Münchener Kommentar zur ZPO Art. 23 note 2; *Kropholler/von Hein* Art. 23 note 3; *Layton/Mercer* para. 20.006.

89　*Kropholler/von Hein* Art. 23 note 3; *Layton/Mercer* para. 20.006; but see *contra* Cassaz. RDIPP 1999, 1012.

to only one Member State as for instance where parties of a purely internal transaction conferred jurisdiction on another Member State or where parties with their domiciles in the same Member State agreed on this State's jurisdiction or where one of the parties to such agreement was domiciled in a third state. The strictest view took recourse to national procedural law in all of these cases.[90] A less strict view applied the old Art. 23 if the agreement conferring jurisdiction on the courts of one Member State derogated at the same time from the jurisdiction of another Member State.[91] The widest – and prevailing – view applied Art. 23 of the old Regulation even if the case was connected only with one Member State as long as there was any other 'true' international element.[92] This view therefore determined a jurisdiction agreement according to former Art. 23 even if for instance a party domiciled in Germany agreed with a party domiciled in the United States on the jurisdiction of German courts[93] whereas the two other views would have applied national procedural law in this case.

But even the widest view under the former Regulation did not regard a case as international if it was for instance only the differing nationality of persons domiciled in the same state from which the internationality was inferred.[94] However, if the only internationality of a mere domestic case was the choice of a court in another Member State the opinions were again split whether this turned the case into a 'true' international one.[95]

The formerly prevailing widest view has also to be supported for Art. 25 Brussels Ibis. Under **25** the new Art. 25 only the widest interpretation can be upheld since the new text removed the requirement of at least one party's domicile in an EU Member State. There need to be a link merely to one Member State, namely the choice of a court (or courts) in a Member State. Any requirement of a link to more than one EU State is now inconsistent with the present wording of Art. 25. Moreover, under the wide interpretation of Art. 25 most jurisdiction agreements can be adjudicated according to the uniform standard of this article. This view avoids the disadvantage and practical difficulty that first possibly derogated jurisdictions of

---

90   See Report *Jenard* to Art. 17.

91   *Droz* paras. 186 *et seq.*; *Jung*, Vereinbarungen über die internationale Zuständigkeit nach dem EWG-Gerichtsstands- und Vollstreckungsübereinkommen und nach § 38 Abs. 2 ZPO (1980), p. 64 *et seq.*; *Schack* para. 464.

92   See Rb Leeuwaarden NIPR 2001 Nr. 294; *Aull*, Der Geltungsanspruch des EuGVÜ (1996), p. 113 *et seq.*; *Burgstaller*, JBl 1998, 691 *et seq.*; *Gaudemet-Tallon* para. 134; *Geimer/Schütze* Art. 23 note 45; *Kropholler/von Hein* Art. 23 note 3; *Layton/Mercer* para. 20.006; *Mankowski*, in: Rauscher Art. 23 note 6; *Gottwald*, in: Münchener Kommentar zur ZPO Art. 23 note 7; *Hk-ZPO/Dörner* Art. 23 note 7. The ECJ-judgment in *Andrew Owusu v. Nugent B. Jackson, trading as "Villa Holidays Bal-Inn Villas", Mammee Bay Resorts Ltd., Mammee Bay Club Ltd., The Enchanted Garden Resorts & Spa Ltd., Consulting Services Ltd., Town & Country Resorts Ltd.*, (Case C-281/02) (2005) ECR I-1383 para. 28 points also clearly, though obiter in this direction.

93   Even on the proposition that there are no contacts whatsoever to other Member States of the Regulation.

94   See *Gaudemet-Tallon* para. 134.

95   For internationality in this case: OGH IHR 2007, 245; *Aull*, IPRax 1999, 226; *Gottwald* in: Münchener Kommentar zur ZPO Art. 23 note 2, 5; *Hausmann*, in: Staudinger, Kommentar zum Bürgerlichen Gesetzbuch mit Einführungsgesetz und Nebengesetzen, Internationales Vertragsrecht (14th ed. 2011) IntVertrVerfR note 241; *Hk-ZPO/Dörner* Art. 23 note 6; against internationality in such a case: OGH JBl 2004, 187 with note *Klicka*; OLG Hamm IPRax 1999, 244, 245; *Beraudo* fasc. 3011 no. 5; *Mankowski*, in: Rauscher Art. 23 note 6.

other Member States must be reviewed before any decision on Art. 25 can be taken.[96] Furthermore, every prorogation which originally did not derogate from another Member State's jurisdiction can later on easily turn into such a derogation if, for example, the parties change afterwards the place of performance of their contract so that the jurisdiction under Art. 7 no. 1 would be founded. Any prorogation of a Member State's court is therefore at least a potential derogation of other Member States' courts' jurisdiction. This further supports the contention that except that an international element is required no additional restriction is needed and should therefore not be read into Art. 25. Finally, already under the Brussels Convention the ECJ has very clearly expressed that its provisions do not only concern intra-community conflicts of competence but as well general international conflicts of competence as far as they affect the Community.[97]

26 Where the parties of a purely internal case with no other objective international links whatsoever (in particular with no place of performance in another Member State) have conferred jurisdiction on the courts of another Member State at first glance the view appears convincing that the necessary international element is lacking and that Art. 25 does not cover the case.[98] In addition, this view corresponds with Art. 1 (2) Hague Convention on Choice of Court Agreements which expressly states that in purely domestic cases the choice of a court in another state does not internationalise the case ("regardless of the location of the chosen court"). The desirable consistency of Art. 25 Brussels Ibis Regulation with the Hague Convention would favour a parallel interpretation of Art. 25. Also, Art. 3 (3) Rome I Regulation could be adduced which in a similar way restricts a choice of foreign law in mere internal cases, in order to prevent an unmotivated "flight" from the naturally applicable law.[99] However, the parallel to this latter provision does not meet the point. The inapplicability of Art. 25 Brussels Ibis Regulation would only mean that the national procedural law on choice of court agreements would apply. An "escape" from the natural forum would not, and cannot, be prevented by leaving the decision to the national law. On the contrary, despite the Hague provision it is desirable that EU courts adjudicate as far as possible all jurisdiction agreements according to the same standard.[100] It would be strange if EU Member States-courts had to apply the own national law if parties domiciled in the same EU State chose the jurisdiction of another Member State whereas the courts have to apply Art. 25 where parties from outside the EU – even if domiciled in the same state – have chosen the court(s) in a Member State.[101]

---

[96] See thereto *Samtleben*, RabelsZ 59 (1995), 691.

[97] *Andrew Owusu v. Nugent B. Jackson, trading as "Villa Holidays Bal-Inn Villas", Mammee Bay Resorts Ltd., Mammee Bay Club Ltd., The Enchanted Garden Resorts & Spa Ltd., Consulting Services Ltd., Town & Country Resorts Ltd*, (Case C-281/02) (2005) ECR I-1383, commented on by *Heinze/Dutta*, IPRax 2005, 224 et seq.; in a similar sense already *Group Josi Reinsurance v. Universal General Insurance*, (Case 412/98) (2000) ECR I-5925.

[98] In this sense to the prior Art. 23 Brussels I Regulation: Cass. D. 1986 IR 265 with note *Audit*; *Gaudemet-Tallon* para. 134; *Junker* § 15 note 7; *Kropholler/von Hein* Art. 23 note 2; *Mankowski*, in: Rauscher Art. 23 note 6; similarly *Auer* in: Bülow/Böckstiegel/Geimer/Schütze Art. 23 note 14; in the same sense also the preceding edition; but evidently contra, e.g., OGH IHR 2007, 245 (248).

[99] See *Magnus*, in: Staudinger, BGB, Internationales Vertragsrecht (14th ed. 2011) Art. 3 Rom I-VO note 131; *Martiny*, in: Münchener Kommentar zum BGB (5th ed. 2010) Art. 3 Rom I-VO note 4.

[100] *Samtleben*, in: FS Ansay (2006), p. 343 et seq.

[101] See further below Art. 25 notes 36 et seq. (*Magnus*).

The only exception is the case where parties domiciled in the same Member State choose a court in this state. Such a choice would have the sole effect to designate the competent local court.[102] This choice should be governed by the local law. Art. 25 does not apply. As to how to deal with the case that parties domiciled in the same third state choose a court of that state thereby prorogating from the – in particular exclusive or at least protective – jurisdiction of an EU Member State is problematic.[103] An international character of the case could be hardly denied, though.

VII. Specific requirements for the application of Art. 25

1. In General

Though Art. 25 recognises the private designation of the competent court to a wide extent   **27** the provision provides for a number of requirements which aim at reasonable limits of jurisdiction agreements. Some of these conditions still refer to the scope of application and concern the territorial relationship by which the parties' agreement must be connected with a Member State.[104] Others concern the formation of the agreement and its contents.[105] Since jurisdiction agreements can exclude the general and special jurisdiction provided for by the Regulation, Art. 25 is to be interpreted strictly.[106]

Regularly, international jurisdiction agreements have at the same time two effects: to fix the   **28** jurisdiction of the chosen court (prorogation effect) and, as far as they are exclusive, to oust the jurisdiction of the otherwise competent court (derogation effect). But the parties may also agree on a pure addition of the jurisdiction of further courts without any derogation or even on a mere derogation of the competent courts without the positive choice of the court which should be competent instead. Art. 25 addresses expressly only the prorogation effect, leaving open according to which rules the derogation effect should be determined.

Moreover, for reasons of sovereignty, the Regulation cannot and does not regulate how   **29** states outside the EU have to deal with jurisdiction agreements and whether and when their courts have to accept jurisdiction which the parties have chosen.[107] But by no means does this preclude the Regulation from regulating the effects which such foreign jurisdiction agreements have in EU courts. The new Arts. 33 and 34 serve the purpose to deal with competing proceedings in third states even if the jurisdiction of the court(s) of the third state follows from a jurisdiction agreement. Yet, Brussels I*bis* does not contain special rules on foreign jurisdiction agreements.[108] Despite this fact, a stance has also to be taken where foreign jurisdiction agreements derogate from the jurisdiction of an EU Member State under Brussels I*bis* in particular where this jurisdiction is exclusive or at least protective.[109]

---

[102] In the same sense already *Samtleben*, in: FS Ansay (2006), pp. 356 *et seq.*

[103] See *infra* Art. 25 notes 38 *et seq.* (*Magnus*).

[104] See *supra* Art. 25 notes 23–26 (*Magnus*).

[105] See *infra* Art. 25 note 75 *et seq.* (*Magnus*).

[106] *Mainschifffahrts-Genossenschaft eG (MSG) v. Les Gravières Rhénanes SARL*, (1997) ECR I-911 para. 14; BGH NJW 2001, 1731.

[107] See also *von Hein*, RIW 2013, 104; also already under the Brussels Convention: the ECJ in *Coreck Maritime GmbH v. Handelsveem BV*, (C-387/98) (2000) ECR I-9337, I-9373 para. 19.

[108] With critique thereto *Ratkovic/Zgrabljicrotar*, J.P.I.L. 9 (2013) 245, 248 s.

2. Choice of court(s) in a Member State

a) Explicit prorogation

aa) Prorogation of Member States' courts' jurisdiction

30 The Article deals expressly only with the prorogative effect of a choice of court agreement. It explicitly requires that the parties confer by way of their agreement the jurisdiction on a court or courts of an EU Member State (also including Denmark).[110] Choice of forum agreements intending this prorogation effect are fully covered by Art. 25; the choice of a forum in a Member State always falls under the provision even if none of the parties is domiciled in a Member State. In principle, it does not matter whether or not the parties derogate from a jurisdiction of a court outside the EU at the same time.[111] It is for those third states' courts, if seised, to decide themselves according to their law whether and when they give effect to such derogation.[112] The parties must therefore comply with Art. 25 if they prorogate the jurisdiction either of a certain court in a Member State (e.g., the High Court in London) or more generally of the courts of a certain Member State (e.g., jurisdiction of the courts of France), leaving it in this latter case to the law of that Member State to determine the locally competent court.

31 The prorogated court must be located on the territory of a Member State of the Brussels I*bis* Regulation. The territory of the respective Member State and whether a court is located there is to be determined in accordance with Art. 355 TFEU. Where the parties for instance agree on the jurisdiction of the courts of the Isle of Man or of one of the Channel Islands (Guernsey, Jersey, Sark etc.) these are courts outside the territorial scope of the Regulation.[113] The prorogative effect then cannot be determined according to Art. 25[114] but depends on the national procedural law of the court seised of the lawsuit (as to the derogatory effect see *infra* note 37).

32 Art. 25 applies also where the jurisdiction of courts in a Member State[115] is agreed upon but absent the jurisdiction agreement the courts of the Member States would lack jurisdiction.[116] An example is the above mentioned case[117] that a German seller and a US buyer agree on the jurisdiction of German courts while the place of performance is in the US. If the seller in such a case intends to sue the buyer, without the agreement no Member States' court would

---

[109] See thereto *infra* Art. 25 notes 38 *et seq.* (*Magnus*).

[110] *Kropholler/von Hein* Art. 23 note 14; *Mankowski*, in: Rauscher Art. 23 note 3.

[111] But see *infra* note 133 on the case that the agreement derogates from a foreign protective jurisdiction similar to that under Arts. 15, 19, 23 Brussels I*bis*.

[112] In the same sense *Geimer/Schütze* Art. 23 note 44. However, as to the effects of an agreement selecting a Non-EU jurisdiction see *infra* notes 31 and 36 (*Magnus*).

[113] See Art. 355 TFEU which also applies to secondary EU legislation; also *Briggs/Rees* para. 1.15 (to the Brussels I Convention); *Kropholler/von Hein* Einl note 29; generally to the territorial scope of the Regulation see Introduction note 85 (*Magnus*).

[114] *von Hein*, RIW 2013, 104; under the Brussels Convention: *Coreck Maritime GmbH v. Handelsveem BV*, (C-387/98) (2000) ECR I-9337.

[115] Even if it is the same Member State where the party is domiciled; see *supra* Art. 25 note 24.

[116] *Layton/Mercer* para. 20.012.

[117] See *supra* Art. 25 note 24 (*Magnus*).

be competent to hear the case. However, Art. 25 does not, and should not be understood to, contain an additional condition that without the jurisdiction agreement the courts of a Member State must have had jurisdiction, in particular, since the outcome then would depend on the procedural role of the parties. In the hypothetical case jurisdiction would then only be lacking if the seller sues the buyer but not vice versa. Art. 25, however, generally ignores the procedural role of the parties because at the time the jurisdiction agreement is concluded it is generally not foreseeable which party will be the claimant and which the defendant.

In a similar vein, the admissibility of a jurisdiction agreement and its generally exclusive effect is not affected because the parties agreed on the jurisdiction which the Regulation provides anyway for. It often remains useful to exclude the possible jurisdiction of further courts.[118]

Art. 25 is not only applicable to exclusive but also to optional jurisdiction agreements. Also **33** the latter must comply with the provisions of Art. 25 in order to be procedurally recognised though they do not have an exclusive effect. Despite its wording ("court or courts of *a* Member State") Art. 25 covers and acknowledges agreements as well which confer the jurisdiction on the courts of several Member States (for instance, reciprocal jurisdiction agreements). In *Nikolaus Meeth v. Glacetal*[119] the German-French parties had agreed upon the following clause: "If Meeth sues Glacetal the French Courts alone shall have jurisdiction. If Glacetal sues Meeth the German Courts alone shall have jurisdiction." The ECJ regarded this as a valid (exclusive) jurisdiction clause and felt not bound by the wording "of *a* Con-tracting State" (of then Art. 17 Brussels Convention). The same reasoning must apply where parties confer jurisdiction onto the courts of two or more Member States between which the claimant is allowed to choose.[120] On the other hand, Art. 25 (1) and (2) should also be applied where the parties have agreed on the jurisdiction of a court in a Member State and in a Non-Member State (be the latter a Lugano State like Switzerland or a State outside the Brussels-Lugano regime).[121]

Art. 25 applies also to jurisdiction agreements which are concluded for the benefit of only **34** one of the parties, for instance if all disputes are to be litigated at the place of one party[122] or if one party reserves the right to choose between different courts while the other party has no

---

[118] See already *Nikolaus Meeth v. Glacetal*, (Case 23/78) (1978) ECR 2133 para. 5.

[119] *Nikolaus Meeth v. Glacetal*, (Case 23/78) (1978) ECR 2133.

[120] As to the validity of such clauses see *infra* Art. 23 note 144 (*Magnus*); to their interpretation see *infra* Art. 23 note 71 (*Magnus*).

[121] See *Group Josi Reinsurance v. Universal General Insurance*, (Case 412/98) (2000) ECR I-5925 para. 41 *et seq.*; *Andrew Owusu v. Nugent B. Jackson, trading as "Villa Holidays Bal-Inn Villas", Mammee Bay Resorts Ltd., Mammee Bay Club Ltd., The Enchanted Garden Resorts & Spa Ltd., Consulting Services Ltd., Town & Country Resorts Ltd*, (Case C-281/02) (2005) ECR I-1383 para. 28.

[122] The ECJ decision in *Anterist v. Crédit Lyonnais*, (Case 22/85) (1986) ECR 1951 which concerned Art. 17 (4) Brussels Convention remains still valid. The ECJ stated that the fact that a jurisdiction clause con-ferred jurisdiction on the courts of the Member State where one of the parties was domiciled did not of itself sufficiently evidence that the clause was concluded for the benefit of that party alone.

such right.[123] Such "asymmetric clauses"[124] are principally valid under the Regulation.[125] Redress to national validity law is principally excluded.[126] This has to be inferred from the legislative history of Art. 25. The Brussels Convention still contained a provision (Art. 17 (4)) which expressly dealt with such clauses but allowed the other party to sue in any other jurisdiction provided by the Convention. Evidently, such clauses were admissible under the Convention but had not the effect of an exclusive jurisdiction agreement. With the introduction of the Brussels I Regulation this special provision was deleted. The reason was, however, not to ban such clauses but merely to remove uncertainties which the former formulation had created.[127] It was unclear when a jurisdiction agreement was "to the benefit of only one party".[128] In any event, it is always a matter of construction of the respective clause whether the parties intended an optional or exclusive jurisdiction. That a clause benefits only one of the parties can support the inference of an optional jurisdiction agreement but it need not automatically imply such an inference nor does the lack of a benefit for only one party exclude an optional jurisdiction agreement (for the discussion of the validity of jurisdiction agreements see *infra* notes 77 *et seq.*).

35 As to the case that both parties agree on the jurisdiction of the courts of a Member State but have their domiciles in states outside the territorial scope of the Regulation see *infra* note 53 *et seq.*

bb) Derogation of Member States' courts' jurisdiction; choice of court in a third country
36 Where on the contrary the parties confer by their agreement jurisdiction on a court outside the territory of the Member States of the Regulation then such agreement is not directly dealt with by Art. 25.[129] Accordingly, it is disputed whether, and if so when, such jurisdiction agreements should be treated according to the principles laid down in Art. 25. As a starting point it seems common ground that Art. 25 is inapplicable even by analogy as far as the prorogative effect of such agreements is concerned.[130] The prorogated court has to decide on the prorogation effect of the jurisdiction agreement according to its own law.[131] The EU has no competence to regulate the prorogation of courts outside its boundaries.

---

123 See the case Cass. Civ. 1ère No. 11-26.022, Bull. I No. 176 = D. 2012.2876 with note *Martel*.
124 *Lehmann/Grimm*, ZEuP 2013, 890 *et seq.*
125 Evidently contra: Cass. Civ. 1ère No. 11-26.022, Bull. I No. 176 = D. 2012.2876 with note *Martel*; see thereto, admitting such clauses *Freitag*, in: FS Magnus 419 *et seq.*; *Lehmann/Grimm*, ZEuP 2013, 890 *et seq.*; *Niggemann* IPRax 2014, 194 *et seq.*
126 See further *infra* notes 148 *et seq.* (*Magnus*).
127 See Magnus/Mankowski/*Magnus*1, Brussels I, Art. 23 note 7.
128 See the discussion by *Kropholler*, Eur.ZPR6 Art. 17 note 101 *et seq.*
129 *Coreck Maritime GmbH v. Handelsveem BV*, (C-387/98) (2000) ECR I-9337, I-9373 para. 19; Report *Schlosser* para. 176.
130 As to Brussels *Ibis von Hein*, RIW 2013, 104; in the same sense to the Proposal *Magnus/Mankowski*, ZvglRWiss 110 (2011) 270; *M. Weller*, GPR 2012, 38; *Coreck Maritime GmbH v. Handelsveem BV*, (C-387/98) (2000) ECR I-9337, I-9373 para. 19; Report *Schlosser* para. 176; *Auer* in: Bülow/Böckstiegel/Geimer/Schütze Art. 23 note 17; *Geimer/Schütze* Art. 23 notes 40 *et seq.*; *Kropholler/von Hein* Art. 23 note 14; *Layton/Mercer* para. 20.014; *Mankowski*, in: Rauscher Art. 23 note 3; for analogous application however *Schaper/Eberlein*, RIW 2012, 43.
131 See OGH JBl 1996, 795; *Mankowski*, in: Rauscher Art. 23 note 3.

However, under Art. 17 Brussels Convention and Art. 23 old Brussels I Regulation it was **37**
much disputed whether these provisions were applicable with respect to the derogation
effect of such jurisdiction agreements. Where there is contact with a Member State the
prorogation can be, and often will be, at the same time a derogation from an otherwise
given jurisdiction of a Member State. In particular, it can be the derogation from the exclusive jurisdiction under Art. 24 or from the protective jurisdiction under Art. 15, 19 or 23.
The court practice of the ECJ may have changed over time: in *Coreck Maritime GmbH v.
Handelsveem BV*[132] – a case on the validity of a choice-of-court clause in a bill of lading – the
ECJ held that the former Art. 17 Brussels Convention did not apply to agreements which
chose a foreign court – neither with respect to the prorogation effect nor to the derogation
effect: "… Article 17 of the Convention does not apply to clauses designating a court in a
third country. A court situated in a Contracting State must, if it is seised notwithstanding
such a jurisdiction clause, assess the validity of the clause according to the applicable law,
including conflict of laws rules, where it sits …"[133] The Court stated no qualification whatsoever of that rule. Also some national courts adopted this view.[134] According to this opinion
the jurisdiction had to be determined in accordance with national procedural and private
international law.[135] The contrary was held by the ECJ in the recent case of *Mahamdia v.
Algeria*:[136] in that case the Algerian embassy in Germany dismissed its driver who sued the
Republic of Algeria in Germany although the employment contract provided for the exclusive jurisdiction of Algerian courts. The ECJ without lengthy discussion held that the
agreement was invalid because it violated Art. 21 Brussels I Regulation (the present Art. 23
Brussels I*bis* Regulation) which prohibits jurisdiction agreements which restrict the jurisdiction provided for employees. Under the former law also other national courts[137] and parts
of legal doctrine[138] advocated that where the prorogation of a court outside the EU constitutes at the same time a derogation of the jurisdiction of an otherwise competent EU court
then, such jurisdiction agreements are also covered by the former Art. 23 and must comply
with the requirements of this provision as far as their derogative effect is concerned. This
latter view has also to be adopted for the new Brussels I*bis* Regulation.[139] Only such interpretation avoids that by the choice of a court outside the EU the exclusive (Art. 24) and

---

[132] *Coreck Maritime GmbH v. Handelsveem BV*, (C-387/98) (2000) ECR I-9337, I-9373 para. 19.

[133] *Coreck Maritime GmbH v. Handelsveem BV*, (C-387/98) (2000) ECR I-9337, I-9373 para. 19.

[134] For instance, BGH NJW 1986, 1438 with note *Geimer*; BGH NJW 1989, 1431.

[135] See *Coreck Maritime GmbH v. Handelsveem BV*, (C-387/98) (2000) ECR I-9337, I-9373 para. 19 citing the
       Report *Schlosser* para. 176; also *Kropholler/von Hein* Art. 23 note 14.

[136] *Mahamdia v. Algeria*, (C-154/11) (2012) nyr.

[137] In particular Greek courts: see Areopagos Ell. Dik. 2002, 1042 *et seq.*; Epheteio Peiraios DEE 1999, 771 *et
       seq.*; Epheteio Peiraios END 1997, 52 *et seq.*; see thereto *Vassilakakis* IPRax 2005, 279, 281.

[138] *Burgstaller/Neumayr* Art. 23 note 15 *et seq.* (however applying in addition a more severe national law);
       Geimer/Schütze Art. 23 notes 42 *et seq.*; *Killias*, Die Gerichtsstandsvereinbarung nach dem Lugano-
       Übereinkommen (1993), p. 73 *et seq.*; *Kropholler/von Hein* Art. 23 note 83; *Mankowski*, in: Rauscher
       Art. 23 note 7; *Tiefenthaler*, in: Czernich/Tiefenthaler/Kodek Art. 17 EuGVÜ note 63; partly also *Layton/
       Mercer* para. 20.015 (if without the jurisdiction agreement courts in Member States of the Regulation
       would have jurisdiction); *Schack* para. 467 (if the jurisdiction of at least two Member States is derogated
       from because then the standard of Art. 23 is needed to ensure uniformity among the Member States with
       respect to the interpretation of the jurisdiction agreement); de lege ferenda: *Samtleben*, in: FS Ansay
       (2006), p. 359 *et seq.*; contra (application of national law) for instance *Junker* § 15 note 11.

[139] *Magnus*, in: FS Dieter Martiny (2014), p. 785, 789.

Ulrich Magnus   609

protective jurisdiction rules of the Regulation (Art. 15, 19, 23) are easily outruled. The respective standard of national law does not in all Member States warrant the same level of protection that the Regulation provides. That the Brussels *Ibis* Regulation does not expressly mention agreements on the jurisdiction of third states[140] cannot be taken as a tacit reversal of the ECJ decision in *Mahamdia v. Algeria*.[141] If that had been intended it would have required an express regulation in light of the importance of a decision that then would have given up the protective and exclusive jurisdiction of European courts by a mere choice of a foreign court. Moreover, also the opening of Art. 25 for jurisdiction agreements by parties from third states delivers a further – though only soft – argument for applying the provision to the reflexive effect of the agreed jurisdiction of third states. In addition, Recital 14 sent. 2 can be taken as a hint to subject foreign jurisdiction agreements to the standard of Art. 25 as far as their derogatory effect affects "the protection of consumers and employees" or the "exclusive jurisdiction" within the Member States.

37a It remains open to discussion whether Art. 25 also applies where a European court is faced with a 'foreign' jurisdiction agreement that does *not* oust the protective or exclusive jurisdiction of EU courts though it may or may not oust the 'normal' jurisdiction of European courts. It is strongly supported here that Art. 25 equally applies to such jurisdiction agreements. A first argument is that it may be uncertain whether or not the foreign jurisdiction agreement is exclusive (or violates a protective regime under Brussels *Ibis*). If exclusive it could be contrary to European exclusive jurisdiction and then Art. 25 (4) had to be applied. If not exclusive it would not contradict the European standard. Should then the seised court apply its national standard? It seems hardly convincing that the standard of assessment should vary whether or not the derogatory effect affects only specific (protective or exclusive) jurisdiction rules of Brussels *Ibis*. A second argument is that of practicability. A double standard increases the complexity and difficulties for the court seised, since the court must always examine whether a protective or exclusive jurisdiction under Brussels *Ibis* is affected before it can apply its national law. Moreover, a single standard for dealing with jurisdiction clauses also militates for the solution advocated here.

b) Mere derogation

38 Though they can do so it is rare that parties merely agree that the jurisdiction of certain courts shall be excluded without designating positively the competent court(s). Whether Art. 25 applies to such a case – at least where the jurisdiction of one or more Member States is derogated from – is again doubtful. The prevailing view to the prior provision rightly favoured the application of the old Art. 23 in order to secure as far as possible a uniform treatment of all kinds of jurisdiction agreements and to prevent misuse by excluding jurisdiction.[142] The same consideration is valid for Art. 25 Brussels *Ibis*.[143] It would be inconsistent if the prorogation of another EU court could not oust the protective and exclusive jurisdiction under Brussels *Ibis* while a mere derogation could.

---

[140] See thereto *Pohl*, IPRax 2013, 109, 112.

[141] *Mahamdia v. Algeria*, (C-154/11) (2012) nyr.

[142] *Kohler*, in: Pocar/Viarengo/Villata 204 (to the Recast Proposal); to the former situation: *Gothot/Holleaux* para. 165; *Kropholler/von Hein* Art. 23 note 15; *Mankowski*, in: Rauscher Art. 23 note 7; *Mari*, p. 584.

[143] In particular the ECJ decision in *Mahamdia v. Algeria*, (C-154/11) (2012) nyr. militates in favour of this view.

However, even if Art. 25 applies the parties cannot totally eliminate the originally existing **39** jurisdiction by excluding the jurisdiction of all competent courts – except by an arbitration agreement. This would mean a removal of any access to justice and would offend the underlying principle of the Regulation that jurisdiction must be always available to a defendant at least where s/he is domiciled.[144] And of course, Art. 25 (4) does not permit to derogate from the exclusive and protective jurisdiction provisions of the Regulation. In this respect it does not matter whether the derogation is a pure one or follows from the choice of courts inside or outside the EU.[145]

c) Purely internal case

The Regulation does not intend to interfere with purely domestic relations.[146] It was there- **40** fore widely accepted that in such cases Art. 23 old Brussels I was not applicable.[147] The same must apply for the new Art. 25. However, the problem is when a case is purely internal. Already the derogation from the jurisdiction in another (Member) State turns a domestic jurisdiction agreement into an international one so that Art. 25 applies.[148] Where parties, both domiciled in Germany, agree after an accident in France on the exclusive jurisdiction of German courts, Art. 25 thus applies (derogation of French jurisdiction under Art. 7 (2)). Art. 25 should also apply where the parties of an otherwise purely domestic case have agreed on the jurisdiction of the courts of another EU Member State or of a Non-EU State; this also sufficiently internationalises the case.[149] The reason underlying Art. 3 (3) Rome I Regulation that a mere choice of foreign law cannot change the character of an otherwise purely domestic case to which mandatory internal provisions may apply cannot be adduced here.[150] Art. 3 (3) Rome I Regulation intends, and is able, to secure the mandatory part of the actually applicable law. Art. 25 cannot achieve the same goal. The choice is here only between Art. 25 and the corresponding national provision. The inapplicability of Art. 25 would lead only to

---

[144] See Recital no. 11 of the Regulation; also *Auer*, in: Bülow/Böckstiegel/Geimer/Schütze Art. 23 note 31; *Gottwald* in: Münchener Kommentar zur ZPO Art. 23 note 10a.

[145] *Magnus*, in: FS Dieter Martiny (2014), p. 785, 789; in the same sense with respect to the prior provision: *Gaudemet-Tallon*, in: Liber amicorum Droz 99; *Gottwald*, in: Münchener Kommentar zur ZPO Art. 23 note 12; *Schlosser* Art. 23 note 30.

[146] See Report *Jenard* to Art. 17; Report *Schlosser* para. 174; see also *supra* Art. 25 note 26 (*Magnus*).

[147] OGH JBl 2004, 187 with note *Klicka*; *Aull* (fn. 70), p. 71 *et seq.*, p. 106 *et seq.*; *Bork*, in: Stein/Jonas, Zivilprozessordnung, I: §§ 1-40 ZPO (22nd ed. 2003) § 38 note 24; *Hausmann*, in: Staudinger, IntVertrVerf note 241; *Mankowski*, in: Rauscher Art. 23 note 6; *Schack* para. 464. But partly contra *Geimer/Schütze* Art. 23 notes 46 *et seq.*; also *Frauenberger-Pfeiler*, in: FS Rechberger, p. 130 (Art. 23 covers all jurisdiction agreements which have an international effect).

[148] See also *supra* Art. 25 note 37 (*Magnus*).

[149] *Aull*, IPRax 1999, 226; *Frauenberger-Pfeiler*, in: FS Rechberger, p. 135; *Hausmann*, in: Staudinger, IntVertrVerf note 241; see also *supra* Art. 25 note 26 (*Magnus*); obiter *Andrew Owusu v. Nugent B. Jackson, trading as "Villa Holidays Bal-Inn Villas", Mammee Bay Resorts Ltd., Mammee Bay Club Ltd., The Enchanted Garden Resorts & Spa Ltd., Consulting Services Ltd., Town & Country Resorts Ltd,* (Case C-281/02) (2005) ECR I-1383 para. 28 and OGH IHR 2007, 243 (248); but contra OGH JBl 2004, 187 with note *Klicka*; OLG Hamm IPRax 1999, 244, 245; *Beraudo* fasc. 3011 no. 5; *Mankowski*, in: Rauscher Art. 23 note 6.

[150] But see in this sense OLG Hamm IPRax 1999, 244; *Mankowski*, in: Rauscher Art. 23 note 6; contra *Aull* (fn. 95), p. 125 *et seq.*; *Mankowski*, IPRax 1999, 226; *Hausmann*, in: Staudinger IntVertrVerf note 241.

the applicability of national law which may or may not secure the 'natural' forum.[151] There-fore, the 'uniformity-consideration' should prevail: As far as possible all jurisdiction agreements with a European element should be measured by the yardstick of Art. 25.

As to the relevant point in time for the internationality of a case see *infra* note 64.

d) Choice of place of performance

41 An agreement on the place of performance may in its effect equal a jurisdiction agreement because of Art. 5 (1). But nonetheless Art. 25 does generally not extend to agreements on the place of performance which therefore need not meet any form requirement under the Regulation but are governed in this respect by the applicable national law.[152] Where, however, the agreed place of performance lacks any factual connection to the real place of performance and remains merely abstract or fictitious and where such agreement therefore aims only at the foundation of jurisdiction and would result in a circumvention of the form requirement of Art. 25 (1), then such agreement requires the form of Art. 25 (1) as well or is otherwise invalid.[153]

42 This philosophy cannot be transferred to the case of a party that opts for one of its two or more domiciles, even though such option, if accepted, may result in the same jurisdictional effect as a jurisdiction agreement.[154] But it is for the national court to decide whether and where a person's domicile is established (Art. 62, 63).

e) Choice of law clauses

43 It is more or less implied that the contractual choice of a certain law does not entail the choice of the courts in the country of that law. A choice of the applicable law does even not amount to a tacit choice of court.[155] The reason is that today's courts rather often apply foreign law in international cases. Therefore it can no longer be presumed that a chosen law is solely applied by the courts of the country of that law. A limited and merely transitional exception to this general rule had been allowed to the United Kingdom and Ireland pursuant to Art. 54 (3) Brussels and Lugano Convention. According to this provision the courts of these two countries could accept jurisdiction based on choice of law clauses which the parties had agreed upon before the entry into force of the two Conventions.[156] This complied with the former practice in the two countries. The Regulation does not contain any equivalent provision. However, a choice of law can add to other indicia for a tacit choice of forum.

44 The rule that a choice of law does in itself not indicate a choice of jurisdiction does not operate vice versa. A jurisdiction agreement has often been regarded as a tacit choice of law

---

[151] See already *supra* Art. 25 note 26 (Magnus).

[152] *Siegfried Zelger v. Sebastiano Salinitri*, (Case 56/79) (1980) ECR 89, 97 para. 5.

[153] *Mainschiffahrts-Genossenschaft eG (MSG) v. Les Gravières Rhénanes SARL*, (Case C-106/95) (1997) ECR I-911, I-943 *et seq.* para. 31–35; confirmed by *GIE Groupe Concorde v. Master of the Vessel "Suhadiwarno Panjan"*, (Case C-440/97) (1999) ECR I-6307, I-6351 *et seq.* para. 28; see also BGH NJW-RR 1998, 755; LG Trier IHR 2004, 115, 116; *Geimer/Schütze* Art. 23 note 53; *Kropholler/von Hein* Art. 5 note 29; *Layton/Mercer* para. 20.019; for a full discussion see Art. 7 notes 145 *et seq.* (*Mankowski*).

[154] See for such a case *The Kherson* (1993) I. L. Pr. 358; see thereto *Layton/Mercer* para. 20.019 fn. 83.

[155] Report *Schlosser* para. 175; *Layton/Mercer* para. 20.018.

[156] See thereto *Layton/Mercer* para. 20.018.

according to the maxim *qui eligit iudicem, eligit ius*.[157] This was at least so held where the parties agreed on the exclusive jurisdiction of certain courts and indicated no intention to the contrary with respect to the applicable law.[158]

f) No discretion

Where a jurisdiction agreement is valid under Art. 25 and relied on by one of the parties the **45** court seised has no discretion but to respect it. If a court other than the seised court is chosen the latter has to stay proceedings and finally decline jurisdiction (Art. 31 (2)) and where the seised court has been chosen it must accept jurisdiction even if it were not competent without the agreement.

The agreement must be given effect even if another court, other than the chosen court, is, for **46** factual reasons, in a better position to hear the case. The ECJ has clearly expressed – though in relation to Art. 2 of the old Brussels I Regulation – that the provisions of the Regulation are compulsory and allow no additional discretion.[159] The parties need to know from the conclusion of their jurisdiction agreement on which court will finally decide their disputes. The doctrine of *forum non conveniens* particularly of English law[160] which gives the court certain discretion to decline or accept jurisdiction is not permissible under the Regulation.[161] Only with respect to certain pending proceedings in third countries Arts. 33 and 34 introduce discretion to stay proceedings in the EU.[162]

g) No necessary link to the prorogated court

Within the boundaries of the Regulation the parties are free to choose any court they wish. **47** Art. 25 does not require any objective connection between the chosen court and the parties or their dispute.[163] The choice of a 'neutral' forum with no connection at all to the dispute is

---

[157] For instance BGHZ 104, 268; BGH NJW-RR 1990, 183; BGH NJW 1991, 1420; BGH NJW 1996, 2569; *Egon Oldendorff v. Liberia Corporation* (1996) 1 Lloyd's Rep. 380; see also Recital 12 Rome I Regulation; further *Collins*, in: Dicey/Morris paras. 32–092 *et seq.*; *Magnus*, in: Staudinger Art. 3 Rom-VO note 75 *et seq.*; *Plender/Wilderspin* paras. 5–10 *et seq.*

[158] See, e.g. BGHZ 104, 268; BGH NJW 1996, 2569; *S. Komninos* [1991] Lloyds L.R. 370; *Marabenu Hong Kong and South China Ltd. v. Mongolian Government* [2002] 2 All E.R. 873.

[159] *Andrew Owusu v. Nugent B. Jackson, trading as "Villa Holidays Bal-Inn Villas", Mammee Bay Resorts Ltd., Mammee Bay Club Ltd., The Enchanted Garden Resorts & Spa Ltd., Consulting Services Ltd., Town & Country Resorts Ltd*, (Case C-281/02) (2005) ECR I-1383.

[160] See in particular *Spiliada Maritime Corporation v. Cansulex Ltd.* (1987) A. C. 460 (H. L., per Lord *Goff* of *Chieveley*).

[161] *Andrew Owusu v. Nugent B. Jackson, trading as "Villa Holidays Bal-Inn Villas", Mammee Bay Resorts Ltd., Mammee Bay Club Ltd., The Enchanted Garden Resorts & Spa Ltd., Consulting Services Ltd., Town & Country Resorts Ltd*, (Case C-281/02) (2005) ECR I-1383 para. 37 *et seq.*; see thereto *Heinze/Dutta*, IPRax 2005, 224 *et seq.*

[162] See the comments on Arts. 33 and 34 *infra* (*Fentiman*).

[163] See *Trasporti Castelletti Spedizioni Internazionali SpA v. Hugo Trumpy SpA*, (Case C-159/97) (1999) ECR I-1597, I-1656 para. 50; *Mainschiffahrts-Genossenschaft eG (MSG) v. Les Gravières Rhénanes SARL*, (Case C-106/95) (1997) ECR I-911, I-944 para. 34; *Francesco Benincasa v. Dentalkit Srl*, (Case C-269/95) (1997) ECR I-3767, I-3798 para. 28; *Siegfried Zelger v. Sebastiano Salinitri*, (Case 56/79) (1980) ECR 89, 97 para. 4.

perfectly valid[164] – for instance London jurisdiction for parties domiciled in France and Germany – and might provide the very advantage the parties have intended by their choice.

3. Domicile of one party in Member State no longer required

48　The basic jurisdiction rule of the Regulation requires the defendant's domicile in the EU Member State where the defendant shall be sued (Art. 4).[165] Contrary to that rule, under Art. 25, it is not necessary that even one of the parties is domiciled in a Member State.[166]

49　Under Art. 23 (1) of the prior Brussels I Regulation one of the parties still had to have a domicile in a Member State. However, already the Review Proposal suggested the abolition of this requirement.[167] The procedural role – plaintiff or defendant – of this party did not matter under the former provision. Even if it was only the plaintiff who was domiciled in a Member State s/he could rely on a respective jurisdiction agreement.[168]

50　Now, Brussels *Ibis* has done away with the complications related to the former requirement of domicile. The consented choice of an EU Court has to be respected independently whether all, one or none of the parties are domiciled within the EU.

51　Even if a party to a jurisdiction agreement changes its domicile this does no longer matter – with respect to the prorogatory effect – while under the old provision it was disputed whether the domicile requirement had to be met when the jurisdiction agreement was concluded or when court proceedings were instituted (the latter view prevailed).[169] With respect to the derogatory effect a change of domicile can still be relevant.[170]

52　Under the Lugano Convention the domicile requirement is still alive.[171] The considerations concerning domicile which were necessary under Art. 23 (1) old Brussels I Regulation still apply there.[172]

4. Parties' domicile outside the Member States

53　Under the old Brussels I Regulation, where both parties' domicile was located outside a Member State former Art. 23 was generally inapplicable.[173] However, if in such a situation

---

[164]　See *Stone*, p. 123.

[165]　Except Denmark; but there Art. 4 Brussels *Ibis* applies accordingly.

[166]　See also Art. 6 (1) Brussels *Ibis*.

[167]　The Proposal did not give express reasons for the modification. However, the change would comply with the overall tendency of the Recast to open the scope of the Regulation towards third countries (and their citizens); it would further comply with the regulation in the Hague Convention (Art. 3 (a) and 5 there).

[168]　*Group Josi Reinsurance Co SA v. Universal General Insurance Co (UGIC)*, (Case C-412/98) (2000) ECR I-5925, I-5954 para. 42; *Geimer/Schütze* Art. 23 note 16; *Myass/Reed* European Business Litigation (1998) p. 88; *Mankowski*, in: Rauscher Art. 23 note 2.

[169]　*Kropholler/von Hein* Art. 23 note 11; but contrary *Geimer/Schütze* Art. 23 note 28. See Art. 66; but compare also *infra* Art. 25 note 60 (*Magnus*).

[170]　See *infra* Art. 25 note 61.

[171]　Art. 23 (1) Lugano Convention.

[172]　See thereon *Killias*, in: Dasser/Oberhammer Art. 23 note 8 *et seq.*; *Schnyder/Grolimund* Art. 23 note 4.

the parties had agreed on a forum in a Member State ('a prorogation from outside'), then, the specific provision of former Art. 23 (3) applied. It excluded the (possible) jurisdiction of the courts of all other Member States – from whose jurisdiction the jurisdiction clause might have derogated – unless and until the prorogated forum had decided and had declined its jurisdiction. By this exclusion the former Art. 23 (3) intended to secure that any derogative effect of such 'jurisdiction clause from outside' was dealt with uniformly within the Member States.[174]

The Brussels I Recast has deleted the former Art. 23 (3). Since the new Art. 25 (1) extends to cases where even no party is domiciled in the EU, the old para. (3) was no longer necessary. Art. 25 (1) now covers the choice of a court in the EU by parties from third states anyway. The abolition of the old para. (3) did thus not aim at a restriction of the scope of Art. 25 but just on the contrary at its extension.

Art. 25 (4) Brussels I*bis* does not directly allow prorogated EU courts to decline their jurisdiction if the jurisdiction agreement violates similar or even identical protective or exclusive jurisdiction rules of third states. An analogous application of Art. 25 (4) is doubtful. The Regulation grants certain discretion at least to stay proceedings only if there are proceedings already pending in a third state and if the jurisdiction of the court in the EU is based on Arts. 4, 7–9 Brussels I*bis* (Art. 33 (1) and 34 (1)). Because of this precisely defined regulation it appears hardly possible to extend this discretion by analogy also to cases where jurisdiction is based on the prorogation of an EU court by parties domiciled in third states. The Regulation does, evidently for the sake of legal certainty and foreseeability, therefore not grant any discretion to decline jurisdiction where parties of third states have reached a valid agreement on the jurisdiction of an EU court.

Where parties domiciled in Lugano-EFTA-States choose the jurisdiction of an EU Member State, however, Art. 25 (4) Brussels I*bis* should apply because Art. 23 (5) Lugano Convention contains the same provision. It would be a strange result if both instruments provide for the priority of their protective and exclusive jurisdiction rules but would not apply them to a case where citizens of the Lugano side agree on the jurisdiction of the Brussels side.

Under the old law whether the prorogation of the court(s) of a Member State was valid had **54** to be determined according to the national law of the court seised.[175] Former Art. 23 did not regulate this issue. Now, it is clear from the wording of the new Art. 25 (1) sent. 1 that the question of validity is also covered by this provision; the new conflicts rule in Art. 25 (1) sent. 1 relates to "the agreement" as understood in the preceding part of the sentence and includes all agreements on the jurisdiction of EU courts "regardless of 'the parties' domicile". The prorogation of a court in the EU by parties either from inside or from outside the EU has thus to be adjudged according to the same standard.

---

[173] Hoge Raad NJ 1985 Nr. 698; *Gaudemet-Tallon* para. 127; *Kropholler/von Hein* Art. 23 note 12; *Layton/ Mercer* para. 20.101; *Mankowski*, in: Rauscher Art. 23 note 2.

[174] See Report *Schlosser* para. 177.

[175] *Auer* in: Bülow/Böckstiegel/Geimer/Schütze Art. 23 note 25; *Geimer/Schütze* Art. 23 note 222; *Hausmann*, in: Staudinger IntVertrVerf note 236; *Kropholler/von Hein* Art. 23 note 12; *Layton/Mercer* para. 20.101.

The former Art. 23 (3) gave priority to the prorogated court to decide whether the agreement was valid. Other courts in Member States, even if seised in contradiction to the jurisdiction agreement, had to decline their jurisdiction irrespective whether they had jurisdiction under their national law. They could stay the proceedings or dismiss the claim for lack of jurisdiction. The old Art. 23 (3) allowed them to accept jurisdiction according to their internal law only if they were seised after the prorogated court had finally declined its jurisdiction.[176] However, they could be bound by final and conclusive findings of the prorogated court in cases, for instance, where the jurisdiction agreement was invalid.[177]

55   Now, Art. 31 (2) Brussels I*bis* regulates the situation of concurrent proceedings in EU Member States where an exclusive jurisdiction agreement in favour of a court in a Member State exists, even if parties from outside the EU are involved. The non-prorogated court if seised first must stay proceedings and await the decision of the prorogated court (Art. 31 (2)). The first court can only continue proceedings if the prorogated court has declined its jurisdiction.

56   Where the defendant submits to the jurisdiction of a non-prorogated Member States' court without invoking a jurisdiction agreement that court becomes however competent in any case.[178] The court does not apply the jurisdiction agreement *ex officio*.

5. Relevant point in time

57   The time between the conclusion of a jurisdiction agreement and its actual invocation in court may be considerable and circumstances which are relevant for the application of the agreement may have changed in the meantime. This change may concern either the internationality of the case or the circumstances relevant for the validity of the jurisdiction agreement. Even a change of domicile may still have an effect on a jurisdiction agreement since the kind of the derogatory effect depends on whether the defendant had its domicile within or outside the EU.

58   It is questionable what point in time is the relevant one with respect to the mentioned aspects. The starting point, which is probably in line with most or even all national contract laws, is that a contract is adjudicated according to the circumstances at the time of its conclusion because it is necessary that the parties from that point onwards know their rights and obligations. But since the jurisdiction agreement becomes effective only when invoked in court this starting point may be subject to modifications. The different questions where time may become relevant have therefore to be pursued separately.

a) Relevant point in time for the validity of the jurisdiction agreement
59   The validity of a jurisdiction agreement is partly regulated by Art. 25 itself and partly by the applicable national law. Despite the insertion of the new conflicts rule in Art. 25 (1) sent. 1 the

---

[176]   *Geimer/Schütze* Art. 23 note 222; *Gottwald*, in: Münchener Kommentar zur ZPO Art. 23 EuGVÜ note 9; *Kropholler/von Hein* Art. 23 note 12; *Layton/Mercer* para. 20.101; *Mankowski*, in: Rauscher Art. 23 note 8.
[177]   *Layton/Mercer* para. 20.102.
[178]   *Gottwald*, in: Münchener Kommentar zur ZPO Art. 23 EuGVÜ note 9; *Hausmann*, in: Staudinger IntVertrVerf note 236; *Mankowski*, in: Rauscher Art. 23 note 9; *Tiefenthaler*, in: Czernich/Tiefenthaler/Kodek Art. 17 note 10.

precise borderline between both is still not entirely clear.[179] However, as far as the material validity of a jurisdiction agreement – in particular whether both parties' consent was unimpeded by error, duress or the like[180] – must be determined in accordance with the applicable law then this law decides also at which time the facts relevant for the validity of the contract must be present. In general it is the time when the agreement was concluded.[181] A later change of such circumstances does normally not affect the validity of the jurisdiction agreement.

On the other hand the formal validity of a jurisdiction agreement is regulated by Art. 25 **60** itself. With regard to formal validity the relevant point in time must therefore be fixed autonomously. In *Sanicentral GmbH v. Collin*[182] the ECJ held – though in an intertemporal context of an employment contract when the respective jurisdiction agreement had been concluded before the entering into force of the Brussels Convention – that the circumstances at the time of commencing proceedings were relevant and that it sufficed that the form requirements were then met. The Court stated: "... clauses conferring jurisdiction included in contracts of employment concluded [before the Brussels Convention entered into force] must be considered valid even in cases in which they would have been regarded as void under the national law in force at the time when the contract was entered into."[183] The Court based its decision on the argument that the jurisdiction agreement constitutes only an option as long as court proceedings are not set in motion so that the relevant date is that of the institution of legal proceedings.[184] It is not certain whether the Court's ruling applies to other than transitional cases.[185] But the Court's solution is in line with Art. 66. The principle of that provision that the date of commencing legal proceedings is decisive could be easily generalised and extended to other situations where circumstances have changed between the conclusion of the contract and the beginning of a law suit.[186] It is therefore suggested here that a jurisdiction agreement must comply with the form requirements of Art. 23 at least at the time proceedings are commenced.[187]

b) Relevant point in time for the domicile

With respect to the prorogatory effect of a jurisdiction agreement a change of domicile does **61** no longer matter since Art. 25 covers jurisdiction agreements "regardless of *'the parties'* domicile." However, for the derogatory effect domicile and its change can still be relevant.

---

179 See *Magnus*, in: FS Dieter Martiny (2014), p. 785, 791 *et seq.*; to the former situation *Layton/Mercer* para. 20.035: "very far from clear". For a full discussion see *infra* Art. 25 notes 73–76.

180 As to the law applicable to these questions see *infra* Art. 25 note 83.

181 See, e.g., Principles of European Contract Law: Art. 4:103 (mistake), Art. 4:107 (fraud), Art. 4:108 (threat), Art. 4:109 (unfairness); see thereto with references to almost all European legal systems *Lando/Beale*, Principles of European Contract Law (2000), p. 229 *et seq.*; in the same sense as the text *Auer*, in: Bülow/Böckstiegel/Geimer/Schütze Art. 23 note 36; *Gottwald*, in: Münchener Kommentar zur ZPO Art. 23 note 13; contra – time of instituting proceedings – *Hausmann*, in: Staudinger IntVertrVerf note 242.

182 (Case 25/79) (1979) ECR 3423.

183 *Sanicentral GmbH v. René Collin*, (Case 25/79) (1979) ECR 3423, 3429.

184 *Sanicentral GmbH v. René Collin*, (Case 25/79) (1979) ECR 3423, 3429. For a restrictive interpretation of the decision see *Gaudemet-Tallon* para. 129.

185 See particularly *Gaudemet-Tallon* para. 129.

186 Cautiously in this direction *Kropholler/von Hein* Art. 23 note 11.

187 See in this sense OLG Köln NJW 1988, 2182; OLG Koblenz NJW-RR 1988, 1335; *Mankowski*, in: Rauscher Art. 23 note 14.

The protective jurisdiction rules of Brussels I*bis* protect insured people, consumers and employees who can be solely sued at the place where they have their domicile (in the EU).[188] If, as is advocated here,[189] these jurisdictions cannot be derogated from (Art. 25 (4)) even by the choice of the court(s) of a third state[190] the question has to be answered when the insured, consumer or employee must have its domicile in the EU. It is evidently unproblematic if the defendant had its domicile in an EU State both at the time of the conclusion of the respective jurisdiction agreement and at the time proceedings were instituted.

62 Under the preceding Regulation it was disputed whether its Art. 23 applied if a domicile in a Member State was established only when the contract was concluded but ceased to exist when proceedings were instituted or existed only when proceedings started but was lacking at the time of the conclusion of the contract. The ECJ had not decided the question though it may not be unlikely that the Court would have followed its reasoning in *Sanicentral GmbH v. Collin.*[191] In legal doctrine the views were split Partly the time of conclusion of contract and the parties' interest in foreseeability and certainty was considered essential;[192] partly the time of commencing proceedings had been regarded as finally decisive.[193] And the views varied whether the domicile at the relevant time was only sufficient or whether it was necessary to found jurisdiction under the former Art. 23.[194] It had even been suggested that either point in time should suffice.[195]

63 For the Brussels I*bis* Regulation though the question has lost much of its importance it is suggested here that the protective EU jurisdiction has to be respected despite the agreed jurisdiction of the court(s) of a third state when the defendant's domicile was situated in the EU at the time proceedings in the EU were commenced. If the time of the conclusion of the agreement or the time proceedings in the prorogated foreign court started were taken as points of reference, the protection would be substantially lessened which the protective regimes of the Regulation and its Art. 25 (4) intend, and are designed, to provide.

c) Relevant point in time for the internationality of the case

64 The problems just discussed encounter as well when the question is posed at which point in time the international element of the case[196] must be present. Generally, it has to be the starting point that the time of the conclusion of the contract is decisive.[197] But unless justified

---

[188] See Arttt. 14, 18 (2) and 22 (1) Brussels I*bis* Regulation.

[189] See *supra* Art. 25 note 39.

[190] See under the preceding Regulation *Mahamdia v. Algeria*, (C-154/11) (2012) nyr.

[191] (Case 25/79) (1979) ECR 3423.

[192] *Auer* in: Bülow/Böckstiegel/Geimer/Schütze Art. 23 note 34; *Bork*, in: Stein/Jonas § 38 note 25; *Gaudemet-Tallon* paras. 128 *et seq.*; *Gothot/Holleaux* para. 163 *et seq.*, 168; Hk-ZPO/*Dörner* Art. 23 note 5; *Layton/Mercer* para. 20.044.

[193] *Samtleben*, RabelsZ 59 (1995), 702 *et seq.*; *Schack* para. 465; cautiously also *Kropholler/von Hein* Art. 23 note 11; without clear decision *Geimer/Schütze* Art. 23 notes 26 *et seq.*

[194] Compare for instance the differing views of *Kropholler/von Hein* Art. 23 note 11 and *Layton/Mercer* paras. 20.043 *et seq.*

[195] See *Droz* para. 185.

[196] See thereto *supra* Art. 25 note 23 (*Magnus*).

[197] In the same sense *Gottwald* in: Münchener Kommentar zur ZPO Art. 23 note 13; however, contra – date of instituting proceedings is relevant – OGH IHR 2007, 243 (248).

interests of one of the parties oppose such a solution it is suggested also here that it suffices that the case is international in character at the time proceedings are commenced.[198] On the other hand, an originally international choice of court agreement should not loose this character if afterwards it becomes purely internal. Parties must be able to rely on the fact that a once valid agreement rests valid.

VIII. Admissibility of jurisdiction agreements

In principle jurisdiction agreements of any kind are permitted under Art. 25 as long as they **65** do not violate the Regulation's provisions on compulsory exclusive or protective jurisdiction (Art. 24 and 15, 19, 23).[199] The parties are even free to confer jurisdiction on courts whose jurisdiction would be regarded as exorbitant under the Regulation (Art. 5 (2) in connection with Art. 76).[200] As far as Art. 25 reaches it overrules any eventual national prohibition of jurisdiction agreements. Under the provision, jurisdiction agreements must satisfy a requirement of certainty in order to avoid doubts and disputes over the competent court.[201] The certainty requirement serves also the aim to prevent that by one single jurisdiction clause a party – in particular the stronger trading partner in general contract terms – can force the other (weaker) party generally to litigate in foreign and otherwise actually incompetent courts.[202] Art. 25 therefore requires that a jurisdiction agreement refers to a particular legal relationship and is linked to disputes arising from that relationship.[203] The jurisdiction agreement must also provide certainty with respect to the prorogated court.[204] Furthermore, it has to be questioned whether Art. 25 requires that jurisdiction agreements must satisfy also a certain control test with regard to their reasonableness.[205]

1. Requirement of certainty

a) Certainty as to a particular legal relationship

According to Art. 25 (1) sent. 1 the jurisdiction agreement must refer to "disputes which **66** have arisen or which may arise in connection with a particular legal relationship." It is necessary that the dispute between the parties originates from the legal relationship for which the jurisdiction agreement had been concluded. The ECJ expressed the underlying considerations for the requirement in the following way: "That requirement is intended to limit the scope of an agreement conferring jurisdiction solely to disputes which arise from the legal relationship in connection with which the agreement was entered into. Its purpose is to avoid a party being taken by surprise by the assignment of jurisdiction to a given forum as regards all disputes which may arise out of its relationship with the other party to the

---

198   In the same sense OGH IHR 2007, 243 (248); *Hausmann*, in: Staudinger, IntVertrVerf note 242; *Kropholler/von Hein* Art. 23 note 11.

199   See already *supra* note 39 (*Magnus*).

200   *Beraudo* fasc. 3011 no. 18; *Gaudemet-Tallon* para. 132.

201   See in particular in this sense: *Coreck Maritime GmbH v. Handelsveem BV*, (C-387/98) (2000) ECR I-9337.

202   See *Droz* para. 200; *Geimer/Schütze* Art. 23 note 156; *Kropholler/von Hein* Art. 23 note 69; *Layton/Mercer* para. 20.055; *Pålsson* para. 5. 3. 1.

203   See *infra* Art. 25 note 66 (*Magnus*).

204   See *infra* Art. 25 note 70 (*Magnus*).

205   See *infra* Art. 25 note 73 (*Magnus*).

contract and stem from a relationship other than that in connection with which the agreement conferring jurisdiction was made."[206] A party can therefore not rely on a jurisdiction agreement if the dispute is unconnected with the legal relationship, generally the contract, for which the choice of forum was concluded. However, it is always a matter of construction to which disputes between the parties a jurisdiction clause shall extend.[207] In doubt, the clause will cover concurrent contractual and tortious claims[208] as well as disputes over the validity of the underlying contract.[209] It may be the intention of the parties to carry forward a prior jurisdiction clause to further transactions of the same or similar character, in particular in a continuing business relationship.[210] A jurisdiction clause in a main contract may also extend to annexed contracts which are concluded in connection with, and in performance of, the main contract.[211] But a 'catch all-clause' which covers each and every present and future dispute between the parties must be regarded as invalid.[212] It lacks the connection to a *particular* legal relationship and would deprive a party in an unlimited number of unforeseeable cases with no time limit of the chance to litigate in the actually competent forum. Art. 25 aims at the prevention of such wide jurisdiction agreements.

67 The ECJ further held that a jurisdiction agreement contained in a company's statutes still satisfied the certainty test since the agreement could be construed as being confined to disputes between the company and its shareholders 'as such' meaning those disputes arising out of the position as shareholder of the company.[213]

68 It appears not to be necessary that it is always one single relationship to which the jurisdiction agreement is related. If the parties agree with sufficient certainty that the jurisdiction clause should refer to several – precisely specified – legal relationships, for instance additionally to each single transaction under a distribution agreement, then the certainty requirement is met as well.[214]

b) Certainty as to the dispute
69 The dispute which is covered by a jurisdiction agreement may be one that has already arisen when the agreement is concluded; then it is unlikely that problems of certainty will arise. However, the much more frequent case is the case of a jurisdiction agreement for future

---

[206] *Powell Duffryn plc v. Wolfgang Petereit*, (Case C-214/89) (1992) ECR I-1745, 1777 para. 31.

[207] See also *Gottwald*, in: Münchener Kommentar zur ZPO Art. 23 note 53. As to the methods of interpretation see *infra* Art. 25 note 141 (*Magnus*).

[208] OLG München RIW 1989, 901 (902); Orléans Rev. crit. 2003, 326 with note *Ancel*; LG Berlin IPRspr. 2004 No. 124; *Geimer/Schütze* Art. 23 note 206; *Gottwald*, in: Münchener Kommentar zur ZPO Art. 23 note 53; *Kropholler/von Hein* Art. 23 note 69; *Mankowski*, in: Rauscher Art. 23 note 62a; see also *infra* note 150 *et seq.* (*Magnus*).

[209] *Francesco Benincasa v. Dentalkit Srl* (Case C-269/95) (1997) ECR I-3767 (para. 21 *et seq.*), BGH NJW 2006, 1672 (1673).

[210] *Droz* para. 200; *Layton/Mercer* para. 20.055.

[211] See *Auer*, in: Bülow/Böckstiegel/Geimer/Schütze Art. 23 note 67.

[212] See also *Hausmann*, in: Staudinger IntVertrVerf note 287.

[213] *Powell Duffryn plc v. Wolfgang Petereit*, (Case C-214/89) (1992) ECR I-1745, 1778 paras. 32–34.

[214] See OLG Oldenburg IPRax 1999, 458, 459 *et seq.*; *Geimer/Schütze* Art. 23 note 158; *Kindler/Huneke*, IPRax 1999, 435, 436; see also *Auer* in: Bülow/Böckstiegel/Geimer/Schütze Art. 23 note 67; *Hausmann*, in: Staudinger IntVertrVerf note 287.

disputes. Art. 25 requires only that the dispute must be connected with the relationship for which the agreement has been concluded.[215] This is, for instance, the case where the dispute concerns the contract which contains the jurisdiction agreement.[216] Art. 25 provides for no further time or other requirement for the dispute.

c) Certainty as to the chosen court

In order to be valid a jurisdiction agreement must, too, designate the chosen court with **70** sufficient certainty. According to Art. 25 (1) sent. 1 the agreement must enable the court seised to decide that the parties have agreed upon "a court or courts of a Member State".[217] The expression includes clauses that designate courts in more than one Member State.[218] It is not necessary though advisable that the court is named in the jurisdiction clause as long as the competent court can be clearly gathered from the parties' contract and intentions and from the circumstances as a whole.[219] The clause must only clearly state the criteria according to which the competent court is to be determined.[220] A jurisdiction clause stating that "(a)ny dispute arising under this Bill of Lading shall be decided in the country where the carrier has his principal place of business"[221] is therefore sufficiently precise since when the clause is invoked the court seised can determine the place of business of the carrier and hence the competent court.[222] If the place of business has changed since the conclusion of the contract it is probably the place at the time when proceedings are instituted which counts unless this party has changed its place of business on purpose in order to change jurisdiction only.[223]

Agreements which confer jurisdiction on the courts at the domicile of the respective defen- **71** dant[224] or even of the respective claimant[225] designate the competent court with sufficient certainty since, again, at the time proceedings are instituted it is clear which party is the claimant or the defendant.[226] Equally, a clause which gives the claimant the right to choose

---

[215] *Powell Duffryn plc v. Wolfgang Petereit*, (Case C-214/89) (1992) ECR I-1745, 1777 para. 31.

[216] See *Powell Duffryn plc v. Wolfgang Petereit*, (Case C-214/89) (1992) ECR I-1745, 1777 para. 31; *Dörner*, in: Hk-ZPO Art. 23 note 20; *Kropholler/von Hein* Art. 23 note 69.

[217] See in particular *Coreck Maritime GmbH v. Handelsveem BV* (C-387/98), (2000) ECR I-9337, I-9372 para. 15.

[218] See indirectly *Nikolaus Meeth v. Glacetal*, (Case 23/78) (1978) ECR 2133 where a reciprocal jurisdiction clause – each party could sue in the other's country – was accepted.

[219] See *Coreck Maritime GmbH v. Handelsveem BV*, (C-387/98) (2000) ECR I-9337, I-9372 para. 15; see also OGH EuLF 2005, 82; further *Auer* in: Bülow/Böckstiegel/Geimer/Schütze Art. 23 note 72; *Gottwald*, in: Münchener Kommentar zur ZPO Art. 23 note 55; *Kropholler/von Hein* Art. 23 note 71; *Layton/Mercer* para. 20.047; *Mankowski*, in: Rauscher Art. 23 note 45.

[220] *Coreck Maritime GmbH v. Handelsveem BV*, (C-387/98) (2000) ECR I-9337, I-9372 para. 15.

[221] This was the wording of the jurisdiction agreement in *Coreck Maritime GmbH v. Handelsveem BV*, (C-387/98) (2000) ECR I-9337; see *supra* Art. 23 note 37.

[222] See *Coreck Maritime GmbH v. Handelsveem BV*, (C-387/98) (2000) ECR I-9337, I-9372 para. 15.

[223] As to the relevant time see *supra* Art. 23 notes 57–64.

[224] See *Nikolaus Meeth v. Glacetal*, (Case 23/78) (1978) ECR 2133 (a reciprocal jurisdiction clause).

[225] In this sense see for instance Cass. RCDIP 70 (1981), 134 with note *Gaudemet-Tallon*; Cassaz. Riv. dir. int. 1996, 577.

[226] In the same sense *Kropholler/von Hein* Art. 23 note 71; *Mankowski*, in: Rauscher Art. 23 note 45; probably also *Gaudemet-Tallon* para. 132.

between different courts – for instance between the court where the defendant is domiciled and the court at the place of performance – is sufficiently precise (though such a clause has generally no exclusive effect).[227] However, a jurisdiction agreement lacks the necessary precision if the choice of the competent court is entirely left at the claimant's option.[228] The same is true for a clause that "the courts of the Ship's Flag State" or "the court mutually agreed by the parties" should have jurisdiction since the competent court cannot be precisely determined.[229] Also a clause "jurisdiction: European courts" would be invalid for uncertainty since the ECJ and the Court of First Instance cannot be freely chosen by private persons and with respect to national courts in Europe the clause leaves it completely uncertain the courts of which European country should be competent. On the other hand, a clause "Internationales Handelsgericht in Brüssel" ("international commercial court in Brussels") has been held to be sufficiently precise: though there is no international commercial court in Brussels but only a national commercial court the clause was construed to designate the latter court.[230]

72 The certainty condition does not require the parties to nominate a specific local court. The wording of Art. 25 allows explicitly that they designate the courts of a certain country without specifying the locally competent court (for instance: "French courts alone shall have jurisdiction").[231] It is then for the national law of civil procedure to determine which local court is to have jurisdiction to decide the dispute.[232] If it should happen that the national law does not provide an answer to this question it has been suggested that the claimant may chose where to sue in this country.[233] The better view in such a case is to apply a uniform standard that follows the underlying policies of the Regulation: first to allow the parties to choose the local court; absent such choice, to seise the court where one of the parties is seated (in case both parties have their domicile in that state where the defendant is seated); lastly, to sue in the courts at the seat of the government of the chosen state.[234]

---

[227] *Auer*, in: Bülow/Böckstiegel/Geimer/Schütze Art. 23 note 73; *Kropholler/von Hein* Art. 23 note 73. It is, however, a different question how such clause is to be interpreted, namely whether it has exclusive effect and derogates from the jurisdiction of other courts or whether it provides only the jurisdiction of additional courts; see thereto *infra* Art. 23 note 141.

[228] CA Rouen DMF 2001, 336; LG Braunschweig AWD 1974, 346; *Gaudemet-Tallon* para. 132; *Gottwald*, in: Münchener Kommentar zur ZPO Art. 23 note 55; *Kropholler/von Hein* Art. 23 note 72; *Mankowski*, in: Rauscher Art. 23 note 45; *Spellenberg*, IPRax 2007, 99.

[229] See Rb Rotterdam NIPR 2002 Nr. 212.

[230] See OLG Celle IHR 2004, 125 *et seq.*

[231] As in *Nikolaus Meeth v. Glacetal*, (Case 23/78) (1978) ECR 2133 (though on a reciprocal basis).

[232] LG Mainz WM 2005, 2319 (2322); *Auer*, in: Bülow/Böckstiegel/Geimer/Schütze Art. 23 note 76; *Kropholler/von Hein* Art. 23 note 78; *Layton/Mercer* paras. 20.051 *et seq.* (the authors advocate in fn. 97 that in this respect the English courts still have "a residual *forum conveniens* discretion, purely as a matter of internal U. K. law". However, this seems acceptable only with respect to the jurisdiction of different local courts); *Mankowski*, in: Rauscher Art. 23 note 46; *Gottwald*, in: Münchener Kommentar zur ZPO Art. 23 note 68. *Gothot/Holleaux* note 181 advocate a right of choice for the claimant; see further *infra* notes 166a *et seq.*

[233] See HG Zürich SZIER 1997, 360, 361; *Briggs/Rees* para. 2.93; *Droz* para. 212; *Layton/Mercer* para. 20.052; *Killias*, p. 112 *et seq.*; *Volken*, SZIER 1997, 362, 364; but sceptical *Mankowski*, in: Rauscher Art. 23 note 46.

[234] In a similar sense *Gottwald*, in: Münchener Kommentar zur ZPO Art. 23 note 56; *Kropholler/von Hein* Art. 23 note 78.

2. Reasonableness test, ordre public or similar control test of jurisdiction agreements?

It is disputed, in particular in German legal doctrine[235] but also in France,[236] whether Art. 25 **73** and its predecessor allows for, or even implicitly contains, a general rule that a jurisdiction agreement must be reasonable or at least that its application must not offend public policy. The probably prevailing view is that in this respect Art. 25 – as well as the former Art. 23 – regulates finally and conclusively the validity of jurisdiction agreements.[237] While general questions of the material validity of jurisdiction agreements like questions of capacity, mistake, fraud etc. are governed by the applicable national law[238] it is argued that the admissibility of jurisdiction clauses as such is a matter of Art. 25 and that this provision does not prescribe any further requirement nor allows for any further control than provided in its text.[239] It is advocated that even under the national law on unfair contract terms, which is based on the respective European Directive,[240] no such control is permissible.[241] On the contrary a growing number of supporters favours the view that the Regulation contains an inherent competence to deny the validity of jurisdiction agreements if the agreement constitutes a clear misuse by one party of the freedom granted by Art. 25.[242]

The position of the ECJ on this question is still ambiguous. On the one hand the Court has **74** ruled that "the choice of court in a jurisdiction clause may be assessed only in the light of considerations connected with the requirements laid down in Art. 17 of the [Brussels] Convention."[243] This decision is understood to express that [now] Art. 25 alone and only the requirements mentioned there regulates the question whether a jurisdiction agreement

---

[235] See in particular *Gottschalk/Bressler*, ZeuP 2007, 56 *et seq.*; *Leible/Röder*, RIW 2007, 481 *et seq.*; *Redmann*, Ordre-public-Kontrolle von Gerichtsstandsvereinbarungen (2005).

[236] See Cour de cass. civ. (1ère), D. 2012.2876 with note *Martel*; see thereto also *Niggemann*, IPRax 2014, 194 *et seq.*; further *Bureau*, RCDIP 2013, 256 *et seq.*; *Pataut*, in: Mélanges Calais-Alois 807 *et seq.*; *Remy*, Clunet 2011, 2 *et seq.*

[237] OLG Hamburg NJW 2004, 3126 (3128); LG Mainz WM 2005, 2319 (2322 *et seq.*); *Geimer/Schütze* Art. 23 note 123; *Gottschalk/Breßler*, ZEuP 2007, 56; *Horn*, IPRax 2006, 4; *Mankowski*, in: Rauscher Art. 23 note 12e *et seq.*; *Redmann*, 192; *Weigel/Blankenheim*, WM 2006, 664.

[238] See *infra* Art. 25 note 83 (*Magnus*).

[239] *Geimer/Schütze* Art. 23 note 74, 181; *Mankowski*, in: Rauscher Art. 23 note 12 f; *Pfeiffer*, in: FS Rolf A. Schütze (1999), p. 671, 679; *Redmann* 192; *Schack* para. 475; *Sparka* 133 *et seq.*; also *Kropholler/von Hein* Art. 23 note 86 *et seq.* with respect to the lex lata.

[240] Council Directive 93/13/EEC of 5 April 1993 on unfair terms in consumer contracts, OJ 1993 L 95/29.

[241] See the references in fn. 249.

[242] See for instance *Gottwald*, in: Münchener Kommentar zur ZPO Art. 23 EuGVÜ note 15 and 60; *Hausmann*, in: Staudinger IntVertrVerf note 294; *Hk-ZPO/Dörner* Art. 23 note 23; *Hüßtege*, in: Thomas/Putzo, Art. 23 note 18; *Kropholler/von Hein* Art. 23 note 89 (cautiously); *Leible/Röder*, RIW 2007, 481; *Mankowski*, in: Rauscher Art. 23 note 12 h; *Musielak/Stadler* Art. 23 note 1; *Pfeiffer*, in: FS Rolf A. Schütze (1999), p. 671, 675 *et seq.*; for Art. 25 Brussels Ibis *Magnus*, in: FS Dieter Martiny (2014), p. 785, 801. Perhaps also in this sense Cour de cass. civ. (1ère), D. 2012.2876 with note *Martel*: in this case the French Cour denied the validity of a jurisdiction clause of a bank which provided for exclusive jurisdiction of the courts in Luxembourg and the further right of the bank to sue the client at her domicile or before any other competent court. Since it is not clear on which specific ground the decision is based – missing agreement, too uncertain agreement, consumer protection, unfair contract terms, ordre public violation – the precise position of the Cour remains open.

is permissible.[244] On the other hand in *Océano Grupo Editorial SA v. Rocío Murciano Quintero*[245] and subsequent decisions[246] the Court held that a jurisdiction agreement between a consumer and a professional – though in a merely domestic case – was invalid because it violated provisions originating from the Unfair Contract Terms Directive. It is not easy to reconcile both strings of decisions and it is still open how the ECJ will decide the misuse question in an international case with a jurisdiction agreement and no consumer involved. It can be argued that the ECJ accepted a misuse control test under the respective Directive and might – and in this author's view should – follow this line even more so in international cases.[247] A certain control is provided by the Regulation already since Art. 15, 19 and 23 disallow certain jurisdiction agreements which violate the procedural interests of the weaker party.[248] This reduces the practical importance of the dispute considerably. Nonetheless, there remain cases where a jurisdiction agreement can be clearly unfair, for instance where the jurisdiction clause favours solely the interests of the principal of a commercial agent by choosing a foreign court in a case with no other international contact whatsoever.[249] Despite its impact on legal certainty and foreseeability a misuse control should be possible under the Regulation if the agent is in a consumer- or employee-like position. The mere circumvention of national mandatory rules, for instance on liability, does however not suffice to invalidate a jurisdiction agreement.[250] Also the German Federal Court has applied a misuse control in a recent case that concerned a choice of Dutch law under the heading "Applicable law/jurisdiction" ("Anwendbares Recht/Gerichtsstand") in the standard terms of a Dutch mail-order pharmacy. The Court held that the clause unreasonably disfavoured the interests of (German) consumers and was therefore invalid.[251] Although the standard term only provided for the applicable law, the Court found that the consumer could have the misleading impression from the heading of being obliged to sue exclusively in the Netherlands. A further aspect was that under German law there exist special mandatory information and advice duties for pharmacists and that their violation can lead to bodily injury. The decision leaves little doubt that in that particular case the Federal Court would have invalidated an explicit jurisdiction agreement as well.[252]

---

243 *Trasporti Castelletti Spedizioni Internazionali SpA v. Hugo Trumpy SpA*, (Case C-159/97), (1999) ECR I-1597, I-1656 para. 52.

244 See *Kröll*, ZZP 113 (2000), 135, 149 *et seq.*; *Layton/Mercer* para. 20.035 *et seq.*; *Mankowski*, in: Rauscher Art. 23 note 12.

245 (Cases C-240 – C-244) (2000) ECR I-4941.

246 *Freiburger Kommunalbauten GmbH Baugesellschaft & Co. KG v. Ludger und Ulrike Hofstetter* (Case C-237/02) (2004) ECR I-3403 (para. 23); *Pannon GSM Zrt. v. Erzsébet Sustikné Győrfi* (Case C-243/08) (2009) ECR I-4713; *VB Pénzügyi Lízing Zrt. v. Ferenc Schneider* (Case C-137/08) RIW 2010, 876.

247 See in this sense *Kropholler/von Hein* Art. 23 note 89 (but more restrictively in note 20); *Ansgar Staudinger*, in: Rauscher Art. 17 note 6.

248 See *infra* Art. 25 notes 132–134 (*Magnus*).

249 For a control in such a case OLG München IPRax 2007, 322; critical thereto *Rühl*, IPRax 2007, 294 *et seq.*

250 See *Gottschalk/Breßler*, ZEuP 2007, 56 (67); *Mankowski*, in: Rauscher Art. 23 note 12 e *et seq.* (with intense discussion); *Sparka*, 156 *et seq.* To a certain extent this view is also supported by Art. 71 which only preempts international conventions (concerning jurisdiction) the Member States were already parties to and which may secure a minimum liability. Any later convention – and national law – is not preempted.

251 BGH GRUR 2013, 421 (in this case a consumer association had criticised the respective standard term and instituted the lawsuit).

IX. Agreement

1. Agreement as central requirement

Art. 25 requires that the parties have in fact agreed that their disputes are to be litigated in a   **75**
certain court or courts. The agreement is the central element for the validity of choice of
court clauses.[253] Only if the choice is carried by the parties' free and unimpeded consent is
the procedural effect of such choice justified. The ECJ has stated on several occasions that it
is the main aim of the provision on jurisdiction agreements to give effect to the parties' free
and independent will and also "to ensure that the consensus between the parties is in fact
established."[254] "... Art. 17 [Brussels Convention] imposes upon the Court before which the
matter is brought the duty of examining, first, whether the clause conferring jurisdiction
upon it was in fact subject of a consensus between the parties, which must be clearly and
precisely demonstrated."[255] A jurisdiction agreement is therefore valid only if it satisfies all
formal and material conditions imposed by Art. 25.

2. Applicable law

The material and formal validity of a jurisdiction *agreement* falling within the scope of   **76**
Art. 25 can be assessed either according to the standards autonomously set by Art. 25 itself
or according to the rules of the applicable national law.[256] Unfortunately, although a conflict
of laws provision was added it is not entirely clear – neither from the wording of Art. 25 nor
from the ECJ judgments – which of the two governs the agreement of the parties to which
extent.[257] The starting point must be an autonomous interpretation of Art. 25 as far as
possible in order to ensure uniformity in the application of the provision.[258] That means
that the requirements of a valid agreement should be inferred from the provision itself to the
extent possible. And it is rather clear that Art. 25 itself regulates the form requirements and
hence the formal validity of a jurisdiction agreement. National law is excluded in this
respect.[259] The position is, however, less clear with respect to the material validity of juris-

---

[252] It can be argued that the incriminated clause was an implicit choice of jurisdiction as well because the
heading mentioned "jurisdiction".

[253] For the exception of trust settlements where a one-sided designation of the competent court suffices see
infra Art. 25 notes 165–170.

[254] *Estasis Salotti di Colzani Aimo and Gianmario Colzani v. RÜWA Polstereimaschinen GmbH*, (Case 24/
76) (1976) ECR 1831 (1st sentence of the summary of the decision); *Galeries Segoura SPRL v. Société
Rahim Bonakdarian*, (Case 25/76) (1976) ECR 1851, 1860 para. 6.

[255] *Galeries Segoura SPRL v. Société Rahim Bonakdarian*, (Case 25/76) (1976) ECR 1851, 1860 para. 6.

[256] As to the applicable law again different solutions can be, and are, advocated: see thereto in particular
Gaudemet-Tallon para. 152 with further references; see further *infra* Art. 25 note 77.

[257] See thereto extensively *Kropholler/von Hein* Art. 23 notes 23 *et seq.*; *Layton/Mercer* paras. 20.028 *et seq.*;
also *Gaudemet-Tallon* para. 152.

[258] In the same sense *Auer* in: Bülow/Böckstiegel/Geimer/Schütze Art. 23 note 41; *Hausmann*, in: Staudinger
2005 Anhang II zu Art. 27–27 EGBGB note 180; *Kropholler/von Hein* Art. 23 note 23; *Layton/Mercer*
para. 10.028.

[259] See *Elefanten Schuh GmbH v. Pierre Jacqmain*, (Case 150/80) (1981) ECR 1671, 1688 paras. 25 *et seq.*;
Trasporti Castelletti Spedizioni Internazionali SpA v. Hugo Trumpy SpA, (Case C-159/97), (1999) ECR
I-1597, I-1653 para. 37; further *Auer* in: Bülow/Böckstiegel/Geimer/Schütze Art. 23 note 46; *Kropholler/*

---

diction agreements.[260] Despite the fact that the Recast inserted a conflict of laws rule into Art. 25 (1) sent. 1, it is not clear beyond doubt how far this new clause governs the questions of material validity.[261]

3. Material consent

a) Autonomous scope of Art. 25 and the new conflicts rule

77 Material consent means the consensus of the parties who according to Art. 25 must "have agreed" on the chosen court's jurisdiction. As mentioned above the ECJ reiterated on various occasions that the consensus of the parties is indispensable since it is one of the aims of the provision on jurisdiction agreements to acknowledge the parties' independence and freedom to choose 'their' court.[262] Where a true consensus of the parties is lacking the jurisdiction agreement is invalid and has no effect. It is not clear whether and, if so, how far Art. 25 regulates the material consent in an autonomous way or refers to applicable national law. The insertion of the new conflict of laws clause in Art. 25 (1) sent. 1 has brought some but no full clarification.

78 The wording of the former Art. 23 Brussels I Regulation was even less supportive in this respect. Nevertheless, under the old Regulation it was widely accepted that the basic requirement of the consensus could be inferred from the Article through an autonomous interpretation.[263] According to the case law of the ECJ the fundamental condition that both parties are to be in agreement required that the parties' intentions were the same concerning the choice of a court or courts *(consensus ad idem)* and that this agreement was in some way expressed.[264] Insofar the formal requirements evidenced the material consent. To a certain extent, the consent could be inferred from the observance of the form.[265] Nonetheless, each party must have declared its consent to the conferral of jurisdiction onto a specific court or courts.[266] The agreement needed, however, not be express; implicit consensus sufficed as long as it complied with the form requirements listed in the old Art. 23 (1) – as well as in the new Art. 25 (1) – and as long it was clearly and precisely established.[267] For instance, the

---

von Hein Art. 23 note 30; *Layton/Mercer* para. 20.029; *Mankowski*, in: Rauscher Art. 23 note 14; *Schack* para. 472.

[260] See thereto *infra* Art. 25 note 82.

[261] See *infra* notes 77 *et seq.*; as to the law applicable to the interpretation of jurisdiction agreements see *infra* notes 141 *et seq.*

[262] See in particular *Galeries Segoura SPRL v. Société Rahim Bonakdarian*, (Case 25/76) (1976) ECR 1851, 1860 para. 6; *Trasporti Castelletti Spedizioni Internazionali SpA v. Hugo Trumpy SpA*, (Case C-159/97), (1999) ECR I-1597, I-1656 para. 52.

[263] See for instance *Fentiman*, International Commercial Litigation note 2.33 *et seq.*; *Geimer/Schütze* Art. 23 note 75; *Gottwald*, in: Münchener Kommentar zur ZPO Art. 23 note 14; *Kropholler/von Hein* Art. 23 note 23; *Spellenberg*, IPRax 2010, 466 *et seq.*; cautiously also *Gaudemet-Tallon* para. 152 ("premier pas"); but contra – for full application of the applicable national law – for instance *Stöve*, p. 20 *et seq.*

[264] In *Galeries Segoura SPRL v. Société Rahim Bonakdarian* (Case 25/76), (1976) ECR 1851, 1860 para. 6 the ECJ requests the consensus to be "in fact established."

[265] See OGH IHR 2009, 126; already *Kohler*, IPRax 1983, 268; further *Gebauer*, in: FS vHoffmann 578.

[266] OGH IHR 2009, 126: there is no agreement if a jurisdiction clause (in standard terms) is in a language which the other party does not understand and which was not used in the precontractual negotiations unless the content of the clause was brought to the knowledge of the other party and was accepted by it.

consensus was lacking where the jurisdiction agreement was contained in a mere draft contract which was never ratified by the parties.[268]

Under the old Brussels I Regulation the basic requirement of a true consensus on the   **79** jurisdiction agreement could therefore, and had to, be determined according to the yardstick of the former Art. 23 alone and needed insofar no redress to the applicable national law.[269] Also the question whether a jurisdiction clause had been validly incorporated into a contract did not follow national law but had to be adjudicated according to the standard of the former Art. 23 (1).[270] On the other hand, the autonomous interpretation had the effect that former Art. 23 required nothing more than mere consent. Further requirements constituting or indicating consent – like the consideration of the Common Law – were excluded and needed not be fulfilled.[271]

It is questionable whether the former legal position can still be upheld after the formulation   **79a** "unless the agreement is null and void as to its substantive validity under the law of that Member State." has been appended to Art. 25 (1) sent. 1. This addition followed closely though not entirely Art. 5 (1) Hague Choice-of-Court Agreements Convention.[272] It can be argued that the new formulation now covers all questions of substantive law (in contrast to the law on the form of jurisdiction agreements) including the requirements for an agreement.[273] The new text can thus have withdrawn the basis for the old ECJ case law on the autonomous determination of the material consent. A first counter-argument is, however, the wording: "unless" means that the validity of a choice-of-court agreement is presumed.[274] The agreement must therefore already be valid according to a certain law before the "unless" clause can come into play. And this validity law can only be and should be the autonomous regulation developed by the former ECJ case law. Moreover, the formulation "null and void as to its substantive validity" points in direction of grounds which invalidate an existing agreement and not in direction of the elements which are necessary to conclude an agree-

---

[267] See OLG Köln IHR 2007, 200; *Auer*, in: Bülow/Böckstiegel/Geimer/Schütze Art. 23 note 51; *Geimer/ Schütze* Art. 23 notes 75, 78 *et seq.*; *Gottwald*, in: Münchener Kommentar zur ZPO Art. 23 EuGVÜ note 15; *Hausmann*, in: Staudinger (fn. 64), Anhang II zu Art. 27–27 EGBGB note 183; *Kropholler/von Hein* Art. 23 note 25.

[268] See *Implants International Ltd. v. Stratec Medical* (1999) 2 All ER (Comm.) 933 (Leeds Mercantile Ct.).

[269] *Czernich/Tiefenthaler* Art. 23 note 20; *Geimer/Schütze* Art. 23 note 75; Hk-ZPO/*Dörner* Art. 23 note 13; *Kropholler/von Hein* Art. 23 note 18, 23; *Layton/Mercer* note 20.083 *et seq.*; *Mankowski*, in: Rauscher Art. 23 note 39; *Pfeiffer*, in: Heidelberg Report note 325; but contra, e.g., *Gottwald*, in: Münchener Kommentar zur ZPO Art. 23 note 15; left open in BGHZ 171, 141 (148: in principle, the question whether a jurisdiction agreement meets the requirements of Art. 23 has to be decided in an autonomous way; however, those questions not regulated by Art. 23 must be decided by the applicable national law). In a recent decision the BGH left the question open because even with respect to the applicable law – in that case the CISG – the agreement of the parties was not in doubt; see BGH 7 January 2014, IHR 56 (57).

[270] BGH NJW 1996, 1819, 1820; OLG München WM 1989, 605; *Mankowski*, in: Rauscher Art. 23 note 39; contra – the applicable national law decides – *Layton/Mercer* para. 20.038.

[271] The opinion that the national law decides inevitably brings in such specific national requirements.

[272] The formulation there is "unless null and void under the law of that State." "That State" is the state of the prorogated court.

[273] In this sense probably *von Hein*, RIW 2013, 105.

[274] See *Lenaerts/Stapper*, RabelsZ 78 (2014) 282; *Weller*, GPR 2012, 41.

ment. The most important argument is, however, that there are no signs whatsoever that the drafters intended to change the former and long-standing jurisprudence of the ECJ on an autonomous material formation concept. If this had been intended this would mean that peculiarities of national law such as the consideration of the Common Law would revive. This would be a deplorable step backwards.[275] As there are no signs for such drawback, it should not be read into the new conflicts rule. The new rule should therefore be understood to leave the former ECJ case law on the material consent intact. The basic essentials of an agreement are therefore to be autonomously taken from Art. 25 itself in its interpretation through the ECJ case law. According to it a real consensus between the parties is needed which generally can be inferred from the compliance with one of the form requirements listed in Art. 25 (1).[276]

80 Despite this limited autonomous scope of Art. 25 with respect to the material consent the precise demarcation line between it and the scope of the new conflicts rule remains still vague. One reason is the already mentioned wording of the new clause which seems to restrict its scope exclusively to grounds that invalidate a contract. Another reason is the fact that the ECJ has decided on the 'interpretative' validity of jurisdiction agreements without any redress to national law. This concerns questions such as whether an agreement is at all a jurisdiction agreement falling under Art. 25,[277] whether it is sufficiently definite[278] and whether it is exclusive.[279] Again, the genesis of Art. 25 does not signal that the case law of the ECJ on these questions should be reversed. It is advocated here that the new conflicts rule in no way hinders to continue this autonomous interpretation of jurisdiction agreements. Such interpretation is all the more required as the text of Art. 25 (1) refers to a "connection with a particular legal relationship" thus necessitating the (autonomous) construction of this formulation.

81 Between the autonomous scope of Art. 25 and the new conflicts clause (understood as comprising merely grounds invalidating a contract) remain several further questions such as agency, assignment, capacity, subrogation, waiver, partly construction etc. Under the former Regulation it was widely accepted that these issues had to be determined according to the conflicts rules of the forum seised with the case.[280] This was partly the lex contractus, partly the specific conflicts rule applicable to the special question.[281] Where preliminary

---

[275] See *Gebauer*, in: FS vHoffmann 587 (to the Proposal); *Magnus*, in: FS Dieter Martiny (2014), p. 785, 792.

[276] See thereto *infra* notes 88 *et seq.*

[277] In particular *Nikolaus Meeth v. Glacetal* (Case 23/78) (1978) ECR 2133.

[278] For instance *Coreck Maritime GmbH v. Handelsveem BV a.o.* (Case C-387/98) (2000) ECR I-9337.

[279] See e.g. *Nikolaus Meeth v. Glacetal* (Case 23/78) (1978) ECR 2133; *Rudolf Anterist v. Credit Lyonnais* (Case 22/85) (1986) ECR 1951; *Mahamdia v. Algeria* (Case C-154/11) nyr.

[280] See *Francesco Benincasa v. Dentalkit srl*, (Case C-269/95) (1997) ECR I-3767, I-3797 para. 25; *Auer* in: Bülow/Böckstiegel/Geimer/Schütze Art. 23 note 48; *Beaumont/Yüksel*, in: FS Siehr, p. 563 (574); *Droz* para. 214; *Gothot/Holleaux* Clunet 1971, 764; *Kropholler/von Hein* Art. 23 note 28; *Layton/Mercer* para. 20.038; *Mankowski*, in: Rauscher Art. 23 note 41; *Spellenberg* IPRax 2010, 467. This is also the solution under the 2005 Hague Convention (Art. 5 (1) and Art. 6 (a)). But see *Fentiman*, International Commercial Litigation note 2.44 *et seq.* who favours the development of a good faith concept of Community Law that contains autonomous solutions for all these additional issues. A party who tried to rely on a choice of court agreement that was achieved by fraud or duress would act in bad faith and could not enforce the agreement; in the same sense *Heinig* 374 *et seq.*; *Merrett*, Int. Comp.L.Q. 2009, 559 *et seq.*

---

questions had to be dealt with separately it was the conflicts rule governing the respective question.[282]

First, the range of the new conflicts clause must be determined. A first point of doubt is **81a** whether the new clause refers to the substantive law at the *forum prorogatum* or to its private international law rules. Recital 20 Brussels I*bis* expressly states that the reference includes the conflict of laws-rules. The Recital is evidently inspired by the comment in the Explanatory Report to the Hague Convention on Choice of Court Agreements which also expresses that the reference to the law of the *forum prorogatum* in Art. 5 (1) Hague Convention includes the conflicts rules.[283] Although both sources have no statutory weight they nevertheless are relevant statements and militate strongly in favour of an inclusion of the conflicts rules.[284] Further, the inclusion would in this respect maintain the former solution. Moreover, the redress to private international law would – at least in theory – always lead to the same substantive law.[285] The disadvantage of the inclusion is that there are no uniform conflicts rules on jurisdiction agreements in Europe.[286] The Rome I Regulation expressly excludes them from its scope (Art. 1 (2) (e)) as already did the Rome Convention of 1980 (Art. 1 (2) (d)). Dogmatically correct, then the conflicts rules would have to be applied which existed before or besides the Rome instruments. They varied considerably among the EU Member States and are in some Member States abolished since years.[287] The most reasonable way out is the analogous application of the Rome I provisions[288] which is also supported here. This would secure a uniform standard on the private international law level. It would mean that first the parties' explicit or implicit choice of law counts (regularly the choice for the main contract);[289] in the absence of a choice the law at the seat of the characteristically performing party would apply (Art. 4 (2) Rome I); and if the determination of that law would be impossible the most closely connected law would be applicable (Art. 4 (4) Rome I).

A further point of discussion is that the conflicts rule of Art. 25 Brussels I*bis* deviates insofar **81b** from the former situation as only the law (including conflicts rules) at the prorogated court has to be applied whereas formerly it was the law of the court seised with the case even if that was not the prorogated court. Yet, looking at the final outcome, there would be no deviation

---

[281] See the references in the preceding note.

[282] See *infra* Art. 25 note 84 (*Magnus*).

[283] *Hartley/Dogauchi*, Explanatory Report para. 125.

[284] In this sense also *von Hein*, RIW 2013, 105; *Magnus*, in: FS Dieter Martiny (2014), p. 785, 793; *Pohl*, IPRax 2013, 111. Critical towards the inclusion of the choice of law rules and in particular a possible renvoi: *Pocar*, in: Essays in honour of M. Bogdan 475 *et seq.*; *Queirolo*, in: Pocar/Viarengo/Villata 190 *et seq.* (to the Proposal); *Ratkovic/Zgrabljicrotar*, J.P.I.L. 9 (2013) 257 *et seq.* and 267.

[285] See also *Hartley*, L.Q.Rev. 129 (2013) 315 (supporting the conflicts approach).

[286] See also *von Hein*, RIW 2013, 105 *et seq.*

[287] For instance in Germany, the former conflicts rules for contracts were abolished when the Rome I Regulation became applicable on 17 December 2009.

[288] *von Hein*, RIW 2013, 105; *Magnus*, in: FS Dieter Martiny (2014), p. 785, 793 *et seq.*

[289] The new Art. 25 (5) – the mutual independance of the main contract and the jurisdiction agreement – provides no counter-argument. Rather often 'infects' the choice of law clause in one of two or more closely linked contracts the other contracts. Moreover, it is extremely rare that parties agree on a separate choice of law for the jurisdiction agreement.

if one follows the suggestion to apply by analogy the Rome I Regulation which had unified the conflicts rules already under the former law.

81c As mentioned above it is further not entirely clear which questions fall under the scope of the new conflicts clause. It is advocated here that the clause merely covers such legal regulations that – as error, mistake, fraud, threat, duress – can invalidate an agreement. There are several reasons for this position: (1) the wording speaks only of "null and void as to its substantive validity". The expression "null and void" is generally used with respect to legal instruments that invalidate an otherwise legally valid act. It would be uncommon if the expression were intended to include all requirements for a legally binding agreement. On the other hand should the wording not be taken too verbally: it should not only include grounds which make an agreement void (directly invalid) but also those which make it merely voidable (invalid only if the ground is invoked by the aggrieved party).[290] (2) Grounds that make an agreement "null and void" in a strict sense require the pre-existence of a valid agreement that can be invalidated. They therefore do not refer to the conditions for the conclusion of a valid agreement. (3) The requirements for an agreement which are autonomously inferred from Art. 25 necessitate a demarcation-line anyway. In the interest of the widest possible uniformity in the application of Art. 25 it is preferable to give the autonomously interpreted part of the provision a wide range and rather to restrict the ambit of those parts which via private international law lead to finally differing national law.

81d The new clause applies not only where the jurisdiction agreement is exclusive but also where the agreement is non-exclusive and merely offers further jurisdictions. In the former case Art. 31 (2) Brussels *Ibis* secures that only the prorogated court decides on the validity of the agreement[291] according to the law referred to by the conflicts clause in Art. 25 (1) sent. 1.[292]

81e Where on the contrary the jurisdiction agreement is non-exclusive, Art. 31 (2) does not apply. The provision refers expressly to exclusive jurisdiction agreements; an analogous application can hardly be advocated. Thus, in such a case, the prorogated court has no monopoly to decide alone on the validity of the agreement conferring jurisdiction. Any other court seised can decide on this question according to the own private international law (as advocated here: according to the Rome I Regulation). Insofar, nothing changed for non-exclusive jurisdiction agreements as compared with the former law. However, under practical aspects a court seised will not deal with the non-exclusive prorogation of another court but merely examine the own jurisdiction which may be based also on an agreed jurisdiction or on other grounds. In result, even where a jurisdiction agreement is non-exclusive there appears to be no danger that a court examines the validity of a prorogation in accordance with other than the own private international law rules as provided for in Art. 25 (1) sent. 1. However, it should be taken into account that non-exclusive jurisdiction clauses do not hinder the incriminated torpedo tactics since the general priority rule of Art. 29 applies.

81f It is questionable which effect the new conflicts clause has if there is a valid and exclusive choice of courts in two different Member States as in *Nikolaus Meeth v. Glacetal*.[293] There,

---

[290] *Magnus*, in: FS Dieter Martiny (2014), p. 785, 793.

[291] See *Pocar*, in: Essays in honour of M. Bogdan 474.

[292] Critical towards the inclusion of the choice of law rules and in particular a possible renvoi: *Pocar* ibid. 475 *et seq.*; *Ratkovic/Zgrabljicrotar*, J.P.I.L. 9 (2013) 257 *et seq.* and 267.

the French and German parties agreed on the exclusive jurisdiction of the French courts for suits against the French party and on the exclusive jurisdiction of the German courts for suits against the German party. In such a case the new conflicts clause would actually refer to two prorogated courts and their private international law. This could lead to irreconcilable results unless both courts would apply the same substantive law. If both courts would, as is advocated here, apply the provisions of the Rome I Regulation, at least in theory this would lead to the same substantive law. This is another argument for the analogous application of the Rome I Regulation to the validity aspect of jurisdiction agreements which the new clause covers. The same solution should be followed if the parties agreed on the non-exclusive jurisdiction in several Member States. Then, each prorogated court should, if seised, analogously apply the Rome I provisions.

In sum, the new conflicts clause has a limited original scope and should be confined to those **81g** legal institutes that can invalidate an otherwise entirely valid agreement either because the free will of a party is impaired (error, mistake, fraud, threat, duress) or because good morals are violated. The clause should further be read as to refer to the conflicts rules of the prorogated court; for the applicable conflicts rules the Rome I Regulation should be applied by analogy.

Whether the new conflicts clause should be extended by analogy to all remaining questions **81h** which are neither covered by the autonomous ambit of Art. 25 nor are those of substantive invalidity of an agreement is discussed below.

b) Specific matters

There remain certain matters which do not concern the material validity of jurisdiction **82** agreements in its strict sense which, however, can neither be decided in an autonomous way nor relate to grounds which invalidate the agreement. As far as these matters are no separate preliminary questions but are closely linked with the jurisdiction agreement they must be governed by their own law which – it is suggested here – should again be designated by the conflicts rules of the prorogated court and in cases of non-exclusive jurisdiction agreements by the conflicts rules of the court seised (be it the prorogated or another court). If the above suggestion is followed to apply the Rome I Regulation[294] by way of analogy the respective conflicts rules are almost identical[295] for all Member States under this Regulation and lead – at least in theory – to the same applicable national law. A further advantage is that the main contract and the jurisdiction agreement are governed by the same applicable law.

The analogous application of Rome I would mean that first the law chosen by the parties **82a** would be applicable. A clear – explicit or implicit – choice in the main contract should suffice. It is no counter-argument that the main contract and the jurisdiction agreement are independent of each other (Art. 25 (5)). Rather often a choice of law in one of two or more closely linked contracts determines the applicable law for all contracts. This is particularly

---

[293] *Nikolaus Meeth v. Glacetal* (Case 23/78) (1978) ECR 2133.

[294] Again, the Rome I Regulation should be applied; though it does not cover choice of court agreements (Art. 1 (2) (e)), it covers matters like assignment and transfer of contracts. Moreover, its provisions can and should apply as far as other conflict rules are lacking.

[295] Thus far, in Denmark the Rome Convention still applies which however is almost identical with the Rome I Regulation.

suitable for jurisdiction agreements which generally are merely one clause among others in an integral contract; a separate choice of law for the jurisdiction agreement is entirely unusual. In the absence of a choice generally the law at the seat of the party applies that executes the characteristic performance (Art. 4 (1) and (2) Rome I). Also the special provision on contracts of carriage (Art. 5 Rome I) must be observed whereas the special provisions of Rome I for consumer, employment and insurance contracts[296] need not be taken into account since Arts. 15, 19 and 23 Brussels I*bis* already exclude any anti-protective effect of jurisdiction clauses in these areas.

82b Where no characteristic performance can be determined the law of the country governs with which the closest connection exists (Art. 4 (4) Rome I). This may result in ephemeral and casual contacts determining the applicable law (place of contract formation, if there is one, etc). In order to avoid this situation the parties should determine the applicable law in their contract.

82c Art. 25 (5) provides for the independence of the jurisdiction agreement from the main contract. If the main contract is invalid this does not, at least not automatically affect the jurisdiction agreement.[297] It is questionable whether a choice of law in an invalid main contract becomes invalid as well or whether the choice remains valid with respect to the jurisdiction agreement. Arts. 3 (5) and 10 (1) Rome I Regulation support the view that the choice of law should still be recognised for the jurisdiction agreement even if the main contract – and actually also the choice of law – are invalid.[298] A similar principle of survival can be found in Art. 81 (1) sent. 2 CISG under which "(a)voidance does not affect any provision of the contract for the settlement of disputes".

83 The ECJ had already decided that certain matters are governed by the law applicable to the main contract to which the jurisdiction agreement is annexed, namely:
- whether a third party has validly succeeded to the rights and obligations of a contract party and is therefore also subject to the original jurisdiction agreement;[299]
- whether a contract for a fixed period of time is prolonged with the effect that also the accompanying jurisdiction agreement is prolonged;[300]
- whether later parties of a contract, in particular persons who become shareholders of an already existing company, are bound by the original contract and its jurisdiction clause.[301]
- However, as Art. 25 (5) sent. 2 now provides a jurisdiction agreement which is valid under Art. 25 is not tainted by the alleged or formal invalidity of the main contract.[302]

---

[296] Arts. 6–8 Rome I.

[297] See *infra* note 140.

[298] See to Art. 3 (5) Rome I *Magnus*, in *Staudinger* Art. 3 Rom I-VO note 171 *et seq.*; to Art. 10 Rome I *Hausmann*, in: Staudinger Art. 10 Rom I-VO notes 12 *et seq.*

[299] *Partenreederei ms "Tilly Russ" and Ernst Russ v. NV Haven- en Vervoerbedrijf Nova and NV Goeminne Hout*, (Case 71/83) (1984) ECR 2417, 2433 para. 24; *Trasporti Castelletti Spedizioni Internazionali SpA v. Hugo Trumpy SpA*, (Case C-159/97), (1999) ECR I-1597, I-1656 para. 52; *Coreck Maritime GmbH v. Handelsveem BV*, (Case C-387/98) (2000) ECR I-9337, I-9373 paras. 22 *et seq.*

[300] *SpA Iveco Fiat v. van Hool NV*, (Case 313/85) (1986) ECR 3337, 3355 paras. 7 *et seq.*

[301] *Powell Duffryn plc v. Wolfgang Petereit*, (Case C-214/89) (1992) ECR I-1745, I-1775 paras. 19, 21.

A number of questions are not governed by the law applicable to the main contract but by **84** their own conflicts rule:[303]
- the capacity of the parties[304] (mainly governed by the law of the party's domicile, residence, place of business or place of incorporation);
- questions of principal and agent[305] (the connecting factor is often the place of business of the [professional] agent or the place where the agent acted).

For matters which are concerned with the direct declaration of consent, like for instance the **85** revocability of a party's declaration or the possible need for consideration, it could be argued that Art. 25 does cover them since the provision requires nothing else but the mere expression of will. The consideration doctrine appears to be no part of the "agreement" envisaged by the provision. With respect to revocability it could be inferred from several EU Directives, which provide for specific rights of revocation or withdrawal, that under the EU *aquis communautaire* concerning general contract law a party can generally not revoke its declaration. Nevertheless the prevailing view, particularly in the UK, seems again to favour the application of the law designated by the conflicts rules.[306]

c) The 'language risk'

It is probably not only a question of formal but of material validity whether the partner of a **86** jurisdiction agreement could, or was obliged to, understand the language in which the other party offered the clause.[307] Where dealt with[308] the question is answered in an autonomous way without redress to the applicable national law.[309] It has been rightly held that a jurisdiction agreement contained in standard contract terms and offered in a language neither known to the other party nor agreed upon as the contractual language becomes binding only if the contract partner has agreed to the contract terms after having been informed in a language understood by him that the terms were part of the contract.[310] The contract partner must be able to understand languagewise that the contract is offered on the basis of general

---

[302] In the same sense already *Francesco Benincasa v. Dentalkit Srl*, (Case C-269/95) (1997) ECR I-3767, I-3798 para. 28.

[303] Also *von Hein*, RIW 2013, 106; already to the proposal: *Gebauer*, in: FS vHoffmann 585 *et seq*. Thus far these conflicts rules are not unified in Europe.

[304] See *Auer*, in: Bülow/Böckstiegel/Geimer/Schütze Art. 23 note 48; *Kropholler/von Hein* Art. 23 note 28; *Layton/Mercer* para. 20.037; *Mankowski*, in: Rauscher Art. 23 note 41.

[305] *Kropholler/von Hein* Art. 23 note 28; *Mankowski*, in: Rauscher Art. 23 note 43.

[306] See for instance *Layton/Mercer* para. 20.038; *Stone*, p. 124 *et seq*.

[307] Explicitly in this sense *Spellenberg*, IPRax 2010, 465.

[308] The ECJ was called on but finally need not to decide on the language risk in *Custom Made Commercial Ltd. v. Stawa Metallbau GmbH*, (Case C-288/92) (1994) ECR I-2913.

[309] *Kropholler/von Hein* Art. 23 note 37; *Mankowski*, in: Rauscher Art. 23 note 40; *Spellenberg*, IPRax 2010, 469; *Stone*, p. 122; for the application of the law designated by the conflicts rules probably *Gaudemet-Tallon* para. 145; as to the relationship between form and substance see in general *Kohler*, Dir. comm. int. 1990, 611 *et seq*.

[310] BGH IPRax 1991, 326; thereto *Kohler*, IPRax 1991, 299; OLG Hamm NJW-RR 1995, 189; OGH JBl. 2000, 121; OGH ecolex 2009, 403; citing the decisions with approval *Kropholler/von Hein* Art. 23 note 37; *Mankowski*, in: Rauscher Art. 23 note 40; see also *Auer*, in: Bülow/Böckstiegel/Geimer/Schütze Art. 23 note 99.

conditions and what the content of these conditions is.[311] If he then consents it is his own risk that the contract contains an unfavourable jurisdiction clause. Otherwise no valid jurisdiction agreement is concluded. Partly, it has been advocated that merchants in international trade must always understand English irrespective of whether English was the language of the main contract.[312] This goes too far; only if the offeree in fact understands English does this language suffice.

d) Factual impediments like illegibility etc.

87 Also factual impediments like, e.g., the illegibility of a jurisdiction clause in very small print, may affect the validity of the jurisdiction agreement. Again, the question must be answered whether Art. 25 provides an autonomous solution or whether the applicable law designated by the conflicts rules should decide. It is suggested here that an autonomous solution should be sought.[313] As a factual question the court seised should be allowed to decide without further redress to national law whether or not a jurisdiction clause could have been read or was illegible and for this reason invalid.[314] If the clause was illegible again the necessary consensus is lacking. However, Art. 25 does not require that the clause must be specifically highlighted (in red ink or the like).[315]

4. Form

88 It is common ground that Art. 25 (1) covers the form requirements for jurisdiction agreements and excludes insofar any redress to national law.[316] In particular with a view to the form requirements the ECJ has stated that the wording of [the former Art. 17 Brussels Convention] must be construed strictly because of the serious consequences a valid jurisdiction agreement may have for a defendant who may lose the access to the courts which normally would be competent for his disputes.[317] Furthermore, the Article's provisions on

---

[311] OGH RdW 1999, 723; OGH IHR 2009, 126 (127: contract terms in Italian are invalid if addressee does not understand Italian and contract negotiations were led in German); *Kohler*, IPRax 1991, 299, 301; *Tiefenthaler*, in: Czernich/Kodek/Tiefenthaler Art. 23 note 33. *Spellenberg*, IPRax 2010, 469 requests that the jurisdiction clause itself must be in a language understood by the other party.

[312] See *Auer*, in: Bülow/Böckstiegel/Geimer/Schütze Art. 23 note 212; contra, e.g., *Spellenberg*, IPRax 2007, 102.

[313] In the same sense *Mankowski*, in: Rauscher Art. 23 note 39; also without redress to the applicable law *Schack* para. 472; evidently also *Spellenberg*, IPRax 2010, 465.

[314] See Cass. RCDIP 85 (1996), 731; Cass. RCDIP 85 (1996), 732 with note *Gaudemet-Tallon*; CA Grenoble RCDIP 86 (1997), 756, 759; in the same sense *Auer*, in: Bülow/Böckstiegel/Geimer/Schütze Art. 23 note 101.

[315] Cass. D. 2008, 490.

[316] See *Elefanten Schuh GmbH v. Pierre Jacqmain*, (Case 150/80) (1981) ECR 1671, 1688 para. 25 *et seq.*; *Trasporti Castelletti Spedizioni Internazionali SpA v. Hugo Trumpy SpA*, (Case C-159/97), (1999) ECR I-1597, I-1653 para. 37; further *Hausmann*, in: Staudinger IntVertrVerf note 265; *Kropholler/von Hein* Art. 23 note 30; *Layton/Mercer* para. 20.029; *Mankowski*, in: Rauscher Art. 23 note 14; *Schack* para. 472; *Spellenberg*, IPRax 2010, 465.

[317] *Estasis Salotti di Colzani Aimo and Gianmario Colzani v. RÜWA Polstereimaschinen GmbH*, (Case 24/76) (1976) ECR 1831, 1841 para. 7; *Galeries Segoura SPRL v. Société Rahim Bonakdarian*, (Case 25/76) (1976) ECR 1851, 1860 para. 6.

form have to be interpreted in an autonomous way without redress to any national law or concept.[318]

If the ECJ judgments[319] on the form of jurisdiction clauses and in particular on their in-   **89**
corporation into a binding agreement between the parties are taken as a whole it is rather evident that they do not only formulate formal but also material rules of formation of a contract.[320] Indeed, these rules could easily be generalised as model for the formation of a contract and the incorporation of general conditions into a contract. It has been suggested that contrary to the ECJ decisions the incorporation problem should be better left to the applicable national law.[321] In support of this view it has been argued that an autonomous solution would raise difficulties. It would, for instance, disregard, where English law would be the proper law of contract, a lack of consideration that could invalidate a jurisdiction clause which under the 'form requirements' of Art. 25 would be valid. This would, it is said, be contrary to the aim of Art. 25 "to impose tighter requirements on jurisdiction clauses than on other clauses."[322] However, Art. 25 aims as well at a unification of the standards according to which jurisdiction clauses are to be adjudicated in the Member States; and this aim militates rather in favour of, than against, a wider scope of Art. 25. Moreover, the argument neglects the fact that the validity of the jurisdiction agreement and validity of the main contract are separate subjects and independent of each other as Art. 25 (5) now expressly states.[323]

The purpose also of the form requirements is "to ensure that the consensus between the   **90**
parties is in fact established."[324] The form serves to evidence that a true consensus was reached but does not substitute the agreement.[325] Where an agreement is lacking the form alone does not suffice.

The Article permits five different forms: an agreement either in writing or evidenced in   **91**
writing or shown by practices among the parties or by international trade usage or communicated by electronic means. The listed requirements are alternative conditions of which

---

[318] See *Auer*, in: Bülow/Böckstiegel/Geimer/Schütze Art. 23 note 84, 86; *Geimer/Schütze* Art. 23 note 97; *Kropholler/von Hein* Art. 23 note 30.

[319] See in particular *Estasis Salotti di Colzani Aimo and Gianmario Colzani v. RÜWA Polstereimaschinen GmbH*, (Case 24/76) (1976) ECR 1831; *Galeries Segoura SPRL v. Société Rahim Bonakdarian*, (Case 25/76) (1976) ECR 1851; *Partenreederei ms "Tilly Russ" and Ernst Russ v. NV Haven- en Vervoerbedrijf Nova and NV Goeminne Hout*, (Case 71/83) (1984) ECR 2417; *Trasporti Castelletti Spedizioni Internazionali SpA v. Hugo Trumpy SpA*, (Case C-159/97), (1999) ECR I 1597; *Coreck Maritime GmbH v. Handelsveem BV*, (Case C-387/98) (2000) ECR I-9337.

[320] See also *Kropholler/von Hein* Art. 23 note 27; *Layton/Mercer* para. 20.083 *et seq.*; *Herbert Roth*, ZZP 93 (1980), 156, 162.

[321] See *Layton/Mercer* para. 20.084.

[322] *Layton/Mercer* para. 20.084.

[323] See thereto *supra* Art. 25 note 82.

[324] *Estasis Salotti di Colzani Aimo and Gianmario Colzani v. RÜWA Polstereimaschinen GmbH*, (Case 24/76) (1976) ECR 1831 (1st sentence of the summary of the decision); *Galeries Segoura SPRL v. Société Rahim Bonakdarian*, (Case 25/76) (1976) ECR 1851, 1860 para. 6.

[325] OGH IHR 2009, 126 *et seq.*

only one must be satisfied. If however none of them is satisfied the jurisdiction agreement is invalid and does not confer jurisdiction onto the chosen court.[326]

92 The decisive point in time when a choice of court clause must meet the form requirements listed in Art. 25 (1) and (2) is the commencement of proceedings. At least then the form must be fulfilled.[327]

93 Since their first formulation in Art. 17 Brussels Convention of 1968[328] the form requirements underwent considerable modifications until they were given their present form in Art. 25 (1) and (2). In particular the form in accordance with practices of the parties or with international trade usages was later added in reaction to preceding decisions of the ECJ.[329] Para. (2) was only added by the Regulation in 2002.

94 It is now only of historical interest that certain stricter form requirements applied until 2008 with respect to transactions whose final place of destination was Luxembourg.[330]

a) In writing, (par. 1) (a) 1st alt.

aa) Meaning of 'writing'

95 A jurisdiction agreement satisfies the form of 'writing' as required by Art. 25 (1) (a) if both (and if more, all) parties have expressed their consent to a specific jurisdiction clause in written and authorised form. Authorisation requires, generally, the signature of the person making the declaration. However, a signature is unnecessary where the kind of the writing (telegram, telefax etc.) does not allow a handwritten signature.[331] Then, it is sufficient if the author of the document is identifiable.[332] Art. 25 (2) has now eased the signature requirement also for electronic communication like email.[333] Too, signing with the initials will do if the person signing can be identified.[334] A single written document containing the jurisdiction clause and signed by all parties generally suffices as do also separate documents containing, or expressly referring to, the same jurisdiction clause and signed each by the respective party alone.[335] Even the mere exchange of letters, faxes, telegrams from both sides

---

[326] *Geimer/Schütze* Art. 23 note 102; *Kropholler/von Hein* Art. 23 note 32; *Mankowski*, in: Rauscher Art. 23 note 14; *Simotta*, in: Fasching, Kommentar zu den Zivilprozessgesetzen I (2nd ed. 2000) § 104 Jurisdiktionsnorm note 242; left open by Report *Jenard* to Art. 17.

[327] See thereto OGH IHR 2007, 243 (248) and *supra* Art. 25 note 59.

[328] The original text of 1968 mentioned only "writing and evidenced in writing" as form requirement.

[329] The form which accords with international trade usages was introduced in 1978 after the ECJ in *Galeries Segoura SPRL v. Société Rahim Bonakdarian*, (Case 25/76) (1976) ECR 1851 had decided that a jurisdiction clause in general contract terms annexed to a confirmation letter needed a further written confirmation of the other party in order to become binding on this party. The form which accords with practices between the parties was introduced in 1989 after the ECJ also in *Galeries Segoura SPRL v. Société Rahim Bonakdarian*, (Case 25/76) (1976) ECR 1851, 1861 para. 11 had already decided in a similar way.

[330] See *infra* Art. 25 note 139 (*Magnus*).

[331] BGH NJW 2001, 1731; *Gottwald*, in: Münchener Kommentar zur ZPO Art. 23 note 25.

[332] *Geimer/Schütze* Art. 23 note 105; *Hausmann*, in: Staudinger IntVertrVerf note 267.

[333] See thereto in detail *infra* Art. 25 note 129 (*Magnus*).

[334] OGH ZfRV 2007, 38.

[335] See BGH NJW 1994, 2700; OGH JBl 2001, 117, 119; *7E Communications Ltd. v. Vertex Antennentechnik*

constitutes "writing."[336] Electronic communications like e-mails which allow a durable record are now a full equivalent to "writing" (Art. 25 (2)). However, the form of 'writing' is not complied with where only one of the parties has signed the document even if the document is a standard form document of the other party.[337] The same is true where the contract obliges only the party who alone has signed it, for instance, a contract of suretyship; the signature of the surety alone does not suffice.[338] Also where a jurisdiction agreement was contained in a draft contract which remained unsigned though was later on referred to by the parties as "the contract" the form of writing is lacking.[339] The same solution applies where the jurisdiction clause was contained in a draft which was deleted before the draft became the contract.[340] Where the parties orally prolong a written contract, which contained a formally valid jurisdiction clause and which expired, the form requirement is complied with.[341]

An agreement in writing is also lacking where the offeror signs the offer – even electronically by email or click on an active website of the offeree and even accepting the offeree's standard terms with a jurisdiction clause – and the offeree merely confirms the receipt of the offer. It is not rare that the offeree (the manufacturer, seller etc.) wants to remain free from any contractual obligation until delivery when s/he can be sure that not too many offers have been received and delivery or other performance is possible. The form of writing is then only met when the offeree sends a signed or otherwise authorised communication that confirms the contract.

bb) 'Writing' and standard contract terms

A most important and frequent practical problem concerns the question of when a juris- **96** diction clause, which is contained in general contract terms, is validly incorporated into a contract which the parties have concluded in writing. Again, the question has to be decided autonomously according to Art. 25 without any redress to national law.[342] The ECJ has developed a body of specific rules for the incorporation which in essence are based on the following principle: jurisdiction clauses are validly incorporated into a written contract and hence validly agreed upon only if the party using them has clearly indicated that the contract terms – with the jurisdiction clause – should apply and if the other party had the reasonable

---

GmbH (2007) 2 Lloyd's Rep. 411 (C.A.); also *Auer*, in: Bülow/Böckstiegel/Geimer/Schütze Art. 23 note 91; *Kropholler/von Hein* Art. 23 note 33; *Mankowski*, in: Rauscher Art. 23 note 15.

[336] OGH JBl 2001, 117, 119; OGH ZfRV 1999, 150; OLG Karlsruhe IPRspr 1977 no. 122; also *Kropholler/von Hein* Art. 23 note 33; *Mankowski*, in: Rauscher Art. 23 note 15.

[337] See BGH NJW 2001, 1731 (signature of the surety on the stamped contract form of the bank (with a jurisdiction clause), but no signature of the bank: no 'writing'); Cassaz. IHR 2009, 74; OLG Celle IHR 2010, 81; LG Aachen IHR 2011, 82; see also BGH RIW 2004, 938 (to Art. 17 Lugano Convention 1988).

[338] See BGH (preceding fn.); also *Kropholler/von Hein* Art. 23 note 33; but contra *Auer*, in: Bülow/Böckstiegel/Geimer/Schütze Art. 23 note 116; *Schlosser* Art. 23 note 19.

[339] See *Implants International Ltd. v. Stratec Medical* (1999) 2 All ER (Comm.) 933 (Leeds Mercantile Ct.) (jurisdiction clause in draft contract: no consensus of the parties).

[340] See Rb Amsterdam, NIPR 2001 Nr. 210.

[341] *Iveco Fiat S. p. A. v. N. V. van Hool*, (Case 313/85) (1986) ECR 3337; *Auer*, in: Bülow/Böckstiegel/Geimer/Schütze Art. 23 note 118; *Kropholler/von Hein* Art. 23 note 39; for further discussion of this case see *infra* note 113.

[342] See *Layton/Mercer* para. 20.071; *Mankowski*, in: Rauscher Art. 23 note 16; *Schack* para. 472.

chance to check the terms and the clause.[343] Qualifications to this principle with less strict form requirements are provided for in Art. 25 (1) (b) and (c).

97   It is therefore, in general, not essential that the jurisdiction clause is in fact part of the text of the contract. A mere reference to standard contract terms, which is contained in a contract signed by both parties, can suffice.[344] However, the reference must be clear and precise: "(A) clause conferring jurisdiction … printed among the general conditions of one of the parties on the reverse of a contract drawn up on the commercial paper of that party does not of itself satisfy the requirements of Article 17 [Brussels Convention], since no guarantee is thereby given that the other party has really consented to the clause waiving the normal jurisdiction."[345] The signed contract itself – or, as the case may be, the offer to which in turn the contract explicitly refers[346] – must contain an express reference to the general conditions containing the jurisdiction clause. The ECJ established the further qualification that the general conditions with the jurisdiction clause had to be communicated to the other party together with the offer to which reference is made so that the reference – and the general conditions – "can be checked by a party exercising reasonable care."[347] On the other hand, "the requirement of a writing in Article 17 [Brussels Convention] would not be fulfilled in the case of indirect or implied references to earlier correspondence, since that would not yield any certainty that the clause conferring jurisdiction was in fact part of the subject matter of the contract properly so-called."[348] The rules stated by the Court intend to ensure that the jurisdiction clause could not slip a reasonable party's attention. Only if this is ensured then can it be safely inferred from the whole process of concluding the contract as evidenced by the form that the jurisdiction clause became part of a true agreement of the parties on the choice of one or more particular courts.

98   In consequence of the statements of the ECJ national courts have decided that in cases where no further practices of the parties nor international trade usages play a role it is an insufficient form if:
      – a jurisdiction clause is printed on the back of invoices.[349] An invoice – with whatever conditions – sent after the contract had already been concluded can as such[350] in any case not incorporate a jurisdiction clause into the contract[351] since the contents of the contract

---

343   See the references in the following notes.
344   *Estasis Salotti di Colzani Aimo and Gianmario Colzani v. RÜWA Polstereimaschinen GmbH*, (Case 24/ 76) (1976) ECR 1831, 1841 para. 9.
345   *Estasis Salotti di Colzani Aimo and Gianmario Colzani v. RÜWA Polstereimaschinen GmbH*, (Case 24/ 76) (1976) ECR 1831, 1841 para. 9.
346   *Estasis Salotti di Colzani Aimo and Gianmario Colzani v. RÜWA Polstereimaschinen GmbH*, (Case 24/ 76) (1976) ECR 1831, 1842 para. 12.
347   *Estasis Salotti di Colzani Aimo and Gianmario Colzani v. RÜWA Polstereimaschinen GmbH*, (Case 24/ 76) (1976) ECR 1831, 1842 para. 12.
348   *Estasis Salotti di Colzani Aimo and Gianmario Colzani v. RÜWA Polstereimaschinen GmbH*, (Case 24/ 76) (1976) ECR 1831, 1842 para. 12.
349   Cassaz. Riv. dir. int. priv. e proc. 2007, 759 (see thereto *Ferrari* Giust. Civ. 2007, 1397 *et seq.*; *Rüfner*, ZEuP 2008, 165 *et seq.*); Trib. Milano Riv.dir.int. 1978, 843; in the same sense *Kropholler/von Hein* Art. 23 note 35.
350   The solution may be otherwise where a party has always accepted invoices with general conditions in a long-standing business relationship; see thereto *infra* Art. 25 note 111 (*Magnus*).

stands as fixed at the time of its conclusion unless changed later on by the consent of both parties;
- the general conditions with the jurisdiction clause are only handed over or attached without any express reference to the fact that they should become part of the contract;[352]
- the contract is concluded by telexes which do not mention general conditions and one party sends afterwards its general conditions;[353]
- a party accepts in writing the written offer of the other party but attaches the own standard contract terms with a jurisdiction clause. Again, the consent "in writing" of the offeror to the standard contract terms is then lacking (unless the offeror now again consents in writing to the terms with their jurisdiction clause);[354]
- a special reference to a jurisdiction clause was given and the required form was observed but in fact the contract contained an arbitration clause;[355]
- the offeror refers in its offer to its general conditions which contain a jurisdiction clause and the parties perform the contract;[356]
- a party sends an unsigned draft contract containing general conditions with a jurisdiction clause and the other party remits a signed declaration that it was aware of the jurisdiction clause. Again, it has been held that this practice does not satisfy the requirement of "writing".[357] It was argued that the practice was not reconcilable with the strict interpretation of the provision. If such a practice would be allowed under the provision a one-sided declaration of the offeree alone would satisfy the form; moreover, whether the form requirement was fulfilled would then depend on the uncertain fact whether the offeree's declaration reached the offeror;[358]
- the parties conclude a contract via faxes; the fax confirming the contract refers to standard terms including a jurisdiction clause. An acceptance with reference to the own jurisdiction clause does not suffice. A further reason stated here was that the standard terms were not attached but were available only on the internet and in the business office of this party;[359]
- the standard contract terms which contained a jurisdiction clause were neither attached to the offer[360] nor accessible in a reproducible form.[361]

---

[351] Hof 's-Hertogenbosch NIPR 2000 Nr. 138; OLG Oldenburg IHR 2008, 112 (even if the other party asked for the – later – sending of the standard terms).

[352] See OLG Hamm IPRspr 1977 Nr. 118; *Kropholler/von Hein* Art. 23 note 35; *Mankowski*, in: Rauscher Art. 23 note 16.

[353] *Unidare Plc v. James Scott Ltd.* (1991) 2 I. R. 88 (S. C.); similarly OLG Oldenburg IHR 2008, 112.

[354] See BGH NJW 1994, 2699; Cassaz. Riv. dir. int. 1997, 414.

[355] Hof Leeuwarden NJ 2003 Nr. 289.

[356] Cassaz. Riv. dir. int. 2002, 697, 699; Trib. Lecco Riv. dir. int. 1998, 881.

[357] BGH EuLF 2004, 230 *et seq.* (with respect to Art. 17 Lugano Convention).

[358] BGH EuLF 2004, 230, 231.

[359] OLG Celle RIW 2010, 164; similarly LG Landshut IHR 2008, 184.

[360] OLG Düsseldorf RIW 2001, 63; OLG Oldenburg IHR 2008, 112; LG Landshut IHR 2008, 184; in the same sense *Hausmann*, in: Staudinger IntVertrVerf note 270; Hk-ZPO/*Dörner* Art. 23 note 32; *Kropholler/von Hein* Art. 233 note 35; contra – for merchants attachment unnecessary – *Polskie Ratownictwo v. Rallo Vito* (2010) 1 Lloyd's Rep. 384 (388); *Gottwald*, in: Münchener Kommentar zur ZPO Art. 23 note 29; *Schlosser* Art. 23 note 20.

[361] OLG Celle RIW 2010, 164 (the decision is not based on this argument).

99   On the other hand the form requirement of "writing" has been held to have been complied with for instance in the following situations:
- where the jurisdiction clause appears on the frontpage of the contract form which both parties have signed[362] or is affixed on the frontpage of such contract by a particular sticker containing the jurisdiction clause;[363]
- where a party signs specifically ("read and accepted") the general contract terms of the other party who has signed its offer or the contract;[364]
- where a clear reference on the frontpage refers to attached general contract terms or to terms on the back;[365] it is not necessary that the reference mentions the jurisdiction clause specifically nor that the general conditions themselves emphasize the jurisdiction clause in a particular print or any other way;[366]
- where parties agree on a written contract which contains a clear reference to general conditions but those conditions refer to other general conditions which contain the jurisdiction clause and which are not attached;[367] however, this decision has been disapproved of by legal doctrine;[368]
- where parties conclude a contract which on the frontpage, although below the signatures of both parties, contains a clear reference to general conditions on the back of this page the form of "writing" is complied with;[369]
- where both parties acting through agents express their agreement to a contract in writing referring to a prior document which in turn refers to the general conditions containing a jurisdiction clause while both parties or their agents know that one party – a P & I Club (an insurer) to which the other party wanted to become an insured member – concludes contracts exclusively on the basis of its general conditions which contain as also is widely known a jurisdiction clause (English jurisdiction) though in fact the general conditions had not been attached nor shown at the time when the contract was concluded.[370]

100   Special attention deserves the case when both parties tried to incorporate their general conditions but that the conditions contained contradicting jurisdiction clauses. It has been rightly suggested that then the necessary consensus – the 'agreement' of the parties – on the choice of a certain court is lacking[371] (unless later on one party has clearly accepted the general conditions of the other party including the jurisdiction of the court which the other party proposed).[372]

---

362   OLG München RIW 1982, 281, 282.
363   OLG Düsseldorf NJW-RR 1989, 1330.
364   OLG München RIW 1989, 901, 902.
365   Cassaz. Riv. dir. int. 1988, 711, 713; OGH JBl 2000, 121; BayObLG BB 2001, 1498.
366   See OLG Düsseldorf RIW 2001, 63, 64; OLG Karlsruhe RIW 2001, 621, 622; BayObLG BB 2001, 1498.
367   BGH RIW 1987, 998.
368   See *Gottwald*, in: Münchener Kommentar zur ZPO Art. 23 note 27; *Hausmann*, in: Reithmann/Martiny note 6441; *Mankowski*, in: Rauscher Art. 23 note 18; *Rauscher*, ZZP 104 (1991), 271, 288.
369   LG Hamburg RIW 1977, 424 with note *Magnus*.
370   *Standard Steamship Owners' Protection and Indemnity Association (Bermuda) Ltd. v. GIE Vision Bail and others* (2005) 1 All ER (Comm.) 618 (Q.B.D.). *Cooke* J. held that "the agreement to the jurisdiction clause was made in writing or at least evidenced in writing" (at p. 631).
371   See *Mankowski*, in: Rauscher Art. 23 note 19.
372   See BGH NJW 2001, 1731; Hof 's-Hertogenbosch NIPR 2003 no. 43; see also *Kropholler/von Hein* Art. 23 note 42; *Mankowski*, in: Rauscher Art. 23 note 22.

The consensus is also lacking where the text of the jurisdiction clause in general conditions is **101**
illegible[373] or where it is formulated in a language which the addressee does not, and is not
obliged to, understand and which is as well not the contract language.[374]

b) Evidenced in writing, (par. 1) (a) 2nd alt.

The alternative requirement of "evidenced in writing" in Art. 25 (1) (a) slightly eases the **102**
rather strict form of "writing". But nonetheless a mere oral agreement on the jurisdiction of
one or more certain courts does not suffice. Certain writing is still necessary. The English
version "evidenced in writing" is less clear in this respect than the French,[375] German[376] or
Spanish[377] versions. Each of the latter versions expresses that an oral (jurisdiction) agreement with a subsequent written confirmation by the other party is required. Therefore if
there is written consent only by one of the parties this satisfies the necessary form if it
confirms a preceding oral agreement. This form of 'half writing' thus presupposes two
elements: an oral agreement and a subsequent confirmation.

aa) Oral agreement

The oral agreement of the parties must include a consensus specifically concerning the **103**
jurisdiction of the chosen court.[378] This consent need not be express; implicit consent is
sufficient.[379] Consent can be inferred for instance from the fact that the parties shortly before
or after concluded further contracts with an identical jurisdiction clause in formal writing
(signed by both parties).[380] Likewise consent is given where the oral contract is concluded on
the basis of general conditions which were produced or handed over prior to the conclusion
of the contract and which contain a jurisdiction clause. Then it is ensured that a party could,
by the exercise of reasonable care, have checked the clause.[381] Where the oral agreement
refers to general conditions which both parties know and also know that a certain jurisdiction clause is contained in the conditions this suffices as well.[382]

By contrast, the necessary oral agreement on the jurisdiction clause is not satisfied if at the **104**
oral conclusion of the contract a party states that it wishes to rely on its general conditions
(with the jurisdiction clause) but annexes the general conditions only to a later letter of

---

[373] See already *supra* Art. 25 note 87 (*Magnus*).

[374] See thereto *supra* Art. 25 note 86 (*Magnus*).

[375] "verbalement avec confirmation écrite".

[376] "mündlich mit schriftlicher Bestätigung".

[377] "verbalmente con confirmación escrita".

[378] See *Partenreederei ms "Tilly Russ" and Ernst Russ v. NV Haven- en Vervoerbedrijf Nova and NV Goeminne Hout*, (Case 71/83) (1984) ECR 2417, 2433 para. 17: "a prior oral agreement between the parties expressly relating to the jurisdiction clause"; Hoge Raad NIPR 2000 Nr. 39; OLG Karlsruhe NJOZ 2009, 2282; see also *Gaudemet-Tallon* para. 142.

[379] OLG Saarbrücken IHR 2008, 55; LG Aachen IHR 2011, 82 (83); *Hausmann*, in: Staudinger Art. 23 note 273; *Kropholler/von Hein* Art. 23 note 42.

[380] OLG Saarbrücken IHR 2008, 55 (58).

[381] BGH NJW 1996, 1819; in the same sense *Bork*, in: Stein/Jonas § 38 note 28; *Kropholler/von Hein* Art. 23 note 42; *Saenger*, ZEuP 2000, 656, 670.

[382] See *Standard Steamship Owners' Protection and Indemnity Association (Bermuda) Ltd. v. GIE Vision Bail and others* (2005) 1 All ER (Comm.) 618, 631 (Q.B.D., *Cooke* J.).

---

confirmation.[383] "(S)ubsequent notification of general conditions containing such a [juris-diction] clause is not capable of altering the terms agreed between the parties, except if those conditions are expressly accepted in writing by the purchaser [the other party]."[384] The outcome may be otherwise where practices between the parties or international trade usages exist which provide that oral consent or mere silence suffices.[385] But without any such practices or usages it cannot be deemed as consent if a buyer remains silent on the con-firmation letter sent by the vendor, which refers for the first time to the vendor's general conditions.[386] "… it cannot be presumed that one of the parties waives the advantage of the provisions of the [Brussels] Convention conferring jurisdiction."[387] Absent particular cir-cumstances like a continuing business relationship the addressee of the confirmation letter is not even bound to object to the incorporation of the general conditions and the jurisdiction clause.[388] Where a party declares nothing more than its intention to conclude the contract under terms containing a jurisdiction clause this is no (oral) agreement at all.[389] In any event, standard terms which contain the jurisdiction clause must be made available – handed over, produced, downloadable – for the other party at the time of the oral agreement.[390] Their attachment to a later confirmation letter does not suffice.[391]

bb) Confirmation in writing

105 An oral agreement on a choice of court which alone is ineffective in cases not falling under Art. 25 (1) (b) or (c) becomes effective if one of the parties confirms the agreement in writing. However, there must exist a prior agreement; if no agreement had been reached there is nothing to confirm.[392] The confirmation must further comply fully with the prior agreement; if the confirmation introduces new conditions they are validly incorporated only if they were in turn accepted by the other party again in written form.[393] Also where the parties have only agreed on single parts of a contract but not on the whole and in particular not on the incorporation of general conditions which contain a jurisdiction clause then the subsequent confirmation of the single parts cannot result in the incorporation of the juris-diction clause since an agreement on it is lacking.[394] A mere invoice or notice on other issues even designated as 'confirmation' does not constitute a valid confirmation if and because it

---

[383] See *Galeries Segoura SPRL v. Société Rahim Bonakdarian*, (Case 25/76) (1976) ECR 1851, 1860 para. 7; see also BGH NJW 1994, 2099.

[384] *Galeries Segoura SPRL v. Société Rahim Bonakdarian*, (Case 25/76) (1976) ECR 1851, 1861 para. 10; in the same sense Cass. Gaz. Pal. 1986, 385 with note *Piedelievre*; *Kropholler/von Hein* Art. 23 note 43; *Layton/Mercer* para. 20.088.

[385] See thereto *infra* Art. 25 notes 124–128 (*Magnus*).

[386] *Galeries Segoura SPRL v. Société Rahim Bonakdarian*, (Case 25/76) (1976) ECR 1851.

[387] *Galeries Segoura SPRL v. Société Rahim Bonakdarian*, (Case 25/76) (1976) ECR 1851, 1860 *et seq.* para. 8.

[388] This is the clear outcome of *Galeries Segoura SPRL v. Société Rahim Bonakdarian*, (Case 25/76) (1976) ECR 1851; see also OLG Frankfurt NJW 1977, 506.

[389] Also *Hausmann*, in: Staudinger Art. 23 note 273; see also BGH NJW 2001, 1731 (mere contract negotia-tions).

[390] See, e.g., OLG Düsseldorf WM 2000, 2192 (2193); OLG Oldenburg IHR 2008, 112 (117).

[391] BGH NJW 1994, 2699 (2700); LG Aachen IHR 2011, 82 (83); Hk-ZPO/*Dörner* Art. 23 note 37.

[392] See BGH NJW 1994, 2699.

[393] See again *Galeries Segoura SPRL v. Société Rahim Bonakdarian*, (Case 25/76) (1976) ECR 1851, 1860 *et seq.* para. 8.

[394] See BGH IHR 2004, 221 *et seq.*

does not pretend to confirm a prior oral agreement.[395] The frequent confirmation merely of the offeror's offer (not of the contract) does also not constitute a confirmation as required by Art. 25 (1) (a) 2nd alt.[396]

The confirmation can be made by either party. It is not necessary that it is made by the party **106** disfavoured by the jurisdiction clause.[397] It has been suggested that the confirmation must be made within a reasonable time after the conclusion of the oral agreement.[398] The confirmation is valid if received, and not objected to, by the other party.[399] This party may raise objections but can do so only within a reasonable time after the reception of the confirmation.[400] The ECJ stated that "(i)t would be a breach of good faith for a party who did not raise any objection subsequently to contest the application of the oral agreement."[401] The Court did, however, not decide which objections could be raised. Moreover, the effect of an objection is still unclear. It is probably an indication that the required agreement is lacking but does not necessarily, and in any event, lead to the invalidity of the jurisdiction clause.[402]

The confirmation may take any form of writing including fax or telex[403] but now also **107** electronic mails. Such signature or authorisation as is usual for the respective forms of communication appears to be necessary.

The party who claims that a prior oral agreement has been concluded must prove it.[404] **108**

c) Practices between the parties, (par. 1) (b)

This alternative[405] allows the inference from practices between the parties that the parties **109**

---

[395] See OLG Hamburg IPRax 1985, 281; see thereto *Samtleben*, IPRax 1985, 261; *Mankowski*, in: Rauscher Art. 23 note 25.

[396] See also *supra* note 95 (*Magnus*).

[397] See *Partenreederei MS "Tilly Russ" and Ernst Russ v. NV Haven- en Vervoerbedrijf Nova and NV Goeminne Hout*, (Case 71/83) (1984) ECR 2417, 2433 para. 17; *F. Berghoefer GmbH & Co KG v. ASA SA*, (Case 221/84) (1985) ECR 2699, 2708 *et seq.*, para. 15; cited with approval by *Gaudemet-Tallon* para. 143; *Kropholler/von Hein* Art. 23 note 48; *Layton/Mercer* para. 20.086; *Mankowski*, in: Rauscher Art. 23 note 24.

[398] See OLG Düsseldorf IPRax 1999, 38 and thereto *Hau*, IPrax 1999, 24; also *Auer*, in: Bülow/Böckstiegel/Geimer/Schütze Art. 23 note 110; *Geimer/Schütze* Art. 23 note 110; *Kropholler/von Hein* Art. 23 note 44; *Mankowski*, in: Rauscher Art. 23 note 24.

[399] *F. Berghoefer GmbH & Co KG v. ASA SA*, (Case 221/84) (1985) ECR 2699, 2708 *et seq.*, para. 15.

[400] See *F. Berghoefer GmbH & Co KG v. ASA SA*, (Case 221/84) (1985) ECR 2699, 2708 *et seq.*, para. 15.

[401] *F. Berghoefer GmbH & Co KG v. ASA SA*, (Case 221/84) (1985) ECR 2699, 2708 *et seq.*, para. 15.

[402] In this sense also *Geimer/Schütze* Art. 23 note 110; *Kropholler/von Hein* Art. 23 note 44; *Mankowski*, in: Rauscher Art. 23 note 24; but contra *Auer* in: Bülow/Böckstiegel/Geimer/Schütze Art. 23 note 115 (objection within reasonable time makes jurisdiction agreement invalid).

[403] OGH JBl 2001, 117.

[404] See BGH IPRspr 1993 Nr. 137 (a party alleging amendments of the jurisdiction clause must prove that the parties agreed on them); see also *Hausmann*, in: Staudinger Art. 23 note 273; *Hk-ZPO/Dörner* Art. 23 note 38; *Mankowski*, in: Rauscher Art. 23 note 24.

[405] The alternative was inserted in 1989 in the Brussels Convention, and retained by the Regulation, in order to codify the rules stated by the ECJ in *Galeries Segoura SPRL v. Société Rahim Bonakdarian*, (Case 25/76) (1976) ECR 1851; see Report *Almeida Cruz/Desantes Real/Jenard* para. 26. The alternative follows the

implicitly agreed on the jurisdiction of a certain court or courts. Nonetheless it is necessary to establish with sufficient certainty the parties' consensus with respect to the jurisdiction of a particular court or courts.[406] A practice alone which the parties have established between themselves does not substitute the agreement.[407]

110 Practices between the parties require that the parties used to conduct their transactions regularly in a specific way and that this practice had lasted a certain time[408] and had taken place several times.[409] The regularity of the conduct must be such that it appears as justified that a party relies on it. It suffices that this is the case at the time when proceedings were instituted.[410] But it should be remembered that like all form requirements listed in Art. 23 the practices exception is to be also construed strictly.

111 Therefore, (1) (b) is not complied with where the parties used to conclude their contracts – for instance the purchase of cattle – orally and send invoices with standard terms containing a jurisdiction clause only after the conclusion of each respective contract, in particular, when the parties deviated in their past practice in other respects from what the standard conditions prescribed.[411] It is not certain in such a case that the parties in fact originally agreed on the jurisdiction clause contained in the standard terms.

112 Even where a party sends its jurisdiction clause several times this cannot as such establish a relevant practice between the parties if there was no original consensus that the jurisdiction clause was to form part of the contract.[412] Only where in a continuing business relationship a party never objected to the other party's habitual sending and/or referring to its general conditions (including a jurisdiction clause) "so that it is established that the dealings taken as a whole are governed by the general conditions … it would be contrary to good faith for the recipient of the confirmation to deny the existence of a jurisdiction conferred by consent".[413]

113 But where a written contract containing a valid jurisdiction clause has expired the clause

---

rather similar formulation of Art. 9 (1) Vienna Sales Convention of 1980 (CISG) which also acknowledges that practices between the parties have priority over non-mandatory provisions of that Convention; see further *Magnus*, in: Staudinger, Kommentar zum Bürgerlichen Gesetzbuch mit Einführungsgesetz und Nebengesetzen. Wiener UN-Kaufrecht – CISG (revised ed. 2013), Art. 9 CISG notes 6 *et seq.* Decisions and legal doctrine on that provision can and should be used for the interpretation of Art. 25 (1) (b) Regulation.

[406] *Mainschiffahrts-Genossenschaft eG (MSG) v. Les Gravières Rhénanes SARL*, (Case C-106/95) (1997) ECR I-911; BGH IHR 2004, 125; BGH NJW-RR 2005, 150 (152).

[407] See BGH IHR 2004, 221, 222; LG Landshut IHR 2008, 184 (186).

[408] See *Auer* in: Bülow/Böckstiegel/Geimer/Schütze Art. 23 note 122; *Geimer/Schütze* Art. 23 note 118; *Kropholler/von Hein* Art. 23 note 50.

[409] See OLG Celle IPRax 1985, 286; thereto *Duintjer Tebbens*, IPRax 1985, 262; OLG Köln RIW 1988, 555 (557); OLG Karlsruhe NJOZ 2009, 2282 (2285); further *Hausmann*, in: Staudinger Art. 23 note 277; *Mankowski*, in: Rauscher Art. 23 note 26 and 27; see also OLG Dresden EuLF 2009 II, 68 (70: two preceding contracts can suffice).

[410] LG Karlsruhe RIW 2001, 702; also *Auer*, in: Bülow/Böckstiegel/Geimer/Schütze Art. 23 note 125.

[411] BGH IHR 2004, 221; see also LG Landshut IHR 2008, 184 (186).

[412] BGH IHR 2004, 221, 222.

[413] *Galeries Segoura SPRL v. Société Rahim Bonakdarian*, (Case 25/76) (1976) ECR 1851, 1861 para. 11.

may remain valid if the parties tacitly prolong the contract. The ECJ had to deal with a particular case of that kind in *Iveco Fiat S. p. A. v. N. V. van Hool*.[414] In that case the contract provided expressly that it could only be renewed in written form. After the expiry of the original contract no such written renewal occurred but nonetheless the parties continued their distributorship contract for further 20 years. When a dispute arose and the jurisdiction clause was invoked the Court in a reference procedure held that national law was applicable to decide whether the contract survived despite the lack of formal renewal. If according to national law the contract had been validly prolonged by conduct the jurisdiction clause also had survived; if national law considered the contract as finally at an end at the expiry date then the jurisdiction clause needed to be confirmed anew in writing.[415]

d) International usage, (par. 1) (c)

aa) The principle

Art. 25 (1) (c) recognises agreements conferring jurisdiction also if they are concluded in a **114** form which does not comply with the ordinary form required under Art. 25 (1) (a) but accords with a less strict form of concluding a contract which is habitually used in international trade and commerce. Where such an international trade usage exists and where the contract is concluded in accordance with it the "consensus on the part of the contracting parties as to the jurisdiction clause is presumed".[416] However, it must be a usage which in the trade concerned is widely known and observed. Moreover, it is required that the parties of the dispute are or ought to have been aware of the usage.

The purpose of this form alternative which was inserted in the Brussels Convention text in **115** 1978 was to relax the form requirements provided for by (1) (a).[417] The insertion of (c) was a reaction to the already mentioned ECJ decision in *Galeries Segoura SPRL v. Société Rahim Bonakdarian*[418] which forces parties generally to confirm a jurisdiction clause (and also the general conditions) in writing after reception. In international trade where general conditions are often first made available as attachment to a letter of confirmation a further written confirmation was regarded as inappropriate because it impedes the rapidity and simplicity of such transactions.[419]

The text of (1) (c) has been rather closely drafted according to the model of Art. 9 (2) **116** CISG.[420] Therefore, also decisions and legal doctrine concerning Art. 9 (2) CISG can – and

---

[414] (Case 313/85) (1986) ECR 3337.

[415] *Iveco Fiat S. p. A. v. N. V. van Hool*, (Case 313/85) (1986) ECR 3337.

[416] *Mainschiffahrts-Genossenschaft eG (MSG) v. Les Gravières Rhénanes SARL*, (Case C-106/95) (1997) ECR I-911, I-940 para. 19.

[417] The addition to the original text of Art. 17 Brussels Convention was mainly prompted by the United Kingdom which intended to ease the use of standard contract terms (containing jurisdiction clauses) in international trade and commerce; see *Layton/Mercer* para. 20.094.

[418] (Case 25/76) (1976) ECR 1851; see thereto *supra* Art. 23 note 75.

[419] See Report *Schlosser* para. 179.

[420] See Report *Jenard/Möller* no. 58; *Kohler*, IPRax 1991, 305. Though the addition to Art. 17 Brussels Convention was introduced in 1978 while the CISG was finally accepted only in 1980 the draft of Art. 9 (2) CISG had already been prepared and published in its almost final form in 1976; see *Magnus*, in: Staudinger (fn. 414), Art. 9 CISG notes 4 *et seq.*

should – be made use of,[421] all the more so since almost all Member States bound by the Regulation are also Member States of the CISG.[422]

bb) International trade usage

117 An international trade usage exists if it is established that "a particular course of conduct is generally and regularly followed by operators in that branch".[423] The usage must first be related to international trade or commerce. An autonomous and wide understanding of these terms is to be applied.[424] A contract between parties established in different countries on the charter of a vessel for transport on the Rhine[425] or international insurance transactions therefore certainly belong to the field of international trade and commerce.[426] A transaction is international if it concerns crossborder supply or takes place between persons whose habitual residence or place of business is located in different states[427] while a different nationality of the parties does not transform an otherwise purely domestic transaction into an international one.[428] Though Art. 25 (1) (c) addresses trade and commerce this does not mean that the provision extends only to persons who qualify as merchant in a formal sense under the applicable national law.[429] It is sufficient that the persons involved act for professional and not for private purposes.

118 A usage further requires that a certain kind of dealing is habitually observed by most of those who are active in the specific branch. The majority of persons involved in a branch which is dealing with transborder transactions or transactions between parties based in different countries must "generally and regularly"[430] observe a certain course of dealing. A usage comes into existence therefore only after some time during which it was observed.

---

[421] In this sense also *Auer*, in: Bülow/Böckstiegel/Geimer/Schütze Art. 23 note 128; *Kropholler/von Hein* Art. 23 note 51; *Mankowski*, in: Rauscher Art. 23 note 31.

[422] Out of the 28 EU States only Ireland, Malta, Portugal and the United Kingdom have not yet ratified the CISG.

[423] *Trasporti Castelletti Spedizioni Internazionali SpA v. Hugo Trumpy SpA*, (Case C-159/97), (1999) ECR I-1597, I-1651 para. 30.

[424] See for instance *Standard Steamship Owners' Protection and Indemnity Association (Bermuda) Ltd. v. GIE Vision Bail and others*, (2005) 1 All ER (Comm.) 618, 631 (Q.B.D., *Cooke* J.); further *Kropholler/von Hein* Art. 23 note 54.

[425] *Mainschiffahrts-Genossenschaft eG (MSG) v. Les Gravières Rhénanes SARL*, (Case C-106/95) (1997) ECR I-911.

[426] *Standard Steamship Owners' Protection and Indemnity Association (Bermuda) Ltd. v. GIE Vision Bail and others* (2005) 1 All ER (Comm.) 618, 631 (Q.B.D., *Cooke* J.).

[427] See for instance *Mainschiffahrts-Genossenschaft eG (MSG) v. Les Gravières Rhénanes SARL*, (Case C-106/95) (1997) ECR I-911 (charter of an inland-waterway vessel between parties based in France and Germany).

[428] In the same sense *Kohler*, Dir. comm. int. 1990, 617, 620; *Kropholler/von Hein* Art. 23 note 54; *Mankowski*, in: Rauscher Art. 23 note 32; *Stöve*, Gerichtsstandsvereinbarungen nach Handelsbrauch, Art. 17 EuGVÜ und § 38 ZPO (1993), p. 69.

[429] See Cass. JCP 1997 IV 747; *Hausmann*, in: Staudinger IntVertrVerf note 280; *Huet*, Clunet 125 (1998), 138, 139; *Kropholler/von Hein* Art. 23 note 54; *Mankowski*, in: Rauscher Art. 23 note 30.

[430] *Trasporti Castelletti Spedizioni Internazionali SpA v. Hugo Trumpy SpA*, (Case C-159/97) (1999) ECR I 1597, 1651 para. 30.

The usage need exist only with respect to the trade the parties are involved in. It is not **119**
necessary that the usage is established worldwide or in specific countries or in all countries in
which the Regulation applies.[431] Nor is it indispensable that the usage is at least accepted in
the country where one of the parties is seated.[432] It is only necessary but also sufficient that in
the particular trade or commerce at stake the usage is well established, namely widely known
and regularly observed.[433] "The fact that a practice is generally and regularly observed by
operators in the countries which play a prominent role in the branch of international trade
or commerce in question can be evidence which helps to prove that a usage exists. The
determining factor remains, however, whether the course of conduct in question is generally
and regularly followed by operators in the branch of international trade in which the parties
to the contract operate."[434] Usual practices in countries which are important for international trade or practices which are accepted by leading operators may provide evidence for
usages but matter only if the same practice is recognised in the particular field the parties are
concerned with.

The usages relevant for Art. 25 (1) (c) must be those which concern the conclusion of **120**
contracts. It must be "a particular course of conduct ... generally and regularly followed
in the conclusion of a particular type of contract".[435] On the other hand, it is not necessary
that a usage is established which specifically concerns the conclusion of a jurisdiction agreement or the incorporation of a jurisdiction clause into a contract.[436]

The party who claims that an international trade usage exists has to prove it.[437] The standard **121**
according to which the existence of an international usage in trade or commerce is adjudicated is exclusively set by Art. 25 (1) (c). National law which may set other standards in this
respect is excluded.[438] But it is for the national courts to decide whether an international
usage has been established.[439] A usage can often only be proven by expert evidence or
information from chambers of commerce.

---

[431] *Trasporti Castelletti Spedizioni Internazionali SpA v. Hugo Trumpy SpA*, (Case C-159/97) (1999) ECR I
1597, 1651 para. 30; see also *Hausmann*, in: Staudinger IntVertrVerf note 280; Hk-ZPO/*Dörner* Art. 23
note 42; *Kröll* ZZP 113 (2000) 135 (154).

[432] Contra Hk-ZPO/*Dörner* Art. 23 note 42; *Kröll*, ZZP 113 (2000) 135 (154). The requirement that the
parties should be able to have known the usage supports the view that not only usages in the country of at
least one party should be covered but also usages outside the countries of the parties' seats.

[433] See also *Gaudemet-Tallon* para. 147; *Kropholler/von Hein* Art. 23 note 55; *Mankowski*, in: Rauscher
Art. 23 note 31.

[434] See *Trasporti Castelletti Spedizioni Internazionali SpA v. Hugo Trumpy SpA*, (Case C-159/97) (1999) ECR
I 1597, 1650 para. 27.

[435] See *Trasporti Castelletti Spedizioni Internazionali SpA v. Hugo Trumpy SpA*, (Case C-159/97) (1999) ECR
I 1597, 1659 ruling 4.

[436] See *Mankowski*, in: Rauscher Art. 23 note 29.

[437] Hof 's-Hertogenbosch NIPR 1998 Nr. 125; OLG Hamburg IPRax 1997, 420 and thereto *Harald Koch*,
IPRax 1997, 405; CA Paris RCDIP 84 (1995), 573 with note *Kessedjian*; further *Mankowski*, in: Rauscher
Art. 23 note 33.

[438] *Trasporti Castelletti Spedizioni Internazionali SpA v. Hugo Trumpy SpA*, (Case C-159/97) (1999) ECR I
1597, 1653 paras. 37 *et seq*.

[439] See *Trasporti Castelletti Spedizioni Internazionali SpA v. Hugo Trumpy SpA*, (Case C-159/97), (1999)
ECR I 1597, 1653 para. 36.

cc) Subjective element

122 If a usage exists a party can rely on it as against the other party only if the usage is one which the other party also knew or ought have known. This subjective element intends – as the same element in Art. 9 (2) CISG does – to protect those parties who could not be aware of certain usages which apply at local places to the international transactions conducted there.[440] In principle, where a person is doing business in a certain branch it must be expected of him that he knows the relevant international usages. But the party must only be aware of "widely known" usages, even if the party is a newcomer to the market. Local usages of limited notoriety, although used for international transactions at the local place, need not be known to parties from other countries and can therefore not be invoked.[441] On the contrary, awareness of a specific usage can be presumed where a party had previous trade relations with a party operating under that – well established – usage.[442]

123 Athough the usage must be so widely known that an operator should be expected to know it as well, nonetheless no formal publication of the usage is required.[443]

dd) Usages as to letters of confirmation and incorporation of general conditions

124 In practice international trade usages play a role mainly with respect to silence on letters of confirmation and with respect to the incorporation of jurisdiction clauses towards third parties. But generally the hurdle is very high to establish an international usage.

125 The ECJ has stated that silence on a commercial letter of confirmation containing for the first time general conditions with a jurisdiction clause amounts to consent where an international usage to that effect exists and the parties ought to have been aware of it.[444] A respective usage – that the letter of confirmation with its annexures then fixes the final contents of the contract unless the other party objects – is acknowledged for instance in Germany,[445] Belgium and Switzerland while many other countries, e.g. Austria,[446] do not recognise such a practice. It is therefore necessary that the parties either have their seats in countries which allow this usage or that the parties are doing business in a field where this usage is observed and the parties are or should be aware of this usage. Where the respective international usage that silence amounts to consent cannot be proven there is no valid

---

[440] See in this sense with respect to Art. 9 (2) CISG: *Ferrari*, in: Ferrari/Flechtner/Brand (eds.), The Draft UNCITRAL Digest and Beyond: Cases, Analysis and Unresolved Issues in the U. N. Sales Convention (2004), p. 191 *et seq.*; *Magnus*, in: Staudinger[2013], Art. 9 CISG note 24.

[441] See references in the preceeding fn.; see further *Kropholler/von Hein* Art. 23 note 58.

[442] *Mainschiffahrts-Genossenschaft eG (MSG) v. Les Gravières Rhénanes SARL*, (Case C-106/95) (1997) ECR I-911 para. 24.

[443] See *Trasporti Castelletti Spedizioni Internazionali SpA v. Hugo Trumpy SpA*, (Case C-159/97), (1999) ECR I 1597, 1659 ruling 4.

[444] *Mainschiffahrts-Genossenschaft eG (MSG) v. Les Gravières Rhénanes SARL*, (Case C-106/95) (1997) ECR I-911, 940 para. 20; see also BGH NJW-RR 1998, 755; Rb Zutphen NIPR 1998 Nr. 110; see also *Geimer/ Schütze* Art. 23 note 121; *Gottwald*, in: Münchener Komentar zur ZPO Art. 23 note 45; *Hausmann*, in: Staudinger IntVertrVerf note 282; *Musielak/Stadler* Art. 23 note 11.

[445] See, e.g., BGH RIW 1995, 410; however, the conditions stated in the letter of confirmation must not deviate to an unreasonable extent from what was agreed or assumed to have been agreed before; moreover, this usage applies only with respect to merchants or professional operators.

[446] Compare *Bollenberger*, in: Koziol/Bydlinski/Bollenberger (eds.), ABGB (4th ed. 2014) § 861 ABGB note 9.

jurisdiction agreement. It is inadmissible then to retreat to the applicable national law and determine the effect of the silence according to that law.[447] There is however no international usage that silence on a written confirmation of an offer (with a jurisdiction clause) amounts to assent.[448] There is no usage in the international car trade that a mere reference incorporates standard terms into the contract even if the terms were never sent or made available.[449] There exists also no international usage that standard terms including a jurisdiction clause that are printed on the back of transmitted invoices become part of the contract. Even if the addressee pays the invoiced amount this generally does not mean assent to such jurisdiction clause.[450]

In sea transport it is general practice that bills of lading contain general conditions including   **126** a jurisdiction clause. The final holder of the bill will often not have signed the bill nor specifically agreed to its conditions but is nevertheless bound by it.[451] This practice is so generally accepted that every operator doing business in this field must know it.[452]

Also in international insurance transactions certain usages may lead to the incorporation of   **127** a jurisdiction clause without express, let alone written consent of the other party. Thus, where both parties know that P & I Clubs contract only on the basis of jurisdiction in London such a clause becomes part of the contract without further consent.[453] However, insofar as one party as a member of a P & I Club qualifies as an insured and the Club as an insurer Art. 15 of the Regulation has to be taken into account. In another international insurance case it was held that where an international insurance broker includes a jurisdiction clause into a contract note this can accord with a usage which both parties to the contract ought to have been aware of.[454]

Also a jurisdiction clause in the general conditions of an international auctioneer of art-   **128** works has been held to be incorporated into the respective contract through international usage.[455]

---

[447]   In this sense, however, *Auer*, in: Bülow/Böckstiegel/Geimer/Schütze Art. 23 note 133.

[448]   BGH NJW 1994, 2699 (2700); *Gottwald*, in: Münchener Kommentar zur ZPO Art. 23 note 45; *Hausmann*, in: Staudinger IntVertrVerf note 282.

[449]   OLG Oldenburg IHR 2008, 112 (117 *et seq.*); *Hausmann*, in: Staudinger IntVertrVerf note 282.

[450]   Cassaz. Riv. dir. int. priv. e proc. 2007, 759; *Mankowski*, in: Rauscher Art. 23 note 35; *Rüfner* ZEuP 2008, 165 (172); *Schlosser* Art. 23 note 23.

[451]   This is the effect of the ECJ decision in *Trasporti Castelletti Spedizioni Internazionali SpA v. Hugo Trumpy SpA*, (Case C-159/97) (1999) ECR I 1597; see also BGH NJW 2007, 2036; OLG Stuttgart TranspR 2004, 406. Extensively on jurisdiction clauses in bills of lading *Mankowski*, Seerechtliche Vertragsverhältnisse im Internationalen Privatrecht (1995), 232 *et seq.*; see also *infra* note 137 (*Magnus*).

[452]   BGHZ 171, 141 (149); *Girsberger*, IPRax 2000, 87, 89; *Gottwald*, in: Münchener Kommentar zur ZPO Art. 23 note 47; *Kropholler/von Hein* Art. 23 note 62; *Mankowski*, in: Rauscher Art. 23 note 33; *Sparka* 102.

[453]   *Standard Steamship Owners' Protection and Indemnity Association (Bermuda) Ltd. v. GIE Vision Bail and others* (2005) 1 All ER 618 (Comm.) (Q.B.D., *Cooke* J.).

[454]   Pres. Rb. Haarlem S & S 1992 Nr. 124. For international insurance contracts see further *infra* Art. 25 note 134.

[455]   Rb Amsterdam NIPR 1994 Nr. 159; but critical thereto – because the persons who are involved regularly buy or sell only once and do therefore not know such usage – *Mankowski*, in: Rauscher Art. 23 note 37.

e) Electronic communication, (par. 2)

129 Art. 25 (2) was only inserted in the former Brussels I Regulation and had no predecessor in the Brussels Convention. The provision pays tribute to the development of electronic communication[456] and ranks electronic messages as equivalent to "writing" under Art. 25 (1) if the message can be reproduced in durable form. The provision accords, too, with the objectives of the E-Commerce Directive[457] which requests the Member States to enable in their legal system the conclusion of contracts by electronic means.[458] According to its wording and purpose the provision merely requires that the electronic communication can be durably stored, for instance in the recipient's mailbox, on disc, usb-stick or the like, so that it can be reproduced in its original form at any time. In what form it is then reproduced – on the screen, on paper or in another form – should not matter.[459] However, the provision appears not to require that the message is in fact so stored. The recipient should have the choice to store the message; if he fails to do so it might become difficult to prove the contents of the original message but it does not question the electronic form being equivalent to writing.[460]

130 Electronic communication which allows durable reproduction covers in particular e-mails.[461] These messages can be easily stored in the recipient's mailbox or can be downloaded onto the personal computer or can be printed. E-mails therefore satisfy the writing requirement either for the whole contract or for the necessary confirmation. So do fax or telex.[462] But for the incorporation of a jurisdiction clause nonetheless the ordinary requirements must be observed: if as usual the jurisdiction clause is contained in the general conditions the clause is incorporated into the contract only if a clear reference to the general conditions is contained in the e-mail and if further the general conditions can be as well easily downloaded and printed at the same time as the e-mail. The e-mail or other electronic message must also be authorised – generally signed with the printed name – though a qualified signature[463] is not required.[464]

131 Art. 25 (2) does, however, not extend to messages on websites which cannot be downloaded but remain in the sphere of the offeror and can therefore be freely modified by him or her.[465] A mere message on the screen is no equivalent to writing.[466] The same is true for voice

---

[456] See the Explanatory Report COM 1999 (348) final p. 20.

[457] Directive 2000/31/EC of 8 June 2000 on certain legal aspects of information society services, in particular electronic commerce, in the Internal Market, OJ EC 2000 L 172/1.

[458] See Art. 9 (1) e-commerce-Directive.

[459] Partly it is requested that the electronic mail need be reproducable on paper; see *Auer*, in: Bülow/Böckstiegel/Geimer/Schütze Art. 23 note 141.

[460] See in this sense *Gaudemet-Tallon* para. 138.

[461] See OLG Dresden EuLF 2009 II-68 (70); *Gottwald*, in: Münchener Kommentar zur ZPO Art. 23 note 40; *Hausmann*, in: Staudinger IntVertrVerf note 271; *Kropholler/von Hein* Art. 23 note 41; *Layton/Mercer* para. 20.100; *Mankowski*, in: Rauscher Art. 23 note 38.

[462] *Geimer/Schütze* Art. 23 note 105; *Layton/Mercer* para. 20.100.

[463] For instance according to the Directive 1999/93/EC of 13 December 1999.

[464] In the same sense *Mankowski*, in: Rauscher Art. 23 note 38.

[465] See *Hausmann*, in: Reithmann/Martiny para. 3010 fn. 4; *Mankowski*, in: Rauscher Art. 23 note 38.

[466] *Auer*, in: Bülow/Böckstiegel/Geimer/Schütze Art. 23 note 142; *Kropholler/von Hein* Art. 23 note 41; similarly *Geimer/Schütze* Art. 23 note 105.

mails,[467] video conferences[468] and other electronic communication not in writing. SMS-messages on mobile phones, though these messages appear in writing, are also insufficient unless they can be reproduced on paper at any time.[469]

Special problems may result from the use of active websites. Many businesses offer the possibility to directly buy a book, book a flight etc. by merely filling and clicking on the website. The user must then generally confirm by special click that the standard conditions of the business (regularly containing a jurisdiction clause) apply. Unless stated otherwise in most cases the offer of the business will be a mere *invitatio ad offerendum* and the user's order is the offer. For, the business normally does not intend to be bound by the order because it could be impossible to meet all orders, bookings etc. The business then often confirms the offer by email. In many cases this is no acceptance but the mere confirmation that the offer was received and will be dealt with. The contract is often concluded only when the business sends the goods, expressly agrees to the booking etc. If this is accompanied by signed writing or email the form of Art. 25 is satisfied if and only if the user had the possibility to print the standard terms when having clicked on them.[470] Whether s/he in fact printed them is however irrelevant.

X. Specific situations

1. Jurisdiction clauses in consumer, insurance and employment contracts (par. 4)

a) In general

Even a jurisdiction agreement which is valid under Art. 25 (1) and (2) cannot oust the   **132** protective and exclusive jurisdiction foreseen by Art. 15, 19, 23 and 24. Therefore, jurisdiction agreements which are contrary to the cited provisions are insofar without any legal effect (see Art. 25 (4)). They do not confer the jurisdiction onto the chosen court. However, insofar as they do not contradict Art. 15, 19, 23 and 24 jurisdiction agreements remain valid and can be relied on if they comply with the form requirements of Art. 25. In consumer, insurance and employment contracts jurisdiction agreements remain valid as long as they operate in favour of the consumer, insured (or policyholder or beneficiary) or employee and allow them to bring proceedings in courts other than those ordinarily provided for by the Regulation or if the jurisdiction agreement has been concluded after the dispute has arisen.[471] In cases falling under Art. 24 a deviating jurisdiction agreement is invalid with respect to the international jurisdiction but might still be valid with respect to the local jurisdiction within the Member State designated by Art. 24 if the applicable national law so allows.[472] In situations other than those listed by Art. 25 (4) the Regulation does not restrict the effect of a jurisdiction agreement. This is even true if a similar need for the protection of one of the parties – like in consumer, insurance or employment contracts – may exist as can be the case in principal-agent-relationships. A similar need existed with respect to maintenance claims.

---

[467] *Layton/Mercer* para. 20.100.

[468] *Mankowski*, in: Rauscher Art. 23 note 38.

[469] See also *Gottwald*, in: Münchener Kommentar zur ZPO Art. 23 note 45; *Kropholler/von Hein* Art. 23 note 41; *Layton/Mercer* note 20.100.

[470] To the same avail *Kropholler/von Hein* Art. 23 note 41.

[471] See Art. 15 (1), (2), Art. 19 (1), (2) and Art. 23 (1), (2).

[472] See thereto *Kropholler/von Hein* Art. 23 note 76; *Layton/Mercer* para. 20.109.

The jurisdiction under Art. 5 no. 2 old Brussels I Regulation could be ousted by agreement. However, this has been changed by the European Maintenance Regulation.[473]

133 It is disputed whether Art. 25 (4) refers to jurisdiction agreements only if they prorogate a court in a Member State or also where a court in a third state is prorogated. The prevailing view favours – in the present author's view rightly – a wide application of par. 4. According to this view the exclusive and protective jurisdiction granted by the Regulation cannot be derogated from by the choice of a court in a third country.[474] It would be a strange result if the 'mandatory' jurisdiction rules of the Regulation could not be overridden by the choice of a court within a Member State but by the choice of a court outside a Member State.[475] However, since the Regulation extends only to its Member States it cannot hinder a prorogated court of a third state to decide a respective suit in violation of Arts. 15, 19, 23 and 24 of the Regulation. Also with respect to the recognition and enforcement of such a judgment, the Regulation, in particular Art. 45 (1), does not come into play[476] since this provision requires that the judgment has been rendered by the courts of a Member State (Art. 36). Whether the Member States may deny the recognition and enforcement of third state judgments if the latter offend the protective[477] and exclusive jurisdiction provisions of the Regulation is questionable.[478]

b) Jurisdiction clauses in insurance contracts
134 It has to be noted that jurisdiction clauses if validly incorporated into insurance contracts may have effect also towards certain third persons, in particular towards beneficiaries of the insurance contract.[479] This means in turn that the limits set by Art. 25 (4) operate also in favour of those persons who benefit from the insurance contract but are no direct party to it.[480] It is unnecessary that the beneficiary has personally consented to, or signed, the insurance contract and its general conditions.[481]

---

[473] Regulation 4/2009 of 18 December 2008, OJ 2009 No. L 7 p. 1. This Regulation is in force since 18 June 2011. Its Art. 4 restricts jurisdiction agreements in maintenance matters drastically.

[474] See OLG Dresden IPRax 2006, 44 with note *von Hein*, IPRax 2006, 16; *Auer*, in: Bülow/Böckstiegel/Geimer/Schütze Art. 23 note 78; *Droz* para. 217; *Gaudemet-Tallon* para. 150; *Gottwald*, in: Münchener Kommentar zur ZPO Art. 23 note 12; *Hausmann*, in: Reithmann/Martiny para. 6486 *et seq.*; Hk-ZPO/*Dörner* Art. 23 note 22; *Kropholler/von Hein* Art. 23 note 81 *et seq.*; probably also *Hess*, Europäisches Zivilprozessrecht note § 6-133; compare also *supra* Art. 25 notes 36–37; but see contra for instance *Jung*, p. 68 *et seq.*, 80.

[475] See *Kropholler/von Hein* Art. 23 note 83.

[476] This is advocated by *Auer*, in: Bülow/Böckstiegel/Geimer/Schütze Art. 23 note 78.

[477] In contrast to the old Brussels I Regulation where the disregard of the protective jurisdiction for employees did not hinder the recognition of a respective judgment, now Art. 45 (1) (e) (i) Brussels I*bis* established this also as a ground for non-recognition.

[478] It is however argued that the Regulation governs the recognition and enforcement of judgments from third states if such judgment violates the Regulation's provision on exclusive jurisdiction (now Art. 24); see *Geimer/Schütze* Einl. note 245; *Kropholler/von Hein* Art. 32 note 19.

[479] See *infra* Art. 25 note 158 (*Magnus*).

[480] *Gottwald*, in: Münchener Kommentar zur ZPO Art. 23 note 51; *Kropholler/von Hein* Art. 23 note 80.

[481] *Gerling v. Amministrazione del Tesoro dello Stato*, (Case 201/82) (1983) ECR 2503.

2. Jurisdiction clauses in statutes of companies

The statutes of a company (the articles of association or the memorandum of association) do   **135**
not infrequently contain a jurisdiction clause which generally intends to cover disputes
between the company and its members and normally concentrates the jurisdiction at the
seat of the company. Though usually only the company founders have subscribed to the
statutes of the company its conditions are deemed to bind all company members even those
who acquired their share later or who voted against the jurisdiction clause.[482] "By becoming
and remaining a shareholder in a company, the shareholder agrees to be subject to all the
conditions appearing in the statutes of the company and to the decisions adopted by the
organs of the company, in accordance with the applicable national law and the statutes, even
if he does not agree with some of those provisions or decisions."[483] The statutes of a company
must, however, be accessible for the shareholder at least either at the company's seat or in a
public register.[484]

To which disputes a jurisdiction clause in a company's statutes extends is always a matter of   **136**
construction of the specific clause.[485] A jurisdiction clause "By subscribing for or acquiring
shares or interim certificates the shareholder submits, with regard to all disputes between
himself and the company or its organs, to the jurisdiction of the courts ordinarily competent
to entertain suits concerning the company"[486] has been held to be definite and precise
enough to confer jurisdiction onto the court at the company's seat for all disputes arising
from the relationship between the company and its shareholder since it had to be construed
as concerning only the relationship between the company and the shareholder in his capacity as company member.[487]

3. Jurisdiction clauses in bills of lading

It has already been mentioned that bills of lading generally contain jurisdiction clauses.[488]   **137**
The first holder of the bill will often have consented to the jurisdiction clause in a form which
satisfies Art. 25 (1) and (2).[489] The issuer and the first holder are therefore bound by the
jurisdiction clause.

The form requirements of Art. 25 (1) and (2) are less frequently, if ever, satisfied with respect   **138**
to further holders and in particular with respect to the final holder of the bill of lading. The
final holder will often not have signed the bill nor will s/he have specifically agreed to its

---

[482] See *Powell Duffryn plc v. Wolfgang Petereit*, (Case C-214/89) (1992) ECR I-1745, 1775, para. 18; thereto
    Harald Koch, IPRax 1993, 19, 20.
[483] *Powell Duffryn plc v. Wolfgang Petereit*, (Case C-214/89) (1992) ECR I-1745, 1775 para. 19.
[484] *Powell Duffryn plc v. Wolfgang Petereit*, (Case C-214/89) (1992) ECR I-1745, 1777 para. 28.
[485] See generally to the construction of jurisdiction clauses *infra* Art. 25 notes 144 *et seq.*
[486] That was the wording of the jurisdiction clause in *Powell Duffryn plc v. Wolfgang Petereit*, (Case C-214/
    89) (1992) ECR I-1745.
[487] See *Powell Duffryn plc v. Wolfgang Petereit*, (Case C-214/89) (1992) ECR I-1745, 1778 para. 32 and BGHZ
    123, 347 as final national decision in this case.
[488] See *supra* Art. 25 note 126 (*Magnus*).
[489] See *Mankowski*, in: Rauscher Art. 23 note 52.

conditions. Nevertheless, s/he is bound by it.[490] This practice is so generally accepted that it can be regarded as an international trade usage[491] so that every operator doing business in this field must know it.[492] However, the binding effect of the jurisdiction clause towards third parties can only occur if the third party has validly succeeded to the party which has first validly agreed to the clause (though the form requirements of Art. 25 (1) and (2) need not be satisfied with respect to the acquisition of the bill by further holders).[493] The ECJ has stated the principle for the first time in *Partenreederei MS "Tilly Russ" and Ernst Russ v. NV Haven-en Vervoerbedrijf Nova and NV Goeminne Hout*[494] and has affirmed it in *Coreck Maritime GmbH v. Handelsveem BV*.[495] Whether a party has validly succeeded to the first holder of a bill of lading is to be determined by the applicable national law.[496]

4. Transfer of jurisdiction agreements in other cases

139 The solution for bills of lading can be transposed to other situations where a party fully succeeds into the contract of the first party if the second party did know or ought have known that the contract contained a jurisdiction clause. This may be the case where contracts as such are traded as in the commodity trade. However, the solution is different where a manufacturer and a first buyer have agreed on a jurisdiction clause and the manufacturer wants to invoke the clause against direct claims of further subbuyers in a chain of sales. Here, each sale is a separate contract with eventually varying conditions. Thus, unless the subbuyer has not validly agreed to the jurisdiction clause the latter does not bind him or her.[497]

5. Jurisdiction agreements with persons domiciled in Luxembourg

139a Under the former Brussels I Regulation persons domiciled in Luxembourg enjoyed a special privilege concerning jurisdiction agreements when sued in another Member State.[498] How-

---

[490] This is the effect of the ECJ decision in *Trasporti Castelletti Spedizioni Internazionali SpA v. Hugo Trumpy SpA*, (Case C-159/97) (1999) ECR I 1597; see also BGH NJW 2007, 2036; OLG Stuttgart TranspR 2004, 406. Extensively to jurisdiction clauses in bills of lading *Mankowski*, Seerechtliche Vertragsverhältnisse im Internationalen Privatrecht (1995), p. 232 *et seq.*

[491] See BGHZ 171, 141; *Kropholler/von Hein* Art. 23 note 67; but contra *Mankowski*, in: Rauscher Art. 23 note 53.

[492] *Girsberger*, IPRax 2000, 87, 89; *Kropholler/von Hein* Art. 23 note 62; *Mankowski*, in: Rauscher Art. 23 note 33 and *supra* Art. 25 note 126 (*Magnus*).

[493] See *Mankowski*, in: Rauscher Art. 23 note 53 *et seq.*; *Mankowski*, Seerechtliche Vertragsverhältnisse im Internationalen Privatrecht, p. 253 *et seq.*; *Mankowski*, ZZP 108 (1995) 272, 279.

[494] (Case 71/83) (1984) ECR 2417, 2435, para. 24 *et seq.*

[495] (Case C-387/98) (2000) ECR I-9337, 9374, para. 23.

[496] See *Partenreederei MS "Tilly Russ" and Ernst Russ v. NV Haven- en Vervoerbedrijf Nova and NV Goeminne Hout*, (Case 71/83) (1984) ECR 2417, 2435, para. 24 *et seq.*; *Coreck Maritime GmbH v. Handelsveem BV*, (Case C-387/98) (2000) ECR I-9337, 9374, para. 23; *Hausmann*, in: Staudinger IntVertrVerf note 284; Hk-ZPO/*Dörner* Art. 23 note 45; *Kropholler/von Hein* Art. 23 note 67; *Mankowski*, in: Rauscher Art. 23 notes 53, 55.

[497] *Refcomp SpA v. Axa Corporate Solutions Assurance SA, AXA France IARD, Emerson Network, Climaventa SpA*, (Case C-543/10) nyr. para. 32 *et seq.*

[498] See Art. 63 (2) former Brussels I Regulation; for a detailed discussion see *Magnus/Mankowski*, Brussels I Regulation (2nd ed.) Art. 23 note 139 (*Magnus*) and Art. 63 notes 11 *et seq.* (*Mankowski*).

ever, this privilege ended by 29 February 2008.[499] Choice of court agreements that were concluded after that date fall exclusively under the scope of Art. 23 former Brussels I Regulation/Art. 25 Brussels I*bis* and need to comply only with this provision's requirements.[500] Only agreements concluded before that date still have to be adjudicated in accordance with the former Art. 63 (2) Brussels I Regulation.

XI. Effects of a valid jurisdiction agreement

1. Separate validity (par. 5)

A jurisdiction agreement is generally annexed to a main contract, often as a clause among   **140** others in standard contract terms. Nonetheless – as Art. 25 (5) now expressly states – its validity is to be determined separately.[501] Even if the main contract is invalid for instance for lack of the required form the – formal – validity of the jurisdiction agreement has to be adjudicated independently according to the standard of Art. 25.[502] If this standard is met the jurisdiction clause is valid despite the invalidity of the main contract; and any dispute over the existence of the main contract is to be pursued in the chosen court.[503] Likewise, where the main contract is for instance invalid for violation of the ordre public and good morals, a jurisdiction agreement which complies with the requirements of Art. 25 remains intact.[504] Otherwise the mere allegation that the main contract is invalid would suffice to also frustrate the effect of the jurisdiction agreement.[505] This does however not exclude the invocation of grounds which invalidate the jurisdiction agreement as such, for instance the lack of capacity under the applicable national law.[506]

Art. 25 (5) applies both to exclusive as well as non-exclusive jurisdiction agreements.

2. Interpretation of jurisdiction agreements

To determine the scope of a jurisdiction agreement is a matter of construction. In the first   **141** instance the parties' intention and the wording of the jurisdiction agreement determine which disputes the agreement covers. That these elements matter can be autonomously gathered from Art. 25 itself, in particular with respect to the precedence of the parties' intentions ("unless the parties have agreed otherwise").[507] Furthermore, Art. 25 provides

---

[499] See Art. 64 (4) former Brussels I Regulation.

[500] Hk-ZPO/*Dörner* Art. 64 note 1 propagates that the date of instituting the suit is decisive. However, for the jurisdiction agreement as a contract the time of its conclusion must decide.

[501] That was already the position before the Brussels I Recast: see for instance LG Berlin IPRax 2005, 261 with note *Jayme*; *Kaufmann-Kohler*, p. 145 *et seq.*; *Kropholler/von Hein* Art. 23 note 17, 91; *Vischer*, in: FS Erik Jayme II (2004), p. 993, 995.

[502] See thereto, under the former law, *Harris*, (1998) 23 Eur. L. Rev. 279 *et seq.*

[503] *Francesco Benincasa v. Dentalkit srl*, (Case C-269/95) (1997) ECR I-3767.

[504] See also *Kropholler/von Hein* Art. 23 note 91.

[505] Art. 25 (5) subpar. 2 now codifies *Francesco Benincasa v. Dentalkit srl*, (Case C-269/95) (1997) ECR I-3767, 3798 para. 29.

[506] This is expressed by the word "solely" in par. 5 subpar. 2.

[507] Art. 25 itself is based on the recognition of the parties' autonomy with respect to jurisdiction; see also Recital (19) and *supra* Art. 25 notes 1, 5. *Gottwald*, in: Münchener Kommentar zur ZPO Art. 23 note 67

---

specific guidance for the interpretation of a jurisdiction agreement with respect to its exclusive effect (Art. 25 (1) sent. 2). However, Art. 25 does not generally state which method or law governs the interpretation as far as the jurisdiction agreement refers to matters which Art. 25 does not mention. The new conflicts rule expressly concerns the issue of substantive (in)validity alone. It is open to debate whether the new rule can and should be extended by analogy to the interpretation issue as well.[508]

141a   The interpretation issue is of particular relevance to the question whether an agreement includes or excludes other non-contractual claims. According to two decisions of the ECJ – still to the Brussels Convention – the forum seised had to apply the standards applicable there.[509] However, the decisions left it undecided whether the standard was the lex fori with or without its conflicts rules. This and also national peculiarities of interpretation could lead to differing results since the courts of some countries – for instance the English and French courts – tend to construe jurisdiction agreements in a narrower sense than others.[510]

142   Partly it had been argued that the ECJ itself favoured a narrow and strict interpretation of jurisdiction clauses.[511] This view was based on dicta in *Estasis Salotti di Colzani Aimo and Gianmario Colzani v. RÜWA Polstereimaschinen GmbH*[512] and *Galeries Segoura SPRL v. Société Rahim Bonakdarian*[513] where the Court stated in identical passages that "the requirements set out in Article 17 [Brussels Convention] governing the validity of clauses conferring jurisdiction must be strictly construed."[514] But it has been rightly observed that the cited passages did not concern the interpretation of jurisdiction clauses but dealt with the interpretation of the text of Art. 17 Brussels Convention only.[515]

143   It is submitted here that as far as possible an autonomous method of interpretation should be developed and applied. For this purpose any interpretation of a jurisdiction agreement should first make use of the rules enshrined in Art. 25 itself, namely the wording of the jurisdiction clause as the starting point, the precedence of the parties' intentions and the presumed exclusive effect of a jurisdiction agreement. But also any other relevant provision of the Regulation and the ECJ judgments thereto, as for instance on set-off and counterclaim,[516] should be taken into account in order to enable, as far as possible, a uniform

---

bases the interpretation of the jurisdiction agreement primarily on the parties' intentions; see also *Gebauer*, in: FS vHoffmann 587.

[508]   See thereto *supra* notes 77 *et seq.*

[509]   See *Powell Duffryn plc v. Wolfgang Petereit*, (Case C-214/89) (1992) ECR I-1745, 1778 para. 37; *Francesco Benincasa v. Dentalkit srl*, (Case C-269/95) (1997) ECR I-3767, 3798 para. 31.

[510]   See for instance for England: *Dresser UK v. Falcongate Freight Management Ltd.* (1992) Q. B. 502 (the clause "all actions under this document" covers only all contracual claims but not all matters relating to a carriage); for France: Cass. RCDIP 1990, 358 with crit. note *Gaudemet-Tallon* (jurisdiction clause in a frame contract did not extend to contract concluded under the frame contract).

[511]   See for instance *Vischer*, in: FS Erik Jayme II (2004), p. 993, 995.

[512]   (Case 24/76) (1976) ECR 1831.

[513]   (Case 25/76) (1976) ECR 1851.

[514]   *Estasis Salotti di Colzani Aimo and Gianmario Colzani v. RÜWA Polstereimaschinen GmbH*, (Case 24/76) (1976) ECR 1831, 1841 para. 7 and *Galeries Segoura SPRL v. Société Rahim Bonakdarian*, (Case 25/76) (1976) 1851, 1860 para. 6.

[515]   *British Sugar plc v. Fratelli Babbini di Lionello Babbini & CSAS* (2005) 1 All ER 55, 72.

method of interpretation of international jurisdiction agreements. Only if the Regulation does not provide any assistance then in cases of doubt the interpretation rules of the law (including the conflicts rules) apply that governs the jurisdiction agreement.[517] Insofar it is suggested here that the applicable law is to be determined in applying the provisions of the Rome I Regulation by analogy (see *supra* note 81a). In the first place this leads to the law which the parties have chosen, generally in their main contract and even if this contract is invalid. In the absence of any choice the interpretation would be governed by the law that is in force at the seat of the party that executes the characteristic performance. In the rare cases where no such law can be determined the law of the closest connection applies.[518] Thus, regularly the law applicable to the main contract applies to the interpretation of the jurisdiction agreement as well.

3. General scope of jurisdiction agreements

a) Exclusive jurisdiction

Art. 17 (1) sent. 1 Brussels Convention provided, and still provides, that the effect of a **144**
jurisdiction agreement was that "that court or those courts shall have exclusive jurisdiction." Notwithstanding this strict wording it was the prevailing view that the parties could, though, agree otherwise.[519] Art. 25 (1) sent. 2 as well as its predecessor in the old Brussels I Regulation explicitly provides that only absent an agreement of the parties to the contrary a jurisdiction clause confers exclusive jurisdiction onto the chosen court(s). The provision raises a presumption that the parties generally intended an exclusive effect of their jurisdiction agreement.[520] This presumption, though, may be rebutted. In particular, the parties are free to agree on an optional jurisdiction clause and to confer jurisdiction onto one or more courts in addition to those which were originally competent and to leave it to the claimant to choose among these courts. This is perfectly permissible under Art. 25 as long as it is sufficiently certain from the clause which court(s) are to have jurisdiction.[521] The Regulation itself acknowledges such kind of jurisdiction agreements in its Art. 15 no. 2, 19 no. 2 and 23 no. 2. The parties may thus tailor such clause as they wish and need for their purposes.[522] It has already noted before that the new Art. 31 (2) Brussels I*bis* has immensely strengthened

---

[516] See Art. 6 (3) and *Danvaern Production v. Schuhfabriken Otterbeck*, (Case C-341/93) (1995) ECR I-2053.

[517] See – still under the law before the Recast –, e.g., BGH NJW 1997, 397 (399: the applicable national law governs the interpretation of the jurisdiction clause); *British Sugar plc v. Fratelli Babbini di Lionello Babbini & CSAS* (2005) 1 All ER 55, 72 *et seq.* ("... the starting point, at any rate, in the process of construction, is to consider the meaning of the relevant clause under the law which is the proper law of contract."); see also *Hausmann*, in: Staudinger IntVertrVerf note 264. In the same sense with respect to the validity of jurisdiction agreements: *Layton/Mercer* para. 20.038; see also *supra* notes 77 *et seq.*

[518] See *supra* note 81a.

[519] See for instance OLG München RIW 1980, 281; *Kurz v. Stella Musical Veranstaltungs GmbH* (1992) 1 All ER 630 (Ch. D., *Hoffmann* J.); *Gamlestaden plc v. Casa de Suecia S. A. and Thulin* (1994) 1 Lloyd's Rep. 433 (Q.B.D.); *Insured Financial Structures Ltd. v. Electrocieplownia Tychy S. A.* (2003) Q. B. 1260; also *Kropholler/von Hein* Art. 23 note 98 with further references.

[520] *Auer*, in: Bülow/Böckstiegel/Geimer/Schütze Art. 23 note 146; *Geimer/Schütze* Art. 23 note 166; *Kropholler/von Hein* Art. 23 note 92; *Layton/Mercer* para. 20.060.

[521] As to the certainty of the jurisdiction agreement see *supra* Art. 25 note 66.

[522] As to clauses for the benefit of only one of the parties see *infra* Art. 25 note 148.

the importance of exclusive jurisdiction agreements by giving the prorogated court priority jurisdiction whereas all non-exclusive agreements lack this effect.

145 By "exclusive jurisdiction" Art. 25 means that the parties – as far as they are allowed to do so[523] – agree on the jurisdiction of certain courts to the exclusion of the jurisdiction of either all courts or certain courts which would be competent in the absence of the agreement. The exclusive effect is the normal consequence of a jurisdiction agreement. Either party can bring proceedings only in the chosen court(s) and nowhere else unless the other party voluntarily submits to the jurisdiction of another court.

146 Where a jurisdiction agreement is exclusive in character the court or courts chosen have to accept jurisdiction if the agreement is valid and relied upon. Any other court in a Member State that is already seised must stay proceedings (Art. 31 (2)) and decline its jurisdiction if the prorogated court has accepted its jurisdiction (Art. 31 (3)). It is not necessary that the parties confer jurisdiction on one single court. If they agree on the courts of a certain country this suffices. If they agree on several courts in different countries as being competent ("London or Paris courts to decide all disputes in connection with the contract") this can and in case of doubt will mean an exclusive agreement ousting the jurisdiction of the otherwise competent court(s) and not only a mere additional jurisdiction. The ECJ has accepted that a reciprocal jurisdiction agreement – jurisdiction, if the French party sued, in Germany; if the German party sued, in France – had an exclusive effect.[524] However, where there are contradicting jurisdiction clauses they have no exclusive effect[525] if any effect at all.

147 Whether a jurisdiction agreement has exclusive or non-exclusive effect depends on its wording and construction.[526] The parties are entirely free to confer jurisdiction on courts in addition to the jurisdiction of the courts ordinarily competent under the Regulation or to exclude the ordinary jurisdiction. But in case of doubt or where there is any ambiguity in the text of a jurisdiction clause the latter is to be understood as conferring exclusive jurisdiction on the chosen court even if the word "exclusive" has not been used.[527] In consequence, a jurisdiction agreement is non-exclusive only where there is clear indication that this was the parties' intention. For the sake of certainty, it must be in fact unambiguous that the agreed jurisdiction shall not replace, but only add to, the ordinary jurisdiction. Therefore, a reciprocal jurisdiction clause ("The seller can sue the buyer in France; the buyer can sue the seller in Germany")[528] as such confers exclusive jurisdiction on the designated courts unless there are further circumstances which clearly indicate a contrary intention of the parties.[529]

b) Jurisdiction agreements for the benefit of only one of the parties

148 Art. 17 (4) Brussels Convention had provided that "(i)f an agreement conferring jurisdiction was concluded for the benefit of only one of the parties, that party shall retain the right to

---

[523] See the limits prescribed by Art. 25 (4).

[524] In *Nikolaus Meeth v. Glacetal*, (Case 23/78) (1978) ECR 2133.

[525] In particular not with respect to Art. 31 (2); see Recital 22 (2).

[526] As to the method of interpretation see *supra* Art. 25 note 141.

[527] See also *Layton/Mercer* para. 20. 060. *Gaudemet-Tallon* para. 153 fn. 76 fears that the new formulation will also lead to uncertainty as to the competent court.

[528] See for a similar case *Nikolaus Meeth v. Glacetal,* (Case 23/78) (1978) ECR 2133.

[529] Rather in favour of non-exclusivity in such a case *Mankowski*, in: Rauscher Art. 23 note 61.

bring proceedings in any other court which has jurisdiction by virtue of this Convention."[530] The provision has been deleted when the Convention was transformed into the former Brussels I Regulation mainly because of the uncertainty caused when it has to be decided whether a jurisdiction agreement had been concluded for the benefit for only one of the parties.[531] Nonetheless such clauses are admissible under the present Regulation.

Under Art. 25 (1) of the Regulation the parties are perfectly free to exclude the presumed **149** exclusive effect of their jurisdiction agreement for the benefit of one party so that only this party can invoke the agreed jurisdiction whereas the other party is bound to sue in the otherwise competent court(s) or that the favoured party may sue at its option in the chosen or in the ordinary courts while the other party can sue only in the agreed court (at the other party's seat). However, the parties are required to agree so in a clear way in order to rebut the presumption regularly raised by a jurisdiction agreement.[532] With respect still to Art. 17 (4) Brussels Convention the ECJ held that a clause choosing the courts in the country where one party is domiciled is of itself not sufficient to support the conclusion that the clause was for the benefit of this party alone.[533] It must be either expressly stated in the clause itself or be clearly evidenced by the circumstances as a whole that the parties intended to confer a jurisdictional advantage on one of them.[534] Therefore, although an implicit agreement favouring one party alone is permitted it should be accepted only where again there is no ambiguity as to the parties' intentions.[535] Because a clause in favour of one party grants this party a considerable advantage, while the other party would be respectively disfavoured, such a one-sided jurisdiction agreement cannot be presumed. Under Art. 17 (4) Brussels Convention the ECJ stated that a clause granting one of the parties a greater variety of options than the other already constitutes a clause in favour of that party.[536] This consequence can be accepted only with the qualification that the jurisdiction clause itself or the circumstances must clearly indicate the intention to favour one party. It is therefore no such one-sided jurisdiction clause if the parties merely agree in a neutral way on the exclusive jurisdiction of the courts at one party's seat.[537] The same is true if in such a case the clause is accompanied by a choice of law clause that also designates as applicable the law at the chosen court's seat.[538]

c) Contractual and extracontractual claims

Since the scope of a jurisdiction agreement depends primarily on the intention of the parties **150** as expressed by the wording of the clause the parties can extend or limit their jurisdiction agreement with respect to the claims covered as freely as they may wish. Thus, the clause

---

[530] The same text is still contained in Art. 17 (4) Lugano Convention.

[531] See *Gaudemet-Tallon* para. 157.

[532] *Rudolf Anterist v. Crédit Lyonnais*, (Case 22/85) (1986) ECR 1951, 1962 para. 14; see also *supra* Art. 23 note 144.

[533] *Rudolf Anterist v. Crédit Lyonnais*, (Case 22/85) (1986) ECR 1951.

[534] *Rudolf Anterist v. Crédit Lyonnais*, (Case 22/85) (1986) ECR 1951, 1962 para. 14.

[535] See also *Geimer/Schütze* Art. 23 note 169; *Kropholler/von Hein* Art. 23 note 94.

[536] *Rudolf Anterist v. Crédit Lyonnais*, (Case 22/85) (1986) ECR 1951.

[537] *Rudolf Anterist v. Crédit Lyonnais*, (Case 22/85) (1986) ECR 1951. Former German decisions to the contrary (LG Gießen IPRax 1984, 160 with note *Jayme*; OLG Saarbrücken RIW 1984, 478 with note *Tosi-Hesse*) are now overruled.

[538] See also *Hausmann*, in: Staudinger IntVertrVerf note 300; but contra OLG Dresden EuLF 2009 II, 68 (70).

"litiges concernant l'interprétation ou l'exécution du contrat" ("disputes concerning the interpretation and execution of the contract") has been held not to include a claim for the annullation of the contract.[539] But if not otherwise agreed upon a jurisdiction agreement in a contract which indicates only the competent court ("Jurisdiction: London", "Gerichtsstand: Hamburg") covers all disputes arising from the contractual relationship between the parties to which the jurisdiction agreement refers. This includes claims for performance of the contract (as far as admitted in the forum seised) but also claims for damages, termination, price reduction or other remedies in case of non-performance. Claims concerning the annullation or invalidity of the contract fall generally within the scope of the jurisdiction agreement as well.[540]

151 Whether other than contractual claims – for instance connected tort claims – fall within the scope of a jurisdiction agreement depends again in the first instance on the wording of the agreement and on its interpretation. In case of doubt and absent any contrary indication, tortious claims for damages and other extracontractual claims which are connected with the contractual relation are deemed to be included as well.[541] This has been so held for claims for restitution/unjust enrichment and *culpa in contrahendo* as far as they were connected with a contract.[542]

d) Provisional measures

152 It is disputed whether also claims for provisional measures like injunctions with respect to contracts are covered by jurisdiction agreements. If this view would be accepted for both the prorogation and derogation effect of the jurisdiction agreement this solution would in fact limit the scope of Art. 35 (the former Art. 31 Brussels I Regulation) which refers the court seised to its national law concerning provisional measures.[543] With respect to the prorogation effect of the jurisdiction agreement it is submitted here that the agreement confers jurisdiction for provisional measures on the prorogated court.[544] This court becomes competent to decide; but its jurisdiction is not exclusive. In order not to contradict the aims of Art. 35 – to facilitate prompt relief – the jurisdiction agreement should not be given effect to derogate from the jurisdiction courts would have under their national law.[545]

---

[539] Cass. JCP 1983 IV 109.

[540] *Francesco Benincasa v. Dentalkit srl*, (Case C-269/95) (1997) ECR I-3767.

[541] See, e.g., *Continental Bank N. A. v. Aeakos Compania Naviera S. A.* (1994) 1 Lloyd's Rep. 505 (C.A.); OLG Stuttgart EuZW 1991, 326; OLG München RIW 1989, 901 (902); OLG Karlsuhe IPRspr 2006 No. 127; *Auer*, in: Bülow/Böckstiegel/Geimer/Schütze Art. 23 note 147; *Hausmann*, in: Staudinger IntVertrVerf note 302; Hk-ZPO/*Dörner* Art. 23 note 24; *Mankowski*, in: Rauscher Art. 23 note 62; *Schlosser* Art. 23 note 38.

[542] LG Berlin IPRax 2005, 261 with note *Jayme*.

[543] In this sense in fact *Geimer/Schütze* Art. 23 note 192; for a discussion see also *infra* Art. 35 note 15 *et seq.* (*Pertegás Sender*).

[544] In the same sense Cour d'appel Orléans Rev. crit. 2003, 326 with note *Ancel*; *Auer*, in: Bülow/Böckstiegel/Geimer/Schütze Art. 23 note 156; *Collins*, p. 90; *Kaye*, p. 1088 *et seq.*; *Gottwald*, in: Münchener Kommentar zur ZPO Art. 23 note 77; *Hausmann*, in: Staudinger IntVertrVerf note 304; *Hüßtege*, in: Thomas/Putzo Art. 23 EuGVO note 25; *Mankowski*, in: Rauscher Art. 23 note 66; *Schlosser* Art. 23 note 42.

[545] See *Auer*, in: Bülow/Böckstiegel/Geimer/Schütze Art. 23 note 156; *Gottwald*, in: Münchener Kommentar zur ZPO Art. 23 note 77; *Kropholler/von Hein* Art. 23 note 103; *Mankowski*, in: Rauscher Art. 23 note 66; but contra *Geimer/Schütze* Art. 23 note 192.

e) Termination of contract

If the main contract containing a jurisdiction clause is terminated it is questionable whether 153
and if so to which extent the jurisdiction clause to the terminated contract survives. The
question is again one of interpretation of the specific clause which must be construed in the
light of the circumstances.[546] But in case of doubt the jurisdiction clause remains intact even
if the main contract is invalidated.[547]

f) Termination and modification of jurisdiction agreement; submission

The parties may terminate or modify a jurisdiction agreement at any time.[548] After proceedings 154
have been instituted the parties can do so by mere submission of the defendant to the jurisdiction of the court which is seised contrary to a jurisdiction agreement (and if there are no
restrictions for a submission under Art. 24).[549] Before court proceedings have started it is
suggested here that the parties may terminate a jurisdiction agreement by mere consent without the observation of any form requirement since such act merely reinstates the ordinary
jurisdiction rules. If the parties substitute an existing jurisdiction clause by another it is suggested that the form requirements of Art. 25 have to be satisfied because of the serious consequences – the ousting of the ordinary jurisdiction – a jurisdiction agreement regularly has.[550]

g) Counter-claim

It is disputed whether a jurisdiction agreement covers also counter-claims so that they can 155
only be brought in the prorogated forum. If not agreed, or clearly indicated, otherwise a
jurisdiction agreement extends to counter-claims as well.[551] The counter-claim can then
only be raised in the chosen court. If the parties have agreed on a jurisdiction clause in favour
of the claimant granting him the option between several courts[552] then the defendant cannot
bring a counter-claim unless the claimant has instituted proceedings in the court which the
parties have at the same time designated as competent for the defendant's claims.[553]

h) Set-off

It is always a matter of construction whether a jurisdiction agreement excludes a claim 156
which falls under the agreement from being set off in other proceedings. In *Nikolaus Meeth
v. Glacetal*[554] the ECJ held that a reciprocal jurisdiction clause according to which each party

---

[546] In this sense also *Gottwald*, in: FS Wolfram Henckel (1995), p. 295, 303; *Mankowski*, in: Rauscher Art. 23
note 63; *Schlosser* Art. 23 note 38.

[547] See already *supra* note 140.

[548] See *Geimer/Schütze* Art. 23 note 127.

[549] See *Elefanten Schuh GmbH v. Pierre Jacqmain* (Case 150/80) (1981) ECR 1671 para. 11; *Hannelore
Spitzley v. Sommer Exploitation S.A.* (Case 48/84) (1985) ECR 787 para. 25; *Geimer/Schütze* Art. 23
note 128; *Kropholler/von Hein* Art. 24 note 17; *Staudinger*, in: Rauscher Art. 24 note 12; *Schack* note 488;
Schlosser Art. 24 note 1; see further the comments to Art. 24 (*Calvo Caravaca/Carrascosa González*).

[550] *Auer*, in: Bülow/Böckstiegel/Geimer/Schütze Art. 23 note 63 (form requirements of Art. 23 apply to
modifications of a jurisdiction agreement).

[551] OGH ZfRV 2000, 76; Hof Amsterdam NJ 1989 Nr. 233; *Gottwald*, in: Münchener Kommentar zur ZPO
Art. 23 note 75; *Kropholler/von Hein* Art. 23 note 98; *Mankowski*, in: Rauscher Art. 23 note 65; but *contra*
Geimer/Schütze Art. 23 note 195; *Saenger*, ZZP 110 (1997) 477, 496.

[552] As to clauses for the benefit of only one of the parties see *supra* Art. 25 notes 34, 148.

[553] In the same sense *Kropholler/von Hein* Art. 23 note 98.

[554] *Nikolaus Meeth v. Glacetal*, (Case 23/78) (1978) ECR 2133; see thereto *supra* Art. 25 notes 33, 156.

had to be sued in its own country did not prevent the court seised "from taking into account a set-off connected with the legal relationship in dispute."[555] The ECJ based its decision on two arguments, namely "the recognition of the independent will of the parties to a contract in deciding which courts are to have jurisdiction"[556] and on "the need to avoid superfluous procedure".[557] Therefore, unless there is clear indication of the parties' intention to the contrary a jurisdiction agreement does not exclude set-off.[558]

157 It has been suggested that the law governing the interpretation follows the law governing the set-off [559] which is now designated by Art. 17 Rome I Regulation.[560] But since it is only the procedural effect of set-off which is at stake it is submitted that the interpretation rules and methods of the law apply which governs the jurisdiction agreement.

o) Third party proceedings

158 It has been held that a jurisdiction agreement between two parties also prevents a party to sue the other in another than the chosen court by way of third party proceedings, for instance by way of an action on a warranty or guarantee or by any other intervention claim.[561] The jurisdiction according to Art. 8 no. 2, too, is then excluded between the parties by their valid jurisdiction agreement. Similarly, if a party intends to join a party in proceedings whose parties have concluded a valid jurisdiction agreement then for the purposes of these proceedings the joining party should also be bound by the agreement between the parties of the original proceedings. But where a claimant sues several defendants in same proceedings ("Streitgenossen") a jurisdiction agreement can only be invoked by and against the defendant with whom the jurisdiction agreement has been concluded.[562]

159 In case of mere notice of suit to a third party ("Streitverkündung") it is the prevailing and preferable view that the jurisdiction agreement between the original parties does not affect the procedural relationship between the party giving notice and the third party.[563]

---

[555] *Nikolaus Meeth v. Glacetal,* (Case 23/78) (1978) ECR 2133, 2142 para. 9.

[556] *Nikolaus Meeth v. Glacetal,* (Case 23/78) (1978) ECR 2133, 2141 para. 5.

[557] *Nikolaus Meeth v. Glacetal,* (Case 23/78) (1978) ECR 2133, 2142 para. 8.

[558] *Geimer/Schütze* Art. 23 note 194; *Gottwald,* in: Münchener Kommentar zur ZPO Art. 23 note 74; *Kropholler/von Hein* Art. 23 note 99; but contra BGH NJW 1979, 2477 (2478: an agreed jurisdiction is regularly to be interpreted as to exclude set-off (the decision is the final decision in the ECJ case *Nikolaus Meeth v. Glacetal)*); *Auer,* in: Bülow/Böckstiegel/Geimer/Schütze Art. 23 note 169.

[559] *Mankowski,* in: Rauscher Art. 23 note 68.

[560] Art. 17 designates "the law applicable to the claim against which the right of set-off is asserted." See thereto *Magnus,* in: Staudinger Art. 17 Rom I-VO note 1 *et seq.* The ECJ favoured in a prior decision a cumulation of the laws governing both the claim with which and against which set-off is raised: *Commission v. Conseil des communes et régions d'Europe (CCRE),* (Case C-87/01) (2003) ECR I-7617, I-7678 para. 61.

[561] See Cass. RCDIP 1983, 658 with note *Lagarde; * Cass. D. 1989 I. R. 283; *Hough v. P & O Containers Ltd. (Blohm + Voss Holding AG and others, third parties)* (1998) 2 All ER 978, 986 *et seq.* (Q.B.D., *Rix* J.); also *Geimer/Schütze* Art. 23 note 197; *Gottwald,* in: Münchener Kommentar zur ZPO Art. 23 note 76; *Kropholler/von Hein* Art. 23 note 101.

[562] *Auer,* in: Bülow/Böckstiegel/Geimer/Schütze Art. 6 note 7; *Droz* note 90; *Kropholler/von Hein* Art. 6 note 12.

[563] *Auer,* in: Bülow/Böckstiegel/Geimer/Schütze Art. 23 note 172; *Geimer/Schütze* Art. 23 note 196; *Krop-*

p) Effects of jurisdiction agreements on third persons; assignment
In principle a jurisdiction agreement is valid only between the parties to it.[564] But it has   160
already been shown above that jurisdiction agreements can have effect towards third persons who may be bound by, or may rely on, the agreement though they were neither party,
nor expressly consented, to it. This is the case with jurisdiction clauses in bills of lading,[565] in
insurance contracts for the benefit of a third party,[566] in statutes of companies,[567] in trust
instruments[568] and in certain third party proceedings.[569]

However, the effects of jurisdiction agreements on third parties are generally at stake where a   161
claim is assigned for which the original parties had designated the competent court. From
the ECJ judgments in *Gerling Konzern Speziale Kreditversicherungs-AG v. Amministrazione
del tesoro dello Stato*,[570] *Partenreederei MS "Tilly Russ" and Ernst Russ v. NV Haven- en
Vervoerbedrijf Nova and NV Goeminne Hout*,[571] *Trasporti Castelletti Spedizioni Internazionali SpA v. Hugo Trumpy SpA*[572] and *Coreck Maritime GmbH v. Handelsveem BV*[573] the
general principle can be inferred that the original jurisdiction agreement if validly concluded
is equally valid against a successor in title on whom the claim is transferred, provided that
the assignment or other transfer is valid according to the applicable national law and that the
assignee or transferee knew or could have known the jurisdiction agreement.[574] The formal
requirements of Art. 25 (1) and (2) need to be satisfied only by the original jurisdiction
agreement but not by any further assignment or transfer.[575] The assignee or transferee is
then bound by the jurisdiction agreement.[576] Where an international trade usage as to
jurisdiction agreements exists, the knowledge of the assignee or transferee is presumed.
The same rules apply where a party takes over the debt or contract of another if for the
debt or contract originally an exclusive jurisdiction had been agreed.[577] National courts have
further decided that an insurer is bound by a jurisdiction agreement that the insured validly
concluded with a third party against whose acts the insurance was taken out and from whom
the insurer now claims redress.[578]

---

holler/von Hein Art. 23 note 102; *Mankowski*, in: Rauscher Art. 23 note 74; but contra *von Hoffmann/
Hau* RIW 1997, 91 *et seq.*; *Bernd Kraft*, Grenzüberschreitende Streitverkündung und Third Party Notice
(1997), p. 107 *et seq.*; sceptical *Gottwald*, in: Münchener Kommentar zur ZPO Art. 23 note 76.

[564] See for instance Cass. Clunet 2000, 78 (reported by *Huet*); Paris E.C.C. 1988, 291.
[565] See *supra* Art. 25 note 137 (*Magnus*).
[566] See *supra* Art. 25 note 134 (*Magnus*).
[567] See *supra* Art. 25 note 135 (*Magnus*).
[568] See *infra* Art. 25 note 165 (*Magnus*).
[569] See *supra* Art. 23 note 158 (*Magnus*).
[570] (Case 201/82) (1983) ECR 2503.
[571] (Case 71/83) (1984) ECR 2417.
[572] (Case C-159/97) (1999) ECR I-1597.
[573] (Case C-387/98) (2000) ECR I-9337.
[574] In the same sense *Geimer/Schütze* Art. 23 note 201; *Hk-ZPO/Dörner* Art. 23 note 45; *Mankowski*, in:
Rauscher Art. 23 note 71.
[575] See the precited ECJ cases (fn. 593–596).
[576] See, for instance, OLG Hamburg IHR 2008, 108.
[577] OLG Hamburg IHR 2008, 108; *Hk-ZPO/Dörner* Art. 23 note 45.
[578] Cass. EuLF 2013, 23.

162 But a mere connection between contracts does not suffice to carry a jurisdiction agreement from one contract over to the other. Thus, a jurisdiction agreement in a contract between a creditor and debtor does not extend to an accompanying guarantee or suretyship between the creditor (or debtor, as the case may be) and the guarantor or surety.[579] Equally, a chain of contracts does not suffice to extend the effects of a jurisdiction agreement in one of the contracts to all other contracts of the chain.[580] The direct claim ("action directe") which a consumer may have against the producer in particular under French law is therefore not affected by a jurisdiction agreement between the manufacturer and the distributor from whom the consumer has bought.[581]

q) Effects on the prorogated and the derogated court

163 The prorogated court if seised has to accept its jurisdiction under a valid choice of court agreement. It cannot decline its jurisdiction with the *forum non conveniens* argument that another court would be better suited to deal with the dispute.[582] If the prorogated court is seised second and the jurisdiction agreement is exclusive (as is presumed) any other court seised first has to stay proceedings and to finally decline jurisdiction if the prorogated court accepts its jurisdiction (Art. 31 (2) and (3) Brussels I*bis*).[583] This is in sharp contrast to the former solution (Art. 27 old Brussels I Regulation) where the prorogated court if seised second had to stay proceedings until the court first seised whose jurisdiction had been derogated from had denied jurisdiction.[584] Even an excessive and generalised slowness of legal proceedings in the Member State where the court first seised was located did not change this result and allowed the well-known torpedo tactics.[585] The ECJ had even disallowed any antisuit injunction to prevent or stop proceedings which were instituted in violation of the jurisdiction provisions of the Regulation.[586] With respect to exclusive jurisdiction agreements the priority rule of the new Art. 31 (2) has reversed this situation. It prohibits torpedo tactics and makes anti-suit injunctions generally unnecessary because it

---

[579] Rb Rotterdam NIPR 2001 Nr. 56; also *Geimer/Schütze* Art. 23 note 202; *Mankowski*, in: Rauscher Art. 23 note 72.

[580] See thereto *Beaumart*, Haftung in Absatzketten im französischen Recht und im europäischen Zuständigkeitsrecht (1999), p. 148 *et seq.*; *Gebauer*, IPRax 2001, 471, 474 *et seq.*; also *Kropholler/von Hein* Art. 23 note 63; *Mankowski*, in: Rauscher Art. 23 note 72.

[581] *Refcomp SpA v. Axa Corporate Solutions Assurance SA, Axa France IARD, Emerson Network, Climaventa SpA*, (Case C-543/10) ECR nyr.; see also Cass. RCDIP 89 (2000), 224 with note *Leclerc* and the references in the preceding fn.

[582] See *Andrew Owusu v. Nugent B. Jackson, trading as "Villa Holidays Bal-Inn Villas", Mammee Bay Resorts Ltd., Mammee Bay Club Ltd., The Enchanted Garden Resorts & Spa Ltd., Consulting Services Ltd., Town & Country Resorts Ltd.*, (Case C-281/02) (2005) ECR I-1383 para. 37 *et seq.* (denying the doctrine of *forum non conveniens* for the Regulation although not specifically for jurisdiction agreements).

[583] The duty to stay comes into existence only if the party relying on the jurisdiction agreement sues before the prorogated court and has not already submitted to the jurisdiction of the court first seised by not merely contesting the jurisdiction; see *Magnus*, in: FS Dieter Martiny (2014), p. 785, 797 s.; *Pohl*, IPRax 2013, 112.

[584] *Erich Gasser GmbH v. MISAT Srl*, (Case C-116/02) (2003) ECR I-14693, I-14741 para. 54.

[585] *Erich Gasser GmbH v. MISAT Srl*, (Case C-116/02) (2003) ECR I-14693, I-14746 paras. 70–73.

[586] *Gregory Paul Turner v. Felix Fareed Ismail Grovit, Harada Ltd. and Changepoint S.A.* (Case C-159/02) (2004) ECR I-3565; see thereto extensively *Carl*, Einstweiliger Rechtsschutz bei Torpedoklagen (2007); *Dutta/Heinze*, ZEuP 2005, 428 *et seq.*

suffices to approach the prorogated court. Yet, it remains open whether the ECJ will still deny the possibility of an anti-suit injunction against the breach of an exclusive jurisdiction agreement.

With respect to non-exclusive jurisdiction agreements the old solution survives: the court **163a** second seised even if it is a prorogated court has to stay proceedings until the court first seised has decided on its jurisdiction (Art. 29 (1) Brussels I*bis*). And the second court has to decline its jurisdiction if the first court has established its jurisdiction (Art. 29 (3) Brussels I*bis*).[587] Thus, torpedo tactics remain possible under non-exclusive jurisdiction agreements.

The court whose jurisdiction has been validly derogated from must of its own motion reject **164** as inadmissible any proceedings which are contrary to the jurisdiction agreement if it is invoked by the defendant (Art. 28 (1)).

r) Effects on recognition and enforcement of judgments
If a court based its judgment on the erroneous assumption that it had jurisdiction either **165** because it regarded an invalid choice of court agreement incorrectly as valid or a valid agreement as invalid then under the Regulation neither case allows to refuse the recognition and enforcement of the judgment.[588] Art. 45 (1) (e) lists the provisions on jurisdiction whose infringement justifies the refusal of recognition. This list does not include Art. 25. The second court is excluded from reviewing the validity or invalidity of the jurisdiction agreement.[589] It must recognise and enforce such decisions.[590] The Brussels I Recast did not change this situation.

s) Remedies for breach of a jurisdiction agreement
If a party institutes proceedings in a court in breach of a valid jurisdiction agreement the **166** court has to dismiss the action as inadmissible. As mentioned above,[591] the ECJ interpreted the Regulation as not allowing injunctive orders which restrain the right to sue in a certain, here the derogated, court.[592] If the court will uphold this practice also under Brussels I*bis* it is therefore generally necessary that the other party of the jurisdiction agreement must defend itself in the proceedings before the derogated court, primarily by contesting the jurisdiction. This party may thereby incur costs which are not recompensed under the national procedural law of costs. It is disputed whether the party can recover these and further consequential costs as damages for breach of the jurisdiction agreement.[593] Also the recasted Regulation is silent on this aspect. The views are split The decision depends on whether the contractual or the procedural character of choice of court agreements is to be preferred. In particular the Common Law favours the contractual character and allows damages for

---

[587] See *infra* the comment on Art. 29 (*Fentiman*).

[588] See also *infra* the comment to Art. 45 (*Francq/Mankowski*).

[589] Cf. OLG Koblenz NJW 1976, 488; *Kodek*, in: Czernich/Tiefenthaler/Kodek Art. 35 note 9; *Kropholler/von Hein* Art. 35 note 14; *Leible*, in: Rauscher Art. 35 note 13.

[590] See *Magnus*, in: FS Dieter Martiny (2014), p. 785, 802; *Peifer* 396, 398 *et seq.*

[591] See *supra* Art. 25 note 163 (*Magnus*).

[592] *Gregory Paul Turner v. Felix Fareed Ismail Grovit, Harada Ltd. and Changepoint S.A.* (Case C-159/02) (2004) ECR I-3565.

[593] For an intense discussion see *Peifer* 474 *et seq.*

breach of a jurisdiction agreement.[594] In Civil Law the view appears to prevail that such breach can only result in procedural sanctions.[595] Damages or a penalty for such breach are only available if the parties have expressly so stipulated which they are entirely free to do.[596]

t) Locally competent court

166a Art. 25 (1) allows the choice of "a court or the courts of a Member State". Where the parties choose one specific court in a Member State (e.g. "High Court London", "Landgericht Hamburg") the designated court is locally competent, too. It does not matter that under national law another court would be locally or functionally competent. However, unless national law so allows the choice of a court of appeal should be interpreted as a choice of the respective court of first instance (e.g. "Oberlandesgericht Hamburg" as choice of "Landgericht Hamburg").[597]

166b Where the parties choose the courts of a Member State (e.g. "French courts") the locally competent court must be determined in accordance with the national law of procedure.[598] If the national law does not provide a locally competent court – for instance, because of the lack of the required connecting factors – it is partly argued that the jurisdiction agreement is invalid.[599] The prevailing view upholds the agreement and applies respective national rules, if necessary by analogy. The preferable view is an autonomous solution (see thereto already *supra* note 72).

XII. Trust instruments, (par. 3)

167 Specific provisions and requirements apply to trust instruments. Art. 25 (3) accords a jurisdiction clause in a trust instrument the same – exclusive – effect that an ordinary jurisdiction agreement between two parties would have though a private trust is regularly created by a one-sided act of its settlor. The provision was – like the predecessors of Art. 7 (6) and Art. 63 (3) which also deal with trust issues – introduced on the occasion of the accession of the United Kingdom and Ireland to the Brussels Convention in 1978 since the Common Law concept of trust is unknown to continental law and necessitated specific procedural rules.[600] Except the numbering of the paragraph the Brussels I Recast changed nothing. By a

---

[594] See, e.g., *National Westminster Bank plc v. Rabobank Nederland (No. 3)* (2008) All E.R. 266; *Standard Bank plc v. Agrinvest International, Inc.* (2008) 1 Lloyd's Rep. 523; *Tham* (2004) LMCLQ 46 *et seq.*; see also *Briggs* note 8.01 *et seq.*; further *Takahashi* Yb. PIL 10 (2008) 57 *et seq.*; *Takahashi*, Yb. PIL 11 (2009) 73 *et seq.* However, also the Spanish Tribunal Supremo granted damages for the breach of a choice of court agreement: see the report by *Álvarez González* IPRax 2009, 529 *et seq.*

[595] *Dutta/Heinze*, ZEuP 2005, 428 (461); *Gottwald*, in: Münchener Kommentar zur ZPO Art. 23 note 79; *Kropholler*, in: Handbuch des Internationalen Zivilverfahrensrechts I (1982) Kap. III note 168, 586; *Mankowski* IPRax 2009, 27 *et seq.*; *Pfeiffer*, in: FS Lindacher 77; but contra for instance *Carl* (*supra* fn. 586), p. 178.

[596] See the references in the preceding fn.

[597] Under German law parties can only agree on the jurisdiction of courts of first instance; § 38 (1) and (2) ZPO.

[598] LG Mainz WM 2006, 2319 (2322); *Kropholler/von Hein* Art. 23 note 76; MünchKommZPO/*Gottwald* Art. 23 note 68; *Rauscher/Mankowski* Art. 23 note 46; *Reithmann/Martiny/Hausmann* note 6485.

[599] *Jung* 77.

[600] See Report *Schlosser* paras. 109 *et seq.*, 178.

trust the settlor orders that the trust property is held, administered, and disposed of, by a trustee who becomes the legal owner of the trust property but who has to act in the interest and to the benefit of one or more beneficiaries, who have no legal title to the property but become only beneficial or equitable owners. Among the conditions of the trust instrument the settlor may include a jurisdiction clause. It binds the settlor as well as the trustee and the beneficiary. However, in contrast to Art. 25 (1) it is not necessary that the other 'parties' to the trust, the trustee and the beneficiary, have consented to the jurisdiction clause.[601] The settlor can impose it one-sidedly.

Art. 25 (3) states as territorial requirement that the jurisdiction clause in the trust instrument   **168**
must have conferred jurisdiction on the court or courts of a Member State; no further territorial connection with a Member State is expressly required. It was disputed whether any further link was nonetheless necessary. Partly, this was denied;[602] partly, it was suggested that – as in the former Art. 23 (1) Brussels I – at least one of the parties had to be domiciled in a Member State.[603] The preferable view was that no further link was required. The fact that Art. 25 (1) no longer presupposes the domicile of one party in a Member State strongly supports this view. Therefore, the validity of a jurisdiction agreement in a trust instrument has to be determined in accordance with the standards of the Regulation even if the trust has no other connection with a Member State than the choice of the court.

The provision does only apply to trusts in the Common Law sense; it cannot be extended by   **169**
analogy to other one-sided acts. Further, with respect to the material scope of Art. 25 (3) it is more or less self-understanding that the provision extends only to such trust instruments which fall within the general scope of the Regulation (see Art. 1).[604] Trusts with respect to succession or marital property are not covered. Nor do resulting or constructive trusts fall within the scope of Art. 25 (3).[605] These are forms where by legal implication a trust relationship is inferred from the circumstances. In such cases there is generally no explicit jurisdiction clause.

Art. 25 (3) does not prescribe any particular form requirement for jurisdiction clauses in   **170**
trust instruments. It has therefore been suggested that the formal as well as the material validity of a jurisdiction clause in a trust instrument should be determined according to the applicable national law.[606] On the other hand, it can be inferred from the text of Art. 7 (6) that a trust instrument and hence a jurisdiction clause contained in it needs to be in writing or, if made orally, to be evidenced in writing, if it shall be recognised under the Regulation. This seems at least true where the instrument is created by a private settlor and not by

---

[601] See *Gottwald*, in: Münchener Kommentar zur ZPO Art. 23 note 18; *Kropholler/von Hein* Art. 23 note 29; *Layton/Mercer* para. 20.104; *Mankowski*, in: Rauscher Art. 23 note 49; *Hausmann*, in: Simons/Hausmann Art. 23 note 59.

[602] *Layton/Mercer* para. 20.104.

[603] *Conrad*, Qualifikationsfragen des Trust im Europäischen Zivilprozeßrecht (2001), p. 310; *Kropholler/von Hein* Art. 23 note 29.

[604] See Report *Schlosser* para. 112; *Gaudemet-Tallon* para. 158.

[605] *Layton/Mercer* para. 20.106.

[606] *Layton/Mercer* para. 20.104.

operation of statute; and Art. 25 (3) appears to address only the 'private' cases.[607] In such a case then also what has been stated on the form of "writing" or "evidenced in writing" under Art. 25 (1) and (2) can be applied accordingly to jurisdiction clauses in trust instruments[608] with the qualification however, that the trust instrument will normally be one single document only. It is suggested here that it is preferable to determine the formal validity of jurisdiction clauses in accordance with the general standard the Regulation requires for jurisdiction clauses.

171 The jurisdiction conferred by a trust instrument covers only disputes which concern the "internal relationships" under a trust.[609] Proceedings brought against the settlor, trustee or beneficiary fall within the scope of the provision, but only if they concern relationships between these persons or their rights or obligations under the trust. Other – "external" – relationships, for instance a trustee's rights and obligations as against third parties, are not governed by Art. 25 (3) but by the Regulation's general provisions on jurisdiction.[610]

172 Like a jurisdiction agreement in a contract also a jurisdiction clause in a trust instrument cannot oust the protective or exclusive jurisdiction provided for by Art. 15, 19, 23 or 24 (see Art. 25 (4)).

XIII. Specific questions of procedure

1. Invocation of jurisdiction agreement

173 The parties are free to rely on their jurisdiction agreement; if one of the parties invokes it the court seised has to honour a valid jurisdiction agreement: either by dismissing the law suit where the parties agreed on the exclusive jurisdiction of another court or by accepting jurisdiction where the parties had chosen the seised court even if this court originally would have not been competent to hear the case. But where neither party invokes the jurisdiction agreement and on the contrary the defendant submits to the jurisdiction of another court than the chosen one, this submission amounts to a kind of a new though tacit choice of court. The submission (Art. 26) then prevails over the prior agreement.[611] Since the parties may freely agree at any time on the jurisdiction of a certain court it is not for the court seised to apply a prior jurisdiction agreement *ex officio* against the present intentions of the parties. Only if a party invokes a jurisdiction agreement has the court to honour it.[612] However, where a jurisdiction agreement offends Art. 15, 19 or 23 the court is now obliged to "ensure

---

[607] See also *Geimer/Schütze* Art. 23 note 129, referring to Report *Schlosser* para. 178 which does not address the issue but could be understood in the sense mentioned in the text.

[608] In the same sense *Kropholler/von Hein* Art. 23 note 68.

[609] Report *Schlosser* paras. 109 *et seq.*; *Auer*, in: Bülow/Böckstiegel/Geimer/Schütze Art. 23 note 52; *Hausmann*, in: Simons/Hausmann Art. 23 note 59; *Layton/Mercer* para. 20.106.

[610] See *Layton/Mercer* para. 20.106.

[611] See *Elefanten Schuh GmbH v. Pierre Jacqmain* (Case 150/80) (1981) ECR 1671, 1700 para. 10; *Hannelore Spitzley v. Sommer Exploitation S. A.* (Case 48/84) (1985) ECR 787, 800; see also *infra* Art. 26 note 22 (*Calvo Caravaca/Carrascosa González*).

[612] *Calvo Caravaca/Carrascosa González* I p. 93; *Gottwald*, in: Münchener Kommentar zur ZPO Art. 23 note 78.

that the defendant is informed of his right to contest the jurisdiction of the court and of the consequences of entering or not entering an appearance" (Art. 26 (2)).

2. Burden of proof

The party who invokes Art. 25 must prove the facts necessary to establish that Art. 25 is **174** applicable[613] and in particular all facts necessary to establish that a valid jurisdiction clause had been agreed upon and that the parties had reached consensus on the jurisdiction of a certain court or courts.[614] Also where a party relies on the fact that a prior oral agreement had been concluded and was confirmed subsequently in writing this party has to prove the oral agreement.[615] Additionally, the party relying on the fact that an international trade usage provided for a less strict form concerning the conclusion of a contract must prove such a usage.[616]

3. Inquiry into validity of jurisdiction agreement

Whether a jurisdiction agreement on which one or both parties rely is invalid is not a matter **175** involving the burden of proof but must be inquired by the court of its own motion if the jurisdiction depends on the agreement. The court must examine *ex officio* whether the agreement violates Art. 24 (see Art. 27). The same is true in all other cases where the defendant has not submitted to the jurisdiction of the seised derogated court (Art. 28 (1))[617] as long as no proceedings in the prorogated court have been instituted. If that occurs the court first seised has to stay proceedings (Art. 31 (2)) unless the jurisdiction agreement violates the protective jurisdiction rules in Art. 15, 19, 23 (see Art. 31 (4)).

Article 26

1. Apart from jurisdiction derived from other provisions of this Regulation, a court of a Member State before which a defendant enters an appearance shall have jurisdiction. This rule shall not apply where appearance was entered to contest the jurisdiction, or where another court has exclusive jurisdiction by virtue of Article 24.
2. In matters referred to in Sections 3, 4 or 5 where the policyholder, the insured, a beneficiary of the insurance contract, the injured party, the consumer or the employee is the defendant, the court shall, before assuming jurisdiction under paragraph 1, ensure that the defendant is informed of his right to contest the jurisdiction of the court and of the consequences of entering or not entering an appearance.

---

[613] See, e.g., Hof 's-Hertogenbosch NIPR 2001 Nr. 289; *Mankowski*, in: Rauscher Art. 23 note 1.

[614] See, e.g., OGH ZfRV 2001, 113; *Kloeckner & Co AG v. Garoil Overseas Inc.* (1990) 1 Lloyd's Rep. 77 (Q.B. D., *Hirst* J.); *Mankowski*, in: Rauscher Art. 23 note 1.

[615] In this sense in a case where an oral jurisdiction agreement was allegedly modified, see BGH IPRspr 1993 no. 137.

[616] Hof 's-Hertogenbosch NIPR 1998 Nr. 125; OLG Hamburg IPRax 1997, 420 (with note *Harald Koch*, IPRax 1997, 405); CA Paris RCDIP 84 (1995), 573 with note *Kessedjian*; further *Mankowski*, in: Rauscher Art. 23 note 33.

[617] See also *Geimer/Schütze* Art. 23 note 232; *Gottwald*, in: Münchener Kommentar zur ZPO Art. 23 note 78.

Bibliography

Cadet, Le nouveau règlement Bruxelles I ou l'itinéraire d'un enfant "gâté", Clunet 2013, 765

Calvo Caravaca/Carrascosa González, Notas breves sobre la sentencia del TJUE (Sala cuarta) de 20 mayo 2010 *(Bilas*: asunto C-111/09): La sumisión tácita en los litigios internacionales de seguro, "consumo y trabajo", Cuadernos de Derecho Transnacional CDT, 2010, 236

Grusic, Submission and Protective Jurisdiction under the Brussels I Regulation, (2011) 48 C.M.L.Rev. 947

Mankowski, Gerichtsstand der rügelosen Einlassung in europäischen Verbrauchersachen?, IPRax 2001, 310

Mankowski, Besteht der Gerichtsstand der rügelosen Einlassung auch gegen von Schutzregimes besonders geschützte Personen?, RIW 2010, 667

Mankowski, Änderungen im Internationalen Ver-

braucherprozessrecht durch die Neufassung der EuGVVO, RIW 2014, 625

Nuyts, La refonte du règlement Bruxelles I, RCDIP 2013, 1

Rottola, L'accettazione tacita della giurisdizione nella convenzione di Bruxelles del 27 settembre 1968, RDIPP 1978, 521

Sandrock, Die Prorogation der internationalen Zuständigkeit eines Gerichts durch hilfsweise Sacheinlassung des Beklagten, ZvglRWiss 78 (1979), 176

Schulte-Beckhausen, Internationale Zuständigkeit durch rügelose Einlassung im Europäischen Zivilprozeßrecht (1994)

Schütze, Zur internationalen Zuständigkeit aufgrund rügeloser Einlassung, ZZP 90 (1977), 67.

I. Submission: concept

1 Submission is an agreement between two parties in a juridical relationship. By this agreement, both parties determine the court that will have international jurisdiction to decide the controversy faced by the parties. The above mentioned agreement is implicit (i.e. it does not previously exist in any oral form nor in writing), and always takes place before a court during the process. Submission exists when the plaintiff lodges a formal complaint before one court of a Member State and the defendant enters an appearance before this court, unless the appearance was entered to contest international jurisdiction. If the defendant contests the court's international jurisdiction and also raises a subsidiary defense on the substance or a subsidiary counterclaim against the plaintiff, submission does not exist.[1] If the parties de-

---

[1] See *infra* Art. 26 notes 14 and 27–29 (*Calvo Caravaca/Carrascosa Gonzalez*).

termine which court will have international jurisdiction previously to the process, then "submission" does not exist. In which case, such an agreement will be considered as a "choice-of-court clause" (i.e. prorogation of jurisdiction), regulated by Art. 25. For the purposes of this work, "Member State" means a State that participates in the Brussels I-bis Regulation, including Denmark. The current version of Art. 26 covers two different paragraphs. The first one is exactly the same as Art. 24 Brussels I Regulation (2000). The second paragraph has been added in order to introduce the "Bilas jurisprudence" as enacted by the ECJ in the text of Art. 26 and in order to avoid a wrong reading of this judgment.[2]

II. Advantages of submission by the defendant

Submission by the defendant has different advantages for the parties as well as for the courts.　2

1. Jurisdictional unit of litigations

Submission promotes the concentration of different litigations before the same court. This　3 fact fosters the interest of the parties, especially of firms operating in international trade. As a matter of fact, if a court has jurisdiction to decide a specific controversy between two companies, these companies can agree that the same court will have jurisdiction to decide a different controversy. Thereby, the same court will have jurisdiction to decide a plurality of legal differences. That reduces procedural costs, since the parties must not be in dispute before different courts of different countries, but before the same court.

2. Procedural economy for the courts

It is convenient to adopt a specific point of view to understand the reason to support　4 "Submission" as a rule of international jurisdiction: this point of view is that of an economic analysis of International Civil Procedure (i.e. Law and Economics applied to International Civil Procedure). Hence, the fact that the parties can determine the court that will have jurisdiction to decide the controversy can be defined as "efficient". For example, this court is perfectly placed to decide the case in a quick and effective manner because the object of the litigation is located in the country to which the court belongs. At the same time, since submission makes possible to raise more than a controversy before the same court, national judicial expense decreases.

3. Choice of the best court (better court perspective)

Submission allows the parties to confer international jurisdiction to courts specially adapted　5 to decide specific international controversies. Submission may contribute to improve the quality of justice in international trade as far as it creates a sort of "competition" between the courts of the different Member States. As a result, the best court will be the one preferred by the parties.

2　Ceská podnikatelská pojištovna as, Vienna Insurance Group v. Michal Bilas (Case C-111/09), in particular paras. 21–22, 24; OGH ZfRV 2003, 190; OLG Koblenz RIW 2000, 636, 637 = IPRax 2001, 334, 335; OLG Köln RIW 2004, 866; OLGRostock OLG-Report 2006, 271, 272; Grusic, (2011) 48 C.M.L.Rev. 947, 951–953 and BAG AP Nr. 1 zu Art. 18 EuGVVO with critical note by Mankowski. Still preferring the opposite result Art. 17 notes 15–16 (Peter Arnt Nielsen/Peter Mankowski); Mankowski, RIW 2010, 667.

6   For these reasons, the Brussels I Regulation promotes submission as a "point of jurisdiction". The Brussels I Regulation raises scanty limits of substance and form to submission. Submission is contained in Art. 26, as said above. It has been studied and analyzed by many European legal scholars.[3] Art. 26 para. 1 to the letter presents the same wording as its predecessor, Art. 18 of the Brussels Convention, at least in both French and Spanish versions. In fact the rule has never been modified in those languages.[4] Only a minor and merely linguistic change has been made in some versions of Art. 26, such as in the English and Italian versions, as we will see further. From the perspective of the Brussels I Regulation, submission is a special kind of "prorogation of Jurisdiction" (i.e. *stillschweigende Prorogation)* and is not a "procedural unilateral act" (i.e. *einseitige Prozesshandlung).* Para 2 of Art. 26 is brand new as it has been underlined before.

III. Requirements for the existence of submission

7   Submission takes place provided that three different elements are met: a) plaintiff's initial lawsuit before a court of a Member State; b) entering an appearance by the defendant before the above mentioned court, unless appearance was entered to contest international jurisdiction (Art. 26); and c) respect of the limits of submission, which are studied *infra.*[5]

1. Plaintiff's initial lawsuit

8   This requirement appears in an implicit form in Art. 26. Art. 26 requires the defendant's appearance because he has previously been sued by a plaintiff. The plaintiff's initial lawsuit is an indispensable requirement for submission to exist as meant by Art. 26. Therefore, the plaintiff's initial lawsuit must have been "presented" and, logically, it must have been "admitted" by the court. The Brussels I Regulation does not regulate the conditions and requirements of the plaintiff's initial lawsuit. Those must be decided under the International Civil Procedure of the State before which the plaintiff has brought proceedings: it is the famous *lex fori regit processum* principle. The ECJ confirms this answer to the question. International Civil Procedure of the State whose courts have international jurisdiction must govern the procedural aspects of the controversy. These aspects are not regulated by the Brussels I Regulation.[6] The Brussels I Regulation leaves this in the hands of the International Civil Procedure of every single Member State the task of solving any question that is not an object of specific provisions by the Brussels I Regulation. Nevertheless, the application of such International Civil Procedure cannot imply a prejudice to the "useful effect" of the principles contained in the Brussels I Regulation.

---

3   *Staudinger,* in: Rauscher Art. 24 notes 1–3; *Kropholler* Art. 24 notes 1–18; *Gaudemet-Tallon* p. 119–123; *Rottola,* RDIPP 1978, 521–529; *Sandrock,* ZVglRWiss 78 (1979), 117–220; *Schütze,* ZZP 90 (1977), 67–76; *Calvo Caravaca* p. 372–379; *Virgós/Garcimartín,* Derecho procesal civil internacional. Litigación internacional (2nd ed. 2007) p. 304–308; *Mari* p. 690–712; *Salerno* p. 148–150; *Gothot/Holleaux* p. 110–114; *O'Malley/Layton* p. 611; *Kaye* p. 1117.

4   *Gaudemet-Tallon* p. 119.

5   See *infra* Art. 26 notes 15 *et seq.* (*Calvo Caravaca/Carrascosa Gonzalez*).

6   See *P. Capelloni et F. Aquilini v. J. C. J. Pelkmans,* (Case 119/84) (1985) ECR 3147, 3164 paras. 20–21.

2. Entering an appearance by the defendant

Art. 26 expressly requires the appearance of the defendant before the court. The appearance **9** of the defendant before the court in question shows that the defendant wishes that this specific court will have international jurisdiction on a specific controversy. Since the plaintiff has already demonstrated his will to dispute before this court by bringing a lawsuit, Art. 26 accepts that there is a "junction" of wills between plaintiff and defendant in the sense of disputing before a specific court. Therefore, the above mentioned court will have jurisdiction about the controversy in question. Several aspects must be specified with regards to the appearance of the defendant.

What does "appearance" mean? The defendant's appearance presents a "hard nucleus" and **10** an "external sphere". The hard nucleus, i.e. the meaning of "entering an appearance", must be determined in the same way for all the Member States. It is a uniform concept valid for the purposes of the Brussels I Regulation, as many legal experts have pointed out.[7] Hence, "entering an appearance" can be defined as "the legal presence of the defendant in the process, which authorizes the defendant to act as a party in that civil trial". And this is the correct meaning of the "external sphere" of "entering an appearance": the acts that the defendant must do to be considered as a party in a civil trial are governed by the International Civil Procedure of every Member State. For example, in German Civil Procedure the relevant moment is the defendant's "answer to the complaint". It is again *lex fori regit processum*. The ECJ has admitted this answer.[8] Anyway, if there is no "appearance" before the court, submission will never exist and the court will not have international jurisdiction based on Art. 26. In other words, it can be said that there will never exist a judgment rendered "in default of appearance" on the basis of Art. 26.

The defendant can enter an appearance but only with the exclusive purpose of "contesting" **11** the jurisdiction of the court. It is crystal clear that this means that the defendant does not want to be in a dispute before that court. Therefore, in the above mentioned hypothesis, submission will not exist. From this point of view, Art. 26 states that: "This rule shall not apply where appearance was entered to contest the jurisdiction". Art. 26 does not indicate what "type of jurisdiction" the defendant must contest to avoid submission to the court. Interpreting Art. 26 in the rubric of the Council Regulation, affirming that, to avoid any submission, the defendant must contest the international jurisdiction of the court in question, seems to be more correct. If the defendant exclusively contests, for example, the "territorial jurisdiction" of the court, the same defendant is admitting, at least, that he wants to bring the dispute before the courts of the State to which the specific court concerned belongs. Therefore, in this hypothesis, the court in question has international jurisdiction by virtue of Art. 26. Nevertheless, this is not enough for the above mentioned court to have "entire jurisdiction" about the matter: since its territorial jurisdiction has been contested, the effects of such contestation will be decided in accordance with the Code of Civil Procedure of the State to which the court belongs.

The determination of the suitable moment for the defendant to contest the jurisdiction of **12**

---

[7]   *Mari* p. 706; *O'Malley/Layton* p. 611; *Kropholler* Art. 24 note 7; *Kaye* p. 1117; *Layton/Mercer* note 20.125.

[8]   See *P. Capelloni et F. Aquilini v. J. C. J. Pelkmans*, (Case 119/84) (1985) ECR 3147, 3164 paras. 20–21.

the court belongs to international civil procedure of the State of the *forum*.[9] This solution has been supported by the ECJ.[10] Nevertheless, the same ECJ has introduced two "uniform rules of Civil Procedure" on the question of the suitable moment for the defendant to contest international jurisdiction.[11] First rule: as it has been pointed out, the Civil Procedure of each Member State cannot admit the possibility of contesting the jurisdiction of the court once the defendant has made submission on the substance.[12] As the ECJ stated in Case C-1/13, Cartier, 27th February 2014, *"[t]he Court has already held that it is clear from Article 18 of the Brussels Convention, a provision which in essence is identical to Article 24 of Regulation No. 44/2001 [and to Art. 26 Bruxelles I-bis Regulation], that the challenge to jurisdiction may not occur after the making of the submissions which under national procedural law are considered to be the first defence addressed to the court seised"*.[13] Second rule: the Civil Procedure of a Member State governing the procedure must be able to allow that the first procedural act of the defendant be "to contest the court jurisdiction". If this case is not contemplated by Civil Procedure, the defendant must contest the court's international jurisdiction as soon as possible according to Civil Procedure of each Member State.[14]

13   As the Report *Jenard* indicates, the rules on civil procedure of the Member State whose courts probably have international jurisdiction, determine the procedure to be observed by the defendant in order to contest the court's international jurisdiction.

14   The defendant may contest the court's international jurisdiction but he may also, at the same time, raise a subsidiary defense on the substance or a subsidiary counterclaim against the plaintiff. The defendant acts this way because he must be prepared for the eventuality of the court asserting its jurisdiction. In that case, the Civil Procedure of a few Member States denies the defendant the possibility to make any defense on the substance of the action subsequently. In the above mentioned hypothesis (i.e. the defendant contests the court's jurisdiction and, at the same time, makes some subsidiary defence on the substance of the action) there is no submission at all. This statement has again been supported with all clarity and iteration by the ECJ.[15] Nevertheless, the defense on the substance of the action must always be subsidiary (i.e. only operative if the court should assert its international jurisdiction). If the defense on the substance of the action is not subsidiary, there will clearly be an intention on the defendant's behalf that he is willing to bring the dispute before the court in question: there will be undoubtedly submission in the sense of Art. 26. On the other hand, it is necessary to keep in mind that the versions in French language and in Spanish language of Art. 18 of the Brussels Convention – direct predecessor to the current Art. 26 – are both very

---

9   Cf. for example Art. 64 Spanish Civil Procedure Code.

10   See *Elefanten Schuh GmbH v. Pierre Jacqmain*, (Case 150/80) (1981) ECR 1671, 1700.

11   See *Elefanten Schuh GmbH v. Pierre Jacqmain*, (Case 150/80) (1981) ECR 1671, 1700.

12   *Gaudemet-Tallon* p. 123.

13   See also Case 150/80 Elefanten Schuh [1981] ECR 1671, para. 16, and Case C 144/12 Goldbet Sportwetten [2013] ECR, para. 37.

14   *Calvo Caravaca* p. 376.

15   See *Elefanten Schuh GmbH v. Pierre Jacqmain*, (Case 150/80) (1981) ECR 1671, 1700; *Établissements Rohr Société anonyme v. Dina Ossberger*, (Case 27/81) (1981) ECR 2431, 2444; *Hannelore Spitzley v. Sommer Exploitation SA*, (Case 48/84) (1985), ECR 787, 800; *C. H.W v. G. J.H*, (Case 25/81) (1982) ECR 1189, 1210; *Gerling Konzern Speziale Kreditversicherungs-AG et al. v. Amministrazione del Tesoro dello Stato*, (Case 210/82) (1983) ECR 2503, 2524.

clear: there is no submission by the defendant when the appearance was made to contest the court's jurisdiction. Other linguistic versions of Art. 18 of the above mentioned Brussels Convention 1968, indicate that to avoid submission, the appearance of the defendant must have been entered "*solely*" to contest the international jurisdiction of the court. This way, the version in English language and the version in Italian language both contain a reference to the term "*solely*" (i.e. English version) and "*solo*" (i.e. Italian version). Let us take a look at the version of Art. 18 of the Brussels Convention 1968 in English language: "*This rule shall not apply where appearance was entered solely to contest the jurisdiction [...].*" And let us also have a look at the version of Art. 18 of the Brussels Convention 1968 in Italian: "*Tale norma non è applicabile se la comparizione avviene solo per eccepire la incompetenza [...].*" The ECJ has interpreted this provision in the sense we have seen before.[16] Thus, the French and later the Spanish version of Art. 18 of the Brussels Convention were preferred. At the present time, the polemic presents only a historical sense, because the version of Art. 26 in Italian language is clear: "*Tale norma non è applicabile se la comparizione avviene per eccepire l'incompetenza o se esiste un altro giudice esclusivamente competente ai sensi dell'articolo 22*", as it is the version in English language: "*This rule shall not apply where appearance was entered to contest the jurisdiction, or where another court has exclusive jurisdiction by virtue of Art. 22*". To sum up, it is not possible to doubt today that the wording of current Art. 26 in all official languages has followed the sense of Art. 18 of the Brussels Convention in French and Spanish language. Thus, the defendant can contest the court's jurisdiction and, and the same time, can make some defenses on the substance of the action. Not "solely" contest the international jurisdiction of the court. As the ECJ has pointed out, the challenge to jurisdiction made bye the defendant may not occur after the making of the submissions which under national procedural law are considered to be the first defence addressed to the court seised. Anyway, in the case of a subsidiary defense on the substance or a subsidiary counterclaim, both the plaintiff and the court seized should be able to ascertain from the time of the defendant's first defence that it is intended to contest the jurisdiction of the court.[17]

IV. Limits of submission

According to Art. 26, submission must respect the following limits.   **15**

It is only possible to confer international jurisdiction by submission to a court belonging to a   **16** Member State in the Brussels I Regulation. As the ECJ has pointed out in relation with choice-of-court clauses regulated by Art. 25, the parties can designate the court or courts that they consider suitable, at their will. It is not necessary that an objective link exist between the controversy and the court designated by the parties.[18] On the other hand, submission in favour of courts belonging to "third countries" (i.e. Non-Member States), is ruled by the national rules on international civil procedure of the above mentioned "third States", and never by the Brussels I Regulation. An example is provided by the submission by a defendant with domicile in Germany before an American court.

---

[16]   *Elefanten Schuh GmbH v. Pierre Jacqmain*, (Case 150/80) (1981) ECR 1671, 1700 para. 14.

[17]   *Cartier parfums – lunettes SAS, Axa Corporate Solutions assurances SA vs. Ziegler France SA, Montgomery Transports SARL, Inko Trade s.r.o., Jaroslav Matĕja, Groupama Transport*, (Case C-1/13 (2014), para. 37.

[18]   See *Siegfried Zelger v. Sebastiano Salinitri*, (Case 56/79) (1980) ECR 89, 102; *Trasporti Castelletti Spedizioni Internazionali SpA v. Hugo Trumpy SpA*, (Case C-159/97) (1999) ECR 561; *Francesco Benincasa v. Dentalkit Srl*, (Case C-269/95) (1997) ECR 3767.

17 The court that has jurisdiction by submission must be a court that, in other cases, would not have had international jurisdiction under other provisions of the Brussels I Regulation. Thus, the parties "extend" the jurisdiction of the court to cases not covered, *a priori*, by other provisions of the Brussels I Regulation. In other words: according to the objective criteria of the Brussels I Regulation, the court has no jurisdiction at all, the international jurisdiction is rather conferred to the court by the parties. Hence, it can be said that the parties "extend" the court's international jurisdiction.

18 A very complicated problem arises when submission is made in favor of a court in the State of the defendant's domicile. Does this specific court have international jurisdiction about the controversy? To give an example: do the courts of Barcelona (Spain) have international jurisdiction *ex* Art. 26, when submission is made by a defendant domiciled in Madrid (Spain)? Two different positions have been suggested about this matter.

19 First position: the parties can tacitly choose the specific court that they consider suitable to decide their controversy. The courts of Barcelona can be chosen by the parties and submission can also be made in this case. In such case it does not matter where the defendant is domiciled. He could even be domiciled in another place of the same country. This first interpretation seems to be supported by the Spanish version of Art. 26, which does not limit the possibility of the parties at the moment of choosing the court to confer jurisdiction. Thus, Art. 26 is understood as a "blend" of the "international jurisdiction rule" and the "territorial jurisdiction rule". Submission confers not only international jurisdiction but also territorial jurisdiction. Therefore, the parties can tacitly choose a specific court in order to solve the controversy that they face.[19]

20 Second position: It is supported by some legal scholars that Art. 26 is "merely" and "solely" a rule of international jurisdiction. It has nothing to do with territorial jurisdiction.[20] According to Art. 26, submission can be made to the courts of a specific State. But this provision does not allow the parties to confer jurisdiction to a specific court. This is a problem of "territorial jurisdiction" and Art. 26 does not deal with this problem. Thus, the question of which specific court has territorial jurisdiction has to be solved under Civil Procedure of each Member State. The French version of Art. 26 seems to support this second position: *"Outre les cas où sa compétence résulte d'autres dispositions du présent règlement [...]."* Hence, in these authors' opinion, Art. 26, does not regulate the question of "territorial jurisdiction". Hence, in the previous example, if an individual domiciled in Madrid makes submission to a court of Barcelona, Art. 26 does not apply to decide the "territorial jurisdiction" of Barcelona's court. This question can only be solved by the current Spanish Civil Procedure Code (i.e. Ley de Enjuiciamiento Civil 1/2000), since the defendant is domiciled in Spain. Therefore, the effects of the appearance of the defendant before the court of Barcelona are to be determined under the above mentioned current Spanish Code of Civil Procedure. The Spanish Code of Civil Procedure can accept the territorial jurisdiction of the courts of Barcelona or can deny this territorial jurisdiction. But Art. 26 has nothing to say on this problem. To sum up, Art. 26 is only useful to confer jurisdiction in case a submission is made to a court of a Member State that does not have jurisdiction according to the rest of

---

[19] *Kaye* p. 1125; *O'Malley/Layton* p. 610–611.
[20] *Mari* p. 704–705; *Gothot/Holleaux* p. 110–114.

provisions of the Brussels I Regulation (i.e. courts that do not have, *a priori*, international jurisdiction).

Submission cannot be made for the matters covered by Art. 24 (i.e. exclusive jurisdiction), as **21** Art. 26 prescribes. These matters are the object of exclusive jurisdiction because of their "link to the sovereignty" of every Member State. Thus, it is not admitted that the parties can "extend" the international jurisdiction of a foreign court in these cases. For example, under Art. 24, property of immovables located in France are to be decided only by French courts. There is no room for submission by the defendant in favor of a German court, even though both parties are German and domiciled in Germany. There is no way to submission in such cases. Exclusive Jurisdiction is always to be respected. The ECJ has supported this statement.[21]

But what about probable "exclusive jurisdiction" of third States' courts? Can the parties **22** "extend" the international jurisdiction of a Member State court in this case? It is not easy to answer this question because it is closely connected with a very controversial theory: the famous *effet réflexe* of Art. 24. But let us go step by step. Some legal experts defend the famous above mentioned theory: the *effet réflexe* of Art. 24. According to this theory the Brussels I Regulation shall not apply to cases involving "probable exclusive jurisdiction" of third States' courts. Therefore, the internal rules of International Civil Procedure are to be applied in those cases. The conclusion is that those rules can allow submission even if the subject matter of the controversy belongs to the exclusive jurisdiction of a third State's courts. But this position is not convincing at all because it can generate a denial of justice in the UE: the plaintiff's complaint is refused. A second group of legal experts indicate that the Brussels I Regulation applies even to those cases (i.e. exclusive jurisdiction of non-Member States' courts). Hence, the courts of a Member State must decide the controversy if submission is made according to Art. 26. The fact that the subject matter of the controversy belongs to the exclusive jurisdiction of a third State's courts does not count. The Brussels I Regulation does not apply in order to defend third States courts' exclusive jurisdiction.[22] But a third position can be sustained:[23] when the Member State court's judgment can be enforced in a Member State, and should not be enforced in a "third State", submission is to be admitted and Art. 26 is to be applied. *Argumentum*: in this case, there is no denial of justice at all, and the judgment can be enforced in the EU territory. On the contrary, when the Member State court's judgment can only be enforced in the third State, sustaining international jurisdiction of the Member State's courts makes no sense at all. This judgment cannot be enforced in the UE territory and cannot be enforced in the third State territory. Hence, why international jurisdiction of Member States' courts is to be maintained? *Argumentum*: sustaining the international jurisdiction of Member States' courts makes no sense because those judgments will be, surely, not enforceable in any part of the world.

Submission is to be made only when a controversy has already arisen. From this point of **23**

---

[21] See: *Theodorus Engelbertus Sanders v. Ronald van der Putte*, (Case 73/77) (1977) ECR 2383, 2398; *Erich Rösler v. Horst Rottwinkel*, (Case 241/83) (1985) ECR 99, 129; *R. O. E. Scherrens v. M. G. Maenhout et al.*, (Case 158/87) (1988) ECR 3791, 3806; *Dansommer A/S v. Andreas Götz*, (Case C-8/98) (2000) ECR I-393.

[22] Report *Almeida Cruz/Desantes Real/Jenard* p. 35–56.

[23] *Droz*, RCDIP 79 (1990), 1, 21; *Calvo Caravaca/Carrascosa González*, Derecho internacional privado, Vol. I, (12th ed. 2011) p. 153–156.

view, submission is quite different from choice-of-court clauses. Choice-of-court clauses are always previous to the process. On the contrary, submission is always made during the process.

24   Art. 26 applies only to international controversies covered by the material scope of the Brussels I Regulation (see Art. 1). Since submission is only possible when the judicial controversy has arisen, there are no risks for the defendant: the plaintiff cannot "impose" the "obligation" to dispute before a specific court[24] on the defendant. Hence, Art. 26 is to be applied in all matters covered by this legal instrument, even to subject matters with a "weaker party", such as consumer contracts, insurance contracts, employment contracts and alimony or maintenance.[25] There is a strong polemic in the doctrine about the possibility of submission in those fields. Nevertheless, there can be no doubt that submission must be accepted even in these subject matters. Firstly, because there is no express limitation to submission in the Sections 4, 5 and 6, Chapter II of the Brussels I Regulation (i.e. the specific Section of the Brussels I Regulation devoted to "consumer contracts", "insurance contracts" and "employment contracts"). Secondly, because when the consumer, the policyholder or the worker are the defendant, they can always contest the court's international jurisdiction if the plaintiff files a lawsuit before a specific court. Not only the consumer-defendant, the policyholder-defendant or the worker can always contest the jurisdiction, but they can refuse to appear in court, and even in this case, this specific court will not have jurisdiction based on Art. 26.[26] Hence, the consumer-defendant, the policyholder-defendant or the worker will never be "forced" to act before a specific court on the basis of Art. 26. This perspective has been clearly confirmed by the ECJ in *Ceská podnikatelská pojištovna as v. Michal Bilas.*[27] The ECJ has stressed that the grounds of jurisdiction contained in the Brussels I Regulation in the specific sections referred to insurance contracts (section 3), consumer contracts (section 4) and employment contracts (section 5) are not exclusive grounds of international jurisdiction. Hence, these matters are not covered by Art. 24. They are not covered by Art. 26 2nd clause either.[28] The doctrine of the EJC expressed in *Ceská podnikatelská pojištovna as v. Michal Bilas* is not only valid for insurance contracts, but is also applicable to consumer contracts and individual contracts of employment. A judgment which has been pronounced by a court of a Member State in matters of insurance contracts,

---

[24] *Calvo Caravaca* p. 374.

[25] *Gaudemet-Tallon* p. 120; *Calvo Caravaca* p. 378; *Mari* p. 703–704. With regard to maintenance, Brussels I Regulation is not applicable anymore in the case that Council Regulation 4/2009 applies. See *Calvo/Carrascosa*, Cuadernos de Derecho Transnacional, vol. 2, n° 2, 2010, 236–241 (available at www.uc3m.es/cdt).

[26] Cf. *Mankowski*, IPRax 2001, 310.

[27] *Ceská podnikatelská pojištovna as, Vienna Insurance Group v. Michal Bilas* (Case C-111/09), nyr. in particular paras. 21–22-24; OGH ZfRV 2003, 190; OLG Koblenz RIW 2000, 636, 637 = IPRax 2001, 334, 335; OLG Köln RIW 2004, 866; OLG Rostock OLG-Report 2006, 271, 272; *Grusic*, (2011) 48 C.M.L.Rev. 947, 951–953 and BAG AP Nr. 1 zu Art. 18 EuGVVO with critical note by *Mankowski*. Still preferring the opposite result Art. 17 notes 15–16 (*Peter Arnt Nielsen*); *Mankowski*, RIW 2010, 667.

[28] *Ceská podnikatelská pojištovna as and Vienna Insurance Group v. Michal Bilas* (Case C-111/09), nyr. in particular para. 26: "Accordingly, since the rules on jurisdiction set out in Section 3 of Chapter II of Regulation No. 44/2001 are not rules on exclusive jurisdiction, the court seised, where those rules are not complied with, must declare itself to have jurisdiction where the defendant enters an appearance and does not contest that court's jurisdiction."

consumer contracts and individual contracts of employment on the basis of tacit prorogation of jurisdiction or submission by virtue of Art. 26, can be recognized in the other
Member States. Art. 45 (1) (e) will not be an obstacle. The court which pronounced the
judgment on that basis was an internationally competent court under the Brussels I*bis*
Regulation. In the case that a "weaker" party voluntarily entered an appearance before that
court, the specific grounds of jurisdiction included in sections 3, 4 and 5 of the Second
Chapter have been not violated.[29]

V. Choice-of-court clauses and subsequent submission

Subsequent submission prevails over the previous choice-of-court clauses. Every choice-of-   **25**
court clause is modifiable by the parties in the same way the parties in an international
contract can modify their choice-of-law clauses. The ECJ has supported this statement.[30]
The parties can conclude a choice-of-court clause. But if they change their mind later, they
can grant international jurisdiction to a different court through submission. The fact that the
previous choice-of-court clause refers any dispute to a Member State court, to a third State
court or to arbitration is irrelevant.[31]

VI. Submission and reconvention

Art. 26 also applies in case of counterclaim against the plaintiff.[32] In such a case, the plaintiff   **26**
becomes the defendant. According to Art. 26, if this "previous plaintiff" pleads to the merits
of the counterclaim and does not contest the jurisdiction of the court, submission exists. The
court will also have international jurisdiction in this case. The ECJ has also supported this
point of view.[33]

VII. Effects of submission

Submission effects only the parties who submit to the court's jurisdiction. On one hand,   **27**
third parties (i.e. persons who are not party to the lawsuit), are not affected by submission at
all. On the other hand, submission only covers the specific subject matters of the dispute
before the court. Controversies between parties that are not involved by the lawsuit or
possible counterclaims are not affected by submission. Therefore, as it has been pointed
out, in case of plurality of controversies or disputes between the parties *(mehrere Streitge-*

---

[29]   *Ceská podnikatelská pojištovna as and Vienna Insurance Group v. Michal Bilas*, (Case C-111/09) nyr.
   para. 29: "That provision concerns non-recognition of judgments given by a court without jurisdiction
   which has not been seised in accordance with those rules. It is therefore not applicable where the judgment is given by a court with jurisdiction. That is true, inter alia, of a court seised, even though those rules
   on special jurisdiction are not complied with, before which the defendant enters an appearance and does
   not contest that court's jurisdiction. Such a court in fact has jurisdiction on the basis of Article 24 of
   Regulation No. 44/2001. Therefore, Article 35 of that regulation does not prevent the recognition of the
   judgment given by that court."
[30]   See *Elefanten Schuh GmbH v. Pierre Jacqmain*, (Case 150/80) (1981) ECR 1671, 1700; *Hannelore Spitzley
   v. Sommer Exploitation SA*, (Case 48/84) (1985) ECR 787, 800.
[31]   *Gothot/Holleaux* p. 110, 114.
[32]   *Gaudemet-Tallon* p. 121.
[33]   *Hannelore Spitzley v. Sommer Exploitation SA* (Case 48/84) (1985) ECR 787, 800 para. 19.

genstände), the court has only international jurisdiction if the defendant does not contest the court's international jurisdiction and accepts it in relation to each and every one of the disputes, legal differences or controversies.[34]

VIII. The problem of the "scope of application" of Art. 26

28 One of the most controversial questions related to Art. 26 concerns the "scope of application" of this provision. Legal experts, particularly, have examined this question: must one of the parties have their domicile in the territory of a Member State for the purposes of Art. 26? Several positions have been sustained.

1. The so-called "parallel thesis"

29 Some legal experts thought that domicile of, at least, one of the parties should be required "parallel" to Art. 23 Brussels I Regulation (2000). This way, at least one of the parties, the plaintiff or the defendant, it does not matter, must be domiciled in the territory of a Member State.[35] But this position was erroneous and wrong in the past as it was underlined by the ECJ in *Group Josi Reinsurance Company SA v. Universal General Insurance Company UGIC.*

2. The thesis of the defendant's domicile

30 The second position, maintained by some legal scholars, indicates that Art. 26 is to be applied only in the case that the defendant has his domicile in the territory of a Member State.[36] The thesis relies on two arguments. First, the philological argument: the current version of Art. 6 states that, if there is no special provision (see Artt. 24 and 25), the Brussels *Ibis* Regulation is to be applied only if the defendant's domicile is located in the territory of a Member State. There is a difference between the previous original version of Art. 4 of the Brussels Convention of September 27th 1968. This provision was missing in that convention whereas it now appears in the version of Art. 4 Brussels I Regulation (2000). Therefore, current Art. 26 should be applied only if the defendant is domiciled is the territory of a Member State. Second, the anti-fraud argument: not requiring the defendant's domicile in the territory of a Member State would promote fraud. In fact, on many occasions, the defendant does not enter in appearance just for mere ignorance. In such a case, a plaintiff with domicile outside the EU, would obtain a judgment from a court of a Member State. And this judgment would have "free movement" in the EU.[37] Hence the fraud, in these authors' opinion. Nevertheless, this second thesis, more refined and much better constructed than the previous one, is not convincing either. As a matter of fact, even when both parties are domiciled in a non-EU country, they can perfectly foresee the application of

---

34 *Calvo Caravaca* p. 374.

35 *Fernández Rozas/Sánchez Lorenzo*, Derecho internacional privado (3rd ed. 2004), p. 79, 80.

36 Report *Jenard* p. 122, 180; *Clarkson/Hill*, Jaffey on the Conflict of Laws (2nd ed. 2002) p. 79: "Although the Regulation does not expressly state that Art. 24 applies only to defendants who are domiciled in a member state, this conclusion follows from Art. 4 which states that, if the defendant is not domiciled in a member state, the jurisdiction of the courts of each Member State is, subject to Art.s 22 and 23 (but not Art. 24), to be determined by that state's traditional rules."; *Béraudo*, Clunet 128 (2001), 1033, 1084; *Gaudemet-Tallon* p. 119, 120.

37 *Gaudemet-Tallon* p. 120.

Art. 26 for submission before a Member State court. And finally, it should be remembered that the wording of Art. 26 does not require any specific domicile of the parties at all.

3. The "expansive thesis"

Most of the legal scholars who have faced this problem, believe that Art. 26 applies irre- **31** spectively of the domicile of both parties. Therefore, Art. 26 applies even when both parties are domiciled in third States or Non-Member States.[38] The ECJ also shares this point of view in *Group Josi Reinsurance Company SA v. Universal General Insurance Company UGIC*. Let us take a look at para. (44): "Admittedly, under Art. 18 of the Convention, the voluntary appearance of the defendant establishes the jurisdiction of a court of a Contracting State before which the plaintiff has brought proceedings, without the place of the defendant's domicile being relevant".[39] And let us also take a look at number (45): "However, although the court seised must be that of a Contracting State, that provision does not further require that the plaintiff be domiciled in such a State".[40] The explanation of this thesis is clear: Art. 26 does not require the domicile of any of the parties because they can reasonably foresee the application of Art. 26, even if none of the parties is domiciled in a Member State. Hence, "legal predictability" is guaranteed and Art. 26 can be considered as not "imperialist" at all.

Considering the new text of Art. 25, which is applicable irrespective of the parties' domicile, **32** it seems more than clear that this last perspective should be preferred. Hence, Art. 26 applies irrespectively of the domicile of both parties. By doing so, Art. 25 and Art. 26 applies even when both parties or just one of them are domiciled in third States or Non-Member States.

IX. The new paragraph of Art. 26. Protection of weaker party

Art. 26.2 expressly indicates that is perfectly admitted the so called tacit submission or tacit **33** prorogation in case that the defendant is a "weaker party" in the legal situation, normally a contract. It refers to the case that "the policyholder, the insured, a beneficiary of the insurance contract, the injured party, the consumer or the employee" is the defendant. This provision has received the point of view held by ECJ in *Ceská podnikatelská pojišťovna as v. Michal Bilas*.[41] The ECJ indicates the way to be followed. The ECJ makes the rule again.

---

[38] *Gothot/Holleaux* p. 110, 114; *Droz*, Compétence judiciaire et effets des jugements dans le marché commun (Étude de la Convention de Bruxelles du 27 septembre 1968) (1972), p. 230; *Droz/Gaudemet-Tallon*, RCDIP 90 (2001), 601, 652; *Weser* p. 265, 270; *Mayer/Heuzé*, Droit international privé (7ᵗʰ ed. 2001) para. 353; *Audit*, Droit international privé (3ʳᵈ ed. 2000) p. 474, 475; *Calvo Caravaca* p. 372, 379; *Kaye* p. 1125; *Mari* p. 702; *Salerno* p. 148.

[39] See: *Group Josi Reinsurance Company SA v. Universal General Insurance Company UGIC*, (Case C-412/98) (2000) ECR I-5925 para. 44.

[40] See: *Group Josi Reinsurance Company SA v. Universal General Insurance Company UGIC*, (Case C-412/98) (2000) ECR I-5925 para. 45.

[41] *Ceská podnikatelská pojišťovna as, Vienna Insurance Group v. Michal Bilas* (Case C-111/09), nyr. in particular paras. 21–24; OGH ZfRV 2003, 190; OLG Koblenz RIW 2000, 636, 637 = IPRax 2001, 334, 335; OLG Köln RIW 2004, 866; OLG Rostock OLG-Report 2006, 271, 272; *Grusic*, (2011) 48 C.M.L.Rev. 947, 951–953 and BAG AP Nr. 1 zu Art. 18 EuGVVO with critical note by *Mankowski*. Still preferring the opposite result Art. 17 notes 15–16 (*Peter Mankowski/Peter Arnt Nielsen*); *Mankowski*, RIW 2010, 667.

Then the European legislator codifies what the ECJ has stated.[42] Anyway the European legislator went a little further, because in accordance with the legal text, the court has the duty, before assuming jurisdiction under paragraph 1, of "ensuring that the defendant is informed of his right to contest the jurisdiction of the court and of the consequences of entering or not entering an appearance". The ECJ did not establish any duty to the courts of the Member States in regard with the information given to the defendant-weaker party. According to *Mankowski*, the rule of Art. 26, 2nd para. prevails on any national legal provision. In addition to that, it seems that the courts of the Member States have an *ex officio – ex* Art. 26. 2nd para. Bruxelles I-bis Regulation duty to provide the legal information to the defendant weaker party as stated before. This Article nothing states about the obligation or possibility of the defendant of being assisted by a lawyer or legal advisor. Nothing is said about the language of the information that should be given to the defendant weaker party. Hence, both issues should be left to the National Procedural Law of the Member States. The burden of providing the legal information referred in Art. 26.2nd lays on the courts of the Member States. The plaintiff does not provide such information.

34 Nevertheless, in these cases an important caution should be observed so that this tacit submission is valid. Indeed, in these suppositions, the competent court should make sure, before assuming its jurisdiction on the case by virtue of a tacit submission, that the defendant has been informed of its right to contest the jurisdiction of the court and of the consequences of appearing or not.

35 Two additional data are important, as pointed out by *Nuyts*.[43] Firstly, Art. 26 2nd para, does not specify the legal consequence of a lack of information to the weak party with respect to his right to contest the jurisdiction of the seized court. It seems convenient to sustain that, in this case, the defendant's voluntary appearance will not be enough to establish jurisdiction on the basis of Art. 26. Secondly, this lack of information should not constitute a ground for refusing the recognition/enforcement of the judgment in another member State.[44]

---

[42] *Mankowski*, Änderungen im Internationalen Verbraucherprozessrecht durch die Neufassung der Eu-GVVO, RIW 2014, 625.

[43] See *Nuyts*, La refonte du règlement Bruxelles I, RCDIP 2013, 1, 60.

[44] See Ceská podnikatelská pojišťovna as, Vienna Insurance Group v. Michal Bilas (Case C-111/09), in particular para. 29: *"That provision [former Art. 35, current Art. 45.1.e Brussels Ibis Regulation] concerns non-recognition of judgments given by to court without jurisdiction which has not been seised in accordance with those rules. It is therefore not applicable where the judgment is given by to court with jurisdiction. That is true, inter he/she allies, of to court seised, even though those rules on special jurisdiction plows not complied with, before which the defendant enters an appearance and does not contest that court's jurisdiction. Such to court in fact has jurisdiction on the basis of Article 24 of Regulation Not 44/2001. Therefore, Article 35 of that regulation does not prevent the recognition of the judgment given by that court."*

Section 8: **Examination as to jurisdiction and admissibility**

Article 27

Where a court of a Member State is seised of a claim which is principally concerned with a matter over which the courts of another Member State have exclusive jurisdiction by virtue of Article 24, it shall declare of its own motion that it has no jurisdiction.

Bibliography

Arenas García, El control de officio de la competencia judicial internacional (1996)
Arenas García, Las normas sobre verificación de la competencia en los Convenios de Bruselas y de Lugano: *Borrás* 389
Boschiero, Il funzionamento del regolamento Bruxelles I nell'ordinamento internazionale: note sulle modifiche contenute nella proposta di rifusione del 2011, Dir. comm. int. 2012, 271
Franzina, Il coordinamento fra *lex fori* e norme uniformi nell'accertamento del titolo di giurisdizione secondo il Regolamento (CE) n. 44/2001, Riv. dir. int. 2004, 345
Franzina, La garanzia dell' osservanza delle norme sulla competenza giurisdizionale nella proposta di revisione del Regolamento "Bruxelles I", Cuad. der. trans. 2011 (Vol. 3) No. 1, 144
Geimer, Die Prüfung der internationalen Zuständigkeit, WM 1986, 117

Grunsky, Rechtsfolgen des Fehlens der internationalen Zuständigkeit nach dem EuGVÜ, in: FS Hilmar Fenge (1996), 63
Mansi, Il giudice italiano e le controversie europee: dalla Convenzione di Bruxelles del 1968 alla Convenzione di Lugano del 1988 ed al Regolamento (CE) n. 44/2001: competenza giurisdizionale, riconoscimento ed esecuzione delle decisioni (2004), 285
Nielsen, The New Brussels I Regulation, C.M.L. Rev. 2013, 503
Nuyts, La refonte du règlement Bruxelles I, RCDIP 2013, 50
Schoibl, Die Prüfung der internationalen Zuständigkeit und der Zulässigkeit des Verfahrens nach dem Brüsseler und dem Luganer Übereinkommen, in: FS Rolf A. Schütze (1999), 777.

I. Preliminary remarks

Art. 27 has its original predecessor in Art. 19 Brussels Convention, according to which **1** "where a court of a Contracting State is seised of a claim which is principally concerned with a matter over which the courts of another Contracting State have exclusive jurisdiction by virtue of Art. 16, it shall declare of its own motion that it has no jurisdiction". The provision specifies when the conditions arise for the court of a Member State to declare that it has no jurisdiction, in order to ensure compliance with the exclusive jurisdiction rules laid down in European law.

2   This provision is not surprising if seen in the context of the European judicial area, where there is now a complex system of jurisdictional criteria of a general, special or exclusive nature; hence the need to ensure coordination of the judicial function performed in Member States through control of the grounds of jurisdiction. This control is all the more important when these grounds are presented as attributing sole jurisdiction to the court of a specific Member State. The European judicial area, in fact, has focused on identifying the disputes – on the basis of homogeneous and binding criteria throughout the Member States – regarding which there are mandatory grounds that are strong enough to prevail over any other criterion laid down in the Regulation, whether general or special, as well as to invalidate any choice to the contrary made by the parties to the dispute.

3   On one hand, therefore, any court situated within the territory of another Member State must deem itself without jurisdiction over such disputes, and, on the other hand, the court identified on the basis of one of the grounds laid down in Art. 24 must deem that it has exclusive jurisdiction in Europe,[1] so that the violation of an exclusive criterion must be established of its own motion *(ex officio)* by any court seised of the claim (Art. 27) and is an impediment for the recognition and enforcement of judgments in civil and commercial matters in the European judicial area (Art. 45 (1)(e)(ii)).[2] The rule in Art. 27, therefore, should ensure prior compliance with exclusive grounds of jurisdiction and, at the same time, prevent non-recognisable judgments.[3]

II. The original proposal for a recasting of Council Regulation (EC) No. 44/2001 presented by the European Commission in 2010

4   Since proposal for a recasting of the Regulation 44/2001[4] was aimed at facilitating cross-border litigation and further developing the European area of justice by removing the remaining obstacles to the free movement of judicial decisions in line with the principle of mutual recognition,[5] the provision of Article 25 of Brussels I Regulation was not been left untouched.[6]

---

[1]   Cf. Art. 24 note 3 (*Lima Pinheiro*).

[2]   Cf. Art. 45 notes 102–107 (*Francq/Mankowski*).

[3]   *Carrascosa González*, in: Calvo Caravaca Art. 25 note 9.

[4]   COM(2010) 748 final of 14 December 2010.

[5]   Precisely, the document pointed out seven objectives characterising the proposed action: i) the abolition of the intermediate procedure for the recognition and enforcement of judgments (exequatur) with the exception of judgments in defamation cases and judgments given in collective compensatory proceedings; ii) the extension of the jurisdiction rules of the Regulation to disputes involving third country defendants, including regulating the situations where the same issue is pending before a court inside and outside the EU; iii) the enhancement of the effectiveness of choice of court agreements; iv) the improvement of the interface between the Regulation and arbitration; v) a better coordination of proceedings before the courts of Member States; vi) the improvement of access to justice for certain specific disputes;

Therefore in the context of the original recasting proposal new Article 27 stated: "where a   5
court of a Member State is seised of a claim which is principally concerned with a matter
over which it has no jurisdiction under this Regulation, it shall declare of its own motion that
it has no jurisdiction".

The *ratio* of such changing shall be mentioned. The removal of the obstacles to the free   6
movement of decisions implied, in this first perspective, the abolition of the *exequatur*
procedure, which allows the court of the execution's State to check the judgement for the
respect of at least four impedimental requirements; such an abolition implied the improvement of the mechanisms aimed at ensuring the respect of the jurisdiction criteria set forth by
the Regulation, specifically enlarging the powers of the court with reference to the *quaestio
iurisdictionis*.

Therefore, the Commission proposal wanted the court to declare, by his own motion, the   7
lack of jurisdiction each time the plaintiff sued the defendant (by virtue of original Art. 4(2)
of the Proposal it did not matter if he was domiciled within the EU or not) not respecting the
criteria of the Regulation, independently from the fact that the claim which was principally
concerned fell within a matter over which the courts of another Member State have exclusive
jurisdiction *ex* Article 22 Brussels I Regulation. This means that the exceptional rule which
allowed the judge to check for his jurisdiction, irrespective from parties' procedural autonomy, only when exclusive *fora* are concerned, was been converted in a general rule with
reference to all jurisdictional criteria.[7] Obviously the new Article 27 had to be read jointly
with the new Article 28 (previously Article 26) of the Regulation, following which the judge
checks for his jurisdiction by his own motion only when the defendant has not entered an
appearance, and with Section 7 of the Regulation, concerning prorogation of jurisdiction.[8]

---

and vii) the clarification of the conditions under which provisional and protective measures can circulate
in the EU.

6   The proposal was preceded by an extensive consultation of the interested public, Member States, other
institutions and experts on the existing problems of the current system and possible solutions to it. On 21
April 2009, the Commission adopted a report on the application of the Regulation and a Green Paper
putting forward suggestions for its review on which a total of 130 responses was received. The Commission took into account the results of several studies on different aspects of the revision, notably a 2007
study, conducted by Prof. Burkhard Hess of the University of Heidelberg, on the practical application of
the Regulation and a 2006 study, conducted by Prof. Arnaud Nuyts of the University of Brussels, on
residual jurisdiction. Moreover, two further external studies collecting empirical data on the impact of the
different options for reform were requested (see: i) Study on Data Collection and Impact Analysis Certain
Aspects of a Possible Revision of Council Regulation No. 44/2001 on Jurisdiction and the Recognition
and Enforcement of Judgments in civil and Commercial matters, conducted by the Centre for Strategy &
Evaluation Services (CSES), 2010; ii) Study to evaluate the impact of a possible ratification by the
European Community of the 2005 Hague Convention on Choice of-Court Agreements conducted by
GHK, 2007), as well as two conferences on the revision were co-organised by the Commission in 2009
and 2010. Finally, meetings with national experts were held in July, September and October 2010.

7   *Franzina*, Cuad. der. trans. 2011 (Vol. 3) No. 1, 144.

8   Specifically, see new Art. 26(2), following which: "*In matters referred to in Sections 3, 4, and 5 where the
policyholder, the insured, a beneficiary of the insurance contract, the injured party, the consumer or the
employee is the defendant, the court shall, before assuming jurisdiction under paragraph 1, ensure that the*

By virtue of such a combined reading, we can assert that the changing brought by the proposal could be said to be significant but not revolutionary.

8   The main consequence of such a solution related to the relevance of the parties' autonomy in choosing the competent forum. Precisely, the relationship between the rule allowing tacit expression of the parties' intentions, that is to say by an uncontested appearance by the defendant pursuant to Art. 26(1) of the Regulation, and the originally proposed wording of Article 27 should be examined. Whereas no incompatibility between the two provisions existed,[9] it seemed that once the *quaestio iurisdictionis* arised, the court should have concluded for his jurisdiction by reason of the implicit parties' will.[10]

9   Notwithstanding the indicated reasons which suggested such an amendment of the provision on each court *ex officio* control on the ground of its own jurisdiction, during the following debate among the Council and the European Parliament it has been decided not to repeal the content of Art. 25 (now 27). This is almost due to the fact that even the content of the new Art. 4 has eventually been approved with the same formulation of previous Art. 2: the original idea to approve an instrument applicable to the judgments involving defendants domiciled in a third State has been definitely rejected.[11]

III. Implementation conditions

10 As expressly laid down in Art. 27, in order for this provision to be effective, three conditions have to be satisfied, namely: (a) that the court of a Member State, being the one *principally* seised of the matter, sees it *has no jurisdiction* over it; (b) that the claim falls within the scope of those matters governed by exclusive jurisdiction rules laid down in Art. 24 of the Regulation; and (c) that a different court in another Member State has exclusive jurisdiction in the matter.[12]

11 As regards the first requisite, Art. 27 itself states that the court seised is obliged to declare that it has no jurisdiction in favour of a court in another Member State every time it is the "principal", as opposed to purely incidental, court authorised to hear the dispute. Title to

---

defendant is informed of his right to contest the jurisdiction of the court and of the consequences of entering or not entering an appearance".

9   See also Council Regulation (EC) No. 4/2009 of 18 December 2008 on jurisdiction, applicable law, recognition and enforcement of decisions and cooperation in matters relating to maintenance obligations, published in *Official Journal L 007*, of 10 January 2009, p. 1–79, where Article 5 states that "*Apart from jurisdiction derived from other provisions of this Regulation, a court of a Member State before which a defendant enters an appearance shall have jurisdiction. This rule shall not apply where appearance was entered to contest the jurisdiction*", while Article 10 states that "*Where a court of a Member State is seised of a case over which it has no jurisdiction under this Regulation it shall declare of its own motion that it has no jurisdiction*".

10 Being irrelevant if the defendant has his own domicile outside the EU (*Group Josi Reinsurance Company SA v. Universal General Insurance Company – UGIC* (Case C-412/98) [2000] ECR 5925) or if the rules in Sections 3, 4 and 5 apply to the case at stake (*Česká podnikatelská pojišťovna as, Vienna Insurance Group v. Michal Bilas* (Case C-111/09) [2010], para. 21–33.

11 Cf. Art. 4 (*Vlas*).

12 *Mansi* p. 289 fn. 8; *Carbone* p. 179; *Gaudemet-Tallon* p. 256; *O'Malley/Layton* p. 617.

ownership of a property, for example, may be a preliminary matter to establishing the validity of a contract of sale relating to the said property; in this event, nothing would prevent the court seised to hear the preliminary matter, to make an *incidenter tantum* decision limited to these circumstances and thus without the value of a final judgment.[13]

Again, the obligation to decline jurisdiction over a claim exists where the court seised has no **12** jurisdiction under Art. 24.[14] In fact there may be a case in which more than one court has exclusive jurisdiction: under Art. 24 (2), regarding "proceedings which have as their object the validity of the constitution, the nullity or the dissolution of companies or other legal persons or associations of natural or legal persons, or of the validity of the decisions of their organs", exclusive jurisdiction is attributed to the "courts of the Member State in which the company, legal person or association has its seat". Now, since the notion of registered office is not univocal, and must therefore be identified on the basis of the "rules of private inter-national law" of the *lex fori*, this may prove to be located within the scope of more than one legal system, among which that of the court seised. In this case, even if another court which has exclusive jurisdiction exists on the basis of Art. 24, the court first seised is not forced to decline jurisdiction. As expressly laid down in Art. 31,[15] in fact, "where actions come within the exclusive jurisdiction of several courts, any court other than the court first seised shall decline jurisdiction in favour of that court".

As regards the third requisite, on the other hand, the provision expressly rules that the **13** obligation to decline jurisdiction over a claim is limited to circumstances in which "the courts of another Member State have exclusive jurisdiction by virtue of Art. 24". This rule has two consequences. The first is that the court must only declare of its own motion that it has no jurisdiction when the exclusive jurisdiction referred in Art. 24 is violated, without considering any violation of an exclusive jurisdiction arising from a prorogation agreement pursuant to Art. 25 (except for the absence of the defendant, regulated by Art. 28 (1)).[16] The second consequence arises from the fact that Art. 24 cannot, at least on the basis of the express provisions of Art. 27, determine the so-called reflected effect, *i.e.* conferring exclu-sive jurisdiction also on the court of a third Member State, in spite of the comments to the contrary that are to be found in the case law.[17] Art. 27, in fact, does not lay down any obligation to decline jurisdiction where the criteria adopted in Art. 24 lead to locating the dispute outside the European judicial area. This conclusion, moreover, is confirmed by the *Almeida Cruz/Desantes Real/Jenard* Report,[18] as well as by the *Jenard/Möller* Report,[19] in which it is stated that exclusive jurisdiction, with specific reference to Art. 24 (1), is only applied where the immovable property is situated within the territory of a Member State. This conclusion, indeed, would seem to be reasonable taking into account the *ratio* itself of

---

[13] Report *Jenard* p. 39; where it is clarified that "The words 'principally concerned' have the effect that the court is not obliged to declare of its own motion that it has no jurisdiction if an issue which comes within the exclusive jurisdiction of another court is raised only as a preliminary or incidental matter".

[14] *Mankowski*, in: Rauscher Art. 25 note 1; *Kropholler* Art. 25 note 1.

[15] Cf. Art. 31 note 1 (*Fentiman*).

[16] *Mankowski*, in: Rauscher Art. 26 note 8.

[17] See, e.g., *Mansi* p. 288; *Gaudemet-Tallon* p. 256; *Mari* p. 761; *Carrascosa González*, in: Calvo Caravaca Art. 25 note 7; *Gothot/Holleaux* p. 84; *Droz* p. 108.

[18] Report *Almeida Cruz/Desantes Real/Jenard* para. 25.

[19] Report *Jenard/Möller* para. 49.

the European judicial area, which was created in order to allow an integrated judicial system to be set up in which judgments handed down by European courts circulate freely; uniform jurisdictional criteria were laid down to attain this objective, among them those in Art. 24. It would not be consistent with these basic principles to maintain the applicability of the Regulation even if jurisdictional criteria confer jurisdiction on a court in a third State.

IV. The examination as to exclusive jurisdiction and its features

1. The terms of the Regulation

14   According to the provisions of the Regulation, where a court is the principal court seised to hear a claim over which the court of another Member State has jurisdiction by virtue of Art. 24, the former court must declare that it has no jurisdiction. Control over compliance with exclusive jurisdiction rules can only be exercised of its own motion by the court seised, regardless of the relevant application by one of the parties or verification that the defendant has appeared before the court.[20]

15   In brief, the features of the examination as to jurisdiction are: (a) determination by the court, of its own motion, that it has no jurisdiction pursuant to Art. 24; (b) irrelevance of any national procedural rules limiting examination as to jurisdiction, making it conditional on statements by the parties or restricting it to particular stages or instances in actions; (c) irrelevance of the parties' will as regards express acceptance of the jurisdiction of the court seised; and (d) irrelevance of any tacit acceptance of the jurisdiction of the court seised and, therefore, the uncontested appearance by the defendant.

16   As to the means that the court may employ in order to establish the factual elements on which its jurisdiction is grounded, it must avail itself of the instruments envisaged in the procedural rules of its national legal system. Specifically, an "essential factor" in the frame-work of the European judicial area is that "assertions by the parties should not bind the court",[21] which, while assessing jurisdiction, may use all the means envisaged for preliminary investigation by the *lex fori*. After having ascertained the existence of jurisdiction, the court seised may decide the dispute "only if it is completely satisfied of all the facts on which such jurisdiction is based; if it is not so satisfied it can and must request the parties to provide the necessary evidence, in default of which the action will be dismissed as inadmissible".[22]

2. Relevance of rules of the lex fori

17   The Regulation states when the court is to verify jurisdiction of its own motion and when, on the contrary, such exercise is conditional upon an objection raised by one of the parties. It says nothing, however, about the instruments available to the court in order "to investigate

---

[20]   Conflicting opinions have been expressed in regards to the qualification of the decision on the existence of jurisdiction within the scope of application of the Brussels I Regulation. It results that, notwithstanding what internal law provides, the decision on jurisdiction has to be considered as *res judicata*, since it has a decisional character which is able to confer the capacity to be recognised within the European judicial area. Cf. Art. 2 (a) (*Rogerson*).

[21]   Report *Schlosser* para. 22; *O'Malley/Layton*, p. 619.

[22]   Report *Schlosser* para. 22.

the facts relevant to jurisdiction", which, accordingly, are to be found in the *lex fori*.[23] The latter, in turn, might even not make any provision for the court to autonomously act of its own motion, with the effect of imposing "the burden of proof in this respect on the party interested in the jurisdiction".[24] This is not an anomaly in the functioning of the European judicial area because it has always been acknowledged that Community law (today European law) does not want to "unify procedural rules but to determine which court has jurisdiction in disputes relating to civil and commercial matters in intra-Community relations and to facilitate the enforcement of judgments".[25]

The point to be stressed is that national laws cannot operate in this sphere independently of uniform legislation. Specifically, the principles adopted in the European judicial area will bind the court seised in interpreting national legislation if the latter's application has the effect of interfering with the provisions of the Regulation, not to speak of the obligation to safeguard the *effet utile* of European law which makes it impossible to attach any importance to domestic rules that might otherwise endanger the full achievement of the purposes of the European judicial area.   **18**

Quite differently, domestic regulations cannot interfere with issues such as timing and the obligation to establish jurisdiction on the court's own motion. Relevant to this is the ECJ decision in the *Duijnstee* case, after the request for a preliminary ruling submitted by the Dutch Hoge Raad, which was in the position of having to resolve the conflict between Art. 419 (1) of the Dutch Code of Civil Procedure (according to which the Hoge Raad must confine its inquiry "to the grounds on which the appeal is based") and Art. 19 Brussels Convention, corresponding to Art. 27 Brussels I*bis* Regulation, according to which if a Contracting State court is principally seised of a dispute over which the judicial body of another Contracting State has exclusive jurisdiction, it "shall declare of its own motion that it has no jurisdiction".[26] In its decision, the ECJ stated that the provisions of Art. 19 Brussels Convention oblige the national court to act of its own motion to investigate the violation of exclusive jurisdiction pursuant to Art. 16 of the same Convention, irrespective of the fact that a domestic procedural rule may confine the investigation solely to the arguments submitted by the parties, thus impeding consideration of jurisdiction issues if the parties have not raised any objections in this respect. The Court's ruling is based on a more than obvious consideration, namely that European law prevails over domestic legislation if the latter is incompatible therewith. The Court's decision, however, also stated that the obligation laid down by (current Brussels I*bis* Regulation's) Art. 27 applies to all stages and instances of a lawsuit, and that it cannot be limited to certain stages in the proceedings, not even as a consequence of the application of the *res judicata* principle on the basis of national law. Specifically, the ECJ ruled that jurisdiction has to be verified even when the question has first arisen in the context of a submission to the Dutch Hoge Raad and not at the beginning of a legal action or in any event during the merits phase.[27]   **19**

---

23 *Mankowski*, in: Rauscher Art. 25 note 5; *Mansi* p. 289.
24 Report *Schlosser* para. 22.
25 *Kongress Agentur Hagen GmbH v. Zeehaghe BV*, (Case C-365/88) [1990] ECR I-1845.
26 *Ferdinand M. J. J. Duijnstee v. Lodewijk Goderbauer*, (Case 288/82) [1983] ECR I-3663 para. 15.
27 *Ferdinand M. J. J. Duijnstee v. Lodewijk Goderbauer*, (Case 288/82) [1983] ECR I-3663 para. 15. The decision has been followed by national courts: *ex multis* see Italian Cassazione civile S.U., 24 May 2007, n.

3. Irrelevance of the parties' will

20   Art. 27 obliges Member State courts to verify exclusive jurisdiction of their own motion, giving no weight to the parties' will. This is not surprising if one considers the nature of the disputes mentioned in Art. 24 for which European law has envisaged exclusive jurisdiction. This means that the provisions of this Article prevail over all other jurisdictional criteria laid down in the Regulation, and that they are mandatory, meaning that they cannot be over-ruled by any intention to the contrary expressed by the parties to the dispute. The grounds for jurisdiction listed in Art. 24, therefore, prevail over any other jurisdictional criteria mentioned in the Regulation and at the same time represent a limitation on the validity of choice-of-forum clauses, and, more generally, on the free expression of the parties' autonomy in choosing the competent forum. Choice-of-forum clauses that specify the court called upon to settle disputes, outweighing considerations laid down in general or special criteria envisaged in uniform legislation, are, in fact, void if they depart from the exclusive jurisdiction criteria of European law. Specifically, a prorogation clause that conflicts with the provisions of Art. 24 may not be taken into consideration by the selected court, which is obliged to decline its jurisdiction over the claim. At the same time, parties are not allowed to circumvent the provisions of Art. 24 even through a tacit expression of their intentions, that is to say by an uncontested appearance by the defendant pursuant to Art. 26 of the Regulation.[28]

21   This conclusion, which clearly emerges from a reading of the Regulation, is confirmed by the *Duijnstee* decision, in which the ECJ stated that the provisions of Art. 25 of the Brussels I Regulation oblige the national court to act of its own motion to establish the violation of exclusive jurisdiction pursuant to Art. 22 Brussels I Regulation, even if neither party raises an objection to this effect.[29]

V. Verifying the grounds of jurisdiction

22   The provisions in the Regulation specify when the court has to verify jurisdiction of its own motion and when, on the other hand, this examination must be requested by the parties in the proceedings.[30] Specifically, Art. 27 states on what conditions the court seised must verify compliance with exclusive jurisdiction governed by Art. 24 of its own motion. This provision is completed by the following Art. in the Regulation, Art. 28,[31] which deals with examination as to jurisdiction in cases other than those falling within Art. 24, that is to say as regards general and special jurisdiction, or prorogation clauses based on agreements between the parties. Art. 28 states that in such cases the court's declaration of its own motion regarding jurisdiction is limited to the cases in which the defendant is absent.[32] Under other circumstances, an examination as to its jurisdiction by the court seised must be specifically requested by the defendant in the framework of his or her defence.[33]

12067; German OLG Düsseldorf, 22 November 2007; German OLG Karlsruhe, 22 December 2009; Portuguese Supremo Tribunal de Justiça, 29 June 2005.

28   Cf. Art. 26 note 24 (*Calvo Caravaca/Carrascosa González*).

29   *Ferdinand M. J. J. Duijnstee v. Lodewijk Goderbauer*, (Case 288/82) [1983] ECR I-3663 para. 15.

30   *Franzina*, Riv. dir. int. 2004, 345, 372; *Gaudemet-Tallon* p. 256.

31   Cf. Art. 28 (*Queirolo*).

32   *Salerno* p. 178; *Carrascosa González*, in: Calvo Caravaca Art. 25 note 4.

1. Verifying the facts relevant to jurisdiction

Questions arise as regards the powers of the court seised in verifying the grounds of juris- **23** diction in a variety of situations: (i) when the examination is based on factual elements as well as on notions with a legal status; (ii) both when elements that are independent of, and unrelated to, the merits of the dispute have to be analysed and when, on the contrary, the examination is intertwined with hearing and judgment of the merits of the dispute; and finally (iii) when the court has to conduct the examination of its own motion (in the case of exclusive jurisdiction and the defendant's absence) or, as the case may be, at the request of a defendant that has appeared before the court.[34]

In the absence of guidance in European law, the only solution is to consider the provisions of **24** domestic law along with the principles that can be inferred from the uniform law itself.[35] Within the legal systems of the Member States, in fact, debate has been sparked off con- cerning the limits to, and the powers of, the court's examination in the light of the principles deriving from domestic legislation.[36] Notably, a particular conflict has arisen between the so- called *presentation theory*, according to which the court must confine its investigation to the facts that the plaintiff submits in its entry of appearance, and the *full cognisance theory*, according to which the court must consider all the material that is relevant for the purposes of the judgment on the merits, including the possibility to request explanations and addi- tional information in accordance with the procedural rules of its domestic system.[37]

As a matter of fact, neither theory would appear to be fully satisfactory, since while it is true **25** that the powers of the court depend on the specific provisions of the domestic law that is taken into consideration in each case, it is just as true that the specific features of the matter submitted for its consideration, as well as the principles adopted in the Brussels Ibis Regu- lation itself, are also significant. In this regard, the ECJ confines itself to functional and teleological interpretative criteria, which allow the "useful effect" of European law to be pursued to the greatest possible extent, which includes cases in which the Court refrains from adopting uniform solutions in that it refers national courts to domestic laws, which necessarily differ from each other.[38]

In this context, domestic laws regarding the examination of the grounds for jurisdiction are **26** instrumental to the pursuance of the aims of European law, of whose enforcement they are

---

[33] *Gaudemet-Tallon* p. 256.

[34] *Mari* p. 746; *Arenas García* p. 152; *Geimer*, WM 1986, 117.

[35] *Franzina*, Riv. dir. int. 2004, 345, 372.

[36] With reference to the evidence problems, see *Mankowski*, in *Rauscher* Art. 26 notes 6 and 7.

[37] See *Mankowski*, in: Rauscher Art. 26 note 4. On the same point, see also *Mari* p. 746; *Born/Fallon/van Boxstael*, Droit judiciaire international (2001) p. 392; *De Cristofaro*, Il foro delle obbligazioni (1999) p. 276; *Salerno*, in: Scritti degli allievi in memoria di Giuseppe Barile (1995), p. 613; *Geimer/Schütze* p. 471.

[38] *Ferdinand M. J. J. Duijnstee v. Lodewijk Goderbauer*, (Case 288/82) [1983] ECR 3663 para. 14, where the ECJ points out that in order to construe the terms of the Brussel Convention, "it is necessary to consider the aims of the convention" and also that the rules of the uniform law, "which seeks to determine the jurisdiction of the courts of the contracting states in civil matters, must override national provisions which are incompatible with it", even where it refers back to the internal law of member States.

---

contributing within the framework of the Member States' legal systems; where there is an irremediable contrast with principles accepted at European level, the only solution is to disregard domestic provisions.

a) The qualification issue

27 A first aspect to be stressed is that in the framework of the examination as to jurisdiction conducted by the court seised the decisive question may be, rather than the existence or the location of the factual element determining the ground for jurisdiction, its qualification in legal terms. In accordance with the principle *iura novit curia*, the identification itself of the provisions governing jurisdiction and their interpretation are among the duties of the court, which must act independently in two respects: on the one hand, it is not bound by the allegations submitted by the parties and, on the other hand, it must take the above mentioned provisions into consideration in the European context.

28 An example might be that of a party that brings an action for damages as a result of an unjustified breaking-off of negotiations, invoking Art. 7 (1) on contractual liability. Although the case law of the ECJ does not require a contract to have been concluded in order for Art. 7 (1) to be invoked, it does consider it indispensable to identify a specific obligation freely entered into by one party with regard to the other; consequently any liability arising from the failure to conclude a contract cannot be described as being of a contractual nature, but one that falls under the definition of torts, delicts or quasi-delicts pursuant to Art. 7 (3) of the Regulation.

29 The court seised is certainly not expected to define the events on which liability is based according to the plaintiff's arguments, nor can it consider its own domestic law, but must assess these in the light of the interpretative guidelines proper to the European judicial area. We recall, in fact, that in interpreting the provisions of this Regulation the ECJ has worked out actual "autonomous notions" or has employed "Community notions", which are, on the one hand, strictly functional to the specific system of rules created by the Regulation in which they are intended to operate and to be used and, on the other hand, have the purpose of extending to all Member States, beyond any different significance in the various national legal systems, certain connecting factors or qualification criteria that appear to be particularly relevant in the mutual relationships occurring throughout the European judicial area.[39]

30 Every time, therefore, that the elements on which jurisdiction is grounded have to be defined, it is certain that the court seised must assess them independently on the basis of European case law and principles existing in the European judicial area, without considering the arguments submitted by the plaintiff, or rather the parties, in the matter.

b) Verifying the location of jurisdictional grounds

31 It appears that the court seised may arrange – based on the *lex fori* – for all the necessary inquiries to be made without being bound by the assertions of the plaintiff, or rather of the parties, even in identifying the precise location in which the element that constitutes the ground of jurisdiction is situated.[40] An example would be a case involving real property

---

[39]   *GIE Groupe Concorde v. The Master of the vessel "Suhadiwarno Panjan"*, (Case C-440/97) [1999] ECR I-6342 para. 11.

[40]   *Franzina*, Riv. dir. int. 2004, 345, 380.

rights, in which the court should examine the factual element of the place in which the property is situated with all the preliminary investigation instruments that its own legal system provides (Art. 24 (1)). The same conclusion would apply if the subject at issue were the validity of a meeting resolution, in the examination of which the court with exclusive jurisdiction would have to establish where the company's registered office is situated (Art. 24 (2)). Another example is an action involving liability for failure to perform a contractual obligation, brought pursuant to Art. 7 (1), in the State in which the contractual obligation should have been performed. In establishing the place of discharge of the obligation, the court is not bound by the plaintiff's assertions, and may thus pay heed to the defendant if he or she locates the criterion conferring jurisdiction in another Member State, or may arrange for this question to be further inquired into. In this connection, the court shall apply the provisions of the *lex fori*, which lay down the preliminary investigation instruments that are admissible and may be employed by the parties or by the court.

c) Contesting the claim's grounds

A different question arises when examination as to jurisdiction becomes necessary because **32** the grounds for the claim are disputed, for example because the very existence of the law that is the basis of the action is challenged. In these cases, the problem arises of establishing whether the court competent to decide whether the claim is well-founded is the court to which the plaintiff has had recourse, based on his or her asserted right, or whether, on the contrary, the claim must be ruled as being inadmissible.

The position taken up by European case law on this question is clear in that it recognises the **33** court that would have jurisdiction if the claim were justified as that enabled to take cognisance of the grounds of the claim. Specifically, the ECJ has ruled that a dispute regarding the existence of a lease falls within exclusive jurisdiction in the matter of real property rights and leases pursuant to Art. 24 (1).[41] A similar conclusion was reached with regard to Art. 7 (1), establishing that jurisdiction over questions arising from a contract includes the power of considering the existence of the elements constituting the contract itself.[42] In the *Benincasa* judgment, the ECJ ruled that the court specified in the jurisdiction clause of a contract has exclusive jurisdiction even if a request is made for the contract containing the clause to be declared void.[43]

In the cases submitted to the attention of the ECJ, however, the question at issue, rather than **34** the presentation theory, which binds the court to the plaintiff's assertions, has been the adoption of an interpretation rule capable of guaranteeing, on the one hand, certainty of law and, on the other hand, the useful effect of conflict rules relating to jurisdiction, with the purpose of avoiding their easy circumvention as a consequence of a dispute on the grounds for the claim. To consider that the court seised has no jurisdiction, in these circumstances, would be to conclude that "in order to defeat the rule contained in that provision it is sufficient for one of the parties to claim that the contract does not exist. On the contrary, respect for the aims and spirit of the convention demands that that provision should be construed as meaning that the court called upon to decide a dispute arising out of a contract

---

[41] *Theodorus Engelbertus Sanders v. Ronald van Der Putte*, (Case 73/77) [1977] ECR 2383 para. 15.

[42] *Effer S.p.A. v. Hans-Joachim Kanter*, (Case 38/81) [1982] ECR 825 para. 7.

[43] *Francesco Benincasa v. Dentalkit Srl*, (Case C-269/95) [1997] ECR I-3767 paras. 28 and 29.

may examine, of its own motion even, the essential preconditions for its jurisdiction, having regard to conclusive and relevant evidence adduced by the party".[44]

35 It is, however, important to emphasise that where jurisdiction and merits are interwoven, that is to say in a case where the same controversial element is the basis for the decision regarding the claim's admissibility and the grounds for it, a ruling on jurisdiction cannot condition the subsequent judgment on the merits. In other words, even if the court seised states that it has jurisdiction on the assumption of the existence of a specific circumstance that determines its jurisdiction, it does not necessarily follow that the judgment on the merits will acknowledge the existence of this right and guarantee the relevant protection.

36 According to this approach, the doctrine of the "double significance" of the elements determining the existence of jurisdiction would appear to be reasonable, if establishing these elements might also have the effect of prejudicing the decision on the merits.[45] The competent court's domestic legislation could not, then, deny the distinction between the two situations, treating them differently also for evidentiary purposes. In fact, ECJ case law seems to allow that it is enough to assert or present the facts constituting the grounds of jurisdiction envisaged in the Regulation (with those clarifications and remedies, if any, laid down by domestic law, specifically in terms of "probability" of the asserted right) for the purpose of examination as to jurisdiction, while national laws place an actual burden of proof on the plaintiff in order to guarantee him or her the substantial protection of the right invoked for the purposes of the judgment on the merits.[46]

2. The time when the grounds for jurisdiction must be verified

37 An especially delicate question is that of establishing the time the court must refer to in examining the preconditions for jurisdiction. The problem obviously does not arise where the jurisdiction criterion is fixed and cannot vary in the course of time. An example is the situation of a property referred to in Art. 24 (1), which cannot move its location unless there is a change of sovereignty over a particular area.

38 It is a different matter when there is a variable element, such as the registered office of a company, which can be moved. Obviously any legal person may move its registered office from one European State to another, or decide to locate it outside the European judicial area. In this case, to examine the effect of European law the time must first be identified at which the grounds of jurisdiction exist. Two different arguments have been presented in this respect: one theory considers that European law is of no assistance on this point, and refers the matter to the domestic law of the court seised, while the other theory does consider European law, finding principles from which, as a general rule, it may be inferred that the relevant time is that at which the action is initiated.

---

[44] *Effer S.p.A. v. Hans-Joachim Kanter*, (Case 38/81) [1982] ECR 825 para. 7.

[45] *Franzina*, Riv. dir. int. 2004, 345, 356; *Mankowski*, in: Rauscher Art. 26 note 5; *Ost*, Doppelrelevante Tatsachen im Internationalen Zivilverfahrensrecht zur Prüfung der internationalen Zuständigkeit bei den Gerichtsständen des Erfüllungsortes und der unerlaubten Handlung (2002), p. 15; *Mansi* p. 289; *Gaudemet-Tallon* p. 134; *Mari*, p. 746; *Proto Pisani*, Problemi e prospettive in tema di (regolamenti) di giurisdizione e di competenza, (1984-V) Foro it., 99.

[46] *Effer S.p.A. v. Hans-Joachim Kanter*, (Case 38/81) [1982] ECR 825 para. 7.

The ECJ has not taken an express stand on this subject, but in several instances has con- 39
sidered the question of the time at which the preconditions for jurisdiction in the European
judicial area must be found, ruling that this must be "only at the time that a claim in court is
submitted, thus initiating the action".[47] The ECJ's statement would seem to elucidate the
principle that the relevant time for the purposes of the enforcement of the Brussels Ibis
Regulation is the time at the beginning of the proceedings.[48] This corresponds to the general
principle embodied in domestic procedural law systems, according to which jurisdiction and
competence are considered in the light of the actual and legal position existing at the time a
claim is presented.

To conclude, it seems possible to state that the time at which to establish domicile is that of 40
the beginning of the action. According to some commentators there could be no exceptions
to this conclusion, as in the European system any element constituting jurisdiction that may
be presented in the court seised after the proceedings have begun must not be taken into
account.[49]

As a matter of fact, if one argues on the basis of the fundamental principles behind the 41
European judicial area, it seems necessary to consider the relevance of the factual elements
determining a ground of jurisdiction even if such elements have arisen after the beginning of
the proceedings, as this is consistent with the solution adopted in the majority of the
Member States. Practical reasons request that the situation is to be avoided where the court
seised has to decline jurisdiction in favour of a foreign court which has in the meantime lost
its jurisdiction. Such a conclusion appears all the more appropriate when considering that
within the Regulation a specific provision exists on *lis alibi pendens* that is perfectly apt to
avoid the overlapping of simultaneously pending proceedings.

Article 28

1. Where a defendant domiciled in one Member State is sued in a court of another Member State
   and does not enter an appearance, the court shall declare of its own motion that it has no
   jurisdiction unless its jurisdiction is derived from the provisions of this Regulation.
2. The court shall stay the proceedings so long as it is not shown that the defendant has been
   able to receive the document instituting the proceedings or an equivalent document in
   sufficient time to enable him to arrange for his defence, or that all necessary steps have
   been taken to this end.
3. Article 19 of Regulation (EC) No. 1393/2007 of the European Parliament and of the Council of
   13 November 2007 on the service in the Member States of judicial and extrajudicial documents in civil or commercial matters (service of documents)* shall apply instead of paragraph 2 of this Article if the document instituting the proceedings or an equivalent document
   had to be transmitted from one Member State to another pursuant to that Regulation.
4. Where Regulation (EC) No. 1393/2007 is not applicable, Article 15 of the Hague Convention of
   15 November 1965 on the Service Abroad of Judicial and Extrajudicial Documents in Civil or

---

47   *Sanicentral GmbH v. René Collin*, (Case 25/79) [1979], ECR 3423.
48   In this sense, see *Pieri*, in: Studi in memoria di Mario Giuliano (1989), p. 739.
49   *Pocar* p. 19.
*   OJ L 324, 10.12.2007, p. 79.

Commercial Matters shall apply if the document instituting the proceedings or an equivalent document had to be transmitted abroad pursuant to that Convention.

Bibliography

Alvarez Rubio, La regla de especialidad en el Art. 57 del Convenio de Bruselas de 1968 sobre embargo preventivo de buques, Anuario del Derecho Marítimo 1995, 273

Cortese, Regime comunitario della competenza giurisdizionale e rilievo delle convenzioni in materie particolari in caso di mancata comparizione del convenuto: brevi note sulla motivazione delle sentenze della Corte e sulla dottrina dell'*acte clair*, Corr. giur. 2005, 12

Belmonte, Sul coordinamento tra l'art. 57 della Convenzione di Bruxelles del 1968 e le altre convenzioni disciplinanti la competenza giurisdizionale, il riconoscimento e l'esecuzione delle decisioni in materie particolari, Giust. civ. 2005 I, 586

Beraudo, Regards sur le nouveau règlement Bruxelles I sur la compétence judiciaire, la reconnaissance et l'exécution des décisions en matière civile et commerciale, Clunet 2013, 741

Brière, La Convention dite CMR prime sur la Convention de Bruxelles, Recueil Le Dalloz 2005 Jur., 548

Briggs, The Brussels Convention tames the Arrest Convention, LMCLQ 1995, 161

Cadet, Le nouveau règlement Bruxelles I ou l'itinéraire d'un enfant gâté, Clunet 2013, 765

Ybarra Bores, El sistema de notificaciones en la Unión europea en el marco del reglamento 1393/2007 y su aplicación jurisprudencial, Cuad. der. trans. 2013 (Vol. 5) No. 2, 481.

I. Preliminary remarks

1 Art. 28 of the Regulation corresponds to (Brussels I Regulation's Art. 26 and, before it, to) Art. 20 of the 1968 Brussels Convention, which it does not change substantially, apart from the reference to Community Regulation 1393/2007.[1]

---

[1] Taking the occasion of Brussels I Regulation recasting, the former reference to the Regulation 1348/2000 has been switched to the new instrument that has repealed the latter from 13 November 2008, i.e. Regulation 1393/2007/EC.

Examination as to jurisdiction by the court seised is a basic principle that allows the Euro- **2**
pean judicial area to operate properly, and this examination must naturally be conducted
using techniques, and on the basis of principles, laid down directly by European law itself.
These techniques and principles are extremely simple to establish when the parties are
present in the proceedings and the court's jurisdiction is justified by a contractual provision
or by virtue of their specific actions in court, as foreseen in Artt. 25 and 26.[2] If these
circumstances arise, the only aspect to be considered (as specified by Art. 27) is whether
the matter at dispute is one reserved for the exclusive and mandatory jurisdiction of a court
in another Member State pursuant to Art. 24.

On the other hand, when differences of opinion arise, the system created by the European **3**
judicial area allows a defendant that appears in the proceedings to object that the court seised
has no jurisdiction if any jurisdictional criterion envisaged in the Regulation is violated.
When the defendant has not appeared, however, the court seised must verify that it has
jurisdiction of its own motion, also in this case by ascertaining whether any jurisdictional
criterion envisaged in the common system is violated. The examination must be conducted
on the basis of the contents of the available documents or on the basis of what the court
establishes independently, within the limits of preliminary investigation procedures and
subject to the restrictions in, and complying with, any further terms of reference envisaged
in its legal system.[3]

Very briefly indeed, therefore, European rules consist in: (a) the court seised that establishing **4**
its own motion stating lack of jurisdiction if the defendant does not appear or in the event of
disputes mandatorily reserved for the exclusive jurisdiction of a single court pursuant to
Art. 24;[4] and (b) the defendant's obligation to contest the jurisdiction of the court seised, as
specified in Art. 26,[5] in, and not after, his or her first defence statement, in order to prevent
the uncontested appearance to be considered *ex lege* as acceptance of the court chosen by the
plaintiff.[6]

II. Assessing jurisdiction and the relevance of the defendant's appearance

The joint provisions of Artt. 27 and 28 indicate that the court must, of its own motion, **5**
conduct an examination as to jurisdiction both in the cases of exclusive jurisdiction regulated by Art. 24 and in the event of the defendant's failure to appear. In the other cases, the
examination as to jurisdiction is only conducted by the court seised if expressly requested by
a defendant that has appeared, since his or her uncontested appearance is considered equivalent to a tacit acceptance of jurisdiction.

In practice, the situations in which compliance with exclusive jurisdiction has to be exam- **6**
ined of the court's own motion and those in which this examination involves the other
jurisdictional criteria as a result of the defendant's absence, are not exactly the same. It is
only in the first case, indeed, that the court must conduct the examination immediately; in

---

2 Cf. Art. 25 (*Magnus*), Art. 26 (*Calvo Caravaca/Carrascosa González*).
3 Cf. Art. 27 notes 18–21 (*Queirolo*).
4 Cf. Art. 24 (*Lima Pinheiro*).
5 Cf. Art. 26 notes 10–15 (*Calvo Caravaca/Carrascosa González*).
6 *Gaudemet-Tallon* p. 256; *Carbone* p. 173; *Salerno* p. 176.

the second case the failure of the defendant to appear must first be established, and only after this is confirmed will the court be obliged to verify, of its own motion, compliance with the jurisdictional rules laid down in the Regulation.

7 As it has been stressed, however, the Regulation does not specify the terms for the conduct of this examination, that is to say it does not explain "whether a court is itself obliged to investigate the facts relevant to jurisdiction, or whether it can, or must, place the burden of proof in this respect on the party interested in the jurisdiction of the court concerned", since this evaluation "is determined solely by national law". Nor does it clarify the instruments to be used for the purpose if the court is called upon to verify that it has jurisdiction (it makes no difference whether the examination is to be made of the court's own motion or at the request of a party). This does not mean that the application of domestic laws cannot be limited by European law principles.[7]

1. Assessing jurisdiction in the event of the defendant's absence

8 Art. 28 (1) is concerned with rules governing the enquiry as to the jurisdiction of the court seised in civil and commercial matters in relation to disputes not falling within Art. 24 (which are covered by an exclusive jurisdiction clause). In such a case, the enquiry as to jurisdiction must be effected by the court before which proceedings have been instituted through an assessment of the criteria and the factual circumstances so as to exclude (at least in principle) further assessments by other courts. This is particularly true with regard to the recognition of the effects of the consequential decisions on the merits or to the assessment of the so-called *lis alibi pendens* and related actions. In particular, the provision lays down that a court other than that of the defendant's domicile must, of its own motion, decline jurisdiction assessed on the basis of the provisions of the Regulation where the defendant has not appeared. This rule is designed to protect defendants domiciled within the European Union, so they do not find themselves judged by courts other than those indicated in the context of the Regulation where they have not themselves expressly or impliedly manifested their agreement to such jurisdiction.[8]

---

[7]   Cf. Art. 27 note 18 (*Queirolo*).

[8]   The rule, however, is not always correctly interpreted and applied by national Courts: in a case devolved to the jurisdiction of the Paris Court of Appeal, for example, the judge seems to consider that Art. 20 (1) of the Brussels convention rules a jurisdictional plea to be submitted by parties in the first defence act before the appointed Court (even if the Judge finally deems that the details of the jurisdictional plea submitted by the respondent are accomplished in the case, delivering a shareable decision): "*Considérant que la société AR DUE n'a pas compare en première instance; qu'en ne demandant pas expressément la nullité du jugement entrepris, l'appelante n'a pas saisi la cour, d'une déclinatoire de sa compétence au titre de l'article 20 de la Convention de Bruxelles; qu'en revanche, en ayant soulevé dès l'origine dans les premières conclusions (...) l'incompétence du tribunal de grande instance initialement saisi, (...) la société AR DUE soulève implicitement mais nécessairement, l'incompétence de la juridiction d'appel du tribunal initialement saisi; que ce déclinatoire de compétence est recevable devant la cour, comme ayant été soulevé avant toute défense au fond ou fin de non recevoir, puisque l'appelante défaillante devant les premiers juges, n'avait pas antérieurement conclu (...)*" (*Cour d'Appel de Paris, 22 octobre 2003, 2002/06111*). On the other hand, the English High Court of Justice, with an order of 22 August 1990, established its jurisdiction in a case where the respondent, French, defaulted, regardless of the check *ex* Art. 20 (1); consequently,

The provision, thus, requires the court of a Member State to assess its jurisdiction of its own **9** motion in matters in the commercial and civil field, excluding those listed under Art. 24, where certain conditions are satisfied, *viz.*: a) where an action is brought before a court which has no jurisdiction pursuant to the Regulation's provisions; b) another European court has jurisdiction on the basis of any criterion provided for by the Regulation whether this be of a general or a special character or based on the parties' will; c) the defendant has his or her domicile within a European State that is different from the one of the court seised; d) the defendant has failed to appear.[9] Where all the circumstances indicated above exist, the court which has no jurisdiction will refuse to hear the dispute independently of any application by the parties.[10] This means that the defendant will have no obligation to appear in order to contest jurisdiction since such an assessment must be made by any court belonging to a Member State of its own motion.

a) Requirement involving the location of the defendant's domicile within a Member State

The obligation to identify lack of jurisdiction of their own motion is imposed on all courts **10** belonging to Member States in the context of proceedings where a party domiciled in a Member State different from that in which the proceedings are instituted has failed to appear. This condition for the operation of the provision has given rise to considerable uncertainty and academic discussion.

On a first reading, the provision can be easily explained on the basis of the general principles **11** governing the functioning of the European judicial area: European law only applies when the defendant is domiciled within the European Union and leads to the granting of general jurisdiction precisely to the courts of the country where the defendant is domiciled. It is true that provisions of exclusive jurisdiction represent exceptions to the above principles. These, in turn, are dealt with in Art. 27 which requires under all circumstances the assessment of whether they have been complied with.

However, the jurisdiction prorogation clause departs from the logic and consistency of the **12** above reconstruction.[11] In theory, at least, such a clause is capable of attributing exclusive competence to the court first seised with the matter. This is unlike the provisions dealing with special criteria which leave the existence of the general forum in any case intact. In particular, where a clause has been agreed between two parties only one – or no one – of which being domiciled in the EU,[12] this will be subject to the Regulation according to the express provisions of Art. 25 (1). Its correct use is however not sufficiently protected by the uniform provisions. Art. 28 (1), indeed, imposes an obligation on the court to confirm compliance with the criteria used in the Regulation of its own motion only when the

---

French judges, applying Art. 28 (3) of the convention, could not examine jurisdiction in the recognition phase of the foreign decision, being obliged to declare its enforceability.

[9] *Mari* p. 743.

[10] See *Mankowski*, in: Rauscher Art. 26 notes 1 and 4; *Kropholler* Art. 26 note 6.

[11] *Mari* p. 744; *Mankowski*, in: Rauscher Art. 26 note 8; *Zucconi Galli Fonseca*, Competenza (competenza giurisdizionale nella Convenzione di Bruxelles del 1968): Enciclopedia giuridica (1988), para. 5 (1).

[12] Under Art. 25, if the parties, regardless of their domicile, have agreed that a court or the courts of a Member State are to have jurisdiction to settle any disputes which have arisen or which may arise in connection with a particular legal relationship, that court or those courts shall have jurisdiction. Such jurisdiction shall be exclusive unless the parties have agreed otherwise.

defendant is domiciled in a Member State different from that of the court seised. This means that if a defendant not appearing is not domiciled in the EU, a jurisdiction prorogation clause would be rendered ineffective by the contrary interpretation of Art. 28 (1) which requires the court to examine its jurisdiction of its own motion only where the defendant is domiciled in the EU. If this provision is interpreted literally it leads to an infringement of Art. 25 of the Regulation. It also represents a discrimination against parties not domiciled in the European Union, not easily reconcilable with the principle of equality and non-discrimination in the defence of a party's rights which should be guaranteed to all defendants in legal proceedings, irrespective of their place of domicile.[13] The contracting party not domiciled in the European Union, unlike the domiciled party, would be required to appear before the court seised to contrast its jurisdiction without being able to invoke the protection guaranteed under Art. 28 (1).

13   On closer inspection it appears that the provision at issue conflicts with the content of Art. 25 even where the defendant is domiciled in the EU. In such a case, indeed, the party domiciled in a third country could certainly initiate proceedings in the courts indicated in the jurisdiction agreement; it could also do so, however, in the country where the defendant is domiciled and such courts will not be able, of their own motion, to enforce the prorogation clause for the benefit of other Member State courts. This conclusion appears to run contrary to the principles in the field of agreements on jurisdiction which play a role of primary importance in identifying the court with jurisdiction within the European judicial area. Prorogation clauses, the expression of the parties' autonomy, are supposed to prevail over both the general and special criteria set out in the Regulation.[14]

14   For the reasons set out above, different interpretations have been suggested for Art. 28 (1) which adopt diametrically opposed solutions. To avoid discrimination in the enforcement of the Regulation it has been suggested, on the one hand, that the existence of a contractual prorogation may never be identified by the court of its own motion whenever the defendant who has failed to appear is domiciled in another state of the European Union.[15] This means that the failure to appear is to be seen as an implied choice of the defendant not to uphold the jurisdiction of the court chosen under the agreement rather than an overall refusal of the court seised by the plaintiff. On the other hand, according to a preferable line of interpretation, it is possible to argue that the requirement of the domicile in a Member State provided for under Art. 28 (1) does not apply in the event of a prorogation of jurisdiction.[16] This is not only to guarantee the effectiveness of the choice of the parties on the matter but also because of the unacceptable consequences in terms of discriminatory treatment which would otherwise occur.

---

13   *Droz* p. 158.

14   In many cases the ECJ has stated that the agreement conferring jurisdiction "excludes both jurisdiction as determined by the general principle of the defendants courts laid down in Art. 2 and the special jurisdictions provided for in Art. 5 and 6". See *MSG v. Les Gravières Rhénanes SARL*, (Case C-106/95) [1997], ECR I-911 para. 14. As regards older decisions, cf. *Estasis Salotti v. Rüwa*, (Case 24/76) [1976] ECR 1841; *Meeth v. Glacetal*, (Case 23/78) [1978] ECR 2133; *Zelger v. Salinitri*, (Case 56/79) [1980] ECR 89.

15   *Zucconi Galli Fonseca*: Enciclopedia giuridica (1988), para. 5 (1).

16   This principle seems to be expressed by Report *Schlosser* para. 22 "a court must also of its own motion consider whether there exists an agreement on jurisdiction which excludes the court's jurisdiction and which is valid in accordance with Article 17".

b) Relevance of jurisdiction criteria laid down in international conventions

Art. 28 (1) expressly provides that in a case where the defendant domiciled in a different   15
Member State fails to appear before the court seised, such court must, of its own motion,
decline its jurisdiction "unless its jurisdiction is derived from the provisions of this Regulation". It is precisely on the basis of a literal interpretation of the above text that it has been
proposed that the courts of a Member State before which a dispute in civil or commercial
matters is brought should decline jurisdiction if the defendant does not appear even if they
have jurisdiction on the basis of provisions contained in special conventions safeguarded by
European law. Reference is made to the Conventions taken into account by Art. 71[17] of the
Regulation which lays down that the Regulation will not affect agreements to which Member
States are contracting parties governing jurisdictional competence, recognition and enforcement of decisions in specific matters.

In a case brought before the ECJ the need arose to consider jurisdiction deriving from the   16
provisions of the Convention on the contract for the international carriage of goods by road
signed in Geneva on May 19, 1956 (so-called "CMR"), intended to apply to all contracts
involving the transport of goods by road for reward when the place for the receipt of the
goods and the intended place of delivery are located in two different countries of which at
least one is a party to the Convention.[18] According to the express provisions of Art. 28 (1)
(corresponding to Art. 20 (1) of Brussels Convention) in the case of the defendant's absence
or failure to appear before the court, the court seised must declare of its own motion that it
has no jurisdiction unless its jurisdiction is grounded on criteria laid down by the European
law. For this reason the *Landgericht Memmingen* had declined jurisdiction notwithstanding
the fact that it was the competent court under the CMR. An appeal was filed against this
decision to the *Oberlandesgericht München* which referred the matter to the ECJ for preliminary ruling. The latter Court relied on the joint corresponding provisions of Art. 28 (1)
and Art. 71, introducing an exception to the general rule under which European law shall
prevail over other conventions signed by Member States for cases involving special conventions, that is concerned with particular matters in relation to which it is appropriate to
introduce special rules.[19] On this basis it was decided that the courts seised are to accept
jurisdiction also on the basis of international conventions and, in such cases, they are not
forced to decline to settle the dispute. The ECJ decided on this point that jurisdiction
deriving from a special convention is to be included as part of the rules applying in the
European judicial area since it is precisely European law which safeguards jurisdictional
criteria contained in special conventions. For this reason it concluded that in a case in which
a party domiciled in one contracting State has been summoned before the courts of another

---

[17]   Cf. Art. 71 (*Mankowski*).
[18]   *Nürnberger Allgemeine Versicherungs AG v. Portbridge Transport International BV*, (Case C-148/03)
       [2004] ECR I-10327. The very same position can be find, having regard to the national jurisprudence,
       in the Austian case judged by *Bundesgerichtshof* on 27 February 2003, I ZR 58/02, published in *European
       Transport Law* [2003] 652: "*das Berufungsgericht ist weiter rechtsfehlerfrei davon ausgegangen, dass die
       Anwendung der Regelung des Art. 31 CMR nicht durch Art. 57 Abs. 1, 2 i.V.m. Art. 20 EuGVÜ ausges-
       chlossen ist*".
[19]   For a former statement of this principle see *The owners of the cargo lately laden on board the ship "Tatry"*
       v. *The owners of the ship "Maciej Rataj"*, (Case C-406/92) [1994] ECR I-5439 para. 24. For a comment see
       Briggs, Lloyd's Maritime and Commercial Law Quarterly (1995), p. 161; *Alvarez Rubio*, Anuario del
       Derecho Marítimo (1995), p. 273.

contracting State and has failed to appear, the court concerned must take account of the rules on jurisdiction contained in the relevant special convention without being required to decline jurisdiction.[20]

2. Assessing jurisdiction in the case of the defendant's appearance

17   Under the joint provisions of Artt. 26 (1), 27 and 28 the court seised, in disputes where exclusive jurisdiction does not apply and the defendant has appeared, will only be required to deal with the question of its jurisdiction should a specific application be made by one of the parties. The appearance of a defendant not challenging the jurisdiction of the court seised in its initial and main defence is thus deemed to represent a tacit acceptance of such jurisdiction according to the precise wording of Art. 26 (1). The only limit on this provision is compliance with exclusive jurisdiction referred to in Art. 24.[21] Acceptance of jurisdiction prevails over the other criteria set out in the uniform law even superseding provisions contained in a clause concerned with the choice of the competent *forum*. The recognition of the role of the parties' autonomy in the choice of the jurisdictional body leads to weight being given to the parties' will in all its manifestations, whether expressed prior to, or after, the initiation of proceedings. In this context tacit acceptance is recognised as superseding agreements that may have been concluded earlier on due to the fact that such agreements represent a willingness of the parties that is no longer actual when the proceedings are initiated.

18   This means that if a defendant challenges the jurisdiction of the court seised, the court will be required to make the appropriate enquiries and checks on the relevant circumstances to justify its jurisdictional competence. If, however, the defendant does not challenge the chosen court's jurisdictional competence despite entering an appearance, the court seised will be entitled to consider the exercise of its jurisdiction as being legitimate on this ground alone (as clearly stated in Art. 26 (1)) so long as it is not a matter reserved to the exclusive and mandatory jurisdiction of another European court pursuant to Art. 24.

III. Assessing the service of process on the absent defendant

19   The sensitive nature and importance of the failure to appear in the context of the court's enquiry as to its jurisdiction justifies the provisions contained in Art. 28 (2) of the Regulation according to which the court seised will be required to stay proceedings until it has been able to confirm that the defendant not appearing has been given the possibility of receiving the application initiating the proceedings or an equivalent document in sufficient time to be able to present a defence or confirm that everything possible has been done in order to allow him or her to do so.[22]

---

20   *Nürnberger Allgemeine Versicherungs AG v. Portbridge Transport International BV*, (Case C-148/03) [2004] ECR I-10327 para. 18. For a comment see *Cortese*, Il Corriere giuridico (2005), p. 12; *Belmonte*, Giustizia civile (2005), I, p. 586; *Brière*, Recueil Le Dalloz (2005) Jur., p. 548. More recently see *TNT Express Nederland BV v. AXA Versicherung AG*, (Case C-533/08) [2010].

21   On the acceptance of jurisdiction and its difference compared with derogation cf. Art. 25 (*Magnus*) and Art. 26 (*Calvo Caravaca/Carrascosa González*).

22   The reference not only to "the document instituting the proceedings" but also to every "equivalent

The provision is of fundamental importance and it is intended to protect the principle of   20
granting each party the right to controvert in a trial from the beginning and more generally,
the right of defence which may be prejudiced by the incorrect service of the initial documentation.[23] But there is more. The provision must also take account of legitimate practical
reasons, since the protection of the defendant may not be allowed to compromise the
plaintiff's right to jurisdictional protection through the possibility of rendering the notice
or communication concerned ineffective.

The provision has its corollary in Art. 45 (1) (b),[24] which provides that a decision of courts of   21
a contracting State reached in breach of the principle of the right to controvert in a trial, may
not circulate freely across the European judicial area "where it was given in default of
appearance, if the defendant was not served with the document which instituted the proceedings or with an equivalent document in sufficient time and in such a way as to enable
him to arrange for his defence". It must be remembered that according to a consistent line of
case law of the ECJ, the enquiry conducted by the court *(ad quem)* for the recognition of a
judgment, is not bound, on this point, by the results of the enquiry conducted at the
beginning of the proceedings by the first court *(a quo)*. In particular, from the *Klomps*
judgment onwards, the Court has stated that even where the original court has made an
express finding on the correctness and validity of service in terms of compliance with the
rules, the court of the State in which recognition is requested may re-examine the question of
the timely nature of the service in order to assess whether the defendant would have been
able to present its defence.[25]

This decision has been confirmed even in cases where the assessment of whether or not   22
notice was given in good time, was effected on the basis of the provisions of the 1965 Hague
Service Convention. The ECJ has noted that European law seeks to guarantee an effective
protection of the defendant's rights by ensuring that the assessment on the correctness of the
service is first of all entrusted with the courts of the State of origin and then subsequently,
again, with the courts of the State where recognition is requested. The rules on recognition
thus require that the court of the State where recognition is requested carry out a check on
the proper and timely nature of service notwithstanding the decision made by the original
Court in application of Art. 15 of the Hague Service Convention, in order to confirm that a
defendant who has not appeared, had the possibility of receiving the claim in good time to be
able to put forward its own defence.[26]

---

document" has been introduced by Convention of 1978, after the adhesion of United Kingdom and
Ireland.

23   *O'Malley/Layton* p. 622.

24   Cf. Art. 45 (1) (a-d) notes 36–59 *(Francq)*. See *Mansi* p. 292.

25   *Klomps v. Michel*, (Case 166/80) [1981] ECR 1593 para. 11, where the ECJ points out that "even if the
court in which the judgment was given has held, in separate adversary proceedings, that service was duly
effected, Art. 27 (2), still requires the court in which enforcement is sought to examine whether service
was effected in sufficient time to enable the defendant to arrange for his defence".

26   *Pendy Plastic Products BV v. Pluspunkt Handelsgesellschaft mbH*, (Case 228/81) [1982] ECR 2723
paras. 13 and 14: "The provisions of the Brussels Convention are designed to ensure that the defendant's rights are effectively protected. For that reason, jurisdiction to determine whether the document
introducing the proceedings was properly served was conferred both on the court of the original State and
on the court of the State in which enforcement is sought. Thus, (...) the court of the State in which

1. Service of process on the absent defendant "in sufficient time"

23   The double enquiry when effecting a valid process service on the absent defendant by both the court seised and by the court of the state where recognition is requested is also indispensable when considering that the rule laid down under 28 (2) (as that provided by Art. 45 (1) (b)) is expressed in extremely generalised terms. This is thus such as to give the domestic court a discretionary power in its assessment of the adequacy of the time granted to the defendant to draw up its defence following the service or communication of the document instituting proceedings. This is because it is necessary to reconcile two opposing interests. On the one hand there is the plaintiff's requirement for certainty which must be able to count on jurisdictional protection of his or her claims even where the defendant decides not to appear. On the other hand there is the requirement to guarantee the defendant's interests – he/she must be put in a position where he she is not only aware of the claims of the other side but also to prepare such defence she/he thinks best.

24   Moreover, unlike the provisions of the Brussels Convention, it is no longer necessary for the procedures existing in the country in which service or communication has been effected to have been complied with, so long as their breach has not prevented the absent defendant from being informed in good time of the document instituting the proceedings. Under the Convention regime indeed, the assessment regarding service on the absent defendant had a dual importance, being given the express provision laying down the obligation to assess, on the one hand, the correctness of service of the document instituting legal proceedings to be effected on the basis of the *lex fori* and, on the other hand, the granting to the defendant of a sufficient period of time in order for him or her to arrange an appropriate defence (an evaluation that was referred to the court). No doubt had been expressed in relation to the fact that the validity of the service and the obligation to serve the document in good time represented distinct and cumulative guarantees for a defendant not appearing. As a consequence, the absence of one of these two guarantees was sufficient to lead to the refusal of a request for recognition of a foreign judgment.[27]

---

enforcement is sought may, if it considers that the conditions laid down by Art. 27 (2) of the Brussels convention are fulfilled, refuse to grant recognition and enforcement of a judgment even though the court of the State in which the judgment was given regarded it as proven, in accordance with the third paragraph of Art. 20 of that convention in conjunction with Art. 15 of the Hague Convention of 15 November 1965, that the defendant, who failed to enter an appearance, had an opportunity to receive service of the document instituting the proceedings in sufficient time to enable him to make arrangements for his defence." More recently see *ASML Netherlands BV v. Semiconductor Industry Services GmbH (SEMIS)*, (Case C-283/05) [2006] ECR I-12041, par. 30.

[27]   *Minalmet GmbH v. Brandeis Ltd.*, (Case C-123/91) [1992] ECR I-5661. See, in particular, paras. 12 and 13: "It must be borne in mind first of all that Art. 27 Brussels Conventions sets out the conditions for recognition in one contracting State of judgments given in another contracting State. According to Art. 27 (2), recognition must be refused" if the defendant was not duly served with the document which instituted the proceedings or with an equivalent document in sufficient time to enable him to arrange for his defence. "It must next be noted that, in its judgment in *Isabelle Lancray SA v. Peters & Sickert KG*, (Case C-305/88) [1990] ECR I-2725 para. 18, the Court held that due service and service in sufficient time constituted two separate and concurrent safeguards for a defendant who fails to appear. The absence of one of those safeguards is therefore e sufficient ground for refusing to recognize a foreign judgment."

Such a scheme could, however, give added incentive to take the risk of not appearing, since   25
someone could take advantage of the situation which could arise following the incorrect
service of the document instituting the foreign legal proceedings, at least in cases where the
absent defendant only had to fear enforcement of the judgment in countries other than the
one in which such judgment emanated. It was precisely to avoid the situation where the
invalidity of such service could be invoked in cases where it would not have had an effect on
the actual possibility of arranging a defence, that the Regulation eliminated the provision
concerned, stating that the enquiry made for the benefit of the absent defendant must be
limited to confirming the existence of "sufficient time to enable him to arrange for his
defence".

It must finally be recalled that so far as the test of the validity of the service on, or delivery to,   26
the defendant is concerned, Art. 28 (2) expressly states that the document instituting the
proceedings does not necessarily have to be actually communicated to the defendant so long
as everything possible has been done to this effect. There is a similar provision in the Service
Regulation and in the Hague Service Convention.[28]

a) Inapplicability of the provision in the event of provisional measures
It is undisputed that the provision set out in Art. 28 (2), does not apply to actions initiated in   27
order to obtain provisional and protective measures pursuant to Art. 35.[29] On this issue ECJ
case law states that the objection to recognition on the grounds that the introductory
document must be served on, or communicated to, an absent defendant correctly and in
good time to enable him or her to arrange for a defence, was not conceived to be applied to
decisions of a provisional or precautionary nature which, under internal law, may be made
without the presence of the party against whom they are addressed and enforced without
having being communicated prior to the decision.[30] Similar considerations lead one to
exclude the view that the obligation of suspension and assessment of service must be guaranteed during the preliminary assessment of jurisdiction where the *lex fori* provides for the
possibility of granting such measures *inaudita altera parte*. The circumstance that the party
against which the order is directed has not had the opportunity of defending itself may
indeed represent an obstacle to the circulation of the provisional measure but it will not
automatically preclude it.

b) Link between second and first paragraph
The discrimination in the first paragraph between defendants domiciled in the European   28
Union and defendants domiciled in third States is destined to have an effect on the same
Article's second paragraph as well. The court seised is thus required to stay proceedings
while awaiting the completion of the enquiry into the correct service on an absent defendant
only in relation to the first category of defendants, leaving domestic law to lay down the
procedure to be adopted in other cases.

If this discrimination already raises enforcement problems in relation to the limitation of the   29
enquiry into jurisdiction by the court of its own motion, there is greater uncertainty in
relation to the enforcement of the second paragraph. The limitation entails, in particular,

---

[28]   See notes 2 and 3 *supra*.
[29]   Cf. Art. 35 notes 46–57 (*Pertegás Sender*).
[30]   *Bernard Denilauler v. Snc Couchet Freres*, (Case 125/79) [1980] ECR 1553.

two difficulties: the first concerns the operation of the uniform judicial system itself and the second relates to the failure to comply with fundamental defence rights.

30   With respect to the first point, the provision introduces the possibility of emanating decisions in the European Union where the guarantee giving the absent defendant the opportunity to arrange an adequate and timely defence has not been observed. It might be that such a decision is not recognised in other Member States according to Art. 45 (1) (b) which lays down the principle barring the circulation of judgments "if the defendant was not served with the document which instituted the proceedings or with an equivalent document in sufficient time and in such a way as to enable him to arrange for his defence" without this principle being limited to a defendant domiciled within a Member State.

31   In the second place it does not appear justifiable that the court, in the context of a dispute characterised by international elements, should adopt procedures intended to safeguard the right to controvert in a trial in a discriminatory manner according to the defendant's place of domicile. In this regard it should be recalled that a provision of European secondary legislation of the kind contained in Art. 28 must be interpreted consistently with the general principles of European law. There is no doubt that those general principles must include the fundamental rights guaranteed by the constitutional traditions common to the Member States which can also be traced to international treaties relating to the protection of human rights to which the Member States have acceded. Of particular significance among such treaties is that of the European Convention for the Protection of Human Rights and Fundamental Freedoms (ECHR), whose importance in the context of the enforcement of the European judicial area has already been confirmed by the ECJ. Art. 6 ECHR provides that everyone has the right to a fair trial. On the one hand, this is concerned with the speed of proceedings while, on the other hand, it recognises the right to controvert in a trial (Art. 6 (3)). The enforcement of Art. 28 (2) of the Regulation does not therefore appear compatible with Art. 6 ECHR, permitting the court to go ahead with proceedings where the defendant is not domiciled in the EU and has not appeared without a required adjournment to allow enquiries as to the service of the document instituting proceedings and the timing of such service.[31]

2. The implications of Regulation 1393/2007/EC

32   According to Art. 28 (3), the rules provided for by Art. 28 (2) are to be replaced by the provisions of Regulation 1393/2007/EC on service and communication in the Member States for judicial and extrajudicial documents in civil and commercial matters whenever "the document instituting the proceedings or an equivalent document had to be transmitted from one Member State to another pursuant to that[32] Regulation". This latter instrument has replaced, as from 13 November 2008, Regulation 1348/2000 (relatively to present analysis, it

---

[31]   *Franzina*, Riv. dir. int. 2004, 345, 376; *Béraudo* p. 15.

[32]   The formulation of Art. 26 (3) of Regulation 44/2001 was very similar, but it's necessary to underline that it ended with the reference to a document which has to be transmitted, inside the EU, "pursuant to *this* Regulation". The using of the adjective "this" had to be considered a material mistake in the English version of the instrument (shared – among others – by the Italian one, while the correct formulation could already be found in the Spanish linguistic version), since Regulation Brussels I was not intended to provide the specific rules concerning the transmission of documents between two Member States. So, the

should be noted that Articles 19 and 23 of Regulation 1393/2007 exactly correspond to articles 19 and 23 of the former Service Regulation of 2000).[33]

This means that Art. 28 (2) will cede to the provisions in Art. 19 Service Regulation when- **33** ever, in civil or commercial matters, a judicial or extrajudicial document has to be transmitted from one Member State to another to be served on, or communicated to, its intended recipient.[34]

The latter provision requires that the court seised suspends proceedings in order to confirm **34** service whenever the document instituting proceedings has to be served abroad and the defendant has failed to appear. The rule provides in particular that "where a writ of summons or an equivalent document has had to be transmitted to another Member State for the purpose of service, under the provisions of this Regulation, and the defendant has not appeared, judgment shall not be given until it is established that: (a) the document was served by a method prescribed by the internal law of the Member State addressed for the service of documents in domestic actions upon persons who are within its territory; or (b) the document was actually delivered to the defendant or to his residence by another method provided for by this Regulation". In either case, moreover, it is necessary that "the service or the delivery was effected in sufficient time to enable the defendant to defend". The court seised retains therefore, the discretion to enquire as to the sufficiency of the time limit imposed on the defendant enabling it to arrange for its defence independently of the requirements of the domestic law applying to the jurisdiction in which the service has been effected. Compliance with the requirement of correct service or delivery with procedural time limits laid down by the *lex fori* is not be enough, since the defendant must have been given "sufficient" time that is, long enough to arrange for an adequate defence.

This first paragraph is thus particularly strict in confirming that service or delivery has been **35** effected on an absent defendant. This is then mitigated by the second paragraph of Art. 19 which introduces an exception which Member States may decide to take advantage of, allowing proceedings to continue once a particular period of time has passed even in the absence of confirmation that service or delivery has been effected. In particular, it is provided that "each Member State shall be free to make it known, in accordance with Art. 23 (1), that the judge, notwithstanding the provisions of paragraph 1, may give judgment even if no certificate of service or delivery has been received, if all the following conditions are fulfilled: (a) the document was transmitted by one of the methods provided for in this Regulation; (b) a period of time of not less than six months, considered adequate by the judge in the particular case, has elapsed since the date of the transmission of the document; (c) no

---

new amended indication that could be found in Art. 28 (3) of Brussels I*bis* has to be considered the right one: the expression "that Regulation" is now clearly referred to Regulation 1393/2007.

[33] Even if Art. 26 (3) of Brussels I Regulation maintained the reference to Regulation 1348/2000, Art. 25 of Regulation 1393/2007 provides that – since its entry into force – any reference to the Regulation 1348/2000 must be considered as made to its content.

[34] *De Cesari*, Diritto internazionale privato e processuale comunitario (2005) p. 215; *Mansi* p. 294; *Frigo/Fumagalli*, L'assistenza giudiziaria internazionale in materia civile (2003); *Biavati*, Riv. trim. dir. proc. 2002, 501; *Frigo*, Riv. dir. proc., 2002, 102; *Marchal Escalona*, El nuevo régimen de la notificación en el espazio judicial europeo (2002); *Campeis/De Pauli*, Giust. civ., 2001, 238; *Ekelmans*, J. trib. 2001, 481; *Laporte*, JCP G 2000, 1947.

certificate of any kind has been received, even though every reasonable effort has been made to obtain it through the competent authorities or bodies of the Member State addressed".[35] This exception is equivalent to the corresponding exception contained in Art. 28 (2) in which it is stated that service on the defendant may be waived where the claimant is able to show that "all necessary steps have been taken to this end".

36 The majority of Member States have taken advantage of this possibility, informing the Commission of their wish to implement the second paragraph of Art. 19 Service Regulation, permitting the court to carry out the enquiry substituting the certificate confirming service on the absent defendant.[36] Only few countries have expressly stated that they do not wish to take advantage of this power granted by the Service Regulation, those being Italy, Portugal, Finland, Sweden, Malta, Polonia and Bulgaria.[37] In these countries the court will not be permitted to continue proceedings where there is no confirmatory evidence capable of proving the correct service of the related document instituting proceedings on a defendant not appearing where such service is to be effected in another Member State. This choice has been criticised because of the rigorous application of the provision relating to the stay of proceedings in the event of failure to enter an appearance and the need for appropriate documentation proving that service has been properly effected does not protect the interests of a plaintiff in cases where it is physically impossible to produce proof of the valid performance of service applying to a judicial document. However, this is without prejudice to the principle according to which, while waiting for confirmation of valid service on, or delivery to, an absent defendant, the court seised "may order, in case of urgency, any provisional or protective measures."

37 Under its Art. 19 (4) the Service Regulation makes further provisions to the effect that, even though an absent defendant may have been correctly served, the court is required to assess, outside cases of "judgments concerning status or capacity of persons", whether to "relieve the defendant from the effects of the expiration of the time for appeal from the judgment if the following conditions are fulfilled: (a) the defendant, without any fault on his part, did not have knowledge of the document in sufficient time to defend, or knowledge of the judgment in sufficient time to appeal; and (b) the defendant has disclosed a *prima facie* defence to the action on the merits". This is however qualified by the following statement: "an application for relief may be filed only within a reasonable time after the defendant has knowledge of the judgment".

38 In this latter case, each Member State "may make it known, in accordance with Art. 23 (1) Service Regulation, that such application will not be entertained if it is filed after the expiration of a time to be stated by it in that communication, but which shall in no case be less than one year following the date of the judgment". The Member States which have already informed the Commission of the manner of enforcement of Art. 19 (4) Service Regulation

---

[35] *Mansi* p. 296.

[36] *Mankowski*, in: Rauscher Art. 26 notes 10 and 11.

[37] Information shall be communicated by Member States under Art. 23 of Regulation (EC) No. 1393/2007 of 13 November 2007 on the service in the Member States of judicial and extrajudicial documents in civil or commercial matters (service of documents), OJ 2007 L 324/79. Concerning the choice of new Member States (Croatia, last of all) on this issue, it is easy to imagine that the behaviour (i.e. the declaration requested by Art. 23 Service Regulation) will be consistent with the Hague Service Convention of 1965.

have opted for a variety of different solutions. Thus it is that while Malta has provided a time limit of only three months, Belgium, Spain, France, the Netherlands, Scotland, Portugal, Cyprus, Estonia, Lithuania, Hungary, Slovenia, Bulgaria and Romania have laid down that the application to remove the bar on the presentation of an appeal may be made within one year from the decision and, on the opposite side, Greece has extended this time limit to three years. England, Wales and Northern Ireland require compliance with the time limit for the challenge as set down in relevant domestic legislation; Ireland and Luxemburg have given the court the task of enquiring whether the application has been made by the absent defendant within a reasonable time starting from the date when he or she first knew of the decision and, finally, Austria, Latvia and Czech Republic have expressly stated that it will not impose any time-limit for the filing of the application to remove the bar.

3. The Hague Service Convention of November 15, 1965

Where service or delivery is not governed by the Service Regulation 1393/2007/EC, the **39** Convention of 15 November 1965 on the Service Abroad of Judicial and Extrajudicial Documents in Civil or Commercial Matters will apply.[38] This entered into force on November 10, 1969, and has been ratified by 68 countries. So far as European countries are concerned, only Austria is not party to the Convention which is binding on all other Member States.

Just as with the Service Regulation, the provisions of the Convention are applicable every **40** time that a particular document has to be transmitted from one contracting State to another contracting State. In the same way as under the Service Regulation, Art. 15 of the Convention provides that "where a writ of summons or an equivalent document had to be transmitted abroad for the purpose of service, under the provisions of the present Convention, and the defendant has not appeared, judgment shall not be given until it is established that a) the document was served by a method prescribed by the internal law of the State addressed for the service of documents in domestic actions upon persons who are within its territory, or b) the document was actually delivered to the defendant or to his residence by another method provided for by this Convention". In both cases, however, it remains necessary to satisfy the requirement of transmission "in sufficient time to enable the defendant to defend".

It should also be emphasised that under Art. 15 (2) of the Convention, contracting States **41** have the same power as that provided for under the Service Regulation, being, the provision that the court "may give a judgment even if no certificate of service or delivery has been received, if all the following conditions are fulfilled a) the document was transmitted by one of the methods provided for in this Convention, b) a period of time of not less than six months, considered adequate by the judge in the particular case, has elapsed since the date of the transmission of the document, c) no certificate of any kind has been received, even though every reasonable effort has been made to obtain it through the competent authorities of the State addressed".

The provision does not prevent the possibility that the court seised "may order, in case of **42** urgency, any provisional or protective measures".

---

[38] *Jayme*, IPRax 1997, 195; *Borrás*, REDI 1989, 660; *Delgrange*, Gaz. Pal. 1988, 73; *Costantino/Saravalle*, RDIPP 1984, 451, *Alley*, 1989 Int'l. Bus. Law. 380. For further references see http://www.hcch.net.

Ilaria Queirolo

43 It is no surprise that the same countries that indicated their intention to take advantage of such a power under the Service Regulation have filed similar declarations for the purposes of the enforcement of the Hague Service Convention. In particular, the majority of Member States being parties to the Convention, have taken advantage of the provision, allowing the courts to carry out the enquiry to replace the certificate of service on the absent defendant. Italy, Finland and Sweden have decided to retain the more rigorous position requiring a stay on proceedings where it is impossible to produce proof of the correct performance of the service formalities applying to the document instituting proceedings. It should be noted that Malta, Poland and Romania, among the new Member States, have not filed any declaration stating their intent to use the more elastic system referred to under Art. 15 (2), while Bulgaria, Croatia, Cyprus, the Czech Republic, Estonia, Hungary, Lithuania, Slovakia and Slovenia (like Belgium, Denmark, France, Germany, Greece, Ireland, Luxembourg, the Netherlands, Portugal, Spain and the United Kingdom) have not imposed an obligation on their domestic courts to stay proceedings in the event of the absence of a certificate confirming service on the absent defendant, taking advantage of the provisions set out under Art. 15 (2).

IV. The dismissed 2010 proposal for the recasting of Art. 26

44 The Commission proposal for a recasting of the Regulation COM(2010) 748 also tried to intervene on Article 26 of the Brussels I Regulation (now Art. 28) but, similarly to the previous Art. 27, the discussion on the recasting project was concluded with the dismissing of the proposed changes. This is to say that the current formulation of Art. 28 is (substantially) the same of Art. 26 Brussels I. Anyway, the proposal's original content has to be mentioned, since it was conceived to solve the two main problems that afflicted – and that today are continuing to afflict – the specific rule. According to the dismissed proposal, Art. 28 of the proposal should read as follows:

"(1) Where a defendant is sued in a court of another Member State and does not enter an appearance, the court shall stay the proceedings so long as it is not shown that the defendant has been able to receive the document instituting the proceedings or an equivalent document in sufficient time to enable him to arrange for his defence, or that all necessary steps have been taken to this end.

(2) Article 19, paragraphs 1, 2, and 3 of Regulation (EC) No. 1393/2007 of the European Parliament and of the Council shall apply instead of the provisions of paragraph 2[39] if the document instituting the proceedings or an equivalent document had to be transmitted from one Member State to another pursuant to this Regulation.

(3) Where the provisions of Regulation (EC) No. 1393/2007 are not applicable, Article 15 of the Hague Convention of 15 November 1965 on the Service Abroad of Judicial and Extrajudicial Documents in Civil or Commercial Matters shall apply if the document instituting the proceedings or an equivalent document had to be transmitted pursuant to that Convention."

45 Such a wording of Article 28 was able to solve the two abovementioned problems concerning i) the discrimination among defendants domiciled within the EU and in third countries; and ii) the fact that the lack of jurisdiction should be verified by the judge of a European country

---

[39] This reference should have been correctly moved to paragraph 1, since in the context of the 2010 proposal the two first paragraphs of the former Art. 26 had been combined together.

by his own motion only if the defendant was sued before a court of a State where he had not his own domicile.

With reference to the first issue, it has to be firstly noted that the changing of (the former) **46** Article 26 was due to the general revision of Brussels I Regulation, that had been accused to be Eurocentric, therefore creating relevant discriminations on third countries domiciled persons by the denial of the application of uniform jurisdictional criteria and leaving free scope of application to national rules which also established exorbitant *fora*.[40] Therefore, in compliance with the extension of the subjective scope of application of the Regulation set forth by Art. 2 as originally drafted, the proposal deleted the reference to the need for the defendant to be domiciled in Member State in order to avail himself of the provision that allows the judge to verify by his own motion that his jurisdiction complies with the Regulation's criteria whenever the defendant has not entered an appearance. Such a solution was perfectly in line with the new formulation prorogation clauses (Art. 25), whose principal amendment contained in the 2010 proposal of recasting has been nevertheless kept in the final version of Regulation 1215/2012: the condition following which only prorogation clauses that have been agreed between two parties, one of which being domiciled in the EU, are subject to the Regulation, has been completely deleted. As already said, the combined reading of such a rule with Art. 26(1) of Brussels I Regulation has created an interpretative problem: if a defendant not appearing was a party not domiciled in the EU, a jurisdiction prorogation clause would be rendered ineffective by the contrary interpretation of Art. 26 (1) which required the court to examine its jurisdiction of its own motion only where the defendant was domiciled in the EU.[41] In spite of this, the final version of Regulation Brussels *Ibis* has maintained the original wording of Article 26 (now Article 28), like it did with the rejected amendments to the general provision on the personal scope of application of the instrument set out by Article 2.

Consequently, also the second issue was solved by the changes conceived by the original **47** proposal. In fact, when the defendant did not enter an appearance, Article 28 (in its version presented by the Commission in 2010) clearly erased the reference to the need for the judge to be "of another member State" in respect of the State of the defendant's domicile. On the contrary, following the old wording of Art. 26 that has been finally kept in the new Art. 28 of Regulation Brussels *Ibis*, the judge has to verify his jurisdiction *only if* he's not the judge of the defendant's domicile.

---

[40] See para. 12 *supra*.
[41] See para. 14 *supra*.

Section 9: Lis pendens – related actions

Bibliography

Bäumer, Die ausländische Rechtshängigkeit und ihre Auswirkungen auf das internationale Zivilverfahrensrecht (1999)
Bell, Negative Declarations and Transnational Litigation, (1995) 111 L.Q.R. 674
Brand/Herrup, The 2005 Hague Convention on Choice of Court Agreements: Commentary and Documents (2008)
Bruneau, Litispendance européenne et clause attributive de jurisdiction, D. 2004 Jur. 1046
Cano Bazaga, La litispendencia communitaria (1997)
Crawford, Ferrexpo AG v. Gilson Investments Ltd and ors: a flexible interpretation of the reflexive doctrine (2013) 17 Edin. L.R. 78
De Verneuil Smith/Lasserson/Rymkiewicz, Reflections on Owusu: the radical decision in Ferrexpo (2012) 8 J. Priv. Int. L. 389–405
Di Blase, Connessione e litispendenza nella convenzione di Bruxelles (1993)
Fawcett, ed., Declining Jurisdiction in Private International Law (1995)
Fentiman, Access to Justice and Parallel Proceedings in Europe, (2004) 63 Cambridge L.J. 292
Fentiman, Case C-116/02, Erich Gasser GmbH v. MISAT Srl, (2005) 42 C.M.L. Rev. 241
Fentiman, Parallel Proceedings and Jurisdiction Agreements in Europe, in: de Vareilles-Sommières, ed., Forum Shopping in the European Judicial Area (2007), p. 29
Financial Markets Law Committee, Brussels 1 Regulation Article 25 Cases, Issue 107, Report (Bank of England, July 2008)
Gebauer, Lis Pendens, Negative Declaratory-Judgment Actions and the First-in-Time Principle, in Gottshalk, ed., Conflict of Laws in a Globalized World (2007)
Reinhold Geimer, Windhunde und Torpedos unterwegs in Europa – ist Art. 29 EuGVVO bzw. Art. 21 EuGVÜ/LugÜ anwendbar trotz Parteiverschiedenheit?, IPRax 2004, 505
Goodwin, Reflexive effect and the Brussels I Regulation (2013) 129 L.Q.R. 317

Grothe, Rechtswegverweisung und Rechtshängigkeitserschleichung, IPRax 2004, 83
Hartley, How to Abuse the Law and (Maybe) Come Out on Top: Bad-Faith Proceedings under the Brussels Jurisdiction and Judgments Convention, in: Nafziger & Symeonides, eds., Law and Justice in a Multistate World, Essays in Honor of Arthur T. von Mehren (2002), at p. 73
Hartley, Choice-of-Court Agreements Under the European and International Instruments (2013)
Herzog, Brussels and Lugano, Should You Race to the Courthouse or Race for a Judgment ?, 43 Am. J. Comp. L. 379 (1995)
Idot, Litispendance, Europe 2004 Février Comm. n° 58, 24
Isenburg-Epple, Die Berücksichtigung ausländischer Rechtshängigkeit nach dem Europäischen Gerichtsstands- und Vollstreckungsübereinkommen vom 29.9.1968 (1992)
Kessedjian, Judicial Regulation of Improper Forum Selections, in Goldsmith, ed., International Dispute Regulation: The Regulation of Forum Selection (1997)
Leipold, Internationale Rechtshängigkeit, Streitgegenstand und Rechtsschutzinteresse – Europäisches und Deutsches Zivilprozessrecht im Vergleich, in: GS Peter Arens (1993), p. 251
McLachlan, Lis Pendens in International Litigation, Recueil des cours, vol. 336 (2008)
Marengo, La litispendenza internazionale (2000)
Nuyts, The Enforcement of Jurisdiction Agreements Further to Gasser and the Union Principle of Abuse of Right, in: de Vareilles-Sommières, ed., Forum Shopping in the European Judicial Area (2007), p. 55
Oberhammer, Internationale Rechtshängigkeit, Aufrechnung und objektive Rechtskraftgrenzen in Europa, IPRax 2002, 424
Otte, Umfassende Streitentscheidung durch Beachtung von Sachzusammenhängen (1998)
Prütting, Die Rechtshängigkeit im internationalen Zivilprozessrecht und der Begriff des Streitgegenstandes nach Art. 21 EuGVÜ, in: GS Alexander Lüderitz (2000), p. 625

Rauscher, Unzulässigkeit einer anti-suit injunction unter Brüssel I, IPRax 2004, 405

Saf, International litispendens, JT 2004, 653

Schilling, Internationale Rechtshängigkeit vs. Entscheidung binnen angemessener Frist, IPRax 2004, 294

Stafyla, Die Rechtshängigkeit des EuGVÜ nach der Rechtsprechung des EuGH und der englischen, französischen und deutschen Gerichte (1998)

Taschner, Ausnahmen von der Rechtshängigkeits-sperre nach Art. 29 Abs. 1 EuGVO?, EWS 2004, 494

Thiele, Anderweitige Rechtshängigkeit im Euro-päischen Zivilprozessrecht – Rechtssicherheit vor Einzelfallgerechtigkeit, RIW 2004, 305

Tiefenthaler, Die Streitanhängigkeit nach Art. 21 Lugano-Übereinkommen, ZfRV 1997, 67

Véron, ECJ Restores Torpedo Power, IIC 2004, 638

Wittibschlager, Rechtshängigkeit in internationalen Verhältnissen (1994)

Wittwer, Auch bei italienischer Prozessdauer gilt Art. 21 EuGVÜ, Eur. L. Rptr. 2004, 49

Zeuner, Zum Verhältnis zwischen internationaler Rechtshängigkeit nach Art. 21 EuGVÜ und Rechts-hängigkeit nach den Regeln der ZPO, in: FS Gerhard Lüke (1997), p. 1003.

Introduction to Articles 29–30

I. Summary of Arts. 29–34

1. Parallel proceedings within the EU

Arts. 29 and 30 of the Regulation[1] address the problem of irreconcilable judgments origi-   **1**

---

[1]   Arts. 29 and 32 have evolved from Arts. 21 and 24 of the Brussels and Lugano Conventions. The principal decisions of the Court of Justice on Arts. 21 and 24 are: *Jozef de Wolf v. Harry Cox BV* (Case 42/76), [1976] ECR 1759; *Owens Bank Ltd. v. Fulvio Bracco Industria Chemica SPA* (Case C-129/92), [1994] ECR I-117; *Gubisch Maschinenfabrik KG v. Giulio Palumbo* (Case 144/86), [1987] ECR 4861; *Overseas Union Insurance Ltd v. New Hampshire Insurance Co.* (Case C-351/89), [1991] ECR I-3297; *The owners of the cargo lately laden on board the ship "Tatry" v. The owners of the ship "Maciej Rataj"* (Case C-406/92), [1994] ECR I-5439; *Drouot Assurances SA v. Consolidated Metallurgical Industries* (Case C-351-96), [1998] ECR I-3275; *Gantner Electronic GmbH v. Basch Expolitatie Maatschappij BV* (Case C-111/01), [2003] ECR I-4207; *Erich Gasser GmbH v. MISAT Srl* (Case C-116/02), [2003] ECR I-14693; *Mærsk Olie & Gas A/S v. Firma M. d Haan en W. de Boer* (Case C-39/02), [2004] ECR I-9657.

Richard Fentiman   713

nating in different Member States, by preventing those parallel proceedings which might give rise to such judgments.[2] Both give preference to the court where proceedings are first initiated. They require proceedings in other courts to cease, by requiring the staying or dismissal of any secondary proceedings.

2   Arts. 29 and 30 are each concerned with different aspects of the problem of irreconcilable judgments. Art. 30 is concerned with the generic problem of irreconcilable judgments, and in principle regulates all cases where there is the potential for inconsistent decisions in different Member States. Art. 29 is concerned with the specific problem of irreconcilable judgments which compete for enforcement within Chapter III of the Regulation. Art. 29 is thus concerned to prevent *conflicting* judgments (those having mutually exclusive legal effects). Art. 30 applies to *inconsistent* judgments (those which reach different conclusions, but which are legally compatible). Art. 29 is thus an aspect of the Regulation's regime for the mutual enforcement of judgments between Member States. But Art. 30 serves the broader goal of ensuring the co-ordination of adjudication in the Union, and promoting uniform decisions.[3] As this suggests, although Art. 29 precedes Art. 30, and is often regarded as in some sense primary, this is misleading. Art. 29 in truth regulates a particular aspect of a more general problem addressed by Art. 30.

3   Arts. 29 and 30 seek to avoid irreconcilable judgments by identifying and controlling those cases involving parallel proceedings in which the problem is likely to occur. Art. 29 avoids *conflicting* judgments by regulating cases where the two sets of proceedings are legally *congruent*: those in which the proceedings have the same legal objective, and so may result in competing orders or awards. Art. 30 avoids *inconsistent* judgments by regulating proceedings that are merely *related*: those in which the legal issues are the same, although there is no risk of a competition for enforcement, because the legal objectives are different.

4   Art. 29 gives precedence to the first court in two ways: by requiring (not merely permitting) the second court to decline jurisdiction if the first court asserts jurisdiction; and by requiring the second court to stay its proceedings to allow the first court to determine its competence. Art. 30 permits (but does not require), the second court to stay its proceedings whenever there are related proceedings in two States, and to decline jurisdiction if both actions may be consolidated in the first court.

5   Under Art. 29, the second court has no choice but to desist, if the preconditions for staying or dismissing proceedings are satisfied. By contrast, Art. 30 confers upon the second court discretion to stay or dismiss proceedings. Arguably, there may be in effect a presumption

---

2   *Jozef de Wolf v. Harry Cox BV* (Case 42/76), [1976] ECR 1759, 1767 para. 12 with note *Hartley*, Eur.L. Rptr. 1977, 146; *Gubisch Maschinenfabrik KG v. Giulio Palumbo* (Case 144/86), [1987] ECR 4861, 4874 para. 8; *Overseas Union Insurance Ltd v. New Hampshire Insurance Co.* (Case C-351/89), [1991] ECR I-3297, I-3348 para. 16; *Mærsk Olie & Gas A/S v. Firma M. d Haan en W. de Boer* (Case C-39/02), [2004] ECR I-9657 para. 29; Report *Jenard*, p. 41; Report *Jenard/Möller*, p. 66; Explanatory Memorandum, paras. 1.1, 2.1, 4.5 (Section 9).

3   *The owners of the cargo lately laden on board the ship "Tatry" v. The owners of the ship "Maciej Rataj"* (Case C-406/92), [1994] ECR I-5439, I-5478 *et seq.* para. 54.

that the second proceedings should cease,[4] but the second court may choose to allow its proceedings to continue, if it considers that the 'presumption' in favour of the court first seised is rebutted.

Arts. 29 and 30 do not confer substantive jurisdiction upon the first court (jurisdiction over **6** the substance of any dispute). They merely regulate the behaviour of the court second seised. But in effect, they confer upon the court first seised sole competence to determine in which Member State proceedings should be brought (except it seems where the court second seised has exclusive jurisdiction under Art. 24). If the first court asserts jurisdiction, no other court may hear the case. If it does not, only then may the second court consider its own jurisdiction – only if the first court declines, may the second court assert jurisdiction. In that sense, Arts. 29 and 30 confer procedural jurisdiction upon the first court (jurisdiction to determine jurisdiction). Arts. 29 and 30 are supplemented by Art. 31 (1), which extends deference to the court first seised to cases where both courts have exclusive jurisdiction. The operation of all three provisions is facilitated by Art. 32, which (in effect) defines the moment at which a court becomes seised as that at which the first legally relevant step in the proceedings is taken.

2. Parallel proceedings in a third state

Arts. 33 and 34 regulate the very different situation where parallel proceedings arise in an EU **7** national court and in the courts of a third state. Such cases give rise to distinct issues of policy and principle, and the meaning and scope of Arts. 33 and 34 is problematic, and controversial. Given that the courts of any third state will necessarily not be a party to the reciprocal rules which operate between Member States, a degree of flexibility, with particular regard to questions of access to justice, is built into the mechanism for staying proceedings in favour of such states. Much uncertainty surrounds the principle that a stay may be granted in the interests of the proper administration of justice.[5] Considerable doubt also surrounds whether Arts. 33 and 34 supply an exclusive regime for the allocating disputes between the courts of EU states and third states. It is uncertain, whether, and in what circumstances an EU national court may decline to exercise jurisdiction on the basis that the courts of a third state have exclusive jurisdiction.

II. Irreconcilable judgments in the EU

Arts. 29 and 30 are together the engines of the Regulation's response to parallel proceedings **8** and irreconcilable judgments. But they cannot be seen in isolation. Another component in the regime is the principle of exclusive jurisdiction. Art. 24 confers exclusive jurisdiction on the courts of Member States having a unique interest in determining particular types of dispute, as where proceedings relate to immovable property within a Member State. Art. 25 confers exclusive jurisdiction upon any court to the exclusive jurisdiction of which the parties have agreed. Again, Art. 45(1)(d) offers a different solution to the problem of irreconcilable judgments (which it is the object of Arts. 29 and 30 to prevent), by determining which of two conflicting judgments shall have priority. Normally, the first judgment in time

---

[4]   *Owens Bank Ltd. v. Fulvio Bracco Industria Chemica SPA* (Case C-129/92), [1994] ECR I-117.

[5]   Art. 33 (2)(c); Art. 34(2)(d).

Richard Fentiman

prevails,[6] but where a foreign judgment is inconsistent with one obtained in the country where enforcement is sought, the latter is preferred.[7] The priority accorded to the court first seised is reinforced by the principle that jurisdictional error in the court first seised does not generally justify denying recognition to a judgment obtained there.[8] Only exceptionally does jurisdictional error justify non-recognition, as where the first court asserts jurisdiction in defiance of another court's exclusive jurisdiction under Art. 24.[9]

9 At first sight, it might seem sufficient to have rules for determining which of two conflicting judgments has priority. But Art. 45(1)(d) is no answer to the problem of inconsistent, as distinct from conflicting judgments: those which are irreconcilable but which do not compete for enforcement. And, if Art. 45(1)(d) is a cure for the problem of conflicting judgments, Art. 29 is intended to prevent it from occurring. In the scheme of the European regime, the possibility of resorting to the rules for the non-recognition of conflicting judgments is itself regarded as a problem to be avoided. The importance of the prophylactic role of Art. 29 has been emphasised by the Court of Justice. Art. 29 (in combination with Art. 30), is 'designed to preclude, in so far as possible and from the outset, the possibility of a situation arising such as that referred to in Art. [45(1)(d)], that is to say the non-recognition on account of its irreconcilability with a judgment given in proceedings between the same parties in the State in which recognition is sought'.[10]

10 The interaction between these related techniques for avoiding parallel proceedings may usefully be summarised: (i) The solution provided in Art. 45(1)(d) is to be seen as a last resort, as a problem to be avoided. Arts. 29 and 30 are the primary means to prevent parallel proceedings and irreconcilable judgments.[11] (ii) In the event of parallel proceedings involving a conflict between Arts. 24 and 25, the former prevails by virtue of Art. 25 (5). (iii) In the event of parallel proceedings involving a conflict between Art. 24 and Art. 29, it is likely that the former must prevail.[12] (iv) In the event of parallel proceedings involving a conflict between Art. 25 and Art. 29, the former prevails.[13] (v) In the event of parallel proceedings involving two courts having jurisdiction under Art. 24, the court first seised prevails, by virtue of Art. 31. (vi) In the event of parallel proceedings involving two courts having jurisdiction under Art. 25, the court first seised prevails, by virtue of either Art. 29, or Art. 31. (vii) Generally, a judgment given in the court first seised must be recognised in another Member State, by virtue of Art. 36 (1). (viii) A judgment given in the court first seised in breach of the jurisdictional rules regulating insurance and consumer contracts[14] will not be

---

6   Art. 34 (4).

7   Art. 34 (3).

8   Art. 35.

9   *Overseas Union Insurance Ltd v. New Hampshire Insurance Co.* (Case C-351/89), [1991] ECR I-3297, I-3348 para. 16.

10 *Overseas Union Insurance Ltd v. New Hampshire Insurance Co.* (Case C-351/89), [1991] ECR I-3297, I-3348 para. 16.

11 *Overseas Union Insurance Ltd v. New Hampshire Insurance Co.* (Case C-351/89), [1991] ECR I-3297, I-3348 para. 16.

12 *Droz*, para. 291 *et seq.*; see also *Overseas Union Insurance Ltd v. New Hampshire Insurance Co.* (Case C-351/89), [1991] ECR I-3297, I-3351 para. 29.

13 Art. 31 (2).

14 Contained in Sections 3 and 4 respectively.

recognised in another Member State, by virtue of Art. 45 (1)(e). (9) A judgment given in the court first seised in defiance of another court's exclusive jurisdiction under Art. 24 will not be recognised, by virtue of Art. 45 (1)(e). (10) A judgment given in the court first seised in breach of Art. 25 must be recognised. This is not permitted as a ground of non-recognition by Art. 45 (1).

III. Objectives of Arts. 29–30

1. Preventing irreconcilable judgments

The primary purpose of the provisions of the Brussels Convention concerning parallel **11** proceedings was to prevent irreconcilable judgments originating in different Member States,[15] although the avoidance of such proceedings may be regarded as desirable as an end in itself. The case law on the Convention emphasises that the objective is to remove any risk that the courts of different Member States might render different judgments in the same matter.[16] Reflecting its origins in Art. 240 of the EC Treaty, the mutual recognition and enforcement of judgments between Member States was the function of the Brussels Convention, and the avoidance of irreconcilable judgments its paramount purpose.[17] It is uncertain whether the objective of avoiding inconsistent judgments is paramount in the scheme of the Regulation. The Explanatory Memorandum to Regulation 44/2001 (the Brussels I Regulation) is ambiguous on the point.[18] But the Recitals to that Regulation suggest that the avoidance of irreconcilable judgments is but one objective of Arts. 29–30, the other being the independent goal of 'the harmonious administration of justice'.[19] This is repeated in the recitals to Brussels I*bis*.[20] However, the avoidance of irreconcilable judgments remains a primary objective of Arts. 29–30 of the Regulation, although it may now be one of several objectives of equal status in the pantheon of objectives.

Arts. 29 and 30 are each concerned with different aspects of the problem of irreconcilable **12** judgments. Art. 29 is designed to avoid *conflicting* judgments: those which have mutually exclusive effects, compete for recognition, and are thus subject to the rules for prioritizing between incompatible judgments. Art. 30 is intended to prevent *inconsistent* judgments: those which reach opposite conclusions, but have compatible legal effects and so do not compete for recognition. Thus, the purpose of Art. 29 is to prevent the vices associated with competing judgments: the inefficiency inherent in duplication, and the threat to mutual trust between Member States. The purpose of Art. 30, however, is to serve the independent goal of uniform adjudication within the Union. Thus, the objective of avoiding irreconcilable judgments is broadly conceived. Such judgments are to be avoided not only because they impede the Regulation's processes for the mutual recognition of judgments, but also because inconsistency in itself is intolerable within the European procedural regime.

---

[15] Report *Jenard*, p. 41; Report *Jenard/Möller*, p. 66.

[16] *Gubisch Maschinenfabrik KG v. Giulio Palumbo* (Case 144/86), [1987] ECR 4861, 4874 para. 8; *Overseas Union Insurance Ltd v. New Hampshire Insurance Co.* (Case C-351/89), [1991] ECR I-3297, I-3348 para. 16.

[17] Brussels Convention, Preamble.

[18] Contrast paras. 2.1 and 3.

[19] Recital 15.

[20] Recital 4.

Richard Fentiman

2. Ensuring procedural efficiency

13 Cases concerning the Brussels Convention emphasise the overriding objective of avoiding irreconcilable judgments by preventing parallel proceedings. But from the outset this has been perceived as serving the higher goal of the proper administration of justice within the Union.[21] The Recitals to the Regulation suggest that the avoidance of inconsistent judgments is but one objective of Arts. 29–30, the other being the independent goal of 'the harmonious administration of justice'.[22] Ensuring uniform adjudication is one aspect of procedural efficiency. In *The Tatry*,[23] the Court described the objective underlying what has become Art. 30 in broad terms, which suggest a general commitment to procedural efficiency beyond merely the avoidance of irreconcilable judgments. One of its purposes is 'to improve coordination of the exercise of judicial functions within the Union'.[24] In principle, however, there are certainly advantages in the avoidance of such proceedings for its own sake. It is desirable to avoid the inefficiency of duplicate litigation, and the manipulation of the legal process associated with a 'rush to judgment' in different courts. There is evidence in the case law that what are now Arts. 29–30 are intended to serve the Regulation's wider objective of procedural efficiency, which requires in turn that the Regulation's approach to parallel proceedings should be simple, certain and uniform. Thus, in *Gantner Electronic GmbH v. Basch Expolitatie Maatschappij BV*,[25] the Court held that it was irrelevant in establishing congruence between different actions that a defendant to one of them might have raised in its defence an issue not before the other court. In so ruling, the Court sought to uphold the 'objective and automatic' nature of the Art. 29 mechanism, which would be frustrated if it were to depend on the arguments advanced in defending proceedings.[26]

3. Promoting mutual trust

14 The Recitals to the Regulation and numerous CJEU decisions confirm the importance of mutual trust between Member States in the administration of justice.[27] Arts. 29 and 30 both express and enforce the principle of mutual trust between Member States. They ordain that the court first seised has (in effect) exclusive jurisdiction to determine its own competence, which both requires and implies a degree of trust between States. And they imply, as a consequence, that no other court may speak to the first court's jurisdiction. In *Overseas Union Insurance v. New Hampshire Insurance*,[28] the Court of Justice held that the operation of Art. 29 does not depend upon a finding by the second court that the first court lacks

---

[21] Report *Jenard*, p. 41.

[22] Recital 15.

[23] *The owners of the cargo lately laden on board the ship "Tatry" v. The owners of the ship "Maciej Rataj"* (Case C-406/92), [1994] ECR I-5439.

[24] *The owners of the cargo lately laden on board the ship "Tatry" v. The owners of the ship "Maciej Rataj"* (Case C-406/92), [1994] ECR I-5439, I-5479 para. 55.

[25] *Gantner Electronic GmbH v. Basch Expolitatie Maatschappij BV* (Case C-111/01), [2003] ECR I-4207.

[26] *Gantner Electronic GmbH v. Basch Expolitatie Maatschappij BV* (Case C-111/01), [2003] ECR I-4207, I-4257 para. 32.

[27] Recital 16; *Gregory Paul Turner v. Felix Fareed Ismail Grovit, Harada Ltd. and Changepoint SA* (Case C-159/02), [2004] ECR I-3565.

[28] *Overseas Union Insurance Ltd v. New Hampshire Insurance Co.* (Case C-351/89), [1991] ECR I-3297, I-3350 para. 25; *Briggs*, (1991) 11 YBEL 521.

jurisdiction. The court second seised cannot examine the jurisdiction of the court first seised, with the objective of ousting Art. 29 and asserting jurisdiction itself if the first court lacks jurisdiction.

IV. Arts. 29–30 in practice

The replication of litigation, between the same parties, and involving the same or related **15** issues, may arise in two ways: if a claimant launches parallel litigation in two courts; and if a defendant counterclaims in a different court from that in which a claim is brought. Arts. 29 and 30 address both cases, but it is perhaps their role in the second that is most important in practice. Arts. 29 and 30 are particularly important in practice for three reasons: they may determine the final outcome of a dispute; they encourage tactical litigation; and they have given fresh impetus to the practice of seeking negative declaratory relief.

1. Determining the outcome

It should not be thought that Arts. 29–30 are merely concerned with allocating jurisdiction **16** between Member States. By doing so, these provisions may have a decisive effect, not merely on the venue for proceedings, but on their final outcome. In reality, for most litigants in multi-state litigation, a dispute is won or lost once it is clear where a dispute is to be heard. In most cases, a defendant sued in a disadvantageous forum will capitulate, and a claimant denied access to its preferred court will withdraw. Moreover, in many cases, this will occur not when the court first seised establishes jurisdiction, but as soon as it is seised. The very fact that any issue of jurisdiction is to be determined in the court first seised may be enough to provoke compromise or capitulation. Moreover, the tactical importance of suing first is reinforced by the Regulation's rules concerning the recognition and enforcement of foreign judgments. Only in exceptional cases does jurisdictional error in the court first seised jeopardise the subsequent enforcement in another Member State of a judgment obtained in the court first seised. The effect is that it may almost always be worthwhile to initiate proceedings, and persuade a court of its jurisdiction, given that any judgment will be enforceable (presumably) in the judgment court, and (unavoidably) in any other Member State. The likelihood that the parties will settle or surrender once jurisdiction is determined, or once a court is seised, gives Arts. 29–30 particular importance. Their effect may be to hand final victory to the party who sues first; their role is as much substantive as procedural.

2. Tactical litigation

For this reason, the battle of forums is of decisive importance in litigation. It is especially **17** significant, therefore, that the mechanical nature of Art. 29 allows well-advised litigants the opportunity to win that all-important battle, and thus secure a perhaps decisive tactical advantage. Certainly, the Court of Justice has complied strictly with the logic of Art. 29, such that critics have condemned the Brussels jurisdiction regime as a 'forum shoppers' charter.[29] By commencing proceedings first, a claimant will ensure that a dispute is heard in its

---

[29]   For critique, see *Juenger*, in: Taruffo (ed.), Abuse of Procedural Rights: Comparative Standards of Procedural Fairness (1999), p. 357, 354 *et seq.*; *Kessedjian*, in: Goldsmith (ed.), International Dispute Regulation: The Regulation of Forum Selection (1997), p. 293; *Fawcett*, in: Fawcett (ed.), Declining Jurisdiction in Private International Law (1995), p. 34–39; *Briggs*, (1995) LMCLQ 161; *Fentiman*, (1995) Cambridge

preferred forum, even if merely declaratory relief is sought,[30] and (potentially) even if any contract between the parties submits disputes to the exclusive jurisdiction of another court.[31] It may be especially tempting for claimants to launch a pre-emptive strike by seising their preferred forum first where that forum is one in which a court becomes seised for Art. 32 purposes merely by lodging the claim (as in English law). This may be a relatively harmless precautionary measure if the claimant has a choice whether in due course to serve the claim, and where notice of the lodging of the claim need not be given to the defendant. Again, the effect of Art. 29 is that claimants are now unlikely to warn defendants of the possibility of proceedings, perhaps by sending the traditional 'letter before action', threatening to commence proceedings at the expiry of an ultimatum. To do so is to run the risk that the defendant will launch offensive-defensive proceedings in its preferred court.

18 The particular difficulties associated with tactical, pre-emptive litigation as a means to circumvent a jurisdiction agreement, using negative declaratory relief as a vehicle, have been partially removed by Art. 31(2), which confers exclusive competence on the designated court to determine such an agreement's effect. But Art. 31(2) is incomplete in its coverage, and the problem of tactical forum-shopping remains in cases not involving a jurisdiction agreement. As this suggests, the effect of the Regulation is to encourage a 'race to the courthouse'. Certainly, the importance of suing first is a feature of all cross-border litigation. But outside the Regulation this does not necessarily mean that parallel proceedings elsewhere are prevented. Outside the Regulation, parallel proceedings are the beginning not the end of the battle of forums. By contrast, the Regulation is striking because merely by suing first, the winner takes all. Moreover, the effect of the Regulation may be to encourage litigation which might never have occurred at all. At a time when many national legal systems are seeking to promote less formal means of dispute resolution, and to defer the moment at which the parties' feel compelled to litigate, the importance of winning any battle of forums that may occur, ensures that litigation will often be a weapon of first resort.[32]

3. Negative declarations

19 The practical importance of pre-emptive proceedings has enhanced the importance of negative declaratory relief in the Union.[33] Proceedings for a declaration of non-liability have the same cause and object as an action to establish the same liability between the same parties.[34] In consequence, one party may try to forestall proceedings elsewhere, by applying for a declaration of non-liability in its preferred court. In a sense such relief is no different in

---

L.J. 261; *Davenport*, (1995) 111 L.Q.Rev. 366; *Collins*, (1992) 108 L.Q.Rev. 545; *Gaudemet-Tallon*, RCDIP 77 (1988) 374.

[30] *The owners of the cargo lately laden on board the ship "Tatry"* v. *The owners of the ship "Maciej Rataj"* (Case C-406/92), [1994] ECR I-5439.

[31] *Erich Gasser GmbH v. MISAT Srl*, (Case C-116/02) [2003] ECR I-14693.

[32] A point noted in *Messier Dowty Ltd.* v. *Sabena SA* [2000] 1 Lloyd's Rep. 432, 432 (C.A.).

[33] *Andrea Merzario Ltd v. International Spedition Leitner Gesellschaft GmbH* [2001] 2 Lloyd's Rep. 49 (C. A.). See generally *von Mehren*, in: FS Ulrich Drobnig (1998), p. 409; *Loewenfeld*, (1997) 91 Am. J. Int'l. L. 294, 298 *et seq.*; *Bell*, (1995) 111 L.Q.Rev. 674.

[34] *Gubisch Maschinenfabrik KG v. Giulio Palumbo*, (Case 144/86) [1987] ECR 4861; *The owners of the cargo lately laden on board the ship "Tatry"* v. *The owners of the ship "Maciej Rataj"*, (Case C-406/92) [1994] ECR I-5439.

principle from a counter-claim, nor should it be seen as inherently devious or tactical. And, arguably, it cannot matter (especially in the Union), where a defendant mounts its defence. But intending claimants may find it troubling that a party, who may have no counter-claim, is entitled to select the forum in which a claimant's case is heard, especially if no claim has yet been brought, or even threatened. The tactical utility of negative declarations is underwritten by the ease with which a tactical claimant may engage the jurisdiction of its preferred court when applying for such relief. It is now clear that subject matter jurisdiction derived from Article 7 of Brussels I*bis* (formerly Article 5 of Regulation 44/2001) founds jurisdiction to grant a negative declaration.[35]

Some limit on this practice is provided by the relevant rules of national law governing the **20** circumstances in which negative relief may be sought. These might confine such relief to cases where a claim has been made against the applicant, or at least has been clearly threatened, and are likely to impose safeguards against abusive proceedings. But such limitations may be of little assistance in practice to the wrong-footed claimant. Merely to seek declaratory relief is unlikely to be viewed as inherently suspect. And even those legal systems which have traditionally regarded negative declarations with suspicion may now treat such relief as equivalent to positive claims, requiring no special caution.[36] But it is not merely that negative declaratory relief has become widespread in the Union. It may have a privileged status in the courts of Member States, in so far as the fact that a case falls within the Regulation may influence how any national rules regulating such relief are applied. Certainly, where a declaration is sought in the courts of a Member State, it has been said that this alone ensures that the applicant cannot be accused of forum shopping.[37] By definition, a forum available under the Brussels Regulation is an appropriate forum.

V. Underlying Assumptions

The operation of Arts. 29–30 (and, indeed, of the Regulation) depends upon certain as- **21** sumptions which, must be identified if the Regulation's response to parallel proceedings is to be understood.

1. Certainty not discretion

One assumption, concerning the design of the Regulation's response to parallel proceedings, **22** is that the appropriate forum may be sufficiently identified by the administration of rules, rather than by the exercise of discretion. Although Art. 30 is expressed in permissive terms – the second court may stay its proceedings in the event of related actions – this is unlikely to import anything resembling the common law doctrine of *forum non conveniens*.[38] As this implies, the unstated assumption is that the procedural rights of the parties are best protected by this means, and efficiency in litigation achieved, by a non-discretionary regime.

---

[35]   Case C-133/11 *Folien Fischer AG v. Ritrama SpA* [2013] Q.B. 523; see also, *cf. Boss Group Ltd v. Boss France SA* [1997] 1 WLR 351; *Equitas Ltd v. Wave City Shipping Co Ltd* [2005] EWHC 923 (Comm).

[36]   As in English law: *Messier Dowty Ltd. v. Sabena SA* [2000] 1 Lloyd's Rep. 432 (C.A.).

[37]   *Messier Dowty Ltd. v. Sabena SA* [2000] 1 Lloyd's Rep. 432, 433 (C.A.); *Boss Group v. Boss France SA* [1996] LRLR 403, 406.

[38]   Report *Schlosser*, p. 71, 97; the message of the cases is unclear: e.g. *Owens Bank Ltd. v. Fulvio Bracco Industria Chemica SPA* (Case C-129/92), [1994] ECR I-117.

Richard Fentiman   721

2. Parity between courts

23 A second assumption is that there are no relevant differences between the courts of Member States in terms of the legal and practical implications of litigation. This presumably follows from the automatic, 'blind' operation of Arts. 29 and 30 in particular.[39] Such a scheme cannot rationally operate if it is accepted that it may matter where a case is heard. It is also implicit in the principle of mutual trust between Member States, reflected in the fact that substantive error in proceedings in another Member State is never a ground for non-recognition of a judgment, and the fact that jurisdictional error is rarely such a ground. It is implicit that there is no (material) advantage to be secured by either party in suing (or being sued) in the courts of one Member State rather than another. Each such court is a natural forum. This is not to say that such differences do not exist, rather that they are irrelevant for present purposes.[40] This has important implications. It explains a feature of the operation of Arts. 29 and 30, which may occasion surprise, at least for common lawyers. Because the Regulation commits itself to the assumption of parity between the courts of Member States, the tactical implications of proceeding in one Member State not another are obscured. The possibility that the venue of litigation may dictate the final outcome, because it may provoke settlement or capitulation, becomes irrelevant – as is the possibility that the parties may have cause to sue in one court rather than another for tactical purposes. For this reason, the familiar charge that the Regulation is a 'forum-shopper's charter', even if it has force, mistakes the assumption upon which the Regulation is founded.

3. The threat of irreconcilability

24 A third (and highly significant) assumption is that parallel proceedings and irreconcilable judgments in the same matter are a real threat to the stability of the Regulation, and in particular to the mutual enforcement of judgments between Member States. It is axiomatic that the reality of this threat underwrites Arts. 29–30 – and, indeed, the very existence of the Regulation's jurisdiction regime. It is enough to report that this is the key assumption upon which Arts. 29–30 are founded. But it is unclear that the threat is in fact as serious as is supposed. It is certainly not uncommon for litigants to claim and counter-claim in different jurisdictions. Parallel proceedings concerning jurisdiction are a feature of cross-border litigation. This reflects the importance of venue to the outcome of a dispute, and in particular in inspiring settlement. Nor is it uncommon for litigants to take the initial steps in substantive parallel proceedings, with the objective of obtaining information, or probing the other party's case, or testing their resolve. But the inefficiency and cost of parallel proceedings usually make it unlikely that the parties would pursue parallel proceedings to final judgment. Moreover, the existence of rules for selecting between conflicting judgments (perhaps by favouring the first in time), may themselves ensure that such a conflict will not in fact arise. There will come a time when it is evident which judgment will be obtained first, making any other proceedings pointless, and no doubt causing the claimant in those proceedings to discontinue. This is not to say that irreconcilable judgments may not occur. Arguably, however, the risk is not so great that the problem could not be solved by mechanisms for choosing between those judgments. Certainly, the real mischief in parallel pro-

---

[39] *Gantner Electronic GmbH v. Basch Exploitatie Maatschappij BV* (Case C-111/01), [2003] ECR I-4207.
[40] See the treatment of the 'Italian torpedo' in *Erich Gasser GmbH v. MISAT Srl* (Case C-116/02), [2003] ECR I-14693.

ceedings may not be the threat of irreconcilable judgments, but the inherent inefficiency of parallel proceedings.

4. A theory of procedural justice

A fourth assumption is that the model of litigation embodied in the European jurisdiction **25** regime adequately secures procedural justice.[41] Any defensible regime governing jurisdiction rests implicitly on the belief that it secures the parties' procedural rights, and in particular, the right of access to justice, better than any other. This requirement is made concrete in the case of the Regulation by the principle that Union law shall respect the human rights regime of the European Convention on Human Rights,[42] although the legal relationship between the Convention and Union law remains problematic.[43] Whether Arts. 29–30 cohere with human rights norms is no mere academic question. As the technical interpretation of the Regulation becomes clearer, so litigants are likely to take their battle to a higher level, and seek to exploit the opportunities for argument presented by the Convention.

For some, the suggestion that Arts. 29–30 promote the strongest available theory of proce- **26** dural justice is at first sight puzzling. Notwithstanding the small degree of discretion permitted by Art. 30, defendants are unable to assert that the *forum conveniens* is anywhere but the court first seised. They are denied the opportunity to argue that procedural justice (to both parties) is best served by proceedings elsewhere, the essence of the doctrine of *forum non conveniens*.[44] Courts are unable to allocate proceedings to the court where equality of arms is best achieved, the doctrine's animating concern.[45] But the Regulation rests upon two different assumptions, which make such considerations irrelevant, indeed meaningless. First, resort to the doctrine of *forum non conveniens* is unnecessary because it is axiomatic that procedural justice is served wherever in the Union proceedings are heard. Secondly,

---

[41] See generally *Fentiman*, in Nuyts/Watté (eds.), International Civil Litigation in Europe and Relations With Third States (2005), p. 83, 129; *Nuyts*, in Nuyts/Watté (eds.), International Civil Litigation in Europe and Relations With Third States (2005), p. 157; *Fentiman*, [2004] 63 Cambridge L.J. 292; *Schlosser*, Riv.dir.int. 1991, 5.

[42] Introduced by the Amsterdam Treaty, Art. 6 (2).

[43] The Convention has 'special significance' as a source of Union legal norms, though is not necessarily part of EU law: *Roland Rutili v. Ministre de l'Interieur* (Case 36/75), [1975] ECR 1219; *Elliniki Radiophonia Tileorassi Anonimi Etairia and Panellinia Omospondia Syllogon Prossopikou ERT v. Dimotiki Etairia Pliroforissis, Sotiris Kouvelas, Nicolaos Avdellas et al.* (Case C-260/89), [1991] ECR I-2925. But whether the Convention is dispositive of the applicable norms, or merely suggestive, is uncertain: see e.g. *Criminal Proceedings against Horst Otto Bickel and Ulrich Franz* (Case C-294/96), [1998] ECR I-7637. The status of the Convention within Union law is a distinct issue from whether, in proceedings under the Convention, the Convention or Union law prevails: *Matthews v. United Kingdom* (application No. 24833/94) (suggesting that the Convention is paramount). See further: *Waddam/Mountfield/Edmundson*, in: Blackstone's Guide to the Human Rights Act, 3rd ed Oxford 1998, Ch. 7; *Harlow*, in *Alston* (ed.), The European Union and Human Rights (1999).

[44] As elaborated in *The Spiliada* [1986] A.C. 460 (H.L.). The lack of a discretion to stay inappropriate proceedings has been called 'deplorable', because the 'forum non conveniens doctrine helps level the playing field': *Juenger*, in: Taruffo (ed.), Abuse of Procedural Rights: Comparative Standards of Procedural Fairness (1999), p. 357.

[45] At least as it functions in English law.

justice is best served by a generic not specific approach to access to justice. More precisely, the certainty and efficiency inherent in the strict application of Arts. 29 and 30 is more conducive to access to justice than a case-by-case assessment of the fairness of proceeding in another court. Whatever the justice of particular cases there is thus an overall increase in just outcomes.

VI. The Scope of Arts. 29–30

1. The subject matter of the Regulation

27   Self-evidently, the scope of Arts. 29–30 is limited to proceedings whose subject-matter is within the scope of the Regulation.[46] In *Owens Bank v. Bracco*[47] the successful claimant in proceedings in Saint Vincent sought to enforce the judgment obtained there in both England and Italy simultaneously. In both countries the defendant raised the defence that the judgment had been obtained by fraud. On the assumption that the Italian courts were first seised of that matter, was the English court required to stay its proceedings? The Court of Justice said no.[48] The subject matter of both disputes – the enforcement of a judgment obtained in a non-Member State – was outside the scope of the European regime.

2. Prior proceedings and interim relief

28   Art. 35 provides that application may be made to the courts of a Member State for interim relief 'even if, under this Regulation, the courts of another Member State have jurisdiction as to the substance of the matter'. This ensures that Arts. 29–30 do not regulate parallel proceedings where the second action is merely for interim relief. A court in one Member State may grant such interim relief as may be available under its law, in support of substantive proceedings pending in another such State. Conversely, it appears that a court is not prevented from entertaining substantive proceedings by the fact that related provisional measures have been sought in another Member State.[49]

3. Prior proceedings and national law

29   The role of the Art. 29–30 regime in preventing inconsistent judgments explains why it applies even when the courts of two Member States have asserted jurisdiction under their national law, pursuant to Art. 6. Thus, as was said of Art. 21 of the Brussels Convention, the rules concerning *lis pendens* apply 'both where the jurisdiction of the court is determined by the Convention itself and where it is derived from the legislation of a Contracting State in accordance with Art. 4 of the Convention'.[50] There is thus no requirement that either party be domiciled in a Member State.[51] This is justified because Art. 29 is not limited in terms to cases involving jurisdiction under the Regulation. And it is required because the regime for

---

[46]   *Toepfer v. Société Cargill France* [1998] 1 Lloyd's Rep. 379 (C.A.).

[47]   *Owens Bank Ltd. v. Fulvio Bracco Industria Chemica SPA* (Case C-129/92), [1994] ECR I-117.

[48]   *Owens Bank Ltd. v. Fulvio Bracco Industria Chemica SPA* (Case C-129/92), [1994] ECR I-117, I-155 para. 36.

[49]   *Boss Group Ltd. v. Boss France SA* [1997] 1 WLR 351 (C.A.).

[50]   *Overseas Union Insurance Ltd v. New Hampshire Insurance Co.* (Case C-351/89), [1991] ECR I-3297, I-3348 para. 14; *The Nordglimt* [1988] QB 183 (Q.B.D.); Report *Jenard*, p. 20 *et seq.*

the recognition and enforcement of judgments provided by the Regulation applies irrespective of the source of the judgment court's jurisdiction. So the efficiency and integrity of that regime would be threatened by inconsistent judgments in different Member States whatever the grounds upon which their courts accepted jurisdiction.

Particular issues arise when the rules of national law concerning *lis pendens* derive from a **30** convention and they conflict with the Regulation. In the event of parallel proceedings in two Member States, Arts. 29 and 30 of the Regulation apply notwithstanding that the parties are domiciled in a state which is a party to the Lugano Convention.[52] Where parallel proceedings are regulated by the provisions of a specialist convention pursuant to Art. 71 of the Regulation, and they conflict with Arts. 29 and 30, they may apply provided that they further the free movement of judgments, and mutual trust in the administration of justice in the EU, in a manner at least as favourable under the Regulation.[53]

Article 29

1. Without prejudice to Article 31(2), where proceedings involving the same cause of action and between the same parties are brought in the courts of different Member States, any court other than the court first seised shall of its own motion stay its proceedings until such time as the jurisdiction of the court first seised is established.
2. In cases referred to in paragraph 1, upon request by a court seised of the dispute, any other court seised shall without delay inform the former court of the date when it was seised in accordance with Article 32.
3. Where the jurisdiction of the court first seised is established, any court other than the court first seised shall decline jurisdiction in favour of that court.

I. Introduction

Art. 29[1] is designed to avoid the situation in which a court in one Member State is obliged to **1** deny recognition to a judgment given in another such State by applying the priority rules of

---

[51] *Overseas Union Insurance Ltd v. New Hampshire Insurance Co.* (Case C-351/89), [1991] ECR I-3297, I-3348 para. 14 with notes *Briggs*, (1991) 11 Cambridge Yb.Eur.L. 521; *Hartley*, (1992) 17 Eur.L.Rev. 75.

[52] *Cooper Tire & Rubber Co. Europe Ltd. v. Dow Deutschland Inc.* [2010] Bus. L.R. 1697 (C.A.).

[53] Case-353/08 *TNT Express Nederland BV v. AXA Versicherung AG* [2010] I.L.Pr. 663 (ECJ)(Art. 29 of the 1956 Geneva Convention on the Contract for the International Carriage of Goods by Road).

[1] Brussels and Lugano Conventions, Art. 21; cf. Report *Jenard*, p. 41; Report *Schlosser*, paras. 180–182; Report *Evrigenis/Kerameus*, paras. 63, 103(b); Report *Jenard/Möller*, para. 64; Explanatory Memorandum, p. 19.

Art. 45(1)(d). It is intended to avoid the inefficiency, and subversion of mutual trust between Member States, that would result. Rather than focusing on whether incompatible judgments may arise, however, Art. 29 poses a different, if related question: do the two actions correspond to the extent that incompatible judgments may be obtained? This does not mean, however, that the proceedings need be identical, only that they overlap sufficiently that such a risk arises. Thus, the two sets of proceedings need not be identical, but they must be congruent.

2 Art. 29 is the latest attempt to regulate congruent proceedings within the Union. Although the wording and ordering of the provision has evolved, the essential mechanism of Art. 29 was largely established by Art. 21 of the Brussels Convention. A significant amendment, however, is that the requirement in what is now Art. 29 (1) that the second court shall stay its proceedings, avoiding the possibility that the first court would itself subsequently decline jurisdiction, prejudicing a claimant who might have no alternative but to return to the second court (where, at worst, the action might have become time-barred).[2]

3 Art. 29 operates in two ways. Art. 29 (3) ensures that, if the jurisdiction of the court first seised is established, any other court must cede jurisdiction to that court. The exclusive jurisdiction of the court first seised to resolve any jurisdictional conflict is thus confirmed. Of greater practical importance is Art. 29 (1), which requires any court but that first seised to stay its proceedings until the jurisdiction of the court first seised is established. The purpose of Art. 29 (1) is, in effect, to confer upon the court first seised exclusive jurisdiction to determine in which Member State proceedings might be brought. In this sense, it is a rule concerning jurisdiction – jurisdiction to determine jurisdiction. By contrast, by giving primacy to the established jurisdiction of the court first seised, Art. 29 (3) is, in effect, a rule concerning the recognition of foreign judgments – foreign judgments within the Union establishing jurisdiction.

4 Art. 29 allows the court second seised no discretion, nor does the required stay or dismissal depend upon the defendant's application. It is expressly required that a court must of its own motion stay its proceedings under Art. 29 (1), and it is no doubt implicit in the peremptory language employed that it must of its own motion decline jurisdiction under Art. 29 (3).

5 The operation of Art. 29 thus depends upon the answer to four key questions: (i) When is each court seised? (ii) When are two actions congruent, such that there is a risk of irreconcilable 'decrees, orders or decisions'?[3] (iii) When is a court's jurisdiction established, such that another court can determine whether to lift a stay under Art. 29 (1), or cede jurisdiction under Art. 29 (3)? (iv) What rules of evidence and procedure govern the second court's actions? The first of these questions depends upon the application of Art. 32, and is addressed below. The second, third and fourth require consideration here.

II. The requirement of congruence

6 Art. 29 does not require that the parallel actions be identical in a literal sense. If it did, Art. 29 would affect only cases where a claimant sought identical relief, in identical terms, in more

---

[2]   Report *Jenard/Möller*, para. 64.
[3]   The definition of a judgment in Art. 2(a).

than one Member State. Some flexibility must be permitted to accommodate cases where a defendant in one State counterclaims in another State, those where there are local differences in the legal basis of each action, and those where the subject matter of both actions only partly corresponds. Thus, Art. 29 does not require that the two actions be identical, only that they are materially congruent – that they correspond sufficiently that there is a risk of irreconcilable judgments. To be congruent, both the parties and the substance of the proceedings must be the same.

1. The same parties

a) Principles

It might be thought obvious that Art. 29 applies only to proceedings between the same **7** parties. But two questions arise. First, what if some, but not all, of the parties are the same in both actions? A possible answer is that Art. 29 should not apply at all unless all parties are the same, so that Art. 30 would apply instead. But the Court of Justice has preferred the other possible response. Where some but not all the parties are the same, Art. 29 operates between the common parties.[4] Secondly, what if the parties are different legal persons, but have a common legal interest? The problem arose in *Drouot Assurances SA v. CMI*,[5] concerning the possible identity of interest between insurer and insured. The Court held that whether in any action an insurer and its insured were to be regarded as sharing the same legal interest in proceedings, was a matter for local national law. But the Court indicated that where an insurer had sued in the insured's name under the doctrine of subrogation, 'insurer and insured must be considered to be one and the same party'.[6] Thus, if an insurer is party to one action in its own name, and to another action in the insured's name, it will be a party to both proceedings for Art. 29 purposes.

Where a claim is founded on a contractual right, and that right is assigned, the assignor and **8** assignee are the 'same parties' in relation to that claim. The effect is that a court is seised of the claim when the assignor commences proceedings although its rights are later assigned. This important principle was relied upon by the English Court of Appeal in *Kolden Holdings Ltd. v. Rodette Commerce Ltd.*[7] There C had begun proceedings in England against R for failure to transfer shares pursuant to a share transfer agreement. C then assigned its rights under the agreement to K. R then began proceedings in Cyprus which were identical for Art. 29 purposes. K was then substituted for C as claimant in the English proceedings. R sought a stay of the English proceedings on the ground that new English proceedings commenced with K's substitution. The stay was refused by the Court of Appeal. The sub-

---

4   *The owners of the cargo lately laden on board the ship "Tatry" v. The owners of the ship "Maciej Rataj"* (Case C-406/92), (1994) ECR I-5439, I-5462 para. 2; *Briggs*, (1995) LMCLQ 161; *Collins*, (1992) 108 L.Q. Rev. 545; *Davenport*, (1995) 111 L.Q.Rev. 366.

5   *Drouot Assurances SA v. Consolidated Metallurgical Industries* (Case C-351-96), (1998) ECR I-3075; applied, *Sony Computer Entertainment Ltd. v. RH Freight Services Ltd.* (2007) 2 Lloyd's Rep. 463 (Q.B.D., *Simon* J.); *Seatzu*, (1999) 24 Eur.L.Rev. 540.

6   *Drouot Assurances SA v. Consolidated Metallurgical Industries* (Case C-351-96), (1998) ECR I-3075, I-3097 para. 19.

7   (2008) 1 Lloyd's Rep. 445(1)(d) (C.A.); applied, *Mölnlycke Health Care AB v. BSN Medical Ltd.* (2010 I.L. Pr. 9 (Ch D., Patents Ct., *Floyd* J.); see also to the same effect, Case 16 U 110/02, September 8, 2003, IPRax 2004, 521.

stitution was irrelevant. Although under English law K only became a party to the proceedings when substituted for C, the definition of 'same parties' had an autonomous meaning. Following *Drouot*, it was irrelevant that C and K were separate legal entities. What mattered was whether the interests of both were identical and indissociable. Identity between C and K was established for two reasons. First, any judgment affecting the one would be *res judicata* against the other. There was between them a privity of interest such that C would be bound by any finding relating to the transfer agreement made in proceedings to which the K had been a party. Secondly, *res judicata* aside, the substantive interests of C as assignor and K as assignee were the same in the matter of the contractual claim against R.

9   The test employed in *Drouot* and *Kolden* has considerable practical importance. It begs the question when rights are identical and indissociable such that two parties are the same under Art. 29. By way of example, a member of a cartel whose exposure is substantial does not share a relevant interest with another member of the cartel whose exposure is less. It is irrelevant that both may have a common interest in defending the same proceedings.[8] Again, a licensee and licensor (whose rights are distinct) may lack the necessary identity of interest, by contrast with an assignor and assignee (whose rights are the same).[9]

b) **Parent and subsidiary**

10   An important question in practice is whether one company in a group of companies may avoid a court's jurisdiction by sheltering behind a related company. If a parent is party to proceedings in one Member State, and its subsidiary is a party to proceedings in another such state, when are they the same parties for Article 29 purposes? Suppose, for example, that Xco has sued Yco in England, and Yco seeks to dismiss the proceedings under Article 29 (3) on the basis that Yco had already brought proceedings in Italy against Zco, a company affiliated to Xco, although Yco has not sued Xco in the Italian courts.[10]

11   It is possible that such legally separate entities may be treated as the same parties for Article 29 purposes.[11] Some courts have approached the matter not by asking whether two distinct corporations are in fact or law the same, but by asking whether a party should be permitted to assert or deny that they are the same. It may be relevant that the defendant seeking a stay has conducted its case as if the two companies are distinct, as where it has sued each separately, or has treated them as distinct by seeking to join one in proceedings against the other.[12] Again, a court should be cautious in equating distinct legal entities for this purpose, so as not to expand the scope of Article 29 at the expense of Article 30, and thereby deprive a court of its discretion to determine cases individually.[13] It is unlikely, however, that a parent and its subsidiary will be treated as the same party, unless the parent seeks 'to hide behind the identity of a subsidiary in order to avoid its liabilities'.[14] As this suggests, the problem of identity concerns a party is acting in bad faith in reliance on its corporate

---

[8]   *Cooper Tire & Rubber Co. Europe Ltd. v. Dow Deutschland Inc.* (2010) Bus. L.R. 1697 (C.A.).

[9]   *MölnlyckeHealth CareAB v. BSN Medical Ltd.* (2010 I.L.Pr. 9 (Ch D., Patents Ct.).

[10]   *WMS Gaming Inc v. B Plus Giocolegale Ltd* [2011] EWHC 2620 (Comm).

[11]   *WMS Gaming Inc v. B Plus Giocolegale Ltd* [2011] EWHC 2620 (Comm).

[12]   *WMS Gaming Inc v. B Plus Giocolegale Ltd* [2011] EWHC 2620 (Comm), at [38].

[13]   *WMS Gaming Inc v. B Plus Giocolegale Ltd* [2011] EWHC 2620 (Comm), at [39].

[14]   *WMS Gaming Inc v. B Plus Giocolegale Ltd* [2011] EWHC 2620 (Comm), at [38], per *Simon* J, commenting on the singular decision in *Berkeley Administration Inc v. McClelland* [1995] ILPr 201.

structure so as to achieve a jurisdictional advantage. The power to police such jurisdictional evasion may perhaps properly derive from an autonomous, EU-wide doctrine of good faith in the operation of the Regulation.[15]

2. Objet: the same legal purpose

In *The Tatry*[16] the Court of Justice defined the *objet* of the action as 'the end the action has in **12** view'.[17] The requirement that both actions must have the same object is a requirement that both must concern liability for the infringement of the same legal obligation. Article 29 therefore prevents a claimant from bringing identical proceedings against the same defendant in two courts, and where a claim and counter-claim share the same object, as when there are proceedings for damages in one court, and proceedings in another court for a declaration that the defendant in the other proceedings is not liable in damages.[18]

Beyond such simple cases, however, it is harder to satisfy the requirement of a common **13** object than might be supposed, significantly reducing Article 29's practical impact. The necessary identity of object is absent if the claims in one court lie in tort, but in the other lie in contract.[19] Again, a buyer's claim against a seller for breach of a warranty as to quality is not congruent with a seller's claim against a buyer for non-payment of the purchase price.[20] Although, each party may advance the other's breach in its defence, the object of the two claims is distinct. Again, an action in damages, and proceedings to limit liability, do not share a common objective. The former seeks to establish liability, the latter to limit any liability that may exist.[21] Nor does an action in one court for the tort of passing-off share a common object with an action elsewhere for the infringement of a trade mark.[22] Nor do proceedings in one country for sums due under a contract, and proceedings elsewhere for negligently inducing the claimant to enter into that contract.[23] Nor does an action to enforce a loan agreement, and one to modify the legal status of that agreement, have a common objective;[24] nor an action to enforce an arbitration agreement, and another action to establish the parties' substantive liability;[25] nor an action to recover a sum due from a defendant, and one to establish a proprietary interest in the defendant's assets.[26]

Two general principles govern the test for whether a common object exists. First, regard **14**

---

[15] Cf. Case C-221/84 *Berghöfer v. ASA S.A.* [1985] E.C.R. 2699.

[16] Case C-406/92 [1994] ECR I-5439.

[17] Case C-406/92 [1994] ECR I-5439, at [41].

[18] *The owners of the cargo lately laden on board the ship 'Tatry' v. The owners of the ship 'Maciej Rataj'* (Case C-406/92), [1994] ECR I-5439; *Briggs,* [1995] LMCLQ 161; *Hartley,* (1989) 105 LQR 640.

[19] *Starlight Shipping Co v. Allianz Marine & Aviation Versicherungs AG, 'The Alexandros T'* [2013] UKSC 70.

[20] As assumed apparently in *Smith's Vitamins and Herbs Ltd v. Ceprodi Compagnie Europeenne De Produits Dietetiques SA* [2010] EWHC 1025.

[21] Case C-39/02 *Mærsk Olie & Gas A/S v. Firma M de Haan en W de Boer* [2004] ECR I-9657, at [36].

[22] *Mecklermedia Corp v. DC Congress GmbH* [1998] Ch. 40.

[23] *Sarrio v. Kuwait Investment Authority* [1996] 1 Lloyd's Rep. 650 (CA).

[24] *Gamlestaden Plc v. Case de Suecia* [1994] 1 Lloyd's Rep. 444.

[25] *The Charterers' Mutual Assurance Assn Ltd v. British and Foreign* [1998] ILPr 838.

[26] *Haji-Ioannou v. Frangos* [1999] 2 Lloyd's Rep. 337 (C.A.).

Richard Fentiman   729

should be had to the substance not the form of proceedings. Second, the enquiry is concerned only with the claims made in each court at the time that proceedings are initiated.

15 The focus on substance not form avoids any problem of characterization which may arise because the manner in which each action has proceeded under the local law of the state in question might disguise its essential features. Differences in form, idiom, procedure, and in the remedy sought may conceal the essential similarity between different actions. In *The Tatry*[27] the question was whether two actions are congruent if in one state the proceedings are classified as proceedings *in rem*, and in the other they are classified as *in personam*. The Court held that the classification of a claim under national law is not material for the purposes of establishing congruence. Because the requirements of common cause and object are EU concepts, they 'must therefore be interpreted independently of the specific features of the law in force in each Contracting State'.[28] In consequence, an action for damages in one State is congruent with an action for a declaration of non-liability for the same loss in another State.[29]

Applying this test, proceedings to enforce a contract, and proceedings to annul the same contract, have a common object.[30] The legal objective of both is to establish the enforceability of the contract. Similarly, an application for a declaration of non-liability for negligence has the same objective as a statutory claim for wrongful death,[31] as do cross-proceedings in different countries, concerning responsibility for a collision at sea.[32] Article 29 also engages where different claims in two courts resolve themselves into the single issue of the extent of each party's liability to the other. For example, if X sues Y in one court for an account of profits held by Y, and Y sues X elsewhere for damages, the set-off of each party's liability to the other is the common object of both actions.[33]

16 If a claim for breach of contract in one court has the same object as a claim in another court that the contract is unenforceable,[34] because whether the defendant in the first court is liable for breach is the essential element of both, it might then be supposed that an application for a declaration that any future claims between the parties were released in a settlement agreement has the same object as claims for damages against the applicant. Both concern the applicant's liability for the same alleged wrongs. In *Starlight Shipping Co v. Allianz Marine & Aviation Versicherungs AG (The Alexandros T)*[35] however, a majority of the UK Supreme Court considered that Article 29 did not engage in such a case,[36] notwithstanding compelling arguments to the contrary endorsed by a minority.[37] Reflecting this divergence, the court

---

[27] Case C-406/92 [1994] ECR I-5439.

[28] Case C-406/92 [1994] ECR I-5439, at [45]–[47].

[29] See also, *Glencore International AG v. Shell International Trading and Shipping Co Ltd* [1999] 2 Lloyd's Rep. 692.

[30] Case 144/86 *Gubisch Maschinenfabrik KG v. Giulio Palumbo* [1987] ECR 4861; Hartley (1988) 13 Eur L Rev 216.

[31] *Kinnear v. Falcon Films NV* [1994] ILPr 731.

[32] *The Linda* [1988] 1 Lloyd's Rep. 175.

[33] *Secret Hotels 2 Ltd v. EA Traveller Ltd* [2010] ILPr 616.

[34] *Gubisch Maschinenfabrik KG v. Giulio Palumbo* (Case 144/86), [1987] ECR 486.

[35] [2013] UKSC 70.

[36] Lord *Clarke*, Lord *Sumption* and Lord *Hughes* agreeing, at [55]–[59].

unanimously decided that it would have been necessary to refer the matter to the CJEU had it been material on the facts of the case. Insofar as the difference in view reflects a difference in principle, this presumably concerns whether a court is confined to comparing the direct outcome of each claim. The majority apparently concluded that to determine whether the settlement agreement released the applicant from future claims was to determine (directly) the effect of the agreement, not (indirectly) its liability under those claims. It is likely, however, that the CJEU will (correctly it is submitted) regard the position of the minority in *Starlight Shipping* as correct.

The second principle, that the enquiry is concerned only with the claims made in each court **17** at the time that proceedings are initiated, also has important consequences. In principle, two proceedings may have a different legal objective, but the defence to a claim in one court may replicate the claim in another court. Such proceedings may be related, but they do not share the same objective. For the purposes of establishing congruence between two actions is it relevant that the defendant in one action has raised by way of defence an issue which is not before the other court? The Court of Justice in *Gantner Electronic GmbH v. Basch Exploitatie Maatschappij BV*[38] held that any such defence should be ignored for the purpose of establishing congruence.[39] Congruence existed when two actions shared the same legal object, meaning the same end in view. They would have that common element regardless of any defence raised in either set of proceedings. Moreover, what is now Article 29 operated at the moment of seisin, at the moment proceedings were initiated. So subsequent arguments deployed by the parties, or speculation as to possible arguments, were irrelevant to the application of Article 29.

This principle was applied by the UK Supreme Court in *Starlight Shipping Co v. Allianz* **18** *Marine & Aviation Versicherungs AG (The Alexandros T)*,[40] where an insured shipowner began proceedings against an insurer in Greece, although the parties had concluded a settlement agreement in English proceedings concerning the insured's liability. It was irrelevant that the insurers might advance the settlement agreement, the basis of most of its claims in the English court, as a defence to the Greek claims. The application of Article 29 is concerned only with the claims advanced in different courts, not with possible defences.

The important consequence of this last principle is that it significantly narrows the range of **19** cases which might fall within Article 29. In effect, it restricts Article 29 to cases where one party brings identical claims in two courts, and to those where one court is seised of a claim that a defendant is liable, and another court is seised of a claim that the same defendant is not liable.[41] Significantly, it means that Article 29 does not apply to related actions in which the claim in one court is (or could be) a defence to a claim elsewhere. X may sue Y in France for non-delivery of goods under a contract, and Y may sue X in England for non-payment of the purchase price under the same contract. No doubt non-delivery would be a defence to the claim for the price, but the object of the proceedings is different in each case, involving

---

[37]   Lord *Mance*, at [142]-[160]; Lord *Neuberger*, at [126]–[132].

[38]   Case C-111/01 [2003] ECR I-4207.

[39]   Case C-111/01 [2003] ECR I-4207, at [24]–[32].

[40]   [2013] UKSC 70.

[41]   *Glencore International AG v. Shell International Trading and Shipping Co Ltd* [1999] 2 Lloyd's Rep. 692, at 697.

claims for breach of distinct obligations. They are clearly related under Article 30, but they are not congruent under Article 29.

3. Cause: the same legal and factual basis

20 Article 29 engages only if the two actions rest on the same cause, defined as the same facts and rule of law.[42] Normally, the requirement that both actions should share the same factual and legal basis adds nothing in practice to the requirement that they should have a common object.[43] If two actions have a different *objet* it is irrelevant that they share the same basis, and if they have the same object their basis will be the same. The reality is that the dual requirement of *objet* and *cause* is one, composite requirement that the subject matter of the proceedings must be the same.

21 Difficulty arises where two actions share the same object, because they concern liability for breach of the same obligation, but the governing law is different in each court. If the legal issue is the same but the governing law is different, is the legal basis the same? There are conflicting answers in the case law. Suppose that a claimant in English proceedings seeks to enforce a loan agreement pursuant to English law, the law governing the contract between the parties, although the defendant in those proceedings had initiated pre-emptive proceedings in Germany to establish that the agreement was unenforceable, relying upon German law and public policy.[44] It is possible to conclude that both courts are concerned with the enforcement of the same obligation, whichever law is applied to determine the matter.[45] Arguably, both courts are concerned with the rights and duties of the parties under the loan agreement.[46] Alternatively, it could be said that, even though the object is the same in both proceedings, concerning liability for default under the agreement, the two actions involve distinct inquiries in deciding any liability,[47] and so do not have the same cause.

22 Principle may favour the conclusion that the proceedings in such a case share a common legal and factual basis. It is consistent with the principle, endorsed by the CJEU, that the form in which a claim is advanced should not affect the operation of Article 29. The classification of a claim under national law is irrelevant,[48] and the issue does not depend on 'the specific features of the law in force in each Contracting State'.[49]

4. Bundled claims and lis pendens

23 In all but the simplest cases, a dispute is unlikely to involve merely the same claims in both set of parallel proceedings. In practice, some claims will be common to both actions, but others will not. It is uncertain, however, whether a court may stay or dismiss some, but not all, of the claims before it pursuant to Articles 29. If a partial stay or dismissal is permitted,

---

[42] *The Tatry* (Case C-406/92), [1994] ECR I-5439, at [39].
[43] *Gantner Electronic GmbH v. Basch Exploitatie Maatschappij BV* (Case C-111/01) [2003] ECR I-4207.
[44] *JP Morgan Europe Ltd v. Primacom AG* [2005] 2 Lloyd's Rep. 665, at [47].
[45] *JP Morgan Europe Ltd v. Primacom AG* [2005] 2 Lloyd's Rep. 665, at [45].
[46] *JP Morgan Europe Ltd v. Primacom AG* [2005] 2 Lloyd's Rep. 665, at [45].
[47] *WMS Gaming Inc v. B Plus Giocolegale Ltd* [2011] EWHC 2620 (Comm), at [32].
[48] *The Tatry* (Case C-406/92) [1994] ECR I-5439.
[49] *The Tatry* (Case C-406/92), [1994] ECR I-5439, at [45]–[47].

some claims will be heard in one court and others elsewhere. The decision of the UK Supreme Court in *Starlight Shipping Co v. Allianz Marine & Aviation Versicherungs AG (The Alexandros T)*[50] endorses a claim-specific approach. It was held that the court's task is to consider the claims advanced by the parties separately and, 'in the case of each cause of action relied upon, to consider whether the same cause of action is being relied upon' in the foreign proceedings.[51] It was improper to enquire as to the overall character of the proceedings, rather than the cause and object of each claim.[52]

The court in *Starlight Shipping* regarded the matter as *acte clair*, and declined to refer the   **24** issue to the CJEU. Arguably, however, the question has no clear answer, and it is far from certain that the answer offered by the Supreme Court is correct. Article 29 refers to the staying of 'proceedings', not claims within those proceedings.[53] Such CJEU authority as exists may, however, favour a claim-by-claim approach. In *The Tatry*[54] the CJEU was prepared to stay proceedings in favour of proceedings elsewhere only to the extent that both proceedings concerned the same parties. Despite the disadvantages of fragmentation, a court should decline jurisdiction 'to the extent to which the parties to the proceedings pending before it are also parties to the action previously started before the court of another Contracting State; it does not prevent the proceedings from continuing between the other parties'.[55] A different response is that that a court should look for the 'central or essential issue' in each of the proceedings,[56] but support for such an approach does not exist in the jurisprudence of the CJEU, or in the principles underlying the Regulation, and the test was rejected in *Starlight Shipping*.[57]

5. The application of Art. 29

Some examples illustrate when parallel proceedings will be regarded as congruent. In *The*   **25** *Tatry*,[58] it was held that proceedings in one Member State for damages, and proceedings in another for a declaration that the defendant in the other proceedings was not liable in damages, had the same subject matter. The legal objective of both actions was to establish the defendant's liability in damages. In *Gubisch Maschinenfabrik KG v. Giulio Palumbo*,[59] the Court of Justice held, in effect, that proceedings to enforce a contract in one Member State, and proceedings to annul it in another, have a common object. The legal objective of

---

50   [2013] UKSC 70.

51   [2013] UKSC 70, at [29]–[51].

52   [2013] UKSC 70, at [50]–[52]; see to the same effect, *Alfred C Toepfer GmbH v. Molino Boschi Srl* [1996] 1 Lloyd's Rep. 510, 513; *Bank of Bank of Tokyo-Mitsubishi Ltd v. Baskan Gida Sanayi Ve Pazarlama AS* [2004] EWHC 945 (Ch.), [243].

53   *Evialis SA v. SIAT* [2003] EWHC 863 (Comm), at [132], per *Andrew Smith J.*

54   Case C-406/92 [1994] ECR I-5439.

55   Case C-406/92 [1994] ECR I-5439, at [33].

56   *Underwriting Members of Lloyd's Syndicate 980 v. Sinco SA* [2008] EWHC 1842 (Comm), at [41], [50], following, *Evialis SA v. SIAT* [2003] EWHC 863 (Comm).

57   At [50]–[52].

58   *The owners of the cargo lately laden on board the ship "Tatry" v. The owners of the ship "Maciej Rataj"* (Case C-406/92), (1994) ECR I-5439; *Briggs*, (1995) LMCLQ 161; *Hartley*, (1989) 105 L.Q.Rev. 640.

59   *Gubisch Maschinenfabrik KG v. Giulio Palumbo* (Case 144/86), (1987) ECR 4861 with note *Hartley*, (1988) 13 Eur.L.Rev. 216.

---

both is to establish the enforceability of the contract. Similarly, it has been held that an application for a declaration of non-liability for negligence had the same objective as a statutory claim for wrongful death,[60] as do cross-proceedings in different countries, concerning responsibility for a collision at sea.[61] Art. 29 also engages where distinct claims in different courts resolve themselves into the single issue of the extent of each party's liability to the other. If X sues Y in one court for an account of profits held by Y, and Y sues X elsewhere for damages, the set-off of each party's liability to the other is the common object of both actions.[62]

26   By contrast, a buyer's claim against a seller for breach of a warranty as to the quality of goods is not congruent with a seller's claim against a buyer for non-payment of the purchase price.[63] Each party may advance the other's breach in its defence. But the objective of the two claims is distinct. Again, an action in one country for the tort of passing off, and one elsewhere for the infringement of a trade mark, do not share a common purpose.[64] Nor do proceedings in one country for sums due under a contract, and proceedings elsewhere for negligently inducing the claimant to enter into that contract.[65] Nor does an action to enforce a loan agreement, and one to modify the legal status of that agreement, lack a common objective;[66] nor an action to enforce an arbitration agreement, and another action to establish the parties' substantive liability;[67] nor an action to recover a sum due from a defendant, and one to establish a proprietary interest in the defendant's assets.[68] Again, an action in damages, and proceedings to limit liability, do not share a common objective. The former seeks to establish liability, the latter to limit any liability that may exist.[69]

III. Establishing Jurisdiction

27   The concept of establishing jurisdiction is the fulcrum of Art. 29. The second court must grant a stay under Art. 29 (1) 'until such time as the jurisdiction of the court first seised is established'. Thus, any such stay will be lifted once it is clear that such jurisdiction has *not* been established. Again, under Art. 29 (3) the second court must decline jurisdiction where 'the jurisdiction of the court first seised is established.' If it is established, the second court must decline jurisdiction under Art. 29 (3), and any previous such a stay will be superseded. But when is jurisdiction established, or not established? There is no indication in the Regulation. Presumably, a finding in the first court to the effect that jurisdiction exists or not is sufficient. But consider the position in those Member States whose procedural law permits or requires the parties to argue simultaneously issues concerning both jurisdiction and the

---

60   *Kinnear v. Falcon Films NV* (1994) I.L.Pr. 731 (Q.B.D, *Phillips* J.).

61   *The Linda* (1988) 1 Lloyd's Rep. 175 (Q.B.D, *Sheen* J.).

62   *Secret Hotels 2 Ltd v. EA Traveller Ltd* (2010) I.L.Pr. 616 (Ch. D., *Peter Smith* J.).

63   As assumed apparently in *Smith's Vitamins and Herbs Ltd v. Ceprodi Compagnie Europeenne De Produits Dietetiques SA* (2010) EWHC 1025 (Q.B.D., *Eady* J.).

64   *Mecklermedia Corp. v. DC Congress GmbH* (1998) Ch 40 (Q.B.D, *Jacobs* J.).

65   *Sarrio v. Kuwait Investment Authority* (1996) 1 Lloyd's Rep. 650 (C.A.).

66   *Gamlestaden Plc v. Case de Suecia* (1994) 1 Lloyd's Rep. 433 (Q.B.D, *Potter* J.).

67   *The Charterers' Mutual Assurance Assn. Ltd. v. British and Foreign* (1998) I.L.Pr. 838 (Q.B.D, Judge *Diamond* Q.C.).

68   *Haji-Ioannou v. Frangos* (1999) 2 Lloyd's Rep. 337 (C.A.).

69   *Mærsk Olie & Gas A/S v. Firma M. de Haan en W. de Boer* (Case C-39/02), (2004) ECR I-9657 para. 36.

merits of the case. Presumably, the mere fact that a court has embarked upon consideration of the merits does not mean that its jurisdiction is established. It has been held that jurisdiction is established for this purpose where the court first seised has not declined jurisdiction of its own motion, and where the defendant has not challenged its jurisdiction before advancing a defence on the substance, as defined by the national law of the forum.[70] It is not necessary that the court first seised has implicitly or expressly asserted jurisdiction.

It should be noted that it is incorrect to assume that a stay need only be granted once the **28** jurisdiction of the court first seised is established.[71] Seisin and establishing jurisdiction are distinct operations. As Art. 29 (1) contemplates, the first court may be seised (and a stay required in the second court), although the issue of jurisdiction has not yet been established (or even addressed). Art. 29 (3) operates only once the first court has accepted jurisdiction over the substance of the dispute. But Art. 29 (1) is triggered immediately that proceedings in the first court are initiated.

IV. Procedure in the second court

Whatever the legal requirements for a stay or dismissal under Art. 29, questions remain **29** concerning the procedure to be followed in the second court. Of particular importance is the express requirement in Art. 29 (1) that the second court shall of its own motion stay its proceedings. This phrasing clearly removes from the court the option, formerly permitted by the Brussels Convention, of dismissing rather than staying the action, and ensures that a court can act in the absence of an application by the defendant. But when and how should a court act in the absence of such an application?

Presumably, a defendant may make such application to the court as national law permits, **30** even if the application is that the court itself moves to grant a stay. Again, at a minimum, if the second court's power to act *sua sponte* is to have any content, it must at least be required to examine whether a stay is justified in any case where the circumstances suggest that Art. 29 may be relevant.[72] But is more required? To oblige a court to examine each case before it for indications that Art. 29 may operate would exceed what is necessary to give meaning to the provision, as well as being impractical. Presumably, however, the national procedural law of individual Member States may require courts to make such enquiry when their jurisdiction is invoked, if only perhaps in limited cases, such as those involving parties originating, or events occurring in other Member States. In English law, for example, service of process abroad in a case under the Regulation is permitted only if the claimant states that no proceedings are pending in another Member State.[73] It is perhaps inevitable that such matters are reserved to national law, although some lack of uniformity in the operation of Art. 29 may result.

---

[70]   Case C-1/13, *Cartier parfums–lunettes SAS and Axa Corporate Solutions assurances SA v. Ziegler France SA* (judgment 29 February 2014) nyr.; *Koechel*, IPRax 2014, 5, 394.

[71]   As was wrongly assumed in *Sarrio v. Kuwait Investment Authority* (1997) 1 Lloyd's Rep. 113 (C.A.).

[72]   Report *Jenard*, p. 41.

[73]   CPR 6.19.

Article 30

1. Where related actions are pending in the courts of different Member States, any court other than the court first seised may stay its proceedings.
2. Where the action in the court first seised is pending at first instance, any other court may also, on the application of one of the parties, decline jurisdiction if the court first seised has jurisdiction over the actions in question and its law permits the consolidation thereof.
3. For the purposes of this Article, actions are deemed to be related where they are so closely connected that it is expedient to hear and determine them together to avoid the risk of irreconcilable judgments resulting from separate proceedings.

I. Introduction

1   Art. 30 (1)[1] confers upon the courts of Member States discretion to stay their proceedings if a related action is pending before a court previously seised. In principle, two actions are related when likely to yield inconsistent judgments, although it is unnecessary that they should conflict, in the sense that they each compete for recognition and enforcement. Art. 30 (2) confers a discretion to decline jurisdiction where both actions are pending at first instance, if the procedural law of the court first seised law allows the actions to be consolidated. Importantly, however, it does not require a court to take either course. The second court may opt to allow its proceedings to continue.

2   The rationale underlying Art. 30 (2) is that the second court should in principle dismiss an action which may be consolidated with another action pending in the first court. But, as the requirements for the operation of Art. 30 (2) confirm, this is possible only in particular circumstances. It is feasible only in those cases where the first court has jurisdiction over both actions, and where its proceedings are at first instance, because only then is consolidation possible. There may be, however, a risk of inconsistent judgments beyond cases where consolidation is possible. The same issues may arise, and thus a risk of inconsistency between two court's findings, even if the actions are not capable of consolidation, and even if the first action has reached the appellate stage. So Art. 30 (1) confers a broad power on the second court to stay its proceedings in any case involving related proceedings.

---

[1]   Cf. Report *Jenard*, p. 41; Report *Evrigenis/Kerameus*, para. 68; Explanatory Memorandum, para. 19.

II. The evolution of Art. 30

The origins of Art. 30 lie in Art. 22 of the 1968 Brussels Convention, which established the **3** principle that the second court has discretion to halt proceedings in the event of previous, related proceedings in another court. But in two important ways the operation of Art. 30 is different. First, in the Regulation the requirement that both proceedings should be pending at first instance qualifies only the power to decline jurisdiction under Art. 30 (2), not the power to stay proceedings under Art. 30 (1). In the Brussels Convention it applied to both powers. The reasons for insisting that both proceedings be at first instance are neither clear, nor without difficulty.[2] It is said that in the former situation, if the first action has reached the appeal stage, and the second court declines jurisdiction, it may be difficult for the claimant to commence fresh proceedings in the first court, where the related action is on appeal. But if the second court merely stays its proceedings, there is at least the possibility that a claimant may seek to revive its claim there if proceedings in the first court are indeed prevented. So there is no need to insist that both proceedings are at first instance. Again, it might be thought that Art. 30 should in principle operate when proceedings in the first court have reached the appeal stage, which suggests that the proceedings need not be at first instance. But where the reason for declining jurisdiction is that consolidation is possible in the first court, the benefits of an omnibus action would disappear unless consolidation could be effected at trial. Indeed, consolidation is likely to be impermissible except when proceedings are at first instance.

Secondly, Art. 30 (2) provides that the second court must ensure that the local law of the first **4** court permits consolidation, before the second court declines jurisdiction. This removes an ambiguity present in the wording of the Art. 22 of the Convention, which might be read as requiring that consolidation be permitted in the second court.

III. The purpose of Art. 30

Like Art. 29, Art. 30 is concerned with avoiding irreconcilable judgments by preventing **5** parallel proceedings. But it is broader than Art. 29 in its reach. The subject matter of the proceedings (their basis and object) need not be the same, nor need both proceedings involve the same parties (though they might). It is enough that the proceedings are 'related'.

Art. 30 has a wider ambit than Art. 29 in another sense. The purpose of both is to avoid the **6** risk of 'irreconcilable judgments'. But this conceals an important difference between Arts. 29 and 30. Both are concerned with irreconcilable judgments, defined by Art. 2(a) as contra-dictory decrees, orders or decisions. Art. 29 seeks to avoid resort to the Regulation's rules for allocating priority between conflicting orders or awards. By contrast, the purpose of Art. 30 is to avoid inconsistent decisions, even though the orders made in each case might be capable of separate enforcement without conflict. Thus Art. 29 is concerned with judgments which are *conflicting*, in so far they compete for recognition, while Art. 30 is concerned with those which are *inconsistent*, in the sense that they reach contrary conclusions without competing for recognition. As the CJEU has expressed it, the animating purpose of Art. 30 is 'to improve coordination in the exercise of judicial functions within the Community and

---

[2]   Report *Jenard*, p. 41; *Droz*, para. 323.

Richard Fentiman

to avoid conflicting and contradictory decisions, even where the separate enforcement of each of them is not precluded'.[3]

7 The different spheres of operation of Arts. 29 and 30 may be highlighted by recalling that Art. 30 operates even if the parties in both proceedings are different, or if there is no common cause of action. In such cases, there may no risk of conflicting orders, each requiring enforcement, but the decisions may be inconsistent. This difference, obscured by a common preoccupation with 'irreconcilable judgments', may be illustrated by reference to an example given by Advocate General Darmon.[4] D1 and D2 are accused of joint responsibility for an accident. Each is domiciled in a different Member State, and each is sued in their respective domiciles. One court finds against D1, the other dismisses the action against D2 on the basis that no compensable damage has been suffered. Neither judgment prevents enforcement of the other. But they involve inconsistent judgments on a common issue.

8 Why is it necessary, however, to avoid judgments which, although inconsistent, do not have legally contradictory effects? There is no waste of legal resources if each is effective, and no erosion of the principle of mutual respect between Member States if ultimately each is capable of recognition. One answer is that it is inefficient, and confounds the proper administration of justice, for two courts to address the same issue. But the vices of parallel litigation are not directly the Regulation's concern. Another answer is that uniformity in adjudication is an objective of the Regulation, whether or not the enforcement of conflicting judgments is involved. Such uniformity is implicit in the very idea that a judgment obtained in one Member State should be recognised throughout the Union. Such uniformity is directly subverted, however, if two courts are capable of giving inconsistent judgments in the same matter. In such cases, a stay or dismissal under Art. 30 is 'conducive to the substantive uniformity of judicial decisions', which is 'in conformity with the objectives pursued by the Brussels [Regulation]'.[5]

IV. The operation of Art. 30

9 The operation of Art. 30 is somewhat complex, partly because of differences between its two limbs. Both Art. 30 (1) and Art. 30 (2) confer upon the second court discretion to decline to exercise jurisdiction. But under Art. 30 (1) this takes the form of a stay of the second court's proceedings, while under Art. 30 (2) the second court may dismiss the proceedings. Again, Art. 30 (2) engages only if the related proceedings are both at first instance. Art. 30 (1), however, operates even if the second court is seised after appellate proceedings have started in the first court. A further difference is that Art. 30 (2) operates only if the first court has jurisdiction over both actions, a requirement absent from Art. 30 (1). Moreover, the second court has a different role under each limb. Unlike Art. 30 (1), Art. 30 (2) provides that proceedings may be dismissed on the application of one of the parties. The implication is that the second court may of its own motion stay its proceedings under Art. 30 (1), although in practice it is uncertain how it could be aware of the earlier proceedings unless they are brought to its attention by one of the parties.

---

3 *The owners of the cargo lately laden on board the ship "Tatry" v. The owners of the ship "Maciej Rataj"* (Case C-406/92), (1994) ECR I-5439, I-5479 para. 55.
4 A-G *Darmon*, (1988) ECR 5565, 5575 para. 30.
5 A-G *Tesauro*, (1994) ECR I-5442, I-5457 para. 30.

The particular purpose underlying Art. 30 (2) dictates the more specific preconditions for its **10** operation. Because its objective is to allow the consolidation of all proceedings in the court first seised, it operates only if consolidation is possible in principle – if the first court has jurisdiction over both actions, and if the first court's proceedings are at first instance – and if the local law of the first court otherwise permits consolidation. The particular purpose of Art. 30 (2) also means that the second court may – indeed, must – examine the jurisdiction of the first court, to ensure that the latter has jurisdiction over both actions. In this respect, Art. 30 (2) provides a limited exception to the principle that the courts of one Member State may not examine the jurisdiction of another such State.

The operation of Art. 30 depends principally upon four matters: the concept of pending **11** proceedings; the concept of related proceedings; the nature and scope of the second court's discretion; the relationship between Arts. 30 (1) and (2).

V. Pending proceedings

Art. 30 (1) operates where related actions are pending in different Member States. Art. 30 (2) **12** applies where those actions are 'pending at first instance'. Proceedings are presumably pending for the purposes of Art. 30 (1) when both courts are seised in accordance with Art. 30. But the concept of proceedings pending at first instance is more problematic. Inevitably the courts concerned must be seised under Art. 30. But two further questions arise: when does a court become seised at first instance; when does it cease to be so seised? Neither question is definitively answered by the Regulation, the case law, or in the literature. Presumably, however, whether actions are pending at first instance is a community matter, requiring an autonomous interpretation. Principle suggests that there should be no necessity that the relevant courts have accepted jurisdiction, because the issue of jurisdiction may be in dispute at first instance. But it is uncertain whether a hearing date must have been fixed, or whether mere seisin is sufficient. As to when proceedings cease at first instance, it must be enough that judgment has been given, provided that no further application to the trial court remains possible.

VI. Related proceedings

Central to the operation of both limbs of Art. 30 is the concept of 'related' proceedings (the **13** proper understanding of which explains how Art. 30 differs from Art. 29). Art. 30 (3) provides that 'actions are deemed to be related where they are so closely connected that it is expedient to hear and determine them together to avoid the risk of irreconcilable judgments resulting from separate proceedings'. But the term 'irreconcilable judgments' is ambiguous. It might be understood narrowly, to mean judgments involving inconsistent orders (or awards). Or it might be taken broadly, so as to embrace cases where the findings made in both courts are incompatible, although the terms of the orders made are not. The narrow view, however, would tend to make Art. 30 redundant, by requiring (in effect) that both proceedings have the same legal objective. It would mean that actions are related where they might result in two conflicting judgments, such that the Regulation's rules for conferring priority between such judgments would apply.[6] If, however, Art. 30 is to have an independent role, the concept of relatedness must be broader than the concept of congruence upon

---

[6]   Art. 34 (3) and (4).

which Art. 29 depends. And the definition of 'irreconcilable judgments' in Art. 30 (3) must be wider than that required in Arts. 34 (3) and (4), which regulate priority between inconsistent orders.

14 In *The Tatry*[7] the Court of Justice rejected the argument that proceedings are related only when they disturb the European regime for the enforcement of judgments, by leading to two equally valid but contradictory orders. They defined the term 'irreconcilable judgments' broadly to mean judgments which come to opposite conclusions, but which do not have contradictory effects. As the Court said, the goal of avoiding irreconcilable judgments is in this context the goal of avoiding 'conflicting and contradictory decisions, even where the separate enforcement of each of them is not precluded'.[8]

1. Conceptual problems

15 The test of relatedness remains in some respects uncertain. This stems from the tension between giving Art. 30 a broad interpretation, as required by the Court of Justice,[9] and the difficulties that might arise in doing so. No doubt the goal of avoiding inconsistent judgments is served by taking a broad view, and capturing a wide range of cases within Art. 30. But too broad an approach may undermine the procedural efficiency which is also a goal of the Regulation, by requiring courts to speculate about the likely connectedness of proceedings. Moreover, it is uncertain how broad an approach is actually required. There is a continuing debate about the precise purpose of the provisions: is it intended to prevent any overlap between proceedings, or merely inconsistent decisions, orders and awards? But a more practical problem also underlies Art. 30. Should courts adopt a technical, intricate approach to its operation, or should they take a less refined, more common sense stance? It is perhaps unsurprising that one leading national judgment on the problem of related actions deliberately avoids such intricacy in favour of a less technical, common sense approach.[10] But it is uncertain how cases could in practice be argued and decided without reference to the precise conceptual components of Art. 30.

a) Evaluating the risk of irreconcilability

16 A cluster of conceptually distinct, yet practically intertwined, problems concern the evaluation of the risk of irreconcilable judgments:

17 i) **The degree of risk.** One aspect of the problem concerns the required degree of risk. Is any risk of irreconcilability sufficient? Or is some higher degree of likelihood required? There is no definitive answer. A broad reading of Art. 30 suggests that any risk should be sufficient, however unlikely. And the Court of Justice may favour this view, having stated that the interpretation of Art. 30 'must be broad and cover all cases where there is a risk of conflicting decisions'.[11] But it may be preferable to take a narrow view, and conclude that it must be

---

7   *The owners of the cargo lately laden on board the ship "Tatry" v. The owners of the ship "Maciej Rataj"* (Case C-406/92), (1994) ECR I-5439.

8   *The owners of the cargo lately laden on board the ship "Tatry" v. The owners of the ship "Maciej Rataj"* (Case C-406/92), (1994) ECR I-5439, I-5478 *et seq.* para. 54.

9   *The owners of the cargo lately laden on board the ship "Tatry" v. The owners of the ship "Maciej Rataj"* (Case C-406/92), (1994) ECR I-5439, I-5478 para. 52.

10 *Sarrio SA v. Kuwait Investment Authority* (1999) 1 AC 32 (H.L.).

certain beyond doubt that the second proceedings will lead to irreconcilable judgments. It cannot have been intended that the second court should engage in speculation as to what might transpire, for that subverts the procedural certainty prized under the Regulation. It is surely not intended that the second court should indulge in lengthy examination of the possible arguments and conclusions that might be made in the court first seised. Again, for any risk of irreconcilability to trigger Art. 30 would mean that a stay or dismissal would be granted more often than not. Given that Art. 30 concerns the lesser evil of inconsistent judgments (not the conflicting judgments of Art. 29), it may be doubted that it should be so broadly interpreted.

In *Research in Motion UK Ltd. v. Visto Corp.*[12] the English Court of Appeal held that **18** proceedings are not related merely because a risk of inconsistent judgments exists. It is for the court to determine whether the risk is sufficiently great to make the actions related. In *Visto* an application had been made in English proceedings for a declaration concerning an English patent in connection with a particular product. There were already Italian proceedings concerning other products. There was a risk of inconsistency concerning an allegation of abuse of process in Italy, which was before both courts (in England by way of an action in tort for abuse of process). But the degree of potential conflict was insufficient to make the proceedings related for the purpose of Art. 30. No doubt the court might have reached the same result by exercising its Art. 30(1) discretion in favour of allowing the English proceedings. It chose to do so, however, by denying that the two actions were subject to Art. 30 at all. The effect is to broaden the scope for denying that parallel proceedings in the court first seised affect later proceedings elsewhere.

ii) The standard of proof. Allied to the degree of risk required is the question of what **19** standard of proof is to be applied in determining inconsistency. A *prima facie* case, a strongly arguable case, proof beyond reasonable doubt? There are suggestions that the standard of proof should not be strict.[13] Again, however, perhaps it may be inferred that nothing less than certainty beyond doubt is sufficient, thereby avoiding evidential difficulty, uncertainty, and procedural inefficiency.

iii) The definition of judgment. What precisely is a 'judgment' for Art. 30 purposes? It **20** follows from the fact that Art. 29 is intended to avoid conflict between enforceable judgments, that judgments for Art. 29 purposes are judgments, as defined in Art. 2(a), to which the Regulation's enforcement regime applies. There is some uncertainty as to the meaning of judgment within Art. 2(a), but it embraces a 'decree, order, decision or writ of execution', and determinations of a similar character. Certainly, Art. 29 engages only with such final and enforceable legal decisions. But Art. 30 is not directed at avoiding conflicting enforceable judgments. And the concepts of a 'judgment' is in principle sufficiently broad (and ambiguous) to refer both to a final decision, and to the reasoning which supports it – to the statements made and reasons given by the Court in reaching an enforceable decision. Indeed, as the Advocate General Tesauro has said, Art. 30 is intended to "obviate the danger of

---

[11]   *The owners of the cargo lately laden on board the ship "Tatry" v. The owners of the ship "Maciej Rataj"*
       (Case C-406/92), (1994) ECR I-5439, I-5478 para. 52.
[12]   (2008) I.L.Pr. 34 (C.A.).
[13]   *The owners of the cargo lately laden on board the ship "Tatry" v. The owners of the ship "Maciej Rataj"*
       (Case C-406/92), (1994) ECR I-5439, I-5478 para. 52.

judgments which conflict with each other, albeit only as regards their reasoning".[14] And, as he said, the court second seised should deploy Art. 30 "whenever it considers that the reasoning adopted by the court hearing the earlier proceedings may concern issues likely to be relevant to its own decision".[15]

21 Does this mean that Art. 30 extends to cases in which there is no more than a risk of contradictory reasoning in different courts? A broad view of Art. 30 suggests that it does. But it is surely unlikely that Art. 30 was intended to prevent all conflicting statements by the courts of Member States. Moreover, the Court of Justice in *The Tatry* referred to the role of what is now Art. 30 in preventing "conflicting and contradictory decisions, even where the separate enforcement of each of them is not precluded".[16] This implies that the decisions are of the same nature as those caught by Art. 29, namely those capable of recognition and enforcement (albeit that under Art. 30 both are enforceable without difficulty).

22 **iv) The risk of overlap.** Art. 30 revolves around the risk of irreconcilable judgments. A theoretically distinct, but practically interlinked, question concerns the likelihood that common issues will arise in both proceedings. Is the second court confined to considering only those issues which the first court is required to decide in the course of proceedings? Or may it consider those which might arise? The answer is uncertain, although in a leading English case the latter, broader view was adopted.[17]

23 Distinct as these issues are, however, they are in truth different aspects of the same problem. Presumably, if a court is confined to matters which the second court is required to consider, this is tantamount to saying that it must be certain (not merely possible) that irreconcilability will result. This in turn is presumably equivalent to saying that future irreconcilability must be proved beyond doubt. Alternatively, if a broad view is adopted, any risk, and any evidence of possible irreconcilability is sufficient. Again, although formally distinct issues, it is hard to see in practice how the risk that common issues will arise is different from the risk of irreconcilable judgments.

24 Some of these conceptual difficulties were examined at length in an important but controversial English decision. In *Sarrio v. Kuwait Investment Authority*[18] the claimant had sued the defendant in Spain in 1993, with the object of establishing the defendant's liability for sums owed by another company. It subsequently sued the same defendant in England, this time alleging that it had entered into certain contracts only because of misrepresentations by the defendant. It was apparent that some discussion of the alleged misrepresentation might arise in the Spanish proceedings, but that such issues as might arise were incidental to those proceedings. The Court of Appeal therefore held that the actions were not related, on the basis that proceedings are related only if the proceedings have 'primary' issues in common: those which are central to both actions, and thus bound to arise.[19] The House of Lords

---

14 A-G *Tesauro*, (1994) ECR I-5442, I-5457 para. 30.
15 A-G *Tesauro*, (1994) ECR I-5442, I-5457 para. 30.
16 *The owners of the cargo lately laden on board the ship "Tatry" v. The owners of the ship "Maciej Rataj"* (Case C-406/92), (1994) ECR I-5439, I-5478 *et seq.* para. 54.
17 *Sarrio SA v. Kuwait Investment Authority* (1999) 1 AC 32 (H.L.).
18 (1997) 3 WLR 1143 (H.L.); *Briggs*, (1997) BYIL 339; *Harris*, (1997) LMCLQ 145.
19 (1997) 1 Lloyd's Rep. 113 (C.A.); *Briggs*, (1996) 67 BYIL 592.

rejected this approach, and held the proceedings to be related. It is enough that any common issues might arise. In so deciding, the House of Lords committed itself to a broad definition of a judgment for Art. 30 purposes. In so far as it considered that even issues which might arise in proceedings are relevant, it also by implication subscribed to the view that any risk of irreconcilable judgments is sufficient.

b) Relatedness and connectedness

What is the relationship (if any) between the test of *relatedness* in Art. 30, and the apparently **25** similar concept of connectedness used in Art. 8 (1) which provides that an EU-domiciled co-defendant may be sued in the courts of another co-defendant's domicile 'provided the claims are so closely connected that it is expedient to hear and determine them together to avoid the risk of irreconcilable judgments resulting from separate proceedings'. It is unsurprising that Art. 8 (1), like all the grounds of jurisdiction in the Regulation, should be orientated towards avoiding irreconcilable judgments. And the Court of Justice has conflated the two provisions, using the concept of relatedness in the context of Art. 8 (1).[20] But the significance of the Court's approach is uncertain. Certainly, it does not follow from the parallelism between the provisions, that the tests of relatedness and connectedness are the same. The objective of avoiding irreconcilable judgments in Art. 8 (1) is subject to countervailing considerations which do not impact upon Art. 30. Art. 8 (1) is an exception to Art. 4, and should be interpreted narrowly. And in principle court should not too readily assert jurisdiction over a party merely because it is a co-defendant in pending proceedings. Not only are such considerations absent from Art. 30, but the Court of Justice has indicated that Art. 30 is to be interpreted broadly – how broadly, however, remains uncertain.

c) Relatedness and discretion

What is the relationship between the process whereby a court determines whether proceed- **26** ings are related, and the exercise of discretion? It should be recalled that there is a distinction between a court's determination of whether proceedings are related, and its discretion to stay or dismiss proceedings. In the scheme of Art. 30, the risk of irreconcilable judgments goes to the first operation. But is it also relevant to the second? Advocate General Lenz has suggested that it does.[21] Arguably, therefore, even if any discernible risk of irreconcilability means that proceedings are related, the likelihood of the risk maturing is a relevant consideration in considering whether to stay or dismiss proceedings.

2. Examples of related proceedings

Proceedings will be related when the same legal issue arises in two actions involving different **27** parties. In *The Tatry*,[22] a group of cargo owners brought proceedings in one Member State against a shipowner, for breach of a contract for the carriage of goods by sea. Another group of cargo owners then sued in another Member State, for breach of an independent but identical contract for the carriage of goods, which formed part of the same cargo, carried on

---

[20] *Anastasios Kalfelis v. Bankhaus Schröder Münchmeyer Hengst & Cie.*, (Case 189/87) (1988) ECR 5565, 5584 para. 13.

[21] *Owens Bank Ltd. v. Fulvio Bracco Industria Chemica SPA* (Case C-129/92), (1994) ECR I-117, I-155 para. 36 *et seq.*

[22] *The owners of the cargo lately laden on board the ship "Tatry" v. The owners of the ship "Maciej Rataj"* (Case C-406/92), (1994) ECR I-5439, I-5479 para. 57.

the same vessel. There was no risk of conflicting judgments, because the actions were legally distinct. But the same issues were involved, so there was a risk of inconsistent judgments in the two proceedings.

28 Again, in the following cases it has been held that two parallel actions were related: where one concerned an action for breach of contract, and the other concerned breach of a different but identical contract;[23] where there were criminal proceedings in one country for fraud in connection with certain sums, and an action elsewhere to recover the same sums;[24] where in one action a declaration was sought to enforce an arbitration agreement, and in the other the defence to the substantive claim was that the dispute should be submitted to arbitration;[25] where in one court an action was brought in damages, and in the other there were proceedings to limit any liability that might arise.[26] By contrast, the following parallel actions involving the same parties have been held not to be related: an action concerning the infringement of a trade mark, and another for passing off;[27] an application for an injunction to enforce an arbitration agreement, and proceedings concerning the parties' substantive dispute.[28]

VII. The Art. 30 discretion

29 Art. 30 confers upon the court second seised discretion to decline to exercise jurisdiction. Under Art. 30 (1) the court has discretion to stay its proceedings; under Art. 30 (2) it has discretion to dismiss the action. Difficulty surrounds the circumstances in which the court's discretion may be exercised – difficulty especially evident in cases under Art. 30 (1). Two questions arise. What is the strength of the Art. 30 discretion, and what considerations are relevant to its exercise?

1. Strength of the discretion

30 It is uncertain whether Article 30 contemplates a strong discretion, whereby the judge's evaluation is relatively unconstrained, or a weak discretion, whereby it is restricted by principle. There are four possible approaches to the structure of the Article 30 discretion. First, there may be no true discretion at all in such cases. The optional character of the test may be exhausted once a court has concluded on the facts that proceedings are related. On this view, the permissive 'may' in Article 30(1) means only that the test of relatedness in Article 30(3) may or may not be satisfied in a given case. Some slight support for this position may be derived from the Schlosser report on the Brussels Convention,[29] but this is inconsistent with the words of Article 30(1), which suggest that the existence of related proceedings is but a pre-condition for the exercise of discretion.

---

[23] *IP Metal Ltd. v. Ruote Spa* (1993) 2 Lloyd's Rep. 60 (Q.B.D, *Waller* J.).

[24] *Haji-Ioannu v. Frangos* (1999) 2 Lloyd's Rep. 337 (C.A.).

[25] *Toepfer International GmbH v. Molino Boschi SRL* (1996) 1 Lloyd's Rep. 510 (Q.B.D, *Mance* J.).

[26] *Mærsk Olie & Gas A/S v. Firma M. de Haan en W. de Boer* (Case C-39/02), (2004) ECR I-9657 para. 40.

[27] *Mecklermedia Corp. v. DC Congress GmbH* (1997) I.L.Pr. 629 (Q.B.D., *Jacob* J.).

[28] *Charterers' Mutual Assurance Assn. Ltd. v. British and Foreign* (1998) I.L.Pr 838 (Q.B.D, Judge *Diamond* Q.C.).

[29] [1979] OJ C 59/71, at [76].

Secondly, a court may enjoy a broad discretion to stay proceedings, constrained only by the 31
general principles underlying the Regulation, and the objectives of Article 30 in particular.
This expansive approach, in which the enquiry is largely unstructured, is evident in particular in the English case law.[30]

Thirdly, courts may have such a broad discretion, but subject additionally to the procedural 32
principle that a stay should be granted in the event of doubt. Traces of this approach may be
found in remarks by Advocate-General Lenz in *Owens Bank v. Bracco*,[31] but it is unclear that
he favoured this position.

Fourthly, drawing on A-G Lenz's remarks in *Owens Bank*, it is arguable that the discretion is 33
subject to a presumption in favour of a stay. This view reconciles the language of Article 30,
which confers a discretion to stay, with the broader objective of ensuring procedural certainty. This view finds support a passage in the Jenard Report on the Brussels Convention,
which states that 'the first duty of the court is to stay its proceedings',[32] and in the approach
of A-G Lenz in *Owens Bank*, who endorsed the view, expressed in the English cases, that
there is 'a strong presumption in favour of allowing an application for a stay'.[33] It is not clear,
however, that these statements endorse the existence of formal burden of proof, whereby a
claimant bears the burden of rebutting a presumption in favour of a stay. Certainly, the
existence of such a 'strong' presumption in favour of a stay has since been doubted in some
decided cases,[34] but accepted in others.[35] The existence of such a strong presumption has
been endorsed, however, by the UK Supreme Court in a leading case.[36]

2. Relevant considerations

It is uncertain what considerations are relevant to the exercise of the Article 30 discretion. 34
The enquiry is apparently concerned not merely with avoiding irreconcilable judgments, but
more broadly with ensuring the proper administration of justice. This is consistent with the
test for staying proceedings in favour of alternative proceedings in a third state,[37] and finds
support in the approach of Advocate-General Lenz in *Owens Bank*. Advocate-General Lenz
saw the enquiry as constrained by two general principles. The overriding objective is to

---

[30] *Centro Internationale Bank AG v. Morgan Grenfell Trade Finance Ltd* [1997] CLC 870; *Trademark
Licensing Co v. Leofelis SA* [2010] ILPr 290; *Nordea Bank Norge Asa v. Unicredit Corporate Banking
SPA* [2011] EWHC 30 (Comm), at [87].

[31] Case C-129/92 [1994] QB 509, at [75], citing with approval the approach adopted in *Virgin Aviation Ltd
v. CAD Aviation* [1991] ILPr 79, 88.

[32] *Jenard*, Report on the Convention on jurisdiction and the enforcement of judgments in civil and commercial matters, OJ C 59/1 5.3.79, at 41.

[33] Case C-129/92 [1994] QB 509, at [75], approving the approach of Ognall J in *Virgin Aviation Services Ltd
v. CAD Aviation Services* [1991] ILPr 79, 88.

[34] *Centro Internationale Bank AG v. Morgan Grenfell Trade Finance Ltd* [1997] CLC 870; *Trademark
Licensing Co v. Leofelis SA* [2010] ILPr 290; *Nordea Bank Norge Asa v. Unicredit Corporate Banking
SPA* [2011] EWHC 30 (Comm), at [87].

[35] *JP Morgan Ltd v. Primacom AG* [2005] 2 Lloyd's Rep. 665, at [65].

[36] *Starlight Shipping Co v. Allianz Marine & Aviation Versicherungs AG (The Alexandros T)* [2013] UKSC
70, at [92]-[93].

[37] Brussels I*bis*, Articles 33(1)(b), 34(2)(d).

Richard Fentiman   745

prevent parallel proceedings, and thus conflicting judgments, for which reason there is a presumption in favour of a stay. But the discretion to stay depends, however, on three further considerations: the stage each action has reached; which court is in the best position to decide the questions at issue; which court has the closest proximity to the subject matter of the proceedings.[38]

35   The second of these additional factors clearly concerns the efficient administration of justice. The first relates to the risk of irreconcilable judgments, but in this context may concern instead the inefficiency inherent in replicating foreign proceedings which are substantially advanced. Similarly, the third factor may concern issues of jurisdictional connection, but in this context may reflect the efficiency of hearing a dispute in its natural forum. In that sense, all three factors may be said to relate to the objective of promoting the proper administration of justice.

36   The relationship between these elements in the Article 30 discretion is, however, uncertain. The primacy of the objective of avoiding irreconcilable judgments implies that a stay cannot be granted unless a risk of irreconcilable judgments exists, in which case presumably the presumption in favour of a stay engages. This entails that the proper administration of justice is only relevant when such a risk is found to exist. If that consideration is to have an independent existence, however, there will inevitably be cases where there is a risk of irreconcilable judgments, and a presumption in favour of a stay, in which the proper administration of justice nonetheless requires that a stay is not granted.

37   In practice, the application of these broad principles has generated further, more specific principles. The English courts, for example, have indicated that a stay should not be granted if the foreign proceedings are initiated for tactical reasons, and have denied a stay to avoid rewarding tactical forum shopping by the claimant in the court first seised.[39] They have also concluded that proceedings should be stayed if there is a jurisdiction agreement in favour of the court second seised.[40] In cases involving such a jurisdiction agreement, they have explicitly held that the presumption in favour of a stay is ousted.[41] The justification for this approach is the injustice of permitting breach of such an agreement.[42] Formerly, it is possible that overriding respect for party autonomy was incompatible with the approach of the CJEU, which at one time prized the prevention of parallel proceedings above party autonomy,[43] but the very different approach embodied in Article 31(2) of Brussels *Ibis* requires that party autonomy now has priority.

---

[38]   Case C-129/92 [1994] QB 509, at [79].

[39]   *JP Morgan Europe Ltd v. Primacom AG* [2005] EWHC 508 (Comm) at [65]; *Nordea Bank Norge ASA, Vasonia Shipping Company Limited v. Unicredit Corporate Banking SpA, Banca di Roma SpA* [2011] EWHC 30 (Comm), at [88].

[40]   *JP Morgan Ltd v. Primacom AG* [2005] 2 Lloyd's Rep. 665, at [65]; *Starlight Shipping Co v. Allianz Marine & Aviation Versicherungs AG* [2013] UKSC 70, at [94]; *Nomura International Plc v. Banca Monte Dei Paschi Di Siena SpA* [2013] EWHC 3187 (Comm), at [73]–[83].

[41]   *JP Morgan Ltd v. Primacom AG* [2005] 2 Lloyd's Rep. 665, at [65]; *Starlight Shipping Co v. Allianz Marine & Aviation Versicherungs AG* [2013] UKSC 70, at [93].

[42]   See, however, *Starlight Shipping Co v. Allianz Marine & Aviation Versicherungs AG*, at [96].

[43]   *Starlight Shipping Co v. Allianz Marine & Aviation Versicherungs AG* [2013] UKSC 70, at [95].

3. Discretion: the Article 30 model

These considerations suggest a coherent model for approaching the Article 30 discretion. **38** Principle demands that a court should ask first if there is a risk of irreconcilable judgments, based on the degree of overlap between the issues, and the progress of both actions. If such a risk exists, the Article 30 discretion engages, controlled by a presumption in favour of granting a stay. That presumption may be rebutted in one of two ways. First, there may be an agreement to the jurisdiction of the court second seised. Second, the proper administration of justice may demand that a stay is refused. Whether the proper administration of justice requires that a stay is refused is guided by two general principles. Irreconcilable judgments should be avoided, and tactical litigation in the court first seised should not be rewarded. Subject to those principles, what the proper administration of justice requires depends on which court is best placed to decide the questions at issue, and which court has the closest proximity to the subject matter of the proceedings. As this suggests, the risk of irreconcilable judgments triggers the Article 30 enquiry, and governs its shape by requiring a presumption in favour of a stay, but whether a stay is granted depends on distinct considerations concerning procedural efficiency and justice.

Applying these principles, national courts have considered the practicality and efficiency **39** advantages of allowing proceedings to continue in the face of prior parallel proceedings,[44] they have taken account of the slowness of proceedings in the court first seised when refusing a stay,[45] and they have held that a court is in principle best placed to apply its own law.[46]

VIII. The relationship between Arts. 30 (1) and (2)

Inevitably, there will be cases where the specific requirements of Art. 30 (2) will not be **40** satisfied, so that only the more general provisions of Art. 30 (1) are available. But what if they are satisfied, so that a court has a choice whether to employ Art. 30 (1) or Art. 30 (2)? It is tempting to assume that the broader power to stay proceedings under Art. 30 (1) is residual, available only if the narrower power to dismiss for consolidation under Art. 30 (2) is not. If so, a court should decline jurisdiction where circumstances permit, and only grant a stay if they do not. This natural reading of Art. 30 is supported by the fact that it was originally intended that the only power available is one to decline jurisdiction to allow consolidation in the first court.[47] Alternatively, it is possible that the general power to stay is the primary power, as perhaps suggested by remarks in the Jenard Report.[48] But these remarks, far from suggesting a preference in principle for granting a stay, may mean only the power to decline, because narrower, will in fact be used less often. The arguments for normally declining

---

44 *Cooper Tire & Rubber Company Europe Ltd v. Dow Deutschland Inc* [2010] Bus LR 1697 (CA), following the approach in *Cooper Tire & Rubber Co v. Shell Chemicals UK Ltd* [2009] ILPr 886.

45 *Cooper Tire & Rubber Company Europe Ltd v. Dow Deutschland Inc* [2010] Bus LR 1697 (CA); *Cooper Tire & Rubber Co v. Shell Chemicals UK Ltd* [2009] ILPr 886.

46 *Nordea Bank Norge ASA, Vasonia Shipping Company Limited v. Unicredit Corporate Banking SpA, Banca di Roma SpA* [2011] EWHC 30 (Comm), at [88]; *Starlight Shipping Co v. Allianz Marine & Aviation Versicherungs AG* [2013] UKSC 70, at [96].

47 *Gaudemet-Tallon* para. 300.

48 Report *Jenard*, p. 41.

jurisdiction perhaps cohere better with the logic and history of Art. 30. But this is far from certain and, in truth, no particular ordering is required by the language of Art. 30. If, however, there is no indication as to which power is paramount, and if courts have an untrammelled discretion to select between the alternatives, courts are left in an awkward position. For, although commentators have suggested possible approaches,[49] neither principle nor authority indicates how they should select one or the other.

Article 31

1. Where actions come within the exclusive jurisdiction of several courts, any court other than the court first seised shall decline jurisdiction in favour of that court.
2. Without prejudice to Article 26, where a court of a Member State on which an agreement as referred to in Article 25 confers exclusive jurisdiction is seised, any court of another Member State shall stay the proceedings until such time as the court seised on the basis of the agreement declares that it has no jurisdiction under the agreement.
3. Where the court designated in the agreement has established jurisdiction in accordance with the agreement, any court of another Member State shall decline jurisdiction in favour of that court.
4. Paragraphs 2 and 3 shall not apply to matters referred to in Sections 3, 4 or 5 where the policyholder, the insured, a beneficiary of the insurance contract, the injured party, the consumer or the employee is the claimant and the agreement is not valid under a provision contained within those Sections.

I. Parallel exclusive jurisdiction

1   The Regulation regulates parallel proceedings in two ways: by allocating exclusive jurisdiction to a given court in certain cases, so that no other proceedings are possible; and by allocating competence to the court first seised. But what if more than one court has exclusive jurisdiction? Art. 29 provides that 'any court other than the court first seised shall decline jurisdiction'. The solution is logical, because neither court in such a case may be said to have paramount jurisdiction. But the number of cases in which Art. 29 is likely to be relevant is smaller than might be thought. It is unlikely that two courts could often have jurisdiction on any of the grounds for exclusive jurisdiction under Art. 24, because those grounds are territorially specific. They confer jurisdiction which is not merely legally exclusive, but also factually unique. Consider a case involving Art. 24 (1), which confers exclusive jurisdiction on the courts of the situs in cases concerning title to immovable property. In such a case, it is self-evident that only one court can be seised under Art. 24, because such property can only be located in one place. Parallel proceedings under Art. 24 cannot then occur.

---

[49]   *Briggs/Rees* para. 2.245 *et seq.*

However, two courts might have exclusive jurisdiction under Art. 24 in cases under Art. 24   **2**
(2), which confers exclusive jurisdiction in matters of corporate status upon the courts of the
country where the corporation has its seat. Art. 24 itself provides that each Member State
shall determine the seat of a corporation by reference to 'its rules of private international
law'. This creates the possibility that two or more States might regard a corporation as
located within its jurisdiction, a conflict of jurisdiction that Art. 29 would resolve.

Further difficulties surround the application of Art. 30 to parallel proceedings under Art. 25.   **3**
On the one hand, there is some doubt whether Art. 30 should apply in such cases at all. It is
true that the Regulation uses the language of exclusive jurisdiction in connection with
prorogation of jurisdiction under Art. 25, and such jurisdiction shall be exclusive unless
otherwise agreed. But Art. 25 is included within Section 7 of the Regulation, headed 'prorogation of jurisdiction', not Section 6, headed 'exclusive jurisdiction'. This begs the question
whether Art. 30 only regulates cases under Art. 24. If it does not, however, the result would
be same, because presumably Art. 29 would operate in that event, achieving the same result.

If Art. 30 does properly regulate cases under Art. 25, when will it do so? Two states could   **4**
only have exclusive jurisdiction by agreement when a jurisdiction clause confers jurisdiction
on more than one Member State's courts, and the parties have not agreed that the jurisdiction of each such court is to be non-exclusive. At first sight it might be doubted whether
Art. 30 could in fact apply to two courts purporting to have exclusive jurisdiction under
Art. 25. Arguably, even if the parties have purported to confer 'exclusive' jurisdiction on two
courts, they have in reality agreed to the non-exclusive jurisdiction of both, in which case
Art. 30 is irrelevant. But this is to misunderstand the operation of Art. 25. To confer exclusive
jurisdiction on two courts does not imply that such jurisdiction is non-exclusive, because it
does not mean that any other court having jurisdiction may hear the case. Arguably it means
that the only courts with competence are those nominated, the first seised being that which
hears the case.

It should be noted, however, that Art. 30 is not the only means by which the Regulation   **5**
regulates parallel exclusive jurisdiction. Suppose that one court has exclusive jurisdiction
under Art. 24, and another has exclusive jurisdiction under Art. 25. In that event, Art. 29 is
ousted, because Art. 25 (4) gives priority to the court having jurisdiction under Art. 24.

II. Parallel proceedings and jurisdiction agreements

1. Article 31(2) and preclusive proceedings

Article 31(2) provides that a court in one Member State must stay its proceedings where the   **6**
courts of another such State are seised of a dispute in which jurisdiction is asserted under
Article 25, until such time as the court designated in the agreement declines jurisdiction. The
effect is to confer *competence–competence* to determine the effects of such an agreement on
the designated court. The intention is to ameliorate the consequences if the CJEU's controversial decision in *Erich Gasser GmbH v. MISAT Srl*,[1] which conferred *competence–com-*

---

[1]   Case C-116/02 [2003] ECR I-14693; *Fentiman* (2005) 42 CMLR 241, (2006) Jl. Int. Banking and Financial
     L 304; *Mance* (2004) 120 LQR 357; see generally, *Merrett* (2006) 55 ICLQ 315.

petence on any court first seised of a dispute, not the designated court. The effects of this reform may be partial, however, and Article 31(2) creates difficulties of its own.

7   Article 31 (2) is supplemented by two related provisions. Article 31(3) completes the scheme of protection, by providing that, where the court designated in the agreement has established jurisdiction in accordance with the agreement, any court of another Member State shall decline jurisdiction in favour of that court. The protective regime of Articles 31(2) and (3) do not apply, however, to jurisdiction agreements in contracts where unequal bargaining power is assumed to exist. They do not apply to the special provisions concerning insurance, consumer or employment contracts within Sections 3, 4 or 5 in cases where the policyholder, the insured, a beneficiary of the insurance contract, the injured party, the consumer or the employee is the claimant, and where the agreement is invalid according to the provisions in those Sections.

8   Importantly, Article 31(2) is not the only mechanism for regulating the problem of pre-clusive proceedings in one EU state in breach of a jurisdiction agreement designating the courts of another such state. When applicable, the Hague Convention on Choice of Court Agreements provides protection for jurisdiction agreements in such cases, in substitution for the protection supplied by Article 31(2).[2]

2. The problem in Gasser

9   It was established in *Erich Gasser GmbH v. MISAT Srl*[3] that the priority conferred on the court first seised under Article 27 of Regulation 44/2001 (now Article 29 of Brussels *Ibis*), prevented the designated court from considering or exercising jurisdiction conferred by a jurisdiction agreement pursuant to Article 23 (now Article 25). Chronological priority must be strictly enforced in such cases because of the overriding need to avoid parallel proceed-ings within the EU. The decision in *Gasser* was subjected to considerable criticism, for its lack of practical awareness, and for promoting tactical forum shopping.[4] Its effect is to encourage pre-emptive proceedings in a non-designated court, intended to circumvent the agreed jurisdiction, and perhaps to force a settlement by exposing the defendant in those proceedings to delay, and possibly irrecoverable costs.[5] That risk is exacerbated be-cause Article 27 (now Article 29) engages even where a tactical claimant seeks a declaration of non-liability in the non-designated court concerning an issue identical with that in the designated court.[6] Moreover, the party seeking to enforce any agreement will be unable to restrain such pre-emptive proceedings by injunction,[7] although they might seek to recover its costs in damages, either against the claimant in the foreign proceedings,[8] or against its legal advisers.[9]

---

[2]   The *Hague Convention of 30 June 2005 on Choice of Court Agreements*; Hartley/Dogauchi, Explanatory Report on the 2005 Hague Choice of Court Agreements Convention (HCCH, 2013).

[3]   Case C-116/02 [2003] ECR I-14693.

[4]   *Fentiman* (2005) 42 CMLR 241, (2006) Jl. Int. Banking and Financial L 304; *Mance* (2004) 120 LQR 357; see generally, *Merrett* (2006) 55 ICLQ 315.

[5]   Fentiman, in de Vareilles-Sommières, ed, *Forum Shopping in the European Judicial Area* (2007), 27.

[6]   *JP Morgan Europe Ltd v. Primacom AG* [2005] EWHC 508 (Comm).

[7]   Case C-159 *Turner v. Grovit* [2004] ECR I-3565.

3. The solution in Article 31(2)

Brussels I*bis* addresses the problem created by *Gasser*. Where proceedings are commenced **10** after 10 January 2015, the agreed court has priority in determining the effect of a jurisdiction agreement even if second seised. Article 31(2) states that any court other than that designated, shall stay its proceedings 'until such time as the court seised on the basis of the agreement declares that it has no jurisdiction under the agreement'.

Article 31(2) is augmented by Recital (22), which suggests that the provision has two ele- **11** ments. The non-designated must stay its proceedings immediately the agreed court has been seised, until such time as the agreed court declines jurisdiction, while the agreed court may entertain proceedings once it is seised, irrespective of whether the court first seised has granted a stay. The effect is to solve the problem revealed in *Gasser*, in the way that the majority of practitioners and commentators wished, simply by permitting proceedings in the agreed court. The consequence is that a tactical claimant can no longer secure the advantage of proceedings in its preferred court to the exclusion of proceedings in the agreed court. The solution offered by Article 31(2) and Recital (22) is, however, only partial, and is likely to generate considerable litigation at least until such time as the CJEU addresses its inherent difficulties.

Article 31(2) is problematic for five particular reasons. First, Article 31(2) is triggered only **12** when the designated court is seised. The effect is to create a problem which is the opposite of that revealed in *Gasser*. A tactical claimant wishing to pre-empt proceedings in one EU state might initiate proceedings in its preferred court, alleging the existence of a jurisdiction agreement in favour of that court, engaging Article 31(2), and forcing the defendant to defend the proceedings in the allegedly designated court.[10] In practice, however, the risk of such a 'reverse' torpedo claim might be minimized, depending on the applicable local procedures, insofar as a purely cynical claim to jurisdiction under Article 25 would presumably be struck out as abusive, or penalized by an adverse award of costs against the tactical claimant.

Secondly, it remains unclear at what point the requirement that the non-designated court **13** should stay its proceedings crystallizes. It might be supposed that all that need be established in the court first seised is that the designated court is seised, and that the alleged basis of jurisdiction is Article 25. But the wording of Article 31(2) is different. A stay is conditional on the fact that 'a court of a Member State on which an agreement as referred to in Article 25 confers exclusive jurisdiction is seised'. It is therefore necessary to establish that Art. 25 is engaged, and there is a requirement that the existence and effect of such an agreement must be established, at least provisionally. It cannot be the case that the court first seised must determine whether the designated court has Art. 25 jurisdiction, for that would render Art. 31(2) meaningless. Under Article 31(2) only the designated court has competence to determine the validity and effect of the agreement, matters which cannot be considered in

---

[8]   *Starlight Shipping Company v. Allianz Marine & Aviation Versicherungs AG (The Alexandros T)* [2014] EWCA Civ 1010.

[9]   *AMT Futures Ltd v. Marzillier, Dr Meier & Dr Guntner Rechtsanwaltsgesellschaft mbH* [2014] EWHC 1085.

[10] *Sancho Villa* (2010) 12 Yrbk Priv Intl L 399, 404.

the court first seised.[11] Arguably, however, the court first seised will need to determine at the least the *prima facie* existence of an agreement in favour of the courts of another state, or perhaps the existence of an issue of jurisdiction which should be tried in the designated court. Profound uncertainty therefore surrounds the threshold that must be met before a stay is granted.

14 Thirdly, the reality that a hearing is required to determine whether a stay is necessary has the effect that the risk of tactical litigation in a non-designated court remains. It is unlikely that the party seeking to enforce the agreement could escape entirely the inconvenience and expense of defending proceedings in that court. It is possible, however, that the likelihood of such tactical proceedings will diminish now that the agreed court may entertain proceedings irrespective of proceedings elsewhere. But the risk of tactical forum-shopping in such cases remains.

15 Fourthly, because Article 31(2) assumes the existence of 'a court seised on the basis of the agreement', it engages only if proceedings are commenced in the agreed court, ensuring the survival of the *Gasser* problem in any other case. Any party seeking to rely on Art. 31(2) must therefore initiate proceedings in the agreed court so as to trigger a stay in the court first seised. This has an important practical consequence, by forcing such a party to initiate proceedings in the agreed court, and to incur the costs of doing so, even if does not wish to do so. The effect is to encourage litigation, and to ignore a contracting party's legitimate objection to proceedings in breach of an exclusive jurisdiction agreement whether or not that party is contemplating litigation. As this implies, Article 31(2) is not concerned, as might have been supposed, with enforcing jurisdiction agreements, but with regulating parallel proceedings where the jurisdiction of one court has been agreed.

16 Fifthly, Article 31(2) applies only where Article 25 'confers exclusive jurisdiction', and not where the parties purport to confer non-exclusive jurisdiction on the courts of a Member State. No doubt this is explicable in the context of a bilateral non-exclusive jurisdiction agreement. But it causes difficulty in relation to asymmetric jurisdiction agreements, of the kind ubiquitous in financial transactions.[12] Assuming that such agreements are, in any event, compatible with Article 23,[13] the fact that they operate differently for each party causes difficulty in the context of Article 31(2).

17 Such asymmetric agreements normally require a counterparty, such as a borrower, to submit to the exclusive jurisdiction of a named court, but allow the beneficiary under the agreement, typically a finance party, to bring proceedings there, or in any other court of competent jurisdiction. For the finance party such an agreement is therefore non-exclusive. If X and Y agree to the jurisdiction of the English courts, for example, X alone has the right to sue in any other court of competent jurisdiction. Suppose therefore that Y launches a pre-emptive strike in Germany, and X replies by suing in England. Is Article 31(2) engaged, or

---

[11]   Recital (24).

[12]   *Fentiman* (2013) 72 CLJ 24; *Fentiman, International Commercial Litigation* (2nd ed, 2015), paras. 2.13 *et seq.*, 2.123 *et seq.*

[13]   Doubted in *Ms X v. Banque Edmond de Rothschild.* Cass civ, 1ere, 26.9.2012, No. 11-26.024; *Ancel, Marion, Wynaendts,* Banque & Droit, mars–avril 2013, n°148, 3; *Beale, Clayson* (2013) 28 JIBLR 463; *Briggs* (2013) LMCLQ 138; *Fentiman* (2013) 72 CLJ 24.

does *Gasser* still prevent X from relying on the agreement? If such agreements are not protected by Article 31(2), there remains the potential for a party to an asymmetric agreement to disable the agreement by launching a pre-emptive strike in its preferred court. Principle suggests that a finance party may rely on Article 31(2) in such a case. Such asymmetric agreements, although non-exclusive for the benefit of the 'beneficiary' under the clause, are exclusive against a counterparty.[14] Article 31(2) should therefore engage if a counterparty brings proceedings other than in the designated court in breach of its promise to sue only in that court.

This solution rests, however, on two assumptions. It assumes that the issue is one of the **18** interpretation of the agreement, and that the law applicable to the issue recognizes that such agreements are exclusive against a counterparty. It is clear that, if the nature of the agreement is a matter concerning the interpretation of the clause, it is a matter for the national law of the forum.[15] Moreover, the proposition that the nature and effect of such agreements is a matter of interpretation is supported by the words of Article 25 of the recast Regulation, which effectively defines an exclusive jurisdiction agreement as one which the parties have not agreed should be non-exclusive. The implication is that the character of the agreement is determined by the parties' intentions, and is therefore a matter of interpretation. If so, the effect of such a clause would depend on which law the forum applies to that question. This entails, however, that the effect of the agreement would vary depending on the applicable law. An asymmetric jurisdiction agreement might not be regarded as exclusive against a counterparty in some legal systems, perhaps because under the law governing the agreement only mutually exclusive agreements are regarded as exclusive. In other legal systems, however, as in English law, such an agreement would be regarded as exclusive against a counterparty where the law governing the contract is English. An English court would determine the effect of the agreement by reference to the law applicable to the host contract. If that were English law, the agreement would be treated as an exclusive jurisdiction agreement preventing a counterparty from suing other than in the designated court.[16] Article 31(2) would therefore engage to prevent pre-emptive proceedings in another court.

4. Article 31 and the Hague Convention

In certain cases Article 31(2) cedes its control of preclusive proceedings to the 2005 Con- **19** vention on choice of court agreements.[17] Where the Convention applies, Article 6 imposes an obligation to decline jurisdiction on any court other than the court designated by a jurisdiction agreement. A court other than the designated court shall suspend or dismiss proceedings subject to an exclusive choice of court agreement applies unless: *(a)* the agreement is null and void under the law of the State of the chosen court; *(b)* a party lacked the

---

14   *Continental Bank NA v. Aeakos Compania Naviera SA* [1994] 1 WLR 588 (CA); *Mauritius Commercial Bank Limited v. Hestia Holdings Limited* [2013] EWHC 1328 (Comm).

15   *Powell Duffryn plc v. Wolfgang Petereit* Case C-214/89 [1992] ECR I-1745.

16   *Continental Bank NA v. Aeakos Compania Naviera SA* [1994] 1 WLR 588 (CA); *Mauritius Commercial Bank Limited v. Hestia Holdings Limited* [2013] EWHC 1328 (Comm).

17   The Convention of 30 June 2005 on Choice of Court Agreements (in force since 1 October 2015); *Hartley* and *Dogauchi, Explanatory Report on the 2005 Convention on Choice of Court Agreements* (2007); *Brand & Herrup, The 2005 Hague Convention on Choice of Court Agreements* (2008); *Hartley* (2006) 31 EL Rev 414; *Briggs* (2010) 12 Yb. PIL 311.

---

capacity to conclude the agreement under the law of the State of the court seised; *(c)* giving effect to the agreement would lead to a manifest injustice or would be manifestly contrary to the public policy of the State of the court seised; *(d)* for exceptional reasons beyond the control of the parties, the agreement cannot reasonably be performed; or *(e)* the chosen court has decided not to hear the case.

20 Each EU Member State is a Contracting State under the Convention, by virtue of the fact that the European Council is empowered to approve the Convention on behalf of the Member States.[18] This gives rise to a potential conflict between the regime of the Regulation, embodied in Article 31(2), and that of the Convention, contained in Article 6. This is removed by Article 26(6) of the Convention, which mediates between the two regimes.[19] Article 26(6) provides that the Convention shall not affect the application of the Regulation 'where none of the parties is resident in a Contracting State that is not a Member State'. The effect is that the Convention supplants the Regulation unless either both parties are EU residents, or come from third states which are not parties to the Convention. A company domiciled in Germany may, for example, conclude a contract with a company domiciled in England, which contains an agreement to submit any disputes to the exclusive jurisdiction of the English courts. The German company brings pre-emptive proceedings in Germany, and the English company responds by suing in England in reliance on the agreement. Neither party is resident in a Hague Convention State which is not an EU Member State, so pursuant to Article 26(6) of the Convention, the case is subject to Article 31(2) of the Regulation. The effect is that the Convention reduces the scope of application of the Regulation, but this is warranted by 'the increase in the respect for party autonomy at international level and increased legal certainty for EU companies engaged in trade with third State parties'.[20]

Article 32

1. For the purposes of this Section, a court shall be deemed to be seised:
   (a) at the time when the document instituting the proceedings or an equivalent document is lodged with the court, provided that the claimant has not subsequently failed to take the steps he was required to take to have service effected on the defendant; or
   (b) if the document has to be served before being lodged with the court, at the time when it is received by the authority responsible for service, provided that the claimant has not subsequently failed to take the steps he was required to take to have the document lodged with the court. The authority responsible for service referred to in point (b) shall be the first authority receiving the documents to be served.

---

[18] Proposal for a Council Decision on the approval, on behalf of the European Union, of the Hague Convention of 30 June 2005 on Choice of Court Agreements, Explanatory Memorandum, para. 3.1, COM/2014/046 final – 2014/0021 (NLE).

[19] *Hartley/Dogauchi, Explanatory Report on the 2005 Convention on Choice of Court Agreements* (2007), para. 295 *et seq.*

[20] Proposal for a Council Decision on the approval, on behalf of the European Union, of the Hague Convention of 30 June 2005 on Choice of Court Agreements, Explanatory Memorandum, para. 3.1, COM/2014/046 final – 2014/0021 (NLE).

2. The court, or the authority responsible for service, referred to in paragraph 1, shall note, respectively, the date of the lodging of the document instituting the proceedings or the equivalent document, or the date of receipt of the documents to be served.

I. The definition of seisin

Arts. 29 and 32 depend upon knowing which court is first seised. Art. 32[1] provides a **1** common, community definition of seisin for this purpose. No such common definition exists in connection with the Brussels and Lugano Conventions, seisin being a matter for the internal law of each Contracting State.[2] This approach has obvious flaws, not least lack of uniformity and evidential difficulties, flaws avoided by the common definition provided by Art. 32.

The effect of Art. 32 is that a court is seised of a dispute for Regulation purposes when the **2** first authoritative step is taken in the initiation of proceedings under the national law of the Member State in question. Because the procedures for initiating proceedings are different between Member States, Art. 32 reflects these differences by supplying two mutually exclusive definitions of seisin. Each captures the essence of the two distinct approaches to seisin accepted in different Member States. Art. 32 (1) applies in those Member States where proceedings are initiated by the filing of the claim with the court. It provides that a court is seised 'when the document instituting proceedings or an equivalent document is lodged with the court'. Art. 32 (2) applies in those Member States where service of the claim represents the formal commencement of proceedings. It provides that a court is seised 'when it is received by the authority responsible for service'.

As a deterrent to frivolous or vexatious proceedings, Art. 32 requires that a court will be **3** seised at the time that proceedings were formally initiated only if subsequently the necessary initiation procedures have been completed. Art. 32 (1) provides that a court is only seised by the filing of the claim if subsequently the claim is served. Art. 32 (2) provides that a court is only seised by service of the claim if subsequently the claim is filed. The need for strict compliance with Art. 32 (1) is illustrated by the decision of the English Court of Appeal in *Debt Collect London Ltd. v. SK Slavia Praha-Fotbal AS.*[3] There S, a Czech defendant in English proceedings, argued that those proceedings should be stayed on the basis that a Czech court was first seised. S had not served the claim in the Czech proceedings on D, the claimant in the English proceedings, because S had not paid the necessary court fee. S argued that there was no 'failure' to serve, as contemplated by Art. 32 (1), because S had merely waited for a request to pay by the court, as was the Czech practice. The Court of Appeal held that S had failed to effect service, so that the Czech court was not seised. Importantly, the court saw S's culpability as decisive. There must be a culpable failure to effect service, not a

---

[1]   Explanatory Memorandum, para. 20.

[2]   *Siegfried Zelger v. Sebastiano Salinitri*, (Case 129/83) (1984) ECR 2397; Report *Jenard*, p. 71.

[3]   (2011) 1 WLR 866 (C.A.).

mere omission to do so. But S had a duty to pay the fee, and there was no impediment to doing so. Moreover, it was irrelevant to the question of seisin under Art. 29 that the proceedings were not invalid under Czech law. By contrast, however, there is no failure to take the steps necessary to effect service if a claimant delays service while the parties attempt to negotiate a settlement.[4]

4 The task of ascertaining whether a foreign court is seised, which can involve contested questions of fact and law, is streamlined by Article 29 (2) which provides that, in cases subject to Art. 29 (1), a court seised of a dispute may request another court to indicate, when it was seised in accordance with Article 32, which the requested court must do without delay.

II. Art. 32 in practice

5 Although Art. 32 supplies certainty, its operation is not without difficulty in practice. Art. 32 aspires to ensure that the position of the parties is equivalent wherever proceedings are launched. Despite differences between the rules governing the initiation of proceedings in different Member States, the principle that seisin occurs when the first official step is taken is intended to ensure uniformity. The intention is that a claimant will not be advantaged or disadvantaged by suing in one state rather than another, an especially important consideration if the parties are competing to seise their preferred forum first. But Art. 32 cannot erase every difference in local procedures. Inevitably, the timing, expense, efficiency, and degree of formality involved in different countries may affect which court is first seised. Indeed, it may encourage litigation in countries whose procedures for initiating proceedings are perceived to be most favourable to the claimant. A particular factor may be the extent to which such procedures are 'private' or 'public', in the sense of requiring notice to the other party. Systems where seisin occurs upon the lodging of the originating process may be especially attractive if (as in English law) this does not involve giving immediate notice to the other party. A court may thus be seised although the defendant is unaware of the fact. This contrasts with systems where notice to the defendant triggers seisin. The former approach may be especially attractive to claimants who wish to preserve their legal position by seisin their preferred court, without at the same time publicising the claim, or prompting counter measures from the other party, or being seen to be taking a hostile stance. It may be especially attractive if settlement negotiations are in progress.

III. Problem cases

1. Seisin and extra-judicial proceedings

6 Should initiating a form of alternative dispute resolution constitute seisin of a state's civil courts? It appears that it may, if it has that effect under the law of the state concerned. This may occur where a party requests conciliation as a prelude to court adjudication, where the conciliation authorities are empowered to determine the merits, and where a claimant can proceed to a court hearing only once conciliation fails.[5]

---

[4] *UBS AG v. Kommunale Wasserwerke Leipzig GmbH* (2010) 2 CLC 499 (Q.B.D., *Gloster* J.).

[5] *Lehman Brothers Finance AG v. Klaus Tschira Stiftung GmbH* [2014] EWHC 2982 (Ch).

2. Seisin and amended claims

In complex litigation, particular difficulty arises when a claim is subsequently amended. Are **7** proceedings initiated at the date of the original claim, or the date of any subsequent amendment?[6] One view is that, if a party amends its claim, a court is seised in connection with that amendment from the date when the amendment is made.[7] Alternatively, a court may be seised of the amended claim from the date when the proceedings were originally initiated. The issue becomes significant in cases where, for example, X sues Y in England in January, Y counterclaims in France in February, and X adds an additional claim in the English proceedings in March. Is the court seised of the amended claim in January or March? If in March, the amended claim may be subject to an Article 29 or 32 stay, and X loses its priority. If in January, the English court remains seised, and that priority is maintained.

To conclude that subsequent amendments do not affect the date of seisin is the more **8** straightforward and perhaps more certain solution. It does not require the fragmentation of proceedings into distinct claims, and does not encourage repeated applications for a stay whenever a claim is added. This reflects the language of Recital 11, which states that the Regulation's rules must be 'highly predictable', and of Recital 15, which states that there must be a 'clear and effective mechanism for resolving cases of *lis pendens*'. Moreover, to treat the date of initial seisin as decisive reflects the language of Article 29, which refers not distinct claims, but to 'proceedings involving the same cause of action', and of Article 32(1) (a), which similarly refers to the date when the document instituting the proceedings are lodged.

Two arguments, however, favour treating a court as seised of any amended claim at the date **9** of the amendment. Arguably, the predictability required by the Regulation means that a court can be seised at a given moment only in relation to claims advanced at that moment, not in relation to unanticipated issues. Again, principle suggests that a claimant should not be allowed to treat the issue of the claim as a means of reserving the first court's jurisdiction over claims advanced later, and should be held to the procedural consequences of subsequently changing its case. This fragmented view of a dispute would also appear to be consistent with the position of the UK Supreme Court that the application of Articles 29 and 32 must be related to each claim, not to the proceedings as whole.[8] That view was expressed, however, in the distinct context of the question whether a stay can be granted of only some claims in a bundle of claims.

An alternative, more refined, approach is to differentiate between cases where a new claim **10** concerns facts known at the date of the original proceedings from those where they do not. Arguably, an amended claim arising from the same facts as the original claim might appropriately be consolidated with the original claim, but not where the facts arose subsequently. In the latter case it may be consistent with the expression 'proceedings' to differentiate the claims. Certainly, there may be particular cases in which a court should be regarded as seised when a new claim is added. Suppose X sues Y in England pursuant to an English jurisdiction

---

6   *Grupo Torras SA v. Al-Sabah* [1995] 1 Lloyd's Rep. 374, 431.

7   Referring to: *Briggs* and *Rees*, para. 2.235, *Fentiman*, International Commercial Litigation (2010), at [11.29], *Dicey, Morris*, and *Collins*, paras. 12-060 to 12-069.

8   *Starlight Shipping Co v. Allianz Marine & Aviation Versicherungs AG* [2013] UKSC 70.

agreement, and Y subsequently counter-claims in France. If X then amends its case against Y in England to add an action in damages for breach of the jurisdiction agreement, it would be strange if the amended claim were backdated to the date of original seisin, when it could not have been anticipated at that date.[9]

11 There is some support in the important decision of the UK Supreme Court in *Starlight Shipping Co v. Allianz Marine & Aviation Versicherungs AG*[10] for the view that a court is seised of an amended claim from the date when the proceedings were originally initiated, based primarily on the wording of the Regulation.[11] The Court concluded, however, that the issue was a matter to be referred to the CJEU, were it necessary to do so in the circumstances of any future case.

3. Seisin and discontinuance

12 A distinct question concerns when a court ceases to be seised, a matter not addressed by Article 32. A court may cease to be seised where it dismisses proceedings for want of jurisdiction,[12] or where proceedings are discontinued by the parties, or if the court delivers judgment on the substance of a dispute. But uncertainty arises where a court grants a stay of proceedings. A court might have jurisdiction pursuant to the EU regime, or under its residual rules of national law, but may for example stay its proceedings in favour of the courts of a non-Member State.[13] Alternatively, it might have jurisdiction under its residual rules, compliant with Article 6, and stay its proceedings in favour of proceedings in another Member State.[14] If parallel proceedings are launched subsequently in another Member State, is the first court still seised?

13 Arguably, the answer to this question depends not upon the status of the proceedings under national law, but on an autonomous definition of the concept of seisin. If so, principle suggests that a court cannot remain seised of an action which has been discontinued. An action cannot be regarded as pending if it cannot be continued save on the claimant's application, especially if the court has discretion to refuse. Nor would the objectives of Articles 29 and 32 be promoted if a court remains seised of proceedings which have been suspended, given that there is no risk of parallel proceedings or of inconsistent judgments.[15] As this suggests, the better view may be that a court which has stayed its proceedings is no longer seised. A different approach was taken, however, by the UK Supreme Court in the important case of *Starlight Shipping Co v. Allianz Marine & Aviation Versicherungs AG*.[16] The court held that Article 30 of Regulation 44/2001, now Article 32 of Brussels *Ibis*, gov-

---

[9] *Lloyd's syndicate 980 v. Sinco SA* [2008] ILPr. 49.

[10] [2013] UKSC 70.

[11] At [62].

[12] Eg in English law, where proceedings are vexatious, scurrilous, ill-founded, or otherwise an abuse of process: CPR r 3.4(2)(b).

[13] *Owusu v. Jackson* Case (C-321/02), [2005] ECR I-1383.

[14] *Rofa Sport AG v. DHL (UK) Ltd.* (1989) 1 WLR 902 (C.A.); *The Xin Yang* (1996) 2 Lloyd's Rep. 217 (Q.B. D., *Clarke* J.); *Sarrio SA v. Kuwait Investment Authority* (1997) 1 Lloyd's Rep. 113 (C.A.); *Haji-Ioannou v. Frangos* (1999) 2 Lloyd's Rep. 337 (C.A.); *Newton*, (1997) LMCLQ 337.

[15] The view taken in *Haji-Ioannou v. Frangos* [1999] 2 Lloyd's Rep. 337 (CA).

[16] [2013] UKSC 70.

erned when a court was first seised, not when it ceased to be seised. In consequence, the cessation of seisin was a matter for national procedural law. In English law, a stay of proceedings is not equivalent to dismissal or discontinuance,[17] with the effect that an English court would remain seised of proceedings which had been settled by consent, and would remain first seised in relation to subsequent proceedings in another Member State.

Article 33

1. Where jurisdiction is based on Article 4 or on Articles 7, 8 or 9 and proceedings are pending before a court of a third State at the time when a court in a Member State is seised of an action involving the same cause of action and between the same parties as the proceedings in the court of the third State, the court of the Member State may stay the proceedings if:
   (a) it is expected that the court of the third State will give a judgment capable of recognition and, where applicable, of enforcement in that Member State; and
   (b) the court of the Member State is satisfied that a stay is necessary for the proper administration of justice.
2. The court of the Member State may continue the proceedings at any time if:
   (a) the proceedings in the court of the third State are themselves stayed or discontinued;
   (b) it appears to the court of the Member State that the proceedings in the court of the third State are unlikely to be concluded within a reasonable time; or
   (c) the continuation of the proceedings is required for the proper administration of justice.
3. The court of the Member State shall dismiss the proceedings if the proceedings in the court of the third State are concluded and have resulted in a judgment capable of recognition and, where applicable, of enforcement in that Member State.
4. The court of the Member State shall apply this Article on the application of one of the parties or, where possible under national law, of its own motion.

Article 34

1. Where jurisdiction is based on Article 4 or on Articles 7, 8 or 9 and an action is pending before a court of a third State at the time when a court in a Member State is seised of an action which is related to the action in the court of the third State, the court of the Member State may stay the proceedings if:
   (a) it is expedient to hear and determine the related actions together to avoid the risk of irreconcilable judgments resulting from separate proceedings;
   (b) it is expected that the court of the third State will give a judgment capable of recognition and, where applicable, of enforcement in that Member State; and
   (c) the court of the Member State is satisfied that a stay is necessary for the proper administration of justice.
2. The court of the Member State may continue the proceedings at any time if:
   (a) it appears to the court of the Member State that there is no longer a risk of irreconcilable judgments;
   (b) the proceedings in the court of the third State are themselves stayed or discontinued;

---

[17]   *Rofa Sport AG v. DHLK International (UK) Ltd* [1989] 1 WLR 902, 909H to 910D and 911A-C.

(c) it appears to the court of the Member State that the proceedings in the court of the third State are unlikely to be concluded within a reasonable time; or

(d) the continuation of the proceedings is required for the proper administration of justice.

3. The court of the Member State may dismiss the proceedings if the proceedings in the court of the third State are concluded and have resulted in a judgment capable of recognition and, where applicable, of enforcement in that Member State.

4. The court of the Member State shall apply this Article on the application of one of the parties or, where possible under national law, of its own motion.

I. Introduction

1   Articles 33 and 34 of Brussels *Ibis* regulate, to a limited extent, the allocation of jurisdiction between the courts of EU and third states. Both provisions permit EU national courts seised under the Regulation to stay their proceedings in the event of pending proceedings in a third state. The introduction of this new regime begs important questions of practice and principle which are likely to encourage litigation, and occupy both national courts and the CJEU, for some time. These partly concern the operation of Articles 33 and 34, and in particular how the discretion to stay is to be exercised. Significantly, however, they also concern the scope of the new regime. Is it exclusive, with the effect that national courts cannot decline jurisdiction in other circumstances in favour of proceedings in a third state? Or are cases not expressly subject to Articles 33 and 34 subject to national law? If national law remains applicable in certain cases, in what circumstances may a court decline jurisdiction under its national rules? The problematic scope of the new regime is of particular importance because it regulates only cases involving parallel proceedings in EU and non-EU courts. It is silent as to cases where the courts of a third state may be regarded as having exclusive jurisdiction, either because of their unique interest in the subject matter of the dispute, or pursuant to a jurisdiction agreement.

2   Articles 33 and 34 are a partial attempt to address the difficulties created by the decision in *Owusu v. Jackson*,[1] in which the CJEU held that the allocation of jurisdiction between EU and non-EU courts is not invariably a matter of national law, but did not indicate when, if at all, national law is applicable in such cases. *Owusu* has given rise to numerous cases con-

---

[1]   C-281/02 [2005] ECR I-1383.

cerning, in particular, whether national law may be invoked to stay proceeding, in which jurisdiction derives from EU law, on the basis that parallel proceedings are ongoing in a third state, or because the parties have submitted to the exclusive jurisdiction of the courts of such a state. Cases involving parallel proceedings would now appear to be governed by Articles 33 and 34, but doubt remains as to the role of national law in cases involving jurisdiction agreements designating the courts of third states.

Importantly, however, nothing in Arts. 33 and 34, or in wider principles of EU law, limits the **3** capacity of national courts to stay or dismiss proceedings in favour of proceedings in third states when their jurisdiction derives from national law. In such cases, which are subject to Art. 6, the EU regime remains applicable in principle, and jurisdiction is founded on national law only by a process of remission.[2] This suggests that the conditions under which those rules apply are subject to the objectives of the Regulation and the principles of EU law.[3] Even so, however, it cannot have been intended that national courts are free to assert jurisdiction under national law in cases subject to Art. 6, but constrained in when they decline to exercise that jurisdiction. Rules for declining jurisdiction are as much part of any national law jurisdiction regime as the grounds to asserting jurisdiction.

II. The scope of Articles 33 and 34

It is uncertain whether the Art. 33/34 regime prescribes an exclusive regime for allocating **4** disputes between EU national courts and those of third states.[4] It may be assumed that it provides an exclusive regime for handling cases involving parallel proceedings, but it is unclear what impact it has on other possible grounds for declining jurisdiction. If the Art. 33/ 34 regime is exclusive, no means therefore exist to stay or dismiss proceedings in the event that the courts of a third state have exclusive jurisdiction, a matter not comprehended by Arts. 33 and 34. If it is not exclusive, it is uncertain in what circumstances, and on what basis, jurisdiction may be declined in favour of proceedings in a third state.[5]

III. The structure of Articles 33 and 34

1. Common features

Arts. 33 and 34 allow the courts of EU states to stay proceedings, when identical or related **5** proceedings are pending in the courts of a third state, in the interests of the 'proper administration of justice'. They address the problem of parallel proceedings in a third state, reflecting the provisions of Arts. 29 and 30, applicable between two Member States. Arts. 33 and 34 also partially reflect the operation of Arts. 24 and 25, concerning cases where another EU court has exclusive jurisdiction. Recital 24 states that a court's assessment of whether to grant a stay in favour of proceedings in a third state 'may also include consideration of the question whether the court of the third State has exclusive jurisdiction in the particular case in circumstances where a court of a Member State would have exclusive jurisdiction'. The important consequence is that a court may consider the fact that a court in a third state, had

---

2   Opinion 1/03, request for an opinion pursuant to Art. 300(6) EC (the Lugano Opinion), at [148].

3   Cf. *Barros Mattos Junior v. MacDaniels Ltd* [2005] ILPr 45, at [171].

4   See section V.3.

5   See section V.4.

it been a court in a Member State, would have had exclusive jurisdiction under Art. 25 pursuant to a jurisdiction agreement.

6 Importantly, Articles 33 and 34 engage only if a court's jurisdiction derives from Article 4, 7, 8 and 9. A stay cannot be granted if jurisdiction is exclusive, derived from Articles 24 and 25, preventing a stay where jurisdiction derives from a jurisdiction agreement. This extends even to jurisdiction founded on a non-exclusive jurisdiction agreement, which confers jurisdiction on a designated court under Article 25. Both articles provide that a court in a Member State shall dismiss, rather than stay, proceedings where the foreign proceedings are concluded, and have resulted in a judgment capable of recognition or enforcement in that Member State. A court shall grant a stay under both articles on the application of one of the parties or, where national law permits, of its own motion.

2. The dynamics of Article 33

7 Article 33 applies where identical proceedings, involving the same cause of action and the same parties, are pending in the courts both of a Member State and a third State, in cases equivalent to those involving two EU states and subject to Article 29.[6] In such cases, proceedings before an EU national court may be stayed if (a) it is expected that the court of the third State will give a judgment effective before the court in which a stay is sought; and (b) that court is satisfied that a stay is necessary for the proper administration of justice. Such a stay may be lifted at any time if (a) the proceedings in the court of the third State are themselves stayed or discontinued; or, (b) it appears that those proceedings are unlikely to be concluded within a reasonable time; or (c) the lifting of the stay is required for the proper administration of justice.

8 The practical effect of Article 33 is circumscribed in two ways. First, it is a precondition for granting a stay that the foreign proceedings are likely to give rise to a judgment effective in the court where the stay is sought. Secondly, Article 33 is subject to the perhaps puzzling requirement that a stay may be sought only if an identical action is already pending before the courts of a third State. No power to stay exists if the third-state court is seised subsequently, even if the foreign proceedings are substantially advanced before the application to stay is heard. These limitations are important in principle. They reveal that Article 33's overriding purpose is not to allocate proceedings to the most appropriate forum, despite the reference to the proper administration of justice, but to prevent irreconcilable judgments in the event of *lis pendens*. They also have problematic consequences in practice. The need to establish the likelihood of an effective judgment requires examination of that issue at the jurisdictional stage of proceedings, without any guidance as what standard of proof must be discharged. Again, because Article 33 hinges on the priority between proceedings, it encourages both pre-emptive proceedings in the courts of EU states, and (conversely) pre-emptive proceedings in the courts of third states by those wishing to avoid the torpedo effect of prior proceedings in a Member State. Moreover, the opaque nature of the concept of the 'proper administration of justice' will be a source of considerable litigation, especially at the outset as courts seek to define its content.

---

6   Reg 44/2001 Art. 27.

3. The dynamics of Article 34

Article 34 permits EU national courts to stay their proceedings where a related action is   9
pending in a third state. A stay is permitted, however, only if (a) the courts of a third state are
already seised; (b) it is expedient to hear both the local and foreign actions together to avoid
the risk of irreconcilable judgments resulting from separate proceedings; (c) it is expected
that the foreign will give a judgment effective in the Member State concerned; and, (d) a stay
is necessary for the proper administration of justice. The stay may be lifted, and proceedings
in a Member State reinstated, if: (a) there is no longer a risk of irreconcilable judgments; (b)
the foreign proceedings have been stayed or discontinued; (c) it appears that the foreign
proceedings are unlikely to be concluded within a reasonable time; or (d) continuation of the
proceedings in the relevant Member State is required for the proper administration of
justice.

Like Article 33, Article 34 has problematic consequences in practice, and is likely to en-   10
courage much litigation. It echoes, however, the language and structure of Article 32 of the
recast Regulation, which has been subject to considerable analysis in the case law. Both
provisions turn on the definition of a 'related action', and on whether it is expedient to
consolidate the local and foreign actions so to avoid the risk of irreconcilable judgments in
separate proceedings.

IV. The discretion to stay

1. The proper administration of justice: efficiency

The overriding principle is that a stay under Articles 33 and 34 must be 'necessary for the   11
proper administration of justice'.[7] The test is intended to introduce flexibility. Recital 23
states that the Regulation 'should provide for a flexible mechanism allowing the courts of the
Member States to take into account proceedings pending before the courts of third States'.
Again, Recital 24 states that a court should consider 'all the circumstances in the case before
it'. It is uncertain, however, how these general statements of principle should be understood.
Recitals 23 and 24, and the language of Articles 33 and 34, suggest that the Regulation is
particularly concerned with three matters: *(i)* allocating proceedings to the forum having the
closest factual connection to the dispute; *(ii)* avoiding delay in resolving the dispute; and,
(iii) preventing irreconcilable judgments. The first concern is suggested by Recital 24 which
states that the relevant circumstances 'may include connections between the facts of the case
and the parties and the third State concerned'. The second is evident from the importance
attached in Articles 33 and 34 to whether any foreign proceedings are unlikely to be concluded within a reasonable time. The third is reflected in the language of Recitals 23 and 24,
and of Articles 33 and 34, and their preoccupation with whether any judgment obtained in
the third state would be enforceable, and with when that judgment is likely to be obtained.

The avoidance of delay, and the prevention of irreconcilable judgments, concern procedural   12
efficiency. The allocation of proceedings to the forum having the closest factual connection
to the dispute is distinct, and concerns whether one court or the other is the most appropriate court to resolve the dispute. The relevance of this last consideration was identified in

---

[7]   Art. 33(1)(b).

Owens Bank v. Bracco,[8] where A-G Lenz considered that one factor to be assessed when considering a stay under what was then Article 28 of Regulation 44/2001 was 'the proximity of the courts to the subject matter of the case'.[9] He apparently meant by this that 'regard may be had to the question of which court is in the best position to decide a given question',[10] implying that a court may consider which forum can most appropriately resolve the dispute. Adopting this approach, the English courts have approached their Article 28 discretion by enquiring which law governs the issues arising, on the basis that in principle a court is best placed to apply its own law.[11] The *Bracco* test, may, however, be broader, involving a wider consideration of which forum is most appropriate in terms of efficiency, recalling the enquiry undertaken by common law courts in equivalent circumstances.[12] If, for example, both parties are resident within the foreign court's jurisdiction, or witnesses are present there, this suggests that it would be less costly and time-consuming – and more conducive to the proper administration of justice – to resolve the dispute in that court.

2. The proper administration of justice: justice

13   It is uncertain to what extent, if at all, a court may consider in cases subject to Articles 33 and 34 whether a claimant would be denied access to justice were proceedings stayed. This is an important element in the *forum conveniens* doctrine familiar to common lawyers.[13] It could mean, for example, that a stay should be refused where the injustice lies in personal prejudice to the claimant, as where, by travelling to defend proceedings in foreign country, the claimant would be exposed to personal risk.[14] Again, it may be unjust to grant a stay where the effect of the stay would be force a claimant to litigate where it has no effective redress, as where a claimant would be unable to finance proceedings in foreign court.[15] Alternatively, the injustice may concern the prejudice, amounting to injustice that a claimant would suffer before the foreign court. The claimant might not receive a fair trial in the foreign court, by reason of that court's bias.[16] Or it may be that the foreign court would apply a law different from that applicable in the court where the stay is sought, with the effect that the claimant's claim would fail.[17] Or the foreign proceedings might be subject to unreasonable delay, such that justice delayed would be justice denied.[18]

---

[8]   C-129/92, [1994] ECR I-117.

[9]   At [76].

[10] At [79]. The phrase is echoed by Article 15(1) of Council Regulation (EC) No. 2201/2003 concerning jurisdiction and the recognition and enforcement of judgments in matrimonial matters and the matters of parental responsibility, OJ L 338, 23/12/2003, 1, whereby the courts of a Member State may stay proceedings 'if they consider that a court of another Member State, with which the child has a particular connection, would be better placed to hear the case, or a specific part thereof, and where this is in the best interests of the child'.

[11] *UBS Limited, UBS AG v. Regione Calabria* [2012] EWHC 699 (Comm), [64].

[12] See commentary to Art. 30, para. 34 *et seq.*

[13] See *Fentiman*, International Commercial Litigation (2nd ed, 2015), para. 13.72 *et seq.*

[14] *Fentiman*, para. 13.87.

[15] *Fentiman*, para. 13.87.

[16] *Fentiman*, para. 13.81.

[17] *Fentiman*, para. 13.82.

[18] *Fentiman*, para. 13.88.

Principle suggests that such instances of potential injustice to the claimant should be con- **14**
sidered when applying Articles 33 and 34. As between Member States it may be assumed that
a claimant would obtain justice if required to litigate in the court first seised, but no such
assumption can be made of proceedings in third states. This interpretation is supported by
the fact that both Articles 33 and 34 permit a stay to be lifted if it 'appears to the court of the
Member State that the proceedings in the court of the third State are unlikely to be concluded within a reasonable time'. Unreasonable delay is a familiar ground for denying a stay
on *forum conveniens* grounds,[19] suggesting the relevance of procedural justice in this context.

The role of justice to the claimant in an analogous case arose in *Virgin Aviation Services* **15**
Limited v. CAD Aviation Services,[20] which concerned the discretion to stay under Art. 22 of
the 1968 Brussels Convention, predecessor to Art. 30 of the recast Regulation. The claimant
argued that a stay of English proceedings should be denied because the remedy they sought
was unavailable in the alternative court in the Netherlands. The judge concluded that such a
consideration was inappropriate in the exercise of his discretion, but only because of the
assumption of equality between Member States, an assumption irrelevant in cases subject to
Articles 33 and 34.

Necessarily, a court's ability to refuse a stay by reason of injustice must be governed by **16**
considerations of EU law. It might be confined, for example, to cases in which to grant a stay
would infringe the claimant's rights under Article 6 ECHR, or those in which the grounds for
doing so reflect those on which the courts of one Member State would be permitted to
decline to enforce a judgment given in another Member State on public policy grounds.[21]

3. Discretion and public policy

A stay under Article 33 or Article 34 will be granted only if it is expected that the court of the **17**
third state will give a judgment capable of recognition and, where applicable, of enforcement
in a Member State. In principle, such recognition may be denied where the court before
which a stay is sought considers that any foreign judgment would be ineffective by reason of
public policy. As this suggests, whether or not considerations of justice are directly relevant
to the grant of a stay, there is another route whereby considerations of justice may be
relevant. If grounds of public policy exist for denying effect to the foreign court's judgment,
no stay can be granted. National law governs the grounds on which this would be permitted,
which might include grounds relating to injustice in the foreign proceedings.

4. Exclusive jurisdiction and lis pendens

The fact that the courts of a third state have exclusive jurisdiction may be relevant in two **18**
situations. First, it may bear, uncontroversially, on a court's discretion to stay proceedings
under Articles 33 and 34 in cases of *lis pendens*. Secondly, it may provide an independent
ground for declining to exercise jurisdiction pursuant to national law in cases where the
courts of a third state are not already seised. The second question concerns the scope of the

---

[19] *Fentiman*, para. 13.88.
[20] [1991] ILPr 79.
[21] Pursuant to Art. 45(1)(a).

Regulation, and its possible reflexive effect. The first concerns whether a stay should be granted in cases of *lis pendens*.

19   Articles 33 and 34 regulate cases involving pending proceedings in the courts of a third state where those courts would have had exclusive jurisdiction under the Regulation were it a Member State. Recital 24 permits an EU national court to consider whether the court of the third State would have had exclusive jurisdiction in that event when exercising its discretion to stay. Importantly, a court may therefore consider the fact that a court in a third state would have exclusive jurisdiction under Article 25 pursuant to a jurisdiction agreement. Although Recital 24 therefore recognizes that significance should be attached to the fact that a court in a third state is regarded as having exclusive jurisdiction, the weight to be given to that fact is less than might be supposed. First, even if a third state's courts would have had exclusive jurisdiction under the Regulation, the effect is not to require the courts of a Member State to decline jurisdiction. A court must apply those articles reflexively to the extent that it must ascertain whether the foreign court would have had exclusive jurisdiction *mutatis mutandis* according to those provisions. It must decide, for example, whether a jurisdiction agreement in favour of such a court would have conferred exclusive jurisdiction under Article 25, but at that point the reflexive effect of Article 25 is exhausted. A court is not required to decline jurisdiction as it would under Article 25. Instead, it must exercise its discretion under Articles 33 and 34 having regard to the fact that the foreign court would have had exclusive jurisdiction. Secondly, the Regulation does not apparently attach special weight to the foreign court's perceived exclusive jurisdiction. Recital 24 provides only that the factors relevant in the exercise of discretion 'may also include consideration of the question whether the court of the third State has exclusive jurisdiction', without specifying what weight should be attached to that fact.

20   The practical effect of Recital 24 remains uncertain. If the fact that the courts of a third state would have exclusive jurisdiction provides an independent ground for declining jurisdiction, distinct from Articles 33 and 34, it is unclear when Recital 24 will engage. Presumably, a defendant seeking a stay or dismissal of proceedings would rely upon any such independent ground for declining jurisdiction. Alternatively, Articles 33 and 34 may provide an exclusive regime for allocating jurisdiction between EU and non-EU states, even in cases where the courts of a third state have exclusive jurisdiction, but only in cases of *lis pendens*. If so, even if the existence of such jurisdiction may be an independent ground for declining jurisdiction in other cases, Recital 24 is an important affirmation of the significance of such jurisdiction in cases of *lis pendens*.

V. The exclusive jurisdiction of third states

1. The problem of exclusive jurisdiction

21   The courts of a third state may have exclusive jurisdiction, from the perspective of national law, or by applying Brussels *Ibis* reflexively, in the absence of parallel proceedings in a Member State and a third state. In that event, three difficult questions arise. First, do Articles 33 and 34 prescribe an exclusive regime for allocating disputes between EU national courts and those of third states? If they do, the effect is that EU national courts are in principle powerless to decline jurisdiction on the basis that exclusive jurisdiction resides in the courts of a third state. Secondly, even if Articles 33 and 34 do not forbid any remission

to national law, does EU law apart from those provisions permit such remission? The second question splinters into several others. One is a question of scope. Are cases involving the exclusive jurisdiction of third-state courts subject to EU law at all? If they are not, national law applies uninhibited by the Regulation. If they are, in what circumstances, if at all, may jurisdiction be declined in favour of the exclusive jurisdiction of the courts of a third state? This last question concerns whether, and in what sense Brussels I*bis* has reflexive effect.

Difficulty arises partly from the silence of the Regulation on the issues, but also because of **22** the uncertain implications of Recital 24. Recital 24 permits a court to consider, when addressing cases of *lis pendens*, the fact that the foreign court would have had exclusive jurisdiction had it been an EU state. No separate provision is made for staying or dismissing proceedings in the event that the courts of a third state are perceived by the courts of a Member State as having exclusive jurisdiction. No provision is made for cases where a third-state court has exclusive jurisdiction under the national law of a Member State, nor (more surprisingly) if it would have had such jurisdiction had it been a Member State. It is unclear whether this means that a court is unable decline proceedings on the sole ground that a foreign court has exclusive jurisdiction, but only in the event of a pending action in a third state, or that a power to do so exists independently of the Regulation, presumably deriving from national law.

This uncertainty affects cases where the courts of a third state are perceived as having **23** paramount jurisdiction by virtue of the subject matter of a dispute, in cases equivalent to those where the courts of an EU have jurisdiction derived from Article 24 of Brussels I*bis*. Importantly, it also affects cases where the parties have agreed to the exclusive jurisdiction of the courts of a third state. It is of little assistance to suggest that cases involving third-state jurisdiction agreements will be subject to the Hague Convention on choice of court agreements where the convention applies.[22] Numerous jurisdiction agreements will remain outside the Convention's scope, given that a stay may be granted under the Convention only if the agreed court is that of another Convention state. As this suggests, the absence of any express treatment of third-state jurisdiction agreements in the recast Regulation may create significant problems in practice.

2. Exclusive jurisdiction and the Hague Convention

The operation of Articles 33 and 34 must be understood in the light of the Hague Conven- **24** tion on Choice of Court Agreements.[23] When applicable, this will provide a mechanism for declining jurisdiction where the parties have submitted by prior agreement to the exclusive jurisdiction of a third state, where that state is also a Convention State. Concluded on 30 June 2005, the Convention entered into force on 1 October 2015, following the deposit of the European Union's instrument of approval on 11 June 2015. In consequence the Convention entered into force in all EU States and in Mexico on 1 October 2015, the EU's action being the second implementing act required to activate the Convention.[24] The EU exercises competence on behalf of each Member State (except Denmark) over all the matters governed by

---

[22] Hague Convention on choice of court agreements of 30 June 2005 (in force 1 October 2015).

[23] (COM)(2008) 538 final.

[24] Art. 31.

the Convention, each such state (except Denmark) being bound by the EU's approval.[25] Mexico, the only non-EU state bound by the Convention, previously acceded to the Convention in September 2007. After 1 October 2015 the Convention will enter into force in each state which subsequently acts to implement it, by ratification or accession.[26] The Convention was signed (but not ratified) by the United States on 19 January 2009, and by Singapore on 25 March 2015. Where applicable, the Convention takes priority over the Regulation.[27] The effect in EU states of an exclusive jurisdiction agreement in favour of the courts of a non-EU state is therefore determined by the Convention, provided that such a non-EU state is a party to the Convention.[28]

25 The effect of the Convention is that, if the parties have agreed to the exclusive jurisdiction of the courts of a non-Member State, any court save the designated court must decline jurisdiction, subject to limited exceptions.[29] In such a case, there is no conflict between the Convention and the Regulation, because the Regulation contains no rules concerning third-state jurisdiction agreements. The rules contained in Article 71 of the Convention, mediating in conflicts between the Convention and Regulation, do not therefore apply.

26 In cases involving third-state jurisdiction agreements the Convention's scope is circumscribed in several practically important respects. First, it applies only where the designated court is that of another Convention State.[30] Second, it applies only to agreements concluded after the Convention's entry into force in the designated court.[31] Third, it applies only to exclusive jurisdiction agreements, although the exclusivity of an agreement to the jurisdiction of a Convention State is presumed.[32] Unilaterally exclusive, or 'asymmetric' agreements, are not to be treated as exclusive, however, and are thus outside the scope of the Convention.[33] This has considerable significance. The exclusion affects those asymmetric jurisdiction agreements, almost invariable in cross-border finance, which provide that a borrower must sue only in one court, but a lender may sue in any court of competent jurisdiction.[34]

27 As this suggests, the Hague Convention does not supply a comprehensive solution to the problem of the exclusive jurisdiction of third states. It is irrelevant where the courts of such a state have exclusive jurisdiction on a ground other than the existence of a jurisdiction agreement, and it applies to such jurisdiction agreements only in a limited number of cases.

3. The scope of Arts. 33 and 34

28 The narrow scope of the Hague Convention exposes a significant practical problem. Given

---

[25] Art. 30.

[26] Art. 31.

[27] Brussels Reg Art. 71.

[28] Art. 3 (a).

[29] Art. 6.

[30] Art. 3(a).

[31] Art. 16.

[32] Art. 3(b).

[33] *Hartley* and *Dogauchi, Explanatory Report on the 2005 Convention on Choice of Court Agreements* (2007), para. 106.

[34] *Fentiman*, International Commercial Litigation (2nd ed., 2015), paras. 2.08 *et seq.*, 2.123 *et seq.*

the omission of any treatment of cases involving the exclusive jurisdiction of the courts of a third state does national law occupies the space beyond Articles 33 and 34, and (where it applies) the Hague Convention? This important question itself breaks down into two further questions. Do the language and objectives of Brussels I*bis* foreclose any such remission to national law? If they do not, does the existing jurisprudence of the CJEU prevent it? This second question revives vexed questions concerning the implications of the decision in *Owusu v. Jackson*,[35] and the reflexive effect of the EU jurisdiction regime.

The arguments for preventing recourse to national law in cases subject to Brussels I*bis* are **29** viable, but not compelling. It may be suggested that EU national courts may not stay or dismiss proceedings save under Articles 33 and 34. Arguably, the principle *expressio unius est exclusio alterius* requires that the new regime be treated as exclusive and comprehensive, and the sole regulator of the allocation of disputes between EU and non-EU national courts. Moreover, although the recast does not provide in the body of the text rules governing cases where a third-state would have had exclusive jurisdiction had it been an EU state, such cases are specifically addressed in Recital 24. This permits a court, when exercising its discretion to stay, to consider whether the court of a third State would have had exclusive jurisdiction. The implication may be that cases where a foreign court has exclusive jurisdiction reflexively are therefore comprehended by Articles 33 and 34, but only in cases otherwise subject to those provisions, and that the existence of such jurisdiction is otherwise irrelevant. Indeed, the reference to the exclusive jurisdiction of a third state's courts would appear to rule out any possibility of declining jurisdiction merely on the ground that such jurisdiction exists. If the fact that a foreign court has exclusive jurisdiction were by itself a reason for granting a stay there would no need to refer to this possibility in Recital 24 in the *lis pendens* context. The consequence would appear to be that an EU national court has no power to dismiss or stay proceedings where, for example, the parties have agreed to the exclusive jurisdiction of the courts of a third state.

Several arguments may be deployed against this position, however, and in favour of remit- **30** ting cases of exclusive jurisdiction to national law. First, an important distinction exists between deferring to the exclusive jurisdiction of a foreign court, and allocating disputes between two courts having equivalent jurisdiction. Certainly, Articles 33 and 34 may not be concerned with cases where a foreign court has overriding jurisdiction, but only with cases involving parallel proceedings. If so, the arguments favouring the exclusivity of those provisions fall away. Secondly, it is possible that cases involving a non-EU court's overriding jurisdiction are, and always were, outside the scope of the EU jurisdiction regime. This view has been taken by the English courts in cases under Regulation 44/2001, and arguably by the CJEU.[36] If correct, this explains why the recast Regulation makes no reference to such cases.

It may be objected, however, that the exclusive jurisdiction of a third state's courts are **31** referred to in Recital 24, suggesting that Articles 33 and 34 embrace such cases exclusively. The terms of Recital 24 may be explained, however, if it is recalled that the laws of EU states differ as to when, if at all, jurisdiction should be declined on the ground that the courts of a third state have exclusive jurisdiction, particularly where the ground for the foreign court's exclusive jurisdiction is a jurisdiction agreement. In some states the power to stay may be

---

[35]   Case C-281/02 [2005] ECR I-1383.
[36]   *Coreck Maritime GmbH v. Handelsveem BV* (Case C-387/98), [2000] ECR I-9337.

limited, while in others, as in English law, the discretionary nature of the power (at least in cases involving foreign jurisdiction agreements) means that a court may sometimes accept jurisdiction notwithstanding the presence of such an agreement. In some circumstances, therefore, at least in some Member States, cases where the courts of a third state have exclusive jurisdiction will indeed fall to be determined under Articles 33 and 34, notwithstanding that the exclusive jurisdiction of the courts of a third state may be an independent reason for declining to exercise jurisdiction. In that event, Recital 24 has the role of ensuring that effect may be given to such agreements.

32 If correct, the argument supporting a residual power to decline jurisdiction, in cases other those involving *lis pendens*, has the effect of preserving each state's rules of national law. This conclusion is reinforced by principle, and indeed common sense. If no such power exists the courts of EU states would be obliged to accept jurisdiction notwithstanding the overriding claim of another court to hear the case, and to do so when they would be prohibited from asserting jurisdiction had the alternative forum been located in another EU state. Again, if the fact that a third-state court has exclusive jurisdiction is relevant only where Articles 33 and 34 apply, the curious consequence would be that a party seeking to rely on such jurisdiction would need to initiate pre-emptive proceedings in the third state concerned in order to do so. A party seeking to rely on an agreement to the exclusive jurisdiction of such a court would be required to seise that court as a prelude to vindicating its contractual rights.

4. General principles and third states

33 The European adjudication regime provides no explicit instructions for handling cases in which third states are implicated. What inference should be drawn from this silence? Are its grounds for exercising jurisdiction mandatory unless qualified by the Regulation itself? In the absence of any mechanism for ceding jurisdiction to third states, are Member States entirely prevented from declining jurisdiction in such cases? Or is the allocation of jurisdiction in such cases a matter for national law? Or is resort to national law permitted in some cases but not others?

34 Such questions have long provoked academic controversy,[37] and differences of judicial opinion.[38] How they might be answered is now suggested by the landmark decision of the

---

[37] *Briggs* [1991] LMCLQ 10, (1991) 107 LQR 180; *Briggs*, in *Andenas and Jacobs*, eds, European Community Law in the English Courts (1998), 277; *Briggs* (2005) 121 LQR 535; *Briggs & Rees*, para. 2.217 *et seq.*; *Collins* (1990) 106 LQR 535; *Droz*, Compétence judiciaire et effets des jugements dans le Marché Commun (1972), 58; *Fentiman* (1993) Cornell Int LJ 59; (2000) 3 CYELS 107; International Civil Litigation in Europe and Relations With Third States (*Nuyts* and *Watté* (eds); 2005), 83; *Gaudemet-Tallon* (1991) Rev cr dr int pr 491; *Gaudemet-Tallon*, Les Conventions de Bruxelles et de Lugano (2nd ed 1996), paras. 75, 84, 93, 111; *Hartley*, Civil Jurisdiction and Judgments (1982) 79–80; *Geimer*, Compétence judiciare et des jugements en Europe (1993), 43; *Hartley* (1992) 17 ELRev 553; *Hogan* (1995) ELRev 471; *Huber*, Recht der internationalen Wirtschaft (1993) 977; *Kaye*, Civil Jurisdiction and Enforcement of Foreign Judgments (1987), 1224–1225; *Kennett* (1995) 54 CLJ 552; *Nuyts*, L'Exception de Forum non conveniens (2003), 253 *et seq.*; *Tebbens*, Law and Reality: Essays in Honour of Voskuil (1992), 47.

[38] Contrast *Re Harrods (Buenos Aires) Ltd* [1992] Ch 72 (CA) (jurisdiction may be declined), with *S & W Berisford v. New Hampshire Insurance Co* [1990] 2 QB 631; *Arkwright Mutual Insurance Co v. Bryanston Ince* [1990] 2 QB 649 (jurisdiction may not be declined).

Court of Justice in *Owusu v. Jackson*.[39] There the Court held that an English court, having jurisdiction pursuant to Article 2 of the Brussels Convention, cannot decline to exercise that jurisdiction on the basis that the courts of a third state are the *forum conveniens*.

Read strictly, *Owusu* may ordain that national courts may never decline to exercise juris-   35
diction in favour of proceedings in a third state, even if Brussels I*bis* gives a residual role to such rules. But the English courts have maintained that a stay may be possible, *Owusu* notwithstanding. Of particular importance are those cases where a stay has been sought on the ground that the courts of a third state have exclusive jurisdiction, either because the parties have contractually agreed to the jurisdiction of a third state, or because in principle such a state's courts have paramount jurisdiction.

There are two approaches to the treatment of the paramount jurisdiction of third-state. First,   36
it could be argued that such cases are not, and were never, intended to be, governed by the European regime. Secondly, it can be said that national law applies to the extent that this is consistent with the provisions of the Regulation. This second question in turn begs numerous difficult questions concerning the form that such consistency must take.

5. The scope of the EU regime

If Articles 33 and 34 do not forbid remission to national law in cases involving the exclusive   37
jurisdiction of third-state courts it remains to ask whether, and if so when, general principles of EU law permit such remission. One possibility is that such cases are outside the scope of the EU jurisdiction regime. This argument finds support in a natural reading of the Regulation and its predecessors. Plainly, the Regulation makes no provision for such cases. Yet, given the ubiquity and importance of national rules of law conferring exclusive jurisdiction on the courts of third states it cannot credibly be suggested that this omission implies that a court cannot decline jurisdiction on such grounds. The consequence is that the treatment of cases in which the courts of a third state may have exclusive jurisdiction is remitted to national law, without resort to any concept of reflexive effect. It might be objected that this approach is inconsistent with the CJEU's decision in *Owusu*. But *Owusu* was not a case in which a stay was sought on the basis that the foreign court had superior jurisdiction. Rather it was sought on the basis that it was a more appropriate forum on *forum conveniens* grounds.

This conclusion is supported by the decision of the CJEU in *Coreck Maritime GmbH v.*   38
Handelsveem BV.[40] In *Coreck* the Court of Justice appears to have confirmed that courts may deploy national law to decline jurisdiction in favour of proceedings in a third state. *Coreck* concerned the effect on jurisdiction under the European regime of an agreement to the exclusive jurisdiction of a non-Member State. The Court of Justice was concerned with the relatively narrow question of what law should govern the validity of such an agreement. It concluded that the applicable law was that identified by choice of law rules applicable under the national law of the forum.[41] But this conclusion inescapably implies that a court must have the power to decline jurisdiction if such an agreement is valid. Of particular importance

---

[39]   Case C-281/02 [2005] ECR I-1383.
[40]   Case C-387/98 [2000] ECR I-9337.
[41]   At [19].

is the Court's reliance on a suggestive passage in the Schlosser Report on the Brussels Convention.[42] This concludes that each court should use its local choice of law rules to determine the validity of a third-state jurisdiction agreement. At first sight this is unexceptional, but it implies that such agreements may be effective to oust jurisdiction under the Convention, which in turn suggests that national law regulates such effectiveness (because the Convention itself makes no provision for doing so). A role for national law is confirmed by the following sentence: 'If, when these tests are applied, the agreement is found to be invalid, then the jurisdictional provisions of the 1968 Convention become applicable.'

39   The inference is that if such an agreement is valid, the European regime is inapplicable–allowing a court to decline jurisdiction under national law. Moreover, the implication is not–or is not merely–that such national rules are outside the scope of the European regime because they share its objective of promoting party autonomy. The suggestion is that a situation involving a third-state jurisdiction agreement is immediately outside its scope–whatever the precise objective, and the precise form of the relevant national rule. *Coreck* does not, however, address the issue of third-state jurisdiction agreements in any depth, and its glancing approach to the matter is inconclusive. Despite the endorsement of the Schlosser Report, it did not directly address whether Article 2 jurisdiction was ousted by a valid third-state jurisdiction agreement. Moreover, the Court of Justice in *Owusu* ignored the possible implications of *Coreck* (and the Schlosser Report). This was despite the fact that it might have been relevant even on the assumption that the only question before the Court was the first one posed by the Court of Appeal because it might have suggested that national law always governs cases involving third-state jurisdiction. Its status is thus uncertain.

40   Support for the view that national law governs cases involving the exclusive jurisdiction of third-state courts may be derived from the position adopted in the Proposal for a Council decision on the approval of the 2005 Hague Convention on Choice of Court Agreements.[43] This states that the Brussels I Regulation does not 'govern the enforcement in the Union of choice of court agreements in favor of third State courts'.[44] The justification is presumably that the Regulation contains no rules applicable in such cases, and the implication is that the EU regime does not apply reflexively in such cases. Although confined in terms to cases involving third-state jurisdiction agreements, this conclusion would necessarily extend to exclusive jurisdiction conferred on a third-state court on other grounds.

41   The legal status of the pronouncement in the Proposal is, however, unclear. Not least, to reconcile this position with the decision in *Owusu* is not straightforward, although this can be achieved if a distinction is drawn between declining jurisdiction on grounds of appropriateness, and on the basis that the alternative forum has overriding jurisdiction. Nor are the implications of the statement obvious. It is consistent with a broad view of the reflexive effect of the Regulation, whereby consistency with what is now Article 25 of Brussels *Ibis* justifies remitting such cases to national law.[45] Importantly, moreover, to conclude that national law applies in cases involving EU and non-EU states leaves open the argument that, even if national law applies, it should do so in a manner consistent with principles

---

[42]   [1979] OJ C 59/71, para. 176.

[43]   COM/2014/046 final – 2014/0021 (NLE).

[44]   Explanatory Memorandum, para. 1.3.

[45]   See below para. 46.

endorsed by the Regulation in intra-EU cases. Indeed, the statement in the Proposal may suggest only that the mechanism whereby such agreements are enforced is subject to national law, and that the circumstances in which such enforcement is warranted may be subject to the principle of reflexive effect. This last position has been adopted, for example, by the English courts.[46]

If the correct analysis is that the allocation of jurisdiction between a Member State and a **42** non-Member State is outside the Regulation's scope, cases under Arts. 33–34 aside, this has an important implication. It means that whether the courts of a third state have exclusive jurisdiction is a matter solely for national law. The doctrine of reflexive effect has no role in such cases. It is irrelevant to ask whether, had the non-EU court been an EU court, it would have had exclusive jurisdiction under Arts. 24 or 25. It would also mean that a national court would be permitted to decline jurisdiction if, for example, its national law considers that a foreign court has (in effect) exclusive jurisdiction, even pursuant to a non-exclusive jurisdiction agreement, where proceedings in that court have commenced.[47]

6. The reflexive effect of Brussels I*bis*

a) Reflexive effect in principle
If Articles 33 and 34 do not forbid remission to national law, the unregulated use of national **43** law may be allowed if such cases are outside the scope of the EU jurisdiction regime. Even if they are subject to the regime, however, principle may nonetheless permit resort to national law in certain circumstances. More precisely, the EU regime may have reflexive effect, in the sense that consistency with the rules applicable between EU states may permit (or require) equivalent treatment for cases involving third states.

To say that the Regulation has reflexive effect means that a stay or dismissal of proceedings **44** in favour of the courts of a third state is justified if to do so would be consistent with the operation of the Regulation between Member States. This begs two questions. First, what is the source of the rules for declining jurisdiction in such cases? Secondly, what degree of consistency is required? The second question itself begs two further questions: on what grounds is a court justified in declining jurisdiction; by what mechanism may it do so?

Principle suggests that national law is the only possible source for such rules. Consistency **45** with the Regulation requires remission to national law. To suggest that the Regulation somehow supplies those rules is to posit the existence of a phantom Regulation, parallel to and identical with Brussels I*bis*, whose invisible rules regulate the court's power to decline jurisdiction.

Principle also suggests that consistency with the Regulation concerning the grounds for **46** declining jurisdiction may be measured in several ways. First, consistency may require, and may only require, that the objectives of the Regulation would be served if proceedings are stayed. As Art. 25 indicates, for example, the Regulation demands respect for jurisdiction agreements in favour of the courts of EU states. Arguably, this permits national courts to

---

[46]   See below para. 50 *et seq.*

[47]   As in English law; see *Fentiman*, International Commercial Litigation (2nd ed, 2015), para. 2.236 *et seq.*

Richard Fentiman

deploy any rules available under their national law which serve the same purpose.[48] If national law possesses rules respecting jurisdiction agreements, they may be deployed.

47 Secondly, resort to national law may be justified if a stay would have been required or permitted had the third state in question been a Member State. This second approach requires in effect applying the rules contained in any relevant Article (most importantly, those in Art. 25) to determine if the conditions are present for declining jurisdiction under the Regulation. This approach may, however, take three different forms, with different outcomes in each case. It is possible, once congruence with the grounds for declining jurisdiction is established, that jurisdiction must also be declined strictly in accordance with the Regulation. In any case reflecting Art. 25, this would mean that a court is entitled to decline jurisdiction automatically in favour of the agreed jurisdiction of a third state's court. If this first view prevails, the effect would be that effect could be given to third-state jurisdiction agreements only in those legal systems whose national rules concerning third-state jurisdiction agreements are non-discretionary.

48 Alternatively, once such congruence is established, the consequence may be that national law engages. A court could then decline jurisdiction exactly as it would under national law. This alternative has the effect that a national court having a discretion to stay proceedings under its national could exercise that discretion once it is clear (in a case involving agreed jurisdiction) that the third state's courts would have had jurisdiction under Art. 25 had it been a court in an EU state.[49]

49 To understand the nature of any reflexive effect that Brussels *Ibis* may have, a further consideration is relevant. Whether the Regulation has reflexive effect concerns the ground on which a court might decline to exercise jurisdiction. It might be suggested, however, that the ground on which jurisdiction is asserted under the Regulation is also relevant. In principle, it is hard to see why this should be the case, given that a court's jurisdiction cannot be said to be weaker or stronger depending on whether, say, Art. 4, Art. 7, or Art. 25 is the basis of jurisdiction.[50] In any event, however, if the issue is whether a court must cede jurisdiction to the exclusive jurisdiction of a third state's courts, logic suggests that the existence of such exclusive jurisdiction has the same effect whatever the basis of the EU court's jurisdiction.

b) **Reflexive effect in practice**

50 Although such cases are not unique to English law, the problem of reflexive effect has been intensely addressed in the English courts, a phenomenon explained by the frequency of cases in which stays are sought in favour of the courts of third states. The English courts have approached the problem by employing the doctrine of reflexive effect, rather than by concluding that cases involving third states are beyond its scope. Indeed, in one leading case the judge expressly doubted that the decision in *Coreck* supports the conclusion that the Regulation is inapplicable in cases involving third-state jurisdiction agreements.[51] In deploying the reflexive principle, the English courts, have established three principles. First, reflexive

---

48   *Konkola Copper Mines plc v. Coromin* [2005] 2 Lloyd's Rep. 555.

49   *Ferrexpo v. Gilson Investments* [2012] EWHC 721 (Comm); *De Verneuil Smith, Lasserson, Rymkiewicz* (2012) JPIL 389; *Crawford, Carruthers* (2013) Edin LR 78; (2013) 129 LQR 317.

50   *Gomez v. Gomez-Monche Vives* [2008] 1 All ER (Comm) 973.

51   *Konkola Copper Mines plc v. Coromin* [2005] 2 Lloyd's Rep. 555, at [99], per *Colman* J.

effect should be given to the European regime, in the sense that a court may decline to exercise jurisdiction where to do so would be consistent with the European regime. Secondly, the principle of reflexive effect leads to the conclusion that a court may exercise its existing powers under national law to stay proceedings in favour of the courts of a non-EU state. Thirdly, because national law regulates such cases, the mechanisms available in national law may be deployed, including a discretionary stay. It does not have the effect that a court must stay proceedings in the manner that the Regulation requires in cases to which it applies directly. There is uncertainty, however, as to how such consistency is to be understood, and as to the situations in which a stay under national law is permitted. Two approaches are evident in the English cases, a broad approach, and a narrow approach.

The broad approach to reflexive effect is exemplified by the decision in *Konkola Copper* **51** *Mines plc v. Coromin.*[52] There the judge examined in depth the status of third-state jurisdiction agreements in the European regime. Whether a stay was permitted exposed two connected issues of particular importance in English commercial practice: is it permissible to stay proceedings on the basis that the parties have agreed to the jurisdiction of a third-state's courts; does it matter if a court's approach to declining jurisdiction is discretionary? Endorsing an earlier pair of English decisions,[53] The judge's conclusion that a discretionary stay in such cases was permitted has since been expressly endorsed without further discussion.[54]

Konkola had brought parallel proceedings in both Zambia and England against Coromin, **52** their insurers. Coromin in turn commenced third party proceedings in England against several reinsurers. Each of the latter sought a stay of the third party proceedings on the basis that, by their contract with Coromin, they had agreed to submit any disputes to the jurisdiction of the Zambian courts. Importantly, the judge did not accept that *Owusu* renders any resort to national law impossible. He took for granted that the absence in *Owusu* of any discussion of foreign jurisdiction agreements left the matter open. Authority being lacking, the judge relied upon principle, which he held warranted a stay in such a case. *Konkola* was unlike *Owusu*. A stay founded upon an agreement to a third-state's jurisdiction was materially different from a stay on the generic ground that the most appropriate forum was in such a state (such as that in *Owusu*). Regulation 44.2001, by Article 23, itself required the courts of one Member State to cede jurisdiction to the agreed jurisdiction of another such State. Consistency with the Regulation therefore justified doing so in favour of the agreed jurisdiction of a third state. Moreover, consistency with the European regime means only consistency with objectives embodied in the regime, not with the form and methodology of its rules. The regime promotes party autonomy, by requiring courts to defer to the agreed jurisdiction of another Member State. It is therefore permissible to deploy rules of national law which likewise have the effect of respecting party autonomy, by giving effect to third-state jurisdiction agreements. The effect was that a court was permitted to use national law to grant a stay.[55]

---

[52]   [2005] 2 Lloyd's Rep. 555, affd on other grounds [2006] 1 Lloyd's Rep. 410 (CA)(no appeal from the judge's decision on the implications of *Owusu*).

[53]   *Arkwright Mutual Insurance Co v. Bryanston Insurance Co Ltd* [1990] 2 QB 649; *Berisford plc v. New Hampshire Insurance Co* [1990] 2 QB 631.

[54]   *Winnetka Trading Corporation v. Julius Baer International Ltd* [2008] EWHC 3146 (Ch), at [25].

[55]   At [99].

53   A narrower approach to reflexive effect is evident in *Ferrexpo v. Gilson Investments.*[56] This approach permits a court to decline jurisdiction in circumstances where the foreign court would have had jurisdiction under the Regulation had it been a court in a Member State. This approach in turn has two variants. On one view, a Member State's must then give effect to that jurisdiction just as it would if the Regulation had applied. In cases equivalent to those under Articles 24 and 25 of the Regulation, for example, it would then automatically decline jurisdiction. Alternatively, once a reflexive situation is identified, the court may employ its national law to determine whether a stay should be granted.

54   The narrow view in its second form was endorsed in *Ferrexpo*. There proceedings brought against an English-domiciled defendant were stayed on the ground that the proceedings had as their object the validity of resolutions made by a Ukrainian company. This was because Article 22 of Regulation 44/2001, conferring exclusive jurisdiction on the courts of an EU state in such a case, had reflexive effect in cases involving a non-EU court. This justified the grant of a stay under English national law.

55   *Ferrexpo* concerned the ownership of a Ukrainian mining company. One party, B, had sought in a Ukrainian court a declaration that certain resolutions of the company concerning his shares in the company were invalid, with the effect that he retained control of the company. The other party, Z, then brought proceedings in the English courts (against English-domiciled companies owned by B) for a declaration that he was the lawful owner of the disputed shares. B challenged the English court's jurisdiction, arguing that the Ukrainian courts had exclusive jurisdiction because Article 22 of Regulation 44/2001[57] had reflexive effect. Z argued in response that *Owusu* obliged the court to exercise jurisdiction.

56   *Ferrexpo*.is significant for three principal reasons. It was accepted that Article 22 has reflexive effect. Again, the decision endorsed the general approach adopted in *Konkola v. Coromin*, to the extent that 'reflection' may justify a stay under national law.[58] Finally, the judge adopted a stricter view of reflexive effect that relied upon in *Konkola*, by asking whether Article 22 would have applied in its terms were Ukraine a Member State. The consequence is that a court may stay proceedings if the connection required under the relevant Article of the Regulation is satisfied, but in that event a stay is granted under national law. *Owusu* did not prevent the reflexive application of Article 22. Uniformity, so important in *Owusu*, would not be disturbed because the principles underlying Article 22 were recognized in most legal systems. Nor was there a risk of uncertainty given that Article 22 was relatively certain in its operation.

57   There is therefore a conflict in the English cases, with important practical consequences, between the broad view underlying *Konkola*, and the narrow view endorsed in *Ferrexpo*. If the second is accepted, the effect may be to restrict the cases in which a stay may be sought. It is uncertain, however, whether the narrow approach favoured in *Ferrexpo* is correct in principle, as a later appeal court might conclude. If the mechanism for declining jurisdiction derives from national law, as the decision supposes, it is unclear why the grounds for doing

---

[56]   [2012] EWHC 721 (Comm); *De Verneuil Smith, Lasserson, Rymkiewicz* (2012) JPIL 389; *Crawford, Carruthers* (2013) *Edin* LR 78; (2013) 129 LQR 317; *Goodwin* (2013) 129 L.Q.R. 317.

[57]   Brussels *Ibis* Art. 24.

[58]   At [127].

so should not also derive from national law. Arguably, it is incoherent to apply the Regulation's rule in terms to determine whether consistency with the Regulation warrants a stay, and then to remit to national law whether a stay should in fact be granted.

Both decisions are, however, exposed to the charge that the Regulation cannot permit **58** national courts to employ discretion when declining jurisdiction in favour of proceedings in third states. Even if the elements of the reasoning employed in both cases is correct, a further question arises concerning the methodology which a court may employ when applying its national law. Arguably, even if the Regulation has reflexive effect, this does not permit the exercise of adjudicatory discretion. If this is correct, EU national courts may only decline to exercise jurisdiction if their national law mandates that jurisdiction must be declined in the event that the courts of a third state have exclusive jurisdiction. Principle may support this view for two reasons. First, if the EU regime is to have reflexive effect, this must be complete not partial, and must extend. Secondly, the CJEU in *Owusu* was critical of the use of discretion to stay proceedings subject to the EU regime.

The point was expressly addressed in *Konkola*, and the judge concluded that the methodol- **59** ogy of national law is irrelevant.[59] This may be supported for two reasons. First, if it is indeed correct that national law applies when the Regulation has reflexive effect, it presumably follows that the mechanism for granting a stay is entirely for national law. Secondly, although the European regime formally lacks a doctrine of *forum non conveniens*, it recognizes the possibility of exercising discretion in the service of its goals. Article 28 of Regulation 44/ 2001, in force at the time of *Konkola*, and now Article 30, give courts discretion to stay proceedings in favour of a related action abroad. More importantly, Articles 33 and 34 now explicitly confer a discretion to stay proceedings in cases involving third states. It would be glaringly inconsistent to hold that discretion is possible in some such cases but not others.

Moreover, the discretionary power to stay proceedings in cases involving third-state juris- **60** diction agreements, on the English law model, is justified for a different reason. Where a stay is granted it is because of the overriding claim of the foreign court to hear the dispute. *Forum conveniens* factors are relevant only to justify any conclusion that the English court is on inspection the most appropriate forum.[60] They do not supply a reason for enforcing any jurisdiction agreement. Such considerations are relevant when a stay is refused, but not when it is granted. It is only when a stay is granted, however, that it can be alleged that the Regulation is infringed, because it is only then that jurisdiction conferred by the Regulation is not exercised. The consequence is that there is no sense in which the court's discretionary approach to jurisdiction agreements undermines the Regulation.

VI. Arts. 33–34: summary

The novelty of the Arts. 33–34 regime, and the many uncertainties to which it gives rise, **61** suggest that it will generate considerable, costly litigation. A possible effect may be to deter litigation in EU national courts in cases involving alternative proceedings in a third state. The effect may be to drive litigation into non-EU courts, or further encourage the trend to submit to arbitration major commercial disputes that were once the preserve of national

---

[59]　At [87] *et seq.*

[60]　*Fentiman*, International Commercial Litigation (2nd ed, 2015), para. 2.222 *et seq.*

courts. Certainly, those sued in such courts may exploit these new difficulties to delay or deter proceedings.

62 In several respects, however, the elements of the new regime, and the problems to which it gives rise may be identified. It is clear that Arts. 33–34 govern any case involving parallel proceedings in an EU state and a third state. It is unclear, however, whether the Art. 33–34 regime is the only permitted mechanism for allocating proceedings between such states, other than the 2005 Hague Convention on choice of court agreements, which prevails over the Regulation.[61] The limited scope of the Hague Convention in cases involving third-state jurisdiction agreements, and the possibility that a third state's courts may have exclusive jurisdiction on other grounds makes it necessary to ask whether, and on what basis, a court may rely upon its national law to decline to exercise jurisdiction in favour of the exclusive jurisdiction of the courts of a third state. There are compelling arguments for suggesting that national law governs in such cases, and that the EU regime does not, and was never intended to, govern cases in which the courts of a third state have exclusive jurisdiction under the national law of EU states. If such cases are not, however, beyond the scope of the Regulation, the doctrine of reflexive effect may nonetheless lead to the application of national law. The circumstances in which this may be possible remain, however, controversial.

Section 10: **Provisional, including protective, measures**

Article 35

Application may be made to the courts of a Member State for such provisional, including protective, measures as may be available under the law of that Member State, even if the courts of another Member State have jurisdiction as to the substance of the matter.

Bibliography

Albrecht, Das EuGVÜ und der einstweilige Rechts-
schutz in England und in der Bundesrepublik
Deutschland (1991)
Baglietto Bergmann, Der einstweilige Rechtsschutz
nach der neuen spanischen Zivilprozeßordnung und
der deutschen Zivilprozeßordnung (2007)
Bertrams, De positie van het kort geding in het EEG
Executieverdrag, WPNR 1981, 1, 21, 49
Boularbah, "Les mesures provisoires en droit com-
mercial international: développements récents au
regard des Conventions de Bruxelles et de Lugano",
TBH 1999, 604

Bülow, Vereinheitlichtes internationales Zivilprozessrecht der Europäischen Wirtschaftsgemeinschaft, RabelsZ 29 (1965) 473
Carpi, I provvedimenti provvisori; controversie
transnazionali e prospettive di armonizzazione,
La Cooperazione Giurisdiziaria, Speziale Document
Giustizia 1996, 172
Collins, Provisional Measures, the Conflict of Laws
and the Brussels Convention, (1981) 1 Yb Eur. L. 249
Collins, The Territorial Reach of Mareva Injunctions,
(1989) 105 L. Q. Rev. 262

---

[61]   Brussels *Ibis*, Art. 71.

Collins, Provisional and Protective Measures in International Litigation, RdC 234 (1992-III) 19

Consolo, Avoiding the Risk of Babel after van Uden and Mietz: Perspectives and Proposals, ZZPInt 6 (2001) 49

Collins, The subtle interpretation of the case law of the European Court on provisional remedies, ZSR 124 (2005) 359

Cuniberti, Les mesures conservatoires portant sur des biens situés à l'étranger (2000)

Dalhuisen, Voorlopige em bewarende maatregelen onder het EG Executie Verdrag, WPNR 1982, 365

Dalhuisen, Creditors' Remedies and the Conflicts of Law in the European Community, in: Liber amicorum Riesenfeld (1983) 1

Dedek, Art. 24 EuGVÜ und provisorische Anordnungen zur Leistungserbringung, EWS 2000, 246

Demeyere, Voorlopige en bewarende maatregelen (art. 24 EEX) na het arrest van Uden en het arrest Mietz, R. W. 1999–2000, 1353

Di Blase, Provvedimenti cautelari e convenzione di Bruxelles, Riv dir int 1987, 5

Dickinson, Provisional Measures in the "Brussels I" Review: Disturbing the Status Quo?, Journal of Private International Law, Vol. 6, 519–664

Dickinson, Provisional Measures in the "Brussels I" Review: Disturbing the Status Quo?, IPRax 2010, 203–214

van Drooghenbroeck, Les compétences internationale et territoriale du juge du provisoire (Les mesures provisoires et le litige européen), in: van Compernolle/Tarzia (eds.), Les mesures provisoires en droit belge, français et italien (1998), p. 475

Donzallaz, Les mesures provisoires et conservatoires dans les Conventions de Bruxelles et de Lugano – état des lieux après les A C J C E Mund, Mietz et van Uden, AJP 2000, 956

Dörschner, Beweissicherung im Ausland (2000)

Eilers, Maßnahmen des einstweiligen Rechtsschutzes im europäischen Zivilrechtsverkehr: Internationale Zuständigkeit, Anerkennung und Vollstreckung (1991)

v. Falck, Implementierung offener ausländischer Vollstreckungstitel – Vollstreckbarerklärung ausländischer Titel und inländischer Bestimmtheitsgrundsatz (1998)

Fallon, Le référé international en matière civile et commerciale, Rev. dr. ULB 1993, 43

Franzosi, Weltweite Patentstreitigkeiten und italienisches "Torpedo", MittdPatA 1998, 300

Fuentes Camacho, Las medidas provisionales y cautelares en el espacio judicial europeo (1996)

Garber, Einstweiliger Rechtsschutz nach der EuGVVO (2011)

Garber, Einstweiliger Rechtsschutz nach der revidierten Brüssel I-VO, in: Grimm/Ladler, EU-Recht im Spannungsverhältnis zu den Herausforderungen im Internationalen Wirtschaftsrecht (2012) 191

Garber, Einstweiliger Rechtsschutz nach der neuen EuGVVO, ecolex 2013, 1071

Garcimartin Alférez, Effects of the Brussels Convention upon the Spanish System: Provisional and Protective Measures, in: Hommelhoff/Jayme/Mangold, Europäischer Binnenmarkt: IPR und Rechtsvergleichung (1995) 129

Geimer, Eine neue internationale Zuständigkeitsordnung für Europa, NJW 1976, 441

Geimer, Zur Vereinbarung der ausschließlichen Zuständigkeit eines ausländischen Gerichts, WM 1975, 910

Gerhard, L'exécution forcée transfrontiére des injonctions extraterritoriales non pécuniaires en droit privé (2000)

Gerhard, La compétence du juge d'appui pour prononcer des mesures provisoires extraterritoriales, SZIER 1999, 97

Grabinski, Zur Bedeutung des Europäischen Gerichtsstands- und Vollstreckungsübereinkommens (Brüsseler Übereinkommens) und des Lugano-Übereinkommens in Rechtsstreitigkeiten über Patentverletzungen, GRURInt 2001, 199, 211

Gronstedt, Grenzüberschreitender einstweiliger Rechtsschutz (1994)

Grundmann Anerkennung und Vollstreckung ausländischer einstweiliger Maßnahmen nach IPRG und Lugano-Übereinkommen (1996)

Grunert, Die "world-wide" Mareva Injunction (1998)

Grunsky, Zum Arrestgrund des § 917 Abs. 2 ZPO bei der Vollstreckung ausländischer Urteile, IPRax 1983, 210

Guidicelli, Cross Border Injunctions für Europäische Patente (2001)

Hanisch, Internationale Arrestzuständigkeit und EuGVÜ, IPRax 1991, 215

Hartley, Jurisdiction in Conflict of Laws: Disclosure,

Third-Party Debt and Freezing Orders, LQR 2010, 194, 221

Hartley, Interim measures under the Brussels Jurisdiction and Judgments Convention, EuLR 24 (1999) 674

Hausmann, Zur Anerkennung und Vollstreckung von Maßnahmen des einstweiligen Rechtsschutzes im Rahmen des EG-Gerichtsstands- und Vollstreckungsübereinkommens, IPRax 1981, 79

Hay, The Common Market Preliminary Draft Convention on the Recognition and Enforcement of Judgements: Some Considerations of Policy and Interpretation, Am. J. Comp. L. 16 (1968) 155

Heinze, Internationaler einstweiliger Rechtsschutz: Möglichkeiten und Grenzen am Beispiel der freezing injunction des englischen Rechts, RIW 2003, 922

Heinze, Europäische Urteilsfreizügigkeit von Entscheidungen ohne vorheriges rechtliches Gehör, ZZP 120 (2007) 303

Heinze, Zur Bedeutung des Europäischen Gerichtsstands- und Vollstreckungsübereinkommens (Brüsseler Übereinkommens) und des Lugano-Übereinkommens in Rechtsstreitigkeiten über Patentverletzungen, IPRax 2007, 343

Heinze, Choice of Court Agreements, Coordination of Proceedings and Provisional Measures in the Reform of the Brussels I Regulation, Max Planck Private Law Research Paper No. 11/5

Hess, Die begrenzte Freizügigkeit einstweiliger Maßnahmen im Binnenmarkt II – weitere Klarstellungen des europäischen Gerichtshofes, IPRax 2000, 370

Hess/Vollkommer, Die begrenzte Freizügigkeit einstweiliger Maßnahmen nach Art. 24 EuGVÜ, IPRax 1999, 220

Hess/Zhou, Beweissicherung und Beweisbeschaffung im europäischen Justizraum, IPRax 2007, 183

Hogan, The Judgments Convention and Mareva Injunctions in the United Kingdom and Ireland, EuLR 1989, 191

Honorati, La cross-border prohibitory injunction olandese in materia di contraffazione di brevetti: sulla legittimità dell'inibitoria transfrontaliera alla luce della convenzione di Bruxelles del 1968, Riv dir int priv proc 1997, 301

Honorati, Provisional Measures and the Recast of Brussels I Regulation: A Missed Opportunity for a Better Ruling, RDIPP 2012, 525

Hye-Knudsen, Marken-, Patent- und Urheberrechtsverletzungen im europäischen Internationalen Zivilprozessrecht (2005)

Jametti Greiner, Der vorsorgliche Rechtsschutz im internationalen Verhältnis, ZBernJV 1992, 649

Jametti Greiner, Der Begriff der Entscheidung im schweizerischen internationalen Zivilverfahrensrecht (1998)

Jametti Greiner, Grundsätzliche Probleme des vorsorglichen Rechtsschutzes aus internationaler Sicht, in: Spühler, Vorsorgliche Massnahmen aus internationaler Sicht (2000) 11

Kennett, The Enforcement of Judgments in Europa (2000)

Kerameus, Provisional remedies in transnational litigation, Andolina Transnational Aspects of Procedural Law III (1998) 1169

Kienle, Arreste im internationalen Rechtsverkehr (1991)

Knothe, Einstweiliger Rechtsschutz im deutschen und spanischen Zivilprozeß (1998)

Koch, Grenzüberschreitender einstweiliger Rechtsschutz, in: Heldrich/Komo, Herausforderungen des internationalen Zivilverfahrensrechts (1994) 85

Koch, Neuere Probleme der internationalen Zwangsvollstreckung einschließlich des einstweiligen Rechtsschutzes, in: Schlosser, Materielles Recht und Prozessrecht und die Auswirkungen der Unterscheidung im Recht der internationalen Zwangsvollstreckung (1992) 171

Kodek, Einstweilige Maßnahmen im Europäischen Justizraum – Bilanz und Zukunftsperspektiven, in: Jahrbuch Zivilverfahrensrecht 2010 (2010) 151

Kofmel Ehrenzeller, Vorläufiger Rechtsschutz im internationalen Verhältnis: Regeln der International Law Association (ILA) anlässlich der Helsinki-Konferenz vom August 1996, SZIER 1998, 177

Kofmel Ehrenzeller, Der vorläufige Rechtsschutz im internationalen Verhältnis (2005)

Kramer, De erkenning en tenuitvoerlegging van kortgeding-vonnissen of het EEX: het Mietz-arrest, NIPR 2000, 26

Kramer, Harmonisation of provisional and protective measures in Europe, in *Storme*, Procedural Laws in Europe (2003) 305, *ders*, Het kort geding in internationaal perspectief (2001)

Kramer, Internationale bevoegdheid van de kortgedingrechter, NTBR 1999, 74

Kramer, Het kort geding in internationaal perspectief (2001)

Kruger, Provisional and Protective Measures, in: Nuyts/Watté (eds.), International Civil Litigation and Relations with Third States (2005), p. 311

Maack, Englische antisuit injunctions im europäischen Zivilrechtsverkehr (1999)

Maher/Rodger, Provisional and Protective Remedies: The British Experience and The Brussels Convention, ICLQ 48 (1999) 302

Mähr, Das internationale Zivilprozessrecht Liechtensteins (2002)

Mankowski, Selbständige Beweisverfahren und einstweiliger Rechtsschutz in Europa, JZ 2005, 1144

Mankowski, Die Brüssel I-Verordnung vor der Reform, in: Verschraegen, Interdisziplinäre Studien zur Komparatistik und zum Kollisionsrecht I (2010) 31

Marmisse/Wilderspin, Le régime jurisprudentiel des mesures provisoires à la lumière des arrêts van Uden et Mietz, RCDIP 88 (1999), 669

Meier, Vorsorgliche Maßnahmen und Arrest nach dem Lugano Übereinkommen, in *Schwander*, Das Lugano-Übereinkommen (1990) 157

Meier-Beck, Aktuelle Fragen des Patentverletzungsverfahren, GRUR 2000, 355

Melike, Beweissicherungsverfahren bei Auslandssachverhalten, NJW 1984, 2017

Mennicke, Zum Arrestgrund der Auslandsvollstreckung bei Urteilen aus Vertragsstaaten des EuGVÜ, EWS 1997, 117

Merkt, Les mesures provisoires en droit international privé (1993)

Micklitz/Rott, Vergemeinschaftung des EuGVÜ in der Verordnung (EG) Nr 44/2001, EuZW 2002, 15

Naudi, Die Umsetzung des europäischen Zivilprozessrechts in Spanien: Zuständigkeit, einstweiliger Rechtsschutz, Anerkennung und Vollstreckung (2003)

Nygh, Provisional and Protective Measures in International Litigation: The Helsinki-Principles, RabelsZ 62 (1998) 115

Olivier Merkt, Les mesures provisoires en droit international privé (1993) 219

Otte, Verfahrenskoordination und einstweiliger Rechtsschutz bei der Verletzung eines europäischen Patents, IPRax 1999, 440

Pålsson, Interim Relief under the Brussels and Lugano Conventions, in: Liber amicorum Kurt Siehr (2000) 621

Pertegás Sender, Aanhangigheid, samenhang en voorlopige maatregelen, in: van Houtte/Pertegás Sender (eds.), Europese IPR-verdragen (1997), p. 115

Reiner, Schiedsgerichtsbarkeit, Einstweiliger Rechtsschutz und EuGVÜ, IPRax 2003, 74

Roth, Vollziehung von Arrestbefehlen gegen ausländische Schuldner (§ 929 Abs. 2, 3 ZPO), IPRax 1990, 161

Sandrock, Prejudgment Attachments: Securing international loans or other claims for money, Int Lawyer 21 (1987) 1, 16

Santa Croce, Les mesures provisoires et conservatoires dans le contentieux international, Gaz. Pal. 2000, 384

Schack, Internationale Urheber-, Marken- und Wettbewerbsrechtsverletzungen im Internet – Internationales Zivilprozessrecht, MMR 2000, 135

Schmutz, Massnahmen des vorsorglichen Rechtsschutzes im Lugano-Übereinkommen aus schweizerischer Sicht (1993)

Schrader, Einstweiliger Rechtsschutz von Zahlungsansprüchen des Wirtschaftsverkehrs im spanischen und deutschen Zivilprozeß (1999)

Schulte-Beckhausen, Internationale Zuständigkeit durch rügelose Einlassung im europäischen Zivilprozeßrecht (1994)

Schulz, Einstweilige Maßnahmen nach dem Brüssler Gerichtsstands- und Vollstreckungsübereinkommen in der Rechtsprechung des Gerichtshofs der Europäischen Gemeinschaften (EuGH), ZEuP 2001, 805

Sosnitza, Einstweiliger Rechtsschutz im Europäischen Binnenmarkt, in: Sànchez Lorenzo/Moya Escudero, La cooperatión judicial internacional en materia civil y la unificaciòn del Derecho privado en Europa (2003) 69

Spellenberg/Leible, Die Notwendigkeit vorläufigen Rechtsschutzes bei transnationalen Streitigkeiten, in: Gilles, Transnationales Prozeßrecht (1995) 293

Stadler, Erlaß und Freizügigkeit einstweiliger Maßnahmen im Anwendungsbereich des EuGVÜ: Auswirkungen der EuGH-Rsp auf das Gefüge des europäischen einstweiligen Rechtsschutzes, JZ 1999, 1089

Steenhoff, Internationale bevoegdheid in kort geding, in: Guus Schmidt (ed.), IPR en Kort geding (2000), p. 19

Marta Pertegás Sender/Thomas Garber   781

Stürner, Der einstweilige Rechtsschutz in Europa, in: Liber amicorum Geiß (2000) 199

Treichel, Die französische Saise-contrefaçon im europäischen Patentverletzungsprozeß: Zur Problematik der Beweisbeschaffung im Ausland nach Art. 24 EuGVÜ, GRURInt 2001, 690

de Vareilles-Sommières, La compétence internationale des tribunaux français en matière de mesures provisoires, RCDIP 85 (1996) 397

Verheul-Wade, Prejudgment Attachment of Movables in French, Dutch and English Laws, in: Liber amicorum Voskuil (1992) 377

Willeitner, Vermögensgerichtsstand und einstweiliger Rechtsschutz im deutschen, niederländischen und europäischen Internationalen Zivilverfahrensrecht (2003)

Wolf, Die Anerkennungsfähigkeit von Entscheidungen im Rahmen eines niederländischen kort geding-Verfahrens nach dem EuGVÜ, EuZW 2000, 11

Wolf/Lange, Das europäische System des einstweiligen Rechtsschutzes – doch noch kein System? RIW 2003, 55

Zonderland, Einstweilige Verfügungen in den Niederlanden, ZZP 90 (1977) 225.

I. Preliminary Remarks

Owing to how long civil proceedings often take, there is a danger that a title obtained **1**
through litigation could prove to be useless due to the plaintiff's loss of access to the execution objects, thereby being divested of the actual satisfaction, or because the plaintiff already
suffers serious adverse effects[1] while the proceedings are still underway.[2] For this reason,
even before delivering a final decision, all European procedural systems grant legal assistance to a party whose claims have been violated or are at risk – to the extent evident – in the
form of provisional measures[3] intended to protect the parties to the proceedings from
adverse effects due to the time needed for the final settlement of disputes and to thereby
ensure the effectiveness of State legal protection.

Despite the significance of provisional legal protection in trans-border commerce, the Brus- **2**
sels I*bis* Regulation's governing of international jurisdiction for ordering provisional measures is only very rudimentary. In addition to the heads of jurisdiction contained in Art. 4
and Art. 7 to 26, the Brussels I Regulation foresees a further jurisdiction ground for provisional, including protective, measures in Art. 35. Art. 35 enables the applicant to seek such
measures from a court, even if, under the Regulation, another court has jurisdiction as to the
substance of the case.

---

[1] The party at risk can threaten insolvency due to supply disruption perhaps.
[2] *Garber*, Rechtsschutz 37.
[3] By way of example, a summary is provided by *Dalhuisen* in: Liber amicorum Riesenfeld 3 *et seq.*

3 This specific jurisdiction rule for provisional measures does not preclude the court deciding on the merits to order any provisional or protective measures which may prove necessary. A request for provisional including protective measures may hence be filed at the court dealing with the substance of the case or, alternatively, at the court that may exercise jurisdiction pursuant to Art. 35. Only the latter is bound by the specific requirements set out by this provision; in other words, Art. 35 does not interfere whenever the court dealing with the merits of the case orders provisional or protective measures.

II. Legislative History

4 Predecessors to Art. 35 are Art. 31 Brussels I Regulation, Art. 24 Brussels Convention and Art. 24 Lugano Convention.[4] Art. 24 Brussels Convention and Art. 24 Lugano Convention were referred to by parts of the doctrine as the "weak point"[5] of the Convention; they were regarded as its "stepchild"[6] and as standards that "leave many questions unanswered".[7] As a result of the criticism, Art. 24 Brussels Convention was supposed to be changed back in 1998 in the context of a revision to the Convention.[8] Since the scope of Art. 24 Brussels Convention was concretised and considerably restricted by two decisions of the ECJ[9] during these efforts, the process of making changes to the provision was completely abandoned,[10] and Art. 24 Brussels Convention was adopted with its contents unaltered into the Brussels I Regulation as its Art. 31. Since the decisions of the ECJ concerning Art. 24 Brussels Convention were referred to by parts of the doctrine[11] as "complicated, little contoured and thus highly confusing from a practical point of view", one of the central reform points of the Brussels I Regulation involved regulating provisional legal protection. Both the Heidelberg Report[12] given by order of the Commission as well as the draft regulation submitted by the Commission to amend the Brussels I Regulation[13] contained numerous suggestions for newly regulating provisional legal protection,[14] only some of which, however, found their way into the revised version of the Brussels I Regulation that (categorically) became applicable as of 10.1.2015. Therefore, European legislators once again failed to seize the opportunity to change Art. 31 Brussels I Regulation, adopting the provision with its contents unaltered into the revised version of the Regulation as its Art. 35.[15] With respect to provi-

---

[4]   The Lugano II Convention (or revised Lugano Convention) was concluded on 30 October 2007. And, to date, is in force for the European Union (including Denmark), Norway, Switzerland and Iceland. Article 31 of the Lugano II Convention is the counterpart on provisional measures in the context of this Convention.

[5]   *Kropholler/von Hein*, Art. 1 EuGVO note 1; similarly *Honorati*, RDIPP 2012, 525.

[6]   *Mankowski* in: Verschraegen, Studien 56.

[7]   *Leible* in: Rauscher Art. 31 Brüssel I-VO note 1.

[8]   In this regard, see *Garber*, Rechtsschutz 105.

[9]   *van Uden Maritime BV v. Deco-Line*, (Case C-391/95) (1998) ECR I-3715; *Mietz v. Intership*, (Case C-99/96) (1999) ECR I-2277.

[10] *Kohler* in: Gottwald, Revision 30.

[11] *Geimer/Schütze*, Art. 31 note 2.

[12] *Hess/Pfeiffer/Schlosser*, The Brussels I Regulation (EC) No. 44/2001 (2008).

[13] COM(2010) 748 def.

[14] In this regard, see *Garber* in: Grimm/Ladler, EU-Recht 191; *Kodek* in Jahrbuch Zivilverfahrensrecht 2010, 151.

[15] *Garber* is crit. in this regard in: Grimm/Ladler, EU-Recht 191; *Garber*, ecolex 2013, 1071.

sional legal protection, therefore, the otherwise excluded recourse to domestic law continues to be permissible (in this regard, see note 43 *et seq.*). It would have made sense to independently regulate international jurisdiction for ordering provisional measures – i.e. without recourse to domestic law of the Member States.[16] Such regulation would correspond to Recital no. 4 of the Brussels I*bis* Regulation, according to which the Regulation was intended to harmonise the places of jurisdiction of the Member States in order to ensure the smooth functioning of the Single Market. Furthermore, this would prevent a Member State from being able to exclude international jurisdiction for ordering provisional measures, even though its jurisdiction – such as due to the location of the object of the decree – appears to be particularly pertinent to the matter.[17]

Art. 35, Art. 31 Brussels I Regulation, Art. 24 Brussels Convention and Art. 24 Lugano **5** Convention are drafted in nearly identical terms. Case law and doctrinal writings on the referred Conventions is hence considered to be relevant for the interpretation of Art. 35.[18] The parallel provisions in Art. 20 Brussels II*bis* Regulation, in Art. 14 EU Maintenance Regulation, in Art. 19 EU Succession Regulation and the ECJ case law it generated are of relevance for the interpretation of Art. 35 as well.

III. Review of international jurisdiction for ordering provisional measures

The courts that have jurisdiction to decide the main proceedings according to the provisions **6** of the Brussels I*bis* Regulation are also competent to order provisional measures (in this regard, see also note 21 *et seq.*). However, the court having jurisdiction in the main proceedings does not have exclusive jurisdiction for ordering provisional measures. For, according to Art. 35, even the courts of those Member States that have no jurisdiction to decide the main proceedings according to the Brussels I*bis* Regulation are competent to decide petitions for provisional security and/or regulation, provided that they have jurisdiction in the provisional legal protection proceedings according to their own domestic law (in this regard, see also note 40 *et seq.*). In the scope of provisional legal protection, therefore, the otherwise excluded recourse to national jurisdiction systems is permissible. The result of this – as the ECJ confirmed in the decisions *van Uden v. Deco-Line*[19] and *Mietz v. Intership*[20] – is a two-track jurisdiction system:[21]
– the European Union autonomous jurisdiction system of the European court of the main
  proceedings and
– the domestic jurisdiction system of the Member States.

---

[16] *Kramer* in: Storme, Procedural Laws 305.

[17] *Garber*, Rechtsschutz 182.

[18] Cf. *Fallon*, Rev. dr. ULB 1993, 43; *van Drooghenbroeck* in: van Compernolle/Tarzia, Les mesures provisoires en droit belge, français et italien (1998), 475; *Boularbah*, TBH 1999, 604; *Hess/Vollkommer*, IPRax 1999, 220; *Marmisse/Wilderspin*, RCDIP 1999, 669; *Maher/Rodger*, (1999) 48 ICLQ 302; *Demeyere*, R. W. 1999–2000, 1353; *Steenhoff* in: Guus E. Schmidt, IPR & Kort geding (2000), 19; *van Haersolte-van Hof* in: Guus E. Schmidt, IPR & Kort geding (2000), 32 *et seq.*; *X. E. Kramer*, NIPR 2000, 26; *X. E. Kramer*, NIPR 2003, 240; *Struycken*, AA 2000, 579; *Vandekerckhove* in: Storme/de Leval 119 *et seq.*

[19] *van Uden Maritime BV v. Deco-Line*, (Case C-391/95) (1998) ECR I-3715.

[20] *Mietz v. Intership*, (Case C-99/96) (1999) ECR I-2277.

[21] *Garber*, Rechtsschutz 71 *et seq.*; *Honorati*, RDIPP 2012, 526 ("double track system").

7   The party at risk can choose between the court that has jurisdiction in the main proceedings according to the Brussels *Ibis* Regulation and the court that has jurisdiction according to domestic procedural law.[22]

8   If a differentiation is made according to the time at which the provisional measure is to be ordered, the result is the following three-track jurisdiction system:[23] Having jurisdiction for ordering a provisional measure is/are

  – the court that is actually involved in the main proceedings pursuant to Art. 4 and Art. 7 to 26 (for more information, see note 21 *et seq.* and note 35);

  – the courts for which the main proceedings could have become pending according to Art. 4 and Art. 7 to 26 (for more information, see note 37 *et seq.*);

  – the courts having jurisdiction in the provisional legal protection proceedings according to Art. 35 in conjunction with domestic law of the Member States (for more information, see note 40 *et seq.*).

9   The extension of the places of jurisdiction under Art. 4 and Art. 7 to 26 to include those prescribed by respective domestic law for ordering provisional measures serves to protect the party at risk.[23a] The intent is that a person whose claim is at risk or violated, and who therefore requires legal assistance in the form of provisional measures as quickly as possible, will not be forced to turn to a court of the main proceedings that happens to be far away and with whose court language and procedural rules the person is unfamiliar. Since the provisional measures issued in a Member State are sometimes exempt from being recognised and enforced (in this regard, see Art. 2 notes 18 *et seq.*), the accumulation of places of jurisdiction makes it possible for provisional measures to be ordered in the State in which they eventually are to be enforced. The provision of Art. 35 thus provides for effective provisional legal protection.[24]

10 However, the extension of the places of jurisdiction undertaken in Art. 35 involves the danger that, in choosing the place of jurisdiction, the party at risk will purposely take advantage of existing divergencies in the definition of provisional legal protection in the various Member States to the detriment of the opposing party.[25] In the provisional legal protection proceedings, the possibility of forum shopping is particularly questionable, since the extent of protection of the opponent to the party at risk is less compared to the main proceedings.[26] For instance, the taking of evidence and standard of proof are subject to fewer requirements in the provisional legal protection proceedings than in the main proceedings,[27] and the opponent to the party at risk is frequently granted no right to be heard before the provisional measure is ordered.[28] In its decision in the legal dispute *van Uden v. Deco-Line,*[29]

---

22   *Kofmel Ehrenzeller*, Rechtsschutz 251 *et seq.*

23   *Garber*, Rechtsschutz 72; *Micklitz/Rott*, EuZW 2002, 23; *Pörnbacher* in: Geimer/Schütze, Rechtsverkehr 540 Art. 31 note 9; *Treichel*, GRURInt 2001, 697.

23a *Bülow*, RabelsZ 29 (1965) 502; *H. Koch*, in: *Schlosser*, Materielles Recht 181; *Hausmann*, IPRax 1981, 79; *Kofmel Ehrenzeller*, Rechtsschutz 249; *St. Paul Dairy v. Unibel Exser*, (Case Rs C-104/03) (2005) ECR I-3481.

24   *Garber*, Rechtsschutz 102.

25   *Meier* in: Schwander, Lugano-Übereinkommen 167; *Spellenberg/Leible* in: Gilles, Prozeßrecht 315.

26   *C. Wolf/Lange*, RIW 2003, 59.

27   *Stürner* in: Liber amicorum Geiß 215 *et seq.*

the ECJ therefore limited the scope of Art. 24 Brussels Convention so that a court having jurisdiction according to Art. 24 Brussels Convention may only order a provisional measure if there is the existence of a real connecting link between the subject-matter of the measures sought and the territorial jurisdiction of the Contracting State of the court before which those measures are sought (in this regard, see note 60 *et seq.*).

Moreover, a measure ordering interim payment of a contractual consideration does not **11** constitute a provisional measure within the meaning of that Article unless, first, repayment to the defendant of the sum awarded is guaranteed if the plaintiff is unsuccessful as regards the substance of his claim and, second, the measure sought relates only to specific assets of the defendant located or to be located within the confines of the territorial jurisdiction of the court to which application is made (see note 63 *et seq.*).

IV. Requirements for ordering provisional measures

1. Scope must be established

a) General
Since the Brussel I*bis* Regulation provides no indications of any need to differentiate be- **12** tween definitive and provisional decisions with respect to the scope, it is also necessary – contrary to the view occasionally taken previously[30] – for the Regulation's geographic/personal, temporal and material scope to be established for the area of the provisional legal protection at all times.[31]

b) Geographic scope
Even for ordering provisional measures, international jurisdiction – subject to Art. 24, 25 **13** and 26, 71b and the extension of the geographic scope in matters of insurance, consumers and labour – is only then determined according to the Brussels I*bis* Regulation if the opponent to the party at risk is domiciled in a Member State of the Regulation.[32] If, however, the opponent to the party is domiciled in a third country instead, then international jurisdiction for ordering provisional measures is strictly governed by the domestic law of the State where the court is located.[33]

This also applies for jurisdiction according to Art. 35 in conjunction with domestic law. The **14** ECJ defined Art. 24 Brussels Convention, the predecessor to Art. 35, as "a rule of jurisdiction falling outside the system set out in Art. 2 and 5 to 18, whereby a court may order provisional or protective measures even if it does not have jurisdiction as to the substance of the case".[34] It is therefore questionable whether an independent jurisdiction rule, such as Art. 35, is limited by the territorial limitations that apply to the other jurisdiction rules. In particular, it

---

[28] *Stürner* in: Liber amicorum Geiß 213.

[29] *van Uden Maritime BV v. Deco-Line*, (Case C-391/95) (1998) ECR I-3715.

[30] Cour d'appel de Bruxelles J T 1978, 119 (*Stranart*) = Pasicrisie belge 164 (1978) 206.

[31] *Garber*, Rechtsschutz 58 *et seq.*

[32] *Kofmel Ehrenzeller*, Rechtsschutz 247; *Sandrock*, Int Lawyer 21 (1987) 17.

[33] *Garber*, Rechtsschutz 62; *H. Koch* in: Heldrich/Kono, Herausforderungen 88.

[34] *van Uden Maritime BV v. Deco-Line*, (Case C-391/95) (1998) ECR I-3715. See, in France, Cass. RCDIP 2002, 371 with note *Muir Watt*.

Marta Pertegás Sender/Thomas Garber   787

could be doubted whether the application of Art. 35 is subject to the further condition that the defendant must be domiciled in the European Union. Is it for instance possible for a Belgian claimant to invoke Art. 35 to request provisional measures against a defendant domiciled in the United States?

15 It is submitted that the answer to this question lies in the subtle combination of Art. 6 and Art. 35. It follows that Art. 35 generally encompasses the situation where the defendant is domiciled in a Member State. On the other hand, Art. 35 cannot be invoked where the defendant is not domiciled in the European Union, subject to Art. 24, 25 and 26, 71b and the present extension of the geographic scope in matters of insurance, consumers and labour.[35]

16 It remains uncertain whether the applicability of Art. 35 is conditional upon the existence of an actual and sufficient link with two or more Member States. In that respect, it has been argued that Art. 35 cannot be invoked in purely internal situations, that is where the proceedings on the merits are pending in the same Member State or, at least, when the dispute concerns two parties domiciled in the same Member State.[36]

c) **Material scope**

17 International jurisdiction for ordering provisional measures as well as the recognition and enforcement of provisional measures are only then determined according to the Brussel I*bis* Regulation if the provisional measure is included in the Regulation's material scope. In the first place, this provision only applies to disputes 'in civil and commercial matters', as the Regulation itself does. The ECJ held in its *De Cavel I* judgment that "in relation to the matters covered by the Convention, no legal basis is to be found therein for drawing a distinction between provisional and definitive measures."[37] It follows that Art. 35 does not apply beyond the general delimitation of the Regulation, that is, a civil and commercial matter other than the ones falling outside the scope of the Regulation pursuant to Art. 1, 2. Art. 35 cannot therefore be invoked to request provisional, including protective, measures in disputes that *ratione materiae* are not covered by the Regulation. The ECJ confirmed this in the *W./H.* judgment: "[the specific jurisdiction rule for provisional measures] may not be relied on to bring within the scope of the Convention provisional or protective measures relating to matters which are excluded from it."[38] The matters at stake are those specifically dealt with in the course of the interlocutory proceedings: a provisional claim for maintenance, for instance, falls within the scope of Art. 35, even if the proceedings on the substance are divorce proceedings and hence excluded from the scope of the Brussel I*bis* Regulation.[39]

---

[35] Cf. Art. 4 notes 3 *et seq.* (*Vlas*).

[36] *Gaudemet-Tallon* p. 246.

[37] *Jacques de Cavel v. Louise de Cavel*, (Case 143/78) (1979) ECR 1055 (placing assets under seal in the course of divorce proceedings); *W. v. H.*, (Case 25/81) (1982) ECR 1189 (provisional order to deliver a document to prevent its use as evidence in proceedings concerning the man's administration of his wife's assets).

[38] *W. v. H.* (Case 25/81), (1982) ECR 1189, 1204.

[39] *Louise de Cavel v. Jacques de Cavel*, (Case 125/79) (1980) ECR 731(interim maintenance claim). See, in the same direction, in Belgium: Trib. Nivelles Div. Act. 1995, 78; CA Bruxelles Div. Act. 1996, 57 (interim maintenance claim during divorce proceedings). In the Netherlands: Hoge Raad NIPR 1993, 390 (interim maintenance claim). Provisional including protective measures filed as a result of insolvency fall outside the scope of Art. 24 Brussels Convention (or Art. 31): Trib.comm. Paris Gaz. Pal. 1985, 1, 185.

Art. 35 cannot, however, be relied on to bring other connected provisional measures, requested in the framework of the same proceedings, within the material scope of the Brussels *Ibis* Regulation.[40]

Thus, only if the provisional measure serves to secure or regulate a claim based on civil or **18**
trade law within the meaning of Art. 1 para. 1 and there is no exception according to Art. 1 para. 2 will international jurisdiction for ordering the provisional measure be determined according to the Brussel *Ibis* Regulation. If, however, the provisional measure is based on a claim under public law or specified in Art. 1 para. 2, then the Brussels *Ibis* Regulation is not applicable.[41]

It is not significant in which proceedings the provisional measure is ordered, since the type **19**
of jurisdiction is not relevant according to Art. 1 para. 1. Thus, even provisional measures ordered by criminal courts fall within the material scope of the Brussel *Ibis* Regulation, provided that they only serve to secure or regulate a claim based on civil or trade law (not specified in Art. 1 para. 2).

Even if there is an arbitration agreement, the provisions of the Brussel *Ibis* Regulation apply **20**
to provisional measures if the claim that is to be secured or regulated falls within the Regulation's scope. As for the question of whether the provisions of the Brussel *Ibis* Regulation apply to provisional measures, only the claim based on the measure is decisive. If the claim that is to be secured or regulated is included in the scope of the Brussel *Ibis* Regulation, then the international jurisdiction of State courts for ordering provisional measures is determined according to the Brussel *Ibis* Regulation despite the existing arbitration agreement for the main proceedings. It is generally true that measures of provisional legal protection – independently of whether the main proceedings were conducted before a State court or arbitration tribunal – serve to secure a claim that has been violated or is at risk. If, however, the provisional measure is for the purpose of conducting the arbitration proceedings, then – since the claim that is to be secured in such a case is excluded from the Regulation's scope pursuant to Art. 1 para. 2 lit. d – the provisions of the Brussel *Ibis* Regulation are not applicable.[42] Concerning the question of which State court has international jurisdiction for ordering provisional measures according to the Brussel *Ibis* Regulation if there is an arbitration agreement, see note 78 *et seq.*

V. International jurisdiction for ordering provisional measures according to Art. 4, 7 to 26 Brussel *Ibis* Regulation

1. General

By virtue of European Union law, the court at which the main proceedings are pending or **21**
can become pending according to the rules of international, local and material jurisdiction is authorised to order measures of provisional legal protection.[43]

---

[40]   *Jacques de Cavel v. Louise de Cavel*, (Case 143/78) (1979) ECR 1055 para. 7; Hof Antwerpen AJT 1997-98, 354 with note *Lambein*.
[41]   *Garber*, Rechtsschutz 64.
[42]   *Garber*, Rechtsschutz 66.
[43]   *Garber*, Rechtsschutz 73 *et seq.*

22   The jurisdiction of the court of the main proceedings for ordering provisional measures is not explicitly mandated in the text of the Brussel I*bis* Regulation, although it follows from Recital no. 33 and Art. 2 lit. a Brussel I*bis* Regulation, in which a differentiation is made between provisional measures mandated by the court of the main proceedings and those that are ordered by a court according to Art. 35 in conjunction with domestic law. Since, according to the domestic law of all six original signatories to the Brussels Convention, the court of the main proceedings is always competent for provisional legal protection as well,[44] it is extremely improbable that the (original) signatories to the Brussels Convention would want to exclude the competency of the court of the main proceedings to order provisional measures, as is provided for in their national procedural rules, without expressly standardising this. Furthermore, the jurisdiction of the court of the main proceedings also follows from *a fortiori* argument: If the court of the main proceedings can definitively decide a legal dispute, then – barring provisions to the contrary – it must be all the more authorised to order less extensive regulations such as provisional security for the object in dispute.[45]

23   The primary argument for jurisdiction in provisional legal protection proceedings of the court of the main proceedings is its proximity to the case.[46] Considerations of procedural economy can also be cited in support of the jurisdiction of the court of the main proceedings: Since, as a rule, the court of the main proceedings is already familiar with the facts of the case, it is generally capable of deciding the petition for provisional security and/or regulation more quickly than the court not involved in the main proceedings and, moreover, it can factor in the findings already gathered in the main proceedings when ordering provisional measures.

2. Duty to grant justice

24   As a rule, the States having jurisdiction according to the Brussel I*bis* Regulation are obligated to serve justice (only excepting those cases in which the Brussel I*bis* Regulation – such as in Art. 7 para. 3 – expressly leaves the decision of whether a Member State has international jurisdiction or not up to the Member States).[47] In the area of the provisional legal protection proceedings, the decision also does not fall to the Member States concerning whether or not they want to avail themselves of the power of jurisdiction granted them in the Brussel I*bis* Regulation. Since the jurisdiction of the court of the main proceedings for ordering provisional measures directly follows from the Brussel I*bis* Regulation, the court of the main proceedings – independently of whether it also has jurisdiction for ordering provisional measures according to domestic law[48] – also has the competency to decide petitions for

---

[44]   For Belgium: *Eilers*, Maßnahmen 110 *et seq.*, Germany: *Grunsky* in *Stein/Jonas*, ZPO IX[22] § 919 note 1 *et seq.*, § 942 note 1 *et seq.*, France: *Vareilles-Sommières*, Rev crit 1996, 397, 416 *et seq.*, Italy: *Eilers*, Maßnahmen 130 *et seq.*, Luxembourg: *Eilers*, Maßnahmen 115 *et seq.*, the Netherlands: *Eilers*, Maßnahmen 120 *et seq.*; the legal systems of Great Britain (in this regard, see *Collins*, RdC 234 [1992-III] 50 *et seq.*) and Spain (in this regard, see *Baglietto Bergmann*, Rechtsschutz 180 *et seq.*; *Knothe*, Rechtsschutz 135 *et seq.*) provide for the jurisdiction of the court of the main proceedings for ordering provisional measures as well.

[45]   *Albrecht*, EuGVÜ 87; *Grundmann*, Anerkennung 112.

[46]   *Kropholler/von Hein*, Art. 31 note 10.

[47]   *Garber*, Rechtsschutz 75 *et seq.*

[48]   *Gassmann*, in: Spühler, Maßnahmen 102 *et seq.*

security and/or regulation.[49] National legislators may neither exclude nor restrict the jurisdiction of the court of the main proceedings in the provisional legal protection proceedings.[50] Naturally, the parties may exclude the jurisdiction of the court of the main proceedings by jurisdiction agreements or – to the extent permitted by domestic law – by arbitration agreements (for more information, see 78 *et seq.*).

3. Requirements for the jurisdiction of the court of the main proceedings for ordering provisional measures

The court of the main proceedings can only order provisional measures under the condition **25** that the geographic/personal, material and temporal scope of the Regulation has been established (for more information, see note 12 *et seq.*). Aside from this, the jurisdiction of the court of the main proceedings for ordering provisional measures – unlike the immediate jurisdiction according to Art. 35 based on domestic jurisdiction law – does not depend on any other autonomous requirements of European Union law.[51]

According to the view of the ECJ[52] and one part of the doctrine,[53] the jurisdiction of the court **26** of the main proceedings for ordering measures assumes that it is even possible for a State court to decide the main proceedings. Therefore, according to this point of view, if the parties have concluded an arbitration agreement, the court of the main proceedings should not be authorised to order provisional measures (in this regard, see note 78).

Unlike international jurisdiction according to Art. 35 in conjunction with domestic law, the **27** jurisdiction of the main court of proceedings for ordering provisional measures also does not imply the possibility of the provisional measure being implemented in the sovereign territory of the Member State whose court ordered it. While the court having jurisdiction according to Art. 35 in conjunction with domestic law can only order interim payment if repayment of the amount awarded is guaranteed (see also note 64 *et seq.*), the court of the main proceedings may order specific performance decrees even without assurance of the amount being repaid according to the *lex fori.*[54]

Concerning the question of whether autonomous requirements of European Union law **28** must be fulfilled once the main proceedings are pending, see note 37 *et seq.*

4. International jurisdiction of the main court of proceedings before initiation of the main proceedings

a) General
Unlike with comparable provisions in bilateral and multilateral agreements, it is not re- **29** quired according to Art. 35, which refers to domestic competency law, for the court to

---

[49]   *Geimer/Schütze*, Art. 31 note 4.

[50]   *Garber*, Rechtsschutz 76.

[51]   *Dedek*, EWS 2000, 250; *Geimer/Schütze*, Art. 31 note 4 *et seq.*; *Kropholler/von Hein*, Art. 31 note 12; *Mietz v. Intership*, (Case C-99/96) (1999) ECR I-2277.

[52]   *van Uden Maritime BV v. Deco-Line*, (Case C-391/95) (1998) ECR I-3715; Hoge Raad NJ 2001, 401.

[53]   *Kropholler/von Hein*, Art. 31 EuGVO note 4, 13; *Maher/Rodger*, (1999) 48 ICLQ 302.

[54]   *Schlosser*, Art. 31 note 22, 32; *Stadler*, JZ 1999, 1093; different view in *Pörnbacher*, RIW 1999, 781.

already be involved with the main proceedings, but instead it is sufficient for the court to have jurisdiction in the main proceedings. This ensures that the courts having jurisdiction according to Art. 35 in conjunction with domestic law will be able to order provisional measures even before the main proceedings are initiated. Since the courts having jurisdiction according to Art. 35 in conjunction with domestic law can order provisional measures before the pendency of the main proceedings, it is also necessary for the courts having jurisdiction according to Art. 4, 7 to 25 to be able to decide petitions for provisional security and/or regulation before the main proceedings are pending. If provisional measures could be ordered before the pendency of the main proceedings by the courts having jurisdiction according to the respective domestic law, but not by the courts having jurisdiction according to Art. 4, 7 to 25, the differentiation would not be objectively justifiable.[55]

b) Determining courts of the main proceedings before pendency of the main proceedings

30 Before the pendency of the main proceedings, it is necessary to identify the State that has international jurisdiction in the main proceedings, always assuming that the party at risk will subsequently initiate the main proceedings. For international jurisdiction, therefore, it is not sufficient for a Member State to have international jurisdiction for affirmative action brought by the opponent to the party at risk. Otherwise, the party at risk – contrary to the principles of the Regulation – will always have the possibility of applying for provisional legal protection in the Member State in whose sovereign territory this party is domiciled.[56]

c) Consequences of competing international jurisdiction

31 If several Member States have international jurisdiction in the main proceedings according to the Brussel I*bis* Regulation, then each potential court of the main proceedings can decide the petition for provisional security and/or regulation.[57] Therefore, based on jurisdiction according to Art. 4, 7 to 25 Brussel I*bis* Regulation, virtual jurisdiction is sufficient for ordering provisional measures.

32 In the event of competing jurisdiction – insofar as the parties have not waived the jurisdiction of a State (for more information, see note 69 *et seq.*) – the party at risk can choose at which of the possible courts of the main proceedings to apply for the provisional measure. This involves the danger that the party at risk will apply for a provisional measure at every potential court of the main proceedings in order to test which of the courts appealed to would presumably issue the most favourable decision for the party in subsequent main proceedings. The danger of such "testing" mainly consists of legal action involving competition, since in such cases the court usually does not have to resolve questions of facts, but of law, also basing its legal opinion when deciding the petition for the ordering of a provisional measure on its decision in the main proceedings.

33 It is doubtful how such testing of the courts of the main proceedings could effectively be prevented. A possible solution would be for the party at risk to be required to choose one of the courts having jurisdiction according to the Regulation as the court of the main proceedings before the pendency of the main proceedings and to only be permitted to apply to have a provisional measure ordered at this court. The subsequent main proceedings could only

---

[55]   *Garber*, Rechtschutz 90; s also *van Uden Maritime BV v. Deco-Line*, (Case C-391/95) (1998) ECR I-3715.

[56]   *Garber*, Rechtsschutz 92.

[57]   *Grundmann*, Anerkennung 112; *Hess/Vollkommer*, IPRax 1999, 221 *et seq.*

then be initiated at this court.[58] If the action in the main proceedings would later be brought to a different court than the one where the provisional measure was applied for, the court would have to deny having jurisdiction – even though it would have jurisdiction according to the Regulation – unless it would have international jurisdiction based on Art. 35. However, this solution does not sufficiently consider that the party at risk may have an interest in applying for the provisional measure in the Member State in which it is to be enforced later on, but in which – due to the fact that the courts in another Member State appear to have closer proximity for deciding the main proceedings – the party does not want to initiate the main proceedings.[59] What is more, the party at risk would first have to investigate which court would be most favourable for it to initiate the main proceedings at a time when it is in need of swift legal assistance. Such an investigation, which could be time-consuming under certain circumstances, would not be reconcilable with the purpose of provisional legal protection.[60]

The "testing" of several courts could also be prevented by only permitting the potential court **34** of the main proceedings to have jurisdiction for ordering provisional measures before the pendency of the main proceedings if the restriction to Art. 24 Brussels Convention persists that was developed by the ECJ in the legal matter of *van Uden v. Deco-Line*,[61] requiring there to be an existence of a real connecting link between the subject-matter of the measures sought and the territorial jurisdiction of the Contracting State of the court before which those measures are sought. This would ensure that only one court with competency for the provisional legal protection proceedings would be able to order provisional measures before the pendency of the main proceedings.[62] If the party at risk wants to apply for the provisional measure in a Member State for which there is no real connecting link, the party will need to initiate the main proceedings while still applying for approval of the provisional measure.[63]

5. Jurisdiction of the court of the main proceedings after initiation of the main proceedings in a Member State

If the main proceedings are already pending in a Member State's court, then this court also **35** has jurisdiction for deciding petitions for provisional security and/or regulation.[64] However, the court involved with the main proceedings does not have sole jurisdiction for ordering a provisional measure once the main proceedings are pending. The fact that the main proceedings are already pending does not hinder the courts of another Member State from deciding a petition for provisional security and/or regulation. Art. 29 is not applicable in the relationship between main proceedings and provisional legal protection proceedings (for more information, see note 85 *et seq.*).

---

[58] C. Wolf/Lange, RIW 2003, 60 *et seq.*

[59] Garber, Rechtsschutz 94.

[60] Garber, Rechtsschutz 94.

[61] van Uden Maritime BV v. Deco-Line, (Case C-391/95) (1998) ECR I-3715.

[62] Garber, Rechtsschutz 94.

[63] Garber, Rechtsschutz 94.

[64] Heinze, RIW 2003, 926.

36 In addition to the court actually involved with the main proceedings, it is the general view that the courts having jurisdiction according to Art. 35 Brussel I*bis* Regulation in conjunction with domestic procedural law are authorised to order provisional measures.[65]

37 Despite legal pendency of the main proceedings in a Member State's court, the virtual courts of the main proceedings – those courts that would have jurisdiction for deciding the main proceedings pursuant to Art. 4, 7 to 25 but were not appealed to as courts of the main proceedings – continue to have jurisdiction for ordering provisional measures as well.[66] Thus, the jurisdiction of the court of the main proceedings for the provisional legal protection proceedings does not assume that it would still be appealed to in a specific case; it is sufficient that the court could have been appealed to *in abstracto* in the main proceedings (hypothetical jurisdiction in main proceedings). If the other courts with (virtual) jurisdiction would lose their competency for ordering provisional measures according to the Brussel I*bis* Regulation due to the legal pendency of the main proceedings in a Member State, while the courts having jurisdiction according to Art. 35 in conjunction with domestic law would retain it, then the established (non-unified) domestic places of jurisdiction established would be more enduring than the uniform jurisdictions standardised in the Regulation.[67] Furthermore, the opponent to the party at risk can be prevented from bringing a negative affirmative action at a Member State's court with a system of provisional legal protection more favourable to the opposing party for the purpose of only allowing the party at risk to apply to have a provisional measure ordered at the court having justification according to Art. 35 in conjunction with domestic law.

38 According to prevailing opinion, the courts having jurisdiction according to Art. 4, 7 to 25 that were not appealed to as courts of the main proceedings, i.e. the virtual courts of the main proceedings, can order provisional measures despite the pendency of the main proceedings in another Member State's court, without it being necessary for any other EU-autonomous requirements to be fulfilled.[68] As a result, all courts having jurisdiction according to the Regulation can order provisional measures, even if the main proceedings are already pending. Since this results in the opponent to the party at risk have a very broad court obligation, there are deliberations on how to limit the virtual courts having jurisdiction in the main proceedings. Thus, parts of the doctrine[69] suggest that a virtual court of the main proceedings should not be permitted to order any provisional measures if it regards the court already involved in the main proceedings as being better suited to decide the petition for the ordering of a provisional measure.[70] However, this leads to considerable legal uncertainty, since the parties cannot foresee which State or which State's courts will have jurisdiction for ordering provisional measures, which therefore contradicts Recital no. 15, according to which determinations of jurisdiction need to be foreseeable to a high degree ("highly predictable"). Naturally, such an investigation, which is generally expensive and time-consum-

---

65 *Pörnbacher*, RIW 1999, 781.

66 *Albrecht*, EuGVÜ 98; *Grabinski*, GRURInt 2001, 211; *Heinze*, RIW 2003, 926; *Hess*, IPRax 2000, 374; *Hess/Vollkommer*, IPRax 1999, 224; *Jametti Greiner*, ZBernJV 1992, 650.

67 *Garber*, Rechtsschutz 96 *et seq*.

68 *Albrecht*, EuGVÜ 98; *Hess*, IPRax 2000, 374; *Meier* in: Schwander, Lugano-Übereinkommen 168; *Stadler*, JZ 1999, 1094.

69 *Guidicelli*, Cross Border Injunctions 37; *Heinze*, RIW 2003, 926.

70 *Garber*, Rechtsschutz 99.

ing, is not reconcilable with the purpose of provisional legal protection: namely, to grant legal assistance as quickly as possible.[71] It seems to make more sense to resort to the restrictions to Art. 24 Brussels Convention developed in the legal matter of *van Uden v. Deco-Line*,[72] according to which a virtual court of the main proceedings would only be allowed to order a provisional measure once the main proceedings are pending in another court if there is a real connecting link between the subject-matter of the measures sought and the territorial jurisdiction of the Member State of the court before which those measures are sought.[73] (For more information on what constitutes a real connecting link, see note 60 *et seq.*). This would ensure that those courts not actually involved with the main proceedings – regardless of whether their jurisdiction ensues from the Brussels I*bis* Regulation or from the provisions of domestic law – could only decide petitions for provisional security and/or regulation if the same requirements are fulfilled. For, despite the fact that the places of jurisdiction according to domestic law would be put on equal footing with those according to the Regulation as standardised in Art. 35, it would not be evident that a court having jurisdiction in provisional legal protection proceedings based on domestic procedural law would only be allowed to order provisional measures under certain conditions, while the virtual court of the main proceedings would have unrestricted jurisdiction for approving provisional measures, even though neither the court having jurisdiction in provisional legal protection proceedings according to domestic law nor the virtual court of the main proceedings is permitted to decide *in concreto* on the main issue and the measures they order serve the same purpose – namely, supporting the main proceedings.[74] If the jurisdiction of the virtual courts of the main proceedings is limited by the requirement that there be a real connecting link between the subject-matter of the measures sought and the territorial jurisdiction of the Member State of the court before which those measures are sought, this will lead to a balance between the interest of the party at risk in effective legal protection and the interest of the opponent to the party at risk in not needing to defend itself in all Member States: For it is only in those cases where there is a real connecting link between the subject-matter of the measures sought and the territorial jurisdiction of the Member State of the court before which those measures are sought, that the party at risk is to be permitted any need meriting consideration to also apply for a provisional measure in a State other than the one where the main proceedings are being conducted.[75]

6. International jurisdiction of courts of the main proceedings for ordering provisional measures after the main proceedings have been initiated in a third state

According to one part of the doctrine[76] and case law,[77] if the main proceedings are initiated **39** in a third state, neither the court of the main proceedings nor a court having jurisdiction according to Art. 35 is to be permitted to grant provisional legal protection, since ensuring the enforcement of a foreign main proceedings decision is not the purpose of the Regulation. However, this view must be rejected, since the party at risk has an interest meriting con-

---

71 *Garber*, Rechtsschutz 99.
72 *van Uden Maritime BV v. Deco-Line*, (Case C-391/95) (1998) ECR I-3715.
73 *Garber*, Rechtsschutz 99 *et seq.*
74 *Garber*, Rechtsschutz 100.
75 *Garber*, Rechtsschutz 100.
76 *Gassmann* in: Spühler, Maßnahmen 106; *Schmutz*, Maßnahmen 90.
77 Court of Appeal (UK) AllER 3 (1997) 724; Court of Appeal (UK) AllER 4 (1991) 458.

sideration that a provisional measure be ordered by a Member State's court, especially if the object of the decree is located in a Member State and a provisional measure ordered by the court of the main proceedings would neither be recognised nor enforced in the Member State in which the object of the decree is located. If in such a case a provisional measure could not be ordered by a court of the main proceedings having jurisdiction according to Art. 4, 7 to 25, this would result in a legal loophole.[78] However, even if the provisional measure ordered in the third state would be recognised and enforced in the Member State in which the object of the decree is located, it is better for the party at risk if the provisional measure is not ordered in the third state in which the main proceedings are pending, but instead in the Member State in which the object of the decree is located. If the provisional measure is ordered in the state in which it is to be enforced, the party at risk will be spared what could turn out to be drawn-out and time-consuming enforcement proceedings.[79]

VI. Art. 35 within the jurisdiction system of the Regulation

1. General

40   Art. 35 is an additional jurisdiction rule to request provisional measures and runs as such parallel to the 'general' jurisdictional system of the Brussels *Ibis* Regulation. A claimant can hence request provisional measures pursuant to Art. 35 even if certain jurisdictional rules in the Regulation impose restrictions on the venue of the proceedings on the merits, either by the will of the parties or by the nature of the dispute.

41   The Regulation does not establish any ranking between the court of the main proceedings and the court having jurisdiction according to Art. 35 in conjunction with domestic law. The party at risk can choose whether to have the provisional measure ordered by the court of the main proceedings or by a court having jurisdiction according to Art. 35 Brussel *Ibis* Regulation in conjunction with domestic law.[80] Besides the possibility of enforcement in the State where the court is located, the party at risk can also consider the possibility of other criteria that will ensure a quick court decision when choosing the court, such as being geographically accessible to witnesses or other proofs and evidence. However, it must be borne in mind that provisional measures ordered by the court having jurisdiction according to Art. 35 are excluded from mutual recognition and enforcement.

Since no restrictions to the scope can be derived from the wording of Art. 35, but instead this provision expressly refers to all jurisdiction provisions of the Regulation, a Member State's court can order provisional measures independently of whether another Member State has jurisdiction in the main proceedings according to Art. 4 or Art. 7 to 26. Art. 35 Brussel *Ibis* Regulation therefore applies in matters of insurance, consumers and labour as well as in cases where another Member State has sole jurisdiction for deciding the main proceedings according to Art. 24 (1) to (4).[81]

---

[78]   *Garber*, Rechtsschutz 101.

[79]   *Garber*, Rechtsschutz 101.

[80]   *Guidicelli*, Cross Border Injunctions 36; *Kienle*, Arreste 64; *Kofmel Ehrenzeller*, Rechtsschutz 251 *et seq.*; *Spellenberg/Leible* in: Gilles, Prozeßrecht 313; *Straub*, SZIER 1992, 541.

[81]   *Gronstedt*, Rechtsschutz 24 *et seq.*; *Maher/Rodger*, ICLQ 48 (1999) 308; *Solvay* (Case C-616/10).

According to Art. 24 (5) Brussel I*bis* Regulation, the courts of the Member State in whose **42** sovereign territory the compulsory enforcement is to be executed or will be executed have sole jurisdiction in proceedings involving the matter of compulsory enforcement arising from court decisions ("in proceedings concerned with the enforcement of judgments, the courts of the Member State in which the judgment has been or is to be enforced"). Art. 24 (5) Brussel I*bis* Regulation makes allowance for the principle of international law that a State can only execute sovereign enforcement within its own territory.[82] For this reason, it is necessary – even if the dividing line between the findings part and the enforcement part is fluid – to decide even for provisional measures which part of the order pertains to the findings proceedings and which part to compulsory enforcement law.[83] Sole jurisdiction for orders of provisional legal protection or for parts of such orders entailing compulsory enforcement proceedings pertains to the Member State in which they are to be enforced.[84] The judge having jurisdiction for ordering provisional measures can only effectively order the part of the provisional measure involving enforcement law for the judge's own sovereign territory.

2. Character of Art. 35

According to the predominant opinion in the doctrine[85] and case law,[86] Art. 35 only refers to **43** national jurisdiction law of Member States, i.e. a Member State's courts only have jurisdiction for ordering provisional measures according to Art. 35 under the condition that the domestic procedural law standardises international jurisdiction for ordering provisional measures. According to a different view,[87] however, Art. 35 Brussel I*bis* Regulation is intended to have the effect of substantiating jurisdiction instead, with the courts of the Member States that do not have jurisdiction to decide the main proceedings also being able to order provisional measures without having to resort to the national jurisdiction provisions of the respective Member State.

The latter view must be rejected. Due to the wording of the provision, it can be immediately **44** ruled out that Art. 35 only refers to the provisions of national legal systems.[88] Moreover, Art. 35 does not align itself with the jurisdiction provisions of the Regulation (Art. 4, 7 to 26), but only follows the provisions concerning verification of procedural jurisdiction and admissibility (Art. 27, 28), the pendency of proceedings and connectivity (Art. 29 to 34).[89] The

---

[82] *Geimer*, IZPR[7] note 1221 with further references.
[83] *Meier* in: Schwander, Lugano-Übereinkommen 172.
[84] *Meier* in: Schwander, Lugano-Übereinkommen 172.
[85] *Collins*, Yb Eu L 1981, 254; *Geimer*, NJW 1976, 446; *Grabinski*, GRURInt 2001, 201, 211; *Gronstedt*, Rechtsschutz 18; *Hanisch*, IPRax 1991, 215 *et seq.*; *Jametti Greiner* in: Spühler, Massnahmen 24; *Maher/ Rodger*, ICLQ 48 (1999) 302; *Remien*, WRP 1994, 25; *Sandrock*, Int Lawyer 21 (1987) 17 *et seq.*; *Schack*, MMR 2000, 139 *et seq.*; *Thümmel*, NJW 1996, 1931.
[86] Court of Appeal (UK) AllER 3 (1997) 724; Corte di Cassazione (I) Il massimario del Foro Italiano 1995 Col 563.
[87] *Albrecht*, EuGVÜ 113 *et seq.*; *Garcimartín Alférez* in: Hommelhoff/Jayme/Mangold, Binnenmarkt 131; *Grundmann*, Anerkennung 131 *et seq.*; *Roth*, IPRax 1990, 161; *Schmutz*, Maßnahmen 88 *et seq.*; *Willeitner*, Vermögensgerichtsstand 11, 139 *et seq.*
[88] *Naudi*, Umsetzung 92.
[89] *Grundmann*, Anerkennung 130: "The positioning raises doubts as to whether Art. 24 Lugano Regulation

---

objection that the structure of the argument only involves historical reasons because the provisions in bilateral recognition and enforcement agreements serving as a model for Art. 35 Brussel I*bis* Regulation follow the provisions concerning the pendency of proceedings[90] is not convincing, due to the fact that the agreements do not independently standardise international jurisdiction of the signatories, but instead only establish the requirements for recognising and enforcing foreign decisions. A comparison of Art. 35 and the provisions in bilateral agreements serving as a model for it also seems unconvincing because the regulations serve different purposes – in contrast to Art. 35, the agreements concerned only served the purpose of declaring ineffective the provisions concerning the pendency of proceedings in provisional legal protection proceedings.[91] It can also be derived from Art. 5 para. 1 Brussel I*bis* Regulation, which excludes resorting to national jurisdiction law only for jurisdiction according to Art. 4, 7 to 26 and not for jurisdiction according to Art. 35, that Art. 35 does not have any independent effect substantiating jurisdiction. The opposing view would also entail that all Member States – based on Art. 4, 7 to 26 Brussel I*bis* Regulation or Art. 35 – would have jurisdiction for ordering provisional measures. This contradicts Recital no. 15, which indicates that excessive court obligations on the part of the defendant are to be hindered in the scope of the regulation. Only if Art. 35 Brussel I*bis* Regulation is understood as referring to the national places of jurisdiction of the respective Member State will it be ensured that – at least according to the judgment of national legislators – there is a sufficient relation between the object in dispute or the parties and the forum.

3. Places of jurisdiction established by Art. 35 Brussel I*bis* Regulation

45 The standardised reference in Art. 35 covers all places of jurisdiction according to domestic law that were included in the Brussel I*bis* Regulation, i.e. even those that, pursuant to Art. 5 para. 2, are to be regarded as exorbitant. Accordingly, provisional measures according to Art. 35 in conjunction with domestic law can also be ordered in the places of jurisdiction excluded by Art. 5 para. 2 on account of being exorbitant.[92]

4. Which 'provisional, including protective measures' are viable under Art. 35?

a) General

46 Despite proposals by the Commission to this effect,[93] the Regulation does not contain any definition of the concept of provisional measures. Due to differences in the concept of provisional legal protection in the Member States, formulating such a definition would certainly be difficult, which is why the European legislators refrained from doing so. It is only Recital 25 that expressly standardises that orders for the purpose of gathering or securing evidence within the meaning of Art. 6 and 7 of Directive 2004/48/EC of the European Parliament and of the Council of 29.4.2004 on the enforcement of intellectual property rights are included under the term 'provisional measure'. In *St. Paul Dairy v. Unibel*

---

truly involves a standard of direct jurisdiction whose purpose lies in determining international jurisdiction".

90 *Grundmann*, Anerkennung 130 *et seq.*

91 *Grundmann*, Anerkennung 130 *et seq.*; cf. also *Merkt*, Mesures provisoires 108.

92 *Geimer*, NJW 1976, 446; *Grunsky*, RIW 1977, 7 *et seq.*; *Heinze*, RIW 2003, 926; different view in *Gronstedt*, Rechtsschutz 22 *et seq.*

93 Recital no. 22 to the draft of the Commission (COM[2010] 748 endg 18).

Exser,[94] the ECJ decided that a measure ordering the hearing of a witness for the purpose of enabling the applicant to decide whether to bring a case, determine whether it would be well founded and assess the relevance of evidence which might be adduced in that regard is not covered by the notion of "provisional, including protective, measures".[95]

The concept of provisional measures needs to be interpreted according to autonomous **47** European Union law.[96] This is because Art. 35 results in a suppression of the jurisdiction system standardised in Art. 4, 7 to 26, which is why, for the purpose of avoiding unequal treatment and legal uncertainty, the requirements under which it is permitted to suppress the jurisdiction system must be as uniform and clear as possible.[97] Otherwise, a Member State could liberally interpret the concept of provisional measures in order to substantiate its own international jurisdiction.[98]

As Art. 35 refers to the measures available under national law, it could appear at first sight **48** that any provisional measure available under the national legal system falls within the scope of Art. 35. However, ECJ case law has specified that there are limits to the 'provisional jurisdiction' under the Brussels system. In particular, proceedings allegedly of a provisional nature but leading *de facto* to final measures may fall beyond the limits of that provisional jurisdiction under Art. 35. The ECJ has taken care to emphasise that "the limits provided for in that provision" *(i.e.* then Art. 24 Brussels Convention) must be respected to avoid a circumvention of the other jurisdiction rules in the Brussels system. In other words, certain provisional, including protective, measures available under national law may exceed the Regulation framework for provisional jurisdiction.

What, then, are the limits set out by the ECJ with respect to Art. 35? Art. 35 empowers **49** national courts to grant provisional measures that match the features highlighted by the ECJ in *Reichert II*.[99] In that judgment, the ECJ defined such measures as "measures which, in matters within the scope of the Convention, are intended to preserve a factual or legal situation so as to safeguard rights the recognition of which is sought elsewhere from the court having jurisdiction as to the substance of the matter." The ECJ emphasised in the first place the provisional nature of measures requested on the basis of Art. 35 (or its predecessor Art. 24 Brussels Convention). It is examined below whether the provisional character requires that the proceedings on the merits are already pending and/or presupposes the urgency of the requested measures. Secondly, the ECJ focuses on the purpose of the requested measures: a safeguard function is compulsory to meet the requirements of the provisional forum.

b) Provisional nature
In *Reichert II*, the ECJ contemplated the application of Art. 35 (or its predecessor Art. 24 **50** Brussels Convention) when the proceedings on the merits were already pending. If the provisional forum's purpose is "to safeguard rights the recognition of which is *sought else-*

---

[94] *St. Paul Dairy v. Unibel Exser*, (Case Rs C-104/03) (2005) ECR I-3481.

[95] In this regard, crit *Garber*, Rechtsschutz 149 *et seq.*

[96] *Garber*, Rechtsschutz 124 *et seq.*

[97] *Garber*, Rechtsschutz 125.

[98] *Dörschner*, Beweissicherung 161; *Schmutz*, Maßnahmen 29.

[99] *Reichert and Kockler v. Dresdner Bank AG*, (Case C-261/90) (1992) ECR I-2149.

where", one could assume that the vital cycle of Art. 35 is reduced to the period between the filing of the proceedings on the merits and the rendering of the corresponding judgment. Some commentators argued that this interpretation would be too restrictive.[100] Accordingly, the ECJ acknowledged in recent case law that no strict condition of simultaneity applies. For Art. 35 to be invoked, it is sufficient that proceedings on the merits are available to recognise the rights safeguarded by means of the requested provisional measures.[101]

51   In order to ensure the provisional character of the requested measures, the court must be able to make its order conditional to all limitations guaranteeing the provisional or protective character of the measure ordered. In particular, the court can, in function of the nature of the assets or goods subject to the measures contemplated, require bank guarantees or nominate a sequestrator.[102] In *van Uden v. Deco-Line*[103] and *Mietz v. Intership*,[104] the ECJ had the opportunity to specify in which way the provisional nature of an interim payment could be guaranteed. It stated that such measures fall outside the scope of Art. 35 unless repayment to the defendant of the sum awarded is guaranteed if the plaintiff is unsuccessful as regards the substance of his claim.[105] To prevent the execution of an interlocutory order for payment having irreversible consequences, the court may impose an additional guarantee on the claimant if, for instance, there are doubts about his chances of winning the case on the merits. Some commentators are of the opinion that a systematic request for a claimant deposit may become an excessive burden on the claimant's financial position, which is incompatible with the *ratio legis* of the interim payment itself.[106] It therefore seems appropriate that the court balances the interests of the respective parties, with regards to the specific circumstances of the case, to decide whether the grant of the measures is made conditional upon a security or deposit by the claimant.

c) Safeguarding rights

52   The second element of the definition of provisional measures in *Reichert II* refers to the purpose of such measures: their aim must be to safeguard rights the recognition of which is sought by means of a definitive decision. Protective measures such as the seizure of goods fulfil this condition.[107]

---

100   *Collins*, Rec. des Cours 234 (1992-III), 13, 24 *et seq.*; *Huet*, Clunet 120 (1993), 461.

101   *van Uden Maritime BV v. Deco-Line*, (Case C-391/95) (1998) ECR I-3715. This issue was not explicitly dealt with by the ECJ in the *St. Paul Dairy Industries* case: it is submitted that the ECJ refused the application of Art. 24 Brussels Convention on the basis of the aim of a provisional hearing of witnesses under Dutch law. The fact that such measure would be granted before the proceedings on the merits of the case does not appear to have been decisive for the ECJ to rule out the application of Art. 24 Brussels Convention. Cf. *St. Paul Dairy Industries NV v. Unibel Exser BVBA*, (Case C-104/03) (2005) ECR I-3481 with note *Mankowski*, JZ 2005, 1144 and *van Het Kaar*, NIPR 2006, 383.

102   *Bernard Denilauler v. SNC Couchet Frères*, (Case 120/79) (1980) ECR 1553, 1570.

103   *van Uden Maritime BV v. Deco-Line*, (Case C-391/95) (1998) ECR I-3715.

104   *Mietz v. Intership*, (Case C-99/96) (1999) ECR I-2277.

105   *van Uden Maritime BV v. Deco-Line*, (Case C-391/95) (1998) ECR I-3715; *Mietz v. Intership*, (Case C-99/96) (1999) ECR I-2277. In addition, a territorial limitation was imposed, as discussed *infra* Art. 31 notes 26–29 *(Pertegás Sender)*.

106   *Boularbah*, TBH 1999, 604, 609; *Jerôme Lange*, NJB 1999, 157, 162.

107   OLG Koblenz Digest I-24 B 1; CA Luxembourg Pas. Lux. 1981, 134.

d) Need for urgency

Another issue connected to the provisional nature of the requested measures is whether **53** Art. 35 presupposes the condition of urgency. This question was once submitted to the ECJ.[108] However, the ECJ did not have an opportunity to give a ruling on that point because the question was finally withdrawn by the Hoge Raad.

Whether such measures can be subsumed under the concept of provisional measures within **54** the meaning of Art. 35 is controversial, as particular urgency is required for ordering them.[109] In contrast to Art. 20 para. 1 Brussels II*bis* Regulation (concerning jurisdiction and the recognition and enforcement of judgments in matrimonial matters and the matters of parental responsibility), Art. 35 does not expressly standardise that provisional measures may only be ordered "in urgent cases". Due to the differences in drafting the text of the two provisions, however, it is not possible to compellingly draw the conclusion that provisional measures may also be ordered according to Art. 35 when there is no particular need for urgency. Since it was controversial whether the need for urgency is a conceptual characteristic of provisional measures at the time the Brussels II*bis* Regulation was passed, there is much to support the claim that the express standardisation of the need for urgency in Art. 20 Brussels II*bis* Regulation only arose for reasons of clarification and not because there was an intent to regulate the requirements under which a provisional measure may be ordered in a way deviating from Art. 35. Similarly, the fact that the ECJ did not explicitly incorporate the urgency of the measure into the definition of the concept of provisional measures does not imply that the need for urgency does not constitute a conceptual characteristic of provisional measures.[110] In fact, the question of whether the need for urgency is an additional autonomous conceptual characteristic of provisional measures under Community law within the meaning of Art. 35 was not explicitly raised in the legal matters being decided by the ECJ because the presence of urgency was already required according to the provisions of domestic law.

However, since the court obligation of the opponent to the party at risk was extended **55** considerably by Art. 35 Brussel I*bis* Regulation, it appears necessary in order to protect the opponent to the party at risk to interpret Art. 35 restrictively and only permit a court having jurisdiction according to Art. 35 in conjunction with domestic law to order a provisional measure in urgent cases. This will guarantee that the jurisdiction system of the Brussel I*bis* Regulation is only suppressed in those cases where the court of the main proceedings is not in a position to order provisional measures in time to secure a claim that is at risk or has been violated.[111] If there is no particular need for urgency, then provisional legal protection

---

108 *Saueressig v. Forbo-Krommenie*, (Case C-99/95), removed from the register on 29 April 1996, referral from Hoge Raad NTER 1995, 252 *et seq.*

109 Affirming *Bischoff/Huet*, J d T 1982, 947; *Couchez*, Rev crit 1983, 115; *Dörschner*, Beweissicherung 164 *et seq.*; *Garcimartín Alférez* in: Hommelhoff/Jayme/Mangold, Binnenmarkt 131; *Garber*, Rechtsschutz 129 *et seq.*; *Guidicelli*, Cross Border Injunctions 36; *Heiss*, Rechtsschutz 42 *et seq.*; *Koch* in: Schlosser, Materielles Recht 181; *Spellenberg/Leible*, ZZPInt 4 (1999) 226; *Stadler*, JZ 1999, 1096; as well as – however, only for specific performance decrees – Bundesgericht (CH) BGE 125 III 451; rejecting *Albrecht*, EuGVÜ 106; *Willeitner*, Vermögensgerichtsstand 11, 92; Cour de Cassation (F) Clunet 120 (1993) 156.

110 *Garber*, Rechtsschutz 130.

111 *Besix AG v. Kretzschmar*, (Case C-256/00) (2002) ECR I-1699; *Group Josi Reinsurance Company/Universal General Reinsurance Company*, (Case C-412/98) (2000) ECR I-5925.

Marta Pertegás Sender/Thomas Garber

measures can also be ordered by the court of the main proceedings without there being any danger of the legal position of the party at risk being adversely affected.

56   The cases in which there is a need for urgency must be autonomously determined under European Union law, since an interpretation according to the respective *lex fori* or *lex causae* would lead to differences in how strict the requirements are for ordering provisional measures. Accordingly, there is a need for urgency in those cases for which the party at risk would incur irreparable damages if the provisional measure is not ordered, since the measure from the court of the main proceedings would come too late.[112] Constituting damages are all serious (material and immaterial) adverse effects suffered by the party at risk with respect to its objects of legal protection or assets and which are presently occurring or at least imminent.[113]

57   If the provisions of the respective domestic law do not stipulate a need for urgency for ordering provisional measures, then this requirement appears as an additional autonomous element of fact.

5. Autonomous requirements under European Union law for the ordering of provisional measures by courts having jurisdiction according to Art. 35

a) Existence of geographic/personal, material and temporal scope of the Regulation

58   A court having jurisdiction according to Art. 35 Brussel I*bis* Regulation can only order provisional measures under the condition that the geographic/personal, material and temporal scope of the regulation has been established. In this regard, see note 12 *et seq.*

b) Petition by the party at risk

59   Provisional measures may only be ordered at the request of the party at risk. It is not possible for provisional measures to be ordered *ex officio* according to Art. 35.

c) Existence of a "real connecting link"

60   To ensure a relation to the forum, ECJ case law[114] requires that there be a real connecting link between the subject-matter of the measures sought and the territorial jurisdiction of the Member State of the court before which those measures are sought. This is to guarantee that no court that is unconnected with the matter will be able to decide a petition for security or regulation. The real connecting link requirement applies for all places of jurisdiction by Art. 35 and domestic law. A restriction to special national places of jurisdiction – such as those that are to be regarded as exorbitant pursuant to Art. 5 para. 2 – cannot be derived from the wording of the decision.

61   The real connecting link concept is based on execution law. As such, there is only an actual link between the object of the measure applied for and the territorial jurisdiction of a Member State's courts for the courts of the Member State in whose sovereign territory the provisional measure is to be executed.[115]

---

112   *Garber*, Rechtsschutz 131.
113   *Garber*, Rechtsschutz 131.
114   *van Uden Maritime BV v. Deco-Line*, (Case C-391/95) (1998) ECR I-3715.

There is a real connecting link for provisional measures involving a certain mobile physical **62** or immobile object if the object involved is located in the State where the court is. What is definitive, therefore is the objectively definable location.[116] If the provisional measure involves a debt claim, then the real connecting link is to the State in which the third-party debtor is domiciled.[117] For current account receivables owed by the opponent to the party at risk to its bank, there is thus a real connecting link to the State where the bank has its registered office. For preliminary arrangements of an activity, there is a real connecting link to the Member State in which the activity is to be carried out.[118] For matters of toleration or injunction decrees, there is a real connecting link with the Member State in which the activity is to be tolerated or desisted from.[119] If an activity bound to a certain location is to be prohibited, then the courts of the State whose sovereign territory is involved have jurisdiction.[120]

d) Special autonomous requirements under European Union law for the ordering of specific performance decrees by courts having jurisdiction according to Art. 35 Brussels I*bis* Regulation

aa) General

According to ECJ case law,[121] courts having jurisdiction according to Art. 35 in conjunction **63** with domestic law may also order interim payment if repayment to the defendant of the sum awarded is guaranteed if the plaintiff is unsuccessful as regards the substance of his claim and, second, the measure sought relates only to specific assets of the defendant located or to be located within the confines of the territorial jurisdiction of the court to which application is made.

bb) Repayment of the amount awarded is guaranteed

The requirement that repayment of the amount awarded must be guaranteed results in a **64** balance between the interest of the party at risk in swift access to the assets of the opponent to the party at risk and the interest of the opponent to the party at risk in preventing changes that can no longer be modified.[122] However, the ECJ left the question concerning when repayment of the amount awarded is to be regarded as guaranteed unanswered. To protect the opponent to the party at risk from no longer being given back a monetary amount unjustly awarded to the party at risk, the repayment of the amount awarded can only be regarded as being guaranteed if the amount to be paid to the party at risk is entrusted to the court or if the party at risk has provided a security – such as in the form of a bank guarantee – before repayment is made.[123] Only in such cases is it ensured that the opponent to the party

---

115 *Schulz*, ZEuP 2001, 816; *Spellenberg/Leible*, ZZPInt 4 (1999) 229 *et seq.*; *Stadler*, JZ 1999, 1093; *Willeitner*, Vermögensgerichtsstand 118 *et seq.*; *Wolf*, EWS 2000, 16.

116 *Kofmel Ehrenzeller*, Rechtsschutz 256; *Willeitner*, Vermögensgerichtsstand 118 *et seq.*

117 *Hess*, IPRax 2000, 373; *Willeitner*, Vermögensgerichtsstand 121.

118 *Spellenberg/Leible*, ZZPInt 4 (1999) 231.

119 *Spellenberg/Leible*, ZZPInt 4 (1999) 231.

120 *Hess/Vollkommer*, IPRax 1999, 225.

121 *Mietz v. Intership*, (Case C-99/96) (1999) ECR I-2277; *van Uden Maritime BV v. Deco-Line*, (Case C-391/95) (1998) ECR I-3715.

122 *Garber*, Rechtsschutz 162.

123 *Geimer/Schütze*, Art. 31 note 49; *Willeitner*, Vermögensgerichtsstand 98.

at risk will receive back the amount paid – should the opposing party win in the main proceedings – without having to bear the risk of insolvency. In contrast, repayment of the preliminarily awarded amount is not already guaranteed if the opponent to the party at risk has a claim involving unfair enrichment, damage compensation or other repayment according to domestic law,[124] as repayment of the amount paid is not certain in such cases, since it may fail due to a worsening financial situation (esp. insolvency) of the alleged party at risk. For this reason, making the execution of the main proceedings a condition is not sufficient to guarantee repayment of the preliminarily awarded amount.

65 The previous cases decided by the ECJ only involved provisional measures oriented to the provisional rendering of a "contractual payment". The question of whether the repayment also needs to be guaranteed for payment claims based on non-contractual legal relationships is controversial.[125] Unlike with contractual payment claims, a creditor from a non-contractual legal relationship generally has not chosen its partner and therefore was not able to take the partner's economic capacity into account.[126] In addition to this, a party at risk that is dependent on payment of the monetary amount it has been awarded is frequently in financial distress and thus unable in practice to provide the security deposit.[127] In contrast, contracting parties have the possibility of safeguarding against the risk of "being in need".[128] A differentiation between contractual and non-contractual relationships therefore seems quite justified. For this reason, it is not mandatory to provide security for specific performance decrees to safeguard a payment claim based on non-contractual relationships, but instead it is sufficient to set a deadline for initiating main proceedings to safeguard the preliminary character of the measure.[129]

66 The particulars of the security are left up to national law (especially with regard to how it is provided).[130] Insofar as the judge grants discretion, European regulations overlie national law in the sense that the judge now needs to mandate security.[131]

cc) Geographic relation required between the provisional measure and the court appealed to

67 The ECJ has already placed general restrictions on international jurisdiction according to Art. 35 by requiring a real connecting link. Nevertheless, for specific performance decrees, it demands that the measure sought relates only to specific assets of the defendant located or to be located within the confines of the territorial jurisdiction of the court to which application is made.[132] With the requirement that the measure only involve certain assets located in the

---

[124] Cour de Cassation (F) Clunet 2000, 83.

[125] Affirming *Dedek*, EWS 2000, 250; *Geimer/Schütze*, Art. 31 note 50; *Stadler*, JZ 1999, 1097; rejecting *Garber*, Rechtsschutz 167; *Leible* in: Rauscher, Art. 31 note 12; *Spellenberg/Leible*, ZZPInt 4 (1999) 224 *et seq.*; *Willeitner*, Vermögensgerichtsstand 10, 105 *et seq.*

[126] *Willeitner*, Vermögensgerichtsstand 105.

[127] *Spellenberg/Leible*, ZZPInt 4 (1999) 224.

[128] *Leible* in: Rauscher, Art. 31 note 12; *Willeitner*, Vermögensgerichtsstand 105.

[129] *Willeitner*, Vermögensgerichtsstand 106.

[130] *Garber*, Rechtsschutz 166; *Geimer/Schütze*, Art. 31 note 49; *Hess/Vollkommer*, IPRax 1999, 221.

[131] *Garber*, Rechtsschutz 166; *Geimer/Schütze*, Art. 31 note 49.

[132] *Mietz v. Intership*, (Case C-99/96) (1999) ECR I-2277; *van Uden Maritime BV v. Deco-Line*, (Case C-391/95) (1998) ECR I-3715.

geographic jurisdiction area of the Member State appealed to, the ECJ appears solely to be defining the real connecting link requirement for specific performance decrees more precisely. Unlike with provisional security and/or regulation decrees, it is not sufficient for the opponent to the party at risk to possess assets in the State, thereby making it appear possible to execute the measure in the sovereign territory of the State where the order is made, but instead the party at risk must identify in detail the assets of the opponent to the party at risk that are located in the State and will later be affected by the specific performance decree being executed. Solely the assets identified by the party at risk and included by the court in the tenor of the provisional measure are subject to the subsequent enforcement of the provisional measure.[133] The requirement that the measure only involve the assets identified (by the plaintiff) that are located in the geographic jurisdiction area of the Member State referred to therefore restricts the objective effect of the specific performance decree.

Even though determining a geographic relation for specific performance decrees ordering 68 the payment of a monetary amount may appear difficult, since debts can be satisfied by way of compulsory enforcement from the overall assets of the debtor, the criterion not only applies for specific performance decrees involving defined non-cash benefits,[134] but also for those ordering a payment.

VII. Place of Prorogation of jurisdiction and their effects on provisional legal protection proceedings

1. Admissibility and effectiveness of place of jurisdiction agreements involving provisional legal protection proceedings

According to the Regulation, the parties have the possibility of substantiating the jurisdic- 69 tion of a court without jurisdiction by means of a place of jurisdiction agreement and/or of derogating the jurisdiction of a Member State with jurisdiction according to the Regulation. The requirements for the admissibility and effectiveness of a place of jurisdiction agreement are standardised in Art. 25; besides the formal requirements specified in Art. 25 Brussel I*bis* Regulation, the standardised restrictions in Art. 15, 19 and 23 also need to be observed in matters of insurance, consumers and labour.

Pursuant to Art. 25 para. 4 Brussel I*bis* Regulation, place of jurisdiction agreements only 70 have no legal effect in those cases where they run contrary to the requirements of Art. 15, 19 and 23 or where a State's mandatory jurisdiction according to Art. 24 is intended to be waived. From the converse argument to Art. 25 para. 4, it follows that place of jurisdiction agreements concerning international jurisdiction in provisional legal protection proceedings are generally admissible.[135] The fact that place of jurisdiction agreements are also admissible for provisional legal protection proceedings enables the parties to presume that the same court will have jurisdiction in all disputes, including for the associated provisional measures, by which means above all the broad court obligation of the opponent to the party at risk can be restricted.

---

[133] Cour de Cassation (F) Clunet 2000, 83 (*Huet*).

[134] So *Hess/Vollkommer*, IPRax 1999, 224.

[135] *Garber*, Rechtsschutz 193 *et seq.*; *Grundmann*, Anerkennung 128; *Leible* in: Rauscher, Art. 31 note 33; *Mankowski* in: Rauscher, Art. 23 note 66.

71 As stipulated by Art. 15, 19, 23 and 25, the parties can therefore arrange that a certain court has jurisdiction in the provisional legal protection proceedings instead of or along with the court of the main proceedings. However, they can also expressly waive the jurisdiction of the (or a) court of the main proceedings for ordering provisional measures.

72 It is controversial whether jurisdiction of the national places of jurisdiction established by Art. 35 can also be modified by a place of jurisdiction agreement. Some take the view that derogating the courts with jurisdiction according to Art. 35 in conjunction with domestic law is categorically permissible.[136] If the parties can exclude the jurisdiction of the court of the main proceedings for ordering provisional measures, they would also have to be able to waive the jurisdiction of the courts with jurisdiction according to Art. 35 in conjunction with domestic law. However, since Art. 35 refers to the jurisdiction provisions of national legal systems of Member States for provisional legal protection proceedings, then the question of whether and under what conditions national places of jurisdiction can be changed through an agreement by the parties must be evaluated according to domestic law.[137]

73 The requirements for the admissibility and effectiveness of place of jurisdiction agreements, which directly govern jurisdiction for ordering provisional measures, are solely derived from Art. 15, 19, 23 and 25, since the Regulation does not provide any indications for differentiating between place of jurisdiction agreements involving the definitive legal protection proceedings and those that govern jurisdiction for provisional legal protection proceedings. Since complying with the requirements of legal security and matters of insurance, consumers and labour that are standardised in the aforementioned provisions also serves to protect the weaker party, a deviation would not be legally explicable either.

2. Place of jurisdiction agreements involving the main proceedings – effects on provisional legal protection proceedings

74 If the parties effectively agree upon the jurisdiction of a Member State's court according to Art. 25 for deciding the main proceedings, then the court – provided that the parties have not expressly arranged any deviating regulation – also has jurisdiction for ordering provisional measures.[138] In principle, therefore, the prorogation effect of the agreement also extends to provisional legal protection measures. After all, it would represent a judgment contradiction if the parties would assign a court the competency to definitively decide a legal dispute, but would not also – without expressly agreeing on something else – assign to it the authorisation for ordering less extensive provisional measures, such as the provisional securing of the object in dispute.

75 Since the prorogated court has jurisdiction in the main proceedings, it can order provisional measures without resorting to Art. 35 and national law. In other words, the autonomous requirements by European Union law developed by the ECJ concerning Art. 24 Brussels Convention do not need to be met.

---

[136] *Geimer*, WM 1975, 912; *Grundmann*, Anerkennung 128.

[137] Bundesgericht (CH) BGE 125 III 451.

[138] *Gassmann* in: Spühler, Massnahmen 113.

It is controversial whether the courts whose jurisdiction in the main proceedings has been **76** waived can still order provisional measures. Therefore, due to the divergent points of view, it is advisable in practice to expressly specify in the place of jurisdiction agreement whether it is also intended to refer to provisional legal protection.

According to the majority view,[139] in case of doubt, the derogation effect of a place of **77** jurisdiction agreement also extends to provisional legal protection measures. According to this opinion, a court whose jurisdiction in the main proceedings has been waived is not authorised to order provisional measures. After all, it would go against the expectations of the parties, if, despite an effective jurisdiction agreement, a court whose jurisdiction had been waived for deciding the main proceedings could order provisional measures.[140] However, this view leads to considerable gaps in legal protection. If the claim of one party is at risk or violated, it is frequently the case that effective legal protection can only be ensured by ordering provisional measures.[141] If only the court agreed upon as exclusive had jurisdiction for ordering provisional measures, effective safeguarding of the legal position – such as in those cases where the object of the provisional measure is located in the State whose jurisdiction has been derogated – would often not be possible.[142] It cannot be gathered from a place of jurisdiction agreement that is solely concluded for the main proceedings that one party is waiving the effective safeguarding of a claim.[143] The derogation effect of a place of jurisdiction agreement therefore does not extend to provisional legal protection measures.[144]

VIII. Effects of an arbitration agreement on international jurisdiction for ordering provisional measures

1. Effects of an arbitration agreement for jurisdiction of the court of main proceedings according to Art. 4, 7 to 25

If the parties have effectively agreed on an arbitration settlement, then the State courts are **78** exempted from deciding the main proceedings. According to the view of the ECJ,[145] the arbitration agreement also causes the court with jurisdiction in the main proceedings according to the Regulation to no longer be able to order provisional measures. Thus, the parties are only left with the possibility of applying for provisional measures in the court having jurisdiction according to Art. 35 in conjunction with domestic law. The ECJ therefore ascribes a comprehensive derogation effect to an arbitration agreement. This can be substantiated by the fact that the court of the main proceedings only has jurisdiction for ordering provisional measures due to reasons of procedural economy, namely that it is often already familiar with the subject matter of the proceedings and is thus generally able to decide the petition for provisional security or regulation most quickly. However, if the State court cannot decide the main proceedings at all due to the arbitration agreement, then there is no longer any objective justification for its jurisdiction in provisional legal protection

---

[139] *Geimer*, WM 1975, 912; *Geimer/Schütze*, Art. 31 note 192, 229.

[140] *Meier* in: Schwander, Lugano-Übereinkommen 170; similarly in *Gronstedt*, Rechtsschutz 44.

[141] *Garber*, Rechtsschutz 197.

[142] *Garber*, Rechtsschutz 197; *Mankowski* in: Rauscher, Art. 23 note 66.

[143] *Garber*, Rechtsschutz 197.

[144] *Leible* in: Rauscher, Art. 31 note 33; *Mankowski* in: Rauscher, Art. 23 note 66; *Schlosser*, Art. 23 note 42.

[145] *van Uden Maritime BV v. Deco-Line*, (Case C-391/95) (1998) ECR I-3715.

proceedings. The view of the ECJ is not convincing.[146] If a State indeed has jurisdiction according to the Brussel I*bis* Regulation, then it is also obligated to serve justice, i.e. it is required to decide the main proceedings and the petition for provisional security and/or regulation.[147] Whether and to what extent the State jurisdiction can be derogated by an arbitration agreement is determined according to the procedural statute relevant for the agreement. If State courts have jurisdiction for ordering provisional measures despite there being an arbitration agreement, then the effects of an arbitration agreement are restricted to the main proceedings. The State courts, which would have had jurisdiction without the arbitration agreement, can therefore order provisional measures despite the existence of an arbitration agreement. The court that has jurisdiction for ordering a provisional measure is determined in such cases according to the general jurisdiction rules of the procedural statute, which also include Art. 4, 7 to 26.[148] Also arguing against the opinion of the ECJ that courts whose jurisdiction is based on Art. 35 in conjunction with domestic law, though not on the Brussel I*bis* Regulation, may order provisional measures, is the fact that the result rules out the validity of unified jurisdictions (the Brussel I*bis* Regulation), while the validity of non-unified jurisdiction provisions (of domestic law) increases.

2. Effects of an arbitration agreement if international jurisdiction is based on Art. 35

79 Even if an arbitration agreement has been concluded for the main proceedings, provisional agreements can still be ordered by courts having jurisdiction according to Art. 35 in conjunction with domestic law.[149] While this does not follow from the wording of Art. 35, which only explicitly establishes additional jurisdiction in the event that the court of another Member State has jurisdiction for deciding the main proceedings according to Art. 4, 7 to 26 Brussel I*bis* Regulation, which is certainly due to the protective character that provisional measures have.[150] Moreover, the statutory provisions of the domestic laws, according to which State courts can order provisional measures despite arbitration agreements, would otherwise be groundless.[151]

IX. Effects of not objecting to international jurisdiction for ordering provisional measures

1. Entering into the main proceedings according to Art. 26 without objection

80 If the defendant does not object to entering into the main proceedings before a court that does not have jurisdiction according to the Regulation, then the court also has jurisdiction for ordering provisional measures as of the time the defendant entered into the main proceedings without objection. The court's jurisdiction solely results from Art. 26 Brussel

---

146 *Garber*, Rechtsschutz 199; *Hess/Vollkommer*, IPRax 1999, 222; *Leible* in: Rauscher, Art. 31 note 20; *Pörnbacher* in: Geimer/Schütze, Rechtsverkehr 540 Art. 31 note 11; *Reiner*, IPRax 2003, 75; *Schulz*, ZEuP 2001, 811.

147 *Garber*, Rechtsschutz 199; *Hess/Vollkommer*, IPRax 1999, 222.

148 *Garber*, Rechtsschutz 199; *Hess/Vollkommer*, IPRax 1999, 222.

149 *Reiner*, IPRax 2003, 75 *et seq.*; *Schulz*, ZEuP 2001, 812; *Spellenberg/Leible*, ZZPInt 4 (1999) 227; *van Uden Maritime BV v. Deco-Line*, (Case C-391/95) (1998) ECR I-3715.

150 *Garber*, Rechtsschutz 200.

151 *Garber*, Rechtsschutz 200.

I*bis* Regulation, and thus resorting to the provisions of the domestic legal system is no longer necessary.[152]

If the defendant has not (yet) entered into the main proceedings without objection, then the **81** jurisdiction of the court appealed to can only result from Art. 35 in conjunction with domestic procedural law. If the court that has erroneously been appealed to as the court of the main proceedings does not have jurisdiction for ordering the provisional measure according to Art. 35 in conjunction with domestic procedural law, then it cannot decide the petition for provisional security and/or regulation. In this case, it must suspend the proceedings until it is certain whether the defendant will enter into the main proceedings without objection. If the defendant successfully objects to the lack of international jurisdiction, then the petition for the order of a provisional measure must be rejected due to this lack of international jurisdiction. If the defendant does not enter into the main proceedings, then the court must verify its international jurisdiction *ex officio*. Since it does not have jurisdiction for ordering provisional measures either as the court of the main proceedings or according to Art. 35 in conjunction with domestic law, it must reject the petition for the order of a provisional measure due to a lack of international jurisdiction.[153]

2. Entering into the provisional legal protection proceedings without objection

In its decision *Mietz v. Intership*,[154] the ECJ stated that a court that does not have jurisdiction **82** for ordering provisional measures either according to Art. 4, 7 to 26 or according to Art. 35 in conjunction with domestic law cannot receive jurisdiction, pursuant to Art. 26 Brussel I*bis* Regulation, by the opponent to the party at risk entering into the provisional legal protection proceedings without objection.[155] This view can be substantiated by arguing that the opponent to the opposing party – if an oral hearing is conducted – will always enter into the proceedings to fend off the impending provisional measure in this State.[156] After all, if the opponent to the party at risk does not enter into the proceedings, the opposing party runs the risk of a provisional measure being ordered in this State and assets being confiscated or impounded according to the stipulations of the domestic legal system. In many cases, therefore, the voluntariness to enter in that is necessary for assuming a remedy is lacking in the provisional legal protection proceedings.[157] While the counterargument could be made that the opponent to the party at risk has the possibility of objecting to the lack of international jurisdiction, in practice, however, the opposing party will often not have any opportunity at all to verify whether the court appealed to has jurisdiction for ordering provisional measures due to the time pressure involved in the provisional legal protection proceedings, and thus the party will already submit on the matter before objecting to the lack of international jurisdiction. The view that entering into the proceedings constitutes a remedy for the lack of jurisdiction even in the provisional legal protection proceedings would therefore result in

---

[152] *Garber*, Rechtsschutz 201.

[153] *Garber*, Rechtsschutz 201.

[154] *Mietz v. Intership*, (Case C-99/96) (1999) ECR I-2277.

[155] *Garber*, Rechtsschutz 202; *Spellenberg/Leible*, ZZPInt 4 (1999) 231; different view in *Schulte-Beckhausen*, Zuständigkeit 116 *et seq.*; OLG Düsseldorf IPRspr 1978/138 = WM 1978, 359.

[156] *Garber*, Rechtsschutz 202.

[157] *Garber*, Rechtsschutz 202 *et seq.*; *Leible* in: Rauscher, Art. 31 note 26; *Spellenberg/Leible*, ZZPInt 4 (1999) 231.

the party who is to be protected by the oral hearing being conducted, the opponent to the party at risk, actually having to put up with further adverse effects due to making a defence.[158]

83   If jurisdiction for ordering provisional measures is in accordance with Art. 35 in conjunction with domestic law, and the domestic law expressly provides for the possibility of a remedy for a lack of international jurisdiction, then such a case, since the question of jurisdiction is solely decided on the basis of domestic law, also substantiates jurisdiction by means of entering into the proceedings without objection.

X. Effects of pendency on the international jurisdiction for ordering provisional measures

1. General

84   If there are pending actions due to the same claim between the same parties in courts of different Member States, then, pursuant to Art. 29 para. 1, the court appealed to later must suspend the proceedings *ex officio* until the jurisdiction of the court appealed to first is certain. Pursuant to Art. 29 para. 2, the court appealed to later must declare that it does not have jurisdiction as soon as the jurisdiction of the court appealed to first is certain. This is to avoid contradictory decisions in the European Single Market.[159] It is doubtful whether Art. 29 Brussel I*bis* Regulation is also applicable in cases where main proceedings are pending in one Member State and legal protection proceedings are pending in another Member State or where provisional legal protection proceedings are initiated in several Member States.

2. Effects of pendency in the relationship between main proceedings and provisional legal protection proceedings

85   Art. 29 is not applicable in the relationship between main proceedings and provisional legal protection proceedings, since the proceedings do not involve the "same cause of action" within the meaning of this provision.[160] This is because the object of the provisional legal protection proceedings is not the claim itself, but instead provisional security or regulation for it.[161]

86   If the pendency of provisional legal protection proceedings in a Member State's court prevents the main proceedings from being executed in another Member State, then "provisional" measures would always be definitive, since it would not be possible to verify the claim in subsequent main proceedings in another Member State. Moreover, the jurisdiction system of the Brussel I*bis* Regulation could be circumvented by applying for a provisional measure in a court having jurisdiction according to Art. 35 in conjunction with domestic law. It would then not be possible to conduct the main proceedings in the court having

---

158   *Garber*, Rechtsschutz 202 *et seq.*; *Leible* in: Rauscher, Art. 31 note 26; *Spellenberg/Leible*, ZZPInt 4 (1999) 231.

159   *Tatry/Maciej Rataj*, (Case 406/92) 1998, ECR I-5439.

160   *Mankowski*, JZ 2005, 1148; cf. also *Purrucker v. Vallés Pérez*, (Case C-296/10) (2010) ECR I-7353; see also *Solvay* (Case C-616/10).

161   *Albrecht*, EuGVÜ 176; *Gronstedt*, Rechtsschutz 139; *Grundmann*, Anerkennung 122.

jurisdiction according to the Brussel I*bis* Regulation. A party would therefore have the possibility of divesting the opposing party of the courts of the main proceedings according to the Regulation by applying for a provisional measure.[162]

Conversely, if the main proceedings are already pending in a Member State, both the virtual **87** courts of the main proceedings as well as the courts having jurisdiction according to Art. 35 in conjunction with domestic law may order provisional measures.[163] This is intended to enable a party that initially did not submit a petition for the order of a provisional measure to petition provisional measures in another Member State even after the main proceedings are pending, for instance if it only becomes apparent after this point in time that the main proceedings cannot be executed within a reasonable length of time[164] or if the claim only becomes at risk or is violated once the main proceedings are pending. Moreover, effective provisional legal protection often cannot be guaranteed by provisional measures in other Member States until there is the possibility of supporting and complementing pending main proceedings.[165]

3. Effects of the pendency between multiple provisional legal protection proceedings

It is doubtful whether the provisions concerning pendency are applicable if provisional legal **88** protection proceedings are pending in several Member States. For instance, the question of pendency came up in a case to be decided by the District Court of Kleve:[166] A provisional measure for restoring property was to be effected while a decision was petitioned in Germany with the aim of prohibiting the leaseholder from occupying the facility.

In order to prevent divergent decisions, one part of the doctrine[167] argues that Art. 29 Brussel **89** I*bis* Regulation is categorically applicable in the provisional legal protection proceedings. However, there can only be a claim within the meaning of Art. 29 in those cases where the same assets are used to secure a claim.[168] In contrast, provisional measures involving different objects are not subject to the pendency ban of Art. 29 Brussel I*bis* Regulation. The party at risk can therefore petition the security of its claim multiple times by means of confiscating various assets. Excessive security can be prevented in the provisional legal protection proceedings by negating the need for security that is generally required by the domestic legal systems of the Member States.[169]

Historical deliberations can also be cited in support of the opinion that Art. 29 should also be **90** observed in the provisional legal protection proceedings. According to the provisions in bilateral recognition and enforcement agreements serving as a model for Art. 35, the standards related to pendency for ordering identical provisional measures therefore had to be excluded, since provisional measures were excluded by the mutual recognition and enforce-

---

[162] *Garber*, Rechtsschutz 204 *et seq.*

[163] *Hye-Knudsen*, Urheberrechtsverletzungen 188; *Meier-Beck*, GRUR 2000, 357.

[164] *Hye-Knudsen*, Urheberrechtsverletzungen 186; *Meier-Beck*, GRUR 2000, 357.

[165] *Garber*, Rechtsschutz 206; *Stadler*, JZ 1999, 1095.

[166] IPRax 2000, 546 (*Jayme*).

[167] *Eilers*, Maßnahmen 220 *et seq.*; *von Falck*, MittdPatA 2002, 438, *Franzosi*, MittdPatA 1998, 301.

[168] *Kaye*, Civil Jurisdiction 1193.

[169] *Albrecht*, EuGVÜ 178; *Grundmann*, Anerkennung 123.

ment according to the provisions of said agreements.[170] To ensure effective legal protection, the party at risk therefore had to have the possibility of petitioning provisional measures in all contracting States. This is because the opponent to the party at risk would otherwise have had the opportunity to prevent the measure from being executed by bringing the object of the decree into the sovereign territory of the other contracting State. In contrast, there would be no need in the scope of the Regulation to be able to petition identical provisional measures in several Member States, since the provisional measures ordered in one Member State can in part be recognised and enforced in all other Member States (in this regard, see Art. 2 note 18 *et seq.*). Therefore, in the absence of any territorial restriction of the effect, it is unnecessary to effect provisional measures in several Member States to protect the party at risk. However, the scope of the Regulation does not include all provisional measures of recognition and enforcement. If the requirements for recognising and enforcing a provisional measure are lacking, the party at risk must in any event have the opportunity to be able to petition identical measures in several States at the same time. Otherwise, effective provisional legal protection would not be possible.[171] There may still be a need to execute several parallel provisional legal protection proceedings in different States despite the recognisability and enforceability of the provisional measure – for example, in those cases where it becomes apparent after initiating the first provisional legal protection proceedings that it is taking too long for the provisional measure to be ordered in one State[172] or in cases where the party at risk does not exactly know in which Member State the object of the decree is located. The fact that the interest of the party at risk in being able to effect a provisional measure in several States must be taken into consideration follows from the rationality of Art. 35, which lies in facilitating legal protection for the party whose claims are at risk or have been violated.[173]

91   Thus, the superior reasons speak in favour of Art. 29 not being applied in the event that identical measures are petitioned in several Member States.[174] The problem of divergent decisions can only then be solved at the level of recognition and enforcement.[175]

XI. Prevention or coordinaton of parallel provisional legal protection proceedings

92   The Brussel *Ibis* Regulation does not contain any provisions for preventing or coordinating parallel provisional legal protection proceedings. According to *A. Stadler*,[176] provisional measures should only be ordered in such cases where they are truly necessary for complementing the main proceedings, such as because corresponding orders were denied by the *de facto* court of the main proceedings or cannot be ordered for reasons of domestic law. The decisions of the ECJ do not result in any corresponding restriction, however. What is more, it is often impossible to verify whether the court of the main proceedings is able to order corresponding measures due to the time pressure involved in the provisional legal protection proceedings. The possible solution recommended by *Geimer/Schütze*[177] of coordinating

---

170   *Merkt*, Mesures provisoires 108.
171   *Gronstedt*, Rechtsschutz 149 *et seq.*; *Hausmann*, IPRax 1981, 82.
172   *Grundmann*, Anerkennung 123 *et seq.*
173   *Kropholler/von Hein*, Art. 31 EuGVO note 19.
174   *Garber*, Rechtsschutz 206 *et seq.*
175   *Italian Leather SpA v. WECO Polstermöbel GmbH & Co.*, (Case C-80/00) (2002) ECR I-4995, I-5025.
176   JZ 1999, 1095; similarly also in *Guidicelli*, Cross Border Injunctions 37.

parallel provisional legal protection proceedings by suspending Art. 30 appears quite convincing, but would lead to difficulties in practice, since the courts often have no knowledge that (other) provisional legal protection proceedings are already pending in another Member State due to the one-sidedness of the proceedings. It would therefore make sense for the Member States of the Regulation to swiftly implement the Helsinki Rules.[178,179] According to Z 15 of the Helsinki Rules, the party at risk is under the obligation to inform the court in which a provisional measure is petitioned of the current status of the provisional legal protection proceedings initiated in other States and of the status of the main proceedings.

Chapter III: Recognition and Enforcement

Section 1: Recognition

Article 36

1. A judgment given in a Member State shall be recognised in the other Member States without any special procedure being required.
2. Any interested party may, in accordance with the procedure provided for in Subsection 2 of Section 3, apply for a decision that there are no grounds for refusal of recognition as referred to in Article 45.
3. If the outcome of proceedings in a court of a Member State depends on the determination of an incidental question of refusal of recognition, that court shall have jurisdiction over that question.

I. General outline

Art. 36 establishes the principle of the automatic recognition of foreign judgments. If a question arises as to whether a foreign judgment should be recognized, the issue can be resolved either by proceedings specifically directed to that issue (under Art. 36 (2)) or, if the issue arises incidentally in the framework of other proceedings, pursuant to Art. 36 (3).[1] If an　1

---

[177]　Art. 27 note 47.
[178]　Reprinted in SZIER 1998, 201, cf. *Kofmel Ehrenzeller*, SZIER 1998, 177; *Nygh*, RabelsZ 62 (1998) 115.
[179]　*Kofmel Ehrenzeller*, SZIER 1998, 200.
[1]　Even though Article 36 is rarely applied as such by courts (as noted by *Hess, Pfeiffer, Schlosser*, The

issue arises before an authority other than a court, that authority should also directly address the recognition question.

II. Legislative history

2 Art. 36 already appeared in the original Brussels Convention (Art. 26). The text was taken over in the Brussels I Regulation (as Art. 33), with the reference to the 'Contracting State' replaced by a reference to 'Member State'. The Brussels *Ibis* Regulation took over the text with some slight changes. A similar provision appears in Art. 33 of the revised Lugano Convention.

III. Commentary

1. The concept of 'recognition' of foreign judgments

a) The various effects of judgments

3 The Regulation does not provide a definition of what is meant by 'recognition' of a foreign judgment. The Jenard Report usefully points to the two defining characteristics of the recognition, as follows:

"Recognition must have the result of conferring on judgments the authority and effectiveness accorded to them in the State in which they were given."[2]

4 Although every lawyer will be influenced by its national law when discussing the exact meaning of the recognition under the Regulation,[3] it is possible to state that to recognize a foreign judgment involves accepting to give it several effects.[4] The first one is a positive one. The State addressed accepts to consider that what the court of origin has decided constitutes a valid determination of the rights and obligations of parties.[5] If the court of origin has ordered a party to pay damages because that party has been found in breach of a contract, courts in other Member States should accept that the parties were bound by a contract and that this contract has been breached.[6]

Brussels I-Regulation (EC) No. 44/2001 (2008), 137–138, para. 472), it remains a provision of fundamental importance for the cross-border circulation of jugdments in the EU.

[2] Report *Jenard* p. 43. This definition was quoted by the ECJ in *Horst Ludwig Martin Hoffmann v. Adelheid Krieg*, (Case 145/86) [1988] ECR 645, 666 para. 10.

[3] See the comparative overview by *Stürner* in: FS Rolf Schütze (1999), p. 913 *et seq*.

[4] See in general the discussion by *Kropholler/von Hein* Art. 33 notes 11 *et seq*.; *Gaudemet-Tallon* pp. 391–393; *Layton/Mercer* para. 845–848; *Leible*, in: Rauscher Art. 33 notes 4–10.

[5] This is referred to as the "materiellen Rechtskraft" in the German doctrine and as the "force obligatoire" in the French doctrine. The English concept of "authority" of the judgment appears to constitute a good approximation of these concepts. In general, *Sepperer*, Der Rechtskrafteinwand in den Mitgliedstaaten der EuGVO (2010).

[6] Dickinson refers to this effect as the "dispositive effects" of a judgment, Dickinson, The Effects in the European Community of Judgments in Civil and Commercial Matters: Recognition, Res Judicata and Abuse of Process, Report 2006 3.

Beyond its authority, the judgment can also be invoked in so far as it produces *procedural* 5
effects. Those effects pertain to the exclusion or restriction of the ability of parties, whether
or not participants in the initial legal proceedings, to provoke a new judicial discussion of the
case which has already been decided. The plea of *res judicata* is probably the best known of
these effects.[7] It should, however, be noted that the procedural effects may include a variety
of rules, depending for example on whether the rule precludes the re-opening of claims or of
issues which have already been determined.[8] At the cross-road of the procedural effects and
the substantive effects of a judgment, one may also distinguish the precise order which may
be included in a judgment. A judgment may indeed include a measure or order which
follows necessarily from its dispositive effect.

b) The law applicable to the effects of foreign judgments

The consequences attached to judgments may vary from state to state. The extent to which a 6
judgment may serve as evidence may for example be different in the state of origin than in
the state addressed. Further, the categories of persons bound by a judgment may also vary
between legal systems. This applies in particular to the procedural consequences of a judgment, some of which may extend beyond the immediate parties to the judgment. The
question therefore arises how the Regulation, whose goal it is to guarantee that judgments
may freely circulate among Member States, deals with this diversity.

The *Jenard* Report seems to support the view that the national law of the adjudicating court 7
is decisive to determine the effects of a judgment in the other Member States.[9] The ECJ also
seems to have accepted that the recognition of foreign judgments should follow the model of
the extension of effects. The Court indeed held that "recognition must have the effect, in
principle, of conferring on judgments the authority and effectiveness accorded to them in
the Member State in which they were given".[10] Finally the fact that Art. 54 of the Regulation
creates a specific mechanism allowing the Member State addressed to adapt the order or
measure included in the judgment, also seems to suggest that the Regulation is based on the
mode of the extension of effects.

The precise limits of that approach are, however, far from clear.[11] The ECJ has indeed 8

---

[7]   This is referred to as the "autorité de chose jugée négative" in French doctrine and as the "Präklusions-
      wirkung" in the German doctrine.

[8]   Whether a court may on its own motion rely on the *res judicata* effect of a foreign judgment, appears to be
      a matter for the procedural law of the Member State addressed to decide – see *Leible*, in: Rauscher Art. 33,
      p. 723, para. 4b. EU law may impose limits on the res judicata of national judgments, see *Kornezov* (2014)
      Common Market L. Rev. 809–842.

[9]   This has been referred to as the doctrine of the "Wirkungserstreckung" or "extension of effects", see
      Kropholler/von Hein Art. 33 note 9.

[10] In the context of enforcement proceedings, the Court of Justice has held that a foreign judgment which
      has been recognised must in principle have the same effects in the State in which enforcement is sought as
      it does in the State in which judgment was given: *Horst Ludwig Martin Hoffmann v. Adelheid Krieg*, (Case
      145/86) (1988) ECR 645, 666 para. 11. See more recently to the same effect: *Meletis Apostolides v. David
      Charles Orams et al.*, (Case C-420/07) (2009) ECR 3571 para. 66.

[11] Compare with the position under the Insolvency Regulation, which seems to be more firmly in favor of
      the extension model, see Recital 22 of the Preamble of the Insolvency Regulation, according to which
      "Automatic recognition should therefore mean that the effects attributed to the proceedings by the law of

qualified the doctrine of the extension of a judgment's effects, indicating that there is "no reason" to grant a judgment "effects that a similar judgment given directly in the Member State in which enforcement is sought, would not have".[12] Further, the extension of effects of a foreign judgments may be paralyzed by the public policy exception. It may also be nuanced by a mechanism of adaptation, such as the one introduced by Art. 54. Finally, an older ruling of the ECJ suggests that whether or not the conduct of a party based on a foreign judgment may form the basis of a plea of abuse of process, should be addressed within the framework of the Regulation.[13]

9   It is indeed far from certain that all consequences attached to a foreign judgment should be determined based on the law of the country of origin.[14] A distinction may be made between the substantial effects of a judgment (also called 'dispositive' effects) and its procedural consequences.[15] If a court has found that a contract was void and has, on this basis, refused to hold a party liable for breach of this contract, the substantial effects entail that the contract is void. In order to appreciate how this decision affects the relationship between the parties, *e.g.* whether it means that the contract is deemed never to have existed, reference should be made to the law applied by the court of origin and not to the law of that court. It may, however, be that some of the substantial effects of a judgment should be assessed using the law of the Member State of origin.[16] It remains unclear which law must be applied to determine whether the court's finding (that the contract is void) may be put in question in further proceedings. It seems that some role should be given to the law of the State of origin in this respect, if only to avoid that a decision issued by a court could give rise to more effects in another country than in the country of origin.[17] If reference is made to the effects of

---

the State in which the proceedings were opened extend to all other Member States". See also, in relation with authentic acts, Art. 59(1) of the Succession Regulation, which provides that authentic instruments established in a Member State "shall have the same evidentiary effects" in other Member States, unless this is manifestly contrary to public policy. The provision adds a caveat: the instrument may be granted "the most comparable effects".

[12]   *Meletis Apostolides v. David Charles Orams et al.*, (Case C-420/07) (2009] ECR 3571 para. 66.

[13]   *Jozef de Wolf v. Harry Cox BV*, (Case 42/76) (1976] ECR 1759.

[14]   For a comparative overview of the practice of Member States under the Brussels I Regulation, see *van de Velden & Stefanelli*, The Effect in the EC of Judgments in Civil and Commercial Matters: Recognition, Res Judicata and Abuse of Process -Comparative Report, 2008, p. 55.

[15]   See e.g. as to the recognition of a judgment without any res judicata effect ArbG Berlin 2007 IPRspr. No. 180a.

[16]   Dickinson suggests that this could be the case if a Member State judgment, under its original law, would be treated as merging with or otherwise discharging the obligation, irrespective of the law applicable to the contract or claim: Dickinson, The Effects in the European Community of Judgments in Civil and Commercial Matters: Recognition, Res Judicata and Abuse of Process, Report 2006, 15.

[17]   *Boss Group Ltd. v. Boss France SA* (1997) 1 WLR 351, 359 (holding that a decision issued by a French court in the context of provisional proceedings could not give rise to issue estoppel as the judgment was "in no way binding in France on any court that might deal there with the matter on a substantive basis") and *The Tsaskemolen* (No. 2) [1997] 2 Lloyd's Rep. 47.6. Compare, however, with the decisions of the Court of Appeal in *Berkeley Administration Inc. v. McClelland*, (1995) ILPr 201 (C.A.) and *Berkeley Administration Inc v. Mc Clelland (No. 2)* (1996) ILPr 772 (C.A.) in which the Court of Appeal did not consider it necessary to refer to French law in order to determine the extent to which a French judgment was entitled to recognition. Compare also with Cass. Clunet 138 (2011), 16 (where the French Court of

the judgment in the State of origin to determine whether the judgment qualifies for *res judicata*, estoppel or any other preclusive doctrine in the State addressed, it is not excluded that the law of the State of origin should be combined with the law of the state addressed, the latter being relevant to decide which procedural instrument is triggered by the foreign judgment[18] and whether the judgment may have any effect towards third parties, such as a surety or a guarantee.[19] It has been suggested that if the court of origin has granted the claim, relitigation of the same cause of action in another Member State should be precluded not based on the law of the country addressed, but on a European standard.[20] Other instances of relitigation could be addressed based on the law of the country of origin. The exact extent to which the law of the country of origin applies to determine the preclusive effects of a foreign judgment, is, however, still discussed.[21]

When deciding upon the effects of a judgment, a court will take as a first reference point the **10** terms of the judgment itself.[22] Additional evidence may be admitted but only to clarify the terms of the judgment, not to add to the substance thereof.[23]

A party may also rely on a foreign judgment as evidence of a fact, *e.g.* that a witness appeared **11** before the foreign court on a certain day or that an expert has presented his findings to the court. A foreign judgment holding that a party is the sole owner of specific assets could serve as the basis for a warranty claim in another State. When a foreign judgment is used to serve as evidence, it has been suggested that this should be assessed under the law of the recognizing State.[24]

Finally, it may be that some consequences of foreign judgments fall, outside the framework **12** of the Regulation. Although the Regulation trumps national law, it is submitted that Member States may still resort to their own provisions to determine under what conditions a foreign judgment may entail such consequences, if any.[25]

Cassation accepted to give res judicata effect to a decision whereby a Greek court had denied a request for provisional attachement of a ship, without making, however, any reference to Greek law).

[18] For the distinction between the 'formal' recognition (which effects should be afforded to a foreign judgment) and the recognition 'in practice' (which process of administering the recognised judgment's preclusive effect) should be followed), see *van de Velden & Stefanelli*, The Effect in the EC of Judgments in Civil and Commercial Matters: Recognition, Res Judicata and Abuse of Process – Comparative Report, 2008, p. 58.

[19] In the Report *Schlosser*, the question how to deal with the situation in which a judgment against the principal debtor is effective against a surety in the legal system of the State of origin whereas under the law of the State addressed the surety would not be affected by the judgment, was left open: Report *Schlosser* para. 191.

[20] Dickinson, 17.

[21] See e.g. Audit in Procédures (2007/8) and *Oberhammer* in IPRax (2002) 431.

[22] See *The Tjaskemolen (now named 'Visvliet')* (1997) 2 Lloyd's Rep. 476 (Q.B.D.).

[23] *Landhurst Leasing plc v. Marcq* (1998) I.L.Pr 822 (the court held that evidence that the defendant had submitted to a consent judgment on the basis that the claimant had agreed only to enforce the judgment against the amount in a particular bank account, was not admissible).

[24] *Dickinson*, 16.

[25] See *Gothot/Holleaux* para. 252; *Kropholler/von Hein* Art. 33 note 17.

Patrick Wautelet

2. The principle: automatic recognition

13 Art. 36 (1) provides that judgments issued in one Member State are automatically recognized in other Member States without any prior proceedings or formal steps. This principle, which is one of the cornerstones of the European judicial area, is known as the recognition de plano, 'de plein *droit*' or *ipso iure*.[26] The automatic nature of the recognition does not mean, however, that judgments from other Member States are awarded the same treatment as domestic judgments.

14 To appreciate the extent of this principle, one must remember that judgments issued in other Member States may be refused recognition under the Regulation if this is justified under one of the grounds of refusal.[27] In practice, foreign judgments will therefore be subjected to some form of examination, either in the framework of a principal action for recognition (see hereunder nr. 3) or incidentally (see hereunder nr. 4). Further, the party who relies on a foreign judgment must comply with the formal requirements laid down in the Art. 37 of the Regulation and in particular with the need to produce an authentic copy of the judgment.[28]

15 Hence, the automatic character of the recognition only means that a party who wishes to rely on a foreign judgment must not undergo some formal procedure or have the judgment be registered in the other Member State prior to relying on the foreign judgment. Rather, the judicial intervention is postponed until such moment as the foreign judgment is either presented for recognition (Art. 36 (2)) or relied upon to justify a *res judicata* exception. In this sense, the word 'special' appearing in Art. 36 (1) must be taken to denote any procedure other than that which is provided for in paragraphs 2 and 3 of Art. 36.

16 It has been said that the automatic recognition amounts to "a presumption in favor of recognition, which can be rebutted if one of the grounds for refusal listed in Article [45] is present".[29] The automatic recognition can only be likened to a presumption of this type in so far as the Regulation removes all traditional procedures for recognition which were provided for in the laws of the Member States. In this respect, the recognition granted to judgments from other Member States still differs from that awarded to domestic judgments.

17 A direct consequence of the automatic nature of the recognition is that the foreign judgment is deemed to be effective at the same time in the state of origin as in the other member States.[30] A more indirect consequence is that at least according to the ECJ, a party who has obtained a judgment on the merits in one Member State is precluded from applying to obtain another judgment on the same cause of action and against the same party in another

---

[26] See Cass. (1997) ILPr 173. See, however, *Kaye* pp. 1376–1382 (the author argues at great length that it is inaccurate to refer to the principle laid down in Art. 33 (1) as one of 'automatic' recognition).

[27] Experience has shown that refusal to recognize foreign judgments is under the scheme of the Regulation, the exception, see the data collected by *Hess, Pfeiffer, Schlosser*, The Brussels I-Regulation (EC) No. 44/2001 (2008), 130–135.

[28] Art. 37(1) (b) of the Regulation also requires that the party who relies on the foreign judgment produces a certificate filled by the court of origin.

[29] Report *Jenard* p. 43.

[30] *Geimer/Schütze* Art. 33 note 16.

Member State.[31] In the *de Wolf* case, a party had obtained a judgment in Belgium ordering a company established in the Netherlands to pay an invoice. Instead of requesting the enforcement of this decision, the Belgian plaintiff brought fresh proceedings in the Netherlands in respect of the same cause of action. Although the Court of Justice seemed more concerned with the need to avoid the existence of conflicting decisions, its judgment cannot be explained but by the fact that the authority of the Belgian decision was automatically recognized by the Dutch courts.

3. Declaratory proceedings (Art. 36 (2))

Art. 36 (2) allows an "interested party" to apply to the court for a declaration that a judgment **18** given in another Member State be recognised ("action en déclaration de reconnaissance"/ "Antrag auf positive Feststellung der Anerkennungsfähigkeit"). Experience with the Brussels I Regulation and the texts which have preceded it has shown that the possibility to obtain a declaration on the recognition of a foreign judgment is rarely used.[32] In the vast majority of cases, a foreign judgment will be recognized incidentally in the framework of other proceedings.[33] Nevertheless, a party may have a good reason to pursue such principal action for recognition. This may be the case when uncertainty remains on whether some grounds of refusal are met. As long as the foreign judgment has not been examined by a court in the State addressed, its effects in that State remain subject to a future (negative) decision by a court. As noted by an English court,[34] in an international loan agreement, it may useful for a creditor to seek recognition of a judgment whereby a foreign court has held that the loan debtor defaulted under the loan agreement, in order for the creditor to be allowed to call in the loan. Further, some judgments do not lend themselves to enforcement and may more appropriately be subject to proceedings to obtain a declaration of recognition. This is the case with a judgment awarding a declaration on certain rights or the position of parties (so-called "Feststellungs- und Gestaltungsurteile"). On the contrary, a party may also have an interest in seeking a declaration that a foreign judgment should not be afforded recognition under the Regulation. Obtaining such a declaration is in particular relevant since the Regulation provides that a judgment given in a Member State is as such and without more enforceable in the other Member States (Art. 39).

Art. 36 (2) refers to the procedures provided in subsection 2 of Section 3 of the Regulation. **19** Whereas under the previous version of the Regulation, the procedure on the application was made *ex parte*,[35] the procedure to be followed under Art. 36 (2) should from the start be conducted between the parties to the foreign judgment. The court will undertake to review whether there are grounds for refusal of recognition, without limiting its enquiry to the

---

[31] *Jozef de Wolf v. Harry Cox BV*, (Case 42/76) [1976] ECR 1759.

[32] See, however, *Tavoulearas v. Tsavliris* (2006) EWHC 414 (Comm) (in relation to the recognition in England of a judgment issued by a Greek court, which was eventually denied both in first instance and in appeal).

[33] *Infra* Art. 36 notes 31 *et seq.* (*Wautelet*) on this possibility.

[34] *Landhurst Leasing plc v. Marcq* [1998] ILPr 822 (CA).

[35] See the criticism on the *ex parte* nature of the proceedings by *Geimer/Schütze* Art. 33 note 104. Compare with *Gothot/Holleaux* para. 394 (who argue that *ex parte* proceedings are well suited to the need for a party to obtain within a reasonable time period a decision on the status of the foreign judgment).

formal requirements for recognition.[36] Certain rules of subsection 2 will not prove adapted to a request for a declaration on the recognition of a foreign judgment. This is the case with Art. 51 of the Regulation, which deals with the possibility for the court to stay the proceedings. It is submitted that since the application concerns the recognition of the judgment, Art. 38 should be preferred over Art. 51. Likewise, some provisions of Section 4 may not be relevant when an application under Art. 36 (2) is filed. As has been suggested in relation to previous versions of the Regulation, the petitioner should have the possibility to seize the court of his domicile or of his choice.[37]

20 Art. 36 (2) does not subject the possibility to request a decision on the recognition of a foreign judgment to the existence between parties of a dispute in this respect. This was the case under the previous version of the Regulation. In most cases, an application under Art. 36 (2) will be made when parties disagree on the issue of the recognition of the foreign judgment. This disagreement will be evidenced by the behaviour of one of the parties concerned which is inconsistent with the foreign judgment, such as the fact that the judgment debtor refuses to give effect to a request made by the judgment creditor to obtain payment or to recognize that a contract has been avoided. Even in the absence of such dispute, a party could, however, request a declaration when it entertains doubts as to the status of the foreign judgment.[38] In any case the various procedural requirements existing in national laws – such as the requirement that the petitioner shows an "*intérêt*" or an "*Interesse*" – will prevent a purely hypothetical request.[39]

a) "Any interested party"

21 Art. 36 (2) reserves the right to request a declaration of recognition to a party showing an interest.[40] According to the Jenard Report, the expression 'on the application of any interested party' implies that "any person who is entitled to the benefit of the judgment in the State in which it was given has the right to apply for an order" for its recognition.[41]

22 Although the Court of Justice has yet to rule on this question, it is generally accepted that the circle of interested parties will not be limited to those parties who were directly involved in the proceedings in the state of origin.[42] A party who was not involved in the litigation in the state of origin may indeed have an interest in obtaining a judgement on the status of the foreign decision. This may be the case for the warehouse holding goods which were subject to a dispute between two parties before the courts of another Member State. Although the warehouse has no right to benefit from a judgement as to which party holds title to the

---

[36] Under the previous version of the Regulation, the review of the various refusal grounds was only possible when an appeal was lodged against a decision granting a declaration.

[37] *Kropholler/von Hein* Art. 33 note 8; *Gaudemet-Tallon* para. 439; *Gothot/Holleaux* para. 398.

[38] This was already suggested by *Gothot/Holleaux* para. 395.

[39] *Kropholler/von Hein* argues that the special 'Feststellungsinteresse' required under German law for declaratory proceedings is not necessary to obtain a declaration under Art. 33 (2): *Kropholler/von Hein* Art. 33 note 4.

[40] The same requirement is made for an application under Art. 45 that the recognition of a judgment be refused.

[41] Report *Jenard* p. 49 (this statement concerned the possibility to request the enforcement of a foreign judgment. It is submitted that is applies likewise to requests for recognition).

[42] *Geimer/Schütze* Art. 33 note 94; *Gaudemet-Tallon* para. 440.

goods, there are good reasons why it should be entitled to obtain a declaration on the status of the foreign judgment. Certainly, the category of the persons having an interest within the meaning of Art. 36 (2) is not limited to those parties against whom enforcement is sought.

One should therefore adopt a broad reading of the requirement of interest.[43] It is submitted **23** that in doing so, courts in the State addressed should not look at their national law to define who is entitled to request a declaration on the recognition of a foreign judgment. Whether an applicant's interest qualifies him to obtain a declaration under Art. 36 (2) must be assessed using a European definition.[44] On the other hand, national law remains decisive to determine whether an applicant should fulfil other requirements in order for the application to be admissible.[45]

Using this rule, one may suggest that under a European reading of the required interest, **24** *assignees* of persons who were parties to the original proceedings may request a declaration pursuant to Art. 36 (2). The question whether one person is indeed an assignee will be assessed by reference to national law. Similarly, a surety such as a guarantor of a contractual obligation may also request a declaration to obtain the recognition of a foreign judgment which has held that the guaranteed obligation is void, even though the guarantor has not participated in the proceedings before the court of origin. Finally parties who have been subrogated in the rights of a party to the original proceedings may also request a declaration under Art. 36 (2).[46]

b) Positive declaration
Art. 36 (2) only refers to the possibility to obtain a declaration to the effect that there are "no **25** grounds for refusal of recognition" of a judgment.[47] Under the previous version of the Regulation, the question arose whether there was any room to seek a declaration of non-recognition..[48] This question arose out of an observation found in the Jenard Report, which seemed to imply that the rules put in place by the Regulation could only be used to seek the recognition of foreign judgments.[49] The silence of the Regulation on this issue contrasted with express provisions allowing an application for a declaration of non-recognition under other Regulations.[50] Art. 45 (4) now expressly allows a party to seek a declaration that the

---

[43] *Gaudemet-Tallon* para. 440; *Gothot/Holleaux* para. 395.

[44] See *Layton/Mercer* para. 26.005; *Gaudemet-Tallon* para. 440.

[45] It is unclear whether one should apply the law of the State addressed or look at whichever system of law is indicated by the choice of law rules of the court.

[46] See CA Paris RCDIP 70 (1981), 121.

[47] The previous version of this provision referred to the possibility to "apply for a decision that the judgment be recognised".

[48] TGI Paris Clunet 120 (1993), 599 granted the plaintiff's request for a negative declaration and decided that several Italian decisions were not entitled to recognition in France, in particular because they contradicted earlier judgments issued by the courts of Delaware. In doing so, the court followed the majority opinion in the French literature (see *Gothot/Holleaux* para. 402; *Lagarde*, RCDIP 78 (1989), 534–537; *Pluyette*, Etudes offertes à Pierre Bellet (1991) pp. 443 ff.).

[49] Report Jenard p. 43. See e.g. *van den Broeck v. Ranieri*, Hof Hertogenbosch NIPR 1994, 157 and LG Athen (2005) ILPr 52.

[50] E.g. Art. 21(3) Brussels IIbis Regulation. See on this question, *Geimer/Schütze* Art. 33 note 85; *Leible*, in: Rauscher Art. 33, p. 724, para. 13. *Layton/Mercer* para. 26.009 suggest that a party could seek such a

recognition of a judgment be refused.[51] This possibility will prove helpful since foreign judgments may under the Regulation be enforced without any prior declaration of enforceability being required. A court may hence on the basis of the Regulation examine whether there are any grounds of refusal of recognition and conclude either that there are no grounds, in which case it will decide that the judgment deserves to be recognized (Art. 36 (2)), or that one or more grounds of refusal prohibit the recognition (Art. 45 (4)).

4. Recognition as an incidental issue (Art. 36 (3))

26   Art. 36 (3) indicates that a court seized of a dispute may also decide incidentally on the recognition of a foreign judgment which is relevant for the outcome of the dispute with which the court is principally concerned. In the absence of such a provision, courts could be required to stay their proceedings while they await the outcome of an application for a judgment to be recognized under Art. 36 (2). Although Art. 36 (3) only refers to incidental recognition in the framework of court proceedings, such incidental recognition may also take place when a foreign judgment is invoked before an authority.

27   Art. 36 (3) creates jurisdiction to rule incidentally on the recognition of the foreign judgment both *ratione materiae* as *ratione loci*.[52] Who bears the burden of proof in this respect, must be decided by the national law of the court seized. In contrast to the earlier version of the provision, Art. 36 (3) only refers to the incidental question "of refusal of recognition". The other language versions of Art. 36 are even clearer: the French version refers to the "refus de reconnaissance".[53] This seems to suggest that Art. 36 (3) only creates jurisdiction to decide incidentally that a foreign judgment may not be recognized. A court could therefore under Art. 36 (3) not decide that a judgment should be extended recognition. However, the refusal of recognition is only the negative version of a decision holding that a judgment must be extended recognition. Further, the Regulation is based on the principle that foreign judgments should be extended recognition. Finally, Art. 36 (3) refers in certain language versions in neutral terms to the possibility for the court to decide on the "recognition", without limiting this possibility to the refusal of recognition.[54] Therefore it must be accepted that a court seized of proceedings, may consider an incidental issue relating to a foreign judgment not only when a refusal of recognition is sought, but also when the recognition is sought.

28   Some language versions of the Regulation seem to imply that it is necessary for the existence of that jurisdiction that the incidental issue of recognition be decisive for the proceedings with which the court is principally concerned.[55] Other language versions are more flexible.[56]

---

negative declaration in accordance with the internal law of the court addressed. See also *van de Velden & Stefanelli*, The Effect in the EC of Judgments in Civil and Commercial Matters: Recognition, Res Judicata and Abuse of Process -Comparative Report, 2008, p. 48.

[51]   It is therefore no longer necessary to refer to the national law of the court addressed to justify the possibility to request a negative declaration, as was suggested under the previous version of the Regulation – e.g. *Kropholler/von Hein* Art. 33 note 7; *Kaye* p. 1397.

[52]   *Gothot/Holleaux* para. 388.

[53]   The Dutch version refers to the "weigering van erkenning"; the Italian version to "una richiesta di diniego di riconoscimento".

[54]   This is the case for the German version, which provides that the court may decide "über die Anerkennung".

In any case, a court will refrain to pass a judgment, even incidentally, on a judgment which is wholly unrelated to the proceedings with which it is principally concerned.

While Art. 36 (2) specifically refers to the rules of 'Subsection 2 of Section 3' of Chapter III, a **29** similar reference does not appear in Art. 36 (3). Given that the issue of recognition arises incidentally in the framework of other proceedings, it is not necessary to apply the procedural rules which the Regulation creates for recognition and enforcement proceedings. There is therefore no need to apply the specific rules of procedure laid out in subsection 2 of Section 3, as they are not relevant when the issue of recognition only arises incidentally. The court seized incidentally of an issue of recognition should, however, duly consider the provisions of section 1 (Artt. 36–38) and subsection 1 of Section 3 of Chapter 3 (art. 45). Some provisions of Section 4 may also be relevant when a party claims incidental recognition, such as Arts. 52, 56 and 57.

Before granting incidental recognition, the court will review the various grounds of refusal **30** listed in the Art. 45 of the Regulation.

The question arises whether the decision to grant incidental recognition enjoys itself *res* **31** *judicata*. It is generally said that a court called upon to make a declaration of recognition or to issue an order for enforcement will not necessarily be absolved from considering, on its own motion if need be, whether one of the grounds specified in Art. 45, exists, merely because another court has accorded (or denied) incidental recognition to the judgment[57] Whether a judgment under Art. 36 (3) effectively enjoys res judicata on the issue of recognition, will depend on the national law of the Member State concerned, if the court seized of a request under Art. 36 (2) sits in the same Member State as the court which has dealt incidentally with the recognition. When the question of the res judicata effect of a judgment dealing incidentally with the recognition of another judgment, arises in another Member State, it is submitted that in so far as the court seized incidentally of the recognition issue has verified the requirements for the recognition, its decision should not be ignored by a court subsequently seized of proceedings under Art. 36 (2). To deny it the status of final and conclusive decision on this question would give the party opposing the recognition an undue possibility to challenge the decision.

5. Partial recognition

Although the Regulation does not expressly contemplate this possibility,[58] it is accepted that **32** recognition of a foreign judgment may be limited to part of it.[59] This follows necessarily from the fact that some judgments will contain issues which fall outside the scope of application of the Regulation, while other issues fall within this scope. It also follows from the fact that a

---

[55] This is the case for the Italian, German and English versions of Art. 36 (3).

[56] This is the case for the French and Dutch versions.

[57] See *Layton/Mercer* para. 26.011; *Kropholler/von Hein* Art. 33 note 11.

[58] Art. 48 of the Brussels I Regulation provided a possibility to obtain a partial enforcement of a foreign judgment. This provision has not been taken over in the Brussels I*bis* Regulation.

[59] *Leible*, in: Rauscher Art. 33 para. 11; *Geimer/Schütze* Art. 33 notes 66–67; *Layton/Mercer* para. 24.043; *Kropholler/von Hein* Art. 33 note 10; *Gothot/Holleaux* para. 392; *d'Avout*, Dalloz (2013), 1014, 1017.

judgment may be held to contradict a ground of refusal only for part of the ruling. In all cases, a partial recognition requires that the judgment is severable.

33 When requesting a declaration that there are no grounds of refusal of recognition (Art. 36 (2)), the applicant may limit the scope of its request to part of the foreign judgment.

Article 37

1. A party who wishes to invoke in a Member State a judgment given in another Member State shall produce:
   (a) a copy of the judgment which satisfies the conditions necessary to establish its authenticity; and
   (b) the certificate issued pursuant to Article 53.
2. The court or authority before which a judgment given in another Member State is invoked may, where necessary, require the party invoking it to provide, in accordance with Article 57, a translation or a transliteration of the contents of the certificate referred to in point (b) of paragraph 1. The court or authority may require the party to provide a translation of the judgment instead of a translation of the contents of the certificate if it is unable to proceed without such a translation.

I. General outline

1 Art. 37 lays down the formal requirements which must be met when a party intends to rely on a judgment given in another Member State. This provision brings together elements which were included in various provisions of the Brussels I Regulation (i.e. Art. 53 and Art. 55(2)). In doing so, it introduces a procedural framework which is specific to the recognition of foreign judgments.

II. Legislative history

2 Art. 37 takes over provisions which appeared in Article 53 and 55(2) of the Brussels Regulation. The text is however, duly adapted and amended on certain points.

III. Commentary

3 Art. 37 indicates which documents a party seeking the recognition of a foreign judgment should produce. It also contains indications on the possibility for the court or authority addressed to request a translation of the relevant documents.

1. The copy of the judgment

4 Art. 37 requires in the first place that a person who wishes to invoke in a Member State a

judgment given in another Member State produces a copy[1] of the judgment which satisfies the conditions necessary to establish its authenticity. Art. 42(1)(a) makes a similar requirement when the enforcement of a judgment is sought. This requirement, which is common to all European Regulations dealing with foreign judgments,[2] is meant to allow the court addressed to verify whether the requirements for recognition or enforcement are met.[3]

The requirement to produce an authentic copy cannot be waived. The court or authority **5** may not dispense with the production of the judgment.[4] A court may, however, grant the applicant a new time limit in order to produce a copy which meets the requirement.[5] A summary of the judgment or the operative part of the judgment will prove insufficient.[6]

The copy which must be produced, should satisfy the conditions necessary to establish its **6** authenticity.[7] This requirement was already present in the Brussels Convention (art. 46(1)). It has been taken over by all European Regulations dealing with foreign judgments. The test is whether the judgment satisfies the authenticity in the country of origin.[8] It may be that according to the country of origin, a copy is deemed to be authentic when it bears a specific seal or has been issued by a given authority, such as the clerk of a court.[9] It may be doubted whether a mere handwritten copy will be accepted, even though the law of the country of origin deems such copy sufficient.

It is up to the court addressed to decide whether it keeps the authentic copy or gives it back to **7** the person seeking recognition or enforcement.[10]

---

[1] French: "copie"; German: "Ausfertigung"; Spanish: "copia"; Italian: "copia della decisione", Dutch: "afschrift". In the Brussels I Regulation, some language versions included a stricter requirement, imposing the production of an 'authentic' version of the judgment (in French i.e. "expédition", in Dutch: "expeditie", in Spanish "copia auténtica").

[2] See Art. 37(1) (a) Brussels II*bis* Regulation; Art. 28 (1) (a) Maintenance Regulation; Art. 46 (3) (a) Succession Regulation.

[3] Art. 47(3) of the Regulation provides, however, that in order to file an application for refusal of enforcement, the person against whom enforcement is sought must provide a "copy" ("Ausfertigung") of the judgment, without specifying that this must be an authentic copy.

[4] Compare with Art. 47(3) of the Regulation, which allows a court seized of an application for refusal of enforcement to dispense with the production of the judgment.

[5] *Couwenberg* in: Pertegás Sender et al. (eds.), Betekenen en uitvoeren over de grenzen heen (2008), p. 77, 102, § 235 (with reference to decisions in this sense).

[6] CA Versailles Gaz. Pal. 2005 somm. 2827 (the Court finds that a summary of the foreign judgment with the operative part, does not meet the Regulation's requirement).

[7] The German version inappropriately refers to the "Beweiskraft" of the copy, whereas other language versions refer to the "authenticity" (in Dutch: "echtheid"; in Italian: "autenticitá").

[8] Report *Jenard* p. 55.

[9] See *e.g.* for judgments issued by German courts, § 317 Abs. 4 ZPO; for judgments issued by Belgian courts Art. 790–791 Code Civil Procedure.

[10] See *e.g.* OLG Zweibrücken IPRax 2006, 49 (the Court notes that an authentic copy of the Italian judgment was produced in first instance, but handed back to the applicant after the declaration of enforceability had been issued. The Court indicates that there is no obligation to keep the original copy in the file). In the same sense, BGHZ, 75, 167, 169.

---

8   No difference is made depending on whether the judgment has been rendered by default or following contradictory proceedings. In both cases, the party seeking recognition or enforcement should produce a copy of the judgment. Under previous versions of the Regulation, a party seeking recognition or enforcement of a judgment issued by default was required to produce a document which established that the party in default was served with the document instituting the proceedings. However, the certificate to be issued under Art. 53 does require a specific mention to be made when the judgment has been given in default of appearance. In such case, the certificate should indicate the date on which the document instituting the proceedings (or an equivalent document) was served on the defendant (section 4.3.2 Art. 53 certificate). This is necessary to ascertain whether the documents were served on the defendant in due time (art. 45 (1)(b)).

9   Art. 37 does not specify how a court or authority should react if the party seeking recognition of a judgment, does not produce an authentic copy of the judgment. Art. 45 does not include the absence of an authentic copy among the grounds for refusal of recognition. However, it must be accepted that if a party fails to produce such an authentic copy, the court or competent authority has the discretion to deny recognition.

2. Certificate

10   Since the Brussels I Regulation, the process of mutual recognition and enforcement of judgments has been eased up within the European judicial area following the introduction of the system of standard forms. With these forms, a court seised of a request of recognition is in a position to verify the key elements of the foreign judgment without considering the actual content of the judgment. Whereas the Brussels I Regulation only imposed the production of a certificate when the enforcement of a foreign judgment was sought (Art. 54 (2)),[11] Art. 37 also requires the production of a certificate when recognition is at stake.[12]

11   The certificate must be issued by the court of origin under Art. 53. Annex I of the Regulation provides a form which must be used for the certificate.[13] The certificate may be issued using the online forms available at the European judicial atlas (http://ec.europa.eu/justice_home/judicialatlascivil/html/index_en.htm).

12   When recognition is sought, Art. 37 does not require that the certificate be first served on the person against whom recognition is sought. This requirement is made in case enforcement is sought of a foreign judgment (Art. 43(1)). The certificate which must be produced under Art. 37, should not certify that the judgment is enforceable, as is required by Art. 42(1)(b) when enforcement is sought. Nor should the certificate at this stage include information on the recoverable costs or the calculation of interests.

13   The Brussels *Ibis* Regulation does not contemplate the possibility to replace the certificate with equivalent documents. It does not envisage the possibility for the court or authority

---

11   Compare with the previous edition of this commentary: *Magnus/Mankowski/Wautelet* (2nd ed.), Art. 33, p. 639, n 16.

12   Art. 42 (1) (b) makes a similar requirement when enforcement is sought.

13   Use of the form is compulsory for the issue of the certificate. No form is provided for the request to obtain a certificate (comp. with Art. 65 (2) Successions Regulation).

faced with a request for recognition, to dispense with the submission of the certificate altogether.[14] This was possible under Art. 55(1) of the Brussels I Regulation.[15] As the practice of issuing certificates becomes more and more engrained, it is understandable that no possibility is offered to replace the certificate with alternative documents. Submission of the certificate is therefore compulsory. This does not smack of formalism: the certificate is an essential element of the recognition and enforcement process and not a mere formal document. Further, obtaining such a certificate will not impose an unnecessary and insurmountable burden on the party seeking recognition or enforcement.[16] In order to avoid extreme formalism, it may be accepted, however, that if no certificate has been submitted, the court or authority may impose a new time limit on the party seeking recognition or enforcement to submit a certificate.[17] When doing so, the court should apply its own procedural rules to decide on the time limit.[18] If the applicant does not produce the certificate within the new time limit, the application should be stricken out. Likewise, if the court or authority happens to already possess a copy of the judgment, it is suggested that the court or authority may dispense the applicant of producing it.

It had been suggested to provide in the Regulation that the certificate is binding on the court   **14** or authority addressed on all questions relating to the application of the Regulation.[19] This suggestion has not been expressly taken over in the Brussels I*bis* Regulation. However, the court or authority addressed should *prima facie* trust the certificate and not proceed to examine the foreign judgment. The latter should only be examined for the purpose of deciding on an application for refusal of recognition under Art. 45. When a clear discrepancy appears between the certificate and the foreign decision, it is submitted that the latter should prevail.

3. Translation – transliteration

When a court or authority is faced with a foreign judgment drafted in a foreign language, the   **15** temptation is great to request a translation of the judgment. After all, such translation makes it possible for the court or authority to fully understand not only the scope and consequences of the judgment, but also the reasoning behind it. Requiring a translation causes, however, additional costs for the party wishing to rely on the judgment. These costs may be disproportionate when the matter at stake is of limited value. Experience with the Brussels I Regulation had shown that even though in some cases, no translation will be requested, *e.g.* in border regions where judges may be consonant with the language of the judgment,[20] courts in general regularly requested a full translation of all judgments presented for rec-

---

[14] Compare with Art. 47 (3), which allows a court seized of an application for refusal of enforcement to dispense with the production of the judgment.

[15] See the explanations provided by *Staudinger*, in: Rauscher Art. 55 note 2, with reference to case law.

[16] Compare with Art. 47 (3) which refers to the situation in which a court considers it "unreasonable" to require an applicant seeking the refusal of enforcement, to provide a copy of the judgment.

[17] Solution accepted under the Brussels I Regulation, see e.g. *Staudinger*, in: Rauscher Art. 55 note 1.

[18] In Germany e.g. §§ 139; 142 ZPO.

[19] *Hess/Pfeiffer/Schlosser*, p. 164, § 562.

[20] *Hess/Pfeiffer/Schlosser*, p. 127, § 446. Couwenberg indicates that most courts in Belgium will not require a translation if the judgment is drafted in French, English or German (*Couwenberg* in: Pertegás Sender et al. (eds.), Betekenen en uitvoeren over de grenzen heen (2008), p. 77, 100, § 231.

ognition or enforcement.[21] This constituted an obstacle to the efficient functioning of the exequatur proceedings. Art. 37 attempts to limit the costs and time associated with the need to translate documents, by distinguishing between the translation of the certificate and that of the judgment.

16 As far as the certificate is concerned, Art. 37 provides that the court or authority before which the judgment is invoked may require a translation or a transliteration of the content of the certificate. The choice between translation and transliteration can be explained by the fact that the certificate may be filled using different alphabets.

17 A translation or transliteration of the certificate may be required "where necessary".[22] This implies that there should be first an examination of the certificate. Requiring a translation as a matter of automatism, is contrary to the text of Art. 37. It is only when the court or authority finds that the content of the certificate remains unclear that a translation or transliteration may be required. In this respect, attention should be paid to the fact that the standard form is identical in every official language of the EU. Accordingly, the translation of the certificate as such is not necessary. Only the information included in the certificate by the court of origin may need to be translated.

18 Art. 37 also provides clarification on the circumstances in which a translation of the judgment may be required. The main principle is that such translation may not be required as a matter of automatism. The translation of the foreign judgment must be seen as a subsidiary means, which may be required if the certificate does not make it possible to gather the necessary information. The content of the judgment has indeed been described in quite some details in the certificate. When the certificate does not make it possible to apply the grounds of refusal listed in Art. 45, the court or authority may choose between requesting a translation of the content of the certificate or requesting a translation of the judgment. The court should therefore first proceed to assess whether a translation of the content of the certificate will prove sufficient. If this is not the case, the court may request a translation of the judgment. In other words, the court should avoid first requesting a translation of the content of the certificate to find out afterwards that it also requires a translation of the judgment as such.

19 Echoing suggestions which had been made,[23] Art. 37 adds that a translation may be required if the court or authority "is unable to proceed without such a translation".[24] A mere feeling of discomfort with the foreign language is therefore insufficient to justify the requirement to translate the judgment. This goes further than the solution found in Art. 55 of the Brussels I Regulation, which did not limit the possibility for the court or authority to require a translation.

---

[21] *Hess/Pfeiffer/Schlosser*, p. 131, § 455. For France, see *Pluyette* in: Travaux comité français droit international privé (1988-90), p. 32 (noting that the court systematically requests a translation). See e.g. TGI Paris, 17 November 1981, *JCP*, 1982, IV, 210 (rejecting an application for exequatur on the ground that the applicant had only produced a free translation, whereas the court requested a translation by a person duly authorized to do so).

[22] The same test is included in Art. 42 par. 3 to guide the competent enforcement authority.

[23] *Hess/Pfeiffer/Schlosser*, p. 131, § 455.

[24] The same test is included in Art. 42 par. 4 to guide the competent enforcement authority.

Although Art. 37 does not make a reference to this solution, it may be possible to require a **20**
translation of only part of the judgment, i.e. the operative part, leaving the body (reasoning)
of the judgment not translated. Further, in order to avoid exaggerated formalism, it must be
accepted that a party may file an application under Art. 36 (2) and submit the translation
afterwards.[25]

The translation or transliteration must be provided by the party invoking the judgment. **21**
Translation or transliteration should be done taking into account the various requirements
of Art. 57.

The possibility to request a translation or transliteration of the certificate or the judgment is **22**
not limited to first instance proceedings. A court sitting in appeal may also avail itself of the
possibility offered by Art. 37(2) and request such a translation or transliteration.[26]

The Regulation does not include any rule in relation to the costs of the translation and how **23**
these costs may possibly be shifted to the other party. It falls upon the national law of the
court addressed to decide on this matter.

Article 38

The court or authority before which a judgment given in another Member State is invoked may
suspend the proceedings, in whole or in part, if:
(a) the judgment is challenged in the Member State of origin; or
(b) an application has been submitted for a decision that there are no grounds for refusal of
recognition as referred to in Article 45 or for a decision that the recognition is to be refused on
the basis of one of those grounds.

I. General Outline

Art. 38 grants the court the discretionary power to stay the proceedings in two situations: **1**
first if the judgment is challenged in the country of origin and second if the recognition is
being discussed in a court in the Member State where recognition is sought.

The possibility to stay proceedings in relation to a foreign judgment is also addressed in **2**

---

[25]   See ECJ, *Roger van der Linden v. Berufsgenossenschaft der Feinmechanik und Elektrotechnik*, (Case
C-275/94) (1996) ECR I-1393, I-1413 para. 18 about the possibility of regularizing an application in
the course of appeal preceedings in relation to the requirement of demonstrating proof of service.
[26]   *Kropholler/von Hein* (2002), p. 481, § 3.

Art. 44 and Art. 51. Both provisions concern the enforcement of a foreign judgment and not its recognition. Art. 44 allows a court seized of enforcement proceedings, to suspend such proceedings if an application for refusal of enforcement (Art. 46 *et seq.*) has been filed. Art. 51 relates directly to the proceedings brought in order to obtain a decision denying the enforcement of a foreign judgment. This provision makes it possible to stay the proceedings when the foreign judgment is being challenged in the country of origin. All these provisions pursue a similar goal, i.e. avoid giving effects to a foreign judgment while the possibility still exists that the judgment could be put aside in the country of origin. There are, however, some clear differences between the provisions, which therefore need to be addressed separately. Art. 51 for example makes it possible to stay the proceedings concerning the refusal of enforcement not only when the judgment has been challenged in the country of origin, but also if the time limit for such a challenge has not expired.

II. Legislative history

3   Art. 38 can be traced back to a provision of the original Brussels Convention, i.e. Art. 30. The text had not been modified in the Brussels I Regulation, save for the substitution of the reference to the 'Contracting State' by 'Member State'. A similar provision appeared in Art. 30 Lugano Convention.

4   Art. 38 has been modified to take into account the new procedure which may lead to a refusal of recognition. At the same time, the special provision in relation to judgments from the United Kingdom and Ireland, which was added to the Brussels Convention by Art. 14 of the 1978 Accession Convention, has been deleted. This provision was meant to clarify the concept of 'ordinary appeal' in relation to judgments given in those two Member States. Its purpose disappeared, as Art. 38 no longer makes a reference to ordinary appeals.[1]

III. Purpose

5   Under the Brussels *Ibis* Regulation, unlike in some national legal systems, foreign judgments can be recognised even if they are not *res judicata* in the continental sense of the phrase, i.e. if they are still susceptible of appeal.[2] If the judgment whose recognition is sought is still susceptible to be overturned or otherwise modified in appeal in its country of origin, it may be premature to give it effect in the country in which recognition is sought. Hence the possibility is given to the recognition court to stay the recognition proceedings once the judgment has effectively been challenged in the country of origin.

6   As the Court of Justice has explained in relation to an earlier version of the provision, the purpose of Art. 38 is "to prevent the compulsory recognition or enforcement of judgments […] when the possibility that they might be annulled or amended in the state in which they were given still exists".[3]

---

[1]   A similar provision was kept in Art. 51(2).

[2]   For a comparative overview of the requirements for recognition of foreign judgments, see *Gerhard Walter/Baumgartner*, in: Gerhard Walter (ed.), Recognition and Enforcement of Foreign Judgments Outside the Scope of the Brussels and Lugano Conventions, Civil Procedure in Europe, Vol. III (2000), p. 21.

[3]   *Industrial Diamond Supplies v. Luigi Riva*, (Case 43/77) (1977] ECR 2175, 2188 paras. 30/31.

Art. 38 aims at all situations in which a foreign judgment is invoked. It may apply in **7** proceedings under Art. 36 (3) in which an incidental question of recognition has been raised. In that case, the court before which the foreign judgment is raised, may stay the proceedings. The possibility to suspend the proceedings may also be used when an application has been filed under Art. 36 (2) that there are no grounds for refusal of recognition.[4] Finally, Art. 38 is also directed to the authority before which a foreign judgment is invoked. It is therefore not limited to court proceedings.

IV. When should a stay be considered

The Brussels I Regulation only contemplated the possibility of a stay in case recognition was **8** sought, when the judgment has been subject to an 'ordinary appeal' in the country of origin. Art. 38 goes further and opens the possibility of a stay in two situations

1. The judgment is challenged in the Member State of origin

A court or authority may first stay the recognition proceedings if the judgment has been **9** challenged in the Member State of origin. This contrasts with an earlier version of the provision, which limited the possibility to suspend the proceedings to situations in which an 'ordinary appeal' had been filed against the foreign judgment.[5] The reference to the concept of 'ordinary appeal', which has been kept in Art. 51, gave rise to much discussion. The new version appears to be broader and free from technical constraints related to procedural peculiarities of Member States.

The concept of 'challenge' should be construed autonomously, without reference to the **10** characterization given in the procedural law of the Member State concerned. This was already the case with the previous version of the provision, which referred to the concept of 'ordinary appeal'.[6] The label or characterization given in the law of the Member State of

---

4   Under Art. 37 of the Brussels I Regulation, it was unclear whether the stay could only be granted when the issue of recognition was raised incidentally or also if the judgment creditor applied for a declaration of recognition. The *Jenard*-Report only mentioned the hypothesis of the incidental recognition (Report *Jenard* p. 46). This led some commentators to argue that the possibility of granting a stay should be limited to the hypothesis of an incidental recognition (*Leible*, in: Rauscher Art. 37 para. 2; *Geimer/Schütze* Art. 37 note 1; *Kropholler/von Hein* Art. 37 note 2). However, as the former Art. 37 did not make any distinction between incidental recognition and proceedings under Art. 33 (2) for a declaration of recognition, it had also been suggested that the possibility granted by Art. 37 should receive the broadest application (In this sense, *Gaudemet-Tallon* para. 450 and *Layton/Mercer* p. 944).

5   For further comparative explanations on the various appeals proceedings in the Member States, see *Tsikrikas*, ZZP Int. 4 (1999), 171; *Ferrand*, Cassation française et révision allemande: essai sur le contrôle exercé en matière civile par la Cour de cassation française et par la Cour fédérale de Justice de la République fédérale d'Allemagne (1993); *Geeroms*, 48 Am. J. Comp. L. 201(2000).

6   The Court of Justice has held that this concept of 'ordinary appeal' should receive an autonomous definition. In the *Riva* case, the Court held that "[t]he expression 'ordinary appeal' within the meaning of Articles [37 and 46] must be defined solely within the framework of the system of the Convention itself and not according to the law either of the State in which the judgment was given or of the State in which recognition or enforcement for that judgment is sought": *Industrial Diamond Supplies v. Luigi Riva*, (Case 43/77) (1977) ECR 2175, 2188 para. 28.

Patrick Wautelet   831

origin is therefore not relevant. This applies in particular to the distinction in some Member States between 'ordinary' and 'extraordinary' remedies.

11   Art. 38 indicates that the stay may be contemplated when the judgment "is challenged" (the judgment "est contestée"/ "angefochten wird"/"è impugnata"): this suggests that there must be an effective challenge. No stay may therefore be considered if the time limit for such a challenge has not yet expired.[7]

12   In the absence of a definition in Art. 38, it is submitted that the possibility to suspend the recognition proceedings should be available each time the challenge could lead to a (complete or partial) reversal of the judgment. This test had already been accepted by the Court under the previous version of the provision. According to the Court, the possibility to stay proceedings should indeed be available "whenever reasonable doubts arise with regard to the fate of the decision in the State in which it was given".[8]

13   Accordingly, an 'ordinary appeal' should certainly be construed as being a challenge within the meaning of Art. 38. According to the Court of Justice, an appeal is 'ordinary' in the sense of the Regulation if (i) it may result in the annulment or amendment of the original judgment and (ii) there is a specific time period for appealing which starts by virtue of the judgment.[9] This also covers an appeal to the Court of cassation in France, Belgium or Luxemburg, even though as a matter of French or Belgian internal law, these appeals are considered to be 'extraordinary'.

14   The application of Art. 38 should, however, not be limited to ordinary appeals. Appeals which depend on events unforeseeable at the time of the original trial or on action taken by persons extraneous to the original proceedings that are not bound by the period for making an appeal, may also trigger the application of Art. 38, even though they are not considered an 'ordinary appeal'. One can refer to the '*requête civile*' known in the laws of Belgium and Luxemburg,[10] to the 'révision' known in French law,[11] or to the *Wiederaufnahmeklage* existing under German law.[12] It may be that these appeals do not constitute a normal procedural development which parties may reasonably expect.[13] As Art. 38 only applies if the challenge has effectively been used in the country of origin, there is no reason to exclude such appeals.

15   The question whether an appeal has any suspensive effect on the enforceability of the judgment should, in principle, not be taken into account to decide whether there is a challenge in the sense of Art. 38.[14] This means that an appeal in cassation may trigger the

---

7   Art. 51(1) makes it possible to suspend enforcement proceedings in this hypothesis.
8   *Industrial Diamond Supplies v. Luigi Riva*, (Case 43/77) [1977] ECR 2175, 2188 paras. 33/34.
9   *Industrial Diamond Supplies v. Luigi Riva*, (Case 43/77) [1977] ECR 2175, 2188 *et seq.* paras. 32–41. It may be that under the national law of the Member State the time period starts not when the judgment is issued but when it is notified to the parties.
10 Art. 1132 Belgian Code Judiciaire; Art. 617 Nouveau Code de Procédure Civile in Luxembourg.
11 Arts. 593 ff. NCPC.
12 §§ 578 *et seq.* ZPO.
13 Compare with the definition of ordinary appeals by the Court in *Industrial Diamond Supplies v. Luigi Riva*, (Case 43/77) (1977] ECR 2175, 2189 paras. 35/48.

application of Art. 38. The same may be said of the question whether the appeal is of right or subject to leave of appeal by the court of origin or to any other specific requirement.

Appeal mechanisms which cannot lead to a reversal of the judgment, may not be considered **16** under Art. 38. This is in particular the case for an appeal to the court of cassation 'in the interests of the law', i.e. an appeal introduced by the public prosecutor. The decision of the Court following such an appeal has indeed no effect on the position of the parties, it only serves to redress *in abstracto* what appears to be a legally wrong decision.[15] Likewise, the mere lodging of a complaint with the authorities, against parties who are involved in the proceedings in the country of origin, does not as such constitute a challenge. The same can be said of a request filed with the European Court of Human Rights, as a decision of this Court will not automatically lead to a reversal of the judgment.[16]

2. An application under Art. 45 has been submitted

Art. 38 also allows the court or authority to suspend the proceedings when an application **17** has been submitted under Art. 45 for a decision in relation to the grounds of refusal of recognition. In this case, the challenge is not brought in the country of origin. Rather, the judgment is being scrutinized in the country addressed, using the special procedure provided in Art. 46 ff. In contrast with the previous hypothesis, an application under Art. 45 will not lead to a reversal or annulment of the judgment. However, such application may lead to a decision that the recognition must be denied. This explains why a possibility should exist to suspend the recognition proceedings.

V. Discretion to stay

As the text suggests, Art. 38 only grants the court a discretionary power to stay the proceed- **18** ings. Hence, a party cannot claim to have a right to have the recognition proceedings suspended simply because the judgment has been challenged in the country of origin or because an application under Art. 45 has been filed.

Given the overall goal of the Regulation of achieving a "rapid and simple recognition and **19** enforcement of judgments given in a Member State",[17] it is submitted that courts should use their discretion so as to give *prima facie* effect to the foreign judgment pending the result of the appeal abroad.[18] A stay will therefore only be granted in exceptional cases.[19]

---

[14] This was already the case for the characterization of an appeal as being 'ordinary' under the previous version of Art. 38, see *Leible*, in: Rauscher Art. 37 note 3; *Kropholler/von Hein* Art. 39 note 3.

[15] Art. 1089 Belgian Code Judiciaire. See over this special form of challenge, the opinion of A-G *Reischl*, (Case 43/77) (1977) ECR 2199, 2200.

[16] In a case involving the 1988 Lugano Convention, the Luxemburg Court of Appeal has held that a request to the European Court of Human Rights did not constitute an ordinary appeal (CA Luxemburg, 13 July 2006, *Procedo Capital Corporation v. Sundal Collier & Co ASA*).

[17] Recital (4).

[18] See *Layton/Mercer* para. 26.108 (in relation to an earlier version of the provision).

[19] In *Petereit v. Babcock International Holdings Ltd.* [1990] 1 WLR 350, 358, Judge *Anthony Diamond* Q.C. held that the power to stay was "general and unfettered" but that "the enforcing court should not adopt a general practice of depriving a succesful plaintiff of the fruits of the judgment by the imposition of a more

20 The Court of Justice has indicated in relation to an earlier version of the text that the power to stay should be used "whenever reasonable doubts arise with regard to the fate of the decision in the State in which it was given".[20] It is submitted that this approach is still good law. Assessing how likely the judgment will be reversed in the country of origin requires, however, an examination of the various arguments put forward to substantiate the challenge brought, in the State of origin, against the judgment whose recognition is sought. The Court of Justice seemed to make a reference to the examination of the merits of the appeal when it described the test as based "on the possible effect of the appeal".[21] Needless to say, the court before which recognition is sought is not necessarily equipped to proceed with such an examination.[22] Given the difficulty of this assessment, the court addressed should, however, at most, only take into account the probable outcome of the appeals proceedings when it is clear that the judgment will not stand in appeal or that the appeal is frivolous and will be dismissed without more.

21 In deciding whether the stay should be granted, courts should take into account the degree of prejudice likely to be suffered if the application is or is not stayed.[23]

22 Under a previous version of Art. 51, the Court has held that when deciding whether to grant a stay of proceedings, a court may take into account only such submissions as the party opposing enforcement of a judgment was unable to make before the court of the state in which the judgment was given.[24] Since Art. 51 and 38 pursue the same goal, (i.e. preventing that the potential effects of the appeal in the country of origin from being pre-empted by the judgment being given immediate effect in the Member State in which recognition is sought) it may be that the Court's decision, which has been criticized, should also apply to the court deciding whether or not to stay proceedings on the basis of Art. 38.

---

or less automatic stay, merely on the ground that there is pending an appeal" (this case was decided on the basis of an earlier version of Art. 51). In *Banco Nacional de Comercio Exterior SNC v. Empresa de Telecomunicaciones de Cuba SA* [2007] EWHC 2322, the court referred to a general principle of "general enforceability of judgments without awaiting the outcome of an appeal which is inherent in the permissive nature of the jurisdiction conferred by Articles [38] and [51] ..."

[20] *Industrial Diamond Supplies v. Luigi Riva*, (Case 43/77) [1977] ECR 2175, 2188 paras. 32/34.

[21] *Industrial Diamond Supplies v. Luigi Riva*, (Case 43/77) [1977] ECR 2175, 2189 paras. 35/41.

[22] In one instance, a Belgian court attempted to review the arguments put forward by the party who had challenged the French judgment before the French Cour de cassation: Trib. Comm. Liège JMLB 1984, 289. In another case, a court refused to stay the proceedings because the reasoning given in the foreign judgment appeared serious and logic, so that it was unlikely that it would be overturned in appeal: TGI Nivelles RTD fam. 1995, 70. The nature of the proceedings (enforcement of maintenance orders, where any delay can be catastrophic for the plaintiff) may explain why the court was reluctant to stay proceedings. In *Banco Nacional de Comercio Exterior SNC v. Empresa de Telecomunicaciones de Cuba SA* (2007) EWHC 2322, the court decided not to question the assessment made by the court of origin (Italy) as to the potential prejudice which a party could suffer in the event the foreign decision would be reversed in appeal after it has been enforced.

[23] See e.g. *Petereit v. Babcock International Holdings Ltd.* [1990] 2 All ER 135 = [1990] 1 WLR 350 (Q.B.D., Judge *Anthony Diamond* Q.C.), a case decided on the basis of Art. 51. See also Aix-en-Provence, 26 April 2005, No. 2005-273154 (the court orders a stay in the light of the uncertainty surrounding the fate of an Italian decreto ingiutivo, taking into account the "importance of the amounts at stake").

[24] *B. J. van Dalfsen and others v. B. van Loon and T. Berendsen*, (Case C-183/90) [1991] ECR I-4743.

For the sake of the efficiency of proceedings, courts should be encouraged, before addressing   23
the issue of a possible stay, to consider whether all requirements for recognition are met. It is
only when the answer to this question is positive that the stay should be considered.[25]

VI. How to suspend

The power to stay the recognition may be used *sua sponte*, on its own motion, by the court.   24
There is no need for a party to seek such suspension..[26] The court must, however, be
informed that a challenge has indeed been filed in the Member State of origin or that an
application under Art. 45 has been made. In most cases, the party informing the court will
also request the suspension.

Art. 38 refers to the suspension of the "proceedings". These may be the proceedings on the   25
merits if the issue of the stay is raised while the foreign judgment is incidentally considered
in these proceedings (art. 36 (3)). The suspension may also touch the recognition proceedings under Art. 36 (2). When the recognition of a foreign judgment is raised before an
authority, it is not entirely clear what should be suspended under Art. 38.

Art. 38 makes it possible to suspend the proceedings "in whole or in part". This is in   26
particular relevant when the recognition of a foreign judgment forms an incidental issue
in the framework of proceedings on the merits (art 36 (3)). In that case, the court seized of
proceedings on the merits, must decide whether the issue of the recognition of the judgment
is central to the dispute it must solve or whether it only affects part of this dispute.

Art. 38 does not open the possibility to make the stay conditional on the provision of a   27
security. A mechanism of this type may not be contemplated even if it is allowed under
national law.

When granting a stay, the court will follow the rules of its own law to determine which form   28
the stay should take.[27] It is not necessary to limit the stay in time. Rather, the stay should
extend for the whole duration of the appeal proceedings in the country of origin.

Section 2: **Enforcement**

Bibliography to Section 2

Beaumont/Johnston, Can Exequatur Be Abolished in   Brussels I: Is a Public Policy Defence Necessary for
Brussels I Whilst Retaining a Public Policy Defence?,   the Protection of Human Rights?, IPRax 2010, 105
(2010) 6 JPrIL 1   *Beraudo*, J-Cl. Droit international, fasc. 633 (2014)
Beaumont/Johnston, Abolition of the Exequatur in   *Cristofaro*, The Abolition of Exequatur Proceedings:

---

[25]   In this sense, Report *Jenard* p. 47.
[26]   This was already the case with Art. 37 of the Brussels I Regulation (see *Leible*, in: Rauscher Art. 37 p. 771,
     para. 5).
[27]   In Germany, § 148 ZPO.

Speeding up the Free Movement of Judgments while
Preserving the Rights of the Defense, in: *Pocar/*
Viarengo/Villata (eds), Recasting Brussels I (2012)
Cuniberti/Rueda, Abolition of Exequatur, RabelsZ
75 (2011), 286
Gascón-Inchausti, La reconnaissance et l'exécution
des decisions dans le règlement Bruxelles I*bis*, in:
Guinchard (ed.), Le nouveau règlement Bruxelles
I*bis* (2014), p. 205
Kramer, Cross-Border Enforcement and the Brussels
I-bis Regulation: Towards A New Balance Between
Mutual Trust and National Control over Funda-
mental Rights, NILR 60 (2013), 343
Lopez de Tejada, La disparition de l'exequatur dans
l'espace judiciaire européen (2013)

Marchadier, La suppression de l'exequatur affaiblit-
elle la protection des droits fondamentaux dans l'e-
space judiciaire européen ?, J. Eur. Dr. H. (2013) 348
Oberhammer, The Abolition of Exequatur,
IPRax 30 (2010) 197
Schack, The (Misguided) Abolition of Exequatur
Proceedings in the European Union, in: Festschrift
Tadeusz Erecinski (2011), p. 1345
Schlosser, The Abolition of Exequatur Proceedings –
Including Public Policy Review?, IPRax (2010) 101
Schramm, Enforcement and the abolition of
exequatur under the 2012 Brussels I regulation,
Yb. PIL 15 (2013/2014), p. 143.

Article 39

**A judgment given in a Member State which is enforceable in that Member State shall be enforce-
able in the other Member States without any declaration of enforceability being required.**

I. General

1 One of the main innovations of the Brussels I*bis* Regulation is to abolish the procedural
requirement that foreign judgments be enforceable only after being declared so by an authority of the Member State of enforcement. Art. 39 provides that judgments enforceable in
the Member State in which they were issued are directly enforceable in any other Member
State without any intermediate procedure of declaration of enforceability.

The European Commission had initially advocated a more far reaching abolition of the
exequatur procedure.[1] The objective is only partially achieved. From a procedural standpoint, Art. 39 eliminates the requirement that an authority of the Member State of enforcement declares enforceable the foreign judgment. However, from a substantive standpoint,
judgment debtors will still have the opportunity to resist enforcement of the foreign judgment by relying at a later stage on the same grounds which were previously available under
the Brussels I Regulation. The verification that the foreign judgment complies with these
grounds is postponed to the enforcement stage,[2] and will only take place if the judgment
debtor initiates it.[3]

---

[1]   Commission Proposal Brussels I*bis* Regulation COM (2010) 748/3.

Art. 39 may be seen as a direct expression of the objective of free movement of judgments   **2**
that the European integration process has been striving towards since the adoption of the
Brussels Convention of 17 September 1968. The Brussels Convention was indeed already a
so-called 'double' or 'mixed' convention that regulated both the jurisdiction of the courts of
the Member States and the recognition and enforcement of the judgments issued by these
courts.

As an EU objective, the freedom of movement of judgments has long been subordinated to
the objective of realisation and good functioning of the internal market. It has gained
autonomy with the Amsterdam Treaty (1997). However, autonomy is not independence.
A subsidiary but necessary link remains with the functioning of the internal market – as
evidenced by the wording of Art. 81 TFEU on judicial cooperation in civil matters.

Free movement of judgments constitutes one of the main aspects of the objective of realisation of the area of freedom, security and justice laid down in Art. 3 TEU. It relies significantly on the principle of mutual recognition of judicial decisions in civil matters set out
by Art. 67 TFEU as one of the mechanisms aimed at facilitating access to justice in the EU.
As articulated in Recital (26) of the Brussels I*bis* Regulation, the abolition of *exequatur*
builds on this principle with the purpose of 'making cross-border litigation less time-consuming and costly' by allowing a judgment given in a Member State to be treated in the same
way as a judgment given in its Member State of enforcement.

It is possible to draw an analogy between the function of the free movement of judgments   **3**
within the area of freedom, justice and security and the function of the four fundamental
freedoms of movement (of goods, persons, services and capital) within the internal market.
In this respect, the underlying conception of the EU territory as a legally unified territory is
enhanced by the Brussels I*bis* Regulation since it extends the spatial scope of the new regime
also to Denmark, Ireland and the United Kingdom. Despite their exceptional status in
matters of European private international law, Ireland and the United Kingdom have indeed
notified their decision to adopt and apply the regulation.[4] So has Denmark by letter of 20
December 2012 addressed to the Commission shortly after the adoption of the regulation.[5]
As Denmark, Ireland and the United Kingdom have given up on their exceptional status, the
Brussels I*bis* Regulation represents an improvement over the Brussels I Regulation in terms
of legislative continuity.

II. Legislative history

Art. 220 of the 1957 Rome Treaty establishing the European Community encouraged Mem-   **4**
ber States to enter into negotiations with each other with a view to securing for the benefit of
their nationals the simplification of formalities governing the reciprocal recognition and
enforcement of judgments. The first step taken by Member States was the adoption of the
1968 Brussels Convention which 1) harmonised the intermediate procedure for the enforce-

---

2   See Art. 45.

3   See Art. 46.

4   See Recital 40.

5   See the *Agreement between the European Community and the Kingdom of Denmark on jurisdiction and
    the recognition and enforcement of judgments in civil and commercial matters*, OJ L 79, 21.2.2013, p. 4.

ment of foreign judgments in civil and commercial matters within the then European Economic Community and 2) limited the grounds on which recognition or enforcement could be denied. The second step took place in 2000 with the adoption of the Brussels I Regulation which further simplified the intermediate procedure by prohibiting any assessment of the existence of the grounds for refusal of enforcement in the first instance procedure and postponing it to the appeal stage.

5   At the 1999 Tampere Summit, the European Council called upon the European Commission to further reduce intermediate measures necessary for the recognition and enforcement of judgments within the European Union.[6] In 2000, the Commission and the Council of Ministers issued a programme[7] announcing a gradual abolition of the *exequatur* procedure in three stages. The European Council had already defined the first stage as consisting in the abolition of exequatur "for titles in respect of small consumer or commercial claims and for certain judgments in the field of family litigation (e.g. on maintenance claims and visiting rights)". It was implemented from 2003 to 2009 through the adoption of five regulations which not only suppressed the required *ex ante* procedure of verification of the foreign judgments, but also certain of the grounds available to refuse enforcement under the Brussels I Regulation, in particular the public policy exception. Other grounds were kept, but postponed at the enforcement stage. Regulation 2201/2003 on matrimonial matters and matters of parental responsibility has first abolished exequatur with respect to orders relating to the rights of access or the return of abducted children. Regulations 805/2004 creating a European enforcement order for uncontested claims, 1896/2006 creating a European order for payment and 861/2007 establishing a European small claims procedure also abolished the procedure of exequatur within their scope. Finally, Regulation 4/2009 on maintenance obligations expressly does the same, but for those countries which are bound by the 2007 Hague Protocol on the Law Applicable to Maintenance Obligations. The next stage of the process of abolition of *exequatur* was meant to be the recast of the Brussels I Regulation, but Members States opposed it and eventually only accepted a purely procedural reform.

6   One of the strongest criticisms against the project to fully abolish the exequatur procedure, and more specifically the public policy exception, was that it might violate European human rights law. In *Pellegrini v. Italy*,[8] the European Court of Human Rights (ECtHR) had ruled that contracting states were under the obligation to verify whether foreign judgments rendered by third states complied with the rights afforded by the European Convention on Human Rights before recognising or enforcing them. Scholars debated whether the judgment should also be interpreted as imposing a similar obligation with respect to judgments originating from Contracting states.[9] In the context of Regulation 2201/2003 on matrimonial matters and matters of parental responsibility (Brussels II*bis*), the ECtHR held in *Povse v. Austria*[10] that the obligation of Member States to enforce foreign judgments under the Regulation triggers a presumption of compliance by Member States of the European Union

---

6   Tampere European Council: Presidency Conclusions, 15th and 16th October 1999 (Presidency Conclusions, Nr 200/1/99, 16.10.1999).

7   Programme of measures for implementation of the principle of mutual recognition of decisions in civil and commercial matters, OJ C12, 15.01.2001, p. 1.

8   ECtHR, *Pellegrini v. Italy*, Application no 30882/96.

9   See, among many others, *Kinsch*, The Impact of the Human Rights on the Application of Foreign Law and on the Recognition of Foreign Judgments, in: Einhorn/Sierh (ed.), International Cooperation

with the European Convention on Human Rights. While earlier judgments of the court had ruled that such a presumption could be rebutted if a manifest deficiency could be identified in the system of protection of fundamental rights established by the European Union, the ECtHR ruled in *Povse* that it had not been able to "find any dysfunction in the control mechanisms for the observance of Convention rights",[11] and that the presumption had thus not been rebutted. In *Avotins c. Lettonie*,[12] the ECtHR ruled in the context of the Brussels I Regulation that the obligation of Member States to enforce foreign judgments under the Regulation also triggers the same presumption of compliance by Member States with the European Convention on Human Rights. The obligation to enforce foreign judgments under the Brussels II*bis* Regulation and the Brussels I Regulation is very different, however, as the public policy exception was retained in the second, and thus gives discretion to the courts of the Member States to deny enforcement if a violation of European human rights law is found.[13]

III. Requirements

1. A judgment

Under the Brussels Convention as well as under the Brussels I Regulation, the concept of 'judgment' was defined in a specific Article that served as an introductory Article for the title/chapter dealing with the recognition and enforcement of foreign judgments. In the Brussels I*bis* Regulation, this introductory Article disappears and is replaced by a definition found in Art. 2(a).[14]   **7**

2. A judgment enforceable in its Member State of origin

The purpose of Art. 39 is to extend the enforceability of the judgment to the whole territory of the E.U. It is thus only logical that a requirement for such extension be that the judgment be enforceable in the Member State of origin in the first place.   **8**

Art. 39 – unlike Art. 36 – does not state that the judgment shall be enforced 'without any special procedure being required', but only 'without any declaration of enforceability being required'. This difference of language could be understood as recognizing that enforcement procedures are subject to judicial control – a 'special procedure' in the terms of Art. 36 – that   **9**

Through Private International Law–Essays in Memory of Peter Nygh (2004) 197; *Fawcett*, The Impact of Article 6(1) of the ECHR on Private International Law, ICLQ 56 (2007) 1.

[10]   ECtHR, 18 June 2013, *Povse v. Austria*, application n° 3890/11. On this case, see *Hazelhorst*, NIP (2014) 27, *Cuniberti*, RCDIP (2014) 303.

[11]   ECtHR, 18 June 2013, *Povse v. Austria*, application n° 3890/11, para. 87.

[12]   ECtHR, 25 February 2014, *Avotins c. Lettonie*, application n° 17502/07. On this case, see *Requejo*, forthcoming IPRax (2014); *Marchadier*, RCDIP (2014) 679.

[13]   *Cuniberti*, RCDIP (2014) 324.

[14]   *Supra* Art. 2(a).

may be either required or optional depending on the Member State.[15] Furthermore, Art. 42 (1)(b) requires the applicant seeking enforcement of a judgment in another Member State to provide the competent enforcement authority with the certificate mentioned in Art. 53 of the Regulation and issued by the court of origin of the judgment.

10 Non enforceability should be distinguished from hypotheses of (1) impossible enforcement and (2) paralyzed enforcement. The *Apostolides* case[16] provides an illustration of the first hypothesis. In that case, the European Court of Justice held that the fact that a judgment given by Cypriot courts cannot, as a practical matter, be enforced because it concerns land located in an area of Cyprus over which the Government does not have effective control, does not mean that this judgment is not enforceable under the Brussels I Regulation.[17] Along the same lines, the Court also held that the fact that a judgment has already been complied with in its Member State of origin does not deprive it of its enforceable nature, even if it cannot be enforced in that State anymore.[18]

The second hypothesis is particularly well illustrated by the *Coursier* case,[19] where the Court ruled that the circumstance that the enforcement of a judgment is concretely being paralysed by ongoing insolvency proceedings in the Member State of origin does not deprive that judgment of its enforceability. This only affects the modalities of enforcement of the foreign judgment in its State of origin.[20] It is therefore up to the courts of the Member State addressed to decide, in their jurisdiction, on the effects of the insolvency law rule of the Member State of origin.[21]

11 However, actual modifications in the enforceability status of a judgment in its Member State of origin may have repercussions in the Member State of enforcement.[22] From the perspective of the enforcement authorities of the Member State addressed, the main element taken into account is the certificate mentioned in Art. 53. The certificate states indeed the enforceability status of the judgment to be enforced. Still, judgments that are enforceable in their State of origin may be provisional or appealable, and therefore subject to amendment. It may thus happen that a judgment issued in one Member State is enforced in another Member State, and that later an action is brought against it in its State of origin and deprives

---

[15]   *Cuniberti/Rueda*, RabelsZ (2011) 309–311; *Nuyts*, 102 RCDIP (2013), para. 16.

[16]   *Meletis Apostolides v. David Charles and Linda Elizabeth Orams*, (Case C-420/07) (2009) ECR I-3571.

[17]   See *Meletis Apostolides v. David Charles and Linda Elizabeth Orams*, (Case C-420/07) (2009) ECR I-3571, paras. 64–71.

[18]   See *Prism Investments BV v. Jaap Anne van der Meer, in his capacity as receiver in the liquidation of Arilco Holland BV*, (Case C-139/10) (2011) ECR I-9511, paras. 36–37.

[19]   *Eric Coursier v. Fortis Bank and Martine Coursier, née Bellami*, (Case C-267/97) (1999) ECR I-2543.

[20]   See *Eric Coursier v. Fortis Bank and Martine Coursier, née Bellami*, (Case C-267/97) (1999) ECR I-2543, para. 29.

[21]   See *Eric Coursier v. Fortis Bank and Martine Coursier, née Bellami*, (Case C-267/97) (1999) ECR I-2543, para. 32; also, RCDIP (2000) 236 with note *Droz* and *Kropholler/von Hein* Art. 38 note 9, both observing that the question of the effects of the insolvency law of the Member State of origin on the territory of the Member State addressed is typically solved by application of the rules of private international law of the latter.

[22]   See *Droz* para. 548; *Kerameus*, in: Magnus/Mankowski, Brussels I Regulation, 2011, Art. 38, 10.

it of its enforceability. The legal consequences of such a turn of event would typically be dealt with by the Member State of enforcement of the original judgment.[23]

IV. Exclusive character of the enforcement system set by the Regulation?

After the abolition of exequatur, the enforcement regime established by the Regulation has **12** become remarkably efficient for judgment creditors. While it is unlikely that any national enforcement regime would be more efficient from a procedural standpoint, it could be more liberal with respect to the available grounds for denying enforcement (and recognition).

While the issue was debated under the Brussels Convention and Regulation,[24] most scholars **13** agreed that national regimes did not apply.[25] Some cited the *de Wolf v. Cox* case[26] as support for this proposition.[27]

Recital 33 explains that provisional, including protective measures, which would not satisfy **14** the special requirements for their enforcement under the Regulation can be enforced under national laws.[28] It is hard to see why national enforcement regimes could supplement the Regulation with regard provisional, including protective measures, and not with regard other judgments. The application of more liberal national regimes would be consistent with the objective of free circulation of judgments.

Article 40

An enforceable judgment shall carry with it by operation of law the power to proceed to any protective measures which exist under the law of the Member State addressed.

I. General

Art. 40 affords judgment creditors the right to proceed to protective measures in any Mem- **1** ber State other than the State of origin of the judgment. The right automatically arises from the existence of an enforceable judgment. In most cases, it will not be meaningful, as creditors should prefer to directly enforce their judgment rather than seek first protective measures. However, protective measures might be advantageous in cases where enforcement measures could not be directly carried out, but might require some judicial step, and could thus reveal unfruitful if the debtor was willing to dispose of his assets. Indeed, Art. 43 (1) requires that the judgment creditor serve on the debtor the certificate obtained pursuant to Art. 53 prior to the first enforcement measure.[1]

---

23   See on German law, *Kropholler/von Hein* Art. 38 note 11.
24   See, e.g., *Gaudemet-Tallon*, para. 435 (debate among French scholars).
25   *Gaudemet-Tallon*, para. 435; *Huet*, Clunet (1988) 31; *Kerameus*, in: Magnus/Mankowski, Brussels I Regulation, 2012, Art. 38, 14.
26   *Jozef de Wolf v. Harry Cox BV*, (Case 42/76) ECR 1759, 1767, para. 14.
27   *Kerameus*, in: Magnus/Mankowski, Brussels I Regulation, 2012, Art. 38, 14.
28   *Infra*, Art. 42 note 11 (*Cuniberti/Rueda*).
1   *Infra*, Art. 43 note 1 (*Cuniberti/Rueda*).

Gilles Cuniberti/Isabelle Rueda

II. Legislative history

2 The origin of Art. 40 is to be found in Art. 39 of the Brussels Convention and Art. 47 of the Brussels I Regulation. The rationale of the provision was then to afford creditors with a right to proceed to protective measures during the process of obtaining authorization to enforce the foreign judgment. As foreign judgments are now directly enforceable in other Member States (see Art. 39), the provision has lost most of its significance.

3 Under the Brussels Convention, foreign judgments could only be declared enforceable after being declared so by a court of the enforcing State.[2] If enforcement was granted, an appeal could be lodged against the decision within a month of its service on the judgment debtor.[3] Until the end of this time period and until the appeal would be decided, Art. 39 para. 1 provided that the judgment creditor could not enforce the judgment and could only proceed to protective measures. However, in order to mitigate the effect of the suspension of the enforcement which resulted from such appeal, Art. 39 para. 2 facilitated the taking of conservative measures by granting the creditor a right to obtain such measures in cases where he had successfully obtained an authorization to enforce the foreign judgment from the first instance court. Despite the appeal, the right of the creditor to enforce the foreign judgment had been recognized by the decision of the first instance court and appeared to be more serious than in the absence of any judicial recognition. Art. 39 para. 2 thus provided that "the decision authorizing enforcement shall carry with it the power to proceed to any such protective measures." It implicitly referred to a decision authorizing enforcement, the effect of which had been suspended. As the Court of Justice of the European Communities ruled in 1985, "the obvious purpose of [Art. 39] is to offer the party who has obtained authorization for enforcement, but who cannot yet proceed with measures of enforcement, a means of preventing the party against whom enforcement is sought from disposing of his property in the meantime …"[4]

4 While the Brussels I Regulation simplified the process for declaring foreign judgments enforceable, it retained an intermediate step whereby an authority of the State of enforcement (typically judicial, but not always) had to issue a declaration of enforceability of the foreign judgment.[5] If such declaration was issued, an appeal could be lodged against it in the same conditions as under the Brussels Convention,[6] which would entail the same suspension of enforcement.[7] The rationale behind Art. 39 para. 1 and 2 of the Brussels Convention remained, and the two provisions became respectively Art. 47(3) and (2) of the Brussels I Regulation.

5 Art. 47 of the Brussels I Regulation introduced two innovations, however. The first was to lay down in Art. 47(1) a new rule attaching the right to seek protective measures to the mere recognition of the foreign judgment. Judgment creditors could seek protective measures even before applying for a declaration of enforceability of the foreign judgment. However,

---

[2] Brussels Convention, Art. 31.

[3] Brussels Convention, Art. 36.

[4] *P. Capelloni and F. Aquilini v. J. C. J. Pelkmans*, (Case 119/84) (1985) ECR 3147, 3159 para. 19.

[5] Brussels I Regulation, Art. 38.

[6] Brussels I Regulation, Art. 43.

[7] Brussels I Regulation, Art. 47(3).

contrary to Art. 47(2) which afforded the power to proceed to protective measures to holders of a declaration of enforceability, Art. 47(1) only recognised judgment creditors the right to avail themselves of both provisional and protective measures in accordance with the law of the Member State requested. It is therefore unclear whether Art. 47(1) contributed any autonomous rule.[8] The provision could be interpreted as merely referring to national law on this point, without facilitating the obtaining of provisional, including protective measures. A more convincing view, however, was that the provision should be interpreted as being meaningful, by affording a power to proceed to protective measures similar to the power contemplated by Art. 47(2).[9] The model of the European lawmaker might have been Belgian law, which allows for extra-judicial protective measures to be carried out on the ground of a foreign judgment before it being declared enforceable.[10] The same has long been true of French law.[11]

The second innovation was to invert para. 1 and 2 of Art. 39 of the Brussels Convention, **6** which became respectively Art. 47(3) and (2) of the Brussels I Regulation. As a consequence, and contrary to Art. 39, the power to proceed to protective measures attached to the declaration of enforceability did not appear to be qualified by any previous paragraph and thus limited to cases where the enforceability of the foreign judgment would have been suspended.

III. The power to proceed to protective measures

1. Scope

Contrary to Art. 35, Art. 40 does not refer to provisional, including protective measures, but **7** to protective measures only. While the European Court of Justice has offered a definition of provisional, including protective measures under Art. 35,[12] it has not specifically defined the concept of protective measures falling within the scope of Art. 40 (or its predecessors).

The purpose of Art. 40 being to protect the enforcement of the foreign judgment, protective **8** measures in the meaning of Art. 40 should be defined as any measure aiming at securing enforcement of the judgment. For judgments ordering the payment of money, protective measures will typically be measures preventing the judgment debtor from disposing of his assets, whether directly by freezing them, or indirectly by granting the judgment creditor an in rem right in the assets making it meaningless to dispose of them. For judgments ordering the judgment debtor to behave in a certain way, protective measures could be any measures ensuring that the ordered behaviour will still satisfy the judgment creditor.

2. Content of power

Art. 40 grants an autonomous power to proceed to any protective measures which exist **9**

---

8   *Pålsson*, in: Magnus/Mankowski, Brussels I Regulation, 2011, Art. 47, 4.

9   This interpretation was shared by many French scholars: see *Gaudemet-Tallon/Droz*, RCDIP 2001, 650; *Cuniberti/Normand/Cornette*: Droit international de l'exécution (2010) 309.

10   *Hess/Hub*, IPRax 2003, 93, 94.

11   See *Cuniberti/Normand/Cornette* (fn. 39), 306.

12   *Supra*, Art. 35 note 49 (*Pertegas*).

under the law of the Member State addressed. However, Art. 40 expressly provides that national law remains applicable to define the kind of protective measures available in the Member State addressed.[13] This logically entails the legal effects of the relevant protective measures. The power to proceed to protective measures afforded by Art. 40, therefore, only impacts some of the requirements for obtaining a protective measure provided by national law,[14] which might not apply if their operation would otherwise lead to frustration of the rationale of Art. 40 and the right that it affords.[15]

10 In *Capelloni*,[16] the European Court of Justice found that three requirements of Italian law were incompatible with the power to proceed to protective measures under the Brussels Convention. The first was the obligation to seek a specific authorization to proceed to the contemplated measure by a local court of competent jurisdiction. The Court ruled that then Art. 39 entailed the power to proceed "directly" to protective measures.[17] The ruling was logical in the context of continental provisional attachments, which are typically carried out by non-judicial enforcement authorities. By contrast, it is unclear whether this part of the ruling could apply to freezing orders which are essentially judicial such as English freezing orders. The judgment creditor should apply to the English competent court for such an order.[18]

11 The second requirement of Italian law was the obligation to take the protective measure within a certain non-extendable period. The Court ruled that the autonomous power to proceed to protective measures being expressly granted by then Art. 39 until the end of the appeal procedure,[19] it could not be limited to a shorter period by a national rule.[20] Contrary to Art. 39 of the Brussels Convention, Art. 40 does not contain any time limit. It might be, therefore, that a requirement such as the second one considered in *Capelloni* could be found to be compatible with Art. 40.

12 The third requirement of Italian law was the obligation to seek a confirmatory judgment after the measure was granted. The Court ruled that the purpose of the rule was to mitigate the fact that protective measures were typically granted in summary proceedings, and that such rationale did not exist where the foundation of the protective measure was a decision allowing enforcement.[21] While the foundation of the protective measure under Art. 40 is not the decision of the forum allowing enforcement, it is the foreign judgment which is directly enforceable in the forum. There is no summary assessment of the rights of the creditor, and a

---

[13]   In the words of the English Court of appeal: "It seems to us therefore that an applicant for such measures must take them as he finds them in the jurisdiction where he seeks to enforce his judgment. So, if a particular measure has a certain feature, either the applicant accepts it or chooses not to avail himself of it." *Banco Nacional de Commercio Exterior SNC v. Empresa de Telecomunicaciones de Cuba SA* [2007] EWCA Civ. 662, at para. 44.

[14]   *Gascon-Inchausti*, in: Guinchard, Le nouveau Règlement Bruxelles *Ibis* (2014) 230.

[15]   *P. Capelloni and F. Aquilini v. J. C. J. Pelkmans*, (Case 119/84) (1985) ECR 3147, para. 21.

[16]   *P. Capelloni and F. Aquilini v. J. C. J. Pelkmans*, (Case 119/84) (1985) ECR 3147.

[17]   *Capelloni*, para. 23.

[18]   English CA, *Banco Nacional de Commercio Exterior SNC*, cit., at para. 45; *Briggs/Rees*, para. 7.28, note 9.

[19]   *Supra*, Art. 40 para. 3.

[20]   *Capelloni*, para. 27.

[21]   *Capelloni*, para. 31.

requirement such as the third one considered in *Capelloni* seems equally incompatible with Art. 40.

It seems clear that Art. 40 further excludes the application of the traditional requirements of **13** protective measures, namely the demonstration that the creditor has a good arguable case[22] and that there is a real risk that the judgment may go unsatisfied.[23]

In principle, Art. 40 should leave untouched domestic rules governing liability for loss **14** caused by a protective measure. Thus, the requirement that the judgment provides an undertaking in damages to compensate innocent third parties for loss caused by a protective measure is not excluded by Art. 40.[24] However, a requirement to provide an undertaking or a security to compensate the judgment debtor in case the protective measure would have been wrongfully granted could be regarded as infringing the right and power of the creditor to obtain the measure, insofar as the right to the measure would exclude that it be wrongfully granted.

Art. 40 affords a right to protective measures in the domestic civil procedure of the requested **15** court. It is not concerned, however, with the jurisdiction of the requested court to grant protective measures. Likewise, it is not concerned with the territorial reach of the requested measure. Art. 40 does not impact the jurisdictional rules of the forum and does not afford a right to an extraterritorial protective measure. Each of these issues remains governed by the otherwise applicable rules of the forum.[25]

Article 41

1. Subject to the provisions of this Section, the procedure for the enforcement of judgments given in another Member State shall be governed by the law of the Member State addressed. A judgment given in a Member State which is enforceable in the Member State addressed shall be enforced there under the same conditions as a judgment given in the Member State addressed.
2. Notwithstanding paragraph 1, the grounds for refusal or of suspension of enforcement under the law of the Member State addressed shall apply in so far as they are not incompatible with the grounds referred to in Article 45.
3. The party seeking the enforcement of a judgment given in another Member State shall not be required to have a postal address in the Member State addressed. Nor shall that party be

---

[22] English CA, *Banco Nacional de Commercio Exterior SNC*, cit., at para. 45. This requirement is met for the sole reason that a judgment ruled in favor of the creditor was rendered.
[23] Cf. *Jenard* Report p. 52, emphasising that the applicant does not have to establish that the case calls for prompt action or that there is any risk in delay. See also Rauscher/*Mankowski*, Art. 47, 12; Geimer/*Schütze*, Art. 47, 18.
[24] English CA, *Banco Nacional de Commercio Exterior SNC*, cit., at para. 32–46.
[25] See English CA, *Banco Nacional de Commercio Exterior SNC v. Empresa de Telecomunicaciones de Cuba SA* [2007] EWCA Civ. 662: an English court may still apply its rule according to which it would be inexpedient to grant a worldwide freezing injunction in a case where the debtor is neither resident in England, nor has assets there.

required to have an authorised representative in the Member State addressed unless such a representative is mandatory irrespective of the nationality or the domicile of the parties.

I. General

1 Just as Art. 39 states, as a general principle, that judgments enforceable in their Member State of origin shall be enforceable in all the EU, Art. 41 relies on the idea that free movement of judgments also requires judgments issued in another Member State to be, in principle, subjected to the same procedure of enforcement as domestic judgments.

In this regard, Art. 41 could be considered as inspired by a *principle of assimilation*[1] under which "a judgment given by the courts of a Member State should be treated as if it had been given in the Member State addressed".[2] Each of the three paragraphs of the Article could be analysed as developing an aspect of that principle.

II. Legislative history

2 One may consider that the source of inspiration for Art. 41 is to be found in Art. 40 of the Brussels I Regulation – with some necessary variations though. Old Art. 40 considered the procedure to be followed to make and assess an application for enforcement – or exequatur procedure. In consideration of the fact that one of the main innovations of the Brussels I*bis* Regulation is to abolish exequatur, Art. 41 adopts logically a different focus and considers the enforcement procedure.

3 Art. 41 relies on the same general principle of conflict of laws as old Art. 40, that procedural questions are governed by the *lex fori*,[3] unless the applicable regime has been harmonised.

III. Commentary

1. Law applicable to the procedure of enforcement

4 Under Art. 41(1), the enforcement procedure is governed by the domestic law of the State of enforcement. Under the Brussels Convention, the European Court of Justice had already the opportunity to make clear that "execution itself [...] continues to be governed by the domestic law of the court in which execution is sought".[4]

---

[1] *Nuyts*, 102 RCDIP (2013), para. 15.

[2] See Recital 26.

[3] See for example *Mayer/Heuzé*, Droit international privé, 11th edn, 2014, para. 514; *Dicey & Morris*, 13th edn, para. 7–002.

[4] See *Deutsche Genossenschaftsbank v. SA Brasserie du Pêcheur*, (Case 148/84) (1985) ECR 1981 para. 18;

As a consequence, when the judgment creditor asks the enforcement court/authority for the   5
seizure of the assets of his debtor on the territory of the Member State addressed, he will have
to do so in compliance with the forms and rules used in that State. Furthermore, if the
judgment to be enforced prescribes a measure which is unknown of the enforcement State,
an adaptation will be necessary along the lines of Art. 54.[5] Assimilation will thus require
adaptation.

2. Grounds for refusal or of suspension of enforcement

Art. 41(2) prescribes that the judgment debtor is entitled to rely on the grounds for refusal   6
and of suspension of enforcement provided for in the domestic law of the Member State
addressed, just as a domestic judgment debtor would. He may thus invoke both the grounds
for refusal laid down in Art. 45 and those provided for in the domestic law of the enforcement State.[6] The purpose of the rule is to recognize that the Regulation only governs the
private international law dimension of the enforcement of the foreign judgment in another
Member State. It only affords rules designed to assess whether the judgment should be
denied enforcement on grounds directly related to its origin and the fact that it was made
by a foreign court. By contrast, the Regulation does not regulate other dimensions of enforcement law, which are not related to the foreign origin of the judgment and would apply
to the enforcement of all domestic judgments.[7] Those specific rules of domestic enforcement
law remain applicable, and, as the case may be, affords grounds for refusing enforcement of
the foreign judgment.

Art. 41(2) provides that the grounds for refusal or of suspension of enforcement under the   7
law of the Member State addressed only apply in so far as they are not incompatible with the
grounds referred to in Article 45. This requirement of compatibility excludes all national
grounds directly related to the origin of the foreign judgment, i.e. national rules of the law of
foreign judgments. Art. 45 must be considered as listing exhaustively the grounds of private
international law available to challenge the enforcement of a foreign judgment. By contrast,
the vast majority of the other grounds available in the domestic law of enforcement of the
Member States will be compatible with Art. 45, because they will not be related to the origin
of the judgment. Such grounds affording the right to resist enforcement under the domestic
law of enforcement of the Member States will include prior voluntary payment of the
judgment, immunity protecting specific goods on account of their professional destination,
dispute over the ownership of the attached asset, violation by the enforcement officer of the
procedural rules he was bound to follow to attach a particular asset, etc … It cannot be

---

comp. with the Report *Jenard* subjecting the procedural aspects of the application for exequatur to the law
   of the enforcement State (*Jenard* Report, p. 49).

[5]   See already *DHL Express France SAS v. Chronopost SA*, (Case C-235/09) (2011) ECR 2801 para. 56: "the
   court seized of the case in that Member State must […] attain the objective pursued by the measure by
   having recourse to the relevant provisions of its national law which are such as to ensure that the
   prohibition originally issued is complied with in an equivalent manner".

[6]   See Recital 30.

[7]   *Nuyts*, 102 RCDIP (2013) 27. It is therefore unconvincing to argue that the Regulation has increased the
   number of grounds available to judgment debtors to resist enforcement (*Beraudo*, J-Cl. Droit International, fasc. 633 (2014) no. 9). The domestic grounds referred to in Art. 41(2) were available before, as
   enforcement was always governed by the domestic law of the State of enforcement (*supra*, Art. 41 note 4).

excluded, however, that certain of these domestic grounds might indirectly impair the effectiveness of the scheme of the Regulation: in such a case, they might be found to be incompatible with Art. 45 grounds.[8] Under the Brussels Convention, the European Court of Justice has insisted that "the application, for the purposes of the execution of a judgment, of the procedural rules of the State in which enforcement is sought may not impair the effectiveness of the scheme of the convention [now Regulation] as regards enforcement orders".[9]

8   Art. 41 does not impose that all grounds (whether under Art. 45 or domestic law) be available in the same procedure before the same court.[10] It will therefore be open to Member States either to establish separate procedures for the purpose of allowing judgment debtors to resist enforcement on each series of grounds, or to establish one single procedure for both.[11] As the verification of the existence of the grounds referred to in Art. 45 is postponed to the enforcement stage, some Member States might be tempted to grant jurisdiction in this regard to the court which has jurisdiction to entertain challenges to enforcement under domestic law.

3. Postal address and authorized representative in the Member State addressed

9   Both the Brussels Convention[12] and the Brussels I Regulation[13] required that the party seeking enforcement "give an address for service of process within the area of jurisdiction of the court applied to. However, if the law of the Member State in which enforcement is sought [would] not provide for the furnishing of such an address, the applicant [had to] appoint a representative ad litem". The European Court of Justice ruled that the purpose of this provision was to "enable the party against whom enforcement has been ordered to lodge an appeal under the Convention without having to embark on formalities outside the confines of his home jurisdiction".[14]

10   Art. 41(3) abolishes the requirement of either providing a postal address or appointing a local authorized representative in the Member State of enforcement. In so far as they impacted only parties based outside of the State of enforcement, those requirements were barely compatible with the objective of achieving a single area of justice in the European Union.

11   Art. 41(3) also prevails on any contrary national rules which might require that foreign litigants give a local postal address or hire a local representative. Such rules, in so far as they would only apply to foreign nationals or domiciliaries, would constitute discriminations on the basis of nationality or domicile. However, if they were not solely applicable to foreign litigants but rather to all litigants before the relevant court, they would not raise the same issue and would thus be left untouched. Art. 41(3) provides expressly so for authorized representative, which can be required if the rule applies without discriminating against

---

8   *Nuyts*, 102 RCDIP (2013), para. 16.

9   See *Horst Ludwig Martin Hoffmann v. Adelheid Krieg*, (Case 145/86) (1988) ECR 645, para. 29.

10   See however Recital 26.

11   *Gascon-Inchausti*, in: Guinchard, Le nouveau Règlement Bruxelles *Ibis* (2014) 243.

12   See Art. 33, 2nd paragraph.

13   See Art. 40(2).

14   *Fernand Carron v. Federal Republic of Germany*, (Case 198/85) (1986) ECR 2437, 2444 para. 8.

foreign nationals or domiciliaries. No such exception is provided for the provision of a local postal address, as it necessarily targets foreign based litigants only.

Another way to present and analyse Art. 41(3) could be to consider it as an expression of the **12** consequences *ratione personae* of the abovementioned principle of assimilation. As an expression of the free movement of judgments within the EU, the principle of assimilation would imply not only to subject foreign judgments but also foreign litigants to the same procedure of enforcement as their domestic counterparts. To this extent, one may thus argue that this provision makes the parallel between the concepts and challenges of 'internal market' and 'area of freedom, security and justice' more patent.

Article 42

1. For the purposes of enforcement in a Member State of a judgment given in another Member State, the applicant shall provide the competent enforcement authority with:
   (a) a copy of the judgment which satisfies the conditions necessary to establish its authenticity; and
   (b) the certificate issued pursuant to Article 53, certifying that the judgment is enforceable and containing an extract of the judgment as well as, where appropriate, relevant information on the recoverable costs of the proceedings and the calculation of interest.
2. For the purposes of enforcement in a Member State of a judgment given in another Member State ordering a provisional, including a protective, measure, the applicant shall provide the competent enforcement authority with:
   (a) a copy of the judgment which satisfies the conditions necessary to establish its authenticity;
   (b) the certificate issued pursuant to Article 53, containing a description of the measure and certifying that:
      (i) the court has jurisdiction as to the substance of the matter;
      (ii) the judgment is enforceable in the Member State of origin; and
   (c) where the measure was ordered without the defendant being summoned to appear, proof of service of the judgment.
3. The competent enforcement authority may, where necessary, require the applicant to provide, in accordance with Article 57, a translation or a transliteration of the contents of the certificate.
4. The competent enforcement authority may require the applicant to provide a translation of the judgment only if it is unable to proceed without such a translation.

I. General

1　The general purpose of Art. 42 is to establish the conditions of enforcement of judgments – be they judgements held on the merits or ordering provisional measures. These conditions aim at ensuring that the enforcement authority of the Member State addressed is sufficiently informed to take the relevant steps regarding the enforcement requested by the judgment creditor.

II. Enforcement of judgments on the merits

2　Art. 42(1) requires the judgment creditor to provide two documents: (a) a copy of the judgment which satisfies the conditions necessary to establish its authenticity, and (b) a certificate issued in conformity with Art. 53 by the court of origin of the judgment.

1. Authentic copy of the judgment

3　Art. 42(1)(a) requires the judgment creditor to provide the competent enforcement authority of the Member State addressed with a copy of the foreign judgment which satisfies the conditions necessary to establish its authenticity. The authenticity of the copy must be ascertained according to the national law of the court which issued the judgment.[1] A mere copy, whether by hand, typewriter or photocopier, should not suffice. The authentic copy need not stay in possession of the enforcement authority[2] which should return it to the applicant.[3]

4　Art. 47(3) subpara. 2 provides that, in the case of an application for refusal of enforcement being submitted by a judgement-debtor to the competent court, the court may "dispense with the production of the [copy of the judgement] if it already possesses [it] or if it considers it unreasonable to require the applicant to provide [it]". Art. 42(1)(a) does not grant any similar discretion to the competent enforcement authority. The main rationale for such difference is that assessing whether it would be unreasonable to require the production of a document is a judicial task which should not be entrusted to an enforcement authority. It has also been pointed out that unlike a decision of a court pursuant to Art. 47(3),[4] the decision of the enforcement authority is not adversarial.[5]

5　As a matter of practice, nothing prevents enforcement authorities from conceding time to the applicant to produce the requested copy of the judgment as long as enforcement is thereby delayed.

---

[1]　Report *Jenard*, p. 55; *Vekas* in: Magnus/Mankowski, Brussels I Regulation, 2011, Art. 53, 1.

[2]　See, under the Brussels Convention, BGHZ 75, 167, 179 = NJW 1980, 527 (copy handed to a court).

[3]　*Vekas*, in: Magnus/Mankowski, Brussels I Regulation, 2011, Art. 53, 1.

[4]　See *Beraudo* J.Cl. Droit International, Fasc. 633, 194.

[5]　By contrast, the argument that an application for refusal of enforcement under Art. 47(3) would typically imply that, at a previous point in time, the judgment creditor has submitted an application for enforcement to the relevant enforcement authority and has provided an authentic copy of the judgment to be enforced is unconvincing, as the two relevant authorities would not be the same.

2. Certificate concerning the judgment to be enforced

The second document the judgment debtor is asked to provide to the enforcement authority **6** is a certificate issued pursuant to Art. 53. The certificate shall provide the enforceability status of the judgment to be enforced. It shall also include an extract of the judgment and, if need be, relevant information on recoverable procedural costs and calculation of interest. The form of the certificate aims at enabling domestic enforcement authorities to take rapid but informed decisions, by providing them with the information they may need, in a standardised form based on a common grid, whatever the Member States of origin and of enforcement and whatever the language used.

As compared to the Brussels I certificate, the Brussels I*bis* certificate is more detailed, **7** especially about the content of the judgement. Its formulation builds on the experience accumulated through the application of the Brussels I Regulation. A drawback of this evolution is however that the task of filling the form will have become more demanding and potentially complex for the court of origin of the judgment.[6] Art. 55(1) of the Brussels I Regulation provided that the certificate could be substituted, and that the competent court/ authority could use their discretion to accept other documents, or even dispense with the submission of a certificate if they already had sufficient evidence. This discretion has not been granted to the enforcement authority under the Brussels I*bis* Regulation. The rationale is the same as for the decision not to grant discretion to dispense with the production of an authentic copy of the judgment.[7]

III. Provisional, including protective, measures

1. Documents to be provided to enforcement authorities

As for other judgments, the applicant seeking to enforce a judgment ordering a provisional **8** or a protective measure must provide the enforcement authority with a copy of the judgment which satisfies the conditions necessary to establish its authenticity and a certificate issued pursuant to Art. 53.

More specifically, Art. 42(2)(b) provides that the Art. 53 certificate should contain a de- **9** scription of the provisional or protective measure. The purpose is to assist the enforcement officer in his assessment of the effects that the foreign measure produces in the legal order of origin. Pursuant to Art. 54, the foreign measure should be enforced through the closest equivalent existing in the law of the Member State addressed. The description of the measure should therefore focus on its effects under its law of origin.

2. Additional requirements for the enforcement of provisional, including protective, measures

Art. 42(2) provides for two special requirements for the enforcement of provisional, includ- **10** ing protective, measures. Art. 42(2) (b)(ii) also repeats the requirement that the judgment

---

6   See *Béraudo*, no. 185; *Schramm*, Yb. PIL 15 (2013/2014), p. 157.
7   *Supra*, Art. 42 note 4.

ordering such measures be enforceable in the Member State of origin, which also applies to other judgments.[8]

11   The two special requirements are provided by Art. 42(2)(b)(i) and (c), which mandate that the applicant seeking to enforce a foreign judgment ordering a provisional, including a protective, measure, provides a certificate certifying that the foreign court had jurisdiction as to the substance of the matter and, where the measure was ordered without the defendant being summoned to appear, proof of service of the judgment. Recital 33 of the Preamble to the Regulation explains that non compliance with the two requirements of Art. 42 will result in their effect being confined to the territory of the Member State of origin "under this Regulation" and "should not preclude the recognition and the enforcement of such measures under national law." Provisional measures which do not comply with the two requirements may thus be recognised or enforced under the national rules of private international law of the requested Member State. As the Regulation does not require the court ordering provisional measures to comply with the requirements of Art. 42, it can be concluded that those requirements are no ground for denying recognition or enforcement of foreign provisional measures, but rather conditions defining the scope of application of the European law of foreign judgments (Chapter III of the Regulation).

12   Contrary to the grounds of Art. 45, the judicial procedure established by Art. 46 is unavailable for sanctioning non compliance with the requirements of Art. 42. Art. 42 suggests that it is the competent enforcement authority which is entrusted with the power to refuse to enforce foreign provisional measures failing to comply with the requirements of Art. 42. The decision of the competent enforcement authority will be challengeable under national judicial procedures.[9]

13   Art. 42 is solely concerned with enforcement. Furthermore, none of the requirements of Art. 42 is listed among the grounds for denying recognition of Art. 45. A systematic interpretation of these provisions should lead to the conclusion that the requirements of Art. 42 are only relevant for enforcement purposes, and do not impact recognition. However, Recital 33 of the Preamble to the Regulation explains that the two requirements of Art. 42 control both recognition and enforcement, and more generally the "effect" of foreign provisional measures. There is no doubt that the application of the same requirements to recognition and enforcement would be more sensible, but the language of the Regulation does not support this conclusion.

3. Jurisdiction of the foreign court as to the substance of the matter

14   The origin of the requirement that the foreign court has jurisdiction as to the substance of the matter lies in the *van Uden* judgment of the European Court of Justice.[10] In *van Uden*, the Court ruled that the granting of provisional or protective measures on the basis of Article 24

---

8   *Supra*, Art. 39 note 8 (*Cuniberti/Rueda*).

9   In France, for instance, a special court (*juge de l'exécution*) has jurisdiction over disputes arising out of the carrying out of enforcement or protective measures: see Art. L213-6 of the French Code of judicial organization.

10   *van Uden Maritime BV, trading as van Uden Africa Line v. Kommanditgesellschaft in Firma Deco-Line and Another* (Case C-391/95), (1998) ECR p. I-07091.

of the Brussels Convention (now Art. 35 of the Regulation) was "conditional on, inter alia, the existence of a real connecting link between the subject-matter of the measures sought and the territorial jurisdiction of the Contracting State of the court before which those measures are sought".[11] By contrast, the Court ruled, "the court having jurisdiction as to the substance of a case under one of the heads of jurisdiction laid down in the Convention [now Regulation] also has jurisdiction to order provisional or protective measures, without that jurisdiction being subject to any further conditions, such as [the existence of a real connecting link]".[12] While *van Uden* was concerned with the jurisdiction to grant provisional and protective measures, the Court ruled in *Mietz* that the limitation on the jurisdiction of Art. 24 (now Art. 35) courts ought to be verified by courts of other Member States requested to enforce provisional measures.[13]

The meaning of the requirement of the existence of a real connecting link between the   **15** subject-matter of the measures sought and the territorial jurisdiction of the requested court raised a number of issues of interpretation. The first was whether the relevant link could be other than assets located in the relevant territory, in particular for measures the subject-matter of which was not directly specific assets.[14] With respect to an interim payment order, the Court had explained that the measure ought to relate "only to specific assets of the defendant located or to be located within the confines of the territorial jurisdiction of the court to which application is made".[15] This suggested that the link with the relevant territory should be assets even for measures with a different subject-matter.[16] The French supreme court endorsed such interpretation for a decision appointing a judicial expert.[17] Others writers, however, insisted that the link could be of a different nature. In the United Kingdom, where freezing orders act *in personam*, it was argued that the connecting link could also be the person of the debtor.[18] The second issue of interpretation was whether the requirement, in particular if understood as relating to assets only, ought to be interpreted as preventing any enforcement of such measures in other Member States. The issue was conceptually different from the first,[19] but a number of scholars simply deduced from the territorial requirement laid down by *van Uden* and *Mietz* that measures ordered on the basis of then Art. 24 (now Art. 35) ought to be considered as incapable of being enforced in other Member States.[20]

By requiring that foreign provisional, including protective, measures be ordered by a court   **16** having jurisdiction as to the substance of the matter and thus excluding measures ordered on the basis of Art. 35, Art. 42(2)(b)(i) endorses the most far-reaching interpretation of the case law of the European Court of Justice. As the rule is deduced from the *van Uden/Mietz*

---

[11]   At para. 40.

[12]   At para. 22.

[13]   See *Mietz*, at para. 56.

[14]   *Gaudemet-Tallon*, no 308-2.

[15]   See *van Uden*, at para. 48; *Mietz*, at para. 53.

[16]   See e.g. *Normand*, RCDIP 88 (1999), 340. In certain languages (French for instance), confusion arose out of the use of the word "*real*", which also means "*in rem*".

[17]   See Cass. RCDIP 91 (2002), 371 with note *Muir Watt*.

[18]   *Dicey/Morris/Collins*, 14th ed., no 8-031; *Briggs/Rees*, 5th ed., no 6.10.

[19]   *Dickinson*, JPIL 6 (2010) 519.

[20]   See *Mayer/Heuzé* (9th ed.) no 354; *Tsikrikas/Carpaneto*, 2012, Art. 31 no 32.

requirement of a real connecting link, it is submitted that Art. 42(2)(b)(i) replaces that requirement which becomes, as such, obsolete under the Brussels I*bis* Regulation.

17 Art. 42(2)(b)(i) does not specify the basis for the jurisdiction on the merits of the foreign court. However, Art. 2(a) explains that for recognition and enforcement purposes, the concept of a judgment includes provisional, including protective, measures ordered by a court or a tribunal "which by virtue of this Regulation" has jurisdiction as to the substance of the matter. The origin of this limitation is to be found in the *van Uden* decision,[21] and it seems clear that it implicitly qualifies Art. 42(2)(b)(i).[22] As a result, a court of a Member State having jurisdiction on the merits on the basis of a national jurisdictional ground (for instance, because the defendant would be domiciled in a third State) would appear not to fulfil the requirement of Art. 42(2)(b)(i). This is unfortunate, as 1) the Regulation might still govern the enforcement of the resulting judgments, both on the merits and ordering provisional measures, 2) no court might have jurisdiction on the merits under the Regulation, and 3) Art. 35 might not apply either, and thus might not limit in any way its jurisdiction to grant provisional measures. Art. 42(2)(b)(i) would thus prevent recognition and enforcement of any provisional measure in the European Union, even if granted by the court having jurisdiction on the merits.

18 Where the Regulation will grant jurisdiction on the merits of the case to several courts in the European Union (for instance in contractual or tort matters), the issue will arise as to whether only one court should ultimately be considered as having jurisdiction for the purpose of Art. 42(2)(b)(i). There is no doubt that only one court will eventually decide the merits of the case. However, it does not necessarily follow that only one court should grant provisional measures. It has been argued that the goal of the European lawmaker was to restrict the number of courts having the power to grant extraterritorial measures and to avoid conflicts of judgments.[23] There is more support for the view, however, that the goal was to avoid that courts which did not have jurisdiction on the merits would be allowed to circumvent the jurisdictional rules of the Regulation.[24] This is the reason why efforts were made to limit the scope of Art. 35, which gives power to grant potentially far reaching measures to courts which do not have jurisdiction under the Regulation. The same risk does not exist with courts having jurisdiction under the Regulation. It is therefore submitted that any court designated by the Regulation as having jurisdiction on the merits should be considered as such for the purpose of Art. 42(2)(b)(i) irrespective of the court which will eventually decide the dispute on the merits. Thus, when a party applied for interim relief to a court having jurisdiction on the merits, but which had not been seized in this capacity, seizing another court on the merits does not result in the first court losing its power to grant extraterritorial measures (or having to vary its order to make it territorial). Likewise, while the *lis pendens* rule may prevent a court from exercising its jurisdiction on the merits because another court was seized first, it should not prevent any of the parties from seeking interim relief from any court having jurisdiction on the merits (even if incapable of exercising it). The only limit to the power of any court having jurisdiction on the merits to grant extra-

---

[21] *Supra*, para. 14.

[22] *Nuyts*, 102 RCDIP (2013), 38.

[23] *Nuyts*, 102 RCDIP (2013), 39.

[24] See *van Uden*, para. 46; *Mietz*, para. 47.

territorial interim relief should be the operation of doctrines aiming at avoiding the issuance of conflicting provisional measures.[25]

4. Proof of service of the judgment for ex parte measures

The origin of the requirement that measures ordered without the defendant being sum- **19** moned to appear be served before enforcement in another Member State lies in the *Deni-lauler* judgment of the European Court of Justice.[26] In *Denilauler*, the Court ruled that "judicial decisions authorizing provisional or protective measures, which are delivered without the party against which they are directed having been summoned to appear and which are intended to be enforced without prior service"[27] fall outside of the scope of the part of the Brussels Convention governing recognition and enforcement of foreign judgments (Title III) and may not benefit from the simplified enforcement procedure of the Convention (although they may be enforced under national law). In *Hengst Import*,[28] the Court made clear that the exclusion only concerned *ex parte* judgments, the enforcement of which was sought before service was made on the defendant. Where an *inter partes* hearing could have been held in the State of origin before enforcement because the defendant was served, irrespective of whether the latter availed himself of this possibility, the judgment falls outside of the *Denilauler* exception and thus within the scope of the Brussels Convention.[29]

In its 2010 Proposal for a Brussels I Regulation Recast, the European Commission advocated **20** extending the enforcement regime of the Brussels Regulation to provisional and protective measures granted *ex parte*, and replacing prior service by a right of the defendant to challenge the measure subsequently.[30] It has been argued[31] that the shift from prior service to the verification of the existence of an effective opportunity to be heard had already occurred under the Brussels I Regulation.[32] 42(2)(c) maintains the *Denilauler* exception and codifies it.[33]

A way to bypass Art. 42(2)(c) is to proceed in two steps. A first judgment ordering a **21** protective measure with immediate effect is rendered, with no particular hope of enforcing it in another Member State. The defendant is then served not only with the first judgment, but also with a document summoning him to appear in a hearing aiming at confirming it. A second judgment confirming the first is then made which, taken in isolation from the first, meets the *Denilauler* requirement. A number of English freezing orders issued after such an *inter partes* hearing have been enforced in other Member States.[34] Some English scholars

---

25 For instance, the *lis pendens* or the *res judicata* doctrines. For the application of the *res judicata* doctrine to a provisional attachment, see Cass Clunet (2011) 631 with note *Cuniberti*, IPRax (2012), 88 with note *Schlosser*.

26 B. *Denilauler v. SNC Couchert Frères*, (Case 125/79) (1980) ECR 1553.

27 *Denilauler*, at para. 18.

28 *Hengst Import BV v. A.M. Campese*, (Case 474/93) (1995) ECR I-2113.

29 *Hengst Import*, at para. 14.

30 *Proposal*, Art. 2(a).

31 *Briggs/Rees*, 5th ed., no 6.21.

32 M. *Apostolides v. D.C. and L.E. Orams*, (Case 420/07) (2009) ECR I-3571, at paras. 75–78.

33 *van Drooghenbroeck/de Boe*, in: Guinchard, Le nouveau Règlement Bruxelles I*bis* (2014) 200.

34 See, e.g., Cass RCDIP (2004) 815 with note *Muir Watt*, Clunet (2005) 112 with note *Cuniberti*.

---

argued that the second step of the procedure cured the order from its initial defect[35] as a consequence of the shift from prior service to a right of the defendant to challenge the judgment operated by the Brussels I Regulation.[36] If this shift was ever relevant in the context of provisional, including protective measures, it has been cancelled by Art. 42(2)(c).

22 It has been argued that the requirement of prior service does not apply to protective measures carried out pursuant to Art. 40.[37] This is certainly the case for measures carried out locally without court involvement, as they are not judicial and may not be enforced under the Regulation. However, it is hard to see why protective measures granted by a court under Art. 40[38] would not fall within the scope of Art. 42 should their enforcement be sought in another Member State.

IV. Translation

23 One of the essential purposes for the establishment of a certificate was the use of a form common to all Member States. The common form being available in all official languages of the European Union, it should enable authorities in the Member State addressed to rely on it without translation in most instances, in particular for money judgments. There is thus no obligation to provide the competent enforcement authority with a translation.

24 However, pursuant to Art. 42(3), enforcement authorities are entitled to request a translation or a transliteration of the contents of the certificate. This will clearly be useful for judgments which do not merely order the payment of a sum of money. It is to be hoped that enforcement authorities will not systematically request such translation. Given that translations are in principle not necessary, it would be perfectly acceptable, and indeed advisable, to admit partial translation, which would only aim at providing the enforcement authority with the information it needs.

25 Art. 42(3) expressly provides that such request shall be made "in accordance with Art. 57". As a consequence, such translation or transliteration shall be into the official language or one of the official languages of the Member State concerned,[39] i.e. the Member State of enforcement. If there are several official languages in that Member state,[40] or if the Member State of enforcement has indicated that it would accept other "languages of the institutions of the Union",[41] the translation may also be in any of these languages. The applicant is entitled to choose among the official or accepted languages, which amounts to say that the enforcement authority may not request a translation if the certificate is provided in any of these languages.

26 Finally, Art. 42(4) makes clear that a translation of the judgment should only be requested in exceptional cases, where the certificate does not suffice to enable the enforcement authority

---

[35] *Briggs/Rees*, 5th ed., no 6.21.

[36] *M. Apostolides v. D.C. and L.E. Orams*, (Case 420/07) (2009) ECR I-3571, at paras. 75–78.

[37] *Nuyts*, 102 RCDIP (2013), 44; *vanDrooghenbroeck/deBoe*, in: Guinchard, Le nouveau Règlement Bruxelles *Ibis* (2014) 202.

[38] And thus decisions in the meaning of Art. 2(a)

[39] Art. 57(1).

[40] Art. 57(1).

[41] Art. 57(2).

to proceed. Although Art. 42(4) does not specifically refer to Art. 57, Art. 57 is of general application. The translation may thus only be requested in an official language of the state addressed.[42] Even more than for certificates, partial translations limited to issues relevant for enforcement purposes should be considered as perfectly admissible and indeed advisable.

Neither Art. 42(3) or (4), nor Art. 57 addresses the issue of the costs of any requested **27** translation. There is no doubt that the translation will have to be provided by the applicant seeking enforcement. This does not necessarily mean, however, that he will eventually bear the burden of the translation costs. Pursuant to Art. 41(1), the issue is to be governed by the national law of the place of enforcement which might provide a mechanism for shifting the burden on the judgment debtor.[43]

Article 43

1. Where enforcement is sought of a judgment given in another Member State, the certificate issued pursuant to Article 53 shall be served on the person against whom the enforcement is sought prior to the first enforcement measure. The certificate shall be accompanied by the judgment, if not already served on that person.
2. Where the person against whom enforcement is sought is domiciled in a Member State other than the Member State of origin, he may request a translation of the judgment in order to contest the enforcement if the judgment is not written in or accompanied by a translation into either of the following languages:
    (a) a language which he understands; or
    (b) the official language of the Member State in which he is domiciled or, where there are several official languages in that Member State, the official language or one of the official languages of the place where he is domiciled.
    Where a translation of the judgment is requested under the first subparagraph, no measures of enforcement may be taken other than protective measures until that translation has been provided to the person against whom enforcement is sought.
    This paragraph shall not apply if the judgment has already been served on the person against whom enforcement is sought in one of the languages referred to in the first subparagraph or is accompanied by a translation into one of those languages.
3. This Article shall not apply to the enforcement of a protective measure in a judgment or where the person seeking enforcement proceeds to protective measures in accordance with Article 40.

I. Service of the certificate

Art. 43(1) requires that the certificate issued pursuant to Art. 53 be served on the debtor **1** prior to the first enforcement measure. Recital 32 of the Preamble explains that the purpose is to inform the debtor that enforcement of the judgment will be sought in another Member State. It is unclear why the debtor should be specifically informed of this. Indeed, if such

---

[42] But not in another language that the Member State would have indicated to accept, as Art. 57(2) only applies to the certificate.

[43] Such as Art. 695 and 704, French Code of Civil Procedure; § 91, German ZPO.

Gilles Cuniberti/Isabelle Rueda

information was necessary, it should be more specific and mention in which other Member State enforcement will be sought, which the Art. 53 certificate does not say.

2   A more convincing rationale for the obligation to serve the certificate would be that it is a fundamental procedural right for any party to be informed of the issuance of any judicial document in proceedings to which he is a party. This is even more the case where the document can be issued *ex parte*, as Art. 53 suggests the certificate can be.[1]

3   While a rationale for the service of the certificate can be found, it remains that this step only applies to cross-border enforcement, and that it is thus an additional, intermediate measure necessary for the enforcement of foreign judgments. The purpose of the abolition of exequatur was precisely to abolish all of them, and Recital 26 of the Preamble explains that foreign judgments ought to be treated as local judgments. Art. 43(1) treats them differently.

4   As the certificate does not specifically mention the jurisdiction where enforcement will be sought, it is only necessary to serve it once on the debtor, prior to the first enforcement measure in another Member State. It is not necessary to serve it again if enforcement is sought in a second foreign Member State.

5   Art. 43(1) is silent as to the authority which is meant to serve the certificate. This will arguably be for the national law of the court issuing the certificate to decide whether this step should be completed by the judgment creditor or the issuing court.[2]

6   Art. 43(3) excludes the obligation to serve the certificate for judgments incorporating a protective measure. The purpose might be to allow the judgment creditor to surprise the debtor and prevent the latter from disposing of his assets before the enforcement of the measure in another Member State. While this concern is to be praised, it must be recalled that *ex parte* provisional, including protective measures, are, in principle, denied enforcement under the Regulation.[3] Judgment creditors may only seek enforcement of protective measures in other Member States after serving them first on the judgment debtor.[4]

II. Translation

7   The judgment debtor may request a translation of the judgment in order to contest its enforcement if the judgment is not written, or accompanied with a translation, in either 1) a language that the debtor understands or 2) in the official language of the Member State where he is domiciled. In cases where the judgment will have been served in one of these languages at an earlier stage of the proceedings,[5] the last paragraph of Art. 43(2) expressly provides that it is not necessary to do it again for the purpose of Art. 43.

8   Although the Regulation does not provide so expressly, it seems clear that the judgment

---

[1]   *Gascon-Inchausti*, in: Guinchard, Le nouveau Règlement Bruxelles I*bis* (2014) 227.

[2]   *Gascon-Inchausti*, in: Guinchard, Le nouveau Règlement Bruxelles I*bis* (2014) 232.

[3]   But not under national law: *supra* Art. 42 note 11 (*Cuniberti/Rueda*).

[4]   See Art. 42(2)(c).

[5]   For instance, because service of the judgment would be the starting point of the time period to lodge an appeal, as in France (Art. 528 of the French Code of Civil Procedure).

debtor is entitled, and thus may request, a translation of the entirety of the judgment. As Art. 57(3) provides that "any translation made under this Regulation shall be done by a person qualified to do translations in one of the Member States", it also seems clear that he may demand that the author of the translation be one such person.

However, as Art. 43(2) does not apply if service was already completed in any of the au- **9** thorised languages, it must be concluded that it is for the judgment creditor to choose the language of translation of the judgment in cases where there is an option.[6]

Art. 43(2) limits the right to request a translation to cases where the judgment debtor is **10** domiciled in a Member State other than the Member State of origin. This is only logical, as the judgment debtor would be deemed to understand the language of the judgment other- wise. Art. 43(2) may also be understood as limiting the benefit of the right to judgment debtors domiciled in the European Union.[7]

The right of a party to be served in either of these languages is found in most recent **11** regulations, in particular Regulation 1393/2007 on the service in the Member States of judicial and extrajudicial documents in civil or commercial matters.[8] The case law of the Court of Justice of the European Union on Regulation 1393/2007 is thus presumably re- levant to interpret Art. 43(2).

Art. 43(2) does not address the issue of the costs of the requested translation. As the transla- **12** tion is presented as a right of the judgment debtor, it could be concluded that it is for the judgment creditor to bear the costs of providing it. Alternatively, and more convincingly, the Regulation could be considered as silent on the issue and thus refer to national law[9] (pur- suant to Art. 41(1)).

The request for a translation in an appropriate language suspends the right of the judgment **13** creditor to enforce the judgment, until provision of such translation. In the meantime, however, he may proceed to protective measures.

Article 44

1. In the event of an application for refusal of enforcement of a judgment pursuant to Subsec- tion 2 of Section 3, the court in the Member State addressed may, on the application of the person against whom enforcement is sought:
   (a) limit the enforcement proceedings to protective measures;
   (b) make enforcement conditional on the provision of such security as it shall determine; or
   (c) suspend, either wholly or in part, the enforcement proceedings.
2. The competent authority in the Member State addressed shall, on the application of the person against whom enforcement is sought, suspend the enforcement proceedings where the enforceability of the judgment is suspended in the Member State of origin.

---

6   *Gascon-Inchausti*, in: Guinchard, Le nouveau Règlement Bruxelles I*bis* (2014) 235.
7   *Gascon-Inchausti*, in: Guinchard, Le nouveau Règlement Bruxelles I*bis* (2014) 235.
8   See Art. 8.
9   Including Art. 11 of the Service Regulation.

I. General

1 One of the objectives of the abolition of exequatur was to suppress the delay in enforcement that it entailed.[1] This delay was essentially the consequence of the need for obtaining a declaration of enforceability in the Member State addressed, and of the rule according to which enforcement of the foreign judgment was suspended during the time specified for an appeal against the declaration of enforceability and until such appeal had been determined.[2] The direct enforceability of foreign judgments established by Art. 39 has resulted in the suppression of the declaration of enforceability and, obviously, of the appeal procedure against it. Judgments rendered in civil and commercial matters are immediately enforceable throughout the European Union, where they should be treated as a judgment made by a court of the enforcing State.[3]

2 While the declaration of exequatur has been suppressed, judgment debtors may apply for a refusal of enforcement if one of the grounds of Art. 45 is found to exist.[4] Such application, and more generally the procedure to decide on it, does not suspend the enforceability of the foreign judgment. While the Regulation does not expressly provide so, this conclusion follows from Art. 44(1), which allows the judgment debtor to apply for a limitation or a suspension of the enforcement of the judgment only under certain conditions.[5]

II. Right to seek suspension or limitation of enforcement

3 Under Art. 44(1), the judgment debtor is entitled to apply for a limitation or a suspension of the enforcement of the judgment before a court of the enforcing State. Art. 44(1) only provides for such right in the event of an application for refusal of enforcement as established by the Regulation for verifying if one of the grounds of Art. 45 exists. The right of the judgment debtor must therefore be considered as existing only if such application is pending.

4 Art. 44(1) further provides that the application for a limitation or suspension of enforcement is to be made before "the" court in the Member State addressed which, in this context, must be understood as the court before which the application for refusal of enforcement was made.[6] This court is thus to be considered as the only one having jurisdiction to entertain an application under Art. 44(1).

---

[1]   See Preamble, Recital 26.
[2]   Brussels I Regulation, Art. 47(3).
[3]   See Preamble, Recital 26.
[4]   See Art. 46.
[5]   *Nuyts*, 102 RCDIP (2013), 32.
[6]   See Art. 47(1).

Art. 44(1) give little guidance as to the conditions at which the competent court may decide **5** to limit or suspend enforcement. The use of the term "may" certainly indicates that the remedy sought is not as of right, and that the court has at least some discretion to grant it. The absence of further guidance given by Art. 44(1) could be interpreted in three different was. A first possible interpretation could be considered that Art. 44(1) simply gives unlimited discretion to the court to grant the remedy. Such interpretation would be damaging for the uniform application of the Regulation. It would also likely jeopardize the purpose of the adoption of the new rule, as it could be expected that many courts would be influenced by the old rule (automatic suspension) and easily grant the remedy. A second possible interpretation could be that national law would apply. The court would apply or adapt its domestic rules designed to address the closest issue under national civil procedure, for instance its rules on the suspension of the enforceability of judgments under appeal. As the procedure to limit or suspend enforcement of the foreign judgment is largely merged with the procedure of refusal of enforcement,[7] support for this interpretation could be found in Art. 47(2) which provides that the "procedure for refusal of enforcement shall, in so far as it is not covered by this Regulation, be governed by the law of the Member State addressed".

Finally, an autonomous interpretation could be offered by the Court of Justice of the Euro- **6** pean Court, if and when asked. The basis for such interpretation would be in the existence of Art. 44(1), which supports the view that this aspect of the procedure for refusal of enforcement is covered by the Regulation. It is submitted that one of the rationales of the abolition of exequatur being to suppress delays in enforcement,[8] such autonomous interpretation should be restrictive and limit the discretion of courts to grant such remedies. The test should not be based on an early assessment of the chances of the applicant to succeed in the procedure for refusal of enforcement,[9] but rather on the demonstration of a risk to suffer special harm if he were to pay immediately, for instance because it would jeopardize his financial situation.[10]

III. Remedies available

Under the Brussels Convention and the Brussels I Regulation, the judgment debtor challen- **7** ging the enforcement of a foreign judgment was protected by a mandatory remedy: the suspension of the enforceability of the judgment in the Member State addressed during the appeal procedure. Some flexibility only existed in the special case scenario of a judgment against which an appeal had been lodged in the State of origin.[11] Art. 44(1) lists three remedies that the court entertaining the application for refusal of enforcement may grant to the applicant. It introduces flexibility and grants discretion to the court entertaining the challenge to decide on the appropriate remedy.

---

[7] *Supra*, Art. 44 note 3 and 4 (*Cuniberti/Rueda*).

[8] *Supra*, Art. 44 note 1 (*Cuniberti/Rueda*).

[9] But see *Kessedjian/Gaudemet-Tallon*, RTDE (2013) 453; *Gascon-Inchausti*, in: Guinchard, Le nouveau Règlement Bruxelles I*bis* (2014) 244.

[10] *Cuniberti/Rueda*, RabelsZ (2011) 315.

[11] *Infra*, para. 10.

1. Suspension of enforceability and limitation to protective measures

8 Art. 44(1)(a) and (c) share a common rationale: to avoid enforcement and to allow only protective measures. The purpose of Art. 44(1)(a) is to limit the future steps that the creditor may take by limiting enforcement proceedings to protective measures. The purpose of Art. 44(1)(c) is to suspend the steps already taken by the creditor by suspending enforcement proceedings already initiated. In both cases, enforcement proceedings are made unavailable, and only protective measures may be sought.

9 The remedies under Art. 44(1)(a) and (c) are flexible. The court need not suspend the enforceability of the entire judgment.[12] It may suspend the enforcement proceedings "in whole or in part".[13] It is unclear whether this flexibility allows the court to suspend enforcement proceedings for certain parts of the judgments, and not for others, or to suspend enforcement proceedings over certain assets, and not over others (even for the same parts of the judgment). It is suggested that the answer will vary depending on the test adopted to exercise the power to suspend or limit enforcement.[14] If the test is based on an assessment of the chances of the application to succeed, such assessment may vary depending on the part of the judgment. If the test is based on the financial consequences of the remedy on the applicant, certain enforcement proceedings might be allowed against certain assets, and not against others.

2. Provision of a security

10 Art. 44(1)(b) allows the court to make enforcement conditional on the provision of such security as it shall determine. Under the Brussels Convention[15] and the Brussels I Regulation,[16] such remedy was only available in limited circumstances. It supplemented the mandatory remedy of the suspension of the enforceability of the foreign judgment when it was not available, i.e. after the end of appeal procedure against the decision of the State of enforcement declaring the foreign judgment enforceable.[17] It could then be necessary to grant a remedy in case an appeal lodged against the judgment was still pending in the State of origin. The court in the Member State addressed could make enforcement conditional on the provision of a security after its decision.[18] Under Art. 44(1), the remedy becomes an alternative to the suspension of the enforceability of the foreign judgment.

11 Contrary to the two other remedies afforded by Art. 44(1), the judgment creditor may proceed to enforce the judgment, but only after providing a security. The purpose of the security is to

---

12 This suggests that the remedies are not the two faces of a single remedy which would be the suspension of the enforceability of the judgment.

13 See Art. 44(1)(c).

14 See Art. 44 note 5–6 (*Cuniberti/Rueda*).

15 See Art. 38, third paragraph.

16 See Art. 46(3).

17 And thus only from the date of this judgment: *Calzaturificio Brennero sas v. Wendel GmbH Schuhproduktion International*, (Case 258/83) (1984) ECR 3971.

18 For cases applying these provisions, see Belgium: Rb. Antwerpen in: Digest I-38 B 4; Denmark: ØLD UfR 1989 A 877; Germany: BGH IPRax 1985, 156 note *Prütting* (at p. 137); BGH IPRspr. 1986 Nr. 189 (affirming OLG Hamm IPRspr. 1985 Nr. 187); OLG Köln in: Digest I-38 B 2; OLG Düsseldorf IPRspr. 1984 Nr. 190; OLG Hamm IPRspr. 1993 Nr. 182; OLG Stuttgart IPRspr. 1997 Nr. 182.

guarantee that, should the application for refusal of enforcement succeed, the judgment debtor could easily cancel the enforcement of the judgment by triggering the security.

Art. 44(1)(b) does not grant the power to order the provision of a security, but to make **12** enforcement conditional upon it. The provision of a security requires active participation of the judgment creditor. While a court confident that it would be obeyed could simply order the provision of such security,[19] a safer way might be to rule that enforcement would be suspended until the creditor provides an appropriate security.

Art. 44(1) does not establish any hierarchy between the three remedies it offers. It could **13** therefore be argued that the court has full discretion to order one or the other.[20] Alternatively, it could be considered that the provision of a security being less intrusive in the right of the creditors, it should be preferred.[21]

IV. Loss of enforceability in Member State of origin

The enforceability of a foreign judgment in the Member State of origin is logically an **14** essential condition for its enforcement in another Member State.[22] Should this condition be lacking or disappear, enforcement proceedings should be suspended, in the Member State of origin as in the rest of the European Union. Art. 44(2) grants the judgment debtor a right to the suspension of enforcement proceedings initiated in another Member State if the enforceability of the judgment is suspended in the Member State of origin. The competent authority for enforcing this right will typically not be a court, but the competent enforcement authority, presumably the same which initiated the proceedings in the first place. The use of the word "shall" suggests that, contrary to the remedies contemplated by Art. 44(1), the remedy afforded by Art. 44(2) is not discretionary, but as of right.

Section 3: Refusal of recognition and enforcement

Subsection 1: Refusal of recognition

Article 45

1. On the application of any interested party, the recognition of a judgment shall be refused:
   (a) if such recognition is manifestly contrary to public policy (ordre public) in the Member State addressed;

---

[19] *Gaudemet-Tallon*, 483.

[20] See, with respect to the option available to courts to either make the enforcement conditional upon provision of a security or stay proceedings under the Brussels Convention and Brussels I Regulation, *Petereit v. Babcock International Holdings Ltd.* (1990) 2 All E. R. 135 (Q.B.D.).

[21] A similar line of reasoning existed under the Brussels Convention and Brussels I Regulation (see previous note): see *Geimer/Schütze* Art. 46 note 3; *Kropholler/von Hein* Art. 46 note 1; *Mankowski*, in: Rauscher Art. 46 note 3; *Pålsson*: in: Magnus/Mankowski, Brussels I Regulation, 2011, Art. 46, 20.

[22] See Art. 39, Art. 42(1)(b).

(b) where the judgment was given in default of appearance, if the defendant was not served with the document which instituted the proceedings or with an equivalent document in sufficient time and in such a way as to enable him to arrange for his defence, unless the defendant failed to commence proceedings to challenge the judgment when it was possible for him to do so;

(c) if the judgment is irreconcilable with a judgment given between the same parties in the Member State addressed;

(d) if the judgment is irreconcilable with an earlier judgment given in another Member State or in a third State involving the same cause of action and between the same parties, provided that the earlier judgment fulfils the conditions necessary for its recognition in the Member State addressed; or

(e) if the judgment conflicts with:

  (i) Sections 3, 4 or 5 of Chapter II where the policyholder, the insured, a beneficiary of the insurance contract, the injured party, the consumer or the employee was the defendant; or

  (ii) Section 6 of Chapter II.

2. In its examination of the grounds of jurisdiction referred to point (e) of paragraph 1, the court to which the application was submitted shall be bound by the findings of fact on which the court of origin based its jurisdiction.

3. Without prejudice to point (e) of paragraph 1, the jurisdiction of the court of origin may not be reviewed. The test of public policy referred to in point (a) of paragraph 1 may not be applied to the rules relating to jurisdiction.

4. The application for refusal of recognition shall be made in accordance with the procedures provided for in Subsection 2 and, where appropriate, Section 4.

Bibliography

Bälz/Marienfeld, Missachtung einer Schiedsklausel als Anerkennungshindernis i.S.v. Art. 34–35 Eu-GVVO und § 328 ZPO?, RIW 2003, 51

Ulrich Becker, Grundrechtsschutz bei der Anerkennung und Vollstreckbarerklärung im europäischen Zivilverfahrensrecht (2004)

Geimer, Nachprüfung der internationalen Zuständigkeit des Urteilsstaates in Versicherungs- und Verbrauchersachen, RIW 1980, 305

Geimer, Die Sonderrolle der Versicherungssachen im Brüssel I-System, in: FS Andreas Heldrich (2005), p. 627

Geimer, Das Anerkennungsregime der neuen Brüssel I-Verordnung (EU) Nr 1215/2012, in: FS Hellwig Torggler (Wien 2013), p. 311

Hartley, The Brussels I Regulation and Arbitration (2014) 63 ICLQ 843

Hess/Pfeiffer, Study: Interpretation of the Public Policy Exception as referred to in EU Instruments of Private International and Procedural Law,

PE 453.189, available at: www.europarl.europa.eu/studies

van Hoek, Erkenning van vonnissen in het privaatrecht: een studie naar de grenzen van de wederijdse erkenning, NIPR 2003, 337

Jafferali, "La règlement Bruxelles I dans la jurisprudence des Cours suprêmes (2010–2012): Allemagne, Belgique, France, Pays-Bas et Royaume-Uni", RDC/TBH 2013, 357, 389–390

Kennett, The Enforcement of Judgments in Europe (2000)

Matthias Koch, Unvereinbare Entscheidungen im Sinne des Art. 27 Nr. 3 und 5 EuGVÜ und ihre Vermeidung (1993)

Xandra Kramer, Abolition of exequatur under the Brussels I Regulation: effecting and protecting rights in the European judicial area, NIPR 2011, 633

Lenenbach, Die Behandlung von Unvereinbarkeiten zwischen rechtskräftigen Zivilurteilen nach deutschem und europäischem Zivilprozessrecht (1997)

Lindacher, Europäisches Zustellungsrecht, ZZP 114 (2001), 179

Lopes Pegna, Il nuovo procedimento per l'esecuzione delle decisioni in materia civile e commercial degli Stati membri della Comunità Europea, Riv. dir. int. 2001, 621

Mankowski, Kann ein Schiedsspruch ein Hindernis für die Anerkennung einer ausländischen Entscheidung sein?, 5 SchiedsVZ (2014), 209

Mansel, Vollstreckung eines französischen Garantieurteils bei gesellschaftsrechtlicher Rechtsnachfolge und andere vollstreckungsrechtliche Fragen des EuGVÜ, IPRax 1995, 362

Marchadier, La suppression de l'exequatur affaiblitelle la protection des droits fondamentaux dans l'espace judiciaire européen?, Eur. Human Rights J. 2013, 348

Merlin, Riconoscimento ed esecutività della decisione straniera nel regolamento "Bruxelles I", Riv. dir. proc. 2001, 433

Micklitz/Rott, Vergemeinschaftung des EuGVÜ in der Verordnung (EG) Nr 44/2001 (II), EuZW 2002, 15

Mosconi, Un confronto tra la disciplina del riconoscimento e dell'esecuzione delle decisioni straniere nei recenti regolamenti comunitari, RDIPP 2001, 548

Münch, Ausländische Tenorierungsgewohnheiten kontra inländische Bestimmtheitsanforderungen, RIW 1989, 18

Marie-Laure Niboyet/de Geouffre de la Pradelle, Droit international privé (4th éd. 2013)

Niboyet, Office du juge et déclenchement du raisonnement conflictuel, in: *Azzi/Boskovic* (ed.), Quel avenir pour la théorie générale des conflits de lois (Brussels 2015) 19

Nuyts/Boularbah, Droit international privé européen (2006–2008), J. dr. eur. 2008, 308

Péroz, La réception des jugements étrangers dans l'ordre juridique français (2005)

Reig Fabado, La ejecución en el Convenio de Bruselas: el problema de Derecho aplicable al carácter ejecutorio de la sentencia, La Ley Unión Europea 29 de diciembre de 1999, 1

Requejo Isidro, Sobre ejecución y exequátur, La Ley Unión Europea 30 de septiembre de 1999, 7

Roccati, Le rôle du juge dans l'espace judiciaire européen (Brussels 2013)

Herbert Roth, Herausbildung von Prinzipien im europäischen Vollstreckungsrecht, IPRax 1989, 14

Herbert Roth, Konkretisierung unbestimmter ausländischer Titel, IPRax 1994, 350

Herbert Roth, Anerkennung von Entscheidungen nach Art. 34 Nr. 2 EuGVVO bei Verweigerung der Annahme des zuzustellenden Schriftstücks (Art. 8 EuZVO), IPRax 2005, 438

Herbert Roth, Systembedingt offene Auslandstitel, IPRax 2006, 22

Sánchez Jiménez, Ejecución de sentencias extranjeras en España: Convenio de Bruselas de 1968 y procedimiento interno (1998)

Peter Schlosser, Die transnationale Bedeutung von Vollstreckbarkeitsnuancierungen, in: FS Kostas Beys (Athen 2003) p. 1471

Peter Schlosser, The Abolition of exequatur proceedings – Including public policy review?, IPRax 2010, 101

Michael Johannes Schmidt, Die Einrede der Schiedsgerichtsbarkeit im Vollstreckbarerklärungsverfahren von EuGVÜ und Lugano-Übereinkommen, in: FG Otto Sandrock (1995), p. 205

Rolf A. Schütze, Die Nachprüfung der internationalen Zuständigkeit und die Vollstreckung gerichtlicher Entscheidungen, RIW 1974, 428

Smyrek, Einheitlicher Rechtsraum – nur in der Theorie?, RIW 2005, 695

Stadler, Die Revision des Brüsseler und des Lugano-Übereinkommens über die gerichtliche Zuständigkeit und die Vollstreckung gerichtlicher Entscheidungen in Zivil- und Handelssachen – Vollstreckbarerklärung und internationale Vollstreckung, in: Peter Gottwald (ed.), Revision des EuGVÜ/Neues Schiedsverfahrensrecht (2000), p. 37

Ansgar Staudinger, Der ordre public-Einwand im Europäischen Zivilverfahrensrecht, EuLF 2004, 273

Wastl, Die Vollstreckung deutscher Titel auf der Grundlage des EuGVÜ in Italien (1990).

Stéphanie Francq

I. Purpose and interpretation

Art. 45 enumerates the main grounds for non-recognition or non-enforcement.[1] It should be   **1**
read in relation with Arts. 64 and 71. The nature of the criteria enumerated in Art. 45 could
be discussed: should they be labelled as regularity conditions or as refusal grounds?[2] They are
usually simply referred to as "grounds for refusing recognition or enforcement".[3] The precise qualification does not matter as long as the purpose and the resulting interpretation of
Art. 45 is clear.

The purpose of Art. 45 and of its predecessors, Art. 27 Brussels Convention and 34 Regu-   **2**
lation Brussels I, derives from the general objectives of chapter III (former title III) dedicated
to recognition and enforcement and more generally from the rationale of the regulation
itself, i.e. facilitating the circulation of judgments. This general ambition is to be traced back
to the Brussels Convention which, according to the wording of Art. 220 EEC Treaty (later
Art. 293 EC Treaty, now deleted from the TFEU), was due to achieve the "simplification of
formalities governing the reciprocal recognition and enforcement of judgments of courts or
tribunals and of arbitration awards".[4] The note sent by the Commission to Member States
inviting them to commence negotiations which resulted in the Brussels Convention already
mentioned the role of such an instrument in the internal market: "a true internal market
between the six States will be achieved only if adequate legal protection can be secured. The
economic life of the Community may be subject to disturbances and difficulties unless it is
possible (…) to ensure the recognition and enforcement of the various rights arising from
the existence of a multiplicity of legal relationships".[5] The idea of a direct link between
economic development, legal security and circulation of judgments, as a support to the
achievement of the internal market, has evolved and is now embodied in the conception
of the European Union as an "area of freedom, security and justice in which the free movement of persons is assured and litigants can assert their rights, enjoying facilities equivalent
to those they enjoy in the courts of their own country".[6] The exact meaning of the "area of
freedom, security and justice" provided for in the now Title V of the third part of Treaty on
the functioning of the European Union (TFEU), in which the legal basis of the Regulation is
to be found, as well as its precise implications for the interpretation of the Regulation, are not
quite clear. But one thing is sure: the circulation of judgments is more than ever seen as a
priority and mutual recognition of decisions has become the guiding principle of cooperation in civil matters.[7] During the revision process of the Brussels I Regulation, as the abolition of the *exequatur* procedure was contemplated, the first project was to delete the

---

[1]   *Stéphanie Francq* wishes to thank Mrs *Marie Dechamps* and Mrs *Julie Mary*, both research assistants at
     the Centre Charles de Visscher pour le droit international et européen, for their valuable research
     assistance for the third edition of this contribution.
[2]   *Gaudemet-Tallon*, p. 396, para. 375.
[3]   For instance, *Layton/Mercer* para. 24.011.
[4]   See as well: Report *Jenard* p. 7, 42 (presenting the free circulation of judgments as "the ultimate objective"
     of the Convention and the adoption of rules of direct jurisdiction as one means for achieving this goal).
[5]   Cited in Report *Jenard*, p. 3.
[6]   Commission Proposal COM (1999) 348 final p. 3, 5.
[7]   As stated in the conclusions of the Tampere European Council, "the principle of mutual recognition (…)
     should become the cornerstone of judicial co-operation in both civil and criminal matters within the
     Union" (pt 33). For direct applications, see for instance: Regulation (EC) No. 805/2004 of the European

possibility of raising any refusal grounds in the host country. This project is further discussed bellow. But even if it was not materialised, the implementation of mutual trust and mutual recognition remain an important point on the EU agenda.[8]

3 Following the favour reserved by the regulation to the circulation of judgments, Art. 45, which brings an exception to this principle, is to be strictly construed.[9] An interpretation by analogy of the terms of Art. 45 is therefore excluded.[10] The refusal grounds are limitative.[11] Two consequences derive from the exhaustive character of Art. 45 with regard to the margin of interpretation left to the national judge. On the one hand, the judge may not use any of the enumerated grounds for controlling an issue which is not mentioned in Art. 45: this would occur for instance, if the national judge was controlling the applicable law under the heading of public policy, or the intervention of a compensation after the issuing of the decision.[12] It can already be stated that all grounds for refusal must be interpreted in the light of the prohibition of review as to the substance (Art. 45 (2)), which implies that the control exercised by the judge of the State addressed will take place within the respect of the findings of facts and law made by the judge of origin. On the other hand, he or she has to respect the limits set by the European Court of Justice (hereafter ECJ) in the exercise of its interpretation function. The ECJ has for instance set the frame within which public policy can be called upon.

4 The limitative enumeration provided for by Art. 45 does not exclude the control of condi-

---

Parliament and of the Council of 21 April 2004 creating a European Enforcement Order for uncontested claims, OJ 2004 L 143/15: Recitals 25 and 29 of the revised Regulation (Brussels Ibis).

[8] Communication from the Commission to the European Parliament, the Council, the European Economic and Social Committee and the Committee of Regions, The EU Justice Agenda for 2020: Strengthening Trust Mobility and Growth within the Union, COM (2014) 144 final, p. 2, 4, 9 (showing how trust has been the foundation of the EU justice system, but still needs to be reinforced in particular in regard of parties' procedural rights).

[9] *Solo Kleinmotoren GmbH v. Emilio Boch*, (Case 414/92) (1994) ECR I-2237 para. 20; *Dieter Krombach v. André Bamberski*, (Case C-7/98) (2000) ECR I-1935, para. 21; *Régie nationale des usines Renault SA v. Maxicar SpA et Orazio Formento*, (Case C-38/98) (2000) ECR I-2973, para. 26; Apostolides, (Case C-420/07) (2009) ECR I-3571, para. 55; *Salzgitter Mannesmann Handel GmbH v. SC Laminoroul SA*, (Case 157/12) ECLI:EU:C:2013:597 para. 39.

[10] *Salzgitter Mannesmann Handel GmBH v. SC Laminoroul SA*, (Case 157/12) ECLI:EU:C:2013:597 para. 39.

[11] Commission Proposal COM (1999) 348 final, p. 22, commenting Art. 41 in which the refusal grounds were to be listed: "This Article determines the *sole* grounds on which a court seized of an appeal may refuse or revoke a declaration of enforceability." See also: *flyLAL-Lithuanian Airlines*, (Case C-302/13) ECLI:EU:C:2014:2319 para.46; *Prism Investments*, (Case C-139/10) [2011] ECR I-9511 para. 33 and the opinion of A-G *Kokott*, delivered on 16 June 2011 in Case 139/10 Prism Investments, [2011] ECR I-9514 para. 53 (excluding means of defence as to the merits to be raised at the recognition or enforcement stage due to the exhaustive nature of the refusal grounds listed in Arts. 34 and 35. In this case, the defendant raised a compensation made after the judgment was delivered by the court in the State of origin); BGH, IX ZB 87/11, para. 3. See also *Rolf Wagner*, IPRax 2012, 326, 329. Comp. in the internal context with, with *Mohamed Aziz v. Caixa d'Estalvis de Catalunya, Tarragona i Manresa (Catalunyacaixa)*, (Case 415/11) ECLI:EU:C:2013:164, para. 64.

[12] *Prism Investments*, (Case 139/10) (2011) ECR I-9511, para. 43.

tions that would be imposed by public international law.[13] Limitations imposed on jurisdiction (to adjudicate or to enforce) with regard to immunities are mainly concerned. Should the immunity of the defendant not have been respected in the court of origin, the resulting judgment would not be entitled to recognition in other Member States, although this ground of refusal is not provided for by Art. 45.[14] Similarly, the enforcement requested against a person who has, after the date of the judgment of origin, acquired an immunity of execution, will be refused.[15] It would indeed be difficult to construe the Regulation as aiming at derogating to Public international law, especially since de ECJ has for long stated that European law is submitted to public international law.[16]

Though very limited in number, the refusal grounds are obligatory. Recognition or enforce- 5 ment must be denied if any of the grounds apply.[17] The judge of the requested State has no discretion in this respect and has to verify the refusal grounds alleged by one of the parties.[18] The existence of the certificate provided by Art. 53 and Annex I Brussels I*bis* Regulation (Art. 54 and Annex V Brussels I Regulation) does not limit the scope of the court's control in the requested State.[19] The judge has to verify in fact whether the defaulting defendant was served with the document instituting the proceedings and whether the service was made in such a way and in sufficient time to enable him to organise for his defence.[20] The requested judge is thus free to verify the accuracy of the facts mentioned in the certificate.[21] The

---

[13] *Geimer/Schütze* Art. 34 notes 6–7; *Kropholler/von Hein* Art. 33 note 5.

[14] Trib Civ. Bruxelles, Reprinted in P. d'Argent, Revue belge de droit international 2007/2, n° 43 et al.: deciding, on the basis of Art. 27 (1) of the Brussels Convention, that it "does not have jurisdiction" for enforcing a Greek judgment condemning Germany to pay damages to Greek nationals in regard to acts perpetrated by German armed forces during the Second World War. Comp.: *Eirini Lechouritou and others v. Dimosiotis Omospondiakis Dimokratias tis Germanias*, (Case C-292/05 (2007) ECR I-1519: 'Civil matters' within the meaning of Art. 1 of the Brussels Convention "does not cover a legal action brought by natural persons in a Contracting State against another Contracting State for compensation in respect of the loss or damage suffered by the successors of the victims of acts perpetrated by armed forces in the course of warfare in the territory of the first State" (para. 46)).

[15] *Kropholler/von Hein* Vor Art. 33 note 5 (citing as an example the private person condemned to reimbursement, who later becomes ambassador).

[16] *International Fruit Company NV and others v. Produktschap voor Groenten en Fruit*, (Joined Case 21-24/72) (1972) ECR 1219 paras. 11, 18; *Yvonne van Duyn v. Home Office*, (Case 41/74) (1974) ECR 1337 para. 22; *Anklagemyndigheden v. Peter Michael Poulsen and Diva Navigation Corp.*, (Case C-286/90) (1992) ECR I-6019 para. 9 ("[...] the European Community must respect International Law in the exercise of its powers and that consequently, Art. 6 must be interpreted and its scope limited, in the light of the relevant rules of International Law of the sea"); *Verhoeven*, Droit de la Communauté européenne (2nd ed. 2001), p. 281. The result was already certain under the Brussels Convention: *Geimer/Schütze* Art. 34 notes 6–7; *Kropholler/von Hein* Vor Art. 33 note 5.

[17] See the wording of Art. 45 Brussels I*bis*: "(...) the recognition of a judgment shall be refused". See before Art. 34 Brussels I: "A judgment *shall not* be recognised (...)". In contrast, see the wording of Art. 26 of the Council regulation (EC) No. 1346/2000 of 29 May 2000 on insolvency proceedings, allowing the Member State a discretion whether to refuse recognition: "Any Member State *may* refuse to recognise (...)".

[18] Cass. Fr. 23.10.2013, n° 12-20102;Cass. Fr., 7.11.2012, n°11-19049.

[19] *Trade Agency Ltd v. Seramico Investments Ltd.* (Case 619/10), ECLI:EU:2012:531, para. 34.

[20] *Trade Agency Ltd v. Seramico Investments Ltd.* (Case 619/10), ECLI:EU:2012:531, para. 38.

[21] *Trade Agency Ltd v. Seramico Investments Ltd.* (Case 619/10), ECLI:EU:2012:531, para. 35.

Stéphanie Francq

obligation to verify the refusal grounds, placed on the tribunal of the requested State, raises two question. The first one concerns the subsidiary application of domestic law and the second one the possibility/obligation to raise the refusal grounds ex officio.

6 The first question concerns the subsidiary application of domestic law: when one of the refusal grounds provided for by Art. 45 applies, can the judgment nevertheless be recognised under national law? It has been submitted that the provision should be interpreted "as meaning that the judgment cannot be recognised under the Convention"[22] (i.e. the Regulation), leaving the court free to grant recognition or enforcement under the ordinary law. This interpretation was developed for Art. 27 (4) of the Brussels Convention which instituted a control of the applicable law on some incidental issues decided upon by the court of origin and excluded from the substantive scope of the Convention by Art. 1. The substance of Art. 27 (4) Brussels Convention has been deleted from the Regulation Brussels I. The question remains however the same: can the Regulation, which is due to favour the circulation of judgments within the EU introduce recognition conditions stricter than those relied upon under domestic law? This proposition leads to the application of the most favourable source of law. It cannot be followed as it relies on a confusion between the applicability of the Regulation and the outcome of the application of its provisions, not allowed by the Regulation,[23] contrary to other international instruments concerned with recognition and enforcement.[24] The applicability of chapter III of the Regulation does not depend on Art. 45 but mainly on Arts. 1 and 2, a). None of the provisions of the Regulation suggest that its applicability could depend on a "more favourable" condition. Once the regulation applies,[25] its provisions command entirely the recognition or enforcement process, be the result positive or negative: the application of domestic law is therefore excluded. In this respect, more details are given *infra* as to the proper understanding of the new Art. 41 (2).[26]

7 Under the Brussels I Regulation, another question was raised concerning the role of the judge with respect to the control of the refusal grounds listed in Art. 34 or 35:[27] should or could he raise them of its own motion? Art. 41 of the Regulation Brussels I forbids any review under Article 34 at the first stage of the recognition or enforcement proceedings. Any initiative of the judge is thus excluded even though the first phase of the proceedings is not contradictory.[28] The wording of Art. 41 introduces a fundamental change in comparison

---

22 *Hartley*, p. 88; for a similar opinion, cf. *Gothot/Holleaux* para. 297.

23 For other arguments supporting the exclusion of domestic law (mainly: uniformity of interpretation, legal certainty, general balance of the jurisdiction and recognition regime of the Regulation, respect of the other aims of the Regulation such as the proper administration of justice): *Gaudemet-Tallon* p. 449–450, para. 434–435; *Stone* p. 153; *Layton/Mercer* para. 24.011.

24 Cf. Convention on the Recognition and Enforcement of Foreign Arbitral Awards of 10 June 1958 (United Nations Conference on International Commercial Arbitration, New York 1958) Art. V (1): "Recognition or enforcement of an arbitral award may be refused ..." and Art. V (2): "This provision is usually interpreted as leaving the judge free to rely on the more favourable domestic law."

25 The opinion of the authors cited above (fn. 24) makes perfect sense if they refers to matters normally excluded from the substantive scope of the Convention and indirectly covered by its Art. 27(4).

26 *Infra* Art. 45 note 13a in fine (*Francq*).

27 Of course, the judge has to verify that the formalities listed in Article 53 have been completed and therefore makes formal checks on the documents presented in support of the application.

28 Commission Proposal COM (1999) 348 final p. 21.

with the Brussels Convention. Under Art. 34 Brussels Convention, the application for recognition or enforcement may be refused even though the first stage of the proceedings is unilateral: only the judge can thus raise one of the refusal grounds.[29] Under the Regulation, the judge does not have the discretion any more to control the refusal grounds during the unilateral phase of the recognition or enforcement proceedings.[30] At the second stage of the proceedings, when an appeal is lodged against the decision granting recognition or enforcement, the question remains. Of course, it is likely to be of minor practical importance since one of the parties has, by definition, taken the initiative of raising one or more refusal grounds.[31] But the judge might disagree on the relevance of the refusal ground chosen by the claimant or notice the violation of other grounds. Though the recast organizes for the refusal grounds to be analysed at the initiative of one party (either the defendant contesting the enforcement under Art. 46 Brussels Ibis, or the party seeking for a declaration stating there are no grounds for refusing recognition under Art. 36 (2) Brussels Ibis), the requested judge may have another view than the party on the relevant refusal ground and wonder whether he/she must/may raise the other refusal ground *ex officio*. The question remains thus valid under Brussels Ibis. The obligatory character of the refusal grounds, deriving from the first words of Art. 34 Brussels I/45 Brussels Ibis implies that recognition or enforcement must be refused if any of them applies. This suggests in turn that each of them needs to be controlled on the initiative of either the parties or the judge. However, under the Brussels Convention, which used the same formulation in the first line of Art. 27, it was usually submitted that the judge "could" raise the grounds on its own motion.[32] Indeed the least that can be derived from the wording of Art. 34 Brussels I/45 Brussels Ibis is that the judge may on its own motion take grounds of refusal into consideration.[33] Whether he or she must do so remains uncertain.[34] According to *Kropholler*,[35] some submit that in the absence of any clear statement of the Convention or Regulation on this point, the question is left to national procedural law: the latter could free the judge of any obligation to control the grounds for

---

[29] Report *Schlosser* para. 190 ("(…) the court *may* of its own motion take into account grounds for refusing recognition *if they appear from the judgment or are known to the court*. It may not however make enquires to establish whether such grounds exist (…)"; emphasis added). Thus the role of the court at the first stage was already limited.

[30] For a different view see *Leible*, in: Rauscher Art. 34 note 3 (proposing an exception in case of gross violation of public policy or of the exclusive jurisdiction grounds listed in Art. 35). See also fn. 31.

[31] At this stage, as stated by the Czech Constitutional Court, an appeal court seized with an appeal against a declaration of enforceability of a foreign judgment must control the grounds for refusal of recognition that are explicitly relied upon by the parties, and cannot refuse to do so on the ground that it does not have jurisdiction to review the foreign judgment on the merits: Ústavní soud (2006) I. ÚS 709/05.

[32] See Report *Schlosser* para. 190; *Droz*, Pratique de la Convention de Bruxelles du 27 septembre 1968 (1973) p. 68 note 153; *Dashwood/Halcon/White* p. 39 (the authors do not make any difference between the possibility and the obligation for the court to control the grounds for refusal on its own motion).

[33] For a similar position *Ansgar Staudinger*, EuLF 2004, 273, 280.

[34] Submitting that the judge must refuse recognition on its own motion when it appears from the document laid before him that one of the refusal grounds apply: *Layton/Mercer* paras. 9.007, 24.011 (the authors apparently consider that such an obligation exists at both stages of the proceedings). Considering that the refusal ground of public policy must be raised *ex officio*: BGH (2012), IX ZB183/09, para. 9; BGH (2007) XII ZB 240/05, para. 25.

[35] *Kropholler/von Hein* Vor Art. 33 note 6.

refusal on its own motion.[36] The wording of Art. 45 Brussels I, which describes the role of the judge seized with the appeal, diverges in the various linguistic versions[37] and is therefore of little help. The Explanatory Memorandum of the Commission's Proposal for Regulation Brussels I clearly rules out any obligation imposed on the judge to control the grounds of Art. 45 on its own motion.[38]

8 The allocation of the burden of proof between the judge and the parties is not directly linked with the possibility for the court to raise the grounds of refusal of its own motion. This is made clear by the Report *Schlosser* which states that "the judge may of its own motion take into consideration grounds for refusing recognition if they appear from the judgment or are known to the court".[39] He does not have to search for the elements proving either the regularity or irregularity of the foreign judgment. As a result of the presumption in favour of recognition, it belongs to the party contesting the recognition to prove that one of the grounds for refusal exists.[40]

9 One last point should be underlined in relation with the restrictive nature of the grounds for refusal listed in Art. 45. The limitation of the grounds for refusal is justified by the global regime established by the Regulation, especially its rules on jurisdiction: the mutual trust

---

[36]   The French Cour de cassation, for instance, has held that under the Brussels Convention, the judge does not have to control any grounds of refusal other than those raised by the defending party, even public policy: Cass. RCDIP 89 (2000), 52 with note *Ancel*; Cass. RCDIP 94 (2005), 371 with note *André Huet*. As a result of the presumption in favour of regularity of judgments from other EU countries established by the Cour de cassation, at the first as at the second stage of the recognition or enforcement proceedings, French courts apparently never raise the grounds for refusal of Article 45 on their own motion: *Niboyet/Sinopoli*, Gaz. Pal. 2004, 4, 20–21. However, it is generally considered that under domestic law the judge has to examine grounds for refusal on its own motion when the ordre public procédural (international public policy and certain matters that are not at the parties disposal) is involved; for more detail, cf. *Mayer/Heuzé*, Droit international privé (11th ed. 2014) para. 447–448.

[37]   "The court (…) *shall* refuse or revoke a declaration of enforceability only on (…)"; "La juridiction (…) ne peut refuser ou révoquer que pour l'un des motifs (…)"; "Die Vollstreckbarerklärung darf von dem (…) Gericht nur (…)" (emphasis added). The French and German versions imply a possibility but no obligation.

[38]   Commission Proposal COM (1999) 348 final, p. 21–22. On the question whether national judges should raise EU law ex officio see: *Rocatti*, Le rôle du juge national dans l'espace judiciaire européen (Brussels 2013); *Niboyet*, Office du juge et déclenchement du raisonnement conflictuel, in *Azzi/Boskovic* (ed.), Quel avenir pour la théorie générale des conflits de lois (Brussels 2015) 19.

[39]   Report *Schlosser* para. 190; emphasis added. See as well: *Mayer/Heuzé* para. 449 in fine ("The principle that the judge has to consider the grounds for refusal of its own motion (…) only means that he shall not grant recognition if the regularity of the foreign decision is not established, even if the defending party does not contest it. It does not impose on him the obligation to enquire whether such grounds exist." The translation is ours).

[40]   Report *Jenard* p. 43; *Layton/Mercer* para. 9.018; *Leible*, in: Rauscher Art. 34 note 3; *Kropholler/von Hein* Vor Art. 33 note 7; *Droz* (fn. 34) p. 68 para. 153 in fine. For examples of application of this principle by national courts in Germany: BGH (2003) I.L.Pr 523; in Belgium: Trib. civ. Liège Act. Dr., 1996, 80; Trib. civ. Bruxelles RGDC 1989, 422. Cf. *Geimer/Schütze* Art. 34 note 1 (no presumption in favour or against recognition deriving from the Regulation influences the allocation of the burden of proof between the parties).

---

between courts of the Member States partially relies on the assurance that certain grounds for jurisdiction have been used and that others have been banned in the court of origin. This is not true, however, for judgments that have not been adopted in accordance with the Regulation Brussels I or Brussels I*bis*. They nevertheless benefit from the favourable system of recognition and enforcement of the Regulation Brussels I or Brussels I*bis* whose application depends on the sole condition that the judgment has been rendered by the tribunal of a Member State. As a result, the judgment taken in a Member State against a defendant domiciled in a third Country will benefit from the recognition regime of the Regulation in other Member States, even though the defendant has not been able to take advantage of the protections established by Chapters I and II of the Regulation Brussels I/I*bis*, in particular the exclusion of some national rules on jurisdiction provided for by Art. 5 (2) Brussels I*bis* (Art. 3 (2) Brussels I). This unequal treatment of defendants domiciled in non-Member States is sometimes severely judged.[41] As stated by Art. 45 (3) Regulation Brussels I*bis*, the jurisdiction of the court of origin is never controlled in the requested State, beyond the conditions set by Art. 45 (1) (e) and 45 (2).

II. Legislative history

The legislative history of Art. 45 derives from its purpose. Pursuant to the general aim of the Regulation of facilitating the circulation of judgments, the grounds for refusal have progressively been restricted in two ways: some have been narrowed, other have been abandoned. Simultaneously, the ECJ and the explanatory Reports have sometimes clarified the meaning of the provisions in a way that slightly enlarged their scope. **10**

The 1978 Accession Convention brought major changes.[42] First, it was specified that a document equivalent to the document which normally institutes the proceedings, delivered in sufficient time to enable the defendant to organize his defence, would also satisfy the requirement of Art. 27 (2) concerning due service in case of default judgment (now Art. 45, § 1 (b)). Second, a point 5 was added to Art. 27, later formally amended by the 1989 Accession Convention,[43] which gives priority to an earlier judgment pronounced in a **11**

---

41   *Hartley*, International Commercial Litigation (2009) p. 342; *Briggs/Rees* pp. 427–428 para. 7.04. Generally speaking, the discrimination between litigations involving third State defendants and litigations involving Member State defendants was at the core of the revision process of Regulation Brussels I. The enlargement of the scope of applicability of the Regulation to litigations involving third State defendants was therefore taken into consideration (see: Revision Proposal, COM (2010) 748 final, p. 3) but was finally adopted only for contracts concluded with consumers and workers. Judgment rendered by a Member State court chosen by the parties might also involve a third State defendant (see. Art. 25).

42   Convention on the Accession of 9 October 1978 of the Kingdom of Denmark, of Ireland and of the United Kingdom of Great Britain and Northern Ireland to the Convention on jurisdiction and enforcement of judgments in civil and commercial matters and to the Protocol on its interpretation by the Court of Justice, OJ 1978 L304/1.

43   Convention on the Accession of the Kingdom of Spain and the Portuguese Republic to the Convention on jurisdiction and the enforcement of judgments in civil and commercial matters and to the Protocol on its interpretation by the Court of Justice with the adjustments made to them by the Convention on the accession of the Kingdom of Denmark, of Ireland and of the United Kingdom of Great Britain and Northern Ireland and the adjustments made to them by the Convention on the accession of the Hellenic Republic, OJ 1989 L 285/1.

Stéphanie Francq

non-contracting State involving the same cause of action and the same parties if it qualifies for recognition in the State addressed (now Art. 45, § 1 (d)). Point 5 of Art. 27 should be read in relation to Art. 57 of the Convention (now Art. 71) which underlines that the Convention does not affect other conventions concerning jurisdiction, recognition or enforcement to which the contracting States would be parties (except for those listed in Art. 55 Brussels Convention). But for Art. 27 (5), a judgment given in a third State that would fill the conditions established for its recognition by the domestic law or more importantly, by a bilateral convention signed with that State, would have raised difficult questions when confronted with a later judgment originating from a Member State. The text of the 1968 Convention lacked clarity on this issue and the addition of point 5 avoided diplomatic complications.[44] Since the solution was already evident under international law,[45] it cannot be said that the addition of the last point of Art. 27 Brussels Convention added any extra condition for recognition.

12   The transformation of the Brussels Convention into a Community instrument (Regulation Brussels I) offered the opportunity for other changes. The adverb "manifestly" was introduced to qualify the contradiction between the recognition of the foreign judgment and public policy of the Member State addressed (Art. 34 (1)) Brussels I; Art. 45, § 1 (a) Brussels *Ibis*). Concerning point 2 of Art. 34 (point 2 of Art. 27 Brussels Convention; now. Art. 45, § 1 (b)), on the one hand, the requirement of a service "duly" effected has been abandoned while on the other hand, the new provision states that service must be made not only in sufficient time but also "in such a way as" to enable the defendant to arrange for his defence. Point 2 of Art. 34 Brussels I (now Art. 45, § 1 (b)) is centred on the practical possibility for the defendant to arrange for his defence rather than on the regularity of the service. Simultaneously, it is severely restricted: since the enactment of Regulation Brussels I, an objection to recognition concerning service of the documents instituting the proceedings can only be raised by the defendant who has appealed in the State of origin when he was in a position to do so. Point 4 of Art. 27 Brussels Convention, concerning the difference of rules of Private international law concerning capacity and personal status between the State of origin and the State addressed, has been deleted. The motivation of this modification might be informative on the Commission's projects with regard to conflict of laws rules: it is due to the fact that these rules of Private international law "are gradually being approximated in the Member States".[46] Eventually the question left open by the Brussels Convention concerning the conflict between two judgments given in different Member States and presented for recognition in a third Member State is solved in Art. 34 (4) by giving priority to the earlier judgment (now Art. 45, § 1 (d)).[47] The solution concerning the conflict between an earlier judgment given in a third State and an EU judgment (Art. 27 (5) of the Convention) is simply extended to the conflict between judgments rendered in Member States other than the State addressed. The only point that has not been changed when turning the Convention into a Regulation is point 3 of Art. 34, which literally takes over the solution of Art. 27 (3) concerning the conflict between a judgment given in the State where recognition is sought and a judgment given in another Member State. As the Explanatory Memorandum puts it,

---

[44]   Report *Schlosser* para. 205.
[45]   Art. 30 (4) (b) Vienna Convention on the Law of Treaties.
[46]   Commission Proposal COM (1999) 348 final, p. 23.
[47]   Highlighting the problem: *Kaye* pp. 3249–3250.

the "grounds (for refusal) have been reframed in a restrictive manner to improve the free movement of judgments".[48]

The history of Art. 34 also shows a need for clarification sometimes leading to a compre- **13**
hensive construction of the grounds for refusal. The ground relating to public policy is the best example. Though fraud was considered as a specific ground for non-recognition in the United Kingdom and Ireland, not to be confused with public policy, the Schlosser report states that fraud can constitute an offence against public policy within the meaning of the Regulation.[49] This specification actually encouraged the United Kingdom and Ireland to enlarge their conception of public policy. Another example concerns the comprehensive interpretation finally given by the *Krombach* case.[50] From the beginning, the question whether public policy could cover procedural aspects without overlapping the requirement of due and timely process, that was presented as the sole ground for refusal concerning the procedure, appeared as a difficult question.[51] The Krombach decision stated that public policy could in exceptional circumstances, cover the fundamental principle of the right to a fair hearing.

In December 2010, the Commission submitted a proposal for a revision of the Brussels I   **13a**
Regulation.[52] One of the major innovations of the Proposal was the abolition of *exequatur* for all judgments rendered in a Member State, except for decisions concerning violations of privacy and rights relating to personality (i.e. mainly defamation) and for decisions rendered in collective compensatory proceedings.[53] In accordance with the Proposal, for all judgments (other than judgment dealing with collective redress and privacy) rendered in a Member State, the enforcement could be requested in another Member State without any specific procedure and without seizing a judge. Therefore, the Proposal deleted Art. 34 of the Brussels I Regulation. The Proposal provided however, for three possibilities of opposing recognition or enforcement. First, enforcement could be opposed in the Member State of enforcement, if the foreign judgment was irreconcilable with a judgment rendered in the requested State or with an earlier judgment rendered in another Member State or a third State between the same parties, concerning the same cause of action, provided that the latter judgment fulfils the necessary conditions for its recognition.[54] Second, if the defendant did not enter an appearance before the court of origin, the Commission proposal stated that this defendant had a right to "apply for a review of the judgment before the competent court of that Member State" where "he was not served with the document instituting the proceeding (…) in sufficient time and in such a way as to enable him to arrange for his defence" or where "force majeure" or "extraordinary circumstances without any fault on his part" prevented

---

48   Commission Proposal COM (1999) 348 final, p. 22. Purely formal modifications, such as the replacement of the term "Contracting State" by the term "Member State", have not been mentioned.

49   Report *Schlosser* para. 192. On the limited circumstances under which fraud might be alleged, *infra* Art. 45 note 27 (*Francq*).

50   *Dieter Krombach v. André Bamberski*, (Case C-7/98) (2000) ECR I-1935.

51   *Gothot/Holleaux* para. 256.

52   Proposal, COM (2010) 748 final.

53   Proposal, COM (2010) 748 final p. 5, n° 3.1.

54   Art. 43 Proposal. The refusal ground provided by Article 34 (3) and (4) of the Brussels I Regulation were thus safeguarded.

Stéphanie Francq   875

him from appearing in the initial proceeding.[55] The defendant who "failed to challenge the judgment when it was possible for him to do so" was precluded from requesting the "review" of the judgment before the courts of the State of origin. This ground for contesting the judgment partially resembled the Art. 34 (2) of the Brussels I Regulation. Third, in "cases other than those covered by Article 45", a party was entitled to challenge the recognition or enforcement of a judgment in the State where recognition or enforcement would be sought "where such recognition or enforcement would not be permitted by the fundamental principles underlying the right to a fair trial".[56] The proposed Article 46 covered only part of the scope of the Article 34 (1) of the Brussels I regulation concerning public policy, i.e. its procedural aspects.

The Proposal of the Commission embodied thus mainly two consequences in regard to the Art. 34 of the Brussels I Regulation. First, the refusal ground concerning the circumstances of service of the document instituting the proceeding in case of a default judgment (Art. 34 (2) of the Brussels I Regulation) was to be addressed in the State of origin of the decision, according to an unclear "review" procedure, and could not be raised in the State of enforcement. Second, the possibility to challenge a judgment of a Member State on ground of substantive public policy was abolished. For the rest, other refusal grounds provided for by Art. 34 (3) and (4) of the Brussels I Regulation as well as part of Art. 34 (1) of the Brussels I Regulation were preserved and were to be addressed in the State of enforcement.

The suppression of any possibility of control in regard to public policy raised controversy. Hearings conducted before the European Parliament before the submission of the proposal had already warned the legislator about the difficulties that a general abolition of *exequatur* (concerning all judgment in civil and commercial matters) could raise, especially in regard to the requirement of the ECHR.[57] Many authors were opposed to the abolition of *exequatur* and/or more specifically the absence of (or a limited) review in regard to public policy in the State of enforcement.[58] The Committee on Legal Affairs of the European Parliament re-

---

[55] Art. 45 Proposal.

[56] Art. 46 Proposal.

[57] Hearing of Professor *M.-L. Niboyet* before the Legal Affairs Committee of the European Parliament, Oct 5, 2009, p. 3 (available at: http://www.europarl.europa.eu/document/activities/cont/200910/20091009-ATT62237/20091009ATT62237FR.pdf).

[58] See for instance: *Hess/Pfeiffer/Schlosser*, Report on the Application of Regulation Brussels I in Member States (2007) Study JLS/C4/2005/03 (hereafter: *Hess/Pfeiffer/Schlosser* Report), p. 251–252, para. 562 (stating after reviewing national case law that a reduction of Art. 34 (1) is possible as long as sufficient means of redress are provided for in the State of origin and in the State of enforcement. A limited control of public policy seems necessary); *Dickinson*, "Response to the green paper on the review of the Council Regulation 44/200", para. 12 (against the abolition of *exequatur* and advocating for the confirmation of a refusal ground based on public policy; *Magnus/Mankowski*, "Joint response to the Green Paper on the Review of the Brussels I Regulation", p. 2–3 (advocating in favour of the abolition of exequatur but also in favour of a public policy control at the practical stage of enforcement); both responses are available at: http://ec.europa.eu/justice/newsroom/civil/opinion/090630_en.htm. See also: *Cuniberti/Rueda*, RabelsZ 75 (2011), 287, 313–314 (in favour of abolition of *exequatur* as long as a public policy revision is possible in the State of enforcement and wondering whether the Commission's Proposal for a Revision offers a wide enough control of public policy as it stands). See also, *Peter Schlosser*, IPRax 2010, 101; *Xandra Kramer*, NIPR 2011, 633; *Marchadier*, Eur. Human Rghts J. 2013, 348.

served a cold reception to the Recast Proposal. In regard to recognition and enforcement, the report of the Parliament accepted the abolition of *exequatur* but reintroduced the possibility to contest enforcement in the Member State addressed under the grounds formerly listed in Art. 34 Brussels I.[59] The current Art. 45 basically results from the formulation proposed by the Parliament.

In the end, exequatur has been abolished, but the refusal grounds have been kept.

Art. 34, 35 and 36 of Brussels I Regulation were simply renumbered in Art. 45. Former Art. 34 Brussels I Regulation has become Art. 45 (1) (a) to (d) Brussels I*bis* Regulation. Former Art. 35 Brussels I Regulation is now incorporated into Art. 45 (1) (e), 45 (2) and 45 (3) Brussels I*bis* Regulation. Former Art. 34 is the object of one major modification: the violation of exclusive grounds for jurisdiction (Art. 24, section 6) has become a ground for refusing recognition and enforcement. Former Art. 36 Brussels I Regulation is now Art. 52 Brussels I*bis* Regulation. The new localisation of the interdiction of review on the merits strangely separates the refusal grounds (Art. 45) from their guiding principle of interpretation (Art. 52).

The refusal grounds are identical and keep the same function for recognition and enforcement. In practice, the circumstances of their intervention have been modified by the abolition of exequatur. Recognition occurs *de plano* as was already the case under Brussels I Regulation. Enforcement is not submitted to any "special procedure" any more,[60] but the party against whom enforcement is sought may apply for a refusal of enforcement or recognition in the requested State (Art. 45, (4), Art. 46 Brussels I*bis*). Thus a judge of the Member State addressed may be seized with an application for refusal of recognition or enforcement based on the refusal grounds listed in Art. 45. In addition, Regulation Brussels I*bis* also provides for a preventive action regarding the recognition. Article 36 (2) states that: "Any interested party may, in accordance with the procedure provided for in Subsection 2 of Section 3, apply for a decision that there are no grounds for refusal of recognition as referred to in Article 45". Art. 33 of the Brussels I Regulation offered a similar possibility but subjected it to the existence of a dispute. Jurisdictions of the Member State addressed may have to apply Art. 45 either upon an application for a refusal of recognition or enforcement, or upon an application for a declaratory decision of the absence of refusal grounds. Because the application can be introduced by the defendant or by the claimant, the first words of the Art. 45 state that refusal grounds can be analysed "on the application of any interested party".

Article 41 (2) introduces, at first sight, some confusion about the exclusive nature of the refusal grounds of Article 45. Following Article 41, the enforcement procedure is governed

---

59   Draft Report *Zwiefka*, Draft Report on the proposal for a regulation of the European Parliament and of the Council on jurisdiction and the recognition and enforcement of judgments in civil and commercial matters, delivered on 28 June 2011, 2010/0383(COD); Report on the proposal for a regulation of the European Parliament and of the Council on jurisdiction and the recognition and enforcement of judgments in civil and commercial matters, delivered on 15 Oct. 2012, 2010/0383(COD), see p. 74 and 138.

60   Recital 26 clarifies that the regulation abolishes the "declaration of enforceability prior to the enforcement in the Member State addressed". However, since the foreign decision will be treated like a national judgment, it it submitted to the enforcement procedure of the Member State addressed.

by the law of the requested State and the foreign judgment is assimilated to a national decision. Under Article 41 (2), "the grounds for refusal or of suspension of enforcement under the law of the Member State addressed shall apply in so far as they are not incompatible with the grounds referred to in Article 45". Article 41 (2) cannot be understood as meaning that other refusal grounds provided by the general rules of private international law of the requested state can be introduced as far as they are compatible with those listed in Article 45 of the recast.[61] Obviously as far as national procedural law applies and the foreign judgment is treated as a decision rendered in the requested State, the foreign judgment is also submitted to the conditions provided for the execution of national judgment by the procedural law of the requested State.[62] It is therefore possible to contest the enforcement procedure or to require its suspension under the conditions set for by the procedural law of the requested State. But the question whether the enforceability of the foreign judgment can be definitively refused is solely submitted to the refusal grounds of Article 45.[63]

III. Art. 45 (1), (a): Public policy

14 Pursuant to paragraph 1, (a) of Art. 45, recognition or enforcement might be refused if it is manifestly contrary to public policy in the Member State addressed. The recast did not modify this provision, beyond the introduction between brackets of the French translation of the concept of public policy (ordre public). As mentioned earlier, the abolition of a control of public policy (at least in its substantive dimension) was probably the most controversial aspect of the Commission's recast proposal. The regime of this refusal ground has undergone almost no modification since the conclusion of the Brussels Convention. The content of public policy depends on the national conception of the State where recognition or enforcement is sought (1), which has to respect the limits set by the ECJ (3). The conditions of application of this ground for refusal results similarly from national and European law (2). As the court phrases it repeatedly, "while the Member States remain in principle free, by virtue of the proviso in Article 34 (1) of Regulation No. 44/2001, to determine, according to their own conceptions, what public policy requires, the limits of that concept are a matter of interpretation of that regulation (…). Consequently, while it is not for the Court to define the content of the public policy of a Member State, it is none the less required to review the limits within which the courts of a Member State may have recourse to that concept for the purpose of refusing recognition to a judgment emanating from another Member State (…)".[64]

---

[61] *Nuyts*, RCDIP 102 (2013), 1, 27.

[62] *Gascón-Inchausti*, in: Emmanuel Guinchard (dir), Le nouveau règlement Bruxelles *Ibis* (2014), p. 203, 231, n°28.

[63] For an exemple of this double level of verification under Brussels I Regulation and national procedural law: *Prism Investment v. Jaap Anne van der Meer* (Case C-139/10) (2011) ECR I-9511, paras. 39–40.

[64] *flyLAL-Lithuanian Airlines*, (Case-302/13) ECLI:EU:C:2014:2319, para. 47 and *Trade Agency Ltd v. Seramico Investments Ltd.* (Case 619/10), (2012), not published yet, para. 49, referring to *Dieter Krombach v. André Bamberski* (Case C-7/98), (2000) ECR I-1935 para. 22–23; *Renault SA v. Maxicar SpA and Orazio Formento*, (Case C-38/98) (2000), ECR, I-2973, para. 27–28; *Meletis Apostolides v. David Charles Orams*, (Case C-420/07) (2009) ECR I-3571, para. 56–57.

1. Content

Domestic law determines what principles and rules belong to public policy. The concept is **15**
therefore not uniformly understood among the Member States.[65] However, under the influence of the ECJ, it is likely that striking divergences of national conception can be avoided.[66] The notion of public policy is also submitted to similar interpretations (or guidelines)
under the various regulations on private international law.[67] Being a domestic notion, public
policy will follow the evolution of national conception and be considered at the time when
the recognition of the judgment is requested. This is why foreign decisions infringing the
prohibition on investment in future options or an exchange control law, itself contrary to EC
law, were granted enforcement when they would have once been considered as contrary to
public policy.[68] Though being a national concept, public policy also includes the principles of
Community law, which belong to the "European public policy".[69] Those concepts are progressively identified by the ECJ. Their understanding should indeed not vary from country
to country. Public policy, be it constituted of national and community concepts, may have a
substantive or procedural aspect.[70]

It is only one particular aspect of public policy that comes into consideration under Art. 45 **16**
(1) (a), namely international public policy. This narrow concept does not cover all internal
rules of public policy but only the core principles and values that cannot be derogated from,
even for situations presenting foreign elements. National case law clearly draws the distinction between international and internal public policy[71] and restrains the use of Art. 45 (1) (a)
to defend fundamental principles.[72]

---

[65] For examples see *infra* Art. 45 notes 27, 32–34 (*Francq*). Cass. Fr. 23.10.2013, n° 12-20102 (condemning an
appeal decision which had failed to analyse the public policy ground in regard of the French "ordre public
international" and had merely assessed the compatibility of the German decision with German law).

[66] *Infra* Art. 45 notes 20–32 (*Francq*).

[67] BGH, IX ZB 35/12, para. 7; BGH, IX ZB 120/11, para. 3; *Eurofood IFSC Ltd* (Case C-341/04) (2006) ECR
I-3813, paras. 63 ff.

[68] BGH (1999) I.L.Pr. 758 (applying a bilateral agreement concluded between Austria and Germany and
finding that the prohibition of futures and gaming plea did not form part of German international public
policy anymore as assessed on the date on which the enforceability of the Austrian judgment had to be
decided); *Westpac Banking Corporation v. Dempsey*, (1993) 3 I.R. 331 (H.C.), *Kaye*, p. 3279–3280.

[69] *Renault SA v. Maxicar SpA and Orazio Formento*, (Case 38/98) (2000) ECR I-2973 para. 32.

[70] *Infra* Art. 45 notes 20–34 (*Francq*).

[71] For instance: Hof van Cass. Pas. belge 1985 I 1323 (the principle according to which the civil proceedings
have to be stayed pending criminal proceedings does not belong to international public policy, but only to
internal public policy); Trib.civ. Liège Act. Dr. (1996) 80 (referring to the narrow definition given by the
Belgian Hof van Cass. Pas. belge (1950) I 624); Cass. Fr. D. 1997 IR 92 (French international public policy
does not oppose a judgment including indexation in a currency other than French Frank); Civ Tournai
(Belgium), 18 nov. 2009, Journal des tribunaux (2010), 456 (refusing to take a French rule considered in
France as part of internal public policy into consideration for the application of Belgian international
public policy under Art. 34 (2) Brussels I Regulation when enforcement of a French decision is sought in
Belgium).

[72] Cassaz. Giust. Civ. 1999 I 3009-3012 with note *Simone* (all principles of the Constitution do not belong to
the narrow notion of public policy of Art. 34 (1)); also on the ECJ Website under n° 2000/42: http://curia.
eu.int/common/recdoc/convention/en/index.htm.

16a Accordingly, denying recognition or enforcement can only be based on the identification of a fundamental principle, which would be violated in the State where recognition or enforcement is sought if recognition enforcement were granted.[73] In this respect, in the *Apostolides* case, the Court stated that in absence of allegation of violation of such a (clearly identified) fundamental principle in the legal order of the State where enforcement is sought, there would be no justification for denying recognition or enforcement to a foreign judgment, under Article 34 (1) of Regulation No. 44/2001.[74] In *Apostolides v. Orams*, Mr Apostolides, a Cypriot national, sought to obtain recognition and enforcement, in the United Kingdom, of two Cypriot judgments against Mr and Mrs Orams, a British married couple. In 2002, the Orams purchased an immovable property, situated in the northern area of the Republic of Cyprus, on which the Cypriot Government has not exercised effective control since the invasion of Cypriot territory in 1974 by the Turkish army. Before the Turkish military occupation, the land belonged to Mr Apostolides' family, who, as member of the Greek Cypriot community, was forced to abandon his house. Mr Apostolides brought an action against the Orams, to a Cypriot court established in the Government-controlled area. The Cypriot judgment ordered the Orams to "demolish the villa, swimming pool and fencing which they had erected on the land, deliver immediately to Mr Apostolides free possession of the land, pay to Mr Apostolides various sums by way of special damages and monthly occupation charges (that is, rent) until the judgment was complied with, together with interest, refrain from continuing with the unlawful intervention on the land, whether personally or through their agents, and pay various sums in respect of the costs and expenses of the proceedings (with interest on those sums)".[75] Two later judgments rejected the arguments of Mr and Mrs Orams trying to have the first judgment set aside. The three judgments were declared enforceable in England by order of the English High Court of Justice. Upon appeal from the Orams, revocation of the order was pronounced. Mr Apostolides appealed against that latter order and the Court of appeal referred five questions to the ECJ. The third question was whether the fact that a judgment given by the courts of a Member State, concerning land situated in an area of that State over which its Government does not exercise effective control, cannot, as a practical matter, be enforced where the land is situated, constitutes a ground for refusal of recognition or enforcement under Article 34 (1) of Regulation No. 44/2001. Since the forum State failed to refer to "any fundamental principle within the legal order of the United Kingdom which the recognition or enforcement of the judgments in question would be liable to infringe", the ECJ stated that "no refusal to recognise them would be justified on the ground that a judgment given by the courts of a Member State, concerning land situated in an area of that State over which its Government does not exercise effective control, cannot, as a practical matter, be enforced where the land is situated".[76] Following the reasoning of the Court, the question is still open whether or not refusal to recognise those judgments could be justified on that ground if the English jurisdiction had referred to a fundamental principle. The Commission, followed by the Orams,

---

[73] *FlyLAL-Lithuanian Airlines*, (Case-302/13) ECLI:EU:C:2014:2319, 49; *Trade Agency Ltd v. Seramico Investments Ltd.*, (Case 619/10) (2012) nyr., para. 51; *National Navigation Co v. Endesa Generacion SA*, [2009] EWCA Civ 1397, para. 131 (the fact that the judge of origin considered inexistent an arbitration agreement, which would be held valid under English law, does not breach any essential fundamental principle of English law justifying to set aside a Spanish judgment under Art. 34 Brussels I).

[74] *Meletis Apostolides v. David Charles Orams*, (Case C-420/07) (2009) ECR I-3571, para. 62.

[75] *Meletis Apostolides v. David Charles Orams*, (Case C-420/07) (2009) ECR I-3571, para. 26.

[76] *Meletis Apostolides v. David Charles Orams*, (Case C-420/07) (2009) ECR I-3571, para. 61 and 62.

submitted that the recognition and enforcement of the Cypriot judgment may contravene "international public policy" – as part of the "national public policy" – by undermining the efforts of the international community to find a solution to the Cyprus problem.[77] In her opinion, Advocate General Kokott rejected the idea that the "preservation of peace and the restoration of the territorial integrity of Cyprus" could be considered as a "rule of law regarded as essential in the legal order of the State in which enforcement is sought or of a right recognised as being fundamental within that legal order".[78] Also, enforcement could not be denied, in regard to Art. 38 (1) of Regulation No. 44/2001, on the ground that claimants might encounter difficulties in having judgments enforced in the northern area.[79]

The strict interpretation of public policy and the need to clearly identify a fundamental **17** principle before relying on this refusal ground is coherent with the prevailing interpretation given from the start to Art. 45 (1) (a) by the *Jenard* Report (at the time, Art. 27 of the Brussels Convention) and confirmed at numerous occasions by the ECJ: it should intervene only in exceptional cases.[80] The *Jenard* Report considered the ground for refusal based on public policy as similar to that adopted in "the most recent convention" of the time. Consequently, the adjunction of the adverb "manifestly" in the Regulation cannot be said to have narrowed down the kind of infringement to public policy required under Art. 45 (or 27 of the Convention and 34 of the Brussels I Regulation): the expectation of a manifest contradiction was included from the start[81] and is coherent with the prohibition of review as to the substance. As the Court formulated it repeatedly: "In order for the prohibition of any review of the substance of a judgment of another Member State to be observed, the infringement would have to constitute a manifest breach of a rule of law regarded as essential in the legal order of the State in which enforcement is sought or of a right recognised as being fundamental within that legal order".[82] The restriction of the hypothesis of intervention of public policy to exceptional cases was already prevailing in domestic laws, which considered that public policy should be given an "effet atténué" for those situations constituted abroad.[83]

---

[77] Opinion of Advocate General Kokott, delivered in Case C-420/07, *Meletis Apostolides v. David Charles Orams*, on 18 December 2008, (2009) ECR I-3571, para. 101.

[78] Opinion of Advocate General Kokott, delivered in Case C-420/07, *Meletis Apostolides v. David Charles Orams*, on 18 December 2008, (2009) ECR I-3571, para. 110. The Court of Appeal, in its decision following the ECJ preliminary ruling, decided that the international efforts towards a peace process were not a ground to refuse recognition of the Cypriot decision (Court of Appeal, 19 Jan 2010, *Orams v. Apostolides*, (2010) EWCA Civ 9, available at: http://www.bailii.org/ew/cases/EWCA/Civ/2010/9.html). For a detailed analysis of the Appeal decision and the public policy considerations in the *Apostolides* case, see: Athanassiou, 16 (2010) Maastricht Journal of European and Comparative Law, 423.

[79] *Meletis Apostolides v. David Charles Orams*, (Case C-420/07) (2009) ECR I-3571 para. 70.

[80] Report *Jenard* p. 44; *Horst Ludwig Martin Hoffmann v. Adelheid Krieg*, (Case 145/86), (1988) ECR 645 para. 21; *Bernardus Hendrikman and Maria Feyen v. Magenta Druck & Verlag GmbH*, (Case C-78/95) (1996) ECR I-4943 para. 23; *Dieter Krombach v. André Bamberski* (Case C-7/98), (2000) ECR I-1935 para. 21; *Régie nationale des usines Renault SA v. Maxicar SpA and Orazio Formento*, (Case C-38/98) (2000) ECR I-2973 para. 26; *Trade Agency Ltd v. Seramico Investments Ltd.* (Case 619/10), ECLI:EU: C:2012:531 para. 48; BGH, 14 June 2012, IX ZB, 183/09, para. 10.

[81] *Leible*, in: Rauscher Art. 34 note 4; *Kropholler/von Hein* Art. 34 note 4.

[82] Recently: *flyLAL-Lithuanian Airlines*, (Case-302/13) ECLI:EU:C:2014:2319, para. 49; *Trade Agency Ltd v. Seramico Investments Ltd.*, (Case 619/10) (2012) not published yet, para. 51; *Meletis Apostolides v. David Charles Orams*, (Case C-420/07) (2009) ECR I-3571, para. 59 (and the cited case law).

18 Be it or not named "effet atténué", this narrow conception of the already narrow international public policy has three implications. Firstly, it is the effects of the recognition that will
be appreciated with regard to public policy, not the foreign judgment: the judge of the State
addressed is not supposed to say whether the foreign judgment as such is contrary to public
policy, but rather whether the recognition of such a decision would produce effects adversary to public policy.[84] Secondly, those effects should reach a certain level of gravity: the
fundamental principle infringed as a result of recognition must suffer a substantial offence.[85]
Thirdly, the appreciation of gravity will depend on the existence of rather close links between the situation and the legal order of the State addressed: the closer the links, the easier it
is to prove that recognition of the foreign decision within the legal order of the State
addressed will lead to intolerable breach of fundamental principles.[86] As a result, the examination of public policy will be lead *in concreto*.[87]

2. Conditions of application

19 The conditions of application of Art. 45 (1) (a), be they substantive or procedural, will be set
by domestic law, under the scrutiny of the ECJ. For instance, in France, public policy must be
raised by the defendant, the judge being allowed to restrict his control to the issue raised by
the parties.[88] Among the conditions of application of Art. 45 (1) (a) its residual role should be
underlined. Public policy should only come into consideration when other (more specific)
grounds for refusal do not apply. Grounds for non-recognition are not overlapping.[89] As a
result, Art. 45 (1) (a) can only come into consideration when conditions of application of
other grounds for refusal are not met. This is a simple application of the principle *lex
specialis derogat generalis*. For instance, the ECJ has expressly excluded the intervention
of Art. 45 (1) (a) when Art. 45 (1) (b) or 45 (1) (c) applies.[90] Another condition sometimes
referred to before a party can raise public policy concerns the question whether that party

---

[83] *Gaudemet-Tallon* p. 412, para. 398; *Ansgar Staudinger*, EuLF 2004, 273.

[84] Report *Jenard* p. 44.

[85] *Dieter Krombach v. André Bamberski* (Case C-7/98), (2000) ECR I-1935 para. 37; *Régie nationale des
usines Renault SA v. Maxicar SpA and Orazio Formento*, (Case C-38/98) (2000) ECR I-2973 para. 30
(mentioning the *manifest* breach of *essential* rules or *fundamental* principles of the State addressed). In
this respect, the mere infringement of the european law does not in itself suffice for applying Art. 45, (1),
a) *(Régie nationale des usines Renault SA v. Maxicar SpA et Orazio Formento*, (Case C-38/98) (2000),
ECR, I-2973, para. 32).

[86] *Kropholler/von Hein* Art. 34 note 18 (pursuant to the classic formula of the BGH – BGH IPRax 1994, 350
with note *Herbert Roth* – proposes to check whether taking into consideration the intensity of the links
between the situation and the forum, the concrete result of recognition would lead to intolerable contradiction with German fundamental ideas or conception of justice); *Ansgar Staudinger*, EuLF 2004, 273,
275; *Geimer/Schütze* Art. 34 notes 19–22.

[87] *CA Paris D.* 1994 IR 66; Trib. civ. Liège Act. Dr. (1996) 80.

[88] *Supra* Art. 45 note 7 *(Francq)*.

[89] *Briggs/Rees* p. 440 para. 7.12.

[90] *Horst Ludwig Martin Hoffmann v. Adelheid Krieg*, (Case 145/86) (1988) ECR 645 para. 21; *Bernardus
Hendrikman and Maria Feyen v. Magenta Druck & Verlag GmbH*, (Case C-78/95) (1996) ECR I-4943
para. 23. However, Art. 45 (1) a) and b) can apply simultaneously to various aspects of a decision rendered
in another Member States (*Trade Agency Ltd v. Seramico Investments Ltd.* (Case 619/10), ECLI:EU:
C:2012:531 see the two preliminary questions).

made use of the means of redress that were at his/her disposal in the State of origin or contested the issues later presented to the tribunal in charge of recognition. It is commonly accepted in Germany that the party who could have appealed against violation of his/her right to a fair hearing, but did not do so, later loses the right to raise procedural public policy in front of the court seized with the recognition issue.[91]

3. Applications within the limits set by the ECJ

a) Substantive public policy

Examples of applications of public policy in its substantive aspect are relatively rare. This has **20** two reasons. Firstly, in those civil and commercial matters covered by the Regulation, the legal divergences between the Member States are rarely strong enough to bring a contradiction with public policy.[92] Secondly, the prohibition of review as to the substance confines quite drastically the hypothesis in which the tribunal will be able to consider a contradiction with its substantive public policy.[93] The principle established by Art. 52 explains many of the limits imposed by the ECJ.

The court seized with recognition or enforcement is not allowed to review the accuracy of **21** the findings of law or facts made by the court of the State of origin.[94] As a consequence, any issue already considered by the court of origin will rarely give rise to a valid objection based on public policy.[95] This is of course linked with the narrow interpretation of public policy, the infringement of which should be manifest. Following this line of thought, the ECJ has even provided a general description of the frame within which public policy could be considered to be infringed: "In order for the prohibition of any review of the foreign judgment as to its substance to be observed, the infringement would have to constitute a manifest breach of a rule of law regarded as essential in the legal order of the State in which enforce-

---

[91] *Kropholler/von Hein* Art. 34 note 14 (with numerous references to case law in footnote 29); *Geimer/ Schütze* Art. 34 notes 30; *Leible*, in: Rauscher Art. 34 note 18. In France, stating that the position usually adopted about fraud should be generalized to all refusal grounds which could have been raised before the Court of origin: *Niboyet/Sinopoli*, Gaz.Pal. 2004 IV 31. About fraud, see *infra* Art. 45 note 27 (*Francq*).

[92] *Gaudemet-Tallon* p. 414, para. 400.

[93] A few recent examples: BGH XII ZR 37/09 paras. 16–17 (inquiring whether the enforcement of a German decision could be refused in Austria on grounds of public policy under Regulation Brussels I, underlining that review as to the merits and applicable law is forbidden and, quite paradoxically, that Austrian law contains provisions similar to those of the German applicable law in regards of alimony for children); Cass. Belgium, 29 April 2010, *Goeble & Kuhl Gmbh v. Tops Food* (sanctioning an Appeal decision because it refused enforcement of a German decision under Art. 34 (2) of the Brussels I Regulation with a motivation based on a review as to the substance). Cour d'Appel (Luxembourg), 8e ch., 14 July 2009, n° 31043, Journal des tribunaux Luxembourg (2010), 206 (the refusal ground based on public policy cannot be opposed to a French decision on the sole ground that the criminal offence at the basis of a criminal judgment from which the civil judgment derives is not as such punished under criminal law in Luxembourg where enforcement of the civil judgment is sought).

[94] *Dieter Krombach v. André Bamberski*, (Case C-7/98) (2000) ECR I-1935 para. 36.

[95] Cf. *supra* Art. 45 note 19 (*Francq*) *in fine*. Considering that the question raised had already been judged unfounded by the court of origin and could not therefore justify the application of Article 27 (1) Brussels Convention: Hoge Raad, *Hupperichs v. Dorthu*, in *Kaye* p. 3277.

ment is sought or of a right recognised as being fundamental within that legal order".[96] This frame is valid for the intervention of both substantial and procedural public policy.

21a Because the courts of the requested State is not entitled to review the findings of law and facts made by the court of origin, they may not use public policy to control the jurisdiction of the court of origin. This is expressly stated in Art. 45 (3). However if the judgement conflicts with a limited list of jurisdiction rules (concerning the protection of the weak party or exclusive grounds of jurisdiction provided by Art. 24), recognition and enforcement will be refused under Art. 45 (1) (e). The breach of a choice-of-court agreement is no valid ground for refusing enforcement or recognition of judgment rendered in another Member State, because Art. 45 (1) (e) does not allow to review the jurisdiction of the court of origin in regard of Art. 25 Brussels *Ibis*. The new *lis pendens* regime might reduce the chances of obtaining a judgment in breach of a jurisdiction agreement. Art. 31 (2) obliges the court seized in breach of an alleged choice-of-court agreement to stay proceeding until the court seized on the basis of the agreement declares that it has no jurisdiction.

22 A mere difference of legislation does not amount to an infringement of public policy.[97] Again, denying recognition on the sole ground that the law applied by the court of origin is different from the law of the forum amounts to a review of the first judgment as to its substance. It would also exceed the limits of the control highlighted before: only the result of the recognition or enforcement, not the judgment itself, is appreciated with regard to fundamental principles of the State addressed. The same is true for the interpretation of a convention to which both States would be parties: the stricter interpretation accepted in the country of origin does not offend public policy of the forum.[98] For the same reason, alleged errors, which would have occurred in the application of the law, be it national or Community law, do not justify either the intervention of public policy. The contrary would amount to criticism of the legal reasoning held by the judge of origin. In this respect, the Court has stated that national and Community law are on equal footing in the *Renault v. Maxicar* case and in the *Diageo Brands v. Simiramida* case (*infra*).

23 In *Renault v. Maxicar*, the litigation was between a French company, Renault, and an Italian Company, Maxicar, which was condemned in France for forgery. The Italian Company had manufactured and marketed spare parts for Renault cars in breach of exclusive intellectual property rights conferred on Renault by French Law. Italy did not have a law recognising exclusive intellectual property rights on spare parts of cars. Maxicar was condemned in France to pay damages. When Renault sought to enforce the judgment in Italy (five years

---

[96] *Dieter Krombach v. André Bamberski,* (Case C-7/98) (2000) ECR I-1935 para. 37; *Régie nationale des usines Renault SA v. Maxicar SpA and Orazio Formento,* (Case C-38/98) (2000) ECR I-2973 para. 30; *Meletis Apostolides v. David Charles Orams,* (Case C-420/07) (2009) ECR I-3571 para. 59; *Trade Agency Ltd v. Seramico Investments Ltd.* (Case 619/10), ECLI:EU:C:2012:531 para.51; *flyLAL-Lithuanian Airlines,* (Case-302/13) ECLI:EU:C:2014:2319, para. 49.

[97] *flyLAL-Lithuanian Airlines,* (Case-302/13) ECLI:EU:C:2014:2319, para. 48; *Dieter Krombach v. André Bamberski,* (Case C-7/98) (2000) ECR I-1935 para. 37; *Régie nationale des usines Renault SA v. Maxicar SpA and Orazio Formento,* (Case C-38/98) (2000) ECR I-2973 para. 29. See for national application: BGH (2001) I.L.Pr. 425; BGH (2012), IX ZB, 183/09, para.11 (about procedural public policy and a difference of procedural laws).

[98] OLG Hamburg (1996) I.L.Pr. 497.

later), Maxicar contended that enforcement would be a contradiction of public policy. Basically, Maxicar held that French law was contrary to two fundamental principles of Community law, the free circulation of goods and the prohibition of abuse of dominant position. Therefore the judgment applying such law should be denied enforcement on the ground of Italian public policy which is in tune with fundamental principles of Community law. The Court insisted on the well-established narrow interpretation of public policy: disparities between the law applied by the first court and that which would have been applied by the court seized with enforcement, or alleged errors in the application of the law do not justify the recourse to public policy. As a result, enforcement could not be refused "solely on the ground that national or Community law was misapplied".[99] The Court went on to say that "an error of law such as that alleged in the main proceedings does not constitute a manifest breach of a rule of law regarded as essential in the legal order of the State in which enforcement is sought" and that the judgment recognising the existence of intellectual property rights in body parts for cars could not be considered as contrary to public policy.[100] Therefore, the Court did not address further questions concerning the compatibility of French Law with the EC Treaty.

It is conclusive that the decision of the ECJ establishes the equality between national and **24** Community law as component parts of public policy within the meaning of Art. 45 (1) (a) of the Regulation (at the time, Art. 27 of the Brussels Convention). It also illustrates the principles mentioned earlier: only the result of enforcement should lead to infringement of fundamental principles of the State where recognition or enforcement is sought, not the legal reasoning of the court, which rendered the judgment. But what is more astonishing is the importance attributed by the Court to the principles of Community Law that were at stake, especially with regard to another decision rendered earlier, namely the Eco Swiss China decision.[101] In Eco Swiss China, the ECJ was asked to state whether Art. 85 EC Treaty (now 101 TFEU) was part of public policy which serves as a ground for annulment of arbitration awards in domestic law. Though Art. 45 (1) (a) of the Regulation (or its equivalent under the Brussels Convention or Regulation Brussels I) was not at stake, the ground provided for by the procedural law of the Netherlands was interpreted in a very similar way. The Court decided that "where domestic rules of procedure require a national court to grant an application for annulment of an arbitration award where such an application is founded on failure to observe national rules of public policy, it must also grant such an application where it is founded on failure to comply with the prohibition laid down in Article 85 (1) of the Treaty".[102] Even though "annulment of or refusal to recognise an award should be possible only in exceptional circumstances", "according to Art. 3 (g) of the EC Treaty (now, after amendment, Art. 3 (1) (g) EC), Art. 85 of the Treaty constitutes a fundamental provision which is essential for the accomplishment of the tasks entrusted to the Commu-

---

99   *Régie nationale des usines Renault SA v. Maxicar SpA and Orazio Formento*, (Case C-38/98) (2000) ECR I-2973 para. 33.

100 *Régie nationale des usines Renault SA v. Maxicar SpA and Orazio Formento*, (Case C-38/98) (2000) ECR I-2973 para. 34.

101 *Eco Swiss China Time Ltd. v. Benetton International NV*, (Case 126/97) ECR (1999) I-3055.

102 *Eco Swiss China Time Ltd. v. Benetton International NV*, (Case 126/97) ECR (1999) I-3055 para. 37.

Stéphanie Francq

nity and, in particular, for the functioning of the internal market".[103] The confrontation of the two decisions gives the following results. On the one hand, 101 TFEU (former 85 ECT) belongs to public policy within the meaning of domestic law when it serves to oppose arbitral awards. On the other hand, it is not sure whether 102 TFEU (former 86 ECT) belongs to national conceptions of public policy when it serves to refuse enforcement of judgments rendered in other Member States. Indeed in the Renault Case, the Court states that the alleged misapplication of Art. 86 ECT did not constitute a manifest breach of a rule of law regarded as essential in Italy.[104] As a result, the established misapplication of Art. 85 ECT is contrary to public policy in one context, but the alleged misapplication of Art. 86 ECT cannot be considered as infringing public policy in another context. The explanation of this apparent contradiction must therefore have something to do with the context. And maybe with the provisions at stake. Art. 45 (1) (a) opposes the recognition of judgments rendered in Member States which present two advantages in comparison with arbitral awards. Firstly, they enjoy a presumption of regularity which could explain that the test of public policy should be even lighter in their case. Secondly, they can be submitted to the system of legal remedies organized by the Treaty, especially the preliminary ruling. Such a possibility is not offered in the framework of arbitration and this consideration seems to have puzzled the ECJ in the Eco Swiss Case.[105] From the comparison between Art. 85 and 86 of the EC Treaty (now Art. 101 and 102 TFEU), it comes out that agreements concluded in contradiction with the first one are automatically void, a specification not provided by the latter one. Would this explain why the infringement of Art. 85 ECT (101 TFEU) would amount to a manifest breach of a fundamental principle, when the same is not true for Art. 86 ECT (102 TFEU)? The mutual trust accorded to judgments rendered in Member States and the system of legal remedies offered to the parties in order to raise their claims seems to provide for a more convincing explanation.

24a   Mutual trust in the administration of justice in other Member States lies at the heart of the ECJ decision *Diageo Brands v. Simiramida*,[105a] dealing with a manifest misapplication of EU law by the court of origin. Confirming its decision in *Renault v. Maxicar*, the court decides that "the fact that a judgment given in a Member State is contrary to EU law does not justify that judgment's not being recognised in another Member State on the grounds that it infringes public policy in that Member State where the error of law relied on does not constitute a manifest breach of a rule of law regarded as essential in the EU legal order and therefore in the legal order of the Member State in which recognition is sought or of a right recognised as being fundamental in those legal orders". The Bulgarian lower instance court had manifestly misapplied several provisions of Directive 89/104 on the approximation of Member States laws on trade marks (applicable to the case, even if now replaced by 2008/95 directive) in a litigation opposing the Dutch holder of the brand Johnny Walker (Diageo Brands) and the Bulgarian importer of a large consignment of Johnny Walker bottles coming from a third State. The consignment had been seized in Hungary but Diageo Brands lost on the merits, due to established case law of the cassation court misapplying the directive. The lower instance court followed the last instance court case law, and Diageo

---

[103]   *Eco Swiss China Time Ltd. v. Benetton International NV*, (Case 126/97) ECR (1999) I-3055 para. 35.

[104]   *Régie nationale des usines Renault SA v. Maxicar SpA and Orazio Formento*, (Case C-38/98) (2000) ECR I-2973 para. 34.

[105]   *Eco Swiss China Time Ltd. v. Benetton International NV*, (Case 126/97) ECR (1999) I-3055 paras. 32–34.

[105a]   *Diageo Brands v. Simiramida*, (Case C-681/13), nyr.

Brands did not appeal, assuming that the last instance court would not change its position. When the Bulgarian importer instigated proceedings in the Netherlands in regard of the damage suffered as a result of the seizure, Diageo Brands opposed the recognition of the Bulgarian decision on the merits on the basis of public policy. Upon the preliminary ruling requested by the Hoge Raad, the ECJ restated the limitative interpretation of public policy. Prohibition of reviewing the foreign decision on the merits implies that the mere difference between the legal rules applied or an error of law supposedly committed by the court of the Sate of origin are not as such sufficient grounds for raising the public policy exception (paras. 43 and 50). The ECJ found that despite an error in the application of Directive 89/104, the recognition of the Bulgarian judgement could not be considered as infringing a "fundamental principle" of the EU legal order (paras. 50 and 51). Beyond confirming *Renault v. Maxicar*, the Diageo *Brands v. Simiramida* is interesting in two respects. First, it offers an interesting statement in regard of mutual trust: mutual trust "requires (…) each of those States, save in exceptional circumstances, to consider all the other Member States to be complying with EU law and thus that the administration of justice in the European Union is dealt with in accordance with EU law" (para. 40). This statement, even though not entirely new, seems to establish a sort of "Bosphorus" presumption within the EU legal system in favor of each Member State.[105b] Second, the ruling illustrates the existence of a European public policy. While in *Renault v. Maxicar* (also dealing with misapplication of EU law), the ECJ referred to a "manifest breach of a rule of law regarded as essential in the legal order *of the State* in which enforcement is sought or of a right recognized as being fundamental within that legal order" (para. 30; emphasis added), in *Diageo Brands v. Simiramida*, the ECJ analyses how the enforcement of the judgement would contradict fundamental principles or right of the EU legal order (paras. 50–51).

The mere difference between the PIL rules applied by the judge of origin and those which **25** would have been applied by the judge seized with the recognition does not as such lead to an infringement of public policy. Art. 27 (4) Brussels Convention, by allowing the control of the applicable law for substantial issues excluded from the material scope of the Convention, led to thinking that such a control was excluded in other cases.[106] Truly enough, the *in concreto* appreciation is hardly reconcilable with the control of a conflict rule: as already underlined, it is the result of the enforcement that matters, not the legal reasoning of the foreign judge. Thus it is rather the outcome of the application of the law designated by the foreign conflict rule which might infringe the public policy of the requested State. According to some authors, it can never be dismissed that a foreign conflict rule, as such, may contradict the public policy of the State where recognition is sought.[107] Admitting that examples are difficult to find, they refer to the default of application of domestic rules presenting a particularly strong will of application, i.e. international mandatory rules or "lois de police", in particular national competition rules.[108] One author, dwelling upon arguments from the Ingmar decision,[109] considers that those rules excluding the application of the law of third States contained in consumer protection directives, such as Art. 6 of the former Directive on unfair

---

[105b] *Bosphorus v. Ireland*, Application n° 45036/98, ECHR Grand Chamber decision 30 June 2005.

[106] Report *Jenard* p. 44; *Beraudo* para. 103.

[107] *Contra Peter Schlosser* Art. 34–36 para. 3.

[108] *Geimer/Schütze* Art. 34 note 18; *Leible*, in: Rauscher Art. 34 note 19; *Kropholler/von Hein* Art. 34 notes 12 and 17.

[109] *IngmarGB Ltd v. Eaton Leonard Technologies Inc*, (Case C-381/98) (2000) ECR I-9305.

terms in consumer contract, would trigger the application of the public policy refusal ground when not respected.[110] Their position amounts to considering public policy at the recognition stage as a mean of enforcement of national "lois de police". This raises two questions. Firstly, even if public policy were to protect the application of the "lois de police" of the requested State, would it apply because of a contradiction with the content of the "lois de police", or with the applicability rule expressing the will of application of this rule to such a situation? The margin is so narrow between the content of the rule and the conditions of its applicability that they can hardly be differentiated. Therefore, it is difficult to say that public policy in this case would protect a rule of private international law rather than substantive principles. Second, it is not so sure that public policy and "lois de police" should be so easily confused.[111] At least, all "lois de police" cannot be said to embody principles belonging to international public policy. More fundamentally, the two concepts serve different purposes and cover different kinds of principles, those protected by public policy being more fundamental than those legislative policies protected by "lois de police".[112] Therefore a contradiction between public policy and a foreign conflict rule may be more realistic in a case of an infringement of fundamental principles not necessarily embodied in international mandatory rules, such as the principle of gender equality.

26   A delicate question concerns the fate of those national conflict rules, which could be considered as contrary to European law. This could occur in the case of a conflict rule infringing the prohibition of discrimination or constituting an obstacle to trade or circulation of persons or services, for instance by reserving some advantages to its nationals.[113] Would such a conflict rule then automatically infringe public policy within the meaning of Art. 45 (1), a)? As the Renault v. Maxicar case shows, it depends on the status given by the ECJ to the European principles disregarded by the national conflict rule. Indeed a conflict rule could very well contradict a principle of European law without justifying recourse to public policy against a judgment having applied this conflict rule. The availability of a means of redress in the Member State of origin, such as the preliminary ruling, would certainly come into consideration, as it did in the Renault v. Maxicar case, and reduce the chances of success of an argument based on public policy at the stage of recognition or enforcement.

27   The possibility of invoking that the judgment was obtained by fraud in the State of origin[114]

---

110   *Ansgar Staudinger*, EuLF 2004, 273, 277.

111   Denying recourse to public policy for refusing recognition of a judgment which did not comply with a Belgian "loi de police": Trib. civ. Liège Act. Dr. (1996) 80. For the different situation of arbitral awards, see *Kleinheisterkamp*, The impact of internationally mandatory law on the enforceability of arbitration agreements, World Arbitration & Mediation Review, Vol. 3, p. 91.

112   This does not mean that public policy and "lois de police" are without connection. For more detail cf. *Francq*, L'applicabilité du droit communautaire dérivé au regard des méthodes du droit international privé (2005) p. 35, 553, 607.

113   The ECJ has not yet condemned a conflict rule as such, but the argument has already been raised (*Jutta Johannes v. Hartmut Johannes*, (Case C-430/97) (1999) ECR I-3475) and since the Court controls any kind of legislation, conflict rules cannot as such be excluded from the scope of its control. The question is raised with regard to Article 12 EC (now 18 TFEU) by *Leible*, in: Rauscher Art. 34 note 19. The compatibility of bilateral conflict rules with EU law has been more often discussed in the field of family law than in civil and commercial cases (see for instance: *Carlos Garcia Avello v. Belgian State*, (Case C-148/02) (2003) ECR I-11613).

is also influenced by the availability of means of redress in the first State. Though the question was at first debated, especially after the accession of Ireland and the United Kingdom, the Schlosser report confirmed that fraud would be controlled under the heading of public policy.[115] It also sets the limits of the argument: the judge of the requested State should always ask himself whether breach of its public policy still exists in view of the fact that proceedings for redress can be, or could have been, lodged in the courts of the State of origin against the judgment allegedly obtained by fraud. This position, once more, is coherent with the prohibition of review as to the substance. Of course, the judge seized with recognition will have to apprehend elements, which might have been already submitted to the judge of origin.[116] This derives directly from the mere existence of a ground for refusal based on public policy. But the public policy argument cannot lead to a control of the findings of law and facts made by the judge of origin. As a result, when the fraud has already been alleged before the judge of origin, it is only in very exceptional cases that it could be accepted as a ground for refusing recognition.[117] When fraud has been discovered after the judgment was rendered and could not therefore be controlled by the judge of origin, the fate of the argument at the recognition stage will depend on the availability of means of redress in the first State. If such means exist and have not been exercised, recognition should not be refused.[118] If such means do not exist, recognition should be refused if fraud is proven before the judge of the requested State.[119] Two delicate question remain. First, when means of

---

[114] This conception of fraud is to be distinguished from the "fraude à la loi" existing when factual elements have been manipulated in order to influence the designation of the applicable law. This conception of fraud is usually not considered as part of public policy under Article 45 (1) (a): *Béraudo* para. 109 in fine; *Gothot/Holleaux* note 260 in fine. See however CA Paris Clunet 116 (1989) 102 with note *André Huet*.

[115] Report *Schlosser* para. 192; *Fentiman*, International Commercial Litigation, OUP 2010, 717, note 18.48 (underlining that the scope of fraud is narrower under the European regime of recognition and enforcement that under English common law); *Hill/Chong*, International Commercial Disputes, Hart 2010, 4th ed., 460, para. 13. 3. 15 (fraud can be raised as a refusal ground even when it has been discussed and rejected in the original proceeding); *Mayer/Heuzé*, para. 477, p. 328. For an interesting case of application: Cass. Fr. 23.10.2013, n° 12-20102.

[116] *Gothot/Holleaux* para. 260.

[117] *Béraudo* para. 107; *Gothot/Holleaux* para. 260. The same line of reasoning is basically followed in the United Kingdom: see *Interdesco S.A. v. Nullfire Ltd* (1992) 1 Lloyd's Rep. 180 and the summary in *Kaye* pp. 3268–3276; *Soc d'Information Inc v. Ampersand*, (1994) 5 ILPr 55 (CA)

[118] This explains why the defendant against whom a default judgment was obtained cannot later claim that it was obtained by fraud: he had to raise the argument before the court of the State of origin: Cass. RCDIP 91 (2002), 573 with note *Ancel* = Clunet 130 (2003), 157 with note *André Huet* (a different position should be adopted if fraud was discovered after the expiration of all means of redress in the State of origin). In exceptional circumstances, fraud can be raised at the execution stage by a defendant who did not appeal. Such is the case of a defendant who renounced to introduce appeal because the plaintiff promised him that he would never execute a judgment only due to reassure his (potential) creditors: BGH IPRax 1987, 236, 219 with note *Grunsky* (for later developments in this case see *infra* note 33 (*Francq*) and the BGH decisions cited by *Hess/Pfeiffer/Schlosser* Report). If an appeal is lodged, the judge seized with the execution remains free to refuse to stay proceedings. The BGH confirmed the principle that the defendant who chooses not to appeal in the State of origin on basis of fraud cannot later raise fraud under public policy at the enforcement level in the requested State: BGH (2012), IX ZB 56/10, para. 3.

[119] *Layton/Mercer* para. 26.024; *Béraudo* para. 110; *Gothot/Holleaux* para. 260; refusing to consider the argument of fraud because it would amount to review as to the substance.

Stéphanie Francq

redress, available in the State of origin, have not been exercised yet but are still open, what should the judge of the requested State do? The judge seized with recognition is only allowed to stay proceedings for ordinary appeals (Art. 46 of the Brussels I Regulation).[120] If such recourses fall into the category of extraordinary means of redress, it seems that recognition must be granted.[121] Second, Hartley distinguishes fraud committed in the State of origin from fraud committed by the court of origin.[122] If it were proved that the court of origin was guilty of bias or corruption, it could also be doubted that appeal in the State of origin would be efficient. Therefore, one can wonder whether the possibility to invoke the refusal ground should be submitted to exhaustion of remedies in the State of origin. Reviewing of foreign decision on the ground of alleged bias or corruption, without reviewing the merits of the case, might however prove very difficult.

27a Substantive public policy "seeks to protect legal interests which are expressed through a rule of law, and not purely economic interests".[123] Therefore, the financial consequences of the enforcement do not come into account under Art. 45 (1) (a).[124] In the *flyLAL-Lithuanian Airlines* case, the Court was asked whether the serious economic consequences of the enforcement which would in the end be supported by the Latvian State as the major shareholder of the defendants would justify recourse to the refusal ground based on public policy as the enforcement of the decision would "jeopardise the security of the State".[125] The ECJ carefully underlines that the financial consequences had been discussed before the issuing court and that the Lithuanian decision, as a provisional and protective measure, does not request the payment of a sum, but concerns the monitoring of the defendants assets.[126]

b) Procedural public policy

28 The question whether the provisions currently numbered Art. 45 (1) (a) (and formerly, Art. 34 (1) Brussels I and 27 (1) Brussels Convention) could offer a legal basis for controlling the foreign procedure has been long debated. Both the text of the provision (more precisely, the text of Art. 34 Brussels I and 27 Brussels Convention) and its traditional interpretation led to think that this kind of control should be excluded.[127] Firstly, it was sustained that Art. Art. 34 (2) Brussels I and 27 (2) Brussels Convention (now Art. 45 (1) (b) Brussels *Ibis*) were the only provision devoted to the procedural aspects of the judgment: therefore a control of the foreign procedure could only take place within the narrow conditions set by the second point of Art. 34 Brussels I (or 27 Brussels Convention), now Art. 45 (1) (b). Secondly, the

---

[120] See for the autonomous definition given by the ECJ of the notion of "ordinary" appeal: *Industrial Diamond Supplies v. Luigi Riva*, (Case 43/77) (1977) ECR 2175 para. 42: "any appeal which is such that it may result in the annulment or the amendment of the judgment which is the subject-matter of the procedure for recognition or enforcement under the Convention and the lodging of which is bound, in the State in which judgment was given, to a period which is laid down by the law and starts to run by virtue of that same judgment constitutes an 'ordinary appeal'".

[121] *Gothot/Holleaux* para. 260.

[122] *Hartley*, International Commercial Litigation (2009) pp. 338–339.

[123] *FlyLAL-Lithuanian Airlines*, (Case-302/13) ECLI:EU:C:2014:2319 para. 56. See also A-G *Kokott*, Opinion of 3. July 2014 in Case C-302/13, ECLI:EU:C:2014:2046 paras. 84–85.

[124] *FlyLAL-Lithuanian Airlines*, (Case-302/13) ECLI:EU:C:2014:2319 para. 58.

[125] *FlyLAL-Lithuanian Airlines*, (Case-302/13) ECLI:EU:C:2014:2319 para. 4.

[126] *flyLAL-Lithuanian Airlines*, (Case-302/13) ECLI:EU:C:2014:2319 para. 57.

[127] *Droz* para. 489; *Gothot/Holleaux* paras. 271–273.

ECJ insisted that Art. 34 (2) Brussels I (at the time, Art. 27 (2) Brussels Convention, now 45 (1) (b) Brussels I*bis*) could only be relied on in exceptional circumstances "where the guarantees contained in the law of the State in which the judgment was given and in the Convention itself are insufficient to ensure that the defendant has an opportunity of arranging for his defence before the court in which judgment was given".[128] This statement combined with the restrictive interpretation of Art. 34 (1) Brussels I (now 45 (1) (a) Brussels I*bis*) suggested that the right to a fair hearing belongs only to the second point of Art. 34 Brussels I (now Art. 45 (1) (b)).[129] This position however left the defendant victim of gross violation of his right to a fair hearing, deprived of any protection when the limited conditions of 34 (2) Brussels I (now Art. 45 (1), b)) were not fulfilled.[130] The ECJ has settled the discussion in the Krombach case.[131] One can even wonder whether the obligation of controlling the foreign procedure outside the narrow conditions of Art. 45 (1) (b) was not already imposed on Member State after the Pellegrini case decided by the ECHR.[132] The reference to Art. 6 ECHR is now replaced or corroborated by a reference to Art. 47 of the Charter of Fundamental Rights of the European Union, "which corresponds, as is clear from the explanations relating to that article, to Article 6 (1) of the ECHR".[133]

Krombach v. Bamberski represents an important step in the case law of the ECJ concerning **29** the interpretation of the Brussels Convention and Regulation.[134] Mr Krombach was con-

---

[128] *Peter Klomps v. Karl Michel*, (Case 166/80) (1981) ECR 1593 para. 7.

[129] CA Paris Clunet 116 (1989), 100; Cass. Bull. civ. 1986 I n° 149.

[130] For more detail on the various positions defended in the doctrine, cf. *Gaudemet-Tallon* p. 416–418, para. 403. Different authors had already sustained that a control of the foreign procedure should take place in application of Art. 45 (1) (a). See amongst others *Sinopoli*, Le droit au procès équitable dans les rapports privés internationaux (thèse Paris I 2000).

[131] *Dieter Krombach v. André Bamberski*, (Case C-7/98) (2000) ECR I-1935.

[132] *Pellegrini v. Italy*, (Case 30882/96) (2001) D.R. 480. The ECHR held that the Italian Court had breached Art. 6, § 1 of the European Convention by authorizing enforcement of a judgment of the Roman Rota and holding that the applicant had had a right to a fair hearing before the ecclesiastical courts. The elements that the Italian courts should have controlled with regard to the foreign procedure go far beyond the procedural elements mentioned in Art. 45 (1) (b) of the Brussels I*bis* Regulation. In the context of Brussels I*bis*, this control could only be performed under the heading of Art. 45 (1) (a). Of course, the relationship between the interpretation of Community law (or the interpretation of Convention between Member States) and the interpretation of the ECHR would require more detailed comments. If an appeal is lodged, the judge seized with the execution remains free to refuse to stay proceedings: CA Versailles June 29, 2000, ECJ Website no. 2001/32. Generally speaking, the abolition of exequatur in various European Regulation on private international law and the automatic enforcement of foreign decisions give rise to litigation before the ECHR. For a good overview *Marchadier*, Eur. J. Human Rights 2013, 348–380. See also the following decisions of the ECHR: S. *Povse & D. Povse v. Austria*, Application n° 3890/11 (about Brussels IIa); *Avotiņš v. Lettonie*, (Application. N°17502/07) (about Art. 34 (2) Brussels I; *infra* Art. 45 note 59b (*Francq*)).

[133] *Trade Agency Ltd v. Seramico Investments Ltd.* (Case 619/10), ECLI:EU:C:2012:531 para. 52. See also: *DEB Deutsche Energiehandels- und Beratungsgesellschaft mbH v. Bundesrepublik Deutschland*, (Case C-279/09) (2010) ECR I-13849 para. 10 ("As regards fundamental rights, it is important, since the entry into force of the Lisbon Treaty, to take account of the Charter, which has 'the same legal value as the Treaties' pursuant to the first subparagraph of Article 6 (1) TEU. Article 51 (1) of the Charter states that the provisions thereof are addressed to the Member States when they are implementing EU law.")

Stéphanie Francq

demned by French Courts for violence resulting in the death of a young girl, Kalinka Bamberski. A civil claim was introduced by the father of the victim before the criminal courts whose jurisdiction was based on the French nationality of the victim. The second peculiarity of these proceedings was that since Mr Krombach refused to appear in person before the French criminal court though he was duly summoned to do so, he was reputed to be contemnor and as such prohibited to be represented by a lawyer. Mr. Bamberski later sought to enforce in Germany the civil judgment condemning Mr. Krombach for damages. Upon appeal from Mr. Krombach, the case ended up before the Bundesgerichtshof which referred two questions to the ECJ. The first was whether enforcement could be refused under Art. 45 (1) (a) (at the time Art. 27 (1) Brussels Convention) on the basis that the foreign court accepted jurisdiction on the basis of nationality of the victim, a ground similar to one prohibited by Art. 5 (2) of the Brussels *Ibis* (at the time Art. 3 second indent Brussels Convention); the second was whether public policy could be considered infringed when the defendant was denied the right to be defended by a lawyer during the proceedings in the State of origin. Without surprise, the ECJ confirmed that Art. 45 (1) (a) (at the time Art. 27 (1) Brussels Convention) cannot be used to control the jurisdiction of the Court of origin.[135] Concerning the second question, the Court asserted the general description of application of Art. 45 (1) (a) (at the time Art. 27 (1) Brussels Convention) mentioned earlier:[136] public policy requires the manifest infringement of a rule or principle considered as fundamental in the Member State where recognition or enforcement is sought.[137] According to the Court, there is no doubt that the right to be effectively defended constitutes one of those fundamental rights since it is considered as such by the constitutional traditions common to Member States, by the European Court of Human Rights and EC law.[138] Hence nothing can preclude the requested tribunal to consider that "the refusal to hear the defence of an accused person who is not present at the hearing constitutes a manifest breach of a fundamental right".[139] As the ECJ underlines it, the decision implies that recourse to public policy is possible "in exceptional cases where the guarantees laid down in the legislation of the State of origin and in the Convention itself have been insufficient to protect the defendant from a manifest breach of his right to defend himself before the court of origin, as recognised by the ECHR".[140]

---

[134] The following paragraph refers to the provisions of the Regulation though the decision was concerned with the application of the Convention, namely Art. 27 (1) Brussels Convention and Article II of the Protocol of 27 September 1968 on the interpretation of the Brussels Convention.

[135] *Dieter Krombach v. André Bamberski*, (Case C-7/98) (2000) ECR I-1935 para. 34.

[136] *Supra* Art. 45 note 21 (*Francq*).

[137] *Dieter Krombach v. André Bamberski*, (Case C-7/98) (2000) ECR I-1935 para. 37.

[138] *Dieter Krombach v. André Bamberski*, (Case C-7/98) (2000) ECR I-1935 paras. 24–26, 38–39, 42.

[139] *Dieter Krombach v. André Bamberski*, (Case C-7/98) (2000) ECR I-1935 para. 40. Another point concerned the impact of Art. 61 Brussels I Regulation (Art. II of the Protocol of 27 September 1968 on the interpretation Brussels Convention) which expressly recognises the right for persons prosecuted for unintentional offence in a Member State to be represented by a lawyer when they do not appear in person. This provision could be construed as denying the right to be defended to persons prosecuted for intentional offence. Recalling that the right to a fair hearing is a fundamental principle of Community law, the ECJ refused such an interpretation and thus overruled previous case-law (*Criminal proceedings against Siegfried Ewald Rinkau*, (Case 157/80) (1981) ECR 1391 para. 12) on the argument that the aims of the Convention/regulation, i.e. facilitating the circulation of judgments, could not be reached by undermining such an important right (paras. 42–43).

The later Gambazzi decision of the ECJ offers another example of procedural public policy **29a** under Art. 45 (1) (a) (the case was still concerning Art. 27 (1) Brussels Convention).[141] The facts present some similarities with the Krombach case in the sense that the defendant was forbidden to take part to the proceedings on the merits. Mr Gambazzi was condemned by the English High Court of Justice (England & Wales) to pay damages with interests to the companies DaimlerChrysler and CIBC. Specifically, because Mr Gambazzi did not fully comply with a disclosure order – requesting the disclosure of details of his assets and certain documents in his possession concerning the principal claim – he was held in contempt of court and was excluded from the proceedings ("debarment"). Before excluding Mr Gambazzi from the proceedings, the High Court has made two "unless order" summoning Mr Gambazzi to comply with the disclosure order before he could take part again in the proceedings. Mr Gambazzi had appealed against the "unless" and the "disclosure" orders, but all were rejected. In the end, the High Court entered judgment as if Mr Gambazzi was in default. The companies later sought to enforce the English decision in Italy. The Corte d'appello di Milano declared it enforceable. Upon appeal from Mr Gambazzi, the Corte d'appello di Milano decided to stay the proceedings and to refer to the ECJ the question of whether the fact that the court of the State of origin ruled on the plaintiff's claims without hearing the defendant, who entered appearance before it, but was excluded from the proceedings by an order, on the ground that he had not complied with the obligations imposed by an order adopted at an earlier stage, could be taken into account, with regard to the public policy clause in Art. 45 (1) (b) (i.e Art. 27 (1) Brussels Convention). Broadly referring to the *Krombach* case, the ECJ answered affirmatively by stressing the necessity of making a comprehensive assessment of the proceedings, in order to examine, in the light of all the circumstances, if it appears that the exclusion measure constituted a manifest and disproportionate infringement of the defendant's right to be heard, in compliance with the adversarial principle and the full exercise of the rights of defence.[142] The contribution of this case, in comparison with the *Krombach* case-law, is to stress that fundamental rights, such as the right to be effectively defended, may be subject to restrictions if those comply with "the objectives of public interest pursued by the measure in question" and do "not constitute, with regard to the aim pursued, a manifest or disproportionate breach of the rights thus guaranteed".[143] The State in which enforcement is sought has to assess whether the right to be heard has been violated, in regard to the specific facts of the proceedings, without reviewing the High Court's assessments of the merits.[144] More specifically, the ECJ states that "the referring court must confine itself to identifying the legal remedies which were available to Mr. Gambazzi and to verifying that they offered him the possibility of being heard, in compliance with the adversarial principle and the full exercise of the rights of defence".[145] The application of the public policy clause of Art. 45 (1) (a) (i.e Art. 27 (1) Brussels Con-

---

140 *Dieter Krombach v. André Bamberski*, (Case C-7/98) (2000) ECR I-1935 para. 44.

141 *Marco Gambazzi v. DaimlerChrysler Canada Inc.*, (Case 394/07) (2009) ECR I-2563, para. 25. For a detailed analysis of the case and of its procedural context: *Cuniberti* (2009) RCDIP, 685.

142 *Marco Gambazzi v. DaimlerChrysler Canada Inc.*, (Case 394/07) (2009), ECR I-2563, para. 42, 45, 46. See also, *Trade Agency Ltd v. Seramico Investments Ltd.* (Case 619/10), ECLI:EU:C:2012:531 para. 62 (insisting on the need for a global assessment of the procedure, in regard of all the circumstances, in search of a "a manifest and disproportionate breach of the defendant's right to a fair trial").

143 *Marco Gambazzi v. DaimlerChrysler Canada Inc.*, (Case 394/07) (2009), ECR I-2563, para. 29.

144 *Marco Gambazzi v. DaimlerChrysler Canada Inc.*, (Case 394/07) (2009), ECR I-2563, para. 46.

145 *Marco Gambazzi v. DaimlerChrysler Canada Inc.*, (Case 394/07) (2009), ECR I-2563, para. 46.

Stéphanie Francq   893

vention) has to be understood as giving a margin of appreciation to the court of the State in which enforcement is sought, to assess the degree of infringement of the right to be heard. The requested tribunal thus has to strike a "balance" between the right to be heard and the needs of a "fair and efficient administration of justice" raised by the government of the United Kingdom for justifying the "disclosure order" and "unless order" and the need to ascertain the efficiency of those orders.[146] The Italian court of Appeal found eventually (after the preliminary ruling) that the enforcement of the English decision did not contravene public policy.[147]

29b Similar issues have been raised in the *Trade Agency* decision.[148] The ECJ was asked whether the enforcement of a decision rendered in default of appearance by the High Court (UK) could be considered as violating public policy when the decision "disposes of the substance of the case" but "does not contain any assessment of the subject-matter or the basis of the action and which is devoid of any argument on the merits thereof".[149] The ECJ advises the national judge to balance the right to a fair hearing (especially here the obligation for judgments to be reasoned) versus the need for swift, effective and cost-effective proceedings. Indeed, if the ECJ had already stated that judgments must be reasoned in order for the defendant to be aware of the reasons why the judgment is rendered against him and of the effective means of appeal, such a requirement can be submitted to restrictions, "provided that the restrictions in fact correspond to objectives of general interest pursued by the measure in question and that they do not constitute, with regard to the objectives pursued, a manifest and disproportionate breach of the rights thus guaranteed".[150] In the particular circumstances of the case, a judgment in default of appearance had been rendered against a Latvian defendant who had been served almost a month before the hearing. The English judgment was deprived of any explanation as to the facts and legal reasons supporting the order to pay a sum of money.[151] The Government of the United Kingdom explained that such a judgment could only be delivered after the claimant had filed a claim and the "particulars of claim", i.e. a detailed description of the facts and legal aspects of the plea, and the defendant does not enter an appearance after he has been informed of the proceed-

---

[146] *Marco Gambazzi v. DaimlerChrysler Canada Inc.*, (Case 394/07) (2009), ECR I-2563, para. 46 and 30. The reasoning is very close to an internal market reasoning where the courts considers whether an infringement to one of the fundamental rights granted by the EU Treaty to individuals is proportionate in regard to legitimate goals of public interest pursued by the infringing State.

[147] Corte d'appello Milano, Dec. 14, 2010 cited in *Hess/Pfeiffer*, Study: Interpretation of the Public Policy Exception as referred to in EU Instruments of Private International and Procedural Law, PE 453.189, 58 available at: www.europarl.europa.eu/studies.

[148] *Trade Agency Ltd v. Seramico Investments Ltd.* (Case 619/10), ECLI:EU:C:2012:531, see the second question paras. 47 and ff.

[149] *Trade Agency Ltd v. Seramico Investments Ltd.* (Case 619/10), ECLI:EU:C:2012:531, see the second question para. 47.

[150] *Trade Agency Ltd v. Seramico Investments Ltd.* (Case 619/10), ECLI:EU:C:2012:531 see the second question para. 55.

[151] The English decision was drafted as follows: "You have not replied to the claim form, which was served on you. It is therefore ordered that you must pay the claimant GBP 289 122.10 for debt [and interest to the date of the judgment] and GBP 130.00 for costs. You must pay to the claimant a total of GBP 293 582.98" (*Trade Agency Ltd v. Seramico Investments Ltd.* (Case 619/10), ECLI:EU:C:2012:531 see the second question para. 16).

---

ing.[152] It is thus for the Latvian judge to assess whether in regard of all the circumstances of the case and of the procedural guarantees surrounding the proceeding (notably the question whether and to what extent the defendant had had access to the statement of claim and had been informed of the potential remedies against the High Court decision), "the restriction introduced by the procedural system in England and Wales is not manifestly disproportionate as compared with the aim pursued".[153] In a decision concerning the enforcement of Lithuanian decision relating to damages following a violation of competition law, the ECJ found that as long as "it is possible to follow the line of reasoning which led to the determination of the amount of sums at issue", the decision does not lack reasoning.[154] The parties had been able to litigate and appeal against the Lithuanian decision.

Art. 45 (1) (b) has thereby definitively lost its monopoly in regard to the foreign procedure. **29c** All conditions considered by the ECHR as necessary for a fair trial, which could not be controlled under Art. 45 (1) (b) will thus fall under the first point of the same provision. Together with other developments of ECJ case law, the *Krombach* and *Gambazzi* decisions could even suggest that the distinction between Art. 45 (1) (a) and (b) is eroded since both provisions pursue the same aim: integrating the requirement of Art. 6 of the ECHR in recognition and enforcement procedures, and now Art. 47 of the Charter.[155] National cases show that procedural public policy is now a more frequent ground for refusing enforcement than substantive public policy.[156]

The preceding considerations should not lead to conclude that the control of the foreign **30** procedure under the Brussels Regulation is unlimited. The general limits affecting recourse to public policy explained earlier remain valid with regard to its procedural aspects.[157] In particular, a mere difference of procedure does not amount to infringement of public policy. The control must be lead *in concreto*[158] and in regard to all stages of the proceedings.[159] The

---

[152] *Trade Agency Ltd v. Seramico Investments Ltd.* (Case 619/10), ECLI:EU:C:2012:531 para. 56.

[153] *Trade Agency Ltd v. Seramico Investments Ltd.* (Case 619/10), ECLI:EU:C:2012:531 para. 56. See paras. 60 and 61 on the circumstances to be taken into consideration. For a presciently application of the same principle under Art. 34 (1) Brussels I Reguation: HR, 18.03.2011, LJN BP 0002 à BP 0004, NJ 2011, 218 (note *Polak*) para. 3.2. of case 10/01368 (BP 0002) and 10/01375 (BP 0003), para.15 of case 10/01377 (BP 0004) (stating that the mere absence of motivation cannot as such justify to refuse recognition of a decision from another Member State under Art. 34 (1) Brussels I but that the existence of a violation; the question whether the recognition of such a decision would constitute a violation of public policy depends on the circumstaces of the case and of the way the parties have been able to litigate).

[154] *FlyLAL-Lithuanian Airlines*, (Case-302/13) ECLI:EU:C:2014:2319, para. 53.

[155] See *infra* comments on the ASML decision, note 59a (*Francq*).

[156] *Hess/Pfeiffer*, Study: Interpretation of the Public Policy Exception as referred to in EU Instruments of Private International and Procedural Law, PE 453.189, 49–59, available at: www.europarl.europa.eu/ studies.

[157] *Supra* mainly Art. 45 notes 17–22 (*Francq*).

[158] Those conditions were already respected in the interpretation of the procedural aspect of public policy under domestic law or bilateral conventions in various Member States. See for instance for Germany: BGHZ 48, 327; BGH NJW 1990, 2201; BGHZ 118, 312; for the Netherlands: Hoge Raad NJ 1987 Nr. 481 with note Schultsz.

[159] *Marco Gambazzi v. DaimlerChrysler Canada Inc.*, (Case 394/07) (2009), ECR I-2563, para. 48.

---

residual function of Art. 45 (1) (a) with regard to Art. 45 (1) (b) should also be underlined again.[160]

31   National case law shows that the principle established in the Krombach decision was easily integrated in national legal orders. Domestic judges actually did not wait for the Krombach decision to integrate the requirement of Art. 6 ECHR in the control of public policy within the framework of Art. 45 (1) (a) of the Brussels *Ibis* Regulation.[161] Surprisingly, even among Member States, a control of the foreign procedure under the heading of public policy seems necessary. The case *Maronier v. Larmer* brought before the English Court of Appeal offers a perfect example of a situation where the right to a fair trial was not respected in the State of origin although the procedural requirements set by Art. 45 (1) (b) were complied with.[162] Proceedings pending in the Netherlands against a dentist were reactivated after 12 years of suspension due to health problems and bankruptcy of the claimant. Though the defendant had been properly served at the origin of the proceedings, he had in the meanwhile moved to England and lost all contacts with the law firm which first represented him. The defendant was thus never informed of the reactivation of the proceedings although he had taken care of leaving his new address with the City Hall in Rotterdam and the Dutch association of Dentists. As a result, he was not represented during the second part of the proceedings at the issue of which he was condemned for damages and substantial interests. He was first notified of the proceedings when the claimant sought to enforce the decision in England, long after the period for lodging an appeal had expired. Relying on the Krombach decision, the English court of appeal decided that the defendant did not receive a fair trial in the Netherlands, pursuant to the requirement under Art. 6 of the Human Rights Convention and refused enforcement. This kind of rather unusual situation shows that Art. 45 (1) (b) does not always provide a sufficient protection to the defendant with regard to the right to a fair trial.[163] National case law generally respects the exceptional character of the procedural aspect of public policy. The French and German Supreme courts did not hesitate to grant enforcement when the defendant did not prove a manifest violation of his right to be heard and underlined the active part that the defendant should take during the proceedings in the State of origin to present his defence.[164] In particular, the omission to introduce appeal in the

---

160   *Bernardus Hendrikman and Maria Feyen v. Magenta Druck & Verlag GmbH*, (Case C-78/95) (1996) ECR I-4943 para. 23. *Supra* Art. 45 note 19 (*Francq*).

161   For instance: Cass. (2000) I.L.Pr. 763 (excessive sums fixed for costs due from the plaintiff in a defamation action, which was not even considered on the merits after he could not pay the significant sum imposed as a security for costs, constitute an obstacle to the plaintiff's access to justice contrary to public policy; the court refers to Art. 6 of the ECHR and Art. 27 (1) Brussels Convention). Other examples are cited in: Hess/Pfeiffer, Study: Interpretation of the Public Policy Exception as referred to in EU Instruments of Private International and Procedural Law, PE 453.189, 58–59, available at: www.europarl.europa.eu/studies.

162   *W. Maronier v. Bryan Larmer* (2002) I.L.Pr. 685 (C.A., per Lord *Phillips of Worth Matravers* M.R.).

163   The English Court of Appeal stated that it had no information on how Dutch procedural law could allow reactivation after 12 years, without a fresh service to be effected on the defendant (*W. Maronier v. Bryan Larmer* (2002) I.L.Pr. 685 para. 36 (C.A., per Lord *Phillips of Worth Matravers* M.R.)).

164   Cass. (2005) I.L.Pr. 266 (defendant who had been properly served but did not enter an appearance and was not represented, did not present any elements that prevented him to take part in the original proceedings or to appeal against the English injunction); BGH (2003) I.L.Pr. 523 (although the translation of summons delivered on the German defendant was erroneous, he could at first glance have noticed

State of origin, without any convincing explanation, strongly diminishes the chances of raising the public policy ground for refusal in the requested State.[165] However some instances show that recourse to Art. 45 (1) (a) in regard of the right to a fair trial is necessary.[166]

Some national procedural peculiarities raise regular doubts in other Member States with **32** regard to public policy. Antisuit and Mareva injunctions in particular have attracted the attention of continental courts.[167] The ECJ settled the discussion concerning Antisuit in-

---

that the date of the hearing given in the translation did not match the date given in the summons and make further investigation; the basic right to be heard gives the defendant only a reasonable opportunity to take part in the judicial proceedings but does not exclude the defendant's own obligation to cooperate as soon as he is informed of the proceedings instituted against him abroad). The active role that should be taken by the claimant to comply with the defendant's right to be heard has also been underlined: OLG Düsseldorf (2002) I.L.Pr. 71 (claimant must prove that he has done what is necessary to find the plaintiff's address. Otherwise a service by publication in newspapers, though considered legitimate under Dutch law, would be considered as infringing public policy in Germany).

[165] In *Diageo Brands v. Simiramida* ((Case C-681/13), nyr.; supra Art. 45 note 24b, *Francq*), the defendant invoked procedural public policy for opposing the enforcement of a Bulgarian judgement misapplying EU law. According to the defendant, the Bulgarian court which had rendered a decision on the merits had breached its duty of cooperation by failing to request a preliminary ruling from the ECJ (para. 57). The ECJ underlined that the court of lower instance was not required to refer to the ECJ (para. 60) and that its decision could have been appealed, a procedure which the defendant failed to introduce (paras. 60–61). The ECJ stated that the defendant should have used "all the legal remedies made available by the law of the Member State of origin", "unless specific circumstances make it too difficult or impossible" (para. 64), especially in regard of the fact that the cassation court, as a court of last instance, would have been obliged to refer to the ECJ if a doubt concerning the application of EU law had been raised (para. 66). The defendant had assumed that the cassation court would not modify its (erroneous) interpretation of EU law. For national Case Law, see for instance: *Citibank N.A. v. Rafidian Bank and another* (2003) I.L.Pr. 758 (Q.B.D., *Tugendhat* J.) (two Iraqi State banks were condemned in the Netherlands to pay a substantial debt to Citibank. When Citibank obtained an order for enforcement in England, the defendants failed to appeal within the regular time-limit but applied for its extension on the ground that public policy had been violated in the Netherlands. They claimed that they had been denied access to legal representation because, due to sanctions imposed on Iraq between 1990 and 2003, their assets were frozen. The extension of this time-limit depended a.o. on the chance of success of the appeal against enforcement. The English High Court found that the case of the Iraqi defendant was not strong enough. Indeed at the time of proceedings in the State of origin, the Iraqi banks could have applied for release of their funds and did not do so. Further, no explanation was provided of what were the steps taken to have the Dutch judgment set aside and why they were unsuccessful).

[166] BGH (2010) IX ZB 121/07 para. 7 (considering under the Lugano Convention that a Swiss judgment refusing an appeal conflicts with public policy when appeal has been refused on the sole ground that the appellant did not pay the provision covering the costs of the litigation within a 2 days time limit).

[167] See for instance the facts and legal questions raised in: *Philip Alexander Securities and Futures Limited v. Bamberger, Theele, Kefer, Riedel, Franz and Gilhaus* (1997) I.L.Pr. 73 (Q.B.D., *Waller* J.); *Antonio Gramsci Shipping Corp v. Aivars Lembergs*, (Case C-350/13) (2014) not published yet (the court refused to answer preliminary questions concerning the compatibility of a mareva injunction with public policy, because the freezing order had been set aside after the ruling had been requested; the question concerned the right of third persons who were not parties to the main proceeding but who claimed their rights were infringed by the injunction).

Stéphanie Francq

junctions by declaring them incompatible with the Brussels Convention/Regulation on the ground that injunctions prohibiting one party from bringing an action before the Court of another Member State inevitably constitutes an interference with the jurisdiction of that foreign court.[168] Courts of other Member States would thus legitimately refuse enforcement of such injunctions on the ground of public policy. On the contrary, a Mareva injunction has been held by the French Cour de cassation as constituting a protective measure of a civil nature, which does not prejudice any of the debtor's fundamental rights, nor the foreign sovereignty and as such, does not trigger the application of Art. 45 (1) (a).[169] In France, the lack of motivation of foreign judgments is systematically considered as an infringement of public policy since it renders it impossible for the judge to control whether conditions established by the Brussels Convention/Regulation are met in allowing recognition or enforcement.[170] The only mean of redress is to produce documents equivalent to the failing motivation. This interpretation of public policy has been opposed to Belgian and German judgments.[171]

4. National Case Law and future developments

33   National case law is marked by a rather restrictive attitude. Examples show that an argument based on public policy, though often raised, is generally refused.[172] Concerning the procedural aspect of public policy, neither the lack of indication on the possible means of appeal,[173] nor a notification served upon the lawyer of the defendant according to civil procedure of the State of origin when the defendant has been duly informed of the proceedings,[174] nor the condemnation of the defendant to pay part of the legal costs paid by the claimant to his lawyers,[175] nor the loss of a stage of appeal for non-compliance with the challenged decision,[176] nor the allocation of interim relief much stricter than those found under domestic law,[177] nor the possibility of curing an irregularity which affected the proceedings at its beginning,[178] nor the enforcement of a decision partially based on an arbitration award that

---

[168]   *Gregory Paul Turner v. Felix Fareed Ismail Grovit, Harada Ltd. and Changepoint SA* (Case C-159/02), (2004) ECR I-3565 paras. 27, 31.

[169]   Cass. (2005) I.L.Pr. 266.

[170]   The solution is constant since: Cass. Clunet 106 (1979), 280 with note *Holleaux*. The opposite solution has been adopted in Italy, as long as the procedure in the State of origin was contradictory: Cassaz. January 13, 1995, ECJ Website n° 1997/14.

[171]   *Gaudemet-Tallon* p. 421 para. 405 in fine. *Infra* Art. 45 note 34 (*Francq*).

[172]   *Hess/Pfeiffer/Schlosser* Report, p. 244, para. 548. See also, p. 243–249, para. 545–558 for a review of national case law in regard to public policy. For reviews of the use of public policy exception under Brussels Convention and Brussels I Regulation by national courts, see: *Hess/Pfeiffer*, Study: Interpretation of the Public Policy Exception as referred to in EU Instruments of Private International and Procedural Law, PE 453.189, 49–94, available at: www.europarl.europa.eu/studies; *Jafferali*, TBH 2013, 357, 389–390 para. 55.

[173]   Cass. RCDIP 86 (1997), 85 with note *Muir Watt*. A mistaken indication of the possible means of appeal however has been considered as an infringement of public policy (Cass. France, 2e ch. Civ., 19 Nov. 2009, n° 08-12.134 cited by *Azoulai* (dir.), Europe (2010) 5, 14, para. 38.

[174]   Cass. France 1ᵉ ch. civ., 14 oct. 2009, *France édition v. Arti Grafiche Boccia*, n° 08-14.849.

[175]   Hof Gent Pas. belge 1989, III 162.

[176]   Cassaz. Giust. Civ. (1999) I 3009-3012 with note *Simone*.

[177]   OLG Hamm RIW 1985, 973 with note *Linke*.

had been set aside,[179] nor the fact that the decision has already been enforced in the Member State of origin,[180] nor the mere absence of reasoning of a foreign decision,[181] nor the refusal by the judge of origin to join to the cause the sub-contractors and the clients of the entrepreneur[182] have been considered as contrary to Art. 45 (1) (a). The French Cour de cassation admitted that refusing, under Art. 34 (1) Brussels I Regulation, the enforcement of a German decision on the ground that the German judge refused a cross-examination of the witness and the request for an expertise would amount to a review of the merits of the case.[183] The Belgian Cour de cassation confirmed the appeal decision refusing to consider contrary to public policy a judgment of the High Court condemning the defendant to pay maintenance, after refusing to hear his Belgian lawyer.[184] The defendant had refused to pay the important cost of an English lawyer and did not appeal against the High Court decision. Concerning the substantive aspect of public policy, a judgment rendered in breach of an arbitration agreement,[185] the use of method for calculating lawyers' fees or damages different or un-

---

178   CA Paris RCDIP 84 (1995), 573 with note *Kessedijan*.

179   High Court (England), 11 Oct. 2007, *Banco Nacional de Comercio Exterior v. Empresa*, International Litigation Procedure (1999) 853 (concerning the registration in England of an Italian judgment relating to an escrow agreement. The loan agreement, which was secured by the escrow agreement, had given rise to an arbitration procedure. The award was annulled in France on a jurisdictional point. The Italian judgment had been entered into in consideration of the arbitration award and the defendant to the Italian procedure therefore appealed against the Italian decision. While the appeal was pending, the claimant to the Italian procedure – the creditor – requested registration of the Italian judgment in England. The High Court decided that registration and enforcement of the Italian decision did not infringe English public policy under Art. 34 (1) Brussels I Regulation on the ground that trying to assert the impact of the annulment of the award on the Italian judgment amounted to a review as to the substance prohibited under Art. 36 Brussels I Regulation. The judge said so after having demonstrated that the annulment of the award has probably no direct impact on the Italian judgment …).

180   HR, LJN BK4932, para. 521 cited by *Jafferali*, TBH 2013, 357, 389–390, para. 55. The ECJ has confirmed that compliance with the decision in the State of origin does not preclude the declaration as to its enforceability in the requested State. However during the enforcement process, authorities of the requested State may take into consideration the fact that the decision has already been enforced, if such a fact would be taken into consideration for the enforcement of national decision in the requested State: *Prism Investment v. Jaap Anne van der Meer* (Case 139/10) (2011) ECR I-9511, paras. 39–40.

181   HR, 18.03.2011, LJN BP 0002 à BP 0004 (the national judge should check whether in regard of all circumstances of the case, the enforcement of a German judgment which is not reasoned amounts to a violation of public policy). Comp. with the attitude of the French Cour de cassation *(infra* fn. 191).

182   Cass. Fr. 28.03.2012, n° 11-11.434 (the entrepreneur could introduce a follow up action against the sub-contractors and client).

183   Cass. Fr. 25.11.2009, n° 08-11441.

184   Cass. Bel. 24.02.2012, K.F.S. v. S.W, n° C.11.0394 The written submission of the defendant had apparently been taken in consideration by the High Court.

185   *National Navigation Co v. Endesa Generacion SA*, [2009] EWCA Civ 1397, para. 131: "it cannot be said that the failure on the part of the Spanish court in good faith to give effect in this case to an arbitration agreement imperfectly spelled out in the bill of lading (but in the eyes of English law sufficiently incorporated by reference) would involve a manifest breach of a rule of law regarded as essential in the legal order of the United Kingdom or of a right recognised as being fundamental within that legal order" (on former case law applying Art. 34 (1) Brussels I Regulation to judgment obtained in breach of jurisdiction or arbitration clauses when the clause would be held valid under English law, see *Fentiman*, International

known in the requested State[186] and the refusal of set-off[187] have been considered compatible with public policy under Art. 45 (1) (a).

34 As stated before, public policy has rather rarely been considered infringed. National case law applying Regulation Brussels I or the Brussels Convention offer a few examples of implementation of the refusal ground based on public policy.[188] It can be deduced *a contrario* from different French decisions that a judgment establishing the paternity and condemning the father to pay maintenance would be contrary to public policy if it were only based on the allegations of the mother.[189] Similarly, German public policy conducts to refusing the recognition and enforcement of a Polish judgment establishing the paternity of a German national and condemning him to pay maintenance on the basis of the allegation of the grandmother of the child about his alleged paternity.[190] French public policy is considered infringed by foreign judgments lacking motivation, unless documents are provided to the requested court that are equivalent to the failing motivation.[191] Italian Public Policy was considered infringed by a French decision, which obliged one party to fulfil a distributorship agreement, which had not been authorised under Italian law.[192] Greek public policy has been opposed successfully to a judgment fixing the legal cost at an excessive level and without proportion with the financial consequences of the dispute.[193] The study conducted by Prof. Hess, Pfeiffer and Schlosser in view of a revision of the Brussels I Regulation cites interesting

---

Commercial Litigation, OUP 2010, para. 18.54); *The Wadi Sudr*, [2010] 1 Lloyd's Rep. 193; *Zellner v. Philipp Alexander Securities and Futures Limited* (1997) I.L.Pr. 730 (Q.B.D.); Trib.civ. Liège Act. Dr. 1996, 80.

[186] BGH, (2014) IX ZB 35/12, para. 8; BGHZ 75, 167; Cass. RCDIP 74 (1985), 131 with note *Mezger*.

[187] Trib. civ. Bruxelles Pas. belge 1987, III, 80.

[188] For a few other examples, cf. *Layton/Mercer* p. 890, n° 26.023; *Béraudo* note 94–100; *Jafferali*, "La règlement Bruxelles I dans la jurisprudence des Cours suprêmes (2010–2012): Allemagne, Belgique, France, Pays-Bas et Royaume-Uni", RDC/TBH 2013, 357, 389–390, para. 55; *Hess/Pfeiffer*, Study: Interpretation of the Public Policy Exception as referred to in EU Instruments of Private International and Procedural Law, PE 453.189, 49–94, available at: www.europarl.europa.eu/studies

[189] Cass. D. 1990 IR 108. Later decisions show that the enforcement of the foreign judgment concerning the paternity and maintenance are usually separated, so that the maintenance obligation can be enforced without having regard to the part of the judgment concerning the filiation (Cass, 3.12.2014, n°13-22672; Cass. 13.02.2013, n°11.23451). Since the entry into force of Regulation 4/2009, maintenance obligations arising from family relationship are not dealt with under Brussel I (*Ibis*) any more.

[190] BGH, (2009) XII ZB 169/07.

[191] See a.o.: Cass. France, (1e ch. civ.), 20 Sept. 2006, *Brero c/Blech* (concerning the Lugano Convention) JDI (Clunet) (2007) 139 & ff. note Cuniberti; Cass (1re ch. Civ.), 28 Nov. 2006, *Société Union Discount Limited c/ Casamata* (concerning the Brussels Convention), JDI (Clunet) (2007) 139 ff. note Cuniberti (citing decisions supporting this view dating back to 1979 and critical on the nature of the document that are accepted by the Cour de cassation as a substitute to motivation of the foreign judgment), also commented by H. Péroz together with another decision of the Cour de cassation on the same topic: Cass. 1e ch. Civ. 28 Nov. 2006, *Masson c/Ottow*, JDI (Clunet) (2007) 543; C. Versailles (1e ch. 1e section), 18 Mai 2000, n° 4354-97 (cited by *Hess/Pfeiffer/Schlosser* Report, p. 244, para. 547). Comp.: Corte di Appelo di Milano, 11 Feb. 2006, Rivista di diritto internazionale privato e processuale (2007), 1062. On the policy issues at stake in regard to recognition of foreign judgment lacking motivation: *Cuniberti*, ICLQ 57 (2008) 25.

[192] *See Layton/Mercer* para. 26.023 fn. 8.

---

case law where public policy has been considered infringed by national courts of Member States. For instance, fraudulent behaviour of the claimant has been taken into consideration by German courts[194] even if it was not raised before the court of origin,[195] a position later contradicted by the BGH.[196] A foreign judgment has also been denied enforcement in Germany on the ground that it ordered a teacher to pay damage to the parents of a boy injured as he was under the teacher's custody, while such a claim could under German law only be directed against the federal State.[197]

It has been stated earlier that the ECJ establishes the limits within which national concep-   **35** tions of public policy might be raised. Its influence on the content of the notion should not be underestimated either. By setting limits to national conceptions of public policy, it progressively identifies what might legitimately be considered as fundamental principles belonging to public policy. By defining what belongs to "Community public policy", which is integrated in the national conceptions for the application of Art. 45 (1) (a), the Court also generates the content of national and European public policy.[197a] As a result, a progressive harmonisation of the national conceptions might be expected in the future. The chances for such harmonisation to take place are increased by the fact that the ECJ will be seized with the interpretation of the same notion under different Regulations, among others Brussels II*bis* and Insolvency Regulations. For the sake of coherence in the Community legal order, common guidelines of interpretation will have to be followed. Those guidelines will in turn influence national case law[198] and encourage similar interpretations of public policy also outside the scope of the Regulations. Indeed it will be difficult for national tribunals to hold completely different interpretations of such a notion depending upon the legal basis under which it is raised.

---

[193] Aerios Pagos, 17 Nov. 2006, n° 1829/2006, I.L.Pr. 2 (2008), 97 (also available at: http://curia.europa.eu/jcms/jcms/Jo2_7061/).

[194] *Hess/Pfeiffer/Schlosser* Report p. 243, para. 546 reports of two decisions concerned for the first, with the fraudulent behaviour of the claimant when seeking a default judgment (BGH, 6 May 2004, NJW 2004, 2386 and BGH 15 Dec. 2005, IX ZB 276/04) and for the second with fraudulent misrepresentation (citation difficult to trace). Recently, see: BGH, (2012) IX ZB 144/10, para. 17.

[195] *Hess/Pfeiffer/Schlosser* Report p. 246, para. 552 citing BGH, 29 Apr. 1999, NJW 1999, 3198.

[196] BGH, (2012) IX ZB 56/10, para. 3 (recalling that as a matter of principle fraud cannot be raised in the requested State if the defendant did not appeal on this ground in the Member State where the decision was issued).

[197] *Hess/Pfeiffer/Schlosser* Report p. 244, para. 546 citing BGH 16 Sept. 1993, IX ZB 82/90, BGHZ 123, 268 IPrax 1994, 118 (the report states that this decision has been strongly critised by German authors).

[197a] In the case *Diageo Brands v. Simiramida*, the ECJ indicates that the enforcement of a national judgement could infringe fundamental principles of the EU legal order (rather than those of the national legal system) and also indicates how a breach of EU public policy would infringe public policy of the requested Member State; *supra* Art. 45 note 24b, (*Francq*).

[198] See, for a national decision relying on the Krombach decision in order to construe the notion of public policy under the Insolvency Regulation: *In the matter of Eurofoods IFSC Limited* (2005) I.L.Pr. 37 (S.C.); HR, 18.03.2011, LJN BP 0002 à BP 0004, in particular para. 3.2 of case 10/01368 reproducing almost entirely the general considerations of the ECJ on the use of the public policy ground. For a more detailed analysis of the functions of the public policy exception in the EU legal system: *Francq*, L'ordre public: Limite ou condition de l'autonomie dans l'Union européenne in: Kessedjian (dir.) Autonomie en droit européen (Paris 2013), 223.

IV. Art. 45 (1) (b): Protection of the defaulting defendant

36 The second refusal ground enumerated by Art. 45 is the only one aiming specifically at protecting the right of the defendant to a fair hearing at the stage of recognition or enforcement. If Art. 45 (1) (a) may sometimes protect the rights of the defendant with regard to procedural aspects, it is only in exceptional circumstances and in a subsidiary way, i.e. when the conditions set by Art. 45 (1) (b) are not met.[199] The latter provision, on the contrary, is entirely dedicated to the circumstances enabling the defendant to organize for his defence before the court of origin. This refusal ground is nevertheless submitted to rather strict conditions of application (2 designates here the title 2) (2): the judgment was rendered in default of appearance (2. a); the "defendant was not served with the document which instituted the proceedings or with an equivalent document in sufficient time and in such a way as to enable him to arrange for his defence" (2. b); and he did not fail "to commence proceedings to challenge the judgment when it was possible for him to do so" (2. c). Before analysing those conditions into detail, a few concepts need to be clarified (1).

37 At an earlier stage of the proceedings, another provision protects the defendant from a decision being taken against him by surprise. Art. 45 (1), (b) should indeed be read in relation with Art. 28, which imposes specific duties on the adjudicating court when the defendant does not appear. In particular, this court should be convinced that the defendant has been able to receive the document instituting the proceedings in sufficient time to arrange for his defence, or at least that all necessary steps have been taken to this end. Reference is made to regulation 1393/2007 on the Service in Member States and to the Hague Convention of 15 November 1965 on Service Abroad which both contain provisions on the protection, by the adjudicating court, of the defendant who does not enter an appearance. Art. 28 ensures that special attention is given to the situation of the defendant before the adoption of a default judgment and the delivery of the certificate mentioned in Art. 53.[200] This helps to understand why the conditions of application of Art. 45 (1) (b) are so strict: a similar control has already been exercised before the adoption of the decision. Two points, however, should be made with regard to the relationship between Art. 45 (1) (b) and Art. 28. Firstly, Art. 28 protects only the defendant domiciled in a Member State, whereas the provision of Art. 45 will concern also the defendant domiciled in third States, since chapter III is applicable to all decisions rendered in a Member State independent on the location of the defendant's domicile.[201] Secondly, the two provisions apply independently. As the ECJ puts it, "jurisdiction to determine whether the document introducing the proceedings was properly served was conferred both on the court of the original State and on the court of the State in which enforcement is sought".[202] The court seized with recognition or enforcement is thus not bound by the appreciations of the judge of origin under Art. 28 and may come to opposite conclusions.[203]

---

[199] *Supra* Art. 45 notes 19, 28–30 (*Francq*).

[200] Similarly, see Art. 18 and Art. 41, (2) (a) Regulation No. 2201/2003 of 27 November 2003 concerning jurisdiction and the recognition and enforcement of judgments in matrimonial matters and the matters of parental responsibility, repealing Regulation 1347/2000, OJ 2003 L 338/1.

[201] Cf. Art. 6 (1), Art. 2 (a), Recital 27.

[202] *Pendy Plastic Products BV v. Pluspunkt Handelsgesellschaft mbH*, (Case 228/81) (1982) ECR 2723 para. 13.

[203] In the *Pendy Plastic* case for instance, a certificate indicating that the defendant had not been served, had been issued according to the Provisions of the Hague Convention on Service, but the Dutch adjudicating

The ECJ recently clarified the role of the court in front of which Art. 45 (1) (b) is raised **37a** against the enforcement of a judgment accompanied by the certificate provided for by Annex I Regulation Brussels I*bis* (Annex V Regulation Brussels I). The Court ruled that Article 34 (2) of the Brussels I Regulation (Art. 45 (1) (b) Brussels I*bis*) "read in conjunction with recitals 16 and 17 in the preamble, must be interpreted as meaning that, where the defendant brings an action against the declaration of enforceability of a judgment given in default of appearance in the Member State of origin which is accompanied by the certificate provided for by Article 54 of that regulation, claiming that he has not been served with the document instituting the proceedings, the court of the Member State in which enforcement is sought hearing the action has jurisdiction to verify that the information in that certificate is consistent with the evidence".[204] The court seized in the State where enforcement is sought may thus control all the relevant facts, including the facts stated in the certificate, in order to assess whether the defendant was served in a way enabling him to arrange for his defence. Nothing in Regulation Brussels I or Brussels I*bis* prohibits to verify the accuracy of the facts stated in the certificate.[205] Review of the merits is only prohibited in regard of the judgment. Also "since the court or authority competent to issue that certificate is not necessarily the same as that which gave the judgment whose enforcement is sought, that information can only have prima facie value."[206] Those clarifications are welcomed at the time of entry into force of Regulation Brussels I*bis*, which abolishes exequatur and generalizes the automatic enforcement of other Member States judgment upon production of a certificate (Art. 42).

1. Definitions

a) Document instituting the proceedings or equivalent document

The second condition of Art. 45 (1) (b) focuses on "the document which instituted the **38** proceedings" or according to the enlargement of the concept due to the accession of the United Kingdom and Ireland, "an equivalent document".[207] The ECJ never gave a formal definition of that concept but rather a functional one, which helps to identify the relevant document through its function independently of its designation in the foreign legal order. According to the ECJ, the term "document which instituted the proceedings or … equivalent document" means "the document or documents which must be duly and in due time served on the defendant in order to enable him to assert his rights before an enforceable judgment is given in the State of origin".[208] Two criteria can be deduced from this definition: the document must necessarily be served before an enforceable judgment can be obtained, and it

---

court had been satisfied that all necessary steps to serve the defendant in sufficient time had been taken, after the claimant produced an extract from the German commercial register and a communication from the local German court showing that according to the files in its possession the defendant's address was the one where service was attempted. However the enforcing court found that the plaintiff had not proved to have taken the necessary measures to discover the defendant's address since the commercial register only mentions the town where the company is established and not its full address. In the circumstances of the case, the defendant had not changed town and according to the enforcing court, the plaintiff should have looked for his new address in that town.

[204] *Trade Agency Ltd v. Seramico Investments Ltd.* (Case 619/10) (2012), nyr., para. 46.
[205] *Trade Agency Ltd v. Seramico Investments Ltd.* (Case 619/10) (2012), nyr., para. 35.
[206] *Trade Agency Ltd v. Seramico Investments Ltd.* (Case 619/10) (2012), nyr., para. 36.
[207] Report *Schlosser* p. 125, 128.
[208] *Hengst Import BV v. Anna Maria Campese*, (Case C-474/93) (1995) ECR I-2113 para. 19.

must enable the defendant to decide whether to defend the action. It is actually due to call on the defendant to prepare his defence.

39 This definition explains why documents served later in the proceedings[209] or documents instituting purely unilateral proceedings[210] are not considered to be documents instituting the proceedings. In the first case, the document is not relevant any more to the decision whether the defendant should defend the case.[211] In the second case, an enforceable judgment can be obtained against the defendant without giving him a chance to assert his rights during the proceedings.[212]

40 However, proceedings which are initially unilateral can be transformed into adversary proceedings if the defendant takes the necessary steps therefore, after having been informed of the initiation of the proceedings. If he fails to do so, the claimant may obtain an enforceable title against him. In this case, the act, which informs the defendant of the beginning of the proceedings and thus gives him the opportunity of appearing in court and preparing his defence, is considered as the document instituting the proceedings. In case of unilateral proceeding, the act informing the defendant of the fact that the unilateral proceeding has taken place and that he can contest the decision unilaterally adopted can be considered as the document instituting the proceeding. Art. 2 (a) second paragraph Brussels I*bis* confirms this position by limiting the circulation regime of chapter III to provisional measures rendered after a unilateral proceeding which have been served on the defendant prior to enforcement, thereby enabling the defendant to contest the decision in the Member State where it was adopted.[213] The ECJ has followed these lines of reasoning about the order for payment (*"Zahlungsbefehl"* at the time of the decision, now *"Mahnbescheid"*) which is delivered by the court after a purely unilateral proceeding, but whose service enables the plaintiff to obtain an enforceable decision if the defendant does not raise any objection which would transform the procedure into a contradictory one.[214] On the contrary, the

---

[209] Cass. (2001) I.L.Pr. 717 (Due service of the judgment is not required by Art. 27 (2) Brussels Convention); Epheteio Thessaloniki (2002) I.L.Pr. 165 (The Brussels Convention requires only service of the document instituting the proceedings; the defendant must not be summoned at every stage of the proceedings); *Kropholler/von Hein* Art. 34 note 31 (citing about the extension of the claim: BGH IPRax 2001, 230, 195 with note *Haas*).

[210] *Bernard Denilauler v. SNC Couchet Frères*, (Case 125/79) (1980) ECR 1553 para. 17: excluding from the *scope* of title III Brussels Convention "measures ordered by a court without the party against whom they are directed having been summoned to appear and which are intended to be enforced without prior service on that party". See also Art. 2 (a) second indent of Regulation Brussels I*bis* and recital 33.

[211] *Kropholler/von Hein* Art. 34 note 31.

[212] *Gothot/Holleaux* para. 263.

[213] Art. 2 a) second paragraph of Regulation Brussels I*bis* clarifies the circulation regime of provisional measure and incorporates in the Regulation the ECJ decisions Denilauler (Case 125/79) (1980) ECR 1553) and Mietz (Hans-Hermann Mietz c. Intership Yachting Sneek BV, (Case C-99/96) (1999) ECR I-2277): "For the purposes of Chapter III, 'judgment' includes provisional, including protective, measures ordered by a court or tribunal which by virtue of this Regulation has jurisdiction as to the substance of the matter. It does not include a provisional, including protective, measure which is ordered by such a court or tribunal without the defendant being summoned to appear, unless the judgment containing the measure is served on the defendant prior to enforcement;". See also Recital 33.

[214] *Peter Klomps v. Karl Michel*, (Case C-166/80) (1981) ECR 1593 paras. 9, 11. See already CA Paris RCDIP

enforcement order *("Vollstreckungsbefehl"*, delivered when the order for payment has not been opposed by the defendant) which is in itself enforceable, cannot be considered as a "document instituting the proceedings",[215] even though the defendant holds the right of lodging an objection which will give him access to an adversary proceeding, because such a document must reach the defendant before an enforceable title is obtained.[216] The European order for payment instituted by Regulation 1896/2006 is tailored after the German *Mahnverfahren*: the order becomes enforceable only after it has been served on the defendant and the defendant renounced to lodge a statement of opposition.[217] According to Italian civil procedural law, an order for payment *("decreto ingiuntivo")* must be served on the defendant together with the application for such order, so as to have a period during which the defendant may oppose the order and at the end of which the claimant may obtain an enforceable title if the defendant has not raised any objection. The *decreto ingiuntivo*, together with its application, are to be considered documents instituting the proceedings, as it is their joint service, which enables the defendant to assert his rights and marks the start of the period of time at the end of which the enforceable judgment can be obtained.[218] An order provisionally limiting the liability of a shipowner under the 1957 International Convention relating to the Limitation of the Liability of Owners of Sea-Going Ships (which refers for procedural questions to the law of the State where the fund is constituted) is also considered as a document that is equivalent to a document instituting the proceedings:[219] although in the case submitted to the ECJ, the order was provisionally adopted at the end of a unilateral

---

69 (1980), 124 with note *Mezger*. About the *Mahnbescheid*: Cass. JCP 1989, jurisp. 359; TS (2003) I.L.Pr. 453 (refusing enforcement of a German enforcement order handed down in a summary proceeding *(Mahnverfahren)*, because no evidence was given with respect to the service of the payment order, rendering it impossible for the Spanish court to control whether it fulfilled the conditions of Article 27 (2) Brussels Convention). On the similarity with the appeal against a default judgment ("opposition") raised against order for payment under French Law: *Gothot/Holleaux* note 263 in fine.

215 *Peter Klomps v. Karl Michel*, (Case C-166/80) (1981) ECR 1593 paras. 9, 11.

216 The current formulation of Art. 2 (a) second paragraph raises the question whether an enforceable decision obtained after a unilateral procedure, which has been served on the defendant thereby enabling him to contest the decision, should circulate and whether the service of the (already) enforceable decision constitutes a "document instituting the proceeding". Considering that the the service of the (already) enforceable decision constitutes a "document instituting the proceeding" would contradict former case law and the logic adopted in Regulation 1896/2006 creating a European order for payment procedure.

217 See Art. 18 (1), 16 and 12 (5) of Regulation 1896/2006 creating a European order for payment procedure (2006) OJ L-399/1.

218 *Hengst Import BV v. Anna Maria Campese*, (Case C-474/93) (1995) ECR I-2113 para. 20. The defendant needs to read the two documents together in order to understand the basic elements of the claim and whether the judge has granted the order which indicates that the plaintiff has good chances of success (ibid note 21); BGH, IX ZB 193/07, para. 13 (the fact that the defendant becomes aware of the existence of the decreto at the enforcement stage does not prevent the enforcement if he still has a chance to contest the decision in Italy at this stage). For a decision, which either contradicts the *Hengst* case law, or deals with one the rare instance in which the "decreto ingiuntivo" is enforceable as such, cf. Cass. Fr. Bull. civ. 1994 I n° 176, p. 130. Even if the *"decreto ingiuntivo"* is served (according to Regulation 1393/2007) on the defendant before being declared enforceable in Italy, the French court in front of which the enforcement is contested must verify if the decreto had in fact been served in a way and in sufficient time to enable the defendant to organize his defence: Cass. Fr., 12 avril 2012, n°10-23.023.

219 *Maersk Olie & Gas A/S v. Firma M. de Haan en W. de Boer*, (Case 39/02) (2004) ECR I-9657 para. 59.

procedure, it was notified to the party requesting damages who then had the opportunity of submitting its claim and to transform the procedure into a contradictory one.

41 The two criteria used to identify the document instituting the proceedings seem to have some implications with regard to its content. In order to enable the defendant to assert his rights and to decide whether to defend the action, the document should provide him with some information concerning the most important elements of the claim.[220] This is indeed what is indicated by the ECJ when it states that Art. 45(1) (b) "may not be relied upon where the defendant appeared, at least if he was notified of the elements of the claim and had the opportunity to arrange for his defence".[221] Obviously he does not need a detailed information about the exact amount of the claim and arguments of the plaintiff. In a preliminary ruling concerning the interpretation of Art. 8, para. 1 of Regulation 1348/2000,[222] the ECJ clarified the notion of "document instituting the proceedings" and took argument of the understanding of this concept under the Brussels I Regulation. The Court stated that "such a document must consist of the document or documents, where they are intrinsically linked, enabling the defendant to understand the subject-matter and grounds of the plaintiff's application and to be aware of the existence of legal proceedings in which he may assert his rights".[223] Therefore, a document instituting the proceedings must not include every item of documentary evidence which makes it possible to prove the various facts and points of law on which the application is based, since they are not necessary for the defendant to be aware of the existence of legal proceedings.[224] Though Art. 45 (1) (b) does not state this requirement as such, it derives not only from the functional definition given to the term "document instituting the proceedings" but also from the condition that the defendant should have received this document "in such a way as to enable him to arrange for his defence".

b) Defendant

42 For the purpose of Art. 45 (1) (b), the notion of defendant is to be understood in broader terms than in Art. 28. Indeed it derives from the scope of application of Chapter III and from

---

[220] *Leible*, in: Rauscher Art. 34 note 28; *Kropholler/von Hein* Art. 34 note 30. *ASML Netherlands BV v. Semiconductor Industry Services (SEMIS)*, (Case C-283/05), para. 35: "In order for the defendant to have the opportunity to bring proceedings enabling him to assert his rights, (…), he should be able to acquaint himself with grounds of the default judgment in order to challenge them effectively". The ASML decision concerned the possibility for the defendant to challenge the judgment in the State of origin. The Court held that the defendant should not only be aware that a judgment had been entered into, but also be acquainted with the content of the judgment. As stated by Advocate General Léger, "the exception to application of the ground for non-recognition introduced by Regulation No. 44/2001 leads necessarily to establishing a parallel between the document instituting the proceedings and the judgment delivered in default of appearance" (Opinion of Advocate General Léger Case 283/05) (2006) ECR 12041 para. 65).

[221] *Volker Sonntag v. Hans Waidmann, Elisabeth Waidmann and Stefan Waidmann*, (Case C-172/91) (1993) ECR I-1963 para. 39.

[222] Council Regulation (EC) No. 1348/2000 of 29 May 2000 on the service in the Member States of judicial and extrajudicial documents in civil or commercial matters, OJ (2000) L 160/37, now replaced by Regulation 1393/2007 OJ (2007) L 324/79.

[223] *Ingenieurbüro Michael Weiss und Partner GbR contre Industrie- und Handelskammer Berlin* (Case C-14/07) (2008) ECR I-03367 para. 64.

[224] *Ingenieurbüro Michael Weiss und Partner GbR contre Industrie- und Handelskammer Berlin* (Case C-14/07) (2008) ECR I-03367 para. 68.

the formulation of Art. 45 that this provision benefits defendants domiciled in third State, as well as defendants domiciled in the State where the litigation as to the merits occurred. The latter situation, which is initially purely internal, has been specially addressed by the ECJ in the case *Debaecker*.[225]

c) Judgment

The notion of judgment has to be understood under the terms of Art. 2 (a) which states that a   **43**
"judgment means any judgment given by a court or tribunal of a Member State, whatever the judgment may be called, including a decree, order, decision or writ of execution, as well as the determination of costs or expenses by an officer of the court". The ECJ considers that it is sufficient for decisions to fall within the scope of Art. 2 (a) if they are judicial decisions which, before their recognition and enforcement are sought, "have been, or have been capable of being, the subject in that State of origin and under various procedures, of an inquiry in adversary proceedings".[226] Therefore, only judgments which are likely to be adopted in the context of contradictory proceedings fall into the scope of Art. 45 (1) (b).[227] This does not mean that decisions adopted after one party was not heard cannot qualify as judgments under Arts. 2, a) and 45 of the Brussels *Ibis* Regulation. For instance in the *Gambazzi* case, the Court decided that the fact that the court entered judgment as if the defendant, who had entered appearance, was in default, cannot suffice to deprive those decisions of being qualified as judgments.[228] Also, even if a judgment has been delivered at the conclusion of an initial phase of the proceedings in which both parties were not heard, such a decision has to be regarded as a judgment within the meaning of Art. 2 (a) when it could have been the subject of submissions by both parties before the issue of its recognition or its enforcement is addressed.[229] Moreover, Art. 45 (1) (b) apparently concerns only those judgments adopted in a litigation initiated by a specific document. As a result, accessory rulings, such as those on costs, are not treated as judgments for the purpose of this provision.[230]

---

[225] *Leon Emile Gaston Carlos Debaecker and Berthe Plouvier v. Cornelis Gerrit Bouwman*, (Case 49/84) (1985) ECR 1779 para. 13.

[226] *Bernard Denilauler v. SNC Couchet Frères*, para. 13.

[227] *Supra* Art. 45 notes 39–40 (*Francq*).

[228] *Marco Gambazzi v. DaimlerChrysler Canada Inc.*, para. 25. *Supra* Art. 45 note 29.a and 40 (*Francq*). The question whether Gambazzi is still valid case law after the new formulation of Art. 2.a) second paragraph deserves further consideration: *van Drooghenbroeck*, Mesures provisoires et conservatoires in *Boularbah*, *van Drooghenbroeck* (dir.) De Bruxelles à Bruxelles *Ibis*, JT 2015, 89. JT 2015 (to be published).

[229] *Maersk Olie & Gas A/S v. Firma M. de Haan en W. de Boer*, (Case 39/02) (2004) ECR I-9657 para. 50. The preliminary ruling concerned an order rendered by a Dutch Court provisionally fixing the amount to which the liability of a shipowner would be limited and establishing a fund for this amount, under the 1957 Convention relating to the Limitation of Liability of Owners of Sea-Going Ships. The Dutch order was entered into upon application by the shipwoner, but without hearing of any of the parties. Such an order is then notified to both parties and they have the right to contest its content before the Court which issued it (in regard to the amount of the limited liability as well as in regard to the right of the shipowner to benefit from such a limitation). In addition, they have a right to Appeal on the sole point of the jurisdiction of the Court (see para. 51). See similarly Hoge Raad N.I.Pr. 2006, 290.

[230] *Kropholler/von Hein* Art. 34 para. 26 (raising the question whether the title obtained by the lawyer against his own client should be considered as accessory).

2. Conditions of application

a) Judgment by default

44 The first condition of application of the refusal ground provided for by Art. 45 (1) (b) is that the judgment must have been adopted in default of appearance of the defendant. The attitude of the defendant is thus relevant in order to decide whether he failed to appear. In this respect, the technical terms of national procedural law (and thus the formal qualification of the judgment under national law) are of no importance. The term "default of appearance" must be interpreted autonomously and the ECJ has provided national courts with general guidelines. As *Kropholler* summarizes it, with respect to the aim of Art. 45 (1) (b), the defendant cannot be considered as having failed to appear as soon as he or his counsel presented arguments before the court from which it can be deduced that he had actual knowledge of the proceedings and enjoyed enough time to prepare his defence.[231]

45 The clearest application of this general criterion is provided by the *Hendrikman* case.[232] The litigation as to the merits concerned an unpaid invoice for stationery ordered in the name of Mr and Mrs Hendrikman by two persons who apparently did not have the authority to do so. Mr and Mrs Hendrikman had not been aware of the proceedings and were represented by lawyers instructed by the same two persons, again without their authority. The ECJ decided that "where proceedings are initiated against a person without his knowledge and a lawyer appears before the court first seized on his behalf but without his authority (…), that person must be regarded as a defendant in default of appearance",[233] even though under national procedural law the judgment would not be considered as rendered by default. Indeed in the present case, the defendants were not in a position to actually prepare their defence. The same cannot be said about the defendant in a civil action joined to criminal proceedings, who appeared at the criminal proceedings, not personally but through a counsel he appointed, and defended the criminal case without presenting any plea concerning the civil action for damages.[234] The defendant was aware of the civil-law claim made against him in the context of the civil proceedings and is therefore regarded as having appeared at the "proceedings taken as a whole".[235] In order for the judgment to be given in default of

---

[231] *Kropholler/von Hein* Art. 34 para. 27. This conception of the term "appearance" seems to correspond best to the indications given by the ECJ, see *Volker Sonntag v. Hans Waidmann, Elisabeth Waidmann and Stefan Waidmann,* (Case C-172/91) (1993) ECR I-1963 para. 39; BGH, XII ZB 187/10, para. 19. For a broader conception of the situations in which the defendant made an appearance: *Geimer/Schütze* Art. 34 note 112. For a case of application in France: Cour d'Appel Nancy, 10 fév. 2011, n° 10/01913 (the defendant was represented during the proceedings in the State of origin and cannot oppose recognition and enforcement on the sole ground of an untimely service).

[232] *Bernardus Hendrikman and Maria Feyen v. Magenta Druck & Verlag GmbH,* (Case 78/95) (1996) ECR I-4943.

[233] *Bernardus Hendrikman and Maria Feyen v. Magenta Druck & Verlag GmbH,* (Case 78/95) (1996) ECR I-4943 para. 18.

[234] *Volker Sonntag v. Hans Waidmann, Elisabeth Waidmann and Stefan Waidmann,* (Case C-172/91) (1993) ECR I-1963 para. 44.

[235] *Volker Sonntag v. Hans Waidmann, Elisabeth Waidmann and Stefan Waidmann,* (Case C-172/91) (1993) ECR I-1963 para. 41. For national case law applying these principles see the cases cited by: R. Jafferali, "Le règlement Bruxelles I dans la jurisprudence des cours suprêmes (2010–2012). Allemagne, Belgique, France, Pays-Bas et Royaume-Uni", RDC/TBH, 2013/5, pp. 357 à 393, p. 390 referring to BGH, 12

---

appearance, the defendant must expressly decline to appear in the civil action. Other behaviours are not considered as an appearance in the proceedings. For instance, when the defendant solely contested the jurisdiction of the court which issued a decision at the term of unilateral proceedings (which could have been transformed into contradictory proceedings, had the defendant submitted his claim), he cannot be considered as having entered an appearance.[236] The situation of the defendant who appeared simply in order to contest the way he was informed of the proceedings (for instance, by raising that he was not allowed enough time to prepare for his defence or that the document instituting the proceedings suffers deficiencies which deprived him of the exercise of his right to be heard) is controversial. In Germany, the case-law and the doctrine are divided on this point.[237] Considering that the defendant did not appear when his intervention was limited to the challenge of the service effected upon him encourages defendants to systematically contest the service of the document instituting the proceedings. But a defendant who wants to avail himself of Art. 45 (1) (b) will do so at the latest in appeal since he has to use all possibilities to challenge the judgment in the State where it was rendered. Considering that the defendant appeared when his intervention was limited to the challenge of the service effected upon him means that there will be very few instances where the defendant will manage to meet the two conditions of Art. 45 (1) (b) depending on his behaviour (making no appearance and having used the existing means of redress), when he is actually confronted with a situation in which he was unable to prepare his defence. Besides those opportunity arguments, the ECJ seems to favour a rather broad conception of the term appearance, indicating that in such a situation the judgment would be considered as a default judgment.[238]

b) Service effected in sufficient time and in such a way as to enable the defendant to prepare his defence

The second condition is actually twofold, even though its two aspects are sometimes difficult **46** to distinguish from one another. The document instituting the proceedings must reach the defendant not only in sufficient time to enable him to prepare his defence (aa), but also in such a way as to allow him this possibility (bb). The introduction of this condition corresponds to the removal of the condition concerning the regularity of the service. Together with the third condition (concerning the obligation for the defendant to challenge the

---

January 2012, IX ZB, 14/09, para. 2; BGH, 12 January 2012, IX ZB, 12/09, para. 2; BGH, 12 January 2012, IX ZB, 11/09, para. 2. See also Recital 29 Regulation Brussels Ibis: "When the defendant has been *deprived* of the opportunity to arrange for his defence in a civil proceeding linked to a criminal proceeding and the judgment was rendered in default of appearance, he should be able to raise Art. 45,(1),(b) against the enforcement of this judgment".

236 *Maersk Olie & Gas A/S v. Firma M. de Haan en W. de Boer*, (Case C-39/02) (2004) ECR I-9657 para. 57.

237 Considering the judgment is given in default of appearance: OLG Stuttgart IPRspr. 1983 Nr. 173; OLG Köln IPRax 1991, 114 with note *Linke*; *Kropholler/von Hein* Art. 34 note 27; *Tschauner*, in: Bülow/Böckstiegel/Geimer/ Schütze Art. 34 note 45; considering there is no default of appearance: *Leible*, in: Rauscher Art. 34 note 37 (and the case law cited fn. 142); *Geimer/Schütze* Art. 34 note 112; *Peter Schlosser* Art. 34–36 note 20 (citing case-law backing both positions).

238 *Volker Sonntag v. Hans Waidmann, Elisabeth Waidmann and Stefan Waidmann*, (Case C-172/91) (1993) ECR I-1963 para. 39: Art. 34 (2) "may not be relied upon where the dependant appeared *at least if* he was notified of the elements of the claim and *had the opportunity to arrange his defence*". This statement suggests that where the defendant had no opportunity to arrange his defence, he cannot be considered as having appeared.

Stéphanie Francq   909

judgment in its State of origin), it constitutes a reaction to the former case law of the ECJ which considered that recognition or enforcement should be refused where service was not duly effected even when the defendant became aware of the proceedings in sufficient time to organize his defence.[239] The aim of these modifications is to ensure that "a mere formal irregularity in the service will not debar recognition or enforcement if it has not prevented the debtor from arranging for his defence".[240] The focus is thus placed on the actual *(in concreto)* possibility for the defendant to arrange for his defence.[241] This will serve us as a guideline in the interpretation of the remaining conditions.

aa) A condition of time

47 Determining whether the defendant received the document instituting the proceedings in sufficient time to organise his defence raises two questions: when does the limitation period begin and how long should it be? The beginning and the duration of the limitation period require separate analyses.

48 **Beginning**: It is usually considered that the period of time necessary for the defendant to arrange for his defence starts running "from the date on which service was duly effected" upon him, "at his habitual residence or elsewhere".[242] What is critical is thus the moment when the defendant receives or is supposed to receive the document instituting the proceedings and to become aware of them, not the moment when all formalities are completed at the tribunal.[243] Despite the abolition of the term "duly" from the wording of Art. 45 (1), b), the regularity of the service has thus not lost all relevance. In the case of a service duly effected, one can proceed from the general assumption that the period allowed to the defendant for organizing his defence starts running on the date of the delivery of the documents. It is important for the claimant to be able to rely on this general rule. Otherwise, even when doing everything correctly, he would be totally submitted to the arbitrary behaviour of the defendant who could for instance chose to disappear without leaving any address. Accordingly, the claimant does not have to prove that "the document which instituted the proceedings was actually brought to the knowledge of the defendant".[244] The judge can thus consider that service was effected on time for the defendant to organize his defence even if he never became aware of the proceedings, simply because service was duly effected.[245]

49 If the actual knowledge of the proceedings is not required in the chief of the defendant, it remains the ultimate goal of various provisions of the Regulation – mainly Art. 28 and 45 (1),

---

[239] *Isabelle Lancray SA v. Peters und Sickert KG*, (Case C-305/88) (1990) ECR I-2725 para. 22; *Minalmet GmbH v. Brandeis Ltd.*, (Case C-123/91) (1992) ECR I-5661 paras. 14, 15; *Bernardus Hendrikman and Maria Feyen v. Magenta Druck & Verlag GmbH*, (Case-78/95) (1996) ECR I-4943 paras. 18, 19.

[240] Commission Proposal COM (1999) 348 final, p. 23.

[241] BGH, IX ZB 193/07, para. 13 (the fact that the defendant becomes aware of the existence of the *decreto ingiuntivo* at the enforcement stage does not prevent the enforcement if the defendant still has a chance to contest the decision in Italy at this stage).

[242] *Peter Klomps v. Karl Michel*, (Case 166/80) (1981) ECR 1593 para. 19.

[243] *Leible*, in: Rauscher Art. 34 note 36. Cf. CA Reims Clunet 106 (1979) with note *Holleaux*.

[244] *Peter Klomps v. Karl Michel*, (Case 166/80) (1981) ECR 1593 para. 19.

[245] CA Luxembourg Pas. lux. 2000, 227–234, ECJ Website n° 2001/47 (that the defendant did not know of the proceedings is no sufficient ground for refusal when service was duly effected).

b) – to ensure that the defendant was put in a position to prepare his defence and therefore did receive the documents instituting the proceedings.[246] As a consequence, even though it is not expressly stated in the Regulation, the construction of Art. 45 (1), b) reveals that the claimant is some how expected, though not obliged, to do everything he can to make sure that the documents reach the defendant.[247] The judge seized with recognition remains thus free to appreciate whether, in a particular case, there are "exceptional circumstances which warrant the conclusion that although service was duly effected, it was, however, inadequate for the purposes of enabling the defendant to take steps to arrange for his defence".[248] In this regard, he or she may take all circumstances of the case into account, including the nature of the relationship between the parties and circumstances which arose after service was duly effected. For instance, between professionals, the absence of the defendant at the time of the delivery of service at the place where he carries his business activities does not deprive him of his right to be heard.[249] The appraisal of those circumstances must be lead *in concreto* independently of the procedural law of the adjudicating or enforcing court. This explains why the ECJ may identify circumstances which could be taken into account in assessing whether the service was effected in sufficient time but may not establish a hierarchy between them or measure their impact in the case at hand. In the *Debaecker* case for instance, the Court reassured the national judge that the fact that the plaintiff learned of the defendant's new address after service was duly effected, and the fact that the defendant was responsible for not having been reached by the documents (since he left without giving his new address) were circumstances to be taken into account in assessing whether service was effected in sufficient time.[250] But the final appraisal of those circumstances remains the task of the judge seized with recognition or enforcement, as none of them leads to an automatic conclusion with respect to the time condition.[251]

From those considerations, it derives that a distinction could be drawn between regular and **50** substituted service. In the case of substituted service, such as the "remise au parquet" or the posting of the document on the court's notice board,[252] the defendant has indeed far less of a

---

[246] Before the entry into force of the Brussels I Regulation, the actual knowledge of the defendant concerning the proceedings engaged against him was already considered by French appeal courts as more important than the formal regularity of service: *Niboyet/Sinopoli*, Gaz. Pal. 2004 IV 28.

[247] *Leon Emile Gaston Carlos Debaecker and Berthe Plouvier v. Cornelis Gerrit Bouwman*, (Case 49/84) (1985) ECR 1779 paras. 27 and 28. The ECJ (para. 28) states that the claimant has no obligation to take further steps to inform the defendant of the pending action as a result of circumstances, which arose after service was effected. But those steps would be taken into consideration in assessing whether service was made in sufficient time and notification to the defendant's new address, for instance, prevents the claimant of a refusal judgment at the stage of recognition (paras. 27 *in fine* and 28). This implies that the defendant should, if he wants to avoid bad surprises, take further steps in case there is any doubt with the service effected.

[248] *Peter Klomps v. Karl Michel*, (Case 166/80) (1981) ECR 1593 para. 19.

[249] *Peter Klomps v. Karl Michel*, (Case 166/80) (1981) ECR 1593 para. 20.

[250] *Leon Emile Gaston Carlos Debaecker and Berthe Plouvier v. Cornelis Gerrit Bouwman*, (Case 49/84) (1985) ECR 1779 para. 33.

[251] *Leon Emile Gaston Carlos Debaecker and Berthe Plouvier v. Cornelis Gerrit Bouwman*, (Case 49/84) (1985) ECR 1779 para. 32.

[252] Refusing recognition because the defendant was served by posting of the document on the court's notice board and had no knowledge of the proceedings engaged against him in Germany: CA Colmar 5.4.2001,

chance of being actually aware of the proceedings. The claimant (or the judge seized with the litigation as to the merits) should thus take care of adopting all possible additional steps to reach the defendant and count that the period of time necessary to enable him to prepare his defence starts running only after the completion of those additional steps.[253] On the other hand, in the case of regular service, the defendant has greater chances of being aware of the proceedings and the general assumption mentioned above could be more confidently relied upon.

51 **Duration**: From the date on which the defendant is (or is supposed to be) informed of the proceedings, a period of time long enough to enable him to prepare for his defence should elapse. This period covers all the time during which the defendant has the possibility of stating his arguments, i.e. the time running between the beginning of the limitation period (described above) and the adoption of an enforceable decision.[254] What matters is the possibility given to the defendant to defend his case from the beginning of the proceedings, not the possibility of contesting an enforceable decision already adopted after a unilateral procedure.[255] The court seized with recognition will thus consider the time elapsed between the service of the writ of summons and the first hearing[256] or the time running until the issue of a default judgment, if a valid notice of appearance entered at any time before the issue of that judgment will actually prevent its adoption, even though this period exceeds the time allowed by the court for appearance.[257]

52 Whether this period of time is sufficient to enable the defendant to organise for his defence is a question of facts left to the determination of the court seized with the recognition. This control is lead *in concreto* with respect to all the factual and legal peculiarities of the case at hand and independently of the requirement of the law applied to the service or the law of the State where recognition is requested and of the opinion of the adjudicating court.[258] National

---

n.r., cited in: Niboyet/Sinopoli, Gaz. Pal. 2004 IV 26; stating that as a general rule, in the absence of any special circumstances, the posting of documents instituting the proceedings on the court's notice board cannot satisfy the condition of service in sufficient time: OGH RdW 2001, 154; ECJ Website, nº 2001/16 (in the circumstances of the case, the court analyses whether the defendant should have known that proceedings were likely to be engaged against him and therefore left an address with the court or the claimant). This judgment adopted before the entry into force of the Regulation, actually anticipates the second aspect of the condition about the delivery of service, i.e. that it must reach the defendant in a way that enables him to prepare his defence.

[253] *Gaudemet-Tallon* p. 431 para. 415; *Gothot/Holleaux* para. 268. Such additional steps are mentioned in Art. 19 (2), c) of the Regulation 1348/2000 on Service in the Member States and Art. 15, second line of paragraph. c. of the 1965 Hague Convention on Service Abroad. In both cases, where no certificate of service or delivery is produced, the court will consider whether a period of at least six months has elapsed since the transmission of the documents.

[254] *Peter Klomps v. Karl Michel*, (Case 166/80) (1981) ECR 1593 paras. 10 and 11.

[255] *Peter Klomps v. Karl Michel*, (Case 166/80) (1981) ECR 1593 paras. 10 and 11, *Minalmet GmbH v. Brandeis Ltd*, (Case C-123/91) (1992) ECR I-5661 para. 19.

[256] OLG Düsseldorf (2002) I.L.Pr. 4.

[257] *TSN Kunststoffrecycling GmbH v. Harry M. Jurgens* (2002) I.L.Pr. 599 (C.A., per Walker LJ).

[258] *Leon Emile Gaston Carlos Debaecker and Berthe Plouvier v. Cornelis Gerrit Bouwman*, (Case 49/84) (1985) ECR 1779 para. 27; *Pendy Plastic Products BV v. Pluspunkt Handelsgesellschaft mbH*, (Case 228/81) (1982) ECR 2723 para. 13; Cassaz. Foro it. 1998 Col 993–994 (ECJ Website nº 1999/59); Cass. Clunet

case law reflects the high diversity of factual settings and thus of the assessment of the necessary duration of the time allowing the defendant to organize his defence.[259] For instance, a German Court decided that a period of nine days between the writ and the first hearing was too short for the defendant to obtain a translation of the writ and instruct a lawyer abroad.[260] Other German rulings were satisfied with a period of 7 days considering the special circumstances of the case or the narrow links between the defendant and the State of the adjudicating court.[261] When the document instituting the proceedings have reached the defendant 5 days after the first hearing, the condition of time set by Art. 45 (1) (b) is of course not respected.[262]

bb) A condition concerning the circumstances of service

As stated above, the document instituting the proceedings must not only reach the defen- **53** dant in sufficient time but also in such a way as to enable him to prepare his defence. The two aspects of the condition concerning the considerations that should enable the defendant to prepare his defence are difficult to distinguish from each other: the circumstances surrounding the delivery of the document instituting the proceedings will often determine whether the defendant received it in sufficient time to prepare his defence.[263] For instance, if the documents are delivered in a foreign language, the judge seized with recognition will naturally tend to consider that a longer period of time is necessary for the defendant to organize his defence.[264] The circumstances of the service were thus already the object of a certain control before being singled out as an autonomous condition or a specific aspect of the condition concerning the service by the Brussels I Regulation.[265]

---

108 (1981), 854 with note *Holleaux*; Report *Jenard* p. 40 (about Article 20 Brussels Convention: "The question of sufficient time is obviously a question of fact for the discretion of the court seized of the matter"); *Droz* (fn. 21) p. 70 para. 158 (submitting that the quality of the parties, be they professionals or consumers, should influence the determination of the length of the period needed to prepare one's defence). Cf. OLG Köln NJW 2002, 360; ECJ Website n° 2002/26 (taking as reference the term fixed by the law of the State where recognition is sought).

[259] See the list established by *Layton/Mercer* para. 26.039 fn. 74 concerning cases ranging from 1978 to 2000, from which it can be concluded that a period of one month is normally held sufficient. Below that length of time, it all depends on the facts of the case. A French court decided that a period of 10 days allowed enough time to a French company to prepare its defence in the Netherlands (Cass. Bull. civ. 1977 I n° 401 p. 320), whereas a period of 13 days was held insufficient by a German Court for the protection of a German defendant served in Dutch concerning Belgian Proceedings (BGH NJW 1986, 2197). Among the facts taken into account, holiday seasons seem to justify the need for longer time in order for the defendant to be able to prepare his defence (App. Milano Digest I-27.2-B6.; cf. also TS (2003) I.L.Pr. 11).

[260] OLG Düsseldorf (2002) I.L.Pr. 4.

[261] *Leible*, in: Rauscher Art. 34 note 35 in fine (citing: OLG Düsseldorf RIW 2002, 558; OLG Köln ZMR 2002, 348). Cf. Trib. civ. Liège JMLB 1994, 929.

[262] Cass., 7 April 1998, n° 96-10679, ECJ Website n° 1998/29.

[263] Cass. 1er civ., 12 April 2012, n° 10-23023, RCDIP, 2012, p. 931.

[264] *Kodek*, in: Czernich/Tiefenthalter/Kodek Art. 34 note 24 and 29. The need for a translation should not influence the appreciation of the time necessary to organize one's defence or the circumstances of the service where the parties used that language in former commercial transactions or where the defendant is an international firm which can be supposed to practice that language (*Peter Schlosser* Art. 34–36 note 17b).

[265] The need for a translation was controlled under the heading of the "regularity" of service (*Leible*, in:

Stéphanie Francq   913

54 This condition should not be confused with the formal regularity of service, which is not as such required. However, since the formal conditions of a valid service are due to ensure that the defendant is put in a situation allowing him to prepare his defence, the regularity of service will of course influence the appreciation made of its circumstances. The respect of Regulation 1393/2007 and of the 1965 Hague Convention concerning service abroad remains thus relevant as a kind of presumption of the quality of the service. If the service suffered some kind of irregularity (such as a mistake concerning the place where it should be delivered), this will not prevent the recognition but the judge will have to assess whether the irregularity actually prevented the defendant to organize his defence.[266] Another question is to know whether service occurred at all.[267] Indeed, the Regulation does not refer to the mere knowledge of the proceedings that the defendant should have, but requires service to be effected in such a way as to enable him to prepare his defence. On the one hand, since the notion of service apparently cannot be considered as merely factual, it seems necessary to select the law which will determine whether service did occur.[268] On the other hand, since Art. 45 (1) (b) provides a ground for refusing recognition which is independent of the formal regularity of service and thus of the law that was applied to it, it seems contradictory to refer to the formal definition of service provided by one piece of legislation – be it the law of the State where service was delivered, the law of the State where recognition is sought or even the provisions of an international instrument – which could bar recognition for purely formalistic reasons. The use of a legal notion independently of a reference to its legal content reveals here its ambiguity.

55 The condition concerning the way in which service was effected could find its "effet utile" in cases of substituted service. The impact of this special kind of service was generally assessed with respect to the time left to the defendant to prepare his defence or with respect to the condition concerning the regularity of service,[269] but it actually concerns directly the manner in which service is effected. For instance, the Court of Appeal of Luxembourg granted recognition with regard to the special circumstances of the case even though service was served by posting on the court of origin's notice board.[270] It appeared indeed that the defendant had actual knowledge of the proceedings and could have prepared his defence with his lawyers who were aware of the proceedings but pretended that they had never received mandate to represent their client. On the one hand, the special circumstances of the

---

Rauscher Art. 34 note 33; *Peter Schlosser* Art. 34–36 note 17 b), but the other circumstances concerning the service influenced the assessment of the time to be left to the defendant for organizing his defence.

[266] *Leible*, in: Rauscher Art. 34 note 33; *Kropholler/von Hein* Art. 34 note 40. *ASML Netherlands BV v. Semiconductor Industry Services (SEMIS)*, (Case C-283/05), para. 47. See for instance OLG Koblenz (2005) 2 U 1239/04 (the action together with the summons was duly served on the respondent at its German postal address while it was proven he was living in Spain).

[267] *Layton/Mercer* para. 26.052; *Leible*, in: Rauscher Art. 34 note 33.

[268] High Court (England), 9 March 2006, Peter Tavoulareas v. Tsavliris and Others, EWHC (2006) 414 (referring to the law of the State of origin of the decision and considering that when the defendant is simply informed by his lawyers of the existence of a proceeding, he has not been served according to the requirement of Art. 34 (2) Brussels I Regulation). Comp. referring to the law of the State where Service was effected: BGH, 21 Jan. 2010 – IX ZB 193/07, s. 265, n° 29, commented by *Bach*, IPRax (2006) 241.

[269] *Supra* Art. 34 note 50 (*Francq*).

[270] CA Luxembourg Pas. lux. 2000 227–234; ECJ Website n° 2001/47. Cf. OLG Karlsruhe (2001) I.L.Pr. 208 (severely judging the "remise au parquet").

case can thus influence the decision whether service occurs in a way that enables the defendant to prepare for his defence even though it is unlikely that the notification would effectively reach him.[271] On the other hand, it should be underlined that the abolition of the condition concerning the regularity of service and the introduction of a condition relating to the circumstances of the service do not necessarily simplify the recognition process. Judges were already tempted to assess substituted service with respect to their national conception of a regular service when they were only supposed to consider whether service was regularly effected following the law of the State of origin.[272] Now that the assessment is mainly factual, it can be feared that judges will control even more severely a kind of service which does not exist in their own procedural law even when the claimant did his best to find the defendant who left without leaving any address and when the service, though substituted, is regular.

The necessary content of the documents instituting the proceedings is another issue which   56
might be relevant for assessing the quality of the service.[273] In order to be served in a way which enables him to arrange for his defence, the defendant needs minimal information about the circumstances of the first hearing and the grounds on which the proceedings rely. Such a requirement could probably already be derived from the definition given to the term "document instituting the proceedings", but the modification introduced by Regulation 44/ 2001, by requesting expressly that the service be effected in a way that enables the defendant to prepare his defence, offers now a solid ground for controlling, at least superficially, the content of the document instituting the proceedings. When the document instituting the proceeding is served in a language that defendant does not understand, the judge should control whether he has been able to organize for his defence despite the absence of translation.[274]

c) The obligation for the defendant to challenge the decision in its country of origin

This condition has been introduced when the Brussels Convention was transformed into a   57
Regulation.[275] The text of the Convention did not mention the necessity for the defendant

---

271 For another case anticipating this solution see OGH RdW 2001, 154. See as well: OLG Köln IPRspr. 2000 Nr. 147 p. 322, ECJ Website n. 2003/22 (taking into account for refusing the recognition the fact that the claimant lied about the defendant's address, who was served therefore by means of public notice). Raising the question whether service effected on a defendant domiciled in another Member State following a national procedure according to which it is possible to lodge the document with the public prosecutor is compatible with Article 12 EC: OLG München ECJ Website n. 2004/7. The question was referred to the ECJ but not answered because it became irrelevant with respect to the answer to the other questions of the case: *Scania Finance France SA v. Rockinger Spezialfabrik für Anhängerkupplungen GmbH & Co.*, C-522/ 03 (2005) ECR I-8638.

272 For a good example cf. Aud. Prov. Madrid Recurso de Apelación n° 109/2001, ECJ Website n°. 2003/30 (considering the claimant should have done everything that is reasonably possible in order to find the defendant's address before effecting service by means of public notice and that this is clearly not the case since the defendant was at the time of service already resident in Spain; the court refers at length to Spanish constitutional conception of due service but never considers the conditions set by German law for such a service).

273 *Supra* Art. 45 note 41 (*Francq*).

274 Cass. Fr., 3.04.2013, n° 11-19000.

275 BGH NJW 2004, 3189 (underlining the change introduced by the regulation and the impossibility of construing the Brussels Convention in regard to the Regulation on this point).

who wanted to oppose the recognition of a decision on the ground that his right to a fair hearing had been violated, to have challenged that decision. The conception, expressly endorsed by the ECJ, was that the important moment for the defendant to exercise his right to a fair hearing is the time at which proceedings are instigated. According to the ECJ, "the possibility of having recourse, at a later stage, to a legal remedy against a judgment given in default of appearance, which has already become enforceable, cannot constitute an equally effective alternative to defending the proceedings before judgment is delivered".[276] The Regulation Brussels I introduced thus a shift of logic. The direct consequence is that the defendant who did not challenge the decision in its State of origin loses the possibility of later raising Art. 34 (2) (now 45 (1) (b)) for opposing its recognition.[277] The possibility of obtaining a legal remedy in the State of origin is thus seen as capable of compensating, if not as being equivalent, to the possibility given of organizing one's defence at the beginning of the proceedings. The regulations Brussels I and Brussels I*bis* tend to concentrate most of the litigation in the State of origin:[278] all procedural issues should be examined by priority in the State where the litigation occurred whose courts are better placed for assessing them. There are positive and negative aspects to this choice. On the one hand, the former conception had the disadvantage of favouring the defendant's passivity.[279] Though being actually aware of the proceedings, he could fail to appear and to challenge the decision and simply raise the violation of his right to a fair hearing at the stage of enforcement. On the other hand, the current conception imposes more procedural costs on the defendant who must search for legal remedies in the State of origin and, if he did not succeed in this State, pursue the proceedings later on in the State of enforcement.[280] The financial consequences are also imposed on the claimant who must defend the appeal in the State of origin and before the court seized with the application for refusal of enforcement (under Art. 46 Brussels I*bis*).

58 Art. 45 (1) (b) encourages the defendant to challenge the judgment in its State of origin. Since the provision does not specify the nature of the legal remedies concerned, it should be

---

[276] *Minalmet GmbH v. Brandeis Ltd*, (Case C-123/91) (1992) ECR I-5661 para. 19; OLG Karlsruhe (2001) I. L.Pr. 208 ("the contravention of Article 27 (2) Brussels Convention is not cured if the debtor failed to lodge a possible appeal against the default judgment").

[277] In the *Apostolides* decision, the ECJ insisted that "a default judgment given on the basis of a document instituting proceedings which was not served on the defendant in sufficient time and in such a way as to enable him to arrange for his defence must be recognised if he did not take the initiative to appeal against that judgment when it was possible for him to do so" (*Meletis Apostolides v. David Charles Orams*, (Case C-420/07) (2009) ECR I-3571, para. 77). In that case, the defendant had challenged the default judgment and this fact proved that his right to a fair hearing had been respected (para. 78 and 80). This position of the ECJ questions the possible use of Art. 34 (2): it seems that the only place left to Art. 34 (2) is when the defendant was put in a situation where it was impossible for him to challenge the decision. For a case where challenge of enforcement was refused because the defendant (although he was not properly served and was first aware of the foreign proceedings when enforcement was sought) failed to challenge the decision in the Member State of origin when it was still possible to do so: BGH, 21 Jan. 2010 – IX ZB 193/07, s. 265, n° 29, commented by *Bach*, IPRax (2006) 241.

[278] Commission Proposal COM (1999) 348 final, p. 7 (point 4.2.2.), p. 21 (commentary on section 2), p. 24 (commentary on Article 50–51). See also *supra* Art. 45 note 21 (*Francq*).

[279] This is why the ECJ construction was generally criticized: *Gaudemet-Tallon* p. 435–436 para. 418.

[280] *Kropholler/von Hein* Art. 34 note 42.

understood as referring to all means provided by the law of the State of origin to set aside the judgment, be they ordinary or extraordinary.[281]

The obligation for the defendant to challenge the judgment in its State of origin is only **59** imposed on him "when it was possible for him to do so". The court seized with recognition will have to consider whether the defendant was in fact in a position to appeal in the State of origin. This decision will rely on a combination of legal and factual elements. The procedural law of the State of origin comes firstly into account: the court seized with recognition should be informed of the legal remedies and of the conditions at which they are opened under that foreign law. In this respect, two points should be underlined. First, the explanatory memorandum proposed by the Commission for Regulation Brussels I states that the debtor should have been "in a position to appeal in the State of origin on grounds of a procedural irregularity".[282] As a consequence, only the legal remedies, which can be used to challenge the decision on the ground of procedural irregularity will come into consideration.[283] This influences as well the general assessment of the defendant's attitude during the litigation in the State of origin: if he did challenge the decision without raising the procedural irregularity which prevented him from exercising his rights to a fair hearing, he will later be prevented to rely on Art. 45 (1) (b). Second, the procedural law of the State of origin will set the time limit for introducing an appeal. If the defendant challenged the proceedings but his action was rejected because it was introduced too late, it should probably be considered that he did not comply with the conditions of Art. 45 (1) (b) and is thus prevented to raise it.[284] Indeed, he can be considered responsible for not having respected the limitation period set by the procedural law of the State of origin. However, factual circumstances might explain his attitude and reveal that he was not in a position to challenge the decision in due time. Besides the procedural law of the State of origin, the judge seized with recognition will also consider all factual circumstances of the case, which might show that it was not possible for the defendant to challenge the decision. For instance, if the defendant did not comply with the time limit set to introduce an appeal, it can be because he received the judgment too late or never received it.[285] If a constant line of case law in the State of origin rejects the arguments, which the defendant would have raised to support his appeal concerning his right to a fair hearing, it can be justified to consider that he was not in a position to search for a legal remedy against the decision.

The ECJ has ruled that "it is 'possible' for the defendant to bring proceedings to challenge a **59a** default judgment against him only if he was in fact acquainted with its content, because it was served on him in sufficient time to enable him to arrange for his defence before the courts of the State in which the judgment was given".[286] In this case, summons to the hearing

---

[281] *Layton/Mercer* para. 26.053; *Gaudemet-Tallon* p. 435–436 para. 418. See also, BGH, 21 January 2010, IX ZB, 193/07, para. 14.

[282] Commission Proposal COM (1999) 348 final p. 23 (emphasis added).

[283] *Leible*, in: Rauscher Art. 34 note 40; *Kropholler/von Hein* Art. 34 note 443.

[284] Such is the case as well if the defendant failed to pay the registry costs after he filed an appeal, since this circumstance shows he would have been able to contest the judgment in the State of origin: BGH, IX ZB 144/10, para. 19.

[285] In the system of the Brussels Convention, the due delivery of the judgment is not required (Cass. (2001) I.L.Pr. 717; Epheteio Thessaloniki (2002) I.L.Pr. 165).

[286] *ASML Netherlands BV v. Semiconductor Industry Services SEMIS*, (Case C-283/05) para. 49. For a detailed

---

Stéphanie Francq

had been served on the defendant after the hearing actually took place in the Netherlands. The judgment (rendered in default of appearance) was never served on him. An Austrian order declaring the Dutch judgment "provisionally enforceable" was served on the defendant but did not include a copy of the Dutch judgment. Referring to case law of the ECHR, the ECJ considered that it was only possible for the defendant to challenge the judgment in his country of origin if he was aware of the grounds of that judgment. The ruling of the ECJ implies that the judgment should be served on the defendant.

59b In February 2014, the ECHR has issued a decision concerning the compatibility with Art. 6 (1) ECHR of an enforcement procedure where Art. 34 (2) of the Brussels I Regulation had been raised by the debtor against the enforcement.[287] In this case, the applicant, Avotiņš, resident in Latvia, lodged a complaint with the ECHR against Cyprus and Latvia. Avotiņš, argued that Cyprus disregarded his right to a fair trial by condemning him to pay 100.000 USD, without having been properly served. In addition, he claimed that Latvia infringed his right to a fair trial, since Latvia granted the *exequatur* of the Cyprus judgment in accordance with Brussels I Regulation. The Latvian court considered that Avotiņš was barred from raising Art. 34 (2) because he did not appeal against this judgment in Cyprus. Due to the late lodging of the complaint against the Cyprus decision, the ECHR had no jurisdiction on that matter. The Court was thus only seized of the application against Latvia.[288] One could have expected the ECHR to rule that the court of the Member State addressed has to check, in practice, whether the right to a fair hearing has been respected. However, the ECHR supported the decision of the Latvian court and considered Art. 6 (1) ECHR had not been violated. The ECHR decision is based on three major arguments: (i) the ECHR had already stated in its Bosphorus decision that the fundamental right protection granted in the EU can be considered equivalent to that of the Convention system;[289] (ii) the Latvian Court had an interest in fulfilling its obligations under EU law and thus to grant fast and effective recognition and execution of the Cyprus judgment;[290] (iii) in regard of the fact of the case, Mr Avotiņš had not convinced the ECHR that he had been unable to appeal in Cyprus, when as a professional investment consultant he could have expected litigations in Cyprus after having signed a recognition of debt governed by Cyprus law and submitted to Cyprus court.[291] The ECHR underlined that it is not competent for analyzing the compatibility of the Latvian decision with EU law.[292] The Grand Chamber of the ECHR has recently accepted to hear the case and could thus overturn this decision.[293]

---

analysis of this decision see: *Pataut*, RCDIP (2007) 645 (considering that the ASML decision induces confusion between Art. 45 (1) (a) and (b) since both provisions tends to protect the requirement of Art. 6 ECHR to the point that Art. 45 (1) (b) could be deleted in favour of Art. 45 (1) (a)); *Geimer*, IPRax (2007) 498 (considering the decision as striking an unfair balance between the rights of the defendant and the rights of the plaintiff, and as damaging the sense of the reform introduced by the Regulation Brussels I in regard to Art. 34 (2) at the time (now 45 (1) (b)).

[287] *Avotiņš v. Lettonie*, (Application. N°17502/07)

[288] *Avotiņš v. Lettonie*, (Application. N°17502/07), para. 46.

[289] See *Bosphorus Hava Yolları Turizm ve Ticaret Anonim Şirketi v. Ireland*, (Application N°45036/98), para. 165.

[290] *Avotiņš v. Lettonie*, (Application. N°17502/07), para. 49.

[291] *Avotiņš v. Lettonie*, (Application. N°17502/07), paras. 50–51.

[292] *Avotiņš v. Lettonie*, (Application. N°17502/07), para. 47.

V. Article 45 (1) (c) and (d): Irreconcilable decisions

After important changes introduced by the Regulation Brussels I,[294] Art. 45 (1) (c) and (d)   **60**
considers the situation where two conflicting judgments are submitted to the judge seized
with recognition. The coexistence of both decisions would cause severe disturbance in the
rule of law in the legal order of the State addressed, which Art. 45 (1) (c) and (d) tends to
prevent.[295] This goal is reached under certain conditions which differ according to the origin
of the conflicting decisions (2). Despite these differences, some terms receive a common
understanding in the two points (1).

As for point (b), points (c) and (d) of the first paragraph of Art. 45 are related to other   **61**
provisions of the Regulation which intervene at an earlier stage of the proceedings, namely
Arts. 29 to 32. The latter provision tends to avoid the pursuit of proceedings before the
courts of two Member States when they are either identical or related. Despite the efficient
mechanism set by these provisions, it may occur that decisions, which reveal themselves to
be contradictory are adopted in different Member States. This would typically occur when
the judge is ignorant of the foreign proceedings because the parties do not raise the subject.
Parallel proceedings may then be pursued at the same time in different Member State or a
decision be adopted in one Member State when a decision concerning the same legal dispute
had already been rendered in another Member State. The new *lis pendens* regime has,
however, improved the situation when one of the Member State court has been seized on
the basis of a choice-of-court agreement. Under Art. 31 (2), the court seized on the basis of
the alleged jurisdiction clause has priority over the court of another Member State, even if
the latter was seized first. The specific *lis pendens* rule concerning choice-of-court agreement
should help preventing the situation where the enforcement of two contradictory decisions
is requested in a Member State and the first decision should be given priority under Art. 45
(1) (d) even though it was rendered in breach of a jurisdiction agreement.

The scope of Art. 45 concerning irreconcilable judgments is both narrower and broader than   **61a**
the scope of the provisions concerning *lis pendens* and related actions. It is narrower because
neither point (c), nor point (d) of the first paragraph of Art. 45 cover the case of related
actions. For instance, point (c), whose application is broader than point (d), requires that
both proceedings involve the same parties. Art. 30, which concerns related actions does not
contain such a requirement. The scope of Art. 45 is broader than that of Arts. 29 to 32
because the decision in conflict with the judgment whose recognition is sought, may fall
outside the scope of the Regulation, either because it was rendered in a third State – for
Art. 45 (1) (d) – or because it covers subjects excluded from the material scope of the
Regulation – for Art. 45 (1) (c) and (d).

It should be noted from the start that the grounds for refusal provided for by point c) and d)   **62**
of Art. 45 are mandatory.[296] If the irreconcilability is proven, the judge has no choice but to
refuse recognition. In other words, he does not keep any margin of appreciation in order to

---

[293]   See the ECHR Press release delivered on 9.9.2014. The hearing of the Grand Chamber took place on 8.4.
2015.

[294]   *Supra* Art. 45 notes 10–13 (*Francq*).

[295]   Report *Jenard* p. 45.

[296]   *Italian Leather SpA v. WECO Polstermöbel GmbH & Co.*, (Case C-80/00) (2000) ECR I-4995 para. 52.

assess the level of disturbance caused by the coexistence of the two decisions in its legal order.

1. Definition

a) Judgment

63 Two judgments are involved: one whose recognition is sought under chapter III of the Regulation and another with which the first one is in conflict. The judgment whose recognition is sought should be understood within the meaning given to this term by Art. 2, a) of the Regulation. Concerning the judgment with which a conflict occurs, the Regulation only states that it must have been "given" in the forum, in another Member State or in a third State depending on the factual setting. Proceedings which are merely pending in the State seized with recognition for instance do thus not justify a refusal.

64 This does not solve the question whether the second judgment should have become *res judicata* or not. The Jenard Report explains that the experts left the question to the discretion of the court in which recognition is sought.[297] Since the Regulation merely states that the judgment must have been "given", a requirement as to *res judicata* would add conditions to the provisions.[298] This position is adopted by the ECJ in the *Italian Leather* case where it states that it is "unimportant whether the judgments at issue have been delivered in proceedings for interim measures or in proceedings on the substance. As Art. 27 (3) Brussels Convention, following the example of Art. 25, refers to judgments without further precision, it has general application".[299] In this case, two decisions on interim measures reached opposite solutions: the Italian decision had granted the measures while the German court had refused it. From this decision, it can be deduced that interim decisions are considered as final and conclusive decisions as well as decisions which have *res judicata*.[300] But the ECJ left open the question of whether the irreconcilability between the decisions should be asserted regarding their respective status.[301] Indeed in the Italian Leather case, it was only seized with two decisions of equal status and underlined that an *interim* judgment granting the measure conflicted with an *interim* measure refusing it.[302]

65 The ECJ has had the opportunity to clarify that settlements do not come into consideration in the application of Art. 45 (1) (c). According to the Court, the provision is only concerned with judicial decisions actually given by a court and settlements are excluded from this category because of their "essentially contractual" nature.[303] The same solution should be

---

297 Report *Jenard* p. 45.

298 *Leible*, in: Rauscher Art. 34 note 44; *Gaudemet-Tallon* p. 442 para. 422.

299 *Italian Leather SpA v. WECO Polstermöbel GmbH & Co.*, (Case C-80/00) (2000) ECR I-4995 para. 41.

300 CA Rouen, 24 March 2009, n° 09/01471, *SA Panagia Odigitria v. Sté Bénéteau*, JDI (Clunet) (2010) 864 note Cuniberti (considering that a Greek decision ordering the restoration of a good formerly seized prevented the adoption of a decision in France to seize the same good and applying Art. 36 to the incidental recognition of the *res judicata* of the Greek decision, but after a confusing reasoning based on Art. 45); Cass.1e ch. Civ. (France), 20 June 2006, *AGF Kosmos v. Soc. Surgil Trans Express*, Bull. civ. 2006 I n°. 315; RCDIP 2007 164, note *J.-P. Rémery* (giving priority to a French provisional decision over a foreign decision as to the merits).

301 *Infra* Art. 45 note 69 (*Francq*).

302 *Italian Leather SpA v. WECO Polstermöbel GmbH & Co.*, (Case C-80/00) (2000) ECR I-4995 para. 47.

valid for Art. 45 (1) (d) because the terms of the reasoning apply in the same way for this provision. The Court has indeed underlined that the conflict between decisions is problematical insofar as it involves the solution adopted by a judicial body "on its own authority".[304] In another decision, the ECJ seems to imply that anti-suit injunctions are not covered by Art. 45 (1) c) and d).[305] It is true that the conflict between an anti-suit injunction and a decision on the merits is not solved by point d) of the first paragraph of Art. 45, since the cause of action differs. But such a case could find a solution in point c) of the first paragraph of Art. 45 because this provision only requires the two decisions to be rendered between the same parties. A conflict between two anti-suit injunctions (rather theoretical between Member States because of the limited number of States where such a measure can be obtained) would simply be solved according to the general lines of the last two points of Art. 45. In practice however, anti-suit injunctions are de facto prohibited in the "Brussels system"[306] and such conflict of decisions should therefore never occur.[307]

The conflict which would arise between a Member State judgment and an arbitration award **65a** entitled to recognition in the State addressed is not covered by the Regulation. More precisely, the recognition of another Member State judgment falls within the scope of the Regulation, the recognition and enforcement of the arbitration award does not and is governed by the New York Convention and the conflict between the judgment and the award is not governed by the Regulation.[308] A conflict between the State obligations under the Regulation and under the New York Convention can thus occur. German authors submit that the solution of Art. 45 (1) (d) should be applied by analogy.[309] In practice, several situations should be distinguished.

---

[303] *Solo Kleinmotoren GmbH v. Emilio Boch*, (Case 414/92) (1994) ECR I-2237 para. 18.

[304] *Solo Kleinmotoren GmbH v. Emilio Boch*, (Case 414/92) (1994) ECR I-2237 para. 17.

[305] *Gregory Paul Turner v. Felix Fareed Ismail Grovit, Harada Ltd. and Changepoint SA* (Case C-159/02), (2004) ECR I-3565 para. 30: recourse to such measure "is liable to give rise to situations involving conflicts for which the *Convention contains no rule*" (emphasis added).

[306] *Gregory Paul Turner v. Felix Fareed Ismail Grovit, Harada Ltd. and Changepoint SA* (Case C-159/02), (2004) ECR I-3565 para. 31.

[307] For "anti-suit injunction" issued by arbitrators see: *Gazprom AO*, (Case 536/13), ECLI:EU:C:2015 316 nyr., para. 41. Recognition and enforcement of an arbitral award ordering a party to arbitration proceedings to reduce the scope of the claims formulated in proceedings pending before a court of that Member State, do not fall within the scope of the Regulation (see also Opinion of AG Wathelet, delivered on Dec. 4. 2014, para. 157).

[308] For a more detailed analysis see: *Mankowski*, Kann ein Schiedsspruch ein Hindernis für die Anerkennung einer ausländischen Entscheidung sein?, 5 SchiedsVZ (2014), 209–216. Concerning the reach of the exclusion of arbitration under Regulation Brussels I*bis* in regard of its Recital 12 see also: *Hartley*, The Brussels I Regulation and Arbitration 63 ICLQ (2014) 843; *Nuyts*, Rev. Crit. Dipe (2013), 11–20.

[309] *Kropholler/von Hein* Art. 34 note 60; *Peter Schlosser* Art. 34–36 para. 29. When they do not apply Regulation Brussels I*bis*, courts are free to rely on the logic underlying Art. 45 (1) (c) and (d) Brussels I*bis*. But when they apply the Regulation, the terms of Art. 45 (1) (d) have to be interpreted strictly and cannot be applied by analogy to situations not directly covered by the provisions, see: *Salzgitter Mannesmann Handel GmBH v. SC Laminoroul SA*, (Case 157/12) ECLI:EU:C:2013:597 para. 39 (Art. 34 (4) Brussels I – Art. 45 (1) (d) Brussels I*bis* – does not apply by analogy to the enforcement of conflicting judgments rendered in the same Member State).

(i) A judgment dealing only with the validity of the arbitration agreement falls outside the scope of the Regulation so that a conflict between such a judgment and an award is to be dealt with under the rules on recognition of foreign judgment of the Requested State and the New York Convention, especially its Art. V (1) (a).[310]

(ii) The Regulation is not applicable to the potential contradiction between an internal judgment and a foreign arbitration award because there is no judgment rendered in another Member State. The courts of the issuing State have to deal with this issue under the New York Convention.[311] In such a situation, the enforcement of the award is likely to be refused under Art. V (1) (a) or V (2) (b) of the New York Convention. Of course, even though Brussels I/ *Ibis* does not apply, the logic underlying Art. 45 (1) (c) Brussels *Ibis* could also be taken into consideration and would plead in favour of refusing enforcement of the award.

(iii) In case a judgment rendered in another Member State contradicts an award rendered in the requested State, the award as such cannot be considered as a "judgment" under Brussels *Ibis* that could justify the application of Art. 45 (1) (c) Brussels *Ibis*.[312] If the award is, however, incorporated into a national judgment of the requested State, Art. 45 (1) (c) could apply and lead to refusing the enforcement of the judgment rendered in another member State.[313] When the award has not been turned into a national decision, Brussels I/*Ibis* commands the enforcement of the judgment rendered in the other Member State while the enforcement of the award does not fall within the scope of the New York Convention (as it deals only with foreign awards). Mankowski considers that despite Regulation Brussels I/ *Ibis* does not resolve this issue (the Regulation commands the enforcement of the judgment rendered in another Member State but does not deal with a potential conflict with an award rendered in the requested State), the logic expressed in Art. 45 (1) (c) should be followed in order to give priority to the award rendered in the requested State.[314]

(iv) Brussels *Ibis* governs the recognition and enforcement of a judgment on the merits rendered in another Member State, even if enforcement of an award (rendered in a Member State or a third State) is requested under the New York Convention in the same requested State.[315] However, the second sentence of Recital 12, paragraph 3 underlines that the New York Convention *takes precedence* over the Regulation (this goes further than the wording of Art. 73 (2) Regulation Brussels *Ibis*) and that the recognition of the judgment rendered in another Member State is without prejudice to the competence of the courts of the Member

---

[310] Recital 12, paragraph 2 Brussels *Ibis*. For instance in the UK see: *Dallah Real Estate and Tourism Holding Company (Appellant) v. The Ministry of Religious Affairs, Government of Pakistan (Respondent)*, [2010] UKSC 46, para. 29 (considering – in an *obiter dictum* – that under the principle of issue estoppel a French decision declaring the arbitration agreement invalid would prevent the execution in the UK of an arbitration award; referring to *The Sennar (No. 2)* [1985] 1 WLR 490).

[311] Hartley, 63 ICLQ (2014) 843, 865.

[312] See *Mankowski*, 5 SchiedsVZ (2014), 209, 210 (but considering that the notion of "judgment" could recieve a larger interpretation).

[313] *Hartley*, 63 ICLQ (2014) 843, 866. See *West Tankers v. Allianz* [2012] EWCA Civ 27 (considering that an English arbitration award could be turned into an English judgment so that the parties could benefit from Art. 34 (3) Brussels I).

[314] *Mankowski*, 5 SchiedsVZ (2014), 209, 211; *Hartley*, 63 ICLQ (2014) 843, 865–866.

[315] Recital 12, paragraph 3 Brussels *Ibis*, first sentence.

State requested to decide on the enforcement of the award under the New York Convention. Even if this part of the Recital is particularly unclear, it apparently implies that if the award contradicts the judgment rendered in another Member State, and when both should be enforced (the judgment under Brussels I*bis* and the award under the New York Convention), priority should be given to the award. The heavy debate surrounding the exclusion of arbitration during the recast process will explains why the language is unclear. Recital 12 as a whole attempts to solve what has not been solved in the text of the Regulation, raising thus the usual concerns about the impact of Recitals which cannot add to the text, nor contradict it. It is interesting to note that favouring the award somehow contradicts the assimilation of judgment rendered in other Member States to national judgments and gives arbitration awards more credit than foreign decisions. Therefore, it is debated whether recital 12 paragraph 3, second sentence should be interpreted as meaning that priority should be given to the award, without consideration for the date at which the award has been rendered. The logic of time priority expressed in Art. 45 (1) (d) in case of conflict between two foreign judgments could potentially be transposed to conflicts between an award and a judgment and lead to favour the earlier decision.[316] The reach of recital 12 concerning potential conflict between a judgment and an arbitral award certainly deserves closer consideration in regard of the way in which (and date at which) foreign judgments and awards receive *res judicata* effect in Member States.

As stated before,[317] the judgments referred to by Arts. 45 (1) (c) and (d) do not need to have **66** been rendered pursuant to the Regulation. Concerning the judgment whose recognition is sought, the only condition, due to Arts. 2 (a) and 1 of the Regulation, is that the judgment was adopted in a Member State and covers civil and commercial matters.[318] The same is true concerning the second judgment. If point (c) of the first paragraph of Art. 45 covers the conflict with a decision from the forum, it is not required that the latter decision was adopted in the framework of the "Brussels system".[319] Furthermore, under point (d), the second judgment might come from a third State.

Art. 45, (1) (d) does not cover irreconcilable judgments given by courts of the same Member **66a** State.[320] In a case involving two conflicting judgments rendered in Romania, German courts wondered whether to apply Art. 34 (4) Brussels I (Art. 45 (1) (d) Brussels I*bis*) in order to

---

[316] Contrast *Mankowski*, 5 SchiedsVZ (2014), 209, 212–214 (considering that the principles expressed in Art. 45 (1), d) Brussels I should lead to favouring an earlier award over a later judgment and an earlier judgment over a later award) with *Hartley*, 63 ICLQ (2014) 843, 865 (considering that the award should be given priority even if it was rendered after the judgment).

[317] *Supra* Art. 45 note 60 (*Francq*).

[318] *Unic Centre SARL (A Company) v. The London Borough of Brent & Harrow Trading Standards Service*, I. L.Pr. (2000) 462 (Q.B.D., *Newman* J.): Forfeiture proceedings are a civil matter falling within the scope of the Brussels Convention. A forfeiture order is thus a judgment within the meaning of Article 45 (1) (c) which could potentially be opposed to a foreign judgment on the existence of a trade mark infringement.

[319] See for instance *Horst Ludwig Martin Hoffmann v. Adelheid Krieg*, (Case 145/86) (1988) ECR 645 para. 25, considering the irreconcilability between a maintenance order rendered in a Member State pursuant to the Brussels Convention and a divorce decree rendered in the Member State where recognition was sought.

[320] *Salzgitter Mannesmann Handel GmbH v. SC Laminorul SA*, (Case C-157/12) ECLI:EU:C:2013:597 para. 40.

Stéphanie Francq

refuse the enforcement of the second judgment. Together with Advocate General Wahl, the ECJ underlined the need to interpret Art. 45 (1) (d) strictly. In regard of its wording, the provision can only cover situations where "irreconcilable judgments are given in two different Member States".[321] Any other interpretation would amount to substituting the opinion of the courts of the requested Member State to that of the court of the State of origin and be incompatible with the principle of mutual trust.[322] The question concerning the incompatibility between the two judgments needs to be addressed in the context of the legal remedies established by the Member State where they have been rendered. Those courts are in charge of controlling the lawfulness of the judgment to be enforced.[323]

b) Irreconcilable

67 The refusal grounds set by points (c) and (d) of Art. 45 only apply as long as the decisions are irreconcilable. The meaning of this term is not to be determined with respect to national law. The ECJ provided an autonomous interpretation in the case *Hoffmann v. Krieg*. Two decisions are irreconcilable if they "entail legal consequences that are mutually exclusive".[324] This does not mean that they must concern exactly the same legal problem. For instance, in the case *Hoffmann v. Krieg* referred to the ECJ, the decisions involved concerned maintenance on the one hand and divorce on the other hand, but were judged irreconcilable because the maintenance order necessarily presupposed the existence of the matrimonial link, which was dissolved by the other decision.[325] A difference of substantive or procedural law is not even necessary, nor is it a reason for justifying tolerance towards conflicting judgments.[326] What is to be considered is the effect of the two judgments. Of course, the margin of discretion of the judge is not totally erased since he will have to assess whether from his point of view the legal consequences of the decisions are mutually exclusive. However, the position traditionally adopted in France according to which irreconcilability is a matter totally left to the discretion of the judge of the facts and not submitted to the control of the Cour de cassation can probably no longer be maintained.[327]

68 National case law and Reports on the Brussels Convention provides a few clear examples. The judgment allowing damages for breach of contract is irreconcilable with another judgment declaring the contract invalid.[328] The judgment rendered in a third State dismissing an action against a person domiciled in the EC conflicts with a judgment rendered in a Member State against the same person and concerning the same cause of action.[329] A decision granting maintenance on the ground of paternity conflicts with a decision refusing to recognize

---

[321] *Salzgitter Mannesmann Handel GmbH v. SC Laminorul SA*, (Case C-157/12) ECLI:EU:C:2013:597 para. 30.

[322] *Salzgitter Mannesmann Handel GmbH v. SC Laminorul SA*, (Case C-157/12) ECLI:EU:C:2013:597 para. 36.

[323] *Salzgitter Mannesmann Handel GmbH v. SC Laminorul SA*, (Case C-157/12) ECLI:EU:C:2013:597 para. 33.

[324] *Horst Ludwig Martin Hoffmann v. Adelheid Krieg*, (Case 145/86) (1988) ECR 645 para. 22.

[325] *Horst Ludwig Martin Hoffmann v. Adelheid Krieg*, (Case 145/86) (1988) ECR 645 para. 24.

[326] *Italian Leather SpA v. WECO Polstermöbel GmbH & Co.*, (Case C-80/00) (2000) ECR I-4995 para. 42; *Layton/Mercer* para. 26.060.

[327] *Gaudemet-Tallon* p. 440 (fn. 162) para. 420 referring to Cass. Bull. civ. 1977 I n°. 401.

[328] Report *Jenard* p. 45.

[329] Report *Schlosser* p. 131.

the paternity.[330] Two judgments concerning different contracts between the same parties are not irreconcilable even though it would have made sense to gather the proceedings before one single court.[331] A decision accepting the jurisdiction of the Court of the forum and a foreign decision on the merits are not irreconcilable.[332] The decision requesting the seller to pay damages because of the lack of conformity of the object sold is reconcilable with a foreign decision condemning the purchaser to pay the price: both could be simultaneously executed by way of set-off.[333]

A difficult question is whether the irreconcilability should be assessed in regard of the **69** respective status of the decisions. Indeed, it can be sustained that a provisional decision is not necessarily irreconcilable with a decision on the merits.[334] This is the position adopted by the French Cour de cassation which gave priority to a German decision on the merits rather than to the national provisional decision.[335] But as long as the decisions are irreconcilable, the French Cour de cassation shall give priority to the domestic provisional decision under Art. 45 (1) (c).[336] On the other hand, a foreign provisional decision would probably be considered irreconcilable with a forum decision on the merits. Some authors and case law suggest that the irreconcilability might also depend on whether the decisions are still open for review.[337] Should the final foreign decision or the forum decision receive priority when the latter is still subject to appeal? Surely, once the forum decision has been over-turned, the refusal ground of Art. 45 (1) (c) no longer exists.[338] The question is what should be done in the meantime, especially since Art. 38 does not allow the judge seized with recognition to stay proceedings in such a situation. The same problem arises in the conflict between two Member State decisions. When only one of them is final, should they be considered as irreconcilable knowing that this conflict might disappear after the exercise of the means of appeal? The autonomous interpretation of the ECJ does not yet offer a clear answer and it can be expected that further preliminary rulings will be requested on this question.

2. Conditions of application

a) Conflict with a local judgment: Art. 45 (1) (c)

Besides the conditions deriving from the definition of irreconcilable judgments, Art. 45 (1), **70** (c) actually imposes only one condition in case of a conflict with a judgment rendered in the State seized with recognition: it must have been rendered between the same parties. This condition is to be constructed in the same way as in Art. 29. This should include the person who did not participate in the first litigation but succeeds to the rights of one of the parties.

---

[330] OLG Hamm IPRax 2004, 437 with note *Geimer* (419).

[331] Trib. civ. Liege JMLB 1994, 929.

[332] Cassaz. RDIPP 1995, 732.

[333] This is the judgment on the merits which gave rise to the decision of the Cour de cassation (Cass. Bull. civ. 1977 I n°. 401).

[334] *Layton/Mercer* para. 26.061.

[335] Cass. Bull. civ. 1996 I n°. 201.

[336] Cass.1e ch. Civ. (France), 20 June 2006, *AGF Kosmos v. Soc. Surgil Trans Express*, Bull. civ. 2006 I n°. 315; RCDIP 2007 164, note J.-P. Rémery.

[337] *Layton/Mercer* para. 26.061; *Kropholler/von Hein* Art. 34 note 53 with further references.

[338] OLG Hamm IPRspr. 1981 Nr. 187.

As stated before, the condition will have the effect of excluding from the scope of Art. 45 (1) (c) related actions which would involve different parties or not exactly the same parties.

71 Art. 45 (1) (c) has the effect that the local judgment will be given automatic priority. The local judgment will prevail, irrespective of which judgment was given first or which proceedings were started first.[339] This solution is easy to apply as long as the local judgment exists at the time when the foreign judgment is adopted or its recognition is requested. What should happen when the local judgment is rendered after the foreign judgment? Some authors suggest that the question is not addressed by the Regulation since it requests the local judgment to be "given" at the time when the foreign decision is considered.[340] Furthermore, since the foreign judgment receives automatic recognition under the Regulation, a local judgment given later cannot affect its status. The ECJ, however, favours another position. In the case *Hoffmann v. Krieg*, the Court considered that a local divorce decree was irreconcilable with a maintenance order from another Member State although it was aware of the fact that the local judgment was rendered later.[341] Pursuant to this decision, many authors sustain that the refusal ground set by Art. 45 (1) (c) has *ex nunc* effect from the date of adoption of the local judgment.[342]

72 The conflict between a local judgment and a third State judgment is not addressed by point c) of Art. 45 nor by its point (d). Such a conflict should be solved with respect to national rules of recognition and enforcement of foreign judgments.

b) **Conflict with judgment given in another Member State: Art. 45 (1) (d)**

73 Point (d) of the first paragraph of Art. 45 sets stricter conditions than point c). Indeed, besides the conditions deriving from the definition of irreconcilable judgments, four conditions should be fulfilled before recognition or enforcement can be denied: the conflict occurs with an earlier judgment rendered in another Member State,[343] both judgments involve not only the same parties but also the same cause of action and finally the earlier judgment must fulfil the conditions necessary for its recognition in the Member State addressed. The identity of parties and of the cause of action receives the same meaning as

---

339 *Hess/Pfeiffer/Schlosser* Report, 253, note 564 (proposing to give precedence to the earlier local judgment in order to enhance consistency with Arts. 27 and 28 Brussels I Regulation) The proposition has not been followed by the Commission in its Proposal for a Revision of the Brussels I Regulation (Revision Proposal, COM (2010) 748 final, p. 40 see the wording of the proposed Art. 43).

340 *Heuzé*, "Jugements en matière civile et commerciale (compétence, reconnaissance et exécution)", Juridictionnaire Joly Communautaire (2002) para. 164; *Gothot/Holleaux* para. 280.

341 *Horst Ludwig Martin Hoffmann v. Adelheid Krieg*, (Case 145/86) (1988) ECR 645 paras. 23, 25.

342 *Kropholler/von Hein* Art. 34 note 54; *Layton/Mercer* para. 26.069 (see however p. 926, para. 26.070: when the two are in the same terms and the proceedings which gave rise to the local judgment were started after the adoption of the foreign judgment, priority should be denied to the local judgment because it was given in contradiction with the principle set in the case *Jozef de Wolf v. Harry Cox B.V.*, (Case 42/76) (1976) ECR 1759. The latter case refuses the opportunity to a party who has already obtained a judgment in a Member State to start new proceedings against the same defendant on the same problem in another Member State); *Leible*, in: Rauscher Art. 34 note 43; *Gaudemet-Tallon* p. 443–445, para. 424.

343 One author proposes to apply Art. 45 (1) (d) to cases where both conflicting judgments originate in the same Member State and give rise to issues of recognition or enforcement in another Member State: Müller IPRax (2009), 484.

in Art. 29. The conditions that the earlier judgment must fulfil will be found in the Regulation since both judgments come from Member States and involve the same cause of action. If one of them falls in the spatial and substantive scope of application of chapter III of the Regulation, so does the other one.

Priority is given to the earlier judgment. The moment to be considered in order to assess the **74** anteriority of one of the two judgments is much debated. The date when recognition is sought is irrelevant as both judgments benefit automatic recognition. The date when the proceedings commenced should also be considered irrelevant for two reasons.[344] Firstly, Art. 45 (1) (d) is not a sanction of the violation of Art. 29. Second, the question of the relevant moment should be solved with respect to the logic followed in Art. 36. A judgment cannot produce in the requested State more effects than it has in its State of origin. As a consequence, a judgment cannot be automatically recognised before it produces any legal effect in the State where it was rendered, and two judgments cannot be considered irreconcilable before each of them starts producing its legal effect according to the procedural law of the State of origin. This date, which can coincide with the date when the judgment was rendered but does not necessarily do so, should determine which is the earlier judgment.[345]

The conflict arising between two irreconcilable judgments rendered in two Member States **75** and presented for enforcement in a third Member State is not addressed by the Regulation when these judgments do not involve the same parties and the same cause of action. The question, which should be of minor practical relevance thanks to the mechanism set by Art. 29 to 32 (mainly Art. 30), remains difficult since following the strict wording of the Regulation, both judgments are entitled to recognition.[346]

c) Conflict with judgment given in a third State, Art. 45 (1), (d)

Judgments rendered in third States can also provide a ground for denying recognition to a **76** judgment issued in a Member State when the four conditions mentioned above are fulfilled.[347] The identity of the parties and the cause of action should also be interpreted in regard to Art. 29, despite the foreign origin of one of the decisions. Those terms should indeed keep the same meaning throughout the provisions of the Regulation. The conditions for its recognition that must be fulfilled by the judgment given in a third State will be found in an international convention or in national law. The purpose of this provision was actually to avoid diplomatic complications with third States.[348]

The conflict with a judgment issued in a third State is treated just like the conflict with a **77** judgment given in another Member State. Priority is given to the earlier judgment. This raises again the question of the date to be considered in order to assess the anteriority of the

---

[344] *Kropholler/von Hein* Art. 34 note 57. Comp. *Hess/Pfeiffer/Schlosser* Report, 253, note 565 (proposing to refer to the moment of pendency for determining the anteriority under Art. 45 (1) (c) and (d)).

[345] *Geimer/Schütze* Art. 34 notes 180 and 181; *Kropholler/von Hein* Art. 34 note 57 (not mentioning a possible difference between the date where the judgment is rendered and the moment when it produces legal effects).

[346] *Layton/Mercer* para. 26.081-26.082 (proposing various solutions).

[347] *Supra* Art. 45 note 73 (*Francq*).

[348] Report *Schlosser* para. 205.

foreign judgment but in slightly different terms.[349] Indeed it is not sure that the judgment issued in a third State benefits from automatic recognition in the Member State addressed. Should that foreign judgment be taken into account for the purpose of Art. 45 (1), d) from the date where it benefits recognition or enforcement in the Member State addressed, which will probably occur at the end of specific proceedings?[350] Or from the date when the judgment was given?[351] On the one hand, the first position is coherent with the notion of irreconcilability: it occurs only between two judgments which have legal effects in the Member State addressed. On the other hand, this position obviously favours the judgment adopted in a Member State, which benefits from automatic recognition, and it is not fully in line with the wording of Art. 45 (1), d), which requires the judgment given in a third State to fulfil the conditions necessary for its recognition, not to have actually completed the process of recognition or enforcement. Of course, the anteriority can be assessed in the same way in case of conflict with a judgment issued in a third State, as in the case of a conflict with a judgment rendered in another Member State,[352] when the State addressed offers automatic recognition to all foreign judgments.[353]

VI. Art. 45 (1) (e), (2), (3): Principle of non-review of jurisdiction of the court of origin

1. General purpose

78 Recognition of judgments shall, as a matter of principle, be automatic under the Brussels I regime. With an expeditious recognition, featuring as low a number of grounds of refusal as possible, a general review of whether the original court that had rendered a judgment had in fact jurisdiction to do so, would be irreconcilable. Accordingly, in order to foster and strengthen the principle of automatic recognition Art. 35 very much restricts the possibilities of a review as to jurisdiction.[354] The main rule is contained in (1) (e) by *argumentum e contrario* and expressly reinforced in (3) cl. 1: Only insofar as (1) (e) (or another rule in the Regulation) expressly allows for a review of the original court's jurisdiction by the court which is applied to for recognition. The language employed in (3) cl. 1 ("may" instead of "must") should be regarded not as softening this rule but as a matter of politeness.

79 The direct and principal aim of the Brussels system was initially not to unify the rules of direct jurisdiction. This became merely an adjunct, to ensure the swift and near-automatic recognition and enforcement of judgments rendered in the adhering States. However, the practical result was that the focus shifted away from the court requested to enforce a judgment (as had been the position under traditional *conventions simples* dealing with recognition and enforcement only) to the court initially seised of the original cause of action: An aggrieved party is encouraged to seek redress in the original jurisdiction, not in the recognising or enforcing court.[355] By then it is too late and – as (3), (1) (e) make clear – illegitimate

---

[349] In favour of the date when the judgment was rendered: TGI Pars, 10 Feb. 1993, *Credit Lyonnais v. Parretti*, RCDIP (1993) 664 note *Gaudemet-Tallon*.

[350] In favour of this position *Heuzé* (fn. 364) para. 165; *Gothot/Holleaux* para. 283.

[351] In favour of this position *Gaudemet-Tallon* p. 446–447 para. 429.

[352] *Supra* Art. 45 note 75 (*Francq*).

[353] Such is the case in Belgium: Loi du 16 juillet 2004 portant code de droit international privé, M.B., 27.7. 2004, p. 57344, Art. 22, § 1, second line of paragraph.

[354] *Layton/Mercer* para. 26.085.

to object to the original court's jurisdiction.[356] If a court in a Member State is seised of an action under jurisdictional rules common to all the Member States there is little room for complaint at the subsequent stage of recognition and enforcement.[357] Matters of jurisdiction ought to be finally decided by the court of origin and should not be restaged in the Member State addressed causing delay to prompt enforcement.[358]

The Report *Jenard* succinctly described the *rationale* underlying Art. 35: "The very strict **80** rules of jurisdiction laid down in Title [today: Chapter] II, and the safeguards granted in Art. 20 [today: 26] to defendants who do not enter an appearance, make it possible to dispense with any review, by the court in which recognition or enforcement is sought, of the jurisdiction of the court in which the original judgment was given. The absence of any review of the substance of the case implies complete confidence in the court of the State in which judgment was given; it is similarly to be assumed that this court correctly applied the rules of jurisdiction of the Convention [today: Regulation]. The absence of any review as to whether the court in which the judgment was given had jurisdiction avoids the possibility that an alleged failure to comply with those rules might again be raised as an issue at the enforcement stage."[359]

The *règlement double* is a credible pledge by the Member States to refrain from exercising **81** exorbitant jurisdiction to the detriment of defendants domiciled in other Member States and thus aims at preventing the externalising of the costs of national legislation to the detriment of such defendants.[360]

Art. 35 in its entirety supports and enhances the axiomatic principle laid down in Art. 34: **82** Unless a rule in the Regulation itself expressly permits refusal of recognition on a specific ground recognition has to be granted and the court in the second state is bound to recognise the judgment without reviewing it.[361] But even the exceptions might generate repercussions in the state of origin as was amply demonstrated in the *Gruber*-case: After the ECJ had given judgment[362] the Austrian OGH decided on the distribution which Austrian court it ordered to be competent. But eventually the OGH expressly allowed for the defendant invoking lack of international jurisdiction and for a full review of the jurisdictional rules for consumer contracts in order to avoid these issues to be addressed only in a later stage in another Member State where recognition or enforcement will be sought.[363]

---

[355] *Newton* p. 165.

[356] Cf. only Aud. Prov, Valencia AEDIPr 2004, 764, 765; *Newton* p. 165.

[357] Report *Evrigenis/Kerameus* para. 78; *Newton* p. 165 *et seq.*; *van Hoek*, NIPR 2003, 337, 343.

[358] *Alio*, NJW 2014, 2395, 2397.

[359] Report *Jenard* p. 46.

[360] *Whincop*, (1999) 23 Melbourne U. L. Rev. 416, 425 *et seq.*, 431; *Tung*, 23 Mich. J. Int'l. L. 31, 49 (2001); *Mankowski*, in: Claus Ott/Hans-Bernd Schäfer (eds.), Vereinheitlichung und Diversität des Zivilrechts in transnationalen Wirtschaftsräumen (2002), p. 118, 138 *et seq.*; cf. also *TSN Kunststoffrecycling GmbH v. Jurgens* [2002] 1 All ER (Comm) 282, 284 (C.A., per *Rix* L.J.); *LoPucki*, 84 Cornell L. Rev. 696, 759 (1999).

[361] *Layton/Mercer* para. 26.085.

[362] *Johann Gruber v. BayWa AG*, (Case C- 464/01) [2005] ECR I-439 = RCDIP 94 (2005), 493 with note *Jude*; note by *Mankowski*, IPRax 2005, 503.

[363] OGH JBl 2005, 594, 596 with note *Pfersmann*.

83 Occasionally, attempts to rephrase and to reformulate the content of Art. 35 end up with the assertion that Art. 35 implements a presumption that the court of origin had jurisdiction; in the light of (1) (e) and (3) cl. 1 such a presumption ought to be irrefutable.[364] Yet this approach gives Art. 35 a positive reading whereby a negative rule of non-review would suffice. The said presumption adds nothing of value beyond what can already be discerned from the rules *per se*, and might, in fact, become a possible source of misinterpretation. Thus, for the sake of caution one should refrain from asserting such a presumption. Relying on a mutual trust that the courts in the partner states applied the relevant jurisdictional rules correctly[365] is different from a presumption.

2. Legislative history

84 From the very outset the basic idea underlying (1) (e)-(3), which was formed as Art. 28 Brussels Convention and then transmogrified into Art. 35 Brussels I Regulation, formed part of the substance of the Brussels regime. The cascade of Accession Conventions saw the number of Sections of Chapter II which were referred to on the rise. Insofar as the evolution of the protective sub-regimes progressed they left their marks and traces in the legislative history of the Article, Art. 28 Brussels Convention always followed suit if a special jurisdictional sub-regime called for escort and support at the level of recognition and enforcement.

85 The case is a special one with the 1988 Lugano Convention. Its Art. 28 acquired an additional second paragraph (with consequential renumbering of the following paragraphs to paras. 3 and 4) which does not re-appear either in the subsequent versions of the Brussels Convention nor in the Brussels I Regulation. Art. 28 (2) 1988 Lugano Convention expressly preserved Arts. 54b (3) and 57 (4) 1988 Lugano Convention.[366] Both rules referred to do not have a counterpart in the Brussels regime but are concerned with particularities which can only occur in the Lugano regime: Only the original Lugano regime was confronted with the necessity to define its relationship with the Brussels regime and did so in its Art. 54b. Accordingly, both Arts. 54b (3) and 57 (4) Lugano Convention deal with the specific relationship to the Brussels regime. Art. 28 (2) was deemed appropriate to accompany these other Articles[367] and to address any ensuing problems in the transitional period.[368] A need to mirror this could not possibly arise within the Brussels I system itself. Quite unlike the ordinary grounds of refusal, Art. 28 (2) of the Lugano Convention is discretionary.[369]

The reshuffle from the Brussels I Regulation to the Brussels *Ibis* Regulation brought about some alterations, most of them significant: Firstly (and least importantly), the former Arts. 35; 36 Brussels I Regulation ceased to be separate Articles, but where integrated into an overarching Art. 45. Secondly, employees were put on an equal footing with consumers,

---

[364] E.g. Report *Evrigenis/Kerameus* para. 78; *Jeantet*, CDE 1972, 375, 411; *Bartlett*, (1975) 24 ICLQ 44, 45 *et seq.*; *Weser* para. 285; *Martiny*, in: Handbuch des Internationalen Zivilverfahrensrechts, vol. III/2 (1984), ch. II note 160.

[365] Cf. only Report *Jenard* p. 46; BGH IHR 2005, 259, 260.

[366] For applications in practice see BGE 123 III 374; 127 III 186.

[367] Report *Jenard/Möller* para. 16 sub 5.

[368] *Möller*, in: Jayme (ed.), Ein internationales Zivilverfahrensrecht für Gesamteuropa (1992), p. 300.

[369] Report *Jenard/Möller* para. 82.

policyholders, insured persons and beneficiaries.[370] Thirdly, the important[371] restriction on cases where the protected party was the defendant, was added to what now has become (1) (e). Fourthly, the reference to cases provided for in Art. 72 was not retained in (1) (e).

3. Limited and restricted review of jurisdiction

a) Principle of non-review of jurisdiction

The principle of non-review of jurisdiction is expressly laid down in (3) cl. 1. It applies **86** indiscriminately whether the court of origin based its jurisdiction on grounds taken from the Regulation or on grounds taken from national law.[372] Indirectly, even the incorrect application of national law in cases where by right the Regulation rules should have governed the case, is sanctioned and has to be accepted.[373] But courts who are only asked for recognition must not censure their fellow courts in other Member States unless this is expressly requested. However blatantly wrong the violation of the jurisdictional rules applied or not-applied might be the court addressed with recognition is only permitted to intervene in the limited instances provided by (1) (e) or elsewhere.[374] The judgment debtor must appeal in their state of origin if he wants to challenge the decision on the basis that jurisdiction was lacking.[375] This applies to errors of fact and to errors in law likewise.[376]

The common rules on direct jurisdiction and the rules on recognition and enforcement of **87** the Brussels I*bis* Regulation to do not constitute distinct and autonomous systems but are closely linked; it is on that link that rests the simplified mechanisms of recognition and enforcement which leads to there being no review of the jurisdiction of the court of origin.[377] Generally, confidence and trust must prevail that the court of origin has applied the (mostly uniform) rules on jurisdiction correctly.[378] Trust and confidence as cost-reducing mechanisms[379] shall work their vile also here.[380] This excludes any forum bias improperly favouring judgment debtors who are resident in the state where recognition is sought.[381] In addition, a possible source of misapplication of the Regulation is avoided insofar as review by the

---

[370] *Crawford/Carruthers*, (2014) 63 ICLQ 1, 19.

[371] *Deumier/Laazouzi/Treppoz*, Rev. contrats 2013, 1037, 1065.

[372] *Kodek*, in: Czernich/Tiefenthaler/Kodek, Art. 35 note 2.

[373] *Dieter Krombach v. André Bamberski*, (Case C-7/98) [2000] ECR I-1935, I-1967 para. 32.

[374] *Layton/Mercer* para. 26.087; *Geimer/Schütze* Art. 35 note 3.

[375] *Geimer/Schütze* Art. 35 note 5; *Tschauner*, in: BBGS, Art. 35 note 1 (2005); *Kropholler/von Hein* Art. 35 note 4.

[376] BGH IHR 2005, 259, 260; *Geimer/Schütze* Art. 35 notes 13 *et seq. Kropholler/von Hein* Art. 35 note 1.

[377] *Opinion pursuant to Art. 300 (6) EC: Competence of the Community to conclude the new Lugano Convention on jurisdiction and the recognition and enforcement of judgments in civil and commercial matters*, (Opinion 1/03) [2006] ECR I-1145 para. 163; *Wolf Naturprodukte GmbH v. SEWAR spol. s r.o.* (Case C-514/10), ECLI:EU:2012:367 para. 25; *Gothaer Allgemeine Versicherung AG v. Samskip GmbH* (Case C-456/11), nyr. para. 35.

[378] Cf. only Report *Jenard* p. 46; BGH IHR 2005, 259, 260; *Wolfgang Lüke*, in: FS Rolf A. Schütze (1999), p. 467, 482; *Leipold*, in: FS Akira Ishikawa (2001), p. 221, 228 *et seq.*; *Rosner* p. 171.

[379] Seminal *Ripperger*, Ökonomik des Vertrauens (1998).

[380] *Mankowski* (fn. 6), p. 118, 138.

[381] *Mankowski* (fn. 6), p. 118, 138.

---

court in which recognition is sought, would by no means guaranteed to be of superior quality to the application of the jurisdictional rules by the court of origin.[382]

88 If the court of origin has incorrectly assumed that it has jurisdiction in many instances Art. 26 will be violated simultaneously. Although this second mistake does not carry any additional and independent weight but must be treated as a consequential matter, that is, necessarily flowing from the first mistake as to the assumption of jurisdiction and therefore subject to the principle of non-review by the court addressed.[383] Art. 26 must not be implemented to circumvent the principle of non-review. However, even if this did not follow from (3) cl. 1, it can be derived from Art. 36. In any event the judgment debtor will, beyond the strict limits defined by (1) (e), not be heard with any defence that the court of origin incorrectly assumed international jurisdiction.[384]

89 Jurisdiction in Art. 35 means international jurisdiction. This does not imply, however, that courts before which recognition of a foreign judgment is sought, might feel invited to investigate as to whether the court of origin was competent in terms of local jurisdiction or venue. Such investigation is clearly ruled out by Art. 36 and the limited grounds of refusal of recognition exhaustively listed in Arts. 34; 35.[385] The Hamburg court asked to recognise a Marseille judgment must not care whether instead of the Marseille court it should have been a Toulouse or Bordeaux court to give the judgment.[386]

90 A further exception to the rule of non-review, additional to the exceptions contained in (1) (e) is to be found in the transitional rule of Art. 66 (2).[387] In this way, the *prima facie* assertion that (1) (e) is exhaustive[388] receives some refinement.

b) Reference to Sections 3, 4, 5 and 6 of Chapter II in (1) (e)

aa) Generalities

91 (1) (e) allows for a review of jurisdiction but in very limited instances only.[389] (1) (e) refers only to selected Sections of Chapter II . This list is exhaustive insofar as references to Chapter II are at stake. Other grounds of jurisdiction other than those expressly referred to must not be reviewed. In this regard (3) cl. 1 is unambiguously clear and unequivocal and allows no room for misunderstandings.[390] Art. 52 completes the overall picture. In understanding the

---

[382] *Mankowski* (fn. 6), p. 118, 138.

[383] Cass. 11 April 1995 – D 736/95; *Kodek*, in: Czernich/Tiefenthaler/Kodek, Art. 35 note 1.

[384] Cf. only CA Orléans in: Digest I-28 B-2; *Geimer*, WM 1976, 830, 837; *Born/Fallon*, J. trib. 1983, 181, 230; *Martiny* (fn. 10), ch. II note 162.

[385] Cf. only *Geimer*, WM 1980, 305, 309; *Martiny* (fn. 10), ch. II note 179; *Kodek*, in: Czernich/Tiefenthaler/Kodek, Art. 35 note 2; *Geimer/Schütze* Art. 35 note 44; *Kropholler/von Hein* Art. 35 note 1; *Leible*, in: Rauscher, Art. 35 note 4.

[386] *Kropholler/von Hein* Art. 35 note 1.

[387] Cf. on this rule in detail Art. 66 notes 15–22 (*Mankowski*).

[388] Cf. only Report *Evrigenis/Kerameus* para. 79; *Dieter Krombach v. André Bamberski*, (Case C-7/98) [2000] ECR I-1935, I-1967 para. 31; OLG Zweibrücken OLG-Report Koblenz/Saarbrücken/Zweibrücken 2001, 349, 350; OLG Zweibrücken NJOZ 2004, 785, 787; Rb. Rotterdam NIPR 2001 Nr. 60 p. 126.

[389] Cf. only *Xandra Kramer*, NIPR 2000, 26, 30.

[390] Cf. only Hoge Raad S&S 2007 Nr 1 p. 14.

role of Art. 52 it must be appreciated that (1) (e) confines the court addressed to reviewing questions of jurisdiction only; the court addressed may not go further by reviewing the substance if the judgment.[391]

The court addressed with recognition must review of its own motion, *ex officio*, whether the **92** court of origin has obeyed Sections 3, 4 and 6 of Chapter II.[392] It must not wait for an extra application by the judgment debtor or alike. Insofar, this same standard applies under Art. 34. Yet the court addressed need not conduct an investigation into this matter.[393] It must not even invite the parties to submit their respective facts although, by virtue of (2), the court is permitted to review the factual ground asserted by the court of origin.

Contentions that the review established by (1) (e) will only become effective in higher **93** instances but not at first instance[394] are plainly wrong insofar as simple recognition is concerned. It is not by chance or fortuitously that these contentions refer to Arts. 41; 45 in this context.[395] The differentiation should be clear: Insofar as enforcement is applied, Art. 41 bars any review at first instance. But insofar as simple recognition is at stake, a counterpart to Art. 41 generally does not exist. The case is different, though, where a declaration of recognition is sought after separately, since in this event Art. 33 (2) expressly refers to the rules contained in Sections 2 and 3 of Chapter III. But where recognition is not the formal cause of action, Art. 33 (2) firmly establishes an *argumentum e contrario* that automatic and incidental recognition, as such, does not follow the specific rules particularly designed for enforcement and that thus Arts. 41; 45 are not applicable. This gains ample support if the prospects of an appeal are taken into account: With regard to enforcement, a system of appeals is institutionalised, whereas in the case of automatic and incidental recognition, the ordinary means of appeal remain the popular choice.

The proviso that jurisdiction must be reviewed with regard to Sections 3, 4 and 6 of Chapter **94** II stems from the belief[396] that *insofar*, i.e. to this limited and expressly confined extent, public policy is engaged and touched upon.[397] This is the case only to the extent that the rules referred to are applicable on their own merits. Accordingly, (1) (e) cannot be applied if the recognition of a provisional measure is sought, since in this area of provisional measures Art. 35 establishes a particular regime touching upon, in particular, the generally exclusive nature of Arts. 17–19.[398]

bb) Insurance and consumer cases
The first two Sections of Chapter II referred to are Sections 3 and 4 which concern insurance **95** and consumer cases respectively. The court addressed thus has to review as to whether the

---

[391] *Layton/Mercer* para. 26.086.
[392] OLG Köln RIW 1990, 229 = NJW-RR 1990, 127; *Droz* para. 534; *Martiny* (fn. 10), ch. II note 165; *Layton/Mercer* para. 26.089; *Tschauner*, in: BBGS, Art. 35 note 7 (2005); *Kropholler/von Hein* Art. 35 note 6.
[393] *Layton/Mercer* para. 26.089.
[394] *Geimer*, RIW 1980, 305, 306; *Kodek*, in: Czernich/Tiefenthaler/Kodek, Art. 35 note 5; *Geimer/Schütze* Art. 35 note 16; *Kropholler/von Hein*, Art. 35 note 6; *Leible*, in: Rauscher, Art. 35 note 6.
[395] For references see last fn.
[396] Critically e.g. *Geimer/Schütze* Art. 35 note 9.
[397] *Arthur Bülow*, RabelsZ 29 (1965), 473, 505; *Hans Arnold*, AWD 1969, 89, 92.
[398] *Xandra Kramer*, NIPR 2000, 26, 31.

court of origin assumed its jurisdiction in contradiction to, and in violation of, Arts. 10–16 17–19 or 21–23 respectively.[399] The protective regimes themselves therefore get accompanying protection with a second-tier of recognition and enforcement. They are regarded with such imminent importance, since they grant generally exclusive jurisdiction, that courts should not tamper with them, and that those rules should be reviewed as to whether they have applied these rules correctly. In particular, this sets a high standard for the recognition and enforcement of a default judgment which is entered into against a consumer outside the state where the consumer has his domicile. Circumventing the protective regime by simply suing in a court which is convenient from the entrepreneur's point of view therefore made quite unattractive and an unappealing strategy.

96 Without (1) (e), entrepreneurs would take less caution, if at all, and would feel inclined to adopt the strategy of suing consumers in their (i.e. 'the entrepreneurs') home countries in the expectation that the consumer would not find the away game worth entering into appearance and that claimants in turn would obtain default judgments but for Art. 26. Fellow travelling courts familiar with an enterprise of local and regional importance could then cause severe harm by creating external effects on consumers in other countries. Yet (1) (e) disables such a strategy. The courts in the consumers' home states can step in to protect their countrymen. The externalisation should therefore not occur. Consumers are protected against an own strategy of (only seemingly) rational disinterest[400] turning into irrational if not disastrous apathy. *Mutatis mutandis* the same applies in insurance cases.

97 However, the exception provided for insurance, consumer and employment cases often gets questioned for the alleged lack of a convincing *ratio*.[401] The critics nonetheless overlook the decisive point as spelled out above. They argue for instance, that it appears illogical to review jurisdiction in a simple consumer case, for example one which concerns the purchase of a vacuum-cleaner which does not threaten the consumer's solvency whereas jurisdiction in a multi-million-Euro-lawsuit, the outcome of which could render either party bankrupt, is not reviewed.[402] But the defendant in a – dramatically speaking – life-threatening multi-million-Euro-lawsuit is not very likely to adopt a strategy of rational apathy but will feel inclined to fight the matter to death (if it is permitted to follow on the metaphor), which is quite contrary to the attitude of a consumer-defendant in an ordinary small-claim lawsuit abroad. The consumer might not think it worth the effort – while the defendant in the multi-million-Euro-lawsuit certainly will.

98 Insofar as review of jurisdiction is permitted the court that is addressed ought to make a full assessment as to whether the court of origin had jurisdiction. This involves both defining the

---

[399] Cf. only Cass. RCDIP 101 (2012), 931, 932 note *Lopez de Tejada*; OLG Frankfurt IPRspr. 2001 Nr 169 p. 340–342 (with note *Mankowski*, EWiR Art. 24 EuGVÜ 1/01, 427); OLG Stuttgart NJW-RR 2001, 858.

[400] On rational apathy as consumers' preferred strategy in cross-border cases bearing in mind the ordinarily small amounts at stake, *Mankowski*, MMR-Beilage 7/2000, 22, 32; *Mankowski*, in: Internet und Recht (Wien 2002), p. 191, 212; *Mankowski*, in: Ruth Nielsen/Sandfeld Jacobsen/Trzaskowski (eds.), EU Electronic Commerce Law (København 2004), p. 125, 142–145.

[401] *Schütze*, RIW 1974, 428, 429; *Kaye* p. 1504; *Gottwald*, in: Münchener Kommentar zur ZPO, Art. 28 EuGVÜ notes 9 *et seq.*; *Schack* para. 840; *Geimer/Schütze* Art. 35 note 8; *Geimer*, in: FS Andreas Heldrich (2005), p. 627, 642; *Kropholler/von Hein*, Art. 35 note 7; *Leible*, in: Rauscher, Art. 35 note 6.

[402] *Schütze*, RIW 1974, 428, 429.

respective parts of the jurisdictional rules involved and a proper conclusion for the purposes of the concrete case pursuant to (2) based on the factual findings of the original court. The final decision of the court addressed might become quite extensive since this court has to assess jurisdiction and has to reason its judgment as though it was the original court giving judgment.[403] Nonetheless it should be emphasised that this still does not amount to a direct application of the jurisdictional rules since the court addressed is not itself deciding the case, but only a means of controlling and monitoring the decision rendered by the court of origin.[404]

If the courts in the state where the court of origin is located, had international jurisdiction, it **99** does not matter that the court of origin might not have been competent in terms of local jurisdiction or venue. Local jurisdiction is, with regard to the exception, not a matter of review since the Regulation is only concerned with cross-border cases and will not erect barriers to recognition that is previously unknown to the national laws of the Member States.[405]

cc) Employment cases (Section 5 of Chapter II)

A new and the most recent entry amongst the Section of Chapter II referred to in (1) (e) is **100** Section 5 on employment agreements, now Arts. 20–23. Art. 35 Brussels I Regulation did not contain a like reference and deliberately so. The justification for this omission read that under Section 5 the employee is ordinarily the claimant and therefore would get the better of the rules on recognition and enforcement if the jurisdiction of the court rendering the judgment was not scrutinised.[406]

This reasoning has always been far from convincing.[407] Firstly, it discounts any claims **101** against the employee by the employer, however rare those events might be in practice. In the area of claims for damages, the factual situation might be different, though,[408] if only one is prepared to let such claims fully fall under then Art. 18 Brussels I Regulation.[409] Secondly, it treats employees differently and less favourably than consumer and insurance policy-

---

[403] Fine examples are provided by OLG Frankfurt IPRspr. 2001 Nr 169 p. 340–342 and OLG Stuttgart NJW-RR 2001, 858.

[404] *van Hoek*, NIPR 2003, 337, 343.

[405] *Geimer*, WM 1976, 830, 839; *Geimer*, RIW 1980, 305, 309; *Gottwald*, in: Münchener Kommentar zur ZPO, Art. 28 EuGVÜ note 11; *Geimer/Schütze*, Art. 35 notes 44, 52; *Tschauner*, in: BBGS, Art. 35 note 1 (2005); *Kropholler/von Hein*, Art. 35 note 9; *Leible*, in: Rauscher, Art. 35 note 6.

[406] Commission Proposal, COM (1999) 348 final p. 25. Cited with approval e.g. by *Jonathan Hill/Chong* para. 13.3.5.

[407] *Droz/Gaudemet-Tallon*, RCDIP 90 (2001), 601, 648; *Junker*, RIW 2002, 569, 577; *Rosner* p. 130; cf. also *Leible*, in: Rauscher, Art. 35 note 12; *Geimer/Schütze* Art. 35 note 14; *de Sousa Gonçalves*, in: Estudos em Memória do Professor Doutor António Marques dos Santos (2005), p. 35, 54–59.

[408] *Droz/Gaudemet-Tallon*, RCDIP 90 (2001), 601, 648; *Junker*, RIW 2002, 569, 577; *Rauscher*, Internationales Privatrecht (2nd ed. 2002) p. 438; *Tschauner*, in: BBGS, Art. 35 note 14 (2005); *Leible*, in: Rauscher, Art. 35 note 12.

[409] At least insofar as they can be attributed a contractual nature they are within Artt. 18–21 whereas this is doubtable to say the least insofar as they are based on tort; see in more detail *Mankowski*, in: Rauscher, Art. 18 note 2.

Peter Mankowski   935

holders or insured persons.[410] The parallel nature of the three regimes, which strive for protecting typically weaker parties, in an integral point that undermines the protection granted to employees to a certain extent, perpetuating the inadequate protection the Brussels and Lugano Conventions afforded to employees. It generates a split between the rules on jurisdiction on the one hand and the rules on recognition on the other hand. Whereas, for example, Art. 20 tries to follow Art. 10 and Art. 17 to the letter, even including the badly fitting *caveat* in favour of Art. 7 (5), Art. 35 (1) Brussels I Regulation did not follow this route and deviated from it to the employees' detriment. Thirdly, it stood to reason that it was inappropriate that Art. 35 (1) Brussels I Regulation, in the event that the typically weaker party is the claimant, was not restricted in a like manner in insurance or consumer matters. The correct approach, if one likes to implement such reasoning at all,[411] would have been to restrict Art. 35 (1) Brussels I Regulation generally[412] (and has now been correctly implemented in (1) (e) i) *in fine).* In summary, the suspicion might have been justified that political agreement had simply not been able to be reached as to the inclusion of Section 5 in Art. 35 (1) Brussels I Regulation.[413]

101a (1) (e) i) now corrects this misgiving and includes the protective regime for employment agreements amongst the rules referred to. Employees are put on an equal footing with other weaker parties[414] and benefit from this extension[415] if they have been defendants in the court of origin. Recital (18) emphasises the protection of weaker parties including employees, and (1) (e) i) obliges at the enforcement level.[416]

c) Cases of exclusive jurisdiction under Art. 24

102 Expressly preserved for is also Section 6 of Chapter II, translated into plain English: expressly preserved for are the cases of exclusive jurisdiction under Art. 24. This coincides with the general emphasis on truly exclusive jurisdiction and Art. 24 in particular. The court which disregards Art. 24 and decides a case which should have been exclusively the business of another court in another Member State, must not feel home and dry as to the recognition of the result it reached.

103 One source for possible conflict was often identified with Art. 24 (2) cl. 2:[417] In order to determine the seat of a company each court shall apply its rules of private international law and not the autonomous definition established by Art. 63. Yet in practice, divergence should not occur, at least if courts have been appraised of the recent authorities correctly. After *Centros, Überseering* and *Expire Art*[418] the Member States of the EU have in fact a uniform

---

[410] *Droz/Gaudemet-Tallon*, RCDIP 90 (2001), 601, 648; *Junker*, RIW 2002, 569, 577; *Tschauner*, in: BBGS, Art. 35 note 14 (2005); *Leible*, in: Rauscher, Art. 35 note 12.

[411] *Contra* e.g. *Junker*, RIW 2002, 569, 577.

[412] See previous edition Art. 35 Brussels I Regulation notes 32–35 (*Mankowski*).

[413] *Vlas*, WPNR 6421 (2000), 745, 751; *Rosner* p. 130.

[414] *Crawford/Carruthers*, (2014) 63 ICLQ 1, 19.

[415] *Deumier/Laazouzi/Treppoz* Rev contrats 2013, 1037, 1065.

[416] See *Alio*, NJW 2014, 2395, 2398.

[417] Cf. only *Layton/Mercer* para. 26.091; *Kropholler/von Hein*, Art. 35 note 13.

[418] *Centros Ltd. v. Erhvervs- og Selskabsstyrelse*, (Case C-212/97) [1999] ECR I-1459; *Überseering BV v. Nordic Construction Co. Baumanagement GmbH*, (Case C-208/00) [2002] ECR I-9919; *Kamer voor Koophandel en Fabrieken voor Amsterdam v. Inspire Art Ltd.*, (Case C-167/01) [2003] ECR I-10155.

conflicts rule that determines the seat of companies in intra-Community cases: the place of incorporation and the statutory seat prevail,[419] the *siège réel* vanishes. Art. 24 (2) cl. 2 does not make an exception to this rule.[420] Formerly there was some controversy between the Report *Jenard*[421] and the prevailing opinion in legal writing[422] as to whether a court should be censured for correctly basing its exclusive jurisdiction under the then Art. 16 (2) Brussels Convention in conjunction with its own private international law if the private international law of the state where recognition is sought would identify the seat of the respective company elsewhere. This controversy should not be enlivened anymore.

Sometimes a restrictive interpretation is advocated for: The violation of Art. 24 shall induce   **104** the court to order a mandatory refusal of recognition only in the event that the courts of a third Member State (i.e. another Member State besides the state of origin and the state where recognition is sought) were vested with exclusive jurisdiction under Art. 24; in the event that exclusive jurisdiction was only vested in the courts of the state where recognition is now sought, it is argued that a refusal of recognition should be treated as discretionary since only the jurisdiction to adjudicate of the state presently concerned was at stake and this state is not required to insist on such jurisdiction.[423] This restrictive interpretation is ill fitting with the wording of (1) (e)[424] and is irreconcilable with the emphasis the Regulation has throughout Art. 24. Underling rationale is the respect for the *Community* rule. The single Member State is not entitled to dispose of Art. 24 since it lacks the respective competence as Art. 24 is not a home-made rule which would be at the disposal of national instances.[425]

In the exceptional circumstance that the court of origin having rendered judgment and a   **105** court in another Member State have exclusive jurisdiction under Art. 24 an auxiliary conflicts rule is required. Two approaches are feasible each based on a different rule of the Regulation: The first gives priority to the court first seised[426] drawing firm support from Art. 29. The latter would treat the entire matter outside (1) (e) since the court of origin itself was blessed with exclusive jurisdiction under Art. 24. Recognition could only be refused if the actual judgments collide in which case the yardstick that is applicable clearly should be (1) (c), (d). Since the matter has already generated at least one judgment the latter approach

---

[419] Cf. in detail on these connecting factors *Jochen Hoffmann*, ZVglRWiss 101 (2002), 283.

[420] *Mankowski*, in: Rauscher, Art. 24 note 30; *Benedetelli*, RDIPP 2002, 879, 910 *et seq.*; *Benedetelli*, in: Meeusen/Pertegás/Straetmans (eds), Enforcement of International Contracts in the European Union (2004) para. 8/26; *Benedetelli*, (2005) 16 Eur. Bus. L. Rev. 55, 73; *Gerhard Wagner*, in: Lutter (ed.) Europäische Auslandsgesellschaften in Deutschland (2005), p. 223, 265; *Leible*, in: Hirte/Bücker (eds.), Grenzüberschreitende Gesellschaften (2005), § 11 note 9; *Schillig*, IPRax 2005, 208, 217 *et seq.*; cf. also *Rehm*, in: Eidenmüller (ed.), Ausländische Kapitalgesellschaften im deutschen Recht (2004) § 5 note 120.

[421] Report *Jenard* p. 35.

[422] *Christian Wolf*, in: BBGS, Art. 28 EuGVÜ note 12 (Dec. 1997); *Gottwald*, in: Münchener Kommentar zur ZPO, Art. 28 EuGVÜ note 16; *Schlosser*, Arts. 34–36 note 32; *Kropholler/von Hein*, Art. 35 note 13; *Leible*, in: Rauscher, Art. 35 note 9.

[423] *Geimer*, WM 1976, 830, 838; *Geimer*, in: Zöller, ZPO, Art. 35 note 10; *Geimer/Schütze* Art. 35 notes 56 et seq.

[424] *Gottwald*, in: Münchener Kommentar zur ZPO, Art. 28 EuGVÜ note 15; *Leible*, in: Rauscher, Art. 35 note 7.

[425] So correctly (concrete in another context) *Geimer/Schütze* Art. 35 note 59.

[426] *Kropholler/von Hein*, Art. 35 note 13.

seems preferable. Technically, one could object to the first approach that (1) (e) does make reference to, and does not preserve, Art. 29.

106 The construction of Art. 24 is decisive for another reason with regard to (1) (e): If Art. 24 is read literally it can only vest exclusive jurisdiction in the courts of Member States. Consequentially, recognition must be granted if a non-Member State could claim exclusive jurisdiction based on its national law.[427] The same applies if the courts of the non-Member State were exclusively competent measured by the yardstick found in the national law of the state addressed with recognition.[428] So far everyone is in complete and utter agreement. Yet if one sticks with the literal reading and does not apply Art. 24 by way of analogy to cases where the respective connecting factor is located in a non-Member State,[429] matters will end here. If one however follows the so-called doctrine of *effet réflexe* and is inclined to restore exclusive jurisdiction to the respective non-Member State, where a connecting factor named in Art. 24 is localised,[430] matters could be different. The somewhat striking result of the latter approach could be that recognition of a Member State's judgment may be mandatorily refused if a 'connection' as defined in Art. 24 exists with a non-Member State.[431] Indirectly, a non-Member State would prevail over a Member State. This result heavily militates against the doctrine of *effet réflexe*. An analogy to Art. 24 in favour of non-Member States must not even indirectly and consequentially pierce the principally exhaustive regime of Art. 45.[432]

---

[427] Cf. only *Geimer/Schütze* Art. 35 note 60; *Leible*, in: Rauscher, Art. 35 note 8.

[428] *Geimer/Schütze* Art. 35 note 60.

[429] Cf. only Report *Jenard/Möller* para. 54; Report *Almeida Cruz/Desantes Real/Jenard* para. 25; OGH SZ 74/ 75 = ZfRV 2002, 115 = JAP 2001/2, 246 with note *Frauenberger-Pfeiler*; *Geimer*, NJW 1976, 441, 443; *Mota de Campos*, Doc. Dir. Comp. 22 (1985), 73, 121; *Teixeira de Sousa/Moura Vicente* p. 113 *et seq.*; *Czernich/Tiefenthaler*, wobl 1999, 255, 257 *et seq.*; *Mari* p. 148 *et seq.*; *Rechberger/Frauenberger-Pfeiler*, ZZP Int 6 (2001), 3, 22; *Béraudo* JCl Droit international fasc. 631-50 para. 27 (2002); *Wenner*, in: FS Walter Jagenburg (2002), p. 1013, 1022–1025; *Tiefenthaler*, in: Czernich/Tiefenthaler/Kodek Art. 24 note 7; *Teixeira de Sousa*, IPRax 2003, 320, 322 *et seq.*; *Geimer/Schütze* Art. 24 notes 13 *et seq.*; Art. 25 note 5 (*Queirolo*); *Mankowski*, in: Rauscher Art. 24 notes 2a *et seq.*

[430] Art. 24 note 10 (*Lima Pinheiro*) and *Droz* p. 14 *et seq.*, 108 *et seq.*; *Bariatti*, RDIPP 1982, 484, 502; *Gothot/ Holleaux* para. 37; *Grundmann*, IPRax 1985, 249; *Luzzatto*, Jus 1990, 9, 13 f; *Bernasconi/Gerber*, SZIER 1993, 39, 55; *Hausmann*, in: Wieczorek/Schütze Art. 16 EuGVÜ Rn 7; *Carrascosa González*, in: Calvo Caravaca Art. 25 BC note 7; *Calvo Caravaca/Carrascosa González*, Derecho Internacional Privado I (2002) 119, II (2000) 443; *Gaudemet-Tallon*, in: Liber amicorum Georges A.L. Droz (1996), p. 85, 95 *et seq.*; *Gaudemet-Tallon* Para. 100; *Boschiero*, in: Appunti sulla riforma del sistema italiano di diritto internazional privato (1996), p. 130 *et seq.*; BBGS/*Safferling* Art. 16 EuGVÜ Rn 2 (1997); *Gottwald*, in: Münchener Kommentar zur ZPO, Art. 16 EuGVÜ note 6; *Fasching/Simotta*, Kommentar zu den Zivilprozessgesetzen I² (2000) Vor §§ 83a, 83b JN note 158; *Grolimund*, Drittstaatenproblematik des europäischen Zivilverfahrensrechts (2000) para. 429; *Kropholler/von Hein* Art. 24 note 7; *Kropholler/von Hein*, in: FS Murad Ferid (1988), p. 239, 241 *et seq.*; *Schack* para. 316; *Fernández Arroyo*, in: FS Erik Jayme (2004), p. 169, 178, 186; *Layton/Mercer* para. 19.010; *Bernard Audit*, in: Mélanges en l'honneur de Paul Lagarde (2005), p. 19, 34; *Fentiman* (2005) 64 Cambridge L.J. 303, 304; *Mourre/Lahlou*, RDAI 2005, 509, 519.

[431] Drawing that consequence indeed *Grundmann*, IPRax 1985, 249, 253.

[432] To the same result *Geimer/Schütze*, Internationale Urteilsanerkennung p. 322; *Geimer/Schütze*, Art. 35 notes 63–65; *Gottwald*, in: Münchener Kommentar zur ZPO, Art. 22 EuGVVO note 14; *Rosner* p. 172; *Kropholler/von Hein* Art. 35 note 11.

The opposite phenomenon can be seen in the case in which a court in a non-Member State   107
gave judgment whereas measured by the standards of the Brussels I*bis* Regulation Art. 24
would have vested exclusive jurisdiction in the courts of a certain Member State. Recognition of such a judgment is not governed directly by Arts. 36 *et seq.*, since the judgment in
question is not from a court in any Member State. Yet the policy expressed in (1) (e) should
generate a duty not to recognise such a judgment.[433] This duty is implanted into the national
rules on recognition and enforcement, technically by virtue of Art. 4 (3) EU Treaty.

d) Nexus with Art. 26
(1) (e) must be seen in some triangular context with the Sections referred to on the one hand   108
and to Art. 26 on the other. Insofar as the court of origin could rightfully base its jurisdiction
on Art. 26 because the defendant had entered into an appearance without invoking the lack
of jurisdiction of the court, the respective Sections are not violated. Whether Art. 26 co-
exists as an additional option besides the respective Sections is a question to be answered by
the respective Sections themselves. In this case Art. 24 responds in the negative, as it does
also in regard to the second clause of Art. 26 (1).

The case is more difficult with regard to Sections 3, 4 and 5, though. An express proviso   109
taking account of them is not to be found in the second clause of Art. 26. This silence is often
interpreted as an *argumentum e contrario* that Art. 26 applies fully fledged in consumer or
insurance matters.[434] Whilst there is undeniably some strength in this argument, policy
reasons call for a more differentiating result, namely that Art. 26 should not operate to
the typically weaker party's detriment.[435] Yet the split of opinion on this point should be
recognised.[436] Nonetheless, this divergence of thought is irrelevant in any event where the
judgment debtor had not entered an appearance at all.[437]

In any event Art. 35 relieves the principally protected defendant of any burden to enter an   110
appearance in the court of origin.[438] But if the protected party, as defendant, enters an
appearance he would be better advised if he challenged jurisdiction in his state of origin,
particularly on appeal, therefore complying with the requirements set by Art. 26 and preventing any detrimental consequences.[439]

e) Restriction in cases where the protected party is the claimant
(1) (e) (i) *in fine* is a novelty introduced by the recast process and did not feature in Art. 35   111
(1) Brussels I Regulation. Jurisdiction under the protective regimes is reviewed only and
solely where the policyholder, the insured, a beneficiary of the insurance contract, the
injured party, the consumer or the employee was the defendant. *E contrario*, jurisdiction

---

[433] *Gottwald*, in: Münchener Kommentar zur ZPO, Art. 22 EuGVVO note 14; *Kodek*, in: Czernich/Tiefen-
    thaler/Kodek, Art. 35 note 8; *Kropholler/von Hein*, Art. 35 note 12; *Leible*, in: Rauscher, Art. 35 note 8.
[434] E.g. OLG Koblenz RIW 2000, 636 = IPRax 2001, 334; Art. 26 note 24 (*Calvo Caravaca/Carrascosa
    González*).
[435] *Mankowski*, IPRax 2001, 310. Cf. also Art. 19 note 15 (*Nielsen*).
[436] Cf. also CA Douai Clunet 118 (1991), 160, 161 with note *André Huet*; CA Luxembourg Pas. lux. 1990–
    1992, 157 = [1993] I.L.Pr. 55.
[437] Cf. OLG Stuttgart NJW-RR 2001, 858, 859.
[438] *Geimer/Schütze* Art. 35 note 27.
[439] *Geimer/Schütze* Art. 35 note 28; *Tschauner*, in: BBGS, Art. 35 note 1 (2005).

under the protective regimes is not reviewed where the policyholder, the insured, a beneficiary of the insurance contract, the injured party, the consumer or the employee was the
plaintiff.

This implements policy reasons where the non-review of jurisdiction is in either the consumer's, the policyholder's, the insured's or the beneficiary's favour.[440] If the party protected
by the special regime has obtained a judgment in a *forum* which would not have been open to
him under the special regime then the judgment obtained by the protected party would
receive an unfavourable level of recognition and enforcement if it did not gain recognition
elsewhere. At first glance this would appear strikingly illogical.[441] Additional support might
be drawn from the reasoning by the draftspersons of the Brussels I Regulation why Section 5
(labour cases and employment matters) of Chapter II of the Brussels I Regulation was not
added to the catalogue of reviewable Sections under the Brussels I Regulation, namely that
such addition would disfavour the employee who is the claimant in the vast majority of
cases.[442]

112 Furthermore, the *ratio* behind (1) (e) (i) is to protect the typically weaker party against the
detrimental consequences of rational apathy, i.e. against the consequences of inactivity on
the weaker party's side.[443] With regard to a consumer-claimant he cannot be said to be
inactive at all as he has initiated the proceedings.[444] It appears to amount to a *venire contra
factum proprium* if the protected party first sues in a certain state and afterwards claims that
the courts of this very state lacked jurisdiction.[445] In the event that the protected party's
application was dismissed in the original *forum* this dismissal will ordinarily not represent a
judgment as to the merits of the claim but be seen as procedural decision lacking the power
of dismissing the claim as such although this depends on the procedural rules of the original
forum.

113 On the other hand, the professional party does not need protection by law[446] since it has the
financial means to defend the claim and will always do so where it believes such defence is
worth the effort. Furthermore, professional parties will only occasionally go the extra-mile
to let the typically weaker party apply for recognition or enforcement in another state after
obtaining a judgment elsewhere. In such matters, they will ordinarily comply with the
judgment in order to retain their reputation in the market.

114 In practice, a true conflict will be very rare since Art. 28 operates at least against the
opposition to the protected party. If the entrepreneur or insurer does not invoke a lack of
jurisdiction albeit appearing in court, the special regime would not be violated. Only in the

---

[440] In favour of such an exception *Grunsky*, JZ 1973, 641, 646; *Geimer*, RIW 1980, 305, 306 *et seq.*; *Schlosser*,
      Arts. 34–36 note 32; *Kodek*, in: Czernich/Tiefenthaler/Kodek, Art. 35 note 5; *Geimer/Schütze* Art. 35
      notes 20, 47 *et seq.*; *Layton/Mercer* para. 26.090; *Tschauner*, in: BBGS Art. 35 note 5 (2005); *Leible*, in:
      Rauscher, Art. 35 note 6.
[441] *Layton/Mercer* para. 26.090.
[442] Commission Proposal, COM (1999) 348 final p. 25.
[443] *Supra*, Art. 45 notes 96–98 (*Mankowski*).
[444] To the same avail *Deumier/Laazouzi/Treppoz*, Rev. contrats 2013, 1037, 1066.
[445] *Geimer/Schütze* Art. 35 note 21.
[446] *Geimer/Schütze* Art. 35 note 21.

unlikely and unprofessional event that the professional party did not appear and was not represented in court then a default judgment will raise the issue – and even then only if the consumer etc. does not seize upon the option established in his favour to sue in his home country. The jurisdictional rules benefit the protected party with a *forum actoris* (but for labour cases), and the other, logical option is the defendant's home country, plus the third option to be derived from Art. 19 (1), Art. 20 (1) or Art. 10 (1) respectively in conjunction with Art. 7 (5) of the forum in another State where the defendant has an establishment. Where a well advised consumer in his right mind should sue can only be left to the imagination. Although, the jurisdictional rules are designed and weighed in the protected party's favour that any true conflicts become highly unlikely.[447]

f) Disponibility of the protection granted?

Only one step further from the last issue discussed is whether the wording in Art. 35 must be **115** strictly adhered to, even if a non-review was in the protected party's favour. From this, a seemingly small, but fundamental question arises: Does the typically weaker party, at whose protection Art. 35 is aimed, have the right to waive the protection granted to it pursuant Art. 35?[448]

The answer does not come as a simple conclusion. This is an issue at law to be considered by **116** the court of its own motion without the interference by any party. It is concerned with a teleological reduction of the rule in its entirety and operates at an abstract level independent from the concrete case and the weaker party's mind-set. Although in regards to a possible waiver, the protected party's mind-set would be of considerable importance.

Prima facie it appears convincing to reconsider whether the protected party really wants **117** such protection. An unwarranted protection would seem paternalistic. Yet second thoughts reveal that another time if only at another level the informational problem reappears which is so typical for weaker parties. Only a free and informed waiver could count, and an investigation would be necessary if the party had enough data to make an informed decision (or whether they received adequate counsel). Any right to dispose of the protection on the protected party's side clashes with Art. 35, which is to be applied by the court pursuant to its own motion. This disposal would re-introduce some kind of application if only in the negative. The following scenario would be startling: The court dismisses recognition of its own motion on the basis of the lack of jurisdiction of the original court, and afterwards the consumer-defendant asks the court to waive this issue? Furthermore, a right to waive would introduce a split in (1) (e) since such right will not exist if Art. 24 is at issue.

The opposite approach might argue that Art. 19 (1) indicates that a consumer can dispose of **118** the jurisdictional protection granted to them by way of agreement after an argument has arisen, although the constellation envisaged by Art. 19 (1) is fairly different and easily distinguishable: In this Article no court must operate of its own motion, and it concerns an entirely different matter. The consumer is asked to conclude an agreement, which at most times is in a distinct manner and fashion that will make the consumer think about his

---

447 *Layton/Mercer* para. 26.090.

448 Pro *Geimer*, RIW 1976, 145, 147; *Geimer*, WM 1980, 305, 307; *Geimer*, in: FS Andreas Heldrich (2005), p. 627, 642 *et seq.*; *Geimer/Schütze* Art. 35 notes 17 *et seq.*; tentatively also *Martiny* (fn. 10), ch. II note 180. *Contra Gottwald*, in: Münchener Kommentar zur ZPO, Art. 35 note 10.

opposition's possibly hidden agenda. At least the issue of jurisdiction does not get drowned in a flood of issues. This differs vastly from the situation where recognition is sought. The jurisdictional point will be only one amongst others, where the consumer and his advisers are faced with the task in deciding whether a court in another state properly assumed that it had jurisdiction. This is an *ex post*-situation with its very own features as opposed to the *ex ante*-calculation of feasible options in the situation envisaged by Art. 19 (1).

119 The main argument on which the policy concerning the disposition of the protected party is based, is as follows: Suppose that the original court dismissed the stronger party's claim but did not have jurisdiction to do so. Then, it is argued, that a review and the ensuing non-recognition would give the stronger party a chance to try its luck again in another Member State and to apply for recognition for a second time if it is favourable to obtain a judgment there.[449] Although the convincing power of such an argument disappears at closer inspection as the argument does not properly take into account the limited range of heads of jurisdiction available to the stronger party under the protective regimes. In principle, the only jurisdiction where the stronger party can sue the weaker party is the weaker party's state of domicile pursuant to Arts. 14, 18 (2). A genuine range of options does not exist, and the stronger party could only such at its own risk and peril if it filed its claim elsewhere. Hence, the alleged danger does not have a high probability occurring, that is if it exists at all.

4. Instances not referred to

a) Agreements on jurisdiction (Section 7 of Chapter II)

120 Section 7 of Chapter II and in essence Art. 25 is not referred to in (1) (e). The court concerned with recognition must not scrutinise whether the court rendering the judgment might have neglected addressing an agreement on jurisdiction which purportedly deprived it of jurisdiction.[450] Thus, jurisdiction clauses do not get protection at this level of recognition and enforcement. The claimant who sues the defendant in the "wrong" or "forbidden" forum in breach of the agreement between the parties might get away with it. Insofar the exclusive jurisdiction conferred upon the court chosen by virtue of Art. 23 (1) (e) is of a lesser degree and of lesser dignity than the exclusive jurisdiction vested in a court pursuant to Art. 24. The exclusive jurisdiction under Art. 25 in this case becomes – *sit venia verbo* – of second class. If the court of origin fails to fulfil its duty[451] to give due respect to an agreement on jurisdiction, the defendant's remedy exclusively lies in challenging the jurisdiction in the state of origin, rather than in opposing the recognition and enforcement of the judgment in other Member States.[452] On the other hand, the court addressed must not positively review

---

[449] *Geimer/Schütze* Art. 35 note 18; *Geimer*, in: FS Andreas Heldrich (2005), p. 627, 643 fn. 72.

[450] Report *Schlosser* para. 188; OLG Koblenz NJW 1976, 488 = IPRspr. 1975 Nr 171; App. Milano RDIPP 1979, 518; CA Dijon D.S 1979, 383 with note *Droz* = Clunet 103 (1976), 146 with note *Holleaux*; OLG Stuttgart NJW-RR 2010, 134, 135 = RPfleger 2009, 688 with note *Strasser*; *Mezger*, RIW 1976, 345, 348; *Geimer*, WM 1976, 830, 838; *Kerr*, EuR 1980, 353, 359; *Collins* p. 112; *Martiny* (fn. 10), ch. II note 169; *Kodek*, in: Czernich/Tiefenthaler/Kodek, Art. 35 note 9; *Layton/Mercer* para. 26.089; *Tschauner*, in: BBGS, Art. 35 note 8 (2005); *Kropholler/von Hein*, Art. 35 note 14.

[451] As spelled out e.g. in Report *Schlosser* para. 188.

[452] *Layton/Mercer* para. 26.089; *Geimer/Schütze* Art. 35 note 5.

whether the court of origin could have based international jurisdiction on a jurisdiction clause.[453]

(1) (e) considers it foremost the defendant's obligation and burden to invoke the agreement **121** on jurisdiction. If the defendant enters into appearance without alleging to the court it's of lack jurisdiction due to the derogative effect of the agreement, this will amount to founding jurisdiction under Art. 26.[454] If the defendant decides to fight it in the "wrong" place so be it. On the other hand, it cannot be said that Art. 25 was excluded since it lacked a typically weaker party[455] because this explanation would not cover the exclusion of Art. 26.

b) Conventions under Article 72
Insofar as Art. 72 expresses respect for the bilateral duties resulting from conventions the **122** state has concluded and in good faith, Art. 35 (1) Brussels I Regulation drew the appropriate and logical consequences from such respect. Member States which are bound by treaty towards non-Member States not to recognise can fulfil their obligations under the respective treaties; Art. 35 (1) Brussels I Regulation thus avoided possible conflicts in this regard.[456] The underlying preference had its basis in Art. 72 itself, with this rule retaining what was permitted under Art. 59 Brussels Convention, and the respective exception to the rule of non-review of jurisdiction was only consequential[457] for otherwise Art. 72 would be deprived of any sensible meaning. Since Art. 72 does not permit EU Member States to conclude any further conventions with non-Member States that comprise obligations of non-recognition of Member State judgments, the phenomenon might not be short-lived but is fairly limited to a handful of bilateral conventions.[458] Art. 59 Brussels Convention was only sparely used so that in turn the exception indirectly confirms the rule of automatic recognition.[459]

(1) (e) has not retained an exception preserving Art. 72. Reasons for dropping such excep- **123a** tion are not discernible. Obviously a drafting error occurred.[460] Apparently attention whilst drafting was so focussed on including employment cases in the reference to the protective regimes and on getting the restriction now to be found in (1) (e) (i) *in fine* right that the reference to Art. 72 was overlooked although it would have been an easy task to retain it as a (1) (e) iii). Hence, the way to a correction of this presumably erroneous omission is not barred. A correction is called for by purposive reasons. Art. 72 is retained, even keeping its number. Accordingly, if the *ratio* underlying Art. 72 Brussels I Regulation was good enough to justify an exception from the principle of non-review of jurisdiction the same should follow from the current Art. 72.

---

[453] OLG Koblenz NJW 1976, 488 = IPRspr. 1975 Nr 171; App. Milano DRIPP 1979, 518; *Mezger*, RIW 1976, 345, 348; *Martiny* (fn. 10), ch. II note 169.

[454] *Elefanten Schuh GmbH v. Pierre Jacqmain*, (Case 150/80) [1981] ECR 1671, 1700 para. 10; *Hannelore Sommer v. Spitzley Exploitation SA*, (Case 48/84) [1985] ECR 787, 800 para. 24; *Mankowski*, in: Rauscher, Art. 23 note 1a; Art. 23 note 171 (*Magnus*).

[455] But cf. so *Kodek*, in: Czernich/Tiefenthaler/Kodek, Art. 35 note 9.

[456] *Kodek*, in: Czernich/Tiefenthaler/Kodek, Art. 35 note 10.

[457] *Kropholler/von Hein*, Art. 35 note 15.

[458] Cf. Art. 72 note 1 with fn. 1 (*Mankowski*).

[459] Hof Amsterdam NIPR 2001 Nr 130 p. 261.

[460] *von Hein*, RIW 2013, 97, 109.

123b Furthermore and most importantly, Recital (29) cl. 6 even expressly mentions Art. 59 Brussels Convention (and thus indirectly Art. 72) in the specific context of grounds for refusal of recognition.[461] It reads:

"It should also include the grounds which could be invoked on the basis of an agreement between the Member State addressed and a third State concluded pursuant to Article 59 off the 1968 Brussels Convention."

That this clear statement was not followed up in the operative part of the Regulation amounts to an equally clear drafting error.

123c It does not do any substantial harm to read (1) (e) as though it would still contain a reference to Art. 72. Floodgate arguments cannot possibly prevail given the scarcity with which cases under Art. 72 occur. On the contrary, Member States which are Contracting States to bilateral conventions, concerned will be able to fulfil their obligations under the respective conventions. This mirrors an EU policy expressed by Arts. 71, 73 (3) and Recitals (35), (36). It is amply evidenced that this policy ought to be respected and paid full regard to under the Brussels I*bis* regime.

124 If the state in which the court addressed has assumed a bilateral obligation mentioned in Art. 72 the court will need to consider three issues:
  – whether the defendant was domiciled in the particular non-Member State with which the bilateral convention exists;
  – whether the court of origin could only have founded its jurisdiction on a ground of exorbitant jurisdiction which in intra-Community cases would be disallowed by the list in Art. 3 (2), and
  – whether the jurisdiction of the court of origin was based on the presence of property within the jurisdiction in the circumstances specified in Art. 59 Brussels Convention.[462]

125 Art. 59 Brussels Convention and Art. 72 both require that the exorbitant head of jurisdiction was the *ratio decidendi* of the judgment for which recognition is sought, and that this cannot be substituted with a "sensible" head of jurisdiction. If and insofar jurisdiction could have been based on another head of jurisdiction, not militating against basic standards of fairness in a like manner, (1) (e) does not accordingly come into operation.[463]

c) Exclusive jurisdiction under national law
126 Grounds for exclusive jurisdiction under national law do not constitute an obstacle and hindrance in the way of recognition.[464] Even if the court addressed had exclusive jurisdiction vested in it by the rules of its own law, the Regulation takes strict and absolute precedence and rules out any reference to national law. National law is rendered inapplicable throughout, and hypothetical jurisdiction does not gain any protection and preservation.

---

[461] *von Hein*, RIW 2013, 97, 109.
[462] *Layton/Mercer* para. 26.093.
[463] Report *Jenard* Art. 59; *Martiny* (fn. 10), ch. II note 194; *Kropholler/von Hein* Art. 72 note 2.
[464] Cf. only *Martiny* (fn. 10), ch. II note 166.

d) Disregard of an agreement to arbitrate or else to submit to ADR

(1) (e) does not mention the case in which a judgment conflicts with an arbitration agree- **127** ment. This carries a strong *argumentum e contrario*. That the court of origin paid disrespect to the arbitration agreement shall not matter and shall not constitute a ground for refusal of recognition of its own.[465] The judgment is in any event given by a *court* in a Member State and is not an arbitral award. Accordingly, Art. 1 (2) (d) does not come into operation.[466] The circumvention *via* invoking that public policy of the court of the state addressed with recognition would be violated, is effectively blocked by (3) cl. 2.[467]

Recital (12) attempts at a clarification. It reads in its second paragraph and in the first clause **128** of its third paragraph:

"A ruling by a court of a Member State as to whether or not an arbitration agreement is null and void, inoperative or incapable of being performed should not be subject to the rules on recognition and enforcement laid down in this Regulation, regardless of whether the court decides on this as a principal issue or as an incidental question.

On the other hand, where a court of a Member State, exercising jurisdiction under this Regulation or under national law has determined that an arbitration agreement is null and void, inoperative or incapable of being performed, this should not preclude that court's judgment on the substance of the matter from being recognised or, as the case may be, enforced in accordance with this Regulation."

The fundamental problem with Recital (12) is that it is a mere Recital and not a proper rule.[468] It does not star in the truly operative part of the Brussels I*bis* Regulation. Recitals serve as authoritative explanations, but nonetheless they are not binding and thus exert lesser authority than genuine rules which would have a binding effect.

---

[465] Report *Evrigenis/Kerameus* para. 62; Cass. JCP G 2001 II 10787 with note *Kaplan/Cuniberti* = RCDIP 90 (2001), 172, 173 with note *Muir Watt* = Rev. arb. 2001, 507 with note *Idot* = RGDA 2001, 126 with note *Heuzé*; BGE 127 III 186, 187 *et seq.*; OLG Celle RIW 1979, 191; OLG Hamburg IPRax 1995, 391 (with note *Mansel* at p. 362); OLG Stuttgart IPRax 1987, 369; App. Milano RDIPP 1991, 1040; *The "Heidberg"* [1994] 2 Lloyd's Rep. 287, 310 (Q.B.D., Judge *Diamond* Q.C.); *Hascher*, Rev. arb. 1991, 697, 703; *Michael Johannes Schmidt*, EWS 1993, 388, 395 *et seq.*; *Michael Johannes Schmidt*, in: FG Otto Sandrock (1995), p. 205, 208–212, 218–222; *van Houtte*, (1997) 13 Arb. Int. 85, 88; *Besson*, in: Études en l'honneur de Jean-Francois Poudret (Lausanne 1999), p. 329, 343–345; *Poudret*, in: FS Otto Sandrock (2000), p. 761, 769 f; *Beraudo*, (2001) 18 J. Int. Arb. 13, 22; *Loquin*, RTD com. 2002, 47 *et seq.*; *Bälz/Marienfeld*, RIW 2003, 51, 52; *Schlosser* Art. 1 note 25; *Geimer/Schütze* Art. 35 notes 33–43; *Gómez Jene*, IPRax 2005, 84, 90; *Pörnbacher*, in: BBGS Art. 1 note 21 (2005); cf. also Art. 1 note 41 (*Rogerson*). *Contra Briggs*, (1991) 11 Yb. Eur. L. 521, 529; *Weigand*, EuZW 1992, 529, 531 *et seq.*; cf. also *Hartley*, (1991) 16 Eur. L. Rev. 529, 532.

[466] Cf. only *Geimer/Schütze* Art. 35 note 39; *Geimer*, in: FS Andreas Heldrich (2005), p. 627, 645 *et seq.*; *Mankowski*, in: Rauscher, Art. 1 note 31a.

[467] OLG Celle RIW 1979, 131; *Killias*, (2002) 4 Eur. J. L. Reform 119, 131; *Bälz/Marienfeld*, RIW 2003, 51, 53; *Mankowski*, in: Rauscher, Art. 1 note 31a.

[468] *Estrup Ippolito/Adler-Nissen*, 2013 Arb. 158, 163 *et seq.*; *Steindl*, in: FS Hellwig Torggler (2013), p. 1181, 1187; *Hess*, JZ 2014, 538, 540. Overstating the case of Recital (12) *Camilleri*, (2013) 62 ICLQ 899.

Peter Mankowski

The result advocated for by Recital (12) para. 3 cl. 1 would jeopardise arbitration agreements if the claimant and the court seised are only bold and haphazard enough. It draws severe criticism in particular from the London arbitration market. Yet in law, it is inevitable – if at first sight only. One should throw a second glance and widen the spectrum by taking into account the 1958 UN New York Convention on the Enforcement of Arbitral Awards.[469] Insofar as this Convention claims application in areas where the Brussels Ia Regulation also applies, the Convention takes precedence over the Regulation by virtue of Art. 73 (2). In these cases the outcome depends on the weight attributed to Art. II (3) cl. 1958 New York Convention. Art. II 1958 New York Convention is generally recognised as a rule of uniform substantive law which ought to be applied even beyond the smaller area of enforcement of arbitral awards. If and insofar Art. II (3) cl. 1958 New York Convention obliges the court charged with recognition to take account of the arbitration agreement and to treat the matter as being exclusively transferred to the realm of arbitration, recognition of the judgment given despite the arbitration agreement ought to be refused.[470] Art. II (3) cl. 1958 New York Convention is to be applied directly and without a deviation *via* national public policy.[471] In any event, Art. II (3) cl. 1958 New York Convention must be invoked by either party and is not open for the court applying it of its own motion.[472]

5. Factual ground of review: facts as ascertained by the court of origin, (2)

129 The court concerned with issues of recognition is not entitled to assert the facts as to jurisdiction *de novo*. It is not even entitled to re-examine facts or to discuss newly arisen facts. It may not re-open the findings of fact upon which the original court acted in accepting jurisdiction.[473] This shall prevent the defendant from delaying recognition and enforcement by raising fresh factual issues or challenging factual holdings .[474] Furthermore, it shall avoid recourse to a time-wasting duplication in the exceptional cases where a re-examination of the jurisdiction of the court of origin is permitted.[475]

130 Consequentially, (2) even disallows the parties from submitting new facts to the court addressed at least insofar as they could have been raised in the original proceedings.[476] Insofar (2) exerts a precluding effect. The parties should have argued their respective facts in the original proceedings and are not to re-visit the issues afresh, if the original court had jurisdiction and in front of another court which lacks the power and competence to alter the outcome of the initial proceedings as such. This even encompasses pleadings of facts which would not be contradictory, but only supplementary to the findings of the original court.[477] Unfortunately, the ECJ evaded an answer when the respective question was raised before it

---

469 *Mankowski*, in: Rauscher, Art. 1 Brüssel I-VO note 31c.

470 *Hascher*, (1997) 13 Arb. Int. 43, 60 *et seq.*; *Béraudo*, (2001) 18 J Int Arb 13, 26 (2001); *Mankowski*, in: Rauscher, Art. 1 Brüssel I-VO note 31c; *Hartley* (2014) 63 ICLQ 843, 865; see also *Muir Watt*, RCDIP 90 (2001), 174, 175.

471 Favouring such an alternative approach *Schlosser*, (1991) 7 Arb. Int. 227, 234; *Michael Johannes Schmidt*, in: FG Otto Sandrock (1995), p. 205, 218 *et seq.*; *van Houtte*, (1997) 13 Arb. Int. 85, 88.

472 *Kaplan/Cuniberti*, JCP G 2001, 1797, 1798.

473 *Layton/Mercer* para. 26.086.

474 Report *Jenard* p. 46; *Kodek*, in: Czernich/Tiefenthaler/Kodek, Art. 35 note 11.

475 Report *Jenard* p. 46.

476 *Geimer*, NJW 1975, 1086, 1087; *Geimer*, RIW 1976, 145, 147; *Kropholler/von Hein*, Art. 35 note 21.

concerning whether a court addressed could take account of new evidence which a party sought to rely on to establish that he was a consumer and therefore illustrating that the court of origin had accepted jurisdiction in breach of Section 4 of Chapter II.[478]

For the purposes of (2) it does not matter whether the court addressed under its national **131** rules of proceedings would investigate facts *ex officio* or whether the parties are called upon to submit the facts. Either road is blocked and unavailable to the court addressed.

The factual findings of a court that are not open for review comprise, among others, the **132** defendant's domicile or habitual residence or the content of a contract in question (e.g. which obligations ought to be performed where). On the other hand a place of delivery of goods or of the performance of services or a place where a certain activity was exerted or generated consequences do not matter[479] since they cannot establish jurisdiction under the Sections of Chapter II referred to. The case is different if the findings concern the habitual working place or the direction of marketing activities, features which star amongst the prerequisites of the rules referred to. Relevant facts, for example, are the agreed duration and period of a tenancy (with regard to Art. 24 (1) (e) subpara. (2) or the purpose for which goods or services are acquired by a person (with regard to Art. 15 (1) (e)).[480] Facts are facts, and factual findings are not findings in law. The court of origin must not attempt at overcoming this distinction and at escaping control by expressly characterising findings in law as factual findings.[481]

The wording of (2) does not distinguish between facts which are in favour of, and facts which **133** are opposed to, recognition. Despite the lack of such distinction it is sometimes alleged that (2) should be restricted to the latter class of facts.[482] The underlying argument can be summarised as follows: (2), like (1), altogether attempts at enhancing the prospects of recognition. Accordingly, it would appear reconcilable with the purpose of the rule to allow such argument regarding the existence of facts, which would only enhance and augment such prospects.[483] Methodologically this approach amounts to a teleological reduction of the wording. Whereas it would indeed be compatible with the said purpose, it would run counter to the second purpose of (2), to prevent the court addressed from re-opening the procedure with regard to facts that possibly establish jurisdiction. Accordingly, (2) should be taken literally and not made object of the proposed reduction.[484]

Nonetheless, a careful and cautious reading of (2) is requested: The court addressed is only **134** bound by the finding as to facts. It is by no means bound by the conclusions of law which the

---

[477] A-G *Pierre Léger*, Opinion in Case C-99/96, [1999] ECR I-2280, I-2294 para. 59; *Kropholler/von Hein*, Art. 35 note 21.

[478] *Hans-Hermann Mietz v. Intership Yachting Sneek BV*, (Case C-99/96) [1999] ECR I-2277, I-2319 para. 57.

[479] Not properly recognised by *Layton/Mercer* para. 26.095.

[480] *Leible*, in: Rauscher, Art. 35 note 16.

[481] But cf. *Lopez de Tejada*, RCDIP 101 (2012), 933, 936.

[482] *Geimer*, RIW 1976, 145, 147; *Geimer/Schütze* Art. 35 note 45.

[483] Cf. *Geimer*, NJW 1975, 1086, 1087; *Geimer*, RIW 1976, 145, 147; *Geimer*, WM 1976, 830, 839; *Geimer/Schütze* Art. 35 note 45.

[484] *Martiny*, in: Handbuch des Internationalen Zivilverfahrensrechts, vol. III/2 (1984) ch. II note 175; *Tschauner*, in: BBGS, Art. 35 note 15 (2005); *Kropholler/von Hein* Art. 35 note 23.

court of origin had based its factual findings.[485] Otherwise, Art. 35 would be rendered nugatory and deprived of any sensible meaning. Insofar a strict distinction has to be made between the single and separate steps in the process of legal reasoning: (2) does not govern both the *praemissio* and the *conclusio* as such. Domicile, consumer, insurance cover of specific risk, dissolution of a corporate body, tenancy etc. are legal concepts not facts.[486] The interpretation of contracts should be regarded as an issue concerning facts, though.[487]

135 If and insofar as the court of origin has not asserted the facts underlying its assumption of jurisdiction, particularly because judgment was given in a summary procedure (e.g. as an Austrian *Zahlungsbefehl)* there are no findings as to facts which could possibly be binding in a strict sense.[488]

6. Jurisdiction does not form part of public policy, (3) cl. 2

a) General rule

136 Ingenious minds could feel tempted to think that what cannot be attained at the front door might be gained by the backdoor, i.e. to declare the jurisdictional regime of the Brussels Ia Regulation in its entirety to be part of the public policy of the state of the court addressed. (3) cl. 2 takes care of, and addresses, such an attempt. It firmly shuts and forcefully locks the backdoor. Courts addressed have to respect this policy decision.[489] They are not allowed to submerge jurisdictional issues in (1) (a).[490] Even a review of the substantive reasons for reaching a certain decision on jurisdiction (for instance whether the Standard Terms and Conditions containing a jurisdiction clause are incorporated into a contract) under a restricted public policy standard must not take place.[491]

137 The "victims", to whose detriment (3) cl. 2 operates, are defendants domiciled outside the EU and thus are subjected to jurisdiction pursuant to national rules, including the exorbitant heads of jurisdiction banned in intra-EU cases by Art. 3 (2).[492] (3) cl. 2 guarantees that judgments rendered where the court can base its competence only on such an exorbitant head of jurisdiction are fully recognised within the EU without a further review as to jurisdiction.[493] Insofar (3) cl. 2 does not suffer the slightest exception.[494]

---

[485] BGHZ 74, 248, 252; OGH ZfRV 1999, 75, 78; *Goldman*, RTDE 1971, 1, 33; *Droz* para. 537; *Martiny* (fn. 10), ch. II note 174; *Schlosser* Arts. 34–36 note 33; *Layton/Mercer* para. 26.095; *Geimer*, in: FS Andreas Heldrich (2005), p. 627, 643; *Tschauner*, in: BBGS, Art. 35 note 16 (2005); *Kropholler/von Hein* Art. 35 note 22.

[486] *Droz* para. 537; *Martiny* (fn. 10), ch. II note 174; *Schlosser* Arts. 34–36 note 33.

[487] *Schlosser* Arts. 34–36 note 33.

[488] OLG Stuttgart NJW-RR 2001, 858, 859.

[489] Cf. only Trib. Sup. AEDIPr 2003, 802; BGH IHR 2005, 259, 260; OLG Hamburg ZfJ 1992, 547; OLG Frankfurt IPRax 2002, 523.

[490] CA Luxembourg Pas. lux. 2000, 200, 203; Aud. Prov. Vizcaya AEDIPr 2004, 769, 770; cf. also *Dieter Krombach v. André Bamberski*, (Case C-7/98) [2000] ECR I-1935, I-1967 para. 32.

[491] Cf. tentatively contra OLG Bremen RdTW 2014, 227, 230–231.

[492] Cf. only *van Hoek*, NIPR 2003, 337, 344.

[493] Sharply criticised by *von Mehren*, Rec. des Cours 167 (1980 II), 9, 98 *et seq.*; *von Mehren*, 81 Col. L. Rev. 1044, 1054 *et seq.* (1981).

[494] Cf. only BGH IHR 2005, 259, 260; *Schlosser* Arts. 34–36 note 30c.

b) The human rights issue

If (3) cl. 2 is construed as a strict rule, public policy is excluded even in the event that the **138**
court of origin incorrectly based its jurisdiction on an exorbitant ground of jurisdiction
derived from the national law of the state of origin.[495] Excessive extraterritorial reach ought
to be sanctioned in such cases.

Yet such a strict construction[496] raises major concerns and particularly so if and insofar it **139**
collides with the guarantee of due process expressed by Art. 6 Human Rights Convention.[497]
The Human Rights Convention could be regarded as a fundamental basic and core of a
pan-European public order,[498] which as *lex superior*, takes precedence even over a rule like
(3) cl. 2 established by a Community Regulation. If the Human Rights Convention is
acknowledged to form part of the constitutional law of the European Union[499] as Art. 6
(2) EU Treaty demonstrates[500] it clearly outranks the secondary legislation. Under this
precondition it gains priority and primacy. That under national law the Human Rights
Convention might only have the rank of "simple" legislation must cede to Art. 6 (2) EU
Treaty.[501]

Insofar as the Brussels I*bis* Regulation is concerned it can be said to encompass an inherent **140**
caveat that its rules apply only insofar as they are compatible with the Human Rights
Convention.[502] In addition, if a state violates its obligations under the Human Rights Convention by issuing a judgment exercising unfair jurisdiction contrary to Art. 6 Human
Rights Convention, any other state recognising such judgment can be said to violate its

---

[495] *Dieter Krombach v. André Bamberski*, (Case C-7/98) [2000] ECR I-1935, I-1967 para. 33.

[496] *Gottwald*, in: Münchener Kommentar zur ZPO, Art. 28 EuGVÜ note 3; *Hüßtege*, in: Thomas/Putzo,
Art. 35 note 1. This approach draws quite some support from *Dieter Krombach v. André Bamberski*, (Case
C-7/98) [2000] ECR I-1935, I-1967 para. 33.

[497] *Schlosser*, RabelsZ 47 (1983), 525, 529; *Schlosser*, in: FS Wilfried Kralik (1986), p. 287, 295 *et seq.*; *Schlosser*
IPRax 1992, 141; *Schlosser*, Arts. 34–36 note 30; *Schlosser*, in: FS Andreas Heldrich (2005), p. 1007, 1010;
Bajons, ZfRV 1993, 45, 52; *Matscher*, IPRax 2001, 428, 433; *Kodek*, in: Czernich/Tiefenthaler/Kodek,
Art. 35 note 3; *Leible*, in: Rauscher, Art. 35 note 5.

[498] *Dieter Krombach v. André Bamberski*, (Case C-7/98) [2000] ECR I-1935, I-1965 *et seq.* paras. 25–27;
Sudre, in: Tavernier (ed.), Quelle Europe pour les droits de l'homme (Bruxelles 1996), p. 39; *Nascimbene*,
RDIPP 2002, 659, 664; *Xandra Kramer*, NIPR 2004, 9, 13 *et seq.*; *Thomas Pfeiffer*, in: FS Erik Jayme
(2004), p. 675, 684; *Basedow*, in: FS Hans Jürgen Sonnenberger (2004), p. 297, 311–313; cf. also *Pellegrini
v. Italy*, [2001] ECHR Rep. VIII 369.

[499] *Marguerite Johnston v. Chief Constable of the Royal Ulster Constabulary*, (Case 222/84) [1986] ECR 1651,
1682 para. 18; *Baustahlgewebe GmbH v. Commission*, (Case C-185/95 P) [1998] I-8417, I-8496 paras. 20
et seq.; *Kingdom of the Netherlands and Gerard van der Wal v. Commission*, (Joint Cases C-174/98 P and
C-189/98 P) [2000] ECR I-1, I-61 para. 17; *Dieter Krombach v. André Bamberski*, (Case C-7/98) [2000]
ECR I-1935, I-1965 *et seq.* paras. 25–27.

[500] *Dieter Krombach v. André Bamberski*, (Case C-7/98) [2000] ECR I-1935, I-1966 para. 27; *Leible*, in:
Rauscher, Art. 35 note 5; *Tschauner*, in: BBGS, Art. 35 note 2 (2005).

[501] Doubting *Föhlisch*, Der gemeineuropäische orde public (1997) p. 47; *Voltz*, Menschenrechte und ordre
public im Internationalen Privatrecht (2002) p. 261; *Martiny*, in: FS Hans Jürgen Sonnenberger (2004),
p. 523, 535 *et seq.*

[502] Cf. *Grolimund*, Drittstaatenproblematik im Europäischen Zivilprozessrecht (2000) para. 734; *Schlosser*,
in: FS Andreas Heldrich (2005), p. 1007, 1010.

Peter Mankowski   949

own obligations under Art. 6 Human Rights Convention by deepening and enhancing the resulting injury.[503] An irrefutable presumption that a judgment given in another Member State cannot have resulted from a violation of Art. 6 Human Rights Convention would therefore be untenable.[504] In its consequences and as transmitted by EU law, Art. 6 Human Rights Convention thus amounts to a ground of refusal yet embraced in the terms of public policy.[505] On the other side this exception ought to be handled carefully and must not amount to an overall review by creeping in the back door contrary to Art. 36.[506]

VII. Applicability of the Brussels I*bis* Regulation

141   Art. 45 does not mention expressly that a judgment has to fall within the scope of the Brussels I*bis* Regulation. Yet Art. 45, as central part of the Regulation regime, can only be triggered off if the Regulation as a whole is applicable. Otherwise recognition, as such, is not governed by the Regulation at all, and cases must be handled outside the Regulation regime in accordance with the rules of the national law of the second state. Hence the Regulation cannot prevent the court from considering whether the judgment, which it is called upon to recognise, falls within the scope of the regime and, to this extent too, the court addressed has power to review the original judgment[507] although such leeway is not expressly provided for in Arts. 34; 35. It is indeed important to distinguish between a decision by the court addressed that states the judgment falls outside the Regulation regime altogether and a decision that the court of origin wrongly assumed jurisdiction under the Regulation regime, with only the latter being indicted by (3) cl. 1.[508]

142   As always, with regard to Art. 1, every court addressed is called upon to seize the point of its own motion, although in practice the matter will arise with the highest probability if the judgment debtor alleges the subject matter of the decision, recognition of which is sought, fell outside the scope of the Regulation regime.[509]

VIII. Immunity

143   Immunity and thus jurisdiction over as state or state body defendant in the sense that international law employs, is a matter not dealt with by the Brussels I Regulation and is outside the ambit of the Regulation. It is in fact a prerequisite supposed to exist before one enters into the realm of the Regulation. Technically, it might be said to correspond with Art. 1 (1) (e) to a certain degree. Yet neither (1) (e) nor (3) precludes the court addressed from probing as to whether the defendant was immune and should not have been subjected to the jurisdiction of the original court at all.[510]

---

[503] *Schlosser,* in: FS Andreas Heldrich (2005), p. 1007, 1010 with reference to *Pellegrini v. Italy,* [2001] ECHR Rep. VIII 369 para. 40; *Basedow,* in: FS Hans Jürgen Sonnenberger (2004), p. 297, 311–313.

[504] *Maronier v. Larmer* [2003] 3 All ER 848, 855 (C.A., per Lord *Phillips of Worth Matravers* M.R.); *Thomas Pfeiffer,* in: FS Erik Jayme (2004), p. 675, 684.

[505] To the same result *Christoph Engel,* RabelsZ 53 (1989), 3, 49; *Jayme,* Nationaler ordre public und europäische Integration (2000) p. 23 *et seq.; Jayme/Christian Kohler,* IPRax 2001, 501, 502.

[506] *Maronier v. Larmer* [2003] 3 All ER 848, 855 (C.A., per Lord *Phillips of Worth Matravers* M.R.).

[507] *Kodek,* in: Czernich/Tiefenthaler/Kodek, Art. 35 note 4; *Layton/Mercer* para. 26.087.

[508] *Layton/Mercer* para. 26.087.

[509] Cf. *Layton/Mercer* para. 26.087.

IX. Existence of a decision capable of recognition

The court addressed is also not prevented from scrutinising as to whether the decision for **144** which recognition is sought, is a decision within the bounds defined in Art. 32.[511] This question is not a question of jurisdiction but is related to another prerequisite relating to the regime of recognition and enforcement itself. The restriction gains its relevance in particular with regard to provisional measures obtained *ex parte* since the ECJ[512] does not attribute the quality of a decision falling under Art. 2 (a) to them.[513]

X. Procedure for an isolated application for refusal of recognition, (4)

1. Generalities

As a novelty,[514] (4) states that an application for refusal of recognition shall be made in **145** accordance with the procedures provided for in Subsection 2 and, where appropriate, Section 4. A major clarification is appropriate at the outset: (4) does not undermine the principle of automatic recognition nor Art. 36 (1). Conversely, (4) only deals with separate, isolated, stand-alone applications for refusal of recognition. It is absolutely vital to make this distinction and to pinpoint the restrictive scope of application of (4). Else (4) would be fundamentally misunderstood and would generate complete incoherence within the European system of recognition. The debtor is entitled to invoke every ground of refusal as a defence against an application by the creditor to recognise or enforce the judgment or against any proceedings initiated by the creditor which incidentally and automatically address the issue of recognition.

(4) establishes negative declaratory relief for the judgment debtor. It guarantees the right to **146** such negatory declaratory relief on the EU level without insofar recourse to be had to the national law of the forum as to whether it grants such relief.[515] Yet the national law of the forum steps in for the details. If the national law of the forum is not familiar with negatory declaratory relief or does not contain respective rules they have to be developed within the limits which the methodological principles of the law of the forum allow. Since (4) grants a subjective right stemming from EU law it thus calls for equivalence and effectiveness as a matter of general principle of EU law. The procedure under (4) is necessarily a contradictorial procedure.[516]

The counterpart to (4) establishing positive declaratory relief for the judgment creditor is **147** Art. 36 (2). The debtor's application under (4) is the mirror image of the creditor's applica-

---

[510] *Geimer,* in: Zöller, ZPO, Art. 35 note 32; *Tschauner,* in: BBGS, Art. 35 note 3 (2005); cf. also *Mankowski,* RIW 2004, 587, 596.

[511] *Kodek,* in: Czernich/Tiefenthaler/Kodek, Art. 36 note 2; *Tschauner,* in: BBGS, Art. 36 note 6 (2005).

[512] *Bernard Denilauler v. Couchet Frères SARL,* (Case 125/79) [1980] ECR 1553, 1571 para. 17; *Mærsk Olie & Gas A/S v. Firma M. de Haan en W. de Boer,* (Case C-39/02) [2004] ECR I-9657, I-9702 para. 50.

[513] *Kodek,* in: Czernich/Tiefenthaler/Kodek, Art. 36 note 2; *Tschauner,* in: BBGS, Art. 36 note 6 (2005).

[514] *Beraudo,* Clunet 140 (2013), 741, 761.

[515] *Supra* Art. 36 note 25 fn. 51 (*Wautelet*).

[516] *Lopes Pegna,* Riv. dir. int. 2013, 1206, 1215.

tion under Art. 36 (2). Both kinds of applications have the same cause and action.[517] Both follow the same yardsticks.[518] In particular, both shall be made in accordance with the procedures provided for in Subsection 2 and, where appropriate, Section 4. In this regard, (4) verbally reproduces Art. 36 (2) which in turn is the successor to Art. 33 (2) Brussels I Regulation.

2. Scope of the references in (4)

148 Since the references to "Subsection 2 and, where appropriate, Section 4" are identical in both Art. 45 (4) and Art. 36 (2) national legislators are not at liberty to implement different jurisdictional rules for both types of application respectively under Art. 47 (1).[519] Subsection 2 of Section 3 consists of the rules designed for refusal of enforcement, namely Arts. 46–51. They ought to be applied *mutatis mutandis*.

149 Section 4 comprises so called common provisions for recognition and enforcement alike. The "where appropriate" putting the reference to Section 4 under some kind of condition, making this reference at least not unconditional, relates to the outset that any reference in (4) is only made to the *procedures* provided for in i.a. Section 4. To sort it out, no reference appears to be to Arts. 55 and 56 which are specifically related with enforcement not with recognition. Art. 52 on the other hand is referred to for the verdict on any *révision au fond* is absolutely vital to the system of recognition under the Regulation. Art. 53 is also sure. It is not beyond any doubt whether there is a reference to Art. 54, too. Art. 54 allows for an adaptation of measures unknown in the law of the Member State addressed. An active adaptation fits rather ill with an application for negative declaratory relief. It would be for the creditor to ask for an adaptation in order to make the measure fitting. The debtor is solely on the destructive path and is interested that recognition of the judgment fails without adaptation.

3. Negative declaratory relief for the debtor and application by the creditor

150 (4) vests the debtor with an opportunity to strike preemptively. It permits the debtor to file an application for negative declaratory relief *ex ante*, i.e. before the creditor applies for recognition or enforcement or commences a lawsuit in which recognition would take place.

151 Once the creditor has launched his strike for recognition or enforcement the debtor should not be allowed to use the procedures envisaged by (4) as a counterstrike.[520] The question as to whether the creditor is entitled to recognition or enforcement of his judgment will be answered in the proceedings initiated by the creditor, either in the affirmative when he obtains his aim, or in the negative when he is denied his aim and such denial is based on one of the grounds listed in (1). If an eventual denial is based on another ground not listed in (1) (for instance not complying with the formal requirements of Art. 37 or Art. 42 respectively) the question as to whether material grounds for refusal of recognition as listed in (1) exist in the concrete case is not answered, and thus the debtor might apply for obtaining an answer.

---

[517] *Geimer*, in: FS Hellwig Torggler (2013), p. 311, 322–323.
[518] On these Art. 36 notes 18–25 (*Wautelet*).
[519] *Geimer*, in: FS Hellwig Torggler (2013), p. 311, 322.
[520] See *Geimer*, in: FS Hellwig Torggler (2013), p. 311, 323.

If the creditor has already initiated proceedings, in principle the debtor's application for   **152** negatory declaratory relief should be suspended for want of an interest justifying such relief pursuant to the procedural rules of the *lex fori* for declaratory relief. Matters can be different when the debtor's application would be decided upon in due course whilst the creditor's application would presumably take a longer time to be decided.

If the debtor files an application under (4) and the creditor files a competing application   **153** under Art. 36 (2) the principle of priority as established by Art. 29 for solving cases of *lis alibi pendens* should apply *per analogiam*.[521] The two applications have the same cause and action, and the reversion of party roles does not have an effect to the contrary.[522]

4. Locus standi

The person entitled to apply under (4) is not necessarily the original judgment debtor. Any   **154** successor to the original judgment debtor (who has succeeded in accordance with the law applicable to such succession) is entitled.

Subsection 2: **Refusal of enforcement**

Article 46

On the application of the person against whom enforcement is sought, the enforcement of a judgment shall be refused where one of the grounds referred to in Article 45 is found to exist.

I. General

While the requirement that foreign judgments be declared enforceable by an authority of the   **1** Member State of enforcement was abolished,[1] the Regulation has not suppressed the right of judgment debtors to apply for the assessment of whether a ground referred to in Art. 45 exists. A new procedure is established by the Regulation. It is not mandatory, but conditional upon an application of the person against who enforcement is sought. It is not a pre-requirement for enforcement in the relevant Member State, but a procedure which, in principle, does not even suspend the enforceability of the foreign judgment in the relevant Member State.[2]

The European Commission advocated the abolition of the *exequatur* procedure on the   **2** ground that it was virtually always successful, which suggested that it entailed unnecessary costs and delays for judgment creditors.[3] Independent studies had indeed confirmed that it

---

[521]   *Geimer*, in: FS Hellwig Torggler (2013), p. 311, 323.
[522]   *Geimer*, in: FS Hellwig Torggler (2013), p. 311, 322–323.
[1]   See Art. 39.
[2]   See Art. 44.
[3]   European Commission, Impact Assessment – Accompanying document to the Proposal for a Regulation

rarely resulted in any denial of enforcement.[4] Additionally, it also seemed that declarations of enforceability were rarely appealed against.[5] This suggested that judgment debtors rarely believed that a ground referred to in then Art. 34 and 35 of the Brussels I Regulation (now Art. 45) existed. The hope is thus that judgment debtors will equally no avail themselves of the remedy afforded by Art. 46 to argue that a ground referred to in Art. 45 exists, and that the costs and delays associated with the former procedure will disappear. Even if a judgment debtor does decide to apply for refusal enforcement, his application will not automatically suspend the enforceability of the foreign judgment[6] and might thus not delay enforcement. This might alone significantly reduce the rate of challenges of the enforceability of foreign judgments under Art. 46.

II. Persons eligible to apply for refusal of enforcement

3 Art. 46 affords the right to apply for a refusal of enforcement of the foreign judgment on the grounds referred to in Art. 45 to the person against whom enforcement is sought. Such person is obviously the most interested one to apply for the remedy. Others, however, could be interested as well, such as judgment debtors against whom no enforcement was sought in the relevant Member State at the time of the application. Art. 46 does not grant them the right to apply for a refusal of enforcement.[7] While one could legitimately argue that other interested persons should be granted the right to apply preventively,[8] such persons are entitled to apply for a refusal of recognition under Art. 45, and it is submitted that such refusal would bind a court in the same Member State entertaining an application under Art. 46.

4 A court may not refuse enforcement of a foreign judgment on its own motion.[9]

Article 47

1. The application for refusal of enforcement shall be submitted to the court which the Member State concerned has communicated to the Commission pursuant to point (a) of Article 75 as the court to which the application is to be submitted.
2. The procedure for refusal of enforcement shall, in so far as it is not covered by this Regulation, be governed by the law of the Member State addressed.

---

of the European Parliament and of the Council on jurisdiction and the recognition and enforcement of judgments in civil and commercial matters, Commission Staff Working Paper, 14 December 2010, SEC (2010) 1547 final ("2010 Commission Impact Assessment"), p. 12: applications are successful in 93 % of cases.

[4] Heidelberg Report, para. 52; Center of Strategy and Evaluation Services, Data Collection and Impact Analysis – Certain Aspects of Possible Revision of Council Regulation No. 44/2011 on Jurisdiction and Enforcement of Judgments in Civil and Commercial Matters, 2010, 37; *Muller/Cuniberti*, Clunet (2013) 83.

[5] Heidelberg Report, para. 52; *Muller/Cuniberti*, Clunet (2013) 83.

[6] See Art. 44, 2 (*Cuniberti/Rueda*).

[7] Past judgments of the European Court of Justice on Art. 36 of the Brussels Convention leave little hope that the Court would interpret broadly this provision: *infra*, Art. 49, 4.

[8] See *Schramm*, Yb. PIL 15 (2013/2014), p. 168; *Cadet*, EuZW (2013), p. 222.

[9] *Gascon-Inchausti*, in: Guinchard, Le nouveau Règlement Bruxelles *Ibis* (2014) 242.

3. The applicant shall provide the court with a copy of the judgment and, where necessary, a translation or transliteration of it.

   The court may dispense with the production of the documents referred to in the first sub-paragraph if it already possesses them or if it considers it unreasonable to require the applicant to provide them. In the latter case, the court may require the other party to provide those documents.

4. The party seeking the refusal of enforcement of a judgment given in another Member State shall not be required to have a postal address in the Member State addressed. Nor shall that party be required to have an authorised representative in the Member State addressed unless such a representative is mandatory irrespective of the nationality or the domicile of the parties.

I. Competent court

All Member States were supposed to communicate the Commission by 10 January 2014 he   **1**
courts to which the application for refusal of enforcement is to be submitted pursuant to
Article 47(1).

Recital 30 of the Preamble encourages Member States to enable applicants "to invoke, in the   **2**
same procedure, in addition to the grounds for refusal provided for in this Regulation, the
grounds for refusal available under national law and within the time-limits laid down in that
law." In Member States where different courts had jurisdiction to declare enforceable foreign
judgments and to control the legality of enforcement measures, this might result in a transfer
of the jurisdiction to entertain applications for refusal of enforcement to courts having
jurisdiction to control the legality of enforcement measures.

II. Procedure

Art. 47(2) logically provides that the procedure for refusal of enforcement shall be governed   **3**
by national law in so far as it is not covered by the Regulation. Procedure is traditionally
governed by the law of the forum *(lex fori)*. Unsurprisingly, Art. 47(2) provides that the
applicable national law is the "law of the Member State addressed", i.e. the law of the court to
which the application is submitted.

The regulation governs the grounds for refusal of enforcement (Art. 45), the effect of the   **4**
application on the enforceability of the foreign judgment (Art. 44), the documents which are to
be provided to the court (Art. 47(3)), the right not to have a postal address or an authorized
representative in the State of enforcement (Art. 47(4)), the length of the procedure (Art. 48),
part of the regime to lodge an appeal against the decision on the application (Art. 49–51). All
other issues are governed by the law of the forum. This includes, inter alia, the form of the
application and the time period within which an application may be made.

The Brussels I Regulation provided uniform rules on a number of issues which are now left   **5**
to local civil procedure, such as the time period (including its starting point) within which a
declaration of enforceability could be challenged.[1] The application of national law on these
issues will decrease the uniformity of application of the new regulation.

---

[1]   Brussels I Regulation, Art. 43(5).

III. Documents accompanying the application

6 Contrary to the judgment creditor, who must provide a copy of the judgment which satisfies the conditions necessary to establish its authenticity to the enforcement authority,[2] Art. 47 (3) provides that the applicant for a refusal of enforcement can produce a mere "copy of the judgment". Furthermore, the court may dispense the applicant from producing even a copy of the judgment if it already has one or if it would be unreasonable to require him to provide it. While such leniency can be understood with regard translation, it is much harder to understand with respect to the judgment itself, which is to be the subject-matter of the procedure.

7 Art. 47(3) provides that a translation or a transliteration of the judgment should only be provided where necessary. The purpose of the rule is not to protect the parties,[3] but rather to allow the court to request a translation if it is needed for entertaining the application. If such needs exist, the burden of providing the translation should, and does, lie on the applicant. However, Art. 47(3) enables the court to take into account special circumstances making it unreasonable to put this burden on the applicant to shift it on the other party. A clear imbalance in resources between the parties could constitute such special circumstances.

8 The court may also request a partial translation if it deems it sufficient.[4] Any translation, however, should be made by a person qualified to do so in one of the Member States.[5]

IV. Postal address and authorized representative

9 Art. 47(4) abolishes the requirement of either providing a postal address or appointing a local authorized representative in the Member State of enforcement.[6] Art. 47(4) also prevails on any contrary national rules which might require that foreign litigants give a local postal address or hire a local representative.[7]

Article 48

The court shall decide on the application for refusal of enforcement without delay.

1 Art. 48 encourages courts entertaining applications for refusal of enforcement to decide without delay. Its origin is to be found in Art. 45(1) of the Brussels Regulation,[1] which provided that the court petitioned to rule on an appeal against a declaration of enforceability was similarly to "give its decision without delay". An important difference between the former and the new regimes, however, is that the procedure used to delay enforcement of

---

[2]   See Art. 43.

[3]   Such purpose is served by Art. 43.

[4]   This has long been the practice of the Paris first instance court: see *Gaudemet-Tallon*, para. 443.

[5]   See Art. 57(3).

[6]   *Supra*, Art. 41 note 10 (*Cuniberti/Rueda*).

[7]   *Supra*, Art. 41 note 11 (*Cuniberti/Rueda*).

[1]   And before in Art. 34 of the Brussels Convention.

the foreign judgment, while it should not under the new regime.[2] Art. 48 might have lost most of its significance, if it ever had any.

The time to entertain appeals against declarations of enforceability varied significantly **2** between the different Member States under the former regime. It is hard to see why this would change under Art. 48. Time to deliver judgment is conditional upon a variety of factors, the most important of which being the resources of the relevant courts. It is unlikely that States will dedicate more resources to their judiciary as a consequence of the existence of Art. 48.[3]

Article 49

1. **The decision on the application for refusal of enforcement may be appealed against by either party.**
2. **The appeal is to be lodged with the court which the Member State concerned has communicated to the Commission pursuant to point (b) of Article 75 as the court with which such an appeal is to be lodged.**

I. General

The purpose of Art. 49 is to organise the appeal against decisions on applications for refusal **1** of enforcement. To this end, it establishes (1) the beneficiaries of the right to lodge such an appeal and (2) the court or organ having jurisdiction to hear the appeal.

Art. 49 draws its inspiration from Art. 43 of the Brussels I Regulation and Art. 36 and 37(1) **2** of the Brussels Convention.

II. Commentary

1. Standing

Art. 49(1) provides that either party has standing to lodge an appeal against a decision on an **3** application for refusal of enforcement. The regulation treats both parties equally in this regard and does not introduce any specific requirement depending on whether the appeal is lodged by the party who sought enforcement or the party against whom enforcement was sought.

Under the Brussels Convention, the European Court of Justice held that interested third **4** parties (for instance creditors of the person against who enforcement is sought)[1] had no standing to challenge an enforcement order on the basis of the domestic law of the enforce-

---

[2] *Deutsche Genossenschaftsbank v. SA Brasserie du Pêcheur*, (Case 148/84) (1985) ECR 1981, para. 17;
[3] Indeed, the rule, and the incentive it might give to Member States to allocate more resources to the relevant courts, has existed for more than 50 years.
[1] See *Draka NK Cables Ltd. et al. v. Omnipol Ltd.*, (Case C-167/08) (2009) ECR I-3477, I-3488.

ment State.[2] The rationale behind this position was that the Convention established "an enforcement procedure which [constituted] an autonomous and complete system, including the matter of appeals".[3] The coherence of the system excluded "procedures whereby interested third parties [might have challenged] an enforcement order under domestic law".[4] However, the Court also highlighted that "the Convention merely regulates the procedure for obtaining an order for the enforcement of foreign enforceable instruments and does not deal with execution itself".[5] Since execution is governed by the law of the enforcement State, interested third parties could still rely on the domestic law of that State to challenge execution measures.

5   While the Brussels *Ibis* Regulation has abolished the "enforcement procedure" which applied under the Convention, it offers a number of provisions governing the appeal of first instance decisions ruling on the enforceability of the foreign judgment. Among them, Art. 49 only mentions the parties in the first instance procedure as persons having standing to appeal. As a consequence, Art. 49 must be regarded as being as "complete" as Art. 36 of the Brussels Convention was on the issue of standing.[6] However, Art. 49 could barely be considered as a complete set of rules regulating appeal. It seems therefore clear that the national law of the forum will apply to supplement the autonomous regime of the Regulation.[7]

6   It is unclear whether the distinction offered by the European Court of Justice between procedure, including matters of appeal, and execution[8] remains, as the verification of the existence of grounds referred to in Art. 45 has now been postponed to the enforcement stage. It is submitted that Art. 49 will govern appeals made on the ground of a wrongful application of Art. 45 and exclude any contrary rule of national law, including rules belonging to the national law of enforcement of the relevant state. By contrast, appeals made on the ground of wrongful application of national grounds of refusal of enforcement[9] will be entirely governed by the national rules of the forum.

2. Competent court

7   The Member States were to communicate the Commission by 10 January 2014 the courts with which an appeal against the decision on the application for refusal of enforcement is to be lodged pursuant to Article 49(2).[10]

---

[2]   *Deutsche Genossenschaftsbank v. SA Brasserie du Pêcheur*, (Case 148/84) (1985) ECR 1981, para. 17; *Volker Sonntag v. Hans Waidmann*, (Case C-172/91) (1993) ECR I-1963, I-2000 para. 33; *Draka NK Cables Ltd. et al. v. Omnipol Ltd.*, (Case C-167/08) (2009) ECR I-3477, I-3488, paras. 27–30.

[3]   *Deutsche Genossenschaftsbank v. SA Brasserie du Pêcheur*, (Case 148/84) (1985) ECR 1981, para. 17.

[4]   *Deutsche Genossenschaftsbank v. SA Brasserie du Pêcheur*, (Case 148/84) (1985) ECR 1981, para. 17.

[5]   *Deutsche Genossenschaftsbank v. SA Brasserie du Pêcheur*, (Case 148/84) (1985) ECR 1981, para. 18; also, *Draka NK Cables Ltd. et al. v. Omnipol Ltd.*, (Case C-167/08) (2009) ECR I-3477, I-3488, paras. 29.

[6]   The European Court of Justice had already accepted that its interpretation under the Brussels Convention applied under the Brussels I Regulation: see *Draka NK Cables Ltd. et al. v. Omnipol Ltd.*, (Case C-167/08) (2009) ECR I-3477, I-3488, paras. 21–24.

[7]   Art. 43(3) of the Brussels I Regulation suggested so.

[8]   *Supra*, Art. 49 note 4 (*Cuniberti/Rueda*).

[9]   *Supra*, Art. 41 note 6 (*Cuniberti/Rueda*).

[10] As of 15 September 2014, the Commission had received notifications from almost all Member States. The

3. Timing

Contrary to Art. 43 of the Brussels I Regulation, Art. 49 does not provide any guidance with **8** respect to the time limit within which an appeal may be lodged against a decision. The issue is now left to national law, which will decrease the uniformity of application of the new regulation.[11]

Article 50

The decision given on the appeal may only be contested by an appeal where the courts with which any further appeal is to be lodged have been communicated by the Member State concerned to the Commission pursuant to point (c) of Article 75.

I. General

Art. 50 provides for a second and final level of appeal against the decision of appeal issued on **1** the basis of Art. 49.Pursuant to Art. 75 (c), the Member States were expected to notify the Commission of the competent court by 10 January 2014.

Art. 50 draws its inspiration from Arts 44 of the Brussels I Regulation and 37(2) of the **2** Brussels Convention.

II. Characteristics of the final appeal

1. Mere option for the Member States

The wording of Art. 50 implies that the establishment of a second and final level of appeal is **3** not compulsory but optional for the Member States.[1] Member States failing to notify the Commission of the competent courts under Art. 75(c) will be assumed to have decided not to make the final appeal available to litigants on their territory.

2. Appeal against a judgment on a first appeal

Art. 50 makes it clear that the final appeal is available only against a decision given on an **4** Art. 49 appeal. Under Art. 37(2) of the Brussels Convention, the European Court of Justice had refused to extend the appeal afforded under this provision "so as to enable an appeal in

---

publication of the notifications of all the Member States was expected by the end of 2014, before entry into force of the regulation.

[11] *Nuyts*, 102 RCDIP (2013), 33.

[1] *Schramm*, Yb. PIL 15 (2013/2014), p. 168; *Beraudo* J.Cl. Intern., fasc. 633, no. 197.

cassation to be lodged against a judgment other than that given on the appeal, for instance against a preliminary or interlocutory order requiring preliminary inquiries to be made".[2] The scope of Art. 50 is limited to appeals against decisions made under Art. 49.

3. No limitation to points of law

5 Unlike Art. 37(2) of the Brussels Convention and Annex IV of the Brussels I Regulation, Art. 50 of the Brussels *Ibis* Regulation does not provide for any limit of the final appeal to points of law. The scope of the appeal will therefore be determined by national law. It is to be expected, however, that the vast majority of Member States will designate a court which only hears appeals on points of law. The determining factor in this respect will be the powers of the court notified to the Commission under Art. 75(c) under the civil procedure of the relevant Member State.

4. Standing of interested third parties

6 The status of interested third parties under Art. 50 will logically be the same as under Art. 49.[3] The rationale underlying the limitation of standing to parties to the first instance procedure was expressly extended to the final appeal procedure by the European Court of Justice under the Brussels Convention.[4]

Article 51

1. The court to which an application for refusal of enforcement is submitted or the court which hears an appeal lodged under Article 49 or Article 50 may stay the proceedings if an ordinary appeal has been lodged against the judgment in the Member State of origin or if the time for such an appeal has not yet expired. In the latter case, the court may specify the time within which such an appeal is to be lodged.
2. Where the judgment was given in Ireland, Cyprus or the United Kingdom, any form of appeal available in the Member State of origin shall be treated as an ordinary appeal for the purposes of paragraph 1.

I. General

1 Art. 51 aims at protecting the debtor of a foreign judgment against any damage that would result from its enforcement in the Member State addressed if the foreign judgment is eventually set aside in its Member State of origin. To prevent such a risk, Art. 51 allows the courts dealing either with an application for refusal of enforcement or with an appeal under Arts. 49 or 50, to stay the proceedings until it is clear whether the foreign judgment becomes *res judicata*.[1]

---

[2]   *Calzaturificio Brennero s. a. s. v. Wendel GmbH Schuhproduktion International*, (Case 258/83) (1984) ECR 3971, para. 15; on Art. 44 of the Brussels I Regulation, see *Kerameus*, in: Magnus/Mankowski, Brussels I Regulation, 2011, Art. 44, 5.

[3]   *Supra*, Art. 49 notes 3–6 (*Cuniberti/Rueda*).

[4]   *Volker Sonntag v. Hans Waidmann*, (Case 172/91) (1993) ECR I-1963, I-1999 para. 35.

Art. 51 draws its inspiration from Art. 46 of the Brussels I Regulation. It is worth noticing **2**
that paragraph 3 of Art. 46 has been deleted as redundant. As a second protective measure
for the judgment debtor, this paragraph allowed the courts to make enforcement conditional
on the provision of a security. This measure is now provided for on a broader basis in Art. 44
(1).

II. Power to stay enforcement proceedings

1. Conditions for granting a stay

While the language of Art. 51 might have suggested that the courts of the Member State **3**
addressed have the power to grant a stay irrespective of any application of the judgment
debtor, it seems reasonable to assume that the stay must be applied for by the party against
who enforcement is sought, and that the court may not grant it on its own motion.[2]

The wording of Art. 51clearly indicates that the courts of the Member State addressed may **4**
stay proceedings whenever the foreign judgment to be enforced has been challenged in its
Member State of origin, but are under no obligation to do so.

Art. 51 does not give guidance as to how this discretion should be exercised. However, in the **5**
context of the Brussels Convention, the European Court of Justice ruled that the power to
grant a stay should be strictly interpreted,[3] and accordingly dramatically limited the range of
arguments that may be taken into account. First, it excluded the arguments previously
submitted to the court of the Member State of origin which issued the foreign judgment
on the ground that it would amount to reviewing it as to its substance. Second, it ruled that
the same problem would arise with an assessment of "the chances of success of an ordinary
appeal lodged or to be lodged in the State in which the judgment was given".[4] Furthermore,
the Court ruled that arguments "unknown to the foreign court at the time of its judgment
because the appellant had failed to put them before it" should not be taken into account
either,[5] as the party should be precluded from relying on them at a later stage.[6] As a result,
only arguments related to facts posterior to the foreign judgment, which the judgment
debtor could therefore not have previously submitted to the court of the Member State of
origin, could be made.[7]

---

[1]   *B. J. van Dalfsen and others v. B. van Loon and T. Berendsen*, (Case C-183/90) (1991) ECR I-4743 para. 29
      on the Brussels Convention.
[2]   See *Gaudemet-Tallon* para. 458.
[3]   See *B. J. van Dalfsen and others v. B. van Loon and T. Berendsen*, (Case C-183/90) (1991) ECR I-4743
      para. 30.
[4]   See *van Dalfsen* para. 32.
[5]   See *van Dalfsen* para. 34.
[6]   See *Horst Ludwig Martin Hoffmann v. Adelheid Krieg*, (Case 145/86) (1988) ECR 645, where the Court
      decided that a party who fails to appeal against an enforcement order, will not be allowed, at the stage of
      the enforcement, to rely on arguments he could have pleaded on appeal.
[7]   See, e.g., in France: CA Paris D. 1994 IR 66; CA Paris RCDIP 91 (2002), 362 with note *Pataut*; Germany:
      BGH IPRax 1995, 243 with notes by *Grunsky*; *Pålsson*, in: Magnus/Mankowski, Brussels I Regulation,
      2011, Art. 46, 11.

6 The position of the European Court of Justice is unreasonably restrictive.[8] Relying on the prohibition to review foreign judgments as to their substance is unconvincing in this context. The purpose of the court exercising its discretion under Art. 51 is not to determine whether the foreign court was right when it delivered its judgment, or whether the foreign appeal court would be right to allow the appeal. It is merely to assess the chances of the foreign judgment losing *res judicata* for the purpose of granting interim protection to the judgment debtor by staying enforcement. By making such assessment, an Art. 51 court is not judgmental on what the foreign court has ruled, or will rule; it merely attempts to predict what it will rule.[9] Accordingly, all arguments which would be admissible before the foreign court should be taken into account by an Art. 51 court.[10]

7 As the goal of an Art. 51 Court should be to assess the chances that a foreign court would annul or amend the foreign judgment, the grounds for refusal of recognition listed in Art. 45 are irrelevant, and may thus not be taken into account.[11]

8 The court's discretion extends to the duration of the stay. However, in practice, the stay should logically end with the release of the judgment of appeal issued in the Member State of origin or – if the foreign judgment had not been challenged yet – after the end of the time limit for the appeal to be lodged in that State.[12]

9 Courts of the Member States tend to generally comply with the restrictive policy adopted by the European Court of Justice regarding stays of proceedings. There is anecdotal evidence, however, that they often order the judgment creditor to provide a security rather than staying the proceedings before them.[13]

2. "Ordinary appeal"

10 While the concept of "ordinary appeal" is not defined by the Regulation, it was already used in the Brussels Convention and has been given an autonomous definition by the European Court of Justice which, it is submitted, is still valid. According to the Court, the rationale of the provision is "to enable [the court of the State of enforcement] to stay the proceedings whenever reasonable doubt arises with regard to the fate of the decision in the State in which it was given".[14] The Court thus requires that the appeal (1) "may lead to the annulment or amendment" of the foreign judgment,[15] (2) "forms part of a normal course of an action [and as such] constitutes a procedural development which any party must reasonably expect"[16]

---

8   See *Gaudemet-Tallon* para. 458.

9   Rauscher/*Mankowski*, Art. 46, 13.

10 See *Gaudemet-Tallon* para. 458; *Kropholler/von Hein* Art. 46 note 5.

11 See A-G *Léger*, opinion in Case C-432/93 (1995) ECR I-2269, I-2283 paras. 43–51; *Pålsson*, in: Magnus/Mankowski, Brussels I Regulation, 2011, Art. 46, 12.

12 *Layton/Mercer* para. 27.062; *Pålsson*, in: Magnus/Mankowski, Brussels I Regulation, 2011, Art. 46, 14.

13 For some examples, in Belgium: Rb. Antwerpen in: Digest I-38 B 4; in Denmark: ØLD UfR 1989 A 877; in Germany: BGH IPRax 1985, 156 note *Prütting* (at p. 137); BGH IPRspr. 1986 Nr. 189 (affirming OLG Hamm IPRspr. 1985 Nr. 187); OLG Köln in: Digest I-38 B 2; OLG Düsseldorf IPRspr. 1984 Nr. 190; OLG Hamm IPRspr. 1993 Nr. 182; OLG Stuttgart IPRspr. 1997 Nr. 182.

14 *Industrial Diamond Supplies v. Luigi Riva*, (Case 43/77) (1977) ECR 2175 para. 33.

15 *Industrial Diamond Supplies* para. 34.

and (3) is "bound by the law to a specific period of time which starts to run by virtue of the actual decision whose enforcement is sought".[17]

As a consequence, "appeals which are dependent either upon events which were unforesee- **11** able at the date of the original judgment or upon the action taken by persons who are extraneous to the case, and who are not bound by the period for entering an appeal which starts to run from the date of the original judgment"[18] are not ordinary appeals.

Whether the enforceability of the foreign judgment is affected by the appeal is irrelevant,[19] as **12** is also the question of whether the appeal is of right or subject to some requirement.[20] Likewise, the characterisation of the appeal in its legal order of origin is of no consequence since the definition adopted is autonomous. As a consequence, appeals of cassation, which are traditionally considered as extraordinary in Belgium, France and Luxembourg, will still be considered as ordinary appeals in the sense of Art. 51.[21]

III. Particularity of the status of Ireland, Cyprus and the United Kingdom

The Irish, Cypriot and UK legal systems are characterised by the fact that the distinction **13** made by the regulation between ordinary and extraordinary appeals is not relevant. As a consequence, Art. 51 provides that for judgments issued in Ireland, Cyprus or the United Kingdom, all forms of appeal available are to be considered as ordinary appeals. This extended definition of an ordinary appeal implies an accordingly extended discretion for the competent courts of the Member State addressed to stay proceedings before them. Caution and self-restraint are therefore required from the court in these circumstances.[22]

Section 4: **Common provisions**

Article 52

Under no circumstances may a judgment given in a Member State be reviewed as to its substance in the Member State addressed.

---

[16]   *Industrial Diamond Supplies* para. 37 – depending on the Member State, the starting point of the period may be when the judgment is issued or when it is notified to the parties. *Wautelet*, in: Magnus/Mankowski, Brussels I Regulation, 2011, Art. 37, 11.

[17]   *Industrial Diamond Supplies* para. 38.

[18]   *Industrial Diamond Supplies* para. 39. The French "recours en révision" and the German "*Wiederaufnahmeklage*" may be cited as illustrations: *Kropholler/von Hein* Art. 37 note 3.

[19]   *Kropholler/von Hein* Art. 37 note 3.

[20]   *Wautelet*, in: Magnus/Mankowski, Brussels I Regulation, 2011, Art. 37, 12.

[21]   *Kropholler/von Hein* Art. 37 note 3; *Pålsson*, in: Magnus/Mankowski, Brussels I Regulation, 2011, Art. 46, 9.

[22]   See *Schlosser* para. 204.

I. General purpose

1 Art. 52, the successor to Arts. 36; 45 (2) Brussels I Regulation, strictly prohibits and rules out any kind of *révision au fond*.[1] This is a pivotal rule for any international instrument on recognition and enforcement[2] or else such instrument would lose much of its point. The court must not review whether the court, having rendered judgment, decided the case correctly. Recognition is by no means even the remotest kind of appeal, and the court concerned with recognition is not superior to the court of origin. It would be expensive exercise to position the former court in the latter court's shoes. These shoes would not fit anyhow. The institution of recognition as such demands that review must be restricted and limited if recognition was to make any sense at low cost level. This institution would be rendered meaningless if the court addressed for recognition was entitled to reviewing the judgment as to substance which amounted to deciding the case *de novo*.[3] Any *révision au fond* would be incompatible with the *rationes* underlying recognition, namely procedural economy and international decisional harmony.[4]

2 The court of a State in which recognition of a foreign judgment is sought must not examine the validity of that judgment; it may not substitute its own discretion for that of the foreign court nor refuse recognition if it considers that a point of fact or of law has been wrongly decided.[5] This makes recognition as expeditious as possible and simultaneously enhances legal security.[6]

3 Mutual trust and confidence in the principal validity of decisions rendered by courts in other Member States have supplanted control and serve as a kind of cost-reducing mechanism.[7] Art. 52 is a fundamental expression of this principle of mutual trust.[8] The judiciary in the Member States is deemed equivalent and equally apt to decide cases which assertion in turn vastly disposes of a necessity for review and control. Whereas control freaks and Leninists[9] might go berserk, European ideology demands so.

---

[1] See only OLG Saarbrücken NJW 1988, 3100; OLG Saarbrücken IPRax 1990, 232; OLG Saarbrücken IPRspr. 2001 Nr 181 p. 381; Hof 's-Gravenhage NIPR 2002 Nr 124 p. 252; Rb. Rotterdam NIPR 2002 Nr 129 p. 242; Aud. Prov. Navarra AEDIPr 2004, 758, 759; *Tschauner*, in: BBGS, Art. 36 EuGVVO note 1 (2005).

[2] Report *Jenard* p. 46.

[3] *Geimer/Schütze*, Art. 36 EuGVO note 1; *Regen*, Prozessbetrug als Anerkennungshindernis (2008) para. 180.

[4] *Regen* (fn. 3), para. 180.

[5] Report *Jenard* p. 46.

[6] *Tschauner*, in: BBGS, Art. 36 EuGVVO note 1 (2005).

[7] *Bartlett*, (1975) 24 ICLQ 44, 55; *Borchers*, 40 Am. J. Comp. L. 121, 130 (1992); *Mankowski*, in: Claus Ott/ Hans-Bernd Schäfer (eds.), Vereinheitlichung und Diversität des Zivilrechts in transnationalen Wirtschaftsräumen (2002), p. 118, 138.

[8] *Gothaer Allgemeine Versicherung AG v. Samskip GmbH* (Case C-456/11), ECLI:EU:C:2012:719 para. 37; comments by *Ivo Bach*, EWS 2013, 56; *Kremmel*, Eur. L. Rpter 2013, 199; *Strikwerda*, NJ 2013 Nr 119; *Hartenstein*, RdTW 2013, 267; *Albert Henke*, Dir. comm. int. 27 (2013), 1085; *Herbert Roth*, IPRax 2014, 136.

[9] Remember the famous *dictum* attributed to *Lenin*: "Trust is good, but control is better."

The need for an express rule to avail this arose because of the national procedural rules of **4** some of the original Member States, in particular France, who provided for a *révision au fond*, whilst this institution was unknown in, and did not find favour with, the laws of the other Member States.[10] Irony had it that France judicially abolished the *révision au fond* as early as 1964,[11] well before the Brussels Convention was completed and ever since.

II. Legislative history

Starting with the very beginning, the present rule was formed as Art. 29 of the Brussels **5** Convention and has remained unchanged since 1968. The wording has been retained to the letter. None of the Accession Conventions altered it, nor did the Lugano Convention, nor did the transgression from the Brussels Convention to the Brussels I Regulation or from the Brussels I Regulation to the Brussels I*bis* Regulation. The number of the Article has changed over the times, but not its content. Under the Brussels I Regulation the then Art. 36 was in the close vicinity of, and neighbourhood to, Arts. 34; 35 Brussels I Regulation where it belonged. Art. 36 Brussels I Regulation was applicable only in the theatre of recognition whereas its counterpart in the area of enforcement was Art. 45 (2) Brussels I Regulation.[12] The Brussels I*bis* Regulation rearranged the systematic structure and places the provisions common to recognition and enforcement at the end of Chapter III in an own Section 4 which starts with Art. 52 as some kind of primer.

III. No review as to the procedure, the material result or the applicable law

The court addressed must not question the validity or correctness of the original decision.[13] **6** It must not re-decide the case by stepping into the shoes of the original court. It must not refuse recognition for the simple reason that it would have decided the case differently had it been called upon to decide the case at all.[14] It is not entitled to review the substantive or legal soundness of the conclusions drawn by the original court, neither to refuse recognition if it believes to have discovered a substantive or legal defect.[15] Examples are easily provided: For instance, the court addressed must not hear an objection challenging the quantum of damages[16] or the validity of a guarantee confirmed and enforced by the court of origin,[17] or the existence of a tort[18] or that re-marriage was taken into account for assessing the amount of

---

10   See only *Kropholler/von Hein*, Art. 36 note 1.

11   Cass. JCP 1964 II 13590 with note *Bertrand Ancel* = RCDIP 53 (1964), 454 with note *Batiffol* = Clunet 91 (1964), 302 with note *Goldman*.

12   *Tschauner*, in: BBGS, Art. 36 EuGVVO note 3 (2005).

13   See only Hoge Raad NJ 2014 Nr 37 p. 398; *Layton/Mercer* para. 26.099.

14   *Dieter Krombach v. André Bamberski*, (Case C-7/98) [2000] ECR I-1935, I-1968 para. 52; *Régie nationale des usines Renault SA v. Maxicar SpA and Orazio Formento* (Case C-39/98), [2000] ECR I-2973, I-3021 para. 29; *Meletis Apostolidis v. David Charles Orams and Linda Elizabeth Orams* (Case C-420/07), [2009] ECR I-3571, I-3631 para. 58; A-G *Vlas*, NJ 2014 Nr 37 p. 387, 389.

15   Report *Evrigenis/Kerameus* para. 80; *Tschauner*, in: BBGS, Art. 36 EuGVVO note 4 (2005).

16   CA Paris 21 September 1995 – *SA Société Française BK c. Hatzatz Hae d'Umin*, published in: Kaye, Casebook p. 437.

17   Rb. Haarlem NIPR 2002 Nr 281 p. 468.

18   OLG Zweibrücken NJOZ 2004, 785, 787.

maintenance awarded.[19] Insofar the defendant is precluded with such challenges[20] and might have missed the appropriate point of defending his case in the state of origin.

7 The court addressed is not entitled to scrutinise whether the court of origin applied the correct substantive law, either. It is not to review whether the court of origin reached the proper conclusions as to private international law and as to which law is the *lex causae*,[21] nor is it invited to cross-check whether the court of origin correctly ascertained the *lex causae* found to be applicable.[22] Matters of diverging conflicts rules are completely outside the exhaustive catalogue of grounds of refusal of recognition contained in the Brussels I Regulation. Even Art. 27 (4) Brussels Convention (which however was dead letter law in practice) has been erased.[23]

8 How the court of origin reached its decision is irrelevant. The court addressed must not review the procedure leading to the decision. It must not review which procedural rules the court of origin applied or whether the court of origin mishandled the procedural rules applied. Procedural defects are beyond scrutiny at the stage of recognition.[24]

9 All and any objections going to the substance of the original decision must be dismissed. This also includes objections grounded on findings of substance made on the basis of procedural rules.[25] Such ought to be concluded from the systematic context with Art. 45 (2) where a ground for refusal exceptionally is based on procedural issues. This in turn indicates that procedural issues are also covered by the principle of non-review as expressed in Art. 52 if and insofar as they do not fall under express exceptions like Art. 45 (1) (b). Yet the content or range of such exceptions are a matter of construing the exceptions. Accordingly, dismissing an objection that a judgment was contrary to, and is irreconcilable with, an earlier judgment because the court of origin disrespected the *res iudicata* effect of the earlier judgment[26] might be too summary an action in the light of Art. 45 (1) (c), (d) if the earlier judgment was not a decision rendered by court in the state of origin.[27] If the court of origin reassuringly affirmed that the plaintiff was believed to exist, the judgment debtor might not challenge the judgment in the court addressed with the allegation that the plaintiff company had been dissolved.[28] Furthermore, the court addressed is not called upon to re-interpret the factual setting found by the court of origin.[29]

---

19   CA Liège JMLB 1984, 391.

20   See only OLG Köln IPRspr. 2001 Nr 186 p. 402.

21   See only OLG Saarbrücken IPRspr. 2001 Nr 180 p. 379; *von Bar*, JZ 2000, 725, 726.

22   BGH IPRax 1984, 202, 204.

23   See the *argumentum e contrario* to be drawn from the existence of Art. 27 (4) Brussels Convention e.g. by *Günter H. Roth*, IPRax 1984, 183.

24   *Geimer/Schütze*, Art. 36 EuGVO note 1.

25   See BGH NJW 1992, 627, 628; Aud. Prov. Madrid AEDIPr 2004, 768, 769; *Tschauner*, in: BBGS, Art. 36 EuGVVO note 4 (2005); *Geimer/Schütze*, Art. 36 EuGVO note 1.

26   Rb. Brussels Digest I-29 B-2.

27   See *Layton/Mercer* para. 26.100 fn. 98.

28   BGH NJW 1992, 627, 628.

29   *Tschauner*, in: BBGS, Art. 36 EuGVVO note 4 (2005); *Geimer/Schütze*, Art. 36 EuGVO note 1.

"Wrong" judgments have to be accepted however defective the procedure to them was or   10
how much they might suffer from their defects.[30] Both procedural and substantive defects
are irrelevant as to recognition.[31] "Wrong" foreign decisions have to be accepted like
"wrong" decisions given by courts sitting in the State where recognition is sought, have to
be accepted.[32] *Res iudicata* in the European system is *res iudicata* regardless whether the
decision was rendered by a foreign court or by a domestic court. A simple control test
confirms this result: Any finding that a foreign decision is "wrong" can only be derived after
hypothetically re-assessing the entire case. "Wrong" can only be said as the outcome of a
complete re-evaluation.

Complete or partial compliance by the defendant with the judgment, i.e. ordinarily in the   11
event of a judgment for payment that the judgment debtor has at least partially accomplished payment, is a matter of review not at an isolated early stage of recognition, but ought
to be left to the later stage of execution where all the remedies the law of the state where
execution is sought, are open to the defendant in this regard.[33] This applies even if the
defendant alleges to have paid the substantial part of the judgment debt before the date
when the appellate court in the state of origin had made its decision.[34]

IV. Judgments allegedly obtained by fraud

Judgments allegedly obtained by fraud are the most problematic instances. Strictly applying   12
the principle of non-review to them at first glance appears to conflict with elementary
principles of justice. On the other hand, the mere allegation of fraud should not allow the
defendant to re-open the case effectively, at least in the court addressed. The line of compromise is clear in theory, but rather thin, and ought to be finely tuned in practice:[35] Only
insofar as public policy under Art. 45 (1) (a) is involved and violated recognition might be
refused;[36] beyond that a review is not permitted.[37]

Where the original court in its judgment ruled precisely on the matters in which the de-   13
fendant seeks to review in challenging a judgment on the ground of fraud, the Regulation
precludes the court addressed from reviewing that conclusion of the foreign court.[38] If a
remedy lies in the case of fraud in the state of origin it will normally be appropriate to leave
the defendant to pursue his remedy in that State as the courts there are likely to be better able
to assess whether the original judgment was procured by fraud.[39] Only a by-note might
indicate that the latter might be of little use in the event of a wholesale corrupt judiciary – an
event, of course, one never hopes to encounter in the Member States of the EU.

---

[30] *Geimer*, in: FS Rolf Stürner (2013), p. 1223, 1230.
[31] *Geimer*, in: FS Rolf Stürner (2013), p. 1223, 1230.
[32] *Geimer*, in: FS Rolf Stürner (2013), p. 1223, 1230.
[33] BGH RIW 1983, 615 = WM 1983, 655; BGH RIW 1984, 485 = WM 1984, 750.
[34] BGH RIW 1983, 615 = WM 1983, 655; BGH RIW 1984, 485 = WM 1984, 750.
[35] *In extenso* and most comprehensively researched and argued by *Regen* (fn. 3).
[36] *Layton/Mercer* para. 26.099.
[37] BGHZ 74, 248, 251; OLG Stuttgart 5 November 2013 – 5 W 13/13; *Interdesco SA v. Nullifire Ltd.* [1992] 1
      Lloyd's Rep. 180, 187 (Q.B.D., *Phillips* J.).
[38] *Interdesco SA v. Nullifire Ltd.* [1992] 1 Lloyd's Rep. 180, 187 (Q.B.D., *Phillips* J.).
[39] *Interdesco SA v. Nullifire Ltd.* [1992] 1 Lloyd's Rep. 180, 188 (Q.B.D., *Phillips* J.).

V. Provisional findings of facts for the purpose of provisional measures

14 Provisional findings of facts for the purpose of provisional measures are of a different kind. On their face they bear the hallmarks of inconclusiveness. Accordingly, the court hearing the main action is not bound by them but may review the facts *de novo* and completely afresh as it likes and deems appropriate. This applies even if the findings are directly on point.[40] This is by no means a departure from the principle of non-review since the trial of the main action will normally involve a fresh appraisal and fresh evaluation of the issues and without review of the provisional measure.[41]

Article 53

The court of origin shall, at the request of any interested party, issue the certificate using the form set out in Annex I.

I. Introduction

1 This provision concerns the 'certificate concerning a judgment in civil and commercial matters' required for the recognition and enforcement of a judgment rendered in a Member State in the other Member States. This judgment certificate shall be issued by the court of origin at the request of any interested party. The certificate is a standard form annexed to the Brussels *Ibis* Regulation as Annex I. This mandatory, multi-lingual form provides extensive information and aims to facilitate the recognition and particularly the enforcement by the competent enforcement authority in the Member State addressed. The Brussels I Regulation also referred to the use of a standard form in its Art. 54 (Annex V, which extended to court settlements), but in a less obligatory form, and the Annex had a limited format.

II. Issuing and use of the judgment certificate (Annex I)

2 The certificate concerning a judgment shall be issued by the Member State of origin at the request of any interested party pursuant of Art. 53. As follows from Art. 2(d), the 'Member of origin' is the Member State in which the judgment has been given. In most cases, the certificate will be issued by the court that rendered the judgment, but this is not required. The concept of an 'interested person' is not defined in the Brussels *Ibis* Regulation, but can be widely construed as encompassing the persons directly involved in the litigation leading up to the judgment, and other persons having an interest in the recognition or enforcement of the judgment.

3 The use of the judgment certificate is mandatorily prescribed for the purpose of invoking recognition and seeking enforcement in another Member State. Art. 37 (1) concerning recognition provides that a party who wishes to invoke the judgment shall produce: (a) a copy of the judgment, and (b) the certificate issued pursuant to Art. 53. For the purpose of enforcement, Art. 42 prescribes that the applicant shall provide the competent authority

---

40 *Layton/Mercer* para. 26.100.
41 *Layton/Mercer* para. 26.100.

with: (a) a copy of the judgment, and (b) the certificate issue pursuant to Art. 53, certifying that the judgment is enforceable and containing an extract of the judgment as well as, where appropriate, relevant information on the recoverable costs of the proceedings and the calculation of interest.

The standard form provides data with regard to the court of origin, the parties, and extensive **4** information on the judgment, including whether it was given in default of appearance, its enforceability, the date and language of service, a description of the subject-matter of the case, details of the (monetary) obligations flowing from the judgment, costs and interest. Generally this should provide sufficient information for the purpose of recognizing or enforcing the judgment, though where necessary the court or enforcement authority may also resort to the judgment itself.

For the recognition of judgments, Art. 37 (2) provides further rules on the translation of the **5** certificate. A translation or transliteration may, where necessary, be required from the party invoking recognition. In that case, the certificate needs to be translated or transliterated into the official language (or one of the official languages) or another language that the Member State addressed has indicated to accept, in accordance with Art. 57.

For the purpose of enforcement, Art. 42 (3) prescribes that the competent enforcement **6** authority may, where necessary, require the applicant to provide a translation or transliteration of the content of the certificate in accordance with Art. 57. The certificate needs to be served on the person against whom enforcement is sough prior to the first enforcement measure, pursuant to Art. 43 (1). A translation of the certificate for the purpose of this service seems not to be required, but this is backed up by the fact that the judgment itself needs to be served as well, where necessary accompanied by a translation (Art. 43 (2)).

Article 54

1. If a judgment contains a measure or an order which is not known in the law of the Member State addressed, that measure or order shall, to the extent possible, be adapted to a measure or an order known in the law of that Member State which has equivalent effects attached to it and which pursues similar aims and interests.
Such adaptation shall not result in effects going beyond those provided for in the law of the Member State of origin.
2. Any party may challenge the adaptation of the measure or order before a court.
3. If necessary, the party invoking the judgment or seeking its enforcement may be required to provide a translation or a transliteration of the judgment.

I. Introduction: a new adaptation provision

1   Art. 54 contains a rule requiring the adaption of a measure or order that is not known in the Member State addressed, as far as possible, into a measure having equivalent effects. Apart from the abolition of exequatur, this provision may be may be regarded as the most noteworthy novelty in the enforcement regime of the Brussels I*bis* Regulation. It equally applies to the recognition of judgments, though in practice it might generally be more relevant for the purpose of enforcement.

2   The Brussels I Regulation lacked a similar provision. However, it is in line with the general idea that a judgment given in another Member State should be given effect to the greatest extent possible. In fact, the CJEU already pointed in the direction of the conversion of measures in *DHL Express France* concerning the territorial effect of a measure to protect a right under the Community trade mark Regulation.[1] The specific measure concerned a periodic penalty payment under French law *(astreinte)* in case of violation of the infringement order. The CJEU, referring to the Brussels I Regulation, *inter alia* ruled that where the national law does not contain a coercive measure similar to that ordered by the Community trade mark court, the objective pursued by that measure must be attained by the competent court of the Member State of enforcement by having recourse to the relevant provisions of its national law which are such as to ensure that the prohibition is complied with in an equivalent manner.

3   The current provision more specifically prescribes that if an order or measure is not known in the Member State addressed (usually the Member State of enforcement), that Member State has the duty to transform this order or measure into an equivalent measure that does exist in that Member State (para. 1). That measure shall pursue similar aims or interests as does the one given in the Member State of origin.[2] This rule aims to give the fullest possible effect to unknown types of judgments or specific orders, such as the penalty ordered to enforce the French judgment in the aforementioned *DHL Express France* case,[3] by requiring assimilation into the legal order of the enforcing Member State. In case the adaptation gives rise to disagreements, it may be challenged by either party (para. 2). If necessary, the party invoking the judgment or seeking its enforcement will have to provide a translation or transliteration of the judgment (para. 3).

4   The Commission proposal contained a provision similar to the first paragraph of the current provision, but was restricted to the residual provisions for the two types of judgments that would still require an exequatur under that proposal.[4] This provision was introduced in response to the Heidelberg Report that identified problems in relation to specific types of judgments and provisional and protective measures that are unknown in the Member State of enforcement.[5] Although the declaration of enforceability was eventually abolished for all

---

[1]   *DHL Express France SAS v. Chronopost SA*, (Case C-235/09) [2011] ECR-2801.

[2]   See also Recital (28).

[3]   To enforce a judgment ordering a payment by way of penalty, Art. 55 requires that the amount has been finally determined by the court of origin.

[4]   Art. 66 Commission proposal. In the proposal the exequatur was retained for judgments in defamation cases and in certain mass disputes, see Art. 37 thereof. See more extensively on Art. 66 of the Commission proposal *Dickinson*, in: Lein (ed.), The Brussels I Review Proposal Uncovered (2012), p. 135, 158–159.

judgments covered by this Regulation, the adaptation provision was retained in an amended and extended version, with the aim of enabling the recognition and enforcement of judgments given in other Member States to the fullest extent possible. In several Member States a similar rule was already in place under domestic private international law rules, primarily in the context of the application of foreign law.[6]

II. The adaptation rule

1. Unknown order or measure

Art. 54 applies in all cases where it is clear that a measure or order given in the court of the Member State of origin is unknown in the Member State addressed. The fact that such measure or order is not known may become apparent on the occasion of the recognition of a judgment in subsequent proceedings in that Member State or when enforcement with the enforcement authority is sought in that Member State.   **5**

Art. 54 does not refer to the 'judgment'[7] in its entirety, but only to a 'measure' or an 'order' which is not known in the Member State addressed. The Member State addressed cannot amend the entire judgment as such, but can only adapt a specific measure or order for it to assimilate in the legal order of the Member State. Recital (28) clarifies that the measure or order includes 'any right indicated therein'. The measure or order refers to a specific operative part of the judgment.[8]   **6**

For the adaptation rule to come into operation the measure or order given by the Member State of origin must be unknown in the Member State addressed. This may concern a specific type of order, such as a restraining order, a payment order or search order. Another example that was already mentioned in the context of *DHL Express France*[9] are penalties to be paid to the enforcing party in case for instance an order not to infringe an intellectual property right is violated, as they exist among others under French and Dutch law.   **7**

Also measures relating to rights *in rem (e.g.* usufruct) and certain provisional or protective measures, such as the English freezing injunction, are only known in a limited number of Member States.[10] The recognition or enforcement of such measures not known in the Member State addressed cannot be denied, but should as far as possible be converted in accordance with Art. 54 to assist in their recognition and enforcement.   **8**

---

5 Heidelberg Report paras. 528 and 724.

6 *Fitchen*, in: Dickinson/Lein (eds.), The Brussels I Regulation Recast (2015) para. 13.482, who refers to French and German law. In the Netherlands assimilation *(assimilatie)* is particularly recognised in the context of the applicable law, see *Asser/Vonken*, Internationaal privaatrecht. Algemeen deel IPR (Asser 10-I) (2012) paras. 342–345.

7 See Art. 2 (a) for the definition of 'judgment' for the purpose of the Regulation.

8 *Fitchen*, in: Dickinson/Lein (eds.), The Brussels I Regulation Recast (2015) para. 13.492.

9 See note 1.

10 *Schramm*, Yb. PIL 15 (2013/2014), 143, 148. See also Heidelberg Report paras. 528 and 724.

2. Equivalent effects

9 Where recognition or enforcement is sought of a judgment containing a measure or an order unknown in the Member State addressed that Member State is required to adapt this measure or order to one that is known in that Member State. The known measure or order in the Member State addressed shall have 'equivalent effects attached to it'. It is for the competent authority of the Member State addressed to assess, first, that the measure or order given in the Member State of origin is unknown and, second, to seek for an equivalent measure under its domestic law. Recital (28) clarifies that how the adaptation is to be carried out is to be determined by the Member State addressed.

10 The equivalent measure or order must pursue 'similar aims and interests'. The competent authority thus has to compare the measure or order given with the available ones in the Member State addressed, taking into account that they must have similar aims and interests. For example, when a Dutch enforcement authority is confronted with an English freezing order, which is unknown in the Netherlands, it can proceed as follows. It should assess the aim of the freezing order under English law, which may be described as restraining a party from disposing of and dealing with his assets. The measure that would probably come closest to that under Dutch law would be a leave for an attachment order (under a third person) *(conservatoir (derden) beslag)*.[11] Although the aims are not exactly the same,[12] they may be regarded as having similar aims and interests.[13]

11 It is not required to convert every measure or order that is unknown into one that is known in the Member State addressed. First, if the judgment for instance obliges to the payment of an amount of money, the fact that the specific measure from which the payment arises (a payment order, penalty, etc.) is not known in the Member State addressed, doesn't seems not to be relevant. Only when the judgment entails more specific obligations or effects, adaptation is required. Second, the obligation of conversion is limited by the existing measures and orders in the Member State addressed; Art. 54 (1) states that the adaptation shall take place 'to the extent possible'. If no reasonable equivalent exists in the Member State addressed, recognition and/or enforcement of this (part of the) decision is not possible. In view of the requirements of the free movement of judgments, the prohibition to review the contents of the judgment[14] and the exhaustive grounds of refusal,[15] the denial of the recognition and enforcement of (a part of) a judgment rendered in another Member State should be an *ultimum remedium*.

---

[11] See also *Zilinsky*, NIPR 2014, 4, 10.

[12] *van Rest*, NIPR 2014, 351, 356 points out, among others, that the English (worldwide) freezing order only has effects *in personam* whereas the Dutch *conservatoir (derden)beslag* has an effect similar to rights *in rem*. This author opines, contrary to *Zilinsky*, NIPR 2014, 4, 10 that generally the Dutch *conservatoirbeslag* cannot be regarded as having the same effects, since the Dutch *conservatoirbeslag* is more far-reaching. See further Art. 54 notes 12–13 (*Xandra Kramer*).

[13] I.e. to secure assets, more in particular to restrain a party from disposing of and dealing with assets and, additionally, to obtain information on the assets.

[14] Art. 52.

[15] Arts. 45 and 46.

3. Effects limited by law of Member State of origin

Art. 54 (1), second sentence, provides that the adaptation shall not result in effects 'going **12** beyond those provided for in the law of the Member State of origin'. This addition is intended to assure that the judgment-creditor does not benefit from the absence of the same measure in the Member State where recognition or enforcement is sought, to the detriment of the judgment-debtor. Since this provision only comes into effect when the same measure is non-existent, it is unlikely that an equivalent measure will produce exactly the same effects. In such situation, the competent authority adjusting the measure or order shall ensure that the effects of the equivalent measure or order do not go beyond that of the one given by the court of origin.

In relation to the example given in the previous sub-section, it has been argued in the Dutch **13** literature that the English freezing order and the Dutch *conservatoir (derden)beslag* may not be regarded equivalent since the Dutch measure is more far-reaching.[16] This should then result in the refusal to enforce such a measure. It is submitted that this would be undesirable. In any event the cooperation in the enforcement of a measure that is generally enforceable within the Brussels I*bis* scheme[17] should be the starting point. In order to ensure that the effect of an equivalent measure in the Member State addressed goes substantially beyond that of the one given in the Member State of origin, it should be considered whether adjusting the conditions of the measure to fit the specific aims and interests is possible.[18] Requiring additional security from the judgment-creditor or otherwise limiting the effects of the measure may satisfy the requirement that its effect does not go beyond that provided in the law of the Member State of origin.

4. Competent authority

The question is which authority is competent to make the necessary adaptation when a **14** measure or order is unknown in the Member State addressed. Since the exequatur is abolished in the Brussels I*bis* Regulation, the judge is in principle no longer involved in the enforcement procedure. Recital (28) states that how, and by whom, the adaptation is to be carried out, should be determined by each Member State.[19] Information on who is competent to make adaptation measures is not part of the information package that had to be provided to the Commission pursuant of Art. 75. It is likely that in most Member States the competent enforcement authority within the meaning of Art. 42 – a court (officer), bailiff or other enforcement agency – is given the task to assess whether an equivalent measure exists and to make the necessary adaptation. This may not be an easy task for an enforcement

---

[16] See Art. 54 notes 9–11 (*Xandra Kramer*) and fn. 12.

[17] Taking into account the definition of 'judgment' in Art. 2(a), which does not exclude *ex parte* measures (such as the English freezing injunction), but does exclude measures granted by a court not having jurisdiction as to the substance, as well as the grounds of refusal in Art. 45.

[18] See also *Fitchen*, in: Dickinson/Lein (eds.), The Brussels I Regulation Recast (2015) para. 13.496 who argues that it 'may be that the necessary qualifications can be achieved by tailoring the usual wording of the equivalent measure or order in the Member State addressed'.

[19] A proposal by the German delegation to provide that if the competent authority is not a court and the competent authority is not able itself to carry out the adaptation that it shall of its own motion bring the matter to court, was not adopted. See Council Document 9758/12, 10 May 2012, p. 3.

authority other than a court.[20] In any case, the challenging of an adaptation measure on the basis of Art. 54 (2) must be subjected to a court.[21]

15 In some Member States, such as Germany, where a court has to authorize any judgment (including domestic judgments) before enforcement, this task can where necessary be carried out on the occasion of this authorization.[22] In other Member States the competent enforcement authority will perform this duty, unless a Member State has made other arrangements. In the Netherlands, the bailiff is the competent enforcement authority for the purpose of enforcing judgments under Brussels I*bis*. However, the Dutch Implementation Act provides that the *court* is competent to make the adaptation of measures or orders pursuant to Art. 54.[23] The request for adaptation can (also) be made by the bailiff charged with the enforcement of the judgment.

III. Challenging the adaptation of a measure

16 Pursuant to Art. 54 (2) any party may challenge the adaptation of the measure or order before a court. This balances the freedom that Member States have in regard to how and by whom the required adaptation of an unknown measure or order in the Member State addressed shall take place.[24] A court procedure to appeal a decision taken by either a lower court or any other enforcement authority that has competence in a given Member State will provide the necessary procedural and substantive guarantees to the parties. The challenge procedure as such is subject to the domestic law of the Member State addressed.

17 As the text of Art. 54 (2) specifies, any party can challenge a decision on adaptation. This challenge will take place in the Member State addressed with regard to an adaptation that is made by the competent authority and with which a party disagrees. Any party evidently includes the parties to the dispute underlying the judgment (the judgment-creditor and judgment-debtor). But also other interested parties, including third parties that are affected by the judgment (for instance, a bank) or the enforcement authority charged with the enforcement (not being the authority that made the adaptation) may challenge the adaptation of the measure or order. The outcome of such appeal may be that the adaptation is reversed, amended or approved by the court.

IV. Requirement of translation or transliteration

18 Art. 54 (3) provides that, if necessary, the party invoking the judgment or seeking its enforcement may be required to provide a translation or transliteration. This ties in with Art. 42 (4) which states that the enforcement authority may only require the translation or

---

[20] *Xandra Kramer*, NILR 2014, 343, 356; *Schramm*, Yb. PIL 15 (2013/2014), 143, 148.

[21] See Art. 54 notes 16–17 (*Xandra Kramer*).

[22] *Schramm*, Yb. PIL 15 (2013/2014), 143, 148.

[23] Art. 12 Uitvoeringswet EU-executieverordening en Verdrag van Lugano, act of 22 January 2014, Stb. 2014, 40. The competent court is the court having jurisdiction for enforcement disputes under domestic law. The Explanatory Memorandum does not explicate why the choice was made to give the court competence in this matter.

[24] Recital (28). See also *Fitchen*, in: Dickinson/Lein (eds.), The Brussels I Regulation Recast (2015) para. 13.497.

transliteration of the judgment if it is unable to proceed without such a translation. Generally, the enforcement authority can and should rely on the enforcement certificate within the meaning of Art. 53 (see Annex I) and, if necessary, a translation thereof.[25] Where adaptation is, however, required or where such adaptation is challenged, the enforcement certificate may not contain sufficiently detailed information to assess whether there is an equivalent measure pursuing similar aims and interests. In that case it is the party invoking the recognition or seeking enforcement of the measure or order (not necessarily coinciding with the party seeking an adaptation or challenging such adaptation) that has to provide the translation.

The competent (enforcement) authority or – when it concerns an appeal against adaptation   **19**
– the court of the Member State addressed that may require a translation or transliteration should do so in accordance with Art. 57. Art. 57 (1) provides that when a translation or transliteration is required, this shall be into the official language of the Member State concerned.[26] Where this Member State has more than one official language, the translation should be into (one of) the official language(s) of the place where the judgment is invoked or an application is made, in accordance with the law of that Member State.

Article 55

A judgment given in a Member State which orders a payment by way of a penalty shall be enforceable in the Member State addressed only if the amount of the payment has been finally determined by the court of origin.

I. Introduction

This provision addresses the enforcement of penalties that exist under the domestic law of a   **1**
good number of Member States and may be imposed in case of the violation of a court measure or order. For such penalties to be enforceable in the Member State addressed, the final amount of the payment has to be fixed by the court of origin. Apart from several textual differences reflecting the new enforcement provisions of the Brussels *Ibis* Regulation or clarifying its meaning,[1] Art. 55 is identical to Art. 49 Brussels I Regulation, which by turn copied its forerunner in the Brussels Convention.[2]

---

[25]   Art. 42 (1) (b) and Art. 42 (3).

[26]   Art. 57 (2), which refers to additional languages that Member States have accepted for the purpose of enforcement only applies to the enforcement certificates of Art. 53 and 60, and not to translations of the judgment itself.

[1]   Most notably, unlike its forerunners, the English version of the text no longer refers to'periodic' payments. This inclusion of 'periodic' in the English version has rightly been commented in the Heidelberg Report (fn. 5), no 619 and elsewhere, since penalties does not necessarily take the form of a periodic payment but can also be related to a certain event (*e.g.* the violation of a prohibition order). This seemingly textual mistake in the English version has been corrected in the current provision.

[2]   Art. 43 Brussels Convention. As *Fitchen*, in: Dickinson/Lein (eds.), The Brussels I Regulation Recast (2015) para. 13.502 notes this provision has been relocated from the enforcement provisions in the

2 This provision has not been without problems in practice, as was also noted in the Heidelberg Report.[3] The requirements and modalities of penalty payments differ substantially per Member State and the scope of this provision is not self-evident. As the Heidelberg Report remarked, it seems to presume that the total amount of the penalty is fixed by the court of origin in the initial proceedings, but it may be set only in enforcement proceedings. The Commission proposal introduced a rule stating that the competent court or authority in the Member State of enforcement shall determine the amount of the payment if that amount had not been finally determined by the courts of the Member State of origin.[4] An additional question raised in the Green Paper as to whether penalties collected by the court of fiscal authorities should be included,[5] was again raised during the negotiations, but overtaken by the ECJ ruling in *Realchemie v. BayerCropScience*.[6] The ECJ ruled that penalties by way of a fine payable to the State, but intended to enforce a judgment in a civil or commercial matter, come within the scope of Art. 49 Brussels I Regulation. The same will hold true for the present provision.

II. Comments

1. Payment by way of penalty

3 Several Member States allow the courts to set penalties to be paid to the judgment-creditor if the debtor does not comply with the judgment. These exist particularly in the Benelux countries and in France (in French: *astreinte*, in Dutch: *dwangsom*). The modalities differ slightly between these countries. For example, in the Netherlands such a penalty is not allowed when the main obligation is the payment of an amount of money. It is widely used in relation to judgments to perform or to refrain from certain acts, for instance, the infringement of intellectual property rights. In other countries, such penalties are also allowed in relation to payment orders. On request of the party seeking a measure, the court will set an amount per event or for a certain period of time that the judgment-debtor does not comply with the judgment. These penalties are regarded as highly effective to ensure compliance with the judgment, and for this reason the cross-border enforcement was already foreseen by the Brussels Convention.[7]

4 In most other Member States penalties to enforce compliance with a civil judgment also exist, but these are to be paid to the State (or more specifically, to the court), for instance in Germany *(Zwangsgeld)*. In some Member States, including the United Kingdom, this is framed as 'contempt of court'. The question has always been whether the predecessor of the current provision also includes these type of penalties.[8] In the aforementioned ECJ ruling in *Realchemie v. BayerCropScience* this was answered in the positive.[9] In this case it concerned

---

Brussels I Regulation and the Brussels Convention to the common provisions in the Brussels I*bis* Regulation.

[3]   Heidelberg Report para. 615–617.

[4]   Art. 67 Commission Proposal.

[5]   Green Paper, p. 9 (para. 8.3).

[6]   *Realchemie Nederland BV v. BayerCropScience AG*, (Case C-406/09) [2011] ECR I-9773.

[7]   *Gaudemet-Tallon*, para. 465.

[8]   See only *Kropholler/von Hein*, Art. 49 EuGVO note 1; *Hess*, para. 6.219; Heidelberg Report, para. 615.

[9]   See Section I and note 32.

the enforcement in the Netherlands of a penalty ordered by a German court under German law *(Zwangsgeld)* in relation to an injunction prohibiting the infringement of an intellectual property right. The Dutch Supreme Court had expressed doubts whether this could be regarded as a 'civil and commercial matter' within the Brussels I Regulation since the penalty is not payable to a private party but to the German State and the actual recovery is done by the German judicial authorities. However, the ECJ was clear on the matter. It ruled that the recognition and enforcement of a judgment that contains an order to pay a fine to ensure compliance with a judgment given in a civil and commercial matter is within the scope of the Regulation. The decisive factor is that the fine is imposed to enforce a right that is to be regarded as a civil or commercial matter within the meaning of the Regulation. The nature of the fine itself seems to be wholly irrelevant.

2. Final determination of the amount

Art. 55 requires that the amount of the payment has been finally determined by the court of 5
origin. Only after final determination the payment constitutes an enforceable order under the Regulation. As was the case under Art. 49 Brussels I Regulation, it is not self-evident what is to be understood by the requirement that the payment has been 'finally determined'. For example, in the Netherlands, the court will set an amount for each time the order is violated or for a unit of time of non-compliance, and enforcement of such an order may be sought in another Member State before the total amount of the penalty to be paid to the creditor has been determined. The proposal put forward in the Heidelberg Report and taken over in the Commission proposal that the authorities in the Member State of enforcement can set the final amount if the court of origin had not yet done so, has not been adopted.

The wording of this provision clarifies that the total amount of the penalty to be paid (either 6
to the creditor or the State) has to be fixed by the court of origin.[10] Though the order to which the penalty relates might be enforceable, the imposed penalties are only enforceable when the total amount has been finally determined by the court of origin. A mere setting of a certain amount for each time an order is violated without a consecutive order establishing the total amount based on the number of violations, would not qualify as a final determination. This does not mean, as has also been argued in relation to the Brussels I Regulation, that this determination requires a decision having *res iudicata*.[11] It suffices that it is provisionally enforceable, as is the case for any other judgment.[12]

Article 56

No security, bond or deposit, however described, shall be required of a party who in one Member State applies for the enforcement of a judgment given in another Member State on the ground that he is a foreign national or that he is not domiciled or resident in the Member State addressed.

---

[10]   See already Report *Jenard*, OJ EEC 1979 C 59/1, 54 Art. 43.

[11]   *Fitchen*, in: Dickinson/Lein (eds.), The Brussels I Regulation Recast (2015) para. 13.508. See in relation to the Brussels I Regulation *Kropholler/von Hein*, Art. 49 EuGVO note 1; *Layton/Mercer*, para. 27.094.

[12]   See Art. 39 and also Art. 2 (a) in relation to provisional and protective measures that are equally enforceable under the Brussels *Ibis* Regulation.

1 Art. 56 prohibits Member States from requiring security, bond or deposit for the purpose of enforcement in another Member State on the ground that the applicant is a foreign national or that he is not domiciled or resident in the Member State addressed. The current provision is, with a minor textual amendment to adjust it to the general enforcement scheme of the Brussels I*bis* Regulation,[1] copied from Art. 51 Brussels I Regulation which relied on the corresponding provision in the Brussels Convention.[2] A similar provision also occurs in other EU instruments on the cross-border enforcement of judgments. Under the regime of the Brussels I Regulation and the Brussels Convention, it functioned primarily in the context of obtaining a declaration of enforceability.[3] It was found unnecessary to require security *(cautio iudicatum solvi)* for this purpose. Under the Brussels I*bis* Regulation, it applies to the enforcement procedure with the competent enforcement authority and, as may be assumed, the procedure to invoke the grounds of refusal pursuant of Arts. 46 *et seq.*

2 This provision only applies to Member States requiring security for the purpose of enforcement procedures for a judgment that has been rendered in another Member State in as far as this is based on the foreign nationality or the fact that the applicant is not domiciled or resident in the Member State addressed. This means that Member States may under their domestic law still require security if it is based on other grounds than the foreign nationality, domicile or residence of the party applying for enforcement.[4] Those domestic laws may, in relation to parties having the nationality of one of the other Member States, also not violate the non-discrimination principle laid down in Art. 18 TFEU.[5]

Article 57

1. When a translation or a transliteration is required under this Regulation, such translation or transliteration shall be into the official language of the Member State concerned or, where there are several official languages in that Member State, into the official language or one of the official languages of court proceedings of the place where a judgment given in another Member State is invoked or an application is made, in accordance with the law of that Member State.
2. For the purposes of the forms referred to in Articles 53 and 60, translations or transliterations may also be into any other official language or languages of the institutions of the Union that the Member State concerned has indicated it can accept.
3. Any translation made under this Regulation shall be done by a person qualified to do translations in one of the Member States.

I. Introduction

1 This provision concerns the translation and transliteration of documents, including the

---

[1] As Art. 55, this provision is relocated from the provisions on enforcement to the common provisions in the Brussels I*bis* Regulation.

[2] Art. 45 Brussels Convention.

[3] See also Report *Jenard*, OJ EEC 1979 C 59/54 Comments to Art. 54.

[4] *Layton/Mercer*, para. 27.100.

[5] *Fitchen*, in: Dickinson/Lein (eds.), The Brussels I Regulation Recast (2015) para. 13.515.

judgment for the purpose of enforcement, and of the forms annexed to the Brussels I*bis* Regulation. Art. 57 is a new provision in the Brussels I*bis* Regulation, but in part relies on rules of the Brussels I Regulation. Art. 55 (2) Brussels I Regulation contained a limited rule on translations. It provided that if the court or competent authority so requires, a translation of the documents shall be produced, and that the translation shall be certified by a person qualified to do so in on the Member States. The latter part is, with a minor amendment, copied in Art. 57 (3) of the present Regulation. Several other EU instruments on the cross-border enforcement of judgments include similar rules.

The Commission Proposal introduced the current provision, with a view to problems in **2** practice pointed out in the Heidelberg Report.[1] Part of the Member States usually order a translation of the foreign judgment, and in some Member States lawyers often add a translation to the application for a declaration of enforceability.[2] It was found that according to information obtained from lawyers Member States did not apply Art. 55 (2) Brussels I Regulation correctly, and that most Member States regularly require a translation.[3] The costs of (legal) translations are significant and add substantially to the costs of the cross-border enforcement of judgments.[4] For this reason the Heidelberg Report proposed to make the translation of the judgment exceptional.[5] It was concluded that in most cases the translation of the operative part of the judgment would be sufficient for the purpose of enforcement. Art. 57 should be understood against this background.[6]

II. Translation or transliteration of documents and forms

1. Documents to be translated or transliterated

Art. 57 (1) concerns documents that under this Regulation require a translation or trans- **3** literation.[7] It provides that such translation or transliteration shall be into the official language of the Member State concerned. Where this Member State has more than one official language, the translation should be into (one of) the official language(s) of the place where

---

[1] Art. 69 Commission Proposal. The words 'translation' and 'transliteration' were, however, reversed in this proposal. See on this more in detail *Fitchen*, in: Dickinson/Lein (eds.), The Brussels I Regulation Recast (2015) para. 13.522-15.523.

[2] Heidelberg Report, para. 505. See also *Layton/Mercer*, para. 28.032 (and fn. 83) who refer to the English CPR Pt 74 (1) (b) and 74 (6) that generally impose a requirement of translation of the judgment.

[3] Heidelberg Report, para. 515.

[4] The abolition of the requirement to obtain a declaration of enforceability in the Member State of enforcement (see Art. 39) should substantially reduce the costs of cross-border enforcement. The translation costs will to some extent continue to be incurred. See also Art. 43 for the required translation in relation to the person against whom enforcement is sought and that needs to be served.

[5] Heidelberg Report, para. 515, 526.

[6] The precise proposals put forward in the Heidelberg Report are, however, not fully incorporated.

[7] The meaning of the word 'transliteration' and the apparent distinction between translation and transliteration is not clarified in the context of the Regulation. It is generally understood as the conversion of one writing system to another; however, legal texts are highly conceptual and contextual and would usually require a genuine translation. This may be different for – most parts of – the certificates (Annex I and II) that in more factual terms provide information on the parties, the procedure and the obligations to be enforced.

Xandra Kramer   979

the judgment given in another Member State is invoked or an application is made, in accordance with the law of that Member State.

4 The words 'under this Regulation' in Art. 57 (1) underline that such requirement cannot be imposed by domestic law, but should follow from the Brussels *Ibis* Regulation itself. The purpose is to minimize translations of documents and the costs and delays incurred in relation thereto. The primary document in this regard would be the judgment rendered in another Member State and for which recognition and/or enforcement is sought. Though Art. 57 appears before Arts. 58 and 59 on authentic instruments and court settlements, it extends to the translation of these documents if so required. For authentic instruments this follows from Art. 58 (2), which states that, *inter alia*, the provisions of the current Section 4 of Chapter III shall apply as appropriate. Art. 59 on court settlements by turn refers to the conditions of authentic instruments.

5 Art. 42 (4) lays down rules for the translation of the judgment for the purpose of enforcement. It provides that the competent enforcement authority may require the applicant (usually the judgment-creditor) to provide a translation of the judgment *only if it is unable to proceed without such a translation* (emphasis added). In most cases the rather extensive judgment certificate (see Annex I) would suffice to pursue the enforcement. Art. 42 (2) (a) in any case requires the applicant to provide the enforcement authority with a copy of the judgment; however, this does not need to be translated. It is important to distinguish this provision aimed at the enforcement authority from the translation requirements vis-à-vis the person against whom enforcement is sought. For the latter, Art. 43 (2) provides further rules that should guarantee that the judgment-debtor is able to read and understand the judgment, also with a view to the possibility to challenge the enforcement pursuant to Arts. 46 *et seq.*[8] This means that even where the enforcement authority does not require a translation, for the purpose of serving the judgment to the person against whom enforcement is sought prior to the enforcement, a translation – or a translation into yet another language – may be required.[9]

2. Translation or transliteration of the forms

6 Art. 57 (2) concerns the translation or transliteration of the forms including the certificates for the purpose of enforcing a judgment (Art. 53; Annex I) and the enforcement of authentic instruments and court settlements (Art. 60; Annex II). For the translation or transliteration of the certificates that may be regarded as the 'judicial passport'[10] (along with a copy of the judgment) for the enforcement, generally Art. 57 (1) regarding documents applies. Para 2 adds a rule to this, stating that these forms may also be translated or transliterated into any other official language or languages of the institution of the Union, as far as the Member State concerned has indicated to accept.

---

[8] Generally, the judgment to be served needs to be accompanied by a translation either in a language that addressee understands, or in the official language of the Member State of place within a Member State where he is domiciled.

[9] *Xandra Kramer*, NILR 2013, 344, 358.

[10] Term used in the Heidelberg Report, para. 636.

This paragraph thus enables Member States to accept other languages than its own official 7
language(s) for the purpose of the forms. This may mean that no translation or transliteration is required, since the Member State addressed accepts the language of the form drawn up by the court of origin, or that a translation in another language (for instance: English), that may be easier and less costly to obtain, suffices.[11] The aim evidently is to reduce the need for and costs of translations.

Information as to the additional languages that Member States may accept for the transla- 8
tion or transliteration of these forms had to be communicated to the Commission pursuant to Art. 75(d). This information is available on the e-Justice portal. Reviewing this information on the website showed that only a minority of ten (or, on a closer look, nine[12]) Member States accept additional languages.[13] Five Member States accept English as an alternative language.[14] The other alternative languages in some of these and other Member States that allow other languages are mostly minority languages or a second language used in (parts of) those Member States.

3. Qualified persons to do translations

A provision on the qualification of the translator is included in Art. 57 (3). It specifies that 9
any translation under this Regulation shall be done by a person qualified to do translations in one of the Member States. This rule is derived from Art. 55 (2) Brussels I Regulation, subject to replacing the word 'certified' under the old Regulation to 'done' in the present text. This is in line with the reduction of formalities and the wording in the Brussels I*bis* Regulation. The Jenard Report clarified in relation to the forerunner of this provision in the Brussels Convention that the aim of the provision that a person only needs to be qualified in one of the Member States is to simplify the enforcement procedure.[15]

This provision only refers to translations and not to transliterations. It may be assumed that 10
this is up to national law or may be generally exempted from formal requirements. A translation by the lawyer or party itself, possibly aided by automated means (online translations) may suffice,[16] as long as it is still comprehensible for the purpose of carrying out the enforcement.

---

[11] Similar provision are also included in several other Regulations containing enforcement provisions.
[12] Luxemburg mentions that it accepts French and German as 'additional' languages, which is abundant and not a true alternative, since those are already official languages in that Member State.
[13] Czech Republic (Slovak), Denmark (Finnish, Icelandic, Norwegian and Swedish), Estonia (English), Cyprus (Greek and English), Luxembourg (French and German), Malta (English), Slovenia (Italian and Hungarian in certain courts), Slovakia (Czech), Finland (English) and Sweden (Danish and English).
[14] Estonia, Cyprus, Malta, Finland and Sweden.
[15] Jenard Report, OJ EEC 1979 C 59/1, 56.
[16] See also *Fitchen*, in: Dickinson/Lein (eds.), The Brussels I Regulation Recast (2015) para. 13.528.

Chapter IV: **Authentic Instruments and Court Settlements**

Article 58

1. An authentic instrument which is enforceable in the Member State of origin shall be enforceable in the other Member States without any declaration of enforceability being required. Enforcement of the authentic instrument may be refused only if such enforcement is manifestly contrary to public policy (ordre public) in the Member State addressed.
   The provisions of Section 2, Subsection 2 of Section 3, and Section 4 of Chapter III shall apply as appropriate to authentic instruments.
2. The authentic instrument produced must satisfy the conditions necessary to establish its authenticity in the Member State of origin.

I. Introduction

1 This provision regulates the enforcement of authentic instruments. It provides that an authentic instrument that is enforceable in the Member State of origin shall be enforceable in the other Member States without a declaration of enforceability (exequatur) being required. Its enforcement may only be refused when it manifestly contradicts public policy *(ordre public)*. The Brussels I Regulation also contained a provision on the enforcement of authentic instruments in its Art. 58.

2 The Heidelberg Report did not reveal specific problems in the enforcement of authentic instruments. It did not propose to make any amendment and generally referred to the significance of the European Enforcement Order Regulation,[1] abolishing exequatur for uncontested claims, which contains a definition of 'authentic instrument' in its Art. 4 (3).[2] Following its general approach to court judgments, the Commission proposed to abolish exequatur for the enforcement of authentic judgments along with the abolition of the public policy exception.[3] As the general abolition of public policy was not accepted, it is also retained for authentic instruments in the present provision.

3 Apart from the abolition of exequatur, Art. 58 introduces several changes of a primarily textual and contextual nature in line with other amendments in the enforcement regime. First, a definition of 'authentic instruments' is included in Art. 2 (d). The Brussels I Regulation lacked a definition,[4] but the present definition was not intended as amendment since it relies on case law and is largely derived from the aforementioned provision of the European

---

[1] Regulation (EC) No. 805/2004 creating a European Enforcement Order for uncontested claims 2004, OJ 2004, L 143/12.

[2] Heidelberg Report, para. 625–629.

[3] Art. 70 Commission Proposal.

Enforcement Order Regulation. Second, the reference to the separate Annex including the certificate for authentic instrument in the Brussels I Regulation[5] has been relocated to Art. 60 which applies to both authentic instruments and court settlements and refers to the common Annex II. Third, the paragraph on authentic instruments for maintenance has been deleted due to the exclusion of maintenance obligations from the Brussels scheme following a separate Regulation.[6]

II. Autonomous concept of authentic instrument

The concept of authentic instruments as well as the procedural requirements differs per **4** Member State, and lacks as such in common law systems.[7] These differences became apparent when the number of Member States increased and consequently their legal origins became more diverse. In *Unibank v. Christensen* the ECJ had to interpret the scope of the provision on authentic instruments with regard to a particular instrument under Danish law.[8] The Court outlawed a private deed and ruled that such instrument needs to be produced by a public authority or other competent authority in order to be recognized as an authentic instrument.

Art. 2 (c) now includes an autonomous definition building on this ruling and the definition **5** of authentic instrument in Art. 4 (3) European Enforcement Order Regulation.[9] It means a document which has been formally drawn up or registered as an authentic instrument in the Member State of origin and the authenticity of which: (i) relates to the signature and the content of the instrument; and (ii) has been established by a public authority or other authority empowered for that purpose. The public or other authority designated in a Member State can for instance be a (public) notary or a court. The law of the Member State of origin governs its authenticity and evidentiary status. As Art. 58 (2) clarifies, in order to be enforceable, the authentic instrument produced must satisfy the conditions necessary to establish its authenticity in the Member State of origin.

III. Enforcement of authentic instruments

1. Enforceability in the Member State of origin

According to Art. 58 (1) the enforceability of an authentic instrument in the Member State **6** addressed (where the enforcement is sought[10]) relies on the enforceability in the Member State of origin (where it has been formally drawn up or registered[11]). The domestic law of the

---

4   This is due to the fact that the original six Member States had a consistent understanding of what an authentic instruments is due to their common legal origin on this point. See *Hess*, para. 6.262.

5   Annex VI Brussels I Regulation.

6   This was included in Art. 57 (2). See Council Regulation (EC) No. 4/2009 on jurisdiction, applicable law, recognition and enforcement of decisions and cooperation in matters relating to maintenance obligations, OJ 2009, L 7/1, Art. 48.

7   See extensively *Fitchen*, Yb. PIL 13 (2011), 33, 39–47.

8   *Unibank A.S. v. Flemming G. Christensen*, (Case C-260/97) [1999] ECR I-3715.

9   See Section 1 and note 60.

10   Art. 2 (e).

11   Art. 2 (d).

Member State of origin thus decides on its enforceability. This requirement also applies to judgments under Art. 39. In relation to judgments the ECJ has ruled that this means that it must be enforceable in formal terms and not to all circumstances in which such decisions may be enforced in the Member State of origin.[12] The *rationale* of this rule is that the effect of an authentic instruments cannot be greater in the Member State addressed than it has in the Member State of origin.[13]

7 It should be noted that Art. 58 does not refer to the recognition of authentic instruments. For the purpose of enforcing the obligations flowing from such instrument, its content is **ac-cepted**.[14] However, such instrument does not have *res iudicata* and it not susceptible to recognition similar to the recognition of a judgment.[15]

2. Procedure for enforcement

8 In line with the Brussels *Ibis* enforcement regime for judgments, authentic instruments may be enforced in other Member States without a declaration of enforcement being required, pursuant to Art. 58 (1).The second sentence of this provision declares Section 2, Subsection 2 of Section 3, and Section 4 of Chapter III (Arts. 39–44, 46–51, 52–57) concerning judgments applicable to the enforcement of authentic instruments 'as appropriate'. These provisions are generally suitable to be applied to authentic instruments *mutatis mutandis*, though some of these provisions are specifically aimed at judgments.

9 As regards the enforcement provisions in Arts. 39–43, particularly Arts. 41–44 seem relevant and appropriate, though access to provisional measures pursuant to Art. 40 can, where relevant, also not be denied. The core of Art. 41is that an authentic instrument enforceable in the Member State of origin should be enforced under the same conditions as would a domestic authentic instrument. In absence of authentic instruments, as is the case in England and Wales, the focus should be on the obligation (usually a payment obligation) that is included in such instrument. Whether the national grounds of refusal or suspension, as referenced in Art. 41 (2) are appropriate in relation to authentic instruments, in view of the restriction of the grounds of refusal to public policy, is not clear. However, it seems plausible that the enforcement of a payment obligation flowing from such instrument may be refused on the basis of, for instance, set-off, or other legal or practical limitations to enforcement of monetary obligations in the Member State addressed. Art. 42 lays down the formal requirement of providing a copy of the authentic instrument and the certificate. For authentic instruments the certificate is referred to in Art. 60 and laid down in Annex II. The translation requirements of this Article also apply to authentic instruments. The same will hold true for the service requirements pursuant to Art. 43, as far as service and translation is still necessary, considering the likely earlier involvement of the person against whom enforce-

---

[12] *Eric Coursier v. Fortis Bank and Martine Coursier, née Bellami*, (Case C-267/97) [1999] ECR I-2543.

[13] *Fitchen*, in: Dickinson/Lein (eds.), The Brussels I Regulation Recast (2015) para. 14.18; *Layton/Mercer*, para. 29.007.

[14] The term 'acceptance' is used in Art. 59 of the Succession Regulation; Regulation (EU) No. 650/2012 on jurisdiction, applicable law, recognition and enforcement of decisions and acceptance and enforcement of authentic instruments in matters of succession and on the creation of a European Certificate of Succession, OJ 2012, L 201/107.

[15] *Fitchen*, in: Dickinson/Lein (eds.), The Brussels I Regulation Recast (2015) para. 14.31.

ment is sought. The application of Art. 44 on the refusal or suspension of the enforcement can also be transposed to the enforcement of authentic instruments.

Arts. 46–51 on the refusal of enforcement can generally be applied as well, subject to some **10** amendments. First, Art. 46 refers to the grounds of refusal laid down in Art. 45, but for authentic instruments these are limited to the violation of public policy pursuant of Art. 58. Art. 51 concerns an ordinary appeal in the Member State of origin, and is (likely) not relevant for authentic instruments, unless for instance a procedure to nullify the instrument is initiated. As far as the common provisions laid down in Arts 52-57 are concerned, particularly Art. 52 (prohibition to review the substance), 56 (no security required), and 57 (translation of the authentic instrument and certificate) are relevant.

3. Ground of refusal: public policy

Pursuant to Art. 58 (1) the enforcement of an authentic instrument may be refused only if **11** the enforcement would be manifestly contrary to public policy in the Member State addressed. As follows from the case law of the ECJ concerning the public policy exception in relation to judgments, this ground of refusal should be applied restrictively.[16] Under no circumstances may the court of the Member State addressed review the substance of the authentic instrument (Art. 52). The review in the context of a violation of public policy will be limited to the formal validity.[17] This primarily pertains to the requirements under Art. 58 and particularly Art. 2 (c) regarding the conditions of the instrument and its authenticity.

Article 59

A court settlement which is enforceable in the Member State of origin shall be enforced in the other Member States under the same conditions as authentic instruments.

I. Introduction

This provision concerns the enforcement of court settlements. It aims to ensure that court **1** settlements that are enforceable in the Member State where it has been approved can be enforced in the other Member States. It declares the same conditions as apply to authentic instruments under Art. 58 applicable to court settlements. This means that a declaration of enforceability *(exequatur)* is not required under the Brussels I*bis* Regulation. As for authentic instruments, the only ground of refusal is the manifest contradiction to public policy in the Member State addressed.

This rule replaces Art. 58 Brussels I Regulation, which received very little attention during **2** the discussions on the recast. The Heidelberg Report remarked that the sparse case law

---

16   See notably *Dieter Krombach v. André Bamberski*, (Case C-7/98) [2000] ECR I-1935; *Marco Gambazzi v. DaimlerChrysler Canada Inc. and CIBC Mellon Trust Company*, (Case C-394/07) [2009] ECR I-2563.
17   *Fitchen*, in: Dickinson/Lein (eds.), The Brussels I Regulation Recast (2015) paras. 14.22-14.23; *Mercer/Layton*, para. 29.16.

Xandra Kramer   985

available on the enforcement of court settlements did not indicate noticeable problems.[1] Three minor (textual) differences between the current Art. 59 and its predecessor in the Brussels I Regulation are apparent that aim to clarify its meaning or reflect other amendments in the enforcement system of the Brussels *Ibis* Regulation.[2] First, the definition included in Art. 2(b) slightly diverges from that included in Art. 58 Brussels I Regulation.[3] Second, the present provision states that a settlement that is enforceable in the Member State of origin shall be *enforced* in the other Member States, whereas Art. 58 Brussels I Regulation provided that these are *enforceable* in the Member State addressed. This textual amendment follows from the abolition of the declaration of enforceability; under the Brussels *Ibis* Regulation a party can immediately proceed to enforcement. Third, Art. 59 does not refer to the Annex including a certificate of the settlement as its predecessor did, since Art. 60 contains a joint reference for authentic instruments and courts settlements to Annex II that applies to both acts.[4]

II. Autonomous concept of court settlement

1. Definition in Art. 2(b)

3 In Art. 2(b) the court settlement is defined as a 'settlement, which has been approved by a court of a Member State or concluded before a court of a Member State in the course of proceedings'. This description seems broader than the one included in Art. 58 Brussels I Regulation that, at least in the English version, required that the settlement had been approved by a court in the course of proceedings. In the literature this has led to discussions on the qualification of a decision to declare a mass settlement binding under the Dutch Collective Settlements Act,[5] since the settlement itself is not reached before a court but prior to requesting the court to declare it binding.[6] The wording of Art. 58 Brussels I Regulation was ambiguous in this regard, and there were differences between the language versions of this provision.

4 The present definition in Art. 2 (b) clarifies that both a settlement that has been concluded before a court, usually as a result of a judicial attempt to settle a case brought before the court, and the prior settlement between parties that is in accordance with domestic law formally approved by the court qualify as a court settlement. Evidently, the settlement must relate to a case that comes within the scope of the Regulation, meaning that is must regard a civil or commercial matter.[7] This would exclude, for instance, settlements on maintenance, in bankruptcy proceedings or relating to matrimonial property.

---

[1] Heidelberg Report, paras. 622–624.

[2] See also *Kramer*, in: Dickinson/Lein (eds.), The Brussels I Regulation Recast (2015) paras. 14.34-14.37.

[3] See more in detail Section II.1 below.

[4] The Brussels I Regulation contained a less detailed form for both court judgments and settlements in its Annex V.

[5] Wet Collectieve Afwikkeling Massaschade (WCAM).

[6] See *Stadler*, in: Pohlmann/Reiner Schulze (eds.), Auf dem Weg zu einer europäischen Sammelklage? (2009), p. 150, 163; *van Lith*, The Dutch Collective Settlements Act and Private International Law (2011) pp. 111–115; *Kramer*, in: Hodges/Stadler (eds.), Resolving Mass Disputes. ADR and Settlement of Mass Claims (2013), p. 63, 83 with further references.

[7] See Art. 1.

2. Relation to judgments

Art. 59 does not apply to decisions that are to be regarded as a 'judgment' as defined in Art. 2 **5**
(1), as the ECJ affirmed in *Solo Kleinmotoren*.[8] Some judicial decisions are on the borderline
between judgments and settlements. Examples referenced in doctrine are the English consent judgments and French *jugements d'expédient*.[9] A more challenging example is the
Dutch binding declaration of a WCAM settlement,[10] which has received a great deal of
attention in Europe. In *Solo Kleinmotoren* the Court ruled that in order to be qualified as a
judgment the decision must 'emanate from a judicial body (…) deciding on its own authority on the issues between the parties'.[11]

In the aforementioned examples of the English and French judgments, this requirement is **6**
fulfilled and these are thus to be regarded as a judgment and not as a court settlement within
the meaning of Art. 59. As for the Dutch court decision to declare a mass settlement binding
views diverge, though the dominant view seems to be that it should be considered a court
judgment and not be treated as a settlement under Art. 59.[12] The decision to declare the
settlement binding is not merely a rubber stamp, but requires an active court involvement in
setting procedural requirements and reviewing a range of legal issues, including whether the
settlement amount is reasonable. The interested parties, on whose behalf the settlement is
concluded, are also served and may be heard in the procedure.[13] The main purpose of this
binding declaration is to establish preclusive effect vis-à-vis the interested parties. It may be
concluded that this goes beyond a simple court approval of a private settlement between
parties, as covered by Art. 59, though there is room for doubt.

III. Enforcement of courts settlements

According to Art. 59, court settlements that are enforceable in the Member State of origin **7**
shall be enforced in the other Member States under the same conditions as authentic instruments. The Member State of origin refers in this context to the Member State in which
the 'court settlement has been approved or concluded', as defined in Art. 2 (d). Art. 58 on
authentic instruments provides that these are enforceable without any declaration of enforceability being required.[14] The certificate issued by the Member State of origin pursuant
to Art. 60 and included as Annex II to the Brussels I*bis* Regulation plays a central role in the

---

8   *Solo Kleinmotoren GmbH v. Emilio Boch*, (Case 414/92) [1994] ECR 2237 para. 25.
9   *Hess*, para. 6.256.
10 See Art. 59 notes 1–2 (*Xandra Kramer*).
11 *Solo Kleinmotoren GmbH v. Emilio Boch*, (Case 414/92) [1994] ECR 2237 para. 17.
12 See inter alia Polak, NJB 2006, 2346, 2353; *Stadler*, JZ 2009, 121, 126; *Arons/van Boom*, EBLR 2010, 857,
    880–881; *van Lith*, The Dutch Collective Settlements Act and Private International Law (2011) pp. 114–
    115; *Halfmeier*, NIPR 2012, 176, 178–180; *Xandra Kramer*, Global Business & Development Law Journal
    2014, 236, 265. In doubt: *Hess*, in: Fairgrieve/Lein (eds.), Extraterritoriality and Collective Redress (2012),
    p. 107, 114. See in greater detail *Xandra Kramer*, in: Dickinson/Lein (eds.), The Brussels I Regulation
    Recast (2015) para. 14.41.
13 See also *Xandra Kramer*, Global Business & Development Law Journal 2014, 236, p. 265.
14 Art. 58 further states that the provisions of Section 2, Subsection 2 of Section 3, and Section 4 of Chapter
    III (Arts. 46–57) shall apply as appropriate. See Art. 58 note 10 (*Xandra Kramer*).

enforcement. As is the case for authentic instruments, the provisions included in Chapter III (Section 2, Subsection 2 of Section 3, and Section 4) apply as appropriate.[15]

8 Enforcement of the court settlement may, as follows from Art. 59 in conjunction with Art. 58 (1), only be refused if such enforcement is manifestly against public policy in the Member State addressed. This may relate to the conditions under with the settlement was concluded or approved and, probably, to the substance of the settlement. However, in view of the very strict interpretation of the public policy exception and the prohibition to review the substance of the matter (Art. 52), this review should be restricted.

9 It should be noted that Art. 59 only concerns the enforcement of court settlements and does not explicitly regulate its recognition. It regards the actual enforcement of what has been contractually agreed between the parties. This is also clear from the *Solo Kleinmotoren* ruling of the ECJ, in which the Court emphasized the contractual nature of the settlement.[16] A court settlement as such is generally not attributed *res iudicata* effect.[17] Nevertheless, the enforcement of a court settlement may implicitly be regarded as recognizing the contractually agreed status between parties.

Article 60

The competent authority or court of the Member State of origin shall, at the request of any interested party, issue the certificate using the form set out in Annex II containing a summary of the enforceable obligation recorded in the authentic instrument or of the agreement between the parties recorded in the court settlement.

I. Introduction

1 This provision applies to both authentic instruments and court settlements, and introduced several new elements compared to the Brussels I Regulation. It states that at the request of any interested party, the Member State of origin shall issue the standard form (certificate) that is attached to the Brussels *Ibis* Regulation as Annex II. This mandatory and extended standard form (certificate for authentic instruments/court settlement) aims to facilitate the enforcement in other Member States. The Brussels I Regulation contained two separate provisions and Annexes for these instruments; Art. 57 (4) Brussels I referred to Annex VI for authentic instruments and Art. 58 to Annex V that applied to both judgments and court settlements.

2 Art. 60 is compliant with Art. 53 for judgments that refers to a similar standard form in Annex I (judgment certificate). The 'connection provision' included in Art. 58 declares other provisions applicable to the enforcement procedure of judgments applicable to authentic instruments; Art. 59 extends these to court settlements. This includes Art. 42, 43 and 57 on the use, service and language of the certificate.[1]

---

[15]   Art. 59 in conjunction with Art. 58 (1), second sentence. See Art. 58 note 10 (*Xandra Kramer*).

[16]   See *Solo Kleinmotoren GmbH* v. *Emilio Boch*, (Case 414/92) [1994] ECR 2237 para. 18.

[17]   Heidelberg Report para. 622; *Briggs/Rees*, para. 7.31; *Gaudemet-Tallon*, para. 389.

[1]   See Art. 58 note 10 (*Xandra Kramer*).

II. Issuing and use of the certificate (Annex II)

The certificate concerning an authentic instrument or court settlement shall be issued by the **3** Member State of origin at the request of any interested party. As described in Art. 2(d), the Member State of origin for an authentic instrument means the Member State in which the instrument has been formally drawn up or registered. For court settlements this is the Member State in which the settlement has been approved or concluded. The concept of an 'interested person' is not defined in the Brussels I*bis* Regulation, but can be widely construed as encompassing the persons directly involved as parties to the authentic instrument or court settlement or any other person mentioned in the instrument or having an interest in seeking its enforcement.

The certificate provides information on the court or competent authority issuing the certi- **4** ficate, the authority and registry of the authentic instrument, and for the court settlement, the date and the parties involved, as well as the enforceability of the authentic instrument or court settlement in the Member State of origin, as well as detailed information on the (monetary) obligations that flow from the authentic instrument or court settlement. This should generally suffice for the enforcement authority in the Member State addressed to enforce the obligations.

As follows from Art. 58 (1), second sentence and 59 in conjunction with Art. 42 (1) the **5** applicant needs to provide the enforcement authority with the certificate,[2] along with a copy of the authentic instrument or court settlement itself.[3] Art. 42 (3) prescribes that the enforcement authority may, where necessary, require the applicant to provide a translation or transliteration of the contents of the certificate, in accordance with Art. 57. Pursuant to Art. 43 (1), the certificate needs to be served on the person against whom enforcement is sought prior to the first enforcement measure.

Chapter V: **General Provisions**

Article 61

No legalisation or other similar formality shall be required for documents issued in a Member State in the context of this Regulation.

This provision prohibits Member States from requiring legalization or other similar for- **1** malities for documents, such as a judgment or notarial deed, issued in one Member State for the purpose of using it (for instance for the recognition or enforcement) in another Member State. It is in line with Art. 56 Brussels I Regulation and the corresponding provision in the Brussels Convention.[1] It is thus a long established rule in European procedural law that aims

---

2   Art. 42 (1) (b).
3   Art. 42 (1) (a).
1   Art. 49 Brussels Convention.

Article 62   Brussels *Ibis* Regulation

to ban unnecessary formalities in relation to the traffic of legal documents within the European Union. A minor textual difference is that Art. 56 Brussels I Regulation referred specifically to the copy of the judgment and the judgment certificate for the purpose of the declaration of enforceability. The formulation of the current provision generally refers to all documents that are issued in the context of the Brussels I*bis* Regulation.

Article 62

1. In order to determine whether a party is domiciled in the Member State whose courts are seised of a matter, the court shall apply its internal law.
2. If a party is not domiciled in the Member State whose courts are seised of the matter, then, in order to determine whether the party is domiciled in another Member State, the court shall apply the law of that Member State.

Bibliography

Conrad, Qualifikationsfragen des Trust im Europäischen Zivilprozessrecht (2001)
Haubold, Internationale Zuständigkeit für gesell-schaftsrechtliche und konzernrechtliche Haftungs-ansprüche nach EuGVÜ und LugÜ, IPRax 2000, 375
Hess/Pfeiffer/Schlosser, The Brussels I Regulation 44/2001. Application and Enforcement in the EU (2008)

Rammeloo, Corporations in Private International Law. A European Perspective (2001)
Schillig, Die ausschließliche Zuständigkeit für gesellschaftsrechtliche Streitigkeiten vor dem Hintergrund der Niederlassungsfreiheit, IPRax 2005, 208.

I. Introduction

1 Chapter V of the Brussels I*bis* Regulation contains general provisions (Artt. 61 to 65). Artt. 62 and 63 provide for the determination of the notion 'domicile' within the meaning of the Regulation. Regarding natural persons Art. 62 does not give an autonomous definition of domicile and does not deviate from its predecessors Art. 52 Brussels Convention and Art. 59 Brussels I Regulation. However, Art. 63 provides for an autonomous definition of domicile of a company or other legal person and has not been changed compared to Art. 60 Brussels I Regulation.

2 Art. 62 refers to the internal law of the court seised in order to determine whether a party (natural person) is domiciled in the forum state. Positive or negative jurisdiction disputes cannot be avoided in this way.[1] For instance, positive jurisdiction disputes may arise, if the

---

[1] *Droz* para. 358 seq.

990   September 2015

court seised of the matter determines that according to its national law the defendant is domiciled within the Member State of that court, whereas a court of another Member State might decide that the defendant is domiciled within its territory. Positive jurisdiction conflicts have to be decided by applying Art. 29 *(lis pendens)*. However, Art. 62 does not give rise to many problems in the legal practice of the Member States.[2]

Art. 62 does not refer to the notion of habitual residence *(résidence habituelle)*, which is a **3** frequently used criterion in conventions on private international law in order to determine the personal status. This notion refers to a country with which a person has the closest bonds, where the centre of his social life is situated.[3] Hence, the habitual residence is factual and depends on the circumstances of the case.

According to the laws of some Member States a contractual choice of domicile (address) can **4** be made for particular legal purposes, see e.g. Art. 15 Book 1 of the Dutch Civil Code, Art. 111 of the French Civil Code and Art. 111 of the Belgian Civil Code. According to the Report *Jenard* the notion 'domicile' in the meaning of Art. 52 Brussels Convention does not extend to the legal fiction of an address for service of process.[4] Since Art. 62 Brussels I*bis* Regulation does not deviate from Art. 52 Brussels Convention, choice of domicile (address) cannot be accepted as a basis for jurisdiction in matters which fall within the scope of the Brussels I*bis* Regulation.[5]

II. Moment of domicile

The moment of having domicile in a Member State is of interest for the application of some **5** rules of jurisdiction of the Brussels I*bis* Regulation.[6] Under the Brussels I Regulation the question was pressing with respect to Art. 23 regarding choice of forum agreements. Art. 23 required that at least one of the parties to the choice of forum agreement had to be domiciled in a Member State. Now Art. 25 Brussels I*bis* Regulation applies regardless of the domicile of the parties. In general, the moment of instituting the proceedings is decisive. If the defendant is domiciled in a Member State at the time the proceedings are instituted against him, Art. 4

---

[2]   See also *Hess/Pfeiffer/Schlosser* paras. 172 and 177. The Green Paper on the review of the Brussels I Regulation, 21 April 2009, COM (2009) 175 final, did not question the application of Art. 59 Brussels I Regulation. See also A. *Staudinger*, in: Rauscher Art. 59 note 9, who is in favour of reforming Art. 59 and introducing the notion of habitual residence.

[3]   Cf., on the interpretation of the concept 'habitual residence' under Art. 8 (1) Brussels II A Regulation, (Case C-523/07) ECLI:EU:C:2009:225, (2009) ECR I-2805. The ECJ ruled that this concept must be interpreted 'as meaning that it corresponds to the place which reflects some degree of integration by the child in a social and family environment. To that end, in particular the duration, regularity, conditions and reasons for the stay on the territory of a Member State and the family's move to that State, the child's nationality, the place and conditions of attendance at school, linguistic knowledge and the family and social relationships of the child in that State must be taken into consideration. It is for the national court to establish the habitual residence of the child, taking account of all the circumstances specific to each individual case'.

[4]   Report *Jenard*, OJ 1979 C 59/18.

[5]   See Rechtbank Breda 10 April 2012, ECLI:NL:RBBRE:2012:BW2485. The Rechtbank denied the application of a choice of address in case of jurisdiction in matters of individual contracts of employment.

[6]   *Kruger* para. 2.31; *Kropholler/von Hein*, vor Art. 2, paras. 12–15.

shall apply. The courts of the Member State of the defendant's domicile shall have jurisdiction, even when the defendant moves his domicile during proceedings to another Member State or to a third State. The principle of *perpetuatio fori* is applicable.[7]

III. Article 62 (1): Domicile in the forum State

6   The court of a Member State seised of a matter falling within the scope of the Brussels Ibis Regulation has to apply its internal law in order to determine whether the defendant is domiciled within the forum State. Each Member State will apply its own internal law.[8] The notion 'domicile' differs from country to country.[9] In common law countries the notion 'domicile' has another meaning than in civil law countries. The common law notion of domicile refers to a person's roots "within a territory covered by a particular legal system".[10] Upon their accession to the Brussels Convention, the United Kingdom and Ireland have introduced a separate notion 'domicile' for the purposes of that Convention.[11] This separate notion applies under the Regulation too.

IV. Article 62 (2): Domicile in another Member State

7   The second paragraph of Art. 62 deals with the problem of how to determine whether a party is domiciled in another Member State, if the party is not domiciled in the Member State of the forum. The court seised has to apply the internal law of that other Member State.[12] The court seised is also compelled to apply foreign law in this respect. Art. 4 shall apply, if the court decides that the party is not domiciled in another Member State.

V. Domicile in a third State

8   Art. 62 does of course not provide for a rule regarding how to determine whether a party is domiciled in a third State. The rules of private international law of the court seised shall then apply.[13]

VI. Domicile of dependency

9   Art. 62 does not give a rule regarding the determination of the domicile of dependent persons.[14] The domicile of a dependent person is to be determined according to the appli-

---

[7]   A. Staudinger, in: Rauscher Art. 59 note 3. See also Hoge Raad 19 March 2004, ECLI:NL:HR:2004: AO2785, NJ 2004, 295 note Vlas, Hof Amsterdam 14 April 2005, NIPR 2005, 262.

[8]   See also para. 40 of the ECJ decision *Hypoteční banka a.s. v. Udo Mike Lindner* (Case C-327/10) ECLI:EU: C:2011:745, (2011) ECR I-11543, NJ 2012/225 note *Polak*. Additional comments by *Vlek*, NIPR 2012, 202 and *Grimm*, ZPR 2012, 87.

[9]   *Hess/Pfeiffer/Schlosser* paras. 172–176.

[10] Report *Schlosser* para. 72.

[11] See for the United Kingdom Section 41 of the Civil Jurisdiction and Judgments Act 1982 (as amended) and for Ireland Section 13 of the Jurisdiction of Courts and Enforcement of Judgments (European Communities) Act (Ireland) 1988 (as amended). *Dicey/Morris/Collins* para. 11R-072.

[12] *Hypoteční banka a.s. v. Udo Mike Lindner* (Case C-327/10) ECLI:EU:C:2011:745, (2011) ECR I-11543, para. 41.

[13] Report *Jenard* p. 16.

cable law to the personal status of that person. The rules of private international law of the forum shall apply.[15]

Article 63

1. For the purposes of this Regulation, a company or other legal person or association of natural or legal persons is domiciled at the place where it has its:
   (a) statutory seat;
   (b) central administration; or
   (c) principal place of business.
2. For the purposes of Ireland, Cyprus and the United Kingdom, 'statutory seat' means the registered office or, where there is no such office anywhere, the place of incorporation or, where there is no such place anywhere, the place under the law of which the formation took place.
3. In order to determine whether a trust is domiciled in the Member State whose courts are seised of the matter, the court shall apply its rules of private international law.

I. Introduction

Art. 63 gives a definition of the notion domicile of a company or other legal person or 1 association of natural or legal persons for the purposes of the Brussels I*bis* Regulation. Art. 63 has been unchanged compared to its predecessor Art. 60 Brussels I Regulation. Art. 63 does not refer to the rules of private international law of the forum in order to determine whether the company or legal person is domiciled in a Member State.[1] However, this system is still used in Art. 24 (2) regarding exclusive jurisdiction in certain matters of company law.[2] For all other articles of the Brussels I*bis* Regulation, the domicile of a company or other legal person is to be determined in accordance with Art. 63. Art. 63 does not provide for the decisive moment in order to establish whether the company or other legal person has its domicile (within the meaning of Article 63) in a Member State. However, the decisive moment is the moment of instituting the proceedings.[3]

---

[14] Art. 52 Brussels Convention gave a provision in this respect, which was deleted by the Accession Convention of San Sebastian of 26 May 1989. The provision on domicile of dependency was not adopted in the Lugano Convention of 16 September 1988, see Report *Jenard/Möller* para. 73.

[15] See also *A. Staudinger*, in: Rauscher Art. 59 note 5.

[1] As was the case under the application of Art. 53 Brussels Convention.

[2] See *Schillig*, IPRax 2005, 208, 209.

[3] See also the commentary on Article 62, note 5.

II. Autonomous definition

2 Art. 63 could be seen as an autonomous definition of the notion domicile of a company or other legal person. It mentions three criteria.[4] The company or other legal person is domiciled at the place where it has either its statutory seat, its central administration, or its principal place of business. These criteria are taken from Art. 54 TFEU (former Art. 48 EC).The company or other legal person has its domicile, for the purposes of the Brussels I*bis* Regulation, in the Member States, if one of the places mentioned in Art. 63 is located in one of these States. In this situation the rules of jurisdiction of the Regulation shall then apply. If the company or other legal person is not domiciled in a Member State, the national rules of jurisdiction shall apply according to Art. 6.

III. Criteria used in Article 63

3 There is no hierarchy between the criteria (statutory seat, central administration and principal place of business) mentioned in Art. 63. The criteria are equal, but exhaustive. All places could be located in one and the same Member State, which will be the normal situation, e.g. a Dutch company having not only its statutory seat in Amsterdam, but also its central administration and principal place of business. Other variations are possible. The company could be incorporated according to Dutch law with central administration in Germany and principal place of business in France. In that case the company is domiciled for the purposes of the Regulation in three Member States. The company can be sued in the courts of each of these Member States according to Art. 4. Positive conflicts of jurisdiction – lis pendens – have to be solved by application of Artt. 29 to 32. Avoiding negative conflicts of jurisdiction is the most important reason for the use of the three autonomous criteria. If, for instance, a French company has its central administration in Amsterdam, Dutch courts would not have jurisdiction under the Brussels Convention, since according to Dutch private international law the company is domiciled in France (Art. 53 Brussels Convention). The French courts would not have jurisdiction either, because the company is domiciled in the Netherlands according to the rules of French private international law. These complications are avoided by Art. 63. Under the Brussels I*bis* Regulation the courts of a Member State shall have jurisdiction if one of the criteria is located in that State. Hence, a Liberian corporation having its registered seat in Monrovia (Liberia) and principal place of business in Piraeus (Greece), is domiciled in Greece for the purposes of the Brussels I*bis* Regulation.[5] The courts of other Member States cannot exercise jurisdiction over this corporation on the basis of their national rules of jurisdiction.

4 The notion 'statutory seat' is known in most legal systems of the Member States. If a company or other legal person is incorporated according to the laws of these Member States, the company or other legal person has its statutory seat in that State. For the purposes of the Regulation the company or other legal person is domiciled in that State of incorporation. The statutory seat is a clear criterion and cannot be changed easily. The place where a company or other legal person has its statutory seat can be found in the Articles of Association and in the public registers. However, the notion of 'statutory seat' is unknown in the

---

4   See on this subject also *Vlas*, Rechtspersonen (Corporations), Praktijkreeks IPR, vol. 9 (2009) paras. 178–187; *Kruger* para. 2.24.

5   Cf., under the Brussels Convention, Rechtbank Amsterdam 1 July 1992 NIPR 1992, 439.

legal systems of Cyprus, Ireland and the United Kingdom. Art. 63 (2) has made a special provision in this respect.

The notion 'central administration' (in French: *'administration centrale'*, in German: **5** *'Hauptverwaltung'*, in Dutch: *'hoofdvestiging'*) means the management and control centre (the 'real seat').[6] Although every company or other legal person has a central administration, this notion is less easy to ascertain than the statutory seat. The location of the central administration depends on factual circumstances, which have to be known to the plaintiff in order to decide in which Member State the company or other legal person can be sued. In practice problems could arise in determining the place of central administration.[7] The notion has to be understood in an autonomous way and ought not to be treated identical to the concepts of the national systems of private international law.

The notion 'principal place of business' (in French: *'principal établissement'*, in German: **6** *'Hauptniederlassung'*, in Dutch: *'hoofdvestiging'*) means the place where the main business activities are located. This notion is also factual and could give rise to problems, which have to be solved by the forum.

The notions mentioned in Art. 63 do not have the same content as the notion 'branch, **7** agency or other establishment' used in Art. 7 (5).[8] The notion 'branch, agency or other establishment' refers to a certain degree of dependency between the local entity and the parent body. The ECJ decided that the concept "implies a place of business which has the appearance of permanency, such as the extension of a parent body, has a management and is materially equipped to negotiate business with third parties so that the latter, although knowing that there will if necessary be a legal link with the parent body, the head office of which is abroad, do not have to deal directly with such parent body but may transact business at the place of business constituting the extension".[9]

---

6   The decisions of the ECJ concerning the freedom of establishment under the former Artt. 43 and 48 EC (now Artt. 49 and 54 TFEU) do not affect the application of (now) Art. 63 Brussels I*bis* Regulation (*Centros Ltd v. Erhvervs- og Selskabsstyrelsen*, (Case C-212/97) ECLI:EU:C:1999:126, (1999) ECR I-1459; *Überseering BV v. Nordic Construction Company Baumanagement GmbH (NCC)*, (Case C-208/00) ECLI: EU:C:2002:632, (2002) ECR I-9919; *Kamer van Koophandel en Fabrieken voor Amsterdam v. Inspire Art Ltd*, (Case C-167/01) ECLI:EU:C:2003:512, (2003) ECR I-10155; *Cartesio*, (Case 210/06) ECLI:EU: C:2008:723 (2008) ECR I-9641); VALE Építési (Case C-378/10) ECLI:EU:C:2012:440. See on this subject in general *Rammeloo*, Corporations in Private International Law. A European Perspective (2001) p. 11; *Vlas*, Rechtspersonen (2009), paras. 105–119; *Geimer/Schütze* Art. 60 note 6.

7   Cf., English High Court, Queen's Bench Division, Commercial Court in D. King v. Crown Energy Trading AG and another, (2003) I.L.Pr. 28, p. 489, 494.

8   CA Versailles 26 September 1991, RCDIP 1992 with note *Gaudemet-Tallon* erroneously decided that a branch of a New York bank could be considered as 'domicile' under Article 2 of the Brussels Convention. Cf., Rechtbank Rotterdam 2 April 2008 NIPR 2008, 136: a Belgian company having its central administration in Belgium and a branch in Rotterdam, cannot be considered as having its domicile in the Netherlands under Art. 2 Brussels I Regulation (now Art. 4 Brussels I*bis* Regulation); Rechtbank Noord-Holland 4 June 2013, ECLI:NL:RBNHO:2013:CA1759: a Portuguese company having its registered seat in Portugal and a branch office in the Netherlands, is not domiciled in the Netherlands within the meaning of Artt. 2 and 60 Brussels I Regulation (now Artt. 4 and 63 Brussels I*bis* Regulation).

9   *Somafer SA v. Saar-Ferngas AG*, (Case 33/78) (1978) ECR 2183, 2193 para. 12.

IV. Company or other legal person

8 Art. 63 is applicable to a company or other legal person or association of natural or legal persons. It is also applicable to organisations not having legal personality, such as partnerships according to English law, and the equivalent forms in other legal systems such as the Italian *società semplice*, the German *offene Handelsgesellschaft* and the Dutch *vennootschap onder firma*. Art. 63 also applies to, e.g., the European Economic Interest Grouping (EEIG), the European Company (*Societas Europaea*; SE), and the European Cooperative Society, which are entities governed by the respective EC Regulations.[10]

V. Article 63 (2): special rule

9 In Cyprus, Ireland and the United Kingdom the notion 'statutory seat' is unknown.[11] The Brussels I Regulation had to give a special rule in this respect, which is laid down in Art. 63 (2). For the purposes of Cyprus, Ireland and the United Kingdom, 'statutory seat' means the registered office or, where there is no such office anywhere, the place of incorporation. If there is no place of incorporation 'statutory seat' can also mean the place under the law of which the formation took place.

VI. Relation to the Lugano Convention

10 Companies incorporated in Iceland, Norway or Switzerland could also have their central administration or principal place of business in a Member State. Should Art. 63 Brussels *Ibis* Regulation apply or Art. 60 of the 2007 Lugano Convention, to which these countries are party?[12] Art. 64 (2) 2007 Lugano Convention deals with the relationship between the Brussels I Regulation (and its predecessor the 1968 Brussels Convention) and the 2007 Lugano Convention.[13] Art. 60 of the 2007 Lugano Convention is identical to Art. 63 Brussels *Ibis* Regulation. If a Swiss company, incorporated under Swiss law, has its central administration or principal place of business in Paris, the French courts now have to choose between the application of the Brussels *Ibis* Regulation and the Lugano Convention. According to Art. 73 Brussels *Ibis* Regulation this Regulation shall not affect the application of the 2007 Lugano Convention. Art. 64 of the 2007 Lugano Convention provides for a rule in this respect: the Lugano Convention shall not prejudice the application of the Brussels I Regulation. However, the Lugano Convention shall apply in matters of jurisdiction, where the defendant is domiciled in the territory of a State which is not a member of the European Union (Art. 64

---

10 Council Regulation No. 2137/85/EEC of 25 July 1985 on the European Economic Interest Grouping (EEIG), OJ 1985 L 199/1; Council Regulation No. 2157/2001/EC of 8 October 2001 on the Statute for a European company (SE), OJ 2001 L 294/1; Council Regulation No. 1435/2003 of 22 July 2003 on the Statute for a European Cooperative Society (SCE), OJ 2003 L 207/1.

11 The notion 'statutory seat' is also unknown in the legal system of Malta, but curiously Malta is not mentioned in Art. 63 (3).

12 The Convention on jurisdiction, recognition and enforcement of decisions in civil and commercial matters was concluded at Lugano on 30 October 2007, OJ 2009, L 147. The 2007 Lugano Convention came into force on 1 January 2010 between the EU Member States and Norway,, on 1 January 2011 between these States and Switzerland, and on 1 May 2011 for Iceland. The 2007 Lugano Convention replaces the 1988 Lugano Convention.

13 Art. 64 of the 2007 Lugano Convention refers to the Brussels I Regulation.

(2) of the 2007 Lugano Convention). In the example given, the Swiss company is domiciled in Switzerland as well as in France. The French courts could therefore decide that in matters of jurisdiction the company has its domicile (within the meaning of Art. 63 Brussels I*bis* Regulation) in France. At the same time, a Swiss court could decide that for jurisdictional purposes the company is domiciled in Switzerland. Possible problems concerning *lis pendens* and related actions shall be solved according to Art. 27–30 of the 2007 Lugano Convention (see Art. 64 (2)(b) of the 2007 Lugano Convention).

VII. Article 63 (3): domicile of trusts

Art. 63 (3) provides for the determination of the domicile of a trust. This provision, which **11** already existed in Art. 53 (2) Brussels Convention, is necessary in view of Art. 7 (6) regarding the special jurisdiction for trusts. In order to determine whether a trust is domiciled in the Member State whose courts are seised of the matter, the court shall apply its rules of private international law. The geographical centre of operation can be seen as the domicile of a trust.[14] In common law systems, in which trusts are common, the application of Art. 63 (3) will not lead to problems. In the United Kingdom, for instance, a trust is domiciled in a part of the United Kingdom if and only if the system of law of that part is the system of law with which the trust has its closest and most real connection.[15]

In civil law countries the application of Art. 63 (3) can be more problematic, because rules of **12** private international law regarding trusts could be lacking or not developed as yet, since trusts might not always be recognised in the internal laws of these countries.[16] The Hague Trust Convention can be of some help in this respect.[17] Art. 7 Hague Trust Convention gives a conflicts rule for the applicable law to a trust. Where no applicable law has been chosen, a trust shall be governed by the law with which it is most closely connected. In this respect reference shall be made in particular to "a) the place of administration of the trust designated by the settlor, b) the situs of the assets, c) the place of residence or business of the trustee, d) the objects of the trust and the places where they are to be fulfilled". These criteria can be of any use in determining the domicile of the trust within the meaning of Art. 63 (3).[18]

Article 64

Without prejudice to any more favourable provisions of national laws, persons domiciled in a Member State who are being prosecuted in the criminal courts of another Member State of which they are not nationals for an offence which was not intentionally committed may be defended by persons qualified to do so, even if they do not appear in person. However, the court seised of the matter may order appearance in person; in the case of failure to appear, a judgment given in the

---

[14] See Report *Schlosser* para. 114; *Schlosser* Art. 60 note 7.

[15] See *Dicey/Morris/Collins* para. 11.094.

[16] *Kropholler/von Hein*, Art. 60 note 5.

[17] Convention on the Law Applicable to Trusts and on their Recognition, The Hague, 1 July 1985, *Recueil des Conventions/Collection of Conventions* (1951–2003), Hague Conference on Private International Law, nr. 30. From the EU Member States Italy, Luxemburg, Malta, Netherlands and the United Kingdom are party to the Trust Convention, see also the Hague Conference's website (www.hcch.net).

[18] In the same sense: *Gaudemet-Tallon* p. 63.

civil action without the person concerned having had the opportunity to arrange for his defence need not be recognised or enforced in the other Member States.

Bibliography

Mankowski, Zivilverfahren vor Strafgerichten und die EuGVVO, in: FG Rudolf Machacek und Franz Matscher (2008), p. 785

Schoibl, Adhäsionsverfahren und Europäisches Zivilverfahrensrecht, in: FS Rainer Sprung (2001), p. 321.

I. Ratio legis and general considerations

1   The *ratio legis* underlying Art. 64 is to safeguard certain minimum standards of fairness towards the accused if only minor charges are at stake.[1] His position to defend himself shall be enhanced particularly in regard to traffic offences.[2] The defendant's right to stay personally absent whilst obtaining proper representation diminishes the danger of the defendant being apprehended and detained when appearing in court, whereas his home country would not proliferate him.[3] Furthermore, bargaining for a mild sentence in the criminal proceedings, the defendant could subdue to settlement proposals which he would refuse in an isolated civil proceeding.[4] Art. 64 safeguards and makes truly effective the defendant's ability to defend his civil interests without having to submit personally to the criminal jurisdiction of the court.[5] The first clause of Art. 64 establishes the standard. Thereafter, the second clause draws the appropriate consequences, firstly for the criminal court and secondly for the courts in other Member States before which enforcement of the eventual judgment is sought.

2   Art. 64 is to the very letter the successor to Art. 61 Brussels I Regulation which in turn was the immediate successor to Art. II Protocol to the Brussels Convention which has been integrated almost to the letter into the wording of the present provision. It must be read primarily in conjunction with Art. 5 (4) providing which provides for international jurisdiction in civil annex or ancillary proceedings in criminal courts. Yet it stretches beyond Art. 7 (3) and covers criminal proceedings in the state where the accused is domiciled or where a *forum damni* can be found, too.[6] Insofar it purports at to answering and countering some particularities of the law of criminal proceedings in the Roman countries where someone can be accused in their absence.[7] Also one must bear in mind that in some Member States (for instance in France, Belgium and Luxembourg) a criminal verdict is regarded as

---

[1]   *Mankowski*, in: FG Rudolf Machacek and Franz Matscher (2008), p. 785, 792.

[2]   *Kropholler/von Hein* Art. 64 note 2.

[3]   *Schoibl*, in: FS Rainer Sprung (2001), p. 321, 330; *Mankowski*, in: FG Rudolf Machacek and Franz Matscher (2008), p. 785, 792 *et seq.*

[4]   *Criminal proceedings against Siegfried Ewald Rinkau* (Case 157/80), [1981] ECR 1391, 1402 *et seq.* paras. 20, 21; *Schoibl*, in: FS Rainer Sprung (2001), p. 321, 330.

[5]   Report *Jenard* Art. II Protocol; *Layton/Mercer* para. 30.028.

[6]   *Geimer/Schütze* Art. 64 note 9; *Mankowski*, in: FG Rudolf Machacek and Franz Matscher (2008), p. 785, 793.

[7]   *Schoibl*, in: FS Rainer Sprung (2001), p. 321, 330 *et seq.*

conclusive in subsequent civil proceedings, whereas in others (like the United Kingdom) it may have substantial evidential effect; a defendant may therefore be prejudiced, perhaps irretrievably, in the defence of his civil interests if he is not able to arrange for his defence in at his criminal trial.[8]

The restrictions which Art. 1 imposes on the scope of the application of the entire Brussels **3** Ibis Regulation have also to be borne in mind. Art. 64 must not be misunderstood as intervening in pure criminal proceedings and by ordering the Member States to alter their national rules on criminal proceedings throughout if necessary.[9] In substance, and assessing the impact of Art. 1 (1) appropriately, it appears that its scope of application is limited to criminal proceedings, which include civil liability as their object, or could at least do so at least in the future anyway.[10]

II. Defendant's right to stay away from the proceedings in person

The first sentence permits the accused/defendant in criminal proceedings to let allow a **4** qualified persons to provide for his defence whilst as he is not forced to appear in person and to attend the court proceedings in person. Such qualified persons are of course primarily (but not necessarily) lawyers established in the *forum* state. Two additional prerequisites have to be fulfilled: Firstly, the charges at stake must be for an offence non-intentionally that was unintentionally committed. An autonomous interpretation abstracted from the particularities of the national legal orders of the Member States is required.[11] Insofar the English text is easier to understand and more intelligible than for instance the German text which relates to *"fahrlässig begangene Straftat"*. Any reference to negligence or alike should be avoided having in mind the differences between the national concepts of the law in this particular respect area. Likewise the English "offence" does gives less reason for misinterpretations than the German *"Straftat"*, the latter calling for an answer to the question whether minor offences prosecuted as *Ordnungswidrigkeiten* should be included (and the answer being affirmative). As only minimum standards shall be guaranteed by Art. 64, national standards already in force or later-on introduced as a means of law reform which are more favourable to the accused/defendant, are expressly reserved.[12] In this respect, Art. 64 does in no way thrive for anticipate full harmonisation including the introduction of maximum standards. Yet, it does supersede national law in the event that the national law in question does not comply with the minimum standards envisaged.[13]

Nevertheless, an inconsistency hard to swallow and even harder to explain is why such **5** minimum standards, as provided for by Art. 64 pr., are only required with regard to charges of concerning unintentional offences non-intentionally committed whereas charges of of-

---

[8] *Layton/Mercer* para. 30.028.

[9] *Mankowski*, in: FG Rudolf Machacek and Franz Matscher (2008), p. 785, 793.

[10] *Criminal proceedings against Siegfried Ewald Rinkau* (Case 157/80), [1981] ECR 1391, 1402 paras. 20 *et seq.*; *Ansgar Staudinger*, in: Rauscher Art. 64 note 1.

[11] *Criminal proceedings against Siegfried Ewald Rinkau* (Case 157/80), [1981] ECR 1391, 1400 para. 11; *Gaudemet-Tallon* para. 224; *Geimer/Schütze* Art. 64 note 6.

[12] *Mankowski*, in: FG Rudolf Machacek and Franz Matscher (2008), p. 785, 794.

[13] *Schoibl*, in: FS Rainer Sprung (2001), p. 321, 330; *Mankowski*, in: FG Rudolf Machacek and Franz Matscher (2008), p. 785, 794.

fences and crimes intentionally committed would demand this *a minore ad maius*; in the latter event the need for protection and minimum standards is even higher.[14] The whole matter is intrinsically linked with the right for proper representation by a defence lawyer as an important sub-issue of the right for a fair trial, a fundamental right which can be detected found in the constitutional traditions of all Member States[15] and in the European Convention for the Protection of Human Rights and Fundamental Freedoms. The accused does not dispose off, nor waive, nor in any other way lose such right simply by not appearing in personal in at the trials.[16] Otherwise fugitives, who are accused in their absence, would be deprived of such a right.[17] At least, there should not be an automatic duty of other Member States to recognise and enforce such civil judgment and there should not be any kind of conclusion *e contrario* derived from Art. 64.[18]

6 Another incident calling for improvement in the course of later revisions is the potentially discriminatory restriction to the accused or defendants who are not a nationals of the *forum* state. Insofar Art. 18 TFEU might be violated contemplating the position of *forum* state nationals.[19] But this touches upon the difficult question as to whether EU law inhibits or at all covers reverse discrimination.[20] Generally it is left to national constitution law to fight reverse discrimination.[21]

III. Court orders to appear in person and consequences for recognition and enforcement in other Member States

7 Nevertheless, the court seised of the matter may order an appearance in person. In this regard it is not restricted in the judicial power vested in it by the national law of the *forum* state. Art. 64 does not bleak out such power but expressly recognises it by virtue of the second sentence *in principio*.[22] Depending on its own rules of proceedings, the court may

---

[14] BGH IPRax 1998, 205, 207; *Geimer*, in: Studia in honorem János Németh (2003), p. 229, 240 *et seq.*; *Mankowski*, in: FG Rudolf Machacek and Franz Matscher (2008), p. 785, 794 *et seq.*; *Ansgar Staudinger*, in: Rauscher Art. 64 note 2; *Geimer/Schütze* Art. 64 note 5.

[15] *Dieter Krombach v. André Bamberski* (Case C-7/98), [2000] ECR I-1935, I-1969 para. 40.

[16] ECHR *Poitrimol v. Republic of France* Series A no. 277-A; ECHR *Pedalloah v. Kingdom of the Netherlands* Series B No.297; ECHR January 21, 1999 *van Geyseghem v. Belgium*.

[17] *Mankowski*, in: FG Rudolf Machacek and Franz Matscher (2008), p. 785, 795.

[18] *Hau*, EWiR Art. 27 EuGVÜ 1/2000, 441, 442; *Schoibl*, in: FS Rainer Sprung (2001), p. 321, 334; *Mankowski*, in: FG Rudolf Machacek and Franz Matscher (2008), p. 785, 795.

[19] *Ansgar Staudinger*, in: Rauscher Art. 64 note 2; *Mankowski*, in: FG Rudolf Machacek and Franz Matscher (2008), p. 785, 795.

[20] Thereon e.g. *Hans Hönig v. Stadt Stockach*, (Case C-128/94) [1995] ECR I-3389; *Volker Steen v. Deutsche Post*, (Case C-332/90), [1992] ECR I-341; *Driancourt, Commissioner of police, carrying out the duties of Public Prosecutor v. Michel Cognet*, Case 355/85, [1986] ECR 3231, 3241 paras. 10–12; *Elestina Esselina Christina Morson v. State of the Netherlands and Head of the Plaatselijke Politie within the meaning of the Vriemdelingenwet; Sewradjie Jhanjan v. State of the Netherlands* (Joined Cases 35 and 36/82) [1982] ECR 3723, 3735–3737 paras. 11–18; *Mankowski*, DZWiR 1996, 200.

[21] See only *Oppermann*, Europarecht (3rd ed. 2005) § 25 para. 22; *Streinz*, in: Streinz (ed.), EUV/EGV (2003) Art. 12 EGV note 63; *Hammerl*, Inländerdiskriminierung (1996) p. 161; *Khan*, in: Geiger/Khan/Kotzur, EUV/AEUV 85th ed. 2010) Art. 18 AEUV note 15.

[22] *Mankowski*, in: FG Rudolf Machacek and Franz Matscher (2008), p. 785, 795.

even issue a verdict without hearing counsel for the defence if the accused fails to comply with an order to appear in person.[23]

Although the judgment in the annexed and ancillary civil proceedings might suffer and **8** might not be recognised in other Member States. Art. 64 *in fine* allows for discretion with regard to the recognition and enforcement of such decisions.[24] It should not be interpreted as requiring the courts seised in other Member States to automatically refuse recognition or enforcement automatically.[25] The discretion of the courts may be guided or restricted by their respective national legislation.[26] Seen systematically in the overall context of the Brussels I Regulation in its entirety,

Art. 64 *in fine* relates to Art. 45 and defines another ground on which recognition and **9** enforcement could be denied. Art. 64 *in fine* borrows its wording from Art. 61 *in fine* Brussels I Regulation where "enforced" relates to a different kind of proceedings than those envisaged where the Brussels I*bis* Regulation employs the notion "enforced". In Art. 61 *in fine* Brussels I Regulation "enforced" relates to exequatur proceedings. Exequatur proceedings do not exist anymore under the Brussels I*bis* system. Accordingly, the understanding of Art. 64 *in fine* ought to be adjusted. "Enforced" should be read as relating to enforcement and enforcement proceedings in the same sense as these notions are employed in Chapter III.

For the sake of ultimate clarity it might be added that even Art. 64 *in fine* does not deal with **10** the recognition and enforcement of the criminal verdict as such. Insofar Art. 1 (1) defines a clear and upheld borderline. In spite of the imminent, but not exhaustive links to Art. 7 (3) it should be clear that not only ancillary civil proceedings, in the technical sense, are envisaged.[27] The case of subsequent or separate civil proceedings pose the same question, and safeguarding human rights and establishing minimum standards should not depend on technicalities such as to whether proceedings are joint or not.[28]

Surrounding Art. 64 another issue arises and ought to be solved: Are courts in other Member **11** States bound and obliged to recognise and enforce judgments rendered in civil annex proceedings to criminal trials insofar as Art. 64 is does not applicable apply? Submitted, such an *argumentum e contrario* does not stand. The courts in other Member States are entitled to take full account of Art. 45, in particular, their respective national public policy under Art. 45 (1) (a) if the defendant was tried under for allegations of intentional wrongdoing.[29] If judicial support for this contention is required, it is amply provided by *Krombach v. Bamberski* where the ECJ without doubting the validity of this approach to be permissive for a second, had recourse to Art. 27 (1) Brussels Convention.[30]

---

[23] *Mankowski*, in: FG Rudolf Machacek and Franz Matscher (2008), p. 785, 795 *et seq.*

[24] *Kropholler/von Hein* Art. 64 note 3; *Schlosser* Art. 64 note 2; *Ansgar Staudinger*, in: Rauscher Art. 64 note 2.

[25] *Contra Geimer*, ZIP 2000, 862; *Hüßtege*, in: Thomas/Putzo Art. 64 note 1; *Geimer/Schütze* Art. 64 note 10.

[26] See *Ansgar Staudinger*, in: Rauscher Art. 64 note 2.

[27] Putting the question *Layton/Mercer* para. 30.035.

[28] *Mankowski*, in: FG Rudolf Machacek and Franz Matscher (2008), p. 785, 796.

[29] *Ansgar Staudinger*, in: Rauscher Art. 64 note 3; *Mankowski*, in: FG Rudolf Machacek and Franz Matscher (2008), p. 785, 796 *et seq.*

[30] *André Krombach v. Walter Bamberski* (Case C-7/98), [2000] ECR I-1935, I-1969 *et seq.* paras. 38–45.

Article 65

1. The jurisdiction specified in point 2 of Article 8 and Article 13 in actions on a warranty or guarantee or in any other third-party proceedings may be resorted to in the Member States included in the list established by the Commission pursuant to point (b) of Article 76(1) and Article 76(2) only in so far as permitted under national law. A person domiciled in another Member State may be invited to join the proceedings before the courts of those Member States pursuant to the rules on third-party notice referred to in that list.
2. Judgments given in a Member State by virtue of point 2 of Article 8 or Article 13 shall be recognised and enforced in accordance with Chapter III in any other Member State. Any effects which judgments given in the Member States included in the list referred to in paragraph 1 may have, in accordance with the law of those Member States, on third parties by application of paragraph 1 shall be recognised in all Member States.
3. The Member States included in the list referred to in paragraph 1 shall, within the framework of the European Judicial Network in civil and commercial matters established by Council Decision 2001/470/EC* ('the European Judicial Network') provide information on how to determine, in accordance with their national law, the effects of the judgments referred to in the second sentence of paragraph 2.

Bibliography

Chizzini, Gerichtspflichtigkeit von Dritten: Streit-verkündung und Interventionsklage (Italien), in: Bajons/Mayr/Zeiler (eds.), Die Übereinkommen von Brüssel und Lugano (1997), p. 163

Geimer, Härtetest für deutsche Dienstleister im Ausland, IPRax 1998, 175

von Hoffmann/Hau, Probleme der abredewidrigen Streitverkündung im europäischen Zivilrechtsver-kehr, RIW 1997, 89

Klicka, Die Bindungswirkung bei Streitgenossen-schaft und Streitverkündung, JBl 1997, 611

Köckert, Die Beteiligung Dritter im Internationalen Zivilverfahrensrecht (2010)

Bernd Kraft, Grenzüberschreitende Streitverkün-dung und Third Party Notice (1997)

Mansel, Vollstreckung eines französischen Garan-tieurteils bei gesellschaftsrechtlicher Rechtsnachfol-ge und andere vollstreckungsrechtliche Fragen des EuGVÜ, IPRax 1995, 362

Mansel, Streitverkündung und Interventionsklage im europäischen Internationalen Zivilprozessrecht, in: Hommelhoff/Jayme/Mangold (eds.), Europäi-

scher Binnenmarkt: IPR und Rechtsangleichung (1995), p. 161

Mansel, Gerichtsstandsvereinbarung und Aus-schluss der Streitverkündung, ZZP 109 (1996), 61

Mansel, Gerichtspflichtigkeit von Dritten: Streitver-kündung und Interventionsklage (Deutschland), in: Bajons/Mayr/Zeiler (eds.), Die Übereinkommen von Brüssel und Lugano (1997), p. 177

von Paris, Die Streitverkündung im europäischen Interventionsrecht (2011)

Rechberger, Der österreichische Oberste Gerichtshof als (Ersatz-)Gesetzgeber, in: FS Rolf A. Schütze zum 65. Geb. (1999), p. 711

Herbert Roth, Zur Überprüfung einer Streitverkün-dung im Vorprozess, IPRax 2003, 515

Rolf Stürner, Die erzwungene Intervention Dritter im europäischen Zivilprozess, in: FS Reinhold Gei-mer (2002), p. 1307

Wolfgang Winter, Ineinandergreifen von EuGVVO und nationalem Zivilverfahrensrecht am Beispiel des Gerichtsstands des Sachzusammenhangs (2007).

---

*   OJ L 174, 27.6.2001, p. 25.

I. Ratio legis

In some Member States actions for warranty or guarantee or genuine third party proceed- **1**
ings do not exist as a matter of their procedural codes.[1] Art. 65 pays due attention to this
particularity. This had to be dealt with in two regards, namely jurisdiction on the one hand
and recognition and enforcement on the other hand. The first issue is addressed by (1), the
second by (2). Unlike some other provisions of Chapter V, Art. 65 does not expire at a given
date of time. An implied prerequisite for the application of Art. 65 is that the case is within
the scope of application of the Brussels I*bis* Regulation.[2]

II. Legislative history

Germany being an initial Member State of the original Brussels Convention of 1968, she **2**
requested paying due respect to her national procedural law providing for the *Streitverkündung* only. Accordingly, Art. V Protocol Brussels Convention was drawn up very much
along the same lines, which can still be found in Art. 65. On the occasions of the numerous
accessions some Member States which followed the German model of *Streitverkündung*
joined the list whereas in substance not all alterations were administered to Art. V Protocol
Brussels Convention. Art. 65 is its direct successor *via* Art. 65 Brussels I Regulation. The
most recent new entry is Hungary as of 1 May 2004 added on the occasion of the 2003 Act of
Accession.

Art. 65 is redrafted in some aspects compared to Art. 65 Brussels I Regulation. Whereas **3**
Art. 65 Brussels I Regulation expressly listed the Member States following the German
model of *Streitverkündung* and their respective rules in the wording itself, the respective
list has now been relegated to the list established by the Commission pursuant to Art. 76 (1)
(b), (2) (b). Furthermore, (3) has been added.

III. Member States concerned

Under the Brussels I Regulation only three Member States are officially recognised as fol- **4**
lowing the German model of *Streitverkündung* disposing of actions for warranty, namely
Germany herself, Austria and Hungary. Art. 65 (1) cl. 2 Brussels I Regulation listed these
States as follows:

---

[1]   A comparative survey is conducted e.g. by *Spellenberg*, ZZP 106 (1993), 283; *Rolf Stürner*, in: FS Reinhold
      Geimer (2002), p. 1307.
[2]   *von Paris*, Die Streitverkündung im europäischen Interventionsrecht (2011) p. 69.

"Any person domiciled in another Member State may be sued in the courts:
(a) of Germany, pursuant to Articles 68 and 72 to 74 of the Code of Civil Procedure (Zivil-prozessordnung) concerning third-party notices,
(b) of Austria, pursuant to Article 21 of the Code of Civil Procedure (Zivilprozessordnung) concerning third-party notices,
(c) of Hungary, pursuant to Articles 58 to 60 of the Code of Civil Procedure (Polgári per-rendtartás) concerning third-party notices."

The same three Member States were listed in Art. 65 (2) Brussels I Regulation.

5   Although this list appears to be exhaustive and conclusive at first glance a somewhat puzz-ling case however was Spain: Art. V Protocol No. 1 1988 Lugano Convention featured Spain also whereas Art. V Protocol Brussels Convention even after the Fourth Accession Con-vention of Donostía-San Sebastian did not. The conundrum would be solved in the past by applying Art. V Protocol No. 1 Lugano Convention 1988 by way of analogy.[3] This way, however, is said to be barred in the event of Art. 65 in which Spain is not expressly men-tioned.[4] But the reason for not expressly including Spain in Art. V Protocol Brussels Con-vention simply was through the technical difficulty and the feared asynchrony from the reference since the instrument concerned was introduced into Spanish law not by legislative intervention, but as judge-made law judicially.[5] Considering this, the analogous application was to be the best solution by far (also with regard to Greece and Sweden[6]). The case for an *argumentum e contrario* is less strong and in fact rather weak, quite contrary to the first impression gained. Art. 65 can be taken as an express provision for the countries listed and serves its purpose well without being treated as exhaustive.[7] It must be conceded, though, that the case for an analogy with regard to Spain has lost considerably of its force after Spain has dropped out of Annex IX to the 2007 Lugano Convention, the successor to Annex II to Protocol No. 1 Lugano Convention 1988.[8]

6   The scope of Art. 65 has been extended quasi by the backdoor. Many of the States who became Member States in the EU accession rounds of 2004, 2007 and 2013 follow the Germanic model. The 2007 Lugano Convention already contained a very strong indication in that direction: The EC made a reservation to Art. II Protocol 1 to the 2007 Lugano Convention. It declared that proceedings referred to in Articles 6 (2) and 11 2007 Lugano Convention may not be resorted to in Estonia, Latvia, Lithuania, Poland and Slovenia in addition to the three Member States Germany, Austria and Hungary already mentioned in Annex IX to the 2007 Lugano Convention. Therefore, in accordance with Art. 77 (2) 2007 Lugano Convention the Standing Committee set up by Art. 4 Protocol 2 to the 2007 Lugano

---

3   Report *Almeida Cruz/Desantes Real/Jenard* para. 22; *Mansel*, in: Wieczorek/Schütze, ZPO, Vol. I/2 (3rd ed 1994) § 68 ZPO note 14; *Mansel*, in: Hommelhoff/Jayme/Mangold (eds.), Europäischer Binnenmarkt: IPR und Rechtsangleichung (1995), p. 161, 194–199.

4   *Geimer/Schütze* Art. 65 note 5.

5   Report *Almeida Cruz/Desantes Real/Jenard* para. 22.

6   See *Mansel*, in: Bajons/Mayr/Zeiler (eds.), Die Übereinkommen von Brüssel und Lugano (1997), p. 177, 188.

7   *Mansel* (fn. 3), p. 161, 196.

8   See *Geimer/Schütze* Art. 6 note. 36, Art. 65 note 5; *Rohner/Lerch*, in: Basler Kommentar Art. II Protokoll 1 LugÜ note 4; *von Paris* (fn. 2), p. 67.

Convention should as soon as the 2007 Lugano Convention entered into force be requested to amend Annex IX to the 2007 Lugano Convention. The Standing Committee complied with this request on 3 May 2011, and Annex IX to the 2007 Lugano was amended as of 3 May 2011 accordingly.[9]

The 2011 amendment of Annex IX to the 2007 Lugano Convention added to the entries **7** concerning Germany, Austria and Hungary the following:
– "Estonia: Article 214 (3) and (4) and Article 216 of the Code of Civil Procedure (tsiviilkohtumenetluse seadustik) concerning third-party notices;
– Latvia: Articles 78, 79, 80 and 81 of the Civil Procedure Law (Civilprocesa likums) concerning third-party notices;
– Lithuania: Article 47 of the Code of Civil Procedure (Civilino proceso kodeksas);
– Poland: Articles 84 and 85 of the Code of Civil Procedure (Kodeks postępowania cywilnego) concerning third-party notices (przypozwanie);
– Slovenia: Article 204 of the Civil Procedure Act (Zakon o pravdnem postopku) concerning third-party notices."

Why (1) cl. 2 does not follow explicitly in the footprints of the now amended Annex IX to the 2007 Lugano Convention and is not amended expressly in the same vein begs reason. The missing amendment in the wording does not give rise to an *argumentum e contrario* and thus does not bar anything. Sometimes Greece and Sweden were added on top of that as candidates for an analogous application of Art. 65 Brussels *Ibis* Regulation/2007 Lugano Convention.[10]

Howsoever, the current authority is the one established by List 2 of the information which **8** the Commission published pursuant to Art. 76 (1) (c) in January 2015.[11] This List reads:

"**List 2**

The rules on third party-notice referred to in Article 65 are the following:
– in Belgium, not applicable,
– in Bulgaria, not applicable,
– in Czech Republic, not applicable,
– in Denmark, not applicable,
– in Germany, Sections 68 and 72–74 of the Code of Civil Procedure,
– in Estonia, Sections 212–216 of the Code of Civil Procedure,
– in Greece, not applicable,
– in Spain, not applicable,
– in France, not applicable,
– in Croatia, Article 211 of the Civil Procedure Act,
– in Ireland, not applicable,
– in Italy, not applicable,

---

[9]   AS 2011, 6059.
[10] *von Paris* (fn. 2), p. 67.
[11] The information referring to Article 76 of Regulation (EU) No. 1215/2012 of the European Parliament and of the Ouncil on jurisdiction and recognition and enforcement of judgments in civil and commercial matters, OJ EU 2015 C 4/2.

- in Cyprus, Order 10 of the Civil Procedure Rules on Third Party Procedure,
- in Latvia, Articles 78, 79, 80, 81 and 75 of the Law on civil procedure,
- in Lithuania, Articles 46 and 47 of the Lithuanian Code of Civil Procedure,
- in Luxembourg, not applicable,
- in Hungary, Articles 58–60(a) of Act III of 1952 on the Civil Proceedings Code concerning third-party notices,
- in Malta, Article 960 to 962 of the Code of Organization and Civil Procedure (Chapter 12 of the Laws of Malta),
- in the Netherlands, not applicable,
- in Austria, Article 21 of the Code of Civil Procedure,
- in Poland, Articles 84 and 85 of the Code of Civil Procedure concerning third-party notice,
- in Portugal, not applicable,
- In Romania, not applicable,
- in Slovenia, Article 204 of the Civil Procedure Act, which governs third-party notice,
- in Slovakia, not applicable,
- in Finland, not applicable,
- in Sweden, not applicable,
- in the United Kingdom, not applicable."

9 Most entries are logical and not surprising given the progeny in Annex IX of the 2007 Lugano Convention. The Member States listed ordinarily had some relation or some affinity to the German or Austrian law of civil procedure in the past, if sometimes only in a rather distant past. This applies for instance to Croatia. Spain certifies that it does not regard his own law as a qualifier. Thus any trouble possibly generated by Art. V Protocol No. 1 1988 Lugano Convention[12] has been authoritatively overruled and erased.

10 But two entries are genuine surprises if one takes into account their vicinity to the English legal system, namely Cyprus and Malta. The surprise is the greater since neither of them is listed in Annex IX of the 2007 Lugano Convention which makes for an odd discrepancy begging explanation (or a respective correction of the said Annex in due course). But every Member State can and should be taken by its word as relayed and conveyed by its own government to the Commission. If Cyprus and Malta nominate rules of their national laws respectively as qualifiers for the purposes of Art. 65 they are believed to have the best insight into their own legal system.

IV. *Streitverkündung* (third party notice)

11 The *Streitverkündung* does not add the third party as a true and genuine, full-fledged party to the proceedings, but only elevates it into a special participating role. It has to be distinguished clearly from any motions adding the third party as a true and genuine party like e.g. the *parteierweiternde Widerklage* (which in some instances is permitted under German procedural law). What can be characterised as a *Streitverkündung* or a like third party notice must be answered by the *lex fori* pursuant to a dynamic reference by (1).[13]

12 Procedural requirements and formalities of the *Streitverkündung* are a matter of the national

---

[12] See *supra* Art. 65 note 5 (*Mankowski*).

[13] *Mansel* (fn. 3), p. 161, 191.

law of the *forum*.[14] This even extends to the issue of whether the *Streitverkündung* must be served on the third party; Art. 65 itself does not establish any prerequisite to this aim.[15] Neither is international jurisdiction necessary as though the third party was added as another defendant to the proceedings.[16] The main condition precedent is that the Regulation itself is applicable by virtue of Art. 4 as the defendant (not the third party!) is domiciled in a Member State.[17] The proceedings to which the Regulation must be applicable are the original proceedings not any possible future redress proceedings against the now third party, then defendant.[18] Jurisdiction is guaranteed if the third party is domiciled in another Member State than the forum State,[19] a parallel to Art. 7 pr. Accordingly, Art. 65 is not operable where the third party is domiciled in the forum State.[20]

If and insofar the *lex fori* relates to reasons of substantive law for permitting a third party **13** notice, the PIL of the *lex fori* must lead to the applicable substantive law.[21] Also for the purposes of Art. 65, the *Streitverkündung* is effective without further requirements to be being met and or against any person against to whom it was declared against and to whom it was properly notified, regardless whether this person later joins, and participates in, the proceedings or not if the national law of the *forum* decides so.[22] The *lex fori* establishes under which circumstances a *Streitverkündung* is permitted, in particular which degree of interest either party to the proceedings must have in the third party being drawn in the proceedings.[23] The *lex fori* has also to rule who is entitled to issue a *Streitverkündung*.

Nevertheless, (1) does not apply directly if the third party is domiciled outside the EU.[24] But **14** this is not the end of the line: Although (1) cl. 2 mentions that the third party should have its domicile in a Member State, this can not be a condition precedent. To the contrary, the *rationale* behind Art. 6 (1) indicates that (1) cl. 2 applies *a fortiori* if the third party is domiciled in a non-Member State.[25]

Art. 8 (2) safeguards against any abuse or misuse of third party proceedings. The idea **15** underlying this is a general idea. It can be transferred to Art. 65 (1) cl. 2: If the proceedings

---

14 *Mansel* (fn. 3), p. 161, 186.

15 *Mansel* (fn. 6), p. 177, 184 *et seq.*

16 *Mansel*, in: Wieczorek/Schütze (fn. 3), § 68 ZPO note 14; *Mansel* (fn. 3), p. 161, 188. But cf. *Bernd Kraft*, Grenzüberschreitende Streitverkündung und Third Party Notice (1997) pp. 111–113: jurisdiction necessary, but granted by (now) Art. 65; cf. also *Taupitz*, ZZP 102 (1989), 288, 313 *et seq.*

17 *Mansel* (fn. 3), p. 161, 189; *Mansel* (fn. 6), p. 177, 187; *Wolfgang Winter*, Ineinandergreifen von EuGVVO und nationalem Zivilverfahrensrecht am Beispiel des Gerichtsstands des Sachzusammenhangs (2007) p. 91; see also *von Paris* (fn. 2), pp. 69–70.

18 *Mansel* (fn. 3), p. 161, 190; *Mansel* (fn. 6), p. 177, 187; *Köckert*, Die Beteiligung Dritter im Internationalen Zivilverfahrensrecht (2010) p. 92; *von Paris* (fn. 2), p. 70.

19 *von Paris* (fn. 2), p. 71, 74.

20 *von Paris* (fn. 2), p. 71.

21 *Mansel* (fn. 3), p. 161, 186 *et seq.*

22 OGH TranspR 2004, 251, 254; *Czernich*, in: Czernich/Kodek/Mayr, Art. 8 note 24.

23 *von Paris* (fn. 2), pp. 72–73.

24 *Mansel* (fn. 6), p. 177, 187 *et seq.*

25 *Mansel*, in: Wieczorek/Schütze (fn. 3), § 68 ZPO note 14.

Peter Mankowski

are only instituted in order to drag the third party out of its home jurisdiction, Art. 8 (2) *in fine* should be applied *per analogiam*.[26]

V. Recognition and enforcement

16   With regard to recognition and enforcement the general guideline is crystal-clear: Since Art. 45 (3) prohibits courts in the State where recognition or enforcement is sought, to examine on which grounds or heads the court giving judgment had based its jurisdiction save for Art. 45 (1) (e), it must not matter whether actions for warranty or guarantee on the one hand or *Streitverkündung* on the other hand are known to the former State. Accordingly, states adhering to either system are obliged to recognise and enforce judgments rendered in states of the other system respectively, i.e. regardless whether their own system comprises the other legal institution or not.

17   Courts in the Member States named in List 2 have to recognise and enforce judgments rendered in other Member States where the courts giving judgment based their jurisdiction on Art. 8 (2).[27] The courts in the country where recognition or enforcement is sought are prevented from checking whether the court giving the original judgments applied Art. 8 (2) correctly, by virtue of Art. 45 (3).[28] In the consequences of which, Art. 8 (2) is by no means irrelevant for parties domiciled in states following the Germanic system, but could to the contrary gain rather high relevance for exporters domiciled there, that and delivering to customers in states following the Romanic system[29] (and might generate just another incentive to insert a jurisdiction clause in a contract[30]). Yet the condition of recognition and enforcement under (2) cl. 1 might be differentiated as to the person concerned (defendant or third party).[31]

18   *Au revanche* courts in the other Member States are bound by (2) cl. 2 to recognise the effects of a judgment rendered after a third party notice by a court in state following the Germanic system of *Streitverkündung*.[32] This applies even if that state is not listed in (1).[33] It is not the *Streitverkündung* as such that is recognised but the effects ensuing from it and the judgment reached.[34] This has the important consequence that (2) cl. 2 is applicable even if the third party is domiciled in the *forum* state or in a non-Member State.[35] Recognition must have the result of conferring on judgments the same authority and effectiveness accorded to them in

---

[26]   *Bernd Kraft* (fn. 15), p. 113; *von Paris* (fn. 2), p. 75. But cf. tentatively contra *Mansel*, ZZP 107 (1996), 61, 94.

[27]   See only BGH IPRax 1998, 205; OLG Düsseldorf RIW 1997, 330; *Rechberger*, in: FS Rolf A. Schütze (1999), p. 711, 713.

[28]   *Geimer*, IPRax 1998, 175; *Geimer/Schütze* Art. 65 note 3.

[29]   See only *Geimer*, IPRax 1998, 175; *Neumayr*, EuGVÜ/LGVÜ (1999) p. 39; *Czernich*, in: Czernich/Kodek/Mayr, Art. 8 note 24.

[30]   *Czernich*, in: Czernich/Kodek/Mayr, Art. 8 note 24.

[31]   *Mansel*, in: Wieczorek/Schütze (fn. 3), § 68 ZPO note 46; *Mansel* (fn. 3), p. 161, 249–252; cf. also OLG Hamburg RIW 1975, 499; OLG Hamm IPRspr. 1976 Nr 171; LG Hamburg AWD 1974, 403.

[32]   See only *Herbert Roth*, IPRax 2003, 515, 516.

[33]   *Mansel* (fn. 3), p. 161, 212 *et seq.*

[34]   *Mansel* (fn. 3), p. 161, 210 *et seq.*; *von Paris* (fn. 2), p. 96.

[35]   *Mansel* (fn. 3), p. 161, 213 *et seq.*

the state they were given.[36] Nevertheless some problems might remain if for instance time bars or limitation periods are stopped from running by the applicable substantive law already on a third party notice as such, thus attributing such effect not to the ensuing judgment, but to aforementioned going steps in the procedure.[37]

No further prerequisite exists but the recognition of the judgment against the defendant as **19** such.[38] Although, recognition has to be ascertained in accordance with Art. 45, though.[39] A sound administration of justice might cast some doubt as to whether Art. 45 (3) can be fully applied in relation to the third party.[40] The effects following from the third party notice have to be ascertained pursuant to the national law of the court which has given judgment; insofar (2) contains a reference to this national law.[41] Procedural effects are envisaged, although effects in substantive law are of minor quality but still qualify.[42] If the judiciary seizes upon the opportunity from the advent of Art. 65 to introduce procedural effects in their national law[43] this is entirely within the realm of the national law.[44] For the purposes of recognition and enforcement, it is irrelevant whether the court which decided the case would have had jurisdiction as against the third party if the third party had would have also been sued as a proper defendant, too.[45] Furthermore, the reference to § 74 ZPO, including its third paragraph, implies that recognition and enforcement is mandatory in principle even if the third party did not join the proceedings.[46] The grounds, on which recognition can be refused, are the same as in Art. 45 yet *mutatis mutandis* and appropriately adapted in relation to the third party.[47]

A *lacuna* in the overall system is the recognition of the effects of a judgment rendered after a **20** third party notice in a country which generally follows the Romanic model of actions for warranty or guarantee, but nevertheless allows the third party notice as an additional option. This is the case in Italy *(denuncia di lite)* and in England.[48] Although, the case is different with France *(jugement commun and chose jugée opposable à un tiers et à lui fermer de ce fait la tierce opposition)*, though, since the *appel en déclaration de jugement commun*[49] adds the third party as a proper and genuine party to the proceedings.[50] As (2) evidently aims at safeguarding the recognition (and enforcement) in every possible respect, whichever the

---

36 Report *Jenard* p. 59.

37 *Bernd Kraft* (fn. 15), pp. 294–301.

38 See only *Mansel*, in: Wieczorek/Schütze (fn. 3), § 68 ZPO note 25, 40; *Bernd Kraft* (fn. 15), p. 290; *Rechberger*, in: FS Rolf A. Schütze zum 65. Geb. (1999), p. 711, 715; *von Paris* (fn. 2), p. 94.

39 *Herbert Roth*, IPRax 2003, 515, 516; *von Paris* (fn. 2), p. 94.

40 In detail *von Paris* (fn. 2), pp. 111–129; see also OLG Köln IPRax 2003, 531.

41 *Klicka*, JBl 1997, 611, 612.

42 *Mansel* (fn. 3), p. 161, 210.

43 As 2GH SZ 70/60 = ecolex 1997, 422 with note *Oberhammer* = JAP 1997/98, 41 with note *Chiwitt-Oberhammer* did for Austrian law.

44 Criticising the OGH e.g. *Klicka*, JBl 1997, 611; *Rechberger*, in: FS Rolf A. Schütze (1999), p. 711.

45 *Rechberger*, in: FS Rolf A. Schütze (1999), p. 711, 715.

46 *Mansel* (fn. 3), p. 161, 215.

47 See in full detail *Mansel*, in: Wieczorek/Schütze (fn. 3), § 68 ZPO note 40; *Mansel* (fn. 3), p. 161, 218–223.

48 Parts 20.13, 19.3 (5) CPR 1998 and previously Order 16 r. 4 (4) RSC.

49 Art. 331 (2) ncpc.

50 *Mansel* (fn. 3), p. 161, 237 *et seq.*

model is adopted by the national law of the court giving judgment, the *lacuna* should be filled by applying (2) by way of analogy.[51]

VI. Lis pendens and Streitverkündung

21 Art. 65 is silent about solving the problem of parallel proceedings of which at least one involves a *Streitverkündung*. It does not expressly declare Arts. 29–34 applicable. But the rules on *lis pendens* at their core reflect that a future judgment would be recognised, and (2) deals exactly with the recognition of the effects of a *Streitverkündung*. Accordingly, it is only consequential that Arts. 29–34 should be applied to resolve any ensuing conflicts, either directly or *per analogiam*.[52]

VII. Information duties of the Member States following the Germanic model of Streitverkündung

22 (3) obliges the Member States following the Germanic model of *Streitverkündung* and included in the list referred to in (1), to provide within the framework of the European Judicial Network information on how to determine, in accordance with their national law, the effects of the judgments referred to in (2) cl. 2, i.e. judgments given in other Member States by virtue of Art. 8 (2) or Art. 13. A like rule was not contained in the Brussels I*bis* Proposal.

23 Since the national laws following the Germanic model of *Streitverkündung* generally do not contain any rules on extending an effect of *res iudicata* and even less enforceability to non-parties (in the formal sense) of the initial proceedings the obligation to recognise and enforce respective judgments given in other Member States, imposed by (2) cl. 2 poses quite some difficulty for them. They have to provide for a solution beyond the ordinary. The cases concern judgment creditors from abroad, or more precisely: creditors who are favoured by a judgment given in another Member State. They carry a certain cross-border element, thus. Creditors and parties not privy to knowledge about the particularities of the respective national laws, have a keen interest in reliable information about the ways they can avail themselves of their judgments in the respective jurisdictions.

VIII. Discrimination violating Art. 18 TFEU?

24 Sometimes restricting defendant parties in German, Austrian or Hungarian proceedings to a mere *Streitverkündung* without an opportunity to add third parties as cross-defendants is said to shorten their judicial protection in a discriminatory manner contravening Art. 18 TFEU as they cannot obtain a genuine judgment positively testifying their position and providing a true title, whereas such an opportunity is granted to defendants sued in other Member States under Art. 6 (2).[53] It remains to be seen whether such allegation will eventually find favour with the CJEU. As long as the CJEU has not declared Art. 65 to be in contradiction to Art. 18 TFEU, the former provision must be applied.

---

[51] See *Mansel* (fn. 3), p. 161, 212 *et seq.*; *Rolf Stürner*, in: FS Reinhold Geimer (2002), p. 1307, 1314.

[52] See OLG Hamburg OLGR Hamburg/Schleswig/Bremen 1997, 13; OLG Frankfurt IPRspr. 1989 Nr 210b; LG Frankfurt/Main IPRax 1990, 234; *von Paris* (fn. 2), pp. 141–162.

[53] *Geimer*, IPRax 2002, 69, 74; *Geimer/Schütze* Art. 65 note 6 and Art. 6 note 39. *Contra Schlosser* Art. 6 note 8; *von Paris* (fn. 2), pp. 98–100.

IX. Voluntary third party intervention

Art. 65 deals with the third party notice, i.e. the forced inclusion of a third party forced by the 25
defendant or the plaintiff, exclusively. This follows unambiguously from the provisions of
the national laws which that are referred to. Those laws are solely and strictly concerned with
the said matter. Hence, Art. 65 does not have direct impact on the treatment of a voluntary
third party intervention. The event that a third party voluntarily joins the proceedings on by
its own motion and issues, for instance, an interpleader, is not expressly covered nor envisaged. But this should not mislead to the assumption that an *argumentum e contrario*
succumbs and that Art. 65 could not be applied by way of analogy insofar as it containing a
suitable and appropriate solution. At least (2) should be applied by way of analogy, thus
guaranteeing recognition (and, if suitable, enforcement) of judgments and their effects as
against or in favour of the intervening third party.[54]

Chapter VI: **Transitional Provisions**

Article 66

1. This Regulation shall apply only to legal proceedings instituted, to authentic instruments
   formally drawn up or registered and to court settlements approved or concluded on or after
   10 January 2015.
2. Notwithstanding Article 80, Regulation (EC) No. 44/2001 shall continue to apply to judgments
   given in legal proceedings instituted, to authentic instruments formally drawn up or registered and to court settlements approved or concluded before 10 January 2015 which fall
   within the scope of that Regulation.

Bibliography

Michael Becker/Karla Müller, Intertemporale
Urteilsanerkennung und Art. 66 EuGVO, IPRax
2006, 432
Bonaduce, L'interpretazione della convenzione
di Bruxelles del 1968 alle luce del regolamento
n. 44/2001 nelle pronuncie della Corte di Giustizia,
Riv. dir. int. 2003, 746
Hau, Intertemporale Anwendungsprobleme der
Brüssel II-VO, IPRax 2003, 461
Hess, Gerichtsstandsvereinbarungen zwischen
EuGVÜ und ZPO, IPRax 1992, 358
Hess, Die intertemporale Anwendung des Europä-
ischen Zivilprozessrechts in den Beitrittsstaaten,
IPRax 2004, 374

Martiny/Ulrich Ernst, Der Beitritt Polens zum
Luganer Übereinkommen, IPRax 2001, 29
Moura Vicente, Da aplicação no tempo e no espaço
das Convenções de Bruxelas de 1968 e de Lugano de
1988, Rev. Fac. Dir. Univ. Lisboa 1994, 461
Rauscher, Intertemporale Anwendung des Art. 21
EuGVÜ, IPRax 1999, 80
Schoibl, Zum zeitlichen Anwendungsbereich und
zum Ratifikationsstand des Brüsseler Übereinkom-
mens und zum Konkurrenzverhältnis der beiden
Europäischen Gerichtsstandsübereinkommen
EuGVÜ – LGVÜ, ÖJZ 2000, 481

---

[54]   *Mansel* (fn. 3), p. 161, 199 *et seq.*; *Mansel* (fn. 6), p. 177, 188.

Thomale, Brüssel I und die Osterweiterung – Zum raumzeitlichen Anwendungsbereich der EuGVVO, IPRax 2014, 239

Thorn, Gerichtsstand des Erfüllungsorts und intertemporales Zivilverfahrensrecht, IPRax 2004, 354

Trunk, Erste deutsche Rechtsprechung zum Lugano-Übereinkommen: Gerichtsstandsvereinbarung, Gerichtsstand des Erfüllungsortes und intertemporale Fragen, IPRax 1996, 249

Vlas, De EEX-Verordening en het voergangsrecht, in: Bundel Ingrid Joppe (2002), p. 235

Rolf Wagner, Zum zeitlichen Anwendungsbereich des Lugano Übereinkommens, ZIP 1994, 82

Rolf Wagner, Der Beitritt Österreichs, Finnlands und Schwedens zum Brüsseler Gerichtsstands- und Vollstreckungsübereinkommen vom 27.9.1968, RIW 1998, 590

Rolf Wagner, Zum Inkrafttreten des Lugano-Übereinkommens für Polen, WiRO 2000, 47.

I. General considerations

1 Art. 66 contains the main rule of transition and defines the temporal scope of application of the Brussels I*bis* Regulation. Its predecessor, Art. 66 Brussels I Regulation, aimed at providing for continuity between the Brussels Convention and the Brussels I Regulation as Recital (19) asserts.[1] Therefore the principle of non-retroactivity is implemented but for the exceptions in (2) which extend the even more favourable rules on recognition and enforcement, as implemented by the Regulation under specified circumstances, to judgments given before the Regulation entered into force.[2]

2 Art. 66 follows the path laid out and charted by Art. 54 of the original Brussels Convention of 1968, Art. 34 First Accession Convention of 1978, Art. 12 Second Accession Convention of 1982, Art. 29 Third Accession Convention of 1989, Art. 13 Fourth Accession Convention of 1996 and Art. 66 Brussels I Regulation. The solution developed there has proved highly successful and has not given rise to major problems. Art. 66 has to be observed by courts *ex officio* of their own motion.[3]

3 Yet it might be added that the subsequent Regulation can be an auxiliary means in interpreting the preceding provisions of the Brussels I Regulation. Although not being applicable in the strict sense *ratione temporis*, the amendment might shed some light on the earlier provisions.[4] The ECJ has seised upon, and gratefully endorsed, this approach when called upon to interpret Art. 5 (3) Brussels Convention in *Henkel* and relied on Art. 5 (3) Brussels I Regulation.[5] Nevertheless, caution is necessary: If the Brussels I*bis* Regulation contains a

---

[1] See also Commission Proposal COM (1999) 348 final p. 27.

[2] *Kropholler/von Hein* Art. 66 note 2.

[3] Cass. Bull. civ. 2006 I n° 424 p. 366.

[4] See in particular *Bonaduce*, Riv. dir. int. 2003, 746, 752–758.

[5] *Verein für Konsumenteninformation v. Karl Heinz Henkel* (Case C-167/00), [2002] ECR I-8111, I-8143 para. 49.

substantive amendment of, or a radical alteration compared to, its predecessor, the Brussels I Regulation must be interpreted solely in its own right, as for instance with regard to Art. 27 (2) Brussels Convention whereas Art. 34 (2) Brussels I Regulation aimed at a significant improvement.[6]

II. Rules on jurisdiction

1. In general

Pursuant to (1) the rules on jurisdiction, as established by Arts. 4–24 and 26, apply if the **4** proceedings were instituted on 10 January 2015 or later.[7] The said rules are not applicable if the proceedings were instituted before 10 January 2015, i.e. on 9 January 2015 or earlier.[8] The borderline is clear-cut and in principle easily intelligible. The date when the Regulation becomes applicable pursuant to Art. 81 subpara. 2 marks its scope of application as to the timely extension.

(1) refrains from applying the rules of the Regulation retroactively. Thus the plaintiff's case **5** is lost for lack of jurisdiction if the court seised did not have jurisdiction pursuant to the rules in force when the lawsuit was initiated even if now the Brussels I*bis* Regulation provided a fitting head of jurisdiction rendering the court seised competent if only the proceedings were instituted after the Brussels I*bis* Regulation became applicable.[9] On the other hand, jurisdiction is retained as a matter of *perpetuatio fori* if it existed at the time when the proceedings were instituted before 10 January 2015, pursuant to the then applicable rules, whereas a like head of jurisdiction would not exist under the Brussels I*bis* Regulation.[10] Insofar the balance between the plaintiff's interests and the need to protect the defendant is struck in the plaintiff's favour.[11]

As to when proceedings are instituted is not expressly defined in (1), and an express re- **6** ference to Art. 32 is not contained, either. Nevertheless, to answer the question by applying the yardsticks of Art. 32[12] appears by far the most convincing manner. Methodologically some doubts might remain,[13] but every alternative would be even more imperfect since it

---

6   BGH NJW 2004, 3189 = RIW 2004, 941, 942 = EuLF 2004, 288 with note *Simons*; BGH InVo 2005, 427, 428.
7   See only OLG Düsseldorf March 7, 2003 – 23 U 199/02; OLG Düsseldorf IHR 2004, 108, 109; LG Trier IHR 2004, 115.
8   E.g. OLG Köln IHR 2005, 174, 175 and in the extreme Rb. Arnhem NIPR 2003 Nr 49 p. 101: Brussels I Regulation was held not to be applicable when proceedings were instituted on 27 February 2002.
9   BGHZ 116, 77 = ZZP 105 (1992), 330 with note *Bork*; BGE 119 II 391, 393 = SZIER 1995, 39 with note *Schwander*; *Ansgar Staudinger*, in: Rauscher Art. 66 note 3; *Geimer/Schütze* Art. 66 note 3.
10 A-G *Strikwerda*, NIPR 2004 Nr 98 p. 171.
11 *Contra Thorn*, IPRax 2004, 354, 355.
12 OGH ZfRV 2004, 32; LG Berlin IPRax 2005, 261 with note *Jayme*; *Béraudo*, Clunet 128 (2001), 1033, 1036; *Kropholler/von Hein* Art. 66 note 2; *Briggs/Rees* para. 2.21; *Schlosser* Art. 66 note 11; *Hau*, IPRax 2003, 461; *Geimer/Schütze* Art. 66 note 2; *Mayr*, in: Fasching/Konecny, Kommentar zu den Zivilprozessgesetzen, vol. III (2nd ed. 2004) Vor § 230 ZPO note 49; *Mayr*, RabelsZ 69 (2005), 558, 566.
13 OLG Koblenz 7 March 2003 – Case 23 U 199/02; OLG Düsseldorf IHR 2004, 108, 109; OLG Düsseldorf RIW 2006, 632, 633; *Ansgar Staudinger*, in: Rauscher Art. 66 note 2; *Thorn*, IPRax 2004, 354, 355 fn. 8.

would consist of a recourse to the diverging national laws of the Member States[14] giving the Regulation an uneven start depending on the law of the respective forum state.[15] Seizing upon assistance rendered by Art. 32 has at least the major advantage of being a solution uniform solution at the starting point and in guaranteeing for a single mode of entry into force for the how the Regulation entered into force for all Member States throughout the entire EU[16] (with the exception of Denmark, that is). The third and last sentence of Recital (15) Brussels I Regulation could be read as supporting such a contention. That the wordings of Art. 66 and Art. 32 respectively are not perfectly synchronised as both employ different language should not amount to an obstacle effectively.[17] But at least the case is different compared to the Brussels Convention where the single Accession Conventions entered into force state by state and not at a uniform point of time.[18] An *argumentum e contrario* from the very existence of transitional rules and Recital (19) backing them does not appear conclusive, either.[19]

7 Croatia became a Member State of the EU as of 1 July 2013.[20] It accepted that the *acquis communautaire* would become part of Croatian law by that date. Hence, the Brussels I*bis* Regulation entered into force for Croatia on 1 July 2013. As 1 July 2013 was before 10 January 2015, Art. 66 can apply without any modification or adaptation with regard to Croatia.[21] The case is different from the accessions of 2004 and 2007 where the date set by Art. 66 (1) Brussels I Regulation had already lapsed. Then the respective date of accession was the relevant date for the entry into force and the becoming effective of the Brussels I Regulation with regard to the acceding States.[22] This caused some lack of synchronicity.[23] It generated intricate questions as to whether a judgment given before the entry of the Brussels I Regulation into force for the Member State addressed could be recognised and enforced under Arts. 38 *et seq.* Brussels I Regulation or not.[24]

2. Agreements on jurisdiction and jurisdiction clauses

8 Agreements on jurisdiction and jurisdiction clauses are special. By their means the parties themselves take over and attempt to contract for a certain security in jurisdictional matters. They often reflect the outcome of a struggle in which each party tried to get a home game. If a contracting party is able to concentrate all lawsuits in which it might be involved at one place

---

14 OLG Stuttgart MDR 2003, 350, 351 with note *Stefan Braun*; *Ansgar Staudinger*, in: Rauscher Art. 66 note 2.

15 *Hau*, IPRax 2003, 461. See (for the Brussels Convention which did not comprise an equivalent to the present Art. 32) BGHZ 132, 105, 107.

16 Readily admitted by *Ansgar Staudinger*, in: Rauscher Art. 66 note 2.

17 *Geimer/Schütze* Art. 66 note 2.

18 See there *Trunk*, IPRax 1996, 249, 250.

19 *Contra* OLG Düsseldorf IHR 2004, 108, 109.

20 Treaty of Accession of 24 April 2012, OJ EU 2012 L 112/10.

21 *Babić*, in: Garašić (ur.), Europsko građansko procesno pravo – Izabrane teme (Zagreb 2013), p. 137, 145 *et seq.* Not clear *Thomale*, IPRax 2014, 239, 242.

22 *Wolf Naturprodukte GmbH v. SEWAR spol. s r.o.* (Case C-514/10), nyr. para. 19.

23 *Thomale*, IPRax 2014, 239.

24 In the latter sense *Wolf Naturprodukte GmbH v. SEWAR spol. s r.o.* (Case C-514/10), nyr. paras. 22–35. In the former sense *Thomale*, IPRax 2014, 239, 240–242.

this allows for rationalisation and cost-saving. Jurisdiction agreements are an instrument of calculation. Alterations in the yardsticks against which they are measured deeply concerns their inherent value for the parties. Jurisdiction agreements ordinarily exist long time before the outbreak of an actual lawsuit and actual court proceedings. Hence, applying (1) by the letter would do grave injustice to them and would be inappropriate in all those events where court proceedings are never initiated. It has to be taken into account seriously that the time of their conclusion and the time when they will actually have an effects on court proceedings might differ wildly. As a starting point, for matters of consensus and formation only the former point of time, i.e. when the agreement is concluded, can be relevant.[25] Parties to an agreement are simply not blessed with the benefit of hindsight.

It is hotly debated whether as to the validity of jurisdiction agreements, the time of their **9** formation[26] or the time when a concrete lawsuit is initiated and court proceedings are instituted,[27] is the material point of time. It is submitted that a differentiating answer is the correct one:[28] If a jurisdiction agreement fulfils all requirements which are in force at the time when proceedings are instituted, it is valid in any event.[29] Insofar even a previous invalidity under the then applicable regime could be overcome and cured.[30] Yet if a jurisdiction agreement does not fulfil stricter requirements now in force under the new version, but was valid pursuant to the requirements that which were in force when the parties concluded it, the earlier provisions should prevail. As the parties relied on them and could only use them as the test and guideline available when they needed it, the parties' reliance ought to be protected, the initial validity should be maintained, and the jurisdiction agreement should not be rendered invalid.[31]

Unfortunately the ECJ characterises jurisdiction agreements as an option with regard to **10** jurisdiction only having effect and being actualised from the time proceedings are institu-

---

25   *Mankowski*, in: Rauscher Art. 23 note 75; *Hüßtege*, in: Thomas/Putzo Art. 23 note 19.

26   In favour of this solution *Gothot/Holleaux*, Clunet 98 (1971), 764, 775; *Bork*, in: Stein/Jonas, ZPO, Vol. I (22nd ed. 2003) § 38 ZPO note 25; *Calvo Caravaca*, in: Calvo Caravaca, Art. 17 note 5.

27   In favour of this solution *Sanicentral GmbH v. René Collin* (Case 25/79), [1979] ECR 3423, 3429 *et seq.* paras. 6 *et seq.*; BGH WM 1976, 401; Cassaz. RDIPP 1992, 327; CA Versailles JCP 1991 II 21672 with note *Martin-Serf*; Rb. Breda WPNR 1981, 771; Trib. Milano RDIPP 1988, 745; LG Berlin IPRax 2005, 261 with note *Jayme*; *Droz* no. 190; *Benecke*, Die teleologische Reduktion des räumlich-persönlichen Anwendungsbereichs von Art. 2 ff. und Art. 17 EuGVÜ (1993) p. 86; *Samtleben*, RabelsZ 59 (1995), 670, 703 *et seq.*; *Martiny/Ulrich Ernst*, IPRax 2001, 29; *Schack* para. 465; *Ansgar Staudinger*, in: Rauscher Art. 66 notes 7 *et seq.*; *Geimer/Schütze* Art. 66 note 3.

28   *Mankowski*, in: Rauscher Art. 23 note 76.

29   *Sanicentral GmbH v. René Collin* (Case 25/79), [1979] ECR 3423, 3429 *et seq.* paras. 6 *et seq.*; OGH ZfRV 2005, 32; LG Bochum RIW 2000, 382, 384.

30   *Sanicentral GmbH v. René Collin* (Case 25/79), [1979] ECR 3423, 3429 para. 6; OLG Hamm IPRax 1991, 324, 325; LG Bochum RIW 2000, 382, 384; *Kropholler/von Hein* Art. 66 note 3; *Geimer/Schütze* Art. 66 note 3.

31   *Trunk*, IPRax 1996, 251; *Tiefenthaler*, in: Czernich/Tiefenthaler/Kodek Art. 23 note 19; cf. also *Saenger*, ZZP 110 (1997), 477, 481 *et seq.*; *Kropholler/von Hein* Art. 66 note 3 and Art. 23 note 11. *Contra* BGE 124 III 436, 441 *et seq.*; LG München I IPRax 1996, 266, 267; *Benecke* (fn. 21), p. 86; *Schack* para. 465.

ted.[32] This places far too much emphasis on the restricted perspective of courts and judges.[33] It bluntly and unadvisedly disregards and discounts incentives and steering functions which a jurisdiction agreement exerts without any lawsuit being initiated.[34] It also does harm to the security the parties thrived for when they concluded the agreement. The prospective plaintiff must be able to count on the agreement if he calculates whether suing is worth the while and if so, where.[35] The important result of the approach submitted consisted in the transgression from the Brussels Convention to the Brussels I Regulation in not applying the wider exceptions under Art. 23 (5), if a jurisdiction agreement was concluded before 1 March 2002 and complied with every provision then in force, regardless whether an eventual lawsuit was commenced only after 1 March 2002. The twilight zone where this matters can be found in particular in the difference between Arts. 13; 15 Brussels Convention and Arts. 15; 17 Brussels I Regulation. Consumer protection is necessary, but does not amount to a catch-all, all-inclusive justification.[36] In the transgression from the Brussels I Regulation to the Brussels *Ibis* Regulation problems might occur with regard to the reversal of priority when an exclusive choice of court clause is at stake, in Art. 31 (2), and such problems are not expressly addressed in Art. 66, either.[37]

III. Rules on recognition and enforcement

1. General considerations

11 Judgments given before 10 January 2015 are in any event and by any measure outside the intertemporal scope of the Brussels *Ibis* Regulation.[38] Judgments rendered after the date when the Regulation became applicable are clearly within the Regulation.[39]

12 The notion of "judgment" is the same as in Art. 2 (a) subpara. 1.[40] Hence it is immaterial whether an appeal can be lodged against the judgment or whether appeal proceedings are already pending. Neither formal nor substantive *Rechtskraft* (effect of *res iudicata)* are required.[41] Any other approach would generate a divergence with Art. 2 (a) subpara. 1, although the wording does not compel to do so such a thing and Art. 2 (a) subpara. 1 aims at being a comprehensive definition applicable throughout the entire Regulation, at least in matters of recognition and enforcement. It might be tempting to let formal *Rechtskraft*

---

[32] *Sanicentral GmbH v. René Collin* (Case 25/79), [1979] ECR 3423, 3429 para. 6; applauded e.g. by OGH SZ 73/76; OGH ÖJZ 2004, 388; OGH ZfRV 2005, 32 *et seq.*; *Ansgar Staudinger*, in: Rauscher Art. 66 note 8; *Ratkovic/Zgrabljicrotar* (2013) 9 JPrIL 245, 251.

[33] *Mankowski*, in: Rauscher Art. 23 note 76.

[34] *Mankowski*, in: Rauscher Art. 23 note 76.

[35] *Mankowski*, in: Rauscher Art. 23 note 76.

[36] Tentatively *contra* BGE 126 III 436, 443; LG München I IPRax 1996, 266, 267; *Ansgar Staudinger*, in: Rauscher Art. 66 note 8.

[37] *Beraudo*, Clunet 140 (2013), 741, 753.

[38] See only BGH NJW 2004, 3189 = RIW 2004, 941, 942 = EuLF 2004, 288 with note *Simons*; BGH NJOZ 2005, 1301, 1302; Rb. Middelburg NIPR 2004 Nr 16 p. 38.

[39] See only TS AEDIPr 2000, 809; TS AEDIPr 2001, 926, 927; Rel. Coimbra Rev. Fac. Dir. Univ. Lisboa 1994, 464, 465 with note *Moura Vicente*; *Michael Becker/Karla Müller*, IPRax 2006, 432, 433.

[40] *Ansgar Staudinger*, in: Rauscher Art. 66 note 10.

[41] *Ansgar Staudinger*, in: Rauscher Art. 66 note 10.

acquired after 10 January 2015 suffice[42] but only insofar as the law of the *forum* state does not regard a judgment as "given" only if it acquires formal *Rechtskraft* that this would contravene the correct overall approach.[43] Accords and settlements concluded by the parties before the court are not encompassed by the notion of "judgment".[44]

The Brussels I*bis* Regulation does not comprise rules which would answer trigger a response **13** when a judgment is "given". Accordingly, the *lex fori* of the state of the court deciding must step in as gap-filler: It has to decide when it regards a suit as *res iudicata* in the concrete court.[45]

Since Art. 34 (2) is more favourable to judgment creditors than Art. 27 (2) Brussels Con- **14** vention was, judgment creditors might feel tempted and have every incentive to argue for a timely extension of Art. 34 (2).[46] This might appear the more sympathetic since Art. 27 (2) Brussels Convention has a reputation for being invoked by judgment creditors rather lightly in order to secure some leverage in settlement discussions. Art. 27 (2) Brussels Convention cannot be blamed for being one of the dormant beauties in the Convention regime. Yet, however many kudos Art. 34 (2) should get for improving the overall feature and how much the emphasis placed on continuity might be, there is no leeway for extending Art. 34 to the recognition and enforcement of judgments rendered before 1 March 2002 outside (2).[47] Harmonising Art. 27 (2) Brussels Convention and Art. 34 (2) would overdo any mere interpretation and would move the chain too far for the very reason that Art. 34 (2) disposes off continuity and introduces a substantial improvement.[48]

Art. 66 (2) Brussels I Regulation contained a rather complex rule. It read: **15**
"(2) However, if the proceedings in the Member State of origin were instituted before the entry into force of this Regulation, judgments given after that date shall be recognised and enforced in accordance with Chapter III,
(a) if the proceedings in the Member State of origin were instituted after the entry into force of the Brussels or the Lugano Convention both in the Member State of origin and in the Member State addressed;
(b) in all other cases, if jurisdiction was founded upon rules which accorded with those provided for either in Chapter II or in a convention concluded between the Member State of origin and the Member State addressed which was in force when the proceedings were instituted."

Nothing like this reappears in Art. 66. Three reasons back this greater simplicity, or better: the reasoning behind it appears to be threefold at least: Firstly, the Brussels I*bis* Regulation abandons formal exequatur proceedings. Secondly, the Brussels I regulation by its Art. 80

---

42   To this avail OLG Köln IPRax 2004, 115, 116; *Geimer*, RIW 1976, 147, 149; *Geimer/Schütze* Art. 66 note 6.

43   *Gottwald*, in: Münchener Kommentar zur ZPO Art. 54 EuGVÜ note 4; *Rolf Wagner*, RIW 1998, 590, 591; *Ansgar Staudinger*, in: Rauscher Art. 66 note 10; *Hüßtege*, in: Thomas/Putzo Art. 66 note 4.

44   *Solo Kleinmotoren GmbH v. Emilio Boch* (Case C-414/92), [1994] ECR I-2237, I-2250 paras. 18–20.

45   *Rolf Wagner*, ZIP 1994, 82, 83; *Kropholler/von Hein* Art. 66 note 4; *Schlosser* Art. 66 note 12; *Ansgar Staudinger*, in: Rauscher Art. 66 note 10.

46   Supported by OLG Köln IPRax 2004, 115, 116; *Geimer*, in: Zöller, Art. 34 note 26.

47   BGH RIW 2004, 941, 942; BGH NJOZ 2005, 1301, 1302; *Mankowski*, RIW 2005, 561, 571.

48   BGH RIW 2004, 941, 942; *Mankowski*, RIW 2005, 561, 571.

subpara. 1 repeals the Brussels I Regulation whereas the Brussels I regulation did and could not formally repeal the Brussels and Lugano Conventions. Thirdly, the transgression from the Brussels I to the Brussels I*bis* Regulation brought about less alterations of the rules on jurisdiction than the transgression from the Brussels Convention to the Brussels I Regulation had done.

IV. Rules on *lis pendens*

16 The third body of rules contained in the Brussels I*bis* Regulation and which should not to be overlooked consists of Artt. 29–34 and is concerned with issues of *lis pendens* and inter-related lawsuits, moulded by the newly introduced definition of when proceedings are instituted, in Art. 32. Whether it applies in the period of transition appears to be regulated by (1) if only for the lack of a better alternative appears arguable. The answer is clear-cut in two of three possible situations, though: If both sets of proceedings are instituted after the relevant date, the Regulation applies. And if both sets of proceedings were instituted before the relevant date, the Regulation does not apply.[49]

17 But the most intricate and complicated is the third situation: One set of proceedings is instituted before, the other after the relevant date. Two limbs – and a limping result? In *van Horn v. Cinnamond* the ECJ attempted an answer along the lines of then Art. 54 (2) Brussels Convention.[50] If this is transferred to the Regulation, (2) could come to the rescue.[51] The ensuing solution would read as follows: The court seised second stays the proceedings pending before it pursuant to Art. 29 (1) until the court seised first has decided whether it has jurisdiction. If the court seised first denies its own jurisdiction, the court seised second lifts the stay and commences the trial. If the court seised first declares itself competent, the court seised second ought to countercheck whether this assertion is correct since only in the event that the judgment eventually rendered by the court seised first will have to be recognised pursuant to (2) it is justified that the court seised second declares itself incompetent and dismisses the proceedings pending before it by virtue of Art. 29 (2).[52] This pinches through the rule of now Art. 45 (3), but appears reasonable enough at least if the court seised second exercises its control and countercheck according to yardsticks borrowed from the Brussels or Lugano Conventions or bilateral accords respectively.[53] If the court seised first referred to its national law *via* Art. 6 (1), the court seised second may only control whether Art. 6 (1) was applied correctly.[54] But exceptionally undermining the fortress of Art. 45 (3) appears justified at least insofar as the court seised first was a non-Member State at the time

---

[49] *Miles Platt Ltd. v. Townroe Ltd.* [2003] 1 All ER 561, 562 (C.A., per *Black* J.).

[50] *Elsbeth Freifrau von Horn v. Kevin Cinnamond* (Case C-163/95), [1997] ECR I-5451, I-5474 *et seq.* paras. 15–25.

[51] *Gottwald*, in: Münchener Kommentar zur ZPO Art. 66 note 2; *Ansgar Staudinger*, in: Rauscher Art. 66 note 15. See also for the parallel question under Art. 42 of the original Brussels II Regulation OGH IPRax 2003, 456, 457; *Hau*, IPRax 2003, 461.

[52] *Elsbeth Freifrau von Horn v. Kevin Cinnamond* (Case C-163/95), [1997] ECR I-5451, I-5475 para. 19; *Lapiedra Alcamí*, REDI 1998, 2, 213, 214 *et seq.*

[53] *Elsbeth Freifrau von Horn v. Kevin Cinnamond* (Case C-163/95), [1997] ECR I-5451, I-5477 para. 25.

[54] *Elsbeth Freifrau von Horn v. Kevin Cinnamond* (Case C-163/95), [1997] ECR I-5451, I-5477 para. 25; *Gaudemet-Tallon*, RCDIP 87 (1998), 113, 116; *Ansgar Staudinger*, in: Rauscher Art. 66 note 15.

of seising.[55] No floodgate argument is permissible since the exceptionality of the situation is evident.[56]

If in the foregoing situation Art. 29 was not applied and if the law of the court seised second **18** does not contain alike rules on *lis pendens* (which admittedly would be rather odd and probable in Member States of the Brussels of Lugano Conventions), both sets of proceedings would continue threatening to generate irreconcilable judgments.[57] The solution promoted by the ECJ also avoids the opposite friction that the court seised second had to declare itself incompetent whilst the recognition of the prospective judgment rendered by the court seised first was not guaranteed.[58] However, in the latter scenario one should not omit purposefully and not even for the sake of the argument the possibility of a recognition and enforcement under national law.[59] Generally, the only half-way feasible alternative would be to treat the courts seised first as being located in a non-Member State generally.[60]

A tiny, but obtrusive detail still needs to be clarified: According to which yardsticks shall it be **19** ascertained as to whether proceedings were instituted before or after the relevant date? According to the new yardsticks (in particular Art. 32) or to the old ones, i.e. by the national law of each *forum* concerned respectively?[61] It may be submitted that the former approach ought to be preferred since it augments uniformity and is the more modern approach, more in line and in tune with the Regulation.[62] Generally, intertemporal conflict rules opt for applying the *lex praesens* where possible insofar allowing the *lex praesens* to define its own scope of application.[63] Furthermore, this has the additional advantage of comparative simplicity compared to the alternative that in which the old yardsticks would be applied where the question is whether the proceedings were instituted before the entry into force of the Regulation, and the new ones yardstick where the question is whether the proceedings were instituted after that date. If Art. 32 is to be preferred in the context of (1), it should be consequent and consistent if it is applied in the akin context, too. This should be the more so since once again issues of the institution of proceedings are at stake and a uniform answer as to how to measure this aspect, is clearly preferential.

V. Documents and authentic instruments

Since Art. 58 deals with documents and authentic instruments, it was necessary to include a **20** rule on them in the provisions on transition, too as well. (1) obediently states that the Regulation shall apply only to legal proceedings instituted and to documents formally drawn up or registered as authentic instruments after the entry into force thereof. This subjects authentic instruments to (1) exclusively and prohibits (2) to be applied in this regard.[64]

---

55 *Rauscher*, IPRax 1999, 80, 82.
56 *Adolphsen*, ZZP Int. 3 (1998), 239, 245.
57 *Rauscher*, IPRax 1999, 80 *et seq.*
58 *Droz* n° 340; *Lagarde*, RCDIP 67 (1978), 374; *Rauscher*, IPRax 1999, 80, 81.
59 *Adolphsen*, ZZP Int. 3 (1998), 239, 243.
60 *Adolphsen*, ZZP Int. 3 (1998), 239, 243.
61 To this avail *Rolf Wagner*, ZIP 1994, 81, 82; *Ansgar Staudinger*, in: Rauscher Art. 66 note 2.
62 To the same result *Hess*, IPRax 2004, 374, 375.
63 *Hess*, Intertemporales Privatrecht (1998) p. 340; *Hess*, IPRax 2004, 374, 375.
64 *Hess*, IPRax 2004, 374, 376.

21 As court settlements are to be enforceable under the same conditions as authentic instruments pursuant to Art. 59 they should be treated analogous to authentic instruments with regard to the relevant datelines, too. Albeit not explicitly mentioned in Art. 66, such an analogy appears to be fairly safe.[65] Further support can be gained from Art. 64 (1) Brussels Ibis Regulation where such a rule is explicitly stated.[66] The critical date is the date on which the court settlement receives formal approval by the court or is registered with an entry in the records of the court depending upon the respective rules of the *lex fori*.[67]

VI. Future accessions to the EU

22 With further countries (in particular Serbia, Iceland and possibly Turkey) looking forward to becoming Member States of the EU (with whatever prospects of success), future accessions have a certain probability. The extent to which Art. 66 will be declared applicable to deal with the entry into force of the Brussels I Regulation in relation to such future Member States will depend on the conditions precedent as spelled out in the respective Acts of Accession. Nevertheless, it appears to be a rather safe bet to predict that Art. 66 will be declared applicable *mutatis mutandis* respectively.

Chapter VII: **Relationship with Other Instruments**

Article 67

This Regulation shall not prejudice the application of provisions governing jurisdiction and the recognition and enforcement of judgments in specific matters which are contained in instruments of the Union or in national legislation harmonised pursuant to such instruments.

Bibliography

Donzallaz, Interactions de la directive européenne 93/13 sur les clauses abusives avec la procédure civile interne ainsi qu'avec les CB/CL et le règlement 44/2001, AJP 2004, 1193
Heinig, Die Konkurrenz der EuGVVO mit dem übrigen Gemeinschaftsrecht, GPR 2010, 36

Mankowski, Wie viel Bedeutung verliert die EuGVVO durch den Europäischen Vollstreckungstitel?, in: FS Jan Kropholler (2008), p. 829.

1 Chapter VII deals with the Brussels Ibis Regulation in relation to other legal instruments. The single provisions differentiate in the source and quality of these instruments. Art. 67 starts with the relation to other EU instruments by establishing the principle of *lex specialis*. The other, more special instrument takes priority and precedence over the Brussels Ibis

---

[65] *Layton/Mercer* para. 31.011; *Hess*, IPRax 2004, 374, 376.

[66] *Hess*, IPRax 2004, 374, 376 fn. 26.

[67] *Layton/Mercer* para. 31.011.

Regulation. This is on the basis of the supposition that the other legal instrument contains more specific ideas and interests so that it is better in tune with the relevant field of law than the Brussels I Regulation which is based upon more general thoughts.[1] It is irrelevant if the concerned instruments became effective before or after the Brussels I*bis* Regulation. The principle of *lex posterior derogat legi priori* is not applied.[2] Equally irrelevant is whether the potentially conflicting other act of Union legislation expressly provides for it demanding priority.[3]

The other legal instrument involved prevails and takes precedence under the condition that **2** it deals directly or indirectly with jurisdiction or with the recognition and enforcement of judgment in civil and commercial matters. Otherwise such instruments are not in conflict with the Brussels I*bis* Regulation because the scopes of application, as regards the subject matter, do not overlap.[4] Prominent examples of EU legislation which peacefully co-exist with the Brussels I*bis* Regulation but do not trigger Art. 67 since they operate only in areas which are excluded from the scope of the Brussels I*bis* Regulation by virtue of Art. 1 (2), are the European Insolvency Regulation, the Brussels II*bis* Regulation and the Maintenance Regulation courtesy of Art. 1 (2) (b), (a) and (e) respectively.[5] Art. 4 Regulation EC No. 2271/ 96,[6] implemented as a counter-measure against the US Helms-Burton Act, is another example as it deals with the recognition and enforcement of judgments rendered by Third State courts, an issue which the Brussels I*bis* Regulation does not address.[7] The Enforcement Directive[8] ought to be mentioned in this context for it harmonizes procedural law with little impact on Brussels I issues but possibly provisional measures and Art. 31.[9]

There are only rather few legal instruments gaining relevance for the purposes of Art. 67. The **3** main example with regard to Art. 67 Brussels I Regulation was the Maintenance Regulation[10] which contains its Art. 68 (1), (2) and Recital (44) clarifying its precedence over the Brussels I Regulation.[11] But with Art. 1 (2) (e) expressly excluding maintenance from the scope of the

---

[1] *Mankowski*, in: Rauscher Art. 67 note 1.

[2] *Kropholler/von Hein* Art. 67 note 2 *in fine*.

[3] *Tentatively contra David C. Jackson*, Enforcement of Maritime Claims (3rd ed. 2000) para. 6.6.

[4] *Mankowski*, in: Rauscher Art. 67 note 2.

[5] *Mankowski*, in: Rauscher Art. 67 note 2.

[6] Council Regulation EC No. 2271/96 of 24 November 1996 protecting against the effects of the extraterritorial application of legislation adopted by a third country, and actions based thereon or resulting therefrom, OJ EU 1996 L 309/1. Discussed in detail by *Kayser*, Gegenmaßnahmen im Außenwirtschaftsrecht und das System des europäischen Kollisionsrechts (2001) pp. 120–198; *Lowe*, (1997) 56 Cambridge L.J. 248; *Reinisch*, ecolex 1997, 900 and 991.

[7] *Mankowski*, in: Rauscher Art. 67 note 2.

[8] Directive 2004/48/EC of the European Parliament and of the Council of 29 April 2004 on the enforcement of intellectual property rights, OJ EU 2004 L 157/1, 195/16.

[9] In more detail *Forner Delaygua*, in: Nuyts (ed.), International Litigation in Intellectual Property and Information Technology (2008), p. 257.

[10] Council Regulation (EC) No. 4/2009 of 18 December 2008 on jurisdiction, applicable law, recognition and enforcement of decisions and cooperation in matters relating to maintenance obligations, OJ EU 2009 L 7/1, with Corrigendum, OJ EU 2009 L 131/26.

[11] See only *Marianne Roth/Egger*, ecolex 2009, 818; *Kohler/Pintens*, FamRZ 2009, 1529; *Mansel/Thorn/Rolf Wagner*, IPRax 2010, 1, 7; *Heinig*, GPR 2010, 36, 38.

Brussels I*bis* Regulation no conflict can arise anymore. A second, still valid example is the specific restriction on jurisdiction against consumer for the confirmation as a European Title in Art. 6 (1) (d) EEO Regulation.[12][13] A third example stems from the Regulations on community industrial property rights[14] (which nevertheless establish some complex system of co-operation with the Brussels I*bis* Regulation).[15]

4   Usually the other legal instruments do not regulate such questions of law. Due to respect for the Brussels I*bis* Regulation, formally for the Brussels I Regulation and the Brussels Convention, some of them intentionally even leave the areas of law concerned out of consideration. A prominent example for this technique is Art. 1 (4) var. 2 E-Commerce Directive.[16] But on the other hand some influence may result from other legal instruments – for example with regard to jurisdiction clauses[17] from the Council Directive on Unfair Terms in Consumer Contracts,[18] in particular its Annex (1) (q). Such constellations may be provided for by the application of Art. 67.[19]

5   The scope of the EU instrument in question has to be ascertained by interpretation on its own terms,[20] particularly if it addresses matters relevant for the Brussels I*bis* Regulation at all.[21] Sometimes this might require some art of interpretation or even some differentiation. The prime example in this regard is Art. 6 (2) Payment Order Regulation.[22] Its relation to Art. 22, Art. 23 and the protective regimes respectively is contested. Yet Art. 6 (2) Payment Order Regulation itself serves a protective purpose and should thus gain prevalence as for claims against consumers,[23] even without admitting derogation by way of agreement to the

---

12   Regulation (EC) No. 805/2004 of the European Parliament and of the Council of 21 April 2004 creating a European Enforcement Order for uncontested claims, OJ EU 2004 L 143/15.

13   See in detail *Mankowski*, in: FS Konstantinos D. Kerameus, vol. I (2009), p. 785; *Mankowski*, VuR 2010, 16.

14   Clearly referring to Art. 67 Rb. den Haag, zittingsplaats den Haag NIPR 2014 Nr 177 p. 316.

15   See in more detail *Christian Kohler*, in: FS Ulrich Everling (1995), p. 651; *Seatzu*, RDIPP 2004, 1279; *Heinig*, GPR 2010, 36, 39–41 with further references.

16   Directive 2000/31/EC of the European Parliament and of the Council of 8 June 2000 on certain legal aspects of information society services, in particular electronic commerce, in the Internal Market, OJ 2000 L 178/1.

17   *Océano GrupoEditorial SA v. Roció Murciano Quintero* and *Salvat Editores SA v. José M. Sánchez Alcón Prades, José Luis Copano Badillo, Mohammed Berroane and Emilio Viñas Feliú*, (Joined Cases C-240/98 to C-244/98) [2000] ECR I-4941 paras. 21–24; *Pannon GSM v. Erszébet Sustikné Győrfi*, (Case C-243/08), [2009] ECR I-4713; discussed e.g. by *Heinig*, EuZW 2009, 885; *Pfeiffer*, NJW 2009, 2369; *Christian Mayer*, GPR 2009, 220; *Poissonnier*, D. 2009, 2312; *Paisant*, JCP G N°. 42, 2009, p. 33 and Art. 17 notes 4–7 (*Peter Arnt Nielsen*)

18   Council Directive 93/13/EEC of 5 April 1993 on unfair terms in consumer contracts, OJ 1993 L 95/29.

19   See Aud. Prov. Santa Cruz de Tenerife REDI 2002, 378 with note *Jiménez Blanco*; *Heinig*, GPR 2010, 36, 41.

20   See ArbG Wiesbaden NZA-RR 2000, 321, 322 = IPRspr. 1999 Nr 131 p. 312; *Mankowski*, in: Rauscher Art. 67 note 2.

21   *Garriga Suau*, AEDIPr 2008, 876, 877.

22   Regulation (EC) No. 1896/2006 of the European Parliament and of the Council of 12 December 2006 creating a European order for payment procedure, OJ EU 2006 L 399/1.

23   *Heinig*, GPR 2010, 36, 38.

extent which Art. 17 would allow for.[24] On the other hand, the interests underpinning Art. 22 militate for a precedence of Art. 22 over Art. 6 (2) Payment Order Regulation[25] whereas the *lex specialis* rule would prefer it the other way round.[26] Eventually and on balance, Art. 23 should cede to Art. 6 (2) Payment Order Regulation.[27]

If the other EU Act has only an optional nature the Brussels I*bis* Regulation is not preju- **6** diced. The prime examples in this regard are provided by the EEO Regulation with regard to enforcement mechanisms (Art. 27) and the Small Claims Regulation.[28][29] If the Brussels I*bis* Regulation drops a notch in relevance due to the advent of these Regulations[30] this is the result of competition and contest, not of hierarchy. Another example is Art. 6 of the Directive concerning the posting of workers in the framework of the provision of services.[31][32] The technique employed is different with Art. 6 European Account Preservation Order[33] which are not optional but strive at generally implementing additional heads of jurisdiction on top of those provided for either by other European instruments including the Brussels I*bis* Regulation or by national law.

Special Regulations, Directives and Decisions of the EU institutions can claim precedence. **7** Pursuant to Art. 288 subpara. 3 TFEU (ex-Art. 249 (3) EC Treaty) Directives have to be transformed into national law. Necessarily the national transforming act has to take precedence because otherwise the Directive system would be inferior to the Brussels I*bis* Regulation. Art. 67 takes this into account by giving priority to national legislations harmonized pursuant to the above-mentioned EU instruments. This is meant to cover the national acts implementing the respective directives and transforming them into parts of national law.[34]

---

[24] As *Pernfuß*, Die Effizienz des Europäischen Mahnverfahrens (2009) pp. 117 *et seq.* argues.

[25] *Heinig*, GPR 2010, 36, 37.

[26] *Kodek*, in: Geimer/Schütze, Internationaler Rechtsverkehr Art. 6 VO Nr 1896/2006 note 8 (2007); *Tschütscher/Weber*, ÖJZ 2007, 303, 307; *Kloiber*, ZfRV 2009, 68, 70; *Pernfuß* (fn. 22), p. 114.

[27] *Kodek*, in: Geimer/Schütze, Internationaler Rechtsverkehr Art. 6 VO Nr 1896/2006 note 5 (2007); *Tschütscher/Weber*, ÖJZ 2007, 303, 307; *Kreße*, EWS 2008, 508, 510; *Kloiber*, ZfRV 2009, 68, 70; cf. also *Leible/Freitag*, BB 2008, 2750, 2751. *Contra Pernfuß* (fn. 22), pp. 117 *et seq.*

[28] Regulation (EC) No. 861/2007 of the European Parliament and of the Council of 11 July 2007 establishing a European Small Claims Procedure, OJ EU 2007 L 199/1.

[29] *Heinig*, GPR 2010, 36, 38 with further references.

[30] See the deliberations in *Mankowski*, in: FS Jan Kropholler (2008), p. 829.

[31] Directive 96/71/EC of the European Parliament and of the Council of 16 December 1996 concerning the posting of workers in the framework of the provision of services, OJ 1997 L 18/1.

[32] See for further details *Mankowski*, in: Rauscher Art. 18 note 16; *Heinig*, GPR 2010, 36, 41. But cf. BAG AP Nr 340 zu § 1 TVG Tarifverträge: Bau.

[33] Regulation (EU) no. 655/2014 of the European Parliament and of the Council of 15 May 2014 establishing a European Account Preservation Order to facilitate cross-border debt recovery in civil and commercial matters, OSEU 2014 L 189/59.

[34] *Mankowski*, in: Rauscher Art. 67 note 3; *Garriga Suau*, AEDIPr 2008, 876, 877.

Article 68

1. This Regulation shall, as between the Member States, supersede the 1968 Brussels Convention, except as regards the territories of the Member States which fall within the territorial scope of that Convention and which are excluded from this Regulation pursuant to Article 355 of the TFEU.
2. In so far as this Regulation replaces the provisions of the 1968 Brussels Convention between the Member States, any reference to that Convention shall be understood as a reference to this Regulation.

I. Remaining relevance of the Brussels Convention, (1)

1   Art. 68 regulates the relation between the Brussels *Ibis* Regulation and the Brussels Convention. It repeats what Art. 68 (1) Brussels I Regulation decreed on the relation between the Brussels I Regulation and the Brussels Convention (but for updating the reference to Art. 299 of the EC Treaty as contained in Art. 68 (1) *in fine* Brussels I Regulation to a reference to Art. 355 TFEU). The respective settlement is simple, proper and satisfactory. The Brussels I Regulation does not simply take priority or precedence,[1] but supersedes and replaces the Brussels Convention as between the Member States.[2] The Brussels Convention (all contracting states are members of the EU) loses nearly its entire significance. On the other hand (1) neither repeals the Brussels Convention nor forces the Member States to denounce it.[3]

2   Denmark is a special case. It is not a Member State of the Brussels I Regulation. The bilateral Agreement between the then EC and Denmark[4] of 19 October 2005 which effectively extends the Brussels I regime to Denmark with slight modifications and was concluded by Council Decision 2006/325/EC[5] entered into force on 1 July 2007 by virtue of its Art. 12.[6] In accordance with Art. 3 (2) of the said Agreement, Denmark has by letter of 20 December 2012 notified the Commission of its decision to implement the contents of the Brussels *Ibis* Regulation.[7] This means that the provisions of the Brussels *Ibis* Regulation will be applied to relations between the EU and Denmark.[8] In accordance with Art. 3 (6) of the said Agreement, the Danish notification creates mutual obligations between the EU and Denmark.[9] Thus, the Brussels *Ibis* Regulation constitutes an amendment of the said Agreement and is

---

[1]   To establish the priority of the Brussels I Regulation an own provision would have been unnecessary. The precedence would follow from Art. 57 (3) Brussels Convention.

[2]   See only Rb. Almelo NIPR 2003 Nr 206 p. 310; Trib. Rovereto RDIPP 2005, 162, 163.

[3]   *Mankowski*, in: Rauscher Art. 68 note 1.

[4]   Agreement between the European Community and the Kingdom of Denmark of 19 October 2005 on jurisdiction and the recognition and enforcement of decisions in civil and commercial matters, OJ EC 2005 L 299/62.

[5]   Council Decision 2006/325/EC of 27 April 2006 concerning the conclusion of the Agreement between the European Community and the Kingdom of Denmark on jurisdiction and the recognition and enforcement of decisions in civil and commercial matters, OJ EC 2006 L 120/22.

[6]   OJ EU 2007 L 94/70.

[7]   OJ EU 2013 L 79/4 para. 3.

[8]   OJ EU 2013 L 79/4 para. 3.

[9]   OJ EU 2013 L 79/4 para. 4.

considered annexed thereto.[10] With reference to Article 3 (3) and (4) of the said Agreement, implementation of the Brussels I*bis* Regulation in Denmark can take place by amending existing Danish legislation by decision of the Danish Parliament.[11] In accordance with Art. 3 (5) (b) of the said Agreement, Denmark shall notify the Commission of the date on which such implementing legislative measures enter into force.[12] The Brussels Convention is still important for cases taking place before the entry into force of the Brussels I Regulation and for cases which bear a relation to Denmark. The Regulation is not in effect for Denmark.[13] The legal relationships between the other Member States (including the United Kingdom and Ireland) on the one hand and Denmark on the other hand are regulated and governed further-on by the Brussels Convention which is still effective in this regard.[14] It remains to be seen if a separate treaty relating to international law transposes the provisions of the Brussels I Regulation into this relationship[15] or if the Brussels Convention continues to have effect.

Beyond that, (1) clarifies that the Brussels Convention remains applicable to those territories **3** of the Member States, who are parties of the Brussels Conventions but are exempted from the application of the Union law pursuant to Art. 355 (2), (5) TFEU. The EU secondary legislation draws the necessary conclusions from the imperative primary EU Law. This reservation is prophylactic in case the territorial scope of the Brussels Conventions would turn out to be more extensive.[16] A relevant example[17] may be Aruba:[18] Pursuant to Art. 355 (2) subpara. 1 in conjunction with Annex II TFEU, Aruba is not subject to Union legislation but to the special association system of Arts. 198–204 TFEU. For this reason the Brussels I*bis* Regulation is not in force for Aruba.[19] During the reign of Art. 60 Brussels Convention 1968/ 1982 the Netherlands have extended the scope of application of the Convention by a declaration[20] over Aruba. Although the Third Accession Convention has abolished Art. 60 Brussels Convention 1968/1982 this declaration continues to have effect.[21] It would be more proper to develop the declaration according to international law to the Brussels Convention 1989[22] than to restrict it to the Convention of 1968/1982.[23]

---

10   OJ EU 2013 L 79/4 para. 4.
11   OJ EU 2013 L 79/4 para. 5.
12   OJ EU 2013 L 79/4 para. 5.
13   See only BGH GRUR 2005, 431, 432 – Hotel Maritime. See for further Details *Mankowski*, in: Rauscher Art. 1 note 32 and *Ansgar Staudinger*, in: Rauscher Introduction note 15.
14   *Mankowski*, in: Rauscher Art. 68 note 2.
15   Corresponding indications by *Christian Kohler*, in: FS Reinhold Geimer (2002), p. 461, 470.
16   *Schlosser* Art. 68 note 1.
17   See the statement of the United Kingdom on the special status of Gibraltar, OJ 2001 C 13/1 and BOE 2001, 2508; cf. also *Checa Martinéz*, AEDIPr 2003, 849, 851.
18   See *Czernich*, in: Tiefenthaler/Kodek/Czernich Art. 1 note 6, but they maintain erroneously and without the necessary differentiation that the Brussels I Regulation extends over Aruba.
19   *Kropholler/von Hein* Introduction note 26. But cf. Hof Amsterdam NIPR 2000 Nr 264 p. 424 with regard to the Brussels Convention.
20   BGBl 1986 II 819.
21   Report *Almeida Cruz/Desantes Real/Jenard* para. 36.
22   See *Gaudemet-Tallon*, Les Conventions de Bruxelles et de Lugano (2nd ed 1996) no. 50; *Kropholler/von Hein* Europäisches Zivilprozessrecht (6th ed 1998) Art. 60 EuGVÜ note 5.
23   *Contra Verschuur*, Vrij verkeer van vonnissen (1995) p. 112.

4 According to Art. 355 (3) TFEU, the provisions of the Treaties and consequentially any EU law including the Brussels *Ibis* Regulation apply to those European territories for whose external relations a Member State is responsible. The only instance this relates to at present is Gibraltar[24] (whereas historically the respective rule in the original EEC Treaty related to the Saarland and whilst Art. 33 (3) TFEU applies to Gibraltar only with the modifications sanctioned by Art. 28 1985 Accession Act[25]). The United Kingdom is taken to be the Member State "responsible" for Gibraltar, and arrangements have been put into place to facilitate this in the Context of the TFEU, without prejudice to the respective positions of the United Kingdom and Spain on the issue of sovereignty in relation to Gibraltar.[26] The European micro-States, i.e. the Vatican State, San Marino, Monaco, and Andorra, do not fall under Art. 355 (3) TFEU.[27]

5 The Åland Islands are subject to EU law pursuant to Art. 355 (4) TFEU but for some provisions as contained in Protocol 2 to the Act of Accession of Austria, Finland and Sweden to the then EC.[28] Accordingly, courts on the Åland Islands have to apply the Rome I Regulation.[29]

6 Art. 355 (5) (a) TFEU excludes the application of EU law to the Faeroe Islands. This is not of particular relevance for the Rome I Regulation since Denmark as the motherland of the Faeroe Islands is not Member State of the Rome I Regulation anyway.

7 Art. 355 (5) (b) TFEU in principle excludes the application of EU law to the United Kingdom Sovereign Base Areas of Akrotiri and Dhekelia in Cyprus reflecting some distant remnants from the time when Cyprus was a British territory, and the struggles of the Cypriot fight for independence.[30] The relevance for the Rome I Regulation is marginal if any but it is not in force there.[31]

---

24 See Parliamentary Question N. 655/85 with answer by Jacques Delors, OJ EEC 1985 C 341/8-9; Ministry of Justice, Should the UK Opt In? (January 2009) http://www.justice.gov.uk/consultations/docs/rome-i-consultation-govt-response.pdf; *Schmalenbach*, in: Christian Calliess/Ruffert, EUV/AEUV (4th ed. 2011) Art. 355 AEUV note 9; *Kokott*, in: Streinz, EUV/AEUV (2nd ed. 2012) Art. 355 AEUV note 7; *Dickinson*, [2013] LMCLQ 86, 89.

25 *Meinhard Schröder*, in: von der Groeben/Schwarze, EUV/EGV, vol. IV (6th ed. 2004) Art. 299 EGV note 32.

26 *Dickinson*, [2013] LMCLQ 86, 89.

27 *Meinhard Schröder*, in: von der Groeben/Schwarze, EUV/EGV, vol. IV (6th ed. 2004) Art. 299 EGV notes 33–36; *Jaeckel*, in: Grabitz/Hilf/Nettesheim, Das Recht der Europäischen Union (looseleaf 1993-ongoing) Art. 355 AEUV note 15 (August 2011); *Kokott*, in: Streinz, EUV/AEUV (2nd ed. 2012) Art. 355 AEUV note 8 and in detail *Sack*, EuZW 1997, 45; *Stapper*, Europäische Mikrostaaten und autonome Territorien im Rahmen der EG (1999); *Katrin Friese*, Die europäischen Mikrostaaten und ihre Integration in die Europäische Union: Andorra, Liechtenstein, Monaco, San Marino und Vatikanstadt auf dem Weg in die EU? (2011).

28 In detail *Fagerlund*, in: Hannikainen (ed.), Autonomy and Demilitarisation in Internationale Law (1997), p. 13.

29 *von Hein*, in: Rauscher, Art. 24 note 5.

30 See Protocol No. 3 of the Treaty of Accession of [i.a.] the Republic of Cyprus on the Sovereign Base Areas of the United Kingdom of Great Britain and Northern Ireland in Cyprus.

Of greater relevance is Art. 355 (5) (c) TFEU: EU law applies only to a limited extent to the 8
Channel Islands (Jersey, Guernsey, Alderney and Sark) and the Isle of Man. The limited
extent does not comprise the Brussels I*bis* Regulation[32] as it does not comprise the Rome I
Regulation.[33]

A special case is posed by the so-called Cyprus Problem. As is well known, the Northern part 9
of Cyprus is occupied by Turkish forces and declared itself an independent Turkish Republic
of Northern Cyprus which has not been recognised by any EU Member State under international law. Howsoever, the Government of the Republic of Cyprus does not exercise
effective control in these areas. This is reflected in Art. 1 (1) of Protocol No. 10 of the Treaty
of Accession of the Republic of Cyprus which reads: "The application of the acquis shall be
suspended in those areas of the Republic of Cyprus in which the Government of the Republic of Cyprus does not exercise effective control." This has to be interpreted restrictively,
though, insofar as courts sitting in the Government-controlled area adjudicate the case
regardless where the substrate of the lawsuit ought to be located.[34] But such restriction
would not allow for a court sitting in the Northern area of Cyprus to be bound by the
Brussels I*bis* Regulation. On the other hand, court sin other Member States have to recognise
and enforce every judgment rendered by courts sitting in the Government-controlled area of
Cyprus.[35]

II. References to the Brussels Convention as references to the Brussels I*bis* Regulation, (2)

Some other legal instruments enacted between the passing of the Brussels Convention and 10
the Brussels I*bis* Regulation refer to the Convention. This concern relates mainly to national
legal instruments, but also to some Union instruments like e.g. Art. 25 (1) subpara. 1 of the
original Insolvency Regulation (Regulation 1346/2000/EC). (2) clarifies that such references
shall be understood as references to the Brussels I*bis* Regulation.[36] This clarification in the
Regulation is more practicable than to change all legal instruments referring to the Brussels
Convention. Otherwise such alteration would have been necessary in every case to take the
special constellation of Denmark into account. Yet the other instruments should be read as
though they were altered in the mentioned manner.[37] (2) gains its main relevance from the
reference of Art. 54b Lugano Convention to the Brussels Convention, which now has to be
read as referring to the Brussels I Regulation.[38] Yet it is presupposed that the respective rule is

---

[31] *von Hein*, in: Rauscher, Art. 24 note 10; *Brödermann/Wegen*, in: Prütting/Wegen/Weinreich, Art. 24
     note 3.
[32] See BGH NJW 1995, 264; OLG Zweibrücken NJOZ 2011, 1940 = IPRspr. 2010 Nr 204 S 514; *Balthasar*,
     IPRax 2007, 475.
[33] *von Hein*, in: Rauscher, Art. 24 note 10.
[34] *Meletis Apostolides v. David Charles Orams and Linda Elizabeth Orams* (Case C-420/07), [2009] ECR
     I-3571 paras. 37–38; *Dickinson*, [2013] LMCLQ 86, 89–90.
[35] *Meletis Apostolides v. David Charles Orams and Linda Elizabeth Orams* (Case C-420/07), [2009] ECR
     I-3571 paras. 37–38; *Dickinson*, [2013] LMCLQ 86, 89–90.
[36] See only *Lydia Fuchs*, ÖJZ 2005, 624, 626. Probably overlooked by *Christian Kohler*, in: FS Reinhold
     Geimer (2002), p. 461, 464 *et seq.*
[37] *Lydia Fuchs*, ÖJZ 2005, 624, 626.
[38] *Schlosser* Art. 66 note 2.

---

applicable in its own right; for instance, the Insolvency Regulation is not applicable in relation to Denmark, and insofar (2) does not lead to any alteration.[39]

11 The EU has the jurisdiction for the enactment of the second paragraph, although it is a passing has been passed on from the Brussels Convention because the Member States transferred this competence in the Treaty of Amsterdam. Practitioners however should be reminded that they must be aware that references to the Brussels Convention are not what they appear to be at first sight. Many surprises might be hidden behind that these references for practitioners not familiar with international procedural law.

12 National legislation of its free motion can voluntarily refer to the Brussels Convention or the Brussels I*bis* Regulation for cases which would *per se* be outside the ambit of either act. For instance, distribution as to territorial jurisdiction or venue in a State territorially sub-divided may be instituted by such reference. Insofar as national legislation still refers to the Brussels Convention it is alleged that it should be for the interpretation of that national law following its own yardsticks to determine as to whether the reference should be read as static and petrified, i.e. still to the Brussels Convention, or as a dynamic reference.[40] Yet (2) should be given guiding force for this interpretation, too. Taking (2) into account the reference should be read as dynamic.[41] National legislators are free in deciding whether to refer but not where to refer to.

13 If references are to be found in legislative acts which predate the entry into force of the Brussels I Regulation, there necessarily are to the Brussels Convention and not to the Brussels I Regulation. For instance, Art. 25 (1) subpara. 1 Insolvency Regulation 2000 (Regulation 1346/2000/EC) contains such a relevant reference to the Brussels Convention.[42] With regard to such references to the Brussels Convention, a double transfer is necessary: first from the Brussels Convention to the Brussels I Regulation, and second from the Brussels I Regulation to the Brussels I*bis* Regulation. One has in a first step to apply Art. 68 (1) Brussels I Regulation and then in a second step (which takes the result reached in the first step as its starting point) Art. 80.

Article 69

Subject to Articles 70 and 71, this Regulation shall, as between the Member States, supersede the conventions that cover the same matters as those to which this Regulation applies. In particular, the conventions included in the list established by the Commission pursuant to point (c) of Article 76(1) and Article 76(2) shall be superseded.

---

[39]   See OLG Frankfurt NJOZ 2005, 2532, 2533 *et seq.*

[40]   *Christian Kohler*, in: FS Reinhold Geimer (2002), p. 461, 464; *Geimer/Schütze* Art. 68 note 2.

[41]   *Mankowski*, in: Rauscher, Art. 68 note 6.

[42]   BGH WM 2013, 53, 54 with further references.

Bibliography

Sawczuk, Bilaterale Verträge und das Problem des polnischen Beitritts zum Lugano-Übereinkommen, in: FS Rolf A. Schütze zum 65. Geb. (1999), p. 733

Traest, La relation entre la Convention et le règlement de Bruxelles, d'une part, et les Conventions bilatérales, d'autre part, J. trib. 2010, 520.

In adoption and continuation of Art. 55 Brussels Convention and Art. 69 Brussels I Regulation Art. 69 orders the precedence of the Brussels I*bis* Regulation over bilateral (and in exceptional cases multilateral) agreements and treaties of recognition and enforcement of judgment negotiated and concluded between Member States. On the occasion of the 2003 Accession Act the list of bilateral conventions as contained in Art. 69 Brussels I Regulation was extended by 32 new entries related to the new Member States.[1] Art. 69 now refrains from listing all bilateral conventions concerned in its very wording as Art. 69 Brussels I Regulation had still done. With the list growing after every new entry of a new Member State, it is a prudent measure of legislative drafting to confine collecting the conventions at stake to a list established and complied by the Commission, the more so, since this more informal technique makes it unnecessary to implement an own Regulation once a previously unmentioned bilateral convention unearths.

Art. 69 affects only and exclusively legal relationships between Member States. In contrast to Art. 73 (3) there is no need to pay attention to the interests of further, non-Member States or international institutions or organisations. Bilateral conventions between Member States and non-Member States remain generally unaffected[2] by virtue of Art. 73 (3).

Within its scope of application the Brussels I*bis* Regulation supersedes the bilateral agreements in total and in their entirety.[3] This concerns even the case in which the convention is more advantageous to the parties.[4] For the Brussels I*bis* Regulation is the most advantageous form of enforcement most advantageous known to creditors known at present this pertinent inconsequence is ineffective in practice.[5] The Brussels I*bis* Regulation even claims precedence if it is less precise than the bilateral agreements.[6] But it should be noted that the bilateral agreements are only *superseded* and not *repealed*. Hence, they do still exist but they have to cede wherever the Regulation claims precedence.

As Art. 69 indicates through the reservation in favour of Arts. 70; 71, the bilateral agreements only remain significant in three constellations: in the first place pursuant to Art. 70 (2) as far as the Brussels I*bis* Regulation is pertinently not relevant;[7] in the second place pursuant to Art. 70 (3) as far as the Regulation is irrelevant at that point of time and in the third place pursuant to Art. 66 (2) (b), again due to intertemporal reasons. The two latter constellations

---

[1] *Jayme/Kohler*, IPRax 2004, 481, 485.

[2] *Sawczuk*, in: FS Rolf A. Schütze zum 65. Geb. (1999), p. 733, 743.

[3] See only Hoge Raad NJ 2010 Nr 556 p. 5554; A-G *Strikwerda*, NJ 2010 Nr 556 p. 5551.

[4] BGH NJW 1993, 2688 (with note *Rauscher*, IPRax 1993, 376).

[5] *Mankowski*, in: Rauscher Art. 69 note 2.

[6] Cassaz. RDIPP 1980, 454; App. Torino RDIPP 1979, 84; App. Bari Riv. dir. int. 1980, 545; *Rottola*, Riv. dir. int. 1980, 424.

[7] Hof van Cass. J. trib. 2010, 520; *Sawczuk*, in: FS Rolf A. Schütze zum 65. Geb. (1999), p. 733, 743.

do not have actual relevance, because the Brussels Convention has already superseded the listed conventions.[8] Conventions concluded by the former German Democratic Republic were already repealed on the event at the time of the German re-unification pursuant to Art. 12 Einigungsvertrag.[9]

5 The list of bilateral conventions generally superseded by the Brussels *Ibis* Regulation reads, as promulgated by the Commission in January 2015:[10]

"**List 3**

The Conventions referred to in Article 69 are the following:

in Austria:
- the Convention between Germany and Austria on the Mutual Recognition and Enforcement of Judgments, Settlements and Authentic Instruments in Civil and Commercial Matters, signed at Vienna on 6 June 1959,
- the Agreement between the People's Republic of Bulgaria and the Republic of Austria on Legal Assistance in Civil Matters and Documents, signed at Sofia on 20 October 1967,
- the Convention between Belgium and Austria on the Mutual Recognition and Enforcement of Judgments, Arbitral Awards and Authentic Instruments in Civil and Commercial Matters, signed at Vienna on 16 June 1959,
- the Convention between the United Kingdom and Austria providing for the Mutual Recognition and Enforcement of Judgments in Civil and Commercial Matters, signed at Vienna on 14 July 1961, with amending Protocol signed at London on 6 March 1970,
- the Convention between the Netherlands and Austria on the Mutual Recognition and Enforcement of Judgments and Authentic Instruments in Civil and Commercial Matters, signed at The Hague on 6 February 1963,
- the Convention between France and Austria on the Recognition and Enforcement of Judgments and Authentic Instruments in Civil and Commercial Matters, signed at Vienna on 15 July 1966,
- the Convention between Luxembourg and Austria on the Recognition and Enforcement of Judgments and Authentic Instruments in Civil and Commercial Matters, signed at Luxembourg on 29 July 1971,
- the Convention between Italy and Austria on the Recognition and Enforcement of Judgments in Civil and Commercial Matters, of Judicial Settlements and of Authentic Instruments, signed at Rome on 16 November 1971,
- the Convention between Austria and Sweden on the Recognition and Enforcement of Judgments in Civil Matters, signed at Stockholm on 16 September 1982,
- the Convention between Austria and Spain on the Recognition and Enforcement of Judgments, Settlements and Enforceable Authentic Instruments in Civil and Commercial Matters, signed at Vienna on 17 February 1984,
- the Convention between Finland and Austria on the Recognition and Enforcement of Judgments in Civil Matters, signed at Vienna on 17 November 1986,

---

[8] *Kropholler/von Hein* Art. 69 note 2; *Mankowski*, in: Rauscher Art. 69 note 3.
[9] *Martiny/Ulrich Ernst*, IPRax 2001, 29, 30.
[10] The information referring to Article 76 of Regulation (EU) No. 1215/2012 of the European Parliament and of the Council on jurisdiction and recognition and enforcement of judgments in civil and commercial matters, OJ EU 2015 C 4/2.

- The Treaty between the Federal People's Republic of Yugoslavia and the Republic of Austria on the Mutual Judicial Cooperation, signed at Vienna on 16 December 1954,
- the Convention between People's Republic of Poland and the Republic of Austria on Mutual Relations in Civil Matters and on Documents, signed at Vienna on 11 December 1963,
- the Convention between the Socialist Republic of Romania and the Republic of Austria on Legal Assistance in Civil and Family law and the Validity and Service of Documents and its annexed Protocol, signed at Vienna on 17 November 1965.

in Belgium:
- the Convention between Belgium and France on Jurisdiction and the Validity and Enforcement of Judgments, Arbitration Awards and Authentic Instruments, signed at Paris on 8 July 1899,
- the Convention between Belgium and the Netherlands on Jurisdiction, Bankruptcy, and the Validity and Enforcement of Judgments, Arbitration Awards and Authentic Instruments, signed at Brussels on 28 March 1925,
- the Convention between the United Kingdom and the Kingdom of Belgium providing for the Mutual Enforcement of Judgments in Civil and Commercial Matters, with Protocol, signed at Brussels on 2 May 1934,
- the Convention between Germany and Belgium on the Mutual Recognition and Enforcement of Judgments, Arbitration Awards and Authentic Instruments in Civil and Commercial Matters, signed at Bonn on 30 June 1958,
- the Convention between Belgium and Austria on the Mutual Recognition and Enforcement of Judgments, Arbitral Awards and Authentic Instruments in Civil and Commercial Matters, signed at Vienna on 16 June 1959,
- the Convention between Belgium and Italy on the Recognition and Enforcement of Judgments and other Enforceable Instruments in Civil and Commercial Matters, signed at Rome on 6 April 1962,
- the Treaty between Belgium, the Netherlands and Luxembourg on Jurisdiction, Bankruptcy, and the Validity and Enforcement of Judgments, Arbitration Awards and Authentic Instruments, signed at Brussels on 24 November 1961, in so far as it is in force.

in Bulgaria:
- the Convention between Bulgaria and Belgium on certain Judicial Matters, signed at Sofia on 2 July 1930,
- the Agreement between the People's Republic of Bulgaria and the Federal People's Republic of Yugoslavia on Mutual Legal Assistance, signed at Sofia on 23 March 1956, still in force between Bulgaria, Slovenia and Croatia,
- the Treaty between the People's Republic of Bulgaria and the Romanian People's Republic on Legal Assistance in Civil, Family and Criminal Matters, signed at Sofia on 3 December 1958,
- the Agreement between the People's Republic of Bulgaria and the Polish People's Republic on Legal Assistance and Legal Relations in Civil, Family and Criminal Matters, signed at Warsaw on 4 December 1961,
- the Agreement between the People's Republic of Bulgaria and the People's Republic of Hungary on Legal Assistance in Civil, Family and Criminal Matters, signed at Sofia on 16 May 1966,
- the Agreement between the People's Republic of Bulgaria and the Hellenic Republic on Legal Assistance in Civil and Criminal Matters, signed at Athens on 10 April 1976,
- the Agreement between the People's Republic of Bulgaria and the Czechoslovak Socialist Republic on Legal Assistance and Regulation of Relations in Civil, Family and Criminal Matters, signed at Sofia on 25 November 1976,

- the Agreement between the People's Republic of Bulgaria and the Republic of Cyprus on Legal Assistance in Civil and Criminal Matters, signed at Nicosia on 29 April 1983,
- the Agreement between the Government of the People's Republic of Bulgaria and the Government of the French Republic on Mutual Legal Assistance in Civil Matters, signed at Sofia on 18 January 1989,
- the Agreement between the People's Republic of Bulgaria and the Italian Republic on Legal Assistance and Enforcement of Judgments in Civil Matters, signed at Rome on 18 May 1990,
- the Agreement between the Republic of Bulgaria and the Kingdom of Spain on Mutual Legal Assistance in Civil Matters, signed at Sofia on 23 May 1993,
- the Agreement between the People's Republic of Bulgaria and the Republic of Austria on Legal Assistance in Civil Matters and Documents, signed at Sofia on 20 October 1967.

in Czech Republic:
- the Agreement between the People's Republic of Bulgaria and the Czechoslovak Socialist Republic on Legal Assistance and Regulation of Relations in Civil, Family and Criminal Matters, signed at Sofia on 25 November 1976,
- the Treaty between the Czechoslovak Socialist Republic and the Republic of Cyprus on Legal Assistance in Civil and Criminal Matters, signed at Nicosia on 23 April 1982,
- the Treaty between the Czechoslovak Socialist Republic and the Hellenic Republic on Legal Assistance in Civil and Criminal Matters, signed at Athens on 22 October 1980,
- the Treaty between the Czechoslovak Socialist Republic and the Kingdom of Spain on Legal Assistance, Recognition and Enforcement of Court Judgments in Civil Matters, signed at Madrid on 4 May 1987,
- the Treaty between the Government of the Czechoslovak Socialist Republic and the Government of the Republic of France on Legal Assistance and the Recognition and Enforcement of Judgments in Civil, Family and Commercial Matters, signed at Paris on 10 May 1984,
- the Treaty between the Czechoslovak Socialist Republic and the People's Republic of Hungary on Legal Assistance and Regulation of Legal Relations in Civil, Family and Criminal Matters, signed at Bratislava on 28 March 1989,
- the Treaty between the Czechoslovak Socialist Republic and the Italian Republic on Legal Assistance in Civil and Criminal Matters, signed at Prague on 6 December 1985,
- the Treaty between the Czechoslovak Socialist Republic and the Polish People's Republic on Legal Assistance and Regulation of Legal Relations in Civil, Family, Labour and Criminal Matters, signed at Warsaw on 21 December 1987, within the meaning of the Treaty between the Czech Republic and the Polish Republic amending and supplementing the Treaty between the Czechoslovak Socialist Republic and the Polish People's Republic on Legal Assistance and Regulation of Legal Relations in Civil, Family, Labour and Criminal Matters, signed at Warsaw on 21 December 1987, signed at Mojmírovce on 30 October 2003,
- the Convention between the Czechoslovak Republic and Portugal on the Recognition and Enforcement of Court Judgments, signed at Lisbon on 23 November 1927,
- the Treaty between the Czech Republic and Romania on Legal Assistance in Civil Matters, signed at Bucharest on 11 July 1994,
- the Treaty between the Czechoslovak Socialist Republic and the Socialist Federal Republic of Yugoslavia on Regulation of Legal Relations in Civil, Family and Criminal cases, signed at Belgrade on 20 January 1964,
- the Treaty between the Czech Republic and the Slovak Republic on Legal Assistance provided by Judicial Bodies and on Regulation of Certain Legal Relations in Civil and Criminal Matters, signed at Prague on 29 October 1992.

in Denmark:
- the Convention between Denmark, Finland, Iceland, Norway and Sweden on the Recognition and Enforcement of Judgments in Civil Matters (the Nordic Judgments Convention), signed at Copenhagen on 11 October 1977.

in Germany:
- the Convention between Germany and Italy on the Recognition and Enforcement of Judgments in Civil and Commercial Matters, signed at Rome on 9 March 1936,
- the Convention between Germany and Belgium on the Mutual Recognition and Enforcement of Judgments, Arbitration Awards and Authentic Instruments in Civil and Commercial Matters, signed at Bonn on 30 June 1958,
- the Convention between Germany and Austria on the Mutual Recognition and Enforcement of Judgments, Settlements and Authentic Instruments in Civil and Commercial Matters, signed at Vienna on 6 June 1959,
- the Convention between the United Kingdom and the Federal Republic of Germany for the Mutual Recognition and Enforcement of Judgments in Civil and Commercial Matters, signed at Bonn on 14 July 1960,
- the Convention between the Netherlands and Germany on the Mutual Recognition and Enforcement of Judgments and Other Enforceable Instruments in Civil and Commercial Matters, signed at The Hague on 30 August 1962,
- the Convention between the Kingdom of Greece and the Federal Republic of Germany for the Mutual Recognition and Enforcement of Judgments, Settlements and Authentic Instruments in Civil and Commercial Matters, signed at Athens on 4 November 1961,
- the Convention between Spain and the Federal Republic of Germany on the Recognition and Enforcement of Judgments, Settlements and Enforceable Authentic Instruments in Civil and Commercial Matters, signed at Bonn on 14 November 1983.

in Estonia:
- the Agreement on Legal Assistance and Legal Relations between the Republic of Lithuania, the Republic of Estonia and the Republic of Latvia, signed at Tallinn on 11 November 1992,
- the Agreement between the Republic of Estonia and the Republic of Poland on Legal Assistance and Legal Relations on Civil, Labour and Criminal Matters, signed at Tallinn on 27 November 1998.

in Greece:
- the Convention between the Kingdom of Greece and the Federal Republic of Germany for the Mutual Recognition and Enforcement of Judgments, Settlements and Authentic instruments in Civil and Commercial Matters, signed at Athens on 4 November 1961,
- the Agreement between the Federal People's Republic of Yugoslavia and the Kingdom of Greece on the Mutual Recognition and Enforcement of Judgments, signed at Athens on 18 June 1959,
- the Convention between the People's Republic of Hungary and the Hellenic Republic on Legal Assistance in Civil and Criminal Matters, signed at Budapest on 8 October 1979,
- the Convention between the People's Republic of Poland and the Hellenic Republic on Legal Assistance in Civil and Criminal Matters, signed at Athens on 24 October 1979,
- the Treaty between the Czechoslovak Socialist Republic and the Hellenic Republic on Legal Assistance in Civil and Criminal Matters, signed at Athens on 22 October 1980 and still in force as between the Czech Republic, Slovakia and Greece,
- the Convention between the Republic of Cyprus and the Hellenic Republic on Legal Cooperation in Matters of Civil, Family, Commercial and Criminal Law, signed at Nicosia on 5 March 1984,

Peter Mankowski   1033

- the Convention between the Socialist Republic of Romania and the Kingdom of Greece on Legal Assistance in Civil and Criminal Matters, signed at Bucharest on 19 October 1972,
- the Agreement between the People's Republic of Bulgaria and the Hellenic Republic on Legal Assistance in Civil and Criminal Matters, signed at Athens on 10 April 1976.

in Spain:
- the Convention between Spain and France on the Recognition and Enforcement of Judgments, Arbitration Awards and Authentic Instruments in Civil and Commercial Matters, signed at Paris on 28 May 1969,
- the Agreement of 25 February 1974, in the form of an exchange of notes interpreting Articles 2 and 17 of the Convention between France and Spain on the Recognition and Enforcement of Judgments, Arbitration Awards and Authentic Instruments in Civil and Commercial Matters, signed at Paris on 28 May 1969,
- the Convention between Spain and Italy regarding Legal Assistance and the Recognition and Enforcement of Judgments in Civil and Commercial Matters, signed at Madrid on Tuesday 22 May 1973,
- the Convention between Spain and the Federal Republic of Germany on the Recognition and Enforcement of Judgments, Settlements and Enforceable Authentic Instruments in Civil and Commercial Matters, signed at Bonn on 14 November 1983,
- the Convention between Austria and Spain on the Recognition and Enforcement of Judgments, Settlements and Enforceable Authentic Instruments in Civil and Commercial Matters, signed at Vienna on 17 February 1984,
- the Treaty between the Czechoslovak Socialist Republic and the Kingdom of Spain on Legal Assistance, Recognition and Enforcement of Court Judgments in Civil Matters, signed at Madrid on 4 May 1987, still in force between the Czech Republic, Slovakia and Spain,
- the Agreement between the Republic of Bulgaria and the Kingdom of Spain on Mutual Legal Assistance in Civil Matters, signed at Sofia on 23 May 1993,
- the Convention between Romania and the Kingdom of Spain on Jurisdiction, Recognition and Enforcement of Judgments in Civil and Commercial Matters, signed at Bucharest on 17 November 1997.

in France:
- the Convention between Belgium and France on Jurisdiction and the Validity and Enforcement of Judgments, Arbitration Awards and Authentic Instruments, signed at Paris on 8 July 1899,
- the Agreement between the Government of the People's Republic of Bulgaria and the Government of the French Republic on Mutual Legal Assistance in Civil Matters, signed at Sofia on 18 January 1989,
- the Treaty between the Government of the Republic of France and the Government of the Czechoslovak Socialist Republic on Legal Assistance and the Recognition and Enforcement of Judgments in Civil, Family and Commercial Matters, signed at Paris on 10 May 1984,
- the Convention between France and Spain on the Recognition and Enforcement of Judgments, Arbitration Awards and Authentic Instruments in Civil and Commercial matters, signed at Paris on 28 May 1969,
- the Agreement of 25 February 1974, in the form of an exchange of notes interpreting Articles 2 and 17 of the Convention between France and Spain on the Recognition and Enforcement of Judgments, Arbitration Awards and Authentic Instruments in Civil and Commercial Matters, signed at Paris on 28 May 1969,
- the Convention between the Government of the Socialist Federal Republic of Yugoslavia and the

Government of the Republic of France on the recognition and enforcement of judgments in civil and commercial matters, signed at Paris on 18 May 1971,
- the Convention between the People's Republic of Hungary and the French Republic on Legal Assistance in Civil and Family Law, on the Recognition and Enforcement of Judgments and on Legal Assistance in Criminal Matters and on Extradition, signed at Budapest on 31 July 1980,
- the Convention between France and Italy on the Enforcement of Judgments in Civil and Commercial Matters, signed at Rome on 3 June 1930,
- the Convention between France and Austria on the Recognition and Enforcement of Judgments and Authentic Instruments in Civil and Commercial Matters, signed at Vienna on 15 July 1966,
- the Convention between the Socialist Republic of Romania and the French Republic on Legal Assistance in Civil and Commercial Matters, signed at Paris 5 November 1974,
- the Convention between the United Kingdom and the French Republic providing for the Mutual Enforcement of Judgments in Civil and Commercial Matters, with Protocol, signed at Paris on 18 January 1934.

in Croatia:
- the Agreement between the Federal People's Republic of Yugoslavia and the People's Republic of Bulgaria of 23.3.1956 on Mutual Legal Assistance,
- the Treaty between the Socialist Federal Republic of Yugoslavia and the Czechoslovak Socialist Republic of 20.1.1964 on Regulation of Legal Relations in Civil, Family and Criminal cases,
- the Convention between the Government of the Socialist Federal Republic of Yugoslavia and the Government of the Republic of France of 18.5.1971 on the Recognition and Enforcement of Judgments in Civil and Commercial Matters,
- the Agreement between the Federal People's Republic of Yugoslavia and the Kingdom of Greece of 18.6.1959 on the Mutual Recognition and Enforcement of Judgments,
- the Treaty between the Socialist Federal Republic of Yugoslavia and the People's Republic of Hungary of 7.3.1968 on Mutual Legal Assistance,
- the Treaty between the Federal People's Republic of Yugoslavia and the People's Republic of Poland of 6.2.1960 on Legal Assistance in Civil and Criminal Matters,
- the Treaty between the Romanian People's Republic and the Federal People's Republic of Yugoslavia of 18.10.1960 on Legal Assistance,
- the Convention between the Federal People's Republic of Yugoslavia and the Italian Republic on Mutual Judicial Cooperation in Civil and Administrative Matters, signed at Rome on 3 December 1960,
- the Treaty between the Federal People's Republic of Yugoslavia and the Republic of Austria on the Mutual Judicial Cooperation, signed at Vienna on 16 December 1954,
- the Treaty between the Republic of Croatia and the Republic of Slovenia of 7.2.1994 on Legal Assistance in Civil and Criminal Matters.

in Ireland, none,

in Italy:
- the Convention between France and Italy on the Enforcement of Judgments in Civil and Commercial Matters, signed at Rome on 3 June 1930,
- the Convention between Germany and Italy on the Recognition and Enforcement of Judgments in Civil and Commercial Matters, signed at Rome on 9 March 1936,
- the Convention between the Netherlands and Italy on the Recognition and Enforcement of Judgments in Civil and Commercial Matters, signed at Rome on 17 April 1959,

- the Convention between Belgium and Italy on the Recognition and Enforcement of Judgments and other Enforceable Instruments in Civil and Commercial Matters, signed at Rome on 6 April 1962,
- the Convention between the United Kingdom and the Italian Republic for the Mutual Recognition and Enforcement of Judgments in Civil and Commercial Matters, signed at Rome on 7 February 1964, with amending Protocol signed at Rome on 14 July 1970,
- the Convention between Italy and Austria on the Recognition and Enforcement of Judgments in Civil and Commercial Matters, of Judicial Settlements and of Authentic Instruments, signed at Rome on 16 November 1971,
- the Convention between Spain and Italy regarding Legal Assistance and the Recognition and Enforcement of Judgments in Civil and Commercial Matters, signed at Madrid on 22 May 1973,
- the Treaty between the Czechoslovak Socialist Republic and the Italian Republic on Legal Assistance in Civil and Criminal Matters, signed at Prague on 6 December 1985, still in force between the Czech Republic, Slovakia and Italy,
- the Convention between the Socialist Republic of Romania and the Italian Republic on Legal Assistance in Civil and Criminal Matters, signed at Bucharest on 11 November 1972,
- the Convention between the People's Republic of Poland and the Italian Republic on Legal Assistance and the Recognition and Enforcement of Judgments in Civil Matters, signed at Warsaw on 28 April 1989,
- the Agreement between the People's Republic of Bulgaria and the Italian Republic on Legal Assistance and the Enforcement of Judgments in Civil Matters, signed at Rome on 18 May 1990,
- the Convention between the Federal People's Republic of Yugoslavia and the Italian Republic on Mutual Judicial Cooperation in Civil and Administrative Matters, signed at Rome on 3 December 1960, still in force between Slovenia, Croatia and Italy.

in Cyprus:
- the 1982 Treaty between the Czechoslovak Socialistic Republic and the Republic of Cyprus on Legal Assistance in Civil and Criminal Matters,
- the 1981 Convention between the Republic of Cyprus and the People's Republic of Hungary on Legal Assistance in Civil and Criminal Matters,
- the 1984 Convention between the Republic of Cyprus and the Hellenic Republic on Legal Co-operation in Matters of Civil, Family, Commercial and Criminal Law,
- the 1983 Agreement between the Republic of Cyprus and the People's Republic of Bulgaria on Legal Assistance in Civil and Criminal Matters,
- the 1984 Treaty between the Republic of Cyprus and the Socialist Federal Republic of Yugoslavia on Legal Assistance in Civil and Criminal Matters (to which Slovenia, among others, is a successor),
- the 1996 Convention between the Republic of Cyprus and the Republic of Poland on Legal Cooperation in Civil and Criminal Matters.

in Latvia:
- Agreement of 11 November 1992 on Legal Assistance and Legal Relations between the Republic of Lithuania, the Republic of Estonia and the Republic of Latvia,
- Agreement of 23 February 1994 between the Republic of Latvia and the Republic of Poland on Legal Assistance and Legal Relations in Civil, Family, Labour and Criminal Matters.

in Lithuania:
- the Agreement on Legal Assistance and Legal Relations between the Republic of Lithuania, the Republic of Estonia and the Republic of Latvia, signed in Tallinn on 11 November 1992,

- the Agreement between the Republic of Lithuania and the Republic of Poland on Legal Assistance and Legal Relations in Civil, Family, Labour and Criminal Matters, signed in Warsaw on 26 January 1993.

in Luxembourg:
- the Convention between Luxembourg and Austria on the Recognition and Enforcement of Judgments and Authentic Instruments in Civil and Commercial Matters, signed at Luxembourg on 29 July 1971,
- the Treaty between Belgium, the Netherlands and Luxembourg on Jurisdiction, Bankruptcy, and the Validity and Enforcement of Judgments, Arbitration Awards and Authentic Instruments, signed at Brussels on 24 November 1961, in so far as it is in force,

in Hungary:
- the Agreement between the People's Republic of Hungary and the People's Republic of Bulgaria on Legal Assistance in Civil, Family and Criminal Matters, signed at Sofia on 16 May 1966,
- the Convention between the People's Republic of Hungary and the Republic of Cyprus on Legal Assistance in Civil and Criminal Matters, signed at Budapest on 30 November 1981,
- the Treaty between the Czechoslovak Socialist Republic and the People's Republic of Hungary on Legal Assistance and Regulation of Legal Relations in Civil, Family and Criminal Matters, signed at Bratislava on 28 March 1989, in respect of the Czech Republic and the Slovak Republic,
- the Convention between the People's Republic of Hungary and the French Republic on Legal Assistance in Civil and Family Law, on the Recognition and Enforcement of Judgments and on Legal Assistance in Criminal Matters and on Extradition, signed at Budapest on 31 July 1980,
- the Convention between the People's Republic of Hungary and the Hellenic Republic on Legal Assistance in Civil and Criminal Matters, signed at Budapest on 8 October 1979,
- the Treaty between the People's Republic of Hungary and the Socialist Federal Republic of Yugoslavia on Mutual Legal Assistance, signed on 7 March 1968, in respect of the Republic of Croatia and in the Republic of Slovenia,
- the Convention between the People's Republic of Hungary and the People's Republic of Poland on Legal Assistance in Civil, Family and Criminal Matters, signed at Budapest on 6 March 1959,
- the Treaty between the People's Republic of Hungary and the People's Republic of Romania on Legal Assistance in Civil, Family and Criminal Matters, signed at Bucharest on 7 October 1958.

in Malta, none,

in the Netherlands:
- the Convention between Belgium and the Netherlands on Jurisdiction, Bankruptcy, and the Validity and Enforcement of Judgments, Arbitration Awards and Authentic Instruments, signed at Brussels on 28 March 1925,
- the Convention between the Netherlands and Italy on the Recognition and Enforcement of Judgments in Civil and Commercial Matters, signed at Rome on 17 April 1959,
- the Convention between the Netherlands and Germany on the Mutual Recognition and Enforcement of Judgments and Other Enforceable Instruments in Civil and Commercial Matters, signed at The Hague on 30 August 1962,
- the Convention between the Netherlands and Austria on the Mutual Recognition and Enforcement of Judgments and Authentic Instruments in Civil and Commercial Matters, signed at The Hague on 6 February 1963,
- the Convention between the United Kingdom and the Kingdom of the Netherlands providing for

the mutual recognition and enforcement of judgments in civil matters, signed at The Hague on 17 November 1967,
–   the Treaty between Belgium, the Netherlands and Luxembourg on Jurisdiction, Bankruptcy, and the Validity and Enforcement of Judgments, Arbitration Awards and Authentic Instruments, signed at Brussels on 24 November 1961, in so far as it is in force.

in Poland:
–   the Convention between the People's Republic of Poland and the People's Republic of Hungary on Legal Assistance in Civil, Family and Criminal Matters, signed at Budapest on 6 March 1959,
–   the Convention between the People's Republic of Poland and the Federal People's Republic of Yugoslavia on Legal Assistance in Civil and Criminal Matters, signed at Warsaw on 6 February 1960, currently in force between Poland and Slovenia and between Poland and Croatia,
–   the Agreement between the People's Republic of Bulgaria and the People's Republic of Poland on Legal Assistance and Legal Relations in Civil, Family and Criminal Matters, signed at Warsaw, on 4 December 1961,
–   the Convention between the People's Republic of Poland and the Republic of Austria on Mutual Relations in Civil Law Matters and on Documents, signed at Vienna, on 11 December 1963,
–   the Convention between the People's Republic of Poland and the Hellenic Republic on Legal Assistance in Civil and Criminal Matters, signed at Athens on 24 October 1979,
–   the Treaty between the Czechoslovak Socialist Republic and the People's Republic of Poland on Legal Assistance and Regulation of Legal Relations in Civil, Family, Labour and Criminal Matters, signed at Warsaw on 21 December 1987, still in force in relations between Poland and the Czech Republic and between Poland and Slovakia,
–   the Convention between the People's Republic of Poland and the Italian Republic on Legal Assistance and Recognition and Enforcement of Judgments in Civil Matters, signed at Warsaw on 28 April 1989,
–   the Agreement between the Republic of Poland and the Republic of Lithuania on Legal Assistance and Legal Relations in Civil, Family, Labour and Criminal Matters, signed at Warsaw on 26 January 1993,
–   the Agreement between the Republic of Latvia and the Republic of Poland on Legal Assistance and Legal Relations in Civil, Family, Labour and Criminal Matters, signed at Riga on 23 February 1994,
–   the Convention between the Republic of Cyprus and the Republic of Poland on Legal Cooperation in Civil and Criminal Matters, signed at Nicosia on 14 November 1996,
–   the Agreement between the Republic of Estonia and the Republic of Poland on Legal Assistance and Legal Relations in Civil, Labour and Criminal matters, signed at Tallinn, on 27 November 1998,
–   the Treaty between Romania and the Republic of Poland on Legal Assistance and Legal Relations in Civil Matters, signed at Bucharest on 15 May 1999.
–   in Portugal, the Convention between the Czechoslovak Republic and Portugal on the Recognition and Enforcement of Court Judgments, signed at Lisbon, 23 November 1927.

in Romania:
–   the Treaty between the People's Republic of Bulgaria and the Romanian People's Republic on Legal Assistance in Civil, Family and Criminal Matters, signed at Sofia on 3 December 1958,
–   the Treaty between the Czech Republic and Romania on Legal Assistance in Civil Matters, signed at Bucharest on 11 July 1994,
–   the Convention between the Socialist Republic of Romania and the Kingdom of Greece on Legal Assistance in Civil and Criminal Matters, signed at Bucharest on 19 October 1972,

- the Convention between the Socialist Republic of Romania and the Italian Republic on Legal Assistance in Civil and Criminal Matters, signed at Bucharest on 11 November 1972,
- the Convention between the Socialist Republic of Romania and the French Republic on Legal Assistance in Civil and Commercial Matters, signed at Paris 5 November 1974,
- the Treaty between Romania and the Republic of Poland on Legal Assistance and Legal Relations in Civil Matters, signed at Bucharest on 15 May 1999,
- the Treaty between the Romanian People's Republic and the Federal People's Republic of Yugoslavia (applicable pursuant to the declaration of succession concluded with Slovenia and Croatia) on Legal Assistance, signed at Belgrade on 18 October 1960,
- the Treaty between the Romanian People's Republic and the Czechoslovak Republic (applicable pursuant to the declaration of succession concluded with Slovakia) on Legal Assistance in Civil, Family and Criminal Matters, signed at Prague on 25 October 1958,
- the Convention between Romania and the Kingdom of Spain on Jurisdiction, Recognition and Enforcement of Judgments in Civil and Commercial Matters, signed at Bucharest on 17 November 1997,
- the Treaty between the Romanian People's Republic and the People's Republic of Hungary on Legal Assistance in Civil, Family and Criminal Matters, signed at Bucharest on 7 October 1958,
- the Convention between the Socialist Republic of Romania and the Republic of Austria on Legal Assistance in Civil and Family law and the Validity and Service of Documents and its annexed Protocol, signed at Vienna on 17 November 1965.

in Slovenia:
- the Treaty between the Federal People's Republic of Yugoslavia and the Republic of Austria on the Mutual Judicial Cooperation, signed at Vienna on 16 December 1954,
- the Convention between the Federal People's Republic of Yugoslavia and the Italian Republic on Mutual Judicial Cooperation in Civil and Administrative Matters, signed at Rome on 3 December 1960,
- the Agreement between the Federal People's Republic of Yugoslavia and the Kingdom of Greece on the Mutual Recognition and Enforcement of Judgments, signed at Athens on 18 June 1959,
- the Convention between the Federal People's Republic of Yugoslavia and the People's Republic of Poland on Legal Assistance in Civil and Criminal Matters, signed at Warsaw on 6 February 1960,
- the Treaty between the Socialist Federal Republic of Yugoslavia and the Czechoslovak Socialist Republic on Regulation of Legal Relations in Civil, Family and Criminal Matters, signed at Belgrade on 20 January 1964,
- the Treaty between the Socialist Federal Republic of Yugoslavia and the Republic of Cyprus on Legal Assistance in Civil and Criminal Matters, signed at Nicosia on 19 September 1984,
- the Agreement between the Federal People's Republic of Yugoslavia and the People's Republic of Bulgaria on Mutual Legal Assistance, signed at Sofia on 23 March 1956,
- the Treaty between the Federal People's Republic of Yugoslavia and the Romanian People's Republic on Legal Assistance, signed at Belgrade on 18 October 1960 and its Protocol,
- the Treaty between the Socialist Federal Republic of Yugoslavia and the Hungarian People's Republic on Mutual Legal Assistance, signed at Belgrade on 7 March 1968,
- the Treaty between the Republic of Slovenia and the Republic of Croatia on Legal Assistance in Civil and Criminal Matters, signed at Zagreb on 7 February 1994,
- the Convention between the Government of the Socialist Federal Republic of Yugoslavia and the Government of the Republic of France on the Recognition and Enforcement of Judgments in Civil and Commercial Matters, signed at Paris on 18 May 1971.

in Slovakia:
- the Agreement between the Czechoslovak Socialist Republic and the People's Republic of Bulgaria on Legal Assistance and Regulation of Relations in Civil, Family and Criminal Matters, signed at Sofia on 25 November 1976,
- the Treaty between the Czechoslovak Socialistic Republic and the Republic of Cyprus on Legal Assistance in Civil and Criminal Matters, signed at Nicosia on 23 April 1982,
- the Treaty between the Slovak Republic and the Czech Republic on Legal Assistance provided by Judicial Authorities and on Regulation of Certain Legal Relations in Civil and Criminal Matters, signed at Prague on 29 October 1992,
- the Treaty between the Government of the Czechoslovak Socialist Republic and the Government of the Republic of France on Legal Assistance and the Recognition and Enforcement of Judgments in Civil, Family and Commercial Matters, signed at Paris on 10 May 1984,
- the Treaty between the Czechoslovak Socialist Republic and the Hellenic Republic on Legal Assistance in Civil and Criminal Matters, signed at Athens on 22 October 1980,
- the Treaty between the Czechoslovak Socialist Republic and the Socialist Federal Republic of Yugoslavia on Regulation of Legal Relations in Civil, Family and Criminal Matters, signed at Belgrade on 20 January 1964,
- the Treaty between the Czechoslovak Socialist Republic and the People's Republic of Hungary on Legal Assistance and Regulation of Legal Relations in Civil, Family and Criminal Matters, signed at Bratislava on 28 March 1989,
- the Treaty between the Czechoslovak Socialist Republic and the People's Republic of Poland on Legal Assistance and Regulation of Legal Relations in Civil, Family, Labour and Criminal Matters, signed at Warsaw on 21 December 1987,
- the Treaty between the Romanian People's Republic and the Czechoslovak Republic on Legal Assistance in Civil, Family and Criminal Matters, signed at Prague on 25 October 1958,
- the Treaty between the Czechoslovak Socialist Republic and the Kingdom of Spain on Legal Assistance, Recognition and Enforcement of Court Judgments in Civil Matters, signed at Madrid on 4 May 1987,
- the Treaty between the Czechoslovak Socialist Republic and the Italian Republic on Legal Assistance in Civil and Criminal Matters, signed at Prague on 6 December 1985.

in Finland:
- the Convention between Denmark, Finland, Iceland, Norway and Sweden on the Recognition and Enforcement of Judgments in Civil Matters, signed at Copenhagen on 11 October 1977,
- the Convention between Finland and Austria on the Recognition and Enforcement of Judgments in Civil Matters, signed at Vienna on 17 November 1986,

in Sweden:
- the Convention between Denmark, Finland, Iceland, Norway and Sweden on the Recognition and Enforcement of Judgments in Civil Matters, signed at Copenhagen on 11 October 1977,
- the Convention between Austria and Sweden on the Recognition and Enforcement of Judgments in Civil Matters, signed at Stockholm on 16 September 1982.

in the United Kingdom:
- the Convention between the United Kingdom and the French Republic providing for the Mutual Enforcement of Judgments in Civil and Commercial Matters, with Protocol, signed at Paris on 18 January 1934,

–   the Convention between the United Kingdom and the Kingdom of Belgium providing for the Mutual Enforcement of Judgments in Civil and Commercial Matters, with Protocol, signed at Brussels on 2 May 1934,
–   the Convention between the United Kingdom and the Federal Republic of Germany for the Mutual Recognition and Enforcement of Judgments in Civil and Commercial Matters, signed at Bonn on 14 July 1960,
–   the Convention between the United Kingdom and Austria providing for the Mutual Recognition and Enforcement of Judgments in Civil and Commercial Matters, signed at Vienna on 14 July 1961, with amending Protocol signed at London on 6 March 1970,
–   the Convention between the United Kingdom and the Italian Republic for the Mutual Recognition and Enforcement of Judgments in Civil and Commercial Matters, signed at Rome on 7 February 1964, with Amending Protocol signed at Rome on 14 July 1970,
–   the Convention between the United Kingdom and the Kingdom of the Netherlands providing for the Mutual Recognition and Enforcement of Judgments in Civil Matters, signed at The Hague on 17 November 1967."

The order of the list of Conventions is first by alphabetical order of the Member States in   **6** their respective official language (but for Austria who should have counted as "Österreich" with an O under these auspices[11]). That is why Hungary (Magyarország with an M) features after Luxemburg, or Cyprus (Κυπρος with a K) after Italy, and why Germany (Deutschland with a D) precedes Estonia, or why Spain (España with an Es) is placed between Greece (Ελλας with an El) and France, or why Croatia (Hrvatska with an H) is to be found between France and Ireland, or Finland (Suomi with an S) between Slovakia and Sweden (Sverige with an Sv). This does not transpire that clearly from the English or French or any other version of List 3. The principle appears to be rather confusing, if not outrightly confused. Obviously prestige took the upper hand over workability. The only argument that can be put forward in its favour is that it avoids the List to be rewritten and re-ordered in every single official language.

In the second, lower tier the order is not chronological for the Conventions concluded by the   **7** single Member State at stake, but rather assembled following the alphabetical order of the respective partner state of the single convention. On this tier Austria appears to have been sorted as "Österreich" with an Ö (equalling Oe), though, so that the order on the first and the second tier do not match exactly.[12] The system chosen could be more user-friendly, and the not attendant user will be prone to overlooking information.

The list cures a curiosity surrounding Art. 69 Brussels I Regulation: Whereas Art. 55 Brussels   **8** Convention, since the 1973 Accession Convention, has also listed bilateral Conventions between other Member States and the United Kingdom, Art. 69 Brussels I Regulation refrained from doing so. Originally this was correct since the United Kingdom did not

---

[11]   Austria opens the English version as "Austria" with an A, likewise the Italian and the Spanish versions, plus the French version as "Autriche" and the Polish version as "Austrii". Confusion is rising with the Dutch version opening with "Oostenrijk" and the Swedish version with "Österrike", to be topped by the Czech version and its primer "Rakousku".
[12]   To make the inconsistency perfect, Austria in Lists 1 and 2 is found at a place in the order as though it read "Österreich". So, the first tier of List 3 begs to differ in this regard also from Lists 1 and 2.

become a Member State in the sense of the Regulation automatically. This was due to Art. 69 EC Treaty and the respective Protocol to the EC Treaty – but it was correct only until the United Kingdom opted in.[13]

9   Art. 69 employs a different technique than its predecessors. It does not contain a list of bilateral Conventions superseded in its very wording. Nor does it refer to an Annex. Both, the wording or an Annex, would be a formal part of the Regulation. Instead, it employs a more informal technique namely to refer to a list established by the Commission. This list is established by the Commission pursuant to Art. 76 (1) (c), (2). There are less and fewer formalities to be observed if this list is to be altered than would have to be complied with if the list was an Annex.

10   The list established, and compiled, by the Commission is not exhaustive and constitutive, but only of a declaratory nature. The phrase "in particular" at the beginning of the second clause of Art. 69 clearly evidences that. Hence, if a bilateral agreement is not listed it is nonetheless superseded. The list is only a collection of information only and alleviates access to the relevant data. But it is does transcend that into normative force. Its possible short comings cannot keep alive or even revitalise a "forgotten" convention. Otherwise there would be an unwarranted incentive for a Member State to inform the Commission incorrectly omitting such convention – just to be puzzled by its partner State under the bilateral agreement nominating the convention to the Commission and leaving the user confronted with a choice whether the nomination by the one partner State prevails over the non-nomination by the other.

11   A case of doubt is provided by the BVIE[14] in relation particularly to Arts. 24 (4); 7 (2).[15] That any Benelux Convention is a trilateral, not a bilateral Treaty is not a tiebreaker as can be deducted from Belgium, Luxemburg and the Netherlands unanimously and concurringly listing another Benelux Convention as being superseded by virtue of Art. 69.

Article 70

1.   **The conventions referred to in Article 69 shall continue to have effect in relation to matters to which this Regulation does not apply.**
2.   **They shall continue to have effect in respect of judgments given, authentic instruments formally drawn up or registered and court settlements approved or concluded before the date of entry into force of Regulation (EC) No. 44/2001.**

1   The provision expresses trite law: The Brussels I*bis* Regulation only supersedes bilateral agreements within its area of application and does not abolish or repeal them completely. That is why the agreements continue to have effect in relation to matters to which the Brussels I Regulation does not apply. Otherwise the Regulation would – against its general

---

13   *Droz/Gaudemet-Tallon*, RCDIP 90 (2001), 601, 618.
14   Benelux-verdrag inzake de intellectuele eigendom (merken en tekeningen of modellen).
15   Rb. Den Haag NIPR 2015 Nr 65 pp. 163–164.

target – cause a deteriorations for of the free movement of judgments by repealing the progresses achieved to date without replacing it through with something of the same value.[1]

The matters concerned are first and foremost the those matters exempted by Art. 1 (1).[2]   **2** Some of the bilateral agreements also regulate the recognition and enforcement of judgments in matrimonial matters, in probate cases or of arbitral awards. In this respect they keep importance. Bilateral agreements also continue to have effect as far as they deal with other fields of law other than with civil or commercial matters pursuant to Art. 1 (1).[3] The same expression in bilateral agreements and in Art. 1 (1) may be interpreted differently.[4] In particular, it should be noted that the notion of "civil and commercial matters" will not necessarily carry the same meaning in a bilateral agreement as it has under the Brussels I Regulation so that a wider understanding in the bilateral agreement might fall into the first constellation.[5] Such wider understanding might be generated by a different understanding of the areas in the vicinity of public law, particularly so if one of the Contracting Parties of the bilateral agreement does not recognise a proper notion of public in its own national law.[6]

In exceptional cases a judgment may partly fall under the Brussels I*bis* Regulation and partly   **3** under a bilateral agreement having a more extensive scope. In these cases it is necessary to carry two pertinent different sets of legal rules for enforcement or recognition respectively.[7] The Brussels I*bis* regime must be stretched beyond its self-defined limits and thus applies only to the part of the judgment falling within its scope of application.[8] The further question of whether, if the enforcement proceedings can be joined or else connected, must be answered by the national procedural law of the state where enforcement is sought.[9] Problems might result from different jurisdictional regimes of courts within the judicial system of that state.

The Brussels I*bis* Regulation can only claim precedence within its temporal scope. This is   **4** laid down in (2). It corresponds to Art. 66 therefore that the Brussels I*bis* Regulation is not applied to judgments respectively as public documents which that were issued respectively were taken down in writing before its entry into force. The pertinent corresponding Brussels Convention as pre-predecessor of the Brussels I*bis* Regulation has already superseded the bilateral conventions so that the scope of this intertemporal statement is reduced.[10] Other-

---

1   *Mankowski*, in: Rauscher Art. 70 note 1.
2   *Tiefenthaler*, in: Czernich/Tiefenthaler/Kodek Art. 70 note 1.
3   *Kropholler/von Hein* Art. 70 note 1.
4   *Bavaria Fluggesellschaft Schwabe & Co. KG and Germanair Bedarfluftfahrt GmbH & Co. KG v. Euro-control* (Case 10/77), [1977] ECR 1517, 1526 paras. 6, 7 = NJW 1978, 483 with note *Geimer*; BGH WM 1977, 88; BGH NJW 1978, 1113.
5   *Bavaria Fluggesellschaft Schwabe & Co. KG and Germanair Bedarfluftfahrt GmbH & Co. KG v. Euro-control* (Case 10/77), [1977] ECR 1517, 1526 paras. 6, 7; Hof van Cass. J. trib. 2010, 520; *Traest*, J. trib. 2010, 520, 521, 522.
6   *Traest*, J. trib. 2010, 520, 522.
7   *Droz* para. 637; *Schlafen*, in: Bülow/Böckstiegel Art. 56 EuGVÜ note 2 (1977); *Kropholler/von Hein* Art. 70 note 1.
8   See only *Layton/Mercer* para. 30.015.
9   *Mankowski*, in: Rauscher Art. 70 note 3.
10 *Kropholler/von Hein* Art. 70 note 2; *Mankowski*, in: Rauscher Art. 70 note 4.

wise the absurd result would emerge that the bilateral Conventions would be revived although they have been had long ago been superseded by the Brussels or Lugano Conventions.[11] Yet the very wording of (2) can be criticised for lacking the utmost precision and giving rise to the possibility of misunderstandings by the unwary.[12]

5 Art. 70 resembles Art. 70 Brussels I Regulation but for one tiny detail in (2) *in fine*: The relevant date of entry into force is not that of the actual Regulation as it was in Art. 70 (2) Brussels I Regulation, but the date of entry into force of the Brussels I Regulation, also for the purposes of the Brussels I*bis* Regulation.

Article 71

1. This Regulation shall not affect any conventions to which the Member States are parties and which, in relation to particular matters, govern jurisdiction or the recognition or enforcement of judgments.
2. With a view to its uniform interpretation, paragraph 1 shall be applied in the following manner:
   (a) this Regulation shall not prevent a court of a Member State which is party to a convention on a particular matter from assuming jurisdiction in accordance with that convention, even where the defendant is domiciled in another Member State which is not party to that convention. The court hearing the action shall, in any event, apply Article 28 of this Regulation;
   (b) judgments given in a Member State by a court in the exercise of jurisdiction provided for in a convention on a particular matter shall be recognised and enforced in the other Member States in accordance with this Regulation.
   Where a convention on a particular matter to which both the Member State of origin and the Member State addressed are parties lays down conditions for the recognition or enforcement of judgments, those conditions shall apply. In any event, the provisions of this Regulation on recognition and enforcement of judgments may be applied.

Bibliography

Álvarez Rubio, La regla de especialidad en el artículo 57 del Convenio de Bruselas de 1968, An. Der. Mar. XII (1995), 273

Attal, Droit international privé communautaire et conventions internationales: un délicate articulation, Pétites affiches 2010 no. 238 p. 32

Barnert, Positive Kompetenzkonflikte im internationalen Zivilprozessrecht – Zum Verhältnis zwischen Art. 21 EuGVÜ und Art. 31 CMR, ZZZ 2005, 81

Bělohlávek, Law Applicable to International Carriage: EU Law and International Treaties, Czech Yb. Int. L. 6 (2015), 27

Raphael Brunner, Unterschiedliche Rechtsprechung in Bezug auf die Durchbrechung der Haftungsbeschränkung und die Frage der Sperrwirkung von negativen Feststellungsklagen gemäß CMR im Transportrecht, TranspR 2013, 99

Dörfelt, Gerichtsstand sowie Anerkennung und Vollstreckung nach dem Bunkeröl-Übereinkommen, IPRax 2009, 470

---

[11] *Droz/Gaudemet-Tallon*, RCDIP 90 (2001), 601, 619.
[12] *Droz/Gaudemet-Tallon*, RCDIP 90 (2001), 601, 619.

Domej, Effet utile der EuGVVO und Vorrang von Spezialübereinkommen, in: FS Heinz Mayer (Wien 2011), p. 41

Espinosa Calabuig, ¿La desarmonización de la armonización europea? A propósito del Convenion de Ginebra de 12 de marzo de 1999 sobre embargo preventivo de buques y su relación con los regolamentos Bruselas I y Bruselas I*bis*, RDIPP 2013, 645

Finger, Anerkennung und Vollstreckung ausländischer (Unterhalts-)Urteile im Inland, FuR 2001, 97

Gaja, Sui rapporti fra la Convenzione di Bruxelles e le altre norme concernenti la giurisdizione ed il riconoscimento di sentenze straniere, RDIPP 1991, 253

Geimer, Anerkennung und Vollstreckung polnischer Vaterschaftsurteile mit Annexentscheidung über den Unterhalt etc., IPRax 2004, 419

Grothe, Gerichtsstandsprobleme bei Regressansprüchen von Transportversicherern im internationalen Speditionsgeschäft, in: FS Helmut Schirmer (2005), p. 151

Haak, Naar een vrij verkeer van CMR-vonnissen in Europa?, NTHR 2009, 69

Haak, Europäische Lösung der deutsch-niederländischen Kontroverse in der CMR-Interpretation?, TranspR 2009, 189

Haubold, Internationale Zuständigkeit nach CMR und EuGVÜ/LugÜ, IPRax 2000, 91

Haubold, CMR und Europäisches Zivilverfahrensrecht – Klarstellungen zu internationaler Zuständigkeit und Rechtshängigkeit, IPRax 2006, 224

Hoeks, CMR of EEX? – van samenloop, litispendentie en het vrij verkeer van vonnissen in Europa, NIPR 2011, 468

van der Klooster, Het TNT/AXA-arrest – het oplossing van een problem of het problem van een oplossing, in: IPR in de spiegel van Paul Vlas, 2012, p. 113

Kropholler/Blobel, Unübersichtliche Gemengelagen im IPR durch EF-Verordnungen und Staatsverträge, in: FS Hans Jürgen Sonnenberger (2004), p. 453

Kuijper, The Changing Status of Private International Law Treaties of the Member States in Relation to Regulation No. 44/2001, (2011) 38 Legal Issues Econ. Integration 89

Kuypers, Eenheid en verdeelheid en Europa: EEX-Verordening versus CMR en de vrij verkeer van vonnissen, NTER 2011, 13

Laviani, Coordinamento tra convenzioni internazionali: l'art. 57 della convenzione di Bruxelles del 1968 nelle ipotesi di litispendenza, RDIPP 2004, 157

Legros, Lex conflits de normes en matière de contrats de transports internationaux de marchandises, Clunet 134 (2007), 799 and 1081

Magrone, Trasporto di merci: Convenzione ad hoc applicabile solo se previdibile in grado di limitare liti parallele, Guida dir. 2010 n. 21 p. 96

Majoros, Les conventions internationales en matière de droit privé, Vol. II (1980)

Majoros, Konflikte zwischen Staatsverträgen auf dem Gebiete des Privatrechts, RabelsZ 46 (1982), 84

Mankowski, Spezialabkommen und EuGVÜ, EWS 1996, 301

Mankowski, Im Dschungel der für die Vollstreckbarerklärung ausländischer Unterhaltsentscheidungen einschlägigen Übereinkommen und ihrer Ausführungsgesetze, IPRax 2000, 188

Mankowski, Gelten die bilateralen Staatsverträge der Bundesrepublik Deutschland im Internationalen Erbrecht nach dem Inwirkungtreten der EuErbVO weiter?, ZEV 2013, 529

Mankowski, EuGVVO, Brüssel Ia-VO und Spezialübereinkommen, TranspR 2014, 129

de Miguel Asensio, Convenios internacionales y unificación del Derecho internacional privado de la Unión Europea, in: Liber amciorum José Luis Iglesias Buhigues (2012), p. 57

de Meij, Samenloop van CMR-Verdrag en EEX-Verordening (Deventer 2003)

Pauknerová, International Conventions and Community Law: Harmony and Conflicts, in: Liber Fausto Pocar, vol. II (2009), p. 793

Pesce, Le convenzioni internazionali in materie particolari ed il conflitto con la convenzione di Bruxelles 27 settembre 1968 e con la convenzione di Lugano 16 settembre 1988 in materia di litispendenza, Dir. mar. 95 (1993), 675

Plašil/Kliment, The CMR Convention, Brussels I Regulation and "Empty International Competence": The Determination of Territorial Jurisdiction of National Courts in Disputes Arising out of the International Carriage of Goods, Czech Yb. Int. L. 6 (2015), 169

Ramming, Zur Zuständigkeit deutscher Gerichte für Ansprüche wegen Ölverschmutzungsschäden, TranspR 2007, 13

Ringblom, EU Regulation 44/2001 and Its Implication for the International Maritime Liability Conventions, 35 JMLC 1 (2004)

Rossolillo, Convenzioni concluse dagli Stati membri e diritto processuale civile internazionale dell'Unione europea: interpretazione conforme o rispetto degli obblighi internazionali?, Cuad. Der. Trans. 2 (2) (2010), 305

Thomas Rüfner, Lis alibi pendens under the CMR, [2001] LMCLQ 460

Schinkels, Verhältnis von Art. 31 CMR und EuGVÜ sowie Einbeziehung der ADSp gegenüber einer italienischen AG, IPRax 2003, 517

Patrick Schmidt, Die negative Feststellungsklage im Anwendungsbereich der CMR – grundsätzliche Überlegungen, TranspR 2013, 377

Florian Schulz, Internationale Gerichtszuständigkeit nach der EuGVVO am Beispiel des Transportrechts, HanseLR 2005, 147

H. Stein, Samenloop van executieverdragen, in: Offerhauskring vijfentwintig jaar (1987), p. 185

Strikwerda, Samenloopperikelen in het internationaal procesrecht, in: Bundel opstellen aangeboden aan C.J.H. Brunner (1994), p. 389

Tagaras, L'applicabilité des conventions de La Haye dans le cadre de la Convention de Bruxelles, RBDI 1991, 479

Tuo, Alcune riflessioni sulla portata applicativa della CMR, RDIPP 2004, 193

Tuo, Regolamento Bruxelles I e convenzioni su materie particolari: Tra obblighi internazionale e primauté del diritto dell'Unione Europea, RDIPP 2011, 377

Tuo, Giurisdizione ed efficacia delle decisioni sul sequestro conservativo: tra regolamento Bruxelles I e convenzioni internazionali, Dir. mar. 2011, 1223

Vassali di Dachenhausen, Il coordinamento tra convenzioni di diritto internazionale privato e processuale (1993)

Verschuur, Vrij verkeer van vonnissen (1995)

Vettorel, Una pronuncia della Corte di giustizia sui rapporti fra il regolamento (CE) n. 44/2001 e le convenzioni in materie particolari, Riv. dir. int. 2010, 826

Volken, Konventionskonflikte im internationalen Privatrecht (1977)

Rolf Wagner, Normenkonflikte zwischen den EG-Verordnungen Brüssel I, Rom I und Rom II und transportrechtlichen Rechtsinstrumenten, TranspR 2009, 103

Waldner, Die internationale Zuständigkeit der Schweizer Gerichte zur Beurteilung der Klagen der Opfer nuklearer Zwischenfälle, SZIER 2011, 5

Wesołowski, The Unclear Relation between CMR and European Union Law in Respect of Jurisdiction and Enforcement of Foreign Judgments, ETL 2011, 133.

I. General considerations

1. Ranking rule

Given the rather technical nature of Chapter VII, its most important provision is Art. 71. **1**
Art. 71 has to be seen in a close context with Art. 351 TFEU (ex-Art. 307 EC Treaty).[1] The
objective of Art. 71 is to deal with possible conflicts of law-making treaties.[2] Such conflicts
may arise between the Brussels I Regulation and other eminent conventions in the area of
international procedural law, particularly those concluded with third countries.[3] The focus
lies especially on the multiple conventions of the Hague Conference on Private International
Law as well as on various conventions in the field of international transportation law. The
potential conflict is solved by (1) allowing specialised conventions to take precedence over
the Brussels I*bis* Regulation, in order to ensure compliance with those conventions and to
enable Member States to meet with paramount obligations as arising from international
law.[4] Recital (35) – reiterating and continuing Recital (25) Brussels I Regulation – unambiguously asserts that respect for international commitments entered into by the Member
States means that this Regulation should not affect conventions relating to specific matters
to which the Member States are parties. This respects stems from Art. 30 (4) Vienna Treaty
Convention.[5] Art. 73 (3) and Recital (36) add that such respect extends to bilateral conventions or agreements between a third State and a Member State.

Phrased in the terminology generally prevailing in international law, Art. 71 is a so called **2**
disconnection clause.[6] It is to secure maximum uniformity with respect to the legal order of
individual Member States and their obligations towards Third States.[7] The application of the
Regulation is deemed to be precluded solely in relation to questions governed by a specialised convention.[8] The purpose of the exception is to ensure compliance with the rules on
jurisdiction, *lis pendens* or recognition and enforcement laid down by such specialised
conventions, since when those rules were enacted, account was taken of the specific features
of the matters to which they relate.[9] (1) emulates a *lex specialis* rule.[10] Although the Brussels
I*bis* Regulation generally accounts for an overall approach, this is a proper way to pay due

---

[1] See only *Rossolillo*, Cuad. Der. Trans. 2 (2) (2010), 305, 306; *Mankowski*, ZEV 2013, 529, 533.

[2] *Mankowski*, EWS 1996, 301, 302; *Gaia*, RDIPP 1991, 253, 255.

[3] Conventions concluded solely among Member States do not lie within the scope of Art. 71, but are dealt
with in Art. 69.

[4] See *The "Po"* [1991] 2 Lloyd's Rep. 206, 209 (C.A., per *Lloyd* L.J.).

[5] *Domej*, in: FS Heinz Mayer (2012), p. 41, 44.

[6] *Pauknerová*, in: Liber Fausto Pocar, vol. II (2009), p. 793, 802.

[7] *Pauknerová*, in: Liber Fausto Pocar, vol. II (2009), p. 793, 803.

[8] *The owners of the cargo lately laden on board the ship "Tatry" v. The owners of the ship "Maciej Rataj"*
(Case 406/92), [1994] ECR I-5439, I-5471 para. 24; *The "Anna H"* [1995] 1 Lloyd's Rep. 11, 18 (C.A., per
Hobhouse L.J.); Trib. Lecco RDIPP 1990, 357, 359.

[9] *The owners of the cargo lately laden on board the ship "Tatry" v. The owners of the ship "Maciej Rataj"*
(Case 406/92), [1994] ECR I-5439, I-5471 para. 24; *Nürnberger Allgemeine Versicherungs-AG v. Port-
bridge Transport International BV*, (Case C-148/03) [2004] ECR I-10327, I-10335 para. 14; *TNT Express
Nederland BV v. AXA Versicherung AG* (Case C-533/08), [2010] ECR I-4107 para. 48; A-G *Kokott*,
Opinion of 28 January 2010 in Case C-533/08), [2010] ECR I-4110 para. 34; *Rolf Wagner*, TranspR
2009, 103, 106.

Peter Mankowski

regard of to the particularities of some areas of the law, in particular maritime law.[11] Of course, it is a prerequisite in order for Art. 71 to become operable that the Regulation and the international or bilateral convention at stake contain concurrent rules.[12]

3 National legislation providing for the enforcement and execution of a ratified convention precedes the Brussels I*bis* Regulation to the same extent as the specialised convention itself does.[13] Otherwise the UK and other Member States that considering multilateral conventions as non-binding, with respect to the national legal framework, and relying solely on provisions of a national origin which stem from the convention, would face unwarranted discrimination.[14] On the other hand, national legislation deriving from a convention takes only precedence over the Brussels I Regulation if the convention has been formally ratified.[15] Similarly, national provisions designed for the execution of a ratified convention but clearly exceeding its scope of application may not take any precedence over the Brussels I Regulation.[16]

4 Art. 71 survived the recast process unscathed and is a continuation to the letter of Art. 71 Brussels I Regulation. That a cry for legislative intervention in favour of superseding the frolics introduced by *TNT v. AXA*[17] into Art. 71 Brussels I Regulation emerged from the quarters of the transportation industry[18] and was apparently been heard by the European Parliament's Committee of Legal Affairs,[19] did not matter eventually for it did not succeed finally.

2. Conventions already ratified by the Member States

a) Generalities

5 Although Art. 71 withholds priority of other conventions on specific matters over the general rule of the Regulation, this only applies to conventions to which the Member States are parties at the time of the adoption of the Regulation. There is no reservation in favour of conventions to which Member States "will be" parties.[20] In sharp contrast to Art. 57 (1)

---

10 See only A-G *Strikwerda*, NJ 2008 Nr 623 p. 6446, 6449; *Delebecque*, Rev. trim. dr. com. 2010, 622, 626; *van den Oosterkamp*, SEW 2011, 193.

11 *Pataut*, RCDIP 93 (2005), 129.

12 *TNT Express Nederland BV v. AXA Versicherung AG* (Case C-533/08), [2010] ECR I-4107 para. 46.

13 The *"Po"* [1991] 2 Lloyd's Rep 206 (C.A.); *Mankowski*, in: Rauscher Art. 71 note 2; *Oberhammer*, in: Stein/Jonas Art. 71 note 4; *Gottwald*, in: Münchener Kommentar zur ZPO Art. 71 note 3.

14 *Mankowski*, in: Rauscher Art. 71 note 2.

15 *Mankowski*, Seerechtliche Vertragsverhältnisse im Internationalen Privatrecht (1995) p. 297 *et seq.*; *Mankowski*, EWS 1996, 301, 302.

16 *Philip*, NTIR 46 (1977) 113, 119; *Basedow*, VersR 1978, 495, 502; *Basedow*, in: Handbuch des internationalen Zivilverfahrensrechts, Vol. I (1982) Ch. II note 140; *Lagarde*, RCDIP 68 (1979), 100, 101; *Mankowski*, EWS 1996, 301, 302.

17 *TNT Express Nederland BV v. AXA Versicherung AG* (Case C-533/08), [2010] ECR I-4107.

18 Deutsche Gesellschaft für Transportrecht e.V., Vorschlag zur Neufassung der Brüssel I-Verordnung, 7.6.2011 p. 2, 10–11.

19 Draft Report *Zwiefka*, p. 39 Amendment 55.

20 *Kennett*, (2001) 50 ICLQ 725, 736; *Droz/Gaudemet-Tallon*, RCDIP 90 (2001), 601, 620 *et seq.*; *Laviani*, RDIPP 2004, 157, 190 *et seq.*; *Tuo*, RDIPP 2011, 377, 379.

Brussels Convention, respect for any such new conventions is no longer maintained. This boils down to a remarkable shift of competence to the European Institutions, largely corresponding to the growth of EC legislative activity in the field of international procedural law.[21] According to the so-called AETR doctrine established by the CJEU, the Union alone is in a position to assume and carry out contractual obligations towards third countries, as far as Union rules are promulgated for the attainment of the objectives of the Treaty.[22] On the basis of Art. 81 (a) TFEU (formerly Artt. 61; 65 (c) EC Treaty after Amsterdam), jurisdiction and the recognition and enforcement of judgments fall within the competence of the European Union. It is a competence that has been exercised, as the Brussels I Regulation derives directly from the then new Title IV of the EC Treaty. Therefore individual Member States must not accept international commitments that could affect the Union rules or alter their scope. Exclusive EU competence as acknowledged internally within the Union comes forth externally also and restricts Member States' liberty to negotiate conventions.

(1) does not distinguish between multilateral and bilateral conventions. It covers both kinds **6** indiscriminately. The decisive feature is that at least one non-Member State must be amongst the Contracting States of the respective convention. Bilateral conventions between a Member State and a non-Member State qualify for this criterion.[23] This coincides with the *ratio* underlying (1) for bilateral conventions do not exert lesser binding force under international law than multilateral treaties. A limiting "international" or "multilateral" must not be read into the wider wording of (1).[24] The Report *Schlosser* might only list multilateral conventions,[25] but the list contained in it is not exclusive and exhaustive.[26] In a wider context, (1) should accord with the yardsticks prevailing under Art. 351 TFEU since Art. 351 TFEU provides the backing for (1) and its likes in other Regulations of European PIL and

---

[21] *Takahashi*, (2003) 52 ICLQ 529, 530; *Jonathan Harris*, (2001) 20 Civ. Just. Q. 218, 223; *Tuo*, RDIPP 2011, 377, 380.

[22] *Commission of the European Communities v. Council of the European Communities* (AETR) (Case 22/70), [1971] ECR 263, 275 para. 28; *Cornelis Kramer* (Joined Cases 3, 4 & 6/76), [1976] ECR 1279, 1311 paras. 30–33; *Draft Agreement establishing a European laying-up fund for inland waterway vessels* (Opinion 1/76), [1977] ECR 741, 756 para. 5; *Convention No. 170 of the International Labour institutionization concerning safety in the use of chemicals at work* (Opinion 2/91), [1993] ECR I-1061, I-1079 para. 18; *Competence of the Union to conclude international agreements concerning services and the protection of intellectual property*, (Opinion 1/94) [1994] ECR I-5267, I-5411 para. 76, I-5413 para. 82 *et seq.*, I-5416 para. 95; *Competence of the Union or one of its institutions to participate in the Third Revised Decision of the OECD on national treatment* (Opinion 2/92), [1995] ECR I-521, I-559 paras. 31–33; *Accession by the Union to the European Convention for the Protection of Human Rights and Fundamental Freedoms* (Opinion 2/94), [1996] ECR I-1759, I-1787 paras. 25–27; *Cartagena Protocol* (Opinion 2/00), [2001] ECR I-9713, I-9764 para. 45; *Commission of the European Communities v. Kingdom of Denmark (Open Skies)* (Case C-467/98), [2002] ECR I-9519, I-9556 para. 82.

[23] To the same result Hoge Raad NJB 1980, 40 = S&S 1980 Nr 25; *Geimer/Schütze*, Internationale Urteilsanerkennung I/1, p. 71; *Donzallaz*, para. 212; *Domej*, in: Dasser/Oberhammer, Art. 67 LugÜ 2007 note 2; cf. also *Basedow*, in: Handbuch des Internationalen Zivilverfahrensrechts, vol. I (1982) ch. II note 133; *Klauser*, in: Fasching/Konecny, Art. 71 note 1; *Kropholler/von Hein*, Art. 71 note 1.

[24] *Mankowski*, ZEV 2013, 529, 531.

[25] Report *Schlosser*, OJ EEC 1979 C 59/71 para. 59.

[26] See *Mankowski*, ZEV 2013, 529, 531.

Peter Mankowski

international procedural law.[27] Art. 19 Rome III Regulation even expressly refers to Art. 351 TFEU. Under Art. 351 (1) TFEU it is accepted that this rules gives precedence also to bilateral conventions with a single non-Member State.[28] Further support is rendered by Art. 69 (1) Maintenance Regulation where bilateral conventions are expressly given precedence.[29] But even if Art. 71 was not applicable Art. 73 (3) would save the day for bilateral agreements, supported by Recital (36).

7 Difficulties arise as some conventions on specific matters may not allow for direct EU participation.[30] The EU itself cannot conclude any agreement which lacks an accession clause allowing not only States, but also institutions and organizations to accede.[31] As a solution the Council may authorize Member States to sign and ratify such a convention in the interest of the EU.[32] Such authorization has for instance been provided by a Council Decision (the Bunkers Decision) of 19 September 2002 regarding the International Convention on Civil Liability or Bunker Oil Pollution Damage 2001.[33] Originally a reservation had been considered in favour of applying the Brussels I Regulation if the defendant was domiciled in a Member State and the damage occurred in a Member State,[34] but that was opposed[35] and finally dismissed.[36] The same delegating procedure was employed specifically in the context of private international law and international procedural law when the Council decided in December 2002 to authorize the Member States to sign the Hague Convention on the Protection of Children of 1996.[37] In Recital (4) cl. 1 of this Decision 2003/93/EC the Council on the one hand reserved the exclusive competence of the EC but on the other hand emphasised that such competence would follow the principle of *begrenzte Einzelermächtigung*. Recital (4) cl. 2 Decision 2003/93/EC accordingly acknowledges that the Member States remain competent where the respective convention goes beyond the areas covered by EU law. The Rotterdam Rules (which contain rules on jurisdiction) could possibly become another test case. For now it has become established and common practice that the Member States get authorization by the EU to ratify or accede to Conventions.[38]

---

27 See *Mankowski*, ZEV 2013, 529, 533.

28 *Terhechte*, in: Schwarze, EU-Kommentar (3rd ed. 2012) Art. 351 AEUV note 4; cf. also *Commission v. Austria* (Case C-205/06), [2009] ECR I-1301 para. 33; *Commission v. Sweden* (Case C-249/06), [2009] ECR I-1335 para. 34; *Commission v. Finland* (Case C-118/07), [2009] ECR I-10889 para. 27 where in all three Cases the ECJ applies Art. 307 (1) EC Treaty to Bilateral Investment Treaties without even discussing whether this rule covers bilateral conventions.

29 *Mankowski*, ZEV 2013, 529, 532.

30 *Mankowski*, in: Rauscher Art. 71 note 4.

31 *Takahashi*, (2003) 52 ICLQ 529, 530; *Mankowski*, TranspR 2014, 129, 130.

32 As to the consequences for Art. 71 see *infra* Art. 71 note 7a.

33 Council Decision 2002/762/EC of 19 September 2002 authorising the Member States, in the interest of the Union, to sign, ratify or accede to the International Convention on Civil Liability for Bunker Oil Pollution Damage, 2001 (the Bunkers Convention), OJ 2002 L 256/7.

34 COM (2001) 675 final p. 8.

35 European Parliament A5-0201/2002 final p. 8.

36 *Dörfelt*, IPRax 2009, 470, 471 f.

37 Council Decision 2003/93/EC of 19 December 2002 authorising the Member States, in the interest of the Union, to sign the 1996 Hague Convention on jurisdiction, applicable law, recognition, enforcement and cooperation in respect of parental responsibility and measures for the protection of children, OJ EU 2003 L 48/1.

Insofar competence is returned to the Member States.[39] The EU might even direct respective recommendations to open negotiations towards the Member States (with the ensuing danger of such recommendations being ignored).[40] The second option for a way-out is for the EU to implement parallel EU legislation if it is not allowed to accede as such to an international instrument.[41]

b) Restrictions superimposed by the CJEU in TNT/AXA and Nipponkoa

Even with regard to such Conventions which Member States had already ratified before the   **8** Brussels I Regulation came into force, the CJEU superimposes some additional restrictions.[42] Pursuant to the CJEU the application of such specialised Conventions cannot compromise the principles which underlie judicial cooperation in the EU, such as the principles recalled in then Recitals (6), (11), (12) and (15)-(17) Brussels I Regulation, namely free movement of judgments, predictability as to the courts having jurisdiction, legal certainty for litigants, sound administration of justice, minimisation of the risk of concurrent proceedings, and mutual trust in the administration of justice in the EU,[43] which principles are deemed to be the *raison d'être* of the Brussels I*bis* Regulation.[44] The CJEU restricts Art. 71 for this rule allegedly cannot have a purpose that conflicts with these basic principles.[45] The practical result of this restriction (which is deducted from a very abstract level[46]) is to avoid results which are less favourable for achieving sound operation of the internal market than the results to which the provisions of the Brussels I Regulation would lead.[47] The objectives of EU law are thus held paramount.[48] Methodologically, teleological and purposive means of interpretation gain the upper hand over verbal and textual interpretation.[49] Specialised Conventions have to pass a check whether they are fit enough for European purposes.[50]

---

[38] E.g. Council Decision 2004/246/EC of 2 March 2004, OJ EU 2004 L 78/22, as revised by Council Decision 2004/664/EC of 24 September 2004, OJ EU 2004 L 303/28.

[39] *Ramming*, TranspR 2007, 13, 15; *Mankowski*, in: Rauscher Art. 71 note 4.

[40] *Kuijper*, (2001) 38 Legal Issues Econ. Integr. 89, 97.

[41] *Kuijper*, (2001) 38 Legal Issues Econ. Integr. 89, 97.

[42] See only *Domej*, in: FS Heinz Mayer (2012), 41, 47; *Mankowski*, TranspR 2014, 129, 131.

[43] *TNT Express Nederland BV v. AXA Versicherung AG* (Case C-533/08), [2010] ECR I-4107 para. 49; *Nipponkoa Insurance Co. (Europe) Ltd. v. Inter-Zuid Transport BV* (Case C-452/12), ECLI:EU:C:2013:858 para. 36; *Nickel & Goeldner Spedition GmbH v. "Kintra" UAB* (Case C-157/13), ECLI:EU:C:2014:2145 para. 38.

[44] *TNT Express Nederland BV v. AXA Versicherung AG* (Case C-533/08), [2010] ECR I-4107 para. 50.

[45] *TNT Express Nederland BV v. AXA Versicherung AG* (Case C-533/08), [2010] ECR I-4107 paras. 51, 55; *Nipponkoa Insurance Co. (Europe) Ltd. v. Inter-Zuid Transport BV* (Case C-452/12), ECLI:EU:C:2013:858 paras. 37–38; *Nickel & Goeldner Spedition GmbH v. "Kintra" UAB* (Case C-157/13), ECLI:EU:C:2014:2145 para. 38; following this Rb. Rotterdam NIPR 2015 Nr 75 p. 174.

[46] *van der Klooster*, in: IPR in de spiegel van Paul Vlas (2012), p. 113, 115.

[47] *TNT Express Nederland BV v. AXA Versicherung AG* (Case C-533/08), [2010] ECR I-4107 para. 51; *Nipponkoa Insurance Co. (Europe) Ltd. v. Inter-Zuid Transport BV* (Case C-452/12), ECLI:EU:C:2013:858 para. 37.

[48] *TNT Express Nederland BV v. AXA Versicherung AG* (Case C-533/08), [2010] ECR I-4107 para. 52 with reference to *Ministère public v. Gérard Deserbais* (Case 286/86), [1988] ECR 4907 para. 18; *RTE and IPT v. Commission* (Joined Cases C-241/91P and C-242/91P), [1995] ECR I-743 para. 84; *Irène Bogiatzi, married Ventouras v. Deutscher Luftpool* (Case C-301/08), [2009] ECR I-10185 para. 19.

[49] *Haak*, NJ 2010 Nr 482 p. 4741 *et seq.*; *Mankowski*, TranspR 2014, 129, 131.

9 To this effect, the Brussels I Regulation is taken as establishing some kind of minimum harmonisation with specialised Conventions being only applicable where they enhance the European level already reached.[51] The CJEU emphasizes the paramount nature of the goals identified in Recitals (11), (12) and (15) Brussels I Regulation in the field of jurisdiction including *lis pendens* and identified in Recitals (6), (16) and (17) Brussels I Regulation in the field of recognition and enforcement.[52] To the CJEU this means for instance that rules governing jurisdiction as contained in a Convention apply but only provided that they are highly predictable, facilitate the sound administration of justice and enable the risk of concurring proceedings to be minimised.[53] This is the strictest and least generous way of interpreting Art. 71,[54] doing violence to the wording of Art. 71[55] and having a potentially devastating effect.[56] Legal certainty is damaged by adding unwritten requirements of an unclear ambit.[57] The unity of the EU systems steps upfront as it has done in other respects of Agreements between Member States and third States.[58] But any attempt to educate Member States to pay proper attention to the purposes of EU law[59] is entirely futile if in the respective field only Conventions concluded in the past are concerned.[60]

10 Yet it appears highly questionable that the Recitals take precedence over the wording of the genuine rules as to such far reaching measure. Nothing in the Recitals specifically relates to Art. 71 and solving the possible conflict with conventions on special matters. The specific conflict and the specific weighing of interests involved are dealt with in Art. 71, not in any Recital whatsoever. The Recitals contain general statements and are in no ways meant to restrict even express rules addressing a specific problem. The rules in an Act of EU legislation are normatively binding whereas the Recitals are interpretative means only. The approach implemented by the CJEU switches heads and heels. Furthermore, it undermines and in fact disregards the *ratio* underpinning Art. 71 as evidenced in Recital (35).[61] If the EU legislator had indeed intended to implement some kind of rather strict EU control before in fact delegating regulatory power to the specialised convention it should have established respective safeguards expressly. This has not been done which reversely, gives rise to a strong *argumentum e contrario*. The tension between the restriction of the field of application of the Brussels Ibis Regulation and the fundamental claim to applicability of EU law[62] has been resolved by Art. 71 in a clear manner. Recital (35) adds additional strength. If and insofar EU law itself cedes and gives way it has withdrawn from any struggle for supremacy. This is the

---

[50] *Oberhammer*, in: Stein/Jonas Art. 71 note 18; *Domej*, in: FS Heinz Mayer (2012), 41, 50.

[51] *Kuypers*, NTER 2011, 13, 19.

[52] *TNT Express Nederland BV v. AXA Versicherung AG* (Case C-533/08), [2010] ECR I-4107 paras. 53–54.

[53] *TNT Express Nederland BV v. AXA Versicherung AG* (Case C-533/08), [2010] ECR I-4107 para. 56.

[54] *Haak*, NJ 2010 Nr 482 p. 4741, 4742; cf. also *Tuo*, RDIPP 2011, 377, 391 *et seq.*

[55] *Attal*, Petites affiches n° 238, 30 novembre 2010, p. 32, 36; *Marmisse-d'Abbadie d'Arrast*, Rev. trim. dr. com. 2010, 825, 826; *Kuijper*, (2001) 38 Legal Issues Econ. Integr. 89, 99; *van den Oosterkamp*, SEW 2011, 193; cf. also *Tuo*, RDIPP 2011, 377, 385.

[56] *Tuo*, RDIPP 2011, 377, 388; *Mankowski*, TranspR 2014, 129, 132.

[57] *Mankowski*, TranspR 2014, 129, 132; see also *Tuo*, RDIPP 2011, 377, 391.

[58] *Kuijper*, (2001) 38 Legal Issues Econ. Integr. 89, 98. See the references in fn. 24.

[59] *Marmisse-d'Abbadie d'Arrast*, Rev. trim. dr. com. 2010, 825, 827.

[60] *Mankowski*, TranspR 2014, 129, 132.

[61] *Mankowski*, TranspR 2014, 129, 132.

[62] A-G *Kokott*, Opinion of 28 January 2010 in Case C-533/08), [2010] ECR I-4110, I-4120 para. 35.

---

distinctive feature which should not be overlooked in order to bring the area in line with current practice of the CJEU in other areas (which in itself might be questioned for very good reasons[63]).[64] Continuity is badly disrupted.[65] The CJEU is overstepping its competence for it in fact strives to occupy quasi-legislative power.[66]

Only some – and if ever, rather limited – justification for the CJEU's activism might be found **11** in Art. 351 (2) TFEU (ex-Art. 307 (2) EC Treaty), though, calling upon the Member States to do anything possible in order to reconcile the application of their treaties with their obligations under the TFEU. But Art. 351 (2) TFEU leaves the competence to deal with the situation to the Member States, and in the extreme case that a reconciliation by adaptation is not possible, Art. 351 (3) TFEU imposes an obligation to cancel the respective international agreement upon the Member States. One could even argue that Art. 71 does not contain rules to the same avail as Art. 351 (2) and (3) TFEU.[67] If activity is required, the Member States ought to be the actors anyway,[68] not the EU or one of its institutions, be it the CJEU.[69] Furthermore, Art. 351 TFEU permits an application of a Convention not yet cancelled even if this would collide with EU law.[70] Conversely, *TNT v. AXA* and *Nipponkoa* would consequentially oblige the Member States to breach their obligations towards Third States under international law and commit a tort under international law.[71]

The restrictive approach of the CJEU in *TNT v. AXA*, however irreconcilable it is with the **12** wording of (1), has yet to prove its true and real effectiveness in practice. For instance, it would appear not only far-fetched, but beyond any belief if the heads of jurisdiction as contained in Art. 31 (1) CMR or Art. 33 Montreal Convention were alleged to be unpredictable.[72] Obligingly, even the CJEU upheld Art. 31 (1) CMR in the light of its own interpretation of Art. 7 (1) (b).[73] In practical effect, the CJEU's approach might thus be less subject to criticism than with regard to its theoretical and dogmatic ambition.[74] Practical results might differ less than policy statements. *TNT v. AXA* should be taken as a mere programmatic statement and not a truly operational device.[75] Or else and paradoxically, *TNT v. AXA* itself would amount to a source of uncertainty and unpredictability.[76] Particularly, if differ-

---

[63] See most extensively *Klabbers*, Treaty Conflict and the European Union (2009).

[64] *Vettorel*, Riv. dir. int. 2010, 826, 827 *et seq.*

[65] *Wesołowski*, ETL 2011, 133, 137; *van den Oosterkamp*, SEW 2011, 193.

[66] *Vettorel*, Riv. dir. int. 2010, 826, 829 *et seq.*

[67] *Domej*, in: FS Heinz Mayer (2012), p. 41, 43.

[68] *Domej*, in: FS Heinz Mayer (2012), p. 41, 43.

[69] *Mankowski*, TranspR 2014, 129, 132.

[70] *Domej*, in: FS Heinz Mayer (2012), 41, 51.

[71] *Mankowski*, TranspR 2014, 129, 132.

[72] *Mankowski*, TranspR 2014, 129, 132. See to a similar avail *Rogerson*, in: Dickinson/Lein para. 17.22 and *Kuypers*, NTER 2011, 13, 19 when testing Art. 31 (1) CMR against Art. 6 (1) Brussels I Regulation.

[73] *Nickel & Goeldner Spedition GmbH v. "Kintra" UAB* (Case C-157/13), ECLI:EU:C:2014:2145 paras. 40–42.

[74] To a similar avail *Domej*, in: FS Heinz Mayer (2012), 41, 53–55.

[75] *Mankowski*, TranspR 2014, 129, 132–133.

[76] *Oberhammer*, in: Stein/Jonas Art. 71 note 8; *Domej*, in: FS Heinz Mayer (2012), 41, 52; *Mankowski*, TranspR 2014, 129, 133; *Mankowski*, TranspR 2015, 120; see also *Attal*, Petites affiches n° 238, 30 novembre 2010, p. 32, 35.

ences as to the interpretation of substantive rules as contained in the Convention at stake happen to occur between the courts of the Contracting States this does not affect the procedural rules and even less the rules on jurisdiction. These issues are to be judged quite separately and have no repercussions on Art. 71 which is only applicable with regard to limited aspects of the procedural sphere.[77] Yet in the field of recognition and enforcement results might differ if the CJEU's approach based on *favor executionis* is applied to the letter.[78] Difficulties in combining specialised Conventions and the Brussels I*bis* Regulation will occur and grow after *TNT v. AXA*, though.[79] The answer in *TNT v. AXA* is multi-fold, not clear cut, not black and white, not "yes" or "no".[80] An even more radical alternative would have been to restrict the application of the specialised Conventions to such cases where rights of Third States might be infringed.[81]

3. Specialised Conventions newly ratified by the EU

13 Art. 71 does not specify how the Regulation relates to specialised conventions to which the Union itself will be party in the future. It provides for precedence solely with regard to conventions to which the Member States are parties already. At a first glance, the *lex specialis* rule may apply as well: As far as the convention in respect covers aspects comprised within the Regulation, the specialised convention may precede take precedence. The Union acts on behalf of the Member States, and the effects of direct Union participation may be the same as all Member States participating in the enactment of a specialised convention simultaneously. But there are hints to a deviant approach. Any specialised convention is binding exclusively between its own Member States; and the Union is deemed to act as such a single Member State if it participates in the enactment of the a convention. Then there is no binding effect of such a convention within any of the Member States, and consequently no intra-Union ruling by the convention, for the Union as a whole is treated as a single Member State. This approach benefits from disturbing the Brussels I*bis* Regulation as little as possible compared to any *lex specialis* rule. Technically, two competing avenues are open: The first is an analogy to Art. 71,[82] the second to apply Art. 67 for Conventions ratified by the EU are said to become part of EU law by virtue of Art. 218 (7) TFEU (ex-Art. 300 (7) EC Treaty).[83]

14 The problem of concurring EU conventions will, at a first blow, be tested on the Hague Convention on Choice of Courts Agreements (HCCA)[84] as of 1 October 2015. According to its autonomous conflict rule as laid down in Art. 26 (6) lit. a HCCA, the Hague Convention shall not affect the application of the rules of a Regional Economic Integration where none of the parties to a choice of court agreement is resident in a Contracting State that is not a

---

77   See *Haak*, NTHR 2009, 69, 76.

78   *Hoeks*, NIPR 2011, 469.

79   *Douchy-Oudinot/Guinchard*, Rev. trim. dr. eur. 2010, 421, 428.

80   *van der Klooster*, in: IPR in de spiegel van Paul Vlas (2012), p. 113, 117.

81   *Domej*, in: FS Heinz Mayer (2012), 41, 59.

82   *Florian Schulz*, HanseLR 2005, 147, 154; *Ansgar Staudinger*, RRa 2007, 155, 156; *Michael Lehmann*, NJW 2007, 1500; *Mankowski*, TranspR 2008, 67.

83   *Rolf Wagner*, TranspR 2009, 103, 109.

84   Hague Convention on Choice of Court Agreements of 30 June 2005, available at http://www.hcch.net.

Member State of the Regional Economic Integration. This solution allows for distinguishing several specific settings.[85]

As an entity the EU will, and is bound to, pay attention to not tampering with the scope of **15** the well-adjusted Brussels I*bis* Regulation and its approach to intra-Union matters if participating in the enactment of specialised conventions. Thus, sorting out conflicts of law-making-rules must not be dealt with academically, but is to remain sufficiently flexible. Practical solutions are to be found according to the following schedule: Fundamentally and by virtue of Art. 71, the Regulation leaves it to the specialised convention itself whether it precedes the Brussels I Regulation. Here, one must scrutinize the miscellaneous provisions of the convention in respect, where the Commission is obliged to put up a specific conflict rule. As far as the convention in respect refrains from ruling matters of a solely intra-EU nature, the Regulation applies. As far as the convention in respect claims to be applicable even in intra-community cases, so be it, and the Regulation gives way to the Convention at stake with (2) providing some modifications. Unlike Arts. 25 (2) Rome I Regulation; 28 Rome II Regulation, Art. 71 does not contain an over-all exception from the general principle for intra-EU cases.[86]

4. Specialised Conventions newly ratified by the Member States authorized by the EU

Although in general the EU has the external competence, in practice it is more likely that the **16** EU re-delegates competence to the Member States. This has already happened several times by single Resolutions of the Council.[87] A general framework defining the limits has been implemented by virtue of Regulations (EC) Nos. 662/2009[88] and 664/2009[89] if only for matters outside the scope of the Brussels I*bis* Regulation. If the Member States, authorized and duly empowered by the EU, conclude, sign and ratify new Conventions they do so in their own names and not as agents for the EU. The respective conclusion takes place under the traditional rules of international law, the only particularity being the authorization in the internal relationship between the EU and its Member States. Clinging to the letter, Art. 71 does not cover such Conventions newly ratified by the Member States. Yet it appears advisable to apply it *per analogiam*. Else a call for respective reshaping of Art. 71 would be inevitable. That it did not emerge in the recast process is strong evidence for the contention that a pragmatic approach in practice and reality was and is satisfactory.[90]

---

[85] See *Mankowski*, in: Rauscher Art. 23 notes 77–80.

[86] *Rolf Wagner*, TranspR 2009, 103, 106.

[87] *Supra* Art. 71 note 4 with references.

[88] Regulation (EC) No. 662/2009 of the European Parliament and of the Council of 13 July 2009 establishing a European procedure for the negotiation and conclusion of agreements between Member States and third countries on particular matters concerning the law applicable to contractual and non-contractual obligations, OJ EU 2009 L 200/25.

[89] Regulation (EC) No. 664/2009 of the European Parliament and of the Council of 7 July 2009 establishing a European procedure for the negotiation and conclusion of agreements between Member States and third countries concerning jurisdiction, recognition and enforcement of judgments and decisions in matrimonial matters, matters of parental responsibility and matters relating to maintenance obligations, and the law applicable to matters relating to maintenance obligations, OJ EU 2009 L 200/46.

[90] *Mankowski*, IGKK/IACPIL 1 (2010), 31, 72.

II. Application of specialised conventions

17 Insofar as a specialised convention is applicable pursuant to (1), the Brussels I Regulation is precluded.[91] Whether such a convention actually deals with relevant specific matters that concern jurisdiction, *lis pendens*, recognition or enforcement or with any of those, is left to the convention itself and to its interpretation.[92] This extends to implications not expressly spelt out in the other Convention but to be derived from it,[93] as e.g. in the case of Art. III (8) Hague Rules which can amount to an obstacle in the way of jurisdiction clauses.[94] To the extent to which the convention in respect does not govern one or more of those topics, the Regulation remains applicable without alteration or modification.[95] Similarly, the Regulation remains applicable as far as the rules prescribed in a specialised convention are confined to specific aspects of one of the aforementioned topics.[96] As a whole, Art. 71 (1) intends to integrate (n a non-technical sense) any specialised set of rules into the larger legal framework of the Regulation.[97] Insofar it goes beyond a simple *lex specialis* rule, but tentatively amounts to a rule of coordination;[98] generally, subsidiarity fits the bill better than strict precedence of the other convention.[99] That a specialised Convention governs a topic does not lead to a genuine carve-out of this topic from the scope of the Regulation.[100] Art. 71 is not a scope rule.

18 According to the Report *Schlosser*, the following international conventions governing jurisdiction and the recognition and enforcement of judgments, in particular areas of law are amongst others (the list is not exhaustive!) prior to Union rules according to (1) (ex Art. 57 of the 1968 Brussels Convention):
- The revised Mannheim Convention for the navigation of the Rhine of 17 October 1868

---

[91] *The owners of the cargo lately laden on board the ship "Tatry" v. The owners of the ship "Maciej Rataj"* (Case 406/92), [1994] ECR I-5439, I-5471 para. 24; *TNT Express Nederland BV v. AXA Versicherung AG* (Case C-533/08), [2010] ECR I-4107 para. 48.

[92] *Deaville v. Aeroflot Russian International Airlines* [1997] 2 Lloyd's Rep 67, 71 (Q.B.D., Judge *Brice* Q.C.) (with relation to the Warsaw Convention and *lis pendens*); *Tuo*, RDIPP 2011, 377, 380 *et seq.*; *van der Klooster*, in: IPR in de spiegel van Paul Vlas (2012), p. 113, 118.

[93] *Mankowski* (fn. 9), p. 297 *et seq.*; *Briggs/Rees* para. 2.47; cf. also *David C. Jackson*, Enforcement of Maritime Claims (3rd ed. 2000) para. 6.31. *Contra Baatz*, [2011] LMCLQ 208, 219; *Treitel/Reynolds*, Carver on Bills of Lading (2nd ed. 2005) para. 9.077 fn. 92; *Aikens/Lord/Bools*, Bills of Lading (2006) para. 10.50 fn. 73, para. 14.43 and tentatively *Layton/Mercer* para. 32.021 fn. 48.

[94] Seminally The *"Morviken"* [1983] 1 A.C. 1 (H.L.).

[95] Cassaz. Foro it. 1978 I col. 2240; Cassaz. RDIPP 2004, 245, 251; The *"Anna H"* [1995] 1 Lloyd's Rep. 11, 18 (C.A., per *Hobhouse* L.J.); *Vassalli di Dachenhausen*, Il coordinamento tra convenzioni di diritto internazionale privato e processuale (1993) p. 110 *et seq.*; *Siig*, [1997] LMCLQ 362, 364 *et seq.*; *David C. Jackson* (fn. 50), para. 6.9; *Ramming* TranspR 2007, 13, 16; *Dörfelt* IPRax 2009, 470, 472; *Tiefenthaler*, in: Czernich/Tiefenthaler/Kodek Art. 71 note 2; *van der Klooster*, in: IPR in de spiegel van Paul Vlas (2012), p. 113, 118.

[96] *Kropholler/von Hein* Art. 71 note 5; *Mankowski*, in: Rauscher Art. 71 note 5.

[97] See *Vassalli di Dachenhausen* (fn. 20), p. 108.

[98] *Mari*, Il diritto processuale civile della convenzione die Bruxelles (1999) p. 119 *et seq.*; *Tuo*, RDIPP 2004, 193, 208 *et seq.*

[99] Applauded by *Tuo*, RDIPP 2011, 377, 381.

[100] *Mankowski*, IPRax 2000, 188, 192–193; *Domej*, in: FS Heinz Mayer (2012), 41, 46.

together with the Revised Agreement of 20 November 1963 and the Additional Protocol of 25 October 1972;
– The Warsaw Convention of 12 October 1929 for the unification of certain rules relating to international carriage by air and the Amending Protocol of 28 September 1955 and Supplementary Convention of 18 September 1961 with the Additional Protocols of 8 March 1971 and 25 September 1975;[101]
– The Brussels International Convention of 10 May 1952 on certain rules concerning civil jurisdiction in matters of collision;
– The Brussels International Convention of 10 May 1952 relating to the arrest of seagoing ships;[102]
– The Rome Convention of 7 October 1952 relating to damage caused by foreign aircraft to third parties on the surface;
– The London Agreement of 27 February 1953 on German external debts;
– The Hague Convention of 1 March 1954 on civil procedure;
– The Hague Convention of 15 November 1965 on the service abroad of judicial and extrajudicial documents in civil and commercial matters;
– The Hague Convention of 18 March 1970 on the taking of evidence abroad in civil or commercial matters;
– The Geneva Convention of 19 May 1956 together with its Protocol of Signature on the contract for the international carriage of goods by road (CMR);
– The Convention of 27 October 1956 between the Grand Duchy of Luxembourg, the Federal Republic of Germany and the French Republic on the canalization of the Moselle, with the Additional Protocol of 28 November 1976;
– The Hague Convention of 15 April 1958 on the recognition and enforcement of decisions relating to maintenance obligations in respect of children;
– The Hague Convention of 15 April 1958 on the jurisdiction of the contractual forum in matters relating to the international sale of goods;
– The Paris Convention of 29 July 1960 on third party liability in the field of nuclear energy together with the Paris Additional Protocol of 28 January 1964 and the Brussels Convention and Annex thereto of 31 January 1963 supplementary to the Paris Convention of 29 July 1960 and the Paris Additional Protocol to the Supplementary Convention of 28 January 1964;[103]
– The Supplementary Convention of 26 February 1966 to the International Convention of 25 February 1961 concerning the carriage of passengers and luggage by rail (CIV) on the liability of railways for death or injury to passengers, amended by Protocol II of the Diplomatic Conference for the entry into force of the CIM and CIV International Agreements of 7 February 1970 concerning the extension of the period of validity of the Supplementary Convention of 26 February 1966;
– The Brussels Convention of 25 May 1962 on the liability of operators of nuclear ships and Additional Protocol;
– The Brussels International Convention of 27 May 1967 for the unification of rules relating to the carriage of passengers' luggage by sea;

---

[101] See e.g. CA Orléans Rev. dr. transp. juillet-août 2008, 29.
[102] See e.g. TS AEDIPr 2001, 904, 905 with note *Álvarez Rubio*; The *"Deichland"* [1990] 1 Q.B. 361 (C.A.); Aud. Prov. Palma de Mallorca AEDIPr 2001, 904, 905 with note *Álvarez Rubio*; Rb. Rotterdam S&S 2011 Nr 25 p. 115; Rapport *Potocki*, DMF 2011, 629, 632.
[103] *Waldner*, SZIER 2011, 5, 20.

- The Brussels International Convention of 27 May 1967 for the unification of certain rules relating to maritime liens and mortgages;
- The Brussels International Convention of 29 November 1969 on civil liability for oil pollution damage and the International Convention to supplement that Convention of 18 December 1971 on the establishment of an international fund for compensation for oil pollution damage;
- The Berne International Conventions of 7 February 1970 on the carriage of goods by rail (CIM) and the carriage of passengers and luggage by rail (CIV), together with the Additional Protocol and Protocol I of 9 November 1973 of the Diplomatic Conference for the implementation of the Conventions;
- The Athens Convention of 13 December 1974 on the carriage by sea of passengers and their luggage;
- The European Agreement of 30 September 1957 covering the international carriage of dangerous goods by road (ADR) and the Additional Protocol of 21 August 1975;
- The Geneva Convention of 1 March 1973 on the contract for the international carriage of passengers and baggage by road (CUR);
- The Hague Convention of 2 October 1973 on the recognition and enforcement of decisions relating to maintenance obligations.

19 In addition to this list which as a matter of fact could comprise only conventions already existing at the time when the Report was drawn up (and still misses out e.g. on the 1976 London Liability Convention[104]), the 2002 Protocol to the 1974 Athens Convention on the Carriage by Sea of Passengers and their Luggage, as well as the aforementioned Bunkers Convention, may be considered as specialised conventions. Similarly, the European Convention on State Immunity[105] takes precedence over Union rules.[106] The 1999 Montreal Convention[107] has succeeded the Warsaw Convention for the most part in the area of international air transportation, with its Art. 33 taking precedence over the jurisdictional regime of the Brussels I*bis* Regulation.[108] The Hamburg Rules are another candidate always provided that Member States are Contracting States. The 1999 Arrest Convention,[109] the successor to the 1952 Arrest Convention, might become another example.[110] On the contrary, the Brussels I*bis* Regulation is not precluded, by virtue of (1) from application to copyright infringement by the provisions of the Berne Convention for the Protection of Literary and Artistic Works, as the latter does not purport to govern jurisdiction.[111] Likewise the 1976 London Convention[112] and its 1996 Protocol[113] do not contain procedural rules which would come within (1).[114] But the Benelux Markenwet is also a qualifier.[115] The idea to

---

[104] See Hoge Raad S&S 2007 Nr 1 p. 13; Rb. Groningen NIPR 2003 Nr 52 p. 102.

[105] European Convention of 16 May 1972 on State Immunity, adopted at Basle, ETS 74.

[106] *Hess*, IPRax 1994, 10, 14.

[107] Montreal Convention of 28 May 1999 for the unification of certain rules relating to international carriage by air.

[108] See only *Reuschle*, Montrealer Übereinkommen (2005) Art. 33 MÜ note 4.

[109] International Convention on Arrest of Ships, done at Geneva on 12 March 1999.

[110] On this convention *Francesco Berlingieri*, Dir. Mar. 102 (2000), 1; *Gaskell/Shaw*, [2000] LMCLQ 470.

[111] *Pearce v. Ove Arup Partnership* [1999] I.L.Pr. 442, 466 (C.A., per *Roch* L.J.).

[112] Convention on Limitation of Liability for Maritime Claims, done at London 19 November 1976.

[113] Protocol Amending the Convention on Limitation of Liability for Maritime Claims, done at London 2 May 1996.

expressly list all specialised conventions was ventilated[116] but eventually dropped, unsurprisingly in view of the scale of the task involved.[117]

III. Reference to specialised Conventions

From a methodical point of view, (1) refers to other conventions. As far as other legal **20** instruments are concerned, the Regulation considers itself explicitly as an instrument of reference, but, by referring to other Conventions, does by no means refrain from governing matters of judicial cooperation on a general basis. As a consequence, the Brussels I Regulation is in no way excluded from application if (1) a specialised Convention referred to in Art. 71 (1) fails to govern a matter dealt with in the provisions of the Regulation[118] or (2) if any specialised Convention referred to in Art. 71 (1) re-refers to the procedural law of the forum State.[119] If so, the Brussels I*bis* Regulation happens to supersede any forum State's procedural law due to the general precedence of EU rules. The situation is similar if the specialised Convention follows the principle of *favor negotii* and takes, by means of an alternative reference rule, explicit provisions not to deprive an interested party of any right he may have according to another law or multilateral agreement.[120] The principle of *favor executionis* applied highlights this.[121] The Regulation is excluded from application not in a wholesale manner[122] but only to the extent to which the specialised Convention purports to govern a specific matter exclusively.[123] It follows by way of converse inference in particular from (2) (b) that the Brussels I*bis* Regulation may be relied on where a specialised Convention contains no rules or only incomplete rules.[124] Whether a certain Convention claims

---

114 *Tsimplis*, [2011] LMCLQ 307, 313.

115 Hof Amsterdam NIPR 2007 Nr 297 p. 400.

116 Commission Proposal COM (1999) 348 final p. 26.

117 *Layton/Mercer* para. 32.020 fn. 46.

118 See only *Domej*, in: FS Heinz Mayer (2012), 41, 47.

119 *Mankowski*, TranspR 2014, 129, 131.

120 A-G *Kokott*, Opinion of 28 January 2010 in Case C-533/08), [2010] ECR I-4110 paras. 42 *et seq.*;
    Mankowski, EWS 1996, 301, 304; *Mankowski*, in: Rauscher Art. 71 note 8; *Mankowski*, TranspR 2014,
    129, 131; OLG Köln MDR 1980, 1030; OLG Koblenz EuZW 1990, 486; OLG Frankfurt DAVorm 1989 col.
    102; OLG Hamm IPRax 2004, 437, 438; App. Milano 13 April 1973 (see *Pocar* RDIPP 1978, 655, 676);
    Strikwerda, in: Bundel opstellen aangeboden aan C.J.H. Brunner (1994), p. 389, 395; *de Meij*, Samenloop
    van CMR-Verdrag en EEX-Verordening (2003) p. 144; *Kropholler/Blobel*, in: FS Hans Jürgen Sonnen-
    berger (2004), p. 453, 475; *Mankowski*, in: Rauscher Art. 71 note 8; *Geimer*, IPRax 2004, 419, 420; *Domej*,
    in: FS Heinz Mayer (2012), 41, 46. *Contra* e.g. *H. Stein*, in: Offerhauskring vijfentwintig jaar (1987),
    p. 185, 186 *et seq.*; *Verschuur*, Vrij verkeer van vonnissen (1995) p. 181.

121 A-G *Kokott*, Opinion of 28 January 2010 in Case C-533/08), [2010] ECR I-4110 para. 42; Hoge Raad NJ
    2008 Nr 623 p. 6452; A-G *Strikwerda*, NJ 2008 Nr 623 p. 6446, 6449.

122 *Tuo*, RDIPP 2011, 377, 383.

123 A-G *Kokott*, Opinion of 28 January 2010 in Case C-533/08), [2010] ECR I-4110 paras. 36, 40, 44; CA
    Orléans Rev Scapel 2007, 111, 113; *Mankowski*, EWS 1996, 301, 304; *Cerina*, RDIPP 1991, 953, 959;
    Basedow, VersR 1978, 495, 501; *Basedow* (fn. 10), Ch. II note 144; *de Meij* (fn. 74), pp. 221 *et seq.*; *Haak*,
    NTHR 2009, 69, 70; *Tsimplis*, (2010) 16 JIML 289, 298; *Tuo*, RDIPP 2011, 377, 381 *et seq.*; *van der
    Klooster*, in: IPR in de spiegel van Paul Vlas (2012), p. 113, 119. Sceptical *Haak*, TranspR 2009, 189, 196.

124 A-G *Kokott*, Opinion of 28 January 2010 in Case C-533/08), [2010] ECR I-4110 para. 39; *Wesołowski*,
    ETL 2011, 133, 138; *Tuo*, RDIPP 2011, 377, 382, 385.

exclusivity is a matter of interpretation of that very Convention.[125] For instance, the CMR does not inhibit application of Art. 45 as the CMR does not address the respective issue.[126] The same is true for the Warsaw or the Montreal Conventions with regard to *lis pendens*.[127]

21 Art. 71 is quite often defined as an integration clause designed to embed specialised conventions in the Brussels I*bis* Regulation.[128] It is worthy of being stressed that the concept of reference as laid down in (1) does not aim at full integration of specialised conventions into the Brussels I*bis* Regulation, but resembles a fictitious implantation of single provisions from other conventions into the structure of the European regime of jurisdiction.[129] Any attempt to fully integrate multilateral commitments of the Member States into the Brussels I Regulation would meet severe vicissitudes from the points of view of EU law and international law as well. The scope of application of the Regulation must not hinge upon individual Member States' membership to international conventions.[130] Furthermore, an integrative approach might iniquitously amplify the CJEU's competence of interpretation by extending it to non-EU laws and statutes. Yet in effect the CJEU has – at least *verbatim* – rejected to assume such competence when it refused to interpret the CMR.[131]

IV. Assuring uniform standards of interpretation

22 The concept of reference to specialised conventions as laid down in (1) maintains minimum standards of interplay between the Union regime and other conventions. But reference to those conventions alone does not suffice to guarantee a flawless collaboration of law-making treaties relating to jurisdiction and enforcement. Thus, the basic rule of (1) is refined in (2). Its objective is to warrant uniform standards of application and assure a continuous interpretation of the EU rules in all Member States. (2) mainly[132] relates to situations which are entirely confined within the EU.[133] Conceptually, (2) serves as some kind of explanation and illustration of (1).[134]

23 (2) (a) deviates from the rule in Art. 5 in order to clarify its scope of application with respect to other conventions. It follows that Member States' courts may still base their jurisdiction on a specialised convention's rule if the latter corresponds to neither Brussels I jurisdiction or even would be ousted as an exorbitant head of jurisdiction under the regime of the Brussels I Regulation.[135] (2) (a) cl. 2 secures the application of Art. 28 in any event and thus

---

[125] See only *Haak*, NJ 2010 Nr 482 p. 4741.

[126] Rb Utrecht S&S 2008 Nr 75 S 358.

[127] CA Orléans Rev. Scapel 2007, 111, 113.

[128] See A-G *Tesauro* [1994] ECR I-5442, I-5447 para. 9; *The "Anna H"* [1995] 1 Lloyd's Rep. 11, 21 (C.A., per Hobhouse L.J.); *Haak*, NTHR 2009, 69, 70; *Tsimplis*, (2010) 16 JIML 289, 297.

[129] *Mankowski*, EWS 1996, 301, 303; *Verschuur* (fn. 68), p. 180; *Tuo*, RDIPP 2011, 377, 398; see Report *Schlosser* para. 240.

[130] *Mankowski*, EWS 1996, 301, 303.

[131] *TNT Express Nederland BV v. AXA Versicherung AG* (Case C-533/08), [2010] ECR I-4107 paras. 58–62; *van der Klooster*, in: IPR in de spiegel van Paul Vlas (2012), p. 113, 118.

[132] But see *Domej*, in: FS Heinz Mayer (2012), 41, 50.

[133] *TNT Express Nederland BV v. AXA Versicherung AG* (Case C-533/08), [2010] ECR I-4107 para. 47.

[134] See only A-G *Strikwerda*, NJ 2008 Nr 623 p. 6446, 6449; *Attal*, Petites affiches n° 238, 30 novembre 2010, p. 32, 33.

the defendant's protection and his right to a fair trial. It implements the European basic standard in cases where jurisdiction would be based on a specialised Convention.[136]

By virtue of (2) (b) subpara. 1, judgments given in a Member State by a court in the exercise **24** of jurisdiction provided for in a convention on a particular matter shall be recognised and enforced in the other Member States in accordance with this Regulation. (2) (b) subpara. 1 exemplifies the overarching principle that the application of the Brussels I*bis* regime does not presuppose that the jurisdiction of the country of origin must be based on the jurisdictional rules of the Regulation.[137] In principle, the jurisdictional regime of a specialised Convention should take precedence even if, absent this Convention, one of the protective regimes of the Brussels I*bis* Regulation governed the case.[138] Yet a consequent application of the reasoning by the CJEU in *TNT v. AXA*[139] plants the seed of doubt whether this would be compatible with European standards.[140]

Pursuant to (2) (b) subpara. 2, where a convention on a particular matter to which both the **25** Member State of origin and the Member State addressed are parties lays down conditions for the recognition or enforcement of judgments, those conditions shall apply. In any event, the provisions of this Regulation which concern the procedure for recognition and enforcement of judgments may be applied. In the interests of claimants, (2) (b) subpara. 2 cl. 2 generally maintains Brussels I*bis* standards of recognition and enforcement. This applies regardless of whether a specialised convention referred to in (1) intends to govern these matters exclusively, as such a convention does apply only to the extent to which the Regulation explicitly refers to it.[141] In particular, Art. 45 (1) (e), (3) are applicable since the jurisdictional rules of the specialised Convention are referred to and form substantive part of the Brussels I*bis* system.[142]

Creditors might profit and benefit from the application of Brussels I*bis* standards and **26** procedures particularly after the Brussels I*bis* Regulation has abolished exequatur proceedings and permits for direct enforcement of judgments. This new system and approach is more favourable to creditors than anything which can be detected in specialised conventions. Since specialised conventions aim at liberating the circulation of judgments among their Contracting States they cannot complain if some Contracting States implement an even more beneficial system than that established by the Convention at stake. The Member States of the EU are not in breach of their obligations under international law if they allow for recognition and enforcement of judgments rendered by courts in other Contracting States who happen to be also Member States of the EU, under better and more favourable terms than the Convention itself. Methodologically, the letter of the Convention can be regarded as teleologically reduced. Convention States fare better than they even negotiated

---

135   *The "Bergen"* [1997] 1 Lloyd's Rep. 380, 383 (Q.B.D., *Clarke* J.).

136   *Oberhammer*, in: Stein/Jonas Art. 71 note 13.

137   *Oberhammer*, in: Stein/Jonas Art. 71 note 14; *Domej*, in: FS Heinz Mayer (2012), p. 41, 45.

138   *Oberhammer*, in: Stein/Jonas Art. 71 note 15.

139   *TNT Express Nederland BV v. AXA Versicherung AG* (Case C-533/08), [2010] ECR I-4107 para. 49.

140   *Oberhammer*, in: Stein/Jonas Art. 71 note 15.

141   *Rauch*, IPRax 1981, 199, 201; *Mankowski*, IPRax 2000, 188, 189.

142   See *Thomale*, IPRax 2014, 239, 241.

for. The *favor executionis* advocated for by the CJEU in *TNT v. AXA*[143] could not possibly gain better momentum.

V. Relationship with Art. 31 CMR

26a The Geneva Convention on the Contract for the International Carriage of Goods by Road of 19 May 1956, generally known as the CMR Convention, is of paramount importance for the carriage of goods by road in the whole of Europe. Pursuant to Art. 31 CMR, any legal proceeding arising out of carriage under the Convention must be brought in a court or tribunal of a Contracting State designated by agreement between the parties, or in the courts or tribunals of a country within whose territory the defendant is ordinarily resident, or has his principal place of business, or the branch or agency through which the contract of carriage was made; or the place where the goods were taken over by the carrier or the place designated for delivery is situated. This general precedence over the Brussels I Regulation is commonly unquestioned.[144] Nevertheless, the exact borderline between CMR jurisdiction and the Brussels I*bis* Regulation may, on behalf of some special issues, remain unclear. At least Art. 31 CMR is not applicable in the event of judgments only preliminarily enforceable whereas these judgments are covered by the Regulation.[145]

1. Form of jurisdiction agreements

26b According to Art. 31 (1) CMR, agreements conferring jurisdiction do not underlay any formal restrictions. Though Art. 25 (1), (2) Brussels I*bis* Regulation requires jurisdiction agreements to be in a certain form, there is no need to conclude a jurisdiction agreement in writing if the CMR Convention is applicable. Pursuant to (1), Art. 31 CMR takes precedence over the Regulation, so that jurisdiction agreements are not required to be in any form to the extent to which the agreement itself meets with the prerequisites of the CMR Convention.[146] In any case, Art. 25 (1) 3 Brussels I*bis* Regulation is entirely superseded by Art. 31 CMR. It follows that, under the CMR Convention, there are no exclusive jurisdiction agreements at all.[147] The alternative[148] would be to apply the formal requirements of Art. 25 (1) 3 Brussels I*bis* Regulation in a first step, just in order to vitiate any result by virtue of Art. 41 CMR.

---

[143] *TNT Express Nederland BV v. AXA Versicherung AG* (Case C-533/08), [2010] ECR I-4107 paras. 56, 54.

[144] For the precedence of Art. 31 CMR over the jurisdictional rules of the Brussels I Regulation e.g. OGH TranspR 2003, 66; OGH TranspR 2003, 67 with note *Rogov*; Rb. Arnhem NIPR 2005 Nr 53 p. 95; Rb. Rotterdam NIPR 2005 Nr 63 p. 104; Rb. 's-Hertogenbosch S&S 2008 Nr 134 p. 631; Trib. Tortona Dir. mar. 113 (2011), 1299, 1309 with note *Tracco* and lastly *Nickel & Goeldner Spedition GmbH v. "Kintra" UAB* (Case C-157/13), ECLI:EU:C:2014:2145 paras. 40–42.

[145] OGH ZfRV 2005, 32.

[146] LG Aachen RIW 1976, 588, 589; *Fremuth*, TranspR 1983, 35, 37; *Götz Müller/Hök*, RIW 1988, 775, 776. For a different view see Trib. Torino RDIPP 1984, 586; *Kropholler/von Hein* in: Handbuch des internationalen Zivilverfahrensrechts, Vol. I (1982) Ch. III note 406; *Kropholler/von Hein* Art. 71 note 5; *Hausmann*, in: Wieczorek/Schütze, Einl. EuGVÜ note 66; *Haubold*, IPRax 2000, 91, 93 *et seq.*; *Baumbach/Hopt*, HGB (36th ed. 2014) Art. 31 CMR note 1; *Tiefenthaler*, in: Czernich/Tiefenthaler/Kodek Art. 71 note 2.

[147] OLG Oldenburg TranspR 2000, 128; *Kropholler/von Hein* Art. 71 note 5.

[148] As tried by Rb. Rotterdam NIPR 2015 Nr 75 p. 174.

2. Examination as to jurisdiction

The relationship between the Brussels I*bis* Regulation and Art. 31 CMR is easily resolved in **27** the ordinary case in favour of Art. 31 CMR which gains prevalence for instance over Art. 7 (1) of the Regulation[149] (under the approach of the CJEU provided that jurisdiction is highly predictable and the risk of concurrent proceedings is minimised[150] which the CJEU acknowledges for Art. 31 (1) CMR.[151] But it may meet some difficulty if the defendant does not enter an appearance. As to the wording of Art. 71 (2) (a) 2, international jurisdiction depends, by virtue of Art. 28, on jurisdiction being established objectively according to the yardsticks contained in the Brussels I*bis* Regulation.

From a narrow point of view, any examination as to jurisdiction might not comprise juris- **28** diction as established by Art. 31 of the CMR Convention or by any other specialised convention, but relate exclusively to the Brussels I*bis* Regulation.[152] It seems reasonable to assume that any such limitation to general precedence of the Convention would have to be very forcefully justified.[153] Since the defendant may deliberately enter an appearance or chose not to do so, there is some danger that the CMR Convention might be superseded wilfully.[154] The objective of Art. 28, namely, to avoid any need to enter an appearance solely for procedural reasons is by no means depreciated if examination as to jurisdiction focuses on the CMR Convention.[155] Accordingly, jurisdiction of the court must be regarded as derived from the Regulation since Art. 71 specifically states that the rules of jurisdiction laid down by specialised Conventions are not affected by the Regulation.[156] When verifying on its own motion whether it has jurisdiction, the court is bound to apply the rules of jurisdiction laid down in the specialised convention if the defendant fails to enter an ap-

---

[149] See only OGH TranspR 2003, 66; OGH TranspR 2003, 67 with note *Rogov*; HD UfR 2003, 2490, 2495; App. Trieste RDIPP 2004, 243, 244; *Kuypers*, NTER 2011, 13, 19; *Mankowski*, TranspR 2014, 129, 132; *Mankowski*, TranspR 2015, 120.

[150] *TNT Express Nederland BV v. AXA Versicherung AG* (Case C-533/08), [2010] ECR I-4107 para. 51.

[151] *Nickel & Goeldner Spedition GmbH v. "Kintra" UAB* (Case C-157/13), ECLI:EU:C:2014:2145 paras. 40–42.

[152] See OLG Dresden TranspR 1999, 62, 63 = IPRax 2000, 121, 123; OLG München TranspR 2001, 399, 401; LG Oldenburg TranspR 2001, 402 f; LG Flensburg TranspR 2001, 401, 402.

[153] *Nürnberger Allgemeine Versicherungs-AG v. Portbridge Transport International BV*, (Case C-148/03) [2004] ECR I-10327, I-10336 paras. 17–20; BGH TranspR 2003, 302, 303; OLG Hamm TranspR 2001, 397, 399; OLG Schleswig TranspR 2002, 76; OLG Nürnberg TranspR 2002, 402; OLG Karlsruhe NJW-RR 2002, 1722, 1723; OLG Hamburg TranspR 2003, 23, 24; OLG München TranspR 2003, 155; *Haubold*, IPRax 2000, 91; *Gottwald*, in: Münchener Kommentar zur ZPO Art. 57 EuGVÜ note 5; *Dißars*, TranspR 2001, 387, 389; *Heuer*, TranspR 2002, 221, 222 et seq.; *Herber*, TranspR 2003, 19, 20; *Mankowski*, in: Reithmann/Martiny, Internationales Vertragsrecht (6th ed. 2004) note 1424; see also Rb. Rotterdam NIPR 2001 Nr 141 p. 275.

[154] OLG Hamm TranspR 2001, 397, 399; OLG Schleswig TranspR 2002, 76; OLG Karlsruhe NJW-RR 2002, 1722, 1723; OLG Hamburg TranspR 2003, 23, 24 f.

[155] *Haubold*, IPRax 2000, 91, 95; *Dißars*, TranspR 2001, 387, 389; *Mankowski*, in: Reithmann/Martiny (fn. 48), note 1424; *Mankowski*, in: Rauscher Art. 71 note 15.

[156] *Nürnberger Allgemeine Versicherungs-AG v. Portbridge Transport International BV*, (Case C-148/03) [2004] ECR I-10327, I-10336 para. 17.

Peter Mankowski

pearance.[157] The same is true where the defendant, while submitting no pleas on the merits, formally contests the jurisdiction of the national court seised of the case.[158]

3. Lis pendens

29   Art. 31 (2) CMR deals with seisin.[159] The prerequisites regarding *lis pendens* as established by the CMR gain priority over the Brussels I*bis* Regulation.[160] Art. 31 (2) aims at a concept of priority similar to the one provided for in Art. 71. Hence Art. 31 (2) of the CMR butts against the CMR's material provisions, the term "plaintiff" in Art. 31 is to be understood as "claimant".[161] Jurisdiction as established by the CMR generally favours the plaintiff. Thus, under the CMR compared to the Brussels I Regulation, the plaintiff faces no remarkable disadvantage. For jurisdiction, it follows that the postulation of equality does not require shifting the general precedence of the CMR in favour of Art. 29 Brussels I*bis* Regulation.[162]

30   Whether Art. 31 (2) CMR exerts a full and proper *lis pendens* effect barring the lawsuit which was commenced later, has been a matter of debate under the CMR, with the German BGH which argues against such an effect,[163] being confronted with the opposite approach favouring such an effect by English,[164] Austrian[165] and Swiss[166] courts.[167] The CJEU intervened and decreed that the same principles as under Art. 29 Brussels I*bis* Regulation should govern the relation between negative declaratory action and action for specific performance under Art. 31 (2) CMR else the handling of Art. 31 (2) CMR would collide with the principles underlying the Brussels I*bis* system and thus would be ruled out by the doctrine established

---

[157]   *Nürnberger Allgemeine Versicherungs-AG v. Portbridge Transport International BV*, (Case C-148/03) [2004] ECR I-10327, I-10336 para. 18.

[158]   *Nürnberger Allgemeine Versicherungs-AG v. Portbridge Transport International BV*, (Case C-148/03) [2004] ECR I-10327, I-10336 para. 19.

[159]   For details see *Andrea Merzario Ltd. v. Internationale Spedition Leitner GmbH* [2001] 1 Lloyd's Rep. 490 (C.A.); *Thomas Rüfner*, [2001] LMCLQ 460.

[160]   See OLG Düsseldorf TranspR 2002, 237; OLG Köln TranspR 2002, 239, 241; OLG Nürnberg TranspR 2002, 402. For a different view see *Frans Maas Logistics (UK) Ltd. v. CDR Trucking BV* [1999] 2 Lloyd's Rep. 179, 186 (Q.B.D., *Colman* J.). Compare also Hoge Raad NJ 2008 Nr 623 and A-G *Strikwerda*, NJ 2008 Nr 623 p. 6446, 6447; *Haak*, NTHR 2009, 69; *Haak*, TranspR 2009, 189; *Hoeks*, NIPR 2011, 469 explaining the underlying economic background of recent Dutch-German struggles.

[161]   OLG Hamburg TranspR 2003, 25 f; *Herber*, TranspR 1996, 196, 197; *Heuer*, TranspR 2002, 221, 225. For a different view see OLG Düsseldorf TranspR 2002, 237.

[162]   OLG Köln TranspR 2002, 239, 241; OLG Hamburg TranspR 2003, 25 *et seq.*; *Heuer*, TranspR 2002, 221, 225; *Herber* TranspR 2003, 19, 20 *et seq.*; *Mankowski*, in: Rauscher Art. 71 note 16. For a different view see OLG Düsseldorf TranspR 2002, 237; *Basedow*, in: Münchener Kommentar zum HGB, vol. VII (1997) Art. 2 (a) subpara. 1 CMR note 30; *Staub/Helm*, HGB, vol. VI/2 (4th ed. 2002) Art. 31 CMR note 49.

[163]   BGH TranspR 2004, 74; BGH TranspR 2004, 77.

[164]   *Andrea Merzario Ltd. v. Internationale Spedition Leitner GmbH* [2001] 1 Lloyd's Rep. 490 (C.A.); *Frans Maas Logistics (UK) Ltd. v. CDR Trucking BV* [1999] 2 Lloyd's Rep. 179 (Q.B.D., *Colman* J.).

[165]   OGH TranspR 2006, 257.

[166]   BGE 139 III 253.

[167]   The most recent contributions to the ongoing debate in legal writing are *Raphael Brunner*, TranspR 2013, 99, 100–102; *Patrick Schmidt*, TranspR 2013, 377.

in *TNT v. Axa.*[168] The European guidelines as introduced by *The "Tatry"*[169] and *Folien Fischer*[170] are extended to Art. 31 (2) CMR.[171]

Dogmatically, the CJEU is clearly overstepping its competences. The CJEU is not entitled to **31** interpret the CMR. It is not a "CMR court" since the EU has not even implemented a "CMR Regulation".[172] Its rulings cannot be binding upon those Contracting States of the CMR who are not Member States of the EU.[173] On the other hand, not all EU Member States are Contracting States of the CMR. Exceptional or exorbitant competences are not at stake.[174]

VI. Enforcement of maintenance orders

In practice of law, the recognition and enforcement of maintenance orders is of paramount **32** concern. In this context, for a long time quite some difficulty arose from the interplay of the Brussels I Regulation and the 1973 and 1958 Hague Conventions on the recognition and enforcement of decisions relating to maintenance obligations. Any solution of possible conflicts proceeded from Art. 71 as a general reference and bow to other conventions. As specialised conventions, the aforementioned Hague Conventions took precedence over the Brussels I Regulation.[175] Similar to (2) (b) 2, both Hague Conventions cling to the principle of *favor negotii*.[176] By means of an alternative reference rule, the national law of procedure was taken into consideration, but is barred by the general precedence of the Brussels I Regulation.[177] Any bilateral agreements as between the Member States of the Brussels I Regulation were excluded from application by Art. 69.[178]

It followed that the maintenance creditor, by virtue of Art. 71 (2) (b) subpara. 2 Brussels I **33** Regulation, may have opted for recognition and enforcement of a judgment according to the Brussels I Regulation to the extent to which he benefited from the Brussels I Regulation.[179]

---

168 *Nipponkoa Insurance Co. (Europe) Ltd. v. Inter-Zuid Transport BV* (Case C-452/12), ECLI:EU:C:2013:858 para. 48.

169 *The owners of the cargo lately laden on board the ship "Tatry" v. The owners of the ship "Maciej Rataj"* (Case C-406/02), [1994] I-5439 para. 45.

170 *Folien Fischer AG and Fofictec AG v. Ritrama SpA* (Case C-133/11), nyr. para. 49; comments i.a. by *Domej*, ecolex 2013, 123; *Vaneleenhove*, NIPR 2013, 25; *Muir Watt*, RCDIP 102 (2013), 506; *Gebauer*, ZEuP 2013, 874.

171 *Nipponkoa Insurance Co. (Europe) Ltd. v. Inter-Zuid Transport BV* (Case C-452/12), ECLI:EU:C:2013:858 para. 48 with para. 42; *Hoeks*, NIPR 2011, 468, 471; *Kuypers*, NTER 2011, 13, 17; *van der Klooster*, in: IPR in de spiegel van Paul Vlas (2012), p. 113, 120.

172 *Mankowski*, TranspR 2014, 129, 134.

173 *Mankowski*, TranspR 2014, 129, 134.

174 A-G *Kokott*, Opinion in Case C-533/08 of 28 January 2010, [2010] ECR I-4110 paras. 61–69.

175 See only BGH NJW-RR 2010, 1, 2; TS REDI 2001, 501 with note *Michinel Álvarez*. But cf. also *Lara Aguado* AEDIPr 2007, 1070, 1072 *et seq.*

176 See BGHZ 171, 310; BGH NJW 2008, 1531, 1532; OLG München FamRZ 2003, 462.

177 BGHZ 171, 310; BGH NJW 2008, 1531, 1532; BGH NJW-RR 2010, 1, 2; *Mankowski*, IPRax 2000, 188, 192. Apparently *contra Geimer*, IPRax 2004, 419, 420.

178 *Mankowski*, IPRax 2000, 188, 193.

179 See hereon OLG München FamRZ 2003, 462; *Mankowski*, IPRax 2000, 188, 193; *Finger*, FuR 2001, 97, 103; *Geimer*, IPRax 2004, 419, 420; *Martiny*, FamRZ 2008, 1681, 1687.

From the maintenance creditor's point of view, the procedure for a declaration of enforceability under the Brussels I Regulation was the most benign existing, as it contented itself with a minimum amount of prerequisites, formalities and participation of the maintenance debtor. Thus, it was strongly recommended to let maintenance judgments undergo the Brussels I procedure of recognition and declaration of enforceability but to refer to other Conventions only insofar as grounds for non-recognition or other prerequisites for recognition were concerned, if those provisions might exceptionally have benefited the maintenance creditor more than the Brussels I Regulation did.[180]

34 As of 18 June 2011 the overall picture has changed dramatically with the Maintenance Regulation[181] taking central position in the ensuing jigsaw. From that date and provided that the Maintenance Regulation has been generally applicable, the starting point for solving the problem is Art. 69 Maintenance Regulation which, however, operates along lines similar to those which had been prevailing under Art. 71 Brussels I Regulation.

35 The Brussels *Ibis* Regulation and the Maintenance Regulation do not compete anymore with regard to maintenance obligations stemming from marriage, family relationships or equivalent relationships. Insofar Art. 1 (2) (e) declares the Brussels *Ibis* Regulation inapplicable and thus gives way to the Maintenance Regulation.

Article 71a

(1) For the purposes of this Regulation, a court common to several Member States (a "common court") shall be a court of a Member State when, pursuing to the agreement establishing it, it exercises jurisdiction in civil and commercial matters within the meaning of this Regulation.
(2) For the purposes of this Regulation, the following shall each be a common court:
    (a) the Unified Patent Court established by the Agreement on a Unified Patent Court signed on 19 February 2013 (the "UPC Agreement");
    (b) the Benelux Court of Justice established by the Treaty of 31 March 1965 concerning the establishment and statute of a Benelux Court of Justice (the "Benelux Agreement").

Bibliography

Erauw, Relación entre el acuerdo sobre el Tribunal de la Patente Unificada Europea y el nuevo reglamento de Bruselas I sobre competencia y reconocimiento, AEDIPr 2013, 101

Holzer, Da waren es plötzlich drei …, ÖBl 2014, 153

Kur, Durchsetzung gemeinschaftsweiter Schutzrechte: Internationale Zuständigkeit und anwendbares Recht, GRUR Int. 2014, 749

Torsten Bjørn Larsen, Rules of Jurisdiction in the Agreement on a Unified Patent Court, NIR 2014, 358

Luginbühl, Das geplante künftige europäische Patentgericht und sein Verhältnis zum Lugano-

---

[180] OLG Hamm IPRax 2004, 437, 438; *Mankowski*, IPRax 2000, 188, 193; *Finger*, FuR 2001, 97, 103; *Kropholler/von Hein* Art. 71 note 5; *Mankowski*, in: Rauscher Art. 71 note 18; *Geimer*, IPRax 2004, 419, 420.

[181] Council Regulation (EC) No. 4/2009 of 18 December 2008 on jurisdiction, applicable law, recognition and enforcement of decisions and cooperation in matters relating to maintenance obligations, OJ EU 2009 L 7/1, with Corrigendum, OJ EU 2009 L 131/26.

Übereinkommen, in: Calame/Hess-Blumer/Stieger (eds.), Patentgerichtsgesetz (PatGG) (Basel 2013)
ders, The patent package of the European Union: the European Patent with unitary effect (Unitary Patent) and the Unified Patent Court, 8 Kyungpook Nat U IT & L Rev 83 (2014)
Luginbühl/Dieter Stauder, Die Anwendung der revidierten Zuständigkeitsregeln nach der Brüssel I-Verordnung auf Klagen in Patentsachen, GRUR Int. 2014, 885
Mankowski, Die neuen Regeln über gemeinsame Gerichte in Artt. 71a–71d Brüssel Ia-VO, GPR 2014, 330
Marongiu Bonaiuti, L'accordo istitutivo del Tribunale unificato dei brevetti e la sua incidenza sulla disciplina della giurisidizione in materia civile nell'Unione europea, Oss cost Assoc It Cost 2014, 1
de Miguel Asensio, Tribunal Unificado de Patentes: competencia judicial y reconocimiento de resoluciónes, AEDIPr 2013, 73
de Miguel Asensio, The Unifoed Patent Court Agreement and the amendment to the Brussels I Regulation (Recast), in: Honorati (a cura di), Luci e ombre del nuovo sistema UE di tutela brevettuale (2014) 153

Philipp, EuGVVO: Anpassungen im Zusammenhang mit dem Übereinkommen über ein Einheitliches Patentgericht, EuZ 2014, 406
Pinckney, Understanding the Transitional Provisions of the Agreement on the Unified Patent Court, (2015) 37 EIPR 268
Schröer, Einheitspatentgericht – Überlegungen zum Forum-Shopping im Rahmen der alternativen Zuständigkeit nach Art. 83 Abs 1 EPGÜ, GRUR Int. 2013, 1102
Dieter Stauder, Europäische Patentgerichtsbarkeit – Wie geht es weiter nach dem Gutachten 1/09 des EuGH?, sic! 2011, 351
Véron, Extent of the Long-Arm Jurisdiction Conferred upon the Unified Patent Court by Art. 71 (b) (3) of the Brussels I Regulation Amended by Regulation 542/2014 of May 15, 2014: Turkish Delight and a Bit of Swiss Chocolate for the Unified Patent Court, (2015) 37 EIPR 588
Wohlgemuth, Änderungen bei gerichtlichen Zuständigkeiten in grenzüberschreitenden europäischen Patentverletzungsfällen, sic! 2015, 299.

I. Ratio legis and general considerations

Arts. 71a–71d are the outcome of the legislative initiative commenced by COM (2013) 554 **1** final. It was finalised by, and culminated in, Regulation (EU) No. 542/2014[1] of the European Parliament and of the Council of 15 May 2014 amending Regulation No. 1215/2012 as regards the rules to be applied with respect to the Unified Patent Court and the Benelux Court of Justice.[2] This Regulation was the first Regulation amending the Brussels I*bis* Regulation. It was enacted and went into force even before the effective date of the Brussels I*bis* Regulation, but nevertheless after its coming into force.

Art. 71a has a mere definitional character.[3] It specifically aims at extending the expression **2** "court" beyond purely national courts of a single Member State to certain courts common to two or more Member States. It purports at clarifying[4] that the courts listed in (2) are courts

---

[1]   Regulation (EU) No.542/2014 of the European Parliament and of the Council of 15 May 2014 amending Regulation (EU) No. 1215/2012 as regards the rules to be applied to the Unified Patent Court and the Benelux Court, OJ EU 2014 L 163/1.

[2]   OJ EU 2014 L 163/1.

[3]   *Marongiu Bonaiuti*, Oss. cost. Assoc. It. Cost. 2014, 1, 9.

[4]   *Miguel de Asensio*, AEDIPr 2013, 73, 78; but see also *Luginbühl* in: Calame/Hess-Blumer/Stieger (eds. eds.), PatGG (Basel 2013) N 40; *Luginbühl/Dieter Stauder*, GRUR Int. 2014, 885, 886 *et seq.*

within the Brussels I Regulation (such a clarification does not exist with regards to the Lugano Convention of 2007[5]).[6] Since Recital (11) already indicated that courts common to several Member States should be understood as "courts" within the Brussels *Ibis* Regulation and expressly mentions the Benelux Court of Justice in this regard, Art. 71a is by no means revolutionary but only fills out a concept already designed.[7] Common courts are only such courts, which have been set up and given substantive competence by their establishing legal act.[8] For matters beyond their competence these courts are neither competent nor courts for the purpose of the Brussels *Ibis* Regulation. The mode of implementation follows the footprints of Art. 3.[9] Only for the sake of enhanced readability the necessary changes are introduced and combined in four new provisions, namely Arts. 71a–71d.

II. Recitals of the Regulation (EU) No. 542/2014 and Commission's Explanatory Memorandum

3 Within the Recitals to the Regulation (EU) No. 524/2014 the following is stipulated in regard to Art. 71a, on the one hand generally and on the other hand specifically:

(1) On 19 February 2013, the Kingdom of Belgium, the Republic of Bulgaria, the Czech Republic, the Kingdom of Denmark, the Federal Republic of Germany, the Republic of Estonia, Ireland, the Hellenic Republic, the French Republic, the Italian Republic, the Republic of Cyprus, the Republic of Latvia, the Republic of Lithuania, the Grand-Duchy of Luxembourg, Hungary, the Republic of Malta, the Kingdom of the Netherlands, the Republic of Austria, the Portuguese Republic, Romania, the Republic of Slovenia, the Slovak Republic, the Republic of Finland, the Kingdom of Sweden and the United Kingdom of Great Britain and Northern Ireland signed the Agreement on a Unified Patent Court[10] (the 'UPC Agreement'). The UPC Agreement provides for its entry into force not prior to the first day of the fourth month after the date of entry into force of the amendments to Regulation (EU) No. 1215/2012 of the European Parliament and of the Council[11] concerning the relationship of that Regulation with the UPC Agreement.

(2) On 15 October 2012, the Kingdom of Belgium, the Grand-Duchy of Luxembourg and the Kingdom of the Netherlands, parties to the Treaty of 31 March 1965 concerning the establishment and statute of a Benelux Court of Justice (the 'Benelux Court of Justice Treaty'), signed a Protocol amending that Treaty. That Protocol made it possible to transfer jurisdiction to the Benelux Court of Justice in specific matters falling within the scope of Regulation (EU) No. 1215/2012.

(3) It is necessary to regulate the relationship of Regulation (EU) No. 1215/2012 with the UPC Agreement and with the Benelux Court of Justice Treaty by way of amendments to that Regulation.

(4) The Unified Patent Court and the Benelux Court of Justice should be deemed to be courts within the meaning of Regulation (EU) No. 1215/2012 in order to ensure legal certainty and predictability

---

5   *Miguel de Asensio*, AEDIPr 2013, 73, 79.

6   Explanatory Memorandum COM (2013) 554 final p. 3.

7   *Wallner-Friedl*, in: Czernich/Kodek/Mayr, Art. 71d note 3; see Explanatory Memorandum COM (2013) 554 final p. 5.

8   *Marongiu Bonaiuti*, Oss. cost. Assoc. It. Cost. 2014, 1, 9.

9   Explanatory Memorandum COM (2013) 554 final p. 5.

10   OJ C 175, 20.6.2013, p. 1.

11   Regulation (EU) No. 1215/2012 of the European Parliament and of the Council of 12 December 2012 on jurisdiction and the recognition and enforcement of judgments in civil and commercial matters (OJ L 351, 20.12.2012, p. 1).

for defendants who could be sued in those two Courts at a location situated in a Member State other than the one designated by the rules of Regulation (EU) No. 1215/2012.

(5) The amendments to Regulation (EU) No. 1215/2012 provided for in this Regulation with regard to the Unified Patent Court are intended to establish the international jurisdiction of that Court and do not affect the internal allocation of proceedings among the divisions of that Court nor the arrangements laid down in the UPC Agreement concerning the exercise of jurisdiction, including exclusive jurisdiction, during the transitional period provided for in that Agreement.

As explanation for the proposal for Art. 71a the Commission[12] gave the following reasons: **4**

"As a result of the internal division of competences within the Unified Patent Court a defendant could find him/herself before a division which would not be situated in the Member State of the court designated by the rules of the Brussels I Regulation. For instance, a Dutch defendant expecting to be sued at its domicile on the basis of Art. 4(1) of the Brussels I Regulation (recast) may be brought before the competent central, regional or local division which may be situated in France, Germany or the United Kingdom (or any other Member State, depending on where regional or local divisions will be set up). This is also relevant when the defendant is domiciled or habitually resident in a Member State which is not a Contracting Party to the UPC Agreement (e.g. a licensee domiciled in Spain had to perform an obligation under the license agreement in the Netherlands; proceedings are brought before the German central division instead of the Netherlands as place of performance of the obligation). Equally, as a result of the transfer of competences to the Benelux Court of Justice, a defendant, including from a non-Contracting Member State, could find him/herself before a court which would not be situated in the Member State of the court designated by the rules of the Brussels I Regulation. While Article 71 of the Brussels I Regulation allows conventions on particular matters which already exist, it does not allow any such new conventions. As a result, it is necessary to clarify that both the Unified Patent Court and the Benelux Court of Justice are to be considered as courts of a Member State in the sense of the Brussels I Regulation, thus ensuring that the Regulation applies fully to the these courts.

The Brussels I Regulation (recast) does not provide for a definition of the term "court". It limits itself, in Article 3, to include certain specific authorities within the concept of "court" for purposes of the operation of the Brussels I Regulation. Recital 11 does clarify, however, that the term "court" should be understood as including courts or tribunals common to several Member States. Recital 11 explicitly refers to the Benelux Court of Justice when it exercises jurisdiction in matters falling within the scope of the Brussels I Regulation. Recital 11 clarifies that judgments given by such common courts should be recognized and enforced in accordance with the Brussels I Regulation. Nevertheless, a recital does not have binding nature and cannot ensure with a sufficient degree of legal certainty compliance of the respective international agreements with the Brussels I Regulation (recast), in particular Article 71 thereof. A specific legislative amendment is therefore necessary. This amendment follows the approach taken for the Hungarian notary and Swedish enforcement authority in Article 3 of the Regulation; it includes specifically the Unified Patent Court and the Benelux

---

[12] Commission Proposal of 26 July 2013 for a Regulation of the European Parliament and of the Council amending Regulation (EU) No. 1215/2012 on jurisdiction and recognition and enforcement of decisions in civil and commercial matters, COM (2013) 554 final pp. 4–5.

Court of Justice in the concept of "court" of the Regulation. For reasons of readability, all necessary changes relating to the UPC and Benelux Court of Justice Agreements are combined in four new provisions (new Articles 71a to 71d).

By clarifying that both the Unified Patent Court and the Benelux Court of Justice should be considered as "courts" within the meaning of the Brussels I Regulation (recast), it will be ensured that the international jurisdiction of these courts will be determined by the Brussels I Regulation; in particular it will be ensured that defendants which would expect to be sued in a specific Member State on the basis of the rules of the Brussels I Regulation may be sued before either a division of the Unified Patent Court or before the Benelux Court of Justice which is located in another Member State than the national courts designated on the basis of the Brussels I Regulation. Legal certainty and predictability for defendants requires that this change of territorial jurisdiction is set out clearly in the text of the Brussels I Regulation."

III. UPC-Agreement as triggering occasion

5 The occasion for creating Arts. 71a–71d (in record time for an ordinary legislative procedure[13]) was the UPC-Agreement and the institutionalisation of the UPC.[14] The UPC itself[15] is the procedural safeguarding of the Regulation (EU) No. 1257/2012[16] and the Regulation (EU) No. 1260/2012.[17] These Regulations replace the EPC in relation between the participating Member States. The Regulation on a uniform patent and the Regulation on language issues create a European patent with uniform effect.[18] Together with the UPC they represent the European "patent package".[19] The UPC decides on this as well as on the European patent according to the EPC. Furthermore, it can have competences for Supplementary Protection Certificates of pharmaceuticals[20] and plant protection producers.[21,22]

---

[13] *Luginbühl/Dieter Stauder*, GRUR Int. 2014, 885, 886.

[14] See only *Marongiu Bonaiuti*, Oss. cost. Assoc. It. Cost. 2014, 1, 15; *Erauw*, AEDIPr 2013, 101, 103; *Luginbühl/Dieter Stauder*, GRUR Int. 2014, 885, 886; *Wallner-Friedl*, in: Czernich/Kodek/Mayr, Art. 71d notes 1 *et seq.*

[15] On it e.g. *Plesner*, NIR 2015, 90; *Grundén*, NIR 2015, 96; *Ydreskog*, NIR 2015, 103.

[16] Council Regulation (EU) No. 1257/2012 of 17 December 2012 implementing enhanced cooperation in the area of the creation of unitary patent protection, OJ EU 2012 L 361/1.

[17] Council Regulation (EU) No. 1260/2012 of 17 December 2012 implementing enhanced cooperation in the area of the creation of unitary patent protection with regard to the applicable translation arrangements, OJ EU 2012 L 361/89.

[18] In detail for instance *Ohly*, ZGE 2012, 419; *Teschemacher*, MittPat 2013, 153; *Luginbühl*, GRUR Int. 2013, 305; *Luginbühl*, 8 Kyungpook Nat. U. IT & L. Rev. 83 (2014); *Eck*, GRUR Int. 2014, 114; *Ellyne*, (2014) 4 Queen Mary J. IP 57; *Ullrich*, Max Planck Institute for Innovation and Competititon Discussion Paper 2/2014; *Götting*, ZEuP 2014, 349.

[19] In more detail the contributions in: Honorati (a cura di), Luci e ombre del nuovo sistema UE di tutela brevettale (2014) and *Desantes Real*, Cah. dr. eur. 49 (2013) 577.

[20] By virtue of VO (EC) No. 469/2009 of the European Parliament and of the Council of 6. March 2009 concerning the creation of the supplementary protection certificate for medicinal products, OJ EU 2009 L 152/1.

[21] VO (EG) Nr. 1610/96 of the European Parliament and of the Council of 23 July 1996 concerning the creation of a supplementary protection certificate for plant protection products, OJ EC 1996 L 198/30.

[22] *Erauw*, AEDIPr 2013, 101, 105.

The systematic place was chosen on purpose as Arts. 71a–71d were believed to address issues **6** similar to those addressed in Art. 71.[23] In order to create full transparency on the combined and coherent application of the respective Agreements and the Brussels I*bis* Regulation the latter prescribes how its rules on jurisdiction apply to the common courts listed.[24] It does so in a like manner as Art. 71 does for other international conventions on particular matters.[25]

For establishing the UPC, the participating states had to choose the instrument of an in- **7** ternational agreement, as the path for an EU-Regulation was barred. The uniform patent is only the fruit of an enhanced cooperation,[26] on which many EU Member States participate,[27] but not all.[28] Therefore, it was not possible to utilise a regulation for the UPC which would be binding upon all EU Member States. The "standard" courts of the Member States to the convention have, at most, a residual function in the unified area.[29] But generally the UPC has an exclusive competence and jurisdiction, from which the necessity of a fit in into the Brussels I*bis*-system follows.[30] The Regulation (EU) No. 642/2014 is considered to be a mile-stone for the UPC-system.[31]

In particular, it has to be taken into account that only its Contracting States are bound by the **8** respective Agreement and that the other Member States which are not Contracting States, are not so bound. Without specific provision being made for a conceptual extension in the Brussels I*bis* Regulation, the common court would replace national courts only for the respective Contracting States. But the common courts are part of the judiciary systems of

---

[23] Explanatory Memorandum COM (2013) 554 final p. 5.

[24] Explanatory Memorandum COM (2013) 554 final p. 5.

[25] Explanatory Memorandum COM (2013) 554 final p. 5.

[26] Permitted by Council Decision 2011/167/EU of 10 March 2011 authorising enhanced cooperation in the area of the creation of unitary patent protection, OJ EU 2011 L 76/53. In more detail *Lamping*, Int. Rev. IP. & Compet. L. 2011, 879; *Pocar* Riv dir int priv proc 2011, 297, 302 ff; *Marongiu Bonaiuti*, Oss. cost. Assoc. It. Cost. 2014, 1, 2 *et seq.*

[27] Contracting Member States are according to Recital (3) Regulation (EU) No. 1257/2012 Belgium, Bulgaria, the Czech Republic, Denmark, Germany, Estonia, Ireland, Greece, France, Cyprus, Latvia, Lithunania, Luxemburg, Hungary, Malta, the Netherlands, Austria, Poland, Portugal, Rumania, Slovenia, Slovakia, Finland, Sweden und the United Kingdom. But for Italy this coincides with the list of Contracting States of the UPC Agreement. Italy has joined the UPC Agreement without prejudice, but not the enhanced cooperation.

[28] Spain and Italy do not participate. Both have sued against the introduction of the Unified Patent by enhanced cooperation and have lost; *Kingdom of Spain and Italian Republic v. Council* (joined Cases C-274/11 and C-295/11) ECLI:EU:C:2013:240 (on this i.a. *Zeitzmann*, EuZW 2013, 748; *Blumenröder/ Peto*, Eur. L. Rpter 2013, 110; *Speyart*, NTER 2013, 135; *Guillard*, Rev. aff. UE 2013, 355 and 374; *Lamping*, Maastricht J. Eur. & Comp. L. 2013, 589; *Pistoia*, [2014] 51 CML Rev. 247); A-G *Bot*, Opinion in Joined Cases C-274/11 and C-295/11 of 11 December 2012, ECLI:EU:C:2012:782. Spain's second attempt, formally split into two separate Cases one each against every of the two Regulation is still pending as Cases C-146/13 and C-147/13 (on the Spanish position *Desantes Real*, REDI 2013-2, 51). Croatia only joined the EU after the enhanced cooperation was completed and has not signed the UPC Agreement yet.

[29] *Marongiu Bonaiuti*, Oss. cost. Assoc. It. Cost. 2014, 1, 3–5.

[30] *Marongiu Bonaiuti*, Oss. cost. Assoc. It. Cost. 2014, 1, 5–8.

[31] *Miguel de Asensio*, AEDIPr 2013, 73, 74.

---

the Contracting States of the respective Agreement, and thus proper regard to them has to be had in the Brussels *Ibis* Regulation in a sensible and constructive manner.

9 The Regulation (EU) No. 1257/2012, Regulation (EU) No. 1260 and the UPC Agreement are not binding upon such Member States of the EPC, which are no Member States of the EU. This concerns Switzerland, Liechtenstein, Norway, Iceland, Turkey, Monaco, San Marino, Albania, Macedonia and Serbia. The UPC-Convention is not open for access for these named states due to its specific context of union law. It does not fall within the scope of Art. 71. Neither does the reverse of Art. 71 take the competence from the Member States to its conclusion.[32] To what extent a future Lugano Convention III in relation to Switzerland, Iceland and Norway can relieve, is left open.[33]

10 Denmark is a signatory state to the UPC Agreement and is equated to a Member State to the Brussels *Ibis* Regulation also for reasons of the Arts. 71–71d as soon as it has issued the relative declaration of extension for the Regulation (EU) No. 542/2014, an explicit amendment regulation to the Brussels *Ibis* Regulation and indirectly to the Brussels I Regulation under the EU-DK-Agreement.

11 The UPC has its court of first instance in a central division with its seat in Paris and sections in London and Munich according to Art. 7(2)(1) UPC Agreement.

12 The Contracting Member States to the UPC Agreement can set up local and regional divisions of the UPC that shall form a Court of First Instance. These divisions are organisational parts of the UPC. They are subdivisions of the UPC, no independent judiciary bodies. Local and regional divisions are on equal footing with the central division, as results from the indiscriminating, non-hierarchical sequence in Art. 7(1) UPC Agreement. As a result, the possibility of forum shopping and deviations from the system of jurisdictions according to the Brussels *Ibis* Regulation develop.[34]

13 Any Contracting Member State can establish a local division in its area according to Art. 7(1) UPC Agreement, and if necessary additional local divisions pursuant to Art. 7(3) UPC Agreements. The maximum number of local divisions in a Member State is four according to Art. 7(4)(2) UPC Agreement.

14 Upon request, regional divisions shall be set up for two or more Contracting Member States according to Art. 7(5)(1) UPC Agreement. Such Contracting Member States designate the seat of the regional division (Art. 7(5)(2) UPC Agreement). That division can hear cases in multiple locations (Art. 7(5)(3) UPC Agreement). Sweden together with the three Baltic States for example has set up a regional division seated in Stockholm with English as the language of proceedings.[35]

---

[32] Commission Proposal of 26 July 2013 for a Regulation of the European Parliament and of the Council amending Regulation (EU) No. 1215/2012 on jurisdiction and recognition and enforcement of decisions in civil and commercial matters, COM (2013) 554 final p. 3.

[33] See *Luginbühl/Dieter Stauder*, GRUR Int. 2014, 885, 886.

[34] *Schröer*, GRUR Int. 2013, 1102, 1103; *Luginbühl/Dieter Stauder*, GRUR Int. 2014, 885, 886.

[35] *Wolfgang Holzer*, ÖBl 2014, 153.

IV. Benelux Court of Justice

Recital (2) lists the common courts envisaged. For the time, the list contains only two entries, **15** namely (a) the Unified Patent Court established by the Agreement on a Unified Patent Court signed on 19 February 2013 and (b) the Benelux Court of Justice established by the Treaty of 31 March 1965 concerning the establishment and statute of a Benelux Court of Justice. Quite obviously, the former enticed the introduction of Arts. 71a–71d, and the Benelux Court of Justice (which has long been existent before without raising the necessity of any further considerations) accompanies it as some kind of fellow traveller in its own right. The Benelux Court of Justice has been established for decades, set up under the Treaty of 31 May 1965 between the Benelux-States.[36] There have never been serious difficulties with this court in the past. Its express inclusion in Art. 71a–71d serves as a rounding-off and as clarification. It makes use of the opportunity given by the UPC Agreement and the UPC. At the same time, it reacts, as proven by Recital (2) Regulation No. 542/2014, to the Protocol to the Treaty to the Benelux Court of Justice, signed by Belgium, the Netherlands and Luxemburg on 15 October 2012. This Protocol opens up the possibility to allocate jurisdiction to the Benelux Court of Justice for matters which are subject to the Regulation (EU) No. 1215/2012. The involvement of the Benelux Court of Justice was not the primary reason for the creation of Arts. 71a–71d, but so to speak this reason is also piggybacked. This does however not exclude that individual provisions out of the Arts. 71a–71d can gain a greater importance for the Benelux Court of Justice than for the UPC.[37] This applies particularly to Art. 71c and Art. 71d. The Arts. 71–71d must not be constricted to the UPC as their initiative case and moreover not only orientate their interpretation alongside the UPC. Said provisions are no specific provisions for intellectual property rights. Thus, they are not to be orientated along specifics of intellectual property rights.

V. Further common courts to a number of Member States

(2) employs the technique of introducing an open and extendable list to which further **16** common courts can be added effortlessly if the necessity arises. But the list is exhaustive and exclusive. If there were other courts common to a number of Member States which are not listed, though, they do not enjoy the status of common courts and consequentially of proper courts within the Brussels I*bis* system granted by (1). However, it would only need a corresponding amendment in the form of an amending regulation to be able to add new numbers in the amount suitable.[38] Arts. 71a–71d are as regards content sufficiently open and flexible to be applicable to further common courts of several Member States. Also in this respect Arts. 71a–71d liberate themselves from their initiative case concerning the establishment of the UPC. They must not be interpreted merely with regard to the UPC and its particular characteristics.

A common court of several Member States is a court that has been set up on an international **17** law basis or other intergovernmental basis by several Member States. A typical instrument of establishment will be an international treaty. An establishment through means of intergov-

---

[36] Vertrag vom 31. März 1965 zwischen dem Königreich Belgien, dem Großherzogtum Luxemburg und dem Königreich der Niederlande über die Gründung und die Satzung des Benelux-Gerichtshofs.

[37] *Mankowski*, GPR 2014, 330, 333.

[38] *Mankowski*, GPR 2014, 330, 333.

ernmental or administrative agreement does not seem to be excluded from the start.[39] At least two Member States would have to belong to the establishment act; it is not required that at least three Member States would have to be Contracting Member States.[40]

18   On the other hand it is insufficient when several territorial units of the same Member State establish a common court, even if these territorial units in principle each had separate jurisdictions.[41] The Supreme Court of the United Kingdom does not constitute a common court of several Member States, as England, Wales, Scotland and Northern Ireland are no independent states and no independent subjects of international law.

19   Likewise, it does not suffice if only one Member State sets up a common court with a Third State or several Third States. For purposes of the Brussels I*bis* Regulation such a common court between a Member State and Third States would constitute a court of the concerned Member State.[42] To the contrary, a common court of several Member States would be a court, of which several Member States as well as at least one third State belongs to the constitutive act. Certainly, one could ask, if these two cases would not require in each case an amendment or supplementation of the Brussels I*bis* Regulation to clarify, when there is sufficient relation to the union and when, as far as wanted, a third-party dimension shall be excluded.

20   Unproblematic and no case for Arts. 71a–71d is, that the Hoge-Raad of the Netherlands rules in matters concerning the Antilles, even though Aruba does not belong to the EU-territory. This is because the Netherlands Antilles lack of independency under international law and thus are not a Third State.[43] The same applies for the Danish Højesteret and Greenlandic matters.

21   The Commission's Explanatory Memorandum[44] reads (the Recital (11) referred to was a planned alteration that did not make it in the final Amendment Regulation):

"As a result of the internal division of competences within the Unified Patent Court a defendant could find him/herself before a division which would not be situated in the Member State of the court designated by the rules of the Brussels I Regulation. For instance, a Dutch defendant expecting to be sued at its domicile on the basis of Art. 4 (1) of the Brussels I Regulation (recast) may be brought before the competent central, regional or local division which may be situated in France, Germany or the United Kingdom (or any other Member State, depending on where regional or local divisions will be set up). This is also relevant when the defendant is domiciled or habitually resident in a Member State which is not a Contracting Party to the UPC Agreement (e.g. a licensee domiciled in Spain had to perform an obligation under the license agreement in the Netherlands; proceedings are brought before the German central division instead of the Netherlands as place of performance of the obligation). Equally, as a result of the transfer of competences to the Benelux Court of Justice, a defendant, including from a non-Contracting Member State, could find him/herself before a court

---

[39]   *Mankowski*, GPR 2014, 330, 333.

[40]   *Mankowski*, GPR 2014, 330, 333.

[41]   *Mankowski*, GPR 2014, 330, 333.

[42]   *Mankowski*, GPR 2014, 330, 333.

[43]   *Mankowski*, GPR 2014, 330, 333.

[44]   Explanatory Memorandum, COM (2013) 554 final pp. 4–5.

which would not be situated in the Member State of the court designated by the rules of the Brussels I Regulation. While Article 71 of the Brussels I Regulation allows conventions on particular matters which already exist, it does not allow any such new conventions. As a result, it is necessary to clarify that both the Unified Patent Court and the Benelux Court of Justice are to be considered as courts of a Member State in the sense of the Brussels I Regulation, thus ensuring that the Regulation applies fully to the these courts. The Brussels I Regulation (recast) does not provide for a definition of the term "court". It limits itself, in Article 3, to include certain specific authorities within the concept of "court" for purposes of the operation of the Brussels I Regulation. Recital 11 does clarify, however, that the term "court" should be understood as including courts or tribunals common to several Member States. Recital 11 explicitly refers to the Benelux Court of Justice when it exercises jurisdiction in matters falling within the scope of the Brussels I Regulation. Recital 11 clarifies that judgments given by such common courts should be recognized and enforced in accordance with the Brussels I Regulation. Nevertheless, a recital does not have binding nature and cannot ensure with a sufficient degree of legal certainty compliance of the respective international agreements with the Brussels I Regulation (recast), in particular Article 71 thereof. A specific legislative amendment is therefore necessary. This amendment follows the approach taken for the Hungarian notary and Swedish enforcement authority in Article 3 of the Regulation; it includes specifically the Unified Patent Court and the Benelux Court of Justice in the concept of "court" of the Regulation. For reasons of readability, all necessary changes relating to the UPC and Benelux Court of Justice Agreements are combined in four new provisions (new Articles 71a to 71d). By clarifying that both the Unified Patent Court and the Benelux Court of Justice should be considered as "courts" within the meaning of the Brussels I Regulation (recast), it will be ensured that the international jurisdiction of these courts will be determined by the Brussels I Regulation; in particular it will be ensured that defendants which would expect to be sued in a specific Member State on the basis of the rules of the Brussels I Regulation may be sued before either a division of the Unified Patent Court or before the Benelux Court of Justice which is located in another Member State than the national courts designated on the basis of the Brussels I Regulation. Legal certainty and predictability for defendants requires that this change of territorial jurisdiction is set out clearly in the text of the Brussels I Regulation."

Article 71b

The jurisdiction of a common court shall be determined as follows:
1. A common court shall have jurisdiction where, under this Regulation, the courts of a Member State party to the instrument establishing the common court would have jurisdiction in a matter governed by that instrument;
2. Where the defendant is not domiciled in a Member State, and this Regulation does not otherwise confer jurisdiction over him, Chapter II shall apply as appropriate regardless of the defendant's domicile.
   Application may be made to a common court for provisional, including protective, measures even if the courts of a third State have jurisdiction as to the substance of the matter;
3. where a common court has jurisdiction over a defendant under point 2 in a dispute relating to an infringement of a European patent giving rise to damage within the Union, that court may also exercise jurisdiction in relation to damage arising outside the Union from such an infringement.
   Such jurisdiction may only be established if property belonging to the defendant is located in any Member State party to the instrument establishing the common court and the dispute has a sufficient connection with any such Member State.

I. Regulation of international jurisdiction

1 Art. 71b regulates the jurisdiction of common courts. Thereby it has to be differentiated whether the defendant is domiciled in a Member State of the Brussels *Ibis* Regulation or not. If he is domiciled in a Brussels *Ibis*-Member State, No. 1 applies, if he is domiciled outside a Brussels *Ibis*-Member State, No. 2 and possibly No. 3 apply. The plaintiff's domicile is by contrast insignificant. The forums according to Art. 71b are also available for plaintiffs domiciled in third States. Where the defendant is domiciled is to be determined according to Arts. 62; 63. Also in the context of Art. 71b, these provisions imply whether the defendant is domiciled in a Brussels *Ibis*-Member State.

2 The subject matters covered by Art. 71b are, as indicated by its own wording, only "the jurisdiction" of a common court. There are no further qualifying adjectives within the wording of Art. 71b. The jurisdiction addressed is only international jurisdiction. Art. 71b does not deal with venue and the interlocal distribution of local jurisdiction. This can on the one hand be derived from the very nature and purpose of a Common Court which is common to several Member States and not subdivided into local, regional or national sections.

3 As far as the situation is different, the constitutive legal act of the concerned common court has to find a regulation. But this concerns the internal allocation of competences and is no question which the Brussels *Ibis* Regulation must or may accept.[1]

4 On the other hand, Recital (5) explicitly refers solely to "international jurisdiction". The subject matter covered by Art. 31 UPC Agreement is also only the international jurisdiction. Whereas the venue is regulated decidedly by Art. 33 UPC Agreement.[2] According to Recital (5) Regulation (EU) No. 542/2014, the Brussels *Ibis* Regulation does not intend to touch upon this.[3]

II. Recitals of the Regulation (EU) No. 542/2014 and Commission's Explanatory Memorandum

5 The Recitals to the Regulation (EU) No. 542/2014 state with regards to Art. 71b:

---

[1] *Wallner-Friedl*, in: Czernich/Kodek/Mayr, Art. 71d note 4.

[2] *Torsten Bjørn Larsen*, NIR 2014, 358, 361–374.

[3] *Miguel de Asensio*, AEDIPr 2013, 73, 79.

(6) As courts common to several Member States, the Unified Patent Court and the Benelux Court of Justice cannot, unlike a court of one Member State, exercise jurisdiction on the basis of national law with respect to defendants not domiciled in a Member State. To allow those two Courts to exercise jurisdiction with respect to such defendants, the rules of Regulation (EU) No. 1215/2012 should therefore, with regard to matters falling within the jurisdiction of, respectively, the Unified Patent Court and the Benelux Court of Justice, also apply to defendants domiciled in third States. The existing rules of jurisdiction of Regulation (EU) No. 1215/2012 ensure a close connection between proceedings to which that Regulation applies and the territory of the Member States. It is therefore appropriate to extend those rules to proceedings against all defendants regardless of their domicile. When applying the rules of jurisdiction of Regulation (EU) No. 1215/2012, the Unified Patent Court and the Benelux Court of Justice (hereinafter individually referred to as a 'common court') should apply only those rules which are appropriate for the subject-matter for which jurisdiction has been conferred on them.

(7) A common court should be able to hear disputes involving defendants from third States on the basis of a subsidiary rule of jurisdiction in proceedings relating to an infringement of a European patent giving rise to damage both inside and outside the Union. Such subsidiary jurisdiction should be exercised where property belonging to the defendant is located in any Member State party to the instrument establishing the common court and the dispute in question has a sufficient connection with any such Member State, for example because the claimant is domiciled there or the evidence relating to the dispute is available there. In establishing its jurisdiction, the common court should have regard to the value of the property in question, which should not be insignificant and which should be such as to make it possible to enforce the judgment, at least in part, in the Member States parties to the instrument establishing the common court.

The Commission's Explanatory Memorandum[4] reads: 6

3.2. The operation of the rules on jurisdiction in relation to the Unified Patent Court and the Benelux Court of Justice on the one hand and the courts of Member States which are not Contracting Parties to the UPC Agreement or the Protocol to the 1965 Benelux Treaty on the other hand.

"In order to create full transparency on the combined and coherent application of the respective international agreements and the Brussels I Regulation (recast), the latter should prescribe how the jurisdiction rules of the Brussels I Regulation (recast) apply to the Unified Patent Court and Benelux Court of Justice, in the same way as Article 71 of the Brussels I Regulation (recast) does for other international conventions on particular matters. Similar clarifications are also found, for instance, in Articles 64 and 67 of the 2007 Lugano Convention on jurisdiction and the recognition and enforcement of judgments in civil and commercial matters. The new rule in Article 71b, paragraph 1 thus prescribes that the Unified Patent Court and the Benelux Court of Justice will have jurisdiction any time when a national court of one of the respective Contracting Member States would have jurisdiction based on the rules of the Brussels I Regulation. A contrario, the Unified Patent Court and the Benelux Court of Justice will not have jurisdiction when no national court of a Contracting Member State has jurisdiction pursuant to the Brussels I Regulation (for example, when jurisdiction pursuant to the Brussels I Regulation would lie with the courts of a non-Contracting Member State)."

---

[4]   Explanatory Memorandum, COM (2013) 554 final pp. 5–7.

3.3. The completion of the jurisdictional rules in relation to third State defendants

"Article 31 of the UPC Agreement provides that the international jurisdiction of the Unified Patent Court shall be established in accordance with Regulation (EU) No. 1215/2012 or, where applicable, on the basis of the Convention on jurisdiction and the recognition and enforcement of judgments in civil and commercial matters (Lugano Convention). However, insofar as the Brussels I Regulation (recast) and the 2007 Lugano Convention determine jurisdiction by reference to national law (see Article 6 of that Regulation and Article 4 of the Lugano Convention), it is not determined which rules should apply to determine the jurisdiction of courts which are common to several Member States such as the Unified Patent Court and the Benelux Court of Justice. In addition, a reference to the one or the other national law for the several divisions of the Unified Patent Court would create an unequal access to justice in a unified jurisdictional system which could not be justified on any objective reason. A similar problem has already been addressed in the existing Trademark Regulation (Council Regulation (EC) No. 207/2009 on the Community Trade Mark) and Design Regulation (Council Regulation (EC) No. 6/2002 on Community designs), which each do contain a complete set of uniform rules on jurisdiction vis-à-vis third State defendants. It is therefore necessary to complete the jurisdiction rules of the Brussels I Regulation (recast) for matters which will come within the competence of the Unified Patent Court and the Benelux Court of Justice insofar as defendants domiciled in non-European Union States are concerned. Uniform jurisdiction rules already exist in certain situations (such as exclusive jurisdiction with respect to the registration and validity of patents, choice of court agreements), but not in others (such as proceedings concerning the infringement of patents, licensing agreements in the absence of choice of court). The new proposal in Art. 71b, paragraph 2 therefore extends the Regulation's jurisdiction rules to disputes involving third State defendants domiciled in third States. In addition, the Unified Patent Court's and Benelux Court of Justice's jurisdiction to issue provisional, including protective measures is ensured even when the courts of third States have jurisdiction as to the substance of the matter. This extension will apply without prejudice to the 2005 Agreement between the European Community and the Kingdom of Denmark on jurisdiction and the recognition and enforcement of judgments in civil and commercial matters, which already regulates the situation of Danish defendants, and the 2007 Lugano Convention on the same subject matter which already regulates the situation of Swiss, Norwegian, and Icelandic defendants. As a result of this extension, access to the Unified Patent Court and the Benelux Court of Justice will be ensured in situations where the defendant is not domiciled in an EU Member State as access is ensured in situations where the defendant is domiciled in an EU Member State. In addition, such access is ensured independently of which instance or division within the Unified Patent Court is seized of a claim. In addition, the new proposal in Art. 71b, paragraph 3 establishes one additional forum for disputes involving defendants domiciled outside the EU. The proposal provides that a non-EU defendant can be sued at the place where moveable assets belonging to him are located provided their value is not insignificant compared to the value of the claim and that the dispute has a sufficient connection with the Member State of the court seized. The forum of the location of assets balances the absence of the defendant in the Union. Such a rule currently exists in a sizeable group of Member States and has the advantage of ensuring that a judgment can be enforced in the State where it was issued. It is a rule which fits better in the general philosophy of the Brussels I Regulation (recast) than other rules of subsidiary jurisdiction such as those provided for in the Trademark and Design Regulations mentioned above which allow proceedings against third State defendants to be brought, in particular, before the courts of the Member State where the plaintiff is domiciled (forum actoris). An asset-based forum may ensure the jurisdiction of the Unified Patent Court and the Benelux Court of Justice in situations where the Regulation's extended jurisdiction rules would not provide for jurisdiction and where such jurisdiction may be appropriate. For instance, with respect to the Unified

Patent Court, the asset-based jurisdiction would ensure that the Court would have jurisdiction vis-à-vis a Turkish defendant infringing a European patent covering several Member States and Turkey."

III. Principle (No. 1)

According to No. 1, a common court (international) shall have jurisdiction where, under this   **7**
Regulation, the courts of a Member State party to the instrument establishing the common court would have jurisdiction in a matter (international) governed by that instrument. The common court functionally replaces a national court and takes its place. Accordingly, also its jurisdiction has to be determined pursuant to the applicable regulations for the national courts of the Member States of the UPC Agreement or respectively of the Statute of the Benelux.[5]

The Member States are not bound to only have national courts within their court system, but   **8**
they can confer their jurisdiction granted for the national courts so to speak to the common court. This happens to the extent, and only to the extent, that the instrument of constitution for the respective court provides.[6] Art. 32 (1) UPC Agreement declares the UPC to have generally exclusive competence in respect of the national courts of the Contracting Member States to the UPC Agreement as soon as the transition period of Art. 83 (1) UPC Agreement has expired. Only for matters which do not come within the exclusive jurisdiction of the court according to the UPC Agreement, the national courts of the Contracting Member States shall remain competent pursuant Art. 32 (2) UPC Agreement.

This is corresponding with Art. 31 UPC Agreement with the official heading "International   **9**
Jurisdiction".[7] It reads:

"The international jurisdiction of the Court shall be established in accordance with Regulation (EU) No. 1215/2012 or, where applicable, on the basis of the Convention on jurisdiction and the recognition and enforcement of judgments in civil and commercial matters (Lugano Convention).[8]"

Art. 32 UPC Agreement differentiates between international competence and competence in general.[9] It includes a catalogue with the substantively encompassed types of actions which remains – from a perspective of the Brussels I*bis*-Regime – primarily within the scope of Art. 24 (4).[10] If the defendant has his residence in a EU-Member State which is no Contracting Member State to the UPC Agreement or outside the territory of the EU, Art. 33 (1) subpara. 3, 4 UPC Agreement applies and declares the central division of UPC to be competent.[11]

It suffices for the jurisdiction of the common court according to No. 1, when the courts of a   **10**

---

5   *Mankowski*, GPR 2014, 330, 335.
6   *Mankowski*, GPR 2014, 330, 335.
7   Thereon *Erauw*, AEDIPr 2013, 101, 109 f; *Torsten Bjørn Larsen* NIR 2014, 358 (358–361).
8   Convention on jurisdiction and the recognition and enforcement of judgments in civil and commercial matters, done at Lugano on 30 October 2007, including any subsequent amendments.
9   *Marongiu Bonaiuti*, Oss. cost. Assoc. It. Cost. 2014, 1, 7.
10 *Erauw*, AEDIPr 2013, 101, 107.
11 *Erauw*, AEDIPr 2013, 101, 111–113.

Member State party to the UPC Agreement or in the case of a the Benelux Court of Justice a national court of any Benelux State pursuant to the Brussels *Ibis*-Jurisdiction (according to the Brussels *Ibis*-Regulation) especially for the national courts of a certain Contracting State or respectively Benelux State had to be existing.[12] When there is a common court, which by definition has to be a court of several states, there can be no forum state (even if the common court such as the UPC is divided into separate local divisions).[13]

11 It is a pure matter of course that only those rules of the Brussels *Ibis*-Regulation which are appropriate for the subject-matter conferring jurisdiction are to be consulted. Emphasizing this in recital (6) cl. 5 Regulation (EU) No. 542/2014 was actually superfluous. The complete reference does, on the one hand, not change anything regarding the internal differentiation within the Brussels *Ibis*-Regime that has been referred to – let it be based on hierarchy of norms, let it be based on qualification. The scope is rather set by the reference. The reference, on the other hand, is not in the position to break the limits of the subject-matter competence of the concerned common court.[14] If a common court, such as the UPC, may only decide upon certain types of disputes, only jurisdiction for this particular dispute is required. A patent dispute does not convert into a contractual dispute through a reference to the Brussels *Ibis*-Regulation. A patent dispute does not convert into a dispute about the issuance of a cultural asset or about remuneration for salvage and assistance. Or to translate it into rules: Art. 7 (4) or (7) will not suddenly be applicable, because the dispute is pending in a common court, while it would not be applicable in a dispute pending before a "normal" court.

12 No. 1 does not change anything concerning the internal hierarchy of the place of jurisdiction within the referred to chapter II.[15] The reference does not turn a special jurisdiction referred to into a general jurisdiction; and exclusive and half-exclusive jurisdictions furthermore enjoy their inherent precedence. On the other hand, the general jurisdiction further coexists with the special jurisdiction and the special jurisdictions coexist among themselves. Prorogations of jurisdiction have exactly the scope, the effect and the status that Art. 25 attributes them.

13 For actions brought in the UPC many jurisdictions do not come into question, as they are outside the subject-matter competence of the UPC and the subject-matter scope of application of the UPC Agreement. This especially holds true for all jurisdictions for contractual disputes.[16] The jurisdiction for the place of performance of Art. 7 (1) is not opened for disputes concerning non-contractual patent infringements. The less, the protective regime of Arts. 10–16; 17–19; 20–23 can be opened, as they all only cover contractual disputes. The UPC aims with its reference in No. 1 primarily at the jurisdiction of Art. 24 (4),[17] secondary at the jurisdiction of tort of Art. 7 (2)[18] (as always differentiated according to the place where the event giving rise to the damage occurred on the one hand and the place where the damage occurred on the other hand,[19] in the latter option subject to the mosaic principle)

---

[12] *Mankowski*, GPR 2014, 330, 336.

[13] *Mankowski*, GPR 2014, 330, 336.

[14] *Mankowski*, GPR 2014, 330, 336.

[15] *Mankowski*, GPR 2014, 330, 336.

[16] *Mankowski*, GPR 2014, 330, 336.

[17] *Miguel de Asensio*, AEDIPr 2013, 73, 82.

[18] *Erauw*, AEDIPr 2013, 101, 115; *Luginbühl/Dieter Stauder*, GRUR Int. 2014, 885, 890.

and the general jurisdiction of Art. 4, furthermore the jurisdiction for joinder of proceedings of Art. 8 (1),[20] the jurisdiction for operations of branches of Art. 7 (5) and the jurisdiction for counter-claims of Art. 8 (3).[21] Possible are prorogations of jurisdictions and the contention without objections.[22]

IV. Actions against defendants not domiciled in a Member States (No. 2 subpara. 1)

Where the defendant before a common court is not domiciled in a Member State, No. 2 **14** subpara. 1 declares Chapter II of the Brussels I*bis*-Regulation applicable, while notwithstanding the particular jurisdictions regardless of the defendant's domicile. This means an application of the jurisdiction of the law of the Union including the requirements on special jurisdiction in Arts. 7; 8.[23] The requirement of the defendant's domicile in a Member State, which was set up in Art. 7 initially before No. 1, is to be ignored according to No. 2 as explicit special rule.[24] The special jurisdictions of the Brussels I*bis*-Regulation will exceptionally and specially be extended to defendants domiciled in third States. What generally was envisaged in the transition from the Brussels I- to the Brussels I*bis*-Regulation,[25] but ultimately was not realized,[26] is realized here in a very particular area.[27] Thereby it seems an unnecessary friction is introduced into the overall system.[28] This would mean for defendants domiciled in third States, that they could be sued under European law relating to jurisdiction.[29] No. 2 amounts to veritable long-arm jurisdiction.[29a] No. 2 operates only where the common court has jurisdiction and not where a mere national court has jurisdiction.[30]

Art. 6 (1) is not applicable by means of No. 2 subpara. 1. No reference to the national law of **15** the forum state takes place.[31] As either a common court has no clearly determinable *lex fori*, because it is a court of several states,[32] or it is divided into several regional divisions and recourse to the *lex fori* would, contrary to the conception of a common court, lead to

---

[19] In detail *Kur*, GRUR Int. 2014, 749, 751 *et seq.*

[20] *Luginbühl/Dieter Stauder*, GRUR Int. 2014, 885, 890.

[21] *Erauw*, AEDIPr 2013, 101, 116.

[22] *Miguel de Asensio*, AEDIPr 2013, 73, 82.

[23] *Miguel de Asensio*, AEDIPr 2013, 73, 83; *Luginbühl/Dieter Stauder*, GRUR Int. 2014, 885, 887.

[24] See also *Marongiu Bonaiuti*, Oss. cost. Assoc. It. Cost. 2014, 1, 11 *et seq.*

[25] Arts. 5; 6 (but for (1)) Commission Proposal COM (2010) 748/3 final.

[26] Discussed e.g. by *Magnus/Mankowski*, ZvglRWiss 110 (2011), 252, 261–272; *Johannes Weber*, RabelsZ 75 (2011), 619.

[27] Stretching even beyond the Commission Proposal for the Brussels I*bis* Regulation since that Art. 6 (1) Proposal did not go for an extension of jurisdiction against multiple defendants against defendants domiciled in Third States.

[28] *Mankowski*, GPR 2014, 330, 336.

[29] *Luginbühl/Dieter Stauder*, GRUR Int. 2014, 885, 887.

[29a] *Véron*, (2015) 37 EIPR 588, 592–593.

[30] *Luginbühl/Dieter Stauder*, GRUR Int. 2014, 885, 888.

[31] *Mankowski*, GPR 2014, 330, 336.

[32] Commission Proposal of 26 July 2013 for a Regulation of the European Parliament and of the Council amending Regulation (EU) No. 1215/2012 on jurisdiction and recognition and enforcement of decisions in civil and commercial matters, COM (2013) 554 final p. 6.

different legal rules being applicable.[33] No. 2 subpara. 1 prevents that a gap will arise. The European rules relating to jurisdiction are appropriate from a European perspective, and uniform patent protection is not made dependent upon the defendant's domicile.

16 By virtue of its wording, the reference of No. 2 subpara. 1 concerns the entire Chapter II without making exceptions. However, by means of No. 2 subpara. 1 also Art. 4 (1) can be inapplicable.[34] For No. 2 subpara. 1 only applies to defendants, who are not domiciled in a Member State, while Art. 4 (1) only applies to defendants domiciled in a Member State. An intended collective jurisdiction[35] within the proposal of the Amendment Regulation did not become part of the ultimate Amendment Regulation.

V. Provisional measures against defendants domiciled in third States (No. 2 subpara. 2)

17 According to No. 2 subpara. 2 applications for provisional, including protective, measures may be made to a common court even if the courts of a third State have jurisdiction as to the substance of the matter. The provision is evidently modelled upon Art. 35, according to which application may be made to the courts of a Member State for provisional, including protective, measures available under the law of that Member State even if the courts of another Member State have jurisdiction as to the substance of the matter. The proposal went even further and provided for an application by analogy of Art. 35 *expressis verbis*.[36]

18 Therefore, interpretation and application of Art. 35 are to be transferred; to the extent possible and as far as there are no relevant differences. In practical terms, this means that the jurisdiction of the common court for provisional measures on the one hand results from the jurisdiction of the common court as to the substance of the matter, which first and foremost is developed from No. 1 Brussels I*bis*-Regulation, and on the other hand results from the common court being a special jurisdiction for provisional measures according to its own code of procedure. If the code of procedure applicable for the common court does not provide for a special jurisdiction for provisional measures, it remains as it is.

19 However, there are two differences with regards to Art. 35: The first one resulting from the fact, that a common court is faced here. Provisional measures will have to be provided for within the code of procedure of the common court, not within the procedural law of the Contracting State of that legal act, on which the common court is based. Since there is no national law of an individual state, to which one can or may refer to for a common court. This is concerning jurisdiction and competence of the common court, not the national courts.

---

[33] Commission Proposal of 26 July 2013 for a Regulation of the European Parliament and of the Council amending Regulation (EU) No. 1215/2012 on jurisdiction and recognition and enforcement of decisions in civil and commercial matters, COM (2013) 554 final p. 6.

[34] *Mankowski*, GPR 2014, 330, 336.

[35] On this *Miguel de Asensio*, AEDIPr 2013, 73, 83–86.

[36] Commission Proposal of 26 July 2013 for a Regulation of the European Parliament and of the Council amending Regulation (EU) No. 1215/2012 on jurisdiction and recognition and enforcement of decisions in civil and commercial matters, COM (2013) 554 final p. 6.

The second difference concerns that jurisdiction for urgent measures only prevail over No. 2   **20**
subpara. 2 for the rendering of provisional measures against jurisdiction as to the substance
of the matter of courts of third States. Whereas they do not prevail over No. 2 subpara. 2
against subject-matter jurisdiction of courts of Member States. This does not mean they
would not prevail over these at all. On the contrary, such precedence indeed does not result
from No. 2 subpara. 2, but from No. 1 in connection with Art. 35. No. 2 is consequently
designed for the prosecution against defendants domiciled in third States; while the prosecution against defendants domiciled in a Member State is regulated by No. 1. Art. 35 and
No. 2 subpara. 2 supplement each other. They are in a parallel relation to each other such as
Arts. 4–26 and No. 1.

No. 2 subpara. 2 does not comment on the type of admissible provisional measure. This is   **21**
left rather impliedly to the code of procedure of the concerned common court. The UPC
Agreement for example regulated provisional measures within its chapter IV.

VI. Claims for damages against defendants domiciled in third States for infringements of a European patent

1. Limits of cognizance

According to No. 3 subpara. 1, where a common court has jurisdiction over a defendant not   **22**
domiciled in a Member State in a dispute relating to an infringement of a European patent
giving rise to damage within the Union, that court may also exercise jurisdiction in relation
to damages arising outside the Union from such an infringement. Technically, on a closer
look this does not constitute an own element of jurisdiction, but a rule on the scope of the
authority for cognition.

Background for this regulation is Art. 7 (2) in its predominant use:[37] Under Art. 7 (2) a   **23**
jurisdiction of the place where the harmful event occurred in every place of infringement
exists. The individual court at the place where the harmful event occurred, however, according to the predominant mosaic theory, has an authority to cognition only for those damages,
which occurred within the respective forum state.[38] Damages outside the forum state are not
covered by the forum of the place of where the harmful event occurred under Art. 7 (2). His
worldwide total damage, the plaintiff can only liquidate under Art. 7 (2) at the general place
of jurisdiction of the defendant according to Art. 4 or in the place of jurisdiction of where the
event occurred which gave rise to the damage occurred. But the general place of jurisdiction
of the defendant is for defendants not domiciled in a Member State by definition outside the
EU. Strictly speaking, not even Art. 7 (2) would be available, as this sets forth according to
Art. 7 pr, that the defendant is domiciled in a Member State other than the forum state.

This starting point is interrupted by No. 3 subpara. 1 for the place of jurisdiction of where the   **24**
harm arose. No. 3 subpara. 1 extends the authority of cognition of the court.[38a] This authority
now does not only extent to damages in the forum state and the EU, but also to damages that
arose in third States.

---

[37]   See *Miguel de Asensio*, AEDIPr 2013, 73, 88; *Luginbühl/Dieter Stauder*, GRUR Int. 2014, 885, 888.

[38]   Seminal *Fiona Shevill v. Press Alliance SA* (Case C-68/93), [1995] ECR I-415.

[38a]   *Véron*, (2015) 37 EIPR 588, 595.

25 Damages in other EU-Member States than the forum state are not explicitly mentioned. They seem to fall through the net. At a closer look, a gap does however in reality not exist. Since intellectual property rights of the industrial legal protection which were established through Community rules apply across the Community and uniformly in all Member States, even if they are organized as a bundle of individual national patents such as the European patent under the UPC. Their validity is not restricted to the territory of an individual Member State. In this respect the territorial principle does not apply. This principle restricts the validity of protective rights, which are granted on the basis of a certain national law, to the country of protection, this means the territory of that State granting the rights. By contrast, the bundled patent bundles protective rights for every individual Member State and, thus, ultimately for the entire EU-area.

26 The community-wide validity of community protective rights prevents their territorialisation, this means their normative assignment to only one individual Member State. This also holds true for the European patent. Other community protective rights are justifiably not mentioned in No. 3 subpara. 1, as they do not fall within the subject-matter jurisdiction of the Unified Patent Court and this is the only common court in existence until now for the area of intellectual property rights. A damage arising in another Member State other than the forum state does not exist, because any damage occurring union-wide is said to be located in any Member State and, thereby, likewise in the forum state.

27 Legally, the problem is, that the jurisdiction of courts within the EU is extended at the expense of courts in other Contracting States of the UPC. The threat to not recognise or not enforce decisions rendered under quasi-exorbitant European jurisdiction rules, will be of little use for third States, as No. 3 with its additional requirement of the defendant's property is located in any Member State party to the instrument establishing the common court ensures connection and access to the enforcement within the EU-area.[39] Elegant remedy is capable to be created if the extension of the authority for cognition for damages in third States in the particular case is put into the discretion of the UPC.[40]

2. Additional prerequisites for jurisdiction for third States

28 Concerning the last subparagraph, doubts already exist as to what it relates exactly. There are two possibilities of reference: Firstly, it could refer to all previous numbers which would make it subpara. 2 to subpara. 1, encompassing all three numbers. Secondly, it could refer to No. 3 only which would make it No. 3 subpara. 2. Semantically the demonstrative pronoun "such" before "jurisdiction" is not clear, as "such jurisdiction" could also refer to "The jurisdiction" from the introductory sentence before No. 1. In favour of the second understanding is the typographical appearance in the Official Journal: The last paragraph is indented just as far as the previous paragraph under No. 3 and one tabulator indented further than the introductory sentence before No. 1. Typographically, the last paragraph is located on the same level with the second subpara. under No. 2, namely just indented by that one tabulator further. The second subpara. of No. 2 is clearly only within the borders of No. 2 and does clearly not relate to the introductory sentence before No. 1.

---

[39] The author is indebted to Ms *Sabrina Jütte*.
[40] Yet again thanks to Ms *Sabrina Jütte*.

The Commission's Proposal contained an additional, then third point on the following **29** terms:

"3. Where the defendant is not domiciled in a Member State and no court of a Member State has jurisdiction under this Regulation, the defendant may be sued in the common court if:
    a) property belonging to the defendant is located in a Member State party to the agreement establishing the common court;
    b) the value of the property is not insignificant compared to the value of the claim;
    c) the dispute has a sufficient connection with any Member State party to the agreement establishing the common court."

This rule did not make it into the final and official text of Regulation (EU) No. 452/2014 as **30** an independent rule, but obviously left some mark in (3) subpara. 2. Yet the content of the original (b) got dropped on the way and does not reappear. Litt (a) and (c) of this Proposal do find a certain continuation within the last subparagraph. However, in their implemented references they only appear within the last concept convoluted as establishment for jurisdiction, while in No. 3 of the Proposal they were meant to stipulate an extension and an additional option in favour of the plaintiff. Within the Proposal they should clearly positively establish a jurisdiction at the place of property against defendants domiciled in third States.

No. 3 subpara. 2 as a result has an effect of establishing jurisdiction, although at first sight it **31** appears to name restrictions by means of further prerequisites. Without these additional prerequisites, however, no extension of jurisdiction would take place and No. 3 would be superfluous and without an inherent purpose next to No. 2 in connection with Art. 7 No. 2. Legally, the provision was attributed significance for decisions of individual States, if they make use of the possibility of an opt-out according to Art. 83 (3) UPC Agreement.[41]

In the end, due to the modification within the wording and the prefixing of the authority for **32** cognition and its scope in No. 3 one should not allow the continuity to the Proposal be interrupted. Also Recital (7) Regulation (EU) No. 542/2014 talks of a subsidiary jurisdiction for damage claims against defendants not domiciled in Member States.

In the background for No. 3 of the Proposal might have stood the same body of thought that **33** was also underlying the Proposal for the Brussels I*bis*-Regulation:[42] Art. 25 Proposal Brussels I*bis*-Regulation provided for a subsidiary jurisdiction a venue at the place of property, if the value of the property is not disproportionate compared to the value of the claim (lit. a) and the dispute has a sufficient connection with the Member State of the court seised (lit. b).[43] An independent, general place of jurisdiction at the place of property, from whatsoever form and in whatsoever rule, has finally failed and was not realized for the Brussels I*bis*-Regula-

---

[41] *Luginbühl/Dieter Stauder*, GRUR Int. 2014, 885, 888.

[42] *Luginbühl/Dieter Stauder*, GRUR Int. 2014, 885, 888 sowie *Koechel*, IPRax 2014, 312, 316.

[43] Zur dogmatischen und systematischen Einordnung dieses Vorschlags *Magnus/Mankowski*, ZvglRWiss 110 (2011), 252, 266–268; *Ibili* WPNR 6892 (2011), 533, 535; *Johannes Weber*, RabelsZ 75 (2011), 619, 639; *Dickinson* Yb. PIL 12 (2010) 247, 278 *et seq.*; *von Hein* RIW 10/2011 Die erste Seite; *Christian Wolf* FS Daphne-Ariane Simotta (2012) 717; *Koechel*, IPRax 2013, 312, 316.

tion. Contrary to the Commission's allegation made, a jurisdiction at the place of property does not suit the system of the Brussels *Ibis*-Regulation, as in the reform of the Brussels *Ibis*-Regulation is was currently and deliberately decided, not to accept a corresponding proposal. Nevertheless, No. 3 establishes a jurisdiction at the place of property so to speak as catch-all jurisdiction and, thereby, introduces a friction into the overall system of the Brussels *Ibis*-Regulation.[44] Although it is less far-reaching than the Proposal,[45] yet is based on the same body of though which actually is strange to the Brussels *Ibis*-Regulation. It holds a "potential to be exorbitant" inside.[46]

34   In the wording of the provision, the requirement of a certain intrinsic value of the property potentially establishing the place of jurisdiction, as it could be found in No. 3 of the Proposal, can no longer be found. Meanwhile Recital (7) sentence 3 Regulation (EU) No. 452/2014 quite revives that criterion. According to Recital (7) sentence 3 Regulation (EU) No. 452/2014, in establishing its jurisdiction, the common court should have regard to the value of the property in question, which should not be insignificant and which should be such as to make it possible to enforce the judgment, at least in part, in the Member States parties to the instrument establishing the common court.[47]

35   Additionally, a sufficient connection to the Member State of the location of property is required. In the general framework of the Brussels *Ibis*-Reform such a criterion was criticized.[48] Meanwhile, this is given concrete form by Recital (7) sentence 2 Regulation (EU) No. 542/2014 in a way that it becomes manageable and the potentially inherent wideness is partially lost.[49] According to this recital such subsidiary jurisdiction should be exercised where property belonging to the defendant is located in any Member State party to the instrument establishing the common court (rightfully: in the State of location of the property) and the dispute in question has a sufficient connection with any such Member State, for example because the plaintiff is domiciled there or the evidence relating to the dispute is available there. Both is, in principle, appropriate.[50] Though, it loses its acutance, because the short list is, as shown by "for example" is not final, but exemplary. Behind the sufficient connection might be less the protection of the defendant by means of an additional requirement, but rather the international law-criterion of the genuine link.[51]

36   If the infringement of a European patent gives rise to damage in a State party to the UPC as well as in a third State, usually, there will be means of evidence located in that Member State party to the UPC. Restrictively, it should be requested that the means of evidence must relate

---

[44]   See also *Luginbühl/Dieter Stauder*, GRUR Int. 2014, 885, 888.

[45]   *Miguel de Asensio*, AEDIPr 2013, 73, 87.

[46]   *Miguel de Asensio*, AEDIPr 2013, 73, 91 f; *Miguel de Asensio*, in: Honorati (a cura di), Luci e ombre del nuovo sistema UE di tutela brevettuale (2014) 153, 165; *Luginbühl/Dieter Stauder*, GRUR Int. 2014, 885, 888.

[47]   See § 99 (1) 2 JN in Österreich.

[48]   *Joh Weber*, RabelsZ 75 (2011) 619, 639 *et seq.*

[49]   See also *Miguel de Asensio*, AEDIPr 2013, 73, 91.

[50]   See *Magnus/Mankowski*, ZvglRWiss 110 (2011) 252, 266 f; *Joh Weber*, RabelsZ 75 (2011) 619, 639; *Weitz* FS Simotta (2012) 679, 688 *et seq.*

[51]   *Mankowski/Hölscher/Gerhardt* in: Rengeling/Gellermann/Middeke, Handbuch des Rechtsschutzes in der Europäischen Union (3. Aufl 2013) § 38 note 51.

especially to the damage in third States, while it is insufficient that means of evidence are existent in the forum state. When there is a uniform infringing activity, this will not be a high barrier, insofar as the means of evidence relate to the facts of the infringing activity.

In any case, a connection is unlikely to derive from the person of the defendant, as he, in **37** cases of Art. 71b, is domiciled in a third State. At most, if the defendant has a subsidiary in a Member State and this subsidiary is involved in the infringement of the European patent, then the idea of connection of Art. 7 No. 5 could be made useful.

Article 71c

(1) Articles 29 to 32 shall apply when proceedings are brought in a common court and in a court of a Member State not party to the agreement establishing that common court.
(2) Articles 29 to 32 shall apply where during the transitional period referred to in Art. 83 (1) of the UPC Agreement proceedings are brought in the Unified Patent Court and in a court of a Member State party to the UPC Agreement.

Art. 71c contains a regulation for current conflicts of jurisdictions. Art. 71c clarifies that the **1** provisions on *lis pendens* as contained in Arts. 29–32 apply *telles quelles* and without any variations or modifications with regard to conflicting sets of proceedings before a common court on the one hand and courts in Member States not party to the Agreement or Treaty establishing the respective common court. This is only consequential and logical if a "common court" is equated with a court. Thereby it complements Art. 71b, which establishes rules on international jurisdiction, and Art. 71d, which establishes rules for recognition and enforcement of judgements. Art. 71c only addresses conflicting stets of proceedings between common courts and courts of Member States which are no party to the agreement. On the other hand, it deals with procedural conflicts within the scope of the common court, for example between various regional or local divisions of the UPC.[1] Moreover, it does not address conflicting sets of proceedings between a common court and a court in third States outside the EU,[2] as paragraph 1 only refers to Arts. 29–32, but not to Arts. 33; 34.

Yet the provisions on *lis pendens* must not apply when proceedings are brought in a common **2** court and in a court of a Member State party to the Agreement establishing that common court. In that event, the Agreement itself will solve the ensuing conflict by giving precedence to the jurisdiction of the common court as a specialised court and will rule out jurisdiction of any ordinary, national court of its Contracting States.

I. Recitals to the Regulation (EU) No. 542/2014 and the Commission's Explanatory Memorandum

The recitals to the Regulation (EU) No. 542/2014 state for Art. 71c: **3**

---

[1] *Miguel de Asensio*, AEDIPr 2013, 73, 80; *Luginbühl/Dieter Stauder*, GRUR Int. 2014, 885, 891; *Wallner-Friedl*, in: Czernich/Kodek/Mayr, Art. 71d note 9.
[2] *Miguel de Asensio*, AEDIPr 2013, 73, 80.

(8) The rules of Regulation (EU) No. 1215/2012 on lis pendens and related actions, aimed at preventing parallel proceedings and irreconcilable judgments, should apply when proceedings are brought in a common court and in a court of a Member State in which the UPC Agreement or, as the case may be, the Benelux Court of Justice Treaty does not apply.

(9) The rules of Regulation (EU) No. 1215/2012 on lis pendens and related actions should likewise apply where, during the transitional period provided for in the UPC Agreement, proceedings concerning certain types of disputes are brought in, on the one hand, the Unified Patent Court and, on the other hand, a national court of a Member State party to the UPC Agreement.

4 By way of explanation for the Proposal for Art. 71c the Commission[3] states:

"In addition, the new rule in Art. 71c prescribes that the rules on *lis pendens* and related actions of the Brussels I Regulation (recast) apply between the Unified Patent Court or the Benelux Court of Justice on the one hand and the courts of non-Contracting Member States on the other hand. Finally, this Article also prescribes that the rules of the Brussels I Regulation (recast) apply when, during the transitional period referred to in Article 83 (1) UPC Agreement, proceedings are brought before the Unified Patent Court on the one hand and before the national courts of Contracting Member States to that Agreement on the other hand."

II. Parallel proceedings in a common court and in a court of a Member State not party to the agreement establishing that common court (1)

5 If Art. 71b regulates the international jurisdiction of common courts, Art. 71c is dedicated to situations of *lis pendens* in which a common court is involved. (1) chooses the simplest and at the same times most resilient solution: The *lis pendens*-regime of Arts. 29–32 extends to such *lis pendens*-situations without changes or concessions. The common court is treated like a "normal" court for the purpose of *lis pendens*.[4] The prerequisite is however – as always – that both proceedings relate to the same matter in dispute. This is not the case, if the proceedings relate to different parts of a European patent.[5] Neither, identity of the cause of action consists between a main proceeding and an interim proceeding.[6] In contrast, action for declaration of non-infringement and opposed action for performance here involve, as always under Art. 29, to the same cause of action.[7] Action for annulment brought in a national court and infringement action brought in the UPC, in turn, do not involve the same cause of action.[8]

---

[3]   Commission Proposal of 26 July 2013 for a Regulation of the European Parliament and of the Council amending Regulation (EU) No. 1215/2012 on jurisdiction and recognition and enforcement of decisions in civil and commercial matters, COM (2013) 554 final p. 7.

[4]   *Marongiu Bonaiuti*, Oss. cost. Assoc. It. Cost. 2014, 1, 13 *et seq.*

[5]   *Luginbühl/Dieter Stauder*, GRUR Int. 2014, 885, 891 f; *Wallner-Friedl*, in: Czernich/Kodek/Mayr, Art. 71d note 10.

[6]   *Wallner-Friedl*, in: Czernich/Kodek/Mayr, Art. 71d note 12.

[7]   *Luginbühl/Dieter Stauder*, GRUR Int. 2014, 885, 891.

[8]   *Luginbühl/Dieter Stauder*, GRUR Int. 2014, 885, 892.

It makes no difference, if the common court is the court first seised or the one seised 6
subsequently. In both cases, Arts. 29–32 are applicable. According to Art. 29, if a national
court is seised first, the common court has to decline jurisdiction in favour of that court first
seised.[9] As Art. 32 establishes a provision of pendency autonomous from the regulation, the
question of pending before the common court does not depend on the rules of procedure of
the common court.

Theoretically, it would be possible, that for both competitive proceedings a common court is 7
the trial court. According to its wording, (1) does indeed not cover this case. Correctly,
Arts. 29–32 would be applied within it, as there is no equally good alternative option.

Paragraph (1) has greater importance for competitive proceedings, if an action is pending 8
before the Benelux Court of Justice, than when an action is pending before the UPC. As the
number of Brussels I*bis*-Member States, which are not party to the agreement establishing
that common court, is in the case of the Benelux Court of Justice much higher that in the case
of the UPC. With regard to the UPC there are only three Third States still left (out of which
Croatia has decided differently, Poland[10] has at all decided and Spain might give up finally),
whereas at the Benelux Court of Justice, there are by definition and permanently all Brussels
I*bis*-Member States except for the three Benelux States no Contracting States. Thus, there
are not less than 25 Brussels I*bis*-Member States which are and will remain to be no Contracting States.

According to the wording of paragraph (1), only Arts. 29–32 are extended, not Art. 33; 34. 9
Arts. 33; 34 are provisions for conflicts of *lis pendens* between courts in Member States and
courts in third States. On the patent protection of European patents, because of the UPC or
the EU-Regulations, there should arise no conflicts due to the territorial principle. Whereas
in proceedings brought in the Benelux Court of Justice, they do not seem to be excluded.
Therefore, it appears worth considering to continue the idea of (1) and declare Arts. 33; 34 to
be applicable *mutatis mutandis*. In any case, one should not draw a conclusion *a contrario* to
the inapplicability of this provision.

III. Regulations for the transitional period for parallel proceedings brought in a common court and a national court in a country of a Member Stated party to the UPC Agreement, (2)

(2) regulates a special situation: During the transitional period referred to in Art. 83 (1) of 10
the UPC Agreement (seven years from the date of the entry onto force of the UPC Agreement)[11] the Unified Patent Court, as already established common court of the Member
States party to the UPC Agreement, does not have exclusive jurisdiction. Rather, next to its
jurisdiction, there is a jurisdiction of the "normal" courts of a Member State party to the
UPC Agreement existing, according to Art. 83 (1). Parallel proceedings at the one hand
brought in the Unified Patent Court and at the other hand brought in a national "normal"
court of a Member State party to the UPC Agreement can result from this. Paragraph (1)

---

9   *Luginbühl/Dieter Stauder*, GRUR Int. 2014, 885, 891.

10 On the Polish position *Zawdzka* IIC 45 (2014), 383; *Kupzok* [2014] EIPR 418, 425 *et seq.*

11 On this e.g. *Luginbühl*, in: FS Dieter Stauder (2011) p. 148; *Tilmann*, MittPat 2014, 58; *Kupfer/Meiller*,
    Propr. Ind. mei 2014, 24; *Luginbühl/Dieter Stauder*, GRUR Int. 2014, 885, 889.

does not cover this conflict, because it requires that the national court is a court of a third State.

11 After the end of the transitional period referred to in Art. 83 (1) of the UPC Agreement, such competitive situations are no longer possible. Rather, the Unified Patent Court claims an exclusive jurisdiction according to Art. 32 UPC Agreement.

12 Insofar, (2) can be evaluated as an alien to the system, as the corresponding provision should actually be the task of the agreement establishing the concerned common court.[12] Both presently known agreements establishing a common court have not made a finding in this respect. If a future agreement establishing a common court should hold this differently, one could think of the principle of speciality and about granting precedence to the provision in every establishing agreement.

13 Art. 33 (6) UPC Agreement declares an action for declaration of non-infringement pending before the UPC shall be stayed once an infringement action is brought before the UPC. An action for declaration of non-infringement pending before a national court of a Member State party to the agreement is, in contrast, capable of being stayed during the transitional period once a subsequent infringement action is brought before the UPC due to paragraph (2). Torpedos are further possible. Paragraph (2) does not supply any satisfactory solution in this constellation and does not defuse them; however, this defect lies more within the UPC Agreement which does not make any provision. The practice might react by opting out in accordance with Art. 83 (3) UPC Agreement.[13]

Article 71d

This Regulation shall apply to the recognition and enforcement of:
(a) judgments given by a common court which are to be recognised and enforced in a Member State not party to the instrument establishing the common court; and
(b) judgments given by the courts of a Member State not party to the instrument establishing the common court which are to be recognised and enforced in a Member State party to that instrument.
However, where recognition and enforcement of a judgment given by a common court is sought in a Member State party to the instrument establishing the common court, any rules of that instrument on recognition and enforcement shall apply instead of the rules of this Regulation.

1 Art. 71d relates to the recognition and enforcement of judgements. It rounds down and completes what Art. 71b has begun for the jurisdiction and Art. 71c for *lis pendens*. Following the course of legal proceedings, it stands in order behind the other two. Art. 71d clarifies that the provisions on recognition and enforcement as contained in Arts. 36 *et seq.* apply *telles quelles* and without any variations or modifications with regard to judgments rendered by common courts. This is only consequential and logical if a "common court" is equated

---

12   Stellungnahme des Deutschen Anwaltvereins durch den Ausschuss Geistiges Eigentum zum Vorschlag KOM (2013) 554 endg vom 26.7.2013, Stellungnahmen-Nr 51/2013 p. 5.
13   *Sabrina Jütte* is to be credited for this thought.

with a court. Art. 71d does not relate to recognition and declaration of enforceability or enforcement of judgements of a common court in a Member State party to the agreement establishing that common court, but leaves the regulation of this to that establishing agreement, for example Art. 34 UPC Agreement.[1]

I. Recitals Regulation (EU) No. 542/2014 and Commission's Explanatory Memorandum

The Recitals of Regulation (EU) No. 542/2014 state for Art. 71d: 2

(10) Judgments given by the Unified Patent Court or by the Benelux Court of Justice should be recognised and enforced in accordance with Regulation (EU) No. 1215/2012 in a Member State not party to, as the case may be, the UPC Agreement or the Benelux Court of Justice Treaty.
(11) Judgments given by the courts of a Member State not party to, as the case may be, the UPC Agreement or the Benelux Court of Justice Treaty should be recognised and enforced in another Member State in accordance with Regulation (EU) No. 1215/2012.

By way of reasoning the Proposal for Art. 71d the Commission[2] states: 3

"3.5 The operation of the rules on recognition and enforcement in relation between Member States that have ratified the UPC Agreement and the Member States that have not ratified the UPC Agreement."

"In order to create full transparency on the combined and coherent application of the respective international agreements and the Brussels I Regulation (recast), the latter should prescribe how the rules on recognition and enforcement of the Brussels I Regulation (recast) will apply in the relations between the Member States Contracting Parties to the respective international agreements and the Member States which are not Contracting Parties to those agreements. Similar provisions are found in Article 71 of the Brussels I Regulation (recast) with respect to other international conventions on particular matters and Articles 64 and 67 of the 2007 Lugano Convention on jurisdiction and the recognition and enforcement of judgments in civil and commercial matters. The new Art. 71d thus regulates the recognition and enforcement of judgments of the Unified Patent Court and the Benelux Court of Justice in Member States which are not Contracting Parties to the respective international agreements, as well as the recognition and enforcement of judgments given in Member States which are not Contracting Parties to these agreements in matters governed by such agreements which need to be recognised and enforced in Member States Contracting Parties to the international agreements."

The natural consequence flowing from this is that the other Member States are obliged to 4 recognise and enforce any judgment given by a common court listed as if such judgment was rendered by an "ordinary" municipal court. When common courts are equivalent with municipal courts this must also hold true under the auspices of recognition and enforcement. (a) draws this consequence obliquely and duly.

---

[1]   See *Erauw*, AEDIPr 2013, 101, 117 sowie *Miguel de Asensio*, AEDIPr 2013, 73, 93 *et seq.*
[2]   Commission Proposal of 26 July 2013 for a Regulation of the European Parliament and of the Council amending Regulation (EU) No. 1215/2012 on jurisdiction and recognition and enforcement of decisions in civil and commercial matters, COM (2013) 554 final p. 8.

5   It might have been helpful to add a few lines to Art. 2 (f) and the definition of "court of origin" although that would not be strictly necessary. If a common court renders a judgment, the common court is the court of origin for this particular judgment. The common court has to issue the certificate under Art. 53 on the claimant's request. The common court has to safeguard the defendant's right to a fair trial. Accordingly, the common court is the court of origin for the purposes of Art. 45 (1) (b), too. Insofar as jurisdiction of the court of origin is subjected to the limited examination under Art. 45 (1) (e) the logical and consequential solution is to be derived from Art. 71a. The rule governing jurisdiction for common courts does matter in this context also.[3]

6   Subpara. 1 has a greater importance, the smaller the circle of Contracting States is, which bear the concerned common court. It, therefore, has a greater importance in the sphere of the Benelux Court of Justice, which only has three Contracting States (just those three Benelux States), than in the sphere of the UPC, to which almost all Member States to the Brussels *Ibis*-Regulation belong to, with (currently) only three exceptions, namely Spain, Poland and (still) Croatia.[4]

II. Recognition or enforcement of judgements given by a common court in a Member States not party to the instrument establishing the common court (subpara. 1 lit. a)

7   Subpara. 1 lit. (a) submits the judgement given by a common court to the recognition and enforcement of the Brussels *Ibis*-Regime in a third State, those Member States not party to the instrument establishing the common court.[5] It equates judgements given by the common court with judgements given by national courts. It treats them as if they were judgements given by national courts.[6] Contracting States are and remain Member States to the Regulation. Common courts are part of the court system of their Contracting State. Excluding their judgements from recognition or enforcement or treating them worse in relation to recognition and enforcement than judgements of "ordinary" national courts would be an unjustifiable break with the system. Subpara. 1 lit. (a) is merely a logical consequence resulting from the fact that common courts are courts of the Member States. Subpara. 1 lit. (a) actually has a mere declaratory meaning, because its content could already be derived from Art. 71a. Under Art. 45 (1) lit. (e) one might want to argue, subpara. 1 lit. (a) clarifies, that the recognition does not fail due to the UPC claiming a jurisdiction which might be perceived as exorbitant.[7]

III. Recognition and enforcement of judgements given by the courts of a Member State not party to the instrument establishing the common court (subpara. 1 lit. b)

8   (b) is far more puzzling. It relates to the converse constellation. It imposes an obligation to recognise and enforce judgments given by courts of other Member States, on those Member States which are Contracting States to an Agreement establishing a common court. Insofar as recognition and enforcement by "ordinary" municipal courts is at stake, such obligation

---

3   *Miguel de Asensio*, AEDIPr 2013, 73, 95.

4   *Miguel de Asensio*, AEDIPr 2013, 73, 75; *Erauw*, AEDIPr 2013, 101, 104.

5   *Erauw*, AEDIPr 2013, 101, 119.

6   *Marongiu Bonaiuti*, Oss. cost. Assoc. It. Cost. 2014, 1, 14–15.

7   *Miguel de Asensio*, AEDIPr 2013, 73, 95.

to recognise and enforce already flows from Arts. 36 *et seq.* Insofar, there would not have been a genuine need to introduce a rule like (b) which if it was restricted to such cases, would only be prone to become a source of misunderstandings and misgivings. It, yet, gains importance insofar as in Contracting States the common court has jurisdiction for recognition and enforcement. But apparently, (b) does not envisage this scenario, but goes for some kind of *quid pro quo* and reciprocity: If the other Member States accept the common court as an institutional part of the judicial system of the Contracting States, in turn the Contracting States have to subscribe expressly to recognition and enforcement of judgments rendered by the "ordinary" courts of these other Member States. Moreover, (b) clarifies the relation to the exclusive jurisdiction of the UPC and prevents that these will arise to an automatically ground for refusal of recognition beyond Art. 45 (1) lit. (e).[8]

IV. Recognition and enforcement of a judgement given by a common court sought in a Member States party to the instrument establishing the common court (subpara. 2)

Subpara. 2 is a logical formation of the principle of speciality: Between Contracting States, **9** the special agreement shall apply, not the general Brussels I*bis*-Regulation. Subpara. 2 envisages the factual setting that a decision rendered by a common court shall be recognised and enforced in a Contracting State of the respective Agreement. In this scenario, recognition and enforcement shall be governed by the rules on these topics as the respective Agreement may contain. If the respective Agreement does not contain any rules on recognition and enforcement or insofar as it does not contain such rules the Brussels I*bis* Regulation applies as a fall-back solution and a default regime. This is a concrete application of the principle *lex specialis derogat legi generali.* The Brussels I*bis* Regulation cedes, and gives way, to the Agreement to the extent that the Agreement demands so.

Recital (3) Regulation (EU) No. 542/2014 emphasises this limited objective, which is reflected in subpara. 2. If one wanted to regulate the recognition and enforcement between Contracting States, hereby one would intervene contrary to the system with the concerned agreement. This holds true even when the rules for recognition and enforcement of the agreement were less favourable than those of the Brussels I*bis*-Regulation. Then it would be a matter for the agreement to open itself via a principle of favourability to the Brussels I*bis*-Regulation.

Article 72

This Regulation shall not affect agreements by which Member States, prior to the entry into force of Regulation (EC) No. 44/2001, undertook pursuant to Article 59 of the 1968 Brussels Convention not to recognise judgments given, in particular in other Contracting States to that Convention, against defendants domiciled or habitually resident in a third State where, in cases provided for in Article 4 of that Convention, the judgment could only be founded on a ground of jurisdiction specified in the second paragraph of Article 3 of that Convention.

---

[8]   See *Erauw,* AEDIPr 2013, 101, 120.

1   Art. 72 deals with a rather odd special problem, which is part of the general matter of the
    discriminating against Third States by the European international civil procedural law. In a
    few agreements relating to international law Member States covenanted with other states
    not to recognize issued judgment under certain circumstances.[1] For the respective Member
    States a contractual obligation of non-recognition exists relating to international law. This
    can conflict with the obligation of recognition pursuant to the Brussels *Ibis* Regulation as far
    as it concerns non-recognitions of judgments from other Member States of the EU.

2   Art. 59 Brussels Convention permitted the Member States expressly to conclude conven-
    tions about the non-recognitions of judgments of Member States as far as the judgments
    were issued in a jurisdiction exorbitant to the third states pursuant to Art. 3 Abs 2 Brussels
    Convention. After the entry into force of the Brussels I Regulation the Member States do not
    have the competence to conclude new agreements standing in contradiction to the Regu-
    lation anymore.[2] Any competence in this regard has been wrestled away from them and
    conferred upon the EC.[3] But Member States may not be forced to break international law so
    already existing agreements had are to be taken into account.[4] What was permitted under
    Art. 59 Brussels Conventions must be respected now and may not be incriminated *ex post*.[5]
    Art. 72 aims at preserving for the future the effect of conventions concluded under Art. 59
    Brussels Convention but not more.[6] In general Art. 59 Brussels Convention was only rarely
    used and indirectly served as a confirmation of the principle of automatic recognition.[7]

3   There is only one slight alteration in the wording Art. 72 compared to Art. 72 Brussels I
    Regulation: In the latter the relevant event is the entry into force of "this Regulation", i.e. the
    Brussels I Regulation. In Art. 72 the wording relates to the entry into force of Regulation
    (EC) No. 44/2001. As to substance, both rules relate to 1 March 2002. This date marks the
    deadline after which the empowerment contained in Art. 59 Brussels Convention became
    ineffective. The Brussels *Ibis* Regulation does not reanimate what the Brussels I Regulation
    has already killed.

---

[1]   I.e. British-Australian Convention of 23 August 1990 and Art. IX British-Canadian Convention of 24
      April 1984 (amended by Exchange of Nottes dated 7 November 1994 and 17 February 1995) as forming
      Schedules to the Reciprocal Enforcement of Foreign Judgments (Australia) Order 1994, S.I. 1994
      No. 1901, and the Reciprocal Enforcement of Foreign Judgments (Canada) Order 1987, S.I. 1987
      No. 468, as amended by the Reciprocal Enforcement of Foreign Judgments (Canada) (Amendment)
      Order 1995, S.I. 1995 No. 2708; see for further details *Kaye* p. 1524 *et seq.*; *O'Malley/Layton* 874 *et seq.*;
      Layton/Mercer paras. 32.045 *et seq.* The German-Norwegian Convention of 17 June 1977, BGBl. 1981 II
      342, which *Layton/Mercer* para. 26.092 add to the list, contains an obligation of non-recognition as to
      third state decisions in its Art. 23 but has been superseded by Art. 55 Lugano Convention; *Geimer/
      Schütze* Art. 72 note 4; *Mankowski*, in: Rauscher, Art. 72 note 1. But cf. incorrectly *Kropholler/von Hein*
      Art. 72 note 1 who asserts that Germany had not concluded any respective Convention.
[2]   See only *Kennett*, (2001) 50 ICLQ 725, 736; *North*, (2002) 55 CLP 395, 414 *et seq.* But cf. also *Droz/
      Gaudemet-Tallon*, RCDIP 90 (2001), 601, 622.
[3]   See in detail e.g. *Kotuby*, NILR 2001, 1; *Wannemacher*, Die Außenkompetenzen der EG im Bereich des
      internationalen Zivilverfahrensrechts (2003).
[4]   *Kropholler/von Hein* Art. 72 note 1.
[5]   *Mankowski*, in: Rauscher Art. 72 note 2.
[6]   *Layton/Mercer* para. 32.040.
[7]   Hof Amsterdam NIPR 2001 Nr 130 p. 261.

On the occasion of passing the Brussels I Regulation and as some *amelioratum* for effectively   **4**
repealing of Art. 59 Brussels Convention[8] the Council and the Commission made the following Joint Statement:[9]

"It follows from Article 4 in conjunction with chapter III of the Regulation that, where a
court in a Member State delivers a judgment which is founded on a ground of jurisdiction
drawn from that Member State's national law, against a defendant who is not domiciled in
the territory of a Member State, that judgment will be recognised an enforced in the other
Member States pursuant to the Regulation.

In some cases this rule may be disadvantageous to persons who are not domiciled in a
territory of a Member state. In the Brussels Convention of 27 September 1968, the situation
was mitigated by Article 59, which allowed Contraction States to conclude agreements with
third States not to recognise judgments founded on certain national grounds of jurisdiction
drawn from national law.

The Council and the Commission will pay particular attention to the possibility of engaging
in negotiations with a view to the conclusion of international agreements that would mitigate the consequences of Chapter III of the Regulation for persons domiciled in third States,
in respect of judgments founded on certain grounds of jurisdiction."

Since Art. 72 perseveres Art. 72 Brussels I Regulation this policy statement should still be
valid.

Article 73

1. **This Regulation shall not affect the application of the 2007 Lugano Convention.**
2. **This Regulation shall not affect the application of the 1958 New York Convention.**
3. **This Regulation shall not affect the application of bilateral conventions and agreements**
   between a third State and a Member State concluded before the date of entry into force
   of Regulation (EC) No. 44/2001 which concern matters governed by this Regulation.

Bibliography

Carducci, The New EU Regulation 1215/2012 of 12
December 2012 on Jurisdiction and International
Arbitration, (2013) 29 Arb. Int. 467
Furrer, The Brussels I Review Proposal: Challenges
for the Lugano Convention, in: Lein (ed.), The
Brussels I Review Proposal Uncovered
(2012), p. 165

Salerno, Il coordinamento tra arbitrato e giustizia
civile nel regolamento (UE) n. 1215/2012, Riv. dir.
int. 2013, 1146.

---

[8]   *Layton/Mercer* para. 32.040.
[9]   JUSTCIV137, 14139/00 and 14139/00cor2, i.a. published in: IPRax 2001, 260.

I. Relation with the 2007 Lugano Convention, Art. 73 (1)

1 Pursuant to (1), the Brussels *Ibis* Regulation shall not affect the application of the 2007 Lugano Convention. This complements Art. 64 (1) 2007 Lugano Convention. According to this rule, the 2007 Lugano Convention shall not prejudice the application by the Member States of the EU of the Brussels I Regulation as well as any amendment thereof. Art. 64 (1) 2007 Lugano Convention is an exception from the EU principle that generally international law takes precedence[1] as it is evidenced in particular by Art. 71.

2 But Art. 64 (2) 2007 Lugano Convention is at the core of the matter and the most relevant rule for practical purposes:

"However, this Convention shall in any event be applied:
a) in matters of jurisdiction, where the defendant is domiciled in the territory of a State where this Convention but non an instrument referred to in paragraph 1 of this Article applies, or where Articles 22 or 23 of this Convention confer jurisdictions on the courts of such a State;
b) in relation to lis pendens or to related actions as provided for in Articles 27 and 28, when proceedings are instituted in a State where this Convention but non an instrument referred to in paragraph 1 of this Article applies and in State where this Convention as well as an instrument referred to in paragraph 1 of this Article apply;
c) in matters of recognition and enforcement, where either the State of origin or the State addressed is not applying an instrument referred to in paragraph 1 of this Article."

3 (1) leaves the application of the 2007 Lugano Convention unaffected, and consequentially, this includes that (1) leaves Art. 64 (2) 2007 Lugano Convention unaffected. (1) is not to intervene with any single rule of the 2007 Lugano Convention, and the least with that rule which tries to circumscribe the applicability of the 2007 Lugano Convention in practical terms *vis-à-vis* the Brussels regime. The Brussels regime itself steps back, and this opens the floor for the 2007 Lugano Convention which gratefully seizes upon the opportunity.

4 In practice, the combination of Art. 64 (2) 2007 Lugano Convention and (1) results in the following: The Brussels *Ibis* Regulation is applicable in the relations between States which are only Member States of the Brussels *Ibis* Regulation;[2] the 2007 Lugano Convention is applicable in the relations between Member States of the Brussels *Ibis* Regulation and States which are solely Contracting States of the 2007 Lugano Convention.[3] In such scenarios, the Member States of the Brussels *Ibis* Regulation are obliged to apply the 2007 Lugano Convention.[4] If a relevant connecting factor leads to a Member State solely of the 2007 Lugano Convention this suffices to render the 2007 Lugano Convention applicable *vis-à-vis* Member States of the Brussels *Ibis* Regulation.[5]

---

[1]   *Furrer*, in: Lein (ed.), The Brussels I Review Proposal Uncovered (2012), p. 165, 172.

[2]   BGE 125 III 108; *Domej*, in: Dasser/Oberhammer, Art. 64 LugÜ note 3; *Oetiker/Weibel*, in: Basler Kommentar zum LugÜ, Art. 64 LugÜ note 5. BGE 124 III 134 states a different opinion.

[3]   Report *Pocar* para. 19; *Rolf Wagner/Janzen*, IPRax 2010, 298, 307; *Domej*, in: Dasser/Oberhammer, Art. 64 LugÜ note 1.

[4]   *Siehr*, in: Schnyder, Art. 64 LugÜ note 4.

[5]   BGE 127 III 186; *Oetiker/Weibel*, in: Basler Kommentar zum LugÜ, Art. 64 LugÜ note 6.

With the Brussels I*bis* Regulation abandoning exequatur, the importance and relevance of 5
the 2007 Lugano Convention which fundamentally differs in this aspect, has risen again with
regard to the recognition and enforcement of judgments.[6] The 2007 Lugano Convention is
applicable whenever recognition or enforcement of a decision rendered by a court of a
Member State solely of the 2007 Lugano Convention is sought after in a Member State of
the Brussels I*bis* Regulation.[7] Both instruments do not collide or clash in this regard since the
Brussels I*bis* Regulation is concerned only with the recognition and enforcement of judgments form courts of Member States of the Brussels I*bis* Regulation in other Member States
of the Brussels I*bis* Regulation.

II. Relation with the 1958 New York Convention, Art. 73 (2)

Pursuant to (2), the Brussels I*bis* Regulation shall not affect the application of the 1958 New 6
York Convention.

(2) is a new entry. It has no predecessor in the Brussels I Regulation. It was called into 7
existence as part of a package: Art. 1 (2) (d) remained unaltered and still excludes "arbitration" from the scope of application of the Brussels I*bis* regime. The wording of this rule is the
very same that Art. 1 (2) (d) had. An immensely rich discussion on the extent of this
exemption did not produce an immediate result where it really would have mattered. The
newly introduced and extensive Recital (12) is small consolation. Another part of the consolation package is (2). It tries to soften the opposition and dismay of those who preferred an
express and explicit clarification of the interface between the Brussels I*bis* Regulation and all
aspects of arbitration. (2) clarifies that the Brussels I*bis* Regulation materially does not
invade into the territory of arbitration and does not have any ambition to do so.[8] But (2)
might be felt necessary for formally they might be some overlap[9] generating the need for
such clarification.

The New York Convention on the Recognition and Enforcement of Arbitral Awards of 10 8
June 1958 takes precedence over the Brussels I*bis* Regulation. Insofar (2) is unambiguous
and a small, but welcome clarification indeed. (2) did not yet appear in the Brussels I*bis*
Proposal. It made its first appearance in a Note from the Presidency[10] of 1 June 2012, in some
kind of exchange for Art. 29 (4) Brussels I*bis* Proposal which would have required courts in
Member States to stay proceedings and allow issues relating to arbitration to be dealt with by
the courts at the seat of the arbitration.[11] From there it made its way into the Report of the

---

6   *Domej*, in: Dasser/Oberhammer, Art. 64 LugÜ note 2 fn. 3; *Bonomi*, in: Dickinson/Lein paras. 17.79–
     17.81.
7   *Domej*, in: Dasser/Oberhammer, Art. 64 LugÜ note 7; *Oetiker/Weibel*, in: Basler Kommentar zum LugÜ,
     Art. 64 LugÜ note 11.
8   *Gaudemet-Tallon/Kessedjian*, RTDE 2013, 435, 437.
9   *Salerno*, Riv. dir. int. 2013, 1146, 1162.
10   Addendum to the Note from the Presidency to the Council on the Proposal for a Regulation of the
     European Parliament and of the Council on jurisdiction and the recognition and enforcement of judg-
     ments in civil and commercial matters (Recast) – First reading, 10609/12 ADD 1 JUSTCIV 209 CODEC
     1495.
11   *Ronald A. Brand*, RdC 358 (2011), 9, 186.

Committee on Legal Affairs of the European Parliament.[12][13] (2) was part of some kind of consolation package, a political compromise also comprising Recital (12) as substitute for a proper rule addressing the interface between the Brussels *Ibis* system and arbitration as comprehensively as possible on the one hand and for dropping the Commission's attempt to establish a rule on *lis pendens* solving the collision of court proceedings and arbitration in Art. 29 (4) Proposal.[14] The proposed rule had been the No. 1 brainchild of the Expert Group on Arbitration and the Brussels I Regulation which was installed by the Commission and consisted of experts with their personal background in arbitration.[15]

9   Recital (35) which expresses the respect for international commitments entered into by the Member States and explaining that the Brussels *Ibis* Regulation should not affect conventions relating to specific matters to which the Member States are parties. Recital (35) gives the *rationale* behind Art. 71. This derives from the fact that it verbally repeats Recital (25) Brussels I Regulation which backed Art. 71 Brussels I Regulation whereas the Brussels I Regulation did not contain a rule resembling (2) and consequentially did not contain any Recital in this regard, either. This is some kind of basis behind (2).[16] (2) can indeed be viewed as rather a clarification than a genuine amendment.[17]

10   Recital (12) subpara. 3 cl. 2 contains the specific parallel with regard to (2). It expressly underlines and emphasises that there should not be any prejudice to the competence of the courts of the Member States to decide on the recognition and enforcement of arbitral awards in accordance with the 1958 New York Convention "which *takes precedence* over this Regulation."[18] The consequence of this is that an instrument which the courts of each Contracting State are free to interpret for themselves imposes a limit on the application of an EU measure.[19] Yet it is likely that the CJEU imposes outer boundaries of Member State jurisdiction in this regard in order to avoid an open-ended escape mechanism, analogous to the boundaries put to the public policy exception[20] to recognition and enforcement.[21]

11   (2) does not answer all questions arising. Its precise meaning is not clear, even less its impact. Whether it is the *West Tankers* fix hoped for in certain quarters remains to be seen.[22] As to substance, (2) does not add too much to what one would have to derive from Art. 71 anyway.[23] (2) as part of the Brussels *Ibis* Regulation operates only within the scope of the

---

[12]   Report of the Committee on Legal Affairs of the European Parliament of 15 October 2012, 2010/0383 (COD) 140.

[13]   *Steindl*, in: FS Hellwig Torggler (2013), p. 1181, 1195.

[14]   Art. 29 (4) Proposal could muster a number of advantages; in detail *Magnus/Mankowski*, ZvglRWiss 110 (2011), 252, 258–260; *Carducci*, (2011) 27 Arb. Int. 171, 191.

[15]   *Illmer*, RabelsZ 75 (2011), 645, 657–658.

[16]   See *Ronald A. Brand*, RdC 358 (2011), 9, 187.

[17]   *Gustaf Möller*, in: Essays in Honour of Michael Bogdan (2013), p. 373, 381.

[18]   Emphasis added.

[19]   *Hartley*, (2014) 63 ICLQ 843, 859.

[20]   See there *André Krombach v. Walter Bamberski* (Case C-7/98), [2000] ECR I-1935; *Mario Gambazzi v. Daimler Chrysler Canada Inc.* (Case C-394/07), [2009] ECR I-2563.

[21]   *Hartley*, (2014) 63 ICLQ 843, 859.

[22]   *Ronald A. Brand*, RdC 358 (2011), 9, 187.

[23]   See Heidelberg Report paras. 122, 131; *Carducci*, (2011) 27 Arb. Int. 171, 189–190, 194; *Carducci*, (2013)

Brussels I Regulation and thus within the limits sketched by Art. 1 (2) (d). (2) is the ultimate safety valve that the Brussels I*bis* Regulation and the 1958 New York Convention cannot collide as far as the 1958 New York Convention reaches.[24] It safeguards and guarantees that Arts. II (3), III 1958 New York Convention are unaffected.[25] The 1958 New York Convention mainly limits its own scope of application to the recognition and enforcement of arbitral awards, an area which is not covered by the Brussels I*bis* Regulation whereas the latter contains rules on jurisdiction an area which in turn the 1958 New York Convention does not cover.[26] The area of true conflicts thus is rather small. Nonetheless, (2) indirectly introduces a precondition for the recognition of a judgment namely that a *prima facie* contradicting arbitration clause is invalid.[27] The precedence of the 1958 New York Convention must not lead to infer the prevalence of an award over an judgment in the area of recognition and enforcement.[28]

Read literally, (2) is a reservation solely in favour of the New York Convention. It does not **12** mention the European Convention on International Commercial Arbitration of 21 April 1961.[29] But there would not be any sound, and even less any convincing justification to treat this Convention differently from the 1958 New York Convention. Hence, (2) should be extended *per analogiam* to preserve the application of this Convention, too. If (2) is regarded as having a declaratory nature only this would even go without saying. If one is not prepared to extend (2) *per analogiam*, Art. 71 would step in and govern the relationship between the Brussels I*bis* Regulation and the 1961 European Arbitration Convention.[30]

III. Relation with bilateral conventions and agreements between a third State and a Member State concluded before 1 March 2002

Pursuant to (3), the Brussels I*bis* Regulation shall not affect the application of bilateral **13** conventions and agreements between a third State and a Member State concluded before the date of entry into force of the Brussels I Regulation which concern matters governed by the Brussels I*bis* Regulation. (3) is a novelty without predecessor in the Brussels I Regulation.[31] It is a welcome clarification of Art. 71 insofar as it unambiguously puts beyond any doubt that *bilateral* Conventions and Agreements with third States also enjoy precedence over the Brussels I*bis* Regulation, given that they have been concluded before 1 March 2002.

---

29 Arb. Int. 467, 478; *Hauberg Wilhelmsen*, (2014) 30 Arb Int 169, 182; *Malatesta*, RDIPP 2014, 5, 6; *Hess*, JZ 2014, 538, 539; *Hartley*, (2014) 63 ICLQ 843, 858. *Markus*, AJP 2014, 800, 805 alleges (2) to have a merely declaratory nature.

24   *Carducci*, (2013) 29 Arb. Int. 467, 478 doubts as to whether even absent (2) there would be any true conflict of rules between the Brussels I*bis* Regulation and the New York Convention.

25   *Markus*, AJP 2014, 800, 805; see also *Malatesta*, RDIPP 2014, 5, 9.

26   *Steindl*, in: FS Hellwig Torggler (2013), p. 1181, 1188.

27   *Salerno*, Riv. dir. int. 2013, 1146, 1186.

28   *Peter Arnt Nielsen*, (2013) 50 CML Rev. 503, 510–511; *Camilleri*, (2013) 62 ICLQ 899, 912; *Carducci*, (2013) 29 Arb. Int. 467, 476; *Leandro* [2015] J Int Disp Sett 1, 4–5. *Contra Clifford/O. Browne*, LW in Practice – The London Dispute Newsletter April 2013; *Salerno*, Riv. dir. int. 2013, 1146, 1185.

29   UNTS 484, 349.

30   See *Hess*, in: FS Bernd von Hoffmann (2011), p. 648, 655 fn. 47.

31   *Mankowski*, ZEV 2013, 529, 532.

14 Recital (36) confirms and supports this:

(36) Without prejudice of the obligations of the Member States under the Treaties, this Regulation should not affect the application of bilateral conventions and agreements between a third State and a Member State concluded before the date of entry into force of Regulation (EC) No. 44/ 2001 which concerns matters governed by this Regulation.

The welcome clarification is the express precedence of bilateral Conventions and Agreements whereas Art. 71 could still leave some doubt as to whether it would only cover multilateral Conventions.

15 In the overall system of European PIL, (3) is a solitary and does not find a companion. *Stricto sensu*, (3) might be said to be superfluous and redundant for its content could already be found in Art. 71. Yet a reduplication is neither inhibited nor detrimental, but has a clarifying effect. (3) exists in its own right insofar as it draws the borderline between bilateral Conventions and Agreements concluded before and after 1 March 2002, the date when the Brussels I Regulation entered into force.[32] One could also argue that the express proviso at the beginning of Recital (36) which gives precedence to TFEU and EU treaty over the bilateral agreements with third States concluded by the single Member States, goes beyond what Art. 71 (1) and Recital (35) establish. But given the line of argument which the CJEU follows with regard to Art. 71 (1)[33] a material difference between Art. 71 (1) and Recital (36) does not exist for practical purposes in this aspect.

Chapter VIII: **Final Provisions**

Article 74

The Member States shall provide, within the framework of the European Judicial Network and with a view to making the information available to the public, a description of national rules and procedures concerning enforcement, including authorities competent for enforcement, and information on any limitations on enforcement, in particular debtor protection rules and limitation or prescription periods.
The Member States shall keep this information permanently updated.

1 Art. 74 is a novelty and has no predecessor either in the Brussels I Regulation or in the 2007 Lugano Convention. It has some kind of service function for the interested public. It intends to help overcome informational difficulties and to make relevant information more accessible and more readily available. It wants to reduce information costs for judgment creditors and to make enforcement easier and less deterring. The means employed are already at hand

---

[32]   *Mankowski*, ZEV 2013, 529, 532.

[33]   *TNT Express Nederland BV v. AXA Versicherung AG* (Case C-533/08), [2010] ECR I-4107 paras. 49 *et seq.*; *Nipponkoa Insurance Co. (Europe) Ltd. v. Inter-Zuid Transport BV* (Case C-452/12), ECLI:EU: C:2013:858 paras. 36 *et seq.*

and need not to be established incurring extra costs. The European Judicial Network is based on a Council Decision already of 2001.[1] Its purpose is outlined in Art. 3 of the said Council Decision. It depends on the willingness of the Member States to provide the necessary information. Subpara (1) goes one technical step beyond that insofar as it imposes a proper obligation on the Member States which could in case of need enforced by the Commission.

Subpara. (2) is intended to safeguard and assure that the information available for public access is up-to-date and current at any given point of time. It is to prevent that it is frozen as it was when it was first promulgated which might have become dated by the time it is accessed. Given the relative reluctance which the Member States have shown even in notifying the international treaties and conventions to which they are Contracting Parties respectively, subpara. 2 announces quite some program. Furthermore, subpara. 2 does not provide for strict rules as for the intervals in which the Member States have to actualise the information but for the "permanently".   **2**

Article 75

By 10 January 2014, the Member States shall communicate to the Commission:
(a) the courts to which the application for refusal of enforcement is to be submitted pursuant to Article 47(1);
(b) the courts with which an appeal against the decision on the application for refusal of enforcement is to be lodged pursuant to Article 49(2);
(c) the courts with which any further appeal is to be lodged pursuant to Article 50; and
(d) the languages accepted for translations of the forms as referred to in Article 57(2).
The Commission shall make the information publicly available through any appropriate means, in particular through the European Judicial Network.

I. Member States' obligation to communicate to the Commission

Art. 75 obliges the Member States to communicate to the Commission the necessary data about the competent authorities or the accepted languages respectively. The required objects of the information to be communicated to the Commission are in detail (a) the courts to which the application for refusal of enforcement is to be submitted pursuant to Art. 47 (1); (b) the courts with which an appeal against the decision on the application for refusal of enforcement is to be lodged pursuant to Art. 49 (2); (c) the courts with which any further appeal is to be lodged pursuant to Art. 50; and (d) the languages accepted for translations of the forms as referred to in Art. 57 (2).   **1**

The Regulation respects the sovereignty of the Member States with regard to institutional and organisational aspects of their judicial system. It does not superimpose European structures, and thus is dependent on the Member States organising apt judicial structures. The single Member State knows best about the intricacies of its own judicial system and where to   **2**

---

[1]   Council Decision 2001/470/EC of 28 May 2001 establishing a European Judicial Network in Civil and Commercial Matters, OJ EC 2001 L 174/25; Council Decision 2008/976/JHA of 18 December 2008 on the European Judicial Network, OJ EC 2008 L 348/130.

establish the competences vested in it by the Regulation within that judicial system. The Member State only has to make the details known to interest parties resident whether they are domiciled in the respective Member State or abroad (and regardless whether they are resident in the EU or in Third States). Art. 75 provides the means for that feat and channels communication to the public *via* Brussels.

3   The basic information was to be provided by 10 January 2014, exactly one year before the bulk and the operative part of the Regulation became effective. Art. 81 subpara. 2 reflects this duly.

4   Unlike Art. 76 (3), Art. 75 subpara. 1 on its face does not implement a two-step tier and does not extend to subsequent alterations and amendments. There is no sound justification discernible why amendments and alterations should not be communicated to the Commission. The best way to cure this shortcoming appears to apply Art. 76 (3) *per analogiam*. Accordingly the Member States shall notify the Commission of any subsequent amendments related to the four topics listed in subpara. 1, and the Commission shall amend its publications in due course.

5   Sanctions in the event that single Member States do not comply with their obligation to communicate necessary data to the Commission, are not spelt out. Since subpara. 1 imposes upon them an obligation by EU law the appropriate sanction appears to be damage for breach of EU law.

II. Commission's obligation to make the information publicly available

6   The relay of information is centralised with the Commission acting as the collector and communicator of the relevant data. Interested parties do not have to check national sources for every single Member State but only the sources provided for by the Commission. Member States provide the data as cheapest information gatherer, and the Commission serves as an intermediate. The overall system is at zero cost for the interested parties (but for the billing of their own legal advisors).

7   The European Judicial Network gets express mention as a possible channel of communication. Despite all its undeniable merits, one should not overestimate its possibilities, though. In particular, it is designed for communication between the judicial systems of the different Member States. It aims less at communicating to, and with, the other legal professions. Informing the judges is one thing, informing the lawyers concerned with cases falling under Brussels *Ibis* Regulation is quite another thing. General public is not privy to the EJN.

8   The Commission does not comply with its duty if it solely uses the European Judicial Network. Interested parties who need the information might live outside the EU and are equally entitled to proper information as EU residents are. But the EJN will most likely not reach them.

9   A separate website of the Directorate General Home and Justice appears to be a sensible means. As to distribution of responsibilities within the Commission, this DG is the one competent to render services required by the Brussels *Ibis* Regulation.

Why Art. 75 does not adopt the very same channels of communication which Art. 76 adopts   **10**
is not ultimately clear. Official lists officially published by the Commission in the Official
Journal of the EU as envisaged by Art. 76 (4) clearly are appropriate means of communication in both areas. The difficulty for the Commission stems from collecting the necessary
information, not from the publication of the information once it has been collected. Apparently, the drafters were content with subpara. 2 coinciding with Art. 76 (5) and overlooked Art. 76 (4).

Details as to *when* the Commission has to publish information received are not to be found   **11**
in subpara. 2. The optimal account of information is provided if the Commission commu-
nicates every information to the public as soon as it has received it, without undue delay. But
it appears to be within the Commission's discretion to collect a number of information
before publicising the whole bunch. Yet the Commission after receiving one bit of information would have to speculate, to predict and to surmise when the next bit was about to drop
in. This would be rather uncertain, and thus proper use of discretion leads to instant publication of every information by the time it is received without waiting for other information
to drop in.

Subpara. 2 does not say anything about the language in which the Commission has to make   **12**
the information publicly available, either. Since exact denominations of the courts designated are necessary under subpara. 1 litt. (a)-(c) those denominations have to be published
in the very language of the respective Member State communicating them to the Commission. This would be in the tradition of the Annexes to the Brussels I Regulation, too. As to the
accompanying text and the necessary announcements, the question is whether publication
in English and French would suffice or whether a publication in all official languages is
required. Once again, the tradition of the Annexes to the Brussels I Regulation would favour
the latter approach. Given that these would be standard text of few words translation costs
are low if not negligible.

Article 76

1. The Member States shall notify the Commission of:
    (a) the rules of jurisdiction referred to in Articles 5(2) and 6(2);
    (b) the rules on third-party notice referred to in Article 65; and
    (c) the conventions referred to in Article 69.
2. The Commission shall, on the basis of the notifications by the Member States referred to in
    paragraph 1, establish the corresponding lists.
3. The Member States shall notify the Commission of any subsequent amendments required to
    be made to those lists. The Commission shall amend those lists accordingly.
4. The Commission shall publish the lists and any subsequent amendments made to them in
    the Official Journal of the European Union.
5. The Commission shall make all information notified pursuant to paragraphs 1 and 3 publicly
    available through any other appropriate means, in particular through the European Judicial
    Network.

I. Listing technique

1 In some instances, the Brussels *Ibis* Regulation makes reference to rules of the national laws of the Member States which fulfil certain qualifications. The Regulation rules set a framework, and the Member State have to name and nominate the respective qualifiers from their national laws. European institutions are not omniscient, and the Member States are the cheapest information providers with regard to the respective rules of their national laws. Recipient of the information to be provided is the Commission, functionally acting as some kind of Notary of the Brussels *Ibis* Regulation. As for the initial information, Art. 81 cl. 2 obliged the Member States to provide it by 10 January 2014 as some kind of preparatory work before a year later the main body of the Brussels *Ibis* Regulation became effective

2 The instances when information is required which rules from national laws qualify respectively, are listed in (1). The list is exhaustive. It comprises:
   – the rules of jurisdiction referred to in Art. 5 (2), i.e. the rules granting exorbitant jurisdiction to be blacklisted (a, first case);
   – correspondingly, the rules of jurisdiction referred to in Art. 6 (2) in conjunction with Art. 5 (2), i.e. the rules of exorbitant jurisdiction to be possibly applied if the defendant is not domiciled in any Member State (a, second case);
   – the rules on third-party notice referred to in Art. 65 (b), clarifying whether a certain Member States regards itself as follower of the Germanic model of *Streitverkündung* (b);
   – the bilateral Conventions and Agreements concluded between Member States as are superseded by the Brussels *Ibis* Regulation within the latter's scope of application (c).

3 Whereas (1) obliges the Member States to provide the necessary information (2) obliges the Commission to collect and compile the information received. (4) decrees the primary mode of publication, namely that the Commission shall publish the lists compiled in the Official Journal of the European Union. This is mandatory. Publication correctly should be in Part L of the OJ since the lists are based on the Brussels *Ibis* Regulation, a proper Regulation, and since their publication is mandatorily required. The Commission chose Part C. It complied with its initial obligation in OJ EU 2015 C 4/2.[1]

4 (5) goes even a step further. It obliges the Commission to make all information notified pursuant to (1) and (3) publicly available through any other appropriate means, in particular through the European Judicial Network. It is not said whether publication in the EJN shall take place prior to, simultaneously with, or only after the publication in the Official Journal.

5 Neither (4) nor (5) expressly addresses the issue of time. Neither of them states how much time the Commission might take before eventually publishing a list. Neither of them clarifies whether the lists have to be re-published in regular or irregular intervals. Neither of them clarifies whether the lists can be published separately or only jointly. The former ought to be preferred. For the initial lists the Commission opted for a joint publication, but differently

---

[1] The information referring to Article 76 of Regulation (EU) No. 1215/2012 of the European Parliament and of the Ouncil on jurisdiction and recognition and enforcement of judgments in civil and commercial matters, OJ EU 2015 C 4/2.

numbered lists.[2] In the future, List 1, 2 or 3 might be published separately. List 1 is devoted to the rules referred to in Art. 5 (2) and in Art. 6 (2) in conjunction with Art. 5 (2), List 2 to the rules on third-party notice, and List 3 to the bilateral Conventions.[3]

The Commission's obligation to publish the lists is not expressly sanctioned. This could **6** become a possible theoretical shortcoming, but without grave consequences for practice anyway.

II. Subsequent amendments

Pursuant to (3), the Member States shall notify the Commission of any subsequent amend- **7** ments required to be made to those lists. The Commission shall amend those lists accordingly Once again, neither the issue of time nor the possible sanctions are addressed. It is not clear how much time a Member State is permitted to take longest before informing the Commission of a change in its national legislation. It is not clarified whether the Commission has to publish each single information in a piecemeal fashion once it has dropped it, or whether it can collect a number of data in order to reach a minimum threshold (and how high a possible threshold should be), either. Pragmatism might solve the matter. Plain handling calls for a publication in due course after the Commission has received an information for no-one can predict when the next information will drop in.

III. Contrast to Art. 74 Brussels I Regulation and Art. 75 2007 Lugano Convention

The remarkable issue about Art. 76 is the contrast to Art. 74 Brussels I Regulation and Art. 75 **8** 2007 Lugano Convention, and the difference in the technique employed. Art. 74 Brussels I Regulation relied on Annexes to the Regulation which in turn were formal parts of the Regulation. Art. 75 2007 Lugano Convention mirrors that and also uses Annexes (subpara. 1) which are declared a formal part of the Convention (subpara. 2). Art. 76 resorts to a more informal mode. According to (4) the Commission shall publish the lists and any subsequent amendments made to them in the Official Journal of the European Union. This is an official communication and can be easily and effortlessly accessed by all persons concerned or interested.

But it does not elevate the list to the formal rank and level of Annexes. That is deliberately so. **9** Every alteration of an Annex would prompt a necessity for an Amendment Regulation. This would be time-consuming and costly. The alternative would be that keeping track with the information gathered would be delayed until a certain number of notifications has been collected an the Commission thought it worth the effort to initiate the process leading to an Amendment Regulation. The technique employed by (4) avoids either of these: The Commission is put in a position that it could announce every single notification at will.

---

2   The information referring to Article 76 of Regulation (EU) No. 1215/2012 of the European Parliament and of the Ouncil on jurisdiction and recognition and enforcement of judgments in civil and commercial matters, OJ EU 2015 C 4/2.
3   The information referring to Article 76 of Regulation (EU) No. 1215/2012 of the European Parliament and of the Ouncil on jurisdiction and recognition and enforcement of judgments in civil and commercial matters, OJ EU 2015 C 4/2.

Article 77

The Commission shall be empowered to adopt delegated acts in accordance with Article 78 concerning the amendment of Annexes I and II.

1 Annex I contains the Certificate concerning a Judgment in Civil and Commercial Matters, as it is provided for in Art. 53, and Annex II contains the Certificate concerning an Authentic Instrument/Court Settlement in Civil and Commercial Matters, as it is provided for in Art. 60. These are technical and bureaucratic issues. Altering them does not require full scale EU legislation with its immense and time-consuming effort. The European Parliament and the Council need not to be bothered with such nitty-gritty. Accordingly, the respective tasks are left to the Commission. The Commission is the institution of the EU which is best equipped for an appropriately speedy reaction if such reaction is required. The basis for the idea and the terminology used is Art. 290 (1) TFEU.[1]

2 Recital (37) explains: "In order to ensure that the certificates to be used in connection with the recognition or enforcement of judgments, authentic instruments and court settlements under this Regulation are kept up-to-date, the power to adopt acts in accordance with Article 290 of the TFEU should be delegated to the Commission in respect of amendments of Annexes I and II to this Regulation. It is of particular importance that the Commission carry out appropriate consultations during its preparatory work, including at expert level. The Commission, when preparing and drawing up delegated acts, should ensure a simultaneous, timely and appropriate transmission of relevant documents to the European Parliament and to the Council."

3 As the Annexes are integral parts of the Brussels I Regulation, it is necessary, though, to expressly empower the Commission to act in an area legislatively covered by European Parliament and Council. Recital (37) cl. 3 is a safeguard that the European Parliament and the Council as the delegators are kept informed.

4 Recital (37) cl. 2 obliges the Commission to carry out consultations before it proceeds to the drafting stage. Experts are one group to be consulted, stakeholders (who are not expressly mentioned) might be another. This consultation process is some kind of replacement for the abandonment of an advisory committee to the Commission as such committee was institutionalised by Art. 75 (1) Brussels I Regulation. Such institutionalised body has not been retained in the Brussels I regulation which indulges into more informal procedures, and rightly so since the committee provided for by Art. 75 (1) Brussels I Regulation lacked a genuine function and real importance.

Article 78

1. **The power to adopt delegated acts is conferred on the Commission subject to the conditions laid down in this Article.**

---

[1]   *Staudinger*, in: Rauscher, Art. 77 Brussels *Ibis* Regulation note 1.

2. The power to adopt delegated acts referred to in Article 77 shall be conferred on the Commission for an indeterminate period of time from 9 January 2013.
3. The delegation of power referred to in Article 77 may be revoked at any time by the European Parliament or by the Council. A decision to revoke shall put an end to the delegation of the power specified in that decision. It shall take effect the day following the publication of the decision in the Official Journal of the European Union or at a later date specified therein. It shall not affect the validity of any delegated acts already in force.
4. As soon as it adopts a delegated act, the Commission shall notify it simultaneously to the European Parliament and to the Council.
5. A delegated act adopted pursuant to Article 77 shall enter into force only if no objection has been expressed either by the European Parliament or the Council within a period of two months of notification of that act to the European Parliament and the Council or if, before the expiry of that period, the European Parliament and the Council have both informed the Commission that they will not object. That period shall be extended by two months at the initiative of the European Parliament or of the Council.

Art. 78 defines the conditions and limits within which the power to adopt delegated acts ins **1** conferred upon the Commission. Thereby, it defines the relationship between the Commission as the delegee and the legislative powers of the EU, the European Parliament and the Council, as the delegators. To a certain extent, it solves the principal-agent-conflict inherent in any delegation of power by a principal to an agent.

(1) effectively repeats and reiterates what Art. 77 already says. Without (1), the outcome **2** would not be different: The Commission is empowered to adopt delegates acts, but only within the limits set by Art. 78. The Commission is not the genuine legislator of the EU and it can only act as legislator if and insofar as the genuine legislative institutions of the EU, the European Parliament and the Council, have empowered it so. (2) fortifies that the Commission was vested with the power for a preliminarily unrestricted time.

(3) expresses a general principle of delegation: The delegator vests the power in the delegee – **3** and the delegator can wrestle away the same power from the delegee. He who gives the power can withdraw it at any time unless he is bound otherwise.

The Proposal contained more detailed specification for the procedure to reach a revocation. **4** Art. 90 (1) Brussels I*bis* Proposal was concerned with communication between the institutions of the EU: "The institution which has commenced an internal an internal procedure for deciding whether to revoke the delegation of power shall endeavour to inform the other institution and the Commission within a reasonable time before the final decision is taken, indicating the delegated powers which could be subject to revocation and possible reasons for a revocation".

In order to exercise their respective rights under (5), the European Parliament and the **5** Council must be informed which delegated acts the Commission has adopted. Insofar they have to overcome informational asymmetries. (4) Thus imposes an obligation on the Commission to notify the European Parliament and the Council of any delegated act it adopts. Equal treatment demands that one institution must not be preferred to the other and accordingly (4) calls for simultaneous notification to the two institutions. The Commission has to notify as soon as it adopts a delegated act, i.e. immediately, without any reasonable delay, after the adoption of a delegated act. Entry into force of the delegated act is not the relevant mark of reference since (5) delays if for a period of two months after notification.

6   There is a slight contradiction between (4) and Recital (37) cl. 3. (4) obliges the Commission to notify a delegated act adopted whereas Recital (37) cl. 3 asserts that the Commission when preparing and drawing up delegated acts, should ensure a simultaneous, timely and appropriate transmission of relevant documents to the European Parliament and to the Council. Such an obligation both wider than, and different in content form, that provided for in (4) has not been transformed into any rule of the Brussels *Ibis* Regulation that would be binding upon the Commission.

7   A direct sanction in the event that the Commission does not comply with its obligation under (4), is not to be found in (4), though.

8   (5) gives the European Parliament and the Council respectively an own right to object to delegated acts adopted by the Commission within a certain period. In order to make this right effective the regular entry into force of the delegated act is delayed until the said period has expired without any objection being expressed.

9   It is not clear whether an objecting institution must give reasons for raising the objection. Art. 91 (3) cl. 2 Brussels *Ibis* Proposal provided that the institution which objects shall state the reasons for objecting to the delegated act. This proposal has not made its way in the final text of the Brussels *Ibis* Regulation. This might be taken as the ground for an *argumentum e contrario*. The objecting institution might be hampered in its liberty to object if it had to make the effort to give reasons for its objection. The opposite result is more convincing and more appealing, though. General standards of government militate in favour of that reasons should be given.

Article 79

By 11 January 2022 the Commission shall present a report to the European Parliament, to the Council and to the European Economic and Social Committee on the application of this Regulation. That report shall include an evaluation of the possible need for a further extension of the rules on jurisdiction to defendants not domiciled in a Member State, taking into account the operation of this Regulation and possible developments at international level. Where appropriate, the report shall be accompanied by a proposal for amendment of this Regulation.

I. Future Commission report and its content

1   Pursuant to Art. 17 EU Treaty the Commission is obliged to monitor, survey and control the application of Union law in the Member States and to adopt measures for the effective implementation of Union law. This general obligation is *in concreto* mirrored in Art. 79 with particular regard to the Brussels *Ibis* Regulation.[1] By 11 January 2022 the Commission has to

---

[1]   Commission Proposal COM (1999) 348 final p. 29; *Layton/Mercer* para. 33.004.

present a report on the application of the Regulation in the Member States. Addressees of this report are the European Parliament, the Council and the Economic and Social Committee. If necessary, i.e. if major difficulties or divergences in the application of single provisions of the Regulation have arisen and can be evidenced by the report, the Commission shall propose appropriate adaptations to the provisions in question and shall thus initiate law reform.

The report the Commission is obliged to produce shall be a general report on all issues **2** related to the Regulation. But one item is expressly mentioned: The report shall include an evaluation of the possible need for a further extension of the rules on jurisdiction to defendants not domiciled in a Member State, taking into account the operation of this Regulation and possible developments at international level. This is part of political compromise surrounding Arts. 6–8 in particular. The Brussels I*bis* Regulation has drawn back from full-scale engagement in the international arena as it had been proposed by the Commission in Arts. 5; 6 Proposal Brussels I*bis* and was subject to heavy and heated discussion.[2] Major Member State raised concerns and were politically victorious.[3] But this step back is only for the time being, and there is not doubt that this will be a topic of considerable on-going debate.[4] Any Commission report whether in 2022 as scheduled or later will certainly stir further debate.

II. Time frame and schedule

Astonishingly and contrary to the over-all scheme, Art. 79 does not yet provide for a repeat **3** report every five years but at least *verbatim* sticks to a seemingly single report after the first seven years after the Regulation became effective. Perhaps Art. 79 might be subject to an adaptation in this direction after the first report. Art. 65 Brussels II*bis* Regulation already provides for such a repeat report.

With regard to Art. 73 Brussels I Regulation, the Commission insisted on a five year period **4** before the (first) report. It did not accept a proposal by the Parliament to shorten this down to two years since it would be impossible, given the duration of judicial procedures in the

---

[2]   *Bonomi*, RDIPP 2007, 313; *Borrás*, AEDIPr 2010, 797; *Borrás*, in: Lein (ed), The Brussels I Review Proposal Uncovered (2012), p. 57; *Boschiero*, AEDIPr 2009, 35; *Buhr*, in: Bonomi/Cristina Schmid (eds.), Die Revision der Verordnung 44/2001 (Brüssel I) – Welche Folgen für das Lugano-Übereinkommen? (2010), p. 11; *Fallon*, in: Liber amicorum Hélène Gaudemet-Tallon (2008), p. 241; *Fallon*, in: Fallon/Lagarde/Poillot-Perruzzetto (dir), Quelle architecture pour un code européen de droit international privé (2011), p. 137; *Fallon/Kruger*, Yb. PIL 14 (2012/13), 1; *Furrer*, in: Lein (ed), The Brussels I Review Proposal Uncovered (2012), p. 165; *Gaudemet-Tallon*, in: Mélanges en l'honneur de Serge Guinchard (2010), p. 465; *Grolimund*, ZVR-Jb 2010, 79; *Hau*, in: FS Bernd von Hoffmann (2011), p. 617; *Luzzatto*, in: Pocar/Viarengo/Villata (eds), Recasting Brussels I (Padova 2012), p. 111; *Markus*, in: Pocar/Viarengo/Villata (eds), Recasting Brussels I (Padova 2012), p. 123; *Nuyts*, Study on residual jurisdiction, 3 September 2007 http:ec.europa.eu/justice_home/doc_centre/civil/studies/doc/study_residual_jurisdiction. en; *Pocar*, in: Liber amicorum Hélène Gaudemet-Tallon (2008), p. 573; *Takahashi*, (2012) 8 JPrIL 1; *de Vareilles-Sommières*, in: Liber amicorum Hélène Gaudemet-Tallon (2008), p. 397; *Johannes Weber*, RabelsZ 75 (2011), 619; *Weitz*, in: FS Daphne-Ariane Simotta (2012), p. 679.

[3]   *Mankowski*, in: Rauscher, Art. 6 Brüssel Ia-VO note 10.

[4]   *Crawford/Carruthers*, (2014) 63 ICLQ 1, 29.

Peter Mankowski   1109

Member States, to accumulate the necessary statistics and number of judgments under the Regulation to prepare a proper report.[5] Although the Commission accepted the proposal by the Parliament to let the report pay specific attention to small and medium enterprises and business,[6] this has not been reflected in the wording eventually. Art. 79 now extends the time until the (first) report has to be presented, to seven years after the date when the Regulation became effective in its entirety pursuant to Art. 66 (1).

5   In a Joint Statement[7] the Commission and the Council have initially announced to pay particular attention to the effects of the Brussels I Regulation on small and medium enterprises. The main focus was be on Art. 15 (1) (c) Brussels I Regulation, today substituted with Art. 17 (1) (c) Brussels *Ibis* Regulation, and its effects on cross-border electronic commerce. The said Joint Statement reads:

"1.   The Council and the Commission are aware that the development of electronic commerce in the information society facilitates the economic growth of undertakings. Union law is an essential if citizens, economic operators and consumers are to benefit from the possibilities afforded by electronic commerce.

    They consider that the development of new distance marketing techniques based on the use of the Internet depends in part on the mutual confidence which may grow up between undertakings and consumers. One of the major elements in this confidence is the opportunity offered to consumers by Article 16 of the Regulation to bring possible disputes before the courts of the Member States in which they reside, where the contract concluded by the consumer is covered by Article 15 of the Regulation.

    The Council and the Commission point out in this connection that for Article 15(1)(c) to be applicable it is not sufficient for an undertaking to target its activities at the Member State of the consumer's residence, or at a number of Member States including that Member State; a contract must also be concluded within the framework of its activities. This provision relates to a number of marketing methods, including contracts concluded at a distance through the Internet. In this context, the Council and the Commission stress that the mere fact that an Internet site is accessible is not sufficient for Article 15 to be applicable, although a factor will be that this Internet site solicits the conclusion of distance contracts and that a contract has actually been concluded at a distance, by whatever means. In this respect, the language or currency which a website uses does not constitute a relevant factor.

2.   The Council and the Commission take the view that in general it is in the interest of consumers and undertakings to try to settle their disputes amicably before resorting to the courts.

    The Council and the Commission stress in this connection that the purpose of the Regulation, and in particular of Articles 15 and 17 thereof, is not to prohibit the parties from making use of alternative methods of dispute settlement.

    The Council and the Commission accordingly wish to reiterate how important it is that work on alternative methods of dispute settlement in civil and commercial matters should continue at European Union level, in keeping with the Council's conclusions of 29 May 2000.

    They are aware of the great significance of this work and stress the useful complementary role represented by alternative methods of dispute settlement in civil and commercial matters, in particular with regard to electronic commerce.

---

5   Amended Commission Proposal COM (2000) 689 final p. 4.
6   Amended Commission Proposal COM (2000) 689 final p. 4.
7   OJ EC 2001 L 12/1.

3. Pursuant to Article 73 of the Regulation, the Commission is to submit a report on the application of the Regulation, accompanied, if need be, by proposals for adaptations, to the European Parliament, the Council and the Economic and Social Committee.
   The Council and the Commission consider that in preparing the report especial attention should be paid to the application of the provisions of the Regulation relating to consumers and small and medium-sized undertakings, in particular with respect to electronic commerce. For this purpose, the Commission will, where appropriate, propose amendments to the Regulation before the expiry of the period referred to in Article 73 of the Regulation."

Art. 73 Brussels I Regulation obliged the Commission to present a report five years after the **6** entry into force of the Brussels I Regulation at latest. The Commission did not comply with this obligation, but only set out to commission the preparatory academic reports on which the official report would be based, around the time when according to the letter an official report would have been due. Five years are only a rather short span of time. In five year time only very few, if any cases, and requests for preliminary rulings on the Regulation will have reached the CJEU. A steady case-law of the CJEU is given small opportunity only to develop with regard to the interpretation of the newly implemented rules. Five years are simply too short to issue a sensible and substantive review report. The ten years after the entry into force opted for by Art. 79 are far more realistic and sensible.

Article 80

This Regulation shall repeal Regulation (EC) No. 44/2001. References to the repealed Regulation shall be construed as references to this Regulation and shall be read in accordance with the correlation table set out in Annex III.

Art. 80 regulates the relation between the Brussels I*bis* Regulation and its predecessor, the **1** Brussels I Regulation. The respective settlement is simple, proper and satisfactory. The Brussels I*bis* dos not only supersede and replace the Brussels Convention as between the Member States. It goes even further and repeals the Brussels I Regulation in an outright manner.

The Brussels I Regulation is still important for cases where the events took place before the **2** Brussels I*bis* Regulation became effective.

Some other legal instruments enacted between the entry into force of the Brussels I Regu- **3** lation on the one hand and the Brussels I*bis* Regulation becoming effective on the other hand refer to the Brussels I Regulation. This concerns both EU and national legal instruments. (2) clarifies that such references shall be understood as references to the Brussels I*bis* Regulation.[1] To insert this clarification in the Brussels I*bis* Regulation is more practicable than to change all legal instruments referring to the Brussels I Regulation. Otherwise such alteration would have been necessary in every case to take into account the special constellation of Denmark. Yet the other instruments should be read as though they were altered in the

---

[1] See only *Lydia Fuchs*, ÖJZ 2005, 624, 626. Probably overlooked by *Christian Kohler*, in: FS Reinhold Geimer (2002), p. 461, 464 *et seq.*

mentioned manner.[2] The Correlation Table in Annex III and expressly pointed at in cl. 2 *in fine* is an excellent and most useful means in order to achieve the re-construction of the references covered.

4   Cl. 2 gains its main relevance from the reference of Art. 64 Lugano Convention 2007 to the Brussels I Regulation, which now has to be read as referring to the Brussels I*bis* Regulation.[3] Yet it is presupposed that the respective rule is applicable in its own right; for instance, the Insolvency Regulation is not applicable in relation to Denmark, and insofar (2) does not lead to any alteration.[4]

5   Practitioners however should be reminded that they must be aware that references to the Brussels I Regulation are not what they seem to be at first sight. Many surprises might be hidden behind these references for practitioners not familiar with international procedural law.

6   National legislation of its free motion can voluntarily refer to the Brussels I Regulation for cases which would *per se* be outside the ambit of this Act. For instance, distribution as to interlocal jurisdiction in a State territorially sub-divided may be instituted by such reference. Insofar as national legislation still refers to the Brussels I Regulation it is alleged that it should be for the interpretation of that national law following its own yardsticks to determine as to whether the reference should be read as static and petrified, i.e. still to the Brussels I Regulation, or as a dynamic reference.[5] Yet cl. 2 should be given guiding force for this interpretation, too. Taking (2) into account the reference should be read as dynamic.[6] National legislators are free in deciding whether to refer but not where to refer to.

7   Art. 80 differs in some respects from the techniques employed by Art. 68 which regulates the relation between the Brussels I*bis* Regulation and the Brussels Convention. These differences stem from the fact that the Brussels Convention is not a legislative Act of the then EEC, but a Treaty between the Contracting States. The differences are the following: Firstly, the Brussels I Regulation only superseded the Brussels Convention whereas the Brussels I*bis* Regulation repeals the Brussels I Regulation. Secondly, both Regulations apply within the territorial confines of the TFEU or the EU Treaty respectively whereas the Brussels Convention had an own territorial scope extending to some territories of the Contracting States which fall outside the ambit of TFEU or the EU Treaty respectively.

8   Yet functionally, Art. 80 supplements Art. 68 in an important regard: It unambiguously clarifies the relation between the Brussels I*bis* Regulation and its immediate predecessor. Systematically, Art. 80 might be said to be inserted in the wrong place within the Brussels I*bis* Regulation. It would have found a more appropriate place if it featured as an Art. 69. Its optimal place would be among, and concluding, the rules dealing with the relationship between the Brussels I*bis* Regulation and other legal instruments. It correct place ought to be in Chapter VII, not in Chapter VIII.

---

[2]   *Lydia Fuchs*, ÖJZ 2005, 624, 626.

[3]   *Schlosser* Art. 66 note 2.

[4]   See OLG Frankfurt NJOZ 2005, 2532, 2533 *et seq.*

[5]   *Christian Kohler*, in: FS Reinhold Geimer (2002), p. 461, 464; *Geimer/Schütze* Art. 68 note 2.

[6]   *Mankowski*, in: Rauscher, Art. 68 note 6.

Article 81

This Regulation shall enter into force on the twentieth day following that of its publication in the Official Journal of the European Union.
It shall apply from 10 January 2015, with the exception of Articles 75 and 76, which shall apply from 10 January 2014.

Unlike its predecessor, Art. 76 Brussels I Regulation, Art. 81 establishes a two-step tier and **1** distinguishes between entry into force and application. Application equates becoming practically effective. The role model for the roughly 18 month's gap between entry into force and applicability obviously is Art. 29 Rome I Regulation. Art. 81 follows in its footprints, not in those of Art. 76 Brussels I Regulation and Art. 2 (a) subpara. 1 Rome II Regulation. Art. 76 Maintenance Regulation follows in the same vein as do Art. 18 Rome III Regulation and Art. 84 Successions Regulation. The European legislator has adopted a policy of giving practitioners one and a half year of time to prepare for the novelties whilst they are already in force with a binding text easily accessible in the Official Journal. Problems and differences of opinion which arose under Arts. 31; 32 Rome II Regulation[1] (and had to be authoritatively resolved by the ECJ in *Homawoo*[2]) cannot arise under Art. 81.[3]

Articles 75 and 76 became effective one year before the remainder, or better: the bulk, of the **2** Brussels I*bis* Regulation. They relate to obligations by the Member States to convey certain information to the Commission and are only relevant in the interaction between the Member States and the Commission, but not as for, or against, private parties. The data already collected by the Commission should be available for interested persons when the operative part of the Brussels I*bis* Regulation became effectively applicable. A respective data base should be available and accessible form the very start of the Brussels I*bis* Regulation by 10 January 2015.

Art. 76 (2) Brussels I Regulation read: "This Regulation is binding in its entirety and directly **3** applicable in the Member States in accordance with the Treaty establishing the European Union." This declaratorily re-iterated the direct effect which is germane to every Regulation. Even without Art. 76 (2) Brussels I Regulation the very same result would have followed necessarily from Art. 288 (2) TFEU (formerly Art. 249 (2) EC Treaty).[4]

Croatia became a Member State of the EU as of 1 July 2013. It accepted that the *acquis* **4** *communautaire* would become part of Croatian law by that date.[5] Hence, the Brussels I*bis* Regulation entered into force for Croatia on 1 July 2013. As 1 July 2013 was before both 10

---

[1] See only *Glöckner*, IPRax 2009, 121; *Bücken*, IPRax 2009, 125; further references are provided by *Junker*, in: Münchener Kommentar zum BGB, vol. 10 (6th ed. 2015) Arts. 31, 32 Rom II-VO note 4.

[2] *Deo Antoine Homawoo v. GMF Assurances SA* (Case C-412/10), [2011] ECR I-11603 paras. 24, 34, 37; noted i.a. by *Illmer*, GPR 2012, 82; *Matthias Lehmann/Duczek*, JuS 2012, 681; *Brière*, Clunet 139 (2012), 693; *Rolf Wagner*, NJW 2012, 1333; *Sendmeyer*, ZEuP 2013, 685; *Torga*, Juridica 2014, 406.

[3] *Ansgar Staudinger*, in: Rauscher Art. 81 Brussels I*bis* Regulation note 1.

[4] *Ansgar Staudinger*, in: Rauscher Art. 76 note 1.

[5] Art. 2 Act concerning the conditions of the accession of the Republic of Croatia and the adjustments to the Treaty on European Union, the Treaty on the Functioning of the European Union and the Treaty establishing the European Atomic Energy Community, OJ EU 2012 L 112/21.

January 2014 and 10 January 2015, Art. 81 subpara. 2 can apply without any modification or adaptation with regard to Croatia.

5 Denmark is a special case. It is not a Member State of the Brussels I Regulation. The bilateral Agreement between the then EC and Denmark[6] of 19 October 2005 which effectively extends the Brussels I regime to Denmark with slight modifications and was concluded by Council Decision 2006/325/EC,[7] entered into force on 1 July 2007 by virtue of its Art. 12.[8] In accordance with Art. 3 (2) of the said Agreement, Denmark has by letter of 20 December 2012 notified the Commission of its decision to implement the contents of the Brussels I*bis* Regulation.[9] This means that the provisions of the Brussels I*bis* Regulation will be applied to relations between the EU and Denmark.[10] In accordance with Art. 3 (6) of the said Agreement, the Danish notification creates mutual obligations between the EU and Denmark.[11] Thus, the Brussels I*bis* Regulation constitutes an amendment of the said Agreement and is considered annexed thereto.[12] With reference to Article 3 (3) and (4) of the said Agreement, implementation of the Brussels I*bis* Regulation in Denmark can take place by amending existing Danish legislation by decision of the Danish Parliament.[13] In accordance with Art. 3 (5) (b) of the said Agreement, Denmark shall notify the Commission of the date on which such implementing legislative measures enter into force.[14]

This Regulation shall be binding in its entirety and directly applicable in the Member States in accordance with the Treaties.

Done at Strasbourg, 12 December 2012

For the European Parliament
The President
M. Schulz

For the Council
The President
A.D. Mavroyiannis

---

6 Agreement between the European Community and the Kingdom of Denmark of 19 October 2005 on jurisdiction and the recognition and enforcement of decisions in civil and commercial matters, OJ EU 2005 L 299/62.

7 Council Decision 2006/325/EC of 27 April 2006 concerning the conclusion of the Agreement between the European Community and the Kingdom of Denmark on jurisdiction and the recognition and enforcement of decisions in civil and commercial matters, OJ EC 2006 L 120/22.

8 OJ EU 2007 L 94/70.

9 OJ EU 2013 L 79/4 para. 3.

10 OJ EU 2013 L 79/4 para. 3.

11 OJ EU 2013 L 79/4 para. 4.

12 OJ EU 2013 L 79/4 para. 4.

13 OJ EU 2013 L 79/4 para. 5.

14 OJ EU 2013 L 79/4 para. 5.

COMMISSION DELEGATED REGULATION (EU) 2015/281 of 26 November 2014

replacing Annexes I and II of Regulation (EU) No. 1215/2012 of the European Parliament and of the Council on jurisdiction and the recognition and enforcement of judgments in civil and commercial matters

THE EUROPEAN COMMISSION,

Having regard to the Treaty on the Functioning of the European Union,

Having regard to Regulation (EU) No. 1215/2012 of the European Parliament and of the Council of 12 December 2012 on jurisdiction and the recognition and enforcement of judgments in civil and commercial matters (¹), and in particular Article 77 thereof,

Whereas:

(1) Regulation (EU) No. 1215/2012 provides for the circulation of judgments, authentic instruments and court settlements in the Union. It will start to apply on 10 January 2015.

(2) Regulation (EU) No. 1215/2012 established, in Annexes I and II, a form of the certificate concerning a judgment in civil and commercial matters and a form of the certificate concerning an authentic instrument/court settlement in civil and commercial matters.

(3) Latvia adopted the euro as from 1 January 2014. Therefore, all the references to the former currency of Latvia should be deleted from the forms. Lithuania will adopt the euro as from 1 January 2015. Therefore, all the references to the currency of Lithuania should be deleted from the forms.

(4) Croatia joined the Union as from 1 July 2013. Therefore, the references to Croatia and its currency should be included in the forms.

(5) In accordance with Articles 1 and 2 of Protocol (No. 22) on the position of Denmark, annexed to the Treaty on European Union and to the Treaty on the Functioning of the European Union, Denmark did not take part in the adoption of Regulation (EU) No. 1215/2012 and it is not bound by it or subject to its application.

(6) However, in accordance with Article 3(2) of the Agreement between the European Union and Denmark, Denmark has, by letter of 20 December 2012, notified (²) the Commission of its decision to implement the contents of Regulation (EU) No. 1215/2012. Therefore the references to Denmark and its currency should be included in the forms.

(7) For reasons of clarity it is appropriate to replace Annexes I and II.

---

¹ OJ L 351, 20.12.2012, p. 1.
² OJ L 79, 21.3.2013, p. 4.

(8) Regulation (EU) No. 1215/2012 should therefore be amended accordingly,

HAS ADOPTED THIS REGULATION:

Article 1

Annexes I and II to Regulation (EU) No. 1215/2012 are replaced by the text in the Annex to this Regulation.

Article 2

This Regulation shall enter into force on the day following the date of its publication in the Official Journal of the European Union.

This Regulation shall be binding in its entirety and directly applicable in the Member States in accordance with the Treaties.

Done at Brussels, 26 November 2014.

For the Commission

The President

Jean-Claude JUNCKER

Annex I

CERTIFICATE CONCERNING A JUDGMENT IN CIVIL AND COMMERCIAL MATTERS

Article 53 of Regulation (EU) No 1215/2012 of the European Parliament and of the Council on
jurisdiction and the recognition and enforcement of judgments in civil and commercial matters

.	COURT OF ORIGIN
.1.	Name:
.2.	Address:
.2.1.	Street and number/PO box:
.2.2.	Place and postal code:
.2.3.	Member State:

AT ☐ BE ☐ BG ☐ CY ☐ CZ ☐ DK ☐ DE ☐ EE ☐ EL ☐ ES ☐ FI ☐ FR ☐ HR ☐ HU ☐ IE ☐ IT ☐ LT
LU ☐ LV ☐ MT ☐ NL ☐ PL ☐ PT ☐ RO ☐ SE ☐ SI ☐ SK ☐ UK ☐

.3.	Telephone:
.4.	Fax:
.5.	E-mail (if available):
.	CLAIMANT(S) (¹)
.1.	Surname and given name(s)/name of company or organisation:
.2.	Identification number (if applicable and if available):
.3.	Date (dd/mm/yyyy) and place of birth or, if legal person, of incorporation/formation/registration (if releva and if available):
.4.	Address:
.4.1.	Street and number/PO box:
.4.2.	Place and postal code:
.4.3.	Country:

AT ☐ BE ☐ BG ☐ CY ☐ CZ ☐ DK ☐ DE ☐ EE ☐ EL ☐ ES ☐ FI ☐ FR ☐ HR ☐ HU ☐ IE ☐ IT ☐ LT
LU ☐ LV ☐ MT ☐ NL ☐ PL ☐ PT ☐ RO ☐ SE ☐ SI ☐ SK ☐ UK ☐ Other (please specify (ISO-code)) ☐

.5.	E-mail (if available):
.	DEFENDANT(S) (²)
.1.	Surname and given name(s)/name of company or organisation:
.2.	Identification number (if applicable and if available):
.3.	Date (dd/mm/yyyy) and place of birth or, if legal person, of incorporation/formation/registration (if releva and if available):
.4.	Address:
.4.1.	Street and number/PO box:
.4.2.	Place and postal code:
.4.3.	Country:

AT ☐ BE ☐ BG ☐ CY ☐ CZ ☐ DK ☐ DE ☐ EE ☐ EL ☐ ES ☐ FI ☐ FR ☐ HR ☐ HU ☐ IE ☐ IT ☐ LT
LU ☐ LV ☐ MT ☐ NL ☐ PL ☐ PT ☐ RO ☐ SE ☐ SI ☐ SK ☐ UK ☐ Other (please specify (ISO-code)) ☐

.5.	E-mail (if available):

THE JUDGMENT

.1.   Date (dd/mm/yyyy) of the judgment:

.2.   Reference number of the judgment:

.3.   The judgment was given in default of appearance:

.3.1.   ☐ No

.3.2.   ☐ Yes (please indicate the date (dd/mm/yyyy) on which the document instituting the proceedings or an equivalent document was served on the defendant):

.4.   The judgment is enforceable in the Member State of origin without any further conditions having to be met:

.4.1.   ☐ Yes (please indicate the date (dd/mm/yyyy) on which the judgment was declared enforceable, if applicable):

.4.2.   ☐ Yes, but only against the following person(s) (please specify):

.4.3.   ☐ Yes, but limited to part(s) of the judgment (please specify):

.4.4.   ☐ The judgment does not contain an enforceable obligation

.5.   As of the date of issue of the certificate, the judgment has been served on the defendant(s):

.5.1.   ☐ Yes (please indicate the date of service (dd/mm/yyyy) if known):

.5.1.1.   The judgment was served in the following language(s):

BG ☐ ES ☐ CS ☐ DK ☐ DE ☐ ET ☐ EL ☐ EN ☐ FR ☐ HR ☐ GA ☐ IT ☐ LV ☐ LT ☐ HU ☐ MT ☐ NL ☐ PL ☐ PT ☐ RO ☐ SK ☐ SL ☐ FI ☐ SV ☐ Other (please specify (ISO-code)) ☐

.5.2.   ☐ Not to the knowledge of the court

.6.   Terms of the judgment and interest:

.6.1.   Judgment on a monetary claim (^{3})

.6.1.1.   Short description of the subject-matter of the case:

.6.1.2.   The court has ordered:

.... (surname and given name(s)/name of company or organisation) (^{4})

to make a payment to:

.... (surname and given name(s)/name of company or organisation)

.6.1.2.1.   If more than one person has been held liable for one and the same claim, the whole amount may be collected from any one of them:

.6.1.2.1.1.   ☐ Yes

.6.1.2.1.2.   ☐ No

.6.1.3.   Currency:

☐ euro (EUR) ☐ Bulgarian lev (BGN) ☐ Czech koruna (CZK) ☐ Danish krone (DKK) ☐ kuna (HRK) ☐ Hungarian forint (HUF) ☐ Polish zloty (PLN) ☐ pound sterling (GBP) ☐ Romanian leu (RON) ☐ Swedish krona (SEK) ☐ other (please specify (ISO code)):

.6.1.4.   Principal amount:

.6.1.4.1.   ☐ Amount to be paid in one sum

.6.1.4.2. ☐ Amount to be paid in instalments (⁵)

Due date (dd/mm/yyyy)	Amount

.6.1.4.3. ☐ Amount to be paid regularly

.6.1.4.3.1. ☐ per day

.6.1.4.3.2. ☐ per week

.6.1.4.3.3. ☐ other (state frequency):

.6.1.4.3.4. From date (dd/mm/yyyy) or event:

.6.1.4.3.5. If applicable, until (date (dd/mm/yyyy) or event):

.6.1.5. Interest, if applicable:

.6.1.5.1. Interest:

.6.1.5.1.1. ☐ Not specified in the judgment

.6.1.5.1.2. ☐ Yes, specified in the judgment as follows:

.6.1.5.1.2.1. Amount:

or:

.6.1.5.1.2.2. Rate ... %

.6.1.5.1.2.3. Interest due from .... (date (dd/mm/yyyy) or event) to .... (date (dd/mm/yyyy) or event) (⁶)

.6.1.5.2. ☐ Statutory interest (if applicable) to be calculated in accordance with (please specify relevant statute):

.6.1.5.2.1. Interest due from .... (date (dd/mm/yyyy) or event) to .... (date (dd/mm/yyyy) or event) (⁶)

.6.1.5.3. ☐ Capitalisation of interest (if applicable, please specify):

.6.2. Judgment ordering a provisional, including a protective, measure:

.6.2.1. Short description of the subject matter of the case and the measure ordered:

.6.2.2. The measure was ordered by a court having jurisdiction as to the substance of the matter:

.6.2.2.1. ☐ Yes

.6.3. Other type of judgment:

.6.3.1. Short description of the subject-matter of the case and the ruling by the court:

.7. Costs (⁷):

.7.1. Currency:

☐ euro (EUR) ☐ Bulgarian lev (BGN) ☐ Czech koruna (CZK) ☐ Danish krone (DKK) ☐ kuna (HRK) ☐ Hungarian forint (HUF) ☐ Polish zloty (PLN) ☐ pound sterling (GBP) ☐ Romanian leu (RON) ☐ Swedish krona (SEK) ☐ other (please specify (ISO code)):

.7.2. The following person(s) against whom enforcement is sought has/have been ordered to bear the costs:

.7.2.1. Surname and given name(s)/name of company or organisation: (⁸)

.7.2.2. If more than one person has been ordered to bear the costs, the whole amount may be collected from any one of them:

4.7.2.2.1. ☐ Ja

4.7.2.2.2. ☐ Nein

4.7.3. Folgende Kosten werden geltend gemacht: ([⁵])

4.7.3.1. ☐ Die Kosten wurden in der Entscheidung in Form eines Gesamtbetrags festgesetzt (bitte Betrag angeben):

4.7.3.2. ☐ Die Kosten wurden in der Entscheidung in Form eines Prozentsatzes der Gesamtkosten festgesetzt (bitte Prozentsatz der Gesamtkosten angeben):

4.7.3.3. ☐ Die Haftung für die Kosten wurde in der Entscheidung festgelegt, und es handelt sich um folgende Beträge:

4.7.3.3.1. ☐ Gerichtsgebühren:

4.7.3.3.2. ☐ Rechtsanwaltsgebühren:

4.7.3.3.3. ☐ Zustellungskosten:

4.7.3.3.4. ☐ Sonstige Kosten:

4.7.3.4. ☐ Sonstige (bitte angeben):

4.7.4. Zinsen auf Kosten:

4.7.4.1. ☐ Nicht zutreffend

4.7.4.2. ☐ In der Entscheidung angegebene Zinsen

4.7.4.2.1. ☐ Betrag:

oder

4.7.4.2.2. ☐ Zinssatz ... %

4.7.4.2.2.1. Zinsen sind fällig ab .... (Datum (TT/MM/JJJJ) oder Ereignis) bis .... (Datum (TT/MM/JJJJ) oder Ereignis) ([⁶])

4.7.4.3. ☐ Gesetzliche Zinsen (falls zutreffend), zu berechnen gemäß (bitte entsprechendes Gesetz angeben):

4.7.4.3.1. Zinsen sind fällig ab .... (Datum (TT/MM/JJJJ) oder Ereignis) bis .... (Datum (TT/MM/JJJJ) oder Ereignis) ([⁶])

4.7.4.4. ☐ Kapitalisierung der Zinsen (falls zutreffend, bitte angeben):

Geschehen zu: ...

Unterschrift und/oder Dienstsiegel des Ursprungsgerichts:

([¹]) Betrifft die Entscheidung mehr als einen Kläger, sind die betreffenden Angaben für sämtliche Kläger einzutragen.
([²]) Betrifft die Entscheidung mehr als einen Beklagten, sind die betreffenden Angaben für sämtliche Beklagten einzutragen.
([³]) Betrifft die Entscheidung allein eine Kostenfeststellung im Zusammenhang mit einem Anspruch, der Gegenstand einer vorherigen Entscheidung war, ist Ziffer 4.6.1 nicht auszufüllen und zu Ziffer 4.7 überzugehen.
([⁴]) Wurde mehr als eine Person angewiesen, eine Zahlung zu leisten, sind die betreffenden Angaben für sämtliche Personen einzutragen.
([⁵]) Es sind die betreffenden Angaben für die einzelnen Ratenzahlungen einzutragen.
([⁶]) Bei mehr als einem Zinszeitraum sind die betreffenden Angaben für sämtliche Zinszeiträume einzutragen.
([⁷]) Dieser Punkt betrifft auch Fälle, in denen die Kosten in einer gesonderten Entscheidung zugesprochen werden.
([⁸]) Bei mehr als einer Person sind die betreffenden Angaben für sämtliche Personen einzutragen.
([⁹]) Falls mehrere Personen für die Kosten in Anspruch genommen werden können, ist die Aufschlüsselung für jede Person gesondert einzutragen.

Annex II

CERTIFICATE CONCERNING AN AUTHENTIC INSTRUMENT/COURT SETTLEMENT (¹) IN CIVIL AND
COMMERCIAL MATTERS

Article 60 of Regulation (EU) No 1215/2012 of the European Parliament and of the Council on
jurisdiction and the recognition and enforcement of judgments in civil and commercial matters

1.	COURT OR COMPETENT AUTHORITY ISSUING THE CERTIFICATE
1.1.	Name:
1.2.	Address:
1.2.1.	Street and number/PO box:
1.2.2.	Place and postal code:
1.2.3.	Member State:

AT ☐ BE ☐ BG ☐ CY ☐ CZ ☐ DK ☐ DE ☐ EE ☐ EL ☐ ES ☐ FI ☐ FR ☐ HR ☐ HU ☐ IE ☐ IT ☐ LT ☐
LU ☐ LV ☐ MT ☐ NL ☐ PL ☐ PT ☐ RO ☐ SE ☐ SI ☐ SK ☐ UK ☐

1.3.	Telephone:
1.4.	Fax:
1.5.	E-mail (if available):
2.	AUTHENTIC INSTRUMENT
2.1.	Authority which has drawn up the authentic instrument (if different from the authority issuing the certificate)
2.1.1.	Name and designation of authority:
2.1.2.	Address:
2.2.	Date (dd/mm/yyyy) on which the authentic instrument was drawn up by the authority referred to in point 2.1:
2.3.	Reference number of the authentic instrument (if applicable):
2.4.	Date (dd/mm/yyyy) on which the authentic instrument was registered in the Member State of origin (to be filled in only if the date of registration determines the legal effect of the instrument and this date is different from the date indicated in point 2.2):
2.4.1.	Reference number in the register (if applicable):
3.	COURT SETTLEMENT
3.1.	Court which approved the court settlement or before which the court settlement was concluded (if different from the court issuing the certificate)
3.1.1.	Name of court:
3.1.2.	Address:
3.2.	Date (dd/mm/yyyy) of the court settlement:
3.3.	Reference number of the court settlement:
4.	PARTIES TO THE AUTHENTIC INSTRUMENT/COURT SETTLEMENT:
4.1.	Name(s) of creditor(s) (surname and given name(s)/name of company or organisation) (²):
4.1.1.	Identification number (if applicable and if available):
4.1.2.	Date (dd/mm/yyyy) and place of birth or, if legal person, of incorporation/formation/registration (if relevant and if available):
4.2.	Name(s) of debtor(s) (surname and given name(s)/name of company or organisation) (³):
4.2.1.	Identification number (if applicable and if available):
4.2.2.	Date (dd/mm/yyyy) and place of birth or, if legal person, of incorporation/formation/registration (if relevant and if available):
4.3.	Name of other parties, if any (surname and given name(s)/name of company or organisation) (⁴):

4.3.1.   Identification number (if applicable and if available):

4.3.2.   Date (dd/mm/yyyy) and place of birth or, if legal person, of incorporation/formation/registration (if relevant and if available):

5.   ENFORCEABILITY OF THE AUTHENTIC INSTRUMENT/COURT SETTLEMENT IN THE MEMBER STATE OF ORIGIN

5.1.   The authentic instrument/court settlement is enforceable in the Member State of origin:

5.1.1.   ☐ Yes

5.2.   Terms of the authentic instrument/court settlement and interest

5.2.1.   Authentic instrument/court settlement relating to a monetary claim

5.2.1.1.   Short description of the subject matter:

5.2.1.2.   Under the authentic instrument/court settlement:

.... (surname and given name(s)/name of company or organisation) (^{5})

has to make a payment to:

.... (surname and given name(s)/name of company or organisation)

5.2.1.2.1. If more than one person has been held liable for one and the same claim, the whole amount may be collected from any one of them:

5.2.1.2.1.1. ☐ Yes

5.2.1.2.1.2. ☐ No

5.2.1.3.   Currency:

☐ euro (EUR) ☐ Bulgarian lev (BGN) ☐ Czech koruna (CZK) ☐ Danish krone (DKK) ☐ kuna (HRK) ☐ Hungarian forint (HUF) ☐ Polish zloty (PLN) ☐ pound sterling (GBP) ☐ Romanian leu (RON) ☐ Swedish krona (SEK) ☐ other (please specify (ISO code)):

5.2.1.4.   Principal amount:

5.2.1.4.1. ☐ Amount to be paid in one sum

5.2.1.4.2. ☐ Amount to be paid in instalments (^{6})

Due date (dd/mm/yyyy)	Amount

5.2.1.4.3.   ☐ Amount to be paid regularly

5.2.1.4.3.1. ☐ per day

5.2.1.4.3.2. ☐ per week

5.2.1.4.3.3. ☐ other (state frequency):

5.2.1.4.3.4. From date (dd/mm/yyyy) or event:

5.2.1.4.3.5. If applicable, until .... (date (dd/mm/yyyy) or event)

5.2.1.5.   Interest, if applicable

5.2.1.5.1.   Interest:

5.2.1.5.1.1. ☐ Not specified in the authentic instrument/court settlement

5.2.1.5.1.2. ☐ Yes, specified in the authentic instrument/court settlement as follows:

5.2.1.5.1.2.1. Amount:

or

5.2.1.5.1.2.2. Rate ... %

5.2.1.5.1.2.3. Interest due from .... (date (dd/mm/yyyy) or event) to .... (date (dd/mm/yyyy) or event) ([7])

5.2.1.5.2. ☐ Statutory interest (if applicable) to be calculated in accordance with (please specify relevant statute):

5.2.1.5.2.1. Interest due from .... (date (dd/mm/yyyy) or event) to .... (date (dd/mm/yyyy) or event) ([7])

5.2.1.5.3. ☐ Capitalisation of interest (if applicable, please specify):

5.2.2. Authentic instrument/court settlement relating to a non-monetary enforceable obligation:

5.2.2.1. Short description of the enforceable obligation

5.2.2.2. The obligation referred to in point 5.2.2.1. is enforceable against the following person(s) ([8]) (surname and given name(s)/name of company or organisation):

Done at: ...

Signature and/or stamp of the court or competent authority issuing the certificate:

([1]) Delete as appropriate throughout the certificate.
([2]) Insert information for all creditors if more than one.
([3]) Insert information for all debtors if more than one.
([4]) Insert information for other parties (if any).
([5]) If more than one person has been ordered to make a payment, insert information for all persons.
([6]) Insert information for each instalment.
([7]) Insert information for all periods if more than one.
([8]) Insert information for all persons if more than one.'

Annex III

Correlation Table

Regulation (EC) No 44/2001	This Regulation
Article 1(1)	Article 1(1)
Article 1(2), introductory words	Article 1(2), introductory words
Article 1(2) point (a)	Article 1(2), points (a) and (f)
Article 1(2), points (b) to (d)	Article 1(2), points (b) to (d)
–	Article 1(2), point (e)
Article 1(3)	–
–	Article 2
Article 2	Article 4
Article 3	Article 5
Article 4	Article 6
Article 5, introductory words	Article 7, introductory words
Article 5, point (1)	Article 7, point (1)
Article 5, point (2)	–
Article 5, points (3) and (4)	Article 7, points (2) and (3)
–	Article 7, point (4)
Article 5, points (5) to (7)	Article 7, points (5) to (7)
Article 6	Article 8
Article 7	Article 9
Article 8	Article 10
Article 9	Article 11
Article 10	Article 12
Article 11	Article 13
Article 12	Article 14
Article 13	Article 15
Article 14	Article 16
Article 15	Article 17
Article 16	Article 18
Article 17	Article 19
Article 18	Article 20
Article 19, points (1) and (2)	Article 21(1)
–	Article 21(2)
Article 20	Article 22
Article 21	Article 23
Article 22	Article 24
Article 23(1) and (2)	Article 25(1) and (2)
Article 23(3)	–
Article 23(4) and (5)	Article 25(3) and (4)
–	Article 25(5)
Article 24	Article 26(1)
–	Article 26(2)
Article 25	Article 27

Article 26	Article 28
Article 27(1)	Article 29(1)
–	Article 29(2)
Article 27(2)	Article 29(3)
Article 28	Article 30
Article 29	Article 31(1)
–	Article 31(2)
–	Article 31(3)
–	Article 31(4)
Article 30	Article 32(1), points (a) and (b)
–	Article 32(1), second subparagraph
–	Article 32(2)
–	Article 33
–	Article 34
Article 31	Article 35
Article 32	Article 2, point (a)
Article 33	Article 36
–	Article 37
–	Article 39
–	Article 40
–	Article 41
–	Article 42
–	Article 43
–	Article 44
Article 34	Article 45(1), points (a) to (d)
Article 35(1)	Article 45(1), point (e)
Article 35(2)	Article 45(2)
Article 35(3)	Article 45(3)
–	Article 45(4)
Article 36	Article 52
Article 37(1)	Article 38, point (a)
Article 38	–
Article 39	–
Article 40	–
Article 41	–
Article 42	–
Article 43	–
Article 44	–
Article 45	–
Article 46	–
Article 47	–
Article 48	–
–	Article 46
–	Article 47
–	Article 48
–	Article 49
–	Article 50

–	Article 51
–	Article 54
Article 49	Article 55
Article 50	–
Article 51	Article 56
Article 52	–
Article 53	–
Article 54	Article 53
Article 55(1)	–
Article 55(2)	Article 37(2), Article 47(3) and Article 57
Article 56	Article 61
Article 57(1)	Article 58(1)
Article 57(2)	–
Article 57(3)	Article 58(2)
Article 57(4)	Article 60
Article 58	Article 59 and Article 60
Article 59	Article 62
Article 60	Article 63
Article 61	Article 64
Article 62	Article 3
Article 63	–
Article 64	–
Article 65	Article 65(1) and (2)
–	Article 65(3)
Article 66	Article 66
Article 67	Article 67
Article 68	Article 68
Article 69	Article 69
Article 70	Article 70
Article 71	Article 71
Article 72	Article 72
–	Article 73
Article 73	Article 79
Article 74(1)	Article 75, first paragraph, points (a), (b) and (c), and Article 76(1), point (a)
Article 74(2)	Article 77
–	Article 78
–	Article 80
Article 75	–
Article 76	Article 81
Annex I	Article 76(1), point (a)
Annex II	Article 75, point (a)
Annex III	Article 75, point (b)
Annex IV	Article 75, point (c)
Annex V	Annex I and Annex II
Annex VI	Annex II
–	Annex III

Table of Cases
European Court of Justice

The first number indicates the relevant article, the second number relates to the respective note within the commentary on this article.

Short	Name	Case	Date	Reported in	Quotations
	Draft Agreement establishing a European laying-up fund for inland waterway vessels	Opinion 1/76	26 April 1977	[1977] ECR 741	Introduction/40, 71/3
	Convention No.170 of the International Labour Organization concerning safety in the use of chemicals at work	Opinion 2/91	19 March 1993	[1993] ECR I-1061	71/3
	Competence of the Community to conclude international agreements concerning services and the protection of intellectual property	Opinion 1/94	15 November 1994	[1994] ECR I-5267	71/3
	Competence of the Community or one of its institutions to participate in the Third Revised Decision of the OECD on national treatment	Opinion 2/92	24 March 1995	[1995] ECR I-521	71/3
	Accession by the Community to the European Convention for the Protection of Human Rights and Fundamental Freedoms	Opinion 2/94	28 March 1996	[1996] ECR I-1759	71/3
	Cartagena Protocol	Opinion 2/00	6 December 2001	[2001] ECR I-9713	71/3
Allianz	Allianz SpA, Generali Assicurazioni Generali Spa v. West Tankers Inc.	C-185/07	10 February 2009	[2009] ECR I-663	1/2, 1/3, 1/7, 1/23, 1/27, 1/42, 1/43, 1/52, 1/56, 25/2
Anklagemyndigheden v. Poulsen	Anklagemyndigheden v. Peter Michael Poulsen and Diva Navigation Corp.	C-286/90	24 November 1992	[1992] ECR I-6019	45/4
Anterist v. Credit Lyonnais	Rudolf Anterist v. Credit Lyonnais	22/85	24 June 1986	[1986] ECR 1951	25/34, 25/80, 25/149
Antonio Gramsci Shipping Corp. v. Lembergs	Antonio Gramsci Shipping Corp. v. Aivars Lembergs	C-350/13	5 June 2014	ECLI:EU:C:2014:1516	45/32

Peter Mankowski

Short	Name	Case	Date	Reported in	Quotations
Apostolides	Meletis Apostolides v. David Charles Orams and Linda Elizabeth Orams	C-420/07	28 April 2009	[2009] ECR I-3571	1/16, 2/32, 24/16, 36/11-12, 39/10, 42/20, 45/3, 45/14, 45/16a, 45/21, 45/57, 52/6, 68/10
Arcado v. Haviland	SPRL Arcado v. SA Haviland	9/87	8 March 1988	[1988] ECR 1539	Introduction/93-94, Introduction/103, 7/38, 7/44
AS-Autoteile v. Malhe	AS-Autoteile Service GmbH v. Pierre Malhe	220/84	4 July 1985	[1985] ECR 2267	4/3, 24/75, 24/79
Asturcom Telecomunicaciones	Asturcom Telecomunicaciones SL gegen Cristina Rodriguez Nogueira	C-40/08	6 October 2009	[2009] ECR I-9579	19/56
ASML Netherlands v. SEMIS	ASML Netherlands BV v. Semiconductor Industry Services GmbH (SEMIS)	C-283/05	14 December 2006	[2006] ECR I-12041	45/41, 45/46, 45/57, 45/59a
Baustahlgewerbe v. Commission	Baustahlgewebe GmbH v. Commission of the European Communities	C-185/95 P	17 December 1998	[1998] ECR I-8417	45/139
Bavaria Fluggesellschaft and Germanair v. Eurocontrol	Bavaria Fluggesellschaft Schwabe & Co. KG and Germanair Bedarfslluftfahrt GmbH & Co. KG v. Eurocontrol	9 and 10/77	14 July 1977	[1977] ECR 1517	1/9, 1/16, 1/20, 70/2
Benincasa v. Dentalkit	Francesco Benincasa v. Dentalkit Srl.	C-269/95	3 July 1997	[1997] ECR I-3767	Introduction 17-19/6, Introduction 17-19/45, 17/25, 17/26, 17/32, 25/14, 25/47, 25/66, 25/67, 25/81, 25/83, 25140–141, 25/150, 26/16, 27/33
Berghoefer v. ASA	F. Berghoefer GmbH & Co KG v. ASA SA	221/84	11 July 1985	[1985] ECR 2699	25/106-107, 29/11
Bertrand v. Ott	Societe Bertrand v. Paul Ott KG	150/77	21 June 1978	[1978] ECR 1431	Introduction 17-19/6, Introduction 17-19/11, 17/19, 17/43, 17/54
Besix v. Kretzschmar	Besix SA v. Wasserreinigungsbau Alfred Kretzschmar GmbH & Co. KG (WABAG) and Pla-	C-256/00	19 February 2002	[2002] ECR I-1699	Introduction/4, 7/1, 7/2, 7/24, 7/157, 7/203, 17/9

Short	Name	Case	Date	Reported in	Quotations
	nungs- und Forschungsgesellschaft Dipl. Ing. W. Kretzschmar GmbH & KG (Plafog)				
BIAO v. Finanzamt für Großunternehmen in Hamburg	Banque internationale pour l'Afrique occidentale SA (BIAO) v. Finanzamt für Großunternehmen in Hamburg	C-306/99	7 January 2003	[2003] ECR I-1	Introduction/113
Bier v. Mines de Potasse d'Alsace	Handelskwekerij G. J. Bier BV v. Mines de Potasse d'Alsace SA	21/76	30 November 1976	[1976] ECR 1735	Introduction/108, 7/240, 7/244, 7/251, 7/253, 7/319, 12/12
Blanckaert & Willems v. Trost	Blanckaert & Willems PVBA v. Luise Trost	139/80	18 March 1981	[1981] ECR 819	7/425, 7/431, 7/444, 7/445, 17/124
Bouchereau	Regina v. Pierre Bouchereau	30/77	27 October 1977	[1977] ECR 1999	Introduction/101
Brenner and Noller v. Witter Reynolds	Wolfgang Brenner and Peter Noller v. Dean Witter Reynolds Inc.	C-318/93	15 September 1994	[1994] ECR I-4275	17/129, 18/6, 15/41, 16/5
Brennero v. Wendel	Calzaturificio Brennero SAS v. Wendel GmbH Schuhproduktion International	258/83	27 November 1984	[1984] ECR 3971	44/10, 50/4
Brogsitter	Marc Brogsitter v. Fabrication de Montres Normandes EURL and Karsten Fräßdorf	C-548/12	13 March 2014	ECLI:EU:C:2014:148	7/27, 7/36, 7/37, 7/38, 7/48, 7/50, 7/238, 17/15
BVG	Berliner Verkehrsbetriebe (BVG) Anstalt des öffentlichen Rechts v. JP Morgan Chase Bank NV, Frankfurt Branch	C-144/10	12 May 2011	[2011] ECR I-3961	7/26, 8/64, 24/14, 24/46
C	Re C	C-435-06	27 November 2007	[2007] ECR I-10141	1/12, 1/14
Capelloni v. Pelkmans	P. Capelloni and F. Aquilini v. J. C. J. Pelkmans	119/84	3 October 1985	[1985] ECR 3147	26/8, 26/10, 24/8, 24/10, 43/9, 477-8, 47/11, 47/13
Cartier parfums	Cartier parfums – lunettes SAS, Axa Corporate Solutions assurances SA v. Ziegler France SA, Montgomery Transpors SARL, Inko Trade s.r.o., Jaroslaw Mateja, Groupama Transport	C-1/13	27 February 2013	ECLI:EU:C:2014:109	26/14
Car Trim	Car Trim GmbH v. KeySafety Systems Srl,	C-381/08	25 February 2010	[2010] ECR I-1255	7/1, 7/91, 7/92, 7/93, 7/123, 7/127, 7/132, 7/

Short	Name	Case	Date	Reported in	Quotations
					139, 7/143, 7/145, 7/150
Carron v. Germany	Fernand Carron v. Federal Republic of Germany	198/85	10 July 1986	[1986] ECR 2437	40/9
Centros	Centros Ltd. v. Erhvervs- og Selskabsstyrelsen	C-212/97	9 March 1999	[1999] ECR I-1459	1/39, 24/41, 45/103, 62/5
Č PP Vienna Insurance Group	Českápodnikatelskápojišťovna as, Vienna Insurance Group v. Michal Bilas	C-111/09	20 May 2010	[2010] ECR I-4545	15/03, 19/48, 26/1, 26/24, 26/33, 26/35, 27/8
Českáspořitelna	Českáspořitelna as v. Gerald Feichter	C-419/11	14 March 2013	ECLI:EU:C:2013:165	7/43, 7/205, 7/216, Introduction 17-19/3, 17/21, 17/32, 17/39, 17/41
CEŽ	Land Oberösterreich v.Č EŽas	C-343/04	18 May 2006	[2006] ECR I-4557	1/9, 1/21, 24/25, 24/26
CILFIT v. Ministry of Health	Srl CILFIT and Lanificio di Gavardo SpA v. Ministry of Health	283/81	6 October 1982	[1982] ECR 3415	Introduction/111, Introduction/122, Introduction/ 124-125
Collins v. Imtrat Handelsgesellschaft mbH and Kraul v. Emi Electrola GmbH	Phil Collins v. Imtrat Handelsgesellschaft mbH and Patricia Im- und Export Verwaltungsgesellschaft mbH and Leif Emanuel Kraul v. Emi Electrola GmbH	C-92 and 392/92	10 October 1993	[1993] ECR I-5145	Introduction/109
Color Drack v. Lexx	Color Drack GmbH v. Lexx International Vertriebs GmbH	C-386/05	3 May 2007	[2007] ECR I-03699	1/5, 7/1, 7/2, 7/127, 7/130, 7/156, 7/159, 7/161, 7/163
Commission v. CCRE	Commission of the European Communities v. Conseil des communes et regions d' Europe (CCRE)	C-87/01	10 July 2003	[2003] ECR I-7617	25/157
Commission v. Council	Commission of the European Communities v. Council of the European Communities (AETR)	22/70	31 March 1971	[1971] ECR 263	Introduction/40, 71/3
Commission v. Denmark	Commission of the European Communities v. Kingdom of Denmark (Open Skies)	C-467/98	5 November 2002	[2002] ECR I-9519	71/3
Commission v. Italien Republic	Commission of the European Communities v. Italian Republic	C-279/00	7 February 2002	[2002] ECR I-1425	21/16

Short	Name	Case	Date	Reported in	Quotations
Coreck Maritime v. Handelsveem	Coreck Maritime GmbH v. Handelsveem BV and Others	C-387/98	9 November 2000	[2000] ECR I-9337	25/5, 25/29, 25/31, 25/36, 25/37, 25/65, 25/70, 25/80, 25/83, 25/88, 25/138, 25/161, Arts. 33-34/30, Arts. 33-34/38
Corman-Collins	Corman-Collins SA v. La Maison du Whisky SA	C-9/12		ECLI:EU:C:2013:860	4/6, 7/36, 7/37, 7/116, 7/117, 7/118, 7/120, 7/122, 7/127, 25/23
Coty Germany	Coty Germany GmbH v. First Note Perfumes NV	C-360/12	5 June 2014	ECLI:EU:C:2014:1318	7/26, 7/27, 7/248, 7/251, 7/282, 7/283, 7/284, 7/290, 7/319, 7/390, 7/391, 7/394
Coursier v. Fortis Bank	Eric Coursier v. Fortis Bank and Martine Coursier, née Bellami	C-267/97	29 April 1999	[1999] ECR I-2543	1/35, 39/10, 58/6
Criminal Proceedings against Bickel and Franz	Criminal Proceedings against Horst Otto Bickel and Ulrich Franz	C-274/96	24 November 1998	[1998] ECR I-7637	Introduction to Arts. 27-30//28
Criminal proceedings against Lyckeskog	Criminal proceedings against Kenny Roland Lyckeskog	C-99/00	4 June 2002	[2002] ECR I-4839	Introduction/119
Criminal proceedings against Rinkau	Criminal proceedings against Siegfried Ewald Rinkau	157/80	26 May 1981	[1981] ECR 1391	Introduction/108, 34/29, 61/1, 61/3-4
Custom Made Commercial v. Stawa Metallbau	Custom Made Commercial Ltd. v. Stawa Metallbau GmbH	C-288/92	29 June 1994	[1994] ECR I-2913	7/1, 7/2, 7/27, 7/205, 7/209, 24/64, 25/86
Da Costa en Schaake NV et al. v. Netherlands Inland Revenue Administration	Da Costa en Schaake NV, Jacob Meijer NV, HoechstHolland NV v. Netherlands Inland Revenue Administration	28-30/62	27 March 1963	[1963] ECR 63	Introduction/124, Introduction/127
Dansommer v. Götz	Dansommer A/S v. Andreas Götz	C-8/98	27 January 2000	[2000] ECR I-393	24/14, 24/29, 26/21, 22/14, 22/29, 24/21
Danværn Production v.		C-341/93	13 July 1995	[1995] ECR I-2053	8/55, 8/59, 8/60, 25/143

Short	Name	Case	Date	Reported in	Quotations
Schuhfabriken Otterbeck	Danvaern Production A/S v. Schuhfabriken Otterbeck GmbH & Co.	C-43/95	26 September 1996	[1996] ECR I-4661	Introduction/109, 51/1
Data Delecta Aktiebolag v. MSL Dynamics	Data Delecta Aktiebolag and Ronny Forsberg v. MSL Dynamics Ltd.	14/76	6 October 1976	[1976] ECR 1497	7/7, 7/198, 7/443, 21/11
De Bloos v. Bouyer	A. de Bloos SPRL v. Societe en commandite par actions Bouyer				
De Cavel v. De Cavel (1)	Jacques de Cavel v. Louise de Cavel	143/78	27 March 1979	[1979] ECR 1055	1/25-26, 31/10
De Cavel v. De Cavel (2)	Louise de Cavel v. Jacques de Cavel	120/79	6 March 1980	[1980] ECR 731	1/53, 1/56, 1/57, 35/17
De Wolf v. Cox	Jozef de Wolf v. Harry Cox BV	42/76	30 November 1976	[1976] ECR 1759	Introduction/100, Introduction/106, Introduction to Arts. 29-34/1, 36/8, 36/17, 39/13, 45/71
Debaecker v. Bouwman	Leon Emile Gaston Carlos Debaecker and Berthe Plouvier v. Cornelis Gerrit Bouwman	49/84	11 June 1985	[1985] ECR 1779	45/42, 45/49
Denilauler v. Couchet Frères	Bernard Denilauler v. SNC Couchet Frères	125/79	21 May 1980	[1980] ECR 1553	24/77, 28/27, 35/51, 42/19, 45/39-40, 45/43, 45/144
Deutsche Genossenschaftsbank v. Brasserie du Pécheur	Deutsche Genossenschaftsbank v. SA Brasserie du Pécheur	148/84	2 July 1985	[1985] ECR 1981	41/4, 49/4
Di Pinto	Criminal proceedings against Patrice Di Pinto	C-361/89	14 March 1991	[1991] ECR I-1189	7/20
DFDS Torline v. SEKO	Danmarks Rederiforening, acting on behalf of DFDS Torline A/S v. LO Landsorganisationen i Sverige, acting on behalf of SEKO Sjöfolk Facket för Service och Kommunikation	C-18/02	5 February 2004	[2004] ECR I-1417	7/2, 7/244, 7/250, 7/251, 7/267, 7/319, 7/345
DHL Express France)	DHL Express France SAS v.Chronopost SA	C-235/09	12 April 2011	[2011] ECR-2801	54/2, 54/3, 54/7
Drouot v. CMI	Drouot assurances SA v. Consolidated metallurgical industries (CMI industrial sites), Protea as-	C-351/96	19 May 1998	[1998] ECR I-3075	Introduction to Arts. 29-34/1, 29/7

Short	Name	Case	Date	Reported in	Quotations
	surance and Groupement d'interbt economique (GIE) Reunion europeenne				
Duijnstee v. Goderbauer	Ferdinand M. J. J. Duijnstee v. Lodewijk Goderbauer	288/82	15 November 1983	[1983] ECR 3663	27/19, 27/21, 27/25
Dumez France	Dumez France SA and Tracoba SARL v. Hessische Landesbank	C-220/88	11 January 1990	[1990] ECR I-49	7/1, 7/251, 7/323, 7/326
Eco Swiss	Eco Swiss China Time Ltd. v. Benetton International NV	C-126/97	1 June 1999	[1999] ECR I-3055	Introduction/116, 34/24
eDate	eDate Advertising v. X and Olivier Martinez and Robert Martinez v. MGN Ltd.	C-509/09 and C-161/10	25 October 2011	[2011] ECR I-10269	7/251, 7/350, 7/351, 7/364, 7/365, 7/366, 7/367, /368, 7/369, 7/370, 7/371, 7/372, 7/373, 17/94
Effer v. Kantner	Effer SpA v. Hans-Joachim Kantner	38/81	4 March 1982	[1982] ECR 825	7/55, 27/33-34, 27/36
Electrosteel	Electrosteel Europe SA v. Edil Centro SpA.	C-87/10	9 June 2011	[2011] ECR I-4987 ECLI:EU:C:2011:375	7/132, 7/133, 7/134, 7/135, 7/139, 7/140, 7/143, 7/147
Elefanten Schuh v. Jacquemain	Elefanten Schuh GmbH v. Pierre Jacquemain	150/80	24 June 1981	[1981] ECR 1671	8/12, 25/75, 25/88, 25/154, 25/173, 26/12, 26/14, 26/25, 45/121
Elliniki Radiophonia Tileorassi Anonimi Etairia v. Dimotiki Etairia Pliroforissis	Elliniki Radiophonia Tileorassi Anonimi Etairia and Panellinia Omospondia Syllogon Prossopikou ERT v. Dimotiki Etairia Piliroforissis, Sotiris Kouvelas, Nicolaos Avdellas and others	C-260/89	18 June 1991	[1991] ECR 1-2925	Introduction to Arts. 29-34/27
Emrek	Lokman Emrek v. Vlado Sabranovic	C-218/12	17 October 2013	ECLI:EU:C:2013:666	Introduction 17-19/1, Introduction 17-19/3, 17/68, 17/99, 17/107, 17/108, 17/113
Engler	Petra Engler v. Janus Versand GmbH	C- 27/02	20 January 2005	[2005] ECR [-48l	7/27, 7/42, 7/43, 7/51, 7/52, 7/53, 7/54, 7/64, 7/73, Introduction 17-

Short	Name	Case	Date	Reported in	Quotations
					19/3, Introduction 17-19/7, 17/07, 17/11, 17/32
Estasis Salotti v. RÜWA	Estasis Salotti di Colzani Aimo and Cianmario Colzani v. RÜWA Polstereimaschinen GmbH	24/76	14 December 1976	[1976] ECR 1831	8/34, 8/50, 25/5, 25/75, 25/88, 25/90, 25/97, 25/142, 28/13
Eurofood	Eurofood IFSC Ltd.	C-341/04	2 May 2006	[2006] ECR I-3813	1/3
Falco Privatstiftung and Rabisch	Falco Privatstiftung and Thomas Rabitsch v. Gisela Weller-Lindhorst,	C-533/07	23 April 2009	[2009] ECR I-3327 ECLI:EU:C:2009:257	7/26, 7/36, 7/39, 7/111, 7/112, 7/113, 7/116, 7/118, 7/195, 7/196, 7/198, 7/199, 7/205, 7/206
Farrell v. Long	Jackie Farrell v. James Long	C-295/95	20 March 1997	[1997] ECR I-1683	Introduction/93, 5/155, 5/165-166, 5/173
Feakins	Robin John Feakins gegen The Scottish Ministers.	C-335/13	6 November 2014	ECLI:EU:C:2014:2343	7/87
Finanzamt Köln-Altstadt v. Schumacker	Finanzamt Köln-Altstadt v. Roland Schumacker	C-279/93	14 February 1995	[1995] ECR I-225	5/183
FlyLAL-Lithuanian Airlines	flyLAL-Lithuanian Airlines AS v. Starptautiskāli-dosta Riga VAS and Air Baltic Corporation AS	C-302/13	23 October 2014	ECLI:EU:C:2014:2319	45/3, 45/14, 45/16a, 45/21, 45/22, 45/27a, 45/29b
Folien Fischer	Folien Fischer AG und Fofitec AG gegen Ritrama SpA	C-133/11	15 October 2012	ECLI:EU:C:2012:664	7/26, 7/228, 7/229, 7/230, 7/233, 7/365
Football Dataco	Football Dataco Ltd. v. Sportradar GmbH	C-173/11	18 October 2012	ECLI:EU:C:2012:642	7/351
Frahuil v. Assitalia	Frahuil SA v. Assitalia SpA	C-265/02	5 February 2004	[2004] ECR I-1543	1/24, 7/2, 7/27, 7/38, 7/43, 7/83 1/19, 5/1, 5/14, 5/26, 5/29, 5/67-68
Freeport	Freeport plc v. Olle Arnoldsson	C-98/06	11 October 2007	[2007] I-8319 ECLI:EU:C:2007:595	1/7

Short	Name	Case	Date	Reported in	Quotations
Freiburger Kommunal-bauten	Freiburger Kommunalbauten GmbH Baugesell-schaft & Co. KG v. Ludger und Ulrike Hofstetter	C-237/02	1 April 2004	[2004] 2004 I-3403 ECLI:EU:C:2004:209	25/74
Freistaat Bayern v. Blij-denstein	Freistaat Bayern v. Jan Blijdenstein	C-433/01	15 January 2004	[2004] ECR I-981	1/17, 5/14, 5/67, 5/177, 1/20, 7/27, 7/87
FBTO v. Odenbreit	FBTO Schadeverzekeringen NV v. Jack Odenbreit	C-463/06	13 December 2007	[2007] ECR I-11321 ECLI:EU:C:2007:792	13/08
F-Tex	F-Tex SIA v.Lietuvos-Anglijos UAB Jadecloud-Vil-ma	C-213/10	10 April 2012	ECLI:EU:C:2012:215	1/34, 1/38
Gabriel	Rudolf Gabriel	C-96/00	11 July 2002	[2002] ECR I-6367	Introduction 17-19/7, Introduction 17-19/28, Introduction 17-19/39, 17/6, 17/7, 17/9, 17/66, 17/77 5/36, 5/193, Introduc-tion to Arts.15-17/7, 15/5-8, 15/33, 15/36
Caillard v. Chekili	Richard Gaillard v. Alaya Chekili	C-518/99	5 April 2001	[2001] ECR I-2771	24/26 22/26
G v. Cornelius de Visser	G v. Cornelius de Visser	C-292/10	15 March 2012	ECLI:EU:C:2012:142	6/8,
Gambazzi	Marco Gambazzi v. DaimlerChrysler Canada Inc. and CIBC Mellon Trust Company	C-394/07	2 April 2009	[2009] ECR I-2563	58/11
Gambelli	Criminal proceedings against Piergiorgio Gambelli and Others	C-243/01	6 November 2003	[2003] ECR I-13031 ECLI:EU:C:2003:597	1/21
Gantner Electronic v. Basch Exploitatie Maatschappij	Gantner Electronic GmbH v. Basch Exploitatie Maatschappij BV	C-III/01	8 May 2003	[2003] ECR I-4207	Introduction/121, In-troduction/126, Intro-duction to Arts. 27-30/1, Introduction to Arts. 27-30/13, Introduction to Arts. 27-30/26, 27/8, 27/12-13, 27/21

Short	Name	Case	Date	Reported in	Quotations
Gasser v. MISAT	Erich Gasser GmbH v. MISAT Srl.	C-1 16/02	9 December 2003	[2003] ECR I-14693	1/3, 1/49, 25/2, 25/8, 25/16, 25/163 Introduction/2; 1/3, 23/16, 23/163, Introduction to Arts. 27-30/1, Introduction to Arts. 27-30/5, Introduction to Arts. 27-30/10, Introduction to Arts. 27-30/17, Introduction to Arts. 27-30/21, Introduction to Arts. 27-30/26, Introduction to Arts. 27-30/30-45, Introduction to Arts. 27-30/49-55
GAT v. Luk	GAT Gesellschaft für Antriebstechnik mbH & Co. KG v. Luk Lamellen- und Kupplungsbau Beteiligungs KG	C-4/03	13 July 2006	[2006] ECR I-6509	24/67 22/66-67
Gemeente Steenbergen v. Baten	Gemeente Steenbergen v. Luc Baten	C-271/00	14 November 2002	[2002] ECR I-10489	Introduction/93-94, Introduction/103, Introduction/108, 1/11, 1/16, 1/35, 1/45, 5/176
Gerling v. Amministrazione del Tesoro dello Stato	Gerling Konzern Speziale Kreditversicherungs-AG et al. v. Amministrazione del Tesoro dello Stato	210/82	14 July 1983	[1983] ECR 2503	10/1, 15/12, 15/14, 25/161, 26/14 Introduction Arts. 8-14/1 13/12-13, 23/134, 23/161, 24/14
Germany v. European Parliament and Council	Federal Republic of Germany v. European Parliament and Council of the European Union	C-376/98	5 October 2000	[2000] I-8419	Introduction/36
German Graphis Graphische Maschinen	German Graphics Graphische Maschinen GmbH v. Alice van de Schee	C-292/08	10 September 2009	[2009] ECR I-8421 ECLI:EU:C:2009:544	1/34
	Arnoud Gerritse v. Finanzamt Neukölln-Nord	C-234/01	12 June 2003	[2003] ECR I-5933	5/183

Short	Name	Case	Date	Reported in	Quotations
Gerritse v. Finanzamt Neukölln-Nord					
GIE Groupe Concorde v. Master of the vessel "Suhadiwarno Panjan"	GIE Groupe Concorde v. Master of the vessel "Suhadiwarno Panjan"	C-440/97	28 September 1999	[1999] I-6307	7/24, 7/205, 7/206, 7/207, 7/215, 7/216, 7/217, 25/41, 27/29 Introduction/4, Introduction/93, Introduction/103, 5/11,
					5/138-140, 5/145-147, 23/41, 25/23
GIE Reunion europeenne v. Zurich Espaça, Soptrans	Groupement d'interêt economique (GIE) Reunion europeenne et al. v. Zurich Espaça, Societe pyreneenne de transit d'automobiles (Soptrans)	C-77/04	26 May 2005	[2005] ECR I-4509	8/5, 8/14, 8/15, 8/39, 8/47, 8/49, 10/7 6/1, 6/4, 6/16, 6/28, 6/35, 6/37, 8/6
Glaxosmithkline	Glaxosmithkline Laboratoires v. Jean-Pierre Rouard	C-462/06	22 May 2008	[2008] ECR I-3965 ECLI:EU:C:2008:299	8/13, 8/25, 8/36, 8/37, Introduction 17-19/48, 17/7
Google France	Google France SARL and Google, Inc. v. Louis Vuitton Malletier SA; Google France SARL v. Viaticum SA and Luteicel SARL; Google France SARL v. Centre national de recherche en relations humaines (CNRRH)	C-236/08 to C-238/08	23 March 2010	[2010] ECR I-2417	7/391
Gothaer Allgemeine Versicherungen	Gothaer Allgemeine Versicherung AG v. Samskip GmbH	C-456/11	15 November 2012	ECLI:EU:C:2012:719	
Goldbet Sportwetten	Goldbet Sportwetten GmbH v. Massimo Sperindeo	C-144/12	13 June 2013	ECLI:EU:C:2013:393	26/12
Gourdain v. Nadler	Henri Gourdain v. Franz Nadler	133/78	22 February 1979	[1979] ECR 733	Introduction/108, 1/30, 1/45 1/11, 1/19, 1/33, 1/40, 1/57

Short	Name	Case	Date	Reported in	Quotations
Gruber v. Bay Wa	Johann Gruber v. Bay Wa AG	C-464/01	20 January 2005	[2005] ECR I-439	Introduction 17-19/3, introduction 17-19/6, Introduction 17-19/44, 17/32, 7/34, 7/35
Gubisch Maschinenfabrik v. Palumbo	Gubisch Maschinenfabrik KG v. Giulio Palumbo	144/86	8 December 1987	[1987] ECR 4861	Introduction/100, Introduction/106, Introduction/108, Introduction 27-30/1, Introduction 27-30/11, Introduction 27-30/19, 27/10, 27/12, 27/17
Hacker v. Euro-Relais	Elisabeth Hacker v. Euro-Relais GmbH	C-280/90	26 February 1992	[1992] ECR -1111	24/30, 24/31 22/30
Handte v. TMCS	Jakob Handte & Co. GmbH v. Traitements Mecano-chimiques des surfaces SA	C-26/91	17 June 1992	[1992] ECR I-3967	7/2, 7/24, 7/27, 7/38 7/43 Introduction/4, 5/2, 5/11, 5/14, 5/26, 5/29, 5/67
Hassett v. Doherty	Hassett v. MDU Services	C-372/07	2 October 2008	[2008] ECR I-7403 ECLI:EU:C:2008:534,	4/11, 24/46
Hayes v. Kronenberger	David Charles Hayes and Jeannette Karen Hayes v. Kronenberger GmbH	C-323/95	20 March 1997	[1997] ECR I-1711	51/1
Heijduk	Pez Hejduk gegen EnergieAgentur.NRW GmbH	C-441/13	22 January 2015	ECLI:EU:C:2015:28	7/350, 7/351, 7/370
Hendrikman and Feyen v. Magenta Druck	Bernardus Hendrikman and Maria Feyen v. Magenta Druck & Verlag GmbH	C-78/95	10 October 1996	[1996] ECR I-4943	34/17 34/19, 34/30, 34/45
Hengst Import v. Campese	Hengst Import BV v. Anna Maria Campese	C-474/93	13 July 1995	[1995] ECR I-2113	32/24, 34/38, 34/40
Hi Hotel v. Spoering	Hi Hotel HCF SARL v. Uwe Spoering	C-387/12	3 April 2014	ECLI:EU:C:2014:215	7/26, 7/248, 7/251, 7/253, 7/282, 7/393
Hoffmann v. Krieg	Horst Ludwig Martin Hoffmann v. Adelheid Krieg	145/86	4 February 1988	[1988] ECR 645	36/3, 36/7 41/7, 45/17,

Short	Name	Case	Date	Reported in	Quotations
					45/19, 45/66-67, 45/71, 51/5
Homawoo	Deo Antoine Homawoo v. GMF Assurances SA	C-412/10	17 November 2011	[2011] ECR I-11603	81/1
HSB-Wohnbau GmbH	HSB-Wohnbau GmbH	C-86/00	10 July 2001	[2001] ECR I-5353	Introduction/115
Hubbard v. Hamburger	Anthony Hubbard (Testamentvollstrecker) v. Peter Hamburger	C-20/92	1 July 1993	[1993] ECR I-3777	Introduction/109
Hypotecni banka	Hypotečníbanka a.s v. Udo Mike Lindner,	C-327/10	17 November 2011	ECLI:EU:C:2011:745	4/6, Introduction 17-19/23, Introduction 17-19/24, 18/3, 18/14, 25/23, 62/6-7
Ilsinger v. Dreschers	Renate Ilsinger v. Martin Dreschers acting as administrator in the insolvency of Schlank & Schick GmbH	C-180/06	14 May 2009	[2009] ECR I-3561 ECLI:EU:C:2009:303	7/51, 7/53, 7/54, Introduction 17-19/6, Introduction 17-19/7, Introduction 17-19/28, Introduction 17-19/39, 17/7, 17/12, 17/13, 17/14, 17/60
Industrial Diamond Supplies v. Riva	Industrial Diamond Supplies v. Luigi Riva	43/77	22 November 1977	[1977] ECR 2175	Introduction/108, 45/27, 51/10-11
Ingmar GB Ltd. v. Eaton Leonard Technologies Inc.	Ingmar GB Ltd. v. Eaton Leonard Technologies Inc.	C-381/98	9 November 2000	[2000] ECR I-9305	Introduction/36, 45/25
Inspire Art	Kamer van Koophandel en Fabrieken voor Amsterdam v. Inspire Art Ltd.	C-167/01	30 September 2003	[2003] ECR I-10155	1/39, 24/41, 45/103, 63/5
International Fruit Company v. Produktschap voor Groenten en Fruit	International Fruit Company NV and others v. Produktschap voor Groenten en Fruit	21-24/72	12 December 1972	[1972] ECR 1219	45/4
Italian Leather v. WECO	Italian Leather SpA v. WECO Polstermöbel GmbH & Co.	C-80/00	6 June 2002	[2002] ECR I-4995	24/77, 35/91, 45/62, 45/64, 45/67

Short	Name	Case	Date	Reported in	Quotations
Iveco Fiat v. Van Hool	SpA Iveco Fiat v. Van Hool NV	313/85	11 November 1986	[1986] ECR 3337	25/83, 25/114
Ivenel	Roger Ivenel v. Helmut Schwab	133/81	26 May 1982	[1982] ECR 1891	1/26, 7/7, 20/1, 21/11
Johannes v. Johannes	Jutta Johannes v. Hartmut Johannes	C-430/97	10 June 1999	[1999] ECR I-3475	45/26
Johnston v. Chief Constable	Marguerite Johnston v. Chief Constable of the Royal Ulster Constabulary	222/84	15 May 1986	[1986] ECR 1651	45/139
Kainz v. Pantherwerke	Andreas Kainz v. Pantherwerke AG	C-45/13	16 January 2014	ECLI:EU:C:2014:7	7/26, 7/27, 7/230, 7/251, 7/307, 7/309
Kalfelis v. Schröder	Anastasios Kalfelis v. Bankhaus Schröder Münchmeyer Hengst and Co. et al.	189/87	27 September 1988	[1988] ECR 5565	7/27, 7/34, 7/35, 7/49. 7/238, 7/245, 8/3, 8/4, 8/7, 8/22, 8/25, 8/26, 8/32, 8/47, 8/57, 30/25
Kingdom of the Netherlands and van der Wal v. Commission	Kingdom of the Netherlands and Gerard van der Wal v. Commission of the European Communities	C-174/98 P and C-189/98 P	11 January 2000	[2000] ECR I-1	35/61
Klein v. Rhodos Management	Brigitte and Marcus Klein v. Rhodos Management Ltd.	C-73/04	13 October 2005	[2005] ECR I-8667	22/33, 24/33
Kleinwort Benson v. City of Glasgow	Kleinwort Benson Ltd. v. City of Glasgow District Council	C-346/93	28 March 1995	[1995] ECR I-615	Introduction/113, 1/4
Klomps v. Michel	Peter Klomps v. Karl Michel	166/80	16 June 1981	[1981] ECR 1593	28/21, 45/28, 45/40, 45/48-49, 45/51-52
Koelzsch	Heiko Koelzsch v. État du Grand Duchy of Luxemburg	C-29/10	15 March 2011	[2011] I-1595	21/13, 21/22, 21/27,
Kolassa v. Barclays	Harald Kolassa v. Barclays Bank plc.	C-375/13	28 January 2015	ECLI:EU:C:2015:37	7/87, 7/248, 7/253, 17/15, 17/53
Kongress Agentur Hagen v. Zeehaghe	Kongress Agentur Hagen GmbH v. Zeehaghe BV	C-365/88	15 May 1990	[1990] ECR I-1845	1/7, 8/4, 8/14, 8/35, 8/41, 8/42, 8/47, 8/51, 8/66, 27/17
Kramer	Cornelis Kramer and others	3, 4 and 6/76	14 July 1976	[1976] ECR 1279	71/3
		C-469/12	14 November 2013	ECLI:EU:C:2013:788	7/115, 7/116

Short	Name	Case	Date	Reported in	Quotations
Krejci Lager & Umschlagbetrieb	Krejci Lager & Umschlagbetriebs GmbH v. Olbrich Transport und Logistik GmbH,				
Krombach v. Bamberski	Dieter Krombach v. Andre Bamberski	C-7/98	28 March 2000	[2000] ECR I-1935	Introduction/110, Introduction/113, 45/3, 45/13, 45/14, 45/18, 45/21, 45/22, 45/28-29, 48/17, 45/86, 45/90, 45/136, 45/138-139, 52/6, 58/11, 64/5, 64/11, 73/10
Kronhofer v. Maier	Rudolf Kronhofer v. Marianne Maier	C-168/02	10 June 2004	[2004] ECR I-6009	7/1, 7/24, 7/26, 7/27, 7/251, 7/323, 7/330, 7/332, 8/30
Lancray v. Peters	Isabelle Lancray SA v. Peters und Sickert KG	C-305/88	3 July 1990	[1990] ECR I-2725	28/24, 45/46
Leathertex v. Bodetex	Leathertex Divisione Sintetici SpA v. Bodetex BVBA	C-420/97	5 October 1999	[1999] ECR I-6747	7/198, 7/199, 7/200, 7/203, 7/205
Lechouritou v. Germany	Eirini Lechouritou, Vasileios Karkoulias, Georgios Pavlopoulos, Panagiotis Brätsikas, Dimitrios Sotiropoulos, Ceorgios Dimopoulos v. Dimosio tis Omospondiakis Dimokratias tis Cermanias	C-292/05	15 February 2007	[2007] ECR I-1519	1/8, 1/9, 1/11, 45/4
Leffler	Götz Leffler v. Berlin Chemie AG	C-443/03	8 November 2005	[2005] ECR I-9611	1/1, 1/2
Lieber v. Göbel	Norbert Lieber v. Willi S. Göbel and Siegrid Göbel	C-292/93	9 June 1994	[1994] ECR I-2535	24/26
L' Oreal v. eBay	L' Oréal SA v. eBay International AG	C-324/09	12 July 2011	[2011] ECR I-6011	7/391
Lloyd's Register of Shipping v. Campenon Bernard	Lloyd's Register of Shipping v. Société Campenon Bernard	C-439/93	6 April 1995	[1995] ECR I-961	7/1, 7/425, 7/452, 11/21, 17/124
LT U v. Eurocontrol	LT U Lufttransportunternehmen GmbH & Co. KG v. Eurocontrol	29/76	14 October 1976	[1976] ECR 1541	Introduction/108, 1/8, 1/13, 1/17
Maersk Olie	Maersk Olie & Gas A v. S v. Firma M. de Haan en W. de Boer	C-39/02	14 Octobre 2004	[2004] ECR I-9657	Introduction 29-34/1, 29/, 29/26, 30/28,

Short	Name	Case	Date	Reported in	Quotations
					45/40, 45/43, 45/45, 45/144
Mahamdia	Mahamdia v. People's Democratic Republic of Algeria	C-154/11	19 Juli 2012	ECLI:EU:C:2012:491	1/1, 1/26, 7/425, 7/429, 19/23, 19/25, 20/16, 23/8, 23/9, 25/37, 25/38, 25/80
Maletic	Armin Maletic, Marianne Maletic v. lastminute.com GmbH, TUI Österreich GmbH	C-478/12	14 November 2013	ECLI:EU:C:2013:735	4/6, Intrduction 17-19/1, Introduction 17-19/23, Introduction 17-19/25, Introduction 17-19/26
Marc Rich	Marc Rich & Co. AG v. Società Italiana Impianti PA	C-190/89	25 July 1991	[1991] ECR I-3855	1/18, 1/22, 1/38-39, 1/44
Marinari v. Lloyd's Bank	Antonio Marinari v. Lloyd's Bank plc and Zubaidi Trading Co.	C-364/93	19 September 1995	[1995] ECR I-2719	7/1, 7/24, 7/251, 7/319, 7/323
Marseille Fret	Marseille Fret SA .v. Seatrano Shipping Company Ltd.	C-24/02	22 March 2002	[2002] ECR I-3383	Introduction/120
Meeth v. Glacetal	Nikolaus Meeth v. Glacetal	23/78	9 November 1978	[1978] ECR 2133	8/34, 8/50, 8/60, 8/63, 25/32, 25/33, 25/70, 25/71, 25/72, 25/80, 25/81f, 25/146-147, 25/156, 28/13
Melzer	Melzer v. MF Global UK Ltd	C-228/11	16 May 2013	ECLI:EU:C:2013:305	7/27, 7/228, 7/251, 7/282, 7/283, 7/284, 7/286, 7/287, 7/290, 7/330, 8/4, 8/28, 8/30
Mietz	Hans-Hermann Mietz v. Intership Yachting Sneek BV	C-99/96	27 April 1999	[1999] ECR I-2277	Introduction 17-19/6, 17/52, 17/55, 17/58, 35/4, 35/6, 35/25, 35/51, 35/63, 35/67, 35/82, 42/14-15, 42/18, 45/40, 45/130

Short	Name	Case	Date	Reported in	Quotations
Minalmet v. Brandeis	Minalmet GmbH v. Brandeis Ltd.	C-123/91	12 November 1992	[1992] ECR I-5661	28/24, 45/46, 45/51, 45/57
Mitteldeutsche Flugha- fen	Mitteldeutsche Flughafen AG and Flughafen Leipzig-Halle GmbH v. Commission	C-288/11	19 December 2012	ECLI:EU:C:2012:821	7/26
Mostaza Claro	Elisa Maria Mostaza Claro v. Centro Móvil Milenium SL	C-168/05	26 October 2006	[2006] ECR I-10421	15/6, 19/56
MSG v. Les Gravieres Rhenanes	Mainschifffahrts-Genossenschaft eG (MSG) v. Les Gravieres Rhenanes SARL	C-106/95	20 February 1997	[1997] ECR I-911	7/27, 7/215, 7/216, 7/217, 25/14, 25/41, 25/47, 25/109, 25/114, 25/117, 25/122, 25/125, 28/13
Mulox v. Geels	Mulox IBC Ltd. v. Hendrick Geels	C-125/92	13 July 1993	[1993] ECR I-4075	7/1, 20/4, 21/12, 21/15, 21/17, 21/18, 21/19, 21/27, 21/31
Mund & Fester	Mund & Fester v. Hatrex Internationaal Transport	C-398/92	10 February 1994	[1994] ECR I-467	2/12
Netherlands v. Rüffer	Netherlands State v. Reinhold Rüffer	814/79	16 December 1980	[1980] ECR 3807	Introduction/108, 1/9, 1/14, 1/17
Nickel & Goeldner	Nickel & Goeldner Spedition GmbH v. "Kintra" UAB	C-157/13	4 September 2014	ECLI:EU:C:2014:2145	71/8, 71/12, 71/25, 71/27
Mühlleitner	Daniela Mühlleitner v. Ahmad Yusufi and Wadat Yusufi	C-190/11	6 September 2012	ECLI:EU:C:2012:542	Introduction 17-19/1, 17/61, 17/68, 17/69, 17/70, 17/99
Nipponkoa	Nipponkoa Insurance Co. (Europe) Ltd v. Inter-Zuid Transport BV	C-452/12	19 December 2013	ECLI:EU:C:2013:858	71/8, 71/11, 71/30, 73/15
Nordsee v. Nordstern	Nordsee Deutsche Hochseefischerei GmbH v. Reederei Mond Hochseefischerei Nordstern AG & Co. KG and Reederei Friedrich Busse Hochseefischerei Nordstern AG & Co. KG,	102/81	23 March 1982	[1982] ECR 1095	Introduction/116
Nürnberger Allge-	Nürnberger Allgemeine Versicherungs AG v. Portbridge Transport International BV	C-148/03	28 October 2004	[2004] ECR I-10327	25/11, 25/12, 28/16

Short	Name	Case	Date	Reported in	Quotations
meine Versicherungs AG					23/11-12, 26/16, 71/1, 71/15
Océano Grupo	Océano Grupo Editorial SA v. Roció Murciano Quintero and Salvat Editores SA v. Jose M. Sánchez Alcón Prades, Jose Luis Copano Badillo, Mohammed Berroane and Emilio Viças Feliffl	C-240/98 to C-244/98	27 June 2000	[2000] ECR I-4941	17/52, 19/7, 19/8, 19/34, 19/56, 25/74
OTP Bank v. Hochtief	OTP Bank Nyilvánosan MüködöRészvénytársaság v. Hochtief Solution AG	C-519/12	17 October 2013	ECLI:EU:C:2013:674	7/43, 7/73, 7/195, 7/238
Overseas Insurance v. New Hampshire Insurance	Overseas Union Insurance Ltd. and Deutsche Ruck UK Reinsurance Ltd. and Pine Top Insurance Company Ltd. v. New Hampshire Insurance Company	C-351/89	27 June 1991	[1991] ECR I-3317	10/6, Introduction to Arts. 29-34/1, Introduction to Arts. 29-34/5, Introduction to Arts. 29-34/8-11,
Owens Bank v. Bracco	Owens Bank Ltd. v. Fulvio Bracco and Bracco Industria Chimica SpA	C-129/92	20 January 1994	[1994] ECR I-117	1/23, 1/27, 1/56, 24/79 Introduction to Arts.29-34/1, Introduction to Arts. 29-34/5, Introduction to Arts. 27-34/22, Introduction to Arts. 29-34/25, Introduction to Arts. 29-34/27, 30/26 30/32-34, Arts. 33-34/ 12
Owusu	Andrew Owusu v. Nugent B. Jackson, trading as "Villa Holidays Bal-Inn Villas", Mammee Bay Resorts Ltd., Mammee Bay Club Ltd., The Enchanted Garden Resorts & Spa Ltd., Consulting Services Ltd., Town & Country Resorts Ltd.	C-281/02	1 March 2005	[2005] ECR I-1383	1/2, 1/10, 4/5, 8/16, 8/18, Introduction 17-19/23, 21/6, 25/24, 25/25, 25/33, 25/50, 25/46, 25/163, 32/12, Introduction to Arts. 33-34/1, Arts. 33-34/28, Arts. 33-34/34
ÖFAB	ÖFAB Östergötlands Fastigheter AB v. Frank Koot and Evergreen Investments BV	C-147/12	18 July 2013	ECLI:EU:C:2013:490	7/26, 7/27, 7/43, 7/69,

Short	Name	Case	Date	Reported in	Quotations
Painer	Eva-Maria Painer v. Standard Verlags GmbH and others	C-145/10	7 March 2013	ECLI:EU:C:2013:138	7/70, 7/236, 7/237, 7/238, 7/251
					8/4, 8/28, 8/29
Pammer	Peter Pammer v. Reederei Karl Schlüter GmbH & Co. KG; Hotel Alpenhof GmbH v. Oliver Heller	C-585/08 and C-144/09	7 December 2010	[2010] ECR I-12527 ECLI:EU:C:2010:740	7/382, 7/383, 17/73, 17/ 75, 17/78, 17/79, 17/87, 17/88, 17/89, 17/90, 17/ 99, 17/100, 17/122
Pannon GSM	Pannon GSM Zrt. v. Erzsébet Sustikné Győrfi	C-243/08	4 June 2009	[2009] I-4713 ECLI:EU:C:2009:350	19/56, 25/74, 67/4
Pendy Plastic v. Plus-punkt	Pendy Plastic Products B. V. v. Pluspunkt Han-delsgesellschaft mbH	228/81	15 July 1982	[1982] ECR 2723	28/22, 45/37, 45/52
Peters	Martin Peters Bauunternehmung GmbH v. Zuid Nederlandse Aannemers Vereniging	34/82	22 March 1983	[1983] ECR 987	7/1, 7/39, 7/64, 7/65, 7/66
Pinkney	Peter Pinckney v. KDG Mediatech AG	C-170/12	3 October 2013	ECLI:EU:C:2013:635	7/26, 7/27, 7/248, 7/ 251, 7/253, 7/264, 7/ 265, 7/301, 7/350, 7/ 351, 7/355, 7/370, 7/ 393, 8/30
Powell Duffryn	Powell Duffryn plc v. Wolfgang Petereit	C-214/89	10 March 1992	[1992] ECR I-1745	1/33, 7/64, 25/66, 25/ 69, 25/83, 25/135-136, 25/141, 35/18
Preservatrice fonciere TIARD v. Staat der Ne-derlanden	Preservatrice fonciere TIARD SA v. Staat der Ne-derlanden	C-266/01	15 May 2003	[2003] ECR I-4867	1/20, 1/22, 1/24, 1/54, 1/57
Prism Investments	Prism Investments BV v. Jaap Anne van der Meer	C-139/10	13 October 2011	[2011] ECR I-9511	39/10-11, 45/3, 45/13a, 45/33
Profit Investment v. Ossi and Commerz-bank	Profit Investment SIM SpA v. Stefano Ossi and Commerzbank AG	C-366/13	pending	pending	7/56

Short	Name	Case	Date	Reported in	Quotations
Pugliese	Giulia Pugliese v. Finmeccanica SpA, Betriebsteil Alenia Aerospazio	C-437/00	10 April 2003	[2003] ECR I-3573	8/37, 20/5, 21/29
Radziejewski	Ulf Kazimierz Radziéjewski v. Kronofogdemyndigheten i Stockholm	C-461/11	8 November 2012	ECLI:EU:C:2012:704	3/7
Realchemie Nederland	Realchemie Nederland BV v.BayerCropScience AG	C-406/09	18 October 2011	[2011] ECR I-9773	1/22, 55/2, 55/4
Rehder	Peter Rehder v. Baltic Air Corporation	C-204/08	9 July 2009	[2009] ECR I-6073	7/1, 7/130, /7189, 7/190, 7/193
Refcomp	Refcomp SpA v. Axa Corporate Solutions Assurance SA, AXA France IARD, Emerson Network, Climaventa SpA	C-543/10	7 February 2013	ECLI:EU:C:2013:62	25/139, 25/162
Reichert v. Dresdner Bank I	Mario P. A. Reichert, Hans-Heinz Reichert and Ingeborg Kockler v. Dresdner Bank	C-115/88	10 January 1990	[1990] ECR I-27	1/37, 24/14, 24/23, 24/25, 24/26, 24/27, 24/76, 28/13
Reichert v. Dresdner Bank II	Mario Reichert, Hans-Heinz Reichert and Ingeborg Kockler v. Dresdner Bank AG	C-261/90	26 March 1992	[1992] ECR I-2149	1/37, 7/238, 35/49
Reisch Montage	Reisch Montage AG v. Kiesel Baumaschinen Handels GmbH	C-103/05	13 July 2006	[2006] ECR I-6827	8/15, 8/35
Renault v. Maxicar	Regie nationale des usines Renault SA v. Maxicar SpA and Orazio Formento	C-38/98	11 May 2000	[2000] ECR I-2973	Introduction/113, 34/15, 34/17-18, 34/21-24, 39/5, 45/2
Reunion europeenne v. Spliethoffs Bevrachtingskantoor	Reunion europeenne SA v. Spliethoffs Bevrachtingskantoor BV and Master of the vessel "Alblasgracht 002"	C-51/97	27 October 1998	[1998] ECR I-6511	7/1, 7/27, 7/34, 7/35, 7/38, 7/43, 7/79, 7/87, 7/238, 7/248, 7/251, 7/323, 7/326, 7/340, 7/341, 8/7, 8/12, 8/21, 8/22, 8/26, 8/32, 8/33, 8/34, 8/43, 8/44, 8/45
Roche Nederland BV v. Primus and Goldenberg	Roche Nederland BV, Roche Diagnostic Systems Inc., Roche NV, Hoffman-La Roche AG, Produits Roch SA, Roche Products Ltd, F. Hoffmann-La	C-539/03	13 July 2006	[2006] ECR I-6535	8/10, 8/27, 8/28, 8/32, 24/67

Short	Name	Case	Date	Reported in	Quotations
	Roche AG, Hoffman-La Roche Wien GmbH, Roche AB v. Frederick Primus, Milton Goldenberg				
Roda Golf & Beach Resort	Roda Golf & Beach Resort SL	C-14/08	25 June 2009	[2009] I-5439	1/1
Rohr v. Ossberger	Etablissements Rohr Societe anonyme v. Dina Ossberger	27/81	22 October 1981	[1981] ECR 2431	26/14
Rösler v. Rottwinkel	Erich Rösler v. Horst Rottwinkel	241/83	15 January 1985	[1985] ECR 99	8/64, 24/29, 24/31, 26/16
Royer	Jean Noel Royer	48/75	8 April 1976	[1976] ECR 497	Introduction/107
Rutili v. Ministre de l' Interieur	Roland Rutili v. Ministre de l' Interieur	36/75	28 October 1975	[1975] ECR 1219	Introduction to Arts. 27-30/28
Rutten v. Cross Medical	Petrus Wilhelmus Rutten v. Cross Medical Ltd.	C-383/95	9 January 1997	[1997] ECR I-57	20/5, 21/19, 21/20
Saldanha v. Hiross Holding	Stephen Austin Saldanha and MTS Securities Corporation v. Hiross Holding AG	C-122/96	2 October 1997	[1997] ECR I-5325	Introduction/109, 51/1
Sapir	Land Berlin v. Ellen Mirjam Sapir et al.	C-645/11	11 April 2013	ECLI:EU:C:2013:228	1/15, 8/8, 8/21, 8/23, 8/28, 8/31
Sanders v. van der Putte	Theodorus Engelbertus Sanders v. Ronald van der Putte	73/77	14 December 1977	[1977] ECR 2383	24/14, 24/30, 24/31, 26/21, 27/33
Sanicentral v. Collin	Sanicentral GmbH v. Rene Collin	25/79	13 November 1979	[1979] ECR 3423	1/26, 23/4, 25/21, 25/60, 27/39, 66/9-10
Scania Finance France SA v. Rockinger GmbH & Co.	Scania Finance France SA v. Rockinger Spezialfabrik für Anhängerkupplungen GmbH & Co.	C-522/03	13 October 2005	[2005] ECR I-8638	45/55
Scherrens v. Maenhout	R.O. E. Scherrens v. M. G. Maenhout, R. A. M. Van Poucke and L. M. L. Van Poucke	158/87	6 July 1988	[1988] ECR 3791	24/34, 26/21
Schneider	Siegfried János Schneider	C-386/12	3 October 2013	ECLI:EU:C:2013:633	1/9, 1/11, 1/29, 24/27
Schotte v. Parfums Rothschild	SAR Schotte GmbH v. Parfums Rothschild SARL	218/86	9 December 1987	[1987] ECR 4905	7/1, 7/425, 7/433,

Short	Name	Case	Date	Reported in	Quotations
SCT Industri	SCT Industri AB ilikvidation v. Alpenblume AB	C-111/08	2 July 2009	[2009] ECR I-5655	7/436, 7/438, 11/19, 17/124, 17/125
Seagon	Seagonv.Deko Marty Belgium NV Case	C-339/07	12 February 2009	[2009] ECR I-767	1/35, 1/36, 1/37, 1/57
Segoura v. Bonakdarian	Galeries Segoura SPRL v. Societe Rahim Bonakdarian	25/76	14 December 1976	[1976] ECR 1851	25/75, 25/77, 25/78, 25/88, 25/90, 25/93, 25/104-105, 25/109, 25/113, 25/115, 25/142
SFIP v. Axa Belgium	Societe financiere et industrielle du Peloux v. Axa Belgium et al.	C-1 12/03	12 May 2005	[2005] ECR I-3707	Introduction/100, Introduction/106, 9/7, 13/16
Shearson v. TVB Treuhandgesellschaft	Shearson Lehman Hutton, Inc. v. TVB Treuhandgesellschaft für Vermögensverwaltung und Beteiligungen mbH	C- 89/91	19 January 1993	[1993] ECR I-139	7/87, Introduction 17-19/6, 17/19, 17/32, 17/39, 17/43, 17/107
Shenavai v. Kreischer	Hassan Shenavai v. Klaus Kreischer	266/85	15 January 1987	[1987] ECR 239	7/1, 7/199, 20/3, 20/4, 21/6, 21/15
SiSRO v. Ampersand	Societe d' Informatique Service Realisation Organisation v. Ampersand Software BV	C-432/93	11 August 1995	[1995] ECR I-2269	43/ 9, 46/4, 46/16
Six Constructions v. Humbert	Six Constructions Ltd. v. Paul Humbert	32/88	15 February 1989	[1989] ECR 341	7/7, 21/13
Société financière v. Axa Belgium	Société financière et industrielle du Peloux v. Axa Belgium et al.	C-112/03	12 May 2005	[2005] ECR I-3707 ECLI:EU:C:2005:280	15/15, 19/22, 19/26
Solo Kleinmotoren v. Boch	Solo Kleinmotoren GmbH v. Emilio Boch	C-414/92	2 June 1994	[1994] ECR I-2237	45/3, 45/65, 59/5, 59/9, 66/12
Solvay v. Honeywell	Solvay SA v. Honeywell Fluorine Products Europe BV et al.	C-616/10	12 July 2012	ECLI:EU:C:2012:445	8/4, 8/29, 8/30, 24/15, 24/67
Somafer v. Saar-Ferngas	Somafer SA v. Saar-Ferngas AG	33/78	22 November 1978	[1978] ECR 2183	17/124, 20/10, 63/7
Sonntag v. Waidmann	Sonntag v. Waidmann	C-172/91	21 April 1993	[1993] ECR I-1963	Introduction/108, 1/15,

Short	Name	Case	Date	Reported in	Quotations
	Volker Sonntag v. Hans Waidmann, Elisabeth Waidmann and Stefan Waidmann				1/20, 45/41, 45/44-45, 49/4, 50/6
Spain and Italy v. Council	Kingdom of Spain and Italian Republic v. Council of the European Union	C-274/11 and C-295/11	16 April 2013	ECLI:EU:C:2013:240	71a/5
Spain v. Parliament and Council	Spain v. Parliament and Council	C-146/13	pending	pending	71a/5
Spain v. Council	Spain v. Council	C-147/13	pending	pending	71a/5
Spitzley v. Sommer	Hannelore Spitzley v. Sommer Exploitation SA	48/84	7 March 1985	[1985] ECR 787	25/154, 25/173, 26/14, 26/25-26 23/172, 24/14, 24/25-26, 45/121
St. Paul Dairy	St. Paul Dairy Industries NV v. Unibel Exser BVBA	C-104/03	28 April 2005	[2005] ECR I-3481	35/9, 35/46, 35/50
Sunico	Revenue and Customs Commissioners v. Sunico ApS	C-49/12	12 September 2013	ECLI:EU:C:2013:545	1/22, 1/24, 1/25
Svensson and Gustavsson	Peter Svensson and Lena Gustavsson v. Ministre de Logement et de l' Urbanisme	C-484/93	14 November 1995	[1995] ECR I-3955	7/125
Tacconi v. HWS	Fonderie Officine Meccaniche Tacconi SpA v. Heinrich Wagner Sinto Maschinenfabrik GmbH (HWS)	C-334/00	17 September 2002	[2002] ECR I-7375	7/2, 7/43, 7/73, 7/77
The "Tatry"	The owners of the cargo lately laden on board the ship "Tatry" v. the owners of the ship "Maciej Rataj"	C-406/92	6 December 1994	[1994] ECR I-5439	Introduction/93, Introduction/108, Introduction/113, 7/1, 7/205, 28/16, Introduction to Arts. 29-34/1-2, Introduction to 29-30/13, Introduction to Arts. 29-34/17, Introduction to Arts. 29-34/19, 29/7, 29/10-11, 29/15, 29/20, 29/22, 29/24-25, 30/6,

Short	Name	Case	Date	Reported in	Quotations
Trade Agency v. Seramico Investments	Trade Agency Ltd v. Seramico Investments Ltd	C-619/10	6 September 2012	ECLI:EU:C:2012:531	30/14-15, 30/17, 30/19, 30/21, 30/27, 71/1
TNT Express Nederland	TNT Express Nederland BV gegen AXA Versicherung AG	C.533/08	4 May 2010	[2010] I-4107	45/5, 45/14, 45/16a, 45/17, 45/19, 45/21, 45/28, 45/29a-29b, 45/37a
Trade Agency v. Seramico Investments	Trade Agency Ltd v. Seramico Investments Ltd	C-619/10	6 September 2012	ECLI:EU:C:2012:531	25/11, 25/12, 28/16, 71/2, 71/4, 71/9, 71/11-12, 71/24, 71/26-27
Trasporti Castelletti v. Trumpy	Trasporti Castelletti Spedizioni Internazionali SpA v. Hugo Trumpy SpA	C-159/97	16 March 1999	[1999] ECR I-1597	25/14, 25/47, 25/74, 25/75, 25/77, 25/83, 25/88, 25/117, 25/118-121, 25/123, 25/126, 25/138, 25/161, 26/16
Turner v. Grovit	Gregory Paul Turner v. Felix Fareed Ismail Grovit, Harada Ltd. and Changepoint SA	C-159/02	27 April 2004	[2004] ECR I-3565	1/3, 1/49, 1/5, 25/163, 25/166, Introduction to Art. 29-34/17, 31/9, 45/32, 45/65
Überseering	Überseering BV v. Nordic Construction Company Baumanagement GmbH (NCC)	C-208/00	5 November 2002	[2002] ECR I-9919	1/39, 24/41, 1/34, 35/24, 63/5
Unibank v. Christensen	Unibank A/S v. Flemming G. Christensen	C-260/97	17 June 1999	[1999] ECR I-3715	2/39, 2/40 38/5, 39/7-8, 58/4
VALE Építési	VALE Építési kft.	C-378/10	12 July 2012	ECLI:EU:C:2012:440	24/41
Van Dalfsen v. van Loon	B. J. van Dalfsen and others v. B. van Loon and T. Berendsen	C-183/90	4 October 1991	[1991] ECR I-4743	38/22, 51/1, 51/5
Van den Boogaard v. Laumen	Antonius van den Boogaard v. Paula Laumen	C-220/95	27 February 1997	[1997] ECR I-1147	1/27
Van der Linden v.		C-275/94	14 March 1996	[1996] ECR I-1393	37/20

Short	Name	Case	Date	Reported in	Quotations
Berufsgenossenschaft Feinmechanik	Roger van der Linden v. Berufsgenossenschaft der Feinmechanik und Elektrotechnik				
van Duyn v. Home Office	Yvonne van Duyn v. Home Office	41/74	4 December 1974	[1974] ECR 1337	45/4
Vapenik v. Thurner	Walter Vapenik v. Josef Thurner	C-508/12	5 December 2013	ECLI:EU:C:2013:790	17/44
VB Pénzügyi Lízing	VB Pénzügyi Lízing Zrt. v. Ferenc Schneider	C-137/08	9 November 2010	[2010] I-10847	25/74
Vereniging Nationaal Overlegorgaan Sociale Werkvoorziening u.a.	Vereniging Nationaal Overlegorgaan Sociale Werkvoorziening u.a.	Joined cases C-383/06 to 385/06	13 March 2008	[2008] ECR I-1561	1/1
Von Horn v. Cinnamond	Elsbeth Freifrau von Horn v. Kevin Cinnamond	C-163/95	9 October 1997	[1997] ECR I-5451	66/24
Voogsgeerd v. Navimer	Voogsgeerd v. Navimer SA	C-384/10	15 December 2011	[2011] ECR I-13275	7/425, 7/429, 21/32
Vorarlberger Gebietskrankenkasse	Vorarlberger Gebietskrankenkasse v. WGV-Schwäbische Allgemeine Versicherungs AG	C-347/08	17 September 2009	[2009] ECR I-8661	10/7, 13/8
W. v. H.	C.H. W. v. G. J. H.	25/81	31 March 1982	[1982] ECR 1189	1/30, 26/14 1/25, 24/14, 31/10
Wallentin v. Riksskatteverket	Florian W. Wallentin v. Riksskatteverket	C-169/03	1 July 2004	[2004] ECR I-6443	5/183
Webb v. Webb	George Lawrence Webb v. Lawrence Desmond Webb	C-294/92	17 May 1994	[1994] ECR I-1717	22/26
Weber v. Universal Ogden Services	Herbert Weber v. Universal Ogden Services Ltd.	C-37/00	27 February 2002	[2002] ECR I-2013	7/272, 20/5, 21/17, 21/ 21, 21/25, 21/30, 24/27
West Tankers	Allianz SpA, Generali Assicurazioni Generali Spa v. West Tankers Inc.	C-185/07	10 February 2009	[2009] ECR I-663	1/2, 1/3, 1/7, 1/23, 1/27 1/42, 1/43, 1/52, 1/56, 25/2
Wood Floor Solutions Andreas Domberger	Wood Floor Solutions Andreas Domberger GmbH v. Silva Trade SA	C-19/09	11 March 2010	[2010] ECR I-2121	7/1, 7/127, 7/163, 7/164, 7/165, 7/167, 7/172

Short	Name	Case	Date	Reported in	Quotations
Zelger v. Salinitri (1)	Siegfried Zelger v. Sebastiano Salinitri	56/79	17 January 1980	[1980] ECR 89	7/1, 7/215, 7/216, 7/219, 25/14, 25/51, 25/47, 26/16, 28/13
Zelger v. Salinitri (2)	Siegfried Zelger v. Sebastiano Salinitri	129/83	7 June 1984	[1984] ECR 2397	Introduction/108
Zuid Chemie	Zuid-Chemie v. Philippo's Mineralenfabriek NV/ SA.	C-189/08	16 July 2009	[2009] ECR I-6917	7/26, 7/27, 7/230, 7/248, 7/251, 7/257, 7/307, 7/386, 7/387, 7/388

Index

The first number indicates the relevant article, the second number relates to the respective note with the commentary on this article.